# Congressional Roll Call 2005

# Congressional Roll Call 2005

A Chronology and Analysis of Votes in the House and Senate
109th Congress, First Session

CQ PRESS

A Division of
Congressional Quarterly Inc.
1255 22nd Street, NW, Suite 400
Washington, DC 20037

# CQ Press

CQ Press is the nation's leading publisher of comprehensive, in-depth, and topical books and electronic information about the politics, policies, and people of government. With a fifty-year history of focus on American national government and elections, CQ Press is a world-class publisher of reference works, college texts, and directories. CQ Press has increasingly expanded its scope to include state government and international affairs and, through the weekly *CQ Researcher,* current topical social and political issues. CQ Press information is now available online through the CQ Electronic Library (www.cqpress.com and http://library.cqpress.com).

CQ Press is a division of Congressional Quarterly Inc., a publishing and information services company that is the recognized national leader in political journalism. CQ serves clients in the fields of business, government, news, and education with complete, timely, and nonpartisan information on Congress, politics, and national issues. With more than 100 reporters, editors, and researchers covering Capitol Hill, CQ keeps readers updated in print and online on a weekly, daily, and real-time basis.

The library and reference group at CQ Press publishes a wide range of volumes on the institutions, processes, and policies of government to serve the needs of librarians and library patrons. Major reference titles include comprehensive guides to Congress, elections, the Supreme Court, and the presidency; legislative history through the *Congress and the Nation* series; and election data through the *America Votes* series and related volumes. The college group at CQ Press publishes textbooks across the political science discipline and is the leading publisher of titles on American government and public policy. The government and professional group at CQ Press publishes comprehensive and current federal, congressional, judicial, and world government contact information, in print and online directories, that serves the needs of government and professional markets.

All of the content available through CQ Press books and on the Web is known for its objectivity, breadth and depth of coverage, and high standards of editorial excellence.

CQ Press
1255 22nd Street, NW, Suite 400
Washington, DC 20037

Phone: 202-729-1900; toll-free, 1-866-4CQ-PRESS (1-866-427-7737)

Web: www.cqpress.com

♾ The paper used in this publication exceeds the requirements of the American National Standard for Information Sciences—Permanence of Paper for Printed Library Materials, ANSI Z39.48-1992.

Printed and bound in the United States of America

10   09   08   07   06        1   2   3   4   5

ISBN 0-87289-308-1
ISSN 0191-1473

# Table of Contents

**Editor's Note:** *Congressional Roll Call 2005* provides a member-by-member survey and analysis of votes in the House and Senate during the first session of the 109th Congress.

After the introductory legislative summary, the book is divided into three sections. The first section contains Congressional Quarterly's special voting studies. These studies examine votes on which a majority of Democrats opposed a majority of Republicans, congressional support of the president's position on specific votes, and the percentage of all recorded votes on which members voted or took stands. Summaries and charts of the key votes are included in the second section.

The third section of the book contains a compilation of roll call votes in the House and Senate in 2005, followed by indexes of the roll call votes and bills on which roll call votes were taken.

# Congressional Roll Call 2005

# INTRODUCTION

# Supreme Court Nominees, Katrina, War Weariness Reshape Agenda

REPUBLICANS OPENED the 109th Congress brimming with confidence from their 2004 election victories, which gave President Bush a second term and expanded the party's majorities in both chambers. "We begin the new Congress with a sense of purpose and optimism. It's been a long time since Republicans have had this much power in Washington," David Dreier, R-Calif., chairman of the House Rules Committee, told his colleagues Jan. 4, the first day of the session.

The leadership promised an activist agenda focused on issues such as border security, curbs on civil-liability lawsuits, indefinitely extending the Bush tax cuts and simplifying the tax code. Republicans also anticipated one or more Supreme Court vacancies during the year, which would allow them to help shape the high court for years to come.

Democratic leaders, though in the minority, vowed to press for more funding for education and first-responders, expanded health care, a higher minimum wage, and the importation of cheaper prescription drugs from Canada.

The Republicans came out of the 2004 elections with 232 seats or 53 percent in the House, the largest number of seats won by GOP candidates since just after World War II. In the Senate, a four-seat gain gave Republicans a solid 55-seat majority that the leadership believed would allow them to overcome the nearly united Democrats, who had managed to to block several top Republican priorities in the last Congress.

During the first half of the session, the leadership delivered on its promise to clear a string of bills that had been hung up in Congress, including a six-year surface transportation bill, an energy overhaul sought by Bush since 2001 and a rewrite of bankruptcy law that had been stalled for eight years. Congress also cleared a bill to limit class action lawsuits and legislation to implement Bush's top trade priority, the Central American Free Trade Agreement (CAFTA).

But the new majorities were not enough to ensure the sweeping changes GOP leaders had hoped for. Democrats reacted by becoming more unified than ever, and the Republican leadership often found itself navigating between conservatives and the party's small moderate wing.

The second half of the session, beginning after the August recess and lasting into Christmas week, was dominated by factors outside the control of any party leaders. First and most dramatic were hurricanes Katrina and Rita and their costly aftermath. At the same time, lawmakers were feeling the public's growing disillusionment with the war in Iraq and the way it was being conducted, worries over the economy, their president's declining popularity and the mounting ethical problems of House Majority Leader Tom DeLay, R-Texas.

By the end of the session, the Republican caucus seemed to be unraveling, and Democrats looked forward to the 2006 elections when they hoped to unseat enough Republicans to get their turn again at running at least one chamber.

But Republican leaders also emerged with more victories to add to those of the first six months. They confirmed a new chief justice to the Supreme Court, won enactment of the first reduction in mandatory spending since 1997, cleared all 11 of the regular appropriations bills without having to resort to an omnibus package, provided $102.7 billion to support U.S. forces in Iraq and Afghanistan, and took innumerable steps to assist Gulf Coast states in recovering from the hurricanes.

## REPUBLICANS COME OUT FIGHTING

Emboldened by the party's increased hold on the Senate, Majority Leader Bill Frist, R-Tenn., used his opening speech on Jan. 4 to warn Democrats to "exercise self-restraint and do not filibuster judicial nominees" or expect him to follow through on threats to diminish the power of the minority. Democrats had used filibusters to halt action on 10 appellate court nominees in the 108th Congress.

On the other side of the Capitol, J. Dennis Hastert, R-Ill., was re-elected Speaker of the House over Nancy Pelosi of California, in her second term as House Democratic leader, 226-199. Hastert, who was catapulted to the position from chief deputy whip in 1999, was on track to become the longest-serving Republican Speaker. "The 109th Congress will be the Reform Congress," an ebullient Hastert told the House on Jan. 4. "In this Congress, big plans will stir men's blood."

The House also adopted a leadership rules package for the 109th Congress on a 220-195 party-line vote. Democrats were particularly angered by a rules change that allowed ethics complaints to lapse without investigation unless a majority of the evenly divided Committee on Standards of Official Conduct agreed to proceed.

Under pressure from their own members, Republican leaders had abandoned plans for an additional change that would have significantly curtailed the power of the ethics committee, and they agreed to reverse a November decision — aimed at protecting DeLay — that would have let GOP leaders keep party posts even if they were criminally indicted.

Democrats and congressional watchdog groups had vigorously criticized the proposed change, and individual Republicans had gotten an earful from the folks back home. "It's never a good idea to tie your shoelaces together right out of the gate," said J.D. Hayworth, R-Ariz., praising the leadership's responsiveness to the rank and file.

# Congressional Leaders: 109th Congress, 1st Session

## HOUSE

Speaker of the House — J. Dennis Hastert, R-Ill.

### REPUBLICANS
Majority Leader — Tom DeLay, Texas[1]
Majority Whip — Roy Blunt, Mo.
Conference Chairwoman — Deborah Pryce, Ohio
Conference Vice Chairman — Jack Kingston, Ga.
Conference Secretary — John T. Doolittle, Calif.
Policy Committee Chairman — John Shadegg, Ariz.
Chairman, National Republican Congressional Committee —
    Thomas M. Reynolds, N.Y.
Chief Deputy Majority Whip — Eric Cantor, Va.

### DEMOCRATS
Minority Leader — Nancy Pelosi, Calif.
Minority Whip — Steny H. Hoyer, Md.
Caucus Chairman — Robert Menendez, N.J.
Caucus Vice Chairman — James E. Clyburn, S.C.
Assistant to the Minority Leader — John M. Spratt Jr., S.C.
Chairman, Democratic Congressional Campaign Committee —
    Rahm Emanuel, Ill.
Senior Chief Deputy Minority Whip — John Lewis, Ga.

## SENATE

President Pro Tempore — Ted Stevens, R-Alaska

### REPUBLICANS
Majority Leader — Bill Frist, Tenn.
Majority Whip — Mitch McConnell, Ky.
Conference Chairman — Rick Santorum, Pa.
Conference Vice Chairwoman — Kay Bailey Hutchison, Texas
Policy Committee Chairman — Jon Kyl, Ariz.
Chairwoman, National Republican Senatorial Committee
    Elizabeth Dole, N.C.
Chief Deputy Majority Whip — Robert F. Bennett, Utah

### DEMOCRATS
Minority Leader — Harry Reid, Nev.
Minority Whip — Richard J. Durbin, Ill.
Conference Secretary — Debbie Stabenow, Mich.
Policy Committee Chairman — Byron L. Dorgan, N.D.
Steering & Outreach Committee Chairwoman —
    Hillary Rodham Clinton, N.Y.
Chairman, Democratic Senatorial Campaign Committee —
    Charles E. Schumer, N.Y.
Chief Deputy Minority Whip — Barbara Boxer, Calif.

[1]DeLay was required by GOP Conference rules to temporarily vacate the position after his Sept. 28 indictment in Texas on campaign finance charges. Speaker J. Dennis Hastert, Ill., named Roy Blunt, Mo., to act as majority leader for the remainder of the session.

House leaders also made it clear they would punish party members who were not sufficiently loyal, starting with Christopher H. Smith, R-N.J., who was removed as chairman of the Veterans' Affairs Committee on the first day of the session, to be replaced by Steve Buyer, R-Ind. Smith had frequently clashed with GOP leaders in his bid to increase funding levels for veterans' programs. It was the first time since Republicans took power a decade before that they deposed a sitting chairman.

Smith was followed not long after by Joel Hefley, R-Colo., who was replaced as chairman of the ethics committee by Doc Hastings, R-Wash. The move was punishment for the panel's admonishments of DeLay for ethical lapses in 2004. In one other change, Jerry Lewis, R-Calif., took the helm in the Appropriations Committee, succeeding C.W. Bill Young, R-Fla., who stepped down due to GOP-imposed term limits.

On the Senate side, committees for the first time felt the impact of the GOP term limits for chairmen. Four senators — Alaska's Ted Stevens on Appropriations, Arizona's John McCain on Commerce, Science and Transportation, Utah's Orrin G. Hatch on Judiciary and Pennsylvania's Arlen Specter on Veterans' Affairs — had to move to other positions. The resulting musical chairs left a total of nine committees under new chairmen.

### CONFIRMING CABINET MEMBERS AND JUDGES

The Senate began the year by confirming all but one of Bush's nominees for high-level jobs in his second term. The exception was John R. Bolton, whose nomination as ambassador to the United Nations was blocked by Senate Democrats. Senators twice voted against invoking cloture, which would have allowed a vote on Bolton's nomination. Bush

later used his constitutional recess appointment powers to install Bolton at the U.N. during Congress' August recess.

The newly confirmed Cabinet members included Alberto R. Gonzales, the first Hispanic to serve as attorney general; Condoleezza Rice, the national security adviser in Bush's first term, who took over the State Department; and Michael Chertoff, who became the second head of the Department of Homeland Security.

When it came to Bush's court nominees, however, the Senate seemed headed toward a showdown. Frist set a date for a test vote in May and appeared ready to follow through on his threat to employ an arcane parliamentary maneuver, dubbed the "nuclear option," to deny Democrats the ability to continue filibustering Bush's picks as they had done in the 108th Congress. But the confrontation some conservatives had hoped for was averted at the last minute, when a group of seven senators from each party took matters in their own hands. The group, which became known as the Gang of 14, struck a deal to let all but a few whom the Democrats considered the most objectionable judges win confirmation. When the test came May 24, the deal held and the Senate agreed to limit debate on the nomination of Priscilla R. Owen by a vote of 81-18. The deal remained in effect throughout the year.

### LEGISLATIVE TO-DO LIST

Topping the Republicans' legislative agenda were bills that had languished in prior years, mainly in the Senate.

On Feb. 17, the House cleared a business-backed bill that limited plaintiffs' ability to pursue class action lawsuits in sympathetic state courts (PL 109-2). A centerpiece of the GOP "tort reform" agenda for years, the legislation also was high on Bush's second-term wish list for

Congress. Frist had pulled the bill in 2004 when he was unable to get the 60 votes needed to halt a Democratic filibuster. This time, the 55-vote majority enabled him to fend off Democratic amendments and send a clean bill to the House.

The enlarged Senate majority also enabled Frist to defeat an amendment that had prevented enactment of a bankruptcy overhaul prized by the credit card and financial services industries. Supporters had been trying to clear the legislation for eight years.

The law, enacted in April (PL 109-8), applied a means test to force more individuals filing for bankruptcy to repay their debts over several years, rather than having much of their debts discharged. The obstacle to enactment in recent years had been an amendment by Sen. Charles E. Schumer, D-N.Y., to prevent violent protesters, particularly anti-abortion protesters, from filing for bankruptcy protection to escape court-ordered fines. The amendment was anathema to conservatives and the Bush White House. This time, the amendment failed, 46-53, enabling the Senate to pass the bill and send it to the House, where it easily cleared.

The Senate had been the graveyard in 2004 for another top Republican priority: an energy policy overhaul that Bush had been seeking since 2001. The Senate easily cleared the bill in late July (PL 109-58), but this time the real turn-around came in the House. At White House insistence, DeLay backed off a demand that the bill protect manufacturers of the gasoline additive methyl tertiary butyl ether, or MTBE, from liability lawsuits over water contamination. The MTBE liability waiver had been the deal breaker in the Senate the previous year.

After a legislative struggle that spanned two years and two Congresses, lawmakers also cleared a $286.5 billion, six-year surface transportation bill in late July (PL 109-59). The legislation had been left stranded at the end of the 108th Congress, mainly because of a conflict with the White House over how much money to provide and the related regional issue of how much each state would get back from the excise taxes it contributed to the highway fund.

A change in the tax treatment of ethanol fuels in 2004 (PL 108-357) that channeled more money into the trust fund paved the way for the administration to increase its six-year total for transportation spending to $284 billion in early 2005. House and Senate conferees had tentatively settled on $299 billion in 2004. This time, they agreed on an amount $2.5 billion over Bush's number, close enough to win White House acceptance. The total was sufficient to guarantee all states enough of an increase in highway aid to get the bill to Bush's desk.

In a major victory for Bush's free-trade policy, legislation to implement a free-trade agreement with five Central American countries and the Dominican Republic cleared in late July (PL 109-53). But the bitter battle and narrow House tally also underscored growing skepticism about the benefits of free trade. The largely unified Democratic opposition forced Republican leaders and the White House to make deals to win solid backing from their own party.

## BUDGET DISCIPLINE

Getting a budget resolution in place was another top priority for the leadership, which was determined to avoid a politically embarrassing repeat of 2004, when Republicans were unable to agree on a budget.

On April 28, both chambers signed off on a fiscal 2006 budget resolution (H Con Res 95) that mirrored the budget request Bush had sent to Congress on Feb. 7, the most stringent fiscal blueprint of his presi-

dency. The budget resolution gave appropriators an $843 billion limit on discretionary spending, as Bush proposed. It also included instructions for writing two reconciliation bills later in the year — one to extend expiring portions of Bush's 2001 and 2003 tax cuts (PL 107-16, PL 108-27), and the other to make the first reductions in nearly a decade in politically sacrosanct entitlement programs such as Medicaid and crop subsidies.

The reconciliation instructions were a critical step because they protected tax and savings bills from filibusters in the Senate. That meant Republicans could prevail with a simple majority, rather than the 60 votes needed to cut off debate. The instructions included protection for another long-stymied GOP goal: opening portions of Alaska's Arctic National Wildlife Refuge (ANWR) to oil and gas drilling.

The leadership put off writing the actual reconciliation bills until the fall; the appropriations process was a more immediate priority. But before the appropriators could get started on the fiscal 2006 spending bills, they had to finish a fiscal 2005 supplemental spending bill requested by Bush to fund operations in Iraq and Afghanistan. The $82 billion measure, cleared May 10 (PL 109-13), brought total appropriations for Iraq and Afghanistan and related expenses since Sept. 11, 2001, to $350.6 billion, according to the Congressional Research Service.

Lewis and the other House appropriators kept their chamber on a tight schedule, passing all 11 regular fiscal 2006 appropriations bills before the July Fourth recess. Thad Cochran, R-Miss., who took over as Senate Appropriations chairman, proceeded at a slower pace, though the Senate amended and passed five of the bills before the August recess. Congress cleared two of the bills — for the Interior Department and EPA (PL 109-54) and the legislative branch (PL 109-55) before leaving.

## NO SILVER LINING

Republicans left Washington for the August recess with an ample list of bragging rights — and a full agenda for the fall.

When they returned, they would have nine annual appropriations bills left to complete, a package of mandatory spending cuts to write, a defense authorization bill, an extension of Bush's tax cuts and renewal of the 2001 anti-terrorism law known as the Patriot Act. On top of that would be the confirmation of a new Supreme Court justice. On July 1, Justice Sandra Day O'Connor, the first woman on the high court, announced her retirement. On July 19, Bush announced his choice of John G. Roberts Jr. to replace O'Connor. The Senate Judiciary Committee scheduled confirmation hearings to begin Sept. 6.

Yet for the GOP leadership there also were signs of trouble that would become increasingly pronounced in the second half of the session.

Republicans had made party unity a hallmark of their control of Congress, and they maintained that pattern in the House, actually increasing their party loyalty a bit over 2004, though not quite matching the record high they set in 1995. But in the Senate, Republicans fell off the pace in 2005, dropping well below the level of partisan cohesion they had reached in the highly partisan 2003 session.

Democrats, meanwhile, were taking a leaf from the GOP playbook and demanding strict adherence to party discipline. As a result, House Democrats were more unified in 2005 than at any time in the previous half-century. Senate Democrats were almost as united as they had been at their high point in 1989. Overall, congressional Republicans maintained a 90 percent unity rate on party unity votes, while Democrats were close behind at 88 percent.

As a result, Republicans could not automatically translate their larg-

# Highlights: 109th Congress, First Session

## CONGRESS DID

- Confirm John G. Roberts Jr. as the first new chief justice of the United States since 1986.
- Complete work on all 11 fiscal 2006 appropriations bills.
- Appropriate $102.7 billion for the military operations in Iraq and Afghanistan but dictated that 2006 be a year of "significant transition" to Iraqi sovereignty and required quarterly reports from President Bush on progress toward that goal.
- Appropriate $62.3 billion, provided about $19 billion in tax relief and altered federal policies on many fronts to assist Gulf Coast states in recovering from Hurricane Katrina, the most economically damaging storm in U.S. history.
- Revise the bankruptcy code to require more debt repayment.
- Overhaul federal energy policy, with an emphasis on enhanced production, four years after a similar plan was proposed by the president.
- Authorize $286.5 billion for federal highway, mass transit and road safety programs through 2009.
- Bar cruel, inhuman or degrading treatment of enemy detainees, but limited access to federal courts by prisoners at Guantánamo Bay, Cuba.
- Provide $3.8 billion for preparations against a potential flu pandemic and shield makers of flu vaccine from liability.
- Implement a free-trade agreement between the United States and five Central American countries and the Dominican Republic.
- Require uniform national standards for state-issued driver's licenses and tighten limits on people seeking asylum.
- Shield gun and ammunition manufacturers, distributors and dealers from civil liability when third parties misuse their products.
- Limit class action litigation by shifting more such cases to federal court.
- Speed the process for reconstituting the House after a catastrophic attack.

## CONGRESS DID NOT

- Complete work on a bill to reduce expected entitlement spending over the next five years by $38.8 billion.
- Take any action in response to the president's top second-term domestic initiative, an overhaul of the Social Security program to allow future beneficiaries to divert some of their payroll taxes to investment accounts.
- Extend 16 expiring provisions of a 2001 law, known as the Patriot Act, that had enhanced law enforcement powers to investigate suspected terrorists.
- Enact or extend any tax reductions, the first year since 2000 without a new tax cut.
- Open the Arctic National Wildlife Refuge in Alaska to energy exploration.
- Create a compensation pool for victims of asbestos exposure.
- Expand the federal role in embryonic stem cell research, although it did fund research on umbilical cord blood cells.
- Update federal policy toward immigrant workers and the treatment of businesses that violate immigration law.
- Confirm John R. Bolton as ambassador to the United Nations; Bush instead used his recess appointment power to install that envoy.
- Reauthorize programs run by the Homeland Security and State departments, the Coast Guard and the Army Corps of Engineers.
- Update the Head Start early childhood education program.
- Reauthorize the federal law regulating higher education policy.
- Revamp governance of the U.S. Postal Service.
- Advance a constitutional amendment to ban gay marriage.
- Reach bipartisan agreement to increase the federally guaranteed minimum wage above $5.15, which was set in 1997.
- Rewrite the Clean Air Act to enact the president's "Clear Skies" initiative to curb power plant emissions.

er majorities into victory, particularly in the Senate. With Democrats united in opposition, GOP leaders had to keep their caucus in tight lock step — a feat they could not always accomplish, especially toward the end of the year when the Republican caucus was badly fragmented.

Troubles of another kind were also brewing for Republicans: a steady accumulation of questions and doubts about DeLay's ethics problems and the party's efforts to sidestep them. In March, the media began to raise questions about the majority leader's connections with Washington lobbyist Jack Abramoff, who was already under investigation.

Democrats on the ethics committee had responded to the January rules changes, the deposing of Hefley and the subsequent firing of several committee staff, by refusing to approve operating rules for the committee itself. That effectively shut down the panel at a time of rising reports of ethics problems. On April 27, the House voted overwhelmingly to reverse all of the rules changes, though the committee remained largely moribund for the rest of the session.

## KATRINA AND IRAQ: AN AGENDA TRANSFORMED

Before lawmakers could return to Washington and start on their burgeoning fall agenda, Hurricane Katrina ripped through coastal areas of Louisiana, Mississippi and Alabama on Aug. 29, leaving staggering problems in its wake. The levees that protected New Orleans were breached and the rising water flooded 80 percent of the city. The federal government was caught flat-footed, and Americans watched round-the-clock coverage as tens of thousands of people sought help that did not come. The public seemed to know more about the deteriorating conditions than the federal government did. Disillusionment and anger grew over the government's slow response at all levels.

Lawmakers cut short their vacations and dashed back to Washington to a congressional agenda turned upside down by forces beyond their control. Everything lawmakers would do for the rest of the year would be colored in some way by Katrina and by Hurricane Rita, which hit the Gulf Coast Sept. 24, doing major damage to the nation's oil and natural gas infrastructure.

Republicans faced the added danger that public dismay over the federal response to the calamity would converge with the growing disillusionment over war in Iraq and anger at the climbing cost of gasoline to create a perfect storm for the party. For nearly two years, public opinion polls had shown growing dissatisfaction with the war and with the direction the country was headed. Bush's own approval rating fell from just above 50 percent in January to the low 40s in September.

With midterm elections coming in 2006, GOP lawmakers, whether moderate or conservative, began looking to their own political futures, and fissures in the party burst into the open. Republicans were left scrambling for direction and a unified message.

It did not help that DeLay had to step aside as majority leader Sept. 28, following his indictment by a Texas grand jury in a fundraising scandal. Majority Whip Roy Blunt, R-Mo., took over as acting majority

leader, but DeLay vowed to return to power after clearing his name of what he said were baseless charges.

The immediate task in early September, however, was obvious: Within 10 days of the disaster, two supplemental spending bills totaling $62.3 billion were enacted (PL 109-61, PL 109-62). In addition, lawmakers introduced dozens of bills aimed at cutting red tape and addressing myriad problems — from providing education for relocated students, to health care problems of poor people who no longer had addresses, to issues such as the need to relocate federal courts and provide temporary identification for those whose possessions were lost in the disaster. Many of the bills were enacted individually; dozens more were tucked into other bills that became law.

On Sept. 2, Frist announced that he had asked Susan Collins, R-Maine, chairwoman of the Senate Homeland Security and Governmental Affairs Committee, to hold oversight hearings on the responses of the federal government, the Federal Emergency Management Agency and the Department of Homeland Security. In the House, the leadership announced a select committee to investigate government actions before and after Katrina. Democrats boycotted the panels, arguing that an outside commission should be created. "The Republican Congress will not investigate this Republican administration," predicted House Minority Leader Pelosi.

## RESHAPING THE SUPREME COURT

Amid the preoccupation with Katrina, the Judiciary Committee prepared to open its hearing on Roberts' nomination to the Supreme Court. Then on Sept. 3, three days before the hearing was to begin, ailing Chief Justice William H. Rehnquist died after 20 years in the office. Bush quickly nominated Roberts to serve as the 17th chief justice. After a six-day delay, Roberts delivered a flawless performance at his confirmation hearing and was easily confirmed by the Senate on Sept. 29. He was sworn in later the same day.

Roberts' smooth confirmation was a much-needed victory for Bush, but within days, the president undercut himself. On Oct. 3, he announced his selection of White House counsel Harriet Miers to take O'Connor's place on the high court. Miers, a Texas lawyer before she followed Bush to the White House in 2001, had little in her background to indicate where she stood on most issues. The nomination generated criticism and outrage from the political right, which was counting on Bush to pick a proven conservative with a clear record on issues such as abortion. On Oct. 27, with the nomination clearly unsustainable, Bush withdrew Miers' name.

It was the most emphatic rejection yet from a Republican-run Congress that had mostly deferred to Bush and his agenda throughout his presidency. The implosion of Miers' nomination also revealed disarray and divisions within the broader GOP coalition, with Bush looking more and more like a lame duck. Democrats mostly sat back and watched the show.

On Oct. 31, Bush moved to assuage his allies on the right by tapping conservative federal appellate judge Samuel A. Alito Jr. to replace O'Connor. Conservatives rejoiced; liberals promised to closely scrutinize Alito's lengthy legal record. The White House hoped to have Alito in place by the end of the year, but Judiciary Chairman Specter announced that the confirmation hearing would begin Jan. 9, 2006.

## WAR WEARINESS

In no area was the growing disconnect between Bush and congressional Republicans more evident than on the conduct of the war in Iraq.

On Nov. 15, the Senate voted 79-19 to adopt an amendment by Frist and John W. Warner, R-Va., chairman of the Armed Services Committee, requiring the president to send Congress quarterly unclassified reports on the course of the war and on progress toward drawing down U.S. forces. It also stated that 2006 should be a turning point in the war. The amendment to the defense authorization bill was offered as an alternative to a Democratic proposal that was nearly identical except for an additional provision requiring the Pentagon to set a schedule for a phased withdrawal from Iraq. The Democratic amendment was rejected.

Still, the Frist-Warner amendment was the most powerful statement of congressional oversight on Iraq policy since the 2003 invasion. "Congress got back in the game," said Jeremy Rosner, a Democratic pollster specializing in foreign affairs. House negotiators agreed to include most of the language in the conference report on the bill.

"Members are feeling the heat, and they want to weigh in more aggressively on what we're doing," said Pennsylvania's Curt Weldon, the second-ranking Republican on House Armed Services.

On Nov. 17, two days after the Senate vote, Rep. John P. Murtha of Pennsylvania, the ranking Democrat on the House Defense Appropriations Subcommittee and a decorated former Marine who had voted for the Iraq War, called for a withdrawal of troops over the next six months. "The military has done everything that has been asked of them. The U.S. cannot accomplish anything further in Iraq militarily," Murtha said. "It is time to bring them home."

Meanwhile, reports of abuse at military detention centers had prompted the Senate in early October, to add language to the fiscal 2006 Defense appropriations bill calling for a ban on "cruel, inhuman or degrading" treatment of detainees. Amendment author McCain, who had been held as a prisoner of war in North Vietnam, also succeeded in attaching the language to the defense authorization bill. Despite intense White House pressure, including a visit by Vice President Dick Cheney, McCain refused to back down.

With House leaders opposed to the amendment and the White House threatening to veto any legislation that contained it, Senate leaders held the two defense bills back. Then on Dec. 14, the House supported McCain's amendment in an overwhelming vote of 308-122. The next day, Bush reversed course and accepted the language in an Oval Office meeting with McCain and Warner. McCain agreed to add protections for U.S. interrogators who were performing "officially authorized" actions.

Lawmakers also were growing dissatisfied with the level of administration secrecy about the war on terrorism. On Nov. 10, the Senate voted to demand a classified report on U.S.-run secret detention facilities overseas. The move came in response to a Washington Post report about a secret overseas system of CIA prisons for terrorists. In a non-binding ballot Dec. 16, the House voted to include the provision in the final defense authorization bill. However, it was dropped in conference as outside the jurisdiction of the Armed Services committees.

The New York Times on Dec. 16 ran a story revealing that the president in 2002 had authorized the National Security Agency to monitor overseas telephone calls by U.S. citizens without court permission. Angry reaction spilled into Senate debate on a bill to reauthorize expiring provisions of the Patriot Act that focused on enhanced surveillance powers. The House adopted the conference report on the reauthorization bill (HR 3199), but four Republicans joined nearly all Democrats in the Senate to reject cloture, blocking a vote on the conference report in that chamber. Frist switched his vote to "no" so he could move to reconsider the vote later.

With the provisions set to expire Dec. 31, Bush and Frist reversed an

# 109th Congress, 1st Session: By the Numbers

The first session of the 109th Congress began, as the Constitution and federal law required, at noon Jan. 3, 2005. Under the terms of the adjournment resolution (H Con Res 326), the House adjourned sine die at 4:36 p.m. Dec. 22; the Senate adjourned sine die at 8:04 p.m. the same day. Following are some statistical comparisons of the two chambers over the past decade:

| | | 2005 | 2004 | 2003 | 2002 | 2001 | 2000 | 1999 | 1998 | 1997 | 1996 |
|---|---|---|---|---|---|---|---|---|---|---|---|
| **Days in Session** | Senate | 159 | 133 | 167 | 149 | 173 | 141 | 162 | 143 | 153 | 132 |
| | House | 140 | 110 | 133 | 123 | 142 | 135 | 137 | 119 | 132 | 122 |
| **Time in Session** | Senate | 1,222 | 1,032 | 1,454 | 1,043 | 1,236 | 1,018 | 1,184 | 1,095 | 1,093 | 1,037 |
| (hours) | House | 1,067 | 879 | 1,015 | 772 | 922 | 1,054 | 1,125 | 999 | 1,004 | 919 |
| **Average Length of** | Senate | 7.7 | 7.8 | 8.7 | 7.0 | 7.1 | 7.2 | 7.3 | 7.7 | 7.1 | 7.9 |
| **Daily Session** (hours) | House | 7.6 | 8.0 | 7.6 | 6.3 | 6.5 | 7.8 | 8.2 | 8.4 | 7.6 | 7.5 |
| **Public Laws Enacted**[1] | | 147 | 300 | 198 | 241 | 136 | 410 | 170 | 241 | 153 | 245 |
| **Bills and Resolutions** | Senate | 2,616 | 1,318 | 2,398 | 1,558 | 2,212 | 1,546 | 2,352 | 1,321 | 1,840 | 860 |
| **Introduced** | House | 5,703 | 2,338 | 4,616 | 2,711 | 4,318 | 2,701 | 4,241 | 2,254 | 3,728 | 1,899 |
| | **Total** | **8,319** | **3,656** | **7,014** | **4,269** | **6,530** | **4,247** | **6,593** | **3,575** | **5,568** | **2,759** |
| **Recorded Votes** | Senate | 366 | 216 | 459 | 253 | 380 | 298 | 374 | 314 | 298 | 306 |
| | House[2] | 671 | 544 | 677 | 484 | 512 | 603 | 611 | 547 | 640 | 455 |
| | **Total** | **1,037** | **760** | **1,136** | **737** | **892** | **901** | **985** | **861** | **938** | **761** |
| **Vetoes** | | 0 | 0 | 0 | 0 | 0 | 7[3] | 5 | 5 | 3[4] | 6 |

SOURCE: Congressional Record

[1] Bills signed into law during congressional session   [2] Includes quorum calls   [3] Includes pocket vetoes   [4] Does not include line-item vetoes

earlier refusal to consider a short-term bill and settle for a five-week extension (PL 109-160).

"For a long time, the Republican majority has been willing to simply be foot soldiers for the president," Thomas E. Mann, a political scholar at the Brookings Institution in Washington, said near the end of the session. "Enough has happened that you're beginning to see them act in a more natural fashion, to reflect public opinion, to be a little more insistent on real congressional oversight."

### FINISHING THE APPROPRIATIONS BILLS

After a brief hiatus, lawmakers went back to work on the appropriations bills, clearing all but two of the remaining nine bills by the Thanksgiving break. The last two did not clear until Dec. 21. Appropriators had made the job slightly easier by a shifting about $6 billion from defense to other programs; the defense funds could be made up in the next supplemental. Still, when all the spending bills were finished, Congress had made the first reduction in non-defense discretionary spending since the Reagan administration.

The tight spending limits made it particularly difficult to muster support for the Labor, Health and Human Services (HHS), and Education spending bill (PL 109-149). House leaders suffered an embarrassing defeat shortly before Thanksgiving, when 22 Republicans joined Democrats in rejecting the Labor-HHS conference report. Members were angry over the elimination of their individual earmarks and reduced spending for health care and education. The House accepted a slightly modified conference report Dec. 14, but there was so much opposition in the Senate that GOP leaders had to wait until the last moment when they could push the conference

report through as part of the final flurry of business.

The Defense spending bill (PL 109-48) was held up until mid-December by the fight over the McCain amendment. Also, GOP leaders held it as a must-pass vehicle to carry $3.8 billion in emergency appropriations to prepare for a possible flu pandemic, a year-end installment on hurricane relief, and a 1 percent across-the-board cut in virtually all fiscal 2006 discretionary spending, a top demand of the fiscal conservatives. The cut did not apply to veterans' programs or emergency war spending.

### SPENDING AND TAX CUTS ALIVE

The leadership had planned to handle the budget and tax reconciliation bills outlined in the budget resolution in the crowded end of the session. By that point, however, the Gulf Coast hurricanes, the war in Iraq and the president's growing unpopularity had changed the dynamic. Fiscal conservatives looked at a yawning federal deficit and demanded offsets for all hurricane spending. They honed in on earmarks — projects inserted into bills by individual members — scolding lawmakers for taking money home that was needed in the Gulf Coast.

On the other side, moderate Republicans such as Olympia J. Snowe of Maine fought against spending cuts in mandatory programs such as Medicaid, the federal-state health program for the poor, and food stamps. They cited the poor in New Orleans whose suffering had captured the nation's attention and reminded Americans of the continuing need to respond to poverty in their midst.

With Democrats almost unanimous in their opposition to the mandatory spending cuts, GOP leaders in both chambers had to walk a narrow path between their own conservative and moderate wings. The Senate passed a bill with a net $35 billion in savings over five years. Fis-

cal conservatives wanted deeper cuts, but influential moderates including Gordon H. Smith of Oregon refused to support more than $10 billion in reductions to Medicaid and held fast against other cuts to programs for the poor. Senate leaders did, however, have enough votes to keep ANWR provisions in the bill.

House leaders just barely got $49.9 billion in net savings through their chamber, but they had to drop ANWR along with some of their proposed cuts to Medicaid and food stamps. In conference, the cuts to Medicaid, which were at the heart of the negotiations, were whittled down to $4.8 billion, less than half what the House sought and a fraction of the $60 billion over 10 years that the White House requested in February.

The final bill was expected to cut mandatory spending by a net $38.8 billion over five years. While the total was far less than fiscal conservatives had hoped for, they could point to having helped force the first cut in entitlement spending since 1997. The biggest savings came from changes to federal student loan programs, Medicare and Medicaid. The bill also required higher premiums for the federal pension guarantee agency and counted on additional funds from auctioning portions of the electromagnetic spectrum. Those funds were used to offset some mandatory spending and to help pay for new expenditures that were included in the bill.

Republicans put off plans to complete the second reconciliation bill aimed at extending Bush's tax cuts. The House passed a version of the bill focused on tax breaks for dividend and capital gains income, while the Senate concentrated on modifying the alternative minimum tax. In addition to the difficulty of finding time for a conference in the crowded end-of-year schedule, many members were uncomfortable voting for tax cuts in tandem with the cuts to entitlement programs.

With the big package put on hold, lawmakers broke out $7.8 billion in additional tax incentives for the Gulf Coast and cleared it Dec. 16 (PL 109-135). At the insistence of House social conservatives, Senate tax writers agreed to limit the breaks that would flow to certain businesses such as casinos, racetracks and liquor stores.

## CHAOTIC END TO THE SESSION

As the session dragged into December, it became increasingly chaotic. Democrats remained united on vote after vote, leaving the interim Republican leadership under Blunt to assemble separate majorities for each roll call, trading provisions in one bill for votes on another. The budget-reconciliation package, the Defense appropriations and authorization bills, the Labor-HHS-Education bill, and the Patriot Act reauthorization all were pulled at one point or another into a massive round of deal making.

An unexpected addition to the year-end mix was an immigration bill, introduced Dec. 6 by Judiciary Committee Chairman James F. Sensenbrenner Jr., R-Wis., and marked up by his committee two days later. The bill (HR 4437), which the House passed Dec. 16, focused on border security and criminal penalties for illegal immigrants and those who aided them. It was the subject of a raucous floor debate and highlighted deep divisions within the GOP. While House passage was a win for the Immigration Reform Caucus, a group of more than 90 House conservatives, many other Republicans argued that border control had to be paired with a plan to allow "guest worker" visas and give some illegal immigrants already in the country a pathway to legal immigration.

The defense authorization and the Labor-HHS-Education measure, the largest of all the appropriations bills, cleared by voice vote four days before Christmas. The Defense spending bill cleared the same day.

Senate Democrats successfully challenged several provisions of the budget reconciliation bill on procedural grounds, causing the conference report to fall on a point of order. Only the vote of the vice president, which broke a 50-50 tie, allowed the Senate to send an amended version of the bill back to the House for final action in 2006. The bill was signed Feb. 8 (PL 109-171)

Indicative of the horse-trading and rapid change of fortunes in the last days of the session, provisions to open parts of ANWR to drilling were sacrificed to get other high-priority legislation through. The Senate-passed version of the budget reconciliation bill included ANWR. But House leaders concluded they could not get enough votes from moderate Republicans to get the conference report through their chamber as long as the provisions remained.

Stevens, a tireless proponent of opening the wildlife refuge to drilling, agreed to move the provisions to the conference report on the fiscal 2006 defense appropriations bill. That angered enough senators to halt work on the conference report, leaving the leadership with no choice but to drop the language. In a fitting coda to the year, a bitter Stevens told his Senate colleagues, "I'm going to go to every one of your states, and I'm going to tell them what you've done."

# VOTE STUDIES

# Bush Boosts His Success Rate Even While Retreating on Key Issues

B Y ONE MEASURE, President Bush can rightfully claim that 2005 was a successful year for getting his legislative agenda through Congress: He prevailed on 78 percent of the roll call votes on which his administration took a clear position. That is a strong statistic in any year, but even more noteworthy because it was logged during the fifth year of Bush's presidency.

Over the five decades that Congressional Quarterly has analyzed roll call votes in Congress, the longer presidents stay in office, generally the less well they have done at getting what they want.

Not so for Bush.

For the fifth year of a presidency, only the administration of Lyndon B. Johnson (who logged a 74.5 percent success rate) comes close to Bush's score. Even Ronald Reagan, in his fifth year in the White House, won on only 59.9 percent of the votes where he took a position. And Reagan's fellow Republicans voted against his positions about a fourth of the time.

This high presidential success score, though, is at odds with what is generally viewed as a complex relationship between Bush and the Republican-led Congress. The White House during 2005 often had to work hard to get its way against push-back from a unified wall of Democrats and defiant Republican dissenters.

While the president made sizable progress on his agenda early in the year, that was followed by a series of retreats and defeats — on treatment of military detainees, drilling in the Arctic, and renewal of the Patriot Act — late in the session. And there were some issues on Bush's agenda, such as a Social Security overhaul and another round of tax cuts, that didn't make it to a vote at all.

Finally, Bush's support in congressional voting is also based on an extraordinarily low number of votes on which the president could be seen as having a definitive position. Of 669 votes in the House, CQ could determine a Bush position for only 46 of them. That was true for just 45 of 366 votes in the Senate.

That is not because this administration does not have firm positions or convictions, but it does reflect a certain reluctance to get involved in the dirty details of legislative deal making. This has been the case for this administration for each of the five years of Bush's presidency, and it has been in stark contrast to his predecessor, Bill Clinton, who used the "statement of administration policy" more frequently as a tool to lay down markers for the GOP-led Congress. He also used the presidential veto 37 times in his two terms. Bush has not used it even once.

The fact that the administration's tentacles on the Hill are not very long or deep could combine with Bush's low approval rating as well as midterm election pressures to cause more defections in the ranks, analysts say. Those defections are likely to come one issue at a time among those considered marginal allies of the president.

With many public opinion polls showing the president's popularity below 50 percent for much of the second half of the year, Republican lawmakers face a dilemma, said Paul S. Herrnson, director of the Center for American Politics and Citizenship at the University of Maryland.

"As the elections get closer, Republicans in close districts will have to vote against the president's policies when their constituents are strongly opposed," he said.

Said Daniel J. Mattoon, a GOP strategist with Podesta Mattoon in Washington: "I think you have a situation where members are going to start looking out for themselves."

At a time when the parties are jockeying for advantage, and seeking to present a unified front in advance of this fall's elections, the possibility of an every-man-for-himself environment will force House and Senate leaders to adopt what Mattoon calls "a more nuanced leadership."

Those potentially clashing impulses have already begun playing out on such issues as immigration reform, and will develop more fully if Congress decides to take on personal accounts or other major Social Security changes, he said.

## 'A GOOD RELATIONSHIP'

The legislative victories that made Bush's fifth year stand out from those of his modern White House predecessors were largely clustered in the early part of 2005, before Congress' attention became diverted by other demands: hurricane disaster relief; the Iraq death count and public questioning about whether the United States has an end game for the war; and the shakeup in House leadership following the September indictment of Majority Leader Tom DeLay on campaign finance-related charges in his home state of Texas.

The foundation of Bush's success score was built on enactment of long-sought limits on class action lawsuits and bankruptcy filings; an energy bill; a highway and transit bill that closely fit the administration's budget parameters; and the Central American Free Trade Agreement.

In addition, the Senate confirmed more of the judges that Bush wanted on the bench, and without much foot-dragging allowed John G. Roberts Jr. to become chief justice of the United States.

All of these, in addition to being tests of the president's clout, turned out to be picks by CQ's editors as "key votes" for the year. The

# Bush Continues His Run of Victories

Graph illustrates the percentage of the time in the past 53 years that the president won on roll call votes on which he took a clear position. Graph shows House and Senate figures combined. *(Data for each year, p. B-15)*

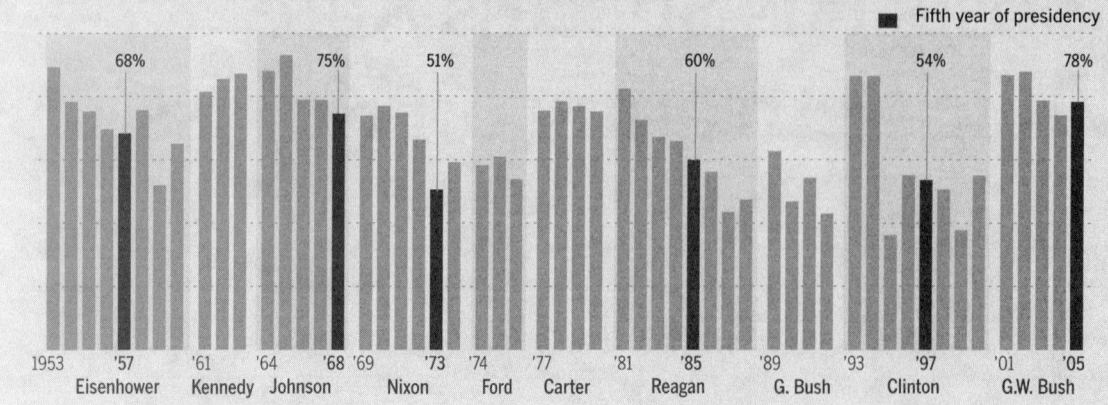

■ Fifth year of presidency

68%  75%  51%  60%  54%  78%

1953  '57  '61  '64  '68  '69  '73  '74  '77  '81  '85  '89  '93  '97  '01  '05

Eisenhower  Kennedy  Johnson  Nixon  Ford  Carter  Reagan  G. Bush  Clinton  G.W. Bush

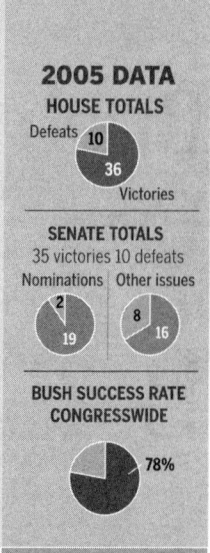

**2005 DATA**

HOUSE TOTALS

Defeats 10
36
Victories

SENATE TOTALS
35 victories 10 defeats

Nominations  Other issues
2  8
19  16

BUSH SUCCESS RATE
CONGRESSWIDE

78%

FOR MORE INFORMATION

| Top scorers | B-7 |
|---|---|
| Background | B-14 |
| List of votes | B-15 |
| House members' scores | B-16 |
| Senators' scores | B-18 |

class action, bankruptcy and trade votes also show up as roll calls that pitted the two political parties against each other on Capitol Hill. *(Party unity, p. B-8; key votes, p. C-3)*

As far as congressional Republican leaders are concerned, backing up Bush on those major initiatives made 2005 a resoundingly successful year. Communication between the White House and Capitol Hill was constant, said House Republican Whip Roy Blunt of Missouri, who had at least temporarily taken the indicted DeLay's place.

And that paid off in major bills that became law, Blunt said. "Your study's indication that our support of the president's proposals is at least equal to what it was in 2004 is an indication that it continues to be a good relationship," he said.

Deborah Pryce of Ohio, chairwoman of the House Republican Conference, acknowledged that the relationship between GOP members and the White House "hasn't always been a bed of roses," but they shared a common goal, she said, and "those people appreciate what's at stake."

"I have seen the Speaker angry with the president. I have seen [White House Chief of Staff Andrew H. Card Jr.] get angry with the Speaker. But they work it out, and they don't do it on the front page, and that makes for trust," Pryce said.

Herrnson at the University of Maryland said the administration has shown that "Republicans can rule, in the sense that they have majorities in Congress and the White House and are pushing their agenda full-speed ahead, rather than governing democratically by reaching out to the other side."

House Speaker J. Dennis Hastert of Illinois has had a longstanding policy of trying to ensure that differences between the White House and lawmakers don't result in floor confrontations where either the Bush administration or GOP leaders lose face. That goes a long way toward shaping Bush's success in Congress.

"We are not going to play unless we play to win," said Ron Bonjean, Hastert's spokesman. "We want to have public discourse and debate, but we want our position to prevail."

In the case of the fiscal 2006 defense authorization bill, that meant keeping the legislation bottled up for months rather than risk a House floor vote on language — attached in the Senate by Arizona Republican John McCain — banning torture, or worse provoking the first presidential veto. Democrats protested loudly but to no avail.

"They are much more interested in partisan advantage than they are in substantial policy, and it is a shame because America is losing because of that," said House Democratic Whip Steny H. Hoyer of Maryland.

Early in the year, when it was clear that a majority of House Republicans were eager to follow the lead of Don Young of Alaska, chairman of the Transportation and Infrastructure Committee, and vote for a highway bill that would break the administration's spending limits, Hastert said he wouldn't allow such a bill onto the floor. Senate Majority Leader Bill Frist of Tennessee made the same commitment and Republicans had to amend the measure on the Senate floor to get around that line in the sand.

## RETREATS AND DEFEATS

Several significant legislative retreats not reflected in House or Senate votes came during a flurry of legislative horse-trading in the last days of the first session of the 109th Congress.

Bush found himself making an about-face and embracing compromise language on the use of torture against U.S. terrorist detainees after both the House and Senate — responding to reports of prisoner abuse at clandestine U.S. detention facilities — added language to the defense authorization bill calling on the administration to report to Congress on conditions in those facilities. And the Senate had added McCain's torture ban not only to the authorization measure but also to the more critical fiscal 2006 Defense spending bill.

House Republican leaders had also kept the conference report on the appropriations bill off the floor in order to avoid facing a vote on the language. But resistance proved to be futile, and on Dec. 15, Bush was standing in the Oval Office with his one-time rival McCain, saying, "We've been happy to work with him to achieve a common objective, and that is to make it clear to the world that this government does not torture and that we adhere to the international convention of torture, whether it be here, at home or abroad."

A day later, Bush retreated again when Congress didn't follow his script and failed to clear a bill that renewed expiring parts of the 2001 anti-terrorism law known as the Patriot Act. He was forced to sign a five-week extension of the expiring provisions that was passed by the House and Senate as Congress was about to adjourn for the year, and after insisting that he wanted a full renewal, not a stopgap of any length.

With the cameras rolling as Bush left the White House for his Christmas vacation, he chose to cast the extension vote as a win rather than a defeat. "It appears to me that Congress understands we've got to keep the Patriot Act in place, that we're still under threat," Bush told reporters.

That sound bite did not, and could not, convey the extent of White House resistance and how just two days earlier Bush's press secretary, Scott McClellan, had pointed a finger at "obstructionist politics" of Senate Democrats and equated their refusal to support a long-term renewal to "putting politics above our nation's security." Also left unsaid: Four Republican senators had voted with 41 Democrats against bringing to a vote the conference report that would reauthorize the law's provisions, and eight Republicans had undermined the president's position by signing a petition calling for a shorter-term extension.

Perhaps the year's biggest retreat was a tactical decision to scrap the Supreme Court nomination of White House Counsel Harriet Miers in the midst of loud outcries from conservatives. Withdrawing the nomination averted the possibility of an embarrassing loss on the Senate floor. And the move also made it impossible to include what clearly was an administration failure in the CQ presidential success scorecard.

Also not on the list of presidential defeats: Congress didn't complete work on a tax cut package — again in the face of bipartisan resistance — and it didn't make any headway on changing the Social Security system to create individual accounts, both White House priorities. Overhauling Social Security had been at the top of Bush's legislative to-do list as 2005 began, but with Democrats solidly united against the proposal and with Republicans not in agreement on whether to buck widespread public opposition, the plan was quietly shelved.

### VETO THREATS

Even with leadership efforts to keep intraparty fights out of the public's eye, the White House intermittently chose to use the whip

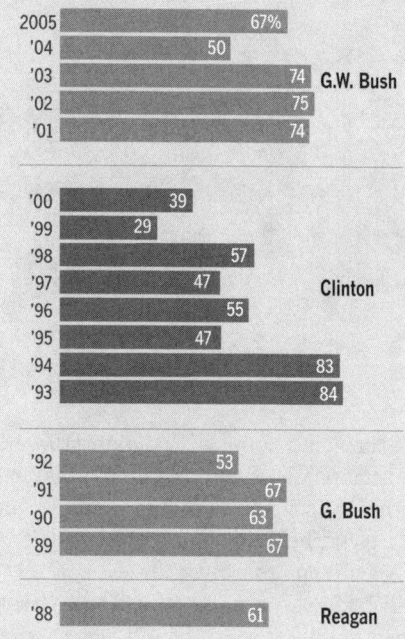

## Senate Support, Minus Nominations

Graph shows the percentage of the time the president won on Senate roll call votes — other than nominations — on which he took a clear position. Data for this series is calculated dating back only to 1988.

|  |  | |
|---|---|---|
| 2005 | 67% | |
| '04 | 50 | |
| '03 | 74 | G.W. Bush |
| '02 | 75 | |
| '01 | 74 | |
| '00 | 39 | |
| '99 | 29 | |
| '98 | 57 | |
| '97 | 47 | Clinton |
| '96 | 55 | |
| '95 | 47 | |
| '94 | 83 | |
| '93 | 84 | |
| '92 | 53 | |
| '91 | 67 | |
| '90 | 63 | G. Bush |
| '89 | 67 | |
| '88 | 61 | Reagan |

of a veto threat.

The Bush administration issued 79 statements of administration policy during 2005, more than the 61 of a year earlier but fewer than the 90 issued in 2003. In 2005, those statements included a raft of veto threats including opposition to Medicare language in a spending cut bill, a bid to lift a ban on imported prescription drugs from Canada in the fiscal 2006 Agriculture appropriations bill, and a Defense department spending bill whose levels the administration deemed to be too low.

The White House also objected to three parts of the fiscal 2006 Transportation-Treasury-Housing spending bill — Amtrak funding, language that would lift a ban on travel to Cuba and an amendment that would restrict the administration's ability to "outsource" federal jobs to private companies. It threatened vetoes on language in the Senate's fiscal 2006 foreign aid spending bill that would overturn the administration's ban on the use of money for abortion counseling, and on a bill that would expand federally financed medical research using embryonic stem cells.

And the White House issued threats over a measure that would overturn the administration's easing of import restrictions on Canadian beef and over provisions in the highway bill.

In spite of those threats, the House defied the administration by supporting stem cell research and limits on federal job outsourcing. In the Senate, the administration lost votes on Canadian beef restrictions and on abortion counseling, often referred to as the "Mexico City policy."

Of the 46 roll call votes in the House and the 45 in the Senate on which the White House had expressed a clear position, according to CQ's editors, Bush lost on 20 — 10 in each chamber. Often, however, where lawmakers defied the administration's wishes and tempted a

## CQ Vote Study Guide

Congressional Quarterly has conducted studies analyzing the voting behavior of members of Congress since 1945. This is how the studies are carried out:

● **SELECTING VOTES.** CQ bases its vote studies on all roll call votes on which members were asked to vote "yea" or "nay." In 2005, there were 669 such votes in the House and 366 in the Senate. The totals exclude quorum calls (there were two in the House in 2005), because they require only that members vote "present."

The totals do include House votes to approve the Journal (eight in 2005) and Senate votes to instruct the sergeant at arms to request members' presence in the chamber (two in 2005).

The presidential support and party unity studies are based on votes selected from the total according to the criteria described on pages B-14 and B-19.

● **INDIVIDUAL SCORES.** Members' scores in the accompanying charts are based only on the votes each member actually cast. That has the effect of making individual support and opposition scores add to 100 percent. The same method is used for identifying the leading scorers on pages B-7 and B-11.

● **OVERALL SCORES.** For consistency with previous years, calculations of average scores by chamber, party and region are based on all eligible yea-or-nay votes, whether or not all members participated. As a result, a member's failure to vote reduces the average support and opposition scores. Therefore, averages are not strictly comparable to individual member scores.

● **ROUNDING.** Scores in the tables for the full House and Senate membership are rounded to the nearest percentage point, although rounding is not used to increase any score to 100 percent or to reduce any score to zero. Scores for party and chamber support and opposition leaders are reported to 1 decimal point to more precisely rank them.

# Frequency of Presidential Support Votes Remains Low

The House and Senate combined for 91 roll call votes in 2005 on which the editors of *CQ Weekly* determined that President Bush took a clear position. That exceeded the 84 so-called presidential support votes cast in 2004, which was the fewest since 1972.

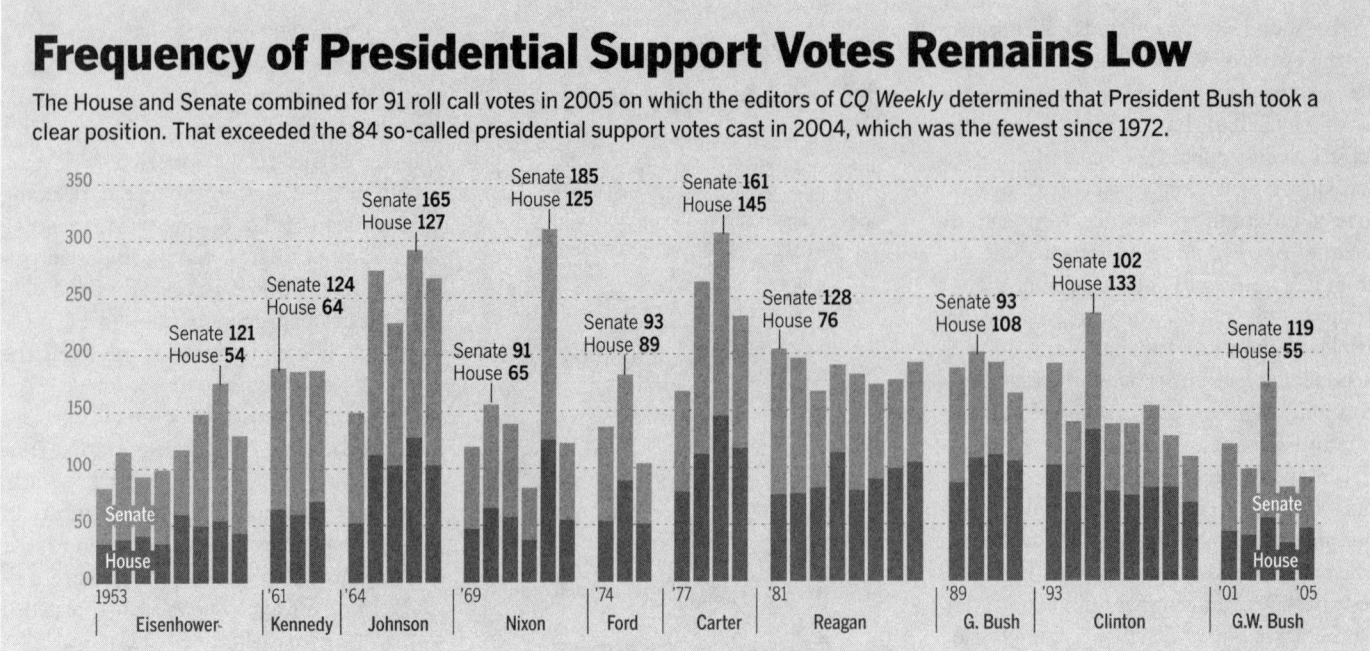

veto, the offending language died in a House-Senate conference committee, as with the outsourcing limits, or the administration was able to claim a compromise, as with the McCain anti-torture language.

"On the major issues, we have been in support of the president," Bonjean said. Where members will differ, he said, "is when it comes to parochial issues, the issues that are more below the radar."

The intraparty debate saw Republican divisions not only along regional lines, but also between groups of increasingly restless conservatives and moderates. Tensions exploded during the debate on the spending cut bill in both the House and Senate.

Congress' most fiscally conservative members began to openly criticize the White House and their Republican colleagues for allowing spending increases that helped widen the federal deficit, and GOP moderates balked at efforts by their partisan brethren to curb spending on such programs as heating assistance for the poor and student aid.

Still, for the most part, fiscal conservatives remained loyal to the White House.

Of Bush's most loyal House members — 13 who had presidential support scores of 93 percent or higher — 10 are publicly identified with the Republican Study Committee, a group of more than 100 lawmakers who champion reduced government spending, tax cuts and conservative social policies. The group claims 19 of the 34 members with support scores of 91 percent or higher. But five members of the group are among the 35 House Republicans who supported the president 75 percent of the time or less. That list includes Jeff Flake of Arizona, an outspoken critic of the administration's refusal to veto certain spending bills and an opponent of Bush's Cuba policy.

Eighteen of those House GOP lawmakers who were least supportive of the president belong to the Republican Main Street Partnership, a group of moderates who were swing votes in some of the administration's 2005 defeats, such as the May 24 vote on stem cells.

Conservatives can also be found at both ends of the spectrum in the Senate, with John Cornyn of Texas supporting the president on 44 of the 45 votes in 2005 on which Bush took a clear position, and Judd Gregg of New Hampshire, chairman of the Budget Committee and a consistent critic of government spending, among the 10 Republicans in the chamber who were least supportive.

Among those Senate Republicans with the lowest presidential support scores were four persistent administration critics: McCain, Susan Collins and Olympia J. Snowe of Maine, and Lincoln Chafee of Rhode Island.

## PARSING THE PERCENTAGES

Though the president set a new standard for fifth-year success, his percentage of winning votes in 2005 is less than it was during his first two years in office. He won on 86.7 percent of the roll call votes in 2001 on which he took a position and 87.8 percent in 2002.

Similarly, while Bush's average support score among House Republicans was 81 percent, a percentage point higher than the previous year, it was lower than any other year of his presidency. And the average Senate GOP support score of 86 percent is his lowest ever.

Democrats, meanwhile, sided with Bush less than ever, supporting his position 38 percent of the time in the Senate and 24 percent of the time in the House. During 2002, Bush's best year among Democrats, his Senate average support score was 71 percent and in the House it was 32 percent on votes where he took a position.

The lack of appeal to Democrats has been intentional. "The president decided after the last election to run an almost Republican-only strategy," said Mattoon.

One case in point was the reauthorization of the Patriot Act. Senate Democratic Whip Richard J. Durbin of Illinois said the administration and Senate GOP leaders might have won the Dec. 16 roll call in which they failed to get the 60 votes needed to invoke cloture and end the filibuster. All the White House had to do was make "a few strategic changes," Durbin said. "They wouldn't hear it. They just said take it or leave it."

## BIGGER FIGHTS, SMALLER VICTORIES

Whether by partisan design or political circumstance, the upshot is that the White House and Republican leaders have to fight harder and sometimes settle for narrower victories.

That was the case when the Senate on March 16 rejected, 49-51, an effort by Washington Democrat Maria Cantwell to strike procedural language in the budget resolution designed to make it more difficult to challenge legislation authorizing oil and natural gas drilling in part

# Leading Scorers: Presidential Support

| | SUPPORT | | | OPPOSITION | |
|---|---|---|---|---|---|

Support indicates those who in 2005 voted most often for President Bush's position. Opposition shows those who voted most often against his position. Scores are based on actual votes cast. Members who missed half or more of the votes are not listed. Scores are rounded to 1 decimal point; those with identical scores are listed alphabetically. *(Complete scores, pp. B-16, B-18)*

### SUPPORT

| Republicans | | Democrats | | Republicans | |
|---|---|---|---|---|---|
| Cornyn, Texas | 97.8% | Nelson, Ben, Neb. | 75.6% | Chafee, R.I. | 44.4% |
| Allard, Colo. | 97.7 | Landrieu, La. | 64.4 | Collins, Maine | 37.8 |
| Allen, Va. | 95.6 | Pryor, Ark. | 57.8 | Snowe, Maine | 33.3 |
| Cochran, Miss. | 95.6 | Lincoln, Ark. | 50.0 | DeWine, Ohio | 24.4 |
| Hutchison, Texas | 95.6 | Salazar, Colo. | 48.9 | McCain, Ariz. | 22.5 |
| Santorum, Pa. | 95.3 | Conrad, N.D. | 47.6 | Smith, Ore. | 21.4 |
| Bond, Mo. | 93.3 | Nelson, Bill, Fla. | 46.5 | Sununu, N.H. | 18.6 |
| Brownback, Kan. | 93.3 | Lieberman, Conn. | 46.3 | Gregg, N.H. | 18.2 |
| Dole, N.C. | 93.3 | Johnson, S.D. | 45.5 | Craig, Idaho | 17.8 |
| McConnell, Ky. | 93.3 | Kohl, Wis. | 45.5 | Coleman, Minn. | 16.3 |
| Bennett, Utah | 93.2 | Baucus, Mont. | 45.2 | Enzi, Wyo. | 15.9 |
| Hatch, Utah | 93.2 | Byrd, W.Va. | 44.4 | | |

### SUPPORT (House)

| Democrats | | Republicans | | Democrats | | Republicans | |
|---|---|---|---|---|---|---|---|
| Wyden, Ore. | 74.4% | Shadegg, Ariz. | 95.6% | Cramer, Ala. | 65.9% | Paul, Texas | 62.2% |
| Kennedy, Mass. | 73.8 | Aderholt, Ala. | 93.5 | Boren, Okla. | 65.2 | Leach, Iowa | 51.1 |
| Harkin, Iowa | 72.7 | Blackburn, Tenn. | 93.5 | Davis, Tenn. | 65.2 | Johnson, Ill. | 45.7 |
| Lautenberg, N.J. | 72.7 | Bonilla, Texas | 93.5 | Skelton, Mo. | 61.4 | Shays, Conn. | 43.5 |
| Biden, Del. | 72.5 | Culberson, Texas | 93.5 | Marshall, Ga. | 58.7 | Johnson, Conn. | 41.3 |
| Corzine, N.J. | 72.2 | Hensarling, Texas | 93.5 | Cuellar, Texas | 57.1 | Smith, N.J. | 40.0 |
| Reed, R.I. | 71.1 | Barrett, S.C. | 93.3 | McIntyre, N.C. | 56.8 | Boehlert, N.Y. | 39.1 |
| Boxer, Calif. | 70.5 | Carter, Texas | 93.3 | Peterson, Minn. | 54.3 | Fitzpatrick, Pa. | 39.1 |
| Clinton, N.Y. | 68.9 | Thornberry, Texas | 93.3 | Edwards, Texas | 52.2 | Jones, N.C. | 38.6 |
| Dayton, Minn. | 68.9 | Johnson, Texas | 93.2 | Holden, Pa. | 52.2 | Bartlett, Md. | 35.6 |
| Sarbanes, Md. | 68.9 | | | Melancon, La. | 52.2 | Simmons, Conn. | 34.9 |
| Schumer, N.Y. | 68.9 | | | Chandler, Ky. | 50.0 | Castle, Del. | 34.8 |
| | | | | Ross, Ark. | 48.7 | Hostettler, Ind. | 33.3 |

of the Arctic National Wildlife Refuge (ANWR) in Alaska. Seven Republicans voted against the administration's position, while three Democrats voted with the president.

Then, in late December, the earlier narrow ANWR victory turned to defeat when the issue surfaced again on the fiscal 2006 Defense spending bill. That time, three Republicans voted against the president's position and refused to end a Democratic filibuster. And then seven Republicans again voted with all but one Democrat to strike the drilling language from the bill.

Just over 53 percent of the House is Republican, and on several close votes GOP leaders had to work extra hard to keep their members in line — as they did during a Nov. 18 vote on the spending cut bill — or woo Democrats to offset Republican defections, as during the July 28 vote on the Central American trade pact. To prevail on that vote, GOP leaders had to count on the votes of 15 Democrats to help offset 27 Republican defectors.

"They are still, at the end of the day, able to twist enough arms to pass their agenda," said House Minority Leader Nancy Pelosi of California. "It appears to be harder for them to do, but they prevail."

"What we are finding is that more and more Republicans are questioning some of the basic tenets of the Bush administration," Durbin said.

To the long-frustrated minority party, what seems to stand out about Bush's success with Congress over the year that just concluded is not how often Republicans had to scramble to deliver victories but how infrequently the president had to walk away empty-handed.

Hoyer expressed surprise that the president's success score wasn't higher. "This president is the first president that I know of who has never vetoed a bill," Hoyer said. "Why? Because this Congress is complacent and complicit and if [Bush] doesn't want it sent down there, if they [administration officials] don't want it passed, they don't pass it."

Bush does have that unbroken no-veto record. If it continues, he will be in the company of Thomas Jefferson, the only two-term president

never to return a bill to Congress.

During the 2006 congressional elections, Democrats want to turn that record into a liability for vulnerable Republicans. "What we'll say is if you want an independent representative for your district, vote Democratic. If you want a rubber stamp, vote Republican," Pelosi said.

Complaints of excess partisanship flow both ways and Republican leaders say that reaching out to Democrats is too often a waste of their time. After being repeatedly rebuffed across the aisle, several GOP leaders said, they became more determined to defend administration initiatives that might otherwise get a more critical reception.

"There has been an unusual and disappointing level of partisanship coming from the Democratic minority, and it has made it more difficult to bring issues together," said Bob Stevenson, a spokesman for

Frist. "In some ways that has galvanized the Republican majority."

Sen. Trent Lott agreed. "Every time Republicans get mad with the administration, the Democrats misplay or overplay their hand and make us mad and drive us right back into the arms of the president," the Mississippi Republican said.

That has been especially true on issues related to the administration's actions in Iraq and its anti-terrorism effort, Lott said. "They don't leave the Republicans any running room to maneuver away from what the president is trying to do," he said.

Whatever the causes, the effects are clear. "Especially in the House, Republicans understand that in order to pass major pieces of legislation, they need to stick together," said GOP strategist Mattoon. "They will get very little help from the Democrats."

# House Democrats Reach Record Unity

THERE WAS A TIME when to be a Democrat in Congress was akin to belonging to a luncheon club just so you could eat the food and enjoy the people. Staying for the program wasn't such a priority. No longer. Democrats on Capitol Hill are relying more on what has been the GOP political playbook, staying in step and sometimes getting tough with those who miss a beat.

A decade after Republicans determined there was value in strict adherence to party discipline, the message has sunk in on the other side of the aisle, and 2005 was a breakout year. Over the past half-century, Democrats in the House were never more unified, an analysis of roll call votes by Congressional Quarterly shows. And only twice before, in 1999 and 2001, were Senate Democrats more united than in 2005.

At the same time, House Republicans, who have played at this game much longer, increased their party loyalty a bit over 2004, though they didn't quite meet the record they set in 1995 — the year they took command of the chamber for the first time in four decades — and reached twice since in 2001 and 2003. Only Senate Republicans fell off the pace in 2005, dropping well below the level of partisan cohesion they reached in 2003. That year, in fact, still appears to have been the most partisan in Congress since World War II.

One manifestation of the leaders' demand for loyalty is a rising number of roll call votes on which a majority of Republicans line up against a majority of Democrats: These are party unity votes as defined by CQ. Almost half of the 669 recorded House votes in 2005 met this definition, as did almost two-thirds of the 366 Senate roll calls. Overall, party unity scores show Congress is becoming more divided on more issues more often, leaving little room for compromise on major issues.

Moreover, rising Democratic unity has forced the majority Republicans to work harder to win — and resulted in a few high-profile GOP defeats that also jeopardized the legislative agenda of President Bush.

An utter lack of Democratic support, for example, required Republican leaders to twist arms and make promises to preserve very narrow victories in both chambers on a spending cut bill that still must survive one more test in the House in 2006. Likewise, most Democrats refused to vote for the Central American Free Trade Agreement (CAFTA) — the centerpiece of Bush's trade agenda — leaving Republicans to scramble to win sufficient support from within their own ranks. And when House Democrats held tighter than the Republicans on a bill to permit federally financed medical research using embryonic stem cells, the GOP and the president both suffered a loss.

It's no coincidence that all three of those votes show up in a companion CQ analysis of the president's influence and were picked by CQ's editors as among the 28 "key votes" of 2005. (Presidential support, p. B-3; key votes, p. C-3)

"Democrats are emboldened," said Sarah Binder, a senior fellow at the Brookings Institution in Washington. "Democrats . . . are going to be more cohesive when they're in the minority when they think they have an incentive to regain the majority."

House Democratic Leader Nancy Pelosi of California showed that she has learned from former House Majority Leader Tom DeLay of Texas and other GOP practitioners of strong-arm tactics to keep her caucus aligned. So serious have Democrats become about catching up — both at the ballot box and in party discipline — that in mid-December, Pelosi lambasted Edolphus Towns of New York for being absent during a crucial roll call on the spending cut bill that Republicans won by two votes.

Pelosi threatened to yank Towns' seat on the Energy and Commerce Committee, which would ordinarily be a high price to pay for a single missed roll call. But Towns was a repeat offender in Pelosi's book, having helped the opposition by voting in favor of the Central American trade pact in July. Then, as well, the GOP had prevailed by two votes.

"Traditionally we haven't been this unified," said Rep. Jim McDermott, D-Wash., who voted with his party colleagues 99 percent of the time in 2005.

He gave credit to Pelosi, a liberal Californian who critics said early on would be too out of step with the mainstream to be an effective leader. "It's primarily a reflection of Nancy's leadership as a persuasive voice to people all across the board," he said. "You can't dismiss her as some wild-eyed San Francisco liberal."

The evidence of rising unity is in the numbers: House Democrats voted with their party colleagues a record 88 percent of the time in 2005, just below the 90 percent average party support score House Republicans posted. The previous high for House Democrats was 87 percent in 2003; House Republicans reached 91 percent that year, in 2001 and in 1995.

In the Senate, both parties stuck together 88 percent of the time in 2005. For Democrats, that was a jump from an 83 percent average party support score in 2004, and just a hair below their record of 89 percent set in 1999 and 2001. For Senate Republicans, the drop in support from a record 94 percent in 2003 and a 90 percent score in 2004 helps

# Partisanship High as Democrats Still Lag Behind GOP

House Democrats were more unified than ever in 2005, voting on average with the party majority 88 percent of the time. House Republicans remained the most united group in Congress, with a 90 percent party unity score, close to an all-time high. In the Senate, Republicans supported the party position slightly less often than a year earlier, while Democrats rallied together more frequently.

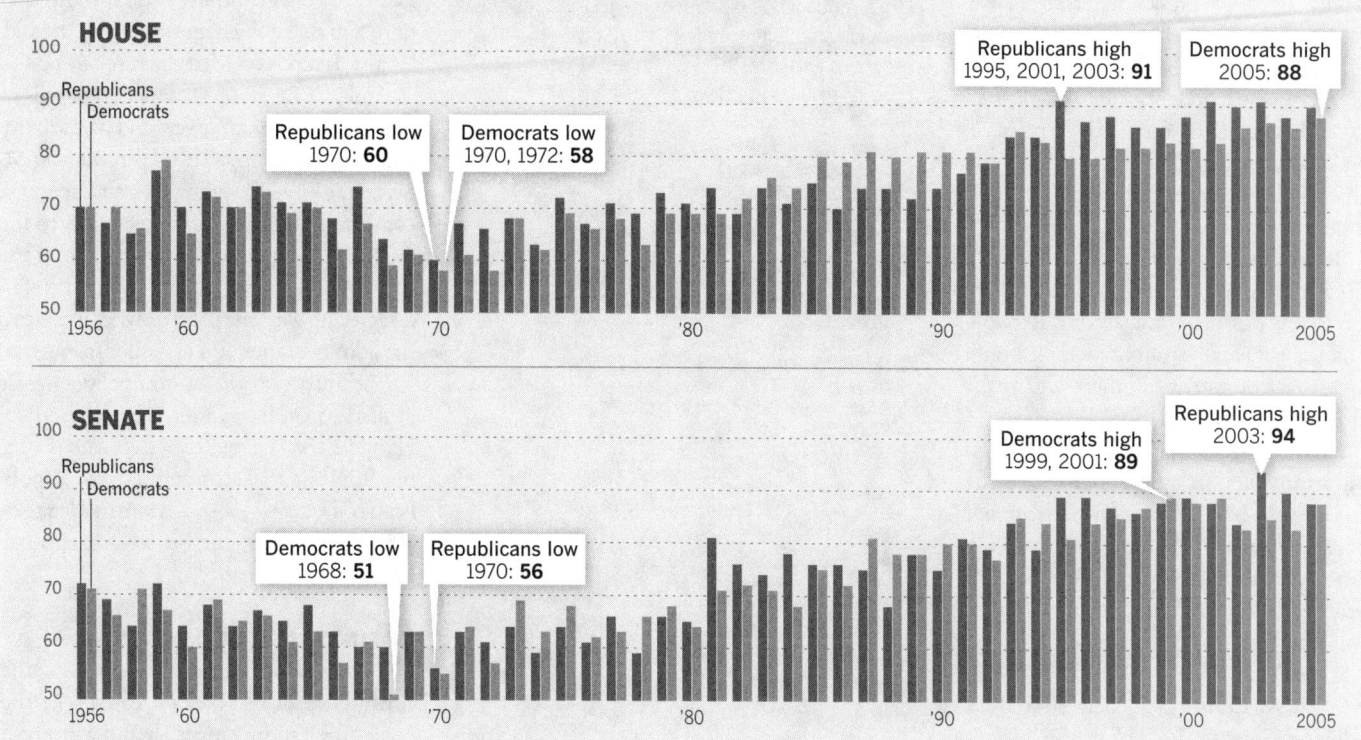

explain why they lost several critical votes in the days before Congress adjourned for the year.

"In the last six months, it's clearly been a more partisan place," said Todd Akin of Missouri, one of five House Republicans who voted with his party more than 99 percent of the time in 2005. "It's a precursor to a rigorous election season."

Still, GOP leaders scoff at the idea that Democrats are making any headway. And Republicans say they have remained remarkably unified considering the political pressures that accompany public sentiment about the war in Iraq and the task of running Congress in the face of increasingly aggressive tactics by the minority Democrats.

"On the issues that are most important to the American people, the Republicans have been united," said Amy Call, a spokeswoman for Senate Majority Leader Bill Frist of Tennessee, who at times has struggled to control his chamber.

## IT'S UNANIMOUS

Rising Democratic unity can also be seen in the frequency with which lawmakers voted unanimously on party unity roll calls. For years, GOP leader have managed often to squelch defections in their ranks — and in the notable partisan year of 2003, Republicans on both sides of the Capitol were unanimous on 239 party unity votes.

Democrats rose to the occasion, voting unanimously 82 times in the House and 69 times in the Senate. Those totals essentially matched the 91 times that Republicans voted unanimously in the House and the 59 times they did so in the Senate.

"I can't remember as many votes with 100 percent Democrats as we've had in the past couple of months," said House Minority Whip Steny H. Hoyer of Maryland.

Hoyer attributed the cohesion of his party's caucus to a coming of age of Pelosi's leadership — which has been under fire as Democrats struggled the past few years — and to what he termed "an exclusively partisan agenda" on the part of GOP leaders. "Whether you are conservative, liberal or moderate you find yourself disagreeing with the Republicans," he said.

He may have a point that is borne out in declining individual party unity scores for at least a dozen moderates in the Republican Party who feel alienated, as well as for some fiscal conservatives in the House who voted against Republican spending initiatives they thought were too expensive. At the same time, party unity scores for some moderate Democrats also fell in 2005, suggesting that disaffection with the deeper partisan strains of the leadership extends across the aisle.

The shift by moderates was especially evident among blue-state Republican senators, such as Susan Collins and Olympia J. Snowe of Maine, who have found it increasingly difficult to stick with their party on close votes. Collins' support score declined 19 points to 59 percent, and Snowe's score dropped 15 points to 56 percent.

Their defections, like that of Lincoln Cha-

### 2005 DATA
**AVERAGE PARTY UNITY SCORE**

All Republicans: 90 percent
All Democrats: 88 percent

**HOUSE**
Republicans    Democrats
90%            88%

**SENATE**
Republicans    Democrats
88%            88%

**VOTES**

|  | SENATE | HOUSE |
|---|---|---|
| PARTISAN VOTES | 229 | 328 |
| TOTAL | 366 | 669 |
|  | 63% | 49% |

**FOR MORE INFORMATION**

| Top scorers | B-11 |
|---|---|
| Background | B-19 |
| History | B-20 |
| Senators' scores | B-24 |
| House members' scores | B-26 |

fee of Rhode Island, who backed his party less than half the time in 2005, will undoubtedly make it harder for Frist to accomplish his goals. Next year is Frist's last to make his mark as a legislator and a leader in preparation for a possible presidential run in 2008. He will not seek re-election to the Senate when his term ends in 2006.

Chafee, who represents a state that Democratic Sen. John Kerry carried by 20 points in the 2004 presidential election, says he isn't ashamed that he stayed with his party on only 47 percent of the party unity votes.

"I strive for consistency," he said with a chuckle when informed that his party support score was dead last among Republicans for the sixth straight year. "I would hope that consistency is there and that's what Rhode Islanders want."

Senate moderates have always been an important bloc in a chamber where the minority can block almost any legislation if they can muster 40 votes to sustain a filibuster. But over the past year, GOP moderates became a more significant voting bloc in the House, too.

Michael N. Castle of Delaware, Christopher Shays of Connecticut, Mark Steven Kirk of Illinois, Sherwood Boehlert of New York and Nancy L. Johnson of Connecticut are among a handful whose party support scores dropped. While moderates have often been ignored by conservative leaders in the House, their power was on display briefly when they blocked passage of the spending cut measure and demanded that a provision be removed that would have allowed oil and natural gas drilling in the Arctic National Wildlife Refuge.

"Moderate Republicans represent that old silent majority," said Wayne T. Gilchrest of Maryland, whose party support score dropped to 80 percent from 85 percent. "This is the dawning of a new day."

Some moderate Senate Democrats also shied from their party. Thomas R. Carper of Delaware, Mary L. Landrieu of Louisiana, Ben Nelson of Nebraska and Kent Conrad of North Dakota all voted with Republicans more often in 2005 than in 2004. Nelson was last among Democrats, voting with his party only 46 percent of the time.

### ELECTION WORRIES

And while Nelson's supporters in the strongly Republican state of Nebraska may remain comfortable with his record of defections, some GOP senators facing tough re-election fights in 2006 are finding similar reasons to occasionally abandon their party.

Mike DeWine of Ohio, who has trailed in his 2006 re-election campaign in some public opinion polls, saw his party support score drop to 70 percent from 79 percent. Chafee, who already has a primary challenger, dropped to 47 percent from 65 percent. Even the reliably conservative Rick Santorum, who trails in Pennsylvania surveys, dropped

## Unanimous Votes Are More Common

This graph shows the number of times that members of one party unanimously opposed a majority of the other party on roll call votes. Unanimous votes have become more frequent. That is especially true for Democrats, who recorded a record 151 unanimous roll calls in both chambers in 2005.

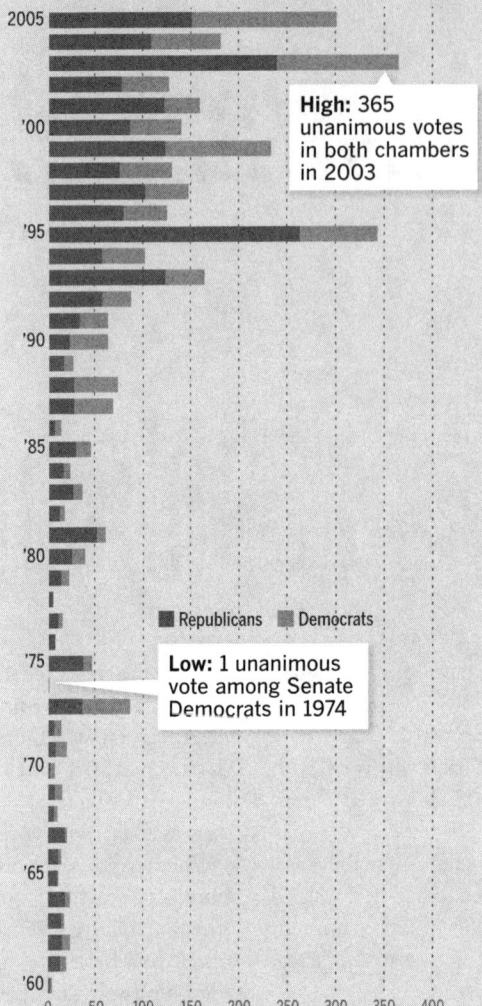

**High:** 365 unanimous votes in both chambers in 2003

■ Republicans  ■ Democrats

**Low:** 1 unanimous vote among Senate Democrats in 1974

to 92 percent in his party support score from 96 percent. That put the chairman of the Republican Conference in the middle of the pack among fellow GOP senators.

Santorum dismissed his decline in party loyalty as having nothing to do with his election. "I'm sure it fluctuates every year," he said. "It just depends on what the votes are on."

And Jim Talent of Missouri, who trails in early public opinion surveys and whose party support score dropped to 84 percent from 96 percent, said he is willing to stand apart on core issues and that his overall loyalty to the GOP is not in question. "I'm not aware of the [party unity] scores, but I am aware when I'm disagreeing with my party or when I criticize the administration" on an issue, Talent said.

The impact of election-year politics wasn't limited to GOP senators. Democratic Rep. Harold E. Ford Jr. of Tennessee, who is running for Frist's Senate seat in a firmly Republican state, came across as more moderate in 2005, as his party support score dropped 7 points to 83 percent.

### OPTIMISTIC DEMOCRATS

Rising Democratic unity is boosting the confidence of the party's leaders. In the Senate, by banding together and winning a few GOP allies, Democrats derailed renewal of the 2001 anti-terrorism law known as the Patriot Act. In fact, they closed the year by winning seven of the last eight party unity votes.

In the House, Democrats rarely win major votes because they are badly outnumbered and the Republicans closely control the debate. But Pelosi has made her GOP counterparts work harder to win. "When I became leader, the Democrats were sort of a co-op. It was an amalgamation of ideas," Pelosi said. "We've decided to define ourselves and our priorities."

On the CAFTA vote, for example, House Republican leaders had to hold the roll call open after midnight July 27 while cajoling some of their more hesitant rank-and-file members to vote for the trade agreement. And on Nov. 17, the first time House leaders brought the conference agreement on the fiscal 2006 Labor/Health and Human Services spending bill up for a vote, all 201 Democrats voted against it, joined by 22 Republicans. Together, they temporarily killed the measure until it could be retooled and brought back to the House floor.

Republicans, meanwhile, have been working to instill party discipline in the next generation of House leaders — freshmen such as Patrick T. McHenry of North Carolina and Bobby Jindal of Louisiana. McHenry backed his party 99 percent of the time on party unity votes. Jindal voted with Republicans 97 percent of the time, and emphasized the few occasions he did not go along with party marching orders. "More important than the number is looking at the particular issue," Jindal said. "There have been times where I voted against the party, like CAFTA."

# Leading Scorers: Party Unity

| SUPPORT | | OPPOSITION | |
|---|---|---|---|

**Support** indicates those who in 2005 voted most often with a majority of their party against a majority of the other party. **Opposition** shows those who voted most often against their party's majority on such party unity votes. Scores are based on actual votes cast. Members who missed half or more of the votes are not listed. Scores are rounded to 1 decimal point; those with identical scores are listed alphabetically. *(Complete scores, pp. B-21, B-22)*

| Republicans | | Democrats | | Republicans | |
|---|---|---|---|---|---|
| McConnell, Ky. | 98.7% | Kennedy, Mass. | 100.0% | Chafee, R.I. | 52.6% |
| Bunning, Ky. | 98.2 | Boxer, Calif. | 98.7 | Snowe, Maine | 44.1 |
| Kyl, Ariz. | 97.8 | Durbin, Ill. | 98.7 | Collins, Maine | 41.0 |
| Allard, Colo. | 96.9 | Sarbanes, Md. | 98.7 | Specter, Pa. | 31.4 |
| Cochran, Miss. | 96.9 | Lautenberg, N.J. | 98.2 | DeWine, Ohio | 29.8 |
| Sessions, Ala. | 96.9 | Mikulski, Md. | 98.1 | Coleman, Minn. | 23.2 |
| Brownback, Kan. | 96.5 | Harkin, Iowa | 97.8 | Smith, Ore. | 17.8 |
| DeMint, S.C. | 96.5 | Reed, R.I. | 97.8 | Talent, Mo. | 16.2 |
| Frist, Tenn. | 96.5 | Kerry, Mass. | 96.9 | McCain, Ariz. | 16.0 |
| Bennett, Utah | 96.4 | Leahy, Vt. | 96.9 | Voinovich, Ohio | 15.8 |
| Grassley, Iowa | 95.6 | Levin, Mich. | 96.9 | Lugar, Ind. | 15.6 |
| Hatch, Utah | 95.6 | Obama, Ill. | 96.9 | Warner, Va. | 13.7 |

| SUPPORT | | OPPOSITION | |
|---|---|---|---|

| Democrats | | Republicans | | Democrats | | Republicans | |
|---|---|---|---|---|---|---|---|
| Nelson, Ben, Neb. | 53.9% | Akin, Mo. | 99.7% | Schakowsky, Ill. | 99.7% | Leach, Iowa | 37.4% |
| Baucus, Mont. | 25.7 | Neugebauer, Texas | 99.4 | Miller, Calif. | 99.4 | Shays, Conn. | 32.9 |
| Conrad, N.D. | 23.6 | Blackburn, Tenn. | 99.1 | Lewis, Ga. | 99.3 | Paul, Texas | 28.4 |
| Landrieu, La. | 23.5 | McHenry, N.C. | 99.1 | Payne, N.J. | 99.3 | Simmons, Conn. | 25.6 |
| Carper, Del. | 23.1 | Musgrave, Colo. | 99.1 | Meehan, Mass. | 99.1 | Fitzpatrick, Pa. | 24.3 |
| Pryor, Ark. | 19.7 | Barrett, S.C. | 99.0 | Van Hollen, Md. | 99.1 | Castle, Del. | 23.6 |
| Lincoln, Ark. | 18.8 | Sessions, Texas | 99.0 | Becerra, Calif. | 99.0 | Johnson, Ill. | 23.3 |
| Johnson, S.D. | 17.0 | Foxx, N.C. | 98.8 | McDermott, Wash. | 99.0 | Boehlert, N.Y. | 23.1 |
| Nelson, Bill, Fla. | 16.2 | Hayes, N.C. | 98.8 | Baldwin, Wis. | 98.8 | Ehlers, Mich. | 21.6 |
| Salazar, Colo. | 16.2 | Cantor, Va. | 98.5 | McGovern, Mass. | 98.8 | Smith, N.J. | 21.4 |
| Byrd, W.Va. | 15.9 | Franks, Ariz. | 98.5 | Pelosi, Calif. | 98.8 | Johnson, Conn. | 20.9 |
| Bingaman, N.M. | 14.6 | Garrett, N.J. | 98.5 | Sanchez, Linda, Calif. | 98.8 | Ramstad, Minn. | 20.1 |
| | | King, Iowa | 98.5 | Woolsey, Calif. | 98.8 | Gilchrest, Md. | 20.0 |
| | | Ryun, Kan. | 98.5 | | | Kirk, Ill. | 19.6 |

## THE MORE THINGS CHANGE . . .

Despite a handful of significant partisan departures, several reliable trends continued in 2005.

For instance, Southern Democrats representing Republican states were the least loyal to their party, while Northern Republicans parted ways with the GOP more often than colleagues from other regions. And strong delegation-wide support for their parties was logged by Texas Republicans, California Democrats and Massachusetts Democrats.

There was no reason to expect the divisive atmosphere in either chamber would change in the second session, with an election coming up and Capitol Hill captivated by the latest installment in the saga of superlobbyist-turned-confessed-criminal Jack Abramoff, whose Jan. 3, 2006, guilty plea rattled the ranks of lawmakers and lobbyists alike.

"Parties aren't letting up," said Binder, the Brookings scholar. "They may look even more partisan in an election year. The minority won't have much incentive to hand victories to the majority."

The GOP majority, in turn, is likely to be highly motivated to stay unified as it strives to give its members opportunities to show a record of accomplishment to the voters who will decide how many Republicans return to Congress next year.

As 2005 wound down, Blunt reflected on the first session of the 109th Congress and public opinion polls showing a negative opinion of the legislative branch, and he professed to see a silver lining in those clouds: the expectation of a positive reaction to the session-closing votes to trim government spending, provide funding for military operations, and provide help for the states devastated by hurricanes Katrina and Rita.

"People's dissatisfaction with gas prices and the war has had an effect," he said. "What we've done over the last three weeks will have a positive impact on people's view of Congress."

# Second Most Roll Calls in a Decade

SENATORS AND HOUSE MEMBERS made more frequent appearances on the floors of their respective chambers in 2005 to cast "yea" or "nay" votes on the issue of the day than in any of the prior three years — reversing a recent trend of declining roll calls and diminished attendance.

House bells rang 669 times in 2005 signaling that members were being asked to cast a vote. That was just shy of the 675 roll calls in 2003 and the second most since 1995, when the House took 867 recorded votes. And while House members were being called to the floor more often, they were also more likely to show up. On average, House members actually cast votes 95.9 percent of the time — the highest percentage since 2001. Moreover, the voting percentage in the House was higher than the chamber's average for the past decade. The Senate was hardly less busy. On 366 occasions in 2005, the Senate clerk called the roll and recorded senators' positions. That was up from a 43-year low of 216 recorded votes in 2004 and a bit above the chamber's 50-year average. Senators, too, were more responsive than in the recent past, voting on average 97.4 percent of the time, above the 95.5 percent for 2004.

Still, while perfect attendance at roll calls is sometimes used by lawmakers as a badge of honor — and while overall the voting percentage for Congress is several percentage points higher during the last decade than it was in the previous 40 or so years — fewer and fewer members seem to make it to the floor for every vote. Only seven senators and nine House members cast ballots on every roll call in 2005, down from 18 senators and 11 House members the year before. Sen. Charles E. Grassley, R-Iowa, has the longest running perfect attendance record of any member of the 109th Congress; the last roll call he missed was in July 1993.

## Perfect Attendance

The following were the only lawmakers who cast "yea" or "nay" votes on every roll call ballot conducted in 2005:

**SENATE**
**Republicans**
Susan Collins of Maine
Charles E. Grassley of Iowa
Olympia J. Snowe of Maine
Jim Talent of Missouri

**Democrats**
Thomas R. Carper of Delaware
Harry Reid of Nevada
Ken Salazar of Colorado

**HOUSE**
**Republicans**
Robert B. Aderholt of Alabama
John J. "Jimmy" Duncan Jr. of Tennessee
Robert W. Goodlatte of Virginia
Mark Kennedy of Minnesota
John Kline of Minnesota
Ralph Regula of Ohio
Fred Upton of Michigan

**Democrats**
Dale E. Kildee of Michigan
Brad Miller of North Carolina

Congressional Quarterly gives lawmakers credit for voting only when they cast a "yea" or a "nay" during a roll call. Very occasionally, members will vote "present" either to avoid a perceived conflict of interest or to stage some form of protest. Often, these votes aren't explained, but regardless of explanation, members who vote present aren't counted by CQ as having participated in the vote.

For Congress as a whole, voting statistics for 2005 were exceptional. The 1,035 roll calls in both chambers made up the third highest total in a quarter-century, and the collective participation rate of 96.1 percent was the fourth highest in that time.

In part, the increase in roll call votes can be explained by a jump in work days. The House was in session 140 days, compared with 110 during the election year of 2004 and 133 in 2003. The Senate met on 159 calendar days in 2005, up from 133 the year before, though fewer than the 167 in 2003.

Especially for the House, sessions on the weekend, Monday or Friday were more prevalent than in the recent past. For several years, House leaders have regularly postponed floor votes for early in the week until after 6 p.m. on Tuesdays and have rarely scheduled Friday sessions, so members would have time to travel to their districts. The House met once on Saturday and twice on Sunday, the first time since 1995 there was more than one Sunday session in a year. Even so, the House met only 11 times on Friday all year long, and just 25 times on Monday.

The Senate, meantime, held two Saturday sessions and two on Sunday, the same as in 2004.

## Lawmakers Answer the Bell More Frequently

Lawmakers were more likely to show up on the floor and vote in 2005 than in the previous year, which was a 12-year low in voting participation for the Senate and matched a 12-year low for the House. Senators voted on average 97.4 percent of the time last year, and House members voted 95.9 percent of the time. For Congress as a whole, the participation rate was 96.1 percent, the highest in four years.

# Voting Participation History

These tables show the number of roll call votes and average participation rates for Congress as a whole and for each chamber since 1953.

| YEAR | ROLL CALLS | RATE | YEAR | ROLL CALLS | RATE | YEAR | ROLL CALLS | RATE |
|---|---|---|---|---|---|---|---|---|
| 2005 | 1,035 | 96.1% | 2005 | 669 | 95.9% | 2005 | 366 | 97.4% |
| 2004 | 759 | 94.2 | 2004 | 543 | 94.1 | 2004 | 216 | 95.5 |
| 2003 | 1,134 | 95.7 | 2003 | 675 | 95.6 | 2003 | 459 | 96.1 |
| 2002 | 736 | 94.8 | 2002 | 483 | 94.6 | 2002 | 253 | 96.3 |
| 2001 | 887 | 96.5 | 2001 | 507 | 96.2 | 2001 | 380 | 98.2 |
| 2000 | 898 | 94.4 | 2000 | 600 | 94.1 | 2000 | 298 | 96.9 |
| 1999 | 983 | 96.6 | 1999 | 609 | 96.5 | 1999 | 374 | 97.9 |
| 1998 | 847 | 95.7 | 1998 | 533 | 95.5 | 1998 | 314 | 97.4 |
| 1997 | 931 | 96.5 | 1997 | 633 | 96.3 | 1997 | 298 | 98.7 |
| 1996 | 760 | 95.8 | 1996 | 454 | 95.5 | 1996 | 306 | 98.2 |
| 1995 | 1,480 | 96.5 | 1995 | 867 | 96.4 | 1995 | 613 | 97.1 |
| 1994 | 826 | 95.0 | 1994 | 497 | 95.0 | 1994 | 329 | 97.0 |
| 1993 | 992 | 96.0 | 1993 | 597 | 96.0 | 1993 | 395 | 97.6 |
| 1992 | 743 | 93.4 | 1992 | 473 | 93.0 | 1992 | 270 | 95.0 |
| 1991 | 708 | 95.0 | 1991 | 428 | 95.0 | 1991 | 280 | 97.0 |
| 1990 | 862 | 95.0 | 1990 | 536 | 94.0 | 1990 | 326 | 97.0 |
| 1989 | 680 | 95.0 | 1989 | 368 | 94.0 | 1989 | 312 | 98.0 |
| 1988 | 830 | 92.0 | 1988 | 451 | 92.0 | 1988 | 379 | 92.0 |
| 1987 | 908 | 93.0 | 1987 | 488 | 93.0 | 1987 | 420 | 94.0 |
| 1986 | 805 | 93.0 | 1986 | 451 | 92.0 | 1986 | 354 | 95.0 |
| 1985 | 820 | 94.0 | 1985 | 439 | 94.0 | 1985 | 381 | 95.0 |
| 1984 | 683 | 91.0 | 1984 | 408 | 91.0 | 1984 | 275 | 91.0 |
| 1983 | 869 | 92.0 | 1983 | 498 | 92.0 | 1983 | 371 | 92.0 |
| 1982 | 924 | 90.0 | 1982 | 459 | 89.0 | 1982 | 465 | 94.0 |
| 1981 | 836 | 92.0 | 1981 | 353 | 91.0 | 1981 | 483 | 93.0 |
| 1980 | 1,135 | 87.0 | 1980 | 604 | 88.0 | 1980 | 531 | 87.0 |
| 1979 | 1,169 | 89.0 | 1979 | 672 | 89.0 | 1979 | 497 | 90.0 |
| 1978 | 1,350 | 87.0 | 1978 | 834 | 87.0 | 1978 | 516 | 87.0 |
| 1977 | 1,341 | 90.0 | 1977 | 706 | 91.0 | 1977 | 635 | 88.0 |
| 1976 | 1,349 | 86.0 | 1976 | 661 | 87.0 | 1976 | 688 | 83.0 |
| 1975 | 1,214 | 91.0 | 1975 | 612 | 91.0 | 1975 | 602 | 89.0 |
| 1974 | 1,081 | 87.0 | 1974 | 537 | 87.0 | 1974 | 544 | 86.0 |
| 1973 | 1,135 | 89.0 | 1973 | 541 | 89.0 | 1973 | 594 | 87.0 |
| 1972 | 861 | 82.0 | 1972 | 329 | 83.0 | 1972 | 532 | 80.0 |
| 1971 | 743 | 85.0 | 1971 | 320 | 86.0 | 1971 | 423 | 83.0 |
| 1970 | 684 | 79.0 | 1970 | 266 | 80.0 | 1970 | 418 | 78.0 |
| 1969 | 422 | 86.0 | 1969 | 177 | 86.0 | 1969 | 245 | 86.0 |
| 1968 | 514 | 80.0 | 1968 | 233 | 82.0 | 1968 | 281 | 77.0 |
| 1967 | 560 | 85.0 | 1967 | 245 | 86.0 | 1967 | 315 | 82.0 |
| 1966 | 428 | 79.0 | 1966 | 193 | 80.0 | 1966 | 235 | 79.0 |
| 1965 | 459 | 87.0 | 1965 | 201 | 87.0 | 1965 | 258 | 86.0 |
| 1964 | 418 | 85.0 | 1964 | 113 | 85.0 | 1964 | 305 | 86.0 |
| 1963 | 348 | 84.0 | 1963 | 119 | 85.0 | 1963 | 229 | 83.0 |
| 1962 | 348 | 82.0 | 1962 | 124 | 83.0 | 1962 | 224 | 80.0 |
| 1961 | 320 | 88.0 | 1961 | 116 | 89.0 | 1961 | 204 | 87.0 |
| 1960 | 300 | 87.0 | 1960 | 93 | 89.0 | 1960 | 207 | 82.0 |
| 1959 | 302 | 89.0 | 1959 | 87 | 90.0 | 1959 | 215 | 89.0 |
| 1958 | 293 | 87.0 | 1958 | 93 | 88.0 | 1958 | 200 | 86.0 |
| 1957 | 207 | 88.0 | 1957 | 100 | 89.0 | 1957 | 107 | 86.0 |
| 1956 | 203 | 88.0 | 1956 | 73 | 88.0 | 1956 | 130 | 89.0 |
| 1955 | 163 | 88.0 | 1955 | 76 | 89.0 | 1955 | 87 | 86.0 |
| 1954 | 247 | 84.0 | 1954 | 76 | 84.0 | 1954 | 171 | 85.0 |
| 1953 | 160 | 87.4 | 1953 | 71 | 88.2 | 1953 | 89 | 84.3 |

# Presidential Support Background

Congressional Quarterly selects the roll call votes used for its presidential support study based on explicit statements made by the president or his authorized spokesmen. **Support** scores show the percentage of roll calls on which members voted in agreement with the president. **Opposition** scores show the percentage of roll calls on which members voted against the president's position. **Success** shows the percentage of the selected votes on which the president prevailed. A member's failure to vote reduces the average scores for his party and chamber.

**Economic affairs** includes votes on trade and on omnibus and supplemental spending bills, which may fund both domestic and defense/foreign policy programs. **Confirmation** votes in the Senate are included only in chamber average scores.

|  | Defense/Foreign Policy | | Domestic | | Economic Affairs | | Overall | |
|---|---|---|---|---|---|---|---|---|
|  | 2005 | 2004 | 2005 | 2004 | 2005 | 2004 | 2005 | 2004 |
| Senate | 67% | 100% | 64% | 31% | 75% | 100% | 78% | 74% |
| House | 73 | 50 | 85 | 78 | 67 | 75 | 78 | 71 |
| Congress | 71 | 60 | 78 | 58 | 69 | 82 | 78 | 73 |

| | Support | | | | | Opposition | | | |
|---|---|---|---|---|---|---|---|---|---|
| | Republicans | | Democrats | | | Republicans | | Democrats | |
| | 2005 | 2004 | 2005 | 2004 | | 2005 | 2004 | 2005 | 2004 |
| Senate | 86% | 91% | 38% | 60% | Senate | 12% | 7% | 59% | 35% |
| House | 81 | 80 | 24 | 30 | House | 17 | 16 | 74 | 66 |

| | Support | | | | | | | | Opposition | | | | | | | |
|---|---|---|---|---|---|---|---|---|---|---|---|---|---|---|---|---|
| | East | | West | | South | | Midwest | | | East | | West | | South | | Midwest | |
| | 2005 | 2004 | 2005 | 2004 | 2005 | 2004 | 2005 | 2004 | | 2005 | 2004 | 2005 | 2004 | 2005 | 2004 | 2005 | 2004 |
| **Republicans** | | | | | | | | | **Republicans** | | | | | | | | |
| Senate | 73% | 85% | 85% | 91% | 90% | 93% | 87% | 91% | Senate | 24% | 12% | 12% | 6% | 8% | 6% | 12% | 7% |
| House | 75 | 74 | 83 | 82 | 83 | 82 | 79 | 81 | House | 24 | 18 | 15 | 14 | 14 | 12 | 18 | 16 |
| **Democrats** | | | | | | | | | | | | | | | | | |
| Senate | 32 | 56 | 31 | 59 | 54 | 64 | 39 | 62 | Senate | 63 | 35 | 59 | 37 | 44 | 27 | 58 | 38 |
| House | 20 | 26 | 19 | 26 | 33 | 39 | 24 | 28 | House | 79 | 70 | 78 | 70 | 63 | 56 | 75 | 67 |

Annual **success** rate combining the results of votes in both chambers of Congress

| Eisenhower | | Johnson | | Ford | | 1984 | 65.8% | 1995 | 36.2% |
|---|---|---|---|---|---|---|---|---|---|
| 1953 | 89.2% | 1964 | 87.9% | 1974 | 58.2% | 1985 | 59.9 | 1996 | 55.1 |
| 1954 | 78.3 | 1965 | 93.1 | 1975 | 61.0 | 1986 | 56.1 | 1997 | 53.6 |
| 1955 | 75.3 | 1966 | 78.9 | 1976 | 53.8 | 1987 | 43.5 | 1998 | 50.6 |
| 1956 | 69.7 | 1967 | 78.8 | | | 1988 | 47.4 | 1999 | 37.8 |
| 1957 | 68.4 | 1968 | 74.5 | **Carter** | | | | 2000 | 55.0 |
| 1958 | 75.7 | | | 1977 | 75.4% | **G. Bush** | | | |
| 1959 | 52.0 | **Nixon** | | 1978 | 78.3 | 1989 | 62.6% | **G.W. Bush** | |
| 1960 | 65.1 | 1969 | 73.9% | 1979 | 76.8 | 1990 | 46.8 | 2001 | 86.7% |
| | | 1970 | 76.9 | 1980 | 75.1 | 1991 | 54.2 | 2002 | 87.8 |
| **Kennedy** | | 1971 | 74.8 | **Reagan** | | 1992 | 43.0 | 2003 | 78.7 |
| 1961 | 81.4% | 1972 | 66.3 | 1981 | 82.4% | **Clinton** | | 2004 | 72.6 |
| 1962 | 85.4 | 1973 | 50.6 | 1982 | 72.4 | 1993 | 86.4% | 2005 | 78.0 |
| 1963 | 87.1 | 1974 | 59.6 | 1983 | 67.1 | 1994 | 86.4 | | |

# 2005 House Presidential Position Votes

Following is a list of 46 House roll call votes in 2005 on which the president took a clear position, based on his statements or those from authorized spokesmen. Votes are listed by roll call number in broad categories and identified by topic.

## Economic Affairs and Trade

| VOTE NUMBER | DESCRIPTION |
|---|---|
| **6 Victories** | |
| 102 | Estate tax repeal |
| 443 | Trade (Central America) |
| 601 | Spending cuts |
| 616 | Trade (Bahrain) |
| 621 | Tax cuts |
| 670 | Spending cuts |
| **3 Defeats** | |
| 430 | Postal Service |
| 547 | Financial regulation |
| 612 | Terrorism insurance |

## Defense and Foreign Policy

| VOTE NUMBER | DESCRIPTION |
|---|---|
| **8 Victories** | |
| 219 | Base closures |
| 254 | Cuba embargo |
| 326 | Aid to Egypt |
| 329 | Andean drug offensive |
| 345 | Cuba travel |
| 346 | Cuba travel |
| 348 | Cuba embargo |
| 548 | Base closures |
| **3 Defeats** | |
| 73 | Iraq embassy |
| 282 | U.N. overhaul |
| 630 | Detainee abuse |

## Domestic Policy

| VOTE NUMBER | DESCRIPTION |
|---|---|
| **22 Victories** | |
| 31 | Immigration |
| 35 | Broadcast indecency |
| 38 | Class action overhaul |
| 46 | Faith-based hiring |
| 121 | Auto fuel economy |
| 122 | ANWR oil drilling |
| 132 | Energy policy |
| 144 | Abortion notification |
| 205 | Stem cell research |
| 216 | Abortions (military) |
| 319 | Privacy (Medicare information-sharing) |
| 414 | Patriot Act renewal |
| 426 | Small-business health plans |
| 445 | Energy policy |
| 449 | Medical malpractice |
| 492 | Faith-based hiring |
| 493 | Head Start renewal |
| 533 | Food industry liability |
| 534 | Gunmaker liability |
| 553 | Frivolous lawsuits |
| 627 | Patriot Act renewal |
| 661 | Immigration |
| **4 Defeats** | |
| 204 | Stem cell research |
| 258 | Privacy (library records) |
| 347 | Federal outsourcing |
| 357 | Federal outsourcing |

### House Success Score

| | |
|---|---|
| Victories | 36 |
| Defeats | 10 |
| Total | 46 |
| Success rate | 78.3% |

# 2005 Senate Presidential Position Votes

The following is a list of 45 Senate roll call votes in 2005 on which the president took a clear position, based on his statements or those from authorized spokesmen. Votes are listed by roll call number in broad categories and identified by topic.

## Economic Affairs and Trade

| VOTE NUMBER | DESCRIPTION |
|---|---|
| **3 Victories** | |
| 170 | Trade (Central America) |
| 303 | Spending cuts |
| 363 | Spending cuts |
| **1 Defeat** | |
| 19 | Trade (Canada beef) |

## Defense and Foreign Policy

| VOTE NUMBER | DESCRIPTION |
|---|---|
| **4 Victories** | |
| 104 | Iraq embassy |
| 167 | Cuba travel |
| 171 | Nuclear weapons |
| 309 | Detainee abuse |
| **2 Defeats** | |
| 83 | International family planning |
| 249 | Detainee standards |

## Domestic Policy

| VOTE NUMBER | DESCRIPTION |
|---|---|
| **9 Victories** | |
| 9 | Class action overhaul |
| 52 | ANWR oil drilling |
| 148 | Climate Change |
| 157 | Auto fuel economy |
| 158 | Energy policy |
| 213 | Energy policy |
| 219 | Gunmaker liability |
| 225 | Mercury emissions |
| 288 | ANWR oil drilling |
| **5 Defeats** | |
| 125 | Highway spending |
| 149 | Climate change |
| 175 | First responder grants |
| 358 | Patriot Act renewal |
| 364 | ANWR oil drilling |

## Nominations

| VOTE NUMBER | DESCRIPTION |
|---|---|
| **19 Victories** | |
| 2 | Condoleezza Rice |
| 3 | Alberto R. Gonzales |
| 10 | Michael Chertoff |
| 87 | Paul A. Crotty |
| 107 | John D. Negroponte |
| 111 | J. Michael Seabright |
| 128 | Priscilla Owen |
| 131 | Janice Rogers Brown |
| 133 | William H. Pryor Jr. |
| 134 | Richard A. Griffin |
| 135 | David W. McKeague |
| 136 | Thomas B. Griffith |
| 190 | Lester M. Crawford |
| 198 | Thomas C. Dorr |
| 245 | John G. Roberts Jr. |
| 265 | Brian Edward Sandoval |
| 266 | Harry Sandlin Mattice Jr. |
| 276 | John Richard Smoak |
| 277 | Susan Bicke Neilson |
| **2 Defeats** | |
| 129 | John R. Bolton (cloture) |
| 142 | John R. Bolton (cloture) |

### Senate Success Score

| | |
|---|---|
| Victories | 35 |
| Defeats | 10 |
| Total | 45 |
| Success rate | 77.8% |
| Success rate, minus nominations | 66.7% |

# HOUSE

**1. Presidential Support.** Percentage of recorded votes cast in 2005 on which President Bush took a position and on which the member voted "yea" or "nay" in agreement with the president's position. Failure to vote does not lower an individual's score.

**2. Presidential Opposition.** Percentage of recorded votes cast in 2005 on which President Bush took a position and on which the member voted "yea" or "nay" in disagreement with the president's position. Failure to vote does not lower an individual's score.

**3. Participation in Presidential Support Votes.** Percentage of the 46 recorded House votes on which President Bush took a position and on which the member was present and voted "yea" or "nay."

[1] Rep. Doris Matsui, D-Calif., was sworn in March 10, 2005. The first vote for which she was eligible was vote 62. She was eligible for 42 presidential support votes in 2005.

[2] Rep. John Campbell, R-Calif., was sworn in Dec. 7, 2005, to replace Republican Christopher Cox, who resigned effective Aug. 2. The first vote for which Campbell was eligible was vote 619; he was eligible for five presidential support votes in 2005. The last vote for which Cox was eligible was vote 453; he was eligible for 31 presidential support votes in 2005. His presidential support score was 90 percent; presidential opposition score, 10 percent; participation rate, 94 percent.

[3] Rep. Randy "Duke" Cunningham, R-Calif., resigned effective Dec. 1, 2005. The last vote for which he was eligible was vote 608. He was eligible for 39 presidential support votes in 2005.

[4] The Speaker votes only at his discretion, usually to break a tie or to emphasize the importance of a matter.

[5] Rep. Jean Schmidt, R-Ohio, was sworn in Sept. 6, 2005, to replace Republican Rob Portman, who resigned effective April 29. The first vote for which Schmidt was eligible was vote 454; she was eligible for 15 presidential support votes in 2005. The last vote for which Portman was eligible was vote 150; he was eligible for 10 presidential support votes in 2005. His presidential support score was 100 percent; presidential opposition score, zero; participation rate, 100 percent.

| | 1 | 2 | 3 | | | 1 | 2 | 3 |
|---|---|---|---|---|---|---|---|---|
| **ALABAMA** | | | | | 50 **Cunningham**[3] | 89 | 11 | 97 |
| 1 **Bonner** | 83 | 17 | 100 | | 51 Filner | 15 | 85 | 100 |
| 2 **Everett** | 85 | 15 | 89 | | 52 **Hunter** | 89 | 11 | 98 |
| 3 **Rogers** | 83 | 17 | 89 | | 53 Davis | 20 | 80 | 100 |
| 4 **Aderholt** | 93 | 7 | 100 | | **COLORADO** | | | |
| 5 Cramer | 66 | 34 | 89 | | 1 DeGette | 16 | 84 | 98 |
| 6 **Bachus** | 88 | 12 | 89 | | 2 Udall | 20 | 80 | 100 |
| 7 Davis | 46 | 54 | 100 | | 3 Salazar | 46 | 54 | 100 |
| **ALASKA** | | | | | 4 **Musgrave** | 89 | 11 | 98 |
| AL **Young** | 78 | 22 | 98 | | 5 **Hefley** | 84 | 16 | 96 |
| **ARIZONA** | | | | | 6 **Tancredo** | 80 | 20 | 100 |
| 1 **Renzi** | 91 | 9 | 100 | | 7 **Beauprez** | 87 | 13 | 100 |
| 2 **Franks** | 91 | 9 | 98 | | **CONNECTICUT** | | | |
| 3 **Shadegg** | 96 | 4 | 98 | | 1 Larson | 15 | 85 | 100 |
| 4 Pastor | 15 | 85 | 100 | | 2 **Simmons** | 65 | 35 | 93 |
| 5 **Hayworth** | 85 | 15 | 100 | | 3 DeLauro | 9 | 91 | 100 |
| 6 **Flake** | 74 | 26 | 100 | | 4 **Shays** | 57 | 43 | 100 |
| 7 Grijalva | 13 | 87 | 100 | | 5 **Johnson** | 59 | 41 | 100 |
| 8 **Kolbe** | 77 | 23 | 96 | | **DELAWARE** | | | |
| **ARKANSAS** | | | | | AL **Castle** | 65 | 35 | 100 |
| 1 Berry | 37 | 63 | 100 | | **FLORIDA** | | | |
| 2 Snyder | 33 | 67 | 100 | | 1 **Miller** | 85 | 15 | 100 |
| 3 **Boozman** | 77 | 23 | 96 | | 2 Boyd | 42 | 58 | 98 |
| 4 Ross | 49 | 51 | 85 | | 3 Brown | 16 | 84 | 93 |
| **CALIFORNIA** | | | | | 4 **Crenshaw** | 89 | 11 | 100 |
| 1 Thompson | 18 | 82 | 98 | | 5 **Brown-Waite** | 83 | 17 | 87 |
| 2 **Herger** | 85 | 15 | 100 | | 6 **Stearns** | 87 | 13 | 98 |
| 3 **Lungren** | 91 | 9 | 100 | | 7 **Mica** | 91 | 9 | 98 |
| 4 **Doolittle** | 86 | 14 | 96 | | 8 **Keller** | 84 | 16 | 96 |
| 5 Matsui, D.[1] | 14 | 86 | 100 | | 9 **Bilirakis** | 84 | 16 | 98 |
| 6 Woolsey | 13 | 87 | 100 | | 10 **Young** | 82 | 18 | 98 |
| 7 Miller, George | 16 | 84 | 98 | | 11 Davis | 26 | 74 | 91 |
| 8 Pelosi | 16 | 84 | 96 | | 12 **Putnam** | 89 | 11 | 100 |
| 9 Lee | 13 | 87 | 100 | | 13 **Harris** | 79 | 21 | 91 |
| 10 Tauscher | 18 | 82 | 96 | | 14 **Mack** | 80 | 20 | 96 |
| 11 **Pombo** | 85 | 15 | 100 | | 15 **Weldon** | 91 | 9 | 100 |
| 12 Lantos | 15 | 85 | 100 | | 16 Foley | 79 | 21 | 93 |
| 13 Stark | 11 | 89 | 98 | | 17 Meek | 26 | 74 | 100 |
| 14 Eshoo | 19 | 81 | 93 | | 18 **Ros-Lehtinen** | 79 | 21 | 93 |
| 15 Honda | 18 | 82 | 98 | | 19 Wexler | 22 | 78 | 89 |
| 16 Lofgren | 13 | 87 | 100 | | 20 Wasserman-Schultz | 24 | 76 | 100 |
| 17 Farr | 18 | 82 | 98 | | 21 **Diaz-Balart, L.** | 81 | 19 | 93 |
| 18 Cardoza | 39 | 61 | 100 | | 22 **Shaw** | 81 | 19 | 93 |
| 19 **Radanovich** | 86 | 14 | 96 | | 23 Hastings | 21 | 79 | 93 |
| 20 Costa | 42 | 58 | 98 | | 24 **Feeney** | 89 | 11 | 96 |
| 21 **Nunes** | 87 | 13 | 98 | | 25 **Diaz-Balart, M.** | 87 | 13 | 87 |
| 22 **Thomas** | 82 | 18 | 98 | | **GEORGIA** | | | |
| 23 Capps | 11 | 89 | 100 | | 1 **Kingston** | 85 | 15 | 85 |
| 24 **Gallegly** | 85 | 15 | 100 | | 2 Bishop | 47 | 53 | 87 |
| 25 **McKeon** | 89 | 11 | 100 | | 3 Marshall | 59 | 41 | 100 |
| 26 **Dreier** | 89 | 11 | 100 | | 4 McKinney | 16 | 84 | 98 |
| 27 Sherman | 15 | 85 | 100 | | 5 Lewis | 9 | 91 | 96 |
| 28 Berman | 18 | 82 | 98 | | 6 **Price** | 87 | 13 | 100 |
| 29 Schiff | 24 | 76 | 89 | | 7 **Linder** | 89 | 11 | 98 |
| 30 Waxman | 16 | 84 | 96 | | 8 **Westmoreland** | 90 | 10 | 89 |
| 31 Becerra | 16 | 84 | 98 | | 9 **Norwood** | 85 | 15 | 100 |
| 32 Solis | 17 | 83 | 100 | | 10 **Deal** | 87 | 13 | 100 |
| 33 Watson | 9 | 91 | 98 | | 11 **Gingrey** | 87 | 13 | 98 |
| 34 Roybal-Allard | 15 | 85 | 87 | | 12 Barrow | 47 | 53 | 98 |
| 35 Waters | 14 | 86 | 96 | | 13 Scott | 43 | 57 | 91 |
| 36 Harman | 26 | 74 | 93 | | **HAWAII** | | | |
| 37 Millender-McD. | 13 | 87 | 87 | | 1 Abercrombie | 15 | 85 | 100 |
| 38 Napolitano | 14 | 86 | 96 | | 2 Case | 48 | 52 | 100 |
| 39 Sánchez, Linda | 13 | 87 | 100 | | **IDAHO** | | | |
| 40 **Royce** | 89 | 11 | 98 | | 1 **Otter** | 70 | 30 | 100 |
| 41 **Lewis** | 89 | 11 | 100 | | 2 **Simpson** | 91 | 9 | 100 |
| 42 **Miller, Gary** | 89 | 11 | 98 | | **ILLINOIS** | | | |
| 43 Baca | 34 | 66 | 96 | | 1 Rush | 20 | 80 | 100 |
| 44 **Calvert** | 89 | 11 | 100 | | 2 Jackson | 13 | 87 | 100 |
| 45 **Bono** | 80 | 20 | 96 | | 3 Lipinski | 43 | 57 | 100 |
| 46 **Rohrabacher** | 80 | 20 | 100 | | 4 Gutierrez | 18 | 82 | 96 |
| 47 Sanchez, Loretta | 24 | 76 | 98 | | 5 Emanuel | 24 | 76 | 91 |
| 48 **Campbell**[2] | 100 | 0 | 100 | | 6 **Hyde** | 90 | 10 | 87 |
| 49 **Issa** | 89 | 11 | 98 | | 7 Davis | 20 | 80 | 100 |
| | | | | | 8 Bean | 48 | 52 | 100 |
| | | | | | 9 Schakowsky | 9 | 91 | 96 |
| | | | | | 10 **Kirk** | 67 | 33 | 100 |
| | | | | | 11 **Weller** | 86 | 14 | 96 |
| | | | | | 12 Costello | 37 | 63 | 100 |

**KEY**    **Republicans**    Democrats    *Independents*

| | | | |
|---|---|---|---|
| 13 Biggert | 72 | 28 | 100 |
| 14 Hastert [4] | 100 | 0 | 28 |
| 15 Johnson | 54 | 46 | 100 |
| 16 Manzullo | 70 | 30 | 100 |
| 17 Evans | 11 | 89 | 98 |
| 18 LaHood | 69 | 31 | 98 |
| 19 Shimkus | 80 | 20 | 100 |
| **INDIANA** | | | |
| 1 Visclosky | 26 | 74 | 100 |
| 2 Chocola | 91 | 9 | 100 |
| 3 Souder | 87 | 13 | 100 |
| 4 Buyer | 86 | 14 | 93 |
| 5 Burton | 89 | 11 | 98 |
| 6 Pence | 91 | 9 | 96 |
| 7 Carson | 16 | 84 | 96 |
| 8 Hostettler | 67 | 33 | 98 |
| 9 Sodrel | 85 | 15 | 100 |
| **IOWA** | | | |
| 1 Nussle | 85 | 15 | 100 |
| 2 Leach | 49 | 51 | 98 |
| 3 Boswell | 39 | 61 | 83 |
| 4 Latham | 87 | 13 | 100 |
| 5 King | 87 | 13 | 100 |
| **KANSAS** | | | |
| 1 Moran | 76 | 24 | 100 |
| 2 Ryun | 87 | 13 | 100 |
| 3 Moore | 30 | 70 | 100 |
| 4 Tiahrt | 91 | 9 | 100 |
| **KENTUCKY** | | | |
| 1 Whitfield | 87 | 13 | 98 |
| 2 Lewis | 89 | 11 | 100 |
| 3 Northup | 87 | 13 | 100 |
| 4 Davis | 87 | 13 | 100 |
| 5 Rogers | 91 | 9 | 100 |
| 6 Chandler | 50 | 50 | 100 |
| **LOUISIANA** | | | |
| 1 Jindal | 85 | 15 | 100 |
| 2 Jefferson | 26 | 74 | 100 |
| 3 Melancon | 52 | 48 | 100 |
| 4 McCrery | 89 | 11 | 100 |
| 5 Alexander | 89 | 11 | 100 |
| 6 Baker | 91 | 9 | 93 |
| 7 Boustany | 86 | 14 | 96 |
| **MAINE** | | | |
| 1 Allen | 13 | 87 | 100 |
| 2 Michaud | 18 | 82 | 98 |
| **MARYLAND** | | | |
| 1 Gilchrest | 72 | 28 | 100 |
| 2 Ruppersberger | 35 | 65 | 100 |
| 3 Cardin | 22 | 78 | 100 |
| 4 Wynn | 27 | 73 | 98 |
| 5 Hoyer | 24 | 76 | 100 |
| 6 Bartlett | 64 | 36 | 98 |
| 7 Cummings | 17 | 83 | 100 |
| 8 Van Hollen | 15 | 85 | 100 |
| **MASSACHUSETTS** | | | |
| 1 Olver | 15 | 85 | 100 |
| 2 Neal | 15 | 85 | 100 |
| 3 McGovern | 15 | 85 | 100 |
| 4 Frank | 15 | 85 | 100 |
| 5 Meehan | 15 | 85 | 100 |
| 6 Tierney | 13 | 87 | 100 |
| 7 Markey | 15 | 85 | 100 |
| 8 Capuano | 17 | 83 | 100 |
| 9 Lynch | 16 | 84 | 93 |
| 10 Delahunt | 9 | 91 | 98 |
| **MICHIGAN** | | | |
| 1 Stupak | 28 | 72 | 93 |
| 2 Hoekstra | 91 | 9 | 100 |
| 3 Ehlers | 67 | 33 | 100 |
| 4 Camp | 83 | 17 | 91 |
| 5 Kildee | 22 | 78 | 100 |
| 6 Upton | 76 | 24 | 100 |
| 7 Schwarz | 72 | 28 | 100 |
| 8 Rogers | 87 | 13 | 100 |
| 9 Knollenberg | 89 | 11 | 100 |
| 10 Miller | 85 | 15 | 100 |
| 11 McCotter | 78 | 22 | 100 |
| 12 Levin | 20 | 80 | 100 |
| 13 Kilpatrick | 17 | 83 | 100 |
| 14 Conyers | 15 | 85 | 100 |
| 15 Dingell | 26 | 74 | 100 |

| | | | |
|---|---|---|---|
| **MINNESOTA** | | | |
| 1 Gutknecht | 78 | 22 | 100 |
| 2 Kline | 89 | 11 | 100 |
| 3 Ramstad | 67 | 33 | 100 |
| 4 McCollum | 11 | 89 | 100 |
| 5 Sabo | 13 | 87 | 100 |
| 6 Kennedy | 87 | 13 | 100 |
| 7 Peterson | 54 | 46 | 100 |
| 8 Oberstar | 23 | 77 | 96 |
| **MISSISSIPPI** | | | |
| 1 Wicker | 84 | 16 | 98 |
| 2 Thompson | 17 | 83 | 100 |
| 3 Pickering | 82 | 18 | 98 |
| 4 Taylor | 45 | 55 | 96 |
| **MISSOURI** | | | |
| 1 Clay | 16 | 84 | 96 |
| 2 Akin | 91 | 9 | 100 |
| 3 Carnahan | 22 | 78 | 100 |
| 4 Skelton | 61 | 39 | 96 |
| 5 Cleaver | 22 | 78 | 98 |
| 6 Graves | 86 | 14 | 96 |
| 7 Blunt | 91 | 9 | 98 |
| 8 Emerson | 68 | 32 | 96 |
| 9 Hulshof | 83 | 17 | 100 |
| **MONTANA** | | | |
| AL Rehberg | 83 | 17 | 100 |
| **NEBRASKA** | | | |
| 1 Fortenberry | 87 | 13 | 100 |
| 2 Terry | 85 | 15 | 100 |
| 3 Osborne | 76 | 24 | 100 |
| **NEVADA** | | | |
| 1 Berkley | 28 | 72 | 100 |
| 2 Gibbons | 80 | 20 | 96 |
| 3 Porter | 80 | 20 | 100 |
| **NEW HAMPSHIRE** | | | |
| 1 Bradley | 70 | 30 | 100 |
| 2 Bass | 67 | 33 | 100 |
| **NEW JERSEY** | | | |
| 1 Andrews | 23 | 77 | 85 |
| 2 LoBiondo | 70 | 30 | 100 |
| 3 Saxton | 80 | 20 | 100 |
| 4 Smith | 60 | 40 | 98 |
| 5 Garrett | 84 | 16 | 96 |
| 6 Pallone | 17 | 83 | 100 |
| 7 Ferguson | 87 | 13 | 98 |
| 8 Pascrell | 15 | 85 | 100 |
| 9 Rothman | 29 | 71 | 100 |
| 10 Payne | 7 | 93 | 96 |
| 11 Frelinghuysen | 83 | 17 | 100 |
| 12 Holt | 11 | 89 | 100 |
| 13 Menendez | 24 | 76 | 100 |
| **NEW MEXICO** | | | |
| 1 Wilson | 70 | 30 | 96 |
| 2 Pearce | 87 | 13 | 100 |
| 3 Udall | 11 | 89 | 98 |
| **NEW YORK** | | | |
| 1 Bishop | 15 | 85 | 100 |
| 2 Israel | 24 | 76 | 100 |
| 3 King | 83 | 17 | 100 |
| 4 McCarthy | 22 | 78 | 98 |
| 5 Ackerman | 24 | 76 | 100 |
| 6 Meeks | 32 | 68 | 96 |
| 7 Crowley | 15 | 85 | 100 |
| 8 Nadler | 13 | 87 | 98 |
| 9 Weiner | 15 | 85 | 100 |
| 10 Towns | 33 | 67 | 98 |
| 11 Owens | 11 | 89 | 100 |
| 12 Velázquez | 18 | 82 | 98 |
| 13 Fossella | 83 | 17 | 100 |
| 14 Maloney | 17 | 83 | 100 |
| 15 Rangel | 16 | 84 | 96 |
| 16 Serrano | 9 | 91 | 100 |
| 17 Engel | 26 | 74 | 100 |
| 18 Lowey | 13 | 87 | 100 |
| 19 Kelly | 72 | 28 | 93 |
| 20 Sweeney | 82 | 18 | 96 |
| 21 McNulty | 26 | 74 | 100 |
| 22 Hinchey | 11 | 89 | 98 |
| 23 McHugh | 78 | 22 | 98 |
| 24 Boehlert | 61 | 39 | 100 |
| 25 Walsh | 86 | 14 | 96 |
| 26 Reynolds | 80 | 20 | 98 |
| 27 Higgins | 29 | 71 | 98 |
| 28 Slaughter | 14 | 86 | 100 |
| 29 Kuhl | 85 | 15 | 100 |

| | | | |
|---|---|---|---|
| **NORTH CAROLINA** | | | |
| 1 Butterfield | 30 | 70 | 100 |
| 2 Etheridge | 24 | 76 | 98 |
| 3 Jones | 61 | 39 | 96 |
| 4 Price | 16 | 84 | 98 |
| 5 Foxx | 87 | 13 | 100 |
| 6 Coble | 78 | 22 | 100 |
| 7 McIntyre | 57 | 43 | 96 |
| 8 Hayes | 89 | 11 | 96 |
| 9 Myrick | 89 | 11 | 96 |
| 10 McHenry | 87 | 13 | 100 |
| 11 Taylor | 84 | 16 | 96 |
| 12 Watt | 16 | 84 | 98 |
| 13 Miller | 26 | 74 | 100 |
| **NORTH DAKOTA** | | | |
| AL Pomeroy | 41 | 59 | 100 |
| **OHIO** | | | |
| 1 Chabot | 89 | 11 | 100 |
| 2 Schmidt [5] | 87 | 13 | 100 |
| 3 Turner | 85 | 15 | 100 |
| 4 Oxley | 91 | 9 | 96 |
| 5 Gillmor | 88 | 12 | 93 |
| 6 Strickland | 22 | 78 | 100 |
| 7 Hobson | 87 | 13 | 100 |
| 8 Boehner | 91 | 9 | 96 |
| 9 Kaptur | 23 | 77 | 96 |
| 10 Kucinich | 11 | 89 | 100 |
| 11 Jones | 20 | 80 | 100 |
| 12 Tiberi | 71 | 29 | 98 |
| 13 Brown | 7 | 93 | 100 |
| 14 LaTourette | 71 | 29 | 98 |
| 15 Pryce | 84 | 16 | 98 |
| 16 Regula | 85 | 15 | 100 |
| 17 Ryan | 30 | 70 | 100 |
| 18 Ney | 72 | 28 | 100 |
| **OKLAHOMA** | | | |
| 1 Sullivan | 89 | 11 | 98 |
| 2 Boren | 65 | 35 | 100 |
| 3 Lucas | 87 | 13 | 100 |
| 4 Cole | 91 | 9 | 96 |
| 5 Istook | 89 | 11 | 96 |
| **OREGON** | | | |
| 1 Wu | 29 | 71 | 98 |
| 2 Walden | 80 | 20 | 100 |
| 3 Blumenauer | 11 | 89 | 96 |
| 4 DeFazio | 17 | 83 | 100 |
| 5 Hooley | 18 | 82 | 98 |
| **PENNSYLVANIA** | | | |
| 1 Brady | 18 | 82 | 98 |
| 2 Fattah | 11 | 89 | 98 |
| 3 English | 85 | 15 | 100 |
| 4 Hart | 89 | 11 | 100 |
| 5 Peterson | 83 | 17 | 87 |
| 6 Gerlach | 69 | 31 | 98 |
| 7 Weldon | 84 | 16 | 98 |
| 8 Fitzpatrick | 61 | 39 | 100 |
| 9 Shuster | 87 | 13 | 100 |
| 10 Sherwood | 87 | 13 | 100 |
| 11 Kanjorski | 39 | 61 | 100 |
| 12 Murtha | 38 | 62 | 98 |
| 13 Schwartz | 17 | 83 | 100 |
| 14 Doyle | 28 | 72 | 100 |
| 15 Dent | 78 | 22 | 100 |
| 16 Pitts | 85 | 15 | 100 |
| 17 Holden | 52 | 48 | 100 |
| 18 Murphy | 80 | 20 | 100 |
| 19 Platts | 80 | 20 | 100 |
| **RHODE ISLAND** | | | |
| 1 Kennedy | 22 | 78 | 98 |
| 2 Langevin | 20 | 80 | 100 |
| **SOUTH CAROLINA** | | | |
| 1 Brown | 83 | 17 | 91 |
| 2 Wilson | 91 | 9 | 100 |
| 3 Barrett | 93 | 7 | 98 |
| 4 Inglis | 76 | 24 | 100 |
| 5 Spratt | 27 | 73 | 98 |
| 6 Clyburn | 25 | 75 | 96 |
| **SOUTH DAKOTA** | | | |
| AL Herseth | 39 | 61 | 100 |
| **TENNESSEE** | | | |
| 1 Jenkins | 78 | 22 | 100 |
| 2 Duncan | 72 | 28 | 100 |

| | | | |
|---|---|---|---|
| 3 Wamp | 87 | 13 | 100 |
| 4 Davis | 65 | 35 | 100 |
| 5 Cooper | 38 | 62 | 91 |
| 6 Gordon | 46 | 54 | 100 |
| 7 Blackburn | 93 | 7 | 100 |
| 8 Tanner | 38 | 62 | 98 |
| 9 Ford | 35 | 65 | 100 |
| **TEXAS** | | | |
| 1 Gohmert | 88 | 12 | 91 |
| 2 Poe | 81 | 19 | 93 |
| 3 Johnson, Sam | 93 | 7 | 96 |
| 4 Hall, R. | 84 | 16 | 96 |
| 5 Hensarling | 93 | 7 | 100 |
| 6 Barton | 87 | 13 | 98 |
| 7 Culberson | 93 | 7 | 100 |
| 8 Brady | 91 | 9 | 93 |
| 9 Green, A. | 20 | 80 | 100 |
| 10 McCaul | 85 | 15 | 100 |
| 11 Conaway | 87 | 13 | 100 |
| 12 Granger | 91 | 9 | 100 |
| 13 Thornberry | 93 | 7 | 98 |
| 14 Paul | 38 | 62 | 98 |
| 15 Hinojosa | 37 | 63 | 89 |
| 16 Reyes | 39 | 61 | 83 |
| 17 Edwards | 52 | 48 | 100 |
| 18 Jackson-Lee | 28 | 72 | 100 |
| 19 Neugebauer | 87 | 13 | 100 |
| 20 Gonzalez | 26 | 74 | 100 |
| 21 Smith | 89 | 11 | 100 |
| 22 DeLay | 91 | 9 | 93 |
| 23 Bonilla | 93 | 7 | 100 |
| 24 Marchant | 89 | 11 | 100 |
| 25 Doggett | 13 | 87 | 100 |
| 26 Burgess | 89 | 11 | 98 |
| 27 Ortiz | 45 | 55 | 87 |
| 28 Cuellar | 57 | 43 | 91 |
| 29 Green, G. | 35 | 65 | 93 |
| 30 Johnson, E.B. | 14 | 86 | 96 |
| 31 Carter | 93 | 7 | 98 |
| 32 Sessions | 90 | 10 | 91 |
| **UTAH** | | | |
| 1 Bishop | 78 | 22 | 98 |
| 2 Matheson | 43 | 57 | 100 |
| 3 Cannon | 87 | 13 | 100 |
| **VERMONT** | | | |
| AL Sanders | 15 | 85 | 100 |
| **VIRGINIA** | | | |
| 1 Davis, Jo Ann | 79 | 21 | 93 |
| 2 Drake | 89 | 11 | 100 |
| 3 Scott | 13 | 87 | 100 |
| 4 Forbes | 89 | 11 | 100 |
| 5 Goode | 84 | 16 | 98 |
| 6 Goodlatte | 85 | 15 | 100 |
| 7 Cantor | 89 | 11 | 100 |
| 8 Moran | 24 | 76 | 100 |
| 9 Boucher | 33 | 67 | 100 |
| 10 Wolf | 84 | 16 | 98 |
| 11 Davis, T. | 80 | 20 | 96 |
| **WASHINGTON** | | | |
| 1 Inslee | 17 | 83 | 100 |
| 2 Larsen | 28 | 72 | 100 |
| 3 Baird | 18 | 82 | 98 |
| 4 Hastings | 87 | 13 | 83 |
| 5 McMorris | 89 | 11 | 100 |
| 6 Dicks | 24 | 76 | 100 |
| 7 McDermott | 14 | 86 | 96 |
| 8 Reichert | 86 | 14 | 96 |
| 9 Smith | 24 | 76 | 100 |
| **WEST VIRGINIA** | | | |
| 1 Mollohan | 36 | 64 | 98 |
| 2 Capito | 75 | 25 | 96 |
| 3 Rahall | 33 | 67 | 98 |
| **WISCONSIN** | | | |
| 1 Ryan | 80 | 20 | 100 |
| 2 Baldwin | 13 | 87 | 100 |
| 3 Kind | 23 | 77 | 96 |
| 4 Moore | 11 | 89 | 96 |
| 5 Sensenbrenner | 81 | 19 | 93 |
| 6 Petri | 80 | 20 | 100 |
| 7 Obey | 18 | 82 | 96 |
| 8 Green | 85 | 15 | 100 |
| **WYOMING** | | | |
| AL Cubin | 80 | 20 | 100 |

# SENATE

**1. Presidential Support.** Percentage of recorded votes cast in 2005 on which President Bush took a position and on which the senator voted "yea" or "nay" in agreement with the president's position. Failure to vote does not lower an individual's score.

**2. Presidential Opposition.** Percentage of recorded votes cast in 2005 on which President Bush took a position and on which the senator voted "yea" or "nay" in disagreement with the president's position. Failure to vote does not lower an individual's score.

**3. Participation in Presidential Support Votes.** Percentage of the 45 recorded Senate votes on which President Bush took a position and on which the senator was present and voted "yea" or "nay."

| | 1 | 2 | 3 | | 1 | 2 | 3 |
|---|---|---|---|---|---|---|---|
| **ALABAMA** | | | | **MONTANA** | | | |
| Shelby | 89 | 11 | 100 | Baucus | 45 | 55 | 93 |
| Sessions | 90 | 10 | 93 | Burns | 88 | 12 | 93 |
| **ALASKA** | | | | **NEBRASKA** | | | |
| Stevens | 93 | 7 | 98 | Hagel | 89 | 11 | 100 |
| Murkowski | 87 | 13 | 89 | Nelson | 76 | 24 | 100 |
| **ARIZONA** | | | | **NEVADA** | | | |
| McCain | 77 | 23 | 89 | Reid | 38 | 62 | 100 |
| Kyl | 89 | 11 | 100 | Ensign | 89 | 11 | 100 |
| **ARKANSAS** | | | | **NEW HAMPSHIRE** | | | |
| Lincoln | 50 | 50 | 98 | Gregg | 82 | 18 | 98 |
| Pryor | 58 | 42 | 100 | Sununu | 81 | 19 | 96 |
| **CALIFORNIA** | | | | **NEW JERSEY** | | | |
| Feinstein | 40 | 60 | 96 | Corzine | 28 | 72 | 80 |
| Boxer | 30 | 70 | 98 | Lautenberg | 27 | 73 | 98 |
| **COLORADO** | | | | **NEW MEXICO** | | | |
| Allard | 98 | 2 | 98 | Domenici | 89 | 11 | 98 |
| Salazar | 49 | 51 | 100 | Bingaman | 43 | 57 | 98 |
| **CONNECTICUT** | | | | **NEW YORK** | | | |
| Dodd | 33 | 67 | 93 | Schumer | 31 | 69 | 100 |
| Lieberman | 46 | 54 | 91 | Clinton | 31 | 69 | 100 |
| **DELAWARE** | | | | **NORTH CAROLINA** | | | |
| Biden | 27 | 73 | 89 | Dole | 93 | 7 | 100 |
| Carper | 38 | 62 | 100 | Burr | 89 | 11 | 100 |
| **FLORIDA** | | | | **NORTH DAKOTA** | | | |
| Nelson | 47 | 53 | 96 | Conrad | 48 | 52 | 93 |
| **Martinez** | 91 | 9 | 98 | Dorgan | 40 | 60 | 93 |
| **GEORGIA** | | | | **OHIO** | | | |
| **Chambliss** | 91 | 9 | 100 | DeWine | 76 | 24 | 100 |
| **Isakson** | 91 | 9 | 100 | Voinovich | 87 | 13 | 100 |
| **HAWAII** | | | | **OKLAHOMA** | | | |
| Inouye | 44 | 56 | 80 | Inhofe | 91 | 9 | 100 |
| Akaka | 40 | 60 | 100 | Coburn | 91 | 9 | 96 |
| **IDAHO** | | | | **OREGON** | | | |
| **Craig** | 82 | 18 | 100 | Wyden | 26 | 74 | 96 |
| **Crapo** | 84 | 16 | 100 | Smith | 79 | 21 | 93 |
| **ILLINOIS** | | | | **PENNSYLVANIA** | | | |
| Durbin | 33 | 67 | 100 | Specter | 85 | 15 | 91 |
| Obama | 33 | 67 | 96 | **Santorum** | 95 | 5 | 96 |
| **INDIANA** | | | | **RHODE ISLAND** | | | |
| **Lugar** | 84 | 16 | 100 | Reed | 29 | 71 | 100 |
| Bayh | 36 | 64 | 100 | **Chafee** | 56 | 44 | 100 |
| **IOWA** | | | | **SOUTH CAROLINA** | | | |
| **Grassley** | 89 | 11 | 100 | Graham | 89 | 11 | 100 |
| Harkin | 27 | 73 | 98 | DeMint | 91 | 9 | 100 |
| **KANSAS** | | | | **SOUTH DAKOTA** | | | |
| **Brownback** | 93 | 7 | 100 | Johnson | 45 | 55 | 98 |
| **Roberts** | 93 | 7 | 98 | Thune | 86 | 14 | 96 |
| **KENTUCKY** | | | | **TENNESSEE** | | | |
| **McConnell** | 93 | 7 | 100 | Frist | 87 | 13 | 100 |
| **Bunning** | 91 | 9 | 98 | Alexander | 88 | 12 | 96 |
| **LOUISIANA** | | | | **TEXAS** | | | |
| Landrieu | 64 | 36 | 100 | **Hutchison** | 96 | 4 | 100 |
| **Vitter** | 89 | 11 | 100 | **Cornyn** | 98 | 2 | 100 |
| **MAINE** | | | | **UTAH** | | | |
| **Snowe** | 67 | 33 | 100 | **Hatch** | 93 | 7 | 98 |
| **Collins** | 62 | 38 | 100 | **Bennett** | 93 | 7 | 98 |
| **MARYLAND** | | | | **VERMONT** | | | |
| Sarbanes | 31 | 69 | 100 | Leahy | 36 | 64 | 100 |
| Mikulski | 35 | 65 | 96 | *Jeffords* | 36 | 64 | 87 |
| **MASSACHUSETTS** | | | | **VIRGINIA** | | | |
| Kennedy | 26 | 74 | 93 | **Warner** | 89 | 11 | 100 |
| Kerry | 34 | 66 | 98 | **Allen** | 96 | 4 | 100 |
| **MICHIGAN** | | | | **WASHINGTON** | | | |
| Levin | 41 | 59 | 98 | Murray | 33 | 67 | 100 |
| Stabenow | 33 | 67 | 100 | Cantwell | 36 | 64 | 100 |
| **MINNESOTA** | | | | **WEST VIRGINIA** | | | |
| Dayton | 31 | 69 | 100 | Byrd | 44 | 56 | 100 |
| **Coleman** | 84 | 16 | 96 | Rockefeller | 40 | 60 | 93 |
| **MISSISSIPPI** | | | | **WISCONSIN** | | | |
| **Cochran** | 96 | 4 | 100 | Kohl | 45 | 55 | 98 |
| **Lott** | 93 | 7 | 96 | Feingold | 37 | 63 | 96 |
| **MISSOURI** | | | | **WYOMING** | | | |
| **Bond** | 93 | 7 | 100 | **Thomas** | 84 | 16 | 100 |
| **Talent** | 91 | 9 | 100 | **Enzi** | 84 | 16 | 98 |

**KEY**   **Republicans**   Democrats   *Independents*

# Party Unity Background

Roll call votes used for the party unity study are those on which a majority of voting Democrats opposed a majority of voting Republicans. **Support** indicates the percentage of the time that members voted in agreement with a majority of their party on party unity votes. **Opposition** indicates the percentage of the time members voted against a majority of their party. In calculating **average** scores by party, chamber and region, a member's failure to vote lowers the score for the group. The tables below also show the number of party unity votes on which each party was victorious, and the number of instances where each party voted unanimously.

## Average 2005 Party Unity Scores by Chamber

|  | HOUSE | | SENATE | | CONGRESS | |
|---|---|---|---|---|---|---|
|  | SUPPORT | OPPOSITION | SUPPORT | OPPOSITION | SUPPORT | OPPOSITION |
| Republicans | 90% | 7% | 88% | 10% | 90% | 7% |
| Democrats | 88 | 9 | 88 | 10 | 88 | 9 |

## Average 2005 Support/Opposition Scores by Party and Region

| SENATE | SUPPORT | OPPOSITION | HOUSE | SUPPORT | OPPOSITION |
|---|---|---|---|---|---|
| Northern Republicans | 85% | 13% | Northern Republicans | 89% | 8% |
| Southern Republicans | 93 | 6 | Southern Republicans | 92 | 4 |
| Northern Democrats | 88 | 9 | Northern Democrats | 90 | 7 |
| Southern Democrats | 80 | 19 | Southern Democrats | 81 | 15 |

* Southern Democrats and Southern Republicans are those from Ala., Ark., Fla., Ga., Ky., La., Miss., N.C., Okla., S.C., Tenn., Texas and Va. All others are considered Northern.

## Victories in Party Unity Votes

|  | HOUSE | | SENATE | | CONGRESS | |
|---|---|---|---|---|---|---|
|  | REPUBLICANS | DEMOCRATS | REPUBLICANS | DEMOCRATS | REPUBLICANS | DEMOCRATS |
| 2005 | 278 | 50 | 182 | 47 | 460 | 97 |
| 2004 | 213 | 42 | 85 | 28 | 298 | 70 |
| 2003 | 310 | 39 | 250 | 56 | 560 | 95 |
| 2002 | 170 | 39 | 73 | 42 | 243 | 81 |
| 2001 | 177 | 27 | 115 | 95 | 292 | 122 |
| 2000 | 182 | 77 | 114 | 31 | 296 | 108 |
| 1999 | 177 | 58 | 211 | 77 | 388 | 135 |
| 1998 | 216 | 80 | 114 | 61 | 330 | 141 |
| 1997 | 261 | 58 | 104 | 46 | 365 | 104 |
| 1996 | 208 | 48 | 132 | 59 | 340 | 107 |
| 1995 | 561 | 74 | 345 | 77 | 906 | 151 |
| 1994 | 50 | 257 | 41 | 129 | 91 | 386 |
| 1993 | 62 | 329 | 66 | 199 | 128 | 528 |
| 1992 | 54 | 251 | 61 | 82 | 115 | 333 |
| 1991 | 39 | 197 | 57 | 81 | 96 | 278 |

## Unanimous Voting by Parties

|  | HOUSE | | SENATE | | CONGRESS | |
|---|---|---|---|---|---|---|
|  | REPUBLICANS | DEMOCRATS | REPUBLICANS | DEMOCRATS | REPUBLICANS | DEMOCRATS |
| 2005 | 91 | 82 | 59 | 69 | 150 | 151 |
| 2004 | 77 | 70 | 31 | 3 | 108 | 73 |
| 2003 | 109 | 94 | 130 | 32 | 239 | 126 |
| 2002 | 54 | 37 | 23 | 12 | 77 | 49 |
| 2001 | 66 | 1 | 55 | 37 | 121 | 38 |
| 2000 | 67 | 1 | 19 | 52 | 86 | 53 |
| 1999 | 59 | 11 | 63 | 100 | 122 | 111 |
| 1998 | 42 | 8 | 33 | 46 | 75 | 54 |
| 1997 | 63 | 11 | 38 | 35 | 101 | 46 |
| 1996 | 32 | 10 | 47 | 35 | 79 | 45 |
| 1995 | 159 | 17 | 104 | 63 | 263 | 80 |
| 1994 | 38 | 7 | 19 | 37 | 57 | 44 |
| 1993 | 65 | 13 | 57 | 29 | 122 | 42 |
| 1992 | 47 | 18 | 10 | 12 | 57 | 30 |
| 1991 | 18 | 11 | 15 | 19 | 33 | 30 |

# Party Unity History

The table below shows how frequently during roll call votes a majority of Democrats aligns against a majority of Republicans. The tables in the center and at the right show the average party unity support score for each party in each chamber.

| Frequency of Unity Votes | | | House Average Scores | | | Senate Average Scores | | |
|---|---|---|---|---|---|---|---|---|
| YEAR | HOUSE | SENATE | YEAR | REPUBLICANS | DEMOCRATS | YEAR | REPUBLICANS | DEMOCRATS |
| 2005 | 49.0% | 62.6% | 2005 | 90% | 88% | 2005 | 88% | 88% |
| 2004 | 47.0 | 52.3 | 2004 | 88 | 86 | 2004 | 90 | 83 |
| 2003 | 51.7 | 66.7 | 2003 | 91 | 87 | 2003 | 94 | 85 |
| 2002 | 43.3 | 45.5 | 2002 | 90 | 86 | 2002 | 84 | 83 |
| 2001 | 40.2 | 55.3 | 2001 | 91 | 83 | 2001 | 88 | 89 |
| 2000 | 43.2 | 48.7 | 2000 | 88 | 82 | 2000 | 89 | 88 |
| 1999 | 47.3 | 62.8 | 1999 | 86 | 83 | 1999 | 88 | 89 |
| 1998 | 55.5 | 55.7 | 1998 | 86 | 82 | 1998 | 86 | 87 |
| 1997 | 50.4 | 50.3 | 1997 | 88 | 82 | 1997 | 87 | 85 |
| 1996 | 56.4 | 62.4 | 1996 | 87 | 80 | 1996 | 89 | 84 |
| 1995 | 73.2 | 68.8 | 1995 | 91 | 80 | 1995 | 89 | 81 |
| 1994 | 61.8 | 51.7 | 1994 | 84 | 83 | 1994 | 79 | 84 |
| 1993 | 65.5 | 67.1 | 1993 | 84 | 85 | 1993 | 84 | 85 |
| 1992 | 64.5 | 53.0 | 1992 | 79 | 79 | 1992 | 79 | 77 |
| 1991 | 55.1 | 49.3 | 1991 | 77 | 81 | 1991 | 81 | 80 |
| 1990 | 49.1 | 54.3 | 1990 | 74 | 81 | 1990 | 75 | 80 |
| 1989 | 56.3 | 35.3 | 1989 | 72 | 81 | 1989 | 78 | 78 |
| 1988 | 47.0 | 42.5 | 1988 | 74 | 80 | 1988 | 68 | 78 |
| 1987 | 63.7 | 40.7 | 1987 | 74 | 81 | 1987 | 75 | 81 |
| 1986 | 56.5 | 52.3 | 1986 | 70 | 79 | 1986 | 76 | 72 |
| 1985 | 61.0 | 49.6 | 1985 | 75 | 80 | 1985 | 76 | 75 |
| 1984 | 47.1 | 40.0 | 1984 | 71 | 74 | 1984 | 78 | 68 |
| 1983 | 55.6 | 43.7 | 1983 | 74 | 76 | 1983 | 74 | 71 |
| 1982 | 36.4 | 43.4 | 1982 | 69 | 72 | 1982 | 76 | 72 |
| 1981 | 37.4 | 47.8 | 1981 | 74 | 69 | 1981 | 81 | 71 |
| 1980 | 37.6 | 45.8 | 1980 | 71 | 69 | 1980 | 65 | 64 |
| 1979 | 47.3 | 46.7 | 1979 | 73 | 69 | 1979 | 66 | 68 |
| 1978 | 33.2 | 45.2 | 1978 | 69 | 63 | 1978 | 59 | 66 |
| 1977 | 42.2 | 42.4 | 1977 | 71 | 68 | 1977 | 66 | 63 |
| 1976 | 35.9 | 37.2 | 1976 | 67 | 66 | 1976 | 61 | 62 |
| 1975 | 48.4 | 47.8 | 1975 | 72 | 69 | 1975 | 64 | 68 |
| 1974 | 29.4 | 44.3 | 1974 | 63 | 62 | 1974 | 59 | 63 |
| 1973 | 41.8 | 39.9 | 1973 | 68 | 68 | 1973 | 64 | 69 |
| 1972 | 27.1 | 36.5 | 1972 | 66 | 58 | 1972 | 61 | 57 |
| 1971 | 37.8 | 41.6 | 1971 | 67 | 61 | 1971 | 63 | 64 |
| 1970 | 27.1 | 35.2 | 1970 | 60 | 58 | 1970 | 56 | 55 |
| 1969 | 31.1 | 36.3 | 1969 | 62 | 61 | 1969 | 63 | 63 |
| 1968 | 35.2 | 32.0 | 1968 | 64 | 59 | 1968 | 60 | 51 |
| 1967 | 36.3 | 34.6 | 1967 | 74 | 67 | 1967 | 60 | 61 |
| 1966 | 41.5 | 50.2 | 1966 | 68 | 62 | 1966 | 63 | 57 |
| 1965 | 52.2 | 41.9 | 1965 | 71 | 70 | 1965 | 68 | 63 |
| 1964 | 54.9 | 35.7 | 1964 | 71 | 69 | 1964 | 65 | 61 |
| 1963 | 48.7 | 47.2 | 1963 | 74 | 73 | 1963 | 67 | 66 |
| 1962 | 46.0 | 41.1 | 1962 | 70 | 70 | 1962 | 64 | 65 |
| 1961 | 50.0 | 62.3 | 1961 | 73 | 72 | 1961 | 68 | 69 |
| 1960 | 52.7 | 36.7 | 1960 | 70 | 65 | 1960 | 64 | 60 |
| 1959 | 55.2 | 47.9 | 1959 | 77 | 79 | 1959 | 72 | 67 |
| 1958 | 39.8 | 43.5 | 1958 | 65 | 66 | 1958 | 64 | 71 |
| 1957 | 59.0 | 35.5 | 1957 | 67 | 70 | 1957 | 69 | 66 |
| 1956 | 43.8 | 53.1 | 1956 | 70 | 70 | 1956 | 72 | 71 |
| 1955 | 40.8 | 29.9 | | | | | | |
| 1954 | 38.2 | 48.0 | | | | | | |
| 1953 | 52.1 | 51.7 | | | | | | |

## Number of Party Unity Votes

In the House in 2005, the two parties aligned against each other on 328 of 669 roll call votes, or 49.0 percent. In the Senate, the parties opposed each other on 229 of 366 roll calls, or 62.6 percent. A list of roll call numbers that were party unity votes is available upon request from Congressional Quarterly.

Calculations of average scores by chamber, party and region are based on all eligible yea-or-nay votes, whether or not all members participated. As a result, a member's failure to vote reduces the average support and opposition scores. Therefore, averages are not strictly comparable to individual member scores.

Also, in the individual member score tables, Sen. James M. Jeffords, I-Vt., and Rep. Bernard Sanders, I-Vt., are treated as if they were Democrats in calculating their support and opposition scores. However, Jeffords' and Sanders' scores are not included in the Democratic Party averages for the Senate and House.

# SENATE

**1. Party Unity.** Percentage of recorded party unity votes in 2005 on which a senator voted "yea" or "nay" in agreement with a majority of his or her party. (Party unity roll calls are those on which a majority of voting Democrats opposed a majority of voting Republicans.) Percentages are based on votes cast; thus, failure to vote does not lower a member's score.

**2. Party Opposition.** Percentage of recorded party unity votes in 2005 on which a senator voted "yea" or "nay" in disagreement with a majority of his or her party. Percentages are based on votes cast; thus, failure to vote does not lower a member's score.

**3. Participation in Party Unity Votes.** Percentage of the 229 recorded Senate party unity votes in 2005 on which a senator was present and voted "yea" or "nay."

| | 1 | 2 | 3 | | 1 | 2 | 3 |
|---|---|---|---|---|---|---|---|
| **ALABAMA** | | | | **MONTANA** | | | |
| **Shelby** | 94 | 6 | 99 | Baucus | 74 | 26 | 99 |
| **Sessions** | 97 | 3 | 99 | **Burns** | 94 | 6 | 98 |
| **ALASKA** | | | | **NEBRASKA** | | | |
| **Stevens** | 95 | 5 | 99 | **Hagel** | 94 | 6 | 99 |
| **Murkowski** | 93 | 7 | 99 | Nelson | 46 | 54 | 99 |
| **ARIZONA** | | | | **NEVADA** | | | |
| **McCain** | 84 | 16 | 96 | Reid | 92 | 8 | 100 |
| **Kyl** | 98 | 2 | 99 | **Ensign** | 94 | 6 | 99 |
| **ARKANSAS** | | | | **NEW HAMPSHIRE** | | | |
| Lincoln | 81 | 19 | 100 | **Gregg** | 91 | 9 | 99 |
| Pryor | 80 | 20 | 99 | **Sununu** | 87 | 13 | 96 |
| **CALIFORNIA** | | | | **NEW JERSEY** | | | |
| Feinstein | 92 | 8 | 98 | Corzine | 97 | 3 | 65 |
| Boxer | 99 | 1 | 97 | Lautenberg | 98 | 2 | 99 |
| **COLORADO** | | | | **NEW MEXICO** | | | |
| **Allard** | 97 | 3 | 99 | **Domenici** | 93 | 7 | 96 |
| Salazar | 84 | 16 | 100 | Bingaman | 85 | 15 | 99 |
| **CONNECTICUT** | | | | **NEW YORK** | | | |
| Dodd | 94 | 6 | 97 | Schumer | 93 | 7 | 99 |
| Lieberman | 90 | 10 | 95 | Clinton | 96 | 4 | 96 |
| **DELAWARE** | | | | **NORTH CAROLINA** | | | |
| Biden | 89 | 11 | 96 | **Dole** | 93 | 7 | 100 |
| Carper | 77 | 23 | 100 | **Burr** | 95 | 5 | 99 |
| **FLORIDA** | | | | **NORTH DAKOTA** | | | |
| Nelson | 84 | 16 | 99 | Conrad | 76 | 24 | 96 |
| **Martinez** | 94 | 6 | 98 | Dorgan | 88 | 12 | 97 |
| **GEORGIA** | | | | **OHIO** | | | |
| **Chambliss** | 95 | 5 | 99 | **DeWine** | 70 | 30 | 99 |
| **Isakson** | 95 | 5 | 99 | **Voinovich** | 84 | 16 | 99 |
| **HAWAII** | | | | **OKLAHOMA** | | | |
| Inouye | 90 | 10 | 86 | **Inhofe** | 94 | 6 | 99 |
| Akaka | 96 | 4 | 100 | **Coburn** | 93 | 7 | 99 |
| **IDAHO** | | | | **OREGON** | | | |
| **Craig** | 93 | 7 | 99 | Wyden | 94 | 6 | 100 |
| **Crapo** | 95 | 5 | 99 | **Smith** | 82 | 18 | 98 |
| **ILLINOIS** | | | | **PENNSYLVANIA** | | | |
| Durbin | 99 | 1 | 99 | **Specter** | 69 | 31 | 97 |
| Obama | 97 | 3 | 99 | **Santorum** | 92 | 8 | 97 |
| **INDIANA** | | | | **RHODE ISLAND** | | | |
| **Lugar** | 84 | 16 | 98 | Reed | 98 | 2 | 99 |
| Bayh | 90 | 10 | 99 | **Chafee** | 47 | 53 | 99 |
| **IOWA** | | | | **SOUTH CAROLINA** | | | |
| **Grassley** | 96 | 4 | 100 | **Graham** | 92 | 8 | 99 |
| Harkin | 98 | 2 | 99 | **DeMint** | 96 | 4 | 99 |
| **KANSAS** | | | | **SOUTH DAKOTA** | | | |
| **Brownback** | 97 | 3 | 100 | Johnson | 83 | 17 | 98 |
| **Roberts** | 94 | 6 | 98 | **Thune** | 87 | 13 | 97 |
| **KENTUCKY** | | | | **TENNESSEE** | | | |
| **McConnell** | 99 | 1 | 99 | **Frist** | 97 | 3 | 100 |
| **Bunning** | 98 | 2 | 99 | **Alexander** | 92 | 8 | 98 |
| **LOUISIANA** | | | | **TEXAS** | | | |
| Landrieu | 76 | 24 | 97 | **Hutchison** | 90 | 10 | 100 |
| **Vitter** | 94 | 6 | 97 | **Cornyn** | 95 | 5 | 98 |
| **MAINE** | | | | **UTAH** | | | |
| **Snowe** | 56 | 44 | 100 | **Hatch** | 96 | 4 | 99 |
| **Collins** | 59 | 41 | 100 | **Bennett** | 96 | 4 | 97 |
| **MARYLAND** | | | | **VERMONT** | | | |
| Sarbanes | 99 | 1 | 100 | Leahy | 97 | 3 | 99 |
| Mikulski | 98 | 2 | 93 | *Jeffords* | 91 | 9 | 96 |
| **MASSACHUSETTS** | | | | **VIRGINIA** | | | |
| Kennedy | 100 | 0 | 98 | **Warner** | 86 | 14 | 99 |
| Kerry | 97 | 3 | 98 | **Allen** | 94 | 6 | 100 |
| **MICHIGAN** | | | | **WASHINGTON** | | | |
| Levin | 97 | 3 | 99 | Murray | 95 | 5 | 99 |
| Stabenow | 95 | 5 | 99 | Cantwell | 92 | 8 | 99 |
| **MINNESOTA** | | | | **WEST VIRGINIA** | | | |
| Dayton | 96 | 4 | 95 | Byrd | 84 | 16 | 99 |
| **Coleman** | 77 | 23 | 96 | Rockefeller | 93 | 7 | 95 |
| **MISSISSIPPI** | | | | **WISCONSIN** | | | |
| **Cochran** | 97 | 3 | 100 | Kohl | 89 | 11 | 99 |
| **Lott** | 95 | 5 | 88 | Feingold | 95 | 5 | 97 |
| **MISSOURI** | | | | **WYOMING** | | | |
| **Bond** | 94 | 6 | 99 | **Thomas** | 94 | 6 | 99 |
| **Talent** | 84 | 16 | 100 | **Enzi** | 94 | 6 | 99 |

**KEY**   **Republicans**   Democrats   *Independents*

# HOUSE

**1. Party Unity.** Percentage of recorded party unity votes in 2005 on which a member voted "yea" or "nay" in agreement with a majority of his or her party. (Party unity votes are those on which a majority of voting Democrats opposed a majority of voting Republicans.) Percentages are based on votes cast; thus, failure to vote does not lower a member's score.

**2. Party Opposition.** Percentage of recorded party unity votes in 2005 on which a member voted "yea" or "nay" in disagreement with a majority of his or her party. Percentages are based on votes cast; thus, failure to vote does not lower a member's score.

**3. Participation in Party Unity Votes.** Percentage of the 328 recorded House party unity votes in 2005 on which a member was present and voted "yea" or "nay."

| | 1 | 2 | 3 | | 1 | 2 | 3 |
|---|---|---|---|---|---|---|---|
| **ALABAMA** | | | | 50 Cunningham[3] | 95 | 5 | 95 |
| 1 Bonner | 96 | 4 | 96 | 51 Filner | 98 | 2 | 98 |
| 2 Everett | 96 | 4 | 95 | 52 Hunter | 97 | 3 | 97 |
| 3 Rogers | 94 | 6 | 94 | 53 Davis | 96 | 4 | 99 |
| 4 Aderholt | 97 | 3 | 100 | **COLORADO** | | | |
| 5 Cramer | 60 | 40 | 96 | 1 DeGette | 96 | 4 | 97 |
| 6 Bachus | 98 | 2 | 95 | 2 Udall | 91 | 9 | 99 |
| 7 Davis | 83 | 17 | 99 | 3 Salazar | 81 | 19 | 99 |
| **ALASKA** | | | | 4 Musgrave | 99 | 1 | 97 |
| AL Young | 91 | 9 | 92 | 5 Hefley | 93 | 7 | 97 |
| **ARIZONA** | | | | 6 Tancredo | 93 | 7 | 95 |
| 1 Renzi | 92 | 8 | 100 | 7 Beauprez | 96 | 4 | 96 |
| 2 Franks | 98 | 2 | 99 | **CONNECTICUT** | | | |
| 3 Shadegg | 98 | 2 | 94 | 1 Larson | 98 | 2 | 91 |
| 4 Pastor | 93 | 7 | 99 | 2 Simmons | 74 | 26 | 95 |
| 5 Hayworth | 95 | 5 | 99 | 3 DeLauro | 98 | 2 | 99 |
| 6 Flake | 91 | 9 | 97 | 4 Shays | 67 | 33 | 95 |
| 7 Grijalva | 98 | 2 | 98 | 5 Johnson | 79 | 21 | 99 |
| 8 Kolbe | 90 | 10 | 96 | **DELAWARE** | | | |
| **ARKANSAS** | | | | AL Castle | 76 | 24 | 99 |
| 1 Berry | 75 | 25 | 100 | **FLORIDA** | | | |
| 2 Snyder | 86 | 14 | 99 | 1 Miller | 96 | 4 | 95 |
| 3 Boozman | 96 | 4 | 96 | 2 Boyd | 75 | 25 | 91 |
| 4 Ross | 78 | 22 | 94 | 3 Brown | 96 | 4 | 91 |
| **CALIFORNIA** | | | | 4 Crenshaw | 97 | 3 | 99 |
| 1 Thompson | 92 | 8 | 99 | 5 Brown-Waite | 91 | 9 | 94 |
| 2 Herger | 97 | 3 | 99 | 6 Stearns | 94 | 6 | 99 |
| 3 Lungren | 97 | 3 | 99 | 7 Mica | 97 | 3 | 99 |
| 4 Doolittle | 97 | 3 | 96 | 8 Keller | 96 | 4 | 97 |
| 5 Matsui, D.[1] | 98 | 2 | 99 | 9 Bilirakis | 94 | 6 | 98 |
| 6 Woolsey | 99 | 1 | 98 | 10 Young | 92 | 8 | 98 |
| 7 Miller, George | 99 | 1 | 99 | 11 Davis | 89 | 11 | 91 |
| 8 Pelosi | 99 | 1 | 98 | 12 Putnam | 97 | 3 | 99 |
| 9 Lee | 98 | 2 | 98 | 13 Harris | 92 | 8 | 93 |
| 10 Tauscher | 95 | 5 | 98 | 14 Mack | 96 | 4 | 98 |
| 11 Pombo | 96 | 4 | 97 | 15 Weldon | 95 | 5 | 98 |
| 12 Lantos | 96 | 4 | 97 | 16 Foley | 90 | 10 | 95 |
| 13 Stark | 98 | 2 | 94 | 17 Meek | 93 | 7 | 98 |
| 14 Eshoo | 97 | 3 | 96 | 18 Ros-Lehtinen | 91 | 9 | 95 |
| 15 Honda | 99 | 1 | 96 | 19 Wexler | 97 | 3 | 94 |
| 16 Lofgren | 97 | 3 | 99 | 20 Wasserman-Schultz | 94 | 6 | 98 |
| 17 Farr | 98 | 2 | 99 | 21 Diaz-Balart, L. | 90 | 10 | 95 |
| 18 Cardoza | 79 | 21 | 98 | 22 Shaw | 93 | 7 | 97 |
| 19 Radanovich | 96 | 4 | 96 | 23 Hastings | 96 | 4 | 91 |
| 20 Costa | 79 | 21 | 97 | 24 Feeney | 98 | 2 | 93 |
| 21 Nunes | 96 | 4 | 98 | 25 Diaz-Balart, M. | 94 | 6 | 88 |
| 22 Thomas | 92 | 8 | 93 | **GEORGIA** | | | |
| 23 Capps | 98 | 2 | 97 | 1 Kingston | 98 | 2 | 94 |
| 24 Gallegly | 97 | 3 | 96 | 2 Bishop | 77 | 23 | 96 |
| 25 McKeon | 97 | 3 | 99 | 3 Marshall | 67 | 33 | 99 |
| 26 Dreier | 96 | 4 | 100 | 4 McKinney | 97 | 3 | 98 |
| 27 Sherman | 95 | 5 | 99 | 5 Lewis | 99 | 1 | 83 |
| 28 Berman | 96 | 4 | 96 | 6 Price | 97 | 3 | 99 |
| 29 Schiff | 94 | 6 | 94 | 7 Linder | 97 | 3 | 99 |
| 30 Waxman | 98 | 2 | 96 | 8 Westmoreland | 98 | 2 | 94 |
| 31 Becerra | 99 | 1 | 95 | 9 Norwood | 97 | 3 | 94 |
| 32 Solis | 99 | 1 | 97 | 10 Deal | 98 | 2 | 98 |
| 33 Watson | 98 | 2 | 96 | 11 Gingrey | 97 | 3 | 98 |
| 34 Roybal-Allard | 97 | 3 | 92 | 12 Barrow | 78 | 22 | 98 |
| 35 Waters | 96 | 4 | 93 | 13 Scott | 79 | 21 | 96 |
| 36 Harman | 90 | 10 | 88 | **HAWAII** | | | |
| 37 Millender-McD. | 98 | 2 | 84 | 1 Abercrombie | 92 | 8 | 97 |
| 38 Napolitano | 98 | 2 | 92 | 2 Case | 78 | 22 | 99 |
| 39 Sánchez, Linda | 99 | 1 | 99 | **IDAHO** | | | |
| 40 Royce | 97 | 3 | 98 | 1 Otter | 91 | 9 | 99 |
| 41 Lewis | 95 | 5 | 99 | 2 Simpson | 94 | 6 | 98 |
| 42 Miller, Gary | 98 | 2 | 96 | **ILLINOIS** | | | |
| 43 Baca | 88 | 12 | 97 | 1 Rush | 97 | 3 | 97 |
| 44 Calvert | 98 | 2 | 99 | 2 Jackson | 98 | 2 | 100 |
| 45 Bono | 93 | 7 | 94 | 3 Lipinski | 86 | 14 | 99 |
| 46 Rohrabacher | 94 | 6 | 98 | 4 Gutierrez | 98 | 2 | 90 |
| 47 Sanchez, Loretta | 93 | 7 | 97 | 5 Emanuel | 95 | 5 | 94 |
| 48 Campbell[2] | 100 | 0 | 100 | 6 Hyde | 96 | 4 | 84 |
| 49 Issa | 95 | 5 | 98 | 7 Davis | 97 | 3 | 98 |
| | | | | 8 Bean | 83 | 17 | 99 |
| | | | | 9 Schakowsky | 99 | 1 | 99 |
| | | | | 10 Kirk | 80 | 20 | 99 |
| | | | | 11 Weller | 94 | 6 | 97 |
| | | | | 12 Costello | 82 | 18 | 99 |

**KEY**   **Republicans**   Democrats   *Independents*

[1] Rep. Doris Matsui, D-Calif., was sworn in March 10, 2005. The first vote for which she was eligible was vote 62. She was eligible for 262 party unity votes in 2005.

[2] Rep. John Campbell, R-Calif., was sworn in Dec. 7, 2005, to replace Republican Christopher Cox, who resigned effective Aug. 2. The first vote for which Campbell was eligible was vote 619; he was eligible for 32 party unity votes in 2005. The last vote for which Cox was eligible was vote 453; he was eligible for 244 party unity votes in 2005. His party unity score was 95 percent; party opposition score, 5 percent; participation rate, 89 percent.

[3] Rep. Randy "Duke" Cunningham, R-Calif., resigned effective Dec. 1, 2005. The last vote for which he was eligible was vote 608. He was eligible for 295 party unity votes in 2005.

[4] The Speaker votes only at his discretion, usually to break a tie or to emphasize the importance of a matter.

[5] Rep. Jeanne Schmidt, R-Ohio, was sworn in Sept. 6, 2005, to replace Republican Rob Portman, who resigned effective April 29, 2005. The first vote for which Schmidt was eligible was vote 454; she was eligible for 84 party unity votes in 2005. The last vote for which Portman was eligible was vote 150; he was eligible for 86 party unity votes in 2005. His party unity score was 99 percent; party opposition score, 1 percent; participation rate, 91 percent.

| | | 1 | 2 | 3 |
|---|---|---|---|---|
| 13 | Biggert | 87 | 13 | 99 |
| 14 | Hastert[4] | 100 | 0 | 13 |
| 15 | Johnson | 77 | 23 | 99 |
| 16 | Manzullo | 94 | 6 | 99 |
| 17 | Evans | 98 | 2 | 98 |
| 18 | LaHood | 89 | 11 | 93 |
| 19 | Shimkus | 92 | 8 | 99 |
| **INDIANA** | | | | |
| 1 | Visclosky | 91 | 9 | 100 |
| 2 | Chocola | 97 | 3 | 99 |
| 3 | Souder | 97 | 3 | 97 |
| 4 | Buyer | 98 | 2 | 96 |
| 5 | Burton | 97 | 3 | 97 |
| 6 | Pence | 98 | 2 | 98 |
| 7 | Carson | 97 | 3 | 94 |
| 8 | Hostettler | 91 | 9 | 98 |
| 9 | Sodrel | 96 | 4 | 100 |
| **IOWA** | | | | |
| 1 | Nussle | 96 | 4 | 99 |
| 2 | Leach | 63 | 37 | 95 |
| 3 | Boswell | 82 | 18 | 86 |
| 4 | Latham | 96 | 4 | 100 |
| 5 | King | 98 | 2 | 100 |
| **KANSAS** | | | | |
| 1 | Moran | 92 | 8 | 98 |
| 2 | Ryun | 98 | 2 | 99 |
| 3 | Moore | 85 | 15 | 99 |
| 4 | Tiahrt | 97 | 3 | 99 |
| **KENTUCKY** | | | | |
| 1 | Whitfield | 94 | 6 | 98 |
| 2 | Lewis | 96 | 4 | 99 |
| 3 | Northup | 96 | 4 | 97 |
| 4 | Davis | 96 | 4 | 99 |
| 5 | Rogers | 96 | 4 | 99 |
| 6 | Chandler | 80 | 20 | 100 |
| **LOUISIANA** | | | | |
| 1 | Jindal | 97 | 3 | 98 |
| 2 | Jefferson | 90 | 10 | 96 |
| 3 | Melancon | 71 | 29 | 96 |
| 4 | McCrery | 97 | 3 | 97 |
| 5 | Alexander | 97 | 3 | 97 |
| 6 | Baker | 98 | 2 | 97 |
| 7 | Boustany | 96 | 4 | 97 |
| **MAINE** | | | | |
| 1 | Allen | 97 | 3 | 98 |
| 2 | Michaud | 92 | 8 | 99 |
| **MARYLAND** | | | | |
| 1 | Gilchrest | 80 | 20 | 99 |
| 2 | Ruppersberger | 89 | 11 | 99 |
| 3 | Cardin | 95 | 5 | 97 |
| 4 | Wynn | 87 | 13 | 99 |
| 5 | Hoyer | 93 | 7 | 99 |
| 6 | Bartlett | 89 | 11 | 98 |
| 7 | Cummings | 97 | 3 | 97 |
| 8 | Van Hollen | 99 | 1 | 99 |
| **MASSACHUSETTS** | | | | |
| 1 | Olver | 98 | 2 | 97 |
| 2 | Neal | 97 | 3 | 96 |
| 3 | McGovern | 99 | 1 | 99 |
| 4 | Frank | 96 | 4 | 98 |
| 5 | Meehan | 99 | 1 | 99 |
| 6 | Tierney | 98 | 2 | 99 |
| 7 | Markey | 98 | 2 | 99 |
| 8 | Capuano | 96 | 4 | 99 |
| 9 | Lynch | 92 | 8 | 97 |
| 10 | Delahunt | 99 | 1 | 91 |
| **MICHIGAN** | | | | |
| 1 | Stupak | 87 | 13 | 95 |
| 2 | Hoekstra | 96 | 4 | 99 |
| 3 | Ehlers | 78 | 22 | 98 |
| 4 | Camp | 95 | 5 | 95 |
| 5 | Kildee | 91 | 9 | 100 |
| 6 | Upton | 87 | 13 | 100 |
| 7 | Schwarz | 85 | 15 | 98 |
| 8 | Rogers | 94 | 6 | 97 |
| 9 | Knollenberg | 95 | 5 | 98 |
| 10 | Miller | 94 | 6 | 100 |
| 11 | McCotter | 89 | 11 | 98 |
| 12 | Levin | 95 | 5 | 100 |
| 13 | Kilpatrick | 96 | 4 | 96 |
| 14 | Conyers | 97 | 3 | 95 |
| 15 | Dingell | 92 | 8 | 98 |

| | | 1 | 2 | 3 |
|---|---|---|---|---|
| **MINNESOTA** | | | | |
| 1 | Gutknecht | 93 | 7 | 99 |
| 2 | Kline | 97 | 3 | 100 |
| 3 | Ramstad | 80 | 20 | 97 |
| 4 | McCollum | 98 | 2 | 99 |
| 5 | Sabo | 96 | 4 | 98 |
| 6 | Kennedy | 92 | 8 | 100 |
| 7 | Peterson | 64 | 36 | 98 |
| 8 | Oberstar | 93 | 7 | 93 |
| **MISSISSIPPI** | | | | |
| 1 | Wicker | 97 | 3 | 97 |
| 2 | Thompson | 93 | 7 | 100 |
| 3 | Pickering | 94 | 6 | 94 |
| 4 | Taylor | 65 | 35 | 94 |
| **MISSOURI** | | | | |
| 1 | Clay | 96 | 4 | 90 |
| 2 | Akin | 99 | 1 | 97 |
| 3 | Carnahan | 94 | 6 | 100 |
| 4 | Skelton | 76 | 24 | 97 |
| 5 | Cleaver | 96 | 4 | 98 |
| 6 | Graves | 95 | 5 | 98 |
| 7 | Blunt | 98 | 2 | 98 |
| 8 | Emerson | 90 | 10 | 96 |
| 9 | Hulshof | 93 | 7 | 96 |
| **MONTANA** | | | | |
| AL | Rehberg | 95 | 5 | 99 |
| **NEBRASKA** | | | | |
| 1 | Fortenberry | 95 | 5 | 99 |
| 2 | Terry | 94 | 6 | 99 |
| 3 | Osborne | 93 | 7 | 98 |
| **NEVADA** | | | | |
| 1 | Berkley | 92 | 8 | 95 |
| 2 | Gibbons | 91 | 9 | 97 |
| 3 | Porter | 90 | 10 | 99 |
| **NEW HAMPSHIRE** | | | | |
| 1 | Bradley | 87 | 13 | 99 |
| 2 | Bass | 87 | 13 | 99 |
| **NEW JERSEY** | | | | |
| 1 | Andrews | 92 | 8 | 91 |
| 2 | LoBiondo | 81 | 19 | 100 |
| 3 | Saxton | 85 | 15 | 99 |
| 4 | Smith | 79 | 21 | 98 |
| 5 | Garrett | 98 | 2 | 99 |
| 6 | Pallone | 97 | 3 | 99 |
| 7 | Ferguson | 89 | 11 | 99 |
| 8 | Pascrell | 93 | 7 | 98 |
| 9 | Rothman | 93 | 7 | 92 |
| 10 | Payne | 99 | 1 | 89 |
| 11 | Frelinghuysen | 89 | 11 | 98 |
| 12 | Holt | 97 | 3 | 99 |
| 13 | Menendez | 93 | 7 | 95 |
| **NEW MEXICO** | | | | |
| 1 | Wilson | 82 | 18 | 95 |
| 2 | Pearce | 96 | 4 | 97 |
| 3 | Udall | 97 | 3 | 96 |
| **NEW YORK** | | | | |
| 1 | Bishop | 95 | 5 | 99 |
| 2 | Israel | 94 | 6 | 98 |
| 3 | King | 89 | 11 | 98 |
| 4 | McCarthy | 93 | 7 | 95 |
| 5 | Ackerman | 98 | 3 | 98 |
| 6 | Meeks | 93 | 7 | 91 |
| 7 | Crowley | 97 | 3 | 99 |
| 8 | Nadler | 98 | 2 | 98 |
| 9 | Weiner | 99 | 1 | 97 |
| 10 | Towns | 93 | 7 | 94 |
| 11 | Owens | 98 | 2 | 98 |
| 12 | Velázquez | 98 | 2 | 97 |
| 13 | Fossella | 90 | 10 | 98 |
| 14 | Maloney | 98 | 2 | 98 |
| 15 | Rangel | 98 | 2 | 95 |
| 16 | Serrano | 96 | 4 | 98 |
| 17 | Engel | 93 | 7 | 99 |
| 18 | Lowey | 98 | 2 | 99 |
| 19 | Kelly | 85 | 15 | 94 |
| 20 | Sweeney | 88 | 12 | 92 |
| 21 | McNulty | 93 | 7 | 99 |
| 22 | Hinchey | 98 | 2 | 96 |
| 23 | McHugh | 89 | 11 | 98 |
| 24 | Boehlert | 77 | 23 | 99 |
| 25 | Walsh | 92 | 8 | 96 |
| 26 | Reynolds | 94 | 6 | 97 |
| 27 | Higgins | 89 | 11 | 98 |
| 28 | Slaughter | 97 | 3 | 95 |
| 29 | Kuhl | 93 | 7 | 99 |

| | | 1 | 2 | 3 |
|---|---|---|---|---|
| **NORTH CAROLINA** | | | | |
| 1 | Butterfield | 93 | 7 | 98 |
| 2 | Etheridge | 88 | 12 | 99 |
| 3 | Jones | 81 | 19 | 93 |
| 4 | Price | 96 | 4 | 99 |
| 5 | Foxx | 99 | 1 | 99 |
| 6 | Coble | 94 | 6 | 98 |
| 7 | McIntyre | 71 | 29 | 98 |
| 8 | Hayes | 99 | 1 | 98 |
| 9 | Myrick | 97 | 3 | 94 |
| 10 | McHenry | 99 | 1 | 99 |
| 11 | Taylor | 97 | 3 | 97 |
| 12 | Watt | 98 | 2 | 98 |
| 13 | Miller | 93 | 7 | 100 |
| **NORTH DAKOTA** | | | | |
| AL | Pomeroy | 80 | 20 | 97 |
| **OHIO** | | | | |
| 1 | Chabot | 95 | 5 | 99 |
| 2 | Schmidt[5] | 98 | 2 | 100 |
| 3 | Turner | 92 | 8 | 99 |
| 4 | Oxley | 97 | 3 | 93 |
| 5 | Gillmor | 94 | 6 | 94 |
| 6 | Strickland | 91 | 9 | 95 |
| 7 | Hobson | 94 | 6 | 98 |
| 8 | Boehner | 97 | 3 | 98 |
| 9 | Kaptur | 93 | 7 | 98 |
| 10 | Kucinich | 98 | 2 | 98 |
| 11 | Jones | 96 | 4 | 91 |
| 12 | Tiberi | 95 | 5 | 97 |
| 13 | Brown | 97 | 3 | 98 |
| 14 | LaTourette | 86 | 14 | 94 |
| 15 | Pryce | 94 | 6 | 99 |
| 16 | Regula | 92 | 8 | 100 |
| 17 | Ryan | 91 | 9 | 98 |
| 18 | Ney | 91 | 9 | 97 |
| **OKLAHOMA** | | | | |
| 1 | Sullivan | 97 | 3 | 95 |
| 2 | Boren | 59 | 41 | 99 |
| 3 | Lucas | 97 | 3 | 97 |
| 4 | Cole | 98 | 2 | 98 |
| 5 | Istook | 98 | 2 | 90 |
| **OREGON** | | | | |
| 1 | Wu | 92 | 8 | 99 |
| 2 | Walden | 92 | 8 | 99 |
| 3 | Blumenauer | 97 | 3 | 97 |
| 4 | DeFazio | 91 | 9 | 98 |
| 5 | Hooley | 93 | 7 | 98 |
| **PENNSYLVANIA** | | | | |
| 1 | Brady | 93 | 7 | 95 |
| 2 | Fattah | 96 | 4 | 95 |
| 3 | English | 93 | 7 | 99 |
| 4 | Hart | 96 | 4 | 100 |
| 5 | Peterson | 95 | 5 | 92 |
| 6 | Gerlach | 82 | 18 | 99 |
| 7 | Weldon | 85 | 15 | 96 |
| 8 | Fitzpatrick | 76 | 24 | 99 |
| 9 | Shuster | 98 | 2 | 99 |
| 10 | Sherwood | 95 | 5 | 99 |
| 11 | Kanjorski | 80 | 20 | 99 |
| 12 | Murtha | 76 | 24 | 99 |
| 13 | Schwartz | 92 | 8 | 99 |
| 14 | Doyle | 90 | 10 | 97 |
| 15 | Dent | 89 | 11 | 100 |
| 16 | Pitts | 97 | 3 | 99 |
| 17 | Holden | 75 | 25 | 99 |
| 18 | Murphy | 91 | 9 | 97 |
| 19 | Platts | 84 | 16 | 97 |
| **RHODE ISLAND** | | | | |
| 1 | Kennedy | 96 | 4 | 98 |
| 2 | Langevin | 92 | 8 | 100 |
| **SOUTH CAROLINA** | | | | |
| 1 | Brown | 96 | 4 | 93 |
| 2 | Wilson | 97 | 3 | 99 |
| 3 | Barrett | 99 | 1 | 96 |
| 4 | Inglis | 93 | 7 | 99 |
| 5 | Spratt | 88 | 12 | 99 |
| 6 | Clyburn | 92 | 8 | 97 |
| **SOUTH DAKOTA** | | | | |
| AL | Herseth | 79 | 21 | 95 |
| **TENNESSEE** | | | | |
| 1 | Jenkins | 96 | 4 | 97 |
| 2 | Duncan | 93 | 7 | 100 |

| | | 1 | 2 | 3 |
|---|---|---|---|---|
| 3 | Wamp | 94 | 6 | 98 |
| 4 | Davis | 67 | 33 | 99 |
| 5 | Cooper | 80 | 20 | 96 |
| 6 | Gordon | 74 | 26 | 98 |
| 7 | Blackburn | 99 | 1 | 99 |
| 8 | Tanner | 74 | 26 | 98 |
| 9 | Ford | 83 | 17 | 97 |
| **TEXAS** | | | | |
| 1 | Gohmert | 95 | 5 | 95 |
| 2 | Poe | 94 | 6 | 96 |
| 3 | Johnson, Sam | 98 | 2 | 97 |
| 4 | Hall, R. | 96 | 4 | 97 |
| 5 | Hensarling | 98 | 2 | 99 |
| 6 | Barton | 96 | 4 | 89 |
| 7 | Culberson | 98 | 2 | 97 |
| 8 | Brady | 98 | 2 | 95 |
| 9 | Green, A. | 93 | 7 | 100 |
| 10 | McCaul | 96 | 4 | 97 |
| 11 | Conaway | 96 | 4 | 96 |
| 12 | Granger | 97 | 3 | 97 |
| 13 | Thornberry | 98 | 2 | 99 |
| 14 | Paul | 72 | 28 | 95 |
| 15 | Hinojosa | 84 | 16 | 85 |
| 16 | Reyes | 81 | 19 | 90 |
| 17 | Edwards | 75 | 25 | 99 |
| 18 | Jackson-Lee | 93 | 7 | 91 |
| 19 | Neugebauer | 99 | 1 | 100 |
| 20 | Gonzalez | 86 | 14 | 99 |
| 21 | Smith | 98 | 2 | 97 |
| 22 | DeLay | 98 | 2 | 95 |
| 23 | Bonilla | 98 | 2 | 99 |
| 24 | Marchant | 98 | 2 | 98 |
| 25 | Doggett | 97 | 3 | 96 |
| 26 | Burgess | 97 | 3 | 99 |
| 27 | Ortiz | 78 | 22 | 94 |
| 28 | Cuellar | 70 | 30 | 95 |
| 29 | Green, G. | 82 | 18 | 96 |
| 30 | Johnson, E.B. | 96 | 4 | 97 |
| 31 | Carter | 98 | 2 | 95 |
| 32 | Sessions | 99 | 1 | 92 |
| **UTAH** | | | | |
| 1 | Bishop | 97 | 3 | 97 |
| 2 | Matheson | 69 | 31 | 100 |
| 3 | Cannon | 96 | 4 | 98 |
| **VERMONT** | | | | |
| AL | Sanders | 97 | 3 | 99 |
| **VIRGINIA** | | | | |
| 1 | Davis, Jo Ann | 93 | 7 | 93 |
| 2 | Drake | 98 | 2 | 100 |
| 3 | Scott | 95 | 5 | 99 |
| 4 | Forbes | 95 | 5 | 99 |
| 5 | Goode | 93 | 7 | 98 |
| 6 | Goodlatte | 96 | 4 | 100 |
| 7 | Cantor | 98 | 2 | 99 |
| 8 | Moran | 92 | 8 | 95 |
| 9 | Boucher | 83 | 17 | 97 |
| 10 | Wolf | 90 | 10 | 99 |
| 11 | Davis, T. | 88 | 12 | 93 |
| **WASHINGTON** | | | | |
| 1 | Inslee | 97 | 3 | 99 |
| 2 | Larsen | 93 | 7 | 98 |
| 3 | Baird | 92 | 8 | 93 |
| 4 | Hastings | 96 | 4 | 92 |
| 5 | McMorris | 98 | 2 | 99 |
| 6 | Dicks | 92 | 8 | 99 |
| 7 | McDermott | 99 | 1 | 95 |
| 8 | Reichert | 88 | 12 | 98 |
| 9 | Smith | 90 | 10 | 99 |
| **WEST VIRGINIA** | | | | |
| 1 | Mollohan | 78 | 22 | 98 |
| 2 | Capito | 90 | 10 | 97 |
| 3 | Rahall | 87 | 13 | 98 |
| **WISCONSIN** | | | | |
| 1 | Ryan | 94 | 6 | 99 |
| 2 | Baldwin | 99 | 1 | 100 |
| 3 | Kind | 89 | 11 | 96 |
| 4 | Moore | 97 | 3 | 97 |
| 5 | Sensenbrenner | 93 | 7 | 98 |
| 6 | Petri | 88 | 12 | 99 |
| 7 | Obey | 95 | 5 | 95 |
| 8 | Green | 89 | 11 | 100 |
| **WYOMING** | | | | |
| AL | Cubin | 94 | 6 | 94 |

# HOUSE

**1.** **Voting Participation.** Percentage of 669 recorded votes in 2005 on which a representative voted "yea" or "nay."

**2.** **Voting Participation (without Journal votes).** Percentage of 661 recorded votes in 2005 on which a member voted "yea" or "nay." In this version of the study, eight votes on approval of the House Journal were excluded.

*Absences because of illness.* Congressional Quarterly no longer designates members who missed votes because of illness. In the past, notations to that effect were based on official statements published in the Congressional Record, but these were found to be inconsistently used.

*Rounding.* Scores are rounded to the nearest percentage, except that no scores are rounded up to 100 percent. Members with a 100 percent score participated in all recorded votes for which they were eligible.

[1] Rep. Doris Matsui, D-Calif., was sworn in March 10, 2005. The first vote for which she was eligible was vote 62.

[2] Rep. John Campbell, R-Calif., was sworn in Dec. 7, 2005, to replace Republican Christopher Cox, who resigned effective Aug. 2. The first vote for which Campbell was eligible was vote 619. The last vote for which Cox was eligible was vote 453; his participation rate was 87 percent.

[3] Rep. Randy "Duke" Cunningham, R-Calif., resigned effective Dec. 1, 2005. The last vote for which he was eligible was vote 608.

[4] The Speaker votes only at his discretion, usually to break a tie or to emphasize the importance of a matter.

[5] Rep. Jean Schmidt, R-Ohio, was sworn in Sept. 6, 2005, to replace Republican Rob Portman, who resigned effective April 29. The first vote for which Schmidt was eligible was vote 454. The last vote for which Portman was eligible was vote 150; his participation rate was 91 percent.

| | | 1 | 2 |
|---|---|---|---|
| **ALABAMA** | | | |
| 1 | Bonner | 97 | 97 |
| 2 | Everett | 94 | 94 |
| 3 | Rogers | 96 | 96 |
| 4 | Aderholt | 100 | 100 |
| 5 | Cramer | 95 | 95 |
| 6 | Bachus | 95 | 95 |
| 7 | Davis | 98 | 98 |
| **ALASKA** | | | |
| AL | Young | 90 | 90 |
| **ARIZONA** | | | |
| 1 | Renzi | 99 | 99 |
| 2 | Franks | 99 | 98 |
| 3 | Shadegg | 95 | 95 |
| 4 | Pastor | 99 | 99 |
| 5 | Hayworth | 99 | 99 |
| 6 | Flake | 97 | 97 |
| 7 | Grijalva | 97 | 98 |
| 8 | Kolbe | 96 | 96 |
| **ARKANSAS** | | | |
| 1 | Berry | 99 | 99 |
| 2 | Snyder | 99 | 99 |
| 3 | Boozman | 97 | 97 |
| 4 | Ross | 94 | 94 |
| **CALIFORNIA** | | | |
| 1 | Thompson | 99 | 99 |
| 2 | Herger | 99 | 99 |
| 3 | Lungren | 99 | 99 |
| 4 | Doolittle | 94 | 94 |
| 5 | Matsui, D.[1] | 99 | 99 |
| 6 | Woolsey | 99 | 99 |
| 7 | Miller, George | 97 | 97 |
| 8 | Pelosi | 94 | 94 |
| 9 | Lee | 96 | 96 |
| 10 | Tauscher | 98 | 98 |
| 11 | Pombo | 95 | 95 |
| 12 | Lantos | 96 | 96 |
| 13 | Stark | 87 | 87 |
| 14 | Eshoo | 94 | 94 |
| 15 | Honda | 96 | 96 |
| 16 | Lofgren | 99 | 99 |
| 17 | Farr | 99 | 98 |
| 18 | Cardoza | 98 | 98 |
| 19 | Radanovich | 94 | 94 |
| 20 | Costa | 97 | 97 |
| 21 | Nunes | 98 | 98 |
| 22 | Thomas | 95 | 95 |
| 23 | Capps | 96 | 96 |
| 24 | Gallegly | 93 | 93 |
| 25 | McKeon | 98 | 98 |
| 26 | Dreier | 99 | 99 |
| 27 | Sherman | 99 | 98 |
| 28 | Berman | 92 | 92 |
| 29 | Schiff | 93 | 93 |
| 30 | Waxman | 96 | 96 |
| 31 | Becerra | 93 | 93 |
| 32 | Solis | 96 | 95 |
| 33 | Watson | 94 | 94 |
| 34 | Roybal-Allard | 90 | 90 |
| 35 | Waters | 90 | 89 |
| 36 | Harman | 89 | 89 |
| 37 | Millender-McD. | 83 | 83 |
| 38 | Napolitano | 93 | 93 |
| 39 | Sánchez, Linda | 98 | 98 |
| 40 | Royce | 97 | 97 |
| 41 | Lewis | 99 | 99 |
| 42 | Miller, Gary | 95 | 95 |
| 43 | Baca | 96 | 96 |
| 44 | Calvert | 97 | 97 |
| 45 | Bono | 94 | 94 |
| 46 | Rohrabacher | 98 | 98 |
| 47 | Sanchez, Loretta | 95 | 95 |
| 48 | Campbell[2] | 100 | 100 |
| 49 | Issa | 97 | 97 |

| | | 1 | 2 |
|---|---|---|---|
| 50 | Cunningham[3] | 93 | 93 |
| 51 | Filner | 97 | 97 |
| 52 | Hunter | 94 | 94 |
| 53 | Davis | 99 | 99 |
| **COLORADO** | | | |
| 1 | DeGette | 96 | 96 |
| 2 | Udall | 98 | 98 |
| 3 | Salazar | 99 | 99 |
| 4 | Musgrave | 97 | 97 |
| 5 | Hefley | 95 | 95 |
| 6 | Tancredo | 94 | 95 |
| 7 | Beauprez | 97 | 97 |
| **CONNECTICUT** | | | |
| 1 | Larson | 91 | 91 |
| 2 | Simmons | 94 | 94 |
| 3 | DeLauro | 99 | 99 |
| 4 | Shays | 95 | 95 |
| 5 | Johnson | 98 | 98 |
| **DELAWARE** | | | |
| AL | Castle | 99 | 99 |
| **FLORIDA** | | | |
| 1 | Miller | 94 | 94 |
| 2 | Boyd | 92 | 92 |
| 3 | Brown | 86 | 86 |
| 4 | Crenshaw | 99 | 99 |
| 5 | Brown-Waite | 88 | 89 |
| 6 | Stearns | 99 | 99 |
| 7 | Mica | 99 | 98 |
| 8 | Keller | 96 | 96 |
| 9 | Bilirakis | 97 | 97 |
| 10 | Young | 85 | 85 |
| 11 | Davis | 84 | 84 |
| 12 | Putnam | 99 | 99 |
| 13 | Harris | 91 | 91 |
| 14 | Mack | 99 | 99 |
| 15 | Weldon | 96 | 96 |
| 16 | Foley | 95 | 95 |
| 17 | Meek | 96 | 96 |
| 18 | Ros-Lehtinen | 93 | 93 |
| 19 | Wexler | 90 | 90 |
| 20 | Wasserman-Schultz | 96 | 96 |
| 21 | Diaz-Balart, L. | 91 | 91 |
| 22 | Shaw | 96 | 96 |
| 23 | Hastings | 87 | 87 |
| 24 | Feeney | 92 | 92 |
| 25 | Diaz-Balart, M. | 85 | 85 |
| **GEORGIA** | | | |
| 1 | Kingston | 92 | 92 |
| 2 | Bishop | 95 | 95 |
| 3 | Marshall | 98 | 98 |
| 4 | McKinney | 96 | 96 |
| 5 | Lewis | 86 | 86 |
| 6 | Price | 99 | 99 |
| 7 | Linder | 97 | 97 |
| 8 | Westmoreland | 94 | 94 |
| 9 | Norwood | 93 | 93 |
| 10 | Deal | 97 | 97 |
| 11 | Gingrey | 97 | 97 |
| 12 | Barrow | 98 | 98 |
| 13 | Scott | 96 | 96 |
| **HAWAII** | | | |
| 1 | Abercrombie | 97 | 97 |
| 2 | Case | 98 | 98 |
| **IDAHO** | | | |
| 1 | Otter | 98 | 98 |
| 2 | Simpson | 97 | 97 |
| **ILLINOIS** | | | |
| 1 | Rush | 91 | 91 |
| 2 | Jackson | 99 | 99 |
| 3 | Lipinski | 99 | 99 |
| 4 | Gutierrez | 84 | 84 |
| 5 | Emanuel | 95 | 95 |
| 6 | Hyde | 87 | 87 |
| 7 | Davis | 98 | 98 |
| 8 | Bean | 99 | 99 |
| 9 | Schakowsky | 97 | 97 |
| 10 | Kirk | 97 | 97 |
| 11 | Weller | 96 | 96 |
| 12 | Costello | 97 | 97 |

**KEY**   Republicans   Democrats   *Independents*

| District | Name | | |
|---|---|---|---|
| 13 | **Biggert** | 99 | 99 |
| 14 | **Hastert**[4] | 9 | 9 |
| 15 | **Johnson** | 98 | 98 |
| 16 | **Manzullo** | 97 | 97 |
| 17 | Evans | 97 | 97 |
| 18 | LaHood | 93 | 93 |
| 19 | **Shimkus** | 97 | 97 |
| **INDIANA** | | | |
| 1 | Visclosky | 99 | 99 |
| 2 | **Chocola** | 99 | 99 |
| 3 | **Souder** | 96 | 96 |
| 4 | **Buyer** | 93 | 93 |
| 5 | **Burton** | 96 | 96 |
| 6 | **Pence** | 96 | 96 |
| 7 | Carson | 93 | 93 |
| 8 | **Hostettler** | 97 | 97 |
| 9 | **Sodrel** | 99 | 99 |
| **IOWA** | | | |
| 1 | **Nussle** | 97 | 97 |
| 2 | Leach | 95 | 95 |
| 3 | Boswell | 79 | 79 |
| 4 | **Latham** | 99 | 99 |
| 5 | **King** | 99 | 99 |
| **KANSAS** | | | |
| 1 | **Moran** | 98 | 98 |
| 2 | **Ryun** | 99 | 99 |
| 3 | Moore | 99 | 99 |
| 4 | **Tiahrt** | 98 | 98 |
| **KENTUCKY** | | | |
| 1 | **Whitfield** | 96 | 96 |
| 2 | **Lewis** | 98 | 98 |
| 3 | **Northup** | 97 | 97 |
| 4 | **Davis** | 99 | 99 |
| 5 | **Rogers** | 99 | 99 |
| 6 | Chandler | 99 | 99 |
| **LOUISIANA** | | | |
| 1 | **Jindal** | 97 | 97 |
| 2 | Jefferson | 95 | 95 |
| 3 | Melancon | 95 | 95 |
| 4 | **McCrery** | 96 | 96 |
| 5 | **Alexander** | 99 | 99 |
| 6 | **Baker** | 95 | 95 |
| 7 | **Boustany** | 97 | 97 |
| **MAINE** | | | |
| 1 | Allen | 99 | 98 |
| 2 | Michaud | 99 | 99 |
| **MARYLAND** | | | |
| 1 | **Gilchrest** | 98 | 98 |
| 2 | Ruppersberger | 99 | 98 |
| 3 | Cardin | 95 | 95 |
| 4 | Wynn | 99 | 98 |
| 5 | Hoyer | 99 | 98 |
| 6 | **Bartlett** | 98 | 98 |
| 7 | Cummings | 96 | 96 |
| 8 | Van Hollen | 99 | 99 |
| **MASSACHUSETTS** | | | |
| 1 | Olver | 94 | 94 |
| 2 | Neal | 93 | 94 |
| 3 | McGovern | 99 | 99 |
| 4 | Frank | 98 | 98 |
| 5 | Meehan | 98 | 98 |
| 6 | Tierney | 98 | 98 |
| 7 | Markey | 99 | 99 |
| 8 | Capuano | 97 | 97 |
| 9 | Lynch | 95 | 95 |
| 10 | Delahunt | 89 | 89 |
| **MICHIGAN** | | | |
| 1 | Stupak | 93 | 93 |
| 2 | **Hoekstra** | 97 | 97 |
| 3 | **Ehlers** | 97 | 97 |
| 4 | **Camp** | 95 | 95 |
| 5 | Kildee | 100 | 100 |
| 6 | **Upton** | 100 | 100 |
| 7 | **Schwarz** | 97 | 97 |
| 8 | **Rogers** | 98 | 98 |
| 9 | **Knollenberg** | 98 | 98 |
| 10 | **Miller** | 99 | 99 |
| 11 | **McCotter** | 98 | 98 |
| 12 | Levin | 99 | 99 |
| 13 | Kilpatrick | 93 | 93 |
| 14 | Conyers | 95 | 95 |
| 15 | Dingell | 96 | 96 |

| District | Name | | |
|---|---|---|---|
| **MINNESOTA** | | | |
| 1 | **Gutknecht** | 98 | 98 |
| 2 | **Kline** | 100 | 100 |
| 3 | **Ramstad** | 98 | 98 |
| 4 | McCollum | 98 | 98 |
| 5 | Sabo | 97 | 97 |
| 6 | **Kennedy** | 100 | 100 |
| 7 | Peterson | 98 | 98 |
| 8 | Oberstar | 93 | 93 |
| **MISSISSIPPI** | | | |
| 1 | **Wicker** | 96 | 97 |
| 2 | Thompson | 99 | 99 |
| 3 | **Pickering** | 94 | 94 |
| 4 | Taylor | 91 | 91 |
| **MISSOURI** | | | |
| 1 | Clay | 89 | 89 |
| 2 | **Akin** | 98 | 98 |
| 3 | Carnahan | 99 | 99 |
| 4 | Skelton | 97 | 97 |
| 5 | Cleaver | 98 | 98 |
| 6 | **Graves** | 96 | 96 |
| 7 | **Blunt** | 98 | 98 |
| 8 | **Emerson** | 95 | 95 |
| 9 | **Hulshof** | 97 | 97 |
| **MONTANA** | | | |
| AL | **Rehberg** | 99 | 99 |
| **NEBRASKA** | | | |
| 1 | **Fortenberry** | 99 | 99 |
| 2 | **Terry** | 97 | 97 |
| 3 | **Osborne** | 99 | 98 |
| **NEVADA** | | | |
| 1 | Berkley | 94 | 94 |
| 2 | **Gibbons** | 95 | 95 |
| 3 | **Porter** | 99 | 99 |
| **NEW HAMPSHIRE** | | | |
| 1 | **Bradley** | 99 | 99 |
| 2 | **Bass** | 98 | 98 |
| **NEW JERSEY** | | | |
| 1 | Andrews | 89 | 89 |
| 2 | **LoBiondo** | 99 | 99 |
| 3 | **Saxton** | 99 | 99 |
| 4 | **Smith** | 99 | 99 |
| 5 | **Garrett** | 99 | 99 |
| 6 | Pallone | 98 | 98 |
| 7 | **Ferguson** | 98 | 98 |
| 8 | Pascrell | 96 | 96 |
| 9 | Rothman | 91 | 92 |
| 10 | Payne | 86 | 87 |
| 11 | **Frelinghuysen** | 98 | 98 |
| 12 | Holt | 99 | 99 |
| 13 | Menendez | 94 | 94 |
| **NEW MEXICO** | | | |
| 1 | **Wilson** | 97 | 97 |
| 2 | **Pearce** | 97 | 97 |
| 3 | Udall | 96 | 96 |
| **NEW YORK** | | | |
| 1 | Bishop | 99 | 99 |
| 2 | Israel | 98 | 98 |
| 3 | **King** | 98 | 98 |
| 4 | McCarthy | 94 | 94 |
| 5 | Ackerman | 96 | 95 |
| 6 | Meeks | 90 | 90 |
| 7 | Crowley | 96 | 96 |
| 8 | Nadler | 97 | 97 |
| 9 | Weiner | 94 | 94 |
| 10 | Towns | 88 | 88 |
| 11 | Owens | 96 | 96 |
| 12 | Velázquez | 96 | 96 |
| 13 | **Fossella** | 96 | 96 |
| 14 | Maloney | 97 | 97 |
| 15 | Rangel | 94 | 94 |
| 16 | Serrano | 97 | 97 |
| 17 | Engel | 98 | 98 |
| 18 | Lowey | 99 | 99 |
| 19 | **Kelly** | 96 | 96 |
| 20 | **Sweeney** | 89 | 89 |
| 21 | McNulty | 98 | 98 |
| 22 | Hinchey | 94 | 94 |
| 23 | **McHugh** | 97 | 97 |
| 24 | **Boehlert** | 98 | 98 |
| 25 | Walsh | 94 | 94 |
| 26 | Reynolds | 96 | 96 |
| 27 | Higgins | 96 | 97 |
| 28 | Slaughter | 94 | 94 |
| 29 | **Kuhl** | 99 | 99 |

| District | Name | | |
|---|---|---|---|
| **NORTH CAROLINA** | | | |
| 1 | Butterfield | 97 | 97 |
| 2 | Etheridge | 97 | 97 |
| 3 | Jones | 94 | 94 |
| 4 | Price | 98 | 98 |
| 5 | Foxx | 99 | 99 |
| 6 | Coble | 97 | 97 |
| 7 | McIntyre | 97 | 97 |
| 8 | Hayes | 97 | 97 |
| 9 | Myrick | 95 | 95 |
| 10 | McHenry | 99 | 99 |
| 11 | Taylor | 96 | 96 |
| 12 | Watt | 96 | 96 |
| 13 | Miller | 100 | 100 |
| **NORTH DAKOTA** | | | |
| AL | Pomeroy | 97 | 97 |
| **OHIO** | | | |
| 1 | **Chabot** | 99 | 99 |
| 2 | **Schmidt**[5] | 100 | 100 |
| 3 | **Turner** | 98 | 98 |
| 4 | **Oxley** | 92 | 92 |
| 5 | **Gillmor** | 94 | 94 |
| 6 | Strickland | 90 | 90 |
| 7 | **Hobson** | 97 | 97 |
| 8 | **Boehner** | 97 | 97 |
| 9 | Kaptur | 97 | 97 |
| 10 | Kucinich | 98 | 98 |
| 11 | Jones | 91 | 91 |
| 12 | **Tiberi** | 97 | 97 |
| 13 | Brown | 96 | 95 |
| 14 | **LaTourette** | 94 | 94 |
| 15 | **Pryce** | 96 | 96 |
| 16 | **Regula** | 100 | 100 |
| 17 | Ryan | 98 | 98 |
| 18 | **Ney** | 97 | 97 |
| **OKLAHOMA** | | | |
| 1 | **Sullivan** | 95 | 95 |
| 2 | Boren | 99 | 99 |
| 3 | **Lucas** | 97 | 97 |
| 4 | **Cole** | 97 | 98 |
| 5 | **Istook** | 87 | 87 |
| **OREGON** | | | |
| 1 | Wu | 99 | 99 |
| 2 | **Walden** | 99 | 98 |
| 3 | Blumenauer | 95 | 95 |
| 4 | DeFazio | 97 | 97 |
| 5 | Hooley | 97 | 97 |
| **PENNSYLVANIA** | | | |
| 1 | Brady | 93 | 93 |
| 2 | Fattah | 89 | 90 |
| 3 | **English** | 98 | 98 |
| 4 | **Hart** | 99 | 99 |
| 5 | **Peterson** | 92 | 92 |
| 6 | **Gerlach** | 98 | 98 |
| 7 | **Weldon** | 95 | 95 |
| 8 | **Fitzpatrick** | 99 | 99 |
| 9 | **Shuster** | 99 | 99 |
| 10 | **Sherwood** | 99 | 99 |
| 11 | Kanjorski | 99 | 99 |
| 12 | Murtha | 90 | 90 |
| 13 | Schwartz | 99 | 99 |
| 14 | Doyle | 96 | 96 |
| 15 | **Dent** | 99 | 99 |
| 16 | **Pitts** | 99 | 99 |
| 17 | Holden | 99 | 98 |
| 18 | Murphy | 97 | 97 |
| 19 | **Platts** | 97 | 97 |
| **RHODE ISLAND** | | | |
| 1 | Kennedy | 96 | 96 |
| 2 | Langevin | 99 | 99 |
| **SOUTH CAROLINA** | | | |
| 1 | **Brown** | 92 | 92 |
| 2 | **Wilson** | 99 | 99 |
| 3 | **Barrett** | 95 | 95 |
| 4 | **Inglis** | 99 | 99 |
| 5 | Spratt | 98 | 98 |
| 6 | Clyburn | 96 | 96 |
| **SOUTH DAKOTA** | | | |
| AL | Herseth | 96 | 96 |
| **TENNESSEE** | | | |
| 1 | **Jenkins** | 92 | 92 |
| 2 | **Duncan** | 100 | 100 |

| District | Name | | |
|---|---|---|---|
| 3 | **Wamp** | 98 | 98 |
| 4 | Davis | 98 | 98 |
| 5 | Cooper | 96 | 96 |
| 6 | Gordon | 97 | 97 |
| 7 | **Blackburn** | 99 | 99 |
| 8 | Tanner | 98 | 98 |
| 9 | Ford | 92 | 92 |
| **TEXAS** | | | |
| 1 | **Gohmert** | 94 | 94 |
| 2 | **Poe** | 96 | 96 |
| 3 | **Johnson, Sam** | 96 | 96 |
| 4 | **Hall, R.** | 97 | 97 |
| 5 | **Hensarling** | 99 | 99 |
| 6 | **Barton** | 91 | 91 |
| 7 | **Culberson** | 96 | 96 |
| 8 | **Brady** | 92 | 92 |
| 9 | Green, A. | 99 | 99 |
| 10 | **McCaul** | 98 | 98 |
| 11 | **Conaway** | 94 | 94 |
| 12 | **Granger** | 96 | 96 |
| 13 | **Thornberry** | 99 | 99 |
| 14 | **Paul** | 94 | 94 |
| 15 | Hinojosa | 85 | 85 |
| 16 | Reyes | 86 | 86 |
| 17 | Edwards | 97 | 97 |
| 18 | Jackson-Lee | 91 | 92 |
| 19 | **Neugebauer** | 99 | 98 |
| 20 | Gonzalez | 98 | 98 |
| 21 | **Smith** | 97 | 97 |
| 22 | **DeLay** | 95 | 95 |
| 23 | **Bonilla** | 99 | 99 |
| 24 | **Marchant** | 97 | 97 |
| 25 | Doggett | 97 | 97 |
| 26 | **Burgess** | 99 | 99 |
| 27 | Ortiz | 92 | 92 |
| 28 | Cuellar | 95 | 95 |
| 29 | Green, G. | 96 | 96 |
| 30 | Johnson, E.B. | 97 | 97 |
| 31 | **Carter** | 96 | 96 |
| 32 | **Sessions** | 90 | 90 |
| **UTAH** | | | |
| 1 | **Bishop** | 96 | 96 |
| 2 | Matheson | 99 | 99 |
| 3 | **Cannon** | 98 | 98 |
| **VERMONT** | | | |
| AL | *Sanders* | 97 | 97 |
| **VIRGINIA** | | | |
| 1 | **Davis, Jo Ann** | 93 | 93 |
| 2 | **Drake** | 99 | 99 |
| 3 | Scott | 97 | 97 |
| 4 | **Forbes** | 99 | 99 |
| 5 | **Goode** | 98 | 98 |
| 6 | **Goodlatte** | 100 | 100 |
| 7 | **Cantor** | 98 | 98 |
| 8 | Moran | 95 | 95 |
| 9 | Boucher | 96 | 96 |
| 10 | **Wolf** | 99 | 99 |
| 11 | **Davis, T.** | 94 | 94 |
| **WASHINGTON** | | | |
| 1 | Inslee | 99 | 99 |
| 2 | Larsen | 97 | 97 |
| 3 | Baird | 92 | 92 |
| 4 | Hastings | 93 | 93 |
| 5 | **McMorris** | 98 | 98 |
| 6 | Dicks | 97 | 97 |
| 7 | McDermott | 94 | 94 |
| 8 | **Reichert** | 98 | 98 |
| 9 | Smith | 98 | 98 |
| **WEST VIRGINIA** | | | |
| 1 | Mollohan | 97 | 97 |
| 2 | **Capito** | 97 | 97 |
| 3 | Rahall | 97 | 97 |
| **WISCONSIN** | | | |
| 1 | **Ryan** | 98 | 98 |
| 2 | Baldwin | 99 | 99 |
| 3 | Kind | 96 | 95 |
| 4 | Moore | 97 | 97 |
| 5 | **Sensenbrenner** | 98 | 98 |
| 6 | **Petri** | 99 | 99 |
| 7 | Obey | 95 | 95 |
| 8 | **Green** | 99 | 99 |
| **WYOMING** | | | |
| AL | **Cubin** | 93 | 92 |

# SENATE

**1. Voting Participation.** Percentage of 366 recorded votes in 2005 on which a senator voted "yea" or "nay."

**2. Voting Participation (without motions to instruct).** Percentage of 364 recorded votes in 2005 on which a senator voted "yea" or "nay." In this version of the study, two votes to instruct the sergeant at arms to request the attendance of absent senators were excluded.

*Absences because of illness.* Congressional Quarterly no longer designates members who missed votes because of illness. In the past, notations to that effect were based on official statements published in the Congressional Record, but these were found to be inconsistently used.

*Rounding.* Scores are rounded to the nearest percentage point, except that no scores are rounded up to 100 percent. Senators with a 100 percent score participated in all recorded votes for which they were eligible.

| | 1 | 2 | | | 1 | 2 |
|---|---|---|---|---|---|---|
| **ALABAMA** | | | | **MONTANA** | | |
| Shelby | 99 | 99 | | Baucus | 98 | 98 |
| Sessions | 98 | 98 | | Burns | 97 | 97 |
| **ALASKA** | | | | **NEBRASKA** | | |
| Stevens | 99 | 99 | | Hagel | 99 | 99 |
| Murkowski | 96 | 96 | | Nelson | 99 | 99 |
| **ARIZONA** | | | | **NEVADA** | | |
| McCain | 91 | 91 | | Reid | 100 | 100 |
| Kyl | 99 | 99 | | Ensign | 98 | 98 |
| **ARKANSAS** | | | | **NEW HAMPSHIRE** | | |
| Lincoln | 99 | 99 | | Gregg | 98 | 98 |
| Pryor | 99 | 99 | | Sununu | 96 | 96 |
| **CALIFORNIA** | | | | **NEW JERSEY** | | |
| Feinstein | 98 | 98 | | Corzine | 63 | 63 |
| Boxer | 96 | 96 | | Lautenberg | 98 | 98 |
| **COLORADO** | | | | **NEW MEXICO** | | |
| Allard | 99 | 99 | | Domenici | 96 | 96 |
| Salazar | 100 | 100 | | Bingaman | 99 | 99 |
| **CONNECTICUT** | | | | **NEW YORK** | | |
| Dodd | 95 | 95 | | Schumer | 99 | 99 |
| Lieberman | 94 | 94 | | Clinton | 97 | 97 |
| **DELAWARE** | | | | **NORTH CAROLINA** | | |
| Biden | 92 | 92 | | Dole | 99 | 99 |
| Carper | 100 | 100 | | Burr | 98 | 98 |
| **FLORIDA** | | | | **NORTH DAKOTA** | | |
| Nelson | 99 | 99 | | Conrad | 97 | 97 |
| Martinez | 96 | 96 | | Dorgan | 97 | 97 |
| **GEORGIA** | | | | **OHIO** | | |
| Chambliss | 97 | 97 | | DeWine | 99 | 99 |
| Isakson | 99 | 99 | | Voinovich | 99 | 99 |
| **HAWAII** | | | | **OKLAHOMA** | | |
| Inouye | 86 | 87 | | Inhofe | 98 | 98 |
| Akaka | 99 | 99 | | Coburn | 99 | 99 |
| **IDAHO** | | | | **OREGON** | | |
| Craig | 98 | 98 | | Wyden | 99 | 99 |
| Crapo | 99 | 99 | | Smith | 98 | 98 |
| **ILLINOIS** | | | | **PENNSYLVANIA** | | |
| Durbin | 99 | 99 | | Specter | 97 | 97 |
| Obama | 98 | 98 | | Santorum | 96 | 96 |
| **INDIANA** | | | | **RHODE ISLAND** | | |
| Lugar | 98 | 98 | | Reed | 99 | 99 |
| Bayh | 98 | 98 | | Chafee | 99 | 99 |
| **IOWA** | | | | **SOUTH CAROLINA** | | |
| Grassley | 100 | 100 | | Graham | 97 | 97 |
| Harkin | 98 | 98 | | DeMint | 98 | 98 |
| **KANSAS** | | | | **SOUTH DAKOTA** | | |
| Brownback | 99 | 99 | | Johnson | 98 | 98 |
| Roberts | 98 | 98 | | Thune | 96 | 96 |
| **KENTUCKY** | | | | **TENNESSEE** | | |
| McConnell | 99 | 99 | | Frist | 99 | 99 |
| Bunning | 99 | 99 | | Alexander | 96 | 96 |
| **LOUISIANA** | | | | **TEXAS** | | |
| Landrieu | 96 | 96 | | Hutchison | 99 | 99 |
| Vitter | 95 | 95 | | Cornyn | 98 | 98 |
| **MAINE** | | | | **UTAH** | | |
| Snowe | 100 | 100 | | Hatch | 99 | 99 |
| Collins | 100 | 100 | | Bennett | 97 | 97 |
| **MARYLAND** | | | | **VERMONT** | | |
| Sarbanes | 99 | 99 | | Leahy | 99 | 99 |
| Mikulski | 93 | 93 | | *Jeffords* | 96 | 96 |
| **MASSACHUSETTS** | | | | **VIRGINIA** | | |
| Kennedy | 97 | 98 | | Warner | 99 | 99 |
| Kerry | 98 | 98 | | Allen | 99 | 99 |
| **MICHIGAN** | | | | **WASHINGTON** | | |
| Levin | 99 | 99 | | Murray | 99 | 99 |
| Stabenow | 99 | 99 | | Cantwell | 98 | 98 |
| **MINNESOTA** | | | | **WEST VIRGINIA** | | |
| Dayton | 95 | 96 | | Byrd | 98 | 98 |
| Coleman | 97 | 97 | | Rockefeller | 92 | 92 |
| **MISSISSIPPI** | | | | **WISCONSIN** | | |
| Cochran | 99 | 99 | | Kohl | 99 | 99 |
| Lott | 90 | 90 | | Feingold | 98 | 98 |
| **MISSOURI** | | | | **WYOMING** | | |
| Bond | 99 | 99 | | Thomas | 98 | 98 |
| Talent | 100 | 100 | | Enzi | 98 | 98 |

**KEY**    Republicans    Democrats    *Independents*

# KEY VOTES

# Votes Test Fealty Amid Quests To Further the GOP Agenda

IT IS TEMPTING TO SAY that the most important vote of 2005 occurred in November 2004 — when Americans went to the polls and handed congressional Republicans slightly bigger majorities in both the House and Senate. In particular, by increasing their Senate majority to a solid 55 from a tenuous 51, GOP leaders assumed they could more easily thwart a united phalanx of Democrats who had more and more been able to muster just enough votes to sidetrack prominent pieces of the Republican agenda.

On some level, it did work out that way. Bills restricting class action lawsuits, overhauling bankruptcy rules, granting liability protection to gunmakers and rewriting federal energy policy — all blocked by Senate Democrats in the past few years — became law in 2005.

Senate Republicans had to give up on a class action bill in July 2004 after they lost a vote on a motion to invoke cloture and break a Democratic filibuster. That roll call was deemed to have been one of two dozen "key votes" of that year. Some six months later, in February 2005, the Senate easily passed an almost identical bill as one of the first acts of the 109th Congress.

The editors of Congressional Quarterly selected 16 from among 366 roll calls in the Senate and and 12 from among 669 roll calls in the House as the key votes for 2005. For 60 years, this has been an annual exercise intended to illustrate legislative turning points and significant controversies, and to focus attention on how both the institution and the individual lawmakers acted.

Limiting plaintiffs from using multiple state courts to bring class action lawsuits had been a central component of the Republican "tort reform" agenda for years and was high on President Bush's second-term wish list from Congress. That made Senate passage of the bill a prime candidate to be picked as a key vote. The same can be said for bankruptcy overhaul, which became law after an eight-year effort.

Other easy selections included passage of the Central American

## How CQ Picks Key Votes

Since its founding in 1945, Congressional Quarterly has selected a series of key votes for both the House and Senate on major issues of the year.

A vote is judged to be key by the extent to which it represents:

- a matter of major controversy.
- a matter of presidential or political power.
- a matter of potentially great impact on the nation and lives of Americans.

For each group of related votes in each chamber on an issue, one key vote is usually chosen — one that, in the opinion of CQ editors, was the most important in determining the outcome of the issue for the year or best reflected the views of the individual members on that issue.

Free-Trade Agreement at a time of rising apprehension on Capitol Hill about globalization and weakening support for free-trade measures, enactment of a five-year highway and mass transit authorization after years of struggle over how to carve up a too-small pie among needy states, and confirmation of John G. Roberts Jr. as the first new chief justice of the United States in 19 years.

### INDEPENDENTLY INCLINED

On the other hand, if the president and his Republican allies thought the rightward shifting ideological sands that helped lead to swift enactment of the class action and bankruptcy laws portended sweeping success in 2005, they were very wrong. Two-thirds of the key votes of the year involved tests of the president's power to persuade Congress — and he lost on almost half of them. And that was as true in the typically lockstep House as it was in the more minority-friendly Senate.

Passage of the Republicans' marquee spending-cut package required careful vote counting and enforced party discipline in the House and the tie-breaking vote of Vice President Dick Cheney in the Senate. Rank-and-file GOP support for the president broke down over concern about the nation's standing in the world and protection of individual liberties. Both chambers stood up to White House pressure and insisted on clear standards for treatment of military detainees that barred torture, forcing Bush to cut a deal in order to save face. Both chambers insisted, over the president's objections, on limiting the reach of federal investigative powers. In the case of expiring parts of the anti-terrorism law known as the Patriot Act, he was compelled to accept the very sort of short-term extension that he had vowed to resist.

The House also dealt a blow to the president and the Republican majority leadership when it voted to permit limited federal research into the use of embryonic stem cells as a source of medical treatment. And the Senate took a step toward pushing the United States to impose limits on emissions of carbon dioxide and other greenhouse gases.

On the following pages are stories describing each of the key votes of 2005. They are listed in the order of their original vote numbers.

# SENATE VOTES

## 9 Class Action Lawsuits

**Passage of legislation to curb class action litigation by shifting jurisdiction over many such cases into federal court.**

For six years, business interests lobbied for restrictions on class action lawsuits, only to be thwarted by opponents in the Senate. But the 2004 elections, which boosted the number of Republicans in that chamber from 51 to 55, showed demonstrably that elections matter and that their outcome can change public policy.

When the new Congress convened, GOP leaders moved quickly to a class action bill that would give federal courts jurisdiction over cases involving at least 100 plaintiffs if at least $5 million was at stake and two-thirds of the plaintiffs lived in different states.

Majority Leader Bill Frist, R-Tenn., who is contemplating a 2008 presidential run, wanted an early victory to flex his political muscle and demonstrate that he could get things done. He had pulled the class action bill from the Senate floor in 2004 when a cloture motion fell 16 votes short of cutting off debate. Frist had some help. He had enough Democratic support that opponents could not mount a filibuster or use parliamentary delays to stop passage of the bill, as they have in past years.

Five Democratic amendments to the bill were defeated by wide margins. Supporters argued that adopting any of the amendments would derail the Senate compromise on the bill and complicate House passage. "We negotiated a pretty significant package," said Democrat Christopher J. Dodd of Connecticut. "If the bill changes, then all bets are off."

Democratic leaders were resigned to the fact that passage of the class action bill was not in doubt, but asserted that it would be the "high-water mark" for Republican efforts to change the civil justice system to limit some types of lawsuits, such as establishing an asbestos trust fund (S 852) and limiting damage awards in medical malpractice suits (HR 5). They proved to be mostly right. Those two bills could not get enough support to reach the Senate floor, but legislation (PL 109-92) to shield gun manufacturers and dealers from being sued when third parties misuse their products was cleared by Congress later in the year.

Without strong opposition from their leadership, 18 Democrats voted for the class action measure. No Republican voted against it. The bill was passed Feb. 10, 72-26: R 53-0; D 18-26 (ND 16-24, SD 2-2); I 1-0. The House easily cleared the measure the next week, giving President Bush his first major legislative accomplishment of his second term. *(Senate vote 9, p. C-26)*

Democratic supporters included Sen. Blanche Lincoln of Arkansas, home of retail giant Wal-Mart Stores Inc., which has been the defendant in major class action suits. Another key supporter was Dodd, whose home state is headquarters to many insurance companies.

In the aftermath of the vote, the Association of Trial Lawyers of America, a vocal opponent of the measure and a major source of campaign funds for Democratic candidates, ramped up its outreach efforts to Republican lawmakers.

## 28 Bankruptcy Law Overhaul

**Defeat of an amendment that would have prevented violent protesters from escaping court-ordered fines or judgments by filing for bankruptcy protection.**

With an increased majority in the Senate and several Democratic defections, Senate Republican leaders were able to defeat a controversial amendment that had become the critical obstacle to enacting a bankruptcy overhaul bill. The defeat of the amendment, offered by Democrat Charles E. Schumer of New York., all but guaranteed a victory for the banking and credit card industries and their congressional supporters, who had pushed for eight years to revamp the bankruptcy code.

The Senate passed the bill, 74-25, on March 10. The House followed suit on April 14, by a 302-126 vote.

That most likely would not have happened if Schumer had prevailed. House Republican leaders had made clear they would not take up the Senate-passed bankruptcy bill if it included the amendment, which would have prevented violent protesters from avoiding fines by filing for bankruptcy protection. In earlier versions, the amendment had specifically targeted anti-abortion protesters. In 2002, negotiations between Schumer and a group of House Republicans resulted in the language being changed to include all violent protesters, but the amendment was still anathema to conservative Republicans.

Worries that the Schumer amendment could stop the overhaul bill were not unfounded. During the 106th Congress, President Bill Clinton pocket vetoed a bankruptcy overhaul measure after the Schumer language was dropped from the bill. The amendment continued to plague overhaul advocates in the 107th and 108th Congresses. In 2004, Senate GOP leaders refused to bring the bill to the floor rather than risk having the language adopted.

Aware of the potential implications, Senate GOP leaders aggressively whipped their members to vote against the amendment. This time, Senate Republicans had more factors working in their favor. The most important was control of 55 seats in the chamber. That gave them greater leeway to allow some moderate caucus members to vote for the amendment without its defeat being jeopardized.

They also could rely on the support of the more conservative Democrats who oppose abortion rights and did not want to vote for a provision aimed at clamping down on abortion protesters. Finally, the clout of the credit card and finance industries, which donated $29.5 million to federal candidates during the eight years it took to enact the bankruptcy overhaul, could not have hurt.

Schumer called on the Senate not to "protect those who use violence," telling his colleagues that a vote against his proposal was a vote "against the rule of law." He stressed that the language would apply to any violent protester, not just those who oppose abortion rights. "If violent atheists burn down a church, it would apply to them," Schumer told his colleagues.

Senate Republicans attacked the amendment on two fronts. They said it was unnecessary and, more immediately, that it would once again prevent Congress from overhauling federal bankruptcy laws.

"Let's don't add this amendment, jeopardizing passage of this bill," Jeff Sessions, R-Ala., implored during the floor debate. He characterized the amendment as the "most perfect example of a poison pill" he had ever seen. Sessions was joined by Orrin G. Hatch, R-Utah, who argued that bankruptcy courts have made clear they will not allow

debtors to escape fines and judgments for willful, violent actions.

In the end, Republican efforts were enough to take down the amendment March 8. The Senate voted against it 46-53; R 4-51; D 41-2 (ND 37-2, SD 4-0); I 1-0. *(Senate vote 28, p. C-26)*

## 127 Confirmation of Judge Owen

**Vote to invoke cloture, or limit debate, on the nomination of Priscilla Owen to be a judge on the U.S. Court of Appeals for the 5th Circuit.**

Texas Supreme Court Justice Priscilla Owen was among the first candidates for the federal bench that President Bush submitted in 2001. But her nomination languished for more than four years before the Senate voted to confirm her in May.

Owen was perhaps the most ideologically controversial of the 10 appellate court nominees whom Democrats filibustered in the Republican-controlled Senate in the 108th Congress. Her opponents worried that she would be hostile to abortion rights as a federal judge. Bush renominated Owen and six of the other previously filibustered candidates in February. Still, the Senate Democratic caucus opposed an up-or-down vote until a group of senators — seven Republicans and seven Democrats — brokered a deal on judicial nominations in May, agreeing not to oppose cloture on the nomination.

A potential showdown over judicial nominations escalated in January, when Majority Leader Bill Frist, R-Tenn., went to the Senate floor on the first day of the 109th Congress to warn that he would not tolerate further Democratic filibusters of appellate court nominees. For the first few months of the year, Frist repeatedly threatened to execute an esoteric procedural gambit, dubbed the "nuclear option," to end minority filibusters of judicial nominees.

Frist and Minority Leader Harry Reid, D-Nev., exchanged half-hearted proposals and rhetorical potshots, to no avail. Finally, Frist scheduled a vote on cloture, which would cut off debate and lead to a vote on Owen's nomination, for May 24.

On May 23, Frist went before a battery of cameras outside the chamber to announce that if the cloture vote fell short of the 60-vote threshold for the motion to succeed, Vice President Dick Cheney would preside over the Senate while Frist made a point of order that there should be a finite amount of debate time for an appellate or a Supreme Court nominee. If Cheney upheld Frist's point of order and Democrats challenged the ruling, a simple majority was all Republicans would need to sustain Cheney's ruling.

Later that day, the group that became known as the "gang of 14" emerged from the Capitol Hill office of Arizona Republican John McCain with the deal that thwarted Frist, but also guaranteed the confirmation of Owen and several other contentious nominees. The 14 senators also agreed that judicial nominees should be filibustered only under "extraordinary circumstances," a term that was left to each group member to define.

The cloture vote on Owen the next day demonstrated that the 14 senators had defused what had promised to be a dramatic parliamentary showdown on judicial nominations, effectively taking control of the issue away from Senate leaders. The Senate agreed to the motion to invoke cloture on an 81-18 vote, which easily exceeded the 60 votes needed: R 55-0; D 26-17 (ND 23-16, SD 3-1); I 0-1. *(Senate vote 127, p. C-26)*

Owen was confirmed the next day with the support of only two Democrats. But the fact that more than half the Democrats had

voted to limit debate was a sign of their relief that the "gang of 14" had given the Senate a way to back away from a showdown over rules that could have fundamentally undermined the power of the minority party in the chamber.

## 129 Confirmation of Bolton as U.N. Ambassador

**Defeat of an attempt to invoke cloture and thereby move to a vote on the nomination of John R. Bolton to be U.S. ambassador to the United Nations.**

Bolton's nomination was in trouble from the moment President Bush announced him as his pick for the top job at the United Nations. Viewed as abrasive, confrontational and willing to run roughshod over his peers at the State Department while he was an undersecretary of State, Bolton faced serious opposition from Democrats and some moderate Republicans.

Several former colleagues testified against Bolton during his confirmation hearings. In public testimony, former State Department official Carl Ford Jr. provided the Senate Foreign Relations Committee with a damaging portrait of the nominee, describing him as a "quintessential kiss-up, kick down sort of guy." Bolton's nomination emerged from the committee in May "without recommendation" — not an outright rejection, but a cautionary message that the nominee would have trouble winning approval from the full Senate.

Democrats threatened to filibuster the Bolton nomination as it headed to the Senate floor. In public and private testimony, Bolton's critics accused him of verbally abusing subordinates and trying to manipulate intelligence appraised by State Department analysts regarding Iraq's weapons of mass destruction programs. In an attempt to end debate, Majority Leader Bill Frist, R-Tenn., made a motion to invoke cloture, which requires 60 votes.

But on May 26 the Senate rejected the motion, 56-42: R 53-1; D 3-40 (ND 1-38, SD 2-2); I 0-1. That was a major setback for the Bush administration and a blow to Bolton, who had routinely criticized the United Nations and vowed to push for changes at the institution. *(Senate vote 129, p. C-26)*

The cloture vote not only showed that Democrats were prepared to obstruct Bush's nominees; it also reflected the tenuous hold Republicans had on their majority in the Senate. Several moderate Republicans, such as Lincoln Chafee of Rhode Island, George V. Voinovich of Ohio and Chuck Hagel of Nebraska, remained undecided on Bolton throughout the nomination process, making it that much harder for Frist to bring home a victory for Bush on the controversial nomination.

Democrats contended that Bolton was unworthy of going to the United Nations to represent the U.S. government. They said they would allow a vote only if the White House released a series of intelligence documents showing how Bolton had handled information regarding Syria's weapons programs. Bolton was also accused of requesting National Security Agency intercepts so he could snoop on subordinates at the State Department.

The White House was not forthcoming with the documents, and Democrats refused to budge. The Senate held a second cloture vote June 20, but the result was so apparent that many senators skipped the vote, and cloture failed by even more votes than it did the first time, 54-38.

None of the Senate's parliamentary delays ended up mattering in the end. Bush bypassed the Senate and installed Bolton at the United Nations with a recess appointment on the first day of the August recess.

Bolton has been working at the United Nations for five months. His recess appointment will expire in January 2007, when he would have to be renominated.

## 149 Global Warming Policy

**Rejection of a motion to table a global warming resolution endorsing the need for mandatory federal greenhouse gas regulations, paving the way for adoption of the resolution.**

Since 1997, when the Senate voted 95-0 to condemn the international global warming agreement signed in Kyoto, Japan, Congress has resisted every effort to set mandatory limits on emissions of carbon dioxide and other gases that are widely blamed for contributing to worldwide climate change.

The Bush administration and, for the most part, Congress have argued that the Kyoto accord would hamstring the U.S. economy while letting off the hook developing nations that are projected to soon emit more greenhouse gases than the United States. There also remains a core of lawmakers who reject the premise of global warming, led by Senate Environment and Public Works Chairman James M. Inhofe, R-Okla., who has called climate change theories "phony science" and a "hoax."

An attempt in 2005 by Sens. John McCain, R-Ariz., and Joseph I. Lieberman, D-Conn., to mandate a reduction in greenhouse gas emissions to 2000 levels by 2010 actually lost ground, winning just 38 votes in favor after garnering 43 votes in 2003.

In a change from past practice, however, the Senate went on record for the first time ever as recognizing that climate change is a significant problem and endorsing the need for mandatory emission limits. While largely symbolic, the action, in support of a resolution offered by Jeff Bingaman, D-N.M., signaled a shift in the political landscape.

McCain and Lieberman offered their proposal in June to a comprehensive energy bill (HR 6). Their plan, which they had promoted for several years, would establish a domestic cap-and-trade model similar to the Kyoto approach. Such market-based programs cap overall pollution while allowing businesses to buy and sell permits in order to meet their obligations.

In a bid to attract more votes this time, senators embraced nuclear energy as an energy source that emits no greenhouse gases. The tactic backfired, angering environmentalists and losing the support of several liberal Democrats who had backed the legislation in 2003. The Senate did approve, 66-29, a separate amendment by Chuck Hagel, R-Neb., to offer economic incentives for businesses to reduce emissions of carbon dioxide and other greenhouse gases. The voluntary approach appealed to many Republicans, but critics derided it as inadequate.

Bingaman sought to bridge the gap between the McCain-Lieberman proposal to mandate a reduction in emissions and the laissez-faire model advanced by Hagel. He proposed tying emissions caps to economic growth and allowing the government to sell more permits to companies that failed to meet the targets once the market price for credits reached a certain level. This "safety valve" would give businesses economic certainty, but would allow emissions to rise in the future, albeit at a slower rate.

As the ranking Democrat on the Energy and Natural Resources Committee, Bingaman has a cooperative relationship with the panel's GOP chairman, fellow New Mexican Pete V. Domenici, and the two discussed the idea of jointly offering Bingaman's plan as an amendment to the energy bill. In the end, Domenici backed off, saying he feared splitting Republicans, alienating the White House and jeopardizing the

energy bill's prospects. But he agreed to hold hearings on the idea and to support an amendment expressing the sense of the Senate that climate change is a problem and endorsing mandatory, market-based measures to "slow, stop and reverse" emissions.

Inhofe moved to table Bingaman's resolution, sparking a showdown over the fundamental question of whether global warming is for real, and illustrating the shifting sentiments on the issue among some Republican senators.

"Climate change is here," said Mike DeWine, R-Ohio, who voted against the McCain-Lieberman amendment. "I am confident that we can draft a bill that will own up to our obligations to our children and our grandchildren and at the same time have dates that are practical." Domenici, who also had voted against McCain-Lieberman, also expressed his conviction that the science now shows that global warming is occurring and must be addressed.

Bingaman's resolution was adopted by voice vote June 22, after the Senate rejected Inhofe's motion to table the proposal 44-53; R 42-12; D 2-40 (ND 2-36, SD 0-4); I 0-1 *(Senate vote 149, p. C-26)*

In addition to the six Republicans who had voted for McCain-Lieberman, six more Republicans voted against the attempt to kill Bingaman's resolution. With that vote, 53 became a magic number in the Senate's global warming debate, offering a new baseline for potential support and a list of lawmakers who would, in principle, support climate change legislation. It also laid the groundwork for Bingaman, backed by Domenici, to pursue an alternative to the McCain-Lieberman plan in 2006.

## 170 Central American Trade Liberalization

**Passage of a bill to implement tariff reductions and other changes to U.S. trade law that were part of a free-trade agreement negotiated between the United States and five Central American countries, plus the Dominican Republic.**

President Bush has made expansion of trade with Western Hemisphere countries a hallmark of his administration from his first election. In 2004, after several fits and starts, his administration secured an agreement to relax trade barriers between the United States and Costa Rica, El Salvador, Guatemala, Honduras and Nicaragua. A parallel agreement was reached with the Dominican Republic.

The Constitution gives Congress explicit authority for trade pacts, but for several decades, lawmakers have allowed the president to negotiate agreements that are then sent to Congress for approval on up-or-down votes. Because no amendments are allowed in committee or on the floor, the White House often has to make side promises to lawmakers to win their votes on trade agreements.

That was the case with the Central American agreement, also known as CAFTA. The name evoked echoes of NAFTA, the 1993 North American Free-Trade Agreement with Mexico and Canada, which many members of the House and Senate thought had not been as beneficial for the United States as promised.

Since NAFTA (PL 103-182) was enacted, trade agreements have been an increasingly tough sell on Capitol Hill, and CAFTA was the first in more than a decade with low-wage countries that are seen as magnets for U.S. jobs. So supporters of the Central American pact decided to press for a vote first in the Senate, where its prospects were considered better than the House. In fact, House Republican leaders were uncertain they had the votes to win in that chamber, and it was hoped that a Senate vote to pass a bill implementing the agreement would give

the House an incentive to do the same.

Trade votes are generally easier in the Senate because senators have more diverse constituencies and the luxury of a six-year term to explain an unpopular vote. But even the Senate was reluctant to pass the CAFTA implementing bill (S 1307), and agreed to do so only after several weeks of administration efforts to address senators' concerns about sugar imports, labor rights in Central America and general uneasiness about the effects of globalization.

When the Senate finally voted late in the evening of June 30, as Congress was trying to get out of town for its July Fourth recess, the vote was an uncharacteristically tight 54-45: R 43-12; D 10-33 (ND 7-32, SD 3-1); I 1-0. *(Senate vote 170, p. C-26)*

The closeness of the vote illustrates a shift in sentiment among lawmakers of both parties on trade issues, though it is especially evident among Democrats, and may portend trouble for future accords.

To win Senate approval, the Bush administration first had to secure a majority in the Senate Finance Committee. Several of the panel's typically pro-trade members from both parties were concerned about the effect of the accord on jobs in their states from additional imports of sugar that would be permitted.

To address their concerns, U.S. Trade Representative Rob Portman and Agriculture Secretary Mike Johanns pledged to use provisions allowed under commodity trading rules to keep sugar imports permitted under CAFTA and other trade deals out of the U.S. market for the remaining two years of the current farm bill (PL 107-171). They also agreed to study the feasibility of government initiatives to spur production of ethanol made from sugar.

That helped win over Agriculture Chairman Saxby Chambliss, R-Ga., and Norm Coleman, R-Minn. But Max Baucus of Montana, the ranking Democrat on Finance, Idaho Republicans Michael D. Crapo and Larry E. Craig, and Conrad Burns R-Mont., were not convinced. They allowed the implementing bill to get out of committee on June 29, but voted against the measure on the floor the following day.

Faced with opposition from GOP sugar-state senators, the administration tried to entice wavering Democrats with a pledge of a multi-year commitment to beef up enforcement and monitoring of labor and environmental standards in Central America and to aid farmers in the region. That helped win the votes of Jeff Bingaman, D-N.M., and James M. Jeffords, I-Vt. But Christopher J. Dodd, D-Conn., who had hoped to support CAFTA, voted no with a "very, very heavy heart," citing concerns that labor protections in the agreement should have been stronger.

The Senate vote had the desired effect and gave impetus to the House, although that chamber came very close to rejecting the pact before voting yes in the end. The Senate had to vote again to clear the separate House-passed bill (HR 3045). The July 28 vote was almost identical to the early tally — 55-45. *(House CAFTA key vote, p. C-16)*

## 213  Energy Policy Overhaul

**Final passage of legislation that includes incentives for greater domestic production of oil, gas, coal and nuclear power, encouragement for conservation and a reduction in regulation of the electric power industry.**

In the culmination of a four-year debate on energy policy, the Senate agreed to a compromise measure that followed the outlines of the energy plan President Bush proposed not long after taking office in 2001 but without the centerpiece of his proposal — drilling for oil and

gas in Alaska's Arctic National Wildlife Refuge (ANWR). That proved too difficult for Republican leaders to force through.

Negotiators also dropped from the final bill liability protection for companies that make the fuel additive methyl tertiary butyl ether (MTBE), an issue that prevented passage for two consecutive years.

The vote showed the broad support for energy legislation once ANWR and MTBE were set aside. More than half of the Senate's Democrats supported the final conference version, with only six Republicans opposed to it. The Senate easily cleared the measure July 29, 74-26: R 49-6; D 25-19 (ND 22-18, SD 3-1); I 0-1. *(Senate vote 213, p. C-27)*

The bill was a mixed success for the Bush administration and GOP leaders, who were intent on increasing domestic production of oil, gas and nuclear power as a way of reducing U.S. dependence on foreign fuels. They also opposed requiring Americans to conserve energy.

Opening the coastal plain of ANWR to energy exploration had been the main feature of Bush's energy plan but a rallying point for environmentalists trying to protect one of the nation's most pristine and remote wilderness areas. Dropping the provision was a GOP defeat.

Under pressure to deliver a bill, Republican leaders — particularly in the House — also had to give up on a contentious liability waiver for MTBE makers that had blocked final action on the bill in the Senate for two years. *(House energy key vote, p. C-16)*

The chemical, used at low levels since 1979, became more prevalent when refiners had to meet fuel standards established under the 1990 Clean Air Act amendments (PL 101-549) that aimed to reduce smog. But the additive had since been found to contaminate groundwater in some areas, including the Northeast and West Coast. Lawmakers from those areas worried that giving liability protection for manufacturers might leave states responsible for cleaning up MTBE in the ground

The new energy law (PL 109-58) includes tax incentives for both traditional and alternative energy producers. It authorizes $14.6 billion in tax breaks and credits between 2005 and 2015, including: $2.8 billion for fossil fuel production; $2.7 billion to extend the renewable electricity production credit; $1.6 billion for investments in plants designed to use cleaner-burning coal; $1.3 billion for conservation and energy efficiency; and $1.3 billion for alternative-fuel motor vehicles and fuels.

Some effects of the law might not be known for years. For instance, it makes major changes in the regulation of electricity markets, including repealing the 1935 Public Utility Holding Company Act, which has restricted many large power companies to certain geographic areas and lines of business. Lawmakers decided that the Federal Energy Regulatory Commission would be better able to examine electric utility books and have the power to block mergers. The new requirements will probably lead to a spate of mergers.

## 219  Gun Industry Liability Shield

**Passage of legislation that protects gun manufacturers and dealers from being sued when third parties misuse their products.**

A priority of the National Rifle Association (NRA) and business groups that want to limit product liability lawsuits in general, legislation to protect gunmakers and dealers had previously stalled in the Senate because of Democratic opposition.

Majority Leader Bill Frist, R-Tenn., sought to avoid a replay of a similar bill's fate in 2004 when Republicans spiked the entire measure rather than allow it to pass with three amendments attached by Democrats, including a renewal of the assault weapons ban.

When the new bill (S 397) reached the floor in July, Frist filed a succession of amendments — a legislative procedure known as "filling the amendment tree" — that allowed him to control what amendments could be brought up for debate. He allowed consideration only of those proposals he thought were harmless or easy to defeat on the floor, thus thwarting any potential Democratic efforts to add gun-control language.

Republicans easily defeated Democratic amendments that would have allowed individuals, but not municipalities, to sue gunmakers; preserved the right of police officers or minors injured by firearms to sue for damages; and blocked the sale of so-called cop-killer bullets. Instead, the Senate adopted a Republican alternative amendment requiring a study of a uniform standard for testing projectiles against body armor and increasing the penalties for violent or drug-trafficking crimes in which the perpetrator uses or possesses armor-piercing ammunition.

The Senate adopted only one Democratic amendment, by Herb Kohl of Wisconsin, to require that child safety locks be sold with all handguns.

The final vote July 29 was a victory for GOP leaders, who had promised to push the legislation through before the August recess, and showed the power of the gun rights lobby led by the NRA. The vote was 65-31: R 50-2; D 14-29 (ND 10-29, SD 4-0); I 1-0. *(Senate vote 219, p. C-27)*

The 14 Democrats who voted for the bill were all from states with large rural areas where hunting is popular. Independent James M. Jeffords of Vermont also voted for the legislation, while two Republicans — Lincoln Chafee of Rhode Island and Mike DeWine of Ohio — voted against it.

The House cleared the bill, 283-144, in October. The measure prohibits civil liability actions from being brought in any state or federal court against manufacturers, distributors, dealers or importers of firearms and ammunition. Trade groups also are protected, and all pending legal action against gunmakers will be dismissed.

The statute does not protect anyone who sells or transfers a firearm knowing it is intended to be used for a crime of violence or drug trafficking, or anyone who knowingly violates state or federal laws applicable to the marketing or sale of firearms, when the violation results in harm. It also exempts cases in which proper use results in physical injury, death or property damage because of a defect in the firearm.

## 220 | Surface Transportation Spending

**Final passage of a six-year reauthorization of highway and transit programs that was more expensive than the Bush administration wanted but not as generous as many in Congress had demanded.**

For the second straight year, Majority Leader Bill Frist, R-Tenn., had to contain open defiance within his caucus at the administration's transportation spending policy. Even fiscal conservatives such as James M. Inhofe of Oklahoma, chairman of the Environment and Public Works Committee, and Charles E. Grassley of Iowa, who chairs the Finance Committee, wanted to spend more on highway programs than the administration said it would allow.

The long impasse and the vote accepting the eventual compromise showed the enduring power of public works projects for members of Congress, irrespective of their party. Frist was able to claim a victory of

sorts for fiscal responsibility because the final conference version of the bill (HR 3) exceeded the administration's request by just $2.5 billion. But the administration had made the task easier at the beginning of 2005 by increasing its request from $256 billion to $284 billion. Also, the bill included an $8.5 billion rescission of prior contract authority that becomes available at the end of fiscal 2009, boosting the available total contract authority at that point, and increasing the cost of the bill, to $295 billion. The authorization is good through fiscal 2009 and is retroactive to fiscal 2004.

Frist attempted to set the parameters early by saying that he stood by the administration's $284 billion request and threatening to bar anything more expensive from coming to the floor. But Inhofe said the nation's legitimate transportation needs required far more money and that transportation was one of the few areas where he, as a conservative, felt increased federal spending was justified. His committee sent to the floor a $284 billion package, but supported amending it to increase the authorization to $295 billion.

Grassley put together a package of tax changes and measures designed to crack down on fuel fraud that supporters claimed fully paid for the additional spending. Grassley's package came under immediate attack from other fiscal conservatives, such as Republican Judd Gregg of New Hampshire, the chairman of the Budget Committee, who said the administration's call for fiscal restraint was "being run over by a bulldozer."

Grassley's proposals also drew a veto threat from the White House and warnings from House Republican leaders that they would not survive conference negotiations.

Those negotiations were predictably difficult. The Senate took a different approach from the House in determining how much highway money each state would receive and in resolving longstanding complaints from the states that collect significantly more in gasoline taxes than they receive back from the government for transportation projects. The final bill was virtually the same as the Senate approach, guaranteeing each state a bonus to ensure by fiscal 2008 a return of at least 92 cents on each dollar contributed to the Highway Trust Fund.

Several senators were critical of the House for its long list of earmarks in the bill. The Senate version was more restrained. But once the measure went into conference, senators demanded the right to determine half of all "high-priority program" highway earmarks.

While it was generally understood that senators would be allocated some earmarks in conference, notwithstanding their public criticism, the scale of their demands in the context of the narrow fiscal margins negotiators were working with threw already difficult discussions into turmoil. It took marathon staff work and sometimes impromptu discussions among top conferees to reach agreement in the final moments before Congress departed for its summer recess.

The House adopted the conference report, 412-8, the morning of July 29 and sent it to the Senate. A little more than an hour later, the Senate cleared the measure 91-4: R 48-4; D 42-0 (ND 38-0, SD 4-0); I 1-0. *(Senate vote 220, p, C-27; House surface transportation key vote, p. C-17)*

## 245 | Confirmation of Roberts as Chief Justice

**Confirmation of John G. Roberts Jr. as the 17th chief justice of the United States.**

After President Bush took office in 2001, conservative and liberal activists alike braced themselves for a cataclysmic Senate showdown

over his first Supreme Court nominee.

But by the time the nomination of John G. Roberts Jr. to succeed William H. Rehnquist as chief justice reached the Senate floor in September, there was no suspense about the outcome.

Roberts, an accomplished appellate lawyer and federal appeals court judge, was originally nominated to replace centrist Justice Sandra Day O'Connor, who announced her retirement July 1 contingent upon her successor's confirmation. But after Rehnquist died Sept. 3, Bush instead nominated Roberts to succeed the chief justice.

Roberts performed brilliantly in his Senate Judiciary Committee confirmation hearing. Given that, and the fact that he was to replace the conservative Rehnquist, many Democrats chose not to heed the urging of liberal activists to vote against him.

The vote on Roberts marked a turning point in the judicial nomination war that had raged in the Senate since 2003. The filibuster-proof tally was a clear sign that many Senate Democrats lacked the appetite to oppose Bush's pick for the high court for ideological reasons.

Still, the Sept. 29 vote was historic, infused with more than a little sense of drama. It was the first Senate action on a chief justice nominee since 1986. Many senators had never voted on a Supreme Court nominee; the last high court vacancy occurred in 1994.

In recognition of the rarity of the moment, senators voted from their desks as the roll was called, rather than by their usual method of casting their votes in the well. Jane Roberts, the nominee's wife, watched from the gallery.

Robert C. Byrd, the 88-year-old West Virginia Democrat seeking a ninth term in 2006, walked to his desk with the aid of two canes. Judiciary Chairman Arlen Specter, R-Pa., took a seat next to his predecessor as committee chairman, Orrin G. Hatch, R-Utah. Hatch patted Specter on the back, and the two men shook hands.

Not all 100 senators were at their desks at the start of the roll call, however. A few stragglers — most notably New York Democrat Charles E. Schumer, one of Bush's main antagonists on judges — arrived late.

Twenty-two Democrats and Independent James M. Jeffords of Vermont joined all 55 Republicans in supporting Roberts. The vote was 78-22: R 55-0; D 22-22 (ND 18-22, SD 4-0); I 1-0. (*Senate vote 245, p. C-27*)

The 50-year-old Roberts, who is the youngest chief justice since John Marshall, was sworn in at the White House by Justice John Paul Stevens later the same day.

## 249 Treatment of Military Detainees

**Adoption of an amendment to the fiscal 2006 Defense appropriations bill banning cruel, inhuman or degrading treatment of enemy combatants and requiring military interrogators to rely on an Army field manual that complies with the Geneva Conventions.**

No proposal caused more waves in Congress during the fall than legislation championed by John McCain, R-Ariz., to regulate the treatment of enemy combatants captured and detained by U.S. military forces or law enforcement. The proposal resulted in the delay of two major defense bills, a veto threat and frequent personal visits and phone calls to key lawmakers by Vice President Dick Cheney. The White House repeatedly told lawmakers they must not pass any legislation that would tie the president's hands in the war on terror.

The Republican-controlled Senate responded, but not with the outcome the White House wanted. On Oct. 5, the Senate adopted McCain's amendment 90-9; R 46-9; D 43-0 (ND 39-0; SD 4-0); I 1-0. (*Senate vote 249, p. C-27*)

With such strong bipartisan support, the vote was the most direct slap to the administration on the moral conduct of the war on terrorism since it began four years ago. After a string of prison abuse scandals and questions over the legal rights of detainees, lawmakers agreed with McCain that the policy on handling military detainees should be decided by Congress.

McCain's amendment, adopted as part of the fiscal 2006 Defense appropriations bill (HR 2863), banned cruel, inhuman or degrading treatment of detainees. It also required military interrogators to use an Army field manual when trying to extract intelligence from suspects. The field manual, under revision at the time of the vote, outlines specific interrogation techniques that comply with the Geneva Conventions. President Bush has argued that the Geneva standards apply to state-sponsored, uniformed soldiers, but not to terrorists.

McCain, who as a Navy flier during the Vietnam War was shot down, captured and tortured for five and a half years, told his colleagues that banning the abuse of suspected terrorists was necessary. "They don't deserve our sympathy. But this isn't about who they are. This is about who we are. These are the values that distinguish us from our enemies." Terrorists do not adhere to anti-torture treaties, McCain said, "but 'we're better than them, and we are the stronger for our faith."

A member of the Armed Services Committee, McCain initially proposed the language as an amendment to the fiscal 2006 defense authorization bill (S 1042), which was on the Senate floor in July. But Majority Leader Bill Frist, R-Tenn., pulled the authorization bill, citing more than 200 pending amendments. Frist said debate would take too long, and the Senate turned its attention to legislation that would shield gunmakers from liability lawsuits. McCain, however, insisted that his proposal was the primary reason the bill was pulled.

In October, McCain sought to attach the detainee requirements to the must-pass Defense appropriations bill. Frist was among the Republicans who voted in favor of the anti-abuse proposal. McCain subsequently won voice vote approval to add the language to the defense authorization bill as well.

After the House expressed strong support for the amendment in mid-December, Bush backed away from his veto threat. The amendment, with a relatively minor change, was cleared as part of both Defense bills. (*House detainee key vote, p. C-18*)

Democrats were quick to portray the move as a proxy vote on Bush's conduct of the war in Iraq. But Republicans — including McCain — were just as insistent that the vote contained no wider message.

"This does not have anything to do with [presidential] leadership," he said. "It has to do with treatment of [detainees] and human rights. And that message is wide enough."

## 262 Redirection of Lawmakers' Earmarks

**Rejection of an amendment to the fiscal 2006 Transportation-Treasury-Housing spending bill that would have denied money for the construction of two "bridges to nowhere" in Alaska.**

The Senate was embarrassed by news coverage of its multimillion-dollar appropriations for "bridges to nowhere" on the coast of Alaska,

but not enough to threaten the congressional tradition of members earmarking federal projects and programs for their own states.

Not long after Rep. Don Young, R-Alaska, included the bridge projects at Ketchikan and Anchorage in a highway authorization bill (PL 109-59), someone noticed that they would connect to lightly settled areas — the Ketchikan bridge would link the town to an island with 50 residents and an airport — and dubbed them bridges to nowhere.

Freshman Republican Tom Coburn of Oklahoma, a staunch fiscal conservative, decided to take action when the fiscal 2006 Transportation-Treasury-Housing appropriations bill came to the Senate floor. "What I am here to tell you is that the rumble against spending is getting louder. People are fed up," Coburn told his colleagues. "All across the country, Americans are rising up against government overspending."

Coburn proposed removing the $454 million for the bridges and spending it instead to reconstruct a Mississippi River bridge in New Orleans damaged by Hurricane Katrina.

Alaska Republican Ted Stevens, former chairman of the Senate Appropriations Committee, was incensed at this challenge to the earmark system. "This amendment is an offense to me," Stevens thundered. "It is not only an offense to me, it is a threat to every person in my state. . . . It is wrong to do this to any state."

If Coburn's amendment were adopted, then money might be shifted from one state to another at will. "I will put the Senate on notice — and I don't kid people," Stevens said later. "If the Senate decides to discriminate against our state and take money only from our state, I will resign from this body. This is not the Senate I came to. This is not the Senate I devoted 37 years to. If one senator can decide he will take all the money from one state to solve a problem of another, that is not a union. That is not equality and is not treating my state the way I have seen it treated for 37 years."

The Senate agreed, and the Oct. 20 vote was a lopsided 15-82: R 11-43; D 4-38 (ND 3-35, SD 1-3); I 0-1. *(Senate vote 262, p. C-28)*

Although the amendment was defeated, it had at least in part the effect Coburn wanted. Media attention to the Alaska bridges increased the pressure on Congress to do something about them. Conferees on the appropriations bill quietly removed the specific funding for the two bridges as part of the final agreement. Instead, the conference report redirected the money to a general fund that the state of Alaska could spend on transportation projects at its discretion.

This achieved two goals: enabling Coburn and those who campaigned against such projects to declare a victory, while also allowing Stevens and his Alaskan colleagues to save face by keeping the money in their state.

There was nothing in the final bill that would prevent the state from simply deciding to allocate money to the two bridges.

## 323 Conduct of the War in Iraq

**Adoption of an amendment to the fiscal 2006 defense authorization bill requiring the president to send Congress quarterly reports on progress toward meeting conditions for the withdrawal of U.S. forces from Iraq.**

More than any legislation passed since the invasion of Iraq in 2003, the Senate vote Nov. 15 sent a strong message to President Bush that Republicans were losing patience with his "stay the course" rhetoric and were watching the decline in public support for the war with increasing wariness as the 2006 midterm elections approached. The vote also

represented Congress' most forceful assertion since the war began that it has authority equal to the administration's in overseeing the conduct of the conflict.

The vote was on an amendment to the fiscal 2006 defense authorization bill (S 1042), offered by Majority Leader Bill Frist, R-Tenn., and John W. Warner, R-Va., chairman of the Armed Services Committee. Its stated purpose was "to clarify and recommend changes to the policy of the United States on Iraq and to require reports on certain matters related to Iraq."

The amendment, which was included in the final bill, requires the Bush administration to set a schedule for meeting preconditions for a pullout of U.S. troops from Iraq, such as the training of Iraqi security forces. It requires quarterly reports to Congress, in which the administration defines the criteria for success in Iraq, including details on the number of Iraqi battalions that must be able to fight independently before U.S. troops can withdraw.

In addition, in non-binding "sense of the Senate" language, the amendment declares 2006 as the year that Iraqis should take the lead on their security. It calls on the administration to tell Iraqi leaders to make the compromises necessary for political progress, and to explain to the American people what the president has called his "strategy for success." The Senate adopted the amendment 79-19: R 41-13; D 37-6. (ND 33-6, SD 4-0); I 1-0. *(Senate vote 323, p. C-28)*

Previous legislation had required the administration to provide Congress with reports on its progress in Iraq, but now the White House will have to describe — in unclassified reports that the public will be allowed to read — how conditions in Iraq are tied to goals for withdrawing U.S. troops. The measure also requires classified reports for lawmakers.

The GOP proposal was nearly identical to a Democratic plan sponsored by Carl Levin of Michigan, ranking member on Armed Services. The only significant difference was that Republicans rejected Democratic language that called for "estimated dates for the phased redeployment of the United States Armed Forces from Iraq." On Nov. 15, Republicans defeated Levin's version of the amendment, 40-58.

But given the public's growing disenchantment with the war, Republicans knew they could not just vote down the Democratic amendment without coming up with a solution of their own. "It's politically very difficult to say, 'I just voted against Levin,'" said Sen. Lincoln Chafee, R-R.I. "Now, you can say, 'But I voted for Warner.'"

Frist rejected as "absurd" the suggestion by some Democrats that his amendment represented a challenge to the president. But the vote did indicate a change in the political temperature — a shift driven by declining public support for the president's stewardship of the war, its rising costs and the more than 2,000 U.S. soldiers killed in the conflict so far. Members are feeling the heat, and they want to weigh in more aggressively on what we're doing," Rep. Curt Weldon, R-Pa., a senior member of the House Armed Services Committee, said of the Senate vote.

The vote on the Frist-Warner amendment came in the context of an increasingly fractious debate in Congress over how the war started and its possible denouement. That debate, which began after the 2004 presidential election, was rekindled in November, when Democrats accused Bush of misleading Congress and the nation about the intelligence he had cited to justify the Iraq war. Bush, backed by Republicans on Capitol Hill, responded that such charges were a partisan attempt to rewrite the Democrats' own history of support for the use of force against Iraq.

The Frist-Warner Iraq amendment avoided placing blame on the administration for its conduct of the war. But in its measured and subtle way, it indicated that Senate Republicans would no longer be acquiescent about the president's Iraq policy.

## 358 Anti-Terrorism Law Reauthorization

**Defeat of an effort to limit debate, and thereby move to a final vote, on the conference report on legislation extending 16 expiring provisions of the 2001 anti-terrorism law known as the Patriot Act.**

All year long, a small band of Senate Republicans worked closely with their Democratic colleagues to increase restrictions on surveillance powers granted to the executive branch under the 2001 anti-terrorism law (PL 107-56). But when it became clear that GOP leaders in the House and Senate, working with the White House, would not go far enough to satisfy critics' concerns about civil liberties protections, a nearly unanimous bloc of Democrats stuck with the small group of libertarian-leaning Republicans and refused to end a filibuster of the conference report on a bill (HR 3199) to reauthorize 16 provisions of the law that were set to expire Dec. 31.

On Dec. 16, two days after the House had adopted the conference report, the Senate defeated a motion to invoke cloture, or limit debate, on the report. The action forced President Bush and GOP leaders to do something they vowed they would never do: accept a short-term extension of the law to give negotiators more time to resolve their differences.

More telling, the vote illustrated that four years after the Sept. 11 terrorist attacks, the mood of lawmakers had shifted toward recognizing public concerns about civil liberties and the extent of police powers exercised in the fight against terrorism. The vote was taken on the same day The New York Times reported that Bush had authorized warrantless monitoring of international phone calls placed by U.S. citizens.

The motion to invoke cloture and limit debate on the conference report fell eight votes short of the 60 required for it to succeed. The vote was 52-47: R 50-5; D 2-41(ND 2-37, SD 0-4); I 0-1. Majority Leader Bill Frist, R-Tenn., switched his vote to "no" in a procedural tactic so he could move to reconsider the vote later. (*Senate vote 358, p. C-28*)

Republicans John E. Sununu of New Hampshire, Larry E. Craig of Idaho, Lisa Murkowski of Alaska and Chuck Hagel of Nebraska joined 41 Democrats and the Senate's lone independent, James M. Jeffords of Vermont, in voting against cloture.

Two Democrats — Ben Nelson of Nebraska and Tim Johnson of South Dakota — voted with the Republicans.

The House had adopted the conference report by a vote of 251-174, with the support of 44 Democrats.

After the cloture motion failed, Vermont Sen. Patrick J. Leahy, the ranking Democrat on the Judiciary Committee, immediately introduced a three-month extension of the current law with the intention of continuing negotiations so that additional restrictions might be placed on the expiring provisions. He wanted a bill that hewed closer to the one the Senate passed by voice vote in July.

Frist objected, saying he would not support a short-term extension and that Bush would not sign one. But as the days passed with no resolution in sight and senators anxious to close out the first session, Frist and Leahy came up with a last-minute compromise to extend the current law until July 1. The Senate passed that bill (S 2167) by voice vote Dec. 21.

The deal did not sit well with House Judiciary Chairman F. James Sensenbrenner Jr., R-Wis., who had fought any attempts at a short-term extension. He reduced the extension to five weeks, expiring on Feb. 3, and the Senate concurred. Bush signed the extension Dec. 30, while still urging Congress to reauthorize the law as soon as possible in 2006.

## 363 Cuts in Mandatory Spending

**Agreeing to a House amendment to a $38.8 billion budget savings package, with an amendment — an act that sent the bill back to the House.**

Clearing the $38.8 billion budget reconciliation package (S 1932) was a top priority for President Bush and Republican leaders of both chambers. The only thing standing in the way as the Senate entered the last real day of the session was adoption of the conference report. In the end, the spending-cut measure survived, more or less intact, although Vice President Dick Cheney had to cut short a trip to the Middle East to cast a tie-breaking vote.

But Democrats spoiled what Republicans had hoped would be a pre-adjournment victory on the first package of savings from entitlement programs such as Medicare, Medicaid and student loans since 1997. The measure was kicked back to the House, and final action was put off until after the first of the year.

Before the final Senate vote on the measure Dec. 21, Kent Conrad, D-N.D., frustrated GOP leaders and succeeded in deleting three minor provisions from the language of the conference agreement on the grounds that they violated the so-called Byrd Rule. That rule prohibits the inclusion of items in a reconciliation bill that have only an incidental budgetary effect, and 60 votes are required to override it. An attempt by Budget Chairman Judd Gregg, R-N.H., to waive the rule — and preserve the conference agreement without change — failed on a 52-48 vote.

But more important, once the Byrd Rule was invoked, the conference report was no longer valid for floor action, and the Senate was put in the unusual position of amending the bill and returning it to the House, which would then have to accept the Senate's changes in order to clear the measure for the president.

One of the stricken provisions would have granted hospitals immunity from malpractice lawsuits if they chose not to treat Medicaid recipients who could not afford co-payments. Two other provisions were essentially technical in nature.

The language of the conference agreement was virtually unchanged, but, in the House, Minority Leader Nancy Pelosi, D-Calif., insisted on a roll call vote. Because most House members had already headed home for the holidays, Republican leaders had little choice but to put off the vote on the slightly altered package until early 2006.

It was yet another obstacle in the path of a bill whose journey had been perilous from the outset. Still, House and Senate leaders thought they had successfully navigated all of the shoals.

They set the stage for the cuts in the fiscal 2006 budget resolution (H Con Res 95), which called for a reconciliation bill that would save $34.7 billion from mandatory spending programs over five years. That qualified the bill for special treatment in the Senate, allowing it to pass with 51 votes instead of the 60 typically needed when opponents threatened to mount a filibuster.

With fiscal conservatives demanding deeper cuts, and Democrats and some moderate Republicans trying to protect programs for the poor, GOP leaders put off the work of writing the bill until after the August recess. At that point the human and fiscal costs of Hurricane Katrina caused both sides to dig in.

By mid-November, the House had passed a $50 billion package, and the Senate had passed a $35 billion version. To get a conference report, GOP leaders had to bridge differences over spending and overcome dis-

agreements within Republican ranks over whether to allow drilling in Alaska's Arctic National Wildlife Refuge (ANWR), whether to cut Medicare, and how much to cut funds for Medicaid, student loans, food stamps and child support enforcement.

The way was cleared in the House when Sen. Ted Stevens, R-Alaska, agreed to remove the Senate's ANWR provisions and attach them instead to the final Defense appropriations bill. The House narrowly adopted the conference report, 212-206, on Dec. 19. *(Senate ANWR key vote, below; House mandatory cuts key vote, p. C-18)*

Conferees had made changes to satisfy Senate supporters as well. Majority Leader Bill Frist, R-Tenn., cut a deal with Norm Coleman, R-Minn., to remove cuts to sugar subsidies in conference. Coleman had voted against the original Senate bill.

Frist and House Speaker J. Dennis Hastert, R-Ill., also appeased Sen. George V. Voinovich, R-Ohio, by reducing planned cuts to Medicare equipment subsidies by $1.9 billion. That protected a major Ohio manufacturer of oxygen tanks for the elderly, but also reduced the planned savings for the entire package. The Coleman flip offset a switch from "yes" to "no" from Gordon H. Smith of Oregon, who along with four other moderate Senate Republicans — Olympia J. Snowe and Susan Collins of Maine, Mike DeWine of Ohio and Lincoln Chafee of Rhode Island — objected to increased costs for Medicaid recipients that were included in the conference agreement.

Before the vote could be held, however, Conrad raised his objections. Democrats had figured out that invoking the Byrd Rule was a means to sidetrack the bill even when they weren't permitted to mount a filibuster. Moreover, the Byrd Rule change gave opponents of the savings package yet another chance to modify or kill it.

The Senate adopted a motion to concur to the House version of the bill, with an amendment that amounted to the original conference agreement minus the three stricken provisions. The motion was agreed to, with Vice President Cheney casting a "yea" vote to break the tie, 50-50: R 50-5; D 0-44 (ND 0-40, SD 0-4); I 0-1. *(Senate vote 363, p. C-28)*

At a news conference afterward, Senate GOP leaders declared victory and vowed to continue their budget-cutting efforts in 2006. Frist dismissed the Democratic maneuver as a "a childish antic," but it denied Republicans the chance to attain their budget-cutting goal by year's end.

## 364  ANWR Oil Drilling

**Defeat of an effort to invoke cloture, thus limiting debate, on the 2006 Defense appropriations bill because of a controversial amendment that would have opened Alaska's Arctic National Wildlife Refuge to oil and gas exploration.**

Legislation enacted in 1980 (PL 96-487) left it up to Congress, not the White House, to decide whether to open part of the Arctic National Wildlife Refuge (ANWR) to oil and gas development. Lawmakers rejected ANWR drilling measures over the next several years, until a Republican-led Congress included a provision in a 1995 budget-saving measure to allow energy development in the area. President Bill Clinton vetoed the bill, and a decade later the fight over developing ANWR — fueled by record gasoline prices — was as fierce as ever.

In the past few years, the Senate has been the graveyard for any ANWR drilling efforts. But Republican gains in the November 2004 election provided the votes needed to keep an ANWR provision in

the fiscal 2006 budget resolution (H Con Res 95). A Democratic attempt to delete it was defeated 49-51 in March. That allowed Republicans to include ANWR drilling in a budget savings bill (S 1932) that was subject to special rules in the Senate. Those rules protect a so-called budget reconciliation bill from a filibuster, which means supporters need only 50 votes to prevail — not the 60 normally needed to overcome a filibuster.

"This is the first step," Sen. Ted Stevens, R-Alaska, said after the March vote. The 82-year-old chairman of the Senate Defense Appropriations Subcommittee has argued persistently that Alaskans know what is best for the remote wildlife refuge. "I've been on this track like a white rat for 24 years," he said at the time.

But this time, Stevens and fellow ANWR supporters ran into difficulty in the House, where moderates insisted the language be stripped out of that chamber's version of the reconciliation bill. House GOP leaders said they could not get enough votes for the conference report on the bill if the ANWR provision was included.

So Stevens agreed to include the provision in the separate conference report on the fiscal 2006 Defense spending bill (HR 2863). That measure, which provided $453.5 billion for military spending, including $50 billion for operations in Iraq and Afghanistan, was considered legislation Congress had to clear before adjourning for the year.

In a bid to ensure that the ANWR provision would stick, Stevens tied billions of dollars in expected revenue from ANWR to additional hurricane relief and homeland security programs. He dared Democrats, in effect, to vote against funding for the troops and other popular spending items. The House adopted the conference report, 308-106, on Dec. 19.

Many senators, though, were furious with the treatment given the appropriations bill in conference, where it gained not only the ANWR language, but a number of other provisions as well. Because it was no longer protected by Senate budget rules, the ANWR language was now vulnerable to a filibuster, and Democrats made it clear they would not accept it. So Majority Leader Bill Frist, R-Tenn., scheduled a vote to invoke cloture, or limit debate, on the measure.

The motion came up four votes short of the 60 required for it to succeed. The Dec. 21 vote was 56-44: R 52-3; D 4-40 (ND 3-37, SD 1-3); I 0-1. *(Senate vote 364, p. C-28)*

All but four Democrats — Hawaiians Daniel K. Akaka and Daniel K. Inouye; Mary L. Landrieu of Louisiana and Ben Nelson of Nebraska — voted against cloture. They were joined by Republicans Lincoln Chafee of Rhode Island and Mike DeWine of Ohio, as well as Frist, who changed his vote to "no" at the last minute to preserve the option of seeking reconsideration of the vote.

After an hours-long quorum call, during which leaders worked off the floor to come up with a way to complete work on the Defense bill, Frist announced a deal in which the Senate would clear the measure, but would also pass a separate enrolling resolution (S Con Res 74) under which the ANWR language would be removed from the bill. After adopting the resolution, 48-45, the Senate cleared the spending bill 93-0 on Dec. 21. President Bush signed the appropriations bill — without ANWR leasing language — into law Dec. 30.

"This has been the saddest day of my life," Stevens told his colleagues. "I'm going to go to every one of your states, and I'm going to tell them what you've done."

"This issue is too important to our consumers and our economy to accept defeat," said Pete V. Domenici, R-N.M., another drilling advocate. "We will try again."

# HOUSE VOTES

## 31 Immigration Policy Changes

**Passage of legislation making it more difficult for illegal immigrants to get driver's licenses and identity cards or to claim asylum, and authorizing the completion of a security fence along the border with Mexico near San Diego.**

Immigration emerged early as one of the year's biggest issues, and supporters of tighter borders won an early victory when House Judiciary Chairman F. James Sensenbrenner Jr., R-Wis., revived provisions dropped from intelligence overhaul legislation at the end of the 108th Congress and pushed them through to enactment.

That he did so with 42 House Democrats backing the measure was a demonstration that even with the Republicans split on some aspects of the immigration debate, the goal of securing the border was a relatively easy sell on both sides of the aisle.

To pass the bill (HR 418), which among other things imposed new requirements for those seeking driver's licenses and state ID cards, Republicans set aside their talk of states' rights, citing the higher priority of homeland security.

The driver's license provision and others were included in a version of an intelligence overhaul measure in the 108th Congress, but were dropped in conference. Sensenbrenner was the only House conferee not to sign the conference agreement, and he won assurances that the provisions would be among the first items of business in the 109th Congress — either as a stand-alone bill or attached to another measure.

In addition to the driver's license and asylum provisions, the immigration bill included language giving the secretary of Homeland Security the power to pre-empt state and federal laws if need be to construct physical barriers and roads designed to curb illegal border crossings. The provision was intended to spur completion of a fence along the U.S.-Mexico border near San Diego.

"We were able to win World War II quicker than we were able to complete this fence," Sensenbrenner quipped.

Critics said the provision was wildly out of proportion to the problem. The pre-emption applied to any local, state or federal laws — whether governing child labor, competition for federal contracts or environmental protection — that would impede physical barriers to curb illegal border crossings.

An attempt by Sam Farr, D-Calif., to remove the provision was rejected, 179-243.

Some members, echoing the concerns of state governors, also complained that the driver's license requirement was an unfunded mandate and would draw states into the expensive role of enforcing immigration laws.

But concerns for national security and outrage over the leaky southern border ruled the day. The House passed Sensenbrenner's bill, Feb. 10, 261-161: R 219-8; D 42-152 (ND 18-127; SD 24-25); I 0-1. Most of the measure was subsequently incorporated into the fiscal 2005 emergency supplemental appropriations bill (PL 109-13), which Bush signed into law in May. *(House vote 31, p. C-20)*

## 90 Federal Intervention in Schiavo Litigation

**Passage of legislation allowing the parents of Terri Schiavo, a brain-damaged Florida woman, access to federal courts to appeal state court decisions that her husband could have her feeding tube removed.**

Three days into Congress' spring recess, House Speaker J. Dennis Hastert, R-Ill., summoned members back to Washington for a gut-wrenching vote that would become a touchstone in the culture war of social conservatives vs. liberals and libertarians. It also stoked public dissatisfaction with Congress.

In 1990, a Florida woman, Terri Schiavo, suffered severe brain damage after her heart briefly stopped. Doctors declared her to be in a persistent vegetative state, and her husband, Michael Schiavo, tried to stop life support, saying it was in accordance with her wishes.

But Terri Schiavo had left no living will, a document outlining her treatment preferences. A legal battle ensued between Michael Schiavo and his wife's parents, Robert and Mary Schindler, who believed she might recover. After various Florida courts considered and rejected the Schindlers' arguments over a seven-year span, Terri Schiavo's feeding tube was removed March 18.

But the case had become a cause célèbre for social conservatives. They argued that Schiavo, much like a fetus, was a person with a "right to life" but incapable of speaking for herself and deserving of the government's protection. Enter congressional Republicans.

As Schiavo's condition began to deteriorate after removal of her feeding tube, the Senate zipped through a bill (S 686) that would have given the Schindlers access to federal courts for a final consideration of their daughter's case. The Senate passed the bill by voice vote March 20 — which was Palm Sunday.

A handful of House Democrats, disgusted with Congress' intervention into what they saw as a family matter, objected to a voice vote in that chamber. Republican leaders called members back to town for a roll call vote the morning of March 21.

President Bush, expecting that the House would clear the bill, returned to Washington from his ranch in Crawford, Texas, to sign it, increasing the public focus.

As the vote neared its conclusion, Republican members clapped when the tally reached 218 — a quorum, ensuring that enough members were present to pass the bill. The final tally was 203-58: R 156-5; D 47-53 (ND 27-38, SD 20-15); I 0-0. Many Democrats, wary of the 2004 elections in which social issues such as gay marriage were perceived to have played a major role, voted for the bill while expressing discomfort with the precedent it set. *(House vote 90, p. C-20)*

Bush signed the bill into law (PL 109-3) an hour later. But the Republicans' effort would prove to be for naught — substantively and politically. Schiavo's case quickly made its way to the Supreme Court, which on March 24 declined to hear the case. She died a week later.

GOP leaders found themselves the focus of a political backlash. Senate Majority Leader Bill Frist, R-Tenn., had questioned Schiavo's diagnosis on the Senate floor after watching a videotape of her apparently responding to "visual stimuli" such as a floating balloon, but an autopsy confirmed that she was not only severely brain-damaged, but also blind.

Polls showed that most Americans, including a majority of Republicans, disapproved of Congress' action in the case.

## 145 House Ethics Regulations

**Adoption of a resolution to repeal three rules changes Republicans made at the start of the session giving House members new rights in ethics investigations.**

In an unusual retreat in the face of Democratic criticism, House Republicans on April 27 voted to reverse three changes in ethics rules they had pushed through on the opening day of the session. The changes had been made to help lawmakers such as Majority Leader Tom DeLay, R-Texas, who had been admonished three times by the ethics committee in the previous Congress. But it was the growing number of questions about DeLay's conduct, and the political damage it might cause his party, that led Republicans to reverse their decision.

The short-lived rules changes specified that any complaint against a House member would die after 45 days unless the committee had voted by then to proceed with an investigation. Previously, the ethics panel, known formally as the Committee on Standards of Official Conduct, had to make a decision on a complaint for it to either expire or proceed.

The House in January also gave members who were the object of an investigation the right to respond to the committee's conclusions before a decision was made final or publicly announced. Republicans said they devised this change to prevent the ethics committee from catching a member off-guard with an admonishment or other punishment.

A third change codified what had been an occasional practice of permitting one attorney to represent multiple members involved in an ethics case. Democrats on the committee wanted to prohibit such a move, saying it allowed the subject of a complaint to collaborate with witnesses via a single attorney and made it impossible for the panel to properly investigate a charge.

Democrats condemned the changes as soon as they were made in January, but Republicans largely ignored their objections.

Then, in March, Democrats on the evenly divided ethics committee refused to vote for a proposed set of procedural rules for the 109th Congress, leaving the panel in procedural limbo and unable to conduct investigations.

The committee's ranking Democrat, Alan B. Mollohan of West Virginia, had meanwhile gathered 208 co-sponsors, including three Republicans, for a resolution (H Res 131) to reverse the three ethics rule changes. Mollohan threatened to file a discharge petition that, if he could get 218 signatures, would bring his resolution directly to the floor.

At that point, Republican leaders decided the ethics impasse and bad publicity were not worth the fight. At a conference meeting with rank-and-file members the morning of April 27, House Speaker J. Dennis Hastert, R-Ill., defended the rules changes as "fair for all members," but said, "We need to move the ethics process forward." Republicans leaving the conference said Hastert told them the best course of action would be to reverse the rules changes.

Almost all of them ultimately agreed. Many said they simply followed the direction of Hastert, who told them it was time to end the stalemate. Other Republicans said they had come to oppose some or all of the rules changes.

By a vote of 406-20, the House adopted a resolution (H Res 241) governing floor debate on a second resolution (H Res 240) that actually rolled back the three rules changes: R 208-20; D 197-0 (ND 148-0, SD 49-0); I 1-0. (*House vote 145, p. C-20*)

The vote was one of the first of a series of strategic victories for Democrats. On June 30, they forced Republicans on the ethics committee to retreat once again on disputed staffing issues. Democrats prevailed in an effort to hire only nonpartisan professionals to work on the committee.

## 204 Federal Research on Stem Cells

**Passage of a bill that would expand federal funding for research on stem cells taken from surplus embryos at in vitro fertilization clinics.**

Republican moderates held Majority Leader Tom DeLay, R-Texas, to a promise that he would hold a vote before summer on a bill (HR 810) by Michael N. Castle, R-Del., to expand the number of stem cell lines available to federally funded researchers by allowing them to work on lines derived from surplus embryos at invitro fertilization clinics.

An executive order issued by President Bush on Aug. 21, 2001, allows federally funded scientists to conduct research only on stem cell lines that existed before that date. The National Institutes of Health estimates 22 such lines are viable for research, though they are contaminated and probably would not be usable for medical treatments.

Supporters of the bill campaigned among their colleagues, stressing that days-old embryos, which have the ability to morph into almost any other kind of cell in the body, show great promise for cures for diseases such as Parkinson's and some cancers.

In an effort to derail the legislation, GOP leaders and conservatives who oppose the research because it requires the destruction of an embryo backed an alternative bill (HR 2520) by Christopher H. Smith, R-N.J. Smith's bill encouraged the use of stem cells, sometimes referred to as "adult stem cells," taken from umbilical cords after birth. Stem cells found in umbilical cord blood are less elastic because they come from specific tissue and are used mainly in treating blood disorders.

House leaders hoped Smith's bill would enable members who faced pressure from their constituents to cast a "pro-stem cell" vote without relaxing Bush's restrictions on research using embryos.

Backers of the Castle bill said they did not oppose Smith's measure, but that it did not address the need for funding research on embryonic cells. The moderate Republican Main Street Partnership launched a multimillion-dollar advertising campaign in support of Castle's bill that highlighted former first lady Nancy Reagan's support for embryonic research.

The floor debate May 24 showcased the emotion and personal experiences that influenced members' votes and led many Republicans to disregard their leadership and support Castle's bill.

Joe L. Barton, R-Texas, noted that his anti-abortion voting record stood at 100 percent until 2005, but said he backed the embryonic stem cell bill because of his father, who has diabetes, and a brother, who had liver cancer. "Maybe the breakthrough will come in adult stem cells. I hope it does. But maybe, just maybe, it's going to come because of embryonic stem cells. Let's look at all avenues."

Anti-abortion Democrat Jim Langevin of Rhode Island, who was paralyzed as a teenager, and Lane Evans, D-Ill., who has Parkinson's disease, made personal pleas to allow federal funding for embryonic research.

Opponents made equally emotional appeals. Twenty-one children were escorted around the Capitol to illustrate the use of surplus embryos to help infertile couples. The youths were born to mothers from surplus frozen embryos donated by other couples.

"The best one can say about embryonic stem cell research is it is a scientific exploration into the potential benefits of killing human

beings," said DeLay, who along with the rest of the House GOP leadership voted against Castle's bill.

Although Bush had reiterated his veto threat, Majority Whip Roy Blunt, R-Mo., said leaders wanted members to vote their consciences. When the vote was finished, 50 Republicans had broken with their leadership. The House passed Castle's bill, 238-194: R 50-180; D 187-14 (ND 140-10, SD 47-4); I 1-0. (*House vote 204, p. C-20*)

The tally fell short of the 290 votes that would be needed to override a veto if all members of the House were present and voting, but supporters expressed hope that a compromise could be reached.

Although the Senate did not take up the Castle bill in the first session, the cord blood bill was subsequently cleared (PL 109-129).

## 258 | Limits on Federal Search Powers

**Adoption of an amendment to the fiscal 2006 Commerce-Justice-Science spending bill to prohibit the FBI from gaining access to library and bookstore records under the 2001 anti-terrorism law known as the Patriot Act.**

Weeks before the House took up legislation to reauthorize expiring provisions of the Patriot Act (PL 107-56), a cadre of Republicans joined every House Democrat save one in making a bold — though ultimately symbolic — gesture toward limiting one of the law's most contentious provisions.

Section 215 of the Patriot Act allows FBI investigators to seize "any tangible things (including books, records, papers, documents and other items)" as part of a terrorism investigation once they get a warrant from a top-secret court established under the Foreign Intelligence Surveillance Act, or FISA (PL 95-511).

The section is one of 16 provisions of the anti-terrorism law that were scheduled to expire at the end of 2005. The White House pressed Congress to make all 16 permanent as part of a bill reauthorizing the act.

Civil liberties advocates, the American Conservative Union, librarians, doctors, business groups, gun rights advocates and former Georgia GOP Rep. Bob Barr (1995-2003) spent much of the year lobbying hard to keep the provision out of the Patriot Act reauthorization or, short of that, to exempt certain records and minimize access.

On June 15, the administration's effort suffered a bipartisan blow during House debate on the fiscal 2006 Commerce-Justice-Science appropriations bill (HR 2862). Not waiting for the Patriot Act debate, Vermont independent Bernard Sanders offered an amendment to bar use of money in the bill to seek a FISA court order to seize library circulation records, library patron lists, book sales records or book customer lists.

Defying a White House veto threat, 38 Republicans and 199 Democrats supported Sanders, pushing his amendment to adoption by a vote of 238-187: R 38-186; D 199-1(ND 150-0; SD 49-1); I 1-0. Dan Boren of Oklahoma was the only Democrat who voted against the amendment. (*House vote 258, p. C-22*)

Sanders garnered more votes than he had with a similar amendment the previous year, when he lost, 210-210. He noted that the 2004 amendment had drawn some opposition from members who did not like the fact that it would have barred FBI access to library Internet records. Sanders dropped that provision in the 2005 version.

The vote was perceived as a snub to the White House and a small victory for those arguing for more balance between the need to flush out terrorists and the desire to protect civil liberties. "A number of conservatives voted conservatively today, and 'conservative' means limited gov-

ernment," said Sanders, one of the most liberal members of the House, who pumped his arm in the air to applause as he left the chamber.

The provision was short-lived: When the House passed a bill (HR 3199) in July to renew the 16 expiring Patriotic Act provisions, the power to seize library and bookstore records was intact. It survived in conference, though the provision was one of two that were accorded a four-year extension; the rest were made permanent.

Still, the vote on Sanders' amendment was a clear indication that reauthorizing the Patriot Act would be no simple matter. With the conference report now stalled by a Senate filibuster, the portent proved accurate. (*Senate anti-terrorism act key vote, p. C-11*)

## 374 | Policy Toward China

**Defeat of a bill that would have imposed new trade restrictions on countries that allow the sale of arms and defense-related technology to China.**

The intense, last-minute lobbying around what had been a non-controversial bill to tighten sanctions on illegal arms sales to China highlighted Congress' continued dilemma on China policy: how to punish the Asian nation's anti-competitive business practices and arms trade while not jeopardizing U.S. commerce with it.

The bill (HR 3100) was designed to discourage European countries from lifting their embargoes on military trade with China. "The bill is not intended to be punitive; its primary purpose is deterrence," said Henry J. Hyde, R-Ill., chairman of the International Relations Committee and the bill's sponsor. It would have required the administration to annually report the names of countries that permit trade in military material with China and would have required an export license before any U.S. company could send military goods to such countries. The president could apply a range of sanctions against countries selling arms to China, including denying licenses for "dual use" goods — those that have both civilian and potential military applications — barring their participation in research projects or prohibiting them from owning U.S. defense companies.

Both Republicans and Democrats initially supported the legislation, and House leaders brought it to the floor under a suspension of the rules, a procedure used for non-controversial bills that requires a two-thirds vote for passage. Just two weeks earlier, the House had overwhelmingly adopted an amendment and a resolution expressing concern that the China National Offshore Oil Corp. Ltd. was trying to buy Unocal, a U.S. oil company, for $18.5 billion.

But House leaders underestimated the opposition from the defense industry, which has companies and manufacturing plants in many congressional districts. Defense manufacturers said the bill could end up punishing companies for selling dual-use products to China. Essentially, defense contractors such as Boeing Co. did not want to be punished for selling aircraft parts to commercial companies in China if those parts ended up on military jets.

When the roll call began July 14, the bill appeared headed for easy passage. But Donald Manzullo, R-Ill., the chairman of the Small Business Committee, was at work on the floor, trying to persuade his colleagues to change their votes.

Manzullo, whose district includes aircraft and machine parts manufacturers, worked both sides of the aisle, telling members that the legislation was a bad deal. He circulated a flyer drawn up by defense contractors saying "passage of this bill means that Boeing and other

aircraft manufacturers will sell fewer planes overseas."

In rapid sequence, dozens of lawmakers, worried that the bill could unintentionally punish defense contractors who do business with European companies that in turn sell to China, began to change their votes. What had been scheduled as a five-minute vote was held open for 23 minutes, but the measure failed to get the necessary two-thirds majority. The vote was 215-203: R 118-106; D 96-97 (ND 70-73, SD 26-24); I 1-0. *(House vote 374, p. C-22)*

A toned-down version of the measure was later attached to the State Department authorization bill (HR 2601) passed by the House in July. The amended version would still monitor European governments or companies that sell military hardware or technology to China, but would punish U.S. companies only if they knew their products would ultimately be used for military purposes. The bill went no further.

## 443 Central American Trade Liberalization

**Passage of a bill to implement tariff reductions and other changes to U.S. trade law that were part of a free-trade agreement negotiated between the United States and five Central American countries, plus the Dominican Republic.**

Hours before leaving for a monthlong August recess, the House voted to pass a bill implementing a free-trade accord between the United States and Costa Rica, El Salvador, Guatemala, Honduras and Nicaragua, plus a parallel agreement with the Dominican Republic.

The vote on the Central American accord, or CAFTA, was a referendum on U.S. trade policy, and a test both of the president's power and GOP party loyalty amid growing congressional partisanship and skepticism on trade.

Although the bill (HR 3045) was a marquee piece of President Bush's trade agenda, it took all of the wiles of then-Majority Leader Tom DeLay, R-Texas, to twist enough arms to eke out a two-vote victory margin. The close vote suggests that GOP members are increasingly wary about trade pacts, carefully weighing the potential impact on their own districts with the goals and desires of the president. Bush even made a rare appearance before the House Republican Conference the morning of the vote, and several members of the Cabinet spent part of the day on Capitol Hill helping to convince reluctant lawmakers.

Democratic support for CAFTA was all but non-existent, which many see as evidence of a backlash that Democrats have felt since a large number from their party supported NAFTA, the North American Free-Trade Agreement, in 1993 (PL 103-182).

The Senate had gone first to give momentum to the House, but even there the vote was a relatively close 54-45. *(Senate CAFTA key vote, p. C-7)*

The voting began in the House shortly after 11 p.m. on July 27, and did not end until well after midnight when the bill passed 217-215; R 202-27; D 15-187 (ND 7-144, SD 8-43); I 0-1. *(House vote 443, p. C-22)*

Almost until the end, a small but vital bloc of Republicans remained concerned that beleaguered domestic textile and apparel makers would be wiped out by imports of Chinese-made goods that they said could slip into the United States duty-free under CAFTA.

The administration had argued vigorously that, if anything, CAFTA would strengthen the bond between U.S. textile mills and Central American apparel factories. Just the same, U.S. Trade Representative Rob Portman promised to go back into the accord later to amend three textile provisions to prevent circumvention by the Chinese, winning over a handful of textile state members just days before the vote.

Additional maneuvering was required even as debate got under way. Robert B. Aderholt, R-Ala., received a letter from Portman and Commerce Secretary Carlos Gutierrez pledging administration help to protect sock makers from import surges possible under CAFTA and other trade pacts, support for an application by the Hosiery Technology Center for a Commerce Department export grant, and a commitment to work with the Pentagon to encourage purchase of U.S.-made socks only.

Another trouble spot was the concern that a modest increase in sugar imports permitted by CAFTA would undermine domestic producers and cost U.S. jobs. An administration proposal to use commodity swaps to contain additional sugar imports for the remaining two years of the current farm bill (PL 107-171) and to undertake a study of government initiatives to spur production of ethanol made from sugar helped win the votes of Dave Camp, R-Mich., Adam H. Putnam, R-Fla., and Mark Kennedy, R-Minn., among others. But Mark Foley, R-Fla., and several Louisiana lawmakers remained skeptical. Foley called his eventual decision to vote for the CAFTA bill a "gut wrencher."

One final issue involved demonstrating more resolve in countering unfair trade practices by China. Phil English, R-Pa., pressed for floor action on a bill (HR 3283) to strengthen U.S. enforcement of trade rules against China. He estimated that as many as 10 Republicans agreed to vote for CAFTA after the House passed the China bill earlier in the day.

A half-hour after the nominal 15-minute roll call vote on the CAFTA bill began, the count froze at 214-211 in favor. Eight Republicans who had either expressed opposition to CAFTA or said they were reluctant to support it had not cast their votes. About midnight, DeLay and GOP leaders persuaded Robin Hayes of North Carolina to switch his vote from no to yes. DeLay then persuaded two of the hesitant Republicans to vote for the trade agreement and allowed the rest to cast last-minute votes against it.

Only 15 Democrats voted yes, a sharp contrast to the 102 Democrats who had answered President Bill Clinton's call to vote for NAFTA more than a decade earlier. Democrats' opposition was based in part on their concerns about what they regarded as a lost opportunity to improve on the NAFTA model and raise labor and environmental standards in developing countries. But Republicans claimed that those "no" votes were simply a partisan effort to weaken Bush.

## 445 Energy Policy Overhaul

**Final passage of legislation that includes incentives for greater domestic production of oil, gas, coal and nuclear power, encouragement for conservation and a reduction in regulation of the electric power industry.**

It took four years, but record fuel prices gave Congress the motivation to pass energy legislation similar to what the Bush administration first proposed in 2001. The final bill (HR 6) emphasized greater production of domestic energy, as President Bush wanted. But to get the bill through the Senate, the White House had to forgo the centerpiece of its energy plan, drilling for oil and natural gas in Alaska's Arctic National Wildlife Refuge (ANWR). And House Republican leaders gave up one of their top priorities, liability protection for the oil companies that make the fuel additive MTBE (methyl tertiary buytl ether), which has been found to contaminate some groundwater.

For two years running, MTBE liability had defeated the energy bill

as House members from oil-producing states, led by then-Majority Leader Tom DeLay, R-Texas, demanded that it be included, while a coalition of Democrats and moderate Republicans demanded that it be dropped.

Though the administration lost on energy exploration in the Alaska wilderness, it was successful in reducing the cost of tax breaks and other incentives in the legislation to about half what GOP congressional leaders have sought in past years.

In one of the most significant energy votes in decades, the House adopted the conference report on the omnibus energy bill July 28, 275-156: R 200-31; D 75-124 (ND 41-107, SD 34-17); I 0-1. *(House vote 445, p. C-22)*

The House had passed other energy bills several times dating back to 2001 only to see them bog down in the Senate, where sponsors had trouble winning the 60 votes necessary to beat filibuster threats from senators upset by what they considered a bias in the legislation toward energy companies. *(Senate energy key vote, p. C-7)*

But this year DeLay and fellow Texas Republican Joe L. Barton, the chairman of the Energy and Commerce Committee, dropped their insistence that the bill include liability relief for the makers of MTBE, which has been used since the 1970s but became more prevalent after federal clean fuel requirements in the early 1990s. Like ethanol, MTBE helps gasoline burn more completely, helping to lower harmful tailpipe emissions. But it also has been found to contaminate groundwater where it has leaked from storage tanks. Some lawmakers, including northeastern Republicans, worried that the liability protection would leave their states to pay for the cleanup.

Unlike previous years, House leaders also won support for the measure by holding down the cost of its tax incentives, which in past years had exceeded $30 billion. That had been a point of criticism from fiscal conservatives and the White House this year. The conference agreement provides for $14.6 billion in tax breaks and credits between 2005 and 2015.

To help deliver the bill, House Republicans agreed to drop language that would have opened ANWR to energy exploration. GOP leaders shifted the provision to other legislation, first a spending-cut package (S 1932) and later a Defense appropriations bill (HR 2863), but those maneuvers also failed.

Even with the House vote and the subsequent Senate action, Congress may not be through with energy legislation. Just weeks after Bush signed the bill, energy supply disruptions from hurricanes Katrina and Rita triggered calls by some House GOP leaders, including Barton, for a new energy bill. On Oct. 7, the House narrowly passed a measure (HR 3893) that would ease environmental reviews and take other steps to encourage the construction of new or expanded refineries. The Senate did not take up the bill and is not expected to do so in 2006. Once again, it is opposed by a coalition of Democrats and moderate Republicans.

## 453 Surface Transportation Spending

**Final passage of a six-year reauthorization of highway and transit programs after more than two years of negotiations and concessions by the White House and Congress.**

It took more than two years and two Congresses, but the House on July 29 adopted the conference report on a bill (HR 3) reauthorizing the nation's highway and public transit programs. The House and Senate had reached the conference stage on a six-year reauthorization bill in 2004, but the negotiators could not get beyond disputes among mem-

bers over how to divide up highway money, and with the White House over the total cost of the bill.

In 2005, Congress finally settled for less money than it wanted; the Bush administration settled for more. The agreement gave a larger share of highway funds to fast-growing states, mainly in the South and Southwest, that argued they had been shortchanged by the previous highway law. In another victory for those states, the House agreed to deduct from each state's formula highway funds any money it received for earmarked projects — a blow to influential lawmakers such as Don Young, R-Alaska, the chairman of the Transportation and Infrastructure Committee — who are adroit at getting such projects for their states.

The final $286.5 billion bill contained more than 5,100 earmarks, demonstrating why highway spending is perennially popular among lawmakers. While the overwhelming majority were for road projects, some were for museums and other amenities not related to traffic. Watchdog groups and fiscal conservatives used the bill and the vote as symbols of the inability of either Republicans or Democrats to exercise self-restraint when it comes to home-state public works projects.

President Bush had for two years demanded that Congress authorize no more than $256 billion for surface transportation programs, while lawmakers were thinking more in the range of $319 billion to as much as $375 billion. The administration made a deal more realistic early in 2005 when it lifted its bottom-line demand to $284 billion — close to the compromise amount conferees had been negotiating in 2004 and just $2.5 billion away from the final figure.

Befitting the tortuous path the legislation had followed since the previous surface transportation law (PL 105-178) expired in September 2003, the final days of negotiations featured marathon sessions to draft language and frustrating snags that developed each time the bill drew close to final action.

Only eight dissidents were prepared to vote against the conference report when it reached the House floor July 29. Six of them were members of the Republican Study Committee, a group of fiscal and social conservatives frustrated with GOP leaders and the White House over spending issues The House adopted the conference report and sent it to the Senate, 412-8: R 217-8; D 194-0 (ND 144-0, SD 50-0); I 1-0. *(House vote 453, p. C-24; Senate transportation key vote, p. C-8)*

The dispute over earmarks resurfaced three months later. Bowing to public criticism of pork barrel spending in light of mounting hurricane-relief costs and pressure to rein in budget deficits, conferees on the transportation appropriations bill (HR 3058) redirected $454 million that had been earmarked in the highway bill for two bridges, dubbed "bridges to nowhere," in Alaska.

The action on the fiscal 2006 Transportation-Treasury-Housing spending bill was largely symbolic because Alaska will still get the money to use at its discretion. *(Senate earmarks key vote, p. C-9)*

## 506 Endangered Species Policy Rewrite

**Passage of a major revision of the 1973 Endangered Species Act that would remove a requirement that the government designate and protect habitat critical to threatened animal and plant species, which has been the source of frequent litigation.**

Rep. Richard W. Pombo, R-Calif., has been fighting environmentalists for years over the Endangered Species Act, arguing that it harms pri-

vate property owners while doing little to aid the recovery of threatened animal and plant species. In 2005, Pombo changed course somewhat and found a new, albeit limited, source of support among Democrats, many of them from Western states where the endangered species program has faced considerable opposition. As a result, Pombo persuaded the House to pass the most extensive changes to the species protection program since the law was reauthorized in 1988.

As chairman of the House Resources Committee, Pombo spent several months negotiating with committee Democrats before releasing a detailed bill (HR 3824) in September. The bipartisan effort paid off Sept. 22, when eight Democrats joined all but two Republicans to approve the bill in committee.

The bill would require the use of peer-reviewed science in federal regulatory decisions and require compensation for landowners affected by federal conservation efforts. It also would eliminate a requirement that the government designate and protect critical habitat for within a year of listing a species as endangered. Instead, the government would have to come up with a recovery plan, keeping in mind habitat and cost.

Opponents of the bill worry that the recovery plans might not be enforceable on private landowners or other government agencies. Environmental groups, which for years have sued the government for failing to designate critical habitat as required under current law, said habitat protection is a critical component of any long-term recovery plan. They declared the bill a frontal assault on a landmark law that, despite its problems, has kept alive most of the species it aims to protect.

Democrats attracted some bipartisan support for a substitute amendment that emphasized recovery planning on federal lands, while promoting technical assistance and grants for private property owners who cooperate on federal conservation programs. Twenty-nine Republicans joined Democrats on the vote, but the amendment failed, 206-216.

In the end, Pombo succeeded in offsetting the Republican votes he lost with support by 36 Democrats, many from Western and Midwestern states. The bill passed Sept. 29, 229-193: R 193-34; D 36-158 (ND 15-129, SD 21-29); I 0-1. *(House vote 506, p. C-24)*

The bill did not advance in the Senate. It was sent to an Environment and Public Works subcommittee chaired by Lincoln Chafee, a Rhode Island Republican who often sides with Democrats on environmental issues. Chafee chose to wait for the results of an independent study he and other senators had requested on the critical habitat question, expected in February.

## 630 Treatment of Military Detainees

**Agreement to a motion to instruct conferees on the fiscal 2006 Defense appropriations bill to support a Senate provision banning abusive treatment of detainees in U.S. custody.**

In an overwhelming vote Dec. 14, the House demonstrated its support for a proposal by Sen. John McCain, R-Ariz., to ban the use of torture on prisoners held in U.S. custody. The timing of the vote and the compelling margin of victory appeared to force President Bush to back down from his months-long opposition to McCain's initiative.

The president's compromise with McCain ended an internecine battle in Republican ranks over how to respond to reports of abuse that had tarnished America's image and complicated efforts to win the war of ideas against radical Islamic terrorists. The political conflict in Washington pitted the president against lawmakers who ordinarily stood with him, including popular McCain, himself a victim of torture in Vietnam and the man Bush had defeated for the Republican nomination in the hard-fought primaries of 2000.

McCain's amendment banned "cruel, inhuman or degrading" treatment of detainees, and made an Army field manual on interrogations the standard for Defense Department handling of prisoners.

The House was voting on a "motion to instruct" its conferees on the fiscal 2006 Defense appropriations bill (HR 2863) to retain McCain's provision. Such motions are not binding, but the force of this one was undeniable. In a House where Republicans typically move in lockstep, more than 100 of them defied the president on the torture vote. The motion was agreed to 308-122: R 107-121; D 200-1 (ND 150-0, SD 50-1); I 1-0. *(House vote 630, p. C-24)*

McCain had won a 90-9 vote in early October to attach the language to the Senate version of the spending bill. For good measure, the Senate agreed by voice vote in early November to add it to the defense authorization bill (HR 1815) as well. *(Senate detainee key vote, p. C-9)*

Bush was so opposed to the amendment that he threatened to veto the two military bills in the middle of a bloody and costly war. Bush dispatched Vice President Dick Cheney to try to persuade McCain to create an exemption for the CIA, but the lobbying campaign backfired. It created the impression that the administration was in favor of torture, or at least opposed to Congress passing a law against it.

National Security Adviser Stephen J. Hadley soon replaced Cheney in the talks with McCain, and Bush spoke with the senator about the amendment on several occasions. Meanwhile, McCain negotiated with Duncan Hunter, R-Calif., chairman of the House Armed Services Committee, who sided with the administration and had his own ideas on changes he thought could improve McCain's amendment in the defense authorization bill.

With all of those talks, described by one aide as "a three-ring circus," going nowhere, the two massive defense bills were stalled going into December. On Dec. 14, House Republican leaders finally named conferees on the appropriations bill, clearing the way for John P. Murtha, D-Pa., to offer his motion to instruct the conferees.

The day after the highly publicized House vote, Bush invited McCain and Sen. John W. Warner, R-Va., to the White House to announce a compromise on the detainee amendment. McCain had not budged on his provision. But he agreed to additional language allowing U.S. interrogators—whether they work for the Defense Department, the CIA, the FBI or a contractor—to have the same legal protections that U.S. military personnel are accorded.

The language was cleared as part of both the defense spending and defense authorization bills.

## 670 Cuts in Mandatory Spending

**Adoption of the conference report on a $38.8 billion budget savings package.**

At the start of 2005, Republican leaders vowed to slow the growth of mandatory entitlement programs such as Medicare, Medicaid and student loans for the first time since 1997, and the House brought them close to achieving their goal. Despite having no Democratic support, they put themselves in position to clear a $38.8 billion savings package (S 1932) in early 2006.

The effort was hanging in the balance in the pre-dawn hours of

Dec. 19. House and Senate negotiators had labored into the night to reconcile a $35 billion Senate plan and a far different $50 billion House package. A deal was announced, then altered, as new objections arose and leaders sought to ensure they had enough support before a final vote.

Negotiations had been stalled for days because of an impasse over efforts to open Alaska's Arctic National Wildlife Refuge (ANWR) to drilling. House Republican moderates vowed to oppose any bill with the ANWR provision, and Sen. Ted Stevens, R-Alaska, a member of the conference committee, vowed to oppose any bill without it.

Stevens relented during a final weekend of negotiations once House and Senate leaders agreed to try to enact the ANWR provisions by attaching them to the fiscal 2006 Defense Appropriations bill (HR 2863) instead, a plan that ultimately failed. *(Senate ANWR key vote, p. C-12)*

On the evening of Dec. 18, House Speaker J. Dennis Hastert, R-Ill., announced that conferees had agreed on a $41.6 billion budget savings package. But after midnight, Hastert and Senate negotiators had to shrink the package to $38.8 billion to secure the votes of Ohio lawmakers who threatened to scuttle the overall deal unless oxygen tank manufacturers, including a major Ohio company, were protected from planned cuts to Medicare. The 774-page conference report was filed well after midnight. The vote came shortly after 6 a.m. on Dec. 19, with a number of lawmakers in both parties already having left town for the winter recess.

But with the backing of enough moderates, GOP leaders managed a 212-206 victory: R 212-9; D 0-196 (ND 0-146, SD 0-50); I 0-1. The vote turned out to be largely devoid of suspense, even though all of the Democrats who showed up voted no. *(House vote 670, p. C-24)*

House leaders had won a narrower 217-215 vote shortly before 2 a.m. Nov. 18 on their original package, which contained deeper cuts

and fewer spending plums.

The final vote was a triumph for the House leadership team, which overcame months of doubt about its ability to deliver votes for the budget package in the face of the criminal indictment of former Majority Leader Tom DeLay, R-Texas, low poll ratings, carping by some moderates and unusually united Democratic opposition.

Yet the victory came at a cost, with House leaders unable to deliver on the $45 billion savings goal they had announced for the conference report. House and Senate moderates had forced leaders to abandon plans to cut off 250,000 recipients from food stamps, and to shrink cuts planned for child support enforcement and welfare. Meanwhile, House leaders refused to go along with a Senate plan to eliminate a $10 billion subsidy for companies included as part of the new Medicare drug benefit. The Senate cut had prompted a veto threat.

Alongside the budget cuts came a number of sweeteners to win votes, including $7.3 billion to prevent doctors from receiving a 4.4 percent Medicare pay cut, $2.1 billion to extend Medicaid to hurricane victims, $1 billion to continue a milk subsidy for two years, $1 billion in home heating subsidies for the poor, and $1.5 billion for digital television converters for analog televisions.

The bill did not clear, however. A procedural maneuver by Senate Democrats required an additional vote in the House. House Minority Leader Nancy Pelosi, D-Calif., refused a quick voice vote before the holidays, saying she wanted to force a vote "in the light of day." *(Senate budget key vote, p. C-11)*

Democrats and their allies vowed to renew pressure on House GOP moderates who supported the conference report to change their minds. Still, after a long night of waiting and deal making, GOP leaders declared victory and pledged to continue the belt-tightening in the new year.

# HOUSE 31, 90, 145, 204

**31.** **HR 418. Immigration Standards/Passage.** Passage of the bill that would tighten national standards for state driver's licenses and identity cards, make it more difficult for foreign nationals to claim asylum and authorize the completion of a security fence along the U.S.-Mexico border. It would allow immigration judges to weigh the credibility of asylum applicants in a variety of proceedings and remove the annual cap of 10,000 refugees who may become permanent residents. It also would require the Homeland Security Department to include in aviation security screening databases information on anyone convicted of using a false driver's license to board an airplane. Passed 261-161: R 219-8; D 42-152 (ND 18-127, SD 24-25); I 0-1. A "yea" was a vote in support of the president's position. Feb. 10, 2005. *(Story, p. C-13)*

**90.** **S 686. Schiavo Medical Care/Passage.** Sensenbrenner, R-Wis., motion to suspend the rules and pass the bill that would give the parents of Theresa Marie Schiavo, a severely brain-damaged Florida woman, the right to file a lawsuit in the U.S. District Court for the Middle District of Florida alleging that Schiavo's rights related to life-sustaining medical treatment have been violated under the Constitution or federal law. Motion agreed to, thus clearing the bill for the president, 203-58: R 156-5; D 47-53 (ND 27-38, SD 20-15); I 0-0. A two-thirds majority of those present and voting (174 in this case) is required for passage under suspension of the rules. March 21, 2005 (in the session that began and the Congressional Record dated March 20, 2005). *(Story, p. C-13)*

**145.** **H Res 240. House Rules/Adoption.** Adoption of the self-executing rule (H Res 241) under which the House would automatically adopt a resolution repealing three changes to the Rules of the House dealing with ethics committee procedures that were made at the start of the 109th Congress, including a rule that allowed the automatic dismissal of an ethics complaint that is not disposed of by the committee within 45 days. Adopted 406-20: R 208-20; D 197-0 (ND 148-0, SD 49-0); I 1-0. April 27, 2005. *(Story, p. C-14)*

**204.** **HR 810. Embryonic Stem Cell Research/Passage.** Passage of the bill that would allow the use of federal funds in research on embryonic stem cell lines derived from surplus embryos at invitro fertilization clinics, but only if donors give their consent and are not paid for the embryos. The bill would authorize the Health and Human Services Department to conduct and support research involving human embryonic stem cells that meet certain criteria, regardless of when the stem cells were derived from a human embryo. Passed 238-194: R 50-180; D 187-14 (ND 140-10, SD 47-4); I 1-0. A "nay" was a vote in support of the president's position. May 24, 2005. *(Story, p. C-14)*

[1] Rep. Doris Matsui, D-Calif., was sworn in March 10, 2005. The first vote for which she was eligible was vote 62.

[2] The Speaker votes only at his discretion, usually to break a tie or to emphasize the importance of a matter.

[3] Rep. Rob Portman, R-Ohio, resigned effective April 29. The last vote for which he was eligible was vote 150.

| | 31 | 90 | 145 | 204 |
|---|---|---|---|---|
| **ALABAMA** | | | | |
| 1 Bonner | Y | Y | Y | N |
| 2 Everett | Y | ? | Y | N |
| 3 Rogers | Y | Y | Y | N |
| 4 Aderholt | Y | Y | Y | N |
| 5 Cramer | Y | Y | Y | N |
| 6 Bachus | Y | Y | Y | N |
| 7 Davis | Y | ? | Y | Y |
| **ALASKA** | | | | |
| AL Young | N | ? | Y | Y |
| **ARIZONA** | | | | |
| 1 Renzi | Y | Y | Y | N |
| 2 Franks | Y | Y | Y | N |
| 3 Shadegg | Y | ? | Y | N |
| 4 Pastor | N | ? | Y | Y |
| 5 Hayworth | Y | Y | Y | N |
| 6 Flake | Y | ? | Y | N |
| 7 Grijalva | N | ? | Y | Y |
| 8 Kolbe | Y | ? | Y | Y |
| **ARKANSAS** | | | | |
| 1 Berry | Y | Y | Y | Y |
| 2 Snyder | N | Y | Y | Y |
| 3 Boozman | Y | ? | Y | N |
| 4 Ross | Y | Y | Y | Y |
| **CALIFORNIA** | | | | |
| 1 Thompson | N | ? | Y | Y |
| 2 Herger | Y | ? | Y | N |
| 3 Lungren | Y | ? | Y | N |
| 4 Doolittle | Y | Y | Y | N |
| 5 Matsui, D.[1] | | N | Y | Y |
| 6 Woolsey | N | ? | Y | Y |
| 7 Miller, George | N | ? | Y | Y |
| 8 Pelosi | N | ? | Y | Y |
| 9 Lee | N | ? | ? | Y |
| 10 Tauscher | N | ? | Y | Y |
| 11 Pombo | N | ? | Y | N |
| 12 Lantos | N | ? | Y | Y |
| 13 Stark | N | ? | Y | Y |
| 14 Eshoo | ? | ? | Y | Y |
| 15 Honda | – | ? | Y | Y |
| 16 Lofgren | N | ? | Y | Y |
| 17 Farr | N | ? | Y | Y |
| 18 Cardoza | Y | ? | Y | Y |
| 19 Radanovich | Y | ? | Y | N |
| 20 Costa | Y | ? | Y | Y |
| 21 Nunes | Y | ? | Y | N |
| 22 Thomas | Y | ? | Y | N |
| 23 Capps | N | ? | Y | Y |
| 24 Gallegly | Y | ? | Y | N |
| 25 McKeon | Y | ? | Y | Y |
| 26 Dreier | Y | Y | Y | N |
| 27 Sherman | N | ? | Y | Y |
| 28 Berman | N | ? | Y | Y |
| 29 Schiff | N | N | Y | Y |
| 30 Waxman | N | ? | ? | Y |
| 31 Becerra | N | – | Y | Y |
| 32 Solis | N | ? | Y | Y |
| 33 Watson | N | ? | Y | Y |
| 34 Roybal-Allard | N | ? | Y | Y |
| 35 Waters | N | ? | Y | Y |
| 36 Harman | N | ? | Y | Y |
| 37 Millender-McD. | N | ? | Y | ? |
| 38 Napolitano | N | ? | Y | Y |
| 39 Sánchez, Linda | N | ? | Y | Y |
| 40 Royce | Y | ? | Y | N |
| 41 Lewis | Y | Y | Y | Y |
| 42 Miller, Gary | Y | ? | Y | N |
| 43 Baca | N | ? | Y | Y |
| 44 Calvert | Y | ? | Y | Y |
| 45 Bono | Y | ? | Y | Y |
| 46 Rohrabacher | Y | ? | Y | Y |
| 47 Sanchez, Loretta | ? | ? | Y | Y |
| 48 Cox | Y | Y | Y | N |
| 49 Issa | Y | + | Y | N |

| | 31 | 90 | 145 | 204 |
|---|---|---|---|---|
| 50 Cunningham | Y | ? | Y | Y |
| 51 Filner | N | ? | Y | Y |
| 52 Hunter | Y | Y | Y | N |
| 53 Davis | N | ? | Y | Y |
| **COLORADO** | | | | |
| 1 DeGette | N | ? | Y | Y |
| 2 Udall | N | ? | Y | Y |
| 3 Salazar | Y | ? | Y | Y |
| 4 Musgrave | Y | Y | Y | N |
| 5 Hefley | Y | Y | Y | N |
| 6 Tancredo | Y | Y | Y | N |
| 7 Beauprez | Y | Y | Y | N |
| **CONNECTICUT** | | | | |
| 1 Larson | N | N | Y | Y |
| 2 Simmons | Y | ? | Y | Y |
| 3 DeLauro | N | ? | Y | Y |
| 4 Shays | Y | N | Y | Y |
| 5 Johnson | Y | ? | Y | Y |
| **DELAWARE** | | | | |
| AL Castle | Y | N | Y | Y |
| **FLORIDA** | | | | |
| 1 Miller | Y | Y | Y | N |
| 2 Boyd | Y | ? | Y | Y |
| 3 Brown | N | ? | ? | Y |
| 4 Crenshaw | Y | Y | Y | N |
| 5 Brown-Waite | Y | N | Y | N |
| 6 Stearns | Y | ? | Y | N |
| 7 Mica | Y | ? | Y | N |
| 8 Keller | Y | ? | Y | N |
| 9 Bilirakis | Y | Y | Y | N |
| 10 Young | Y | ? | Y | Y |
| 11 Davis | Y | N | Y | Y |
| 12 Putnam | Y | Y | Y | N |
| 13 Harris | Y | Y | Y | N |
| 14 Mack | Y | Y | Y | Y |
| 15 Weldon | Y | Y | N | N |
| 16 Foley | Y | Y | Y | Y |
| 17 Meek | N | Y | Y | Y |
| 18 Ros-Lehtinen | N | Y | Y | Y |
| 19 Wexler | N | N | Y | Y |
| 20 Wasserman-Schultz | N | N | Y | Y |
| 21 Diaz-Balart, L. | N | Y | Y | Y |
| 22 Shaw | Y | ? | Y | Y |
| 23 Hastings | N | N | Y | Y |
| 24 Feeney | ? | Y | Y | N |
| 25 Diaz-Balart, M. | N | Y | Y | N |
| **GEORGIA** | | | | |
| 1 Kingston | Y | Y | Y | N |
| 2 Bishop | Y | Y | Y | Y |
| 3 Marshall | Y | Y | Y | N |
| 4 McKinney | N | N | Y | Y |
| 5 Lewis | N | N | Y | Y |
| 6 Price | Y | Y | N | N |
| 7 Linder | Y | Y | Y | N |
| 8 Westmoreland | Y | ? | – | N |
| 9 Norwood | Y | ? | Y | N |
| 10 Deal | Y | ? | Y | N |
| 11 Gingrey | Y | Y | Y | N |
| 12 Barrow | Y | Y | Y | Y |
| 13 Scott | Y | Y | Y | Y |
| **HAWAII** | | | | |
| 1 Abercrombie | N | ? | Y | Y |
| 2 Case | Y | ? | Y | Y |
| **IDAHO** | | | | |
| 1 Otter | Y | Y | N | N |
| 2 Simpson | Y | Y | N | N |
| **ILLINOIS** | | | | |
| 1 Rush | N | ? | Y | Y |
| 2 Jackson | N | Y | Y | Y |
| 3 Lipinski | Y | Y | Y | N |
| 4 Gutierrez | N | N | Y | Y |
| 5 Emanuel | N | ? | Y | Y |
| 6 Hyde | Y | ? | Y | N |
| 7 Davis | N | ? | Y | Y |
| 8 Bean | Y | Y | Y | Y |
| 9 Schakowsky | N | ? | Y | Y |
| 10 Kirk | Y | Y | Y | Y |
| 11 Weller | Y | ? | Y | N |
| 12 Costello | Y | Y | Y | N |

**KEY** Republicans Democrats *Independents*

| | | | |
|---|---|---|---|
| Y Voted for (yea) | X Paired against | C Voted "present" to avoid possible conflict of interest |
| # Paired for | – Announced against | |
| + Announced for | P Voted "present" | ? Did not vote or otherwise make a position known |
| N Voted against (nay) | | |

| | 31 | 90 | 145 | 204 |
|---|---|---|---|---|
| 13 Biggert | Y | Y | Y | Y |
| 14 Hastert[2] | | Y | | N |
| 15 Johnson | Y | Y | Y | N |
| 16 Manzullo | Y | Y | Y | N |
| 17 Evans | N | N | Y | Y |
| 18 LaHood | Y | Y | Y | N |
| 19 Shimkus | Y | ? | Y | N |
| **INDIANA** | | | | |
| 1 Visclosky | N | N | Y | Y |
| 2 Chocola | Y | Y | Y | N |
| 3 Souder | Y | Y | P | N |
| 4 Buyer | Y | N | Y | N |
| 5 Burton | Y | Y | N | N |
| 6 Pence | Y | Y | N | N |
| 7 Carson | N | N | Y | Y |
| 8 Hostettler | Y | ? | Y | N |
| 9 Sodrel | Y | Y | Y | N |
| **IOWA** | | | | |
| 1 Nussle | Y | Y | Y | N |
| 2 Leach | Y | Y | Y | Y |
| 3 Boswell | N | ? | Y | Y |
| 4 Latham | Y | Y | Y | N |
| 5 King | Y | Y | N | N |
| **KANSAS** | | | | |
| 1 Moran | Y | ? | Y | N |
| 2 Ryun | Y | Y | Y | N |
| 3 Moore | N | - | Y | Y |
| 4 Tiahrt | Y | Y | N | N |
| **KENTUCKY** | | | | |
| 1 Whitfield | Y | Y | Y | N |
| 2 Lewis | Y | Y | Y | N |
| 3 Northup | Y | Y | Y | N |
| 4 Davis | Y | Y | Y | N |
| 5 Rogers | Y | ? | Y | N |
| 6 Chandler | Y | Y | Y | Y |
| **LOUISIANA** | | | | |
| 1 Jindal | Y | Y | Y | N |
| 2 Jefferson | N | ? | Y | Y |
| 3 Melancon | Y | ? | Y | N |
| 4 McCrery | Y | ? | Y | N |
| 5 Alexander | Y | Y | Y | N |
| 6 Baker | Y | Y | Y | N |
| 7 Boustany | Y | ? | Y | N |
| **MAINE** | | | | |
| 1 Allen | N | ? | Y | Y |
| 2 Michaud | N | Y | Y | Y |
| **MARYLAND** | | | | |
| 1 Gilchrest | Y | Y | Y | Y |
| 2 Ruppersberger | N | ? | Y | Y |
| 3 Cardin | N | N | Y | Y |
| 4 Wynn | N | Y | Y | Y |
| 5 Hoyer | N | N | Y | Y |
| 6 Bartlett | ? | Y | Y | N |
| 7 Cummings | N | Y | Y | Y |
| 8 Van Hollen | N | N | Y | Y |
| **MASSACHUSETTS** | | | | |
| 1 Olver | N | N | Y | Y |
| 2 Neal | N | ? | Y | Y |
| 3 McGovern | N | ? | Y | Y |
| 4 Frank | N | N | Y | Y |
| 5 Meehan | N | ? | Y | Y |
| 6 Tierney | N | ? | Y | Y |
| 7 Markey | N | ? | Y | Y |
| 8 Capuano | N | N | Y | Y |
| 9 Lynch | N | Y | Y | Y |
| 10 Delahunt | N | ? | Y | Y |
| **MICHIGAN** | | | | |
| 1 Stupak | ? | Y | Y | N |
| 2 Hoekstra | Y | ? | Y | N |
| 3 Ehlers | Y | Y | Y | N |
| 4 Camp | Y | Y | Y | N |
| 5 Kildee | N | Y | Y | Y |
| 6 Upton | Y | Y | Y | Y |
| 7 Schwarz | Y | Y | Y | Y |
| 8 Rogers | Y | ? | Y | N |
| 9 Knollenberg | Y | ? | Y | N |
| 10 Miller | Y | Y | Y | N |
| 11 McCotter | Y | Y | Y | N |
| 12 Levin | N | N | Y | Y |
| 13 Kilpatrick | N | ? | Y | Y |
| 14 Conyers | N | N | Y | Y |
| 15 Dingell | N | ? | Y | Y |

| | 31 | 90 | 145 | 204 |
|---|---|---|---|---|
| **MINNESOTA** | | | | |
| 1 Gutknecht | Y | ? | Y | N |
| 2 Kline | Y | Y | Y | N |
| 3 Ramstad | Y | Y | Y | N |
| 4 McCollum | N | ? | Y | Y |
| 5 Sabo | N | ? | Y | Y |
| 6 Kennedy | Y | Y | Y | N |
| 7 Peterson | Y | ? | Y | N |
| 8 Oberstar | N | Y | Y | Y |
| **MISSISSIPPI** | | | | |
| 1 Wicker | Y | + | ? | N |
| 2 Thompson | N | N | Y | Y |
| 3 Pickering | Y | Y | Y | N |
| 4 Taylor | Y | ? | Y | N |
| **MISSOURI** | | | | |
| 1 Clay | N | N | Y | Y |
| 2 Akin | Y | Y | Y | N |
| 3 Carnahan | N | N | Y | Y |
| 4 Skelton | Y | Y | Y | Y |
| 5 Cleaver | N | N | Y | Y |
| 6 Graves | Y | Y | Y | N |
| 7 Blunt | Y | Y | Y | N |
| 8 Emerson | Y | Y | Y | Y |
| 9 Hulshof | Y | Y | Y | N |
| **MONTANA** | | | | |
| AL Rehberg | Y | Y | Y | N |
| **NEBRASKA** | | | | |
| 1 Fortenberry | Y | Y | Y | N |
| 2 Terry | Y | Y | Y | N |
| 3 Osborne | Y | ? | Y | N |
| **NEVADA** | | | | |
| 1 Berkley | N | N | Y | Y |
| 2 Gibbons | Y | ? | Y | Y |
| 3 Porter | Y | Y | Y | Y |
| **NEW HAMPSHIRE** | | | | |
| 1 Bradley | Y | ? | Y | Y |
| 2 Bass | Y | Y | Y | Y |
| **NEW JERSEY** | | | | |
| 1 Andrews | N | ? | Y | Y |
| 2 LoBiondo | Y | Y | Y | N |
| 3 Saxton | Y | Y | Y | N |
| 4 Smith | N | Y | Y | N |
| 5 Garrett | Y | Y | Y | N |
| 6 Pallone | N | N | Y | Y |
| 7 Ferguson | + | Y | Y | N |
| 8 Pascrell | N | N | Y | Y |
| 9 Rothman | N | N | ? | Y |
| 10 Payne | N | N | Y | Y |
| 11 Frelinghuysen | Y | ? | Y | Y |
| 12 Holt | N | N | Y | Y |
| 13 Menendez | N | ? | Y | Y |
| **NEW MEXICO** | | | | |
| 1 Wilson | N | ? | Y | Y |
| 2 Pearce | Y | Y | Y | N |
| 3 Udall | N | ? | Y | Y |
| **NEW YORK** | | | | |
| 1 Bishop | N | N | Y | Y |
| 2 Israel | N | N | Y | Y |
| 3 King | Y | ? | Y | N |
| 4 McCarthy | N | ? | Y | Y |
| 5 Ackerman | N | ? | Y | Y |
| 6 Meeks | N | ? | Y | Y |
| 7 Crowley | N | ? | Y | Y |
| 8 Nadler | N | N | Y | Y |
| 9 Weiner | N | N | Y | Y |
| 10 Towns | N | ? | Y | Y |
| 11 Owens | N | ? | Y | Y |
| 12 Velázquez | N | ? | Y | Y |
| 13 Fossella | Y | Y | Y | Y |
| 14 Maloney | N | ? | Y | Y |
| 15 Rangel | N | ? | Y | Y |
| 16 Serrano | N | Y | Y | Y |
| 17 Engel | N | Y | Y | Y |
| 18 Lowey | N | ? | Y | Y |
| 19 Kelly | Y | Y | Y | Y |
| 20 Sweeney | Y | ? | Y | Y |
| 21 McNulty | Y | Y | Y | Y |
| 22 Hinchey | ? | ? | Y | Y |
| 23 McHugh | Y | Y | Y | N |
| 24 Boehlert | Y | ? | Y | Y |
| 25 Walsh | Y | Y | Y | Y |
| 26 Reynolds | Y | ? | Y | Y |
| 27 Higgins | N | Y | Y | Y |
| 28 Slaughter | N | ? | Y | Y |
| 29 Kuhl | Y | Y | Y | N |

| | 31 | 90 | 145 | 204 |
|---|---|---|---|---|
| **NORTH CAROLINA** | | | | |
| 1 Butterfield | Y | N | Y | Y |
| 2 Etheridge | N | Y | Y | Y |
| 3 Jones | Y | Y | Y | N |
| 4 Price | N | N | Y | Y |
| 5 Foxx | Y | Y | Y | N |
| 6 Coble | Y | + | Y | Y |
| 7 McIntyre | Y | Y | Y | N |
| 8 Hayes | Y | Y | Y | N |
| 9 Myrick | Y | Y | Y | N |
| 10 McHenry | Y | Y | Y | N |
| 11 Taylor | Y | Y | Y | N |
| 12 Watt | N | N | Y | Y |
| 13 Miller | N | N | Y | Y |
| **NORTH DAKOTA** | | | | |
| AL Pomeroy | N | Y | Y | Y |
| **OHIO** | | | | |
| 1 Chabot | Y | Y | Y | N |
| 2 Portman[3] | Y | Y | Y | |
| 3 Turner | Y | Y | Y | N |
| 4 Oxley | Y | ? | Y | N |
| 5 Gillmor | Y | Y | N | N |
| 6 Strickland | Y | N | Y | Y |
| 7 Hobson | Y | Y | Y | N |
| 8 Boehner | Y | Y | Y | N |
| 9 Kaptur | N | N | Y | N |
| 10 Kucinich | N | ? | Y | Y |
| 11 Jones | N | ? | Y | Y |
| 12 Tiberi | Y | Y | Y | N |
| 13 Brown | N | ? | Y | Y |
| 14 LaTourette | Y | ? | Y | Y |
| 15 Pryce | Y | Y | Y | N |
| 16 Regula | Y | Y | Y | Y |
| 17 Ryan | Y | ? | Y | Y |
| 18 Ney | Y | Y | Y | N |
| **OKLAHOMA** | | | | |
| 1 Sullivan | Y | Y | Y | N |
| 2 Boren | Y | Y | Y | Y |
| 3 Lucas | Y | Y | Y | N |
| 4 Cole | Y | Y | Y | N |
| 5 Istook | Y | Y | Y | N |
| **OREGON** | | | | |
| 1 Wu | N | N | Y | Y |
| 2 Walden | Y | ? | Y | Y |
| 3 Blumenauer | N | ? | Y | Y |
| 4 DeFazio | Y | ? | Y | Y |
| 5 Hooley | Y | ? | Y | Y |
| **PENNSYLVANIA** | | | | |
| 1 Brady | N | Y | Y | Y |
| 2 Fattah | N | ? | Y | Y |
| 3 English | Y | Y | Y | N |
| 4 Hart | Y | Y | Y | N |
| 5 Peterson | Y | Y | Y | N |
| 6 Gerlach | Y | ? | Y | Y |
| 7 Weldon | Y | Y | Y | N |
| 8 Fitzpatrick | Y | Y | Y | N |
| 9 Shuster | Y | Y | Y | N |
| 10 Sherwood | Y | Y | Y | N |
| 11 Kanjorski | Y | Y | Y | Y |
| 12 Murtha | N | N | Y | Y |
| 13 Schwartz | N | N | Y | Y |
| 14 Doyle | N | N | Y | Y |
| 15 Dent | Y | N | Y | Y |
| 16 Pitts | Y | Y | Y | N |
| 17 Holden | Y | Y | Y | N |
| 18 Murphy | Y | Y | Y | N |
| 19 Platts | Y | Y | Y | N |
| **RHODE ISLAND** | | | | |
| 1 Kennedy | N | N | Y | Y |
| 2 Langevin | N | Y | Y | Y |
| **SOUTH CAROLINA** | | | | |
| 1 Brown | Y | ? | Y | N |
| 2 Wilson | Y | Y | Y | N |
| 3 Barrett | Y | Y | Y | N |
| 4 Inglis | Y | Y | Y | N |
| 5 Spratt | N | N | Y | Y |
| 6 Clyburn | N | N | Y | Y |
| **SOUTH DAKOTA** | | | | |
| AL Herseth | Y | Y | Y | Y |
| **TENNESSEE** | | | | |
| 1 Jenkins | Y | Y | Y | N |
| 2 Duncan | Y | Y | Y | N |

| | 31 | 90 | 145 | 204 |
|---|---|---|---|---|
| 3 Wamp | Y | Y | Y | N |
| 4 Davis | Y | Y | Y | N |
| 5 Cooper | Y | ? | Y | Y |
| 6 Gordon | Y | ? | Y | Y |
| 7 Blackburn | Y | Y | N | N |
| 8 Tanner | Y | Y | Y | Y |
| 9 Ford | Y | Y | Y | Y |
| **TEXAS** | | | | |
| 1 Gohmert | Y | Y | N | N |
| 2 Poe | Y | Y | N | N |
| 3 Johnson, Sam | Y | ? | Y | N |
| 4 Hall, R. | Y | Y | Y | N |
| 5 Hensarling | Y | Y | Y | N |
| 6 Barton | Y | ? | N | Y |
| 7 Culberson | Y | Y | N | N |
| 8 Brady | Y | ? | Y | N |
| 9 Green, A. | N | Y | Y | Y |
| 10 McCaul | Y | Y | Y | N |
| 11 Conaway | Y | Y | Y | N |
| 12 Granger | Y | ? | Y | Y |
| 13 Thornberry | Y | Y | N | N |
| 14 Paul | N | ? | Y | N |
| 15 Hinojosa | - | ? | Y | Y |
| 16 Reyes | N | ? | Y | Y |
| 17 Edwards | Y | Y | Y | Y |
| 18 Jackson-Lee | N | ? | Y | Y |
| 19 Neugebauer | Y | Y | Y | N |
| 20 Gonzalez | N | ? | Y | Y |
| 21 Smith | Y | Y | Y | N |
| 22 DeLay | Y | Y | Y | N |
| 23 Bonilla | Y | ? | Y | N |
| 24 Marchant | Y | Y | Y | N |
| 25 Doggett | N | ? | Y | Y |
| 26 Burgess | Y | Y | N | N |
| 27 Ortiz | N | ? | Y | Y |
| 28 Cuellar | Y | Y | Y | Y |
| 29 Green, G. | ? | ? | Y | Y |
| 30 Johnson, E.B. | N | ? | Y | Y |
| 31 Carter | + | Y | N | N |
| 32 Sessions | Y | ? | Y | N |
| **UTAH** | | | | |
| 1 Bishop | Y | ? | Y | N |
| 2 Matheson | Y | Y | Y | Y |
| 3 Cannon | Y | Y | Y | N |
| **VERMONT** | | | | |
| AL Sanders | N | ? | Y | Y |
| **VIRGINIA** | | | | |
| 1 Davis, Jo Ann | Y | Y | Y | N |
| 2 Drake | Y | Y | Y | N |
| 3 Scott | N | N | Y | Y |
| 4 Forbes | Y | Y | Y | N |
| 5 Goode | Y | Y | Y | N |
| 6 Goodlatte | Y | Y | Y | N |
| 7 Cantor | Y | Y | Y | N |
| 8 Moran | N | N | Y | Y |
| 9 Boucher | Y | ? | ? | Y |
| 10 Wolf | Y | ? | Y | N |
| 11 Davis, T. | Y | Y | Y | Y |
| **WASHINGTON** | | | | |
| 1 Inslee | N | ? | Y | Y |
| 2 Larsen | N | ? | Y | Y |
| 3 Baird | N | Y | Y | Y |
| 4 Hastings | Y | Y | Y | ? |
| 5 McMorris | Y | ? | Y | N |
| 6 Dicks | N | N | Y | Y |
| 7 McDermott | N | N | Y | Y |
| 8 Reichert | Y | N | Y | N |
| 9 Smith | N | ? | Y | Y |
| **WEST VIRGINIA** | | | | |
| 1 Mollohan | N | Y | Y | N |
| 2 Capito | Y | Y | Y | Y |
| 3 Rahall | N | ? | Y | N |
| **WISCONSIN** | | | | |
| 1 Ryan | Y | Y | Y | N |
| 2 Baldwin | N | N | Y | Y |
| 3 Kind | N | ? | Y | Y |
| 4 Moore | N | N | Y | Y |
| 5 Sensenbrenner | Y | Y | Y | N |
| 6 Petri | Y | ? | Y | N |
| 7 Obey | N | ? | Y | Y |
| 8 Green | Y | Y | Y | N |
| **WYOMING** | | | | |
| AL Cubin | Y | ? | N | N |

# HOUSE 258, 374, 443, 445

**258.** **HR 2862. Fiscal 2006 Commerce-Justice-Science Appropriations/ Surveillance of Library Records.** Sanders, I-Vt., amendment that would prohibit the use of funds in the bill to make an application under the Foreign Intelligence Surveillance Act to acquire library circulation records, library patron lists, bookseller sales records or bookseller customer lists. Adopted 238-187: R 38-186; D 199-1 (ND 150-0, SD 49-1); I 1-0. A "nay" was a vote in support of the president's position. June 15, 2005. *(Story, p. C-15)*

**374.** **HR 3100. Arms Sales to China/Passage.** Hyde, R-Ill., motion to suspend the rules and pass the bill that would require the president to report to Congress 180 days after the bill's enactment, and yearly thereafter, identifying European or other entities that have exported any arms or dual-use technology to China for military use since Jan. 1, 2005. Motion rejected 215-203: R 118-106; D 96-97 (ND 70-73, SD 26-24); I 1-0. A two-thirds majority of those present and voting (279 in this case) is required for passage under suspension of the rules. July 14, 2005. *(Story, p. C-15)*

**443.** **HR 3045. Central American Free-Trade Agreement/Passage.** Passage of the bill that would implement a free-trade agreement between the United States and Costa Rica, El Salvador, Guatemala, Honduras and Nicaragua and a separate pact with the Dominican Republic. It also would eliminate customs duties on all originating goods traded among the participating nations within 10 days. Passed 217-215: R 202-27; D 15-187 (ND 7-144, SD 8-43); I 0-1. A "yea" was a vote in support of the president's position. July 28, 2005 (in the session that began and the Congressional Record dated July 27, 2005). *(Story, p. C-16)*

**445.** **HR 6. Energy Policy/Conference Report.** Adoption of the conference report on the bill that would overhaul the nation's energy policy and provide for $14.6 billion in energy-related tax incentives. It would allow lawsuits involving the gasoline additive methyl tertiary butyl ether to be moved to a federal district court and require refiners to annually use 7.5 billion gallons of renewable fuels by 2012. The measure would grant the Federal Energy Regulatory Commission (FERC) jurisdiction over reliability standards for electricity transmission networks and extend daylight-saving time by one month. It would allow FERC to approve the construction, expansion or operation of any facility that imports or processes natural gas, including liquefied natural gas. Adopted (thus sent to the Senate) 275-156: R 200-31; D 75-124 (ND 41-107, SD 34-17); I 0-1. A "yea" was a vote in support of the president's position. July 28, 2005. *(Story, p. C-16)*

*\* The Speaker votes only at his discretion, usually to break a tie or to emphasize the importance of a matter.*

| | 258 | 374 | 443 | 445 |
|---|---|---|---|---|
| **ALABAMA** | | | | |
| 1 Bonner | N | N | Y | N |
| 2 Everett | N | N | Y | Y |
| 3 Rogers | N | Y | Y | Y |
| 4 Aderholt | N | Y | Y | Y |
| 5 Cramer | Y | N | N | Y |
| 6 Bachus | N | Y | Y | Y |
| 7 Davis | Y | Y | N | Y |
| **ALASKA** | | | | |
| AL Young | Y | N | Y | Y |
| **ARIZONA** | | | | |
| 1 Renzi | N | N | Y | Y |
| 2 Franks | N | Y | Y | Y |
| 3 Shadegg | N | Y | Y | N |
| 4 Pastor | Y | N | N | N |
| 5 Hayworth | N | Y | Y | Y |
| 6 Flake | Y | Y | Y | N |
| 7 Grijalva | Y | Y | N | N |
| 8 Kolbe | N | N | Y | Y |
| **ARKANSAS** | | | | |
| 1 Berry | Y | N | N | Y |
| 2 Snyder | Y | N | Y | N |
| 3 Boozman | Y | Y | Y | Y |
| 4 Ross | Y | Y | N | Y |
| **CALIFORNIA** | | | | |
| 1 Thompson | Y | N | N | N |
| 2 Herger | N | Y | Y | Y |
| 3 Lungren | N | Y | Y | Y |
| 4 Doolittle | N | Y | Y | Y |
| 5 Matsui, D. | Y | Y | N | N |
| 6 Woolsey | Y | N | N | N |
| 7 Miller, George | Y | N | N | N |
| 8 Pelosi | Y | N | N | N |
| 9 Lee | Y | N | N | N |
| 10 Tauscher | Y | N | N | N |
| 11 Pombo | N | Y | Y | Y |
| 12 Lantos | Y | Y | N | N |
| 13 Stark | Y | N | N | N |
| 14 Eshoo | Y | N | N | N |
| 15 Honda | Y | N | N | N |
| 16 Lofgren | Y | N | N | N |
| 17 Farr | Y | Y | N | N |
| 18 Cardoza | Y | Y | N | Y |
| 19 Radanovich | N | Y | Y | Y |
| 20 Costa | Y | Y | N | Y |
| 21 Nunes | N | N | Y | Y |
| 22 Thomas | N | N | Y | Y |
| 23 Capps | Y | + | N | N |
| 24 Gallegly | N | + | Y | Y |
| 25 McKeon | N | N | Y | Y |
| 26 Dreier | N | N | Y | Y |
| 27 Sherman | Y | N | N | N |
| 28 Berman | Y | N | N | N |
| 29 Schiff | Y | Y | N | N |
| 30 Waxman | Y | N | N | N |
| 31 Becerra | Y | N | N | N |
| 32 Solis | Y | N | N | N |
| 33 Watson | Y | Y | N | N |
| 34 Roybal-Allard | Y | Y | N | N |
| 35 Waters | Y | N | N | N |
| 36 Harman | Y | N | N | N |
| 37 Millender-McD. | Y | N | N | N |
| 38 Napolitano | Y | N | N | N |
| 39 Sánchez, Linda | Y | Y | N | N |
| 40 Royce | N | Y | Y | Y |
| 41 Lewis | N | N | Y | Y |
| 42 Miller, Gary | N | Y | Y | Y |
| 43 Baca | Y | N | N | Y |
| 44 Calvert | N | N | Y | Y |
| 45 Bono | ? | N | Y | Y |
| 46 Rohrabacher | N | Y | Y | N |
| 47 Sanchez, Loretta | Y | N | N | N |
| 48 Cox | N | Y | Y | Y |
| 49 Issa | N | N | Y | Y |

| | 258 | 374 | 443 | 445 |
|---|---|---|---|---|
| 50 Cunningham | N | ? | Y | Y |
| 51 Filner | Y | Y | N | N |
| 52 Hunter | N | Y | N | Y |
| 53 Davis | Y | N | N | N |
| **COLORADO** | | | | |
| 1 DeGette | Y | Y | N | N |
| 2 Udall | Y | N | N | N |
| 3 Salazar | Y | N | N | Y |
| 4 Musgrave | Y | Y | Y | Y |
| 5 Hefley | N | Y | Y | Y |
| 6 Tancredo | N | N | N | Y |
| 7 Beauprez | N | N | Y | Y |
| **CONNECTICUT** | | | | |
| 1 Larson | Y | Y | N | N |
| 2 Simmons | N | ? | N | Y |
| 3 DeLauro | Y | Y | N | N |
| 4 Shays | N | N | Y | N |
| 5 Johnson | N | N | Y | Y |
| **DELAWARE** | | | | |
| AL Castle | Y | Y | Y | N |
| **FLORIDA** | | | | |
| 1 Miller | Y | + | Y | N |
| 2 Boyd | Y | Y | N | N |
| 3 Brown | Y | Y | N | N |
| 4 Crenshaw | N | N | Y | N |
| 5 Brown-Waite | N | Y | Y | Y |
| 6 Stearns | N | Y | Y | Y |
| 7 Mica | N | N | Y | Y |
| 8 Keller | N | Y | Y | N |
| 9 Bilirakis | N | Y | Y | Y |
| 10 Young | N | ? | Y | N |
| 11 Davis | Y | Y | N | N |
| 12 Putnam | N | Y | Y | N |
| 13 Harris | Y | N | Y | N |
| 14 Mack | N | Y | N | N |
| 15 Weldon | N | Y | Y | N |
| 16 Foley | N | Y | Y | N |
| 17 Meek | Y | N | N | N |
| 18 Ros-Lehtinen | Y | N | N | N |
| 19 Wexler | Y | N | N | N |
| 20 Wasserman-Schultz | Y | Y | N | N |
| 21 Diaz-Balart, L. | N | Y | Y | N |
| 22 Shaw | N | Y | Y | N |
| 23 Hastings | Y | N | N | N |
| 24 Feeney | N | Y | Y | N |
| 25 Diaz-Balart, M. | N | Y | Y | N |
| **GEORGIA** | | | | |
| 1 Kingston | Y | N | Y | Y |
| 2 Bishop | Y | Y | N | Y |
| 3 Marshall | Y | N | N | Y |
| 4 McKinney | Y | N | N | N |
| 5 Lewis | Y | N | N | N |
| 6 Price | N | Y | Y | Y |
| 7 Linder | N | Y | Y | Y |
| 8 Westmoreland | N | Y | Y | Y |
| 9 Norwood | N | Y | N | Y |
| 10 Deal | N | Y | Y | Y |
| 11 Gingrey | N | Y | Y | Y |
| 12 Barrow | Y | Y | N | Y |
| 13 Scott | Y | Y | N | Y |
| **HAWAII** | | | | |
| 1 Abercrombie | Y | Y | N | N |
| 2 Case | Y | Y | N | N |
| **IDAHO** | | | | |
| 1 Otter | Y | N | N | Y |
| 2 Simpson | N | N | N | Y |
| **ILLINOIS** | | | | |
| 1 Rush | Y | N | N | Y |
| 2 Jackson | Y | N | N | N |
| 3 Lipinski | Y | N | N | Y |
| 4 Gutierrez | Y | + | N | N |
| 5 Emanuel | Y | N | N | N |
| 6 Hyde | – | Y | Y | Y |
| 7 Davis | Y | N | N | N |
| 8 Bean | Y | N | Y | Y |
| 9 Schakowsky | Y | N | N | ? |
| 10 Kirk | Y | N | Y | Y |
| 11 Weller | N | N | Y | Y |
| 12 Costello | Y | N | N | Y |

**KEY**   Republicans   Democrats   *Independents*

| | | | |
|---|---|---|---|
| **Y** Voted for (yea) | **X** Paired against | **C** Voted "present" to avoid possible conflict of interest |
| **#** Paired for | **–** Announced against | |
| **+** Announced for | **P** Voted "present" | **?** Did not vote or otherwise make a position known |
| **N** Voted against (nay) | | |

| | 258 | 374 | 443 | 445 |
|---|---|---|---|---|
| 13 Biggert | N | N | Y | Y |
| 14 Hastert* | | | Y | Y |
| 15 Johnson | Y | Y | Y | Y |
| 16 Manzullo | Y | N | Y | Y |
| 17 Evans | Y | Y | N | Y |
| 18 LaHood | Y | N | Y | Y |
| 19 Shimkus | N | N | Y | Y |
| **INDIANA** | | | | |
| 1 Visclosky | Y | N | N | Y |
| 2 Chocola | N | Y | Y | Y |
| 3 Souder | N | Y | Y | Y |
| 4 Buyer | N | Y | Y | Y |
| 5 Burton | N | Y | Y | Y |
| 6 Pence | N | Y | Y | Y |
| 7 Carson | Y | ? | N | Y |
| 8 Hostettler | N | Y | N | Y |
| 9 Sodrel | N | N | Y | Y |
| **IOWA** | | | | |
| 1 Nussle | N | N | Y | Y |
| 2 Leach | Y | N | Y | Y |
| 3 Boswell | Y | N | N | Y |
| 4 Latham | N | N | Y | Y |
| 5 King | N | N | Y | Y |
| **KANSAS** | | | | |
| 1 Moran | Y | N | Y | Y |
| 2 Ryun | N | N | Y | Y |
| 3 Moore | Y | N | Y | Y |
| 4 Tiahrt | N | N | Y | Y |
| **KENTUCKY** | | | | |
| 1 Whitfield | Y | N | Y | Y |
| 2 Lewis | N | N | Y | Y |
| 3 Northup | N | Y | Y | Y |
| 4 Davis | N | N | Y | Y |
| 5 Rogers | N | Y | Y | Y |
| 6 Chandler | Y | Y | N | N |
| **LOUISIANA** | | | | |
| 1 Jindal | N | Y | N | Y |
| 2 Jefferson | Y | N | Y | Y |
| 3 Melancon | Y | Y | N | Y |
| 4 McCrery | N | Y | Y | Y |
| 5 Alexander | N | Y | Y | Y |
| 6 Baker | N | N | Y | Y |
| 7 Boustany | N | N | N | Y |
| **MAINE** | | | | |
| 1 Allen | Y | Y | N | N |
| 2 Michaud | Y | Y | N | N |
| **MARYLAND** | | | | |
| 1 Gilchrest | N | N | Y | Y |
| 2 Ruppersberger | Y | N | N | Y |
| 3 Cardin | Y | ? | N | N |
| 4 Wynn | Y | N | N | Y |
| 5 Hoyer | Y | N | N | Y |
| 6 Bartlett | N | N | Y | N |
| 7 Cummings | Y | Y | N | N |
| 8 Van Hollen | Y | N | N | N |
| **MASSACHUSETTS** | | | | |
| 1 Olver | Y | N | N | N |
| 2 Neal | Y | N | N | N |
| 3 McGovern | Y | N | N | N |
| 4 Frank | Y | Y | N | N |
| 5 Meehan | Y | N | N | N |
| 6 Tierney | Y | Y | N | N |
| 7 Markey | Y | Y | N | N |
| 8 Capuano | Y | N | N | N |
| 9 Lynch | Y | N | N | N |
| 10 Delahunt | Y | N | N | N |
| **MICHIGAN** | | | | |
| 1 Stupak | Y | Y | N | Y |
| 2 Hoekstra | N | N | Y | Y |
| 3 Ehlers | Y | N | Y | Y |
| 4 Camp | N | N | Y | Y |
| 5 Kildee | Y | Y | N | Y |
| 6 Upton | N | N | Y | Y |
| 7 Schwarz | Y | Y | Y | Y |
| 8 Rogers | N | Y | Y | Y |
| 9 Knollenberg | N | Y | Y | Y |
| 10 Miller | N | Y | Y | Y |
| 11 McCotter | N | Y | Y | Y |
| 12 Levin | Y | N | N | Y |
| 13 Kilpatrick | Y | + | N | N |
| 14 Conyers | Y | N | N | N |
| 15 Dingell | Y | Y | N | Y |

| | 258 | 374 | 443 | 445 |
|---|---|---|---|---|
| **MINNESOTA** | | | | |
| 1 Gutknecht | N | N | N | Y |
| 2 Kline | N | N | Y | Y |
| 3 Ramstad | N | Y | Y | Y |
| 4 McCollum | Y | N | N | N |
| 5 Sabo | Y | N | N | N |
| 6 Kennedy | N | N | Y | Y |
| 7 Peterson | Y | Y | N | Y |
| 8 Oberstar | + | ? | N | Y |
| **MISSISSIPPI** | | | | |
| 1 Wicker | N | Y | Y | Y |
| 2 Thompson | Y | Y | N | Y |
| 3 Pickering | N | Y | Y | Y |
| 4 Taylor | Y | Y | N | N |
| **MISSOURI** | | | | |
| 1 Clay | Y | N | N | N |
| 2 Akin | N | Y | Y | Y |
| 3 Carnahan | Y | Y | N | N |
| 4 Skelton | Y | N | Y | Y |
| 5 Cleaver | Y | Y | N | N |
| 6 Graves | N | Y | Y | Y |
| 7 Blunt | N | Y | Y | Y |
| 8 Emerson | Y | Y | Y | Y |
| 9 Hulshof | N | N | Y | Y |
| **MONTANA** | | | | |
| AL Rehberg | Y | N | N | Y |
| **NEBRASKA** | | | | |
| 1 Fortenberry | N | Y | Y | Y |
| 2 Terry | N | Y | Y | Y |
| 3 Osborne | N | Y | Y | Y |
| **NEVADA** | | | | |
| 1 Berkley | Y | Y | N | N |
| 2 Gibbons | N | N | Y | Y |
| 3 Porter | Y | Y | Y | Y |
| **NEW HAMPSHIRE** | | | | |
| 1 Bradley | N | Y | Y | N |
| 2 Bass | N | N | Y | Y |
| **NEW JERSEY** | | | | |
| 1 Andrews | Y | Y | N | N |
| 2 LoBiondo | N | N | N | N |
| 3 Saxton | N | N | Y | N |
| 4 Smith | N | Y | N | N |
| 5 Garrett | - | N | N | Y |
| 6 Pallone | Y | N | N | N |
| 7 Ferguson | N | N | Y | Y |
| 8 Pascrell | Y | Y | N | N |
| 9 Rothman | Y | Y | N | N |
| 10 Payne | Y | N | N | ? |
| 11 Frelinghuysen | N | N | Y | Y |
| 12 Holt | Y | N | N | N |
| 13 Menendez | Y | N | N | N |
| **NEW MEXICO** | | | | |
| 1 Wilson | N | N | Y | Y |
| 2 Pearce | N | Y | Y | Y |
| 3 Udall | Y | N | N | Y |
| **NEW YORK** | | | | |
| 1 Bishop | Y | Y | N | N |
| 2 Israel | Y | N | N | N |
| 3 King | N | Y | Y | Y |
| 4 McCarthy | Y | N | N | N |
| 5 Ackerman | Y | Y | N | N |
| 6 Meeks | Y | N | Y | N |
| 7 Crowley | Y | Y | N | N |
| 8 Nadler | Y | Y | N | N |
| 9 Weiner | Y | ? | N | N |
| 10 Towns | Y | N | N | N |
| 11 Owens | Y | Y | N | N |
| 12 Velázquez | Y | N | N | N |
| 13 Fossella | N | N | Y | Y |
| 14 Maloney | Y | Y | N | N |
| 15 Rangel | Y | N | N | N |
| 16 Serrano | Y | Y | N | N |
| 17 Engel | Y | Y | N | N |
| 18 Lowey | Y | Y | N | N |
| 19 Kelly | N | Y | Y | N |
| 20 Sweeney | N | N | Y | Y |
| 21 McNulty | Y | N | N | N |
| 22 Hinchey | Y | N | N | N |
| 23 McHugh | N | N | Y | Y |
| 24 Boehlert | Y | Y | N | N |
| 25 Walsh | N | Y | Y | Y |
| 26 Reynolds | N | Y | Y | Y |
| 27 Higgins | Y | Y | N | N |
| 28 Slaughter | Y | N | N | N |
| 29 Kuhl | N | N | Y | Y |

| | 258 | 374 | 443 | 445 |
|---|---|---|---|---|
| **NORTH CAROLINA** | | | | |
| 1 Butterfield | Y | Y | N | Y |
| 2 Etheridge | Y | N | N | Y |
| 3 Jones | Y | Y | N | N |
| 4 Price | Y | N | N | N |
| 5 Foxx | N | Y | N | Y |
| 6 Coble | N | N | Y | Y |
| 7 McIntyre | Y | ? | N | Y |
| 8 Hayes | N | Y | Y | Y |
| 9 Myrick | N | Y | Y | Y |
| 10 McHenry | N | Y | N | Y |
| 11 Taylor | Y | Y | - | Y |
| 12 Watt | Y | N | N | N |
| 13 Miller | Y | N | N | N |
| **NORTH DAKOTA** | | | | |
| AL Pomeroy | Y | N | N | Y |
| **OHIO** | | | | |
| 1 Chabot | N | Y | Y | Y |
| 2 Vacant | | | | |
| 3 Turner | N | N | Y | Y |
| 4 Oxley | N | Y | Y | Y |
| 5 Gillmor | Y | Y | Y | Y |
| 6 Strickland | Y | N | Y | Y |
| 7 Hobson | N | N | Y | Y |
| 8 Boehner | Y | N | Y | Y |
| 9 Kaptur | Y | Y | N | N |
| 10 Kucinich | Y | N | N | N |
| 11 Jones | Y | N | N | N |
| 12 Tiberi | N | N | Y | Y |
| 13 Brown | Y | Y | N | N |
| 14 LaTourette | Y | N | Y | Y |
| 15 Pryce | N | N | Y | Y |
| 16 Regula | N | N | Y | Y |
| 17 Ryan | Y | N | N | Y |
| 18 Ney | Y | Y | N | Y |
| **OKLAHOMA** | | | | |
| 1 Sullivan | ? | N | Y | Y |
| 2 Boren | N | N | N | Y |
| 3 Lucas | N | Y | Y | Y |
| 4 Cole | N | Y | Y | Y |
| 5 Istook | N | Y | Y | Y |
| **OREGON** | | | | |
| 1 Wu | Y | N | N | N |
| 2 Walden | Y | Y | Y | Y |
| 3 Blumenauer | Y | N | N | N |
| 4 DeFazio | Y | Y | N | N |
| 5 Hooley | Y | N | N | N |
| **PENNSYLVANIA** | | | | |
| 1 Brady | Y | Y | N | ? |
| 2 Fattah | Y | Y | N | N |
| 3 English | N | N | Y | Y |
| 4 Hart | N | N | Y | Y |
| 5 Peterson | Y | Y | Y | Y |
| 6 Gerlach | N | Y | Y | Y |
| 7 Weldon | ? | Y | Y | Y |
| 8 Fitzpatrick | Y | Y | N | N |
| 9 Shuster | N | N | Y | Y |
| 10 Sherwood | N | Y | Y | Y |
| 11 Kanjorski | Y | Y | N | Y |
| 12 Murtha | Y | N | Y | Y |
| 13 Schwartz | Y | Y | N | N |
| 14 Doyle | Y | Y | N | Y |
| 15 Dent | N | Y | Y | Y |
| 16 Pitts | N | Y | Y | Y |
| 17 Holden | Y | N | Y | Y |
| 18 Murphy | N | N | Y | Y |
| 19 Platts | Y | Y | N | Y |
| **RHODE ISLAND** | | | | |
| 1 Kennedy | Y | Y | N | N |
| 2 Langevin | Y | Y | N | N |
| **SOUTH CAROLINA** | | | | |
| 1 Brown | N | N | Y | Y |
| 2 Wilson | N | Y | Y | Y |
| 3 Barrett | N | Y | Y | Y |
| 4 Inglis | N | Y | Y | Y |
| 5 Spratt | Y | Y | N | Y |
| 6 Clyburn | Y | N | N | N |
| **SOUTH DAKOTA** | | | | |
| AL Herseth | Y | N | N | Y |
| **TENNESSEE** | | | | |
| 1 Jenkins | N | N | Y | Y |
| 2 Duncan | Y | Y | Y | Y |

| | 258 | 374 | 443 | 445 |
|---|---|---|---|---|
| 3 Wamp | N | Y | N | Y |
| 4 Davis | Y | Y | N | Y |
| 5 Cooper | Y | Y | Y | N |
| 6 Gordon | Y | N | N | Y |
| 7 Blackburn | N | Y | Y | Y |
| 8 Tanner | Y | Y | Y | Y |
| 9 Ford | Y | Y | N | Y |
| **TEXAS** | | | | |
| 1 Gohmert | N | N | Y | Y |
| 2 Poe | Y | N | Y | Y |
| 3 Johnson, Sam | N | Y | Y | Y |
| 4 Hall, R. | N | N | Y | Y |
| 5 Hensarling | N | N | Y | Y |
| 6 Barton | N | Y | Y | Y |
| 7 Culberson | N | Y | Y | Y |
| 8 Brady | N | Y | Y | Y |
| 9 Green, A. | Y | Y | N | Y |
| 10 McCaul | N | Y | Y | Y |
| 11 Conaway | N | Y | Y | Y |
| 12 Granger | N | Y | Y | Y |
| 13 Thornberry | N | N | Y | Y |
| 14 Paul | Y | N | N | N |
| 15 Hinojosa | Y | Y | Y | Y |
| 16 Reyes | Y | N | Y | Y |
| 17 Edwards | Y | Y | N | Y |
| 18 Jackson-Lee | Y | Y | N | Y |
| 19 Neugebauer | N | N | Y | Y |
| 20 Gonzalez | Y | N | N | Y |
| 21 Smith | N | N | Y | Y |
| 22 DeLay | N | Y | Y | Y |
| 23 Bonilla | N | N | Y | Y |
| 24 Marchant | N | Y | Y | Y |
| 25 Doggett | Y | N | N | N |
| 26 Burgess | Y | N | Y | Y |
| 27 Ortiz | Y | N | N | Y |
| 28 Cuellar | ? | N | Y | Y |
| 29 Green, G. | Y | Y | N | Y |
| 30 Johnson, E.B. | Y | Y | N | Y |
| 31 Carter | N | N | Y | Y |
| 32 Sessions | ? | N | Y | Y |
| **UTAH** | | | | |
| 1 Bishop | Y | Y | Y | Y |
| 2 Matheson | Y | Y | Y | Y |
| 3 Cannon | N | N | Y | Y |
| **VERMONT** | | | | |
| AL Sanders | Y | Y | N | N |
| **VIRGINIA** | | | | |
| 1 Davis, Jo Ann | N | Y | - | Y |
| 2 Drake | N | Y | Y | Y |
| 3 Scott | Y | N | N | Y |
| 4 Forbes | N | Y | Y | Y |
| 5 Goode | N | Y | N | Y |
| 6 Goodlatte | N | N | Y | Y |
| 7 Cantor | N | Y | Y | Y |
| 8 Moran | Y | N | Y | N |
| 9 Boucher | Y | N | N | Y |
| 10 Wolf | N | Y | Y | Y |
| 11 Davis, T. | N | N | Y | Y |
| **WASHINGTON** | | | | |
| 1 Inslee | Y | N | N | N |
| 2 Larsen | Y | N | N | Y |
| 3 Baird | Y | N | N | N |
| 4 Hastings | N | Y | Y | Y |
| 5 McMorris | N | Y | Y | Y |
| 6 Dicks | Y | N | N | Y |
| 7 McDermott | Y | N | N | N |
| 8 Reichert | N | N | Y | Y |
| 9 Smith | Y | N | N | N |
| **WEST VIRGINIA** | | | | |
| 1 Mollohan | Y | N | Y | Y |
| 2 Capito | N | Y | N | Y |
| 3 Rahall | Y | N | N | Y |
| **WISCONSIN** | | | | |
| 1 Ryan | N | N | Y | Y |
| 2 Baldwin | Y | Y | N | N |
| 3 Kind | Y | N | N | N |
| 4 Moore | Y | N | N | N |
| 5 Sensenbrenner | N | N | Y | Y |
| 6 Petri | Y | N | Y | Y |
| 7 Obey | Y | ? | N | N |
| 8 Green | N | Y | Y | Y |
| **WYOMING** | | | | |
| AL Cubin | Y | ? | N | Y |

# HOUSE 453, 506, 630, 670

**453.** HR 3. Surface Transportation Reauthorization/Conference Report. Adoption of the conference report on the bill that would bring total authorization for federal highway, mass transit, safety and research programs, including fiscal 2004 funding, to $286.5 billion through 2009. The bill would increase the rate of return to states on their Highway Trust Fund contributions to 92 percent by fiscal 2008. It would make the Transportation Department the lead agency in the environmental review process for transportation projects. Adopted (thus sent to the Senate) 412-8: R 217-8; D 194-0 (ND 144-0, SD 50-0); I 1-0. July 29, 2005. (Story, p. C-17)

**506.** HR 3824. Endangered Species Act Overhaul/Passage. Passage of the bill that would overhaul and reauthorize the Endangered Species Act through 2010. It would replace the critical habitat designation with expanded authority to develop recovery plans for species. The Interior Department would be required to reimburse landowners who are not allowed to develop their land because of protections for endangered species. It also would authorize grants for private landowners to protect endangered species. Passed 229-193: R 193-34; D 36-158 (ND 15-129, SD 21-29); I 0-1. Sept. 29, 2005. (Story, p. C-17)

**630.** HR 2863. Fiscal 2006 Defense Appropriations/Motion to Instruct. Murtha, D-Pa., motion to instruct House conferees to include Senate-passed language that would establish the U.S. Army Field Manual on Intelligence Interrogation as the uniform standard for interrogating persons detained by the Department of Defense, and prohibit cruel, inhuman or degrading treatment of any prisoner detained by the U.S. government. Motion agreed to 308-122: R 107-121; D 200-1 (ND 150-0, SD 50-1); I 1-0. A "nay" was a vote in support of the president's position. Dec. 14, 2005. (Story, p. C-18)

**670.** S 1932. Budget Reconciliation/Conference Report. Adoption of the conference report on the bill that would make changes to programs for a net savings of $38.8 billion over five years. The total includes savings of roughly $12.7 billion from the student loan program, $1.5 billion from aid to states to enforce child support payments and $4.8 billion from Medicaid. The bill would provide $2.1 billion in hurricane assistance, authorize an additional $1 billion for low-income energy assistance and provide $7.3 billion to avoid a scheduled Medicare reimbursement cut to physicians. Adopted (thus sent to the Senate) 212-206: R 212-9; D 0-196 (ND 0-146, SD 0-50); I 0-1. A "yea" was a vote in support of the president's position. Dec. 19, 2005 (in the session that began and the Congressional Record dated Dec. 18, 2005). (Story, p. C-18)

[1] Rep. John Campbell, R-Calif., was sworn in Dec. 7, 2005, to replace Republican Christopher Cox, who resigned effective Aug. 2. The first vote for which Campbell was eligible was vote 619. The last vote for which Cox was eligible was vote 453, on which he voted "yea."

[2] Rep. Randy "Duke" Cunningham, R-Calif., resigned effective Dec. 1, 2005. The last vote for which he was eligible was vote 608.

[3] The Speaker votes only at his discretion, usually to break a tie or to emphasize the importance of a matter.

[4] Rep. Jean Schmidt, R-Ohio, was sworn in Sept. 6, 2005, to replace Republican Rob Portman, who resigned effective April 29. The first vote for which Schmidt was eligible was vote 454.

| | 453 | 506 | 630 | 670 |
|---|---|---|---|---|
| **ALABAMA** | | | | |
| 1 Bonner | Y | Y | N | Y |
| 2 Everett | Y | Y | N | Y |
| 3 Rogers | Y | Y | N | Y |
| 4 Aderholt | Y | Y | N | Y |
| 5 Cramer | Y | Y | Y | N |
| 6 Bachus | Y | Y | Y | Y |
| 7 Davis | Y | Y | Y | N |
| **ALASKA** | | | | |
| AL Young | Y | Y | N | Y |
| **ARIZONA** | | | | |
| 1 Renzi | Y | Y | N | Y |
| 2 Franks | Y | Y | N | Y |
| 3 Shadegg | N | Y | N | Y |
| 4 Pastor | Y | N | Y | N |
| 5 Hayworth | Y | Y | N | Y |
| 6 Flake | N | Y | Y | Y |
| 7 Grijalva | Y | N | Y | N |
| 8 Kolbe | Y | Y | Y | ? |
| **ARKANSAS** | | | | |
| 1 Berry | Y | Y | Y | N |
| 2 Snyder | Y | N | Y | N |
| 3 Boozman | Y | Y | Y | Y |
| 4 Ross | Y | Y | Y | N |
| **CALIFORNIA** | | | | |
| 1 Thompson | Y | N | Y | N |
| 2 Herger | Y | Y | N | Y |
| 3 Lungren | Y | Y | N | Y |
| 4 Doolittle | Y | Y | N | Y |
| 5 Matsui, D. | Y | N | Y | N |
| 6 Woolsey | Y | N | Y | N |
| 7 Miller, George | ? | N | Y | N |
| 8 Pelosi | Y | N | Y | N |
| 9 Lee | Y | N | Y | N |
| 10 Tauscher | Y | N | Y | N |
| 11 Pombo | + | Y | Y | Y |
| 12 Lantos | Y | N | Y | N |
| 13 Stark | ? | N | Y | N |
| 14 Eshoo | Y | N | Y | N |
| 15 Honda | Y | N | Y | N |
| 16 Lofgren | Y | N | Y | N |
| 17 Farr | Y | N | Y | N |
| 18 Cardoza | Y | Y | Y | N |
| 19 Radanovich | Y | Y | N | ? |
| 20 Costa | Y | Y | + | N |
| 21 Nunes | Y | Y | N | Y |
| 22 Thomas | Y | Y | Y | Y |
| 23 Capps | + | N | Y | N |
| 24 Gallegly | Y | Y | N | Y |
| 25 McKeon | Y | Y | N | Y |
| 26 Dreier | Y | Y | N | Y |
| 27 Sherman | Y | N | Y | N |
| 28 Berman | Y | N | Y | N |
| 29 Schiff | Y | N | Y | N |
| 30 Waxman | Y | N | Y | N |
| 31 Becerra | Y | N | Y | N |
| 32 Solis | Y | N | Y | N |
| 33 Watson | Y | N | Y | N |
| 34 Roybal-Allard | Y | N | Y | ? |
| 35 Waters | Y | N | Y | N |
| 36 Harman | Y | - | Y | ? |
| 37 Millender-McD. | Y | N | Y | N |
| 38 Napolitano | Y | N | Y | N |
| 39 Sánchez, Linda | Y | N | Y | N |
| 40 Royce | N | Y | N | Y |
| 41 Lewis | Y | Y | N | Y |
| 42 Miller, Gary | Y | Y | N | ? |
| 43 Baca | Y | Y | Y | ? |
| 44 Calvert | Y | Y | N | Y |
| 45 Bono | Y | Y | N | Y |
| 46 Rohrabacher | Y | Y | N | Y |
| 47 Sanchez, Loretta | Y | N | Y | N |
| 48 Campbell[1] | | | N | Y |
| 49 Issa | Y | Y | Y | Y |

| | 453 | 506 | 630 | 670 |
|---|---|---|---|---|
| 50 Cunningham[2] | Y | Y | | |
| 51 Filner | Y | N | Y | N |
| 52 Hunter | Y | Y | N | Y |
| 53 Davis | Y | N | Y | N |
| **COLORADO** | | | | |
| 1 DeGette | Y | N | Y | N |
| 2 Udall | Y | N | Y | N |
| 3 Salazar | Y | Y | Y | N |
| 4 Musgrave | Y | Y | N | Y |
| 5 Hefley | Y | Y | N | Y |
| 6 Tancredo | Y | Y | Y | Y |
| 7 Beauprez | Y | Y | Y | Y |
| **CONNECTICUT** | | | | |
| 1 Larson | Y | N | Y | N |
| 2 Simmons | Y | N | Y | Y |
| 3 DeLauro | Y | N | Y | N |
| 4 Shays | Y | N | Y | Y |
| 5 Johnson | Y | N | Y | Y |
| **DELAWARE** | | | | |
| AL Castle | Y | N | Y | Y |
| **FLORIDA** | | | | |
| 1 Miller | Y | Y | N | Y |
| 2 Boyd | Y | Y | Y | N |
| 3 Brown | Y | N | Y | N |
| 4 Crenshaw | Y | Y | N | Y |
| 5 Brown-Waite | Y | Y | Y | Y |
| 6 Stearns | Y | N | N | Y |
| 7 Mica | ? | Y | N | Y |
| 8 Keller | Y | Y | N | Y |
| 9 Bilirakis | Y | Y | N | Y |
| 10 Young | Y | Y | N | Y |
| 11 Davis | Y | ? | Y | N |
| 12 Putnam | Y | Y | N | Y |
| 13 Harris | Y | Y | N | Y |
| 14 Mack | Y | Y | Y | Y |
| 15 Weldon | Y | Y | N | Y |
| 16 Foley | Y | N | Y | Y |
| 17 Meek | Y | N | Y | N |
| 18 Ros-Lehtinen | Y | Y | Y | Y |
| 19 Wexler | ? | N | Y | N |
| 20 Wasserman-Schultz | Y | N | Y | N |
| 21 Diaz-Balart, L. | Y | Y | Y | Y |
| 22 Shaw | Y | N | Y | Y |
| 23 Hastings | Y | N | Y | N |
| 24 Feeney | Y | Y | Y | Y |
| 25 Diaz-Balart, M. | Y | Y | + | Y |
| **GEORGIA** | | | | |
| 1 Kingston | Y | Y | N | Y |
| 2 Bishop | Y | Y | Y | N |
| 3 Marshall | Y | N | N | N |
| 4 McKinney | Y | N | Y | N |
| 5 Lewis | Y | N | Y | N |
| 6 Price | Y | Y | N | Y |
| 7 Linder | Y | Y | N | Y |
| 8 Westmoreland | Y | Y | N | Y |
| 9 Norwood | Y | Y | N | Y |
| 10 Deal | Y | Y | N | Y |
| 11 Gingrey | Y | Y | N | Y |
| 12 Barrow | Y | Y | Y | N |
| 13 Scott | Y | Y | Y | N |
| **HAWAII** | | | | |
| 1 Abercrombie | Y | Y | Y | N |
| 2 Case | Y | N | Y | N |
| **IDAHO** | | | | |
| 1 Otter | Y | Y | Y | Y |
| 2 Simpson | Y | Y | N | Y |
| **ILLINOIS** | | | | |
| 1 Rush | Y | N | Y | N |
| 2 Jackson | Y | N | Y | N |
| 3 Lipinski | Y | N | Y | N |
| 4 Gutierrez | Y | - | Y | ? |
| 5 Emanuel | Y | N | Y | ? |
| 6 Hyde | Y | Y | + | ? |
| 7 Davis | Y | N | Y | N |
| 8 Bean | Y | N | Y | N |
| 9 Schakowsky | ? | N | Y | N |
| 10 Kirk | Y | N | Y | Y |
| 11 Weller | Y | Y | Y | Y |
| 12 Costello | Y | Y | Y | N |

| KEY | Republicans | Democrats | Independents | | |
|---|---|---|---|---|---|
| Y | Voted for (yea) | X | Paired against | C | Voted "present" to avoid possible conflict of interest |
| # | Paired for | - | Announced against | | |
| + | Announced for | P | Voted "present" | ? | Did not vote or otherwise make a position known |
| N | Voted against (nay) | | | | |

| | 453 | 506 | 630 | 670 |
|---|---|---|---|---|
| 13 Biggert | Y | N | Y | Y |
| 14 Hastert[3] | Y | | | Y |
| 15 Johnson | Y | N | Y | N |
| 16 Manzullo | Y | Y | Y | Y |
| 17 Evans | Y | N | Y | N |
| 18 LaHood | Y | N | N | Y |
| 19 Shimkus | Y | Y | Y | Y |
| **INDIANA** | | | | |
| 1 Visclosky | Y | N | Y | N |
| 2 Chocola | Y | Y | Y | Y |
| 3 Souder | Y | Y | N | Y |
| 4 Buyer | Y | Y | Y | N |
| 5 Burton | Y | Y | N | Y |
| 6 Pence | Y | Y | Y | Y |
| 7 Carson | Y | N | Y | N |
| 8 Hostettler | Y | Y | N | ? |
| 9 Sodrel | Y | Y | Y | Y |
| **IOWA** | | | | |
| 1 Nussle | Y | Y | Y | Y |
| 2 Leach | Y | N | Y | N |
| 3 Boswell | Y | ? | Y | N |
| 4 Latham | Y | Y | Y | Y |
| 5 King | Y | Y | N | Y |
| **KANSAS** | | | | |
| 1 Moran | Y | Y | Y | Y |
| 2 Ryun | Y | Y | N | Y |
| 3 Moore | Y | N | Y | N |
| 4 Tiahrt | Y | Y | N | Y |
| **KENTUCKY** | | | | |
| 1 Whitfield | Y | Y | Y | Y |
| 2 Lewis | Y | Y | N | Y |
| 3 Northup | Y | Y | Y | Y |
| 4 Davis | Y | Y | N | Y |
| 5 Rogers | Y | Y | N | Y |
| 6 Chandler | Y | N | Y | N |
| **LOUISIANA** | | | | |
| 1 Jindal | Y | Y | N | Y |
| 2 Jefferson | Y | N | Y | N |
| 3 Melancon | Y | Y | Y | N |
| 4 McCrery | Y | Y | Y | Y |
| 5 Alexander | Y | Y | Y | Y |
| 6 Baker | Y | Y | N | Y |
| 7 Boustany | Y | Y | Y | Y |
| **MAINE** | | | | |
| 1 Allen | Y | N | Y | N |
| 2 Michaud | Y | N | Y | N |
| **MARYLAND** | | | | |
| 1 Gilchrest | Y | N | Y | Y |
| 2 Ruppersberger | Y | N | Y | N |
| 3 Cardin | Y | N | Y | N |
| 4 Wynn | Y | Y | Y | N |
| 5 Hoyer | Y | N | Y | N |
| 6 Bartlett | Y | Y | Y | Y |
| 7 Cummings | Y | N | Y | N |
| 8 Van Hollen | Y | N | Y | N |
| **MASSACHUSETTS** | | | | |
| 1 Olver | Y | N | Y | N |
| 2 Neal | Y | N | Y | N |
| 3 McGovern | Y | N | Y | N |
| 4 Frank | Y | N | Y | N |
| 5 Meehan | Y | N | Y | N |
| 6 Tierney | Y | N | Y | N |
| 7 Markey | Y | N | Y | N |
| 8 Capuano | Y | N | Y | N |
| 9 Lynch | Y | N | Y | N |
| 10 Delahunt | ? | N | Y | N |
| **MICHIGAN** | | | | |
| 1 Stupak | Y | N | Y | N |
| 2 Hoekstra | Y | Y | N | Y |
| 3 Ehlers | Y | N | Y | Y |
| 4 Camp | Y | Y | Y | Y |
| 5 Kildee | Y | N | Y | N |
| 6 Upton | Y | N | Y | Y |
| 7 Schwarz | ? | N | Y | Y |
| 8 Rogers | Y | Y | N | Y |
| 9 Knollenberg | Y | Y | N | Y |
| 10 Miller | Y | Y | Y | Y |
| 11 McCotter | Y | Y | Y | Y |
| 12 Levin | Y | N | Y | N |
| 13 Kilpatrick | Y | N | Y | N |
| 14 Conyers | Y | N | Y | N |
| 15 Dingell | Y | N | Y | N |

| | 453 | 506 | 630 | 670 |
|---|---|---|---|---|
| **MINNESOTA** | | | | |
| 1 Gutknecht | Y | Y | Y | Y |
| 2 Kline | Y | Y | Y | Y |
| 3 Ramstad | Y | N | Y | Y |
| 4 McCollum | Y | N | Y | N |
| 5 Sabo | Y | N | Y | N |
| 6 Kennedy | Y | Y | Y | Y |
| 7 Peterson | Y | Y | Y | N |
| 8 Oberstar | Y | N | Y | N |
| **MISSISSIPPI** | | | | |
| 1 Wicker | Y | Y | N | Y |
| 2 Thompson | Y | Y | Y | N |
| 3 Pickering | Y | Y | Y | Y |
| 4 Taylor | Y | Y | Y | N |
| **MISSOURI** | | | | |
| 1 Clay | Y | N | Y | N |
| 2 Akin | Y | Y | N | Y |
| 3 Carnahan | Y | N | Y | N |
| 4 Skelton | Y | Y | Y | N |
| 5 Cleaver | Y | N | Y | N |
| 6 Graves | Y | Y | N | Y |
| 7 Blunt | Y | Y | N | Y |
| 8 Emerson | Y | Y | N | Y |
| 9 Hulshof | Y | Y | Y | Y |
| **MONTANA** | | | | |
| AL Rehberg | Y | Y | N | Y |
| **NEBRASKA** | | | | |
| 1 Fortenberry | Y | Y | Y | Y |
| 2 Terry | Y | Y | N | Y |
| 3 Osborne | Y | Y | Y | Y |
| **NEVADA** | | | | |
| 1 Berkley | Y | N | Y | N |
| 2 Gibbons | Y | Y | Y | Y |
| 3 Porter | Y | Y | Y | Y |
| **NEW HAMPSHIRE** | | | | |
| 1 Bradley | Y | N | Y | Y |
| 2 Bass | Y | N | Y | Y |
| **NEW JERSEY** | | | | |
| 1 Andrews | Y | N | Y | N |
| 2 LoBiondo | Y | N | Y | Y |
| 3 Saxton | Y | N | Y | N |
| 4 Smith | Y | N | Y | N |
| 5 Garrett | Y | Y | N | Y |
| 6 Pallone | Y | N | Y | N |
| 7 Ferguson | Y | N | Y | N |
| 8 Pascrell | Y | N | Y | N |
| 9 Rothman | Y | N | Y | N |
| 10 Payne | Y | ? | Y | N |
| 11 Frelinghuysen | Y | N | N | Y |
| 12 Holt | Y | N | Y | N |
| 13 Menendez | Y | N | Y | N |
| **NEW MEXICO** | | | | |
| 1 Wilson | Y | Y | Y | N |
| 2 Pearce | Y | Y | N | Y |
| 3 Udall | Y | N | Y | N |
| **NEW YORK** | | | | |
| 1 Bishop | Y | N | Y | N |
| 2 Israel | Y | N | Y | N |
| 3 King | Y | Y | N | Y |
| 4 McCarthy | Y | N | Y | N |
| 5 Ackerman | Y | N | Y | N |
| 6 Meeks | Y | N | Y | N |
| 7 Crowley | Y | N | Y | N |
| 8 Nadler | Y | N | Y | N |
| 9 Weiner | Y | N | Y | N |
| 10 Towns | Y | ? | Y | N |
| 11 Owens | Y | N | Y | N |
| 12 Velázquez | Y | N | Y | N |
| 13 Fossella | Y | Y | N | Y |
| 14 Maloney | Y | N | Y | N |
| 15 Rangel | Y | N | Y | N |
| 16 Serrano | Y | N | Y | N |
| 17 Engel | Y | N | Y | N |
| 18 Lowey | Y | N | Y | N |
| 19 Kelly | Y | N | Y | Y |
| 20 Sweeney | Y | Y | Y | Y |
| 21 McNulty | Y | N | Y | N |
| 22 Hinchey | Y | N | Y | N |
| 23 McHugh | Y | Y | Y | N |
| 24 Boehlert | Y | N | Y | Y |
| 25 Walsh | Y | N | Y | Y |
| 26 Reynolds | Y | Y | Y | Y |
| 27 Higgins | Y | N | Y | N |
| 28 Slaughter | Y | N | Y | N |
| 29 Kuhl | Y | Y | Y | Y |

| | 453 | 506 | 630 | 670 |
|---|---|---|---|---|
| **NORTH CAROLINA** | | | | |
| 1 Butterfield | Y | N | Y | N |
| 2 Etheridge | Y | N | Y | N |
| 3 Jones | N | Y | Y | ? |
| 4 Price | Y | N | Y | N |
| 5 Foxx | Y | Y | N | Y |
| 6 Coble | Y | Y | N | Y |
| 7 McIntyre | Y | Y | Y | N |
| 8 Hayes | Y | Y | N | Y |
| 9 Myrick | Y | Y | N | ? |
| 10 McHenry | Y | Y | N | Y |
| 11 Taylor | Y | Y | Y | Y |
| 12 Watt | Y | N | Y | N |
| 13 Miller | Y | N | Y | N |
| **NORTH DAKOTA** | | | | |
| AL Pomeroy | Y | Y | Y | N |
| **OHIO** | | | | |
| 1 Chabot | Y | Y | N | Y |
| 2 Schmidt[4] | | Y | N | Y |
| 3 Turner | Y | Y | N | Y |
| 4 Oxley | Y | Y | Y | Y |
| 5 Gillmor | Y | Y | Y | Y |
| 6 Strickland | Y | N | Y | N |
| 7 Hobson | Y | ? | N | Y |
| 8 Boehner | N | Y | N | Y |
| 9 Kaptur | Y | N | Y | N |
| 10 Kucinich | Y | N | Y | N |
| 11 Jones | Y | N | Y | N |
| 12 Tiberi | Y | Y | Y | Y |
| 13 Brown | Y | N | Y | N |
| 14 LaTourette | Y | N | Y | Y |
| 15 Pryce | Y | Y | Y | Y |
| 16 Regula | Y | Y | Y | Y |
| 17 Ryan | Y | N | Y | N |
| 18 Ney | Y | N | Y | Y |
| **OKLAHOMA** | | | | |
| 1 Sullivan | Y | Y | N | Y |
| 2 Boren | Y | Y | Y | N |
| 3 Lucas | Y | Y | N | Y |
| 4 Cole | Y | Y | N | Y |
| 5 Istook | Y | Y | N | ? |
| **OREGON** | | | | |
| 1 Wu | Y | N | Y | N |
| 2 Walden | Y | Y | Y | Y |
| 3 Blumenauer | Y | N | Y | N |
| 4 DeFazio | Y | N | Y | N |
| 5 Hooley | Y | N | Y | N |
| **PENNSYLVANIA** | | | | |
| 1 Brady | ? | N | Y | N |
| 2 Fattah | ? | – | Y | N |
| 3 English | Y | Y | Y | Y |
| 4 Hart | Y | Y | N | Y |
| 5 Peterson | Y | Y | Y | Y |
| 6 Gerlach | Y | N | Y | Y |
| 7 Weldon | Y | N | Y | Y |
| 8 Fitzpatrick | Y | N | Y | Y |
| 9 Shuster | Y | Y | N | Y |
| 10 Sherwood | Y | Y | Y | Y |
| 11 Kanjorski | Y | N | Y | N |
| 12 Murtha | Y | Y | Y | N |
| 13 Schwartz | Y | N | Y | N |
| 14 Doyle | Y | N | Y | N |
| 15 Dent | Y | Y | Y | Y |
| 16 Pitts | ? | Y | Y | Y |
| 17 Holden | Y | Y | Y | N |
| 18 Murphy | Y | Y | Y | Y |
| 19 Platts | Y | N | Y | Y |
| **RHODE ISLAND** | | | | |
| 1 Kennedy | Y | N | Y | N |
| 2 Langevin | Y | N | Y | N |
| **SOUTH CAROLINA** | | | | |
| 1 Brown | Y | Y | N | Y |
| 2 Wilson | Y | Y | N | Y |
| 3 Barrett | Y | Y | N | Y |
| 4 Inglis | Y | Y | Y | Y |
| 5 Spratt | Y | N | Y | N |
| 6 Clyburn | Y | N | Y | N |
| **SOUTH DAKOTA** | | | | |
| AL Herseth | Y | Y | Y | N |
| **TENNESSEE** | | | | |
| 1 Jenkins | Y | Y | Y | Y |
| 2 Duncan | Y | Y | Y | Y |

| | 453 | 506 | 630 | 670 |
|---|---|---|---|---|
| 3 Wamp | Y | Y | Y | Y |
| 4 Davis | Y | Y | Y | N |
| 5 Cooper | Y | N | Y | N |
| 6 Gordon | Y | N | Y | N |
| 7 Blackburn | Y | Y | N | Y |
| 8 Tanner | Y | Y | Y | N |
| 9 Ford | Y | Y | Y | N |
| **TEXAS** | | | | |
| 1 Gohmert | Y | Y | N | Y |
| 2 Poe | Y | Y | N | Y |
| 3 Johnson, Sam | ? | Y | N | ? |
| 4 Hall, R. | Y | Y | N | Y |
| 5 Hensarling | N | Y | N | Y |
| 6 Barton | Y | Y | N | Y |
| 7 Culberson | Y | ? | N | Y |
| 8 Brady | Y | Y | N | Y |
| 9 Green, A. | Y | N | Y | N |
| 10 McCaul | Y | Y | Y | Y |
| 11 Conaway | Y | Y | N | Y |
| 12 Granger | Y | Y | Y | Y |
| 13 Thornberry | N | Y | N | Y |
| 14 Paul | ? | ? | Y | N |
| 15 Hinojosa | Y | Y | Y | N |
| 16 Reyes | Y | N | Y | ? |
| 17 Edwards | Y | Y | Y | N |
| 18 Jackson-Lee | Y | N | Y | N |
| 19 Neugebauer | Y | Y | N | Y |
| 20 Gonzalez | Y | N | Y | N |
| 21 Smith | Y | Y | N | Y |
| 22 DeLay | Y | Y | N | Y |
| 23 Bonilla | Y | Y | N | Y |
| 24 Marchant | Y | Y | N | Y |
| 25 Doggett | Y | N | Y | N |
| 26 Burgess | Y | Y | N | Y |
| 27 Ortiz | Y | Y | Y | N |
| 28 Cuellar | Y | Y | Y | N |
| 29 Green, G. | Y | N | Y | N |
| 30 Johnson, E.B. | Y | N | Y | N |
| 31 Carter | Y | Y | N | Y |
| 32 Sessions | Y | Y | N | Y |
| **UTAH** | | | | |
| 1 Bishop | Y | Y | N | Y |
| 2 Matheson | Y | Y | Y | N |
| 3 Cannon | Y | Y | N | Y |
| **VERMONT** | | | | |
| AL Sanders | Y | N | Y | N |
| **VIRGINIA** | | | | |
| 1 Davis, Jo Ann | Y | Y | Y | ? |
| 2 Drake | Y | Y | N | Y |
| 3 Scott | Y | N | Y | N |
| 4 Forbes | Y | Y | Y | Y |
| 5 Goode | Y | Y | N | Y |
| 6 Goodlatte | Y | Y | Y | Y |
| 7 Cantor | Y | Y | N | Y |
| 8 Moran | Y | N | Y | N |
| 9 Boucher | Y | N | Y | N |
| 10 Wolf | Y | N | Y | Y |
| 11 Davis, T. | Y | N | Y | Y |
| **WASHINGTON** | | | | |
| 1 Inslee | Y | N | Y | N |
| 2 Larsen | Y | N | Y | N |
| 3 Baird | Y | N | Y | N |
| 4 Hastings | Y | Y | N | Y |
| 5 McMorris | Y | Y | Y | Y |
| 6 Dicks | Y | N | Y | N |
| 7 McDermott | Y | N | Y | N |
| 8 Reichert | Y | N | Y | Y |
| 9 Smith | Y | N | Y | N |
| **WEST VIRGINIA** | | | | |
| 1 Mollohan | Y | Y | Y | N |
| 2 Capito | Y | Y | Y | Y |
| 3 Rahall | Y | N | Y | N |
| **WISCONSIN** | | | | |
| 1 Ryan | Y | Y | Y | Y |
| 2 Baldwin | Y | N | Y | N |
| 3 Kind | Y | N | Y | N |
| 4 Moore | Y | N | Y | N |
| 5 Sensenbrenner | N | Y | Y | Y |
| 6 Petri | Y | Y | Y | Y |
| 7 Obey | Y | N | Y | N |
| 8 Green | Y | Y | Y | Y |
| **WYOMING** | | | | |
| AL Cubin | Y | Y | N | Y |

# SENATE 9, 28, 127, 129, 149, 170

**9.** **S 5. Class Action Overhaul/Passage.** Passage of the bill that would give federal courts jurisdiction over class action cases involving at least 100 plaintiffs if at least $5 million was at stake and two-thirds of the plaintiffs lived in different states. It would require judges to review all non-cash settlements, such as coupons for goods and services, and limit attorney's fees paid in such settlements. It also would prohibit federal judges from approving a net loss settlement without finding that the loss is outweighed by non-monetary benefits. Passed 72-26: R 53-0; D 18-26 (ND 16-24, SD 2-2); I 1-0. A "yea" was a vote in support of the president's position. Feb. 10, 2005. *(Story, p. C-4)*

**28.** **S 256. Bankruptcy Overhaul/Violent Protesters.** Schumer, D-N.Y., amendment that would prohibit violent protesters, such as anti-abortion activists, from escaping court-ordered fines or judgments by filing for bankruptcy protection. It would bar such debtors from discharging debts, such as damages, court fines, penalties, citations or attorney fees, incurred from acts of violence or potential acts of violence. Rejected 46-53: R 4-51; D 41-2 (ND 37-2, SD 4-0); I 1-0. March 8, 2005. *(Story, p. C-4)*

**127.** **Owen Nomination/Cloture.** Motion to invoke cloture (thus limiting debate) on President Bush's nomination of Priscilla R. Owen of Texas to be a judge for the U.S. Court of Appeals for the 5th Circuit. Motion agreed to 81-18: R 55-0; D 26-17 (ND 23-16, SD 3-1); I 0-1. Three-fifths of the total Senate (60) is required to invoke cloture. May 24, 2005. *(Story, p. C-5)*

**129.** **Bolton Nomination/Cloture.** Motion to invoke cloture (thus limiting debate) on President Bush's nomination of John R. Bolton of Maryland to be the permanent U.S. representative to the United Nations. Motion rejected 56-42: R 53-1; D 3-40 (ND 1-38, SD 2-2); I 0-1. Three-fifths of the total Senate (60) is required to invoke cloture. A "yea" was a vote in support of the president's position. May 26, 2005. *(Story, p. C-5)*

**149.** **HR 6. Energy Policy/Climate Change.** Inhofe, R-Okla., motion to table (kill) the Bingaman, D-N.M., amendment that would express the sense of the Senate that Congress should enact a national program of mandatory, market-based limits and incentives on greenhouse gas emissions that slow, stop and reverse their growth at a rate that would not harm the economy, and would encourage comparable action by other nations. Motion rejected 44-53: R 42-12; D 2-40 (ND 2-36, SD 0-4); I 0-1. (Subsequently, the amendment was adopted by voice vote.) A "yea" was a vote in support of the president's position. June 22, 2005. *(Story, p. C-6)*

**170.** **S 1307. Central American Free-Trade Agreement/Passage.** Passage of the bill that would implement a free-trade agreement between the United States and Costa Rica, El Salvador, Guatemala, Honduras, Nicaragua and a separate pact with the Dominican Republic. It also would eliminate customs duties on all originating goods traded among the participating nations within 10 days. Passed 54-45: R 43-12; D 10-33 (ND 7-32, SD 3-1); I 1-0. A "yea" was a vote in support of the president's position. June 30, 2005. *(Story, p. C-6)*

| | 9 | 28 | 127 | 129 | 149 | 170 | | 9 | 28 | 127 | 129 | 149 | 170 |
|---|---|---|---|---|---|---|---|---|---|---|---|---|---|
| **ALABAMA** | | | | | | | **MONTANA** | | | | | | |
| Shelby | Y | N | Y | Y | Y | N | Baucus | N | Y | Y | N | Y | N |
| Sessions | Y | N | Y | Y | Y | Y | Burns | Y | N | Y | Y | Y | N |
| **ALASKA** | | | | | | | **NEBRASKA** | | | | | | |
| Stevens | Y | N | Y | Y | Y | Y | Hagel | Y | N | Y | Y | Y | Y |
| Murkowski | Y | N | Y | Y | Y | Y | Nelson | Y | N | Y | Y | Y | Y |
| **ARIZONA** | | | | | | | **NEVADA** | | | | | | |
| McCain | Y | N | Y | Y | Y | Y | Reid | N | Y | Y | N | Y | N |
| Kyl | Y | N | Y | Y | Y | Y | Ensign | Y | N | Y | Y | Y | Y |
| **ARKANSAS** | | | | | | | **NEW HAMPSHIRE** | | | | | | |
| Lincoln | Y | Y | N | N | Y | N | Gregg | Y | N | Y | Y | Y | Y |
| Pryor | N | Y | Y | N | Y | Y | Sununu | ? | N | Y | Y | Y | Y |
| **CALIFORNIA** | | | | | | | **NEW JERSEY** | | | | | | |
| Feinstein | Y | Y | Y | N | N | Y | Corzine | N | ? | N | N | N | N |
| Boxer | N | Y | N | N | N | N | Lautenberg | N | Y | N | N | N | N |
| **COLORADO** | | | | | | | **NEW MEXICO** | | | | | | |
| Allard | Y | N | Y | Y | Y | Y | Domenici | Y | N | Y | Y | Y | Y |
| Salazar | Y | Y | Y | N | N | Y | Bingaman | Y | Y | Y | N | N | N |
| **CONNECTICUT** | | | | | | | **NEW YORK** | | | | | | |
| Dodd | Y | Y | Y | N | N | N | Schumer | Y | Y | Y | N | N | N |
| Lieberman | Y | Y | Y | N | N | ? | Clinton | N | Y | N | N | N | N |
| **DELAWARE** | | | | | | | **NORTH CAROLINA** | | | | | | |
| Biden | N | Y | N | N | N | N | Dole | Y | N | Y | Y | Y | Y |
| Carper | Y | Y | Y | N | N | Y | Burr | Y | N | Y | Y | Y | Y |
| **FLORIDA** | | | | | | | **NORTH DAKOTA** | | | | | | |
| Nelson | N | Y | Y | N | N | N | Conrad | Y | Y | Y | N | ? | N |
| Martinez | Y | N | Y | Y | Y | Y | Dorgan | N | Y | N | N | ? | N |
| **GEORGIA** | | | | | | | **OHIO** | | | | | | |
| Chambliss | Y | N | Y | Y | Y | Y | DeWine | Y | Y | Y | Y | N | Y |
| Isakson | Y | N | Y | Y | Y | Y | Voinovich | Y | N | Y | Y | Y | Y |
| **HAWAII** | | | | | | | **OKLAHOMA** | | | | | | |
| Inouye | N | Y | ? | ? | N | N | Inhofe | Y | N | Y | Y | Y | N |
| Akaka | N | Y | Y | N | N | N | Coburn | Y | N | Y | Y | Y | N |
| **IDAHO** | | | | | | | **OREGON** | | | | | | |
| Craig | Y | N | Y | Y | Y | N | Wyden | N | Y | Y | N | N | N |
| Crapo | Y | N | Y | Y | Y | N | Smith | Y | N | Y | Y | Y | Y |
| **ILLINOIS** | | | | | | | **PENNSYLVANIA** | | | | | | |
| Durbin | N | Y | N | N | N | N | Specter | Y | Y | Y | ? | N | N |
| Obama | Y | Y | N | N | N | N | Santorum | ? | N | Y | Y | Y | Y |
| **INDIANA** | | | | | | | **RHODE ISLAND** | | | | | | |
| Lugar | Y | N | Y | Y | N | Y | Reed | Y | Y | N | N | N | N |
| Bayh | Y | Y | Y | N | N | N | Chafee | Y | Y | Y | N | N | Y |
| **IOWA** | | | | | | | **SOUTH CAROLINA** | | | | | | |
| Grassley | Y | N | Y | Y | Y | Y | Graham | Y | N | Y | Y | N | N |
| Harkin | N | Y | Y | N | N | N | DeMint | Y | N | Y | Y | N | N |
| **KANSAS** | | | | | | | **SOUTH DAKOTA** | | | | | | |
| Brownback | Y | N | Y | Y | Y | Y | Johnson | Y | Y | Y | N | N | N |
| Roberts | Y | N | Y | Y | Y | Y | Thune | Y | Y | Y | Y | N | N |
| **KENTUCKY** | | | | | | | **TENNESSEE** | | | | | | |
| McConnell | Y | N | Y | Y | Y | Y | Frist | Y | N | Y | Y | Y | Y |
| Bunning | Y | N | Y | Y | Y | Y | Alexander | Y | N | Y | Y | N | Y |
| **LOUISIANA** | | | | | | | **TEXAS** | | | | | | |
| Landrieu | Y | Y | Y | N | N | N | Hutchison | Y | N | Y | Y | Y | Y |
| Vitter | Y | N | Y | Y | N | N | Cornyn | Y | N | Y | Y | Y | Y |
| **MAINE** | | | | | | | **UTAH** | | | | | | |
| Snowe | Y | Y | Y | N | N | N | Hatch | Y | N | Y | Y | Y | Y |
| Collins | Y | Y | Y | N | N | N | Bennett | Y | N | Y | Y | Y | Y |
| **MARYLAND** | | | | | | | **VERMONT** | | | | | | |
| Sarbanes | N | Y | N | N | N | N | Leahy | N | Y | N | N | N | N |
| Mikulski | N | Y | N | N | N | N | Jeffords | Y | Y | N | N | N | N |
| **MASSACHUSETTS** | | | | | | | **VIRGINIA** | | | | | | |
| Kennedy | N | Y | N | N | N | N | Warner | Y | N | Y | Y | N | Y |
| Kerry | N | Y | N | N | N | N | Allen | Y | N | Y | Y | Y | Y |
| **MICHIGAN** | | | | | | | **WASHINGTON** | | | | | | |
| Levin | N | Y | N | N | N | N | Murray | N | Y | N | N | N | N |
| Stabenow | N | Y | N | N | N | N | Cantwell | Y | Y | N | N | N | Y |
| **MINNESOTA** | | | | | | | **WEST VIRGINIA** | | | | | | |
| Dayton | N | Y | N | N | N | N | Byrd | N | N | Y | N | N | N |
| Coleman | Y | N | Y | Y | – | Y | Rockefeller | Y | Y | N | N | N | N |
| **MISSISSIPPI** | | | | | | | **WISCONSIN** | | | | | | |
| Cochran | Y | N | Y | Y | Y | Y | Kohl | Y | Y | N | N | N | Y |
| Lott | Y | N | Y | Y | Y | Y | Feingold | N | Y | N | N | N | N |
| **MISSOURI** | | | | | | | **WYOMING** | | | | | | |
| Bond | Y | N | Y | Y | Y | Y | Thomas | Y | N | Y | Y | Y | N |
| Talent | Y | N | Y | Y | Y | Y | Enzi | Y | N | Y | Y | Y | N |

**KEY**    Republicans    Democrats    *Independents*

| | | | | | |
|---|---|---|---|---|---|
| Y | Voted for (yea) | X | Paired against | C | Voted "present" to avoid possible conflict of interest |
| # | Paired for | – | Announced against | | |
| + | Announced for | P | Voted "present" | ? | Did not vote or otherwise make a position known |
| N | Voted against (nay) | | | | |

# SENATE 213, 219, 220, 245, 249

**213.** **HR 6. Energy Policy/Conference Report.** Adoption of the conference report on the bill that would overhaul the nation's energy policy and provide for $14.6 billion in energy-related tax incentives. It would allow lawsuits involving the gasoline additive methyl tertiary butyl ether (MTBE) to be moved to a federal district court and require refiners to annually use 7.5 billion gallons of renewable fuels by 2012. The measure would grant the Federal Energy Regulatory Commission (FERC) jurisdiction over reliability standards for electricity transmission networks and extend daylight-saving time by one month. It would allow FERC to approve the construction, expansion or operation of any facility that imports or processes natural gas, including liquefied natural gas. Adopted (thus cleared for the president) 74-26: R 49-6; D 25-19 (ND 22-18, SD 3-1); I 0-1. A "yea" was a vote in support of the president's position. July 29, 2005. *(Story, p. C-7)*

**219.** **S 397. Gun Liability/Passage.** Passage of the bill that would bar certain civil lawsuits against manufacturers, distributors, dealers and importers of firearms and ammunition, principally those lawsuits aimed at making them liable for gun violence. Trade groups also would be protected and all pending legal action against gunmakers would be dismissed. It also would, with certain exceptions, make it unlawful for licensed gun importers, manufacturers or dealers to sell, deliver or transfer handguns without a secure gun storage or safety device. Passed 65-31: R 50-2; D 14-29 (ND 10-29, SD 4-0); I 1-0. A "yea" was a vote in support of the president's position. July 29, 2005. *(Story, p. C-7)*

**220.** **HR 3. Fiscal 2006 Surface Transportation Reauthorization/ Conference Report.** Adoption of the conference report on the bill that would bring total authorization for federal highway, mass transit, safety and research programs, including fiscal 2004 funding, to $286.5 billion through 2009. The bill would increase the rate of return to states on their Highway Trust Fund contributions to 92 percent by fiscal 2008. It would make the Transportation Department the lead agency in the environmental review process for transportation projects. Adopted (thus cleared for the president) 91-4: R 48-4; D 42-0 (ND 38-0, SD 4-0); I 1-0. July 29, 2005. *(Story, p. C-8)*

**245.** **Roberts Nomination/Confirmation.** Confirmation of President Bush's nomination of John G. Roberts Jr. of Maryland to be chief justice of the United States. Confirmed 78-22: R 55-0; D 22-22 (ND 18-22, SD 4-0); I 1-0. A "yea" was a vote in support of the president's position. Sept. 29, 2005. *(Story, p. C-8)*

**249.** **HR 2863. Fiscal 2006 Defense Appropriations/Detainee Standards.** McCain, R-Ariz., amendment that would establish the U.S. Army Field Manual on Intelligence Interrogation as the uniform standard for interrogating persons detained by the Department of Defense and prohibit cruel, inhuman or degrading treatment of any prisoner detained by the U.S. government. Adopted 90-9: R 46-9; D 43-0 (ND 39-0, SD 4-0); I 1-0. A "nay" was a vote in support of the president's position. Oct. 5, 2005. *(Story, p. C-9)*

| | 213 | 219 | 220 | 245 | 249 |
|---|---|---|---|---|---|
| **ALABAMA** | | | | | |
| Shelby | Y | Y | Y | Y | Y |
| Sessions | Y | Y | Y | Y | N |
| **ALASKA** | | | | | |
| Stevens | Y | Y | Y | Y | N |
| Murkowski | Y | Y | Y | Y | Y |
| **ARIZONA** | | | | | |
| McCain | N | Y | N | Y | Y |
| Kyl | N | Y | N | Y | Y |
| **ARKANSAS** | | | | | |
| Lincoln | Y | Y | Y | Y | Y |
| Pryor | Y | Y | Y | Y | Y |
| **CALIFORNIA** | | | | | |
| Feinstein | N | – | + | N | Y |
| Boxer | N | N | + | N | Y |
| **COLORADO** | | | | | |
| Allard | Y | Y | Y | Y | N |
| Salazar | Y | Y | Y | Y | Y |
| **CONNECTICUT** | | | | | |
| Dodd | N | N | Y | N | Y |
| Lieberman | Y | N | Y | Y | Y |
| **DELAWARE** | | | | | |
| Biden | N | N | Y | N | Y |
| Carper | N | N | Y | Y | Y |
| **FLORIDA** | | | | | |
| Nelson | N | Y | Y | Y | Y |
| Martinez | N | Y | Y | Y | Y |
| **GEORGIA** | | | | | |
| Chambliss | Y | Y | Y | Y | Y |
| Isakson | Y | Y | Y | Y | Y |
| **HAWAII** | | | | | |
| Inouye | Y | N | Y | N | Y |
| Akaka | Y | N | Y | N | Y |
| **IDAHO** | | | | | |
| Craig | Y | Y | Y | Y | N |
| Crapo | Y | Y | Y | Y | Y |
| **ILLINOIS** | | | | | |
| Durbin | Y | N | Y | N | Y |
| Obama | Y | N | Y | N | Y |
| **INDIANA** | | | | | |
| Lugar | Y | Y | Y | Y | Y |
| Bayh | Y | N | Y | N | Y |
| **IOWA** | | | | | |
| Grassley | Y | Y | Y | Y | Y |
| Harkin | Y | N | Y | N | Y |
| **KANSAS** | | | | | |
| Brownback | Y | Y | Y | Y | Y |
| Roberts | Y | + | + | Y | N |
| **KENTUCKY** | | | | | |
| McConnell | Y | Y | Y | Y | Y |
| Bunning | Y | Y | Y | Y | Y |
| **LOUISIANA** | | | | | |
| Landrieu | Y | Y | Y | Y | Y |
| Vitter | Y | Y | Y | Y | Y |
| **MAINE** | | | | | |
| Snowe | Y | Y | Y | Y | Y |
| Collins | Y | Y | Y | Y | Y |
| **MARYLAND** | | | | | |
| Sarbanes | N | N | Y | N | Y |
| Mikulski | Y | N | Y | N | Y |
| **MASSACHUSETTS** | | | | | |
| Kennedy | N | N | Y | N | Y |
| Kerry | N | N | Y | N | Y |
| **MICHIGAN** | | | | | |
| Levin | Y | N | Y | N | Y |
| Stabenow | Y | N | Y | N | Y |
| **MINNESOTA** | | | | | |
| Dayton | Y | N | Y | N | Y |
| Coleman | Y | Y | Y | Y | Y |
| **MISSISSIPPI** | | | | | |
| Cochran | Y | Y | Y | Y | N |
| Lott | Y | Y | Y | Y | Y |
| **MISSOURI** | | | | | |
| Bond | Y | Y | Y | Y | N |
| Talent | Y | Y | Y | Y | Y |
| **MONTANA** | | | | | |
| Baucus | Y | Y | Y | Y | Y |
| Burns | Y | Y | Y | Y | Y |
| **NEBRASKA** | | | | | |
| Hagel | Y | Y | Y | Y | Y |
| Nelson | Y | Y | Y | Y | Y |
| **NEVADA** | | | | | |
| Reid | N | Y | Y | N | Y |
| Ensign | Y | Y | Y | Y | Y |
| **NEW HAMPSHIRE** | | | | | |
| Gregg | N | Y | N | Y | Y |
| Sununu | N | ? | ? | Y | Y |
| **NEW JERSEY** | | | | | |
| Corzine | N | N | Y | N | ? |
| Lautenberg | N | N | Y | N | Y |
| **NEW MEXICO** | | | | | |
| Domenici | Y | Y | Y | Y | Y |
| Bingaman | Y | N | Y | Y | Y |
| **NEW YORK** | | | | | |
| Schumer | N | N | Y | N | Y |
| Clinton | N | N | Y | N | Y |
| **NORTH CAROLINA** | | | | | |
| Dole | Y | Y | Y | Y | Y |
| Burr | Y | Y | Y | Y | Y |
| **NORTH DAKOTA** | | | | | |
| Conrad | Y | Y | Y | Y | Y |
| Dorgan | Y | Y | Y | Y | Y |
| **OHIO** | | | | | |
| DeWine | Y | N | Y | Y | Y |
| Voinovich | Y | Y | Y | Y | Y |
| **OKLAHOMA** | | | | | |
| Inhofe | Y | Y | Y | Y | N |
| Coburn | Y | Y | Y | Y | N |
| **OREGON** | | | | | |
| Wyden | N | N | Y | Y | Y |
| Smith | Y | + | + | Y | Y |
| **PENNSYLVANIA** | | | | | |
| Specter | Y | Y | Y | Y | Y |
| Santorum | Y | Y | Y | Y | Y |
| **RHODE ISLAND** | | | | | |
| Reed | N | N | Y | N | Y |
| Chafee | N | N | Y | Y | Y |
| **SOUTH CAROLINA** | | | | | |
| Graham | Y | Y | Y | Y | Y |
| DeMint | Y | Y | Y | Y | Y |
| **SOUTH DAKOTA** | | | | | |
| Johnson | Y | Y | Y | Y | Y |
| Thune | Y | Y | Y | Y | Y |
| **TENNESSEE** | | | | | |
| Frist | Y | Y | Y | Y | Y |
| Alexander | Y | Y | Y | Y | Y |
| **TEXAS** | | | | | |
| Hutchison | Y | Y | Y | Y | Y |
| Cornyn | Y | Y | N | Y | N |
| **UTAH** | | | | | |
| Hatch | Y | Y | Y | Y | Y |
| Bennett | Y | Y | Y | Y | Y |
| **VERMONT** | | | | | |
| Leahy | N | N | Y | Y | Y |
| Jeffords | N | N | Y | Y | Y |
| **VIRGINIA** | | | | | |
| Warner | Y | Y | Y | Y | Y |
| Allen | Y | Y | Y | Y | Y |
| **WASHINGTON** | | | | | |
| Murray | N | N | Y | N | Y |
| Cantwell | Y | N | Y | N | Y |
| **WEST VIRGINIA** | | | | | |
| Byrd | Y | Y | Y | Y | Y |
| Rockefeller | Y | Y | Y | Y | Y |
| **WISCONSIN** | | | | | |
| Kohl | Y | Y | Y | Y | Y |
| Feingold | N | N | Y | Y | Y |
| **WYOMING** | | | | | |
| Thomas | Y | Y | Y | Y | Y |
| Enzi | Y | Y | Y | Y | Y |

**KEY**  Republicans  Democrats  *Independents*

| | | | |
|---|---|---|---|
| Y | Voted for (yea) | X | Paired against |
| # | Paired for | – | Announced against |
| + | Announced for | P | Voted "present" |
| N | Voted against (nay) | | |

| | |
|---|---|
| C | Voted "present" to avoid possible conflict of interest |
| ? | Did not vote or otherwise make a position known |

# SENATE 262, 323, 358, 363, 364

**262. HR 3058. Fiscal 2006 Transportation-Treasury-Housing Appropriations/Bridge Funding.** Coburn, R-Okla., amendment that would transfer $125 million in funding from the Ketchikan-Gravina and Kink Arm bridge projects in Alaska to the reconstruction of the Twin Spans Bridge connecting New Orleans and Slidell, La. It would place remaining Alaska bridge funds into a general highway fund for Alaska. Rejected 15-82: R 11-43; D 4-38 (ND 3-35, SD 1-3); I 0-1. (By unanimous consent, the Senate agreed to raise the majority requirement for adoption of the Coburn amendment to 60 votes.) Oct. 20, 2005. *(Story, p. C-9)*

**323. S 1042. Fiscal 2006 Defense Authorization/Iraq Withdrawal.** Warner, R-Va., amendment that would require the president to submit an unclassified report to Congress 90 days after the bill's enactment and every three months thereafter on U.S. policy and operations in Iraq. It would also state that 2006 should be a period of significant transition to Iraqi sovereignty; that U.S. forces should not remain in Iraq any longer than necessary; and that the administration needs to explain to Congress and the American public the strategy for the completion of the Iraq mission. Adopted 79-19: R 41-13; D 37-6 (ND 33-6, SD 4-0); I 1-0. Nov. 15, 2005. *(Story, p. C-10)*

**358. HR 3199. "Patriot Act" Reauthorization/Cloture.** Motion to invoke cloture (thus limiting debate) on the conference report on the bill that would reauthorize the law known as the Patriot Act, and make permanent 14 of the 16 provisions of the act set to expire at the end of the year, and extend for four years the two provisions on access to business and other records and "roving" wiretaps. Motion rejected 52-47: R 50-5; D 2-41 (ND 2-37, SD 0-4); I 0-1. Three-fifths of the total Senate (60) is required to invoke cloture. A "yea" was a vote in support of the president's position. Dec. 16, 2005. *(Story, p. C-11)*

**363. S 1932. Budget Reconciliation/Motion to Concur.** Gregg, R-N.H., motion to concur in the House amendment with a Senate amendment on the bill that would make changes to programs for a net savings of $38.8 billion over five years. The Senate amendment would strike two reporting requirements and language that would allow for a Medicaid liability treatment provision regarding hospitals that deny treatment to low-income individuals unable to pay. Motion agreed to, with Vice President Cheney casting a "yea" vote to break the tie, 50-50: R 50-5; D 0-44 (ND 0-40, SD 0-4); I 0-1. A "yea" was a vote in support of the president's position. Dec. 21, 2005. *(Story, p. C-11)*

**364. HR 2863. Fiscal 2006 Defense Appropriations/Cloture.** Motion to invoke cloture (thus limiting debate) on the conference report on the bill that would appropriate $453.5 billion for defense spending in fiscal 2006, including $50 billion for operations in Iraq and Afghanistan. It also would require a 1 percent across-the-board cut to all fiscal 2006 discretionary spending except Veterans Administration funding that was added to the legislation. It would provide $29 billion for disaster assistance to hurricane-damaged areas and $3.8 billion for flu preparedness. It would allow oil and gas leasing in the Arctic National Wildlife Refuge. Motion rejected 56-44: R 52-3; D 4-40 (ND 3-37, SD 1-3); I 0-1. Three-fifths of the total Senate (60) is required to invoke cloture. A "yea" was a vote in support of the president's position. Dec. 21, 2005. *(Story, p. C-12)*

| | 262 | 323 | 358 | 363 | 364 | | 262 | 323 | 358 | 363 | 364 |
|---|---|---|---|---|---|---|---|---|---|---|---|
| **ALABAMA** | | | | | | **MONTANA** | | | | | |
| Shelby | N | Y | Y | Y | Y | Baucus | N | Y | N | N | N |
| Sessions | Y | N | Y | Y | Y | Burns | N | Y | Y | Y | Y |
| **ALASKA** | | | | | | **NEBRASKA** | | | | | |
| Stevens | N | Y | N | Y | Y | Hagel | N | Y | N | Y | Y |
| Murkowski | N | Y | N | Y | Y | Nelson | N | Y | Y | N | Y |
| **ARIZONA** | | | | | | **NEVADA** | | | | | |
| McCain | ? | N | Y | Y | Y | Reid | N | Y | N | N | N |
| Kyl | Y | N | Y | Y | Y | Ensign | N | Y | Y | Y | Y |
| **ARKANSAS** | | | | | | **NEW HAMPSHIRE** | | | | | |
| Lincoln | N | Y | N | N | N | Gregg | N | Y | Y | Y | Y |
| Pryor | N | Y | N | N | N | Sununu | Y | Y | N | Y | Y |
| **CALIFORNIA** | | | | | | **NEW JERSEY** | | | | | |
| Feinstein | N | Y | N | N | N | Corzine | ? | ? | N | N | N |
| Boxer | N | Y | N | N | N | Lautenberg | N | Y | N | N | N |
| **COLORADO** | | | | | | **NEW MEXICO** | | | | | |
| Allard | Y | Y | Y | Y | Y | Domenici | N | Y | Y | Y | Y |
| Salazar | N | Y | N | N | N | Bingaman | N | Y | N | N | N |
| **CONNECTICUT** | | | | | | **NEW YORK** | | | | | |
| Dodd | N | Y | ? | N | N | Schumer | ? | Y | N | N | N |
| Lieberman | N | Y | N | N | N | Clinton | N | Y | N | N | N |
| **DELAWARE** | | | | | | **NORTH CAROLINA** | | | | | |
| Biden | N | Y | N | N | N | Dole | N | Y | Y | Y | Y |
| Carper | N | Y | N | N | N | Burr | Y | N | Y | Y | Y |
| **FLORIDA** | | | | | | **NORTH DAKOTA** | | | | | |
| Nelson | N | Y | N | N | N | Conrad | Y | N | N | N | N |
| Martinez | N | Y | Y | Y | Y | Dorgan | N | Y | N | N | N |
| **GEORGIA** | | | | | | **OHIO** | | | | | |
| Chambliss | N | N | Y | Y | Y | DeWine | Y | Y | Y | Y | Y |
| Isakson | N | N | Y | Y | Y | Voinovich | N | Y | Y | Y | Y |
| **HAWAII** | | | | | | **OKLAHOMA** | | | | | |
| Inouye | N | Y | N | N | Y | Inhofe | N | Y | Y | Y | Y |
| Akaka | N | Y | N | N | Y | Coburn | Y | N | Y | Y | Y |
| **IDAHO** | | | | | | **OREGON** | | | | | |
| Craig | N | Y | N | Y | Y | Wyden | N | Y | N | N | N |
| Crapo | N | Y | Y | Y | Y | Smith | N | Y | N | N | Y |
| **ILLINOIS** | | | | | | **PENNSYLVANIA** | | | | | |
| Durbin | N | Y | N | N | N | Specter | N | Y | Y | Y | Y |
| Obama | N | Y | N | N | N | Santorum | N | Y | Y | Y | Y |
| **INDIANA** | | | | | | **RHODE ISLAND** | | | | | |
| Lugar | N | Y | Y | Y | Y | Reed | N | Y | N | N | N |
| Bayh | Y | Y | N | N | N | Chafee | N | Y | N | N | N |
| **IOWA** | | | | | | **SOUTH CAROLINA** | | | | | |
| Grassley | N | Y | Y | Y | Y | Graham | Y | N | Y | Y | Y |
| Harkin | N | N | N | N | N | DeMint | Y | N | Y | Y | Y |
| **KANSAS** | | | | | | **SOUTH DAKOTA** | | | | | |
| Brownback | N | Y | Y | Y | Y | Johnson | N | Y | Y | N | N |
| Roberts | N | Y | Y | Y | Y | Thune | N | N | Y | Y | Y |
| **KENTUCKY** | | | | | | **TENNESSEE** | | | | | |
| McConnell | N | Y | Y | Y | Y | Frist | N | Y | N | Y | Y |
| Bunning | N | N | Y | Y | Y | Alexander | N | + | Y | Y | Y |
| **LOUISIANA** | | | | | | **TEXAS** | | | | | |
| Landrieu | Y | Y | N | N | Y | Hutchison | N | Y | Y | Y | Y |
| Vitter | Y | N | Y | Y | Y | Cornyn | N | Y | Y | Y | Y |
| **MAINE** | | | | | | **UTAH** | | | | | |
| Snowe | N | Y | Y | N | Y | Hatch | N | Y | Y | Y | Y |
| Collins | N | Y | N | Y | Y | Bennett | N | Y | Y | Y | Y |
| **MARYLAND** | | | | | | **VERMONT** | | | | | |
| Sarbanes | N | Y | N | N | N | Leahy | N | N | N | N | N |
| Mikulski | N | Y | N | N | N | Jeffords | N | Y | N | N | N |
| **MASSACHUSETTS** | | | | | | **VIRGINIA** | | | | | |
| Kennedy | N | N | N | N | N | Warner | N | Y | Y | Y | Y |
| Kerry | N | N | N | N | N | Allen | Y | Y | Y | Y | Y |
| **MICHIGAN** | | | | | | **WASHINGTON** | | | | | |
| Levin | N | Y | N | N | N | Murray | N | Y | N | N | N |
| Stabenow | N | Y | N | N | N | Cantwell | N | Y | N | N | N |
| **MINNESOTA** | | | | | | **WEST VIRGINIA** | | | | | |
| Dayton | N | Y | N | N | N | Byrd | N | N | N | N | N |
| Coleman | N | Y | Y | Y | Y | Rockefeller | N | Y | N | N | N |
| **MISSISSIPPI** | | | | | | **WISCONSIN** | | | | | |
| Cochran | N | Y | Y | Y | Y | Kohl | N | Y | N | N | N |
| Lott | N | Y | Y | Y | Y | Feingold | Y | Y | N | N | N |
| **MISSOURI** | | | | | | **WYOMING** | | | | | |
| Bond | N | Y | Y | Y | Y | Thomas | N | Y | Y | Y | Y |
| Talent | N | Y | Y | Y | Y | Enzi | N | Y | Y | Y | Y |

| **KEY** | **Republicans** | Democrats | *Independents* | | |
|---|---|---|---|---|---|
| Y | Voted for (yea) | X | Paired against | C | Voted "present" to avoid possible conflict of interest |
| # | Paired for | – | Announced against | | |
| + | Announced for | P | Voted "present" | ? | Did not vote or otherwise make a position known |
| N | Voted against (nay) | | | | |

# HOUSE
# ROLL CALL
# VOTES

# House Roll Call Index By Bill Number

# IN THE HOUSE | By Vote Number

**1.*** **Quorum Call.** 424 members responded. Jan. 4, 2005.

**2.** **Election of the Speaker.** Nomination of J. Dennis Hastert, R-Ill., and Nancy Pelosi, D-Calif., for Speaker of the House of Representatives for the 109th Congress. Hastert elected, 226-199: R 226-0; D 0-198 (ND 0-148, SD 0-50); I 0-1. A "Y" on the chart represents a vote for Hastert; an "N" represents a vote for Pelosi, except in the case of Gene Taylor, D-Miss., who voted for John P. Murtha, D-Pa. A majority of the votes cast for a person by name (214 in this case) is needed for election. All members-elect are eligible to vote on the election of the Speaker. Jan. 4, 2005.

**3.** **H Res 5. House Organizing Resolution/Motion to Consider.** Baird, D-Wash., motion to consider the resolution that would set the rules for the 109th Congress. Motion agreed to 224-192: R 223-0; D 1-191 (ND 0-142, SD 1-49); I 0-1. Jan. 4, 2005.

**4.** **H Res 5. House Organizing Resolution/Previous Question.** Dreier, R-Calif., motion to order the previous question (thus ending debate and possibility of amendment) on adoption of the resolution that would set the rules for the 109th Congress. Motion agreed to 222-196: R 222-0; D 0-195 (ND 0-144, SD 0-51); I 0-1. Jan. 4, 2005.

**5.** **H Res 5. House Organizing Resolution/Motion to Commit.** Slaughter, D-N.Y., motion to commit the resolution that would set the rules for the 109th Congress to a select committee comprised of the majority and minority leader with instructions that it be reported back after adding sections that would set post-employment restrictions for members and require a two-thirds vote to waive the three day lay-over rule. Motion rejected 196-219: R 1-219; D 194-0 (ND 143-0, SD 51-0); I 1-0. Jan. 4, 2005.

**6.** **H Res 5. House Organizing Resolution/Adoption.** Adoption of the resolution that would set the rules for the 109th Congress. The rules would create a permanent Homeland Security Committee, allow lawmakers to pay for certain office-related expenses with campaign funds and outline procedures for operating with a provisional quorum after widespread death or incapacitation. Adopted 220-195: R 220-0; D 0-194 (ND 0-143, SD 0-51); I 0-1. Jan. 4, 2005.

**7.** **Electoral Vote Count.** Rep. Stephanie Tubbs Jones, D-Ohio, and Sen. Barbara Boxer, D-Calif., objection to the certification of the Ohio electoral votes to protest voting irregularities in that state. Rejected 31-267: R 0-178; D 31-88 (ND 23-60, SD 8-28); I 0-1. Jan. 6, 2005.

---

\* CQ does not include quorum calls in its vote charts.

[1] Reps. Michael M. Honda, D-Calif.; Luis V. Gutierrez, D-Ill.; Tom Osborne, R-Neb.; and Chris Cannon, R-Utah, had not yet been sworn in, and thus were ineligible to vote except for the vote for Speaker. Reps. John Shadegg, R-Ariz., and Charlie Norwood, R-Ga., were sworn in Jan. 6, making them eligible for both the vote for Speaker and for vote 7.

[2] Rep. Robert T. Matsui, D-Calif., died Jan. 1, 2005. A special election for his replacement will be announced by Jan. 15.

[3] In the case of Rep. Gene Taylor, D-Miss., an "N" on vote 2 represents a vote for John P. Murtha, D-Pa.

| | 2 | 3 | 4 | 5 | 6 | 7 |
|---|---|---|---|---|---|---|
| **ALABAMA** | | | | | | |
| 1 Bonner | Y | Y | Y | N | Y | N |
| 2 Everett | Y | Y | Y | N | Y | ? |
| 3 Rogers | Y | Y | Y | N | Y | ? |
| 4 Aderholt | Y | Y | Y | N | Y | N |
| 5 Cramer | N | N | N | Y | N | N |
| 6 Bachus | Y | Y | Y | N | Y | N |
| 7 Davis | N | N | N | Y | N | N |
| **ALASKA** | | | | | | |
| AL Young | Y | Y | Y | N | Y | N |
| **ARIZONA** | | | | | | |
| 1 Renzi | Y | Y | Y | N | Y | N |
| 2 Franks | Y | Y | Y | N | Y | N |
| 3 Shadegg[1] | ? | I | I | I | I | N |
| 4 Pastor | N | N | N | Y | N | N |
| 5 Hayworth | Y | Y | Y | N | Y | N |
| 6 Flake | Y | Y | Y | N | Y | ? |
| 7 Grijalva | N | N | N | Y | N | Y |
| 8 Kolbe | Y | Y | Y | N | Y | ? |
| **ARKANSAS** | | | | | | |
| 1 Berry | N | N | N | Y | N | ? |
| 2 Snyder | N | N | N | Y | N | N |
| 3 Boozman | Y | Y | Y | N | Y | N |
| 4 Ross | N | N | N | Y | N | N |
| **CALIFORNIA** | | | | | | |
| 1 Thompson | N | N | N | Y | N | ? |
| 2 Herger | Y | Y | Y | N | Y | N |
| 3 Lungren | Y | Y | Y | N | Y | N |
| 4 Doolittle | Y | Y | Y | N | Y | ? |
| 5 Vacant[2] | | | | | | |
| 6 Woolsey | N | N | N | Y | N | Y |
| 7 Miller, George | N | N | N | Y | N | N |
| 8 Pelosi | N | N | N | Y | N | N |
| 9 Lee | N | N | N | Y | N | N |
| 10 Tauscher | N | N | N | Y | N | ? |
| 11 Pombo | Y | Y | Y | N | Y | N |
| 12 Lantos | N | N | N | Y | N | ? |
| 13 Stark | N | N | N | Y | N | ? |
| 14 Eshoo | N | N | N | Y | N | N |
| 15 Honda[1] | ? | I | I | I | I | I |
| 16 Lofgren | N | N | N | Y | N | ? |
| 17 Farr | N | N | N | Y | N | Y |
| 18 Cardoza | N | N | N | Y | N | N |
| 19 Radanovich | Y | Y | Y | N | Y | N |
| 20 Costa | N | N | N | Y | N | N |
| 21 Nunes | Y | Y | Y | N | Y | N |
| 22 Thomas | Y | Y | Y | N | Y | N |
| 23 Capps | N | – | – | + | – | ? |
| 24 Gallegly | Y | Y | Y | N | Y | – |
| 25 McKeon | Y | Y | Y | N | Y | N |
| 26 Dreier | Y | Y | Y | N | Y | N |
| 27 Sherman | N | N | N | Y | N | N |
| 28 Berman | N | N | N | Y | N | – |
| 29 Schiff | N | N | N | Y | N | ? |
| 30 Waxman | N | N | N | Y | N | Y |
| 31 Becerra | N | N | N | Y | N | Y |
| 32 Solis | N | – | N | Y | N | N |
| 33 Watson | N | N | ? | ? | ? | Y |
| 34 Roybal-Allard | N | N | N | Y | N | – |
| 35 Waters | N | N | N | Y | N | Y |
| 36 Harman | N | N | N | Y | N | Y |
| 37 Millender-McD. | N | ? | N | Y | N | ? |
| 38 Napolitano | N | N | N | Y | N | N |
| 39 Sánchez, Linda | N | N | N | Y | N | N |
| 40 Royce | Y | Y | Y | N | Y | N |
| 41 Lewis | Y | Y | Y | N | Y | N |
| 42 Miller, Gary | Y | Y | ? | ? | ? | ? |
| 43 Baca | N | N | N | Y | N | ? |
| 44 Calvert | Y | Y | Y | N | Y | N |
| 45 Bono | Y | Y | Y | N | Y | ? |
| 46 Rohrabacher | Y | P | N | Y | Y | ? |
| 47 Sanchez, Loretta | N | N | N | Y | N | ? |
| 48 Cox | + | Y | Y | N | Y | N |
| 49 Issa | Y | Y | Y | N | Y | N |

| | 2 | 3 | 4 | 5 | 6 | 7 |
|---|---|---|---|---|---|---|
| 50 Cunningham | Y | Y | Y | N | Y | ? |
| 51 Filner | N | N | N | Y | N | Y |
| 52 Hunter | Y | Y | Y | N | Y | N |
| 53 Davis | N | N | N | Y | N | N |
| **COLORADO** | | | | | | |
| 1 DeGette | N | N | N | Y | N | N |
| 2 Udall | N | N | N | Y | N | ? |
| 3 Salazar | N | N | N | Y | N | N |
| 4 Musgrave | Y | Y | Y | N | Y | N |
| 5 Hefley | Y | Y | Y | N | Y | ? |
| 6 Tancredo | Y | Y | Y | N | Y | ? |
| 7 Beauprez | Y | Y | Y | N | Y | N |
| **CONNECTICUT** | | | | | | |
| 1 Larson | N | N | N | Y | N | N |
| 2 Simmons | Y | ? | Y | N | Y | N |
| 3 DeLauro | N | N | N | Y | N | N |
| 4 Shays | Y | Y | Y | Y | Y | – |
| 5 Johnson | Y | ? | Y | N | Y | ? |
| **DELAWARE** | | | | | | |
| AL Castle | Y | Y | Y | N | Y | N |
| **FLORIDA** | | | | | | |
| 1 Miller | Y | Y | Y | N | Y | ? |
| 2 Boyd | N | N | N | Y | N | ? |
| 3 Brown | N | N | N | Y | N | N |
| 4 Crenshaw | Y | Y | Y | N | Y | N |
| 5 Brown-Waite | Y | Y | Y | N | Y | N |
| 6 Stearns | Y | Y | Y | N | Y | N |
| 7 Mica | Y | Y | Y | N | Y | – |
| 8 Keller | Y | Y | Y | N | Y | N |
| 9 Bilirakis | Y | Y | Y | N | Y | ? |
| 10 Young | Y | Y | Y | N | Y | N |
| 11 Davis | N | N | N | Y | N | N |
| 12 Putnam | Y | Y | Y | N | Y | N |
| 13 Harris | Y | Y | Y | N | Y | N |
| 14 Mack | Y | Y | Y | N | Y | N |
| 15 Weldon | Y | Y | Y | N | Y | N |
| 16 Foley | Y | Y | Y | N | Y | N |
| 17 Meek | N | N | N | Y | N | N |
| 18 Ros-Lehtinen | Y | Y | Y | N | Y | N |
| 19 Wexler | N | N | N | Y | N | ? |
| 20 Wasserman-Schultz | N | N | N | Y | N | N |
| 21 Diaz-Balart, L. | Y | Y | Y | N | Y | N |
| 22 Shaw | Y | Y | Y | N | Y | N |
| 23 Hastings | N | ? | ? | ? | ? | Y |
| 24 Feeney | Y | ? | ? | ? | ? | N |
| 25 Diaz-Balart, M. | Y | Y | Y | N | Y | N |
| **GEORGIA** | | | | | | |
| 1 Kingston | Y | Y | Y | N | Y | N |
| 2 Bishop | N | N | N | Y | N | N |
| 3 Marshall | N | N | N | Y | N | N |
| 4 McKinney | N | N | N | Y | N | Y |
| 5 Lewis | N | N | N | Y | N | N |
| 6 Price | Y | Y | Y | N | Y | N |
| 7 Linder | Y | Y | Y | N | Y | N |
| 8 Westmoreland | Y | Y | Y | N | Y | N |
| 9 Norwood[1] | ? | I | I | I | I | N |
| 10 Deal | Y | Y | Y | N | Y | N |
| 11 Gingrey | Y | Y | Y | N | Y | N |
| 12 Barrow | N | – | N | Y | N | N |
| 13 Scott | N | N | N | Y | N | N |
| **HAWAII** | | | | | | |
| 1 Abercrombie | N | N | N | Y | N | + |
| 2 Case | N | N | N | Y | N | N |
| **IDAHO** | | | | | | |
| 1 Otter | Y | Y | Y | N | Y | ? |
| 2 Simpson | Y | Y | Y | N | Y | N |
| **ILLINOIS** | | | | | | |
| 1 Rush | N | N | N | Y | N | ? |
| 2 Jackson | N | N | N | Y | N | Y |
| 3 Lipinski | N | N | N | Y | N | N |
| 4 Gutierrez[1] | ? | I | I | I | I | ? |
| 5 Emanuel | N | N | N | Y | N | N |
| 6 Hyde | Y | Y | Y | N | Y | N |
| 7 Davis | N | N | N | Y | N | N |
| 8 Bean | N | N | N | Y | N | N |
| 9 Schakowsky | N | N | N | Y | N | N |
| 10 Kirk | Y | Y | Y | N | Y | N |
| 11 Weller | Y | Y | Y | N | Y | N |
| 12 Costello | N | N | N | Y | N | ? |

| KEY | Republicans | Democrats | *Independents* | | | |
|---|---|---|---|---|---|---|
| Y | Voted for (yea) | X | Paired against | C | Voted "present" to avoid possible conflict of interest |
| # | Paired for | – | Announced against | | |
| + | Announced for | P | Voted "present" | ? | Did not vote or otherwise make a position known |
| N | Voted against (nay) | | | | |

| | 2 | 3 | 4 | 5 | 6 | 7 |
|---|---|---|---|---|---|---|
| 13 **Biggert** | Y | Y | Y | N | Y | ? |
| 14 **Hastert** | | Y | | | | N |
| 15 **Johnson** | Y | Y | Y | N | Y | – |
| 16 **Manzullo** | Y | Y | Y | N | Y | N |
| 17 Evans | N | N | N | Y | N | Y |
| 18 **LaHood** | Y | Y | Y | N | Y | ? |
| 19 **Shimkus** | Y | Y | Y | N | Y | ? |
| **INDIANA** | | | | | | |
| 1 Visclosky | N | N | N | Y | N | N |
| 2 **Chocola** | Y | Y | Y | N | Y | N |
| 3 **Souder** | Y | Y | Y | N | Y | ? |
| 4 **Buyer** | Y | Y | Y | N | Y | N |
| 5 **Burton** | Y | Y | Y | N | Y | N |
| 6 **Pence** | Y | Y | Y | N | Y | N |
| 7 Carson | N | N | N | Y | N | Y |
| 8 **Hostettler** | Y | Y | Y | N | Y | N |
| 9 **Sodrel** | Y | Y | Y | N | Y | N |
| **IOWA** | | | | | | |
| 1 **Nussle** | Y | Y | Y | N | Y | N |
| 2 **Leach** | Y | Y | Y | N | Y | ? |
| 3 Boswell | N | N | N | Y | N | ? |
| 4 **Latham** | Y | Y | Y | N | Y | N |
| 5 **King** | Y | Y | Y | N | Y | N |
| **KANSAS** | | | | | | |
| 1 **Moran** | Y | Y | Y | N | Y | ? |
| 2 **Ryun** | Y | Y | Y | N | Y | N |
| 3 Moore | N | N | N | Y | N | N |
| 4 **Tiahrt** | Y | Y | Y | N | Y | N |
| **KENTUCKY** | | | | | | |
| 1 **Whitfield** | Y | Y | Y | N | Y | N |
| 2 **Lewis** | Y | Y | Y | N | Y | N |
| 3 **Northup** | + | Y | ? | ? | ? | N |
| 4 **Davis** | Y | Y | Y | N | Y | N |
| 5 **Rogers** | Y | Y | Y | N | Y | N |
| 6 Chandler | N | N | N | Y | N | N |
| **LOUISIANA** | | | | | | |
| 1 **Jindal** | Y | Y | Y | N | Y | N |
| 2 Jefferson | N | N | N | Y | N | ? |
| 3 Melancon | N | N | N | Y | N | N |
| 4 **McCrery** | Y | Y | Y | N | Y | N |
| 5 **Alexander** | Y | Y | Y | N | Y | N |
| 6 **Baker** | Y | Y | Y | N | Y | ? |
| 7 **Boustany** | Y | Y | Y | N | Y | N |
| **MAINE** | | | | | | |
| 1 Allen | N | N | N | Y | N | ? |
| 2 Michaud | N | N | N | Y | N | ? |
| **MARYLAND** | | | | | | |
| 1 **Gilchrest** | Y | Y | Y | N | Y | ? |
| 2 Ruppersberger | N | N | N | Y | N | ? |
| 3 Cardin | N | N | N | Y | N | ? |
| 4 Wynn | N | N | N | Y | N | ? |
| 5 Hoyer | N | N | N | Y | N | ? |
| 6 **Bartlett** | Y | Y | Y | N | Y | N |
| 7 Cummings | N | N | N | Y | N | N |
| 8 Van Hollen | N | N | N | Y | N | N |
| **MASSACHUSETTS** | | | | | | |
| 1 Olver | N | N | N | Y | N | Y |
| 2 Neal | N | N | N | Y | N | ? |
| 3 McGovern | N | N | N | Y | N | N |
| 4 Frank | N | N | N | Y | N | ? |
| 5 Meehan | N | N | N | Y | N | N |
| 6 Tierney | N | N | N | Y | N | N |
| 7 Markey | N | N | N | Y | N | Y |
| 8 Capuano | N | N | N | Y | N | ? |
| 9 Lynch | N | N | N | Y | N | ? |
| 10 Delahunt | N | N | N | Y | N | ? |
| **MICHIGAN** | | | | | | |
| 1 Stupak | N | N | N | Y | N | ? |
| 2 **Hoekstra** | Y | Y | Y | N | Y | N |
| 3 **Ehlers** | Y | Y | Y | N | Y | N |
| 4 **Camp** | Y | Y | Y | N | Y | N |
| 5 Kildee | N | N | N | Y | N | N |
| 6 **Upton** | Y | Y | Y | N | Y | N |
| 7 **Schwarz** | Y | Y | Y | N | Y | N |
| 8 **Rogers** | Y | Y | Y | N | Y | N |
| 9 **Knollenberg** | Y | Y | Y | N | Y | N |
| 10 **Miller** | Y | Y | Y | N | Y | N |
| 11 **McCotter** | Y | Y | Y | N | Y | N |
| 12 Levin | N | N | N | Y | N | N |
| 13 Kilpatrick | N | N | N | Y | N | Y |
| 14 Conyers | N | N | N | Y | N | Y |
| 15 Dingell | N | N | N | Y | N | N |

| | 2 | 3 | 4 | 5 | 6 | 7 |
|---|---|---|---|---|---|---|
| **MINNESOTA** | | | | | | |
| 1 **Gutknecht** | Y | Y | Y | N | Y | ? |
| 2 **Kline** | Y | Y | Y | N | Y | N |
| 3 **Ramstad** | Y | Y | Y | N | Y | N |
| 4 McCollum | N | N | N | Y | N | N |
| 5 Sabo | N | N | N | Y | N | N |
| 6 **Kennedy** | Y | Y | Y | N | Y | N |
| 7 Peterson | N | N | N | Y | N | N |
| 8 Oberstar | N | N | N | Y | N | N |
| **MISSISSIPPI** | | | | | | |
| 1 **Wicker** | Y | Y | Y | N | Y | N |
| 2 Thompson | N | N | N | Y | N | Y |
| 3 **Pickering** | Y | Y | Y | N | Y | ? |
| 4 Taylor[3] | N | N | N | Y | N | N |
| **MISSOURI** | | | | | | |
| 1 Clay | N | N | N | Y | N | Y |
| 2 **Akin** | Y | Y | Y | N | Y | N |
| 3 Carnahan | N | N | N | Y | N | N |
| 4 Skelton | N | N | N | Y | N | ? |
| 5 Cleaver | N | N | N | Y | N | N |
| 6 **Graves** | Y | Y | Y | N | Y | – |
| 7 **Blunt** | Y | Y | Y | N | Y | N |
| 8 **Emerson** | Y | Y | Y | N | Y | N |
| 9 **Hulshof** | Y | Y | Y | N | Y | N |
| **MONTANA** | | | | | | |
| AL **Rehberg** | Y | Y | Y | N | Y | N |
| **NEBRASKA** | | | | | | |
| 1 **Fortenberry** | Y | Y | Y | – | Y | N |
| 2 **Terry** | Y | Y | Y | N | Y | ? |
| 3 **Osborne**[1] | Y | I | I | I | I | I |
| **NEVADA** | | | | | | |
| 1 Berkley | N | N | N | Y | N | ? |
| 2 **Gibbons** | Y | Y | Y | N | Y | N |
| 3 **Porter** | Y | Y | Y | N | Y | N |
| **NEW HAMPSHIRE** | | | | | | |
| 1 **Bradley** | Y | Y | Y | N | Y | N |
| 2 **Bass** | Y | Y | Y | N | Y | ? |
| **NEW JERSEY** | | | | | | |
| 1 Andrews | N | N | N | Y | N | N |
| 2 **LoBiondo** | Y | Y | Y | N | Y | N |
| 3 **Saxton** | Y | Y | Y | N | Y | N |
| 4 **Smith** | Y | Y | Y | N | Y | N |
| 5 **Garrett** | Y | Y | Y | N | Y | N |
| 6 Pallone | N | N | N | Y | N | Y |
| 7 **Ferguson** | Y | Y | Y | N | Y | N |
| 8 Pascrell | N | ? | N | Y | N | – |
| 9 Rothman | N | N | N | Y | N | N |
| 10 Payne | N | N | N | Y | N | Y |
| 11 **Frelinghuysen** | Y | Y | Y | N | Y | N |
| 12 Holt | N | N | N | Y | N | N |
| 13 Menendez | N | N | N | Y | N | – |
| **NEW MEXICO** | | | | | | |
| 1 **Wilson** | Y | Y | Y | N | Y | N |
| 2 **Pearce** | Y | Y | Y | N | Y | ? |
| 3 Udall | N | N | N | Y | N | N |
| **NEW YORK** | | | | | | |
| 1 Bishop | N | N | N | Y | N | ? |
| 2 Israel | N | N | N | Y | N | N |
| 3 **King** | Y | Y | Y | N | Y | N |
| 4 McCarthy | N | N | N | Y | N | – |
| 5 Ackerman | N | N | N | Y | N | ? |
| 6 Meeks | N | N | N | Y | N | ? |
| 7 Crowley | N | N | N | Y | N | ? |
| 8 Nadler | N | N | N | Y | N | N |
| 9 Weiner | N | N | N | Y | N | N |
| 10 Towns | N | N | N | Y | N | ? |
| 11 Owens | N | N | N | Y | N | Y |
| 12 Velázquez | N | N | N | Y | N | ? |
| 13 **Fossella** | Y | Y | Y | N | Y | ? |
| 14 Maloney | N | N | N | Y | N | ? |
| 15 Rangel | N | N | N | Y | N | ? |
| 16 Serrano | N | ? | ? | ? | ? | ? |
| 17 Engel | N | N | N | Y | N | N |
| 18 Lowey | N | N | N | Y | N | ? |
| 19 **Kelly** | Y | Y | Y | N | Y | ? |
| 20 **Sweeney** | Y | Y | Y | N | Y | ? |
| 21 McNulty | N | N | N | Y | N | N |
| 22 Hinchey | N | N | N | Y | N | Y |
| 23 **McHugh** | Y | Y | ? | ? | ? | N |
| 24 **Boehlert** | Y | Y | Y | N | Y | N |
| 25 **Walsh** | Y | Y | Y | N | Y | ? |
| 26 **Reynolds** | Y | Y | Y | N | Y | N |
| 27 Higgins | N | N | N | Y | N | ? |
| 28 Slaughter | N | N | N | Y | N | ? |
| 29 **Kuhl** | Y | Y | Y | N | Y | N |

| | 2 | 3 | 4 | 5 | 6 | 7 |
|---|---|---|---|---|---|---|
| **NORTH CAROLINA** | | | | | | |
| 1 Butterfield | N | N | N | Y | N | N |
| 2 Etheridge | N | N | N | Y | N | N |
| 3 **Jones** | Y | Y | ? | ? | ? | ? |
| 4 Price | N | N | N | Y | N | N |
| 5 **Foxx** | Y | Y | Y | N | Y | N |
| 6 **Coble** | Y | Y | Y | N | Y | ? |
| 7 McIntyre | N | N | N | Y | N | ? |
| 8 **Hayes** | Y | Y | Y | N | Y | N |
| 9 **Myrick** | Y | Y | Y | N | Y | N |
| 10 **McHenry** | Y | Y | Y | N | Y | N |
| 11 **Taylor** | Y | Y | Y | N | Y | N |
| 12 Watt | N | N | N | Y | N | N |
| 13 Miller | N | Y | N | Y | N | N |
| **NORTH DAKOTA** | | | | | | |
| AL Pomeroy | N | N | N | Y | N | N |
| **OHIO** | | | | | | |
| 1 **Chabot** | Y | Y | Y | N | Y | N |
| 2 **Portman** | Y | Y | Y | N | Y | N |
| 3 **Turner** | Y | Y | Y | N | Y | N |
| 4 **Oxley** | Y | Y | Y | N | Y | N |
| 5 **Gillmor** | Y | Y | Y | N | Y | ? |
| 6 Strickland | N | N | N | Y | N | N |
| 7 **Hobson** | Y | Y | Y | N | Y | N |
| 8 **Boehner** | Y | Y | Y | N | Y | N |
| 9 Kaptur | N | N | N | Y | N | N |
| 10 Kucinich | N | N | N | Y | N | Y |
| 11 Jones | N | N | N | Y | N | Y |
| 12 **Tiberi** | Y | Y | Y | N | Y | N |
| 13 Brown | N | N | N | Y | N | N |
| 14 **LaTourette** | Y | Y | Y | N | Y | N |
| 15 **Pryce** | Y | Y | Y | N | Y | N |
| 16 **Regula** | Y | Y | Y | N | Y | N |
| 17 Ryan | N | N | N | Y | N | N |
| 18 **Ney** | Y | Y | Y | N | Y | N |
| **OKLAHOMA** | | | | | | |
| 1 **Sullivan** | Y | Y | Y | N | Y | ? |
| 2 Boren | N | N | N | Y | N | N |
| 3 **Lucas** | Y | Y | Y | N | Y | N |
| 4 **Cole** | Y | ? | Y | N | Y | N |
| 5 **Istook** | Y | Y | Y | N | Y | N |
| **OREGON** | | | | | | |
| 1 Wu | N | N | N | Y | N | N |
| 2 **Walden** | Y | Y | Y | N | Y | – |
| 3 Blumenauer | N | N | N | Y | N | ? |
| 4 DeFazio | N | N | N | Y | N | ? |
| 5 Hooley | N | N | N | Y | N | N |
| **PENNSYLVANIA** | | | | | | |
| 1 Brady | N | N | N | Y | N | ? |
| 2 Fattah | N | N | N | Y | N | ? |
| 3 **English** | Y | Y | Y | N | Y | N |
| 4 **Hart** | Y | Y | Y | N | Y | N |
| 5 **Peterson** | Y | Y | Y | ? | ? | N |
| 6 **Gerlach** | Y | Y | Y | N | Y | N |
| 7 **Weldon** | Y | Y | Y | N | Y | N |
| 8 **Fitzpatrick** | Y | Y | Y | N | Y | N |
| 9 **Shuster** | Y | Y | Y | N | Y | N |
| 10 **Sherwood** | Y | Y | Y | N | Y | N |
| 11 Kanjorski | N | N | N | Y | N | N |
| 12 Murtha | N | N | N | Y | N | N |
| 13 Schwartz | N | N | N | Y | N | N |
| 14 Doyle | N | N | N | ? | ? | ? |
| 15 **Dent** | Y | Y | Y | N | Y | N |
| 16 **Pitts** | Y | Y | Y | N | Y | N |
| 17 Holden | N | N | N | Y | N | ? |
| 18 **Murphy** | Y | Y | Y | N | Y | N |
| 19 **Platts** | Y | Y | Y | N | Y | N |
| **RHODE ISLAND** | | | | | | |
| 1 Kennedy | N | N | N | Y | N | N |
| 2 Langevin | N | N | N | Y | N | ? |
| **SOUTH CAROLINA** | | | | | | |
| 1 **Brown** | Y | Y | Y | N | Y | N |
| 2 **Wilson** | Y | Y | Y | N | Y | ? |
| 3 **Barrett** | Y | Y | Y | N | Y | N |
| 4 **Inglis** | Y | Y | Y | N | Y | N |
| 5 Spratt | N | N | N | Y | N | N |
| 6 Clyburn | N | N | N | Y | N | Y |
| **SOUTH DAKOTA** | | | | | | |
| AL Herseth | N | N | N | Y | N | N |
| **TENNESSEE** | | | | | | |
| 1 **Jenkins** | Y | Y | Y | N | Y | ? |
| 2 **Duncan** | Y | Y | Y | N | Y | N |

| | 2 | 3 | 4 | 5 | 6 | 7 |
|---|---|---|---|---|---|---|
| 3 **Wamp** | Y | Y | Y | N | Y | N |
| 4 Davis | N | N | N | Y | N | ? |
| 5 Cooper | N | N | N | Y | N | ? |
| 6 Gordon | N | N | N | Y | N | N |
| 7 **Blackburn** | Y | Y | Y | N | Y | N |
| 8 Tanner | N | N | N | Y | N | ? |
| 9 Ford | N | N | N | Y | N | ? |
| **TEXAS** | | | | | | |
| 1 **Gohmert** | Y | Y | Y | N | Y | N |
| 2 **Poe** | Y | Y | Y | N | Y | N |
| 3 **Johnson, S.** | Y | Y | Y | N | Y | N |
| 4 **Hall** | Y | Y | Y | N | Y | N |
| 5 **Hensarling** | Y | Y | Y | N | Y | N |
| 6 **Barton** | Y | Y | Y | N | Y | N |
| 7 **Culberson** | Y | Y | Y | N | Y | N |
| 8 **Brady** | Y | Y | Y | N | Y | N |
| 9 Green, A. | N | N | N | Y | N | N |
| 10 **McCaul** | Y | Y | Y | N | Y | N |
| 11 **Conaway** | Y | Y | Y | N | Y | N |
| 12 **Granger** | Y | Y | Y | N | Y | ? |
| 13 **Thornberry** | Y | Y | Y | N | Y | N |
| 14 **Paul** | Y | Y | Y | N | Y | ? |
| 15 Hinojosa | N | N | N | Y | N | ? |
| 16 Reyes | N | N | N | Y | N | N |
| 17 Edwards | N | N | N | Y | N | ? |
| 18 Jackson-Lee | N | N | N | Y | N | Y |
| 19 **Neugebauer** | Y | Y | Y | N | Y | N |
| 20 Gonzalez | N | N | N | Y | N | ? |
| 21 **Smith** | Y | Y | Y | N | Y | N |
| 22 **DeLay** | Y | Y | Y | N | Y | N |
| 23 **Bonilla** | Y | Y | Y | N | Y | N |
| 24 **Marchant** | Y | Y | Y | N | Y | N |
| 25 Doggett | N | N | N | Y | N | ? |
| 26 **Burgess** | Y | Y | Y | N | Y | N |
| 27 Ortiz | N | N | N | Y | N | ? |
| 28 Cuellar | N | N | N | Y | N | N |
| 29 Green, G. | N | N | N | Y | N | N |
| 30 Johnson, E. | N | N | N | Y | N | Y |
| 31 **Carter** | Y | Y | Y | N | Y | N |
| 32 **Sessions** | Y | Y | Y | N | Y | N |
| **UTAH** | | | | | | |
| 1 **Bishop** | Y | Y | Y | N | Y | N |
| 2 Matheson | N | N | N | Y | N | ? |
| 3 **Cannon**[1] | ? | I | I | I | I | I |
| **VERMONT** | | | | | | |
| AL *Sanders* | N | N | N | Y | N | N |
| **VIRGINIA** | | | | | | |
| 1 **Davis, J.** | Y | Y | Y | N | Y | N |
| 2 **Drake** | Y | Y | Y | N | Y | N |
| 3 Scott | N | N | N | Y | N | N |
| 4 **Forbes** | Y | Y | Y | N | Y | ? |
| 5 **Goode** | Y | Y | Y | N | Y | ? |
| 6 **Goodlatte** | Y | Y | Y | N | Y | N |
| 7 **Cantor** | Y | Y | Y | N | Y | N |
| 8 Moran | N | N | N | Y | N | N |
| 9 Boucher | N | N | N | Y | N | ? |
| 10 **Wolf** | Y | Y | Y | N | Y | N |
| 11 **Davis, T.** | Y | Y | Y | N | Y | N |
| **WASHINGTON** | | | | | | |
| 1 Inslee | N | N | N | Y | N | ? |
| 2 Larsen | N | ? | ? | ? | ? | ? |
| 3 Baird | N | N | N | Y | N | ? |
| 4 **Hastings** | Y | Y | Y | N | ? | N |
| 5 **McMorris** | Y | Y | Y | N | Y | N |
| 6 Dicks | N | N | N | Y | N | N |
| 7 McDermott | N | N | N | Y | N | ? |
| 8 **Reichert** | Y | Y | Y | N | Y | N |
| 9 Smith | N | N | N | Y | N | ? |
| **WEST VIRGINIA** | | | | | | |
| 1 Mollohan | N | N | N | Y | N | N |
| 2 **Capito** | Y | Y | Y | N | Y | N |
| 3 Rahall | N | N | N | Y | N | N |
| **WISCONSIN** | | | | | | |
| 1 **Ryan** | Y | Y | Y | N | Y | N |
| 2 Baldwin | N | N | N | Y | N | ? |
| 3 Kind | N | N | N | Y | N | ? |
| 4 Moore | N | N | N | Y | N | N |
| 5 **Sensenbrenner** | Y | Y | Y | N | Y | N |
| 6 **Petri** | Y | Y | Y | N | Y | N |
| 7 Obey | N | N | N | Y | N | N |
| 8 **Green** | Y | Y | Y | N | Y | N |
| **WYOMING** | | | | | | |
| AL **Cubin** | Y | Y | Y | N | Y | N |

# IN THE HOUSE | By Vote Number

**8.** **H Con Res 16. Ukraine Elections/Adoption.** Hyde, R-Ill., motion to suspend the rules and adopt the concurrent resolution that would congratulate the people and government of Ukraine for ensuring a free and fair run-off presidential election Dec. 26, 2004. It also would express continuing support for the efforts of Ukraine to establish a full democracy, rule of law and respect for human rights. Motion agreed to 392-1: R 210-1; D 181-0 (ND 131-0, SD 50-0); I 1-0. A two-thirds majority of those present and voting (262 in this case) is required for adoption under suspension of the rules. Jan. 25, 2005.

**9.** **H Res 39. Liberation of Auschwitz 60th Anniversary/Adoption.** Hyde, R-Ill., motion to suspend the rules and adopt the resolution that would commend foreign countries, the United Nations and international organizations for marking the 60th anniversary of the liberation of Auschwitz on Jan. 27, 1945. Motion agreed to 393-0: R 211-0; D 181-0 (ND 132-0, SD 49-0); I 1-0. A two-thirds majority of those present and voting (262 in this case) is required for adoption under suspension of the rules. Jan. 25, 2005.

**10.** **HR 54. Congressional Gold Medals/Limit Increase.** Crowley, D-N.Y., amendment that would increase the limit on the number of congressional gold medals permitted under the bill from two per year to six per Congress, with no limit on how many of the six medals could be awarded in either year of a Congress. Rejected 189-212: R 1-209; D 187-3 (ND 139-2, SD 48-1); I 1-0. Jan. 26, 2005.

**11.** **HR 54. Congressional Gold Medals/Award Requirements.** Crowley, D-N.Y., amendment that would stipulate that no more than half of the congressional gold medals permitted under the bill could be awarded based on legislation sponsored by members of the same political party. Rejected 182-211: R 0-209; D 181-2 (ND 133-1, SD 48-1), I 1-0. Jan. 26, 2005.

**12.** **HR 54. Congressional Gold Medals/Recommit.** Crowley, D-N.Y., motion to recommit the bill to the Financial Services Committee with instructions to insert language preventing the Treasury secretary from striking a congressional gold medal for presentation posthumously in behalf of any individual except during the 20-year period beginning five years after the individual's death, unless the authorization for the medal was enacted before the individual's death. Motion rejected 187-217: R 0-215; D 186-2 (ND 137-2, SD 49-0); I 1-0. Jan. 26, 2005.

**13.** **HR 54. Congressional Gold Medals/Passage.** Passage of the bill that would limit the number of congressional gold medals that may be struck by the Treasury Department in any calendar year to two, effective as of the date of enactment. The medals could be awarded only to individuals, and could not be presented posthumously unless the recipient had been deceased for five years and then only for 20 years after that milestone. Passed 231-173: R 211-3; D 20-169 (ND 14-126, SD 6-43); I 0-1. Jan. 26, 2005.

| | 8 | 9 | 10 | 11 | 12 | 13 |
|---|---|---|---|---|---|---|
| **ALABAMA** | | | | | | |
| 1 Bonner | Y | Y | N | N | N | Y |
| 2 Everett | Y | Y | N | N | N | Y |
| 3 Rogers | Y | Y | N | N | N | Y |
| 4 Aderholt | Y | Y | N | N | N | Y |
| 5 Cramer | Y | Y | Y | Y | Y | N |
| 6 Bachus | Y | Y | N | N | N | Y |
| 7 Davis | Y | Y | Y | Y | Y | N |
| **ALASKA** | | | | | | |
| AL Young | Y | Y | N | N | N | Y |
| **ARIZONA** | | | | | | |
| 1 Renzi | Y | Y | N | N | N | Y |
| 2 Franks | Y | Y | N | N | N | Y |
| 3 Shadegg | Y | Y | N | N | N | Y |
| 4 Pastor | Y | Y | Y | Y | Y | N |
| 5 Hayworth | Y | Y | N | N | N | Y |
| 6 Flake | Y | Y | N | N | N | Y |
| 7 Grijalva | Y | Y | Y | ? | Y | N |
| 8 Kolbe | Y | Y | N | N | N | Y |
| **ARKANSAS** | | | | | | |
| 1 Berry | Y | Y | Y | Y | Y | N |
| 2 Snyder | Y | Y | Y | Y | Y | N |
| 3 Boozman | Y | Y | N | N | N | Y |
| 4 Ross | Y | Y | Y | Y | Y | N |
| **CALIFORNIA** | | | | | | |
| 1 Thompson | Y | Y | Y | Y | Y | N |
| 2 Herger | Y | Y | N | N | N | Y |
| 3 Lungren | Y | Y | N | N | N | Y |
| 4 Doolittle | Y | Y | N | N | N | Y |
| 5 Vacant | | | | | | |
| 6 Woolsey | Y | Y | Y | Y | Y | N |
| 7 Miller, George | Y | Y | Y | Y | Y | N |
| 8 Pelosi | Y | Y | Y | Y | Y | N |
| 9 Lee | + | + | Y | Y | Y | N |
| 10 Tauscher | Y | Y | Y | Y | Y | N |
| 11 Pombo | ? | ? | N | N | N | Y |
| 12 Lantos | + | + | ? | ? | ? | ? |
| 13 Stark | ? | ? | Y | Y | Y | N |
| 14 Eshoo | Y | Y | Y | Y | Y | Y |
| 15 Honda | Y | Y | Y | Y | Y | N |
| 16 Lofgren | Y | Y | Y | Y | Y | N |
| 17 Farr | Y | Y | Y | Y | Y | N |
| 18 Cardoza | Y | Y | Y | Y | Y | N |
| 19 Radanovich | Y | Y | N | N | N | Y |
| 20 Costa | ? | ? | ? | ? | ? | ? |
| 21 Nunes | Y | Y | N | N | N | Y |
| 22 Thomas | Y | Y | N | N | N | Y |
| 23 Capps | Y | Y | Y | Y | Y | N |
| 24 Gallegly | ? | ? | ? | ? | ? | ? |
| 25 McKeon | Y | Y | N | N | N | Y |
| 26 Dreier | Y | Y | N | N | N | Y |
| 27 Sherman | Y | Y | Y | Y | Y | N |
| 28 Berman | Y | Y | Y | Y | Y | N |
| 29 Schiff | Y | Y | Y | + | + | – |
| 30 Waxman | Y | Y | Y | Y | Y | N |
| 31 Becerra | Y | Y | Y | Y | Y | N |
| 32 Solis | Y | Y | Y | Y | Y | N |
| 33 Watson | ? | ? | Y | Y | Y | N |
| 34 Roybal-Allard | ? | ? | ? | ? | ? | ? |
| 35 Waters | Y | Y | ? | Y | Y | N |
| 36 Harman | Y | Y | Y | ? | Y | N |
| 37 Millender-McD. | Y | Y | Y | Y | Y | N |
| 38 Napolitano | Y | Y | Y | Y | Y | N |
| 39 Sánchez, Linda | Y | Y | Y | Y | Y | N |
| 40 Royce | ? | ? | N | N | N | Y |
| 41 Lewis | Y | Y | N | N | N | Y |
| 42 Miller, Gary | Y | Y | N | ? | N | Y |
| 43 Baca | Y | Y | Y | Y | Y | N |
| 44 Calvert | Y | Y | N | N | N | Y |
| 45 Bono | ? | ? | ? | ? | ? | ? |
| 46 Rohrabacher | ? | ? | ? | ? | ? | ? |
| 47 Sanchez, Loretta | Y | Y | N | Y | N | Y |
| 48 Cox | Y | Y | ? | N | N | Y |
| 49 Issa | Y | Y | N | N | N | Y |
| 50 Cunningham | Y | Y | N | N | N | Y |
| 51 Filner | Y | Y | Y | Y | Y | N |
| 52 Hunter | ? | Y | N | N | N | Y |
| 53 Davis | Y | Y | Y | Y | Y | N |
| **COLORADO** | | | | | | |
| 1 DeGette | Y | Y | Y | Y | Y | N |
| 2 Udall | Y | Y | Y | Y | Y | N |
| 3 Salazar | Y | Y | Y | Y | Y | N |
| 4 Musgrave | Y | Y | N | N | N | Y |
| 5 Hefley | Y | Y | N | N | N | Y |
| 6 Tancredo | Y | Y | N | N | N | Y |
| 7 Beauprez | Y | Y | N | N | N | Y |
| **CONNECTICUT** | | | | | | |
| 1 Larson | Y | Y | Y | Y | Y | N |
| 2 Simmons | Y | Y | N | N | N | Y |
| 3 DeLauro | Y | Y | Y | Y | Y | N |
| 4 Shays | + | + | – | – | – | + |
| 5 Johnson | Y | Y | N | N | N | Y |
| **DELAWARE** | | | | | | |
| AL Castle | Y | Y | N | N | N | Y |
| **FLORIDA** | | | | | | |
| 1 Miller | Y | Y | N | N | N | Y |
| 2 Boyd | Y | Y | Y | Y | Y | Y |
| 3 Brown | ? | ? | Y | Y | Y | N |
| 4 Crenshaw | Y | Y | N | N | N | Y |
| 5 Brown-Waite | Y | Y | N | N | N | Y |
| 6 Stearns | Y | Y | N | N | N | Y |
| 7 Mica | Y | Y | N | N | N | Y |
| 8 Keller | Y | Y | N | N | N | Y |
| 9 Bilirakis | + | ? | ? | ? | ? | ? |
| 10 Young | Y | Y | N | N | N | Y |
| 11 Davis | Y | Y | ? | ? | Y | N |
| 12 Putnam | Y | Y | N | N | N | Y |
| 13 Harris | Y | Y | N | N | N | Y |
| 14 Mack | Y | Y | N | N | N | Y |
| 15 Weldon | Y | Y | N | N | N | Y |
| 16 Foley | ? | ? | ? | ? | ? | ? |
| 17 Meek | Y | Y | Y | Y | Y | N |
| 18 Ros-Lehtinen | Y | Y | N | ? | N | Y |
| 19 Wexler | Y | Y | Y | Y | Y | N |
| 20 Wasserman-Schultz | Y | Y | Y | Y | Y | N |
| 21 Diaz-Balart, L. | Y | Y | N | N | N | Y |
| 22 Shaw | Y | Y | N | N | N | Y |
| 23 Hastings | Y | Y | Y | Y | Y | N |
| 24 Feeney | Y | Y | ? | N | N | Y |
| 25 Diaz-Balart, M. | Y | Y | N | N | N | Y |
| **GEORGIA** | | | | | | |
| 1 Kingston | Y | Y | N | N | N | Y |
| 2 Bishop | Y | Y | Y | Y | Y | Y |
| 3 Marshall | Y | Y | N | N | Y | Y |
| 4 McKinney | Y | Y | Y | Y | Y | N |
| 5 Lewis | Y | Y | Y | Y | Y | N |
| 6 Price | Y | Y | N | N | N | Y |
| 7 Linder | Y | Y | N | N | N | Y |
| 8 Westmoreland | Y | Y | N | N | N | Y |
| 9 Norwood | Y | Y | N | N | N | Y |
| 10 Deal | Y | Y | N | N | N | Y |
| 11 Gingrey | Y | Y | N | N | N | Y |
| 12 Barrow | Y | Y | Y | Y | Y | N |
| 13 Scott | Y | Y | Y | Y | Y | N |
| **HAWAII** | | | | | | |
| 1 Abercrombie | Y | Y | Y | Y | Y | N |
| 2 Case | Y | Y | Y | Y | Y | Y |
| **IDAHO** | | | | | | |
| 1 Otter | Y | N | N | N | N | Y |
| 2 Simpson | Y | Y | ? | ? | ? | ? |
| **ILLINOIS** | | | | | | |
| 1 Rush | ? | ? | Y | Y | Y | N |
| 2 Jackson | Y | Y | Y | Y | Y | N |
| 3 Lipinski | Y | Y | Y | Y | Y | N |
| 4 Gutierrez | Y | Y | Y | Y | Y | N |
| 5 Emanuel | Y | Y | Y | Y | Y | N |
| 6 Hyde | Y | Y | N | N | N | Y |
| 7 Davis | Y | Y | Y | Y | Y | N |
| 8 Bean | Y | Y | Y | Y | Y | N |
| 9 Schakowsky | Y | Y | Y | Y | Y | N |
| 10 Kirk | Y | Y | N | N | N | Y |
| 11 Weller | Y | Y | N | N | N | Y |
| 12 Costello | Y | Y | Y | Y | Y | N |

| KEY | Republicans | Democrats | *Independents* |
|---|---|---|---|

| | | |
|---|---|---|
| Y Voted for (yea) | X Paired against | C Voted "present" to avoid possible conflict of interest |
| # Paired for | – Announced against | |
| + Announced for | P Voted "present" | ? Did not vote or otherwise make a position known |
| N Voted against (nay) | | |

| | 8 | 9 | 10 | 11 | 12 | 13 |
|---|---|---|---|---|---|---|
| 13 **Biggert** | Y | Y | N | N | N | Y |
| 14 **Hastert** | | | | | | |
| 15 **Johnson** | Y | Y | N | N | N | Y |
| 16 **Manzullo** | ? | ? | ? | ? | ? | ? |
| 17 Evans | Y | Y | Y | Y | Y | N |
| 18 **LaHood** | Y | Y | N | N | N | Y |
| 19 **Shimkus** | Y | Y | N | N | N | Y |
| **INDIANA** | | | | | | |
| 1 Visclosky | Y | Y | Y | Y | Y | N |
| 2 **Chocola** | Y | Y | N | N | N | Y |
| 3 **Souder** | Y | Y | N | N | N | Y |
| 4 **Buyer** | Y | Y | N | N | N | Y |
| 5 **Burton** | ? | + | – | – | – | + |
| 6 **Pence** | Y | Y | N | N | N | Y |
| 7 Carson | Y | Y | Y | Y | Y | N |
| 8 **Hostettler** | Y | Y | N | N | N | Y |
| 9 **Sodrel** | Y | Y | N | N | N | Y |
| **IOWA** | | | | | | |
| 1 **Nussle** | Y | Y | N | N | N | Y |
| 2 **Leach** | Y | Y | N | N | N | Y |
| 3 Boswell | Y | Y | Y | Y | Y | N |
| 4 **Latham** | Y | Y | N | N | N | Y |
| 5 **King** | Y | Y | N | N | N | Y |
| **KANSAS** | | | | | | |
| 1 **Moran** | Y | Y | N | N | N | Y |
| 2 **Ryun** | Y | Y | N | N | N | Y |
| 3 Moore | Y | Y | Y | ? | Y | N |
| 4 **Tiahrt** | Y | Y | N | N | N | Y |
| **KENTUCKY** | | | | | | |
| 1 **Whitfield** | Y | Y | N | N | N | Y |
| 2 **Lewis** | Y | Y | N | N | N | Y |
| 3 **Northup** | Y | Y | N | N | N | Y |
| 4 **Davis** | Y | Y | N | N | N | Y |
| 5 **Rogers** | Y | Y | N | N | N | Y |
| 6 Chandler | Y | Y | Y | Y | Y | N |
| **LOUISIANA** | | | | | | |
| 1 **Jindal** | Y | Y | N | N | N | Y |
| 2 Jefferson | Y | Y | Y | Y | Y | N |
| 3 Melancon | Y | Y | Y | Y | Y | N |
| 4 **McCrery** | Y | Y | N | N | N | Y |
| 5 **Alexander** | Y | Y | N | N | N | Y |
| 6 **Baker** | Y | Y | N | N | N | Y |
| 7 **Boustany** | Y | Y | ? | ? | N | Y |
| **MAINE** | | | | | | |
| 1 Allen | Y | Y | Y | Y | Y | N |
| 2 Michaud | Y | Y | Y | Y | Y | N |
| **MARYLAND** | | | | | | |
| 1 **Gilchrest** | Y | Y | N | N | N | Y |
| 2 Ruppersberger | Y | Y | Y | Y | Y | N |
| 3 Cardin | Y | Y | Y | Y | Y | N |
| 4 Wynn | Y | Y | Y | Y | Y | N |
| 5 Hoyer | Y | Y | Y | Y | Y | N |
| 6 **Bartlett** | Y | Y | N | N | N | Y |
| 7 Cummings | Y | Y | Y | Y | N | N |
| 8 Van Hollen | Y | Y | Y | Y | Y | N |
| **MASSACHUSETTS** | | | | | | |
| 1 Olver | Y | Y | Y | Y | Y | N |
| 2 Neal | Y | Y | Y | Y | Y | N |
| 3 McGovern | Y | Y | Y | Y | Y | N |
| 4 Frank | ? | ? | ? | ? | ? | ? |
| 5 Meehan | Y | Y | Y | Y | Y | N |
| 6 Tierney | Y | Y | Y | Y | Y | N |
| 7 Markey | Y | Y | Y | Y | Y | N |
| 8 Capuano | Y | Y | Y | Y | Y | N |
| 9 Lynch | Y | Y | Y | Y | Y | N |
| 10 Delahunt | ? | ? | ? | ? | ? | ? |
| **MICHIGAN** | | | | | | |
| 1 Stupak | Y | Y | Y | Y | Y | Y |
| 2 **Hoekstra** | Y | Y | N | N | N | Y |
| 3 **Ehlers** | ? | ? | ? | ? | ? | ? |
| 4 **Camp** | Y | Y | N | N | N | Y |
| 5 Kildee | Y | Y | Y | Y | Y | N |
| 6 **Upton** | Y | Y | N | N | N | Y |
| 7 **Schwarz** | Y | Y | N | N | N | Y |
| 8 **Rogers** | Y | Y | N | N | N | Y |
| 9 **Knollenberg** | Y | Y | N | N | N | Y |
| 10 **Miller** | Y | Y | N | N | N | Y |
| 11 **McCotter** | ? | ? | ? | ? | ? | ? |
| 12 Levin | Y | Y | Y | Y | Y | N |
| 13 Kilpatrick | Y | Y | Y | Y | Y | N |
| 14 Conyers | Y | Y | Y | Y | Y | N |
| 15 Dingell | Y | Y | Y | Y | Y | N |
| **MINNESOTA** | | | | | | |
| 1 **Gutknecht** | Y | Y | N | N | N | Y |
| 2 **Kline** | Y | Y | N | N | N | Y |
| 3 **Ramstad** | Y | Y | N | N | N | Y |
| 4 McCollum | ? | ? | Y | Y | Y | N |
| 5 Sabo | Y | Y | Y | Y | Y | N |
| 6 **Kennedy** | Y | Y | N | N | N | Y |
| 7 Peterson | Y | Y | Y | Y | Y | Y |
| 8 Oberstar | Y | Y | Y | Y | Y | N |
| **MISSISSIPPI** | | | | | | |
| 1 **Wicker** | Y | Y | N | N | N | Y |
| 2 Thompson | Y | Y | Y | Y | Y | N |
| 3 **Pickering** | Y | Y | N | N | N | Y |
| 4 Taylor | Y | Y | Y | Y | Y | Y |
| **MISSOURI** | | | | | | |
| 1 Clay | Y | Y | Y | Y | Y | N |
| 2 **Akin** | Y | Y | N | N | N | Y |
| 3 Carnahan | Y | Y | Y | Y | Y | N |
| 4 Skelton | Y | Y | Y | Y | Y | N |
| 5 Cleaver | Y | Y | Y | Y | Y | N |
| 6 **Graves** | ? | ? | ? | ? | ? | ? |
| 7 **Blunt** | Y | Y | N | N | N | Y |
| 8 **Emerson** | Y | Y | N | N | N | Y |
| 9 **Hulshof** | Y | Y | N | N | N | N |
| **MONTANA** | | | | | | |
| AL **Rehberg** | Y | Y | N | N | N | Y |
| **NEBRASKA** | | | | | | |
| 1 **Fortenberry** | Y | Y | N | N | N | Y |
| 2 **Terry** | Y | Y | N | N | N | Y |
| 3 **Osborne** | Y | Y | N | N | N | Y |
| **NEVADA** | | | | | | |
| 1 Berkley | + | + | + | + | + | + |
| 2 **Gibbons** | Y | Y | – | – | N | N |
| 3 **Porter** | Y | Y | N | N | N | Y |
| **NEW HAMPSHIRE** | | | | | | |
| 1 **Bradley** | Y | Y | N | N | N | Y |
| 2 **Bass** | Y | Y | N | N | N | Y |
| **NEW JERSEY** | | | | | | |
| 1 Andrews | Y | Y | Y | Y | Y | N |
| 2 **LoBiondo** | Y | Y | N | N | N | Y |
| 3 **Saxton** | Y | Y | N | N | N | Y |
| 4 **Smith** | Y | Y | N | N | N | Y |
| 5 **Garrett** | Y | Y | N | N | N | Y |
| 6 Pallone | Y | Y | Y | Y | Y | N |
| 7 **Ferguson** | Y | Y | N | N | N | Y |
| 8 Pascrell | Y | Y | Y | Y | Y | N |
| 9 Rothman | Y | Y | Y | Y | Y | N |
| 10 Payne | Y | Y | Y | Y | Y | N |
| 11 **Frelinghuysen** | Y | Y | N | N | N | Y |
| 12 Holt | Y | Y | N | Y | Y | Y |
| 13 Menendez | Y | Y | Y | Y | Y | N |
| **NEW MEXICO** | | | | | | |
| 1 **Wilson** | Y | Y | N | N | N | Y |
| 2 **Pearce** | Y | Y | N | N | N | Y |
| 3 Udall | Y | Y | Y | Y | Y | N |
| **NEW YORK** | | | | | | |
| 1 Bishop | Y | Y | Y | Y | Y | N |
| 2 Israel | ? | ? | ? | ? | ? | ? |
| 3 **King** | Y | Y | N | N | N | N |
| 4 McCarthy | Y | Y | Y | Y | Y | N |
| 5 Ackerman | Y | Y | Y | Y | Y | N |
| 6 Meeks | Y | Y | Y | Y | Y | N |
| 7 Crowley | Y | Y | Y | Y | Y | N |
| 8 Nadler | Y | Y | Y | Y | Y | N |
| 9 Weiner | Y | Y | Y | Y | Y | N |
| 10 Towns | ? | ? | Y | Y | Y | N |
| 11 Owens | Y | Y | Y | Y | Y | N |
| 12 Velázquez | Y | Y | Y | Y | Y | N |
| 13 **Fossella** | Y | Y | ? | N | N | Y |
| 14 Maloney | Y | Y | Y | Y | Y | N |
| 15 Rangel | Y | Y | Y | ? | Y | N |
| 16 Serrano | Y | Y | Y | Y | Y | N |
| 17 Engel | Y | Y | Y | Y | Y | N |
| 18 Lowey | Y | Y | Y | Y | Y | N |
| 19 **Kelly** | Y | Y | N | N | N | Y |
| 20 **Sweeney** | Y | Y | N | N | N | Y |
| 21 McNulty | Y | Y | Y | N | Y | N |
| 22 Hinchey | Y | Y | Y | Y | Y | N |
| 23 **McHugh** | Y | Y | N | N | N | Y |
| 24 **Boehlert** | Y | Y | N | N | N | Y |
| 25 **Walsh** | Y | Y | N | N | N | Y |
| 26 **Reynolds** | Y | Y | N | N | N | Y |
| 27 Higgins | Y | Y | Y | Y | Y | N |
| 28 Slaughter | Y | Y | Y | Y | Y | N |
| 29 **Kuhl** | Y | Y | N | N | N | Y |
| **NORTH CAROLINA** | | | | | | |
| 1 Butterfield | Y | Y | Y | Y | Y | N |
| 2 Etheridge | Y | Y | Y | Y | Y | N |
| 3 **Jones** | Y | Y | N | N | N | Y |
| 4 Price | Y | Y | Y | Y | Y | N |
| 5 **Foxx** | Y | Y | N | N | N | Y |
| 6 **Coble** | Y | Y | N | N | N | Y |
| 7 McIntyre | Y | Y | Y | Y | Y | N |
| 8 **Hayes** | Y | Y | N | ? | N | Y |
| 9 **Myrick** | Y | Y | N | N | N | Y |
| 10 **McHenry** | Y | Y | N | N | N | Y |
| 11 **Taylor** | Y | Y | N | N | N | Y |
| 12 Watt | Y | ? | Y | Y | Y | N |
| 13 Miller | Y | Y | Y | Y | Y | N |
| **NORTH DAKOTA** | | | | | | |
| AL Pomeroy | Y | Y | Y | Y | N | N |
| **OHIO** | | | | | | |
| 1 **Chabot** | Y | Y | N | N | N | Y |
| 2 **Portman** | Y | Y | – | N | N | Y |
| 3 **Turner** | Y | Y | N | N | N | Y |
| 4 **Oxley** | Y | Y | N | N | N | Y |
| 5 **Gillmor** | Y | ? | N | N | N | Y |
| 6 Strickland | Y | Y | Y | Y | Y | N |
| 7 **Hobson** | Y | Y | N | N | N | Y |
| 8 **Boehner** | ? | ? | N | N | N | Y |
| 9 Kaptur | Y | Y | Y | Y | ? | Y |
| 10 Kucinich | Y | Y | Y | Y | Y | N |
| 11 Jones | Y | Y | Y | Y | Y | N |
| 12 **Tiberi** | Y | Y | N | N | N | Y |
| 13 Brown | Y | Y | Y | Y | Y | N |
| 14 **LaTourette** | Y | Y | N | N | N | Y |
| 15 **Pryce** | Y | Y | N | N | N | Y |
| 16 **Regula** | Y | Y | N | N | N | Y |
| 17 Ryan | ? | Y | Y | Y | Y | N |
| 18 **Ney** | Y | Y | N | N | N | Y |
| **OKLAHOMA** | | | | | | |
| 1 **Sullivan** | ? | ? | ? | ? | ? | ? |
| 2 Boren | Y | Y | Y | Y | Y | N |
| 3 **Lucas** | Y | Y | N | N | N | Y |
| 4 **Cole** | Y | Y | N | N | N | Y |
| 5 **Istook** | Y | Y | N | N | N | Y |
| **OREGON** | | | | | | |
| 1 Wu | Y | Y | Y | Y | Y | N |
| 2 **Walden** | Y | Y | N | N | N | Y |
| 3 Blumenauer | Y | Y | Y | Y | Y | N |
| 4 DeFazio | ? | ? | ? | ? | ? | ? |
| 5 Hooley | Y | Y | Y | Y | Y | N |
| **PENNSYLVANIA** | | | | | | |
| 1 Brady | Y | Y | Y | Y | Y | Y |
| 2 Fattah | ? | ? | Y | Y | Y | Y |
| 3 **English** | Y | Y | N | N | N | Y |
| 4 **Hart** | Y | Y | N | N | N | Y |
| 5 **Peterson** | Y | Y | N | N | N | Y |
| 6 **Gerlach** | Y | Y | N | N | N | Y |
| 7 **Weldon** | Y | Y | N | N | N | Y |
| 8 **Fitzpatrick** | Y | Y | N | N | N | Y |
| 9 **Shuster** | Y | Y | N | N | N | Y |
| 10 **Sherwood** | Y | Y | N | N | N | Y |
| 11 Kanjorski | Y | Y | Y | Y | Y | Y |
| 12 Murtha | ? | ? | Y | Y | Y | Y |
| 13 Schwartz | Y | Y | Y | Y | Y | Y |
| 14 Doyle | Y | Y | Y | Y | Y | N |
| 15 **Dent** | Y | Y | N | N | N | Y |
| 16 **Pitts** | Y | Y | N | N | N | Y |
| 17 Holden | Y | Y | Y | Y | Y | Y |
| 18 **Murphy** | Y | Y | N | N | N | Y |
| 19 **Platts** | ? | ? | N | N | N | Y |
| **RHODE ISLAND** | | | | | | |
| 1 Kennedy | Y | Y | Y | Y | Y | N |
| 2 Langevin | Y | Y | Y | Y | Y | N |
| **SOUTH CAROLINA** | | | | | | |
| 1 **Brown** | Y | Y | N | N | N | Y |
| 2 **Wilson** | Y | Y | N | N | N | Y |
| 3 **Barrett** | Y | Y | N | N | N | Y |
| 4 **Inglis** | Y | Y | N | N | N | Y |
| 5 Spratt | Y | Y | Y | Y | Y | N |
| 6 Clyburn | Y | Y | Y | Y | Y | N |
| **SOUTH DAKOTA** | | | | | | |
| AL Herseth | Y | Y | Y | Y | Y | N |
| **TENNESSEE** | | | | | | |
| 1 **Jenkins** | ? | ? | ? | ? | ? | ? |
| 2 **Duncan** | Y | Y | N | N | N | Y |
| 3 **Wamp** | ? | ? | N | N | N | Y |
| 4 Davis | Y | Y | Y | Y | Y | Y |
| 5 Cooper | Y | Y | Y | Y | Y | N |
| 6 Gordon | Y | Y | Y | Y | Y | N |
| 7 **Blackburn** | Y | Y | N | N | – | Y |
| 8 Tanner | Y | Y | Y | Y | Y | N |
| 9 Ford | Y | Y | Y | Y | Y | N |
| **TEXAS** | | | | | | |
| 1 **Gohmert** | Y | Y | N | ? | N | Y |
| 2 **Poe** | Y | Y | N | N | N | Y |
| 3 **Johnson, S.** | Y | Y | N | N | N | Y |
| 4 **Hall** | Y | Y | N | N | N | Y |
| 5 **Hensarling** | Y | Y | N | N | N | Y |
| 6 **Barton** | Y | Y | N | N | N | Y |
| 7 **Culberson** | Y | Y | N | N | N | Y |
| 8 **Brady** | Y | Y | N | N | N | Y |
| 9 Green, A. | Y | Y | Y | Y | Y | N |
| 10 **McCaul** | Y | Y | N | N | N | Y |
| 11 **Conaway** | Y | Y | N | N | N | Y |
| 12 **Granger** | ? | ? | ? | ? | ? | ? |
| 13 **Thornberry** | Y | Y | N | N | N | Y |
| 14 **Paul** | N | Y | N | N | N | Y |
| 15 Hinojosa | Y | Y | Y | Y | Y | N |
| 16 Reyes | Y | Y | Y | Y | Y | N |
| 17 Edwards | Y | Y | Y | Y | Y | Y |
| 18 Jackson-Lee | Y | Y | Y | Y | Y | N |
| 19 **Neugebauer** | Y | Y | N | N | N | Y |
| 20 Gonzalez | Y | Y | Y | Y | Y | N |
| 21 **Smith** | Y | Y | N | N | N | Y |
| 22 **DeLay** | Y | Y | N | N | N | Y |
| 23 **Bonilla** | Y | Y | N | N | N | Y |
| 24 **Marchant** | Y | Y | N | N | N | Y |
| 25 Doggett | Y | Y | Y | Y | Y | N |
| 26 **Burgess** | Y | Y | N | N | N | Y |
| 27 Ortiz | Y | Y | Y | Y | Y | N |
| 28 Cuellar | Y | Y | Y | Y | Y | N |
| 29 Green, G. | Y | Y | Y | Y | Y | Y |
| 30 Johnson, E. | Y | Y | Y | Y | Y | N |
| 31 **Carter** | Y | Y | N | N | N | ? |
| 32 **Sessions** | Y | Y | N | N | N | Y |
| **UTAH** | | | | | | |
| 1 **Bishop** | Y | Y | N | N | N | Y |
| 2 Matheson | Y | Y | Y | Y | Y | N |
| 3 **Cannon** | Y | Y | N | N | N | Y |
| **VERMONT** | | | | | | |
| AL *Sanders* | Y | Y | Y | Y | Y | N |
| **VIRGINIA** | | | | | | |
| 1 **Davis, J.** | Y | Y | N | N | N | ? |
| 2 **Drake** | Y | Y | N | N | N | Y |
| 3 Scott | Y | Y | Y | Y | Y | N |
| 4 **Forbes** | Y | Y | N | N | N | Y |
| 5 **Goode** | Y | Y | N | N | N | Y |
| 6 **Goodlatte** | Y | Y | N | N | N | Y |
| 7 **Cantor** | Y | Y | N | N | N | Y |
| 8 Moran | Y | Y | ? | ? | ? | ? |
| 9 Boucher | Y | Y | Y | Y | Y | N |
| 10 **Wolf** | Y | Y | N | N | N | Y |
| 11 **Davis, T.** | Y | Y | N | N | N | Y |
| **WASHINGTON** | | | | | | |
| 1 Inslee | Y | Y | Y | Y | Y | N |
| 2 Larsen | Y | Y | Y | Y | Y | N |
| 3 Baird | Y | Y | ? | ? | ? | ? |
| 4 **Hastings** | Y | Y | N | N | N | Y |
| 5 **McMorris** | Y | Y | N | N | N | Y |
| 6 Dicks | Y | Y | Y | Y | Y | N |
| 7 McDermott | + | + | Y | Y | Y | N |
| 8 **Reichert** | Y | Y | N | N | N | Y |
| 9 Smith | Y | Y | Y | Y | Y | Y |
| **WEST VIRGINIA** | | | | | | |
| 1 Mollohan | Y | Y | Y | Y | Y | N |
| 2 **Capito** | Y | Y | N | N | N | Y |
| 3 Rahall | ? | ? | Y | Y | Y | N |
| **WISCONSIN** | | | | | | |
| 1 **Ryan** | Y | Y | N | N | N | Y |
| 2 Baldwin | Y | Y | Y | Y | Y | N |
| 3 Kind | Y | Y | Y | Y | Y | N |
| 4 Moore | Y | Y | Y | + | Y | N |
| 5 **Sensenbrenner** | Y | Y | N | N | N | Y |
| 6 **Petri** | Y | Y | N | N | N | Y |
| 7 Obey | Y | Y | Y | Y | Y | N |
| 8 **Green** | Y | Y | N | N | N | Y |
| **WYOMING** | | | | | | |
| AL **Cubin** | Y | Y | N | ? | N | Y |

# IN THE HOUSE | By Vote Number

**14.** **H Res 23. Catholic Schools Tribute/Adoption.** Boehner, R-Ohio, motion to suspend the rules and adopt the resolution that would express support for Catholic Schools Week and congratulate Catholic schools, students, parents and teachers for their roles in promoting a brighter and stronger future for the United States. Motion agreed to 408-0: R 218-0; D 189-0 (ND 143-0, SD 46-0); I 1-0. A two-thirds majority of those present and voting (272 in this case) is required for adoption under suspension of the rules. Feb. 1, 2005.

**15.** **HR 120. Dalip Singh Saund Post Office/Passage.** Issa, R-Calif., motion to suspend the rules and pass the bill that would designate a post office in Temecula, Calif., after former Rep. Dalip Singh Saund, D-Calif. (1957-63), the first Asian Indian-American elected to Congress. Motion agreed to 410-0: R 221-0; D 188-0 (ND 142-0, SD 46-0); I 1-0. A two-thirds majority of those present and voting (274 in this case) is required for passage under suspension of the rules. Feb. 1, 2005.

**16.** **H Con Res 36. Access for Military Recruiters/Adoption.** Adoption of the concurrent resolution that would express the sense of the Congress that the executive branch should aggressively challenge any decision that impedes the implementation of an existing ban on most federal funding for universities that do not grant equal access to military recruiters. Adopted 327-84: R 223-0; D 104-83 (ND 67-73, SD 37-10); I 0-1. Feb. 2, 2005.

**17.** **H Res 56. Palestinian Elections/Adoption.** Ros-Lehtinen, R-Fla., motion to suspend the rules and adopt the resolution that would commend the Palestinian people for conducting a free and fair presidential election on Jan. 9, 2005. It also would strongly condemn terrorism and urge the new president to take immediate steps to dismantle the Palestinian terrorist infrastructure. Motion agreed to 415-1: R 223-1; D 191-0 (ND 142-0, SD 49-0); I 1-0. A two-thirds majority of those present and voting (278 in this case) is required for adoption under suspension of the rules. Feb. 2, 2005.

**18.** **H Res 57. EU Arms Sales to China/Adoption.** Gallegly, R-Calif., motion to suspend the rules and adopt the resolution that would deplore the recent increase in arms sales by European Union (EU) member states to China, as well as the European Council's decision to lift its arms embargo on China. A two-thirds majority of those present and voting (276 in this case) is required for adoption under suspension of the rules. Motion agreed to 411-3: R 220-1; D 190-2 (ND 142-1, SD 48-1); I 1-0. Feb. 2, 2005.

**19.** **H Res 60. Iraqi Elections/Adoption.** Adoption of the resolution that would congratulate the Iraqi people for participating in the elections on Jan. 30, 2005. Adopted 404-9: R 223-1; D 180-8 (ND 134-7, SD 46-1); I 1-0. Feb. 2, 2005.

| | 14 | 15 | 16 | 17 | 18 | 19 |
|---|---|---|---|---|---|---|
| **ALABAMA** | | | | | | |
| 1 Bonner | Y | Y | Y | Y | Y | Y |
| 2 Everett | Y | Y | Y | Y | Y | Y |
| 3 Rogers | Y | Y | Y | Y | Y | Y |
| 4 Aderholt | Y | Y | Y | Y | Y | Y |
| 5 Cramer | Y | Y | Y | Y | Y | Y |
| 6 Bachus | ? | ? | Y | Y | Y | Y |
| 7 Davis | Y | Y | Y | Y | Y | Y |
| **ALASKA** | | | | | | |
| AL Young | Y | Y | Y | Y | Y | Y |
| **ARIZONA** | | | | | | |
| 1 Renzi | Y | Y | Y | Y | Y | Y |
| 2 Franks | Y | Y | Y | Y | Y | Y |
| 3 Shadegg | Y | Y | Y | Y | Y | Y |
| 4 Pastor | Y | Y | N | Y | Y | Y |
| 5 Hayworth | Y | Y | Y | Y | Y | Y |
| 6 Flake | Y | Y | Y | Y | Y | Y |
| 7 Grijalva | Y | Y | N | Y | Y | Y |
| 8 Kolbe | Y | Y | Y | Y | Y | Y |
| **ARKANSAS** | | | | | | |
| 1 Berry | Y | Y | Y | Y | Y | Y |
| 2 Snyder | Y | Y | Y | Y | Y | Y |
| 3 Boozman | Y | Y | Y | Y | Y | Y |
| 4 Ross | Y | Y | Y | Y | Y | Y |
| **CALIFORNIA** | | | | | | |
| 1 Thompson | Y | Y | N | Y | Y | Y |
| 2 Herger | Y | Y | Y | Y | Y | Y |
| 3 Lungren | Y | Y | Y | Y | Y | Y |
| 4 Doolittle | Y | Y | Y | Y | Y | Y |
| 5 Vacant | | | | | | |
| 6 Woolsey | Y | Y | N | Y | N | N |
| 7 Miller, George | Y | Y | N | Y | Y | Y |
| 8 Pelosi | Y | Y | N | Y | Y | Y |
| 9 Lee | Y | Y | N | Y | N | N |
| 10 Tauscher | Y | Y | Y | Y | Y | Y |
| 11 Pombo | Y | Y | Y | Y | Y | Y |
| 12 Lantos | Y | Y | Y | Y | Y | Y |
| 13 Stark | Y | Y | N | Y | N | N |
| 14 Eshoo | ? | ? | ? | ? | ? | ? |
| 15 Honda | Y | Y | N | Y | Y | Y |
| 16 Lofgren | Y | Y | Y | Y | Y | Y |
| 17 Farr | Y | Y | N | Y | Y | Y |
| 18 Cardoza | Y | Y | Y | Y | Y | Y |
| 19 Radanovich | Y | Y | Y | Y | Y | Y |
| 20 Costa | Y | Y | Y | Y | Y | Y |
| 21 Nunes | Y | Y | Y | Y | Y | Y |
| 22 Thomas | Y | Y | Y | Y | Y | Y |
| 23 Capps | Y | Y | N | Y | Y | Y |
| 24 Gallegly | Y | Y | Y | Y | Y | Y |
| 25 McKeon | Y | Y | Y | Y | Y | Y |
| 26 Dreier | Y | Y | Y | Y | Y | Y |
| 27 Sherman | Y | Y | Y | Y | Y | Y |
| 28 Berman | Y | Y | N | Y | Y | Y |
| 29 Schiff | Y | Y | Y | Y | Y | Y |
| 30 Waxman | Y | Y | N | Y | Y | Y |
| 31 Becerra | Y | Y | N | Y | Y | Y |
| 32 Solis | Y | Y | N | Y | Y | Y |
| 33 Watson | Y | Y | N | Y | Y | N |
| 34 Roybal-Allard | Y | Y | N | Y | Y | Y |
| 35 Waters | Y | Y | N | Y | Y | N |
| 36 Harman | Y | Y | Y | Y | Y | Y |
| 37 Millender-McD. | Y | Y | Y | Y | Y | Y |
| 38 Napolitano | Y | Y | Y | Y | Y | Y |
| 39 Sánchez, Linda | Y | Y | N | Y | Y | Y |
| 40 Royce | Y | Y | ? | Y | Y | Y |
| 41 Lewis | Y | Y | Y | Y | Y | Y |
| 42 Miller, Gary | Y | Y | Y | Y | Y | Y |
| 43 Baca | Y | Y | Y | Y | Y | Y |
| 44 Calvert | Y | Y | Y | Y | Y | Y |
| 45 Bono | Y | Y | Y | Y | Y | Y |
| 46 Rohrabacher | Y | Y | Y | Y | Y | Y |
| 47 Sanchez, Loretta | Y | Y | Y | Y | Y | Y |
| 48 Cox | ? | ? | Y | Y | Y | Y |
| 49 Issa | Y | Y | Y | Y | Y | Y |

| | 14 | 15 | 16 | 17 | 18 | 19 |
|---|---|---|---|---|---|---|
| 50 Cunningham | Y | Y | Y | Y | Y | Y |
| 51 Filner | Y | Y | N | Y | Y | Y |
| 52 Hunter | ? | ? | Y | Y | Y | Y |
| 53 Davis | Y | Y | Y | Y | Y | Y |
| **COLORADO** | | | | | | |
| 1 DeGette | Y | Y | N | Y | Y | Y |
| 2 Udall | Y | Y | Y | Y | Y | Y |
| 3 Salazar | Y | Y | Y | Y | Y | Y |
| 4 Musgrave | Y | Y | Y | Y | Y | Y |
| 5 Hefley | Y | Y | Y | Y | Y | Y |
| 6 Tancredo | Y | Y | Y | Y | Y | Y |
| 7 Beauprez | Y | Y | Y | Y | Y | Y |
| **CONNECTICUT** | | | | | | |
| 1 Larson | Y | Y | Y | Y | Y | Y |
| 2 Simmons | Y | Y | Y | Y | Y | Y |
| 3 DeLauro | Y | Y | N | Y | Y | Y |
| 4 Shays | Y | Y | Y | Y | Y | Y |
| 5 Johnson | Y | Y | Y | Y | Y | Y |
| **DELAWARE** | | | | | | |
| AL Castle | Y | Y | Y | Y | Y | Y |
| **FLORIDA** | | | | | | |
| 1 Miller | Y | Y | Y | Y | Y | Y |
| 2 Boyd | Y | Y | Y | Y | Y | Y |
| 3 Brown | ? | ? | ? | ? | ? | ? |
| 4 Crenshaw | Y | Y | Y | Y | Y | Y |
| 5 Brown-Waite | Y | Y | Y | Y | Y | Y |
| 6 Stearns | Y | Y | Y | Y | Y | Y |
| 7 Mica | Y | Y | Y | Y | Y | Y |
| 8 Keller | Y | Y | Y | Y | Y | Y |
| 9 Bilirakis | ? | ? | ? | ? | ? | ? |
| 10 Young | Y | Y | Y | Y | Y | Y |
| 11 Davis | Y | Y | Y | Y | Y | Y |
| 12 Putnam | Y | Y | Y | Y | Y | Y |
| 13 Harris | Y | Y | Y | Y | Y | Y |
| 14 Mack | Y | Y | Y | Y | Y | Y |
| 15 Weldon | ? | ? | Y | Y | Y | Y |
| 16 Foley | Y | Y | Y | Y | Y | Y |
| 17 Meek | Y | Y | Y | Y | Y | Y |
| 18 Ros-Lehtinen | Y | Y | Y | Y | Y | Y |
| 19 Wexler | Y | Y | N | Y | Y | Y |
| 20 Wasserman-Schultz | Y | Y | N | Y | Y | Y |
| 21 Diaz-Balart, L. | Y | Y | Y | Y | Y | Y |
| 22 Shaw | Y | Y | Y | Y | Y | Y |
| 23 Hastings | Y | Y | N | Y | Y | Y |
| 24 Feeney | Y | Y | Y | Y | Y | Y |
| 25 Diaz-Balart, M. | ? | ? | ? | ? | ? | ? |
| **GEORGIA** | | | | | | |
| 1 Kingston | Y | Y | Y | Y | Y | Y |
| 2 Bishop | Y | Y | Y | Y | Y | Y |
| 3 Marshall | Y | Y | Y | Y | Y | Y |
| 4 McKinney | Y | Y | N | Y | N | N |
| 5 Lewis | Y | Y | N | Y | Y | P |
| 6 Price | Y | Y | Y | Y | Y | Y |
| 7 Linder | Y | Y | Y | Y | Y | Y |
| 8 Westmoreland | Y | Y | Y | Y | Y | Y |
| 9 Norwood | Y | Y | Y | Y | Y | Y |
| 10 Deal | Y | Y | Y | Y | Y | Y |
| 11 Gingrey | Y | Y | Y | Y | Y | Y |
| 12 Barrow | Y | Y | Y | Y | Y | Y |
| 13 Scott | Y | Y | Y | Y | Y | Y |
| **HAWAII** | | | | | | |
| 1 Abercrombie | Y | Y | N | Y | Y | Y |
| 2 Case | Y | Y | Y | Y | Y | Y |
| **IDAHO** | | | | | | |
| 1 Otter | Y | Y | Y | Y | Y | Y |
| 2 Simpson | Y | Y | Y | Y | Y | Y |
| **ILLINOIS** | | | | | | |
| 1 Rush | ? | ? | ? | ? | ? | ? |
| 2 Jackson | Y | Y | N | Y | Y | Y |
| 3 Lipinski | Y | Y | Y | Y | Y | Y |
| 4 Gutierrez | Y | Y | N | Y | Y | Y |
| 5 Emanuel | Y | Y | N | Y | Y | Y |
| 6 Hyde | + | + | + | + | + | + |
| 7 Davis | Y | Y | N | Y | Y | Y |
| 8 Bean | Y | Y | Y | Y | Y | Y |
| 9 Schakowsky | Y | Y | N | Y | Y | Y |
| 10 Kirk | Y | Y | Y | Y | Y | Y |
| 11 Weller | Y | Y | Y | Y | Y | Y |
| 12 Costello | Y | Y | Y | Y | Y | Y |

**KEY**     **Republicans**     Democrats     *Independents*

| | | | | | |
|---|---|---|---|---|---|
| **Y** | Voted for (yea) | **X** | Paired against | **C** | Voted "present" to avoid possible conflict of interest |
| **#** | Paired for | **–** | Announced against | | |
| **+** | Announced for | **P** | Voted "present" | **?** | Did not vote or otherwise make a position known |
| **N** | Voted against (nay) | | | | |

| | 14 | 15 | 16 | 17 | 18 | 19 |
|---|---|---|---|---|---|---|
| 13 **Biggert** | Y | Y | Y | Y | Y | Y |
| 14 **Hastert** | | | | | | Y |
| 15 **Johnson** | Y | Y | Y | Y | Y | Y |
| 16 **Manzullo** | ? | Y | Y | Y | ? | Y |
| 17 Evans | Y | Y | Y | Y | Y | Y |
| 18 **LaHood** | Y | Y | Y | Y | Y | Y |
| 19 **Shimkus** | Y | Y | Y | Y | Y | Y |
| **INDIANA** | | | | | | |
| 1 Visclosky | Y | Y | Y | Y | Y | Y |
| 2 **Chocola** | Y | Y | Y | Y | Y | Y |
| 3 **Souder** | Y | Y | Y | Y | Y | Y |
| 4 **Buyer** | Y | Y | Y | Y | Y | Y |
| 5 **Burton** | Y | Y | Y | Y | Y | Y |
| 6 **Pence** | Y | Y | Y | Y | Y | Y |
| 7 Carson | Y | Y | - | Y | Y | Y |
| 8 **Hostettler** | Y | Y | Y | Y | Y | Y |
| 9 **Sodrel** | Y | Y | Y | Y | Y | Y |
| **IOWA** | | | | | | |
| 1 **Nussle** | Y | Y | Y | Y | Y | Y |
| 2 **Leach** | Y | Y | Y | Y | Y | Y |
| 3 Boswell | Y | Y | Y | Y | Y | Y |
| 4 **Latham** | Y | Y | Y | Y | Y | Y |
| 5 **King** | Y | Y | Y | Y | Y | Y |
| **KANSAS** | | | | | | |
| 1 **Moran** | Y | Y | ? | ? | ? | ? |
| 2 **Ryun** | Y | Y | Y | Y | Y | Y |
| 3 Moore | Y | Y | Y | Y | Y | Y |
| 4 **Tiahrt** | Y | Y | Y | Y | + | Y |
| **KENTUCKY** | | | | | | |
| 1 **Whitfield** | Y | Y | Y | Y | Y | Y |
| 2 **Lewis** | Y | Y | Y | Y | Y | Y |
| 3 **Northup** | + | + | + | + | + | + |
| 4 **Davis** | Y | Y | Y | Y | + | Y |
| 5 **Rogers** | Y | Y | Y | Y | Y | Y |
| 6 Chandler | Y | Y | Y | Y | Y | Y |
| **LOUISIANA** | | | | | | |
| 1 **Jindal** | Y | Y | Y | Y | Y | Y |
| 2 Jefferson | Y | Y | Y | Y | Y | Y |
| 3 Melancon | Y | Y | Y | Y | Y | Y |
| 4 **McCrery** | Y | Y | Y | Y | Y | Y |
| 5 **Alexander** | Y | Y | Y | Y | Y | Y |
| 6 **Baker** | Y | Y | Y | Y | Y | Y |
| 7 **Boustany** | Y | Y | Y | Y | Y | Y |
| **MAINE** | | | | | | |
| 1 Allen | Y | Y | N | ? | Y | Y |
| 2 Michaud | Y | Y | N | Y | Y | Y |
| **MARYLAND** | | | | | | |
| 1 **Gilchrest** | Y | Y | Y | Y | Y | Y |
| 2 Ruppersberger | Y | Y | Y | Y | Y | Y |
| 3 Cardin | Y | Y | Y | Y | Y | Y |
| 4 Wynn | Y | Y | Y | Y | Y | Y |
| 5 Hoyer | Y | Y | Y | Y | Y | Y |
| 6 **Bartlett** | Y | Y | Y | Y | Y | Y |
| 7 Cummings | Y | Y | N | Y | Y | Y |
| 8 Van Hollen | Y | Y | Y | Y | Y | Y |
| **MASSACHUSETTS** | | | | | | |
| 1 Olver | Y | Y | N | Y | Y | Y |
| 2 Neal | Y | Y | N | Y | Y | Y |
| 3 McGovern | Y | Y | N | Y | Y | Y |
| 4 Frank | Y | Y | N | Y | Y | Y |
| 5 Meehan | Y | Y | N | Y | Y | Y |
| 6 Tierney | Y | Y | N | Y | Y | Y |
| 7 Markey | Y | Y | N | Y | Y | Y |
| 8 Capuano | Y | Y | N | Y | Y | Y |
| 9 Lynch | Y | Y | N | Y | Y | Y |
| 10 Delahunt | Y | Y | N | Y | Y | Y |
| **MICHIGAN** | | | | | | |
| 1 Stupak | ? | ? | ? | ? | ? | ? |
| 2 **Hoekstra** | Y | Y | Y | Y | Y | Y |
| 3 **Ehlers** | Y | Y | Y | Y | Y | Y |
| 4 **Camp** | Y | Y | Y | Y | Y | Y |
| 5 Kildee | Y | Y | Y | Y | Y | Y |
| 6 **Upton** | Y | Y | Y | Y | Y | Y |
| 7 **Schwarz** | Y | Y | Y | Y | Y | Y |
| 8 **Rogers** | Y | Y | Y | Y | + | Y |
| 9 **Knollenberg** | Y | Y | Y | Y | Y | Y |
| 10 **Miller** | Y | Y | Y | Y | Y | Y |
| 11 **McCotter** | Y | Y | Y | Y | Y | Y |
| 12 Levin | Y | Y | N | Y | Y | Y |
| 13 Kilpatrick | Y | Y | N | Y | Y | Y |
| 14 Conyers | Y | Y | N | Y | Y | Y |
| 15 Dingell | Y | Y | ? | ? | ? | ? |

| | 14 | 15 | 16 | 17 | 18 | 19 |
|---|---|---|---|---|---|---|
| **MINNESOTA** | | | | | | |
| 1 **Gutknecht** | Y | Y | Y | Y | Y | Y |
| 2 **Kline** | Y | Y | Y | Y | Y | Y |
| 3 **Ramstad** | Y | Y | Y | Y | Y | Y |
| 4 McCollum | Y | Y | Y | Y | Y | Y |
| 5 Sabo | Y | Y | N | Y | Y | Y |
| 6 **Kennedy** | Y | Y | Y | Y | Y | Y |
| 7 Peterson | Y | Y | Y | Y | Y | Y |
| 8 Oberstar | Y | Y | N | Y | N | Y |
| **MISSISSIPPI** | | | | | | |
| 1 **Wicker** | Y | Y | Y | Y | Y | Y |
| 2 Thompson | Y | Y | Y | Y | Y | Y |
| 3 **Pickering** | Y | Y | Y | Y | Y | Y |
| 4 Taylor | Y | Y | Y | Y | Y | Y |
| **MISSOURI** | | | | | | |
| 1 Clay | Y | Y | N | Y | Y | Y |
| 2 **Akin** | Y | Y | Y | Y | Y | Y |
| 3 Carnahan | Y | Y | Y | Y | Y | Y |
| 4 Skelton | Y | Y | Y | Y | Y | Y |
| 5 Cleaver | Y | Y | Y | Y | Y | Y |
| 6 **Graves** | Y | Y | Y | Y | Y | Y |
| 7 **Blunt** | Y | Y | Y | Y | Y | Y |
| 8 **Emerson** | Y | Y | Y | Y | Y | Y |
| 9 **Hulshof** | Y | Y | Y | Y | Y | Y |
| **MONTANA** | | | | | | |
| AL **Rehberg** | Y | Y | Y | Y | Y | Y |
| **NEBRASKA** | | | | | | |
| 1 **Fortenberry** | Y | Y | Y | Y | Y | Y |
| 2 **Terry** | Y | Y | Y | Y | Y | Y |
| 3 **Osborne** | Y | Y | Y | Y | Y | Y |
| **NEVADA** | | | | | | |
| 1 Berkley | Y | Y | Y | Y | Y | Y |
| 2 **Gibbons** | Y | Y | Y | Y | Y | Y |
| 3 **Porter** | Y | Y | Y | Y | Y | Y |
| **NEW HAMPSHIRE** | | | | | | |
| 1 **Bradley** | Y | Y | Y | Y | Y | Y |
| 2 **Bass** | Y | Y | Y | Y | Y | Y |
| **NEW JERSEY** | | | | | | |
| 1 Andrews | Y | Y | Y | Y | Y | Y |
| 2 **LoBiondo** | Y | Y | Y | Y | Y | Y |
| 3 **Saxton** | Y | Y | Y | Y | Y | Y |
| 4 **Smith** | Y | Y | ? | Y | Y | Y |
| 5 **Garrett** | Y | Y | Y | Y | Y | Y |
| 6 Pallone | Y | Y | N | Y | Y | Y |
| 7 **Ferguson** | Y | Y | Y | Y | Y | Y |
| 8 Pascrell | Y | Y | N | Y | Y | Y |
| 9 Rothman | Y | Y | ? | ? | ? | ? |
| 10 Payne | Y | Y | N | Y | Y | P |
| 11 **Frelinghuysen** | Y | Y | Y | Y | Y | Y |
| 12 Holt | Y | Y | N | Y | Y | Y |
| 13 Menendez | Y | Y | Y | Y | Y | Y |
| **NEW MEXICO** | | | | | | |
| 1 **Wilson** | Y | Y | Y | Y | Y | Y |
| 2 **Pearce** | Y | Y | Y | Y | Y | Y |
| 3 Udall | ? | ? | ? | ? | ? | ? |
| **NEW YORK** | | | | | | |
| 1 Bishop | Y | Y | Y | Y | Y | Y |
| 2 Israel | Y | Y | Y | Y | Y | Y |
| 3 **King** | Y | Y | Y | Y | Y | Y |
| 4 McCarthy | Y | Y | Y | Y | Y | Y |
| 5 Ackerman | Y | Y | N | Y | Y | Y |
| 6 Meeks | ? | ? | N | Y | Y | Y |
| 7 Crowley | Y | Y | N | Y | Y | Y |
| 8 Nadler | Y | Y | N | Y | Y | Y |
| 9 Weiner | Y | Y | N | Y | Y | Y |
| 10 Towns | ? | ? | ? | ? | ? | ? |
| 11 Owens | Y | Y | N | Y | Y | P |
| 12 Velázquez | Y | Y | N | Y | Y | Y |
| 13 **Fossella** | Y | Y | Y | Y | Y | Y |
| 14 Maloney | Y | Y | N | Y | Y | Y |
| 15 Rangel | Y | Y | N | Y | Y | Y |
| 16 Serrano | Y | Y | N | Y | Y | Y |
| 17 Engel | Y | Y | N | Y | Y | Y |
| 18 Lowey | Y | Y | Y | Y | Y | Y |
| 19 **Kelly** | Y | Y | Y | Y | Y | ? |
| 20 **Sweeney** | ? | ? | Y | Y | Y | ? |
| 21 McNulty | Y | Y | Y | Y | Y | Y |
| 22 Hinchey | Y | Y | N | Y | Y | Y |
| 23 **McHugh** | Y | Y | Y | Y | Y | Y |
| 24 **Boehlert** | Y | Y | Y | Y | Y | Y |
| 25 **Walsh** | Y | Y | Y | Y | Y | Y |
| 26 **Reynolds** | Y | Y | Y | Y | Y | Y |
| 27 Higgins | Y | Y | Y | Y | Y | Y |
| 28 Slaughter | Y | Y | Y | Y | Y | Y |
| 29 **Kuhl** | Y | Y | Y | Y | Y | Y |

| | 14 | 15 | 16 | 17 | 18 | 19 |
|---|---|---|---|---|---|---|
| **NORTH CAROLINA** | | | | | | |
| 1 Butterfield | Y | Y | Y | Y | Y | Y |
| 2 Etheridge | Y | Y | Y | Y | Y | Y |
| 3 **Jones** | Y | Y | Y | Y | Y | Y |
| 4 Price | Y | Y | Y | Y | Y | Y |
| 5 **Foxx** | Y | Y | Y | Y | Y | Y |
| 6 **Coble** | Y | Y | Y | Y | Y | Y |
| 7 McIntyre | Y | Y | Y | Y | Y | Y |
| 8 **Hayes** | Y | Y | Y | Y | Y | Y |
| 9 **Myrick** | Y | Y | Y | Y | Y | Y |
| 10 **McHenry** | Y | Y | Y | Y | Y | Y |
| 11 **Taylor** | Y | Y | Y | Y | Y | Y |
| 12 Watt | Y | Y | N | Y | Y | Y |
| 13 Miller | Y | Y | Y | Y | Y | Y |
| **NORTH DAKOTA** | | | | | | |
| AL Pomeroy | Y | Y | Y | Y | Y | Y |
| **OHIO** | | | | | | |
| 1 **Chabot** | Y | Y | Y | Y | Y | Y |
| 2 **Portman** | Y | Y | Y | Y | Y | Y |
| 3 **Turner** | Y | Y | Y | Y | Y | Y |
| 4 **Oxley** | Y | Y | Y | Y | Y | Y |
| 5 **Gillmor** | Y | Y | Y | Y | Y | Y |
| 6 Strickland | Y | Y | Y | Y | Y | Y |
| 7 **Hobson** | Y | Y | Y | Y | Y | Y |
| 8 **Boehner** | Y | Y | Y | Y | Y | Y |
| 9 Kaptur | Y | Y | Y | Y | Y | Y |
| 10 Kucinich | Y | Y | N | Y | Y | N |
| 11 Jones | Y | Y | Y | Y | Y | Y |
| 12 **Tiberi** | Y | Y | Y | Y | Y | Y |
| 13 Brown | Y | Y | N | Y | Y | Y |
| 14 **LaTourette** | Y | Y | Y | Y | Y | Y |
| 15 **Pryce** | Y | Y | Y | Y | Y | Y |
| 16 **Regula** | Y | Y | Y | Y | Y | Y |
| 17 Ryan | Y | Y | Y | Y | Y | Y |
| 18 **Ney** | Y | Y | Y | Y | Y | Y |
| **OKLAHOMA** | | | | | | |
| 1 **Sullivan** | Y | Y | Y | Y | Y | Y |
| 2 Boren | Y | Y | Y | Y | Y | Y |
| 3 **Lucas** | Y | Y | Y | Y | Y | Y |
| 4 **Cole** | Y | Y | Y | Y | Y | Y |
| 5 **Istook** | Y | Y | Y | Y | Y | Y |
| **OREGON** | | | | | | |
| 1 Wu | Y | Y | Y | Y | Y | Y |
| 2 **Walden** | Y | Y | Y | Y | Y | Y |
| 3 Blumenauer | Y | Y | N | Y | Y | Y |
| 4 DeFazio | Y | Y | Y | Y | Y | Y |
| 5 Hooley | Y | Y | Y | Y | Y | Y |
| **PENNSYLVANIA** | | | | | | |
| 1 Brady | Y | Y | N | Y | Y | Y |
| 2 Fattah | ? | ? | N | Y | Y | Y |
| 3 **English** | Y | Y | Y | Y | Y | Y |
| 4 **Hart** | Y | Y | Y | Y | Y | Y |
| 5 **Peterson** | ? | Y | Y | Y | Y | Y |
| 6 **Gerlach** | Y | Y | Y | Y | Y | Y |
| 7 **Weldon** | ? | ? | ? | ? | ? | ? |
| 8 **Fitzpatrick** | Y | Y | Y | Y | Y | Y |
| 9 **Shuster** | Y | Y | Y | Y | Y | Y |
| 10 **Sherwood** | Y | Y | Y | Y | Y | Y |
| 11 Kanjorski | Y | Y | Y | Y | Y | Y |
| 12 Murtha | Y | Y | Y | Y | Y | Y |
| 13 Schwartz | Y | Y | Y | Y | Y | Y |
| 14 Doyle | Y | Y | Y | Y | Y | Y |
| 15 **Dent** | + | Y | Y | Y | Y | Y |
| 16 **Pitts** | Y | Y | Y | Y | Y | Y |
| 17 Holden | Y | Y | Y | Y | Y | Y |
| 18 **Murphy** | Y | Y | Y | Y | Y | Y |
| 19 **Platts** | Y | Y | Y | Y | Y | Y |
| **RHODE ISLAND** | | | | | | |
| 1 Kennedy | Y | Y | Y | Y | Y | Y |
| 2 Langevin | Y | Y | Y | Y | Y | Y |
| **SOUTH CAROLINA** | | | | | | |
| 1 **Brown** | Y | Y | Y | Y | Y | Y |
| 2 **Wilson** | Y | Y | Y | Y | Y | Y |
| 3 **Barrett** | Y | Y | Y | Y | Y | Y |
| 4 **Inglis** | Y | Y | Y | Y | Y | Y |
| 5 Spratt | Y | Y | ? | Y | Y | Y |
| 6 Clyburn | Y | Y | Y | Y | Y | Y |
| **SOUTH DAKOTA** | | | | | | |
| AL Herseth | Y | Y | Y | Y | Y | Y |
| **TENNESSEE** | | | | | | |
| 1 **Jenkins** | Y | Y | Y | Y | Y | Y |
| 2 **Duncan** | Y | Y | Y | Y | Y | Y |

| | 14 | 15 | 16 | 17 | 18 | 19 |
|---|---|---|---|---|---|---|
| 3 **Wamp** | Y | Y | Y | Y | Y | Y |
| 4 Davis | Y | Y | Y | Y | Y | Y |
| 5 Cooper | Y | Y | Y | Y | Y | Y |
| 6 Gordon | Y | Y | Y | Y | Y | ? |
| 7 **Blackburn** | Y | Y | Y | Y | Y | Y |
| 8 Tanner | Y | Y | Y | Y | Y | Y |
| 9 Ford | ? | ? | ? | Y | Y | Y |
| **TEXAS** | | | | | | |
| 1 **Gohmert** | Y | Y | Y | Y | Y | Y |
| 2 **Poe** | Y | Y | Y | Y | Y | Y |
| 3 **Johnson, Sam** | Y | Y | Y | Y | Y | Y |
| 4 **Hall, R.** | Y | Y | Y | Y | Y | Y |
| 5 **Hensarling** | Y | Y | Y | Y | Y | Y |
| 6 **Barton** | Y | Y | Y | Y | Y | Y |
| 7 **Culberson** | Y | Y | Y | Y | Y | Y |
| 8 **Brady** | Y | Y | Y | + | Y | Y |
| 9 Green, A. | Y | Y | N | Y | Y | Y |
| 10 **McCaul** | Y | Y | Y | Y | Y | Y |
| 11 **Conaway** | Y | Y | Y | Y | Y | Y |
| 12 **Granger** | Y | Y | Y | Y | Y | Y |
| 13 **Thornberry** | Y | Y | Y | Y | Y | Y |
| 14 **Paul** | Y | Y | Y | N | N | N |
| 15 Hinojosa | Y | Y | Y | Y | Y | Y |
| 16 Reyes | Y | Y | Y | Y | Y | Y |
| 17 Edwards | ? | ? | Y | Y | Y | Y |
| 18 Jackson-Lee | Y | Y | N | Y | Y | Y |
| 19 **Neugebauer** | Y | Y | Y | Y | Y | Y |
| 20 Gonzalez | Y | Y | Y | Y | Y | Y |
| 21 **Smith** | Y | Y | Y | Y | Y | Y |
| 22 **DeLay** | Y | Y | Y | Y | Y | Y |
| 23 **Bonilla** | Y | Y | Y | Y | Y | Y |
| 24 **Marchant** | Y | Y | Y | Y | Y | Y |
| 25 Doggett | Y | Y | Y | Y | Y | Y |
| 26 **Burgess** | Y | Y | Y | Y | Y | Y |
| 27 Ortiz | Y | Y | Y | Y | Y | Y |
| 28 Cuellar | Y | Y | Y | Y | Y | Y |
| 29 Green, G. | ? | ? | ? | ? | ? | ? |
| 30 Johnson, E.B. | Y | Y | N | Y | Y | Y |
| 31 **Carter** | Y | Y | Y | Y | Y | Y |
| 32 **Sessions** | Y | Y | Y | Y | Y | Y |
| **UTAH** | | | | | | |
| 1 **Bishop** | Y | Y | Y | Y | Y | Y |
| 2 Matheson | Y | Y | Y | Y | Y | Y |
| 3 **Cannon** | Y | Y | Y | Y | Y | Y |
| **VERMONT** | | | | | | |
| AL *Sanders* | Y | Y | N | Y | Y | Y |
| **VIRGINIA** | | | | | | |
| 1 **Davis, Jo Ann** | Y | Y | Y | Y | Y | Y |
| 2 **Drake** | Y | Y | Y | Y | Y | Y |
| 3 Scott | Y | Y | N | Y | Y | Y |
| 4 **Forbes** | Y | Y | Y | Y | Y | Y |
| 5 **Goode** | Y | Y | Y | Y | Y | Y |
| 6 **Goodlatte** | Y | Y | Y | Y | Y | Y |
| 7 **Cantor** | Y | Y | Y | Y | Y | Y |
| 8 Moran | Y | Y | Y | Y | Y | Y |
| 9 Boucher | ? | ? | Y | Y | Y | Y |
| 10 **Wolf** | Y | Y | Y | Y | Y | Y |
| 11 **Davis, T.** | Y | Y | Y | Y | Y | Y |
| **WASHINGTON** | | | | | | |
| 1 Inslee | Y | Y | Y | Y | Y | Y |
| 2 Larsen | Y | Y | Y | Y | Y | Y |
| 3 Baird | Y | Y | Y | Y | Y | Y |
| 4 **Hastings** | Y | Y | Y | Y | Y | Y |
| 5 **McMorris** | Y | Y | Y | Y | Y | Y |
| 6 Dicks | Y | Y | Y | Y | Y | Y |
| 7 McDermott | Y | Y | N | Y | Y | N |
| 8 **Reichert** | Y | Y | Y | Y | Y | Y |
| 9 Smith | Y | Y | Y | Y | Y | Y |
| **WEST VIRGINIA** | | | | | | |
| 1 Mollohan | Y | ? | N | Y | Y | Y |
| 2 **Capito** | Y | Y | Y | Y | Y | Y |
| 3 Rahall | Y | Y | N | Y | Y | Y |
| **WISCONSIN** | | | | | | |
| 1 **Ryan** | Y | Y | Y | Y | Y | Y |
| 2 Baldwin | Y | Y | N | Y | Y | Y |
| 3 Kind | Y | Y | Y | Y | Y | Y |
| 4 Moore | Y | Y | - | Y | Y | Y |
| 5 **Sensenbrenner** | Y | Y | Y | Y | Y | Y |
| 6 **Petri** | Y | Y | Y | Y | Y | Y |
| 7 Obey | Y | Y | ? | Y | Y | Y |
| 8 **Green** | Y | Y | Y | Y | Y | Y |
| **WYOMING** | | | | | | |
| AL **Cubin** | Y | Y | Y | Y | Y | Y |

# IN THE HOUSE | By Vote Number

**20.** **H Res 46. National Mentoring Month/Adoption.** Osborne, R-Neb., motion to suspend the rules and adopt the resolution that would support the goals and ideals of National Mentoring Month and praise the millions of adults who mentor children. Motion agreed to 414-0: R 227-0; D 186-0 (ND 139-0, SD 47-0); I 1-0. A two-thirds majority of those present and voting (276 in this case) is required for adoption under suspension of the rules. Feb. 8, 2005.

**21.** **HR 315. John Milton Bryan Simpson Courthouse/Passage.** Shuster, R-Pa., motion to suspend the rules and pass the bill that would name a federal courthouse in Jacksonville, Fla., after the late John Milton Bryan Simpson, a former judge who ordered the desegregation of public schools in Florida. Motion agreed to 412-0: R 225-0; D 186-0 (ND 138-0, SD 48-0); I 1-0. A two-thirds majority of those present and voting (275 in this case) is required for passage under suspension of the rules. Feb. 8, 2005.

**22.** **HR 548. Tony Hall Tribute/Passage.** Shuster, R-Pa., motion to suspend the rules and pass the bill that would name a federal building and courthouse in Dayton, Ohio, after former Rep. Tony P. Hall, D-Ohio (1979-2002). Motion agreed to 404-0: R 220-0; D 183-0 (ND 136-0, SD 47-0); I 1-0. A two-thirds majority of those present and voting (270 in this case) is required for passage under suspension of the rules. Feb. 8, 2005.

**23.** **HR 418. Immigration Standards/Question of Consideration.** Question of whether the House should consider the rule (H Res 71) to provide for House floor consideration of the bill that would tighten national standards for state driver's licenses and identity cards, make it more difficult for foreign nationals to claim asylum, and authorize the completion of a security fence on the U.S.-Mexico border. Agreed to consider 228-191: R 227-0; D 1-190 (ND 0-141, SD 1-49); I 0-1. (Jackson-Lee, D-Texas, had raised a point of order that the rule provided for an unfunded mandate in violation of section 426(a) of the Congressional Budget Act.) Feb. 9, 2005.

**24.** **H Con Res 6. Support of Boy Scouts/Adoption.** Hefley, R-Colo., motion to suspend the rules and adopt the concurrent resolution that would express the sense of Congress that the Defense Department should continue to support the activities of the Boy Scouts of America. Motion agreed to 418-7: R 229-0; D 188-7 (ND 139-7, SD 49-0); I 1-0. A two-thirds majority of those present and voting (284 in this case) is required for adoption under suspension of the rules. Feb. 9, 2005.

**25.** **H Con Res 26. Tuskegee Airmen Tribute/Adoption.** Rogers, R-Ala., motion to suspend the rules and adopt the concurrent resolution that would honor the Tuskegee Airmen, a group of African-American fighter pilots who fought in the U.S. Army Air Corps during World War II. Motion agreed to 423-0: R 228-0; D 194-0 (ND 146-0, SD 48-0); I 1-0. A two-thirds majority of those present and voting (282 in this case) is required for adoption under suspension of the rules. Feb. 9, 2005.

| | 20 | 21 | 22 | 23 | 24 | 25 |
|---|---|---|---|---|---|---|
| **ALABAMA** | | | | | | |
| 1 Bonner | Y | Y | Y | Y | Y | Y |
| 2 Everett | Y | Y | Y | Y | Y | Y |
| 3 Rogers | Y | Y | Y | Y | Y | Y |
| 4 Aderholt | Y | Y | Y | Y | Y | Y |
| 5 Cramer | Y | Y | Y | N | Y | Y |
| 6 Bachus | Y | Y | Y | Y | Y | Y |
| 7 Davis | Y | Y | Y | N | Y | Y |
| **ALASKA** | | | | | | |
| AL Young | Y | Y | Y | Y | Y | Y |
| **ARIZONA** | | | | | | |
| 1 Renzi | Y | Y | Y | Y | Y | Y |
| 2 Franks | Y | Y | Y | Y | Y | Y |
| 3 Shadegg | Y | Y | Y | Y | Y | Y |
| 4 Pastor | Y | Y | Y | N | Y | Y |
| 5 Hayworth | Y | Y | Y | Y | Y | Y |
| 6 Flake | Y | Y | Y | Y | Y | Y |
| 7 Grijalva | Y | Y | Y | N | Y | Y |
| 8 Kolbe | Y | Y | Y | Y | Y | Y |
| **ARKANSAS** | | | | | | |
| 1 Berry | Y | Y | Y | N | Y | Y |
| 2 Snyder | ? | ? | ? | ? | ? | ? |
| 3 Boozman | Y | Y | Y | Y | Y | Y |
| 4 Ross | Y | Y | Y | N | Y | Y |
| **CALIFORNIA** | | | | | | |
| 1 Thompson | Y | Y | Y | N | Y | Y |
| 2 Herger | Y | Y | Y | Y | Y | Y |
| 3 Lungren | Y | Y | Y | Y | Y | Y |
| 4 Doolittle | Y | Y | Y | Y | Y | Y |
| 5 Vacant | | | | | | |
| 6 Woolsey | Y | Y | Y | N | N | Y |
| 7 Miller, George | Y | Y | Y | N | Y | Y |
| 8 Pelosi | Y | Y | Y | N | Y | Y |
| 9 Lee | Y | Y | Y | N | N | Y |
| 10 Tauscher | Y | Y | Y | N | Y | Y |
| 11 Pombo | Y | Y | Y | Y | Y | Y |
| 12 Lantos | Y | Y | Y | N | Y | Y |
| 13 Stark | Y | Y | Y | N | N | Y |
| 14 Eshoo | ? | ? | ? | ? | ? | ? |
| 15 Honda | Y | Y | Y | N | Y | Y |
| 16 Lofgren | Y | Y | Y | N | Y | Y |
| 17 Farr | Y | Y | Y | N | Y | Y |
| 18 Cardoza | Y | Y | Y | N | Y | Y |
| 19 Radanovich | Y | Y | Y | Y | Y | Y |
| 20 Costa | Y | Y | Y | N | Y | Y |
| 21 Nunes | Y | Y | Y | Y | Y | Y |
| 22 Thomas | Y | Y | Y | Y | Y | Y |
| 23 Capps | Y | Y | Y | N | Y | Y |
| 24 Gallegly | Y | Y | Y | Y | Y | Y |
| 25 McKeon | Y | Y | Y | Y | Y | Y |
| 26 Dreier | Y | Y | Y | Y | Y | Y |
| 27 Sherman | Y | Y | Y | N | Y | Y |
| 28 Berman | Y | Y | Y | N | Y | Y |
| 29 Schiff | Y | Y | Y | – | Y | Y |
| 30 Waxman | Y | Y | Y | N | Y | Y |
| 31 Becerra | Y | Y | Y | N | Y | Y |
| 32 Solis | Y | Y | Y | N | Y | Y |
| 33 Watson | ? | ? | ? | N | Y | Y |
| 34 Roybal-Allard | Y | Y | Y | N | Y | Y |
| 35 Waters | Y | Y | Y | N | Y | Y |
| 36 Harman | Y | Y | Y | N | Y | Y |
| 37 Millender-McD. | Y | Y | Y | N | Y | Y |
| 38 Napolitano | Y | Y | ? | N | Y | Y |
| 39 Sánchez, Linda | Y | Y | Y | N | Y | Y |
| 40 Royce | Y | Y | Y | Y | Y | Y |
| 41 Lewis | Y | Y | Y | Y | Y | Y |
| 42 Miller, Gary | Y | Y | Y | Y | Y | Y |
| 43 Baca | Y | Y | Y | N | Y | Y |
| 44 Calvert | Y | Y | Y | Y | Y | Y |
| 45 Bono | Y | Y | Y | Y | Y | Y |
| 46 Rohrabacher | Y | Y | Y | Y | Y | Y |
| 47 Sanchez, Loretta | Y | Y | Y | N | Y | Y |
| 48 Cox | Y | Y | Y | Y | Y | Y |
| 49 Issa | Y | Y | Y | Y | Y | Y |

| | 20 | 21 | 22 | 23 | 24 | 25 |
|---|---|---|---|---|---|---|
| 50 Cunningham | Y | Y | Y | Y | Y | Y |
| 51 Filner | Y | Y | Y | N | Y | Y |
| 52 Hunter | Y | Y | Y | Y | Y | Y |
| 53 Davis | Y | Y | Y | N | Y | Y |
| **COLORADO** | | | | | | |
| 1 DeGette | ? | ? | ? | ? | Y | Y |
| 2 Udall | Y | Y | Y | N | Y | Y |
| 3 Salazar | Y | Y | Y | N | Y | Y |
| 4 Musgrave | Y | Y | Y | Y | Y | Y |
| 5 Hefley | Y | Y | Y | Y | Y | Y |
| 6 Tancredo | Y | Y | Y | Y | Y | Y |
| 7 Beauprez | Y | Y | Y | Y | Y | Y |
| **CONNECTICUT** | | | | | | |
| 1 Larson | Y | Y | Y | N | Y | Y |
| 2 Simmons | Y | Y | Y | Y | Y | Y |
| 3 DeLauro | Y | Y | Y | N | Y | Y |
| 4 Shays | Y | Y | Y | Y | Y | Y |
| 5 Johnson | Y | Y | Y | Y | Y | Y |
| **DELAWARE** | | | | | | |
| AL Castle | Y | Y | Y | Y | Y | Y |
| **FLORIDA** | | | | | | |
| 1 Miller | Y | Y | Y | Y | Y | Y |
| 2 Boyd | Y | Y | Y | N | Y | Y |
| 3 Brown | Y | Y | Y | N | Y | Y |
| 4 Crenshaw | Y | Y | Y | Y | Y | Y |
| 5 Brown-Waite | Y | Y | Y | Y | Y | Y |
| 6 Stearns | Y | Y | ? | Y | Y | Y |
| 7 Mica | Y | Y | Y | Y | Y | + |
| 8 Keller | Y | Y | Y | Y | Y | Y |
| 9 Bilirakis | Y | Y | Y | Y | Y | Y |
| 10 Young | Y | Y | Y | Y | Y | Y |
| 11 Davis | ? | Y | Y | N | Y | Y |
| 12 Putnam | Y | Y | Y | Y | Y | Y |
| 13 Harris | Y | Y | Y | Y | Y | Y |
| 14 Mack | Y | Y | Y | Y | Y | Y |
| 15 Weldon | Y | Y | Y | Y | Y | Y |
| 16 Foley | Y | Y | Y | Y | Y | Y |
| 17 Meek | Y | Y | Y | N | Y | Y |
| 18 Ros-Lehtinen | Y | Y | Y | ? | ? | ? |
| 19 Wexler | ? | ? | ? | N | Y | Y |
| 20 Wasserman-Schultz | Y | Y | Y | N | Y | Y |
| 21 Diaz-Balart, L. | Y | Y | Y | Y | Y | Y |
| 22 Shaw | Y | Y | Y | Y | Y | Y |
| 23 Hastings | Y | Y | Y | N | Y | Y |
| 24 Feeney | ? | ? | ? | ? | ? | ? |
| 25 Diaz-Balart, M. | Y | Y | Y | Y | Y | Y |
| **GEORGIA** | | | | | | |
| 1 Kingston | Y | Y | Y | Y | Y | Y |
| 2 Bishop | Y | Y | Y | N | Y | Y |
| 3 Marshall | Y | Y | Y | N | Y | Y |
| 4 McKinney | Y | Y | Y | N | Y | Y |
| 5 Lewis | Y | Y | Y | N | Y | Y |
| 6 Price | Y | Y | Y | Y | Y | Y |
| 7 Linder | Y | Y | Y | Y | Y | Y |
| 8 Westmoreland | Y | Y | Y | Y | Y | Y |
| 9 Norwood | Y | Y | Y | ? | Y | Y |
| 10 Deal | Y | Y | Y | Y | Y | Y |
| 11 Gingrey | Y | Y | Y | Y | Y | Y |
| 12 Barrow | Y | Y | Y | N | Y | Y |
| 13 Scott | Y | Y | Y | N | Y | Y |
| **HAWAII** | | | | | | |
| 1 Abercrombie | Y | Y | Y | N | Y | Y |
| 2 Case | Y | Y | Y | N | Y | Y |
| **IDAHO** | | | | | | |
| 1 Otter | Y | Y | Y | Y | Y | Y |
| 2 Simpson | Y | Y | Y | Y | Y | Y |
| **ILLINOIS** | | | | | | |
| 1 Rush | Y | Y | Y | N | ? | ? |
| 2 Jackson | Y | Y | Y | N | Y | Y |
| 3 Lipinski | Y | Y | Y | ? | Y | Y |
| 4 Gutierrez | + | + | + | N | Y | Y |
| 5 Emanuel | Y | Y | Y | N | Y | Y |
| 6 Hyde | Y | Y | Y | Y | Y | Y |
| 7 Davis | Y | Y | Y | ? | Y | Y |
| 8 Bean | Y | Y | Y | N | Y | Y |
| 9 Schakowsky | Y | Y | Y | N | Y | Y |
| 10 Kirk | Y | Y | ? | Y | Y | Y |
| 11 Weller | Y | Y | Y | Y | Y | Y |
| 12 Costello | Y | Y | Y | N | Y | Y |

**KEY**  Republicans  Democrats  *Independents*

| Y | Voted for (yea) | X | Paired against | C | Voted "present" to avoid possible conflict of interest |
|---|---|---|---|---|---|
| # | Paired for | – | Announced against | | |
| + | Announced for | P | Voted "present" | ? | Did not vote or otherwise make a position known |
| N | Voted against (nay) | | | | |

| | 20 | 21 | 22 | 23 | 24 | 25 |
|---|---|---|---|---|---|---|
| 13 **Biggert** | Y | Y | Y | Y | Y | Y |
| 14 **Hastert** | Y | | | | | |
| 15 **Johnson** | Y | Y | Y | Y | Y | Y |
| 16 **Manzullo** | Y | Y | Y | Y | Y | Y |
| 17 Evans | Y | Y | Y | N | Y | Y |
| 18 **LaHood** | Y | Y | Y | Y | Y | Y |
| 19 **Shimkus** | Y | Y | Y | Y | Y | Y |
| **INDIANA** | | | | | | |
| 1 Visclosky | Y | Y | Y | N | Y | Y |
| 2 **Chocola** | Y | Y | Y | Y | Y | Y |
| 3 **Souder** | Y | Y | Y | Y | Y | Y |
| 4 **Buyer** | Y | Y | Y | Y | Y | Y |
| 5 **Burton** | Y | Y | Y | Y | Y | Y |
| 6 **Pence** | Y | Y | Y | ? | Y | Y |
| 7 Carson | Y | Y | Y | N | Y | Y |
| 8 **Hostettler** | Y | Y | Y | Y | Y | Y |
| 9 **Sodrel** | Y | Y | Y | Y | Y | Y |
| **IOWA** | | | | | | |
| 1 **Nussle** | Y | Y | Y | Y | Y | Y |
| 2 **Leach** | Y | Y | Y | Y | Y | Y |
| 3 Boswell | Y | Y | Y | N | Y | Y |
| 4 **Latham** | Y | Y | Y | Y | Y | Y |
| 5 **King** | Y | Y | Y | Y | Y | Y |
| **KANSAS** | | | | | | |
| 1 **Moran** | Y | Y | Y | Y | Y | Y |
| 2 **Ryun** | Y | Y | Y | Y | Y | Y |
| 3 Moore | Y | Y | Y | N | Y | Y |
| 4 **Tiahrt** | Y | Y | Y | Y | Y | Y |
| **KENTUCKY** | | | | | | |
| 1 **Whitfield** | Y | Y | Y | Y | Y | Y |
| 2 **Lewis** | Y | Y | Y | Y | Y | Y |
| 3 **Northup** | Y | Y | Y | Y | Y | Y |
| 4 **Davis** | Y | Y | Y | Y | Y | Y |
| 5 **Rogers** | Y | Y | Y | Y | Y | Y |
| 6 Chandler | Y | Y | Y | N | Y | Y |
| **LOUISIANA** | | | | | | |
| 1 **Jindal** | Y | Y | Y | Y | Y | Y |
| 2 Jefferson | Y | Y | Y | N | Y | Y |
| 3 Melancon | Y | Y | Y | N | Y | Y |
| 4 **McCrery** | Y | Y | Y | Y | Y | Y |
| 5 **Alexander** | Y | Y | Y | Y | Y | Y |
| 6 **Baker** | Y | Y | Y | Y | Y | Y |
| 7 **Boustany** | Y | Y | Y | Y | Y | Y |
| **MAINE** | | | | | | |
| 1 Allen | Y | Y | Y | N | Y | Y |
| 2 Michaud | Y | Y | Y | N | Y | Y |
| **MARYLAND** | | | | | | |
| 1 **Gilchrest** | Y | Y | Y | Y | Y | Y |
| 2 Ruppersberger | Y | Y | Y | N | Y | Y |
| 3 Cardin | Y | Y | Y | N | Y | Y |
| 4 Wynn | Y | Y | Y | N | Y | Y |
| 5 Hoyer | Y | Y | Y | N | Y | Y |
| 6 **Bartlett** | Y | Y | Y | Y | Y | Y |
| 7 Cummings | Y | Y | Y | N | Y | Y |
| 8 Van Hollen | Y | Y | Y | N | Y | Y |
| **MASSACHUSETTS** | | | | | | |
| 1 Olver | Y | Y | Y | N | Y | Y |
| 2 Neal | Y | Y | Y | N | Y | Y |
| 3 McGovern | Y | Y | Y | N | Y | Y |
| 4 Frank | Y | Y | Y | N | N | Y |
| 5 Meehan | Y | Y | Y | N | Y | Y |
| 6 Tierney | Y | Y | Y | N | Y | Y |
| 7 Markey | Y | Y | Y | N | Y | Y |
| 8 Capuano | Y | Y | Y | N | Y | Y |
| 9 Lynch | ? | ? | ? | N | Y | Y |
| 10 Delahunt | Y | Y | Y | N | Y | Y |
| **MICHIGAN** | | | | | | |
| 1 Stupak | ? | ? | ? | ? | ? | ? |
| 2 **Hoekstra** | Y | Y | Y | Y | Y | Y |
| 3 **Ehlers** | Y | Y | Y | Y | Y | Y |
| 4 **Camp** | Y | Y | Y | Y | Y | Y |
| 5 Kildee | Y | Y | Y | N | Y | Y |
| 6 **Upton** | Y | Y | Y | Y | Y | Y |
| 7 **Schwarz** | Y | Y | Y | Y | Y | Y |
| 8 **Rogers** | Y | Y | Y | Y | Y | Y |
| 9 **Knollenberg** | Y | Y | Y | Y | Y | Y |
| 10 **Miller** | Y | Y | Y | Y | Y | Y |
| 11 **McCotter** | Y | Y | Y | Y | Y | Y |
| 12 Levin | Y | Y | Y | N | Y | Y |
| 13 Kilpatrick | Y | Y | Y | N | Y | Y |
| 14 Conyers | Y | Y | Y | N | Y | Y |
| 15 Dingell | Y | Y | Y | N | Y | Y |

| | 20 | 21 | 22 | 23 | 24 | 25 |
|---|---|---|---|---|---|---|
| **MINNESOTA** | | | | | | |
| 1 **Gutknecht** | Y | Y | Y | Y | Y | Y |
| 2 **Kline** | Y | Y | Y | Y | Y | Y |
| 3 **Ramstad** | Y | Y | Y | Y | Y | Y |
| 4 McCollum | Y | Y | Y | N | Y | Y |
| 5 Sabo | ? | ? | ? | N | Y | Y |
| 6 **Kennedy** | Y | Y | Y | Y | Y | Y |
| 7 Peterson | Y | Y | Y | N | Y | Y |
| 8 Oberstar | Y | Y | Y | N | Y | Y |
| **MISSISSIPPI** | | | | | | |
| 1 **Wicker** | Y | Y | Y | Y | Y | Y |
| 2 Thompson | Y | Y | Y | N | Y | Y |
| 3 **Pickering** | Y | Y | Y | Y | Y | Y |
| 4 Taylor | Y | Y | Y | N | Y | Y |
| **MISSOURI** | | | | | | |
| 1 Clay | Y | Y | Y | N | Y | Y |
| 2 **Akin** | Y | Y | Y | Y | Y | Y |
| 3 Carnahan | Y | Y | Y | N | Y | Y |
| 4 Skelton | Y | Y | Y | N | Y | Y |
| 5 Cleaver | Y | Y | Y | N | Y | Y |
| 6 **Graves** | Y | Y | Y | Y | Y | Y |
| 7 **Blunt** | Y | Y | Y | Y | Y | Y |
| 8 **Emerson** | ? | ? | ? | Y | Y | Y |
| 9 **Hulshof** | Y | Y | Y | Y | Y | Y |
| **MONTANA** | | | | | | |
| AL **Rehberg** | Y | Y | Y | Y | Y | Y |
| **NEBRASKA** | | | | | | |
| 1 **Fortenberry** | Y | Y | Y | Y | Y | Y |
| 2 **Terry** | Y | Y | Y | Y | Y | Y |
| 3 **Osborne** | Y | Y | Y | Y | Y | Y |
| **NEVADA** | | | | | | |
| 1 Berkley | Y | Y | Y | N | Y | Y |
| 2 **Gibbons** | Y | Y | Y | Y | Y | Y |
| 3 **Porter** | Y | Y | Y | Y | Y | Y |
| **NEW HAMPSHIRE** | | | | | | |
| 1 **Bradley** | Y | Y | Y | Y | Y | Y |
| 2 **Bass** | Y | Y | Y | Y | Y | Y |
| **NEW JERSEY** | | | | | | |
| 1 Andrews | Y | Y | Y | N | Y | Y |
| 2 **LoBiondo** | + | + | + | Y | Y | Y |
| 3 **Saxton** | Y | Y | Y | Y | Y | Y |
| 4 **Smith** | Y | Y | Y | Y | Y | Y |
| 5 **Garrett** | Y | Y | Y | Y | Y | Y |
| 6 Pallone | Y | Y | Y | N | Y | Y |
| 7 **Ferguson** | Y | Y | Y | Y | Y | Y |
| 8 Pascrell | Y | Y | Y | N | Y | Y |
| 9 Rothman | Y | Y | Y | N | Y | Y |
| 10 Payne | ? | ? | ? | N | Y | Y |
| 11 **Frelinghuysen** | Y | Y | Y | Y | Y | Y |
| 12 Holt | Y | ? | ? | N | Y | Y |
| 13 Menendez | Y | Y | Y | N | Y | Y |
| **NEW MEXICO** | | | | | | |
| 1 **Wilson** | Y | Y | Y | Y | Y | Y |
| 2 **Pearce** | Y | Y | Y | Y | Y | Y |
| 3 Udall | Y | Y | Y | N | Y | Y |
| **NEW YORK** | | | | | | |
| 1 Bishop | Y | Y | Y | N | Y | Y |
| 2 Israel | Y | Y | Y | N | Y | Y |
| 3 **King** | Y | Y | Y | Y | Y | Y |
| 4 McCarthy | Y | Y | Y | N | Y | Y |
| 5 Ackerman | ? | ? | ? | N | Y | Y |
| 6 Meeks | Y | Y | Y | N | Y | Y |
| 7 Crowley | Y | Y | Y | N | Y | Y |
| 8 Nadler | Y | Y | Y | N | Y | Y |
| 9 Weiner | Y | Y | Y | N | Y | Y |
| 10 Towns | Y | Y | Y | N | Y | Y |
| 11 Owens | Y | Y | Y | N | Y | Y |
| 12 Velázquez | Y | Y | Y | N | Y | Y |
| 13 **Fossella** | Y | Y | Y | Y | Y | Y |
| 14 Maloney | Y | Y | Y | N | Y | Y |
| 15 Rangel | Y | Y | Y | N | Y | Y |
| 16 Serrano | Y | Y | Y | N | Y | Y |
| 17 Engel | Y | Y | Y | N | Y | Y |
| 18 Lowey | Y | Y | Y | N | Y | Y |
| 19 **Kelly** | Y | Y | Y | Y | Y | Y |
| 20 **Sweeney** | Y | Y | Y | Y | Y | Y |
| 21 McNulty | Y | Y | Y | N | Y | Y |
| 22 Hinchey | ? | ? | ? | ? | ? | ? |
| 23 **McHugh** | Y | Y | Y | Y | Y | Y |
| 24 **Boehlert** | Y | Y | Y | Y | Y | Y |
| 25 **Walsh** | Y | Y | Y | Y | Y | Y |
| 26 **Reynolds** | Y | Y | Y | Y | Y | Y |
| 27 Higgins | Y | Y | Y | N | Y | Y |
| 28 Slaughter | Y | Y | Y | N | Y | Y |
| 29 **Kuhl** | Y | Y | Y | Y | Y | Y |

| | 20 | 21 | 22 | 23 | 24 | 25 |
|---|---|---|---|---|---|---|
| **NORTH CAROLINA** | | | | | | |
| 1 Butterfield | Y | Y | Y | N | Y | Y |
| 2 Etheridge | ? | ? | ? | N | Y | Y |
| 3 **Jones** | Y | Y | Y | ? | Y | Y |
| 4 Price | Y | Y | Y | N | Y | Y |
| 5 **Foxx** | Y | Y | Y | Y | Y | Y |
| 6 **Coble** | Y | Y | Y | Y | Y | Y |
| 7 McIntyre | Y | Y | Y | N | Y | Y |
| 8 **Hayes** | Y | Y | Y | Y | Y | Y |
| 9 **Myrick** | Y | Y | Y | Y | Y | Y |
| 10 **McHenry** | Y | Y | Y | Y | Y | Y |
| 11 **Taylor** | Y | Y | ? | Y | Y | Y |
| 12 Watt | Y | Y | Y | N | Y | Y |
| 13 Miller | Y | Y | Y | N | Y | Y |
| **NORTH DAKOTA** | | | | | | |
| AL Pomeroy | Y | Y | Y | N | Y | Y |
| **OHIO** | | | | | | |
| 1 **Chabot** | Y | Y | Y | Y | Y | Y |
| 2 **Portman** | Y | Y | Y | Y | Y | Y |
| 3 **Turner** | Y | Y | Y | Y | Y | Y |
| 4 **Oxley** | Y | Y | Y | Y | Y | Y |
| 5 **Gillmor** | Y | Y | Y | Y | Y | Y |
| 6 Strickland | Y | Y | Y | N | Y | Y |
| 7 **Hobson** | Y | Y | Y | Y | Y | Y |
| 8 **Boehner** | Y | Y | Y | Y | Y | Y |
| 9 Kaptur | Y | Y | Y | N | Y | Y |
| 10 Kucinich | Y | Y | Y | N | N | Y |
| 11 Jones | Y | Y | Y | N | Y | Y |
| 12 **Tiberi** | Y | Y | Y | Y | Y | Y |
| 13 Brown | Y | Y | Y | N | Y | Y |
| 14 **LaTourette** | Y | Y | Y | Y | Y | Y |
| 15 **Pryce** | Y | Y | Y | Y | Y | Y |
| 16 **Regula** | Y | Y | Y | Y | Y | Y |
| 17 Ryan | Y | Y | Y | N | Y | Y |
| 18 **Ney** | + | + | + | Y | Y | Y |
| **OKLAHOMA** | | | | | | |
| 1 **Sullivan** | Y | Y | Y | Y | Y | Y |
| 2 Boren | Y | Y | Y | N | Y | Y |
| 3 **Lucas** | Y | Y | Y | Y | Y | Y |
| 4 **Cole** | Y | Y | Y | Y | Y | Y |
| 5 **Istook** | Y | Y | Y | Y | Y | Y |
| **OREGON** | | | | | | |
| 1 Wu | Y | Y | Y | N | Y | Y |
| 2 **Walden** | Y | Y | Y | Y | Y | Y |
| 3 Blumenauer | Y | Y | Y | N | N | Y |
| 4 DeFazio | Y | Y | Y | N | Y | Y |
| 5 Hooley | Y | Y | Y | N | Y | Y |
| **PENNSYLVANIA** | | | | | | |
| 1 Brady | Y | Y | Y | N | Y | Y |
| 2 Fattah | Y | Y | Y | N | Y | Y |
| 3 **English** | Y | Y | Y | Y | Y | Y |
| 4 **Hart** | Y | Y | Y | Y | Y | Y |
| 5 **Peterson** | Y | Y | Y | Y | Y | Y |
| 6 **Gerlach** | Y | ? | ? | Y | Y | Y |
| 7 **Weldon** | Y | Y | Y | Y | Y | Y |
| 8 **Fitzpatrick** | Y | Y | Y | Y | Y | Y |
| 9 **Shuster** | Y | Y | Y | Y | Y | Y |
| 10 **Sherwood** | Y | Y | Y | Y | Y | Y |
| 11 Kanjorski | Y | Y | Y | N | Y | Y |
| 12 Murtha | Y | Y | Y | N | Y | Y |
| 13 Schwartz | Y | Y | Y | N | Y | Y |
| 14 Doyle | Y | Y | Y | N | Y | Y |
| 15 **Dent** | Y | Y | Y | Y | Y | Y |
| 16 **Pitts** | Y | Y | Y | Y | Y | Y |
| 17 Holden | Y | Y | Y | N | Y | Y |
| 18 **Murphy** | Y | Y | Y | Y | Y | Y |
| 19 **Platts** | Y | Y | Y | Y | Y | Y |
| **RHODE ISLAND** | | | | | | |
| 1 Kennedy | Y | Y | Y | N | Y | Y |
| 2 Langevin | Y | Y | Y | N | Y | Y |
| **SOUTH CAROLINA** | | | | | | |
| 1 **Brown** | Y | Y | Y | Y | Y | Y |
| 2 **Wilson** | Y | Y | ? | Y | Y | Y |
| 3 **Barrett** | Y | Y | Y | Y | Y | Y |
| 4 **Inglis** | Y | Y | Y | Y | Y | Y |
| 5 Spratt | Y | Y | Y | N | Y | Y |
| 6 Clyburn | Y | Y | ? | N | Y | Y |
| **SOUTH DAKOTA** | | | | | | |
| AL Herseth | Y | Y | Y | N | Y | Y |
| **TENNESSEE** | | | | | | |
| 1 **Jenkins** | Y | Y | Y | Y | Y | Y |
| 2 **Duncan** | Y | Y | Y | Y | Y | Y |

| | 20 | 21 | 22 | 23 | 24 | 25 |
|---|---|---|---|---|---|---|
| 3 **Wamp** | Y | Y | Y | Y | Y | Y |
| 4 Davis | Y | Y | Y | Y | Y | Y |
| 5 Cooper | Y | Y | Y | N | Y | Y |
| 6 Gordon | Y | Y | Y | N | Y | ? |
| 7 **Blackburn** | Y | Y | Y | Y | Y | Y |
| 8 Tanner | Y | Y | Y | N | Y | Y |
| 9 Ford | Y | Y | Y | N | Y | Y |
| **TEXAS** | | | | | | |
| 1 **Gohmert** | Y | Y | Y | Y | Y | Y |
| 2 **Poe** | Y | Y | Y | Y | Y | Y |
| 3 **Johnson, S.** | Y | Y | Y | Y | Y | Y |
| 4 **Hall** | Y | Y | Y | Y | Y | Y |
| 5 **Hensarling** | Y | Y | Y | Y | Y | Y |
| 6 **Barton** | Y | Y | Y | Y | Y | Y |
| 7 **Culberson** | Y | Y | Y | Y | Y | Y |
| 8 **Brady** | Y | Y | Y | Y | Y | Y |
| 9 Green, A. | Y | Y | Y | N | Y | Y |
| 10 **McCaul** | Y | Y | Y | Y | Y | Y |
| 11 **Conaway** | Y | Y | Y | Y | Y | Y |
| 12 **Granger** | Y | Y | ? | Y | Y | Y |
| 13 **Thornberry** | Y | Y | Y | Y | Y | Y |
| 14 **Paul** | Y | Y | Y | Y | Y | Y |
| 15 Hinojosa | Y | Y | Y | N | + | + |
| 16 Reyes | Y | Y | Y | N | Y | Y |
| 17 Edwards | Y | Y | Y | N | Y | Y |
| 18 Jackson-Lee | Y | Y | Y | N | Y | Y |
| 19 **Neugebauer** | + | + | + | Y | Y | Y |
| 20 Gonzalez | Y | Y | Y | N | Y | Y |
| 21 **Smith** | Y | Y | Y | Y | Y | Y |
| 22 **DeLay** | Y | Y | Y | Y | Y | Y |
| 23 **Bonilla** | Y | Y | Y | Y | Y | Y |
| 24 **Marchant** | Y | Y | Y | Y | Y | Y |
| 25 Doggett | Y | Y | Y | N | Y | Y |
| 26 **Burgess** | Y | Y | Y | Y | Y | Y |
| 27 Ortiz | Y | Y | Y | N | Y | Y |
| 28 Cuellar | Y | Y | Y | N | Y | Y |
| 29 Green, G. | Y | Y | Y | N | Y | Y |
| 30 Johnson, E. | Y | Y | Y | N | Y | Y |
| 31 **Carter** | Y | Y | Y | Y | Y | Y |
| 32 **Sessions** | Y | Y | Y | Y | Y | Y |
| **UTAH** | | | | | | |
| 1 **Bishop** | Y | Y | Y | Y | Y | Y |
| 2 Matheson | Y | Y | Y | N | Y | Y |
| 3 **Cannon** | Y | Y | Y | Y | Y | Y |
| **VERMONT** | | | | | | |
| AL *Sanders* | Y | Y | Y | N | Y | Y |
| **VIRGINIA** | | | | | | |
| 1 **Davis, J.** | Y | Y | Y | Y | Y | Y |
| 2 **Drake** | Y | Y | Y | Y | Y | Y |
| 3 Scott | Y | Y | Y | N | Y | Y |
| 4 **Forbes** | Y | Y | Y | Y | Y | Y |
| 5 **Goode** | Y | Y | Y | Y | Y | Y |
| 6 **Goodlatte** | Y | Y | Y | Y | Y | Y |
| 7 **Cantor** | Y | Y | Y | Y | Y | Y |
| 8 Moran | Y | Y | Y | N | Y | Y |
| 9 Boucher | Y | Y | Y | N | Y | Y |
| 10 **Wolf** | Y | Y | Y | Y | Y | Y |
| 11 **Davis, T.** | Y | Y | Y | Y | Y | Y |
| **WASHINGTON** | | | | | | |
| 1 Inslee | Y | Y | Y | N | Y | Y |
| 2 Larsen | Y | Y | Y | N | Y | Y |
| 3 Baird | ? | ? | ? | N | Y | Y |
| 4 **Hastings** | Y | Y | Y | Y | Y | Y |
| 5 **McMorris** | Y | Y | Y | Y | Y | Y |
| 6 Dicks | Y | Y | Y | ? | Y | Y |
| 7 McDermott | Y | Y | Y | N | N | Y |
| 8 **Reichert** | Y | Y | Y | Y | Y | Y |
| 9 Smith | Y | Y | Y | N | Y | Y |
| **WEST VIRGINIA** | | | | | | |
| 1 Mollohan | Y | Y | Y | N | Y | Y |
| 2 **Capito** | Y | Y | Y | Y | Y | Y |
| 3 Rahall | Y | Y | Y | N | Y | Y |
| **WISCONSIN** | | | | | | |
| 1 **Ryan** | Y | Y | Y | Y | Y | Y |
| 2 Baldwin | Y | Y | Y | N | Y | Y |
| 3 Kind | Y | Y | Y | N | Y | Y |
| 4 Moore | Y | Y | Y | N | Y | Y |
| 5 **Sensenbrenner** | Y | Y | Y | Y | Y | Y |
| 6 **Petri** | Y | Y | Y | Y | Y | Y |
| 7 Obey | Y | Y | Y | ? | Y | Y |
| 8 **Green** | Y | Y | Y | Y | Y | Y |
| **WYOMING** | | | | | | |
| AL **Cubin** | Y | Y | Y | Y | Y | Y |

# IN THE HOUSE | By Vote Number

**26.** H Con Res 30. National Black HIV/AIDS Awareness Day/Adoption. Deal, R-Ga., motion to suspend the rules and adopt the concurrent resolution that would express congressional support for the goals and ideals of National Black HIV/AIDS Awareness Day and recognize its fifth anniversary. Motion agreed to 422-0: R 227-0; D 194-0 (ND 145-0, SD 49-0); I 1-0. A two-thirds majority of those present and voting (282 in this case) is required for adoption under suspension of the rules. Feb. 9, 2005.

**27.** HR 418. Immigration Standards/Rule. Adoption of the rule (H Res 75) to provide for further House floor consideration of the bill that would tighten national standards for state driver's licenses and identity cards, make it more difficult for foreign nationals to claim asylum, and authorize the completion of a security fence along the U.S.-Mexico border. Adopted 228-198: R 228-0; D 0-197 (ND 0-147, SD 0-50); I 0-1. Feb. 10, 2005.

**28.** HR 418. Immigration Standards/Asylum Provisions. Nadler, D-N.Y., amendment that would strike the section of the bill modifying conditions for granting asylum to foreign nationals. Rejected 185-236: R 10-216; D 174-20 (ND 140-5, SD 34-15); I 1-0. Feb. 10, 2005.

**29.** HR 418. Immigration Standards/Border Security. Farr, D-Calif., amendment that would strike language in the bill that would authorize the Homeland Security secretary to waive laws impeding construction of physical barriers and roads designed to curb illegal border crossings, including the completion of a fortified fence along the U.S.-Mexico border close to San Diego, Calif. Rejected 179-243: R 8-220; D 170-23 (ND 137-7, SD 33-16); I 1-0. Feb. 10, 2005.

**30.** HR 418. Immigration Standards/Recommit. Reyes, D-Texas, motion to recommit the bill to the Judiciary Committee with instructions to add language stating that a state's motor vehicle database could not include any information that would conflict with rights guaranteed under the First, Second or 14th Amendments. Motion rejected 195-229: R 2-227; D 192-2 (ND 144-1, SD 48-1); I 1-0. Feb. 10, 2005.

**31.** HR 418. Immigration Standards/Passage. Passage of the bill that would tighten national standards for state driver's licenses and identity cards, make it more difficult for foreign nationals to claim asylum, and authorize the completion of a security fence along the U.S.-Mexico border. It would allow immigration judges to weigh the credibility of asylum applicants in a variety of proceedings and remove the annual cap of 10,000 refugees who may become permanent residents. Passed 261-161: R 219-8; D 42-152 (ND 18-127, SD 24-25); I 0-1. A "yea" was a vote in support of the president's position. Feb. 10, 2005.

| | 26 | 27 | 28 | 29 | 30 | 31 |
|---|---|---|---|---|---|---|
| **ALABAMA** | | | | | | |
| 1 Bonner | Y | Y | N | N | N | Y |
| 2 Everett | Y | Y | N | N | N | Y |
| 3 Rogers | Y | Y | N | N | N | Y |
| 4 Aderholt | Y | Y | N | N | N | Y |
| 5 Cramer | Y | N | N | N | Y | Y |
| 6 Bachus | Y | Y | N | N | N | Y |
| 7 Davis | Y | N | Y | N | Y | Y |
| **ALASKA** | | | | | | |
| AL Young | Y | Y | N | N | N | N |
| **ARIZONA** | | | | | | |
| 1 Renzi | Y | Y | N | N | N | Y |
| 2 Franks | Y | Y | N | N | N | Y |
| 3 Shadegg | Y | Y | N | N | N | Y |
| 4 Pastor | Y | N | Y | Y | Y | N |
| 5 Hayworth | Y | Y | N | N | N | Y |
| 6 Flake | Y | Y | N | N | N | Y |
| 7 Grijalva | Y | N | Y | Y | Y | N |
| 8 Kolbe | Y | Y | N | N | N | Y |
| **ARKANSAS** | | | | | | |
| 1 Berry | Y | N | Y | N | Y | Y |
| 2 Snyder | ? | N | Y | Y | Y | N |
| 3 Boozman | Y | Y | N | N | N | Y |
| 4 Ross | Y | N | Y | Y | Y | Y |
| **CALIFORNIA** | | | | | | |
| 1 Thompson | Y | N | N | Y | Y | N |
| 2 Herger | Y | Y | N | N | N | Y |
| 3 Lungren | Y | Y | N | N | N | Y |
| 4 Doolittle | Y | Y | N | N | N | Y |
| 5 Vacant | | | | | | |
| 6 Woolsey | Y | N | Y | Y | Y | N |
| 7 Miller, George | Y | N | Y | Y | Y | N |
| 8 Pelosi | Y | N | Y | Y | Y | N |
| 9 Lee | Y | N | Y | Y | Y | N |
| 10 Tauscher | Y | N | Y | Y | Y | N |
| 11 Pombo | Y | Y | N | N | N | Y |
| 12 Lantos | Y | N | Y | Y | Y | N |
| 13 Stark | Y | N | Y | Y | Y | N |
| 14 Eshoo | ? | ? | ? | ? | ? | ? |
| 15 Honda | Y | N | + | + | + | - |
| 16 Lofgren | Y | N | Y | Y | Y | N |
| 17 Farr | Y | N | Y | Y | Y | N |
| 18 Cardoza | Y | N | Y | Y | Y | Y |
| 19 Radanovich | Y | ? | N | N | N | Y |
| 20 Costa | Y | N | N | Y | Y | Y |
| 21 Nunes | Y | Y | N | N | N | Y |
| 22 Thomas | Y | Y | N | N | N | Y |
| 23 Capps | Y | N | Y | Y | Y | N |
| 24 Gallegly | Y | Y | N | N | N | Y |
| 25 McKeon | Y | Y | N | N | N | Y |
| 26 Dreier | Y | Y | N | N | N | Y |
| 27 Sherman | Y | N | Y | Y | Y | N |
| 28 Berman | Y | N | Y | Y | Y | N |
| 29 Schiff | Y | N | Y | Y | Y | N |
| 30 Waxman | Y | N | Y | Y | Y | N |
| 31 Becerra | Y | N | Y | Y | Y | N |
| 32 Solis | Y | N | Y | Y | Y | N |
| 33 Watson | Y | N | Y | Y | Y | N |
| 34 Roybal-Allard | Y | N | Y | Y | Y | N |
| 35 Waters | Y | N | Y | Y | Y | N |
| 36 Harman | Y | N | Y | Y | Y | N |
| 37 Millender-McD. | Y | N | Y | Y | Y | N |
| 38 Napolitano | Y | N | Y | Y | Y | N |
| 39 Sánchez, Linda | Y | N | Y | Y | Y | N |
| 40 Royce | Y | Y | N | N | N | Y |
| 41 Lewis | Y | Y | N | N | N | Y |
| 42 Miller, Gary | Y | Y | N | N | N | Y |
| 43 Baca | Y | N | Y | Y | Y | N |
| 44 Calvert | Y | Y | N | N | N | Y |
| 45 Bono | Y | Y | N | N | N | Y |
| 46 Rohrabacher | Y | Y | N | N | N | Y |
| 47 Sanchez, Loretta | Y | N | ? | ? | ? | ? |
| 48 Cox | Y | Y | N | N | N | Y |
| 49 Issa | Y | Y | N | N | N | Y |

| | 26 | 27 | 28 | 29 | 30 | 31 |
|---|---|---|---|---|---|---|
| 50 Cunningham | Y | Y | N | N | N | Y |
| 51 Filner | Y | N | Y | Y | Y | N |
| 52 Hunter | Y | Y | N | N | N | Y |
| 53 Davis | Y | N | Y | Y | Y | N |
| **COLORADO** | | | | | | |
| 1 DeGette | Y | N | Y | Y | Y | N |
| 2 Udall | Y | N | Y | Y | Y | N |
| 3 Salazar | Y | N | Y | Y | Y | N |
| 4 Musgrave | Y | Y | N | N | N | Y |
| 5 Hefley | Y | Y | N | N | N | Y |
| 6 Tancredo | Y | Y | N | N | N | Y |
| 7 Beauprez | Y | Y | N | N | N | Y |
| **CONNECTICUT** | | | | | | |
| 1 Larson | Y | N | Y | Y | Y | N |
| 2 Simmons | Y | Y | Y | N | N | Y |
| 3 DeLauro | Y | N | Y | Y | Y | N |
| 4 Shays | Y | Y | N | N | N | Y |
| 5 Johnson | ? | Y | N | N | N | Y |
| **DELAWARE** | | | | | | |
| AL Castle | Y | Y | N | N | N | Y |
| **FLORIDA** | | | | | | |
| 1 Miller | Y | Y | N | N | N | Y |
| 2 Boyd | Y | N | Y | Y | Y | Y |
| 3 Brown | Y | N | Y | Y | Y | N |
| 4 Crenshaw | Y | Y | N | N | N | Y |
| 5 Brown-Waite | Y | Y | N | N | N | Y |
| 6 Stearns | Y | Y | N | N | N | Y |
| 7 Mica | Y | Y | N | N | N | Y |
| 8 Keller | Y | Y | N | N | N | Y |
| 9 Bilirakis | Y | Y | N | N | N | Y |
| 10 Young | Y | Y | N | N | N | Y |
| 11 Davis | Y | N | Y | Y | Y | N |
| 12 Putnam | Y | Y | N | N | N | Y |
| 13 Harris | Y | Y | N | N | N | Y |
| 14 Mack | Y | Y | N | N | N | Y |
| 15 Weldon | Y | Y | N | N | N | Y |
| 16 Foley | Y | Y | N | N | N | Y |
| 17 Meek | Y | N | Y | Y | Y | N |
| 18 Ros-Lehtinen | ? | Y | N | N | N | N |
| 19 Wexler | Y | N | Y | Y | Y | N |
| 20 Wasserman-Schultz | Y | N | Y | Y | Y | N |
| 21 Diaz-Balart, L. | Y | Y | N | N | N | N |
| 22 Shaw | Y | Y | N | N | N | Y |
| 23 Hastings | Y | N | Y | Y | Y | N |
| 24 Feeney | ? | ? | ? | ? | ? | ? |
| 25 Diaz-Balart, M. | Y | Y | Y | N | N | N |
| **GEORGIA** | | | | | | |
| 1 Kingston | Y | Y | N | N | N | Y |
| 2 Bishop | Y | N | Y | N | N | Y |
| 3 Marshall | Y | N | N | N | N | Y |
| 4 McKinney | Y | N | Y | Y | Y | N |
| 5 Lewis | Y | N | Y | Y | Y | N |
| 6 Price | Y | Y | N | N | N | Y |
| 7 Linder | Y | Y | N | N | N | Y |
| 8 Westmoreland | Y | Y | N | N | N | Y |
| 9 Norwood | Y | Y | N | N | N | Y |
| 10 Deal | Y | Y | N | N | N | Y |
| 11 Gingrey | Y | Y | N | N | N | Y |
| 12 Barrow | Y | N | N | N | N | Y |
| 13 Scott | Y | N | Y | Y | Y | N |
| **HAWAII** | | | | | | |
| 1 Abercrombie | Y | N | Y | Y | Y | N |
| 2 Case | Y | N | N | Y | N | Y |
| **IDAHO** | | | | | | |
| 1 Otter | Y | Y | N | N | N | Y |
| 2 Simpson | Y | Y | N | N | N | Y |
| **ILLINOIS** | | | | | | |
| 1 Rush | Y | N | Y | Y | Y | N |
| 2 Jackson | Y | N | Y | Y | Y | N |
| 3 Lipinski | Y | N | Y | Y | Y | N |
| 4 Gutierrez | Y | N | Y | Y | Y | N |
| 5 Emanuel | Y | N | Y | Y | Y | N |
| 6 Hyde | Y | Y | N | N | N | Y |
| 7 Davis | Y | N | Y | Y | Y | N |
| 8 Bean | Y | N | Y | N | Y | Y |
| 9 Schakowsky | Y | N | Y | Y | Y | N |
| 10 Kirk | Y | Y | N | N | N | Y |
| 11 Weller | Y | Y | N | N | N | Y |
| 12 Costello | Y | N | Y | Y | Y | Y |

**KEY**   Republicans   Democrats   *Independents*

| | | | |
|---|---|---|---|
| Y | Voted for (yea) | X | Paired against |
| # | Paired for | - | Announced against |
| + | Announced for | P | Voted "present" |
| N | Voted against (nay) | | |
| C | Voted "present" to avoid possible conflict of interest | | |
| ? | Did not vote or otherwise make a position known | | |

| | 26 | 27 | 28 | 29 | 30 | 31 |
|---|---|---|---|---|---|---|
| 13 **Biggert** | Y | Y | N | N | N | Y |
| 14 **Hastert** | | | | | | |
| 15 **Johnson** | Y | Y | Y | Y | N | Y |
| 16 **Manzullo** | Y | Y | N | N | N | Y |
| 17 Evans | Y | N | Y | Y | Y | N |
| 18 **LaHood** | Y | Y | N | N | N | Y |
| 19 **Shimkus** | Y | Y | N | N | N | Y |
| **INDIANA** | | | | | | |
| 1 Visclosky | Y | N | Y | Y | Y | N |
| 2 **Chocola** | Y | Y | N | N | N | Y |
| 3 **Souder** | Y | Y | N | N | N | Y |
| 4 **Buyer** | Y | Y | N | N | N | Y |
| 5 **Burton** | Y | Y | N | N | N | Y |
| 6 **Pence** | Y | Y | N | N | N | Y |
| 7 Carson | Y | N | Y | Y | Y | N |
| 8 **Hostettler** | Y | Y | N | N | N | Y |
| 9 **Sodrel** | Y | Y | N | N | N | Y |
| **IOWA** | | | | | | |
| 1 **Nussle** | Y | Y | N | N | N | Y |
| 2 **Leach** | Y | Y | Y | N | N | Y |
| 3 Boswell | Y | N | Y | Y | Y | N |
| 4 **Latham** | Y | Y | N | N | N | Y |
| 5 **King** | Y | Y | N | N | N | Y |
| **KANSAS** | | | | | | |
| 1 **Moran** | Y | Y | N | N | N | Y |
| 2 **Ryun** | Y | Y | N | N | N | Y |
| 3 Moore | Y | N | Y | Y | Y | N |
| 4 **Tiahrt** | Y | Y | N | N | N | Y |
| **KENTUCKY** | | | | | | |
| 1 **Whitfield** | Y | Y | N | N | N | Y |
| 2 **Lewis** | Y | Y | N | N | N | Y |
| 3 **Northup** | Y | Y | N | N | N | Y |
| 4 **Davis** | Y | Y | N | N | N | Y |
| 5 **Rogers** | Y | Y | N | N | N | Y |
| 6 Chandler | Y | N | N | N | Y | Y |
| **LOUISIANA** | | | | | | |
| 1 **Jindal** | Y | Y | N | N | N | Y |
| 2 Jefferson | Y | N | N | Y | Y | N |
| 3 Melancon | Y | N | N | N | Y | Y |
| 4 **McCrery** | Y | Y | N | N | N | Y |
| 5 **Alexander** | Y | Y | N | N | N | Y |
| 6 **Baker** | Y | Y | N | N | N | Y |
| 7 **Boustany** | Y | Y | N | N | N | Y |
| **MAINE** | | | | | | |
| 1 Allen | Y | N | Y | Y | Y | N |
| 2 Michaud | Y | N | Y | Y | Y | N |
| **MARYLAND** | | | | | | |
| 1 **Gilchrest** | Y | Y | N | N | N | Y |
| 2 Ruppersberger | Y | N | Y | Y | Y | N |
| 3 Cardin | Y | N | Y | Y | Y | N |
| 4 Wynn | Y | N | Y | Y | Y | N |
| 5 Hoyer | Y | N | Y | Y | Y | N |
| 6 **Bartlett** | Y | Y | Y | N | N | ? |
| 7 Cummings | Y | N | Y | Y | Y | N |
| 8 Van Hollen | Y | N | Y | Y | Y | N |
| **MASSACHUSETTS** | | | | | | |
| 1 Olver | Y | N | Y | Y | Y | N |
| 2 Neal | Y | N | Y | Y | Y | N |
| 3 McGovern | Y | N | Y | Y | Y | N |
| 4 Frank | Y | N | Y | Y | Y | N |
| 5 Meehan | Y | N | Y | Y | Y | N |
| 6 Tierney | Y | N | Y | Y | Y | N |
| 7 Markey | Y | N | Y | Y | Y | N |
| 8 Capuano | Y | N | Y | Y | Y | N |
| 9 Lynch | Y | N | Y | Y | Y | N |
| 10 Delahunt | Y | N | Y | Y | Y | N |
| **MICHIGAN** | | | | | | |
| 1 Stupak | ? | ? | ? | ? | ? | ? |
| 2 **Hoekstra** | Y | Y | N | N | N | Y |
| 3 **Ehlers** | Y | Y | N | Y | N | Y |
| 4 **Camp** | Y | Y | N | N | N | Y |
| 5 Kildee | Y | N | Y | Y | Y | N |
| 6 **Upton** | Y | Y | N | N | N | Y |
| 7 **Schwarz** | Y | Y | N | N | N | Y |
| 8 **Rogers** | Y | Y | N | N | N | Y |
| 9 **Knollenberg** | Y | Y | N | N | N | Y |
| 10 **Miller** | Y | Y | N | N | N | Y |
| 11 **McCotter** | Y | Y | N | N | N | Y |
| 12 Levin | Y | N | Y | Y | Y | N |
| 13 Kilpatrick | Y | N | Y | Y | Y | N |
| 14 Conyers | Y | N | Y | Y | Y | N |
| 15 Dingell | Y | N | Y | Y | Y | N |
| **MINNESOTA** | | | | | | |
| 1 **Gutknecht** | Y | Y | N | N | N | Y |
| 2 **Kline** | Y | Y | N | N | N | Y |
| 3 **Ramstad** | Y | Y | N | N | N | Y |
| 4 McCollum | Y | N | Y | Y | Y | N |
| 5 Sabo | Y | N | Y | Y | Y | N |
| 6 **Kennedy** | Y | Y | N | N | N | Y |
| 7 Peterson | Y | N | N | Y | Y | Y |
| 8 Oberstar | Y | N | Y | Y | Y | N |
| **MISSISSIPPI** | | | | | | |
| 1 **Wicker** | Y | Y | N | N | N | Y |
| 2 Thompson | Y | N | Y | Y | Y | N |
| 3 **Pickering** | Y | Y | ? | N | N | Y |
| 4 Taylor | Y | N | N | N | Y | Y |
| **MISSOURI** | | | | | | |
| 1 Clay | Y | N | Y | Y | Y | N |
| 2 **Akin** | Y | Y | N | N | N | Y |
| 3 Carnahan | Y | N | Y | Y | Y | N |
| 4 Skelton | Y | N | N | Y | Y | Y |
| 5 Cleaver | Y | N | Y | Y | Y | N |
| 6 **Graves** | Y | Y | N | N | N | Y |
| 7 **Blunt** | Y | Y | N | N | N | Y |
| 8 **Emerson** | Y | Y | N | N | N | Y |
| 9 **Hulshof** | Y | Y | N | N | N | Y |
| **MONTANA** | | | | | | |
| AL **Rehberg** | Y | Y | N | N | N | Y |
| **NEBRASKA** | | | | | | |
| 1 **Fortenberry** | Y | Y | N | N | N | Y |
| 2 **Terry** | Y | Y | N | N | N | Y |
| 3 **Osborne** | Y | Y | N | N | N | Y |
| **NEVADA** | | | | | | |
| 1 Berkley | Y | N | Y | Y | Y | N |
| 2 **Gibbons** | Y | Y | N | N | N | Y |
| 3 **Porter** | Y | Y | N | N | N | Y |
| **NEW HAMPSHIRE** | | | | | | |
| 1 **Bradley** | Y | Y | N | N | N | Y |
| 2 **Bass** | Y | Y | – | N | N | Y |
| **NEW JERSEY** | | | | | | |
| 1 Andrews | Y | N | Y | Y | Y | N |
| 2 **LoBiondo** | Y | Y | N | Y | N | Y |
| 3 **Saxton** | Y | Y | N | Y | N | Y |
| 4 **Smith** | Y | Y | Y | N | N | N |
| 5 **Garrett** | Y | Y | N | N | N | Y |
| 6 Pallone | Y | N | Y | Y | Y | N |
| 7 **Ferguson** | Y | Y | N | N | N | + |
| 8 Pascrell | Y | N | Y | Y | Y | N |
| 9 Rothman | Y | N | Y | Y | Y | N |
| 10 Payne | Y | N | Y | Y | Y | N |
| 11 **Frelinghuysen** | Y | Y | N | N | N | Y |
| 12 Holt | Y | N | Y | Y | Y | N |
| 13 Menendez | Y | N | Y | Y | Y | N |
| **NEW MEXICO** | | | | | | |
| 1 **Wilson** | Y | Y | Y | Y | N | N |
| 2 **Pearce** | Y | Y | N | N | N | Y |
| 3 Udall | Y | N | Y | Y | Y | N |
| **NEW YORK** | | | | | | |
| 1 Bishop | Y | N | Y | Y | Y | N |
| 2 Israel | Y | N | Y | Y | Y | N |
| 3 **King** | Y | Y | N | N | N | Y |
| 4 McCarthy | Y | N | Y | Y | Y | N |
| 5 Ackerman | Y | N | Y | Y | Y | N |
| 6 Meeks | Y | N | Y | Y | Y | N |
| 7 Crowley | Y | N | Y | Y | Y | N |
| 8 Nadler | Y | N | Y | Y | Y | N |
| 9 Weiner | Y | N | Y | ? | Y | N |
| 10 Towns | Y | N | Y | Y | Y | N |
| 11 Owens | Y | N | Y | Y | Y | N |
| 12 Velázquez | Y | N | Y | Y | Y | N |
| 13 **Fossella** | Y | Y | N | N | N | Y |
| 14 Maloney | Y | N | Y | Y | Y | N |
| 15 Rangel | Y | N | Y | Y | Y | N |
| 16 Serrano | Y | N | Y | Y | Y | N |
| 17 Engel | Y | N | Y | Y | Y | N |
| 18 Lowey | Y | N | Y | Y | Y | N |
| 19 **Kelly** | Y | Y | N | N | N | Y |
| 20 **Sweeney** | Y | Y | N | N | N | Y |
| 21 McNulty | Y | N | Y | N | Y | Y |
| 22 Hinchey | ? | ? | ? | ? | ? | ? |
| 23 **McHugh** | ? | Y | N | N | N | Y |
| 24 **Boehlert** | Y | Y | N | Y | N | Y |
| 25 **Walsh** | Y | Y | Y | N | N | Y |
| 26 **Reynolds** | Y | Y | N | N | N | Y |
| 27 Higgins | Y | N | Y | Y | Y | N |
| 28 Slaughter | Y | N | Y | Y | Y | N |
| 29 **Kuhl** | Y | Y | N | N | N | Y |
| **NORTH CAROLINA** | | | | | | |
| 1 Butterfield | Y | N | Y | Y | Y | Y |
| 2 Etheridge | Y | N | Y | Y | Y | N |
| 3 **Jones** | Y | Y | N | N | N | Y |
| 4 Price | Y | N | Y | Y | Y | N |
| 5 **Foxx** | Y | Y | N | N | N | Y |
| 6 **Coble** | Y | Y | N | N | N | Y |
| 7 McIntyre | Y | N | Y | N | Y | Y |
| 8 **Hayes** | Y | Y | N | N | N | Y |
| 9 **Myrick** | Y | Y | N | N | N | Y |
| 10 **McHenry** | Y | Y | N | N | N | Y |
| 11 **Taylor** | Y | Y | N | N | N | Y |
| 12 Watt | Y | N | Y | Y | Y | N |
| 13 Miller | Y | N | Y | Y | Y | N |
| **NORTH DAKOTA** | | | | | | |
| AL Pomeroy | Y | N | Y | Y | Y | N |
| **OHIO** | | | | | | |
| 1 **Chabot** | Y | Y | N | N | N | Y |
| 2 **Portman** | Y | Y | N | N | N | Y |
| 3 **Turner** | Y | Y | N | N | N | Y |
| 4 **Oxley** | Y | Y | ? | ? | N | Y |
| 5 **Gillmor** | Y | Y | N | N | N | Y |
| 6 Strickland | Y | N | Y | Y | Y | Y |
| 7 **Hobson** | Y | Y | N | N | N | Y |
| 8 **Boehner** | Y | Y | N | N | N | Y |
| 9 Kaptur | Y | N | Y | Y | Y | N |
| 10 Kucinich | ? | N | Y | Y | Y | N |
| 11 Jones | Y | N | Y | Y | Y | N |
| 12 **Tiberi** | Y | Y | N | N | N | Y |
| 13 Brown | Y | N | Y | Y | Y | N |
| 14 **LaTourette** | Y | Y | N | N | N | Y |
| 15 **Pryce** | Y | Y | N | N | N | Y |
| 16 **Regula** | Y | Y | N | N | N | Y |
| 17 Ryan | Y | N | Y | Y | Y | Y |
| 18 **Ney** | Y | Y | N | N | N | Y |
| **OKLAHOMA** | | | | | | |
| 1 **Sullivan** | Y | Y | N | N | N | Y |
| 2 Boren | Y | N | N | N | Y | Y |
| 3 **Lucas** | Y | Y | N | N | N | Y |
| 4 **Cole** | Y | Y | N | N | N | Y |
| 5 **Istook** | Y | Y | N | N | N | Y |
| **OREGON** | | | | | | |
| 1 Wu | Y | N | Y | Y | Y | N |
| 2 **Walden** | Y | Y | N | N | N | Y |
| 3 Blumenauer | Y | N | Y | Y | Y | N |
| 4 DeFazio | Y | N | Y | Y | Y | Y |
| 5 Hooley | Y | N | Y | Y | Y | Y |
| **PENNSYLVANIA** | | | | | | |
| 1 Brady | Y | N | Y | Y | Y | N |
| 2 Fattah | ? | N | Y | Y | Y | N |
| 3 **English** | Y | Y | N | N | N | Y |
| 4 **Hart** | Y | Y | N | N | N | Y |
| 5 **Peterson** | Y | Y | N | N | N | Y |
| 6 **Gerlach** | Y | Y | N | N | N | Y |
| 7 **Weldon** | Y | Y | N | N | N | Y |
| 8 **Fitzpatrick** | Y | Y | N | N | N | Y |
| 9 **Shuster** | Y | Y | N | N | N | Y |
| 10 **Sherwood** | Y | Y | N | N | N | Y |
| 11 Kanjorski | Y | N | Y | Y | Y | Y |
| 12 Murtha | Y | N | Y | Y | Y | N |
| 13 Schwartz | Y | N | Y | Y | Y | N |
| 14 Doyle | Y | N | Y | Y | Y | N |
| 15 **Dent** | Y | Y | N | N | N | Y |
| 16 **Pitts** | Y | Y | N | N | N | Y |
| 17 Holden | Y | N | N | N | Y | Y |
| 18 **Murphy** | Y | Y | N | N | N | Y |
| 19 **Platts** | Y | Y | N | N | N | Y |
| **RHODE ISLAND** | | | | | | |
| 1 Kennedy | Y | N | Y | Y | Y | N |
| 2 Langevin | Y | N | Y | Y | Y | N |
| **SOUTH CAROLINA** | | | | | | |
| 1 **Brown** | Y | Y | N | N | N | Y |
| 2 **Wilson** | Y | Y | N | N | N | Y |
| 3 **Barrett** | Y | Y | N | N | N | Y |
| 4 **Inglis** | Y | Y | N | N | N | Y |
| 5 Spratt | Y | N | Y | Y | Y | N |
| 6 Clyburn | Y | N | Y | Y | Y | N |
| **SOUTH DAKOTA** | | | | | | |
| AL Herseth | Y | N | Y | N | Y | Y |
| **TENNESSEE** | | | | | | |
| 1 **Jenkins** | Y | Y | N | N | N | Y |
| 2 **Duncan** | Y | Y | N | N | Y | Y |
| 3 **Wamp** | Y | Y | N | N | N | Y |
| 4 Davis | Y | N | N | N | N | Y |
| 5 Cooper | Y | N | N | N | Y | Y |
| 6 Gordon | Y | N | N | Y | Y | Y |
| 7 **Blackburn** | Y | Y | N | N | N | Y |
| 8 Tanner | Y | N | N | Y | Y | Y |
| 9 Ford | Y | N | N | Y | Y | Y |
| **TEXAS** | | | | | | |
| 1 **Gohmert** | Y | Y | N | N | N | Y |
| 2 **Poe** | Y | Y | N | N | N | Y |
| 3 **Johnson, S.** | Y | Y | N | N | N | Y |
| 4 **Hall** | Y | Y | N | N | N | Y |
| 5 **Hensarling** | Y | Y | N | N | N | Y |
| 6 **Barton** | Y | Y | N | N | N | Y |
| 7 **Culberson** | Y | Y | N | N | N | Y |
| 8 **Brady** | Y | Y | N | N | N | Y |
| 9 Green, A. | Y | N | Y | Y | Y | N |
| 10 **McCaul** | Y | Y | N | N | N | Y |
| 11 **Conaway** | Y | Y | N | N | N | Y |
| 12 **Granger** | Y | Y | N | N | N | Y |
| 13 **Thornberry** | Y | Y | N | N | N | Y |
| 14 **Paul** | Y | Y | N | Y | Y | N |
| 15 Hinojosa | + | – | + | + | + | – |
| 16 Reyes | Y | N | Y | N | Y | N |
| 17 Edwards | Y | N | N | Y | Y | Y |
| 18 Jackson-Lee | Y | N | Y | Y | Y | N |
| 19 **Neugebauer** | Y | Y | N | N | N | Y |
| 20 Gonzalez | Y | N | Y | Y | Y | N |
| 21 **Smith** | Y | Y | N | N | N | Y |
| 22 **DeLay** | Y | Y | N | N | N | Y |
| 23 **Bonilla** | Y | Y | N | N | N | Y |
| 24 **Marchant** | Y | Y | N | N | N | Y |
| 25 Doggett | Y | N | Y | Y | Y | N |
| 26 **Burgess** | Y | Y | N | N | N | Y |
| 27 Ortiz | Y | N | Y | Y | Y | N |
| 28 Cuellar | Y | N | Y | Y | Y | Y |
| 29 Green, G. | Y | N | ? | ? | ? | ? |
| 30 Johnson, E. | Y | N | Y | Y | Y | N |
| 31 **Carter** | Y | ? | – | – | – | + |
| 32 **Sessions** | Y | Y | N | N | N | Y |
| **UTAH** | | | | | | |
| 1 **Bishop** | Y | Y | N | N | N | Y |
| 2 Matheson | Y | N | N | N | Y | Y |
| 3 **Cannon** | Y | Y | N | N | N | Y |
| **VERMONT** | | | | | | |
| AL *Sanders* | Y | N | Y | Y | Y | N |
| **VIRGINIA** | | | | | | |
| 1 **Davis, J.** | Y | Y | N | N | N | Y |
| 2 **Drake** | Y | Y | N | N | N | Y |
| 3 Scott | Y | N | Y | Y | Y | N |
| 4 **Forbes** | Y | Y | N | N | N | Y |
| 5 **Goode** | Y | Y | N | N | N | Y |
| 6 **Goodlatte** | Y | Y | N | N | N | Y |
| 7 **Cantor** | Y | Y | N | N | N | Y |
| 8 Moran | Y | N | Y | Y | Y | N |
| 9 Boucher | Y | N | Y | N | Y | Y |
| 10 **Wolf** | Y | Y | N | N | N | Y |
| 11 **Davis, T.** | Y | Y | N | N | N | Y |
| **WASHINGTON** | | | | | | |
| 1 Inslee | Y | N | Y | Y | Y | N |
| 2 Larsen | Y | N | Y | Y | Y | N |
| 3 Baird | Y | N | Y | Y | Y | N |
| 4 **Hastings** | Y | Y | N | N | N | Y |
| 5 **McMorris** | Y | Y | N | N | N | Y |
| 6 Dicks | Y | N | Y | Y | Y | N |
| 7 McDermott | Y | N | Y | Y | Y | N |
| 8 **Reichert** | Y | Y | N | N | N | Y |
| 9 Smith | Y | N | Y | Y | Y | N |
| **WEST VIRGINIA** | | | | | | |
| 1 Mollohan | Y | N | Y | Y | Y | N |
| 2 **Capito** | Y | Y | N | N | N | Y |
| 3 Rahall | Y | N | Y | Y | Y | N |
| **WISCONSIN** | | | | | | |
| 1 **Ryan** | Y | Y | N | N | N | Y |
| 2 Baldwin | Y | N | Y | Y | Y | N |
| 3 Kind | Y | N | Y | Y | Y | N |
| 4 Moore | Y | N | Y | Y | Y | N |
| 5 **Sensenbrenner** | Y | Y | N | N | N | Y |
| 6 **Petri** | Y | Y | N | N | N | Y |
| 7 Obey | Y | N | Y | Y | Y | N |
| 8 **Green** | Y | Y | N | N | N | Y |
| **WYOMING** | | | | | | |
| AL **Cubin** | Y | Y | N | N | N | Y |

# IN THE HOUSE | By Vote Number

**32.** **H Con Res 25. Greensboro Four Tribute/Adoption.** Dent, R-Pa., motion to suspend the rules and adopt the concurrent resolution that would applaud the valor and courage of four African-American college freshmen, known as the "Greensboro Four," who challenged segregation in Greensboro, N.C., on Feb. 1, 1960. Motion agreed to 424-0: R 228-0; D 195-0 (ND 144-0, SD 51-0); I 1-0. A two-thirds majority of those present and voting (283 in this case) is required for adoption under suspension of the rules. Feb. 15, 2005.

**33.** **HR 324. Arthur Stacey Mastrapa Post Office/Passage.** Dent, R-Pa., motion to suspend the rules and pass the bill that would designate a post office in Altamonte Springs, Fla., for Arthur Stacey Mastrapa, a postal worker and Army Reservist killed in Iraq. Motion agreed to 420-0: R 228-0; D 191-0 (ND 140-0, SD 51-0); I 1-0. A two-thirds majority of those present and voting (280 in this case) is required for passage under suspension of the rules. Feb. 15, 2005.

**34.** **HR 310. Broadcast Indecency/Previous Question.** Capito, R-W.Va., motion to order the previous question (thus ending debate and possibility of amendment) on adoption of the rule (H Res 95) to provide for House floor consideration of the bill that would increase the maximum fines for sexually explicit or vulgar broadcast programming. Motion agreed to 230-198: R 229-0; D 1-197 (ND 1-146, SD 0-51); I 0-1. Subsequently, the rule was adopted by voice vote. Feb. 16, 2005.

**35.** **HR 310. Broadcast Indecency/Passage.** Passage of the bill that would increase to $500,000 per violation the maximum fines that the Federal Communications Commission (FCC) could levy on broadcasters for airing indecent, obscene or profane material. The bill would require the FCC to consider revoking a license after three or more indecency-related offenses. Passed 389-38: R 228-1; D 161-36 (ND 114-32, SD 47-4); I 0-1. A "yea" was a vote in support of the president's position. Feb. 16, 2005.

**36** **S 5. Class Action Overhaul/Substitute.** Conyers, D-Mich., substitute amendment to the bill that would give federal courts jurisdiction over certain class action cases. It would allow for several exemptions and would prohibit federal district courts from denying certification of a class action suit if the laws of more than one state apply. Rejected 178-247: R 0-228; D 177-19 (ND 140-5, SD 37-14); I 1-0. Feb. 17, 2005.

**37.** **S 5. Class Action Overhaul/Motion to Commit.** Brown, D-Ohio, motion to commit the bill to the Judiciary Committee with instructions to add language specifying that the term "class action" does not include suits arising from the use of the drug Vioxx. Motion rejected 175-249: R 0-227; D 174-22 (ND 138-7, SD 36-15); I 1-0. Feb. 17, 2005.

**38.** **S 5. Class Action Overhaul/Passage.** Passage of the bill that would give federal courts jurisdiction over class action cases involving at least 100 plaintiffs if at least $5 million was at stake and two-thirds of the plaintiffs lived in different states. It would require judges to review all non-cash settlements and limit attorney's fees in such settlements. Passed 279-149: R 229-1; D 50-147 (ND 27-119, SD 23-28); I 0-1. A "yea" was a vote in support of the president's position. Feb. 17, 2005.

**39.** **H Res 91. Rafik Hariri Tribute/Adoption.** Issa, R-Calif., motion to suspend the rules and adopt the resolution that would condemn the killing of the former Lebanese prime minister in Beirut on Feb. 14, 2005. A two-thirds majority of those present and voting (273 in this case) is required for adoption under suspension of the rules. Motion agreed to 409-0: R 222-0; D 187-0 (ND 137-0, SD 50-0); I 0-0. Feb. 17, 2005.

| | 32 | 33 | 34 | 35 | 36 | 37 | 38 | 39 |
|---|---|---|---|---|---|---|---|---|
| **ALABAMA** | | | | | | | | |
| 1 Bonner | Y | Y | Y | Y | N | N | Y | Y |
| 2 Everett | Y | Y | Y | Y | N | N | Y | Y |
| 3 Rogers | Y | Y | Y | Y | N | N | Y | Y |
| 4 Aderholt | Y | Y | Y | Y | N | N | Y | Y |
| 5 Cramer | Y | Y | N | Y | N | N | Y | Y |
| 6 Bachus | Y | Y | Y | Y | N | N | Y | Y |
| 7 Davis | Y | Y | N | Y | Y | N | Y | Y |
| **ALASKA** | | | | | | | | |
| AL Young | Y | Y | Y | Y | N | N | Y | Y |
| **ARIZONA** | | | | | | | | |
| 1 Renzi | Y | Y | Y | Y | N | N | Y | Y |
| 2 Franks | Y | Y | Y | Y | N | N | Y | Y |
| 3 Shadegg | Y | Y | Y | Y | N | ? | Y | Y |
| 4 Pastor | Y | Y | N | Y | Y | N | Y | Y |
| 5 Hayworth | Y | Y | Y | Y | N | N | Y | Y |
| 6 Flake | Y | Y | Y | Y | N | N | Y | Y |
| 7 Grijalva | Y | Y | N | N | Y | Y | N | Y |
| 8 Kolbe | Y | Y | Y | Y | N | N | Y | Y |
| **ARKANSAS** | | | | | | | | |
| 1 Berry | Y | Y | N | Y | Y | Y | Y | Y |
| 2 Snyder | Y | Y | N | Y | Y | Y | Y | Y |
| 3 Boozman | Y | Y | Y | Y | N | N | Y | Y |
| 4 Ross | Y | Y | N | Y | N | Y | N | Y |
| **CALIFORNIA** | | | | | | | | |
| 1 Thompson | Y | Y | N | Y | Y | Y | N | Y |
| 2 Herger | Y | Y | Y | Y | N | N | Y | Y |
| 3 Lungren | Y | Y | Y | Y | N | N | Y | Y |
| 4 Doolittle | Y | Y | Y | Y | N | N | N | Y |
| 5 Vacant | | | | | | | | |
| 6 Woolsey | Y | Y | N | N | Y | Y | N | Y |
| 7 Miller, George | Y | Y | N | Y | Y | Y | N | Y |
| 8 Pelosi | Y | Y | N | Y | Y | Y | N | Y |
| 9 Lee | Y | Y | N | N | Y | Y | N | Y |
| 10 Tauscher | Y | Y | N | Y | Y | Y | Y | Y |
| 11 Pombo | Y | Y | Y | Y | N | N | Y | Y |
| 12 Lantos | Y | Y | N | Y | Y | Y | N | Y |
| 13 Stark | ? | ? | N | N | Y | Y | N | Y |
| 14 Eshoo | ? | ? | ? | ? | ? | ? | ? | ? |
| 15 Honda | Y | Y | N | Y | Y | Y | N | Y |
| 16 Lofgren | Y | Y | N | N | Y | Y | N | Y |
| 17 Farr | Y | Y | N | N | ? | ? | ? | Y |
| 18 Cardoza | Y | Y | N | Y | Y | Y | N | Y |
| 19 Radanovich | Y | Y | Y | Y | N | N | Y | ? |
| 20 Costa | Y | Y | N | Y | Y | Y | Y | Y |
| 21 Nunes | Y | Y | Y | Y | N | N | Y | Y |
| 22 Thomas | Y | Y | Y | Y | ? | N | Y | Y |
| 23 Capps | Y | Y | N | Y | Y | Y | N | Y |
| 24 Gallegly | Y | Y | Y | Y | N | Y | Y | ? |
| 25 McKeon | Y | Y | Y | Y | N | N | Y | Y |
| 26 Dreier | Y | Y | Y | Y | N | Y | Y | Y |
| 27 Sherman | Y | Y | N | N | Y | Y | N | Y |
| 28 Berman | Y | Y | N | N | Y | Y | N | Y |
| 29 Schiff | Y | Y | N | Y | Y | Y | N | Y |
| 30 Waxman | Y | Y | N | Y | Y | Y | N | Y |
| 31 Becerra | Y | Y | N | Y | Y | Y | N | Y |
| 32 Solis | Y | Y | N | Y | Y | Y | N | Y |
| 33 Watson | Y | Y | N | N | Y | Y | N | Y |
| 34 Roybal-Allard | Y | Y | N | Y | Y | Y | N | Y |
| 35 Waters | ? | ? | N | N | Y | Y | N | ? |
| 36 Harman | Y | Y | N | N | Y | Y | Y | Y |
| 37 Millender-McD. | Y | Y | N | Y | Y | Y | N | Y |
| 38 Napolitano | Y | Y | N | Y | Y | Y | N | Y |
| 39 Sánchez, Linda | Y | Y | N | N | Y | Y | N | Y |
| 40 Royce | Y | Y | Y | Y | N | N | Y | Y |
| 41 Lewis | Y | Y | Y | Y | N | N | Y | Y |
| 42 Miller, Gary | Y | Y | Y | Y | N | N | Y | Y |
| 43 Baca | Y | Y | N | Y | Y | Y | N | Y |
| 44 Calvert | Y | Y | Y | Y | N | N | Y | Y |
| 45 Bono | Y | Y | Y | Y | N | N | Y | Y |
| 46 Rohrabacher | Y | Y | Y | Y | N | N | Y | Y |
| 47 Sanchez, Loretta | Y | Y | N | Y | Y | Y | N | ? |
| 48 Cox | Y | Y | Y | Y | N | ? | Y | Y |
| 49 Issa | Y | Y | Y | Y | N | N | Y | Y |
| 50 Cunningham | Y | Y | Y | Y | N | N | Y | Y |
| 51 Filner | Y | Y | N | Y | Y | Y | N | Y |
| 52 Hunter | Y | Y | Y | Y | N | N | Y | Y |
| 53 Davis | Y | Y | N | Y | Y | Y | N | Y |
| **COLORADO** | | | | | | | | |
| 1 DeGette | Y | ? | N | Y | Y | Y | N | Y |
| 2 Udall | Y | Y | N | Y | Y | Y | N | Y |
| 3 Salazar | Y | Y | N | Y | Y | Y | N | Y |
| 4 Musgrave | Y | Y | Y | Y | N | N | Y | Y |
| 5 Hefley | Y | Y | Y | Y | N | N | Y | Y |
| 6 Tancredo | Y | Y | Y | Y | N | N | Y | Y |
| 7 Beauprez | Y | Y | Y | Y | N | N | Y | Y |
| **CONNECTICUT** | | | | | | | | |
| 1 Larson | Y | Y | N | Y | Y | Y | N | Y |
| 2 Simmons | Y | Y | Y | Y | N | N | Y | Y |
| 3 DeLauro | Y | Y | N | Y | Y | Y | N | Y |
| 4 Shays | Y | Y | Y | Y | N | N | Y | Y |
| 5 Johnson | Y | Y | Y | Y | N | N | Y | Y |
| **DELAWARE** | | | | | | | | |
| AL Castle | Y | Y | Y | Y | N | N | Y | Y |
| **FLORIDA** | | | | | | | | |
| 1 Miller | ? | ? | Y | Y | N | N | Y | Y |
| 2 Boyd | Y | Y | N | Y | N | N | Y | Y |
| 3 Brown | Y | Y | N | Y | Y | N | Y | Y |
| 4 Crenshaw | Y | Y | Y | Y | N | N | Y | Y |
| 5 Brown-Waite | Y | Y | Y | Y | N | N | Y | Y |
| 6 Stearns | Y | Y | Y | Y | N | N | Y | Y |
| 7 Mica | Y | Y | Y | Y | N | N | Y | Y |
| 8 Keller | Y | Y | Y | Y | N | N | Y | Y |
| 9 Bilirakis | Y | Y | Y | Y | N | N | Y | Y |
| 10 Young | Y | Y | Y | ? | N | N | Y | Y |
| 11 Davis | Y | Y | N | Y | Y | N | Y | Y |
| 12 Putnam | Y | Y | Y | Y | N | N | Y | Y |
| 13 Harris | Y | Y | Y | Y | N | N | Y | Y |
| 14 Mack | Y | Y | Y | Y | N | N | Y | Y |
| 15 Weldon | Y | Y | Y | Y | N | N | Y | Y |
| 16 Foley | Y | Y | Y | Y | N | N | Y | Y |
| 17 Meek | Y | Y | N | Y | Y | Y | N | Y |
| 18 Ros-Lehtinen | Y | Y | Y | Y | N | N | Y | Y |
| 19 Wexler | Y | Y | N | Y | Y | Y | N | Y |
| 20 Wasserman-Schultz | Y | Y | N | N | Y | Y | N | Y |
| 21 Diaz-Balart, L. | Y | Y | Y | Y | N | N | Y | Y |
| 22 Shaw | Y | Y | Y | Y | N | N | Y | Y |
| 23 Hastings | Y | Y | N | N | Y | Y | N | Y |
| 24 Feeney | Y | Y | Y | Y | N | N | Y | ? |
| 25 Diaz-Balart, M. | Y | Y | Y | Y | N | N | Y | Y |
| **GEORGIA** | | | | | | | | |
| 1 Kingston | Y | Y | Y | Y | N | N | Y | Y |
| 2 Bishop | Y | Y | N | Y | N | Y | N | Y |
| 3 Marshall | Y | Y | N | Y | N | Y | Y | Y |
| 4 McKinney | Y | Y | N | Y | Y | Y | N | Y |
| 5 Lewis | Y | Y | N | N | Y | Y | N | Y |
| 6 Price | Y | Y | Y | Y | N | N | Y | Y |
| 7 Linder | Y | Y | Y | Y | N | N | Y | Y |
| 8 Westmoreland | Y | Y | Y | Y | N | N | Y | Y |
| 9 Norwood | Y | Y | Y | Y | N | N | Y | Y |
| 10 Deal | Y | Y | Y | Y | N | N | Y | Y |
| 11 Gingrey | Y | Y | Y | Y | N | N | Y | Y |
| 12 Barrow | Y | Y | N | Y | N | Y | Y | Y |
| 13 Scott | Y | Y | N | N | N | N | Y | Y |
| **HAWAII** | | | | | | | | |
| 1 Abercrombie | Y | Y | N | N | Y | Y | N | Y |
| 2 Case | Y | Y | N | N | N | N | Y | Y |
| **IDAHO** | | | | | | | | |
| 1 Otter | Y | Y | Y | Y | N | N | Y | Y |
| 2 Simpson | Y | Y | Y | Y | N | N | Y | Y |
| **ILLINOIS** | | | | | | | | |
| 1 Rush | Y | Y | N | Y | Y | Y | N | Y |
| 2 Jackson | Y | Y | N | Y | Y | Y | N | Y |
| 3 Lipinski | Y | Y | N | Y | Y | Y | N | Y |
| 4 Gutierrez | Y | Y | N | Y | Y | Y | N | Y |
| 5 Emanuel | Y | Y | N | Y | Y | Y | Y | Y |
| 6 Hyde | Y | Y | Y | Y | N | N | Y | Y |
| 7 Davis | Y | Y | N | Y | ? | Y | N | Y |
| 8 Bean | Y | Y | N | Y | N | Y | Y | Y |
| 9 Schakowsky | Y | Y | N | N | Y | Y | N | Y |
| 10 Kirk | Y | Y | Y | Y | N | N | Y | ? |
| 11 Weller | Y | Y | Y | Y | N | N | Y | Y |
| 12 Costello | Y | Y | N | Y | Y | Y | N | Y |

| KEY | Republicans | Democrats | Independents |
|---|---|---|---|
| **Y** Voted for (yea) | **X** Paired against | | **C** Voted "present" to avoid possible conflict of interest |
| **#** Paired for | **–** Announced against | | |
| **+** Announced for | **P** Voted "present" | | **?** Did not vote or otherwise make a position known |
| **N** Voted against (nay) | | | |

| | 32 | 33 | 34 | 35 | 36 | 37 | 38 | 39 |
|---|---|---|---|---|---|---|---|---|
| 13 **Biggert** | Y | Y | Y | Y | N | N | Y | Y |
| 14 **Hastert** | | | | | N | N | Y | |
| 15 **Johnson** | Y | Y | Y | Y | N | N | Y | Y |
| 16 **Manzullo** | Y | Y | Y | Y | N | N | Y | Y |
| 17 Evans | Y | Y | N | Y | Y | Y | N | Y |
| 18 **LaHood** | Y | Y | Y | Y | N | N | Y | Y |
| 19 **Shimkus** | Y | Y | Y | Y | N | N | Y | Y |
| INDIANA | | | | | | | | |
| 1 Visclosky | Y | Y | N | Y | Y | Y | N | Y |
| 2 **Chocola** | Y | Y | Y | Y | N | N | Y | Y |
| 3 **Souder** | Y | Y | Y | Y | N | N | Y | Y |
| 4 **Buyer** | Y | Y | Y | Y | N | ? | Y | Y |
| 5 **Burton** | Y | Y | Y | Y | N | N | Y | Y |
| 6 **Pence** | Y | Y | Y | Y | N | N | Y | Y |
| 7 Carson | Y | Y | N | Y | Y | Y | N | Y |
| 8 **Hostettler** | Y | Y | Y | Y | N | N | Y | Y |
| 9 **Sodrel** | Y | Y | Y | Y | N | N | Y | Y |
| IOWA | | | | | | | | |
| 1 **Nussle** | Y | Y | Y | Y | N | N | Y | Y |
| 2 **Leach** | Y | Y | Y | Y | N | N | Y | Y |
| 3 Boswell | Y | Y | N | Y | Y | Y | N | Y |
| 4 **Latham** | Y | Y | Y | Y | N | N | Y | Y |
| 5 **King** | Y | Y | Y | Y | N | N | Y | Y |
| KANSAS | | | | | | | | |
| 1 **Moran** | Y | Y | Y | Y | N | N | Y | Y |
| 2 **Ryun** | Y | Y | Y | Y | N | N | Y | Y |
| 3 Moore | Y | Y | N | Y | Y | Y | Y | Y |
| 4 **Tiahrt** | Y | Y | Y | Y | N | N | Y | Y |
| KENTUCKY | | | | | | | | |
| 1 **Whitfield** | Y | Y | Y | Y | N | N | Y | Y |
| 2 **Lewis** | Y | Y | Y | Y | N | N | Y | Y |
| 3 **Northup** | Y | Y | Y | Y | N | N | Y | Y |
| 4 **Davis** | Y | Y | Y | Y | N | N | Y | Y |
| 5 **Rogers** | Y | Y | Y | Y | N | N | Y | Y |
| 6 Chandler | Y | Y | N | Y | Y | Y | Y | Y |
| LOUISIANA | | | | | | | | |
| 1 **Jindal** | Y | Y | Y | Y | N | N | Y | Y |
| 2 Jefferson | Y | Y | N | Y | Y | Y | N | Y |
| 3 Melancon | Y | Y | N | Y | Y | Y | Y | Y |
| 4 **McCrery** | Y | Y | Y | Y | N | N | Y | Y |
| 5 **Alexander** | Y | Y | Y | Y | N | N | Y | Y |
| 6 **Baker** | Y | Y | Y | Y | N | N | ? | ? |
| 7 **Boustany** | Y | Y | Y | Y | N | N | Y | Y |
| MAINE | | | | | | | | |
| 1 Allen | Y | Y | N | Y | Y | Y | N | Y |
| 2 Michaud | Y | Y | N | Y | Y | Y | Y | Y |
| MARYLAND | | | | | | | | |
| 1 **Gilchrest** | Y | Y | Y | Y | N | N | Y | Y |
| 2 Ruppersberger | Y | Y | N | Y | Y | Y | Y | ? |
| 3 Cardin | Y | Y | N | Y | Y | Y | N | Y |
| 4 Wynn | Y | Y | ? | ? | Y | Y | N | Y |
| 5 Hoyer | Y | Y | N | Y | Y | Y | N | Y |
| 6 **Bartlett** | Y | Y | Y | Y | N | N | Y | Y |
| 7 Cummings | Y | Y | N | Y | Y | Y | N | Y |
| 8 Van Hollen | Y | Y | N | Y | Y | Y | N | Y |
| MASSACHUSETTS | | | | | | | | |
| 1 Olver | Y | Y | N | Y | Y | Y | N | Y |
| 2 Neal | Y | Y | N | Y | Y | Y | N | Y |
| 3 McGovern | Y | Y | N | Y | Y | Y | N | Y |
| 4 Frank | Y | Y | N | N | Y | Y | N | Y |
| 5 Meehan | Y | Y | N | Y | Y | Y | N | Y |
| 6 Tierney | Y | Y | N | Y | Y | Y | N | Y |
| 7 Markey | Y | Y | N | Y | Y | Y | N | Y |
| 8 Capuano | Y | Y | N | Y | Y | Y | N | Y |
| 9 Lynch | Y | Y | N | Y | Y | Y | N | Y |
| 10 Delahunt | Y | Y | N | N | Y | Y | N | Y |
| MICHIGAN | | | | | | | | |
| 1 Stupak | ? | ? | ? | ? | ? | ? | ? | ? |
| 2 **Hoekstra** | Y | Y | Y | Y | N | N | Y | Y |
| 3 **Ehlers** | Y | Y | Y | Y | N | N | Y | Y |
| 4 **Camp** | Y | Y | Y | Y | N | N | Y | Y |
| 5 Kildee | Y | Y | N | Y | Y | Y | N | Y |
| 6 **Upton** | Y | Y | Y | Y | N | N | Y | Y |
| 7 **Schwarz** | Y | Y | Y | Y | N | N | Y | Y |
| 8 **Rogers** | Y | Y | Y | Y | N | N | Y | Y |
| 9 **Knollenberg** | Y | Y | Y | Y | N | N | Y | Y |
| 10 **Miller** | Y | Y | Y | Y | N | N | Y | Y |
| 11 **McCotter** | Y | Y | Y | Y | N | N | Y | Y |
| 12 Levin | Y | Y | N | Y | Y | Y | N | Y |
| 13 Kilpatrick | Y | Y | N | Y | Y | Y | N | Y |
| 14 Conyers | Y | Y | N | N | Y | Y | N | Y |
| 15 Dingell | Y | Y | Y | Y | Y | Y | N | Y |
| MINNESOTA | | | | | | | | |
| 1 **Gutknecht** | Y | Y | Y | Y | N | N | Y | Y |
| 2 **Kline** | Y | Y | Y | Y | N | N | Y | Y |
| 3 **Ramstad** | Y | Y | Y | Y | N | N | Y | Y |
| 4 McCollum | Y | Y | N | Y | Y | Y | N | Y |
| 5 Sabo | Y | Y | N | N | Y | Y | N | ? |
| 6 **Kennedy** | Y | Y | Y | Y | N | N | Y | Y |
| 7 Peterson | Y | Y | N | Y | N | N | Y | Y |
| 8 Oberstar | Y | Y | N | Y | Y | Y | N | Y |
| MISSISSIPPI | | | | | | | | |
| 1 **Wicker** | Y | Y | Y | Y | N | N | Y | Y |
| 2 Thompson | Y | Y | N | Y | Y | Y | N | Y |
| 3 **Pickering** | Y | Y | Y | Y | N | N | Y | Y |
| 4 Taylor | Y | Y | N | Y | N | Y | Y | Y |
| MISSOURI | | | | | | | | |
| 1 Clay | Y | Y | N | N | Y | Y | N | Y |
| 2 **Akin** | Y | Y | Y | Y | N | N | Y | Y |
| 3 Carnahan | Y | Y | N | Y | Y | Y | N | Y |
| 4 Skelton | Y | Y | N | Y | Y | Y | N | ? |
| 5 Cleaver | Y | Y | N | Y | Y | Y | N | Y |
| 6 **Graves** | Y | Y | Y | Y | N | N | Y | Y |
| 7 **Blunt** | Y | Y | Y | Y | N | N | Y | Y |
| 8 **Emerson** | Y | Y | Y | Y | N | N | Y | Y |
| 9 **Hulshof** | ? | ? | Y | Y | N | N | Y | Y |
| MONTANA | | | | | | | | |
| AL **Rehberg** | Y | Y | Y | Y | N | N | Y | Y |
| NEBRASKA | | | | | | | | |
| 1 **Fortenberry** | Y | Y | Y | Y | N | N | Y | Y |
| 2 **Terry** | Y | Y | Y | Y | N | N | Y | Y |
| 3 **Osborne** | Y | Y | Y | Y | N | N | Y | Y |
| NEVADA | | | | | | | | |
| 1 Berkley | Y | Y | N | Y | Y | Y | N | Y |
| 2 **Gibbons** | Y | Y | Y | Y | N | N | Y | Y |
| 3 **Porter** | Y | Y | Y | Y | N | N | Y | Y |
| NEW HAMPSHIRE | | | | | | | | |
| 1 **Bradley** | Y | Y | Y | Y | N | N | Y | Y |
| 2 **Bass** | Y | Y | Y | Y | N | N | Y | Y |
| NEW JERSEY | | | | | | | | |
| 1 Andrews | ? | ? | N | Y | Y | Y | N | Y |
| 2 **LoBiondo** | Y | Y | Y | Y | N | N | Y | Y |
| 3 **Saxton** | Y | Y | Y | Y | N | N | Y | Y |
| 4 **Smith** | Y | Y | Y | Y | N | N | Y | Y |
| 5 **Garrett** | Y | Y | Y | Y | N | N | Y | Y |
| 6 Pallone | Y | Y | N | Y | Y | Y | N | Y |
| 7 **Ferguson** | Y | Y | Y | Y | N | N | Y | Y |
| 8 Pascrell | Y | Y | N | Y | Y | Y | N | ? |
| 9 Rothman | Y | Y | N | Y | Y | Y | N | Y |
| 10 Payne | Y | Y | N | N | Y | Y | N | Y |
| 11 **Frelinghuysen** | Y | Y | Y | Y | N | N | Y | Y |
| 12 Holt | Y | Y | N | Y | Y | Y | N | Y |
| 13 Menendez | Y | Y | N | Y | Y | Y | N | Y |
| NEW MEXICO | | | | | | | | |
| 1 **Wilson** | Y | Y | Y | Y | N | N | Y | Y |
| 2 **Pearce** | Y | Y | Y | Y | N | N | Y | Y |
| 3 Udall | Y | Y | N | Y | Y | Y | N | Y |
| NEW YORK | | | | | | | | |
| 1 Bishop | Y | Y | N | Y | Y | Y | N | Y |
| 2 Israel | Y | Y | N | Y | Y | Y | N | Y |
| 3 **King** | Y | Y | Y | Y | N | N | Y | Y |
| 4 McCarthy | Y | Y | N | Y | Y | Y | N | Y |
| 5 Ackerman | Y | Y | N | N | Y | Y | N | Y |
| 6 Meeks | Y | Y | N | Y | Y | Y | Y | Y |
| 7 Crowley | Y | ? | N | Y | Y | Y | N | Y |
| 8 Nadler | Y | Y | N | N | Y | Y | N | Y |
| 9 Weiner | Y | Y | N | Y | Y | Y | N | Y |
| 10 Towns | Y | Y | N | Y | Y | Y | N | Y |
| 11 Owens | Y | Y | N | N | Y | Y | N | Y |
| 12 Velázquez | Y | Y | N | N | Y | Y | N | Y |
| 13 **Fossella** | Y | Y | Y | Y | N | N | Y | Y |
| 14 Maloney | Y | Y | N | Y | Y | Y | N | Y |
| 15 Rangel | Y | Y | N | Y | ? | ? | ? | ? |
| 16 Serrano | Y | Y | N | N | Y | Y | N | Y |
| 17 Engel | Y | Y | N | Y | Y | N | N | Y |
| 18 Lowey | Y | Y | N | Y | Y | Y | N | Y |
| 19 **Kelly** | Y | Y | Y | Y | N | N | Y | Y |
| 20 **Sweeney** | Y | Y | Y | Y | N | N | Y | Y |
| 21 McNulty | Y | Y | N | Y | Y | Y | N | Y |
| 22 Hinchey | Y | Y | N | N | Y | Y | N | Y |
| 23 **McHugh** | Y | Y | Y | Y | N | N | Y | Y |
| 24 **Boehlert** | Y | Y | Y | Y | N | N | Y | Y |
| 25 **Walsh** | Y | Y | Y | Y | N | N | Y | Y |
| 26 **Reynolds** | Y | Y | Y | Y | N | N | Y | Y |
| 27 Higgins | Y | Y | N | Y | Y | Y | Y | Y |
| 28 Slaughter | Y | Y | N | Y | Y | Y | N | Y |
| 29 **Kuhl** | Y | Y | Y | Y | N | N | Y | Y |
| NORTH CAROLINA | | | | | | | | |
| 1 Butterfield | Y | Y | N | Y | Y | Y | N | Y |
| 2 Etheridge | Y | Y | N | Y | Y | Y | N | Y |
| 3 **Jones** | Y | Y | Y | Y | N | N | Y | Y |
| 4 Price | Y | Y | N | Y | Y | Y | N | Y |
| 5 **Foxx** | Y | Y | Y | Y | N | N | Y | Y |
| 6 **Coble** | Y | Y | Y | Y | N | N | Y | Y |
| 7 McIntyre | Y | Y | N | Y | Y | Y | N | ? |
| 8 **Hayes** | Y | Y | Y | Y | N | N | Y | Y |
| 9 **Myrick** | Y | Y | Y | Y | N | N | Y | Y |
| 10 **McHenry** | Y | Y | Y | Y | N | N | Y | Y |
| 11 **Taylor** | Y | Y | Y | Y | N | N | Y | ? |
| 12 Watt | Y | Y | N | Y | Y | Y | N | Y |
| 13 Miller | Y | Y | N | Y | Y | Y | N | Y |
| NORTH DAKOTA | | | | | | | | |
| AL Pomeroy | Y | Y | N | Y | Y | N | Y | Y |
| OHIO | | | | | | | | |
| 1 **Chabot** | Y | Y | Y | Y | N | N | Y | Y |
| 2 **Portman** | Y | Y | Y | Y | N | N | Y | Y |
| 3 **Turner** | Y | Y | Y | Y | N | N | Y | Y |
| 4 **Oxley** | Y | Y | ? | Y | N | N | Y | Y |
| 5 **Gillmor** | Y | Y | Y | Y | N | N | Y | Y |
| 6 Strickland | Y | Y | N | Y | Y | Y | N | Y |
| 7 **Hobson** | Y | Y | Y | Y | N | N | Y | Y |
| 8 **Boehner** | Y | Y | Y | Y | N | N | Y | ? |
| 9 Kaptur | Y | Y | N | ? | Y | Y | N | ? |
| 10 Kucinich | Y | Y | N | N | Y | Y | N | Y |
| 11 Jones | Y | Y | N | Y | Y | ? | N | Y |
| 12 **Tiberi** | Y | Y | Y | Y | N | N | Y | Y |
| 13 Brown | Y | Y | N | Y | Y | Y | N | Y |
| 14 **LaTourette** | Y | Y | Y | Y | N | N | Y | Y |
| 15 **Pryce** | Y | Y | Y | Y | N | N | Y | Y |
| 16 **Regula** | Y | Y | Y | Y | N | N | Y | Y |
| 17 Ryan | Y | Y | N | Y | Y | Y | N | Y |
| 18 **Ney** | Y | Y | Y | Y | N | N | Y | Y |
| OKLAHOMA | | | | | | | | |
| 1 **Sullivan** | Y | Y | Y | Y | ? | N | Y | Y |
| 2 Boren | Y | Y | N | Y | N | N | Y | Y |
| 3 **Lucas** | Y | Y | Y | Y | N | N | Y | Y |
| 4 **Cole** | Y | Y | Y | + | N | N | Y | Y |
| 5 **Istook** | Y | Y | Y | Y | N | N | Y | Y |
| OREGON | | | | | | | | |
| 1 Wu | Y | Y | N | Y | Y | Y | Y | Y |
| 2 **Walden** | Y | Y | Y | Y | N | N | Y | Y |
| 3 Blumenauer | Y | Y | N | Y | Y | Y | N | Y |
| 4 DeFazio | Y | Y | N | Y | Y | Y | N | Y |
| 5 Hooley | Y | Y | N | Y | Y | Y | N | Y |
| PENNSYLVANIA | | | | | | | | |
| 1 Brady | Y | Y | N | Y | Y | Y | N | Y |
| 2 Fattah | Y | ? | N | N | Y | Y | N | Y |
| 3 **English** | Y | Y | Y | Y | N | N | Y | Y |
| 4 **Hart** | Y | Y | Y | Y | N | N | Y | Y |
| 5 **Peterson** | Y | Y | Y | Y | N | N | Y | Y |
| 6 **Gerlach** | Y | Y | Y | Y | N | N | Y | Y |
| 7 **Weldon** | Y | Y | Y | Y | N | N | Y | Y |
| 8 **Fitzpatrick** | Y | Y | Y | Y | N | N | Y | Y |
| 9 **Shuster** | Y | Y | Y | Y | N | N | Y | Y |
| 10 **Sherwood** | Y | Y | Y | Y | N | N | Y | Y |
| 11 Kanjorski | Y | Y | N | Y | Y | Y | Y | Y |
| 12 Murtha | Y | ? | N | Y | N | N | Y | Y |
| 13 Schwartz | Y | Y | N | Y | Y | Y | N | Y |
| 14 Doyle | Y | Y | N | Y | Y | Y | N | Y |
| 15 **Dent** | Y | Y | Y | Y | N | N | Y | Y |
| 16 **Pitts** | Y | Y | Y | Y | N | N | Y | Y |
| 17 Holden | Y | Y | N | Y | N | N | Y | Y |
| 18 **Murphy** | Y | Y | Y | Y | N | N | Y | Y |
| 19 **Platts** | Y | Y | Y | Y | N | N | Y | Y |
| RHODE ISLAND | | | | | | | | |
| 1 Kennedy | Y | Y | N | Y | Y | Y | N | Y |
| 2 Langevin | Y | Y | N | Y | Y | Y | N | Y |
| SOUTH CAROLINA | | | | | | | | |
| 1 **Brown** | Y | Y | Y | Y | N | N | Y | Y |
| 2 **Wilson** | Y | Y | Y | Y | N | N | Y | Y |
| 3 **Barrett** | Y | Y | Y | Y | N | N | Y | Y |
| 4 **Inglis** | Y | Y | Y | Y | N | ? | Y | Y |
| 5 Spratt | Y | Y | N | Y | Y | N | N | Y |
| 6 Clyburn | Y | Y | N | Y | Y | Y | N | Y |
| SOUTH DAKOTA | | | | | | | | |
| AL Herseth | Y | Y | N | Y | Y | Y | N | Y |
| TENNESSEE | | | | | | | | |
| 1 **Jenkins** | Y | Y | Y | Y | N | N | Y | Y |
| 2 **Duncan** | Y | Y | Y | Y | N | N | Y | Y |
| 3 **Wamp** | ? | ? | Y | Y | N | N | Y | Y |
| 4 Davis | Y | Y | N | Y | N | N | Y | Y |
| 5 Cooper | Y | Y | N | Y | N | N | Y | Y |
| 6 Gordon | Y | Y | N | Y | N | N | Y | Y |
| 7 **Blackburn** | Y | Y | Y | Y | N | N | Y | Y |
| 8 Tanner | Y | Y | N | Y | N | N | Y | Y |
| 9 Ford | Y | Y | N | Y | N | N | Y | Y |
| TEXAS | | | | | | | | |
| 1 **Gohmert** | Y | Y | Y | Y | N | N | Y | Y |
| 2 **Poe** | Y | Y | Y | Y | N | N | Y | Y |
| 3 **Johnson, S.** | Y | Y | Y | Y | N | N | Y | Y |
| 4 **Hall** | Y | Y | Y | Y | N | N | Y | Y |
| 5 **Hensarling** | Y | Y | Y | Y | N | N | Y | Y |
| 6 **Barton** | Y | Y | Y | Y | N | N | Y | Y |
| 7 **Culberson** | Y | Y | Y | Y | N | N | Y | Y |
| 8 **Brady** | Y | Y | Y | Y | N | N | Y | Y |
| 9 Green, A. | Y | Y | N | Y | Y | Y | N | Y |
| 10 **McCaul** | Y | Y | Y | Y | N | N | Y | Y |
| 11 **Conaway** | Y | Y | Y | Y | N | N | Y | Y |
| 12 **Granger** | Y | Y | Y | Y | N | N | Y | Y |
| 13 **Thornberry** | Y | Y | Y | Y | N | N | Y | Y |
| 14 **Paul** | Y | Y | Y | N | N | N | Y | Y |
| 15 Hinojosa | Y | Y | N | Y | Y | Y | Y | Y |
| 16 Reyes | Y | Y | N | Y | Y | Y | Y | Y |
| 17 Edwards | Y | Y | N | Y | Y | Y | Y | Y |
| 18 Jackson-Lee | Y | Y | N | Y | Y | Y | N | Y |
| 19 **Neugebauer** | Y | Y | Y | Y | N | N | Y | Y |
| 20 Gonzalez | Y | Y | N | Y | Y | Y | Y | Y |
| 21 **Smith** | Y | Y | Y | Y | N | N | Y | Y |
| 22 **DeLay** | Y | Y | Y | Y | N | N | Y | Y |
| 23 **Bonilla** | Y | Y | Y | Y | N | N | Y | Y |
| 24 **Marchant** | Y | Y | Y | Y | N | N | Y | Y |
| 25 Doggett | Y | Y | N | Y | Y | Y | N | Y |
| 26 **Burgess** | Y | Y | Y | Y | N | N | Y | Y |
| 27 Ortiz | Y | Y | N | Y | Y | Y | N | Y |
| 28 Cuellar | Y | Y | N | Y | N | N | Y | Y |
| 29 Green, G. | Y | Y | N | Y | Y | Y | N | Y |
| 30 Johnson, E. | Y | Y | N | Y | Y | Y | N | Y |
| 31 **Carter** | Y | Y | Y | Y | N | N | Y | Y |
| 32 **Sessions** | Y | Y | Y | Y | N | N | Y | Y |
| UTAH | | | | | | | | |
| 1 **Bishop** | Y | Y | Y | Y | N | N | Y | Y |
| 2 Matheson | Y | Y | N | Y | N | N | Y | Y |
| 3 **Cannon** | Y | Y | Y | Y | N | N | Y | Y |
| VERMONT | | | | | | | | |
| AL *Sanders* | Y | Y | N | N | Y | Y | N | ? |
| VIRGINIA | | | | | | | | |
| 1 **Davis, J.** | Y | Y | Y | Y | N | N | Y | Y |
| 2 **Drake** | Y | Y | Y | Y | N | N | Y | Y |
| 3 Scott | Y | Y | N | N | Y | Y | N | Y |
| 4 **Forbes** | Y | Y | Y | Y | N | N | Y | Y |
| 5 **Goode** | Y | Y | Y | Y | N | N | Y | Y |
| 6 **Goodlatte** | Y | Y | Y | Y | N | N | Y | Y |
| 7 **Cantor** | Y | Y | Y | Y | N | N | Y | Y |
| 8 Moran | Y | Y | N | Y | N | N | Y | Y |
| 9 Boucher | Y | Y | N | Y | N | N | Y | Y |
| 10 **Wolf** | Y | Y | Y | Y | N | N | Y | Y |
| 11 **Davis, T.** | Y | Y | Y | Y | N | N | Y | Y |
| WASHINGTON | | | | | | | | |
| 1 Inslee | Y | Y | N | Y | Y | Y | N | Y |
| 2 Larsen | Y | Y | N | Y | Y | Y | Y | Y |
| 3 Baird | ? | ? | N | N | Y | Y | Y | Y |
| 4 **Hastings** | Y | Y | Y | Y | N | N | Y | Y |
| 5 **McMorris** | Y | Y | Y | Y | N | N | Y | Y |
| 6 Dicks | Y | Y | N | Y | Y | Y | N | Y |
| 7 McDermott | Y | Y | N | N | Y | Y | N | Y |
| 8 **Reichert** | Y | Y | ? | ? | ? | ? | + | + |
| 9 Smith | Y | Y | N | Y | Y | Y | Y | Y |
| WEST VIRGINIA | | | | | | | | |
| 1 Mollohan | Y | Y | N | Y | Y | Y | N | ? |
| 2 **Capito** | Y | Y | Y | Y | N | N | Y | ? |
| 3 Rahall | Y | Y | N | Y | Y | Y | Y | Y |
| WISCONSIN | | | | | | | | |
| 1 **Ryan** | Y | Y | Y | Y | N | N | Y | Y |
| 2 Baldwin | Y | Y | N | Y | Y | Y | N | Y |
| 3 Kind | Y | Y | N | Y | Y | Y | Y | ? |
| 4 Moore | Y | Y | N | Y | Y | Y | N | Y |
| 5 **Sensenbrenner** | Y | Y | Y | Y | N | N | Y | Y |
| 6 **Petri** | Y | Y | Y | Y | N | N | Y | Y |
| 7 Obey | Y | Y | N | Y | Y | Y | N | Y |
| 8 **Green** | Y | Y | Y | Y | N | N | Y | Y |
| WYOMING | | | | | | | | |
| AL **Cubin** | Y | Y | Y | Y | N | N | Y | Y |

# IN THE HOUSE | By Vote Number

**40.** H Con Res 5. Sarah Winnemucca Statue/Adoption. Ney, R-Ohio, motion to suspend the rules and adopt the concurrent resolution that would accept a statue of American Indian rights advocate Sarah Winnemucca into the National Statuary Hall in the Capitol. It also would authorize the state of Nevada to use the Capitol Rotunda for a presentation ceremony March 9, 2005. Motion agreed to 418-0: R 226-0; D 191-0 (ND 142-0, SD 49-0); I 1-0. A two-thirds majority of those present and voting (279 in this case) is required for adoption under suspension of the rules. March 1, 2005.

**41.** H Con Res 63. Holocaust Remembrance/Adoption. Ney, R-Ohio, motion to suspend the rules and adopt the concurrent resolution that would authorize the use of the Capitol Rotunda for a ceremony on May 5, 2005, to commemorate victims of the Holocaust. Motion agreed to 416-0: R 226-0; D 189-0 (ND 141-0, SD 48-0); I 1-0. A two-thirds majority of those present and voting (278 in this case) is required for adoption under suspension of the rules. March 1, 2005.

**42.** HR 27. Job Training Reauthorization/Rule. Adoption of the rule (H Res 126) to provide for House floor consideration of the bill that would reauthorize the Workforce Investment Act, consolidate several programs into block grants for states and allow faith-based providers of job training activities to use religion as a factor in hiring decisions. Adopted 227-191: R 226-0; D 1-191 (ND 0-141, SD 1-50); I 0-0. March 2, 2005.

**43.** HR 912. Abuse Safeguards for Aid Organizations/Passage. Smith, R-N.J., motion to suspend the rules and pass the bill that would require humanitarian aid organizations to adopt safeguards to protect women and children from sexual exploitation and abuse before receiving U.S. disaster assistance. The bill would require the president to provide Congress with a detailed report on the implementation of the bill. Motion agreed to 416-0: R 226-0; D 190-0 (ND 140-0, SD 50-0); I 0-0. A two-thirds majority of those present and voting (278 in this case) is required for passage under suspension of the rules. March 2, 2005.

**44.** HR 27. Job Training Reauthorization/Youth Employment Programs. Kildee, D-Mich., amendment that would strike the provision in the bill that would limit the portion of a state's funds used for youth employment programs to 30 percent of its allotment. Rejected 200-222: R 5-222; D 194-0 (ND 143-0, SD 51-0); I 1-0. March 2, 2005.

**45.** HR 27. Job Training Reauthorization/Small Business Loans. Velázquez, D-N.Y., amendment that would allow unemployed workers to use funds from personal re-employment accounts to cover the borrower guarantee costs of 7(a) loans used to start a small business. Rejected 202-221: R 8-219; D 193-2 (ND 142-2, SD 51-0); I 1-0. March 2, 2005.

**46.** HR 27. Job Training Reauthorization/Religious Preferences. Scott, D-Va., amendment that would strike the provision in the bill that would permit faith-based organizations to use religion as a factor in hiring decisions. Rejected 186-239: R 3-225; D 182-14 (ND 139-6, SD 43-8); I 1-0. A "nay" was a vote in support of the president's position. March 2, 2005.

| | 40 | 41 | 42 | 43 | 44 | 45 | 46 |
|---|---|---|---|---|---|---|---|
| **ALABAMA** | | | | | | | |
| 1 Bonner | Y | Y | Y | Y | N | N | N |
| 2 Everett | Y | Y | Y | Y | N | N | N |
| 3 Rogers | Y | Y | Y | Y | N | N | N |
| 4 Aderholt | Y | Y | Y | Y | N | N | N |
| 5 Cramer | Y | Y | N | Y | Y | Y | N |
| 6 Bachus | Y | Y | Y | Y | N | N | N |
| 7 Davis | Y | Y | N | Y | Y | Y | Y |
| **ALASKA** | | | | | | | |
| AL Young | Y | Y | Y | N | N | N | N |
| **ARIZONA** | | | | | | | |
| 1 Renzi | Y | Y | Y | Y | N | Y | N |
| 2 Franks | Y | Y | Y | Y | N | N | N |
| 3 Shadegg | Y | Y | Y | Y | N | N | N |
| 4 Pastor | Y | Y | N | Y | Y | Y | Y |
| 5 Hayworth | Y | Y | Y | Y | N | N | N |
| 6 Flake | Y | Y | Y | Y | N | N | N |
| 7 Grijalva | Y | Y | N | Y | Y | Y | Y |
| 8 Kolbe | Y | Y | Y | Y | N | N | N |
| **ARKANSAS** | | | | | | | |
| 1 Berry | Y | Y | N | Y | Y | Y | Y |
| 2 Snyder | Y | Y | Y | Y | Y | Y | Y |
| 3 Boozman | Y | Y | Y | Y | N | N | N |
| 4 Ross | Y | Y | N | Y | Y | Y | Y |
| **CALIFORNIA** | | | | | | | |
| 1 Thompson | Y | Y | N | Y | Y | Y | Y |
| 2 Herger | Y | Y | Y | Y | N | N | N |
| 3 Lungren | Y | Y | Y | Y | N | N | N |
| 4 Doolittle | Y | Y | Y | Y | N | N | N |
| 5 Vacant | | | | | | | |
| 6 Woolsey | Y | Y | N | Y | Y | Y | Y |
| 7 Miller, George | Y | Y | N | Y | Y | Y | Y |
| 8 Pelosi | Y | Y | N | Y | Y | Y | Y |
| 9 Lee | Y | Y | N | Y | Y | Y | Y |
| 10 Tauscher | Y | Y | N | Y | Y | Y | Y |
| 11 Pombo | Y | Y | Y | Y | N | N | N |
| 12 Lantos | Y | Y | N | Y | Y | Y | Y |
| 13 Stark | ? | ? | N | Y | Y | Y | Y |
| 14 Eshoo | Y | Y | N | Y | Y | Y | Y |
| 15 Honda | Y | Y | N | Y | Y | Y | Y |
| 16 Lofgren | Y | Y | N | Y | Y | Y | Y |
| 17 Farr | Y | Y | N | Y | Y | Y | Y |
| 18 Cardoza | Y | Y | N | Y | Y | Y | Y |
| 19 Radanovich | Y | Y | Y | Y | N | N | N |
| 20 Costa | Y | Y | N | Y | Y | Y | Y |
| 21 Nunes | Y | Y | Y | Y | N | N | N |
| 22 Thomas | Y | Y | Y | Y | N | N | N |
| 23 Capps | Y | Y | N | Y | Y | Y | Y |
| 24 Gallegly | Y | Y | Y | Y | N | N | N |
| 25 McKeon | Y | Y | Y | Y | N | N | N |
| 26 Dreier | Y | Y | Y | Y | N | N | N |
| 27 Sherman | Y | Y | N | Y | Y | Y | Y |
| 28 Berman | Y | Y | N | Y | Y | Y | Y |
| 29 Schiff | Y | Y | N | Y | Y | Y | Y |
| 30 Waxman | Y | Y | N | Y | Y | Y | Y |
| 31 Becerra | Y | Y | N | Y | Y | Y | Y |
| 32 Solis | Y | Y | N | Y | Y | Y | Y |
| 33 Watson | ? | ? | N | Y | Y | Y | Y |
| 34 Roybal-Allard | Y | Y | N | Y | Y | Y | Y |
| 35 Waters | Y | Y | N | Y | Y | Y | Y |
| 36 Harman | Y | Y | N | Y | Y | Y | Y |
| 37 Millender-McD. | ? | ? | ? | ? | ? | ? | ? |
| 38 Napolitano | ? | ? | ? | ? | ? | ? | ? |
| 39 Sánchez, Linda | Y | Y | N | Y | Y | Y | Y |
| 40 Royce | Y | Y | Y | Y | N | N | N |
| 41 Lewis | Y | Y | Y | Y | N | N | N |
| 42 Miller, Gary | Y | Y | Y | Y | N | N | N |
| 43 Baca | Y | Y | N | Y | Y | Y | Y |
| 44 Calvert | Y | Y | Y | Y | N | N | N |
| 45 Bono | Y | Y | Y | Y | N | N | N |
| 46 Rohrabacher | Y | Y | Y | Y | N | N | N |
| 47 Sanchez, Loretta | Y | Y | N | Y | Y | Y | Y |
| 48 Cox | Y | Y | Y | Y | N | N | N |
| 49 Issa | Y | Y | Y | Y | N | N | N |
| 50 Cunningham | Y | Y | Y | Y | N | N | N |
| 51 Filner | Y | Y | N | Y | Y | Y | Y |
| 52 Hunter | Y | Y | Y | Y | N | N | N |
| 53 Davis | Y | Y | N | Y | Y | Y | Y |
| **COLORADO** | | | | | | | |
| 1 DeGette | Y | Y | N | Y | Y | Y | Y |
| 2 Udall | Y | Y | N | Y | Y | Y | Y |
| 3 Salazar | Y | Y | N | Y | Y | Y | Y |
| 4 Musgrave | Y | Y | Y | Y | N | N | N |
| 5 Hefley | Y | Y | Y | Y | N | N | N |
| 6 Tancredo | Y | Y | Y | Y | N | N | N |
| 7 Beauprez | Y | Y | Y | Y | N | Y | N |
| **CONNECTICUT** | | | | | | | |
| 1 Larson | Y | Y | N | Y | Y | Y | Y |
| 2 Simmons | Y | Y | Y | Y | Y | N | Y |
| 3 DeLauro | Y | Y | N | Y | Y | Y | Y |
| 4 Shays | Y | Y | Y | Y | Y | N | Y |
| 5 Johnson | Y | Y | Y | Y | Y | N | Y |
| **DELAWARE** | | | | | | | |
| AL Castle | Y | Y | Y | N | N | N | N |
| **FLORIDA** | | | | | | | |
| 1 Miller | Y | Y | Y | Y | N | N | N |
| 2 Boyd | Y | Y | N | Y | Y | Y | Y |
| 3 Brown | ? | ? | N | Y | Y | Y | Y |
| 4 Crenshaw | Y | Y | Y | Y | N | N | N |
| 5 Brown-Waite | Y | Y | Y | Y | N | N | N |
| 6 Stearns | Y | Y | Y | Y | N | N | N |
| 7 Mica | Y | Y | Y | Y | N | N | N |
| 8 Keller | Y | Y | Y | Y | N | N | N |
| 9 Bilirakis | Y | Y | Y | Y | N | N | N |
| 10 Young | Y | Y | Y | Y | N | N | N |
| 11 Davis | Y | Y | N | ? | Y | Y | Y |
| 12 Putnam | Y | Y | Y | Y | N | N | N |
| 13 Harris | ? | ? | ? | ? | ? | ? | ? |
| 14 Mack | Y | Y | Y | Y | N | N | N |
| 15 Weldon | Y | Y | Y | Y | N | N | N |
| 16 Foley | Y | Y | Y | ? | ? | N | N |
| 17 Meek | Y | Y | N | Y | Y | Y | Y |
| 18 Ros-Lehtinen | Y | Y | Y | Y | N | N | N |
| 19 Wexler | Y | Y | N | Y | Y | Y | Y |
| 20 Wasserman-Schultz | Y | Y | N | Y | Y | Y | Y |
| 21 Diaz-Balart, L. | Y | Y | Y | Y | N | N | N |
| 22 Shaw | Y | Y | Y | Y | N | N | N |
| 23 Hastings | Y | Y | N | Y | Y | Y | Y |
| 24 Feeney | Y | Y | Y | Y | N | N | N |
| 25 Diaz-Balart, M. | Y | Y | Y | Y | N | N | N |
| **GEORGIA** | | | | | | | |
| 1 Kingston | ? | ? | Y | Y | N | N | N |
| 2 Bishop | Y | Y | N | Y | Y | Y | Y |
| 3 Marshall | Y | Y | Y | Y | Y | Y | Y |
| 4 McKinney | Y | Y | N | Y | Y | Y | Y |
| 5 Lewis | Y | Y | N | Y | Y | Y | Y |
| 6 Price | Y | Y | Y | Y | N | N | N |
| 7 Linder | Y | Y | Y | Y | N | N | N |
| 8 Westmoreland | Y | Y | Y | Y | N | N | N |
| 9 Norwood | Y | Y | Y | Y | N | N | N |
| 10 Deal | Y | Y | Y | Y | N | N | N |
| 11 Gingrey | Y | Y | Y | Y | N | N | N |
| 12 Barrow | Y | Y | N | Y | Y | Y | Y |
| 13 Scott | Y | Y | N | Y | Y | Y | Y |
| **HAWAII** | | | | | | | |
| 1 Abercrombie | Y | Y | N | Y | Y | Y | Y |
| 2 Case | Y | Y | N | Y | Y | Y | Y |
| **IDAHO** | | | | | | | |
| 1 Otter | Y | Y | Y | Y | N | N | N |
| 2 Simpson | Y | Y | Y | Y | N | N | N |
| **ILLINOIS** | | | | | | | |
| 1 Rush | ? | ? | N | Y | Y | Y | Y |
| 2 Jackson | Y | Y | N | Y | Y | Y | Y |
| 3 Lipinski | Y | Y | N | Y | Y | Y | N |
| 4 Gutierrez | ? | ? | N | Y | Y | Y | Y |
| 5 Emanuel | Y | Y | N | Y | Y | Y | Y |
| 6 Hyde | Y | Y | Y | Y | N | N | N |
| 7 Davis | Y | Y | N | Y | Y | Y | Y |
| 8 Bean | Y | Y | N | Y | Y | Y | Y |
| 9 Schakowsky | Y | Y | N | Y | Y | Y | Y |
| 10 Kirk | Y | Y | Y | Y | N | N | N |
| 11 Weller | Y | Y | Y | Y | N | N | N |
| 12 Costello | Y | Y | N | Y | Y | Y | Y |

**KEY**    Republicans    Democrats    *Independents*

| | | | | |
|---|---|---|---|---|
| **Y** Voted for (yea) | **X** Paired against | **C** Voted "present" to avoid possible conflict of interest |
| **#** Paired for | **–** Announced against | |
| **+** Announced for | **P** Voted "present" | **?** Did not vote or otherwise make a position known |
| **N** Voted against (nay) | | |

| | 40 | 41 | 42 | 43 | 44 | 45 | 46 |
|---|---|---|---|---|---|---|---|
| 13 **Biggert** | Y | Y | Y | Y | N | N | N |
| 14 **Hastert** | | | | | | | |
| 15 **Johnson** | Y | Y | Y | Y | N | Y | N |
| 16 **Manzullo** | Y | Y | Y | Y | N | N | N |
| 17 Evans | Y | Y | N | Y | Y | Y | Y |
| 18 **LaHood** | Y | Y | Y | Y | N | N | N |
| 19 **Shimkus** | Y | Y | Y | Y | N | N | N |
| **INDIANA** | | | | | | | |
| 1 Visclosky | Y | Y | N | Y | Y | Y | Y |
| 2 **Chocola** | Y | Y | Y | Y | N | N | N |
| 3 **Souder** | Y | Y | Y | Y | N | N | N |
| 4 **Buyer** | Y | Y | Y | Y | N | N | N |
| 5 **Burton** | Y | Y | Y | Y | N | N | N |
| 6 **Pence** | Y | Y | Y | Y | N | N | N |
| 7 Carson | ? | ? | ? | ? | ? | ? | ? |
| 8 **Hostettler** | Y | Y | Y | Y | N | N | N |
| 9 **Sodrel** | Y | Y | Y | Y | N | N | N |
| **IOWA** | | | | | | | |
| 1 **Nussle** | Y | Y | Y | Y | N | N | N |
| 2 **Leach** | Y | Y | Y | Y | Y | N | N |
| 3 Boswell | Y | Y | N | Y | Y | Y | Y |
| 4 **Latham** | Y | Y | Y | Y | N | N | N |
| 5 **King** | Y | Y | Y | Y | N | N | N |
| **KANSAS** | | | | | | | |
| 1 **Moran** | Y | Y | Y | Y | N | N | N |
| 2 **Ryun** | Y | Y | Y | Y | N | N | N |
| 3 Moore | Y | Y | N | Y | Y | Y | Y |
| 4 **Tiahrt** | Y | Y | Y | Y | N | N | N |
| **KENTUCKY** | | | | | | | |
| 1 **Whitfield** | Y | Y | Y | Y | N | N | N |
| 2 **Lewis** | Y | Y | Y | Y | N | N | N |
| 3 **Northup** | Y | Y | Y | Y | N | N | N |
| 4 **Davis** | Y | Y | Y | Y | N | N | N |
| 5 **Rogers** | Y | Y | Y | Y | N | N | N |
| 6 Chandler | Y | Y | N | Y | Y | Y | N |
| **LOUISIANA** | | | | | | | |
| 1 **Jindal** | Y | Y | Y | Y | N | N | N |
| 2 Jefferson | Y | Y | N | Y | Y | Y | Y |
| 3 Melancon | Y | ? | N | Y | Y | Y | Y |
| 4 **McCrery** | Y | Y | Y | Y | ? | ? | N |
| 5 **Alexander** | Y | Y | Y | Y | N | N | N |
| 6 **Baker** | Y | Y | Y | Y | N | N | N |
| 7 **Boustany** | Y | Y | Y | Y | N | N | N |
| **MAINE** | | | | | | | |
| 1 Allen | Y | Y | N | ? | Y | Y | Y |
| 2 Michaud | Y | Y | N | Y | Y | Y | Y |
| **MARYLAND** | | | | | | | |
| 1 **Gilchrest** | Y | Y | Y | Y | N | N | N |
| 2 Ruppersberger | Y | Y | N | Y | Y | Y | Y |
| 3 Cardin | Y | Y | N | Y | Y | Y | Y |
| 4 Wynn | Y | Y | N | Y | Y | Y | Y |
| 5 Hoyer | Y | Y | N | Y | Y | Y | Y |
| 6 **Bartlett** | Y | Y | Y | Y | N | N | N |
| 7 Cummings | Y | Y | N | Y | Y | Y | Y |
| 8 Van Hollen | Y | Y | N | Y | Y | Y | Y |
| **MASSACHUSETTS** | | | | | | | |
| 1 Olver | Y | Y | N | Y | Y | Y | Y |
| 2 Neal | Y | Y | ? | Y | Y | Y | Y |
| 3 McGovern | Y | Y | ? | ? | Y | Y | Y |
| 4 Frank | Y | Y | N | Y | Y | Y | Y |
| 5 Meehan | Y | Y | N | Y | Y | Y | Y |
| 6 Tierney | Y | Y | N | Y | Y | Y | Y |
| 7 Markey | Y | Y | ? | ? | Y | Y | Y |
| 8 Capuano | Y | Y | ? | ? | Y | Y | Y |
| 9 Lynch | Y | Y | N | Y | Y | Y | Y |
| 10 Delahunt | Y | Y | N | Y | Y | Y | Y |
| **MICHIGAN** | | | | | | | |
| 1 Stupak | Y | Y | N | Y | Y | Y | Y |
| 2 **Hoekstra** | Y | Y | Y | Y | N | N | N |
| 3 **Ehlers** | Y | Y | Y | Y | N | N | N |
| 4 **Camp** | Y | Y | Y | Y | N | N | N |
| 5 Kildee | Y | Y | N | Y | Y | Y | Y |
| 6 **Upton** | Y | Y | Y | Y | N | N | N |
| 7 **Schwarz** | Y | Y | Y | Y | N | N | N |
| 8 **Rogers** | Y | Y | Y | Y | N | N | N |
| 9 **Knollenberg** | Y | Y | Y | ? | N | N | N |
| 10 **Miller** | Y | Y | Y | Y | N | N | N |
| 11 **McCotter** | Y | Y | Y | Y | N | N | N |
| 12 Levin | Y | Y | N | Y | Y | Y | Y |
| 13 Kilpatrick | Y | Y | N | Y | Y | Y | Y |
| 14 Conyers | Y | Y | N | Y | Y | Y | Y |
| 15 Dingell | Y | Y | N | Y | Y | Y | Y |
| **MINNESOTA** | | | | | | | |
| 1 **Gutknecht** | Y | Y | Y | Y | N | N | N |
| 2 **Kline** | Y | Y | Y | Y | N | N | N |
| 3 **Ramstad** | Y | Y | ? | Y | N | N | N |
| 4 McCollum | Y | Y | N | P | Y | Y | Y |
| 5 Sabo | Y | Y | N | Y | Y | Y | Y |
| 6 **Kennedy** | Y | Y | Y | Y | N | N | N |
| 7 Peterson | Y | Y | N | Y | Y | N | N |
| 8 Oberstar | Y | Y | N | Y | Y | Y | Y |
| **MISSISSIPPI** | | | | | | | |
| 1 **Wicker** | Y | Y | Y | Y | N | N | N |
| 2 Thompson | Y | Y | N | Y | Y | Y | Y |
| 3 **Pickering** | Y | Y | Y | Y | N | N | N |
| 4 Taylor | Y | Y | N | Y | Y | Y | N |
| **MISSOURI** | | | | | | | |
| 1 Clay | Y | Y | N | Y | Y | Y | Y |
| 2 **Akin** | Y | Y | Y | Y | N | N | N |
| 3 Carnahan | Y | Y | N | Y | Y | Y | Y |
| 4 Skelton | Y | Y | N | Y | Y | Y | N |
| 5 Cleaver | Y | Y | ? | ? | ? | ? | ? |
| 6 **Graves** | Y | Y | Y | Y | N | N | N |
| 7 **Blunt** | Y | Y | Y | Y | N | N | N |
| 8 **Emerson** | Y | Y | Y | Y | N | N | N |
| 9 **Hulshof** | Y | Y | Y | Y | N | N | N |
| **MONTANA** | | | | | | | |
| AL **Rehberg** | Y | Y | Y | Y | N | N | N |
| **NEBRASKA** | | | | | | | |
| 1 **Fortenberry** | Y | Y | Y | Y | N | N | N |
| 2 **Terry** | Y | Y | Y | Y | N | N | N |
| 3 **Osborne** | Y | Y | Y | Y | N | N | N |
| **NEVADA** | | | | | | | |
| 1 Berkley | Y | Y | N | Y | Y | Y | Y |
| 2 **Gibbons** | Y | Y | Y | Y | N | N | N |
| 3 **Porter** | Y | Y | Y | Y | N | N | N |
| **NEW HAMPSHIRE** | | | | | | | |
| 1 **Bradley** | Y | Y | Y | Y | N | N | N |
| 2 **Bass** | Y | Y | Y | Y | N | N | N |
| **NEW JERSEY** | | | | | | | |
| 1 Andrews | Y | Y | N | Y | Y | Y | Y |
| 2 **LoBiondo** | Y | Y | Y | Y | N | N | N |
| 3 **Saxton** | Y | Y | Y | Y | N | N | N |
| 4 **Smith** | Y | Y | Y | Y | N | N | N |
| 5 **Garrett** | Y | Y | Y | Y | N | N | N |
| 6 Pallone | Y | Y | N | Y | Y | Y | Y |
| 7 **Ferguson** | Y | Y | ? | ? | N | N | N |
| 8 Pascrell | Y | Y | N | Y | Y | Y | Y |
| 9 Rothman | Y | Y | N | Y | Y | Y | Y |
| 10 Payne | Y | Y | N | Y | Y | Y | Y |
| 11 **Frelinghuysen** | Y | Y | Y | Y | N | N | N |
| 12 Holt | Y | Y | N | Y | Y | Y | Y |
| 13 Menendez | Y | Y | N | Y | Y | Y | Y |
| **NEW MEXICO** | | | | | | | |
| 1 **Wilson** | Y | Y | Y | Y | N | N | N |
| 2 **Pearce** | Y | Y | Y | Y | N | Y | N |
| 3 Udall | Y | Y | N | Y | Y | Y | Y |
| **NEW YORK** | | | | | | | |
| 1 Bishop | Y | Y | N | Y | Y | Y | Y |
| 2 Israel | Y | Y | N | Y | Y | Y | Y |
| 3 **King** | Y | Y | Y | Y | N | N | N |
| 4 McCarthy | Y | Y | N | Y | Y | Y | Y |
| 5 Ackerman | Y | Y | N | Y | Y | Y | Y |
| 6 Meeks | ? | ? | ? | ? | ? | ? | ? |
| 7 Crowley | Y | Y | N | Y | Y | Y | Y |
| 8 Nadler | Y | Y | N | Y | Y | Y | Y |
| 9 Weiner | Y | Y | N | Y | Y | Y | Y |
| 10 Towns | Y | Y | N | Y | Y | Y | Y |
| 11 Owens | Y | Y | N | Y | Y | Y | Y |
| 12 Velázquez | Y | Y | N | Y | Y | Y | Y |
| 13 **Fossella** | Y | Y | Y | Y | N | Y | N |
| 14 Maloney | Y | Y | N | Y | Y | Y | Y |
| 15 Rangel | Y | Y | N | Y | Y | Y | Y |
| 16 Serrano | Y | Y | N | Y | Y | Y | Y |
| 17 Engel | Y | Y | N | Y | Y | Y | Y |
| 18 Lowey | Y | Y | N | Y | Y | Y | Y |
| 19 **Kelly** | Y | Y | Y | Y | N | N | N |
| 20 **Sweeney** | Y | ? | Y | Y | N | Y | N |
| 21 McNulty | Y | Y | N | Y | Y | Y | Y |
| 22 Hinchey | Y | Y | N | Y | Y | Y | Y |
| 23 **McHugh** | Y | Y | Y | Y | N | N | N |
| 24 **Boehlert** | Y | Y | Y | Y | N | N | N |
| 25 **Walsh** | Y | Y | Y | Y | N | N | N |
| 26 **Reynolds** | Y | Y | Y | Y | ? | ? | ? |
| 27 Higgins | Y | Y | N | Y | Y | Y | Y |
| 28 Slaughter | Y | Y | N | Y | Y | Y | Y |
| 29 **Kuhl** | Y | Y | Y | Y | N | N | N |
| **NORTH CAROLINA** | | | | | | | |
| 1 Butterfield | Y | Y | N | Y | Y | Y | Y |
| 2 Etheridge | Y | Y | N | Y | Y | Y | Y |
| 3 **Jones** | Y | Y | Y | Y | N | N | N |
| 4 Price | Y | Y | N | Y | Y | Y | Y |
| 5 **Foxx** | Y | Y | Y | Y | N | N | N |
| 6 **Coble** | Y | Y | Y | Y | N | N | N |
| 7 McIntyre | Y | Y | N | Y | Y | Y | N |
| 8 **Hayes** | Y | Y | Y | Y | N | N | N |
| 9 **Myrick** | Y | Y | Y | Y | N | N | N |
| 10 **McHenry** | Y | Y | Y | Y | N | N | N |
| 11 **Taylor** | Y | Y | Y | Y | N | N | N |
| 12 Watt | ? | ? | N | Y | Y | Y | Y |
| 13 Miller | Y | Y | N | Y | Y | Y | Y |
| **NORTH DAKOTA** | | | | | | | |
| AL Pomeroy | Y | Y | N | Y | Y | Y | Y |
| **OHIO** | | | | | | | |
| 1 **Chabot** | Y | Y | Y | Y | N | N | N |
| 2 **Portman** | Y | Y | Y | Y | N | N | N |
| 3 **Turner** | Y | Y | Y | Y | N | N | N |
| 4 **Oxley** | Y | Y | Y | Y | N | N | N |
| 5 **Gillmor** | ? | ? | ? | ? | ? | ? | ? |
| 6 Strickland | Y | Y | N | Y | Y | Y | Y |
| 7 **Hobson** | Y | Y | Y | Y | N | N | N |
| 8 **Boehner** | Y | Y | Y | Y | N | N | N |
| 9 Kaptur | Y | Y | N | Y | Y | Y | Y |
| 10 Kucinich | Y | Y | N | Y | Y | Y | Y |
| 11 Jones | Y | Y | N | Y | ? | ? | Y |
| 12 **Tiberi** | Y | Y | Y | Y | N | N | N |
| 13 Brown | Y | Y | N | Y | Y | Y | Y |
| 14 **LaTourette** | Y | Y | Y | Y | N | N | N |
| 15 **Pryce** | Y | Y | Y | Y | N | N | N |
| 16 **Regula** | Y | Y | Y | Y | N | N | N |
| 17 Ryan | Y | Y | N | Y | ? | Y | Y |
| 18 **Ney** | Y | Y | Y | Y | N | N | N |
| **OKLAHOMA** | | | | | | | |
| 1 **Sullivan** | Y | Y | Y | Y | N | N | N |
| 2 Boren | Y | Y | N | Y | Y | Y | Y |
| 3 **Lucas** | Y | Y | Y | Y | N | N | N |
| 4 **Cole** | Y | Y | Y | Y | N | N | N |
| 5 **Istook** | ? | Y | Y | Y | N | N | N |
| **OREGON** | | | | | | | |
| 1 Wu | Y | Y | N | Y | Y | Y | Y |
| 2 **Walden** | Y | Y | Y | Y | N | N | N |
| 3 Blumenauer | Y | Y | N | Y | Y | Y | Y |
| 4 DeFazio | Y | Y | N | Y | Y | N | Y |
| 5 Hooley | Y | Y | N | Y | Y | Y | Y |
| **PENNSYLVANIA** | | | | | | | |
| 1 Brady | Y | Y | N | Y | Y | Y | Y |
| 2 Fattah | Y | Y | N | Y | Y | Y | Y |
| 3 **English** | Y | Y | Y | Y | N | N | N |
| 4 **Hart** | Y | Y | Y | Y | N | N | N |
| 5 **Peterson** | ? | Y | Y | Y | N | N | N |
| 6 **Gerlach** | Y | Y | Y | Y | N | N | N |
| 7 **Weldon** | Y | Y | Y | Y | N | N | N |
| 8 **Fitzpatrick** | Y | Y | Y | Y | N | N | N |
| 9 **Shuster** | Y | Y | Y | Y | N | N | N |
| 10 **Sherwood** | Y | Y | Y | Y | N | N | N |
| 11 Kanjorski | Y | Y | N | Y | Y | Y | Y |
| 12 Murtha | Y | ? | N | Y | Y | Y | Y |
| 13 Schwartz | Y | Y | N | Y | Y | Y | Y |
| 14 Doyle | Y | Y | N | Y | Y | Y | Y |
| 15 **Dent** | Y | Y | Y | Y | N | N | N |
| 16 **Pitts** | Y | Y | Y | Y | N | N | N |
| 17 Holden | Y | Y | N | Y | Y | Y | Y |
| 18 **Murphy** | Y | Y | Y | Y | N | N | N |
| 19 **Platts** | Y | Y | Y | Y | N | N | N |
| **RHODE ISLAND** | | | | | | | |
| 1 Kennedy | Y | Y | N | Y | Y | Y | Y |
| 2 Langevin | Y | Y | N | Y | Y | Y | Y |
| **SOUTH CAROLINA** | | | | | | | |
| 1 **Brown** | Y | Y | Y | Y | N | N | N |
| 2 **Wilson** | Y | Y | Y | Y | N | N | N |
| 3 **Barrett** | Y | Y | Y | Y | N | N | N |
| 4 **Inglis** | Y | Y | Y | Y | N | N | N |
| 5 Spratt | Y | Y | N | Y | Y | Y | Y |
| 6 Clyburn | Y | Y | N | Y | Y | Y | Y |
| **SOUTH DAKOTA** | | | | | | | |
| AL Herseth | Y | Y | N | Y | Y | Y | N |
| **TENNESSEE** | | | | | | | |
| 1 **Jenkins** | Y | ? | Y | Y | N | N | N |
| 2 **Duncan** | Y | Y | Y | Y | N | N | N |
| 3 **Wamp** | Y | Y | Y | Y | N | N | N |
| 4 Davis | Y | Y | N | Y | Y | Y | N |
| 5 Cooper | Y | Y | N | Y | Y | Y | Y |
| 6 Gordon | Y | Y | N | Y | Y | Y | N |
| 7 **Blackburn** | Y | Y | Y | Y | N | N | N |
| 8 Tanner | Y | Y | N | Y | Y | Y | Y |
| 9 Ford | Y | Y | N | Y | Y | Y | Y |
| **TEXAS** | | | | | | | |
| 1 **Gohmert** | Y | Y | Y | Y | N | N | N |
| 2 **Poe** | Y | Y | Y | Y | N | N | N |
| 3 **Johnson, S.** | Y | Y | Y | Y | N | N | N |
| 4 **Hall** | Y | Y | Y | Y | N | N | N |
| 5 **Hensarling** | Y | Y | Y | Y | N | N | N |
| 6 **Barton** | Y | Y | Y | Y | N | N | N |
| 7 **Culberson** | Y | Y | Y | Y | N | N | N |
| 8 **Brady** | Y | Y | Y | Y | N | N | N |
| 9 Green | Y | Y | N | Y | Y | Y | Y |
| 10 **McCaul** | Y | Y | Y | Y | N | N | N |
| 11 **Conaway** | Y | Y | Y | Y | N | N | N |
| 12 **Granger** | Y | Y | Y | Y | N | N | N |
| 13 **Thornberry** | Y | Y | Y | Y | N | N | N |
| 14 **Paul** | Y | Y | Y | Y | Y | Y | N |
| 15 Hinojosa | Y | Y | Y | Y | Y | Y | Y |
| 16 Reyes | Y | Y | N | Y | Y | Y | Y |
| 17 Edwards | Y | Y | N | Y | Y | Y | Y |
| 18 Jackson-Lee | Y | Y | N | Y | Y | Y | Y |
| 19 **Neugebauer** | Y | Y | Y | Y | N | N | N |
| 20 Gonzalez | Y | Y | N | Y | Y | Y | Y |
| 21 **Smith** | Y | Y | Y | Y | N | N | N |
| 22 **DeLay** | Y | Y | Y | Y | N | N | N |
| 23 **Bonilla** | Y | Y | Y | Y | N | N | N |
| 24 **Marchant** | Y | Y | Y | Y | N | N | N |
| 25 Doggett | Y | Y | N | Y | Y | Y | Y |
| 26 **Burgess** | Y | Y | Y | Y | N | N | N |
| 27 Ortiz | Y | Y | N | Y | Y | Y | Y |
| 28 Cuellar | Y | Y | N | Y | Y | Y | Y |
| 29 Green | Y | Y | N | Y | Y | Y | Y |
| 30 Johnson, E. | Y | Y | N | Y | Y | Y | Y |
| 31 **Carter** | Y | Y | Y | Y | N | N | N |
| 32 **Sessions** | Y | Y | Y | Y | N | N | N |
| **UTAH** | | | | | | | |
| 1 **Bishop** | Y | Y | Y | Y | N | N | N |
| 2 Matheson | Y | Y | N | Y | Y | Y | Y |
| 3 **Cannon** | Y | Y | Y | Y | N | N | N |
| **VERMONT** | | | | | | | |
| AL *Sanders* | Y | Y | ? | ? | Y | Y | Y |
| **VIRGINIA** | | | | | | | |
| 1 **Davis, J.** | Y | Y | Y | Y | N | N | N |
| 2 **Drake** | Y | Y | Y | Y | N | N | N |
| 3 Scott | Y | Y | N | Y | Y | Y | Y |
| 4 **Forbes** | Y | Y | Y | Y | N | N | N |
| 5 **Goode** | Y | Y | Y | Y | N | N | N |
| 6 **Goodlatte** | Y | Y | Y | Y | N | N | N |
| 7 **Cantor** | Y | Y | Y | Y | N | N | N |
| 8 Moran | Y | Y | N | Y | Y | Y | Y |
| 9 Boucher | Y | Y | N | Y | Y | Y | Y |
| 10 **Wolf** | Y | Y | Y | Y | N | N | N |
| 11 **Davis, T.** | Y | Y | Y | Y | N | N | N |
| **WASHINGTON** | | | | | | | |
| 1 Inslee | Y | Y | N | Y | Y | Y | Y |
| 2 Larsen | Y | Y | N | Y | Y | Y | Y |
| 3 Baird | Y | Y | N | Y | Y | Y | Y |
| 4 **Hastings** | Y | Y | Y | Y | N | N | N |
| 5 **McMorris** | Y | Y | Y | Y | N | N | N |
| 6 Dicks | Y | Y | N | Y | Y | Y | Y |
| 7 McDermott | Y | Y | N | Y | Y | Y | Y |
| 8 **Reichert** | Y | Y | Y | Y | N | N | N |
| 9 Smith | Y | Y | N | Y | Y | Y | Y |
| **WEST VIRGINIA** | | | | | | | |
| 1 Mollohan | Y | Y | N | Y | Y | Y | N |
| 2 **Capito** | Y | Y | Y | Y | N | N | N |
| 3 Rahall | Y | Y | N | Y | Y | Y | N |
| **WISCONSIN** | | | | | | | |
| 1 **Ryan** | Y | Y | Y | Y | N | N | N |
| 2 Baldwin | Y | Y | N | Y | Y | Y | Y |
| 3 Kind | Y | Y | N | Y | Y | Y | Y |
| 4 Moore | Y | Y | N | Y | Y | Y | Y |
| 5 **Sensenbrenner** | Y | Y | Y | Y | N | N | N |
| 6 **Petri** | Y | Y | Y | Y | N | N | N |
| 7 Obey | Y | Y | N | Y | Y | Y | Y |
| 8 **Green** | Y | Y | Y | Y | N | N | N |
| **WYOMING** | | | | | | | |
| AL **Cubin** | Y | Y | Y | Y | N | N | N |

# IN THE HOUSE | By Vote Number

**47.** **HR 27. Job Training Reauthorization/Recommit.** Kildee, D-Mich., motion to recommit the bill to the Education and the Workforce Committee with instructions to add language that would provide financial assistance equal to the trade adjustment assistance program for job training, job searching or relocation costs for veterans returning from active duty in Iraq and to workers who are unemployed because their jobs were moved offshore. Motion rejected 197-228: R 0-228; D 196-0 (ND 145-0, SD 51-0); I 1-0. March 2, 2005.

**48.** **HR 27. Job Training Reauthorization/Passage.** Passage of a bill that would reauthorize the Workforce Investment Act, consolidate several programs into block grants for states and allow faith-based providers of job training activities to use religion as a factor in hiring decisions. It would combine the funding for adults, dislocated workers and employment services into a single $3 billion block grant program. The measure would authorize a demonstration program to create personal unemployment accounts under which an unemployed individual would receive a voucher worth up to $3,000 for job-training and other services. Passed 224-200: R 220-8; D 4-191 (ND 1-143, SD 3-48); I 0-1. March 2, 2005.

**49.** **HR 841. Continuity of Congress/Sixty-Day Election Deadline.** Millender-McDonald, D-Calif., amendment that would extend the deadline for conducting special elections under the bill from 45 days to 60 days after the Speaker's announcement. Rejected 192-229: R 1-225; D 190-4 (ND 142-3, SD 48-1); I 1-0. March 3, 2005.

**50.** **HR 841. Continuity of Congress/Lawsuit Deadline.** Jackson-Lee, D-Texas, amendment that would require that any lawsuit challenging the Speaker's announcement that more than 100 vacancies in the House exist must be filed within five days, rather than two days, of the announcement. It would allow any citizen of the district, or any group of citizens, to intervene in support or opposition to the challenge. Rejected 183-239: R 1-226; D 181-13 (ND 137-8, SD 44-5); I 1-0. March 3, 2005.

**51.** **HR 841. Continuity of Congress/Recommit.** Conyers, D-Mich., motion to recommit the bill to the House Administration Committee with instructions to add language that would require states to distribute election personnel and equipment equally when conducting special elections. Motion rejected 196-223: R 0-223; D 195-0 (ND 146-0, SD 49-0); I 1-0. March 3, 2005.

**52.** **HR 841. Continuity of Congress/Passage.** Passage of the bill that would require special elections to fill vacant House seats within 49 days of a catastrophe that kills at least 100 House members. If a regularly scheduled election is planned to fill a vacant House seat within 75 days of the House Speaker's announcement of the vacancies, then no special election for that seat is required. Parties would be required to nominate their candidates within 10 days of the House Speaker's announcement. Passed 329-68: R 206-3; D 122-65 (ND 88-52, SD 34-13); I 1-0. March 3, 2005.

| | 47 | 48 | 49 | 50 | 51 | 52 |
|---|---|---|---|---|---|---|
| **ALABAMA** | | | | | | |
| 1 Bonner | ? | ? | N | N | N | Y |
| 2 Everett | N | Y | N | N | N | Y |
| 3 Rogers | N | Y | N | N | N | Y |
| 4 Aderholt | N | Y | N | N | N | Y |
| 5 Cramer | Y | Y | Y | Y | Y | ? |
| 6 Bachus | N | Y | N | N | N | Y |
| 7 Davis | Y | N | Y | Y | Y | N |
| **ALASKA** | | | | | | |
| AL Young | N | Y | ? | ? | ? | ? |
| **ARIZONA** | | | | | | |
| 1 Renzi | N | Y | N | N | N | Y |
| 2 Franks | N | Y | N | N | N | Y |
| 3 Shadegg | N | Y | N | N | N | Y |
| 4 Pastor | Y | N | Y | Y | Y | Y |
| 5 Hayworth | N | Y | N | N | N | Y |
| 6 Flake | N | N | N | N | N | N |
| 7 Grijalva | Y | N | Y | Y | Y | N |
| 8 Kolbe | N | Y | N | N | N | Y |
| **ARKANSAS** | | | | | | |
| 1 Berry | Y | N | Y | Y | Y | N |
| 2 Snyder | Y | N | Y | Y | Y | Y |
| 3 Boozman | N | Y | N | N | N | Y |
| 4 Ross | Y | N | Y | Y | Y | Y |
| **CALIFORNIA** | | | | | | |
| 1 Thompson | Y | N | Y | N | Y | Y |
| 2 Herger | N | Y | N | N | N | Y |
| 3 Lungren | N | Y | N | N | N | Y |
| 4 Doolittle | N | Y | N | N | N | Y |
| 5 Vacant | | | | | | |
| 6 Woolsey | Y | N | Y | Y | Y | N |
| 7 Miller, George | Y | N | Y | Y | Y | N |
| 8 Pelosi | Y | ? | Y | Y | Y | N |
| 9 Lee | Y | N | Y | Y | Y | N |
| 10 Tauscher | Y | N | Y | Y | Y | N |
| 11 Pombo | N | Y | N | N | N | ? |
| 12 Lantos | Y | N | Y | Y | Y | Y |
| 13 Stark | Y | N | Y | Y | Y | N |
| 14 Eshoo | Y | N | Y | Y | Y | N |
| 15 Honda | Y | N | Y | Y | Y | N |
| 16 Lofgren | Y | N | Y | Y | Y | N |
| 17 Farr | Y | N | Y | Y | Y | N |
| 18 Cardoza | Y | N | Y | Y | Y | Y |
| 19 Radanovich | N | Y | N | N | N | Y |
| 20 Costa | Y | N | Y | Y | Y | Y |
| 21 Nunes | N | Y | N | N | N | Y |
| 22 Thomas | N | Y | N | N | N | Y |
| 23 Capps | Y | N | Y | Y | Y | Y |
| 24 Gallegly | N | Y | N | N | N | ? |
| 25 McKeon | N | Y | N | N | N | Y |
| 26 Dreier | N | Y | N | N | N | Y |
| 27 Sherman | Y | N | Y | Y | Y | Y |
| 28 Berman | Y | N | Y | Y | Y | Y |
| 29 Schiff | Y | N | Y | Y | Y | Y |
| 30 Waxman | Y | N | Y | Y | Y | Y |
| 31 Becerra | Y | N | Y | Y | Y | Y |
| 32 Solis | Y | N | Y | Y | Y | Y |
| 33 Watson | Y | N | Y | Y | Y | N |
| 34 Roybal-Allard | Y | N | Y | Y | Y | Y |
| 35 Waters | Y | N | Y | Y | Y | N |
| 36 Harman | Y | N | Y | N | Y | Y |
| 37 Millender-McD. | ? | ? | Y | Y | Y | N |
| 38 Napolitano | ? | ? | ? | ? | ? | ? |
| 39 Sánchez, Linda | N | Y | Y | Y | Y | N |
| 40 Royce | N | Y | N | N | N | Y |
| 41 Lewis | N | Y | N | N | N | Y |
| 42 Miller, Gary | N | Y | N | N | N | Y |
| 43 Baca | N | Y | Y | Y | Y | Y |
| 44 Calvert | N | Y | N | N | N | Y |
| 45 Bono | N | Y | N | N | N | Y |
| 46 Rohrabacher | N | Y | N | N | N | N |
| 47 Sanchez, Loretta | Y | N | Y | Y | Y | Y |
| 48 Cox | N | Y | N | N | N | Y |
| 49 Issa | N | Y | N | N | ? | ? |

| | 47 | 48 | 49 | 50 | 51 | 52 |
|---|---|---|---|---|---|---|
| 50 Cunningham | N | Y | ? | ? | ? | ? |
| 51 Filner | Y | N | Y | Y | Y | N |
| 52 Hunter | N | Y | N | N | N | N |
| 53 Davis | Y | N | Y | Y | Y | N |
| **COLORADO** | | | | | | |
| 1 DeGette | Y | N | Y | Y | Y | Y |
| 2 Udall | Y | N | Y | Y | Y | Y |
| 3 Salazar | Y | N | Y | Y | Y | Y |
| 4 Musgrave | N | Y | N | N | N | Y |
| 5 Hefley | N | Y | N | Y | N | Y |
| 6 Tancredo | N | N | N | N | N | N |
| 7 Beauprez | N | Y | N | N | N | Y |
| **CONNECTICUT** | | | | | | |
| 1 Larson | Y | N | Y | Y | Y | N |
| 2 Simmons | N | Y | N | N | N | Y |
| 3 DeLauro | Y | N | Y | Y | Y | N |
| 4 Shays | N | Y | N | N | N | Y |
| 5 Johnson | N | Y | N | N | N | Y |
| **DELAWARE** | | | | | | |
| AL Castle | N | Y | N | N | N | Y |
| **FLORIDA** | | | | | | |
| 1 Miller | N | Y | N | N | N | Y |
| 2 Boyd | Y | N | Y | Y | Y | Y |
| 3 Brown | Y | N | Y | Y | Y | Y |
| 4 Crenshaw | N | Y | N | N | N | Y |
| 5 Brown-Waite | N | Y | N | N | N | ? |
| 6 Stearns | N | Y | N | N | N | Y |
| 7 Mica | N | Y | N | N | N | ? |
| 8 Keller | N | Y | N | N | N | Y |
| 9 Bilirakis | N | Y | N | N | N | Y |
| 10 Young | N | Y | N | N | N | Y |
| 11 Davis | Y | N | Y | Y | Y | Y |
| 12 Putnam | N | Y | N | N | N | Y |
| 13 Harris | ? | ? | ? | ? | ? | ? |
| 14 Mack | N | Y | N | N | N | Y |
| 15 Weldon | N | Y | N | N | N | Y |
| 16 Foley | N | Y | N | N | N | Y |
| 17 Meek | Y | N | Y | Y | Y | Y |
| 18 Ros-Lehtinen | N | Y | N | ? | ? | ? |
| 19 Wexler | Y | N | Y | Y | Y | Y |
| 20 Wasserman-Schultz | Y | N | Y | Y | Y | Y |
| 21 Diaz-Balart, L. | N | Y | N | N | N | Y |
| 22 Shaw | N | Y | N | N | N | Y |
| 23 Hastings | N | Y | Y | Y | Y | N |
| 24 Feeney | N | Y | N | N | N | ? |
| 25 Diaz-Balart, M. | N | Y | N | N | N | Y |
| **GEORGIA** | | | | | | |
| 1 Kingston | N | Y | N | N | ? | ? |
| 2 Bishop | Y | N | Y | Y | Y | Y |
| 3 Marshall | Y | Y | Y | Y | Y | Y |
| 4 McKinney | Y | N | Y | Y | Y | N |
| 5 Lewis | Y | N | ? | ? | ? | Y |
| 6 Price | N | Y | N | N | N | Y |
| 7 Linder | N | Y | N | N | N | Y |
| 8 Westmoreland | N | Y | N | N | N | N |
| 9 Norwood | N | Y | N | N | N | Y |
| 10 Deal | N | Y | N | N | N | Y |
| 11 Gingrey | N | Y | N | N | N | Y |
| 12 Barrow | Y | N | Y | Y | Y | Y |
| 13 Scott | Y | N | Y | Y | Y | ? |
| **HAWAII** | | | | | | |
| 1 Abercrombie | Y | N | Y | Y | Y | N |
| 2 Case | Y | N | Y | N | Y | Y |
| **IDAHO** | | | | | | |
| 1 Otter | N | Y | N | N | N | Y |
| 2 Simpson | N | Y | N | N | N | Y |
| **ILLINOIS** | | | | | | |
| 1 Rush | Y | N | Y | Y | Y | N |
| 2 Jackson | Y | N | Y | Y | Y | N |
| 3 Lipinski | Y | N | Y | Y | Y | Y |
| 4 Gutierrez | Y | N | Y | Y | Y | N |
| 5 Emanuel | Y | N | Y | Y | Y | N |
| 6 Hyde | N | Y | N | N | N | Y |
| 7 Davis | Y | N | Y | Y | Y | N |
| 8 Bean | Y | N | Y | Y | Y | N |
| 9 Schakowsky | Y | N | Y | Y | Y | N |
| 10 Kirk | N | Y | N | N | N | Y |
| 11 Weller | N | Y | N | N | N | Y |
| 12 Costello | Y | N | Y | Y | Y | Y |

**KEY**  Republicans   Democrats   *Independents*

| | | | |
|---|---|---|---|
| Y | Voted for (yea) | X | Paired against |
| # | Paired for | – | Announced against |
| + | Announced for | P | Voted "present" |
| N | Voted against (nay) | | |

| | |
|---|---|
| C | Voted "present" to avoid possible conflict of interest |
| ? | Did not vote or otherwise make a position known |

| | 47 | 48 | 49 | 50 | 51 | 52 |
|---|---|---|---|---|---|---|
| 13 **Biggert** | N | Y | N | N | N | Y |
| 14 **Hastert** | | | | | N | Y |
| 15 **Johnson** | N | Y | N | N | N | Y |
| 16 **Manzullo** | N | Y | N | N | N | Y |
| 17 Evans | Y | N | Y | Y | Y | Y |
| 18 **LaHood** | N | Y | N | N | N | Y |
| 19 **Shimkus** | N | Y | N | N | N | Y |
| **INDIANA** | | | | | | |
| 1 Visclosky | Y | N | Y | Y | Y | Y |
| 2 **Chocola** | N | Y | N | N | N | Y |
| 3 **Souder** | N | Y | N | N | N | Y |
| 4 **Buyer** | N | Y | N | N | N | Y |
| 5 **Burton** | N | Y | N | N | N | Y |
| 6 **Pence** | N | Y | N | N | N | Y |
| 7 Carson | ? | ? | ? | ? | ? | ? |
| 8 **Hostettler** | N | N | N | N | N | Y |
| 9 **Sodrel** | N | Y | N | N | N | Y |
| **IOWA** | | | | | | |
| 1 **Nussle** | N | Y | N | N | N | Y |
| 2 **Leach** | N | Y | ? | ? | ? | ? |
| 3 Boswell | Y | N | Y | Y | Y | Y |
| 4 **Latham** | N | Y | N | N | N | Y |
| 5 **King** | N | Y | N | N | N | Y |
| **KANSAS** | | | | | | |
| 1 **Moran** | N | Y | N | N | N | Y |
| 2 **Ryun** | N | Y | N | N | N | Y |
| 3 Moore | Y | N | Y | N | Y | Y |
| 4 **Tiahrt** | N | Y | N | N | N | Y |
| **KENTUCKY** | | | | | | |
| 1 **Whitfield** | N | Y | N | N | N | Y |
| 2 **Lewis** | N | Y | N | N | N | Y |
| 3 **Northup** | N | Y | N | N | N | Y |
| 4 **Davis** | N | Y | N | N | N | Y |
| 5 **Rogers** | N | Y | N | N | N | Y |
| 6 Chandler | Y | N | Y | Y | Y | Y |
| **LOUISIANA** | | | | | | |
| 1 **Jindal** | N | Y | N | N | N | Y |
| 2 Jefferson | Y | N | Y | Y | Y | N |
| 3 Melancon | Y | N | Y | Y | Y | Y |
| 4 **McCrery** | N | Y | N | N | N | Y |
| 5 **Alexander** | N | Y | N | N | N | Y |
| 6 **Baker** | N | Y | N | N | N | Y |
| 7 **Boustany** | N | Y | N | N | N | Y |
| **MAINE** | | | | | | |
| 1 Allen | Y | N | Y | Y | Y | Y |
| 2 Michaud | Y | N | N | Y | Y | Y |
| **MARYLAND** | | | | | | |
| 1 **Gilchrest** | N | Y | N | N | N | Y |
| 2 Ruppersberger | Y | N | Y | Y | Y | Y |
| 3 Cardin | Y | N | Y | Y | Y | Y |
| 4 Wynn | Y | N | Y | Y | Y | Y |
| 5 Hoyer | Y | N | Y | Y | Y | Y |
| 6 **Bartlett** | N | Y | N | N | N | Y |
| 7 Cummings | Y | N | Y | Y | Y | Y |
| 8 Van Hollen | Y | N | Y | Y | Y | N |
| **MASSACHUSETTS** | | | | | | |
| 1 Olver | Y | N | Y | Y | Y | N |
| 2 Neal | Y | N | Y | Y | Y | Y |
| 3 McGovern | Y | N | Y | Y | Y | N |
| 4 Frank | Y | N | Y | Y | Y | Y |
| 5 Meehan | Y | N | Y | Y | Y | ? |
| 6 Tierney | Y | N | Y | Y | Y | N |
| 7 Markey | Y | N | Y | Y | Y | N |
| 8 Capuano | Y | N | Y | Y | Y | Y |
| 9 Lynch | Y | N | Y | Y | Y | N |
| 10 Delahunt | Y | N | Y | Y | Y | ? |
| **MICHIGAN** | | | | | | |
| 1 Stupak | Y | N | Y | Y | Y | Y |
| 2 **Hoekstra** | N | Y | N | N | N | Y |
| 3 **Ehlers** | N | Y | N | N | N | Y |
| 4 **Camp** | N | Y | N | N | N | Y |
| 5 Kildee | Y | N | Y | Y | Y | Y |
| 6 **Upton** | N | Y | N | N | N | Y |
| 7 **Schwarz** | N | Y | N | N | N | Y |
| 8 **Rogers** | N | Y | N | N | N | Y |
| 9 **Knollenberg** | N | Y | N | N | N | Y |
| 10 **Miller** | N | Y | N | N | N | Y |
| 11 **McCotter** | N | Y | N | N | Y | Y |
| 12 Levin | Y | N | Y | Y | Y | Y |
| 13 Kilpatrick | Y | N | Y | Y | Y | Y |
| 14 Conyers | Y | N | Y | Y | Y | N |
| 15 Dingell | Y | N | Y | Y | Y | Y |

| | 47 | 48 | 49 | 50 | 51 | 52 |
|---|---|---|---|---|---|---|
| **MINNESOTA** | | | | | | |
| 1 **Gutknecht** | N | Y | N | N | N | Y |
| 2 **Kline** | N | Y | N | N | N | Y |
| 3 **Ramstad** | N | Y | N | N | N | Y |
| 4 McCollum | Y | N | Y | Y | Y | N |
| 5 Sabo | Y | N | Y | Y | Y | Y |
| 6 **Kennedy** | N | Y | N | N | N | Y |
| 7 Peterson | Y | Y | Y | Y | Y | Y |
| 8 Oberstar | Y | N | Y | Y | Y | N |
| **MISSISSIPPI** | | | | | | |
| 1 **Wicker** | N | Y | N | N | N | Y |
| 2 Thompson | Y | N | Y | Y | Y | Y |
| 3 **Pickering** | N | Y | N | N | N | Y |
| 4 Taylor | Y | Y | Y | N | Y | N |
| **MISSOURI** | | | | | | |
| 1 Clay | Y | N | Y | Y | Y | Y |
| 2 **Akin** | N | Y | N | N | N | Y |
| 3 Carnahan | Y | N | Y | Y | Y | Y |
| 4 Skelton | Y | N | Y | Y | Y | Y |
| 5 Cleaver | ? | ? | Y | Y | Y | Y |
| 6 **Graves** | N | Y | N | N | N | ? |
| 7 **Blunt** | N | Y | N | N | N | Y |
| 8 **Emerson** | N | Y | N | N | N | ? |
| 9 **Hulshof** | N | Y | N | N | N | Y |
| **MONTANA** | | | | | | |
| AL **Rehberg** | N | Y | N | N | N | Y |
| **NEBRASKA** | | | | | | |
| 1 **Fortenberry** | N | Y | N | N | N | Y |
| 2 **Terry** | N | Y | N | N | N | ? |
| 3 **Osborne** | N | Y | N | N | N | Y |
| **NEVADA** | | | | | | |
| 1 Berkley | Y | N | Y | Y | Y | Y |
| 2 **Gibbons** | N | Y | N | N | N | Y |
| 3 **Porter** | N | Y | N | N | N | Y |
| **NEW HAMPSHIRE** | | | | | | |
| 1 **Bradley** | N | Y | N | N | N | Y |
| 2 **Bass** | N | Y | N | N | N | Y |
| **NEW JERSEY** | | | | | | |
| 1 Andrews | Y | N | Y | Y | Y | N |
| 2 **LoBiondo** | N | Y | N | N | N | Y |
| 3 **Saxton** | N | Y | N | N | N | Y |
| 4 **Smith** | N | Y | N | N | N | Y |
| 5 **Garrett** | N | Y | N | N | N | Y |
| 6 Pallone | Y | N | Y | Y | Y | N |
| 7 **Ferguson** | N | Y | N | N | N | Y |
| 8 Pascrell | Y | N | N | Y | Y | Y |
| 9 Rothman | Y | N | ? | ? | ? | ? |
| 10 Payne | Y | N | Y | Y | Y | N |
| 11 **Frelinghuysen** | N | Y | N | N | N | Y |
| 12 Holt | Y | N | Y | Y | Y | N |
| 13 Menendez | Y | N | Y | Y | Y | N |
| **NEW MEXICO** | | | | | | |
| 1 **Wilson** | N | Y | N | N | N | Y |
| 2 **Pearce** | N | Y | N | N | N | Y |
| 3 Udall | Y | N | Y | Y | Y | Y |
| **NEW YORK** | | | | | | |
| 1 Bishop | Y | N | Y | Y | Y | Y |
| 2 Israel | Y | N | Y | Y | Y | Y |
| 3 **King** | N | Y | N | N | N | Y |
| 4 McCarthy | Y | N | Y | Y | Y | Y |
| 5 Ackerman | Y | N | Y | Y | Y | Y |
| 6 Meeks | ? | ? | ? | ? | ? | ? |
| 7 Crowley | Y | N | Y | Y | Y | Y |
| 8 Nadler | Y | N | Y | Y | Y | N |
| 9 Weiner | Y | N | Y | Y | Y | Y |
| 10 Towns | Y | N | Y | Y | Y | Y |
| 11 Owens | Y | N | Y | Y | Y | N |
| 12 Velázquez | Y | N | Y | Y | Y | Y |
| 13 **Fossella** | N | Y | N | N | N | Y |
| 14 Maloney | Y | N | Y | Y | Y | Y |
| 15 Rangel | Y | N | Y | Y | Y | Y |
| 16 Serrano | Y | N | Y | Y | Y | Y |
| 17 Engel | Y | N | Y | Y | Y | Y |
| 18 Lowey | Y | N | Y | Y | Y | Y |
| 19 **Kelly** | N | Y | N | N | N | Y |
| 20 **Sweeney** | N | Y | N | N | N | Y |
| 21 McNulty | Y | N | Y | Y | Y | Y |
| 22 Hinchey | Y | N | Y | Y | Y | N |
| 23 **McHugh** | N | Y | N | N | N | Y |
| 24 **Boehlert** | N | Y | N | N | N | ? |
| 25 **Walsh** | N | Y | N | N | N | Y |
| 26 **Reynolds** | N | Y | N | N | N | Y |
| 27 Higgins | Y | N | N | Y | Y | Y |
| 28 Slaughter | Y | N | Y | Y | Y | ? |
| 29 **Kuhl** | N | Y | N | N | N | ? |

| | 47 | 48 | 49 | 50 | 51 | 52 |
|---|---|---|---|---|---|---|
| **NORTH CAROLINA** | | | | | | |
| 1 Butterfield | Y | N | Y | Y | Y | Y |
| 2 Etheridge | Y | N | Y | Y | Y | Y |
| 3 **Jones** | N | Y | N | N | N | N |
| 4 Price | Y | N | Y | Y | Y | Y |
| 5 **Foxx** | N | Y | N | N | N | Y |
| 6 **Coble** | N | Y | N | N | N | Y |
| 7 McIntyre | Y | N | Y | Y | Y | Y |
| 8 **Hayes** | N | Y | N | N | N | Y |
| 9 **Myrick** | N | Y | N | N | N | Y |
| 10 **McHenry** | N | Y | N | N | N | Y |
| 11 **Taylor** | N | Y | N | N | N | Y |
| 12 Watt | Y | N | Y | Y | Y | Y |
| 13 Miller | Y | N | Y | Y | Y | N |
| **NORTH DAKOTA** | | | | | | |
| AL Pomeroy | Y | N | Y | Y | Y | Y |
| **OHIO** | | | | | | |
| 1 **Chabot** | N | Y | N | N | N | Y |
| 2 **Portman** | N | Y | N | N | N | Y |
| 3 **Turner** | N | Y | N | N | N | Y |
| 4 **Oxley** | N | Y | N | N | N | Y |
| 5 **Gillmor** | ? | ? | N | N | N | Y |
| 6 Strickland | Y | N | Y | Y | Y | N |
| 7 **Hobson** | N | Y | N | N | N | Y |
| 8 **Boehner** | N | Y | N | N | N | Y |
| 9 Kaptur | Y | N | Y | Y | Y | Y |
| 10 Kucinich | Y | N | Y | Y | Y | N |
| 11 Jones | Y | N | Y | Y | Y | N |
| 12 **Tiberi** | N | Y | N | N | N | ? |
| 13 Brown | Y | N | ? | ? | Y | Y |
| 14 **LaTourette** | N | Y | N | N | N | ? |
| 15 **Pryce** | N | Y | N | N | N | Y |
| 16 **Regula** | N | Y | N | N | N | Y |
| 17 Ryan | Y | N | Y | Y | Y | N |
| 18 **Ney** | N | Y | N | N | N | Y |
| **OKLAHOMA** | | | | | | |
| 1 **Sullivan** | N | Y | N | N | N | Y |
| 2 Boren | Y | N | Y | N | Y | Y |
| 3 **Lucas** | N | Y | N | N | N | Y |
| 4 **Cole** | N | Y | N | N | N | Y |
| 5 **Istook** | N | Y | N | N | N | Y |
| **OREGON** | | | | | | |
| 1 Wu | Y | N | Y | Y | Y | Y |
| 2 **Walden** | N | Y | N | N | N | Y |
| 3 Blumenauer | Y | N | Y | Y | Y | Y |
| 4 DeFazio | Y | N | Y | Y | Y | Y |
| 5 Hooley | Y | N | Y | Y | Y | Y |
| **PENNSYLVANIA** | | | | | | |
| 1 Brady | Y | N | Y | Y | Y | Y |
| 2 Fattah | Y | N | Y | Y | Y | Y |
| 3 **English** | N | Y | N | N | N | Y |
| 4 **Hart** | N | Y | N | N | N | Y |
| 5 **Peterson** | N | Y | N | N | N | Y |
| 6 **Gerlach** | N | Y | N | N | N | Y |
| 7 **Weldon** | N | Y | N | N | N | ? |
| 8 **Fitzpatrick** | N | Y | N | N | N | Y |
| 9 **Shuster** | N | Y | N | N | N | Y |
| 10 **Sherwood** | N | Y | N | N | N | Y |
| 11 Kanjorski | Y | N | Y | Y | Y | Y |
| 12 Murtha | Y | N | Y | Y | Y | Y |
| 13 Schwartz | Y | N | Y | Y | Y | Y |
| 14 Doyle | Y | N | Y | Y | Y | Y |
| 15 **Dent** | N | Y | N | N | N | Y |
| 16 **Pitts** | N | Y | N | N | N | Y |
| 17 Holden | Y | N | Y | Y | Y | Y |
| 18 **Murphy** | N | Y | N | N | N | Y |
| 19 **Platts** | N | Y | N | N | N | Y |
| **RHODE ISLAND** | | | | | | |
| 1 Kennedy | Y | N | Y | Y | Y | N |
| 2 Langevin | Y | N | Y | Y | Y | N |
| **SOUTH CAROLINA** | | | | | | |
| 1 **Brown** | N | Y | N | N | N | Y |
| 2 **Wilson** | N | Y | N | N | N | Y |
| 3 **Barrett** | N | Y | N | N | N | Y |
| 4 **Inglis** | N | Y | ? | N | N | Y |
| 5 Spratt | Y | N | Y | Y | Y | ? |
| 6 Clyburn | Y | N | Y | Y | Y | N |
| **SOUTH DAKOTA** | | | | | | |
| AL Herseth | Y | N | Y | N | Y | Y |
| **TENNESSEE** | | | | | | |
| 1 **Jenkins** | N | Y | N | N | N | Y |
| 2 **Duncan** | N | N | N | N | N | N |

| | 47 | 48 | 49 | 50 | 51 | 52 |
|---|---|---|---|---|---|---|
| 3 **Wamp** | N | N | N | N | ? | ? |
| 4 Davis | Y | N | Y | N | Y | Y |
| 5 Cooper | Y | N | Y | Y | Y | Y |
| 6 Gordon | Y | N | Y | Y | Y | N |
| 7 **Blackburn** | N | Y | N | N | N | Y |
| 8 Tanner | Y | N | Y | Y | Y | Y |
| 9 Ford | Y | N | ? | ? | ? | ? |
| **TEXAS** | | | | | | |
| 1 **Gohmert** | N | Y | N | N | N | Y |
| 2 **Poe** | N | Y | N | N | N | Y |
| 3 **Johnson, S.** | N | Y | N | N | N | Y |
| 4 **Hall** | N | Y | N | N | N | Y |
| 5 **Hensarling** | N | N | N | N | N | Y |
| 6 **Barton** | N | Y | N | N | N | Y |
| 7 **Culberson** | N | Y | N | N | N | Y |
| 8 **Brady** | N | Y | N | N | N | Y |
| 9 Green, A. | Y | N | Y | Y | Y | Y |
| 10 **McCaul** | N | Y | N | N | N | Y |
| 11 **Conaway** | N | Y | N | N | N | Y |
| 12 **Granger** | N | Y | N | N | N | Y |
| 13 **Thornberry** | N | Y | N | N | N | Y |
| 14 **Paul** | N | N | N | N | N | Y |
| 15 Hinojosa | Y | N | Y | Y | Y | Y |
| 16 Reyes | Y | N | Y | Y | Y | Y |
| 17 Edwards | Y | N | Y | Y | Y | Y |
| 18 Jackson-Lee | Y | N | Y | Y | Y | N |
| 19 **Neugebauer** | N | Y | N | N | N | Y |
| 20 Gonzalez | Y | N | Y | Y | Y | N |
| 21 **Smith** | N | Y | N | N | N | Y |
| 22 **DeLay** | N | Y | N | N | N | Y |
| 23 **Bonilla** | N | Y | N | N | N | Y |
| 24 **Marchant** | N | Y | N | N | N | Y |
| 25 Doggett | Y | N | Y | Y | Y | Y |
| 26 **Burgess** | N | Y | N | N | N | Y |
| 27 Ortiz | Y | N | Y | Y | Y | Y |
| 28 Cuellar | Y | N | N | Y | Y | Y |
| 29 Green, G. | Y | N | Y | Y | Y | Y |
| 30 Johnson, E. | Y | N | Y | Y | Y | Y |
| 31 **Carter** | N | Y | N | N | N | Y |
| 32 **Sessions** | N | Y | N | N | N | Y |
| **UTAH** | | | | | | |
| 1 **Bishop** | N | Y | N | N | N | Y |
| 2 Matheson | Y | N | Y | N | Y | Y |
| 3 **Cannon** | N | Y | N | N | N | Y |
| **VERMONT** | | | | | | |
| AL *Sanders* | Y | N | Y | Y | Y | Y |
| **VIRGINIA** | | | | | | |
| 1 **Davis, J.** | N | Y | N | N | N | Y |
| 2 **Drake** | N | Y | N | N | N | Y |
| 3 Scott | Y | N | Y | Y | Y | N |
| 4 **Forbes** | N | Y | N | N | N | Y |
| 5 **Goode** | N | Y | N | N | N | Y |
| 6 **Goodlatte** | N | Y | N | N | N | Y |
| 7 **Cantor** | N | Y | N | N | N | Y |
| 8 Moran | Y | N | Y | Y | Y | N |
| 9 Boucher | Y | N | Y | Y | Y | Y |
| 10 **Wolf** | N | Y | N | N | N | Y |
| 11 **Davis, T.** | N | Y | N | N | N | Y |
| **WASHINGTON** | | | | | | |
| 1 Inslee | Y | N | Y | Y | Y | N |
| 2 Larsen | Y | N | Y | Y | Y | N |
| 3 Baird | Y | N | Y | Y | Y | N |
| 4 **Hastings** | N | Y | N | N | N | Y |
| 5 **McMorris** | N | Y | N | N | N | Y |
| 6 Dicks | Y | N | Y | Y | Y | N |
| 7 McDermott | Y | N | Y | Y | Y | ? |
| 8 **Reichert** | N | Y | N | N | N | Y |
| 9 Smith | Y | N | Y | Y | Y | Y |
| **WEST VIRGINIA** | | | | | | |
| 1 Mollohan | Y | N | Y | Y | Y | N |
| 2 **Capito** | N | Y | N | N | N | Y |
| 3 Rahall | Y | N | Y | Y | Y | Y |
| **WISCONSIN** | | | | | | |
| 1 **Ryan** | N | Y | N | N | N | Y |
| 2 Baldwin | Y | N | Y | Y | Y | N |
| 3 Kind | Y | N | Y | Y | Y | Y |
| 4 Moore | Y | N | Y | Y | Y | Y |
| 5 **Sensenbrenner** | N | N | N | N | N | Y |
| 6 **Petri** | N | Y | N | N | N | Y |
| 7 Obey | Y | N | Y | Y | Y | ? |
| 8 **Green** | N | Y | N | N | N | Y |
| **WYOMING** | | | | | | |
| AL **Cubin** | N | Y | N | N | N | Y |

# IN THE HOUSE | By Vote Number

**53. Procedural Motion/Journal.** Approval of the House Journal of Monday, March 7, 2005. Approved 378-29: R 220-8; D 157-21 (ND 112-18, SD 45-3); I 1-0. March 8, 2005.

**54. H Res 133. Committee Funding Extension/Adoption.** Ney, R-Ohio, motion to suspend the rules and adopt the resolution that would extend funding authority for House committees at current levels from April 1 through April 30. Motion agreed to 406-0: R 228-0; D 178-0 (ND 130-0, SD 48-0); I 0-0. A two-thirds majority of those present and voting (271 in this case) is required for adoption under suspension of the rules. March 8, 2005.

**55. H Res 122. Language Study/Adoption.** Porter, R-Nev., motion to suspend the rules and adopt the resolution that would express the sense of the House that language study contributes to the intellectual and social development of a student, as well as of the economy and security of the nation. Motion agreed to 396-0: R 223-0; D 173-0 (ND 126-0, SD 47-0); I 0-0. A two-thirds majority of those present and voting (264 in this case) is required for adoption under suspension of the rules. March 8, 2005.

**56. HR 3. Surface Transportation Reauthorization/Oil and Gas Hours-of-Service Exemptions.** Conaway, R-Texas, amendment that would exempt commercial drivers working in field operations for the natural gas and oil industry from hours-of-service rules issued by the Federal Motor Carrier Safety Administration in 2003. Rejected 198-226: R 185-43; D 13-182 (ND 6-139, SD 7-43); I 0-1. March 9, 2005.

**57. HR 3. Surface Transportation Reauthorization/Agriculture Hours-of-Service Exemptions.** Moran, R-Kan., amendment that would expand exemptions from hours-of-service rules for drivers of trucks transporting agricultural commodities to include livestock, food, feed, fiber and other farm products. Adopted 257-167: R 214-14; D 43-152 (ND 18-127, SD 25-25); I 0-1. March 9, 2005.

**58. HR 3. Surface Transportation Reauthorization/Vehicle Length Exemption.** Osborne, R-Neb., amendment that would exempt Nebraska from vehicle length restrictions of 65 feet and increase the limit to 81.5 feet for custom harvesters operating in the state during the harvesting of certain crops. Adopted 236-184: R 201-25; D 34-159 (ND 17-126, SD 17-33); I 1-0. March 9, 2005.

**59. HR 3. Surface Transportation Reauthorization/New Interstate Tolls.** Kennedy, R-Minn., amendment that would authorize new tolls on any existing toll road or newly constructed lane on the interstate system to manage congestion or address air pollution problems. It also would allow an unlimited number of new, toll-eligible express traffic lanes. Rejected 155-265: R 134-92; D 21-172 (ND 11-133, SD 10-39); I 0-1. March 9, 2005.

| | 53 | 54 | 55 | 56 | 57 | 58 | 59 |
|---|---|---|---|---|---|---|---|
| **ALABAMA** | | | | | | | |
| 1 Bonner | Y | Y | Y | Y | Y | Y | Y |
| 2 Everett | Y | Y | Y | Y | Y | Y | Y |
| 3 Rogers | Y | Y | Y | N | Y | Y | Y |
| 4 Aderholt | Y | Y | Y | Y | Y | Y | Y |
| 5 Cramer | Y | Y | Y | Y | Y | N | Y |
| 6 Bachus | Y | Y | Y | Y | Y | Y | N |
| 7 Davis | Y | Y | Y | N | Y | N | N |
| **ALASKA** | | | | | | | |
| AL Young | Y | Y | Y | N | N | N | N |
| **ARIZONA** | | | | | | | |
| 1 Renzi | Y | Y | Y | Y | Y | Y | Y |
| 2 Franks | Y | Y | Y | Y | Y | Y | Y |
| 3 Shadegg | Y | Y | Y | Y | Y | Y | Y |
| 4 Pastor | N | Y | Y | N | N | N | Y |
| 5 Hayworth | Y | Y | Y | Y | Y | Y | Y |
| 6 Flake | Y | Y | Y | Y | Y | Y | Y |
| 7 Grijalva | Y | Y | Y | N | N | N | N |
| 8 Kolbe | Y | Y | Y | Y | Y | Y | Y |
| **ARKANSAS** | | | | | | | |
| 1 Berry | Y | Y | Y | N | Y | N | N |
| 2 Snyder | Y | Y | Y | N | Y | N | N |
| 3 Boozman | Y | Y | Y | Y | Y | Y | Y |
| 4 Ross | Y | Y | Y | N | Y | N | N |
| **CALIFORNIA** | | | | | | | |
| 1 Thompson | Y | Y | Y | N | N | N | N |
| 2 Herger | Y | Y | Y | Y | Y | Y | N |
| 3 Lungren | Y | Y | Y | Y | Y | Y | Y |
| 4 Doolittle | Y | Y | Y | Y | Y | Y | |
| 5 Vacant | | | | | | | |
| 6 Woolsey | Y | Y | Y | N | N | N | N |
| 7 Miller, George | N | Y | Y | N | N | N | N |
| 8 Pelosi | Y | Y | Y | N | N | N | N |
| 9 Lee | ? | ? | ? | N | N | N | N |
| 10 Tauscher | Y | Y | Y | N | N | N | N |
| 11 Pombo | Y | Y | Y | Y | Y | Y | N |
| 12 Lantos | Y | Y | Y | N | N | N | N |
| 13 Stark | ? | ? | ? | N | N | N | N |
| 14 Eshoo | Y | Y | Y | N | N | N | N |
| 15 Honda | Y | Y | Y | N | N | N | N |
| 16 Lofgren | Y | Y | Y | N | N | N | N |
| 17 Farr | Y | Y | Y | N | N | N | N |
| 18 Cardoza | Y | Y | Y | N | Y | Y | N |
| 19 Radanovich | Y | Y | Y | Y | Y | Y | N |
| 20 Costa | Y | Y | Y | N | Y | Y | N |
| 21 Nunes | Y | Y | Y | Y | Y | Y | N |
| 22 Thomas | Y | Y | Y | Y | Y | Y | N |
| 23 Capps | Y | Y | Y | N | N | N | N |
| 24 Gallegly | Y | Y | Y | Y | N | Y | N |
| 25 McKeon | Y | Y | Y | Y | Y | Y | N |
| 26 Dreier | Y | Y | Y | Y | Y | Y | N |
| 27 Sherman | Y | Y | Y | N | N | N | N |
| 28 Berman | Y | Y | Y | N | N | N | N |
| 29 Schiff | Y | Y | Y | N | N | N | N |
| 30 Waxman | Y | Y | Y | N | N | N | N |
| 31 Becerra | Y | Y | Y | N | N | N | N |
| 32 Solis | Y | Y | Y | N | N | N | N |
| 33 Watson | Y | Y | Y | N | N | N | N |
| 34 Roybal-Allard | Y | Y | Y | N | N | N | N |
| 35 Waters | N | Y | Y | N | N | N | N |
| 36 Harman | Y | Y | Y | N | N | N | N |
| 37 Millender-McD. | Y | Y | Y | N | N | N | N |
| 38 Napolitano | Y | Y | Y | N | N | N | N |
| 39 Sánchez, Linda | Y | Y | Y | N | N | N | N |
| 40 Royce | Y | Y | Y | Y | Y | ? | Y |
| 41 Lewis | Y | Y | Y | Y | Y | Y | Y |
| 42 Miller, Gary | Y | Y | Y | Y | Y | Y | Y |
| 43 Baca | Y | Y | Y | N | Y | Y | N |
| 44 Calvert | Y | Y | Y | Y | Y | Y | N |
| 45 Bono | Y | Y | Y | Y | Y | Y | N |
| 46 Rohrabacher | Y | Y | Y | Y | Y | Y | N |
| 47 Sanchez, Loretta | Y | Y | Y | N | N | Y | N |
| 48 Cox | Y | Y | Y | Y | Y | Y | N |
| 49 Issa | Y | Y | Y | Y | Y | Y | N |
| 50 Cunningham | N | Y | Y | N | N | N | N |
| 51 Filner | N | Y | Y | N | N | N | N |
| 52 Hunter | Y | Y | ? | Y | Y | Y | Y |
| 53 Davis | Y | Y | Y | N | N | N | N |
| **COLORADO** | | | | | | | |
| 1 DeGette | Y | Y | Y | N | N | N | N |
| 2 Udall | N | Y | Y | Y | Y | Y | N |
| 3 Salazar | Y | Y | Y | Y | Y | Y | N |
| 4 Musgrave | Y | Y | Y | Y | Y | Y | Y |
| 5 Hefley | N | Y | Y | Y | Y | Y | N |
| 6 Tancredo | Y | Y | Y | N | Y | Y | Y |
| 7 Beauprez | Y | Y | Y | Y | Y | Y | Y |
| **CONNECTICUT** | | | | | | | |
| 1 Larson | Y | Y | Y | N | N | N | N |
| 2 Simmons | Y | Y | Y | N | Y | Y | N |
| 3 DeLauro | Y | Y | Y | N | N | N | N |
| 4 Shays | Y | Y | Y | N | Y | N | N |
| 5 Johnson | Y | Y | ? | N | Y | Y | N |
| **DELAWARE** | | | | | | | |
| AL Castle | Y | Y | Y | Y | Y | Y | N |
| **FLORIDA** | | | | | | | |
| 1 Miller | Y | Y | Y | Y | Y | Y | Y |
| 2 Boyd | Y | Y | Y | N | Y | Y | Y |
| 3 Brown | Y | Y | Y | N | N | N | N |
| 4 Crenshaw | Y | Y | Y | Y | Y | Y | Y |
| 5 Brown-Waite | Y | Y | Y | Y | Y | Y | N |
| 6 Stearns | Y | Y | Y | Y | Y | Y | N |
| 7 Mica | Y | Y | Y | Y | Y | Y | Y |
| 8 Keller | Y | Y | Y | Y | Y | Y | Y |
| 9 Bilirakis | Y | Y | Y | Y | Y | N | Y |
| 10 Young | Y | Y | Y | N | Y | Y | N |
| 11 Davis | Y | Y | Y | N | N | N | N |
| 12 Putnam | Y | Y | Y | Y | Y | Y | Y |
| 13 Harris | Y | Y | Y | Y | Y | Y | Y |
| 14 Mack | Y | Y | Y | Y | Y | Y | Y |
| 15 Weldon | Y | Y | Y | N | N | Y | Y |
| 16 Foley | Y | Y | Y | Y | Y | Y | N |
| 17 Meek | Y | Y | Y | N | N | N | N |
| 18 Ros-Lehtinen | Y | Y | Y | N | Y | Y | N |
| 19 Wexler | Y | Y | Y | N | N | N | N |
| 20 Wasserman-Schultz | ? | ? | ? | N | N | N | N |
| 21 Diaz-Balart, L. | Y | Y | Y | Y | Y | Y | Y |
| 22 Shaw | Y | Y | Y | Y | Y | Y | N |
| 23 Hastings | N | Y | Y | N | N | N | N |
| 24 Feeney | Y | Y | Y | Y | Y | Y | Y |
| 25 Diaz-Balart, M. | Y | Y | Y | Y | Y | Y | Y |
| **GEORGIA** | | | | | | | |
| 1 Kingston | Y | Y | Y | Y | Y | Y | Y |
| 2 Bishop | Y | Y | Y | N | Y | Y | N |
| 3 Marshall | Y | Y | Y | N | Y | Y | N |
| 4 McKinney | Y | Y | Y | N | N | N | N |
| 5 Lewis | Y | Y | Y | N | N | N | N |
| 6 Price | Y | Y | Y | Y | Y | Y | Y |
| 7 Linder | Y | Y | Y | Y | Y | Y | Y |
| 8 Westmoreland | Y | Y | Y | Y | Y | Y | N |
| 9 Norwood | Y | Y | Y | Y | Y | Y | N |
| 10 Deal | Y | Y | Y | Y | Y | Y | Y |
| 11 Gingrey | Y | Y | Y | Y | Y | Y | Y |
| 12 Barrow | ? | ? | ? | N | N | N | N |
| 13 Scott | Y | Y | Y | N | N | N | N |
| **HAWAII** | | | | | | | |
| 1 Abercrombie | Y | Y | Y | N | N | Y | N |
| 2 Case | Y | Y | Y | N | Y | N | N |
| **IDAHO** | | | | | | | |
| 1 Otter | N | Y | Y | Y | Y | Y | N |
| 2 Simpson | Y | Y | ? | Y | Y | Y | Y |
| **ILLINOIS** | | | | | | | |
| 1 Rush | Y | Y | Y | N | N | N | N |
| 2 Jackson | Y | Y | Y | N | N | N | N |
| 3 Lipinski | Y | Y | Y | N | N | N | N |
| 4 Gutierrez | Y | Y | ? | N | N | N | N |
| 5 Emanuel | Y | Y | Y | N | N | N | N |
| 6 Hyde | Y | Y | Y | Y | Y | Y | Y |
| 7 Davis | Y | Y | Y | N | N | N | N |
| 8 Bean | + | + | + | N | N | N | N |
| 9 Schakowsky | N | Y | ? | N | N | N | N |
| 10 Kirk | Y | Y | Y | N | N | N | N |
| 11 Weller | N | Y | Y | Y | Y | Y | N |
| 12 Costello | Y | Y | Y | N | Y | Y | N |

| | 53 | 54 | 55 | 56 | 57 | 58 | 59 |
|---|---|---|---|---|---|---|---|
| 13 **Biggert** | Y | Y | Y | N | N | N | N |
| 14 **Hastert** | | | | | | | |
| 15 **Johnson** | Y | Y | Y | Y | Y | Y | Y |
| 16 **Manzullo** | Y | Y | Y | Y | Y | Y | Y |
| 17 Evans | Y | Y | Y | N | N | N | N |
| 18 **LaHood** | Y | Y | Y | Y | Y | Y | Y |
| 19 **Shimkus** | Y | Y | Y | Y | Y | Y | Y |
| **INDIANA** | | | | | | | |
| 1 Visclosky | Y | Y | Y | N | N | N | N |
| 2 **Chocola** | Y | Y | Y | Y | Y | Y | N |
| 3 **Souder** | Y | Y | Y | Y | Y | Y | Y |
| 4 **Buyer** | Y | Y | Y | Y | Y | Y | Y |
| 5 **Burton** | Y | Y | Y | Y | Y | Y | Y |
| 6 **Pence** | Y | Y | Y | Y | Y | Y | Y |
| 7 Carson | ? | ? | ? | N | N | N | N |
| 8 **Hostettler** | Y | Y | Y | Y | Y | Y | Y |
| 9 **Sodrel** | Y | Y | Y | Y | Y | Y | N |
| **IOWA** | | | | | | | |
| 1 **Nussle** | Y | Y | Y | N | Y | Y | Y |
| 2 **Leach** | ? | ? | ? | N | Y | N | Y |
| 3 Boswell | Y | Y | Y | N | Y | Y | N |
| 4 **Latham** | N | Y | Y | Y | Y | Y | Y |
| 5 **King** | Y | Y | Y | Y | Y | Y | Y |
| **KANSAS** | | | | | | | |
| 1 **Moran** | Y | Y | Y | Y | Y | Y | Y |
| 2 **Ryun** | Y | Y | Y | Y | Y | Y | N |
| 3 Moore | Y | Y | Y | Y | Y | Y | Y |
| 4 **Tiahrt** | Y | Y | Y | Y | Y | Y | N |
| **KENTUCKY** | | | | | | | |
| 1 **Whitfield** | Y | Y | Y | Y | Y | Y | Y |
| 2 **Lewis** | Y | Y | Y | Y | Y | Y | N |
| 3 **Northup** | Y | Y | Y | Y | Y | Y | Y |
| 4 **Davis** | Y | Y | Y | Y | Y | Y | N |
| 5 **Rogers** | Y | Y | Y | Y | Y | Y | Y |
| 6 Chandler | Y | Y | Y | N | N | N | N |
| **LOUISIANA** | | | | | | | |
| 1 **Jindal** | Y | Y | Y | Y | Y | Y | Y |
| 2 Jefferson | Y | Y | Y | Y | N | N | ? |
| 3 Melancon | Y | Y | Y | Y | Y | Y | Y |
| 4 **McCrery** | Y | Y | Y | Y | Y | Y | N |
| 5 **Alexander** | Y | Y | Y | Y | Y | Y | Y |
| 6 **Baker** | Y | Y | Y | Y | Y | Y | N |
| 7 **Boustany** | Y | Y | Y | Y | Y | Y | Y |
| **MAINE** | | | | | | | |
| 1 Allen | Y | Y | Y | N | N | N | N |
| 2 Michaud | Y | Y | Y | N | N | N | Y |
| **MARYLAND** | | | | | | | |
| 1 **Gilchrest** | Y | Y | Y | N | Y | Y | N |
| 2 Ruppersberger | Y | Y | Y | N | Y | N | N |
| 3 Cardin | Y | Y | Y | N | N | N | N |
| 4 Wynn | Y | Y | ? | N | N | N | N |
| 5 Hoyer | Y | Y | Y | N | N | N | N |
| 6 **Bartlett** | Y | Y | Y | Y | Y | Y | N |
| 7 Cummings | Y | Y | Y | N | N | N | N |
| 8 Van Hollen | Y | Y | Y | N | N | N | N |
| **MASSACHUSETTS** | | | | | | | |
| 1 Olver | N | Y | Y | N | N | N | N |
| 2 Neal | Y | Y | Y | N | N | N | N |
| 3 McGovern | Y | Y | Y | N | N | N | N |
| 4 Frank | Y | Y | Y | N | N | Y | N |
| 5 Meehan | Y | Y | Y | N | N | N | N |
| 6 Tierney | Y | Y | Y | N | N | N | N |
| 7 Markey | Y | Y | Y | N | N | N | N |
| 8 Capuano | N | Y | Y | N | N | N | N |
| 9 Lynch | Y | Y | Y | N | N | Y | N |
| 10 Delahunt | Y | Y | Y | N | N | N | N |
| **MICHIGAN** | | | | | | | |
| 1 Stupak | ? | ? | ? | ? | ? | ? | ? |
| 2 **Hoekstra** | Y | Y | Y | N | Y | Y | Y |
| 3 **Ehlers** | Y | Y | Y | Y | Y | N | Y |
| 4 **Camp** | Y | Y | Y | Y | Y | Y | N |
| 5 Kildee | Y | Y | Y | N | N | N | N |
| 6 **Upton** | Y | Y | Y | N | Y | Y | Y |
| 7 **Schwarz** | Y | Y | Y | Y | Y | Y | N |
| 8 **Rogers** | Y | Y | Y | Y | Y | Y | N |
| 9 **Knollenberg** | Y | Y | Y | Y | Y | Y | N |
| 10 **Miller** | Y | Y | Y | N | Y | Y | N |
| 11 **McCotter** | Y | Y | Y | N | N | N | Y |
| 12 Levin | Y | Y | Y | N | N | N | N |
| 13 Kilpatrick | Y | Y | Y | N | N | N | N |
| 14 Conyers | Y | Y | ? | N | N | N | N |
| 15 Dingell | Y | Y | Y | N | N | Y | N |

| | 53 | 54 | 55 | 56 | 57 | 58 | 59 |
|---|---|---|---|---|---|---|---|
| **MINNESOTA** | | | | | | | |
| 1 **Gutknecht** | N | Y | Y | Y | Y | Y | Y |
| 2 **Kline** | Y | Y | Y | Y | Y | Y | Y |
| 3 **Ramstad** | ? | ? | ? | ? | ? | ? | ? |
| 4 McCollum | Y | Y | Y | N | N | N | N |
| 5 Sabo | N | Y | Y | N | N | N | N |
| 6 **Kennedy** | Y | Y | Y | Y | Y | Y | Y |
| 7 Peterson | N | Y | Y | N | Y | Y | N |
| 8 Oberstar | N | Y | Y | N | N | N | N |
| **MISSISSIPPI** | | | | | | | |
| 1 **Wicker** | Y | Y | Y | Y | Y | Y | Y |
| 2 Thompson | N | Y | Y | N | N | N | N |
| 3 **Pickering** | Y | Y | Y | Y | Y | Y | Y |
| 4 Taylor | N | Y | Y | N | N | Y | N |
| **MISSOURI** | | | | | | | |
| 1 Clay | ? | ? | ? | ? | ? | ? | ? |
| 2 **Akin** | Y | Y | Y | Y | Y | Y | Y |
| 3 Carnahan | Y | Y | Y | N | N | N | N |
| 4 Skelton | Y | Y | Y | Y | Y | Y | N |
| 5 Cleaver | + | + | + | N | N | N | N |
| 6 **Graves** | Y | Y | Y | Y | Y | Y | N |
| 7 **Blunt** | Y | Y | Y | Y | Y | Y | Y |
| 8 **Emerson** | Y | Y | Y | Y | Y | Y | Y |
| 9 **Hulshof** | Y | Y | Y | Y | Y | Y | N |
| **MONTANA** | | | | | | | |
| AL **Rehberg** | Y | Y | Y | Y | Y | Y | Y |
| **NEBRASKA** | | | | | | | |
| 1 **Fortenberry** | Y | Y | Y | Y | Y | Y | N |
| 2 **Terry** | Y | Y | Y | Y | Y | Y | N |
| 3 **Osborne** | Y | Y | Y | Y | Y | Y | N |
| **NEVADA** | | | | | | | |
| 1 Berkley | ? | ? | ? | N | N | N | N |
| 2 **Gibbons** | Y | Y | Y | Y | Y | + | + |
| 3 **Porter** | Y | Y | Y | Y | Y | Y | N |
| **NEW HAMPSHIRE** | | | | | | | |
| 1 **Bradley** | Y | Y | Y | Y | Y | Y | Y |
| 2 **Bass** | ? | ? | ? | Y | N | Y | Y |
| **NEW JERSEY** | | | | | | | |
| 1 Andrews | Y | Y | Y | N | N | N | Y |
| 2 **LoBiondo** | N | Y | Y | N | Y | N | Y |
| 3 **Saxton** | Y | Y | Y | Y | Y | Y | N |
| 4 **Smith** | Y | Y | Y | N | Y | N | Y |
| 5 **Garrett** | Y | Y | Y | Y | Y | Y | Y |
| 6 Pallone | Y | Y | Y | N | N | N | N |
| 7 **Ferguson** | Y | Y | Y | N | Y | N | Y |
| 8 Pascrell | Y | Y | Y | N | N | N | N |
| 9 Rothman | Y | Y | Y | ? | ? | ? | ? |
| 10 Payne | Y | Y | Y | N | N | ? | ? |
| 11 **Frelinghuysen** | Y | Y | Y | N | Y | Y | N |
| 12 Holt | Y | Y | Y | N | N | N | N |
| 13 Menendez | Y | Y | Y | N | N | N | N |
| **NEW MEXICO** | | | | | | | |
| 1 **Wilson** | Y | Y | Y | N | Y | Y | Y |
| 2 **Pearce** | Y | Y | Y | Y | Y | Y | Y |
| 3 Udall | N | Y | Y | Y | Y | N | N |
| **NEW YORK** | | | | | | | |
| 1 Bishop | Y | Y | Y | N | N | N | N |
| 2 Israel | Y | Y | Y | N | N | N | N |
| 3 **King** | Y | Y | Y | N | Y | Y | Y |
| 4 McCarthy | ? | ? | ? | N | N | N | N |
| 5 Ackerman | Y | Y | Y | N | N | N | N |
| 6 Meeks | ? | ? | ? | N | Y | N | Y |
| 7 Crowley | ? | ? | ? | N | N | N | N |
| 8 Nadler | Y | Y | Y | N | N | N | N |
| 9 Weiner | ? | ? | ? | N | N | N | N |
| 10 Towns | ? | ? | ? | N | N | N | N |
| 11 Owens | Y | Y | Y | N | N | N | N |
| 12 Velázquez | Y | Y | Y | N | N | N | N |
| 13 **Fossella** | N | Y | Y | N | Y | Y | Y |
| 14 Maloney | Y | Y | Y | N | N | N | N |
| 15 Rangel | Y | Y | Y | N | N | N | N |
| 16 Serrano | Y | Y | Y | N | N | N | N |
| 17 Engel | Y | Y | Y | N | N | N | N |
| 18 Lowey | Y | Y | Y | N | N | N | N |
| 19 **Kelly** | Y | Y | Y | N | Y | N | Y |
| 20 **Sweeney** | Y | Y | Y | N | Y | Y | Y |
| 21 McNulty | Y | Y | Y | N | N | N | N |
| 22 Hinchey | N | Y | Y | N | N | ? | N |
| 23 **McHugh** | Y | Y | Y | N | Y | Y | Y |
| 24 **Boehlert** | Y | Y | Y | Y | Y | N | Y |
| 25 **Walsh** | Y | Y | Y | N | N | Y | N |
| 26 **Reynolds** | Y | Y | Y | N | Y | Y | Y |
| 27 Higgins | ? | ? | ? | N | N | N | N |
| 28 Slaughter | Y | Y | Y | N | N | Y | N |
| 29 **Kuhl** | Y | Y | Y | Y | Y | Y | N |

| | 53 | 54 | 55 | 56 | 57 | 58 | 59 |
|---|---|---|---|---|---|---|---|
| **NORTH CAROLINA** | | | | | | | |
| 1 Butterfield | Y | Y | Y | N | N | N | N |
| 2 Etheridge | Y | Y | Y | N | Y | Y | N |
| 3 **Jones** | Y | Y | Y | Y | Y | N | Y |
| 4 Price | Y | Y | Y | N | N | N | N |
| 5 **Foxx** | Y | Y | Y | Y | Y | Y | Y |
| 6 **Coble** | Y | Y | Y | N | Y | N | Y |
| 7 McIntyre | Y | Y | Y | Y | Y | Y | N |
| 8 **Hayes** | Y | Y | Y | Y | Y | Y | Y |
| 9 **Myrick** | Y | Y | Y | Y | Y | Y | N |
| 10 **McHenry** | Y | Y | Y | Y | Y | Y | Y |
| 11 **Taylor** | Y | Y | Y | Y | Y | Y | Y |
| 12 Watt | Y | Y | Y | N | N | N | N |
| 13 Miller | Y | Y | Y | N | N | N | N |
| **NORTH DAKOTA** | | | | | | | |
| AL Pomeroy | Y | Y | Y | N | Y | Y | N |
| **OHIO** | | | | | | | |
| 1 **Chabot** | Y | Y | Y | Y | Y | Y | Y |
| 2 **Portman** | Y | Y | Y | Y | Y | Y | Y |
| 3 **Turner** | Y | Y | Y | N | Y | Y | N |
| 4 **Oxley** | Y | Y | Y | Y | Y | Y | Y |
| 5 **Gillmor** | Y | Y | Y | N | Y | N | Y |
| 6 Strickland | Y | Y | Y | N | N | N | Y |
| 7 **Hobson** | Y | Y | Y | ? | ? | ? | ? |
| 8 **Boehner** | Y | Y | Y | Y | Y | Y | Y |
| 9 Kaptur | Y | Y | Y | N | N | N | N |
| 10 Kucinich | N | Y | Y | N | N | N | N |
| 11 Jones | Y | Y | Y | N | N | N | N |
| 12 **Tiberi** | Y | Y | Y | ? | ? | ? | ? |
| 13 Brown | Y | Y | Y | N | N | N | N |
| 14 **LaTourette** | Y | Y | Y | N | N | N | N |
| 15 **Pryce** | Y | Y | Y | Y | Y | Y | Y |
| 16 **Regula** | Y | Y | Y | Y | Y | Y | N |
| 17 Ryan | Y | Y | Y | N | N | N | N |
| 18 **Ney** | Y | Y | Y | Y | Y | Y | Y |
| **OKLAHOMA** | | | | | | | |
| 1 **Sullivan** | Y | Y | Y | Y | Y | Y | Y |
| 2 Boren | Y | Y | Y | Y | Y | Y | Y |
| 3 **Lucas** | Y | Y | Y | Y | Y | Y | N |
| 4 **Cole** | Y | Y | Y | Y | Y | Y | Y |
| 5 **Istook** | Y | Y | Y | Y | Y | Y | Y |
| **OREGON** | | | | | | | |
| 1 Wu | Y | Y | Y | N | N | N | N |
| 2 **Walden** | Y | Y | ? | Y | Y | Y | N |
| 3 Blumenauer | Y | Y | ? | N | N | N | N |
| 4 DeFazio | Y | Y | Y | N | N | N | N |
| 5 Hooley | N | Y | Y | N | N | N | N |
| **PENNSYLVANIA** | | | | | | | |
| 1 Brady | ? | ? | ? | N | N | N | N |
| 2 Fattah | Y | Y | Y | N | N | N | N |
| 3 **English** | N | Y | Y | N | N | Y | Y |
| 4 **Hart** | Y | Y | Y | Y | N | Y | Y |
| 5 **Peterson** | Y | Y | Y | Y | Y | Y | Y |
| 6 **Gerlach** | Y | Y | Y | N | Y | Y | N |
| 7 **Weldon** | Y | Y | Y | N | Y | N | Y |
| 8 **Fitzpatrick** | Y | Y | Y | N | Y | N | N |
| 9 **Shuster** | Y | Y | Y | Y | Y | Y | Y |
| 10 **Sherwood** | Y | Y | Y | Y | Y | Y | N |
| 11 Kanjorski | ? | ? | ? | N | N | N | N |
| 12 Murtha | Y | Y | Y | N | N | N | N |
| 13 Schwartz | Y | Y | Y | N | N | N | N |
| 14 Doyle | Y | Y | Y | N | N | N | N |
| 15 **Dent** | Y | Y | Y | Y | Y | Y | Y |
| 16 **Pitts** | Y | Y | Y | Y | Y | Y | Y |
| 17 Holden | Y | Y | Y | N | N | N | N |
| 18 **Murphy** | Y | Y | Y | N | N | N | N |
| 19 **Platts** | Y | Y | Y | N | Y | Y | Y |
| **RHODE ISLAND** | | | | | | | |
| 1 Kennedy | ? | ? | Y | N | N | Y | N |
| 2 Langevin | Y | Y | Y | N | N | N | N |
| **SOUTH CAROLINA** | | | | | | | |
| 1 **Brown** | Y | Y | Y | Y | Y | Y | Y |
| 2 **Wilson** | Y | Y | Y | Y | Y | Y | Y |
| 3 **Barrett** | Y | Y | Y | Y | Y | Y | Y |
| 4 **Inglis** | Y | Y | Y | Y | Y | Y | Y |
| 5 Spratt | Y | Y | Y | N | Y | N | Y |
| 6 Clyburn | Y | Y | Y | N | N | N | N |
| **SOUTH DAKOTA** | | | | | | | |
| AL Herseth | ? | ? | ? | ? | ? | ? | ? |
| **TENNESSEE** | | | | | | | |
| 1 **Jenkins** | Y | Y | Y | Y | Y | Y | Y |
| 2 **Duncan** | Y | Y | Y | Y | Y | Y | Y |

| | 53 | 54 | 55 | 56 | 57 | 58 | 59 |
|---|---|---|---|---|---|---|---|
| 3 **Wamp** | Y | Y | Y | Y | Y | Y | Y |
| 4 Davis | Y | Y | Y | N | Y | Y | N |
| 5 Cooper | Y | Y | Y | N | Y | N | Y |
| 6 Gordon | Y | Y | Y | N | Y | Y | Y |
| 7 **Blackburn** | Y | Y | Y | Y | Y | Y | Y |
| 8 Tanner | Y | Y | Y | Y | Y | N | Y |
| 9 Ford | Y | Y | Y | N | Y | Y | N |
| **TEXAS** | | | | | | | |
| 1 **Gohmert** | Y | Y | Y | Y | Y | Y | N |
| 2 **Poe** | Y | Y | Y | Y | Y | Y | N |
| 3 **Johnson, S.** | Y | Y | Y | Y | Y | Y | N |
| 4 **Hall** | Y | Y | Y | Y | Y | Y | N |
| 5 **Hensarling** | Y | Y | Y | Y | Y | Y | Y |
| 6 **Barton** | Y | Y | Y | Y | Y | Y | N |
| 7 **Culberson** | Y | Y | Y | Y | Y | Y | N |
| 8 **Brady** | Y | Y | Y | Y | Y | Y | N |
| 9 Green, A. | Y | Y | Y | N | N | N | N |
| 10 **McCaul** | Y | Y | Y | Y | Y | Y | Y |
| 11 **Conaway** | Y | Y | Y | Y | Y | Y | N |
| 12 **Granger** | Y | Y | Y | Y | Y | Y | N |
| 13 **Thornberry** | Y | Y | Y | Y | Y | Y | Y |
| 14 **Paul** | Y | Y | Y | Y | Y | Y | Y |
| 15 Hinojosa | Y | Y | Y | N | Y | N | Y |
| 16 Reyes | Y | Y | Y | N | Y | N | Y |
| 17 Edwards | Y | Y | Y | N | Y | N | N |
| 18 Jackson-Lee | Y | Y | ? | ? | ? | ? | ? |
| 19 **Neugebauer** | Y | Y | Y | Y | Y | Y | Y |
| 20 Gonzalez | Y | Y | Y | N | N | Y | N |
| 21 **Smith** | Y | Y | Y | Y | Y | Y | Y |
| 22 **DeLay** | Y | Y | Y | Y | Y | Y | N |
| 23 **Bonilla** | Y | Y | Y | Y | Y | Y | N |
| 24 **Marchant** | Y | Y | Y | Y | Y | Y | N |
| 25 Doggett | Y | Y | Y | N | N | N | Y |
| 26 **Burgess** | Y | Y | Y | Y | Y | Y | N |
| 27 Ortiz | Y | Y | Y | N | Y | N | N |
| 28 Cuellar | Y | Y | Y | N | Y | Y | N |
| 29 Green, G. | Y | Y | Y | N | N | Y | N |
| 30 Johnson, E. | Y | Y | Y | N | N | N | N |
| 31 **Carter** | Y | Y | Y | Y | Y | Y | N |
| 32 **Sessions** | Y | Y | Y | Y | Y | Y | Y |
| **UTAH** | | | | | | | |
| 1 **Bishop** | Y | Y | Y | Y | Y | Y | ? |
| 2 Matheson | Y | Y | Y | Y | Y | N | N |
| 3 **Cannon** | Y | Y | Y | Y | Y | Y | Y |
| **VERMONT** | | | | | | | |
| AL *Sanders* | Y | ? | ? | N | N | Y | N |
| **VIRGINIA** | | | | | | | |
| 1 **Davis, J.** | Y | Y | Y | Y | N | Y | N |
| 2 **Drake** | Y | Y | Y | Y | Y | Y | Y |
| 3 Scott | Y | Y | Y | N | N | N | N |
| 4 **Forbes** | Y | Y | Y | Y | Y | Y | N |
| 5 **Goode** | Y | Y | Y | Y | Y | Y | Y |
| 6 **Goodlatte** | Y | Y | Y | Y | Y | Y | N |
| 7 **Cantor** | Y | Y | Y | Y | Y | Y | Y |
| 8 Moran | Y | Y | Y | N | N | N | N |
| 9 Boucher | ? | ? | ? | N | Y | N | N |
| 10 **Wolf** | Y | Y | ? | N | N | N | N |
| 11 **Davis, T.** | Y | Y | Y | Y | Y | N | N |
| **WASHINGTON** | | | | | | | |
| 1 Inslee | Y | Y | Y | N | N | N | N |
| 2 Larsen | N | Y | Y | N | N | N | N |
| 3 Baird | ? | ? | ? | ? | ? | ? | ? |
| 4 **Hastings** | Y | Y | Y | Y | Y | Y | Y |
| 5 **McMorris** | Y | Y | Y | Y | Y | Y | N |
| 6 Dicks | Y | Y | Y | N | N | N | N |
| 7 McDermott | N | Y | Y | N | N | N | N |
| 8 **Reichert** | Y | Y | Y | Y | Y | Y | N |
| 9 Smith | Y | Y | Y | N | N | N | Y |
| **WEST VIRGINIA** | | | | | | | |
| 1 Mollohan | Y | Y | Y | N | Y | N | Y |
| 2 **Capito** | Y | Y | Y | Y | Y | Y | N |
| 3 Rahall | Y | Y | Y | N | N | N | Y |
| **WISCONSIN** | | | | | | | |
| 1 **Ryan** | Y | Y | Y | Y | Y | Y | Y |
| 2 Baldwin | N | Y | Y | N | N | N | N |
| 3 Kind | Y | Y | Y | N | Y | Y | Y |
| 4 Moore | + | + | + | N | N | N | N |
| 5 **Sensenbrenner** | Y | Y | Y | Y | Y | N | Y |
| 6 **Petri** | Y | Y | Y | N | N | N | N |
| 7 Obey | Y | Y | Y | N | N | Y | N |
| 8 **Green** | Y | Y | Y | Y | Y | N | Y |
| **WYOMING** | | | | | | | |
| AL **Cubin** | Y | Y | Y | Y | Y | Y | Y |

# IN THE HOUSE | By Vote Number

**60.** **HR 3. Surface Transportation Reauthorization/Rental Company Liability.** Graves, R-Mo., amendment that would bar so-called vicarious liability under state law for car- and truck-rental companies for injuries and damage caused by vehicles they rent, provided there is no negligence or criminal wrongdoing by the company. Adopted 218-201: R 203-22; D 15-178 (ND 5-138, SD 10-40); I 0-1. March 9, 2005.

**61.** **Procedural Motion/Journal.** Approval of the House Journal of Wednesday, March 9, 2005. Approved 365-39: R 206-10; D 159-29 (ND 118-23, SD 41-6); I 0-0. March 10, 2005.

**62.** **HR 3. Surface Transportation Reauthorization/Low-Income Toll Reductions.** T. Davis, R-Va., amendment that would eliminate provisions in the bill that would require states to allow low-income individuals to pay reduced tolls on high-occupancy vehicle (HOV) lanes if they participate in HOV, congestion-pricing or construction toll programs. Adopted 224-201: R 214-11; D 10-189 (ND 4-144, SD 6-45); I 0-1. March 10, 2005.

**63.** **HR 3. Surface Transportation Reauthorization/Urban Area Grants.** Pitts, R-Pa., amendment that would authorize urban areas with populations that recently exceeded 200,000 to use grants under the Urbanized Area Formula Grants mass transit program to cover 50 percent of equipment and facilities operating costs in fiscal 2005 through 2007, and 25 percent for such costs in fiscal 2008 and 2009. Adopted 228-197: R 159-67; D 69-129 (ND 38-109, SD 31-20); I 0-1. March 10, 2005.

**64.** **HR 3. Surface Transportation Reauthorization/Recommit.** Higgins, D-N.Y., motion to recommit the bill to the House Transportation and Infrastructure and Ways and Means committees with instructions to add language that would increase funding in the bill to $318 billion, while providing offsets by eliminating certain tax provisions for companies that move jobs and operations offshore. Motion rejected 190-235: R 0-227; D 189-8 (ND 143-3, SD 46-5); I 1-0. March 10, 2005.

**65.** **HR 3. Surface Transportation Reauthorization/Passage.** Passage of the bill that would authorize $283.9 billion for federal aid highway, mass transit, safety and research programs from fiscal 2004 to 2009. The funding total includes $225.5 billion in guaranteed funding for highways, $52.4 billion for mass transit and other public transportation programs and $11.1 billion for members' projects. The bill, as amended, would include 92.6 percent of total highway funding in the calculation of a state's minimum guarantee of rate-of-return on their contributions to the Highway Trust Fund. Passed 417-9: R 218-9; D 198-0 (ND 147-0, SD 51-0); I 1-0. A "nay" was a vote in support of the president's position. March 10, 2005.

| | 60 | 61 | 62 | 63 | 64 | 65 |
|---|---|---|---|---|---|---|
| **ALABAMA** | | | | | | |
| 1 Bonner | Y | Y | Y | Y | N | Y |
| 2 Everett | Y | Y | N | Y | N | Y |
| 3 Rogers | N | ? | ? | ? | ? | Y |
| 4 Aderholt | Y | Y | Y | Y | N | Y |
| 5 Cramer | Y | Y | Y | Y | Y | Y |
| 6 Bachus | Y | ? | Y | N | N | Y |
| 7 Davis | N | Y | N | Y | N | Y |
| **ALASKA** | | | | | | |
| AL Young | N | Y | N | N | N | Y |
| **ARIZONA** | | | | | | |
| 1 Renzi | Y | Y | Y | Y | N | Y |
| 2 Franks | Y | Y | Y | Y | N | Y |
| 3 Shadegg | Y | Y | Y | Y | N | N |
| 4 Pastor | N | Y | N | N | Y | Y |
| 5 Hayworth | Y | Y | Y | Y | N | Y |
| 6 Flake | N | Y | Y | Y | N | N |
| 7 Grijalva | N | Y | N | N | Y | Y |
| 8 Kolbe | Y | Y | Y | Y | N | Y |
| **ARKANSAS** | | | | | | |
| 1 Berry | N | Y | N | N | Y | Y |
| 2 Snyder | N | Y | N | Y | N | Y |
| 3 Boozman | Y | Y | Y | Y | N | Y |
| 4 Ross | N | Y | N | N | Y | Y |
| **CALIFORNIA** | | | | | | |
| 1 Thompson | N | N | N | N | Y | Y |
| 2 Herger | Y | Y | ? | Y | N | Y |
| 3 Lungren | Y | Y | Y | N | N | Y |
| 4 Doolittle | N | Y | Y | N | N | Y |
| 5 Matsui, D.* | | | N | N | Y | Y |
| 6 Woolsey | N | Y | N | N | Y | Y |
| 7 Miller, George | N | Y | N | N | Y | Y |
| 8 Pelosi | N | Y | N | N | Y | Y |
| 9 Lee | N | Y | N | N | Y | Y |
| 10 Tauscher | N | Y | N | Y | Y | Y |
| 11 Pombo | Y | Y | Y | Y | N | Y |
| 12 Lantos | N | Y | N | N | Y | Y |
| 13 Stark | N | Y | N | N | Y | Y |
| 14 Eshoo | N | Y | N | N | Y | Y |
| 15 Honda | N | Y | N | N | Y | Y |
| 16 Lofgren | N | Y | N | N | Y | Y |
| 17 Farr | N | Y | N | N | Y | Y |
| 18 Cardoza | Y | ? | N | N | Y | Y |
| 19 Radanovich | Y | Y | Y | Y | N | Y |
| 20 Costa | Y | Y | N | Y | Y | Y |
| 21 Nunes | Y | Y | Y | Y | N | Y |
| 22 Thomas | ? | Y | Y | Y | N | Y |
| 23 Capps | N | Y | N | N | Y | Y |
| 24 Gallegly | Y | Y | Y | N | N | Y |
| 25 McKeon | Y | Y | Y | Y | N | Y |
| 26 Dreier | Y | Y | Y | Y | N | Y |
| 27 Sherman | N | Y | N | N | Y | Y |
| 28 Berman | N | Y | N | N | Y | Y |
| 29 Schiff | N | Y | N | Y | N | Y |
| 30 Waxman | N | Y | N | N | Y | Y |
| 31 Becerra | N | Y | N | N | Y | Y |
| 32 Solis | N | Y | N | N | Y | Y |
| 33 Watson | N | Y | N | N | Y | Y |
| 34 Roybal-Allard | N | Y | N | N | Y | Y |
| 35 Waters | N | N | N | N | Y | Y |
| 36 Harman | N | Y | N | N | Y | Y |
| 37 Millender-McD. | N | Y | N | N | Y | Y |
| 38 Napolitano | N | Y | N | N | Y | Y |
| 39 Sánchez, Linda | N | Y | N | N | Y | Y |
| 40 Royce | Y | Y | Y | N | N | Y |
| 41 Lewis | Y | Y | Y | N | N | Y |
| 42 Miller, Gary | Y | Y | Y | N | N | Y |
| 43 Baca | N | Y | N | N | Y | Y |
| 44 Calvert | Y | Y | Y | N | N | Y |
| 45 Bono | Y | Y | Y | N | N | Y |
| 46 Rohrabacher | Y | Y | Y | N | N | Y |
| 47 Sanchez, Loretta | N | Y | N | N | Y | Y |
| 48 Cox | Y | ? | Y | N | N | Y |
| 49 Issa | Y | Y | Y | Y | N | Y |

| | 60 | 61 | 62 | 63 | 64 | 65 |
|---|---|---|---|---|---|---|
| 50 Cunningham | Y | Y | Y | Y | N | Y |
| 51 Filner | N | N | N | N | Y | Y |
| 52 Hunter | Y | Y | Y | Y | N | Y |
| 53 Davis | N | Y | N | N | Y | Y |
| **COLORADO** | | | | | | |
| 1 DeGette | ? | Y | N | N | Y | Y |
| 2 Udall | N | N | N | Y | Y | Y |
| 3 Salazar | N | Y | N | N | Y | Y |
| 4 Musgrave | Y | Y | Y | Y | N | Y |
| 5 Hefley | Y | N | Y | N | N | Y |
| 6 Tancredo | N | P | Y | N | Y | Y |
| 7 Beauprez | Y | Y | Y | Y | N | Y |
| **CONNECTICUT** | | | | | | |
| 1 Larson | N | Y | N | N | Y | Y |
| 2 Simmons | + | Y | Y | Y | N | Y |
| 3 DeLauro | N | Y | N | N | Y | Y |
| 4 Shays | Y | Y | Y | Y | N | Y |
| 5 Johnson | Y | Y | Y | Y | N | Y |
| **DELAWARE** | | | | | | |
| AL Castle | N | Y | N | N | N | N |
| **FLORIDA** | | | | | | |
| 1 Miller | Y | Y | Y | Y | N | Y |
| 2 Boyd | Y | Y | N | N | Y | Y |
| 3 Brown | N | Y | N | N | Y | Y |
| 4 Crenshaw | Y | Y | Y | Y | N | Y |
| 5 Brown-Waite | Y | Y | Y | N | N | Y |
| 6 Stearns | Y | Y | Y | N | N | Y |
| 7 Mica | Y | Y | Y | Y | N | Y |
| 8 Keller | Y | Y | Y | Y | N | Y |
| 9 Bilirakis | Y | Y | Y | Y | N | Y |
| 10 Young | N | Y | Y | Y | N | N |
| 11 Davis | N | Y | N | Y | Y | Y |
| 12 Putnam | Y | Y | Y | Y | N | Y |
| 13 Harris | Y | Y | Y | Y | N | Y |
| 14 Mack | Y | Y | Y | N | N | Y |
| 15 Weldon | Y | Y | Y | Y | ? | Y |
| 16 Foley | Y | Y | Y | Y | N | Y |
| 17 Meek | N | Y | N | N | Y | Y |
| 18 Ros-Lehtinen | Y | Y | Y | Y | N | Y |
| 19 Wexler | N | ? | N | N | Y | Y |
| 20 Wasserman-Schultz | N | Y | N | N | Y | Y |
| 21 Diaz-Balart, L. | N | Y | Y | Y | N | Y |
| 22 Shaw | Y | Y | Y | N | N | Y |
| 23 Hastings | N | N | N | Y | Y | Y |
| 24 Feeney | Y | Y | Y | Y | N | Y |
| 25 Diaz-Balart, M. | Y | Y | Y | Y | N | Y |
| **GEORGIA** | | | | | | |
| 1 Kingston | Y | Y | Y | Y | N | Y |
| 2 Bishop | N | Y | N | Y | Y | Y |
| 3 Marshall | N | N | N | Y | Y | Y |
| 4 McKinney | N | N | N | Y | Y | Y |
| 5 Lewis | N | N | N | Y | Y | Y |
| 6 Price | Y | Y | Y | Y | N | Y |
| 7 Linder | Y | Y | Y | Y | N | Y |
| 8 Westmoreland | Y | Y | Y | Y | N | Y |
| 9 Norwood | Y | ? | Y | N | N | Y |
| 10 Deal | Y | Y | Y | N | N | Y |
| 11 Gingrey | Y | Y | Y | Y | N | Y |
| 12 Barrow | N | Y | N | N | Y | Y |
| 13 Scott | N | ? | N | N | Y | Y |
| **HAWAII** | | | | | | |
| 1 Abercrombie | N | Y | Y | N | Y | Y |
| 2 Case | N | Y | N | N | Y | Y |
| **IDAHO** | | | | | | |
| 1 Otter | N | Y | Y | Y | N | N |
| 2 Simpson | Y | Y | Y | N | N | Y |
| **ILLINOIS** | | | | | | |
| 1 Rush | N | Y | N | N | Y | Y |
| 2 Jackson | N | Y | N | N | Y | Y |
| 3 Lipinski | N | Y | N | N | Y | Y |
| 4 Gutierrez | N | Y | N | N | Y | Y |
| 5 Emanuel | N | Y | N | N | Y | Y |
| 6 Hyde | Y | ? | Y | N | N | Y |
| 7 Davis | N | Y | N | N | Y | Y |
| 8 Bean | N | Y | N | N | Y | Y |
| 9 Schakowsky | N | N | N | N | Y | Y |
| 10 Kirk | Y | Y | Y | N | N | Y |
| 11 Weller | Y | N | Y | N | N | Y |
| 12 Costello | N | N | N | N | Y | Y |

**KEY**    **Republicans**    Democrats    *Independents*

| | | |
|---|---|---|
| Y   Voted for (yea) | X   Paired against | C   Voted "present" to avoid possible conflict of interest |
| #   Paired for | –   Announced against | |
| +   Announced for | P   Voted "present" | ?   Did not vote or otherwise make a position known |
| N   Voted against (nay) | | |

* Rep. Doris Matsui, D-Calif., was sworn in March 10, 2005. The first vote for which she was eligible was vote 62.

| | 60 | 61 | 62 | 63 | 64 | 65 |
|---|---|---|---|---|---|---|
| 13 **Biggert** | Y | Y | Y | N | N | Y |
| 14 **Hastert** | Y | | | | N | Y |
| 15 **Johnson** | N | Y | N | N | N | Y |
| 16 **Manzullo** | N | Y | Y | Y | N | Y |
| 17 Evans | N | Y | ? | ? | ? | ? |
| 18 **LaHood** | Y | Y | Y | Y | N | Y |
| 19 **Shimkus** | Y | Y | N | Y | N | Y |
| **INDIANA** | | | | | | |
| 1 Visclosky | N | Y | N | N | Y | Y |
| 2 **Chocola** | Y | Y | Y | Y | N | Y |
| 3 **Souder** | Y | Y | Y | Y | N | Y |
| 4 **Buyer** | Y | Y | Y | Y | N | Y |
| 5 **Burton** | Y | Y | Y | N | N | Y |
| 6 **Pence** | Y | Y | Y | Y | N | Y |
| 7 Carson | N | Y | N | N | Y | Y |
| 8 **Hostettler** | Y | Y | Y | Y | N | Y |
| 9 **Sodrel** | Y | Y | Y | N | N | Y |
| **IOWA** | | | | | | |
| 1 **Nussle** | Y | Y | Y | Y | N | Y |
| 2 **Leach** | Y | Y | Y | Y | N | Y |
| 3 Boswell | N | Y | N | N | Y | Y |
| 4 **Latham** | Y | N | Y | Y | N | Y |
| 5 **King** | Y | Y | Y | Y | N | Y |
| **KANSAS** | | | | | | |
| 1 **Moran** | Y | Y | Y | Y | N | Y |
| 2 **Ryun** | Y | Y | Y | Y | N | Y |
| 3 Moore | N | Y | N | Y | N | Y |
| 4 **Tiahrt** | Y | Y | Y | Y | N | Y |
| **KENTUCKY** | | | | | | |
| 1 **Whitfield** | Y | Y | Y | Y | N | Y |
| 2 **Lewis** | Y | Y | Y | Y | N | Y |
| 3 **Northup** | Y | ? | ? | ? | ? | ? |
| 4 **Davis** | Y | Y | Y | N | N | Y |
| 5 **Rogers** | Y | Y | Y | N | N | Y |
| 6 Chandler | N | Y | N | N | Y | Y |
| **LOUISIANA** | | | | | | |
| 1 **Jindal** | Y | Y | Y | Y | N | Y |
| 2 Jefferson | N | ? | N | Y | Y | Y |
| 3 Melancon | N | Y | N | Y | Y | Y |
| 4 **McCrery** | Y | Y | Y | N | N | Y |
| 5 **Alexander** | Y | Y | Y | Y | N | Y |
| 6 **Baker** | Y | Y | Y | Y | N | Y |
| 7 **Boustany** | Y | Y | Y | Y | N | Y |
| **MAINE** | | | | | | |
| 1 Allen | N | Y | N | N | Y | Y |
| 2 Michaud | N | Y | N | N | Y | Y |
| **MARYLAND** | | | | | | |
| 1 **Gilchrest** | Y | Y | Y | N | N | Y |
| 2 Ruppersberger | N | Y | N | Y | Y | Y |
| 3 Cardin | N | Y | N | Y | Y | Y |
| 4 Wynn | N | Y | N | Y | Y | Y |
| 5 Hoyer | N | Y | N | Y | Y | Y |
| 6 **Bartlett** | Y | Y | Y | Y | N | Y |
| 7 Cummings | N | ? | N | N | Y | Y |
| 8 Van Hollen | N | Y | N | N | Y | Y |
| **MASSACHUSETTS** | | | | | | |
| 1 Olver | N | N | N | Y | Y | Y |
| 2 Neal | N | Y | N | Y | Y | Y |
| 3 McGovern | N | N | N | Y | Y | Y |
| 4 Frank | N | Y | N | Y | Y | Y |
| 5 Meehan | N | Y | N | Y | Y | Y |
| 6 Tierney | N | ? | N | Y | Y | Y |
| 7 Markey | N | Y | N | Y | Y | Y |
| 8 Capuano | N | N | N | N | Y | Y |
| 9 Lynch | N | Y | N | Y | Y | Y |
| 10 Delahunt | N | ? | N | Y | Y | Y |
| **MICHIGAN** | | | | | | |
| 1 Stupak | ? | ? | ? | ? | ? | ? |
| 2 **Hoekstra** | Y | Y | Y | N | N | Y |
| 3 **Ehlers** | Y | Y | N | N | N | Y |
| 4 **Camp** | Y | Y | Y | N | N | Y |
| 5 Kildee | N | Y | N | N | Y | Y |
| 6 **Upton** | Y | Y | Y | N | N | Y |
| 7 **Schwarz** | Y | Y | Y | Y | N | Y |
| 8 **Rogers** | Y | Y | Y | Y | N | Y |
| 9 **Knollenberg** | N | Y | Y | N | N | Y |
| 10 **Miller** | Y | Y | Y | N | N | Y |
| 11 **McCotter** | Y | Y | Y | Y | N | Y |
| 12 Levin | N | Y | N | N | Y | Y |
| 13 Kilpatrick | N | Y | N | N | Y | Y |
| 14 Conyers | N | Y | N | N | Y | Y |
| 15 Dingell | N | Y | N | N | Y | Y |

| | 60 | 61 | 62 | 63 | 64 | 65 |
|---|---|---|---|---|---|---|
| **MINNESOTA** | | | | | | |
| 1 **Gutknecht** | Y | N | Y | Y | N | Y |
| 2 **Kline** | Y | Y | Y | Y | N | Y |
| 3 **Ramstad** | ? | ? | ? | ? | ? | ? |
| 4 McCollum | N | Y | N | N | Y | Y |
| 5 Sabo | N | N | N | N | ? | Y |
| 6 **Kennedy** | Y | N | Y | Y | N | Y |
| 7 Peterson | Y | N | N | N | Y | Y |
| 8 Oberstar | N | N | N | N | Y | Y |
| **MISSISSIPPI** | | | | | | |
| 1 **Wicker** | Y | N | Y | N | N | Y |
| 2 Thompson | N | ? | N | N | Y | Y |
| 3 **Pickering** | Y | Y | Y | N | N | Y |
| 4 Taylor | N | N | N | Y | N | Y |
| **MISSOURI** | | | | | | |
| 1 Clay | ? | ? | N | Y | Y | Y |
| 2 **Akin** | Y | Y | Y | Y | N | Y |
| 3 Carnahan | N | Y | N | Y | Y | Y |
| 4 Skelton | N | Y | N | Y | Y | Y |
| 5 Cleaver | N | Y | N | Y | Y | Y |
| 6 **Graves** | Y | Y | Y | Y | N | Y |
| 7 **Blunt** | Y | Y | Y | Y | N | Y |
| 8 **Emerson** | Y | Y | Y | Y | N | Y |
| 9 **Hulshof** | Y | Y | Y | Y | N | Y |
| **MONTANA** | | | | | | |
| AL **Rehberg** | Y | Y | Y | Y | N | Y |
| **NEBRASKA** | | | | | | |
| 1 **Fortenberry** | Y | Y | Y | Y | N | Y |
| 2 **Terry** | N | Y | Y | Y | N | Y |
| 3 **Osborne** | Y | Y | Y | Y | N | Y |
| **NEVADA** | | | | | | |
| 1 Berkley | N | Y | N | N | Y | Y |
| 2 **Gibbons** | Y | N | Y | Y | N | Y |
| 3 **Porter** | Y | Y | Y | Y | N | Y |
| **NEW HAMPSHIRE** | | | | | | |
| 1 **Bradley** | Y | Y | Y | Y | N | Y |
| 2 **Bass** | Y | Y | Y | Y | N | Y |
| **NEW JERSEY** | | | | | | |
| 1 Andrews | N | Y | N | N | Y | Y |
| 2 **LoBiondo** | Y | N | Y | N | N | Y |
| 3 **Saxton** | ? | Y | Y | N | N | Y |
| 4 **Smith** | Y | Y | Y | N | N | Y |
| 5 **Garrett** | Y | Y | Y | Y | N | Y |
| 6 Pallone | N | Y | N | N | Y | Y |
| 7 **Ferguson** | Y | Y | Y | N | N | Y |
| 8 Pascrell | N | Y | N | N | Y | Y |
| 9 Rothman | ? | Y | N | N | Y | Y |
| 10 Payne | ? | ? | N | N | Y | Y |
| 11 **Frelinghuysen** | Y | Y | Y | Y | N | Y |
| 12 Holt | N | N | N | N | Y | Y |
| 13 Menendez | N | Y | N | N | Y | Y |
| **NEW MEXICO** | | | | | | |
| 1 **Wilson** | Y | Y | Y | Y | N | Y |
| 2 **Pearce** | Y | Y | Y | N | N | Y |
| 3 Udall | N | N | N | Y | Y | Y |
| **NEW YORK** | | | | | | |
| 1 Bishop | N | Y | N | N | Y | Y |
| 2 Israel | N | Y | N | N | Y | Y |
| 3 **King** | N | Y | Y | Y | N | Y |
| 4 McCarthy | N | Y | N | N | Y | Y |
| 5 Ackerman | N | Y | N | N | Y | Y |
| 6 Meeks | N | Y | N | N | Y | Y |
| 7 Crowley | N | Y | N | N | Y | Y |
| 8 Nadler | N | Y | N | N | Y | Y |
| 9 Weiner | N | Y | N | N | Y | Y |
| 10 Towns | N | Y | N | N | Y | Y |
| 11 Owens | N | Y | N | N | Y | Y |
| 12 Velázquez | N | Y | N | N | Y | Y |
| 13 **Fossella** | Y | ? | Y | Y | N | Y |
| 14 Maloney | N | Y | N | Y | Y | Y |
| 15 Rangel | N | Y | N | N | Y | Y |
| 16 Serrano | N | Y | N | N | Y | Y |
| 17 Engel | N | Y | N | Y | Y | Y |
| 18 Lowey | N | Y | N | Y | Y | Y |
| 19 **Kelly** | Y | Y | Y | Y | N | Y |
| 20 **Sweeney** | Y | Y | Y | Y | N | Y |
| 21 McNulty | N | N | N | N | Y | Y |
| 22 Hinchey | N | Y | N | N | Y | Y |
| 23 **McHugh** | Y | ? | Y | N | N | Y |
| 24 **Boehlert** | Y | Y | N | Y | N | Y |
| 25 **Walsh** | Y | Y | Y | N | N | Y |
| 26 **Reynolds** | Y | Y | Y | Y | N | Y |
| 27 Higgins | N | Y | N | N | Y | Y |
| 28 Slaughter | N | Y | N | ? | ? | ? |
| 29 **Kuhl** | Y | Y | Y | N | N | Y |

| | 60 | 61 | 62 | 63 | 64 | 65 |
|---|---|---|---|---|---|---|
| **NORTH CAROLINA** | | | | | | |
| 1 Butterfield | N | Y | N | N | Y | Y |
| 2 Etheridge | N | Y | N | Y | Y | Y |
| 3 **Jones** | Y | Y | Y | Y | N | ? |
| 4 Price | N | Y | N | Y | Y | Y |
| 5 **Foxx** | Y | Y | Y | Y | N | Y |
| 6 **Coble** | Y | Y | Y | Y | N | Y |
| 7 McIntyre | Y | Y | N | Y | Y | Y |
| 8 **Hayes** | Y | Y | Y | Y | N | Y |
| 9 **Myrick** | Y | Y | Y | Y | N | Y |
| 10 **McHenry** | Y | ? | Y | Y | N | Y |
| 11 **Taylor** | Y | Y | Y | N | N | Y |
| 12 Watt | N | Y | N | Y | Y | Y |
| 13 Miller | N | Y | N | Y | Y | Y |
| **NORTH DAKOTA** | | | | | | |
| AL Pomeroy | N | Y | N | N | Y | Y |
| **OHIO** | | | | | | |
| 1 **Chabot** | Y | Y | Y | Y | N | Y |
| 2 **Portman** | Y | Y | Y | Y | N | Y |
| 3 **Turner** | N | Y | Y | Y | N | Y |
| 4 **Oxley** | Y | ? | Y | Y | N | Y |
| 5 **Gillmor** | Y | Y | Y | Y | N | Y |
| 6 Strickland | N | N | N | N | Y | Y |
| 7 **Hobson** | ? | Y | Y | N | N | Y |
| 8 **Boehner** | Y | Y | Y | Y | N | N |
| 9 Kaptur | N | Y | N | Y | Y | Y |
| 10 Kucinich | N | N | N | N | Y | Y |
| 11 Jones | N | Y | N | N | Y | Y |
| 12 **Tiberi** | ? | Y | Y | N | N | Y |
| 13 Brown | N | Y | N | Y | Y | Y |
| 14 **LaTourette** | N | Y | Y | N | N | Y |
| 15 **Pryce** | Y | Y | Y | N | N | Y |
| 16 **Regula** | Y | Y | Y | Y | N | Y |
| 17 Ryan | N | N | N | N | Y | Y |
| 18 **Ney** | Y | Y | Y | N | N | Y |
| **OKLAHOMA** | | | | | | |
| 1 **Sullivan** | Y | Y | Y | Y | N | Y |
| 2 Boren | Y | Y | Y | Y | N | Y |
| 3 **Lucas** | Y | Y | Y | Y | N | Y |
| 4 **Cole** | Y | + | Y | Y | N | Y |
| 5 **Istook** | N | Y | Y | Y | N | Y |
| **OREGON** | | | | | | |
| 1 Wu | N | N | N | Y | Y | Y |
| 2 **Walden** | Y | Y | Y | N | N | Y |
| 3 Blumenauer | N | Y | N | N | Y | Y |
| 4 DeFazio | N | Y | N | N | Y | Y |
| 5 Hooley | N | Y | N | Y | Y | Y |
| **PENNSYLVANIA** | | | | | | |
| 1 Brady | N | N | N | N | Y | Y |
| 2 Fattah | N | ? | N | N | Y | Y |
| 3 **English** | Y | N | Y | Y | N | Y |
| 4 **Hart** | Y | N | Y | Y | N | Y |
| 5 **Peterson** | Y | Y | Y | Y | N | Y |
| 6 **Gerlach** | Y | Y | Y | Y | N | Y |
| 7 **Weldon** | Y | Y | + | + | N | Y |
| 8 **Fitzpatrick** | N | Y | N | N | N | Y |
| 9 **Shuster** | Y | Y | Y | Y | N | Y |
| 10 **Sherwood** | Y | Y | Y | Y | N | Y |
| 11 Kanjorski | N | Y | N | N | Y | Y |
| 12 Murtha | N | Y | N | N | Y | Y |
| 13 Schwartz | N | Y | N | Y | Y | Y |
| 14 Doyle | N | Y | N | N | Y | Y |
| 15 **Dent** | Y | Y | Y | Y | N | Y |
| 16 **Pitts** | Y | Y | Y | Y | N | Y |
| 17 Holden | Y | Y | N | Y | Y | Y |
| 18 **Murphy** | Y | Y | Y | Y | N | Y |
| 19 **Platts** | Y | Y | Y | Y | N | Y |
| **RHODE ISLAND** | | | | | | |
| 1 Kennedy | N | Y | N | N | Y | Y |
| 2 Langevin | N | Y | N | N | Y | Y |
| **SOUTH CAROLINA** | | | | | | |
| 1 **Brown** | Y | Y | Y | N | N | Y |
| 2 **Wilson** | Y | Y | Y | N | N | Y |
| 3 **Barrett** | Y | Y | Y | N | N | Y |
| 4 **Inglis** | Y | Y | Y | N | N | Y |
| 5 Spratt | N | Y | N | N | Y | Y |
| 6 Clyburn | N | Y | N | N | Y | Y |
| **SOUTH DAKOTA** | | | | | | |
| AL Herseth | ? | Y | Y | N | Y | Y |
| **TENNESSEE** | | | | | | |
| 1 **Jenkins** | N | Y | Y | Y | N | Y |
| 2 **Duncan** | Y | Y | Y | Y | N | Y |

| | 60 | 61 | 62 | 63 | 64 | 65 |
|---|---|---|---|---|---|---|
| 3 **Wamp** | Y | Y | Y | Y | N | Y |
| 4 Davis | Y | N | N | N | Y | Y |
| 5 Cooper | Y | N | N | Y | N | Y |
| 6 Gordon | Y | Y | N | N | Y | Y |
| 7 **Blackburn** | Y | Y | Y | N | N | Y |
| 8 Tanner | Y | Y | N | N | Y | Y |
| 9 Ford | N | Y | N | N | Y | Y |
| **TEXAS** | | | | | | |
| 1 **Gohmert** | Y | Y | Y | Y | N | Y |
| 2 **Poe** | Y | Y | Y | Y | N | Y |
| 3 **Johnson, S.** | Y | Y | Y | N | N | Y |
| 4 **Hall** | Y | Y | Y | Y | N | Y |
| 5 **Hensarling** | Y | Y | Y | Y | N | Y |
| 6 **Barton** | Y | Y | Y | Y | N | Y |
| 7 **Culberson** | Y | Y | Y | Y | N | Y |
| 8 **Brady** | Y | Y | Y | Y | N | Y |
| 9 Green, A. | N | Y | N | Y | Y | Y |
| 10 **McCaul** | Y | Y | Y | Y | N | Y |
| 11 **Conaway** | Y | ? | Y | N | N | Y |
| 12 **Granger** | Y | Y | Y | Y | N | Y |
| 13 **Thornberry** | Y | Y | Y | Y | N | N |
| 14 **Paul** | N | Y | Y | Y | N | N |
| 15 Hinojosa | N | Y | N | Y | Y | Y |
| 16 Reyes | N | Y | N | Y | Y | Y |
| 17 Edwards | N | Y | Y | Y | Y | Y |
| 18 Jackson-Lee | ? | Y | N | N | Y | Y |
| 19 **Neugebauer** | Y | Y | Y | Y | N | Y |
| 20 Gonzalez | N | Y | N | Y | Y | Y |
| 21 **Smith** | Y | Y | Y | Y | N | Y |
| 22 **DeLay** | Y | ? | ? | ? | ? | ? |
| 23 **Bonilla** | Y | Y | Y | Y | N | Y |
| 24 **Marchant** | Y | Y | Y | Y | N | Y |
| 25 Doggett | N | Y | N | Y | Y | Y |
| 26 **Burgess** | Y | Y | Y | Y | N | Y |
| 27 Ortiz | N | Y | N | Y | Y | Y |
| 28 Cuellar | Y | Y | N | Y | Y | Y |
| 29 Green, G. | N | Y | N | Y | Y | Y |
| 30 Johnson, E. | N | Y | N | N | Y | Y |
| 31 **Carter** | Y | Y | Y | Y | N | Y |
| 32 **Sessions** | Y | Y | Y | Y | N | Y |
| **UTAH** | | | | | | |
| 1 **Bishop** | ? | Y | Y | Y | N | Y |
| 2 Matheson | Y | Y | N | N | N | Y |
| 3 **Cannon** | Y | Y | Y | N | N | Y |
| **VERMONT** | | | | | | |
| AL *Sanders* | N | ? | N | N | Y | Y |
| **VIRGINIA** | | | | | | |
| 1 **Davis, J.** | Y | Y | Y | Y | N | Y |
| 2 **Drake** | Y | Y | Y | Y | N | Y |
| 3 Scott | N | Y | N | Y | Y | Y |
| 4 **Forbes** | Y | Y | Y | Y | N | Y |
| 5 **Goode** | Y | Y | Y | Y | N | Y |
| 6 **Goodlatte** | Y | Y | Y | Y | N | Y |
| 7 **Cantor** | Y | Y | Y | Y | N | Y |
| 8 Moran | N | Y | Y | N | Y | Y |
| 9 Boucher | Y | Y | N | N | Y | Y |
| 10 **Wolf** | Y | Y | Y | Y | N | Y |
| 11 **Davis, T.** | Y | Y | Y | Y | N | Y |
| **WASHINGTON** | | | | | | |
| 1 Inslee | N | Y | Y | Y | Y | Y |
| 2 Larsen | N | N | N | N | Y | Y |
| 3 Baird | ? | ? | ? | ? | ? | ? |
| 4 **Hastings** | Y | Y | Y | N | N | Y |
| 5 **McMorris** | Y | Y | Y | Y | N | Y |
| 6 Dicks | N | Y | N | N | Y | Y |
| 7 McDermott | N | N | N | N | Y | Y |
| 8 **Reichert** | Y | Y | N | N | N | Y |
| 9 Smith | N | Y | N | N | Y | Y |
| **WEST VIRGINIA** | | | | | | |
| 1 Mollohan | N | Y | N | N | Y | Y |
| 2 **Capito** | Y | Y | Y | N | N | Y |
| 3 Rahall | N | Y | N | N | Y | Y |
| **WISCONSIN** | | | | | | |
| 1 **Ryan** | Y | Y | Y | Y | N | Y |
| 2 Baldwin | N | N | N | Y | Y | Y |
| 3 Kind | N | Y | N | N | Y | Y |
| 4 Moore | N | Y | N | Y | Y | Y |
| 5 **Sensenbrenner** | Y | Y | Y | N | N | N |
| 6 **Petri** | N | Y | N | N | N | Y |
| 7 Obey | N | Y | N | N | Y | Y |
| 8 **Green** | Y | Y | Y | Y | N | Y |
| **WYOMING** | | | | | | |
| AL **Cubin** | Y | Y | Y | N | N | Y |

# IN THE HOUSE | By Vote Number

**66.** **H Res 135. Democracy Commission/Adoption.** Barrett, R-S.C., motion to suspend the rules and adopt the resolution that would establish the House Democracy Assistance Commission to provide advice to members and staff of newly formed parliaments in emerging democracies. Motion agreed to 386-2: R 208-1; D 177-1 (ND 133-0, SD 44-1); I 1-0. A two-thirds majority of those present and voting (259 in this case) is required for adoption under suspension of the rules. March 14, 2005.

**67.** **H Res 101. Hezbollah Terrorist Designation/Adoption.** Barrett, R-S.C., motion to suspend the rules and adopt the resolution that would urge the European Union to classify Hezbollah as a terrorist organization and prohibit funding to the group. Motion agreed to 380-3: R 208-1; D 171-2 (ND 126-2, SD 45-0); I 1-0. A two-thirds majority of those present and voting (259 in this case) is required for adoption under suspension of the rules. March 14, 2005.

**68.** **S 384. Interagency Working Group Extension/Passage.** Shays, R-Conn., motion to suspend the rules and pass the bill that would extend through December 2006 the term of the Nazi War Crimes and Japanese Imperial Government Records Interagency Working Group, which works to locate and declassify Nazi war criminal records. Motion agreed to 391-0: R 211-0; D 179-0 (ND 133-0, SD 46-0); I 1-0. A two-thirds majority of those present and voting (261 in this case) is required for passage under suspension of the rules. March 14, 2005.

**69.** **HR 1268. Fiscal 2005 Supplemental Appropriations/Previous Question.** Cole, R-Okla., motion to order the previous question (thus ending debate and possibility of amendment) on adoption of the rule (H Res 151) and a Cole amendment to the rule. The rule would provide for House floor consideration of the bill that would appropriate $81.3 billion in fiscal 2005 supplemental spending. The amendment would waive points of order against provisions on life insurance and death benefits for U.S. troops. Motion agreed to 220-195: R 220-1; D 0-193 (ND 0-144, SD 0-49); I 0-1. (Subsequently, the Cole amendment and the rule were adopted by voice vote.) March 15, 2005.

**70.** **H Res 153. Ethics Task Force/Motion to Table.** Lewis, R-Calif., motion to table (kill) the Pelosi, D-Calif., privileged resolution that would require the Speaker of the House to appoint a bipartisan task force, with equal representation of Republicans and Democrats, to make recommendations, by May 2, 2005, to restore public confidence in the House ethics process. Motion agreed to 223-194: R 223-1; D 0-192 (ND 0-145, SD 0-47); I 0-1. March 15, 2005.

**71.** **HR 1268. Fiscal 2005 Supplemental Appropriations/Ruling of the Chair.** Motion to sustain the ruling of the chair that upheld the Lewis, R-Calif., point of order against the Filner, D-Calif., amendment on grounds that it would constitute unauthorized legislation on an appropriations bill. The Filner amendment would provide an additional $3.1 billion for the Veterans Health Administration and designate it as emergency spending. Motion agreed to 224-200: R 223-0; D 1-199 (ND 1-148, SD 0-51); I 0-1. March 15, 2005.

**72.** **HR 1268. Fiscal 2005 Supplemental Appropriations/Contracting Investigation.** Tierney, D-Mass., amendment that would provide $5 million to establish a select committee to investigate reconstruction efforts in Iraq and Afghanistan. Rejected 191-236: R 0-226; D 190-10 (ND 140-9, SD 50-1); I 1-0. March 15, 2005.

**73.** **HR 1268. Fiscal 2005 Supplemental Appropriations/Embassy Funding.** Upton, R-Mich., amendment to prohibit use of funds in the bill for the security, construction and maintenance of U.S. embassies. The underlying bill would provide $592 million to construct a new embassy in Baghdad. Adopted 258-170: R 119-107; D 138-63 (ND 98-52, SD 40-11); I 1-0. A "nay" was a vote in support of the president's position. March 15, 2005.

| | 66 | 67 | 68 | 69 | 70 | 71 | 72 | 73 |
|---|---|---|---|---|---|---|---|---|
| **ALABAMA** | | | | | | | | |
| 1 Bonner | Y | Y | Y | Y | Y | Y | N | Y |
| 2 Everett | Y | Y | Y | Y | Y | Y | N | N |
| 3 Rogers | Y | Y | Y | Y | Y | Y | N | N |
| 4 Aderholt | Y | Y | Y | Y | Y | Y | N | N |
| 5 Cramer | ? | Y | Y | N | N | N | N | N |
| 6 Bachus | Y | Y | Y | Y | Y | Y | ? | ? |
| 7 Davis | ? | ? | ? | N | N | N | Y | N |
| **ALASKA** | | | | | | | | |
| AL Young | Y | Y | Y | Y | ? | Y | N | Y |
| **ARIZONA** | | | | | | | | |
| 1 Renzi | Y | Y | Y | Y | Y | Y | N | N |
| 2 Franks | Y | ? | Y | Y | Y | Y | N | Y |
| 3 Shadegg | Y | Y | Y | Y | Y | Y | N | Y |
| 4 Pastor | Y | Y | Y | N | N | N | N | Y |
| 5 Hayworth | Y | Y | Y | Y | Y | Y | N | N |
| 6 Flake | ? | ? | ? | Y | Y | Y | N | Y |
| 7 Grijalva | Y | Y | Y | N | N | N | Y | Y |
| 8 Kolbe | Y | Y | Y | Y | Y | Y | N | N |
| **ARKANSAS** | | | | | | | | |
| 1 Berry | Y | Y | Y | N | N | N | Y | Y |
| 2 Snyder | Y | Y | Y | N | N | N | Y | Y |
| 3 Boozman | Y | Y | Y | Y | Y | Y | N | N |
| 4 Ross | Y | Y | Y | N | N | N | N | N |
| **CALIFORNIA** | | | | | | | | |
| 1 Thompson | Y | Y | Y | N | N | N | Y | Y |
| 2 Herger | Y | Y | Y | Y | Y | Y | N | N |
| 3 Lungren | Y | Y | Y | Y | Y | Y | N | N |
| 4 Doolittle | Y | Y | Y | Y | Y | Y | N | N |
| 5 Matsui, D. | Y | Y | Y | N | N | N | Y | Y |
| 6 Woolsey | Y | Y | Y | N | N | N | Y | Y |
| 7 Miller, George | ? | ? | ? | N | N | N | Y | Y |
| 8 Pelosi | ? | Y | Y | N | N | N | Y | Y |
| 9 Lee | Y | Y | Y | N | N | N | Y | Y |
| 10 Tauscher | Y | Y | Y | N | N | N | Y | Y |
| 11 Pombo | Y | Y | Y | Y | Y | Y | N | Y |
| 12 Lantos | Y | Y | Y | N | N | N | Y | Y |
| 13 Stark | Y | P | Y | N | N | N | Y | Y |
| 14 Eshoo | Y | Y | Y | N | N | N | Y | Y |
| 15 Honda | Y | Y | Y | N | N | N | Y | Y |
| 16 Lofgren | Y | Y | Y | N | N | N | Y | Y |
| 17 Farr | Y | Y | Y | N | N | N | Y | Y |
| 18 Cardoza | Y | Y | Y | N | N | N | Y | Y |
| 19 Radanovich | Y | Y | Y | Y | Y | Y | N | Y |
| 20 Costa | Y | Y | Y | N | N | N | Y | Y |
| 21 Nunes | Y | Y | Y | Y | Y | Y | N | Y |
| 22 Thomas | Y | Y | Y | Y | Y | Y | N | Y |
| 23 Capps | Y | Y | Y | N | N | N | Y | Y |
| 24 Gallegly | Y | Y | Y | Y | Y | Y | N | Y |
| 25 McKeon | Y | Y | Y | Y | Y | Y | N | N |
| 26 Dreier | Y | Y | Y | Y | Y | Y | N | N |
| 27 Sherman | Y | Y | Y | N | N | N | Y | Y |
| 28 Berman | Y | Y | Y | N | N | N | Y | Y |
| 29 Schiff | Y | Y | Y | N | N | N | Y | Y |
| 30 Waxman | Y | Y | Y | N | N | N | Y | Y |
| 31 Becerra | ? | ? | ? | N | N | N | Y | Y |
| 32 Solis | Y | Y | Y | N | N | N | Y | Y |
| 33 Watson | Y | N | Y | N | N | N | Y | Y |
| 34 Roybal-Allard | Y | Y | Y | N | N | N | Y | Y |
| 35 Waters | Y | P | Y | ? | ? | ? | ? | ? |
| 36 Harman | Y | Y | Y | N | N | ? | Y | Y |
| 37 Millender-McD. | Y | Y | Y | N | N | ? | Y | Y |
| 38 Napolitano | Y | Y | Y | N | N | N | Y | Y |
| 39 Sánchez, Linda | ? | ? | ? | N | N | N | Y | Y |
| 40 Royce | Y | Y | Y | Y | Y | Y | N | Y |
| 41 Lewis | Y | Y | Y | Y | Y | Y | N | N |
| 42 Miller, Gary | Y | Y | Y | Y | Y | Y | N | N |
| 43 Baca | Y | Y | Y | N | N | N | Y | Y |
| 44 Calvert | Y | Y | Y | Y | Y | Y | N | N |
| 45 Bono | Y | Y | Y | Y | Y | Y | N | N |
| 46 Rohrabacher | Y | Y | Y | Y | Y | Y | N | N |
| 47 Sanchez, Loretta | Y | Y | Y | N | N | N | Y | Y |
| 48 Cox | Y | Y | Y | Y | Y | Y | N | N |
| 49 Issa | Y | Y | Y | Y | Y | Y | N | N |
| 50 Cunningham | Y | Y | Y | Y | Y | Y | N | N |
| 51 Filner | Y | Y | Y | N | N | N | Y | N |
| 52 Hunter | ? | ? | ? | Y | Y | Y | N | N |
| 53 Davis | Y | Y | Y | N | N | N | Y | N |
| **COLORADO** | | | | | | | | |
| 1 DeGette | Y | Y | Y | N | N | N | Y | Y |
| 2 Udall | Y | Y | Y | N | N | N | Y | Y |
| 3 Salazar | Y | Y | Y | N | N | N | Y | Y |
| 4 Musgrave | Y | Y | Y | Y | Y | Y | N | Y |
| 5 Hefley | ? | ? | ? | Y | N | Y | N | Y |
| 6 Tancredo | Y | Y | Y | N | Y | N | N | Y |
| 7 Beauprez | Y | Y | Y | Y | Y | Y | N | N |
| **CONNECTICUT** | | | | | | | | |
| 1 Larson | Y | Y | Y | N | N | N | N | Y |
| 2 Simmons | Y | Y | Y | N | N | N | N | Y |
| 3 DeLauro | Y | Y | Y | N | N | N | N | Y |
| 4 Shays | Y | Y | Y | Y | Y | Y | N | N |
| 5 Johnson | Y | Y | Y | Y | Y | Y | N | N |
| **DELAWARE** | | | | | | | | |
| AL Castle | Y | Y | Y | Y | Y | Y | N | Y |
| **FLORIDA** | | | | | | | | |
| 1 Miller | Y | Y | Y | Y | Y | Y | N | N |
| 2 Boyd | Y | Y | Y | N | N | N | Y | Y |
| 3 Brown | ? | ? | ? | ? | N | N | Y | Y |
| 4 Crenshaw | Y | Y | Y | Y | Y | Y | N | N |
| 5 Brown-Waite | + | + | + | Y | Y | Y | N | N |
| 6 Stearns | Y | Y | Y | Y | Y | Y | N | N |
| 7 Mica | Y | Y | Y | Y | Y | Y | N | N |
| 8 Keller | Y | Y | Y | Y | Y | Y | N | N |
| 9 Bilirakis | Y | Y | Y | Y | Y | Y | N | N |
| 10 Young | Y | Y | Y | Y | Y | Y | N | N |
| 11 Davis | ? | ? | ? | N | ? | N | Y | Y |
| 12 Putnam | Y | Y | Y | Y | Y | Y | N | N |
| 13 Harris | Y | Y | Y | Y | Y | Y | N | N |
| 14 Mack | Y | Y | Y | Y | Y | Y | N | N |
| 15 Weldon | Y | Y | Y | Y | Y | Y | N | N |
| 16 Foley | Y | Y | Y | Y | Y | Y | N | N |
| 17 Meek | Y | Y | N | N | N | N | Y | Y |
| 18 Ros-Lehtinen | Y | Y | Y | Y | Y | Y | N | N |
| 19 Wexler | ? | ? | ? | N | N | N | Y | Y |
| 20 Wasserman-Schultz | Y | Y | Y | N | N | N | Y | Y |
| 21 Diaz-Balart, L. | Y | Y | Y | Y | Y | Y | N | N |
| 22 Shaw | Y | Y | Y | ? | Y | Y | N | N |
| 23 Hastings | Y | Y | Y | N | N | N | Y | Y |
| 24 Feeney | ? | ? | ? | Y | Y | Y | N | Y |
| 25 Diaz-Balart, M. | Y | Y | Y | Y | Y | Y | N | N |
| **GEORGIA** | | | | | | | | |
| 1 Kingston | Y | Y | Y | N | N | N | Y | Y |
| 2 Bishop | Y | Y | Y | N | N | N | Y | Y |
| 3 Marshall | Y | Y | Y | N | N | N | Y | Y |
| 4 McKinney | N | P | N | N | N | N | Y | Y |
| 5 Lewis | Y | Y | Y | N | N | N | Y | Y |
| 6 Price | Y | Y | Y | Y | Y | Y | N | N |
| 7 Linder | Y | Y | Y | Y | Y | Y | N | N |
| 8 Westmoreland | Y | Y | Y | ? | Y | Y | N | N |
| 9 Norwood | Y | Y | Y | ? | Y | Y | N | N |
| 10 Deal | Y | Y | Y | Y | Y | Y | N | N |
| 11 Gingrey | Y | Y | Y | Y | Y | Y | N | N |
| 12 Barrow | Y | Y | Y | N | N | N | Y | Y |
| 13 Scott | Y | Y | Y | N | N | N | Y | Y |
| **HAWAII** | | | | | | | | |
| 1 Abercrombie | Y | Y | Y | ? | N | N | Y | Y |
| 2 Case | Y | Y | Y | N | N | N | Y | N |
| **IDAHO** | | | | | | | | |
| 1 Otter | Y | Y | Y | Y | ? | Y | N | Y |
| 2 Simpson | ? | ? | ? | Y | Y | Y | N | N |
| **ILLINOIS** | | | | | | | | |
| 1 Rush | Y | Y | Y | N | N | N | Y | Y |
| 2 Jackson | Y | Y | Y | N | N | N | Y | Y |
| 3 Lipinski | Y | Y | Y | N | N | N | Y | Y |
| 4 Gutierrez | ? | ? | ? | N | N | N | Y | Y |
| 5 Emanuel | Y | Y | Y | N | N | N | Y | Y |
| 6 Hyde | Y | Y | Y | Y | Y | ? | N | N |
| 7 Davis | Y | Y | Y | N | N | N | Y | Y |
| 8 Bean | Y | Y | Y | N | N | N | Y | Y |
| 9 Schakowsky | Y | Y | Y | N | N | N | Y | Y |
| 10 Kirk | Y | Y | Y | Y | Y | Y | N | N |
| 11 Weller | Y | Y | Y | N | N | N | Y | Y |
| 12 Costello | Y | Y | Y | N | N | N | Y | Y |

| KEY | Republicans | Democrats | *Independents* | | |
|---|---|---|---|---|---|
| Y | Voted for (yea) | X | Paired against | C | Voted "present" to avoid possible conflict of interest |
| # | Paired for | – | Announced against | | |
| + | Announced for | P | Voted "present" | ? | Did not vote or otherwise make a position known |
| N | Voted against (nay) | | | | |

| | 66 | 67 | 68 | 69 | 70 | 71 | 72 | 73 |
|---|---|---|---|---|---|---|---|---|
| 13 **Biggert** | Y | Y | Y | Y | Y | Y | N | N |
| 14 **Hastert** | | | | | | | | |
| 15 **Johnson** | Y | Y | Y | Y | Y | Y | N | N |
| 16 **Manzullo** | Y | Y | Y | Y | Y | Y | N | Y |
| 17 Evans | ? | ? | ? | N | N | N | Y | Y |
| 18 **LaHood** | ? | ? | ? | Y | Y | Y | N | N |
| 19 **Shimkus** | Y | Y | Y | Y | Y | Y | N | Y |
| **INDIANA** | | | | | | | | |
| 1 Visclosky | Y | Y | Y | N | N | N | Y | N |
| 2 **Chocola** | Y | Y | Y | Y | Y | Y | N | Y |
| 3 **Souder** | Y | Y | Y | Y | Y | Y | N | N |
| 4 **Buyer** | Y | Y | ? | Y | Y | Y | N | Y |
| 5 **Burton** | Y | Y | Y | Y | Y | Y | N | N |
| 6 **Pence** | ? | ? | ? | Y | Y | Y | N | Y |
| 7 Carson | Y | Y | Y | N | N | N | Y | Y |
| 8 **Hostettler** | Y | Y | Y | Y | Y | Y | N | Y |
| 9 **Sodrel** | Y | Y | Y | Y | Y | Y | N | Y |
| **IOWA** | | | | | | | | |
| 1 **Nussle** | ? | ? | ? | Y | Y | Y | N | Y |
| 2 **Leach** | Y | Y | Y | Y | Y | ? | ? | ? |
| 3 Boswell | ? | ? | ? | N | N | N | Y | N |
| 4 **Latham** | Y | Y | Y | Y | Y | Y | N | N |
| 5 **King** | Y | Y | Y | Y | Y | Y | N | Y |
| **KANSAS** | | | | | | | | |
| 1 **Moran** | Y | Y | Y | Y | Y | Y | N | Y |
| 2 **Ryun** | Y | Y | Y | Y | Y | Y | N | Y |
| 3 Moore | Y | Y | Y | N | N | N | Y | Y |
| 4 **Tiahrt** | Y | Y | Y | Y | Y | Y | N | N |
| **KENTUCKY** | | | | | | | | |
| 1 **Whitfield** | Y | Y | Y | Y | Y | Y | N | Y |
| 2 **Lewis** | Y | Y | Y | Y | Y | Y | N | N |
| 3 **Northup** | Y | Y | Y | Y | Y | Y | N | N |
| 4 **Davis** | Y | Y | Y | Y | Y | Y | N | N |
| 5 **Rogers** | Y | Y | Y | Y | Y | Y | N | N |
| 6 Chandler | Y | Y | Y | N | N | N | Y | Y |
| **LOUISIANA** | | | | | | | | |
| 1 **Jindal** | Y | Y | Y | Y | Y | Y | N | N |
| 2 Jefferson | Y | Y | Y | N | ? | N | Y | Y |
| 3 Melancon | Y | Y | Y | N | N | N | Y | Y |
| 4 **McCrery** | Y | Y | Y | Y | Y | Y | N | N |
| 5 **Alexander** | ? | ? | ? | Y | Y | Y | N | N |
| 6 **Baker** | Y | Y | Y | Y | Y | Y | N | N |
| 7 **Boustany** | ? | ? | ? | Y | Y | Y | N | N |
| **MAINE** | | | | | | | | |
| 1 Allen | Y | Y | Y | N | N | N | Y | N |
| 2 Michaud | Y | Y | Y | N | N | N | Y | Y |
| **MARYLAND** | | | | | | | | |
| 1 **Gilchrest** | Y | Y | Y | Y | Y | Y | N | N |
| 2 Ruppersberger | Y | Y | ? | ? | N | N | Y | N |
| 3 Cardin | Y | Y | Y | N | N | N | Y | Y |
| 4 Wynn | Y | Y | Y | N | N | N | Y | Y |
| 5 Hoyer | Y | Y | Y | N | N | N | Y | Y |
| 6 **Bartlett** | Y | Y | Y | Y | Y | Y | N | Y |
| 7 Cummings | Y | Y | Y | N | N | N | Y | Y |
| 8 Van Hollen | Y | ? | Y | N | N | N | Y | Y |
| **MASSACHUSETTS** | | | | | | | | |
| 1 Olver | Y | Y | Y | N | N | N | Y | Y |
| 2 Neal | Y | Y | Y | N | N | N | Y | Y |
| 3 McGovern | Y | Y | Y | N | N | N | Y | Y |
| 4 Frank | Y | Y | Y | N | N | N | Y | Y |
| 5 Meehan | Y | Y | Y | N | N | N | Y | Y |
| 6 Tierney | Y | Y | Y | N | N | N | Y | Y |
| 7 Markey | Y | Y | Y | N | N | N | Y | Y |
| 8 Capuano | ? | ? | ? | N | N | N | Y | N |
| 9 Lynch | Y | Y | Y | N | N | N | Y | Y |
| 10 Delahunt | Y | Y | Y | N | N | N | Y | Y |
| **MICHIGAN** | | | | | | | | |
| 1 Stupak | Y | Y | Y | N | N | N | Y | N |
| 2 **Hoekstra** | Y | Y | Y | Y | Y | Y | N | N |
| 3 **Ehlers** | Y | Y | Y | Y | Y | Y | N | Y |
| 4 **Camp** | Y | Y | Y | Y | Y | Y | N | Y |
| 5 Kildee | Y | Y | Y | N | N | N | Y | Y |
| 6 **Upton** | Y | Y | Y | Y | Y | Y | N | Y |
| 7 **Schwarz** | ? | Y | Y | Y | Y | Y | N | N |
| 8 **Rogers** | Y | Y | Y | + | Y | Y | N | Y |
| 9 **Knollenberg** | ? | ? | ? | ? | Y | Y | N | N |
| 10 **Miller** | Y | Y | Y | Y | Y | Y | N | Y |
| 11 **McCotter** | Y | Y | Y | Y | Y | Y | N | Y |
| 12 Levin | Y | Y | Y | N | N | N | Y | Y |
| 13 Kilpatrick | ? | ? | ? | N | N | N | Y | Y |
| 14 Conyers | Y | Y | Y | N | N | N | Y | Y |
| 15 Dingell | Y | Y | Y | N | N | N | Y | Y |

| | 66 | 67 | 68 | 69 | 70 | 71 | 72 | 73 |
|---|---|---|---|---|---|---|---|---|
| **MINNESOTA** | | | | | | | | |
| 1 **Gutknecht** | Y | Y | Y | Y | Y | Y | N | Y |
| 2 **Kline** | Y | Y | Y | Y | Y | Y | N | N |
| 3 **Ramstad** | Y | Y | Y | Y | Y | Y | N | Y |
| 4 McCollum | Y | Y | Y | N | N | N | Y | Y |
| 5 Sabo | Y | Y | Y | N | N | N | Y | Y |
| 6 **Kennedy** | Y | Y | Y | Y | Y | Y | N | N |
| 7 Peterson | ? | ? | ? | N | N | N | N | Y |
| 8 Oberstar | Y | Y | Y | N | N | N | Y | Y |
| **MISSISSIPPI** | | | | | | | | |
| 1 **Wicker** | Y | Y | Y | Y | Y | Y | N | Y |
| 2 Thompson | Y | Y | Y | N | N | N | Y | Y |
| 3 **Pickering** | Y | Y | Y | Y | Y | Y | N | Y |
| 4 Taylor | Y | Y | Y | N | N | N | Y | Y |
| **MISSOURI** | | | | | | | | |
| 1 Clay | Y | Y | Y | ? | ? | N | Y | Y |
| 2 **Akin** | Y | Y | Y | Y | Y | Y | N | N |
| 3 Carnahan | Y | Y | Y | N | N | N | Y | Y |
| 4 Skelton | Y | Y | Y | N | N | N | Y | N |
| 5 Cleaver | Y | Y | Y | N | N | N | Y | Y |
| 6 **Graves** | Y | Y | Y | Y | Y | Y | N | N |
| 7 **Blunt** | Y | Y | Y | Y | Y | Y | N | N |
| 8 **Emerson** | ? | ? | ? | Y | Y | Y | N | N |
| 9 **Hulshof** | Y | Y | Y | Y | Y | Y | N | Y |
| **MONTANA** | | | | | | | | |
| AL **Rehberg** | Y | Y | Y | Y | ? | Y | N | N |
| **NEBRASKA** | | | | | | | | |
| 1 **Fortenberry** | Y | Y | Y | Y | Y | Y | N | N |
| 2 **Terry** | Y | Y | Y | Y | Y | ? | N | Y |
| 3 **Osborne** | Y | Y | Y | Y | Y | Y | N | Y |
| **NEVADA** | | | | | | | | |
| 1 Berkley | Y | Y | Y | N | N | N | Y | N |
| 2 **Gibbons** | Y | Y | Y | Y | Y | Y | N | Y |
| 3 **Porter** | Y | Y | Y | Y | Y | Y | N | Y |
| **NEW HAMPSHIRE** | | | | | | | | |
| 1 **Bradley** | Y | Y | Y | Y | Y | Y | N | Y |
| 2 **Bass** | Y | Y | Y | Y | Y | Y | N | Y |
| **NEW JERSEY** | | | | | | | | |
| 1 Andrews | Y | Y | Y | N | N | N | Y | Y |
| 2 **LoBiondo** | Y | Y | Y | Y | Y | Y | N | Y |
| 3 **Saxton** | Y | Y | Y | ? | Y | Y | N | N |
| 4 **Smith** | Y | Y | Y | Y | Y | Y | N | N |
| 5 **Garrett** | Y | Y | Y | Y | Y | Y | N | Y |
| 6 Pallone | ? | ? | ? | N | N | N | Y | Y |
| 7 **Ferguson** | Y | Y | Y | Y | Y | Y | N | N |
| 8 Pascrell | ? | ? | ? | ? | N | N | N | Y |
| 9 Rothman | Y | Y | Y | N | N | N | Y | N |
| 10 Payne | ? | ? | ? | N | N | N | Y | Y |
| 11 **Frelinghuysen** | Y | Y | Y | Y | Y | Y | N | N |
| 12 Holt | Y | Y | Y | N | N | N | Y | Y |
| 13 Menendez | + | + | + | N | N | N | Y | Y |
| **NEW MEXICO** | | | | | | | | |
| 1 **Wilson** | Y | Y | Y | N | Y | Y | N | N |
| 2 **Pearce** | Y | Y | Y | Y | Y | Y | N | N |
| 3 Udall | Y | Y | Y | N | N | N | Y | Y |
| **NEW YORK** | | | | | | | | |
| 1 Bishop | Y | Y | Y | N | N | N | Y | Y |
| 2 Israel | Y | Y | Y | N | ? | N | Y | N |
| 3 **King** | Y | Y | Y | Y | Y | Y | N | Y |
| 4 McCarthy | ? | ? | ? | N | N | N | Y | N |
| 5 Ackerman | Y | Y | Y | N | N | N | Y | N |
| 6 Meeks | Y | Y | Y | N | N | N | Y | Y |
| 7 Crowley | Y | Y | Y | N | N | N | Y | N |
| 8 Nadler | Y | Y | Y | N | N | N | Y | N |
| 9 Weiner | Y | Y | Y | N | N | N | Y | Y |
| 10 Towns | Y | Y | Y | N | N | N | Y | Y |
| 11 Owens | Y | Y | Y | N | ? | N | Y | Y |
| 12 Velázquez | Y | Y | Y | N | N | N | Y | Y |
| 13 **Fossella** | Y | Y | Y | Y | Y | Y | N | Y |
| 14 Maloney | Y | Y | Y | N | N | N | Y | Y |
| 15 Rangel | ? | ? | ? | N | N | N | Y | Y |
| 16 Serrano | Y | Y | Y | N | N | N | Y | Y |
| 17 Engel | Y | Y | Y | N | N | N | Y | N |
| 18 Lowey | Y | Y | Y | N | N | N | Y | Y |
| 19 **Kelly** | ? | ? | ? | Y | Y | Y | N | N |
| 20 **Sweeney** | Y | Y | Y | ? | ? | ? | ? | ? |
| 21 McNulty | Y | Y | Y | N | N | N | Y | N |
| 22 Hinchey | Y | P | Y | N | N | N | Y | N |
| 23 **McHugh** | Y | Y | Y | Y | Y | Y | N | N |
| 24 **Boehlert** | Y | Y | Y | ? | Y | Y | N | Y |
| 25 **Walsh** | ? | ? | ? | ? | ? | ? | ? | ? |
| 26 **Reynolds** | Y | Y | Y | Y | Y | Y | N | Y |
| 27 Higgins | Y | Y | Y | N | N | N | Y | N |
| 28 Slaughter | Y | Y | Y | N | N | N | Y | Y |
| 29 **Kuhl** | Y | Y | Y | Y | Y | Y | N | Y |

| | 66 | 67 | 68 | 69 | 70 | 71 | 72 | 73 |
|---|---|---|---|---|---|---|---|---|
| **NORTH CAROLINA** | | | | | | | | |
| 1 Butterfield | Y | Y | Y | N | N | N | Y | Y |
| 2 Etheridge | Y | Y | Y | N | N | N | Y | Y |
| 3 **Jones** | Y | Y | Y | Y | Y | Y | N | Y |
| 4 Price | Y | Y | Y | N | N | N | Y | Y |
| 5 **Foxx** | Y | Y | Y | Y | Y | Y | N | Y |
| 6 **Coble** | Y | Y | Y | Y | Y | Y | N | Y |
| 7 McIntyre | Y | Y | Y | N | N | N | Y | Y |
| 8 **Hayes** | Y | Y | Y | Y | Y | Y | N | N |
| 9 **Myrick** | Y | Y | Y | Y | Y | Y | N | Y |
| 10 **McHenry** | Y | Y | Y | Y | Y | Y | N | N |
| 11 **Taylor** | ? | Y | Y | Y | Y | Y | N | N |
| 12 Watt | Y | Y | Y | N | N | N | Y | Y |
| 13 Miller | Y | Y | Y | N | N | N | Y | Y |
| **NORTH DAKOTA** | | | | | | | | |
| AL Pomeroy | Y | Y | Y | N | N | N | Y | N |
| **OHIO** | | | | | | | | |
| 1 **Chabot** | Y | ? | Y | Y | ? | Y | N | Y |
| 2 **Portman** | Y | Y | Y | Y | Y | Y | N | N |
| 3 **Turner** | Y | Y | Y | Y | Y | Y | N | Y |
| 4 **Oxley** | Y | Y | Y | Y | Y | ? | N | N |
| 5 **Gillmor** | Y | Y | Y | Y | Y | Y | N | N |
| 6 Strickland | Y | Y | Y | N | N | N | Y | Y |
| 7 **Hobson** | Y | Y | Y | Y | Y | Y | N | N |
| 8 **Boehner** | Y | Y | Y | Y | Y | Y | N | Y |
| 9 Kaptur | Y | Y | Y | N | N | N | Y | N |
| 10 Kucinich | Y | Y | Y | N | N | N | Y | Y |
| 11 Jones | ? | ? | ? | ? | ? | N | Y | N |
| 12 **Tiberi** | Y | Y | Y | Y | Y | Y | N | Y |
| 13 Brown | Y | Y | Y | N | N | N | Y | Y |
| 14 **LaTourette** | Y | Y | Y | Y | Y | Y | N | Y |
| 15 **Pryce** | ? | ? | ? | Y | Y | Y | N | N |
| 16 **Regula** | Y | Y | Y | Y | Y | Y | N | N |
| 17 Ryan | Y | Y | Y | N | N | N | Y | N |
| 18 **Ney** | Y | Y | Y | Y | Y | Y | N | Y |
| **OKLAHOMA** | | | | | | | | |
| 1 **Sullivan** | Y | Y | Y | Y | Y | ? | N | Y |
| 2 Boren | Y | Y | Y | N | N | N | Y | N |
| 3 **Lucas** | Y | Y | Y | Y | Y | Y | N | N |
| 4 **Cole** | Y | Y | Y | Y | Y | Y | N | N |
| 5 **Istook** | Y | Y | Y | Y | Y | ? | N | Y |
| **OREGON** | | | | | | | | |
| 1 Wu | Y | Y | Y | N | N | N | Y | Y |
| 2 **Walden** | Y | Y | Y | Y | Y | Y | N | Y |
| 3 Blumenauer | Y | Y | Y | N | N | N | Y | Y |
| 4 DeFazio | Y | Y | Y | N | N | N | Y | Y |
| 5 Hooley | Y | Y | Y | N | N | N | Y | Y |
| **PENNSYLVANIA** | | | | | | | | |
| 1 Brady | Y | Y | Y | N | N | N | N | N |
| 2 Fattah | Y | Y | Y | N | N | N | Y | N |
| 3 **English** | Y | Y | Y | Y | Y | Y | N | N |
| 4 **Hart** | Y | Y | Y | Y | Y | Y | N | N |
| 5 **Peterson** | ? | ? | ? | Y | Y | Y | N | Y |
| 6 **Gerlach** | Y | Y | Y | Y | Y | Y | N | N |
| 7 **Weldon** | Y | Y | Y | Y | Y | Y | N | N |
| 8 **Fitzpatrick** | Y | Y | Y | Y | Y | Y | N | Y |
| 9 **Shuster** | Y | Y | Y | Y | Y | Y | N | Y |
| 10 **Sherwood** | Y | Y | Y | Y | Y | Y | N | N |
| 11 Kanjorski | Y | Y | Y | N | N | N | Y | N |
| 12 Murtha | Y | Y | Y | N | N | N | N | N |
| 13 Schwartz | Y | Y | Y | N | N | N | Y | N |
| 14 Doyle | Y | Y | Y | N | N | N | N | N |
| 15 **Dent** | Y | Y | Y | Y | Y | Y | N | Y |
| 16 **Pitts** | Y | Y | Y | Y | Y | Y | N | Y |
| 17 Holden | Y | Y | Y | N | N | N | N | N |
| 18 **Murphy** | Y | Y | Y | Y | Y | Y | N | N |
| 19 **Platts** | Y | Y | Y | Y | Y | Y | N | Y |
| **RHODE ISLAND** | | | | | | | | |
| 1 Kennedy | Y | Y | Y | N | N | N | ? | N |
| 2 Langevin | Y | Y | Y | N | N | N | Y | Y |
| **SOUTH CAROLINA** | | | | | | | | |
| 1 **Brown** | Y | Y | Y | Y | Y | Y | N | Y |
| 2 **Wilson** | Y | Y | Y | Y | Y | Y | N | N |
| 3 **Barrett** | Y | Y | Y | Y | Y | Y | N | N |
| 4 **Inglis** | Y | Y | Y | Y | Y | Y | N | Y |
| 5 Spratt | Y | Y | Y | N | N | N | Y | Y |
| 6 Clyburn | Y | Y | Y | N | N | N | Y | Y |
| **SOUTH DAKOTA** | | | | | | | | |
| AL Herseth | Y | Y | Y | N | N | N | Y | N |
| **TENNESSEE** | | | | | | | | |
| 1 **Jenkins** | Y | Y | Y | Y | Y | Y | N | Y |
| 2 **Duncan** | Y | Y | Y | Y | Y | Y | N | Y |

| | 66 | 67 | 68 | 69 | 70 | 71 | 72 | 73 |
|---|---|---|---|---|---|---|---|---|
| 3 **Wamp** | Y | Y | Y | Y | Y | Y | N | N |
| 4 Davis | Y | Y | Y | N | N | N | Y | N |
| 5 Cooper | Y | Y | Y | N | N | N | Y | Y |
| 6 Gordon | Y | Y | Y | N | N | N | Y | Y |
| 7 **Blackburn** | ? | ? | ? | Y | Y | Y | N | Y |
| 8 Tanner | Y | Y | Y | N | N | N | Y | Y |
| 9 Ford | Y | Y | Y | N | N | N | Y | N |
| **TEXAS** | | | | | | | | |
| 1 **Gohmert** | Y | Y | Y | Y | Y | Y | N | Y |
| 2 **Poe** | Y | Y | Y | Y | Y | Y | N | Y |
| 3 **Johnson, S.** | Y | Y | Y | Y | Y | Y | N | Y |
| 4 **Hall** | Y | Y | Y | Y | Y | Y | N | Y |
| 5 **Hensarling** | Y | Y | Y | Y | Y | Y | N | Y |
| 6 **Barton** | Y | Y | Y | Y | Y | Y | N | Y |
| 7 **Culberson** | ? | ? | ? | Y | Y | Y | N | N |
| 8 **Brady** | Y | Y | Y | Y | Y | Y | N | Y |
| 9 Green, A. | Y | Y | Y | N | N | N | Y | Y |
| 10 **McCaul** | Y | Y | Y | Y | Y | Y | N | Y |
| 11 **Conaway** | Y | Y | Y | Y | Y | Y | N | Y |
| 12 **Granger** | Y | Y | Y | Y | Y | Y | N | N |
| 13 **Thornberry** | Y | Y | Y | Y | Y | Y | ? | ? |
| 14 **Paul** | N | N | Y | Y | Y | Y | N | Y |
| 15 Hinojosa | ? | ? | ? | – | – | N | Y | Y |
| 16 Reyes | Y | Y | Y | N | ? | N | Y | Y |
| 17 Edwards | Y | Y | Y | N | N | N | Y | N |
| 18 Jackson-Lee | Y | Y | Y | N | N | N | Y | N |
| 19 **Neugebauer** | Y | Y | Y | Y | Y | Y | N | Y |
| 20 Gonzalez | Y | Y | Y | N | N | N | Y | Y |
| 21 **Smith** | Y | Y | Y | Y | Y | Y | N | Y |
| 22 **DeLay** | Y | Y | Y | Y | Y | Y | N | N |
| 23 **Bonilla** | Y | Y | Y | Y | Y | Y | N | N |
| 24 **Marchant** | Y | Y | Y | Y | Y | Y | N | Y |
| 25 Doggett | Y | Y | Y | N | N | N | Y | Y |
| 26 **Burgess** | Y | Y | Y | ? | Y | Y | N | Y |
| 27 Ortiz | Y | Y | Y | N | N | N | Y | Y |
| 28 Cuellar | Y | Y | Y | N | N | N | Y | Y |
| 29 Green, G. | Y | Y | Y | N | N | N | Y | Y |
| 30 Johnson, E. | Y | Y | Y | N | N | N | Y | Y |
| 31 **Carter** | Y | Y | Y | Y | Y | Y | N | N |
| 32 **Sessions** | ? | ? | Y | Y | Y | Y | N | Y |
| **UTAH** | | | | | | | | |
| 1 **Bishop** | Y | Y | Y | Y | Y | Y | N | N |
| 2 Matheson | Y | Y | Y | N | N | N | Y | Y |
| 3 **Cannon** | Y | Y | Y | Y | Y | Y | N | Y |
| **VERMONT** | | | | | | | | |
| AL *Sanders* | Y | Y | Y | N | N | N | Y | Y |
| **VIRGINIA** | | | | | | | | |
| 1 **Davis, J.** | Y | Y | Y | Y | Y | Y | N | Y |
| 2 **Drake** | Y | Y | Y | Y | Y | Y | N | N |
| 3 Scott | Y | Y | Y | N | N | N | Y | Y |
| 4 **Forbes** | Y | Y | Y | Y | Y | Y | N | N |
| 5 **Goode** | Y | Y | Y | Y | Y | Y | N | Y |
| 6 **Goodlatte** | Y | Y | Y | Y | Y | Y | N | Y |
| 7 **Cantor** | Y | Y | Y | Y | Y | Y | N | N |
| 8 Moran | Y | Y | Y | N | N | N | Y | Y |
| 9 Boucher | Y | Y | Y | N | N | N | Y | Y |
| 10 **Wolf** | Y | Y | Y | Y | Y | Y | N | N |
| 11 **Davis, T.** | Y | Y | Y | Y | Y | Y | N | N |
| **WASHINGTON** | | | | | | | | |
| 1 Inslee | Y | Y | Y | N | N | N | Y | Y |
| 2 Larsen | Y | Y | Y | N | N | N | Y | Y |
| 3 Baird | ? | ? | ? | ? | ? | N | Y | Y |
| 4 **Hastings** | Y | Y | Y | Y | Y | Y | N | N |
| 5 **McMorris** | Y | Y | Y | Y | Y | Y | N | N |
| 6 Dicks | Y | Y | Y | N | N | N | Y | N |
| 7 McDermott | Y | P | Y | N | N | N | Y | Y |
| 8 **Reichert** | Y | Y | Y | Y | Y | Y | N | Y |
| 9 Smith | Y | Y | Y | N | N | N | Y | N |
| **WEST VIRGINIA** | | | | | | | | |
| 1 Mollohan | Y | Y | Y | N | N | N | N | N |
| 2 **Capito** | Y | Y | Y | Y | Y | Y | N | N |
| 3 Rahall | Y | N | Y | N | N | N | N | N |
| **WISCONSIN** | | | | | | | | |
| 1 **Ryan** | Y | Y | Y | Y | Y | Y | N | Y |
| 2 Baldwin | Y | Y | Y | N | N | N | Y | Y |
| 3 Kind | Y | Y | Y | N | N | N | Y | Y |
| 4 Moore | Y | Y | Y | N | N | N | Y | Y |
| 5 **Sensenbrenner** | Y | Y | Y | Y | Y | Y | N | Y |
| 6 **Petri** | Y | Y | Y | Y | Y | Y | N | Y |
| 7 Obey | Y | Y | Y | N | N | N | Y | Y |
| 8 **Green** | Y | Y | Y | Y | Y | Y | N | Y |
| **WYOMING** | | | | | | | | |
| AL **Cubin** | Y | Y | Y | Y | Y | Y | N | N |

# IN THE HOUSE | By Vote Number

**74.** **HR 1268. Fiscal 2005 Supplemental Appropriations/Aid for Saudi Arabia.** Weiner, D-N.Y., amendment that would prohibit the use of funds in the bill for assistance to Saudi Arabia. Rejected 196-231: R 39-187; D 156-44 (ND 121-28, SD 35-16); I 1-0. March 15, 2005.

**75.** **HR 1268. Fiscal 2005 Supplemental Appropriations/Torture Policy.** Markey, D-Mass., amendment that would prohibit the use of funds in the bill to contravene U.S. laws implementing the U.N. Convention Against Torture. Adopted 420-2: R 222-2; D 197-0 (ND 148-0, SD 49-0); I 1-0. March 16, 2005.

**76.** **HR 1268. Fiscal 2005 Supplemental Appropriations/Recommit.** Hooley, D-Ore., motion to recommit the bill to the Appropriations Committee with instructions to add language that would increase funding for military health care by $100 million and for transitional job training for military personnel by $50 million. Motion rejected 200-229: R 2-226; D 197-3 (ND 146-3, SD 51-0); I 1-0. March 16, 2005.

**77.** **HR 1268. Fiscal 2005 Supplemental Appropriations/Passage.** Passage of the bill that would appropriate $81.4 billion in fiscal 2005 supplemental spending for military operations and reconstruction in Iraq and Afghanistan and for disaster assistance to victims of the December 2004 tsunami in South Asia. The bill would provide $15.5 billion for military personnel, $37.5 billion for operations and maintenance, $18.2 billion for procurement, $1.3 billion for reconstruction in Afghanistan and $4.6 billion for new combat brigades under the Army's force-restructuring plan. It also would provide $656 million for tsunami relief and recovery, and $222 million to reimburse the U.S. military for its tsunami-relief operations. Passed 388-43: R 226-3; D 162-39 (ND 115-35, SD 47-4); I 0-1. March 16, 2005.

**78.** **H Con Res 95. Fiscal 2006 Budget Resolution/Previous Question.** Putnam, R-Fla., motion to order the previous question (thus ending debate and possibility of amendment) on adoption of the rule (H Res 154) to provide for House floor consideration of the concurrent resolution that would set broad spending and revenue targets over the next five years. Motion agreed to 230-202: R 229-0; D 1-201 (ND 0-151, SD 1-50); I 0-1. March 16, 2005.

**79.** **H Con Res 95. Fiscal 2006 Budget Resolution/Rule.** Adoption of the rule (H Res 154) to provide for House floor consideration of the concurrent resolution that would set broad spending and revenue targets over the next five years. Adopted 228-196: R 227-0; D 1-195 (ND 1-147, SD 0-48); I 0-1. March 16, 2005.

**80.** **HR 1270. Leaking Underground Storage Tanks/Passage.** Chocola, R-Ind., motion to suspend the rules and pass the bill that would extend the 0.1-cent tax rate on motor vehicle fuels sold in the United States to fund the Leaking Underground Storage Tank Trust Fund through Oct. 1, 2005. Motion agreed to 431-1: R 228-1; D 202-0 (ND 151-0, SD 51-0); I 1-0. A two-thirds majority of those present and voting (288 in this case) is required for passage under suspension of the rules. March 16, 2005.

**81.** **H Con Res 98. China-Taiwan Relations/Adoption.** Smith, R-N.J., motion to suspend the rules and adopt the concurrent resolution that would express the sense of Congress that the March 14, 2005, passage of an anti-secession law by China is of grave concern to the United States because it provides a legal justification for the use of force against Taiwan. Motion agreed to 424-4: R 226-1; D 197-3 (ND 147-3, SD 50-0); I 1-0. A two-thirds majority of those present and voting (286 in this case) is required for adoption under suspension of the rules. March 16, 2005.

| | 74 | 75 | 76 | 77 | 78 | 79 | 80 | 81 |
|---|---|---|---|---|---|---|---|---|
| **ALABAMA** | | | | | | | | |
| 1 Bonner | N | Y | N | Y | Y | Y | Y | Y |
| 2 Everett | N | Y | N | Y | Y | Y | Y | Y |
| 3 Rogers | Y | Y | N | Y | Y | Y | Y | Y |
| 4 Aderholt | N | Y | N | Y | Y | Y | Y | Y |
| 5 Cramer | Y | Y | Y | N | N | Y | N | Y |
| 6 Bachus | ? | Y | N | Y | Y | Y | Y | Y |
| 7 Davis | N | Y | Y | Y | N | N | Y | Y |
| **ALASKA** | | | | | | | | |
| AL Young | N | Y | N | Y | Y | Y | Y | Y |
| **ARIZONA** | | | | | | | | |
| 1 Renzi | N | Y | N | Y | Y | Y | Y | Y |
| 2 Franks | N | Y | N | Y | Y | Y | Y | Y |
| 3 Shadegg | N | Y | N | Y | Y | Y | Y | Y |
| 4 Pastor | N | Y | Y | N | N | Y | N | Y |
| 5 Hayworth | Y | Y | N | Y | Y | Y | Y | Y |
| 6 Flake | N | Y | N | Y | Y | Y | Y | Y |
| 7 Grijalva | Y | Y | Y | N | N | N | Y | Y |
| 8 Kolbe | N | Y | N | Y | Y | Y | Y | Y |
| **ARKANSAS** | | | | | | | | |
| 1 Berry | Y | Y | Y | Y | N | N | Y | Y |
| 2 Snyder | N | Y | Y | Y | N | N | Y | Y |
| 3 Boozman | N | Y | N | Y | Y | Y | Y | Y |
| 4 Ross | Y | Y | Y | Y | N | N | Y | Y |
| **CALIFORNIA** | | | | | | | | |
| 1 Thompson | Y | Y | Y | N | N | N | Y | Y |
| 2 Herger | N | Y | N | Y | Y | Y | Y | Y |
| 3 Lungren | N | Y | N | Y | Y | Y | Y | Y |
| 4 Doolittle | Y | Y | Y | Y | N | Y | Y | Y |
| 5 Matsui, D. | Y | Y | Y | N | N | N | Y | Y |
| 6 Woolsey | Y | Y | Y | N | N | N | Y | Y |
| 7 Miller, George | Y | Y | Y | N | N | N | Y | Y |
| 8 Pelosi | Y | Y | Y | N | N | N | Y | Y |
| 9 Lee | Y | Y | Y | N | N | N | Y | Y |
| 10 Tauscher | Y | Y | Y | N | N | N | Y | Y |
| 11 Pombo | N | Y | N | Y | Y | Y | Y | Y |
| 12 Lantos | Y | Y | Y | N | N | N | Y | Y |
| 13 Stark | N | Y | Y | N | N | N | Y | Y |
| 14 Eshoo | Y | Y | Y | N | N | N | Y | Y |
| 15 Honda | Y | Y | Y | N | ? | N | Y | Y |
| 16 Lofgren | Y | Y | Y | N | N | N | Y | Y |
| 17 Farr | Y | Y | Y | N | N | N | Y | Y |
| 18 Cardoza | Y | Y | Y | N | N | N | Y | Y |
| 19 Radanovich | N | Y | N | Y | ? | ? | Y | Y |
| 20 Costa | Y | Y | Y | Y | N | N | Y | Y |
| 21 Nunes | N | Y | N | Y | Y | Y | Y | Y |
| 22 Thomas | N | Y | N | Y | Y | Y | Y | Y |
| 23 Capps | Y | Y | Y | N | N | N | Y | Y |
| 24 Gallegly | N | Y | N | Y | Y | Y | Y | Y |
| 25 McKeon | N | Y | N | Y | Y | Y | Y | Y |
| 26 Dreier | N | Y | N | Y | Y | Y | Y | Y |
| 27 Sherman | Y | Y | Y | N | N | N | Y | Y |
| 28 Berman | Y | Y | Y | N | N | N | Y | Y |
| 29 Schiff | Y | Y | Y | N | N | N | Y | Y |
| 30 Waxman | Y | Y | Y | N | N | N | Y | Y |
| 31 Becerra | Y | Y | Y | N | N | N | Y | Y |
| 32 Solis | Y | Y | Y | N | N | N | Y | Y |
| 33 Watson | Y | Y | Y | N | ? | N | Y | Y |
| 34 Roybal-Allard | N | ? | ? | Y | N | N | Y | Y |
| 35 Waters | ? | Y | Y | N | N | N | Y | Y |
| 36 Harman | Y | Y | Y | N | N | N | Y | Y |
| 37 Millender-McD. | Y | Y | Y | N | N | N | Y | Y |
| 38 Napolitano | Y | Y | Y | N | N | N | Y | Y |
| 39 Sánchez, Linda | Y | Y | Y | N | N | N | Y | Y |
| 40 Royce | Y | Y | N | Y | Y | Y | Y | Y |
| 41 Lewis | N | Y | N | Y | Y | Y | Y | Y |
| 42 Miller, Gary | Y | Y | N | Y | Y | Y | Y | Y |
| 43 Baca | Y | Y | Y | N | N | N | Y | Y |
| 44 Calvert | N | Y | N | Y | Y | Y | Y | Y |
| 45 Bono | N | Y | N | Y | Y | Y | Y | Y |
| 46 Rohrabacher | Y | P | N | Y | Y | Y | Y | Y |
| 47 Sanchez, Loretta | Y | Y | Y | N | N | N | Y | Y |
| 48 Cox | Y | Y | Y | N | Y | Y | Y | Y |
| 49 Issa | N | Y | N | Y | Y | Y | Y | Y |
| 50 Cunningham | N | Y | N | Y | Y | Y | Y | Y |
| 51 Filner | Y | Y | Y | N | N | N | Y | Y |
| 52 Hunter | N | Y | N | Y | Y | Y | Y | Y |
| 53 Davis | Y | Y | Y | Y | N | N | Y | Y |
| **COLORADO** | | | | | | | | |
| 1 DeGette | N | Y | Y | N | N | N | Y | Y |
| 2 Udall | Y | Y | Y | N | N | N | Y | Y |
| 3 Salazar | Y | Y | Y | N | N | N | Y | Y |
| 4 Musgrave | N | Y | N | Y | Y | Y | Y | Y |
| 5 Hefley | N | Y | N | Y | Y | Y | Y | Y |
| 6 Tancredo | Y | Y | N | Y | Y | Y | Y | Y |
| 7 Beauprez | N | Y | N | Y | Y | Y | Y | Y |
| **CONNECTICUT** | | | | | | | | |
| 1 Larson | Y | Y | Y | N | N | N | Y | Y |
| 2 Simmons | Y | Y | Y | N | Y | Y | Y | Y |
| 3 DeLauro | Y | Y | Y | N | N | N | Y | Y |
| 4 Shays | N | Y | N | Y | Y | Y | Y | Y |
| 5 Johnson | N | Y | N | Y | Y | Y | Y | Y |
| **DELAWARE** | | | | | | | | |
| AL Castle | N | Y | N | Y | Y | Y | Y | Y |
| **FLORIDA** | | | | | | | | |
| 1 Miller | N | Y | N | Y | Y | Y | Y | Y |
| 2 Boyd | Y | Y | Y | N | N | N | Y | Y |
| 3 Brown | Y | Y | Y | N | N | N | Y | Y |
| 4 Crenshaw | N | Y | N | Y | Y | Y | Y | Y |
| 5 Brown-Waite | N | Y | N | Y | Y | Y | Y | Y |
| 6 Stearns | Y | Y | N | Y | Y | Y | Y | Y |
| 7 Mica | N | Y | N | Y | Y | Y | Y | Y |
| 8 Keller | N | Y | N | Y | Y | Y | Y | Y |
| 9 Bilirakis | Y | Y | N | Y | Y | Y | Y | Y |
| 10 Young | N | Y | N | Y | Y | Y | Y | Y |
| 11 Davis | Y | Y | Y | N | N | N | Y | Y |
| 12 Putnam | N | Y | N | Y | Y | Y | Y | Y |
| 13 Harris | N | Y | N | Y | Y | Y | Y | Y |
| 14 Mack | N | Y | N | Y | Y | Y | Y | Y |
| 15 Weldon | Y | Y | N | Y | Y | ? | Y | Y |
| 16 Foley | Y | Y | N | Y | Y | Y | Y | Y |
| 17 Meek | Y | Y | Y | N | N | N | Y | Y |
| 18 Ros-Lehtinen | N | Y | N | Y | Y | Y | Y | Y |
| 19 Wexler | Y | Y | Y | N | N | N | Y | Y |
| 20 Wasserman-Schultz | Y | Y | Y | N | N | N | Y | Y |
| 21 Diaz-Balart, L. | N | Y | N | Y | Y | Y | Y | Y |
| 22 Shaw | N | Y | N | Y | Y | Y | Y | Y |
| 23 Hastings | Y | Y | Y | N | N | N | Y | Y |
| 24 Feeney | N | Y | N | Y | Y | Y | Y | Y |
| 25 Diaz-Balart, M. | N | Y | N | Y | Y | Y | Y | Y |
| **GEORGIA** | | | | | | | | |
| 1 Kingston | N | Y | N | Y | Y | Y | Y | Y |
| 2 Bishop | N | Y | Y | N | N | N | Y | Y |
| 3 Marshall | Y | Y | Y | N | N | N | Y | Y |
| 4 McKinney | N | ? | Y | N | N | N | Y | Y |
| 5 Lewis | Y | Y | Y | N | N | N | Y | Y |
| 6 Price | N | P | Y | Y | Y | Y | Y | Y |
| 7 Linder | N | Y | N | Y | Y | Y | Y | Y |
| 8 Westmoreland | N | P | N | Y | Y | Y | Y | Y |
| 9 Norwood | N | Y | N | Y | Y | Y | Y | Y |
| 10 Deal | N | Y | N | Y | Y | Y | Y | Y |
| 11 Gingrey | N | Y | N | Y | Y | Y | Y | Y |
| 12 Barrow | Y | Y | Y | N | N | N | Y | Y |
| 13 Scott | N | Y | Y | N | N | N | Y | Y |
| **HAWAII** | | | | | | | | |
| 1 Abercrombie | N | Y | Y | N | N | N | Y | Y |
| 2 Case | N | Y | Y | N | N | N | Y | Y |
| **IDAHO** | | | | | | | | |
| 1 Otter | Y | Y | N | Y | Y | Y | Y | Y |
| 2 Simpson | N | Y | N | Y | Y | Y | Y | Y |
| **ILLINOIS** | | | | | | | | |
| 1 Rush | N | Y | Y | N | ? | N | Y | Y |
| 2 Jackson | N | Y | Y | N | N | N | Y | Y |
| 3 Lipinski | Y | Y | Y | N | N | N | Y | Y |
| 4 Gutierrez | Y | Y | Y | N | N | N | Y | Y |
| 5 Emanuel | N | Y | Y | N | N | N | Y | Y |
| 6 Hyde | N | Y | N | Y | Y | Y | Y | Y |
| 7 Davis | Y | Y | Y | N | N | N | Y | Y |
| 8 Bean | Y | Y | Y | N | N | N | Y | Y |
| 9 Schakowsky | Y | Y | Y | N | N | N | Y | Y |
| 10 Kirk | N | Y | N | Y | Y | Y | Y | Y |
| 11 Weller | N | Y | N | Y | Y | Y | Y | Y |
| 12 Costello | N | Y | N | Y | N | N | Y | Y |

**KEY**    Republicans    Democrats    *Independents*

| | | |
|---|---|---|
| Y   Voted for (yea) | X   Paired against | C   Voted "present" to avoid possible conflict of interest |
| #   Paired for | –   Announced against | ?   Did not vote or otherwise make a position known |
| +   Announced for | P   Voted "present" | |
| N   Voted against (nay) | | |

| | 74 | 75 | 76 | 77 | 78 | 79 | 80 | 81 |
|---|---|---|---|---|---|---|---|---|
| 13 **Biggert** | N | Y | N | Y | Y | Y | Y | Y |
| 14 **Hastert** | | | | | | | | |
| 15 **Johnson** | Y | Y | N | Y | Y | Y | Y | Y |
| 16 **Manzullo** | N | Y | N | Y | Y | Y | Y | Y |
| 17 Evans | Y | Y | Y | Y | N | N | Y | Y |
| 18 **LaHood** | N | Y | N | Y | Y | Y | Y | Y |
| 19 **Shimkus** | N | Y | N | Y | Y | Y | Y | Y |
| **INDIANA** | | | | | | | | |
| 1 Visclosky | N | Y | Y | Y | N | N | Y | Y |
| 2 **Chocola** | N | Y | N | Y | Y | Y | Y | Y |
| 3 **Souder** | Y | N | N | Y | Y | Y | Y | Y |
| 4 **Buyer** | N | Y | N | Y | Y | Y | Y | Y |
| 5 **Burton** | Y | Y | N | Y | Y | Y | Y | Y |
| 6 **Pence** | Y | Y | N | Y | Y | Y | Y | Y |
| 7 Carson | Y | Y | Y | Y | N | N | Y | Y |
| 8 **Hostettler** | Y | Y | N | Y | Y | ? | ? | Y |
| 9 **Sodrel** | N | Y | N | Y | Y | Y | Y | Y |
| **IOWA** | | | | | | | | |
| 1 **Nussle** | N | Y | N | Y | Y | Y | Y | Y |
| 2 **Leach** | ? | Y | N | Y | Y | Y | Y | Y |
| 3 Boswell | Y | Y | Y | Y | N | N | Y | Y |
| 4 **Latham** | N | Y | N | Y | Y | Y | Y | Y |
| 5 **King** | N | Y | N | Y | Y | Y | Y | Y |
| **KANSAS** | | | | | | | | |
| 1 **Moran** | Y | Y | N | Y | Y | Y | Y | Y |
| 2 **Ryun** | Y | Y | N | Y | Y | Y | Y | Y |
| 3 Moore | Y | Y | Y | Y | N | N | Y | Y |
| 4 **Tiahrt** | N | Y | N | Y | Y | Y | Y | ? |
| **KENTUCKY** | | | | | | | | |
| 1 **Whitfield** | N | Y | N | Y | Y | Y | Y | Y |
| 2 **Lewis** | N | Y | N | Y | Y | Y | Y | Y |
| 3 **Northup** | N | Y | N | Y | Y | Y | Y | Y |
| 4 **Davis** | N | Y | N | Y | Y | Y | Y | Y |
| 5 **Rogers** | N | Y | N | Y | Y | Y | Y | Y |
| 6 Chandler | Y | Y | Y | Y | N | N | Y | Y |
| **LOUISIANA** | | | | | | | | |
| 1 **Jindal** | N | Y | N | Y | Y | Y | Y | Y |
| 2 Jefferson | Y | Y | Y | Y | N | ? | Y | Y |
| 3 Melancon | Y | Y | Y | Y | N | ? | Y | ? |
| 4 **McCrery** | N | Y | N | Y | Y | Y | Y | Y |
| 5 **Alexander** | N | Y | N | Y | Y | Y | Y | Y |
| 6 **Baker** | N | ? | N | Y | Y | Y | Y | Y |
| 7 **Boustany** | N | Y | N | Y | Y | Y | Y | Y |
| **MAINE** | | | | | | | | |
| 1 Allen | N | Y | Y | Y | N | N | Y | Y |
| 2 Michaud | Y | Y | Y | Y | N | N | Y | Y |
| **MARYLAND** | | | | | | | | |
| 1 **Gilchrest** | N | Y | N | Y | Y | Y | Y | ? |
| 2 Ruppersberger | N | Y | Y | Y | N | N | Y | Y |
| 3 Cardin | Y | Y | Y | Y | N | N | Y | Y |
| 4 Wynn | Y | Y | Y | Y | N | N | Y | Y |
| 5 Hoyer | Y | Y | Y | Y | N | N | Y | Y |
| 6 **Bartlett** | N | Y | N | Y | Y | Y | Y | Y |
| 7 Cummings | Y | Y | Y | Y | N | N | Y | Y |
| 8 Van Hollen | Y | Y | Y | Y | N | N | Y | Y |
| **MASSACHUSETTS** | | | | | | | | |
| 1 Olver | Y | Y | Y | Y | N | N | Y | Y |
| 2 Neal | Y | Y | Y | Y | N | N | Y | ? |
| 3 McGovern | Y | Y | Y | N | N | N | Y | Y |
| 4 Frank | Y | Y | Y | N | N | N | Y | Y |
| 5 Meehan | Y | Y | Y | N | N | N | Y | Y |
| 6 Tierney | Y | Y | Y | N | N | N | Y | Y |
| 7 Markey | Y | Y | Y | N | N | N | Y | Y |
| 8 Capuano | Y | Y | Y | N | N | N | Y | Y |
| 9 Lynch | Y | Y | Y | Y | N | N | Y | Y |
| 10 Delahunt | Y | Y | Y | Y | N | N | Y | Y |
| **MICHIGAN** | | | | | | | | |
| 1 Stupak | Y | Y | Y | Y | N | N | Y | Y |
| 2 **Hoekstra** | N | Y | N | Y | Y | Y | Y | Y |
| 3 **Ehlers** | N | Y | N | Y | Y | Y | Y | Y |
| 4 **Camp** | N | Y | N | Y | Y | Y | Y | Y |
| 5 Kildee | N | Y | Y | Y | N | N | Y | Y |
| 6 **Upton** | N | Y | N | Y | Y | Y | Y | Y |
| 7 **Schwarz** | N | Y | N | Y | Y | Y | Y | Y |
| 8 **Rogers** | Y | Y | N | Y | Y | Y | Y | Y |
| 9 **Knollenberg** | N | Y | N | Y | Y | Y | Y | Y |
| 10 **Miller** | N | Y | N | Y | Y | Y | Y | Y |
| 11 **McCotter** | Y | Y | N | Y | Y | Y | Y | Y |
| 12 Levin | Y | Y | Y | Y | N | N | Y | Y |
| 13 Kilpatrick | N | Y | Y | Y | N | N | Y | Y |
| 14 Conyers | Y | Y | Y | Y | N | N | Y | Y |
| 15 Dingell | N | Y | Y | Y | N | N | Y | Y |

| | 74 | 75 | 76 | 77 | 78 | 79 | 80 | 81 |
|---|---|---|---|---|---|---|---|---|
| **MINNESOTA** | | | | | | | | |
| 1 **Gutknecht** | N | Y | N | Y | Y | Y | Y | Y |
| 2 **Kline** | N | Y | N | Y | Y | Y | Y | Y |
| 3 **Ramstad** | Y | Y | N | Y | Y | Y | Y | Y |
| 4 McCollum | Y | Y | Y | N | N | N | Y | N |
| 5 Sabo | Y | Y | Y | Y | N | N | Y | Y |
| 6 **Kennedy** | Y | Y | N | Y | Y | Y | Y | Y |
| 7 Peterson | Y | Y | Y | Y | N | N | Y | Y |
| 8 Oberstar | Y | Y | Y | Y | N | N | Y | N |
| **MISSISSIPPI** | | | | | | | | |
| 1 **Wicker** | N | Y | N | Y | Y | Y | Y | Y |
| 2 Thompson | N | Y | Y | Y | N | N | Y | Y |
| 3 **Pickering** | N | Y | N | Y | Y | Y | Y | Y |
| 4 Taylor | N | Y | Y | Y | N | N | Y | Y |
| **MISSOURI** | | | | | | | | |
| 1 Clay | Y | Y | Y | N | N | N | Y | Y |
| 2 **Akin** | N | Y | N | Y | Y | Y | Y | Y |
| 3 Carnahan | Y | Y | Y | Y | N | N | Y | Y |
| 4 Skelton | N | Y | Y | Y | N | N | Y | Y |
| 5 Cleaver | Y | Y | Y | Y | N | N | Y | Y |
| 6 **Graves** | Y | Y | N | Y | Y | Y | Y | Y |
| 7 **Blunt** | N | Y | N | Y | Y | Y | Y | Y |
| 8 **Emerson** | N | Y | N | Y | Y | Y | Y | Y |
| 9 **Hulshof** | N | Y | N | Y | Y | Y | Y | Y |
| **MONTANA** | | | | | | | | |
| AL **Rehberg** | N | Y | N | Y | Y | Y | Y | Y |
| **NEBRASKA** | | | | | | | | |
| 1 **Fortenberry** | N | Y | N | Y | Y | Y | Y | Y |
| 2 **Terry** | N | Y | N | Y | Y | Y | Y | Y |
| 3 **Osborne** | N | Y | N | Y | Y | Y | Y | Y |
| **NEVADA** | | | | | | | | |
| 1 Berkley | Y | Y | Y | Y | N | N | Y | Y |
| 2 **Gibbons** | N | Y | N | Y | Y | Y | Y | Y |
| 3 **Porter** | Y | Y | N | Y | Y | Y | Y | Y |
| **NEW HAMPSHIRE** | | | | | | | | |
| 1 **Bradley** | N | Y | N | Y | Y | Y | Y | Y |
| 2 **Bass** | N | Y | N | Y | Y | Y | Y | Y |
| **NEW JERSEY** | | | | | | | | |
| 1 Andrews | Y | Y | Y | Y | N | N | Y | Y |
| 2 **LoBiondo** | N | Y | N | Y | Y | Y | Y | Y |
| 3 **Saxton** | N | Y | N | Y | Y | Y | Y | Y |
| 4 **Smith** | N | Y | ? | Y | Y | Y | Y | Y |
| 5 **Garrett** | N | Y | N | Y | Y | Y | Y | Y |
| 6 Pallone | Y | Y | Y | N | N | N | Y | Y |
| 7 **Ferguson** | Y | Y | N | Y | Y | Y | Y | Y |
| 8 Pascrell | Y | Y | Y | Y | N | N | Y | Y |
| 9 Rothman | Y | Y | Y | Y | N | N | Y | Y |
| 10 Payne | Y | Y | Y | N | N | N | Y | Y |
| 11 **Frelinghuysen** | N | Y | N | Y | Y | Y | Y | Y |
| 12 Holt | Y | Y | Y | N | N | N | Y | Y |
| 13 Menendez | Y | Y | Y | Y | N | N | Y | Y |
| **NEW MEXICO** | | | | | | | | |
| 1 **Wilson** | N | Y | N | Y | Y | Y | Y | Y |
| 2 **Pearce** | N | Y | N | Y | Y | Y | Y | Y |
| 3 Udall | Y | Y | Y | Y | N | N | Y | Y |
| **NEW YORK** | | | | | | | | |
| 1 Bishop | Y | Y | Y | Y | N | N | Y | Y |
| 2 Israel | Y | Y | Y | Y | N | N | Y | Y |
| 3 **King** | N | Y | N | Y | Y | Y | Y | Y |
| 4 McCarthy | Y | Y | Y | Y | N | N | Y | Y |
| 5 Ackerman | N | Y | Y | Y | N | N | Y | Y |
| 6 Meeks | Y | Y | Y | Y | N | N | Y | Y |
| 7 Crowley | Y | Y | Y | Y | N | N | Y | Y |
| 8 Nadler | Y | Y | Y | Y | N | N | Y | Y |
| 9 Weiner | Y | Y | Y | N | N | N | Y | Y |
| 10 Towns | Y | Y | Y | N | N | N | Y | Y |
| 11 Owens | Y | Y | Y | N | N | N | Y | Y |
| 12 Velázquez | Y | Y | Y | N | N | N | Y | Y |
| 13 **Fossella** | N | Y | N | Y | Y | Y | Y | Y |
| 14 Maloney | Y | Y | Y | N | N | N | Y | Y |
| 15 Rangel | Y | Y | Y | N | N | N | Y | Y |
| 16 Serrano | Y | Y | Y | N | N | N | Y | Y |
| 17 Engel | Y | Y | Y | Y | N | N | Y | Y |
| 18 Lowey | Y | Y | Y | Y | N | N | Y | Y |
| 19 **Kelly** | N | Y | N | Y | Y | Y | Y | Y |
| 20 **Sweeney** | ? | ? | ? | ? | Y | Y | Y | Y |
| 21 McNulty | Y | Y | Y | Y | N | N | Y | Y |
| 22 Hinchey | Y | Y | Y | N | N | N | Y | Y |
| 23 **McHugh** | N | Y | N | Y | Y | Y | Y | Y |
| 24 **Boehlert** | N | Y | N | Y | Y | Y | Y | Y |
| 25 **Walsh** | ? | Y | N | Y | Y | Y | Y | Y |
| 26 **Reynolds** | N | Y | N | Y | Y | Y | Y | Y |
| 27 Higgins | Y | Y | Y | Y | N | N | Y | Y |
| 28 Slaughter | Y | Y | Y | Y | N | N | Y | Y |
| 29 **Kuhl** | N | Y | N | Y | Y | Y | Y | Y |

| | 74 | 75 | 76 | 77 | 78 | 79 | 80 | 81 |
|---|---|---|---|---|---|---|---|---|
| **NORTH CAROLINA** | | | | | | | | |
| 1 Butterfield | Y | Y | Y | Y | N | N | Y | Y |
| 2 Etheridge | N | Y | Y | Y | N | N | Y | Y |
| 3 **Jones** | Y | Y | Y | Y | Y | Y | Y | Y |
| 4 Price | N | Y | Y | Y | N | N | Y | Y |
| 5 **Foxx** | N | Y | N | Y | Y | Y | Y | Y |
| 6 **Coble** | N | Y | N | N | Y | Y | Y | Y |
| 7 McIntyre | Y | Y | Y | Y | N | N | Y | Y |
| 8 **Hayes** | N | N | N | Y | Y | Y | Y | Y |
| 9 **Myrick** | N | Y | N | Y | Y | Y | Y | Y |
| 10 **McHenry** | N | Y | N | Y | Y | Y | Y | Y |
| 11 **Taylor** | N | Y | N | Y | Y | Y | Y | Y |
| 12 Watt | Y | Y | Y | Y | N | ? | Y | Y |
| 13 Miller | Y | Y | Y | Y | N | N | Y | Y |
| **NORTH DAKOTA** | | | | | | | | |
| AL Pomeroy | N | Y | Y | Y | N | N | Y | Y |
| **OHIO** | | | | | | | | |
| 1 **Chabot** | Y | Y | N | Y | Y | Y | Y | Y |
| 2 **Portman** | N | ? | N | Y | Y | Y | Y | Y |
| 3 **Turner** | N | Y | N | Y | Y | Y | Y | Y |
| 4 **Oxley** | N | Y | N | Y | Y | Y | Y | Y |
| 5 **Gillmor** | N | Y | N | Y | Y | Y | Y | Y |
| 6 Strickland | Y | Y | Y | Y | N | N | Y | Y |
| 7 **Hobson** | N | Y | N | Y | Y | Y | Y | Y |
| 8 **Boehner** | N | Y | N | Y | Y | Y | Y | Y |
| 9 Kaptur | N | Y | Y | Y | N | N | Y | Y |
| 10 Kucinich | N | Y | Y | N | N | N | Y | Y |
| 11 Jones | Y | Y | Y | Y | N | N | Y | Y |
| 12 **Tiberi** | N | Y | N | Y | Y | Y | Y | Y |
| 13 Brown | Y | Y | Y | Y | N | N | Y | Y |
| 14 **LaTourette** | N | Y | N | Y | Y | Y | Y | Y |
| 15 **Pryce** | N | Y | N | Y | Y | Y | Y | Y |
| 16 **Regula** | N | Y | N | Y | Y | Y | Y | Y |
| 17 Ryan | Y | Y | Y | Y | N | N | Y | Y |
| 18 **Ney** | N | Y | N | Y | Y | Y | Y | Y |
| **OKLAHOMA** | | | | | | | | |
| 1 **Sullivan** | Y | Y | N | Y | Y | Y | Y | Y |
| 2 Boren | Y | Y | Y | Y | N | N | Y | Y |
| 3 **Lucas** | N | Y | N | Y | Y | Y | Y | Y |
| 4 **Cole** | N | Y | N | Y | Y | Y | Y | Y |
| 5 **Istook** | N | Y | N | Y | Y | Y | Y | Y |
| **OREGON** | | | | | | | | |
| 1 Wu | Y | Y | Y | Y | N | N | Y | Y |
| 2 **Walden** | N | Y | N | Y | Y | Y | Y | Y |
| 3 Blumenauer | Y | Y | Y | N | N | N | Y | Y |
| 4 DeFazio | Y | Y | Y | Y | N | N | Y | Y |
| 5 Hooley | Y | Y | Y | Y | N | N | Y | Y |
| **PENNSYLVANIA** | | | | | | | | |
| 1 Brady | Y | Y | N | Y | N | N | Y | Y |
| 2 Fattah | Y | Y | Y | Y | N | N | Y | Y |
| 3 **English** | N | Y | N | Y | Y | Y | Y | Y |
| 4 **Hart** | N | Y | N | Y | Y | Y | Y | Y |
| 5 **Peterson** | N | Y | N | Y | Y | Y | Y | Y |
| 6 **Gerlach** | N | Y | N | Y | Y | Y | Y | Y |
| 7 **Weldon** | N | Y | N | Y | Y | Y | Y | Y |
| 8 **Fitzpatrick** | N | Y | N | Y | Y | Y | Y | Y |
| 9 **Shuster** | N | Y | N | Y | Y | Y | Y | Y |
| 10 **Sherwood** | N | Y | N | Y | Y | Y | Y | Y |
| 11 Kanjorski | N | Y | N | Y | N | N | Y | Y |
| 12 Murtha | N | Y | N | Y | N | N | Y | Y |
| 13 Schwartz | Y | Y | Y | Y | N | N | Y | Y |
| 14 Doyle | N | Y | Y | Y | N | N | Y | Y |
| 15 **Dent** | Y | Y | N | Y | Y | Y | Y | Y |
| 16 **Pitts** | N | Y | N | Y | Y | Y | Y | Y |
| 17 Holden | Y | Y | Y | Y | N | N | Y | Y |
| 18 **Murphy** | N | Y | N | Y | Y | Y | Y | Y |
| 19 **Platts** | Y | Y | N | Y | Y | Y | Y | Y |
| **RHODE ISLAND** | | | | | | | | |
| 1 Kennedy | Y | Y | Y | Y | N | N | Y | Y |
| 2 Langevin | Y | Y | Y | Y | N | N | Y | Y |
| **SOUTH CAROLINA** | | | | | | | | |
| 1 **Brown** | Y | Y | N | Y | Y | Y | Y | Y |
| 2 **Wilson** | N | Y | N | Y | Y | Y | Y | Y |
| 3 **Barrett** | N | Y | N | Y | Y | Y | Y | Y |
| 4 **Inglis** | N | Y | N | Y | Y | Y | Y | Y |
| 5 Spratt | Y | Y | Y | Y | N | N | Y | Y |
| 6 Clyburn | Y | Y | Y | Y | N | N | Y | Y |
| **SOUTH DAKOTA** | | | | | | | | |
| AL Herseth | Y | Y | Y | Y | N | N | Y | Y |
| **TENNESSEE** | | | | | | | | |
| 1 **Jenkins** | N | Y | N | Y | Y | Y | Y | Y |
| 2 **Duncan** | N | Y | N | N | Y | Y | Y | Y |

| | 74 | 75 | 76 | 77 | 78 | 79 | 80 | 81 |
|---|---|---|---|---|---|---|---|---|
| 3 **Wamp** | N | Y | N | Y | Y | Y | Y | Y |
| 4 Davis | Y | Y | Y | Y | N | N | Y | Y |
| 5 Cooper | Y | Y | Y | Y | N | N | Y | Y |
| 6 Gordon | Y | Y | Y | Y | N | N | Y | Y |
| 7 **Blackburn** | N | Y | N | Y | Y | Y | Y | Y |
| 8 Tanner | N | Y | Y | Y | N | N | Y | Y |
| 9 Ford | Y | Y | Y | Y | N | N | Y | Y |
| **TEXAS** | | | | | | | | |
| 1 **Gohmert** | N | Y | N | Y | Y | Y | Y | Y |
| 2 **Poe** | N | Y | N | Y | Y | Y | Y | Y |
| 3 **Johnson, S.** | N | Y | N | Y | Y | Y | Y | ? |
| 4 **Hall** | Y | Y | N | Y | Y | Y | Y | Y |
| 5 **Hensarling** | N | Y | N | Y | Y | Y | Y | Y |
| 6 **Barton** | N | Y | N | Y | Y | Y | Y | Y |
| 7 **Culberson** | N | Y | N | Y | Y | Y | Y | Y |
| 8 **Brady** | N | Y | N | Y | Y | Y | Y | Y |
| 9 Green, A. | Y | Y | Y | Y | N | N | Y | Y |
| 10 **McCaul** | N | Y | N | Y | Y | Y | Y | Y |
| 11 **Conaway** | N | Y | N | Y | Y | Y | Y | Y |
| 12 **Granger** | N | Y | N | Y | Y | Y | Y | Y |
| 13 **Thornberry** | ? | Y | N | Y | Y | Y | Y | Y |
| 14 **Paul** | Y | Y | Y | N | Y | Y | N | N |
| 15 Hinojosa | N | Y | Y | Y | N | N | Y | Y |
| 16 Reyes | Y | Y | Y | Y | N | N | Y | Y |
| 17 Edwards | Y | Y | Y | Y | N | N | Y | Y |
| 18 Jackson-Lee | N | Y | Y | N | N | N | Y | Y |
| 19 **Neugebauer** | N | Y | N | Y | Y | Y | Y | Y |
| 20 Gonzalez | N | Y | Y | Y | N | N | Y | Y |
| 21 **Smith** | N | Y | N | Y | Y | Y | Y | Y |
| 22 **DeLay** | N | Y | N | Y | Y | Y | Y | Y |
| 23 **Bonilla** | N | Y | N | Y | Y | Y | Y | Y |
| 24 **Marchant** | N | Y | N | Y | Y | Y | Y | Y |
| 25 Doggett | Y | Y | Y | Y | N | N | Y | Y |
| 26 **Burgess** | N | Y | N | Y | Y | Y | Y | Y |
| 27 Ortiz | Y | Y | Y | Y | N | N | Y | Y |
| 28 Cuellar | N | Y | Y | Y | N | N | Y | Y |
| 29 Green, G. | Y | Y | Y | Y | N | N | Y | Y |
| 30 Johnson, E. | Y | Y | Y | Y | N | N | Y | Y |
| 31 **Carter** | N | Y | N | Y | Y | Y | Y | Y |
| 32 **Sessions** | N | Y | N | Y | Y | Y | Y | Y |
| **UTAH** | | | | | | | | |
| 1 **Bishop** | N | Y | N | Y | Y | Y | Y | Y |
| 2 Matheson | Y | Y | Y | Y | N | N | Y | Y |
| 3 **Cannon** | N | Y | N | Y | Y | Y | Y | Y |
| **VERMONT** | | | | | | | | |
| AL *Sanders* | Y | Y | Y | N | N | N | Y | Y |
| **VIRGINIA** | | | | | | | | |
| 1 **Davis, J.** | Y | Y | N | Y | Y | Y | Y | Y |
| 2 **Drake** | N | Y | N | Y | Y | Y | Y | Y |
| 3 Scott | Y | Y | Y | Y | N | N | Y | Y |
| 4 **Forbes** | N | Y | N | Y | Y | Y | Y | Y |
| 5 **Goode** | Y | Y | N | Y | Y | Y | Y | Y |
| 6 **Goodlatte** | N | Y | N | Y | Y | Y | Y | Y |
| 7 **Cantor** | N | Y | N | Y | Y | Y | Y | Y |
| 8 Moran | N | Y | Y | Y | N | N | Y | Y |
| 9 Boucher | N | ? | Y | Y | N | N | Y | Y |
| 10 **Wolf** | N | Y | N | Y | Y | Y | Y | Y |
| 11 **Davis, T.** | N | Y | N | Y | Y | Y | Y | Y |
| **WASHINGTON** | | | | | | | | |
| 1 Inslee | Y | Y | Y | Y | N | N | Y | Y |
| 2 Larsen | Y | ? | Y | Y | N | N | Y | Y |
| 3 Baird | Y | ? | ? | ? | N | N | Y | Y |
| 4 **Hastings** | N | Y | N | Y | Y | Y | Y | Y |
| 5 **McMorris** | N | Y | N | Y | Y | Y | Y | Y |
| 6 Dicks | Y | Y | Y | Y | N | N | Y | Y |
| 7 McDermott | Y | Y | Y | N | N | N | Y | N |
| 8 **Reichert** | N | Y | N | Y | Y | Y | Y | Y |
| 9 Smith | ? | Y | Y | Y | N | N | Y | Y |
| **WEST VIRGINIA** | | | | | | | | |
| 1 Mollohan | N | Y | Y | Y | N | N | Y | Y |
| 2 **Capito** | N | Y | N | Y | Y | Y | Y | Y |
| 3 Rahall | N | Y | Y | Y | N | N | Y | Y |
| **WISCONSIN** | | | | | | | | |
| 1 **Ryan** | N | Y | N | Y | Y | Y | Y | Y |
| 2 Baldwin | N | Y | Y | N | N | N | Y | Y |
| 3 Kind | Y | Y | Y | Y | N | N | Y | Y |
| 4 Moore | Y | Y | Y | Y | N | N | Y | Y |
| 5 **Sensenbrenner** | Y | Y | N | Y | Y | Y | Y | Y |
| 6 **Petri** | Y | Y | N | Y | Y | Y | Y | Y |
| 7 Obey | N | Y | Y | Y | N | Y | Y | Y |
| 8 **Green** | Y | Y | N | Y | Y | Y | Y | Y |
| **WYOMING** | | | | | | | | |
| AL **Cubin** | N | ? | ? | ? | ? | ? | ? | ? |

# IN THE HOUSE | By Vote Number

**82.** **H Con Res 95. Fiscal 2006 Budget Resolution/Increased Spending.**
Obey, D-Wis., amendment that would increase fiscal 2006 spending by a total of $15.8 billion, including $8 billion for education, training and social services programs, $2 billion for health care, and $2.9 billion for veterans' health care. It also would increase fiscal 2006 revenue by $25.8 billion by reducing tax cuts for those earning more than $1 million. Rejected 180-242: R 3-218; D 176-24 (ND 137-12, SD 39-12); I 1-0. March 17, 2005.

**83.** **H Con Res 95. Fiscal 2006 Budget Resolution/Republican Study Committee Substitute.** Hensarling, R-Texas, substitute that would call for an extra $58 billion in mandatory spending cuts over five years. It would reduce non-defense and non-homeland discretionary spending by 2 percent. It would provide reconciliation protection for $106 billion in tax cuts, establish new budgetary points of order and require roll call votes on legislation authorizing or appropriating more than $50 million. Rejected 102-320: R 101-122; D 1-197 (ND 1-148, SD 0-49); I 0-1. March 17, 2005.

**84.** **H Con Res 32. Syrian Occupation of Lebanon/Adoption.** Ros-Lehtinen, R-Fla., motion to suspend the rules and adopt the concurrent resolution that would express the sense of Congress that Lebanon is a captive country and that its occupation by Syria represents a long-term threat to the security of the Middle East. Motion agreed to 419-1: R 221-1; D 197-0 (ND 147-0, SD 50-0); I 1-0. A two-thirds majority of those present and voting (280 in this case) is required for adoption under suspension of the rules. March 17, 2005.

**85.** **H Con Res 95. Fiscal 2006 Budget Resolution/Congressional Black Caucus Substitute.** Watt, D-N.C., substitute that would increase fiscal 2006 spending by $36.3 billion, including $23.9 billion for education and job training and $7.8 billion for homeland security and veterans' programs. It would call for action to rescind tax cuts for wealthy individuals, close several tax loopholes and reduce funding for the ballistic missile defense program. Rejected 134-292: R 1-225; D 132-67 (ND 104-45, SD 28-22); I 1-0. March 17, 2005.

**86.** **H Con Res 95. Fiscal 2006 Budget Resolution/Motion to Rise.**
Blumenauer, D-Ore., motion to rise from the Committee of the Whole. Motion rejected 101-313: R 0-224; D 100-89 (ND 83-58, SD 17-31); I 1-0. March 17, 2005.

| | 82 | 83 | 84 | 85 | 86 |
|---|---|---|---|---|---|
| **ALABAMA** | | | | | |
| 1 Bonner | N | Y | Y | N | N |
| 2 Everett | N | N | Y | N | N |
| 3 Rogers | N | N | Y | N | N |
| 4 Aderholt | N | N | Y | N | N |
| 5 Cramer | N | N | Y | N | N |
| 6 Bachus | N | N | Y | N | N |
| 7 Davis | Y | N | Y | Y | Y |
| **ALASKA** | | | | | |
| AL Young | N | N | Y | N | N |
| **ARIZONA** | | | | | |
| 1 Renzi | N | N | Y | N | N |
| 2 Franks | N | Y | Y | N | N |
| 3 Shadegg | N | Y | Y | N | N |
| 4 Pastor | Y | N | Y | Y | Y |
| 5 Hayworth | N | Y | Y | N | N |
| 6 Flake | N | Y | Y | N | N |
| 7 Grijalva | Y | N | Y | Y | Y |
| 8 Kolbe | N | N | Y | N | N |
| **ARKANSAS** | | | | | |
| 1 Berry | Y | N | Y | N | Y |
| 2 Snyder | Y | N | Y | N | N |
| 3 Boozman | N | Y | Y | N | N |
| 4 Ross | Y | N | Y | N | N |
| **CALIFORNIA** | | | | | |
| 1 Thompson | N | N | Y | N | N |
| 2 Herger | N | Y | Y | N | N |
| 3 Lungren | N | Y | Y | N | N |
| 4 Doolittle | N | N | Y | N | ? |
| 5 Matsui, D. | Y | N | Y | Y | Y |
| 6 Woolsey | Y | N | Y | Y | ? |
| 7 Miller, George | Y | N | Y | Y | Y |
| 8 Pelosi | Y | N | Y | Y | Y |
| 9 Lee | Y | N | Y | Y | Y |
| 10 Tauscher | Y | N | Y | N | N |
| 11 Pombo | N | Y | Y | N | N |
| 12 Lantos | Y | N | Y | Y | N |
| 13 Stark | Y | N | Y | Y | ? |
| 14 Eshoo | Y | N | Y | Y | Y |
| 15 Honda | Y | N | Y | Y | N |
| 16 Lofgren | Y | N | Y | Y | N |
| 17 Farr | Y | N | Y | Y | Y |
| 18 Cardoza | N | N | Y | N | ? |
| 19 Radanovich | N | Y | Y | N | N |
| 20 Costa | N | N | Y | N | N |
| 21 Nunes | N | N | Y | N | N |
| 22 Thomas | N | N | Y | N | N |
| 23 Capps | Y | N | Y | N | N |
| 24 Gallegly | N | N | Y | N | N |
| 25 McKeon | N | N | Y | N | N |
| 26 Dreier | N | N | Y | N | N |
| 27 Sherman | Y | N | Y | Y | Y |
| 28 Berman | Y | N | Y | Y | N |
| 29 Schiff | Y | N | Y | N | N |
| 30 Waxman | Y | N | Y | Y | ? |
| 31 Becerra | Y | N | Y | Y | Y |
| 32 Solis | Y | N | Y | Y | Y |
| 33 Watson | Y | N | Y | Y | Y |
| 34 Roybal-Allard | Y | N | Y | Y | Y |
| 35 Waters | Y | N | Y | Y | Y |
| 36 Harman | N | N | Y | N | N |
| 37 Millender-McD. | Y | N | Y | Y | Y |
| 38 Napolitano | Y | N | Y | Y | Y |
| 39 Sánchez, Linda | Y | N | Y | Y | Y |
| 40 Royce | N | Y | Y | N | N |
| 41 Lewis | N | N | Y | N | N |
| 42 Miller, Gary | N | Y | Y | N | N |
| 43 Baca | Y | N | Y | N | N |
| 44 Calvert | N | N | Y | N | N |
| 45 Bono | N | N | Y | N | N |
| 46 Rohrabacher | N | Y | Y | N | N |
| 47 Sanchez, Loretta | Y | N | Y | N | N |
| 48 Cox | N | Y | Y | N | N |
| 49 Issa | N | N | Y | N | N |

| | 82 | 83 | 84 | 85 | 86 |
|---|---|---|---|---|---|
| 50 Cunningham | N | N | Y | N | N |
| 51 Filner | Y | N | Y | Y | Y |
| 52 Hunter | N | N | Y | N | N |
| 53 Davis | Y | N | Y | N | N |
| **COLORADO** | | | | | |
| 1 DeGette | Y | N | Y | N | N |
| 2 Udall | Y | N | Y | N | Y |
| 3 Salazar | N | N | Y | N | N |
| 4 Musgrave | N | Y | Y | N | N |
| 5 Hefley | N | N | Y | N | N |
| 6 Tancredo | N | Y | Y | N | N |
| 7 Beauprez | N | Y | Y | N | N |
| **CONNECTICUT** | | | | | |
| 1 Larson | ? | ? | Y | Y | Y |
| 2 Simmons | N | N | Y | N | N |
| 3 DeLauro | Y | N | Y | Y | Y |
| 4 Shays | N | N | Y | N | N |
| 5 Johnson | N | N | Y | N | N |
| **DELAWARE** | | | | | |
| AL Castle | N | N | Y | N | N |
| **FLORIDA** | | | | | |
| 1 Miller | N | Y | Y | N | N |
| 2 Boyd | Y | N | Y | N | Y |
| 3 Brown | Y | N | Y | Y | Y |
| 4 Crenshaw | N | Y | Y | N | N |
| 5 Brown-Waite | N | Y | Y | N | N |
| 6 Stearns | N | Y | Y | N | N |
| 7 Mica | N | Y | Y | N | N |
| 8 Keller | N | Y | Y | N | N |
| 9 Bilirakis | Y | N | Y | N | N |
| 10 Young | ? | ? | ? | ? | ? |
| 11 Davis | Y | N | Y | Y | Y |
| 12 Putnam | N | Y | Y | N | N |
| 13 Harris | N | Y | Y | N | N |
| 14 Mack | N | Y | Y | N | N |
| 15 Weldon | N | N | Y | N | N |
| 16 Foley | – | – | + | N | N |
| 17 Meek | Y | N | Y | Y | Y |
| 18 Ros-Lehtinen | N | N | Y | N | N |
| 19 Wexler | Y | N | Y | Y | Y |
| 20 Wasserman-Schultz | Y | N | Y | Y | Y |
| 21 Diaz-Balart, L. | ? | ? | Y | N | N |
| 22 Shaw | N | N | Y | N | N |
| 23 Hastings | Y | N | Y | Y | Y |
| 24 Feeney | N | Y | Y | N | N |
| 25 Diaz-Balart, M. | ? | Y | Y | N | N |
| **GEORGIA** | | | | | |
| 1 Kingston | N | N | Y | N | N |
| 2 Bishop | Y | N | Y | Y | N |
| 3 Marshall | N | N | Y | N | N |
| 4 McKinney | Y | N | P | Y | Y |
| 5 Lewis | Y | N | Y | Y | Y |
| 6 Price | N | Y | Y | N | N |
| 7 Linder | N | Y | Y | N | N |
| 8 Westmoreland | N | Y | Y | N | N |
| 9 Norwood | N | Y | Y | N | N |
| 10 Deal | N | Y | Y | N | N |
| 11 Gingrey | N | Y | Y | N | N |
| 12 Barrow | N | N | Y | N | N |
| 13 Scott | Y | N | Y | N | N |
| **HAWAII** | | | | | |
| 1 Abercrombie | Y | N | Y | Y | Y |
| 2 Case | N | Y | Y | N | N |
| **IDAHO** | | | | | |
| 1 Otter | N | Y | Y | N | N |
| 2 Simpson | N | N | Y | N | N |
| **ILLINOIS** | | | | | |
| 1 Rush | Y | N | Y | Y | Y |
| 2 Jackson | Y | N | Y | Y | Y |
| 3 Lipinski | Y | N | Y | N | N |
| 4 Gutierrez | Y | N | Y | Y | Y |
| 5 Emanuel | Y | N | Y | Y | Y |
| 6 Hyde | N | N | Y | N | N |
| 7 Davis | Y | N | Y | Y | Y |
| 8 Bean | N | N | Y | N | N |
| 9 Schakowsky | Y | N | Y | Y | Y |
| 10 Kirk | N | N | Y | N | N |
| 11 Weller | N | Y | Y | N | N |
| 12 Costello | Y | N | Y | N | N |

| | 82 | 83 | 84 | 85 | 86 |
|---|---|---|---|---|---|
| 13 Biggert | N | N | Y | N | N |
| 14 Hastert | | | | | |
| 15 Johnson | N | N | Y | N | N |
| 16 Manzullo | N | Y | Y | N | N |
| 17 Evans | Y | N | Y | Y | Y |
| 18 LaHood | N | N | Y | N | N |
| 19 Shimkus | N | Y | Y | N | N |
| **INDIANA** | | | | | |
| 1 Visclosky | Y | N | Y | N | N |
| 2 Chocola | N | Y | Y | N | N |
| 3 Souder | N | N | Y | N | N |
| 4 Buyer | N | N | Y | N | N |
| 5 Burton | N | N | Y | N | N |
| 6 Pence | N | Y | Y | N | N |
| 7 Carson | Y | N | Y | Y | Y |
| 8 Hostettler | N | Y | Y | N | N |
| 9 Sodrel | N | Y | Y | N | N |
| **IOWA** | | | | | |
| 1 Nussle | N | N | Y | N | N |
| 2 Leach | N | N | Y | N | N |
| 3 Boswell | N | N | Y | N | N |
| 4 Latham | N | N | Y | N | N |
| 5 King | N | Y | Y | N | N |
| **KANSAS** | | | | | |
| 1 Moran | | N | Y | N | N |
| 2 Ryun | N | Y | Y | N | N |
| 3 Moore | N | N | Y | N | N |
| 4 Tiahrt | N | Y | Y | N | N |
| **KENTUCKY** | | | | | |
| 1 Whitfield | N | N | Y | N | N |
| 2 Lewis | N | N | Y | N | N |
| 3 Northup | N | N | Y | N | N |
| 4 Davis | N | N | Y | N | N |
| 5 Rogers | N | N | Y | N | N |
| 6 Chandler | Y | N | Y | N | N |
| **LOUISIANA** | | | | | |
| 1 Jindal | N | Y | Y | N | N |
| 2 Jefferson | Y | ? | Y | Y | N |
| 3 Melancon | N | ? | Y | N | N |
| 4 McCrery | N | N | Y | N | N |
| 5 Alexander | N | N | Y | N | N |
| 6 Baker | N | N | Y | N | N |
| 7 Boustany | N | N | Y | N | N |
| **MAINE** | | | | | |
| 1 Allen | Y | N | Y | N | Y |
| 2 Michaud | Y | N | Y | N | N |
| **MARYLAND** | | | | | |
| 1 Gilchrest | N | N | Y | N | N |
| 2 Ruppersberger | Y | N | Y | Y | N |
| 3 Cardin | Y | N | Y | Y | N |
| 4 Wynn | Y | N | Y | Y | N |
| 5 Hoyer | Y | N | Y | Y | N |
| 6 Bartlett | N | Y | Y | N | N |
| 7 Cummings | Y | N | Y | Y | ? |
| 8 Van Hollen | Y | N | Y | Y | Y |
| **MASSACHUSETTS** | | | | | |
| 1 Olver | Y | N | Y | Y | ? |
| 2 Neal | Y | N | Y | Y | Y |
| 3 McGovern | Y | N | Y | Y | Y |
| 4 Frank | Y | N | Y | Y | Y |
| 5 Meehan | Y | N | Y | Y | Y |
| 6 Tierney | Y | N | Y | Y | Y |
| 7 Markey | Y | N | Y | Y | Y |
| 8 Capuano | Y | N | Y | P | Y |
| 9 Lynch | Y | N | Y | Y | N |
| 10 Delahunt | ? | ? | ? | ? | ? |
| **MICHIGAN** | | | | | |
| 1 Stupak | Y | N | Y | N | N |
| 2 Hoekstra | N | N | Y | N | N |
| 3 Ehlers | N | N | Y | N | N |
| 4 Camp | N | N | Y | N | N |
| 5 Kildee | Y | N | Y | N | N |
| 6 Upton | N | N | Y | N | N |
| 7 Schwarz | N | N | Y | N | N |
| 8 Rogers | N | Y | Y | N | N |
| 9 Knollenberg | N | N | Y | N | N |
| 10 Miller | N | N | Y | N | N |
| 11 McCotter | N | Y | Y | N | N |
| 12 Levin | Y | N | Y | N | N |
| 13 Kilpatrick | Y | N | Y | Y | N |
| 14 Conyers | Y | N | Y | Y | Y |
| 15 Dingell | Y | N | Y | Y | N |

| | 82 | 83 | 84 | 85 | 86 |
|---|---|---|---|---|---|
| **MINNESOTA** | | | | | |
| 1 Gutknecht | N | Y | Y | N | N |
| 2 Kline | N | Y | Y | N | N |
| 3 Ramstad | N | N | Y | N | N |
| 4 McCollum | Y | N | Y | Y | N |
| 5 Sabo | Y | N | Y | Y | Y |
| 6 Kennedy | N | Y | Y | N | N |
| 7 Peterson | N | N | Y | N | N |
| 8 Oberstar | Y | N | Y | Y | Y |
| **MISSISSIPPI** | | | | | |
| 1 Wicker | N | N | Y | N | N |
| 2 Thompson | Y | N | Y | Y | Y |
| 3 Pickering | N | N | Y | N | N |
| 4 Taylor | N | N | Y | N | Y |
| **MISSOURI** | | | | | |
| 1 Clay | Y | N | Y | Y | Y |
| 2 Akin | N | Y | Y | N | N |
| 3 Carnahan | Y | N | Y | N | Y |
| 4 Skelton | N | N | Y | N | N |
| 5 Cleaver | Y | N | Y | Y | Y |
| 6 Graves | N | N | Y | N | N |
| 7 Blunt | N | Y | Y | N | N |
| 8 Emerson | N | N | Y | N | N |
| 9 Hulshof | N | N | Y | N | N |
| **MONTANA** | | | | | |
| AL Rehberg | N | N | Y | N | N |
| **NEBRASKA** | | | | | |
| 1 Fortenberry | N | N | Y | N | N |
| 2 Terry | N | Y | Y | N | N |
| 3 Osborne | N | N | Y | N | N |
| **NEVADA** | | | | | |
| 1 Berkley | Y | N | Y | N | Y |
| 2 Gibbons | N | Y | Y | N | N |
| 3 Porter | N | N | Y | N | N |
| **NEW HAMPSHIRE** | | | | | |
| 1 Bradley | N | N | Y | N | N |
| 2 Bass | N | N | Y | N | N |
| **NEW JERSEY** | | | | | |
| 1 Andrews | Y | N | Y | Y | Y |
| 2 LoBiondo | N | N | Y | N | N |
| 3 Saxton | N | N | Y | N | N |
| 4 Smith | N | N | Y | N | N |
| 5 Garrett | N | Y | Y | N | N |
| 6 Pallone | Y | N | Y | Y | N |
| 7 Ferguson | Y | N | Y | N | N |
| 8 Pascrell | Y | N | Y | Y | N |
| 9 Rothman | Y | N | Y | Y | Y |
| 10 Payne | Y | N | Y | Y | Y |
| 11 Frelinghuysen | N | N | Y | N | N |
| 12 Holt | Y | N | Y | Y | Y |
| 13 Menendez | Y | N | Y | Y | N |
| **NEW MEXICO** | | | | | |
| 1 Wilson | Y | N | Y | N | N |
| 2 Pearce | N | N | Y | N | N |
| 3 Udall | Y | N | Y | Y | N |
| **NEW YORK** | | | | | |
| 1 Bishop | Y | N | Y | Y | Y |
| 2 Israel | Y | N | Y | N | Y |
| 3 King | ? | ? | ? | Y | N |
| 4 McCarthy | Y | N | Y | N | N |
| 5 Ackerman | Y | N | Y | Y | Y |
| 6 Meeks | Y | N | Y | Y | Y |
| 7 Crowley | Y | N | Y | Y | Y |
| 8 Nadler | Y | N | Y | Y | Y |
| 9 Weiner | Y | N | Y | Y | N |
| 10 Towns | Y | N | Y | Y | Y |
| 11 Owens | Y | N | Y | Y | Y |
| 12 Velázquez | Y | N | Y | Y | Y |
| 13 Fossella | N | N | Y | N | N |
| 14 Maloney | Y | N | Y | Y | Y |
| 15 Rangel | Y | N | Y | Y | Y |
| 16 Serrano | Y | N | Y | Y | Y |
| 17 Engel | Y | N | Y | Y | Y |
| 18 Lowey | Y | N | Y | Y | N |
| 19 Kelly | N | N | Y | N | N |
| 20 Sweeney | N | N | Y | N | N |
| 21 McNulty | Y | N | Y | Y | N |
| 22 Hinchey | Y | N | P | Y | Y |
| 23 McHugh | N | N | Y | N | N |
| 24 Boehlert | N | N | Y | N | N |
| 25 Walsh | N | N | Y | N | N |
| 26 Reynolds | ? | Y | Y | N | N |
| 27 Higgins | Y | N | Y | Y | Y |
| 28 Slaughter | Y | N | Y | Y | Y |
| 29 Kuhl | N | Y | Y | N | N |

| | 82 | 83 | 84 | 85 | 86 |
|---|---|---|---|---|---|
| **NORTH CAROLINA** | | | | | |
| 1 Butterfield | Y | N | Y | Y | Y |
| 2 Etheridge | Y | N | Y | Y | N |
| 3 Jones | Y | N | Y | N | N |
| 4 Price | Y | N | Y | Y | N |
| 5 Foxx | N | Y | Y | N | N |
| 6 Coble | - | + | + | - | - |
| 7 McIntyre | N | N | Y | N | N |
| 8 Hayes | N | N | Y | N | N |
| 9 Myrick | N | Y | Y | N | N |
| 10 McHenry | N | Y | Y | N | N |
| 11 Taylor | N | N | Y | N | N |
| 12 Watt | Y | N | Y | Y | ? |
| 13 Miller | Y | N | Y | Y | N |
| **NORTH DAKOTA** | | | | | |
| AL Pomeroy | Y | N | Y | N | N |
| **OHIO** | | | | | |
| 1 Chabot | N | Y | Y | N | N |
| 2 Portman | ? | ? | ? | N | N |
| 3 Turner | N | N | Y | N | N |
| 4 Oxley | N | N | Y | N | N |
| 5 Gillmor | N | N | Y | N | N |
| 6 Strickland | Y | N | Y | N | Y |
| 7 Hobson | N | N | Y | N | N |
| 8 Boehner | N | Y | Y | N | ? |
| 9 Kaptur | Y | N | Y | Y | Y |
| 10 Kucinich | Y | N | P | Y | Y |
| 11 Jones | Y | N | Y | Y | Y |
| 12 Tiberi | N | N | Y | N | N |
| 13 Brown | Y | N | Y | Y | Y |
| 14 LaTourette | N | N | Y | Y | N |
| 15 Pryce | N | N | Y | N | N |
| 16 Regula | N | N | Y | N | N |
| 17 Ryan | Y | N | Y | Y | Y |
| 18 Ney | N | N | Y | N | ? |
| **OKLAHOMA** | | | | | |
| 1 Sullivan | N | Y | Y | N | ? |
| 2 Boren | N | N | Y | N | N |
| 3 Lucas | N | N | Y | N | N |
| 4 Cole | N | Y | Y | N | N |
| 5 Istook | N | Y | Y | N | N |
| **OREGON** | | | | | |
| 1 Wu | Y | N | Y | Y | N |
| 2 Walden | N | N | Y | N | N |
| 3 Blumenauer | Y | N | Y | Y | Y |
| 4 DeFazio | Y | N | Y | Y | Y |
| 5 Hooley | Y | N | Y | N | Y |
| **PENNSYLVANIA** | | | | | |
| 1 Brady | Y | N | Y | Y | N |
| 2 Fattah | Y | N | Y | Y | Y |
| 3 English | N | Y | Y | N | N |
| 4 Hart | N | N | Y | N | N |
| 5 Peterson | N | N | Y | N | N |
| 6 Gerlach | N | N | Y | N | N |
| 7 Weldon | N | N | Y | N | N |
| 8 Fitzpatrick | N | N | Y | N | N |
| 9 Shuster | N | Y | Y | N | N |
| 10 Sherwood | N | N | Y | N | N |
| 11 Kanjorski | Y | N | Y | Y | N |
| 12 Murtha | Y | N | Y | Y | N |
| 13 Schwartz | Y | N | Y | Y | Y |
| 14 Doyle | Y | N | Y | Y | N |
| 15 Dent | N | N | Y | N | N |
| 16 Pitts | N | Y | Y | N | N |
| 17 Holden | Y | N | Y | N | N |
| 18 Murphy | N | N | Y | N | N |
| 19 Platts | N | N | Y | N | N |
| **RHODE ISLAND** | | | | | |
| 1 Kennedy | Y | N | Y | Y | Y |
| 2 Langevin | Y | N | Y | N | N |
| **SOUTH CAROLINA** | | | | | |
| 1 Brown | N | N | Y | N | N |
| 2 Wilson | N | Y | Y | N | N |
| 3 Barrett | N | Y | Y | N | N |
| 4 Inglis | N | Y | Y | N | N |
| 5 Spratt | Y | N | Y | N | N |
| 6 Clyburn | Y | N | Y | N | N |
| **SOUTH DAKOTA** | | | | | |
| AL Herseth | Y | N | Y | N | N |
| **TENNESSEE** | | | | | |
| 1 Jenkins | N | Y | Y | N | N |
| 2 Duncan | N | Y | Y | N | N |

| | 82 | 83 | 84 | 85 | 86 |
|---|---|---|---|---|---|
| 3 Wamp | N | Y | Y | N | N |
| 4 Davis | N | N | Y | N | N |
| 5 Cooper | N | N | Y | N | N |
| 6 Gordon | N | N | Y | N | N |
| 7 Blackburn | N | Y | Y | N | N |
| 8 Tanner | N | N | Y | N | N |
| 9 Ford | N | N | Y | P | N |
| **TEXAS** | | | | | |
| 1 Gohmert | N | Y | Y | ? | N |
| 2 Poe | N | Y | Y | N | N |
| 3 Johnson, S. | N | Y | Y | N | N |
| 4 Hall | N | Y | Y | N | N |
| 5 Hensarling | N | Y | Y | N | N |
| 6 Barton | N | Y | Y | N | N |
| 7 Culberson | N | Y | Y | N | N |
| 8 Brady | N | Y | Y | N | N |
| 9 Green, A. | Y | N | Y | Y | Y |
| 10 McCaul | N | Y | Y | N | N |
| 11 Conaway | N | Y | Y | N | N |
| 12 Granger | N | N | Y | N | N |
| 13 Thornberry | N | Y | Y | N | N |
| 14 Paul | N | Y | N | N | N |
| 15 Hinojosa | Y | N | Y | Y | ? |
| 16 Reyes | Y | N | Y | N | N |
| 17 Edwards | Y | N | Y | Y | N |
| 18 Jackson-Lee | Y | N | Y | Y | ? |
| 19 Neugebauer | N | Y | Y | N | N |
| 20 Gonzalez | Y | N | Y | Y | N |
| 21 Smith | N | N | Y | N | N |
| 22 DeLay | N | N | ? | N | N |
| 23 Bonilla | N | N | Y | N | N |
| 24 Marchant | N | Y | Y | N | N |
| 25 Doggett | Y | N | Y | Y | N |
| 26 Burgess | N | Y | Y | N | N |
| 27 Ortiz | Y | N | Y | Y | N |
| 28 Cuellar | Y | N | Y | Y | N |
| 29 Green, G. | Y | N | Y | Y | N |
| 30 Johnson, E. | Y | N | Y | Y | Y |
| 31 Carter | N | Y | Y | N | N |
| 32 Sessions | N | Y | Y | N | N |
| **UTAH** | | | | | |
| 1 Bishop | N | Y | Y | N | N |
| 2 Matheson | N | N | Y | N | N |
| 3 Cannon | N | Y | Y | N | N |
| **VERMONT** | | | | | |
| AL *Sanders* | Y | N | Y | Y | Y |
| **VIRGINIA** | | | | | |
| 1 Davis, J. | N | N | Y | P | N |
| 2 Drake | N | Y | Y | N | N |
| 3 Scott | Y | N | Y | Y | N |
| 4 Forbes | ? | ? | ? | N | N |
| 5 Goode | N | N | Y | N | N |
| 6 Goodlatte | N | Y | Y | N | N |
| 7 Cantor | N | Y | Y | N | N |
| 8 Moran | Y | N | Y | Y | Y |
| 9 Boucher | Y | N | Y | N | N |
| 10 Wolf | N | N | Y | N | N |
| 11 Davis, T. | N | N | Y | N | N |
| **WASHINGTON** | | | | | |
| 1 Inslee | Y | N | Y | N | Y |
| 2 Larsen | Y | N | Y | N | ? |
| 3 Baird | Y | N | Y | N | N |
| 4 Hastings | N | N | Y | N | N |
| 5 McMorris | N | Y | Y | N | N |
| 6 Dicks | Y | N | Y | N | N |
| 7 McDermott | Y | N | P | Y | ? |
| 8 Reichert | N | N | Y | N | N |
| 9 Smith | Y | N | Y | N | Y |
| **WEST VIRGINIA** | | | | | |
| 1 Mollohan | Y | N | Y | N | N |
| 2 Capito | N | N | Y | N | N |
| 3 Rahall | Y | N | Y | N | N |
| **WISCONSIN** | | | | | |
| 1 Ryan | N | N | Y | N | N |
| 2 Baldwin | Y | N | Y | Y | Y |
| 3 Kind | Y | N | Y | N | Y |
| 4 Moore | Y | N | Y | Y | Y |
| 5 Sensenbrenner | N | Y | Y | N | N |
| 6 Petri | N | Y | Y | N | N |
| 7 Obey | Y | N | Y | Y | P |
| 8 Green | N | N | Y | N | N |
| **WYOMING** | | | | | |
| AL Cubin | ? | ? | ? | ? | N |

# IN THE HOUSE | By Vote Number

**87.** **H Con Res 95. Fiscal 2006 Budget Resolution/Democratic Substitute.** Spratt, D-S.C., substitute that would institute pay-as-you-go rules requiring tax cuts and mandatory spending increases be offset, while eliminating $68.6 billion in cuts to mandatory spending. It would add $4.5 billion more for education and training, $1.6 billion for veterans and $2.9 billion for environmental protection and conservation. It also would call for spending levels that produce a balanced budget by fiscal 2012. Rejected 165-264: R 0-228; D 164-36 (ND 130-19, SD 34-17); I 1-0. March 17, 2005.

**88.** **H Con Res 95. Fiscal 2006 Budget Resolution/Adoption.** Adoption of the concurrent resolution that would allow up to $843 billion in discretionary spending in fiscal 2006, plus $50 billion for operations in Iraq. It would call for mandatory spending cuts of $68.6 billion over five years and tax cuts totaling $106 billion, $45 billion of it protected by reconciliation rules. Defense spending would increase by 4 percent over fiscal 2005, to $439 billion, and non-defense spending would be cut by 1 percent, to $404 billion. Adopted 218-214: R 218-12; D 0-201 (ND 0-150, SD 0-51); I 0-1. March 17, 2005.

**89.** **H Con Res 18. Syrian Human Rights Abuses/Adoption.** Smith, R-N.J., motion to suspend the rules and adopt the concurrent resolution that would condemn the Syrian government for gross violations of internationally recognized human rights. Motion agreed to 402-3: R 217-1; D 184-2 (ND 135-1, SD 49-1); I 1-0. A two-thirds majority of those present and voting (270 in this case) is required for adoption under suspension of the rules. March 17, 2005.

**90.** **S 686. Schiavo Medical Care/Passage.** Sensenbrenner, R-Wis., motion to suspend the rules and pass the bill that would give the parents of Theresa Marie Schiavo, a severely brain-damaged Florida woman, the right to file a lawsuit in the U.S. District Court for the Middle District of Florida alleging that Schiavo's rights related to life-sustaining medical treatment have been violated under the Constitution or federal law. Motion agreed to, thus cleared for the president, 203-58: R 156-5; D 47-53 (ND 28-37, SD 19-16); I 0-0. A two-thirds majority of those present and voting (174 in this case) is required for passage under suspension of the rules. March 21, 2005 (in the session that began and the Congressional Record dated March 20, 2005).

| | 87 | 88 | 89 | 90 |
|---|---|---|---|---|
| **ALABAMA** | | | | |
| 1 Bonner | N | Y | Y | Y |
| 2 Everett | N | Y | Y | ? |
| 3 Rogers | N | Y | Y | Y |
| 4 Aderholt | N | Y | Y | Y |
| 5 Cramer | N | N | Y | Y |
| 6 Bachus | N | Y | Y | Y |
| 7 Davis | Y | N | Y | ? |
| **ALASKA** | | | | |
| AL Young | N | Y | Y | ? |
| **ARIZONA** | | | | |
| 1 Renzi | N | Y | Y | Y |
| 2 Franks | N | Y | Y | Y |
| 3 Shadegg | N | Y | Y | ? |
| 4 Pastor | Y | N | Y | ? |
| 5 Hayworth | N | Y | Y | Y |
| 6 Flake | N | Y | Y | ? |
| 7 Grijalva | Y | N | Y | ? |
| 8 Kolbe | N | Y | Y | ? |
| **ARKANSAS** | | | | |
| 1 Berry | N | N | Y | Y |
| 2 Snyder | Y | N | Y | Y |
| 3 Boozman | N | Y | Y | ? |
| 4 Ross | N | N | Y | Y |
| **CALIFORNIA** | | | | |
| 1 Thompson | N | N | ? | ? |
| 2 Herger | N | Y | Y | ? |
| 3 Lungren | N | Y | Y | ? |
| 4 Doolittle | N | Y | Y | Y |
| 5 Matsui, D. | Y | N | Y | N |
| 6 Woolsey | N | N | Y | ? |
| 7 Miller, George | Y | N | Y | ? |
| 8 Pelosi | Y | N | Y | ? |
| 9 Lee | N | N | Y | ? |
| 10 Tauscher | Y | N | Y | ? |
| 11 Pombo | N | Y | Y | ? |
| 12 Lantos | Y | N | Y | ? |
| 13 Stark | N | N | Y | ? |
| 14 Eshoo | Y | N | Y | ? |
| 15 Honda | Y | N | Y | ? |
| 16 Lofgren | Y | N | ? | ? |
| 17 Farr | Y | N | Y | ? |
| 18 Cardoza | N | N | Y | ? |
| 19 Radanovich | N | Y | Y | ? |
| 20 Costa | N | N | Y | ? |
| 21 Nunes | N | Y | Y | ? |
| 22 Thomas | N | Y | Y | ? |
| 23 Capps | Y | N | ? | ? |
| 24 Gallegly | N | Y | ? | ? |
| 25 McKeon | N | Y | Y | ? |
| 26 Dreier | N | Y | Y | Y |
| 27 Sherman | Y | N | Y | ? |
| 28 Berman | Y | N | ? | ? |
| 29 Schiff | Y | N | Y | N |
| 30 Waxman | Y | N | Y | ? |
| 31 Becerra | Y | N | ? | – |
| 32 Solis | Y | N | Y | ? |
| 33 Watson | Y | N | Y | ? |
| 34 Roybal-Allard | Y | N | Y | ? |
| 35 Waters | Y | N | Y | ? |
| 36 Harman | Y | N | Y | ? |
| 37 Millender-McD. | Y | N | Y | ? |
| 38 Napolitano | Y | N | ? | ? |
| 39 Sánchez, Linda | Y | N | Y | ? |
| 40 Royce | N | Y | Y | Y |
| 41 Lewis | N | Y | Y | Y |
| 42 Miller, Gary | N | Y | ? | ? |
| 43 Baca | Y | N | ? | Y |
| 44 Calvert | N | Y | ? | Y |
| 45 Bono | N | Y | ? | Y |
| 46 Rohrabacher | N | Y | Y | ? |
| 47 Sanchez, Loretta | N | N | Y | ? |
| 48 Cox | N | Y | Y | Y |
| 49 Issa | N | Y | Y | + |

| | 87 | 88 | 89 | 90 |
|---|---|---|---|---|
| 50 Cunningham | N | Y | Y | ? |
| 51 Filner | Y | N | Y | ? |
| 52 Hunter | N | Y | Y | ? |
| 53 Davis | Y | N | Y | ? |
| **COLORADO** | | | | |
| 1 DeGette | Y | N | ? | ? |
| 2 Udall | Y | N | Y | ? |
| 3 Salazar | N | N | Y | ? |
| 4 Musgrave | N | Y | Y | Y |
| 5 Hefley | N | Y | Y | Y |
| 6 Tancredo | N | Y | Y | Y |
| 7 Beauprez | N | Y | Y | Y |
| **CONNECTICUT** | | | | |
| 1 Larson | Y | N | Y | N |
| 2 Simmons | N | N | Y | ? |
| 3 DeLauro | Y | N | Y | ? |
| 4 Shays | N | N | Y | N |
| 5 Johnson | N | Y | Y | ? |
| **DELAWARE** | | | | |
| AL Castle | N | Y | Y | N |
| **FLORIDA** | | | | |
| 1 Miller | N | Y | Y | Y |
| 2 Boyd | N | N | Y | ? |
| 3 Brown | Y | N | Y | Y |
| 4 Crenshaw | N | Y | Y | Y |
| 5 Brown-Waite | N | Y | ? | N |
| 6 Stearns | N | Y | Y | ? |
| 7 Mica | N | Y | Y | ? |
| 8 Keller | N | Y | Y | ? |
| 9 Bilirakis | N | Y | Y | Y |
| 10 Young | ? | ? | ? | ? |
| 11 Davis | Y | N | Y | N |
| 12 Putnam | N | Y | Y | Y |
| 13 Harris | N | Y | ? | Y |
| 14 Mack | N | Y | Y | Y |
| 15 Weldon | N | Y | Y | Y |
| 16 Foley | N | Y | Y | Y |
| 17 Meek | Y | N | Y | ? |
| 18 Ros-Lehtinen | N | Y | Y | Y |
| 19 Wexler | Y | N | Y | N |
| 20 Wasserman-Schultz | Y | N | Y | N |
| 21 Diaz-Balart, L. | N | Y | Y | Y |
| 22 Shaw | N | Y | Y | ? |
| 23 Hastings | Y | N | Y | N |
| 24 Feeney | N | Y | Y | Y |
| 25 Diaz-Balart, M. | N | Y | Y | Y |
| **GEORGIA** | | | | |
| 1 Kingston | N | Y | Y | Y |
| 2 Bishop | Y | N | Y | Y |
| 3 Marshall | N | N | Y | Y |
| 4 McKinney | Y | N | N | N |
| 5 Lewis | N | N | Y | N |
| 6 Price | N | Y | Y | Y |
| 7 Linder | N | Y | Y | Y |
| 8 Westmoreland | N | Y | Y | Y |
| 9 Norwood | N | Y | Y | ? |
| 10 Deal | N | Y | Y | ? |
| 11 Gingrey | N | Y | Y | Y |
| 12 Barrow | N | N | Y | Y |
| 13 Scott | Y | N | Y | Y |
| **HAWAII** | | | | |
| 1 Abercrombie | Y | N | Y | ? |
| 2 Case | N | N | Y | ? |
| **IDAHO** | | | | |
| 1 Otter | N | Y | Y | Y |
| 2 Simpson | N | Y | Y | Y |
| **ILLINOIS** | | | | |
| 1 Rush | Y | N | Y | ? |
| 2 Jackson | Y | N | Y | Y |
| 3 Lipinski | N | N | Y | Y |
| 4 Gutierrez | Y | N | Y | N |
| 5 Emanuel | Y | N | Y | ? |
| 6 Hyde | N | Y | Y | ? |
| 7 Davis | Y | N | Y | ? |
| 8 Bean | N | N | Y | Y |
| 9 Schakowsky | Y | N | Y | Y |
| 10 Kirk | N | Y | Y | Y |
| 11 Weller | N | Y | Y | ? |
| 12 Costello | Y | N | Y | Y |

**KEY** **Republicans** Democrats *Independents*

| | | | |
|---|---|---|---|
| **Y** Voted for (yea) | **X** Paired against | **C** Voted "present" to avoid possible conflict of interest |
| **#** Paired for | **–** Announced against | |
| **+** Announced for | **P** Voted "present" | **?** Did not vote or otherwise make a position known |
| **N** Voted against (nay) | | |

| | 87 | 88 | 89 | 90 |
|---|---|---|---|---|
| 13 Biggert | N | Y | Y | Y |
| 14 Hastert | | Y | | Y |
| 15 Johnson | N | N | Y | Y |
| 16 Manzullo | N | Y | Y | Y |
| 17 Evans | Y | N | ? | N |
| 18 LaHood | N | Y | Y | Y |
| 19 Shimkus | N | Y | Y | ? |
| **INDIANA** | | | | |
| 1 Visclosky | Y | N | Y | N |
| 2 Chocola | N | Y | Y | Y |
| 3 Souder | N | Y | Y | Y |
| 4 Buyer | N | Y | Y | Y |
| 5 Burton | N | Y | Y | Y |
| 6 Pence | N | Y | Y | Y |
| 7 Carson | Y | N | Y | N |
| 8 Hostettler | N | N | Y | ? |
| 9 Sodrel | N | Y | Y | Y |
| **IOWA** | | | | |
| 1 Nussle | N | Y | Y | Y |
| 2 Leach | N | Y | ? | Y |
| 3 Boswell | N | N | Y | ? |
| 4 Latham | N | Y | Y | Y |
| 5 King | N | Y | Y | Y |
| **KANSAS** | | | | |
| 1 Moran | N | Y | Y | ? |
| 2 Ryun | - | Y | Y | Y |
| 3 Moore | N | N | Y | - |
| 4 Tiahrt | N | Y | Y | Y |
| **KENTUCKY** | | | | |
| 1 Whitfield | N | Y | Y | Y |
| 2 Lewis | N | Y | Y | Y |
| 3 Northup | N | Y | Y | Y |
| 4 Davis | N | Y | Y | Y |
| 5 Rogers | N | Y | Y | ? |
| 6 Chandler | N | N | Y | Y |
| **LOUISIANA** | | | | |
| 1 Jindal | N | Y | Y | Y |
| 2 Jefferson | Y | N | Y | ? |
| 3 Melancon | N | N | Y | Y |
| 4 McCrery | N | Y | Y | ? |
| 5 Alexander | N | Y | Y | Y |
| 6 Baker | N | Y | Y | Y |
| 7 Boustany | N | Y | Y | Y |
| **MAINE** | | | | |
| 1 Allen | Y | N | Y | ? |
| 2 Michaud | N | N | Y | Y |
| **MARYLAND** | | | | |
| 1 Gilchrest | N | Y | Y | Y |
| 2 Ruppersberger | Y | N | Y | ? |
| 3 Cardin | Y | N | Y | N |
| 4 Wynn | Y | N | Y | Y |
| 5 Hoyer | Y | N | Y | N |
| 6 Bartlett | N | Y | Y | Y |
| 7 Cummings | Y | N | Y | Y |
| 8 Van Hollen | Y | N | Y | N |
| **MASSACHUSETTS** | | | | |
| 1 Olver | Y | N | Y | N |
| 2 Neal | Y | N | Y | ? |
| 3 McGovern | Y | N | Y | ? |
| 4 Frank | Y | N | Y | N |
| 5 Meehan | Y | N | Y | ? |
| 6 Tierney | Y | N | Y | ? |
| 7 Markey | Y | N | ? | ? |
| 8 Capuano | P | N | Y | N |
| 9 Lynch | Y | N | Y | Y |
| 10 Delahunt | ? | ? | ? | ? |
| **MICHIGAN** | | | | |
| 1 Stupak | Y | N | Y | Y |
| 2 Hoekstra | N | Y | Y | ? |
| 3 Ehlers | N | Y | Y | Y |
| 4 Camp | N | Y | Y | Y |
| 5 Kildee | Y | N | Y | Y |
| 6 Upton | N | Y | Y | Y |
| 7 Schwarz | N | Y | Y | Y |
| 8 Rogers | N | Y | Y | ? |
| 9 Knollenberg | N | Y | Y | ? |
| 10 Miller | N | Y | Y | Y |
| 11 McCotter | N | Y | Y | Y |
| 12 Levin | Y | N | Y | N |
| 13 Kilpatrick | Y | N | Y | ? |
| 14 Conyers | Y | N | Y | N |
| 15 Dingell | Y | N | Y | ? |

| | 87 | 88 | 89 | 90 |
|---|---|---|---|---|
| **MINNESOTA** | | | | |
| 1 Gutknecht | N | N | Y | ? |
| 2 Kline | N | Y | Y | Y |
| 3 Ramstad | N | Y | Y | Y |
| 4 McCollum | Y | N | Y | ? |
| 5 Sabo | Y | N | Y | ? |
| 6 Kennedy | N | Y | Y | Y |
| 7 Peterson | N | N | Y | ? |
| 8 Oberstar | Y | N | Y | Y |
| **MISSISSIPPI** | | | | |
| 1 Wicker | N | Y | Y | + |
| 2 Thompson | Y | N | Y | N |
| 3 Pickering | N | Y | Y | Y |
| 4 Taylor | N | N | Y | ? |
| **MISSOURI** | | | | |
| 1 Clay | Y | N | Y | N |
| 2 Akin | N | Y | Y | Y |
| 3 Carnahan | Y | N | Y | N |
| 4 Skelton | Y | N | Y | Y |
| 5 Cleaver | Y | N | Y | N |
| 6 Graves | N | Y | Y | Y |
| 7 Blunt | N | Y | Y | Y |
| 8 Emerson | N | N | Y | Y |
| 9 Hulshof | N | Y | Y | Y |
| **MONTANA** | | | | |
| AL Rehberg | N | Y | Y | Y |
| **NEBRASKA** | | | | |
| 1 Fortenberry | N | Y | Y | Y |
| 2 Terry | N | Y | Y | Y |
| 3 Osborne | N | Y | Y | ? |
| **NEVADA** | | | | |
| 1 Berkley | Y | N | Y | N |
| 2 Gibbons | N | Y | Y | ? |
| 3 Porter | N | Y | Y | Y |
| **NEW HAMPSHIRE** | | | | |
| 1 Bradley | N | Y | Y | ? |
| 2 Bass | N | Y | Y | Y |
| **NEW JERSEY** | | | | |
| 1 Andrews | Y | N | Y | ? |
| 2 LoBiondo | N | Y | Y | Y |
| 3 Saxton | N | Y | Y | Y |
| 4 Smith | N | N | Y | Y |
| 5 Garrett | N | Y | ? | Y |
| 6 Pallone | Y | N | Y | N |
| 7 Ferguson | N | Y | Y | Y |
| 8 Pascrell | Y | N | Y | N |
| 9 Rothman | Y | N | Y | N |
| 10 Payne | Y | N | Y | N |
| 11 Frelinghuysen | N | Y | ? | ? |
| 12 Holt | Y | N | Y | N |
| 13 Menendez | Y | N | Y | ? |
| **NEW MEXICO** | | | | |
| 1 Wilson | N | Y | Y | ? |
| 2 Pearce | N | Y | Y | Y |
| 3 Udall | Y | N | Y | ? |
| **NEW YORK** | | | | |
| 1 Bishop | Y | N | Y | N |
| 2 Israel | Y | N | Y | N |
| 3 King | N | Y | Y | ? |
| 4 McCarthy | Y | N | Y | ? |
| 5 Ackerman | Y | N | Y | ? |
| 6 Meeks | Y | N | Y | ? |
| 7 Crowley | Y | N | Y | ? |
| 8 Nadler | Y | N | ? | N |
| 9 Weiner | Y | N | Y | N |
| 10 Towns | Y | N | Y | ? |
| 11 Owens | Y | N | Y | ? |
| 12 Velázquez | Y | N | Y | ? |
| 13 Fossella | N | Y | Y | Y |
| 14 Maloney | Y | N | Y | ? |
| 15 Rangel | Y | N | Y | ? |
| 16 Serrano | Y | N | Y | Y |
| 17 Engel | Y | N | Y | ? |
| 18 Lowey | Y | N | Y | ? |
| 19 Kelly | N | Y | Y | Y |
| 20 Sweeney | N | Y | Y | ? |
| 21 McNulty | Y | N | Y | ? |
| 22 Hinchey | Y | N | ? | ? |
| 23 McHugh | N | Y | Y | Y |
| 24 Boehlert | N | Y | Y | Y |
| 25 Walsh | N | Y | Y | ? |
| 26 Reynolds | N | Y | Y | ? |
| 27 Higgins | Y | N | Y | ? |
| 28 Slaughter | Y | N | Y | ? |
| 29 Kuhl | N | Y | Y | Y |

| | 87 | 88 | 89 | 90 |
|---|---|---|---|---|
| **NORTH CAROLINA** | | | | |
| 1 Butterfield | Y | N | Y | N |
| 2 Etheridge | Y | N | Y | Y |
| 3 Jones | N | N | Y | Y |
| 4 Price | Y | N | Y | N |
| 5 Foxx | N | Y | Y | Y |
| 6 Coble | - | + | + | + |
| 7 McIntyre | N | N | Y | Y |
| 8 Hayes | N | Y | Y | Y |
| 9 Myrick | N | Y | Y | Y |
| 10 McHenry | N | Y | Y | Y |
| 11 Taylor | N | Y | Y | Y |
| 12 Watt | Y | N | Y | N |
| 13 Miller | Y | N | Y | N |
| **NORTH DAKOTA** | | | | |
| AL Pomeroy | Y | N | Y | Y |
| **OHIO** | | | | |
| 1 Chabot | N | Y | Y | Y |
| 2 Portman | N | Y | ? | Y |
| 3 Turner | N | Y | Y | Y |
| 4 Oxley | N | Y | Y | ? |
| 5 Gillmor | N | Y | Y | Y |
| 6 Strickland | Y | N | Y | N |
| 7 Hobson | N | Y | Y | Y |
| 8 Boehner | N | Y | Y | Y |
| 9 Kaptur | Y | N | Y | N |
| 10 Kucinich | N | N | N | ? |
| 11 Jones | Y | N | Y | ? |
| 12 Tiberi | N | Y | Y | Y |
| 13 Brown | Y | N | Y | ? |
| 14 LaTourette | N | Y | Y | ? |
| 15 Pryce | N | Y | Y | Y |
| 16 Regula | N | Y | Y | Y |
| 17 Ryan | Y | N | Y | ? |
| 18 Ney | N | Y | Y | Y |
| **OKLAHOMA** | | | | |
| 1 Sullivan | N | Y | Y | Y |
| 2 Boren | N | N | Y | Y |
| 3 Lucas | N | Y | Y | Y |
| 4 Cole | N | Y | Y | Y |
| 5 Istook | N | Y | Y | Y |
| **OREGON** | | | | |
| 1 Wu | Y | N | Y | N |
| 2 Walden | N | Y | Y | ? |
| 3 Blumenauer | Y | N | Y | ? |
| 4 DeFazio | Y | N | Y | ? |
| 5 Hooley | Y | N | Y | ? |
| **PENNSYLVANIA** | | | | |
| 1 Brady | Y | N | Y | Y |
| 2 Fattah | Y | N | Y | Y |
| 3 English | N | Y | Y | Y |
| 4 Hart | N | Y | Y | Y |
| 5 Peterson | N | Y | Y | Y |
| 6 Gerlach | N | N | Y | ? |
| 7 Weldon | N | Y | Y | Y |
| 8 Fitzpatrick | N | Y | Y | Y |
| 9 Shuster | N | Y | Y | ? |
| 10 Sherwood | N | Y | Y | Y |
| 11 Kanjorski | N | N | Y | Y |
| 12 Murtha | N | N | Y | N |
| 13 Schwartz | Y | N | Y | N |
| 14 Doyle | Y | N | Y | N |
| 15 Dent | N | Y | Y | N |
| 16 Pitts | N | Y | Y | Y |
| 17 Holden | Y | N | Y | Y |
| 18 Murphy | N | Y | Y | Y |
| 19 Platts | N | Y | Y | Y |
| **RHODE ISLAND** | | | | |
| 1 Kennedy | Y | N | Y | N |
| 2 Langevin | Y | N | Y | Y |
| **SOUTH CAROLINA** | | | | |
| 1 Brown | N | Y | Y | ? |
| 2 Wilson | N | Y | Y | Y |
| 3 Barrett | N | Y | Y | Y |
| 4 Inglis | N | Y | Y | Y |
| 5 Spratt | Y | N | Y | N |
| 6 Clyburn | Y | N | Y | N |
| **SOUTH DAKOTA** | | | | |
| AL Herseth | N | N | Y | Y |
| **TENNESSEE** | | | | |
| 1 Jenkins | N | Y | Y | Y |
| 2 Duncan | N | Y | Y | Y |

| | 87 | 88 | 89 | 90 |
|---|---|---|---|---|
| 3 Wamp | N | Y | Y | Y |
| 4 Davis | N | N | Y | Y |
| 5 Cooper | N | N | Y | ? |
| 6 Gordon | N | N | Y | ? |
| 7 Blackburn | N | Y | Y | Y |
| 8 Tanner | N | N | Y | Y |
| 9 Ford | N | N | Y | Y |
| **TEXAS** | | | | |
| 1 Gohmert | N | Y | Y | Y |
| 2 Poe | N | Y | Y | Y |
| 3 Johnson, S. | N | Y | Y | ? |
| 4 Hall | N | Y | Y | Y |
| 5 Hensarling | N | Y | Y | Y |
| 6 Barton | N | Y | Y | ? |
| 7 Culberson | N | Y | Y | Y |
| 8 Brady | N | Y | Y | ? |
| 9 Green, A. | Y | N | Y | Y |
| 10 McCaul | N | Y | Y | Y |
| 11 Conaway | N | Y | Y | Y |
| 12 Granger | N | Y | Y | ? |
| 13 Thornberry | N | Y | Y | Y |
| 14 Paul | N | N | N | ? |
| 15 Hinojosa | Y | N | Y | ? |
| 16 Reyes | Y | N | Y | ? |
| 17 Edwards | Y | N | Y | ? |
| 18 Jackson-Lee | Y | N | Y | ? |
| 19 Neugebauer | N | Y | Y | Y |
| 20 Gonzalez | Y | N | Y | ? |
| 21 Smith | N | Y | Y | Y |
| 22 DeLay | N | Y | Y | Y |
| 23 Bonilla | N | Y | Y | Y |
| 24 Marchant | N | Y | Y | Y |
| 25 Doggett | Y | N | Y | ? |
| 26 Burgess | N | Y | Y | Y |
| 27 Ortiz | Y | N | Y | ? |
| 28 Cuellar | Y | N | Y | ? |
| 29 Green, G. | Y | N | Y | ? |
| 30 Johnson, E. | Y | N | Y | ? |
| 31 Carter | N | Y | Y | Y |
| 32 Sessions | N | Y | Y | ? |
| **UTAH** | | | | |
| 1 Bishop | N | Y | Y | ? |
| 2 Matheson | N | N | Y | Y |
| 3 Cannon | N | Y | Y | Y |
| **VERMONT** | | | | |
| AL *Sanders* | Y | N | Y | ? |
| **VIRGINIA** | | | | |
| 1 Davis, J. | N | Y | ? | Y |
| 2 Drake | N | Y | Y | Y |
| 3 Scott | Y | N | Y | N |
| 4 Forbes | N | Y | Y | Y |
| 5 Goode | N | Y | Y | Y |
| 6 Goodlatte | N | Y | Y | Y |
| 7 Cantor | N | Y | Y | Y |
| 8 Moran | Y | N | Y | N |
| 9 Boucher | Y | N | ? | ? |
| 10 Wolf | N | Y | Y | ? |
| 11 Davis, T. | N | Y | Y | Y |
| **WASHINGTON** | | | | |
| 1 Inslee | Y | N | Y | ? |
| 2 Larsen | Y | N | Y | ? |
| 3 Baird | Y | N | Y | Y |
| 4 Hastings | N | Y | Y | Y |
| 5 McMorris | N | Y | Y | ? |
| 6 Dicks | Y | N | ? | N |
| 7 McDermott | Y | N | Y | N |
| 8 Reichert | N | Y | Y | N |
| 9 Smith | Y | N | ? | ? |
| **WEST VIRGINIA** | | | | |
| 1 Mollohan | N | Y | Y | Y |
| 2 Capito | N | Y | Y | Y |
| 3 Rahall | Y | N | Y | ? |
| **WISCONSIN** | | | | |
| 1 Ryan | N | Y | Y | Y |
| 2 Baldwin | Y | N | Y | N |
| 3 Kind | Y | N | Y | Y |
| 4 Moore | Y | N | Y | ? |
| 5 Sensenbrenner | N | Y | Y | Y |
| 6 Petri | N | Y | Y | ? |
| 7 Obey | Y | N | Y | ? |
| 8 Green | N | Y | Y | Y |
| **WYOMING** | | | | |
| AL Cubin | N | Y | Y | ? |

# IN THE HOUSE | By Vote Number

**91.** **H Res 108. Zurab Zhvania Tribute/Adoption.** McCotter, R-Mich., motion to suspend the rules and adopt the resolution that would express the sympathy of the House of Representatives to the family of Zurab Zhvania and the people of the Republic of Georgia for the death of their prime minister. Motion agreed to 402-0: R 214-0; D 187-0 (ND 138-0, SD 49-0); I 1-0. A two-thirds majority of those present and voting (268 in this case) is required for adoption under suspension of the rules. April 5, 2005.

**92.** **H Res 120. Tsunami Response/Adoption.** McCotter, R-Mich., motion to suspend the rules and adopt the resolution commending the efforts by the armed forces and civilian employees of the State Department and the U.S. Agency for International Development in response to the earthquake and tsunami in South Asia of Dec. 26, 2004. Motion agreed to 401-0: R 214-0; D 186-0 (ND 138-0, SD 48-0); I 1-0. A two-thirds majority of those present and voting (268 in this case) is required for adoption under suspension of the rules. April 5, 2005.

**93.** **H Con Res 34. Yogi Bhajan Tribute/Adoption.** McCotter, R-Mich., motion to suspend the rules and adopt the concurrent resolution that would honor the life and contributions of Yogi Bhajan, a leader of Sikhs, and would express condolences to the Sikh community on his death. Motion agreed to 405-0: R 215-0; D 189-0 (ND 141-0, SD 48-0); I 1-0. A two-thirds majority of those present and voting (270 in this case) is required for adoption under suspension of the rules. April 5, 2005.

**94.** **H Res 190. Pope John Paul II Tribute/Adoption.** Adoption of a resolution that would honor the life and achievements of Pope John Paul II and express profound sorrow on his death. Adopted 415-0: R 222-0; D 192-0 (ND 142-0, SD 50-0); I 1-0. April 6, 2005.

**95.** **H Res 148. Financial Literacy Month/Adoption.** Gutknecht, R-Minn., motion to suspend the rules and adopt the resolution that would express support for the goals and ideals of Financial Literacy Month. Motion agreed to 409-2: R 216-2; D 192-0 (ND 143-0, SD 49-0); I 1-0. A two-thirds majority of those present and voting (274 in this case) is required for adoption under suspension of the rules. April 6, 2005.

| | 91 | 92 | 93 | 94 | 95 |
|---|---|---|---|---|---|
| **ALABAMA** | | | | | |
| 1 Bonner | Y | Y | Y | Y | Y |
| 2 Everett | Y | Y | Y | Y | Y |
| 3 Rogers | Y | Y | Y | Y | Y |
| 4 Aderholt | Y | Y | Y | Y | Y |
| 5 Cramer | Y | Y | Y | Y | Y |
| 6 Bachus | Y | Y | Y | Y | Y |
| 7 Davis | Y | Y | Y | Y | Y |
| **ALASKA** | | | | | |
| AL Young | Y | Y | Y | Y | Y |
| **ARIZONA** | | | | | |
| 1 Renzi | Y | Y | ? | Y | Y |
| 2 Franks | Y | Y | Y | Y | Y |
| 3 Shadegg | Y | Y | Y | Y | Y |
| 4 Pastor | Y | Y | Y | Y | Y |
| 5 Hayworth | Y | Y | Y | Y | Y |
| 6 Flake | Y | Y | Y | Y | N |
| 7 Grijalva | ? | Y | Y | Y | Y |
| 8 Kolbe | Y | Y | Y | Y | Y |
| **ARKANSAS** | | | | | |
| 1 Berry | Y | Y | Y | Y | Y |
| 2 Snyder | Y | Y | Y | Y | Y |
| 3 Boozman | Y | Y | Y | Y | Y |
| 4 Ross | Y | Y | Y | Y | Y |
| **CALIFORNIA** | | | | | |
| 1 Thompson | Y | Y | Y | Y | Y |
| 2 Herger | Y | Y | Y | Y | Y |
| 3 Lungren | Y | Y | Y | Y | Y |
| 4 Doolittle | Y | Y | Y | Y | Y |
| 5 Matsui, D. | Y | Y | Y | Y | Y |
| 6 Woolsey | Y | Y | Y | Y | Y |
| 7 Miller, George | Y | Y | Y | Y | Y |
| 8 Pelosi | Y | Y | Y | Y | Y |
| 9 Lee | Y | Y | Y | Y | Y |
| 10 Tauscher | Y | Y | Y | Y | Y |
| 11 Pombo | Y | Y | Y | Y | Y |
| 12 Lantos | Y | Y | Y | Y | Y |
| 13 Stark | Y | Y | Y | Y | Y |
| 14 Eshoo | Y | Y | Y | Y | Y |
| 15 Honda | Y | Y | Y | Y | Y |
| 16 Lofgren | Y | Y | Y | Y | Y |
| 17 Farr | Y | Y | Y | Y | Y |
| 18 Cardoza | Y | Y | Y | Y | Y |
| 19 Radanovich | Y | Y | Y | Y | Y |
| 20 Costa | ? | Y | Y | Y | Y |
| 21 Nunes | Y | Y | Y | Y | Y |
| 22 Thomas | Y | Y | Y | Y | Y |
| 23 Capps | Y | Y | Y | Y | Y |
| 24 Gallegly | Y | Y | Y | Y | Y |
| 25 McKeon | Y | Y | Y | Y | Y |
| 26 Dreier | Y | Y | Y | Y | Y |
| 27 Sherman | Y | Y | Y | Y | Y |
| 28 Berman | Y | ? | Y | Y | Y |
| 29 Schiff | Y | Y | Y | Y | Y |
| 30 Waxman | Y | Y | Y | Y | Y |
| 31 Becerra | Y | Y | Y | Y | Y |
| 32 Solis | Y | Y | Y | Y | Y |
| 33 Watson | ? | ? | ? | ? | ? |
| 34 Roybal-Allard | Y | Y | Y | Y | Y |
| 35 Waters | ? | ? | ? | ? | ? |
| 36 Harman | Y | ? | Y | Y | Y |
| 37 Millender-McD. | ? | ? | ? | ? | ? |
| 38 Napolitano | Y | Y | Y | + | Y |
| 39 Sánchez, Linda | Y | Y | Y | Y | Y |
| 40 Royce | Y | Y | Y | Y | Y |
| 41 Lewis | Y | Y | Y | Y | Y |
| 42 Miller, Gary | Y | Y | Y | Y | Y |
| 43 Baca | Y | Y | Y | Y | Y |
| 44 Calvert | ? | ? | ? | Y | Y |
| 45 Bono | Y | Y | Y | Y | Y |
| 46 Rohrabacher | Y | Y | Y | Y | Y |
| 47 Sanchez, Loretta | Y | Y | Y | Y | Y |
| 48 Cox | Y | Y | Y | Y | Y |
| 49 Issa | Y | Y | Y | Y | Y |
| 50 Cunningham | Y | Y | Y | Y | Y |
| 51 Filner | Y | Y | Y | Y | Y |
| 52 Hunter | ? | ? | ? | Y | Y |
| 53 Davis | Y | Y | Y | Y | Y |
| **COLORADO** | | | | | |
| 1 DeGette | Y | Y | Y | Y | Y |
| 2 Udall | Y | Y | Y | Y | Y |
| 3 Salazar | Y | Y | Y | Y | Y |
| 4 Musgrave | Y | Y | Y | Y | Y |
| 5 Hefley | Y | Y | Y | Y | Y |
| 6 Tancredo | Y | Y | Y | Y | Y |
| 7 Beauprez | Y | Y | Y | Y | Y |
| **CONNECTICUT** | | | | | |
| 1 Larson | Y | Y | Y | Y | Y |
| 2 Simmons | Y | Y | Y | Y | Y |
| 3 DeLauro | Y | Y | Y | Y | Y |
| 4 Shays | Y | Y | Y | Y | ? |
| 5 Johnson | Y | Y | Y | Y | Y |
| **DELAWARE** | | | | | |
| AL Castle | Y | Y | Y | Y | Y |
| **FLORIDA** | | | | | |
| 1 Miller | Y | Y | Y | Y | Y |
| 2 Boyd | Y | Y | Y | Y | Y |
| 3 Brown | Y | Y | Y | Y | Y |
| 4 Crenshaw | Y | Y | Y | Y | Y |
| 5 Brown-Waite | Y | Y | Y | Y | Y |
| 6 Stearns | Y | Y | Y | Y | Y |
| 7 Mica | Y | Y | Y | Y | Y |
| 8 Keller | Y | ? | Y | Y | Y |
| 9 Bilirakis | Y | Y | Y | Y | Y |
| 10 Young | ? | ? | ? | ? | ? |
| 11 Davis | Y | Y | Y | Y | Y |
| 12 Putnam | Y | Y | Y | Y | Y |
| 13 Harris | Y | Y | Y | Y | Y |
| 14 Mack | Y | Y | Y | Y | Y |
| 15 Weldon | Y | Y | Y | Y | Y |
| 16 Foley | Y | Y | Y | Y | Y |
| 17 Meek | Y | Y | Y | Y | Y |
| 18 Ros-Lehtinen | Y | Y | Y | Y | Y |
| 19 Wexler | Y | Y | Y | Y | Y |
| 20 Wasserman-Schultz | Y | Y | Y | Y | Y |
| 21 Diaz-Balart, L. | Y | Y | Y | Y | Y |
| 22 Shaw | Y | Y | Y | Y | Y |
| 23 Hastings | Y | Y | Y | Y | Y |
| 24 Feeney | Y | Y | Y | Y | Y |
| 25 Diaz-Balart, M. | Y | Y | Y | Y | Y |
| **GEORGIA** | | | | | |
| 1 Kingston | Y | Y | Y | ? | ? |
| 2 Bishop | Y | Y | Y | Y | Y |
| 3 Marshall | Y | Y | Y | Y | Y |
| 4 McKinney | Y | Y | Y | Y | Y |
| 5 Lewis | Y | Y | Y | Y | Y |
| 6 Price | Y | Y | Y | Y | Y |
| 7 Linder | Y | Y | Y | Y | Y |
| 8 Westmoreland | Y | Y | Y | Y | Y |
| 9 Norwood | Y | Y | Y | Y | Y |
| 10 Deal | Y | Y | Y | Y | Y |
| 11 Gingrey | Y | Y | Y | Y | Y |
| 12 Barrow | Y | Y | P | Y | Y |
| 13 Scott | Y | ? | Y | Y | Y |
| **HAWAII** | | | | | |
| 1 Abercrombie | Y | Y | Y | Y | Y |
| 2 Case | Y | Y | Y | Y | Y |
| **IDAHO** | | | | | |
| 1 Otter | Y | Y | Y | Y | ? |
| 2 Simpson | Y | Y | Y | Y | Y |
| **ILLINOIS** | | | | | |
| 1 Rush | Y | Y | Y | Y | Y |
| 2 Jackson | Y | Y | Y | Y | Y |
| 3 Lipinski | Y | Y | Y | Y | Y |
| 4 Gutierrez | Y | Y | Y | + | + |
| 5 Emanuel | Y | Y | Y | Y | Y |
| 6 Hyde | Y | Y | Y | Y | Y |
| 7 Davis | Y | Y | Y | Y | Y |
| 8 Bean | Y | Y | Y | Y | Y |
| 9 Schakowsky | Y | Y | Y | Y | Y |
| 10 Kirk | Y | ? | Y | Y | Y |
| 11 Weller | Y | Y | Y | Y | Y |
| 12 Costello | ? | ? | ? | Y | Y |

**KEY**   Republicans   Democrats   *Independents*

| | | |
|---|---|---|
| Y Voted for (yea) | X Paired against | C Voted "present" to avoid possible conflict of interest |
| # Paired for | – Announced against | |
| + Announced for | P Voted "present" | ? Did not vote or otherwise make a position known |
| N Voted against (nay) | | |

| | 91 | 92 | 93 | 94 | 95 |
|---|---|---|---|---|---|
| 13 Biggert | Y | Y | Y | Y | Y |
| 14 Hastert | | | | | |
| 15 Johnson | Y | Y | Y | Y | Y |
| 16 Manzullo | Y | Y | Y | Y | Y |
| 17 Evans | ? | Y | Y | Y | ? |
| 18 LaHood | Y | Y | Y | Y | Y |
| 19 Shimkus | ? | ? | ? | ? | ? |
| **INDIANA** | | | | | |
| 1 Visclosky | Y | Y | Y | Y | Y |
| 2 Chocola | Y | Y | Y | Y | Y |
| 3 Souder | ? | ? | ? | ? | ? |
| 4 Buyer | Y | Y | Y | Y | Y |
| 5 Burton | Y | Y | Y | Y | Y |
| 6 Pence | Y | Y | Y | Y | Y |
| 7 Carson | Y | Y | Y | Y | Y |
| 8 Hostettler | ? | ? | ? | ? | Y |
| 9 Sodrel | Y | Y | Y | Y | Y |
| **IOWA** | | | | | |
| 1 Nussle | Y | Y | Y | Y | Y |
| 2 Leach | Y | Y | Y | Y | Y |
| 3 Boswell | Y | Y | Y | Y | Y |
| 4 Latham | Y | Y | Y | Y | Y |
| 5 King | Y | Y | Y | Y | Y |
| **KANSAS** | | | | | |
| 1 Moran | Y | Y | | | Y |
| 2 Ryun | Y | Y | Y | Y | Y |
| 3 Moore | Y | Y | Y | Y | Y |
| 4 Tiahrt | Y | Y | Y | Y | Y |
| **KENTUCKY** | | | | | |
| 1 Whitfield | Y | Y | Y | Y | Y |
| 2 Lewis | + | + | + | Y | Y |
| 3 Northup | Y | Y | Y | Y | Y |
| 4 Davis | Y | Y | Y | Y | Y |
| 5 Rogers | Y | Y | Y | Y | Y |
| 6 Chandler | Y | Y | Y | Y | Y |
| **LOUISIANA** | | | | | |
| 1 Jindal | Y | Y | Y | Y | Y |
| 2 Jefferson | Y | Y | Y | Y | ? |
| 3 Melancon | Y | Y | Y | Y | Y |
| 4 McCrery | Y | Y | Y | Y | Y |
| 5 Alexander | ? | ? | ? | Y | Y |
| 6 Baker | Y | Y | Y | Y | Y |
| 7 Boustany | Y | Y | Y | Y | Y |
| **MAINE** | | | | | |
| 1 Allen | Y | Y | Y | Y | Y |
| 2 Michaud | Y | Y | Y | Y | Y |
| **MARYLAND** | | | | | |
| 1 Gilchrest | Y | Y | Y | Y | Y |
| 2 Ruppersberger | Y | Y | Y | Y | Y |
| 3 Cardin | Y | Y | Y | Y | Y |
| 4 Wynn | Y | Y | Y | Y | Y |
| 5 Hoyer | Y | Y | Y | Y | Y |
| 6 Bartlett | Y | Y | Y | Y | Y |
| 7 Cummings | Y | Y | Y | Y | Y |
| 8 Van Hollen | Y | Y | Y | Y | Y |
| **MASSACHUSETTS** | | | | | |
| 1 Olver | Y | Y | Y | Y | Y |
| 2 Neal | Y | Y | Y | Y | Y |
| 3 McGovern | Y | Y | Y | Y | Y |
| 4 Frank | Y | Y | Y | Y | Y |
| 5 Meehan | Y | Y | Y | Y | Y |
| 6 Tierney | Y | Y | Y | Y | Y |
| 7 Markey | Y | Y | Y | Y | Y |
| 8 Capuano | Y | Y | Y | Y | Y |
| 9 Lynch | Y | Y | Y | ? | Y |
| 10 Delahunt | Y | Y | Y | Y | Y |
| **MICHIGAN** | | | | | |
| 1 Stupak | Y | ? | Y | Y | Y |
| 2 Hoekstra | ? | ? | ? | ? | ? |
| 3 Ehlers | ? | ? | ? | Y | Y |
| 4 Camp | Y | Y | Y | Y | Y |
| 5 Kildee | Y | Y | Y | Y | Y |
| 6 Upton | Y | Y | Y | Y | Y |
| 7 Schwarz | Y | Y | Y | Y | Y |
| 8 Rogers | Y | Y | Y | Y | Y |
| 9 Knollenberg | Y | Y | Y | Y | Y |
| 10 Miller | Y | Y | Y | Y | Y |
| 11 McCotter | Y | Y | Y | Y | Y |
| 12 Levin | Y | Y | Y | Y | Y |
| 13 Kilpatrick | Y | Y | ? | Y | Y |
| 14 Conyers | Y | ? | Y | Y | Y |
| 15 Dingell | Y | Y | Y | Y | Y |

| | 91 | 92 | 93 | 94 | 95 |
|---|---|---|---|---|---|
| **MINNESOTA** | | | | | |
| 1 Gutknecht | Y | Y | Y | Y | Y |
| 2 Kline | Y | Y | Y | Y | Y |
| 3 Ramstad | Y | Y | Y | Y | Y |
| 4 McCollum | Y | Y | Y | Y | Y |
| 5 Sabo | Y | Y | Y | Y | Y |
| 6 Kennedy | Y | Y | Y | Y | Y |
| 7 Peterson | Y | Y | Y | Y | Y |
| 8 Oberstar | Y | Y | Y | Y | Y |
| **MISSISSIPPI** | | | | | |
| 1 Wicker | Y | Y | Y | Y | Y |
| 2 Thompson | Y | Y | Y | Y | Y |
| 3 Pickering | Y | Y | Y | Y | Y |
| 4 Taylor | Y | Y | Y | Y | Y |
| **MISSOURI** | | | | | |
| 1 Clay | Y | Y | Y | Y | Y |
| 2 Akin | Y | Y | Y | Y | Y |
| 3 Carnahan | Y | Y | Y | Y | Y |
| 4 Skelton | Y | Y | Y | Y | Y |
| 5 Cleaver | Y | Y | Y | Y | Y |
| 6 Graves | Y | Y | Y | Y | Y |
| 7 Blunt | Y | Y | Y | Y | Y |
| 8 Emerson | Y | Y | Y | Y | Y |
| 9 Hulshof | Y | Y | Y | Y | Y |
| **MONTANA** | | | | | |
| AL Rehberg | Y | Y | Y | Y | Y |
| **NEBRASKA** | | | | | |
| 1 Fortenberry | Y | Y | Y | Y | Y |
| 2 Terry | Y | Y | Y | Y | Y |
| 3 Osborne | Y | Y | Y | Y | Y |
| **NEVADA** | | | | | |
| 1 Berkley | Y | Y | Y | Y | Y |
| 2 Gibbons | Y | Y | Y | Y | Y |
| 3 Porter | Y | Y | Y | Y | Y |
| **NEW HAMPSHIRE** | | | | | |
| 1 Bradley | Y | Y | Y | Y | Y |
| 2 Bass | Y | Y | Y | Y | Y |
| **NEW JERSEY** | | | | | |
| 1 Andrews | Y | Y | Y | Y | Y |
| 2 LoBiondo | Y | Y | Y | Y | Y |
| 3 Saxton | Y | Y | Y | Y | Y |
| 4 Smith | Y | Y | Y | Y | Y |
| 5 Garrett | Y | Y | Y | Y | Y |
| 6 Pallone | Y | Y | Y | Y | Y |
| 7 Ferguson | ? | ? | ? | Y | Y |
| 8 Pascrell | Y | Y | Y | Y | Y |
| 9 Rothman | Y | Y | Y | Y | Y |
| 10 Payne | ? | ? | ? | Y | Y |
| 11 Frelinghuysen | Y | Y | Y | Y | Y |
| 12 Holt | Y | Y | Y | Y | Y |
| 13 Menendez | Y | Y | Y | Y | Y |
| **NEW MEXICO** | | | | | |
| 1 Wilson | Y | Y | Y | Y | Y |
| 2 Pearce | Y | Y | Y | Y | Y |
| 3 Udall | Y | Y | Y | Y | Y |
| **NEW YORK** | | | | | |
| 1 Bishop | Y | Y | Y | Y | Y |
| 2 Israel | Y | Y | Y | Y | Y |
| 3 King | Y | Y | Y | Y | Y |
| 4 McCarthy | Y | Y | Y | Y | Y |
| 5 Ackerman | Y | Y | Y | Y | Y |
| 6 Meeks | Y | Y | Y | Y | Y |
| 7 Crowley | Y | Y | Y | Y | Y |
| 8 Nadler | Y | Y | Y | Y | Y |
| 9 Weiner | Y | Y | Y | Y | Y |
| 10 Towns | Y | Y | Y | Y | Y |
| 11 Owens | Y | Y | Y | Y | Y |
| 12 Velázquez | Y | Y | Y | Y | Y |
| 13 Fossella | Y | Y | Y | Y | Y |
| 14 Maloney | Y | Y | Y | Y | Y |
| 15 Rangel | ? | ? | ? | ? | ? |
| 16 Serrano | Y | Y | Y | Y | Y |
| 17 Engel | Y | Y | Y | Y | Y |
| 18 Lowey | Y | Y | Y | Y | Y |
| 19 Kelly | Y | Y | Y | Y | Y |
| 20 Sweeney | Y | Y | Y | Y | Y |
| 21 McNulty | Y | Y | Y | Y | Y |
| 22 Hinchey | Y | Y | Y | Y | Y |
| 23 McHugh | Y | Y | Y | Y | Y |
| 24 Boehlert | Y | Y | Y | Y | Y |
| 25 Walsh | Y | Y | Y | Y | Y |
| 26 Reynolds | Y | Y | Y | Y | Y |
| 27 Higgins | Y | Y | Y | Y | Y |
| 28 Slaughter | Y | Y | Y | Y | Y |
| 29 Kuhl | Y | Y | Y | Y | Y |

| | 91 | 92 | 93 | 94 | 95 |
|---|---|---|---|---|---|
| **NORTH CAROLINA** | | | | | |
| 1 Butterfield | Y | Y | Y | Y | Y |
| 2 Etheridge | Y | Y | Y | Y | Y |
| 3 Jones | Y | Y | Y | Y | ? |
| 4 Price | Y | Y | Y | Y | Y |
| 5 Foxx | Y | Y | Y | Y | Y |
| 6 Coble | ? | ? | ? | Y | Y |
| 7 McIntyre | Y | Y | Y | Y | Y |
| 8 Hayes | Y | Y | Y | Y | Y |
| 9 Myrick | Y | Y | Y | Y | Y |
| 10 McHenry | Y | Y | Y | Y | Y |
| 11 Taylor | Y | Y | Y | Y | Y |
| 12 Watt | Y | Y | Y | Y | Y |
| 13 Miller | Y | Y | Y | Y | Y |
| **NORTH DAKOTA** | | | | | |
| AL Pomeroy | Y | Y | Y | Y | Y |
| **OHIO** | | | | | |
| 1 Chabot | Y | Y | Y | Y | Y |
| 2 Portman | Y | Y | Y | Y | Y |
| 3 Turner | Y | Y | Y | Y | Y |
| 4 Oxley | Y | Y | Y | Y | Y |
| 5 Gillmor | Y | Y | Y | Y | Y |
| 6 Strickland | Y | Y | Y | Y | Y |
| 7 Hobson | Y | Y | Y | ? | ? |
| 8 Boehner | ? | Y | Y | Y | Y |
| 9 Kaptur | Y | Y | Y | Y | Y |
| 10 Kucinich | Y | Y | Y | Y | Y |
| 11 Jones | Y | Y | Y | Y | Y |
| 12 Tiberi | Y | Y | Y | Y | Y |
| 13 Brown | ? | ? | ? | ? | ? |
| 14 LaTourette | Y | ? | Y | Y | Y |
| 15 Pryce | Y | Y | Y | Y | Y |
| 16 Regula | Y | Y | Y | Y | Y |
| 17 Ryan | ? | Y | Y | Y | Y |
| 18 Ney | Y | Y | Y | Y | Y |
| **OKLAHOMA** | | | | | |
| 1 Sullivan | Y | Y | Y | Y | Y |
| 2 Boren | Y | Y | Y | Y | Y |
| 3 Lucas | Y | Y | Y | Y | Y |
| 4 Cole | Y | Y | Y | Y | Y |
| 5 Istook | Y | Y | Y | + | Y |
| **OREGON** | | | | | |
| 1 Wu | Y | Y | Y | Y | Y |
| 2 Walden | Y | Y | Y | Y | Y |
| 3 Blumenauer | Y | Y | Y | Y | Y |
| 4 DeFazio | Y | Y | Y | Y | Y |
| 5 Hooley | Y | Y | Y | Y | Y |
| **PENNSYLVANIA** | | | | | |
| 1 Brady | Y | Y | Y | Y | Y |
| 2 Fattah | ? | ? | ? | Y | Y |
| 3 English | Y | Y | Y | Y | Y |
| 4 Hart | Y | Y | Y | Y | Y |
| 5 Peterson | Y | Y | Y | Y | Y |
| 6 Gerlach | Y | Y | Y | Y | Y |
| 7 Weldon | Y | Y | Y | Y | Y |
| 8 Fitzpatrick | Y | Y | Y | Y | Y |
| 9 Shuster | Y | Y | Y | Y | Y |
| 10 Sherwood | Y | Y | Y | Y | Y |
| 11 Kanjorski | Y | Y | Y | Y | Y |
| 12 Murtha | Y | Y | Y | Y | Y |
| 13 Schwartz | Y | Y | Y | Y | Y |
| 14 Doyle | Y | Y | Y | Y | Y |
| 15 Dent | Y | Y | Y | Y | Y |
| 16 Pitts | Y | Y | Y | Y | Y |
| 17 Holden | Y | Y | Y | Y | Y |
| 18 Murphy | Y | Y | Y | Y | Y |
| 19 Platts | ? | Y | Y | Y | Y |
| **RHODE ISLAND** | | | | | |
| 1 Kennedy | Y | Y | Y | Y | Y |
| 2 Langevin | Y | Y | Y | Y | Y |
| **SOUTH CAROLINA** | | | | | |
| 1 Brown | Y | Y | Y | Y | Y |
| 2 Wilson | Y | Y | Y | Y | Y |
| 3 Barrett | Y | Y | Y | Y | Y |
| 4 Inglis | Y | Y | Y | Y | Y |
| 5 Spratt | Y | Y | Y | Y | Y |
| 6 Clyburn | Y | Y | Y | ? | ? |
| **SOUTH DAKOTA** | | | | | |
| AL Herseth | Y | Y | Y | Y | Y |
| **TENNESSEE** | | | | | |
| 1 Jenkins | Y | Y | Y | Y | Y |
| 2 Duncan | Y | Y | Y | Y | Y |

| | 91 | 92 | 93 | 94 | 95 |
|---|---|---|---|---|---|
| 3 Wamp | Y | Y | Y | Y | Y |
| 4 Davis | Y | Y | Y | Y | Y |
| 5 Cooper | Y | Y | Y | Y | Y |
| 6 Gordon | Y | Y | Y | Y | Y |
| 7 Blackburn | Y | Y | Y | Y | Y |
| 8 Tanner | Y | Y | Y | Y | Y |
| 9 Ford | Y | Y | Y | Y | Y |
| **TEXAS** | | | | | |
| 1 Gohmert | Y | Y | ? | Y | ? |
| 2 Poe | Y | Y | Y | Y | Y |
| 3 Johnson, S. | Y | Y | Y | Y | Y |
| 4 Hall | Y | Y | Y | Y | Y |
| 5 Hensarling | Y | Y | Y | Y | Y |
| 6 Barton | Y | Y | Y | Y | Y |
| 7 Culberson | ? | Y | Y | Y | Y |
| 8 Brady | Y | Y | Y | Y | Y |
| 9 Green | Y | Y | Y | Y | Y |
| 10 McCaul | Y | Y | Y | Y | Y |
| 11 Conaway | Y | Y | Y | Y | Y |
| 12 Granger | ? | ? | ? | Y | Y |
| 13 Thornberry | Y | Y | Y | Y | Y |
| 14 Paul | Y | Y | Y | Y | N |
| 15 Hinojosa | Y | Y | Y | Y | Y |
| 16 Reyes | Y | Y | Y | Y | Y |
| 17 Edwards | Y | Y | Y | Y | Y |
| 18 Jackson-Lee | + | + | + | Y | Y |
| 19 Neugebauer | + | + | + | Y | Y |
| 20 Gonzalez | Y | Y | Y | Y | Y |
| 21 Smith | Y | Y | Y | Y | Y |
| 22 DeLay | Y | Y | Y | Y | ? |
| 23 Bonilla | Y | Y | Y | Y | Y |
| 24 Marchant | Y | Y | Y | Y | Y |
| 25 Doggett | Y | Y | Y | Y | Y |
| 26 Burgess | Y | Y | Y | Y | Y |
| 27 Ortiz | Y | Y | Y | Y | Y |
| 28 Cuellar | Y | Y | Y | Y | Y |
| 29 Green | Y | Y | Y | Y | Y |
| 30 Johnson, E. | Y | Y | Y | Y | Y |
| 31 Carter | Y | Y | Y | Y | Y |
| 32 Sessions | Y | Y | Y | Y | Y |
| **UTAH** | | | | | |
| 1 Bishop | Y | Y | Y | Y | Y |
| 2 Matheson | Y | Y | Y | Y | Y |
| 3 Cannon | Y | Y | Y | Y | Y |
| **VERMONT** | | | | | |
| AL *Sanders* | Y | Y | Y | Y | Y |
| **VIRGINIA** | | | | | |
| 1 Davis, J. | Y | Y | Y | Y | Y |
| 2 Drake | Y | Y | Y | Y | Y |
| 3 Scott | ? | ? | ? | Y | Y |
| 4 Forbes | Y | Y | Y | ? | ? |
| 5 Goode | Y | Y | Y | Y | Y |
| 6 Goodlatte | Y | Y | Y | Y | Y |
| 7 Cantor | Y | Y | Y | Y | Y |
| 8 Moran | Y | Y | Y | Y | Y |
| 9 Boucher | Y | Y | Y | Y | Y |
| 10 Wolf | Y | Y | Y | Y | Y |
| 11 Davis, T. | Y | Y | Y | Y | Y |
| **WASHINGTON** | | | | | |
| 1 Inslee | Y | Y | Y | Y | Y |
| 2 Larsen | Y | Y | Y | Y | Y |
| 3 Baird | ? | ? | ? | ? | ? |
| 4 Hastings | Y | Y | Y | Y | Y |
| 5 McMorris | Y | Y | Y | Y | Y |
| 6 Dicks | Y | Y | Y | Y | Y |
| 7 McDermott | Y | Y | Y | Y | Y |
| 8 Reichert | Y | Y | Y | Y | Y |
| 9 Smith | Y | Y | Y | Y | Y |
| **WEST VIRGINIA** | | | | | |
| 1 Mollohan | Y | Y | Y | Y | Y |
| 2 Capito | Y | Y | Y | Y | Y |
| 3 Rahall | Y | Y | Y | Y | Y |
| **WISCONSIN** | | | | | |
| 1 Ryan | Y | Y | Y | Y | Y |
| 2 Baldwin | Y | Y | Y | Y | Y |
| 3 Kind | Y | Y | Y | Y | Y |
| 4 Moore | Y | Y | Y | Y | Y |
| 5 Sensenbrenner | Y | Y | Y | Y | Y |
| 6 Petri | Y | Y | Y | Y | Y |
| 7 Obey | Y | Y | Y | Y | Y |
| 8 Green | Y | Y | Y | Y | Y |
| **WYOMING** | | | | | |
| AL Cubin | Y | Y | Y | ? | ? |

# IN THE HOUSE | By Vote Number

**96.** **HR 135. Water Commission/Passage.** Duncan, R-Tenn., motion to suspend the rules and pass the bill that would authorize $9 million to establish the 21st Century Water Commission, responsible for projecting future water supply and demand as well as studying current public and private water management programs, and developing recommendations for a comprehensive water strategy. Motion agreed to 402-22: R 204-22; D 197-0 (ND 148-0, SD 49-0); I 1-0. A two-thirds majority of those present and voting (283 in this case) is required for passage under suspension of the rules. April 12, 2005.

**97.** **HR 541. Nevada Land Conveyance/Passage.** Duncan, R-Tenn., motion to suspend the rules and pass the bill that would convey 8.75 acres from Kingston Cemetery to go to Lander County, Nev., and 10 acres from Maiden's Grave Cemetery to Eureka County, Nev., and would require that the land be used as a cemetery. Motion agreed to 423-0: R 225-0; D 197-0 (ND 148-0, SD 49-0); I 1-0. A two-thirds majority of those present and voting (282 in this case) is required for passage under suspension of the rules. April 12, 2005.

**98.** **HR 1463. Justin W. Williams Tribute/Passage.** Shuster, R-Pa., motion to suspend the rules and pass the bill that would designate a portion of a federal building in Alexandria, Va., after the late Justin W. Williams, an attorney who worked in the Justice Department for many years. Motion agreed to 427-0: R 227-0; D 199-0 (ND 149-0, SD 50-0); I 1-0. A two-thirds majority of those present and voting (285 in this case) is required for passage under suspension of the rules. April 13, 2005.

**99.** **HR 787. Robert T. Matsui Courthouse/Passage.** Shuster, R-Pa., motion to suspend the rules and pass the bill that would name a federal courthouse in Sacramento, Calif., after former Rep. Robert T. Matsui, D-Calif. (1979-2005), who died Jan. 1 after 26 years in office. Motion agreed to 426-0: R 225-0; D 200-0 (ND 150-0, SD 50-0); I 1-0. A two-thirds majority of those present and voting (284 in this case) is required for passage under suspension of the rules. April 13, 2005.

**100.** **HR 8. Estate Tax Permanent Repeal/Previous Question.** Hastings, R-Wash., motion to order the previous question (thus ending debate and possibility of amendment) on adoption of the rule (H Res 202) to provide for House floor consideration of the bill that would permanently repeal the estate tax. Motion agreed to 237-195: R 230-0; D 7-194 (ND 3-147, SD 4-47); I 0-1. (Subsequently, the rule was adopted by voice vote.) April 13, 2005.

**101.** **HR 8. Estate Tax Permanent Repeal/Democratic Substitute.** Pomeroy, D-N.D., substitute amendment that would increase the estate tax exemption to $3 million for individuals and $6 million for married couples in 2006. In 2009, the exemption would increase to $3.5 million for individuals and $7 million for married couples. The substitute would freeze the maximum estate tax at the current rate of 47 percent and reinstate the 5 percent surtax on estates valued at more than $10 million that was repealed under the 2001 tax law. Rejected 194-238: R 1-228; D 193-9 (ND 145-6, SD 48-3); I 0-1. April 13, 2005.

**102.** **HR 8. Estate Tax Permanent Repeal/Passage.** Passage of the bill that would make permanent the repeal of the estate tax contained in the 2001 tax cut law (PL 107-16) and which is set to expire after 2010. Passed 272-162: R 230-1; D 42-160 (ND 23-128, SD 19-32); I 0-1. A "yea" was a vote in support of the president's position. April 13, 2005.

| | 96 | 97 | 98 | 99 | 100 | 101 | 102 |
|---|---|---|---|---|---|---|---|
| **ALABAMA** | | | | | | | |
| 1 Bonner | Y | Y | Y | Y | Y | N | Y |
| 2 Everett | Y | Y | Y | Y | Y | N | Y |
| 3 Rogers | Y | Y | Y | Y | Y | N | Y |
| 4 Aderholt | Y | Y | Y | Y | Y | N | Y |
| 5 Cramer | Y | Y | Y | Y | Y | N | Y |
| 6 Bachus | Y | Y | Y | Y | Y | N | Y |
| 7 Davis | Y | Y | Y | Y | N | Y | Y |
| **ALASKA** | | | | | | | |
| AL Young | Y | Y | Y | Y | Y | N | Y |
| **ARIZONA** | | | | | | | |
| 1 Renzi | Y | Y | Y | Y | Y | N | Y |
| 2 Franks | Y | Y | Y | Y | Y | N | Y |
| 3 Shadegg | Y | Y | Y | Y | Y | N | Y |
| 4 Pastor | Y | Y | Y | Y | N | N | N |
| 5 Hayworth | Y | Y | Y | Y | Y | N | Y |
| 6 Flake | N | Y | Y | Y | Y | N | Y |
| 7 Grijalva | Y | Y | Y | Y | N | Y | N |
| 8 Kolbe | Y | Y | Y | Y | Y | N | Y |
| **ARKANSAS** | | | | | | | |
| 1 Berry | Y | Y | Y | Y | N | Y | Y |
| 2 Snyder | Y | Y | Y | Y | N | Y | N |
| 3 Boozman | Y | Y | Y | Y | Y | N | Y |
| 4 Ross | Y | Y | Y | Y | N | Y | Y |
| **CALIFORNIA** | | | | | | | |
| 1 Thompson | Y | Y | Y | Y | N | Y | N |
| 2 Herger | Y | Y | Y | Y | Y | N | Y |
| 3 Lungren | Y | Y | Y | Y | Y | N | Y |
| 4 Doolittle | Y | Y | + | + | Y | N | Y |
| 5 Matsui, D. | Y | Y | Y | Y | N | Y | N |
| 6 Woolsey | Y | Y | Y | Y | N | Y | N |
| 7 Miller, George | Y | ? | Y | Y | N | Y | N |
| 8 Pelosi | Y | Y | Y | Y | N | Y | N |
| 9 Lee | Y | Y | Y | Y | N | Y | N |
| 10 Tauscher | Y | Y | Y | Y | N | Y | N |
| 11 Pombo | Y | Y | Y | Y | Y | N | Y |
| 12 Lantos | Y | Y | Y | Y | N | Y | N |
| 13 Stark | ? | ? | Y | Y | N | Y | N |
| 14 Eshoo | Y | Y | Y | Y | N | Y | N |
| 15 Honda | Y | Y | Y | Y | N | Y | N |
| 16 Lofgren | Y | Y | Y | Y | N | Y | N |
| 17 Farr | Y | Y | Y | Y | N | Y | Y |
| 18 Cardoza | Y | Y | Y | Y | N | Y | N |
| 19 Radanovich | Y | Y | Y | Y | Y | N | Y |
| 20 Costa | Y | Y | Y | Y | N | Y | Y |
| 21 Nunes | Y | Y | Y | Y | Y | N | Y |
| 22 Thomas | Y | Y | Y | Y | Y | N | Y |
| 23 Capps | Y | Y | Y | Y | N | Y | N |
| 24 Gallegly | Y | Y | Y | Y | Y | N | Y |
| 25 McKeon | Y | Y | Y | Y | Y | N | Y |
| 26 Dreier | Y | Y | Y | Y | Y | N | Y |
| 27 Sherman | Y | Y | Y | Y | N | Y | N |
| 28 Berman | Y | Y | Y | Y | N | Y | N |
| 29 Schiff | Y | Y | Y | Y | N | Y | N |
| 30 Waxman | Y | Y | Y | Y | N | Y | N |
| 31 Becerra | Y | Y | Y | Y | N | Y | N |
| 32 Solis | Y | Y | Y | Y | N | Y | N |
| 33 Watson | Y | Y | Y | Y | N | Y | N |
| 34 Roybal-Allard | Y | Y | Y | Y | N | Y | N |
| 35 Waters | Y | Y | Y | Y | N | Y | N |
| 36 Harman | Y | Y | Y | Y | N | Y | N |
| 37 Millender-McD. | Y | Y | Y | Y | N | Y | N |
| 38 Napolitano | Y | Y | Y | Y | N | Y | N |
| 39 Sánchez, Linda | Y | Y | Y | Y | N | Y | N |
| 40 Royce | Y | Y | Y | Y | Y | N | Y |
| 41 Lewis | Y | Y | Y | Y | Y | N | Y |
| 42 Miller, Gary | Y | Y | Y | Y | Y | N | Y |
| 43 Baca | Y | Y | Y | Y | N | Y | N |
| 44 Calvert | Y | Y | Y | ? | Y | N | Y |
| 45 Bono | Y | Y | Y | Y | Y | N | Y |
| 46 Rohrabacher | Y | Y | Y | Y | Y | N | Y |
| 47 Sanchez, Loretta | Y | Y | Y | Y | N | Y | N |
| 48 Cox | Y | Y | Y | Y | Y | N | Y |
| 49 Issa | Y | Y | Y | Y | Y | N | Y |

| | 96 | 97 | 98 | 99 | 100 | 101 | 102 |
|---|---|---|---|---|---|---|---|
| 50 Cunningham | Y | Y | Y | Y | Y | N | Y |
| 51 Filner | Y | Y | Y | Y | N | Y | N |
| 52 Hunter | Y | Y | ? | Y | Y | N | Y |
| 53 Davis | Y | Y | Y | Y | N | Y | N |
| **COLORADO** | | | | | | | |
| 1 DeGette | Y | Y | Y | Y | N | Y | N |
| 2 Udall | Y | Y | Y | Y | N | Y | N |
| 3 Salazar | Y | Y | Y | Y | N | Y | Y |
| 4 Musgrave | Y | Y | Y | Y | Y | N | Y |
| 5 Hefley | Y | Y | Y | Y | Y | N | Y |
| 6 Tancredo | Y | Y | Y | Y | Y | N | Y |
| 7 Beauprez | Y | Y | Y | Y | Y | N | Y |
| **CONNECTICUT** | | | | | | | |
| 1 Larson | Y | Y | Y | Y | N | Y | N |
| 2 Simmons | Y | Y | Y | Y | Y | N | Y |
| 3 DeLauro | Y | Y | Y | Y | N | Y | N |
| 4 Shays | Y | Y | Y | Y | Y | N | Y |
| 5 Johnson | Y | Y | Y | Y | Y | N | Y |
| **DELAWARE** | | | | | | | |
| AL Castle | Y | Y | Y | Y | Y | Y | Y |
| **FLORIDA** | | | | | | | |
| 1 Miller | N | Y | Y | Y | Y | N | Y |
| 2 Boyd | Y | Y | Y | Y | N | Y | N |
| 3 Brown | Y | Y | Y | Y | N | Y | N |
| 4 Crenshaw | Y | Y | Y | Y | Y | N | Y |
| 5 Brown-Waite | Y | Y | Y | Y | Y | N | Y |
| 6 Stearns | Y | Y | Y | Y | Y | N | Y |
| 7 Mica | Y | Y | Y | Y | Y | N | Y |
| 8 Keller | Y | Y | Y | ? | Y | N | Y |
| 9 Bilirakis | Y | Y | Y | Y | Y | N | Y |
| 10 Young | Y | Y | Y | Y | Y | N | Y |
| 11 Davis | Y | Y | Y | Y | N | Y | N |
| 12 Putnam | Y | Y | Y | Y | Y | N | Y |
| 13 Harris | Y | Y | Y | Y | Y | N | Y |
| 14 Mack | Y | Y | Y | Y | Y | N | Y |
| 15 Weldon | Y | Y | Y | Y | Y | N | Y |
| 16 Foley | Y | Y | Y | Y | Y | N | Y |
| 17 Meek | Y | Y | Y | Y | N | Y | N |
| 18 Ros-Lehtinen | Y | Y | Y | Y | Y | N | Y |
| 19 Wexler | Y | Y | Y | Y | N | Y | N |
| 20 Wasserman-Schultz | Y | Y | Y | Y | N | Y | N |
| 21 Diaz-Balart, L. | Y | Y | Y | Y | Y | N | Y |
| 22 Shaw | Y | Y | Y | Y | Y | N | Y |
| 23 Hastings | Y | Y | Y | Y | N | Y | N |
| 24 Feeney | Y | Y | Y | Y | Y | N | Y |
| 25 Diaz-Balart, M. | Y | Y | Y | Y | Y | N | Y |
| **GEORGIA** | | | | | | | |
| 1 Kingston | Y | Y | Y | Y | Y | N | Y |
| 2 Bishop | Y | Y | Y | Y | N | Y | Y |
| 3 Marshall | Y | Y | Y | Y | N | Y | Y |
| 4 McKinney | Y | Y | Y | Y | N | Y | N |
| 5 Lewis | Y | Y | Y | Y | N | Y | N |
| 6 Price | Y | Y | Y | Y | Y | N | Y |
| 7 Linder | Y | Y | Y | Y | Y | N | Y |
| 8 Westmoreland | Y | Y | Y | Y | Y | N | Y |
| 9 Norwood | Y | Y | Y | ? | Y | N | Y |
| 10 Deal | Y | Y | Y | ? | Y | N | Y |
| 11 Gingrey | Y | Y | Y | Y | Y | N | Y |
| 12 Barrow | Y | Y | Y | Y | N | Y | Y |
| 13 Scott | Y | Y | Y | Y | N | Y | N |
| **HAWAII** | | | | | | | |
| 1 Abercrombie | Y | Y | Y | Y | N | N | N |
| 2 Case | Y | Y | Y | Y | N | Y | N |
| **IDAHO** | | | | | | | |
| 1 Otter | N | Y | Y | Y | Y | N | Y |
| 2 Simpson | Y | Y | Y | Y | Y | N | Y |
| **ILLINOIS** | | | | | | | |
| 1 Rush | Y | Y | Y | Y | Y | N | N |
| 2 Jackson | Y | Y | Y | Y | N | Y | N |
| 3 Lipinski | Y | Y | Y | Y | N | Y | N |
| 4 Gutierrez | Y | Y | Y | Y | N | Y | N |
| 5 Emanuel | Y | Y | Y | Y | N | Y | N |
| 6 Hyde | Y | Y | Y | Y | Y | N | Y |
| 7 Davis | Y | Y | Y | Y | N | Y | N |
| 8 Bean | Y | Y | Y | Y | N | Y | Y |
| 9 Schakowsky | Y | Y | Y | Y | N | Y | N |
| 10 Kirk | Y | Y | Y | Y | Y | N | Y |
| 11 Weller | Y | Y | Y | Y | Y | N | Y |
| 12 Costello | Y | Y | Y | Y | N | Y | N |

**KEY**    Republicans    Democrats    *Independents*

| | | | | | |
|---|---|---|---|---|---|
| Y | Voted for (yea) | X | Paired against | C | Voted "present" to avoid possible conflict of interest |
| # | Paired for | – | Announced against | | |
| + | Announced for | P | Voted "present" | ? | Did not vote or otherwise make a position known |
| N | Voted against (nay) | | | | |

| | 96 | 97 | 98 | 99 | 100 | 101 | 102 |
|---|---|---|---|---|---|---|---|
| 13 **Biggert** | Y | Y | Y | Y | Y | N | Y |
| 14 **Hastert** | | | | | | | Y |
| 15 **Johnson** | Y | Y | Y | Y | Y | N | Y |
| 16 **Manzullo** | N | Y | Y | Y | Y | N | Y |
| 17 Evans | Y | Y | Y | Y | N | Y | N |
| 18 **LaHood** | N | Y | Y | Y | Y | N | Y |
| 19 **Shimkus** | Y | Y | Y | Y | Y | N | Y |
| **INDIANA** | | | | | | | |
| 1 Visclosky | Y | Y | Y | Y | N | Y | N |
| 2 **Chocola** | Y | Y | Y | ? | Y | N | Y |
| 3 **Souder** | Y | Y | Y | Y | Y | N | Y |
| 4 **Buyer** | Y | Y | Y | Y | Y | N | Y |
| 5 **Burton** | Y | Y | Y | Y | Y | N | Y |
| 6 **Pence** | N | Y | Y | Y | Y | N | Y |
| 7 Carson | Y | Y | Y | Y | N | Y | N |
| 8 **Hostettler** | Y | Y | Y | Y | Y | N | Y |
| 9 **Sodrel** | Y | Y | Y | Y | Y | N | Y |
| **IOWA** | | | | | | | |
| 1 **Nussle** | Y | Y | Y | Y | Y | N | Y |
| 2 **Leach** | Y | Y | Y | Y | Y | N | N |
| 3 Boswell | Y | Y | Y | Y | N | Y | Y |
| 4 **Latham** | Y | Y | Y | Y | Y | N | Y |
| 5 **King** | Y | Y | Y | Y | Y | N | Y |
| **KANSAS** | | | | | | | |
| 1 **Moran** | Y | Y | Y | Y | Y | N | Y |
| 2 **Ryun** | Y | Y | Y | Y | Y | N | Y |
| 3 Moore | Y | Y | Y | Y | N | Y | N |
| 4 **Tiahrt** | Y | Y | Y | Y | Y | N | Y |
| **KENTUCKY** | | | | | | | |
| 1 **Whitfield** | Y | Y | Y | Y | Y | N | Y |
| 2 **Lewis** | + | + | Y | Y | Y | N | Y |
| 3 **Northup** | Y | Y | Y | Y | Y | N | Y |
| 4 **Davis** | Y | Y | Y | Y | Y | N | Y |
| 5 **Rogers** | Y | Y | Y | Y | Y | N | Y |
| 6 Chandler | Y | Y | Y | Y | N | Y | Y |
| **LOUISIANA** | | | | | | | |
| 1 **Jindal** | Y | Y | Y | Y | Y | - | Y |
| 2 Jefferson | Y | Y | Y | Y | N | Y | Y |
| 3 Melancon | Y | Y | Y | Y | N | Y | Y |
| 4 **McCrery** | Y | Y | Y | Y | Y | N | Y |
| 5 **Alexander** | Y | Y | Y | Y | Y | N | Y |
| 6 **Baker** | Y | Y | Y | Y | Y | N | Y |
| 7 **Boustany** | Y | Y | Y | Y | Y | N | Y |
| **MAINE** | | | | | | | |
| 1 Allen | Y | Y | Y | Y | N | Y | N |
| 2 Michaud | Y | Y | Y | Y | N | Y | N |
| **MARYLAND** | | | | | | | |
| 1 **Gilchrest** | Y | Y | Y | Y | Y | N | Y |
| 2 Ruppersberger | Y | Y | Y | Y | N | Y | Y |
| 3 Cardin | Y | Y | Y | Y | N | Y | N |
| 4 Wynn | Y | Y | Y | Y | N | Y | Y |
| 5 Hoyer | Y | Y | Y | Y | N | Y | N |
| 6 **Bartlett** | Y | Y | Y | Y | Y | N | Y |
| 7 Cummings | Y | Y | Y | Y | N | Y | N |
| 8 Van Hollen | Y | Y | Y | Y | N | Y | N |
| **MASSACHUSETTS** | | | | | | | |
| 1 Olver | Y | Y | Y | Y | N | N | N |
| 2 Neal | Y | Y | Y | Y | N | Y | N |
| 3 McGovern | Y | Y | Y | Y | N | Y | N |
| 4 Frank | Y | Y | Y | Y | N | Y | N |
| 5 Meehan | Y | Y | Y | Y | N | Y | N |
| 6 Tierney | Y | Y | Y | Y | N | Y | N |
| 7 Markey | Y | Y | Y | Y | N | Y | N |
| 8 Capuano | Y | Y | Y | Y | N | Y | N |
| 9 Lynch | Y | Y | Y | Y | N | Y | N |
| 10 Delahunt | Y | Y | Y | Y | N | Y | N |
| **MICHIGAN** | | | | | | | |
| 1 Stupak | Y | Y | Y | Y | N | Y | N |
| 2 **Hoekstra** | Y | Y | Y | Y | Y | N | Y |
| 3 **Ehlers** | Y | Y | Y | Y | Y | N | Y |
| 4 **Camp** | Y | Y | Y | Y | Y | N | Y |
| 5 Kildee | Y | Y | Y | Y | N | Y | N |
| 6 **Upton** | Y | Y | Y | Y | Y | N | Y |
| 7 **Schwarz** | Y | Y | Y | Y | Y | N | Y |
| 8 **Rogers** | Y | Y | Y | Y | Y | N | Y |
| 9 **Knollenberg** | Y | Y | Y | Y | Y | N | Y |
| 10 **Miller** | N | Y | Y | Y | Y | N | Y |
| 11 **McCotter** | Y | Y | Y | Y | Y | N | Y |
| 12 Levin | Y | Y | Y | Y | N | Y | N |
| 13 Kilpatrick | Y | Y | Y | Y | N | Y | N |
| 14 Conyers | Y | Y | Y | Y | N | Y | N |
| 15 Dingell | Y | Y | Y | Y | N | Y | N |
| **MINNESOTA** | | | | | | | |
| 1 **Gutknecht** | N | Y | Y | Y | Y | N | Y |
| 2 **Kline** | Y | Y | Y | Y | Y | N | Y |
| 3 **Ramstad** | Y | Y | Y | Y | Y | N | Y |
| 4 McCollum | Y | Y | Y | Y | N | Y | N |
| 5 Sabo | Y | Y | Y | Y | N | Y | N |
| 6 **Kennedy** | Y | Y | Y | Y | Y | N | Y |
| 7 Peterson | Y | Y | Y | Y | N | Y | Y |
| 8 Oberstar | Y | Y | Y | Y | N | Y | N |
| **MISSISSIPPI** | | | | | | | |
| 1 **Wicker** | Y | Y | Y | Y | Y | N | Y |
| 2 Thompson | Y | Y | Y | Y | N | Y | N |
| 3 **Pickering** | Y | Y | Y | Y | Y | N | Y |
| 4 Taylor | Y | Y | Y | Y | N | Y | N |
| **MISSOURI** | | | | | | | |
| 1 Clay | Y | Y | Y | Y | N | Y | Y |
| 2 **Akin** | Y | Y | Y | Y | Y | N | Y |
| 3 Carnahan | Y | Y | Y | Y | N | Y | N |
| 4 Skelton | Y | Y | Y | Y | N | Y | Y |
| 5 Cleaver | Y | Y | Y | Y | N | Y | N |
| 6 **Graves** | Y | Y | Y | Y | Y | N | Y |
| 7 **Blunt** | Y | Y | Y | Y | Y | N | Y |
| 8 **Emerson** | N | Y | Y | Y | Y | N | Y |
| 9 **Hulshof** | Y | Y | Y | Y | Y | N | Y |
| **MONTANA** | | | | | | | |
| AL **Rehberg** | Y | Y | Y | Y | Y | N | Y |
| **NEBRASKA** | | | | | | | |
| 1 **Fortenberry** | Y | Y | Y | Y | Y | N | Y |
| 2 **Terry** | Y | Y | Y | Y | Y | N | Y |
| 3 **Osborne** | Y | Y | Y | Y | Y | N | Y |
| **NEVADA** | | | | | | | |
| 1 Berkley | Y | Y | Y | Y | N | Y | Y |
| 2 **Gibbons** | Y | Y | Y | Y | Y | N | Y |
| 3 **Porter** | Y | Y | Y | Y | Y | N | Y |
| **NEW HAMPSHIRE** | | | | | | | |
| 1 **Bradley** | Y | Y | Y | Y | Y | N | Y |
| 2 **Bass** | Y | Y | Y | Y | Y | N | Y |
| **NEW JERSEY** | | | | | | | |
| 1 Andrews | Y | Y | Y | Y | N | Y | N |
| 2 **LoBiondo** | Y | Y | Y | Y | Y | N | Y |
| 3 **Saxton** | Y | Y | Y | Y | Y | N | Y |
| 4 **Smith** | Y | Y | Y | Y | Y | N | Y |
| 5 **Garrett** | Y | Y | Y | Y | Y | N | Y |
| 6 Pallone | Y | Y | Y | Y | N | Y | N |
| 7 **Ferguson** | Y | Y | Y | Y | Y | N | Y |
| 8 Pascrell | Y | Y | Y | Y | N | Y | N |
| 9 Rothman | Y | Y | Y | Y | N | Y | N |
| 10 Payne | Y | Y | Y | Y | N | Y | N |
| 11 **Frelinghuysen** | Y | Y | ? | Y | Y | N | Y |
| 12 Holt | Y | Y | Y | Y | N | Y | N |
| 13 Menendez | Y | Y | Y | Y | N | Y | N |
| **NEW MEXICO** | | | | | | | |
| 1 **Wilson** | Y | Y | Y | Y | Y | N | Y |
| 2 **Pearce** | Y | Y | Y | Y | Y | N | Y |
| 3 Udall | Y | Y | Y | Y | N | Y | N |
| **NEW YORK** | | | | | | | |
| 1 Bishop | Y | Y | Y | Y | N | Y | N |
| 2 Israel | Y | Y | Y | Y | N | Y | Y |
| 3 **King** | Y | Y | Y | Y | Y | N | Y |
| 4 McCarthy | Y | Y | Y | Y | N | Y | Y |
| 5 Ackerman | Y | Y | Y | Y | N | Y | N |
| 6 Meeks | Y | Y | ? | Y | N | Y | N |
| 7 Crowley | Y | Y | Y | Y | N | Y | N |
| 8 Nadler | Y | Y | Y | Y | N | Y | N |
| 9 Weiner | Y | Y | Y | Y | N | Y | N |
| 10 Towns | Y | Y | Y | Y | N | Y | Y |
| 11 Owens | Y | Y | Y | Y | N | Y | N |
| 12 Velázquez | Y | Y | Y | Y | N | Y | N |
| 13 **Fossella** | Y | Y | Y | Y | Y | N | Y |
| 14 Maloney | Y | Y | Y | Y | N | Y | N |
| 15 Rangel | Y | Y | Y | Y | N | Y | N |
| 16 Serrano | Y | Y | Y | Y | N | Y | N |
| 17 Engel | Y | Y | Y | Y | N | Y | N |
| 18 Lowey | Y | Y | Y | Y | N | Y | N |
| 19 **Kelly** | Y | Y | Y | Y | Y | N | Y |
| 20 **Sweeney** | Y | Y | Y | Y | Y | N | Y |
| 21 McNulty | Y | Y | Y | Y | N | Y | N |
| 22 Hinchey | Y | Y | Y | Y | N | Y | N |
| 23 **McHugh** | Y | Y | Y | Y | Y | N | Y |
| 24 **Boehlert** | Y | Y | Y | Y | Y | N | Y |
| 25 **Walsh** | Y | Y | Y | Y | Y | N | Y |
| 26 **Reynolds** | Y | Y | Y | Y | Y | N | Y |
| 27 Higgins | Y | Y | Y | Y | N | Y | N |
| 28 Slaughter | Y | Y | Y | Y | N | Y | N |
| 29 **Kuhl** | Y | Y | Y | Y | Y | N | Y |
| **NORTH CAROLINA** | | | | | | | |
| 1 Butterfield | Y | Y | Y | Y | N | Y | Y |
| 2 Etheridge | Y | Y | Y | Y | N | Y | N |
| 3 **Jones** | N | Y | Y | Y | Y | N | Y |
| 4 Price | Y | Y | Y | Y | N | Y | N |
| 5 **Foxx** | N | Y | Y | Y | Y | N | Y |
| 6 **Coble** | N | Y | Y | Y | Y | N | Y |
| 7 McIntyre | Y | Y | Y | Y | N | Y | Y |
| 8 **Hayes** | Y | Y | Y | Y | Y | N | Y |
| 9 **Myrick** | N | Y | Y | Y | Y | N | Y |
| 10 **McHenry** | Y | Y | Y | Y | Y | N | Y |
| 11 **Taylor** | Y | Y | Y | Y | Y | N | Y |
| 12 Watt | Y | Y | Y | Y | N | Y | N |
| 13 Miller | Y | Y | Y | Y | N | Y | N |
| **NORTH DAKOTA** | | | | | | | |
| AL Pomeroy | Y | Y | Y | Y | N | Y | N |
| **OHIO** | | | | | | | |
| 1 **Chabot** | Y | Y | Y | Y | Y | N | Y |
| 2 **Portman** | Y | Y | Y | Y | Y | N | Y |
| 3 **Turner** | Y | Y | Y | Y | Y | N | Y |
| 4 **Oxley** | Y | Y | Y | Y | Y | N | Y |
| 5 **Gillmor** | ? | ? | ? | ? | ? | ? | ? |
| 6 Strickland | Y | Y | Y | Y | N | Y | N |
| 7 **Hobson** | Y | Y | Y | Y | Y | N | Y |
| 8 **Boehner** | Y | Y | Y | Y | Y | N | Y |
| 9 Kaptur | Y | Y | Y | Y | N | Y | N |
| 10 Kucinich | Y | Y | Y | Y | N | Y | N |
| 11 Jones | Y | Y | Y | Y | N | Y | N |
| 12 **Tiberi** | Y | Y | Y | Y | Y | N | Y |
| 13 Brown | Y | Y | Y | Y | N | Y | N |
| 14 **LaTourette** | Y | Y | Y | Y | Y | N | Y |
| 15 **Pryce** | Y | Y | Y | Y | Y | N | Y |
| 16 **Regula** | Y | Y | Y | Y | Y | N | Y |
| 17 Ryan | Y | Y | Y | Y | N | Y | Y |
| 18 **Ney** | Y | Y | Y | Y | Y | N | Y |
| **OKLAHOMA** | | | | | | | |
| 1 **Sullivan** | Y | Y | Y | Y | Y | N | Y |
| 2 Boren | Y | Y | Y | Y | N | Y | Y |
| 3 **Lucas** | Y | Y | Y | Y | Y | N | Y |
| 4 **Cole** | Y | Y | Y | Y | Y | N | Y |
| 5 **Istook** | N | Y | Y | Y | Y | N | Y |
| **OREGON** | | | | | | | |
| 1 Wu | Y | Y | Y | Y | N | Y | N |
| 2 **Walden** | Y | Y | Y | Y | Y | N | Y |
| 3 Blumenauer | Y | Y | Y | Y | N | Y | N |
| 4 DeFazio | Y | Y | Y | Y | N | Y | N |
| 5 Hooley | Y | Y | Y | Y | N | Y | Y |
| **PENNSYLVANIA** | | | | | | | |
| 1 Brady | Y | Y | Y | Y | N | N | N |
| 2 Fattah | ? | Y | Y | Y | N | Y | N |
| 3 **English** | Y | Y | Y | Y | Y | N | Y |
| 4 **Hart** | Y | Y | Y | Y | Y | N | Y |
| 5 **Peterson** | Y | Y | Y | Y | Y | N | Y |
| 6 **Gerlach** | Y | Y | Y | Y | Y | N | Y |
| 7 **Weldon** | Y | Y | Y | Y | Y | N | Y |
| 8 **Fitzpatrick** | Y | Y | Y | Y | Y | N | Y |
| 9 **Shuster** | Y | Y | Y | Y | Y | N | Y |
| 10 **Sherwood** | Y | Y | Y | Y | Y | N | Y |
| 11 Kanjorski | Y | Y | Y | Y | N | Y | N |
| 12 Murtha | Y | Y | Y | Y | N | N | N |
| 13 Schwartz | Y | Y | Y | Y | N | Y | N |
| 14 Doyle | Y | Y | Y | Y | N | Y | N |
| 15 **Dent** | Y | Y | Y | Y | Y | N | Y |
| 16 **Pitts** | Y | Y | Y | Y | Y | N | Y |
| 17 Holden | Y | Y | Y | Y | N | Y | N |
| 18 **Murphy** | Y | Y | Y | Y | Y | N | Y |
| 19 **Platts** | Y | Y | Y | Y | Y | N | Y |
| **RHODE ISLAND** | | | | | | | |
| 1 Kennedy | Y | Y | Y | Y | N | Y | N |
| 2 Langevin | Y | Y | Y | Y | N | Y | N |
| **SOUTH CAROLINA** | | | | | | | |
| 1 **Brown** | Y | Y | Y | Y | Y | N | Y |
| 2 **Wilson** | Y | Y | Y | Y | Y | N | Y |
| 3 **Barrett** | Y | Y | Y | Y | Y | N | Y |
| 4 **Inglis** | ? | ? | Y | Y | Y | N | Y |
| 5 Spratt | Y | Y | Y | Y | N | Y | N |
| 6 Clyburn | Y | Y | Y | Y | N | Y | N |
| **SOUTH DAKOTA** | | | | | | | |
| AL Herseth | Y | Y | Y | Y | N | Y | N |
| **TENNESSEE** | | | | | | | |
| 1 **Jenkins** | ? | ? | Y | Y | Y | N | Y |
| 2 **Duncan** | Y | Y | Y | Y | Y | N | Y |
| 3 **Wamp** | Y | Y | Y | Y | Y | N | Y |
| 4 Davis | Y | Y | ? | Y | N | Y | Y |
| 5 Cooper | Y | Y | Y | Y | N | Y | N |
| 6 Gordon | Y | Y | Y | Y | Y | N | Y |
| 7 **Blackburn** | N | Y | Y | Y | Y | N | Y |
| 8 Tanner | Y | Y | Y | Y | N | N | N |
| 9 Ford | ? | ? | Y | Y | N | Y | N |
| **TEXAS** | | | | | | | |
| 1 **Gohmert** | Y | Y | Y | Y | Y | N | Y |
| 2 **Poe** | Y | Y | Y | Y | Y | N | Y |
| 3 **Johnson, S.** | N | Y | Y | Y | Y | N | Y |
| 4 **Hall** | Y | Y | Y | Y | Y | N | Y |
| 5 **Hensarling** | N | Y | Y | Y | Y | N | Y |
| 6 **Barton** | Y | Y | Y | Y | Y | N | Y |
| 7 **Culberson** | N | Y | Y | Y | Y | N | Y |
| 8 **Brady** | Y | Y | Y | Y | Y | N | Y |
| 9 Green | Y | Y | Y | Y | N | Y | N |
| 10 **McCaul** | Y | Y | Y | Y | Y | N | Y |
| 11 **Conaway** | Y | Y | Y | Y | Y | N | Y |
| 12 **Granger** | Y | Y | Y | Y | Y | N | Y |
| 13 **Thornberry** | Y | ? | Y | Y | Y | N | Y |
| 14 **Paul** | N | Y | Y | Y | Y | N | Y |
| 15 Hinojosa | Y | Y | Y | Y | N | Y | Y |
| 16 Reyes | Y | Y | Y | ? | N | Y | N |
| 17 Edwards | ? | ? | Y | Y | N | Y | Y |
| 18 Jackson-Lee | Y | Y | Y | Y | N | Y | Y |
| 19 **Neugebauer** | Y | Y | Y | Y | Y | N | Y |
| 20 Gonzalez | Y | Y | Y | Y | N | Y | N |
| 21 **Smith** | Y | Y | Y | Y | Y | N | Y |
| 22 **DeLay** | Y | Y | Y | Y | Y | N | Y |
| 23 **Bonilla** | Y | Y | Y | Y | Y | N | Y |
| 24 **Marchant** | Y | Y | Y | Y | Y | N | Y |
| 25 Doggett | Y | Y | Y | Y | N | Y | N |
| 26 **Burgess** | Y | Y | Y | Y | Y | N | Y |
| 27 Ortiz | Y | Y | Y | Y | N | Y | N |
| 28 Cuellar | Y | Y | Y | Y | N | Y | Y |
| 29 Green | Y | Y | Y | Y | N | Y | N |
| 30 Johnson, E. | Y | Y | Y | Y | N | Y | N |
| 31 **Carter** | + | + | Y | Y | Y | N | Y |
| 32 **Sessions** | Y | Y | Y | Y | Y | N | Y |
| **UTAH** | | | | | | | |
| 1 **Bishop** | Y | Y | Y | Y | Y | N | Y |
| 2 Matheson | Y | Y | Y | Y | N | Y | Y |
| 3 **Cannon** | Y | Y | Y | Y | Y | N | Y |
| **VERMONT** | | | | | | | |
| AL *Sanders* | Y | Y | Y | Y | N | N | N |
| **VIRGINIA** | | | | | | | |
| 1 **Davis, J.** | N | Y | Y | Y | Y | N | Y |
| 2 **Drake** | Y | Y | Y | Y | Y | N | Y |
| 3 Scott | Y | Y | Y | Y | N | Y | N |
| 4 **Forbes** | Y | Y | Y | Y | Y | N | Y |
| 5 **Goode** | N | Y | Y | Y | Y | N | Y |
| 6 **Goodlatte** | Y | Y | Y | Y | Y | N | Y |
| 7 **Cantor** | Y | Y | Y | Y | Y | N | Y |
| 8 Moran | Y | Y | Y | Y | N | Y | N |
| 9 Boucher | Y | Y | Y | Y | N | Y | Y |
| 10 **Wolf** | Y | Y | Y | Y | Y | N | Y |
| 11 **Davis, T.** | Y | Y | Y | Y | Y | N | Y |
| **WASHINGTON** | | | | | | | |
| 1 Inslee | Y | Y | Y | Y | N | Y | N |
| 2 Larsen | Y | Y | Y | Y | N | Y | N |
| 3 Baird | Y | Y | ? | ? | ? | Y | N |
| 4 **Hastings** | Y | Y | Y | Y | Y | N | Y |
| 5 **McMorris** | Y | Y | Y | Y | Y | N | Y |
| 6 Dicks | Y | Y | Y | Y | N | Y | N |
| 7 McDermott | Y | Y | Y | Y | N | Y | N |
| 8 **Reichert** | Y | Y | Y | Y | Y | N | Y |
| 9 Smith | ? | ? | Y | Y | N | Y | N |
| **WEST VIRGINIA** | | | | | | | |
| 1 Mollohan | Y | Y | Y | Y | N | Y | N |
| 2 **Capito** | Y | Y | Y | Y | Y | N | Y |
| 3 Rahall | Y | Y | Y | Y | Y | Y | Y |
| **WISCONSIN** | | | | | | | |
| 1 **Ryan** | Y | Y | Y | Y | Y | N | Y |
| 2 Baldwin | Y | Y | Y | Y | N | Y | N |
| 3 Kind | Y | Y | Y | Y | N | Y | N |
| 4 Moore | Y | Y | Y | Y | N | Y | N |
| 5 **Sensenbrenner** | Y | Y | Y | Y | Y | N | Y |
| 6 **Petri** | Y | Y | Y | Y | Y | N | Y |
| 7 Obey | Y | Y | Y | Y | N | Y | N |
| 8 **Green** | Y | Y | Y | Y | Y | N | Y |
| **WYOMING** | | | | | | | |
| AL **Cubin** | N | Y | Y | Y | Y | N | Y |

# IN THE HOUSE | By Vote Number

**103.** **Procedural Motion/Adjourn.** Woolsey, D-Calif., motion to adjourn. Motion rejected 49-371: R 1-220; D 48-150 (ND 40-107, SD 8-43); I 0-1. April 14, 2005.

**104.** **S 256. Bankruptcy Overhaul/Previous Question.** Gingrey, R-Ga., motion to order the previous question (thus ending debate and possibility of amendment) on adoption of the rule (H Res 211) to provide for House floor consideration of the bill that would overhaul bankruptcy laws. Motion agreed to 227-199: R 227-0; D 0-198 (ND 0-148, SD 0-50); I 0-1. April 14, 2005.

**105.** **S 256. Bankruptcy Overhaul/Rule.** Adoption of the rule (H Res 211) to provide for House floor consideration of the bill that would overhaul bankruptcy laws. Adopted 227-196: R 225-0; D 2-195 (ND 1-147, SD 1-48); I 0-1. April 14, 2005.

**106.** **H Res 213. Ethics Task Force/Motion to Table.** Sensenbrenner, R-Wis., motion to table (kill) the Pelosi, D-Calif., privileged resolution that would require the Speaker of the House to appoint a bipartisan task force, with equal representation of Republicans and Democrats, to make recommendations, by June 1, 2005, to restore public confidence in the House ethics process. Motion agreed to 218-195: R 218-2; D 0-192 (ND 0-144, SD 0-48); I 0-1. April 14, 2005.

**107.** **S 256. Bankruptcy Overhaul/Recommit.** Schakowsky, D-Ill., motion to recommit the bill to the House Judiciary Committee with instructions to exempt members of the National Guard and Reserve from the means test in the bill if their debt was a result of active duty service or was incurred within two years of returning home from their service. Motion rejected 200-229: R 1-228; D 198-1 (ND 148-0, SD 50-1); I 1-0. April 14, 2005.

**108.** **S 256. Bankruptcy Overhaul/Passage.** Passage of the bill that would create a means test tied to the median incomes of individual states to determine whether personal bankruptcy filers were able to repay some or all of their debts. Those deemed able to pay would be pushed into Chapter 13 bankruptcy, which results in a court-ordered repayment plan; those with insufficient assets would be allowed to file under Chapter 7, which erases debts after the forfeiture of certain assets. The bill would exempt disabled veterans from the means test if their debts were incurred primarily when they were on active duty or performing homeland defense duties. It also would make a number of debts non-dischargeable, including student loans, child support, alimony and luxury payments over $500 made within three months of a bankruptcy filing. Passed (thus cleared for the president) 302-126: R 229-0; D 73-125 (ND 41-106, SD 32-19); I 0-1. April 14, 2005.

| | 103 | 104 | 105 | 106 | 107 | 108 |
|---|---|---|---|---|---|---|
| **ALABAMA** | | | | | | |
| 1 **Bonner** | N | Y | Y | Y | N | Y |
| 2 **Everett** | N | Y | Y | Y | N | Y |
| 3 **Rogers** | N | Y | Y | Y | N | Y |
| 4 **Aderholt** | N | Y | Y | Y | N | Y |
| 5 Cramer | N | N | Y | N | Y | Y |
| 6 **Bachus** | N | Y | Y | Y | N | Y |
| 7 Davis | N | N | N | N | Y | Y |
| **ALASKA** | | | | | | |
| AL **Young** | N | Y | Y | ? | N | Y |
| **ARIZONA** | | | | | | |
| 1 **Renzi** | N | Y | Y | Y | N | Y |
| 2 **Franks** | N | Y | Y | Y | N | Y |
| 3 **Shadegg** | N | Y | Y | Y | N | Y |
| 4 Pastor | N | N | N | N | Y | Y |
| 5 **Hayworth** | N | Y | Y | Y | N | Y |
| 6 **Flake** | N | Y | Y | Y | N | Y |
| 7 Grijalva | N | N | N | N | Y | N |
| 8 **Kolbe** | N | Y | Y | Y | N | Y |
| **ARKANSAS** | | | | | | |
| 1 Berry | N | N | N | N | Y | Y |
| 2 Snyder | N | N | N | N | Y | N |
| 3 **Boozman** | N | Y | Y | Y | N | Y |
| 4 Ross | N | N | N | N | Y | Y |
| **CALIFORNIA** | | | | | | |
| 1 Thompson | N | N | N | N | Y | Y |
| 2 **Herger** | ? | Y | Y | Y | N | Y |
| 3 **Lungren** | N | Y | Y | Y | N | Y |
| 4 **Doolittle** | N | Y | Y | Y | N | Y |
| 5 Matsui, D. | N | N | N | N | Y | N |
| 6 Woolsey | Y | N | N | N | Y | N |
| 7 Miller, George | Y | N | N | N | Y | N |
| 8 Pelosi | N | N | N | N | Y | N |
| 9 Lee | Y | N | N | N | Y | N |
| 10 Tauscher | N | N | N | N | Y | Y |
| 11 **Pombo** | N | Y | Y | Y | N | Y |
| 12 Lantos | N | N | N | N | Y | ? |
| 13 Stark | Y | N | N | N | Y | N |
| 14 Eshoo | N | N | N | N | Y | N |
| 15 Honda | N | N | N | N | Y | N |
| 16 Lofgren | N | N | N | - | Y | N |
| 17 Farr | N | N | N | N | Y | N |
| 18 Cardoza | N | N | N | N | Y | Y |
| 19 **Radanovich** | N | Y | Y | Y | N | Y |
| 20 Costa | N | N | N | N | Y | Y |
| 21 **Nunes** | N | Y | Y | Y | N | Y |
| 22 **Thomas** | ? | Y | Y | Y | N | Y |
| 23 Capps | Y | N | N | N | Y | N |
| 24 **Gallegly** | N | Y | Y | Y | N | Y |
| 25 **McKeon** | N | Y | Y | Y | N | Y |
| 26 **Dreier** | N | Y | Y | Y | N | Y |
| 27 Sherman | N | N | N | N | Y | N |
| 28 Berman | Y | N | N | N | Y | N |
| 29 Schiff | N | N | N | N | Y | N |
| 30 Waxman | Y | N | N | N | Y | N |
| 31 Becerra | N | N | N | N | Y | N |
| 32 Solis | + | - | - | - | + | N |
| 33 Watson | N | N | N | N | Y | N |
| 34 Roybal-Allard | N | N | N | N | Y | N |
| 35 Waters | N | N | N | N | Y | N |
| 36 Harman | N | N | N | N | Y | Y |
| 37 Millender-McD. | N | N | N | N | Y | N |
| 38 Napolitano | N | N | N | N | Y | N |
| 39 Sánchez, Linda | Y | N | N | N | Y | N |
| 40 **Royce** | N | Y | Y | Y | N | Y |
| 41 **Lewis** | N | Y | Y | Y | N | Y |
| 42 **Miller, Gary** | N | Y | Y | Y | N | Y |
| 43 Baca | N | N | N | N | Y | Y |
| 44 **Calvert** | N | Y | Y | Y | N | Y |
| 45 **Bono** | N | Y | Y | Y | N | Y |
| 46 **Rohrabacher** | N | Y | Y | Y | N | Y |
| 47 Sanchez, Loretta | N | N | N | N | Y | N |
| 48 **Cox** | N | Y | Y | Y | N | Y |
| 49 **Issa** | N | Y | Y | Y | N | Y |
| 50 **Cunningham** | N | Y | Y | Y | N | Y |
| 51 Filner | Y | N | N | N | Y | N |
| 52 **Hunter** | N | Y | Y | N | N | Y |
| 53 Davis | N | N | N | N | Y | N |
| **COLORADO** | | | | | | |
| 1 DeGette | N | N | N | N | Y | N |
| 2 Udall | N | N | N | N | Y | Y |
| 3 Salazar | N | N | N | N | Y | Y |
| 4 **Musgrave** | N | Y | Y | Y | N | Y |
| 5 **Hefley** | N | Y | Y | Y | N | Y |
| 6 **Tancredo** | N | Y | Y | ? | N | Y |
| 7 **Beauprez** | N | Y | Y | Y | N | Y |
| **CONNECTICUT** | | | | | | |
| 1 Larson | N | N | N | N | Y | N |
| 2 **Simmons** | N | Y | Y | Y | N | Y |
| 3 DeLauro | Y | N | N | N | Y | N |
| 4 **Shays** | N | Y | Y | Y | N | Y |
| 5 **Johnson** | N | Y | Y | Y | N | Y |
| **DELAWARE** | | | | | | |
| AL **Castle** | N | Y | Y | Y | N | Y |
| **FLORIDA** | | | | | | |
| 1 **Miller** | N | Y | Y | Y | N | Y |
| 2 Boyd | N | N | N | N | Y | Y |
| 3 Brown | N | N | N | ? | Y | N |
| 4 **Crenshaw** | N | Y | Y | Y | N | Y |
| 5 **Brown-Waite** | N | Y | Y | Y | N | Y |
| 6 **Stearns** | N | Y | Y | Y | N | Y |
| 7 **Mica** | N | Y | Y | Y | N | Y |
| 8 **Keller** | N | Y | Y | Y | N | Y |
| 9 **Bilirakis** | ? | Y | Y | Y | N | Y |
| 10 **Young** | N | Y | Y | Y | N | Y |
| 11 Davis | N | N | N | N | Y | N |
| 12 **Putnam** | N | Y | Y | Y | N | Y |
| 13 **Harris** | N | Y | Y | Y | N | Y |
| 14 **Mack** | N | Y | Y | Y | N | Y |
| 15 **Weldon** | N | Y | Y | Y | ? | Y |
| 16 **Foley** | N | Y | Y | Y | N | Y |
| 17 Meek | N | N | N | N | Y | N |
| 18 **Ros-Lehtinen** | N | Y | Y | Y | N | Y |
| 19 Wexler | N | N | N | N | Y | N |
| 20 Wasserman-Schultz | N | N | N | N | Y | N |
| 21 **Diaz-Balart, L.** | N | Y | Y | Y | N | Y |
| 22 **Shaw** | N | Y | Y | Y | N | Y |
| 23 Hastings | N | N | N | N | Y | N |
| 24 **Feeney** | N | Y | ? | Y | N | Y |
| 25 **Diaz-Balart, M.** | N | Y | Y | Y | N | Y |
| **GEORGIA** | | | | | | |
| 1 **Kingston** | N | Y | Y | Y | N | Y |
| 2 Bishop | N | N | N | N | Y | Y |
| 3 Marshall | N | N | N | N | Y | Y |
| 4 McKinney | N | N | N | N | Y | N |
| 5 Lewis | N | N | N | N | Y | N |
| 6 **Price** | N | Y | Y | Y | N | Y |
| 7 **Linder** | N | Y | Y | Y | N | Y |
| 8 **Westmoreland** | N | Y | Y | Y | N | Y |
| 9 **Norwood** | N | Y | Y | ? | N | Y |
| 10 **Deal** | N | Y | Y | Y | N | Y |
| 11 **Gingrey** | N | Y | Y | Y | N | Y |
| 12 Barrow | N | N | N | N | Y | Y |
| 13 Scott | N | N | N | N | Y | Y |
| **HAWAII** | | | | | | |
| 1 Abercrombie | N | N | N | N | Y | N |
| 2 Case | N | N | N | N | Y | N |
| **IDAHO** | | | | | | |
| 1 **Otter** | N | Y | Y | Y | N | Y |
| 2 **Simpson** | N | Y | Y | Y | N | Y |
| **ILLINOIS** | | | | | | |
| 1 Rush | N | N | N | N | Y | N |
| 2 Jackson | N | N | N | N | Y | N |
| 3 Lipinski | N | N | N | N | Y | N |
| 4 Gutierrez | N | N | N | N | ? | ? |
| 5 Emanuel | N | N | N | N | Y | N |
| 6 **Hyde** | N | Y | Y | ? | N | Y |
| 7 Davis | N | N | N | N | Y | N |
| 8 Bean | N | N | N | N | Y | Y |
| 9 Schakowsky | Y | N | N | N | Y | N |
| 10 **Kirk** | N | Y | Y | Y | N | Y |
| 11 **Weller** | N | Y | Y | Y | N | Y |
| 12 Costello | N | N | N | N | Y | N |

**KEY**    **Republicans**    Democrats    *Independents*

| | | | |
|---|---|---|---|
| **Y** Voted for (yea) | **X** Paired against | **C** Voted "present" to avoid possible conflict of interest |
| **#** Paired for | **−** Announced against | |
| **+** Announced for | **P** Voted "present" | **?** Did not vote or otherwise make a position known |
| **N** Voted against (nay) | | |

| | 103 | 104 | 105 | 106 | 107 | 108 |
|---|---|---|---|---|---|---|
| 13 **Biggert** | N | Y | Y | Y | N | Y |
| 14 **Hastert** | | | | | N | Y |
| 15 **Johnson** | N | Y | Y | Y | Y | Y |
| 16 **Manzullo** | ? | Y | Y | Y | N | Y |
| 17 Evans | Y | N | N | ? | Y | N |
| 18 **LaHood** | N | ? | ? | ? | ? | ? |
| 19 **Shimkus** | N | Y | Y | Y | N | Y |
| **INDIANA** | | | | | | |
| 1 Visclosky | N | N | N | N | Y | N |
| 2 **Chocola** | N | Y | Y | Y | N | Y |
| 3 **Souder** | N | Y | Y | ? | N | Y |
| 4 **Buyer** | ? | Y | Y | Y | N | Y |
| 5 **Burton** | N | Y | Y | Y | N | Y |
| 6 **Pence** | N | Y | Y | Y | N | Y |
| 7 Carson | N | N | N | N | Y | N |
| 8 **Hostettler** | N | Y | Y | Y | N | Y |
| 9 **Sodrel** | N | Y | Y | Y | N | Y |
| **IOWA** | | | | | | |
| 1 **Nussle** | N | Y | Y | Y | N | Y |
| 2 **Leach** | N | Y | Y | N | N | Y |
| 3 Boswell | N | N | N | N | Y | Y |
| 4 **Latham** | N | Y | Y | Y | N | Y |
| 5 **King** | N | Y | Y | Y | N | Y |
| **KANSAS** | | | | | | |
| 1 **Moran** | N | Y | Y | Y | N | Y |
| 2 **Ryun** | N | Y | Y | Y | N | Y |
| 3 Moore | N | N | N | N | Y | Y |
| 4 **Tiahrt** | N | Y | Y | Y | N | Y |
| **KENTUCKY** | | | | | | |
| 1 **Whitfield** | N | Y | Y | Y | N | Y |
| 2 **Lewis** | N | Y | Y | Y | N | Y |
| 3 **Northup** | N | Y | Y | Y | N | Y |
| 4 **Davis** | N | Y | Y | Y | N | Y |
| 5 **Rogers** | N | Y | Y | Y | N | Y |
| 6 Chandler | N | N | N | N | Y | Y |
| **LOUISIANA** | | | | | | |
| 1 **Jindal** | N | Y | Y | Y | N | Y |
| 2 Jefferson | N | N | N | N | Y | Y |
| 3 Melancon | N | N | N | N | Y | Y |
| 4 **McCrery** | ? | Y | Y | Y | N | Y |
| 5 **Alexander** | N | Y | Y | Y | N | Y |
| 6 **Baker** | N | Y | Y | Y | N | Y |
| 7 **Boustany** | N | Y | Y | Y | N | Y |
| **MAINE** | | | | | | |
| 1 Allen | Y | N | N | ? | Y | N |
| 2 Michaud | N | N | N | N | Y | Y |
| **MARYLAND** | | | | | | |
| 1 **Gilchrest** | N | Y | Y | Y | N | Y |
| 2 Ruppersberger | N | N | N | N | Y | Y |
| 3 Cardin | N | N | N | N | Y | N |
| 4 Wynn | N | N | N | N | Y | Y |
| 5 Hoyer | N | N | N | N | Y | Y |
| 6 **Bartlett** | N | Y | Y | Y | N | Y |
| 7 Cummings | N | N | N | N | Y | N |
| 8 Van Hollen | N | N | N | N | Y | N |
| **MASSACHUSETTS** | | | | | | |
| 1 Olver | Y | N | N | ? | Y | N |
| 2 Neal | N | N | N | N | Y | N |
| 3 McGovern | Y | N | N | N | Y | N |
| 4 Frank | Y | N | N | N | Y | N |
| 5 Meehan | Y | N | N | N | Y | N |
| 6 Tierney | Y | N | N | N | Y | N |
| 7 Markey | Y | N | N | N | Y | N |
| 8 Capuano | Y | N | N | N | Y | N |
| 9 Lynch | N | N | N | N | Y | N |
| 10 Delahunt | Y | N | N | N | Y | N |
| **MICHIGAN** | | | | | | |
| 1 Stupak | N | N | N | N | Y | N |
| 2 **Hoekstra** | N | Y | Y | Y | N | Y |
| 3 **Ehlers** | N | Y | Y | Y | N | Y |
| 4 **Camp** | N | Y | Y | Y | N | Y |
| 5 Kildee | N | N | N | N | Y | N |
| 6 **Upton** | N | Y | Y | Y | N | Y |
| 7 **Schwarz** | N | Y | Y | Y | N | Y |
| 8 **Rogers** | N | Y | Y | Y | N | Y |
| 9 **Knollenberg** | N | Y | Y | Y | N | Y |
| 10 **Miller** | N | Y | Y | Y | N | Y |
| 11 **McCotter** | N | Y | Y | Y | N | Y |
| 12 Levin | N | N | N | N | Y | N |
| 13 Kilpatrick | Y | N | N | N | Y | N |
| 14 Conyers | Y | N | N | N | Y | N |
| 15 Dingell | Y | N | N | N | Y | N |

| | 103 | 104 | 105 | 106 | 107 | 108 |
|---|---|---|---|---|---|---|
| **MINNESOTA** | | | | | | |
| 1 **Gutknecht** | N | Y | ? | Y | N | Y |
| 2 **Kline** | N | Y | Y | Y | N | Y |
| 3 **Ramstad** | N | Y | Y | Y | N | Y |
| 4 McCollum | N | N | N | N | Y | N |
| 5 Sabo | N | N | N | N | Y | N |
| 6 **Kennedy** | N | Y | Y | Y | N | Y |
| 7 Peterson | N | N | Y | N | Y | Y |
| 8 Oberstar | Y | N | N | N | Y | N |
| **MISSISSIPPI** | | | | | | |
| 1 **Wicker** | N | Y | Y | Y | N | Y |
| 2 Thompson | Y | N | N | N | Y | N |
| 3 **Pickering** | N | Y | Y | Y | N | Y |
| 4 Taylor | N | N | N | N | Y | Y |
| **MISSOURI** | | | | | | |
| 1 Clay | Y | N | N | N | Y | N |
| 2 **Akin** | N | Y | Y | Y | N | Y |
| 3 Carnahan | N | N | N | N | Y | N |
| 4 Skelton | N | N | N | N | Y | Y |
| 5 Cleaver | N | N | N | N | Y | Y |
| 6 **Graves** | N | Y | Y | Y | N | Y |
| 7 **Blunt** | N | Y | Y | Y | N | Y |
| 8 **Emerson** | N | Y | Y | Y | N | Y |
| 9 **Hulshof** | N | Y | Y | Y | N | Y |
| **MONTANA** | | | | | | |
| AL **Rehberg** | N | Y | Y | Y | N | Y |
| **NEBRASKA** | | | | | | |
| 1 **Fortenberry** | N | Y | Y | Y | N | Y |
| 2 **Terry** | N | Y | Y | Y | N | Y |
| 3 **Osborne** | N | Y | Y | Y | N | Y |
| **NEVADA** | | | | | | |
| 1 Berkley | ? | ? | ? | ? | ? | ? |
| 2 **Gibbons** | N | Y | Y | Y | N | Y |
| 3 **Porter** | N | Y | Y | Y | N | Y |
| **NEW HAMPSHIRE** | | | | | | |
| 1 **Bradley** | N | Y | Y | Y | N | Y |
| 2 **Bass** | N | Y | Y | Y | N | Y |
| **NEW JERSEY** | | | | | | |
| 1 Andrews | N | N | N | N | Y | Y |
| 2 **LoBiondo** | N | Y | Y | Y | N | Y |
| 3 **Saxton** | N | Y | Y | Y | N | Y |
| 4 **Smith** | N | Y | Y | Y | N | Y |
| 5 **Garrett** | N | Y | Y | Y | N | Y |
| 6 Pallone | N | N | N | N | Y | N |
| 7 **Ferguson** | N | Y | Y | Y | N | Y |
| 8 Pascrell | N | N | N | N | Y | N |
| 9 Rothman | N | N | N | N | Y | Y |
| 10 Payne | Y | ? | N | N | Y | N |
| 11 **Frelinghuysen** | N | Y | Y | Y | N | Y |
| 12 Holt | Y | N | N | N | Y | N |
| 13 Menendez | N | N | N | N | Y | Y |
| **NEW MEXICO** | | | | | | |
| 1 **Wilson** | N | Y | Y | Y | N | Y |
| 2 **Pearce** | N | Y | Y | Y | N | Y |
| 3 Udall | N | N | N | N | Y | N |
| **NEW YORK** | | | | | | |
| 1 Bishop | N | N | N | N | Y | N |
| 2 Israel | N | N | N | N | Y | Y |
| 3 **King** | N | Y | Y | Y | N | Y |
| 4 McCarthy | N | N | N | N | Y | Y |
| 5 Ackerman | N | N | N | N | Y | N |
| 6 Meeks | N | N | N | N | Y | Y |
| 7 Crowley | N | N | N | N | Y | Y |
| 8 Nadler | Y | N | N | N | Y | N |
| 9 Weiner | N | N | N | N | Y | N |
| 10 Towns | ? | N | N | N | Y | N |
| 11 Owens | Y | N | N | N | Y | N |
| 12 Velázquez | N | N | N | N | Y | N |
| 13 **Fossella** | N | Y | Y | Y | N | Y |
| 14 Maloney | N | N | N | N | Y | N |
| 15 Rangel | Y | N | ? | ? | Y | N |
| 16 Serrano | ? | N | N | N | Y | N |
| 17 Engel | N | N | N | N | Y | N |
| 18 Lowey | N | N | N | N | Y | N |
| 19 **Kelly** | N | Y | Y | Y | N | Y |
| 20 **Sweeney** | N | Y | Y | Y | N | Y |
| 21 McNulty | N | N | N | N | Y | N |
| 22 Hinchey | Y | N | N | N | Y | N |
| 23 **McHugh** | N | Y | Y | Y | N | Y |
| 24 **Boehlert** | N | Y | Y | Y | N | Y |
| 25 **Walsh** | N | Y | Y | Y | N | Y |
| 26 **Reynolds** | N | Y | Y | Y | N | Y |
| 27 Higgins | N | N | N | N | Y | Y |
| 28 Slaughter | N | N | N | N | Y | N |
| 29 **Kuhl** | N | Y | Y | Y | N | Y |

| | 103 | 104 | 105 | 106 | 107 | 108 |
|---|---|---|---|---|---|---|
| **NORTH CAROLINA** | | | | | | |
| 1 Butterfield | Y | N | N | N | Y | N |
| 2 Etheridge | N | N | N | N | Y | Y |
| 3 **Jones** | N | Y | Y | Y | N | Y |
| 4 Price | N | N | N | N | Y | Y |
| 5 **Foxx** | N | Y | Y | Y | N | Y |
| 6 **Coble** | N | Y | Y | Y | N | Y |
| 7 McIntyre | N | N | N | N | Y | Y |
| 8 **Hayes** | N | Y | Y | ? | N | Y |
| 9 **Myrick** | N | Y | Y | ? | N | Y |
| 10 **McHenry** | N | Y | Y | Y | N | Y |
| 11 **Taylor** | N | Y | Y | ? | N | Y |
| 12 Watt | N | N | N | N | Y | N |
| 13 Miller | N | N | N | N | Y | N |
| **NORTH DAKOTA** | | | | | | |
| AL Pomeroy | N | N | N | N | Y | Y |
| **OHIO** | | | | | | |
| 1 **Chabot** | N | Y | Y | Y | N | Y |
| 2 **Portman** | N | Y | Y | Y | N | Y |
| 3 **Turner** | N | Y | Y | Y | N | Y |
| 4 **Oxley** | N | Y | Y | ? | N | Y |
| 5 **Gillmor** | ? | ? | ? | ? | ? | ? |
| 6 Strickland | N | N | N | N | Y | Y |
| 7 **Hobson** | N | Y | Y | Y | N | Y |
| 8 **Boehner** | N | Y | Y | Y | N | Y |
| 9 Kaptur | Y | N | N | N | Y | N |
| 10 Kucinich | Y | N | N | N | Y | N |
| 11 Jones | Y | N | N | N | Y | N |
| 12 **Tiberi** | N | Y | Y | Y | N | Y |
| 13 Brown | N | N | N | N | Y | N |
| 14 **LaTourette** | N | Y | Y | Y | N | Y |
| 15 **Pryce** | N | Y | Y | Y | N | Y |
| 16 **Regula** | N | Y | Y | Y | N | Y |
| 17 Ryan | N | N | N | N | Y | N |
| 18 **Ney** | N | Y | Y | Y | N | Y |
| **OKLAHOMA** | | | | | | |
| 1 **Sullivan** | N | Y | Y | Y | N | Y |
| 2 Boren | N | N | N | N | Y | Y |
| 3 **Lucas** | N | Y | Y | Y | N | Y |
| 4 **Cole** | N | Y | Y | Y | N | Y |
| 5 **Istook** | ? | Y | Y | Y | N | Y |
| **OREGON** | | | | | | |
| 1 Wu | N | N | N | N | Y | Y |
| 2 **Walden** | N | Y | Y | Y | N | Y |
| 3 Blumenauer | N | N | N | N | Y | N |
| 4 DeFazio | N | N | N | N | Y | N |
| 5 Hooley | N | N | N | N | Y | Y |
| **PENNSYLVANIA** | | | | | | |
| 1 Brady | Y | N | N | N | Y | N |
| 2 Fattah | Y | N | N | N | Y | N |
| 3 **English** | N | Y | Y | Y | N | Y |
| 4 **Hart** | N | Y | Y | Y | N | Y |
| 5 **Peterson** | N | Y | Y | Y | N | Y |
| 6 **Gerlach** | N | Y | Y | Y | N | Y |
| 7 **Weldon** | N | Y | Y | Y | N | Y |
| 8 **Fitzpatrick** | N | Y | Y | Y | N | Y |
| 9 **Shuster** | N | Y | Y | Y | N | Y |
| 10 **Sherwood** | N | Y | Y | Y | N | Y |
| 11 Kanjorski | N | N | N | N | Y | N |
| 12 Murtha | N | N | N | N | Y | Y |
| 13 Schwartz | N | N | N | N | Y | Y |
| 14 Doyle | N | N | N | N | Y | N |
| 15 **Dent** | N | Y | Y | Y | N | Y |
| 16 **Pitts** | N | Y | Y | Y | N | Y |
| 17 Holden | N | N | N | N | Y | Y |
| 18 **Murphy** | N | Y | Y | Y | N | Y |
| 19 **Platts** | N | Y | Y | Y | N | Y |
| **RHODE ISLAND** | | | | | | |
| 1 Kennedy | Y | N | N | N | Y | N |
| 2 Langevin | N | N | N | N | Y | N |
| **SOUTH CAROLINA** | | | | | | |
| 1 **Brown** | N | Y | Y | Y | N | Y |
| 2 **Wilson** | N | Y | Y | Y | N | Y |
| 3 **Barrett** | N | Y | Y | Y | N | Y |
| 4 **Inglis** | N | Y | Y | Y | N | Y |
| 5 Spratt | N | N | N | N | Y | Y |
| 6 Clyburn | Y | N | N | N | Y | N |
| **SOUTH DAKOTA** | | | | | | |
| AL Herseth | N | N | N | N | Y | Y |
| **TENNESSEE** | | | | | | |
| 1 **Jenkins** | N | Y | ? | Y | N | Y |
| 2 **Duncan** | N | Y | Y | Y | N | Y |

| | 103 | 104 | 105 | 106 | 107 | 108 |
|---|---|---|---|---|---|---|
| 3 **Wamp** | ? | ? | Y | Y | N | Y |
| 4 Davis | N | N | N | N | Y | Y |
| 5 Cooper | Y | ? | ? | N | Y | Y |
| 6 Gordon | N | N | ? | ? | Y | Y |
| 7 **Blackburn** | N | Y | Y | Y | N | Y |
| 8 Tanner | N | N | N | N | Y | Y |
| 9 Ford | N | N | N | N | Y | Y |
| **TEXAS** | | | | | | |
| 1 **Gohmert** | N | Y | Y | Y | N | Y |
| 2 **Poe** | N | Y | Y | Y | N | Y |
| 3 **Johnson, S.** | N | Y | Y | Y | N | Y |
| 4 **Hall** | N | Y | Y | Y | N | Y |
| 5 **Hensarling** | N | Y | Y | Y | N | Y |
| 6 **Barton** | N | Y | Y | Y | N | Y |
| 7 **Culberson** | N | Y | Y | Y | N | Y |
| 8 **Brady** | N | Y | Y | Y | N | Y |
| 9 Green | Y | N | N | N | Y | Y |
| 10 **McCaul** | N | Y | Y | Y | N | Y |
| 11 **Conaway** | N | Y | Y | Y | N | Y |
| 12 **Granger** | N | Y | Y | Y | N | Y |
| 13 **Thornberry** | N | Y | Y | Y | N | Y |
| 14 **Paul** | Y | Y | Y | Y | N | Y |
| 15 Hinojosa | N | N | N | N | Y | Y |
| 16 Reyes | N | N | N | N | Y | Y |
| 17 Edwards | N | N | N | N | Y | Y |
| 18 Jackson-Lee | Y | N | N | N | Y | N |
| 19 **Neugebauer** | N | Y | Y | Y | N | Y |
| 20 Gonzalez | N | N | N | N | Y | Y |
| 21 **Smith** | N | Y | Y | Y | N | Y |
| 22 **DeLay** | N | Y | Y | Y | N | Y |
| 23 **Bonilla** | N | Y | Y | Y | N | Y |
| 24 **Marchant** | N | Y | Y | Y | N | Y |
| 25 Doggett | Y | N | N | N | Y | N |
| 26 **Burgess** | N | Y | Y | Y | N | Y |
| 27 Ortiz | N | N | N | N | Y | Y |
| 28 Cuellar | N | N | N | N | Y | Y |
| 29 Green | N | N | N | N | Y | N |
| 30 Johnson, E. | N | N | N | ? | Y | N |
| 31 **Carter** | N | Y | Y | Y | N | Y |
| 32 **Sessions** | N | Y | Y | Y | N | Y |
| **UTAH** | | | | | | |
| 1 **Bishop** | N | Y | Y | Y | N | Y |
| 2 Matheson | N | N | N | N | Y | Y |
| 3 **Cannon** | N | Y | Y | Y | N | Y |
| **VERMONT** | | | | | | |
| AL *Sanders* | N | N | N | N | Y | N |
| **VIRGINIA** | | | | | | |
| 1 **Davis, J.** | N | Y | Y | Y | N | Y |
| 2 **Drake** | N | Y | Y | Y | N | Y |
| 3 Scott | N | N | N | N | Y | N |
| 4 **Forbes** | N | Y | Y | Y | N | Y |
| 5 **Goode** | N | Y | Y | Y | N | Y |
| 6 **Goodlatte** | N | Y | Y | Y | N | Y |
| 7 **Cantor** | N | Y | Y | Y | N | Y |
| 8 Moran | N | N | N | N | Y | Y |
| 9 Boucher | N | N | N | N | Y | Y |
| 10 **Wolf** | N | Y | Y | Y | N | Y |
| 11 **Davis, T.** | ? | ? | ? | Y | N | Y |
| **WASHINGTON** | | | | | | |
| 1 Inslee | N | N | N | N | Y | N |
| 2 Larsen | N | N | N | N | Y | Y |
| 3 Baird | N | N | N | N | Y | Y |
| 4 **Hastings** | N | Y | Y | Y | N | Y |
| 5 **McMorris** | N | Y | Y | Y | N | Y |
| 6 Dicks | N | N | N | N | Y | N |
| 7 McDermott | Y | N | N | N | Y | N |
| 8 **Reichert** | N | Y | Y | Y | N | Y |
| 9 Smith | N | N | N | N | Y | N |
| **WEST VIRGINIA** | | | | | | |
| 1 Mollohan | N | N | N | N | Y | Y |
| 2 **Capito** | N | Y | Y | Y | N | Y |
| 3 Rahall | N | N | N | N | Y | Y |
| **WISCONSIN** | | | | | | |
| 1 **Ryan** | N | Y | Y | Y | N | Y |
| 2 Baldwin | Y | N | N | N | Y | N |
| 3 Kind | N | N | N | N | Y | Y |
| 4 Moore | N | N | N | N | Y | N |
| 5 **Sensenbrenner** | N | Y | Y | Y | N | Y |
| 6 **Petri** | N | Y | Y | Y | N | Y |
| 7 Obey | N | N | N | N | Y | N |
| 8 **Green** | N | Y | Y | Y | N | Y |
| **WYOMING** | | | | | | |
| AL **Cubin** | N | Y | Y | Y | N | Y |

# IN THE HOUSE | By Vote Number

**109.** **HR 683. Trademark Protection/Passage.** Sensenbrenner, R-Wis., motion to suspend the rules and pass the bill that would allow trademark owners to seek an injunction against the use of similar trademarks that might harm a company's reputation or confuse consumers. Motion agreed to 411-8: R 220-3; D 190-5 (ND 140-5, SD 50-0); I 1-0. A two-thirds majority of those present and voting (280 in this case) is required for passage under suspension of the rules. April 19, 2005.

**110.** **H J Res 19. Citizen Regent For Smithsonian Institution/Passage.** Ney, R-Ohio, motion to suspend the rules and pass the joint resolution that would appoint Shirley Ann Jackson of New York as a citizen regent of the Smithsonian Institution. Motion agreed to 417-0: R 222-0; D 194-0 (ND 144-0, SD 50-0); I 1-0. A two-thirds majority of those present and voting (278 in this case) is required for passage under suspension of the rules. April 19, 2005.

**111.** **H J Res 20. Citizen Regent For Smithsonian Institution/Passage.** Ney, R-Ohio, motion to suspend the rules and pass the joint resolution that would appoint Robert P. Kogod of the District of Columbia as a citizen regent of the Smithsonian Institution. Motion agreed to 412-0: R 222-0; D 190-0 (ND 141-0, SD 49-0); I 0-0. A two-thirds majority of those present and voting (275 in this case) is required for passage under suspension of the rules. April 19, 2005.

**112.** **HR 6. Energy Policy/Question of Consideration.** Question of whether the House should consider the rule (H Res 219) to provide for House floor consideration of the bill that would overhaul the nation's energy policy. Agreed to consider 231-193: R 224-0; D 7-192 (ND 1-147, SD 6-45); I 0-1. (McGovern, D-Mass., had raised a point of order that the rule would waive points of order against an unfunded mandate in the bill in violation of section 426(a) of the Congressional Budget Act.) April 20, 2005.

**113.** **H Con Res 126. Red Lake School Shooting/Adoption.** Kline, R-Minn., motion to suspend the rules and adopt the concurrent resolution that would express condolences to the families and friends of victims of the school shootings in Red Lake, Minn. Motion agreed to 424-0: R 224-0; D 199-0 (ND 148-0, SD 51-0); I 1-0. A two-thirds majority of those present and voting (283 in this case) is required for adoption under suspension of the rules. April 20, 2005.

**114.** **H Res 208. Polio Vaccine Anniversary/Adoption.** Murphy, R-Pa., motion to suspend the rules and adopt the resolution to recognize the University of Pittsburgh, Dr. Jonas Salk and others on the 50th anniversary of the discovery of the polio vaccine. Motion agreed to 422-0: R 223-0; D 198-0 (ND 147-0, SD 51-0); I 1-0. A two-thirds majority of those present and voting (282 in this case) is required for adoption under suspension of the rules. April 20, 2005.

**115.** **HR 6. Energy Policy/Refinery Approval Process.** Solis, D-Calif., amendment that would strike a provision in the bill that would allow an expedited review and approval process to open refineries in areas that have experienced manufacturing-sector layoffs and have unemployment rates that exceed the national average by at least 10 percent. Rejected 182-248: R 15-215; D 166-33 (ND 137-11, SD 29-22); I 1-0. April 20, 2005.

**116.** **HR 6. Energy Policy/Strategic Petroleum Reserve.** Kaptur, D-Ohio, amendment that would rename the Strategic Petroleum Reserve the Strategic Fuels Reserve, and would give the Energy Department authority to include alternate fuels, such as ethanol and biodiesel, in the reserve. Rejected 186-239: R 12-214; D 173-25 (ND 139-8, SD 34-17); I 1-0. April 20, 2005.

| | 109 | 110 | 111 | 112 | 113 | 114 | 115 | 116 |
|---|---|---|---|---|---|---|---|---|
| **ALABAMA** | | | | | | | | |
| 1 Bonner | Y | Y | Y | Y | Y | Y | N | N |
| 2 Everett | Y | Y | Y | Y | Y | Y | N | N |
| 3 Rogers | Y | Y | Y | Y | Y | Y | N | N |
| 4 Aderholt | Y | Y | Y | Y | Y | Y | N | N |
| 5 Cramer | Y | Y | Y | N | Y | Y | N | Y |
| 6 Bachus | Y | Y | Y | Y | ? | ? | N | ? |
| 7 Davis | Y | Y | Y | N | Y | Y | N | N |
| **ALASKA** | | | | | | | | |
| AL Young | ? | ? | ? | Y | Y | ? | N | N |
| **ARIZONA** | | | | | | | | |
| 1 Renzi | Y | Y | Y | Y | Y | Y | N | N |
| 2 Franks | Y | Y | Y | Y | Y | Y | N | N |
| 3 Shadegg | Y | Y | Y | Y | Y | Y | N | N |
| 4 Pastor | Y | Y | Y | N | Y | Y | Y | Y |
| 5 Hayworth | Y | Y | Y | Y | Y | Y | N | N |
| 6 Flake | N | Y | Y | Y | Y | Y | N | N |
| 7 Grijalva | Y | Y | Y | N | Y | Y | Y | ? |
| 8 Kolbe | Y | Y | Y | Y | Y | Y | N | N |
| **ARKANSAS** | | | | | | | | |
| 1 Berry | Y | Y | Y | N | Y | Y | N | Y |
| 2 Snyder | Y | Y | Y | N | Y | Y | Y | Y |
| 3 Boozman | Y | Y | Y | Y | Y | Y | N | N |
| 4 Ross | Y | Y | Y | N | Y | Y | N | Y |
| **CALIFORNIA** | | | | | | | | |
| 1 Thompson | Y | Y | Y | N | Y | Y | Y | Y |
| 2 Herger | Y | Y | Y | Y | Y | Y | N | N |
| 3 Lungren | Y | Y | Y | Y | Y | Y | N | N |
| 4 Doolittle | ? | ? | ? | Y | Y | Y | Y | N |
| 5 Matsui, D. | Y | Y | Y | N | Y | Y | Y | Y |
| 6 Woolsey | Y | Y | Y | N | Y | Y | Y | Y |
| 7 Miller, George | Y | Y | Y | N | Y | Y | Y | Y |
| 8 Pelosi | Y | Y | Y | N | Y | Y | Y | Y |
| 9 Lee | Y | Y | Y | N | Y | Y | Y | Y |
| 10 Tauscher | Y | Y | Y | N | Y | Y | Y | Y |
| 11 Pombo | Y | Y | Y | Y | Y | Y | N | N |
| 12 Lantos | Y | Y | Y | N | Y | Y | Y | Y |
| 13 Stark | Y | Y | Y | N | Y | Y | Y | Y |
| 14 Eshoo | Y | Y | ? | N | Y | Y | Y | Y |
| 15 Honda | Y | Y | Y | N | Y | Y | Y | Y |
| 16 Lofgren | Y | Y | Y | N | Y | Y | Y | Y |
| 17 Farr | Y | Y | Y | N | Y | Y | Y | Y |
| 18 Cardoza | Y | Y | Y | N | Y | Y | N | N |
| 19 Radanovich | Y | Y | Y | Y | Y | Y | N | N |
| 20 Costa | Y | Y | Y | N | Y | Y | N | Y |
| 21 Nunes | Y | Y | Y | Y | Y | Y | N | N |
| 22 Thomas | Y | Y | Y | Y | Y | Y | N | N |
| 23 Capps | Y | Y | Y | N | Y | Y | Y | Y |
| 24 Gallegly | Y | Y | Y | Y | Y | Y | N | N |
| 25 McKeon | Y | Y | Y | Y | Y | Y | N | N |
| 26 Dreier | Y | Y | Y | Y | Y | Y | N | N |
| 27 Sherman | Y | Y | Y | N | Y | Y | Y | Y |
| 28 Berman | Y | Y | Y | N | Y | Y | Y | Y |
| 29 Schiff | Y | Y | Y | N | Y | Y | Y | Y |
| 30 Waxman | Y | Y | Y | N | Y | Y | Y | Y |
| 31 Becerra | Y | Y | Y | N | Y | Y | Y | Y |
| 32 Solis | Y | Y | Y | N | Y | Y | Y | Y |
| 33 Watson | Y | Y | Y | N | Y | Y | Y | Y |
| 34 Roybal-Allard | Y | Y | Y | N | Y | Y | Y | Y |
| 35 Waters | Y | Y | Y | N | Y | Y | Y | Y |
| 36 Harman | Y | Y | Y | N | Y | Y | N | Y |
| 37 Millender-McD. | Y | Y | Y | N | Y | Y | Y | Y |
| 38 Napolitano | Y | Y | Y | N | Y | Y | Y | Y |
| 39 Sánchez, Linda | Y | Y | Y | N | Y | Y | Y | Y |
| 40 Royce | Y | Y | Y | Y | Y | Y | N | N |
| 41 Lewis | Y | Y | Y | Y | Y | Y | N | N |
| 42 Miller, Gary | Y | Y | Y | Y | Y | Y | N | N |
| 43 Baca | Y | Y | Y | N | Y | Y | N | N |
| 44 Calvert | Y | Y | Y | Y | Y | Y | N | N |
| 45 Bono | Y | Y | Y | Y | Y | Y | N | N |
| 46 Rohrabacher | Y | Y | Y | Y | Y | Y | N | N |
| 47 Sanchez, Loretta | Y | Y | Y | N | Y | Y | Y | Y |
| 48 Cox | Y | Y | Y | Y | Y | Y | N | Y |
| 49 Issa | Y | Y | Y | Y | Y | Y | N | N |
| 50 Cunningham | Y | Y | Y | Y | Y | Y | N | N |
| 51 Filner | N | Y | Y | N | Y | Y | Y | Y |
| 52 Hunter | Y | Y | Y | Y | Y | Y | N | ? |
| 53 Davis | Y | Y | Y | N | Y | Y | Y | Y |
| **COLORADO** | | | | | | | | |
| 1 DeGette | ? | ? | ? | ? | ? | ? | Y | Y |
| 2 Udall | Y | Y | Y | N | Y | Y | Y | Y |
| 3 Salazar | Y | Y | Y | N | Y | Y | Y | N |
| 4 Musgrave | Y | Y | Y | Y | Y | Y | N | N |
| 5 Hefley | Y | Y | Y | Y | Y | Y | N | N |
| 6 Tancredo | Y | Y | Y | Y | Y | Y | N | N |
| 7 Beauprez | Y | Y | Y | Y | Y | Y | N | N |
| **CONNECTICUT** | | | | | | | | |
| 1 Larson | Y | Y | Y | N | Y | Y | Y | Y |
| 2 Simmons | Y | Y | Y | Y | Y | Y | Y | Y |
| 3 DeLauro | Y | Y | Y | Y | Y | Y | Y | Y |
| 4 Shays | Y | Y | Y | Y | Y | Y | Y | Y |
| 5 Johnson | Y | Y | Y | Y | Y | Y | Y | N |
| **DELAWARE** | | | | | | | | |
| AL Castle | Y | Y | Y | Y | Y | Y | Y | N |
| **FLORIDA** | | | | | | | | |
| 1 Miller | Y | Y | Y | Y | Y | Y | N | N |
| 2 Boyd | Y | Y | Y | N | Y | Y | N | Y |
| 3 Brown | Y | Y | Y | N | Y | Y | N | Y |
| 4 Crenshaw | Y | Y | Y | Y | Y | Y | N | N |
| 5 Brown-Waite | Y | Y | Y | Y | Y | Y | N | N |
| 6 Stearns | Y | Y | Y | Y | Y | Y | N | N |
| 7 Mica | Y | Y | Y | Y | Y | Y | N | N |
| 8 Keller | Y | Y | Y | Y | Y | Y | N | N |
| 9 Bilirakis | Y | Y | Y | Y | Y | Y | N | N |
| 10 Young | ? | ? | ? | ? | ? | ? | N | N |
| 11 Davis | Y | Y | Y | N | Y | Y | Y | Y |
| 12 Putnam | Y | Y | Y | Y | Y | Y | N | N |
| 13 Harris | Y | Y | Y | Y | Y | Y | N | N |
| 14 Mack | Y | Y | Y | Y | Y | Y | N | N |
| 15 Weldon | Y | Y | Y | Y | Y | Y | N | N |
| 16 Foley | Y | Y | Y | Y | Y | Y | N | N |
| 17 Meek | Y | Y | Y | N | Y | Y | Y | Y |
| 18 Ros-Lehtinen | Y | Y | Y | Y | Y | Y | N | N |
| 19 Wexler | ? | ? | ? | N | Y | Y | Y | Y |
| 20 Wasserman-Schultz | Y | Y | Y | N | Y | Y | N | N |
| 21 Diaz-Balart, L. | ? | ? | ? | ? | ? | ? | N | N |
| 22 Shaw | Y | Y | Y | Y | Y | Y | N | N |
| 23 Hastings | Y | Y | Y | N | Y | Y | N | N |
| 24 Feeney | Y | Y | Y | Y | Y | Y | N | N |
| 25 Diaz-Balart, M. | Y | Y | Y | Y | Y | Y | N | N |
| **GEORGIA** | | | | | | | | |
| 1 Kingston | Y | Y | Y | Y | Y | Y | N | N |
| 2 Bishop | Y | Y | Y | N | Y | Y | N | N |
| 3 Marshall | Y | Y | Y | N | Y | Y | Y | Y |
| 4 McKinney | Y | Y | Y | N | Y | Y | Y | Y |
| 5 Lewis | Y | Y | Y | N | Y | Y | Y | Y |
| 6 Price | Y | Y | Y | Y | Y | Y | N | N |
| 7 Linder | Y | Y | Y | Y | Y | Y | N | N |
| 8 Westmoreland | Y | Y | Y | Y | Y | Y | N | N |
| 9 Norwood | Y | Y | Y | Y | Y | Y | N | N |
| 10 Deal | ? | ? | ? | Y | Y | Y | N | N |
| 11 Gingrey | Y | Y | Y | Y | Y | Y | N | N |
| 12 Barrow | Y | Y | Y | N | Y | Y | N | Y |
| 13 Scott | Y | Y | ? | N | Y | Y | N | N |
| **HAWAII** | | | | | | | | |
| 1 Abercrombie | Y | Y | Y | N | Y | Y | Y | Y |
| 2 Case | Y | Y | Y | ? | ? | ? | Y | Y |
| **IDAHO** | | | | | | | | |
| 1 Otter | Y | Y | Y | Y | Y | Y | N | N |
| 2 Simpson | Y | Y | Y | Y | Y | Y | N | N |
| **ILLINOIS** | | | | | | | | |
| 1 Rush | ? | ? | ? | N | Y | Y | Y | Y |
| 2 Jackson | Y | Y | Y | N | Y | Y | Y | Y |
| 3 Lipinski | Y | Y | Y | N | Y | Y | Y | Y |
| 4 Gutierrez | Y | Y | Y | N | Y | Y | Y | Y |
| 5 Emanuel | Y | Y | Y | N | Y | Y | ? | ? |
| 6 Hyde | Y | Y | Y | Y | Y | Y | N | N |
| 7 Davis | Y | Y | Y | N | Y | Y | Y | Y |
| 8 Bean | Y | Y | Y | Y | Y | Y | Y | Y |
| 9 Schakowsky | Y | Y | Y | N | Y | Y | Y | Y |
| 10 Kirk | Y | Y | Y | Y | Y | Y | N | N |
| 11 Weller | Y | Y | Y | Y | Y | ? | N | N |
| 12 Costello | N | Y | Y | N | Y | Y | N | Y |

| KEY | Republicans | Democrats | *Independents* |
|---|---|---|---|
| Y | Voted for (yea) | X Paired against | C Voted "present" to avoid possible conflict of interest |
| # | Paired for | – Announced against | |
| + | Announced for | P Voted "present" | ? Did not vote or otherwise make a position known |
| N | Voted against (nay) | | |

| | 109 | 110 | 111 | 112 | 113 | 114 | 115 | 116 |
|---|---|---|---|---|---|---|---|---|
| 13 **Biggert** | Y | Y | Y | Y | Y | Y | N | N |
| 14 **Hastert** | | | | | | | | |
| 15 **Johnson** | Y | Y | Y | Y | Y | Y | Y | N |
| 16 **Manzullo** | Y | Y | Y | Y | Y | Y | N | N |
| 17 Evans | Y | Y | ? | N | Y | Y | Y | Y |
| 18 **LaHood** | Y | Y | Y | Y | Y | Y | N | N |
| 19 **Shimkus** | Y | Y | Y | Y | Y | Y | N | N |
| **INDIANA** | | | | | | | | |
| 1 Visclosky | Y | Y | Y | N | Y | Y | Y | Y |
| 2 **Chocola** | Y | Y | ? | Y | Y | Y | N | N |
| 3 **Souder** | Y | Y | Y | Y | Y | Y | N | Y |
| 4 **Buyer** | Y | Y | Y | Y | Y | Y | N | N |
| 5 **Burton** | Y | Y | Y | Y | Y | Y | N | N |
| 6 **Pence** | Y | Y | Y | Y | Y | Y | N | N |
| 7 Carson | Y | Y | Y | N | Y | Y | Y | Y |
| 8 **Hostettler** | Y | Y | Y | Y | Y | Y | N | Y |
| 9 **Sodrel** | Y | Y | Y | Y | Y | Y | N | N |
| **IOWA** | | | | | | | | |
| 1 **Nussle** | Y | Y | ? | Y | Y | Y | N | Y |
| 2 **Leach** | Y | Y | Y | Y | Y | Y | Y | Y |
| 3 Boswell | Y | Y | Y | N | Y | Y | N | Y |
| 4 **Latham** | Y | Y | Y | Y | Y | Y | N | N |
| 5 **King** | Y | Y | Y | Y | Y | Y | N | N |
| **KANSAS** | | | | | | | | |
| 1 **Moran** | Y | Y | Y | Y | Y | Y | N | N |
| 2 **Ryun** | Y | Y | Y | Y | Y | Y | N | N |
| 3 Moore | Y | Y | Y | N | Y | Y | Y | Y |
| 4 **Tiahrt** | Y | Y | Y | Y | Y | Y | N | N |
| **KENTUCKY** | | | | | | | | |
| 1 **Whitfield** | Y | Y | Y | Y | Y | Y | N | N |
| 2 **Lewis** | Y | Y | Y | Y | Y | Y | N | N |
| 3 **Northup** | Y | Y | Y | Y | Y | Y | N | N |
| 4 **Davis** | Y | Y | Y | Y | Y | Y | N | N |
| 5 **Rogers** | Y | Y | Y | Y | Y | Y | N | N |
| 6 Chandler | Y | Y | Y | N | Y | Y | Y | Y |
| **LOUISIANA** | | | | | | | | |
| 1 **Jindal** | Y | Y | Y | Y | Y | Y | N | N |
| 2 Jefferson | Y | Y | Y | N | Y | Y | Y | N |
| 3 Melancon | Y | Y | Y | Y | Y | Y | N | N |
| 4 **McCrery** | Y | Y | Y | Y | Y | Y | N | N |
| 5 **Alexander** | Y | Y | Y | Y | Y | Y | N | N |
| 6 **Baker** | Y | Y | Y | Y | Y | Y | N | N |
| 7 **Boustany** | Y | Y | Y | Y | Y | Y | N | N |
| **MAINE** | | | | | | | | |
| 1 Allen | Y | Y | Y | N | Y | Y | Y | N |
| 2 Michaud | Y | Y | Y | N | Y | Y | Y | Y |
| **MARYLAND** | | | | | | | | |
| 1 **Gilchrest** | Y | Y | Y | Y | Y | Y | Y | Y |
| 2 Ruppersberger | Y | Y | Y | N | Y | Y | N | Y |
| 3 Cardin | Y | Y | Y | N | Y | Y | Y | Y |
| 4 Wynn | Y | Y | Y | N | Y | Y | Y | Y |
| 5 Hoyer | Y | Y | Y | N | Y | Y | Y | Y |
| 6 **Bartlett** | Y | Y | Y | Y | Y | Y | N | N |
| 7 Cummings | Y | Y | Y | N | Y | Y | Y | Y |
| 8 Van Hollen | Y | Y | Y | N | Y | Y | Y | Y |
| **MASSACHUSETTS** | | | | | | | | |
| 1 Olver | Y | Y | Y | N | Y | Y | Y | Y |
| 2 Neal | Y | Y | Y | N | Y | Y | Y | Y |
| 3 McGovern | Y | Y | Y | N | Y | Y | Y | Y |
| 4 Frank | Y | Y | Y | N | Y | Y | Y | Y |
| 5 Meehan | Y | Y | Y | N | Y | Y | Y | Y |
| 6 Tierney | Y | Y | Y | N | Y | Y | Y | Y |
| 7 Markey | Y | Y | Y | N | Y | Y | Y | Y |
| 8 Capuano | Y | Y | Y | N | Y | Y | Y | Y |
| 9 Lynch | Y | Y | Y | N | Y | Y | Y | Y |
| 10 Delahunt | Y | Y | Y | N | Y | Y | ? | Y |
| **MICHIGAN** | | | | | | | | |
| 1 Stupak | Y | Y | Y | N | Y | Y | Y | Y |
| 2 **Hoekstra** | Y | Y | Y | Y | Y | Y | N | N |
| 3 **Ehlers** | Y | Y | Y | Y | Y | Y | Y | Y |
| 4 **Camp** | Y | Y | Y | Y | Y | Y | N | N |
| 5 Kildee | Y | Y | Y | N | Y | Y | Y | Y |
| 6 **Upton** | Y | Y | Y | Y | Y | Y | N | N |
| 7 **Schwarz** | Y | Y | Y | Y | Y | Y | N | N |
| 8 **Rogers** | Y | Y | Y | Y | Y | Y | N | N |
| 9 **Knollenberg** | Y | Y | Y | Y | Y | Y | N | N |
| 10 **Miller** | Y | Y | Y | Y | Y | Y | N | N |
| 11 **McCotter** | Y | Y | Y | Y | Y | Y | N | N |
| 12 Levin | Y | Y | Y | N | Y | Y | Y | N |
| 13 Kilpatrick | Y | Y | Y | N | Y | Y | Y | Y |
| 14 Conyers | Y | Y | Y | N | Y | Y | Y | Y |
| 15 Dingell | Y | Y | Y | N | Y | Y | Y | N |

| | 109 | 110 | 111 | 112 | 113 | 114 | 115 | 116 |
|---|---|---|---|---|---|---|---|---|
| **MINNESOTA** | | | | | | | | |
| 1 **Gutknecht** | Y | Y | Y | Y | Y | Y | N | Y |
| 2 **Kline** | Y | Y | Y | Y | Y | Y | N | N |
| 3 **Ramstad** | Y | Y | Y | Y | Y | Y | Y | N |
| 4 McCollum | Y | Y | Y | N | Y | Y | Y | Y |
| 5 Sabo | Y | Y | Y | N | Y | Y | Y | Y |
| 6 **Kennedy** | Y | Y | Y | Y | Y | Y | N | Y |
| 7 Peterson | Y | Y | Y | N | Y | Y | N | Y |
| 8 Oberstar | Y | Y | Y | N | Y | Y | Y | Y |
| **MISSISSIPPI** | | | | | | | | |
| 1 **Wicker** | Y | Y | Y | Y | Y | Y | N | N |
| 2 Thompson | Y | Y | Y | N | Y | Y | Y | Y |
| 3 **Pickering** | Y | Y | Y | Y | Y | Y | N | ? |
| 4 Taylor | Y | Y | Y | N | Y | Y | N | Y |
| **MISSOURI** | | | | | | | | |
| 1 Clay | Y | Y | Y | N | Y | Y | Y | Y |
| 2 **Akin** | Y | Y | Y | Y | Y | Y | N | N |
| 3 Carnahan | Y | Y | Y | N | Y | Y | Y | Y |
| 4 Skelton | Y | Y | Y | N | Y | Y | Y | Y |
| 5 Cleaver | Y | Y | Y | N | Y | Y | Y | Y |
| 6 **Graves** | Y | Y | Y | Y | Y | Y | N | N |
| 7 **Blunt** | Y | Y | Y | Y | Y | Y | N | N |
| 8 **Emerson** | Y | Y | Y | Y | Y | Y | N | Y |
| 9 **Hulshof** | Y | Y | Y | Y | Y | Y | N | N |
| **MONTANA** | | | | | | | | |
| AL **Rehberg** | Y | Y | Y | Y | Y | Y | N | N |
| **NEBRASKA** | | | | | | | | |
| 1 **Fortenberry** | Y | Y | Y | Y | Y | Y | N | N |
| 2 **Terry** | Y | Y | Y | Y | Y | Y | N | N |
| 3 **Osborne** | Y | Y | Y | Y | Y | Y | N | N |
| **NEVADA** | | | | | | | | |
| 1 Berkley | Y | Y | Y | N | Y | Y | Y | Y |
| 2 **Gibbons** | Y | Y | Y | Y | Y | Y | N | N |
| 3 **Porter** | Y | Y | Y | Y | Y | Y | N | N |
| **NEW HAMPSHIRE** | | | | | | | | |
| 1 **Bradley** | Y | + | Y | Y | Y | Y | N | N |
| 2 **Bass** | Y | Y | Y | Y | Y | Y | N | N |
| **NEW JERSEY** | | | | | | | | |
| 1 Andrews | Y | Y | Y | N | Y | Y | ? | ? |
| 2 **LoBiondo** | Y | Y | Y | Y | Y | Y | Y | N |
| 3 **Saxton** | Y | Y | Y | Y | Y | Y | Y | N |
| 4 **Smith** | Y | Y | Y | Y | Y | Y | Y | N |
| 5 **Garrett** | Y | Y | Y | Y | Y | Y | N | N |
| 6 Pallone | ? | ? | ? | N | Y | Y | Y | Y |
| 7 **Ferguson** | Y | Y | Y | Y | Y | Y | N | N |
| 8 Pascrell | Y | Y | ? | N | Y | Y | Y | Y |
| 9 Rothman | Y | Y | Y | N | Y | Y | Y | Y |
| 10 Payne | Y | Y | Y | N | Y | Y | Y | Y |
| 11 **Frelinghuysen** | Y | Y | Y | Y | Y | Y | N | N |
| 12 Holt | Y | Y | Y | N | Y | Y | Y | Y |
| 13 Menendez | + | + | + | N | Y | Y | Y | Y |
| **NEW MEXICO** | | | | | | | | |
| 1 **Wilson** | Y | Y | Y | Y | Y | Y | Y | N |
| 2 **Pearce** | Y | Y | Y | Y | Y | Y | N | N |
| 3 Udall | Y | Y | Y | N | Y | Y | Y | Y |
| **NEW YORK** | | | | | | | | |
| 1 Bishop | Y | Y | Y | N | Y | Y | Y | Y |
| 2 Israel | Y | Y | Y | N | Y | Y | Y | Y |
| 3 **King** | Y | Y | Y | Y | Y | Y | N | N |
| 4 McCarthy | Y | Y | Y | N | Y | Y | Y | Y |
| 5 Ackerman | Y | Y | Y | N | Y | Y | Y | Y |
| 6 Meeks | Y | Y | Y | N | Y | Y | Y | Y |
| 7 Crowley | Y | Y | Y | N | Y | Y | Y | Y |
| 8 Nadler | Y | Y | Y | N | Y | Y | Y | Y |
| 9 Weiner | Y | Y | Y | N | Y | Y | Y | Y |
| 10 Towns | Y | Y | Y | N | Y | Y | Y | N |
| 11 Owens | Y | Y | Y | N | Y | Y | Y | Y |
| 12 Velázquez | Y | Y | Y | N | Y | Y | Y | Y |
| 13 **Fossella** | + | Y | Y | Y | Y | Y | N | N |
| 14 Maloney | Y | Y | Y | N | Y | Y | Y | Y |
| 15 Rangel | Y | Y | Y | N | Y | Y | Y | Y |
| 16 Serrano | Y | Y | Y | N | Y | Y | Y | Y |
| 17 Engel | Y | Y | Y | N | Y | Y | Y | Y |
| 18 Lowey | Y | Y | Y | N | Y | Y | Y | Y |
| 19 **Kelly** | Y | Y | Y | ? | ? | ? | ? | ? |
| 20 **Sweeney** | Y | Y | Y | ? | ? | ? | N | N |
| 21 McNulty | Y | Y | Y | N | Y | Y | Y | Y |
| 22 Hinchey | Y | Y | Y | N | Y | Y | Y | Y |
| 23 **McHugh** | Y | Y | Y | Y | Y | Y | N | N |
| 24 **Boehlert** | Y | Y | Y | Y | Y | Y | Y | N |
| 25 **Walsh** | Y | Y | Y | Y | Y | Y | N | N |
| 26 **Reynolds** | Y | Y | Y | Y | Y | Y | N | N |
| 27 Higgins | Y | Y | Y | N | Y | Y | Y | Y |
| 28 Slaughter | Y | Y | Y | N | Y | Y | Y | Y |
| 29 **Kuhl** | Y | Y | Y | ? | Y | Y | N | N |

| | 109 | 110 | 111 | 112 | 113 | 114 | 115 | 116 |
|---|---|---|---|---|---|---|---|---|
| **NORTH CAROLINA** | | | | | | | | |
| 1 Butterfield | Y | Y | Y | N | Y | Y | Y | Y |
| 2 Etheridge | Y | Y | Y | N | Y | Y | Y | Y |
| 3 **Jones** | Y | Y | Y | Y | Y | Y | N | N |
| 4 Price | Y | Y | Y | N | Y | Y | Y | Y |
| 5 **Foxx** | Y | Y | Y | + | + | Y | N | N |
| 6 **Coble** | Y | Y | Y | Y | Y | Y | N | N |
| 7 McIntyre | Y | Y | Y | N | Y | Y | Y | Y |
| 8 **Hayes** | Y | Y | Y | Y | Y | Y | N | N |
| 9 **Myrick** | Y | Y | Y | Y | Y | Y | N | N |
| 10 **McHenry** | Y | Y | Y | Y | Y | Y | N | N |
| 11 **Taylor** | Y | Y | Y | Y | Y | Y | N | N |
| 12 Watt | Y | Y | Y | N | Y | Y | Y | Y |
| 13 Miller | Y | Y | Y | N | Y | Y | Y | Y |
| **NORTH DAKOTA** | | | | | | | | |
| AL Pomeroy | Y | Y | Y | N | Y | Y | N | Y |
| **OHIO** | | | | | | | | |
| 1 **Chabot** | Y | Y | Y | Y | Y | Y | N | N |
| 2 **Portman** | Y | Y | Y | ? | Y | Y | N | N |
| 3 **Turner** | Y | Y | Y | Y | Y | Y | N | N |
| 4 **Oxley** | Y | Y | Y | Y | Y | Y | N | N |
| 5 **Gillmor** | Y | Y | Y | Y | Y | Y | N | N |
| 6 Strickland | Y | Y | Y | N | Y | ? | Y | Y |
| 7 **Hobson** | Y | Y | Y | Y | Y | Y | N | N |
| 8 **Boehner** | Y | Y | Y | Y | Y | Y | N | N |
| 9 Kaptur | Y | Y | Y | N | Y | Y | Y | Y |
| 10 Kucinich | Y | Y | Y | N | Y | Y | Y | Y |
| 11 Jones | Y | Y | Y | N | Y | Y | Y | Y |
| 12 **Tiberi** | Y | Y | Y | Y | Y | Y | N | N |
| 13 Brown | Y | Y | Y | N | Y | Y | Y | Y |
| 14 **LaTourette** | Y | Y | Y | Y | Y | Y | N | Y |
| 15 **Pryce** | Y | Y | Y | Y | Y | Y | N | N |
| 16 **Regula** | Y | Y | Y | Y | Y | Y | N | N |
| 17 Ryan | Y | Y | Y | N | Y | Y | Y | Y |
| 18 **Ney** | Y | Y | Y | Y | Y | Y | N | N |
| **OKLAHOMA** | | | | | | | | |
| 1 **Sullivan** | Y | Y | Y | Y | Y | Y | N | N |
| 2 Boren | Y | Y | Y | N | Y | Y | N | N |
| 3 **Lucas** | Y | Y | Y | Y | Y | Y | N | N |
| 4 **Cole** | Y | Y | Y | Y | Y | Y | N | N |
| 5 **Istook** | ? | ? | ? | Y | Y | Y | N | N |
| **OREGON** | | | | | | | | |
| 1 Wu | N | Y | Y | N | Y | Y | Y | Y |
| 2 **Walden** | Y | Y | Y | Y | Y | Y | N | N |
| 3 Blumenauer | Y | Y | Y | N | Y | Y | Y | Y |
| 4 DeFazio | N | Y | Y | N | Y | Y | Y | Y |
| 5 Hooley | Y | Y | Y | N | Y | Y | Y | Y |
| **PENNSYLVANIA** | | | | | | | | |
| 1 Brady | Y | Y | Y | N | Y | Y | Y | Y |
| 2 Fattah | ? | ? | ? | N | Y | Y | Y | Y |
| 3 **English** | Y | Y | Y | Y | Y | Y | N | N |
| 4 **Hart** | Y | Y | Y | Y | Y | Y | N | N |
| 5 **Peterson** | Y | Y | Y | Y | Y | Y | N | N |
| 6 **Gerlach** | Y | ? | Y | Y | Y | Y | Y | N |
| 7 **Weldon** | Y | Y | Y | Y | Y | Y | N | N |
| 8 **Fitzpatrick** | Y | Y | Y | Y | Y | Y | Y | N |
| 9 **Shuster** | Y | Y | Y | Y | Y | Y | N | N |
| 10 **Sherwood** | Y | Y | Y | Y | Y | Y | N | N |
| 11 Kanjorski | Y | Y | Y | N | Y | Y | Y | Y |
| 12 Murtha | Y | ? | ? | N | Y | Y | Y | Y |
| 13 Schwartz | Y | Y | Y | N | Y | Y | Y | Y |
| 14 Doyle | Y | Y | Y | N | Y | Y | Y | Y |
| 15 **Dent** | Y | Y | Y | Y | Y | Y | N | N |
| 16 **Pitts** | Y | Y | Y | Y | Y | Y | N | N |
| 17 Holden | Y | Y | Y | N | Y | Y | Y | Y |
| 18 **Murphy** | Y | Y | Y | Y | Y | Y | N | N |
| 19 **Platts** | Y | Y | Y | Y | Y | Y | N | N |
| **RHODE ISLAND** | | | | | | | | |
| 1 Kennedy | ? | ? | ? | ? | ? | ? | Y | Y |
| 2 Langevin | Y | Y | Y | N | Y | Y | Y | Y |
| **SOUTH CAROLINA** | | | | | | | | |
| 1 **Brown** | Y | Y | Y | Y | Y | Y | N | N |
| 2 **Wilson** | Y | Y | Y | Y | Y | Y | N | N |
| 3 **Barrett** | Y | Y | Y | Y | Y | Y | N | N |
| 4 **Inglis** | Y | Y | Y | Y | Y | Y | N | N |
| 5 Spratt | Y | Y | Y | N | Y | Y | Y | Y |
| 6 Clyburn | Y | Y | Y | N | Y | Y | Y | Y |
| **SOUTH DAKOTA** | | | | | | | | |
| AL Herseth | Y | Y | Y | N | Y | Y | N | Y |
| **TENNESSEE** | | | | | | | | |
| 1 **Jenkins** | ? | ? | ? | Y | Y | Y | N | N |
| 2 **Duncan** | N | Y | Y | Y | Y | Y | N | N |

| | 109 | 110 | 111 | 112 | 113 | 114 | 115 | 116 |
|---|---|---|---|---|---|---|---|---|
| 3 **Wamp** | Y | Y | Y | Y | Y | Y | N | N |
| 4 Davis | Y | Y | Y | N | Y | Y | N | Y |
| 5 Cooper | Y | Y | Y | N | Y | Y | N | N |
| 6 Gordon | Y | Y | Y | N | Y | Y | N | Y |
| 7 **Blackburn** | Y | Y | Y | Y | Y | Y | N | N |
| 8 Tanner | Y | Y | Y | N | Y | Y | N | Y |
| 9 Ford | Y | Y | Y | N | Y | Y | N | Y |
| **TEXAS** | | | | | | | | |
| 1 **Gohmert** | Y | Y | Y | Y | Y | + | N | ? |
| 2 **Poe** | Y | Y | Y | Y | Y | Y | N | N |
| 3 **Johnson, S.** | Y | Y | Y | Y | Y | Y | N | N |
| 4 **Hall** | Y | Y | Y | Y | Y | Y | N | N |
| 5 **Hensarling** | Y | Y | Y | Y | Y | Y | N | N |
| 6 **Barton** | Y | Y | Y | Y | Y | Y | N | N |
| 7 **Culberson** | Y | Y | Y | Y | Y | Y | N | N |
| 8 **Brady** | Y | Y | Y | Y | Y | Y | N | N |
| 9 Green | Y | Y | Y | N | Y | Y | Y | N |
| 10 **McCaul** | Y | Y | Y | Y | Y | Y | N | N |
| 11 **Conaway** | Y | Y | Y | Y | Y | Y | N | N |
| 12 **Granger** | Y | Y | Y | Y | Y | Y | N | N |
| 13 **Thornberry** | Y | Y | Y | Y | Y | Y | N | N |
| 14 **Paul** | N | Y | Y | Y | Y | Y | N | N |
| 15 Hinojosa | Y | Y | Y | Y | Y | Y | N | N |
| 16 Reyes | Y | Y | Y | Y | Y | Y | N | N |
| 17 Edwards | Y | Y | Y | N | Y | Y | N | N |
| 18 Jackson-Lee | Y | Y | Y | N | Y | Y | Y | N |
| 19 **Neugebauer** | Y | Y | Y | Y | Y | Y | N | N |
| 20 Gonzalez | Y | Y | Y | Y | Y | Y | Y | N |
| 21 **Smith** | Y | Y | Y | Y | Y | Y | N | N |
| 22 **DeLay** | Y | Y | Y | Y | Y | Y | N | N |
| 23 **Bonilla** | Y | Y | Y | Y | Y | Y | N | N |
| 24 **Marchant** | Y | Y | Y | Y | Y | Y | N | N |
| 25 Doggett | Y | Y | Y | N | Y | Y | Y | N |
| 26 **Burgess** | Y | Y | Y | Y | Y | Y | N | N |
| 27 Ortiz | Y | Y | Y | Y | Y | Y | N | N |
| 28 Cuellar | Y | Y | Y | N | Y | Y | N | N |
| 29 Green | Y | Y | Y | Y | Y | Y | N | N |
| 30 Johnson, E. | Y | Y | Y | N | Y | Y | Y | N |
| 31 **Carter** | Y | Y | Y | Y | Y | Y | N | N |
| 32 **Sessions** | Y | Y | Y | Y | ? | Y | N | N |
| **UTAH** | | | | | | | | |
| 1 **Bishop** | Y | Y | Y | Y | Y | Y | N | N |
| 2 Matheson | Y | Y | Y | N | Y | Y | N | N |
| 3 **Cannon** | Y | Y | Y | Y | Y | Y | N | N |
| **VERMONT** | | | | | | | | |
| AL *Sanders* | Y | Y | ? | N | Y | Y | Y | Y |
| **VIRGINIA** | | | | | | | | |
| 1 **Davis, J.** | Y | Y | Y | Y | Y | Y | N | N |
| 2 **Drake** | Y | Y | Y | Y | Y | Y | N | N |
| 3 Scott | Y | Y | Y | N | Y | Y | Y | Y |
| 4 **Forbes** | Y | Y | Y | Y | Y | Y | N | N |
| 5 **Goode** | Y | Y | Y | Y | Y | Y | N | N |
| 6 **Goodlatte** | Y | Y | Y | Y | Y | Y | N | N |
| 7 **Cantor** | Y | Y | Y | Y | Y | Y | N | N |
| 8 Moran | Y | Y | Y | N | Y | Y | Y | Y |
| 9 Boucher | Y | Y | Y | N | Y | Y | N | Y |
| 10 **Wolf** | Y | Y | Y | Y | Y | Y | N | N |
| 11 **Davis, T.** | Y | Y | Y | Y | Y | Y | N | N |
| **WASHINGTON** | | | | | | | | |
| 1 Inslee | Y | Y | Y | N | Y | Y | Y | Y |
| 2 Larsen | Y | Y | Y | N | Y | Y | Y | Y |
| 3 Baird | Y | Y | Y | N | Y | Y | Y | Y |
| 4 **Hastings** | Y | Y | Y | Y | Y | Y | N | N |
| 5 **McMorris** | Y | Y | Y | Y | Y | Y | N | N |
| 6 Dicks | Y | Y | Y | N | Y | Y | Y | Y |
| 7 McDermott | Y | Y | Y | N | Y | Y | Y | Y |
| 8 **Reichert** | Y | Y | Y | Y | Y | Y | N | N |
| 9 Smith | Y | Y | Y | N | Y | Y | Y | Y |
| **WEST VIRGINIA** | | | | | | | | |
| 1 Mollohan | Y | Y | Y | N | Y | Y | Y | ? |
| 2 **Capito** | Y | Y | Y | Y | Y | Y | N | N |
| 3 Rahall | Y | Y | Y | N | Y | Y | Y | Y |
| **WISCONSIN** | | | | | | | | |
| 1 **Ryan** | Y | Y | Y | Y | Y | Y | N | N |
| 2 Baldwin | Y | Y | Y | N | Y | Y | Y | Y |
| 3 Kind | Y | Y | Y | N | Y | Y | Y | Y |
| 4 Moore | N | Y | Y | N | Y | Y | Y | Y |
| 5 **Sensenbrenner** | Y | Y | Y | Y | Y | Y | N | N |
| 6 **Petri** | Y | Y | Y | Y | Y | Y | N | N |
| 7 Obey | Y | Y | Y | N | Y | Y | Y | Y |
| 8 **Green** | Y | Y | Y | Y | Y | Y | N | Y |
| **WYOMING** | | | | | | | | |
| AL **Cubin** | Y | Y | Y | Y | Y | Y | N | N |

# IN THE HOUSE | By Vote Number

**117.** **HR 6. Energy Policy/Oil Demand Reduction.** Waxman, D-Calif., amendment that would require federal agencies to develop steps to reduce demand for oil by 1 million barrels per day by 2013. Rejected 166-262: R 18-210; D 147-52 (ND 123-25, SD 24-27); I 1-0. April 20, 2005.

**118.** **HR 6. Energy Policy/Energy Dependence Reduction.** Bishop, D-N.Y., amendment that would require electric utility companies to reduce dependence on non-renewable energy sources and authorize $50 million over 10 years for the development of new electricity reliability standards for bulk-power. It would provide tax benefits for energy-efficient homes and other energy-efficient buildings, and prohibit oil and gas drilling in the Great Lakes. Rejected 170-259: R 4-226; D 165-33 (ND 137-10, SD 28-23); I 1-0. April 20, 2005.

**119.** **HR 6. Energy Policy/Fuel Economy Testing.** Rogers, R-Mich., amendment to the Johnson, R-Conn., amendment. The Rogers amendment would direct the EPA to revise certain federal vehicle fuel-economy measure-ment standards to factor in higher speed limits, variations in temperature and other fuel-depleting features to provide consumers with accurate fuel economy data on new vehicle labels. The Johnson amendment would require the EPA's fuel economy test procedures to reflect current driving patterns and conditions, and provide consumers with fuel economy information. Adopted 259-172: R 189-41; D 70-130 (ND 38-111, SD 32-19); I 0-1. April 20, 2005.

**120.** **HR 6. Energy Policy/Fuel Economy Testing.** Johnson, R-Conn., amendment to direct the EPA to revise certain federal vehicle fuel-economy measurement standards to factor in higher speed limits, variations in temperature and other fuel-depleting features to provide consumers with accurate fuel economy data on new vehicle labels. Adopted 346-85: R 225-5; D 121-79 (ND 74-75, SD 47-4); I 0-1. April 20, 2005.

**121.** **HR 6 Energy Policy/CAFE Standards.** Boehlert, R-N.Y., amendment to require the Transportation Department to issue regulations by model year 2007 that would increase fuel efficiency standards to at least 33 miles per gallon in automobiles manufactured by model year 2015. Rejected 177-254: R 36-194; D 140-60 (ND 118-31, SD 22-29); I 1-0. A "nay" was a vote in support of the president's position. April 20, 2005.

**122.** **HR 6. Energy Policy/ANWR Drilling.** Markey, D-Mass., amendment to strike the provision in the bill that would allow leases for oil and gas exploration, development and production in Alaska's Arctic National Wildlife Refuge. Rejected 200-231: R 29-201; D 170-30 (ND 138-11, SD 32-19); I 1-0. A "nay" was a vote in support of the president's position. April 20, 2005.

**123.** **HR 6. Energy Policy/Power Act Violations.** Dingell, D-Mich., amendment to authorize the Federal Energy Regulatory Commission to refund electricity overcharges and increase the penalties for violations of the Federal Power Act. It would strike a provision in the bill repealing the Public Utility Holding Company Act (PUHCA), and direct the Securities and Exchange Commission to review utility companies' compliance with PUHCA. Rejected 188-243: R 6-224; D 181-19 (ND 143-6, SD 38-13); I 1-0. April 20, 2005.

**124.** **HR 6. Energy Policy/Uranium Mining.** Udall, D-N.M., amendment to strike the provision in the bill that would authorize $10 million annually from fiscal 2006-08 for a program to seek improved technologies for mining uranium and for environmental restoration of uranium-mine sites. Rejected 204-225: R 24-202; D 179-23 (ND 143-8, SD 36-15); I 1-0. April 21, 2005.

| Member | 117 | 118 | 119 | 120 | 121 | 122 | 123 | 124 |
|---|---|---|---|---|---|---|---|---|
| **ALABAMA** | | | | | | | | |
| 1 Bonner | N | N | Y | Y | N | N | N | N |
| 2 Everett | N | N | Y | Y | N | N | N | N |
| 3 Rogers | N | N | Y | Y | N | N | N | N |
| 4 Aderholt | N | N | Y | Y | N | N | N | N |
| 5 Cramer | N | N | Y | Y | N | Y | N | N |
| 6 Bachus | ? | N | Y | Y | N | N | N | N |
| 7 Davis | Y | Y | Y | Y | N | N | N | Y |
| **ALASKA** | | | | | | | | |
| AL Young | N | N | Y | Y | N | N | N | N |
| **ARIZONA** | | | | | | | | |
| 1 Renzi | N | N | Y | Y | N | N | N | Y |
| 2 Franks | N | N | Y | Y | N | N | N | ? |
| 3 Shadegg | N | N | Y | Y | N | N | N | Y |
| 4 Pastor | Y | Y | Y | Y | Y | Y | Y | Y |
| 5 Hayworth | N | N | Y | Y | N | N | N | N |
| 6 Flake | N | N | Y | Y | N | N | N | Y |
| 7 Grijalva | Y | Y | N | N | Y | Y | Y | Y |
| 8 Kolbe | N | N | N | Y | N | N | N | N |
| **ARKANSAS** | | | | | | | | |
| 1 Berry | N | N | Y | Y | N | N | N | N |
| 2 Snyder | Y | Y | N | Y | Y | Y | Y | Y |
| 3 Boozman | N | N | Y | Y | N | N | N | N |
| 4 Ross | N | N | Y | Y | N | Y | N | N |
| **CALIFORNIA** | | | | | | | | |
| 1 Thompson | Y | Y | N | N | Y | Y | Y | Y |
| 2 Herger | N | N | Y | Y | N | N | N | N |
| 3 Lungren | N | N | Y | Y | N | N | N | N |
| 4 Doolittle | N | N | Y | Y | N | N | N | N |
| 5 Matsui, D. | Y | Y | N | N | Y | Y | Y | Y |
| 6 Woolsey | Y | Y | N | N | Y | Y | Y | Y |
| 7 Miller, George | Y | Y | N | N | Y | Y | Y | Y |
| 8 Pelosi | Y | Y | N | N | Y | Y | Y | Y |
| 9 Lee | Y | Y | N | N | Y | Y | Y | Y |
| 10 Tauscher | Y | Y | N | N | Y | Y | Y | Y |
| 11 Pombo | N | N | Y | Y | N | N | N | N |
| 12 Lantos | Y | Y | N | N | Y | Y | Y | Y |
| 13 Stark | Y | Y | N | N | Y | Y | Y | Y |
| 14 Eshoo | Y | Y | N | N | Y | Y | Y | Y |
| 15 Honda | Y | Y | N | N | Y | Y | Y | Y |
| 16 Lofgren | Y | Y | N | N | Y | Y | Y | Y |
| 17 Farr | Y | Y | N | N | Y | Y | Y | Y |
| 18 Cardoza | Y | Y | N | N | Y | Y | Y | Y |
| 19 Radanovich | N | N | Y | Y | N | N | N | N |
| 20 Costa | Y | N | N | Y | N | Y | Y | N |
| 21 Nunes | N | N | Y | Y | N | N | N | N |
| 22 Thomas | N | N | Y | Y | N | N | N | N |
| 23 Capps | Y | Y | N | N | Y | Y | Y | Y |
| 24 Gallegly | N | N | Y | Y | N | N | N | N |
| 25 McKeon | N | N | Y | Y | N | N | N | N |
| 26 Dreier | N | N | Y | Y | N | N | N | N |
| 27 Sherman | Y | Y | N | N | Y | Y | Y | Y |
| 28 Berman | Y | Y | N | N | Y | Y | Y | Y |
| 29 Schiff | Y | Y | N | N | Y | Y | Y | Y |
| 30 Waxman | Y | Y | N | N | Y | Y | Y | Y |
| 31 Becerra | Y | Y | N | N | Y | Y | Y | Y |
| 32 Solis | Y | Y | N | N | Y | Y | Y | Y |
| 33 Watson | Y | Y | N | N | Y | Y | Y | Y |
| 34 Roybal-Allard | Y | Y | N | N | Y | Y | Y | Y |
| 35 Waters | Y | Y | N | N | Y | Y | Y | Y |
| 36 Harman | Y | Y | N | N | Y | Y | Y | Y |
| 37 Millender-McD. | Y | Y | N | N | Y | Y | Y | Y |
| 38 Napolitano | Y | Y | N | N | Y | Y | Y | Y |
| 39 Sánchez, Linda | Y | Y | N | N | Y | Y | Y | Y |
| 40 Royce | N | N | Y | Y | N | N | N | N |
| 41 Lewis | N | N | Y | Y | N | N | N | N |
| 42 Miller, Gary | N | N | Y | Y | N | N | N | N |
| 43 Baca | N | Y | Y | N | Y | N | N | Y |
| 44 Calvert | N | N | Y | Y | N | N | N | N |
| 45 Bono | N | N | Y | Y | N | N | N | N |
| 46 Rohrabacher | N | N | Y | Y | N | N | N | Y |
| 47 Sanchez, Loretta | Y | Y | N | Y | Y | Y | Y | Y |
| 48 Cox | N | N | Y | Y | N | N | N | N |
| 49 Issa | N | N | Y | Y | N | N | N | N |
| 50 Cunningham | N | N | Y | Y | N | N | N | N |
| 51 Filner | Y | Y | N | Y | Y | Y | Y | Y |
| 52 Hunter | N | N | Y | Y | N | N | N | N |
| 53 Davis | Y | Y | N | Y | Y | Y | Y | Y |
| **COLORADO** | | | | | | | | |
| 1 DeGette | Y | Y | N | N | Y | Y | Y | Y |
| 2 Udall | Y | Y | N | N | Y | Y | Y | Y |
| 3 Salazar | N | Y | Y | N | Y | Y | Y | Y |
| 4 Musgrave | N | N | Y | Y | N | N | N | N |
| 5 Hefley | N | N | N | Y | N | N | N | N |
| 6 Tancredo | N | N | Y | Y | N | N | N | N |
| 7 Beauprez | N | N | Y | Y | N | N | N | N |
| **CONNECTICUT** | | | | | | | | |
| 1 Larson | Y | Y | N | Y | Y | Y | Y | Y |
| 2 Simmons | N | N | N | Y | N | Y | N | N |
| 3 DeLauro | Y | Y | N | Y | Y | Y | Y | Y |
| 4 Shays | Y | Y | Y | Y | Y | Y | Y | Y |
| 5 Johnson | N | N | N | Y | Y | N | N | N |
| **DELAWARE** | | | | | | | | |
| AL Castle | N | N | N | Y | N | N | Y | N |
| **FLORIDA** | | | | | | | | |
| 1 Miller | N | N | Y | Y | N | N | N | N |
| 2 Boyd | N | N | Y | Y | N | Y | N | Y |
| 3 Brown | Y | Y | N | Y | Y | Y | Y | Y |
| 4 Crenshaw | N | N | Y | Y | N | N | N | N |
| 5 Brown-Waite | N | N | Y | Y | N | N | N | N |
| 6 Stearns | N | N | Y | Y | N | N | N | N |
| 7 Mica | N | N | Y | N | N | N | N | N |
| 8 Keller | N | N | Y | Y | N | N | N | N |
| 9 Bilirakis | N | N | Y | Y | N | N | N | N |
| 10 Young | N | N | Y | Y | N | Y | N | ? |
| 11 Davis | Y | Y | N | Y | Y | Y | Y | Y |
| 12 Putnam | N | N | Y | Y | N | N | N | N |
| 13 Harris | N | N | Y | Y | N | N | N | Y |
| 14 Mack | N | N | Y | Y | N | N | N | N |
| 15 Weldon | N | N | Y | Y | N | N | N | N |
| 16 Foley | N | N | Y | Y | N | N | N | N |
| 17 Meek | N | Y | Y | Y | Y | N | Y | Y |
| 18 Ros-Lehtinen | N | N | Y | Y | N | N | N | N |
| 19 Wexler | Y | Y | N | Y | Y | Y | Y | Y |
| 20 Wasserman-Schultz | Y | Y | N | Y | Y | Y | Y | Y |
| 21 Diaz-Balart, L. | N | N | Y | Y | N | N | N | N |
| 22 Shaw | N | N | Y | Y | N | N | N | N |
| 23 Hastings | Y | Y | Y | Y | Y | Y | Y | Y |
| 24 Feeney | N | N | Y | Y | N | N | N | N |
| 25 Diaz-Balart, M. | N | N | Y | Y | N | N | N | N |
| **GEORGIA** | | | | | | | | |
| 1 Kingston | N | N | Y | Y | N | N | N | N |
| 2 Bishop | N | Y | Y | Y | N | N | N | Y |
| 3 Marshall | N | N | N | Y | N | Y | N | Y |
| 4 McKinney | Y | Y | Y | Y | Y | Y | Y | Y |
| 5 Lewis | Y | Y | N | Y | Y | Y | Y | Y |
| 6 Price | N | N | Y | Y | N | N | N | N |
| 7 Linder | N | N | Y | Y | N | N | N | N |
| 8 Westmoreland | N | N | Y | Y | N | N | N | N |
| 9 Norwood | N | N | Y | Y | N | N | N | N |
| 10 Deal | N | N | Y | Y | N | N | N | N |
| 11 Gingrey | N | N | Y | Y | N | N | N | N |
| 12 Barrow | Y | Y | N | Y | Y | Y | Y | Y |
| 13 Scott | N | N | Y | Y | N | N | N | Y |
| **HAWAII** | | | | | | | | |
| 1 Abercrombie | Y | Y | N | N | Y | Y | Y | Y |
| 2 Case | Y | Y | N | N | Y | Y | Y | Y |
| **IDAHO** | | | | | | | | |
| 1 Otter | N | N | Y | Y | N | N | N | N |
| 2 Simpson | N | N | Y | Y | N | N | N | N |
| **ILLINOIS** | | | | | | | | |
| 1 Rush | Y | Y | Y | Y | N | Y | Y | Y |
| 2 Jackson | Y | Y | N | N | Y | Y | Y | Y |
| 3 Lipinski | Y | Y | N | N | Y | Y | Y | Y |
| 4 Gutierrez | Y | Y | N | N | Y | Y | Y | Y |
| 5 Emanuel | ? | ? | ? | ? | ? | ? | ? | Y |
| 6 Hyde | N | N | N | Y | N | N | N | N |
| 7 Davis | Y | Y | Y | Y | Y | Y | Y | Y |
| 8 Bean | Y | Y | N | Y | Y | Y | Y | Y |
| 9 Schakowsky | Y | Y | N | N | Y | Y | Y | Y |
| 10 Kirk | Y | Y | N | Y | N | Y | N | Y |
| 11 Weller | N | N | Y | Y | N | N | N | N |
| 12 Costello | Y | N | Y | Y | Y | Y | Y | Y |

**KEY**   Republicans   Democrats   *Independents*

| | | | |
|---|---|---|---|
| Y | Voted for (yea) | X Paired against | C Voted "present" to avoid possible conflict of interest |
| # | Paired for | – Announced against | |
| + | Announced for | P Voted "present" | ? Did not vote or otherwise make a position known |
| N | Voted against (nay) | | |

| | 117 | 118 | 119 | 120 | 121 | 122 | 123 | 124 |
|---|---|---|---|---|---|---|---|---|
| 13 **Biggert** | N | N | N | Y | Y | N | N | N |
| 14 **Hastert** | | | | | | | | |
| 15 **Johnson** | Y | N | N | Y | Y | Y | N | Y |
| 16 **Manzullo** | N | N | Y | Y | N | N | N | N |
| 17 Evans | Y | Y | N | N | Y | Y | Y | Y |
| 18 **LaHood** | N | N | N | Y | Y | N | N | N |
| 19 **Shimkus** | N | N | Y | Y | N | N | N | N |
| **INDIANA** | | | | | | | | |
| 1 Visclosky | N | Y | Y | Y | N | Y | N | Y |
| 2 **Chocola** | N | N | Y | Y | N | N | N | N |
| 3 **Souder** | N | N | Y | Y | N | N | N | N |
| 4 **Buyer** | N | N | Y | Y | N | N | N | N |
| 5 **Burton** | N | N | Y | Y | N | N | N | N |
| 6 **Pence** | N | N | Y | Y | N | N | N | N |
| 7 Carson | Y | Y | Y | Y | Y | Y | Y | Y |
| 8 **Hostettler** | N | N | Y | Y | N | N | N | N |
| 9 **Sodrel** | N | N | Y | Y | N | N | N | N |
| **IOWA** | | | | | | | | |
| 1 **Nussle** | N | N | Y | Y | N | N | N | N |
| 2 **Leach** | Y | N | N | Y | Y | Y | N | Y |
| 3 Boswell | N | Y | Y | Y | N | Y | N | Y |
| 4 **Latham** | N | N | Y | Y | N | N | N | N |
| 5 **King** | N | N | Y | Y | N | N | N | N |
| **KANSAS** | | | | | | | | |
| 1 **Moran** | N | N | Y | Y | N | N | N | N |
| 2 **Ryun** | N | N | Y | Y | N | N | N | N |
| 3 Moore | N | Y | N | Y | N | Y | Y | Y |
| 4 **Tiahrt** | N | N | Y | Y | N | N | N | N |
| **KENTUCKY** | | | | | | | | |
| 1 **Whitfield** | N | N | Y | Y | N | N | N | N |
| 2 **Lewis** | N | N | Y | Y | N | N | N | N |
| 3 **Northup** | N | N | Y | Y | N | N | N | N |
| 4 **Davis** | N | N | Y | Y | N | N | N | N |
| 5 **Rogers** | N | N | Y | Y | N | N | N | N |
| 6 Chandler | N | Y | Y | Y | N | Y | N | Y |
| **LOUISIANA** | | | | | | | | |
| 1 **Jindal** | N | N | Y | Y | N | N | N | N |
| 2 Jefferson | N | Y | Y | Y | N | N | Y | Y |
| 3 Melancon | N | N | Y | Y | N | N | N | N |
| 4 **McCrery** | N | N | Y | Y | N | N | N | N |
| 5 **Alexander** | N | N | Y | Y | N | N | N | N |
| 6 **Baker** | N | N | Y | N | N | N | N | N |
| 7 **Boustany** | N | N | Y | Y | N | N | N | N |
| **MAINE** | | | | | | | | |
| 1 Allen | Y | Y | N | N | Y | Y | Y | Y |
| 2 Michaud | Y | Y | N | Y | Y | Y | Y | Y |
| **MARYLAND** | | | | | | | | |
| 1 **Gilchrest** | Y | N | N | Y | Y | Y | N | Y |
| 2 Ruppersberger | N | Y | Y | Y | N | Y | Y | Y |
| 3 Cardin | Y | Y | N | Y | Y | Y | Y | Y |
| 4 Wynn | N | Y | Y | Y | N | Y | Y | N |
| 5 Hoyer | Y | Y | Y | Y | N | Y | Y | Y |
| 6 **Bartlett** | Y | N | N | Y | Y | Y | N | N |
| 7 Cummings | Y | Y | Y | Y | N | Y | Y | Y |
| 8 Van Hollen | Y | Y | N | N | Y | Y | Y | Y |
| **MASSACHUSETTS** | | | | | | | | |
| 1 Olver | Y | Y | N | N | Y | Y | Y | Y |
| 2 Neal | Y | Y | N | Y | Y | Y | Y | Y |
| 3 McGovern | Y | Y | N | N | Y | Y | Y | Y |
| 4 Frank | Y | Y | N | N | Y | Y | Y | Y |
| 5 Meehan | Y | Y | N | N | Y | Y | Y | Y |
| 6 Tierney | Y | Y | N | N | Y | Y | Y | Y |
| 7 Markey | Y | Y | N | N | Y | Y | Y | Y |
| 8 Capuano | Y | Y | N | N | Y | Y | Y | Y |
| 9 Lynch | Y | Y | N | Y | Y | Y | Y | Y |
| 10 Delahunt | Y | Y | N | Y | Y | Y | Y | Y |
| **MICHIGAN** | | | | | | | | |
| 1 Stupak | N | Y | Y | Y | N | Y | Y | N |
| 2 **Hoekstra** | N | N | Y | Y | N | N | N | N |
| 3 **Ehlers** | Y | N | N | Y | Y | Y | Y | Y |
| 4 **Camp** | N | N | Y | Y | N | N | N | N |
| 5 Kildee | N | Y | Y | Y | N | Y | Y | Y |
| 6 **Upton** | N | N | Y | Y | N | N | N | N |
| 7 **Schwarz** | N | N | Y | Y | N | Y | N | N |
| 8 **Rogers** | N | N | Y | Y | N | N | N | N |
| 9 **Knollenberg** | N | N | Y | Y | N | N | N | N |
| 10 **Miller** | N | N | Y | Y | N | N | N | N |
| 11 **McCotter** | N | N | Y | Y | N | N | N | N |
| 12 Levin | N | Y | Y | Y | N | Y | Y | Y |
| 13 Kilpatrick | Y | Y | Y | Y | N | Y | Y | Y |
| 14 Conyers | Y | Y | Y | Y | N | Y | Y | Y |
| 15 Dingell | N | Y | Y | Y | N | Y | Y | Y |
| **MINNESOTA** | | | | | | | | |
| 1 **Gutknecht** | N | N | Y | Y | Y | N | N | N |
| 2 **Kline** | N | N | Y | Y | N | N | N | N |
| 3 **Ramstad** | Y | N | N | Y | Y | Y | N | N |
| 4 McCollum | Y | Y | N | N | Y | Y | Y | Y |
| 5 Sabo | Y | Y | N | Y | Y | Y | Y | Y |
| 6 **Kennedy** | N | N | Y | Y | N | Y | N | N |
| 7 Peterson | N | N | Y | Y | Y | N | Y | Y |
| 8 Oberstar | Y | Y | N | Y | Y | Y | Y | Y |
| **MISSISSIPPI** | | | | | | | | |
| 1 **Wicker** | N | N | Y | Y | N | N | N | N |
| 2 Thompson | Y | Y | Y | Y | N | Y | Y | Y |
| 3 **Pickering** | N | N | Y | Y | N | N | N | N |
| 4 Taylor | Y | N | Y | Y | Y | N | Y | Y |
| **MISSOURI** | | | | | | | | |
| 1 Clay | N | ? | Y | Y | N | Y | Y | Y |
| 2 **Akin** | N | N | Y | Y | N | N | N | N |
| 3 Carnahan | Y | Y | N | Y | Y | Y | Y | Y |
| 4 Skelton | Y | N | N | Y | Y | N | Y | Y |
| 5 Cleaver | N | Y | Y | Y | N | Y | Y | Y |
| 6 **Graves** | N | N | Y | Y | N | N | Y | N |
| 7 **Blunt** | N | N | Y | Y | N | N | N | N |
| 8 **Emerson** | N | N | Y | Y | N | N | N | N |
| 9 **Hulshof** | N | N | Y | Y | N | N | N | N |
| **MONTANA** | | | | | | | | |
| AL **Rehberg** | N | N | Y | Y | N | N | N | N |
| **NEBRASKA** | | | | | | | | |
| 1 **Fortenberry** | N | N | Y | Y | N | N | N | N |
| 2 **Terry** | N | N | Y | Y | N | N | N | N |
| 3 **Osborne** | N | N | Y | Y | N | N | N | N |
| **NEVADA** | | | | | | | | |
| 1 Berkley | Y | Y | N | Y | Y | Y | Y | Y |
| 2 **Gibbons** | N | N | Y | Y | N | N | N | N |
| 3 **Porter** | N | N | Y | Y | N | N | N | N |
| **NEW HAMPSHIRE** | | | | | | | | |
| 1 **Bradley** | Y | N | N | Y | N | Y | N | N |
| 2 **Bass** | Y | N | Y | Y | N | Y | N | N |
| **NEW JERSEY** | | | | | | | | |
| 1 Andrews | ? | ? | ? | ? | ? | ? | ? | Y |
| 2 **LoBiondo** | Y | N | N | N | Y | Y | N | Y |
| 3 **Saxton** | Y | N | N | N | Y | Y | N | Y |
| 4 **Smith** | Y | N | N | N | Y | Y | N | Y |
| 5 **Garrett** | N | N | N | Y | N | N | N | N |
| 6 Pallone | Y | Y | N | N | Y | Y | Y | Y |
| 7 **Ferguson** | N | N | N | Y | N | Y | N | N |
| 8 Pascrell | Y | Y | N | N | Y | Y | Y | Y |
| 9 Rothman | Y | Y | N | Y | Y | Y | Y | Y |
| 10 Payne | Y | Y | N | N | Y | Y | Y | Y |
| 11 **Frelinghuysen** | N | N | N | Y | Y | Y | N | N |
| 12 Holt | Y | Y | N | N | Y | Y | Y | Y |
| 13 Menendez | Y | Y | N | N | Y | Y | Y | Y |
| **NEW MEXICO** | | | | | | | | |
| 1 **Wilson** | N | N | Y | Y | N | N | N | Y |
| 2 **Pearce** | N | N | Y | Y | N | N | N | N |
| 3 Udall | Y | Y | N | N | Y | Y | Y | Y |
| **NEW YORK** | | | | | | | | |
| 1 Bishop | Y | Y | N | N | Y | Y | Y | Y |
| 2 Israel | Y | Y | N | N | Y | Y | Y | Y |
| 3 **King** | N | N | N | Y | Y | N | N | N |
| 4 McCarthy | Y | Y | N | N | Y | Y | Y | Y |
| 5 Ackerman | Y | Y | N | N | Y | Y | Y | Y |
| 6 Meeks | N | N | Y | N | N | Y | Y | Y |
| 7 Crowley | Y | Y | Y | Y | Y | Y | Y | Y |
| 8 Nadler | Y | Y | N | N | Y | Y | Y | Y |
| 9 Weiner | Y | Y | N | N | Y | Y | Y | Y |
| 10 Towns | N | N | N | Y | N | N | Y | Y |
| 11 Owens | Y | Y | N | Y | Y | Y | Y | Y |
| 12 Velázquez | Y | Y | N | N | Y | Y | Y | Y |
| 13 **Fossella** | N | N | N | Y | N | N | N | N |
| 14 Maloney | Y | Y | N | N | Y | Y | Y | Y |
| 15 Rangel | Y | Y | Y | N | Y | Y | Y | Y |
| 16 Serrano | Y | Y | N | Y | Y | Y | Y | Y |
| 17 Engel | Y | Y | N | N | Y | Y | Y | Y |
| 18 Lowey | Y | Y | N | N | Y | Y | Y | Y |
| 19 **Kelly** | ? | ? | ? | ? | ? | ? | ? | ? |
| 20 **Sweeney** | N | N | N | Y | N | N | N | N |
| 21 McNulty | Y | Y | N | N | Y | Y | Y | Y |
| 22 Hinchey | Y | Y | N | N | Y | Y | Y | Y |
| 23 **McHugh** | N | N | Y | Y | N | N | N | N |
| 24 **Boehlert** | Y | N | N | Y | Y | Y | Y | Y |
| 25 **Walsh** | Y | N | Y | Y | N | Y | N | N |
| 26 **Reynolds** | N | N | Y | Y | Y | N | N | N |
| 27 Higgins | Y | Y | N | N | Y | Y | Y | Y |
| 28 Slaughter | ? | Y | N | N | Y | Y | Y | Y |
| 29 **Kuhl** | N | N | Y | Y | N | N | N | N |
| **NORTH CAROLINA** | | | | | | | | |
| 1 Butterfield | Y | Y | N | Y | Y | Y | Y | Y |
| 2 Etheridge | Y | Y | N | Y | Y | Y | Y | Y |
| 3 **Jones** | N | N | Y | Y | N | N | N | N |
| 4 Price | Y | Y | N | Y | Y | Y | Y | Y |
| 5 **Foxx** | N | N | Y | Y | N | N | N | N |
| 6 **Coble** | N | N | Y | Y | N | N | N | N |
| 7 McIntyre | Y | N | Y | Y | N | Y | N | Y |
| 8 **Hayes** | N | N | Y | Y | N | N | N | N |
| 9 **Myrick** | N | N | Y | Y | N | N | N | N |
| 10 **McHenry** | N | N | Y | Y | N | N | N | N |
| 11 **Taylor** | N | N | Y | Y | N | N | N | N |
| 12 Watt | Y | Y | Y | Y | Y | Y | Y | Y |
| 13 Miller | Y | Y | N | N | Y | Y | Y | Y |
| **NORTH DAKOTA** | | | | | | | | |
| AL Pomeroy | Y | N | N | Y | N | Y | N | Y |
| **OHIO** | | | | | | | | |
| 1 **Chabot** | N | N | Y | Y | N | N | N | Y |
| 2 **Portman** | N | N | Y | Y | N | N | N | ? |
| 3 **Turner** | N | N | Y | Y | N | N | N | N |
| 4 **Oxley** | N | N | Y | Y | N | N | N | N |
| 5 **Gillmor** | N | N | Y | Y | N | N | N | N |
| 6 Strickland | N | Y | Y | Y | N | Y | Y | Y |
| 7 **Hobson** | N | N | Y | Y | N | N | N | N |
| 8 **Boehner** | N | N | Y | Y | N | N | N | N |
| 9 Kaptur | Y | Y | N | Y | N | Y | Y | Y |
| 10 Kucinich | Y | Y | N | N | Y | Y | Y | Y |
| 11 Jones | Y | Y | Y | Y | N | Y | Y | Y |
| 12 **Tiberi** | N | N | Y | Y | Y | N | N | N |
| 13 Brown | Y | Y | N | Y | Y | Y | Y | Y |
| 14 **LaTourette** | ? | Y | Y | Y | Y | N | N | N |
| 15 **Pryce** | N | N | Y | Y | N | N | N | N |
| 16 **Regula** | N | N | N | Y | N | N | N | N |
| 17 Ryan | Y | Y | Y | Y | Y | Y | Y | Y |
| 18 **Ney** | N | N | Y | Y | N | N | N | N |
| **OKLAHOMA** | | | | | | | | |
| 1 **Sullivan** | N | N | Y | Y | N | N | N | N |
| 2 Boren | N | N | Y | Y | N | N | N | N |
| 3 **Lucas** | N | N | Y | Y | N | N | N | N |
| 4 **Cole** | N | N | Y | Y | N | N | N | N |
| 5 **Istook** | N | N | Y | Y | N | N | N | N |
| **OREGON** | | | | | | | | |
| 1 Wu | Y | Y | N | Y | Y | Y | Y | Y |
| 2 **Walden** | N | N | Y | Y | N | N | N | N |
| 3 Blumenauer | Y | Y | N | N | Y | Y | Y | Y |
| 4 DeFazio | Y | Y | N | N | Y | Y | Y | Y |
| 5 Hooley | Y | Y | N | Y | Y | Y | Y | Y |
| **PENNSYLVANIA** | | | | | | | | |
| 1 Brady | N | Y | Y | Y | Y | N | Y | Y |
| 2 Fattah | Y | Y | N | Y | Y | Y | Y | Y |
| 3 **English** | N | N | N | Y | Y | N | N | N |
| 4 **Hart** | N | N | Y | Y | N | N | N | N |
| 5 **Peterson** | N | N | N | Y | N | N | N | N |
| 6 **Gerlach** | N | N | N | Y | Y | Y | N | N |
| 7 **Weldon** | N | N | N | Y | Y | N | N | N |
| 8 **Fitzpatrick** | Y | N | N | Y | Y | Y | N | Y |
| 9 **Shuster** | N | N | Y | Y | N | N | N | N |
| 10 **Sherwood** | N | N | N | Y | N | N | N | N |
| 11 Kanjorski | N | Y | Y | Y | N | N | N | N |
| 12 Murtha | N | Y | Y | Y | N | N | Y | N |
| 13 Schwartz | Y | Y | N | N | Y | Y | Y | Y |
| 14 Doyle | N | Y | Y | Y | N | Y | Y | N |
| 15 **Dent** | N | N | Y | Y | N | N | N | N |
| 16 **Pitts** | N | N | Y | Y | N | N | N | N |
| 17 Holden | N | Y | Y | Y | N | Y | N | N |
| 18 **Murphy** | N | N | Y | Y | N | N | N | N |
| 19 **Platts** | Y | Y | N | Y | Y | N | N | ? |
| **RHODE ISLAND** | | | | | | | | |
| 1 Kennedy | Y | Y | N | N | Y | Y | Y | Y |
| 2 Langevin | Y | Y | N | N | Y | Y | Y | Y |
| **SOUTH CAROLINA** | | | | | | | | |
| 1 **Brown** | N | N | Y | Y | N | N | N | N |
| 2 **Wilson** | N | N | Y | Y | N | N | N | N |
| 3 **Barrett** | N | N | Y | Y | N | N | N | N |
| 4 **Inglis** | N | N | Y | Y | Y | Y | N | N |
| 5 Spratt | Y | Y | N | Y | Y | Y | Y | Y |
| 6 Clyburn | Y | Y | Y | Y | N | Y | Y | Y |
| **SOUTH DAKOTA** | | | | | | | | |
| AL Herseth | Y | N | Y | Y | Y | N | N | N |
| **TENNESSEE** | | | | | | | | |
| 1 **Jenkins** | N | N | Y | Y | N | N | N | N |
| 2 **Duncan** | N | N | Y | Y | N | N | N | N |
| 3 **Wamp** | N | N | N | Y | N | N | N | N |
| 4 Davis | N | N | Y | Y | N | N | Y | Y |
| 5 Cooper | Y | Y | N | Y | Y | Y | Y | Y |
| 6 Gordon | N | N | Y | Y | N | Y | Y | N |
| 7 **Blackburn** | N | N | Y | Y | N | N | N | N |
| 8 Tanner | N | N | Y | Y | N | N | Y | Y |
| 9 Ford | Y | Y | N | Y | Y | Y | Y | Y |
| **TEXAS** | | | | | | | | |
| 1 **Gohmert** | N | N | Y | Y | N | N | N | N |
| 2 **Poe** | N | N | Y | Y | N | N | N | N |
| 3 **Johnson, S.** | N | N | Y | Y | N | N | N | N |
| 4 **Hall** | N | N | Y | Y | N | N | N | N |
| 5 **Hensarling** | N | N | Y | Y | N | N | N | N |
| 6 **Barton** | N | N | Y | Y | N | N | N | N |
| 7 **Culberson** | N | N | Y | Y | N | N | N | N |
| 8 **Brady** | N | N | Y | Y | N | N | N | N |
| 9 Green | N | N | Y | Y | N | N | Y | Y |
| 10 **McCaul** | N | N | Y | Y | N | N | N | N |
| 11 **Conaway** | N | N | Y | Y | N | N | N | N |
| 12 **Granger** | N | N | Y | Y | N | N | N | N |
| 13 **Thornberry** | N | N | Y | Y | N | N | N | N |
| 14 **Paul** | N | N | Y | Y | N | N | N | Y |
| 15 Hinojosa | N | N | N | Y | N | N | N | N |
| 16 Reyes | N | N | Y | Y | N | N | N | N |
| 17 Edwards | N | N | Y | Y | N | N | N | N |
| 18 Jackson-Lee | N | N | Y | Y | N | Y | Y | Y |
| 19 **Neugebauer** | N | N | Y | Y | N | N | N | N |
| 20 Gonzalez | N | N | Y | Y | N | Y | Y | N |
| 21 **Smith** | N | N | Y | Y | N | N | N | N |
| 22 **DeLay** | N | N | Y | Y | N | N | N | N |
| 23 **Bonilla** | N | N | Y | Y | N | N | N | N |
| 24 **Marchant** | N | N | Y | Y | N | N | N | N |
| 25 Doggett | Y | Y | N | N | Y | Y | Y | Y |
| 26 **Burgess** | N | N | Y | Y | N | N | N | N |
| 27 Ortiz | N | N | Y | Y | N | N | N | N |
| 28 Cuellar | N | N | Y | Y | N | N | N | N |
| 29 Green | N | N | Y | Y | N | N | N | Y |
| 30 Johnson, E. | N | Y | Y | Y | Y | Y | Y | Y |
| 31 **Carter** | N | N | Y | Y | N | N | N | N |
| 32 **Sessions** | N | N | Y | Y | N | N | N | N |
| **UTAH** | | | | | | | | |
| 1 **Bishop** | N | N | Y | Y | N | N | N | N |
| 2 Matheson | N | N | N | Y | Y | Y | Y | Y |
| 3 **Cannon** | N | N | Y | Y | N | N | N | N |
| **VERMONT** | | | | | | | | |
| AL *Sanders* | Y | Y | N | N | Y | Y | Y | Y |
| **VIRGINIA** | | | | | | | | |
| 1 **Davis, J.** | N | N | Y | Y | N | N | N | N |
| 2 **Drake** | N | N | Y | Y | N | N | N | N |
| 3 Scott | Y | Y | Y | Y | N | Y | Y | Y |
| 4 **Forbes** | N | N | Y | Y | N | N | N | N |
| 5 **Goode** | N | N | Y | Y | N | N | N | N |
| 6 **Goodlatte** | N | N | Y | Y | N | N | N | N |
| 7 **Cantor** | N | N | Y | Y | N | N | N | N |
| 8 Moran | Y | Y | N | Y | Y | Y | Y | Y |
| 9 Boucher | N | N | Y | Y | N | Y | Y | N |
| 10 **Wolf** | N | N | N | N | Y | N | N | N |
| 11 **Davis, T.** | Y | N | N | Y | Y | Y | N | N |
| **WASHINGTON** | | | | | | | | |
| 1 Inslee | Y | Y | N | N | Y | Y | Y | Y |
| 2 Larsen | Y | Y | N | N | Y | Y | Y | Y |
| 3 Baird | Y | Y | N | Y | Y | Y | Y | Y |
| 4 **Hastings** | N | N | Y | Y | N | N | N | N |
| 5 **McMorris** | N | N | Y | Y | N | N | N | N |
| 6 Dicks | Y | Y | N | Y | Y | Y | Y | Y |
| 7 McDermott | Y | ? | N | N | Y | Y | Y | Y |
| 8 **Reichert** | N | N | Y | Y | N | Y | N | N |
| 9 Smith | Y | Y | N | Y | Y | Y | Y | Y |
| **WEST VIRGINIA** | | | | | | | | |
| 1 Mollohan | N | Y | Y | Y | N | N | Y | N |
| 2 **Capito** | N | N | Y | Y | N | N | N | N |
| 3 Rahall | N | Y | Y | Y | N | Y | Y | Y |
| **WISCONSIN** | | | | | | | | |
| 1 **Ryan** | N | N | Y | Y | N | N | N | N |
| 2 Baldwin | Y | Y | N | N | Y | Y | Y | Y |
| 3 Kind | Y | Y | N | N | Y | Y | Y | Y |
| 4 Moore | Y | Y | N | N | Y | Y | Y | Y |
| 5 **Sensenbrenner** | N | N | Y | Y | N | Y | Y | Y |
| 6 **Petri** | N | N | N | Y | Y | Y | Y | Y |
| 7 Obey | Y | Y | N | N | Y | Y | Y | Y |
| 8 **Green** | N | N | Y | Y | N | N | N | Y |
| **WYOMING** | | | | | | | | |
| AL **Cubin** | N | N | Y | Y | N | N | N | N |

# IN THE HOUSE | By Vote Number

**125.** **HR 6. Energy Policy/Renewable Fuels.** Engel, D-N.Y., amendment that would make producers of all renewable fuels approved by the Energy Department eligible for grants to build renewable fuel production facilities. Adopted 239-190: R 45-181; D 193-9 (ND 147-4, SD 46-5); I 1-0. April 21, 2005.

**126.** **HR 6. Energy Policy/Gas Company Consolidation.** Israel, D-N.Y., amendment that would direct the comptroller general to study and report to Congress within one year on the impact of the consolidation of gasoline refiners, importers, producers, and wholesalers on the retail gasoline market. Adopted 302-128: R 102-126; D 199-2 (ND 150-0, SD 49-2); I 1-0. April 21, 2005.

**127.** **HR 6. Energy Policy/Mustard Seed Feasibility.** Kucinich, D-Ohio, amendment that would authorize a study by the National Academy of Sciences on the feasibility of mustard seed as a feedstock for biodiesel. Adopted 259-171: R 68-161; D 190-10 (ND 144-5, SD 46-5); I 1-0. April 21, 2005.

**128.** **HR 6. Energy Policy/Royalty Payments.** Grijalva, D-Ariz., amendment that would strike a provision in the bill authorizing the Interior Department to suspend collection of royalties for certain gas wells leased in the deep waters of the Gulf of Mexico. Rejected 203-227: R 29-200; D 173-27 (ND 141-9, SD 32-18); I 1-0. April 21, 2005.

**129.** **HR 6. Energy Policy/MTBE Liability.** Capps, D-Calif., motion to strike a provision in the bill that would provide liability protection for manufacturers of the gasoline additive methyl tertiary butyl ether (MTBE). Motion rejected 213-219: R 25-205; D 187-14 (ND 148-2, SD 39-12); I 1-0. April 21, 2005.

**130.** **HR 6. Energy Policy/Environmental Justice.** Hastings, D-Fla., amendment that would expand the definition of environmental justice, direct each federal agency to establish an office of environmental justice and re-establish the interagency federal working group on environmental justice. Rejected 185-243: R 2-224; D 182-19 (ND 143-7, SD 39-12); I 1-0. April 21, 2005.

**131.** **HR 6. Energy Policy/Natural Gas Facilities.** Castle, R-Del., amendment that would strike a provision in the bill specifying that the Federal Energy Regulatory Commission, instead of state agencies, would have the authority to approve the construction, expansion or operation of any facility that imports or processes natural gas, including liquefied natural gas. Rejected 194-237: R 35-194; D 158-43 (ND 132-18, SD 26-25); I 1-0. April 21, 2005.

**132.** **HR 6. Energy Policy/Passage.** Passage of the bill that would overhaul the nation's energy policy and provide for approximately $8 billion in energy-related tax incentives. It also would authorize the Interior Department to hold a lease sale for oil and gas exploration, development, and production in the Arctic National Wildlife Refuge in Alaska, on a total of about 1.6 million acres. Makers of the gasoline additive methyl tertiary butyl ether would be protected from liability, but would have to cease production of the additive by 2015. The bill would grant the Federal Energy Regulatory Commission jurisdiction over reliability standards for electricity transmission networks and extend daylight-saving time by two months. Passed 249-183: R 208-22; D 41-160 (ND 20-130, SD 21-30); I 0-1. A "yea" was a vote in support of the president's position. April 21, 2005.

| | 125 | 126 | 127 | 128 | 129 | 130 | 131 | 132 |
|---|---|---|---|---|---|---|---|---|
| **ALABAMA** | | | | | | | | |
| 1 Bonner | N | Y | N | N | N | N | Y | Y |
| 2 Everett | N | Y | N | N | N | N | N | Y |
| 3 Rogers | N | N | Y | N | N | N | N | Y |
| 4 Aderholt | N | Y | N | N | N | N | N | Y |
| 5 Cramer | Y | Y | N | N | N | N | N | Y |
| 6 Bachus | N | N | N | N | N | N | N | Y |
| 7 Davis | Y | Y | Y | Y | Y | Y | N | Y |
| **ALASKA** | | | | | | | | |
| AL Young | N | N | N | N | N | N | N | Y |
| **ARIZONA** | | | | | | | | |
| 1 Renzi | N | Y | Y | N | N | N | N | Y |
| 2 Franks | ? | N | N | N | N | N | N | Y |
| 3 Shadegg | N | N | N | N | N | N | N | Y |
| 4 Pastor | Y | Y | Y | Y | Y | Y | Y | N |
| 5 Hayworth | N | Y | N | N | N | N | N | Y |
| 6 Flake | N | N | N | N | N | N | N | N |
| 7 Grijalva | Y | Y | Y | Y | Y | Y | Y | N |
| 8 Kolbe | N | Y | N | N | N | N | N | Y |
| **ARKANSAS** | | | | | | | | |
| 1 Berry | Y | Y | Y | Y | Y | N | N | N |
| 2 Snyder | Y | Y | Y | Y | N | Y | N | Y |
| 3 Boozman | N | N | N | N | N | N | N | Y |
| 4 Ross | Y | Y | N | N | Y | Y | N | Y |
| **CALIFORNIA** | | | | | | | | |
| 1 Thompson | Y | Y | N | Y | Y | Y | Y | N |
| 2 Herger | N | N | N | N | N | N | N | Y |
| 3 Lungren | N | Y | N | N | N | N | N | Y |
| 4 Doolittle | N | N | Y | N | N | N | N | Y |
| 5 Matsui, D. | Y | Y | Y | Y | Y | Y | Y | N |
| 6 Woolsey | Y | Y | Y | Y | Y | Y | Y | N |
| 7 Miller, George | Y | Y | Y | Y | Y | Y | Y | N |
| 8 Pelosi | Y | Y | Y | Y | Y | Y | Y | N |
| 9 Lee | Y | Y | Y | Y | Y | Y | Y | N |
| 10 Tauscher | Y | Y | Y | Y | Y | Y | Y | N |
| 11 Pombo | N | Y | N | N | N | N | N | Y |
| 12 Lantos | Y | Y | Y | Y | Y | Y | Y | N |
| 13 Stark | Y | Y | Y | Y | Y | Y | Y | N |
| 14 Eshoo | Y | Y | Y | Y | Y | Y | Y | N |
| 15 Honda | Y | Y | Y | Y | Y | Y | Y | N |
| 16 Lofgren | Y | Y | N | Y | Y | Y | Y | N |
| 17 Farr | Y | Y | Y | Y | Y | Y | Y | N |
| 18 Cardoza | Y | Y | N | Y | Y | Y | Y | N |
| 19 Radanovich | N | N | N | N | N | N | N | Y |
| 20 Costa | N | Y | N | Y | N | Y | N | Y |
| 21 Nunes | N | N | N | N | N | N | N | Y |
| 22 Thomas | N | N | N | N | N | N | N | Y |
| 23 Capps | Y | Y | Y | Y | Y | Y | N | N |
| 24 Gallegly | N | Y | N | N | N | N | N | Y |
| 25 McKeon | N | N | N | N | N | N | N | Y |
| 26 Dreier | N | N | N | N | N | N | N | Y |
| 27 Sherman | Y | Y | Y | Y | Y | Y | Y | N |
| 28 Berman | Y | Y | ? | Y | Y | Y | Y | N |
| 29 Schiff | Y | Y | Y | Y | Y | Y | Y | N |
| 30 Waxman | Y | Y | Y | Y | Y | Y | Y | N |
| 31 Becerra | Y | Y | Y | Y | Y | Y | Y | N |
| 32 Solis | Y | Y | Y | Y | Y | Y | Y | N |
| 33 Watson | Y | Y | Y | Y | Y | Y | Y | N |
| 34 Roybal-Allard | Y | Y | Y | Y | Y | Y | Y | N |
| 35 Waters | Y | Y | Y | Y | Y | Y | Y | N |
| 36 Harman | Y | Y | Y | Y | Y | Y | Y | N |
| 37 Millender-McD. | Y | Y | Y | Y | Y | Y | Y | N |
| 38 Napolitano | Y | Y | Y | Y | Y | Y | Y | N |
| 39 Sánchez, Linda | Y | Y | Y | Y | Y | Y | Y | N |
| 40 Royce | N | Y | N | N | N | N | N | Y |
| 41 Lewis | N | N | N | N | N | N | N | Y |
| 42 Miller, Gary | N | N | N | N | N | N | N | Y |
| 43 Baca | Y | Y | Y | Y | Y | Y | Y | N |
| 44 Calvert | N | N | N | N | N | N | N | Y |
| 45 Bono | Y | Y | N | N | N | N | N | Y |
| 46 Rohrabacher | N | Y | N | N | N | N | N | Y |
| 47 Sanchez, Loretta | Y | Y | Y | Y | Y | Y | Y | N |
| 48 Cox | N | Y | N | N | N | N | N | Y |
| 49 Issa | Y | Y | N | N | N | N | N | Y |

| | 125 | 126 | 127 | 128 | 129 | 130 | 131 | 132 |
|---|---|---|---|---|---|---|---|---|
| 50 Cunningham | Y | N | Y | N | N | N | N | Y |
| 51 Filner | Y | Y | Y | Y | Y | Y | Y | N |
| 52 Hunter | N | Y | Y | N | N | N | N | Y |
| 53 Davis | Y | Y | Y | Y | Y | Y | Y | N |
| **COLORADO** | | | | | | | | |
| 1 DeGette | Y | Y | Y | Y | Y | Y | Y | N |
| 2 Udall | Y | Y | Y | Y | Y | Y | N | N |
| 3 Salazar | Y | Y | Y | N | Y | Y | N | Y |
| 4 Musgrave | N | N | N | N | N | N | N | Y |
| 5 Hefley | N | N | Y | N | N | N | N | Y |
| 6 Tancredo | N | Y | N | N | N | N | N | Y |
| 7 Beauprez | N | N | N | N | N | N | N | Y |
| **CONNECTICUT** | | | | | | | | |
| 1 Larson | Y | Y | Y | Y | Y | Y | Y | N |
| 2 Simmons | Y | Y | Y | Y | Y | N | Y | Y |
| 3 DeLauro | Y | Y | Y | Y | Y | Y | Y | N |
| 4 Shays | Y | Y | N | Y | Y | + | Y | N |
| 5 Johnson | Y | Y | Y | Y | Y | N | Y | N |
| **DELAWARE** | | | | | | | | |
| AL Castle | Y | Y | N | Y | Y | N | Y | N |
| **FLORIDA** | | | | | | | | |
| 1 Miller | Y | N | N | N | N | Y | N | Y |
| 2 Boyd | N | Y | Y | Y | Y | Y | Y | N |
| 3 Brown | Y | Y | Y | ? | Y | Y | Y | N |
| 4 Crenshaw | N | N | N | N | N | N | N | Y |
| 5 Brown-Waite | Y | Y | N | N | N | N | N | Y |
| 6 Stearns | N | Y | N | N | N | N | N | Y |
| 7 Mica | N | N | N | ? | N | N | N | Y |
| 8 Keller | N | N | N | ? | N | Y | N | Y |
| 9 Bilirakis | N | Y | Y | N | N | N | N | Y |
| 10 Young | ? | Y | Y | N | N | N | N | Y |
| 11 Davis | Y | Y | Y | Y | Y | Y | Y | N |
| 12 Putnam | N | N | N | N | N | N | N | Y |
| 13 Harris | Y | Y | N | N | N | N | N | Y |
| 14 Mack | N | N | N | N | N | N | N | Y |
| 15 Weldon | Y | Y | N | N | N | N | N | Y |
| 16 Foley | N | N | N | N | N | N | N | Y |
| 17 Meek | Y | Y | Y | Y | Y | Y | Y | N |
| 18 Ros-Lehtinen | N | N | N | N | N | N | N | Y |
| 19 Wexler | Y | Y | Y | Y | Y | Y | Y | N |
| 20 Wasserman-Schultz | Y | Y | Y | Y | Y | Y | Y | N |
| 21 Diaz-Balart, L. | N | Y | N | N | N | N | N | Y |
| 22 Shaw | N | Y | N | N | N | N | Y | Y |
| 23 Hastings | Y | Y | Y | Y | Y | Y | Y | N |
| 24 Feeney | N | N | N | N | N | N | N | Y |
| 25 Diaz-Balart, M. | N | N | N | N | N | N | N | Y |
| **GEORGIA** | | | | | | | | |
| 1 Kingston | N | Y | N | N | N | N | N | Y |
| 2 Bishop | N | Y | Y | N | Y | Y | N | Y |
| 3 Marshall | N | Y | Y | Y | Y | N | N | N |
| 4 McKinney | Y | Y | Y | Y | Y | Y | Y | N |
| 5 Lewis | Y | Y | Y | Y | Y | Y | Y | N |
| 6 Price | N | N | N | N | N | N | N | Y |
| 7 Linder | N | N | N | N | N | N | Y | Y |
| 8 Westmoreland | N | N | N | N | N | N | N | Y |
| 9 Norwood | N | N | N | N | N | N | N | Y |
| 10 Deal | N | N | N | N | N | N | N | Y |
| 11 Gingrey | N | Y | N | N | N | N | N | Y |
| 12 Barrow | Y | Y | Y | Y | Y | Y | Y | N |
| 13 Scott | N | Y | N | Y | N | Y | N | Y |
| **HAWAII** | | | | | | | | |
| 1 Abercrombie | Y | Y | Y | N | Y | Y | Y | N |
| 2 Case | Y | Y | Y | Y | Y | N | Y | N |
| **IDAHO** | | | | | | | | |
| 1 Otter | N | N | Y | N | N | N | N | Y |
| 2 Simpson | N | N | Y | N | N | N | N | Y |
| **ILLINOIS** | | | | | | | | |
| 1 Rush | Y | Y | Y | Y | Y | Y | N | Y |
| 2 Jackson | Y | Y | Y | Y | Y | Y | Y | Y |
| 3 Lipinski | Y | Y | Y | Y | Y | Y | Y | Y |
| 4 Gutierrez | Y | Y | Y | Y | Y | Y | Y | Y |
| 5 Emanuel | Y | Y | Y | Y | Y | Y | Y | N |
| 6 Hyde | N | N | N | N | N | N | N | Y |
| 7 Davis | Y | Y | Y | N | Y | Y | Y | N |
| 8 Bean | Y | Y | Y | Y | Y | Y | Y | Y |
| 9 Schakowsky | Y | Y | Y | Y | Y | Y | Y | N |
| 10 Kirk | Y | Y | Y | Y | Y | N | Y | N |
| 11 Weller | N | N | N | N | N | N | N | Y |
| 12 Costello | Y | Y | Y | Y | Y | Y | Y | N |

**KEY**  Republicans   Democrats   *Independents*

| | 125 | 126 | 127 | 128 | 129 | 130 | 131 | 132 |
|---|---|---|---|---|---|---|---|---|
| 13 **Biggert** | N | N | N | N | N | N | N | Y |
| 14 **Hastert** | | | | | N | | | Y |
| 15 **Johnson** | N | Y | N | Y | Y | Y | N | Y |
| 16 **Manzullo** | N | Y | Y | N | N | N | N | Y |
| 17 Evans | Y | Y | Y | Y | Y | Y | Y | N |
| 18 **LaHood** | Y | Y | Y | Y | N | N | N | Y |
| 19 **Shimkus** | N | Y | Y | N | N | N | N | Y |
| **INDIANA** | | | | | | | | |
| 1 Visclosky | Y | Y | Y | Y | Y | Y | N | Y |
| 2 **Chocola** | N | Y | N | N | N | N | N | Y |
| 3 **Souder** | N | N | N | N | N | N | ? | Y |
| 4 **Buyer** | N | N | N | N | N | N | N | Y |
| 5 **Burton** | N | N | Y | N | N | N | N | Y |
| 6 **Pence** | N | N | N | N | N | N | N | Y |
| 7 Carson | Y | Y | Y | N | Y | Y | Y | N |
| 8 **Hostettler** | N | Y | N | N | N | N | N | Y |
| 9 **Sodrel** | N | N | N | N | N | N | N | Y |
| **IOWA** | | | | | | | | |
| 1 **Nussle** | N | N | N | N | N | N | N | Y |
| 2 **Leach** | N | Y | Y | Y | Y | N | N | N |
| 3 Boswell | Y | Y | Y | N | Y | Y | N | Y |
| 4 **Latham** | N | N | N | N | N | N | N | Y |
| 5 **King** | N | N | N | N | N | N | N | Y |
| **KANSAS** | | | | | | | | |
| 1 **Moran** | N | Y | N | N | N | N | N | Y |
| 2 **Ryun** | N | N | N | N | N | N | N | Y |
| 3 Moore | Y | Y | Y | Y | Y | Y | Y | N |
| 4 **Tiahrt** | N | N | Y | N | N | N | N | Y |
| **KENTUCKY** | | | | | | | | |
| 1 **Whitfield** | N | N | N | N | N | N | N | Y |
| 2 **Lewis** | N | Y | N | N | N | N | N | Y |
| 3 **Northup** | N | Y | N | N | N | N | N | Y |
| 4 **Davis** | N | N | Y | N | N | N | N | Y |
| 5 **Rogers** | N | N | N | N | N | N | N | Y |
| 6 Chandler | Y | Y | Y | Y | Y | Y | Y | N |
| **LOUISIANA** | | | | | | | | |
| 1 **Jindal** | N | N | N | N | N | N | N | Y |
| 2 Jefferson | Y | Y | Y | N | Y | Y | N | Y |
| 3 Melancon | Y | Y | Y | N | N | Y | N | Y |
| 4 **McCrery** | N | N | N | N | N | N | N | Y |
| 5 **Alexander** | N | N | N | N | N | N | N | Y |
| 6 **Baker** | N | N | N | N | N | N | N | Y |
| 7 **Boustany** | N | N | N | N | N | N | N | Y |
| **MAINE** | | | | | | | | |
| 1 Allen | Y | Y | Y | Y | Y | Y | Y | N |
| 2 Michaud | Y | Y | Y | Y | Y | Y | Y | N |
| **MARYLAND** | | | | | | | | |
| 1 **Gilchrest** | Y | Y | Y | N | Y | N | Y | N |
| 2 Ruppersberger | Y | Y | Y | Y | Y | Y | Y | N |
| 3 Cardin | Y | Y | Y | Y | Y | Y | Y | N |
| 4 Wynn | Y | Y | Y | Y | Y | Y | N | Y |
| 5 Hoyer | Y | Y | Y | Y | Y | Y | Y | N |
| 6 **Bartlett** | Y | Y | Y | N | N | N | N | N |
| 7 Cummings | Y | Y | Y | Y | Y | Y | N | N |
| 8 Van Hollen | Y | Y | Y | Y | Y | Y | Y | N |
| **MASSACHUSETTS** | | | | | | | | |
| 1 Olver | Y | Y | Y | Y | Y | Y | Y | N |
| 2 Neal | Y | Y | Y | Y | Y | Y | Y | N |
| 3 McGovern | Y | Y | Y | Y | Y | Y | Y | N |
| 4 Frank | Y | Y | Y | Y | Y | Y | Y | N |
| 5 Meehan | Y | Y | Y | Y | Y | Y | Y | N |
| 6 Tierney | Y | Y | Y | Y | Y | Y | Y | N |
| 7 Markey | Y | Y | Y | Y | Y | Y | Y | N |
| 8 Capuano | Y | Y | N | Y | Y | Y | Y | N |
| 9 Lynch | Y | Y | N | Y | Y | Y | Y | N |
| 10 Delahunt | Y | Y | Y | Y | Y | Y | Y | N |
| **MICHIGAN** | | | | | | | | |
| 1 Stupak | N | Y | Y | Y | Y | Y | Y | N |
| 2 **Hoekstra** | Y | Y | N | N | N | N | N | Y |
| 3 **Ehlers** | N | Y | N | Y | N | N | Y | N |
| 4 **Camp** | N | Y | N | N | N | N | N | Y |
| 5 Kildee | Y | Y | Y | Y | Y | Y | Y | N |
| 6 **Upton** | N | Y | Y | Y | N | N | N | Y |
| 7 **Schwarz** | N | Y | Y | N | N | N | N | N |
| 8 **Rogers** | Y | Y | Y | N | N | N | N | Y |
| 9 **Knollenberg** | N | N | N | N | N | N | N | Y |
| 10 **Miller** | N | Y | Y | N | N | N | N | Y |
| 11 **McCotter** | Y | Y | Y | N | N | N | N | Y |
| 12 Levin | Y | Y | Y | Y | Y | Y | Y | N |
| 13 Kilpatrick | Y | Y | Y | Y | Y | Y | N | N |
| 14 Conyers | Y | Y | Y | Y | Y | Y | Y | N |
| 15 Dingell | Y | Y | Y | Y | Y | Y | Y | N |
| **MINNESOTA** | | | | | | | | |
| 1 **Gutknecht** | N | Y | N | N | N | N | Y | Y |
| 2 **Kline** | N | N | N | N | N | N | N | Y |
| 3 **Ramstad** | Y | Y | Y | Y | Y | N | Y | Y |
| 4 McCollum | Y | Y | Y | Y | Y | Y | Y | N |
| 5 Sabo | Y | Y | Y | Y | Y | Y | Y | N |
| 6 **Kennedy** | N | Y | Y | Y | N | N | N | Y |
| 7 Peterson | Y | Y | Y | N | Y | N | N | Y |
| 8 Oberstar | Y | Y | Y | Y | Y | Y | Y | N |
| **MISSISSIPPI** | | | | | | | | |
| 1 **Wicker** | Y | Y | N | N | N | N | N | Y |
| 2 Thompson | Y | Y | Y | Y | Y | Y | Y | N |
| 3 **Pickering** | N | Y | N | N | N | N | N | Y |
| 4 Taylor | Y | Y | Y | Y | Y | N | Y | N |
| **MISSOURI** | | | | | | | | |
| 1 Clay | Y | Y | Y | Y | Y | Y | Y | N |
| 2 **Akin** | N | N | N | N | N | N | N | Y |
| 3 Carnahan | Y | Y | Y | Y | Y | N | Y | N |
| 4 Skelton | Y | Y | Y | Y | Y | N | N | Y |
| 5 Cleaver | Y | Y | Y | Y | Y | Y | Y | N |
| 6 **Graves** | Y | N | N | N | N | N | N | Y |
| 7 **Blunt** | N | N | N | N | N | N | N | Y |
| 8 **Emerson** | N | Y | Y | N | N | N | Y | Y |
| 9 **Hulshof** | N | Y | Y | N | N | N | N | Y |
| **MONTANA** | | | | | | | | |
| AL **Rehberg** | N | N | N | N | N | N | N | Y |
| **NEBRASKA** | | | | | | | | |
| 1 **Fortenberry** | N | Y | Y | N | N | N | N | Y |
| 2 **Terry** | N | N | N | N | N | N | N | Y |
| 3 **Osborne** | N | N | Y | N | N | N | N | Y |
| **NEVADA** | | | | | | | | |
| 1 Berkley | Y | Y | Y | Y | Y | Y | Y | N |
| 2 **Gibbons** | N | Y | Y | N | N | N | N | Y |
| 3 **Porter** | N | Y | Y | N | N | N | N | Y |
| **NEW HAMPSHIRE** | | | | | | | | |
| 1 **Bradley** | N | Y | N | Y | Y | N | N | N |
| 2 **Bass** | N | Y | N | Y | N | N | N | Y |
| **NEW JERSEY** | | | | | | | | |
| 1 Andrews | Y | Y | Y | Y | Y | Y | Y | N |
| 2 **LoBiondo** | Y | Y | Y | Y | Y | N | Y | N |
| 3 **Saxton** | Y | Y | Y | Y | Y | N | Y | N |
| 4 **Smith** | Y | Y | Y | Y | Y | N | Y | N |
| 5 **Garrett** | N | N | N | N | N | N | N | Y |
| 6 Pallone | Y | Y | Y | Y | Y | Y | Y | N |
| 7 **Ferguson** | Y | N | Y | Y | N | N | N | Y |
| 8 Pascrell | Y | Y | Y | Y | Y | Y | Y | N |
| 9 Rothman | Y | Y | Y | Y | Y | Y | Y | N |
| 10 Payne | Y | Y | Y | Y | Y | Y | Y | N |
| 11 **Frelinghuysen** | Y | N | Y | Y | Y | N | Y | Y |
| 12 Holt | Y | Y | Y | Y | Y | Y | Y | N |
| 13 Menendez | Y | Y | Y | Y | Y | Y | Y | N |
| **NEW MEXICO** | | | | | | | | |
| 1 **Wilson** | N | Y | Y | N | N | Y | N | Y |
| 2 **Pearce** | N | N | N | N | N | N | N | Y |
| 3 Udall | Y | Y | Y | Y | Y | Y | Y | N |
| **NEW YORK** | | | | | | | | |
| 1 Bishop | Y | Y | Y | Y | Y | Y | Y | N |
| 2 Israel | Y | Y | Y | Y | Y | Y | Y | N |
| 3 **King** | Y | Y | N | N | N | N | Y | Y |
| 4 McCarthy | Y | Y | Y | Y | Y | Y | Y | N |
| 5 Ackerman | Y | Y | Y | Y | Y | Y | Y | N |
| 6 Meeks | Y | Y | Y | Y | Y | Y | Y | Y |
| 7 Crowley | Y | Y | Y | Y | Y | Y | Y | N |
| 8 Nadler | Y | Y | Y | Y | Y | Y | Y | N |
| 9 Weiner | Y | Y | Y | Y | Y | Y | Y | N |
| 10 Towns | Y | Y | Y | N | Y | Y | N | Y |
| 11 Owens | Y | Y | Y | Y | Y | Y | N | N |
| 12 Velázquez | Y | Y | ? | ? | ? | ? | ? | ? |
| 13 **Fossella** | Y | Y | ? | N | N | N | Y | Y |
| 14 Maloney | Y | Y | Y | Y | Y | Y | Y | N |
| 15 Rangel | Y | Y | Y | Y | Y | Y | Y | N |
| 16 Serrano | Y | Y | Y | Y | Y | Y | Y | N |
| 17 Engel | Y | Y | Y | Y | Y | Y | Y | N |
| 18 Lowey | Y | Y | Y | Y | Y | Y | Y | N |
| 19 **Kelly** | ? | ? | ? | ? | ? | ? | ? | ? |
| 20 **Sweeney** | Y | Y | Y | N | Y | N | N | Y |
| 21 McNulty | Y | Y | Y | Y | Y | Y | Y | N |
| 22 Hinchey | Y | Y | Y | Y | Y | Y | Y | N |
| 23 **McHugh** | Y | Y | Y | N | N | N | N | Y |
| 24 **Boehlert** | Y | Y | Y | Y | Y | N | Y | N |
| 25 **Walsh** | Y | N | N | N | N | N | N | Y |
| 26 **Reynolds** | Y | Y | N | N | N | N | N | Y |
| 27 Higgins | Y | Y | Y | Y | Y | Y | Y | N |
| 28 Slaughter | Y | Y | Y | Y | Y | Y | Y | N |
| 29 **Kuhl** | N | N | N | N | N | N | N | Y |
| **NORTH CAROLINA** | | | | | | | | |
| 1 Butterfield | Y | Y | Y | Y | Y | Y | Y | N |
| 2 Etheridge | Y | Y | Y | Y | Y | Y | Y | N |
| 3 **Jones** | N | Y | N | N | N | N | Y | N |
| 4 Price | Y | Y | Y | Y | Y | Y | Y | N |
| 5 **Foxx** | N | N | N | N | N | N | N | Y |
| 6 **Coble** | N | N | Y | N | N | N | N | Y |
| 7 McIntyre | Y | Y | Y | Y | Y | Y | N | N |
| 8 **Hayes** | N | N | N | N | N | N | N | Y |
| 9 **Myrick** | N | N | N | N | N | N | N | Y |
| 10 **McHenry** | N | N | N | N | N | N | N | Y |
| 11 **Taylor** | N | N | Y | N | N | N | N | Y |
| 12 Watt | Y | Y | Y | Y | Y | Y | Y | N |
| 13 Miller | Y | Y | Y | Y | Y | Y | Y | N |
| **NORTH DAKOTA** | | | | | | | | |
| AL Pomeroy | N | Y | Y | Y | Y | N | N | Y |
| **OHIO** | | | | | | | | |
| 1 **Chabot** | N | Y | N | N | N | N | N | Y |
| 2 **Portman** | ? | ? | Y | N | N | N | N | Y |
| 3 **Turner** | N | Y | N | N | N | N | N | Y |
| 4 **Oxley** | N | ? | N | N | N | N | N | Y |
| 5 **Gillmor** | N | N | N | N | N | N | N | Y |
| 6 Strickland | N | Y | Y | Y | Y | Y | Y | N |
| 7 **Hobson** | N | Y | N | N | N | N | N | Y |
| 8 **Boehner** | N | N | N | N | N | N | N | Y |
| 9 Kaptur | Y | Y | Y | Y | Y | Y | Y | N |
| 10 Kucinich | Y | Y | Y | Y | Y | Y | Y | N |
| 11 Jones | Y | Y | Y | Y | Y | Y | N | N |
| 12 **Tiberi** | N | Y | N | N | N | N | N | Y |
| 13 Brown | Y | Y | Y | Y | Y | Y | Y | N |
| 14 **LaTourette** | Y | Y | Y | N | N | N | N | Y |
| 15 **Pryce** | N | Y | N | N | N | N | N | Y |
| 16 **Regula** | Y | Y | Y | N | N | N | N | Y |
| 17 Ryan | Y | Y | Y | Y | Y | Y | Y | N |
| 18 **Ney** | Y | Y | N | N | N | N | N | Y |
| **OKLAHOMA** | | | | | | | | |
| 1 **Sullivan** | N | N | Y | N | N | N | N | Y |
| 2 Boren | Y | N | N | N | N | N | N | Y |
| 3 **Lucas** | N | N | N | N | N | N | N | Y |
| 4 **Cole** | N | N | N | N | N | N | N | Y |
| 5 **Istook** | N | N | N | N | N | N | N | Y |
| **OREGON** | | | | | | | | |
| 1 Wu | Y | Y | Y | Y | Y | Y | Y | N |
| 2 **Walden** | N | Y | Y | N | N | N | N | Y |
| 3 Blumenauer | Y | Y | Y | Y | Y | Y | Y | N |
| 4 DeFazio | Y | Y | Y | Y | Y | Y | Y | N |
| 5 Hooley | Y | Y | Y | Y | Y | Y | Y | N |
| **PENNSYLVANIA** | | | | | | | | |
| 1 Brady | Y | Y | Y | Y | Y | Y | Y | Y |
| 2 Fattah | Y | Y | Y | Y | Y | Y | Y | N |
| 3 **English** | Y | Y | N | N | N | ? | N | Y |
| 4 **Hart** | N | N | N | N | N | N | N | Y |
| 5 **Peterson** | N | Y | N | N | N | N | N | Y |
| 6 **Gerlach** | Y | Y | Y | Y | N | N | Y | N |
| 7 **Weldon** | Y | Y | Y | Y | Y | N | Y | Y |
| 8 **Fitzpatrick** | Y | Y | Y | Y | Y | N | N | N |
| 9 **Shuster** | N | N | Y | N | N | N | N | Y |
| 10 **Sherwood** | N | Y | N | N | N | N | N | Y |
| 11 Kanjorski | Y | Y | Y | Y | Y | Y | N | N |
| 12 Murtha | Y | Y | Y | Y | Y | Y | N | Y |
| 13 Schwartz | Y | Y | Y | Y | Y | Y | Y | N |
| 14 Doyle | Y | Y | Y | Y | Y | Y | N | Y |
| 15 **Dent** | N | Y | Y | N | N | N | N | Y |
| 16 **Pitts** | N | N | N | N | N | N | N | Y |
| 17 Holden | Y | Y | Y | Y | Y | Y | N | Y |
| 18 **Murphy** | N | Y | Y | N | N | N | N | Y |
| 19 **Platts** | Y | Y | Y | Y | Y | N | Y | Y |
| **RHODE ISLAND** | | | | | | | | |
| 1 Kennedy | Y | Y | Y | Y | Y | Y | Y | N |
| 2 Langevin | Y | Y | Y | Y | Y | Y | Y | N |
| **SOUTH CAROLINA** | | | | | | | | |
| 1 **Brown** | N | N | N | N | N | N | Y | Y |
| 2 **Wilson** | N | N | N | N | N | N | N | Y |
| 3 **Barrett** | N | N | N | N | N | N | N | Y |
| 4 **Inglis** | N | N | N | Y | N | N | N | N |
| 5 Spratt | Y | Y | Y | Y | Y | Y | Y | N |
| 6 Clyburn | Y | Y | Y | Y | Y | Y | Y | N |
| **SOUTH DAKOTA** | | | | | | | | |
| AL Herseth | Y | Y | Y | Y | Y | Y | N | Y |
| **TENNESSEE** | | | | | | | | |
| 1 **Jenkins** | N | N | N | N | N | N | Y | Y |
| 2 **Duncan** | N | N | N | N | N | N | N | Y |
| 3 **Wamp** | Y | N | Y | N | N | N | N | N |
| 4 Davis | Y | Y | Y | Y | Y | N | N | Y |
| 5 Cooper | Y | Y | N | Y | Y | N | N | N |
| 6 Gordon | Y | Y | Y | Y | Y | N | N | Y |
| 7 **Blackburn** | N | N | N | N | N | N | N | Y |
| 8 Tanner | Y | Y | Y | Y | Y | N | Y | N |
| 9 Ford | Y | Y | Y | Y | Y | Y | Y | Y |
| **TEXAS** | | | | | | | | |
| 1 **Gohmert** | Y | N | N | N | N | N | N | Y |
| 2 **Poe** | N | N | N | N | N | N | N | Y |
| 3 **Johnson, S.** | N | N | N | N | N | N | N | Y |
| 4 **Hall** | N | N | Y | N | N | ? | N | Y |
| 5 **Hensarling** | N | N | N | N | N | N | N | Y |
| 6 **Barton** | N | N | Y | N | N | N | N | Y |
| 7 **Culberson** | N | N | N | N | N | N | N | Y |
| 8 **Brady** | N | N | Y | N | N | N | N | Y |
| 9 Green | Y | Y | Y | N | N | Y | N | Y |
| 10 **McCaul** | Y | N | N | N | N | N | N | Y |
| 11 **Conaway** | N | N | N | N | N | N | N | Y |
| 12 **Granger** | N | N | N | N | N | N | N | Y |
| 13 **Thornberry** | N | N | N | N | N | N | N | Y |
| 14 **Paul** | N | N | N | N | N | N | Y | N |
| 15 Hinojosa | Y | Y | Y | N | N | Y | N | Y |
| 16 Reyes | Y | Y | Y | N | N | Y | N | Y |
| 17 Edwards | Y | Y | Y | N | N | N | N | Y |
| 18 Jackson-Lee | Y | Y | Y | N | N | Y | N | Y |
| 19 **Neugebauer** | N | N | N | N | N | N | N | Y |
| 20 Gonzalez | Y | Y | Y | N | N | Y | N | Y |
| 21 **Smith** | N | N | N | N | N | N | N | Y |
| 22 **DeLay** | N | N | Y | N | N | N | N | Y |
| 23 **Bonilla** | N | N | N | N | N | N | N | Y |
| 24 **Marchant** | N | N | N | N | N | N | N | Y |
| 25 Doggett | Y | Y | N | Y | Y | Y | Y | N |
| 26 **Burgess** | N | N | Y | N | N | N | N | Y |
| 27 Ortiz | Y | Y | Y | N | N | Y | N | Y |
| 28 Cuellar | Y | N | Y | N | N | Y | N | Y |
| 29 Green | N | Y | Y | N | N | Y | N | Y |
| 30 Johnson, E. | Y | Y | Y | Y | Y | Y | Y | N |
| 31 **Carter** | N | N | N | N | N | N | N | Y |
| 32 **Sessions** | N | N | N | N | N | N | N | ? |
| **UTAH** | | | | | | | | |
| 1 **Bishop** | N | N | N | N | N | N | N | Y |
| 2 Matheson | Y | Y | N | N | Y | Y | N | Y |
| 3 **Cannon** | ? | N | N | N | N | N | N | Y |
| **VERMONT** | | | | | | | | |
| AL *Sanders* | Y | Y | Y | Y | Y | Y | Y | N |
| **VIRGINIA** | | | | | | | | |
| 1 **Davis, J.** | N | Y | N | N | N | N | Y | Y |
| 2 **Drake** | N | Y | N | N | N | N | N | Y |
| 3 Scott | Y | Y | Y | Y | Y | Y | Y | N |
| 4 **Forbes** | N | Y | N | N | N | N | N | Y |
| 5 **Goode** | N | Y | N | N | Y | N | N | Y |
| 6 **Goodlatte** | N | Y | N | N | N | N | N | Y |
| 7 **Cantor** | N | N | N | N | N | N | N | Y |
| 8 Moran | Y | Y | Y | Y | Y | Y | N | N |
| 9 Boucher | Y | Y | Y | N | Y | N | N | Y |
| 10 **Wolf** | N | Y | N | N | Y | N | Y | Y |
| 11 **Davis, T.** | N | Y | N | N | Y | N | N | Y |
| **WASHINGTON** | | | | | | | | |
| 1 Inslee | Y | Y | Y | Y | Y | Y | Y | N |
| 2 Larsen | Y | Y | Y | Y | Y | Y | Y | N |
| 3 Baird | Y | ? | Y | Y | Y | Y | Y | N |
| 4 **Hastings** | N | N | N | N | N | N | N | Y |
| 5 **McMorris** | N | N | N | N | N | N | N | Y |
| 6 Dicks | Y | Y | Y | Y | Y | Y | Y | N |
| 7 McDermott | Y | Y | Y | Y | Y | Y | Y | N |
| 8 **Reichert** | N | N | N | N | Y | N | N | Y |
| 9 Smith | Y | Y | Y | Y | Y | Y | Y | N |
| **WEST VIRGINIA** | | | | | | | | |
| 1 Mollohan | Y | Y | Y | N | Y | Y | Y | Y |
| 2 **Capito** | Y | Y | N | N | N | N | N | Y |
| 3 Rahall | Y | Y | Y | Y | Y | Y | Y | N |
| **WISCONSIN** | | | | | | | | |
| 1 **Ryan** | N | N | N | N | Y | N | N | Y |
| 2 Baldwin | Y | Y | Y | Y | Y | Y | Y | N |
| 3 Kind | Y | Y | Y | Y | Y | Y | Y | N |
| 4 Moore | Y | Y | Y | Y | Y | Y | Y | N |
| 5 **Sensenbrenner** | N | Y | N | Y | Y | N | N | Y |
| 6 **Petri** | N | Y | N | Y | N | N | N | Y |
| 7 Obey | Y | Y | Y | Y | Y | Y | Y | N |
| 8 **Green** | N | Y | N | Y | Y | N | N | Y |
| **WYOMING** | | | | | | | | |
| AL **Cubin** | N | N | N | N | N | ? | N | Y |

# IN THE HOUSE | By Vote Number

**133.** **HR 1268. Fiscal 2005 Supplemental Appropriations/Motion to Instruct.** Obey, D-Wis., motion to instruct House conferees to insist on a conference report that would include the highest possible funding for additional border patrol agents and increase funds for other immigration and law-enforcement programs, and accept the Senate provision that future funding for military operations in Afghanistan and Iraq be included in the president's annual budget. Motion agreed to 417-4: R 220-4; D 196-0 (ND 146-0, SD 50-0); I 1-0. April 26, 2005.

**134.** **H Con Res 95. Fiscal 2006 Budget Resolution/Motion to Instruct.** Herseth, D-S.D., motion to instruct House conferees to insist on a conference report that would reject cuts to the Medicaid program and instruct conferees to include a $1.5 million reserve fund for the creation of a bipartisan Medicaid commission. Motion agreed to 348-72: R 152-72; D 195-0 (ND 145-0, SD 50-0); I 1-0. April 26, 2005.

**135.** **Procedural Motion/Journal.** Approval of the House Journal of Tuesday, April 26, 2005. Approved 371-47: R 213-12; D 157-35 (ND 115-28, SD 42-7); I 1-0. April 27, 2005.

**136.** **HR 902. Commemorative Coins/Passage.** Castle, R-Del., motion to suspend the rules and pass the bill that would authorize the U.S. Mint to issue a new $1 coin to commemorate U.S. presidents and a series of $10 gold bullion coins to honor first ladies. It also would authorize the Mint to redesign the back of the penny that will be issued in 2009 to commemorate the 200th anniversary of President Abraham Lincoln's birth. Motion agreed to 422-6: R 226-2; D 195-4 (ND 145-4, SD 50-0); I 1-0. A two-thirds majority of those present and voting (286 in this case) is required for passage under suspension of the rules. April 27, 2005.

**137.** **H Con Res 81. Cuba Human Rights Condemnation/Adoption.** Smith, R-N.J., motion to suspend the rules and adopt the concurrent resolution that would condemn the arrest of more than 75 journalists, labor union organizers, civic leaders, librarians and human rights activists as Cuban political prisoners in March 2003. Motion agreed to 398-27: R 226-1; D 171-26 (ND 125-23, SD 46-3); I 1-0. A two-thirds majority of those present and voting (284 in this case) is required for passage under suspension of the rules. April 27, 2005.

**138.** **H Res 235. Small Business Bill of Rights/Previous Question.** Capito, R-W.Va., motion to order the previous question (thus ending debate and possibility of amendment) on adoption of the rule (H Res 235) to provide for House floor consideration of the bill that would express the sense of the House that small businesses should have a bill of rights. Motion agreed to 228-201: R 228-0; D 0-200 (ND 0-150, SD 0-50); I 0-1. (Subsequently, the rule was adopted by voice vote.) April 27, 2005.

| | 133 | 134 | 135 | 136 | 137 | 138 |
|---|---|---|---|---|---|---|
| **ALABAMA** | | | | | | |
| 1 Bonner | Y | Y | Y | Y | Y | Y |
| 2 Everett | Y | Y | Y | Y | Y | Y |
| 3 Rogers | Y | Y | Y | Y | Y | Y |
| 4 Aderholt | Y | Y | Y | Y | Y | Y |
| 5 Cramer | Y | Y | Y | Y | Y | N |
| 6 Bachus | Y | Y | Y | Y | ? | Y |
| 7 Davis | Y | Y | Y | Y | Y | N |
| **ALASKA** | | | | | | |
| AL Young | Y | Y | Y | Y | Y | Y |
| **ARIZONA** | | | | | | |
| 1 Renzi | Y | Y | Y | Y | Y | Y |
| 2 Franks | Y | N | Y | Y | Y | Y |
| 3 Shadegg | Y | N | Y | Y | Y | Y |
| 4 Pastor | Y | Y | Y | Y | Y | N |
| 5 Hayworth | Y | N | Y | Y | Y | Y |
| 6 Flake | Y | N | Y | Y | Y | Y |
| 7 Grijalva | Y | Y | N | Y | N | N |
| 8 Kolbe | Y | N | Y | Y | Y | Y |
| **ARKANSAS** | | | | | | |
| 1 Berry | Y | Y | Y | Y | Y | N |
| 2 Snyder | Y | Y | Y | Y | Y | N |
| 3 Boozman | Y | Y | Y | Y | Y | Y |
| 4 Ross | Y | Y | Y | Y | Y | N |
| **CALIFORNIA** | | | | | | |
| 1 Thompson | Y | Y | N | Y | Y | N |
| 2 Herger | Y | N | Y | Y | Y | Y |
| 3 Lungren | Y | Y | Y | Y | Y | Y |
| 4 Doolittle | Y | Y | Y | Y | Y | Y |
| 5 Matsui, D. | Y | Y | Y | Y | Y | N |
| 6 Woolsey | Y | Y | Y | N | N | N |
| 7 Miller, George | Y | Y | N | Y | N | N |
| 8 Pelosi | Y | Y | Y | Y | Y | N |
| 9 Lee | + | + | Y | Y | N | N |
| 10 Tauscher | Y | Y | Y | Y | Y | N |
| 11 Pombo | Y | Y | Y | Y | Y | Y |
| 12 Lantos | Y | Y | Y | Y | Y | N |
| 13 Stark | Y | Y | Y | N | N | N |
| 14 Eshoo | Y | Y | Y | Y | Y | N |
| 15 Honda | Y | Y | Y | Y | Y | N |
| 16 Lofgren | Y | Y | Y | Y | Y | N |
| 17 Farr | Y | Y | Y | Y | N | N |
| 18 Cardoza | Y | Y | Y | Y | Y | N |
| 19 Radanovich | Y | N | Y | Y | Y | Y |
| 20 Costa | Y | Y | Y | Y | Y | N |
| 21 Nunes | Y | N | Y | Y | Y | Y |
| 22 Thomas | Y | N | Y | Y | Y | Y |
| 23 Capps | Y | Y | Y | Y | Y | N |
| 24 Gallegly | Y | Y | Y | Y | Y | Y |
| 25 McKeon | Y | Y | Y | Y | Y | Y |
| 26 Dreier | Y | Y | Y | Y | Y | Y |
| 27 Sherman | Y | Y | Y | N | N | N |
| 28 Berman | Y | Y | Y | Y | N | N |
| 29 Schiff | Y | Y | Y | Y | Y | N |
| 30 Waxman | Y | Y | Y | Y | Y | N |
| 31 Becerra | Y | Y | Y | Y | Y | N |
| 32 Solis | Y | Y | Y | Y | Y | N |
| 33 Watson | Y | Y | ? | Y | Y | N |
| 34 Roybal-Allard | Y | Y | Y | Y | Y | N |
| 35 Waters | Y | Y | N | N | N | N |
| 36 Harman | Y | Y | Y | Y | Y | N |
| 37 Millender-McD. | Y | Y | Y | Y | Y | N |
| 38 Napolitano | Y | Y | Y | Y | Y | N |
| 39 Sánchez, Linda | Y | Y | Y | Y | Y | N |
| 40 Royce | Y | N | Y | Y | Y | Y |
| 41 Lewis | Y | Y | Y | Y | Y | Y |
| 42 Miller, Gary | Y | Y | Y | Y | Y | Y |
| 43 Baca | Y | Y | Y | Y | Y | N |
| 44 Calvert | Y | Y | Y | Y | Y | Y |
| 45 Bono | Y | Y | Y | Y | Y | Y |
| 46 Rohrabacher | Y | N | Y | Y | Y | Y |
| 47 Sanchez, Loretta | Y | Y | N | Y | Y | N |
| 48 Cox | Y | Y | Y | Y | Y | Y |
| 49 Issa | Y | Y | Y | Y | Y | Y |

| | 133 | 134 | 135 | 136 | 137 | 138 |
|---|---|---|---|---|---|---|
| 50 Cunningham | Y | Y | Y | Y | Y | Y |
| 51 Filner | Y | Y | N | Y | Y | N |
| 52 Hunter | Y | N | ? | Y | Y | Y |
| 53 Davis | Y | Y | Y | Y | Y | N |
| **COLORADO** | | | | | | |
| 1 DeGette | Y | Y | Y | Y | Y | N |
| 2 Udall | Y | Y | N | Y | Y | N |
| 3 Salazar | Y | Y | Y | Y | Y | N |
| 4 Musgrave | Y | N | Y | Y | Y | Y |
| 5 Hefley | Y | Y | N | Y | Y | Y |
| 6 Tancredo | Y | N | P | Y | Y | Y |
| 7 Beauprez | Y | Y | Y | Y | Y | Y |
| **CONNECTICUT** | | | | | | |
| 1 Larson | Y | Y | N | Y | Y | N |
| 2 Simmons | Y | Y | Y | Y | Y | Y |
| 3 DeLauro | Y | Y | Y | Y | Y | N |
| 4 Shays | Y | Y | Y | Y | Y | Y |
| 5 Johnson | Y | Y | Y | Y | Y | Y |
| **DELAWARE** | | | | | | |
| AL Castle | Y | Y | Y | Y | Y | Y |
| **FLORIDA** | | | | | | |
| 1 Miller | Y | N | Y | Y | Y | Y |
| 2 Boyd | Y | Y | Y | Y | Y | N |
| 3 Brown | ? | ? | ? | ? | ? | ? |
| 4 Crenshaw | Y | Y | Y | Y | Y | Y |
| 5 Brown-Waite | Y | Y | Y | Y | Y | Y |
| 6 Stearns | Y | N | Y | Y | Y | Y |
| 7 Mica | Y | Y | Y | Y | Y | Y |
| 8 Keller | Y | Y | Y | Y | Y | Y |
| 9 Bilirakis | Y | Y | Y | Y | Y | Y |
| 10 Young | Y | Y | ? | Y | Y | Y |
| 11 Davis | Y | Y | Y | Y | Y | N |
| 12 Putnam | Y | Y | Y | Y | Y | Y |
| 13 Harris | ? | ? | Y | Y | Y | Y |
| 14 Mack | Y | N | Y | N | Y | Y |
| 15 Weldon | Y | N | Y | Y | Y | Y |
| 16 Foley | Y | Y | Y | Y | Y | Y |
| 17 Meek | Y | Y | Y | Y | Y | N |
| 18 Ros-Lehtinen | Y | Y | Y | Y | Y | Y |
| 19 Wexler | Y | Y | Y | Y | Y | N |
| 20 Wasserman-Schultz | Y | Y | Y | Y | Y | N |
| 21 Diaz-Balart, L. | ? | ? | Y | Y | Y | Y |
| 22 Shaw | Y | Y | Y | Y | Y | Y |
| 23 Hastings | Y | Y | N | Y | N | N |
| 24 Feeney | N | N | Y | Y | Y | Y |
| 25 Diaz-Balart, M. | ? | ? | Y | Y | Y | Y |
| **GEORGIA** | | | | | | |
| 1 Kingston | Y | N | Y | Y | Y | Y |
| 2 Bishop | Y | Y | Y | Y | Y | N |
| 3 Marshall | Y | Y | N | Y | Y | N |
| 4 McKinney | Y | Y | Y | Y | N | N |
| 5 Lewis | Y | Y | Y | Y | Y | N |
| 6 Price | Y | Y | Y | Y | Y | Y |
| 7 Linder | Y | N | Y | Y | Y | Y |
| 8 Westmoreland | ? | ? | ? | ? | ? | ? |
| 9 Norwood | Y | Y | Y | Y | Y | Y |
| 10 Deal | Y | N | Y | Y | Y | Y |
| 11 Gingrey | Y | N | Y | Y | Y | Y |
| 12 Barrow | Y | Y | Y | Y | Y | N |
| 13 Scott | Y | Y | Y | Y | Y | N |
| **HAWAII** | | | | | | |
| 1 Abercrombie | Y | Y | Y | Y | Y | N |
| 2 Case | Y | Y | Y | Y | Y | N |
| **IDAHO** | | | | | | |
| 1 Otter | Y | N | Y | Y | Y | Y |
| 2 Simpson | Y | Y | Y | Y | Y | Y |
| **ILLINOIS** | | | | | | |
| 1 Rush | Y | Y | Y | Y | N | N |
| 2 Jackson | Y | Y | Y | Y | N | N |
| 3 Lipinski | Y | Y | Y | Y | Y | N |
| 4 Gutierrez | + | + | ? | Y | Y | N |
| 5 Emanuel | Y | Y | Y | Y | Y | N |
| 6 Hyde | Y | Y | Y | Y | Y | Y |
| 7 Davis | Y | Y | Y | Y | N | N |
| 8 Bean | Y | Y | Y | Y | Y | N |
| 9 Schakowsky | Y | Y | N | Y | N | N |
| 10 Kirk | Y | Y | Y | Y | Y | Y |
| 11 Weller | Y | Y | N | Y | Y | Y |
| 12 Costello | Y | Y | N | Y | Y | N |

**KEY**    Republicans    Democrats    *Independents*

| | | | |
|---|---|---|---|
| **Y** Voted for (yea) | **X** Paired against | **C** Voted "present" to avoid possible conflict of interest |
| **#** Paired for | **–** Announced against | |
| **+** Announced for | **P** Voted "present" | **?** Did not vote or otherwise make a position known |
| **N** Voted against (nay) | | |

| | 133 | 134 | 135 | 136 | 137 | 138 |
|---|---|---|---|---|---|---|
| 13 **Biggert** | Y | Y | Y | Y | Y | Y |
| 14 **Hastert** | | | | | | |
| 15 **Johnson** | Y | Y | Y | Y | Y | Y |
| 16 **Manzullo** | Y | Y | Y | Y | Y | Y |
| 17 Evans | Y | Y | Y | Y | Y | N |
| 18 **LaHood** | Y | Y | Y | Y | Y | Y |
| 19 **Shimkus** | Y | Y | Y | Y | Y | Y |
| **INDIANA** | | | | | | |
| 1 Visclosky | Y | Y | Y | Y | Y | N |
| 2 **Chocola** | Y | Y | Y | Y | Y | Y |
| 3 **Souder** | Y | N | Y | Y | Y | Y |
| 4 **Buyer** | Y | N | Y | Y | Y | Y |
| 5 **Burton** | Y | Y | Y | Y | Y | Y |
| 6 **Pence** | Y | N | Y | Y | Y | Y |
| 7 Carson | Y | Y | Y | Y | N | N |
| 8 **Hostettler** | Y | N | Y | Y | Y | Y |
| 9 **Sodrel** | Y | Y | Y | Y | Y | Y |
| **IOWA** | | | | | | |
| 1 **Nussle** | Y | Y | Y | Y | Y | Y |
| 2 **Leach** | Y | Y | Y | Y | Y | Y |
| 3 Boswell | Y | Y | Y | Y | Y | N |
| 4 **Latham** | Y | Y | N | Y | Y | Y |
| 5 **King** | Y | N | Y | Y | Y | Y |
| **KANSAS** | | | | | | |
| 1 **Moran** | Y | Y | N | Y | Y | Y |
| 2 **Ryun** | Y | Y | Y | Y | Y | Y |
| 3 Moore | Y | Y | Y | Y | Y | N |
| 4 **Tiahrt** | N | N | Y | Y | Y | Y |
| **KENTUCKY** | | | | | | |
| 1 **Whitfield** | Y | Y | N | Y | Y | Y |
| 2 **Lewis** | Y | Y | Y | Y | Y | Y |
| 3 **Northup** | Y | Y | Y | Y | Y | Y |
| 4 **Davis** | Y | Y | Y | Y | Y | Y |
| 5 **Rogers** | Y | Y | Y | Y | Y | Y |
| 6 Chandler | Y | Y | Y | Y | Y | N |
| **LOUISIANA** | | | | | | |
| 1 **Jindal** | Y | Y | Y | Y | Y | Y |
| 2 Jefferson | Y | Y | Y | Y | Y | N |
| 3 Melancon | Y | Y | Y | Y | Y | N |
| 4 **McCrery** | Y | Y | Y | Y | Y | Y |
| 5 **Alexander** | Y | Y | Y | Y | Y | Y |
| 6 **Baker** | Y | N | Y | Y | Y | Y |
| 7 **Boustany** | Y | N | Y | Y | Y | Y |
| **MAINE** | | | | | | |
| 1 Allen | Y | Y | Y | Y | Y | N |
| 2 Michaud | Y | Y | Y | Y | Y | N |
| **MARYLAND** | | | | | | |
| 1 **Gilchrest** | Y | Y | Y | Y | Y | Y |
| 2 Ruppersberger | Y | Y | Y | Y | Y | N |
| 3 Cardin | Y | Y | Y | Y | Y | N |
| 4 Wynn | Y | Y | Y | Y | N | N |
| 5 Hoyer | Y | Y | Y | Y | Y | N |
| 6 **Bartlett** | Y | N | Y | Y | Y | Y |
| 7 Cummings | Y | Y | Y | Y | Y | N |
| 8 Van Hollen | Y | Y | Y | Y | Y | N |
| **MASSACHUSETTS** | | | | | | |
| 1 Olver | Y | Y | Y | Y | N | N |
| 2 Neal | Y | Y | Y | Y | Y | N |
| 3 McGovern | Y | Y | Y | Y | Y | N |
| 4 Frank | Y | Y | Y | Y | Y | N |
| 5 Meehan | Y | Y | Y | Y | Y | N |
| 6 Tierney | Y | Y | Y | Y | Y | N |
| 7 Markey | Y | Y | Y | Y | Y | N |
| 8 Capuano | Y | Y | N | N | Y | N |
| 9 Lynch | Y | Y | Y | Y | Y | N |
| 10 Delahunt | Y | Y | Y | Y | Y | N |
| **MICHIGAN** | | | | | | |
| 1 Stupak | Y | Y | N | Y | Y | N |
| 2 **Hoekstra** | Y | Y | Y | Y | Y | Y |
| 3 **Ehlers** | Y | Y | Y | Y | Y | Y |
| 4 **Camp** | Y | Y | Y | Y | Y | Y |
| 5 Kildee | Y | Y | Y | Y | Y | N |
| 6 **Upton** | Y | Y | Y | Y | Y | Y |
| 7 **Schwarz** | Y | Y | Y | Y | Y | Y |
| 8 **Rogers** | Y | N | Y | Y | Y | Y |
| 9 **Knollenberg** | Y | Y | Y | Y | Y | Y |
| 10 **Miller** | Y | Y | Y | Y | Y | Y |
| 11 **McCotter** | Y | Y | N | Y | Y | Y |
| 12 Levin | Y | Y | Y | Y | Y | N |
| 13 Kilpatrick | Y | ? | Y | Y | N | N |
| 14 Conyers | Y | Y | Y | Y | Y | N |
| 15 Dingell | Y | Y | Y | Y | Y | N |

| | 133 | 134 | 135 | 136 | 137 | 138 |
|---|---|---|---|---|---|---|
| **MINNESOTA** | | | | | | |
| 1 **Gutknecht** | Y | N | N | Y | Y | Y |
| 2 **Kline** | Y | Y | Y | Y | Y | Y |
| 3 **Ramstad** | Y | Y | N | Y | Y | Y |
| 4 McCollum | Y | Y | Y | Y | Y | N |
| 5 Sabo | Y | Y | N | Y | Y | N |
| 6 **Kennedy** | Y | Y | Y | Y | Y | Y |
| 7 Peterson | Y | Y | N | Y | Y | N |
| 8 Oberstar | Y | Y | N | Y | Y | N |
| **MISSISSIPPI** | | | | | | |
| 1 **Wicker** | ? | ? | ? | ? | ? | ? |
| 2 Thompson | Y | Y | N | Y | N | N |
| 3 **Pickering** | Y | Y | Y | Y | Y | Y |
| 4 Taylor | Y | Y | N | Y | Y | N |
| **MISSOURI** | | | | | | |
| 1 Clay | Y | Y | Y | Y | N | N |
| 2 **Akin** | Y | N | Y | Y | Y | Y |
| 3 Carnahan | Y | Y | Y | Y | Y | N |
| 4 Skelton | Y | Y | Y | Y | Y | N |
| 5 Cleaver | Y | Y | Y | Y | Y | N |
| 6 **Graves** | Y | Y | Y | Y | Y | Y |
| 7 **Blunt** | Y | Y | Y | Y | Y | Y |
| 8 **Emerson** | Y | Y | Y | Y | Y | Y |
| 9 **Hulshof** | Y | Y | Y | Y | Y | Y |
| **MONTANA** | | | | | | |
| AL **Rehberg** | Y | Y | Y | Y | Y | Y |
| **NEBRASKA** | | | | | | |
| 1 **Fortenberry** | Y | Y | Y | Y | Y | Y |
| 2 **Terry** | Y | N | Y | Y | Y | Y |
| 3 **Osborne** | Y | Y | Y | Y | Y | Y |
| **NEVADA** | | | | | | |
| 1 Berkley | Y | Y | Y | Y | Y | N |
| 2 **Gibbons** | Y | Y | Y | Y | Y | Y |
| 3 **Porter** | Y | Y | Y | Y | Y | Y |
| **NEW HAMPSHIRE** | | | | | | |
| 1 **Bradley** | Y | Y | Y | Y | Y | Y |
| 2 **Bass** | Y | Y | Y | Y | Y | Y |
| **NEW JERSEY** | | | | | | |
| 1 Andrews | Y | Y | Y | Y | Y | N |
| 2 **LoBiondo** | Y | Y | N | Y | Y | Y |
| 3 **Saxton** | Y | Y | Y | Y | Y | Y |
| 4 **Smith** | Y | Y | Y | Y | Y | Y |
| 5 **Garrett** | Y | N | Y | Y | Y | Y |
| 6 Pallone | Y | Y | Y | Y | Y | N |
| 7 **Ferguson** | Y | N | Y | Y | Y | Y |
| 8 Pascrell | Y | Y | Y | Y | Y | N |
| 9 Rothman | ? | ? | ? | ? | ? | ? |
| 10 Payne | Y | Y | Y | Y | N | N |
| 11 **Frelinghuysen** | Y | Y | Y | Y | Y | Y |
| 12 Holt | Y | Y | N | Y | Y | N |
| 13 Menendez | Y | Y | ? | Y | Y | N |
| **NEW MEXICO** | | | | | | |
| 1 **Wilson** | Y | Y | Y | Y | Y | Y |
| 2 **Pearce** | Y | N | Y | Y | Y | Y |
| 3 Udall | Y | Y | N | Y | Y | N |
| **NEW YORK** | | | | | | |
| 1 Bishop | Y | Y | Y | Y | Y | N |
| 2 Israel | Y | Y | Y | Y | Y | N |
| 3 **King** | Y | Y | Y | Y | Y | Y |
| 4 McCarthy | Y | Y | Y | Y | Y | N |
| 5 Ackerman | Y | Y | Y | Y | Y | N |
| 6 Meeks | Y | Y | Y | Y | N | N |
| 7 Crowley | Y | Y | Y | Y | Y | N |
| 8 Nadler | Y | Y | N | Y | Y | N |
| 9 Weiner | Y | Y | Y | Y | Y | N |
| 10 Towns | Y | Y | Y | Y | N | N |
| 11 Owens | Y | Y | Y | Y | Y | N |
| 12 Velázquez | Y | Y | ? | Y | N | N |
| 13 **Fossella** | Y | Y | N | Y | Y | Y |
| 14 Maloney | Y | Y | Y | Y | Y | N |
| 15 Rangel | Y | Y | Y | Y | N | N |
| 16 Serrano | Y | Y | Y | Y | N | N |
| 17 Engel | Y | Y | Y | Y | Y | N |
| 18 Lowey | Y | Y | Y | Y | Y | N |
| 19 **Kelly** | Y | Y | Y | Y | Y | Y |
| 20 **Sweeney** | Y | Y | Y | Y | Y | Y |
| 21 McNulty | Y | Y | Y | Y | Y | N |
| 22 Hinchey | Y | Y | N | Y | N | N |
| 23 **McHugh** | Y | Y | Y | Y | Y | Y |
| 24 **Boehlert** | Y | Y | Y | Y | Y | Y |
| 25 **Walsh** | Y | Y | Y | Y | Y | Y |
| 26 **Reynolds** | Y | Y | Y | Y | Y | Y |
| 27 Higgins | Y | Y | Y | Y | Y | N |
| 28 Slaughter | Y | Y | Y | Y | Y | N |
| 29 **Kuhl** | Y | Y | Y | Y | Y | Y |

| | 133 | 134 | 135 | 136 | 137 | 138 |
|---|---|---|---|---|---|---|
| **NORTH CAROLINA** | | | | | | |
| 1 Butterfield | Y | Y | Y | Y | Y | N |
| 2 Etheridge | Y | Y | Y | Y | Y | N |
| 3 **Jones** | Y | Y | Y | Y | Y | Y |
| 4 Price | Y | Y | Y | Y | Y | N |
| 5 **Foxx** | Y | N | Y | Y | Y | Y |
| 6 **Coble** | N | Y | Y | Y | Y | Y |
| 7 McIntyre | Y | Y | Y | Y | Y | N |
| 8 **Hayes** | Y | Y | Y | Y | Y | Y |
| 9 **Myrick** | Y | N | Y | Y | Y | Y |
| 10 **McHenry** | Y | N | Y | Y | Y | Y |
| 11 **Taylor** | Y | N | Y | Y | Y | Y |
| 12 Watt | Y | Y | Y | Y | P | N |
| 13 Miller | Y | Y | Y | Y | Y | N |
| **NORTH DAKOTA** | | | | | | |
| AL Pomeroy | Y | Y | Y | Y | Y | N |
| **OHIO** | | | | | | |
| 1 **Chabot** | Y | N | Y | Y | Y | Y |
| 2 **Portman** | Y | Y | Y | + | + | + |
| 3 **Turner** | Y | Y | Y | Y | Y | Y |
| 4 **Oxley** | Y | Y | Y | Y | Y | Y |
| 5 **Gillmor** | Y | Y | Y | Y | Y | Y |
| 6 Strickland | Y | Y | N | N | Y | N |
| 7 **Hobson** | Y | Y | Y | Y | Y | Y |
| 8 **Boehner** | Y | Y | Y | Y | Y | Y |
| 9 Kaptur | Y | Y | Y | Y | Y | N |
| 10 Kucinich | Y | Y | N | Y | N | N |
| 11 Jones | Y | Y | Y | Y | ? | N |
| 12 **Tiberi** | N | N | N | Y | Y | Y |
| 13 Brown | Y | Y | Y | Y | Y | N |
| 14 **LaTourette** | Y | Y | Y | Y | Y | Y |
| 15 **Pryce** | Y | Y | Y | Y | Y | Y |
| 16 **Regula** | Y | Y | Y | Y | Y | Y |
| 17 Ryan | Y | Y | Y | Y | Y | N |
| 18 **Ney** | Y | Y | Y | Y | Y | Y |
| **OKLAHOMA** | | | | | | |
| 1 **Sullivan** | Y | Y | Y | Y | Y | Y |
| 2 Boren | Y | Y | Y | Y | Y | N |
| 3 **Lucas** | Y | Y | Y | Y | Y | Y |
| 4 **Cole** | Y | Y | Y | Y | Y | Y |
| 5 **Istook** | Y | N | Y | Y | Y | Y |
| **OREGON** | | | | | | |
| 1 Wu | Y | Y | N | Y | Y | N |
| 2 **Walden** | Y | Y | Y | Y | Y | Y |
| 3 Blumenauer | Y | Y | Y | Y | Y | N |
| 4 DeFazio | Y | Y | N | N | P | N |
| 5 Hooley | ? | ? | ? | Y | Y | N |
| **PENNSYLVANIA** | | | | | | |
| 1 Brady | Y | Y | N | Y | Y | N |
| 2 Fattah | Y | Y | ? | Y | Y | N |
| 3 **English** | Y | Y | ? | Y | Y | Y |
| 4 **Hart** | Y | Y | N | Y | Y | Y |
| 5 **Peterson** | Y | Y | Y | Y | Y | Y |
| 6 **Gerlach** | Y | Y | Y | Y | Y | Y |
| 7 **Weldon** | Y | Y | Y | Y | Y | Y |
| 8 **Fitzpatrick** | Y | Y | Y | Y | Y | Y |
| 9 **Shuster** | Y | Y | Y | Y | Y | Y |
| 10 **Sherwood** | Y | Y | Y | Y | Y | Y |
| 11 Kanjorski | Y | Y | Y | Y | Y | N |
| 12 Murtha | ? | ? | Y | Y | Y | N |
| 13 Schwartz | Y | Y | Y | Y | Y | N |
| 14 Doyle | Y | Y | Y | Y | Y | N |
| 15 **Dent** | Y | Y | Y | Y | Y | Y |
| 16 **Pitts** | Y | N | Y | Y | Y | Y |
| 17 Holden | Y | Y | Y | Y | Y | N |
| 18 **Murphy** | Y | N | Y | Y | Y | Y |
| 19 **Platts** | Y | Y | Y | Y | Y | Y |
| **RHODE ISLAND** | | | | | | |
| 1 Kennedy | Y | Y | ? | Y | Y | N |
| 2 Langevin | Y | Y | Y | Y | Y | N |
| **SOUTH CAROLINA** | | | | | | |
| 1 **Brown** | Y | Y | Y | Y | Y | Y |
| 2 **Wilson** | Y | Y | Y | Y | Y | Y |
| 3 **Barrett** | Y | N | Y | Y | Y | Y |
| 4 **Inglis** | Y | N | Y | Y | Y | Y |
| 5 Spratt | Y | Y | ? | Y | Y | N |
| 6 Clyburn | Y | Y | Y | Y | Y | N |
| **SOUTH DAKOTA** | | | | | | |
| AL Herseth | Y | Y | Y | Y | Y | N |
| **TENNESSEE** | | | | | | |
| 1 **Jenkins** | ? | ? | Y | Y | Y | Y |
| 2 **Duncan** | Y | N | Y | Y | Y | Y |

| | 133 | 134 | 135 | 136 | 137 | 138 |
|---|---|---|---|---|---|---|
| 3 **Wamp** | Y | N | Y | Y | Y | Y |
| 4 Davis | Y | Y | Y | Y | Y | N |
| 5 Cooper | Y | Y | Y | Y | Y | N |
| 6 Gordon | Y | Y | Y | Y | Y | N |
| 7 **Blackburn** | Y | N | Y | Y | Y | Y |
| 8 Tanner | Y | Y | N | Y | Y | N |
| 9 Ford | Y | Y | N | Y | Y | N |
| **TEXAS** | | | | | | |
| 1 **Gohmert** | Y | Y | Y | Y | Y | Y |
| 2 **Poe** | Y | N | Y | N | Y | Y |
| 3 **Johnson, S.** | Y | N | Y | Y | Y | Y |
| 4 **Hall** | Y | Y | Y | Y | Y | Y |
| 5 **Hensarling** | Y | N | Y | Y | Y | Y |
| 6 **Barton** | Y | N | Y | Y | Y | Y |
| 7 **Culberson** | Y | N | Y | Y | Y | Y |
| 8 **Brady** | + | – | Y | Y | Y | Y |
| 9 Green | Y | Y | Y | Y | Y | N |
| 10 **McCaul** | Y | Y | Y | Y | Y | Y |
| 11 **Conaway** | Y | N | Y | Y | Y | Y |
| 12 **Granger** | Y | Y | Y | Y | Y | Y |
| 13 **Thornberry** | Y | N | Y | Y | Y | Y |
| 14 **Paul** | Y | N | Y | Y | N | Y |
| 15 Hinojosa | Y | Y | Y | Y | Y | N |
| 16 Reyes | Y | Y | Y | Y | Y | N |
| 17 Edwards | Y | Y | Y | Y | Y | N |
| 18 Jackson-Lee | Y | Y | Y | Y | Y | N |
| 19 **Neugebauer** | Y | N | Y | Y | Y | Y |
| 20 Gonzalez | Y | Y | Y | Y | Y | N |
| 21 **Smith** | Y | Y | Y | Y | Y | Y |
| 22 **DeLay** | Y | Y | Y | Y | Y | Y |
| 23 **Bonilla** | Y | N | Y | Y | Y | Y |
| 24 **Marchant** | Y | N | Y | Y | Y | Y |
| 25 Doggett | Y | Y | Y | Y | Y | N |
| 26 **Burgess** | Y | N | Y | Y | Y | Y |
| 27 Ortiz | Y | Y | Y | Y | Y | N |
| 28 Cuellar | Y | Y | Y | Y | Y | N |
| 29 Green | Y | Y | N | Y | Y | N |
| 30 Johnson, E. | Y | Y | Y | Y | N | N |
| 31 **Carter** | Y | N | Y | Y | Y | Y |
| 32 **Sessions** | Y | N | Y | Y | Y | Y |
| **UTAH** | | | | | | |
| 1 **Bishop** | Y | N | Y | Y | Y | Y |
| 2 Matheson | Y | Y | Y | Y | Y | N |
| 3 **Cannon** | Y | N | Y | Y | Y | Y |
| **VERMONT** | | | | | | |
| AL *Sanders* | Y | Y | Y | Y | Y | N |
| **VIRGINIA** | | | | | | |
| 1 **Davis, J.** | Y | Y | Y | Y | Y | Y |
| 2 **Drake** | Y | Y | Y | Y | Y | Y |
| 3 Scott | Y | Y | Y | Y | Y | N |
| 4 **Forbes** | Y | Y | Y | Y | Y | Y |
| 5 **Goode** | Y | Y | Y | Y | Y | Y |
| 6 **Goodlatte** | Y | Y | Y | Y | Y | Y |
| 7 **Cantor** | Y | Y | Y | Y | Y | Y |
| 8 Moran | Y | Y | Y | Y | Y | N |
| 9 Boucher | Y | Y | Y | Y | Y | N |
| 10 **Wolf** | Y | Y | Y | Y | Y | Y |
| 11 **Davis, T.** | Y | Y | Y | Y | Y | Y |
| **WASHINGTON** | | | | | | |
| 1 Inslee | Y | Y | Y | Y | Y | N |
| 2 Larsen | Y | Y | N | Y | Y | N |
| 3 Baird | Y | Y | N | Y | Y | N |
| 4 **Hastings** | Y | Y | Y | Y | Y | Y |
| 5 **McMorris** | Y | Y | Y | Y | Y | Y |
| 6 Dicks | Y | Y | Y | Y | Y | N |
| 7 McDermott | Y | Y | N | Y | N | N |
| 8 **Reichert** | Y | Y | Y | Y | Y | Y |
| 9 Smith | Y | Y | Y | ? | Y | N |
| **WEST VIRGINIA** | | | | | | |
| 1 Mollohan | Y | Y | Y | Y | Y | N |
| 2 **Capito** | Y | Y | Y | Y | Y | Y |
| 3 Rahall | Y | Y | Y | Y | Y | N |
| **WISCONSIN** | | | | | | |
| 1 **Ryan** | Y | Y | Y | Y | Y | Y |
| 2 Baldwin | Y | Y | N | Y | Y | N |
| 3 Kind | Y | Y | Y | Y | Y | N |
| 4 Moore | Y | Y | Y | Y | Y | N |
| 5 **Sensenbrenner** | Y | Y | Y | Y | Y | Y |
| 6 **Petri** | Y | Y | Y | Y | Y | Y |
| 7 Obey | Y | Y | Y | Y | Y | N |
| 8 **Green** | Y | Y | Y | Y | Y | Y |
| **WYOMING** | | | | | | |
| AL **Cubin** | Y | Y | Y | Y | Y | Y |

# IN THE HOUSE | By Vote Number

**139.** **HR 748. Abortion Notification/Previous Question.** Gingrey, R-Ga., motion to order the previous question (thus ending debate and possibility of amendment) on adoption of the rule (H Res 236) to provide for House floor consideration of the bill that would make it a crime to transport a minor across state lines with the intent to obtain an abortion and circumvent state parental-consent laws. Motion agreed to 234-192: R 226-0; D 8-191 (ND 4-145, SD 4-46); I 0-1. (Subsequently, the rule was adopted by voice vote.) April 27, 2005.

**140.** **H Res 22. "Small Business Bill of Rights"/Recommit.** Velázquez, D-N.Y., motion to recommit the resolution to the House Small Business Committee. Motion rejected 188-222: R 0-212; D 187-10 (ND 141-8, SD 46-2); I 1-0. (Subsequently, the resolution was adopted by voice vote.) April 27, 2005.

**141.** **HR 748. Abortion Notification/Professional Transportation and Medical Provider Exemption.** Scott, D-Va., amendment that would exempt taxicab drivers, bus drivers and others in the professional transportation business, as well as doctors, nurses and other medical providers or their staff from criminal liability under the transportation provisions in the bill. Rejected 179-245: R 15-211; D 163-34 (ND 129-19, SD 34-15); I 1-0. April 27, 2005.

**142.** **HR 748. Abortion Notification/Grandparent and Clergy Exemption.** Jackson-Lee, D-Texas., amendment that would exempt from prosecution the grandparents of the minor or a member of the clergy who transports a minor across state lines for the purposes of obtaining an abortion. Rejected 177-252: R 13-215; D 163-37 (ND 129-21, SD 34-16); I 1-0. April 27, 2005.

**143.** **HR 748. Abortion Notification/Recommit.** Nadler, D-N.Y., motion to recommit the bill to the House Judiciary Committee with instructions to include language which would bar fathers who have committed rape or incest against a minor that resulted in a pregnancy from being able to sue the doctor who performed the abortion. Motion rejected 183-245: R 10-218; D 172-27 (ND 135-15, SD 37-12); I 1-0. April 27, 2005.

**144.** **HR 748. Abortion Notification/Passage.** Passage of the bill that would bar the transportation of a minor girl across state lines to obtain an abortion without the consent of a parent, guardian or judge. The bill would authorize fines and/or up to a year in prison for individuals who transport a minor to a state without a parental consent law in an attempt to circumvent parents' involvement. Doctors who perform such abortions also would be subject to the penalties. Abortion providers in states without parental consent laws would be required to try to notify a parent or legal guardian, either personally or by certified mail, before performing an abortion on a minor who was a resident of another state. Passed 270-157: R 216-11; D 54-145 (ND 27-122, SD 27-23); I 0-1. A "yea" was a vote in support of the president's position. April 27, 2005.

| | 139 | 140 | 141 | 142 | 143 | 144 |
|---|---|---|---|---|---|---|
| **ALABAMA** | | | | | | |
| 1 Bonner | Y | N | N | N | N | Y |
| 2 Everett | Y | N | N | N | N | Y |
| 3 Rogers | Y | N | N | N | N | Y |
| 4 Aderholt | Y | N | N | N | N | Y |
| 5 Cramer | N | Y | N | N | N | Y |
| 6 Bachus | Y | N | N | N | N | Y |
| 7 Davis | N | Y | Y | Y | Y | Y |
| **ALASKA** | | | | | | |
| AL Young | Y | N | N | N | N | Y |
| **ARIZONA** | | | | | | |
| 1 Renzi | Y | N | N | N | N | Y |
| 2 Franks | Y | N | N | N | N | Y |
| 3 Shadegg | Y | ? | N | N | N | Y |
| 4 Pastor | N | Y | Y | Y | Y | N |
| 5 Hayworth | Y | N | N | N | N | Y |
| 6 Flake | Y | ? | N | N | N | Y |
| 7 Grijalva | N | Y | ? | Y | Y | N |
| 8 Kolbe | Y | N | Y | N | Y | Y |
| **ARKANSAS** | | | | | | |
| 1 Berry | Y | Y | N | N | N | Y |
| 2 Snyder | N | Y | N | N | Y | Y |
| 3 Boozman | Y | N | N | N | N | Y |
| 4 Ross | N | Y | Y | Y | Y | Y |
| **CALIFORNIA** | | | | | | |
| 1 Thompson | N | Y | Y | Y | Y | N |
| 2 Herger | Y | N | N | N | N | Y |
| 3 Lungren | Y | N | N | N | N | Y |
| 4 Doolittle | Y | ? | N | N | N | Y |
| 5 Matsui, D. | N | Y | Y | Y | Y | N |
| 6 Woolsey | N | Y | Y | Y | Y | N |
| 7 Miller, George | N | Y | Y | Y | Y | N |
| 8 Pelosi | N | Y | Y | Y | Y | N |
| 9 Lee | N | Y | Y | Y | Y | N |
| 10 Tauscher | N | Y | Y | Y | Y | N |
| 11 Pombo | Y | N | N | N | N | Y |
| 12 Lantos | N | Y | Y | Y | Y | N |
| 13 Stark | N | Y | Y | Y | Y | N |
| 14 Eshoo | N | Y | Y | Y | Y | N |
| 15 Honda | N | Y | Y | Y | Y | N |
| 16 Lofgren | N | Y | Y | Y | Y | N |
| 17 Farr | N | Y | Y | Y | Y | N |
| 18 Cardoza | N | Y | Y | Y | Y | Y |
| 19 Radanovich | Y | N | N | N | N | Y |
| 20 Costa | N | N | Y | Y | Y | Y |
| 21 Nunes | Y | N | N | N | N | Y |
| 22 Thomas | Y | N | N | N | N | Y |
| 23 Capps | N | Y | Y | Y | Y | N |
| 24 Gallegly | Y | N | N | N | N | Y |
| 25 McKeon | Y | N | N | N | N | Y |
| 26 Dreier | Y | N | N | N | N | Y |
| 27 Sherman | N | Y | Y | Y | Y | N |
| 28 Berman | N | Y | Y | Y | Y | N |
| 29 Schiff | N | Y | Y | Y | Y | N |
| 30 Waxman | N | Y | Y | Y | Y | N |
| 31 Becerra | N | Y | Y | Y | Y | N |
| 32 Solis | N | Y | Y | Y | Y | N |
| 33 Watson | N | Y | Y | Y | Y | N |
| 34 Roybal-Allard | N | Y | Y | Y | Y | N |
| 35 Waters | N | Y | Y | Y | Y | N |
| 36 Harman | N | Y | Y | Y | Y | N |
| 37 Millender-McD. | N | Y | Y | Y | Y | N |
| 38 Napolitano | N | Y | Y | Y | Y | N |
| 39 Sánchez, Linda | N | Y | Y | Y | Y | N |
| 40 Royce | Y | N | N | N | N | Y |
| 41 Lewis | Y | N | N | N | N | Y |
| 42 Miller, Gary | Y | N | N | N | N | Y |
| 43 Baca | N | Y | N | N | Y | Y |
| 44 Calvert | Y | N | N | N | N | Y |
| 45 Bono | Y | N | N | N | N | Y |
| 46 Rohrabacher | Y | N | N | N | N | Y |
| 47 Sanchez, Loretta | N | Y | Y | Y | Y | N |
| 48 Cox | Y | N | N | N | N | Y |
| 49 Issa | Y | N | N | N | N | Y |

| | 139 | 140 | 141 | 142 | 143 | 144 |
|---|---|---|---|---|---|---|
| 50 Cunningham | Y | N | N | N | N | Y |
| 51 Filner | N | Y | Y | Y | Y | Y |
| 52 Hunter | Y | N | N | N | N | Y |
| 53 Davis | N | Y | Y | Y | Y | Y |
| **COLORADO** | | | | | | |
| 1 DeGette | N | Y | Y | Y | Y | N |
| 2 Udall | N | Y | Y | Y | Y | N |
| 3 Salazar | N | N | Y | N | N | Y |
| 4 Musgrave | Y | ? | N | N | N | Y |
| 5 Hefley | Y | N | N | N | N | Y |
| 6 Tancredo | Y | N | N | N | N | Y |
| 7 Beauprez | Y | N | N | N | N | Y |
| **CONNECTICUT** | | | | | | |
| 1 Larson | N | Y | Y | Y | Y | N |
| 2 Simmons | Y | N | Y | Y | Y | N |
| 3 DeLauro | N | Y | Y | Y | Y | N |
| 4 Shays | Y | N | Y | Y | Y | N |
| 5 Johnson | Y | N | Y | Y | Y | N |
| **DELAWARE** | | | | | | |
| AL Castle | Y | N | Y | Y | Y | N |
| **FLORIDA** | | | | | | |
| 1 Miller | Y | N | N | N | N | Y |
| 2 Boyd | N | Y | Y | Y | Y | Y |
| 3 Brown | ? | ? | ? | ? | ? | ? |
| 4 Crenshaw | Y | N | N | N | N | Y |
| 5 Brown-Waite | Y | ? | N | N | N | Y |
| 6 Stearns | Y | N | N | N | N | Y |
| 7 Mica | Y | N | N | N | N | Y |
| 8 Keller | Y | N | N | N | N | Y |
| 9 Bilirakis | Y | N | N | N | N | Y |
| 10 Young | Y | N | N | N | N | Y |
| 11 Davis | N | Y | Y | Y | Y | N |
| 12 Putnam | Y | N | N | N | N | Y |
| 13 Harris | Y | N | N | N | N | Y |
| 14 Mack | Y | N | N | N | N | Y |
| 15 Weldon | Y | N | N | N | N | Y |
| 16 Foley | Y | N | N | N | N | Y |
| 17 Meek | N | Y | Y | Y | Y | N |
| 18 Ros-Lehtinen | Y | N | N | N | N | Y |
| 19 Wexler | N | Y | Y | Y | Y | N |
| 20 Wasserman-Schultz | N | Y | Y | Y | Y | N |
| 21 Diaz-Balart, L. | Y | N | N | N | N | Y |
| 22 Shaw | Y | N | N | N | N | Y |
| 23 Hastings | N | Y | Y | Y | Y | N |
| 24 Feeney | Y | ? | N | N | N | Y |
| 25 Diaz-Balart, M. | Y | N | N | N | N | Y |
| **GEORGIA** | | | | | | |
| 1 Kingston | Y | N | N | N | N | Y |
| 2 Bishop | N | Y | Y | Y | ? | Y |
| 3 Marshall | N | Y | N | N | Y | Y |
| 4 McKinney | N | Y | Y | Y | Y | N |
| 5 Lewis | N | Y | Y | Y | Y | N |
| 6 Price | Y | N | N | N | N | Y |
| 7 Linder | Y | N | N | N | N | Y |
| 8 Westmoreland | ? | ? | ? | ? | ? | ? |
| 9 Norwood | Y | N | N | N | N | Y |
| 10 Deal | Y | N | N | N | N | Y |
| 11 Gingrey | Y | N | N | N | N | Y |
| 12 Barrow | N | Y | Y | Y | Y | N |
| 13 Scott | N | ? | Y | Y | Y | N |
| **HAWAII** | | | | | | |
| 1 Abercrombie | N | Y | Y | Y | Y | N |
| 2 Case | N | Y | Y | Y | Y | N |
| **IDAHO** | | | | | | |
| 1 Otter | Y | N | N | N | N | Y |
| 2 Simpson | Y | N | N | N | N | Y |
| **ILLINOIS** | | | | | | |
| 1 Rush | N | Y | Y | Y | Y | N |
| 2 Jackson | N | Y | Y | Y | Y | N |
| 3 Lipinski | Y | N | N | N | N | Y |
| 4 Gutierrez | N | Y | Y | Y | Y | N |
| 5 Emanuel | N | Y | Y | N | N | Y |
| 6 Hyde | Y | N | N | N | N | Y |
| 7 Davis | N | Y | Y | Y | Y | N |
| 8 Bean | N | Y | Y | Y | Y | Y |
| 9 Schakowsky | N | Y | Y | Y | Y | N |
| 10 Kirk | Y | N | Y | Y | Y | N |
| 11 Weller | Y | N | N | N | N | Y |
| 12 Costello | N | Y | N | N | N | Y |

**KEY** Republicans Democrats *Independents*

| | | | |
|---|---|---|---|
| **Y** Voted for (yea) | | **X** Paired against | **C** Voted "present" to avoid possible conflict of interest |
| **#** Paired for | | **–** Announced against | |
| **+** Announced for | | **P** Voted "present" | **?** Did not vote or otherwise make a position known |
| **N** Voted against (nay) | | | |

| | 139 | 140 | 141 | 142 | 143 | 144 |
|---|---|---|---|---|---|---|
| 13 **Biggert** | Y | N | Y | Y | N | N |
| 14 **Hastert** | | | | | | |
| 15 **Johnson** | Y | N | N | N | N | Y |
| 16 **Manzullo** | Y | N | N | N | N | Y |
| 17 Evans | N | Y | Y | Y | Y | N |
| 18 **LaHood** | Y | N | N | N | N | Y |
| 19 **Shimkus** | Y | N | N | N | N | Y |
| **INDIANA** | | | | | | |
| 1 Visclosky | N | Y | Y | Y | Y | N |
| 2 **Chocola** | Y | N | N | N | N | Y |
| 3 **Souder** | Y | ? | N | N | N | Y |
| 4 **Buyer** | Y | N | N | N | N | Y |
| 5 **Burton** | Y | ? | N | N | N | Y |
| 6 **Pence** | Y | ? | N | N | N | Y |
| 7 Carson | N | Y | Y | Y | Y | N |
| 8 **Hostettler** | Y | N | N | N | N | Y |
| 9 **Sodrel** | Y | N | N | N | N | Y |
| **IOWA** | | | | | | |
| 1 **Nussle** | Y | N | N | N | N | Y |
| 2 **Leach** | Y | N | Y | Y | Y | Y |
| 3 Boswell | N | Y | Y | Y | Y | Y |
| 4 **Latham** | Y | N | N | N | N | Y |
| 5 **King** | Y | N | N | N | N | Y |
| **KANSAS** | | | | | | |
| 1 **Moran** | Y | N | N | N | N | Y |
| 2 **Ryun** | Y | N | N | N | N | Y |
| 3 Moore | N | Y | Y | N | Y | N |
| 4 **Tiahrt** | Y | N | N | N | N | Y |
| **KENTUCKY** | | | | | | |
| 1 **Whitfield** | Y | N | N | N | N | Y |
| 2 **Lewis** | Y | N | N | N | N | Y |
| 3 **Northup** | Y | N | N | N | N | Y |
| 4 **Davis** | Y | N | N | N | N | Y |
| 5 **Rogers** | Y | N | N | N | N | Y |
| 6 Chandler | N | Y | N | N | Y | Y |
| **LOUISIANA** | | | | | | |
| 1 **Jindal** | Y | N | N | N | N | Y |
| 2 Jefferson | N | Y | Y | Y | Y | N |
| 3 Melancon | N | Y | N | N | N | Y |
| 4 **McCrery** | Y | N | N | N | N | Y |
| 5 **Alexander** | Y | N | N | N | N | Y |
| 6 **Baker** | Y | N | N | N | N | Y |
| 7 **Boustany** | Y | N | N | N | N | Y |
| **MAINE** | | | | | | |
| 1 Allen | N | Y | Y | Y | Y | N |
| 2 Michaud | N | Y | Y | Y | Y | N |
| **MARYLAND** | | | | | | |
| 1 **Gilchrest** | Y | N | N | Y | N | N |
| 2 Ruppersberger | N | Y | Y | Y | Y | N |
| 3 Cardin | N | Y | Y | Y | Y | N |
| 4 Wynn | N | Y | Y | Y | Y | N |
| 5 Hoyer | N | Y | Y | Y | Y | N |
| 6 **Bartlett** | Y | N | N | N | N | Y |
| 7 Cummings | N | Y | Y | Y | Y | N |
| 8 Van Hollen | N | Y | Y | Y | Y | N |
| **MASSACHUSETTS** | | | | | | |
| 1 Olver | N | Y | + | Y | Y | N |
| 2 Neal | N | Y | Y | Y | Y | N |
| 3 McGovern | N | Y | Y | Y | Y | N |
| 4 Frank | N | Y | Y | Y | Y | N |
| 5 Meehan | N | Y | Y | Y | Y | N |
| 6 Tierney | N | Y | Y | Y | Y | N |
| 7 Markey | N | Y | Y | Y | Y | N |
| 8 Capuano | N | Y | Y | Y | Y | N |
| 9 Lynch | N | ? | Y | N | Y | Y |
| 10 Delahunt | N | Y | Y | Y | Y | N |
| **MICHIGAN** | | | | | | |
| 1 Stupak | Y | Y | N | N | N | Y |
| 2 **Hoekstra** | Y | N | N | N | N | Y |
| 3 **Ehlers** | Y | N | N | N | Y | Y |
| 4 **Camp** | Y | N | N | N | N | ? |
| 5 Kildee | N | N | N | N | N | Y |
| 6 **Upton** | Y | N | N | N | N | Y |
| 7 **Schwarz** | Y | N | Y | N | N | Y |
| 8 **Rogers** | Y | N | N | N | N | Y |
| 9 **Knollenberg** | Y | N | N | N | N | Y |
| 10 **Miller** | Y | N | N | N | N | Y |
| 11 **McCotter** | Y | N | N | N | N | Y |
| 12 Levin | N | Y | Y | Y | Y | N |
| 13 Kilpatrick | N | Y | Y | Y | Y | N |
| 14 Conyers | N | N | Y | Y | Y | N |
| 15 Dingell | N | Y | Y | Y | Y | N |

| | 139 | 140 | 141 | 142 | 143 | 144 |
|---|---|---|---|---|---|---|
| **MINNESOTA** | | | | | | |
| 1 **Gutknecht** | Y | N | N | N | N | Y |
| 2 **Kline** | Y | N | N | N | N | Y |
| 3 **Ramstad** | Y | N | N | N | N | Y |
| 4 McCollum | N | Y | Y | Y | Y | N |
| 5 Sabo | N | Y | Y | Y | Y | N |
| 6 **Kennedy** | Y | N | N | N | N | Y |
| 7 Peterson | N | Y | N | N | N | Y |
| 8 Oberstar | N | Y | N | N | N | Y |
| **MISSISSIPPI** | | | | | | |
| 1 **Wicker** | ? | ? | ? | ? | ? | ? |
| 2 Thompson | N | Y | Y | Y | Y | N |
| 3 **Pickering** | Y | N | N | N | N | Y |
| 4 Taylor | Y | N | N | N | N | Y |
| **MISSOURI** | | | | | | |
| 1 Clay | N | Y | Y | Y | Y | Y |
| 2 **Akin** | Y | N | N | N | N | Y |
| 3 Carnahan | N | Y | Y | Y | Y | N |
| 4 Skelton | N | Y | N | N | N | Y |
| 5 Cleaver | N | Y | Y | Y | Y | N |
| 6 **Graves** | Y | N | N | N | N | Y |
| 7 **Blunt** | Y | N | N | N | N | Y |
| 8 **Emerson** | Y | N | N | N | N | Y |
| 9 **Hulshof** | Y | N | N | N | N | Y |
| **MONTANA** | | | | | | |
| AL **Rehberg** | Y | N | N | N | N | Y |
| **NEBRASKA** | | | | | | |
| 1 **Fortenberry** | Y | N | N | N | N | Y |
| 2 **Terry** | Y | N | N | N | N | Y |
| 3 **Osborne** | Y | N | N | N | N | Y |
| **NEVADA** | | | | | | |
| 1 Berkley | N | Y | Y | Y | Y | N |
| 2 **Gibbons** | Y | N | N | N | N | Y |
| 3 **Porter** | Y | N | N | N | N | Y |
| **NEW HAMPSHIRE** | | | | | | |
| 1 **Bradley** | Y | N | N | N | N | Y |
| 2 **Bass** | Y | N | Y | Y | Y | N |
| **NEW JERSEY** | | | | | | |
| 1 Andrews | N | Y | Y | Y | Y | N |
| 2 **LoBiondo** | Y | N | N | N | N | Y |
| 3 **Saxton** | Y | N | N | N | N | Y |
| 4 **Smith** | Y | N | N | N | N | Y |
| 5 **Garrett** | Y | N | N | N | N | Y |
| 6 Pallone | N | Y | Y | Y | Y | N |
| 7 **Ferguson** | Y | N | N | N | N | Y |
| 8 Pascrell | N | Y | N | N | Y | N |
| 9 Rothman | ? | ? | ? | ? | ? | ? |
| 10 Payne | N | Y | Y | Y | Y | N |
| 11 **Frelinghuysen** | Y | N | N | N | N | Y |
| 12 Holt | N | Y | Y | Y | Y | N |
| 13 Menendez | N | Y | Y | Y | Y | N |
| **NEW MEXICO** | | | | | | |
| 1 **Wilson** | ? | N | N | N | N | ? |
| 2 **Pearce** | Y | N | ? | N | N | Y |
| 3 Udall | N | Y | Y | Y | Y | N |
| **NEW YORK** | | | | | | |
| 1 Bishop | N | Y | Y | Y | Y | N |
| 2 Israel | N | Y | Y | Y | Y | N |
| 3 **King** | Y | N | N | N | N | Y |
| 4 McCarthy | N | Y | Y | Y | Y | N |
| 5 Ackerman | N | Y | Y | Y | Y | N |
| 6 Meeks | N | Y | Y | Y | Y | N |
| 7 Crowley | N | Y | Y | Y | Y | N |
| 8 Nadler | N | Y | Y | Y | Y | N |
| 9 Weiner | N | Y | Y | Y | Y | N |
| 10 Towns | N | Y | Y | Y | Y | N |
| 11 Owens | N | Y | Y | Y | Y | N |
| 12 Velázquez | N | Y | Y | Y | Y | N |
| 13 **Fossella** | Y | N | N | N | N | Y |
| 14 Maloney | N | Y | Y | Y | Y | N |
| 15 Rangel | N | Y | Y | Y | Y | N |
| 16 Serrano | N | Y | Y | Y | Y | N |
| 17 Engel | N | Y | Y | Y | Y | N |
| 18 Lowey | N | Y | Y | Y | Y | N |
| 19 **Kelly** | Y | N | Y | N | N | Y |
| 20 **Sweeney** | Y | N | Y | N | N | Y |
| 21 McNulty | N | Y | N | N | Y | Y |
| 22 Hinchey | N | Y | Y | Y | Y | N |
| 23 **McHugh** | Y | N | N | N | N | Y |
| 24 **Boehlert** | Y | N | Y | Y | Y | N |
| 25 **Walsh** | Y | N | N | N | N | Y |
| 26 **Reynolds** | Y | N | N | N | N | Y |
| 27 Higgins | N | Y | Y | Y | Y | N |
| 28 Slaughter | N | Y | Y | Y | Y | N |
| 29 **Kuhl** | Y | N | N | N | N | Y |

| | 139 | 140 | 141 | 142 | 143 | 144 |
|---|---|---|---|---|---|---|
| **NORTH CAROLINA** | | | | | | |
| 1 Butterfield | N | Y | Y | Y | Y | N |
| 2 Etheridge | N | Y | Y | Y | Y | Y |
| 3 **Jones** | Y | N | N | N | N | Y |
| 4 Price | N | Y | Y | Y | Y | N |
| 5 **Foxx** | Y | N | N | N | N | Y |
| 6 **Coble** | Y | N | N | N | N | Y |
| 7 McIntyre | N | Y | N | N | N | Y |
| 8 **Hayes** | Y | N | N | N | N | Y |
| 9 **Myrick** | Y | ? | N | N | N | Y |
| 10 **McHenry** | Y | N | N | N | N | Y |
| 11 **Taylor** | Y | N | N | N | N | Y |
| 12 Watt | N | Y | Y | Y | Y | N |
| 13 Miller | N | Y | Y | Y | Y | N |
| **NORTH DAKOTA** | | | | | | |
| AL Pomeroy | N | Y | N | N | N | Y |
| **OHIO** | | | | | | |
| 1 **Chabot** | Y | N | N | N | N | Y |
| 2 **Portman** | + | N | N | N | N | Y |
| 3 **Turner** | Y | N | N | N | N | Y |
| 4 **Oxley** | Y | N | N | N | N | Y |
| 5 **Gillmor** | Y | N | N | N | N | Y |
| 6 Strickland | N | Y | Y | N | Y | Y |
| 7 **Hobson** | Y | N | N | N | N | Y |
| 8 **Boehner** | Y | N | N | N | N | Y |
| 9 Kaptur | N | Y | Y | Y | Y | N |
| 10 Kucinich | N | Y | Y | Y | Y | N |
| 11 Jones | N | Y | Y | Y | Y | N |
| 12 **Tiberi** | Y | N | N | N | N | Y |
| 13 Brown | N | Y | Y | Y | Y | N |
| 14 **LaTourette** | Y | N | N | N | N | Y |
| 15 **Pryce** | Y | N | N | N | N | Y |
| 16 **Regula** | Y | N | N | N | N | Y |
| 17 Ryan | N | Y | N | N | N | Y |
| 18 **Ney** | Y | N | N | N | N | Y |
| **OKLAHOMA** | | | | | | |
| 1 **Sullivan** | Y | N | N | N | N | Y |
| 2 Boren | Y | N | N | N | N | Y |
| 3 **Lucas** | Y | N | N | N | N | Y |
| 4 **Cole** | Y | N | N | N | N | Y |
| 5 **Istook** | Y | ? | N | ? | N | Y |
| **OREGON** | | | | | | |
| 1 Wu | N | Y | Y | Y | Y | N |
| 2 **Walden** | Y | N | N | N | N | Y |
| 3 Blumenauer | N | Y | Y | Y | Y | ? |
| 4 DeFazio | N | Y | Y | Y | Y | N |
| 5 Hooley | N | Y | Y | Y | Y | N |
| **PENNSYLVANIA** | | | | | | |
| 1 Brady | N | Y | Y | Y | Y | N |
| 2 Fattah | N | Y | Y | Y | Y | N |
| 3 **English** | Y | N | ? | N | N | Y |
| 4 **Hart** | Y | N | N | N | N | Y |
| 5 **Peterson** | Y | N | N | N | N | Y |
| 6 **Gerlach** | Y | N | N | N | N | Y |
| 7 **Weldon** | Y | N | N | N | N | Y |
| 8 **Fitzpatrick** | Y | N | N | N | N | Y |
| 9 **Shuster** | Y | N | N | N | N | Y |
| 10 **Sherwood** | Y | N | N | N | N | Y |
| 11 Kanjorski | N | Y | N | Y | N | Y |
| 12 Murtha | N | Y | N | N | N | Y |
| 13 Schwartz | N | Y | Y | Y | Y | N |
| 14 Doyle | N | Y | N | Y | Y | Y |
| 15 **Dent** | Y | N | Y | Y | N | Y |
| 16 **Pitts** | Y | ? | N | N | N | Y |
| 17 Holden | Y | Y | N | N | N | Y |
| 18 **Murphy** | Y | N | N | N | N | N |
| 19 **Platts** | Y | N | N | N | N | Y |
| **RHODE ISLAND** | | | | | | |
| 1 Kennedy | N | Y | Y | Y | Y | N |
| 2 Langevin | Y | Y | N | N | Y | Y |
| **SOUTH CAROLINA** | | | | | | |
| 1 **Brown** | Y | N | N | N | N | Y |
| 2 **Wilson** | Y | N | N | N | N | Y |
| 3 **Barrett** | Y | N | N | N | N | Y |
| 4 **Inglis** | Y | N | N | N | N | Y |
| 5 Spratt | N | Y | Y | Y | Y | Y |
| 6 Clyburn | N | Y | Y | Y | Y | N |
| **SOUTH DAKOTA** | | | | | | |
| AL Herseth | N | Y | Y | Y | Y | N |
| **TENNESSEE** | | | | | | |
| 1 **Jenkins** | Y | N | N | N | N | Y |
| 2 **Duncan** | Y | N | N | N | N | Y |

| | 139 | 140 | 141 | 142 | 143 | 144 |
|---|---|---|---|---|---|---|
| 3 **Wamp** | Y | N | N | N | N | Y |
| 4 Davis | Y | Y | N | N | N | Y |
| 5 Cooper | N | Y | Y | Y | Y | Y |
| 6 Gordon | N | Y | N | N | N | Y |
| 7 **Blackburn** | Y | N | N | N | N | Y |
| 8 Tanner | N | Y | N | Y | N | Y |
| 9 Ford | N | Y | Y | Y | N | Y |
| **TEXAS** | | | | | | |
| 1 **Gohmert** | Y | N | N | N | N | Y |
| 2 **Poe** | Y | N | N | N | N | Y |
| 3 **Johnson, S.** | Y | ? | N | N | N | Y |
| 4 **Hall** | Y | N | N | N | N | Y |
| 5 **Hensarling** | Y | ? | N | N | N | Y |
| 6 **Barton** | Y | N | N | Y | N | Y |
| 7 **Culberson** | Y | N | N | N | N | Y |
| 8 **Brady** | Y | – | N | N | ? | Y |
| 9 Green | N | Y | Y | Y | Y | N |
| 10 **McCaul** | Y | N | N | N | N | Y |
| 11 **Conaway** | Y | N | N | N | N | Y |
| 12 **Granger** | Y | N | N | N | N | Y |
| 13 **Thornberry** | Y | N | N | N | N | Y |
| 14 **Paul** | Y | N | Y | Y | N | N |
| 15 Hinojosa | N | + | Y | Y | Y | Y |
| 16 Reyes | N | Y | Y | N | Y | Y |
| 17 Edwards | N | Y | N | N | Y | Y |
| 18 Jackson-Lee | N | Y | Y | Y | Y | N |
| 19 **Neugebauer** | Y | N | N | N | N | Y |
| 20 Gonzalez | N | Y | Y | Y | Y | N |
| 21 **Smith** | ? | N | N | N | N | Y |
| 22 **DeLay** | Y | N | N | N | N | Y |
| 23 **Bonilla** | Y | N | N | N | N | Y |
| 24 **Marchant** | Y | N | N | N | N | Y |
| 25 Doggett | N | Y | Y | Y | Y | N |
| 26 **Burgess** | Y | N | N | N | N | Y |
| 27 Ortiz | N | Y | N | N | N | Y |
| 28 Cuellar | N | Y | N | N | N | Y |
| 29 Green | N | Y | ? | Y | Y | N |
| 30 Johnson, E. | N | Y | Y | Y | Y | N |
| 31 **Carter** | Y | N | N | N | N | Y |
| 32 **Sessions** | Y | N | N | N | N | Y |
| **UTAH** | | | | | | |
| 1 **Bishop** | Y | N | N | N | N | Y |
| 2 Matheson | N | Y | N | N | Y | Y |
| 3 **Cannon** | Y | N | N | N | N | Y |
| **VERMONT** | | | | | | |
| AL *Sanders* | N | Y | Y | Y | Y | N |
| **VIRGINIA** | | | | | | |
| 1 **Davis, J.** | Y | N | N | N | N | Y |
| 2 **Drake** | Y | N | N | N | N | Y |
| 3 Scott | N | Y | Y | Y | Y | N |
| 4 **Forbes** | Y | N | N | N | N | Y |
| 5 **Goode** | Y | N | N | N | N | Y |
| 6 **Goodlatte** | Y | N | N | N | N | Y |
| 7 **Cantor** | Y | N | N | N | N | Y |
| 8 Moran | N | Y | Y | Y | Y | N |
| 9 Boucher | N | Y | Y | Y | Y | N |
| 10 **Wolf** | Y | N | N | N | N | Y |
| 11 **Davis, T.** | Y | N | N | N | N | Y |
| **WASHINGTON** | | | | | | |
| 1 Inslee | N | Y | Y | Y | Y | N |
| 2 Larsen | N | Y | Y | Y | Y | N |
| 3 Baird | N | Y | Y | Y | Y | N |
| 4 **Hastings** | Y | N | N | N | N | Y |
| 5 **McMorris** | Y | N | N | N | N | Y |
| 6 Dicks | N | Y | Y | Y | Y | N |
| 7 McDermott | ? | Y | Y | Y | Y | N |
| 8 **Reichert** | Y | N | N | N | N | Y |
| 9 Smith | N | Y | Y | Y | Y | N |
| **WEST VIRGINIA** | | | | | | |
| 1 Mollohan | N | Y | N | N | N | Y |
| 2 **Capito** | Y | N | N | N | N | Y |
| 3 Rahall | N | N | N | N | N | Y |
| **WISCONSIN** | | | | | | |
| 1 **Ryan** | Y | – | N | N | N | Y |
| 2 Baldwin | N | Y | Y | Y | Y | N |
| 3 Kind | N | N | Y | Y | Y | N |
| 4 Moore | N | Y | Y | Y | Y | N |
| 5 **Sensenbrenner** | Y | N | N | N | N | Y |
| 6 **Petri** | Y | N | N | N | N | Y |
| 7 Obey | N | N | Y | Y | Y | Y |
| 8 **Green** | Y | N | N | N | N | Y |
| **WYOMING** | | | | | | |
| AL **Cubin** | Y | ? | N | N | N | Y |

# IN THE HOUSE | By Vote Number

**145.** **H Res 240. House Rules/Adoption.** Adoption of the self-executing rule (H Res 241) under which the House would automatically adopt a resolution repealing three changes to the Rules of the House dealing with ethics committee procedures that were made at the start of the 109th Congress, including a rule that allowed the automatic dismissal of an ethics complaint that is not disposed of by the committee within 45 days. Adopted 406-20: R 208-20; D 197-0 (ND 148-0, SD 49-0); I 1-0. April 27, 2005.

**146.** **H Con Res 95. Fiscal 2006 Budget Resolution/Same-Day Consideration.** Adoption of the resolution (H Res 242) that would waive the two-thirds majority vote requirement for same-day consideration of the rule to provide for House floor consideration of the conference report on the fiscal 2006 budget resolution (H Con Res 95). Adopted 230-199: R 230-0; D 0-198 (ND 0-149, SD 0-49); I 0-1. April 28, 2005.

**147.** **H Con Res 95 . Fiscal 2006 Budget Resolution/Previous Question.** Putnam, R-Fla., motion to order the previous question (thus ending debate and possibility of amendment) on adoption of the rule (H Res 248) to provide for House floor consideration of the conference report on the concurrent resolution that would set broad spending and revenue targets over the next five years. Motion agreed to 228-196: R 228-0; D 0-195 (ND 0-148, SD 0-47); I 0-1. (Subsequently, the rule was adopted by voice vote.) April 28, 2005.

**148.** **Procedural Motion/Journal.** Approval of the House Journal of Wednesday April 27, 2005. Approved 345-75: R 201-23; D 143-52 (ND 105-43, SD 38-9); I 1-0. April 28, 2005.

**149.** **H Con Res 95. Fiscal 2006 Budget Resolution/Conference Report.** Adoption of the conference report on the concurrent resolution that would set broad spending and revenue targets for five years, limit discretionary spending to $843 billion in fiscal 2006, and provide instructions for reconciliation bills that would achieve $70 billion in tax cuts and $34.7 billion in savings to mandatory programs, including $10 billion in Medicaid savings. Adopted (thus sent to the Senate) 214-211: R 214-15; D 0-195 (ND 0-148, SD 0-47); I 0-1. April 28, 2005.

**150.** **H Res 210. Intellectual Property Day/Adoption.** Sensenbrenner, R-Wis., motion to suspend the rules and adopt the resolution that would support the goals of World Intellectual Property Day, to promote, inform and teach the importance of intellectual property. Motion agreed to 315-0: R 176-0; D 139-0 (ND 107-0, SD 32-0); I 0-0. A two-thirds majority of those present and voting (210 in this case) is required for adoption under suspension of the rules. April 28, 2005.

| | 145 | 146 | 147 | 148 | 149 | 150 |
|---|---|---|---|---|---|---|
| **ALABAMA** | | | | | | |
| 1 Bonner | Y | Y | Y | Y | Y | ? |
| 2 Everett | Y | Y | Y | Y | Y | ? |
| 3 Rogers | Y | Y | Y | Y | Y | ? |
| 4 Aderholt | Y | Y | Y | Y | Y | Y |
| 5 Cramer | Y | N | N | Y | N | Y |
| 6 Bachus | Y | Y | Y | Y | Y | Y |
| 7 Davis | Y | N | N | Y | N | Y |
| **ALASKA** | | | | | | |
| AL Young | Y | Y | Y | Y | Y | Y |
| **ARIZONA** | | | | | | |
| 1 Renzi | Y | Y | Y | Y | Y | Y |
| 2 Franks | Y | Y | Y | Y | Y | Y |
| 3 Shadegg | Y | Y | Y | Y | Y | ? |
| 4 Pastor | Y | N | N | Y | N | Y |
| 5 Hayworth | Y | Y | Y | Y | Y | Y |
| 6 Flake | Y | Y | ? | ? | ? | ? |
| 7 Grijalva | Y | N | N | N | N | Y |
| 8 Kolbe | Y | Y | Y | Y | Y | Y |
| **ARKANSAS** | | | | | | |
| 1 Berry | Y | N | N | N | N | Y |
| 2 Snyder | Y | N | N | Y | N | Y |
| 3 Boozman | Y | Y | Y | Y | Y | Y |
| 4 Ross | Y | N | N | Y | N | Y |
| **CALIFORNIA** | | | | | | |
| 1 Thompson | Y | N | N | N | N | Y |
| 2 Herger | Y | Y | Y | Y | Y | Y |
| 3 Lungren | Y | Y | Y | Y | Y | Y |
| 4 Doolittle | Y | Y | Y | Y | Y | Y |
| 5 Matsui, D. | Y | N | N | Y | N | Y |
| 6 Woolsey | Y | N | N | Y | N | Y |
| 7 Miller, George | Y | N | N | Y | N | Y |
| 8 Pelosi | Y | N | N | Y | N | ? |
| 9 Lee | ? | N | N | Y | N | Y |
| 10 Tauscher | Y | N | N | N | N | Y |
| 11 Pombo | Y | Y | Y | Y | Y | Y |
| 12 Lantos | Y | N | N | N | N | Y |
| 13 Stark | Y | ? | N | N | N | ? |
| 14 Eshoo | Y | N | N | Y | N | Y |
| 15 Honda | Y | N | N | Y | N | ? |
| 16 Lofgren | Y | N | N | Y | N | Y |
| 17 Farr | Y | N | N | Y | N | Y |
| 18 Cardoza | Y | N | N | Y | N | Y |
| 19 Radanovich | Y | Y | Y | Y | Y | ? |
| 20 Costa | Y | N | N | Y | N | Y |
| 21 Nunes | Y | Y | Y | Y | Y | Y |
| 22 Thomas | Y | Y | Y | Y | Y | Y |
| 23 Capps | Y | N | N | Y | N | ? |
| 24 Gallegly | Y | Y | Y | Y | Y | ? |
| 25 McKeon | Y | Y | Y | Y | Y | ? |
| 26 Dreier | Y | Y | Y | Y | Y | Y |
| 27 Sherman | Y | N | N | Y | N | Y |
| 28 Berman | Y | N | N | Y | N | ? |
| 29 Schiff | Y | N | N | Y | N | Y |
| 30 Waxman | ? | N | N | Y | N | Y |
| 31 Becerra | Y | N | N | N | N | ? |
| 32 Solis | Y | N | N | Y | N | Y |
| 33 Watson | Y | N | N | Y | N | Y |
| 34 Roybal-Allard | Y | N | N | Y | N | Y |
| 35 Waters | Y | N | N | N | N | Y |
| 36 Harman | Y | N | N | Y | N | Y |
| 37 Millender-McD. | Y | N | N | Y | N | ? |
| 38 Napolitano | Y | N | N | Y | N | Y |
| 39 Sánchez, Linda | Y | N | N | Y | N | Y |
| 40 Royce | Y | Y | Y | Y | Y | Y |
| 41 Lewis | Y | Y | Y | Y | Y | Y |
| 42 Miller, Gary | Y | Y | Y | Y | Y | ? |
| 43 Baca | Y | N | N | Y | N | ? |
| 44 Calvert | Y | Y | Y | Y | Y | Y |
| 45 Bono | Y | Y | Y | Y | Y | Y |
| 46 Rohrabacher | Y | Y | Y | Y | Y | Y |
| 47 Sanchez, Loretta | Y | N | N | N | N | ? |
| 48 Cox | Y | Y | Y | Y | Y | ? |
| 49 Issa | Y | Y | Y | N | Y | Y |

| | 145 | 146 | 147 | 148 | 149 | 150 |
|---|---|---|---|---|---|---|
| 50 Cunningham | Y | Y | ? | ? | ? | ? |
| 51 Filner | Y | N | – | – | – | + |
| 52 Hunter | Y | Y | Y | Y | Y | Y |
| 53 Davis | Y | N | N | Y | N | Y |
| **COLORADO** | | | | | | |
| 1 DeGette | Y | N | N | Y | N | Y |
| 2 Udall | Y | N | N | N | N | Y |
| 3 Salazar | Y | N | N | Y | N | Y |
| 4 Musgrave | Y | Y | Y | Y | Y | Y |
| 5 Hefley | Y | Y | Y | N | Y | Y |
| 6 Tancredo | Y | Y | Y | P | Y | Y |
| 7 Beauprez | Y | Y | Y | Y | Y | Y |
| **CONNECTICUT** | | | | | | |
| 1 Larson | Y | N | N | N | N | ? |
| 2 Simmons | Y | Y | Y | Y | N | ? |
| 3 DeLauro | Y | N | N | Y | N | ? |
| 4 Shays | Y | Y | Y | Y | N | ? |
| 5 Johnson | Y | Y | Y | Y | N | ? |
| **DELAWARE** | | | | | | |
| AL Castle | Y | Y | Y | Y | N | Y |
| **FLORIDA** | | | | | | |
| 1 Miller | Y | Y | Y | Y | Y | Y |
| 2 Boyd | Y | N | N | Y | N | ? |
| 3 Brown | ? | ? | N | Y | N | Y |
| 4 Crenshaw | Y | Y | Y | Y | Y | Y |
| 5 Brown-Waite | Y | Y | Y | Y | Y | Y |
| 6 Stearns | Y | Y | Y | Y | Y | Y |
| 7 Mica | Y | Y | Y | Y | Y | Y |
| 8 Keller | Y | Y | Y | Y | Y | Y |
| 9 Bilirakis | Y | Y | Y | Y | Y | Y |
| 10 Young | Y | Y | Y | Y | Y | Y |
| 11 Davis | Y | N | N | Y | N | ? |
| 12 Putnam | Y | Y | Y | Y | Y | Y |
| 13 Harris | Y | Y | Y | Y | Y | ? |
| 14 Mack | Y | Y | Y | Y | Y | Y |
| 15 Weldon | N | Y | Y | Y | Y | Y |
| 16 Foley | Y | Y | Y | Y | Y | Y |
| 17 Meek | Y | N | N | Y | N | Y |
| 18 Ros-Lehtinen | Y | Y | Y | Y | Y | Y |
| 19 Wexler | Y | N | N | N | N | Y |
| 20 Wasserman-Schultz | Y | N | N | Y | N | Y |
| 21 Diaz-Balart, L. | Y | Y | Y | Y | Y | Y |
| 22 Shaw | Y | Y | Y | Y | Y | ? |
| 23 Hastings | Y | N | N | N | N | Y |
| 24 Feeney | Y | Y | Y | Y | Y | Y |
| 25 Diaz-Balart, M. | Y | Y | Y | Y | Y | Y |
| **GEORGIA** | | | | | | |
| 1 Kingston | Y | Y | Y | Y | | Y |
| 2 Bishop | Y | N | N | Y | N | ? |
| 3 Marshall | Y | N | N | N | N | ? |
| 4 McKinney | Y | N | N | Y | N | ? |
| 5 Lewis | Y | N | N | Y | N | ? |
| 6 Price | N | Y | Y | Y | Y | Y |
| 7 Linder | Y | Y | Y | Y | Y | ? |
| 8 Westmoreland | ? | Y | Y | N | Y | Y |
| 9 Norwood | Y | Y | Y | N | Y | Y |
| 10 Deal | Y | Y | Y | Y | Y | ? |
| 11 Gingrey | Y | Y | Y | Y | Y | ? |
| 12 Barrow | Y | N | N | Y | N | Y |
| 13 Scott | Y | N | N | Y | N | Y |
| **HAWAII** | | | | | | |
| 1 Abercrombie | Y | N | N | Y | N | Y |
| 2 Case | Y | N | N | Y | N | Y |
| **IDAHO** | | | | | | |
| 1 Otter | N | Y | Y | N | Y | Y |
| 2 Simpson | N | Y | Y | Y | Y | Y |
| **ILLINOIS** | | | | | | |
| 1 Rush | Y | N | N | Y | N | Y |
| 2 Jackson | Y | N | N | Y | N | Y |
| 3 Lipinski | Y | N | N | Y | N | Y |
| 4 Gutierrez | Y | N | N | Y | N | Y |
| 5 Emanuel | Y | N | N | Y | N | ? |
| 6 Hyde | Y | ? | Y | Y | Y | Y |
| 7 Davis | Y | N | N | Y | N | Y |
| 8 Bean | Y | N | N | Y | N | Y |
| 9 Schakowsky | Y | N | N | N | N | ? |
| 10 Kirk | Y | Y | Y | Y | Y | Y |
| 11 Weller | Y | Y | Y | Y | Y | Y |
| 12 Costello | Y | N | N | N | N | Y |

**KEY**  **Republicans**  Democrats  *Independents*

| | | | |
|---|---|---|---|
| Y | Voted for (yea) | X | Paired against |
| # | Paired for | – | Announced against |
| + | Announced for | P | Voted "present" |
| N | Voted against (nay) | | |

| | |
|---|---|
| C | Voted "present" to avoid possible conflict of interest |
| ? | Did not vote or otherwise make a position known |

| | 145 | 146 | 147 | 148 | 149 | 150 |
|---|---|---|---|---|---|---|
| 13 **Biggert** | Y | Y | Y | Y | Y | Y |
| 14 **Hastert** | | | | Y | Y | |
| 15 **Johnson** | Y | Y | Y | Y | N | ? |
| 16 **Manzullo** | Y | Y | Y | Y | Y | Y |
| 17 Evans | Y | N | N | Y | N | Y |
| 18 **LaHood** | Y | Y | Y | Y | Y | ? |
| 19 **Shimkus** | Y | Y | Y | Y | Y | Y |
| **INDIANA** | | | | | | |
| 1 Visclosky | Y | N | N | N | N | Y |
| 2 **Chocola** | Y | Y | Y | Y | Y | Y |
| 3 **Souder** | P | Y | Y | Y | Y | Y |
| 4 **Buyer** | N | Y | Y | Y | Y | ? |
| 5 **Burton** | N | Y | Y | Y | Y | ? |
| 6 **Pence** | N | Y | Y | Y | Y | Y |
| 7 Carson | Y | N | N | Y | N | Y |
| 8 **Hostettler** | Y | Y | Y | Y | Y | Y |
| 9 **Sodrel** | Y | Y | Y | Y | Y | Y |
| **IOWA** | | | | | | |
| 1 **Nussle** | Y | Y | Y | Y | Y | Y |
| 2 **Leach** | Y | Y | Y | Y | N | Y |
| 3 Boswell | Y | N | N | Y | N | Y |
| 4 **Latham** | Y | Y | Y | N | Y | Y |
| 5 **King** | N | Y | Y | Y | Y | Y |
| **KANSAS** | | | | | | |
| 1 **Moran** | Y | Y | Y | Y | Y | Y |
| 2 **Ryun** | Y | Y | Y | Y | Y | Y |
| 3 Moore | Y | N | N | N | N | Y |
| 4 **Tiahrt** | N | Y | Y | Y | Y | Y |
| **KENTUCKY** | | | | | | |
| 1 **Whitfield** | Y | Y | Y | Y | Y | Y |
| 2 **Lewis** | Y | Y | Y | Y | Y | Y |
| 3 **Northup** | Y | Y | Y | Y | Y | ? |
| 4 **Davis** | Y | Y | Y | Y | Y | Y |
| 5 **Rogers** | Y | Y | Y | Y | Y | ? |
| 6 Chandler | Y | N | N | Y | N | ? |
| **LOUISIANA** | | | | | | |
| 1 **Jindal** | Y | Y | Y | Y | Y | Y |
| 2 Jefferson | Y | N | N | ? | ? | ? |
| 3 Melancon | Y | N | N | Y | N | Y |
| 4 **McCrery** | Y | Y | Y | Y | Y | Y |
| 5 **Alexander** | Y | Y | Y | Y | Y | Y |
| 6 **Baker** | Y | Y | Y | Y | Y | ? |
| 7 **Boustany** | Y | Y | Y | Y | Y | Y |
| **MAINE** | | | | | | |
| 1 Allen | Y | N | N | Y | N | ? |
| 2 Michaud | Y | N | N | Y | N | Y |
| **MARYLAND** | | | | | | |
| 1 **Gilchrest** | Y | Y | Y | Y | Y | Y |
| 2 Ruppersberger | Y | N | N | Y | N | Y |
| 3 Cardin | Y | N | N | Y | N | Y |
| 4 Wynn | Y | N | N | Y | N | Y |
| 5 Hoyer | Y | N | N | Y | N | Y |
| 6 **Bartlett** | Y | Y | Y | Y | Y | Y |
| 7 Cummings | Y | N | N | Y | N | Y |
| 8 Van Hollen | Y | N | N | Y | N | Y |
| **MASSACHUSETTS** | | | | | | |
| 1 Olver | Y | N | N | N | N | ? |
| 2 Neal | Y | N | N | N | N | ? |
| 3 McGovern | Y | N | N | N | N | Y |
| 4 Frank | Y | N | N | Y | N | Y |
| 5 Meehan | Y | N | N | Y | N | ? |
| 6 Tierney | Y | N | N | Y | N | ? |
| 7 Markey | Y | N | N | N | N | Y |
| 8 Capuano | Y | N | N | N | N | ? |
| 9 Lynch | Y | N | N | Y | N | ? |
| 10 Delahunt | Y | N | N | Y | N | ? |
| **MICHIGAN** | | | | | | |
| 1 Stupak | Y | N | N | N | N | Y |
| 2 **Hoekstra** | Y | Y | Y | Y | Y | Y |
| 3 **Ehlers** | Y | Y | Y | Y | Y | Y |
| 4 **Camp** | Y | Y | Y | Y | Y | Y |
| 5 Kildee | Y | N | N | Y | N | Y |
| 6 **Upton** | Y | Y | Y | Y | Y | Y |
| 7 **Schwarz** | Y | Y | Y | Y | Y | Y |
| 8 **Rogers** | Y | Y | Y | Y | Y | Y |
| 9 **Knollenberg** | Y | Y | Y | Y | Y | Y |
| 10 **Miller** | Y | Y | Y | Y | Y | Y |
| 11 **McCotter** | Y | Y | Y | N | Y | Y |
| 12 Levin | Y | N | N | N | N | Y |
| 13 Kilpatrick | Y | N | N | Y | N | Y |
| 14 Conyers | Y | N | N | Y | N | Y |
| 15 Dingell | Y | N | N | Y | N | Y |

| | 145 | 146 | 147 | 148 | 149 | 150 |
|---|---|---|---|---|---|---|
| **MINNESOTA** | | | | | | |
| 1 **Gutknecht** | Y | Y | Y | N | N | Y |
| 2 **Kline** | Y | Y | Y | Y | Y | Y |
| 3 **Ramstad** | Y | Y | Y | N | N | Y |
| 4 McCollum | Y | N | N | Y | N | Y |
| 5 Sabo | Y | N | N | N | N | Y |
| 6 **Kennedy** | Y | Y | Y | N | Y | Y |
| 7 Peterson | Y | N | N | N | N | Y |
| 8 Oberstar | Y | N | N | N | N | Y |
| **MISSISSIPPI** | | | | | | |
| 1 **Wicker** | ? | Y | Y | Y | Y | Y |
| 2 Thompson | Y | N | N | N | N | Y |
| 3 **Pickering** | Y | Y | Y | Y | Y | Y |
| 4 Taylor | Y | N | N | N | N | Y |
| **MISSOURI** | | | | | | |
| 1 Clay | Y | N | N | Y | N | ? |
| 2 **Akin** | Y | Y | Y | Y | Y | Y |
| 3 Carnahan | Y | N | N | Y | N | Y |
| 4 Skelton | Y | N | N | Y | N | Y |
| 5 Cleaver | Y | N | N | Y | N | Y |
| 6 **Graves** | Y | Y | Y | N | Y | ? |
| 7 **Blunt** | Y | Y | Y | Y | Y | Y |
| 8 **Emerson** | Y | Y | Y | Y | Y | Y |
| 9 **Hulshof** | Y | Y | Y | N | Y | Y |
| **MONTANA** | | | | | | |
| AL **Rehberg** | Y | Y | Y | Y | Y | Y |
| **NEBRASKA** | | | | | | |
| 1 **Fortenberry** | Y | Y | Y | Y | Y | Y |
| 2 **Terry** | Y | Y | Y | Y | Y | Y |
| 3 **Osborne** | Y | Y | Y | Y | Y | Y |
| **NEVADA** | | | | | | |
| 1 Berkley | Y | N | N | ? | N | ? |
| 2 **Gibbons** | Y | Y | Y | N | Y | Y |
| 3 **Porter** | Y | Y | Y | Y | Y | Y |
| **NEW HAMPSHIRE** | | | | | | |
| 1 **Bradley** | Y | Y | Y | Y | Y | Y |
| 2 **Bass** | Y | Y | Y | Y | N | ? |
| **NEW JERSEY** | | | | | | |
| 1 Andrews | Y | N | N | Y | N | Y |
| 2 **LoBiondo** | Y | Y | Y | N | N | Y |
| 3 **Saxton** | Y | Y | Y | Y | N | Y |
| 4 **Smith** | Y | Y | Y | Y | Y | Y |
| 5 **Garrett** | Y | Y | Y | Y | Y | Y |
| 6 Pallone | Y | N | N | Y | N | Y |
| 7 **Ferguson** | Y | Y | Y | Y | Y | Y |
| 8 Pascrell | Y | N | N | Y | N | Y |
| 9 Rothman | ? | ? | ? | ? | ? | ? |
| 10 Payne | Y | N | N | Y | N | Y |
| 11 **Frelinghuysen** | Y | Y | Y | Y | Y | Y |
| 12 Holt | Y | N | N | Y | N | Y |
| 13 Menendez | Y | N | N | Y | N | ? |
| **NEW MEXICO** | | | | | | |
| 1 **Wilson** | Y | Y | Y | Y | Y | Y |
| 2 **Pearce** | Y | Y | Y | Y | Y | ? |
| 3 Udall | Y | N | N | N | N | Y |
| **NEW YORK** | | | | | | |
| 1 Bishop | Y | N | N | Y | N | ? |
| 2 Israel | Y | N | N | Y | N | ? |
| 3 **King** | Y | Y | Y | ? | Y | ? |
| 4 McCarthy | Y | N | N | N | N | Y |
| 5 Ackerman | Y | N | N | Y | N | ? |
| 6 Meeks | Y | N | ? | Y | N | Y |
| 7 Crowley | Y | N | N | N | N | Y |
| 8 Nadler | Y | N | N | N | N | ? |
| 9 Weiner | Y | N | N | N | N | Y |
| 10 Towns | Y | N | N | Y | ? | ? |
| 11 Owens | Y | N | N | Y | N | Y |
| 12 Velázquez | Y | N | N | Y | N | ? |
| 13 **Fossella** | Y | Y | Y | N | Y | Y |
| 14 Maloney | Y | N | N | Y | N | ? |
| 15 Rangel | Y | N | N | Y | N | ? |
| 16 Serrano | Y | N | N | Y | N | Y |
| 17 Engel | Y | N | N | Y | N | Y |
| 18 Lowey | Y | N | N | Y | N | ? |
| 19 **Kelly** | Y | Y | Y | N | Y | Y |
| 20 **Sweeney** | Y | Y | Y | Y | Y | Y |
| 21 McNulty | Y | N | N | N | N | Y |
| 22 Hinchey | Y | N | N | N | N | ? |
| 23 **McHugh** | Y | Y | Y | Y | Y | ? |
| 24 **Boehlert** | Y | Y | Y | Y | N | ? |
| 25 **Walsh** | Y | Y | Y | Y | Y | ? |
| 26 **Reynolds** | Y | Y | Y | Y | Y | Y |
| 27 Higgins | Y | N | N | Y | N | Y |
| 28 Slaughter | Y | N | N | N | N | ? |
| 29 **Kuhl** | Y | Y | Y | Y | Y | Y |

| | 145 | 146 | 147 | 148 | 149 | 150 |
|---|---|---|---|---|---|---|
| **NORTH CAROLINA** | | | | | | |
| 1 Butterfield | Y | N | N | Y | N | ? |
| 2 Etheridge | Y | N | N | Y | N | ? |
| 3 **Jones** | Y | Y | Y | N | N | Y |
| 4 Price | Y | N | N | Y | N | ? |
| 5 **Foxx** | Y | Y | Y | Y | Y | Y |
| 6 **Coble** | Y | Y | Y | Y | Y | Y |
| 7 McIntyre | Y | N | N | Y | N | Y |
| 8 **Hayes** | Y | Y | Y | Y | Y | ? |
| 9 **Myrick** | Y | Y | Y | Y | Y | Y |
| 10 **McHenry** | N | Y | Y | Y | Y | Y |
| 11 **Taylor** | Y | Y | Y | Y | Y | ? |
| 12 Watt | Y | N | N | Y | N | ? |
| 13 Miller | Y | N | N | Y | N | Y |
| **NORTH DAKOTA** | | | | | | |
| AL Pomeroy | Y | N | N | Y | N | Y |
| **OHIO** | | | | | | |
| 1 **Chabot** | Y | Y | Y | Y | Y | Y |
| 2 **Portman** | Y | Y | Y | Y | Y | Y |
| 3 **Turner** | Y | Y | Y | Y | Y | ? |
| 4 **Oxley** | Y | Y | Y | Y | Y | ? |
| 5 **Gillmor** | N | Y | Y | Y | Y | Y |
| 6 Strickland | Y | N | N | N | N | ? |
| 7 **Hobson** | Y | Y | Y | Y | Y | Y |
| 8 **Boehner** | Y | Y | Y | ? | Y | Y |
| 9 Kaptur | Y | N | N | Y | N | Y |
| 10 Kucinich | Y | N | N | N | N | Y |
| 11 Jones | Y | N | N | Y | N | ? |
| 12 **Tiberi** | Y | Y | Y | N | Y | ? |
| 13 Brown | Y | N | N | Y | N | ? |
| 14 **LaTourette** | Y | Y | Y | Y | Y | Y |
| 15 **Pryce** | Y | Y | Y | N | Y | Y |
| 16 **Regula** | Y | Y | Y | Y | Y | Y |
| 17 Ryan | Y | N | N | Y | N | ? |
| 18 **Ney** | Y | Y | Y | Y | Y | Y |
| **OKLAHOMA** | | | | | | |
| 1 **Sullivan** | Y | Y | Y | ? | Y | Y |
| 2 Boren | Y | N | N | Y | N | Y |
| 3 **Lucas** | Y | Y | Y | Y | Y | Y |
| 4 **Cole** | Y | Y | Y | Y | Y | Y |
| 5 **Istook** | Y | Y | Y | Y | Y | Y |
| **OREGON** | | | | | | |
| 1 Wu | Y | N | N | N | N | Y |
| 2 **Walden** | Y | Y | Y | Y | Y | Y |
| 3 Blumenauer | Y | N | N | Y | N | Y |
| 4 DeFazio | Y | N | N | N | N | ? |
| 5 Hooley | Y | N | N | Y | N | Y |
| **PENNSYLVANIA** | | | | | | |
| 1 Brady | Y | N | N | N | N | Y |
| 2 Fattah | Y | N | N | Y | N | Y |
| 3 **English** | Y | Y | Y | N | Y | Y |
| 4 **Hart** | Y | Y | Y | N | Y | Y |
| 5 **Peterson** | Y | Y | Y | Y | Y | ? |
| 6 **Gerlach** | Y | Y | Y | Y | Y | Y |
| 7 **Weldon** | Y | Y | Y | Y | Y | Y |
| 8 **Fitzpatrick** | Y | Y | Y | N | Y | Y |
| 9 **Shuster** | Y | Y | Y | Y | Y | Y |
| 10 **Sherwood** | Y | Y | Y | Y | Y | Y |
| 11 Kanjorski | Y | N | N | Y | N | Y |
| 12 Murtha | Y | N | N | Y | N | Y |
| 13 Schwartz | Y | N | N | Y | N | Y |
| 14 Doyle | Y | N | N | Y | N | ? |
| 15 **Dent** | Y | Y | Y | Y | Y | Y |
| 16 **Pitts** | Y | Y | Y | Y | Y | Y |
| 17 Holden | Y | N | N | Y | N | Y |
| 18 **Murphy** | Y | Y | Y | Y | Y | ? |
| 19 **Platts** | Y | Y | Y | N | Y | Y |
| **RHODE ISLAND** | | | | | | |
| 1 Kennedy | Y | N | N | N | N | Y |
| 2 Langevin | Y | N | N | Y | N | Y |
| **SOUTH CAROLINA** | | | | | | |
| 1 **Brown** | Y | Y | Y | Y | Y | ? |
| 2 **Wilson** | Y | Y | Y | Y | Y | Y |
| 3 **Barrett** | Y | Y | Y | Y | Y | ? |
| 4 **Inglis** | Y | Y | Y | Y | Y | ? |
| 5 Spratt | Y | N | N | Y | N | Y |
| 6 Clyburn | Y | N | ? | ? | ? | ? |
| **SOUTH DAKOTA** | | | | | | |
| AL Herseth | Y | N | N | Y | N | Y |
| **TENNESSEE** | | | | | | |
| 1 **Jenkins** | Y | Y | Y | Y | Y | Y |
| 2 **Duncan** | Y | Y | Y | Y | Y | Y |

| | 145 | 146 | 147 | 148 | 149 | 150 |
|---|---|---|---|---|---|---|
| 3 **Wamp** | Y | Y | Y | Y | Y | ? |
| 4 Davis | Y | N | N | Y | N | ? |
| 5 Cooper | Y | N | N | Y | N | ? |
| 6 Gordon | Y | N | N | Y | N | ? |
| 7 **Blackburn** | N | Y | Y | Y | Y | Y |
| 8 Tanner | Y | N | N | N | N | Y |
| 9 Ford | Y | ? | ? | ? | ? | ? |
| **TEXAS** | | | | | | |
| 1 **Gohmert** | N | Y | Y | Y | Y | Y |
| 2 **Poe** | N | Y | Y | Y | Y | Y |
| 3 **Johnson, S.** | Y | Y | Y | Y | Y | Y |
| 4 **Hall** | Y | Y | Y | Y | Y | Y |
| 5 **Hensarling** | Y | Y | Y | Y | Y | Y |
| 6 **Barton** | N | Y | Y | Y | Y | Y |
| 7 **Culberson** | N | Y | Y | Y | Y | Y |
| 8 **Brady** | Y | Y | Y | Y | Y | Y |
| 9 Green | Y | N | N | Y | N | Y |
| 10 **McCaul** | Y | Y | Y | Y | Y | Y |
| 11 **Conaway** | Y | Y | Y | Y | Y | Y |
| 12 **Granger** | Y | Y | Y | Y | Y | Y |
| 13 **Thornberry** | N | Y | Y | Y | Y | Y |
| 14 **Paul** | Y | Y | ? | ? | ? | ? |
| 15 Hinojosa | Y | N | N | Y | N | Y |
| 16 Reyes | Y | N | N | Y | N | ? |
| 17 Edwards | Y | N | N | Y | N | Y |
| 18 Jackson-Lee | Y | N | N | N | N | Y |
| 19 **Neugebauer** | Y | Y | Y | Y | Y | ? |
| 20 Gonzalez | Y | N | N | Y | N | Y |
| 21 **Smith** | Y | Y | Y | Y | Y | Y |
| 22 **DeLay** | Y | Y | Y | Y | Y | Y |
| 23 **Bonilla** | Y | Y | Y | ? | Y | Y |
| 24 **Marchant** | Y | Y | Y | Y | Y | Y |
| 25 Doggett | Y | N | ? | ? | ? | ? |
| 26 **Burgess** | N | Y | Y | Y | Y | Y |
| 27 Ortiz | Y | N | N | Y | N | Y |
| 28 Cuellar | Y | N | N | Y | N | Y |
| 29 Green | Y | N | N | N | N | Y |
| 30 Johnson, E. | Y | N | N | Y | N | Y |
| 31 **Carter** | N | Y | Y | Y | Y | Y |
| 32 **Sessions** | Y | Y | Y | Y | Y | Y |
| **UTAH** | | | | | | |
| 1 **Bishop** | Y | Y | Y | Y | Y | Y |
| 2 Matheson | Y | N | N | Y | N | Y |
| 3 **Cannon** | Y | Y | Y | Y | Y | ? |
| **VERMONT** | | | | | | |
| AL *Sanders* | Y | N | N | Y | N | ? |
| **VIRGINIA** | | | | | | |
| 1 **Davis, J.** | Y | Y | Y | Y | Y | ? |
| 2 **Drake** | Y | Y | Y | Y | Y | Y |
| 3 Scott | Y | N | N | N | N | Y |
| 4 **Forbes** | Y | Y | Y | Y | Y | Y |
| 5 **Goode** | Y | Y | Y | Y | N | ? |
| 6 **Goodlatte** | Y | Y | Y | Y | Y | Y |
| 7 **Cantor** | Y | Y | Y | Y | Y | Y |
| 8 Moran | Y | N | – | Y | N | Y |
| 9 Boucher | ? | N | N | Y | N | Y |
| 10 **Wolf** | Y | Y | Y | Y | Y | Y |
| 11 **Davis, T.** | Y | Y | Y | Y | Y | ? |
| **WASHINGTON** | | | | | | |
| 1 Inslee | Y | N | N | Y | N | Y |
| 2 Larsen | Y | N | N | N | N | ? |
| 3 Baird | Y | N | N | N | N | Y |
| 4 **Hastings** | Y | Y | Y | Y | Y | Y |
| 5 **McMorris** | Y | Y | Y | Y | Y | Y |
| 6 Dicks | Y | N | N | Y | N | ? |
| 7 McDermott | Y | N | N | N | N | Y |
| 8 **Reichert** | Y | Y | Y | Y | Y | Y |
| 9 Smith | Y | N | N | Y | N | Y |
| **WEST VIRGINIA** | | | | | | |
| 1 Mollohan | Y | N | N | Y | N | Y |
| 2 **Capito** | Y | Y | Y | Y | Y | ? |
| 3 Rahall | Y | N | N | Y | N | Y |
| **WISCONSIN** | | | | | | |
| 1 **Ryan** | Y | Y | Y | Y | Y | ? |
| 2 Baldwin | Y | N | N | N | N | Y |
| 3 Kind | Y | N | N | N | N | Y |
| 4 Moore | Y | N | N | N | N | Y |
| 5 **Sensenbrenner** | Y | Y | Y | Y | Y | Y |
| 6 **Petri** | Y | Y | Y | Y | Y | Y |
| 7 Obey | Y | N | N | Y | N | Y |
| 8 **Green** | Y | Y | Y | Y | N | Y |
| **WYOMING** | | | | | | |
| AL **Cubin** | N | Y | Y | Y | Y | Y |

# IN THE HOUSE | By Vote Number

**151. HR 748. House Judiciary Committee Report/Motion to Table.**
Sensenbrenner, R-Wis., motion to table (kill) the Conyers, D-Mich., privileged resolution (H Res 253) that would direct the chairman of the Judiciary Committee to provide a supplement to the committee report that would describe Democratic committee amendments with objective language for the interstate abortion notification bill. Motion agreed to 220-196: R 220-0; D 0-195 (ND 0-146, SD 0-49); I 0-1. May 3, 2005.

**152. H Res 228. Vietnamese Americans Tribute/Adoption.** Fortenberry, R-Neb., motion to suspend the rules and adopt the resolution that would celebrate the contributions of Vietnamese Americans, honor all members of the U.S. and South Vietnamese armed forces who fought in the Vietnam conflict and observe the 30th anniversary of the fall of the Republic of Vietnam to the Communist forces of North Vietnam on April 30, 1975. Motion agreed to 416-0: R 222-0; D 193-0 (ND 145-0, SD 48-0); I 1-0. A two-thirds majority of those present and voting (278 in this case) is required for adoption under suspension of the rules. May 3, 2005.

**153. HR 366. Vocational and Technical Education/Recommit.** Miller, D-Calif., motion to recommit the bill to the House Education and the Workforce Committee with instructions to include language that would bar the use of Education Department funds to pay journalists or commentators to espouse points of view and would require on-air disclosure if prepackaged news segments were paid for with federal funds. Motion rejected 197-224: R 1-223; D 195-1 (ND 146-1, SD 49-0); I 1-0. May 4, 2005.

**154. HR 366. Vocational and Technical Education/Passage.** Passage of the bill that would reauthorize the Perkins vocational and technical education program for $1.3 billion in fiscal 2006 and such funds as necessary in fiscal 2007-11. The bill would merge Perkins funding with Tech-Prep, a program that provides specialized math and science courses to ease the transition of high school students to vocational school or community college. It also would provide federal grants to states for supplemental programs, such as courses in emerging technologies. Passed 416-9: R 218-9; D 197-0 (ND 147-0, SD 50-0); I 1-0. May 4, 2005.

**155. H Con Res 127. Charles Ghankay Taylor Condemnation/Adoption.**
Smith, R-N.J., motion to suspend the rules and adopt the concurrent resolution that would call on the government of Nigeria to transfer Charles Ghankay Taylor, former president of Liberia, to a United Nations special court to be tried for war crimes and other violations of international humanitarian law. Motion agreed to 421-1: R 223-1; D 197-0 (ND 148-0, SD 49-0); I 1-0. A two-thirds majority of those present and voting (282 in this case) is required for adoption under suspension of the rules. May 4, 2005.

**156. H Res 195. Victory in Europe Anniversary/Adoption.** Smith, R-N.J., motion to suspend the rules and adopt the resolution that would recognize the 60th anniversary of the liberation of Western Bohemia by Allied military forces, and honor those individuals who gave their lives during the liberation. Motion agreed to 419-0: R 224-0; D 194-0 (ND 145-0, SD 49-0); I 1-0. A two-thirds majority of those present and voting (280 in this case) is required for adoption under suspension of the rules. May 4, 2005.

| | 151 | 152 | 153 | 154 | 155 | 156 |
|---|---|---|---|---|---|---|
| **ALABAMA** | | | | | | |
| 1 Bonner | Y | Y | N | Y | Y | Y |
| 2 Everett | Y | Y | N | Y | Y | Y |
| 3 Rogers | Y | Y | N | Y | Y | Y |
| 4 Aderholt | Y | Y | N | Y | Y | Y |
| 5 Cramer | N | Y | Y | Y | Y | Y |
| 6 Bachus | Y | Y | N | Y | Y | Y |
| 7 Davis | N | Y | Y | Y | Y | Y |
| **ALASKA** | | | | | | |
| AL Young | Y | Y | N | Y | Y | Y |
| **ARIZONA** | | | | | | |
| 1 Renzi | Y | Y | N | Y | Y | Y |
| 2 Franks | Y | Y | N | N | Y | Y |
| 3 Shadegg | Y | Y | N | Y | Y | Y |
| 4 Pastor | N | Y | Y | Y | Y | Y |
| 5 Hayworth | Y | Y | N | Y | Y | Y |
| 6 Flake | Y | Y | N | Y | Y | Y |
| 7 Grijalva | N | Y | Y | Y | Y | Y |
| 8 Kolbe | Y | Y | N | Y | Y | Y |
| **ARKANSAS** | | | | | | |
| 1 Berry | N | ? | Y | Y | Y | Y |
| 2 Snyder | N | Y | Y | Y | Y | Y |
| 3 Boozman | Y | Y | N | Y | Y | Y |
| 4 Ross | N | Y | Y | Y | Y | Y |
| **CALIFORNIA** | | | | | | |
| 1 Thompson | N | Y | Y | Y | Y | Y |
| 2 Herger | Y | Y | N | Y | Y | Y |
| 3 Lungren | Y | Y | N | Y | Y | Y |
| 4 Doolittle | Y | Y | N | Y | Y | Y |
| 5 Matsui, D. | N | Y | Y | Y | Y | Y |
| 6 Woolsey | N | Y | Y | Y | Y | ? |
| 7 Miller, George | N | Y | Y | Y | Y | Y |
| 8 Pelosi | N | Y | Y | Y | Y | Y |
| 9 Lee | N | Y | Y | Y | Y | Y |
| 10 Tauscher | N | Y | Y | Y | Y | Y |
| 11 Pombo | Y | Y | N | Y | Y | Y |
| 12 Lantos | N | Y | Y | Y | Y | Y |
| 13 Stark | N | Y | Y | Y | Y | Y |
| 14 Eshoo | N | Y | Y | Y | Y | Y |
| 15 Honda | N | Y | Y | Y | Y | Y |
| 16 Lofgren | N | Y | Y | Y | Y | Y |
| 17 Farr | N | Y | Y | Y | Y | Y |
| 18 Cardoza | N | Y | Y | Y | Y | Y |
| 19 Radanovich | Y | Y | N | Y | Y | Y |
| 20 Costa | N | Y | Y | Y | Y | Y |
| 21 Nunes | Y | Y | N | Y | Y | Y |
| 22 Thomas | Y | Y | N | Y | Y | Y |
| 23 Capps | N | Y | Y | Y | Y | Y |
| 24 Gallegly | Y | Y | N | Y | Y | Y |
| 25 McKeon | Y | Y | N | Y | Y | Y |
| 26 Dreier | Y | Y | N | Y | Y | Y |
| 27 Sherman | N | Y | Y | Y | Y | Y |
| 28 Berman | N | Y | Y | Y | Y | Y |
| 29 Schiff | N | Y | Y | Y | Y | Y |
| 30 Waxman | N | Y | Y | Y | Y | Y |
| 31 Becerra | N | Y | Y | Y | Y | Y |
| 32 Solis | N | Y | Y | Y | Y | Y |
| 33 Watson | N | Y | Y | Y | Y | Y |
| 34 Roybal-Allard | N | Y | Y | Y | Y | Y |
| 35 Waters | N | Y | Y | Y | Y | Y |
| 36 Harman | N | Y | Y | Y | Y | Y |
| 37 Millender-McD. | N | Y | Y | Y | Y | Y |
| 38 Napolitano | N | Y | Y | Y | Y | Y |
| 39 Sánchez, Linda | N | Y | Y | Y | Y | Y |
| 40 Royce | Y | Y | N | Y | Y | Y |
| 41 Lewis | Y | Y | N | Y | Y | Y |
| 42 Miller, Gary | Y | Y | N | Y | Y | Y |
| 43 Baca | N | Y | Y | Y | Y | Y |
| 44 Calvert | Y | Y | N | Y | Y | Y |
| 45 Bono | Y | Y | N | Y | Y | Y |
| 46 Rohrabacher | Y | Y | N | Y | Y | Y |
| 47 Sanchez, Loretta | N | Y | + | Y | Y | Y |
| 48 Cox | Y | Y | N | Y | Y | Y |
| 49 Issa | Y | Y | N | Y | Y | Y |
| 50 Cunningham | Y | Y | N | Y | Y | Y |
| 51 Filner | N | Y | Y | Y | Y | Y |
| 52 Hunter | Y | Y | N | Y | Y | Y |
| 53 Davis | N | Y | Y | Y | Y | Y |
| **COLORADO** | | | | | | |
| 1 DeGette | N | Y | Y | Y | Y | Y |
| 2 Udall | N | Y | Y | Y | Y | Y |
| 3 Salazar | N | Y | Y | Y | Y | Y |
| 4 Musgrave | Y | Y | N | Y | Y | Y |
| 5 Hefley | Y | Y | N | Y | Y | Y |
| 6 Tancredo | Y | Y | N | Y | Y | Y |
| 7 Beauprez | Y | Y | N | Y | Y | Y |
| **CONNECTICUT** | | | | | | |
| 1 Larson | − | + | + | + | + | + |
| 2 Simmons | Y | Y | N | Y | Y | Y |
| 3 DeLauro | N | Y | Y | Y | Y | Y |
| 4 Shays | ? | Y | N | Y | Y | Y |
| 5 Johnson | ? | Y | Y | Y | Y | Y |
| **DELAWARE** | | | | | | |
| AL Castle | Y | Y | N | Y | Y | Y |
| **FLORIDA** | | | | | | |
| 1 Miller | Y | Y | N | Y | Y | Y |
| 2 Boyd | N | Y | Y | Y | Y | Y |
| 3 Brown | N | Y | Y | Y | Y | Y |
| 4 Crenshaw | Y | Y | N | Y | Y | Y |
| 5 Brown-Waite | Y | Y | N | Y | Y | Y |
| 6 Stearns | Y | Y | N | Y | Y | Y |
| 7 Mica | Y | Y | N | Y | Y | Y |
| 8 Keller | Y | Y | N | Y | Y | Y |
| 9 Bilirakis | Y | Y | N | Y | Y | Y |
| 10 Young | Y | Y | N | Y | Y | Y |
| 11 Davis | ? | ? | Y | Y | Y | Y |
| 12 Putnam | Y | Y | N | Y | Y | Y |
| 13 Harris | Y | Y | N | Y | Y | Y |
| 14 Mack | Y | Y | N | Y | Y | Y |
| 15 Weldon | ? | ? | Y | Y | Y | Y |
| 16 Foley | Y | Y | N | Y | Y | Y |
| 17 Meek | N | Y | Y | Y | Y | Y |
| 18 Ros-Lehtinen | Y | Y | N | Y | Y | Y |
| 19 Wexler | N | Y | Y | Y | Y | Y |
| 20 Wasserman-Schultz | N | Y | Y | Y | Y | Y |
| 21 Diaz-Balart, L. | ? | ? | ? | ? | ? | ? |
| 22 Shaw | Y | Y | N | Y | Y | Y |
| 23 Hastings | N | Y | Y | Y | Y | Y |
| 24 Feeney | Y | Y | N | N | Y | Y |
| 25 Diaz-Balart, M. | ? | ? | ? | ? | ? | ? |
| **GEORGIA** | | | | | | |
| 1 Kingston | Y | Y | N | Y | Y | Y |
| 2 Bishop | N | Y | Y | Y | Y | Y |
| 3 Marshall | N | Y | Y | Y | Y | Y |
| 4 McKinney | N | Y | Y | Y | Y | Y |
| 5 Lewis | N | Y | Y | Y | Y | Y |
| 6 Price | Y | Y | N | Y | Y | Y |
| 7 Linder | Y | Y | N | Y | Y | Y |
| 8 Westmoreland | Y | Y | N | Y | Y | Y |
| 9 Norwood | Y | Y | N | Y | Y | Y |
| 10 Deal | Y | Y | N | Y | Y | Y |
| 11 Gingrey | Y | Y | N | Y | Y | Y |
| 12 Barrow | N | Y | Y | Y | Y | Y |
| 13 Scott | N | Y | Y | Y | Y | Y |
| **HAWAII** | | | | | | |
| 1 Abercrombie | N | Y | Y | Y | Y | ? |
| 2 Case | N | Y | Y | Y | Y | Y |
| **IDAHO** | | | | | | |
| 1 Otter | ? | ? | N | Y | Y | Y |
| 2 Simpson | ? | ? | N | Y | Y | Y |
| **ILLINOIS** | | | | | | |
| 1 Rush | N | Y | Y | Y | Y | Y |
| 2 Jackson | N | Y | Y | Y | Y | Y |
| 3 Lipinski | N | Y | Y | Y | Y | Y |
| 4 Gutierrez | N | Y | Y | Y | Y | Y |
| 5 Emanuel | N | Y | Y | Y | Y | Y |
| 6 Hyde | Y | Y | N | Y | Y | Y |
| 7 Davis | N | Y | Y | Y | Y | Y |
| 8 Bean | N | Y | Y | Y | Y | Y |
| 9 Schakowsky | N | Y | Y | Y | Y | Y |
| 10 Kirk | Y | Y | N | Y | ? | Y |
| 11 Weller | Y | Y | N | Y | Y | Y |
| 12 Costello | N | Y | Y | Y | Y | Y |

| KEY | **Republicans** | Democrats | *Independents* | | |
|---|---|---|---|---|---|
| Y | Voted for (yea) | X | Paired against | C | Voted "present" to avoid possible conflict of interest |
| # | Paired for | − | Announced against | | |
| + | Announced for | P | Voted "present" | ? | Did not vote or otherwise make a position known |
| N | Voted against (nay) | | | | |

*Rep. Rob Portman, R-Ohio, resigned effective April 29, 2005. The last vote for which he was eligible was vote 150.

| | 151 | 152 | 153 | 154 | 155 | 156 |
|---|---|---|---|---|---|---|
| 13 **Biggert** | ? | Y | N | Y | Y | Y |
| 14 **Hastert** | | | | | | |
| 15 **Johnson** | Y | Y | N | Y | Y | Y |
| 16 **Manzullo** | Y | Y | N | Y | Y | Y |
| 17 Evans | N | Y | Y | Y | Y | Y |
| 18 **LaHood** | Y | Y | N | Y | Y | Y |
| 19 **Shimkus** | Y | Y | N | Y | Y | Y |
| **INDIANA** | | | | | | |
| 1 Visclosky | N | Y | Y | Y | Y | Y |
| 2 **Chocola** | Y | Y | N | Y | Y | Y |
| 3 **Souder** | Y | Y | N | Y | Y | Y |
| 4 **Buyer** | Y | Y | N | Y | Y | Y |
| 5 **Burton** | Y | Y | N | Y | Y | Y |
| 6 **Pence** | Y | Y | N | Y | Y | Y |
| 7 Carson | N | Y | Y | Y | Y | Y |
| 8 **Hostettler** | Y | Y | N | N | Y | Y |
| 9 **Sodrel** | Y | Y | N | Y | Y | Y |
| **IOWA** | | | | | | |
| 1 **Nussle** | Y | Y | N | Y | Y | Y |
| 2 **Leach** | Y | Y | N | Y | Y | Y |
| 3 Boswell | N | Y | Y | Y | Y | Y |
| 4 **Latham** | Y | Y | N | Y | Y | Y |
| 5 **King** | Y | Y | N | Y | Y | Y |
| **KANSAS** | | | | | | |
| 1 **Moran** | Y | Y | N | Y | Y | Y |
| 2 **Ryun** | Y | Y | N | Y | Y | Y |
| 3 Moore | N | Y | Y | Y | Y | ? |
| 4 **Tiahrt** | Y | Y | N | Y | Y | Y |
| **KENTUCKY** | | | | | | |
| 1 **Whitfield** | Y | Y | N | Y | Y | ? |
| 2 **Lewis** | Y | Y | N | Y | Y | Y |
| 3 **Northup** | Y | Y | N | Y | Y | Y |
| 4 **Davis** | Y | Y | N | Y | Y | Y |
| 5 **Rogers** | Y | Y | N | Y | Y | Y |
| 6 Chandler | N | Y | Y | Y | Y | Y |
| **LOUISIANA** | | | | | | |
| 1 **Jindal** | Y | Y | N | Y | Y | Y |
| 2 Jefferson | N | Y | Y | Y | Y | Y |
| 3 Melancon | N | Y | ? | Y | Y | Y |
| 4 **McCrery** | Y | Y | N | Y | Y | Y |
| 5 **Alexander** | Y | Y | N | Y | Y | Y |
| 6 **Baker** | Y | Y | N | Y | Y | Y |
| 7 **Boustany** | Y | Y | N | Y | Y | Y |
| **MAINE** | | | | | | |
| 1 Allen | N | Y | Y | Y | Y | Y |
| 2 Michaud | N | Y | Y | Y | Y | Y |
| **MARYLAND** | | | | | | |
| 1 **Gilchrest** | Y | Y | N | Y | Y | Y |
| 2 Ruppersberger | N | Y | Y | Y | Y | Y |
| 3 Cardin | N | Y | Y | Y | Y | Y |
| 4 Wynn | N | Y | Y | Y | Y | Y |
| 5 Hoyer | ? | ? | Y | Y | Y | Y |
| 6 **Bartlett** | Y | Y | N | N | Y | Y |
| 7 Cummings | N | Y | Y | Y | Y | Y |
| 8 Van Hollen | N | Y | Y | Y | Y | Y |
| **MASSACHUSETTS** | | | | | | |
| 1 Olver | N | Y | Y | Y | Y | Y |
| 2 Neal | N | Y | Y | Y | Y | Y |
| 3 McGovern | N | Y | Y | Y | Y | Y |
| 4 Frank | N | Y | Y | Y | Y | Y |
| 5 Meehan | N | Y | Y | Y | Y | Y |
| 6 Tierney | N | Y | Y | Y | Y | Y |
| 7 Markey | N | Y | Y | Y | Y | Y |
| 8 Capuano | N | Y | Y | Y | Y | Y |
| 9 Lynch | N | Y | Y | Y | Y | Y |
| 10 Delahunt | N | Y | Y | Y | Y | Y |
| **MICHIGAN** | | | | | | |
| 1 Stupak | N | Y | Y | Y | Y | Y |
| 2 **Hoekstra** | Y | Y | N | Y | Y | Y |
| 3 **Ehlers** | Y | Y | N | Y | Y | Y |
| 4 **Camp** | Y | Y | N | Y | Y | Y |
| 5 Kildee | N | Y | Y | Y | Y | Y |
| 6 **Upton** | Y | Y | N | Y | Y | Y |
| 7 **Schwarz** | Y | Y | N | Y | Y | Y |
| 8 **Rogers** | Y | Y | ? | Y | Y | Y |
| 9 **Knollenberg** | Y | Y | N | Y | Y | Y |
| 10 **Miller** | Y | Y | N | Y | Y | Y |
| 11 **McCotter** | Y | Y | N | Y | Y | Y |
| 12 Levin | N | Y | Y | Y | Y | Y |
| 13 Kilpatrick | N | Y | Y | Y | Y | Y |
| 14 Conyers | N | Y | Y | Y | Y | Y |
| 15 Dingell | N | Y | Y | Y | Y | Y |

| | 151 | 152 | 153 | 154 | 155 | 156 |
|---|---|---|---|---|---|---|
| **MINNESOTA** | | | | | | |
| 1 **Gutknecht** | Y | Y | ? | Y | Y | Y |
| 2 **Kline** | Y | Y | N | Y | Y | Y |
| 3 **Ramstad** | Y | Y | Y | Y | Y | Y |
| 4 McCollum | N | Y | Y | Y | Y | Y |
| 5 Sabo | N | Y | Y | Y | Y | Y |
| 6 **Kennedy** | Y | Y | N | Y | Y | Y |
| 7 Peterson | N | Y | Y | Y | Y | Y |
| 8 Oberstar | N | Y | Y | Y | Y | Y |
| **MISSISSIPPI** | | | | | | |
| 1 **Wicker** | Y | Y | N | Y | Y | Y |
| 2 Thompson | N | Y | Y | Y | Y | Y |
| 3 **Pickering** | Y | Y | N | Y | Y | Y |
| 4 Taylor | N | Y | Y | Y | Y | Y |
| **MISSOURI** | | | | | | |
| 1 Clay | ? | ? | Y | Y | Y | Y |
| 2 **Akin** | Y | Y | N | Y | Y | Y |
| 3 Carnahan | N | Y | Y | Y | Y | Y |
| 4 Skelton | N | Y | Y | Y | Y | Y |
| 5 Cleaver | N | Y | Y | Y | Y | Y |
| 6 **Graves** | Y | Y | N | Y | Y | Y |
| 7 **Blunt** | Y | Y | N | Y | Y | Y |
| 8 **Emerson** | Y | Y | N | Y | Y | Y |
| 9 **Hulshof** | Y | Y | N | Y | Y | Y |
| **MONTANA** | | | | | | |
| AL **Rehberg** | Y | Y | N | Y | Y | Y |
| **NEBRASKA** | | | | | | |
| 1 **Fortenberry** | Y | Y | N | Y | Y | Y |
| 2 **Terry** | Y | Y | N | Y | Y | Y |
| 3 **Osborne** | Y | Y | N | Y | Y | Y |
| **NEVADA** | | | | | | |
| 1 Berkley | N | Y | Y | Y | Y | Y |
| 2 **Gibbons** | Y | Y | N | Y | Y | Y |
| 3 **Porter** | Y | Y | N | Y | Y | Y |
| **NEW HAMPSHIRE** | | | | | | |
| 1 **Bradley** | Y | Y | N | Y | Y | Y |
| 2 **Bass** | Y | Y | N | Y | Y | Y |
| **NEW JERSEY** | | | | | | |
| 1 Andrews | N | Y | N | Y | Y | Y |
| 2 **LoBiondo** | Y | Y | N | Y | Y | Y |
| 3 **Saxton** | Y | Y | N | Y | Y | Y |
| 4 **Smith** | Y | Y | N | Y | Y | Y |
| 5 **Garrett** | Y | Y | N | N | Y | Y |
| 6 Pallone | N | Y | Y | Y | Y | Y |
| 7 **Ferguson** | Y | Y | N | Y | Y | Y |
| 8 Pascrell | N | Y | Y | Y | Y | Y |
| 9 Rothman | N | Y | Y | Y | Y | Y |
| 10 Payne | N | Y | Y | Y | Y | Y |
| 11 **Frelinghuysen** | Y | Y | N | Y | Y | Y |
| 12 Holt | N | Y | Y | Y | Y | Y |
| 13 Menendez | N | Y | Y | Y | Y | Y |
| **NEW MEXICO** | | | | | | |
| 1 **Wilson** | Y | Y | N | Y | Y | Y |
| 2 **Pearce** | Y | Y | N | Y | Y | Y |
| 3 Udall | N | Y | Y | Y | Y | Y |
| **NEW YORK** | | | | | | |
| 1 Bishop | N | Y | Y | Y | Y | Y |
| 2 Israel | N | Y | Y | Y | Y | Y |
| 3 **King** | Y | Y | N | Y | Y | Y |
| 4 McCarthy | N | Y | Y | Y | Y | Y |
| 5 Ackerman | N | Y | Y | Y | Y | Y |
| 6 Meeks | N | Y | Y | Y | Y | Y |
| 7 Crowley | N | Y | Y | Y | Y | Y |
| 8 Nadler | N | Y | Y | Y | Y | Y |
| 9 Weiner | N | Y | ? | ? | ? | ? |
| 10 Towns | N | Y | Y | ? | Y | Y |
| 11 Owens | N | Y | Y | Y | Y | Y |
| 12 Velázquez | N | Y | Y | Y | Y | Y |
| 13 **Fossella** | Y | Y | N | Y | Y | Y |
| 14 Maloney | N | Y | Y | Y | Y | Y |
| 15 Rangel | N | Y | Y | Y | Y | Y |
| 16 Serrano | N | Y | Y | Y | Y | Y |
| 17 Engel | N | Y | Y | Y | Y | Y |
| 18 Lowey | N | Y | Y | Y | Y | Y |
| 19 **Kelly** | Y | Y | N | Y | Y | Y |
| 20 **Sweeney** | Y | Y | N | Y | Y | Y |
| 21 McNulty | N | Y | Y | Y | Y | Y |
| 22 Hinchey | N | Y | Y | Y | Y | Y |
| 23 **McHugh** | Y | Y | N | Y | Y | Y |
| 24 **Boehlert** | Y | Y | N | Y | Y | Y |
| 25 **Walsh** | ? | ? | N | Y | Y | Y |
| 26 **Reynolds** | Y | Y | N | Y | Y | Y |
| 27 Higgins | N | Y | Y | Y | Y | Y |
| 28 Slaughter | N | Y | Y | Y | Y | Y |
| 29 **Kuhl** | Y | Y | N | Y | Y | Y |

| | 151 | 152 | 153 | 154 | 155 | 156 |
|---|---|---|---|---|---|---|
| **NORTH CAROLINA** | | | | | | |
| 1 Butterfield | N | Y | Y | Y | Y | Y |
| 2 Etheridge | N | Y | Y | Y | Y | Y |
| 3 **Jones** | Y | Y | N | Y | Y | Y |
| 4 Price | N | Y | Y | Y | Y | Y |
| 5 **Foxx** | Y | Y | N | Y | Y | Y |
| 6 **Coble** | Y | Y | N | Y | Y | Y |
| 7 McIntyre | N | Y | Y | Y | Y | Y |
| 8 **Hayes** | Y | Y | N | Y | Y | Y |
| 9 **Myrick** | Y | Y | N | Y | Y | Y |
| 10 **McHenry** | Y | Y | N | Y | Y | Y |
| 11 **Taylor** | Y | Y | N | Y | Y | Y |
| 12 Watt | N | Y | Y | Y | Y | Y |
| 13 Miller | N | Y | Y | Y | Y | Y |
| **NORTH DAKOTA** | | | | | | |
| AL Pomeroy | N | Y | Y | Y | Y | Y |
| **OHIO** | | | | | | |
| 1 **Chabot** | Y | Y | N | Y | Y | Y |
| 2 Vacant* | | | | | | |
| 3 **Turner** | Y | Y | N | Y | Y | Y |
| 4 **Oxley** | Y | Y | N | Y | Y | Y |
| 5 **Gillmor** | Y | Y | N | Y | Y | Y |
| 6 Strickland | N | Y | Y | Y | Y | Y |
| 7 **Hobson** | Y | Y | N | Y | Y | Y |
| 8 **Boehner** | Y | Y | N | Y | Y | Y |
| 9 Kaptur | N | Y | Y | Y | Y | Y |
| 10 Kucinich | N | Y | Y | Y | Y | Y |
| 11 Jones | N | Y | Y | Y | Y | Y |
| 12 **Tiberi** | Y | Y | N | Y | Y | Y |
| 13 Brown | ? | ? | ? | ? | ? | ? |
| 14 **LaTourette** | Y | Y | N | Y | Y | Y |
| 15 **Pryce** | Y | Y | N | Y | Y | Y |
| 16 **Regula** | Y | Y | N | Y | Y | Y |
| 17 Ryan | N | Y | Y | Y | Y | Y |
| 18 **Ney** | Y | Y | N | Y | Y | Y |
| **OKLAHOMA** | | | | | | |
| 1 **Sullivan** | Y | ? | N | Y | ? | Y |
| 2 Boren | N | Y | Y | Y | Y | Y |
| 3 **Lucas** | Y | Y | N | Y | Y | Y |
| 4 **Cole** | Y | Y | N | Y | Y | Y |
| 5 **Istook** | Y | Y | N | Y | Y | Y |
| **OREGON** | | | | | | |
| 1 Wu | N | Y | Y | Y | Y | Y |
| 2 **Walden** | Y | Y | N | Y | Y | Y |
| 3 Blumenauer | N | Y | Y | Y | Y | Y |
| 4 DeFazio | N | Y | Y | Y | Y | Y |
| 5 Hooley | N | Y | Y | Y | Y | Y |
| **PENNSYLVANIA** | | | | | | |
| 1 Brady | N | Y | Y | Y | Y | Y |
| 2 Fattah | ? | ? | Y | Y | Y | Y |
| 3 **English** | Y | Y | N | Y | Y | Y |
| 4 **Hart** | Y | Y | N | Y | Y | Y |
| 5 **Peterson** | Y | Y | N | Y | Y | Y |
| 6 **Gerlach** | Y | Y | N | Y | Y | Y |
| 7 **Weldon** | Y | Y | – | + | + | + |
| 8 **Fitzpatrick** | Y | Y | N | Y | Y | Y |
| 9 **Shuster** | Y | Y | N | Y | Y | Y |
| 10 **Sherwood** | Y | Y | N | Y | Y | Y |
| 11 Kanjorski | N | Y | Y | Y | Y | Y |
| 12 Murtha | N | ? | Y | Y | Y | Y |
| 13 Schwartz | N | Y | Y | Y | Y | Y |
| 14 Doyle | N | Y | Y | Y | Y | Y |
| 15 **Dent** | Y | Y | N | Y | Y | Y |
| 16 **Pitts** | Y | Y | N | Y | Y | Y |
| 17 Holden | N | Y | Y | Y | Y | Y |
| 18 **Murphy** | Y | Y | N | Y | Y | Y |
| 19 **Platts** | Y | Y | N | Y | Y | Y |
| **RHODE ISLAND** | | | | | | |
| 1 Kennedy | N | Y | Y | Y | Y | Y |
| 2 Langevin | N | Y | Y | Y | Y | Y |
| **SOUTH CAROLINA** | | | | | | |
| 1 **Brown** | Y | Y | N | Y | Y | Y |
| 2 **Wilson** | Y | Y | N | Y | Y | Y |
| 3 **Barrett** | Y | Y | N | Y | Y | Y |
| 4 **Inglis** | Y | Y | N | Y | Y | Y |
| 5 Spratt | N | Y | Y | Y | Y | Y |
| 6 Clyburn | N | Y | Y | Y | Y | Y |
| **SOUTH DAKOTA** | | | | | | |
| AL Herseth | N | Y | Y | Y | Y | Y |
| **TENNESSEE** | | | | | | |
| 1 **Jenkins** | Y | Y | N | Y | Y | Y |
| 2 **Duncan** | Y | Y | N | Y | Y | Y |

| | 151 | 152 | 153 | 154 | 155 | 156 |
|---|---|---|---|---|---|---|
| 3 **Wamp** | Y | Y | N | Y | Y | Y |
| 4 Davis | N | Y | Y | Y | Y | Y |
| 5 Cooper | N | Y | Y | Y | Y | Y |
| 6 Gordon | N | Y | Y | Y | Y | ? |
| 7 **Blackburn** | Y | Y | N | Y | Y | Y |
| 8 Tanner | N | Y | Y | Y | Y | Y |
| 9 Ford | N | Y | Y | Y | Y | Y |
| **TEXAS** | | | | | | |
| 1 **Gohmert** | Y | Y | N | Y | Y | Y |
| 2 **Poe** | Y | Y | N | Y | Y | Y |
| 3 **Johnson, S.** | Y | Y | N | Y | Y | Y |
| 4 **Hall** | Y | Y | N | Y | Y | Y |
| 5 **Hensarling** | Y | Y | N | N | Y | Y |
| 6 **Barton** | Y | Y | N | Y | Y | Y |
| 7 **Culberson** | ? | ? | N | Y | Y | Y |
| 8 **Brady** | Y | Y | N | Y | Y | Y |
| 9 Green | N | Y | Y | Y | Y | Y |
| 10 **McCaul** | Y | Y | N | Y | Y | Y |
| 11 **Conaway** | Y | Y | N | Y | Y | Y |
| 12 **Granger** | Y | Y | N | Y | Y | Y |
| 13 **Thornberry** | Y | Y | N | Y | Y | Y |
| 14 **Paul** | Y | Y | N | N | N | Y |
| 15 Hinojosa | N | Y | Y | Y | Y | Y |
| 16 Reyes | N | Y | Y | Y | Y | Y |
| 17 Edwards | ? | ? | Y | Y | Y | Y |
| 18 Jackson-Lee | N | Y | Y | Y | ? | Y |
| 19 **Neugebauer** | Y | Y | N | Y | ? | Y |
| 20 Gonzalez | N | Y | Y | Y | Y | Y |
| 21 **Smith** | Y | Y | ? | Y | Y | Y |
| 22 **DeLay** | Y | Y | N | Y | Y | Y |
| 23 **Bonilla** | Y | Y | N | Y | Y | Y |
| 24 **Marchant** | Y | Y | N | Y | Y | Y |
| 25 Doggett | N | Y | Y | Y | Y | Y |
| 26 **Burgess** | Y | Y | N | Y | Y | Y |
| 27 Ortiz | N | Y | Y | Y | Y | Y |
| 28 Cuellar | N | Y | Y | Y | Y | Y |
| 29 Green | N | Y | Y | Y | Y | Y |
| 30 Johnson, E. | N | Y | Y | Y | Y | Y |
| 31 **Carter** | Y | Y | N | Y | Y | Y |
| 32 **Sessions** | Y | Y | N | Y | Y | Y |
| **UTAH** | | | | | | |
| 1 **Bishop** | Y | Y | N | Y | Y | Y |
| 2 Matheson | N | Y | Y | Y | Y | Y |
| 3 **Cannon** | Y | Y | N | Y | Y | Y |
| **VERMONT** | | | | | | |
| AL *Sanders* | N | Y | Y | Y | Y | Y |
| **VIRGINIA** | | | | | | |
| 1 **Davis, J.** | Y | Y | N | Y | Y | Y |
| 2 **Drake** | Y | Y | N | Y | Y | Y |
| 3 Scott | N | Y | ? | ? | ? | ? |
| 4 **Forbes** | Y | Y | N | Y | Y | Y |
| 5 **Goode** | Y | Y | N | Y | Y | Y |
| 6 **Goodlatte** | Y | Y | N | Y | Y | Y |
| 7 **Cantor** | Y | Y | N | Y | Y | Y |
| 8 Moran | N | Y | Y | Y | Y | Y |
| 9 Boucher | N | Y | Y | Y | Y | Y |
| 10 **Wolf** | Y | Y | N | Y | Y | Y |
| 11 **Davis, T.** | Y | Y | N | Y | Y | Y |
| **WASHINGTON** | | | | | | |
| 1 Inslee | N | Y | Y | Y | Y | Y |
| 2 Larsen | N | Y | Y | Y | Y | Y |
| 3 Baird | N | Y | Y | Y | Y | Y |
| 4 **Hastings** | Y | Y | N | Y | Y | Y |
| 5 **McMorris** | Y | Y | N | Y | Y | ? |
| 6 Dicks | N | Y | Y | Y | Y | Y |
| 7 McDermott | N | Y | Y | Y | Y | Y |
| 8 **Reichert** | Y | Y | N | Y | Y | Y |
| 9 Smith | N | Y | Y | Y | Y | Y |
| **WEST VIRGINIA** | | | | | | |
| 1 Mollohan | N | Y | Y | Y | Y | Y |
| 2 **Capito** | Y | Y | N | Y | Y | Y |
| 3 Rahall | N | Y | Y | Y | Y | Y |
| **WISCONSIN** | | | | | | |
| 1 **Ryan** | Y | Y | N | Y | Y | Y |
| 2 Baldwin | N | Y | Y | Y | Y | Y |
| 3 Kind | N | Y | Y | Y | Y | Y |
| 4 Moore | N | Y | Y | Y | Y | Y |
| 5 **Sensenbrenner** | Y | Y | N | N | Y | Y |
| 6 **Petri** | Y | Y | N | Y | Y | Y |
| 7 Obey | N | Y | Y | Y | Y | Y |
| 8 **Green** | Y | Y | N | Y | Y | Y |
| **WYOMING** | | | | | | |
| AL **Cubin** | Y | Y | N | Y | Y | Y |

# IN THE HOUSE | By Vote Number

**157.** **HR 1185. Federal Deposit Insurance Limit/Passage.** Passage of the bill that would increase to $130,000 from $100,000 the ceiling on bank deposits guaranteed by the Federal Deposit Insurance Corporation and index the limit to inflation thereafter. It would merge the FDIC's Bank Insurance Fund and the Savings Association Insurance Fund. The FDIC would be able to set risk-based premiums for insured institutions and double to $260,000 the coverage limits for certain types of retirement accounts. Passed 413-10: R 219-5; D 194-4 (ND 147-2, SD 47-2); I 0-1. May 4, 2005.

**158.** **H Res 233. Victory in Europe Anniversary/Adoption.** Smith, R-N.J., motion to suspend the rules and adopt the resolution that would recognize the 60th anniversary of the end of World War II in Europe and that would express respect and appreciation to the men and women who served in Europe during World War II. Motion agreed to 423-0: R 225-0; D 197-0 (ND 148-0, SD 49-0); I 1-0. A two-thirds majority of those present and voting (282 in this case) is required for adoption under suspension of the rules. May 4, 2005.

**159.** **HR 1268. Fiscal 2005 Supplemental Appropriations/Previous Question.** Cole, R-Okla., motion to order the previous question (thus ending debate and possibility of amendment) on adoption of the rule (H Res 258) to provide for House floor consideration of the conference report on the bill that would appropriate $82 billion in fiscal 2005 supplemental spending for military operations and reconstruction in Iraq and Afghanistan and for disaster assistance to victims of the December 2004 tsunami. The rule also would allow for the chairman of the Judiciary Committee to file a supplemental report to the interstate abortion notification bill (HR 748). Motion agreed to 224-196: R 224-1; D 0-194 (ND 0-144, SD 0-50); I 0-1. (Subsequently, the rule was adopted by voice vote.) May 5, 2005.

**160.** **HR 1268. Fiscal 2005 Supplemental Appropriations/Recommit.** Obey, D-Wis., motion to recommit the bill to the conference committee with instructions to include Senate language that would provide for the highest levels of funding for immigration and customs enforcement. Motion rejected 201-225: R 2-225; D 198-0 (ND 147-0, SD 51-0); I 1-0. May 5, 2005.

**161.** **HR 1268. Fiscal 2005 Supplemental Appropriations/Adoption.** Adoption of the conference report on the bill that would appropriate $82 billion in fiscal 2005 supplemental spending for military operations and reconstruction in Iraq and Afghanistan and for disaster assistance to victims of the December 2004 tsunami. It also would establish national driver's license standards, stiffen asylum requirements and speed completion of a fence on the U.S.-Mexico border. Adopted (thus sent to the Senate) 368-58: R 225-3; D 143-54 (ND 98-48, SD 45-6); I 0-1. May 5, 2005.

| | 157 | 158 | 159 | 160 | 161 |
|---|---|---|---|---|---|
| **ALABAMA** | | | | | |
| 1 **Bonner** | Y | Y | Y | N | Y |
| 2 **Everett** | Y | Y | Y | N | Y |
| 3 **Rogers** | Y | Y | Y | N | Y |
| 4 **Aderholt** | Y | Y | Y | N | Y |
| 5 Cramer | Y | Y | N | Y | Y |
| 6 **Bachus** | Y | Y | Y | N | Y |
| 7 Davis | Y | Y | N | Y | Y |
| **ALASKA** | | | | | |
| AL **Young** | Y | Y | Y | N | Y |
| **ARIZONA** | | | | | |
| 1 **Renzi** | Y | Y | Y | N | Y |
| 2 **Franks** | + | + | Y | N | Y |
| 3 **Shadegg** | Y | Y | Y | N | Y |
| 4 Pastor | Y | Y | N | Y | N |
| 5 **Hayworth** | Y | Y | Y | N | Y |
| 6 **Flake** | N | Y | Y | N | Y |
| 7 Grijalva | Y | Y | N | Y | N |
| 8 **Kolbe** | Y | Y | Y | N | Y |
| **ARKANSAS** | | | | | |
| 1 Berry | Y | Y | N | Y | Y |
| 2 Snyder | Y | Y | N | Y | Y |
| 3 **Boozman** | Y | Y | Y | N | Y |
| 4 Ross | Y | Y | N | Y | Y |
| **CALIFORNIA** | | | | | |
| 1 Thompson | Y | Y | N | Y | N |
| 2 **Herger** | + | Y | Y | N | Y |
| 3 **Lungren** | Y | Y | Y | N | Y |
| 4 **Doolittle** | Y | Y | Y | ? | Y |
| 5 Matsui, D. | Y | Y | N | Y | P |
| 6 Woolsey | Y | Y | N | Y | N |
| 7 Miller, George | Y | Y | N | Y | N |
| 8 Pelosi | Y | Y | N | Y | Y |
| 9 Lee | Y | Y | N | Y | N |
| 10 Tauscher | Y | Y | N | Y | Y |
| 11 **Pombo** | Y | Y | Y | N | Y |
| 12 Lantos | Y | Y | N | + | + |
| 13 Stark | N | Y | N | Y | N |
| 14 Eshoo | Y | Y | N | Y | Y |
| 15 Honda | Y | Y | N | Y | N |
| 16 Lofgren | Y | Y | N | Y | Y |
| 17 Farr | Y | Y | N | Y | N |
| 18 Cardoza | Y | Y | N | Y | Y |
| 19 **Radanovich** | Y | Y | Y | N | Y |
| 20 Costa | Y | Y | N | Y | Y |
| 21 **Nunes** | Y | Y | Y | N | Y |
| 22 **Thomas** | Y | Y | Y | N | Y |
| 23 Capps | Y | Y | - | + | + |
| 24 **Gallegly** | Y | Y | Y | N | Y |
| 25 **McKeon** | Y | Y | Y | N | Y |
| 26 **Dreier** | Y | Y | Y | N | Y |
| 27 Sherman | Y | Y | N | Y | Y |
| 28 Berman | Y | Y | N | Y | Y |
| 29 Schiff | Y | Y | N | Y | Y |
| 30 Waxman | Y | Y | N | Y | Y |
| 31 Becerra | Y | Y | N | Y | Y |
| 32 Solis | Y | Y | ? | Y | Y |
| 33 Watson | Y | Y | N | Y | Y |
| 34 Roybal-Allard | Y | Y | N | Y | Y |
| 35 Waters | Y | Y | N | Y | N |
| 36 Harman | Y | Y | N | Y | Y |
| 37 Millender-McD. | Y | Y | N | Y | Y |
| 38 Napolitano | Y | Y | N | Y | N |
| 39 Sánchez, Linda | Y | Y | N | Y | Y |
| 40 **Royce** | N | Y | Y | N | Y |
| 41 **Lewis** | Y | Y | Y | N | Y |
| 42 **Miller, Gary** | Y | Y | N | Y | Y |
| 43 Baca | Y | Y | N | Y | Y |
| 44 **Calvert** | Y | Y | Y | N | Y |
| 45 **Bono** | Y | Y | Y | N | Y |
| 46 **Rohrabacher** | N | Y | Y | N | Y |
| 47 Sanchez, Loretta | Y | Y | N | Y | Y |
| 48 **Cox** | Y | Y | Y | N | Y |
| 49 **Issa** | Y | Y | Y | N | Y |

| | 157 | 158 | 159 | 160 | 161 |
|---|---|---|---|---|---|
| 50 **Cunningham** | Y | Y | Y | N | Y |
| 51 Filner | Y | Y | Y | N | N |
| 52 **Hunter** | Y | Y | Y | N | Y |
| 53 Davis | Y | Y | N | Y | Y |
| **COLORADO** | | | | | |
| 1 DeGette | Y | Y | N | Y | Y |
| 2 Udall | Y | Y | N | Y | Y |
| 3 Salazar | Y | Y | Y | N | Y |
| 4 **Musgrave** | Y | Y | Y | N | Y |
| 5 **Hefley** | Y | Y | Y | N | Y |
| 6 **Tancredo** | Y | ? | Y | N | Y |
| 7 **Beauprez** | Y | Y | Y | N | Y |
| **CONNECTICUT** | | | | | |
| 1 Larson | + | + | - | + | + |
| 2 **Simmons** | Y | Y | Y | N | Y |
| 3 DeLauro | Y | Y | N | Y | Y |
| 4 **Shays** | Y | Y | Y | N | Y |
| 5 **Johnson** | Y | Y | Y | N | Y |
| **DELAWARE** | | | | | |
| AL **Castle** | Y | Y | Y | N | Y |
| **FLORIDA** | | | | | |
| 1 **Miller** | Y | Y | Y | N | Y |
| 2 Boyd | Y | Y | N | Y | Y |
| 3 Brown | Y | Y | N | Y | Y |
| 4 **Crenshaw** | Y | Y | Y | N | Y |
| 5 **Brown-Waite** | Y | Y | Y | N | Y |
| 6 **Stearns** | Y | Y | Y | N | Y |
| 7 **Mica** | Y | Y | Y | N | Y |
| 8 **Keller** | Y | Y | Y | N | Y |
| 9 **Bilirakis** | Y | Y | Y | N | Y |
| 10 **Young** | Y | Y | Y | N | Y |
| 11 Davis | Y | Y | N | Y | Y |
| 12 **Putnam** | Y | Y | Y | N | Y |
| 13 **Harris** | Y | Y | Y | N | Y |
| 14 **Mack** | Y | Y | Y | N | Y |
| 15 **Weldon** | Y | Y | Y | N | Y |
| 16 **Foley** | Y | Y | Y | N | Y |
| 17 Meek | Y | Y | N | Y | Y |
| 18 **Ros-Lehtinen** | Y | Y | Y | N | Y |
| 19 Wexler | Y | Y | N | Y | N |
| 20 Wasserman-Schultz | Y | Y | N | Y | Y |
| 21 **Diaz-Balart, L.** | ? | ? | ? | ? | ? |
| 22 **Shaw** | Y | Y | Y | N | Y |
| 23 Hastings | Y | Y | N | Y | Y |
| 24 **Feeney** | Y | Y | Y | N | Y |
| 25 **Diaz-Balart, M.** | ? | ? | ? | ? | ? |
| **GEORGIA** | | | | | |
| 1 **Kingston** | Y | Y | Y | N | Y |
| 2 Bishop | Y | Y | N | Y | Y |
| 3 Marshall | Y | Y | N | Y | Y |
| 4 McKinney | Y | Y | N | Y | N |
| 5 Lewis | Y | Y | N | Y | N |
| 6 **Price** | Y | Y | Y | N | Y |
| 7 **Linder** | Y | Y | Y | N | Y |
| 8 **Westmoreland** | Y | Y | Y | N | Y |
| 9 **Norwood** | Y | Y | Y | N | Y |
| 10 **Deal** | Y | Y | Y | N | Y |
| 11 **Gingrey** | Y | Y | Y | N | Y |
| 12 Barrow | Y | Y | N | Y | Y |
| 13 Scott | Y | Y | N | Y | Y |
| **HAWAII** | | | | | |
| 1 Abercrombie | Y | Y | N | Y | N |
| 2 Case | Y | Y | N | Y | Y |
| **IDAHO** | | | | | |
| 1 **Otter** | Y | Y | Y | N | Y |
| 2 **Simpson** | Y | Y | Y | N | Y |
| **ILLINOIS** | | | | | |
| 1 Rush | Y | Y | N | Y | Y |
| 2 Jackson | Y | Y | N | Y | Y |
| 3 Lipinski | Y | Y | N | Y | Y |
| 4 Gutierrez | Y | Y | N | Y | N |
| 5 Emanuel | Y | Y | N | Y | Y |
| 6 **Hyde** | Y | Y | ? | N | Y |
| 7 Davis | Y | Y | N | Y | N |
| 8 Bean | Y | Y | N | Y | Y |
| 9 Schakowsky | Y | Y | N | Y | N |
| 10 **Kirk** | Y | Y | Y | N | Y |
| 11 **Weller** | Y | Y | Y | N | Y |
| 12 Costello | Y | Y | N | Y | Y |

| KEY | Republicans | Democrats | *Independents* | | |
|---|---|---|---|---|---|
| **Y** Voted for (yea) | | **X** Paired against | | **C** Voted "present" to avoid possible conflict of interest | |
| **#** Paired for | | **–** Announced against | | | |
| **+** Announced for | | **P** Voted "present" | | **?** Did not vote or otherwise make a position known | |
| **N** Voted against (nay) | | | | | |

| | 157 | 158 | 159 | 160 | 161 |
|---|---|---|---|---|---|
| 13 Biggert | Y | Y | Y | N | Y |
| 14 Hastert | | | | | |
| 15 Johnson | Y | Y | Y | N | Y |
| 16 Manzullo | Y | Y | Y | N | Y |
| 17 Evans | Y | Y | N | Y | Y |
| 18 LaHood | Y | Y | Y | N | Y |
| 19 Shimkus | Y | Y | Y | N | Y |
| **INDIANA** | | | | | |
| 1 Visclosky | Y | Y | N | Y | Y |
| 2 Chocola | Y | Y | Y | N | Y |
| 3 Souder | Y | Y | Y | N | Y |
| 4 Buyer | Y | Y | Y | N | Y |
| 5 Burton | Y | Y | Y | N | Y |
| 6 Pence | Y | Y | Y | N | Y |
| 7 Carson | Y | Y | N | Y | N |
| 8 Hostettler | Y | Y | Y | N | Y |
| 9 Sodrel | Y | Y | Y | N | Y |
| **IOWA** | | | | | |
| 1 Nussle | Y | Y | Y | N | Y |
| 2 Leach | Y | Y | N | N | Y |
| 3 Boswell | Y | Y | N | Y | Y |
| 4 Latham | Y | Y | Y | N | Y |
| 5 King | Y | Y | Y | N | Y |
| **KANSAS** | | | | | |
| 1 Moran | Y | Y | Y | N | Y |
| 2 Ryun | Y | Y | Y | N | Y |
| 3 Moore | Y | Y | N | Y | Y |
| 4 Tiahrt | Y | Y | Y | N | Y |
| **KENTUCKY** | | | | | |
| 1 Whitfield | Y | Y | Y | N | Y |
| 2 Lewis | Y | Y | Y | N | Y |
| 3 Northup | Y | Y | Y | N | Y |
| 4 Davis | Y | Y | Y | N | Y |
| 5 Rogers | Y | Y | Y | N | Y |
| 6 Chandler | Y | Y | N | Y | Y |
| **LOUISIANA** | | | | | |
| 1 Jindal | Y | Y | Y | N | Y |
| 2 Jefferson | Y | Y | N | Y | Y |
| 3 Melancon | Y | Y | N | Y | Y |
| 4 McCrery | Y | Y | Y | N | Y |
| 5 Alexander | Y | Y | Y | N | Y |
| 6 Baker | Y | Y | Y | N | Y |
| 7 Boustany | Y | Y | Y | N | Y |
| **MAINE** | | | | | |
| 1 Allen | Y | Y | N | Y | Y |
| 2 Michaud | Y | Y | N | Y | Y |
| **MARYLAND** | | | | | |
| 1 Gilchrest | Y | Y | Y | N | Y |
| 2 Ruppersberger | Y | Y | N | Y | Y |
| 3 Cardin | Y | Y | N | Y | Y |
| 4 Wynn | Y | Y | N | Y | Y |
| 5 Hoyer | Y | Y | N | Y | Y |
| 6 Bartlett | Y | Y | Y | N | Y |
| 7 Cummings | Y | Y | N | Y | Y |
| 8 Van Hollen | Y | Y | N | Y | Y |
| **MASSACHUSETTS** | | | | | |
| 1 Olver | Y | Y | N | Y | N |
| 2 Neal | Y | Y | N | Y | Y |
| 3 McGovern | Y | Y | N | Y | N |
| 4 Frank | Y | Y | N | Y | N |
| 5 Meehan | Y | Y | N | Y | N |
| 6 Tierney | Y | Y | N | Y | N |
| 7 Markey | Y | Y | N | Y | N |
| 8 Capuano | Y | Y | N | Y | N |
| 9 Lynch | Y | Y | N | Y | Y |
| 10 Delahunt | Y | Y | N | Y | N |
| **MICHIGAN** | | | | | |
| 1 Stupak | Y | Y | N | Y | Y |
| 2 Hoekstra | Y | Y | Y | N | Y |
| 3 Ehlers | Y | Y | Y | N | Y |
| 4 Camp | Y | Y | Y | N | Y |
| 5 Kildee | Y | Y | N | Y | Y |
| 6 Upton | Y | Y | Y | N | Y |
| 7 Schwarz | Y | Y | Y | N | Y |
| 8 Rogers | Y | Y | Y | N | Y |
| 9 Knollenberg | Y | Y | Y | N | Y |
| 10 Miller | Y | Y | Y | N | Y |
| 11 McCotter | Y | Y | Y | N | Y |
| 12 Levin | Y | Y | N | Y | Y |
| 13 Kilpatrick | Y | Y | N | Y | Y |
| 14 Conyers | Y | Y | N | Y | N |
| 15 Dingell | Y | Y | N | Y | Y |

| | 157 | 158 | 159 | 160 | 161 |
|---|---|---|---|---|---|
| **MINNESOTA** | | | | | |
| 1 Gutknecht | Y | Y | Y | N | Y |
| 2 Kline | Y | Y | Y | N | Y |
| 3 Ramstad | Y | Y | Y | N | Y |
| 4 McCollum | Y | Y | N | Y | N |
| 5 Sabo | Y | Y | N | Y | Y |
| 6 Kennedy | Y | Y | Y | N | Y |
| 7 Peterson | Y | Y | N | Y | Y |
| 8 Oberstar | Y | Y | N | Y | N |
| **MISSISSIPPI** | | | | | |
| 1 Wicker | Y | Y | Y | N | Y |
| 2 Thompson | Y | Y | N | Y | Y |
| 3 Pickering | Y | Y | Y | N | Y |
| 4 Taylor | N | Y | N | Y | Y |
| **MISSOURI** | | | | | |
| 1 Clay | Y | Y | ? | Y | N |
| 2 Akin | Y | Y | Y | N | Y |
| 3 Carnahan | Y | Y | N | Y | Y |
| 4 Skelton | Y | Y | N | Y | Y |
| 5 Cleaver | Y | Y | N | Y | Y |
| 6 Graves | Y | Y | Y | N | Y |
| 7 Blunt | Y | Y | Y | N | Y |
| 8 Emerson | Y | Y | Y | N | Y |
| 9 Hulshof | Y | Y | Y | N | Y |
| **MONTANA** | | | | | |
| AL Rehberg | Y | Y | Y | N | Y |
| **NEBRASKA** | | | | | |
| 1 Fortenberry | Y | Y | Y | N | Y |
| 2 Terry | Y | Y | Y | N | Y |
| 3 Osborne | Y | Y | Y | N | Y |
| **NEVADA** | | | | | |
| 1 Berkley | Y | Y | N | Y | Y |
| 2 Gibbons | Y | Y | Y | N | Y |
| 3 Porter | Y | Y | Y | N | Y |
| **NEW HAMPSHIRE** | | | | | |
| 1 Bradley | Y | Y | Y | N | Y |
| 2 Bass | Y | Y | Y | N | Y |
| **NEW JERSEY** | | | | | |
| 1 Andrews | Y | Y | N | Y | Y |
| 2 LoBiondo | Y | Y | Y | N | Y |
| 3 Saxton | Y | Y | Y | N | Y |
| 4 Smith | Y | Y | Y | N | Y |
| 5 Garrett | Y | Y | Y | N | Y |
| 6 Pallone | Y | Y | N | Y | N |
| 7 Ferguson | Y | Y | Y | N | Y |
| 8 Pascrell | Y | Y | N | Y | Y |
| 9 Rothman | Y | Y | N | Y | Y |
| 10 Payne | Y | Y | N | Y | Y |
| 11 Frelinghuysen | Y | Y | N | Y | Y |
| 12 Holt | Y | Y | N | Y | N |
| 13 Menendez | Y | Y | N | Y | Y |
| **NEW MEXICO** | | | | | |
| 1 Wilson | Y | Y | Y | N | Y |
| 2 Pearce | Y | Y | Y | N | Y |
| 3 Udall | Y | Y | N | Y | Y |
| **NEW YORK** | | | | | |
| 1 Bishop | Y | Y | N | Y | Y |
| 2 Israel | Y | Y | N | Y | Y |
| 3 King | Y | Y | Y | N | Y |
| 4 McCarthy | Y | Y | N | Y | Y |
| 5 Ackerman | Y | Y | N | Y | Y |
| 6 Meeks | Y | Y | N | Y | N |
| 7 Crowley | Y | Y | N | Y | Y |
| 8 Nadler | Y | Y | N | Y | Y |
| 9 Weiner | Y | Y | N | Y | N |
| 10 Towns | Y | Y | N | Y | Y |
| 11 Owens | Y | Y | N | Y | Y |
| 12 Velázquez | Y | Y | N | Y | N |
| 13 Fossella | Y | Y | Y | N | Y |
| 14 Maloney | Y | Y | N | Y | Y |
| 15 Rangel | Y | Y | N | Y | N |
| 16 Serrano | Y | Y | N | Y | N |
| 17 Engel | Y | Y | N | Y | Y |
| 18 Lowey | Y | Y | N | Y | Y |
| 19 Kelly | Y | Y | Y | N | Y |
| 20 Sweeney | Y | Y | Y | N | Y |
| 21 McNulty | Y | Y | N | Y | Y |
| 22 Hinchey | Y | Y | N | Y | N |
| 23 McHugh | Y | Y | Y | N | Y |
| 24 Boehlert | Y | Y | Y | N | Y |
| 25 Walsh | Y | Y | Y | N | Y |
| 26 Reynolds | Y | Y | Y | N | Y |
| 27 Higgins | Y | Y | N | Y | Y |
| 28 Slaughter | Y | Y | N | Y | N |
| 29 Kuhl | Y | Y | Y | N | Y |

| | 157 | 158 | 159 | 160 | 161 |
|---|---|---|---|---|---|
| **NORTH CAROLINA** | | | | | |
| 1 Butterfield | Y | Y | N | Y | Y |
| 2 Etheridge | Y | Y | N | Y | Y |
| 3 Jones | Y | Y | Y | Y | Y |
| 4 Price | Y | Y | N | Y | Y |
| 5 Foxx | Y | Y | Y | N | Y |
| 6 Coble | Y | Y | Y | N | N |
| 7 McIntyre | Y | Y | N | Y | Y |
| 8 Hayes | Y | Y | Y | N | Y |
| 9 Myrick | Y | Y | Y | N | Y |
| 10 McHenry | Y | Y | Y | N | Y |
| 11 Taylor | Y | Y | Y | N | Y |
| 12 Watt | Y | Y | N | Y | N |
| 13 Miller | Y | Y | N | Y | Y |
| **NORTH DAKOTA** | | | | | |
| AL Pomeroy | Y | Y | N | Y | Y |
| **OHIO** | | | | | |
| 1 Chabot | Y | Y | Y | N | Y |
| 2 Vacant | | | | | |
| 3 Turner | Y | Y | Y | N | Y |
| 4 Oxley | Y | Y | Y | N | Y |
| 5 Gillmor | Y | Y | Y | N | Y |
| 6 Strickland | Y | Y | N | Y | Y |
| 7 Hobson | Y | Y | Y | N | Y |
| 8 Boehner | Y | Y | Y | N | Y |
| 9 Kaptur | Y | ? | ? | Y | Y |
| 10 Kucinich | Y | Y | N | Y | N |
| 11 Jones | Y | Y | ? | Y | N |
| 12 Tiberi | Y | Y | Y | N | Y |
| 13 Brown | ? | ? | ? | ? | ? |
| 14 LaTourette | Y | Y | Y | N | Y |
| 15 Pryce | Y | Y | Y | N | Y |
| 16 Regula | Y | Y | Y | N | Y |
| 17 Ryan | Y | Y | N | Y | Y |
| 18 Ney | Y | Y | Y | N | Y |
| **OKLAHOMA** | | | | | |
| 1 Sullivan | Y | Y | Y | N | Y |
| 2 Boren | Y | Y | N | Y | Y |
| 3 Lucas | Y | Y | Y | N | Y |
| 4 Cole | Y | Y | Y | N | Y |
| 5 Istook | Y | Y | ? | N | Y |
| **OREGON** | | | | | |
| 1 Wu | Y | Y | N | Y | Y |
| 2 Walden | Y | Y | Y | N | Y |
| 3 Blumenauer | Y | Y | N | Y | N |
| 4 DeFazio | N | Y | N | Y | Y |
| 5 Hooley | Y | Y | N | Y | Y |
| **PENNSYLVANIA** | | | | | |
| 1 Brady | Y | Y | N | Y | Y |
| 2 Fattah | Y | Y | N | Y | Y |
| 3 English | Y | Y | Y | N | Y |
| 4 Hart | Y | Y | Y | N | Y |
| 5 Peterson | Y | Y | Y | N | Y |
| 6 Gerlach | Y | Y | Y | N | Y |
| 7 Weldon | Y | Y | Y | N | Y |
| 8 Fitzpatrick | Y | Y | Y | N | Y |
| 9 Shuster | Y | Y | Y | N | Y |
| 10 Sherwood | Y | Y | Y | N | Y |
| 11 Kanjorski | Y | Y | N | Y | Y |
| 12 Murtha | Y | Y | N | Y | Y |
| 13 Schwartz | Y | Y | N | Y | Y |
| 14 Doyle | Y | Y | N | Y | Y |
| 15 Dent | Y | Y | Y | N | Y |
| 16 Pitts | Y | Y | Y | N | Y |
| 17 Holden | Y | Y | N | Y | Y |
| 18 Murphy | Y | Y | Y | N | Y |
| 19 Platts | Y | Y | ? | N | Y |
| **RHODE ISLAND** | | | | | |
| 1 Kennedy | Y | Y | N | Y | Y |
| 2 Langevin | Y | Y | N | Y | Y |
| **SOUTH CAROLINA** | | | | | |
| 1 Brown | Y | Y | Y | N | Y |
| 2 Wilson | Y | Y | Y | N | Y |
| 3 Barrett | Y | Y | Y | N | Y |
| 4 Inglis | Y | Y | Y | N | Y |
| 5 Spratt | Y | Y | N | Y | Y |
| 6 Clyburn | Y | Y | N | Y | Y |
| **SOUTH DAKOTA** | | | | | |
| AL Herseth | Y | Y | N | Y | Y |
| **TENNESSEE** | | | | | |
| 1 Jenkins | Y | Y | Y | N | Y |
| 2 Duncan | Y | Y | Y | N | N |

| | 157 | 158 | 159 | 160 | 161 |
|---|---|---|---|---|---|
| 3 Wamp | Y | Y | Y | N | Y |
| 4 Davis | Y | Y | N | Y | Y |
| 5 Cooper | N | Y | N | Y | Y |
| 6 Gordon | Y | Y | ? | Y | N |
| 7 Blackburn | Y | Y | Y | N | Y |
| 8 Tanner | Y | Y | N | Y | Y |
| 9 Ford | Y | Y | N | Y | Y |
| **TEXAS** | | | | | |
| 1 Gohmert | Y | Y | Y | N | Y |
| 2 Poe | Y | Y | Y | N | Y |
| 3 Johnson, S. | Y | Y | Y | N | Y |
| 4 Hall | Y | Y | Y | N | Y |
| 5 Hensarling | Y | Y | Y | N | Y |
| 6 Barton | Y | Y | Y | N | Y |
| 7 Culberson | Y | Y | Y | N | Y |
| 8 Brady | Y | Y | Y | N | Y |
| 9 Green | Y | Y | N | Y | Y |
| 10 McCaul | Y | Y | Y | N | Y |
| 11 Conaway | Y | Y | Y | N | Y |
| 12 Granger | Y | Y | Y | N | Y |
| 13 Thornberry | Y | Y | Y | N | Y |
| 14 Paul | N | Y | Y | N | N |
| 15 Hinojosa | Y | Y | N | Y | Y |
| 16 Reyes | Y | Y | N | Y | Y |
| 17 Edwards | Y | Y | N | Y | Y |
| 18 Jackson-Lee | + | + | N | Y | N |
| 19 Neugebauer | Y | Y | Y | N | Y |
| 20 Gonzalez | Y | Y | N | Y | Y |
| 21 Smith | Y | Y | Y | N | Y |
| 22 DeLay | Y | Y | Y | N | Y |
| 23 Bonilla | Y | Y | Y | N | Y |
| 24 Marchant | Y | Y | Y | N | Y |
| 25 Doggett | Y | Y | N | Y | Y |
| 26 Burgess | Y | Y | Y | N | Y |
| 27 Ortiz | Y | Y | N | Y | Y |
| 28 Cuellar | Y | Y | N | Y | Y |
| 29 Green | Y | Y | N | Y | Y |
| 30 Johnson, E. | Y | Y | N | Y | Y |
| 31 Carter | Y | Y | Y | N | Y |
| 32 Sessions | Y | Y | Y | N | Y |
| **UTAH** | | | | | |
| 1 Bishop | Y | Y | Y | N | Y |
| 2 Matheson | Y | Y | N | Y | Y |
| 3 Cannon | Y | Y | Y | N | Y |
| **VERMONT** | | | | | |
| AL Sanders | N | Y | N | Y | N |
| **VIRGINIA** | | | | | |
| 1 Davis, J. | N | Y | Y | N | Y |
| 2 Drake | + | Y | Y | N | Y |
| 3 Scott | ? | ? | N | Y | Y |
| 4 Forbes | Y | Y | Y | N | Y |
| 5 Goode | Y | Y | Y | Y | Y |
| 6 Goodlatte | Y | Y | Y | N | Y |
| 7 Cantor | Y | Y | Y | N | Y |
| 8 Moran | Y | Y | N | Y | Y |
| 9 Boucher | Y | Y | N | Y | Y |
| 10 Wolf | Y | Y | Y | N | Y |
| 11 Davis, T. | Y | Y | Y | N | Y |
| **WASHINGTON** | | | | | |
| 1 Inslee | Y | Y | N | Y | Y |
| 2 Larsen | Y | Y | N | Y | Y |
| 3 Baird | Y | Y | N | Y | Y |
| 4 Hastings | ? | ? | Y | N | Y |
| 5 McMorris | Y | Y | Y | N | Y |
| 6 Dicks | Y | Y | N | Y | Y |
| 7 McDermott | Y | Y | N | Y | N |
| 8 Reichert | Y | Y | Y | N | Y |
| 9 Smith | Y | Y | N | Y | Y |
| **WEST VIRGINIA** | | | | | |
| 1 Mollohan | Y | Y | N | Y | Y |
| 2 Capito | Y | Y | Y | N | Y |
| 3 Rahall | Y | Y | N | Y | Y |
| **WISCONSIN** | | | | | |
| 1 Ryan | Y | Y | Y | N | Y |
| 2 Baldwin | Y | Y | N | Y | N |
| 3 Kind | Y | Y | N | Y | Y |
| 4 Moore | Y | Y | N | Y | N |
| 5 Sensenbrenner | Y | Y | Y | N | Y |
| 6 Petri | Y | Y | Y | N | Y |
| 7 Obey | Y | Y | N | Y | Y |
| 8 Green | Y | Y | Y | N | Y |
| **WYOMING** | | | | | |
| AL Cubin | Y | Y | Y | N | Y |

## IN THE HOUSE | By Vote Number

**162.** **H Res 193. Democracy in Cuba/Adoption.** Ros-Lehtinen, R-Fla., motion to suspend the rules and adopt the resolution that would ask the international community to support the Assembly to Promote the Civil Society in Cuba's mission to bring democracy to that country and would urge the administration and international community to actively oppose any attempts by the Castro regime to repress or punish the organizers of and participants in the assembly. Motion agreed to 392-22: R 223-1; D 169-21 (ND 120-20, SD 49-1); I 0-0. A two-thirds majority of those present and voting (276 in this case) is required for adoption under suspension of the rules. May 10, 2005.

**163.** **H Res 142. Rotary International Tribute/Adoption.** Ros-Lehtinen, R-Fla., motion to suspend the rules and adopt the resolution that would recognize Rotary International on its Feb. 23, 2005, anniversary for 100 years of service throughout the world. Motion agreed to 413-0: R 223-0; D 190-0 (ND 140-0, SD 50-0); I 0-0. A two-thirds majority of those present and voting (276 in this case) is required for adoption under suspension of the rules. May 10, 2005.

**164.** **HR 1279. Gang Deterrence/Previous Question.** Gingrey, R-Ga., motion to order the previous question (thus ending debate and possibility of amendment) on adoption of the rule (H Res 268) to provide for House floor consideration of the bill that would create new federal criminal penalties for crimes committed by gang members and increase criminal penalties for certain violent crimes. Motion agreed to 227-198: R 227-0; D 0-197 (ND 0-148, SD 0-49); I 0-1. (Subsequently, the rule was adopted by voice vote.) May 11, 2005.

**165.** **HR 1279. Gang Deterrence/Illegal Aliens.** Goodlatte, R-Va., amendment that would add five years to any sentence for violent crime or drug trafficking when the offender is an illegal alien. It would add 15 years to a sentence if the alien has previously been deported for criminal offenses and has re-entered the country. Adopted 266-159: R 215-13; D 51-145 (ND 31-117, SD 20-28); I 0-1. May 11, 2005.

**166.** **HR 1279. Gang Deterrence/Gang Membership Study.** Norwood, R-Ga., amendment that would require the Justice and Homeland Security departments to conduct a joint study and report to Congress within one year on the connection between illegal immigration and gang membership. Adopted 395-31: R 229-0; D 165-31 (ND 118-30, SD 47-1); I 1-0. May 11, 2005.

| | 162 | 163 | 164 | 165 | 166 |
|---|---|---|---|---|---|
| **ALABAMA** | | | | | |
| 1 Bonner | Y | Y | Y | Y | Y |
| 2 Everett | Y | Y | Y | Y | Y |
| 3 Rogers | Y | Y | Y | Y | Y |
| 4 Aderholt | Y | Y | Y | Y | Y |
| 5 Cramer | Y | Y | N | Y | Y |
| 6 Bachus | Y | ? | Y | Y | Y |
| 7 Davis | Y | Y | N | N | Y |
| **ALASKA** | | | | | |
| AL Young | Y | Y | Y | Y | Y |
| **ARIZONA** | | | | | |
| 1 Renzi | Y | Y | Y | Y | Y |
| 2 Franks | Y | Y | Y | Y | Y |
| 3 Shadegg | Y | Y | Y | Y | Y |
| 4 Pastor | Y | Y | N | N | Y |
| 5 Hayworth | Y | Y | Y | Y | Y |
| 6 Flake | Y | Y | Y | N | Y |
| 7 Grijalva | Y | Y | N | N | N |
| 8 Kolbe | Y | Y | Y | Y | Y |
| **ARKANSAS** | | | | | |
| 1 Berry | Y | Y | N | Y | Y |
| 2 Snyder | Y | Y | N | Y | Y |
| 3 Boozman | Y | Y | Y | Y | Y |
| 4 Ross | Y | Y | N | Y | Y |
| **CALIFORNIA** | | | | | |
| 1 Thompson | Y | Y | N | N | Y |
| 2 Herger | Y | Y | Y | Y | Y |
| 3 Lungren | Y | Y | Y | Y | Y |
| 4 Doolittle | Y | Y | Y | Y | Y |
| 5 Matsui, D. | Y | Y | N | N | Y |
| 6 Woolsey | N | Y | N | N | Y |
| 7 Miller, George | Y | Y | N | N | Y |
| 8 Pelosi | Y | Y | N | N | Y |
| 9 Lee | N | Y | N | N | N |
| 10 Tauscher | Y | Y | N | Y | Y |
| 11 Pombo | Y | Y | Y | Y | Y |
| 12 Lantos | ? | ? | N | N | Y |
| 13 Stark | N | Y | N | N | N |
| 14 Eshoo | Y | Y | N | N | Y |
| 15 Honda | Y | Y | N | N | N |
| 16 Lofgren | Y | Y | N | N | Y |
| 17 Farr | N | Y | N | N | Y |
| 18 Cardoza | Y | Y | N | Y | Y |
| 19 Radanovich | Y | Y | Y | Y | Y |
| 20 Costa | Y | Y | N | Y | Y |
| 21 Nunes | Y | Y | Y | Y | Y |
| 22 Thomas | Y | Y | Y | Y | Y |
| 23 Capps | Y | Y | N | N | Y |
| 24 Gallegly | Y | Y | Y | Y | Y |
| 25 McKeon | Y | Y | Y | Y | Y |
| 26 Dreier | Y | Y | Y | Y | Y |
| 27 Sherman | Y | Y | N | Y | Y |
| 28 Berman | Y | Y | N | N | Y |
| 29 Schiff | ? | ? | N | Y | Y |
| 30 Waxman | Y | Y | N | N | Y |
| 31 Becerra | Y | Y | N | N | Y |
| 32 Solis | Y | Y | N | N | Y |
| 33 Watson | Y | Y | N | N | Y |
| 34 Roybal-Allard | Y | Y | N | N | Y |
| 35 Waters | N | Y | N | N | Y |
| 36 Harman | Y | Y | N | Y | Y |
| 37 Millender-McD. | ? | ? | ? | ? | ? |
| 38 Napolitano | Y | Y | N | N | Y |
| 39 Sánchez, Linda | Y | Y | N | N | N |
| 40 Royce | Y | Y | Y | Y | Y |
| 41 Lewis | Y | Y | Y | Y | Y |
| 42 Miller, Gary | Y | Y | Y | Y | Y |
| 43 Baca | Y | Y | N | N | Y |
| 44 Calvert | Y | Y | Y | Y | Y |
| 45 Bono | Y | Y | Y | Y | Y |
| 46 Rohrabacher | Y | Y | Y | Y | Y |
| 47 Sanchez, Loretta | Y | Y | N | Y | Y |
| 48 Cox | Y | Y | Y | Y | Y |
| 49 Issa | Y | Y | Y | Y | Y |
| **50 Cunningham** | Y | Y | Y | Y | Y |
| 51 Filner | Y | Y | N | N | N |
| 52 Hunter | Y | Y | Y | Y | Y |
| 53 Davis | Y | Y | N | N | Y |
| **COLORADO** | | | | | |
| 1 DeGette | Y | Y | N | N | Y |
| 2 Udall | Y | Y | N | Y | Y |
| 3 Salazar | Y | Y | N | Y | Y |
| 4 Musgrave | ? | ? | ? | ? | ? |
| 5 Hefley | Y | Y | Y | Y | Y |
| 6 Tancredo | Y | Y | Y | Y | Y |
| 7 Beauprez | Y | Y | Y | Y | Y |
| **CONNECTICUT** | | | | | |
| 1 Larson | + | + | – | – | + |
| 2 Simmons | Y | Y | Y | Y | Y |
| 3 DeLauro | Y | Y | N | N | Y |
| 4 Shays | Y | Y | Y | Y | Y |
| 5 Johnson | Y | Y | Y | Y | Y |
| **DELAWARE** | | | | | |
| AL Castle | Y | Y | Y | N | Y |
| **FLORIDA** | | | | | |
| 1 Miller | Y | Y | Y | Y | Y |
| 2 Boyd | Y | Y | N | Y | Y |
| 3 Brown | Y | Y | N | N | Y |
| 4 Crenshaw | Y | Y | Y | Y | Y |
| 5 Brown-Waite | Y | Y | Y | Y | Y |
| 6 Stearns | Y | Y | Y | Y | Y |
| 7 Mica | Y | Y | Y | Y | Y |
| 8 Keller | ? | Y | Y | Y | Y |
| 9 Bilirakis | Y | Y | Y | Y | Y |
| 10 Young | Y | Y | Y | Y | Y |
| 11 Davis | Y | Y | N | N | Y |
| 12 Putnam | Y | Y | Y | Y | Y |
| 13 Harris | Y | ? | Y | Y | Y |
| 14 Mack | Y | Y | Y | Y | Y |
| 15 Weldon | Y | Y | Y | Y | Y |
| 16 Foley | Y | Y | N | N | Y |
| 17 Meek | Y | Y | N | N | Y |
| 18 Ros-Lehtinen | Y | Y | N | N | Y |
| 19 Wexler | Y | Y | N | N | Y |
| 20 Wasserman-Schultz | Y | Y | N | ? | ? |
| 21 Diaz-Balart, L. | Y | Y | Y | N | Y |
| 22 Shaw | Y | Y | Y | Y | Y |
| 23 Hastings | ? | ? | ? | ? | ? |
| 24 Feeney | Y | Y | Y | Y | Y |
| 25 Diaz-Balart, M. | Y | Y | Y | N | Y |
| **GEORGIA** | | | | | |
| 1 Kingston | Y | Y | Y | Y | Y |
| 2 Bishop | Y | Y | N | Y | Y |
| 3 Marshall | Y | Y | N | Y | Y |
| 4 McKinney | N | Y | N | N | N |
| 5 Lewis | Y | Y | N | N | N |
| 6 Price | Y | Y | Y | Y | Y |
| 7 Linder | Y | Y | Y | Y | Y |
| 8 Westmoreland | Y | Y | Y | Y | Y |
| 9 Norwood | Y | Y | Y | Y | Y |
| 10 Deal | Y | Y | Y | Y | Y |
| 11 Gingrey | Y | Y | Y | Y | Y |
| 12 Barrow | Y | Y | N | Y | Y |
| 13 Scott | Y | Y | N | N | Y |
| **HAWAII** | | | | | |
| 1 Abercrombie | Y | Y | N | Y | N |
| 2 Case | Y | Y | N | Y | Y |
| **IDAHO** | | | | | |
| 1 Otter | ? | ? | Y | Y | Y |
| 2 Simpson | Y | Y | Y | Y | Y |
| **ILLINOIS** | | | | | |
| 1 Rush | Y | Y | N | N | Y |
| 2 Jackson | Y | Y | N | N | Y |
| 3 Lipinski | Y | Y | N | Y | Y |
| 4 Gutierrez | ? | ? | N | N | N |
| 5 Emanuel | Y | Y | N | N | Y |
| 6 Hyde | Y | Y | ? | Y | Y |
| 7 Davis | Y | Y | N | N | N |
| 8 Bean | Y | Y | N | Y | Y |
| 9 Schakowsky | Y | Y | N | N | N |
| 10 Kirk | Y | Y | Y | Y | Y |
| 11 Weller | Y | Y | Y | Y | Y |
| 12 Costello | ? | Y | N | Y | Y |

**KEY**  Republicans  Democrats  *Independents*

| | | |
|---|---|---|
| Y  Voted for (yea) | X  Paired against | C  Voted "present" to avoid possible conflict of interest |
| #  Paired for | –  Announced against | |
| +  Announced for | P  Voted "present" | ?  Did not vote or otherwise make a position known |
| N  Voted against (nay) | | |

| | 162 | 163 | 164 | 165 | 166 |
|---|---|---|---|---|---|
| 13 Biggert | Y | Y | Y | Y | Y |
| 14 Hastert | | | | | |
| 15 Johnson | Y | Y | Y | Y | Y |
| 16 Manzullo | Y | Y | Y | Y | Y |
| 17 Evans | Y | Y | N | N | Y |
| 18 LaHood | Y | Y | Y | Y | Y |
| 19 Shimkus | Y | Y | Y | Y | Y |
| **INDIANA** | | | | | |
| 1 Visclosky | Y | Y | N | N | Y |
| 2 Chocola | Y | Y | Y | Y | Y |
| 3 Souder | Y | Y | Y | Y | Y |
| 4 Buyer | Y | Y | Y | Y | Y |
| 5 Burton | Y | Y | Y | Y | Y |
| 6 Pence | Y | Y | Y | Y | Y |
| 7 Carson | Y | Y | N | N | Y |
| 8 Hostettler | Y | Y | Y | Y | Y |
| 9 Sodrel | Y | Y | Y | Y | Y |
| **IOWA** | | | | | |
| 1 Nussle | Y | Y | Y | Y | Y |
| 2 Leach | Y | Y | Y | N | Y |
| 3 Boswell | Y | Y | N | Y | Y |
| 4 Latham | Y | Y | Y | Y | Y |
| 5 King | Y | Y | Y | Y | Y |
| **KANSAS** | | | | | |
| 1 Moran | Y | Y | Y | Y | Y |
| 2 Ryun | Y | Y | Y | Y | Y |
| 3 Moore | Y | Y | N | Y | Y |
| 4 Tiahrt | Y | Y | Y | Y | Y |
| **KENTUCKY** | | | | | |
| 1 Whitfield | Y | Y | Y | Y | Y |
| 2 Lewis | Y | Y | Y | Y | Y |
| 3 Northup | Y | Y | Y | Y | Y |
| 4 Davis | Y | Y | Y | Y | Y |
| 5 Rogers | Y | Y | Y | Y | Y |
| 6 Chandler | Y | Y | N | Y | Y |
| **LOUISIANA** | | | | | |
| 1 Jindal | Y | Y | Y | Y | Y |
| 2 Jefferson | Y | Y | N | N | Y |
| 3 Melancon | Y | Y | N | N | Y |
| 4 McCrery | Y | Y | Y | Y | Y |
| 5 Alexander | Y | Y | Y | Y | Y |
| 6 Baker | Y | Y | Y | Y | Y |
| 7 Boustany | Y | Y | Y | Y | Y |
| **MAINE** | | | | | |
| 1 Allen | Y | Y | N | N | Y |
| 2 Michaud | Y | Y | N | Y | Y |
| **MARYLAND** | | | | | |
| 1 Gilchrest | Y | ? | Y | Y | Y |
| 2 Ruppersberger | Y | Y | N | Y | Y |
| 3 Cardin | Y | Y | N | N | Y |
| 4 Wynn | Y | Y | N | N | Y |
| 5 Hoyer | Y | Y | N | N | Y |
| 6 Bartlett | Y | Y | Y | Y | Y |
| 7 Cummings | Y | Y | N | N | Y |
| 8 Van Hollen | Y | Y | N | N | Y |
| **MASSACHUSETTS** | | | | | |
| 1 Olver | N | Y | N | N | N |
| 2 Neal | Y | Y | N | N | Y |
| 3 McGovern | Y | Y | N | N | N |
| 4 Frank | Y | ? | N | N | Y |
| 5 Meehan | Y | Y | N | N | Y |
| 6 Tierney | ? | ? | N | N | Y |
| 7 Markey | Y | Y | N | N | Y |
| 8 Capuano | Y | Y | N | N | Y |
| 9 Lynch | Y | Y | N | N | Y |
| 10 Delahunt | Y | Y | N | N | N |
| **MICHIGAN** | | | | | |
| 1 Stupak | Y | Y | N | N | Y |
| 2 Hoekstra | Y | Y | Y | Y | Y |
| 3 Ehlers | Y | Y | Y | Y | Y |
| 4 Camp | Y | Y | Y | Y | Y |
| 5 Kildee | Y | Y | N | N | Y |
| 6 Upton | Y | Y | Y | N | Y |
| 7 Schwarz | Y | Y | Y | Y | Y |
| 8 Rogers | Y | Y | Y | Y | Y |
| 9 Knollenberg | Y | Y | Y | Y | Y |
| 10 Miller | Y | Y | Y | Y | Y |
| 11 McCotter | Y | Y | Y | Y | Y |
| 12 Levin | Y | Y | N | N | Y |
| 13 Kilpatrick | N | Y | N | N | N |
| 14 Conyers | N | ? | N | N | N |
| 15 Dingell | ? | ? | N | N | N |
| **MINNESOTA** | | | | | |
| 1 Gutknecht | Y | Y | Y | Y | Y |
| 2 Kline | Y | Y | Y | Y | Y |
| 3 Ramstad | Y | Y | Y | Y | Y |
| 4 McCollum | Y | Y | N | N | Y |
| 5 Sabo | Y | Y | N | N | Y |
| 6 Kennedy | Y | Y | Y | Y | Y |
| 7 Peterson | Y | Y | N | N | Y |
| 8 Oberstar | Y | Y | N | N | N |
| **MISSISSIPPI** | | | | | |
| 1 Wicker | Y | Y | Y | Y | Y |
| 2 Thompson | Y | Y | N | N | Y |
| 3 Pickering | Y | Y | Y | Y | Y |
| 4 Taylor | Y | Y | Y | N | Y |
| **MISSOURI** | | | | | |
| 1 Clay | Y | Y | N | N | Y |
| 2 Akin | Y | Y | Y | Y | Y |
| 3 Carnahan | Y | Y | N | N | Y |
| 4 Skelton | Y | Y | N | Y | Y |
| 5 Cleaver | Y | Y | N | N | Y |
| 6 Graves | Y | Y | Y | Y | Y |
| 7 Blunt | Y | Y | Y | Y | Y |
| 8 Emerson | Y | Y | Y | Y | Y |
| 9 Hulshof | ? | ? | Y | Y | Y |
| **MONTANA** | | | | | |
| AL Rehberg | Y | Y | Y | Y | Y |
| **NEBRASKA** | | | | | |
| 1 Fortenberry | Y | Y | Y | Y | Y |
| 2 Terry | Y | Y | Y | Y | Y |
| 3 Osborne | Y | Y | Y | Y | Y |
| **NEVADA** | | | | | |
| 1 Berkley | ? | ? | ? | ? | ? |
| 2 Gibbons | Y | Y | Y | Y | Y |
| 3 Porter | Y | Y | Y | Y | Y |
| **NEW HAMPSHIRE** | | | | | |
| 1 Bradley | Y | Y | Y | Y | Y |
| 2 Bass | Y | Y | Y | Y | Y |
| **NEW JERSEY** | | | | | |
| 1 Andrews | Y | Y | N | N | Y |
| 2 LoBiondo | Y | Y | Y | Y | Y |
| 3 Saxton | Y | Y | Y | Y | Y |
| 4 Smith | Y | Y | Y | Y | Y |
| 5 Garrett | Y | Y | Y | Y | Y |
| 6 Pallone | Y | Y | N | N | N |
| 7 Ferguson | ? | Y | Y | Y | Y |
| 8 Pascrell | Y | Y | N | N | Y |
| 9 Rothman | Y | Y | N | N | Y |
| 10 Payne | N | Y | N | N | N |
| 11 Frelinghuysen | Y | Y | Y | Y | Y |
| 12 Holt | Y | Y | N | N | Y |
| 13 Menendez | Y | Y | N | N | Y |
| **NEW MEXICO** | | | | | |
| 1 Wilson | Y | Y | Y | N | Y |
| 2 Pearce | Y | Y | Y | Y | Y |
| 3 Udall | N | Y | N | N | Y |
| **NEW YORK** | | | | | |
| 1 Bishop | Y | Y | N | Y | Y |
| 2 Israel | Y | Y | N | N | Y |
| 3 King | Y | Y | Y | Y | Y |
| 4 McCarthy | Y | Y | N | Y | Y |
| 5 Ackerman | Y | Y | N | N | Y |
| 6 Meeks | N | Y | N | N | Y |
| 7 Crowley | Y | Y | N | N | Y |
| 8 Nadler | Y | Y | N | N | Y |
| 9 Weiner | ? | ? | N | N | Y |
| 10 Towns | N | Y | N | N | Y |
| 11 Owens | Y | Y | N | N | Y |
| 12 Velázquez | N | Y | N | N | Y |
| 13 Fossella | Y | Y | Y | Y | Y |
| 14 Maloney | Y | Y | N | N | Y |
| 15 Rangel | N | Y | N | N | Y |
| 16 Serrano | N | Y | N | N | N |
| 17 Engel | Y | Y | N | N | Y |
| 18 Lowey | Y | Y | N | N | Y |
| 19 Kelly | Y | Y | Y | Y | Y |
| 20 Sweeney | Y | Y | Y | N | Y |
| 21 McNulty | Y | Y | N | N | Y |
| 22 Hinchey | N | Y | N | N | Y |
| 23 McHugh | Y | Y | Y | Y | Y |
| 24 Boehlert | Y | Y | Y | Y | Y |
| 25 Walsh | Y | Y | Y | Y | Y |
| 26 Reynolds | Y | Y | Y | Y | Y |
| 27 Higgins | Y | Y | N | N | Y |
| 28 Slaughter | Y | Y | N | N | Y |
| 29 Kuhl | Y | Y | Y | Y | Y |
| **NORTH CAROLINA** | | | | | |
| 1 Butterfield | Y | Y | N | N | Y |
| 2 Etheridge | Y | Y | N | Y | Y |
| 3 Jones | Y | Y | N | N | Y |
| 4 Price | Y | Y | N | N | Y |
| 5 Foxx | Y | Y | Y | Y | Y |
| 6 Coble | Y | Y | Y | Y | Y |
| 7 McIntyre | Y | Y | N | Y | Y |
| 8 Hayes | Y | Y | Y | Y | Y |
| 9 Myrick | Y | Y | Y | Y | Y |
| 10 McHenry | Y | Y | Y | Y | Y |
| 11 Taylor | Y | Y | Y | Y | Y |
| 12 Watt | Y | Y | N | N | Y |
| 13 Miller | Y | Y | N | N | Y |
| **NORTH DAKOTA** | | | | | |
| AL Pomeroy | Y | Y | N | Y | Y |
| **OHIO** | | | | | |
| 1 Chabot | Y | Y | Y | Y | Y |
| 2 Vacant | | | | | |
| 3 Turner | Y | Y | Y | Y | Y |
| 4 Oxley | Y | Y | Y | Y | Y |
| 5 Gillmor | Y | Y | Y | Y | Y |
| 6 Strickland | Y | Y | N | N | Y |
| 7 Hobson | Y | Y | Y | Y | Y |
| 8 Boehner | Y | Y | Y | Y | Y |
| 9 Kaptur | Y | Y | N | N | Y |
| 10 Kucinich | N | N | N | N | N |
| 11 Jones | N | N | N | N | Y |
| 12 Tiberi | Y | Y | Y | Y | Y |
| 13 Brown | Y | Y | N | N | Y |
| 14 LaTourette | Y | Y | N | N | Y |
| 15 Pryce | Y | Y | Y | Y | Y |
| 16 Regula | Y | Y | Y | Y | Y |
| 17 Ryan | Y | Y | N | N | Y |
| 18 Ney | Y | Y | Y | Y | Y |
| **OKLAHOMA** | | | | | |
| 1 Sullivan | Y | Y | Y | Y | Y |
| 2 Boren | Y | Y | N | Y | Y |
| 3 Lucas | Y | Y | Y | Y | Y |
| 4 Cole | Y | Y | Y | Y | Y |
| 5 Istook | Y | Y | Y | Y | Y |
| **OREGON** | | | | | |
| 1 Wu | Y | Y | N | Y | Y |
| 2 Walden | Y | Y | Y | Y | Y |
| 3 Blumenauer | Y | Y | N | N | Y |
| 4 DeFazio | Y | Y | N | Y | Y |
| 5 Hooley | Y | Y | N | Y | Y |
| **PENNSYLVANIA** | | | | | |
| 1 Brady | Y | Y | N | N | Y |
| 2 Fattah | Y | Y | N | N | Y |
| 3 English | Y | Y | Y | Y | Y |
| 4 Hart | Y | Y | Y | Y | Y |
| 5 Peterson | Y | Y | Y | Y | Y |
| 6 Gerlach | Y | Y | Y | Y | Y |
| 7 Weldon | Y | Y | Y | Y | Y |
| 8 Fitzpatrick | Y | Y | Y | Y | Y |
| 9 Shuster | Y | Y | Y | Y | Y |
| 10 Sherwood | Y | Y | Y | Y | Y |
| 11 Kanjorski | Y | Y | N | N | Y |
| 12 Murtha | Y | Y | N | N | Y |
| 13 Schwartz | Y | Y | N | N | Y |
| 14 Doyle | Y | Y | N | N | Y |
| 15 Dent | Y | Y | Y | Y | Y |
| 16 Pitts | Y | Y | Y | Y | Y |
| 17 Holden | Y | Y | N | Y | Y |
| 18 Murphy | Y | Y | Y | Y | Y |
| 19 Platts | Y | Y | Y | Y | Y |
| **RHODE ISLAND** | | | | | |
| 1 Kennedy | Y | Y | N | N | Y |
| 2 Langevin | Y | Y | N | N | Y |
| **SOUTH CAROLINA** | | | | | |
| 1 Brown | Y | Y | Y | Y | Y |
| 2 Wilson | + | + | Y | Y | Y |
| 3 Barrett | Y | Y | Y | Y | Y |
| 4 Inglis | Y | Y | Y | Y | Y |
| 5 Spratt | Y | Y | N | Y | Y |
| 6 Clyburn | Y | Y | N | N | Y |
| **SOUTH DAKOTA** | | | | | |
| AL Herseth | Y | Y | N | Y | Y |
| **TENNESSEE** | | | | | |
| 1 Jenkins | Y | Y | Y | Y | Y |
| 2 Duncan | Y | Y | Y | Y | Y |
| 3 Wamp | Y | Y | Y | Y | Y |
| 4 Davis | Y | Y | N | N | Y |
| 5 Cooper | Y | Y | N | N | Y |
| 6 Gordon | Y | Y | N | Y | Y |
| 7 Blackburn | Y | Y | Y | Y | Y |
| 8 Tanner | Y | Y | N | N | Y |
| 9 Ford | Y | Y | N | N | Y |
| **TEXAS** | | | | | |
| 1 Gohmert | Y | Y | Y | Y | Y |
| 2 Poe | Y | Y | Y | Y | Y |
| 3 Johnson, S. | Y | Y | Y | Y | Y |
| 4 Hall | Y | Y | Y | Y | Y |
| 5 Hensarling | Y | Y | Y | Y | Y |
| 6 Barton | Y | Y | Y | Y | Y |
| 7 Culberson | Y | Y | Y | Y | Y |
| 8 Brady | Y | Y | Y | Y | Y |
| 9 Green | Y | Y | N | N | Y |
| 10 McCaul | Y | Y | Y | Y | Y |
| 11 Conaway | Y | Y | Y | Y | Y |
| 12 Granger | Y | Y | Y | Y | Y |
| 13 Thornberry | Y | Y | Y | Y | Y |
| 14 Paul | N | Y | Y | N | Y |
| 15 Hinojosa | Y | Y | N | N | Y |
| 16 Reyes | Y | Y | N | N | Y |
| 17 Edwards | Y | Y | N | N | Y |
| 18 Jackson-Lee | Y | Y | N | N | Y |
| 19 Neugebauer | Y | Y | Y | Y | Y |
| 20 Gonzalez | Y | Y | N | N | Y |
| 21 Smith | Y | Y | Y | Y | Y |
| 22 DeLay | Y | Y | Y | Y | Y |
| 23 Bonilla | Y | Y | Y | Y | Y |
| 24 Marchant | Y | Y | Y | Y | Y |
| 25 Doggett | Y | Y | N | N | Y |
| 26 Burgess | Y | Y | Y | Y | Y |
| 27 Ortiz | Y | Y | N | N | Y |
| 28 Cuellar | Y | Y | N | N | Y |
| 29 Green | Y | Y | N | N | Y |
| 30 Johnson, E. | Y | Y | N | N | Y |
| 31 Carter | Y | Y | Y | Y | Y |
| 32 Sessions | Y | Y | Y | Y | Y |
| **UTAH** | | | | | |
| 1 Bishop | Y | Y | Y | ? | Y |
| 2 Matheson | Y | Y | N | Y | Y |
| 3 Cannon | Y | Y | Y | Y | Y |
| **VERMONT** | | | | | |
| AL Sanders | ? | ? | N | N | Y |
| **VIRGINIA** | | | | | |
| 1 Davis, J. | Y | Y | Y | Y | Y |
| 2 Drake | Y | Y | Y | Y | Y |
| 3 Scott | Y | Y | N | N | Y |
| 4 Forbes | Y | Y | Y | Y | Y |
| 5 Goode | Y | Y | ? | Y | Y |
| 6 Goodlatte | Y | Y | Y | Y | Y |
| 7 Cantor | Y | Y | Y | Y | Y |
| 8 Moran | Y | Y | ? | ? | ? |
| 9 Boucher | Y | Y | N | N | Y |
| 10 Wolf | Y | Y | Y | Y | Y |
| 11 Davis, T. | Y | Y | Y | Y | Y |
| **WASHINGTON** | | | | | |
| 1 Inslee | Y | Y | N | N | Y |
| 2 Larsen | Y | Y | N | N | Y |
| 3 Baird | Y | Y | N | N | Y |
| 4 Hastings | Y | Y | Y | Y | Y |
| 5 McMorris | Y | Y | Y | Y | Y |
| 6 Dicks | Y | Y | N | N | Y |
| 7 McDermott | N | Y | N | N | N |
| 8 Reichert | Y | Y | Y | Y | Y |
| 9 Smith | Y | Y | N | N | Y |
| **WEST VIRGINIA** | | | | | |
| 1 Mollohan | Y | Y | N | N | Y |
| 2 Capito | Y | Y | Y | Y | Y |
| 3 Rahall | Y | Y | N | N | Y |
| **WISCONSIN** | | | | | |
| 1 Ryan | Y | Y | Y | Y | Y |
| 2 Baldwin | Y | Y | N | N | N |
| 3 Kind | Y | Y | N | N | Y |
| 4 Moore | P | Y | N | N | N |
| 5 Sensenbrenner | Y | Y | Y | Y | Y |
| 6 Petri | Y | Y | Y | Y | Y |
| 7 Obey | Y | Y | N | N | Y |
| 8 Green | Y | Y | Y | Y | Y |
| **WYOMING** | | | | | |
| AL Cubin | Y | Y | Y | Y | Y |

# IN THE HOUSE | By Vote Number

**167. HR 1279. Gang Deterrence/Recommit.** Tierney, D-Mass., motion to recommit the bill to the House Judiciary Committee with instructions to include language that would prohibit profiteering and fraud in connection with the war and reconstruction efforts in Iraq. Motion rejected 198-227: R 2-227; D 195-0 (ND 147-0, SD 48-0); I 1-0. May 11, 2005.

**168. HR 1279. Gang Deterrence/Passage.** Passage of the bill that would increase penalties for crimes committed by "criminal street gangs." Certain gang-related offenses would be subject to mandatory minimum sentences, including 30 years or more in prison for cases of kidnapping, aggravated sexual assault or maiming. It would authorize $438 million over five years for federal, state and local law enforcement efforts against violent gangs and for law enforcement efforts to share intelligence and jointly investigate violent gangs. The bill would also add 94 assistant U.S. attorneys, 100 inspectors and 100 agents to work on gang activity. Passed 279-144: R 208-20; D 71-123 (ND 44-102, SD 27-21); I 0-1. May 11, 2005.

**169. HR 1544. First-Responder Funding/Urban Area Security Initiative.** Weiner, D-N.Y., amendment that would limit to 50 the number of grants provided under the Urban Area Security Initiative. Rejected 88-331: R 0-228; D 88-102 (ND 80-60, SD 8-42); I 0-1. May 12, 2005.

**170. HR 1544. First-Responder Funding/Passage.** Passage of the bill that would change the distribution of certain first-responder grants provided by the Homeland Security Department to require that grants be distributed primarily based on threat levels. Each state would be guaranteed at least 0.25 percent of the total funding available, or 0.45 percent for states that have an international border or that are on a body of water with an international border. It also would require state governments to develop three-year homeland security plans for enhancing their preparedness and response capabilities. Passed 409-10: R 227-1; D 181-9 (ND 134-6, SD 47-3); I 1-0. May 12, 2005.

| | 167 | 168 | 169 | 170 |
|---|---|---|---|---|
| **ALABAMA** | | | | |
| 1 Bonner | N | Y | N | Y |
| 2 Everett | N | Y | N | Y |
| 3 Rogers | N | Y | N | Y |
| 4 Aderholt | N | Y | N | Y |
| 5 Cramer | Y | Y | N | Y |
| 6 Bachus | N | Y | N | Y |
| 7 Davis | Y | Y | N | N |
| **ALASKA** | | | | |
| AL Young | N | Y | N | Y |
| **ARIZONA** | | | | |
| 1 Renzi | N | Y | N | Y |
| 2 Franks | N | Y | N | Y |
| 3 Shadegg | N | N | N | Y |
| 4 Pastor | Y | N | N | Y |
| 5 Hayworth | N | Y | N | Y |
| 6 Flake | N | N | N | Y |
| 7 Grijalva | Y | N | N | Y |
| 8 Kolbe | N | Y | N | Y |
| **ARKANSAS** | | | | |
| 1 Berry | Y | Y | N | N |
| 2 Snyder | Y | N | N | Y |
| 3 Boozman | N | Y | N | Y |
| 4 Ross | Y | Y | N | N |
| **CALIFORNIA** | | | | |
| 1 Thompson | Y | N | N | Y |
| 2 Herger | N | Y | N | Y |
| 3 Lungren | N | Y | N | Y |
| 4 Doolittle | N | Y | N | Y |
| 5 Matsui, D. | Y | N | N | Y |
| 6 Woolsey | Y | N | Y | Y |
| 7 Miller, George | Y | N | Y | Y |
| 8 Pelosi | Y | N | Y | Y |
| 9 Lee | Y | N | Y | Y |
| 10 Tauscher | Y | N | N | Y |
| 11 Pombo | N | Y | N | Y |
| 12 Lantos | Y | Y | Y | Y |
| 13 Stark | Y | N | Y | Y |
| 14 Eshoo | Y | N | Y | Y |
| 15 Honda | Y | N | ? | Y |
| 16 Lofgren | Y | N | N | Y |
| 17 Farr | Y | N | Y | Y |
| 18 Cardoza | Y | Y | N | Y |
| 19 Radanovich | N | Y | N | Y |
| 20 Costa | Y | Y | N | Y |
| 21 Nunes | N | Y | N | Y |
| 22 Thomas | N | Y | N | Y |
| 23 Capps | Y | N | Y | Y |
| 24 Gallegly | N | Y | N | Y |
| 25 McKeon | N | Y | N | Y |
| 26 Dreier | N | Y | N | Y |
| 27 Sherman | Y | N | Y | Y |
| 28 Berman | Y | N | ? | ? |
| 29 Schiff | Y | N | Y | Y |
| 30 Waxman | Y | N | ? | ? |
| 31 Becerra | Y | N | ? | ? |
| 32 Solis | Y | N | + | + |
| 33 Watson | Y | Y | ? | ? |
| 34 Roybal-Allard | Y | N | ? | ? |
| 35 Waters | Y | N | Y | Y |
| 36 Harman | Y | Y | N | Y |
| 37 Millender-McD. | ? | ? | ? | ? |
| 38 Napolitano | Y | N | Y | Y |
| 39 Sánchez, Linda | Y | N | N | Y |
| 40 Royce | N | Y | N | Y |
| 41 Lewis | N | Y | N | Y |
| 42 Miller, Gary | N | Y | N | Y |
| 43 Baca | Y | Y | N | Y |
| 44 Calvert | N | Y | N | Y |
| 45 Bono | N | Y | N | Y |
| 46 Rohrabacher | N | Y | N | Y |
| 47 Sanchez, Loretta | Y | N | – | + |
| 48 Cox | N | Y | N | Y |
| 49 Issa | N | Y | N | Y |

| | 167 | 168 | 169 | 170 |
|---|---|---|---|---|
| 50 Cunningham | N | Y | N | Y |
| 51 Filner | Y | N | Y | Y |
| 52 Hunter | N | Y | N | Y |
| 53 Davis | Y | N | Y | Y |
| **COLORADO** | | | | |
| 1 DeGette | Y | N | N | Y |
| 2 Udall | Y | N | Y | Y |
| 3 Salazar | Y | Y | N | Y |
| 4 Musgrave | ? | ? | ? | ? |
| 5 Hefley | N | Y | N | Y |
| 6 Tancredo | N | Y | N | Y |
| 7 Beauprez | N | Y | N | Y |
| **CONNECTICUT** | | | | |
| 1 Larson | + | – | – | + |
| 2 Simmons | N | Y | N | Y |
| 3 DeLauro | Y | N | N | Y |
| 4 Shays | N | Y | N | Y |
| 5 Johnson | N | Y | N | Y |
| **DELAWARE** | | | | |
| AL Castle | N | Y | N | Y |
| **FLORIDA** | | | | |
| 1 Miller | N | Y | N | Y |
| 2 Boyd | Y | Y | N | Y |
| 3 Brown | Y | N | N | Y |
| 4 Crenshaw | N | Y | N | Y |
| 5 Brown-Waite | N | Y | N | Y |
| 6 Stearns | N | Y | N | Y |
| 7 Mica | N | Y | N | Y |
| 8 Keller | N | Y | N | Y |
| 9 Bilirakis | N | Y | N | Y |
| 10 Young | N | Y | N | Y |
| 11 Davis | Y | N | N | Y |
| 12 Putnam | N | Y | N | Y |
| 13 Harris | N | Y | N | Y |
| 14 Mack | N | Y | N | Y |
| 15 Weldon | N | Y | N | Y |
| 16 Foley | N | Y | N | Y |
| 17 Meek | Y | N | Y | Y |
| 18 Ros-Lehtinen | N | Y | N | Y |
| 19 Wexler | Y | N | N | Y |
| 20 Wasserman-Schultz | ? | ? | N | Y |
| 21 Diaz-Balart, L. | N | Y | N | Y |
| 22 Shaw | N | Y | N | Y |
| 23 Hastings | ? | ? | ? | ? |
| 24 Feeney | N | ? | N | Y |
| 25 Diaz-Balart, M. | N | Y | N | Y |
| **GEORGIA** | | | | |
| 1 Kingston | N | Y | ? | ? |
| 2 Bishop | Y | Y | N | Y |
| 3 Marshall | Y | Y | N | Y |
| 4 McKinney | Y | N | N | Y |
| 5 Lewis | Y | N | Y | Y |
| 6 Price | N | Y | N | Y |
| 7 Linder | N | Y | N | Y |
| 8 Westmoreland | N | Y | N | Y |
| 9 Norwood | N | Y | N | Y |
| 10 Deal | N | Y | N | Y |
| 11 Gingrey | N | Y | N | Y |
| 12 Barrow | Y | Y | N | Y |
| 13 Scott | Y | Y | Y | Y |
| **HAWAII** | | | | |
| 1 Abercrombie | Y | N | Y | Y |
| 2 Case | Y | Y | N | Y |
| **IDAHO** | | | | |
| 1 Otter | N | Y | N | Y |
| 2 Simpson | N | Y | N | Y |
| **ILLINOIS** | | | | |
| 1 Rush | Y | N | Y | Y |
| 2 Jackson | Y | N | Y | Y |
| 3 Lipinski | Y | Y | Y | Y |
| 4 Gutierrez | Y | N | Y | Y |
| 5 Emanuel | Y | Y | Y | Y |
| 6 Hyde | N | Y | N | Y |
| 7 Davis | Y | N | Y | Y |
| 8 Bean | Y | Y | Y | Y |
| 9 Schakowsky | Y | N | Y | Y |
| 10 Kirk | N | Y | N | Y |
| 11 Weller | N | Y | N | Y |
| 12 Costello | Y | Y | Y | Y |

| | | 167 | 168 | 169 | 170 |
|---|---|---|---|---|---|
| 13 | Biggert | N | Y | N | Y |
| 14 | Hastert | | | | |
| 15 | Johnson | N | Y | N | Y |
| 16 | Manzullo | N | N | N | Y |
| 17 | Evans | Y | ? | N | Y |
| 18 | LaHood | N | Y | N | Y |
| 19 | Shimkus | N | Y | N | Y |
| **INDIANA** | | | | | |
| 1 | Visclosky | Y | Y | N | Y |
| 2 | Chocola | N | Y | N | Y |
| 3 | Souder | N | Y | N | Y |
| 4 | Buyer | N | Y | N | Y |
| 5 | Burton | N | Y | N | Y |
| 6 | Pence | N | Y | N | Y |
| 7 | Carson | Y | N | N | Y |
| 8 | Hostettler | N | N | N | Y |
| 9 | Sodrel | N | Y | N | Y |
| **IOWA** | | | | | |
| 1 | Nussle | N | Y | N | Y |
| 2 | Leach | Y | Y | N | Y |
| 3 | Boswell | Y | Y | N | Y |
| 4 | Latham | N | Y | N | Y |
| 5 | King | N | Y | N | Y |
| **KANSAS** | | | | | |
| 1 | Moran | N | Y | N | Y |
| 2 | Ryun | N | Y | N | Y |
| 3 | Moore | Y | Y | Y | Y |
| 4 | Tiahrt | N | Y | N | Y |
| **KENTUCKY** | | | | | |
| 1 | Whitfield | N | Y | N | Y |
| 2 | Lewis | N | Y | N | Y |
| 3 | Northup | N | Y | N | Y |
| 4 | Davis | N | Y | N | Y |
| 5 | Rogers | N | Y | N | Y |
| 6 | Chandler | Y | Y | N | Y |
| **LOUISIANA** | | | | | |
| 1 | Jindal | N | Y | N | Y |
| 2 | Jefferson | Y | N | Y | Y |
| 3 | Melancon | Y | Y | Y | Y |
| 4 | McCrery | N | Y | N | Y |
| 5 | Alexander | N | Y | N | Y |
| 6 | Baker | N | Y | N | Y |
| 7 | Boustany | N | Y | N | Y |
| **MAINE** | | | | | |
| 1 | Allen | Y | N | N | N |
| 2 | Michaud | Y | N | N | N |
| **MARYLAND** | | | | | |
| 1 | Gilchrest | N | Y | N | Y |
| 2 | Ruppersberger | Y | Y | Y | Y |
| 3 | Cardin | Y | Y | Y | Y |
| 4 | Wynn | Y | Y | N | Y |
| 5 | Hoyer | Y | Y | Y | Y |
| 6 | Bartlett | N | N | N | Y |
| 7 | Cummings | Y | N | N | Y |
| 8 | Van Hollen | Y | Y | Y | Y |
| **MASSACHUSETTS** | | | | | |
| 1 | Olver | Y | N | Y | Y |
| 2 | Neal | Y | N | Y | Y |
| 3 | McGovern | Y | N | Y | Y |
| 4 | Frank | Y | N | Y | Y |
| 5 | Meehan | Y | N | Y | Y |
| 6 | Tierney | Y | N | Y | Y |
| 7 | Markey | Y | N | Y | Y |
| 8 | Capuano | Y | N | Y | Y |
| 9 | Lynch | Y | N | Y | Y |
| 10 | Delahunt | Y | N | Y | Y |
| **MICHIGAN** | | | | | |
| 1 | Stupak | Y | Y | N | Y |
| 2 | Hoekstra | N | Y | N | Y |
| 3 | Ehlers | N | N | N | Y |
| 4 | Camp | N | Y | N | Y |
| 5 | Kildee | Y | N | N | Y |
| 6 | Upton | N | Y | N | Y |
| 7 | Schwarz | N | Y | N | Y |
| 8 | Rogers | N | Y | N | Y |
| 9 | Knollenberg | N | Y | N | Y |
| 10 | Miller | N | Y | N | Y |
| 11 | McCotter | N | Y | N | Y |
| 12 | Levin | Y | N | N | Y |
| 13 | Kilpatrick | Y | N | N | Y |
| 14 | Conyers | Y | N | N | Y |
| 15 | Dingell | Y | N | N | Y |

| | | 167 | 168 | 169 | 170 |
|---|---|---|---|---|---|
| **MINNESOTA** | | | | | |
| 1 | Gutknecht | N | N | N | Y |
| 2 | Kline | N | Y | N | Y |
| 3 | Ramstad | N | Y | N | Y |
| 4 | McCollum | Y | N | N | Y |
| 5 | Sabo | Y | N | Y | N |
| 6 | Kennedy | N | Y | N | Y |
| 7 | Peterson | Y | Y | N | Y |
| 8 | Oberstar | Y | N | N | Y |
| **MISSISSIPPI** | | | | | |
| 1 | Wicker | N | Y | N | Y |
| 2 | Thompson | Y | N | N | Y |
| 3 | Pickering | N | Y | N | Y |
| 4 | Taylor | Y | Y | N | Y |
| **MISSOURI** | | | | | |
| 1 | Clay | Y | N | Y | Y |
| 2 | Akin | N | Y | N | Y |
| 3 | Carnahan | Y | N | Y | Y |
| 4 | Skelton | Y | Y | Y | Y |
| 5 | Cleaver | Y | N | Y | Y |
| 6 | Graves | N | Y | N | Y |
| 7 | Blunt | N | Y | N | Y |
| 8 | Emerson | N | Y | N | Y |
| 9 | Hulshof | N | Y | N | Y |
| **MONTANA** | | | | | |
| AL | Rehberg | N | Y | N | Y |
| **NEBRASKA** | | | | | |
| 1 | Fortenberry | N | Y | N | Y |
| 2 | Terry | N | Y | N | Y |
| 3 | Osborne | N | Y | N | Y |
| **NEVADA** | | | | | |
| 1 | Berkley | ? | ? | ? | ? |
| 2 | Gibbons | N | Y | N | Y |
| 3 | Porter | N | Y | N | Y |
| **NEW HAMPSHIRE** | | | | | |
| 1 | Bradley | N | Y | N | Y |
| 2 | Bass | N | Y | N | Y |
| **NEW JERSEY** | | | | | |
| 1 | Andrews | Y | N | Y | Y |
| 2 | LoBiondo | N | Y | N | Y |
| 3 | Saxton | N | Y | N | Y |
| 4 | Smith | N | Y | N | Y |
| 5 | Garrett | N | N | N | Y |
| 6 | Pallone | Y | N | Y | Y |
| 7 | Ferguson | N | Y | N | Y |
| 8 | Pascrell | Y | Y | N | Y |
| 9 | Rothman | Y | N | Y | Y |
| 10 | Payne | Y | N | Y | Y |
| 11 | Frelinghuysen | N | Y | N | Y |
| 12 | Holt | Y | N | Y | Y |
| 13 | Menendez | Y | N | Y | Y |
| **NEW MEXICO** | | | | | |
| 1 | Wilson | N | Y | N | Y |
| 2 | Pearce | N | Y | N | Y |
| 3 | Udall | Y | N | N | Y |
| **NEW YORK** | | | | | |
| 1 | Bishop | Y | Y | Y | Y |
| 2 | Israel | Y | Y | Y | Y |
| 3 | King | Y | Y | N | Y |
| 4 | McCarthy | Y | Y | N | Y |
| 5 | Ackerman | Y | N | Y | Y |
| 6 | Meeks | ? | ? | Y | Y |
| 7 | Crowley | Y | N | Y | Y |
| 8 | Nadler | Y | N | Y | Y |
| 9 | Weiner | Y | N | Y | Y |
| 10 | Towns | Y | N | Y | Y |
| 11 | Owens | Y | N | Y | Y |
| 12 | Velázquez | Y | N | Y | Y |
| 13 | Fossella | N | Y | N | Y |
| 14 | Maloney | Y | N | Y | Y |
| 15 | Rangel | Y | N | Y | Y |
| 16 | Serrano | Y | N | Y | Y |
| 17 | Engel | Y | N | Y | Y |
| 18 | Lowey | Y | N | Y | Y |
| 19 | Kelly | N | Y | N | Y |
| 20 | Sweeney | N | N | N | Y |
| 21 | McNulty | Y | N | Y | Y |
| 22 | Hinchey | Y | N | Y | Y |
| 23 | McHugh | N | Y | N | Y |
| 24 | Boehlert | N | Y | N | Y |
| 25 | Walsh | N | Y | N | Y |
| 26 | Reynolds | N | Y | N | Y |
| 27 | Higgins | Y | Y | Y | Y |
| 28 | Slaughter | Y | Y | Y | Y |
| 29 | Kuhl | N | Y | N | Y |

| | | 167 | 168 | 169 | 170 |
|---|---|---|---|---|---|
| **NORTH CAROLINA** | | | | | |
| 1 | Butterfield | Y | N | N | Y |
| 2 | Etheridge | Y | Y | N | Y |
| 3 | Jones | Y | N | N | Y |
| 4 | Price | Y | N | N | Y |
| 5 | Foxx | N | Y | N | Y |
| 6 | Coble | N | Y | N | Y |
| 7 | McIntyre | Y | Y | N | Y |
| 8 | Hayes | N | Y | N | Y |
| 9 | Myrick | N | Y | N | Y |
| 10 | McHenry | N | Y | N | Y |
| 11 | Taylor | N | Y | N | Y |
| 12 | Watt | Y | N | N | Y |
| 13 | Miller | Y | Y | N | Y |
| **NORTH DAKOTA** | | | | | |
| AL | Pomeroy | Y | Y | N | Y |
| **OHIO** | | | | | |
| 1 | Chabot | N | Y | N | Y |
| 2 | Vacant | | | | |
| 3 | Turner | N | Y | N | Y |
| 4 | Oxley | N | Y | N | Y |
| 5 | Gillmor | N | Y | N | Y |
| 6 | Strickland | Y | N | N | Y |
| 7 | Hobson | N | Y | N | Y |
| 8 | Boehner | N | Y | N | Y |
| 9 | Kaptur | Y | Y | N | Y |
| 10 | Kucinich | Y | N | N | Y |
| 11 | Jones | Y | N | N | Y |
| 12 | Tiberi | N | Y | N | Y |
| 13 | Brown | Y | N | N | Y |
| 14 | LaTourette | N | N | N | Y |
| 15 | Pryce | N | Y | N | Y |
| 16 | Regula | N | Y | N | Y |
| 17 | Ryan | Y | Y | N | Y |
| 18 | Ney | N | Y | N | Y |
| **OKLAHOMA** | | | | | |
| 1 | Sullivan | N | Y | N | Y |
| 2 | Boren | Y | Y | N | Y |
| 3 | Lucas | N | Y | N | Y |
| 4 | Cole | N | Y | N | Y |
| 5 | Istook | N | Y | N | Y |
| **OREGON** | | | | | |
| 1 | Wu | Y | Y | Y | Y |
| 2 | Walden | N | Y | N | Y |
| 3 | Blumenauer | Y | N | Y | Y |
| 4 | DeFazio | Y | Y | N | Y |
| 5 | Hooley | Y | Y | N | Y |
| **PENNSYLVANIA** | | | | | |
| 1 | Brady | Y | N | Y | Y |
| 2 | Fattah | Y | N | Y | Y |
| 3 | English | N | Y | N | Y |
| 4 | Hart | N | Y | N | Y |
| 5 | Peterson | N | Y | N | Y |
| 6 | Gerlach | N | Y | N | Y |
| 7 | Weldon | N | Y | N | Y |
| 8 | Fitzpatrick | N | Y | N | Y |
| 9 | Shuster | N | Y | N | Y |
| 10 | Sherwood | N | N | N | Y |
| 11 | Kanjorski | Y | Y | N | Y |
| 12 | Murtha | Y | Y | N | Y |
| 13 | Schwartz | Y | Y | Y | Y |
| 14 | Doyle | Y | Y | Y | Y |
| 15 | Dent | N | Y | N | Y |
| 16 | Pitts | N | N | N | Y |
| 17 | Holden | Y | Y | N | Y |
| 18 | Murphy | N | Y | N | Y |
| 19 | Platts | N | Y | N | Y |
| **RHODE ISLAND** | | | | | |
| 1 | Kennedy | Y | N | N | Y |
| 2 | Langevin | Y | Y | N | Y |
| **SOUTH CAROLINA** | | | | | |
| 1 | Brown | N | Y | N | Y |
| 2 | Wilson | N | Y | N | Y |
| 3 | Barrett | N | Y | N | Y |
| 4 | Inglis | N | N | N | Y |
| 5 | Spratt | Y | Y | N | Y |
| 6 | Clyburn | Y | N | N | Y |
| **SOUTH DAKOTA** | | | | | |
| AL | Herseth | Y | Y | N | N |
| **TENNESSEE** | | | | | |
| 1 | Jenkins | N | Y | N | Y |
| 2 | Duncan | N | N | N | Y |

| | | 167 | 168 | 169 | 170 |
|---|---|---|---|---|---|
| 3 | Wamp | N | N | N | Y |
| 4 | Davis | Y | Y | N | Y |
| 5 | Cooper | Y | Y | N | Y |
| 6 | Gordon | Y | Y | N | Y |
| 7 | Blackburn | N | Y | N | Y |
| 8 | Tanner | Y | N | N | Y |
| 9 | Ford | Y | Y | N | Y |
| **TEXAS** | | | | | |
| 1 | Gohmert | N | Y | N | Y |
| 2 | Poe | N | Y | N | Y |
| 3 | Johnson, S. | N | Y | N | Y |
| 4 | Hall | N | Y | N | Y |
| 5 | Hensarling | N | N | N | Y |
| 6 | Barton | N | Y | N | Y |
| 7 | Culberson | N | Y | N | Y |
| 8 | Brady | N | Y | N | Y |
| 9 | Green | Y | N | Y | Y |
| 10 | McCaul | N | Y | N | Y |
| 11 | Conaway | N | Y | N | Y |
| 12 | Granger | N | Y | N | Y |
| 13 | Thornberry | N | Y | N | Y |
| 14 | Paul | N | N | N | Y |
| 15 | Hinojosa | Y | N | N | Y |
| 16 | Reyes | Y | Y | N | Y |
| 17 | Edwards | Y | Y | N | Y |
| 18 | Jackson-Lee | Y | N | N | Y |
| 19 | Neugebauer | N | Y | N | Y |
| 20 | Gonzalez | Y | Y | N | Y |
| 21 | Smith | N | Y | N | Y |
| 22 | DeLay | N | Y | N | Y |
| 23 | Bonilla | N | Y | N | Y |
| 24 | Marchant | N | Y | N | Y |
| 25 | Doggett | Y | N | N | Y |
| 26 | Burgess | N | Y | N | Y |
| 27 | Ortiz | Y | Y | N | Y |
| 28 | Cuellar | Y | Y | N | Y |
| 29 | Green | Y | N | Y | Y |
| 30 | Johnson, E. | Y | N | Y | Y |
| 31 | Carter | N | Y | N | Y |
| 32 | Sessions | N | Y | N | Y |
| **UTAH** | | | | | |
| 1 | Bishop | N | Y | N | Y |
| 2 | Matheson | Y | Y | N | Y |
| 3 | Cannon | N | Y | N | Y |
| **VERMONT** | | | | | |
| AL | *Sanders* | Y | N | N | Y |
| **VIRGINIA** | | | | | |
| 1 | Davis, J. | N | Y | N | Y |
| 2 | Drake | N | Y | N | Y |
| 3 | Scott | Y | N | N | Y |
| 4 | Forbes | N | Y | N | Y |
| 5 | Goode | N | Y | N | Y |
| 6 | Goodlatte | N | Y | N | Y |
| 7 | Cantor | N | Y | N | Y |
| 8 | Moran | ? | ? | Y | Y |
| 9 | Boucher | Y | Y | N | Y |
| 10 | Wolf | N | Y | N | Y |
| 11 | Davis, T. | N | Y | N | Y |
| **WASHINGTON** | | | | | |
| 1 | Inslee | Y | N | Y | Y |
| 2 | Larsen | Y | N | N | Y |
| 3 | Baird | Y | N | N | Y |
| 4 | Hastings | N | Y | N | Y |
| 5 | McMorris | N | Y | N | Y |
| 6 | Dicks | Y | N | N | Y |
| 7 | McDermott | Y | N | Y | N |
| 8 | Reichert | N | Y | N | Y |
| 9 | Smith | Y | N | N | Y |
| **WEST VIRGINIA** | | | | | |
| 1 | Mollohan | Y | N | N | Y |
| 2 | Capito | N | Y | N | Y |
| 3 | Rahall | Y | N | N | Y |
| **WISCONSIN** | | | | | |
| 1 | Ryan | N | Y | N | Y |
| 2 | Baldwin | Y | N | N | Y |
| 3 | Kind | Y | N | N | Y |
| 4 | Moore | Y | N | N | Y |
| 5 | Sensenbrenner | N | Y | N | Y |
| 6 | Petri | N | Y | N | Y |
| 7 | Obey | Y | N | N | Y |
| 8 | Green | N | Y | N | Y |
| **WYOMING** | | | | | |
| AL | Cubin | N | N | N | N |

# IN THE HOUSE | By Vote Number

**171.** **HR 627. Linda White-Epps Post Office/Passage.** Miller, R-Mich., motion to suspend the rules and pass the bill that would name a post office in Hamden, Conn., for Linda White-Epps, who founded the cancer-survivor support group "Sisters' Journey" in Connecticut. Motion agreed to 390-0: R 213-0; D 176-0 (ND 134-0, SD 42-0); I 1-0. A two-thirds majority of those present and voting (260 in this case) is required for passage under suspension of the rules. May 16, 2005.

**172.** **H Res 266. Peace Officers Memorial Day/Adoption.** Miller, R-Mich., motion to suspend the rules and adopt the resolution that would support the goals and ideals of Peace Officers Memorial Day and ask the public to observe the day with appropriate ceremonies and respect. Motion agreed to 391-0: R 213-0; D 177-0 (ND 135-0, SD 42-0); I 1-0. A two-thirds majority of those present and voting (261 in this case) is required for adoption under suspension of the rules. May 16, 2005.

**173.** **HR 2107. Law Enforcement Officers Memorial Fund/Passage.** Renzi, R-Ariz., motion to suspend the rules and pass the bill that would transfer control of the National Law Enforcement Memorial Maintenance Fund from the National Park Service to the National Law Enforcement Officers Memorial Fund Inc., a nonprofit corporation that operates and maintains the National Law Enforcement Officers Memorial. Motion agreed to 392-0: R 214-0; D 177-0 (ND 135-0, SD 42-0); I 1-0. A two-thirds majority of those present and voting (262 in this case) is required for passage under suspension of the rules. May 16, 2005.

**174.** **HR 2360. Fiscal 2006 Homeland Security Appropriations/Previous Question.** Sessions, R-Texas, motion to order the previous question (thus ending debate and possibility of further amendment) on adoption of the rule (H Res 278) to provide for House floor consideration of the bill that would appropriate $31.9 billion in fiscal 2006 for the Department of Homeland Security. Motion agreed to 223-185: R 223-0; D 0-184 (ND 0-134, SD 0-50); I 0-1. May 17, 2005.

**175.** **HR 2360. Fiscal 2006 Homeland Security Appropriations/Rule.** Adoption of the rule (H Res 278), as amended, to provide for House floor consideration of the bill that would appropriate $31.9 billion in fiscal 2006 for the Department of Homeland Security. Adopted 222-185: R 221-1; D 1-183 (ND 1-134, SD 0-49); I 0-1. May 17, 2005.

**176.** **HR 2360. Fiscal 2006 Homeland Security Appropriations/Chemical Plant Security.** Menendez, D-N.J., amendment that would increase funding by $50 million for state and local grant programs to improve security of chemical plants. The amendment would be offset by a $50 million cut to the Office of the Undersecretary for Management. Adopted 225-198: R 35-193; D 189-5 (ND 142-3, SD 47-2); I 1-0. May 17, 2005.

**177.** **HR 2360. Fiscal 2006 Homeland Security Appropriations/Immigration.** Tancredo, R-Colo., amendment that would prohibit the use of funds to assist state or local governments that have restrictions on exchanging information with the Bureau of Immigration and Customs Enforcement on an individual's citizenship or immigration status. Rejected 165-258: R 163-65; D 2-192 (ND 0-145, SD 2-47); I 0-1. May 17, 2005.

| | 171 | 172 | 173 | 174 | 175 | 176 | 177 |
|---|---|---|---|---|---|---|---|
| **ALABAMA** | | | | | | | |
| 1 Bonner | Y | Y | Y | Y | Y | N | Y |
| 2 Everett | Y | Y | Y | Y | Y | N | Y |
| 3 Rogers | Y | Y | Y | Y | Y | N | Y |
| 4 Aderholt | Y | Y | Y | Y | Y | N | Y |
| 5 Cramer | Y | Y | Y | N | N | Y | N |
| 6 Bachus | Y | Y | Y | Y | Y | N | Y |
| 7 Davis | ? | ? | ? | N | N | Y | N |
| **ALASKA** | | | | | | | |
| AL Young | Y | Y | Y | Y | Y | N | N |
| **ARIZONA** | | | | | | | |
| 1 Renzi | Y | Y | Y | Y | Y | N | Y |
| 2 Franks | Y | Y | Y | Y | Y | N | Y |
| 3 Shadegg | Y | Y | Y | Y | Y | N | Y |
| 4 Pastor | Y | Y | Y | N | N | Y | N |
| 5 Hayworth | Y | Y | Y | Y | Y | N | Y |
| 6 Flake | Y | Y | Y | Y | Y | N | Y |
| 7 Grijalva | Y | Y | Y | N | N | Y | N |
| 8 Kolbe | Y | Y | Y | Y | Y | N | Y |
| **ARKANSAS** | | | | | | | |
| 1 Berry | Y | Y | Y | N | N | Y | N |
| 2 Snyder | Y | Y | Y | N | N | Y | N |
| 3 Boozman | Y | Y | Y | Y | Y | N | Y |
| 4 Ross | Y | Y | Y | N | N | Y | N |
| **CALIFORNIA** | | | | | | | |
| 1 Thompson | Y | Y | Y | N | N | Y | N |
| 2 Herger | Y | Y | Y | Y | Y | N | Y |
| 3 Lungren | Y | Y | Y | Y | Y | N | Y |
| 4 Doolittle | Y | Y | Y | Y | Y | N | Y |
| 5 Matsui, D. | Y | Y | Y | N | N | Y | N |
| 6 Woolsey | Y | Y | Y | N | N | Y | N |
| 7 Miller, George | Y | Y | Y | N | N | Y | N |
| 8 Pelosi | Y | Y | Y | N | N | Y | N |
| 9 Lee | Y | Y | Y | N | N | Y | N |
| 10 Tauscher | Y | Y | Y | N | N | Y | N |
| 11 Pombo | Y | Y | Y | Y | Y | N | Y |
| 12 Lantos | ? | ? | ? | N | N | Y | N |
| 13 Stark | Y | Y | Y | N | N | Y | N |
| 14 Eshoo | Y | Y | Y | N | N | Y | N |
| 15 Honda | Y | Y | Y | N | ? | Y | N |
| 16 Lofgren | Y | Y | Y | N | N | Y | N |
| 17 Farr | Y | Y | Y | N | N | Y | N |
| 18 Cardoza | Y | Y | Y | N | N | Y | N |
| 19 Radanovich | Y | Y | Y | Y | Y | N | Y |
| 20 Costa | + | Y | Y | N | N | Y | N |
| 21 Nunes | Y | Y | Y | Y | Y | N | Y |
| 22 Thomas | Y | Y | Y | ? | Y | N | N |
| 23 Capps | Y | Y | ? | N | N | Y | N |
| 24 Gallegly | Y | Y | Y | Y | Y | N | Y |
| 25 McKeon | Y | Y | Y | Y | Y | N | Y |
| 26 Dreier | Y | Y | Y | Y | Y | N | Y |
| 27 Sherman | Y | Y | Y | N | N | Y | N |
| 28 Berman | Y | Y | Y | N | N | Y | N |
| 29 Schiff | Y | Y | Y | N | N | Y | N |
| 30 Waxman | Y | Y | Y | N | N | Y | N |
| 31 Becerra | Y | Y | Y | N | N | Y | N |
| 32 Solis | Y | Y | Y | N | N | Y | N |
| 33 Watson | Y | Y | Y | N | N | Y | N |
| 34 Roybal-Allard | Y | Y | Y | N | N | Y | N |
| 35 Waters | ? | ? | ? | ? | ? | Y | N |
| 36 Harman | Y | Y | Y | N | N | Y | N |
| 37 Millender-McD. | ? | ? | ? | ? | ? | ? | ? |
| 38 Napolitano | Y | Y | Y | N | N | Y | N |
| 39 Sánchez, Linda | Y | Y | Y | N | N | Y | N |
| 40 Royce | Y | Y | Y | Y | Y | N | Y |
| 41 Lewis | Y | Y | Y | Y | Y | N | Y |
| 42 Miller, Gary | Y | Y | Y | Y | Y | N | Y |
| 43 Baca | Y | Y | Y | N | N | Y | N |
| 44 Calvert | Y | Y | Y | Y | Y | N | Y |
| 45 Bono | Y | Y | Y | Y | Y | N | Y |
| 46 Rohrabacher | Y | Y | Y | Y | Y | N | Y |
| 47 Sanchez, Loretta | Y | Y | Y | N | N | Y | N |
| 48 Cox | Y | Y | Y | Y | Y | N | Y |
| 49 Issa | Y | Y | Y | Y | Y | N | Y |
| 50 Cunningham | Y | Y | Y | Y | Y | N | Y |
| 51 Filner | Y | Y | Y | N | N | Y | N |
| 52 Hunter | Y | Y | Y | Y | Y | N | Y |
| 53 Davis | Y | Y | Y | N | N | Y | N |
| **COLORADO** | | | | | | | |
| 1 DeGette | Y | Y | Y | N | N | Y | N |
| 2 Udall | Y | Y | Y | N | N | Y | N |
| 3 Salazar | Y | Y | Y | N | N | Y | N |
| 4 Musgrave | Y | Y | Y | Y | Y | N | Y |
| 5 Hefley | Y | Y | Y | Y | Y | N | Y |
| 6 Tancredo | Y | Y | Y | Y | Y | N | Y |
| 7 Beauprez | Y | Y | Y | Y | Y | N | Y |
| **CONNECTICUT** | | | | | | | |
| 1 Larson | ? | ? | ? | – | – | + | – |
| 2 Simmons | Y | Y | Y | Y | Y | N | Y |
| 3 DeLauro | Y | Y | Y | N | N | Y | N |
| 4 Shays | Y | Y | Y | Y | Y | Y | Y |
| 5 Johnson | Y | Y | Y | Y | Y | N | N |
| **DELAWARE** | | | | | | | |
| AL Castle | Y | Y | Y | Y | Y | N | N |
| **FLORIDA** | | | | | | | |
| 1 Miller | Y | Y | Y | Y | Y | – | + |
| 2 Boyd | Y | Y | Y | N | N | Y | N |
| 3 Brown | ? | ? | ? | N | N | Y | N |
| 4 Crenshaw | Y | Y | Y | Y | Y | N | Y |
| 5 Brown-Waite | Y | Y | Y | Y | Y | N | Y |
| 6 Stearns | Y | Y | Y | Y | Y | N | Y |
| 7 Mica | Y | Y | Y | Y | Y | N | Y |
| 8 Keller | Y | Y | Y | Y | Y | N | Y |
| 9 Bilirakis | Y | Y | Y | Y | Y | N | Y |
| 10 Young | ? | ? | ? | ? | ? | ? | ? |
| 11 Davis | Y | Y | Y | N | N | Y | N |
| 12 Putnam | Y | Y | Y | Y | Y | N | Y |
| 13 Harris | Y | Y | Y | Y | Y | N | Y |
| 14 Mack | Y | Y | Y | Y | Y | N | Y |
| 15 Weldon | ? | ? | ? | Y | Y | N | Y |
| 16 Foley | Y | Y | Y | Y | Y | N | Y |
| 17 Meek | ? | Y | ? | N | N | Y | N |
| 18 Ros-Lehtinen | ? | ? | ? | Y | Y | N | Y |
| 19 Wexler | Y | Y | Y | N | N | ? | ? |
| 20 Wasserman-Schultz | ? | ? | ? | N | N | Y | N |
| 21 Diaz-Balart, L. | ? | ? | ? | Y | Y | N | Y |
| 22 Shaw | Y | Y | Y | Y | Y | N | Y |
| 23 Hastings | Y | Y | Y | N | N | Y | N |
| 24 Feeney | Y | Y | Y | Y | Y | N | Y |
| 25 Diaz-Balart, M. | ? | ? | ? | Y | Y | N | Y |
| **GEORGIA** | | | | | | | |
| 1 Kingston | Y | Y | Y | Y | Y | N | Y |
| 2 Bishop | Y | Y | Y | N | N | Y | N |
| 3 Marshall | ? | ? | ? | N | N | Y | N |
| 4 McKinney | Y | Y | Y | N | N | Y | N |
| 5 Lewis | ? | ? | ? | N | N | ? | ? |
| 6 Price | Y | Y | Y | Y | Y | N | Y |
| 7 Linder | Y | Y | Y | Y | Y | N | Y |
| 8 Westmoreland | Y | Y | Y | Y | Y | N | Y |
| 9 Norwood | Y | Y | Y | Y | Y | N | Y |
| 10 Deal | Y | Y | Y | Y | Y | N | Y |
| 11 Gingrey | Y | Y | Y | Y | Y | Y | Y |
| 12 Barrow | Y | Y | Y | N | N | Y | N |
| 13 Scott | Y | Y | Y | N | N | Y | N |
| **HAWAII** | | | | | | | |
| 1 Abercrombie | Y | Y | Y | N | N | Y | N |
| 2 Case | Y | Y | Y | N | N | Y | N |
| **IDAHO** | | | | | | | |
| 1 Otter | Y | Y | Y | Y | Y | N | Y |
| 2 Simpson | Y | Y | Y | Y | Y | N | Y |
| **ILLINOIS** | | | | | | | |
| 1 Rush | Y | Y | Y | N | N | Y | N |
| 2 Jackson | Y | Y | Y | N | N | Y | N |
| 3 Lipinski | Y | Y | Y | N | N | Y | N |
| 4 Gutierrez | + | + | + | N | N | Y | N |
| 5 Emanuel | Y | Y | Y | N | N | Y | N |
| 6 Hyde | Y | Y | Y | Y | Y | N | Y |
| 7 Davis | ? | ? | ? | ? | ? | Y | N |
| 8 Bean | Y | Y | Y | N | N | Y | N |
| 9 Schakowsky | Y | Y | Y | N | N | Y | N |
| 10 Kirk | Y | Y | Y | Y | Y | N | Y |
| 11 Weller | Y | Y | Y | Y | Y | N | Y |
| 12 Costello | Y | Y | Y | N | N | Y | N |

**KEY**  Republicans  Democrats  *Independents*

| | | |
|---|---|---|
| **Y** Voted for (yea) | **X** Paired against | **C** Voted "present" to avoid possible conflict of interest |
| **#** Paired for | **–** Announced against | |
| **+** Announced for | **P** Voted "present" | **?** Did not vote or otherwise make a position known |
| **N** Voted against (nay) | | |

| | 171 | 172 | 173 | 174 | 175 | 176 | 177 |
|---|---|---|---|---|---|---|---|
| 13 **Biggert** | Y | Y | Y | Y | Y | N | N |
| 14 **Hastert** | | | | | | | |
| 15 **Johnson** | Y | Y | Y | Y | Y | N | N |
| 16 **Manzullo** | ? | ? | ? | Y | Y | N | Y |
| 17 Evans | Y | Y | Y | N | N | Y | N |
| 18 **LaHood** | Y | Y | Y | Y | Y | N | N |
| 19 **Shimkus** | Y | Y | Y | Y | Y | N | Y |
| **INDIANA** | | | | | | | |
| 1 Visclosky | Y | Y | Y | N | N | N | N |
| 2 **Chocola** | Y | Y | Y | Y | Y | N | N |
| 3 **Souder** | ? | ? | ? | Y | Y | N | Y |
| 4 **Buyer** | Y | Y | Y | Y | Y | N | Y |
| 5 **Burton** | + | + | + | ? | ? | N | Y |
| 6 **Pence** | Y | Y | Y | Y | Y | N | Y |
| 7 Carson | ? | ? | ? | ? | ? | Y | N |
| 8 **Hostettler** | Y | Y | Y | Y | Y | Y | Y |
| 9 **Sodrel** | Y | Y | Y | Y | Y | N | Y |
| **IOWA** | | | | | | | |
| 1 **Nussle** | Y | Y | Y | Y | Y | N | Y |
| 2 **Leach** | Y | Y | Y | Y | Y | Y | N |
| 3 Boswell | Y | Y | Y | N | N | Y | N |
| 4 **Latham** | Y | Y | Y | Y | Y | N | N |
| 5 **King** | Y | Y | Y | Y | Y | N | Y |
| **KANSAS** | | | | | | | |
| 1 **Moran** | Y | Y | Y | Y | Y | N | Y |
| 2 **Ryun** | Y | Y | Y | Y | Y | N | Y |
| 3 Moore | Y | Y | Y | N | N | Y | N |
| 4 **Tiahrt** | Y | Y | Y | Y | Y | N | Y |
| **KENTUCKY** | | | | | | | |
| 1 **Whitfield** | Y | Y | Y | Y | Y | N | Y |
| 2 **Lewis** | Y | Y | Y | Y | Y | N | Y |
| 3 **Northup** | Y | Y | Y | Y | Y | N | N |
| 4 **Davis** | Y | Y | Y | Y | Y | N | Y |
| 5 **Rogers** | Y | Y | Y | Y | Y | N | Y |
| 6 Chandler | Y | Y | Y | N | N | Y | N |
| **LOUISIANA** | | | | | | | |
| 1 **Jindal** | Y | Y | Y | Y | Y | N | Y |
| 2 Jefferson | Y | Y | Y | N | N | Y | N |
| 3 Melancon | Y | Y | Y | N | N | Y | N |
| 4 **McCrery** | Y | Y | Y | Y | Y | N | Y |
| 5 **Alexander** | Y | Y | Y | Y | Y | N | Y |
| 6 **Baker** | Y | Y | Y | Y | Y | N | Y |
| 7 **Boustany** | Y | Y | Y | Y | Y | N | Y |
| **MAINE** | | | | | | | |
| 1 Allen | Y | Y | Y | N | N | Y | N |
| 2 Michaud | Y | Y | Y | N | N | Y | N |
| **MARYLAND** | | | | | | | |
| 1 **Gilchrest** | ? | ? | ? | Y | Y | Y | N |
| 2 Ruppersberger | Y | Y | Y | N | N | Y | N |
| 3 Cardin | Y | Y | Y | N | N | Y | N |
| 4 Wynn | Y | Y | Y | N | N | Y | N |
| 5 Hoyer | Y | Y | Y | N | N | Y | N |
| 6 **Bartlett** | Y | Y | Y | Y | Y | N | Y |
| 7 Cummings | Y | Y | Y | N | N | Y | N |
| 8 Van Hollen | Y | Y | Y | N | N | Y | N |
| **MASSACHUSETTS** | | | | | | | |
| 1 Olver | Y | Y | Y | N | N | Y | N |
| 2 Neal | ? | ? | ? | ? | ? | Y | N |
| 3 McGovern | Y | Y | Y | N | N | Y | N |
| 4 Frank | Y | Y | Y | N | N | Y | N |
| 5 Meehan | Y | Y | Y | N | N | Y | N |
| 6 Tierney | Y | Y | Y | N | N | Y | N |
| 7 Markey | Y | Y | Y | N | N | Y | N |
| 8 Capuano | Y | Y | Y | N | N | Y | N |
| 9 Lynch | Y | Y | Y | N | N | Y | N |
| 10 Delahunt | Y | Y | Y | N | N | Y | N |
| **MICHIGAN** | | | | | | | |
| 1 Stupak | Y | Y | Y | N | N | Y | N |
| 2 **Hoekstra** | Y | Y | Y | Y | Y | N | Y |
| 3 **Ehlers** | Y | Y | Y | Y | Y | N | N |
| 4 **Camp** | Y | Y | Y | Y | Y | N | Y |
| 5 Kildee | Y | Y | Y | N | N | Y | N |
| 6 **Upton** | Y | Y | Y | Y | Y | Y | Y |
| 7 **Schwarz** | Y | Y | Y | Y | Y | Y | N |
| 8 **Rogers** | Y | Y | Y | Y | Y | N | Y |
| 9 **Knollenberg** | Y | Y | Y | Y | Y | N | N |
| 10 **Miller** | Y | Y | Y | Y | Y | N | Y |
| 11 **McCotter** | Y | Y | Y | Y | Y | N | Y |
| 12 Levin | Y | Y | Y | N | N | Y | N |
| 13 Kilpatrick | + | + | + | – | – | + | – |
| 14 Conyers | Y | Y | Y | N | N | Y | N |
| 15 Dingell | Y | Y | Y | ? | ? | Y | N |
| **MINNESOTA** | | | | | | | |
| 1 **Gutknecht** | Y | Y | Y | Y | Y | N | Y |
| 2 **Kline** | Y | Y | Y | Y | Y | N | Y |
| 3 **Ramstad** | Y | Y | Y | Y | Y | Y | Y |
| 4 McCollum | Y | Y | Y | N | N | Y | N |
| 5 Sabo | Y | Y | Y | N | N | N | N |
| 6 **Kennedy** | Y | Y | Y | Y | Y | N | N |
| 7 Peterson | Y | Y | Y | ? | N | N | N |
| 8 Oberstar | Y | Y | Y | N | N | Y | N |
| **MISSISSIPPI** | | | | | | | |
| 1 **Wicker** | ? | ? | ? | ? | ? | N | Y |
| 2 Thompson | Y | Y | Y | N | N | Y | N |
| 3 **Pickering** | Y | Y | Y | Y | Y | N | Y |
| 4 Taylor | ? | ? | ? | N | N | Y | Y |
| **MISSOURI** | | | | | | | |
| 1 Clay | ? | ? | ? | N | N | Y | N |
| 2 **Akin** | Y | Y | Y | Y | Y | N | Y |
| 3 Carnahan | Y | Y | Y | N | N | Y | N |
| 4 Skelton | Y | Y | Y | N | N | Y | N |
| 5 Cleaver | Y | Y | Y | N | N | Y | N |
| 6 **Graves** | + | + | + | Y | Y | N | Y |
| 7 **Blunt** | Y | Y | Y | Y | Y | N | N |
| 8 **Emerson** | Y | Y | Y | Y | P | N | Y |
| 9 **Hulshof** | Y | Y | Y | Y | Y | N | Y |
| **MONTANA** | | | | | | | |
| AL **Rehberg** | Y | Y | Y | Y | Y | N | Y |
| **NEBRASKA** | | | | | | | |
| 1 **Fortenberry** | Y | Y | Y | Y | Y | N | N |
| 2 **Terry** | Y | Y | Y | Y | Y | N | N |
| 3 **Osborne** | Y | Y | Y | Y | Y | N | N |
| **NEVADA** | | | | | | | |
| 1 Berkley | Y | Y | Y | N | N | Y | N |
| 2 **Gibbons** | Y | Y | Y | Y | Y | N | Y |
| 3 **Porter** | Y | Y | Y | Y | Y | Y | N |
| **NEW HAMPSHIRE** | | | | | | | |
| 1 **Bradley** | Y | Y | Y | Y | Y | Y | Y |
| 2 **Bass** | Y | Y | Y | Y | Y | Y | Y |
| **NEW JERSEY** | | | | | | | |
| 1 Andrews | Y | Y | Y | N | N | Y | N |
| 2 **LoBiondo** | Y | Y | Y | Y | Y | Y | N |
| 3 **Saxton** | Y | Y | Y | Y | Y | Y | N |
| 4 **Smith** | Y | Y | Y | Y | Y | Y | N |
| 5 **Garrett** | Y | Y | Y | Y | Y | N | Y |
| 6 Pallone | Y | Y | Y | N | N | Y | N |
| 7 **Ferguson** | Y | Y | Y | Y | Y | Y | N |
| 8 Pascrell | Y | Y | Y | N | N | Y | N |
| 9 Rothman | Y | Y | Y | N | N | Y | N |
| 10 Payne | Y | Y | Y | N | N | ? | ? |
| 11 **Frelinghuysen** | Y | Y | Y | Y | Y | N | N |
| 12 Holt | Y | Y | Y | N | N | Y | N |
| 13 Menendez | Y | Y | Y | N | N | Y | N |
| **NEW MEXICO** | | | | | | | |
| 1 **Wilson** | Y | Y | Y | Y | Y | Y | N |
| 2 **Pearce** | Y | Y | Y | Y | Y | N | N |
| 3 Udall | Y | Y | Y | N | N | Y | N |
| **NEW YORK** | | | | | | | |
| 1 Bishop | Y | Y | Y | N | N | Y | N |
| 2 Israel | Y | Y | Y | N | N | Y | N |
| 3 **King** | Y | Y | Y | Y | Y | Y | N |
| 4 McCarthy | Y | Y | Y | N | N | Y | N |
| 5 Ackerman | ? | ? | ? | ? | ? | ? | ? |
| 6 Meeks | Y | Y | Y | N | N | Y | N |
| 7 Crowley | Y | Y | Y | N | N | Y | N |
| 8 Nadler | Y | Y | Y | N | N | Y | N |
| 9 Weiner | Y | Y | Y | N | N | Y | N |
| 10 Towns | Y | Y | Y | N | N | Y | N |
| 11 Owens | Y | Y | Y | ? | ? | Y | N |
| 12 Velázquez | Y | Y | Y | N | N | Y | N |
| 13 **Fossella** | Y | Y | Y | Y | Y | Y | N |
| 14 Maloney | Y | Y | Y | N | N | Y | N |
| 15 Rangel | Y | Y | Y | N | N | Y | N |
| 16 Serrano | Y | Y | Y | N | N | Y | N |
| 17 Engel | Y | Y | Y | N | N | Y | N |
| 18 Lowey | Y | Y | Y | N | N | Y | N |
| 19 **Kelly** | Y | Y | Y | Y | Y | Y | Y |
| 20 **Sweeney** | ? | ? | ? | ? | ? | N | Y |
| 21 McNulty | Y | Y | Y | N | N | Y | N |
| 22 Hinchey | Y | Y | Y | N | N | Y | N |
| 23 **McHugh** | Y | Y | Y | Y | Y | N | Y |
| 24 **Boehlert** | Y | Y | Y | Y | Y | N | N |
| 25 **Walsh** | Y | Y | Y | Y | Y | N | N |
| 26 **Reynolds** | Y | Y | Y | Y | Y | N | N |
| 27 Higgins | Y | Y | Y | N | N | Y | N |
| 28 Slaughter | Y | Y | Y | – | N | Y | N |
| 29 **Kuhl** | Y | Y | Y | Y | Y | N | N |
| **NORTH CAROLINA** | | | | | | | |
| 1 Butterfield | Y | Y | Y | N | N | Y | N |
| 2 Etheridge | Y | Y | Y | N | N | Y | N |
| 3 **Jones** | Y | Y | Y | Y | Y | N | Y |
| 4 Price | Y | Y | Y | N | N | Y | N |
| 5 **Foxx** | Y | Y | Y | Y | Y | N | Y |
| 6 **Coble** | Y | Y | Y | Y | Y | N | Y |
| 7 McIntyre | Y | Y | Y | N | N | Y | N |
| 8 **Hayes** | Y | Y | Y | Y | Y | N | Y |
| 9 **Myrick** | Y | Y | Y | Y | Y | N | Y |
| 10 **McHenry** | Y | Y | Y | Y | Y | N | Y |
| 11 **Taylor** | Y | Y | Y | Y | Y | N | Y |
| 12 Watt | Y | Y | Y | N | N | Y | N |
| 13 Miller | Y | Y | Y | N | N | Y | N |
| **NORTH DAKOTA** | | | | | | | |
| AL Pomeroy | Y | Y | Y | N | N | Y | N |
| **OHIO** | | | | | | | |
| 1 **Chabot** | Y | Y | Y | Y | Y | N | Y |
| 2 Vacant | | | | | | | |
| 3 **Turner** | Y | Y | Y | Y | Y | N | N |
| 4 **Oxley** | Y | Y | Y | Y | Y | N | N |
| 5 **Gillmor** | Y | Y | Y | Y | Y | N | Y |
| 6 Strickland | Y | Y | Y | N | N | Y | N |
| 7 **Hobson** | Y | Y | Y | Y | Y | N | N |
| 8 **Boehner** | Y | Y | Y | Y | Y | N | Y |
| 9 Kaptur | Y | ? | Y | N | N | Y | N |
| 10 Kucinich | Y | Y | Y | N | N | Y | N |
| 11 Jones | Y | Y | Y | N | N | Y | N |
| 12 **Tiberi** | Y | Y | Y | Y | Y | N | N |
| 13 Brown | Y | Y | Y | N | N | Y | N |
| 14 **LaTourette** | Y | Y | Y | Y | Y | N | N |
| 15 **Pryce** | ? | ? | ? | Y | Y | N | N |
| 16 **Regula** | Y | Y | Y | Y | Y | N | N |
| 17 Ryan | Y | Y | Y | N | N | Y | N |
| 18 **Ney** | Y | Y | Y | Y | Y | N | Y |
| **OKLAHOMA** | | | | | | | |
| 1 **Sullivan** | Y | Y | Y | Y | Y | N | Y |
| 2 Boren | Y | Y | Y | N | N | Y | N |
| 3 **Lucas** | Y | Y | Y | Y | Y | N | Y |
| 4 **Cole** | Y | Y | Y | Y | Y | N | N |
| 5 **Istook** | ? | ? | ? | Y | P | N | Y |
| **OREGON** | | | | | | | |
| 1 Wu | Y | Y | Y | N | N | Y | N |
| 2 **Walden** | Y | Y | Y | Y | Y | N | Y |
| 3 Blumenauer | Y | Y | Y | N | N | Y | N |
| 4 DeFazio | Y | Y | Y | N | N | Y | N |
| 5 Hooley | Y | Y | Y | N | N | Y | N |
| **PENNSYLVANIA** | | | | | | | |
| 1 Brady | Y | Y | Y | ? | ? | ? | ? |
| 2 Fattah | Y | Y | Y | ? | ? | Y | N |
| 3 **English** | Y | Y | Y | Y | Y | N | N |
| 4 **Hart** | Y | Y | Y | Y | Y | N | N |
| 5 **Peterson** | Y | Y | Y | Y | Y | N | Y |
| 6 **Gerlach** | Y | Y | Y | Y | Y | Y | Y |
| 7 **Weldon** | Y | Y | Y | Y | Y | Y | Y |
| 8 **Fitzpatrick** | Y | Y | Y | Y | Y | Y | N |
| 9 **Shuster** | Y | Y | Y | Y | Y | N | Y |
| 10 **Sherwood** | Y | Y | Y | Y | Y | N | N |
| 11 Kanjorski | ? | ? | ? | ? | ? | Y | N |
| 12 Murtha | Y | Y | Y | N | N | Y | N |
| 13 Schwartz | Y | Y | Y | N | N | Y | N |
| 14 Doyle | ? | ? | ? | ? | ? | Y | N |
| 15 **Dent** | Y | Y | Y | Y | Y | Y | Y |
| 16 **Pitts** | Y | Y | Y | Y | Y | N | Y |
| 17 Holden | ? | ? | ? | N | N | Y | N |
| 18 **Murphy** | Y | Y | Y | Y | Y | Y | N |
| 19 **Platts** | Y | Y | Y | Y | Y | Y | Y |
| **RHODE ISLAND** | | | | | | | |
| 1 Kennedy | Y | Y | Y | N | N | Y | N |
| 2 Langevin | Y | Y | Y | N | N | Y | N |
| **SOUTH CAROLINA** | | | | | | | |
| 1 **Brown** | Y | Y | Y | Y | Y | N | Y |
| 2 **Wilson** | Y | Y | Y | Y | Y | N | Y |
| 3 **Barrett** | + | + | + | Y | Y | N | Y |
| 4 **Inglis** | Y | Y | Y | Y | Y | N | Y |
| 5 Spratt | Y | Y | Y | N | N | Y | N |
| 6 Clyburn | Y | Y | Y | N | N | Y | N |
| **SOUTH DAKOTA** | | | | | | | |
| AL Herseth | Y | Y | Y | N | N | Y | N |
| **TENNESSEE** | | | | | | | |
| 1 **Jenkins** | Y | Y | Y | Y | Y | N | Y |
| 2 **Duncan** | Y | Y | Y | Y | Y | N | Y |
| 3 **Wamp** | Y | Y | Y | Y | Y | N | Y |
| 4 Davis | Y | Y | Y | N | N | Y | N |
| 5 Cooper | Y | Y | Y | N | N | Y | N |
| 6 Gordon | Y | Y | Y | N | N | Y | N |
| 7 **Blackburn** | Y | Y | Y | Y | Y | N | Y |
| 8 Tanner | Y | Y | Y | N | N | Y | N |
| 9 Ford | Y | Y | ? | N | N | Y | N |
| **TEXAS** | | | | | | | |
| 1 **Gohmert** | ? | ? | ? | ? | ? | N | Y |
| 2 **Poe** | Y | Y | Y | Y | Y | N | Y |
| 3 **Johnson, S.** | Y | Y | Y | Y | Y | N | Y |
| 4 **Hall** | Y | Y | Y | Y | Y | N | Y |
| 5 **Hensarling** | Y | Y | Y | Y | Y | N | N |
| 6 **Barton** | Y | Y | Y | Y | Y | N | Y |
| 7 **Culberson** | Y | Y | Y | Y | Y | N | Y |
| 8 **Brady** | ? | ? | ? | Y | Y | N | Y |
| 9 Green | Y | Y | Y | N | N | Y | N |
| 10 **McCaul** | Y | Y | Y | Y | Y | N | Y |
| 11 **Conaway** | Y | Y | Y | Y | Y | N | Y |
| 12 **Granger** | Y | Y | Y | Y | Y | Y | Y |
| 13 **Thornberry** | Y | Y | Y | Y | Y | N | Y |
| 14 **Paul** | Y | Y | Y | Y | Y | N | Y |
| 15 Hinojosa | Y | Y | Y | N | N | Y | N |
| 16 Reyes | Y | Y | Y | N | N | Y | N |
| 17 Edwards | Y | Y | Y | N | N | N | N |
| 18 Jackson-Lee | Y | Y | Y | N | N | Y | N |
| 19 **Neugebauer** | Y | Y | Y | Y | Y | N | Y |
| 20 Gonzalez | Y | Y | Y | N | N | Y | N |
| 21 **Smith** | Y | Y | Y | Y | Y | N | Y |
| 22 **DeLay** | Y | Y | Y | Y | Y | N | Y |
| 23 **Bonilla** | Y | Y | Y | Y | Y | N | Y |
| 24 **Marchant** | Y | Y | Y | Y | Y | N | Y |
| 25 Doggett | Y | Y | Y | N | N | Y | N |
| 26 **Burgess** | Y | Y | Y | Y | Y | N | Y |
| 27 Ortiz | Y | Y | Y | N | N | Y | N |
| 28 Cuellar | Y | Y | Y | N | N | Y | N |
| 29 Green | Y | Y | Y | N | N | Y | N |
| 30 Johnson, E. | Y | Y | Y | N | N | Y | N |
| 31 **Carter** | Y | Y | Y | Y | Y | N | Y |
| 32 **Sessions** | Y | Y | Y | Y | Y | N | Y |
| **UTAH** | | | | | | | |
| 1 **Bishop** | Y | Y | Y | Y | Y | N | Y |
| 2 Matheson | Y | Y | Y | N | N | Y | N |
| 3 **Cannon** | Y | Y | Y | Y | Y | N | N |
| **VERMONT** | | | | | | | |
| AL *Sanders* | Y | Y | Y | N | N | Y | N |
| **VIRGINIA** | | | | | | | |
| 1 **Davis, J.** | Y | Y | Y | Y | Y | N | Y |
| 2 **Drake** | Y | Y | Y | Y | Y | N | Y |
| 3 Scott | Y | Y | Y | N | ? | Y | N |
| 4 **Forbes** | Y | Y | Y | Y | Y | N | Y |
| 5 **Goode** | Y | Y | Y | Y | Y | N | Y |
| 6 **Goodlatte** | Y | Y | Y | Y | Y | N | Y |
| 7 **Cantor** | Y | Y | Y | Y | Y | N | Y |
| 8 Moran | ? | ? | ? | N | N | N | N |
| 9 Boucher | Y | Y | Y | ? | ? | Y | N |
| 10 **Wolf** | Y | Y | Y | Y | Y | N | Y |
| 11 **Davis, T.** | Y | Y | Y | Y | Y | N | N |
| **WASHINGTON** | | | | | | | |
| 1 Inslee | Y | Y | Y | N | N | Y | N |
| 2 Larsen | ? | ? | ? | N | N | Y | N |
| 3 Baird | Y | Y | Y | ? | ? | Y | N |
| 4 **Hastings** | Y | Y | Y | Y | Y | N | N |
| 5 **McMorris** | Y | Y | Y | Y | Y | N | N |
| 6 Dicks | Y | Y | Y | N | Y | Y | N |
| 7 McDermott | Y | Y | Y | N | N | Y | N |
| 8 **Reichert** | Y | Y | Y | Y | Y | N | N |
| 9 Smith | ? | Y | Y | N | N | Y | N |
| **WEST VIRGINIA** | | | | | | | |
| 1 Mollohan | Y | Y | Y | N | N | Y | N |
| 2 **Capito** | Y | Y | Y | Y | Y | Y | N |
| 3 Rahall | Y | Y | Y | N | N | Y | N |
| **WISCONSIN** | | | | | | | |
| 1 **Ryan** | Y | Y | Y | Y | Y | Y | N |
| 2 Baldwin | Y | Y | Y | N | N | Y | N |
| 3 Kind | Y | Y | Y | N | N | Y | N |
| 4 Moore | Y | Y | Y | N | N | Y | N |
| 5 **Sensenbrenner** | Y | Y | Y | Y | Y | N | Y |
| 6 **Petri** | Y | Y | Y | Y | Y | N | N |
| 7 Obey | Y | Y | Y | N | N | Y | N |
| 8 **Green** | Y | Y | Y | Y | Y | Y | N |
| **WYOMING** | | | | | | | |
| AL **Cubin** | Y | Y | Y | ? | ? | N | Y |

# IN THE HOUSE | By Vote Number

**178.** HR 2360. Fiscal 2006 Homeland Security Appropriations/**Detention Centers.** Meeks, D-N.Y., amendment that would prohibit the use of funds in the bill to close any detention facility operated by or on behalf of U.S. Immigration and Customs Enforcement that has been operational in 2005. Rejected 199-223: R 22-205; D 176-18 (ND 133-12, SD 43-6); I 1-0. May 17, 2005.

**179.** HR 2360. Fiscal 2006 Homeland Security Appropriations/**Driver's License Standards.** Obey, D-Wis., amendment that would provide $100 million for states to comply with new national driver's license standards, offset with cuts spread through the bill. Adopted 226-198: R 32-196; D 193-2 (ND 144-2, SD 49-0); I 1-0. May 17, 2005.

**180.** HR 2360. Fiscal 2006 Homeland Security Appropriations/**Passage.** Passage of the bill that would provide $31.9 billion in fiscal 2006 for the Homeland Security Department, including $22 billion for security, enforcement and investigation activities; $5.7 billion for the Transportation Security Administration, and $3.6 billion for state and local grant programs. It would withhold more than $310 million pending improvements in air cargo screening and deployment of more explosive-detection technologies at airports. Passed 424-1: R 229-1; D 194-0 (ND 145-0, SD 49-0); I 1-0. May 17, 2005.

**181.** HR 1817. Fiscal 2006 Homeland Security Authorization/**Previous Question.** Sessions, R-Texas, motion to order the previous question (thus ending debate and possibility of amendment) on adoption of the rule (H Res 283) that would provide for House floor consideration of the bill that would authorize $34.2 billion in fiscal 2006 for the Department of Homeland Security. Motion agreed to 226-199: R 226-0; D 0-198 (ND 0-148, SD 0-50); I 0-1. May 18, 2005.

**182.** HR 1817. Fiscal 2006 Homeland Security Authorization/**Rule.** Adoption of the rule (H Res 283) to provide for House floor consideration of the bill that would authorize $34.2 billion in fiscal 2006 for the Department of Homeland Security. Adopted 284-124: R 221-0; D 63-124 (ND 43-96, SD 20-28); I 0-0. May 18, 2005.

**183.** HR 1817. Fiscal 2006 Homeland Security Authorization/**Inspector General Funding.** Meek, D-Fla., amendment that would increase funding for the Department of Homeland Security Office of Inspector General to $200 million. Rejected 184-244: R 2-226; D 181-18 (ND 136-13, SD 45-5); I 1-0. May 18, 2005.

**184.** HR 1817. Fiscal 2006 Homeland Security Authorization/**Airline Passenger Fees.** Hooley, D-Ore., amendment that would bar any funds authorized by the bill to come from an increase in the aviation security passenger fee. Adopted 363-65: R 176-52; D 186-13 (ND 141-8, SD 45-5); I 1-0. May 18, 2005.

**185.** HR 1817. Fiscal 2006 Homeland Security Authorization/**State and Local Law Enforcement Duties.** Norwood, R-Ga., amendment that would clarify the existing authority for state and local enforcement personnel to apprehend, detain, remove and transport illegal aliens in the routine course of duty. It also would require the Homeland Security Department to establish a manual for training personnel to enforce immigration laws and set guidelines for making the training available. Adopted 242-185: R 216-11; D 26-173 (ND 14-135, SD 12-38); I 0-1. May 18, 2005.

| | 178 | 179 | 180 | 181 | 182 | 183 | 184 | 185 |
|---|---|---|---|---|---|---|---|---|
| **ALABAMA** | | | | | | | | |
| 1 Bonner | N | N | Y | Y | Y | N | Y | Y |
| 2 Everett | N | Y | Y | Y | Y | N | N | Y |
| 3 Rogers | N | N | Y | Y | Y | N | Y | Y |
| 4 Aderholt | N | N | Y | Y | Y | N | Y | Y |
| 5 Cramer | N | Y | Y | N | Y | N | Y | Y |
| 6 Bachus | N | N | Y | Y | Y | N | Y | Y |
| 7 Davis | Y | Y | Y | N | N | Y | Y | N |
| **ALASKA** | | | | | | | | |
| AL Young | N | Y | Y | Y | Y | N | N | Y |
| **ARIZONA** | | | | | | | | |
| 1 Renzi | N | N | Y | Y | Y | N | Y | Y |
| 2 Franks | N | N | Y | Y | Y | N | N | Y |
| 3 Shadegg | N | N | Y | Y | Y | N | Y | Y |
| 4 Pastor | Y | Y | Y | N | N | N | Y | N |
| 5 Hayworth | N | N | Y | Y | Y | N | Y | Y |
| 6 Flake | N | N | Y | Y | Y | N | Y | Y |
| 7 Grijalva | N | N | Y | N | N | Y | Y | N |
| 8 Kolbe | N | N | Y | Y | Y | N | Y | N |
| **ARKANSAS** | | | | | | | | |
| 1 Berry | Y | Y | Y | N | Y | Y | N | N |
| 2 Snyder | Y | Y | Y | N | N | Y | Y | N |
| 3 Boozman | N | N | Y | Y | Y | N | Y | Y |
| 4 Ross | Y | Y | Y | N | Y | Y | Y | N |
| **CALIFORNIA** | | | | | | | | |
| 1 Thompson | Y | Y | Y | N | Y | Y | Y | N |
| 2 Herger | N | N | Y | Y | Y | N | Y | Y |
| 3 Lungren | N | N | Y | Y | Y | N | N | Y |
| 4 Doolittle | Y | N | Y | Y | Y | N | Y | Y |
| 5 Matsui, D. | Y | Y | Y | N | N | Y | Y | N |
| 6 Woolsey | Y | Y | Y | N | N | Y | Y | N |
| 7 Miller, George | Y | Y | Y | N | ? | Y | Y | N |
| 8 Pelosi | Y | Y | Y | N | N | Y | Y | N |
| 9 Lee | Y | Y | Y | N | N | Y | Y | N |
| 10 Tauscher | Y | Y | Y | N | Y | Y | Y | N |
| 11 Pombo | N | N | Y | Y | Y | N | N | Y |
| 12 Lantos | Y | Y | Y | N | N | Y | Y | N |
| 13 Stark | Y | Y | Y | N | ? | Y | Y | N |
| 14 Eshoo | Y | Y | Y | N | ? | Y | Y | N |
| 15 Honda | Y | Y | Y | N | N | Y | Y | N |
| 16 Lofgren | N | Y | Y | N | N | Y | Y | N |
| 17 Farr | Y | Y | Y | N | N | Y | Y | N |
| 18 Cardoza | Y | Y | Y | N | ? | Y | Y | N |
| 19 Radanovich | N | N | Y | Y | Y | N | N | Y |
| 20 Costa | N | Y | Y | N | N | N | Y | N |
| 21 Nunes | N | N | Y | Y | Y | N | Y | Y |
| 22 Thomas | N | N | Y | Y | Y | N | Y | Y |
| 23 Capps | Y | Y | Y | N | N | Y | Y | N |
| 24 Gallegly | N | N | Y | Y | Y | N | Y | Y |
| 25 McKeon | N | Y | Y | ? | Y | N | Y | Y |
| 26 Dreier | N | Y | Y | N | Y | N | Y | Y |
| 27 Sherman | N | Y | Y | N | N | Y | Y | N |
| 28 Berman | N | Y | Y | N | ? | Y | Y | N |
| 29 Schiff | N | Y | Y | N | Y | Y | Y | N |
| 30 Waxman | Y | Y | Y | N | N | Y | Y | N |
| 31 Becerra | Y | Y | Y | N | ? | Y | Y | N |
| 32 Solis | Y | Y | Y | N | N | Y | Y | N |
| 33 Watson | Y | Y | Y | N | N | Y | Y | N |
| 34 Roybal-Allard | Y | Y | Y | N | N | Y | Y | N |
| 35 Waters | Y | Y | Y | N | N | Y | Y | N |
| 36 Harman | Y | Y | Y | N | N | Y | Y | N |
| 37 Millender-McD. | ? | ? | ? | ? | ? | ? | ? | ? |
| 38 Napolitano | Y | Y | Y | N | ? | Y | Y | N |
| 39 Sánchez, Linda | Y | Y | Y | N | Y | Y | Y | N |
| 40 Royce | N | Y | Y | Y | Y | N | Y | Y |
| 41 Lewis | N | Y | Y | Y | Y | N | Y | Y |
| 42 Miller, Gary | N | N | Y | Y | Y | N | Y | Y |
| 43 Baca | Y | Y | Y | N | Y | Y | Y | N |
| 44 Calvert | N | N | Y | Y | Y | N | Y | Y |
| 45 Bono | N | N | Y | Y | Y | N | Y | Y |
| 46 Rohrabacher | N | N | Y | Y | Y | N | N | Y |
| 47 Sanchez, Loretta | Y | Y | Y | N | N | Y | Y | N |
| 48 Cox | N | N | Y | Y | Y | N | Y | Y |
| 49 Issa | N | N | Y | Y | Y | N | Y | Y |
| 50 Cunningham | N | N | Y | Y | Y | N | Y | Y |
| 51 Filner | Y | Y | Y | N | N | Y | Y | N |
| 52 Hunter | N | N | Y | Y | Y | N | Y | Y |
| 53 Davis | Y | Y | Y | N | N | Y | Y | N |
| **COLORADO** | | | | | | | | |
| 1 DeGette | Y | Y | Y | N | N | Y | Y | N |
| 2 Udall | Y | Y | Y | N | N | Y | Y | N |
| 3 Salazar | Y | Y | Y | N | N | Y | Y | N |
| 4 Musgrave | N | N | Y | Y | Y | N | Y | Y |
| 5 Hefley | N | N | Y | Y | Y | N | Y | Y |
| 6 Tancredo | N | N | Y | ? | ? | ? | ? | ? |
| 7 Beauprez | N | N | Y | Y | Y | N | Y | Y |
| **CONNECTICUT** | | | | | | | | |
| 1 Larson | + | + | + | – | – | + | + | – |
| 2 Simmons | N | N | Y | Y | Y | N | Y | Y |
| 3 DeLauro | N | N | Y | Y | Y | N | Y | N |
| 4 Shays | N | N | Y | Y | Y | N | N | Y |
| 5 Johnson | N | N | Y | Y | Y | N | Y | Y |
| **DELAWARE** | | | | | | | | |
| AL Castle | N | N | Y | Y | Y | N | Y | Y |
| **FLORIDA** | | | | | | | | |
| 1 Miller | – | N | Y | Y | Y | N | Y | Y |
| 2 Boyd | Y | Y | Y | N | Y | Y | Y | Y |
| 3 Brown | Y | Y | Y | N | N | Y | Y | N |
| 4 Crenshaw | N | N | Y | Y | Y | N | Y | Y |
| 5 Brown-Waite | N | Y | Y | Y | Y | N | Y | Y |
| 6 Stearns | N | N | Y | Y | Y | N | Y | Y |
| 7 Mica | N | N | Y | Y | Y | N | N | Y |
| 8 Keller | N | N | Y | Y | Y | N | Y | Y |
| 9 Bilirakis | N | N | Y | Y | Y | N | Y | Y |
| 10 Young | ? | ? | Y | Y | Y | N | Y | Y |
| 11 Davis | Y | Y | Y | N | Y | Y | Y | N |
| 12 Putnam | N | N | Y | Y | Y | N | Y | Y |
| 13 Harris | N | N | Y | Y | Y | N | Y | Y |
| 14 Mack | N | N | Y | Y | Y | N | Y | Y |
| 15 Weldon | N | N | Y | Y | Y | N | Y | Y |
| 16 Foley | N | Y | Y | ? | ? | N | Y | Y |
| 17 Meek | Y | Y | Y | N | N | Y | Y | N |
| 18 Ros-Lehtinen | N | N | Y | Y | Y | N | Y | N |
| 19 Wexler | ? | ? | ? | N | Y | Y | Y | N |
| 20 Wasserman-Schultz | Y | Y | Y | N | N | Y | Y | N |
| 21 Diaz-Balart, L. | N | N | Y | Y | Y | N | N | Y |
| 22 Shaw | N | N | Y | Y | Y | N | Y | Y |
| 23 Hastings | Y | Y | Y | N | Y | Y | Y | N |
| 24 Feeney | N | N | Y | Y | Y | N | Y | Y |
| 25 Diaz-Balart, M. | N | N | Y | Y | Y | N | Y | N |
| **GEORGIA** | | | | | | | | |
| 1 Kingston | N | N | Y | Y | Y | N | N | Y |
| 2 Bishop | Y | Y | Y | N | N | Y | Y | N |
| 3 Marshall | N | Y | Y | N | Y | N | Y | N |
| 4 McKinney | Y | Y | Y | N | N | Y | Y | N |
| 5 Lewis | ? | ? | ? | ? | ? | ? | ? | ? |
| 6 Price | N | N | Y | Y | Y | N | Y | N |
| 7 Linder | Y | N | Y | Y | Y | N | Y | Y |
| 8 Westmoreland | N | N | Y | Y | Y | N | N | Y |
| 9 Norwood | N | N | Y | Y | Y | N | N | Y |
| 10 Deal | N | N | Y | Y | Y | N | Y | Y |
| 11 Gingrey | N | N | Y | Y | Y | N | Y | N |
| 12 Barrow | Y | Y | Y | N | Y | Y | Y | N |
| 13 Scott | Y | Y | Y | N | Y | Y | Y | N |
| **HAWAII** | | | | | | | | |
| 1 Abercrombie | Y | Y | Y | N | Y | Y | Y | N |
| 2 Case | N | Y | Y | N | ? | N | Y | Y |
| **IDAHO** | | | | | | | | |
| 1 Otter | N | Y | Y | Y | Y | N | N | Y |
| 2 Simpson | N | N | Y | Y | Y | N | Y | Y |
| **ILLINOIS** | | | | | | | | |
| 1 Rush | Y | Y | Y | N | N | Y | Y | N |
| 2 Jackson | Y | Y | Y | N | N | Y | Y | N |
| 3 Lipinski | Y | Y | Y | N | N | Y | Y | N |
| 4 Gutierrez | Y | N | Y | N | N | Y | Y | N |
| 5 Emanuel | Y | Y | Y | N | N | Y | Y | N |
| 6 Hyde | N | Y | Y | ? | ? | N | Y | Y |
| 7 Davis | Y | Y | Y | N | N | Y | Y | N |
| 8 Bean | Y | Y | Y | N | N | Y | Y | N |
| 9 Schakowsky | Y | Y | Y | N | N | Y | Y | N |
| 10 Kirk | N | N | Y | Y | Y | N | Y | Y |
| 11 Weller | N | N | Y | Y | Y | N | N | Y |
| 12 Costello | Y | Y | Y | N | N | Y | Y | N |

**KEY**　Republicans　Democrats　*Independents*

| | | | |
|---|---|---|---|
| Y | Voted for (yea) | X | Paired against |
| # | Paired for | – | Announced against |
| + | Announced for | P | Voted "present" |
| N | Voted against (nay) | | |

C　Voted "present" to avoid possible conflict of interest

?　Did not vote or otherwise make a position known

| | 178 | 179 | 180 | 181 | 182 | 183 | 184 | 185 |
|---|---|---|---|---|---|---|---|---|
| 13 **Biggert** | N | N | Y | Y | Y | N | Y | Y |
| 14 **Hastert** | | | | | | | | |
| 15 **Johnson** | N | Y | Y | Y | Y | N | Y | Y |
| 16 **Manzullo** | N | N | Y | Y | Y | N | Y | Y |
| 17 Evans | Y | Y | Y | N | Y | N | Y | N |
| 18 **LaHood** | N | N | Y | Y | Y | N | Y | Y |
| 19 **Shimkus** | N | N | Y | Y | Y | N | Y | Y |
| **INDIANA** | | | | | | | | |
| 1 Visclosky | Y | Y | Y | N | N | Y | Y | N |
| 2 **Chocola** | N | N | Y | Y | Y | N | Y | Y |
| 3 **Souder** | Y | N | Y | Y | Y | N | N | Y |
| 4 **Buyer** | N | N | Y | Y | ? | N | N | Y |
| 5 **Burton** | Y | N | Y | Y | Y | N | Y | Y |
| 6 **Pence** | N | N | Y | Y | Y | N | N | Y |
| 7 Carson | Y | Y | Y | N | N | Y | Y | N |
| 8 **Hostettler** | Y | Y | Y | Y | Y | N | Y | Y |
| 9 **Sodrel** | N | N | Y | Y | Y | N | Y | Y |
| **IOWA** | | | | | | | | |
| 1 **Nussle** | N | N | Y | Y | Y | N | Y | Y |
| 2 **Leach** | N | N | Y | Y | Y | N | Y | Y |
| 3 Boswell | Y | Y | Y | N | N | Y | Y | Y |
| 4 **Latham** | N | N | Y | Y | Y | N | Y | Y |
| 5 **King** | N | N | Y | Y | Y | N | N | Y |
| **KANSAS** | | | | | | | | |
| 1 **Moran** | N | N | Y | Y | Y | N | N | Y |
| 2 **Ryun** | N | N | Y | Y | Y | N | N | Y |
| 3 Moore | Y | Y | Y | N | N | Y | Y | N |
| 4 **Tiahrt** | N | N | Y | Y | Y | N | Y | Y |
| **KENTUCKY** | | | | | | | | |
| 1 **Whitfield** | N | N | Y | Y | Y | N | N | Y |
| 2 **Lewis** | N | N | Y | Y | Y | N | Y | Y |
| 3 **Northup** | N | N | Y | Y | Y | N | Y | Y |
| 4 **Davis** | N | N | Y | Y | Y | N | Y | Y |
| 5 **Rogers** | N | N | Y | Y | Y | N | Y | Y |
| 6 Chandler | Y | Y | Y | N | Y | Y | Y | Y |
| **LOUISIANA** | | | | | | | | |
| 1 **Jindal** | N | N | Y | Y | Y | N | Y | Y |
| 2 Jefferson | Y | Y | Y | N | ? | Y | Y | N |
| 3 Melancon | Y | Y | Y | N | Y | Y | Y | N |
| 4 **McCrery** | N | N | Y | Y | Y | N | Y | Y |
| 5 **Alexander** | N | N | Y | Y | Y | N | Y | Y |
| 6 **Baker** | N | N | Y | Y | Y | N | Y | Y |
| 7 **Boustany** | N | N | Y | Y | Y | N | N | Y |
| **MAINE** | | | | | | | | |
| 1 Allen | Y | Y | Y | N | Y | Y | Y | N |
| 2 Michaud | Y | Y | Y | N | Y | Y | Y | N |
| **MARYLAND** | | | | | | | | |
| 1 **Gilchrest** | N | N | Y | Y | Y | N | Y | Y |
| 2 Ruppersberger | Y | Y | Y | N | Y | Y | Y | Y |
| 3 Cardin | Y | Y | Y | N | Y | Y | Y | N |
| 4 Wynn | Y | Y | Y | N | N | Y | Y | N |
| 5 Hoyer | Y | Y | Y | N | N | Y | Y | N |
| 6 **Bartlett** | N | N | Y | Y | Y | N | N | Y |
| 7 Cummings | Y | Y | Y | N | N | Y | Y | N |
| 8 Van Hollen | Y | Y | Y | N | N | Y | Y | N |
| **MASSACHUSETTS** | | | | | | | | |
| 1 Olver | Y | Y | Y | N | N | Y | Y | N |
| 2 Neal | Y | Y | Y | N | N | Y | Y | N |
| 3 McGovern | Y | Y | Y | N | N | Y | Y | N |
| 4 Frank | Y | Y | Y | N | N | Y | N | N |
| 5 Meehan | Y | Y | Y | N | N | Y | Y | N |
| 6 Tierney | Y | Y | Y | N | N | N | N | N |
| 7 Markey | Y | Y | Y | ? | N | Y | Y | N |
| 8 Capuano | N | Y | Y | N | Y | Y | Y | N |
| 9 Lynch | Y | Y | Y | N | N | Y | Y | N |
| 10 Delahunt | Y | Y | Y | N | N | Y | Y | N |
| **MICHIGAN** | | | | | | | | |
| 1 Stupak | Y | Y | Y | N | Y | Y | Y | N |
| 2 **Hoekstra** | N | N | Y | Y | Y | N | N | Y |
| 3 **Ehlers** | N | Y | Y | Y | Y | N | N | N |
| 4 **Camp** | N | Y | Y | Y | Y | N | Y | Y |
| 5 Kildee | Y | Y | Y | N | N | Y | Y | N |
| 6 **Upton** | N | N | Y | Y | Y | N | Y | Y |
| 7 **Schwarz** | N | N | Y | Y | Y | N | Y | Y |
| 8 **Rogers** | N | N | Y | Y | Y | N | Y | Y |
| 9 **Knollenberg** | N | N | Y | Y | ? | N | Y | Y |
| 10 **Miller** | N | N | Y | Y | Y | N | N | Y |
| 11 **McCotter** | N | Y | Y | Y | Y | N | Y | Y |
| 12 Levin | Y | Y | Y | N | Y | Y | Y | N |
| 13 Kilpatrick | + | + | + | N | N | Y | Y | N |
| 14 Conyers | Y | Y | Y | N | N | Y | Y | N |
| 15 Dingell | Y | Y | Y | N | N | Y | Y | N |
| **MINNESOTA** | | | | | | | | |
| 1 **Gutknecht** | N | N | Y | Y | Y | N | N | Y |
| 2 **Kline** | N | N | Y | Y | Y | N | Y | Y |
| 3 **Ramstad** | N | N | Y | Y | Y | N | Y | Y |
| 4 McCollum | Y | Y | Y | N | ? | Y | Y | N |
| 5 Sabo | Y | Y | Y | N | N | Y | N | N |
| 6 **Kennedy** | N | N | Y | Y | Y | N | Y | Y |
| 7 Peterson | Y | Y | Y | N | Y | Y | N | Y |
| 8 Oberstar | Y | Y | Y | N | N | Y | Y | N |
| **MISSISSIPPI** | | | | | | | | |
| 1 **Wicker** | N | N | Y | Y | Y | N | N | Y |
| 2 Thompson | Y | Y | Y | N | N | Y | Y | N |
| 3 **Pickering** | N | N | Y | Y | Y | N | Y | Y |
| 4 Taylor | N | Y | Y | N | N | N | N | Y |
| **MISSOURI** | | | | | | | | |
| 1 Clay | Y | Y | Y | N | N | Y | Y | N |
| 2 **Akin** | N | ? | Y | Y | Y | N | Y | Y |
| 3 Carnahan | Y | Y | Y | N | Y | Y | Y | N |
| 4 Skelton | N | Y | Y | N | Y | N | Y | Y |
| 5 Cleaver | Y | Y | Y | N | N | Y | Y | N |
| 6 **Graves** | N | N | Y | Y | Y | N | Y | Y |
| 7 **Blunt** | N | N | Y | Y | Y | N | N | Y |
| 8 **Emerson** | N | N | Y | Y | Y | N | Y | Y |
| 9 **Hulshof** | N | N | Y | Y | Y | N | Y | Y |
| **MONTANA** | | | | | | | | |
| AL **Rehberg** | N | N | Y | Y | Y | N | Y | Y |
| **NEBRASKA** | | | | | | | | |
| 1 **Fortenberry** | N | N | Y | Y | Y | N | Y | Y |
| 2 **Terry** | Y | N | Y | Y | Y | N | Y | Y |
| 3 **Osborne** | Y | N | Y | Y | Y | N | Y | Y |
| **NEVADA** | | | | | | | | |
| 1 Berkley | Y | Y | Y | N | N | Y | Y | N |
| 2 **Gibbons** | N | N | Y | Y | Y | N | Y | Y |
| 3 **Porter** | N | N | Y | Y | Y | N | Y | Y |
| **NEW HAMPSHIRE** | | | | | | | | |
| 1 **Bradley** | N | N | Y | Y | Y | N | Y | Y |
| 2 **Bass** | N | N | Y | Y | Y | N | Y | Y |
| **NEW JERSEY** | | | | | | | | |
| 1 Andrews | Y | Y | Y | N | N | Y | Y | N |
| 2 **LoBiondo** | N | Y | Y | Y | Y | N | Y | Y |
| 3 **Saxton** | N | N | Y | Y | Y | N | Y | Y |
| 4 **Smith** | N | Y | Y | Y | Y | N | Y | Y |
| 5 **Garrett** | N | N | Y | Y | Y | N | Y | Y |
| 6 Pallone | Y | Y | Y | N | N | Y | Y | N |
| 7 **Ferguson** | N | N | Y | Y | Y | N | Y | Y |
| 8 Pascrell | Y | Y | Y | N | – | Y | Y | N |
| 9 Rothman | Y | Y | Y | N | N | Y | Y | N |
| 10 Payne | ? | ? | ? | N | N | Y | Y | N |
| 11 **Frelinghuysen** | N | N | Y | Y | Y | N | Y | N |
| 12 Holt | Y | Y | Y | N | Y | Y | Y | N |
| 13 Menendez | Y | Y | Y | N | N | Y | Y | N |
| **NEW MEXICO** | | | | | | | | |
| 1 **Wilson** | N | N | Y | Y | Y | N | Y | N |
| 2 **Pearce** | N | N | Y | Y | Y | N | Y | Y |
| 3 Udall | Y | Y | Y | N | N | Y | Y | N |
| **NEW YORK** | | | | | | | | |
| 1 Bishop | Y | Y | Y | N | Y | Y | Y | Y |
| 2 Israel | Y | Y | Y | N | N | Y | Y | Y |
| 3 **King** | Y | N | Y | Y | Y | N | Y | Y |
| 4 McCarthy | Y | Y | Y | N | Y | Y | Y | Y |
| 5 Ackerman | ? | Y | Y | N | N | Y | Y | N |
| 6 Meeks | Y | Y | Y | N | N | Y | Y | N |
| 7 Crowley | Y | Y | Y | N | Y | Y | Y | N |
| 8 Nadler | Y | Y | Y | N | N | Y | N | N |
| 9 Weiner | Y | Y | Y | N | N | Y | Y | N |
| 10 Towns | Y | Y | Y | N | N | Y | Y | N |
| 11 Owens | Y | Y | Y | N | N | Y | Y | N |
| 12 Velázquez | Y | Y | Y | N | N | Y | Y | N |
| 13 **Fossella** | Y | N | Y | Y | Y | N | Y | Y |
| 14 Maloney | Y | Y | Y | N | N | Y | Y | N |
| 15 Rangel | Y | Y | Y | N | N | Y | Y | N |
| 16 Serrano | Y | Y | Y | N | Y | Y | Y | N |
| 17 Engel | Y | Y | Y | N | N | Y | Y | N |
| 18 Lowey | Y | Y | Y | N | N | Y | Y | N |
| 19 **Kelly** | Y | N | Y | Y | Y | N | Y | Y |
| 20 **Sweeney** | Y | N | Y | Y | Y | N | Y | Y |
| 21 McNulty | Y | Y | Y | N | N | Y | Y | N |
| 22 Hinchey | Y | Y | Y | N | Y | Y | Y | N |
| 23 **McHugh** | Y | Y | Y | Y | Y | N | Y | Y |
| 24 **Boehlert** | N | N | Y | Y | Y | N | Y | Y |
| 25 **Walsh** | Y | N | Y | Y | Y | N | Y | Y |
| 26 **Reynolds** | Y | N | Y | Y | Y | N | Y | Y |
| 27 Higgins | Y | Y | Y | N | N | Y | Y | Y |
| 28 Slaughter | Y | Y | Y | N | N | Y | Y | N |
| 29 **Kuhl** | N | Y | Y | Y | Y | N | Y | Y |
| **NORTH CAROLINA** | | | | | | | | |
| 1 Butterfield | Y | Y | Y | N | N | Y | Y | N |
| 2 Etheridge | Y | Y | Y | N | N | Y | Y | N |
| 3 **Jones** | N | Y | Y | Y | Y | N | Y | Y |
| 4 Price | Y | Y | Y | N | N | Y | Y | N |
| 5 **Foxx** | N | N | Y | Y | Y | N | Y | Y |
| 6 **Coble** | N | N | Y | Y | Y | N | Y | Y |
| 7 McIntyre | Y | Y | Y | N | Y | Y | Y | Y |
| 8 **Hayes** | N | N | Y | Y | Y | N | N | Y |
| 9 **Myrick** | N | Y | Y | Y | ? | N | Y | Y |
| 10 **McHenry** | N | N | Y | Y | Y | N | Y | Y |
| 11 **Taylor** | N | N | Y | Y | Y | N | Y | N |
| 12 Watt | Y | Y | Y | N | N | Y | Y | N |
| 13 Miller | Y | Y | Y | N | N | Y | Y | N |
| **NORTH DAKOTA** | | | | | | | | |
| AL Pomeroy | Y | Y | Y | N | N | Y | Y | N |
| **OHIO** | | | | | | | | |
| 1 **Chabot** | N | N | Y | Y | Y | N | Y | Y |
| 2 Vacant | | | | | | | | |
| 3 **Turner** | N | N | Y | Y | ? | N | Y | Y |
| 4 **Oxley** | N | N | Y | Y | Y | N | Y | Y |
| 5 **Gillmor** | N | Y | Y | Y | Y | N | N | Y |
| 6 Strickland | Y | Y | Y | N | Y | Y | Y | N |
| 7 **Hobson** | N | N | Y | Y | Y | N | Y | Y |
| 8 **Boehner** | N | N | Y | Y | Y | N | Y | Y |
| 9 Kaptur | Y | Y | Y | N | N | Y | Y | N |
| 10 Kucinich | Y | Y | Y | N | N | Y | Y | N |
| 11 Jones | Y | Y | Y | N | N | Y | Y | N |
| 12 **Tiberi** | N | N | Y | Y | Y | N | Y | Y |
| 13 Brown | Y | Y | Y | N | Y | Y | Y | N |
| 14 **LaTourette** | N | N | Y | Y | Y | N | N | Y |
| 15 **Pryce** | N | N | Y | Y | Y | N | Y | Y |
| 16 **Regula** | N | N | Y | Y | Y | N | Y | Y |
| 17 Ryan | Y | Y | Y | N | Y | Y | Y | N |
| 18 **Ney** | N | N | Y | Y | Y | N | N | Y |
| **OKLAHOMA** | | | | | | | | |
| 1 **Sullivan** | Y | N | Y | Y | Y | N | Y | ? |
| 2 Boren | Y | Y | Y | N | Y | N | Y | Y |
| 3 **Lucas** | N | N | Y | Y | Y | ? | ? | ? |
| 4 **Cole** | N | N | Y | Y | Y | N | N | Y |
| 5 **Istook** | N | N | Y | Y | Y | N | N | Y |
| **OREGON** | | | | | | | | |
| 1 Wu | Y | Y | Y | N | Y | Y | Y | N |
| 2 **Walden** | N | N | Y | Y | Y | N | Y | Y |
| 3 Blumenauer | N | Y | Y | N | Y | Y | Y | N |
| 4 DeFazio | Y | Y | Y | N | Y | Y | Y | Y |
| 5 Hooley | Y | Y | Y | N | Y | Y | Y | Y |
| **PENNSYLVANIA** | | | | | | | | |
| 1 Brady | ? | ? | ? | N | Y | Y | Y | N |
| 2 Fattah | Y | Y | Y | N | Y | Y | Y | N |
| 3 **English** | N | N | Y | Y | Y | N | N | Y |
| 4 **Hart** | N | N | Y | Y | Y | N | Y | Y |
| 5 **Peterson** | N | N | Y | Y | Y | N | Y | Y |
| 6 **Gerlach** | N | Y | Y | Y | Y | N | Y | Y |
| 7 **Weldon** | N | N | Y | Y | Y | N | Y | Y |
| 8 **Fitzpatrick** | N | Y | Y | ? | Y | N | Y | Y |
| 9 **Shuster** | N | N | Y | Y | Y | N | N | Y |
| 10 **Sherwood** | N | N | Y | Y | Y | N | Y | Y |
| 11 Kanjorski | Y | Y | Y | N | Y | N | Y | Y |
| 12 Murtha | Y | Y | Y | N | Y | N | Y | N |
| 13 Schwartz | Y | Y | Y | N | Y | Y | Y | N |
| 14 Doyle | Y | Y | Y | N | Y | Y | Y | N |
| 15 **Dent** | N | Y | Y | Y | Y | N | Y | Y |
| 16 **Pitts** | Y | N | Y | Y | Y | N | Y | Y |
| 17 Holden | Y | Y | Y | N | Y | Y | Y | Y |
| 18 **Murphy** | N | Y | Y | Y | Y | N | Y | Y |
| 19 **Platts** | N | Y | Y | Y | Y | N | N | Y |
| **RHODE ISLAND** | | | | | | | | |
| 1 Kennedy | Y | Y | Y | N | N | Y | Y | N |
| 2 Langevin | Y | Y | Y | N | N | Y | Y | N |
| **SOUTH CAROLINA** | | | | | | | | |
| 1 **Brown** | N | N | Y | Y | Y | N | Y | Y |
| 2 **Wilson** | N | N | Y | Y | Y | N | Y | Y |
| 3 **Barrett** | N | N | Y | Y | Y | N | Y | Y |
| 4 **Inglis** | N | N | Y | Y | Y | N | Y | Y |
| 5 Spratt | Y | Y | Y | N | Y | Y | Y | N |
| 6 Clyburn | Y | Y | Y | N | N | Y | Y | N |
| **SOUTH DAKOTA** | | | | | | | | |
| AL Herseth | Y | Y | Y | N | N | Y | Y | N |
| **TENNESSEE** | | | | | | | | |
| 1 **Jenkins** | N | N | Y | Y | Y | N | Y | Y |
| 2 **Duncan** | N | N | Y | Y | Y | N | Y | Y |
| 3 **Wamp** | N | N | Y | Y | Y | N | Y | Y |
| 4 Davis | N | Y | Y | N | N | Y | Y | Y |
| 5 Cooper | Y | Y | Y | N | N | Y | N | N |
| 6 Gordon | Y | Y | Y | N | N | Y | Y | Y |
| 7 **Blackburn** | N | N | Y | Y | Y | N | Y | Y |
| 8 Tanner | N | Y | Y | N | Y | Y | Y | Y |
| 9 Ford | Y | Y | Y | N | N | Y | N | N |
| **TEXAS** | | | | | | | | |
| 1 **Gohmert** | Y | Y | Y | Y | Y | N | Y | Y |
| 2 **Poe** | N | N | Y | Y | Y | N | Y | Y |
| 3 **Johnson, S.** | N | N | Y | Y | Y | N | N | Y |
| 4 **Hall** | Y | N | Y | Y | Y | N | Y | Y |
| 5 **Hensarling** | N | N | Y | Y | Y | N | N | Y |
| 6 **Barton** | N | N | Y | Y | Y | N | Y | Y |
| 7 **Culberson** | N | N | Y | Y | Y | N | Y | Y |
| 8 **Brady** | N | N | Y | Y | Y | N | Y | Y |
| 9 Green | Y | Y | Y | N | N | Y | Y | N |
| 10 **McCaul** | N | Y | Y | Y | Y | N | Y | Y |
| 11 **Conaway** | N | N | Y | Y | Y | N | Y | Y |
| 12 **Granger** | N | N | Y | Y | Y | N | Y | Y |
| 13 **Thornberry** | N | N | Y | Y | Y | N | N | Y |
| 14 **Paul** | Y | N | N | Y | Y | N | Y | Y |
| 15 Hinojosa | Y | Y | Y | N | Y | Y | Y | N |
| 16 Reyes | Y | Y | Y | N | Y | Y | Y | N |
| 17 Edwards | Y | Y | Y | N | N | Y | Y | N |
| 18 Jackson-Lee | Y | Y | Y | N | N | Y | Y | N |
| 19 **Neugebauer** | N | N | Y | Y | Y | N | Y | Y |
| 20 Gonzalez | Y | Y | Y | N | N | Y | Y | N |
| 21 **Smith** | N | N | Y | Y | Y | N | N | Y |
| 22 **DeLay** | N | N | Y | Y | Y | N | Y | Y |
| 23 **Bonilla** | ? | N | Y | Y | Y | N | N | Y |
| 24 **Marchant** | N | N | Y | Y | ? | N | N | Y |
| 25 Doggett | Y | Y | Y | N | N | Y | Y | N |
| 26 **Burgess** | N | N | Y | Y | Y | N | Y | Y |
| 27 Ortiz | Y | Y | Y | N | Y | Y | Y | N |
| 28 Cuellar | Y | Y | Y | N | Y | Y | Y | N |
| 29 Green | Y | Y | Y | N | N | Y | Y | N |
| 30 Johnson, E. | Y | Y | Y | N | N | Y | Y | N |
| 31 **Carter** | N | N | Y | Y | Y | N | Y | Y |
| 32 **Sessions** | Y | N | Y | Y | Y | N | N | Y |
| **UTAH** | | | | | | | | |
| 1 **Bishop** | N | N | Y | Y | Y | N | Y | Y |
| 2 Matheson | Y | Y | Y | N | Y | N | Y | Y |
| 3 **Cannon** | N | N | Y | Y | Y | N | N | N |
| **VERMONT** | | | | | | | | |
| AL *Sanders* | Y | Y | Y | N | ? | Y | Y | N |
| **VIRGINIA** | | | | | | | | |
| 1 **Davis, J.** | N | Y | Y | Y | Y | N | Y | Y |
| 2 **Drake** | N | N | Y | Y | Y | N | Y | Y |
| 3 Scott | Y | Y | Y | N | Y | Y | Y | N |
| 4 **Forbes** | N | N | Y | Y | Y | N | Y | Y |
| 5 **Goode** | N | N | Y | Y | Y | N | Y | Y |
| 6 **Goodlatte** | N | N | Y | Y | Y | N | Y | Y |
| 7 **Cantor** | N | N | Y | Y | Y | N | N | Y |
| 8 Moran | Y | Y | Y | N | N | Y | Y | N |
| 9 Boucher | Y | Y | Y | N | ? | N | Y | N |
| 10 **Wolf** | N | N | Y | Y | Y | N | Y | Y |
| 11 **Davis, T.** | N | N | Y | Y | Y | N | Y | Y |
| **WASHINGTON** | | | | | | | | |
| 1 Inslee | Y | Y | Y | N | N | Y | Y | N |
| 2 Larsen | Y | Y | Y | N | Y | Y | Y | N |
| 3 Baird | Y | Y | Y | N | N | N | N | N |
| 4 **Hastings** | N | N | Y | Y | Y | N | Y | Y |
| 5 **McMorris** | N | N | Y | Y | Y | N | Y | Y |
| 6 Dicks | Y | Y | Y | N | N | Y | Y | N |
| 7 McDermott | Y | Y | Y | N | N | Y | Y | N |
| 8 **Reichert** | N | N | Y | Y | Y | N | Y | N |
| 9 Smith | Y | Y | ? | N | N | Y | Y | N |
| **WEST VIRGINIA** | | | | | | | | |
| 1 Mollohan | Y | Y | Y | N | Y | N | Y | N |
| 2 **Capito** | N | Y | Y | Y | Y | N | Y | Y |
| 3 Rahall | Y | Y | Y | N | Y | Y | Y | N |
| **WISCONSIN** | | | | | | | | |
| 1 **Ryan** | N | Y | Y | Y | Y | N | N | Y |
| 2 Baldwin | Y | Y | Y | N | N | Y | Y | N |
| 3 Kind | Y | Y | Y | N | Y | Y | Y | N |
| 4 Moore | N | Y | Y | N | N | Y | Y | N |
| 5 **Sensenbrenner** | Y | Y | Y | Y | Y | N | N | Y |
| 6 **Petri** | Y | Y | Y | Y | Y | N | N | Y |
| 7 Obey | Y | Y | Y | N | N | Y | N | N |
| 8 **Green** | N | Y | Y | Y | Y | N | Y | Y |
| **WYOMING** | | | | | | | | |
| AL **Cubin** | N | N | Y | Y | Y | N | Y | Y |

# IN THE HOUSE | By Vote Number

**186.** HR 1817. Fiscal 2006 Homeland Security Authorization/Border Violence Activity. Jackson-Lee, D-Texas, amendment that would require the Homeland Security secretary to submit a report to Congress on border violence activity that includes the number and types of activities that have occurred, a description of victim categories and a description of the steps the agency is taking and plans to prevent these activities. Rejected 182-245: R 2-225; D 179-20 (ND 136-13, SD 43-7); I 1-0. May 18, 2005.

**187.** HR 1817. Fiscal 2006 Homeland Security Authorization/Democratic Substitute. Thompson, D-Miss., substitute amendment that would authorize $41 billion in fiscal 2006 for the Department of Homeland Security, including $6.5 billion for grants to state and local governments, $1.8 billion for science and technology programs and $3.3 billion for emergency preparedness and response activities. The substitute also would authorize $2.8 billion for a three-year grant program to reduce the vulnerability of transit systems to terrorist attacks and more than $1 billion for rail security. It would require that 100 percent of air cargo on passenger planes be screened within three years. Rejected 196-230: R 1-227; D 194-3 (ND 147-0, SD 47-3); I 1-0. May 8, 2005.

**188.** HR 1817. Fiscal 2006 Homeland Security Authorization/Recommit. Thompson, D-Miss., motion to recommit the bill to the House Homeland Security Committee with instructions to include language that would authorize $400 million in fiscal 2006 for in-line checked baggage screening system installations as well as require that all air cargo on passenger planes be screened within three years. Motion rejected 199-228: R 1-226; D 197-2 (ND 147-2, SD 50-0); I 1-0. May 18, 2005.

**189.** HR 1817. Fiscal 2006 Homeland Security Authorization/Passage. Passage of the bill that would authorize $34.2 billion in fiscal 2006 for the Department of Homeland Security, including $6.9 billion for Customs and Border Protection and $2 billion for grants to state and local governments for terrorism preparedness. It also would authorize the hiring of 2,000 new border patrol agents and create an assistant secretary for cybersecurity to oversee the National Cyber Security Division and the National Communications System. The bill would refine the color-coded threat alert system by requiring any alerts or advisories to include information on appropriate protective measures and limit the scope to a specific region, locality, or economic sector. Passed 424-4: R 227-1; D 196-3 (ND 146-3, SD 50-0); I 1-0. May 18, 2005.

**190.** HR 2361. Fiscal 2006 Interior and Environment Appropriations/Previous Question. Bishop, R-Utah, motion to order the previous question (thus ending debate and possibility of amendment) on adoption of the rule H Res 287) to provide for House floor consideration of the bill that would appropriate $26.2 billion in fiscal 2006 for the Department of Interior, the EPA and related agencies. Motion agreed to 215-194: R 215-0; D 0-193 (ND 0-144, SD 0-49); I 0-1. Subsequently, the rule was adopted by voice vote. May 19, 2005.

**191.** HR 2361. Fiscal 2006 Interior and Environment Appropriations/Payments in Lieu of Taxes. Hefley, R-Colo., amendment that would increase the bill's appropriations by $4.8 million for payments in lieu of taxes while reducing funding for the National Endowment for the Arts by $15 million. Rejected 109-311: R 102-121; D 7-189 (ND 5-142, SD 2-47); I 0-1. May 19, 2005.

| | 186 | 187 | 188 | 189 | 190 | 191 |
|---|---|---|---|---|---|---|
| **ALABAMA** | | | | | | |
| 1 Bonner | N | N | N | Y | Y | Y |
| 2 Everett | N | N | N | Y | Y | Y |
| 3 Rogers | N | N | N | Y | Y | Y |
| 4 Aderholt | N | N | N | Y | Y | Y |
| 5 Cramer | N | Y | Y | Y | N | N |
| 6 Bachus | N | N | N | Y | Y | Y |
| 7 Davis | Y | Y | Y | Y | N | N |
| **ALASKA** | | | | | | |
| AL Young | N | N | N | Y | Y | Y |
| **ARIZONA** | | | | | | |
| 1 Renzi | N | N | N | Y | Y | N |
| 2 Franks | N | N | N | Y | Y | Y |
| 3 Shadegg | N | N | N | Y | Y | N |
| 4 Pastor | Y | Y | N | Y | N | N |
| 5 Hayworth | N | N | N | Y | Y | Y |
| 6 Flake | N | N | N | Y | Y | Y |
| 7 Grijalva | Y | Y | Y | Y | N | N |
| 8 Kolbe | N | N | N | Y | Y | N |
| **ARKANSAS** | | | | | | |
| 1 Berry | N | Y | Y | Y | Y | N |
| 2 Snyder | Y | Y | Y | Y | N | N |
| 3 Boozman | N | N | N | Y | Y | Y |
| 4 Ross | Y | Y | Y | Y | N | N |
| **CALIFORNIA** | | | | | | |
| 1 Thompson | N | Y | Y | Y | N | N |
| 2 Herger | N | N | N | Y | Y | N |
| 3 Lungren | N | N | N | Y | Y | Y |
| 4 Doolittle | N | N | N | Y | Y | Y |
| 5 Matsui, D. | Y | Y | Y | Y | ? | ? |
| 6 Woolsey | Y | Y | Y | Y | N | N |
| 7 Miller, George | Y | Y | Y | Y | N | N |
| 8 Pelosi | Y | Y | Y | Y | N | N |
| 9 Lee | Y | Y | Y | Y | N | N |
| 10 Tauscher | Y | Y | Y | Y | N | N |
| 11 Pombo | N | N | N | Y | Y | Y |
| 12 Lantos | Y | Y | Y | Y | N | N |
| 13 Stark | Y | Y | Y | Y | N | N |
| 14 Eshoo | Y | Y | Y | Y | N | N |
| 15 Honda | Y | Y | Y | Y | N | N |
| 16 Lofgren | Y | Y | Y | Y | N | N |
| 17 Farr | Y | Y | Y | Y | N | N |
| 18 Cardoza | N | Y | Y | Y | N | N |
| 19 Radanovich | N | N | N | Y | Y | N |
| 20 Costa | N | Y | Y | Y | N | N |
| 21 Nunes | N | N | N | Y | Y | Y |
| 22 Thomas | N | N | N | Y | Y | Y |
| 23 Capps | Y | Y | Y | Y | N | N |
| 24 Gallegly | N | N | N | Y | Y | N |
| 25 McKeon | N | N | N | Y | Y | N |
| 26 Dreier | N | N | N | Y | Y | N |
| 27 Sherman | Y | Y | Y | Y | N | N |
| 28 Berman | Y | Y | Y | Y | N | N |
| 29 Schiff | Y | Y | Y | Y | N | N |
| 30 Waxman | Y | Y | Y | Y | N | N |
| 31 Becerra | Y | Y | Y | Y | N | N |
| 32 Solis | Y | Y | Y | Y | N | N |
| 33 Watson | Y | Y | Y | Y | N | N |
| 34 Roybal-Allard | Y | Y | Y | Y | N | N |
| 35 Waters | Y | Y | Y | Y | N | N |
| 36 Harman | Y | Y | Y | Y | ? | ? |
| 37 Millender-McD. | ? | ? | ? | ? | ? | ? |
| 38 Napolitano | Y | Y | Y | Y | N | N |
| 39 Sánchez, Linda | Y | Y | Y | Y | N | N |
| 40 Royce | N | N | N | Y | Y | N |
| 41 Lewis | N | N | N | Y | Y | N |
| 42 Miller, Gary | N | N | N | Y | Y | Y |
| 43 Baca | Y | Y | Y | Y | N | N |
| 44 Calvert | N | N | N | Y | Y | N |
| 45 Bono | N | N | N | Y | Y | N |
| 46 Rohrabacher | N | N | N | Y | Y | Y |
| 47 Sanchez, Loretta | Y | Y | Y | Y | N | N |
| 48 Cox | N | N | N | Y | Y | N |
| 49 Issa | N | N | N | Y | Y | N |
| 50 Cunningham | N | N | N | Y | Y | N |
| 51 Filner | Y | Y | Y | Y | N | N |
| 52 Hunter | N | N | N | Y | Y | N |
| 53 Davis | Y | Y | Y | Y | N | N |
| **COLORADO** | | | | | | |
| 1 DeGette | Y | Y | Y | Y | N | N |
| 2 Udall | Y | Y | Y | Y | ? | N |
| 3 Salazar | Y | Y | Y | Y | N | Y |
| 4 Musgrave | N | N | N | Y | Y | Y |
| 5 Hefley | N | N | N | Y | Y | Y |
| 6 Tancredo | ? | ? | ? | ? | ? | ? |
| 7 Beauprez | N | N | N | Y | Y | Y |
| **CONNECTICUT** | | | | | | |
| 1 Larson | + | + | + | + | – | – |
| 2 Simmons | N | N | N | Y | Y | N |
| 3 DeLauro | Y | Y | Y | Y | N | N |
| 4 Shays | N | Y | Y | Y | ? | N |
| 5 Johnson | N | N | N | Y | Y | N |
| **DELAWARE** | | | | | | |
| AL Castle | N | N | N | Y | Y | N |
| **FLORIDA** | | | | | | |
| 1 Miller | N | N | N | Y | Y | Y |
| 2 Boyd | N | Y | Y | Y | N | N |
| 3 Brown | Y | Y | Y | Y | N | N |
| 4 Crenshaw | N | N | N | Y | Y | N |
| 5 Brown-Waite | N | N | N | Y | Y | Y |
| 6 Stearns | N | N | N | Y | Y | Y |
| 7 Mica | N | N | N | Y | Y | Y |
| 8 Keller | N | N | N | Y | ? | N |
| 9 Bilirakis | N | N | N | Y | Y | N |
| 10 Young | N | N | N | Y | Y | N |
| 11 Davis | Y | Y | Y | Y | N | N |
| 12 Putnam | N | N | N | Y | Y | Y |
| 13 Harris | N | N | N | Y | Y | N |
| 14 Mack | N | N | N | Y | Y | Y |
| 15 Weldon | N | N | N | Y | ? | Y |
| 16 Foley | N | N | N | Y | Y | N |
| 17 Meek | N | N | N | Y | Y | N |
| 18 Ros-Lehtinen | N | N | N | Y | Y | N |
| 19 Wexler | Y | Y | Y | Y | N | N |
| 20 Wasserman-Schultz | Y | Y | Y | Y | N | N |
| 21 Diaz-Balart, L. | N | N | N | Y | Y | N |
| 22 Shaw | N | N | N | Y | Y | N |
| 23 Hastings | Y | Y | Y | Y | N | N |
| 24 Feeney | N | N | ? | Y | Y | N |
| 25 Diaz-Balart, M. | N | N | N | Y | Y | N |
| **GEORGIA** | | | | | | |
| 1 Kingston | N | N | N | Y | Y | N |
| 2 Bishop | Y | Y | Y | Y | N | N |
| 3 Marshall | Y | Y | Y | Y | N | N |
| 4 McKinney | Y | Y | Y | Y | N | N |
| 5 Lewis | ? | ? | ? | ? | ? | ? |
| 6 Price | N | N | N | Y | Y | N |
| 7 Linder | N | N | N | Y | Y | N |
| 8 Westmoreland | N | N | N | Y | Y | Y |
| 9 Norwood | N | N | N | Y | Y | Y |
| 10 Deal | N | N | N | Y | Y | Y |
| 11 Gingrey | N | N | N | Y | ? | Y |
| 12 Barrow | Y | Y | Y | Y | N | N |
| 13 Scott | N | Y | Y | Y | N | N |
| **HAWAII** | | | | | | |
| 1 Abercrombie | Y | Y | Y | Y | N | N |
| 2 Case | Y | Y | Y | Y | N | N |
| **IDAHO** | | | | | | |
| 1 Otter | N | N | N | Y | Y | Y |
| 2 Simpson | N | N | N | Y | Y | Y |
| **ILLINOIS** | | | | | | |
| 1 Rush | Y | Y | Y | Y | N | N |
| 2 Jackson | Y | Y | Y | Y | N | N |
| 3 Lipinski | Y | Y | Y | Y | N | N |
| 4 Gutierrez | Y | Y | Y | N | N | N |
| 5 Emanuel | Y | Y | Y | Y | N | N |
| 6 Hyde | N | N | N | Y | Y | N |
| 7 Davis | Y | Y | Y | Y | N | N |
| 8 Bean | Y | Y | Y | Y | N | N |
| 9 Schakowsky | Y | Y | Y | Y | N | N |
| 10 Kirk | N | N | N | Y | Y | N |
| 11 Weller | N | N | N | Y | Y | Y |
| 12 Costello | Y | Y | Y | Y | N | N |

| KEY | Republicans | Democrats | Independents |
|---|---|---|---|

| | | | | | |
|---|---|---|---|---|---|
| Y | Voted for (yea) | X | Paired against | C | Voted "present" to avoid possible conflict of interest |
| # | Paired for | – | Announced against | | |
| + | Announced for | P | Voted "present" | ? | Did not vote or otherwise make a position known |
| N | Voted against (nay) | | | | |

| | 186 | 187 | 188 | 189 | 190 | 191 |
|---|---|---|---|---|---|---|
| 13 **Biggert** | N | N | N | Y | Y | N |
| 14 **Hastert** | | | | | | |
| 15 **Johnson** | N | N | N | Y | Y | N |
| 16 **Manzullo** | N | N | N | Y | Y | Y |
| 17 Evans | Y | Y | Y | Y | N | N |
| 18 **LaHood** | N | N | N | Y | Y | N |
| 19 **Shimkus** | N | N | N | Y | Y | N |
| **INDIANA** | | | | | | |
| 1 Visclosky | Y | Y | Y | Y | N | N |
| 2 **Chocola** | N | N | N | Y | Y | N |
| 3 **Souder** | N | N | N | Y | Y | N |
| 4 **Buyer** | N | N | N | Y | Y | Y |
| 5 **Burton** | N | N | N | Y | Y | Y |
| 6 **Pence** | N | N | N | Y | Y | Y |
| 7 Carson | Y | Y | Y | Y | N | N |
| 8 **Hostettler** | Y | N | N | Y | Y | Y |
| 9 **Sodrel** | N | N | N | Y | Y | N |
| **IOWA** | | | | | | |
| 1 **Nussle** | N | N | N | Y | Y | N |
| 2 **Leach** | Y | N | N | Y | Y | ? |
| 3 Boswell | Y | Y | Y | Y | N | N |
| 4 **Latham** | N | N | N | Y | Y | N |
| 5 **King** | N | N | N | Y | Y | Y |
| **KANSAS** | | | | | | |
| 1 **Moran** | N | N | N | Y | Y | N |
| 2 **Ryun** | N | N | N | Y | Y | Y |
| 3 Moore | Y | Y | Y | Y | N | N |
| 4 **Tiahrt** | N | N | N | Y | ? | Y |
| **KENTUCKY** | | | | | | |
| 1 **Whitfield** | N | N | N | Y | Y | N |
| 2 **Lewis** | N | N | N | Y | Y | Y |
| 3 **Northup** | N | N | N | Y | Y | N |
| 4 **Davis** | N | N | N | Y | Y | N |
| 5 **Rogers** | N | N | N | Y | Y | N |
| 6 Chandler | Y | Y | Y | Y | N | N |
| **LOUISIANA** | | | | | | |
| 1 **Jindal** | N | N | N | Y | Y | N |
| 2 Jefferson | Y | Y | Y | Y | N | N |
| 3 Melancon | Y | Y | Y | Y | N | N |
| 4 **McCrery** | N | N | N | Y | Y | N |
| 5 **Alexander** | N | N | N | Y | Y | N |
| 6 **Baker** | N | N | N | Y | Y | N |
| 7 **Boustany** | N | N | N | Y | ? | N |
| **MAINE** | | | | | | |
| 1 Allen | Y | Y | Y | Y | N | N |
| 2 Michaud | Y | Y | Y | Y | N | N |
| **MARYLAND** | | | | | | |
| 1 **Gilchrest** | N | N | N | Y | Y | N |
| 2 Ruppersberger | Y | Y | Y | Y | N | N |
| 3 Cardin | Y | Y | Y | Y | N | N |
| 4 Wynn | Y | Y | Y | Y | N | N |
| 5 Hoyer | Y | Y | Y | Y | N | N |
| 6 **Bartlett** | N | N | N | Y | Y | Y |
| 7 Cummings | Y | Y | Y | Y | N | N |
| 8 Van Hollen | Y | Y | Y | Y | N | N |
| **MASSACHUSETTS** | | | | | | |
| 1 Olver | Y | Y | Y | Y | N | N |
| 2 Neal | Y | Y | Y | Y | N | N |
| 3 McGovern | Y | Y | Y | Y | N | N |
| 4 Frank | Y | Y | Y | Y | N | N |
| 5 Meehan | Y | Y | Y | Y | N | N |
| 6 Tierney | N | Y | Y | Y | N | N |
| 7 Markey | Y | Y | Y | N | N | N |
| 8 Capuano | Y | Y | Y | Y | N | N |
| 9 Lynch | Y | Y | Y | Y | N | N |
| 10 Delahunt | Y | Y | Y | Y | N | N |
| **MICHIGAN** | | | | | | |
| 1 Stupak | Y | Y | Y | Y | N | N |
| 2 **Hoekstra** | N | N | N | Y | Y | Y |
| 3 **Ehlers** | N | N | N | Y | Y | N |
| 4 **Camp** | N | N | N | Y | Y | N |
| 5 Kildee | Y | Y | Y | Y | N | N |
| 6 **Upton** | N | N | N | Y | Y | N |
| 7 **Schwarz** | N | N | N | Y | Y | N |
| 8 **Rogers** | N | N | N | Y | Y | N |
| 9 **Knollenberg** | N | N | N | Y | Y | N |
| 10 **Miller** | N | N | N | Y | Y | N |
| 11 **McCotter** | N | N | N | Y | Y | N |
| 12 Levin | Y | Y | Y | Y | N | N |
| 13 Kilpatrick | Y | Y | Y | Y | N | N |
| 14 Conyers | Y | Y | Y | Y | N | N |
| 15 Dingell | Y | Y | Y | Y | N | N |

| | 186 | 187 | 188 | 189 | 190 | 191 |
|---|---|---|---|---|---|---|
| **MINNESOTA** | | | | | | |
| 1 **Gutknecht** | N | N | N | Y | Y | Y |
| 2 **Kline** | N | N | N | Y | Y | Y |
| 3 **Ramstad** | N | N | N | Y | Y | N |
| 4 McCollum | Y | Y | Y | Y | N | N |
| 5 Sabo | Y | Y | Y | Y | N | N |
| 6 **Kennedy** | N | N | N | Y | Y | N |
| 7 Peterson | N | Y | Y | Y | N | Y |
| 8 Oberstar | Y | Y | Y | Y | N | N |
| **MISSISSIPPI** | | | | | | |
| 1 **Wicker** | N | N | N | Y | Y | N |
| 2 Thompson | Y | Y | Y | Y | N | N |
| 3 **Pickering** | N | N | N | Y | Y | N |
| 4 Taylor | N | N | Y | Y | N | Y |
| **MISSOURI** | | | | | | |
| 1 Clay | Y | Y | Y | Y | N | N |
| 2 **Akin** | N | N | N | Y | Y | Y |
| 3 Carnahan | Y | Y | Y | Y | N | N |
| 4 Skelton | N | Y | Y | Y | N | Y |
| 5 Cleaver | Y | Y | Y | Y | N | N |
| 6 **Graves** | N | N | N | Y | Y | Y |
| 7 **Blunt** | N | N | N | Y | Y | Y |
| 8 **Emerson** | N | N | N | Y | Y | Y |
| 9 **Hulshof** | N | N | N | Y | Y | Y |
| **MONTANA** | | | | | | |
| AL **Rehberg** | N | N | N | Y | Y | N |
| **NEBRASKA** | | | | | | |
| 1 **Fortenberry** | N | N | N | Y | Y | N |
| 2 **Terry** | N | N | N | Y | Y | N |
| 3 **Osborne** | N | N | N | Y | Y | N |
| **NEVADA** | | | | | | |
| 1 Berkley | Y | Y | Y | Y | N | Y |
| 2 **Gibbons** | N | N | N | Y | Y | Y |
| 3 **Porter** | N | N | N | Y | Y | N |
| **NEW HAMPSHIRE** | | | | | | |
| 1 **Bradley** | N | N | N | Y | Y | N |
| 2 **Bass** | N | N | N | Y | Y | N |
| **NEW JERSEY** | | | | | | |
| 1 Andrews | Y | Y | Y | Y | N | N |
| 2 **LoBiondo** | N | N | N | Y | Y | N |
| 3 **Saxton** | N | N | N | Y | Y | N |
| 4 **Smith** | N | N | N | Y | Y | N |
| 5 **Garrett** | N | N | N | Y | Y | Y |
| 6 Pallone | Y | Y | Y | Y | N | N |
| 7 **Ferguson** | N | N | N | Y | Y | N |
| 8 Pascrell | Y | Y | Y | Y | N | N |
| 9 Rothman | Y | Y | Y | Y | N | N |
| 10 Payne | Y | Y | Y | Y | N | N |
| 11 **Frelinghuysen** | N | N | N | Y | Y | N |
| 12 Holt | Y | Y | Y | Y | N | N |
| 13 Menendez | Y | Y | Y | Y | N | N |
| **NEW MEXICO** | | | | | | |
| 1 **Wilson** | N | N | N | Y | Y | Y |
| 2 **Pearce** | N | N | N | Y | Y | N |
| 3 Udall | Y | Y | Y | Y | N | N |
| **NEW YORK** | | | | | | |
| 1 Bishop | Y | Y | Y | Y | N | N |
| 2 Israel | Y | Y | Y | Y | N | N |
| 3 **King** | N | N | N | Y | Y | N |
| 4 McCarthy | Y | Y | Y | Y | N | N |
| 5 Ackerman | Y | Y | Y | Y | N | N |
| 6 Meeks | Y | Y | Y | Y | N | N |
| 7 Crowley | Y | Y | Y | Y | N | N |
| 8 Nadler | Y | Y | Y | Y | N | N |
| 9 Weiner | Y | Y | Y | Y | N | N |
| 10 Towns | Y | Y | Y | Y | N | N |
| 11 Owens | Y | Y | Y | Y | N | N |
| 12 Velázquez | Y | Y | Y | Y | N | N |
| 13 **Fossella** | N | N | N | Y | Y | N |
| 14 Maloney | Y | Y | Y | Y | N | N |
| 15 Rangel | Y | Y | Y | Y | N | N |
| 16 Serrano | Y | Y | Y | Y | N | N |
| 17 Engel | Y | Y | Y | Y | N | N |
| 18 Lowey | Y | Y | Y | Y | N | N |
| 19 **Kelly** | N | N | N | Y | Y | N |
| 20 **Sweeney** | N | N | N | Y | Y | N |
| 21 McNulty | Y | Y | Y | Y | N | N |
| 22 Hinchey | Y | Y | Y | Y | N | N |
| 23 **McHugh** | N | N | N | Y | Y | N |
| 24 **Boehlert** | N | N | N | Y | Y | N |
| 25 **Walsh** | N | N | N | Y | Y | N |
| 26 **Reynolds** | N | N | N | Y | Y | N |
| 27 Higgins | Y | Y | Y | Y | N | N |
| 28 Slaughter | Y | Y | Y | Y | N | N |
| 29 **Kuhl** | N | N | N | Y | Y | Y |

| | 186 | 187 | 188 | 189 | 190 | 191 |
|---|---|---|---|---|---|---|
| **NORTH CAROLINA** | | | | | | |
| 1 Butterfield | Y | Y | Y | Y | N | N |
| 2 Etheridge | Y | Y | Y | Y | N | N |
| 3 **Jones** | N | N | N | Y | Y | Y |
| 4 Price | Y | Y | Y | Y | N | N |
| 5 **Foxx** | N | N | N | Y | Y | Y |
| 6 **Coble** | N | N | N | Y | Y | N |
| 7 McIntyre | Y | Y | Y | Y | N | N |
| 8 **Hayes** | N | N | N | Y | Y | Y |
| 9 **Myrick** | N | N | N | Y | Y | Y |
| 10 **McHenry** | N | N | N | Y | Y | Y |
| 11 **Taylor** | ? | N | N | Y | Y | N |
| 12 Watt | Y | Y | Y | Y | N | N |
| 13 Miller | Y | Y | Y | Y | N | N |
| **NORTH DAKOTA** | | | | | | |
| AL Pomeroy | N | Y | Y | Y | N | Y |
| **OHIO** | | | | | | |
| 1 **Chabot** | N | N | N | Y | Y | Y |
| 2 Vacant | | | | | | |
| 3 **Turner** | N | N | N | Y | Y | N |
| 4 **Oxley** | N | N | N | Y | Y | N |
| 5 **Gillmor** | N | N | N | Y | Y | N |
| 6 Strickland | N | Y | Y | Y | ? | ? |
| 7 **Hobson** | N | N | N | Y | Y | N |
| 8 **Boehner** | N | N | N | Y | Y | Y |
| 9 Kaptur | Y | ? | Y | Y | N | N |
| 10 Kucinich | Y | Y | Y | Y | N | N |
| 11 Jones | Y | Y | Y | Y | N | N |
| 12 **Tiberi** | N | N | N | Y | Y | N |
| 13 Brown | Y | Y | Y | Y | N | N |
| 14 **LaTourette** | N | N | N | Y | Y | ? |
| 15 **Pryce** | N | N | N | Y | Y | N |
| 16 **Regula** | N | N | N | Y | Y | N |
| 17 Ryan | Y | Y | Y | Y | N | N |
| 18 **Ney** | N | N | N | Y | ? | N |
| **OKLAHOMA** | | | | | | |
| 1 **Sullivan** | N | N | N | Y | ? | Y |
| 2 Boren | N | N | Y | Y | N | N |
| 3 **Lucas** | ? | ? | ? | ? | ? | ? |
| 4 **Cole** | N | N | N | Y | Y | N |
| 5 **Istook** | N | N | N | Y | Y | Y |
| **OREGON** | | | | | | |
| 1 Wu | Y | Y | Y | Y | N | N |
| 2 **Walden** | N | N | N | Y | Y | N |
| 3 Blumenauer | N | Y | Y | Y | N | N |
| 4 DeFazio | Y | Y | Y | Y | N | N |
| 5 Hooley | Y | Y | Y | Y | N | N |
| **PENNSYLVANIA** | | | | | | |
| 1 Brady | Y | Y | Y | Y | N | N |
| 2 Fattah | Y | Y | Y | Y | ? | N |
| 3 **English** | N | N | N | Y | Y | N |
| 4 **Hart** | N | N | N | Y | Y | N |
| 5 **Peterson** | N | N | N | Y | Y | N |
| 6 **Gerlach** | N | N | N | Y | Y | N |
| 7 **Weldon** | N | N | N | Y | ? | ? |
| 8 **Fitzpatrick** | N | N | N | Y | Y | N |
| 9 **Shuster** | N | N | N | Y | Y | Y |
| 10 **Sherwood** | N | N | N | Y | Y | N |
| 11 Kanjorski | Y | Y | Y | Y | N | N |
| 12 Murtha | N | Y | Y | Y | N | N |
| 13 Schwartz | Y | Y | Y | Y | N | N |
| 14 Doyle | Y | Y | Y | Y | N | N |
| 15 **Dent** | N | N | N | Y | Y | N |
| 16 **Pitts** | N | N | N | Y | Y | Y |
| 17 Holden | Y | Y | Y | Y | N | N |
| 18 **Murphy** | N | N | N | Y | Y | N |
| 19 **Platts** | N | N | N | Y | Y | N |
| **RHODE ISLAND** | | | | | | |
| 1 Kennedy | Y | Y | Y | Y | N | N |
| 2 Langevin | Y | Y | Y | Y | N | N |
| **SOUTH CAROLINA** | | | | | | |
| 1 **Brown** | N | N | N | Y | Y | N |
| 2 **Wilson** | N | N | N | Y | Y | Y |
| 3 **Barrett** | N | N | N | Y | Y | Y |
| 4 **Inglis** | N | N | N | Y | Y | N |
| 5 Spratt | Y | Y | Y | Y | N | N |
| 6 Clyburn | Y | Y | Y | Y | N | N |
| **SOUTH DAKOTA** | | | | | | |
| AL Herseth | N | Y | Y | Y | N | N |
| **TENNESSEE** | | | | | | |
| 1 **Jenkins** | N | N | N | Y | Y | Y |
| 2 **Duncan** | N | N | N | Y | Y | N |

| | 186 | 187 | 188 | 189 | 190 | 191 |
|---|---|---|---|---|---|---|
| 3 **Wamp** | N | N | N | Y | Y | N |
| 4 Davis | Y | Y | Y | Y | N | N |
| 5 Cooper | Y | Y | Y | Y | N | N |
| 6 Gordon | Y | Y | Y | Y | N | N |
| 7 **Blackburn** | N | N | N | Y | Y | Y |
| 8 Tanner | N | Y | Y | Y | N | Y |
| 9 Ford | Y | Y | Y | Y | N | N |
| **TEXAS** | | | | | | |
| 1 **Gohmert** | N | N | N | Y | Y | Y |
| 2 **Poe** | N | N | N | Y | Y | Y |
| 3 **Johnson, S.** | N | N | N | Y | Y | Y |
| 4 **Hall** | N | N | N | Y | Y | Y |
| 5 **Hensarling** | N | N | N | Y | Y | Y |
| 6 **Barton** | N | N | N | Y | Y | Y |
| 7 **Culberson** | N | N | N | Y | Y | Y |
| 8 **Brady** | N | N | N | Y | Y | Y |
| 9 Green | Y | Y | Y | Y | N | N |
| 10 **McCaul** | N | N | N | Y | Y | Y |
| 11 **Conaway** | N | N | N | Y | Y | + |
| 12 **Granger** | N | N | N | Y | Y | N |
| 13 **Thornberry** | N | N | N | Y | Y | Y |
| 14 **Paul** | N | N | N | N | Y | Y |
| 15 Hinojosa | Y | Y | Y | Y | N | N |
| 16 Reyes | Y | Y | Y | Y | N | N |
| 17 Edwards | Y | Y | Y | Y | N | N |
| 18 Jackson-Lee | Y | Y | Y | Y | ? | ? |
| 19 **Neugebauer** | N | N | N | Y | Y | Y |
| 20 Gonzalez | Y | Y | Y | Y | N | N |
| 21 **Smith** | N | N | N | Y | Y | N |
| 22 **DeLay** | N | N | N | Y | Y | Y |
| 23 **Bonilla** | N | N | N | Y | Y | N |
| 24 **Marchant** | N | N | N | Y | Y | Y |
| 25 Doggett | Y | Y | Y | Y | N | N |
| 26 **Burgess** | N | N | N | Y | ? | Y |
| 27 Ortiz | Y | Y | Y | Y | N | N |
| 28 Cuellar | Y | Y | Y | Y | N | N |
| 29 Green | Y | N | Y | Y | N | N |
| 30 Johnson, E. | Y | Y | Y | Y | N | N |
| 31 **Carter** | N | N | N | Y | Y | N |
| 32 **Sessions** | N | N | N | Y | Y | Y |
| **UTAH** | | | | | | |
| 1 **Bishop** | N | N | N | Y | Y | Y |
| 2 Matheson | Y | Y | Y | Y | N | N |
| 3 **Cannon** | N | N | N | Y | Y | Y |
| **VERMONT** | | | | | | |
| AL *Sanders* | Y | Y | Y | Y | N | N |
| **VIRGINIA** | | | | | | |
| 1 **Davis, J.** | N | N | N | Y | Y | Y |
| 2 **Drake** | N | N | N | Y | Y | N |
| 3 Scott | Y | Y | Y | Y | N | N |
| 4 **Forbes** | N | N | N | Y | Y | Y |
| 5 **Goode** | N | N | N | Y | Y | Y |
| 6 **Goodlatte** | N | N | N | Y | Y | Y |
| 7 **Cantor** | N | N | N | Y | ? | N |
| 8 Moran | Y | Y | Y | Y | N | N |
| 9 Boucher | Y | Y | Y | Y | N | N |
| 10 **Wolf** | N | N | N | Y | Y | N |
| 11 **Davis, T.** | N | N | N | Y | Y | N |
| **WASHINGTON** | | | | | | |
| 1 Inslee | Y | Y | Y | Y | N | N |
| 2 Larsen | Y | Y | Y | Y | N | N |
| 3 Baird | Y | Y | N | Y | N | N |
| 4 **Hastings** | N | N | N | Y | Y | Y |
| 5 **McMorris** | N | N | N | Y | Y | Y |
| 6 Dicks | Y | Y | Y | Y | N | N |
| 7 McDermott | Y | ? | Y | Y | N | N |
| 8 **Reichert** | N | N | N | Y | Y | N |
| 9 Smith | Y | Y | Y | Y | N | N |
| **WEST VIRGINIA** | | | | | | |
| 1 Mollohan | N | Y | Y | Y | N | N |
| 2 **Capito** | N | N | N | Y | Y | N |
| 3 Rahall | N | Y | Y | Y | N | N |
| **WISCONSIN** | | | | | | |
| 1 **Ryan** | N | N | N | Y | ? | Y |
| 2 Baldwin | Y | Y | Y | Y | N | N |
| 3 Kind | Y | Y | Y | Y | N | N |
| 4 Moore | Y | Y | Y | Y | N | N |
| 5 **Sensenbrenner** | N | N | N | Y | Y | Y |
| 6 **Petri** | N | N | N | Y | Y | Y |
| 7 Obey | Y | Y | Y | N | N | N |
| 8 **Green** | N | N | N | Y | Y | Y |
| **WYOMING** | | | | | | |
| AL **Cubin** | N | N | N | Y | Y | Y |

# IN THE HOUSE | By Vote Number

**192.** HR 2361. Fiscal 2006 Interior and Environment Appropriations/ **Natural Gas Moratorium.** Peterson, R-Pa., amendment that would lift the moratorium on natural gas production in the Outer Continental Shelf. Rejected 157-262: R 130-93; D 27-168 (ND 8-138, SD 19-30); I 0-1. May 19, 2005.

**193.** HR 2361. Fiscal 2006 Interior and Environment Appropriations/ **Hazardous Substance Superfund.** Terry, R-Neb., amendment that would increase funding for the superfund hazardous waste cleanup program by $130 million, offset by a cut in the EPA's Science and Technology account. Rejected 76-344: R 42-181; D 34-162 (ND 28-119, SD 6-43); I 0-1. May 19, 2005.

**194.** HR 2361. Fiscal 2006 Interior and Environment Appropriations/ **Clean Water Revolving Fund.** Obey, D-Wis., amendment that would increase the Clean Water State Revolving Fund by $100 million, offset by a cut in state and tribal assistance grants. Rejected 186-235: R 6-218; D 179-17 (ND 133-14, SD 46-3); I 1-0. May 19, 2005.

**195.** HR 2361. Fiscal 2006 Interior and Environment Appropriations/ **Forest Service Funding.** Beauprez, R-Colo., amendment that would increase funding for the Forest Service by $27.5 million, offset by reducing funds for the National Endowment for the Arts by $30 million. Rejected 122-298: R 116-108; D 6-189 (ND 4-143, SD 2-46); I 0-1. May 19, 2005.

**196.** HR 2361. Fiscal 2006 Interior and Environment Appropriations/ **Wild Horses and Burros.** Rahall, D-W.Va., amendment that would prohibit the use of funds in the bill for the sale or slaughter of wild horses and burros. Adopted 249-159: R 78-140; D 170-19 (ND 132-11, SD 38-8); I 1-0. May 19, 2005.

**197.** HR 2361. Fiscal 2006 Interior and Environment Appropriations/ **Across-the-Board Cut.** Hefley, R-Colo., amendment that would require a 1 percent across-the-board cut to discretionary spending. Rejected 90-326: R 87-134; D 3-191 (ND 1-144, SD 2-47); I 0-1. May 19, 2005.

**198.** HR 2361. Fiscal 2006 Interior and Environment Appropriations/ **Recommit.** Obey, D-Wis., motion to recommit the bill to the House Appropriations Committee with instructions to include language that would add $242 million for the Clean Water State Revolving Fund and $110 million for State and Tribal Assistance Grants. Motion rejected 191-228: R 0-223; D 190-5 (ND 141-5, SD 49-0); I 1-0. May 19, 2005.

**199.** HR 2361. Fiscal 2006 Interior and Environment Appropriations/ **Passage.** Passage of the bill that would provide $26.2 billion in fiscal 2006 for the Department of Interior, the EPA and related agencies. The bill would provide $9.8 billion for the Interior Department, $7.7 billion for the EPA, $4.2 billion for the Forest Service and $3.1 billion for the Indian Health Service. The National Endowment for the Arts would receive $131 million and the National Endowment for the Humanities would be funded at $143 million. It would maintain the moratorium on natural gas production in the Outer Continental Shelf. Passed 329-89: R 214-8; D 115-80 (ND 75-71, SD 40-9); I 0-1. May 19, 2005.

| | 192 | 193 | 194 | 195 | 196 | 197 | 198 | 199 |
|---|---|---|---|---|---|---|---|---|
| **ALABAMA** | | | | | | | | |
| 1 Bonner | Y | N | N | N | N | N | N | Y |
| 2 Everett | Y | N | N | N | Y | Y | N | Y |
| 3 Rogers | N | N | N | N | N | N | N | Y |
| 4 Aderholt | Y | N | N | N | Y | N | N | Y |
| 5 Cramer | Y | N | Y | N | Y | N | Y | Y |
| 6 Bachus | Y | N | N | Y | N | N | N | Y |
| 7 Davis | N | N | Y | N | Y | N | Y | Y |
| **ALASKA** | | | | | | | | |
| AL Young | Y | N | N | Y | ? | ? | ? | ? |
| **ARIZONA** | | | | | | | | |
| 1 Renzi | Y | N | N | Y | N | N | N | Y |
| 2 Franks | Y | N | N | Y | Y | Y | N | N |
| 3 Shadegg | Y | N | N | Y | N | Y | N | Y |
| 4 Pastor | N | N | Y | N | Y | N | Y | Y |
| 5 Hayworth | Y | Y | N | Y | N | Y | N | Y |
| 6 Flake | Y | Y | N | Y | N | Y | N | N |
| 7 Grijalva | N | N | Y | N | Y | N | Y | N |
| 8 Kolbe | Y | ? | N | N | N | N | N | Y |
| **ARKANSAS** | | | | | | | | |
| 1 Berry | Y | N | Y | N | Y | N | Y | N |
| 2 Snyder | N | N | Y | N | Y | N | Y | Y |
| 3 Boozman | Y | N | N | N | N | N | N | Y |
| 4 Ross | Y | N | Y | N | N | N | Y | Y |
| **CALIFORNIA** | | | | | | | | |
| 1 Thompson | N | N | Y | N | Y | N | Y | Y |
| 2 Herger | Y | N | N | Y | N | N | N | Y |
| 3 Lungren | Y | N | N | Y | N | N | N | Y |
| 4 Doolittle | Y | N | N | N | N | N | N | Y |
| 5 Matsui, D. | N | Y | Y | N | Y | N | Y | N |
| 6 Woolsey | N | N | Y | N | Y | N | Y | N |
| 7 Miller, George | N | N | Y | N | Y | N | Y | N |
| 8 Pelosi | N | N | Y | N | Y | N | Y | N |
| 9 Lee | N | N | Y | N | Y | N | Y | N |
| 10 Tauscher | N | N | Y | N | Y | N | Y | Y |
| 11 Pombo | N | N | N | N | N | N | N | Y |
| 12 Lantos | N | N | Y | N | Y | N | Y | N |
| 13 Stark | N | N | Y | N | Y | N | Y | N |
| 14 Eshoo | N | N | Y | N | Y | N | Y | N |
| 15 Honda | N | N | Y | N | Y | N | Y | N |
| 16 Lofgren | N | N | Y | N | Y | N | Y | N |
| 17 Farr | N | N | Y | N | Y | N | Y | Y |
| 18 Cardoza | N | N | Y | N | N | N | Y | Y |
| 19 Radanovich | N | N | N | ? | ? | ? | ? | ? |
| 20 Costa | N | N | Y | N | N | Y | Y | Y |
| 21 Nunes | Y | N | N | Y | N | N | N | Y |
| 22 Thomas | Y | N | N | N | N | N | N | Y |
| 23 Capps | N | N | Y | N | Y | N | Y | N |
| 24 Gallegly | N | N | N | Y | Y | N | N | Y |
| 25 McKeon | N | N | N | N | N | N | N | Y |
| 26 Dreier | N | N | N | Y | Y | N | N | Y |
| 27 Sherman | N | N | Y | N | Y | N | Y | N |
| 28 Berman | N | N | Y | N | Y | N | Y | N |
| 29 Schiff | N | N | Y | N | Y | N | Y | Y |
| 30 Waxman | N | N | Y | N | Y | N | Y | N |
| 31 Becerra | N | N | Y | N | Y | N | Y | N |
| 32 Solis | N | N | Y | N | Y | N | Y | N |
| 33 Watson | N | N | Y | N | Y | N | Y | N |
| 34 Roybal-Allard | N | N | Y | N | Y | N | Y | N |
| 35 Waters | N | N | Y | N | Y | N | Y | N |
| 36 Harman | ? | ? | ? | ? | ? | ? | ? | ? |
| 37 Millender-McD. | ? | ? | ? | ? | ? | ? | ? | ? |
| 38 Napolitano | N | N | N | N | Y | N | Y | N |
| 39 Sánchez, Linda | N | N | Y | N | Y | N | Y | N |
| 40 Royce | N | N | N | Y | N | N | N | Y |
| 41 Lewis | N | N | N | Y | N | N | N | Y |
| 42 Miller, Gary | Y | Y | N | Y | N | Y | N | Y |
| 43 Baca | N | N | Y | N | Y | N | Y | Y |
| 44 Calvert | N | N | N | Y | N | N | N | Y |
| 45 Bono | N | N | N | N | Y | N | N | Y |
| 46 Rohrabacher | Y | N | N | Y | N | Y | N | N |
| 47 Sanchez, Loretta | N | N | Y | N | Y | N | Y | Y |
| 48 Cox | N | N | Y | N | ? | N | Y | Y |
| 49 Issa | N | N | N | Y | Y | N | N | Y |

| | 192 | 193 | 194 | 195 | 196 | 197 | 198 | 199 |
|---|---|---|---|---|---|---|---|---|
| 50 Cunningham | N | N | Y | Y | N | N | Y | |
| 51 Filner | N | N | Y | N | Y | N | Y | Y |
| 52 Hunter | Y | N | N | Y | N | N | N | Y |
| 53 Davis | N | N | Y | N | Y | N | Y | Y |
| **COLORADO** | | | | | | | | |
| 1 DeGette | N | N | Y | N | Y | N | Y | N |
| 2 Udall | N | N | Y | Y | Y | N | Y | N |
| 3 Salazar | Y | Y | Y | Y | N | N | Y | N |
| 4 Musgrave | Y | Y | N | Y | N | Y | N | Y |
| 5 Hefley | Y | N | N | Y | N | Y | N | Y |
| 6 Tancredo | ? | ? | ? | ? | ? | ? | ? | ? |
| 7 Beauprez | Y | N | N | Y | N | Y | N | Y |
| **CONNECTICUT** | | | | | | | | |
| 1 Larson | – | – | + | – | + | – | + | – |
| 2 Simmons | N | N | N | N | Y | N | N | Y |
| 3 DeLauro | N | N | Y | N | Y | N | Y | N |
| 4 Shays | ? | ? | ? | ? | ? | ? | ? | ? |
| 5 Johnson | Y | N | Y | N | N | N | N | Y |
| **DELAWARE** | | | | | | | | |
| AL Castle | N | N | N | N | Y | N | N | Y |
| **FLORIDA** | | | | | | | | |
| 1 Miller | N | Y | N | Y | N | Y | N | Y |
| 2 Boyd | N | N | Y | N | N | N | Y | Y |
| 3 Brown | N | N | Y | N | Y | N | Y | Y |
| 4 Crenshaw | N | N | N | N | N | N | N | Y |
| 5 Brown-Waite | N | N | N | N | Y | N | Y | Y |
| 6 Stearns | N | N | Y | N | Y | N | Y | N |
| 7 Mica | Y | N | N | N | N | N | N | Y |
| 8 Keller | N | N | Y | Y | Y | Y | N | Y |
| 9 Bilirakis | N | N | N | Y | Y | N | N | Y |
| 10 Young | N | N | N | Y | N | N | N | Y |
| 11 Davis | N | N | N | N | N | N | N | Y |
| 12 Putnam | N | N | N | N | N | N | N | Y |
| 13 Harris | N | N | N | N | N | N | N | Y |
| 14 Mack | N | N | N | N | N | N | N | Y |
| 15 Weldon | N | N | N | N | Y | N | N | Y |
| 16 Foley | N | N | N | Y | Y | Y | N | Y |
| 17 Meek | N | N | Y | N | Y | N | Y | Y |
| 18 Ros-Lehtinen | N | N | N | N | N | N | N | Y |
| 19 Wexler | N | N | Y | N | Y | N | Y | N |
| 20 Wasserman-Schultz | N | N | Y | N | Y | N | Y | N |
| 21 Diaz-Balart, L. | N | N | N | N | N | N | N | Y |
| 22 Shaw | N | N | N | N | N | N | N | Y |
| 23 Hastings | N | N | Y | N | Y | N | Y | Y |
| 24 Feeney | N | N | Y | N | Y | N | Y | Y |
| 25 Diaz-Balart, M. | N | N | Y | Y | Y | N | Y | |
| **GEORGIA** | | | | | | | | |
| 1 Kingston | N | N | Y | N | N | N | N | Y |
| 2 Bishop | N | N | Y | N | Y | N | Y | Y |
| 3 Marshall | Y | N | Y | N | N | N | Y | Y |
| 4 McKinney | N | N | Y | N | Y | N | Y | N |
| 5 Lewis | ? | ? | ? | ? | ? | ? | ? | ? |
| 6 Price | Y | N | N | Y | N | Y | N | Y |
| 7 Linder | N | N | Y | Y | Y | Y | N | Y |
| 8 Westmoreland | Y | N | Y | N | Y | N | Y | Y |
| 9 Norwood | Y | Y | N | Y | Y | N | N | Y |
| 10 Deal | Y | Y | N | Y | N | Y | N | Y |
| 11 Gingrey | Y | N | Y | N | N | N | N | Y |
| 12 Barrow | N | Y | Y | N | + | N | Y | Y |
| 13 Scott | N | N | N | N | Y | N | Y | Y |
| **HAWAII** | | | | | | | | |
| 1 Abercrombie | Y | N | Y | N | N | N | Y | Y |
| 2 Case | N | N | Y | N | Y | N | Y | Y |
| **IDAHO** | | | | | | | | |
| 1 Otter | Y | N | N | Y | N | Y | N | Y |
| 2 Simpson | Y | N | N | N | N | N | N | Y |
| **ILLINOIS** | | | | | | | | |
| 1 Rush | N | N | Y | N | Y | N | Y | Y |
| 2 Jackson | N | N | Y | N | Y | N | Y | N |
| 3 Lipinski | N | N | Y | N | Y | N | Y | Y |
| 4 Gutierrez | ? | Y | Y | N | Y | N | Y | N |
| 5 Emanuel | N | N | Y | N | Y | N | Y | Y |
| 6 Hyde | Y | N | N | N | N | N | N | Y |
| 7 Davis | N | N | Y | N | Y | N | Y | N |
| 8 Bean | N | Y | Y | N | Y | Y | Y | Y |
| 9 Schakowsky | N | N | Y | N | Y | N | Y | N |
| 10 Kirk | N | N | N | N | Y | N | N | Y |
| 11 Weller | Y | Y | N | Y | Y | Y | N | Y |
| 12 Costello | N | Y | Y | N | Y | N | Y | N |

**KEY** | Republicans | Democrats | *Independents*

| | | | |
|---|---|---|---|
| Y | Voted for (yea) | X | Paired against |
| # | Paired for | – | Announced against |
| + | Announced for | P | Voted "present" |
| N | Voted against (nay) | | |
| C | Voted "present" to avoid possible conflict of interest |
| ? | Did not vote or otherwise make a position known |

| | 192 | 193 | 194 | 195 | 196 | 197 | 198 | 199 |
|---|---|---|---|---|---|---|---|---|
| 13 **Biggert** | N | N | N | N | Y | N | N | Y |
| 14 **Hastert** | | | | | | | | |
| 15 **Johnson** | N | N | Y | N | Y | N | N | Y |
| 16 **Manzullo** | Y | N | N | Y | N | Y | N | Y |
| 17 Evans | N | N | Y | N | Y | N | Y | Y |
| 18 **LaHood** | N | N | N | N | N | N | N | Y |
| 19 **Shimkus** | Y | Y | N | Y | N | Y | N | Y |
| **INDIANA** | | | | | | | | |
| 1 Visclosky | N | N | Y | N | Y | N | Y | Y |
| 2 **Chocola** | Y | Y | N | N | N | Y | N | Y |
| 3 **Souder** | Y | N | N | Y | N | N | N | Y |
| 4 **Buyer** | Y | N | N | Y | N | Y | N | Y |
| 5 **Burton** | Y | N | N | Y | N | Y | N | Y |
| 6 **Pence** | Y | Y | N | Y | Y | Y | N | Y |
| 7 Carson | N | N | Y | N | Y | N | Y | Y |
| 8 **Hostettler** | Y | Y | N | Y | Y | Y | N | N |
| 9 **Sodrel** | Y | N | N | N | N | N | N | Y |
| **IOWA** | | | | | | | | |
| 1 **Nussle** | N | N | N | Y | N | N | N | Y |
| 2 **Leach** | ? | ? | ? | ? | ? | ? | ? | ? |
| 3 Boswell | N | N | Y | N | N | N | Y | Y |
| 4 **Latham** | N | N | N | Y | N | N | N | Y |
| 5 **King** | Y | Y | N | Y | N | Y | N | Y |
| **KANSAS** | | | | | | | | |
| 1 **Moran** | Y | Y | N | N | N | Y | N | Y |
| 2 **Ryun** | Y | N | N | Y | N | Y | N | Y |
| 3 Moore | N | N | Y | N | Y | N | Y | Y |
| 4 **Tiahrt** | Y | N | N | Y | N | N | N | Y |
| **KENTUCKY** | | | | | | | | |
| 1 **Whitfield** | N | N | N | N | Y | N | N | Y |
| 2 **Lewis** | Y | N | N | Y | N | Y | N | Y |
| 3 **Northup** | Y | N | N | N | N | N | N | Y |
| 4 **Davis** | N | N | N | N | N | N | N | Y |
| 5 **Rogers** | Y | N | N | N | N | N | N | Y |
| 6 Chandler | N | N | Y | N | N | N | Y | N |
| **LOUISIANA** | | | | | | | | |
| 1 **Jindal** | Y | Y | N | N | N | Y | N | Y |
| 2 Jefferson | Y | N | Y | N | Y | N | Y | Y |
| 3 Melancon | Y | N | Y | N | N | N | Y | Y |
| 4 **McCrery** | Y | N | N | N | N | N | N | Y |
| 5 **Alexander** | Y | N | N | N | N | N | N | Y |
| 6 **Baker** | Y | N | N | N | N | Y | N | Y |
| 7 **Boustany** | Y | N | N | Y | N | N | N | Y |
| **MAINE** | | | | | | | | |
| 1 Allen | N | N | Y | N | Y | N | Y | N |
| 2 Michaud | N | N | Y | N | Y | N | Y | N |
| **MARYLAND** | | | | | | | | |
| 1 **Gilchrest** | N | N | N | N | N | N | N | Y |
| 2 Ruppersberger | N | Y | Y | N | Y | N | Y | Y |
| 3 Cardin | N | N | Y | N | Y | N | Y | N |
| 4 Wynn | N | Y | Y | N | Y | N | Y | Y |
| 5 Hoyer | N | N | Y | N | Y | N | Y | N |
| 6 **Bartlett** | N | N | N | Y | Y | Y | N | Y |
| 7 Cummings | N | N | Y | N | Y | N | Y | Y |
| 8 Van Hollen | N | N | Y | N | Y | N | Y | N |
| **MASSACHUSETTS** | | | | | | | | |
| 1 Olver | N | N | N | N | Y | N | Y | Y |
| 2 Neal | N | N | Y | N | Y | N | Y | N |
| 3 McGovern | N | N | Y | N | Y | N | Y | N |
| 4 Frank | N | Y | Y | N | ? | N | Y | N |
| 5 Meehan | N | N | Y | N | Y | N | Y | Y |
| 6 Tierney | N | N | Y | N | Y | N | Y | N |
| 7 Markey | N | Y | Y | N | Y | N | Y | N |
| 8 Capuano | N | Y | N | N | Y | N | N | Y |
| 9 Lynch | N | N | Y | N | ? | N | Y | Y |
| 10 Delahunt | N | N | Y | N | Y | N | Y | Y |
| **MICHIGAN** | | | | | | | | |
| 1 Stupak | N | Y | N | N | Y | N | Y | Y |
| 2 **Hoekstra** | Y | N | N | Y | N | Y | N | Y |
| 3 **Ehlers** | N | N | N | N | Y | N | N | Y |
| 4 **Camp** | N | Y | N | N | N | N | N | Y |
| 5 Kildee | N | N | Y | N | Y | N | Y | Y |
| 6 **Upton** | Y | N | N | N | Y | N | N | Y |
| 7 **Schwarz** | N | N | N | N | N | N | N | Y |
| 8 **Rogers** | N | N | N | N | Y | Y | N | Y |
| 9 **Knollenberg** | N | N | N | N | N | N | N | Y |
| 10 **Miller** | N | N | N | N | Y | N | N | Y |
| 11 **McCotter** | N | N | N | N | Y | Y | N | Y |
| 12 Levin | N | N | Y | N | Y | N | Y | Y |
| 13 Kilpatrick | N | N | Y | N | Y | N | Y | Y |
| 14 Conyers | N | N | Y | N | Y | N | Y | N |
| 15 Dingell | N | Y | Y | N | N | N | Y | N |

| | 192 | 193 | 194 | 195 | 196 | 197 | 198 | 199 |
|---|---|---|---|---|---|---|---|---|
| **MINNESOTA** | | | | | | | | |
| 1 **Gutknecht** | Y | N | N | Y | N | Y | N | Y |
| 2 **Kline** | Y | N | N | Y | N | N | N | Y |
| 3 **Ramstad** | N | Y | Y | N | Y | Y | N | Y |
| 4 McCollum | N | N | Y | N | Y | N | Y | N |
| 5 Sabo | Y | N | Y | N | N | N | Y | Y |
| 6 **Kennedy** | N | Y | Y | Y | Y | Y | N | Y |
| 7 Peterson | Y | N | Y | N | N | N | Y | Y |
| 8 Oberstar | Y | N | Y | N | N | N | Y | N |
| **MISSISSIPPI** | | | | | | | | |
| 1 **Wicker** | Y | N | N | Y | N | N | N | Y |
| 2 Thompson | N | N | Y | N | Y | N | Y | Y |
| 3 **Pickering** | Y | N | N | Y | N | N | N | Y |
| 4 Taylor | Y | Y | Y | Y | Y | Y | Y | N |
| **MISSOURI** | | | | | | | | |
| 1 Clay | N | N | Y | N | ? | ? | ? | ? |
| 2 **Akin** | Y | Y | N | Y | N | Y | N | Y |
| 3 Carnahan | N | N | Y | N | Y | N | Y | Y |
| 4 Skelton | N | N | Y | N | Y | N | Y | Y |
| 5 Cleaver | N | N | Y | N | Y | N | Y | Y |
| 6 **Graves** | Y | N | N | Y | N | Y | N | Y |
| 7 **Blunt** | N | N | N | N | N | N | N | Y |
| 8 **Emerson** | Y | N | N | Y | N | N | N | Y |
| 9 **Hulshof** | Y | N | N | N | N | N | N | Y |
| **MONTANA** | | | | | | | | |
| AL **Rehberg** | N | N | N | N | N | N | N | Y |
| **NEBRASKA** | | | | | | | | |
| 1 **Fortenberry** | Y | Y | N | N | N | N | N | Y |
| 2 **Terry** | Y | Y | N | N | N | Y | N | Y |
| 3 **Osborne** | Y | Y | N | N | N | N | N | Y |
| **NEVADA** | | | | | | | | |
| 1 Berkley | N | N | Y | N | Y | N | Y | N |
| 2 **Gibbons** | Y | N | N | Y | N | Y | N | Y |
| 3 **Porter** | Y | N | N | Y | N | N | N | Y |
| **NEW HAMPSHIRE** | | | | | | | | |
| 1 **Bradley** | N | Y | N | N | Y | N | N | Y |
| 2 **Bass** | N | N | N | N | Y | N | N | Y |
| **NEW JERSEY** | | | | | | | | |
| 1 Andrews | N | N | Y | N | Y | N | Y | Y |
| 2 **LoBiondo** | N | Y | N | N | Y | N | N | Y |
| 3 **Saxton** | N | Y | N | N | Y | N | N | Y |
| 4 **Smith** | N | N | N | N | Y | N | N | Y |
| 5 **Garrett** | Y | N | N | Y | N | Y | N | Y |
| 6 Pallone | N | Y | Y | N | Y | N | Y | N |
| 7 **Ferguson** | N | N | N | N | Y | N | N | Y |
| 8 Pascrell | N | Y | Y | N | Y | N | Y | N |
| 9 Rothman | N | N | Y | N | Y | N | Y | Y |
| 10 Payne | N | N | Y | N | Y | N | Y | N |
| 11 **Frelinghuysen** | N | N | N | N | Y | N | N | Y |
| 12 Holt | N | N | Y | N | Y | N | Y | N |
| 13 Menendez | N | Y | Y | N | Y | N | Y | N |
| **NEW MEXICO** | | | | | | | | |
| 1 **Wilson** | Y | N | N | Y | Y | N | N | Y |
| 2 **Pearce** | Y | Y | N | N | N | N | N | Y |
| 3 Udall | N | N | Y | N | Y | N | Y | Y |
| **NEW YORK** | | | | | | | | |
| 1 Bishop | N | N | Y | N | Y | N | Y | N |
| 2 Israel | N | N | Y | N | Y | N | Y | N |
| 3 **King** | N | Y | N | N | Y | N | N | Y |
| 4 McCarthy | N | N | Y | N | Y | N | Y | N |
| 5 Ackerman | N | N | Y | N | Y | N | Y | N |
| 6 Meeks | N | N | Y | N | Y | N | Y | Y |
| 7 Crowley | N | N | Y | N | Y | N | Y | Y |
| 8 Nadler | N | Y | Y | N | Y | N | Y | N |
| 9 Weiner | N | N | Y | N | Y | N | Y | Y |
| 10 Towns | N | N | Y | N | Y | N | Y | N |
| 11 Owens | N | N | Y | N | Y | N | Y | N |
| 12 Velázquez | N | N | Y | N | Y | N | Y | N |
| 13 **Fossella** | N | N | N | N | Y | N | N | Y |
| 14 Maloney | N | Y | Y | N | Y | N | Y | N |
| 15 Rangel | N | N | Y | N | Y | N | Y | N |
| 16 Serrano | N | N | Y | N | Y | N | Y | N |
| 17 Engel | N | N | Y | N | Y | N | Y | Y |
| 18 Lowey | N | N | N | N | Y | N | Y | Y |
| 19 **Kelly** | N | Y | Y | N | Y | N | N | Y |
| 20 **Sweeney** | N | N | N | N | Y | N | N | Y |
| 21 McNulty | N | N | Y | N | Y | N | Y | Y |
| 22 Hinchey | N | Y | Y | N | Y | N | Y | Y |
| 23 **McHugh** | Y | N | N | N | Y | N | N | Y |
| 24 **Boehlert** | N | N | N | N | N | N | N | Y |
| 25 **Walsh** | N | N | N | N | Y | N | N | Y |
| 26 **Reynolds** | N | N | N | N | Y | N | N | Y |
| 27 Higgins | N | N | Y | N | Y | N | Y | Y |
| 28 Slaughter | N | N | Y | N | Y | N | Y | Y |
| 29 **Kuhl** | Y | N | N | Y | Y | N | N | Y |

| | 192 | 193 | 194 | 195 | 196 | 197 | 198 | 199 |
|---|---|---|---|---|---|---|---|---|
| **NORTH CAROLINA** | | | | | | | | |
| 1 Butterfield | N | N | Y | ? | Y | N | Y | Y |
| 2 Etheridge | N | N | Y | N | Y | N | Y | N |
| 3 **Jones** | N | N | N | Y | Y | Y | N | N |
| 4 Price | N | N | Y | N | Y | N | Y | Y |
| 5 **Foxx** | Y | N | N | Y | N | Y | N | Y |
| 6 **Coble** | Y | N | N | Y | N | N | N | Y |
| 7 McIntyre | N | N | N | N | N | N | Y | Y |
| 8 **Hayes** | Y | N | N | Y | N | N | N | Y |
| 9 **Myrick** | Y | N | N | Y | Y | Y | N | Y |
| 10 **McHenry** | Y | N | N | Y | N | Y | N | Y |
| 11 **Taylor** | N | N | N | N | N | N | N | Y |
| 12 Watt | N | N | Y | N | Y | N | Y | Y |
| 13 Miller | N | N | Y | N | Y | N | Y | Y |
| **NORTH DAKOTA** | | | | | | | | |
| AL Pomeroy | N | N | Y | N | N | N | Y | Y |
| **OHIO** | | | | | | | | |
| 1 **Chabot** | N | N | N | Y | Y | Y | N | Y |
| 2 Vacant | | | | | | | | |
| 3 **Turner** | N | N | N | N | Y | N | N | Y |
| 4 **Oxley** | Y | N | N | N | N | N | N | Y |
| 5 **Gillmor** | N | N | N | N | N | N | N | Y |
| 6 Strickland | ? | ? | ? | ? | ? | ? | ? | ? |
| 7 **Hobson** | N | N | N | N | Y | N | N | Y |
| 8 **Boehner** | Y | Y | N | Y | N | N | N | Y |
| 9 Kaptur | N | N | Y | N | Y | N | Y | Y |
| 10 Kucinich | N | N | Y | N | Y | N | Y | N |
| 11 Jones | N | N | N | N | Y | ? | Y | N |
| 12 **Tiberi** | Y | N | N | N | N | N | N | Y |
| 13 Brown | N | N | Y | N | ? | N | Y | N |
| 14 **LaTourette** | ? | ? | ? | ? | ? | ? | ? | ? |
| 15 **Pryce** | N | N | N | N | N | N | N | Y |
| 16 **Regula** | Y | N | N | N | N | N | N | Y |
| 17 Ryan | N | N | Y | N | Y | N | Y | N |
| 18 **Ney** | Y | N | N | Y | N | N | N | Y |
| **OKLAHOMA** | | | | | | | | |
| 1 **Sullivan** | Y | N | ? | Y | N | Y | N | Y |
| 2 Boren | Y | Y | Y | Y | N | N | Y | Y |
| 3 **Lucas** | ? | ? | ? | ? | ? | ? | ? | ? |
| 4 **Cole** | Y | N | N | Y | N | N | N | Y |
| 5 **Istook** | Y | N | N | Y | N | ? | N | Y |
| **OREGON** | | | | | | | | |
| 1 Wu | N | Y | Y | N | Y | N | Y | Y |
| 2 **Walden** | N | N | N | N | N | N | N | Y |
| 3 Blumenauer | N | N | Y | N | Y | N | Y | N |
| 4 DeFazio | N | Y | Y | Y | Y | N | Y | Y |
| 5 Hooley | N | N | Y | N | Y | N | Y | Y |
| **PENNSYLVANIA** | | | | | | | | |
| 1 Brady | N | Y | N | N | Y | N | Y | Y |
| 2 Fattah | N | Y | Y | N | Y | N | Y | Y |
| 3 **English** | Y | N | N | N | Y | N | N | Y |
| 4 **Hart** | Y | N | N | N | N | Y | N | Y |
| 5 **Peterson** | Y | ? | N | N | N | N | N | Y |
| 6 **Gerlach** | N | N | N | N | ? | N | N | Y |
| 7 **Weldon** | ? | N | N | N | Y | N | N | Y |
| 8 **Fitzpatrick** | N | Y | N | N | Y | N | N | Y |
| 9 **Shuster** | Y | Y | N | Y | N | Y | N | Y |
| 10 **Sherwood** | Y | N | N | N | N | N | N | Y |
| 11 Kanjorski | N | Y | N | N | Y | N | N | Y |
| 12 Murtha | N | N | N | N | Y | N | N | Y |
| 13 Schwartz | N | Y | N | N | Y | N | Y | Y |
| 14 Doyle | Y | Y | N | N | Y | N | N | Y |
| 15 **Dent** | Y | N | N | N | Y | N | N | Y |
| 16 **Pitts** | Y | Y | N | Y | Y | Y | N | Y |
| 17 Holden | Y | Y | N | N | Y | N | N | Y |
| 18 **Murphy** | Y | Y | N | N | Y | N | N | Y |
| 19 **Platts** | N | N | N | N | Y | N | N | Y |
| **RHODE ISLAND** | | | | | | | | |
| 1 Kennedy | N | N | Y | N | Y | N | Y | Y |
| 2 Langevin | N | N | Y | N | Y | N | Y | Y |
| **SOUTH CAROLINA** | | | | | | | | |
| 1 **Brown** | Y | N | N | N | N | N | N | Y |
| 2 **Wilson** | Y | N | N | Y | N | Y | N | Y |
| 3 **Barrett** | Y | N | N | Y | N | Y | N | Y |
| 4 **Inglis** | N | N | N | N | N | Y | N | Y |
| 5 Spratt | N | N | Y | N | Y | N | Y | Y |
| 6 Clyburn | N | N | Y | N | Y | N | Y | Y |
| **SOUTH DAKOTA** | | | | | | | | |
| AL Herseth | N | N | Y | Y | Y | N | Y | Y |
| **TENNESSEE** | | | | | | | | |
| 1 **Jenkins** | Y | Y | N | N | N | Y | N | Y |
| 2 **Duncan** | Y | N | N | N | N | Y | N | Y |

| | 192 | 193 | 194 | 195 | 196 | 197 | 198 | 199 |
|---|---|---|---|---|---|---|---|---|
| 3 **Wamp** | N | N | N | N | Y | N | N | Y |
| 4 Davis | Y | N | Y | N | Y | N | Y | Y |
| 5 Cooper | Y | N | Y | N | Y | N | Y | Y |
| 6 Gordon | N | N | Y | N | Y | N | Y | Y |
| 7 **Blackburn** | Y | N | N | Y | N | Y | N | Y |
| 8 Tanner | Y | N | Y | N | Y | Y | Y | N |
| 9 Ford | N | N | Y | N | Y | N | Y | Y |
| **TEXAS** | | | | | | | | |
| 1 **Gohmert** | Y | N | N | Y | N | N | N | Y |
| 2 **Poe** | N | Y | N | Y | ? | Y | N | Y |
| 3 **Johnson, S.** | Y | Y | N | Y | N | Y | N | Y |
| 4 **Hall** | Y | Y | N | Y | Y | Y | N | Y |
| 5 **Hensarling** | Y | Y | N | Y | N | Y | N | Y |
| 6 **Barton** | Y | N | N | N | N | N | N | Y |
| 7 **Culberson** | Y | N | N | Y | ? | N | N | Y |
| 8 **Brady** | Y | N | N | Y | N | Y | N | Y |
| 9 Green | Y | N | Y | N | Y | N | Y | Y |
| 10 **McCaul** | Y | N | N | Y | Y | N | N | Y |
| 11 **Conaway** | + | N | N | N | N | N | N | Y |
| 12 **Granger** | Y | N | N | N | N | N | N | Y |
| 13 **Thornberry** | Y | N | N | Y | N | Y | N | Y |
| 14 **Paul** | Y | N | N | Y | ? | Y | N | N |
| 15 Hinojosa | Y | N | Y | N | – | N | Y | Y |
| 16 Reyes | Y | N | Y | N | Y | N | Y | Y |
| 17 Edwards | Y | N | N | N | Y | N | Y | Y |
| 18 Jackson-Lee | ? | ? | ? | ? | ? | ? | ? | ? |
| 19 **Neugebauer** | Y | N | N | Y | N | Y | N | Y |
| 20 Gonzalez | Y | N | Y | N | Y | N | Y | Y |
| 21 **Smith** | Y | N | N | N | N | N | N | Y |
| 22 **DeLay** | N | N | N | Y | N | N | N | Y |
| 23 **Bonilla** | Y | N | N | Y | N | N | N | Y |
| 24 **Marchant** | Y | N | N | Y | ? | N | N | ? |
| 25 Doggett | N | Y | Y | N | Y | N | Y | Y |
| 26 **Burgess** | Y | N | N | Y | Y | Y | N | Y |
| 27 Ortiz | Y | N | Y | N | Y | N | Y | Y |
| 28 Cuellar | Y | N | Y | N | Y | N | Y | Y |
| 29 Green | Y | Y | Y | N | Y | N | Y | Y |
| 30 Johnson, E. | N | N | Y | N | Y | N | Y | Y |
| 31 **Carter** | Y | N | N | Y | N | N | N | Y |
| 32 **Sessions** | Y | N | N | Y | N | Y | N | Y |
| **UTAH** | | | | | | | | |
| 1 **Bishop** | Y | Y | N | ? | N | N | N | Y |
| 2 Matheson | N | N | Y | N | N | N | Y | N |
| 3 **Cannon** | Y | Y | N | Y | N | Y | N | Y |
| **VERMONT** | | | | | | | | |
| AL *Sanders* | N | N | Y | N | Y | N | Y | N |
| **VIRGINIA** | | | | | | | | |
| 1 **Davis, J.** | N | N | N | Y | Y | Y | N | Y |
| 2 **Drake** | N | N | N | N | N | N | N | Y |
| 3 Scott | N | N | Y | N | Y | N | Y | Y |
| 4 **Forbes** | N | N | N | N | Y | N | N | Y |
| 5 **Goode** | Y | N | N | Y | Y | N | N | Y |
| 6 **Goodlatte** | Y | N | N | Y | N | Y | N | Y |
| 7 **Cantor** | N | N | N | Y | N | N | N | Y |
| 8 Moran | N | N | Y | N | + | N | Y | Y |
| 9 Boucher | N | N | Y | N | Y | N | Y | Y |
| 10 **Wolf** | N | N | N | N | N | N | N | Y |
| 11 **Davis, T.** | N | N | N | N | Y | N | N | Y |
| **WASHINGTON** | | | | | | | | |
| 1 Inslee | N | N | Y | N | Y | N | Y | N |
| 2 Larsen | N | N | Y | N | Y | N | Y | Y |
| 3 Baird | N | N | N | N | Y | N | Y | N |
| 4 **Hastings** | Y | N | N | Y | N | N | N | Y |
| 5 **McMorris** | Y | N | N | Y | N | N | N | Y |
| 6 Dicks | N | N | Y | N | Y | N | Y | Y |
| 7 McDermott | N | N | Y | N | Y | N | Y | N |
| 8 **Reichert** | N | N | N | N | N | N | N | Y |
| 9 Smith | N | Y | Y | N | Y | N | Y | Y |
| **WEST VIRGINIA** | | | | | | | | |
| 1 Mollohan | Y | N | N | N | Y | N | N | Y |
| 2 **Capito** | N | N | N | N | Y | N | N | Y |
| 3 Rahall | N | N | Y | N | Y | N | Y | N |
| **WISCONSIN** | | | | | | | | |
| 1 **Ryan** | N | Y | N | Y | N | Y | N | Y |
| 2 Baldwin | N | N | Y | N | Y | N | Y | N |
| 3 Kind | N | N | Y | N | Y | N | Y | N |
| 4 Moore | N | Y | Y | N | Y | N | Y | N |
| 5 **Sensenbrenner** | Y | N | N | Y | N | Y | N | Y |
| 6 **Petri** | N | N | N | Y | N | Y | N | Y |
| 7 Obey | N | N | Y | N | Y | N | Y | N |
| 8 **Green** | N | N | Y | Y | Y | Y | N | Y |
| **WYOMING** | | | | | | | | |
| AL **Cubin** | Y | Y | N | Y | N | Y | N | Y |

# IN THE HOUSE | By Vote Number

**200. HR 744. "Spyware" Programs/Passage.** Sensenbrenner, R-Wis., motion to suspend the rules and pass the bill that would establish criminal penalties, including up to two years in prison, for intentionally gaining unauthorized access to a computer to steal information or damage the machine. Intentionally gaining access in furtherance of a federal crime could mean up to five years in prison. Motion agreed to 395-1: R 207-1; D 187-0 (ND 137-0, SD 50-0); I 1-0. A two-thirds majority of those present and voting (264 in this case) is required for passage under suspension of the rules. May 23, 2005.

**201. HR 29. "Spyware" Programs/Passage.** Barton, R-Texas., motion to suspend the rules and pass the bill that would require software companies to obtain permission from computer users before installing programs that can collect personal information and distribute it to third parties. Violators would be subject to fines of up to $3 million. Motion agreed to 393-4: R 207-1; D 185-3 (ND 136-2, SD 49-1); I 1-0. A two-thirds majority of those present and voting (265 in this case) is required for passage under suspension of the rules. May 23, 2005.

**202. H Con Res 149. Israel Independence Tribute/Adoption.** Ros-Lehtinen, R-Fla., motion to suspend the rules and adopt the concurrent resolution that would recognize that Israel's independence provided a refuge and homeland for the Jewish people and congratulate the Israeli people on the country's 57th anniversary of independence. Motion agreed to 397-0: R 208-0; D 188-0 (ND 138-0, SD 50-0); I 1-0. A two-thirds majority of those present and voting (265 in this case) is required for adoption under suspension of the rules. May 23, 2005.

**203. HR 2419. Fiscal 2006 Energy and Water Appropriations/Previous Question.** L. Diaz-Balart, R-Fla., motion to order the previous question (thus ending debate and possibility of amendment) on adoption of the rule (H Res 291) to provide for House floor consideration of the bill that would appropriate $29.7 billion in fiscal 2006 for energy and water development projects. Motion agreed to 219-190: R 218-0; D 1-189 (ND 1-141, SD 0-48); I 0-1. (Subsequently, the rule was adopted by voice vote.) May 24, 2005.

**204. HR 810. Embryonic Stem Cell Research/Passage.** Passage of the bill to allow the use of federal funds in research on embryonic stem cell lines derived from surplus embryos at in-vitro fertilization clinics, but only if donors give their consent and are not paid for the embryos. The bill would authorize the Health and Human Services Department to conduct and support research involving human embryonic stem cells that meet certain criteria, regardless of when the stem cells were derived from a human embryo. Passed 238-194: R 50-180; D 187-14 (ND 140-10, SD 47-4); I 1-0. A "nay" was a vote in support of the president's position. May 24, 2005.

**205. HR 2520. Cord Blood Stem Cell Research/Passage.** Barton, R-Texas, motion to suspend the rules and pass the bill to create a new federal program to collect and store umbilical-cord-blood stem cells. The bill would reauthorize and expand the current bone-marrow registry program to both bone-marrow and cord-blood transplants. It would authorize $156 million over five years for the program. Motion agreed to 431-1: R 229-1; D 201-0 (ND 150-0, SD 51-0); I 1-0. A two-thirds majority of those present and voting (288 in this case) is required for passage under suspension of the rules. A "yea" was a vote in support of the president's position. May 24, 2005.

| | 200 | 201 | 202 | 203 | 204 | 205 |
|---|---|---|---|---|---|---|
| **ALABAMA** | | | | | | |
| 1 Bonner | Y | Y | Y | Y | N | Y |
| 2 Everett | Y | Y | Y | Y | N | Y |
| 3 Rogers | Y | Y | Y | Y | N | Y |
| 4 Aderholt | Y | Y | Y | Y | N | Y |
| 5 Cramer | Y | Y | Y | N | Y | Y |
| 6 Bachus | Y | Y | Y | Y | N | Y |
| 7 Davis | ? | ? | ? | N | Y | Y |
| **ALASKA** | | | | | | |
| AL Young | ? | ? | ? | Y | Y | Y |
| **ARIZONA** | | | | | | |
| 1 Renzi | Y | Y | Y | Y | N | Y |
| 2 Franks | Y | Y | Y | Y | N | Y |
| 3 Shadegg | Y | Y | Y | Y | N | Y |
| 4 Pastor | Y | Y | Y | N | Y | Y |
| 5 Hayworth | Y | Y | Y | Y | N | Y |
| 6 Flake | Y | Y | Y | Y | N | Y |
| 7 Grijalva | Y | Y | Y | N | Y | Y |
| 8 Kolbe | Y | Y | Y | Y | Y | Y |
| **ARKANSAS** | | | | | | |
| 1 Berry | Y | Y | Y | N | Y | Y |
| 2 Snyder | Y | Y | Y | N | Y | Y |
| 3 Boozman | Y | Y | Y | Y | N | Y |
| 4 Ross | Y | Y | Y | N | Y | Y |
| **CALIFORNIA** | | | | | | |
| 1 Thompson | Y | Y | Y | N | Y | Y |
| 2 Herger | Y | Y | Y | Y | N | Y |
| 3 Lungren | Y | Y | Y | Y | N | Y |
| 4 Doolittle | Y | Y | Y | Y | N | Y |
| 5 Matsui, D. | Y | Y | Y | N | Y | Y |
| 6 Woolsey | Y | Y | Y | N | Y | Y |
| 7 Miller, George | Y | Y | Y | N | Y | Y |
| 8 Pelosi | Y | Y | Y | N | Y | Y |
| 9 Lee | Y | Y | Y | N | Y | Y |
| 10 Tauscher | Y | Y | Y | N | Y | Y |
| 11 Pombo | Y | Y | Y | Y | N | Y |
| 12 Lantos | Y | Y | Y | N | Y | Y |
| 13 Stark | ? | ? | ? | N | Y | Y |
| 14 Eshoo | Y | Y | Y | N | Y | Y |
| 15 Honda | Y | Y | Y | N | Y | Y |
| 16 Lofgren | Y | N | Y | N | Y | Y |
| 17 Farr | Y | Y | Y | N | Y | Y |
| 18 Cardoza | Y | Y | Y | ? | Y | Y |
| 19 Radanovich | Y | Y | Y | Y | N | Y |
| 20 Costa | Y | Y | Y | N | Y | Y |
| 21 Nunes | Y | Y | Y | Y | N | Y |
| 22 Thomas | Y | Y | Y | Y | N | Y |
| 23 Capps | Y | Y | Y | N | Y | Y |
| 24 Gallegly | + | + | + | Y | N | Y |
| 25 McKeon | Y | Y | Y | Y | Y | Y |
| 26 Dreier | Y | Y | Y | Y | N | Y |
| 27 Sherman | Y | Y | Y | N | Y | Y |
| 28 Berman | Y | Y | Y | N | Y | Y |
| 29 Schiff | Y | Y | Y | N | Y | Y |
| 30 Waxman | Y | Y | Y | N | Y | Y |
| 31 Becerra | ? | ? | ? | N | Y | Y |
| 32 Solis | Y | Y | Y | N | Y | Y |
| 33 Watson | Y | Y | Y | N | Y | Y |
| 34 Roybal-Allard | Y | Y | Y | N | Y | Y |
| 35 Waters | Y | Y | Y | N | Y | Y |
| 36 Harman | Y | Y | Y | N | Y | Y |
| 37 Millender-McD. | ? | ? | ? | ? | ? | ? |
| 38 Napolitano | Y | Y | Y | N | Y | Y |
| 39 Sánchez, Linda | Y | Y | Y | N | Y | Y |
| 40 Royce | Y | Y | Y | Y | N | Y |
| 41 Lewis | Y | Y | Y | Y | Y | Y |
| 42 Miller, Gary | Y | Y | Y | Y | N | Y |
| 43 Baca | Y | Y | Y | N | Y | Y |
| 44 Calvert | Y | Y | Y | Y | N | Y |
| 45 Bono | Y | Y | Y | Y | Y | Y |
| 46 Rohrabacher | Y | Y | Y | Y | Y | Y |
| 47 Sanchez, Loretta | ? | ? | ? | ? | Y | Y |
| 48 Cox | Y | Y | Y | Y | N | Y |
| 49 Issa | Y | Y | Y | Y | Y | Y |

| | 200 | 201 | 202 | 203 | 204 | 205 |
|---|---|---|---|---|---|---|
| 50 Cunningham | Y | Y | Y | Y | Y | Y |
| 51 Filner | Y | Y | Y | N | Y | Y |
| 52 Hunter | Y | Y | Y | Y | N | Y |
| 53 Davis | Y | Y | Y | N | Y | Y |
| **COLORADO** | | | | | | |
| 1 DeGette | Y | Y | Y | N | Y | Y |
| 2 Udall | Y | Y | Y | N | Y | Y |
| 3 Salazar | Y | Y | Y | N | Y | Y |
| 4 Musgrave | Y | Y | Y | Y | N | Y |
| 5 Hefley | Y | Y | Y | Y | N | Y |
| 6 Tancredo | Y | Y | Y | Y | N | Y |
| 7 Beauprez | Y | Y | Y | Y | N | Y |
| **CONNECTICUT** | | | | | | |
| 1 Larson | Y | Y | Y | N | Y | Y |
| 2 Simmons | Y | Y | Y | Y | Y | Y |
| 3 DeLauro | Y | Y | Y | N | Y | Y |
| 4 Shays | + | + | + | Y | Y | Y |
| 5 Johnson | Y | Y | Y | Y | Y | Y |
| **DELAWARE** | | | | | | |
| AL Castle | Y | Y | Y | Y | Y | Y |
| **FLORIDA** | | | | | | |
| 1 Miller | Y | Y | Y | N | Y | Y |
| 2 Boyd | Y | Y | Y | N | Y | Y |
| 3 Brown | Y | Y | Y | N | Y | Y |
| 4 Crenshaw | Y | Y | Y | Y | N | Y |
| 5 Brown-Waite | Y | Y | Y | Y | Y | Y |
| 6 Stearns | Y | Y | Y | Y | N | Y |
| 7 Mica | Y | Y | Y | Y | N | Y |
| 8 Keller | Y | Y | Y | Y | Y | Y |
| 9 Bilirakis | Y | Y | Y | Y | Y | Y |
| 10 Young | Y | Y | Y | Y | Y | Y |
| 11 Davis | Y | Y | Y | N | Y | Y |
| 12 Putnam | Y | Y | Y | Y | N | Y |
| 13 Harris | Y | Y | Y | Y | N | Y |
| 14 Mack | Y | Y | Y | Y | N | Y |
| 15 Weldon | Y | Y | Y | Y | N | Y |
| 16 Foley | Y | Y | Y | Y | Y | Y |
| 17 Meek | Y | Y | Y | ? | Y | Y |
| 18 Ros-Lehtinen | Y | Y | Y | Y | N | Y |
| 19 Wexler | Y | Y | Y | ? | Y | Y |
| 20 Wasserman-Schultz | Y | Y | Y | N | Y | Y |
| 21 Diaz-Balart, L. | Y | Y | Y | Y | N | Y |
| 22 Shaw | ? | ? | ? | Y | Y | Y |
| 23 Hastings | Y | Y | Y | N | Y | Y |
| 24 Feeney | Y | Y | Y | Y | N | Y |
| 25 Diaz-Balart, M. | Y | Y | Y | Y | N | Y |
| **GEORGIA** | | | | | | |
| 1 Kingston | ? | ? | ? | Y | N | Y |
| 2 Bishop | Y | Y | Y | N | Y | Y |
| 3 Marshall | Y | Y | Y | N | Y | Y |
| 4 McKinney | Y | Y | Y | N | Y | Y |
| 5 Lewis | Y | Y | Y | N | Y | Y |
| 6 Price | Y | Y | Y | Y | N | Y |
| 7 Linder | Y | Y | Y | Y | N | Y |
| 8 Westmoreland | Y | Y | Y | Y | N | Y |
| 9 Norwood | Y | Y | Y | Y | N | Y |
| 10 Deal | Y | Y | Y | Y | N | Y |
| 11 Gingrey | Y | Y | Y | Y | N | Y |
| 12 Barrow | Y | Y | Y | N | Y | Y |
| 13 Scott | Y | Y | Y | N | Y | Y |
| **HAWAII** | | | | | | |
| 1 Abercrombie | Y | Y | Y | N | Y | Y |
| 2 Case | Y | Y | Y | N | Y | Y |
| **IDAHO** | | | | | | |
| 1 Otter | Y | Y | Y | Y | N | Y |
| 2 Simpson | Y | Y | Y | Y | N | Y |
| **ILLINOIS** | | | | | | |
| 1 Rush | ? | ? | ? | ? | Y | Y |
| 2 Jackson | Y | Y | Y | N | Y | Y |
| 3 Lipinski | Y | Y | Y | N | Y | Y |
| 4 Gutierrez | Y | Y | Y | N | Y | Y |
| 5 Emanuel | Y | Y | Y | N | Y | Y |
| 6 Hyde | Y | Y | Y | Y | N | Y |
| 7 Davis | Y | Y | Y | N | Y | Y |
| 8 Bean | Y | Y | Y | N | Y | Y |
| 9 Schakowsky | Y | Y | Y | N | Y | Y |
| 10 Kirk | Y | Y | Y | Y | Y | Y |
| 11 Weller | Y | Y | Y | Y | N | Y |
| 12 Costello | Y | Y | Y | N | Y | Y |

| KEY | Republicans | Democrats | Independents |
|---|---|---|---|
| Y Voted for (yea) | X Paired against | C Voted "present" to avoid possible conflict of interest | |
| # Paired for | − Announced against | | |
| + Announced for | P Voted "present" | ? Did not vote or otherwise make a position known | |
| N Voted against (nay) | | | |

| | 200 | 201 | 202 | 203 | 204 | 205 |
|---|---|---|---|---|---|---|
| 13 **Biggert** | Y | Y | Y | Y | Y | Y |
| 14 **Hastert** | | | | | N | Y |
| 15 **Johnson** | Y | Y | Y | Y | N | Y |
| 16 **Manzullo** | Y | Y | Y | Y | N | Y |
| 17 Evans | Y | Y | Y | N | Y | Y |
| 18 **LaHood** | Y | Y | Y | Y | N | Y |
| 19 **Shimkus** | ? | ? | ? | Y | N | Y |
| **INDIANA** | | | | | | |
| 1 Visclosky | Y | Y | Y | N | Y | Y |
| 2 **Chocola** | Y | Y | Y | Y | N | Y |
| 3 **Souder** | Y | Y | Y | Y | N | Y |
| 4 **Buyer** | ? | ? | ? | Y | N | Y |
| 5 **Burton** | + | + | + | ? | N | Y |
| 6 **Pence** | Y | Y | Y | Y | N | Y |
| 7 Carson | Y | Y | Y | N | Y | Y |
| 8 **Hostettler** | Y | Y | Y | Y | N | Y |
| 9 **Sodrel** | Y | Y | Y | Y | N | Y |
| **IOWA** | | | | | | |
| 1 **Nussle** | Y | Y | Y | Y | N | Y |
| 2 **Leach** | Y | Y | Y | Y | Y | Y |
| 3 Boswell | Y | Y | Y | N | Y | Y |
| 4 **Latham** | Y | Y | Y | Y | N | Y |
| 5 **King** | Y | Y | Y | Y | N | Y |
| **KANSAS** | | | | | | |
| 1 **Moran** | Y | Y | Y | Y | N | Y |
| 2 **Ryun** | Y | Y | Y | Y | N | Y |
| 3 Moore | ? | Y | Y | N | Y | Y |
| 4 **Tiahrt** | Y | Y | Y | Y | N | Y |
| **KENTUCKY** | | | | | | |
| 1 **Whitfield** | Y | Y | Y | Y | N | Y |
| 2 **Lewis** | Y | Y | Y | Y | N | Y |
| 3 **Northup** | Y | Y | Y | Y | N | Y |
| 4 **Davis** | Y | Y | Y | Y | N | Y |
| 5 **Rogers** | Y | Y | Y | Y | N | Y |
| 6 Chandler | Y | Y | Y | N | Y | Y |
| **LOUISIANA** | | | | | | |
| 1 **Jindal** | Y | Y | Y | Y | N | Y |
| 2 Jefferson | Y | Y | Y | N | Y | Y |
| 3 Melancon | Y | Y | Y | N | Y | Y |
| 4 **McCrery** | ? | ? | ? | Y | N | Y |
| 5 **Alexander** | Y | Y | Y | Y | N | Y |
| 6 **Baker** | Y | Y | Y | Y | N | Y |
| 7 **Boustany** | Y | Y | Y | Y | N | Y |
| **MAINE** | | | | | | |
| 1 Allen | Y | Y | Y | N | Y | Y |
| 2 Michaud | Y | Y | Y | N | Y | Y |
| **MARYLAND** | | | | | | |
| 1 **Gilchrest** | Y | Y | Y | Y | Y | Y |
| 2 Ruppersberger | Y | Y | Y | N | Y | Y |
| 3 Cardin | Y | Y | Y | N | Y | Y |
| 4 Wynn | Y | Y | Y | N | Y | Y |
| 5 Hoyer | Y | Y | Y | N | Y | Y |
| 6 **Bartlett** | Y | Y | Y | Y | N | Y |
| 7 Cummings | Y | Y | Y | N | Y | Y |
| 8 Van Hollen | Y | Y | Y | N | Y | Y |
| **MASSACHUSETTS** | | | | | | |
| 1 Olver | Y | Y | Y | N | Y | Y |
| 2 Neal | Y | Y | Y | N | Y | Y |
| 3 McGovern | Y | Y | Y | N | Y | Y |
| 4 Frank | Y | Y | Y | N | Y | Y |
| 5 Meehan | Y | Y | Y | N | Y | Y |
| 6 Tierney | Y | Y | Y | N | Y | Y |
| 7 Markey | Y | Y | Y | N | Y | Y |
| 8 Capuano | Y | Y | Y | N | Y | Y |
| 9 Lynch | ? | ? | ? | N | Y | Y |
| 10 Delahunt | ? | ? | ? | ? | Y | Y |
| **MICHIGAN** | | | | | | |
| 1 Stupak | Y | Y | Y | N | N | Y |
| 2 **Hoekstra** | Y | Y | Y | Y | N | Y |
| 3 **Ehlers** | Y | Y | Y | Y | N | Y |
| 4 **Camp** | Y | Y | Y | Y | N | Y |
| 5 Kildee | Y | Y | Y | N | N | Y |
| 6 **Upton** | Y | Y | Y | Y | Y | Y |
| 7 **Schwarz** | Y | Y | Y | Y | Y | Y |
| 8 **Rogers** | Y | Y | Y | Y | N | Y |
| 9 **Knollenberg** | Y | Y | Y | Y | N | Y |
| 10 **Miller** | ? | ? | ? | Y | N | Y |
| 11 **McCotter** | Y | Y | Y | Y | N | Y |
| 12 Levin | Y | Y | Y | N | Y | Y |
| 13 Kilpatrick | Y | Y | Y | N | Y | Y |
| 14 Conyers | Y | Y | Y | N | Y | Y |
| 15 Dingell | Y | Y | Y | ? | Y | Y |

| | 200 | 201 | 202 | 203 | 204 | 205 |
|---|---|---|---|---|---|---|
| **MINNESOTA** | | | | | | |
| 1 **Gutknecht** | Y | Y | Y | Y | N | Y |
| 2 **Kline** | Y | Y | Y | Y | N | Y |
| 3 **Ramstad** | Y | Y | Y | Y | Y | Y |
| 4 McCollum | Y | Y | Y | N | Y | Y |
| 5 Sabo | Y | Y | Y | N | Y | Y |
| 6 **Kennedy** | Y | Y | Y | Y | N | Y |
| 7 Peterson | Y | Y | Y | Y | N | Y |
| 8 Oberstar | Y | Y | Y | N | N | Y |
| **MISSISSIPPI** | | | | | | |
| 1 **Wicker** | Y | Y | Y | Y | N | Y |
| 2 Thompson | Y | Y | Y | N | Y | Y |
| 3 **Pickering** | Y | Y | Y | Y | N | Y |
| 4 Taylor | Y | Y | Y | N | N | Y |
| **MISSOURI** | | | | | | |
| 1 Clay | ? | ? | ? | N | Y | Y |
| 2 **Akin** | Y | Y | Y | Y | N | Y |
| 3 Carnahan | Y | Y | Y | N | Y | Y |
| 4 Skelton | Y | Y | Y | N | Y | Y |
| 5 Cleaver | Y | Y | Y | N | Y | Y |
| 6 **Graves** | Y | Y | Y | Y | N | Y |
| 7 **Blunt** | Y | Y | Y | Y | N | Y |
| 8 **Emerson** | Y | Y | Y | Y | Y | Y |
| 9 **Hulshof** | Y | Y | Y | Y | N | Y |
| **MONTANA** | | | | | | |
| AL **Rehberg** | Y | Y | Y | Y | N | Y |
| **NEBRASKA** | | | | | | |
| 1 **Fortenberry** | Y | Y | Y | Y | N | Y |
| 2 **Terry** | Y | Y | Y | Y | N | Y |
| 3 **Osborne** | Y | Y | Y | Y | N | Y |
| **NEVADA** | | | | | | |
| 1 Berkley | Y | Y | Y | N | Y | Y |
| 2 **Gibbons** | + | + | + | Y | Y | Y |
| 3 **Porter** | Y | Y | Y | Y | Y | Y |
| **NEW HAMPSHIRE** | | | | | | |
| 1 **Bradley** | Y | Y | Y | Y | Y | Y |
| 2 **Bass** | Y | Y | Y | Y | Y | Y |
| **NEW JERSEY** | | | | | | |
| 1 Andrews | Y | Y | Y | N | Y | Y |
| 2 **LoBiondo** | Y | Y | Y | Y | N | Y |
| 3 **Saxton** | Y | Y | Y | Y | N | Y |
| 4 **Smith** | Y | Y | Y | Y | N | Y |
| 5 **Garrett** | Y | Y | Y | Y | N | Y |
| 6 Pallone | Y | Y | Y | N | Y | Y |
| 7 **Ferguson** | ? | ? | ? | Y | N | Y |
| 8 Pascrell | Y | Y | Y | N | Y | Y |
| 9 Rothman | Y | Y | Y | N | Y | Y |
| 10 Payne | Y | Y | Y | N | Y | Y |
| 11 **Frelinghuysen** | Y | Y | Y | Y | Y | Y |
| 12 Holt | Y | Y | Y | N | Y | Y |
| 13 Menendez | Y | Y | Y | N | Y | Y |
| **NEW MEXICO** | | | | | | |
| 1 **Wilson** | Y | Y | Y | Y | Y | Y |
| 2 **Pearce** | Y | Y | Y | Y | N | Y |
| 3 Udall | Y | Y | Y | N | Y | Y |
| **NEW YORK** | | | | | | |
| 1 Bishop | Y | Y | Y | N | Y | Y |
| 2 Israel | Y | Y | Y | N | Y | Y |
| 3 **King** | Y | Y | Y | Y | N | Y |
| 4 McCarthy | Y | Y | Y | N | Y | Y |
| 5 Ackerman | Y | Y | Y | N | Y | Y |
| 6 Meeks | ? | ? | ? | ? | Y | Y |
| 7 Crowley | Y | Y | Y | N | Y | Y |
| 8 Nadler | Y | Y | Y | N | Y | Y |
| 9 Weiner | Y | Y | Y | N | Y | Y |
| 10 Towns | Y | Y | Y | N | Y | Y |
| 11 Owens | Y | Y | Y | N | Y | Y |
| 12 Velázquez | ? | ? | ? | N | Y | Y |
| 13 **Fossella** | Y | Y | Y | Y | Y | Y |
| 14 Maloney | Y | Y | Y | N | Y | Y |
| 15 Rangel | Y | Y | Y | N | Y | Y |
| 16 Serrano | Y | Y | Y | N | Y | Y |
| 17 Engel | Y | Y | Y | N | Y | Y |
| 18 Lowey | Y | Y | Y | N | Y | Y |
| 19 **Kelly** | Y | Y | Y | Y | Y | Y |
| 20 **Sweeney** | Y | Y | Y | Y | Y | Y |
| 21 McNulty | Y | Y | Y | N | Y | Y |
| 22 Hinchey | Y | Y | Y | N | Y | Y |
| 23 **McHugh** | Y | Y | Y | Y | N | Y |
| 24 **Boehlert** | Y | Y | Y | ? | Y | Y |
| 25 **Walsh** | Y | Y | Y | ? | N | Y |
| 26 **Reynolds** | Y | Y | Y | ? | N | Y |
| 27 Higgins | Y | Y | Y | N | Y | Y |
| 28 Slaughter | Y | Y | Y | N | Y | Y |
| 29 **Kuhl** | Y | Y | Y | ? | N | Y |

| | 200 | 201 | 202 | 203 | 204 | 205 |
|---|---|---|---|---|---|---|
| **NORTH CAROLINA** | | | | | | |
| 1 Butterfield | Y | Y | Y | N | Y | Y |
| 2 Etheridge | Y | Y | Y | N | Y | Y |
| 3 **Jones** | Y | Y | Y | ? | N | Y |
| 4 Price | Y | Y | Y | N | Y | Y |
| 5 **Foxx** | Y | Y | Y | Y | N | Y |
| 6 **Coble** | Y | Y | Y | Y | Y | Y |
| 7 McIntyre | Y | Y | Y | N | N | Y |
| 8 **Hayes** | Y | Y | Y | Y | N | Y |
| 9 **Myrick** | Y | Y | Y | Y | N | Y |
| 10 **McHenry** | Y | Y | Y | Y | N | Y |
| 11 **Taylor** | Y | Y | Y | Y | N | Y |
| 12 Watt | Y | Y | Y | ? | Y | Y |
| 13 Miller | Y | Y | Y | N | Y | Y |
| **NORTH DAKOTA** | | | | | | |
| AL Pomeroy | Y | Y | Y | N | Y | Y |
| **OHIO** | | | | | | |
| 1 **Chabot** | Y | Y | Y | Y | N | Y |
| 2 Vacant | | | | | | |
| 3 **Turner** | Y | Y | Y | Y | N | Y |
| 4 **Oxley** | Y | Y | Y | Y | N | Y |
| 5 **Gillmor** | Y | Y | Y | Y | N | Y |
| 6 Strickland | Y | Y | Y | N | Y | Y |
| 7 **Hobson** | Y | Y | Y | Y | N | Y |
| 8 **Boehner** | Y | Y | Y | Y | N | Y |
| 9 Kaptur | Y | Y | Y | N | N | Y |
| 10 Kucinich | Y | Y | Y | N | Y | Y |
| 11 Jones | Y | Y | Y | N | Y | Y |
| 12 **Tiberi** | Y | Y | Y | Y | N | Y |
| 13 Brown | ? | ? | ? | N | Y | Y |
| 14 **LaTourette** | ? | ? | ? | Y | Y | Y |
| 15 **Pryce** | ? | ? | ? | ? | Y | Y |
| 16 **Regula** | Y | Y | Y | Y | Y | Y |
| 17 Ryan | Y | Y | Y | N | Y | Y |
| 18 **Ney** | Y | Y | Y | Y | N | Y |
| **OKLAHOMA** | | | | | | |
| 1 **Sullivan** | Y | Y | Y | Y | N | Y |
| 2 Boren | Y | Y | Y | N | Y | Y |
| 3 **Lucas** | Y | Y | Y | Y | N | Y |
| 4 **Cole** | Y | Y | Y | Y | N | Y |
| 5 **Istook** | ? | ? | ? | ? | N | Y |
| **OREGON** | | | | | | |
| 1 Wu | Y | N | Y | ? | Y | Y |
| 2 **Walden** | Y | Y | Y | Y | Y | Y |
| 3 Blumenauer | Y | Y | Y | N | Y | Y |
| 4 DeFazio | Y | Y | Y | N | Y | Y |
| 5 Hooley | Y | Y | Y | N | Y | Y |
| **PENNSYLVANIA** | | | | | | |
| 1 Brady | Y | Y | Y | N | Y | Y |
| 2 Fattah | ? | ? | ? | N | Y | Y |
| 3 **English** | ? | ? | ? | Y | N | Y |
| 4 **Hart** | Y | Y | Y | Y | N | Y |
| 5 **Peterson** | Y | Y | Y | Y | N | Y |
| 6 **Gerlach** | Y | Y | Y | Y | Y | Y |
| 7 **Weldon** | Y | Y | Y | Y | N | Y |
| 8 **Fitzpatrick** | Y | Y | Y | Y | N | Y |
| 9 **Shuster** | Y | Y | Y | Y | N | Y |
| 10 **Sherwood** | Y | Y | Y | Y | N | Y |
| 11 Kanjorski | Y | Y | Y | N | Y | Y |
| 12 Murtha | Y | Y | Y | N | Y | Y |
| 13 Schwartz | Y | Y | Y | N | Y | Y |
| 14 Doyle | Y | Y | Y | N | Y | Y |
| 15 **Dent** | Y | Y | Y | Y | Y | Y |
| 16 **Pitts** | Y | Y | Y | Y | N | Y |
| 17 Holden | Y | Y | Y | N | N | Y |
| 18 **Murphy** | Y | Y | Y | Y | N | Y |
| 19 **Platts** | Y | Y | Y | Y | Y | Y |
| **RHODE ISLAND** | | | | | | |
| 1 Kennedy | + | + | + | N | Y | Y |
| 2 Langevin | Y | Y | Y | N | Y | Y |
| **SOUTH CAROLINA** | | | | | | |
| 1 **Brown** | Y | Y | Y | Y | N | Y |
| 2 **Wilson** | Y | Y | Y | Y | N | Y |
| 3 **Barrett** | + | + | + | Y | N | Y |
| 4 **Inglis** | Y | Y | Y | Y | N | Y |
| 5 Spratt | Y | Y | Y | N | Y | Y |
| 6 Clyburn | Y | Y | Y | N | Y | Y |
| **SOUTH DAKOTA** | | | | | | |
| AL Herseth | Y | Y | Y | N | Y | Y |
| **TENNESSEE** | | | | | | |
| 1 **Jenkins** | Y | Y | Y | Y | N | Y |
| 2 **Duncan** | Y | Y | Y | Y | N | Y |

| | 200 | 201 | 202 | 203 | 204 | 205 |
|---|---|---|---|---|---|---|
| 3 **Wamp** | Y | Y | Y | Y | N | Y |
| 4 Davis | Y | Y | Y | N | N | Y |
| 5 Cooper | Y | Y | Y | N | Y | Y |
| 6 Gordon | Y | Y | Y | N | Y | Y |
| 7 **Blackburn** | Y | Y | Y | Y | N | Y |
| 8 Tanner | Y | Y | Y | N | Y | Y |
| 9 Ford | Y | Y | Y | N | Y | Y |
| **TEXAS** | | | | | | |
| 1 **Gohmert** | ? | ? | ? | ? | N | Y |
| 2 **Poe** | + | + | + | + | N | Y |
| 3 **Johnson, S.** | Y | Y | Y | Y | N | Y |
| 4 **Hall** | Y | Y | Y | Y | N | Y |
| 5 **Hensarling** | Y | Y | Y | Y | N | Y |
| 6 **Barton** | Y | Y | Y | Y | Y | Y |
| 7 **Culberson** | Y | Y | Y | Y | N | Y |
| 8 **Brady** | Y | Y | Y | ? | N | Y |
| 9 Green | Y | Y | Y | N | Y | Y |
| 10 **McCaul** | Y | Y | Y | Y | N | Y |
| 11 **Conaway** | Y | Y | Y | Y | N | Y |
| 12 **Granger** | Y | Y | Y | Y | Y | Y |
| 13 **Thornberry** | Y | Y | Y | Y | N | Y |
| 14 **Paul** | N | N | Y | Y | N | N |
| 15 Hinojosa | Y | Y | Y | N | Y | Y |
| 16 Reyes | Y | Y | Y | N | Y | Y |
| 17 Edwards | Y | Y | Y | N | Y | Y |
| 18 Jackson-Lee | Y | N | Y | N | Y | Y |
| 19 **Neugebauer** | Y | Y | Y | Y | N | Y |
| 20 Gonzalez | Y | Y | Y | N | Y | Y |
| 21 **Smith** | Y | Y | Y | Y | N | Y |
| 22 **DeLay** | Y | Y | Y | Y | N | Y |
| 23 **Bonilla** | Y | Y | Y | Y | N | Y |
| 24 **Marchant** | Y | Y | Y | Y | N | Y |
| 25 Doggett | Y | Y | Y | N | Y | Y |
| 26 **Burgess** | Y | Y | Y | Y | N | Y |
| 27 Ortiz | Y | Y | Y | N | Y | Y |
| 28 Cuellar | Y | Y | Y | N | Y | Y |
| 29 Green | Y | Y | Y | N | Y | Y |
| 30 Johnson, E. | Y | Y | Y | N | Y | Y |
| 31 **Carter** | Y | Y | Y | Y | N | Y |
| 32 **Sessions** | ? | ? | ? | Y | N | Y |
| **UTAH** | | | | | | |
| 1 **Bishop** | Y | Y | Y | Y | N | Y |
| 2 Matheson | Y | Y | Y | N | Y | Y |
| 3 **Cannon** | Y | Y | Y | Y | N | Y |
| **VERMONT** | | | | | | |
| AL *Sanders* | Y | Y | Y | N | Y | Y |
| **VIRGINIA** | | | | | | |
| 1 **Davis, J.** | Y | Y | Y | Y | N | Y |
| 2 **Drake** | Y | Y | Y | Y | N | Y |
| 3 Scott | Y | Y | Y | N | Y | Y |
| 4 **Forbes** | Y | Y | Y | Y | N | Y |
| 5 **Goode** | Y | Y | Y | Y | N | Y |
| 6 **Goodlatte** | Y | Y | Y | Y | N | Y |
| 7 **Cantor** | Y | Y | Y | Y | N | Y |
| 8 Moran | Y | Y | Y | N | Y | Y |
| 9 Boucher | Y | Y | Y | N | Y | Y |
| 10 **Wolf** | Y | Y | Y | Y | N | Y |
| 11 **Davis, T.** | Y | Y | Y | Y | Y | Y |
| **WASHINGTON** | | | | | | |
| 1 Inslee | Y | Y | Y | N | Y | Y |
| 2 Larsen | Y | Y | Y | N | Y | Y |
| 3 Baird | Y | Y | Y | N | Y | Y |
| 4 **Hastings** | ? | ? | ? | ? | ? | ? |
| 5 **McMorris** | Y | Y | Y | Y | N | Y |
| 6 Dicks | Y | Y | Y | N | Y | Y |
| 7 McDermott | Y | Y | Y | ? | Y | Y |
| 8 **Reichert** | Y | Y | Y | Y | N | Y |
| 9 Smith | Y | Y | Y | N | Y | Y |
| **WEST VIRGINIA** | | | | | | |
| 1 Mollohan | Y | Y | Y | N | N | Y |
| 2 **Capito** | Y | Y | Y | Y | Y | Y |
| 3 Rahall | Y | Y | Y | N | N | Y |
| **WISCONSIN** | | | | | | |
| 1 **Ryan** | Y | Y | Y | Y | N | Y |
| 2 Baldwin | Y | Y | Y | N | Y | Y |
| 3 Kind | Y | Y | Y | N | Y | Y |
| 4 Moore | Y | Y | Y | N | Y | Y |
| 5 **Sensenbrenner** | Y | Y | Y | Y | N | Y |
| 6 **Petri** | Y | Y | Y | Y | N | Y |
| 7 Obey | Y | Y | Y | N | Y | Y |
| 8 **Green** | Y | Y | Y | Y | N | Y |
| **WYOMING** | | | | | | |
| AL **Cubin** | ? | ? | ? | Y | N | Y |

# IN THE HOUSE | By Vote Number

**206.** HR 1224. Business Checking Accounts/Passage. Kelly, R-N.Y., motion to suspend the rules and pass the bill that would allow banks, thrifts and certain industrial loan companies to pay interest on balances held in business checking accounts. Motion agreed to 424-1: R 226-0; D 197-1 (ND 146-1, SD 51-0); I 1-0. A two-thirds majority of those present and voting (284 in this case) is required for passage under suspension of the rules. May 24, 2005.

**207.** HR 2419. Fiscal 2006 Energy and Water Appropriations/Energy Efficiency and Conservation. Markey, D-Mass., amendment that would transfer $15.5 million from interim storage and reprocessing and direct the funds towards energy efficiency and conservation. Rejected 110-312: R 1-223; D 108-89 (ND 96-51, SD 12-38); I 1-0. May 24, 2005.

**208.** HR 2419. Fiscal 2006 Energy and Water Appropriations/Army Corps of Engineers Funding. Jones, R-N.C., amendment that would increase funding for the Army Corps of Engineers by $20 million, offset by an equal cut for the Energy Department's administration account. Rejected 152-275: R 43-183; D 109-91 (ND 81-68, SD 28-23); I 0-1. May 24, 2005.

**209.** HR 2419. Fiscal 2006 Energy and Water Appropriations/Strategic Petroleum Reserve. Stupak, D-Mich., amendment that would bar the use of funds in the bill to accept oil deliveries to the Strategic Petroleum Reserve. Rejected 174-253: R 12-215; D 161-38 (ND 132-16, SD 29-22); I 1-0. May 24, 2005.

**210.** HR 2419. Fiscal 2006 Energy and Water Appropriations/Recommit. Etheridge, D-N.C., motion to recommit the bill to the Appropriations Committee with instructions to include language that would direct $500,000 toward a study on imported oil and provide $1 million for the Energy secretary to conduct a conference with OPEC nations on oil prices. Motion rejected 167-261: R 1-226; D 165-35 (ND 125-24, SD 40-11); I 1-0. May 24, 2005.

**211.** HR 2419. Fiscal 2006 Energy and Water Appropriations/Passage. Passage of the bill that would provide $29.7 billion in fiscal 2006 for energy and water development projects, including $4.7 billion for the Army Corps of Engineers and $8.8 billion for the National Nuclear Security Administration. It also would provide $661 million for the Yucca Mountain nuclear waste repository, including $10 million for the department to begin accepting waste for interim storage at one or more facilities by fiscal 2006. Passed 416-13: R 219-8; D 196-5 (ND 146-4, SD 50-1); I 1-0. May 24, 2005.

**212.** HR 1815. Fiscal 2006 Defense Authorization/Previous Question. Cole, R-Okla., motion to order the previous question (thus ending debate and possibility of amendment) on adoption of the rule (H Res 293) to provide for House floor consideration of the bill that would authorize $441.6 billion in fiscal 2006 for the Department of Defense and an additional $49.1 billion in emergency supplemental spending. Motion agreed to 225-200: R 225-0; D 0-199 (ND 0-148, SD 0-51); I 0-1. May 25, 2005.

**213.** HR 1815. Fiscal 2006 Defense Authorization/Rule. Adoption of the rule (H Res 293) to provide for House floor consideration of the bill that would authorize $441.6 billion in fiscal 2006 for the Department of Defense and $49.1 billion in emergency supplemental spending. Adopted 225-198: R 223-0; D 2-197 (ND 2-146, SD 0-51); I 0-1. May 25, 2005.

| | 206 | 207 | 208 | 209 | 210 | 211 | 212 | 213 |
|---|---|---|---|---|---|---|---|---|
| **ALABAMA** | | | | | | | | |
| 1 Bonner | Y | N | N | N | N | Y | Y | Y |
| 2 Everett | Y | N | N | N | N | Y | Y | Y |
| 3 Rogers | Y | N | Y | N | N | Y | Y | Y |
| 4 Aderholt | Y | N | N | N | N | Y | Y | Y |
| 5 Cramer | Y | N | N | N | Y | N | N | N |
| 6 Bachus | Y | N | N | N | N | Y | Y | Y |
| 7 Davis | Y | N | N | Y | Y | Y | N | N |
| **ALASKA** | | | | | | | | |
| AL Young | Y | ? | ? | ? | ? | ? | Y | Y |
| **ARIZONA** | | | | | | | | |
| 1 Renzi | Y | N | Y | N | N | Y | Y | Y |
| 2 Franks | Y | N | N | N | N | N | Y | Y |
| 3 Shadegg | Y | N | N | N | N | Y | Y | Y |
| 4 Pastor | Y | N | N | N | + | Y | N | N |
| 5 Hayworth | Y | N | Y | N | N | Y | Y | Y |
| 6 Flake | Y | N | N | Y | N | N | Y | Y |
| 7 Grijalva | Y | Y | Y | Y | Y | Y | N | N |
| 8 Kolbe | Y | N | N | N | N | Y | Y | Y |
| **ARKANSAS** | | | | | | | | |
| 1 Berry | Y | N | N | N | N | Y | N | N |
| 2 Snyder | Y | N | N | N | Y | N | N | N |
| 3 Boozman | Y | N | N | N | N | Y | Y | Y |
| 4 Ross | Y | N | N | Y | Y | Y | N | N |
| **CALIFORNIA** | | | | | | | | |
| 1 Thompson | Y | Y | Y | Y | Y | Y | N | N |
| 2 Herger | Y | N | N | N | N | Y | Y | Y |
| 3 Lungren | Y | N | Y | N | N | Y | Y | Y |
| 4 Doolittle | Y | N | N | N | N | Y | Y | Y |
| 5 Matsui, D. | Y | N | N | Y | Y | Y | N | N |
| 6 Woolsey | Y | Y | Y | Y | Y | Y | N | N |
| 7 Miller, George | Y | Y | N | Y | Y | Y | N | N |
| 8 Pelosi | Y | Y | N | Y | Y | Y | N | N |
| 9 Lee | Y | Y | Y | ? | Y | Y | N | N |
| 10 Tauscher | Y | N | N | Y | Y | Y | N | N |
| 11 Pombo | Y | N | N | N | N | Y | Y | Y |
| 12 Lantos | Y | N | Y | N | Y | Y | N | N |
| 13 Stark | Y | Y | Y | Y | Y | Y | N | N |
| 14 Eshoo | Y | Y | N | Y | Y | Y | N | N |
| 15 Honda | Y | Y | Y | Y | Y | Y | N | N |
| 16 Lofgren | Y | Y | N | Y | Y | Y | N | N |
| 17 Farr | Y | Y | N | Y | Y | Y | N | N |
| 18 Cardoza | Y | N | Y | Y | Y | N | N | N |
| 19 Radanovich | Y | N | N | N | N | Y | Y | Y |
| 20 Costa | Y | N | Y | Y | Y | Y | N | N |
| 21 Nunes | Y | N | N | N | N | Y | Y | Y |
| 22 Thomas | Y | N | N | N | N | Y | Y | Y |
| 23 Capps | Y | Y | N | Y | Y | Y | N | N |
| 24 Gallegly | Y | N | N | N | N | Y | Y | N |
| 25 McKeon | Y | N | N | N | N | Y | Y | Y |
| 26 Dreier | Y | N | N | N | N | Y | Y | Y |
| 27 Sherman | Y | Y | Y | Y | Y | Y | N | N |
| 28 Berman | Y | Y | N | Y | Y | Y | N | N |
| 29 Schiff | Y | Y | N | Y | Y | Y | N | N |
| 30 Waxman | Y | Y | N | Y | Y | Y | N | N |
| 31 Becerra | Y | Y | N | Y | Y | Y | N | N |
| 32 Solis | Y | Y | N | Y | Y | Y | N | N |
| 33 Watson | Y | Y | Y | Y | Y | Y | N | N |
| 34 Roybal-Allard | Y | Y | N | Y | Y | Y | N | N |
| 35 Waters | Y | N | N | N | Y | Y | N | N |
| 36 Harman | Y | Y | N | Y | Y | Y | N | N |
| 37 Millender-McD. | ? | ? | ? | ? | ? | ? | ? | ? |
| 38 Napolitano | Y | Y | Y | Y | Y | Y | N | N |
| 39 Sánchez, Linda | Y | Y | Y | Y | Y | Y | N | N |
| 40 Royce | Y | N | N | N | N | Y | Y | Y |
| 41 Lewis | Y | N | N | N | N | Y | Y | Y |
| 42 Miller, Gary | Y | N | Y | N | N | Y | Y | Y |
| 43 Baca | Y | N | Y | Y | Y | Y | N | N |
| 44 Calvert | Y | N | N | N | N | Y | Y | Y |
| 45 Bono | Y | N | N | N | N | Y | Y | Y |
| 46 Rohrabacher | Y | N | N | N | N | Y | Y | Y |
| 47 Sanchez, Loretta | Y | Y | N | Y | Y | Y | N | N |
| 48 Cox | Y | N | N | N | N | Y | Y | Y |
| 49 Issa | Y | N | N | N | N | Y | Y | Y |
| 50 Cunningham | Y | N | N | N | Y | Y | Y | Y |
| 51 Filner | Y | Y | N | Y | Y | Y | N | N |
| 52 Hunter | Y | N | N | N | N | Y | Y | Y |
| 53 Davis | Y | Y | Y | Y | Y | Y | N | N |
| **COLORADO** | | | | | | | | |
| 1 DeGette | Y | Y | Y | Y | Y | Y | N | N |
| 2 Udall | Y | Y | Y | Y | N | Y | N | N |
| 3 Salazar | Y | N | Y | Y | Y | Y | N | N |
| 4 Musgrave | Y | N | N | N | N | Y | Y | ? |
| 5 Hefley | Y | N | N | N | N | Y | Y | Y |
| 6 Tancredo | Y | N | Y | N | N | Y | Y | Y |
| 7 Beauprez | Y | N | N | N | N | Y | Y | Y |
| **CONNECTICUT** | | | | | | | | |
| 1 Larson | Y | Y | N | Y | Y | Y | N | N |
| 2 Simmons | Y | N | N | N | N | Y | Y | Y |
| 3 DeLauro | Y | Y | Y | N | Y | Y | N | N |
| 4 Shays | Y | N | N | N | Y | Y | Y | Y |
| 5 Johnson | Y | N | N | N | N | Y | Y | Y |
| **DELAWARE** | | | | | | | | |
| AL Castle | Y | N | N | N | N | Y | ? | Y |
| **FLORIDA** | | | | | | | | |
| 1 Miller | Y | N | N | N | N | Y | Y | Y |
| 2 Boyd | Y | N | N | N | N | Y | N | N |
| 3 Brown | Y | Y | Y | Y | Y | Y | N | N |
| 4 Crenshaw | Y | N | N | N | N | Y | Y | Y |
| 5 Brown-Waite | Y | N | N | N | N | Y | Y | Y |
| 6 Stearns | Y | N | N | N | N | N | Y | Y |
| 7 Mica | Y | N | N | N | N | Y | Y | Y |
| 8 Keller | Y | N | N | N | N | Y | Y | Y |
| 9 Bilirakis | Y | N | N | N | N | Y | Y | Y |
| 10 Young | Y | N | N | N | N | Y | Y | Y |
| 11 Davis | Y | N | N | N | Y | Y | N | N |
| 12 Putnam | Y | N | N | N | N | Y | Y | Y |
| 13 Harris | Y | N | N | N | N | Y | Y | Y |
| 14 Mack | Y | N | N | N | N | Y | Y | Y |
| 15 Weldon | Y | N | N | N | N | Y | Y | Y |
| 16 Foley | Y | N | N | N | N | Y | Y | Y |
| 17 Meek | Y | N | N | N | Y | Y | N | N |
| 18 Ros-Lehtinen | Y | N | N | N | N | Y | Y | Y |
| 19 Wexler | Y | Y | Y | Y | Y | Y | N | N |
| 20 Wasserman-Schultz | Y | Y | Y | Y | Y | Y | N | N |
| 21 Diaz-Balart, L. | Y | N | N | N | N | Y | Y | Y |
| 22 Shaw | Y | N | N | N | N | Y | Y | Y |
| 23 Hastings | Y | Y | Y | Y | Y | Y | N | N |
| 24 Feeney | Y | N | N | N | N | Y | Y | Y |
| 25 Diaz-Balart, M. | Y | N | N | N | N | Y | Y | Y |
| **GEORGIA** | | | | | | | | |
| 1 Kingston | Y | N | N | N | N | Y | Y | Y |
| 2 Bishop | Y | N | N | Y | N | Y | N | N |
| 3 Marshall | Y | N | N | Y | N | Y | N | N |
| 4 McKinney | Y | Y | N | Y | Y | Y | N | N |
| 5 Lewis | Y | Y | N | Y | Y | Y | N | N |
| 6 Price | Y | N | N | N | N | Y | Y | Y |
| 7 Linder | ? | N | N | N | N | Y | Y | Y |
| 8 Westmoreland | Y | N | N | N | N | Y | Y | Y |
| 9 Norwood | Y | N | N | N | N | Y | Y | Y |
| 10 Deal | Y | N | N | N | N | Y | Y | Y |
| 11 Gingrey | Y | N | N | N | N | Y | ? | ? |
| 12 Barrow | Y | Y | Y | Y | Y | Y | N | N |
| 13 Scott | Y | N | N | N | Y | Y | N | N |
| **HAWAII** | | | | | | | | |
| 1 Abercrombie | Y | Y | Y | N | N | Y | N | N |
| 2 Case | Y | N | Y | N | Y | Y | N | N |
| **IDAHO** | | | | | | | | |
| 1 Otter | Y | N | N | N | N | Y | Y | Y |
| 2 Simpson | Y | N | N | N | N | Y | Y | Y |
| **ILLINOIS** | | | | | | | | |
| 1 Rush | Y | N | N | Y | Y | Y | N | N |
| 2 Jackson | Y | Y | N | Y | Y | Y | N | N |
| 3 Lipinski | Y | Y | Y | Y | Y | N | N | N |
| 4 Gutierrez | Y | Y | N | Y | Y | Y | N | N |
| 5 Emanuel | Y | Y | N | Y | Y | Y | N | N |
| 6 Hyde | Y | N | N | N | N | Y | Y | Y |
| 7 Davis | Y | N | Y | Y | Y | Y | N | N |
| 8 Bean | Y | – | Y | N | Y | Y | N | N |
| 9 Schakowsky | Y | Y | N | Y | Y | Y | N | N |
| 10 Kirk | Y | N | N | N | N | Y | Y | Y |
| 11 Weller | Y | N | N | N | N | Y | Y | Y |
| 12 Costello | Y | N | N | Y | N | Y | N | N |

**KEY**   Republicans    Democrats    *Independents*

| | | |
|---|---|---|
| Y Voted for (yea) | X Paired against | C Voted "present" to avoid possible conflict of interest |
| # Paired for | – Announced against | |
| + Announced for | P Voted "present" | ? Did not vote or otherwise make a position known |
| N Voted against (nay) | | |

| | 206 | 207 | 208 | 209 | 210 | 211 | 212 | 213 |
|---|---|---|---|---|---|---|---|---|
| 13 **Biggert** | Y | N | N | N | N | Y | Y | Y |
| 14 **Hastert** | | | | | | | | |
| 15 **Johnson** | Y | N | Y | Y | N | Y | Y | Y |
| 16 **Manzullo** | Y | N | N | N | N | Y | Y | Y |
| 17 Evans | Y | Y | Y | Y | Y | Y | N | N |
| 18 **LaHood** | Y | N | N | N | N | Y | Y | Y |
| 19 **Shimkus** | Y | N | Y | N | N | Y | Y | Y |
| **INDIANA** | | | | | | | | |
| 1 Visclosky | Y | N | N | Y | N | Y | N | N |
| 2 **Chocola** | Y | N | N | N | N | Y | Y | Y |
| 3 **Souder** | Y | N | N | N | N | Y | Y | Y |
| 4 **Buyer** | Y | N | N | N | N | Y | Y | Y |
| 5 **Burton** | Y | N | N | N | N | Y | Y | Y |
| 6 **Pence** | Y | ? | N | N | N | Y | Y | Y |
| 7 Carson | Y | Y | Y | Y | Y | Y | N | N |
| 8 **Hostettler** | Y | N | Y | N | N | Y | Y | Y |
| 9 **Sodrel** | Y | N | N | N | N | Y | Y | Y |
| **IOWA** | | | | | | | | |
| 1 **Nussle** | Y | N | Y | N | N | Y | Y | Y |
| 2 **Leach** | Y | N | Y | Y | N | Y | Y | Y |
| 3 Boswell | ? | Y | Y | Y | Y | Y | N | N |
| 4 **Latham** | Y | N | N | N | N | Y | Y | Y |
| 5 **King** | Y | N | N | N | N | Y | Y | Y |
| **KANSAS** | | | | | | | | |
| 1 **Moran** | Y | N | N | N | N | Y | Y | Y |
| 2 **Ryun** | Y | N | N | N | N | Y | Y | Y |
| 3 Moore | Y | N | Y | Y | Y | Y | N | N |
| 4 **Tiahrt** | Y | N | N | N | N | Y | Y | Y |
| **KENTUCKY** | | | | | | | | |
| 1 **Whitfield** | Y | N | N | N | N | Y | Y | Y |
| 2 **Lewis** | Y | N | N | N | N | Y | Y | Y |
| 3 **Northup** | Y | N | N | N | N | Y | Y | Y |
| 4 **Davis** | Y | N | N | N | N | Y | Y | Y |
| 5 **Rogers** | Y | N | N | N | N | Y | Y | Y |
| 6 Chandler | Y | Y | Y | Y | Y | Y | N | N |
| **LOUISIANA** | | | | | | | | |
| 1 **Jindal** | Y | N | N | N | N | Y | Y | Y |
| 2 Jefferson | Y | N | Y | N | Y | Y | N | N |
| 3 Melancon | Y | N | Y | N | Y | Y | N | N |
| 4 **McCrery** | Y | ? | N | N | N | Y | Y | Y |
| 5 **Alexander** | Y | N | N | N | N | Y | Y | Y |
| 6 **Baker** | Y | N | N | N | N | Y | Y | Y |
| 7 **Boustany** | Y | N | N | N | N | Y | Y | Y |
| **MAINE** | | | | | | | | |
| 1 Allen | Y | + | + | + | Y | Y | N | N |
| 2 Michaud | Y | Y | Y | Y | Y | Y | N | N |
| **MARYLAND** | | | | | | | | |
| 1 **Gilchrest** | Y | N | N | N | N | Y | Y | Y |
| 2 Ruppersberger | Y | N | Y | Y | Y | Y | N | N |
| 3 Cardin | Y | N | N | Y | Y | Y | N | N |
| 4 Wynn | Y | N | Y | Y | Y | Y | N | N |
| 5 Hoyer | Y | N | N | Y | Y | Y | N | N |
| 6 **Bartlett** | Y | N | Y | N | N | Y | Y | Y |
| 7 Cummings | Y | N | Y | Y | Y | Y | N | N |
| 8 Van Hollen | Y | Y | N | Y | Y | Y | N | N |
| **MASSACHUSETTS** | | | | | | | | |
| 1 Olver | Y | Y | N | Y | Y | Y | N | N |
| 2 Neal | Y | Y | Y | Y | Y | Y | N | N |
| 3 McGovern | Y | Y | Y | Y | Y | Y | N | N |
| 4 Frank | Y | Y | Y | Y | Y | Y | N | N |
| 5 Meehan | Y | Y | Y | Y | Y | Y | N | N |
| 6 Tierney | Y | Y | Y | Y | N | Y | N | N |
| 7 Markey | Y | Y | Y | Y | Y | Y | N | N |
| 8 Capuano | Y | Y | N | Y | N | Y | N | N |
| 9 Lynch | Y | Y | Y | Y | N | Y | N | N |
| 10 Delahunt | Y | Y | Y | Y | Y | Y | N | N |
| **MICHIGAN** | | | | | | | | |
| 1 Stupak | Y | N | N | Y | N | Y | N | N |
| 2 **Hoekstra** | Y | N | N | N | N | Y | Y | Y |
| 3 **Ehlers** | Y | N | N | N | N | Y | Y | Y |
| 4 **Camp** | Y | N | N | N | N | Y | Y | Y |
| 5 Kildee | Y | N | Y | Y | Y | Y | N | N |
| 6 **Upton** | Y | N | N | N | N | Y | Y | Y |
| 7 **Schwarz** | Y | N | N | N | N | Y | Y | Y |
| 8 **Rogers** | Y | N | N | N | N | Y | Y | Y |
| 9 **Knollenberg** | Y | N | N | N | N | Y | Y | Y |
| 10 **Miller** | Y | N | N | N | N | Y | Y | Y |
| 11 **McCotter** | Y | N | N | N | N | Y | Y | Y |
| 12 Levin | Y | N | N | Y | Y | Y | N | N |
| 13 Kilpatrick | Y | N | N | Y | Y | Y | N | N |
| 14 Conyers | Y | Y | Y | Y | Y | Y | N | N |
| 15 Dingell | ? | N | N | N | Y | Y | N | N |

| | 206 | 207 | 208 | 209 | 210 | 211 | 212 | 213 |
|---|---|---|---|---|---|---|---|---|
| **MINNESOTA** | | | | | | | | |
| 1 **Gutknecht** | Y | N | Y | Y | N | Y | Y | Y |
| 2 **Kline** | Y | N | N | N | N | Y | Y | Y |
| 3 **Ramstad** | Y | N | N | N | N | Y | Y | Y |
| 4 McCollum | Y | Y | N | Y | Y | Y | N | N |
| 5 Sabo | Y | Y | N | N | N | Y | N | N |
| 6 **Kennedy** | Y | N | N | N | N | Y | Y | Y |
| 7 Peterson | Y | N | Y | Y | N | Y | N | N |
| 8 Oberstar | Y | Y | Y | Y | N | Y | N | N |
| **MISSISSIPPI** | | | | | | | | |
| 1 **Wicker** | ? | N | N | N | N | Y | Y | Y |
| 2 Thompson | Y | N | N | N | Y | Y | N | N |
| 3 **Pickering** | Y | ? | ? | ? | ? | ? | ? | ? |
| 4 Taylor | Y | N | Y | Y | N | Y | N | N |
| **MISSOURI** | | | | | | | | |
| 1 Clay | Y | Y | Y | Y | Y | Y | ? | ? |
| 2 **Akin** | Y | N | N | N | N | Y | Y | Y |
| 3 Carnahan | Y | N | Y | Y | Y | Y | N | N |
| 4 Skelton | Y | N | Y | N | Y | Y | N | N |
| 5 Cleaver | Y | N | N | Y | Y | Y | N | N |
| 6 **Graves** | Y | N | N | N | N | Y | Y | Y |
| 7 **Blunt** | Y | N | N | N | N | Y | Y | Y |
| 8 **Emerson** | Y | N | N | N | N | Y | ? | ? |
| 9 **Hulshof** | Y | N | Y | N | N | Y | Y | Y |
| **MONTANA** | | | | | | | | |
| AL **Rehberg** | Y | N | N | N | N | Y | Y | Y |
| **NEBRASKA** | | | | | | | | |
| 1 **Fortenberry** | Y | N | Y | N | N | Y | Y | Y |
| 2 **Terry** | Y | N | Y | Y | N | Y | Y | Y |
| 3 **Osborne** | ? | N | N | N | N | Y | Y | Y |
| **NEVADA** | | | | | | | | |
| 1 Berkley | Y | Y | Y | Y | N | N | N | N |
| 2 **Gibbons** | Y | Y | Y | N | N | N | Y | Y |
| 3 **Porter** | Y | N | Y | N | N | N | Y | Y |
| **NEW HAMPSHIRE** | | | | | | | | |
| 1 **Bradley** | Y | N | N | N | N | Y | Y | Y |
| 2 **Bass** | Y | N | N | N | N | Y | Y | Y |
| **NEW JERSEY** | | | | | | | | |
| 1 Andrews | Y | N | N | Y | Y | Y | N | Y |
| 2 **LoBiondo** | Y | N | N | N | N | Y | Y | Y |
| 3 **Saxton** | Y | N | N | N | N | Y | Y | Y |
| 4 **Smith** | Y | N | N | N | N | Y | Y | Y |
| 5 **Garrett** | Y | N | N | N | N | Y | Y | Y |
| 6 Pallone | Y | Y | Y | Y | Y | Y | N | N |
| 7 **Ferguson** | Y | N | N | N | N | Y | Y | Y |
| 8 Pascrell | Y | N | N | Y | Y | Y | N | N |
| 9 Rothman | Y | N | N | Y | Y | Y | N | N |
| 10 Payne | Y | Y | Y | Y | Y | Y | N | N |
| 11 **Frelinghuysen** | Y | N | N | N | N | Y | Y | Y |
| 12 Holt | Y | Y | N | Y | N | Y | N | N |
| 13 Menendez | Y | Y | Y | Y | Y | Y | N | N |
| **NEW MEXICO** | | | | | | | | |
| 1 **Wilson** | Y | N | N | N | N | Y | Y | Y |
| 2 **Pearce** | Y | N | N | N | N | Y | Y | Y |
| 3 Udall | Y | Y | Y | Y | N | Y | N | N |
| **NEW YORK** | | | | | | | | |
| 1 Bishop | Y | Y | Y | Y | Y | Y | N | N |
| 2 Israel | Y | Y | Y | Y | Y | Y | N | N |
| 3 **King** | Y | N | Y | N | N | Y | Y | Y |
| 4 McCarthy | Y | N | N | Y | Y | Y | N | N |
| 5 Ackerman | Y | Y | Y | Y | Y | Y | N | N |
| 6 Meeks | ? | N | N | Y | Y | Y | N | N |
| 7 Crowley | Y | Y | N | Y | Y | Y | N | N |
| 8 Nadler | Y | Y | N | Y | Y | Y | N | N |
| 9 Weiner | Y | Y | Y | Y | Y | Y | N | N |
| 10 Towns | Y | N | Y | Y | Y | Y | N | N |
| 11 Owens | Y | Y | N | Y | Y | Y | N | N |
| 12 Velázquez | Y | Y | N | Y | Y | Y | N | N |
| 13 **Fossella** | Y | N | Y | N | N | Y | Y | Y |
| 14 Maloney | Y | Y | Y | Y | Y | Y | N | N |
| 15 Rangel | Y | Y | Y | Y | Y | Y | N | N |
| 16 Serrano | Y | Y | N | Y | Y | Y | N | N |
| 17 Engel | Y | N | Y | Y | Y | Y | N | N |
| 18 Lowey | Y | Y | Y | Y | Y | Y | N | N |
| 19 **Kelly** | Y | N | N | Y | N | Y | Y | Y |
| 20 **Sweeney** | Y | N | N | N | N | Y | Y | Y |
| 21 McNulty | Y | Y | N | Y | Y | Y | N | N |
| 22 Hinchey | Y | Y | N | Y | N | Y | N | N |
| 23 **McHugh** | Y | N | N | N | N | Y | Y | Y |
| 24 **Boehlert** | Y | N | N | N | N | Y | Y | Y |
| 25 **Walsh** | Y | N | N | N | N | Y | Y | Y |
| 26 **Reynolds** | Y | N | N | N | N | Y | Y | Y |
| 27 Higgins | Y | N | Y | Y | Y | Y | N | N |
| 28 Slaughter | Y | Y | Y | Y | Y | Y | N | N |
| 29 **Kuhl** | Y | N | N | N | N | Y | Y | Y |

| | 206 | 207 | 208 | 209 | 210 | 211 | 212 | 213 |
|---|---|---|---|---|---|---|---|---|
| **NORTH CAROLINA** | | | | | | | | |
| 1 Butterfield | Y | N | Y | Y | Y | Y | N | N |
| 2 Etheridge | Y | N | Y | Y | Y | N | N | N |
| 3 **Jones** | Y | N | Y | Y | Y | Y | Y | ? |
| 4 Price | Y | N | Y | Y | Y | Y | N | N |
| 5 **Foxx** | Y | N | N | N | N | Y | Y | Y |
| 6 **Coble** | Y | N | Y | N | N | Y | Y | Y |
| 7 McIntyre | Y | N | Y | Y | Y | Y | N | N |
| 8 **Hayes** | Y | N | N | N | N | Y | Y | Y |
| 9 **Myrick** | Y | N | N | N | N | Y | Y | Y |
| 10 **McHenry** | Y | N | N | N | N | Y | Y | Y |
| 11 **Taylor** | Y | N | N | N | N | Y | Y | Y |
| 12 Watt | Y | N | Y | Y | Y | Y | N | N |
| 13 Miller | Y | N | N | Y | Y | Y | N | N |
| **NORTH DAKOTA** | | | | | | | | |
| AL Pomeroy | Y | N | Y | Y | Y | Y | N | N |
| **OHIO** | | | | | | | | |
| 1 **Chabot** | Y | N | N | N | N | Y | Y | Y |
| 2 Vacant | | | | | | | | |
| 3 **Turner** | Y | N | N | N | N | Y | Y | Y |
| 4 **Oxley** | Y | N | N | N | N | Y | Y | Y |
| 5 **Gillmor** | Y | N | N | N | N | Y | Y | Y |
| 6 Strickland | Y | N | Y | Y | Y | Y | N | N |
| 7 **Hobson** | Y | N | N | N | N | Y | Y | Y |
| 8 **Boehner** | Y | N | Y | N | N | Y | Y | Y |
| 9 Kaptur | Y | N | N | N | N | Y | N | N |
| 10 Kucinich | Y | Y | Y | Y | Y | N | N | N |
| 11 Jones | Y | N | N | Y | Y | Y | N | N |
| 12 **Tiberi** | Y | N | N | N | N | Y | Y | Y |
| 13 Brown | Y | Y | Y | Y | Y | Y | N | N |
| 14 **LaTourette** | Y | N | N | N | N | Y | Y | Y |
| 15 **Pryce** | Y | N | N | N | N | Y | Y | Y |
| 16 **Regula** | Y | N | N | N | N | Y | Y | Y |
| 17 Ryan | Y | Y | N | Y | Y | Y | N | N |
| 18 **Ney** | Y | N | N | N | N | Y | Y | Y |
| **OKLAHOMA** | | | | | | | | |
| 1 **Sullivan** | Y | N | N | N | N | Y | Y | Y |
| 2 Boren | Y | N | N | N | N | Y | N | N |
| 3 **Lucas** | Y | N | N | N | N | Y | Y | Y |
| 4 **Cole** | Y | N | N | N | N | Y | Y | Y |
| 5 **Istook** | Y | N | N | N | N | Y | Y | Y |
| **OREGON** | | | | | | | | |
| 1 Wu | Y | Y | N | Y | Y | Y | N | N |
| 2 **Walden** | Y | N | N | N | N | Y | Y | Y |
| 3 Blumenauer | Y | Y | N | N | N | Y | N | N |
| 4 DeFazio | N | Y | Y | Y | Y | Y | N | N |
| 5 Hooley | Y | Y | Y | Y | Y | Y | N | N |
| **PENNSYLVANIA** | | | | | | | | |
| 1 Brady | Y | N | N | Y | Y | Y | N | N |
| 2 Fattah | Y | N | N | Y | Y | Y | N | N |
| 3 **English** | Y | N | N | N | N | Y | Y | Y |
| 4 **Hart** | Y | N | N | N | N | Y | Y | Y |
| 5 **Peterson** | Y | N | N | N | N | Y | Y | Y |
| 6 **Gerlach** | Y | N | Y | N | N | Y | Y | Y |
| 7 **Weldon** | Y | N | N | N | N | Y | Y | Y |
| 8 **Fitzpatrick** | Y | N | N | N | N | Y | Y | Y |
| 9 **Shuster** | Y | N | N | N | N | Y | Y | Y |
| 10 **Sherwood** | Y | N | N | N | N | Y | Y | Y |
| 11 Kanjorski | Y | N | N | N | N | Y | N | N |
| 12 Murtha | Y | N | N | N | N | Y | ? | ? |
| 13 Schwartz | Y | Y | N | Y | Y | Y | N | N |
| 14 Doyle | Y | N | N | Y | Y | Y | N | N |
| 15 **Dent** | Y | N | N | N | N | Y | Y | Y |
| 16 **Pitts** | Y | N | N | N | N | Y | Y | Y |
| 17 Holden | Y | N | N | Y | N | Y | N | N |
| 18 **Murphy** | Y | N | Y | N | N | Y | Y | Y |
| 19 **Platts** | Y | N | N | N | N | Y | Y | Y |
| **RHODE ISLAND** | | | | | | | | |
| 1 Kennedy | Y | Y | Y | Y | Y | Y | N | N |
| 2 Langevin | Y | Y | Y | Y | Y | Y | N | N |
| **SOUTH CAROLINA** | | | | | | | | |
| 1 **Brown** | Y | N | N | N | N | Y | Y | Y |
| 2 **Wilson** | Y | N | Y | N | N | Y | Y | Y |
| 3 **Barrett** | Y | N | N | N | N | Y | Y | Y |
| 4 **Inglis** | Y | N | N | N | N | Y | Y | Y |
| 5 Spratt | Y | Y | N | Y | Y | Y | N | N |
| 6 Clyburn | Y | N | N | N | Y | Y | N | N |
| **SOUTH DAKOTA** | | | | | | | | |
| AL Herseth | Y | N | Y | Y | Y | Y | N | N |
| **TENNESSEE** | | | | | | | | |
| 1 **Jenkins** | Y | N | Y | N | N | Y | Y | Y |
| 2 **Duncan** | Y | N | Y | N | N | Y | Y | Y |

| | 206 | 207 | 208 | 209 | 210 | 211 | 212 | 213 |
|---|---|---|---|---|---|---|---|---|
| 3 **Wamp** | Y | ? | ? | N | N | Y | Y | Y |
| 4 Davis | Y | N | Y | N | Y | Y | N | N |
| 5 Cooper | Y | Y | N | N | Y | Y | N | N |
| 6 Gordon | Y | N | N | Y | Y | Y | N | N |
| 7 **Blackburn** | Y | N | N | N | N | Y | Y | Y |
| 8 Tanner | Y | N | Y | Y | Y | Y | N | N |
| 9 Ford | Y | Y | Y | N | Y | Y | N | N |
| **TEXAS** | | | | | | | | |
| 1 **Gohmert** | Y | N | N | N | N | Y | Y | Y |
| 2 **Poe** | Y | N | Y | N | N | Y | Y | Y |
| 3 **Johnson, S.** | Y | N | Y | N | N | Y | Y | Y |
| 4 **Hall** | Y | N | N | N | N | Y | Y | Y |
| 5 **Hensarling** | Y | N | N | N | N | Y | Y | Y |
| 6 **Barton** | Y | N | N | N | N | Y | Y | Y |
| 7 **Culberson** | Y | N | N | N | N | Y | Y | Y |
| 8 **Brady** | Y | N | N | N | N | Y | Y | Y |
| 9 Green | Y | N | Y | Y | Y | Y | N | N |
| 10 **McCaul** | Y | N | Y | N | N | Y | Y | Y |
| 11 **Conaway** | Y | N | N | N | N | Y | Y | Y |
| 12 **Granger** | Y | N | N | N | N | Y | Y | Y |
| 13 **Thornberry** | Y | N | N | N | N | Y | Y | Y |
| 14 **Paul** | Y | N | Y | Y | N | N | Y | Y |
| 15 Hinojosa | Y | N | Y | N | Y | Y | N | N |
| 16 Reyes | Y | N | Y | N | N | Y | N | N |
| 17 Edwards | Y | N | N | Y | N | Y | N | N |
| 18 Jackson-Lee | Y | N | Y | Y | Y | Y | N | N |
| 19 **Neugebauer** | Y | N | N | N | N | Y | Y | Y |
| 20 Gonzalez | Y | N | Y | N | N | Y | N | N |
| 21 **Smith** | Y | N | N | N | N | Y | Y | Y |
| 22 **DeLay** | Y | N | N | N | N | Y | Y | Y |
| 23 **Bonilla** | Y | N | N | N | N | Y | Y | Y |
| 24 **Marchant** | Y | N | N | N | N | Y | Y | Y |
| 25 Doggett | Y | ? | N | Y | Y | Y | N | N |
| 26 **Burgess** | Y | N | N | N | N | Y | Y | Y |
| 27 Ortiz | Y | N | Y | N | N | Y | N | N |
| 28 Cuellar | Y | N | N | N | Y | Y | N | N |
| 29 Green | Y | N | Y | N | N | Y | N | N |
| 30 Johnson, E. | Y | Y | Y | Y | Y | Y | N | N |
| 31 **Carter** | Y | N | N | N | N | Y | Y | Y |
| 32 **Sessions** | Y | N | Y | N | N | Y | Y | Y |
| **UTAH** | | | | | | | | |
| 1 **Bishop** | Y | N | Y | N | N | Y | Y | Y |
| 2 Matheson | Y | Y | Y | Y | Y | N | N | N |
| 3 **Cannon** | Y | N | Y | N | N | Y | Y | Y |
| **VERMONT** | | | | | | | | |
| AL *Sanders* | Y | Y | N | Y | Y | Y | N | N |
| **VIRGINIA** | | | | | | | | |
| 1 **Davis, J.** | Y | N | Y | Y | N | Y | Y | Y |
| 2 **Drake** | Y | N | N | N | N | Y | Y | Y |
| 3 Scott | Y | N | Y | Y | Y | Y | N | N |
| 4 **Forbes** | Y | N | Y | Y | N | Y | Y | Y |
| 5 **Goode** | Y | N | Y | N | N | Y | Y | Y |
| 6 **Goodlatte** | Y | N | N | Y | N | Y | Y | Y |
| 7 **Cantor** | Y | N | N | N | N | Y | Y | Y |
| 8 Moran | Y | N | Y | Y | Y | Y | N | N |
| 9 Boucher | Y | N | N | Y | Y | Y | N | N |
| 10 **Wolf** | Y | N | N | N | N | Y | Y | Y |
| 11 **Davis, T.** | Y | N | N | N | N | Y | Y | Y |
| **WASHINGTON** | | | | | | | | |
| 1 Inslee | Y | Y | Y | Y | Y | N | N | N |
| 2 Larsen | Y | Y | Y | Y | Y | Y | N | N |
| 3 Baird | Y | Y | Y | Y | Y | Y | N | N |
| 4 **Hastings** | ? | ? | ? | ? | ? | ? | ? | ? |
| 5 **McMorris** | Y | N | N | N | N | Y | Y | Y |
| 6 Dicks | Y | Y | N | Y | Y | Y | N | N |
| 7 McDermott | Y | Y | Y | Y | N | Y | N | N |
| 8 **Reichert** | Y | N | N | N | N | Y | Y | Y |
| 9 Smith | Y | Y | Y | N | N | Y | N | N |
| **WEST VIRGINIA** | | | | | | | | |
| 1 Mollohan | Y | N | N | N | N | Y | N | N |
| 2 **Capito** | Y | N | N | N | N | Y | Y | Y |
| 3 Rahall | Y | Y | Y | Y | Y | Y | N | N |
| **WISCONSIN** | | | | | | | | |
| 1 **Ryan** | Y | N | N | N | N | Y | Y | Y |
| 2 Baldwin | Y | Y | N | Y | Y | Y | N | N |
| 3 Kind | Y | N | Y | Y | N | Y | N | N |
| 4 Moore | Y | + | Y | Y | Y | Y | N | N |
| 5 **Sensenbrenner** | Y | N | N | N | N | N | Y | Y |
| 6 **Petri** | Y | N | Y | N | N | Y | Y | Y |
| 7 Obey | Y | Y | N | Y | Y | Y | N | N |
| 8 **Green** | Y | N | Y | Y | N | N | Y | Y |
| **WYOMING** | | | | | | | | |
| AL **Cubin** | Y | N | N | N | N | Y | Y | Y |

# IN THE HOUSE | By Vote Number

**214.** **HR 1815. Fiscal 2006 Defense Authorization/Border Security.**
Goode, R-Va., amendment that would authorize the Defense secretary to assign military personnel to assist the Homeland Security Department with border security under certain circumstances. Adopted 245-184: R 214-13; D 31-170 (ND 15-135, SD 16-35); I 0-1. May 25, 2005.

**215.** **HR 1815. Fiscal 2006 Defense Authorization/Boy Scouts.** J. Davis, R-Va., amendment that would require the Defense Department to provide the minimum level of support it provided the Boy Scouts and similar youth groups in the previous four fiscal years. Support would be defined as holding meetings, camping events, or other activities on Defense property and hosting any official event of the youth organization. Adopted 413-16: R 227-0; D 185-16 (ND 135-15, SD 50-1); I 1-0. May 25, 2005.

**216.** **HR 1815. Fiscal 2006 Defense Authorization/Abortion at Military Facilities.** Davis, D-Calif., amendment that would allow overseas military facilities to provide privately funded abortions for women who are in the military or are military dependents. Rejected 194-233: R 22-203; D 171-30 (ND 131-19, SD 40-11); I 1-0. A "nay" was a vote in support of the president's position. May 25, 2005.

**217.** **HR 1815. Fiscal 2006 Defense Authorization/Women in Combat.** Hunter, R-Calif., amendment that would require the Defense Department to provide Congress with a detailed report on policy regarding women in combat by March 31, 2006. The Pentagon would be required to give Congress at least 60 legislative days advance notice before opening or closing any jobs to women. It would extend veterans' preference to individuals who served on active duty in the armed forces for more than 180 consecutive days between Sept. 11, 2001, and the end of Operation Iraqi Freedom and who were discharged under honorable conditions. Adopted 428-1: R 227-0; D 200-1 (ND 149-1, SD 51-0); I 1-0. May 25, 2005.

**218.** **HR 1815. Fiscal 2006 Defense Authorization/ROTC Programs.** Stearns, R-Fla., amendment that would express the sense of Congress that any college or university that denies equal access or discriminates against Reserve Officer Training Corps (ROTC) programs or military recruiters should be denied certain federal taxpayer support, especially funding for military and defense programs. The amendment would require the Defense secretary to report to Congress on the colleges and universities that are denying equal access to military recruiters and ROTC programs. Adopted 336-92: R 227-0; D 109-91 (ND 70-80, SD 39-11); I 0-1. May 25, 2005.

**219.** **HR 1815. Fiscal 2006 Defense Authorization/BRAC Closures.** Bradley, R-N.H., amendment that would postpone the 2005 Base Realignment and Closure recommendations until one year after the Defense secretary has implemented recommendations of the Review of Overseas Military Facility Structure; a substantial number of U.S. troops return from Iraq; congressional committees receive the quadrennial defense review; the National Maritime Security Strategy is implemented; and the Homeland Defense and Civil Support Directive is implemented. Rejected 112-316: R 40-186; D 72-129 (ND 49-101, SD 23-28); I 0-1. A "nay" was a vote in support of the president's position. May 25, 2005.

**220.** **HR 1815. Fiscal 2006 Defense Authorization/Withdrawal From Iraq.** Woolsey, D-Calif., amendment to express the sense of Congress that the president should develop a plan for withdrawing U.S. military forces from Iraq and submit it to the appropriate congressional committees. Rejected 128-300: R 5-221; D 122-79 (ND 101-49, SD 21-30); I 1-0. May 25, 2005.

| | 214 | 215 | 216 | 217 | 218 | 219 | 220 |
|---|---|---|---|---|---|---|---|
| **ALABAMA** | | | | | | | |
| 1 Bonner | Y | Y | N | Y | Y | N | N |
| 2 Everett | Y | Y | N | Y | Y | N | N |
| 3 Rogers | Y | Y | N | Y | Y | N | N |
| 4 Aderholt | Y | Y | N | Y | Y | N | N |
| 5 Cramer | Y | Y | Y | Y | Y | N | N |
| 6 Bachus | Y | Y | N | Y | Y | N | N |
| 7 Davis | N | Y | Y | Y | Y | Y | N |
| **ALASKA** | | | | | | | |
| AL Young | Y | Y | N | Y | Y | N | N |
| **ARIZONA** | | | | | | | |
| 1 Renzi | Y | Y | N | Y | Y | N | N |
| 2 Franks | Y | Y | N | Y | Y | N | N |
| 3 Shadegg | Y | Y | N | Y | Y | N | N |
| 4 Pastor | N | Y | Y | Y | N | N | Y |
| 5 Hayworth | Y | Y | N | Y | Y | N | N |
| 6 Flake | N | Y | N | Y | N | N | N |
| 7 Grijalva | N | Y | Y | Y | N | N | Y |
| 8 Kolbe | Y | Y | Y | Y | Y | N | N |
| **ARKANSAS** | | | | | | | |
| 1 Berry | N | Y | N | Y | Y | N | N |
| 2 Snyder | N | Y | Y | Y | Y | N | N |
| 3 Boozman | Y | Y | N | Y | Y | Y | N |
| 4 Ross | N | Y | N | Y | Y | N | N |
| **CALIFORNIA** | | | | | | | |
| 1 Thompson | N | Y | Y | Y | N | N | Y |
| 2 Herger | Y | Y | N | Y | Y | N | N |
| 3 Lungren | Y | Y | N | Y | Y | N | N |
| 4 Doolittle | Y | Y | N | Y | Y | N | N |
| 5 Matsui, D. | N | Y | Y | Y | N | N | Y |
| 6 Woolsey | N | N | Y | Y | N | N | Y |
| 7 Miller, George | N | Y | Y | Y | N | N | Y |
| 8 Pelosi | N | Y | Y | N | N | N | Y |
| 9 Lee | N | N | Y | Y | N | N | Y |
| 10 Tauscher | N | Y | Y | Y | Y | N | N |
| 11 Pombo | Y | Y | N | Y | Y | N | N |
| 12 Lantos | N | Y | Y | Y | Y | N | N |
| 13 Stark | N | N | Y | N | N | N | Y |
| 14 Eshoo | N | Y | Y | Y | N | N | Y |
| 15 Honda | N | Y | Y | Y | N | N | Y |
| 16 Lofgren | N | Y | Y | Y | N | N | Y |
| 17 Farr | N | Y | Y | Y | N | N | Y |
| 18 Cardoza | Y | Y | Y | Y | Y | Y | N |
| 19 Radanovich | Y | Y | N | Y | Y | N | N |
| 20 Costa | N | Y | Y | Y | Y | N | N |
| 21 Nunes | Y | Y | N | Y | Y | N | N |
| 22 Thomas | Y | Y | N | Y | Y | N | N |
| 23 Capps | N | Y | Y | Y | N | Y | Y |
| 24 Gallegly | Y | Y | N | Y | Y | N | N |
| 25 McKeon | Y | Y | N | Y | Y | N | N |
| 26 Dreier | N | Y | N | Y | Y | N | N |
| 27 Sherman | N | Y | Y | Y | Y | N | N |
| 28 Berman | N | Y | Y | Y | Y | N | N |
| 29 Schiff | N | Y | Y | Y | Y | N | N |
| 30 Waxman | N | Y | Y | Y | N | N | Y |
| 31 Becerra | N | Y | Y | Y | N | N | Y |
| 32 Solis | N | N | Y | Y | N | N | Y |
| 33 Watson | N | Y | Y | Y | N | Y | Y |
| 34 Roybal-Allard | N | Y | Y | Y | N | N | Y |
| 35 Waters | N | Y | Y | Y | N | N | Y |
| 36 Harman | N | Y | Y | Y | Y | N | N |
| 37 Millender-McD. | ? | ? | ? | ? | ? | ? | ? |
| 38 Napolitano | N | Y | Y | Y | N | N | Y |
| 39 Sánchez, Linda | N | N | Y | Y | N | N | Y |
| 40 Royce | Y | Y | N | Y | Y | N | N |
| 41 Lewis | Y | Y | N | Y | Y | N | N |
| 42 Miller, Gary | Y | Y | N | Y | Y | N | N |
| 43 Baca | N | Y | Y | Y | Y | N | N |
| 44 Calvert | Y | Y | N | Y | Y | N | N |
| 45 Bono | Y | Y | N | Y | Y | N | N |
| 46 Rohrabacher | Y | Y | N | Y | Y | N | N |
| 47 Sanchez, Loretta | N | Y | Y | Y | Y | N | N |
| 48 Cox | Y | Y | N | Y | Y | N | N |
| 49 Issa | Y | Y | N | Y | Y | N | N |
| 50 Cunningham | Y | Y | N | Y | Y | N | N |
| 51 Filner | N | Y | Y | Y | N | N | Y |
| 52 Hunter | Y | Y | N | Y | Y | N | N |
| 53 Davis | N | Y | Y | Y | Y | N | N |
| **COLORADO** | | | | | | | |
| 1 DeGette | N | Y | Y | Y | N | N | Y |
| 2 Udall | Y | Y | Y | Y | Y | N | N |
| 3 Salazar | N | Y | N | Y | Y | N | N |
| 4 Musgrave | Y | Y | N | Y | Y | N | N |
| 5 Hefley | Y | Y | N | Y | Y | N | N |
| 6 Tancredo | Y | Y | N | Y | Y | N | N |
| 7 Beauprez | Y | Y | N | Y | Y | N | N |
| **CONNECTICUT** | | | | | | | |
| 1 Larson | N | Y | Y | Y | N | Y | Y |
| 2 Simmons | N | Y | Y | Y | Y | Y | Y |
| 3 DeLauro | N | Y | Y | Y | N | Y | Y |
| 4 Shays | Y | Y | Y | Y | Y | N | N |
| 5 Johnson | Y | Y | Y | Y | Y | N | N |
| **DELAWARE** | | | | | | | |
| AL Castle | Y | Y | Y | Y | Y | N | N |
| **FLORIDA** | | | | | | | |
| 1 Miller | Y | Y | N | Y | Y | N | N |
| 2 Boyd | Y | Y | N | Y | Y | N | N |
| 3 Brown | N | Y | Y | Y | Y | N | N |
| 4 Crenshaw | Y | Y | N | Y | Y | N | N |
| 5 Brown-Waite | Y | Y | N | Y | Y | N | N |
| 6 Stearns | Y | Y | N | Y | Y | N | N |
| 7 Mica | Y | Y | – | Y | Y | N | N |
| 8 Keller | Y | Y | N | Y | Y | N | N |
| 9 Bilirakis | Y | Y | N | Y | Y | N | N |
| 10 Young | Y | Y | N | Y | Y | N | N |
| 11 Davis | N | Y | Y | Y | Y | N | N |
| 12 Putnam | N | Y | N | Y | Y | N | N |
| 13 Harris | Y | Y | N | Y | Y | N | N |
| 14 Mack | Y | Y | N | Y | Y | N | N |
| 15 Weldon | Y | Y | N | Y | Y | Y | N |
| 16 Foley | Y | Y | N | Y | Y | N | N |
| 17 Meek | N | Y | Y | Y | N | N | Y |
| 18 Ros-Lehtinen | Y | Y | N | Y | Y | N | N |
| 19 Wexler | N | Y | Y | Y | N | N | Y |
| 20 Wasserman-Schultz | N | Y | Y | Y | N | Y | Y |
| 21 Diaz-Balart, L. | Y | Y | N | Y | Y | N | N |
| 22 Shaw | Y | Y | N | Y | Y | N | N |
| 23 Hastings | N | Y | Y | Y | N | N | Y |
| 24 Feeney | Y | Y | N | Y | Y | N | N |
| 25 Diaz-Balart, M. | Y | Y | N | Y | Y | N | N |
| **GEORGIA** | | | | | | | |
| 1 Kingston | Y | Y | N | Y | Y | N | N |
| 2 Bishop | Y | Y | Y | Y | Y | N | N |
| 3 Marshall | Y | Y | N | Y | Y | N | N |
| 4 McKinney | N | Y | Y | Y | N | N | Y |
| 5 Lewis | N | Y | Y | Y | N | N | Y |
| 6 Price | Y | Y | N | Y | Y | N | N |
| 7 Linder | Y | Y | N | Y | Y | N | N |
| 8 Westmoreland | Y | Y | N | Y | Y | N | N |
| 9 Norwood | Y | Y | N | Y | Y | N | N |
| 10 Deal | Y | Y | N | Y | Y | N | N |
| 11 Gingrey | Y | Y | N | Y | Y | Y | N |
| 12 Barrow | Y | Y | Y | Y | Y | Y | N |
| 13 Scott | N | Y | Y | Y | Y | Y | N |
| **HAWAII** | | | | | | | |
| 1 Abercrombie | N | Y | Y | Y | Y | Y | Y |
| 2 Case | Y | Y | Y | Y | N | N | N |
| **IDAHO** | | | | | | | |
| 1 Otter | Y | Y | N | Y | Y | N | N |
| 2 Simpson | Y | Y | N | Y | Y | N | N |
| **ILLINOIS** | | | | | | | |
| 1 Rush | N | Y | Y | Y | N | N | Y |
| 2 Jackson | N | Y | Y | Y | N | N | Y |
| 3 Lipinski | N | Y | N | Y | Y | N | N |
| 4 Gutierrez | N | Y | Y | Y | N | N | Y |
| 5 Emanuel | N | Y | Y | Y | N | N | Y |
| 6 Hyde | Y | Y | N | Y | Y | N | N |
| 7 Davis | N | Y | Y | Y | N | N | Y |
| 8 Bean | N | Y | Y | Y | Y | N | N |
| 9 Schakowsky | N | N | Y | Y | N | N | Y |
| 10 Kirk | Y | Y | Y | Y | Y | N | N |
| 11 Weller | Y | Y | N | Y | Y | N | N |
| 12 Costello | N | Y | N | Y | Y | N | N |

| | 214 | 215 | 216 | 217 | 218 | 219 | 220 |
|---|---|---|---|---|---|---|---|
| 13 **Biggert** | Y | Y | Y | Y | Y | N | N |
| 14 **Hastert** | | | | | | | |
| 15 **Johnson** | Y | Y | N | Y | Y | N | N |
| 16 **Manzullo** | Y | Y | N | Y | Y | Y | N |
| 17 Evans | N | Y | Y | Y | Y | Y | Y |
| 18 **LaHood** | Y | Y | N | Y | Y | Y | N |
| 19 **Shimkus** | Y | Y | N | Y | Y | Y | N |
| **INDIANA** | | | | | | | |
| 1 Visclosky | N | Y | Y | Y | Y | N | N |
| 2 **Chocola** | Y | Y | N | Y | Y | N | N |
| 3 **Souder** | N | Y | N | Y | Y | N | N |
| 4 **Buyer** | N | Y | ? | Y | Y | N | N |
| 5 **Burton** | Y | Y | N | Y | Y | N | N |
| 6 **Pence** | Y | Y | N | Y | Y | N | N |
| 7 Carson | N | Y | Y | Y | N | N | Y |
| 8 **Hostettler** | Y | Y | N | Y | Y | N | N |
| 9 **Sodrel** | Y | Y | N | Y | Y | N | N |
| **IOWA** | | | | | | | |
| 1 **Nussle** | Y | Y | N | Y | Y | N | N |
| 2 **Leach** | Y | Y | Y | Y | Y | N | Y |
| 3 Boswell | Y | Y | Y | Y | Y | N | Y |
| 4 **Latham** | Y | Y | N | Y | Y | N | N |
| 5 **King** | Y | Y | N | Y | Y | N | N |
| **KANSAS** | | | | | | | |
| 1 **Moran** | Y | Y | N | Y | Y | N | N |
| 2 **Ryun** | Y | Y | N | Y | Y | N | N |
| 3 Moore | Y | Y | Y | Y | Y | N | N |
| 4 **Tiahrt** | Y | Y | N | Y | Y | N | N |
| **KENTUCKY** | | | | | | | |
| 1 **Whitfield** | Y | Y | N | Y | Y | N | N |
| 2 **Lewis** | Y | Y | N | Y | Y | N | N |
| 3 **Northup** | Y | Y | N | Y | Y | N | N |
| 4 **Davis** | Y | Y | N | Y | Y | N | N |
| 5 **Rogers** | Y | Y | N | Y | Y | N | N |
| 6 Chandler | Y | Y | Y | Y | ? | N | N |
| **LOUISIANA** | | | | | | | |
| 1 **Jindal** | Y | Y | N | Y | Y | Y | N |
| 2 Jefferson | N | Y | Y | Y | Y | Y | Y |
| 3 Melancon | N | Y | N | Y | N | Y | Y |
| 4 **McCrery** | Y | Y | N | Y | Y | N | N |
| 5 **Alexander** | Y | Y | N | Y | Y | N | N |
| 6 **Baker** | Y | Y | N | Y | Y | N | N |
| 7 **Boustany** | Y | Y | N | Y | Y | N | N |
| **MAINE** | | | | | | | |
| 1 Allen | N | Y | Y | Y | N | Y | Y |
| 2 Michaud | N | Y | N | Y | N | Y | Y |
| **MARYLAND** | | | | | | | |
| 1 **Gilchrest** | Y | Y | Y | Y | Y | N | N |
| 2 Ruppersberger | N | Y | Y | Y | Y | N | N |
| 3 Cardin | N | Y | Y | Y | Y | N | N |
| 4 Wynn | N | Y | Y | Y | Y | N | Y |
| 5 Hoyer | N | Y | Y | Y | Y | N | N |
| 6 **Bartlett** | Y | Y | N | Y | Y | N | N |
| 7 Cummings | N | Y | Y | Y | Y | N | Y |
| 8 Van Hollen | N | Y | Y | Y | Y | N | Y |
| **MASSACHUSETTS** | | | | | | | |
| 1 Olver | N | Y | Y | Y | N | N | Y |
| 2 Neal | N | Y | Y | Y | N | N | Y |
| 3 McGovern | N | Y | Y | Y | N | N | Y |
| 4 Frank | N | N | Y | Y | N | N | Y |
| 5 Meehan | N | Y | Y | Y | N | N | Y |
| 6 Tierney | N | Y | Y | Y | N | N | Y |
| 7 Markey | N | Y | Y | Y | N | N | Y |
| 8 Capuano | N | Y | Y | Y | Y | N | Y |
| 9 Lynch | N | Y | N | Y | Y | Y | Y |
| 10 Delahunt | N | Y | Y | Y | Y | Y | Y |
| **MICHIGAN** | | | | | | | |
| 1 Stupak | N | Y | N | Y | Y | N | N |
| 2 **Hoekstra** | Y | Y | N | Y | Y | N | N |
| 3 **Ehlers** | N | Y | N | Y | Y | Y | N |
| 4 **Camp** | Y | Y | N | Y | Y | N | N |
| 5 Kildee | N | Y | N | Y | Y | N | N |
| 6 **Upton** | Y | Y | N | Y | Y | N | N |
| 7 **Schwarz** | Y | Y | N | Y | Y | Y | N |
| 8 **Rogers** | Y | Y | N | Y | Y | N | N |
| 9 **Knollenberg** | Y | Y | N | Y | Y | N | N |
| 10 **Miller** | Y | Y | N | Y | Y | N | N |
| 11 **McCotter** | Y | Y | N | Y | Y | Y | N |
| 12 Levin | N | Y | Y | Y | N | N | N |
| 13 Kilpatrick | N | Y | Y | Y | N | N | Y |
| 14 Conyers | N | N | Y | Y | N | N | Y |
| 15 Dingell | N | Y | Y | Y | N | N | N |

| | 214 | 215 | 216 | 217 | 218 | 219 | 220 |
|---|---|---|---|---|---|---|---|
| **MINNESOTA** | | | | | | | |
| 1 **Gutknecht** | Y | Y | N | Y | Y | N | N |
| 2 **Kline** | N | Y | N | Y | Y | N | N |
| 3 **Ramstad** | Y | Y | Y | Y | Y | N | N |
| 4 McCollum | N | Y | Y | Y | N | Y | Y |
| 5 Sabo | N | Y | Y | Y | Y | N | Y |
| 6 **Kennedy** | Y | Y | N | Y | Y | N | N |
| 7 Peterson | Y | Y | N | Y | Y | N | N |
| 8 Oberstar | N | Y | N | Y | N | Y | Y |
| **MISSISSIPPI** | | | | | | | |
| 1 **Wicker** | Y | Y | N | Y | Y | Y | N |
| 2 Thompson | N | Y | Y | Y | Y | Y | Y |
| 3 **Pickering** | Y | Y | N | Y | Y | Y | N |
| 4 Taylor | Y | Y | N | Y | Y | Y | N |
| **MISSOURI** | | | | | | | |
| 1 Clay | N | Y | Y | Y | Y | Y | Y |
| 2 **Akin** | Y | Y | N | Y | Y | N | N |
| 3 Carnahan | N | Y | Y | Y | Y | N | Y |
| 4 Skelton | N | Y | N | Y | Y | N | N |
| 5 Cleaver | N | Y | Y | Y | Y | N | Y |
| 6 **Graves** | Y | Y | N | Y | Y | N | N |
| 7 **Blunt** | Y | Y | N | Y | Y | N | N |
| 8 **Emerson** | ? | ? | ? | ? | ? | ? | ? |
| 9 **Hulshof** | Y | Y | N | Y | Y | N | N |
| **MONTANA** | | | | | | | |
| AL **Rehberg** | Y | Y | N | Y | Y | Y | N |
| **NEBRASKA** | | | | | | | |
| 1 **Fortenberry** | Y | Y | N | Y | Y | N | N |
| 2 **Terry** | Y | Y | N | Y | Y | N | N |
| 3 **Osborne** | Y | Y | N | Y | Y | N | N |
| **NEVADA** | | | | | | | |
| 1 Berkley | N | Y | Y | Y | Y | N | N |
| 2 **Gibbons** | Y | Y | N | Y | Y | Y | N |
| 3 **Porter** | Y | Y | N | Y | Y | N | ? |
| **NEW HAMPSHIRE** | | | | | | | |
| 1 **Bradley** | Y | Y | Y | Y | Y | Y | N |
| 2 **Bass** | Y | Y | Y | Y | Y | Y | N |
| **NEW JERSEY** | | | | | | | |
| 1 Andrews | N | Y | Y | Y | Y | N | N |
| 2 **LoBiondo** | Y | Y | N | Y | Y | N | N |
| 3 **Saxton** | Y | Y | N | Y | Y | N | N |
| 4 **Smith** | Y | Y | N | Y | Y | Y | N |
| 5 **Garrett** | Y | Y | N | Y | Y | N | N |
| 6 Pallone | N | Y | Y | Y | N | Y | Y |
| 7 **Ferguson** | Y | Y | N | Y | Y | N | N |
| 8 Pascrell | N | Y | Y | Y | N | Y | Y |
| 9 Rothman | N | Y | Y | Y | N | Y | Y |
| 10 Payne | N | Y | Y | Y | N | Y | Y |
| 11 **Frelinghuysen** | Y | Y | Y | Y | Y | N | N |
| 12 Holt | N | Y | Y | Y | N | Y | Y |
| 13 Menendez | N | Y | Y | Y | Y | Y | Y |
| **NEW MEXICO** | | | | | | | |
| 1 **Wilson** | N | Y | N | Y | Y | Y | N |
| 2 **Pearce** | N | Y | N | Y | Y | Y | N |
| 3 Udall | N | Y | Y | Y | N | Y | Y |
| **NEW YORK** | | | | | | | |
| 1 Bishop | Y | Y | Y | Y | Y | N | N |
| 2 Israel | Y | Y | Y | Y | Y | N | N |
| 3 **King** | Y | Y | N | Y | Y | N | N |
| 4 McCarthy | Y | Y | Y | Y | Y | N | N |
| 5 Ackerman | N | N | Y | Y | N | N | N |
| 6 Meeks | N | Y | Y | Y | N | N | Y |
| 7 Crowley | N | Y | Y | Y | N | Y | N |
| 8 Nadler | N | Y | Y | Y | N | N | Y |
| 9 Weiner | N | Y | Y | Y | N | N | Y |
| 10 Towns | N | Y | Y | Y | Y | N | Y |
| 11 Owens | N | Y | Y | Y | N | Y | Y |
| 12 Velázquez | N | Y | Y | Y | N | Y | Y |
| 13 **Fossella** | Y | Y | N | Y | Y | N | N |
| 14 Maloney | N | Y | Y | N | N | N | Y |
| 15 Rangel | N | Y | Y | Y | N | N | Y |
| 16 Serrano | N | Y | Y | Y | N | Y | Y |
| 17 Engel | N | Y | Y | Y | Y | N | N |
| 18 Lowey | N | Y | Y | Y | N | Y | N |
| 19 **Kelly** | Y | Y | Y | Y | Y | N | N |
| 20 **Sweeney** | Y | Y | N | Y | Y | N | N |
| 21 McNulty | N | Y | N | Y | N | Y | Y |
| 22 Hinchey | N | Y | Y | Y | N | Y | Y |
| 23 **McHugh** | Y | Y | N | Y | Y | N | N |
| 24 **Boehlert** | Y | Y | Y | Y | Y | N | N |
| 25 **Walsh** | Y | Y | N | Y | Y | N | N |
| 26 **Reynolds** | Y | Y | N | Y | Y | Y | N |
| 27 Higgins | N | Y | Y | Y | Y | Y | N |
| 28 Slaughter | N | Y | Y | Y | N | Y | Y |
| 29 **Kuhl** | Y | Y | N | Y | Y | N | N |

| | 214 | 215 | 216 | 217 | 218 | 219 | 220 |
|---|---|---|---|---|---|---|---|
| **NORTH CAROLINA** | | | | | | | |
| 1 Butterfield | N | Y | N | Y | Y | N | N |
| 2 Etheridge | Y | Y | Y | Y | Y | N | N |
| 3 **Jones** | Y | Y | N | Y | Y | Y | Y |
| 4 Price | N | Y | Y | Y | Y | N | Y |
| 5 **Foxx** | Y | Y | N | Y | Y | N | N |
| 6 **Coble** | Y | Y | N | Y | Y | N | Y |
| 7 McIntyre | Y | Y | N | Y | Y | N | N |
| 8 **Hayes** | Y | Y | N | Y | Y | N | N |
| 9 **Myrick** | Y | Y | N | Y | Y | N | N |
| 10 **McHenry** | Y | Y | N | Y | Y | N | N |
| 11 **Taylor** | Y | Y | N | Y | Y | N | N |
| 12 Watt | N | Y | Y | Y | N | N | Y |
| 13 Miller | N | Y | Y | Y | Y | N | Y |
| **NORTH DAKOTA** | | | | | | | |
| AL Pomeroy | Y | Y | Y | Y | Y | N | N |
| **OHIO** | | | | | | | |
| 1 **Chabot** | Y | Y | N | Y | Y | N | N |
| 2 Vacant | | | | | | | |
| 3 **Turner** | Y | Y | N | Y | Y | N | N |
| 4 **Oxley** | Y | Y | N | Y | Y | N | N |
| 5 **Gillmor** | Y | Y | N | Y | Y | N | N |
| 6 Strickland | N | Y | Y | Y | Y | Y | Y |
| 7 **Hobson** | Y | Y | N | Y | Y | N | N |
| 8 **Boehner** | Y | Y | N | Y | Y | N | N |
| 9 Kaptur | N | Y | Y | Y | N | N | Y |
| 10 Kucinich | N | N | Y | Y | N | Y | Y |
| 11 Jones | N | Y | Y | Y | N | Y | Y |
| 12 **Tiberi** | Y | Y | N | Y | Y | N | N |
| 13 Brown | N | Y | Y | Y | N | Y | Y |
| 14 **LaTourette** | Y | Y | N | Y | Y | Y | N |
| 15 **Pryce** | Y | Y | Y | Y | Y | N | N |
| 16 **Regula** | Y | Y | N | Y | Y | N | N |
| 17 Ryan | Y | Y | N | Y | Y | N | Y |
| 18 **Ney** | Y | Y | N | Y | Y | N | N |
| **OKLAHOMA** | | | | | | | |
| 1 **Sullivan** | Y | Y | N | Y | Y | N | N |
| 2 Boren | Y | Y | N | Y | Y | N | N |
| 3 **Lucas** | Y | Y | N | Y | Y | N | N |
| 4 **Cole** | Y | Y | N | Y | Y | N | N |
| 5 **Istook** | Y | Y | N | Y | Y | N | N |
| **OREGON** | | | | | | | |
| 1 Wu | N | Y | Y | Y | N | Y | Y |
| 2 **Walden** | Y | Y | Y | Y | Y | N | N |
| 3 Blumenauer | N | N | Y | Y | N | N | Y |
| 4 DeFazio | Y | Y | Y | Y | Y | Y | Y |
| 5 Hooley | Y | Y | Y | Y | Y | Y | Y |
| **PENNSYLVANIA** | | | | | | | |
| 1 Brady | N | Y | Y | Y | N | Y | Y |
| 2 Fattah | N | Y | Y | Y | Y | Y | Y |
| 3 **English** | Y | Y | N | Y | Y | N | N |
| 4 **Hart** | Y | Y | N | Y | Y | Y | N |
| 5 **Peterson** | Y | Y | N | Y | Y | N | N |
| 6 **Gerlach** | Y | Y | N | Y | Y | Y | N |
| 7 **Weldon** | Y | Y | N | Y | Y | N | N |
| 8 **Fitzpatrick** | Y | Y | N | Y | Y | Y | N |
| 9 **Shuster** | Y | Y | N | Y | Y | N | N |
| 10 **Sherwood** | Y | Y | N | Y | Y | N | N |
| 11 Kanjorski | N | Y | N | Y | Y | N | N |
| 12 Murtha | N | Y | N | Y | Y | Y | N |
| 13 Schwartz | N | Y | Y | Y | Y | Y | Y |
| 14 Doyle | N | Y | N | Y | Y | Y | Y |
| 15 **Dent** | Y | Y | Y | Y | Y | N | N |
| 16 **Pitts** | Y | Y | N | Y | Y | N | N |
| 17 Holden | N | Y | N | Y | Y | N | N |
| 18 **Murphy** | Y | Y | N | Y | Y | Y | N |
| 19 **Platts** | Y | Y | N | Y | Y | N | N |
| **RHODE ISLAND** | | | | | | | |
| 1 Kennedy | N | Y | Y | Y | Y | N | N |
| 2 Langevin | N | Y | N | Y | Y | Y | N |
| **SOUTH CAROLINA** | | | | | | | |
| 1 **Brown** | ? | ? | ? | ? | ? | ? | ? |
| 2 **Wilson** | Y | Y | N | Y | Y | N | N |
| 3 **Barrett** | Y | Y | N | Y | Y | N | N |
| 4 **Inglis** | Y | Y | N | Y | Y | N | N |
| 5 Spratt | Y | Y | Y | Y | Y | N | N |
| 6 Clyburn | N | Y | Y | Y | Y | N | Y |
| **SOUTH DAKOTA** | | | | | | | |
| AL Herseth | N | Y | Y | Y | Y | Y | N |
| **TENNESSEE** | | | | | | | |
| 1 **Jenkins** | Y | Y | N | Y | Y | Y | N |
| 2 **Duncan** | Y | Y | N | Y | Y | N | Y |

| | 214 | 215 | 216 | 217 | 218 | 219 | 220 |
|---|---|---|---|---|---|---|---|
| 3 **Wamp** | Y | Y | N | Y | Y | N | N |
| 4 Davis | Y | Y | N | Y | Y | N | N |
| 5 Cooper | N | Y | Y | Y | Y | N | N |
| 6 Gordon | Y | Y | Y | Y | Y | Y | Y |
| 7 **Blackburn** | Y | Y | N | Y | Y | N | N |
| 8 Tanner | Y | Y | Y | Y | Y | N | N |
| 9 Ford | Y | Y | Y | Y | Y | Y | N |
| **TEXAS** | | | | | | | |
| 1 **Gohmert** | Y | Y | N | Y | Y | Y | N |
| 2 **Poe** | Y | Y | N | Y | Y | Y | N |
| 3 **Johnson, S.** | Y | Y | N | Y | Y | N | N |
| 4 **Hall** | Y | Y | N | Y | Y | Y | N |
| 5 **Hensarling** | Y | Y | N | Y | Y | N | N |
| 6 **Barton** | Y | Y | N | Y | Y | N | N |
| 7 **Culberson** | Y | Y | N | Y | Y | N | N |
| 8 **Brady** | Y | Y | N | Y | Y | N | N |
| 9 Green | N | Y | Y | Y | N | Y | Y |
| 10 **McCaul** | Y | Y | N | Y | Y | N | N |
| 11 **Conaway** | Y | Y | N | Y | Y | N | N |
| 12 **Granger** | Y | Y | N | Y | Y | N | N |
| 13 **Thornberry** | N | Y | N | Y | Y | N | N |
| 14 **Paul** | N | Y | N | Y | Y | Y | Y |
| 15 Hinojosa | N | Y | Y | Y | Y | Y | Y |
| 16 Reyes | N | Y | Y | Y | Y | N | N |
| 17 Edwards | N | Y | Y | Y | Y | N | N |
| 18 Jackson-Lee | N | Y | Y | Y | N | Y | Y |
| 19 **Neugebauer** | Y | Y | N | Y | Y | N | N |
| 20 Gonzalez | N | Y | Y | Y | Y | Y | N |
| 21 **Smith** | Y | Y | N | Y | Y | N | N |
| 22 **DeLay** | Y | Y | N | Y | Y | N | N |
| 23 **Bonilla** | Y | Y | N | Y | Y | N | N |
| 24 **Marchant** | Y | Y | N | Y | Y | N | N |
| 25 Doggett | N | Y | Y | Y | Y | N | Y |
| 26 **Burgess** | Y | Y | N | Y | Y | N | N |
| 27 Ortiz | N | Y | N | Y | Y | Y | N |
| 28 Cuellar | N | Y | N | Y | Y | Y | N |
| 29 Green | N | Y | Y | Y | Y | Y | Y |
| 30 Johnson, E. | N | Y | Y | Y | Y | N | Y |
| 31 **Carter** | Y | Y | N | Y | Y | N | N |
| 32 **Sessions** | Y | Y | N | Y | Y | N | N |
| **UTAH** | | | | | | | |
| 1 **Bishop** | Y | Y | N | Y | Y | ? | N |
| 2 Matheson | Y | Y | Y | Y | Y | N | N |
| 3 **Cannon** | Y | Y | N | Y | Y | N | N |
| **VERMONT** | | | | | | | |
| AL *Sanders* | N | Y | Y | Y | N | N | Y |
| **VIRGINIA** | | | | | | | |
| 1 **Davis, J.** | Y | Y | N | Y | Y | Y | N |
| 2 **Drake** | Y | Y | N | Y | Y | N | N |
| 3 Scott | N | Y | Y | Y | N | Y | Y |
| 4 **Forbes** | Y | Y | N | Y | Y | N | N |
| 5 **Goode** | Y | Y | N | Y | Y | N | N |
| 6 **Goodlatte** | Y | Y | N | Y | Y | N | N |
| 7 **Cantor** | Y | Y | N | Y | Y | N | N |
| 8 Moran | N | Y | Y | Y | N | Y | Y |
| 9 Boucher | Y | Y | Y | Y | Y | N | N |
| 10 **Wolf** | Y | Y | N | Y | Y | Y | N |
| 11 **Davis, T.** | Y | Y | N | Y | Y | Y | N |
| **WASHINGTON** | | | | | | | |
| 1 Inslee | N | Y | Y | Y | Y | N | Y |
| 2 Larsen | N | Y | Y | Y | Y | N | N |
| 3 Baird | N | Y | Y | Y | Y | Y | Y |
| 4 **Hastings** | ? | ? | ? | ? | ? | ? | ? |
| 5 **McMorris** | Y | Y | N | Y | Y | N | N |
| 6 Dicks | N | Y | Y | Y | Y | N | N |
| 7 McDermott | N | N | Y | Y | N | N | Y |
| 8 **Reichert** | Y | Y | N | Y | Y | N | N |
| 9 Smith | N | Y | Y | Y | Y | N | Y |
| **WEST VIRGINIA** | | | | | | | |
| 1 Mollohan | N | Y | N | Y | N | Y | N |
| 2 **Capito** | Y | Y | Y | Y | Y | Y | N |
| 3 Rahall | N | Y | N | Y | N | Y | Y |
| **WISCONSIN** | | | | | | | |
| 1 **Ryan** | Y | Y | N | Y | Y | N | N |
| 2 Baldwin | N | N | Y | Y | N | N | Y |
| 3 Kind | Y | Y | Y | Y | Y | N | N |
| 4 Moore | N | N | Y | Y | N | Y | Y |
| 5 **Sensenbrenner** | Y | Y | N | Y | Y | N | N |
| 6 **Petri** | Y | Y | N | Y | Y | N | N |
| 7 Obey | N | Y | Y | Y | N | N | Y |
| 8 **Green** | Y | Y | N | Y | Y | N | N |
| **WYOMING** | | | | | | | |
| AL **Cubin** | Y | Y | N | Y | Y | N | N |

# IN THE HOUSE | By Vote Number

**221.** **HR 1815. Fiscal 2006 Defense Authorization/Recommit.** Taylor, D-Miss., motion to recommit the bill to the House Armed Services Committee with instructions to extend access to the military's Tricare health insurance program to all reservists and National Guard members. Motion rejected 211-218: R 9-218; D 201-0 (ND 150-0, SD 51-0); I 1-0. May 25, 2005.

**222.** **HR 1815. Fiscal 2006 Defense Authorization/Passage.** Passage of the bill that would authorize $441.6 billion for defense programs and $49.1 billion in emergency supplemental spending for fiscal 2006. The Pentagon would be required to notify Congress within 60 consecutive legislative days if it intends to open to women military jobs closed under a 1994 policy that restricts women from serving in units that are sent into direct ground combat, such as infantry, armor and special forces. Passed 390-39: R 225-2; D 164-37 (ND 117-33, SD 47-4); I 1-0. May 25, 2005.

**223.** **HR 2528 Fiscal 2006 Military Quality of Life and Veterans Affairs Appropriations/Previous Question.** Gingrey, R-Ga., motion to order the previous question (thus ending debate and possibility of amendment) on adoption of the rule (H Res 298) to provide for House floor consideration of the bill that would appropriate $121.8 billion in fiscal 2006 for the Department of Veterans Affairs, military construction and military housing. Motion agreed to 223-194: R 223-0; D 0-193 (ND 0-144, SD 0-49); I 0-1. Subsequently, the rule was adopted by voice vote. May 26, 2005.

**224.** **HR 2528. Fiscal 2006 Military Quality of Life and Veterans Affairs Appropriations/Veterans Health.** Melancon, D-La., amendment that would add $53 million for veterans' health care and to process claims for compensation and pensions. It would be offset by a $169 million cut to the 2005 Base Realignment and Closure account. Rejected 213-214: R 19-210; D 193-4 (ND 145-2, SD 48-2); I 1-0. May 26, 2005.

**225.** **HR 2528. Fiscal 2006 Military Quality of Life and Veterans Affairs Appropriations/Environmental Remediation.** Blumenauer, D-Ore., amendment to add $351 million to complete all environmental remediation at bases closed during the 1988 round of base closings, offset by a $351 million cut to the 2005 Base Realignment and Closure account. Rejected 171-254: R 13-214; D 157-40 (ND 128-19, SD 29-21); I 1-0. May 26, 2005.

**226.** **HR 2528. Fiscal 2006 Military Quality of Life and Veterans Affairs Appropriations/Passage.** Passage of the bill that would provide $121.8 billion in fiscal 2006 for the Department of Veterans Affairs, military construction and military housing. The bill would provide $68.1 billion for the Department of Veterans Affairs, including $28.8 billion for the Veterans' Health Administration. It also would provide $5.8 billion for military construction, $4.2 billion for military family housing and $1.6 billion for the latest round of base closures. Passed 425-1: R 228-0; D 196-1 (ND 146-1, SD 50-0); I 1-0. May 26, 2005.

**227.** **HR 3. Surface Transportation Reauthorization/Motion to Instruct.** Oberstar, D-Minn., motion to instruct House conferees to insist on a conference report that would authorize additional funds for highway, transit and safety programs to increase the guaranteed rate of return for states to at least 92 percent, without reducing the amount each state was provided by the $283.9 billion, six-year bill. Motion rejected 189-223: R 2-222; D 186-1 (ND 138-1, SD 48-0); I 1-0. May 26, 2005.

| | 221 | 222 | 223 | 224 | 225 | 226 | 227 |
|---|---|---|---|---|---|---|---|
| **ALABAMA** | | | | | | | |
| 1 Bonner | N | Y | Y | N | N | Y | N |
| 2 Everett | N | Y | Y | N | N | Y | N |
| 3 Rogers | N | Y | Y | N | N | Y | N |
| 4 Aderholt | N | Y | Y | N | N | Y | N |
| 5 Cramer | Y | Y | N | N | N | Y | ? |
| 6 Bachus | N | Y | Y | N | N | Y | N |
| 7 Davis | Y | Y | N | Y | N | Y | Y |
| **ALASKA** | | | | | | | |
| AL Young | N | Y | Y | N | N | Y | N |
| **ARIZONA** | | | | | | | |
| 1 Renzi | N | Y | Y | N | N | Y | N |
| 2 Franks | N | Y | Y | N | N | Y | N |
| 3 Shadegg | N | Y | Y | N | N | N | N |
| 4 Pastor | Y | Y | N | Y | N | Y | Y |
| 5 Hayworth | N | Y | Y | N | N | Y | N |
| 6 Flake | N | Y | Y | N | N | N | N |
| 7 Grijalva | Y | N | N | Y | Y | Y | Y |
| 8 Kolbe | N | Y | Y | N | N | Y | N |
| **ARKANSAS** | | | | | | | |
| 1 Berry | Y | Y | N | Y | N | Y | Y |
| 2 Snyder | Y | Y | N | Y | Y | Y | Y |
| 3 Boozman | N | Y | Y | N | N | Y | N |
| 4 Ross | Y | Y | N | Y | N | Y | Y |
| **CALIFORNIA** | | | | | | | |
| 1 Thompson | Y | Y | N | Y | Y | Y | Y |
| 2 Herger | N | Y | Y | N | N | Y | N |
| 3 Lungren | N | Y | Y | N | N | Y | N |
| 4 Doolittle | N | Y | Y | N | N | Y | N |
| 5 Matsui, D. | Y | Y | N | Y | Y | Y | Y |
| 6 Woolsey | Y | N | N | Y | Y | Y | Y |
| 7 Miller, George | Y | Y | N | Y | Y | Y | Y |
| 8 Pelosi | Y | Y | N | Y | Y | Y | Y |
| 9 Lee | Y | N | N | Y | Y | Y | Y |
| 10 Tauscher | Y | Y | N | Y | Y | Y | Y |
| 11 Pombo | N | Y | Y | N | N | Y | N |
| 12 Lantos | Y | Y | N | Y | Y | Y | Y |
| 13 Stark | Y | N | N | Y | Y | N | Y |
| 14 Eshoo | Y | Y | N | Y | Y | Y | Y |
| 15 Honda | Y | Y | N | Y | Y | Y | Y |
| 16 Lofgren | Y | Y | N | Y | Y | Y | Y |
| 17 Farr | Y | Y | N | Y | Y | Y | Y |
| 18 Cardoza | Y | Y | N | Y | Y | Y | Y |
| 19 Radanovich | N | Y | Y | N | N | Y | N |
| 20 Costa | Y | Y | N | Y | Y | Y | Y |
| 21 Nunes | N | Y | Y | N | N | Y | N |
| 22 Thomas | N | Y | Y | N | N | Y | N |
| 23 Capps | Y | Y | N | Y | Y | Y | Y |
| 24 Gallegly | N | Y | Y | N | N | Y | N |
| 25 McKeon | N | Y | Y | N | N | Y | N |
| 26 Dreier | N | Y | Y | N | N | Y | N |
| 27 Sherman | Y | Y | N | Y | N | Y | Y |
| 28 Berman | Y | Y | N | Y | Y | Y | Y |
| 29 Schiff | Y | Y | N | Y | Y | Y | Y |
| 30 Waxman | Y | Y | N | Y | Y | Y | Y |
| 31 Becerra | Y | Y | N | Y | Y | Y | Y |
| 32 Solis | Y | N | N | Y | Y | Y | Y |
| 33 Watson | Y | Y | N | Y | Y | Y | Y |
| 34 Roybal-Allard | Y | Y | N | Y | Y | Y | Y |
| 35 Waters | Y | N | N | Y | Y | Y | Y |
| 36 Harman | Y | Y | N | Y | Y | Y | Y |
| 37 Millender-McD. | ? | ? | ? | ? | ? | ? | ? |
| 38 Napolitano | Y | Y | N | Y | Y | Y | Y |
| 39 Sánchez, Linda | Y | Y | N | Y | Y | Y | Y |
| 40 Royce | N | Y | Y | N | N | Y | N |
| 41 Lewis | N | Y | Y | N | N | Y | N |
| 42 Miller, Gary | N | Y | Y | N | N | Y | N |
| 43 Baca | Y | Y | N | Y | Y | Y | Y |
| 44 Calvert | N | Y | Y | N | N | Y | N |
| 45 Bono | N | Y | Y | N | N | Y | N |
| 46 Rohrabacher | N | Y | Y | N | N | Y | N |
| 47 Sanchez, Loretta | Y | Y | N | Y | Y | Y | Y |
| 48 Cox | N | Y | Y | N | ? | Y | N |
| 49 Issa | N | Y | Y | N | N | Y | N |

| | 221 | 222 | 223 | 224 | 225 | 226 | 227 |
|---|---|---|---|---|---|---|---|
| 50 Cunningham | N | Y | Y | N | N | Y | ? |
| 51 Filner | Y | N | – | + | + | – | + |
| 52 Hunter | N | Y | Y | N | N | Y | N |
| 53 Davis | Y | Y | N | Y | N | Y | Y |
| **COLORADO** | | | | | | | |
| 1 DeGette | Y | Y | N | Y | Y | Y | Y |
| 2 Udall | Y | Y | N | Y | Y | Y | Y |
| 3 Salazar | Y | Y | N | Y | Y | Y | Y |
| 4 Musgrave | N | Y | Y | N | N | Y | N |
| 5 Hefley | N | Y | Y | N | N | Y | N |
| 6 Tancredo | N | Y | Y | N | N | Y | N |
| 7 Beauprez | N | Y | Y | N | Y | Y | N |
| **CONNECTICUT** | | | | | | | |
| 1 Larson | Y | Y | N | Y | Y | Y | Y |
| 2 Simmons | N | Y | Y | N | N | Y | N |
| 3 DeLauro | Y | Y | N | Y | Y | Y | Y |
| 4 Shays | Y | Y | Y | N | N | Y | N |
| 5 Johnson | N | Y | Y | N | N | Y | N |
| **DELAWARE** | | | | | | | |
| AL Castle | N | Y | Y | N | N | Y | N |
| **FLORIDA** | | | | | | | |
| 1 Miller | N | Y | Y | N | N | Y | N |
| 2 Boyd | Y | Y | N | N | N | Y | Y |
| 3 Brown | Y | Y | N | Y | Y | Y | Y |
| 4 Crenshaw | N | Y | Y | N | N | Y | N |
| 5 Brown-Waite | Y | Y | Y | N | N | Y | N |
| 6 Stearns | N | Y | Y | N | N | Y | N |
| 7 Mica | N | Y | Y | N | N | Y | N |
| 8 Keller | N | Y | Y | N | N | Y | N |
| 9 Bilirakis | N | Y | Y | N | N | Y | N |
| 10 Young | N | Y | ? | N | N | Y | N |
| 11 Davis | Y | Y | N | Y | N | Y | Y |
| 12 Putnam | N | Y | Y | N | N | Y | N |
| 13 Harris | N | Y | Y | N | N | Y | N |
| 14 Mack | N | Y | Y | N | N | N | N |
| 15 Weldon | N | Y | Y | N | N | Y | N |
| 16 Foley | N | Y | Y | N | N | Y | N |
| 17 Meek | Y | Y | N | Y | Y | Y | Y |
| 18 Ros-Lehtinen | N | Y | Y | N | N | Y | N |
| 19 Wexler | Y | Y | N | Y | Y | Y | Y |
| 20 Wasserman-Schultz | Y | Y | N | Y | Y | Y | Y |
| 21 Diaz-Balart, L. | N | Y | Y | N | N | Y | N |
| 22 Shaw | N | Y | Y | N | N | Y | N |
| 23 Hastings | Y | N | N | Y | Y | Y | Y |
| 24 Feeney | N | Y | Y | N | N | Y | N |
| 25 Diaz-Balart, M. | N | Y | Y | N | N | Y | N |
| **GEORGIA** | | | | | | | |
| 1 Kingston | N | Y | Y | N | N | Y | N |
| 2 Bishop | Y | Y | N | Y | N | Y | Y |
| 3 Marshall | Y | Y | N | Y | N | Y | Y |
| 4 McKinney | Y | N | ? | Y | Y | Y | Y |
| 5 Lewis | Y | N | N | Y | Y | Y | Y |
| 6 Price | N | Y | Y | N | N | N | N |
| 7 Linder | N | Y | Y | N | N | Y | N |
| 8 Westmoreland | N | Y | Y | N | N | N | N |
| 9 Norwood | N | Y | ? | N | N | Y | N |
| 10 Deal | N | Y | Y | N | N | Y | ? |
| 11 Gingrey | N | Y | Y | N | N | Y | N |
| 12 Barrow | Y | Y | N | Y | N | Y | Y |
| 13 Scott | Y | Y | N | Y | N | Y | Y |
| **HAWAII** | | | | | | | |
| 1 Abercrombie | Y | Y | N | Y | Y | Y | Y |
| 2 Case | Y | Y | N | Y | Y | Y | Y |
| **IDAHO** | | | | | | | |
| 1 Otter | N | Y | Y | N | N | Y | N |
| 2 Simpson | N | Y | Y | N | N | Y | N |
| **ILLINOIS** | | | | | | | |
| 1 Rush | Y | N | N | Y | Y | Y | Y |
| 2 Jackson | Y | N | N | Y | Y | Y | Y |
| 3 Lipinski | Y | Y | N | Y | Y | Y | Y |
| 4 Gutierrez | Y | N | N | Y | Y | Y | Y |
| 5 Emanuel | Y | Y | N | Y | Y | Y | Y |
| 6 Hyde | N | Y | ? | N | N | Y | N |
| 7 Davis | Y | N | N | Y | Y | Y | Y |
| 8 Bean | Y | Y | N | Y | Y | Y | Y |
| 9 Schakowsky | Y | N | N | Y | Y | Y | Y |
| 10 Kirk | N | Y | Y | N | N | Y | N |
| 11 Weller | N | Y | Y | N | N | Y | N |
| 12 Costello | Y | Y | N | Y | Y | Y | Y |

| | 221 | 222 | 223 | 224 | 225 | 226 | 227 |
|---|---|---|---|---|---|---|---|
| 13 **Biggert** | N | Y | Y | N | N | Y | N |
| 14 **Hastert** | | | | N | | | |
| 15 **Johnson** | N | Y | Y | N | Y | Y | N |
| 16 **Manzullo** | N | Y | Y | N | Y | Y | N |
| 17 Evans | Y | Y | N | Y | Y | Y | Y |
| 18 **LaHood** | N | Y | Y | N | N | Y | N |
| 19 **Shimkus** | N | Y | Y | N | N | Y | N |
| **INDIANA** | | | | | | | |
| 1 Visclosky | Y | Y | N | Y | N | Y | Y |
| 2 **Chocola** | N | Y | Y | N | N | Y | N |
| 3 **Souder** | N | Y | Y | N | N | Y | N |
| 4 **Buyer** | N | Y | Y | N | N | Y | N |
| 5 **Burton** | N | Y | Y | N | N | Y | N |
| 6 **Pence** | N | Y | Y | N | N | Y | N |
| 7 Carson | Y | Y | N | Y | Y | Y | Y |
| 8 **Hostettler** | N | Y | Y | N | N | Y | N |
| 9 **Sodrel** | N | Y | Y | N | Y | Y | N |
| **IOWA** | | | | | | | |
| 1 **Nussle** | N | Y | Y | N | N | Y | N |
| 2 **Leach** | Y | Y | Y | Y | N | Y | N |
| 3 Boswell | Y | Y | N | Y | Y | Y | Y |
| 4 **Latham** | Y | Y | Y | N | N | Y | N |
| 5 **King** | N | Y | Y | N | N | Y | N |
| **KANSAS** | | | | | | | |
| 1 **Moran** | N | Y | Y | N | N | Y | N |
| 2 **Ryun** | N | Y | Y | N | N | Y | N |
| 3 Moore | Y | Y | N | Y | Y | Y | Y |
| 4 **Tiahrt** | N | Y | Y | N | N | Y | N |
| **KENTUCKY** | | | | | | | |
| 1 **Whitfield** | N | Y | Y | N | N | Y | N |
| 2 **Lewis** | N | Y | Y | N | N | Y | N |
| 3 **Northup** | N | Y | Y | N | N | Y | N |
| 4 **Davis** | N | Y | Y | N | N | Y | N |
| 5 **Rogers** | N | Y | Y | N | N | Y | N |
| 6 Chandler | Y | Y | N | Y | Y | Y | Y |
| **LOUISIANA** | | | | | | | |
| 1 **Jindal** | N | Y | Y | N | N | Y | N |
| 2 Jefferson | Y | Y | N | Y | Y | Y | Y |
| 3 Melancon | Y | Y | N | Y | Y | Y | Y |
| 4 **McCrery** | N | Y | Y | N | N | Y | N |
| 5 **Alexander** | N | Y | Y | N | N | Y | N |
| 6 **Baker** | N | Y | Y | N | N | Y | N |
| 7 **Boustany** | N | Y | Y | N | N | Y | N |
| **MAINE** | | | | | | | |
| 1 Allen | Y | Y | N | Y | Y | Y | Y |
| 2 Michaud | Y | Y | N | Y | N | Y | Y |
| **MARYLAND** | | | | | | | |
| 1 **Gilchrest** | N | Y | Y | N | N | Y | N |
| 2 Ruppersberger | Y | Y | N | Y | Y | Y | Y |
| 3 Cardin | Y | Y | N | Y | Y | Y | Y |
| 4 Wynn | Y | Y | N | Y | Y | Y | Y |
| 5 Hoyer | Y | Y | N | Y | N | Y | Y |
| 6 **Bartlett** | N | Y | Y | N | N | Y | N |
| 7 Cummings | Y | Y | N | Y | Y | Y | Y |
| 8 Van Hollen | Y | Y | N | Y | Y | Y | Y |
| **MASSACHUSETTS** | | | | | | | |
| 1 Olver | Y | N | N | Y | Y | Y | Y |
| 2 Neal | Y | Y | N | Y | Y | Y | Y |
| 3 McGovern | Y | N | N | Y | Y | Y | Y |
| 4 Frank | Y | N | N | Y | N | Y | Y |
| 5 Meehan | Y | Y | N | Y | Y | Y | Y |
| 6 Tierney | Y | N | N | Y | Y | Y | Y |
| 7 Markey | Y | Y | N | Y | Y | Y | Y |
| 8 Capuano | Y | Y | N | Y | Y | Y | Y |
| 9 Lynch | Y | Y | N | Y | Y | Y | Y |
| 10 Delahunt | Y | N | N | Y | Y | Y | ? |
| **MICHIGAN** | | | | | | | |
| 1 Stupak | Y | Y | N | Y | Y | Y | Y |
| 2 **Hoekstra** | N | Y | Y | N | N | Y | N |
| 3 **Ehlers** | N | Y | Y | N | Y | Y | N |
| 4 **Camp** | N | Y | Y | N | N | Y | N |
| 5 Kildee | Y | Y | N | Y | Y | Y | Y |
| 6 **Upton** | N | Y | Y | N | N | Y | N |
| 7 **Schwarz** | N | Y | Y | N | N | Y | N |
| 8 **Rogers** | N | Y | Y | N | N | Y | N |
| 9 **Knollenberg** | N | Y | Y | N | N | Y | N |
| 10 **Miller** | N | Y | Y | N | N | Y | N |
| 11 **McCotter** | N | Y | Y | N | N | Y | N |
| 12 Levin | Y | Y | N | Y | N | Y | Y |
| 13 Kilpatrick | Y | N | N | Y | Y | Y | Y |
| 14 Conyers | Y | N | N | Y | Y | Y | Y |
| 15 Dingell | Y | Y | N | Y | Y | Y | Y |
| **MINNESOTA** | | | | | | | |
| 1 **Gutknecht** | N | Y | Y | N | N | Y | N |
| 2 **Kline** | N | Y | Y | N | N | Y | N |
| 3 **Ramstad** | Y | Y | Y | Y | N | Y | N |
| 4 McCollum | Y | Y | N | Y | Y | Y | Y |
| 5 Sabo | Y | Y | N | Y | Y | Y | Y |
| 6 **Kennedy** | N | Y | Y | Y | N | Y | N |
| 7 Peterson | Y | Y | N | Y | N | Y | Y |
| 8 Oberstar | Y | N | N | Y | Y | Y | Y |
| **MISSISSIPPI** | | | | | | | |
| 1 **Wicker** | N | Y | Y | N | N | Y | N |
| 2 Thompson | Y | Y | N | Y | Y | Y | Y |
| 3 **Pickering** | N | Y | Y | N | N | Y | N |
| 4 Taylor | Y | Y | N | Y | Y | Y | ? |
| **MISSOURI** | | | | | | | |
| 1 Clay | Y | Y | N | Y | Y | Y | Y |
| 2 **Akin** | N | Y | Y | N | N | Y | N |
| 3 Carnahan | Y | Y | N | Y | Y | Y | Y |
| 4 Skelton | Y | Y | N | Y | N | Y | Y |
| 5 Cleaver | Y | Y | N | Y | Y | Y | Y |
| 6 **Graves** | N | Y | Y | N | N | Y | N |
| 7 **Blunt** | N | Y | Y | N | N | Y | N |
| 8 **Emerson** | ? | ? | ? | ? | ? | ? | ? |
| 9 **Hulshof** | N | Y | Y | N | N | Y | N |
| **MONTANA** | | | | | | | |
| AL **Rehberg** | N | Y | Y | N | N | Y | N |
| **NEBRASKA** | | | | | | | |
| 1 **Fortenberry** | N | Y | Y | N | N | Y | N |
| 2 **Terry** | N | Y | Y | N | N | Y | N |
| 3 **Osborne** | N | Y | Y | N | N | Y | N |
| **NEVADA** | | | | | | | |
| 1 Berkley | Y | Y | N | Y | Y | Y | ? |
| 2 **Gibbons** | N | Y | Y | Y | N | Y | N |
| 3 **Porter** | N | Y | Y | Y | N | Y | N |
| **NEW HAMPSHIRE** | | | | | | | |
| 1 **Bradley** | N | Y | Y | N | N | Y | N |
| 2 **Bass** | N | Y | Y | N | N | Y | N |
| **NEW JERSEY** | | | | | | | |
| 1 Andrews | Y | Y | N | Y | Y | Y | Y |
| 2 **LoBiondo** | N | Y | Y | N | N | Y | N |
| 3 **Saxton** | N | Y | Y | N | N | Y | N |
| 4 **Smith** | N | Y | Y | Y | N | Y | N |
| 5 **Garrett** | N | Y | Y | N | N | Y | N |
| 6 Pallone | Y | Y | N | Y | Y | Y | Y |
| 7 **Ferguson** | N | Y | Y | N | N | Y | N |
| 8 Pascrell | Y | Y | N | Y | Y | Y | Y |
| 9 Rothman | Y | Y | N | Y | Y | Y | Y |
| 10 Payne | Y | N | N | Y | Y | Y | Y |
| 11 **Frelinghuysen** | N | Y | ? | N | N | Y | N |
| 12 Holt | Y | Y | N | Y | Y | Y | Y |
| 13 Menendez | Y | Y | ? | ? | ? | ? | ? |
| **NEW MEXICO** | | | | | | | |
| 1 **Wilson** | Y | Y | Y | Y | Y | Y | N |
| 2 **Pearce** | N | Y | Y | N | N | Y | N |
| 3 Udall | Y | Y | N | Y | Y | Y | Y |
| **NEW YORK** | | | | | | | |
| 1 Bishop | Y | Y | N | Y | Y | Y | Y |
| 2 Israel | Y | Y | N | Y | Y | Y | Y |
| 3 **King** | N | Y | Y | N | N | Y | N |
| 4 McCarthy | Y | Y | N | Y | Y | Y | ? |
| 5 Ackerman | Y | Y | N | Y | Y | Y | Y |
| 6 Meeks | Y | Y | N | Y | Y | Y | Y |
| 7 Crowley | Y | Y | N | Y | Y | Y | Y |
| 8 Nadler | Y | Y | N | Y | Y | Y | Y |
| 9 Weiner | Y | Y | N | Y | Y | Y | Y |
| 10 Towns | Y | Y | N | Y | Y | Y | Y |
| 11 Owens | Y | N | N | Y | Y | Y | Y |
| 12 Velázquez | Y | N | N | Y | Y | Y | Y |
| 13 **Fossella** | N | Y | Y | Y | N | Y | N |
| 14 Maloney | Y | Y | N | Y | Y | Y | Y |
| 15 Rangel | Y | N | N | Y | Y | Y | Y |
| 16 Serrano | Y | N | N | Y | Y | Y | Y |
| 17 Engel | Y | Y | N | Y | Y | Y | Y |
| 18 Lowey | Y | Y | N | Y | Y | Y | Y |
| 19 **Kelly** | N | Y | Y | N | N | Y | N |
| 20 **Sweeney** | N | Y | ? | N | N | Y | N |
| 21 McNulty | Y | Y | N | Y | Y | Y | ? |
| 22 Hinchey | Y | N | N | Y | Y | Y | Y |
| 23 **McHugh** | N | Y | Y | N | N | Y | N |
| 24 **Boehlert** | N | Y | Y | N | N | Y | N |
| 25 **Walsh** | N | Y | Y | N | N | Y | N |
| 26 **Reynolds** | N | Y | Y | N | N | Y | N |
| 27 Higgins | Y | Y | N | Y | Y | Y | Y |
| 28 Slaughter | Y | Y | N | Y | Y | Y | Y |
| 29 **Kuhl** | N | Y | Y | N | N | Y | N |
| **NORTH CAROLINA** | | | | | | | |
| 1 Butterfield | Y | Y | N | Y | Y | Y | Y |
| 2 Etheridge | Y | Y | N | Y | Y | Y | Y |
| 3 **Jones** | Y | Y | Y | Y | N | Y | N |
| 4 Price | Y | Y | N | Y | Y | Y | Y |
| 5 **Foxx** | N | Y | Y | N | N | Y | N |
| 6 **Coble** | N | Y | Y | N | N | Y | N |
| 7 McIntyre | Y | Y | N | Y | N | Y | Y |
| 8 **Hayes** | N | Y | Y | N | N | Y | N |
| 9 **Myrick** | N | Y | Y | N | N | Y | N |
| 10 **McHenry** | N | Y | Y | N | N | Y | N |
| 11 **Taylor** | N | Y | Y | N | N | Y | N |
| 12 Watt | Y | N | N | Y | Y | Y | Y |
| 13 Miller | Y | Y | N | Y | Y | Y | Y |
| **NORTH DAKOTA** | | | | | | | |
| AL Pomeroy | Y | Y | N | Y | N | Y | Y |
| **OHIO** | | | | | | | |
| 1 **Chabot** | N | Y | Y | N | N | Y | N |
| 2 Vacant | | | | | | | |
| 3 **Turner** | N | Y | Y | N | N | Y | N |
| 4 **Oxley** | N | Y | Y | N | N | Y | N |
| 5 **Gillmor** | N | Y | Y | N | N | Y | N |
| 6 Strickland | Y | Y | N | Y | Y | Y | Y |
| 7 **Hobson** | N | Y | Y | N | N | Y | N |
| 8 **Boehner** | N | Y | Y | N | N | Y | N |
| 9 Kaptur | Y | Y | N | Y | Y | Y | Y |
| 10 Kucinich | Y | N | N | Y | Y | Y | Y |
| 11 Jones | Y | N | ? | Y | Y | Y | Y |
| 12 **Tiberi** | N | Y | Y | N | N | Y | N |
| 13 Brown | Y | Y | N | Y | Y | Y | Y |
| 14 **LaTourette** | N | Y | Y | N | N | Y | N |
| 15 **Pryce** | N | Y | Y | N | N | Y | N |
| 16 **Regula** | N | Y | Y | N | N | Y | N |
| 17 Ryan | Y | Y | N | Y | Y | Y | Y |
| 18 **Ney** | N | Y | Y | N | N | Y | N |
| **OKLAHOMA** | | | | | | | |
| 1 **Sullivan** | N | Y | Y | N | N | Y | N |
| 2 Boren | Y | Y | N | Y | N | Y | Y |
| 3 **Lucas** | N | Y | Y | N | N | Y | N |
| 4 **Cole** | N | Y | Y | N | N | Y | N |
| 5 **Istook** | N | Y | Y | N | N | Y | N |
| **OREGON** | | | | | | | |
| 1 Wu | Y | N | N | Y | Y | Y | Y |
| 2 **Walden** | N | Y | Y | N | Y | Y | N |
| 3 Blumenauer | Y | N | N | Y | Y | Y | Y |
| 4 DeFazio | Y | Y | N | Y | Y | Y | Y |
| 5 Hooley | Y | Y | N | Y | Y | Y | Y |
| **PENNSYLVANIA** | | | | | | | |
| 1 Brady | Y | Y | N | Y | Y | Y | Y |
| 2 Fattah | Y | Y | N | Y | Y | Y | N |
| 3 **English** | N | Y | Y | N | N | Y | N |
| 4 **Hart** | N | Y | Y | N | N | Y | N |
| 5 **Peterson** | N | Y | Y | N | N | Y | N |
| 6 **Gerlach** | N | Y | Y | Y | N | Y | N |
| 7 **Weldon** | N | Y | Y | N | N | Y | ? |
| 8 **Fitzpatrick** | N | Y | Y | Y | N | Y | N |
| 9 **Shuster** | N | Y | Y | N | N | Y | N |
| 10 **Sherwood** | N | Y | Y | N | N | Y | N |
| 11 Kanjorski | Y | Y | N | Y | N | Y | Y |
| 12 Murtha | Y | Y | ? | N | N | Y | Y |
| 13 Schwartz | Y | Y | N | Y | Y | Y | Y |
| 14 Doyle | Y | Y | ? | ? | ? | ? | ? |
| 15 **Dent** | N | Y | Y | Y | N | Y | N |
| 16 **Pitts** | N | Y | Y | N | N | Y | N |
| 17 Holden | Y | Y | N | Y | N | Y | ? |
| 18 **Murphy** | N | Y | Y | N | N | Y | N |
| 19 **Platts** | N | Y | Y | N | N | Y | N |
| **RHODE ISLAND** | | | | | | | |
| 1 Kennedy | Y | Y | N | Y | N | Y | Y |
| 2 Langevin | Y | Y | N | Y | Y | Y | Y |
| **SOUTH CAROLINA** | | | | | | | |
| 1 **Brown** | ? | ? | Y | N | N | Y | N |
| 2 **Wilson** | N | Y | Y | N | N | Y | N |
| 3 **Barrett** | N | Y | Y | N | N | Y | N |
| 4 **Inglis** | N | Y | Y | N | N | Y | N |
| 5 Spratt | Y | Y | N | Y | N | Y | Y |
| 6 Clyburn | Y | Y | N | Y | Y | Y | Y |
| **SOUTH DAKOTA** | | | | | | | |
| AL Herseth | Y | Y | ? | Y | N | Y | Y |
| **TENNESSEE** | | | | | | | |
| 1 **Jenkins** | N | Y | Y | N | N | Y | ? |
| 2 **Duncan** | N | N | Y | N | N | Y | N |
| 3 **Wamp** | N | Y | Y | N | N | Y | N |
| 4 Davis | Y | Y | N | Y | N | Y | Y |
| 5 Cooper | Y | Y | N | Y | N | Y | Y |
| 6 Gordon | Y | Y | N | Y | Y | Y | Y |
| 7 **Blackburn** | N | Y | Y | N | N | Y | N |
| 8 Tanner | Y | Y | N | Y | N | Y | Y |
| 9 Ford | Y | Y | N | Y | Y | Y | Y |
| **TEXAS** | | | | | | | |
| 1 **Gohmert** | N | Y | Y | N | N | Y | N |
| 2 **Poe** | N | Y | Y | Y | N | Y | N |
| 3 **Johnson, S.** | N | Y | Y | N | N | Y | N |
| 4 **Hall** | N | Y | Y | Y | Y | Y | N |
| 5 **Hensarling** | N | Y | Y | N | N | Y | N |
| 6 **Barton** | N | Y | Y | N | N | Y | N |
| 7 **Culberson** | N | Y | Y | N | N | Y | N |
| 8 **Brady** | N | Y | Y | N | N | Y | N |
| 9 Green | Y | Y | N | Y | Y | Y | Y |
| 10 **McCaul** | N | Y | Y | N | N | Y | N |
| 11 **Conaway** | N | Y | Y | N | N | Y | N |
| 12 **Granger** | N | Y | Y | N | N | Y | N |
| 13 **Thornberry** | N | Y | Y | N | N | Y | N |
| 14 **Paul** | Y | N | Y | Y | Y | Y | Y |
| 15 Hinojosa | Y | Y | N | Y | Y | Y | Y |
| 16 Reyes | Y | Y | N | Y | N | Y | Y |
| 17 Edwards | Y | Y | N | Y | Y | Y | Y |
| 18 Jackson-Lee | Y | Y | N | Y | Y | Y | Y |
| 19 **Neugebauer** | N | Y | Y | N | N | Y | N |
| 20 Gonzalez | Y | Y | N | Y | Y | Y | Y |
| 21 **Smith** | N | Y | Y | N | N | Y | N |
| 22 **DeLay** | N | Y | Y | N | N | Y | N |
| 23 **Bonilla** | N | Y | Y | N | N | Y | N |
| 24 **Marchant** | N | Y | Y | N | N | Y | N |
| 25 Doggett | Y | Y | N | Y | Y | Y | Y |
| 26 **Burgess** | N | Y | Y | N | N | Y | N |
| 27 Ortiz | Y | Y | N | N | N | Y | Y |
| 28 Cuellar | Y | Y | N | Y | N | Y | Y |
| 29 Green | Y | Y | N | Y | N | Y | ? |
| 30 Johnson, E. | Y | Y | – | + | + | + | Y |
| 31 **Carter** | N | Y | Y | N | N | Y | N |
| 32 **Sessions** | N | Y | Y | N | N | Y | N |
| **UTAH** | | | | | | | |
| 1 **Bishop** | N | Y | Y | N | N | Y | N |
| 2 Matheson | Y | Y | N | Y | Y | Y | Y |
| 3 **Cannon** | N | Y | Y | N | N | Y | N |
| **VERMONT** | | | | | | | |
| AL *Sanders* | Y | Y | N | Y | Y | Y | Y |
| **VIRGINIA** | | | | | | | |
| 1 **Davis, J.** | N | Y | Y | Y | Y | Y | N |
| 2 **Drake** | N | Y | Y | N | N | Y | N |
| 3 Scott | Y | Y | N | Y | N | Y | Y |
| 4 **Forbes** | N | Y | Y | N | N | Y | N |
| 5 **Goode** | Y | Y | Y | N | N | Y | N |
| 6 **Goodlatte** | N | Y | Y | N | N | Y | N |
| 7 **Cantor** | N | Y | Y | N | N | Y | N |
| 8 Moran | Y | Y | N | Y | Y | Y | Y |
| 9 Boucher | Y | Y | N | Y | N | Y | Y |
| 10 **Wolf** | N | Y | Y | N | N | Y | N |
| 11 **Davis, T.** | N | Y | Y | N | N | Y | Y |
| **WASHINGTON** | | | | | | | |
| 1 Inslee | Y | Y | N | Y | Y | Y | Y |
| 2 Larsen | Y | Y | N | Y | N | Y | Y |
| 3 Baird | Y | Y | N | Y | Y | Y | Y |
| 4 **Hastings** | ? | ? | ? | ? | ? | ? | ? |
| 5 **McMorris** | N | Y | Y | N | N | Y | N |
| 6 Dicks | Y | Y | N | Y | N | Y | Y |
| 7 McDermott | Y | N | N | Y | Y | Y | ? |
| 8 **Reichert** | N | Y | Y | Y | N | Y | N |
| 9 Smith | Y | Y | N | Y | Y | Y | ? |
| **WEST VIRGINIA** | | | | | | | |
| 1 Mollohan | Y | Y | N | N | N | Y | Y |
| 2 **Capito** | N | Y | Y | Y | N | Y | N |
| 3 Rahall | Y | Y | N | Y | Y | Y | Y |
| **WISCONSIN** | | | | | | | |
| 1 **Ryan** | N | Y | Y | N | N | Y | N |
| 2 Baldwin | Y | N | N | Y | Y | Y | Y |
| 3 Kind | Y | Y | N | Y | Y | Y | ? |
| 4 Moore | Y | N | N | Y | Y | Y | Y |
| 5 **Sensenbrenner** | N | Y | Y | N | N | Y | N |
| 6 **Petri** | N | Y | Y | N | N | Y | N |
| 7 Obey | Y | Y | N | Y | Y | Y | Y |
| 8 **Green** | N | Y | Y | Y | N | Y | N |
| **WYOMING** | | | | | | | |
| AL **Cubin** | N | Y | Y | N | N | Y | N |

# IN THE HOUSE | By Vote Number

**228.** **H Con Res 44. Cinco de Mayo Tribute/Adoption.** Ros-Lehtinen, R-Fla., motion to suspend the rules and adopt the concurrent resolution that would recognize Mexico's struggle for independence from European control and would request the president to issue a proclamation recognizing the fight for Mexican independence. Motion agreed to 405-0: R 220-0; D 184-0 (ND 137-0, SD 47-0); I 1-0. A two-thirds majority of those present and voting (270 in this case) is required for adoption under suspension of the rules. June 7, 2005.

**229.** **H Res 282. Condemnation of Anti-Semitic Statements/Adoption.** Ros-Lehtinen, R-Fla., motion to suspend the rules and adopt the resolution that would call on the United Nations to officially and publicly condemn anti-Semitic statements made at U.N. meetings and by U.N. member states. Motion agreed to 409-2: R 222-1; D 186-1 (ND 141-0, SD 45-1); I 1-0. A two-thirds majority of those present and voting (274 in this case) is required for adoption under suspension of the rules. June 7, 2005.

**230.** **HR 2744. Fiscal 2006 Agriculture Appropriations/Animal and Plant Health Inspection Service.** Weiner, D-N.Y., amendment that would increase funding by $19 million for the Animal and Plant Health Inspection Service, to be offset by a $21 million reduction to the Agriculture Department common computing environment account. Adopted 226-201: R 40-188; D 185-13 (ND 145-4, SD 40-9); I 1-0. June 8, 2005.

**231.** **HR 2744. Fiscal 2006 Agriculture Appropriations/Country-of-Origin Labels.** Rehberg, R-Mont., amendment that would strike a provision that would prohibit the Agriculture Department from using funds in the bill to enforce country-of-origin labels for meat and meat products. Rejected 187-240: R 41-188; D 145-52 (ND 130-19, SD 15-33); I 1-0. June 8, 2005.

**232.** **HR 2744. Fiscal 2006 Agriculture Appropriations/Conflict of Interest Requirement.** Hinchey, D-N.Y., amendment that would prohibit the use of funds in the bill to grant a waiver of financial conflict of interest requirements for a voting member of an advisory committee or panel of the Food and Drug Administration. Adopted 218-210: R 32-198; D 185-12 (ND 143-5, SD 42-7); I 1-0. June 8, 2005.

**233.** **HR 2744. Fiscal 2006 Agriculture Appropriations/Wild Horses.** Sweeney, R-N.Y., amendment that would prohibit use of funds in the bill to pay salaries or expenses of employees to inspect horses and regulate transportation of horses intended for slaughter, including for meat, under the Federal Meat Inspection Act or the Federal Agriculture Improvement and Reform Act. Adopted 269-158: R 104-125; D 164-33 (ND 132-16, SD 32-17); I 1-0. June 8, 2005.

**234.** **HR 2744. Fiscal 2006 Agriculture Appropriations/Sugar Program.** Blumenauer, D-Ore., amendment that would bar use of funds in the bill for salaries or expenses of personnel who make loans in excess of 17 cents per pound for domestically grown raw sugar cane or 21.6 cents per pound for refined beet sugar from domestically grown beets. Rejected 146-280: R 81-148; D 65-131 (ND 57-91, SD 8-40); I 0-1. June 8, 2005.

| | 228 | 229 | 230 | 231 | 232 | 233 | 234 |
|---|---|---|---|---|---|---|---|
| **ALABAMA** | | | | | | | |
| 1 Bonner | Y | Y | N | Y | N | N | N |
| 2 Everett | Y | Y | N | Y | N | Y | N |
| 3 Rogers | Y | Y | N | Y | N | N | N |
| 4 Aderholt | Y | Y | N | N | N | Y | N |
| 5 Cramer | Y | Y | N | Y | N | Y | N |
| 6 Bachus | Y | Y | N | N | N | Y | N |
| 7 Davis | Y | Y | Y | Y | Y | Y | N |
| **ALASKA** | | | | | | | |
| AL Young | ? | ? | N | Y | N | N | N |
| **ARIZONA** | | | | | | | |
| 1 Renzi | Y | Y | Y | N | N | Y | N |
| 2 Franks | Y | Y | N | N | N | N | N |
| 3 Shadegg | Y | Y | N | N | N | N | Y |
| 4 Pastor | Y | Y | N | Y | N | N | N |
| 5 Hayworth | Y | Y | N | N | N | Y | N |
| 6 Flake | Y | Y | N | N | N | N | Y |
| 7 Grijalva | Y | Y | Y | Y | Y | Y | N |
| 8 Kolbe | Y | Y | N | N | N | N | Y |
| **ARKANSAS** | | | | | | | |
| 1 Berry | Y | Y | N | Y | N | Y | N |
| 2 Snyder | Y | Y | N | Y | N | Y | N |
| 3 Boozman | Y | Y | N | Y | N | N | N |
| 4 Ross | Y | Y | N | Y | N | N | N |
| **CALIFORNIA** | | | | | | | |
| 1 Thompson | Y | Y | Y | Y | Y | Y | N |
| 2 Herger | Y | Y | N | N | N | Y | N |
| 3 Lungren | Y | Y | N | N | N | Y | N |
| 4 Doolittle | Y | Y | N | N | N | N | N |
| 5 Matsui, D. | Y | Y | Y | Y | Y | Y | N |
| 6 Woolsey | Y | Y | Y | Y | Y | Y | N |
| 7 Miller, George | Y | Y | Y | Y | Y | Y | N |
| 8 Pelosi | Y | Y | Y | Y | Y | Y | N |
| 9 Lee | Y | Y | Y | Y | Y | Y | N |
| 10 Tauscher | Y | Y | Y | Y | Y | Y | N |
| 11 Pombo | Y | Y | N | N | N | N | N |
| 12 Lantos | Y | Y | Y | Y | Y | Y | N |
| 13 Stark | ? | ? | Y | Y | Y | Y | Y |
| 14 Eshoo | Y | Y | Y | Y | Y | Y | Y |
| 15 Honda | + | + | Y | Y | Y | N | N |
| 16 Lofgren | Y | Y | Y | Y | Y | Y | N |
| 17 Farr | Y | Y | N | N | Y | Y | N |
| 18 Cardoza | Y | Y | Y | Y | Y | Y | N |
| 19 Radanovich | Y | Y | N | N | N | N | N |
| 20 Costa | Y | Y | Y | Y | Y | Y | N |
| 21 Nunes | Y | Y | N | N | N | N | N |
| 22 Thomas | Y | Y | N | N | N | N | N |
| 23 Capps | Y | Y | Y | Y | Y | Y | Y |
| 24 Gallegly | Y | Y | N | Y | N | N | N |
| 25 McKeon | Y | Y | N | N | N | N | N |
| 26 Dreier | Y | Y | N | N | N | Y | N |
| 27 Sherman | Y | Y | Y | Y | Y | Y | N |
| 28 Berman | Y | Y | Y | Y | Y | Y | Y |
| 29 Schiff | + | Y | Y | Y | Y | Y | N |
| 30 Waxman | Y | Y | Y | Y | Y | Y | Y |
| 31 Becerra | Y | Y | Y | Y | Y | Y | N |
| 32 Solis | Y | Y | Y | Y | Y | Y | N |
| 33 Watson | Y | Y | Y | Y | Y | Y | N |
| 34 Roybal-Allard | Y | Y | Y | Y | Y | Y | N |
| 35 Waters | Y | Y | Y | Y | Y | Y | N |
| 36 Harman | Y | Y | Y | Y | Y | Y | N |
| 37 Millender-McD. | Y | Y | Y | Y | Y | Y | N |
| 38 Napolitano | Y | Y | Y | Y | Y | Y | N |
| 39 Sánchez, Linda | Y | Y | Y | Y | Y | Y | N |
| 40 Royce | Y | Y | N | N | N | N | Y |
| 41 Lewis | Y | Y | N | N | N | N | N |
| 42 Miller, Gary | Y | Y | N | N | N | N | N |
| 43 Baca | Y | Y | Y | Y | Y | Y | N |
| 44 Calvert | Y | Y | N | N | N | N | N |
| 45 Bono | Y | Y | N | N | N | N | N |
| 46 Rohrabacher | Y | Y | N | Y | N | N | Y |
| 47 Sanchez, Loretta | + | + | Y | Y | Y | Y | N |
| 48 Cox | Y | Y | ? | ? | ? | ? | ? |
| 49 Issa | Y | Y | N | N | N | Y | N |
| 50 Cunningham | Y | Y | N | N | N | Y | N |
| 51 Filner | Y | Y | Y | Y | Y | Y | N |
| 52 Hunter | Y | Y | N | N | N | Y | N |
| 53 Davis | Y | Y | Y | Y | Y | Y | Y |
| **COLORADO** | | | | | | | |
| 1 DeGette | Y | Y | Y | Y | Y | Y | Y |
| 2 Udall | Y | Y | Y | Y | Y | Y | N |
| 3 Salazar | Y | Y | Y | Y | Y | N | N |
| 4 Musgrave | Y | Y | N | N | N | N | N |
| 5 Hefley | Y | Y | N | N | N | Y | N |
| 6 Tancredo | Y | Y | N | N | N | Y | N |
| 7 Beauprez | Y | Y | N | N | N | N | N |
| **CONNECTICUT** | | | | | | | |
| 1 Larson | Y | Y | Y | Y | Y | Y | ? |
| 2 Simmons | Y | Y | Y | Y | N | Y | Y |
| 3 DeLauro | Y | Y | Y | Y | Y | Y | Y |
| 4 Shays | Y | Y | Y | Y | Y | Y | Y |
| 5 Johnson | Y | Y | N | Y | N | Y | N |
| **DELAWARE** | | | | | | | |
| AL Castle | Y | Y | N | N | N | Y | Y |
| **FLORIDA** | | | | | | | |
| 1 Miller | Y | Y | N | Y | N | N | N |
| 2 Boyd | Y | Y | N | Y | N | N | N |
| 3 Brown | ? | ? | Y | Y | Y | Y | N |
| 4 Crenshaw | Y | Y | N | N | N | Y | N |
| 5 Brown-Waite | Y | Y | N | Y | N | Y | N |
| 6 Stearns | Y | Y | N | N | N | N | N |
| 7 Mica | Y | Y | N | N | N | Y | N |
| 8 Keller | Y | Y | N | N | N | Y | N |
| 9 Bilirakis | Y | Y | N | Y | N | N | N |
| 10 Young | Y | Y | N | Y | N | Y | N |
| 11 Davis | Y | Y | Y | Y | Y | Y | N |
| 12 Putnam | Y | Y | N | N | N | N | N |
| 13 Harris | Y | Y | N | N | N | N | N |
| 14 Mack | Y | Y | N | N | N | N | N |
| 15 Weldon | Y | Y | N | Y | N | Y | N |
| 16 Foley | Y | Y | N | Y | N | Y | N |
| 17 Meek | Y | Y | N | Y | N | Y | N |
| 18 Ros-Lehtinen | Y | Y | N | Y | N | Y | N |
| 19 Wexler | Y | Y | Y | Y | Y | Y | N |
| 20 Wasserman-Schultz | Y | Y | Y | Y | Y | Y | N |
| 21 Diaz-Balart, L. | Y | Y | N | Y | N | Y | Y |
| 22 Shaw | Y | Y | N | Y | N | Y | Y |
| 23 Hastings | ? | ? | ? | ? | ? | ? | ? |
| 24 Feeney | Y | Y | N | N | N | N | N |
| 25 Diaz-Balart, M. | Y | Y | N | Y | N | N | N |
| **GEORGIA** | | | | | | | |
| 1 Kingston | Y | Y | N | N | N | N | Y |
| 2 Bishop | Y | Y | Y | N | Y | Y | N |
| 3 Marshall | Y | Y | N | Y | N | Y | N |
| 4 McKinney | Y | N | Y | Y | Y | N | Y |
| 5 Lewis | Y | Y | Y | Y | Y | Y | Y |
| 6 Price | Y | Y | N | N | N | N | N |
| 7 Linder | Y | Y | N | N | N | N | N |
| 8 Westmoreland | Y | Y | N | N | N | N | N |
| 9 Norwood | Y | Y | N | N | N | N | N |
| 10 Deal | Y | Y | N | N | N | N | N |
| 11 Gingrey | Y | Y | N | N | N | N | N |
| 12 Barrow | Y | Y | Y | Y | Y | Y | N |
| 13 Scott | ? | ? | Y | N | Y | Y | N |
| **HAWAII** | | | | | | | |
| 1 Abercrombie | Y | Y | N | Y | Y | Y | N |
| 2 Case | Y | Y | Y | N | Y | Y | N |
| **IDAHO** | | | | | | | |
| 1 Otter | ? | ? | N | N | N | N | N |
| 2 Simpson | Y | Y | N | N | N | N | N |
| **ILLINOIS** | | | | | | | |
| 1 Rush | ? | ? | ? | ? | ? | ? | ? |
| 2 Jackson | Y | Y | Y | Y | Y | Y | Y |
| 3 Lipinski | Y | Y | Y | Y | Y | Y | N |
| 4 Gutierrez | ? | ? | Y | Y | Y | Y | N |
| 5 Emanuel | Y | Y | Y | Y | Y | Y | Y |
| 6 Hyde | + | + | N | N | N | Y | N |
| 7 Davis | Y | Y | Y | Y | Y | Y | Y |
| 8 Bean | Y | Y | Y | Y | Y | Y | Y |
| 9 Schakowsky | Y | Y | Y | Y | Y | Y | Y |
| 10 Kirk | Y | Y | N | N | Y | Y | N |
| 11 Weller | Y | Y | N | N | N | N | N |
| 12 Costello | Y | Y | Y | Y | Y | Y | N |

**KEY**    Republicans    Democrats    *Independents*

| | | |
|---|---|---|
| **Y** Voted for (yea) | **X** Paired against | **C** Voted "present" to avoid possible conflict of interest |
| **#** Paired for | **−** Announced against | |
| **+** Announced for | **P** Voted "present" | **?** Did not vote or otherwise make a position known |
| **N** Voted against (nay) | | |

| | 228 | 229 | 230 | 231 | 232 | 233 | 234 |
|---|---|---|---|---|---|---|---|
| 13 **Biggert** | Y | Y | Y | N | N | Y | Y |
| 14 **Hastert** | | | | | N | | |
| 15 **Johnson** | Y | Y | N | N | N | Y | N |
| 16 **Manzullo** | Y | Y | N | N | N | N | Y |
| 17 Evans | Y | Y | Y | Y | Y | Y | N |
| 18 **LaHood** | Y | Y | N | N | N | N | N |
| 19 **Shimkus** | Y | Y | N | N | N | N | N |
| **INDIANA** | | | | | | | |
| 1 Visclosky | Y | Y | Y | N | Y | Y | N |
| 2 **Chocola** | Y | Y | N | N | N | N | Y |
| 3 **Souder** | Y | Y | Y | N | N | N | Y |
| 4 **Buyer** | Y | Y | N | N | N | N | N |
| 5 **Burton** | Y | Y | N | N | Y | Y | Y |
| 6 **Pence** | Y | Y | N | N | N | N | Y |
| 7 Carson | Y | Y | Y | Y | Y | N | Y |
| 8 **Hostettler** | Y | Y | N | N | N | Y | Y |
| 9 **Sodrel** | Y | Y | N | N | N | N | N |
| **IOWA** | | | | | | | |
| 1 **Nussle** | ? | ? | N | N | N | N | N |
| 2 **Leach** | Y | Y | N | N | Y | N | N |
| 3 Boswell | Y | Y | Y | Y | Y | N | N |
| 4 **Latham** | Y | Y | N | N | N | N | N |
| 5 **King** | Y | Y | N | N | N | N | N |
| **KANSAS** | | | | | | | |
| 1 **Moran** | Y | Y | N | N | Y | N | N |
| 2 **Ryun** | Y | Y | N | N | N | N | N |
| 3 Moore | Y | Y | Y | N | Y | Y | Y |
| 4 **Tiahrt** | Y | Y | N | N | N | Y | N |
| **KENTUCKY** | | | | | | | |
| 1 **Whitfield** | Y | Y | N | N | N | Y | N |
| 2 **Lewis** | Y | Y | N | N | Y | Y | N |
| 3 **Northup** | Y | Y | N | N | N | Y | N |
| 4 **Davis** | Y | Y | N | N | N | Y | N |
| 5 **Rogers** | Y | Y | N | N | Y | Y | N |
| 6 Chandler | Y | Y | Y | N | Y | Y | N |
| **LOUISIANA** | | | | | | | |
| 1 **Jindal** | Y | Y | Y | N | Y | Y | N |
| 2 Jefferson | Y | Y | Y | N | N | Y | N |
| 3 Melancon | Y | Y | Y | Y | Y | N | N |
| 4 **McCrery** | Y | Y | N | N | N | N | N |
| 5 **Alexander** | Y | Y | N | N | N | N | N |
| 6 **Baker** | Y | Y | N | N | N | N | N |
| 7 **Boustany** | Y | Y | N | N | N | N | N |
| **MAINE** | | | | | | | |
| 1 Allen | Y | Y | Y | Y | Y | Y | Y |
| 2 Michaud | Y | Y | Y | Y | Y | Y | N |
| **MARYLAND** | | | | | | | |
| 1 **Gilchrest** | Y | Y | Y | N | N | Y | N |
| 2 Ruppersberger | Y | Y | Y | Y | Y | Y | N |
| 3 Cardin | Y | Y | Y | Y | Y | Y | N |
| 4 Wynn | Y | Y | Y | N | Y | Y | N |
| 5 Hoyer | Y | Y | Y | Y | Y | Y | N |
| 6 **Bartlett** | Y | Y | N | Y | N | Y | Y |
| 7 Cummings | Y | Y | N | Y | Y | Y | N |
| 8 Van Hollen | Y | Y | Y | Y | Y | Y | Y |
| **MASSACHUSETTS** | | | | | | | |
| 1 Olver | Y | Y | Y | Y | Y | Y | N |
| 2 Neal | Y | Y | Y | Y | Y | Y | N |
| 3 McGovern | Y | Y | Y | Y | Y | Y | N |
| 4 Frank | Y | Y | Y | Y | Y | Y | Y |
| 5 Meehan | Y | Y | Y | Y | Y | Y | Y |
| 6 Tierney | Y | Y | Y | Y | Y | Y | Y |
| 7 Markey | Y | Y | Y | Y | Y | Y | Y |
| 8 Capuano | Y | Y | Y | Y | Y | Y | Y |
| 9 Lynch | Y | Y | Y | Y | Y | Y | N |
| 10 Delahunt | ? | Y | Y | Y | Y | N | Y |
| **MICHIGAN** | | | | | | | |
| 1 Stupak | Y | Y | Y | Y | Y | Y | N |
| 2 **Hoekstra** | Y | Y | Y | N | N | N | N |
| 3 **Ehlers** | Y | Y | Y | N | N | Y | N |
| 4 **Camp** | Y | Y | Y | N | N | N | N |
| 5 Kildee | Y | Y | Y | Y | Y | Y | N |
| 6 **Upton** | Y | Y | Y | Y | N | Y | Y |
| 7 **Schwarz** | Y | Y | Y | N | N | Y | N |
| 8 **Rogers** | Y | Y | Y | N | N | Y | N |
| 9 **Knollenberg** | Y | Y | N | N | N | N | N |
| 10 **Miller** | Y | Y | N | N | N | N | N |
| 11 **McCotter** | Y | Y | Y | N | N | Y | N |
| 12 Levin | Y | Y | Y | Y | Y | Y | N |
| 13 Kilpatrick | Y | Y | Y | Y | Y | Y | N |
| 14 Conyers | ? | Y | Y | Y | Y | Y | Y |
| 15 Dingell | Y | Y | Y | Y | Y | N | N |

| | 228 | 229 | 230 | 231 | 232 | 233 | 234 |
|---|---|---|---|---|---|---|---|
| **MINNESOTA** | | | | | | | |
| 1 **Gutknecht** | Y | Y | N | N | Y | Y | N |
| 2 **Kline** | Y | Y | N | N | N | Y | N |
| 3 **Ramstad** | Y | Y | N | N | N | Y | Y |
| 4 McCollum | ? | ? | Y | Y | Y | Y | N |
| 5 Sabo | Y | Y | Y | Y | Y | Y | N |
| 6 **Kennedy** | Y | Y | N | N | N | Y | N |
| 7 Peterson | Y | Y | Y | Y | Y | N | N |
| 8 Oberstar | Y | Y | Y | Y | Y | N | N |
| **MISSISSIPPI** | | | | | | | |
| 1 **Wicker** | Y | Y | N | N | N | N | N |
| 2 Thompson | Y | Y | Y | N | Y | Y | N |
| 3 **Pickering** | Y | Y | N | Y | N | Y | N |
| 4 Taylor | Y | Y | Y | Y | Y | Y | N |
| **MISSOURI** | | | | | | | |
| 1 Clay | Y | Y | Y | N | Y | Y | N |
| 2 **Akin** | Y | Y | ? | N | N | N | Y |
| 3 Carnahan | Y | Y | Y | N | Y | Y | N |
| 4 Skelton | Y | Y | Y | N | Y | Y | N |
| 5 Cleaver | Y | Y | Y | N | Y | Y | N |
| 6 **Graves** | Y | Y | N | N | N | N | N |
| 7 **Blunt** | Y | Y | N | N | N | N | N |
| 8 **Emerson** | Y | Y | N | N | Y | N | N |
| 9 **Hulshof** | Y | Y | N | N | Y | N | N |
| **MONTANA** | | | | | | | |
| AL **Rehberg** | Y | Y | N | Y | N | N | N |
| **NEBRASKA** | | | | | | | |
| 1 **Fortenberry** | Y | Y | N | Y | N | N | N |
| 2 **Terry** | Y | Y | N | N | N | N | N |
| 3 **Osborne** | Y | Y | N | Y | N | N | N |
| **NEVADA** | | | | | | | |
| 1 Berkley | Y | Y | Y | Y | Y | Y | Y |
| 2 **Gibbons** | Y | Y | Y | N | N | Y | Y |
| 3 **Porter** | Y | Y | Y | N | N | Y | Y |
| **NEW HAMPSHIRE** | | | | | | | |
| 1 **Bradley** | Y | Y | Y | N | Y | Y | Y |
| 2 **Bass** | Y | Y | Y | N | Y | Y | Y |
| **NEW JERSEY** | | | | | | | |
| 1 Andrews | + | + | Y | N | Y | Y | Y |
| 2 **LoBiondo** | Y | Y | Y | Y | N | Y | Y |
| 3 **Saxton** | Y | Y | N | Y | N | Y | N |
| 4 **Smith** | Y | Y | Y | Y | N | Y | Y |
| 5 **Garrett** | Y | Y | N | N | N | N | Y |
| 6 Pallone | Y | Y | Y | Y | Y | Y | Y |
| 7 **Ferguson** | Y | Y | Y | N | N | Y | Y |
| 8 Pascrell | Y | Y | Y | Y | Y | Y | Y |
| 9 Rothman | ? | ? | Y | Y | Y | Y | N |
| 10 Payne | ? | ? | Y | Y | Y | Y | Y |
| 11 **Frelinghuysen** | Y | Y | N | N | N | Y | Y |
| 12 Holt | Y | Y | Y | Y | Y | Y | Y |
| 13 Menendez | Y | Y | ? | ? | ? | ? | ? |
| **NEW MEXICO** | | | | | | | |
| 1 **Wilson** | Y | Y | Y | Y | N | N | N |
| 2 **Pearce** | Y | Y | N | Y | N | N | N |
| 3 Udall | Y | Y | Y | Y | Y | Y | Y |
| **NEW YORK** | | | | | | | |
| 1 Bishop | Y | Y | Y | Y | Y | Y | Y |
| 2 Israel | Y | Y | Y | Y | Y | Y | N |
| 3 **King** | Y | Y | Y | Y | N | Y | N |
| 4 McCarthy | Y | Y | Y | Y | Y | Y | N |
| 5 Ackerman | Y | Y | Y | Y | Y | Y | N |
| 6 Meeks | Y | Y | Y | N | N | Y | N |
| 7 Crowley | Y | Y | Y | Y | Y | Y | N |
| 8 Nadler | Y | Y | Y | Y | Y | Y | Y |
| 9 Weiner | Y | Y | Y | Y | Y | Y | Y |
| 10 Towns | Y | Y | Y | Y | N | Y | N |
| 11 Owens | Y | Y | Y | Y | Y | Y | Y |
| 12 Velázquez | Y | Y | Y | Y | Y | Y | Y |
| 13 **Fossella** | Y | Y | N | N | N | Y | Y |
| 14 Maloney | Y | Y | Y | Y | Y | Y | N |
| 15 Rangel | Y | Y | Y | Y | Y | N | N |
| 16 Serrano | Y | Y | Y | Y | Y | Y | N |
| 17 Engel | Y | Y | Y | Y | Y | Y | N |
| 18 Lowey | Y | Y | Y | Y | Y | Y | Y |
| 19 **Kelly** | Y | Y | Y | Y | Y | Y | Y |
| 20 **Sweeney** | Y | Y | Y | N | N | Y | Y |
| 21 McNulty | Y | Y | Y | N | Y | Y | Y |
| 22 Hinchey | Y | Y | Y | Y | Y | Y | N |
| 23 **McHugh** | Y | Y | N | Y | Y | N | N |
| 24 **Boehlert** | Y | Y | N | Y | Y | Y | Y |
| 25 **Walsh** | Y | Y | N | N | N | N | N |
| 26 **Reynolds** | Y | Y | N | N | N | N | N |
| 27 Higgins | Y | Y | Y | Y | Y | Y | N |
| 28 Slaughter | Y | Y | Y | N | + | + | N |
| 29 **Kuhl** | Y | Y | N | N | N | Y | Y |

| | 228 | 229 | 230 | 231 | 232 | 233 | 234 |
|---|---|---|---|---|---|---|---|
| **NORTH CAROLINA** | | | | | | | |
| 1 Butterfield | Y | Y | Y | N | Y | Y | N |
| 2 Etheridge | Y | Y | Y | N | N | Y | N |
| 3 **Jones** | Y | Y | N | Y | Y | Y | N |
| 4 Price | Y | Y | Y | N | N | Y | N |
| 5 **Foxx** | Y | Y | N | N | N | N | N |
| 6 **Coble** | Y | Y | N | N | N | N | N |
| 7 McIntyre | Y | Y | N | N | Y | Y | N |
| 8 **Hayes** | Y | Y | N | N | N | Y | N |
| 9 **Myrick** | Y | Y | N | Y | N | Y | Y |
| 10 **McHenry** | Y | Y | N | N | N | N | Y |
| 11 **Taylor** | Y | Y | N | N | N | N | N |
| 12 Watt | Y | Y | Y | Y | Y | N | N |
| 13 Miller | Y | Y | Y | N | N | Y | N |
| **NORTH DAKOTA** | | | | | | | |
| AL Pomeroy | Y | Y | Y | Y | Y | N | N |
| **OHIO** | | | | | | | |
| 1 **Chabot** | Y | Y | N | N | N | Y | Y |
| 2 Vacant | | | | | | | |
| 3 **Turner** | Y | Y | N | N | N | Y | N |
| 4 **Oxley** | + | + | N | N | N | N | N |
| 5 **Gillmor** | Y | Y | N | N | N | N | N |
| 6 Strickland | Y | Y | Y | Y | Y | Y | N |
| 7 **Hobson** | Y | Y | N | N | N | N | N |
| 8 **Boehner** | Y | Y | N | N | N | N | N |
| 9 Kaptur | ? | Y | Y | Y | Y | Y | N |
| 10 Kucinich | Y | Y | Y | Y | Y | Y | N |
| 11 Jones | Y | Y | Y | Y | Y | Y | N |
| 12 **Tiberi** | Y | Y | N | N | N | N | Y |
| 13 Brown | Y | Y | Y | Y | Y | Y | N |
| 14 **LaTourette** | Y | Y | N | N | N | Y | N |
| 15 **Pryce** | Y | Y | N | N | N | Y | N |
| 16 **Regula** | Y | Y | N | Y | N | N | N |
| 17 Ryan | Y | Y | Y | Y | Y | Y | N |
| 18 **Ney** | Y | Y | N | N | N | Y | Y |
| **OKLAHOMA** | | | | | | | |
| 1 **Sullivan** | Y | Y | N | N | N | N | N |
| 2 Boren | Y | Y | N | N | Y | N | N |
| 3 **Lucas** | ? | Y | N | N | N | N | N |
| 4 **Cole** | Y | Y | N | N | N | N | N |
| 5 **Istook** | Y | Y | N | Y | N | N | Y |
| **OREGON** | | | | | | | |
| 1 Wu | Y | Y | Y | Y | Y | Y | N |
| 2 **Walden** | Y | Y | N | Y | N | N | N |
| 3 Blumenauer | Y | Y | Y | Y | Y | Y | Y |
| 4 DeFazio | Y | Y | Y | Y | Y | Y | N |
| 5 Hooley | Y | Y | Y | Y | Y | Y | N |
| **PENNSYLVANIA** | | | | | | | |
| 1 Brady | Y | Y | Y | Y | Y | Y | Y |
| 2 Fattah | Y | Y | Y | Y | Y | Y | Y |
| 3 **English** | Y | Y | N | N | N | Y | Y |
| 4 **Hart** | Y | Y | N | N | N | N | N |
| 5 **Peterson** | Y | Y | N | N | Y | N | Y |
| 6 **Gerlach** | Y | Y | N | N | N | Y | Y |
| 7 **Weldon** | ? | Y | Y | Y | Y | Y | N |
| 8 **Fitzpatrick** | Y | Y | Y | N | Y | Y | Y |
| 9 **Shuster** | Y | Y | N | N | N | N | Y |
| 10 **Sherwood** | Y | Y | N | N | N | N | N |
| 11 Kanjorski | Y | Y | Y | Y | Y | Y | N |
| 12 Murtha | Y | Y | Y | Y | Y | Y | N |
| 13 Schwartz | Y | Y | Y | Y | Y | Y | Y |
| 14 Doyle | Y | Y | Y | Y | Y | Y | Y |
| 15 **Dent** | Y | Y | N | N | N | Y | Y |
| 16 **Pitts** | Y | Y | N | N | N | N | Y |
| 17 Holden | Y | Y | Y | Y | Y | Y | N |
| 18 **Murphy** | Y | Y | N | N | N | N | Y |
| 19 **Platts** | ? | ? | N | N | Y | Y | Y |
| **RHODE ISLAND** | | | | | | | |
| 1 Kennedy | + | + | Y | Y | Y | Y | Y |
| 2 Langevin | Y | Y | Y | Y | Y | Y | Y |
| **SOUTH CAROLINA** | | | | | | | |
| 1 **Brown** | Y | Y | N | N | Y | Y | Y |
| 2 **Wilson** | Y | Y | N | N | N | Y | Y |
| 3 **Barrett** | Y | Y | N | N | N | N | N |
| 4 **Inglis** | Y | Y | N | N | N | Y | Y |
| 5 Spratt | Y | Y | Y | N | Y | Y | N |
| 6 Clyburn | Y | Y | Y | N | N | Y | N |
| **SOUTH DAKOTA** | | | | | | | |
| AL Herseth | Y | Y | Y | Y | Y | Y | N |
| **TENNESSEE** | | | | | | | |
| 1 **Jenkins** | ? | ? | N | N | Y | N | N |
| 2 **Duncan** | Y | Y | N | N | Y | N | Y |

| | 228 | 229 | 230 | 231 | 232 | 233 | 234 |
|---|---|---|---|---|---|---|---|
| 3 **Wamp** | Y | Y | N | N | Y | Y | Y |
| 4 Davis | Y | Y | N | N | Y | N | N |
| 5 Cooper | Y | Y | Y | N | N | N | Y |
| 6 Gordon | Y | Y | Y | N | Y | Y | Y |
| 7 **Blackburn** | Y | Y | N | N | N | N | Y |
| 8 Tanner | Y | Y | Y | N | Y | Y | N |
| 9 Ford | Y | Y | Y | ? | Y | Y | N |
| **TEXAS** | | | | | | | |
| 1 **Gohmert** | Y | Y | N | N | N | Y | N |
| 2 **Poe** | Y | Y | N | N | N | Y | Y |
| 3 **Johnson, S.** | Y | Y | N | N | N | N | Y |
| 4 **Hall** | Y | Y | N | N | N | Y | N |
| 5 **Hensarling** | Y | Y | N | N | N | N | Y |
| 6 **Barton** | Y | Y | N | N | N | N | N |
| 7 **Culberson** | Y | Y | N | N | N | N | N |
| 8 **Brady** | Y | Y | N | N | N | N | N |
| 9 Green | Y | Y | Y | Y | Y | Y | N |
| 10 **McCaul** | Y | Y | Y | N | N | Y | N |
| 11 **Conaway** | Y | Y | N | N | N | N | N |
| 12 **Granger** | Y | Y | N | N | N | N | N |
| 13 **Thornberry** | Y | Y | N | N | N | N | N |
| 14 **Paul** | Y | N | Y | Y | Y | Y | Y |
| 15 Hinojosa | Y | Y | Y | N | Y | N | – |
| 16 Reyes | Y | Y | Y | N | Y | N | N |
| 17 Edwards | Y | Y | Y | N | Y | N | N |
| 18 Jackson-Lee | ? | ? | ? | ? | ? | ? | ? |
| 19 **Neugebauer** | Y | Y | N | N | N | N | N |
| 20 Gonzalez | Y | Y | Y | N | Y | Y | N |
| 21 **Smith** | Y | Y | N | N | N | N | N |
| 22 **DeLay** | Y | Y | N | N | N | N | N |
| 23 **Bonilla** | Y | Y | N | N | N | N | N |
| 24 **Marchant** | Y | Y | N | N | N | N | N |
| 25 Doggett | Y | Y | Y | Y | Y | Y | Y |
| 26 **Burgess** | Y | Y | N | N | N | N | Y |
| 27 Ortiz | Y | Y | N | N | Y | Y | N |
| 28 Cuellar | Y | Y | Y | N | Y | N | N |
| 29 Green | Y | ? | N | Y | Y | Y | N |
| 30 Johnson, E. | Y | Y | Y | Y | Y | Y | N |
| 31 **Carter** | Y | Y | N | N | N | N | N |
| 32 **Sessions** | Y | Y | N | N | N | N | Y |
| **UTAH** | | | | | | | |
| 1 **Bishop** | Y | Y | N | N | N | N | N |
| 2 Matheson | Y | Y | Y | Y | N | N | Y |
| 3 **Cannon** | Y | Y | N | N | N | N | N |
| **VERMONT** | | | | | | | |
| AL *Sanders* | Y | Y | Y | Y | Y | Y | N |
| **VIRGINIA** | | | | | | | |
| 1 **Davis, J.** | Y | Y | N | Y | N | Y | Y |
| 2 **Drake** | Y | Y | N | N | N | N | N |
| 3 Scott | Y | Y | Y | Y | Y | Y | Y |
| 4 **Forbes** | Y | Y | N | N | N | Y | Y |
| 5 **Goode** | Y | Y | N | N | N | N | N |
| 6 **Goodlatte** | Y | Y | N | N | N | N | N |
| 7 **Cantor** | Y | Y | N | N | N | N | N |
| 8 Moran | Y | Y | Y | N | Y | Y | Y |
| 9 Boucher | Y | Y | Y | N | Y | N | Y |
| 10 **Wolf** | Y | Y | N | N | N | Y | N |
| 11 **Davis, T.** | Y | Y | N | N | N | Y | Y |
| **WASHINGTON** | | | | | | | |
| 1 Inslee | Y | Y | Y | Y | Y | Y | Y |
| 2 Larsen | Y | Y | Y | N | Y | Y | N |
| 3 Baird | Y | Y | Y | Y | Y | Y | N |
| 4 **Hastings** | Y | Y | N | N | N | N | N |
| 5 **McMorris** | Y | Y | N | Y | N | N | N |
| 6 Dicks | Y | Y | Y | Y | Y | Y | N |
| 7 McDermott | Y | Y | Y | Y | Y | Y | Y |
| 8 **Reichert** | Y | Y | N | N | N | Y | N |
| 9 Smith | Y | Y | Y | Y | Y | N | Y |
| **WEST VIRGINIA** | | | | | | | |
| 1 Mollohan | Y | Y | Y | Y | Y | Y | N |
| 2 **Capito** | Y | Y | N | Y | N | Y | N |
| 3 Rahall | Y | Y | Y | Y | Y | Y | N |
| **WISCONSIN** | | | | | | | |
| 1 **Ryan** | Y | Y | N | N | N | N | Y |
| 2 Baldwin | Y | Y | Y | Y | Y | Y | Y |
| 3 Kind | Y | Y | Y | Y | Y | Y | Y |
| 4 Moore | Y | Y | Y | Y | Y | Y | Y |
| 5 **Sensenbrenner** | Y | Y | N | N | N | Y | Y |
| 6 **Petri** | Y | Y | N | N | N | N | Y |
| 7 Obey | Y | Y | Y | Y | Y | Y | N |
| 8 **Green** | Y | Y | Y | N | N | Y | Y |
| **WYOMING** | | | | | | | |
| AL **Cubin** | + | Y | Y | Y | N | N | N |

# IN THE HOUSE | By Vote Number

**235.** **HR 2744. Fiscal 2006 Agriculture Appropriations/Market Access Program.** Chabot, R-Ohio, amendment that would prohibit the use of funds in the bill to carry out activities of the Market Access Program, which helps fund advertising and marketing for agricultural exports. Rejected 66-356: R 48-178; D 18-177 (ND 16-131, SD 2-46); I 0-1. June 8, 2005.

**236.** **HR 2744. Fiscal 2006 Agriculture Appropriations/Across-the-Board Cut.** Hefley, R-Colo., amendment that would require a 1 percent across-the-board cut in discretionary spending. Rejected 80-335: R 76-144; D 4-190 (ND 2-146, SD 2-44); I 0-1. June 8, 2005.

**237.** **HR 2744. Fiscal 2006 Agriculture Appropriations/Food Stamps.** Garrett, R-N.J., amendment that would prohibit the use of funds under the food stamp program to contravene existing immigration law requiring that sponsors of legal aliens be financially liable for government benefits provided to the aliens. Rejected 169-258: R 162-66; D 7-191 (ND 2-148, SD 5-43); I 0-1. June 8, 2005.

**238.** **HR 2744. Fiscal 2006 Agriculture Appropriations/Passage.** Passage of the bill that would provide $100.3 billion in fiscal 2006 for the Department of Agriculture and related agencies, such as the Food and Drug Administration (FDA). The bill would fund the food stamp program at $40.7 billion and the child nutrition program at $12.4 billion. It would provide $25.7 billion for the Commodity Credit Corporation, $5.3 billion for the Women, Infants and Children program and $1.5 billion for the FDA. Passed 408-18: R 215-13; D 192-5 (ND 145-4, SD 47-1); I 1-0. June 8, 2005.

**239.** **H J Res 27. World Trade Organization Withdrawal/Passage.** Passage of the joint resolution that would withdraw congressional approval of the agreement establishing the World Trade Organization. Rejected 86-338: R 39-185; D 46-153 (ND 39-110, SD 7-43); I 1-0. June 9, 2005.

**240.** **H Res 310. Ethics Committee Staff/Motion to Table.** Blunt, R-Mo., motion to table (kill) the Pelosi, D-Calif., privileged resolution that would direct the Committee on Standards of Official Conduct to appoint a nonpartisan professional staff if a majority of the committee agrees to do so. Motion agreed to 219-199: R 219-0; D 0-198 (ND 0-148, SD 0-50); I 0-1. June 9, 2005.

| | 235 | 236 | 237 | 238 | 239 | 240 |
|---|---|---|---|---|---|---|
| **ALABAMA** | | | | | | |
| 1 Bonner | N | N | Y | Y | N | Y |
| 2 Everett | N | Y | Y | Y | Y | ? |
| 3 Rogers | N | N | Y | Y | N | Y |
| 4 Aderholt | N | N | Y | Y | Y | Y |
| 5 Cramer | N | N | Y | Y | N | N |
| 6 Bachus | Y | N | Y | Y | N | Y |
| 7 Davis | N | N | N | Y | N | N |
| **ALASKA** | | | | | | |
| AL Young | N | ? | ? | ? | N | Y |
| **ARIZONA** | | | | | | |
| 1 Renzi | N | N | Y | Y | N | Y |
| 2 Franks | Y | Y | Y | N | Y | Y |
| 3 Shadegg | Y | Y | Y | Y | N | Y |
| 4 Pastor | N | N | N | Y | Y | N |
| 5 Hayworth | Y | Y | Y | Y | N | Y |
| 6 Flake | Y | Y | Y | N | Y | Y |
| 7 Grijalva | N | N | N | Y | Y | N |
| 8 Kolbe | N | N | Y | Y | N | Y |
| **ARKANSAS** | | | | | | |
| 1 Berry | N | N | Y | Y | N | N |
| 2 Snyder | N | N | N | Y | N | N |
| 3 Boozman | N | N | Y | Y | N | Y |
| 4 Ross | N | N | N | Y | N | N |
| **CALIFORNIA** | | | | | | |
| 1 Thompson | N | N | N | Y | N | N |
| 2 Herger | N | Y | Y | Y | N | Y |
| 3 Lungren | N | Y | Y | Y | N | Y |
| 4 Doolittle | N | N | Y | Y | N | Y |
| 5 Matsui, D. | N | N | N | Y | N | N |
| 6 Woolsey | N | N | N | Y | Y | N |
| 7 Miller, George | N | N | N | Y | N | N |
| 8 Pelosi | N | N | N | Y | N | N |
| 9 Lee | N | N | Y | Y | Y | N |
| 10 Tauscher | N | N | N | Y | N | N |
| 11 Pombo | N | N | Y | Y | Y | Y |
| 12 Lantos | N | N | N | Y | N | N |
| 13 Stark | N | N | N | N | N | N |
| 14 Eshoo | N | N | Y | Y | N | N |
| 15 Honda | N | N | N | Y | N | N |
| 16 Lofgren | N | N | N | Y | N | N |
| 17 Farr | N | N | N | Y | Y | N |
| 18 Cardoza | N | N | N | Y | N | N |
| 19 Radanovich | N | Y | Y | Y | N | Y |
| 20 Costa | N | N | N | Y | N | N |
| 21 Nunes | N | N | Y | Y | N | Y |
| 22 Thomas | N | N | Y | Y | N | Y |
| 23 Capps | N | N | N | Y | N | N |
| 24 Gallegly | N | N | Y | Y | N | Y |
| 25 McKeon | N | N | Y | Y | N | Y |
| 26 Dreier | N | N | Y | Y | N | Y |
| 27 Sherman | N | N | N | Y | N | N |
| 28 Berman | N | N | N | Y | N | N |
| 29 Schiff | N | N | N | Y | N | N |
| 30 Waxman | Y | N | N | Y | N | N |
| 31 Becerra | N | N | N | Y | N | N |
| 32 Solis | N | N | N | Y | N | N |
| 33 Watson | N | N | N | Y | N | N |
| 34 Roybal-Allard | N | N | N | Y | N | N |
| 35 Waters | N | N | N | Y | Y | N |
| 36 Harman | N | N | N | Y | N | N |
| 37 Millender-McD. | N | N | N | Y | N | N |
| 38 Napolitano | N | N | N | Y | N | N |
| 39 Sánchez, Linda | N | N | N | Y | Y | N |
| 40 Royce | Y | Y | Y | N | N | Y |
| 41 Lewis | N | N | Y | Y | N | Y |
| 42 Miller, Gary | Y | Y | Y | Y | N | Y |
| 43 Baca | N | N | N | Y | N | N |
| 44 Calvert | N | N | Y | Y | N | Y |
| 45 Bono | N | N | Y | Y | N | ? |
| 46 Rohrabacher | Y | Y | Y | N | Y | Y |
| 47 Sanchez, Loretta | N | N | N | Y | N | N |
| 48 Cox | ? | Y | Y | Y | ? | ? |
| 49 Issa | N | Y | Y | Y | N | Y |

| | 235 | 236 | 237 | 238 | 239 | 240 |
|---|---|---|---|---|---|---|
| 50 Cunningham | N | N | Y | Y | N | Y |
| 51 Filner | N | N | N | Y | N | N |
| 52 Hunter | N | N | Y | Y | Y | Y |
| 53 Davis | N | N | N | Y | N | N |
| **COLORADO** | | | | | | |
| 1 DeGette | Y | N | N | Y | N | N |
| 2 Udall | N | N | N | Y | N | N |
| 3 Salazar | N | N | N | Y | N | N |
| 4 Musgrave | N | N | Y | N | Y | Y |
| 5 Hefley | N | Y | Y | N | N | Y |
| 6 Tancredo | Y | Y | Y | N | Y | Y |
| 7 Beauprez | N | Y | Y | Y | N | Y |
| **CONNECTICUT** | | | | | | |
| 1 Larson | N | N | N | Y | N | N |
| 2 Simmons | N | N | Y | Y | N | N |
| 3 DeLauro | N | N | N | Y | N | N |
| 4 Shays | Y | Y | Y | N | N | Y |
| 5 Johnson | N | N | Y | Y | N | N |
| **DELAWARE** | | | | | | |
| AL Castle | Y | N | N | Y | N | Y |
| **FLORIDA** | | | | | | |
| 1 Miller | N | Y | Y | Y | Y | Y |
| 2 Boyd | N | N | N | Y | N | N |
| 3 Brown | N | N | N | Y | N | N |
| 4 Crenshaw | ? | N | Y | Y | N | Y |
| 5 Brown-Waite | N | N | Y | Y | N | Y |
| 6 Stearns | N | Y | Y | Y | N | Y |
| 7 Mica | N | Y | Y | Y | N | Y |
| 8 Keller | N | Y | Y | Y | N | Y |
| 9 Bilirakis | N | N | Y | Y | N | Y |
| 10 Young | N | N | Y | Y | N | Y |
| 11 Davis | N | N | N | Y | N | N |
| 12 Putnam | N | N | Y | Y | N | Y |
| 13 Harris | N | N | Y | Y | N | Y |
| 14 Mack | N | Y | Y | Y | N | Y |
| 15 Weldon | N | N | Y | Y | N | Y |
| 16 Foley | N | N | Y | Y | N | Y |
| 17 Meek | N | N | N | Y | N | N |
| 18 Ros-Lehtinen | N | N | N | Y | N | Y |
| 19 Wexler | N | N | N | Y | N | N |
| 20 Wasserman-Schultz | N | ? | N | Y | N | N |
| 21 Diaz-Balart, L. | N | N | N | Y | N | Y |
| 22 Shaw | N | Y | Y | Y | N | Y |
| 23 Hastings | ? | ? | ? | ? | ? | ? |
| 24 Feeney | N | Y | Y | Y | Y | Y |
| 25 Diaz-Balart, M. | N | Y | N | Y | N | Y |
| **GEORGIA** | | | | | | |
| 1 Kingston | N | N | Y | Y | N | Y |
| 2 Bishop | N | N | N | Y | N | N |
| 3 Marshall | N | ? | Y | Y | Y | N |
| 4 McKinney | Y | N | N | Y | N | N |
| 5 Lewis | N | N | N | Y | N | N |
| 6 Price | Y | Y | Y | Y | N | Y |
| 7 Linder | Y | Y | Y | Y | N | Y |
| 8 Westmoreland | Y | Y | Y | Y | Y | Y |
| 9 Norwood | N | Y | Y | Y | Y | Y |
| 10 Deal | N | Y | Y | Y | N | Y |
| 11 Gingrey | N | N | Y | Y | N | Y |
| 12 Barrow | N | N | Y | Y | N | N |
| 13 Scott | N | N | N | Y | N | N |
| **HAWAII** | | | | | | |
| 1 Abercrombie | N | N | N | Y | Y | N |
| 2 Case | N | N | N | Y | N | N |
| **IDAHO** | | | | | | |
| 1 Otter | N | N | Y | Y | Y | Y |
| 2 Simpson | N | N | Y | Y | N | Y |
| **ILLINOIS** | | | | | | |
| 1 Rush | ? | ? | N | Y | N | N |
| 2 Jackson | N | N | N | Y | N | N |
| 3 Lipinski | Y | N | N | Y | P | N |
| 4 Gutierrez | N | N | Y | Y | Y | N |
| 5 Emanuel | N | N | N | Y | N | N |
| 6 Hyde | Y | N | Y | Y | N | Y |
| 7 Davis | N | N | N | Y | N | N |
| 8 Bean | N | Y | N | N | N | N |
| 9 Schakowsky | N | N | N | Y | N | N |
| 10 Kirk | N | N | Y | Y | N | Y |
| 11 Weller | N | N | Y | Y | N | Y |
| 12 Costello | N | N | N | Y | N | N |

**KEY**    Republicans    Democrats    *Independents*

| | | | |
|---|---|---|---|
| **Y** | Voted for (yea) | **X** Paired against | **C** Voted "present" to avoid possible conflict of interest |
| **#** | Paired for | **−** Announced against | |
| **+** | Announced for | **P** Voted "present" | **?** Did not vote or otherwise make a position known |
| **N** | Voted against (nay) | | |

| | 235 | 236 | 237 | 238 | 239 | 240 |
|---|---|---|---|---|---|---|
| 13 **Biggert** | N | N | N | Y | N | Y |
| 14 **Hastert** | | | | | | |
| 15 **Johnson** | N | N | N | Y | N | Y |
| 16 **Manzullo** | Y | Y | Y | Y | N | Y |
| 17 Evans | N | N | N | Y | Y | N |
| 18 **LaHood** | N | N | N | Y | ? | ? |
| 19 **Shimkus** | N | Y | N | Y | N | Y |
| **INDIANA** | | | | | | |
| 1 Visclosky | N | N | N | Y | Y | N |
| 2 **Chocola** | N | Y | Y | Y | N | Y |
| 3 **Souder** | N | N | Y | Y | N | Y |
| 4 **Buyer** | N | Y | N | Y | N | Y |
| 5 **Burton** | N | N | Y | Y | N | Y |
| 6 **Pence** | Y | Y | Y | Y | N | Y |
| 7 Carson | Y | N | N | Y | N | N |
| 8 **Hostettler** | Y | Y | Y | Y | Y | Y |
| 9 **Sodrel** | N | N | Y | Y | N | Y |
| **IOWA** | | | | | | |
| 1 **Nussle** | N | N | Y | Y | N | Y |
| 2 **Leach** | N | N | N | Y | N | Y |
| 3 Boswell | N | N | N | Y | N | N |
| 4 **Latham** | N | N | N | Y | N | Y |
| 5 **King** | N | ? | Y | Y | N | Y |
| **KANSAS** | | | | | | |
| 1 **Moran** | N | N | Y | Y | N | Y |
| 2 **Ryun** | N | N | Y | Y | N | Y |
| 3 Moore | ? | N | N | Y | N | N |
| 4 **Tiahrt** | N | N | Y | Y | N | Y |
| **KENTUCKY** | | | | | | |
| 1 **Whitfield** | N | N | Y | Y | Y | Y |
| 2 **Lewis** | N | N | Y | Y | N | Y |
| 3 **Northup** | N | N | Y | Y | N | Y |
| 4 **Davis** | N | N | Y | Y | N | Y |
| 5 **Rogers** | N | N | Y | Y | N | Y |
| 6 Chandler | N | N | N | Y | N | N |
| **LOUISIANA** | | | | | | |
| 1 **Jindal** | N | N | Y | Y | N | Y |
| 2 Jefferson | N | N | N | Y | N | N |
| 3 Melancon | N | N | N | Y | N | N |
| 4 **McCrery** | N | N | Y | Y | N | Y |
| 5 **Alexander** | N | N | N | Y | N | Y |
| 6 **Baker** | N | Y | Y | Y | N | Y |
| 7 **Boustany** | N | N | N | Y | N | Y |
| **MAINE** | | | | | | |
| 1 Allen | N | N | N | Y | N | N |
| 2 Michaud | N | N | N | Y | N | N |
| **MARYLAND** | | | | | | |
| 1 **Gilchrest** | N | N | N | Y | N | Y |
| 2 Ruppersberger | N | N | N | Y | N | N |
| 3 Cardin | N | N | N | Y | N | N |
| 4 Wynn | N | N | N | Y | N | N |
| 5 Hoyer | N | N | N | Y | N | N |
| 6 **Bartlett** | Y | Y | Y | Y | Y | Y |
| 7 Cummings | N | N | N | Y | N | N |
| 8 Van Hollen | Y | N | N | Y | N | N |
| **MASSACHUSETTS** | | | | | | |
| 1 Olver | N | N | N | Y | N | N |
| 2 Neal | N | N | N | Y | N | N |
| 3 McGovern | N | N | N | Y | N | N |
| 4 Frank | N | N | N | Y | Y | N |
| 5 Meehan | N | N | N | Y | N | N |
| 6 Tierney | Y | N | N | Y | Y | N |
| 7 Markey | Y | N | N | Y | N | N |
| 8 Capuano | Y | N | N | Y | N | N |
| 9 Lynch | N | N | N | Y | Y | N |
| 10 Delahunt | N | N | N | Y | N | N |
| **MICHIGAN** | | | | | | |
| 1 Stupak | N | N | N | Y | Y | N |
| 2 **Hoekstra** | N | N | Y | Y | N | Y |
| 3 **Ehlers** | Y | N | N | Y | N | Y |
| 4 **Camp** | ? | N | Y | Y | N | Y |
| 5 Kildee | N | N | N | Y | Y | N |
| 6 **Upton** | N | N | Y | Y | N | Y |
| 7 **Schwarz** | N | N | N | Y | N | Y |
| 8 **Rogers** | N | Y | Y | Y | N | Y |
| 9 **Knollenberg** | N | N | N | Y | N | Y |
| 10 **Miller** | N | N | Y | Y | N | Y |
| 11 **McCotter** | N | Y | Y | Y | Y | Y |
| 12 Levin | N | N | N | Y | N | N |
| 13 Kilpatrick | N | N | N | Y | N | N |
| 14 Conyers | N | N | N | Y | N | N |
| 15 Dingell | N | N | N | Y | N | N |

| | 235 | 236 | 237 | 238 | 239 | 240 |
|---|---|---|---|---|---|---|
| **MINNESOTA** | | | | | | |
| 1 **Gutknecht** | N | Y | Y | Y | N | Y |
| 2 **Kline** | N | N | Y | Y | N | Y |
| 3 **Ramstad** | Y | Y | Y | Y | N | Y |
| 4 McCollum | N | N | N | Y | N | N |
| 5 Sabo | N | N | N | Y | Y | N |
| 6 **Kennedy** | N | N | Y | Y | N | Y |
| 7 Peterson | N | N | N | Y | N | N |
| 8 Oberstar | N | N | N | Y | Y | N |
| **MISSISSIPPI** | | | | | | |
| 1 **Wicker** | N | N | Y | Y | N | Y |
| 2 Thompson | N | N | N | Y | N | N |
| 3 **Pickering** | N | – | + | Y | N | Y |
| 4 Taylor | N | Y | Y | N | Y | N |
| **MISSOURI** | | | | | | |
| 1 Clay | N | N | N | Y | N | N |
| 2 **Akin** | Y | Y | Y | Y | N | Y |
| 3 Carnahan | N | N | N | Y | N | N |
| 4 Skelton | N | N | N | Y | N | N |
| 5 Cleaver | N | N | N | Y | N | N |
| 6 **Graves** | N | Y | Y | Y | N | Y |
| 7 **Blunt** | N | N | Y | Y | N | Y |
| 8 **Emerson** | N | N | Y | Y | N | Y |
| 9 **Hulshof** | N | N | N | Y | ? | ? |
| **MONTANA** | | | | | | |
| AL **Rehberg** | N | N | N | Y | N | Y |
| **NEBRASKA** | | | | | | |
| 1 **Fortenberry** | N | N | N | Y | N | Y |
| 2 **Terry** | N | Y | N | Y | N | ? |
| 3 **Osborne** | N | N | N | Y | N | Y |
| **NEVADA** | | | | | | |
| 1 Berkley | Y | N | N | Y | N | N |
| 2 **Gibbons** | Y | Y | Y | Y | Y | Y |
| 3 **Porter** | N | N | N | Y | N | Y |
| **NEW HAMPSHIRE** | | | | | | |
| 1 **Bradley** | Y | Y | Y | N | N | Y |
| 2 **Bass** | Y | Y | Y | N | N | Y |
| **NEW JERSEY** | | | | | | |
| 1 Andrews | Y | N | N | Y | N | N |
| 2 **LoBiondo** | Y | N | N | Y | N | Y |
| 3 **Saxton** | N | N | N | Y | N | Y |
| 4 **Smith** | Y | N | N | Y | N | Y |
| 5 **Garrett** | Y | Y | Y | Y | Y | Y |
| 6 Pallone | N | N | N | Y | Y | N |
| 7 **Ferguson** | Y | N | N | Y | N | Y |
| 8 Pascrell | N | N | N | Y | Y | N |
| 9 Rothman | N | N | N | Y | N | N |
| 10 Payne | N | ? | N | Y | Y | N |
| 11 **Frelinghuysen** | Y | N | Y | Y | N | Y |
| 12 Holt | N | N | N | Y | N | N |
| 13 Menendez | ? | ? | ? | ? | ? | ? |
| **NEW MEXICO** | | | | | | |
| 1 **Wilson** | N | N | N | Y | N | Y |
| 2 **Pearce** | N | N | Y | Y | N | Y |
| 3 Udall | N | N | N | Y | N | N |
| **NEW YORK** | | | | | | |
| 1 Bishop | N | N | N | Y | N | N |
| 2 Israel | N | N | N | Y | N | N |
| 3 **King** | N | N | N | Y | N | ? |
| 4 McCarthy | N | N | N | Y | N | N |
| 5 Ackerman | N | N | N | Y | N | N |
| 6 Meeks | N | N | N | Y | N | N |
| 7 Crowley | N | N | N | Y | N | N |
| 8 Nadler | N | N | N | Y | N | N |
| 9 Weiner | N | N | N | Y | N | N |
| 10 Towns | N | N | N | Y | N | N |
| 11 Owens | N | N | N | ? | Y | N |
| 12 Velázquez | N | N | N | Y | N | N |
| 13 **Fossella** | Y | Y | Y | N | N | Y |
| 14 Maloney | N | N | N | Y | N | N |
| 15 Rangel | N | N | N | Y | N | N |
| 16 Serrano | N | N | N | Y | N | N |
| 17 Engel | N | N | N | Y | N | N |
| 18 Lowey | N | N | N | Y | N | N |
| 19 **Kelly** | N | N | N | Y | N | Y |
| 20 **Sweeney** | N | N | Y | Y | N | ? |
| 21 McNulty | N | N | N | Y | N | N |
| 22 Hinchey | N | N | N | Y | Y | N |
| 23 **McHugh** | N | N | Y | Y | N | Y |
| 24 **Boehlert** | N | N | N | Y | N | Y |
| 25 **Walsh** | N | N | N | Y | N | Y |
| 26 **Reynolds** | N | ? | N | Y | N | Y |
| 27 Higgins | N | N | N | Y | N | N |
| 28 Slaughter | ? | N | N | Y | N | N |
| 29 **Kuhl** | N | N | Y | Y | N | Y |

| | 235 | 236 | 237 | 238 | 239 | 240 |
|---|---|---|---|---|---|---|
| **NORTH CAROLINA** | | | | | | |
| 1 Butterfield | N | N | N | Y | N | N |
| 2 Etheridge | N | N | N | Y | N | N |
| 3 **Jones** | N | Y | Y | Y | Y | Y |
| 4 Price | N | N | N | Y | N | N |
| 5 **Foxx** | N | Y | Y | Y | Y | Y |
| 6 **Coble** | N | Y | Y | Y | Y | Y |
| 7 McIntyre | N | N | Y | Y | Y | N |
| 8 **Hayes** | N | N | Y | Y | N | Y |
| 9 **Myrick** | Y | Y | Y | Y | N | Y |
| 10 **McHenry** | Y | + | Y | Y | N | Y |
| 11 **Taylor** | N | N | Y | Y | Y | Y |
| 12 Watt | N | N | N | Y | N | N |
| 13 Miller | N | N | N | Y | N | N |
| **NORTH DAKOTA** | | | | | | |
| AL Pomeroy | N | N | N | Y | N | N |
| **OHIO** | | | | | | |
| 1 **Chabot** | Y | Y | Y | Y | N | Y |
| 2 Vacant | | | | | | |
| 3 **Turner** | N | N | N | Y | N | Y |
| 4 **Oxley** | N | N | N | Y | N | Y |
| 5 **Gillmor** | N | N | Y | Y | N | Y |
| 6 Strickland | N | N | N | Y | Y | ? |
| 7 **Hobson** | N | N | N | Y | ? | ? |
| 8 **Boehner** | N | N | N | Y | N | Y |
| 9 Kaptur | N | N | N | Y | Y | N |
| 10 Kucinich | Y | N | N | N | Y | N |
| 11 Jones | N | N | N | Y | Y | N |
| 12 **Tiberi** | Y | N | Y | Y | ? | ? |
| 13 Brown | Y | N | N | Y | Y | N |
| 14 **LaTourette** | N | N | N | Y | Y | Y |
| 15 **Pryce** | N | N | N | Y | N | Y |
| 16 **Regula** | N | N | N | Y | N | Y |
| 17 Ryan | N | N | N | Y | Y | N |
| 18 **Ney** | N | N | Y | Y | Y | Y |
| **OKLAHOMA** | | | | | | |
| 1 **Sullivan** | ? | Y | Y | Y | Y | Y |
| 2 Boren | N | N | N | Y | N | N |
| 3 **Lucas** | N | N | N | Y | N | Y |
| 4 **Cole** | N | N | Y | Y | N | Y |
| 5 **Istook** | Y | ? | Y | Y | Y | Y |
| **OREGON** | | | | | | |
| 1 Wu | N | N | N | Y | N | N |
| 2 **Walden** | N | N | Y | Y | N | Y |
| 3 Blumenauer | N | N | N | Y | N | N |
| 4 DeFazio | N | N | Y | Y | Y | N |
| 5 Hooley | N | N | N | Y | N | N |
| **PENNSYLVANIA** | | | | | | |
| 1 Brady | N | N | N | Y | N | N |
| 2 Fattah | N | N | N | Y | N | N |
| 3 **English** | Y | N | N | Y | N | Y |
| 4 **Hart** | N | N | N | Y | N | Y |
| 5 **Peterson** | N | N | N | Y | N | Y |
| 6 **Gerlach** | N | N | N | Y | N | Y |
| 7 **Weldon** | N | N | N | Y | N | Y |
| 8 **Fitzpatrick** | Y | N | N | Y | N | Y |
| 9 **Shuster** | N | Y | Y | Y | N | Y |
| 10 **Sherwood** | N | N | N | Y | N | Y |
| 11 Kanjorski | N | N | N | Y | N | N |
| 12 Murtha | N | N | N | Y | N | ? |
| 13 Schwartz | N | N | N | Y | N | N |
| 14 Doyle | N | N | N | Y | Y | N |
| 15 **Dent** | Y | Y | Y | Y | N | Y |
| 16 **Pitts** | N | Y | Y | Y | N | Y |
| 17 Holden | N | N | N | Y | N | N |
| 18 **Murphy** | N | N | Y | Y | N | Y |
| 19 **Platts** | N | N | Y | Y | N | Y |
| **RHODE ISLAND** | | | | | | |
| 1 Kennedy | N | N | N | Y | Y | N |
| 2 Langevin | N | N | N | Y | N | N |
| **SOUTH CAROLINA** | | | | | | |
| 1 **Brown** | N | N | Y | Y | N | Y |
| 2 **Wilson** | Y | Y | Y | Y | N | Y |
| 3 **Barrett** | Y | Y | Y | Y | Y | Y |
| 4 **Inglis** | Y | Y | Y | Y | N | Y |
| 5 Spratt | ? | N | N | Y | N | N |
| 6 Clyburn | N | N | N | Y | N | N |
| **SOUTH DAKOTA** | | | | | | |
| AL Herseth | N | N | N | Y | N | N |
| **TENNESSEE** | | | | | | |
| 1 **Jenkins** | N | Y | Y | Y | Y | Y |
| 2 **Duncan** | Y | Y | Y | Y | Y | Y |

| | 235 | 236 | 237 | 238 | 239 | 240 |
|---|---|---|---|---|---|---|
| 3 **Wamp** | N | Y | Y | Y | Y | Y |
| 4 Davis | N | N | N | Y | Y | N |
| 5 Cooper | N | N | N | Y | N | N |
| 6 Gordon | N | ? | ? | ? | N | N |
| 7 **Blackburn** | N | Y | Y | Y | N | Y |
| 8 Tanner | N | Y | N | Y | N | N |
| 9 Ford | N | N | N | Y | N | N |
| **TEXAS** | | | | | | |
| 1 **Gohmert** | N | ? | Y | Y | Y | Y |
| 2 **Poe** | N | N | Y | Y | N | Y |
| 3 **Johnson, S.** | N | ? | Y | Y | N | Y |
| 4 **Hall** | N | N | Y | Y | N | Y |
| 5 **Hensarling** | Y | Y | Y | Y | N | Y |
| 6 **Barton** | N | N | N | Y | N | Y |
| 7 **Culberson** | N | ? | Y | Y | N | Y |
| 8 **Brady** | N | Y | Y | Y | N | Y |
| 9 Green | N | N | N | Y | N | N |
| 10 **McCaul** | N | N | Y | Y | N | Y |
| 11 **Conaway** | N | N | Y | Y | N | Y |
| 12 **Granger** | N | N | Y | Y | N | ? |
| 13 **Thornberry** | N | N | N | Y | N | Y |
| 14 **Paul** | Y | Y | Y | N | Y | Y |
| 15 Hinojosa | N | N | N | Y | N | N |
| 16 Reyes | N | N | N | Y | N | N |
| 17 Edwards | N | N | N | Y | N | N |
| 18 Jackson-Lee | ? | ? | ? | ? | N | N |
| 19 **Neugebauer** | N | N | Y | Y | N | Y |
| 20 Gonzalez | N | N | N | Y | N | N |
| 21 **Smith** | N | N | Y | ? | N | N |
| 22 **DeLay** | N | N | Y | Y | N | Y |
| 23 **Bonilla** | N | N | N | Y | N | Y |
| 24 **Marchant** | N | N | Y | Y | N | Y |
| 25 Doggett | Y | N | N | Y | N | N |
| 26 **Burgess** | Y | Y | Y | Y | N | Y |
| 27 Ortiz | N | N | N | Y | N | N |
| 28 Cuellar | N | N | N | Y | N | N |
| 29 Green | N | N | N | Y | Y | N |
| 30 Johnson, E. | N | N | N | Y | N | N |
| 31 **Carter** | N | N | Y | Y | N | Y |
| 32 **Sessions** | N | Y | Y | Y | N | Y |
| **UTAH** | | | | | | |
| 1 **Bishop** | N | Y | Y | Y | Y | Y |
| 2 Matheson | Y | Y | Y | Y | N | N |
| 3 **Cannon** | N | ? | N | Y | N | Y |
| **VERMONT** | | | | | | |
| AL *Sanders* | N | N | N | Y | Y | N |
| **VIRGINIA** | | | | | | |
| 1 **Davis, J.** | Y | Y | Y | Y | ? | Y |
| 2 **Drake** | N | N | Y | Y | N | Y |
| 3 Scott | N | N | N | Y | N | N |
| 4 **Forbes** | N | N | Y | Y | N | Y |
| 5 **Goode** | N | N | Y | Y | Y | Y |
| 6 **Goodlatte** | N | N | Y | Y | N | Y |
| 7 **Cantor** | N | N | N | Y | N | Y |
| 8 Moran | N | N | N | Y | N | N |
| 9 Boucher | N | N | N | Y | N | N |
| 10 **Wolf** | N | N | N | Y | N | Y |
| 11 **Davis, T.** | N | Y | N | Y | N | Y |
| **WASHINGTON** | | | | | | |
| 1 Inslee | N | N | N | Y | N | N |
| 2 Larsen | N | N | N | Y | N | N |
| 3 Baird | N | N | N | Y | N | N |
| 4 **Hastings** | N | N | N | Y | N | Y |
| 5 **McMorris** | N | N | N | Y | N | Y |
| 6 Dicks | N | N | N | Y | N | N |
| 7 McDermott | Y | N | N | N | N | N |
| 8 **Reichert** | N | N | Y | Y | N | Y |
| 9 Smith | N | N | N | Y | N | N |
| **WEST VIRGINIA** | | | | | | |
| 1 Mollohan | N | N | N | Y | Y | N |
| 2 **Capito** | N | N | Y | Y | N | Y |
| 3 Rahall | N | N | N | Y | Y | N |
| **WISCONSIN** | | | | | | |
| 1 **Ryan** | N | Y | Y | Y | N | Y |
| 2 Baldwin | N | N | N | Y | Y | N |
| 3 Kind | N | N | N | Y | N | N |
| 4 Moore | Y | N | N | Y | N | N |
| 5 **Sensenbrenner** | Y | Y | Y | N | Y | Y |
| 6 **Petri** | N | Y | Y | Y | N | Y |
| 7 Obey | N | N | N | Y | Y | N |
| 8 **Green** | N | N | Y | Y | N | Y |
| **WYOMING** | | | | | | |
| AL **Cubin** | N | Y | Y | Y | N | Y |

# IN THE HOUSE | By Vote Number

**241.** **S 643. State Mediation Programs/Passage.** Lucas, R-Okla., motion to suspend the rules and pass the bill that would authorize $7.5 million in each of fiscal 2006 through 2010 for grants for state agricultural mediation programs. Motion agreed to 371-2: R 205-2; D 165-0 (ND 120-0, SD 45-0); I 1-0. A two-thirds majority of those present and voting (249 in this case) is required for passage under suspension of the rules. June 13, 2005.

**242.** **HR 2326. Floyd Lupton Post Office/Passage.** Duncan, R-Tenn., motion to suspend the rules and pass the bill that would designate a post office in Belhaven, N.C., after Floyd Lupton, who served as chief of staff to the late Rep. Walter B. Jones Sr., D-N.C. (1966-92), for 26 years. Motion agreed to 370-0: R 204-0; D 165-0 (ND 120-0, SD 45-0); I 1-0. A two-thirds majority of those present and voting (247 in this case) is required for passage under suspension of the rules. June 13, 2005.

**243.** **HR 2862. Fiscal 2006 Commerce-Justice-Science Appropriations/ Previous Question.** Gingrey, R-Ga., motion to order the previous question (thus ending debate and possibility of amendment) on adoption of the rule (H Res 314) to provide for House floor consideration of the bill that would appropriate $57.8 billion in fiscal 2006 for the departments of Commerce, Justice and State, as well as various science and other related agencies. Motion agreed to 222-190: R 220-0; D 2-189 (ND 0-142, SD 2-47); I 0-1. (Subsequently, the rule was adopted by voice vote.) June 14, 2005.

**244.** **HR 2862. Fiscal 2006 Commerce-Justice-Science Appropriations/ State and Local Law Enforcement Funding.** Obey, D-Wis., amendment that would add $100 million for justice assistance grants to state and local law enforcement and $100 million for law enforcement grants under the Community Oriented Policing Services program, offset by a $200 million decrease for NASA. Rejected 196-230: R 21-206; D 174-24 (ND 137-11, SD 37-13); I 1-0. June 14, 2005.

**245.** **HR 2862. Fiscal 2006 Commerce-Justice-Science Appropriations/ Justice Assistance Grants.** Terry, R-Neb., amendment that would increase funding for Justice Assistance Grants by $286 million, offset with a 0.448 percent across-the-board cut in discretionary spending. Rejected 175-252: R 91-137; D 84-114 (ND 64-84, SD 20-30); I 0-1. June 14, 2005.

**246.** **HR 2862. Fiscal 2006 Commerce-Justice-Science Appropriations/ Small Business Loan Program.** Velázquez, D-N.Y., amendment that would provide $79 million for the Small Business Administration's 7(a) small business loan program offset by various cuts in the bill. Adopted 234-189: R 36-189; D 197-0 (ND 147-0, SD 50-0); I 1-0. June 14, 2005.

**247.** **HR 2862. Fiscal 2006 Commerce-Justice-Science Appropriations/ Law Enforcement Funding.** Reichert, R-Wash., amendment that would increase funding by $78.3 million for Community Oriented Policing Services programs. It would be offset by reducing funds for salaries and expenses at the FBI and the Drug Enforcement Administration, and reducing funds for international broadcasting operations. Rejected 130-297: R 55-173; D 75-123 (ND 61-87, SD 14-36); I 0-1. June 14, 2005.

| | 241 | 242 | 243 | 244 | 245 | 246 | 247 |
|---|---|---|---|---|---|---|---|
| **ALABAMA** | | | | | | | |
| 1 Bonner | Y | Y | Y | N | N | N | N |
| 2 Everett | Y | Y | ? | N | N | N | N |
| 3 Rogers | Y | Y | Y | N | N | N | N |
| 4 Aderholt | Y | Y | Y | N | N | N | N |
| 5 Cramer | Y | Y | N | N | N | Y | N |
| 6 Bachus | Y | Y | Y | N | Y | N | Y |
| 7 Davis | Y | Y | N | N | N | N | N |
| **ALASKA** | | | | | | | |
| AL Young | Y | Y | Y | N | N | N | Y |
| **ARIZONA** | | | | | | | |
| 1 Renzi | Y | Y | Y | Y | Y | Y | Y |
| 2 Franks | Y | Y | Y | N | Y | N | N |
| 3 Shadegg | Y | Y | Y | N | N | N | N |
| 4 Pastor | Y | Y | N | Y | N | Y | Y |
| 5 Hayworth | Y | Y | Y | N | Y | N | N |
| 6 Flake | N | Y | Y | N | N | N | N |
| 7 Grijalva | Y | Y | N | Y | Y | Y | Y |
| 8 Kolbe | Y | Y | Y | N | N | N | N |
| **ARKANSAS** | | | | | | | |
| 1 Berry | Y | Y | N | Y | N | Y | N |
| 2 Snyder | Y | Y | N | Y | N | Y | N |
| 3 Boozman | Y | + | Y | N | Y | N | N |
| 4 Ross | Y | Y | N | Y | N | Y | N |
| **CALIFORNIA** | | | | | | | |
| 1 Thompson | Y | Y | N | Y | Y | Y | N |
| 2 Herger | Y | Y | Y | N | Y | N | N |
| 3 Lungren | Y | Y | Y | N | N | N | N |
| 4 Doolittle | Y | Y | Y | N | N | N | N |
| 5 Matsui, D. | Y | Y | N | Y | N | Y | Y |
| 6 Woolsey | Y | Y | N | Y | N | Y | Y |
| 7 Miller, George | Y | Y | N | Y | N | Y | N |
| 8 Pelosi | Y | Y | N | Y | N | Y | N |
| 9 Lee | + | + | N | Y | Y | Y | Y |
| 10 Tauscher | Y | Y | N | Y | N | Y | N |
| 11 Pombo | Y | Y | Y | N | N | N | N |
| 12 Lantos | Y | Y | N | Y | N | Y | N |
| 13 Stark | ? | ? | ? | N | Y | Y | Y |
| 14 Eshoo | Y | Y | N | Y | N | Y | Y |
| 15 Honda | Y | Y | N | Y | N | Y | Y |
| 16 Lofgren | Y | Y | N | Y | N | Y | Y |
| 17 Farr | Y | Y | N | Y | N | Y | Y |
| 18 Cardoza | ? | ? | N | Y | Y | Y | N |
| 19 Radanovich | ? | ? | Y | N | Y | N | N |
| 20 Costa | Y | Y | N | Y | Y | Y | Y |
| 21 Nunes | Y | Y | N | N | N | N | N |
| 22 Thomas | Y | Y | ? | N | Y | N | N |
| 23 Capps | Y | Y | N | Y | N | Y | N |
| 24 Gallegly | Y | Y | N | N | N | N | N |
| 25 McKeon | Y | Y | Y | N | N | N | N |
| 26 Dreier | Y | Y | Y | N | N | N | N |
| 27 Sherman | Y | Y | N | Y | N | Y | N |
| 28 Berman | Y | Y | N | Y | N | Y | N |
| 29 Schiff | Y | Y | N | Y | Y | Y | N |
| 30 Waxman | Y | Y | N | Y | N | Y | N |
| 31 Becerra | Y | Y | N | Y | N | Y | N |
| 32 Solis | Y | Y | N | Y | Y | Y | N |
| 33 Watson | Y | Y | N | Y | N | Y | Y |
| 34 Roybal-Allard | Y | Y | N | Y | N | Y | Y |
| 35 Waters | ? | ? | N | N | Y | Y | N |
| 36 Harman | Y | Y | N | Y | N | Y | N |
| 37 Millender-McD. | Y | Y | N | Y | Y | Y | N |
| 38 Napolitano | Y | Y | N | Y | N | Y | N |
| 39 Sánchez, Linda | + | + | N | Y | N | Y | N |
| 40 Royce | Y | Y | Y | N | N | N | N |
| 41 Lewis | Y | Y | N | N | N | N | N |
| 42 Miller, Gary | Y | Y | N | Y | Y | Y | Y |
| 43 Baca | Y | Y | N | Y | Y | Y | N |
| 44 Calvert | Y | Y | N | Y | N | N | N |
| 45 Bono | Y | Y | N | Y | N | N | N |
| 46 Rohrabacher | Y | Y | N | N | N | N | N |
| 47 Sanchez, Loretta | ? | ? | N | Y | N | Y | N |
| 48 Cox | Y | Y | Y | ? | ? | ? | ? |
| 49 Issa | Y | Y | Y | N | N | N | N |

| | 241 | 242 | 243 | 244 | 245 | 246 | 247 |
|---|---|---|---|---|---|---|---|
| 50 Cunningham | Y | Y | Y | N | N | N | N |
| 51 Filner | Y | Y | N | Y | N | Y | Y |
| 52 Hunter | Y | Y | Y | N | N | N | N |
| 53 Davis | Y | Y | N | Y | N | Y | N |
| **COLORADO** | | | | | | | |
| 1 DeGette | Y | Y | N | Y | Y | Y | Y |
| 2 Udall | + | + | N | N | Y | Y | N |
| 3 Salazar | Y | Y | N | Y | N | Y | N |
| 4 Musgrave | Y | Y | Y | N | Y | N | N |
| 5 Hefley | Y | Y | Y | N | N | N | N |
| 6 Tancredo | Y | Y | Y | N | ? | N | N |
| 7 Beauprez | Y | Y | Y | N | Y | N | N |
| **CONNECTICUT** | | | | | | | |
| 1 Larson | Y | Y | - | Y | N | Y | N |
| 2 Simmons | ? | ? | Y | Y | Y | N | Y |
| 3 DeLauro | Y | Y | N | Y | N | Y | N |
| 4 Shays | ? | Y | Y | Y | N | N | N |
| 5 Johnson | Y | Y | Y | N | N | N | N |
| **DELAWARE** | | | | | | | |
| AL Castle | Y | Y | Y | N | N | N | N |
| **FLORIDA** | | | | | | | |
| 1 Miller | Y | Y | Y | N | N | N | N |
| 2 Boyd | Y | Y | N | Y | N | Y | N |
| 3 Brown | Y | Y | N | Y | N | Y | N |
| 4 Crenshaw | Y | Y | Y | N | Y | N | N |
| 5 Brown-Waite | Y | Y | N | Y | N | Y | N |
| 6 Stearns | Y | Y | Y | Y | N | Y | Y |
| 7 Mica | Y | Y | Y | N | N | N | N |
| 8 Keller | ? | ? | Y | N | N | N | N |
| 9 Bilirakis | Y | Y | Y | N | N | N | N |
| 10 Young | ? | ? | ? | N | N | N | N |
| 11 Davis | ? | ? | N | Y | N | Y | N |
| 12 Putnam | Y | Y | Y | N | N | N | N |
| 13 Harris | Y | Y | Y | N | N | N | N |
| 14 Mack | Y | Y | ? | N | N | N | N |
| 15 Weldon | Y | Y | Y | N | N | N | N |
| 16 Foley | Y | Y | Y | N | N | N | N |
| 17 Meek | ? | ? | N | Y | N | Y | Y |
| 18 Ros-Lehtinen | ? | ? | N | Y | N | N | N |
| 19 Wexler | Y | Y | N | Y | N | Y | N |
| 20 Wasserman-Schultz | Y | Y | N | Y | N | Y | N |
| 21 Diaz-Balart, L. | Y | Y | Y | N | N | N | N |
| 22 Shaw | Y | Y | Y | N | N | N | N |
| 23 Hastings | Y | Y | N | Y | N | Y | N |
| 24 Feeney | Y | Y | Y | N | N | N | N |
| 25 Diaz-Balart, M. | Y | Y | Y | N | N | N | N |
| **GEORGIA** | | | | | | | |
| 1 Kingston | Y | Y | Y | N | N | N | N |
| 2 Bishop | Y | Y | N | Y | N | Y | N |
| 3 Marshall | Y | Y | Y | Y | Y | Y | N |
| 4 McKinney | Y | Y | N | Y | N | Y | Y |
| 5 Lewis | ? | ? | N | Y | Y | Y | N |
| 6 Price | Y | Y | Y | N | N | N | N |
| 7 Linder | Y | Y | Y | N | N | N | N |
| 8 Westmoreland | Y | Y | Y | N | N | N | N |
| 9 Norwood | Y | Y | Y | N | N | N | N |
| 10 Deal | Y | Y | Y | N | N | N | N |
| 11 Gingrey | Y | ? | Y | N | N | N | N |
| 12 Barrow | Y | Y | N | Y | Y | Y | N |
| 13 Scott | Y | Y | N | Y | Y | Y | N |
| **HAWAII** | | | | | | | |
| 1 Abercrombie | Y | Y | N | Y | N | Y | N |
| 2 Case | ? | ? | N | Y | Y | Y | N |
| **IDAHO** | | | | | | | |
| 1 Otter | Y | Y | Y | N | Y | N | Y |
| 2 Simpson | Y | Y | Y | N | N | N | N |
| **ILLINOIS** | | | | | | | |
| 1 Rush | ? | ? | N | Y | Y | Y | N |
| 2 Jackson | Y | Y | N | Y | Y | Y | N |
| 3 Lipinski | Y | Y | N | Y | Y | Y | Y |
| 4 Gutierrez | + | + | N | Y | N | Y | N |
| 5 Emanuel | Y | Y | N | Y | N | Y | N |
| 6 Hyde | Y | Y | Y | N | N | N | N |
| 7 Davis | Y | Y | N | Y | N | Y | N |
| 8 Bean | Y | Y | N | Y | N | Y | N |
| 9 Schakowsky | Y | Y | N | Y | N | Y | Y |
| 10 Kirk | Y | Y | Y | N | N | N | N |
| 11 Weller | Y | Y | Y | N | N | N | N |
| 12 Costello | Y | Y | N | Y | Y | Y | Y |

| KEY | Republicans | Democrats | Independents |
|---|---|---|---|

| | | |
|---|---|---|
| Y Voted for (yea) | X Paired against | C Voted "present" to avoid possible conflict of interest |
| # Paired for | − Announced against | |
| + Announced for | P Voted "present" | ? Did not vote or otherwise make a position known |
| N Voted against (nay) | | |

| | 241 | 242 | 243 | 244 | 245 | 246 | 247 |
|---|---|---|---|---|---|---|---|
| 13 **Biggert** | Y | Y | Y | N | N | N | N |
| 14 **Hastert** | | | | | | | |
| 15 **Johnson** | Y | Y | Y | N | Y | N | Y |
| 16 **Manzullo** | Y | Y | Y | N | N | N | N |
| 17 Evans | Y | Y | N | Y | N | Y | Y |
| 18 **LaHood** | ? | ? | Y | N | N | N | N |
| 19 **Shimkus** | ? | ? | Y | N | Y | N | Y |
| **INDIANA** | | | | | | | |
| 1 Visclosky | Y | Y | N | Y | N | Y | N |
| 2 **Chocola** | Y | Y | Y | N | Y | N | Y |
| 3 **Souder** | Y | Y | Y | N | Y | N | Y |
| 4 **Buyer** | ? | ? | ? | N | N | N | N |
| 5 **Burton** | Y | Y | Y | N | Y | N | N |
| 6 **Pence** | Y | ? | Y | N | Y | N | N |
| 7 Carson | Y | Y | N | Y | Y | Y | N |
| 8 **Hostettler** | Y | Y | Y | N | N | N | N |
| 9 **Sodrel** | Y | Y | Y | N | N | N | N |
| **IOWA** | | | | | | | |
| 1 **Nussle** | Y | Y | Y | N | Y | N | N |
| 2 **Leach** | Y | Y | Y | N | Y | Y | N |
| 3 Boswell | ? | ? | N | Y | Y | Y | N |
| 4 **Latham** | Y | Y | Y | Y | Y | N | N |
| 5 **King** | Y | Y | Y | N | Y | N | Y |
| **KANSAS** | | | | | | | |
| 1 **Moran** | Y | Y | Y | N | Y | Y | Y |
| 2 **Ryun** | Y | Y | Y | N | N | N | N |
| 3 Moore | Y | Y | N | Y | Y | Y | N |
| 4 **Tiahrt** | Y | Y | Y | N | N | N | N |
| **KENTUCKY** | | | | | | | |
| 1 **Whitfield** | Y | Y | Y | N | N | Y | N |
| 2 **Lewis** | Y | Y | Y | N | Y | N | N |
| 3 **Northup** | Y | Y | Y | N | N | N | N |
| 4 **Davis** | Y | Y | Y | N | Y | N | Y |
| 5 **Rogers** | Y | Y | Y | N | N | N | N |
| 6 Chandler | Y | Y | N | Y | Y | Y | Y |
| **LOUISIANA** | | | | | | | |
| 1 **Jindal** | Y | Y | Y | N | Y | N | N |
| 2 Jefferson | Y | Y | N | Y | N | Y | Y |
| 3 Melancon | Y | Y | N | Y | Y | Y | Y |
| 4 **McCrery** | Y | Y | ? | Y | Y | ? | Y |
| 5 **Alexander** | Y | Y | Y | N | N | N | N |
| 6 **Baker** | ? | ? | Y | N | Y | N | N |
| 7 **Boustany** | Y | Y | Y | N | Y | N | N |
| **MAINE** | | | | | | | |
| 1 Allen | Y | Y | N | Y | N | Y | Y |
| 2 Michaud | Y | Y | N | Y | N | Y | Y |
| **MARYLAND** | | | | | | | |
| 1 **Gilchrest** | Y | Y | Y | N | N | N | N |
| 2 Ruppersberger | Y | Y | N | Y | Y | Y | N |
| 3 Cardin | Y | Y | N | Y | Y | Y | N |
| 4 Wynn | Y | Y | N | Y | Y | Y | N |
| 5 Hoyer | ? | ? | N | Y | N | Y | N |
| 6 **Bartlett** | Y | Y | Y | N | N | N | N |
| 7 Cummings | Y | Y | ? | Y | Y | Y | N |
| 8 Van Hollen | Y | Y | N | Y | Y | Y | N |
| **MASSACHUSETTS** | | | | | | | |
| 1 Olver | Y | Y | N | Y | N | Y | Y |
| 2 Neal | ? | ? | N | Y | N | Y | Y |
| 3 McGovern | Y | Y | N | Y | N | Y | N |
| 4 Frank | Y | Y | N | Y | N | Y | Y |
| 5 Meehan | Y | Y | N | Y | Y | Y | Y |
| 6 Tierney | Y | Y | N | Y | N | Y | Y |
| 7 Markey | Y | Y | N | Y | N | Y | N |
| 8 Capuano | Y | Y | N | Y | Y | Y | N |
| 9 Lynch | Y | Y | N | Y | Y | Y | N |
| 10 Delahunt | ? | ? | N | Y | Y | Y | N |
| **MICHIGAN** | | | | | | | |
| 1 Stupak | Y | Y | N | Y | Y | Y | N |
| 2 **Hoekstra** | Y | Y | Y | N | N | N | N |
| 3 **Ehlers** | + | + | Y | N | N | N | Y |
| 4 **Camp** | Y | Y | Y | Y | N | N | N |
| 5 Kildee | Y | Y | N | Y | N | Y | N |
| 6 **Upton** | Y | Y | Y | Y | Y | N | Y |
| 7 **Schwarz** | Y | Y | Y | N | N | N | N |
| 8 **Rogers** | Y | Y | Y | N | Y | N | N |
| 9 **Knollenberg** | + | + | + | N | N | N | N |
| 10 **Miller** | Y | Y | Y | N | N | N | N |
| 11 **McCotter** | Y | Y | Y | N | Y | Y | N |
| 12 Levin | Y | Y | N | Y | N | Y | N |
| 13 Kilpatrick | + | + | N | Y | N | Y | N |
| 14 Conyers | Y | Y | N | Y | N | ? | Y |
| 15 Dingell | ? | ? | N | Y | N | Y | N |

| | 241 | 242 | 243 | 244 | 245 | 246 | 247 |
|---|---|---|---|---|---|---|---|
| **MINNESOTA** | | | | | | | |
| 1 **Gutknecht** | Y | Y | Y | N | Y | N | N |
| 2 **Kline** | Y | Y | Y | N | Y | Y | N |
| 3 **Ramstad** | Y | Y | Y | Y | Y | Y | Y |
| 4 McCollum | Y | Y | N | Y | N | Y | N |
| 5 Sabo | Y | Y | N | Y | N | Y | N |
| 6 **Kennedy** | Y | Y | Y | N | Y | Y | Y |
| 7 Peterson | Y | Y | N | Y | N | Y | Y |
| 8 Oberstar | ? | ? | ? | ? | ? | ? | ? |
| **MISSISSIPPI** | | | | | | | |
| 1 **Wicker** | Y | Y | Y | N | N | N | N |
| 2 Thompson | Y | Y | N | Y | N | Y | N |
| 3 **Pickering** | Y | Y | Y | N | N | N | N |
| 4 Taylor | Y | Y | N | N | Y | Y | N |
| **MISSOURI** | | | | | | | |
| 1 Clay | Y | Y | N | Y | N | Y | Y |
| 2 **Akin** | Y | Y | Y | N | N | N | N |
| 3 Carnahan | Y | Y | N | Y | Y | Y | Y |
| 4 Skelton | Y | Y | N | Y | Y | Y | N |
| 5 Cleaver | Y | Y | N | Y | N | Y | N |
| 6 **Graves** | Y | Y | Y | N | Y | Y | N |
| 7 **Blunt** | Y | Y | Y | N | N | N | N |
| 8 **Emerson** | Y | Y | Y | N | Y | N | N |
| 9 **Hulshof** | ? | ? | Y | N | Y | Y | N |
| **MONTANA** | | | | | | | |
| AL **Rehberg** | Y | Y | Y | N | N | N | N |
| **NEBRASKA** | | | | | | | |
| 1 **Fortenberry** | Y | Y | Y | N | Y | N | Y |
| 2 **Terry** | Y | Y | Y | N | Y | N | Y |
| 3 **Osborne** | Y | Y | Y | N | Y | N | Y |
| **NEVADA** | | | | | | | |
| 1 Berkley | ? | ? | N | Y | N | Y | N |
| 2 **Gibbons** | Y | Y | Y | Y | Y | N | N |
| 3 **Porter** | Y | Y | Y | N | Y | Y | Y |
| **NEW HAMPSHIRE** | | | | | | | |
| 1 **Bradley** | Y | Y | Y | N | N | Y | N |
| 2 **Bass** | Y | Y | Y | N | N | N | N |
| **NEW JERSEY** | | | | | | | |
| 1 Andrews | Y | Y | N | Y | N | Y | N |
| 2 **LoBiondo** | Y | Y | Y | N | Y | Y | Y |
| 3 **Saxton** | Y | Y | Y | N | N | N | N |
| 4 **Smith** | Y | Y | Y | Y | N | N | N |
| 5 **Garrett** | Y | Y | Y | N | N | N | N |
| 6 Pallone | Y | Y | N | Y | Y | Y | Y |
| 7 **Ferguson** | Y | Y | Y | N | N | N | N |
| 8 Pascrell | ? | ? | ? | Y | Y | Y | N |
| 9 Rothman | ? | ? | ? | ? | ? | ? | ? |
| 10 Payne | ? | ? | N | Y | N | Y | Y |
| 11 **Frelinghuysen** | Y | Y | Y | N | N | N | N |
| 12 Holt | Y | Y | N | Y | N | Y | N |
| 13 Menendez | Y | Y | N | Y | N | Y | N |
| **NEW MEXICO** | | | | | | | |
| 1 **Wilson** | Y | Y | Y | Y | N | Y | N |
| 2 **Pearce** | Y | Y | Y | N | N | N | N |
| 3 Udall | Y | Y | N | Y | Y | Y | N |
| **NEW YORK** | | | | | | | |
| 1 Bishop | Y | Y | N | Y | Y | Y | Y |
| 2 Israel | Y | Y | N | Y | Y | Y | N |
| 3 **King** | Y | Y | Y | Y | Y | Y | N |
| 4 McCarthy | Y | Y | N | Y | Y | Y | N |
| 5 Ackerman | Y | Y | N | Y | Y | Y | Y |
| 6 Meeks | Y | Y | N | Y | Y | Y | Y |
| 7 Crowley | ? | ? | N | Y | Y | Y | Y |
| 8 Nadler | ? | ? | N | Y | N | Y | Y |
| 9 Weiner | Y | Y | N | Y | Y | Y | Y |
| 10 Towns | ? | ? | N | Y | Y | Y | Y |
| 11 Owens | ? | ? | ? | Y | N | Y | Y |
| 12 Velázquez | Y | Y | N | Y | N | Y | N |
| 13 **Fossella** | + | + | Y | Y | Y | N | N |
| 14 Maloney | Y | Y | N | Y | N | Y | N |
| 15 Rangel | Y | Y | N | Y | N | Y | N |
| 16 Serrano | Y | Y | N | Y | N | Y | N |
| 17 Engel | Y | Y | N | Y | Y | Y | Y |
| 18 Lowey | Y | Y | N | Y | N | Y | N |
| 19 **Kelly** | Y | Y | Y | N | Y | Y | Y |
| 20 **Sweeney** | ? | ? | ? | N | N | N | N |
| 21 McNulty | Y | Y | N | Y | Y | Y | Y |
| 22 Hinchey | Y | Y | N | Y | Y | Y | N |
| 23 **McHugh** | Y | Y | Y | N | N | N | N |
| 24 **Boehlert** | Y | Y | Y | N | N | N | N |
| 25 **Walsh** | Y | Y | Y | N | N | N | N |
| 26 **Reynolds** | Y | Y | Y | N | N | N | Y |
| 27 Higgins | Y | Y | N | Y | N | Y | N |
| 28 Slaughter | Y | Y | N | Y | N | Y | Y |
| 29 **Kuhl** | Y | Y | Y | N | N | Y | N |

| | 241 | 242 | 243 | 244 | 245 | 246 | 247 |
|---|---|---|---|---|---|---|---|
| **NORTH CAROLINA** | | | | | | | |
| 1 Butterfield | Y | Y | N | Y | N | Y | N |
| 2 Etheridge | Y | Y | N | Y | Y | Y | Y |
| 3 **Jones** | Y | Y | Y | N | Y | N | Y |
| 4 Price | Y | Y | N | Y | N | Y | N |
| 5 **Foxx** | Y | Y | Y | N | Y | N | N |
| 6 **Coble** | Y | Y | Y | N | Y | N | N |
| 7 McIntyre | Y | Y | N | Y | Y | Y | N |
| 8 **Hayes** | Y | Y | Y | N | N | Y | Y |
| 9 **Myrick** | Y | Y | Y | N | N | N | Y |
| 10 **McHenry** | Y | Y | Y | N | Y | N | Y |
| 11 **Taylor** | Y | Y | Y | N | N | N | N |
| 12 Watt | Y | Y | N | Y | Y | Y | N |
| 13 Miller | Y | Y | N | N | N | Y | N |
| **NORTH DAKOTA** | | | | | | | |
| AL Pomeroy | Y | Y | N | Y | Y | Y | Y |
| **OHIO** | | | | | | | |
| 1 **Chabot** | Y | Y | Y | Y | Y | N | N |
| 2 Vacant | | | | | | | |
| 3 **Turner** | Y | Y | Y | N | N | Y | N |
| 4 **Oxley** | ? | ? | Y | N | N | N | N |
| 5 **Gillmor** | Y | Y | Y | N | N | N | N |
| 6 Strickland | ? | ? | ? | ? | ? | ? | ? |
| 7 **Hobson** | Y | Y | Y | N | N | N | N |
| 8 **Boehner** | Y | Y | Y | N | N | N | N |
| 9 Kaptur | Y | Y | N | Y | Y | Y | Y |
| 10 Kucinich | Y | Y | N | N | N | Y | N |
| 11 Jones | Y | Y | ? | N | Y | Y | N |
| 12 **Tiberi** | Y | Y | Y | N | N | N | N |
| 13 Brown | Y | Y | N | Y | Y | Y | Y |
| 14 **LaTourette** | Y | Y | Y | N | N | Y | N |
| 15 **Pryce** | Y | Y | Y | N | N | N | N |
| 16 **Regula** | Y | Y | Y | N | N | N | N |
| 17 Ryan | Y | Y | N | Y | Y | Y | N |
| 18 **Ney** | Y | Y | Y | N | Y | Y | N |
| **OKLAHOMA** | | | | | | | |
| 1 **Sullivan** | ? | ? | Y | N | Y | N | N |
| 2 Boren | Y | Y | N | N | Y | Y | N |
| 3 **Lucas** | Y | Y | Y | N | N | N | N |
| 4 **Cole** | Y | Y | Y | N | N | Y | N |
| 5 **Istook** | ? | ? | Y | N | N | N | N |
| **OREGON** | | | | | | | |
| 1 Wu | Y | Y | N | Y | Y | Y | N |
| 2 **Walden** | Y | Y | Y | N | Y | N | Y |
| 3 Blumenauer | Y | Y | N | Y | N | Y | N |
| 4 DeFazio | Y | Y | N | Y | Y | Y | N |
| 5 Hooley | Y | Y | N | Y | Y | Y | Y |
| **PENNSYLVANIA** | | | | | | | |
| 1 Brady | Y | Y | N | N | N | Y | Y |
| 2 Fattah | ? | ? | N | Y | N | Y | Y |
| 3 **English** | Y | Y | Y | N | N | N | Y |
| 4 **Hart** | Y | Y | Y | N | N | N | N |
| 5 **Peterson** | ? | ? | ? | ? | Y | N | N |
| 6 **Gerlach** | Y | Y | Y | Y | Y | N | Y |
| 7 **Weldon** | Y | Y | Y | N | N | Y | N |
| 8 **Fitzpatrick** | Y | Y | Y | Y | Y | N | Y |
| 9 **Shuster** | Y | Y | Y | N | Y | N | N |
| 10 **Sherwood** | Y | Y | Y | N | N | N | N |
| 11 Kanjorski | Y | Y | N | N | N | Y | Y |
| 12 Murtha | ? | ? | N | N | N | Y | Y |
| 13 Schwartz | Y | Y | N | Y | N | Y | Y |
| 14 Doyle | Y | Y | N | N | Y | Y | Y |
| 15 **Dent** | Y | Y | Y | Y | N | N | N |
| 16 **Pitts** | Y | Y | Y | N | Y | N | N |
| 17 Holden | Y | Y | N | Y | Y | Y | Y |
| 18 **Murphy** | Y | Y | Y | N | Y | N | Y |
| 19 **Platts** | Y | Y | Y | Y | Y | Y | Y |
| **RHODE ISLAND** | | | | | | | |
| 1 Kennedy | + | + | N | Y | N | Y | N |
| 2 Langevin | Y | Y | N | Y | N | Y | N |
| **SOUTH CAROLINA** | | | | | | | |
| 1 **Brown** | Y | Y | Y | N | N | N | Y |
| 2 **Wilson** | Y | Y | Y | N | N | N | Y |
| 3 **Barrett** | Y | Y | Y | N | Y | N | N |
| 4 **Inglis** | Y | Y | Y | N | N | N | N |
| 5 Spratt | Y | Y | N | Y | N | Y | N |
| 6 Clyburn | ? | ? | N | Y | N | Y | N |
| **SOUTH DAKOTA** | | | | | | | |
| AL Herseth | Y | Y | N | Y | Y | Y | N |
| **TENNESSEE** | | | | | | | |
| 1 **Jenkins** | ? | ? | Y | N | Y | N | N |
| 2 **Duncan** | Y | Y | Y | N | Y | N | Y |

| | 241 | 242 | 243 | 244 | 245 | 246 | 247 |
|---|---|---|---|---|---|---|---|
| 3 **Wamp** | Y | Y | Y | N | Y | N | Y |
| 4 Davis | Y | Y | N | N | N | Y | N |
| 5 Cooper | ? | ? | N | Y | Y | Y | N |
| 6 Gordon | Y | Y | N | N | N | Y | N |
| 7 **Blackburn** | Y | Y | Y | N | Y | N | N |
| 8 Tanner | Y | Y | N | Y | Y | Y | Y |
| 9 Ford | Y | Y | N | Y | N | Y | Y |
| **TEXAS** | | | | | | | |
| 1 **Gohmert** | Y | Y | Y | Y | Y | Y | N |
| 2 **Poe** | Y | Y | Y | N | Y | N | Y |
| 3 **Johnson, S.** | Y | Y | Y | N | Y | N | N |
| 4 **Hall** | Y | Y | Y | N | N | N | N |
| 5 **Hensarling** | Y | Y | Y | N | N | N | N |
| 6 **Barton** | Y | Y | Y | N | Y | N | N |
| 7 **Culberson** | Y | Y | Y | N | N | N | N |
| 8 **Brady** | Y | Y | Y | N | N | N | N |
| 9 Green, A. | Y | Y | N | N | N | Y | Y |
| 10 **McCaul** | Y | Y | Y | N | N | N | N |
| 11 **Conaway** | Y | Y | Y | N | N | Y | N |
| 12 **Granger** | Y | Y | Y | N | N | N | N |
| 13 **Thornberry** | Y | Y | Y | N | N | N | N |
| 14 **Paul** | N | Y | Y | N | N | Y | Y |
| 15 Hinojosa | ? | ? | ? | ? | ? | ? | ? |
| 16 Reyes | Y | Y | N | N | Y | Y | N |
| 17 Edwards | Y | Y | N | Y | N | Y | N |
| 18 Jackson-Lee | Y | Y | N | N | N | Y | N |
| 19 **Neugebauer** | Y | Y | Y | N | N | N | N |
| 20 Gonzalez | Y | Y | N | N | Y | Y | N |
| 21 **Smith** | Y | Y | Y | N | N | N | N |
| 22 **DeLay** | Y | Y | Y | N | N | N | N |
| 23 **Bonilla** | Y | Y | Y | N | N | N | N |
| 24 **Marchant** | Y | ? | Y | N | Y | Y | N |
| 25 Doggett | Y | Y | N | Y | Y | Y | N |
| 26 **Burgess** | Y | Y | Y | N | N | N | Y |
| 27 Ortiz | Y | Y | N | N | Y | Y | N |
| 28 Cuellar | Y | Y | N | Y | Y | Y | N |
| 29 Green, G. | Y | Y | N | N | Y | Y | Y |
| 30 Johnson, E. | Y | Y | N | Y | N | Y | N |
| 31 **Carter** | Y | Y | Y | N | N | N | N |
| 32 **Sessions** | ? | ? | ? | ? | ? | ? | ? |
| **UTAH** | | | | | | | |
| 1 **Bishop** | Y | Y | Y | N | Y | N | Y |
| 2 Matheson | Y | Y | N | Y | Y | Y | Y |
| 3 **Cannon** | Y | Y | Y | N | Y | N | N |
| **VERMONT** | | | | | | | |
| AL *Sanders* | Y | Y | N | Y | N | Y | N |
| **VIRGINIA** | | | | | | | |
| 1 **Davis, J.** | Y | Y | Y | N | N | N | N |
| 2 **Drake** | Y | Y | Y | N | N | N | N |
| 3 Scott | Y | Y | N | Y | N | Y | N |
| 4 **Forbes** | Y | Y | Y | N | N | N | N |
| 5 **Goode** | Y | Y | Y | N | N | N | N |
| 6 **Goodlatte** | Y | Y | Y | N | N | N | N |
| 7 **Cantor** | Y | Y | Y | N | N | N | N |
| 8 Moran | Y | Y | N | Y | N | Y | Y |
| 9 Boucher | Y | Y | ? | Y | Y | Y | Y |
| 10 **Wolf** | Y | Y | Y | N | N | N | N |
| 11 **Davis, T.** | Y | Y | Y | N | N | N | N |
| **WASHINGTON** | | | | | | | |
| 1 Inslee | Y | Y | N | Y | Y | Y | Y |
| 2 Larsen | ? | ? | N | Y | Y | Y | Y |
| 3 Baird | Y | Y | N | Y | N | Y | N |
| 4 **Hastings** | Y | Y | Y | N | N | N | Y |
| 5 **McMorris** | Y | Y | Y | N | Y | Y | Y |
| 6 Dicks | Y | Y | N | Y | N | Y | N |
| 7 McDermott | Y | Y | N | Y | N | Y | N |
| 8 **Reichert** | Y | Y | Y | N | Y | N | Y |
| 9 Smith | Y | Y | N | Y | Y | Y | Y |
| **WEST VIRGINIA** | | | | | | | |
| 1 Mollohan | Y | Y | N | N | N | Y | N |
| 2 **Capito** | ? | ? | Y | N | N | Y | N |
| 3 Rahall | Y | Y | N | Y | N | Y | Y |
| **WISCONSIN** | | | | | | | |
| 1 **Ryan** | Y | Y | Y | N | Y | ? | Y |
| 2 Baldwin | Y | Y | N | Y | Y | Y | Y |
| 3 Kind | Y | Y | N | Y | N | Y | N |
| 4 Moore | ? | ? | N | Y | Y | Y | Y |
| 5 **Sensenbrenner** | Y | Y | Y | N | Y | N | N |
| 6 **Petri** | Y | Y | Y | N | Y | N | Y |
| 7 Obey | Y | Y | N | Y | N | Y | N |
| 8 **Green** | + | + | Y | Y | Y | Y | Y |
| **WYOMING** | | | | | | | |
| AL **Cubin** | Y | Y | Y | N | Y | Y | Y |

# IN THE HOUSE | By Vote Number

**248.** HR 2862. Fiscal 2006 Commerce-Justice-Science Appropriations/ **Law and Drug Enforcement Funding.** Baird, D-Wash., amendment that would increase funding for Community Oriented Policing Services programs by $10 million and the Drug Enforcement Administration by $10 million. It would be offset by a $10 million cut in funding for the 2010 decennial census and a $10 million decrease for salaries and expenses at the Bureau of the Census. Adopted 260-168: R 96-133; D 163-35 (ND 122-26, SD 41-9); I 1-0. June 14, 2005.

**249.** HR 2862. Fiscal 2006 Commerce-Justice-Science Appropriations/ **Justice Assistance Grants.** Stearns, R-Fla., amendment that would increase funding for Justice Assistance Grants by $10 million, offset by a reduction for the Legal Services Corporation. Rejected 112-316: R 109-120; D 3-195 (ND 0-148, SD 3-47); I 0-1. June 14, 2005.

**250.** HR 2862. Fiscal 2006 Commerce-Justice-Science Appropriations/ **State Criminal Alien Assistance Program.** Dreier, R-Calif., amendment that would increase funding for the State Criminal Alien Assistance Program by $50 million, offset by a reduction for operations, research and facilities at the National Oceanic and Atmospheric Administration. Adopted 231-195: R 178-50; D 53-144 (ND 40-107, SD 13-37); I 0-1. June 14, 2005.

**251.** HR 2862. Fiscal 2006 Commerce-Justice-Science Appropriations/ **Community Oriented Policing Services.** Weiner, D-N.Y., amendment that would increase funding for the Community Oriented Policing Services program by $126.2 million, offset with cuts to the National Science Foundation. Rejected 31-396: R 6-221; D 25-174 (ND 21-129, SD 4-45); I 0-1. June 15, 2005.

**252.** HR 2862. Fiscal 2006 Commerce-Justice-Science Appropriations/ **NOAA Funding.** Inslee, D-Wash., amendment that would increase funding for the National Oceanic and Atmospheric Administration Operations, Research and Facilities account by $5 million, offset by reductions related to export control functions at the Department of Commerce. Rejected 177-248: R 26-200; D 150-48 (ND 117-31, SD 33-17); I 1-0. June 15, 2005.

**253** HR 2862. Fiscal 2006 Commerce-Justice-Science Appropriations/ **U.N. Contribution Decrease.** Hayworth, R-Ariz., amendment that would cut the U.S. contribution to the United Nations by $218 million. Rejected 124-304: R 120-107; D 4-196 (ND 1-149, SD 3-47); I 0-1. June 15. 2005.

**254.** HR 2862. Fiscal 2006 Commerce-Justice-Science Appropriations/ **Cuban Gift and Humanitarian Donations.** Flake, R-Ariz., amendment that would prohibit the use of funds in the bill to implement, administer or enforce regulations related to license exemptions for gift parcels and humanitarian donations for Cuba. Rejected 210-216: R 35-190; D 174-26 (ND 134-16, SD 40-10); I 1-0. A "nay" was a vote in support of the president's position. June 15, 2005.

| | 248 | 249 | 250 | 251 | 252 | 253 | 254 |
|---|---|---|---|---|---|---|---|
| **ALABAMA** | | | | | | | |
| 1 Bonner | Y | N | N | N | N | Y | Y |
| 2 Everett | Y | Y | N | N | N | Y | Y |
| 3 Rogers | Y | N | N | N | N | Y | N |
| 4 Aderholt | N | Y | N | N | N | N | N |
| 5 Cramer | N | N | N | N | N | N | Y |
| 6 Bachus | N | N | ? | N | ? | Y | N |
| 7 Davis | Y | N | N | N | N | N | N |
| **ALASKA** | | | | | | | |
| AL Young | N | N | Y | N | N | Y | N |
| **ARIZONA** | | | | | | | |
| 1 Renzi | Y | N | Y | Y | N | Y | N |
| 2 Franks | N | Y | Y | N | N | Y | N |
| 3 Shadegg | Y | Y | Y | N | N | N | N |
| 4 Pastor | Y | N | Y | N | N | Y | Y |
| 5 Hayworth | Y | N | Y | N | N | Y | N |
| 6 Flake | N | Y | Y | N | N | N | N |
| 7 Grijalva | Y | N | Y | N | Y | N | Y |
| 8 Kolbe | N | N | Y | N | N | N | Y |
| **ARKANSAS** | | | | | | | |
| 1 Berry | N | N | N | N | N | N | Y |
| 2 Snyder | Y | N | N | N | N | N | Y |
| 3 Boozman | Y | Y | Y | N | N | Y | Y |
| 4 Ross | Y | N | N | N | N | N | Y |
| **CALIFORNIA** | | | | | | | |
| 1 Thompson | Y | N | N | N | Y | N | Y |
| 2 Herger | Y | Y | Y | N | N | Y | N |
| 3 Lungren | N | Y | Y | N | N | N | N |
| 4 Doolittle | N | Y | Y | N | N | N | N |
| 5 Matsui, D. | Y | N | N | N | Y | N | Y |
| 6 Woolsey | Y | N | N | N | Y | N | Y |
| 7 Miller, George | Y | N | N | N | Y | N | Y |
| 8 Pelosi | Y | N | N | N | Y | N | Y |
| 9 Lee | N | N | N | N | Y | N | Y |
| 10 Tauscher | Y | N | N | N | Y | N | Y |
| 11 Pombo | Y | Y | Y | N | N | Y | N |
| 12 Lantos | Y | N | N | N | Y | N | Y |
| 13 Stark | N | N | Y | N | Y | N | Y |
| 14 Eshoo | Y | N | N | N | Y | N | Y |
| 15 Honda | Y | N | N | N | Y | N | Y |
| 16 Lofgren | Y | N | N | N | Y | N | Y |
| 17 Farr | Y | N | N | N | Y | N | Y |
| 18 Cardoza | Y | N | Y | N | ? | N | N |
| 19 Radanovich | Y | Y | Y | N | N | N | N |
| 20 Costa | Y | N | N | N | Y | N | N |
| 21 Nunes | N | Y | Y | N | N | N | N |
| 22 Thomas | N | Y | Y | N | N | N | N |
| 23 Capps | N | N | N | N | Y | N | Y |
| 24 Gallegly | N | N | Y | N | N | N | N |
| 25 McKeon | N | N | Y | N | N | N | N |
| 26 Dreier | N | N | Y | N | N | N | N |
| 27 Sherman | Y | N | N | N | Y | N | Y |
| 28 Berman | Y | N | N | N | Y | N | Y |
| 29 Schiff | Y | N | N | N | Y | N | N |
| 30 Waxman | Y | N | N | N | Y | N | Y |
| 31 Becerra | Y | N | N | N | Y | N | Y |
| 32 Solis | Y | N | N | N | Y | N | Y |
| 33 Watson | N | N | N | N | Y | N | Y |
| 34 Roybal-Allard | N | N | Y | N | Y | N | Y |
| 35 Waters | N | N | N | N | Y | N | Y |
| 36 Harman | Y | N | N | N | Y | N | Y |
| 37 Millender-McD. | N | N | N | N | Y | N | Y |
| 38 Napolitano | N | N | N | N | Y | N | Y |
| 39 Sánchez, Linda | Y | N | N | N | Y | N | Y |
| 40 Royce | N | Y | Y | N | N | Y | N |
| 41 Lewis | N | N | Y | N | N | N | N |
| 42 Miller, Gary | N | Y | Y | N | N | N | N |
| 43 Baca | Y | N | Y | N | Y | N | Y |
| 44 Calvert | N | Y | Y | N | N | N | N |
| 45 Bono | N | N | Y | N | N | Y | Y |
| 46 Rohrabacher | N | Y | Y | N | N | Y | N |
| 47 Sanchez, Loretta | N | N | N | N | N | N | Y |
| 48 Cox | N | Y | Y | N | N | ? | N |
| 49 Issa | N | Y | Y | N | N | N | N |

| | 248 | 249 | 250 | 251 | 252 | 253 | 254 |
|---|---|---|---|---|---|---|---|
| 50 Cunningham | N | Y | Y | N | N | Y | N |
| 51 Filner | Y | N | Y | N | Y | N | Y |
| 52 Hunter | N | Y | Y | N | N | Y | N |
| 53 Davis | Y | N | N | N | Y | N | Y |
| **COLORADO** | | | | | | | |
| 1 DeGette | Y | N | N | N | Y | N | Y |
| 2 Udall | Y | N | N | N | N | N | Y |
| 3 Salazar | Y | N | N | N | N | N | N |
| 4 Musgrave | Y | Y | Y | N | N | Y | Y |
| 5 Hefley | Y | N | N | N | Y | N | Y |
| 6 Tancredo | N | Y | Y | N | Y | N | N |
| 7 Beauprez | Y | N | N | N | N | N | N |
| **CONNECTICUT** | | | | | | | |
| 1 Larson | Y | N | N | N | Y | N | Y |
| 2 Simmons | N | N | N | Y | N | N | N |
| 3 DeLauro | Y | N | N | N | Y | N | Y |
| 4 Shays | N | N | N | N | Y | N | Y |
| 5 Johnson | N | N | Y | N | Y | N | Y |
| **DELAWARE** | | | | | | | |
| AL Castle | Y | N | N | N | Y | N | Y |
| **FLORIDA** | | | | | | | |
| 1 Miller | N | Y | Y | – | N | Y | N |
| 2 Boyd | Y | N | N | N | N | Y | N |
| 3 Brown | Y | N | N | N | N | N | N |
| 4 Crenshaw | N | N | Y | N | N | N | N |
| 5 Brown-Waite | Y | N | Y | N | Y | N | N |
| 6 Stearns | Y | Y | Y | N | N | Y | Y |
| 7 Mica | Y | Y | Y | N | N | Y | N |
| 8 Keller | Y | Y | N | N | N | Y | N |
| 9 Bilirakis | Y | Y | Y | N | N | Y | N |
| 10 Young | N | N | N | N | N | Y | N |
| 11 Davis | Y | N | N | N | Y | N | Y |
| 12 Putnam | N | Y | Y | N | N | N | N |
| 13 Harris | Y | N | N | N | Y | N | N |
| 14 Mack | N | Y | Y | N | N | N | N |
| 15 Weldon | N | N | N | N | N | N | N |
| 16 Foley | Y | Y | N | N | N | Y | N |
| 17 Meek | Y | N | N | N | Y | N | Y |
| 18 Ros-Lehtinen | N | N | N | N | N | Y | N |
| 19 Wexler | Y | N | N | N | Y | N | Y |
| 20 Wasserman-Schultz | Y | N | N | N | N | N | Y |
| 21 Diaz-Balart, L. | N | Y | Y | N | N | Y | N |
| 22 Shaw | Y | N | Y | N | N | Y | N |
| 23 Hastings | N | N | N | Y | N | N | Y |
| 24 Feeney | N | Y | N | N | N | Y | N |
| 25 Diaz-Balart, M. | N | N | Y | N | N | N | N |
| **GEORGIA** | | | | | | | |
| 1 Kingston | Y | N | N | N | N | Y | N |
| 2 Bishop | N | N | N | N | N | N | Y |
| 3 Marshall | Y | N | N | N | Y | N | Y |
| 4 McKinney | Y | N | N | N | Y | N | Y |
| 5 Lewis | Y | N | N | N | Y | N | Y |
| 6 Price | Y | Y | N | N | N | Y | N |
| 7 Linder | N | Y | Y | N | N | Y | N |
| 8 Westmoreland | Y | Y | Y | N | N | Y | N |
| 9 Norwood | Y | Y | N | N | N | Y | N |
| 10 Deal | Y | Y | Y | N | N | Y | N |
| 11 Gingrey | Y | Y | Y | N | N | Y | N |
| 12 Barrow | Y | Y | Y | Y | N | Y | N |
| 13 Scott | Y | N | N | N | Y | N | Y |
| **HAWAII** | | | | | | | |
| 1 Abercrombie | Y | N | N | N | Y | N | Y |
| 2 Case | Y | N | N | N | Y | N | N |
| **IDAHO** | | | | | | | |
| 1 Otter | N | Y | Y | N | N | Y | Y |
| 2 Simpson | N | N | Y | N | N | N | N |
| **ILLINOIS** | | | | | | | |
| 1 Rush | Y | N | N | N | Y | N | Y |
| 2 Jackson | Y | N | N | N | Y | N | Y |
| 3 Lipinski | Y | N | Y | N | Y | N | Y |
| 4 Gutierrez | N | N | + | N | Y | N | Y |
| 5 Emanuel | N | N | N | N | Y | N | Y |
| 6 Hyde | N | Y | Y | ? | ? | ? | ? |
| 7 Davis | Y | N | N | N | Y | N | Y |
| 8 Bean | Y | N | N | N | Y | N | Y |
| 9 Schakowsky | N | N | N | N | Y | N | Y |
| 10 Kirk | N | N | N | N | N | N | N |
| 11 Weller | N | N | N | N | N | N | N |
| 12 Costello | Y | N | N | N | Y | N | Y |

| KEY | Republicans | Democrats | *Independents* | | |
|---|---|---|---|---|---|
| Y | Voted for (yea) | X | Paired against | C | Voted "present" to avoid possible conflict of interest |
| # | Paired for | – | Announced against | | |
| + | Announced for | P | Voted "present" | ? | Did not vote or otherwise make a position known |
| N | Voted against (nay) | | | | |

| | 248 | 249 | 250 | 251 | 252 | 253 | 254 |
|---|---|---|---|---|---|---|---|
| 13 **Biggert** | N | N | N | N | N | N | Y |
| 14 **Hastert** | | | | | | | |
| 15 **Johnson** | Y | N | N | N | N | N | Y |
| 16 **Manzullo** | N | N | Y | N | N | Y | N |
| 17 Evans | Y | N | Y | N | N | N | Y |
| 18 **LaHood** | Y | N | Y | N | N | N | Y |
| 19 **Shimkus** | Y | Y | Y | N | ? | N | Y |
| **INDIANA** | | | | | | | |
| 1 Visclosky | N | N | N | N | N | N | Y |
| 2 **Chocola** | Y | Y | Y | N | N | N | N |
| 3 **Souder** | Y | Y | Y | N | N | Y | N |
| 4 **Buyer** | N | Y | Y | N | N | Y | N |
| 5 **Burton** | N | Y | Y | N | N | Y | N |
| 6 **Pence** | N | Y | N | N | N | N | N |
| 7 Carson | Y | N | N | Y | N | N | Y |
| 8 **Hostettler** | N | Y | Y | N | N | Y | Y |
| 9 **Sodrel** | N | Y | N | N | N | Y | N |
| **IOWA** | | | | | | | |
| 1 **Nussle** | Y | Y | Y | N | N | Y | N |
| 2 **Leach** | Y | N | N | N | N | N | Y |
| 3 Boswell | Y | N | Y | Y | N | N | Y |
| 4 **Latham** | N | N | Y | N | N | N | N |
| 5 **King** | Y | Y | Y | N | N | Y | N |
| **KANSAS** | | | | | | | |
| 1 **Moran** | Y | N | N | N | N | Y | Y |
| 2 **Ryun** | N | Y | Y | N | N | N | N |
| 3 Moore | Y | N | Y | N | N | N | Y |
| 4 **Tiahrt** | N | N | Y | N | N | N | N |
| **KENTUCKY** | | | | | | | |
| 1 **Whitfield** | N | Y | Y | N | N | Y | N |
| 2 **Lewis** | Y | Y | Y | N | N | Y | N |
| 3 **Northup** | N | N | Y | N | N | N | N |
| 4 **Davis** | Y | Y | Y | N | N | Y | N |
| 5 **Rogers** | N | N | Y | N | N | N | N |
| 6 Chandler | Y | N | Y | N | N | N | N |
| **LOUISIANA** | | | | | | | |
| 1 **Jindal** | Y | Y | N | N | Y | Y | N |
| 2 Jefferson | N | N | N | N | Y | N | Y |
| 3 Melancon | Y | N | N | - | Y | N | N |
| 4 **McCrery** | Y | N | Y | N | N | N | N |
| 5 **Alexander** | N | N | N | N | N | N | N |
| 6 **Baker** | N | N | N | N | N | Y | N |
| 7 **Boustany** | N | N | N | N | N | N | N |
| **MAINE** | | | | | | | |
| 1 Allen | Y | N | N | N | Y | N | Y |
| 2 Michaud | Y | N | N | N | Y | N | Y |
| **MARYLAND** | | | | | | | |
| 1 **Gilchrest** | N | N | N | N | N | N | N |
| 2 Ruppersberger | Y | N | N | N | Y | N | Y |
| 3 Cardin | N | N | N | N | Y | N | Y |
| 4 Wynn | N | N | N | N | Y | N | Y |
| 5 Hoyer | N | N | N | N | Y | N | Y |
| 6 **Bartlett** | Y | Y | Y | N | N | Y | N |
| 7 Cummings | Y | N | N | N | Y | N | Y |
| 8 Van Hollen | Y | N | N | N | Y | N | Y |
| **MASSACHUSETTS** | | | | | | | |
| 1 Olver | Y | N | N | N | Y | N | Y |
| 2 Neal | Y | N | N | N | Y | N | Y |
| 3 McGovern | Y | N | N | N | Y | N | Y |
| 4 Frank | Y | N | N | N | Y | N | Y |
| 5 Meehan | Y | N | N | N | Y | N | Y |
| 6 Tierney | Y | N | N | N | Y | N | Y |
| 7 Markey | Y | N | N | N | N | N | Y |
| 8 Capuano | Y | N | N | N | Y | N | Y |
| 9 Lynch | Y | N | N | N | N | N | Y |
| 10 Delahunt | Y | N | N | N | Y | N | Y |
| **MICHIGAN** | | | | | | | |
| 1 Stupak | Y | N | N | N | Y | N | Y |
| 2 **Hoekstra** | N | N | Y | N | N | N | N |
| 3 **Ehlers** | Y | N | N | N | Y | N | Y |
| 4 **Camp** | N | Y | Y | N | N | N | Y |
| 5 Kildee | Y | N | N | N | Y | N | Y |
| 6 **Upton** | Y | N | N | N | N | Y | Y |
| 7 **Schwarz** | Y | N | N | N | N | N | Y |
| 8 **Rogers** | N | Y | Y | N | N | N | N |
| 9 **Knollenberg** | N | N | Y | N | N | N | N |
| 10 **Miller** | N | N | Y | N | Y | N | N |
| 11 **McCotter** | Y | N | Y | N | N | Y | N |
| 12 Levin | Y | N | N | N | Y | N | Y |
| 13 Kilpatrick | Y | N | N | N | N | N | Y |
| 14 Conyers | N | N | N | Y | Y | N | Y |
| 15 Dingell | Y | N | N | N | Y | N | Y |

| | 248 | 249 | 250 | 251 | 252 | 253 | 254 |
|---|---|---|---|---|---|---|---|
| **MINNESOTA** | | | | | | | |
| 1 **Gutknecht** | Y | Y | N | N | N | Y | N |
| 2 **Kline** | Y | Y | Y | N | Y | N | N |
| 3 **Ramstad** | Y | N | Y | Y | N | Y | Y |
| 4 McCollum | Y | N | N | N | Y | N | Y |
| 5 Sabo | Y | N | N | N | N | N | Y |
| 6 **Kennedy** | Y | Y | Y | N | Y | N | N |
| 7 Peterson | Y | N | Y | N | Y | Y | Y |
| 8 Oberstar | ? | ? | ? | ? | ? | ? | ? |
| **MISSISSIPPI** | | | | | | | |
| 1 **Wicker** | N | N | Y | N | N | N | N |
| 2 Thompson | Y | N | Y | N | N | N | Y |
| 3 **Pickering** | Y | N | Y | N | N | N | N |
| 4 Taylor | Y | N | N | N | Y | Y | Y |
| **MISSOURI** | | | | | | | |
| 1 Clay | N | N | N | N | Y | N | Y |
| 2 **Akin** | N | Y | Y | N | N | Y | N |
| 3 Carnahan | Y | N | Y | N | N | N | N |
| 4 Skelton | Y | N | N | N | Y | N | N |
| 5 Cleaver | Y | N | N | N | Y | N | N |
| 6 **Graves** | Y | Y | Y | N | N | Y | Y |
| 7 **Blunt** | N | N | Y | N | N | N | N |
| 8 **Emerson** | Y | N | Y | N | N | Y | Y |
| 9 **Hulshof** | Y | N | Y | N | N | Y | N |
| **MONTANA** | | | | | | | |
| AL **Rehberg** | N | N | Y | N | N | N | N |
| **NEBRASKA** | | | | | | | |
| 1 **Fortenberry** | Y | Y | Y | N | N | N | N |
| 2 **Terry** | Y | Y | N | N | N | Y | N |
| 3 **Osborne** | Y | N | Y | N | N | N | Y |
| **NEVADA** | | | | | | | |
| 1 Berkley | Y | N | N | N | N | N | N |
| 2 **Gibbons** | Y | Y | Y | N | N | Y | N |
| 3 **Porter** | N | Y | Y | Y | N | N | N |
| **NEW HAMPSHIRE** | | | | | | | |
| 1 **Bradley** | Y | N | N | Y | Y | N | N |
| 2 **Bass** | N | N | Y | N | Y | N | Y |
| **NEW JERSEY** | | | | | | | |
| 1 Andrews | N | N | N | N | Y | N | N |
| 2 **LoBiondo** | Y | Y | Y | N | Y | Y | N |
| 3 **Saxton** | N | N | N | N | N | N | N |
| 4 **Smith** | Y | N | Y | N | N | Y | N |
| 5 **Garrett** | N | Y | Y | N | N | Y | ? |
| 6 Pallone | Y | N | N | Y | Y | N | N |
| 7 **Ferguson** | Y | N | Y | N | N | N | N |
| 8 Pascrell | N | N | N | Y | Y | N | N |
| 9 Rothman | ? | ? | N | Y | Y | N | N |
| 10 Payne | N | N | N | Y | Y | N | Y |
| 11 **Frelinghuysen** | N | N | Y | N | N | N | N |
| 12 Holt | Y | N | N | N | Y | N | Y |
| 13 Menendez | N | N | N | Y | Y | N | N |
| **NEW MEXICO** | | | | | | | |
| 1 **Wilson** | Y | N | Y | N | N | N | N |
| 2 **Pearce** | N | N | Y | N | N | N | N |
| 3 Udall | Y | N | Y | N | Y | N | Y |
| **NEW YORK** | | | | | | | |
| 1 Bishop | Y | N | N | Y | Y | N | Y |
| 2 Israel | Y | N | N | Y | Y | N | Y |
| 3 **King** | Y | N | Y | N | N | N | N |
| 4 McCarthy | Y | N | N | N | Y | N | Y |
| 5 Ackerman | Y | N | N | Y | Y | N | Y |
| 6 Meeks | Y | N | N | N | Y | N | Y |
| 7 Crowley | Y | N | N | N | Y | N | Y |
| 8 Nadler | Y | N | Y | N | Y | N | Y |
| 9 Weiner | Y | N | Y | Y | Y | N | Y |
| 10 Towns | Y | N | N | Y | Y | N | Y |
| 11 Owens | N | N | N | Y | N | N | Y |
| 12 Velázquez | Y | N | N | Y | Y | N | Y |
| 13 **Fossella** | Y | N | Y | N | Y | Y | N |
| 14 Maloney | N | N | N | N | Y | N | Y |
| 15 Rangel | N | N | N | N | Y | N | Y |
| 16 Serrano | N | N | N | N | N | N | Y |
| 17 Engel | Y | N | Y | N | Y | N | N |
| 18 Lowey | Y | N | N | Y | Y | N | Y |
| 19 **Kelly** | N | N | Y | Y | Y | Y | N |
| 20 **Sweeney** | N | N | Y | N | N | N | N |
| 21 McNulty | Y | N | Y | N | Y | N | Y |
| 22 Hinchey | Y | N | N | N | Y | N | Y |
| 23 **McHugh** | Y | N | Y | N | N | N | N |
| 24 **Boehlert** | Y | N | N | N | N | N | Y |
| 25 **Walsh** | N | N | Y | N | N | N | N |
| 26 **Reynolds** | N | Y | Y | N | N | N | N |
| 27 Higgins | Y | N | Y | Y | Y | N | Y |
| 28 Slaughter | Y | N | N | N | Y | N | Y |
| 29 **Kuhl** | Y | Y | Y | N | N | Y | N |

| | 248 | 249 | 250 | 251 | 252 | 253 | 254 |
|---|---|---|---|---|---|---|---|
| **NORTH CAROLINA** | | | | | | | |
| 1 Butterfield | Y | N | N | N | Y | N | Y |
| 2 Etheridge | Y | N | N | N | N | N | Y |
| 3 **Jones** | Y | Y | Y | N | N | Y | N |
| 4 Price | Y | N | N | N | Y | N | Y |
| 5 **Foxx** | N | N | Y | N | N | Y | N |
| 6 **Coble** | Y | Y | N | N | N | Y | N |
| 7 McIntyre | Y | N | Y | Y | Y | Y | N |
| 8 **Hayes** | N | N | Y | N | N | Y | N |
| 9 **Myrick** | N | Y | Y | N | N | N | N |
| 10 **McHenry** | N | Y | Y | N | N | Y | N |
| 11 **Taylor** | N | N | N | N | N | Y | N |
| 12 Watt | N | N | N | N | Y | N | Y |
| 13 Miller | Y | N | N | N | Y | N | Y |
| **NORTH DAKOTA** | | | | | | | |
| AL Pomeroy | Y | N | N | N | Y | N | Y |
| **OHIO** | | | | | | | |
| 1 **Chabot** | Y | Y | Y | N | N | Y | N |
| 2 Vacant | | | | | | | |
| 3 **Turner** | N | N | Y | N | N | N | N |
| 4 **Oxley** | N | N | Y | N | N | N | N |
| 5 **Gillmor** | N | N | Y | N | N | N | Y |
| 6 Strickland | ? | ? | ? | Y | Y | N | Y |
| 7 **Hobson** | N | N | Y | N | N | N | N |
| 8 **Boehner** | N | Y | N | N | N | N | N |
| 9 Kaptur | Y | N | N | N | Y | N | Y |
| 10 Kucinich | N | N | N | Y | Y | N | Y |
| 11 Jones | Y | N | N | N | ? | N | Y |
| 12 **Tiberi** | N | N | N | N | N | Y | ? |
| 13 Brown | Y | N | Y | N | Y | N | Y |
| 14 **LaTourette** | N | N | N | N | N | N | N |
| 15 **Pryce** | N | N | Y | N | N | N | N |
| 16 **Regula** | N | N | Y | N | N | N | N |
| 17 Ryan | Y | N | Y | N | Y | N | Y |
| 18 **Ney** | Y | N | Y | N | N | Y | Y |
| **OKLAHOMA** | | | | | | | |
| 1 **Sullivan** | N | Y | Y | N | N | N | N |
| 2 Boren | Y | Y | N | N | N | N | Y |
| 3 **Lucas** | N | Y | N | N | N | Y | N |
| 4 **Cole** | N | Y | N | N | N | N | N |
| 5 **Istook** | N | Y | N | N | N | Y | N |
| **OREGON** | | | | | | | |
| 1 Wu | Y | N | N | N | Y | N | N |
| 2 **Walden** | Y | N | Y | N | N | N | N |
| 3 Blumenauer | Y | N | N | N | Y | N | Y |
| 4 DeFazio | Y | N | Y | N | Y | N | Y |
| 5 Hooley | Y | N | N | N | Y | N | Y |
| **PENNSYLVANIA** | | | | | | | |
| 1 Brady | Y | N | N | N | N | N | Y |
| 2 Fattah | Y | N | ? | N | Y | N | Y |
| 3 **English** | N | N | Y | N | N | N | N |
| 4 **Hart** | N | N | Y | N | N | Y | N |
| 5 **Peterson** | Y | N | Y | N | N | Y | Y |
| 6 **Gerlach** | Y | N | Y | N | Y | N | N |
| 7 **Weldon** | Y | N | N | N | Y | N | N |
| 8 **Fitzpatrick** | Y | N | N | N | Y | N | N |
| 9 **Shuster** | N | N | Y | N | N | Y | N |
| 10 **Sherwood** | N | N | Y | N | N | N | N |
| 11 Kanjorski | Y | N | N | N | N | N | Y |
| 12 Murtha | N | N | N | N | N | N | N |
| 13 Schwartz | Y | N | Y | N | Y | N | Y |
| 14 Doyle | Y | N | N | N | Y | N | Y |
| 15 **Dent** | Y | N | Y | N | N | N | N |
| 16 **Pitts** | N | Y | N | N | N | N | N |
| 17 Holden | Y | N | N | Y | N | N | Y |
| 18 **Murphy** | Y | N | Y | Y | N | Y | N |
| 19 **Platts** | Y | N | N | N | Y | Y | N |
| **RHODE ISLAND** | | | | | | | |
| 1 Kennedy | Y | N | N | N | Y | N | Y |
| 2 Langevin | Y | N | N | N | Y | N | Y |
| **SOUTH CAROLINA** | | | | | | | |
| 1 **Brown** | N | N | N | N | N | Y | Y |
| 2 **Wilson** | N | Y | Y | N | N | N | N |
| 3 **Barrett** | N | Y | N | N | N | Y | N |
| 4 **Inglis** | N | N | N | N | N | N | Y |
| 5 Spratt | N | N | N | N | Y | N | Y |
| 6 Clyburn | Y | N | N | N | N | N | Y |
| **SOUTH DAKOTA** | | | | | | | |
| AL Herseth | Y | N | Y | N | N | N | Y |
| **TENNESSEE** | | | | | | | |
| 1 **Jenkins** | N | N | Y | N | N | Y | N |
| 2 **Duncan** | N | Y | Y | N | N | Y | N |

| | 248 | 249 | 250 | 251 | 252 | 253 | 254 |
|---|---|---|---|---|---|---|---|
| 3 **Wamp** | Y | N | Y | N | N | Y | N |
| 4 Davis | Y | Y | N | N | N | N | Y |
| 5 Cooper | Y | N | N | N | N | N | Y |
| 6 Gordon | Y | N | N | N | Y | N | Y |
| 7 **Blackburn** | N | N | Y | N | N | N | N |
| 8 Tanner | Y | N | N | N | Y | N | Y |
| 9 Ford | Y | N | N | N | Y | N | Y |
| **TEXAS** | | | | | | | |
| 1 **Gohmert** | Y | Y | Y | N | N | Y | N |
| 2 **Poe** | Y | Y | Y | N | Y | Y | N |
| 3 **Johnson, S.** | N | Y | Y | N | N | Y | N |
| 4 **Hall** | N | Y | Y | N | N | Y | N |
| 5 **Hensarling** | N | Y | Y | N | N | Y | N |
| 6 **Barton** | N | Y | Y | N | N | Y | N |
| 7 **Culberson** | N | N | Y | N | N | N | N |
| 8 **Brady** | N | Y | Y | N | N | N | ? |
| 9 Green, A. | Y | N | N | N | Y | N | Y |
| 10 **McCaul** | Y | Y | Y | N | Y | Y | N |
| 11 **Conaway** | N | N | Y | N | N | N | N |
| 12 **Granger** | N | N | Y | N | N | N | N |
| 13 **Thornberry** | Y | Y | Y | N | N | Y | N |
| 14 **Paul** | Y | Y | Y | N | N | Y | Y |
| 15 Hinojosa | ? | ? | ? | N | N | N | Y |
| 16 Reyes | Y | N | Y | N | N | N | Y |
| 17 Edwards | Y | N | N | N | Y | N | Y |
| 18 Jackson-Lee | Y | N | N | N | Y | N | Y |
| 19 **Neugebauer** | N | Y | Y | N | N | Y | N |
| 20 Gonzalez | N | N | Y | N | Y | N | Y |
| 21 **Smith** | N | N | Y | N | N | Y | N |
| 22 **DeLay** | N | Y | Y | N | N | N | N |
| 23 **Bonilla** | N | N | Y | N | N | Y | N |
| 24 **Marchant** | N | Y | Y | N | N | Y | N |
| 25 Doggett | Y | N | Y | N | Y | N | Y |
| 26 **Burgess** | N | N | Y | N | N | Y | N |
| 27 Ortiz | Y | N | Y | N | Y | N | Y |
| 28 Cuellar | Y | N | Y | ? | ? | ? | ? |
| 29 Green, G. | Y | N | Y | Y | Y | Y | Y |
| 30 Johnson, E. | N | N | Y | N | Y | N | Y |
| 31 **Carter** | N | N | Y | N | N | Y | N |
| 32 **Sessions** | ? | ? | ? | ? | ? | ? | ? |
| **UTAH** | | | | | | | |
| 1 **Bishop** | N | Y | Y | N | N | Y | N |
| 2 Matheson | Y | N | N | N | N | N | Y |
| 3 **Cannon** | N | N | Y | N | N | Y | N |
| **VERMONT** | | | | | | | |
| AL *Sanders* | Y | N | N | N | Y | N | Y |
| **VIRGINIA** | | | | | | | |
| 1 **Davis, J.** | Y | Y | Y | N | N | Y | N |
| 2 **Drake** | Y | Y | Y | N | N | Y | N |
| 3 Scott | Y | N | N | N | Y | N | Y |
| 4 **Forbes** | Y | Y | Y | N | N | Y | N |
| 5 **Goode** | N | Y | Y | N | N | Y | N |
| 6 **Goodlatte** | N | Y | Y | N | N | Y | N |
| 7 **Cantor** | N | N | Y | N | N | N | N |
| 8 Moran | N | N | N | N | N | N | Y |
| 9 Boucher | Y | N | N | N | Y | N | Y |
| 10 **Wolf** | N | N | Y | N | N | N | N |
| 11 **Davis, T.** | N | N | Y | N | N | N | N |
| **WASHINGTON** | | | | | | | |
| 1 Inslee | Y | N | N | N | Y | N | Y |
| 2 Larsen | Y | N | Y | N | Y | N | Y |
| 3 Baird | Y | N | N | N | Y | N | Y |
| 4 **Hastings** | Y | Y | Y | N | N | Y | N |
| 5 **McMorris** | Y | N | Y | N | N | Y | N |
| 6 Dicks | Y | N | N | N | Y | N | Y |
| 7 McDermott | Y | N | N | N | Y | N | Y |
| 8 **Reichert** | Y | N | N | N | N | N | N |
| 9 Smith | Y | N | Y | N | Y | N | Y |
| **WEST VIRGINIA** | | | | | | | |
| 1 Mollohan | N | N | N | N | N | N | Y |
| 2 **Capito** | Y | N | Y | N | N | N | N |
| 3 Rahall | Y | N | N | N | N | N | Y |
| **WISCONSIN** | | | | | | | |
| 1 **Ryan** | Y | Y | Y | N | N | N | Y |
| 2 Baldwin | Y | N | N | N | Y | N | Y |
| 3 Kind | Y | N | N | N | Y | N | Y |
| 4 Moore | Y | N | N | N | Y | N | Y |
| 5 **Sensenbrenner** | N | Y | Y | N | N | Y | N |
| 6 **Petri** | N | Y | Y | N | N | Y | N |
| 7 Obey | Y | N | N | N | N | N | Y |
| 8 **Green** | Y | Y | Y | N | N | Y | N |
| **WYOMING** | | | | | | | |
| AL **Cubin** | Y | Y | Y | N | N | Y | Y |

# IN THE HOUSE | By Vote Number

**255.** HR 2862. Fiscal 2006 Commerce-Justice-Science Appropriations/ **Medical Marijuana.** Hinchey, D-N.Y., amendment that would prohibit the use of funds in the bill to prevent the implementation of state laws authorizing the use of marijuana for medical reasons in Alaska, California, Colorado, Hawaii, Maine, Montana, Nevada, Oregon, Vermont or Washington state. Rejected 161-264: R 15-210; D 145-54 (ND 123-26, SD 22-28); I 1-0. June 15, 2005.

**256.** HR 2862. Fiscal 2006 Commerce-Justice-Science Appropriations/ **Equal Employment Opportunity Commission.** Jones, D-Ohio, amendment that would prohibit use of funds in the bill to close or consolidate any office of the Equal Employment Opportunity Commission or make any reductions in the number of full-time officers or employees in any commission office as part of workforce repositioning, restructuring or reorganizing. Rejected 201-222: R 2-221; D 198-1 (ND 148-1, SD 50-0); I 1-0. June 15, 2005.

**257.** HR 2862. Fiscal 2006 Commerce-Justice-Science Appropriations/ **Ten Commandments Court Ruling.** Hostettler, R-Ind., amendment that would prohibit the use of funds in the bill to enforce a ruling by the U.S. District Court for the Southern District of Indiana that a monument representing the Ten Commandments must be removed from the county courthouse. Adopted 242-182: R 204-20; D 38-161 (ND 17-133, SD 21-28); I 0-1. June 15, 2005.

**258.** HR 2862. Fiscal 2006 Commerce-Justice-Science Appropriations/ **Surveillance of Library Records.** Sanders, I-Vt., amendment that would prohibit the use of funds in the bill to make an application under the Foreign Intelligence Surveillance Act to acquire library circulation records, library patron lists, bookseller sales records or bookseller customer lists. Adopted 238-187: R 38-186; D 199-1 (ND 150-0, SD 49-1); I 1-0. A "nay" was a vote in support of the president's position. June 15, 2005.

**259.** HR 2862. Fiscal 2006 Commerce-Justice-Science Appropriations/ **U.N. Funding.** Paul, R-Texas, amendment that would prohibit the use of funds in the bill to pay any U.S. contribution to the United Nations or any affiliated agency of the United Nations. Rejected 65-357: R 64-160; D 1-196 (ND 0-149, SD 1-47); I 0-1. June 16, 2005.

**260.** HR 2862. Fiscal 2006 Commerce-Justice-Science Appropriations/ **Across-the-Board Cut.** Hefley, R-Colo., amendment that would require an approximate 1 percent across-the-board cut in discretionary spending. Rejected 91-336: R 87-140; D 4-195 (ND 2-147, SD 2-48); I 0-1. June 16, 2005.

**261.** HR 2862. Fiscal 2006 Commerce-Justice-Science Appropriations/ **U.S. Commitment Against Torture.** Markey, D-Mass., amendment that would reaffirm the U.S. commitment to the U.N. Convention Against Torture. Adopted 415-8: R 215-8; D 199-0 (ND 149-0, SD 50-0); I 1-0. June 16, 2005.

| | 255 | 256 | 257 | 258 | 259 | 260 | 261 |
|---|---|---|---|---|---|---|---|
| **ALABAMA** | | | | | | | |
| 1 Bonner | N | N | Y | N | Y | N | Y |
| 2 Everett | N | N | Y | N | Y | Y | Y |
| 3 Rogers | N | N | Y | N | Y | N | Y |
| 4 Aderholt | N | N | Y | N | N | N | Y |
| 5 Cramer | N | Y | Y | Y | N | N | Y |
| 6 Bachus | N | N | Y | N | Y | Y | Y |
| 7 Davis | N | Y | N | Y | N | N | Y |
| **ALASKA** | | | | | | | |
| AL Young | N | N | Y | Y | N | N | Y |
| **ARIZONA** | | | | | | | |
| 1 Renzi | N | N | Y | N | N | N | Y |
| 2 Franks | N | N | Y | N | Y | Y | Y |
| 3 Shadegg | N | N | Y | N | Y | Y | Y |
| 4 Pastor | Y | Y | N | Y | N | N | Y |
| 5 Hayworth | N | N | Y | N | Y | N | P |
| 6 Flake | Y | N | Y | Y | Y | Y | Y |
| 7 Grijalva | Y | Y | N | Y | N | N | Y |
| 8 Kolbe | N | N | N | N | N | N | Y |
| **ARKANSAS** | | | | | | | |
| 1 Berry | N | Y | Y | Y | N | N | Y |
| 2 Snyder | N | Y | N | Y | N | Y | Y |
| 3 Boozman | N | N | Y | N | N | Y | Y |
| 4 Ross | N | Y | Y | Y | N | N | Y |
| **CALIFORNIA** | | | | | | | |
| 1 Thompson | Y | Y | N | Y | N | N | Y |
| 2 Herger | N | N | Y | N | Y | Y | Y |
| 3 Lungren | N | N | N | N | N | Y | Y |
| 4 Doolittle | N | N | Y | N | Y | N | Y |
| 5 Matsui, D. | Y | Y | N | Y | N | N | Y |
| 6 Woolsey | Y | Y | N | Y | ? | N | Y |
| 7 Miller, George | Y | Y | N | Y | N | N | Y |
| 8 Pelosi | Y | Y | N | Y | N | N | Y |
| 9 Lee | Y | Y | N | Y | N | N | Y |
| 10 Tauscher | Y | Y | N | Y | N | N | Y |
| 11 Pombo | N | N | Y | N | Y | N | Y |
| 12 Lantos | Y | Y | N | Y | N | N | Y |
| 13 Stark | Y | Y | N | Y | N | N | Y |
| 14 Eshoo | Y | Y | N | Y | N | N | Y |
| 15 Honda | Y | Y | N | Y | N | N | Y |
| 16 Lofgren | Y | Y | N | Y | N | N | Y |
| 17 Farr | Y | Y | N | Y | N | N | Y |
| 18 Cardoza | N | Y | Y | Y | N | N | Y |
| 19 Radanovich | N | N | Y | N | Y | Y | Y |
| 20 Costa | Y | Y | N | Y | N | N | Y |
| 21 Nunes | N | N | N | N | N | N | Y |
| 22 Thomas | N | N | N | N | N | N | Y |
| 23 Capps | Y | Y | N | Y | N | N | Y |
| 24 Gallegly | N | N | Y | N | N | N | Y |
| 25 McKeon | N | N | Y | N | N | N | Y |
| 26 Dreier | N | N | Y | N | N | N | Y |
| 27 Sherman | Y | Y | N | Y | N | N | Y |
| 28 Berman | Y | Y | N | Y | N | N | Y |
| 29 Schiff | Y | Y | N | Y | N | N | Y |
| 30 Waxman | Y | Y | N | Y | N | N | Y |
| 31 Becerra | Y | Y | N | Y | N | N | Y |
| 32 Solis | Y | Y | N | Y | N | N | Y |
| 33 Watson | Y | Y | N | Y | N | N | Y |
| 34 Roybal-Allard | Y | Y | N | Y | N | N | Y |
| 35 Waters | Y | Y | N | Y | N | N | ? |
| 36 Harman | Y | Y | N | Y | N | N | Y |
| 37 Millender-McD. | Y | Y | N | Y | N | N | Y |
| 38 Napolitano | Y | + | N | Y | N | N | Y |
| 39 Sánchez, Linda | Y | Y | N | Y | N | N | Y |
| 40 Royce | Y | N | Y | N | Y | Y | Y |
| 41 Lewis | N | N | N | N | N | N | Y |
| 42 Miller, Gary | N | N | Y | N | N | N | Y |
| 43 Baca | Y | Y | Y | N | N | N | Y |
| 44 Calvert | N | N | Y | N | N | N | Y |
| 45 Bono | N | ? | ? | ? | ? | ? | ? |
| 46 Rohrabacher | Y | N | Y | N | Y | Y | Y |
| 47 Sanchez, Loretta | Y | Y | N | Y | N | N | Y |
| 48 Cox | ? | N | Y | N | ? | Y | Y |
| 49 Issa | N | N | Y | N | N | Y | Y |
| **COLORADO** | | | | | | | |
| 50 Cunningham | N | N | Y | N | N | N | Y |
| 51 Filner | Y | Y | N | Y | N | N | Y |
| 52 Hunter | N | N | Y | N | Y | N | Y |
| 53 Davis | Y | Y | N | Y | N | N | Y |
| 1 DeGette | Y | Y | N | Y | N | N | Y |
| 2 Udall | Y | Y | N | Y | N | N | Y |
| 3 Salazar | N | Y | Y | Y | N | N | Y |
| 4 Musgrave | N | N | Y | Y | Y | Y | Y |
| 5 Hefley | N | N | Y | N | Y | Y | Y |
| 6 Tancredo | N | Y | N | Y | Y | Y | Y |
| 7 Beauprez | Y | N | Y | N | N | N | Y |
| **CONNECTICUT** | | | | | | | |
| 1 Larson | Y | Y | N | Y | N | N | Y |
| 2 Simmons | Y | Y | N | Y | N | N | Y |
| 3 DeLauro | Y | Y | N | Y | N | N | Y |
| 4 Shays | N | N | N | N | N | N | Y |
| 5 Johnson | Y | N | N | N | N | N | Y |
| **DELAWARE** | | | | | | | |
| AL Castle | N | N | N | N | N | N | Y |
| **FLORIDA** | | | | | | | |
| 1 Miller | N | N | Y | Y | Y | Y | Y |
| 2 Boyd | N | Y | Y | N | N | N | Y |
| 3 Brown | Y | Y | N | Y | N | N | Y |
| 4 Crenshaw | N | N | Y | N | N | N | Y |
| 5 Brown-Waite | N | N | Y | N | N | N | Y |
| 6 Stearns | N | N | Y | N | Y | Y | Y |
| 7 Mica | N | N | Y | N | N | Y | N |
| 8 Keller | N | N | Y | N | Y | Y | Y |
| 9 Bilirakis | N | N | Y | N | Y | N | Y |
| 10 Young | N | N | N | N | N | N | Y |
| 11 Davis | Y | Y | N | Y | N | N | Y |
| 12 Putnam | N | N | N | N | N | N | Y |
| 13 Harris | N | N | Y | N | Y | Y | Y |
| 14 Mack | N | N | Y | N | N | Y | Y |
| 15 Weldon | N | N | N | N | N | N | Y |
| 16 Foley | N | N | Y | N | N | Y | Y |
| 17 Meek | Y | Y | N | Y | N | N | Y |
| 18 Ros-Lehtinen | N | N | N | N | N | N | Y |
| 19 Wexler | Y | Y | N | Y | N | N | Y |
| 20 Wasserman-Schultz | N | Y | N | Y | N | N | Y |
| 21 Diaz-Balart, L. | N | N | Y | N | N | N | Y |
| 22 Shaw | N | N | Y | N | N | N | Y |
| 23 Hastings | Y | Y | N | Y | N | N | Y |
| 24 Feeney | ? | N | Y | N | Y | Y | N |
| 25 Diaz-Balart, M. | N | N | Y | N | N | Y | Y |
| **GEORGIA** | | | | | | | |
| 1 Kingston | N | N | N | N | Y | N | Y |
| 2 Bishop | Y | Y | Y | Y | N | N | Y |
| 3 Marshall | N | Y | Y | Y | N | N | Y |
| 4 McKinney | Y | Y | Y | ? | N | N | Y |
| 5 Lewis | Y | Y | N | Y | N | N | Y |
| 6 Price | N | N | Y | N | Y | Y | Y |
| 7 Linder | N | N | Y | N | Y | Y | Y |
| 8 Westmoreland | N | N | Y | N | Y | Y | N |
| 9 Norwood | N | N | N | Y | Y | Y | Y |
| 10 Deal | N | N | N | Y | Y | Y | Y |
| 11 Gingrey | N | N | N | N | N | N | Y |
| 12 Barrow | N | Y | Y | Y | N | N | Y |
| 13 Scott | Y | Y | Y | Y | N | N | Y |
| **HAWAII** | | | | | | | |
| 1 Abercrombie | Y | Y | N | Y | N | N | Y |
| 2 Case | Y | Y | N | Y | N | N | Y |
| **IDAHO** | | | | | | | |
| 1 Otter | Y | N | Y | Y | Y | Y | Y |
| 2 Simpson | Y | N | Y | N | Y | N | Y |
| **ILLINOIS** | | | | | | | |
| 1 Rush | Y | Y | N | Y | N | N | Y |
| 2 Jackson | Y | Y | N | Y | N | N | Y |
| 3 Lipinski | N | Y | Y | Y | N | N | Y |
| 4 Gutierrez | Y | Y | N | Y | N | N | Y |
| 5 Emanuel | Y | Y | N | Y | N | N | Y |
| 6 Hyde | ? | ? | ? | ? | ? | N | Y |
| 7 Davis | Y | Y | N | Y | N | N | Y |
| 8 Bean | N | Y | Y | N | Y | Y | Y |
| 9 Schakowsky | Y | Y | N | Y | N | N | Y |
| 10 Kirk | N | N | N | Y | N | N | + |
| 11 Weller | N | N | Y | N | N | N | Y |
| 12 Costello | N | Y | Y | Y | N | Y | Y |

**KEY**  Republicans  Democrats  *Independents*

| | | |
|---|---|---|
| Y Voted for (yea) | X Paired against | C Voted "present" to avoid possible conflict of interest |
| # Paired for | – Announced against | |
| + Announced for | P Voted "present" | ? Did not vote or otherwise make a position known |
| N Voted against (nay) | | |

| | 255 | 256 | 257 | 258 | 259 | 260 | 261 |
|---|---|---|---|---|---|---|---|
| 13 **Biggert** | N | N | Y | N | N | N | Y |
| 14 **Hastert** | | | | | | | |
| 15 **Johnson** | Y | N | Y | Y | N | N | Y |
| 16 **Manzullo** | N | N | Y | Y | Y | Y | Y |
| 17 Evans | Y | Y | N | Y | N | N | Y |
| 18 **LaHood** | N | N | Y | Y | N | N | Y |
| 19 **Shimkus** | N | Y | Y | N | N | Y | Y |
| **INDIANA** | | | | | | | |
| 1 Visclosky | N | Y | N | Y | N | N | Y |
| 2 **Chocola** | N | N | Y | N | N | Y | Y |
| 3 **Souder** | N | N | Y | N | N | N | Y |
| 4 **Buyer** | N | N | Y | N | N | Y | ? |
| 5 **Burton** | N | N | Y | N | Y | Y | Y |
| 6 **Pence** | N | N | Y | N | N | Y | Y |
| 7 Carson | Y | Y | N | Y | N | N | Y |
| 8 **Hostettler** | N | N | Y | N | Y | Y | Y |
| 9 **Sodrel** | N | N | Y | N | N | Y | Y |
| **IOWA** | | | | | | | |
| 1 **Nussle** | N | N | Y | N | N | N | Y |
| 2 **Leach** | N | N | Y | Y | N | N | Y |
| 3 Boswell | N | Y | Y | Y | N | N | Y |
| 4 **Latham** | N | N | Y | N | N | N | Y |
| 5 **King** | N | N | Y | N | Y | Y | Y |
| **KANSAS** | | | | | | | |
| 1 **Moran** | N | N | Y | Y | Y | Y | Y |
| 2 **Ryun** | N | N | Y | N | Y | Y | Y |
| 3 Moore | N | Y | Y | Y | N | N | Y |
| 4 **Tiahrt** | N | N | Y | N | N | N | Y |
| **KENTUCKY** | | | | | | | |
| 1 **Whitfield** | N | N | Y | Y | N | N | Y |
| 2 **Lewis** | N | N | Y | N | Y | Y | Y |
| 3 **Northup** | N | ? | Y | N | N | N | Y |
| 4 **Davis** | N | N | Y | N | Y | N | N |
| 5 **Rogers** | N | N | Y | N | N | N | Y |
| 6 Chandler | N | Y | Y | Y | ? | N | Y |
| **LOUISIANA** | | | | | | | |
| 1 **Jindal** | N | N | Y | N | Y | Y | Y |
| 2 Jefferson | Y | Y | N | Y | N | N | Y |
| 3 Melancon | Y | Y | Y | Y | N | N | Y |
| 4 **McCrery** | N | N | Y | N | ? | N | Y |
| 5 **Alexander** | N | N | Y | N | N | N | Y |
| 6 **Baker** | N | N | Y | N | N | Y | Y |
| 7 **Boustany** | N | N | Y | N | N | N | Y |
| **MAINE** | | | | | | | |
| 1 Allen | Y | Y | N | Y | N | N | Y |
| 2 Michaud | Y | Y | N | Y | N | N | Y |
| **MARYLAND** | | | | | | | |
| 1 **Gilchrest** | Y | N | N | N | N | N | Y |
| 2 Ruppersberger | Y | Y | N | Y | N | N | Y |
| 3 Cardin | Y | Y | N | Y | N | N | Y |
| 4 Wynn | Y | Y | Y | Y | N | N | Y |
| 5 Hoyer | Y | Y | N | Y | N | N | Y |
| 6 **Bartlett** | Y | N | Y | Y | Y | Y | Y |
| 7 Cummings | N | Y | N | Y | N | N | Y |
| 8 Van Hollen | Y | Y | N | Y | N | N | Y |
| **MASSACHUSETTS** | | | | | | | |
| 1 Olver | Y | Y | N | Y | N | N | Y |
| 2 Neal | Y | Y | N | Y | N | N | Y |
| 3 McGovern | Y | Y | N | Y | N | N | Y |
| 4 Frank | Y | Y | N | Y | N | N | Y |
| 5 Meehan | Y | Y | N | Y | N | N | Y |
| 6 Tierney | Y | Y | N | Y | N | N | Y |
| 7 Markey | Y | Y | N | Y | N | N | Y |
| 8 Capuano | Y | Y | N | Y | N | N | Y |
| 9 Lynch | N | Y | Y | Y | N | N | Y |
| 10 Delahunt | Y | Y | N | Y | N | N | Y |
| **MICHIGAN** | | | | | | | |
| 1 Stupak | N | Y | N | Y | N | N | Y |
| 2 **Hoekstra** | N | N | Y | N | N | N | Y |
| 3 **Ehlers** | N | N | Y | Y | N | N | Y |
| 4 **Camp** | N | N | Y | N | N | N | Y |
| 5 Kildee | Y | Y | N | Y | N | N | Y |
| 6 **Upton** | N | N | Y | N | N | N | Y |
| 7 **Schwarz** | N | N | Y | Y | N | N | Y |
| 8 **Rogers** | N | N | Y | N | N | Y | ? |
| 9 **Knollenberg** | N | N | N | N | N | N | Y |
| 10 **Miller** | N | N | Y | N | N | N | Y |
| 11 **McCotter** | N | Y | Y | N | N | Y | Y |
| 12 Levin | N | Y | N | Y | N | N | Y |
| 13 Kilpatrick | Y | Y | N | Y | N | N | Y |
| 14 Conyers | ? | Y | N | Y | N | ? | Y |
| 15 Dingell | N | Y | N | Y | N | N | Y |
| **MINNESOTA** | | | | | | | |
| 1 **Gutknecht** | N | N | Y | N | N | Y | Y |
| 2 **Kline** | N | N | Y | N | N | N | Y |
| 3 **Ramstad** | N | N | Y | N | N | Y | Y |
| 4 McCollum | Y | Y | N | Y | N | N | Y |
| 5 Sabo | Y | Y | N | Y | N | N | Y |
| 6 **Kennedy** | N | N | Y | N | N | N | Y |
| 7 Peterson | N | N | Y | Y | N | N | Y |
| 8 Oberstar | ? | ? | ? | ? | ? | ? | ? |
| **MISSISSIPPI** | | | | | | | |
| 1 **Wicker** | N | N | Y | N | N | N | Y |
| 2 Thompson | N | Y | N | Y | N | N | Y |
| 3 **Pickering** | N | N | Y | N | N | N | Y |
| 4 Taylor | N | Y | Y | Y | Y | Y | Y |
| **MISSOURI** | | | | | | | |
| 1 Clay | Y | Y | N | Y | N | N | Y |
| 2 **Akin** | N | N | Y | N | Y | Y | Y |
| 3 Carnahan | Y | Y | N | Y | N | N | Y |
| 4 Skelton | N | Y | Y | Y | N | N | Y |
| 5 Cleaver | Y | Y | N | Y | N | N | Y |
| 6 **Graves** | N | N | Y | N | N | Y | N |
| 7 **Blunt** | N | N | Y | N | N | N | N |
| 8 **Emerson** | N | N | Y | Y | N | N | Y |
| 9 **Hulshof** | N | N | Y | N | Y | N | Y |
| **MONTANA** | | | | | | | |
| AL **Rehberg** | Y | N | Y | Y | N | N | Y |
| **NEBRASKA** | | | | | | | |
| 1 **Fortenberry** | N | N | Y | N | N | N | Y |
| 2 **Terry** | N | N | Y | N | N | N | Y |
| 3 **Osborne** | N | N | Y | N | N | N | Y |
| **NEVADA** | | | | | | | |
| 1 Berkley | Y | Y | N | Y | N | N | Y |
| 2 **Gibbons** | N | N | Y | N | Y | Y | Y |
| 3 **Porter** | Y | N | Y | Y | N | N | Y |
| **NEW HAMPSHIRE** | | | | | | | |
| 1 **Bradley** | N | N | Y | N | N | N | Y |
| 2 **Bass** | N | N | Y | N | N | Y | Y |
| **NEW JERSEY** | | | | | | | |
| 1 Andrews | Y | Y | N | Y | N | N | Y |
| 2 **LoBiondo** | N | N | Y | N | N | N | Y |
| 3 **Saxton** | N | N | Y | N | N | N | Y |
| 4 **Smith** | N | N | Y | N | N | N | Y |
| 5 **Garrett** | ? | ? | ? | ? | Y | Y | Y |
| 6 Pallone | Y | Y | N | Y | N | N | Y |
| 7 **Ferguson** | N | N | Y | N | N | N | Y |
| 8 Pascrell | Y | Y | N | Y | N | N | Y |
| 9 Rothman | Y | Y | N | Y | N | N | Y |
| 10 Payne | Y | Y | N | Y | N | N | Y |
| 11 **Frelinghuysen** | N | N | Y | N | N | N | Y |
| 12 Holt | Y | Y | N | Y | N | N | Y |
| 13 Menendez | Y | Y | N | Y | N | N | Y |
| **NEW MEXICO** | | | | | | | |
| 1 **Wilson** | N | N | N | N | N | N | Y |
| 2 **Pearce** | N | N | Y | N | N | N | Y |
| 3 Udall | Y | Y | N | Y | N | N | Y |
| **NEW YORK** | | | | | | | |
| 1 Bishop | Y | Y | N | Y | N | N | Y |
| 2 Israel | Y | Y | N | Y | N | N | Y |
| 3 **King** | N | N | Y | N | N | N | Y |
| 4 McCarthy | Y | Y | N | Y | N | N | Y |
| 5 Ackerman | Y | Y | N | Y | N | N | Y |
| 6 Meeks | Y | Y | N | Y | N | N | Y |
| 7 Crowley | Y | Y | N | Y | N | N | Y |
| 8 Nadler | Y | Y | N | Y | N | N | Y |
| 9 Weiner | Y | Y | N | Y | N | N | Y |
| 10 Towns | Y | Y | N | Y | N | N | Y |
| 11 Owens | Y | Y | N | Y | N | N | Y |
| 12 Velázquez | Y | Y | N | Y | N | N | Y |
| 13 **Fossella** | N | N | Y | N | N | Y | Y |
| 14 Maloney | Y | Y | N | Y | N | N | Y |
| 15 Rangel | Y | Y | N | Y | N | N | Y |
| 16 Serrano | Y | Y | N | Y | N | N | Y |
| 17 Engel | Y | Y | N | Y | N | N | Y |
| 18 Lowey | Y | Y | N | Y | N | N | Y |
| 19 **Kelly** | N | N | Y | N | N | N | Y |
| 20 **Sweeney** | N | N | N | N | N | N | Y |
| 21 McNulty | Y | Y | N | Y | N | N | Y |
| 22 Hinchey | Y | Y | N | Y | N | N | Y |
| 23 **McHugh** | N | N | N | N | N | N | Y |
| 24 **Boehlert** | N | N | N | Y | N | N | Y |
| 25 **Walsh** | N | N | Y | N | N | N | Y |
| 26 **Reynolds** | N | N | Y | N | N | N | Y |
| 27 Higgins | Y | Y | Y | Y | N | N | Y |
| 28 Slaughter | Y | Y | N | Y | N | N | Y |
| 29 **Kuhl** | N | N | Y | N | N | N | Y |
| **NORTH CAROLINA** | | | | | | | |
| 1 Butterfield | Y | Y | N | Y | N | N | Y |
| 2 Etheridge | N | Y | Y | Y | N | N | Y |
| 3 **Jones** | N | N | Y | Y | Y | Y | Y |
| 4 Price | Y | Y | N | Y | N | N | Y |
| 5 **Foxx** | N | N | Y | N | Y | Y | Y |
| 6 **Coble** | N | N | Y | N | Y | Y | Y |
| 7 McIntyre | N | Y | Y | Y | N | N | Y |
| 8 **Hayes** | N | N | Y | N | N | N | N |
| 9 **Myrick** | N | N | Y | N | N | Y | Y |
| 10 **McHenry** | N | N | Y | N | Y | Y | Y |
| 11 **Taylor** | N | N | Y | Y | N | N | Y |
| 12 Watt | Y | Y | N | Y | N | N | Y |
| 13 Miller | N | Y | N | Y | N | N | Y |
| **NORTH DAKOTA** | | | | | | | |
| AL Pomeroy | N | Y | Y | Y | N | N | Y |
| **OHIO** | | | | | | | |
| 1 **Chabot** | N | N | Y | N | N | Y | Y |
| 2 Vacant | | | | | | | |
| 3 **Turner** | N | N | Y | N | N | N | Y |
| 4 **Oxley** | N | N | Y | N | N | N | Y |
| 5 **Gillmor** | N | N | Y | Y | N | N | Y |
| 6 Strickland | Y | Y | N | Y | N | N | Y |
| 7 **Hobson** | N | N | Y | N | N | N | Y |
| 8 **Boehner** | N | N | Y | N | N | N | Y |
| 9 Kaptur | Y | Y | Y | Y | N | N | Y |
| 10 Kucinich | Y | Y | N | Y | N | N | Y |
| 11 Jones | Y | Y | N | Y | N | N | Y |
| 12 **Tiberi** | N | N | Y | N | Y | N | Y |
| 13 Brown | Y | Y | N | Y | N | N | Y |
| 14 **LaTourette** | N | N | Y | Y | N | N | Y |
| 15 **Pryce** | N | N | Y | N | ? | N | Y |
| 16 **Regula** | N | N | Y | N | N | N | Y |
| 17 Ryan | Y | Y | N | Y | N | N | Y |
| 18 **Ney** | N | N | Y | Y | Y | N | Y |
| **OKLAHOMA** | | | | | | | |
| 1 **Sullivan** | N | ? | ? | ? | N | N | Y |
| 2 Boren | N | Y | Y | N | N | N | Y |
| 3 **Lucas** | N | N | Y | N | N | N | Y |
| 4 **Cole** | N | N | Y | N | N | N | Y |
| 5 **Istook** | N | N | Y | N | N | N | Y |
| **OREGON** | | | | | | | |
| 1 Wu | Y | Y | N | Y | N | N | Y |
| 2 **Walden** | N | N | Y | Y | N | N | Y |
| 3 Blumenauer | Y | Y | N | Y | N | N | Y |
| 4 DeFazio | Y | Y | N | Y | N | N | Y |
| 5 Hooley | Y | Y | N | Y | N | N | Y |
| **PENNSYLVANIA** | | | | | | | |
| 1 Brady | Y | Y | N | Y | N | N | Y |
| 2 Fattah | Y | Y | N | Y | N | N | Y |
| 3 **English** | N | N | Y | N | N | N | Y |
| 4 **Hart** | N | N | Y | N | N | Y | Y |
| 5 **Peterson** | N | N | Y | Y | Y | N | Y |
| 6 **Gerlach** | N | N | Y | N | N | N | Y |
| 7 **Weldon** | N | ? | ? | ? | N | N | Y |
| 8 **Fitzpatrick** | N | N | Y | Y | N | N | Y |
| 9 **Shuster** | N | N | Y | N | Y | Y | Y |
| 10 **Sherwood** | N | N | Y | N | N | N | Y |
| 11 Kanjorski | Y | Y | N | Y | N | N | Y |
| 12 Murtha | N | Y | N | Y | N | N | Y |
| 13 Schwartz | N | Y | N | Y | N | N | Y |
| 14 Doyle | Y | Y | N | Y | N | N | Y |
| 15 **Dent** | N | N | N | N | N | N | Y |
| 16 **Pitts** | N | N | Y | N | N | ? | Y |
| 17 Holden | N | Y | N | Y | N | N | Y |
| 18 **Murphy** | N | N | Y | N | N | N | Y |
| 19 **Platts** | N | N | Y | N | Y | N | Y |
| **RHODE ISLAND** | | | | | | | |
| 1 Kennedy | Y | Y | N | Y | N | N | Y |
| 2 Langevin | N | Y | Y | Y | N | N | Y |
| **SOUTH CAROLINA** | | | | | | | |
| 1 **Brown** | N | N | Y | N | N | N | Y |
| 2 **Wilson** | N | N | Y | N | Y | Y | Y |
| 3 **Barrett** | N | N | Y | N | Y | Y | Y |
| 4 **Inglis** | N | N | Y | N | N | Y | Y |
| 5 Spratt | N | Y | N | Y | N | N | Y |
| 6 Clyburn | N | Y | N | Y | N | N | Y |
| **SOUTH DAKOTA** | | | | | | | |
| AL Herseth | N | Y | Y | Y | N | N | Y |
| **TENNESSEE** | | | | | | | |
| 1 **Jenkins** | N | N | Y | N | N | Y | Y |
| 2 **Duncan** | N | N | Y | Y | Y | Y | Y |
| 3 **Wamp** | N | N | Y | N | Y | N | Y |
| 4 Davis | N | Y | Y | Y | N | N | Y |
| 5 Cooper | N | Y | N | Y | N | N | Y |
| 6 Gordon | N | Y | Y | Y | N | N | Y |
| 7 **Blackburn** | N | N | Y | N | N | Y | Y |
| 8 Tanner | N | Y | Y | Y | N | Y | Y |
| 9 Ford | N | Y | N | Y | N | N | Y |
| **TEXAS** | | | | | | | |
| 1 **Gohmert** | N | N | Y | N | N | Y | Y |
| 2 **Poe** | N | N | Y | Y | N | Y | Y |
| 3 **Johnson, S.** | N | N | Y | N | Y | Y | Y |
| 4 **Hall** | N | N | Y | N | N | Y | Y |
| 5 **Hensarling** | N | N | Y | N | N | Y | Y |
| 6 **Barton** | N | N | Y | N | N | Y | Y |
| 7 **Culberson** | N | N | Y | N | N | N | Y |
| 8 **Brady** | N | N | Y | N | N | Y | Y |
| 9 Green, A. | Y | Y | N | Y | N | N | Y |
| 10 **McCaul** | N | N | Y | N | N | N | Y |
| 11 **Conaway** | N | N | Y | N | N | N | Y |
| 12 **Granger** | N | N | N | N | N | N | Y |
| 13 **Thornberry** | N | N | Y | N | N | N | Y |
| 14 **Paul** | Y | N | Y | Y | Y | Y | Y |
| 15 Hinojosa | N | Y | Y | Y | N | N | Y |
| 16 Reyes | N | Y | Y | Y | N | N | Y |
| 17 Edwards | N | Y | N | Y | N | N | Y |
| 18 Jackson-Lee | Y | Y | N | Y | N | N | Y |
| 19 **Neugebauer** | N | N | Y | N | Y | Y | Y |
| 20 Gonzalez | Y | Y | N | Y | N | N | Y |
| 21 **Smith** | N | N | Y | N | N | N | Y |
| 22 **DeLay** | N | N | Y | N | N | N | Y |
| 23 **Bonilla** | N | N | Y | N | N | N | N |
| 24 **Marchant** | N | N | Y | N | N | N | Y |
| 25 Doggett | Y | Y | N | Y | N | N | Y |
| 26 **Burgess** | N | N | Y | Y | Y | N | Y |
| 27 Ortiz | N | Y | Y | Y | N | N | Y |
| 28 Cuellar | ? | ? | ? | ? | ? | ? | ? |
| 29 Green, G. | N | Y | Y | Y | N | N | Y |
| 30 Johnson, E. | Y | Y | N | Y | N | N | Y |
| 31 **Carter** | N | N | Y | N | N | N | Y |
| 32 **Sessions** | ? | ? | ? | ? | ? | ? | ? |
| **UTAH** | | | | | | | |
| 1 **Bishop** | N | N | Y | Y | Y | Y | Y |
| 2 Matheson | N | Y | Y | Y | N | N | Y |
| 3 **Cannon** | N | N | Y | N | Y | Y | Y |
| **VERMONT** | | | | | | | |
| AL *Sanders* | Y | Y | N | Y | N | N | Y |
| **VIRGINIA** | | | | | | | |
| 1 **Davis, J.** | N | N | Y | N | Y | N | Y |
| 2 **Drake** | N | N | Y | N | N | N | Y |
| 3 Scott | Y | Y | N | Y | N | N | Y |
| 4 **Forbes** | N | N | Y | N | Y | N | Y |
| 5 **Goode** | N | N | Y | N | Y | N | Y |
| 6 **Goodlatte** | N | N | Y | N | N | N | Y |
| 7 **Cantor** | N | N | Y | N | N | N | ? |
| 8 Moran | Y | Y | N | Y | N | N | Y |
| 9 Boucher | Y | Y | ? | Y | N | N | Y |
| 10 **Wolf** | N | N | N | N | N | N | Y |
| 11 **Davis, T.** | N | N | N | N | ? | N | Y |
| **WASHINGTON** | | | | | | | |
| 1 Inslee | Y | Y | N | Y | N | N | Y |
| 2 Larsen | N | Y | N | Y | N | N | Y |
| 3 Baird | Y | Y | N | Y | N | N | Y |
| 4 **Hastings** | N | N | Y | N | N | N | Y |
| 5 **McMorris** | N | N | Y | N | N | Y | Y |
| 6 Dicks | N | Y | N | Y | N | N | Y |
| 7 McDermott | Y | Y | N | Y | N | N | Y |
| 8 **Reichert** | N | N | Y | N | N | N | Y |
| 9 Smith | Y | Y | N | Y | N | N | Y |
| **WEST VIRGINIA** | | | | | | | |
| 1 Mollohan | N | Y | N | Y | N | N | Y |
| 2 **Capito** | N | N | Y | N | N | N | Y |
| 3 Rahall | N | Y | Y | Y | N | N | Y |
| **WISCONSIN** | | | | | | | |
| 1 **Ryan** | N | N | Y | N | N | Y | Y |
| 2 Baldwin | Y | Y | N | Y | N | N | Y |
| 3 Kind | Y | Y | N | Y | N | N | Y |
| 4 Moore | Y | Y | N | Y | N | N | Y |
| 5 **Sensenbrenner** | N | N | Y | N | N | Y | Y |
| 6 **Petri** | N | N | Y | Y | N | Y | Y |
| 7 Obey | Y | Y | N | Y | N | N | Y |
| 8 **Green** | N | N | Y | N | N | N | Y |
| **WYOMING** | | | | | | | |
| AL **Cubin** | N | N | Y | Y | Y | Y | Y |

# IN THE HOUSE | By Vote Number

**262.** HR 2862. Fiscal 2006 Commerce-Justice-Science Appropriations/ **Immigration Standards.** Tancredo, R-Colo., amendment that would prohibit the use of funds for the State Criminal Alien Assistance Program by any state or local government entity that restricts its officials from transmitting information regarding an individual's citizenship or immigration status to the Department of Homeland Security. Rejected 204-222: R 189-37; D 15-184 (ND 7-142, SD 8-42); I 0-1. June 16, 2005.

**263.** HR 2862. Fiscal 2006 Commerce-Justice-Science Appropriations/ **Immigration and Trade Agreements.** Tancredo, R-Colo., amendment that would prohibit the use of funds in the bill to include provisions in any trade agreement that would increase the number of aliens permitted into the United States as non-immigrants or permanent residents. Rejected 106-322: R 89-139; D 17-182 (ND 11-138, SD 6-44); I 0-1. June 16, 2005.

**264.** HR 2862. Fiscal 2006 Commerce-Justice-Science Appropriations/ **Racial Conviction Distribution.** Jackson-Lee, D-Texas, amendment that would prohibit funds in the bill to be used to fund state or local anti-drug task forces that do not collect and make available data on the racial distribution of convictions. Rejected 183-244: R 2-226; D 180-18 (ND 137-11, SD 43-7); I 1-0. June 16, 2005.

**265.** HR 2862. Fiscal 2006 Commerce-Justice-Science Appropriations/ **Firearms Exportation.** Moran, D-Va., amendment that would prohibit the use of funds in the bill to license the export of non-automatic or semiautomatic. 50 caliber firearms. Rejected 149-278: R 15-212; D 134-65 (ND 114-36, SD 20-29); I 0-1. June 16, 2005.

**266.** HR 2862. Fiscal 2006 Commerce-Justice-Science Appropriations/ **U.N. Population Fund.** Maloney, D-N.Y., amendment that would prohibit the use of funds in the bill to enforce any provision of law that restricts or prohibits funding for the U.N. Population Fund. Rejected 192-233: R 19-209; D 172-24 (ND 132-15, SD 40-9); I 1-0. June 16, 2005.

**267.** HR 2862. Fiscal 2006 Commerce-Justice-Science Appropriations/ **Illegal Immigration.** King, R-Iowa, amendment that would increase by $1 million funds for provisions in current law that allow state or local officials to transmit information regarding an individual's citizenship or immigration status to the Homeland Security Department. It would be offset by a reduction in salaries, expenses and general legal activities at the Justice Department. Adopted 218-208: R 208-20; D 10-187 (ND 3-144, SD 7-43); I 0-1. June 16, 2005.

| | 262 | 263 | 264 | 265 | 266 | 267 |
|---|---|---|---|---|---|---|
| **ALABAMA** | | | | | | |
| 1 Bonner | Y | N | N | N | N | Y |
| 2 Everett | Y | N | N | N | N | Y |
| 3 Rogers | Y | Y | N | N | N | Y |
| 4 Aderholt | Y | Y | N | N | N | Y |
| 5 Cramer | Y | N | N | N | Y | N |
| 6 Bachus | Y | N | N | N | N | Y |
| 7 Davis | N | N | Y | N | Y | N |
| **ALASKA** | | | | | | |
| AL Young | N | N | N | N | N | N |
| **ARIZONA** | | | | | | |
| 1 Renzi | Y | Y | N | N | N | Y |
| 2 Franks | Y | Y | N | N | N | Y |
| 3 Shadegg | Y | N | N | N | N | Y |
| 4 Pastor | N | N | Y | Y | Y | N |
| 5 Hayworth | Y | N | N | N | N | Y |
| 6 Flake | Y | N | N | N | N | N |
| 7 Grijalva | N | N | Y | Y | Y | N |
| 8 Kolbe | Y | N | N | N | Y | N |
| **ARKANSAS** | | | | | | |
| 1 Berry | N | N | Y | N | N | N |
| 2 Snyder | N | N | Y | Y | Y | N |
| 3 Boozman | Y | Y | N | N | N | Y |
| 4 Ross | N | N | Y | N | N | N |
| **CALIFORNIA** | | | | | | |
| 1 Thompson | N | N | Y | N | Y | N |
| 2 Herger | Y | N | N | N | N | Y |
| 3 Lungren | Y | N | N | N | N | Y |
| 4 Doolittle | Y | N | N | N | N | Y |
| 5 Matsui, D. | N | N | Y | Y | Y | N |
| 6 Woolsey | N | N | Y | Y | Y | N |
| 7 Miller, George | N | N | Y | Y | Y | N |
| 8 Pelosi | N | N | Y | Y | Y | N |
| 9 Lee | N | N | Y | Y | Y | N |
| 10 Tauscher | N | N | Y | Y | Y | N |
| 11 Pombo | Y | Y | N | N | N | Y |
| 12 Lantos | N | N | Y | Y | Y | N |
| 13 Stark | N | N | Y | Y | Y | N |
| 14 Eshoo | N | N | Y | Y | Y | N |
| 15 Honda | N | N | Y | Y | Y | N |
| 16 Lofgren | N | N | Y | Y | Y | N |
| 17 Farr | N | N | Y | Y | Y | N |
| 18 Cardoza | N | N | Y | N | Y | N |
| 19 Radanovich | Y | Y | N | N | N | Y |
| 20 Costa | Y | N | Y | N | Y | N |
| 21 Nunes | Y | N | N | N | N | Y |
| 22 Thomas | Y | N | N | N | N | Y |
| 23 Capps | N | N | Y | Y | Y | N |
| 24 Gallegly | Y | N | N | N | N | Y |
| 25 McKeon | Y | N | N | N | N | Y |
| 26 Dreier | Y | N | N | N | N | Y |
| 27 Sherman | N | N | Y | Y | Y | N |
| 28 Berman | N | N | Y | Y | Y | N |
| 29 Schiff | N | N | Y | Y | Y | N |
| 30 Waxman | N | N | Y | Y | Y | N |
| 31 Becerra | N | N | Y | Y | Y | N |
| 32 Solis | N | N | Y | Y | Y | N |
| 33 Watson | N | N | Y | Y | Y | N |
| 34 Roybal-Allard | N | N | Y | Y | Y | N |
| 35 Waters | N | N | Y | Y | Y | ? |
| 36 Harman | N | N | Y | Y | Y | N |
| 37 Millender-McD. | N | N | Y | Y | Y | N |
| 38 Napolitano | N | N | Y | Y | Y | N |
| 39 Sánchez, Linda | N | N | Y | Y | Y | N |
| 40 Royce | Y | Y | N | N | N | Y |
| 41 Lewis | N | N | N | N | N | N |
| 42 Miller, Gary | Y | N | N | N | N | Y |
| 43 Baca | N | N | Y | N | Y | N |
| 44 Calvert | Y | N | N | N | N | Y |
| 45 Bono | ? | ? | ? | ? | ? | ? |
| 46 Rohrabacher | Y | Y | N | N | N | Y |
| 47 Sanchez, Loretta | N | N | Y | Y | Y | N |
| 48 Cox | Y | Y | N | N | N | Y |
| 49 Issa | Y | N | N | N | N | Y |

| | 262 | 263 | 264 | 265 | 266 | 267 |
|---|---|---|---|---|---|---|
| 50 Cunningham | Y | N | N | N | N | Y |
| 51 Filner | N | N | Y | Y | Y | N |
| 52 Hunter | ? | Y | N | N | N | Y |
| 53 Davis | N | N | Y | Y | Y | N |
| **COLORADO** | | | | | | |
| 1 DeGette | N | N | Y | Y | Y | N |
| 2 Udall | N | N | Y | N | Y | N |
| 3 Salazar | N | N | Y | N | N | N |
| 4 Musgrave | Y | N | N | N | N | Y |
| 5 Hefley | Y | Y | N | N | N | Y |
| 6 Tancredo | Y | Y | N | N | N | Y |
| 7 Beauprez | Y | N | N | N | N | Y |
| **CONNECTICUT** | | | | | | |
| 1 Larson | N | N | Y | Y | Y | N |
| 2 Simmons | N | N | N | N | Y | N |
| 3 DeLauro | N | N | Y | Y | Y | N |
| 4 Shays | Y | N | N | Y | Y | N |
| 5 Johnson | Y | N | N | Y | Y | Y |
| **DELAWARE** | | | | | | |
| AL Castle | N | N | N | Y | Y | Y |
| **FLORIDA** | | | | | | |
| 1 Miller | Y | Y | N | N | N | Y |
| 2 Boyd | N | N | N | N | Y | N |
| 3 Brown | N | N | Y | Y | Y | N |
| 4 Crenshaw | Y | N | N | N | N | Y |
| 5 Brown-Waite | Y | N | N | N | N | Y |
| 6 Stearns | Y | Y | N | N | N | Y |
| 7 Mica | Y | Y | N | N | N | Y |
| 8 Keller | Y | Y | N | N | N | Y |
| 9 Bilirakis | Y | Y | N | N | N | Y |
| 10 Young | Y | Y | N | N | N | Y |
| 11 Davis | N | N | Y | Y | Y | N |
| 12 Putnam | Y | N | N | N | N | Y |
| 13 Harris | Y | N | N | N | N | Y |
| 14 Mack | Y | N | N | N | N | Y |
| 15 Weldon | Y | N | N | N | N | Y |
| 16 Foley | + | N | N | N | N | Y |
| 17 Meek | N | N | Y | Y | Y | N |
| 18 Ros-Lehtinen | N | N | N | N | N | Y |
| 19 Wexler | N | N | Y | Y | Y | N |
| 20 Wasserman-Schultz | N | N | Y | Y | Y | N |
| 21 Diaz-Balart, L. | N | N | N | N | N | Y |
| 22 Shaw | N | N | N | N | N | Y |
| 23 Hastings | N | N | Y | Y | Y | N |
| 24 Feeney | Y | N | N | N | N | Y |
| 25 Diaz-Balart, M. | N | N | N | N | N | N |
| **GEORGIA** | | | | | | |
| 1 Kingston | Y | N | N | N | N | Y |
| 2 Bishop | N | N | Y | N | Y | N |
| 3 Marshall | Y | Y | N | Y | Y | Y |
| 4 McKinney | N | N | Y | Y | Y | N |
| 5 Lewis | N | N | Y | Y | Y | N |
| 6 Price | Y | N | N | N | N | Y |
| 7 Linder | Y | N | N | N | N | Y |
| 8 Westmoreland | N | N | N | N | N | Y |
| 9 Norwood | Y | Y | N | N | N | Y |
| 10 Deal | Y | Y | N | N | N | Y |
| 11 Gingrey | Y | Y | N | N | N | Y |
| 12 Barrow | Y | Y | Y | N | Y | Y |
| 13 Scott | N | N | Y | N | Y | N |
| **HAWAII** | | | | | | |
| 1 Abercrombie | N | Y | Y | Y | Y | N |
| 2 Case | Y | Y | N | Y | Y | Y |
| **IDAHO** | | | | | | |
| 1 Otter | Y | Y | N | N | N | Y |
| 2 Simpson | Y | Y | N | N | N | Y |
| **ILLINOIS** | | | | | | |
| 1 Rush | N | N | ? | Y | Y | N |
| 2 Jackson | N | N | Y | Y | Y | N |
| 3 Lipinski | N | N | Y | Y | Y | N |
| 4 Gutierrez | N | N | Y | Y | Y | N |
| 5 Emanuel | N | N | Y | Y | Y | N |
| 6 Hyde | Y | N | N | N | N | Y |
| 7 Davis | N | N | Y | Y | Y | N |
| 8 Bean | N | N | Y | Y | Y | N |
| 9 Schakowsky | N | N | Y | Y | Y | N |
| 10 Kirk | N | N | N | Y | Y | Y |
| 11 Weller | N | N | N | N | N | Y |
| 12 Costello | N | N | Y | N | N | N |

| | 262 | 263 | 264 | 265 | 266 | 267 |
|---|---|---|---|---|---|---|
| 13 **Biggert** | N | N | N | N | Y | N |
| 14 **Hastert** | | | | | | |
| 15 **Johnson** | N | N | N | N | N | Y |
| 16 **Manzullo** | Y | Y | N | N | N | Y |
| 17 Evans | N | N | Y | Y | Y | N |
| 18 **LaHood** | Y | N | N | N | N | Y |
| 19 **Shimkus** | Y | N | N | N | N | Y |
| **INDIANA** | | | | | | |
| 1 Visclosky | N | N | Y | N | Y | N |
| 2 **Chocola** | Y | N | N | N | N | Y |
| 3 **Souder** | Y | N | N | N | N | Y |
| 4 **Buyer** | Y | N | N | N | N | Y |
| 5 **Burton** | Y | N | N | N | N | Y |
| 6 **Pence** | Y | Y | N | N | N | Y |
| 7 Carson | N | N | Y | Y | Y | N |
| 8 **Hostettler** | Y | Y | N | N | N | Y |
| 9 **Sodrel** | Y | Y | N | N | N | Y |
| **IOWA** | | | | | | |
| 1 **Nussle** | Y | N | N | N | N | Y |
| 2 **Leach** | N | N | N | Y | Y | Y |
| 3 Boswell | N | N | N | N | Y | N |
| 4 **Latham** | Y | N | N | N | N | Y |
| 5 **King** | Y | Y | N | N | N | Y |
| **KANSAS** | | | | | | |
| 1 **Moran** | Y | Y | N | N | N | Y |
| 2 **Ryun** | Y | Y | N | N | N | Y |
| 3 Moore | N | N | Y | Y | Y | N |
| 4 **Tiahrt** | Y | N | N | N | N | Y |
| **KENTUCKY** | | | | | | |
| 1 **Whitfield** | Y | Y | N | N | N | Y |
| 2 **Lewis** | Y | N | N | N | N | Y |
| 3 **Northup** | Y | N | N | N | N | Y |
| 4 **Davis** | Y | N | N | N | N | Y |
| 5 **Rogers** | Y | N | N | N | N | Y |
| 6 Chandler | N | N | N | N | Y | Y |
| **LOUISIANA** | | | | | | |
| 1 **Jindal** | Y | N | N | N | N | Y |
| 2 Jefferson | N | N | Y | N | Y | N |
| 3 Melancon | N | Y | N | N | N | N |
| 4 **McCrery** | Y | N | N | N | N | Y |
| 5 **Alexander** | Y | N | N | N | N | Y |
| 6 **Baker** | Y | N | N | N | N | Y |
| 7 **Boustany** | Y | N | N | N | N | Y |
| **MAINE** | | | | | | |
| 1 Allen | N | N | Y | Y | Y | N |
| 2 Michaud | N | N | Y | N | Y | N |
| **MARYLAND** | | | | | | |
| 1 **Gilchrest** | N | N | N | Y | Y | N |
| 2 Ruppersberger | N | N | Y | N | Y | N |
| 3 Cardin | N | N | Y | Y | Y | N |
| 4 Wynn | N | N | Y | Y | Y | N |
| 5 Hoyer | N | N | Y | Y | Y | N |
| 6 **Bartlett** | Y | Y | N | N | N | Y |
| 7 Cummings | N | N | Y | Y | Y | N |
| 8 Van Hollen | N | N | Y | Y | Y | N |
| **MASSACHUSETTS** | | | | | | |
| 1 Olver | N | N | Y | Y | Y | N |
| 2 Neal | N | N | Y | Y | Y | N |
| 3 McGovern | N | N | Y | Y | Y | N |
| 4 Frank | N | N | Y | Y | Y | N |
| 5 Meehan | N | N | Y | Y | Y | N |
| 6 Tierney | ? | N | Y | Y | Y | N |
| 7 Markey | N | N | Y | Y | Y | N |
| 8 Capuano | N | N | Y | Y | Y | N |
| 9 Lynch | N | N | Y | Y | Y | N |
| 10 Delahunt | N | ? | Y | Y | ? | N |
| **MICHIGAN** | | | | | | |
| 1 Stupak | N | N | Y | N | N | N |
| 2 **Hoekstra** | Y | N | N | N | N | Y |
| 3 **Ehlers** | N | N | N | Y | N | N |
| 4 **Camp** | Y | N | N | N | N | Y |
| 5 Kildee | N | N | Y | N | N | N |
| 6 **Upton** | Y | N | N | N | N | Y |
| 7 **Schwarz** | N | N | N | N | N | Y |
| 8 **Rogers** | Y | Y | N | N | N | Y |
| 9 **Knollenberg** | N | N | N | N | N | N |
| 10 **Miller** | Y | Y | N | N | N | Y |
| 11 **McCotter** | Y | Y | N | N | N | Y |
| 12 Levin | N | N | Y | Y | Y | N |
| 13 Kilpatrick | N | N | Y | Y | Y | N |
| 14 Conyers | N | N | Y | Y | ? | N |
| 15 Dingell | N | N | Y | N | Y | N |
| **MINNESOTA** | | | | | | |
| 1 **Gutknecht** | Y | Y | N | N | N | Y |
| 2 **Kline** | Y | N | N | N | N | Y |
| 3 **Ramstad** | Y | N | N | Y | Y | Y |
| 4 McCollum | N | N | Y | Y | Y | N |
| 5 Sabo | N | N | Y | Y | Y | N |
| 6 **Kennedy** | Y | N | N | N | N | Y |
| 7 Peterson | Y | Y | N | N | N | Y |
| 8 Oberstar | ? | ? | ? | ? | ? | ? |
| **MISSISSIPPI** | | | | | | |
| 1 **Wicker** | Y | N | N | N | N | Y |
| 2 Thompson | N | N | Y | Y | Y | N |
| 3 **Pickering** | Y | N | N | N | N | Y |
| 4 Taylor | Y | Y | N | N | N | Y |
| **MISSOURI** | | | | | | |
| 1 Clay | N | N | Y | Y | Y | N |
| 2 **Akin** | Y | Y | N | N | N | Y |
| 3 Carnahan | N | N | Y | Y | Y | N |
| 4 Skelton | Y | Y | Y | N | N | N |
| 5 Cleaver | N | N | Y | Y | Y | N |
| 6 **Graves** | Y | Y | N | N | N | Y |
| 7 **Blunt** | Y | N | N | N | N | Y |
| 8 **Emerson** | Y | Y | N | N | N | Y |
| 9 **Hulshof** | Y | N | N | N | N | Y |
| **MONTANA** | | | | | | |
| AL **Rehberg** | Y | Y | N | N | N | Y |
| **NEBRASKA** | | | | | | |
| 1 **Fortenberry** | Y | N | N | N | N | Y |
| 2 **Terry** | N | N | N | N | N | Y |
| 3 **Osborne** | Y | N | N | N | N | Y |
| **NEVADA** | | | | | | |
| 1 Berkley | N | N | Y | Y | Y | N |
| 2 **Gibbons** | Y | Y | N | N | N | Y |
| 3 **Porter** | N | N | N | N | N | N |
| **NEW HAMPSHIRE** | | | | | | |
| 1 **Bradley** | Y | Y | N | N | Y | Y |
| 2 **Bass** | Y | N | N | N | Y | Y |
| **NEW JERSEY** | | | | | | |
| 1 Andrews | N | N | Y | Y | Y | N |
| 2 **LoBiondo** | N | Y | N | Y | N | Y |
| 3 **Saxton** | N | N | N | N | N | Y |
| 4 **Smith** | Y | N | N | N | N | Y |
| 5 **Garrett** | Y | Y | N | N | N | Y |
| 6 Pallone | N | N | Y | Y | Y | N |
| 7 **Ferguson** | N | N | N | Y | N | N |
| 8 Pascrell | N | Y | Y | Y | Y | N |
| 9 Rothman | N | N | Y | Y | Y | N |
| 10 Payne | N | N | Y | Y | Y | N |
| 11 **Frelinghuysen** | N | N | N | N | Y | Y |
| 12 Holt | N | N | Y | Y | Y | N |
| 13 Menendez | N | N | Y | Y | Y | N |
| **NEW MEXICO** | | | | | | |
| 1 **Wilson** | N | N | N | N | N | N |
| 2 **Pearce** | Y | N | N | N | N | Y |
| 3 Udall | N | N | Y | Y | Y | N |
| **NEW YORK** | | | | | | |
| 1 Bishop | N | N | Y | Y | Y | N |
| 2 Israel | N | N | Y | Y | Y | N |
| 3 **King** | Y | N | N | N | N | Y |
| 4 McCarthy | N | N | Y | Y | Y | N |
| 5 Ackerman | N | N | Y | N | Y | N |
| 6 Meeks | N | N | Y | N | Y | N |
| 7 Crowley | N | N | Y | N | Y | N |
| 8 Nadler | N | N | Y | Y | Y | N |
| 9 Weiner | N | N | Y | Y | Y | N |
| 10 Towns | N | N | Y | Y | Y | N |
| 11 Owens | N | N | Y | Y | Y | N |
| 12 Velázquez | N | N | Y | Y | Y | N |
| 13 **Fossella** | N | N | N | N | N | Y |
| 14 Maloney | N | N | Y | Y | Y | N |
| 15 Rangel | N | N | Y | Y | Y | N |
| 16 Serrano | N | N | Y | Y | Y | N |
| 17 Engel | N | N | Y | Y | Y | N |
| 18 Lowey | N | N | Y | Y | Y | N |
| 19 **Kelly** | N | N | N | N | Y | Y |
| 20 **Sweeney** | Y | Y | N | N | N | Y |
| 21 McNulty | N | N | Y | N | Y | N |
| 22 Hinchey | N | N | Y | Y | ? | ? |
| 23 **McHugh** | Y | Y | N | N | N | Y |
| 24 **Boehlert** | N | N | N | N | Y | Y |
| 25 **Walsh** | Y | N | N | N | N | N |
| 26 **Reynolds** | N | N | N | N | N | Y |
| 27 Higgins | N | N | Y | Y | Y | N |
| 28 Slaughter | N | N | Y | Y | Y | N |
| 29 **Kuhl** | N | N | N | N | N | Y |
| **NORTH CAROLINA** | | | | | | |
| 1 Butterfield | N | N | Y | N | Y | N |
| 2 Etheridge | N | N | Y | N | Y | N |
| 3 **Jones** | Y | Y | N | N | N | Y |
| 4 Price | N | N | Y | Y | Y | N |
| 5 **Foxx** | Y | Y | N | N | N | Y |
| 6 **Coble** | Y | Y | N | N | N | Y |
| 7 McIntyre | N | N | Y | N | N | Y |
| 8 **Hayes** | Y | Y | N | N | N | Y |
| 9 **Myrick** | Y | N | N | N | N | Y |
| 10 **McHenry** | Y | Y | N | N | N | Y |
| 11 **Taylor** | Y | Y | N | N | N | Y |
| 12 Watt | N | N | Y | Y | Y | N |
| 13 Miller | N | N | Y | Y | Y | N |
| **NORTH DAKOTA** | | | | | | |
| AL Pomeroy | N | N | N | N | Y | N |
| **OHIO** | | | | | | |
| 1 **Chabot** | Y | Y | N | N | N | Y |
| 2 Vacant | | | | | | |
| 3 **Turner** | Y | N | N | N | N | Y |
| 4 **Oxley** | Y | N | N | ? | N | Y |
| 5 **Gillmor** | Y | Y | N | N | N | Y |
| 6 Strickland | N | Y | Y | N | Y | N |
| 7 **Hobson** | Y | N | N | N | N | Y |
| 8 **Boehner** | Y | N | N | N | N | Y |
| 9 Kaptur | N | Y | Y | N | N | N |
| 10 Kucinich | N | N | Y | Y | Y | N |
| 11 Jones | N | N | Y | Y | Y | N |
| 12 **Tiberi** | Y | N | N | N | N | Y |
| 13 Brown | N | N | Y | Y | Y | N |
| 14 **LaTourette** | Y | N | N | N | N | Y |
| 15 **Pryce** | Y | N | N | N | N | Y |
| 16 **Regula** | Y | N | N | Y | N | Y |
| 17 Ryan | N | Y | Y | N | N | N |
| 18 **Ney** | Y | Y | N | N | N | Y |
| **OKLAHOMA** | | | | | | |
| 1 **Sullivan** | Y | Y | N | N | N | Y |
| 2 Boren | N | Y | Y | N | N | Y |
| 3 **Lucas** | Y | N | N | N | N | Y |
| 4 **Cole** | Y | N | N | N | N | Y |
| 5 **Istook** | Y | Y | N | N | N | Y |
| **OREGON** | | | | | | |
| 1 Wu | N | N | Y | N | Y | N |
| 2 **Walden** | N | N | N | N | N | Y |
| 3 Blumenauer | N | N | Y | Y | Y | N |
| 4 DeFazio | N | Y | Y | N | Y | N |
| 5 Hooley | N | N | Y | Y | Y | N |
| **PENNSYLVANIA** | | | | | | |
| 1 Brady | N | N | Y | Y | Y | N |
| 2 Fattah | N | N | Y | Y | Y | N |
| 3 **English** | Y | N | N | N | N | Y |
| 4 **Hart** | Y | N | N | N | N | Y |
| 5 **Peterson** | Y | Y | N | N | N | Y |
| 6 **Gerlach** | Y | N | N | N | Y | Y |
| 7 **Weldon** | Y | Y | N | Y | N | Y |
| 8 **Fitzpatrick** | Y | N | N | Y | N | Y |
| 9 **Shuster** | Y | Y | N | N | N | Y |
| 10 **Sherwood** | Y | N | N | N | N | Y |
| 11 Kanjorski | Y | N | N | N | N | N |
| 12 Murtha | Y | N | N | Y | N | N |
| 13 Schwartz | N | N | Y | Y | Y | N |
| 14 Doyle | N | N | Y | Y | N | N |
| 15 **Dent** | Y | N | N | N | Y | Y |
| 16 **Pitts** | Y | Y | N | N | N | Y |
| 17 Holden | Y | Y | N | N | N | N |
| 18 **Murphy** | N | Y | Y | N | N | Y |
| 19 **Platts** | Y | Y | N | N | N | Y |
| **RHODE ISLAND** | | | | | | |
| 1 Kennedy | N | N | Y | Y | Y | N |
| 2 Langevin | N | N | Y | Y | Y | N |
| **SOUTH CAROLINA** | | | | | | |
| 1 **Brown** | Y | N | N | N | N | Y |
| 2 **Wilson** | Y | Y | N | N | N | Y |
| 3 **Barrett** | Y | Y | N | N | N | Y |
| 4 **Inglis** | Y | N | N | N | N | Y |
| 5 Spratt | N | N | Y | Y | Y | N |
| 6 Clyburn | N | N | Y | Y | Y | N |
| **SOUTH DAKOTA** | | | | | | |
| AL Herseth | N | Y | N | N | Y | N |
| **TENNESSEE** | | | | | | |
| 1 **Jenkins** | Y | N | N | N | N | Y |
| 2 **Duncan** | Y | Y | N | N | N | Y |
| 3 **Wamp** | Y | Y | N | N | N | Y |
| 4 Davis | Y | Y | N | N | N | N |
| 5 Cooper | N | N | Y | N | Y | N |
| 6 Gordon | Y | N | Y | N | Y | N |
| 7 **Blackburn** | Y | N | N | N | N | Y |
| 8 Tanner | Y | N | N | N | Y | Y |
| 9 Ford | N | N | Y | N | Y | N |
| **TEXAS** | | | | | | |
| 1 **Gohmert** | Y | Y | N | N | N | Y |
| 2 **Poe** | Y | N | N | N | N | Y |
| 3 **Johnson, S.** | Y | N | N | N | N | Y |
| 4 **Hall** | Y | Y | N | N | N | Y |
| 5 **Hensarling** | Y | N | N | N | N | Y |
| 6 **Barton** | Y | Y | N | N | N | Y |
| 7 **Culberson** | Y | N | N | N | N | Y |
| 8 **Brady** | Y | Y | N | N | N | Y |
| 9 Green, A. | N | N | Y | Y | Y | N |
| 10 **McCaul** | Y | N | N | N | N | Y |
| 11 **Conaway** | Y | N | N | N | N | Y |
| 12 **Granger** | Y | N | N | N | N | Y |
| 13 **Thornberry** | Y | N | N | N | N | Y |
| 14 **Paul** | Y | Y | Y | N | N | Y |
| 15 Hinojosa | N | N | Y | N | Y | N |
| 16 Reyes | N | N | Y | N | Y | N |
| 17 Edwards | N | N | Y | N | Y | N |
| 18 Jackson-Lee | N | N | Y | Y | ? | N |
| 19 **Neugebauer** | Y | N | N | N | N | Y |
| 20 Gonzalez | N | N | Y | N | Y | N |
| 21 **Smith** | Y | Y | N | N | N | Y |
| 22 **DeLay** | Y | N | N | N | N | Y |
| 23 **Bonilla** | Y | N | N | N | N | Y |
| 24 **Marchant** | Y | Y | N | N | N | Y |
| 25 Doggett | N | N | Y | Y | Y | N |
| 26 **Burgess** | Y | Y | N | N | N | Y |
| 27 Ortiz | N | N | Y | N | N | N |
| 28 Cuellar | ? | ? | ? | ? | ? | ? |
| 29 Green, G. | N | N | Y | ? | Y | N |
| 30 Johnson, E. | N | N | Y | Y | Y | N |
| 31 **Carter** | Y | N | N | N | N | Y |
| 32 **Sessions** | ? | ? | ? | ? | ? | ? |
| **UTAH** | | | | | | |
| 1 **Bishop** | Y | N | N | N | N | Y |
| 2 Matheson | N | N | N | N | Y | Y |
| 3 **Cannon** | N | N | N | N | N | Y |
| **VERMONT** | | | | | | |
| AL *Sanders* | N | N | Y | N | Y | N |
| **VIRGINIA** | | | | | | |
| 1 **Davis, J.** | Y | Y | N | N | N | Y |
| 2 **Drake** | Y | Y | N | N | N | Y |
| 3 Scott | N | N | Y | Y | Y | N |
| 4 **Forbes** | Y | Y | N | N | N | Y |
| 5 **Goode** | Y | Y | N | N | N | Y |
| 6 **Goodlatte** | Y | Y | N | N | N | Y |
| 7 **Cantor** | Y | N | N | N | N | Y |
| 8 Moran | N | N | Y | Y | Y | N |
| 9 Boucher | Y | N | Y | N | Y | N |
| 10 **Wolf** | Y | Y | N | Y | N | Y |
| 11 **Davis, T.** | Y | N | N | Y | N | Y |
| **WASHINGTON** | | | | | | |
| 1 Inslee | N | N | Y | Y | Y | N |
| 2 Larsen | N | N | Y | N | Y | N |
| 3 Baird | N | N | N | Y | Y | N |
| 4 **Hastings** | N | N | N | N | N | Y |
| 5 **McMorris** | Y | Y | N | N | N | Y |
| 6 Dicks | N | N | N | Y | Y | N |
| 7 McDermott | N | N | ? | Y | Y | ? |
| 8 **Reichert** | N | N | N | N | N | N |
| 9 Smith | N | N | Y | N | Y | N |
| **WEST VIRGINIA** | | | | | | |
| 1 Mollohan | N | N | Y | N | N | N |
| 2 **Capito** | N | N | N | N | N | Y |
| 3 Rahall | N | N | N | N | N | N |
| **WISCONSIN** | | | | | | |
| 1 **Ryan** | N | N | N | N | N | Y |
| 2 Baldwin | N | N | Y | Y | Y | N |
| 3 Kind | N | N | Y | N | Y | N |
| 4 Moore | N | N | Y | Y | Y | N |
| 5 **Sensenbrenner** | Y | Y | N | N | N | Y |
| 6 **Petri** | Y | N | N | N | N | Y |
| 7 Obey | N | N | Y | N | N | N |
| 8 **Green** | N | Y | N | N | N | Y |
| **WYOMING** | | | | | | |
| AL **Cubin** | Y | N | N | N | N | Y |

# IN THE HOUSE | By Vote Number

**268.** HR 2862. Fiscal 2006 Commerce-Justice-Science Appropriations/ **Passage.** Passage of the bill that would provide $57.8 billion in fiscal 2006 for the Departments of Commerce, Justice and State as well as various science and other related agencies. It would provide $21.8 billion for the Justice Department, $5.8 billion for the Commerce Department, $9.7 billion for the State Department and international broadcasting agencies, $16.5 billion for NASA, and $5.6 billion for the National Science Foundation. It would block the Office of the U.S. Trade Representative from enforcing language in future trade agreements that would make it more difficult to import prescription drugs from the specific countries involved. Passed 418-7: R 221-5; D 196-2 (ND 147-1, SD 49-1); I 1-0. June 16, 2005.

**269.** HR 2863. Fiscal 2006 Defense Appropriations/Previous **Question.** Cole, R-Okla., motion to order the previous question (thus ending debate and possibility of amendment) on adoption of the rule (H Res 315) to provide for House floor consideration of the bill that would appropriate $408.9 billion in fiscal 2006 for the Defense Department. Motion agreed to 223-200: R 223-1; D 0-198 (ND 0-148, SD 0-50); I 0-1. (Subsequently, the rule was adopted by voice vote.) June 16, 2005.

**270.** HR 2745. U.N. Overhaul/Immunity for U.N. Officials. King, R-N.Y., amendment that would instruct the president to direct the U.S. permanent representative to the United Nations to ensure that the Secretary General exercises the right and duty to waive immunity of any U.N. official who is under investigation for, or is charged with, committing a serious criminal offense. Adopted 405-13: R 224-0; D 180-13 (ND 134-10, SD 46-3); I 1-0. June 16, 2005.

**271.** HR 2745. U.N. Overhaul/U.S. Contributions to the United Nations. Poe, R-Texas, amendment that would require the Office of Management and Budget to submit a report to the House International Relations Committee on the U.S. contributions to the United Nations, including assessed, voluntary and in-kind contributions. Adopted 402-14: R 223-0; D 178-14 (ND 131-12, SD 47-2); I 1-0. June 16, 2005.

**272.** HR 2745. U.N. Overhaul/IAEA Resolution. Cantor, R-Va., amendment that would direct the U.S. permanent representative to the International Atomic Energy Agency to ensure that the IAEA adopts a resolution making Iran ineligible to receive any nuclear material, technology, equipment or assistance from any IAEA member state until it is in full compliance with the agency. Adopted 411-9: R 223-1; D 187-8 (ND 139-7, SD 48-1); I 1-0. June 16, 2005.

**273.** H Res 324. House Judiciary Committee Hearing/Motion to Table. DeLay, R-Texas, motion to table (kill) the Nadler, D-N.Y., privileged resolution that would condemn the breaking of House rules by the chairman of the Judiciary Committee during a hearing on the law known as the Patriot Act on June 10, 2005. It would instruct the chairman, in consultation with the ranking Democrat, to schedule another day of hearings with witnesses requested by the minority. Motion agreed to 222-191: R 222-0; D 0-190 (ND 0-142, SD 0-48); I 0-1. June 16, 2005.

| | 268 | 269 | 270 | 271 | 272 | 273 |
|---|---|---|---|---|---|---|
| **ALABAMA** | | | | | | |
| 1 Bonner | Y | Y | Y | Y | Y | Y |
| 2 Everett | Y | Y | Y | Y | Y | Y |
| 3 Rogers | Y | Y | Y | Y | Y | Y |
| 4 Aderholt | Y | Y | Y | Y | Y | Y |
| 5 Cramer | Y | N | Y | Y | Y | N |
| 6 Bachus | Y | Y | Y | Y | Y | Y |
| 7 Davis | Y | N | Y | Y | Y | N |
| **ALASKA** | | | | | | |
| AL Young | Y | Y | ? | ? | ? | ? |
| **ARIZONA** | | | | | | |
| 1 Renzi | Y | Y | Y | Y | Y | Y |
| 2 Franks | Y | Y | Y | Y | Y | Y |
| 3 Shadegg | Y | Y | Y | Y | Y | Y |
| 4 Pastor | Y | N | Y | Y | Y | N |
| 5 Hayworth | Y | Y | Y | Y | Y | Y |
| 6 Flake | N | Y | Y | Y | Y | Y |
| 7 Grijalva | Y | N | Y | Y | Y | N |
| 8 Kolbe | Y | Y | Y | Y | Y | Y |
| **ARKANSAS** | | | | | | |
| 1 Berry | Y | N | Y | Y | Y | N |
| 2 Snyder | Y | N | Y | Y | Y | N |
| 3 Boozman | Y | Y | Y | Y | Y | Y |
| 4 Ross | Y | N | Y | Y | Y | N |
| **CALIFORNIA** | | | | | | |
| 1 Thompson | Y | N | Y | Y | Y | N |
| 2 Herger | Y | Y | Y | Y | Y | Y |
| 3 Lungren | Y | Y | Y | Y | Y | Y |
| 4 Doolittle | Y | Y | Y | Y | Y | Y |
| 5 Matsui, D. | Y | N | Y | Y | Y | N |
| 6 Woolsey | Y | N | N | N | Y | N |
| 7 Miller, George | Y | N | Y | Y | Y | ? |
| 8 Pelosi | Y | N | ? | ? | ? | ? |
| 9 Lee | ? | N | N | N | N | N |
| 10 Tauscher | Y | N | Y | Y | N | N |
| 11 Pombo | Y | Y | Y | Y | Y | Y |
| 12 Lantos | Y | N | Y | Y | Y | N |
| 13 Stark | Y | N | N | N | N | N |
| 14 Eshoo | Y | N | Y | Y | Y | N |
| 15 Honda | Y | N | N | N | Y | N |
| 16 Lofgren | Y | N | Y | Y | Y | N |
| 17 Farr | Y | N | Y | Y | Y | N |
| 18 Cardoza | Y | N | Y | Y | Y | N |
| 19 Radanovich | Y | Y | Y | Y | Y | Y |
| 20 Costa | Y | N | Y | Y | Y | N |
| 21 Nunes | Y | Y | Y | Y | Y | Y |
| 22 Thomas | Y | ? | Y | Y | Y | Y |
| 23 Capps | Y | N | Y | Y | Y | N |
| 24 Gallegly | Y | Y | Y | Y | Y | Y |
| 25 McKeon | Y | Y | Y | Y | Y | Y |
| 26 Dreier | Y | Y | Y | Y | Y | Y |
| 27 Sherman | Y | N | Y | Y | Y | N |
| 28 Berman | Y | N | Y | Y | Y | ? |
| 29 Schiff | Y | N | Y | Y | Y | N |
| 30 Waxman | Y | N | Y | Y | Y | N |
| 31 Becerra | Y | N | Y | Y | Y | N |
| 32 Solis | Y | N | Y | Y | Y | N |
| 33 Watson | Y | N | Y | Y | Y | N |
| 34 Roybal-Allard | Y | N | Y | Y | Y | N |
| 35 Waters | Y | N | P | Y | Y | N |
| 36 Harman | Y | N | Y | Y | Y | N |
| 37 Millender-McD. | Y | N | ? | ? | ? | ? |
| 38 Napolitano | Y | N | Y | Y | Y | N |
| 39 Sánchez, Linda | Y | N | Y | Y | Y | N |
| 40 Royce | Y | Y | Y | Y | Y | Y |
| 41 Lewis | Y | Y | Y | Y | Y | Y |
| 42 Miller, Gary | Y | Y | Y | Y | Y | Y |
| 43 Baca | Y | N | Y | Y | Y | N |
| 44 Calvert | Y | Y | Y | Y | Y | Y |
| 45 Bono | ? | ? | ? | ? | ? | ? |
| 46 Rohrabacher | Y | Y | Y | Y | Y | Y |
| 47 Sanchez, Loretta | Y | N | Y | Y | Y | N |
| 48 Cox | Y | Y | ? | ? | ? | ? |
| 49 Issa | Y | Y | Y | Y | Y | Y |

| | 268 | 269 | 270 | 271 | 272 | 273 |
|---|---|---|---|---|---|---|
| 50 Cunningham | Y | Y | Y | Y | Y | Y |
| 51 Filner | Y | N | Y | Y | Y | N |
| 52 Hunter | Y | Y | Y | Y | Y | Y |
| 53 Davis | Y | N | Y | Y | Y | N |
| **COLORADO** | | | | | | |
| 1 DeGette | Y | N | Y | Y | Y | N |
| 2 Udall | Y | N | Y | Y | Y | N |
| 3 Salazar | Y | N | Y | Y | Y | N |
| 4 Musgrave | Y | Y | Y | Y | Y | Y |
| 5 Hefley | N | Y | Y | Y | Y | Y |
| 6 Tancredo | Y | Y | Y | Y | Y | Y |
| 7 Beauprez | Y | Y | Y | Y | Y | Y |
| **CONNECTICUT** | | | | | | |
| 1 Larson | Y | N | Y | Y | Y | N |
| 2 Simmons | Y | Y | Y | Y | Y | Y |
| 3 DeLauro | Y | N | Y | Y | Y | N |
| 4 Shays | Y | Y | Y | Y | Y | Y |
| 5 Johnson | Y | Y | Y | Y | Y | Y |
| **DELAWARE** | | | | | | |
| AL Castle | Y | Y | Y | Y | Y | Y |
| **FLORIDA** | | | | | | |
| 1 Miller | N | Y | Y | Y | Y | Y |
| 2 Boyd | Y | N | Y | Y | Y | N |
| 3 Brown | Y | N | Y | Y | Y | N |
| 4 Crenshaw | Y | Y | Y | Y | Y | Y |
| 5 Brown-Waite | Y | Y | Y | Y | Y | Y |
| 6 Stearns | Y | Y | Y | Y | Y | Y |
| 7 Mica | Y | Y | Y | Y | Y | Y |
| 8 Keller | Y | Y | Y | Y | Y | Y |
| 9 Bilirakis | Y | Y | Y | Y | Y | Y |
| 10 Young | Y | Y | Y | Y | Y | Y |
| 11 Davis | Y | N | Y | Y | Y | N |
| 12 Putnam | Y | Y | Y | Y | Y | Y |
| 13 Harris | Y | Y | Y | Y | Y | Y |
| 14 Mack | Y | Y | Y | Y | Y | Y |
| 15 Weldon | Y | Y | Y | Y | Y | Y |
| 16 Foley | Y | Y | Y | Y | Y | Y |
| 17 Meek | Y | N | Y | Y | Y | N |
| 18 Ros-Lehtinen | Y | Y | Y | Y | Y | Y |
| 19 Wexler | Y | N | Y | Y | Y | N |
| 20 Wasserman-Schultz | Y | N | Y | Y | Y | N |
| 21 Diaz-Balart, L. | Y | Y | Y | Y | Y | Y |
| 22 Shaw | Y | Y | Y | Y | Y | Y |
| 23 Hastings | Y | N | N | N | Y | N |
| 24 Feeney | Y | Y | Y | Y | Y | Y |
| 25 Diaz-Balart, M. | Y | Y | Y | Y | Y | Y |
| **GEORGIA** | | | | | | |
| 1 Kingston | Y | Y | Y | Y | Y | Y |
| 2 Bishop | Y | N | Y | Y | Y | N |
| 3 Marshall | Y | N | Y | Y | Y | N |
| 4 McKinney | Y | N | N | Y | N | N |
| 5 Lewis | Y | N | Y | Y | Y | N |
| 6 Price | Y | Y | Y | Y | Y | Y |
| 7 Linder | Y | Y | Y | Y | Y | Y |
| 8 Westmoreland | Y | Y | Y | Y | Y | Y |
| 9 Norwood | Y | Y | Y | Y | Y | Y |
| 10 Deal | Y | Y | Y | Y | Y | Y |
| 11 Gingrey | Y | Y | Y | Y | Y | Y |
| 12 Barrow | Y | N | Y | Y | Y | N |
| 13 Scott | Y | N | Y | Y | Y | N |
| **HAWAII** | | | | | | |
| 1 Abercrombie | Y | N | Y | Y | N | N |
| 2 Case | Y | N | Y | Y | Y | N |
| **IDAHO** | | | | | | |
| 1 Otter | Y | Y | Y | Y | Y | Y |
| 2 Simpson | Y | Y | Y | Y | Y | Y |
| **ILLINOIS** | | | | | | |
| 1 Rush | Y | N | Y | Y | N | N |
| 2 Jackson | Y | N | Y | N | Y | N |
| 3 Lipinski | Y | N | Y | Y | Y | N |
| 4 Gutierrez | Y | N | Y | Y | Y | N |
| 5 Emanuel | Y | N | Y | Y | Y | N |
| 6 Hyde | Y | Y | Y | Y | Y | Y |
| 7 Davis | Y | N | Y | Y | Y | N |
| 8 Bean | Y | N | Y | Y | Y | N |
| 9 Schakowsky | Y | N | Y | Y | Y | N |
| 10 Kirk | Y | Y | Y | Y | Y | Y |
| 11 Weller | Y | Y | Y | Y | Y | Y |
| 12 Costello | Y | N | Y | Y | Y | N |

**KEY**  Republicans  Democrats  *Independents*

| | | | |
|---|---|---|---|
| Y | Voted for (yea) | X | Paired against |
| # | Paired for | – | Announced against |
| + | Announced for | P | Voted "present" |
| N | Voted against (nay) | | |

| | |
|---|---|
| C | Voted "present" to avoid possible conflict of interest |
| ? | Did not vote or otherwise make a position known |

| | 268 | 269 | 270 | 271 | 272 | 273 |
|---|---|---|---|---|---|---|
| 13 **Biggert** | Y | Y | Y | Y | Y | Y |
| 14 **Hastert** | | | | | | |
| 15 **Johnson** | Y | Y | Y | Y | Y | Y |
| 16 **Manzullo** | Y | Y | Y | Y | Y | Y |
| 17 Evans | Y | N | Y | Y | Y | N |
| 18 **LaHood** | Y | Y | Y | Y | Y | Y |
| 19 **Shimkus** | Y | Y | Y | Y | Y | Y |
| **INDIANA** | | | | | | |
| 1 Visclosky | Y | N | Y | Y | Y | N |
| 2 **Chocola** | Y | Y | Y | Y | Y | Y |
| 3 **Souder** | Y | Y | Y | Y | Y | Y |
| 4 **Buyer** | Y | Y | Y | ? | Y | Y |
| 5 **Burton** | Y | Y | Y | Y | Y | Y |
| 6 **Pence** | Y | Y | Y | Y | Y | Y |
| 7 Carson | Y | N | Y | N | Y | N |
| 8 **Hostettler** | Y | N | Y | Y | Y | Y |
| 9 **Sodrel** | Y | Y | Y | Y | Y | Y |
| **IOWA** | | | | | | |
| 1 **Nussle** | Y | Y | Y | Y | Y | Y |
| 2 **Leach** | Y | Y | Y | Y | Y | Y |
| 3 Boswell | Y | N | Y | Y | Y | N |
| 4 **Latham** | Y | Y | Y | Y | Y | Y |
| 5 **King** | Y | Y | Y | Y | Y | Y |
| **KANSAS** | | | | | | |
| 1 **Moran** | Y | Y | Y | Y | Y | Y |
| 2 **Ryun** | Y | Y | Y | Y | Y | Y |
| 3 Moore | Y | N | Y | Y | Y | N |
| 4 **Tiahrt** | Y | Y | Y | Y | Y | Y |
| **KENTUCKY** | | | | | | |
| 1 **Whitfield** | ? | Y | Y | Y | Y | Y |
| 2 **Lewis** | Y | Y | Y | Y | Y | Y |
| 3 **Northup** | Y | Y | Y | Y | Y | Y |
| 4 **Davis** | Y | Y | Y | Y | Y | Y |
| 5 **Rogers** | Y | Y | Y | Y | Y | Y |
| 6 Chandler | Y | N | Y | Y | Y | N |
| **LOUISIANA** | | | | | | |
| 1 **Jindal** | Y | Y | Y | Y | Y | Y |
| 2 Jefferson | Y | N | Y | Y | Y | N |
| 3 Melancon | Y | N | Y | Y | Y | N |
| 4 **McCrery** | Y | Y | Y | Y | Y | Y |
| 5 **Alexander** | Y | Y | Y | Y | Y | Y |
| 6 **Baker** | Y | Y | Y | Y | Y | Y |
| 7 **Boustany** | Y | Y | Y | Y | Y | Y |
| **MAINE** | | | | | | |
| 1 Allen | Y | N | Y | Y | Y | N |
| 2 Michaud | Y | N | Y | Y | Y | N |
| **MARYLAND** | | | | | | |
| 1 **Gilchrest** | Y | Y | Y | Y | Y | Y |
| 2 Ruppersberger | Y | N | Y | Y | Y | N |
| 3 Cardin | Y | N | ? | ? | Y | N |
| 4 Wynn | Y | N | Y | Y | Y | N |
| 5 Hoyer | Y | N | Y | Y | Y | N |
| 6 **Bartlett** | Y | Y | Y | Y | Y | Y |
| 7 Cummings | Y | N | Y | Y | Y | N |
| 8 Van Hollen | Y | N | Y | Y | Y | N |
| **MASSACHUSETTS** | | | | | | |
| 1 Olver | Y | N | Y | Y | Y | N |
| 2 Neal | Y | N | Y | Y | Y | N |
| 3 McGovern | Y | N | Y | N | Y | N |
| 4 Frank | Y | N | Y | N | Y | N |
| 5 Meehan | Y | N | Y | Y | Y | N |
| 6 Tierney | Y | N | Y | Y | Y | N |
| 7 Markey | Y | N | Y | Y | Y | N |
| 8 Capuano | Y | N | N | Y | Y | N |
| 9 Lynch | Y | N | Y | Y | Y | N |
| 10 Delahunt | ? | N | Y | Y | Y | ? |
| **MICHIGAN** | | | | | | |
| 1 Stupak | Y | N | Y | Y | Y | N |
| 2 **Hoekstra** | Y | Y | Y | Y | Y | Y |
| 3 **Ehlers** | Y | Y | Y | Y | Y | Y |
| 4 **Camp** | Y | Y | Y | Y | Y | Y |
| 5 Kildee | Y | N | Y | Y | Y | N |
| 6 **Upton** | Y | Y | Y | Y | Y | Y |
| 7 **Schwarz** | Y | Y | Y | Y | Y | Y |
| 8 **Rogers** | Y | Y | Y | Y | Y | Y |
| 9 **Knollenberg** | Y | Y | Y | Y | Y | Y |
| 10 **Miller** | Y | Y | Y | Y | Y | Y |
| 11 **McCotter** | Y | Y | Y | Y | Y | Y |
| 12 Levin | Y | N | Y | Y | Y | N |
| 13 Kilpatrick | Y | N | Y | Y | Y | N |
| 14 Conyers | Y | N | N | ? | N | N |
| 15 Dingell | Y | N | Y | Y | Y | N |

| | 268 | 269 | 270 | 271 | 272 | 273 |
|---|---|---|---|---|---|---|
| **MINNESOTA** | | | | | | |
| 1 **Gutknecht** | Y | Y | Y | Y | Y | Y |
| 2 **Kline** | Y | Y | Y | Y | Y | Y |
| 3 **Ramstad** | Y | Y | Y | Y | Y | Y |
| 4 McCollum | Y | N | Y | Y | Y | N |
| 5 Sabo | Y | N | Y | Y | Y | N |
| 6 **Kennedy** | Y | Y | Y | Y | Y | Y |
| 7 Peterson | Y | N | Y | Y | Y | N |
| 8 Oberstar | ? | ? | ? | ? | ? | ? |
| **MISSISSIPPI** | | | | | | |
| 1 **Wicker** | Y | Y | Y | Y | Y | Y |
| 2 Thompson | Y | N | Y | Y | Y | N |
| 3 **Pickering** | Y | Y | Y | Y | Y | Y |
| 4 Taylor | Y | N | Y | Y | Y | N |
| **MISSOURI** | | | | | | |
| 1 Clay | Y | N | Y | Y | Y | N |
| 2 **Akin** | Y | Y | Y | Y | Y | Y |
| 3 Carnahan | Y | N | Y | Y | Y | N |
| 4 Skelton | Y | N | Y | Y | Y | N |
| 5 Cleaver | Y | N | Y | Y | Y | N |
| 6 **Graves** | Y | Y | Y | Y | Y | Y |
| 7 **Blunt** | Y | Y | Y | Y | Y | Y |
| 8 **Emerson** | Y | Y | Y | Y | Y | Y |
| 9 **Hulshof** | Y | Y | Y | Y | Y | Y |
| **MONTANA** | | | | | | |
| AL **Rehberg** | Y | Y | Y | Y | Y | Y |
| **NEBRASKA** | | | | | | |
| 1 **Fortenberry** | Y | Y | Y | Y | Y | Y |
| 2 **Terry** | Y | Y | Y | Y | Y | Y |
| 3 **Osborne** | Y | Y | Y | Y | Y | Y |
| **NEVADA** | | | | | | |
| 1 Berkley | Y | N | Y | Y | Y | N |
| 2 **Gibbons** | Y | Y | Y | Y | Y | Y |
| 3 **Porter** | Y | Y | Y | Y | Y | Y |
| **NEW HAMPSHIRE** | | | | | | |
| 1 **Bradley** | Y | Y | Y | Y | Y | Y |
| 2 **Bass** | Y | Y | Y | Y | Y | Y |
| **NEW JERSEY** | | | | | | |
| 1 Andrews | Y | N | Y | Y | Y | N |
| 2 **LoBiondo** | Y | Y | Y | Y | Y | Y |
| 3 **Saxton** | Y | Y | Y | Y | Y | Y |
| 4 **Smith** | Y | Y | Y | Y | Y | Y |
| 5 **Garrett** | Y | Y | Y | Y | Y | Y |
| 6 Pallone | Y | N | Y | Y | Y | N |
| 7 **Ferguson** | Y | Y | Y | Y | Y | Y |
| 8 Pascrell | Y | N | Y | Y | Y | N |
| 9 Rothman | Y | N | Y | Y | Y | N |
| 10 Payne | Y | N | Y | N | Y | N |
| 11 **Frelinghuysen** | Y | Y | Y | Y | Y | Y |
| 12 Holt | Y | N | Y | Y | Y | N |
| 13 Menendez | Y | N | Y | Y | Y | N |
| **NEW MEXICO** | | | | | | |
| 1 **Wilson** | Y | Y | Y | Y | Y | Y |
| 2 **Pearce** | Y | Y | Y | Y | Y | Y |
| 3 Udall | Y | N | Y | Y | Y | N |
| **NEW YORK** | | | | | | |
| 1 Bishop | Y | N | Y | Y | Y | N |
| 2 Israel | Y | N | Y | Y | Y | N |
| 3 **King** | Y | Y | Y | Y | Y | Y |
| 4 McCarthy | Y | N | Y | Y | Y | N |
| 5 Ackerman | Y | N | Y | Y | Y | N |
| 6 Meeks | Y | N | Y | Y | Y | N |
| 7 Crowley | Y | N | Y | Y | Y | N |
| 8 Nadler | Y | N | Y | Y | Y | N |
| 9 Weiner | Y | N | Y | Y | Y | N |
| 10 Towns | Y | N | Y | Y | Y | N |
| 11 Owens | Y | N | Y | Y | Y | N |
| 12 Velázquez | Y | N | Y | Y | Y | N |
| 13 **Fossella** | Y | Y | Y | Y | Y | Y |
| 14 Maloney | Y | N | Y | Y | Y | N |
| 15 Rangel | Y | N | N | Y | Y | N |
| 16 Serrano | Y | N | Y | Y | Y | N |
| 17 Engel | Y | N | Y | Y | Y | N |
| 18 Lowey | Y | N | Y | Y | Y | N |
| 19 **Kelly** | Y | Y | Y | Y | Y | Y |
| 20 **Sweeney** | Y | Y | Y | Y | Y | Y |
| 21 McNulty | Y | N | Y | Y | Y | N |
| 22 Hinchey | Y | N | N | Y | Y | N |
| 23 **McHugh** | Y | Y | Y | Y | Y | Y |
| 24 **Boehlert** | Y | Y | Y | Y | Y | Y |
| 25 **Walsh** | Y | Y | Y | Y | Y | Y |
| 26 **Reynolds** | Y | Y | Y | Y | Y | Y |
| 27 Higgins | Y | N | Y | Y | Y | N |
| 28 Slaughter | Y | N | Y | Y | Y | N |
| 29 **Kuhl** | Y | Y | Y | Y | Y | Y |

| | 268 | 269 | 270 | 271 | 272 | 273 |
|---|---|---|---|---|---|---|
| **NORTH CAROLINA** | | | | | | |
| 1 Butterfield | Y | N | Y | Y | Y | N |
| 2 Etheridge | Y | N | Y | Y | Y | N |
| 3 **Jones** | Y | Y | Y | Y | Y | Y |
| 4 Price | Y | N | Y | Y | Y | N |
| 5 **Foxx** | Y | Y | Y | Y | Y | Y |
| 6 **Coble** | Y | Y | Y | Y | Y | Y |
| 7 McIntyre | Y | N | Y | Y | Y | N |
| 8 **Hayes** | Y | Y | Y | Y | Y | Y |
| 9 **Myrick** | Y | Y | Y | Y | Y | Y |
| 10 **McHenry** | Y | Y | Y | Y | Y | Y |
| 11 **Taylor** | Y | Y | Y | Y | Y | Y |
| 12 Watt | Y | N | Y | N | Y | N |
| 13 Miller | Y | N | Y | Y | Y | N |
| **NORTH DAKOTA** | | | | | | |
| AL Pomeroy | Y | N | Y | Y | Y | N |
| **OHIO** | | | | | | |
| 1 **Chabot** | Y | Y | Y | Y | Y | Y |
| 2 Vacant | | | | | | |
| 3 **Turner** | Y | Y | Y | Y | Y | Y |
| 4 **Oxley** | Y | Y | Y | Y | Y | ? |
| 5 **Gillmor** | Y | Y | ? | ? | ? | ? |
| 6 Strickland | Y | N | Y | Y | Y | N |
| 7 **Hobson** | Y | Y | Y | Y | Y | Y |
| 8 **Boehner** | Y | Y | Y | Y | Y | Y |
| 9 Kaptur | Y | N | Y | Y | Y | N |
| 10 Kucinich | Y | N | N | N | N | N |
| 11 Jones | Y | ? | N | Y | Y | N |
| 12 **Tiberi** | Y | Y | Y | Y | Y | Y |
| 13 Brown | Y | N | Y | Y | Y | N |
| 14 **LaTourette** | Y | Y | Y | Y | Y | ? |
| 15 **Pryce** | Y | Y | Y | Y | Y | Y |
| 16 **Regula** | Y | Y | Y | Y | Y | Y |
| 17 Ryan | Y | N | Y | Y | Y | N |
| 18 **Ney** | Y | Y | Y | Y | Y | Y |
| **OKLAHOMA** | | | | | | |
| 1 **Sullivan** | Y | Y | Y | Y | Y | Y |
| 2 Boren | Y | N | Y | Y | Y | N |
| 3 **Lucas** | Y | Y | Y | Y | Y | Y |
| 4 **Cole** | Y | Y | Y | Y | Y | Y |
| 5 **Istook** | Y | Y | Y | Y | Y | Y |
| **OREGON** | | | | | | |
| 1 Wu | Y | N | Y | Y | Y | N |
| 2 **Walden** | Y | Y | Y | Y | Y | Y |
| 3 Blumenauer | Y | N | ? | ? | ? | ? |
| 4 DeFazio | Y | N | Y | Y | Y | N |
| 5 Hooley | Y | N | ? | ? | ? | ? |
| **PENNSYLVANIA** | | | | | | |
| 1 Brady | Y | N | Y | Y | Y | N |
| 2 Fattah | Y | N | Y | Y | Y | N |
| 3 **English** | Y | ? | Y | Y | Y | Y |
| 4 **Hart** | Y | Y | Y | Y | Y | Y |
| 5 **Peterson** | Y | Y | Y | Y | Y | Y |
| 6 **Gerlach** | Y | Y | Y | Y | Y | Y |
| 7 **Weldon** | Y | Y | Y | Y | Y | Y |
| 8 **Fitzpatrick** | Y | Y | Y | Y | Y | Y |
| 9 **Shuster** | Y | Y | Y | Y | Y | Y |
| 10 **Sherwood** | Y | Y | Y | Y | Y | Y |
| 11 Kanjorski | Y | N | Y | Y | Y | N |
| 12 Murtha | Y | N | Y | Y | Y | N |
| 13 Schwartz | Y | N | Y | Y | Y | N |
| 14 Doyle | Y | N | Y | Y | Y | N |
| 15 **Dent** | Y | Y | Y | Y | Y | Y |
| 16 **Pitts** | Y | Y | Y | Y | Y | Y |
| 17 Holden | Y | N | Y | Y | Y | N |
| 18 **Murphy** | Y | Y | Y | Y | Y | Y |
| 19 **Platts** | Y | Y | Y | Y | Y | Y |
| **RHODE ISLAND** | | | | | | |
| 1 Kennedy | Y | ? | Y | Y | Y | N |
| 2 Langevin | Y | N | Y | Y | Y | N |
| **SOUTH CAROLINA** | | | | | | |
| 1 **Brown** | Y | Y | Y | Y | Y | Y |
| 2 **Wilson** | Y | Y | Y | Y | Y | Y |
| 3 **Barrett** | Y | Y | Y | Y | Y | Y |
| 4 **Inglis** | Y | Y | Y | Y | Y | Y |
| 5 Spratt | Y | N | Y | Y | Y | N |
| 6 Clyburn | Y | N | Y | Y | Y | N |
| **SOUTH DAKOTA** | | | | | | |
| AL Herseth | Y | N | Y | Y | Y | N |
| **TENNESSEE** | | | | | | |
| 1 **Jenkins** | Y | Y | Y | Y | Y | Y |
| 2 **Duncan** | N | Y | Y | Y | Y | Y |

| | 268 | 269 | 270 | 271 | 272 | 273 |
|---|---|---|---|---|---|---|
| 3 **Wamp** | Y | Y | Y | Y | Y | Y |
| 4 Davis | Y | N | Y | Y | Y | N |
| 5 Cooper | N | N | Y | Y | Y | N |
| 6 Gordon | Y | N | Y | Y | Y | N |
| 7 **Blackburn** | Y | Y | Y | Y | Y | Y |
| 8 Tanner | Y | N | Y | Y | Y | N |
| 9 Ford | Y | N | Y | Y | Y | N |
| **TEXAS** | | | | | | |
| 1 **Gohmert** | Y | Y | Y | Y | Y | Y |
| 2 **Poe** | Y | Y | Y | Y | Y | Y |
| 3 **Johnson, S.** | Y | Y | Y | Y | Y | Y |
| 4 **Hall** | Y | Y | Y | Y | Y | Y |
| 5 **Hensarling** | Y | Y | Y | Y | Y | Y |
| 6 **Barton** | + | Y | Y | Y | Y | Y |
| 7 **Culberson** | Y | Y | Y | Y | Y | Y |
| 8 **Brady** | Y | Y | Y | Y | Y | Y |
| 9 Green, A. | Y | N | Y | Y | Y | N |
| 10 **McCaul** | Y | Y | Y | Y | Y | Y |
| 11 **Conaway** | Y | Y | Y | Y | Y | Y |
| 12 **Granger** | Y | ? | Y | Y | Y | Y |
| 13 **Thornberry** | Y | Y | Y | Y | Y | Y |
| 14 **Paul** | N | Y | Y | Y | N | Y |
| 15 Hinojosa | Y | N | Y | Y | Y | N |
| 16 Reyes | Y | N | ? | ? | ? | ? |
| 17 Edwards | Y | N | Y | Y | Y | N |
| 18 Jackson-Lee | Y | N | Y | Y | Y | N |
| 19 **Neugebauer** | Y | Y | Y | Y | Y | Y |
| 20 Gonzalez | Y | N | Y | Y | Y | N |
| 21 **Smith** | Y | Y | Y | Y | Y | Y |
| 22 **DeLay** | Y | Y | Y | Y | Y | Y |
| 23 **Bonilla** | Y | Y | Y | Y | Y | Y |
| 24 **Marchant** | Y | Y | Y | Y | Y | Y |
| 25 Doggett | Y | N | Y | Y | Y | N |
| 26 **Burgess** | Y | Y | Y | Y | Y | Y |
| 27 Ortiz | Y | N | Y | Y | Y | N |
| 28 Cuellar | ? | ? | ? | ? | ? | ? |
| 29 Green, G. | Y | N | Y | Y | Y | N |
| 30 Johnson, E. | Y | N | Y | Y | Y | N |
| 31 **Carter** | Y | Y | Y | Y | Y | Y |
| 32 **Sessions** | ? | ? | ? | ? | ? | ? |
| **UTAH** | | | | | | |
| 1 **Bishop** | Y | Y | Y | Y | Y | Y |
| 2 Matheson | N | N | Y | Y | Y | N |
| 3 **Cannon** | Y | Y | Y | Y | Y | Y |
| **VERMONT** | | | | | | |
| AL *Sanders* | Y | N | Y | Y | Y | N |
| **VIRGINIA** | | | | | | |
| 1 **Davis, J.** | Y | Y | Y | Y | Y | Y |
| 2 **Drake** | Y | Y | Y | Y | Y | Y |
| 3 Scott | Y | N | N | Y | Y | N |
| 4 **Forbes** | Y | Y | Y | Y | Y | Y |
| 5 **Goode** | Y | Y | Y | Y | Y | Y |
| 6 **Goodlatte** | Y | Y | Y | Y | Y | Y |
| 7 **Cantor** | Y | Y | Y | Y | Y | Y |
| 8 Moran | Y | N | Y | Y | Y | N |
| 9 Boucher | Y | N | Y | Y | Y | ? |
| 10 **Wolf** | Y | Y | Y | Y | Y | Y |
| 11 **Davis, T.** | Y | ? | ? | ? | ? | ? |
| **WASHINGTON** | | | | | | |
| 1 Inslee | Y | N | Y | ? | Y | N |
| 2 Larsen | Y | N | Y | Y | Y | N |
| 3 Baird | Y | N | Y | Y | Y | N |
| 4 **Hastings** | Y | Y | Y | Y | Y | Y |
| 5 **McMorris** | Y | Y | Y | Y | Y | Y |
| 6 Dicks | Y | N | Y | Y | Y | ? |
| 7 McDermott | Y | N | N | N | N | N |
| 8 **Reichert** | Y | Y | Y | Y | Y | Y |
| 9 Smith | Y | N | Y | Y | Y | N |
| **WEST VIRGINIA** | | | | | | |
| 1 Mollohan | Y | N | Y | Y | Y | N |
| 2 **Capito** | Y | Y | Y | Y | Y | Y |
| 3 Rahall | Y | N | Y | Y | Y | N |
| **WISCONSIN** | | | | | | |
| 1 **Ryan** | Y | Y | Y | Y | Y | Y |
| 2 Baldwin | Y | N | Y | Y | Y | N |
| 3 Kind | Y | N | Y | Y | Y | N |
| 4 Moore | Y | N | Y | N | N | N |
| 5 **Sensenbrenner** | Y | Y | Y | Y | Y | Y |
| 6 **Petri** | Y | Y | Y | Y | Y | Y |
| 7 Obey | Y | N | Y | Y | Y | N |
| 8 **Green** | Y | Y | Y | Y | Y | Y |
| **WYOMING** | | | | | | |
| AL **Cubin** | Y | Y | Y | Y | Y | Y |

# IN THE HOUSE | By Vote Number

**274.** **HR 2745. U.N. Overhaul/Country-Specific Resolutions.** Royce, R-Calif., amendment that would add a statement barring the elimination of country-specific resolutions to the list of changes required of the United Nations in the area of human rights overhaul. Adopted 373-32: R 218-1; D 154-31 (ND 115-25, SD 39-6); I 1-0. June 17, 2005.

**275.** **HR 2745. U.N. Overhaul/Suspension of Member State.** Fortenberry, R-Neb., amendment to direct the U.S. representative to seek the adoption and use of mechanisms to suspend a member state if its government is engaged in, or complicit in, acts of genocide, war crimes or crimes against humanity; to impose an arms and trade embargo, travel restrictions and asset freezes on groups or individuals responsible for such actions; and to deploy peacekeeping forces to halt such actions. Adopted 375-29: R 218-1; D 156-28 (ND 118-22, SD 38-6); I 1-0. June 17, 2005.

**276.** **HR 2745. U.N. Overhaul/Oil-for-Food Program.** Flake, R-Ariz., amendment to require the United Nations to release documents about the Oil-for-Food Program upon request by member states and to waive U.S. immunity of U.N. officials for civil or criminal acts under federal or state law that transpired in the United States in connection with the program. Adopted 366-38: R 220-0; D 145-38 (ND 106-32, SD 39-6); I 1-0. June 17, 2005.

**277.** **HR 2745. U.N. Overhaul/Anti-Semitic Statements.** Chabot, R-Ohio, amendment that would direct the U.S. ambassador to the United Nations to oppose anti-Semitic statements and anti-Israel resolutions in the United Nations. Adopted 405-2: R 219-1; D 185-1 (ND 140-0, SD 45-1); I 1-0. June 17, 2005.

**278.** **HR 2745. U.N. Overhaul/U.N. Assessment Levels.** Pence, R-Ind., amendment to direct the U.S. representative to ensure that the scale of assessments for a permanent member of the Security Council is no more than five times that for any other permanent member. If a permanent member is not in compliance, the U.N. representative would seek to deny that member the use of its veto in the Security Council. Adopted 281-126: R 211-8; D 70-117 (ND 48-93, SD 22-24); I 0-1. June 17, 2005.

**279.** **HR 2745. U.N. Overhaul/U.S. Foreign Assistance.** Gohmert, R-Texas, amendment to bar U.S. aid to countries that oppose the U.S. position on more than 50 percent of U.N. votes. Rejected 108-297: R 106-112; D 2-184 (ND 0-140, SD 2-44); I 0-1. June 17, 2005.

**280.** **HR 2745. U.N. Overhaul/Increase in U.S. Withheld Dues.** Stearns, R-Fla., amendment to increase the amount of regular U.S. dues withheld under the bill to 75 percent, from 50 percent. Rejected 100-306: R 97-122; D 3-183 (ND 1-139, SD 2-44); I 0-1. June 17, 2005.

**281.** **HR 2745. U.N. Overhaul/Democratic Substitute.** Lantos, D-Calif., substitute amendment that would give the secretary of State authority to withhold up to 50 percent of U.S. dues unless the United Nations has complied with 32 of 39 changes by Oct. 1, 2007. The United States also could withhold up to 50 percent of its dues if member states do not make substantial progress in raising voluntary contributions for some programs. Rejected 190-216: R 9-211; D 180-5 (ND 136-3, SD 44-2); I 1-0. June 17, 2005.

| | 274 | 275 | 276 | 277 | 278 | 279 | 280 | 281 |
|---|---|---|---|---|---|---|---|---|
| **ALABAMA** | | | | | | | | |
| 1 Bonner | Y | Y | Y | Y | Y | N | N | N |
| 2 Everett | Y | Y | Y | Y | Y | N | N | N |
| 3 Rogers | Y | Y | Y | Y | Y | N | Y | N |
| 4 Aderholt | Y | Y | Y | Y | Y | N | Y | N |
| 5 Cramer | Y | Y | Y | Y | Y | N | Y | Y |
| 6 Bachus | Y | Y | Y | Y | Y | N | Y | Y |
| 7 Davis | Y | Y | Y | Y | Y | N | N | Y |
| **ALASKA** | | | | | | | | |
| AL Young | Y | Y | Y | Y | Y | Y | N | N |
| **ARIZONA** | | | | | | | | |
| 1 Renzi | Y | Y | Y | Y | Y | N | Y | N |
| 2 Franks | Y | Y | Y | Y | Y | Y | Y | N |
| 3 Shadegg | Y | Y | Y | Y | Y | Y | Y | N |
| 4 Pastor | Y | Y | Y | Y | N | N | N | N |
| 5 Hayworth | Y | Y | Y | Y | Y | Y | Y | Y |
| 6 Flake | Y | Y | Y | Y | Y | Y | Y | N |
| 7 Grijalva | N | N | N | Y | N | N | N | N |
| 8 Kolbe | Y | Y | Y | Y | N | N | N | N |
| **ARKANSAS** | | | | | | | | |
| 1 Berry | Y | Y | Y | Y | Y | N | N | Y |
| 2 Snyder | Y | Y | Y | Y | N | N | N | Y |
| 3 Boozman | Y | Y | Y | Y | Y | N | Y | N |
| 4 Ross | Y | Y | Y | Y | Y | N | N | Y |
| **CALIFORNIA** | | | | | | | | |
| 1 Thompson | Y | Y | Y | Y | Y | N | N | Y |
| 2 Herger | Y | Y | Y | Y | Y | Y | Y | N |
| 3 Lungren | Y | Y | Y | Y | Y | N | N | N |
| 4 Doolittle | Y | Y | Y | Y | Y | N | N | N |
| 5 Matsui, D. | Y | Y | Y | Y | Y | N | N | Y |
| 6 Woolsey | N | N | Y | N | N | N | N | Y |
| 7 Miller, George | Y | N | N | Y | N | N | N | Y |
| 8 Pelosi | ? | ? | ? | ? | ? | ? | ? | ? |
| 9 Lee | N | N | N | Y | N | N | N | N |
| 10 Tauscher | Y | Y | Y | Y | N | N | N | Y |
| 11 Pombo | Y | Y | Y | Y | Y | Y | Y | N |
| 12 Lantos | Y | Y | Y | Y | Y | N | N | Y |
| 13 Stark | ? | ? | ? | ? | ? | ? | ? | ? |
| 14 Eshoo | Y | Y | Y | Y | N | N | N | Y |
| 15 Honda | Y | Y | N | Y | N | N | N | Y |
| 16 Lofgren | Y | Y | Y | Y | N | N | N | Y |
| 17 Farr | Y | Y | N | Y | N | N | N | Y |
| 18 Cardoza | Y | Y | Y | Y | N | N | N | Y |
| 19 Radanovich | Y | Y | Y | Y | Y | N | Y | N |
| 20 Costa | Y | Y | Y | Y | Y | N | N | N |
| 21 Nunes | Y | Y | Y | Y | Y | N | N | N |
| 22 Thomas | Y | Y | Y | Y | Y | N | N | N |
| 23 Capps | Y | Y | Y | Y | N | N | N | Y |
| 24 Gallegly | Y | Y | Y | Y | Y | N | N | N |
| 25 McKeon | Y | Y | Y | Y | Y | Y | Y | N |
| 26 Dreier | Y | Y | Y | Y | Y | N | N | N |
| 27 Sherman | Y | Y | Y | Y | N | N | N | Y |
| 28 Berman | Y | Y | Y | Y | Y | N | N | Y |
| 29 Schiff | Y | Y | Y | Y | N | N | N | Y |
| 30 Waxman | ? | ? | ? | ? | ? | ? | ? | ? |
| 31 Becerra | Y | Y | Y | Y | N | N | N | Y |
| 32 Solis | N | N | N | Y | N | N | N | Y |
| 33 Watson | N | N | N | Y | N | N | N | Y |
| 34 Roybal-Allard | Y | Y | Y | Y | N | N | N | Y |
| 35 Waters | N | N | N | Y | N | N | N | Y |
| 36 Harman | Y | Y | Y | Y | N | N | N | Y |
| 37 Millender-McD. | ? | ? | ? | ? | ? | ? | ? | ? |
| 38 Napolitano | Y | Y | Y | Y | N | N | N | Y |
| 39 Sánchez, Linda | Y | Y | Y | Y | N | N | N | Y |
| 40 Royce | Y | Y | Y | Y | Y | Y | Y | N |
| 41 Lewis | Y | Y | Y | Y | Y | N | N | N |
| 42 Miller, Gary | Y | Y | Y | Y | Y | Y | Y | N |
| 43 Baca | Y | Y | Y | Y | N | N | N | Y |
| 44 Calvert | Y | Y | Y | Y | Y | N | N | N |
| 45 Bono | ? | ? | ? | ? | ? | ? | ? | ? |
| 46 Rohrabacher | Y | Y | Y | Y | Y | Y | Y | N |
| 47 Sanchez, Loretta | Y | Y | Y | Y | N | N | N | Y |
| 48 Cox | Y | Y | Y | Y | Y | N | N | N |
| 49 Issa | + | + | + | + | - | - | - | - |
| 50 Cunningham | Y | Y | Y | Y | N | N | N | N |
| 51 Filner | Y | Y | Y | Y | N | N | N | Y |
| 52 Hunter | Y | Y | Y | Y | N | N | N | N |
| 53 Davis | Y | Y | Y | Y | N | N | N | Y |
| **COLORADO** | | | | | | | | |
| 1 DeGette | Y | Y | N | N | N | N | N | Y |
| 2 Udall | Y | Y | Y | Y | N | N | N | Y |
| 3 Salazar | Y | Y | Y | Y | N | N | N | Y |
| 4 Musgrave | Y | Y | Y | Y | Y | Y | Y | N |
| 5 Hefley | Y | Y | Y | Y | Y | N | N | N |
| 6 Tancredo | Y | Y | Y | Y | Y | N | Y | N |
| 7 Beauprez | Y | Y | Y | Y | Y | N | Y | N |
| **CONNECTICUT** | | | | | | | | |
| 1 Larson | N | N | N | Y | N | N | N | Y |
| 2 Simmons | ? | ? | ? | ? | ? | ? | ? | ? |
| 3 DeLauro | Y | Y | Y | Y | N | N | N | Y |
| 4 Shays | Y | Y | Y | Y | N | N | N | Y |
| 5 Johnson | Y | Y | Y | Y | N | N | N | Y |
| **DELAWARE** | | | | | | | | |
| AL Castle | Y | Y | Y | Y | Y | N | N | Y |
| **FLORIDA** | | | | | | | | |
| 1 Miller | Y | Y | Y | Y | Y | N | Y | N |
| 2 Boyd | Y | Y | Y | Y | N | N | N | Y |
| 3 Brown | ? | ? | ? | ? | ? | ? | ? | ? |
| 4 Crenshaw | Y | Y | Y | Y | Y | N | N | N |
| 5 Brown-Waite | Y | Y | Y | Y | Y | N | N | N |
| 6 Stearns | Y | Y | Y | Y | Y | Y | Y | N |
| 7 Mica | Y | Y | Y | Y | Y | N | N | N |
| 8 Keller | Y | Y | Y | Y | Y | Y | N | N |
| 9 Bilirakis | Y | Y | Y | Y | Y | N | N | N |
| 10 Young | Y | Y | Y | Y | N | N | N | N |
| 11 Davis | Y | Y | Y | Y | N | N | N | Y |
| 12 Putnam | Y | Y | Y | Y | Y | N | N | N |
| 13 Harris | Y | Y | Y | Y | Y | N | N | N |
| 14 Mack | Y | Y | Y | Y | Y | N | N | N |
| 15 Weldon | Y | Y | Y | Y | Y | Y | Y | N |
| 16 Foley | Y | Y | Y | Y | Y | N | N | N |
| 17 Meek | Y | N | N | Y | N | N | N | Y |
| 18 Ros-Lehtinen | Y | Y | Y | Y | Y | N | N | N |
| 19 Wexler | Y | Y | Y | Y | N | N | N | Y |
| 20 Wasserman-Schultz | Y | Y | Y | Y | N | N | N | Y |
| 21 Diaz-Balart, L. | Y | Y | Y | Y | ? | N | N | Y |
| 22 Shaw | Y | Y | Y | Y | N | N | N | N |
| 23 Hastings | N | N | N | Y | N | N | N | Y |
| 24 Feeney | Y | Y | Y | Y | Y | Y | Y | N |
| 25 Diaz-Balart, M. | Y | Y | Y | Y | Y | Y | Y | N |
| **GEORGIA** | | | | | | | | |
| 1 Kingston | Y | Y | Y | Y | Y | Y | Y | N |
| 2 Bishop | ? | ? | ? | ? | ? | ? | ? | ? |
| 3 Marshall | Y | Y | Y | Y | N | N | N | Y |
| 4 McKinney | Y | N | N | N | N | N | N | N |
| 5 Lewis | N | N | N | Y | N | N | N | Y |
| 6 Price | Y | Y | Y | Y | Y | N | N | N |
| 7 Linder | Y | Y | Y | Y | Y | N | N | N |
| 8 Westmoreland | Y | Y | Y | Y | Y | Y | Y | N |
| 9 Norwood | Y | Y | Y | Y | Y | N | N | N |
| 10 Deal | Y | Y | Y | Y | Y | N | N | N |
| 11 Gingrey | ? | ? | ? | ? | ? | ? | ? | ? |
| 12 Barrow | Y | Y | Y | Y | N | N | N | Y |
| 13 Scott | Y | Y | Y | Y | N | N | N | Y |
| **HAWAII** | | | | | | | | |
| 1 Abercrombie | Y | Y | Y | Y | N | N | N | Y |
| 2 Case | Y | Y | Y | Y | N | N | N | Y |
| **IDAHO** | | | | | | | | |
| 1 Otter | Y | Y | Y | Y | Y | Y | Y | N |
| 2 Simpson | Y | Y | Y | Y | N | N | N | N |
| **ILLINOIS** | | | | | | | | |
| 1 Rush | Y | Y | N | Y | N | N | N | Y |
| 2 Jackson | N | N | N | Y | N | N | N | Y |
| 3 Lipinski | Y | Y | Y | Y | N | N | N | Y |
| 4 Gutierrez | N | N | N | Y | N | N | N | Y |
| 5 Emanuel | Y | Y | Y | Y | N | N | N | Y |
| 6 Hyde | Y | Y | Y | Y | Y | N | N | N |
| 7 Davis | Y | N | Y | N | N | N | N | Y |
| 8 Bean | Y | Y | Y | Y | N | N | N | Y |
| 9 Schakowsky | N | Y | N | Y | N | N | N | Y |
| 10 Kirk | Y | Y | Y | Y | N | N | N | N |
| 11 Weller | Y | Y | Y | Y | Y | N | N | N |
| 12 Costello | Y | Y | Y | Y | N | N | N | Y |

**KEY**  Republicans  Democrats  *Independents*

| | | |
|---|---|---|
| Y Voted for (yea) | X Paired against | C Voted "present" to avoid possible conflict of interest |
| # Paired for | - Announced against | |
| + Announced for | P Voted "present" | ? Did not vote or otherwise make a position known |
| N Voted against (nay) | | |

| | 274 | 275 | 276 | 277 | 278 | 279 | 280 | 281 |
|---|---|---|---|---|---|---|---|---|
| 13 **Biggert** | Y | Y | Y | Y | N | N | ? | N |
| 14 **Hastert** | | | | | | | | |
| 15 **Johnson** | Y | Y | Y | Y | Y | N | N | N |
| 16 **Manzullo** | Y | Y | Y | Y | Y | Y | Y | N |
| 17 Evans | Y | Y | Y | Y | N | N | N | Y |
| 18 **LaHood** | Y | Y | Y | Y | Y | N | N | Y |
| 19 **Shimkus** | Y | Y | Y | Y | Y | N | N | N |
| **INDIANA** | | | | | | | | |
| 1 Visclosky | Y | Y | Y | Y | Y | N | N | Y |
| 2 **Chocola** | Y | Y | Y | Y | ? | N | N | N |
| 3 **Souder** | Y | Y | Y | Y | Y | N | Y | N |
| 4 **Buyer** | Y | Y | Y | Y | Y | Y | Y | N |
| 5 **Burton** | Y | Y | Y | Y | Y | Y | Y | N |
| 6 **Pence** | Y | Y | Y | Y | Y | N | N | N |
| 7 Carson | Y | Y | Y | Y | N | N | N | Y |
| 8 **Hostettler** | Y | Y | Y | Y | Y | Y | Y | N |
| 9 **Sodrel** | Y | Y | Y | Y | Y | Y | N | N |
| **IOWA** | | | | | | | | |
| 1 **Nussle** | Y | Y | Y | Y | Y | N | N | N |
| 2 **Leach** | Y | Y | Y | Y | N | N | N | Y |
| 3 Boswell | Y | Y | Y | Y | N | N | N | Y |
| 4 **Latham** | Y | Y | Y | Y | Y | N | N | N |
| 5 **King** | Y | Y | Y | Y | Y | Y | Y | N |
| **KANSAS** | | | | | | | | |
| 1 **Moran** | Y | Y | Y | Y | Y | Y | Y | N |
| 2 **Ryun** | Y | Y | Y | Y | Y | Y | Y | N |
| 3 Moore | Y | Y | Y | Y | Y | N | N | Y |
| 4 **Tiahrt** | Y | Y | Y | Y | Y | Y | Y | N |
| **KENTUCKY** | | | | | | | | |
| 1 **Whitfield** | Y | Y | Y | Y | Y | N | N | N |
| 2 **Lewis** | Y | Y | Y | Y | Y | Y | Y | N |
| 3 **Northup** | Y | Y | Y | Y | Y | N | N | N |
| 4 **Davis** | Y | Y | Y | Y | Y | Y | N | N |
| 5 **Rogers** | Y | Y | Y | Y | Y | N | N | N |
| 6 Chandler | Y | Y | Y | Y | Y | N | N | Y |
| **LOUISIANA** | | | | | | | | |
| 1 **Jindal** | Y | Y | Y | Y | Y | N | Y | N |
| 2 Jefferson | Y | Y | Y | Y | N | N | N | Y |
| 3 Melancon | Y | Y | Y | Y | Y | N | N | Y |
| 4 **McCrery** | Y | Y | Y | Y | Y | Y | Y | N |
| 5 **Alexander** | Y | Y | Y | Y | Y | Y | Y | N |
| 6 **Baker** | Y | Y | Y | Y | Y | Y | Y | N |
| 7 **Boustany** | Y | Y | Y | Y | Y | N | Y | N |
| **MAINE** | | | | | | | | |
| 1 Allen | Y | Y | Y | Y | N | N | N | Y |
| 2 Michaud | Y | Y | Y | Y | N | N | N | Y |
| **MARYLAND** | | | | | | | | |
| 1 **Gilchrest** | Y | Y | Y | Y | N | N | N | N |
| 2 Ruppersberger | Y | Y | Y | Y | Y | N | N | Y |
| 3 Cardin | Y | Y | Y | Y | Y | N | N | Y |
| 4 Wynn | Y | Y | Y | Y | Y | N | N | Y |
| 5 Hoyer | Y | Y | Y | Y | Y | N | N | Y |
| 6 **Bartlett** | Y | Y | Y | Y | Y | Y | Y | N |
| 7 Cummings | Y | Y | Y | Y | N | N | N | Y |
| 8 Van Hollen | Y | Y | Y | Y | N | N | N | Y |
| **MASSACHUSETTS** | | | | | | | | |
| 1 Olver | N | Y | N | Y | N | N | N | Y |
| 2 Neal | Y | Y | Y | Y | N | N | N | Y |
| 3 McGovern | N | Y | N | Y | N | N | N | Y |
| 4 Frank | Y | Y | Y | Y | N | N | N | Y |
| 5 Meehan | Y | Y | Y | Y | N | N | N | Y |
| 6 Tierney | Y | Y | N | Y | N | N | N | Y |
| 7 Markey | N | Y | Y | Y | N | N | N | Y |
| 8 Capuano | N | Y | N | Y | N | N | N | Y |
| 9 Lynch | Y | Y | ? | Y | Y | N | Y | Y |
| 10 Delahunt | N | N | N | Y | N | N | N | Y |
| **MICHIGAN** | | | | | | | | |
| 1 Stupak | Y | Y | Y | Y | N | N | N | Y |
| 2 **Hoekstra** | Y | Y | Y | Y | Y | N | N | N |
| 3 **Ehlers** | Y | Y | Y | Y | Y | N | N | N |
| 4 **Camp** | Y | Y | Y | Y | Y | N | N | N |
| 5 Kildee | Y | Y | Y | Y | N | N | N | Y |
| 6 **Upton** | Y | Y | Y | Y | Y | N | N | N |
| 7 **Schwarz** | Y | Y | Y | Y | Y | N | N | N |
| 8 **Rogers** | Y | Y | Y | Y | Y | N | N | N |
| 9 **Knollenberg** | Y | Y | Y | Y | Y | N | N | N |
| 10 **Miller** | Y | Y | Y | Y | Y | Y | Y | N |
| 11 **McCotter** | Y | Y | Y | Y | Y | N | N | N |
| 12 Levin | Y | Y | Y | Y | N | N | N | Y |
| 13 Kilpatrick | Y | N | N | Y | N | N | N | Y |
| 14 Conyers | N | N | N | Y | N | N | N | Y |
| 15 Dingell | Y | N | N | Y | N | N | N | Y |

| | 274 | 275 | 276 | 277 | 278 | 279 | 280 | 281 |
|---|---|---|---|---|---|---|---|---|
| **MINNESOTA** | | | | | | | | |
| 1 **Gutknecht** | Y | Y | Y | Y | Y | N | N | N |
| 2 **Kline** | Y | Y | Y | Y | Y | N | N | N |
| 3 **Ramstad** | Y | Y | Y | Y | Y | N | N | N |
| 4 McCollum | Y | Y | N | Y | N | N | N | Y |
| 5 Sabo | Y | Y | N | Y | N | N | N | Y |
| 6 **Kennedy** | Y | Y | Y | Y | Y | N | N | N |
| 7 Peterson | Y | Y | Y | Y | Y | N | N | ? |
| 8 Oberstar | Y | Y | N | Y | N | N | N | Y |
| **MISSISSIPPI** | | | | | | | | |
| 1 **Wicker** | Y | Y | Y | Y | Y | N | N | N |
| 2 Thompson | N | Y | N | Y | N | N | N | Y |
| 3 **Pickering** | Y | Y | Y | Y | Y | Y | N | N |
| 4 Taylor | ? | ? | ? | Y | Y | Y | Y | N |
| **MISSOURI** | | | | | | | | |
| 1 Clay | Y | Y | Y | Y | N | N | N | Y |
| 2 **Akin** | Y | Y | Y | Y | Y | Y | Y | N |
| 3 Carnahan | Y | Y | Y | Y | Y | N | N | Y |
| 4 Skelton | ? | ? | ? | ? | ? | ? | ? | ? |
| 5 Cleaver | Y | Y | Y | Y | N | N | N | Y |
| 6 **Graves** | ? | ? | ? | ? | ? | ? | ? | ? |
| 7 **Blunt** | Y | Y | Y | Y | Y | Y | N | N |
| 8 **Emerson** | Y | Y | Y | Y | Y | Y | Y | N |
| 9 **Hulshof** | Y | Y | Y | Y | Y | Y | Y | N |
| **MONTANA** | | | | | | | | |
| AL **Rehberg** | Y | Y | Y | Y | Y | Y | Y | N |
| **NEBRASKA** | | | | | | | | |
| 1 **Fortenberry** | Y | Y | Y | Y | Y | N | N | N |
| 2 **Terry** | Y | Y | Y | Y | Y | N | Y | N |
| 3 **Osborne** | Y | Y | Y | Y | Y | N | N | N |
| **NEVADA** | | | | | | | | |
| 1 Berkley | Y | Y | Y | Y | Y | N | N | Y |
| 2 **Gibbons** | Y | Y | Y | Y | Y | Y | Y | N |
| 3 **Porter** | Y | Y | Y | Y | Y | N | N | N |
| **NEW HAMPSHIRE** | | | | | | | | |
| 1 **Bradley** | Y | Y | Y | Y | Y | N | N | N |
| 2 **Bass** | Y | Y | Y | Y | Y | N | N | Y |
| **NEW JERSEY** | | | | | | | | |
| 1 Andrews | ? | ? | ? | ? | ? | ? | ? | ? |
| 2 **LoBiondo** | Y | Y | Y | Y | Y | N | N | N |
| 3 **Saxton** | Y | Y | Y | Y | Y | N | N | N |
| 4 **Smith** | Y | Y | Y | Y | Y | N | N | N |
| 5 **Garrett** | Y | Y | Y | Y | Y | Y | Y | N |
| 6 Pallone | Y | Y | Y | Y | N | N | N | Y |
| 7 **Ferguson** | Y | Y | Y | Y | Y | N | N | N |
| 8 Pascrell | N | N | Y | Y | N | N | N | Y |
| 9 Rothman | Y | Y | Y | Y | Y | N | N | Y |
| 10 Payne | N | N | N | Y | N | N | N | Y |
| 11 **Frelinghuysen** | Y | Y | Y | Y | Y | N | N | N |
| 12 Holt | Y | Y | Y | Y | N | N | N | Y |
| 13 Menendez | Y | Y | Y | Y | Y | N | N | Y |
| **NEW MEXICO** | | | | | | | | |
| 1 **Wilson** | Y | Y | Y | Y | N | N | N | N |
| 2 **Pearce** | Y | Y | Y | Y | Y | N | N | N |
| 3 Udall | Y | Y | Y | Y | Y | N | N | Y |
| **NEW YORK** | | | | | | | | |
| 1 Bishop | Y | Y | Y | Y | N | N | N | Y |
| 2 Israel | Y | Y | Y | Y | N | N | N | Y |
| 3 **King** | Y | Y | Y | Y | Y | N | N | N |
| 4 McCarthy | Y | Y | Y | Y | Y | N | N | Y |
| 5 Ackerman | Y | Y | Y | Y | N | N | N | Y |
| 6 Meeks | N | N | Y | Y | N | N | N | Y |
| 7 Crowley | Y | Y | Y | Y | N | N | N | Y |
| 8 Nadler | Y | Y | N | Y | N | N | N | Y |
| 9 Weiner | Y | Y | Y | Y | N | N | N | Y |
| 10 Towns | Y | N | Y | Y | N | N | N | Y |
| 11 Owens | Y | Y | N | Y | N | N | N | Y |
| 12 Velázquez | Y | Y | Y | ? | N | N | N | Y |
| 13 **Fossella** | + | Y | Y | Y | Y | N | N | N |
| 14 Maloney | Y | Y | Y | Y | N | N | N | Y |
| 15 Rangel | N | Y | Y | Y | N | N | N | Y |
| 16 Serrano | N | N | N | Y | N | N | N | Y |
| 17 Engel | Y | Y | Y | Y | Y | N | N | Y |
| 18 Lowey | Y | Y | Y | Y | Y | N | N | Y |
| 19 **Kelly** | Y | Y | Y | Y | Y | Y | N | N |
| 20 **Sweeney** | Y | Y | Y | Y | Y | N | N | N |
| 21 McNulty | Y | Y | Y | Y | N | N | N | Y |
| 22 Hinchey | Y | Y | Y | Y | N | N | N | Y |
| 23 **McHugh** | Y | Y | Y | Y | Y | N | N | N |
| 24 **Boehlert** | Y | Y | Y | Y | Y | N | N | Y |
| 25 **Walsh** | ? | ? | ? | ? | ? | ? | ? | ? |
| 26 **Reynolds** | Y | Y | Y | Y | Y | N | N | N |
| 27 Higgins | Y | Y | Y | Y | Y | N | N | Y |
| 28 Slaughter | Y | Y | Y | Y | N | N | N | Y |
| 29 **Kuhl** | Y | Y | Y | Y | Y | N | N | N |

| | 274 | 275 | 276 | 277 | 278 | 279 | 280 | 281 |
|---|---|---|---|---|---|---|---|---|
| **NORTH CAROLINA** | | | | | | | | |
| 1 Butterfield | Y | Y | Y | Y | Y | N | N | Y |
| 2 Etheridge | Y | Y | Y | Y | Y | N | N | Y |
| 3 **Jones** | Y | Y | Y | Y | Y | Y | Y | N |
| 4 Price | Y | Y | Y | Y | N | N | N | Y |
| 5 **Foxx** | Y | Y | Y | Y | Y | Y | Y | N |
| 6 **Coble** | Y | Y | Y | Y | Y | Y | Y | N |
| 7 McIntyre | Y | Y | Y | Y | Y | N | N | Y |
| 8 **Hayes** | Y | Y | Y | Y | Y | Y | Y | N |
| 9 **Myrick** | Y | Y | Y | Y | Y | Y | Y | N |
| 10 **McHenry** | Y | Y | Y | Y | Y | Y | Y | N |
| 11 **Taylor** | Y | Y | Y | Y | Y | Y | N | N |
| 12 Watt | Y | ? | N | Y | N | N | N | Y |
| 13 Miller | Y | Y | Y | Y | N | N | N | Y |
| **NORTH DAKOTA** | | | | | | | | |
| AL Pomeroy | Y | Y | Y | Y | Y | N | N | Y |
| **OHIO** | | | | | | | | |
| 1 **Chabot** | Y | Y | Y | Y | Y | Y | Y | N |
| 2 Vacant | | | | | | | | |
| 3 **Turner** | Y | Y | Y | Y | Y | N | N | N |
| 4 **Oxley** | Y | Y | Y | Y | Y | N | N | N |
| 5 **Gillmor** | ? | ? | ? | ? | ? | ? | ? | ? |
| 6 Strickland | Y | Y | Y | Y | Y | N | N | Y |
| 7 **Hobson** | Y | Y | Y | Y | Y | N | N | N |
| 8 **Boehner** | ? | ? | ? | ? | ? | ? | ? | ? |
| 9 Kaptur | Y | Y | ? | Y | N | N | N | Y |
| 10 Kucinich | N | Y | N | Y | N | N | N | Y |
| 11 Jones | N | Y | N | Y | N | N | N | Y |
| 12 **Tiberi** | Y | Y | Y | Y | Y | Y | Y | N |
| 13 Brown | Y | Y | Y | Y | N | N | N | Y |
| 14 **LaTourette** | Y | Y | Y | Y | N | Y | N | N |
| 15 **Pryce** | Y | Y | Y | Y | Y | N | N | N |
| 16 **Regula** | Y | Y | Y | Y | Y | N | N | N |
| 17 Ryan | Y | Y | Y | Y | Y | N | N | Y |
| 18 **Ney** | Y | Y | Y | Y | Y | Y | Y | N |
| **OKLAHOMA** | | | | | | | | |
| 1 **Sullivan** | Y | Y | Y | Y | Y | Y | Y | N |
| 2 Boren | Y | Y | Y | Y | Y | N | N | Y |
| 3 **Lucas** | Y | Y | Y | Y | Y | Y | Y | N |
| 4 **Cole** | Y | Y | Y | Y | Y | N | N | N |
| 5 **Istook** | Y | Y | Y | Y | Y | ? | Y | N |
| **OREGON** | | | | | | | | |
| 1 Wu | Y | Y | Y | Y | Y | N | N | Y |
| 2 **Walden** | Y | Y | Y | Y | Y | N | N | N |
| 3 Blumenauer | + | - | - | + | - | - | - | + |
| 4 DeFazio | Y | Y | Y | Y | Y | N | N | Y |
| 5 Hooley | ? | ? | ? | ? | ? | ? | ? | ? |
| **PENNSYLVANIA** | | | | | | | | |
| 1 Brady | Y | Y | Y | Y | N | N | N | Y |
| 2 Fattah | Y | Y | Y | Y | N | N | N | Y |
| 3 **English** | Y | Y | Y | Y | Y | N | N | N |
| 4 **Hart** | Y | Y | Y | Y | Y | Y | N | N |
| 5 **Peterson** | Y | Y | Y | Y | Y | Y | N | N |
| 6 **Gerlach** | Y | Y | Y | Y | Y | N | N | N |
| 7 **Weldon** | Y | ? | Y | Y | Y | N | N | N |
| 8 **Fitzpatrick** | Y | Y | Y | Y | Y | N | N | N |
| 9 **Shuster** | Y | Y | Y | Y | Y | Y | Y | N |
| 10 **Sherwood** | Y | Y | Y | Y | Y | N | N | N |
| 11 Kanjorski | N | N | Y | Y | N | N | N | Y |
| 12 Murtha | N | N | Y | Y | N | N | N | N |
| 13 Schwartz | Y | Y | Y | Y | Y | N | N | Y |
| 14 Doyle | Y | Y | Y | Y | Y | N | N | Y |
| 15 **Dent** | Y | Y | Y | Y | Y | N | N | N |
| 16 **Pitts** | Y | Y | Y | Y | Y | Y | N | N |
| 17 Holden | Y | Y | Y | Y | Y | N | N | Y |
| 18 **Murphy** | Y | Y | Y | Y | Y | N | N | N |
| 19 **Platts** | Y | Y | Y | Y | Y | Y | Y | N |
| **RHODE ISLAND** | | | | | | | | |
| 1 Kennedy | Y | Y | Y | Y | N | ? | ? | ? |
| 2 Langevin | Y | Y | Y | Y | Y | N | N | Y |
| **SOUTH CAROLINA** | | | | | | | | |
| 1 **Brown** | Y | Y | Y | Y | Y | Y | Y | N |
| 2 **Wilson** | Y | Y | Y | Y | Y | Y | Y | N |
| 3 **Barrett** | Y | Y | Y | Y | Y | Y | Y | N |
| 4 **Inglis** | Y | Y | Y | Y | Y | N | N | Y |
| 5 Spratt | Y | Y | Y | Y | Y | N | N | Y |
| 6 Clyburn | N | N | Y | Y | N | N | N | Y |
| **SOUTH DAKOTA** | | | | | | | | |
| AL Herseth | Y | Y | Y | Y | Y | N | N | Y |
| **TENNESSEE** | | | | | | | | |
| 1 **Jenkins** | Y | Y | Y | Y | Y | Y | Y | N |
| 2 **Duncan** | Y | Y | Y | Y | Y | Y | Y | N |

| | 274 | 275 | 276 | 277 | 278 | 279 | 280 | 281 |
|---|---|---|---|---|---|---|---|---|
| 3 **Wamp** | Y | Y | Y | Y | Y | Y | Y | N |
| 4 Davis | Y | Y | Y | Y | Y | N | N | Y |
| 5 Cooper | Y | Y | Y | Y | N | N | N | Y |
| 6 Gordon | Y | Y | Y | Y | N | N | N | Y |
| 7 **Blackburn** | Y | Y | Y | Y | Y | N | Y | N |
| 8 Tanner | Y | Y | Y | Y | Y | N | N | Y |
| 9 Ford | Y | Y | Y | Y | Y | N | N | Y |
| **TEXAS** | | | | | | | | |
| 1 **Gohmert** | Y | Y | Y | Y | Y | Y | Y | N |
| 2 **Poe** | Y | Y | Y | Y | Y | Y | N | N |
| 3 **Johnson, S.** | Y | Y | Y | Y | Y | Y | Y | N |
| 4 **Hall** | Y | Y | Y | Y | Y | Y | N | N |
| 5 **Hensarling** | Y | Y | Y | Y | Y | N | N | N |
| 6 **Barton** | Y | Y | Y | Y | Y | Y | Y | N |
| 7 **Culberson** | Y | Y | Y | Y | Y | Y | N | N |
| 8 **Brady** | Y | Y | Y | Y | Y | Y | N | N |
| 9 Green, A. | N | Y | Y | Y | N | N | N | Y |
| 10 **McCaul** | Y | Y | Y | Y | Y | Y | Y | N |
| 11 **Conaway** | Y | Y | Y | Y | Y | Y | Y | N |
| 12 **Granger** | Y | Y | Y | Y | Y | N | N | N |
| 13 **Thornberry** | Y | Y | Y | Y | Y | N | N | N |
| 14 **Paul** | N | N | Y | N | N | Y | Y | N |
| 15 Hinojosa | Y | Y | Y | Y | Y | N | N | Y |
| 16 Reyes | ? | ? | ? | ? | ? | ? | ? | ? |
| 17 Edwards | Y | Y | Y | Y | Y | N | N | Y |
| 18 Jackson-Lee | Y | Y | Y | Y | N | N | N | Y |
| 19 **Neugebauer** | Y | Y | Y | Y | Y | Y | Y | N |
| 20 Gonzalez | Y | Y | Y | Y | N | N | N | Y |
| 21 **Smith** | Y | Y | Y | Y | Y | N | N | N |
| 22 **DeLay** | Y | Y | Y | Y | Y | Y | N | N |
| 23 **Bonilla** | Y | Y | Y | Y | Y | N | N | N |
| 24 **Marchant** | Y | Y | Y | Y | Y | Y | Y | N |
| 25 Doggett | Y | Y | Y | Y | N | N | N | Y |
| 26 **Burgess** | Y | Y | Y | Y | Y | Y | Y | N |
| 27 Ortiz | Y | Y | Y | Y | N | N | N | Y |
| 28 Cuellar | ? | ? | ? | ? | ? | ? | ? | ? |
| 29 Green, G. | Y | Y | Y | Y | Y | Y | Y | Y |
| 30 Johnson, E. | + | + | + | + | - | - | - | + |
| 31 **Carter** | Y | Y | Y | Y | Y | Y | Y | N |
| 32 **Sessions** | ? | ? | ? | ? | ? | ? | ? | ? |
| **UTAH** | | | | | | | | |
| 1 **Bishop** | Y | Y | Y | Y | Y | Y | Y | N |
| 2 Matheson | Y | Y | Y | Y | Y | N | N | Y |
| 3 **Cannon** | Y | Y | Y | Y | Y | Y | Y | N |
| **VERMONT** | | | | | | | | |
| AL *Sanders* | Y | Y | Y | Y | N | N | N | Y |
| **VIRGINIA** | | | | | | | | |
| 1 **Davis, J.** | Y | Y | Y | Y | Y | Y | Y | N |
| 2 **Drake** | Y | Y | Y | Y | Y | Y | Y | N |
| 3 Scott | N | N | N | Y | N | N | N | Y |
| 4 **Forbes** | Y | Y | Y | Y | Y | Y | Y | N |
| 5 **Goode** | Y | Y | Y | Y | Y | Y | Y | N |
| 6 **Goodlatte** | Y | Y | Y | Y | Y | Y | Y | N |
| 7 **Cantor** | Y | Y | Y | Y | Y | Y | N | N |
| 8 Moran | Y | Y | Y | Y | N | N | N | Y |
| 9 Boucher | Y | Y | Y | Y | Y | N | N | Y |
| 10 **Wolf** | Y | Y | Y | Y | Y | N | N | N |
| 11 **Davis, T.** | ? | ? | ? | ? | ? | ? | ? | ? |
| **WASHINGTON** | | | | | | | | |
| 1 Inslee | Y | Y | Y | Y | N | N | N | Y |
| 2 Larsen | Y | Y | Y | Y | N | N | N | Y |
| 3 Baird | ? | ? | ? | ? | ? | ? | ? | ? |
| 4 **Hastings** | Y | Y | Y | Y | Y | N | N | N |
| 5 **McMorris** | Y | Y | Y | Y | Y | Y | N | N |
| 6 Dicks | Y | Y | Y | Y | N | N | N | Y |
| 7 McDermott | ? | ? | ? | ? | ? | ? | ? | ? |
| 8 **Reichert** | Y | Y | Y | Y | Y | N | N | N |
| 9 Smith | ? | ? | Y | Y | N | N | N | Y |
| **WEST VIRGINIA** | | | | | | | | |
| 1 Mollohan | Y | Y | Y | Y | Y | N | N | Y |
| 2 **Capito** | Y | Y | Y | Y | Y | Y | N | N |
| 3 Rahall | Y | N | Y | Y | N | N | N | Y |
| **WISCONSIN** | | | | | | | | |
| 1 **Ryan** | Y | Y | Y | Y | Y | N | N | N |
| 2 Baldwin | Y | Y | Y | Y | N | N | N | Y |
| 3 Kind | Y | Y | Y | Y | N | N | N | Y |
| 4 Moore | Y | Y | Y | Y | Y | N | N | Y |
| 5 **Sensenbrenner** | Y | Y | Y | Y | Y | Y | Y | N |
| 6 **Petri** | Y | Y | Y | Y | Y | N | Y | N |
| 7 Obey | Y | Y | ? | Y | N | N | N | Y |
| 8 **Green** | Y | Y | Y | Y | Y | N | Y | N |
| **WYOMING** | | | | | | | | |
| AL **Cubin** | Y | Y | Y | Y | Y | N | N | N |

# IN THE HOUSE | By Vote Number

**282.** HR 2745. U.N. Overhaul/Passage. Passage of the bill that would withhold up to 50 percent of U.S. dues to the United Nations unless the secretary of State certifies by Oct. 1, 2007, that the United Nations has complied with 32 of 39 changes in its operations, 14 of them mandatory. Overall U.S. contributions would be capped at 22 percent of the regular (non-peacekeeping) U.N. budget. Passed 221-184: R 213-7; D 8-176 (ND 3-136, SD 5-40); I 0-1. A "nay" was a vote in support of the president's position. June 17, 2005.

**283.** HR 2863. Fiscal 2006 Defense Appropriations/Religious **Proselytizing.** Obey, D-Wis., amendment to the Hunter, R-Calif., amendment. The Obey amendment would express the sense of Congress that coercive and abusive religious proselytizing at the Air Force Academy is inconsistent with academy standards. The Hunter amendment would strike similar language in the underlying bill and express the sense of Congress that expression of personal religious faith is welcome in the military and that the Air Force should review issues of religious tolerance at the academy and issue a report. Rejected 198-210: R 8-207; D 189-3 (ND 143-1, SD 46-2); I 1-0. (Subsequently, the Hunter amendment was adopted by voice vote.) June 20, 2005.

**284.** HR 2863. Fiscal 2006 Defense Appropriations/Uzbekistan. Doggett, D-Texas, amendment that would prohibit use of funds in the bill for activities in Uzbekistan. Rejected 84-329: R 1-217; D 82-112 (ND 76-71, SD 6-41); I 1-0. June 20, 2005.

**285.** HR 2863. Fiscal 2006 Defense Appropriations/Military Action **Against Rogue Nations.** DeFazio, D-Ore., amendment to prohibit the administration from initiating military operations without authorization from Congress. Rejected 136-280: R 3-218; D 132-62 (ND 107-40, SD 25-22); I 1-0. June 20, 2005.

**286.** HR 2863. Fiscal 2006 Defense Appropriations/Small Business **Procurement.** Velázquez, D-N.Y., amendment to bar use of funds in the bill for certain procurement policies that effectively exclude small businesses. Rejected 180-235: R 2-219; D 177-16 (ND 138-9, SD 39-7); I 1-0. June 20, 2005.

**287.** HR 2863. Fiscal 2006 Defense Appropriations/Passage. Passage of the bill that would appropriate $408.9 billion for the Department of Defense, including $45.3 billion for operations in Iraq and Afghanistan. The total includes $116.1 billion for operations and maintenance, $76.8 billion for procurement and $71.7 billion for research and development. Passed 398-19: R 219-2; D 178-17 (ND 133-14, SD 45-3); I 1-0. June 20, 2005.

**288.** HR 2475 Fiscal 2006 Intelligence Authorization/Previous **Question.** Putnam, R-Fla., motion to order the previous question (thus ending debate and the possibility of amendment) on adoption of the rule (H Res 331) to provide for House floor consideration of the intelligence authorization bill. Motion agreed to 224-201: R 224-0; D 0-200 (ND 0-150, SD 0-50); I 0-1. (Subsequently, the rule was adopted by voice vote.) June 21, 2005.

**289.** HR 2475. Fiscal 2006 Intelligence Authorization/Recommit. Waxman, D-Calif., motion to recommit the bill to the House Intelligence Committee with instructions to include language that would establish a bipartisan independent commission to investigate the detainee abuses at Abu Ghraib prison and other facilities. Motion rejected 197-228: R 1-223; D 195-5 (ND 148-2, SD 47-3); I 1-0. June 21, 2005.

| | 282 | 283 | 284 | 285 | 286 | 287 | 288 | 289 |
|---|---|---|---|---|---|---|---|---|
| **ALABAMA** | | | | | | | | |
| 1 Bonner | Y | N | N | N | N | Y | Y | N |
| 2 Everett | Y | N | N | N | N | Y | Y | N |
| 3 Rogers | Y | – | N | N | N | Y | Y | N |
| 4 Aderholt | Y | N | N | N | N | Y | Y | N |
| 5 Cramer | N | Y | N | N | Y | Y | N | N |
| 6 Bachus | Y | N | N | N | N | Y | Y | N |
| 7 Davis | N | Y | N | N | N | Y | Y | N |
| **ALASKA** | | | | | | | | |
| AL Young | Y | N | N | N | N | Y | Y | N |
| **ARIZONA** | | | | | | | | |
| 1 Renzi | Y | N | N | N | N | Y | Y | N |
| 2 Franks | Y | N | N | N | N | Y | Y | N |
| 3 Shadegg | Y | N | N | N | N | Y | Y | N |
| 4 Pastor | N | Y | Y | Y | Y | Y | N | Y |
| 5 Hayworth | Y | N | N | N | N | Y | Y | N |
| 6 Flake | Y | ? | ? | ? | ? | ? | Y | N |
| 7 Grijalva | N | Y | Y | Y | Y | Y | N | Y |
| 8 Kolbe | Y | N | N | N | N | Y | Y | N |
| **ARKANSAS** | | | | | | | | |
| 1 Berry | N | Y | N | Y | Y | Y | N | Y |
| 2 Snyder | N | Y | N | N | Y | Y | Y | N |
| 3 Boozman | Y | N | N | N | N | Y | Y | N |
| 4 Ross | N | Y | N | N | Y | Y | N | Y |
| **CALIFORNIA** | | | | | | | | |
| 1 Thompson | N | Y | Y | Y | Y | Y | N | Y |
| 2 Herger | Y | N | N | N | N | Y | Y | N |
| 3 Lungren | Y | N | N | N | N | Y | Y | N |
| 4 Doolittle | Y | N | N | N | N | Y | Y | N |
| 5 Matsui, D. | N | Y | N | Y | Y | Y | N | Y |
| 6 Woolsey | N | Y | Y | Y | Y | N | N | Y |
| 7 Miller, George | N | Y | Y | Y | Y | N | N | Y |
| 8 Pelosi | ? | Y | Y | Y | Y | Y | N | Y |
| 9 Lee | N | Y | Y | Y | Y | N | N | Y |
| 10 Tauscher | N | Y | N | Y | Y | Y | N | Y |
| 11 Pombo | Y | N | N | N | N | Y | Y | N |
| 12 Lantos | N | ? | N | Y | Y | Y | N | Y |
| 13 Stark | ? | Y | Y | Y | Y | N | N | Y |
| 14 Eshoo | N | Y | Y | Y | Y | Y | N | Y |
| 15 Honda | N | Y | Y | Y | Y | Y | N | Y |
| 16 Lofgren | N | Y | Y | Y | Y | Y | N | Y |
| 17 Farr | N | Y | Y | Y | Y | Y | N | Y |
| 18 Cardoza | N | Y | N | N | Y | Y | N | Y |
| 19 Radanovich | Y | N | N | N | N | Y | Y | N |
| 20 Costa | N | Y | N | N | Y | Y | N | Y |
| 21 Nunes | Y | N | N | N | N | Y | Y | N |
| 22 Thomas | Y | N | N | N | N | Y | Y | N |
| 23 Capps | N | Y | Y | Y | Y | Y | N | Y |
| 24 Gallegly | Y | N | N | N | N | Y | Y | N |
| 25 McKeon | Y | N | N | N | N | Y | Y | N |
| 26 Dreier | Y | N | N | N | N | Y | Y | N |
| 27 Sherman | N | Y | N | Y | Y | Y | N | Y |
| 28 Berman | N | Y | Y | N | Y | Y | N | Y |
| 29 Schiff | N | Y | N | N | Y | Y | N | Y |
| 30 Waxman | ? | ? | ? | ? | ? | ? | N | Y |
| 31 Becerra | N | Y | Y | Y | Y | Y | N | Y |
| 32 Solis | N | Y | Y | Y | Y | Y | N | Y |
| 33 Watson | N | Y | Y | Y | Y | Y | N | Y |
| 34 Roybal-Allard | N | Y | Y | Y | Y | Y | N | Y |
| 35 Waters | N | Y | Y | N | Y | N | N | Y |
| 36 Harman | N | Y | N | Y | Y | Y | N | Y |
| 37 Millender-McD. | ? | Y | N | Y | Y | Y | N | Y |
| 38 Napolitano | N | Y | N | Y | Y | Y | N | Y |
| 39 Sánchez, Linda | N | Y | Y | Y | Y | Y | N | Y |
| 40 Royce | Y | N | N | N | N | Y | Y | N |
| 41 Lewis | Y | N | N | N | N | Y | Y | N |
| 42 Miller, Gary | Y | N | N | N | N | Y | Y | N |
| 43 Baca | N | Y | N | N | Y | Y | N | Y |
| 44 Calvert | Y | N | N | N | N | Y | Y | N |
| 45 Bono | ? | N | N | N | N | Y | Y | N |
| 46 Rohrabacher | Y | N | N | N | N | Y | Y | N |
| 47 Sanchez, Loretta | N | Y | N | Y | Y | Y | N | Y |
| 48 Cox | Y | N | N | N | N | Y | Y | N |
| 49 Issa | + | N | N | N | N | Y | Y | N |
| 50 Cunningham | Y | N | N | N | N | Y | Y | N |
| 51 Filner | N | Y | Y | Y | Y | N | N | Y |
| 52 Hunter | Y | N | N | N | N | Y | Y | N |
| 53 Davis | N | Y | N | N | Y | Y | N | Y |
| **COLORADO** | | | | | | | | |
| 1 DeGette | N | Y | Y | Y | Y | Y | N | Y |
| 2 Udall | N | Y | Y | Y | Y | Y | N | Y |
| 3 Salazar | N | Y | N | N | Y | Y | N | Y |
| 4 Musgrave | Y | N | N | N | N | Y | Y | N |
| 5 Hefley | Y | N | N | N | N | Y | Y | N |
| 6 Tancredo | Y | N | N | N | N | Y | Y | N |
| 7 Beauprez | Y | N | N | N | N | Y | Y | N |
| **CONNECTICUT** | | | | | | | | |
| 1 Larson | N | Y | Y | Y | Y | Y | N | Y |
| 2 Simmons | + | N | N | N | Y | Y | N | Y |
| 3 DeLauro | Y | Y | Y | Y | Y | Y | N | Y |
| 4 Shays | N | N | N | N | N | Y | Y | N |
| 5 Johnson | Y | Y | N | N | Y | Y | Y | N |
| **DELAWARE** | | | | | | | | |
| AL Castle | N | Y | N | N | N | Y | Y | N |
| **FLORIDA** | | | | | | | | |
| 1 Miller | Y | N | N | N | N | Y | Y | N |
| 2 Boyd | N | Y | ? | ? | ? | N | Y | N |
| 3 Brown | ? | ? | ? | ? | ? | ? | N | Y |
| 4 Crenshaw | Y | N | ? | ? | ? | ? | Y | N |
| 5 Brown-Waite | Y | N | N | N | N | Y | Y | N |
| 6 Stearns | Y | N | N | N | N | Y | Y | N |
| 7 Mica | Y | N | N | N | N | Y | Y | N |
| 8 Keller | Y | N | N | N | N | Y | Y | N |
| 9 Bilirakis | Y | N | N | N | N | Y | Y | N |
| 10 Young | Y | N | N | N | N | Y | ? | ? |
| 11 Davis | N | Y | Y | Y | Y | Y | N | Y |
| 12 Putnam | Y | N | N | N | N | Y | Y | N |
| 13 Harris | Y | – | – | – | – | + | Y | N |
| 14 Mack | Y | N | N | N | N | Y | Y | N |
| 15 Weldon | Y | N | N | N | N | Y | Y | N |
| 16 Foley | Y | N | N | N | N | Y | Y | N |
| 17 Meek | N | Y | N | Y | Y | Y | N | Y |
| 18 Ros-Lehtinen | Y | N | N | N | N | Y | Y | N |
| 19 Wexler | N | ? | ? | ? | ? | N | Y | N |
| 20 Wasserman-Schultz | N | ? | ? | ? | ? | Y | N | Y |
| 21 Diaz-Balart, L. | Y | N | N | N | N | Y | Y | N |
| 22 Shaw | Y | N | N | N | N | Y | Y | N |
| 23 Hastings | N | Y | N | Y | Y | Y | N | Y |
| 24 Feeney | Y | N | N | N | N | Y | Y | N |
| 25 Diaz-Balart, M. | Y | N | N | N | N | Y | Y | N |
| **GEORGIA** | | | | | | | | |
| 1 Kingston | Y | N | N | N | N | Y | Y | N |
| 2 Bishop | ? | Y | N | Y | Y | Y | N | Y |
| 3 Marshall | Y | N | N | N | Y | Y | N | N |
| 4 McKinney | N | Y | Y | Y | ? | N | N | Y |
| 5 Lewis | N | Y | Y | Y | Y | N | ? | ? |
| 6 Price | Y | N | N | N | N | Y | Y | N |
| 7 Linder | Y | N | N | N | N | Y | Y | N |
| 8 Westmoreland | Y | N | N | N | N | Y | Y | N |
| 9 Norwood | Y | N | N | N | N | Y | Y | N |
| 10 Deal | Y | N | N | N | N | Y | Y | N |
| 11 Gingrey | ? | N | N | N | N | Y | Y | N |
| 12 Barrow | Y | Y | N | N | Y | Y | N | Y |
| 13 Scott | N | Y | N | Y | Y | Y | N | Y |
| **HAWAII** | | | | | | | | |
| 1 Abercrombie | N | Y | Y | Y | N | Y | N | N |
| 2 Case | N | Y | N | Y | Y | Y | N | N |
| **IDAHO** | | | | | | | | |
| 1 Otter | Y | N | N | N | N | Y | Y | N |
| 2 Simpson | Y | N | N | N | N | Y | Y | N |
| **ILLINOIS** | | | | | | | | |
| 1 Rush | N | Y | Y | Y | Y | Y | N | Y |
| 2 Jackson | N | Y | Y | Y | Y | Y | N | Y |
| 3 Lipinski | N | Y | N | N | Y | Y | N | Y |
| 4 Gutierrez | N | Y | Y | Y | Y | Y | N | Y |
| 5 Emanuel | N | Y | Y | Y | Y | Y | N | Y |
| 6 Hyde | Y | N | N | N | N | Y | Y | N |
| 7 Davis | N | Y | Y | Y | Y | Y | N | Y |
| 8 Bean | N | Y | N | N | Y | Y | N | N |
| 9 Schakowsky | N | Y | Y | Y | Y | N | N | Y |
| 10 Kirk | Y | Y | N | N | N | Y | Y | N |
| 11 Weller | Y | N | – | N | N | Y | Y | N |
| 12 Costello | Y | Y | N | Y | Y | Y | N | Y |

**KEY** — Republicans — Democrats — *Independents*

| Y | Voted for (yea) | X | Paired against | C | Voted "present" to avoid possible conflict of interest |
|---|---|---|---|---|---|
| # | Paired for | – | Announced against | | |
| + | Announced for | P | Voted "present" | ? | Did not vote or otherwise make a position known |
| N | Voted against (nay) | | | | |

| | 282 | 283 | 284 | 285 | 286 | 287 | 288 | 289 |
|---|---|---|---|---|---|---|---|---|
| 13 **Biggert** | Y | Y | N | N | N | Y | Y | N |
| 14 **Hastert** | | | | | | | | |
| 15 **Johnson** | Y | N | N | N | N | Y | Y | N |
| 16 **Manzullo** | Y | N | N | N | N | Y | Y | N |
| 17 Evans | N | Y | Y | Y | Y | Y | N | Y |
| 18 **LaHood** | Y | N | N | N | N | Y | Y | N |
| 19 **Shimkus** | Y | ? | N | N | N | Y | Y | N |
| **INDIANA** | | | | | | | | |
| 1 Visclosky | N | Y | N | N | Y | Y | N | Y |
| 2 **Chocola** | Y | N | N | N | N | Y | Y | N |
| 3 **Souder** | Y | ? | ? | ? | ? | ? | Y | N |
| 4 **Buyer** | Y | N | N | N | N | Y | Y | N |
| 5 **Burton** | Y | N | N | N | N | Y | Y | N |
| 6 **Pence** | Y | N | N | N | N | Y | Y | - |
| 7 Carson | N | Y | Y | Y | Y | Y | N | Y |
| 8 **Hostettler** | Y | N | N | N | N | Y | Y | N |
| 9 **Sodrel** | Y | N | N | N | N | Y | Y | N |
| **IOWA** | | | | | | | | |
| 1 **Nussle** | Y | N | N | N | N | Y | Y | N |
| 2 **Leach** | N | Y | N | Y | Y | Y | Y | Y |
| 3 Boswell | N | Y | N | Y | N | Y | N | Y |
| 4 **Latham** | Y | N | N | N | N | Y | Y | N |
| 5 **King** | Y | N | N | N | N | Y | Y | N |
| **KANSAS** | | | | | | | | |
| 1 **Moran** | Y | N | N | N | N | Y | Y | N |
| 2 **Ryun** | Y | N | N | N | N | Y | Y | N |
| 3 Moore | N | Y | N | N | Y | Y | N | Y |
| 4 **Tiahrt** | Y | N | N | N | N | Y | Y | N |
| **KENTUCKY** | | | | | | | | |
| 1 **Whitfield** | Y | N | N | N | N | Y | ? | N |
| 2 **Lewis** | Y | ? | ? | ? | ? | ? | Y | N |
| 3 **Northup** | Y | N | N | N | N | Y | Y | N |
| 4 **Davis** | Y | N | N | N | N | Y | Y | N |
| 5 **Rogers** | Y | N | N | N | N | Y | Y | N |
| 6 Chandler | N | Y | N | Y | Y | Y | N | Y |
| **LOUISIANA** | | | | | | | | |
| 1 **Jindal** | Y | N | N | N | N | Y | Y | N |
| 2 Jefferson | N | Y | N | N | N | Y | N | Y |
| 3 Melancon | N | Y | N | N | N | Y | N | Y |
| 4 **McCrery** | Y | N | N | N | N | Y | Y | N |
| 5 **Alexander** | Y | N | N | N | N | Y | Y | N |
| 6 **Baker** | Y | ? | ? | ? | ? | ? | Y | N |
| 7 **Boustany** | Y | N | N | N | N | Y | Y | N |
| **MAINE** | | | | | | | | |
| 1 Allen | N | Y | Y | N | Y | Y | N | Y |
| 2 Michaud | N | Y | N | Y | Y | Y | N | Y |
| **MARYLAND** | | | | | | | | |
| 1 **Gilchrest** | Y | N | N | N | N | Y | Y | N |
| 2 Ruppersberger | N | Y | N | N | Y | Y | N | Y |
| 3 Cardin | N | Y | Y | Y | Y | Y | N | Y |
| 4 Wynn | N | Y | N | Y | Y | Y | N | Y |
| 5 Hoyer | N | Y | N | N | Y | Y | N | Y |
| 6 **Bartlett** | Y | N | N | N | N | Y | Y | N |
| 7 Cummings | N | Y | N | Y | Y | Y | N | Y |
| 8 Van Hollen | N | Y | Y | Y | Y | Y | N | Y |
| **MASSACHUSETTS** | | | | | | | | |
| 1 Olver | N | Y | Y | Y | Y | Y | N | Y |
| 2 Neal | N | Y | Y | Y | Y | Y | N | Y |
| 3 McGovern | N | Y | Y | Y | Y | Y | N | Y |
| 4 Frank | N | Y | Y | Y | Y | Y | N | Y |
| 5 Meehan | N | Y | Y | Y | Y | Y | N | Y |
| 6 Tierney | N | Y | Y | Y | Y | Y | N | Y |
| 7 Markey | N | Y | Y | Y | Y | Y | N | Y |
| 8 Capuano | N | Y | N | Y | Y | Y | N | Y |
| 9 Lynch | N | Y | N | N | Y | Y | N | Y |
| 10 Delahunt | N | Y | Y | Y | Y | Y | N | Y |
| **MICHIGAN** | | | | | | | | |
| 1 Stupak | N | Y | N | N | Y | Y | N | Y |
| 2 **Hoekstra** | Y | N | N | N | Y | Y | Y | N |
| 3 **Ehlers** | Y | - | N | N | N | Y | Y | N |
| 4 **Camp** | Y | N | N | N | N | Y | Y | N |
| 5 Kildee | N | Y | N | Y | Y | Y | N | Y |
| 6 **Upton** | Y | N | N | N | N | Y | Y | N |
| 7 **Schwarz** | Y | ? | ? | ? | ? | ? | Y | N |
| 8 **Rogers** | Y | N | N | N | N | Y | Y | N |
| 9 **Knollenberg** | Y | ? | N | N | N | Y | Y | N |
| 10 **Miller** | Y | N | N | N | N | Y | Y | N |
| 11 **McCotter** | Y | N | N | N | N | Y | Y | N |
| 12 Levin | N | Y | N | Y | Y | Y | N | Y |
| 13 Kilpatrick | N | ? | N | Y | N | Y | N | Y |
| 14 Conyers | N | ? | Y | Y | Y | N | N | Y |
| 15 Dingell | N | Y | N | Y | Y | Y | N | Y |

| | 282 | 283 | 284 | 285 | 286 | 287 | 288 | 289 |
|---|---|---|---|---|---|---|---|---|
| **MINNESOTA** | | | | | | | | |
| 1 **Gutknecht** | Y | N | N | N | N | Y | Y | N |
| 2 **Kline** | Y | N | N | N | N | Y | Y | N |
| 3 **Ramstad** | Y | N | N | N | N | Y | Y | N |
| 4 McCollum | N | Y | Y | Y | Y | Y | N | Y |
| 5 Sabo | N | Y | Y | Y | Y | Y | N | Y |
| 6 **Kennedy** | Y | N | N | N | N | Y | Y | N |
| 7 Peterson | N | N | N | N | N | Y | N | Y |
| 8 Oberstar | N | Y | Y | Y | Y | Y | N | Y |
| **MISSISSIPPI** | | | | | | | | |
| 1 **Wicker** | Y | N | N | N | N | Y | Y | N |
| 2 Thompson | N | Y | N | Y | N | Y | N | Y |
| 3 **Pickering** | Y | N | N | N | N | Y | Y | N |
| 4 Taylor | Y | N | N | N | Y | Y | N | Y |
| **MISSOURI** | | | | | | | | |
| 1 Clay | N | Y | Y | Y | Y | Y | N | Y |
| 2 **Akin** | Y | N | N | N | N | Y | Y | N |
| 3 Carnahan | N | Y | N | Y | Y | Y | N | Y |
| 4 Skelton | ? | Y | N | N | Y | Y | N | Y |
| 5 Cleaver | N | Y | N | Y | Y | Y | N | Y |
| 6 **Graves** | + | N | N | N | N | Y | Y | N |
| 7 **Blunt** | Y | N | N | N | N | Y | Y | N |
| 8 **Emerson** | Y | N | N | N | N | Y | Y | N |
| 9 **Hulshof** | Y | N | N | N | N | Y | Y | N |
| **MONTANA** | | | | | | | | |
| AL **Rehberg** | Y | N | N | N | N | Y | Y | N |
| **NEBRASKA** | | | | | | | | |
| 1 **Fortenberry** | Y | N | N | N | N | Y | Y | N |
| 2 **Terry** | Y | N | N | N | N | Y | Y | N |
| 3 **Osborne** | Y | N | N | N | N | Y | Y | N |
| **NEVADA** | | | | | | | | |
| 1 Berkley | Y | Y | Y | Y | Y | Y | N | Y |
| 2 **Gibbons** | Y | N | N | N | N | Y | Y | N |
| 3 **Porter** | Y | N | N | N | N | Y | Y | N |
| **NEW HAMPSHIRE** | | | | | | | | |
| 1 **Bradley** | Y | N | N | N | N | Y | Y | N |
| 2 **Bass** | Y | N | N | N | N | Y | Y | N |
| **NEW JERSEY** | | | | | | | | |
| 1 Andrews | - | Y | N | Y | Y | Y | N | Y |
| 2 **LoBiondo** | Y | N | N | N | N | Y | Y | N |
| 3 **Saxton** | Y | N | N | N | N | Y | Y | N |
| 4 **Smith** | Y | N | N | N | N | Y | Y | N |
| 5 **Garrett** | Y | N | N | N | N | Y | Y | N |
| 6 Pallone | N | Y | Y | Y | Y | Y | N | Y |
| 7 **Ferguson** | Y | N | N | N | N | Y | Y | N |
| 8 Pascrell | N | Y | N | Y | Y | Y | N | Y |
| 9 Rothman | N | Y | N | Y | Y | Y | N | Y |
| 10 Payne | N | Y | Y | Y | Y | N | N | Y |
| 11 **Frelinghuysen** | Y | N | N | N | N | Y | Y | N |
| 12 Holt | N | Y | Y | Y | Y | Y | N | Y |
| 13 Menendez | N | Y | N | Y | Y | Y | N | Y |
| **NEW MEXICO** | | | | | | | | |
| 1 **Wilson** | Y | Y | N | N | N | Y | Y | N |
| 2 **Pearce** | Y | N | N | N | N | Y | Y | N |
| 3 Udall | N | Y | Y | Y | Y | Y | N | Y |
| **NEW YORK** | | | | | | | | |
| 1 Bishop | N | Y | N | N | Y | Y | N | Y |
| 2 Israel | N | Y | N | N | Y | Y | N | Y |
| 3 **King** | Y | N | N | N | N | Y | Y | N |
| 4 McCarthy | N | Y | N | N | Y | Y | N | Y |
| 5 Ackerman | N | Y | N | Y | Y | Y | N | Y |
| 6 Meeks | N | Y | Y | Y | Y | Y | N | Y |
| 7 Crowley | N | Y | N | Y | Y | Y | N | Y |
| 8 Nadler | N | Y | Y | Y | Y | Y | N | Y |
| 9 Weiner | N | Y | Y | Y | Y | Y | N | Y |
| 10 Towns | N | ? | ? | ? | ? | ? | N | Y |
| 11 Owens | N | Y | Y | Y | Y | N | N | Y |
| 12 Velázquez | N | Y | Y | Y | Y | Y | N | Y |
| 13 **Fossella** | Y | N | N | N | N | Y | Y | N |
| 14 Maloney | N | Y | N | Y | Y | Y | N | Y |
| 15 Rangel | N | Y | Y | Y | Y | N | N | Y |
| 16 Serrano | N | Y | Y | Y | Y | Y | N | Y |
| 17 Engel | N | Y | N | Y | Y | Y | N | Y |
| 18 Lowey | N | Y | N | Y | Y | Y | N | Y |
| 19 **Kelly** | Y | N | N | N | N | Y | Y | N |
| 20 **Sweeney** | Y | N | N | N | N | Y | Y | N |
| 21 McNulty | N | Y | Y | Y | Y | Y | N | Y |
| 22 Hinchey | N | Y | Y | Y | Y | N | N | Y |
| 23 **McHugh** | Y | N | N | N | N | Y | Y | N |
| 24 **Boehlert** | N | N | N | N | N | Y | Y | N |
| 25 **Walsh** | ? | N | N | N | N | Y | Y | N |
| 26 **Reynolds** | Y | ? | ? | N | N | Y | Y | N |
| 27 Higgins | N | Y | N | Y | Y | Y | N | Y |
| 28 Slaughter | ? | Y | Y | Y | Y | Y | N | Y |
| 29 **Kuhl** | Y | N | N | N | N | Y | Y | N |

| | 282 | 283 | 284 | 285 | 286 | 287 | 288 | 289 |
|---|---|---|---|---|---|---|---|---|
| **NORTH CAROLINA** | | | | | | | | |
| 1 Butterfield | N | Y | N | N | Y | Y | N | Y |
| 2 Etheridge | N | Y | N | N | Y | Y | N | Y |
| 3 **Jones** | Y | N | N | Y | N | Y | Y | N |
| 4 Price | N | Y | N | Y | Y | Y | N | Y |
| 5 **Foxx** | Y | N | N | N | N | Y | Y | N |
| 6 **Coble** | Y | N | N | N | N | Y | Y | N |
| 7 McIntyre | Y | Y | N | N | Y | Y | N | Y |
| 8 **Hayes** | Y | N | N | N | N | Y | Y | N |
| 9 **Myrick** | Y | N | N | N | N | Y | Y | N |
| 10 **McHenry** | Y | N | N | N | N | Y | Y | N |
| 11 **Taylor** | Y | N | N | N | N | Y | Y | N |
| 12 Watt | N | Y | N | Y | Y | N | N | Y |
| 13 Miller | N | Y | N | N | Y | Y | N | Y |
| **NORTH DAKOTA** | | | | | | | | |
| AL Pomeroy | N | Y | Y | N | Y | Y | N | Y |
| **OHIO** | | | | | | | | |
| 1 **Chabot** | Y | N | N | N | N | Y | Y | N |
| 2 Vacant | | | | | | | | |
| 3 **Turner** | Y | N | N | N | N | Y | Y | N |
| 4 **Oxley** | Y | N | N | N | N | Y | Y | N |
| 5 **Gillmor** | ? | N | N | N | N | Y | Y | N |
| 6 Strickland | N | Y | Y | Y | Y | Y | N | Y |
| 7 **Hobson** | Y | N | N | N | N | Y | Y | N |
| 8 **Boehner** | ? | N | N | N | N | Y | Y | N |
| 9 Kaptur | N | Y | N | N | Y | Y | N | Y |
| 10 Kucinich | N | Y | Y | Y | Y | N | N | Y |
| 11 Jones | N | Y | N | N | N | Y | N | Y |
| 12 **Tiberi** | Y | N | N | N | N | Y | Y | N |
| 13 Brown | N | Y | Y | Y | Y | Y | N | Y |
| 14 **LaTourette** | Y | N | N | N | N | Y | Y | N |
| 15 **Pryce** | Y | N | N | N | N | Y | Y | N |
| 16 **Regula** | Y | N | N | N | N | Y | Y | N |
| 17 Ryan | N | Y | N | N | N | Y | N | Y |
| 18 **Ney** | Y | N | N | N | N | Y | Y | N |
| **OKLAHOMA** | | | | | | | | |
| 1 **Sullivan** | Y | N | N | N | N | Y | Y | N |
| 2 Boren | N | Y | N | N | Y | Y | N | Y |
| 3 **Lucas** | Y | N | N | N | N | Y | Y | N |
| 4 **Cole** | Y | N | N | N | N | Y | Y | N |
| 5 **Istook** | Y | ? | ? | ? | ? | ? | Y | N |
| **OREGON** | | | | | | | | |
| 1 Wu | N | Y | N | Y | Y | Y | N | Y |
| 2 **Walden** | Y | N | N | N | N | Y | ? | N |
| 3 Blumenauer | ? | Y | Y | Y | Y | Y | N | Y |
| 4 DeFazio | N | Y | Y | Y | Y | Y | N | Y |
| 5 Hooley | ? | Y | Y | Y | Y | Y | N | Y |
| **PENNSYLVANIA** | | | | | | | | |
| 1 Brady | N | Y | N | N | Y | Y | N | Y |
| 2 Fattah | N | Y | N | N | Y | Y | N | Y |
| 3 **English** | Y | N | N | N | N | Y | Y | N |
| 4 **Hart** | Y | N | N | N | N | Y | Y | N |
| 5 **Peterson** | Y | N | N | N | N | Y | Y | N |
| 6 **Gerlach** | Y | N | N | N | N | Y | Y | N |
| 7 **Weldon** | Y | N | N | N | N | Y | Y | N |
| 8 **Fitzpatrick** | Y | N | N | N | N | Y | Y | N |
| 9 **Shuster** | Y | N | N | N | N | Y | Y | N |
| 10 **Sherwood** | Y | N | N | N | N | Y | Y | N |
| 11 Kanjorski | N | Y | N | N | Y | Y | N | Y |
| 12 Murtha | N | Y | N | N | Y | Y | N | Y |
| 13 Schwartz | N | Y | N | N | Y | Y | N | Y |
| 14 Doyle | N | Y | N | N | Y | Y | N | Y |
| 15 **Dent** | Y | Y | N | N | N | Y | Y | N |
| 16 **Pitts** | Y | N | N | N | N | Y | Y | N |
| 17 Holden | N | Y | N | N | Y | Y | N | Y |
| 18 **Murphy** | Y | N | N | N | N | Y | + | - |
| 19 **Platts** | Y | ? | N | N | N | Y | Y | N |
| **RHODE ISLAND** | | | | | | | | |
| 1 Kennedy | ? | Y | N | N | Y | Y | N | Y |
| 2 Langevin | N | Y | N | N | Y | Y | N | Y |
| **SOUTH CAROLINA** | | | | | | | | |
| 1 **Brown** | Y | N | N | N | N | Y | Y | N |
| 2 **Wilson** | Y | N | N | N | N | Y | Y | N |
| 3 **Barrett** | Y | N | N | N | N | Y | Y | N |
| 4 **Inglis** | Y | N | N | N | N | Y | Y | N |
| 5 Spratt | N | Y | N | N | Y | Y | N | Y |
| 6 Clyburn | N | Y | N | Y | N | Y | N | Y |
| **SOUTH DAKOTA** | | | | | | | | |
| AL Herseth | N | ? | ? | ? | ? | ? | ? | ? |
| **TENNESSEE** | | | | | | | | |
| 1 **Jenkins** | Y | N | N | N | N | Y | Y | N |
| 2 **Duncan** | Y | N | N | N | N | N | Y | N |

| | 282 | 283 | 284 | 285 | 286 | 287 | 288 | 289 |
|---|---|---|---|---|---|---|---|---|
| 3 **Wamp** | Y | - | - | N | N | Y | Y | N |
| 4 Davis | N | Y | N | N | N | Y | N | N |
| 5 Cooper | N | Y | N | N | Y | Y | N | Y |
| 6 Gordon | N | Y | N | N | Y | Y | N | Y |
| 7 **Blackburn** | Y | N | N | N | N | Y | Y | N |
| 8 Tanner | ? | Y | N | N | Y | Y | N | Y |
| 9 Ford | N | Y | N | N | Y | Y | N | Y |
| **TEXAS** | | | | | | | | |
| 1 **Gohmert** | Y | N | N | N | N | Y | Y | N |
| 2 **Poe** | Y | N | N | N | N | Y | Y | N |
| 3 **Johnson, S.** | Y | N | N | N | N | Y | Y | N |
| 4 **Hall** | Y | N | N | N | N | Y | Y | N |
| 5 **Hensarling** | Y | N | N | N | N | Y | Y | N |
| 6 **Barton** | Y | N | N | N | N | Y | Y | N |
| 7 **Culberson** | Y | N | N | N | N | Y | Y | N |
| 8 **Brady** | Y | N | N | N | N | Y | Y | N |
| 9 Green, A. | N | Y | N | Y | Y | Y | N | Y |
| 10 **McCaul** | Y | N | N | N | N | Y | Y | N |
| 11 **Conaway** | Y | N | N | N | N | Y | Y | ? |
| 12 **Granger** | Y | ? | ? | ? | ? | ? | Y | N |
| 13 **Thornberry** | Y | N | N | N | N | Y | Y | N |
| 14 **Paul** | N | N | Y | Y | N | N | Y | N |
| 15 Hinojosa | N | Y | N | Y | Y | Y | N | Y |
| 16 Reyes | ? | Y | N | Y | Y | Y | N | Y |
| 17 Edwards | N | Y | N | Y | Y | Y | N | Y |
| 18 Jackson-Lee | N | Y | Y | Y | Y | Y | N | Y |
| 19 **Neugebauer** | Y | N | N | N | N | Y | Y | N |
| 20 Gonzalez | N | Y | N | Y | Y | Y | N | Y |
| 21 **Smith** | Y | N | N | N | N | Y | Y | N |
| 22 **DeLay** | Y | N | N | N | N | Y | Y | N |
| 23 **Bonilla** | Y | N | N | N | N | Y | Y | N |
| 24 **Marchant** | Y | N | N | N | N | Y | Y | N |
| 25 Doggett | N | Y | Y | Y | Y | Y | N | Y |
| 26 **Burgess** | Y | N | N | N | N | Y | Y | N |
| 27 Ortiz | N | Y | N | Y | Y | Y | N | Y |
| 28 Cuellar | ? | Y | N | N | Y | Y | N | Y |
| 29 Green, G. | Y | Y | N | Y | Y | Y | N | Y |
| 30 Johnson, E. | - | Y | Y | Y | Y | Y | N | Y |
| 31 **Carter** | Y | N | N | N | N | Y | + | - |
| 32 **Sessions** | ? | N | N | N | N | Y | ? | ? |
| **UTAH** | | | | | | | | |
| 1 **Bishop** | Y | N | N | N | N | Y | Y | N |
| 2 Matheson | N | Y | N | N | N | Y | N | N |
| 3 **Cannon** | Y | N | N | N | N | Y | Y | N |
| **VERMONT** | | | | | | | | |
| AL *Sanders* | N | Y | Y | Y | Y | Y | N | Y |
| **VIRGINIA** | | | | | | | | |
| 1 **Davis, J.** | Y | N | N | N | N | Y | Y | N |
| 2 **Drake** | Y | N | N | N | N | Y | Y | N |
| 3 Scott | N | Y | N | Y | N | Y | N | Y |
| 4 **Forbes** | Y | N | N | N | N | Y | Y | N |
| 5 **Goode** | N | N | N | N | N | Y | Y | N |
| 6 **Goodlatte** | Y | N | N | N | N | Y | Y | N |
| 7 **Cantor** | Y | N | N | N | N | Y | Y | N |
| 8 Moran | N | Y | Y | Y | Y | Y | N | Y |
| 9 Boucher | N | Y | N | Y | N | Y | N | Y |
| 10 **Wolf** | Y | N | N | N | N | Y | Y | N |
| 11 **Davis, T.** | ? | N | N | N | N | Y | Y | N |
| **WASHINGTON** | | | | | | | | |
| 1 Inslee | N | Y | Y | Y | Y | Y | N | Y |
| 2 Larsen | N | Y | Y | Y | Y | Y | N | Y |
| 3 Baird | ? | Y | Y | Y | Y | Y | N | Y |
| 4 **Hastings** | Y | N | N | N | N | Y | Y | N |
| 5 **McMorris** | Y | N | N | N | N | Y | Y | N |
| 6 Dicks | N | Y | N | N | Y | Y | N | Y |
| 7 McDermott | - | Y | Y | Y | Y | N | N | Y |
| 8 **Reichert** | N | N | N | N | N | Y | Y | N |
| 9 Smith | N | Y | Y | Y | N | Y | N | Y |
| **WEST VIRGINIA** | | | | | | | | |
| 1 Mollohan | Y | Y | N | N | Y | Y | N | Y |
| 2 **Capito** | Y | N | N | N | N | Y | Y | N |
| 3 Rahall | N | Y | N | Y | Y | Y | N | Y |
| **WISCONSIN** | | | | | | | | |
| 1 **Ryan** | Y | N | N | N | N | Y | Y | N |
| 2 Baldwin | N | Y | Y | Y | Y | N | N | Y |
| 3 Kind | N | Y | N | Y | Y | Y | N | Y |
| 4 Moore | N | ? | ? | ? | ? | ? | N | Y |
| 5 **Sensenbrenner** | Y | Y | N | N | N | Y | Y | N |
| 6 **Petri** | Y | N | N | N | N | Y | Y | N |
| 7 Obey | N | Y | N | Y | Y | Y | N | Y |
| 8 **Green** | Y | N | N | N | N | Y | Y | N |
| **WYOMING** | | | | | | | | |
| AL **Cubin** | Y | N | N | N | N | Y | Y | N |

# IN THE HOUSE | By Vote Number

**290.** **HR 2475. Fiscal 2006 Intelligence Authorization/Passage.** Passage of the bill that would authorize classified amounts in fiscal 2006 for U.S. intelligence activities and agencies including the CIA, the National Security Agency and the Defense Intelligence Agency. Passed 409-16: R 222-2; D 186-14 (ND 137-13, SD 49-1); I 1-0. June 21, 2005.

**291.** **H J Res 52. Myanmar Sanctions/Passage.** Shaw, R-Fla., motion to suspend the rules and pass the joint resolution that would extend for one year import restrictions on products from Myanmar, formerly known as Burma, until the president certifies that the Myanmar government has made significant progress in democracy and human rights. Motion agreed to 423-2: R 222-2; D 200-0 (ND 150-0, SD 50-0); I 1-0. A two-thirds majority of those present and voting (284 in this case) is required for passage under suspension of the rules. June 21, 2005.

**292.** **H Con Res 160. Juneteenth Independence Day Tribute/Adoption.** Brown-Waite, R-Fla., motion to suspend the rules and adopt the concurrent resolution to recognize the historical significance and back the celebration of June 19, 1865, as "Juneteenth," and urge the president to call for the public to observe the day. Motion agreed to 425-0: R 224-0; D 200-0 (ND 150-0, SD 50-0); I 1-0. A two-thirds majority of those present and voting (284 in this case) is required for adoption under suspension of the rules. June 21, 2005.

**293.** **H J Res 10. Flag Desecration Constitutional Amendment/ Democratic Substitute.** Watt, D-N.C., substitute amendment that would grant Congress the power to prohibit the physical desecration of the U.S. flag but only if that is consistent with the First Amendment of the Constitution. Rejected 129-279: R 3-213; D 125-66 (ND 101-44, SD 24-22); I 1-0. June 22, 2005.

**294.** **H J Res 10. Flag Desecration Constitutional Amendment/Appeal Ruling of the Chair.** Sensenbrenner, R-Wis., motion to table (kill) the Taylor, D-Miss., appeal of the ruling of the chair that the Taylor motion to recommit was not germane. The Taylor motion would recommit the bill to the Judiciary Committee with instructions to add language proposing a balanced-budget constitutional amendment. Motion agreed to 222-194: R 221-0; D 1-193 (ND 1-147, SD 0-46); I 0-1. June 22, 2005.

**295.** **H J Res 10. Flag Desecration Constitutional Amendment/Appeal Ruling of the Chair.** Sensenbrenner, R-Wis., motion to table (kill) the Taylor, D-Miss., appeal of the ruling of the chair that the Taylor motion to recommit was not germane. The Taylor motion would recommit the bill to the Judiciary Committee to add language proposing a constitutional amendment to segregate several trust funds from the federal budget. Motion agreed to 222-190: R 220-0; D 2-189 (ND 2-143, SD 0-46); I 0-1. June 22, 2005.

| | 290 | 291 | 292 | 293 | 294 | 295 |
|---|---|---|---|---|---|---|
| **ALABAMA** | | | | | | |
| 1 Bonner | Y | Y | Y | ? | ? | ? |
| 2 Everett | Y | Y | Y | N | Y | Y |
| 3 Rogers | Y | Y | Y | N | Y | Y |
| 4 Aderholt | Y | Y | Y | N | Y | Y |
| 5 Cramer | Y | Y | Y | N | N | N |
| 6 Bachus | Y | Y | Y | N | Y | Y |
| 7 Davis | Y | Y | Y | Y | N | N |
| **ALASKA** | | | | | | |
| AL Young | Y | Y | Y | N | Y | Y |
| **ARIZONA** | | | | | | |
| 1 Renzi | Y | Y | Y | N | Y | Y |
| 2 Franks | Y | Y | Y | N | Y | Y |
| 3 Shadegg | Y | Y | Y | N | Y | Y |
| 4 Pastor | Y | Y | Y | Y | N | N |
| 5 Hayworth | Y | Y | Y | N | Y | Y |
| 6 Flake | Y | N | Y | N | Y | Y |
| 7 Grijalva | Y | Y | Y | Y | N | N |
| 8 Kolbe | Y | Y | Y | N | Y | Y |
| **ARKANSAS** | | | | | | |
| 1 Berry | Y | Y | Y | N | N | N |
| 2 Snyder | Y | Y | Y | Y | N | N |
| 3 Boozman | Y | Y | Y | N | Y | Y |
| 4 Ross | Y | Y | Y | N | N | N |
| **CALIFORNIA** | | | | | | |
| 1 Thompson | Y | Y | Y | Y | N | N |
| 2 Herger | Y | Y | Y | N | Y | Y |
| 3 Lungren | Y | Y | Y | N | Y | Y |
| 4 Doolittle | Y | Y | Y | N | Y | Y |
| 5 Matsui, D. | Y | Y | Y | Y | N | N |
| 6 Woolsey | N | Y | Y | Y | N | N |
| 7 Miller, George | Y | Y | Y | Y | N | N |
| 8 Pelosi | Y | Y | Y | Y | N | N |
| 9 Lee | N | Y | Y | N | N | N |
| 10 Tauscher | Y | Y | Y | Y | N | N |
| 11 Pombo | Y | Y | Y | N | Y | Y |
| 12 Lantos | Y | Y | Y | N | N | N |
| 13 Stark | N | Y | Y | Y | N | N |
| 14 Eshoo | Y | Y | Y | Y | N | N |
| 15 Honda | Y | Y | Y | Y | N | N |
| 16 Lofgren | Y | Y | Y | Y | N | N |
| 17 Farr | Y | Y | Y | Y | N | N |
| 18 Cardoza | Y | Y | Y | N | N | N |
| 19 Radanovich | Y | Y | Y | N | Y | Y |
| 20 Costa | Y | Y | Y | N | Y | N |
| 21 Nunes | Y | Y | Y | N | Y | Y |
| 22 Thomas | Y | Y | Y | ? | ? | ? |
| 23 Capps | Y | Y | Y | Y | N | N |
| 24 Gallegly | Y | Y | Y | N | Y | Y |
| 25 McKeon | Y | Y | Y | N | Y | Y |
| 26 Dreier | Y | Y | Y | N | Y | Y |
| 27 Sherman | Y | Y | Y | N | N | N |
| 28 Berman | Y | Y | Y | N | Y | N |
| 29 Schiff | Y | Y | Y | Y | N | N |
| 30 Waxman | Y | Y | Y | Y | N | N |
| 31 Becerra | Y | Y | Y | + | N | N |
| 32 Solis | Y | Y | Y | Y | N | N |
| 33 Watson | N | Y | Y | Y | N | N |
| 34 Roybal-Allard | Y | Y | Y | Y | N | N |
| 35 Waters | N | Y | Y | N | N | N |
| 36 Harman | Y | Y | Y | N | N | N |
| 37 Millender-McD. | Y | Y | Y | Y | N | N |
| 38 Napolitano | Y | Y | Y | Y | N | N |
| 39 Sánchez, Linda | Y | Y | Y | Y | N | N |
| 40 Royce | Y | Y | Y | N | Y | Y |
| 41 Lewis | Y | Y | Y | N | Y | Y |
| 42 Miller, Gary | Y | Y | Y | N | Y | Y |
| 43 Baca | Y | Y | Y | N | N | N |
| 44 Calvert | Y | Y | Y | N | Y | Y |
| 45 Bono | Y | Y | Y | N | Y | Y |
| 46 Rohrabacher | Y | Y | Y | N | Y | Y |
| 47 Sanchez, Loretta | Y | Y | Y | N | N | N |
| 48 Cox | Y | Y | Y | N | Y | ? |
| 49 Issa | Y | Y | Y | N | Y | Y |

| | 290 | 291 | 292 | 293 | 294 | 295 |
|---|---|---|---|---|---|---|
| 50 Cunningham | Y | Y | Y | N | Y | Y |
| 51 Filner | Y | Y | Y | N | N | N |
| 52 Hunter | Y | Y | Y | N | Y | Y |
| 53 Davis | Y | Y | Y | Y | N | N |
| **COLORADO** | | | | | | |
| 1 DeGette | Y | Y | Y | N | N | N |
| 2 Udall | Y | Y | Y | N | N | N |
| 3 Salazar | Y | Y | Y | N | N | N |
| 4 Musgrave | Y | Y | Y | N | Y | Y |
| 5 Hefley | Y | Y | Y | N | Y | Y |
| 6 Tancredo | Y | Y | Y | N | Y | Y |
| 7 Beauprez | Y | Y | Y | N | Y | Y |
| **CONNECTICUT** | | | | | | |
| 1 Larson | Y | Y | Y | Y | N | N |
| 2 Simmons | Y | Y | Y | Y | N | N |
| 3 DeLauro | Y | Y | Y | Y | N | N |
| 4 Shays | Y | Y | Y | N | Y | N |
| 5 Johnson | Y | Y | Y | N | Y | N |
| **DELAWARE** | | | | | | |
| AL Castle | Y | Y | Y | N | Y | Y |
| **FLORIDA** | | | | | | |
| 1 Miller | Y | Y | Y | N | Y | Y |
| 2 Boyd | Y | Y | Y | ? | ? | ? |
| 3 Brown | Y | Y | Y | N | N | N |
| 4 Crenshaw | Y | Y | Y | N | Y | Y |
| 5 Brown-Waite | Y | Y | Y | ? | Y | Y |
| 6 Stearns | Y | Y | Y | N | Y | Y |
| 7 Mica | Y | Y | Y | N | Y | Y |
| 8 Keller | Y | Y | Y | N | Y | Y |
| 9 Bilirakis | Y | Y | Y | N | Y | Y |
| 10 Young | ? | ? | ? | N | Y | Y |
| 11 Davis | Y | Y | Y | N | N | N |
| 12 Putnam | Y | Y | Y | N | Y | Y |
| 13 Harris | Y | Y | Y | N | Y | Y |
| 14 Mack | Y | Y | Y | N | Y | Y |
| 15 Weldon | Y | Y | Y | N | Y | Y |
| 16 Foley | Y | Y | Y | N | Y | Y |
| 17 Meek | Y | Y | Y | N | N | N |
| 18 Ros-Lehtinen | Y | Y | Y | N | Y | Y |
| 19 Wexler | Y | Y | Y | N | N | N |
| 20 Wasserman-Schultz | Y | Y | Y | Y | N | N |
| 21 Diaz-Balart, L. | Y | Y | Y | N | Y | Y |
| 22 Shaw | Y | Y | Y | N | Y | Y |
| 23 Hastings | Y | Y | Y | N | N | N |
| 24 Feeney | Y | Y | Y | N | Y | Y |
| 25 Diaz-Balart, M. | Y | Y | Y | N | Y | Y |
| **GEORGIA** | | | | | | |
| 1 Kingston | Y | Y | Y | N | Y | Y |
| 2 Bishop | Y | Y | Y | N | N | N |
| 3 Marshall | Y | Y | Y | N | N | N |
| 4 McKinney | N | Y | Y | N | N | N |
| 5 Lewis | ? | ? | ? | ? | ? | ? |
| 6 Price | Y | Y | Y | N | Y | Y |
| 7 Linder | Y | Y | Y | N | Y | Y |
| 8 Westmoreland | Y | Y | Y | N | Y | Y |
| 9 Norwood | Y | Y | Y | N | Y | Y |
| 10 Deal | Y | ? | ? | N | Y | Y |
| 11 Gingrey | Y | Y | Y | N | Y | Y |
| 12 Barrow | Y | Y | Y | N | N | N |
| 13 Scott | Y | Y | Y | N | N | N |
| **HAWAII** | | | | | | |
| 1 Abercrombie | Y | Y | Y | N | N | N |
| 2 Case | Y | Y | Y | N | N | N |
| **IDAHO** | | | | | | |
| 1 Otter | Y | Y | Y | N | Y | Y |
| 2 Simpson | Y | Y | Y | N | Y | Y |
| **ILLINOIS** | | | | | | |
| 1 Rush | Y | Y | Y | Y | N | N |
| 2 Jackson | N | Y | Y | Y | N | N |
| 3 Lipinski | Y | Y | Y | N | N | N |
| 4 Gutierrez | Y | Y | Y | Y | N | N |
| 5 Emanuel | Y | Y | Y | Y | N | N |
| 6 Hyde | Y | Y | Y | N | Y | Y |
| 7 Davis | Y | Y | Y | N | N | N |
| 8 Bean | Y | Y | Y | N | N | N |
| 9 Schakowsky | Y | Y | Y | N | N | N |
| 10 Kirk | Y | Y | Y | N | N | N |
| 11 Weller | Y | Y | Y | N | N | N |
| 12 Costello | Y | Y | Y | N | N | N |

| | 290 | 291 | 292 | 293 | 294 | 295 |
|---|---|---|---|---|---|---|
| 13 **Biggert** | Y | Y | Y | N | Y | Y |
| 14 **Hastert** | | | | | | |
| 15 **Johnson** | Y | Y | Y | N | Y | Y |
| 16 **Manzullo** | Y | Y | Y | N | Y | Y |
| 17 Evans | Y | Y | Y | Y | N | N |
| 18 **LaHood** | Y | Y | Y | N | Y | Y |
| 19 **Shimkus** | Y | Y | Y | N | Y | Y |
| **INDIANA** | | | | | | |
| 1 Visclosky | Y | Y | Y | Y | N | N |
| 2 **Chocola** | Y | Y | Y | N | Y | Y |
| 3 **Souder** | Y | Y | Y | N | Y | Y |
| 4 **Buyer** | Y | Y | Y | N | Y | Y |
| 5 **Burton** | Y | Y | Y | N | Y | Y |
| 6 **Pence** | + | Y | Y | N | Y | Y |
| 7 Carson | Y | Y | Y | Y | N | N |
| 8 **Hostettler** | Y | Y | Y | N | Y | Y |
| 9 **Sodrel** | Y | Y | Y | N | Y | Y |
| **IOWA** | | | | | | |
| 1 **Nussle** | Y | Y | Y | N | Y | Y |
| 2 **Leach** | Y | Y | Y | Y | Y | Y |
| 3 Boswell | Y | Y | Y | N | N | N |
| 4 **Latham** | Y | Y | Y | N | Y | Y |
| 5 **King** | Y | Y | Y | N | Y | Y |
| **KANSAS** | | | | | | |
| 1 **Moran** | Y | Y | Y | N | Y | Y |
| 2 **Ryun** | Y | Y | Y | N | Y | Y |
| 3 Moore | Y | Y | Y | Y | N | N |
| 4 **Tiahrt** | Y | Y | Y | N | Y | Y |
| **KENTUCKY** | | | | | | |
| 1 **Whitfield** | Y | Y | Y | N | Y | Y |
| 2 **Lewis** | Y | Y | Y | N | Y | Y |
| 3 **Northup** | Y | Y | Y | N | Y | Y |
| 4 **Davis** | Y | Y | Y | N | Y | Y |
| 5 **Rogers** | Y | Y | Y | N | Y | Y |
| 6 Chandler | Y | Y | Y | N | N | N |
| **LOUISIANA** | | | | | | |
| 1 **Jindal** | Y | Y | Y | N | Y | Y |
| 2 Jefferson | Y | Y | Y | Y | N | N |
| 3 Melancon | Y | Y | Y | N | N | N |
| 4 **McCrery** | Y | Y | Y | N | Y | Y |
| 5 **Alexander** | Y | Y | Y | N | Y | Y |
| 6 **Baker** | Y | Y | Y | N | Y | Y |
| 7 **Boustany** | Y | Y | Y | N | Y | Y |
| **MAINE** | | | | | | |
| 1 Allen | Y | Y | Y | Y | N | N |
| 2 Michaud | Y | Y | Y | N | N | N |
| **MARYLAND** | | | | | | |
| 1 **Gilchrest** | Y | Y | Y | Y | Y | Y |
| 2 Ruppersberger | Y | Y | Y | Y | N | N |
| 3 Cardin | Y | Y | Y | Y | N | N |
| 4 Wynn | Y | Y | Y | N | N | N |
| 5 Hoyer | Y | Y | Y | N | N | N |
| 6 **Bartlett** | Y | Y | Y | N | Y | Y |
| 7 Cummings | Y | Y | Y | Y | N | N |
| 8 Van Hollen | Y | Y | Y | Y | N | N |
| **MASSACHUSETTS** | | | | | | |
| 1 Olver | Y | Y | Y | Y | N | N |
| 2 Neal | Y | Y | Y | Y | N | N |
| 3 McGovern | Y | Y | Y | Y | N | N |
| 4 Frank | Y | Y | Y | ? | N | Y |
| 5 Meehan | Y | Y | Y | Y | N | N |
| 6 Tierney | Y | Y | Y | Y | N | N |
| 7 Markey | Y | Y | Y | N | N | N |
| 8 Capuano | Y | Y | Y | Y | N | N |
| 9 Lynch | Y | Y | Y | N | N | N |
| 10 Delahunt | Y | Y | Y | N | N | N |
| **MICHIGAN** | | | | | | |
| 1 Stupak | Y | Y | Y | N | N | N |
| 2 **Hoekstra** | Y | Y | Y | N | Y | Y |
| 3 **Ehlers** | Y | Y | Y | N | Y | Y |
| 4 **Camp** | Y | Y | Y | N | Y | Y |
| 5 Kildee | Y | Y | Y | N | N | N |
| 6 **Upton** | Y | Y | Y | N | Y | Y |
| 7 **Schwarz** | Y | Y | Y | N | Y | Y |
| 8 **Rogers** | Y | Y | Y | N | Y | Y |
| 9 **Knollenberg** | Y | Y | Y | N | Y | Y |
| 10 **Miller** | Y | Y | Y | N | Y | Y |
| 11 **McCotter** | Y | Y | Y | N | Y | Y |
| 12 Levin | Y | Y | Y | N | N | N |
| 13 Kilpatrick | Y | Y | Y | N | N | N |
| 14 Conyers | N | Y | Y | Y | N | N |
| 15 Dingell | Y | Y | Y | Y | N | N |

| | 290 | 291 | 292 | 293 | 294 | 295 |
|---|---|---|---|---|---|---|
| **MINNESOTA** | | | | | | |
| 1 **Gutknecht** | Y | Y | Y | N | Y | Y |
| 2 **Kline** | Y | Y | Y | N | Y | Y |
| 3 **Ramstad** | Y | Y | Y | N | Y | Y |
| 4 McCollum | Y | Y | Y | Y | N | N |
| 5 Sabo | Y | Y | Y | Y | Y | Y |
| 6 **Kennedy** | Y | Y | Y | N | Y | Y |
| 7 Peterson | Y | Y | Y | N | N | N |
| 8 Oberstar | N | Y | Y | Y | N | N |
| **MISSISSIPPI** | | | | | | |
| 1 **Wicker** | Y | Y | Y | N | Y | Y |
| 2 Thompson | Y | Y | Y | Y | N | N |
| 3 **Pickering** | Y | Y | Y | ? | Y | Y |
| 4 Taylor | Y | Y | Y | N | N | N |
| **MISSOURI** | | | | | | |
| 1 Clay | Y | Y | Y | Y | N | N |
| 2 **Akin** | Y | Y | Y | N | Y | Y |
| 3 Carnahan | Y | Y | Y | Y | N | N |
| 4 Skelton | Y | Y | Y | N | N | N |
| 5 Cleaver | Y | Y | Y | Y | N | N |
| 6 **Graves** | Y | Y | Y | N | Y | Y |
| 7 **Blunt** | Y | Y | Y | N | Y | Y |
| 8 **Emerson** | Y | Y | Y | N | Y | Y |
| 9 **Hulshof** | Y | Y | Y | N | Y | Y |
| **MONTANA** | | | | | | |
| AL **Rehberg** | Y | Y | Y | N | Y | Y |
| **NEBRASKA** | | | | | | |
| 1 **Fortenberry** | Y | Y | Y | N | Y | Y |
| 2 **Terry** | Y | Y | Y | N | Y | Y |
| 3 **Osborne** | Y | Y | Y | N | Y | Y |
| **NEVADA** | | | | | | |
| 1 Berkley | Y | Y | Y | N | N | N |
| 2 **Gibbons** | Y | Y | Y | N | Y | Y |
| 3 **Porter** | Y | Y | Y | N | Y | Y |
| **NEW HAMPSHIRE** | | | | | | |
| 1 **Bradley** | Y | Y | Y | N | Y | Y |
| 2 **Bass** | Y | Y | Y | N | Y | Y |
| **NEW JERSEY** | | | | | | |
| 1 Andrews | Y | Y | Y | Y | N | N |
| 2 **LoBiondo** | Y | Y | Y | N | Y | Y |
| 3 **Saxton** | Y | Y | Y | N | Y | Y |
| 4 **Smith** | Y | Y | Y | N | Y | Y |
| 5 **Garrett** | Y | Y | Y | N | Y | Y |
| 6 Pallone | Y | Y | Y | Y | N | N |
| 7 **Ferguson** | Y | Y | Y | N | Y | Y |
| 8 Pascrell | Y | Y | Y | N | N | N |
| 9 Rothman | Y | Y | Y | N | N | N |
| 10 Payne | N | Y | Y | Y | N | ? |
| 11 **Frelinghuysen** | Y | Y | Y | N | Y | Y |
| 12 Holt | Y | Y | Y | Y | N | N |
| 13 Menendez | Y | Y | Y | N | N | N |
| **NEW MEXICO** | | | | | | |
| 1 **Wilson** | Y | Y | Y | N | Y | Y |
| 2 **Pearce** | Y | Y | Y | N | Y | Y |
| 3 Udall | Y | Y | Y | Y | N | N |
| **NEW YORK** | | | | | | |
| 1 Bishop | Y | Y | Y | N | N | N |
| 2 Israel | Y | Y | Y | Y | N | N |
| 3 **King** | Y | Y | Y | N | Y | Y |
| 4 McCarthy | Y | Y | Y | N | N | N |
| 5 Ackerman | Y | Y | Y | Y | N | N |
| 6 Meeks | Y | Y | Y | Y | N | N |
| 7 Crowley | Y | Y | Y | N | N | N |
| 8 Nadler | Y | Y | Y | Y | N | N |
| 9 Weiner | Y | Y | Y | Y | N | ? |
| 10 Towns | Y | Y | Y | Y | N | N |
| 11 Owens | N | Y | Y | Y | N | N |
| 12 Velázquez | Y | Y | Y | Y | N | N |
| 13 **Fossella** | Y | Y | Y | N | Y | Y |
| 14 Maloney | Y | Y | Y | Y | N | N |
| 15 Rangel | N | Y | Y | ? | ? | ? |
| 16 Serrano | Y | Y | Y | N | N | N |
| 17 Engel | Y | Y | Y | Y | N | N |
| 18 Lowey | Y | Y | Y | Y | N | N |
| 19 **Kelly** | Y | Y | Y | N | Y | Y |
| 20 **Sweeney** | Y | Y | Y | N | Y | Y |
| 21 McNulty | Y | Y | Y | Y | N | N |
| 22 Hinchey | Y | Y | Y | Y | N | N |
| 23 **McHugh** | Y | Y | Y | N | Y | Y |
| 24 **Boehlert** | Y | Y | Y | N | Y | Y |
| 25 **Walsh** | Y | Y | Y | N | Y | Y |
| 26 **Reynolds** | Y | Y | Y | N | Y | Y |
| 27 Higgins | Y | Y | Y | N | N | N |
| 28 Slaughter | Y | Y | Y | Y | N | N |
| 29 **Kuhl** | Y | Y | Y | N | Y | Y |

| | 290 | 291 | 292 | 293 | 294 | 295 |
|---|---|---|---|---|---|---|
| **NORTH CAROLINA** | | | | | | |
| 1 Butterfield | Y | Y | Y | Y | N | N |
| 2 Etheridge | Y | Y | Y | Y | N | N |
| 3 **Jones** | Y | Y | Y | N | Y | Y |
| 4 Price | Y | Y | Y | Y | N | N |
| 5 **Foxx** | Y | Y | Y | N | Y | Y |
| 6 **Coble** | Y | Y | Y | N | Y | Y |
| 7 McIntyre | Y | Y | Y | N | N | N |
| 8 **Hayes** | Y | Y | Y | N | Y | Y |
| 9 **Myrick** | Y | Y | Y | N | Y | Y |
| 10 **McHenry** | Y | Y | Y | N | Y | Y |
| 11 **Taylor** | Y | Y | Y | N | Y | Y |
| 12 Watt | Y | Y | Y | Y | N | N |
| 13 Miller | Y | Y | Y | Y | N | N |
| **NORTH DAKOTA** | | | | | | |
| AL Pomeroy | Y | Y | Y | ? | ? | ? |
| **OHIO** | | | | | | |
| 1 **Chabot** | Y | Y | Y | N | Y | Y |
| 2 Vacant | | | | | | |
| 3 **Turner** | Y | Y | Y | N | Y | Y |
| 4 **Oxley** | Y | Y | Y | ? | ? | ? |
| 5 **Gillmor** | Y | Y | Y | N | Y | Y |
| 6 Strickland | Y | Y | Y | N | N | N |
| 7 **Hobson** | Y | Y | Y | N | Y | Y |
| 8 **Boehner** | Y | Y | Y | N | Y | Y |
| 9 Kaptur | Y | Y | Y | Y | N | N |
| 10 Kucinich | N | Y | Y | N | N | N |
| 11 Jones | Y | Y | Y | Y | N | N |
| 12 **Tiberi** | Y | Y | Y | N | Y | Y |
| 13 Brown | Y | Y | Y | N | N | N |
| 14 **LaTourette** | Y | Y | Y | N | Y | Y |
| 15 **Pryce** | Y | Y | Y | N | Y | Y |
| 16 **Regula** | Y | Y | Y | N | Y | Y |
| 17 Ryan | Y | Y | Y | Y | N | N |
| 18 **Ney** | Y | Y | Y | ? | ? | ? |
| **OKLAHOMA** | | | | | | |
| 1 **Sullivan** | Y | Y | Y | N | Y | Y |
| 2 Boren | Y | Y | Y | N | N | N |
| 3 **Lucas** | Y | Y | Y | N | Y | Y |
| 4 **Cole** | Y | Y | Y | N | Y | Y |
| 5 **Istook** | Y | Y | Y | N | Y | Y |
| **OREGON** | | | | | | |
| 1 Wu | Y | Y | Y | Y | N | N |
| 2 **Walden** | Y | Y | Y | N | Y | Y |
| 3 Blumenauer | Y | Y | Y | Y | N | N |
| 4 DeFazio | Y | Y | Y | Y | N | N |
| 5 Hooley | Y | Y | Y | Y | N | N |
| **PENNSYLVANIA** | | | | | | |
| 1 Brady | Y | Y | Y | Y | N | N |
| 2 Fattah | Y | Y | Y | Y | N | N |
| 3 **English** | Y | Y | Y | N | Y | Y |
| 4 **Hart** | Y | Y | Y | N | Y | Y |
| 5 **Peterson** | Y | Y | Y | N | Y | Y |
| 6 **Gerlach** | Y | Y | Y | N | Y | Y |
| 7 **Weldon** | Y | Y | Y | N | Y | Y |
| 8 **Fitzpatrick** | Y | Y | Y | N | Y | Y |
| 9 **Shuster** | Y | Y | Y | N | Y | Y |
| 10 **Sherwood** | Y | Y | Y | N | Y | Y |
| 11 Kanjorski | Y | Y | Y | N | N | N |
| 12 Murtha | Y | Y | Y | ? | N | ? |
| 13 Schwartz | Y | Y | Y | N | N | N |
| 14 Doyle | Y | Y | Y | Y | N | N |
| 15 **Dent** | Y | Y | Y | N | Y | Y |
| 16 **Pitts** | Y | Y | Y | N | Y | Y |
| 17 Holden | Y | Y | Y | N | N | N |
| 18 **Murphy** | + | + | ? | N | Y | Y |
| 19 **Platts** | Y | Y | Y | N | Y | Y |
| **RHODE ISLAND** | | | | | | |
| 1 Kennedy | Y | Y | Y | Y | N | N |
| 2 Langevin | Y | Y | Y | N | N | N |
| **SOUTH CAROLINA** | | | | | | |
| 1 **Brown** | Y | Y | Y | N | Y | Y |
| 2 **Wilson** | Y | Y | Y | N | Y | Y |
| 3 **Barrett** | Y | Y | Y | N | Y | Y |
| 4 **Inglis** | Y | Y | Y | N | Y | Y |
| 5 Spratt | Y | Y | Y | Y | N | N |
| 6 Clyburn | Y | Y | Y | Y | N | N |
| **SOUTH DAKOTA** | | | | | | |
| AL Herseth | ? | ? | ? | ? | ? | ? |
| **TENNESSEE** | | | | | | |
| 1 **Jenkins** | Y | Y | Y | N | Y | Y |
| 2 **Duncan** | N | Y | Y | N | Y | Y |

| | 290 | 291 | 292 | 293 | 294 | 295 |
|---|---|---|---|---|---|---|
| 3 **Wamp** | Y | Y | Y | N | Y | Y |
| 4 Davis | Y | Y | Y | N | N | N |
| 5 Cooper | Y | Y | Y | Y | N | N |
| 6 Gordon | Y | Y | Y | N | N | N |
| 7 **Blackburn** | Y | Y | Y | N | Y | Y |
| 8 Tanner | Y | Y | Y | Y | N | N |
| 9 Ford | Y | Y | Y | N | N | N |
| **TEXAS** | | | | | | |
| 1 **Gohmert** | Y | Y | Y | – | Y | Y |
| 2 **Poe** | Y | Y | Y | N | Y | Y |
| 3 **Johnson, S.** | Y | Y | Y | N | Y | Y |
| 4 **Hall** | Y | Y | Y | N | Y | Y |
| 5 **Hensarling** | Y | Y | Y | N | Y | Y |
| 6 **Barton** | Y | Y | Y | ? | ? | ? |
| 7 **Culberson** | Y | Y | Y | N | Y | Y |
| 8 **Brady** | Y | Y | Y | N | Y | Y |
| 9 Green, A. | Y | Y | Y | Y | N | N |
| 10 **McCaul** | Y | Y | Y | ? | ? | ? |
| 11 **Conaway** | + | ? | + | ? | ? | ? |
| 12 **Granger** | Y | Y | Y | N | Y | Y |
| 13 **Thornberry** | Y | Y | Y | N | Y | Y |
| 14 **Paul** | N | N | Y | Y | Y | Y |
| 15 Hinojosa | Y | Y | Y | ? | ? | ? |
| 16 Reyes | Y | Y | Y | N | N | N |
| 17 Edwards | Y | Y | Y | N | N | N |
| 18 Jackson-Lee | Y | Y | Y | ? | ? | ? |
| 19 **Neugebauer** | Y | Y | Y | N | Y | Y |
| 20 Gonzalez | Y | Y | Y | Y | N | N |
| 21 **Smith** | Y | Y | Y | ? | ? | ? |
| 22 **DeLay** | Y | Y | Y | ? | Y | Y |
| 23 **Bonilla** | Y | Y | Y | N | Y | Y |
| 24 **Marchant** | Y | Y | Y | ? | Y | Y |
| 25 Doggett | Y | Y | Y | ? | ? | ? |
| 26 **Burgess** | Y | Y | Y | N | Y | Y |
| 27 Ortiz | Y | Y | Y | N | N | N |
| 28 Cuellar | Y | Y | Y | N | N | N |
| 29 Green, G. | Y | Y | Y | N | N | N |
| 30 Johnson, E. | Y | Y | Y | Y | N | N |
| 31 **Carter** | + | + | + | ? | ? | ? |
| 32 **Sessions** | ? | ? | ? | N | Y | Y |
| **UTAH** | | | | | | |
| 1 **Bishop** | Y | Y | Y | N | Y | Y |
| 2 Matheson | Y | Y | Y | Y | N | N |
| 3 **Cannon** | Y | Y | Y | N | Y | Y |
| **VERMONT** | | | | | | |
| AL *Sanders* | Y | Y | Y | Y | N | N |
| **VIRGINIA** | | | | | | |
| 1 **Davis, J.** | Y | Y | Y | N | Y | Y |
| 2 **Drake** | Y | Y | Y | N | Y | Y |
| 3 Scott | Y | Y | Y | Y | N | N |
| 4 **Forbes** | Y | Y | Y | N | Y | Y |
| 5 **Goode** | Y | Y | Y | N | Y | Y |
| 6 **Goodlatte** | Y | Y | Y | N | Y | Y |
| 7 **Cantor** | Y | Y | Y | N | Y | Y |
| 8 Moran | Y | Y | Y | Y | N | N |
| 9 Boucher | Y | Y | Y | N | N | N |
| 10 **Wolf** | Y | Y | Y | N | Y | Y |
| 11 **Davis, T.** | Y | Y | Y | N | Y | Y |
| **WASHINGTON** | | | | | | |
| 1 Inslee | Y | Y | Y | Y | N | N |
| 2 Larsen | Y | Y | Y | Y | N | N |
| 3 Baird | Y | Y | Y | Y | N | N |
| 4 **Hastings** | Y | Y | Y | N | Y | Y |
| 5 **McMorris** | Y | Y | Y | N | Y | Y |
| 6 Dicks | Y | Y | Y | Y | N | N |
| 7 McDermott | N | Y | Y | Y | N | N |
| 8 **Reichert** | Y | Y | Y | N | Y | Y |
| 9 Smith | Y | Y | Y | N | N | N |
| **WEST VIRGINIA** | | | | | | |
| 1 Mollohan | Y | Y | Y | N | N | N |
| 2 **Capito** | Y | Y | Y | N | Y | Y |
| 3 Rahall | Y | Y | Y | N | N | N |
| **WISCONSIN** | | | | | | |
| 1 **Ryan** | Y | Y | Y | N | Y | Y |
| 2 Baldwin | Y | Y | Y | Y | N | N |
| 3 Kind | Y | Y | Y | Y | N | N |
| 4 Moore | Y | Y | Y | N | N | N |
| 5 **Sensenbrenner** | Y | Y | Y | N | Y | Y |
| 6 **Petri** | Y | Y | Y | N | Y | Y |
| 7 Obey | Y | Y | Y | Y | N | N |
| 8 **Green** | Y | Y | Y | N | Y | Y |
| **WYOMING** | | | | | | |
| AL **Cubin** | Y | Y | Y | N | Y | Y |

# IN THE HOUSE | By Vote Number

**296.** H J Res 10. Flag Desecration Constitutional Amendment/
**Passage.** Passage of the joint resolution to propose a constitutional amendment to state that Congress shall have the power to prohibit the physical desecration of the flag of the United States. Passed 286-130: R 209-12; D 77-117 (ND 50-98, SD 27-19); I 0-1. A two-thirds majority vote of those present and voting (278 in this case) is required to pass a joint resolution proposing a constitutional amendment. June 22, 2005.

**297.** HR 2985. Fiscal 2006 Legislative Branch Appropriations/
**Previous Question.** L. Diaz-Balart, R-Fla., motion to order the previous question (thus ending debate and the possibility of amendment) on adoption of the rule (H Res 334) to provide for House floor consideration of the legislative branch spending bill. Motion agreed to 219-196: R 219-1; D 0-194 (ND 0-148, SD 0-46); I 0-1. June 22, 2005.

**298.** HR 2985. Fiscal 2006 Legislative Branch Appropriations/Rule.
Adoption of the rule (H Res 334) to provide for House floor consideration of the bill that would appropriate $2.9 billion in fiscal 2006 for legislative branch operations, excluding funds for Senate operations. Adopted 220-192: R 220-0; D 0-191 (ND 0-147, SD 0-44); I 0-1. June 22, 2005.

**299.** HR 2985. Fiscal 2006 Legislative Branch Appropriations/
**Continuity of Congress.** Baird, D-Wash., amendment that would strike language in the bill that would require states to hold special elections within 49 days to fill open House seats if more than 100 vacancies occur due to a terrorist attack or other catastrophe. Rejected 143-268: R 1-218; D 141-50 (ND 113-33, SD 28-17); I 1-0. June 22, 2005.

**300.** HR 2985. Fiscal 2006 Legislative Branch Appropriations/Capitol
**Police Horses.** J. Davis, R-Va., amendment that would strike provisions in the bill that would prohibit the Capitol Police from operating a mounted horse unit and require the transfer of the horses and equipment to the U.S. Park Police. Rejected 185-226: R 63-155; D 121-71 (ND 93-54, SD 28-17); I 1-0. June 22, 2005.

**301.** HR 2985. Fiscal 2006 Legislative Branch Appropriations/
**Across-the-Board Cut.** Hefley, R-Colo., amendment that would reduce all discretionary spending in the bill by 1 percent. Rejected 114-294: R 91-125; D 23-168 (ND 14-132, SD 9-36); I 0-1. June 22, 2005.

| | 296 | 297 | 298 | 299 | 300 | 301 |
|---|---|---|---|---|---|---|
| **ALABAMA** | | | | | | |
| 1 Bonner | ? | ? | ? | ? | ? | ? |
| 2 Everett | Y | Y | Y | N | N | Y |
| 3 Rogers | Y | Y | Y | N | N | N |
| 4 Aderholt | Y | Y | Y | N | N | N |
| 5 Cramer | Y | N | N | N | N | N |
| 6 Bachus | Y | Y | Y | N | N | ? |
| 7 Davis | N | N | ? | Y | N | N |
| **ALASKA** | | | | | | |
| AL Young | Y | Y | Y | N | Y | N |
| **ARIZONA** | | | | | | |
| 1 Renzi | Y | Y | Y | N | N | N |
| 2 Franks | Y | Y | Y | N | Y | Y |
| 3 Shadegg | N | Y | N | N | Y | Y |
| 4 Pastor | N | N | N | Y | N | N |
| 5 Hayworth | Y | Y | Y | N | N | Y |
| 6 Flake | N | Y | Y | N | N | Y |
| 7 Grijalva | N | N | N | Y | N | Y |
| 8 Kolbe | N | Y | Y | N | N | N |
| **ARKANSAS** | | | | | | |
| 1 Berry | Y | N | N | Y | N | Y |
| 2 Snyder | N | N | N | N | N | Y |
| 3 Boozman | Y | Y | Y | N | N | Y |
| 4 Ross | Y | N | N | Y | Y | Y |
| **CALIFORNIA** | | | | | | |
| 1 Thompson | N | N | N | Y | Y | N |
| 2 Herger | Y | Y | Y | N | N | Y |
| 3 Lungren | Y | Y | Y | N | N | N |
| 4 Doolittle | Y | Y | Y | N | N | N |
| 5 Matsui, D. | N | N | N | Y | N | N |
| 6 Woolsey | N | N | N | Y | N | N |
| 7 Miller, George | N | N | N | Y | N | N |
| 8 Pelosi | N | N | N | Y | N | N |
| 9 Lee | N | N | N | Y | N | N |
| 10 Tauscher | N | N | N | Y | N | N |
| 11 Pombo | Y | Y | Y | N | N | N |
| 12 Lantos | Y | N | N | Y | N | N |
| 13 Stark | N | N | N | N | N | N |
| 14 Eshoo | N | N | N | Y | N | N |
| 15 Honda | N | N | N | Y | N | N |
| 16 Lofgren | N | N | N | Y | N | N |
| 17 Farr | N | N | N | Y | N | ? |
| 18 Cardoza | Y | N | N | N | N | Y |
| 19 Radanovich | Y | Y | Y | N | N | N |
| 20 Costa | Y | N | N | N | N | N |
| 21 Nunes | Y | Y | Y | N | N | N |
| 22 Thomas | ? | ? | ? | ? | ? | ? |
| 23 Capps | Y | N | N | Y | N | N |
| 24 Gallegly | Y | Y | Y | N | N | N |
| 25 McKeon | Y | Y | Y | N | N | N |
| 26 Dreier | N | Y | Y | N | N | N |
| 27 Sherman | Y | N | N | Y | N | N |
| 28 Berman | N | N | N | Y | N | N |
| 29 Schiff | N | N | N | Y | N | N |
| 30 Waxman | N | N | N | Y | Y | N |
| 31 Becerra | N | N | N | Y | N | N |
| 32 Solis | N | N | N | Y | N | N |
| 33 Watson | N | N | N | ? | Y | N |
| 34 Roybal-Allard | N | N | N | Y | N | N |
| 35 Waters | N | N | N | Y | Y | N |
| 36 Harman | Y | N | N | Y | N | N |
| 37 Millender-McD. | N | N | N | Y | N | N |
| 38 Napolitano | N | N | N | Y | N | N |
| 39 Sánchez, Linda | N | N | N | Y | Y | N |
| 40 Royce | Y | Y | Y | N | N | Y |
| 41 Lewis | Y | Y | Y | N | N | N |
| 42 Miller, Gary | Y | Y | Y | N | N | N |
| 43 Baca | N | N | N | N | N | N |
| 44 Calvert | Y | Y | Y | N | N | N |
| 45 Bono | Y | Y | Y | N | N | N |
| 46 Rohrabacher | Y | Y | Y | N | N | Y |
| 47 Sanchez, Loretta | Y | N | N | Y | N | Y |
| 48 Cox | Y | Y | Y | N | N | Y |
| 49 Issa | Y | Y | Y | N | N | Y |
| 50 Cunningham | Y | Y | Y | N | Y | N |
| 51 Filner | N | N | N | Y | N | N |
| 52 Hunter | Y | Y | Y | N | Y | N |
| 53 Davis | N | N | N | Y | N | N |
| **COLORADO** | | | | | | |
| 1 DeGette | N | N | N | Y | Y | Y |
| 2 Udall | N | N | N | Y | Y | Y |
| 3 Salazar | Y | N | N | Y | Y | N |
| 4 Musgrave | Y | Y | Y | N | N | Y |
| 5 Hefley | Y | Y | Y | N | Y | Y |
| 6 Tancredo | Y | Y | Y | N | Y | Y |
| 7 Beauprez | Y | Y | Y | N | Y | Y |
| **CONNECTICUT** | | | | | | |
| 1 Larson | Y | N | N | Y | Y | N |
| 2 Simmons | Y | Y | Y | N | Y | N |
| 3 DeLauro | N | N | N | Y | Y | N |
| 4 Shays | N | Y | Y | N | Y | N |
| 5 Johnson | Y | Y | Y | N | N | N |
| **DELAWARE** | | | | | | |
| AL Castle | Y | Y | Y | N | N | N |
| **FLORIDA** | | | | | | |
| 1 Miller | Y | Y | Y | N | Y | Y |
| 2 Boyd | ? | ? | ? | ? | ? | ? |
| 3 Brown | Y | N | N | Y | Y | N |
| 4 Crenshaw | Y | Y | Y | N | N | N |
| 5 Brown-Waite | Y | Y | Y | N | Y | Y |
| 6 Stearns | Y | Y | Y | N | Y | Y |
| 7 Mica | Y | Y | Y | N | N | N |
| 8 Keller | Y | Y | Y | N | N | N |
| 9 Bilirakis | Y | Y | Y | N | N | N |
| 10 Young | Y | Y | Y | N | N | N |
| 11 Davis | N | N | N | N | N | N |
| 12 Putnam | Y | Y | Y | N | N | N |
| 13 Harris | Y | Y | Y | N | Y | Y |
| 14 Mack | Y | Y | Y | N | N | Y |
| 15 Weldon | Y | Y | Y | N | N | N |
| 16 Foley | Y | Y | Y | N | N | N |
| 17 Meek | N | N | N | Y | N | N |
| 18 Ros-Lehtinen | Y | Y | Y | N | Y | N |
| 19 Wexler | N | N | N | Y | N | N |
| 20 Wasserman-Schultz | N | N | N | Y | N | N |
| 21 Diaz-Balart, L. | Y | Y | Y | N | N | N |
| 22 Shaw | Y | Y | Y | N | N | N |
| 23 Hastings | N | N | N | Y | N | N |
| 24 Feeney | Y | Y | Y | N | N | Y |
| 25 Diaz-Balart, M. | Y | Y | Y | N | N | N |
| **GEORGIA** | | | | | | |
| 1 Kingston | Y | Y | Y | N | N | N |
| 2 Bishop | Y | N | N | N | N | N |
| 3 Marshall | Y | N | N | Y | Y | Y |
| 4 McKinney | N | N | N | Y | Y | Y |
| 5 Lewis | ? | ? | ? | ? | ? | ? |
| 6 Price | Y | Y | Y | N | Y | Y |
| 7 Linder | Y | Y | Y | N | N | Y |
| 8 Westmoreland | Y | Y | Y | N | Y | Y |
| 9 Norwood | Y | Y | Y | N | N | Y |
| 10 Deal | Y | Y | Y | N | N | Y |
| 11 Gingrey | Y | Y | Y | N | N | N |
| 12 Barrow | Y | N | N | Y | N | N |
| 13 Scott | Y | N | N | Y | N | N |
| **HAWAII** | | | | | | |
| 1 Abercrombie | N | N | N | Y | Y | N |
| 2 Case | N | N | N | N | Y | N |
| **IDAHO** | | | | | | |
| 1 Otter | Y | Y | Y | N | Y | N |
| 2 Simpson | Y | Y | Y | N | Y | N |
| **ILLINOIS** | | | | | | |
| 1 Rush | N | N | N | Y | Y | N |
| 2 Jackson | N | N | N | Y | N | N |
| 3 Lipinski | N | N | N | Y | N | N |
| 4 Gutierrez | N | N | N | Y | N | N |
| 5 Emanuel | N | N | N | Y | N | N |
| 6 Hyde | Y | Y | Y | N | Y | N |
| 7 Davis | N | N | N | Y | N | N |
| 8 Bean | Y | N | N | Y | N | N |
| 9 Schakowsky | N | N | N | Y | Y | N |
| 10 Kirk | Y | Y | Y | N | N | N |
| 11 Weller | Y | Y | Y | N | N | N |
| 12 Costello | N | N | N | Y | N | N |

| KEY | Republicans | Democrats | *Independents* |
|---|---|---|---|

| | | |
|---|---|---|
| Y  Voted for (yea) | X  Paired against | C  Voted "present" to avoid possible conflict of interest |
| #  Paired for | −  Announced against | |
| +  Announced for | P  Voted "present" | ?  Did not vote or otherwise make a position known |
| N  Voted against (nay) | | |

| | 296 | 297 | 298 | 299 | 300 | 301 |
|---|---|---|---|---|---|---|
| 13 **Biggert** | Y | Y | Y | N | N | Y |
| 14 **Hastert** | Y | | | N | | |
| 15 **Johnson** | Y | Y | Y | N | N | N |
| 16 **Manzullo** | Y | Y | Y | N | N | Y |
| 17 Evans | N | N | N | Y | Y | N |
| 18 **LaHood** | Y | Y | Y | N | N | N |
| 19 **Shimkus** | Y | Y | Y | N | N | Y |
| **INDIANA** | | | | | | |
| 1 Visclosky | N | N | N | Y | N | N |
| 2 **Chocola** | Y | Y | Y | N | N | Y |
| 3 **Souder** | Y | Y | Y | N | N | N |
| 4 **Buyer** | Y | Y | Y | N | Y | ? |
| 5 **Burton** | Y | Y | Y | N | Y | Y |
| 6 **Pence** | Y | Y | Y | N | N | Y |
| 7 Carson | N | N | N | Y | N | N |
| 8 **Hostettler** | Y | Y | Y | N | Y | Y |
| 9 **Sodrel** | Y | Y | Y | N | Y | N |
| **IOWA** | | | | | | |
| 1 **Nussle** | Y | Y | Y | N | N | N |
| 2 **Leach** | N | N | Y | N | N | N |
| 3 Boswell | Y | N | N | Y | Y | N |
| 4 **Latham** | Y | Y | Y | N | N | N |
| 5 **King** | Y | Y | Y | N | N | Y |
| **KANSAS** | | | | | | |
| 1 **Moran** | Y | Y | Y | N | N | Y |
| 2 **Ryun** | Y | Y | Y | N | Y | Y |
| 3 Moore | N | N | N | Y | N | N |
| 4 **Tiahrt** | Y | Y | Y | N | N | N |
| **KENTUCKY** | | | | | | |
| 1 **Whitfield** | Y | Y | Y | N | Y | Y |
| 2 **Lewis** | Y | Y | Y | N | N | Y |
| 3 **Northup** | Y | Y | Y | N | N | N |
| 4 **Davis** | Y | Y | Y | N | N | N |
| 5 **Rogers** | Y | Y | Y | N | N | N |
| 6 Chandler | Y | N | N | Y | Y | Y |
| **LOUISIANA** | | | | | | |
| 1 **Jindal** | Y | Y | Y | N | N | Y |
| 2 Jefferson | Y | N | N | Y | Y | N |
| 3 Melancon | Y | N | N | N | Y | N |
| 4 **McCrery** | Y | Y | Y | N | N | N |
| 5 **Alexander** | Y | Y | Y | N | N | N |
| 6 **Baker** | Y | Y | Y | N | N | N |
| 7 **Boustany** | Y | Y | Y | N | Y | N |
| **MAINE** | | | | | | |
| 1 Allen | N | N | N | N | N | N |
| 2 Michaud | Y | N | N | N | Y | Y |
| **MARYLAND** | | | | | | |
| 1 **Gilchrest** | N | Y | Y | N | Y | N |
| 2 Ruppersberger | Y | N | N | Y | Y | N |
| 3 Cardin | N | N | N | N | Y | N |
| 4 Wynn | Y | N | N | N | Y | N |
| 5 Hoyer | N | N | N | Y | N | N |
| 6 **Bartlett** | Y | Y | Y | N | N | Y |
| 7 Cummings | N | N | N | Y | N | N |
| 8 Van Hollen | N | N | N | Y | Y | N |
| **MASSACHUSETTS** | | | | | | |
| 1 Olver | N | N | N | Y | N | N |
| 2 Neal | Y | N | N | N | N | N |
| 3 McGovern | Y | N | N | Y | N | N |
| 4 Frank | N | N | N | Y | N | N |
| 5 Meehan | N | N | N | Y | Y | N |
| 6 Tierney | N | N | N | Y | Y | N |
| 7 Markey | N | N | N | N | Y | N |
| 8 Capuano | N | N | N | Y | Y | N |
| 9 Lynch | Y | N | N | Y | Y | N |
| 10 Delahunt | Y | N | N | N | Y | N |
| **MICHIGAN** | | | | | | |
| 1 Stupak | Y | N | N | N | Y | N |
| 2 **Hoekstra** | N | Y | Y | N | N | N |
| 3 **Ehlers** | N | Y | Y | N | N | N |
| 4 **Camp** | Y | Y | Y | N | N | N |
| 5 Kildee | Y | N | N | Y | N | N |
| 6 **Upton** | Y | Y | Y | N | N | N |
| 7 **Schwarz** | N | Y | Y | N | Y | N |
| 8 **Rogers** | Y | Y | Y | N | N | N |
| 9 **Knollenberg** | Y | Y | Y | N | N | N |
| 10 **Miller** | Y | Y | Y | N | Y | N |
| 11 **McCotter** | Y | Y | Y | N | Y | Y |
| 12 Levin | N | N | N | Y | N | N |
| 13 Kilpatrick | N | N | N | Y | N | N |
| 14 Conyers | N | N | N | Y | N | N |
| 15 Dingell | N | N | N | Y | Y | N |

| | 296 | 297 | 298 | 299 | 300 | 301 |
|---|---|---|---|---|---|---|
| **MINNESOTA** | | | | | | |
| 1 **Gutknecht** | Y | Y | Y | N | N | Y |
| 2 **Kline** | Y | Y | Y | N | N | N |
| 3 **Ramstad** | Y | Y | Y | N | Y | Y |
| 4 McCollum | N | N | N | Y | Y | N |
| 5 Sabo | N | N | ? | Y | N | N |
| 6 **Kennedy** | Y | Y | Y | N | N | Y |
| 7 Peterson | Y | N | N | N | Y | N |
| 8 Oberstar | N | N | N | Y | N | N |
| **MISSISSIPPI** | | | | | | |
| 1 **Wicker** | Y | Y | Y | N | N | N |
| 2 Thompson | Y | N | N | Y | Y | N |
| 3 **Pickering** | Y | Y | Y | N | Y | N |
| 4 Taylor | Y | N | N | Y | N | Y |
| **MISSOURI** | | | | | | |
| 1 Clay | N | N | N | Y | Y | N |
| 2 **Akin** | Y | ? | Y | N | N | Y |
| 3 Carnahan | Y | N | N | Y | Y | N |
| 4 Skelton | Y | N | N | N | Y | N |
| 5 Cleaver | N | N | N | Y | Y | N |
| 6 **Graves** | Y | Y | Y | N | N | Y |
| 7 **Blunt** | Y | Y | Y | N | N | N |
| 8 **Emerson** | Y | Y | Y | N | N | N |
| 9 **Hulshof** | Y | Y | Y | N | N | Y |
| **MONTANA** | | | | | | |
| AL **Rehberg** | Y | Y | Y | N | N | N |
| **NEBRASKA** | | | | | | |
| 1 **Fortenberry** | Y | Y | Y | N | N | N |
| 2 **Terry** | Y | Y | Y | N | N | Y |
| 3 **Osborne** | Y | Y | Y | N | N | N |
| **NEVADA** | | | | | | |
| 1 Berkley | Y | N | N | Y | N | N |
| 2 **Gibbons** | Y | Y | Y | N | N | Y |
| 3 **Porter** | Y | Y | Y | N | Y | N |
| **NEW HAMPSHIRE** | | | | | | |
| 1 **Bradley** | Y | Y | Y | N | N | Y |
| 2 **Bass** | Y | Y | Y | N | N | Y |
| **NEW JERSEY** | | | | | | |
| 1 Andrews | Y | N | N | Y | N | N |
| 2 **LoBiondo** | Y | Y | Y | N | N | Y |
| 3 **Saxton** | Y | Y | Y | N | Y | Y |
| 4 **Smith** | Y | Y | Y | N | Y | N |
| 5 **Garrett** | Y | Y | Y | N | N | Y |
| 6 Pallone | Y | N | N | Y | N | N |
| 7 **Ferguson** | Y | Y | Y | N | N | N |
| 8 Pascrell | Y | N | N | Y | Y | N |
| 9 Rothman | Y | N | N | Y | Y | N |
| 10 Payne | N | N | N | Y | Y | N |
| 11 **Frelinghuysen** | Y | Y | Y | N | N | N |
| 12 Holt | N | N | N | Y | Y | N |
| 13 Menendez | Y | N | N | Y | N | N |
| **NEW MEXICO** | | | | | | |
| 1 **Wilson** | Y | Y | Y | N | N | N |
| 2 **Pearce** | Y | Y | Y | N | N | N |
| 3 Udall | N | N | N | Y | Y | Y |
| **NEW YORK** | | | | | | |
| 1 Bishop | Y | N | N | Y | N | N |
| 2 Israel | N | N | N | N | Y | N |
| 3 **King** | Y | Y | Y | N | Y | N |
| 4 McCarthy | Y | N | N | Y | Y | N |
| 5 Ackerman | N | N | N | Y | Y | N |
| 6 Meeks | N | N | N | Y | Y | N |
| 7 Crowley | Y | N | N | Y | Y | N |
| 8 Nadler | N | N | N | Y | Y | N |
| 9 Weiner | N | N | N | Y | Y | N |
| 10 Towns | Y | N | N | Y | Y | N |
| 11 Owens | N | N | N | Y | Y | N |
| 12 Velázquez | N | N | N | Y | Y | N |
| 13 **Fossella** | Y | Y | Y | N | Y | Y |
| 14 Maloney | N | N | N | Y | Y | Y |
| 15 Rangel | ? | ? | ? | ? | ? | ? |
| 16 Serrano | N | N | N | Y | Y | N |
| 17 Engel | N | N | N | N | Y | N |
| 18 Lowey | N | N | N | Y | Y | N |
| 19 **Kelly** | Y | Y | Y | N | N | N |
| 20 **Sweeney** | Y | Y | Y | N | N | N |
| 21 McNulty | Y | N | N | N | Y | N |
| 22 Hinchey | N | N | N | Y | Y | N |
| 23 **McHugh** | Y | Y | Y | N | N | N |
| 24 **Boehlert** | Y | Y | Y | N | N | N |
| 25 **Walsh** | Y | Y | Y | N | N | N |
| 26 **Reynolds** | Y | Y | Y | N | N | N |
| 27 Higgins | Y | N | N | Y | N | N |
| 28 Slaughter | N | N | N | Y | N | N |
| 29 **Kuhl** | Y | Y | Y | N | N | N |

| | 296 | 297 | 298 | 299 | 300 | 301 |
|---|---|---|---|---|---|---|
| **NORTH CAROLINA** | | | | | | |
| 1 Butterfield | N | N | N | Y | N | N |
| 2 Etheridge | Y | N | N | Y | Y | N |
| 3 **Jones** | Y | Y | Y | N | Y | Y |
| 4 Price | N | N | N | Y | N | N |
| 5 **Foxx** | Y | Y | Y | N | N | Y |
| 6 **Coble** | Y | Y | Y | N | N | Y |
| 7 McIntyre | Y | N | N | N | Y | N |
| 8 **Hayes** | Y | Y | Y | N | N | N |
| 9 **Myrick** | Y | Y | Y | N | N | Y |
| 10 **McHenry** | Y | Y | Y | N | N | Y |
| 11 **Taylor** | Y | Y | Y | N | N | N |
| 12 Watt | N | N | N | Y | N | N |
| 13 Miller | N | N | N | Y | N | N |
| **NORTH DAKOTA** | | | | | | |
| AL Pomeroy | ? | ? | ? | ? | ? | ? |
| **OHIO** | | | | | | |
| 1 **Chabot** | Y | Y | Y | N | Y | Y |
| 2 Vacant | | | | | | |
| 3 **Turner** | Y | Y | Y | N | Y | N |
| 4 **Oxley** | ? | ? | ? | ? | ? | ? |
| 5 **Gillmor** | Y | Y | Y | N | N | N |
| 6 Strickland | Y | N | N | Y | Y | N |
| 7 **Hobson** | Y | Y | Y | N | N | N |
| 8 **Boehner** | Y | Y | Y | N | N | N |
| 9 Kaptur | Y | N | N | Y | Y | N |
| 10 Kucinich | N | ? | ? | ? | ? | ? |
| 11 Jones | N | N | N | ? | ? | ? |
| 12 **Tiberi** | Y | Y | Y | ? | ? | ? |
| 13 Brown | Y | N | N | Y | Y | Y |
| 14 **LaTourette** | Y | Y | Y | ? | ? | ? |
| 15 **Pryce** | Y | Y | Y | N | N | N |
| 16 **Regula** | Y | Y | Y | N | N | N |
| 17 Ryan | N | N | N | Y | Y | N |
| 18 **Ney** | ? | ? | ? | ? | ? | ? |
| **OKLAHOMA** | | | | | | |
| 1 **Sullivan** | Y | Y | Y | N | N | Y |
| 2 Boren | Y | N | N | Y | Y | N |
| 3 **Lucas** | Y | Y | Y | N | N | N |
| 4 **Cole** | Y | Y | Y | ? | ? | ? |
| 5 **Istook** | Y | Y | Y | N | N | N |
| **OREGON** | | | | | | |
| 1 Wu | N | N | N | Y | Y | N |
| 2 **Walden** | Y | Y | Y | N | N | N |
| 3 Blumenauer | N | N | N | Y | N | N |
| 4 DeFazio | N | N | N | Y | Y | N |
| 5 Hooley | N | N | N | Y | N | Y |
| **PENNSYLVANIA** | | | | | | |
| 1 Brady | N | N | N | Y | Y | N |
| 2 Fattah | N | N | N | N | Y | N |
| 3 **English** | Y | Y | Y | N | N | N |
| 4 **Hart** | Y | Y | Y | N | N | Y |
| 5 **Peterson** | Y | Y | Y | N | Y | N |
| 6 **Gerlach** | Y | Y | Y | N | Y | N |
| 7 **Weldon** | Y | Y | Y | N | Y | N |
| 8 **Fitzpatrick** | Y | Y | Y | N | Y | N |
| 9 **Shuster** | Y | Y | Y | N | N | Y |
| 10 **Sherwood** | Y | Y | Y | N | N | N |
| 11 Kanjorski | Y | N | N | N | Y | N |
| 12 Murtha | Y | N | N | N | Y | N |
| 13 Schwartz | N | N | N | N | N | N |
| 14 Doyle | Y | N | N | N | Y | N |
| 15 **Dent** | Y | Y | Y | N | N | N |
| 16 **Pitts** | Y | Y | Y | N | Y | Y |
| 17 Holden | Y | N | N | N | Y | N |
| 18 **Murphy** | Y | Y | Y | N | N | N |
| 19 **Platts** | Y | Y | Y | N | Y | N |
| **RHODE ISLAND** | | | | | | |
| 1 Kennedy | N | N | N | Y | Y | N |
| 2 Langevin | Y | N | N | Y | Y | N |
| **SOUTH CAROLINA** | | | | | | |
| 1 **Brown** | Y | Y | Y | N | N | N |
| 2 **Wilson** | Y | Y | Y | N | Y | Y |
| 3 **Barrett** | Y | Y | Y | N | N | Y |
| 4 **Inglis** | Y | Y | Y | N | Y | Y |
| 5 Spratt | Y | N | N | Y | Y | N |
| 6 Clyburn | Y | N | N | Y | Y | N |
| **SOUTH DAKOTA** | | | | | | |
| AL Herseth | ? | N | N | N | Y | Y |
| **TENNESSEE** | | | | | | |
| 1 **Jenkins** | Y | Y | Y | N | N | Y |
| 2 **Duncan** | Y | Y | Y | N | N | Y |

| | 296 | 297 | 298 | 299 | 300 | 301 |
|---|---|---|---|---|---|---|
| 3 **Wamp** | Y | Y | Y | N | N | N |
| 4 Davis | Y | N | N | ? | ? | ? |
| 5 Cooper | N | N | N | N | Y | Y |
| 6 Gordon | Y | N | N | Y | Y | N |
| 7 **Blackburn** | Y | Y | Y | N | N | Y |
| 8 Tanner | N | N | N | N | N | Y |
| 9 Ford | Y | N | N | N | N | N |
| **TEXAS** | | | | | | |
| 1 **Gohmert** | Y | Y | Y | N | N | Y |
| 2 **Poe** | Y | Y | Y | N | Y | Y |
| 3 **Johnson, S.** | Y | Y | Y | N | N | N |
| 4 **Hall** | Y | Y | Y | N | N | N |
| 5 **Hensarling** | Y | Y | Y | N | Y | Y |
| 6 **Barton** | ? | ? | ? | ? | ? | ? |
| 7 **Culberson** | Y | Y | Y | N | N | N |
| 8 **Brady** | ? | Y | Y | N | N | Y |
| 9 Green, A. | N | N | N | Y | Y | N |
| 10 **McCaul** | ? | ? | ? | ? | ? | ? |
| 11 **Conaway** | + | ? | ? | ? | ? | ? |
| 12 **Granger** | Y | Y | Y | N | N | N |
| 13 **Thornberry** | Y | Y | Y | N | Y | N |
| 14 **Paul** | N | Y | Y | N | N | Y |
| 15 Hinojosa | ? | ? | ? | ? | ? | ? |
| 16 Reyes | Y | N | N | N | Y | N |
| 17 Edwards | Y | N | N | Y | N | Y |
| 18 Jackson-Lee | ? | ? | ? | ? | ? | ? |
| 19 **Neugebauer** | Y | Y | Y | N | N | Y |
| 20 Gonzalez | N | N | N | N | Y | N |
| 21 **Smith** | ? | ? | ? | ? | ? | ? |
| 22 **DeLay** | Y | Y | Y | N | N | N |
| 23 **Bonilla** | Y | Y | Y | N | N | N |
| 24 **Marchant** | Y | Y | Y | N | N | N |
| 25 Doggett | ? | ? | ? | ? | ? | ? |
| 26 **Burgess** | Y | Y | Y | N | N | Y |
| 27 Ortiz | Y | N | N | N | Y | N |
| 28 Cuellar | Y | N | N | N | Y | N |
| 29 Green, G. | Y | N | N | Y | Y | N |
| 30 Johnson, E. | N | N | N | Y | N | N |
| 31 **Carter** | ? | ? | ? | ? | ? | ? |
| 32 **Sessions** | Y | Y | Y | N | N | Y |
| **UTAH** | | | | | | |
| 1 **Bishop** | Y | Y | Y | N | Y | N |
| 2 Matheson | N | N | N | Y | N | Y |
| 3 **Cannon** | Y | Y | Y | N | N | Y |
| **VERMONT** | | | | | | |
| AL *Sanders* | N | N | N | Y | Y | N |
| **VIRGINIA** | | | | | | |
| 1 **Davis, J.** | Y | Y | Y | N | Y | Y |
| 2 **Drake** | Y | Y | Y | N | Y | Y |
| 3 Scott | N | N | N | Y | N | N |
| 4 **Forbes** | Y | Y | Y | N | Y | Y |
| 5 **Goode** | Y | Y | Y | N | Y | N |
| 6 **Goodlatte** | Y | Y | Y | N | Y | N |
| 7 **Cantor** | Y | Y | Y | N | N | N |
| 8 Moran | N | N | N | Y | N | N |
| 9 Boucher | N | N | ? | Y | Y | N |
| 10 **Wolf** | Y | Y | Y | N | N | N |
| 11 **Davis, T.** | Y | Y | ? | N | Y | N |
| **WASHINGTON** | | | | | | |
| 1 Inslee | N | N | N | Y | Y | Y |
| 2 Larsen | N | N | N | Y | Y | N |
| 3 Baird | Y | N | N | Y | N | N |
| 4 **Hastings** | Y | Y | Y | N | N | N |
| 5 **McMorris** | Y | Y | Y | N | N | Y |
| 6 Dicks | N | N | N | Y | N | N |
| 7 McDermott | N | N | N | Y | N | N |
| 8 **Reichert** | Y | Y | Y | N | Y | N |
| 9 Smith | Y | N | N | Y | N | Y |
| **WEST VIRGINIA** | | | | | | |
| 1 Mollohan | Y | N | N | N | Y | N |
| 2 **Capito** | Y | Y | Y | N | N | N |
| 3 Rahall | Y | N | N | N | Y | N |
| **WISCONSIN** | | | | | | |
| 1 **Ryan** | Y | Y | Y | N | N | Y |
| 2 Baldwin | N | N | N | Y | Y | N |
| 3 Kind | N | N | N | Y | N | Y |
| 4 Moore | N | N | N | N | N | N |
| 5 **Sensenbrenner** | Y | Y | Y | N | N | Y |
| 6 **Petri** | N | Y | Y | N | Y | Y |
| 7 Obey | N | N | N | Y | N | N |
| 8 **Green** | Y | Y | Y | N | N | Y |
| **WYOMING** | | | | | | |
| AL **Cubin** | Y | Y | Y | N | N | Y |

# IN THE HOUSE | By Vote Number

**302.** HR 2985. Fiscal 2006 Legislative Branch Appropriations/ **Recommit.** Obey, D-Wis., motion to recommit the bill to the House Appropriations Committee. Motion rejected 180-232: R 0-219; D 179-13 (ND 135-12, SD 44-1); I 1-0. June 22, 2005.

**303.** HR 2985. Fiscal 2006 Legislative Branch Appropriations/ **Passage.** Passage of the bill that would appropriate $2.9 billion in fiscal 2006 for legislative branch operations, excluding funds for Senate operations. It would provide $1.1 billion for operations of the House of Representatives, $543 million for the Library of Congress, $482 million for the Government Accountability Office, $317 million for the Architect of the Capitol and $123 million for the Government Printing Office. Passed 330-82: R 205-14; D 125-67 (ND 96-51, SD 29-16); I 0-1. June 22, 2005.

**304.** HR 3010. Fiscal 2006 Labor-HHS-Education Appropriations/ **Previous Question.** Capito, R-W.Va., motion to order the previous question (thus ending debate and the possibility of amendment) on adoption of the rule (H Res 337) to provide for House floor consideration of the bill that would appropriate $602 billion in fiscal 2006 for the departments of Labor, Health and Human Services and Education and for other various agencies and programs. Motion agreed to 225-194: R 224-0; D 1-193 (ND 0-145, SD 1-48); I 0-1. (Subsequently, the rule was adopted by voice vote.) June 23, 2005.

**305.** HR 3010. Fiscal 2006 Labor-HHS-Education Appropriations/ **Corporation for Public Broadcasting.** Obey, D-Wis., amendment that would add $100 million for the Corporation for Public Broadcasting, offset with cuts to the Department of Labor departmental management and pilot programs, Health Resources and Services Administration program management and Department of Education departmental management and demonstration projects. Adopted 284-140: R 87-140; D 196-0 (ND 148-0, SD 48-0); I 1-0. June 23, 2005.

**306.** HR 3010. Fiscal 2006 Labor-HHS-Education Appropriations/ **Respirator Testing.** Owens, D-N.Y., amendment that would strike a provision in the bill that would bar funds from enforcing an Occupational Safety and Health Administration requirement that hospitals conduct annual testing of respirators for tuberculosis exposure. Rejected 206-216: R 12-214; D 193-2 (ND 147-1, SD 46-1); I 1-0. June 23, 2005.

**307.** HR 3010. Fiscal 2006 Labor-HHS-Education Appropriations/ **Special Education Funding.** Bradley, R-N.H., amendment that would increase funds for special education by $50 million, offset with reductions to the Occupational Safety and Health Administration and Education Department program administration accounts. Rejected 161-262: R 115-111; D 46-150 (ND 30-119, SD 16-31); I 0-1. June 23, 2005.

| | 302 | 303 | 304 | 305 | 306 | 307 |
|---|---|---|---|---|---|---|
| **ALABAMA** | | | | | | |
| 1 Bonner | ? | ? | Y | N | N | N |
| 2 Everett | N | Y | Y | N | N | N |
| 3 Rogers | N | Y | Y | N | N | N |
| 4 Aderholt | N | Y | Y | N | N | N |
| 5 Cramer | Y | Y | N | Y | Y | N |
| 6 Bachus | N | Y | Y | N | N | N |
| 7 Davis | Y | Y | N | Y | Y | N |
| **ALASKA** | | | | | | |
| AL Young | N | Y | Y | Y | N | Y |
| **ARIZONA** | | | | | | |
| 1 Renzi | N | Y | Y | Y | N | Y |
| 2 Franks | N | Y | Y | N | N | Y |
| 3 Shadegg | N | Y | Y | N | N | Y |
| 4 Pastor | Y | N | N | Y | Y | Y |
| 5 Hayworth | N | Y | Y | N | N | Y |
| 6 Flake | N | N | Y | N | N | Y |
| 7 Grijalva | Y | N | N | Y | Y | N |
| 8 Kolbe | N | Y | Y | N | N | N |
| **ARKANSAS** | | | | | | |
| 1 Berry | Y | N | N | Y | Y | N |
| 2 Snyder | Y | N | N | Y | Y | N |
| 3 Boozman | N | Y | Y | Y | N | Y |
| 4 Ross | Y | N | N | Y | Y | N |
| **CALIFORNIA** | | | | | | |
| 1 Thompson | Y | N | N | Y | Y | N |
| 2 Herger | N | Y | Y | N | N | Y |
| 3 Lungren | N | Y | Y | N | N | Y |
| 4 Doolittle | N | Y | Y | N | N | N |
| 5 Matsui, D. | Y | N | N | Y | Y | N |
| 6 Woolsey | Y | N | N | Y | Y | N |
| 7 Miller, George | Y | N | N | Y | Y | N |
| 8 Pelosi | Y | N | N | Y | Y | N |
| 9 Lee | Y | N | N | Y | Y | N |
| 10 Tauscher | Y | Y | N | Y | Y | N |
| 11 Pombo | N | Y | Y | N | N | N |
| 12 Lantos | Y | Y | N | Y | Y | N |
| 13 Stark | Y | N | N | Y | Y | N |
| 14 Eshoo | Y | N | N | Y | Y | N |
| 15 Honda | Y | N | N | Y | Y | N |
| 16 Lofgren | Y | N | N | Y | Y | N |
| 17 Farr | Y | N | N | Y | Y | N |
| 18 Cardoza | Y | N | N | Y | Y | N |
| 19 Radanovich | N | Y | Y | N | N | N |
| 20 Costa | Y | Y | N | Y | Y | N |
| 21 Nunes | N | Y | Y | Y | N | N |
| 22 Thomas | ? | ? | Y | Y | N | N |
| 23 Capps | Y | N | N | Y | Y | N |
| 24 Gallegly | N | Y | Y | N | N | Y |
| 25 McKeon | N | Y | Y | N | N | N |
| 26 Dreier | N | Y | Y | N | N | N |
| 27 Sherman | Y | N | N | Y | Y | N |
| 28 Berman | Y | Y | N | Y | Y | N |
| 29 Schiff | Y | Y | N | Y | Y | N |
| 30 Waxman | Y | N | N | Y | Y | N |
| 31 Becerra | Y | N | N | Y | Y | N |
| 32 Solis | Y | N | N | Y | Y | N |
| 33 Watson | Y | N | N | Y | Y | N |
| 34 Roybal-Allard | Y | Y | N | Y | Y | N |
| 35 Waters | Y | N | N | Y | Y | N |
| 36 Harman | Y | Y | N | ? | ? | Y |
| 37 Millender-McD. | Y | Y | N | Y | Y | N |
| 38 Napolitano | Y | Y | N | Y | Y | N |
| 39 Sánchez, Linda | Y | Y | N | Y | Y | N |
| 40 Royce | N | Y | Y | N | N | N |
| 41 Lewis | N | Y | Y | N | N | N |
| 42 Miller, Gary | N | Y | Y | N | N | Y |
| 43 Baca | Y | Y | N | Y | Y | N |
| 44 Calvert | N | Y | Y | N | N | N |
| 45 Bono | N | Y | Y | N | N | N |
| 46 Rohrabacher | N | Y | Y | N | N | Y |
| 47 Sanchez, Loretta | Y | Y | N | Y | Y | N |
| 48 Cox | N | Y | Y | N | N | N |
| 49 Issa | N | Y | Y | N | N | N |

| | 302 | 303 | 304 | 305 | 306 | 307 |
|---|---|---|---|---|---|---|
| 50 Cunningham | N | Y | Y | Y | N | N |
| 51 Filner | Y | N | N | Y | Y | N |
| 52 Hunter | N | Y | ? | N | N | Y |
| 53 Davis | Y | N | N | Y | Y | Y |
| **COLORADO** | | | | | | |
| 1 DeGette | Y | Y | N | Y | Y | N |
| 2 Udall | Y | N | N | Y | Y | Y |
| 3 Salazar | Y | N | N | Y | Y | N |
| 4 Musgrave | N | Y | Y | N | N | Y |
| 5 Hefley | N | N | Y | N | N | Y |
| 6 Tancredo | N | Y | Y | N | N | N |
| 7 Beauprez | N | Y | Y | N | N | Y |
| **CONNECTICUT** | | | | | | |
| 1 Larson | Y | Y | N | Y | Y | N |
| 2 Simmons | N | Y | Y | Y | N | Y |
| 3 DeLauro | Y | N | N | Y | Y | N |
| 4 Shays | N | N | Y | Y | Y | Y |
| 5 Johnson | N | Y | Y | Y | N | Y |
| **DELAWARE** | | | | | | |
| AL Castle | N | Y | Y | Y | N | N |
| **FLORIDA** | | | | | | |
| 1 Miller | N | Y | Y | N | N | N |
| 2 Boyd | ? | ? | ? | ? | ? | ? |
| 3 Brown | Y | Y | N | Y | Y | N |
| 4 Crenshaw | N | Y | Y | N | N | N |
| 5 Brown-Waite | N | Y | Y | N | N | N |
| 6 Stearns | N | N | Y | N | N | Y |
| 7 Mica | N | Y | Y | N | N | N |
| 8 Keller | N | Y | Y | N | N | N |
| 9 Bilirakis | N | Y | Y | N | N | N |
| 10 Young | N | Y | Y | N | N | N |
| 11 Davis | Y | Y | N | Y | Y | N |
| 12 Putnam | N | Y | Y | N | N | N |
| 13 Harris | N | Y | Y | N | N | N |
| 14 Mack | N | Y | Y | N | N | N |
| 15 Weldon | N | Y | Y | N | N | N |
| 16 Foley | N | Y | Y | Y | N | Y |
| 17 Meek | Y | Y | N | ? | ? | ? |
| 18 Ros-Lehtinen | N | Y | Y | N | N | N |
| 19 Wexler | Y | Y | N | Y | Y | N |
| 20 Wasserman-Schultz | Y | N | N | Y | Y | N |
| 21 Diaz-Balart, L. | N | Y | Y | N | N | N |
| 22 Shaw | N | Y | Y | N | N | N |
| 23 Hastings | Y | N | N | Y | Y | N |
| 24 Feeney | N | Y | Y | N | N | Y |
| 25 Diaz-Balart, M. | N | Y | Y | N | N | N |
| **GEORGIA** | | | | | | |
| 1 Kingston | N | Y | Y | N | N | Y |
| 2 Bishop | N | Y | N | Y | Y | N |
| 3 Marshall | Y | N | N | Y | Y | N |
| 4 McKinney | Y | Y | N | Y | Y | N |
| 5 Lewis | ? | ? | ? | ? | ? | ? |
| 6 Price | N | Y | Y | N | N | Y |
| 7 Linder | N | Y | Y | N | N | N |
| 8 Westmoreland | N | Y | Y | N | N | Y |
| 9 Norwood | N | Y | Y | N | N | N |
| 10 Deal | N | Y | Y | N | N | N |
| 11 Gingrey | N | Y | Y | N | N | N |
| 12 Barrow | Y | N | N | Y | Y | N |
| 13 Scott | Y | N | N | Y | Y | N |
| **HAWAII** | | | | | | |
| 1 Abercrombie | Y | N | N | Y | Y | N |
| 2 Case | N | Y | N | Y | Y | N |
| **IDAHO** | | | | | | |
| 1 Otter | N | N | Y | N | N | Y |
| 2 Simpson | N | Y | Y | N | N | Y |
| **ILLINOIS** | | | | | | |
| 1 Rush | Y | Y | N | Y | Y | N |
| 2 Jackson | Y | Y | N | Y | Y | N |
| 3 Lipinski | Y | N | N | Y | Y | N |
| 4 Gutierrez | Y | Y | N | Y | Y | N |
| 5 Emanuel | Y | Y | N | Y | Y | N |
| 6 Hyde | N | Y | ? | N | N | N |
| 7 Davis | Y | Y | N | Y | Y | N |
| 8 Bean | N | Y | N | Y | Y | Y |
| 9 Schakowsky | Y | N | N | Y | Y | N |
| 10 Kirk | N | Y | Y | Y | N | Y |
| 11 Weller | N | Y | Y | N | N | N |
| 12 Costello | Y | Y | N | Y | Y | N |

**KEY**    Republicans    Democrats    *Independents*

| | | | | |
|---|---|---|---|---|
| **Y** Voted for (yea) | **X** Paired against | **C** Voted "present" to avoid |
| **#** Paired for | **–** Announced against | possible conflict of interest |
| **+** Announced for | **P** Voted "present" | **?** Did not vote or otherwise |
| **N** Voted against (nay) | | make a position known |

| | 302 | 303 | 304 | 305 | 306 | 307 |
|---|---|---|---|---|---|---|
| 13 **Biggert** | N | Y | Y | Y | N | Y |
| 14 **Hastert** | N | Y | | | | |
| 15 **Johnson** | N | Y | Y | Y | Y | Y |
| 16 **Manzullo** | N | Y | Y | N | N | Y |
| 17 Evans | Y | Y | N | Y | Y | N |
| 18 **LaHood** | N | Y | Y | Y | Y | N |
| 19 **Shimkus** | N | Y | Y | Y | Y | N |
| **INDIANA** | | | | | | |
| 1 Visclosky | Y | Y | N | Y | Y | N |
| 2 **Chocola** | N | Y | Y | N | N | Y |
| 3 **Souder** | N | Y | Y | N | N | Y |
| 4 **Buyer** | N | Y | ? | N | N | N |
| 5 **Burton** | N | Y | Y | N | N | Y |
| 6 **Pence** | N | Y | Y | N | N | Y |
| 7 Carson | Y | Y | N | Y | Y | N |
| 8 **Hostettler** | N | Y | Y | N | N | Y |
| 9 **Sodrel** | N | Y | Y | Y | N | N |
| **IOWA** | | | | | | |
| 1 **Nussle** | N | Y | Y | N | N | Y |
| 2 **Leach** | N | Y | Y | Y | N | Y |
| 3 Boswell | Y | N | N | Y | Y | N |
| 4 **Latham** | N | Y | Y | Y | N | Y |
| 5 **King** | N | Y | Y | N | N | Y |
| **KANSAS** | | | | | | |
| 1 **Moran** | N | Y | Y | Y | N | Y |
| 2 **Ryun** | N | Y | Y | N | N | Y |
| 3 Moore | Y | N | N | Y | Y | Y |
| 4 **Tiahrt** | N | Y | Y | N | N | N |
| **KENTUCKY** | | | | | | |
| 1 **Whitfield** | N | Y | Y | Y | N | N |
| 2 **Lewis** | N | Y | Y | Y | N | Y |
| 3 **Northup** | N | Y | Y | N | N | N |
| 4 **Davis** | N | Y | Y | N | N | N |
| 5 **Rogers** | N | Y | Y | Y | N | N |
| 6 Chandler | Y | N | N | Y | Y | Y |
| **LOUISIANA** | | | | | | |
| 1 **Jindal** | N | Y | Y | N | N | Y |
| 2 Jefferson | Y | Y | N | Y | Y | N |
| 3 Melancon | Y | N | N | Y | Y | N |
| 4 **McCrery** | N | Y | Y | N | N | Y |
| 5 **Alexander** | N | Y | Y | Y | N | N |
| 6 **Baker** | N | Y | Y | N | N | N |
| 7 **Boustany** | N | Y | Y | N | N | N |
| **MAINE** | | | | | | |
| 1 Allen | Y | Y | N | Y | Y | N |
| 2 Michaud | Y | Y | N | Y | Y | N |
| **MARYLAND** | | | | | | |
| 1 **Gilchrest** | N | Y | Y | Y | N | N |
| 2 Ruppersberger | Y | Y | N | Y | Y | N |
| 3 Cardin | Y | Y | N | Y | Y | N |
| 4 Wynn | Y | Y | N | Y | Y | N |
| 5 Hoyer | Y | Y | N | Y | Y | N |
| 6 **Bartlett** | N | Y | Y | N | N | N |
| 7 Cummings | Y | Y | N | Y | Y | N |
| 8 Van Hollen | Y | Y | N | Y | Y | N |
| **MASSACHUSETTS** | | | | | | |
| 1 Olver | Y | N | N | Y | Y | N |
| 2 Neal | Y | Y | N | Y | Y | N |
| 3 McGovern | Y | N | N | Y | Y | N |
| 4 Frank | Y | N | N | Y | Y | Y |
| 5 Meehan | Y | N | N | Y | Y | Y |
| 6 Tierney | Y | N | N | Y | Y | Y |
| 7 Markey | Y | Y | N | Y | Y | Y |
| 8 Capuano | Y | Y | N | Y | Y | N |
| 9 Lynch | Y | Y | N | Y | Y | N |
| 10 Delahunt | Y | Y | N | Y | Y | N |
| **MICHIGAN** | | | | | | |
| 1 Stupak | Y | N | N | Y | Y | N |
| 2 **Hoekstra** | N | Y | Y | N | N | Y |
| 3 **Ehlers** | N | Y | Y | Y | N | N |
| 4 **Camp** | N | Y | Y | Y | N | Y |
| 5 Kildee | Y | N | N | Y | Y | N |
| 6 **Upton** | N | Y | Y | Y | N | Y |
| 7 **Schwarz** | N | Y | Y | Y | N | N |
| 8 **Rogers** | N | Y | Y | N | N | N |
| 9 **Knollenberg** | N | Y | Y | N | N | N |
| 10 **Miller** | N | Y | Y | Y | N | Y |
| 11 **McCotter** | N | Y | Y | Y | Y | Y |
| 12 Levin | Y | Y | N | Y | Y | N |
| 13 Kilpatrick | Y | Y | N | Y | Y | N |
| 14 Conyers | Y | N | N | Y | Y | N |
| 15 Dingell | Y | Y | N | Y | Y | N |

| | 302 | 303 | 304 | 305 | 306 | 307 |
|---|---|---|---|---|---|---|
| **MINNESOTA** | | | | | | |
| 1 **Gutknecht** | N | Y | Y | N | N | Y |
| 2 **Kline** | N | Y | Y | N | N | Y |
| 3 **Ramstad** | N | Y | Y | Y | N | Y |
| 4 McCollum | Y | N | N | Y | Y | Y |
| 5 Sabo | Y | Y | N | Y | Y | N |
| 6 **Kennedy** | N | N | Y | Y | N | Y |
| 7 Peterson | Y | Y | ? | Y | N | Y |
| 8 Oberstar | Y | N | N | Y | Y | N |
| **MISSISSIPPI** | | | | | | |
| 1 **Wicker** | N | Y | Y | N | N | N |
| 2 Thompson | Y | Y | N | Y | Y | N |
| 3 **Pickering** | N | Y | Y | Y | N | Y |
| 4 Taylor | Y | N | N | Y | Y | N |
| **MISSOURI** | | | | | | |
| 1 Clay | Y | Y | N | Y | Y | N |
| 2 **Akin** | N | Y | Y | N | N | Y |
| 3 Carnahan | Y | Y | N | Y | Y | N |
| 4 Skelton | Y | Y | N | Y | Y | N |
| 5 Cleaver | Y | N | N | Y | Y | Y |
| 6 **Graves** | N | N | Y | N | N | Y |
| 7 **Blunt** | N | Y | Y | N | N | N |
| 8 **Emerson** | N | Y | Y | N | N | N |
| 9 **Hulshof** | N | N | Y | N | N | Y |
| **MONTANA** | | | | | | |
| AL **Rehberg** | N | Y | Y | N | N | N |
| **NEBRASKA** | | | | | | |
| 1 **Fortenberry** | N | Y | Y | N | N | Y |
| 2 **Terry** | N | Y | Y | N | Y | Y |
| 3 **Osborne** | N | Y | Y | N | N | Y |
| **NEVADA** | | | | | | |
| 1 Berkley | Y | Y | N | Y | Y | N |
| 2 **Gibbons** | N | Y | Y | Y | N | Y |
| 3 **Porter** | N | Y | Y | Y | N | Y |
| **NEW HAMPSHIRE** | | | | | | |
| 1 **Bradley** | N | Y | Y | Y | N | Y |
| 2 **Bass** | N | Y | Y | ? | ? | ? |
| **NEW JERSEY** | | | | | | |
| 1 Andrews | Y | N | N | Y | Y | N |
| 2 **LoBiondo** | N | Y | Y | N | Y | N |
| 3 **Saxton** | N | Y | Y | N | N | N |
| 4 **Smith** | N | Y | Y | Y | N | N |
| 5 **Garrett** | N | Y | Y | N | N | Y |
| 6 Pallone | Y | N | N | Y | Y | N |
| 7 **Ferguson** | N | Y | Y | Y | Y | Y |
| 8 Pascrell | N | Y | N | Y | Y | N |
| 9 Rothman | Y | Y | N | Y | Y | N |
| 10 Payne | Y | N | N | Y | Y | N |
| 11 **Frelinghuysen** | N | Y | Y | Y | N | N |
| 12 Holt | Y | Y | N | Y | Y | N |
| 13 Menendez | Y | N | N | Y | Y | N |
| **NEW MEXICO** | | | | | | |
| 1 **Wilson** | N | Y | Y | ? | ? | ? |
| 2 **Pearce** | N | Y | Y | N | N | Y |
| 3 Udall | Y | N | N | ? | ? | ? |
| **NEW YORK** | | | | | | |
| 1 Bishop | Y | Y | N | Y | Y | Y |
| 2 Israel | Y | Y | N | Y | Y | N |
| 3 **King** | N | Y | Y | Y | N | N |
| 4 McCarthy | Y | Y | N | Y | Y | N |
| 5 Ackerman | Y | Y | N | Y | Y | N |
| 6 Meeks | Y | Y | N | Y | ? | N |
| 7 Crowley | Y | Y | N | Y | Y | N |
| 8 Nadler | Y | Y | N | Y | Y | N |
| 9 Weiner | Y | Y | N | Y | Y | Y |
| 10 Towns | Y | Y | N | Y | Y | N |
| 11 Owens | Y | N | N | Y | Y | N |
| 12 Velázquez | Y | Y | N | Y | Y | N |
| 13 **Fossella** | N | Y | Y | Y | N | Y |
| 14 Maloney | Y | N | N | Y | Y | N |
| 15 Rangel | ? | ? | N | Y | Y | N |
| 16 Serrano | Y | Y | N | Y | Y | N |
| 17 Engel | Y | Y | N | Y | Y | N |
| 18 Lowey | Y | N | N | Y | Y | N |
| 19 **Kelly** | N | Y | Y | Y | N | Y |
| 20 **Sweeney** | N | Y | Y | Y | N | N |
| 21 McNulty | Y | Y | N | Y | Y | N |
| 22 Hinchey | Y | Y | N | Y | Y | N |
| 23 **McHugh** | N | Y | Y | Y | N | N |
| 24 **Boehlert** | N | Y | Y | Y | N | N |
| 25 **Walsh** | N | Y | Y | Y | N | N |
| 26 **Reynolds** | N | Y | Y | Y | N | N |
| 27 Higgins | Y | N | N | Y | Y | N |
| 28 Slaughter | Y | Y | N | Y | Y | N |
| 29 **Kuhl** | N | Y | Y | Y | N | Y |

| | 302 | 303 | 304 | 305 | 306 | 307 |
|---|---|---|---|---|---|---|
| **NORTH CAROLINA** | | | | | | |
| 1 Butterfield | Y | Y | N | Y | Y | Y |
| 2 Etheridge | Y | N | N | Y | Y | Y |
| 3 **Jones** | N | N | Y | N | ? | Y |
| 4 Price | Y | Y | N | Y | Y | Y |
| 5 **Foxx** | N | Y | Y | N | N | Y |
| 6 **Coble** | N | Y | Y | Y | N | Y |
| 7 McIntyre | Y | Y | N | Y | Y | Y |
| 8 **Hayes** | N | Y | Y | N | N | Y |
| 9 **Myrick** | N | Y | Y | N | N | N |
| 10 **McHenry** | N | Y | Y | N | N | Y |
| 11 **Taylor** | N | Y | Y | N | N | Y |
| 12 Watt | Y | N | N | Y | Y | N |
| 13 Miller | Y | Y | N | Y | Y | Y |
| **NORTH DAKOTA** | | | | | | |
| AL Pomeroy | ? | ? | ? | Y | Y | Y |
| **OHIO** | | | | | | |
| 1 **Chabot** | N | Y | Y | N | N | N |
| 2 Vacant | | | | | | |
| 3 **Turner** | N | Y | Y | N | N | N |
| 4 **Oxley** | ? | ? | Y | N | N | N |
| 5 **Gillmor** | N | Y | Y | Y | N | N |
| 6 Strickland | Y | Y | N | Y | Y | N |
| 7 **Hobson** | N | Y | Y | N | N | N |
| 8 **Boehner** | N | Y | Y | N | N | N |
| 9 Kaptur | N | Y | N | Y | Y | N |
| 10 Kucinich | ? | ? | ? | Y | Y | N |
| 11 Jones | ? | ? | ? | Y | Y | N |
| 12 **Tiberi** | ? | ? | Y | Y | N | N |
| 13 Brown | Y | N | N | Y | Y | N |
| 14 **LaTourette** | ? | ? | ? | Y | Y | N |
| 15 **Pryce** | N | Y | Y | Y | N | N |
| 16 **Regula** | N | Y | Y | N | N | N |
| 17 Ryan | Y | Y | ? | ? | Y | Y |
| 18 **Ney** | ? | ? | Y | Y | N | N |
| **OKLAHOMA** | | | | | | |
| 1 **Sullivan** | N | Y | Y | N | N | N |
| 2 Boren | Y | Y | N | Y | Y | Y |
| 3 **Lucas** | N | Y | Y | N | N | N |
| 4 **Cole** | ? | ? | Y | N | N | Y |
| 5 **Istook** | N | Y | Y | N | N | N |
| **OREGON** | | | | | | |
| 1 Wu | Y | N | N | Y | Y | Y |
| 2 **Walden** | N | Y | Y | Y | N | Y |
| 3 Blumenauer | Y | Y | N | Y | Y | Y |
| 4 DeFazio | Y | Y | N | Y | Y | N |
| 5 Hooley | Y | Y | N | Y | Y | Y |
| **PENNSYLVANIA** | | | | | | |
| 1 Brady | N | Y | N | Y | Y | N |
| 2 Fattah | Y | Y | N | Y | Y | N |
| 3 **English** | N | Y | Y | Y | N | Y |
| 4 **Hart** | N | Y | Y | Y | N | Y |
| 5 **Peterson** | N | Y | Y | Y | N | N |
| 6 **Gerlach** | N | Y | Y | Y | N | Y |
| 7 **Weldon** | N | Y | Y | Y | Y | Y |
| 8 **Fitzpatrick** | N | Y | Y | Y | N | Y |
| 9 **Shuster** | N | Y | Y | N | N | N |
| 10 **Sherwood** | N | Y | Y | Y | N | N |
| 11 Kanjorski | N | Y | N | Y | Y | N |
| 12 Murtha | N | Y | N | Y | Y | N |
| 13 Schwartz | Y | Y | N | Y | Y | N |
| 14 Doyle | N | Y | N | Y | Y | N |
| 15 **Dent** | N | Y | Y | Y | N | N |
| 16 **Pitts** | N | Y | Y | N | N | Y |
| 17 Holden | N | Y | N | Y | Y | N |
| 18 **Murphy** | N | Y | Y | Y | Y | Y |
| 19 **Platts** | N | Y | ? | Y | Y | Y |
| **RHODE ISLAND** | | | | | | |
| 1 Kennedy | Y | Y | N | Y | Y | Y |
| 2 Langevin | Y | Y | N | Y | Y | Y |
| **SOUTH CAROLINA** | | | | | | |
| 1 **Brown** | N | Y | Y | N | N | Y |
| 2 **Wilson** | N | Y | Y | N | N | N |
| 3 **Barrett** | N | Y | Y | N | N | ? |
| 4 **Inglis** | N | Y | Y | Y | N | N |
| 5 Spratt | Y | Y | N | Y | Y | N |
| 6 Clyburn | Y | Y | N | Y | Y | N |
| **SOUTH DAKOTA** | | | | | | |
| AL Herseth | Y | N | N | Y | Y | Y |
| **TENNESSEE** | | | | | | |
| 1 **Jenkins** | N | Y | Y | Y | N | Y |
| 2 **Duncan** | N | N | Y | Y | N | Y |

| | 302 | 303 | 304 | 305 | 306 | 307 |
|---|---|---|---|---|---|---|
| 3 **Wamp** | N | Y | Y | Y | N | N |
| 4 Davis | Y | Y | N | Y | Y | Y |
| 5 Cooper | Y | N | N | Y | Y | Y |
| 6 Gordon | ? | ? | N | Y | Y | Y |
| 7 **Blackburn** | N | Y | Y | N | N | N |
| 8 Tanner | Y | N | N | Y | Y | Y |
| 9 Ford | Y | Y | N | Y | Y | Y |
| **TEXAS** | | | | | | |
| 1 **Gohmert** | N | Y | Y | N | N | Y |
| 2 **Poe** | N | Y | Y | N | N | Y |
| 3 **Johnson, S.** | N | Y | Y | N | N | N |
| 4 **Hall** | N | Y | Y | N | N | N |
| 5 **Hensarling** | N | Y | Y | N | N | Y |
| 6 **Barton** | ? | ? | Y | N | N | N |
| 7 **Culberson** | N | Y | Y | N | N | N |
| 8 **Brady** | N | Y | Y | N | N | Y |
| 9 Green, A. | Y | Y | N | Y | Y | Y |
| 10 **McCaul** | ? | ? | Y | Y | N | Y |
| 11 **Conaway** | ? | ? | Y | N | N | N |
| 12 **Granger** | N | Y | Y | N | N | N |
| 13 **Thornberry** | N | Y | Y | N | N | N |
| 14 **Paul** | N | N | Y | Y | N | Y |
| 15 Hinojosa | ? | ? | N | Y | Y | N |
| 16 Reyes | Y | Y | N | Y | ? | ? |
| 17 Edwards | Y | Y | N | Y | Y | Y |
| 18 Jackson-Lee | ? | ? | N | Y | Y | N |
| 19 **Neugebauer** | N | Y | Y | N | N | Y |
| 20 Gonzalez | Y | Y | N | Y | Y | N |
| 21 **Smith** | ? | ? | Y | N | N | N |
| 22 **DeLay** | N | Y | Y | N | N | N |
| 23 **Bonilla** | N | Y | Y | N | N | N |
| 24 **Marchant** | N | Y | Y | Y | N | N |
| 25 Doggett | ? | ? | N | Y | Y | N |
| 26 **Burgess** | N | Y | Y | N | N | N |
| 27 Ortiz | Y | Y | N | Y | Y | N |
| 28 Cuellar | Y | Y | N | Y | Y | N |
| 29 Green, G. | Y | N | N | Y | Y | N |
| 30 Johnson, E. | Y | Y | N | Y | Y | N |
| 31 **Carter** | ? | ? | Y | N | N | N |
| 32 **Sessions** | N | Y | Y | N | N | Y |
| **UTAH** | | | | | | |
| 1 **Bishop** | N | Y | Y | N | N | Y |
| 2 Matheson | Y | N | N | Y | Y | Y |
| 3 **Cannon** | N | Y | Y | N | N | Y |
| **VERMONT** | | | | | | |
| AL *Sanders* | Y | N | N | Y | Y | N |
| **VIRGINIA** | | | | | | |
| 1 **Davis, J.** | N | N | Y | Y | N | Y |
| 2 **Drake** | N | Y | Y | Y | N | Y |
| 3 Scott | Y | N | N | Y | Y | N |
| 4 **Forbes** | N | Y | Y | N | N | Y |
| 5 **Goode** | N | N | Y | N | N | N |
| 6 **Goodlatte** | N | Y | Y | N | N | N |
| 7 **Cantor** | N | Y | Y | N | N | N |
| 8 Moran | Y | Y | N | Y | Y | N |
| 9 Boucher | Y | Y | N | Y | Y | N |
| 10 **Wolf** | N | Y | Y | Y | N | N |
| 11 **Davis, T.** | N | Y | ? | ? | ? | ? |
| **WASHINGTON** | | | | | | |
| 1 Inslee | Y | N | N | Y | Y | Y |
| 2 Larsen | Y | Y | N | Y | Y | N |
| 3 Baird | Y | N | N | Y | Y | N |
| 4 **Hastings** | N | Y | Y | N | N | N |
| 5 **McMorris** | N | Y | Y | N | N | Y |
| 6 Dicks | Y | Y | N | Y | Y | N |
| 7 McDermott | Y | N | N | Y | Y | N |
| 8 **Reichert** | N | Y | Y | Y | N | Y |
| 9 Smith | Y | N | N | Y | Y | Y |
| **WEST VIRGINIA** | | | | | | |
| 1 Mollohan | N | Y | N | Y | Y | N |
| 2 **Capito** | N | Y | Y | Y | N | Y |
| 3 Rahall | N | Y | N | Y | Y | N |
| **WISCONSIN** | | | | | | |
| 1 **Ryan** | N | Y | Y | N | N | Y |
| 2 Baldwin | Y | N | N | Y | Y | N |
| 3 Kind | Y | N | N | Y | Y | Y |
| 4 Moore | Y | Y | ? | Y | Y | N |
| 5 **Sensenbrenner** | N | Y | Y | N | N | Y |
| 6 **Petri** | N | Y | Y | Y | N | Y |
| 7 Obey | Y | N | N | Y | Y | N |
| 8 **Green** | N | N | Y | N | N | Y |
| **WYOMING** | | | | | | |
| AL **Cubin** | N | Y | Y | Y | N | Y |

# IN THE HOUSE | By Vote Number

**308.** HR 3010. Fiscal 2006 Labor-HHS-Education Appropriations/ **AmeriCorps Funding.** Price, R-Ga., amendment that would add $70 million to the Teacher Incentive Fund, offset by a cut in operations funding for AmeriCorps grants. Rejected 102-298: R 101-114; D 1-183 (ND 0-138, SD 1-45); I 0-1. June 24, 2005.

**309.** HR 3010. Fiscal 2006 Labor-HHS-Education Appropriations/ **United Airlines Pensions.** Miller, D-Calif., amendment that would prohibit the use of funds to terminate the United Airlines employees' pension plan. Adopted 219-185: R 31-185; D 187-0 (ND 140-0, SD 47-0); I 1-0. June 24, 2005.

**310.** HR 3010. Fiscal 2006 Labor-HHS-Education Appropriations/ **Medicaid Commission.** Brown, D-Ohio, amendment that would prohibit the use of funds in the bill for the operations of the Medicaid Commission. Rejected 170-237: R 1-218; D 168-19 (ND 128-12, SD 40-7); I 1-0. June 24, 2005.

**311.** HR 3010. Fiscal 2006 Labor-HHS-Education Appropriations/ **Social Security Numbers.** Filner, D-Calif., amendment that would prohibit the use of funds in the bill to place Social Security numbers on identification cards issued to Medicare beneficiaries. Adopted 314-94: R 128-92; D 185-2 (ND 138-2, SD 47-0); I 1-0. June 24, 2005.

**312.** HR 3010. Fiscal 2006 Labor-HHS-Education Appropriations/ **Impotence Prescription Drugs.** King, R-Iowa, amendment that would prohibit the use of funds in the bill to pay for drugs prescribed for the treatment of impotence. Adopted 285-121: R 185-33; D 100-87 (ND 68-72, SD 32-15); I 0-1. June 24, 2005.

**313.** HR 3010. Fiscal 2006 Labor-HHS-Education Appropriations/ **Discretionary Spending Cut.** Hefley, R-Colo., amendment that would reduce discretionary spending in the bill by 1 percent. Rejected 84-323: R 82-137; D 2-185 (ND 1-139, SD 1-46); I 0-1. June 24, 2005.

**314.** HR 3010. Fiscal 2006 Labor-HHS-Education Appropriations/ **Corporation for Public Broadcasting Content.** Hinchey, D-N.Y., amendment that would prohibit the use of funds by any federal department, agency, officer or employee to exercise any direction, supervision, or control over the content or distribution of public telecommunications programs and services. Rejected 187-218: R 3-216; D 183-2 (ND 137-2, SD 46-0); I 1-0. June 24, 2005.

**315.** HR 3010. Fiscal 2006 Labor-HHS-Education Appropriations/ **Tribal Labor Standards.** Hayworth, R-Ariz., amendment that would prohibit the use of funds in the bill for the National Labor Relations Board to exert jurisdiction over tribally owned or operated enterprises on tribal land. Rejected 146-256: R 142-74; D 4-181 (ND 3-135, SD 1-46); I 0-1. June 24, 2005.

| | 308 | 309 | 310 | 311 | 312 | 313 | 314 | 315 |
|---|---|---|---|---|---|---|---|---|
| **ALABAMA** | | | | | | | | |
| 1 Bonner | N | N | N | Y | Y | N | N | Y |
| 2 Everett | N | N | N | Y | Y | N | N | Y |
| 3 Rogers | ? | ? | ? | ? | ? | ? | ? | ? |
| 4 Aderholt | N | N | N | Y | Y | N | N | Y |
| 5 Cramer | N | Y | N | Y | Y | N | Y | N |
| 6 Bachus | N | N | N | N | N | Y | N | Y |
| 7 Davis | N | Y | N | Y | Y | N | Y | N |
| **ALASKA** | | | | | | | | |
| AL Young | N | N | N | Y | N | N | N | N |
| **ARIZONA** | | | | | | | | |
| 1 Renzi | Y | N | N | Y | Y | N | N | Y |
| 2 Franks | Y | N | N | Y | Y | N | Y | N |
| 3 Shadegg | N | N | N | Y | Y | N | N | Y |
| 4 Pastor | N | Y | Y | N | N | Y | N | Y |
| 5 Hayworth | N | N | N | Y | Y | N | N | Y |
| 6 Flake | Y | N | N | Y | Y | N | Y | Y |
| 7 Grijalva | N | Y | Y | Y | N | N | Y | N |
| 8 Kolbe | N | N | N | Y | N | N | N | Y |
| **ARKANSAS** | | | | | | | | |
| 1 Berry | N | Y | Y | Y | Y | N | Y | N |
| 2 Snyder | N | Y | Y | Y | N | N | Y | N |
| 3 Boozman | ? | ? | ? | ? | ? | ? | ? | ? |
| 4 Ross | N | Y | Y | Y | Y | N | Y | N |
| **CALIFORNIA** | | | | | | | | |
| 1 Thompson | N | Y | Y | Y | Y | N | Y | N |
| 2 Herger | Y | N | N | Y | Y | N | Y | Y |
| 3 Lungren | Y | N | N | Y | Y | Y | N | Y |
| 4 Doolittle | N | N | N | Y | Y | N | N | Y |
| 5 Matsui, D. | N | Y | Y | Y | N | N | Y | N |
| 6 Woolsey | N | Y | Y | N | N | N | Y | N |
| 7 Miller, George | N | Y | Y | N | N | N | Y | N |
| 8 Pelosi | N | Y | Y | Y | N | N | Y | N |
| 9 Lee | N | Y | Y | N | N | N | Y | N |
| 10 Tauscher | N | Y | Y | N | N | N | Y | N |
| 11 Pombo | Y | N | N | Y | Y | N | N | N |
| 12 Lantos | N | Y | Y | Y | Y | N | Y | N |
| 13 Stark | N | Y | Y | Y | N | N | Y | N |
| 14 Eshoo | N | Y | Y | Y | N | N | Y | N |
| 15 Honda | ? | Y | Y | Y | N | N | Y | N |
| 16 Lofgren | N | Y | Y | Y | N | N | Y | N |
| 17 Farr | N | Y | Y | Y | N | N | Y | N |
| 18 Cardoza | N | Y | Y | Y | N | N | Y | N |
| 19 Radanovich | Y | N | N | Y | N | N | N | Y |
| 20 Costa | N | Y | Y | Y | Y | N | Y | N |
| 21 Nunes | N | N | N | Y | ? | ? | ? | ? |
| 22 Thomas | N | N | N | N | N | N | N | N |
| 23 Capps | N | Y | Y | Y | N | N | Y | N |
| 24 Gallegly | Y | N | N | Y | Y | N | N | Y |
| 25 McKeon | Y | N | N | Y | Y | N | N | Y |
| 26 Dreier | N | N | N | Y | Y | N | N | Y |
| 27 Sherman | N | Y | Y | Y | N | N | N | N |
| 28 Berman | N | Y | Y | N | N | N | Y | N |
| 29 Schiff | N | Y | Y | Y | Y | N | Y | N |
| 30 Waxman | N | Y | Y | Y | N | N | Y | N |
| 31 Becerra | – | + | + | + | + | – | + | – |
| 32 Solis | N | Y | Y | Y | N | N | Y | N |
| 33 Watson | N | Y | Y | Y | N | N | Y | ? |
| 34 Roybal-Allard | N | Y | Y | Y | N | N | Y | N |
| 35 Waters | N | Y | Y | Y | N | N | Y | N |
| 36 Harman | ? | ? | ? | ? | ? | ? | ? | ? |
| 37 Millender-McD. | N | Y | Y | Y | N | N | Y | N |
| 38 Napolitano | N | Y | Y | Y | N | N | Y | N |
| 39 Sánchez, Linda | N | Y | Y | Y | N | N | Y | N |
| 40 Royce | Y | N | N | Y | Y | N | N | Y |
| 41 Lewis | N | N | N | Y | N | N | N | N |
| 42 Miller, Gary | Y | N | N | Y | N | N | Y | Y |
| 43 Baca | N | Y | Y | Y | N | Y | N | ? |
| 44 Calvert | Y | N | N | Y | N | N | N | Y |
| 45 Bono | N | Y | N | N | N | N | Y | N |
| 46 Rohrabacher | Y | N | N | Y | N | N | Y | Y |
| 47 Sanchez, Loretta | N | Y | Y | Y | N | N | Y | N |
| 48 Cox | Y | ? | N | Y | Y | N | N | Y |
| 49 Issa | N | N | N | Y | Y | N | N | Y |

| | 308 | 309 | 310 | 311 | 312 | 313 | 314 | 315 |
|---|---|---|---|---|---|---|---|---|
| 50 Cunningham | N | N | N | Y | N | N | N | Y |
| 51 Filner | N | Y | Y | Y | N | N | Y | N |
| 52 Hunter | N | N | N | Y | N | N | N | Y |
| 53 Davis | N | Y | Y | Y | N | N | Y | N |
| **COLORADO** | | | | | | | | |
| 1 DeGette | N | Y | Y | Y | N | N | Y | N |
| 2 Udall | N | Y | Y | Y | N | N | Y | N |
| 3 Salazar | N | Y | N | Y | Y | N | Y | N |
| 4 Musgrave | Y | N | N | Y | Y | Y | N | Y |
| 5 Hefley | Y | N | N | Y | Y | Y | N | Y |
| 6 Tancredo | Y | Y | N | Y | Y | Y | N | Y |
| 7 Beauprez | Y | N | N | Y | Y | Y | N | Y |
| **CONNECTICUT** | | | | | | | | |
| 1 Larson | N | Y | Y | Y | N | N | Y | N |
| 2 Simmons | – | + | – | + | – | – | – | N |
| 3 DeLauro | N | Y | Y | Y | Y | N | Y | N |
| 4 Shays | N | Y | N | N | N | Y | N | Y |
| 5 Johnson | Y | N | N | N | N | N | N | N |
| **DELAWARE** | | | | | | | | |
| AL Castle | N | N | N | Y | Y | N | N | Y |
| **FLORIDA** | | | | | | | | |
| 1 Miller | Y | Y | N | Y | Y | Y | N | Y |
| 2 Boyd | ? | ? | ? | ? | ? | ? | ? | ? |
| 3 Brown | N | Y | Y | Y | Y | N | Y | N |
| 4 Crenshaw | N | N | N | N | N | N | N | N |
| 5 Brown-Waite | Y | N | Y | Y | N | N | Y | N |
| 6 Stearns | Y | Y | N | Y | Y | N | N | N |
| 7 Mica | Y | N | N | Y | N | N | Y | N |
| 8 Keller | Y | N | N | Y | N | N | N | Y |
| 9 Bilirakis | Y | Y | N | N | Y | N | N | + |
| 10 Young | ? | ? | ? | ? | ? | ? | ? | N |
| 11 Davis | N | Y | Y | Y | N | N | Y | N |
| 12 Putnam | N | N | N | Y | N | N | Y | N |
| 13 Harris | N | N | N | Y | N | Y | N | ? |
| 14 Mack | Y | N | N | Y | N | N | N | Y |
| 15 Weldon | Y | N | Y | Y | Y | N | N | N |
| 16 Foley | Y | N | N | Y | N | N | Y | N |
| 17 Meek | N | Y | Y | Y | N | N | Y | N |
| 18 Ros-Lehtinen | N | N | N | Y | N | N | N | ? |
| 19 Wexler | N | Y | Y | Y | N | N | Y | N |
| 20 Wasserman-Schultz | N | Y | Y | Y | N | N | Y | N |
| 21 Diaz-Balart, L. | Y | N | N | N | Y | N | N | Y |
| 22 Shaw | N | N | N | Y | N | N | Y | N |
| 23 Hastings | N | Y | Y | Y | N | N | Y | N |
| 24 Feeney | Y | N | Y | Y | N | N | Y | Y |
| 25 Diaz-Balart, M. | N | N | N | Y | Y | N | N | Y |
| **GEORGIA** | | | | | | | | |
| 1 Kingston | ? | ? | N | N | Y | N | N | Y |
| 2 Bishop | N | Y | N | Y | Y | N | Y | N |
| 3 Marshall | N | N | N | Y | Y | N | N | N |
| 4 McKinney | N | Y | Y | Y | N | N | Y | N |
| 5 Lewis | ? | ? | ? | ? | ? | ? | ? | ? |
| 6 Price | Y | N | N | Y | N | N | Y | Y |
| 7 Linder | Y | N | N | Y | Y | Y | N | Y |
| 8 Westmoreland | Y | N | N | Y | Y | Y | N | Y |
| 9 Norwood | Y | N | N | Y | N | N | N | N |
| 10 Deal | Y | N | N | Y | Y | N | N | Y |
| 11 Gingrey | Y | N | Y | Y | Y | Y | N | Y |
| 12 Barrow | N | Y | Y | Y | Y | N | Y | N |
| 13 Scott | N | Y | Y | Y | N | N | Y | N |
| **HAWAII** | | | | | | | | |
| 1 Abercrombie | N | Y | Y | Y | N | N | Y | N |
| 2 Case | N | Y | Y | Y | N | N | Y | N |
| **IDAHO** | | | | | | | | |
| 1 Otter | Y | Y | N | Y | Y | Y | N | Y |
| 2 Simpson | N | N | N | Y | Y | N | N | Y |
| **ILLINOIS** | | | | | | | | |
| 1 Rush | N | Y | Y | Y | N | N | Y | N |
| 2 Jackson | N | Y | Y | Y | N | N | Y | N |
| 3 Lipinski | N | Y | Y | Y | Y | N | Y | N |
| 4 Gutierrez | ? | ? | ? | ? | ? | ? | ? | ? |
| 5 Emanuel | N | Y | Y | Y | N | N | Y | N |
| 6 Hyde | N | N | Y | Y | N | N | N | N |
| 7 Davis | N | Y | Y | Y | N | N | Y | N |
| 8 Bean | N | N | Y | Y | N | Y | N | N |
| 9 Schakowsky | N | Y | Y | Y | N | N | Y | N |
| 10 Kirk | N | N | N | Y | Y | N | N | N |
| 11 Weller | N | N | N | Y | N | N | N | N |
| 12 Costello | N | Y | Y | Y | Y | N | Y | N |

**KEY**   Republicans   Democrats   *Independents*

| Y | Voted for (yea) | X | Paired against | C | Voted "present" to avoid possible conflict of interest |
|---|---|---|---|---|---|
| # | Paired for | – | Announced against | | |
| + | Announced for | P | Voted "present" | ? | Did not vote or otherwise make a position known |
| N | Voted against (nay) | | | | |

| | 308 | 309 | 310 | 311 | 312 | 313 | 314 | 315 |
|---|---|---|---|---|---|---|---|---|
| 13 **Biggert** | N | N | N | N | Y | N | N | Y |
| 14 **Hastert** | | | | | | | | |
| 15 **Johnson** | N | N | N | Y | Y | N | Y | N |
| 16 **Manzullo** | N | N | N | N | Y | Y | N | N |
| 17 Evans | ? | Y | Y | Y | N | N | Y | N |
| 18 **LaHood** | N | Y | N | Y | Y | N | N | N |
| 19 **Shimkus** | N | Y | Y | Y | Y | Y | N | N |
| **INDIANA** | | | | | | | | |
| 1 Visclosky | N | Y | Y | Y | Y | N | Y | N |
| 2 **Chocola** | Y | N | N | N | Y | Y | N | Y |
| 3 **Souder** | Y | N | N | N | Y | N | N | N |
| 4 **Buyer** | Y | N | N | N | Y | N | Y | Y |
| 5 **Burton** | Y | N | N | N | Y | Y | N | Y |
| 6 **Pence** | Y | N | N | Y | Y | Y | N | Y |
| 7 Carson | N | Y | Y | Y | Y | N | Y | N |
| 8 **Hostettler** | Y | N | N | N | Y | Y | N | Y |
| 9 **Sodrel** | Y | N | N | N | Y | N | N | Y |
| **IOWA** | | | | | | | | |
| 1 **Nussle** | N | N | N | Y | Y | N | N | N |
| 2 **Leach** | N | N | N | Y | Y | N | Y | N |
| 3 Boswell | N | Y | Y | Y | Y | N | Y | N |
| 4 **Latham** | N | N | N | Y | N | N | N | Y |
| 5 **King** | Y | N | N | N | Y | Y | N | Y |
| **KANSAS** | | | | | | | | |
| 1 **Moran** | N | N | N | Y | Y | Y | N | N |
| 2 **Ryun** | Y | N | N | Y | Y | Y | N | Y |
| 3 Moore | N | Y | N | Y | Y | N | Y | N |
| 4 **Tiahrt** | Y | N | N | N | Y | N | N | N |
| **KENTUCKY** | | | | | | | | |
| 1 **Whitfield** | ? | ? | N | N | N | N | N | Y |
| 2 **Lewis** | Y | N | N | Y | Y | Y | N | Y |
| 3 **Northup** | N | N | N | Y | Y | N | N | Y |
| 4 **Davis** | Y | N | N | N | Y | N | N | Y |
| 5 **Rogers** | Y | N | N | Y | Y | N | N | Y |
| 6 Chandler | N | Y | Y | Y | Y | N | Y | N |
| **LOUISIANA** | | | | | | | | |
| 1 **Jindal** | Y | N | N | N | Y | Y | N | Y |
| 2 Jefferson | N | Y | Y | Y | N | N | Y | N |
| 3 Melancon | N | Y | Y | Y | Y | N | Y | N |
| 4 **McCrery** | N | N | N | N | N | N | N | Y |
| 5 **Alexander** | N | N | N | N | Y | N | N | N |
| 6 **Baker** | N | N | N | N | Y | N | N | Y |
| 7 **Boustany** | N | N | N | N | Y | N | N | Y |
| **MAINE** | | | | | | | | |
| 1 Allen | N | Y | Y | Y | Y | N | Y | N |
| 2 Michaud | N | Y | Y | Y | Y | N | Y | N |
| **MARYLAND** | | | | | | | | |
| 1 **Gilchrest** | N | N | N | N | N | N | N | Y |
| 2 Ruppersberger | N | Y | Y | Y | N | N | Y | N |
| 3 Cardin | N | Y | Y | Y | Y | N | Y | N |
| 4 Wynn | N | Y | N | Y | N | N | Y | N |
| 5 Hoyer | N | Y | Y | Y | N | N | Y | N |
| 6 **Bartlett** | ? | ? | ? | ? | ? | Y | N | Y |
| 7 Cummings | N | Y | Y | Y | Y | N | Y | N |
| 8 Van Hollen | N | Y | Y | Y | Y | N | Y | N |
| **MASSACHUSETTS** | | | | | | | | |
| 1 Olver | N | Y | Y | Y | Y | N | Y | N |
| 2 Neal | N | Y | Y | Y | N | N | Y | N |
| 3 McGovern | N | Y | Y | Y | Y | N | Y | N |
| 4 Frank | N | Y | Y | Y | Y | N | Y | N |
| 5 Meehan | N | Y | Y | Y | N | N | Y | N |
| 6 Tierney | N | Y | Y | Y | Y | N | Y | N |
| 7 Markey | N | Y | Y | Y | N | N | Y | N |
| 8 Capuano | N | Y | Y | Y | N | N | Y | N |
| 9 Lynch | N | Y | N | Y | N | N | Y | N |
| 10 Delahunt | ? | ? | ? | ? | ? | ? | ? | ? |
| **MICHIGAN** | | | | | | | | |
| 1 Stupak | N | Y | Y | Y | Y | N | Y | N |
| 2 **Hoekstra** | N | N | N | Y | Y | N | N | N |
| 3 **Ehlers** | N | N | N | N | N | N | N | N |
| 4 **Camp** | N | N | N | Y | Y | N | N | ? |
| 5 Kildee | N | Y | Y | Y | N | N | Y | N |
| 6 **Upton** | N | N | N | Y | Y | N | N | N |
| 7 **Schwarz** | N | N | N | Y | N | N | N | N |
| 8 **Rogers** | Y | N | N | Y | Y | Y | N | Y |
| 9 **Knollenberg** | N | N | N | N | Y | N | N | N |
| 10 **Miller** | N | N | N | Y | Y | N | N | N |
| 11 **McCotter** | N | Y | N | Y | Y | Y | N | Y |
| 12 Levin | N | Y | Y | Y | N | N | Y | N |
| 13 Kilpatrick | N | Y | Y | Y | N | N | Y | N |
| 14 Conyers | N | Y | Y | Y | Y | N | Y | N |
| 15 Dingell | N | Y | Y | Y | Y | N | Y | N |

| | 308 | 309 | 310 | 311 | 312 | 313 | 314 | 315 |
|---|---|---|---|---|---|---|---|---|
| **MINNESOTA** | | | | | | | | |
| 1 **Gutknecht** | Y | N | N | N | Y | Y | N | Y |
| 2 **Kline** | Y | N | N | N | Y | N | N | Y |
| 3 **Ramstad** | Y | N | N | Y | Y | N | N | Y |
| 4 McCollum | N | Y | Y | Y | N | N | Y | N |
| 5 Sabo | N | Y | Y | N | N | N | Y | N |
| 6 **Kennedy** | Y | N | N | Y | Y | N | N | Y |
| 7 Peterson | N | Y | N | Y | Y | N | Y | Y |
| 8 Oberstar | N | Y | Y | Y | Y | N | Y | N |
| **MISSISSIPPI** | | | | | | | | |
| 1 **Wicker** | ? | N | N | Y | Y | N | N | Y |
| 2 Thompson | N | Y | Y | Y | Y | N | Y | N |
| 3 **Pickering** | N | ? | N | Y | Y | N | N | Y |
| 4 Taylor | ? | ? | ? | ? | ? | ? | ? | ? |
| **MISSOURI** | | | | | | | | |
| 1 Clay | N | Y | Y | Y | N | N | Y | ? |
| 2 **Akin** | Y | N | N | N | Y | Y | N | Y |
| 3 Carnahan | N | Y | Y | Y | N | N | Y | N |
| 4 Skelton | N | Y | N | Y | Y | N | Y | N |
| 5 Cleaver | N | Y | Y | Y | Y | N | Y | N |
| 6 **Graves** | Y | N | N | Y | Y | Y | N | N |
| 7 **Blunt** | N | N | N | Y | Y | N | N | ? |
| 8 **Emerson** | Y | N | N | Y | Y | N | N | N |
| 9 **Hulshof** | Y | N | N | N | N | N | N | Y |
| **MONTANA** | | | | | | | | |
| AL **Rehberg** | N | N | N | Y | Y | N | N | Y |
| **NEBRASKA** | | | | | | | | |
| 1 **Fortenberry** | Y | N | N | Y | Y | N | N | Y |
| 2 **Terry** | Y | N | N | Y | Y | Y | N | N |
| 3 **Osborne** | N | N | N | N | N | N | N | N |
| **NEVADA** | | | | | | | | |
| 1 Berkley | N | Y | Y | Y | N | N | Y | N |
| 2 **Gibbons** | Y | Y | N | Y | Y | N | N | N |
| 3 **Porter** | N | N | N | N | Y | N | N | N |
| **NEW HAMPSHIRE** | | | | | | | | |
| 1 **Bradley** | N | N | N | Y | Y | N | N | Y |
| 2 **Bass** | N | N | N | N | Y | Y | N | Y |
| **NEW JERSEY** | | | | | | | | |
| 1 Andrews | ? | ? | ? | ? | ? | ? | ? | ? |
| 2 **LoBiondo** | N | Y | N | Y | Y | N | N | N |
| 3 **Saxton** | N | N | N | N | Y | N | N | N |
| 4 **Smith** | N | Y | N | Y | Y | N | N | N |
| 5 **Garrett** | Y | N | N | Y | Y | Y | N | Y |
| 6 Pallone | N | Y | Y | Y | N | N | Y | N |
| 7 **Ferguson** | N | N | N | Y | Y | N | N | N |
| 8 Pascrell | N | Y | Y | Y | Y | N | Y | N |
| 9 Rothman | N | Y | Y | Y | N | N | Y | N |
| 10 Payne | N | Y | Y | Y | N | N | Y | N |
| 11 **Frelinghuysen** | N | N | N | Y | Y | N | N | Y |
| 12 Holt | N | Y | Y | Y | N | N | Y | N |
| 13 Menendez | N | Y | Y | Y | N | N | Y | N |
| **NEW MEXICO** | | | | | | | | |
| 1 **Wilson** | ? | ? | ? | ? | ? | ? | ? | ? |
| 2 **Pearce** | Y | Y | N | N | Y | N | N | Y |
| 3 Udall | ? | ? | ? | ? | ? | ? | ? | ? |
| **NEW YORK** | | | | | | | | |
| 1 Bishop | N | Y | Y | Y | Y | N | Y | N |
| 2 Israel | N | Y | Y | Y | Y | N | Y | N |
| 3 **King** | N | N | N | Y | N | N | N | N |
| 4 McCarthy | N | Y | Y | Y | Y | N | Y | N |
| 5 Ackerman | N | Y | Y | Y | N | N | Y | N |
| 6 Meeks | ? | ? | ? | ? | ? | ? | ? | ? |
| 7 Crowley | N | Y | Y | Y | Y | N | Y | N |
| 8 Nadler | N | Y | Y | Y | Y | N | Y | N |
| 9 Weiner | N | Y | Y | Y | Y | N | Y | N |
| 10 Towns | ? | ? | ? | ? | ? | ? | ? | N |
| 11 Owens | N | Y | Y | Y | N | N | Y | N |
| 12 Velázquez | N | Y | Y | Y | N | N | Y | N |
| 13 **Fossella** | Y | Y | N | Y | N | Y | N | N |
| 14 Maloney | N | Y | Y | Y | N | N | Y | N |
| 15 Rangel | N | Y | Y | Y | N | N | Y | N |
| 16 Serrano | N | Y | Y | Y | N | N | Y | N |
| 17 Engel | N | Y | Y | Y | N | N | Y | N |
| 18 Lowey | N | Y | Y | Y | N | N | Y | N |
| 19 **Kelly** | Y | N | N | Y | N | N | N | Y |
| 20 **Sweeney** | N | Y | N | N | N | N | N | N |
| 21 McNulty | N | Y | Y | Y | N | N | Y | N |
| 22 Hinchey | N | Y | Y | Y | N | N | Y | N |
| 23 **McHugh** | N | Y | N | Y | N | N | N | N |
| 24 **Boehlert** | N | Y | N | Y | N | N | N | N |
| 25 **Walsh** | N | N | N | Y | N | N | N | N |
| 26 **Reynolds** | N | N | N | Y | Y | N | N | N |
| 27 Higgins | N | Y | Y | Y | Y | N | Y | N |
| 28 Slaughter | N | Y | N | Y | Y | N | Y | ? |
| 29 **Kuhl** | N | Y | N | Y | Y | N | N | N |

| | 308 | 309 | 310 | 311 | 312 | 313 | 314 | 315 |
|---|---|---|---|---|---|---|---|---|
| **NORTH CAROLINA** | | | | | | | | |
| 1 Butterfield | N | Y | Y | Y | N | N | Y | N |
| 2 Etheridge | N | Y | Y | Y | Y | N | Y | N |
| 3 **Jones** | ? | ? | ? | ? | ? | ? | ? | ? |
| 4 Price | N | Y | Y | Y | N | N | Y | N |
| 5 **Foxx** | Y | N | N | Y | Y | Y | N | Y |
| 6 **Coble** | Y | N | N | N | Y | Y | N | Y |
| 7 McIntyre | N | Y | N | Y | Y | N | Y | N |
| 8 **Hayes** | Y | N | N | N | Y | N | N | Y |
| 9 **Myrick** | N | N | N | N | Y | Y | N | N |
| 10 **McHenry** | Y | N | N | N | Y | Y | N | Y |
| 11 **Taylor** | ? | N | N | N | Y | N | N | Y |
| 12 Watt | N | Y | Y | Y | N | N | Y | N |
| 13 Miller | N | Y | Y | Y | N | N | Y | N |
| **NORTH DAKOTA** | | | | | | | | |
| AL Pomeroy | N | Y | N | Y | Y | N | Y | Y |
| **OHIO** | | | | | | | | |
| 1 **Chabot** | ? | N | N | Y | Y | Y | N | Y |
| 2 Vacant | | | | | | | | |
| 3 **Turner** | N | N | N | Y | Y | N | N | N |
| 4 **Oxley** | N | N | N | N | Y | N | N | N |
| 5 **Gillmor** | N | N | N | Y | Y | N | N | N |
| 6 Strickland | N | Y | Y | Y | Y | N | Y | N |
| 7 **Hobson** | N | N | N | N | Y | N | N | N |
| 8 **Boehner** | N | N | N | Y | Y | N | N | Y |
| 9 Kaptur | N | Y | Y | Y | Y | N | ? | N |
| 10 Kucinich | N | Y | Y | Y | Y | N | Y | N |
| 11 Jones | N | Y | Y | Y | Y | N | Y | N |
| 12 **Tiberi** | N | N | N | N | Y | N | N | Y |
| 13 Brown | N | Y | Y | Y | N | N | Y | N |
| 14 **LaTourette** | N | Y | N | N | ? | ? | ? | ? |
| 15 **Pryce** | N | N | N | N | Y | N | N | N |
| 16 **Regula** | N | N | N | N | Y | N | N | N |
| 17 Ryan | N | Y | Y | Y | Y | N | Y | ? |
| 18 **Ney** | Y | N | N | Y | Y | N | N | Y |
| **OKLAHOMA** | | | | | | | | |
| 1 **Sullivan** | Y | N | N | N | Y | Y | N | Y |
| 2 Boren | N | Y | N | Y | Y | N | Y | Y |
| 3 **Lucas** | N | N | N | Y | Y | N | N | Y |
| 4 **Cole** | N | N | N | Y | Y | N | N | Y |
| 5 **Istook** | Y | N | N | N | Y | N | N | Y |
| **OREGON** | | | | | | | | |
| 1 Wu | N | Y | Y | Y | Y | N | Y | N |
| 2 **Walden** | N | N | N | N | N | N | N | Y |
| 3 Blumenauer | N | Y | Y | Y | N | N | Y | N |
| 4 DeFazio | N | Y | Y | Y | Y | N | Y | N |
| 5 Hooley | N | Y | Y | Y | N | N | Y | N |
| **PENNSYLVANIA** | | | | | | | | |
| 1 Brady | N | Y | Y | Y | Y | N | Y | N |
| 2 Fattah | ? | ? | ? | ? | ? | ? | ? | ? |
| 3 **English** | Y | N | N | Y | Y | N | N | Y |
| 4 **Hart** | N | N | N | N | Y | N | N | Y |
| 5 **Peterson** | N | N | N | Y | Y | N | N | N |
| 6 **Gerlach** | N | Y | N | Y | Y | N | N | N |
| 7 **Weldon** | N | N | N | Y | Y | N | N | N |
| 8 **Fitzpatrick** | N | Y | N | Y | Y | N | N | N |
| 9 **Shuster** | N | N | N | N | Y | N | N | Y |
| 10 **Sherwood** | N | N | N | Y | Y | N | N | N |
| 11 Kanjorski | N | Y | Y | N | Y | N | Y | N |
| 12 Murtha | N | Y | Y | Y | Y | N | Y | N |
| 13 Schwartz | N | Y | Y | Y | Y | N | Y | N |
| 14 Doyle | N | Y | Y | Y | Y | N | Y | N |
| 15 **Dent** | N | N | N | Y | Y | N | N | N |
| 16 **Pitts** | Y | N | N | N | Y | Y | N | Y |
| 17 Holden | N | Y | Y | Y | Y | N | Y | N |
| 18 **Murphy** | Y | N | N | Y | Y | N | N | N |
| 19 **Platts** | N | N | N | Y | Y | N | N | N |
| **RHODE ISLAND** | | | | | | | | |
| 1 Kennedy | N | Y | Y | Y | N | N | Y | N |
| 2 Langevin | N | Y | Y | Y | N | N | Y | N |
| **SOUTH CAROLINA** | | | | | | | | |
| 1 **Brown** | N | N | N | N | Y | N | N | Y |
| 2 **Wilson** | Y | N | N | N | Y | Y | N | Y |
| 3 **Barrett** | Y | N | N | Y | Y | Y | N | Y |
| 4 **Inglis** | Y | N | N | N | N | Y | N | N |
| 5 Spratt | N | Y | Y | Y | Y | N | Y | N |
| 6 Clyburn | N | Y | Y | Y | Y | N | Y | N |
| **SOUTH DAKOTA** | | | | | | | | |
| AL Herseth | N | Y | N | Y | Y | N | Y | Y |
| **TENNESSEE** | | | | | | | | |
| 1 **Jenkins** | N | N | N | Y | Y | Y | N | Y |
| 2 **Duncan** | N | N | N | Y | Y | Y | N | Y |

| | 308 | 309 | 310 | 311 | 312 | 313 | 314 | 315 |
|---|---|---|---|---|---|---|---|---|
| 3 **Wamp** | N | N | N | Y | Y | N | N | Y |
| 4 Davis | N | Y | Y | Y | Y | N | Y | N |
| 5 Cooper | N | Y | Y | Y | Y | N | Y | N |
| 6 Gordon | N | Y | N | Y | Y | N | Y | N |
| 7 **Blackburn** | Y | N | N | Y | Y | Y | N | Y |
| 8 Tanner | N | Y | Y | Y | Y | Y | Y | N |
| 9 Ford | N | Y | Y | Y | Y | N | Y | N |
| **TEXAS** | | | | | | | | |
| 1 **Gohmert** | ? | ? | ? | ? | ? | ? | ? | ? |
| 2 **Poe** | N | Y | N | Y | Y | Y | N | N |
| 3 **Johnson, S.** | N | N | N | Y | Y | N | N | N |
| 4 **Hall** | Y | N | N | Y | Y | N | N | Y |
| 5 **Hensarling** | N | N | N | Y | Y | Y | N | Y |
| 6 **Barton** | N | N | N | Y | N | Y | N | Y |
| 7 **Culberson** | Y | N | N | Y | Y | N | N | Y |
| 8 **Brady** | Y | N | N | N | Y | Y | N | Y |
| 9 Green, A. | N | Y | Y | Y | Y | N | Y | N |
| 10 **McCaul** | Y | N | N | Y | Y | N | N | Y |
| 11 **Conaway** | N | N | N | Y | Y | N | N | Y |
| 12 **Granger** | N | N | N | Y | Y | N | N | N |
| 13 **Thornberry** | Y | N | N | Y | Y | Y | N | Y |
| 14 **Paul** | Y | Y | N | Y | Y | Y | N | Y |
| 15 Hinojosa | N | Y | Y | Y | Y | N | Y | N |
| 16 Reyes | ? | ? | ? | ? | ? | ? | ? | ? |
| 17 Edwards | N | Y | Y | Y | Y | N | Y | N |
| 18 Jackson-Lee | N | Y | Y | Y | N | N | Y | N |
| 19 **Neugebauer** | Y | N | N | Y | Y | N | N | Y |
| 20 Gonzalez | N | Y | Y | Y | N | N | Y | N |
| 21 **Smith** | Y | N | N | N | Y | N | N | Y |
| 22 **DeLay** | N | N | N | N | Y | N | N | Y |
| 23 **Bonilla** | N | N | N | N | ? | N | N | N |
| 24 **Marchant** | Y | N | ? | Y | Y | N | N | Y |
| 25 Doggett | N | Y | Y | Y | Y | N | Y | N |
| 26 **Burgess** | N | N | N | Y | Y | N | N | Y |
| 27 Ortiz | N | Y | Y | Y | N | N | Y | N |
| 28 Cuellar | Y | Y | Y | Y | Y | N | Y | N |
| 29 Green, G. | N | Y | Y | Y | Y | N | Y | N |
| 30 Johnson, E. | N | Y | Y | Y | Y | N | Y | N |
| 31 **Carter** | Y | N | N | Y | Y | N | N | Y |
| 32 **Sessions** | Y | N | N | Y | Y | Y | N | Y |
| **UTAH** | | | | | | | | |
| 1 **Bishop** | N | N | N | Y | Y | Y | N | N |
| 2 Matheson | N | Y | N | Y | Y | N | Y | N |
| 3 **Cannon** | Y | N | N | Y | Y | Y | N | N |
| **VERMONT** | | | | | | | | |
| AL *Sanders* | N | Y | Y | Y | N | N | Y | N |
| **VIRGINIA** | | | | | | | | |
| 1 **Davis, J.** | Y | N | N | Y | Y | Y | N | Y |
| 2 **Drake** | N | N | N | Y | Y | N | N | N |
| 3 Scott | N | Y | Y | Y | N | N | ? | N |
| 4 **Forbes** | Y | N | N | Y | Y | N | N | Y |
| 5 **Goode** | Y | Y | N | Y | Y | N | N | Y |
| 6 **Goodlatte** | Y | N | N | Y | Y | Y | N | Y |
| 7 **Cantor** | N | N | N | N | Y | N | N | Y |
| 8 Moran | N | Y | Y | Y | Y | N | Y | N |
| 9 Boucher | N | Y | Y | Y | Y | N | Y | N |
| 10 **Wolf** | N | Y | N | N | Y | N | N | N |
| 11 **Davis, T.** | ? | ? | ? | ? | ? | ? | ? | ? |
| **WASHINGTON** | | | | | | | | |
| 1 Inslee | N | Y | Y | Y | N | N | Y | N |
| 2 Larsen | N | Y | Y | Y | Y | N | Y | N |
| 3 Baird | N | Y | Y | Y | N | N | Y | N |
| 4 **Hastings** | N | N | N | N | Y | N | N | Y |
| 5 **McMorris** | N | N | N | Y | Y | N | N | Y |
| 6 Dicks | N | Y | Y | Y | N | N | Y | N |
| 7 McDermott | N | Y | Y | Y | N | N | Y | N |
| 8 **Reichert** | N | Y | N | Y | Y | N | N | Y |
| 9 Smith | N | Y | Y | Y | Y | N | Y | N |
| **WEST VIRGINIA** | | | | | | | | |
| 1 Mollohan | ? | ? | ? | ? | ? | ? | ? | N |
| 2 **Capito** | ? | ? | ? | ? | ? | ? | ? | ? |
| 3 Rahall | – | + | + | + | + | – | + | N |
| **WISCONSIN** | | | | | | | | |
| 1 **Ryan** | Y | N | N | Y | Y | Y | N | Y |
| 2 Baldwin | N | Y | Y | Y | Y | N | Y | N |
| 3 Kind | N | Y | N | Y | Y | N | Y | N |
| 4 Moore | N | Y | Y | Y | N | N | Y | N |
| 5 **Sensenbrenner** | Y | Y | N | Y | Y | Y | N | N |
| 6 **Petri** | Y | N | N | Y | Y | Y | N | N |
| 7 Obey | N | Y | Y | Y | Y | N | Y | N |
| 8 **Green** | Y | Y | N | Y | Y | N | N | Y |
| **WYOMING** | | | | | | | | |
| AL **Cubin** | N | N | N | Y | N | Y | N | N |

# IN THE HOUSE | By Vote Number

**316.** HR 3010. Fiscal 2006 Labor-HHS-Education Appropriations/ **Student Loans.** Van Hollen, D-Md., amendment that would prohibit the use of funds in the bill to pay certain lenders a rate of return on student loans that is 6 percent higher than the return lenders receive on regular student loans. Adopted 224-178: R 42-175; D 181-3 (ND 135-2, SD 46-1); I 1-0. June 24, 2005.

**317.** HR 3010. Fiscal 2006 Labor-HHS-Education Appropriations/ **Mental Health Screening.** Paul, R-Texas, amendment that would prohibit the use of funds in the bill to create or implement any universal mental health screening program. Rejected 97-304: R 93-124; D 4-179 (ND 2-135, SD 2-44); I 0-1. June 24, 2005.

**318.** HR 3010. Fiscal 2006 Labor-HHS-Education Appropriations/ **Wal-Mart Labor Agreement.** DeLauro, D-Conn., amendment that would prohibit use of funds in the bill to carry out a settlement agreement between the Labor Department and Wal-Mart, which would provide Wal-Mart with 15 days' advance notice of any investigation or audit of possible child labor violations. Rejected 165-234: R 3-212; D 161-22 (ND 129-8, SD 32-14); I 1-0. June 24, 2005.

**319.** HR 3010. Fiscal 2006 Labor-HHS-Education Appropriations/ **Beneficiary Personal Information.** Hinchey, D-N.Y., amendment that would prohibit the use of funds in the bill to distribute the personal information of Medicare and Medicaid beneficiaries to private companies for marketing purposes. Rejected 192-210: R 9-207; D 182-3 (ND 137-1, SD 45-2); I 1-0. A "nay" was a vote in support of the president's position. June 24, 2005.

**320.** HR 3010. Fiscal 2006 Labor-HHS-Education Appropriations/ **Recommit.** Obey, D-Wis., motion to recommit the bill to the Appropriations Committee. Motion rejected 185-216: R 0-216; D 184-0 (ND 138-0, SD 46-0); I 1-0. June 24, 2005.

**321.** HR 3010. Fiscal 2006 Labor-HHS-Education Appropriations/ **Passage.** Passage of the bill that would appropriate $601.6 billion in fiscal 2006, including $143 billion in discretionary spending, for the Labor, Health and Human Services, and Education departments and related agencies. The bill would provide $63.7 billion for the Education Department, $14.8 billion for the Labor Department, and $473.8 billion for Health and Human Services. Passed 250-151: R 206-10; D 44-140 (ND 32-106, SD 12-34); I 0-1. June 24, 2005.

**322.** H Res 199. Srebrenica Massacre Remembrance/Adoption. Smith, R-N.J., motion to suspend the rules and adopt the resolution that would express the sense of the House that the victims of the massacre at Srebrenica should be honored and remembered and that the actions of the Serbian forces in Bosnia between 1992 and 1995 meet the criteria of genocide. Motion agreed to 370-1: R 199-1; D 170-0 (ND 128-0, SD 42-0); I 1-0. A two-thirds majority of those present and voting (248 in this case) is required for adoption under suspension of the rules. June 27, 2005.

**323.** H Con Res 155. Albania Parliamentary Elections/Adoption. Smith, R-N.J., motion to suspend the rules and adopt the concurrent resolution that would urge the government of Albania to conduct fair elections in which observers are given unobstructed access to all aspects of the election process. Motion agreed to 369-1: R 200-1; D 168-0 (ND 126-0, SD 42-0); I 1-0. A two-thirds majority of those present and voting (247 in this case) is required for adoption under suspension of the rules. June 27, 2005.

| | 316 | 317 | 318 | 319 | 320 | 321 | 322 | 323 |
|---|---|---|---|---|---|---|---|---|
| **ALABAMA** | | | | | | | | |
| 1 Bonner | N | N | N | N | N | Y | Y | Y |
| 2 Everett | N | Y | N | N | N | Y | Y | Y |
| 3 Rogers | ? | ? | ? | ? | ? | ? | Y | Y |
| 4 Aderholt | N | Y | N | N | N | Y | Y | Y |
| 5 Cramer | Y | N | N | Y | Y | Y | Y | Y |
| 6 Bachus | N | N | N | N | N | Y | Y | Y |
| 7 Davis | Y | N | Y | Y | Y | N | Y | Y |
| **ALASKA** | | | | | | | | |
| AL Young | N | N | N | N | N | Y | Y | Y |
| **ARIZONA** | | | | | | | | |
| 1 Renzi | Y | N | N | N | N | Y | Y | Y |
| 2 Franks | N | Y | N | N | N | N | Y | Y |
| 3 Shadegg | Y | Y | N | N | N | Y | Y | Y |
| 4 Pastor | Y | N | Y | Y | Y | N | Y | Y |
| 5 Hayworth | N | N | N | N | N | Y | Y | Y |
| 6 Flake | N | Y | N | N | N | N | Y | Y |
| 7 Grijalva | Y | N | Y | Y | Y | N | Y | Y |
| 8 Kolbe | N | N | N | N | N | Y | Y | Y |
| **ARKANSAS** | | | | | | | | |
| 1 Berry | N | N | N | Y | Y | N | Y | Y |
| 2 Snyder | Y | N | N | Y | N | Y | Y | Y |
| 3 Boozman | ? | ? | ? | ? | ? | ? | Y | Y |
| 4 Ross | Y | N | N | Y | Y | N | ? | ? |
| **CALIFORNIA** | | | | | | | | |
| 1 Thompson | Y | N | N | Y | Y | Y | Y | Y |
| 2 Herger | N | Y | N | N | N | Y | Y | Y |
| 3 Lungren | N | N | N | N | N | Y | Y | Y |
| 4 Doolittle | N | N | N | N | N | Y | Y | Y |
| 5 Matsui, D. | Y | N | Y | Y | Y | Y | + | + |
| 6 Woolsey | Y | N | Y | Y | Y | N | Y | Y |
| 7 Miller, George | Y | N | Y | Y | Y | N | Y | Y |
| 8 Pelosi | Y | N | Y | Y | Y | N | Y | Y |
| 9 Lee | Y | N | Y | Y | Y | N | Y | Y |
| 10 Tauscher | Y | N | Y | Y | Y | N | Y | Y |
| 11 Pombo | N | N | N | N | N | Y | Y | Y |
| 12 Lantos | Y | N | Y | Y | Y | N | Y | Y |
| 13 Stark | Y | N | Y | Y | Y | N | ? | ? |
| 14 Eshoo | Y | N | Y | Y | Y | N | Y | Y |
| 15 Honda | Y | N | Y | Y | Y | N | ? | ? |
| 16 Lofgren | Y | N | Y | Y | Y | N | Y | Y |
| 17 Farr | Y | N | Y | Y | Y | Y | Y | Y |
| 18 Cardoza | Y | N | Y | Y | Y | N | Y | Y |
| 19 Radanovich | N | N | N | N | N | Y | Y | Y |
| 20 Costa | Y | N | ? | Y | Y | N | Y | Y |
| 21 Nunes | ? | ? | ? | ? | ? | ? | Y | Y |
| 22 Thomas | ? | N | N | N | N | Y | Y | Y |
| 23 Capps | Y | N | Y | Y | Y | N | Y | Y |
| 24 Gallegly | N | Y | N | N | N | Y | Y | Y |
| 25 McKeon | N | N | N | N | N | Y | Y | Y |
| 26 Dreier | N | N | N | N | N | Y | Y | Y |
| 27 Sherman | Y | N | Y | Y | Y | N | Y | Y |
| 28 Berman | Y | N | Y | ? | ? | Y | Y | Y |
| 29 Schiff | Y | N | Y | Y | Y | Y | Y | Y |
| 30 Waxman | Y | N | Y | Y | Y | N | Y | Y |
| 31 Becerra | + | – | + | + | + | – | Y | Y |
| 32 Solis | Y | N | Y | Y | Y | N | Y | Y |
| 33 Watson | ? | ? | ? | ? | ? | ? | Y | Y |
| 34 Roybal-Allard | Y | N | Y | Y | Y | N | Y | Y |
| 35 Waters | Y | N | Y | Y | Y | N | Y | Y |
| 36 Harman | ? | ? | ? | ? | ? | ? | Y | Y |
| 37 Millender-McD. | Y | N | Y | Y | Y | N | Y | Y |
| 38 Napolitano | Y | N | Y | Y | Y | N | Y | Y |
| 39 Sánchez, Linda | Y | N | Y | Y | Y | N | Y | Y |
| 40 Royce | N | Y | N | N | N | Y | Y | Y |
| 41 Lewis | N | N | N | N | N | Y | Y | Y |
| 42 Miller, Gary | N | Y | N | N | N | Y | Y | Y |
| 43 Baca | ? | ? | ? | ? | ? | ? | Y | Y |
| 44 Calvert | N | N | N | N | N | Y | Y | Y |
| 45 Bono | N | N | N | N | N | Y | Y | Y |
| 46 Rohrabacher | N | Y | N | N | N | Y | ? | ? |
| 47 Sanchez, Loretta | N | Y | Y | Y | Y | N | Y | Y |
| 48 Cox | N | N | N | N | N | Y | Y | Y |
| 49 Issa | N | N | N | N | N | Y | Y | Y |
| **50 Cunningham** | N | N | N | N | Y | Y | Y | |
| 51 Filner | Y | N | Y | Y | Y | N | + | + |
| 52 Hunter | N | N | N | N | N | Y | ? | ? |
| 53 Davis | Y | N | Y | Y | Y | N | Y | Y |
| **COLORADO** | | | | | | | | |
| 1 DeGette | Y | N | N | Y | Y | N | Y | Y |
| 2 Udall | Y | N | Y | Y | Y | N | Y | Y |
| 3 Salazar | Y | N | Y | Y | Y | N | Y | Y |
| 4 Musgrave | N | Y | N | N | N | Y | Y | Y |
| 5 Hefley | N | Y | N | N | N | N | Y | Y |
| 6 Tancredo | N | Y | N | N | N | N | Y | Y |
| 7 Beauprez | N | N | N | N | N | Y | Y | Y |
| **CONNECTICUT** | | | | | | | | |
| 1 Larson | Y | N | Y | Y | Y | N | Y | Y |
| 2 Simmons | Y | N | Y | N | N | N | Y | Y |
| 3 DeLauro | Y | N | Y | Y | Y | N | Y | Y |
| 4 Shays | Y | N | Y | N | N | N | Y | Y |
| 5 Johnson | Y | N | N | N | N | Y | Y | Y |
| **DELAWARE** | | | | | | | | |
| AL Castle | N | N | N | N | N | Y | Y | Y |
| **FLORIDA** | | | | | | | | |
| 1 Miller | N | Y | N | N | N | Y | Y | Y |
| 2 Boyd | ? | ? | ? | ? | ? | ? | Y | Y |
| 3 Brown | Y | N | Y | Y | Y | N | ? | ? |
| 4 Crenshaw | N | N | N | N | N | Y | Y | Y |
| 5 Brown-Waite | Y | Y | N | N | N | Y | Y | Y |
| 6 Stearns | Y | Y | N | N | N | N | Y | Y |
| 7 Mica | N | N | N | N | N | Y | Y | Y |
| 8 Keller | N | N | N | N | N | Y | Y | Y |
| 9 Bilirakis | + | + | – | N | Y | Y | Y | |
| 10 Young | N | N | N | N | N | Y | ? | ? |
| 11 Davis | Y | N | Y | Y | N | N | ? | ? |
| 12 Putnam | N | N | N | N | N | Y | Y | Y |
| 13 Harris | ? | ? | ? | ? | ? | ? | ? | ? |
| 14 Mack | N | Y | N | N | N | Y | Y | Y |
| 15 Weldon | N | Y | N | N | N | Y | Y | Y |
| 16 Foley | Y | N | N | N | N | Y | Y | Y |
| 17 Meek | Y | ? | Y | Y | Y | N | Y | Y |
| 18 Ros-Lehtinen | N | N | N | N | N | Y | Y | Y |
| 19 Wexler | Y | N | Y | Y | Y | N | Y | Y |
| 20 Wasserman-Schultz | Y | N | Y | Y | Y | N | Y | Y |
| 21 Diaz-Balart, L. | N | N | N | N | Y | ? | ? | |
| 22 Shaw | N | N | N | N | N | Y | Y | Y |
| 23 Hastings | Y | N | Y | Y | Y | N | Y | Y |
| 24 Feeney | N | Y | N | N | N | Y | Y | Y |
| 25 Diaz-Balart, M. | N | N | N | N | Y | ? | ? | |
| **GEORGIA** | | | | | | | | |
| 1 Kingston | N | Y | N | N | N | Y | ? | ? |
| 2 Bishop | Y | N | Y | Y | Y | Y | Y | Y |
| 3 Marshall | Y | N | Y | Y | Y | Y | Y | Y |
| 4 McKinney | Y | Y | Y | Y | Y | N | Y | Y |
| 5 Lewis | ? | ? | ? | ? | ? | ? | Y | Y |
| 6 Price | N | Y | N | N | N | Y | Y | Y |
| 7 Linder | N | Y | N | N | N | Y | Y | Y |
| 8 Westmoreland | N | Y | N | N | N | N | Y | Y |
| 9 Norwood | N | Y | N | N | N | Y | Y | Y |
| 10 Deal | N | Y | N | N | N | Y | Y | Y |
| 11 Gingrey | Y | Y | N | N | N | Y | Y | Y |
| 12 Barrow | Y | N | Y | Y | Y | N | Y | Y |
| 13 Scott | Y | N | Y | Y | Y | Y | Y | Y |
| **HAWAII** | | | | | | | | |
| 1 Abercrombie | Y | N | Y | Y | Y | Y | ? | ? |
| 2 Case | Y | N | Y | Y | Y | N | Y | Y |
| **IDAHO** | | | | | | | | |
| 1 Otter | Y | Y | N | Y | N | N | Y | Y |
| 2 Simpson | Y | Y | N | N | N | Y | ? | ? |
| **ILLINOIS** | | | | | | | | |
| 1 Rush | Y | N | Y | Y | Y | Y | Y | Y |
| 2 Jackson | Y | N | Y | Y | N | N | Y | Y |
| 3 Lipinski | Y | N | Y | Y | Y | N | Y | Y |
| 4 Gutierrez | + | – | + | + | + | – | + | + |
| 5 Emanuel | Y | N | Y | Y | Y | N | Y | Y |
| 6 Hyde | N | N | N | N | N | Y | Y | Y |
| 7 Davis | Y | N | Y | Y | Y | Y | Y | Y |
| 8 Bean | Y | N | Y | Y | Y | N | Y | Y |
| 9 Schakowsky | Y | N | Y | Y | Y | N | Y | Y |
| 10 Kirk | N | N | N | N | N | Y | + | + |
| 11 Weller | Y | Y | N | N | N | Y | Y | Y |
| 12 Costello | Y | N | Y | Y | Y | Y | Y | Y |

**KEY**    Republicans    Democrats    *Independents*

| | | |
|---|---|---|
| **Y** Voted for (yea) | **X** Paired against | **C** Voted "present" to avoid possible conflict of interest |
| **#** Paired for | **–** Announced against | |
| **+** Announced for | **P** Voted "present" | **?** Did not vote or otherwise make a position known |
| **N** Voted against (nay) | | |

| | 316 | 317 | 318 | 319 | 320 | 321 | 322 | 323 |
|---|---|---|---|---|---|---|---|---|
| 13 **Biggert** | N | Y | N | N | N | Y | Y | Y |
| 14 **Hastert** | | | | | | | | |
| 15 **Johnson** | N | Y | Y | N | N | Y | Y | Y |
| 16 **Manzullo** | N | Y | N | N | N | Y | Y | Y |
| 17 Evans | Y | N | Y | Y | Y | Y | Y | Y |
| 18 **LaHood** | N | N | N | N | N | Y | Y | Y |
| 19 **Shimkus** | Y | Y | N | N | N | Y | ? | ? |
| **INDIANA** | | | | | | | | |
| 1 Visclosky | Y | N | Y | Y | Y | Y | Y | Y |
| 2 **Chocola** | N | Y | N | N | N | Y | Y | Y |
| 3 **Souder** | N | Y | N | N | N | Y | ? | ? |
| 4 **Buyer** | N | N | N | N | N | Y | Y | Y |
| 5 **Burton** | N | Y | N | N | N | Y | + | + |
| 6 **Pence** | N | Y | N | N | N | Y | Y | Y |
| 7 Carson | Y | N | Y | Y | Y | N | + | + |
| 8 **Hostettler** | N | Y | N | Y | N | Y | Y | Y |
| 9 **Sodrel** | N | Y | N | N | N | Y | ? | ? |
| **IOWA** | | | | | | | | |
| 1 **Nussle** | N | N | N | N | N | Y | Y | Y |
| 2 **Leach** | N | N | N | Y | N | Y | Y | Y |
| 3 Boswell | Y | N | Y | Y | Y | Y | Y | Y |
| 4 **Latham** | N | N | N | N | N | Y | Y | Y |
| 5 **King** | N | Y | N | N | N | Y | Y | Y |
| **KANSAS** | | | | | | | | |
| 1 **Moran** | N | Y | N | N | ? | ? | Y | Y |
| 2 **Ryun** | N | Y | N | N | N | Y | Y | Y |
| 3 Moore | Y | N | N | Y | Y | N | Y | Y |
| 4 **Tiahrt** | N | N | N | N | N | Y | Y | Y |
| **KENTUCKY** | | | | | | | | |
| 1 **Whitfield** | N | N | N | N | N | Y | Y | Y |
| 2 **Lewis** | N | Y | N | N | N | Y | Y | Y |
| 3 **Northup** | Y | N | N | N | N | Y | Y | Y |
| 4 **Davis** | Y | Y | N | N | N | Y | Y | Y |
| 5 **Rogers** | N | N | N | N | N | Y | Y | Y |
| 6 Chandler | Y | N | Y | Y | Y | N | Y | Y |
| **LOUISIANA** | | | | | | | | |
| 1 **Jindal** | N | Y | N | N | N | Y | Y | Y |
| 2 Jefferson | Y | N | ? | Y | Y | N | ? | ? |
| 3 Melancon | Y | N | Y | Y | Y | N | Y | Y |
| 4 **McCrery** | N | N | N | N | N | Y | Y | Y |
| 5 **Alexander** | N | N | N | N | N | Y | Y | Y |
| 6 **Baker** | N | N | N | N | N | Y | Y | Y |
| 7 **Boustany** | N | N | N | N | N | Y | Y | Y |
| **MAINE** | | | | | | | | |
| 1 Allen | Y | N | Y | Y | Y | N | Y | Y |
| 2 Michaud | Y | N | Y | Y | Y | N | ? | ? |
| **MARYLAND** | | | | | | | | |
| 1 **Gilchrest** | N | N | N | N | N | Y | Y | Y |
| 2 Ruppersberger | Y | N | Y | Y | Y | Y | ? | ? |
| 3 Cardin | Y | N | Y | Y | Y | N | ? | ? |
| 4 Wynn | Y | N | N | Y | Y | Y | Y | ? |
| 5 Hoyer | Y | N | Y | Y | Y | N | Y | Y |
| 6 **Bartlett** | N | Y | N | N | N | Y | Y | Y |
| 7 Cummings | Y | N | Y | Y | Y | N | Y | Y |
| 8 Van Hollen | Y | N | Y | Y | Y | N | Y | Y |
| **MASSACHUSETTS** | | | | | | | | |
| 1 Olver | Y | N | Y | Y | Y | N | Y | Y |
| 2 Neal | Y | N | Y | Y | Y | Y | Y | Y |
| 3 McGovern | Y | N | Y | Y | Y | N | Y | Y |
| 4 Frank | Y | N | Y | Y | Y | N | Y | Y |
| 5 Meehan | Y | N | Y | Y | Y | Y | Y | Y |
| 6 Tierney | Y | N | Y | Y | Y | N | Y | Y |
| 7 Markey | Y | N | Y | Y | Y | N | Y | Y |
| 8 Capuano | Y | N | Y | Y | Y | N | Y | Y |
| 9 Lynch | Y | N | Y | Y | Y | N | Y | Y |
| 10 Delahunt | ? | ? | ? | ? | ? | ? | Y | Y |
| **MICHIGAN** | | | | | | | | |
| 1 Stupak | Y | N | Y | Y | Y | N | Y | Y |
| 2 **Hoekstra** | N | Y | N | N | N | Y | Y | Y |
| 3 **Ehlers** | N | N | N | N | N | Y | Y | Y |
| 4 **Camp** | ? | ? | ? | ? | ? | ? | Y | Y |
| 5 Kildee | Y | N | Y | Y | Y | Y | Y | Y |
| 6 **Upton** | Y | Y | N | N | N | Y | Y | Y |
| 7 **Schwarz** | Y | N | N | N | N | Y | Y | Y |
| 8 **Rogers** | Y | Y | N | N | N | Y | Y | Y |
| 9 **Knollenberg** | N | N | N | N | N | Y | Y | Y |
| 10 **Miller** | Y | N | N | N | N | Y | Y | Y |
| 11 **McCotter** | Y | Y | N | N | N | Y | Y | Y |
| 12 Levin | Y | N | Y | Y | Y | N | Y | Y |
| 13 Kilpatrick | Y | N | Y | Y | Y | N | + | + |
| 14 Conyers | Y | N | Y | Y | Y | N | Y | Y |
| 15 Dingell | Y | N | Y | Y | Y | N | Y | Y |

| | 316 | 317 | 318 | 319 | 320 | 321 | 322 | 323 |
|---|---|---|---|---|---|---|---|---|
| **MINNESOTA** | | | | | | | | |
| 1 **Gutknecht** | N | Y | N | N | N | Y | Y | Y |
| 2 **Kline** | N | Y | N | N | N | Y | Y | Y |
| 3 **Ramstad** | Y | N | N | N | N | N | Y | Y |
| 4 McCollum | Y | N | Y | Y | Y | N | Y | Y |
| 5 Sabo | Y | N | Y | Y | Y | N | Y | Y |
| 6 **Kennedy** | N | Y | N | N | N | Y | Y | Y |
| 7 Peterson | Y | N | Y | Y | Y | N | Y | Y |
| 8 Oberstar | Y | N | Y | Y | Y | N | Y | Y |
| **MISSISSIPPI** | | | | | | | | |
| 1 **Wicker** | N | N | N | N | N | Y | Y | Y |
| 2 Thompson | Y | N | N | Y | Y | Y | Y | Y |
| 3 **Pickering** | Y | N | N | N | N | Y | Y | Y |
| 4 Taylor | + | + | - | + | + | - | + | + |
| **MISSOURI** | | | | | | | | |
| 1 Clay | ? | ? | ? | Y | Y | N | Y | Y |
| 2 **Akin** | N | Y | N | N | N | Y | Y | Y |
| 3 Carnahan | Y | N | Y | Y | Y | N | Y | Y |
| 4 Skelton | ? | ? | ? | ? | ? | ? | Y | Y |
| 5 Cleaver | Y | N | Y | Y | Y | N | Y | Y |
| 6 **Graves** | Y | Y | N | N | N | Y | Y | Y |
| 7 **Blunt** | N | N | ? | N | N | Y | Y | Y |
| 8 **Emerson** | Y | N | N | N | N | Y | Y | Y |
| 9 **Hulshof** | Y | N | N | N | N | Y | Y | Y |
| **MONTANA** | | | | | | | | |
| AL **Rehberg** | N | N | N | N | N | Y | Y | Y |
| **NEBRASKA** | | | | | | | | |
| 1 **Fortenberry** | N | N | N | N | N | Y | Y | Y |
| 2 **Terry** | N | Y | N | N | N | Y | ? | ? |
| 3 **Osborne** | N | N | N | N | N | Y | Y | Y |
| **NEVADA** | | | | | | | | |
| 1 Berkley | Y | N | Y | Y | Y | N | Y | Y |
| 2 **Gibbons** | N | N | N | N | N | N | Y | Y |
| 3 **Porter** | N | N | N | N | N | Y | Y | Y |
| **NEW HAMPSHIRE** | | | | | | | | |
| 1 **Bradley** | Y | N | N | N | N | Y | Y | Y |
| 2 **Bass** | Y | N | N | N | N | Y | Y | Y |
| **NEW JERSEY** | | | | | | | | |
| 1 Andrews | + | - | + | + | + | - | Y | Y |
| 2 **LoBiondo** | Y | N | N | N | N | Y | Y | Y |
| 3 **Saxton** | N | N | N | N | N | Y | Y | Y |
| 4 **Smith** | Y | N | N | N | N | Y | Y | Y |
| 5 **Garrett** | N | Y | N | N | N | Y | Y | Y |
| 6 Pallone | Y | N | Y | Y | Y | N | Y | Y |
| 7 **Ferguson** | Y | N | N | N | N | Y | Y | Y |
| 8 Pascrell | Y | N | Y | Y | Y | Y | Y | Y |
| 9 Rothman | Y | N | Y | Y | Y | Y | Y | Y |
| 10 Payne | Y | N | Y | Y | Y | N | ? | ? |
| 11 **Frelinghuysen** | N | N | N | N | N | Y | Y | Y |
| 12 Holt | Y | N | Y | Y | Y | Y | Y | Y |
| 13 Menendez | Y | N | Y | Y | Y | N | Y | Y |
| **NEW MEXICO** | | | | | | | | |
| 1 **Wilson** | ? | ? | ? | ? | ? | - | Y | Y |
| 2 **Pearce** | N | N | N | N | N | Y | Y | Y |
| 3 Udall | ? | ? | ? | ? | ? | ? | Y | Y |
| **NEW YORK** | | | | | | | | |
| 1 Bishop | Y | N | Y | Y | Y | N | + | + |
| 2 Israel | Y | N | Y | Y | Y | N | ? | ? |
| 3 **King** | N | N | N | N | N | Y | Y | Y |
| 4 McCarthy | Y | N | Y | Y | Y | N | Y | Y |
| 5 Ackerman | Y | N | Y | Y | Y | N | Y | Y |
| 6 Meeks | ? | ? | ? | ? | ? | ? | Y | Y |
| 7 Crowley | Y | N | Y | Y | Y | N | Y | Y |
| 8 Nadler | Y | N | Y | Y | Y | N | Y | Y |
| 9 Weiner | Y | N | Y | Y | Y | N | ? | ? |
| 10 Towns | Y | N | N | N | Y | Y | Y | Y |
| 11 Owens | Y | N | Y | Y | Y | N | Y | Y |
| 12 Velázquez | Y | N | Y | Y | Y | N | Y | Y |
| 13 **Fossella** | N | N | N | N | N | Y | + | + |
| 14 Maloney | Y | N | Y | Y | Y | N | Y | Y |
| 15 Rangel | Y | N | Y | Y | Y | N | Y | Y |
| 16 Serrano | Y | N | Y | Y | Y | N | Y | Y |
| 17 Engel | Y | N | Y | Y | Y | Y | Y | Y |
| 18 Lowey | Y | N | Y | Y | Y | N | Y | Y |
| 19 **Kelly** | Y | N | N | N | N | Y | Y | Y |
| 20 **Sweeney** | N | N | N | N | N | Y | ? | ? |
| 21 McNulty | Y | N | Y | Y | Y | N | Y | Y |
| 22 Hinchey | Y | Y | Y | Y | Y | N | Y | Y |
| 23 **McHugh** | Y | N | N | N | N | Y | ? | ? |
| 24 **Boehlert** | Y | N | N | N | N | Y | ? | ? |
| 25 **Walsh** | N | N | N | N | N | Y | Y | Y |
| 26 **Reynolds** | N | N | N | N | N | Y | ? | ? |
| 27 Higgins | Y | N | Y | Y | Y | Y | ? | ? |
| 28 Slaughter | + | - | + | + | + | - | + | + |
| 29 **Kuhl** | Y | N | N | N | N | Y | Y | Y |

| | 316 | 317 | 318 | 319 | 320 | 321 | 322 | 323 |
|---|---|---|---|---|---|---|---|---|
| **NORTH CAROLINA** | | | | | | | | |
| 1 Butterfield | Y | N | N | Y | Y | N | Y | Y |
| 2 Etheridge | Y | N | Y | Y | Y | N | + | + |
| 3 **Jones** | ? | ? | ? | ? | ? | ? | Y | Y |
| 4 Price | Y | N | Y | Y | Y | N | Y | Y |
| 5 **Foxx** | N | Y | N | N | N | Y | Y | Y |
| 6 **Coble** | N | N | N | N | N | Y | Y | Y |
| 7 McIntyre | Y | N | Y | Y | Y | N | Y | Y |
| 8 **Hayes** | N | Y | N | N | N | Y | Y | Y |
| 9 **Myrick** | N | Y | N | N | N | Y | Y | Y |
| 10 **McHenry** | N | Y | N | N | N | Y | Y | Y |
| 11 **Taylor** | N | N | ? | ? | ? | ? | Y | Y |
| 12 Watt | Y | N | Y | Y | Y | N | Y | Y |
| 13 Miller | Y | N | Y | Y | Y | N | Y | Y |
| **NORTH DAKOTA** | | | | | | | | |
| AL Pomeroy | N | N | Y | Y | Y | Y | Y | Y |
| **OHIO** | | | | | | | | |
| 1 **Chabot** | Y | Y | N | Y | N | Y | Y | Y |
| 2 Vacant | | | | | | | | |
| 3 **Turner** | Y | N | N | N | N | Y | ? | ? |
| 4 **Oxley** | N | N | N | N | N | Y | + | + |
| 5 **Gillmor** | N | N | N | N | N | Y | Y | Y |
| 6 Strickland | Y | N | Y | Y | Y | N | ? | ? |
| 7 **Hobson** | N | N | N | N | N | Y | ? | ? |
| 8 **Boehner** | N | N | N | N | N | Y | Y | Y |
| 9 Kaptur | Y | N | Y | Y | Y | N | Y | Y |
| 10 Kucinich | Y | N | Y | Y | Y | N | ? | ? |
| 11 Jones | Y | N | Y | Y | Y | N | ? | ? |
| 12 **Tiberi** | N | N | N | N | N | Y | Y | Y |
| 13 Brown | Y | N | Y | Y | Y | N | Y | Y |
| 14 **LaTourette** | ? | ? | ? | ? | ? | ? | ? | ? |
| 15 **Pryce** | N | N | N | N | N | Y | ? | ? |
| 16 **Regula** | N | N | N | N | N | Y | Y | Y |
| 17 Ryan | ? | ? | Y | Y | Y | N | Y | Y |
| 18 **Ney** | N | N | N | N | N | Y | Y | Y |
| **OKLAHOMA** | | | | | | | | |
| 1 **Sullivan** | N | N | N | N | N | Y | Y | Y |
| 2 Boren | Y | N | N | Y | Y | Y | Y | Y |
| 3 **Lucas** | N | N | N | N | N | Y | Y | Y |
| 4 **Cole** | N | Y | N | N | N | Y | Y | Y |
| 5 **Istook** | N | Y | N | N | N | Y | ? | ? |
| **OREGON** | | | | | | | | |
| 1 Wu | Y | N | Y | Y | Y | N | Y | Y |
| 2 **Walden** | N | N | N | N | N | Y | ? | ? |
| 3 Blumenauer | Y | N | Y | Y | Y | N | Y | Y |
| 4 DeFazio | Y | N | Y | Y | Y | N | Y | Y |
| 5 Hooley | Y | N | Y | Y | Y | N | Y | Y |
| **PENNSYLVANIA** | | | | | | | | |
| 1 Brady | Y | N | Y | Y | Y | Y | ? | ? |
| 2 Fattah | ? | ? | ? | ? | ? | ? | ? | ? |
| 3 **English** | N | N | N | N | N | Y | Y | Y |
| 4 **Hart** | N | Y | N | N | N | Y | Y | Y |
| 5 **Peterson** | Y | ? | N | N | N | Y | Y | Y |
| 6 **Gerlach** | N | N | N | N | N | Y | Y | Y |
| 7 **Weldon** | N | N | N | N | N | Y | Y | Y |
| 8 **Fitzpatrick** | N | N | N | Y | N | Y | Y | Y |
| 9 **Shuster** | N | N | N | N | N | Y | Y | Y |
| 10 **Sherwood** | N | N | N | N | N | Y | Y | Y |
| 11 Kanjorski | Y | N | Y | Y | Y | Y | Y | Y |
| 12 Murtha | Y | N | Y | Y | Y | Y | Y | ? |
| 13 Schwartz | Y | N | Y | Y | Y | N | Y | Y |
| 14 Doyle | Y | N | Y | Y | Y | Y | Y | Y |
| 15 **Dent** | N | N | N | N | N | Y | Y | Y |
| 16 **Pitts** | Y | Y | N | N | N | Y | Y | Y |
| 17 Holden | Y | N | Y | Y | Y | Y | Y | Y |
| 18 **Murphy** | Y | N | N | N | N | Y | Y | Y |
| 19 **Platts** | N | N | N | N | N | Y | Y | Y |
| **RHODE ISLAND** | | | | | | | | |
| 1 Kennedy | Y | N | Y | Y | Y | N | Y | Y |
| 2 Langevin | Y | N | Y | Y | Y | N | Y | Y |
| **SOUTH CAROLINA** | | | | | | | | |
| 1 **Brown** | N | N | N | N | N | Y | Y | Y |
| 2 **Wilson** | N | N | N | N | N | Y | Y | Y |
| 3 **Barrett** | N | Y | N | N | N | Y | Y | Y |
| 4 **Inglis** | N | N | N | N | N | Y | Y | Y |
| 5 Spratt | Y | N | Y | Y | Y | N | Y | Y |
| 6 Clyburn | Y | N | N | N | Y | N | Y | Y |
| **SOUTH DAKOTA** | | | | | | | | |
| AL Herseth | Y | N | Y | Y | Y | N | Y | Y |
| **TENNESSEE** | | | | | | | | |
| 1 **Jenkins** | N | Y | N | N | N | Y | ? | ? |
| 2 **Duncan** | N | Y | N | N | N | Y | Y | Y |

| | 316 | 317 | 318 | 319 | 320 | 321 | 322 | 323 |
|---|---|---|---|---|---|---|---|---|
| 3 **Wamp** | N | N | N | N | N | Y | Y | Y |
| 4 Davis | Y | N | Y | Y | Y | Y | Y | Y |
| 5 Cooper | Y | N | Y | Y | Y | N | Y | Y |
| 6 Gordon | Y | N | Y | Y | Y | Y | ? | ? |
| 7 **Blackburn** | N | Y | N | N | N | Y | Y | Y |
| 8 Tanner | Y | N | N | Y | ? | ? | Y | Y |
| 9 Ford | Y | N | N | Y | Y | N | ? | ? |
| **TEXAS** | | | | | | | | |
| 1 **Gohmert** | ? | ? | ? | ? | ? | ? | Y | Y |
| 2 **Poe** | N | Y | N | N | N | Y | Y | Y |
| 3 **Johnson, S.** | N | N | N | N | N | Y | Y | Y |
| 4 **Hall** | N | N | N | N | N | Y | Y | Y |
| 5 **Hensarling** | N | Y | N | N | N | Y | Y | Y |
| 6 **Barton** | N | N | N | N | N | Y | Y | Y |
| 7 **Culberson** | N | Y | N | N | N | Y | ? | ? |
| 8 **Brady** | N | Y | N | N | N | Y | Y | Y |
| 9 Green, A. | Y | N | Y | Y | Y | N | Y | Y |
| 10 **McCaul** | N | N | N | N | N | Y | Y | Y |
| 11 **Conaway** | N | N | N | N | N | Y | Y | Y |
| 12 **Granger** | N | N | N | N | N | Y | Y | Y |
| 13 **Thornberry** | N | Y | N | N | N | Y | Y | Y |
| 14 **Paul** | N | Y | N | Y | N | N | N | N |
| 15 Hinojosa | Y | N | Y | Y | Y | N | Y | Y |
| 16 Reyes | ? | ? | ? | ? | ? | ? | Y | Y |
| 17 Edwards | Y | N | Y | Y | Y | N | Y | Y |
| 18 Jackson-Lee | Y | N | Y | Y | Y | N | Y | Y |
| 19 **Neugebauer** | N | Y | N | N | N | Y | Y | Y |
| 20 Gonzalez | Y | N | N | Y | Y | Y | + | + |
| 21 **Smith** | N | N | N | N | N | Y | Y | Y |
| 22 **DeLay** | N | Y | N | N | N | Y | Y | Y |
| 23 **Bonilla** | N | N | N | N | N | Y | Y | Y |
| 24 **Marchant** | N | Y | N | N | N | Y | Y | Y |
| 25 Doggett | Y | N | Y | Y | Y | N | Y | Y |
| 26 **Burgess** | N | N | N | N | N | Y | Y | Y |
| 27 Ortiz | Y | N | Y | Y | Y | Y | Y | Y |
| 28 Cuellar | Y | N | N | Y | Y | N | Y | Y |
| 29 Green, G. | Y | N | Y | Y | Y | N | Y | Y |
| 30 Johnson, E. | Y | N | Y | Y | Y | N | Y | Y |
| 31 **Carter** | N | N | N | N | N | Y | Y | Y |
| 32 **Sessions** | N | Y | N | N | N | Y | Y | Y |
| **UTAH** | | | | | | | | |
| 1 **Bishop** | N | N | N | N | N | Y | Y | Y |
| 2 Matheson | N | N | N | Y | Y | N | Y | Y |
| 3 **Cannon** | N | Y | N | N | N | Y | Y | Y |
| **VERMONT** | | | | | | | | |
| AL *Sanders* | Y | N | Y | Y | Y | N | Y | Y |
| **VIRGINIA** | | | | | | | | |
| 1 **Davis, J.** | N | Y | N | Y | N | Y | Y | Y |
| 2 **Drake** | N | Y | N | N | N | Y | Y | Y |
| 3 Scott | Y | N | Y | Y | Y | N | Y | Y |
| 4 **Forbes** | N | Y | N | N | N | Y | Y | Y |
| 5 **Goode** | Y | Y | ? | ? | ? | ? | Y | Y |
| 6 **Goodlatte** | N | Y | N | N | N | Y | Y | Y |
| 7 **Cantor** | N | N | N | N | N | Y | Y | Y |
| 8 Moran | Y | N | Y | Y | Y | N | Y | Y |
| 9 Boucher | Y | N | Y | Y | Y | Y | Y | Y |
| 10 **Wolf** | N | N | N | N | N | Y | Y | Y |
| 11 **Davis, T.** | ? | ? | ? | ? | ? | ? | ? | ? |
| **WASHINGTON** | | | | | | | | |
| 1 Inslee | Y | N | Y | Y | Y | N | Y | Y |
| 2 Larsen | Y | N | Y | Y | Y | N | Y | Y |
| 3 Baird | Y | N | Y | Y | Y | N | Y | Y |
| 4 **Hastings** | N | N | N | N | N | Y | Y | Y |
| 5 **McMorris** | N | Y | N | N | N | Y | Y | Y |
| 6 Dicks | Y | N | Y | Y | Y | Y | Y | Y |
| 7 McDermott | Y | N | Y | Y | Y | N | Y | Y |
| 8 **Reichert** | N | N | N | N | N | Y | Y | Y |
| 9 Smith | Y | N | Y | Y | Y | N | Y | Y |
| **WEST VIRGINIA** | | | | | | | | |
| 1 Mollohan | Y | N | Y | Y | Y | Y | Y | Y |
| 2 **Capito** | ? | ? | ? | ? | ? | ? | Y | Y |
| 3 Rahall | Y | N | Y | Y | Y | Y | + | + |
| **WISCONSIN** | | | | | | | | |
| 1 **Ryan** | N | Y | N | N | N | Y | Y | Y |
| 2 Baldwin | Y | N | Y | Y | Y | N | Y | Y |
| 3 Kind | Y | N | N | Y | Y | N | Y | Y |
| 4 Moore | Y | Y | Y | Y | Y | N | Y | Y |
| 5 **Sensenbrenner** | N | Y | N | N | N | Y | Y | Y |
| 6 **Petri** | Y | Y | N | N | N | Y | Y | Y |
| 7 Obey | Y | N | Y | Y | Y | N | Y | Y |
| 8 **Green** | Y | Y | N | N | N | Y | + | Y |
| **WYOMING** | | | | | | | | |
| AL **Cubin** | N | Y | N | N | N | Y | Y | Y |

# IN THE HOUSE | By Vote Number

**324.** **HR 458. Military Personnel Financial Services/Passage.** Davis, R-Ky., motion to suspend the rules and pass the bill that would ban all future sales of contractual plan mutual funds, require greater regulation of insurance sales on military bases and establish requirements for certain loans to service members. Motion agreed to 405-2: R 217-2; D 187-0 (ND 144-0, SD 43-0); I 1-0. A two-thirds majority of those present and voting (272 in this case) is required for passage under suspension of the rules. June 28, 2005.

**325.** **HR 3057. Fiscal 2006 Foreign Operations Appropriations/Previous Question.** L. Diaz-Balart, R-Fla., motion to order the previous question (thus ending debate and the possibility of amendment) on adoption of the rule (H Res 341) to provide for House floor consideration of the bill that would appropriate $20.3 billion in fiscal 2006 for foreign aid and economic assistance. Motion agreed to 217-189: R 217-0; D 0-188 (ND 0-145, SD 0-43); I 0-1. (Subsequently, the rule was adopted by voice vote.) June 28, 2005.

**326.** **HR 3057. Fiscal 2006 Foreign Operations Appropriations/Aid to Egypt.** Pitts, R-Pa., amendment that would transfer $750 million of military aid for Egypt to programs for malaria in Africa. Rejected 87-326: R 53-168; D 34-157 (ND 29-118, SD 5-39); I 0-1. A "nay" was a vote in support of the president's position. June 28, 2005.

**327.** **HR 3058 Fiscal 2006 Transportation-Treasury-Housing Appropriations/Previous Question.** L. Diaz-Balart, R-Fla., motion to order the previous question (thus ending debate and the possibility of amendment) on adoption of the rule (H Res 342) to provide for House floor consideration of the bill that would provide $139.1 billion in fiscal 2006 for the departments of Transportation, Treasury, and Housing and Urban Development as well as the judiciary and the District of Columbia. Motion agreed to 263-152: R 136-87; D 127-64 (ND 101-46, SD 26-18); I 0-1. June 28, 2005.

**328.** **HR 3058. Fiscal 2006 Transportation-Treasury-Housing Appropriations/Rule.** Adoption of the rule (H Res 342) that would provide for House floor consideration of the bill that would provide $139.1 billion in fiscal 2006 for the Departments of Transportation, Treasury, and Housing and Urban Development as well as the judiciary and the District of Columbia. Adopted 219-193: R 219-2; D 0-190 (ND 0-146, SD 0-44); I 0-1. June 28, 2005.

**329.** **HR 3057. Fiscal 2006 Foreign Operations Appropriations/Andean Counterdrug Initiative.** McGovern, D-Mass., amendment that would reduce by $100 million funds for the Andean Counterdrug Initiative. Rejected 189-234: R 19-207; D 169-27 (ND 134-16, SD 35-11); I 1-0. A "nay" was a vote in support of the president's position. June 28, 2005.

**330.** **HR 3057. Fiscal 2006 Foreign Operations Appropriations/Limitation on Foreign Assistance.** Beauprez, R-Colo., amendment that would limit assistance to foreign countries that refuse to extradite to the United States any individual accused in the United States of killing a law enforcement officer. Adopted 327-98: R 208-18; D 119-79 (ND 82-68, SD 37-11); I 0-1. June 28, 2005.

**331.** **HR 3057. Fiscal 2006 Foreign Operations Appropriations/Aid for Saudi Arabia.** Weiner, D-N.Y., amendment that would prohibit use of funds in the bill for assistance to Saudi Arabia. Adopted 293-132: R 121-105; D 171-27 (ND 132-18, SD 39-9); I 1-0. June 28, 2005.

| Member | 324 | 325 | 326 | 327 | 328 | 329 | 330 | 331 |
|---|---|---|---|---|---|---|---|---|
| **ALABAMA** | | | | | | | | |
| 1 Bonner | Y | Y | N | Y | Y | N | Y | N |
| 2 Everett | Y | Y | N | Y | Y | N | Y | N |
| 3 Rogers | Y | Y | Y | N | Y | N | Y | Y |
| 4 Aderholt | Y | Y | N | N | Y | N | Y | N |
| 5 Cramer | Y | N | N | N | N | N | Y | N |
| 6 Bachus | Y | Y | N | Y | Y | N | Y | Y |
| 7 Davis | Y | N | N | Y | N | Y | Y | Y |
| **ALASKA** | | | | | | | | |
| AL Young | Y | Y | N | Y | N | Y | N | N |
| **ARIZONA** | | | | | | | | |
| 1 Renzi | Y | Y | N | Y | N | Y | Y | Y |
| 2 Franks | Y | Y | Y | Y | Y | N | Y | Y |
| 3 Shadegg | Y | Y | N | Y | N | Y | Y | Y |
| 4 Pastor | Y | N | N | Y | N | Y | N | N |
| 5 Hayworth | Y | Y | Y | N | Y | N | Y | Y |
| 6 Flake | N | Y | N | N | Y | Y | Y | Y |
| 7 Grijalva | Y | N | N | Y | N | Y | N | Y |
| 8 Kolbe | Y | Y | N | Y | Y | N | N | N |
| **ARKANSAS** | | | | | | | | |
| 1 Berry | Y | N | Y | N | N | N | Y | N |
| 2 Snyder | Y | N | N | N | N | N | Y | N |
| 3 Boozman | Y | Y | N | N | Y | N | Y | Y |
| 4 Ross | ? | ? | ? | ? | ? | ? | ? | ? |
| **CALIFORNIA** | | | | | | | | |
| 1 Thompson | Y | N | N | Y | N | Y | Y | Y |
| 2 Herger | ? | Y | N | Y | N | Y | Y | Y |
| 3 Lungren | Y | Y | N | Y | Y | N | Y | Y |
| 4 Doolittle | ? | ? | ? | ? | ? | ? | ? | ? |
| 5 Matsui, D. | Y | N | N | Y | N | Y | N | Y |
| 6 Woolsey | Y | N | N | Y | N | Y | N | Y |
| 7 Miller, George | Y | N | N | Y | N | Y | N | Y |
| 8 Pelosi | Y | N | N | Y | N | Y | N | Y |
| 9 Lee | Y | N | N | Y | N | Y | N | Y |
| 10 Tauscher | Y | N | N | Y | N | Y | N | Y |
| 11 Pombo | Y | Y | N | Y | N | Y | Y | Y |
| 12 Lantos | Y | N | Y | Y | N | Y | Y | Y |
| 13 Stark | Y | N | N | Y | ? | Y | N | N |
| 14 Eshoo | Y | N | N | Y | N | Y | N | Y |
| 15 Honda | Y | N | N | Y | N | Y | N | Y |
| 16 Lofgren | Y | N | Y | N | Y | Y | Y | Y |
| 17 Farr | Y | N | N | Y | N | Y | N | Y |
| 18 Cardoza | Y | N | Y | N | N | N | Y | Y |
| 19 Radanovich | Y | Y | N | Y | Y | N | N | N |
| 20 Costa | Y | N | N | N | Y | N | Y | N |
| 21 Nunes | Y | Y | N | Y | Y | N | Y | N |
| 22 Thomas | Y | N | N | N | N | N | N | N |
| 23 Capps | Y | N | N | N | N | N | Y | Y |
| 24 Gallegly | Y | Y | N | Y | Y | N | Y | Y |
| 25 McKeon | Y | Y | N | Y | N | Y | N | N |
| 26 Dreier | Y | Y | N | Y | N | N | N | N |
| 27 Sherman | Y | N | Y | Y | N | Y | N | Y |
| 28 Berman | Y | N | N | Y | N | Y | N | Y |
| 29 Schiff | Y | N | N | N | N | Y | Y | Y |
| 30 Waxman | Y | N | N | Y | N | Y | N | Y |
| 31 Becerra | Y | N | N | Y | N | Y | N | Y |
| 32 Solis | Y | N | N | Y | N | Y | N | Y |
| 33 Watson | Y | N | Y | N | Y | N | Y | Y |
| 34 Roybal-Allard | Y | N | N | N | N | Y | Y | Y |
| 35 Waters | Y | N | N | Y | N | Y | N | Y |
| 36 Harman | Y | N | N | Y | N | Y | N | Y |
| 37 Millender-McD. | Y | N | N | Y | N | Y | N | Y |
| 38 Napolitano | Y | N | Y | N | N | Y | N | Y |
| 39 Sánchez, Linda | Y | N | N | Y | N | Y | N | Y |
| 40 Royce | Y | Y | Y | N | Y | N | Y | Y |
| 41 Lewis | Y | Y | Y | N | Y | Y | N | N |
| 42 Miller, Gary | Y | Y | N | Y | N | Y | N | Y |
| 43 Baca | Y | N | N | N | N | N | Y | Y |
| 44 Calvert | Y | Y | N | Y | Y | N | Y | N |
| 45 Bono | Y | Y | Y | Y | Y | N | Y | Y |
| 46 Rohrabacher | Y | Y | N | Y | Y | Y | Y | Y |
| 47 Sanchez, Loretta | Y | N | N | N | N | Y | N | Y |
| 48 Cox | Y | Y | N | Y | Y | ? | Y | Y |
| 49 Issa | Y | Y | N | Y | Y | N | Y | N |
| 50 Cunningham | Y | Y | N | Y | Y | N | Y | N |
| 51 Filner | Y | N | N | Y | N | Y | N | Y |
| 52 Hunter | Y | Y | ? | Y | Y | N | Y | Y |
| 53 Davis | Y | N | N | N | N | N | Y | Y |
| **COLORADO** | | | | | | | | |
| 1 DeGette | Y | N | N | Y | N | Y | N | Y |
| 2 Udall | Y | N | Y | N | N | Y | N | Y |
| 3 Salazar | Y | N | N | N | N | N | N | Y |
| 4 Musgrave | Y | Y | N | Y | N | Y | Y | Y |
| 5 Hefley | Y | Y | Y | N | Y | N | Y | Y |
| 6 Tancredo | Y | Y | Y | Y | Y | Y | Y | Y |
| 7 Beauprez | Y | ? | Y | Y | Y | N | Y | Y |
| **CONNECTICUT** | | | | | | | | |
| 1 Larson | Y | N | N | Y | N | Y | N | Y |
| 2 Simmons | Y | Y | N | N | Y | N | Y | Y |
| 3 DeLauro | Y | N | N | N | Y | N | Y | Y |
| 4 Shays | ? | ? | N | Y | Y | N | N | ? |
| 5 Johnson | Y | Y | N | N | Y | N | N | N |
| **DELAWARE** | | | | | | | | |
| AL Castle | Y | Y | N | N | Y | N | Y | N |
| **FLORIDA** | | | | | | | | |
| 1 Miller | Y | Y | N | N | Y | N | Y | Y |
| 2 Boyd | Y | N | N | Y | N | Y | Y | Y |
| 3 Brown | Y | N | N | N | Y | N | N | Y |
| 4 Crenshaw | Y | Y | N | N | Y | N | Y | Y |
| 5 Brown-Waite | Y | Y | N | N | Y | N | Y | Y |
| 6 Stearns | Y | Y | Y | N | Y | N | Y | Y |
| 7 Mica | Y | Y | N | N | Y | N | Y | Y |
| 8 Keller | Y | Y | N | N | Y | N | Y | Y |
| 9 Bilirakis | Y | Y | N | N | Y | N | Y | Y |
| 10 Young | Y | Y | Y | N | Y | N | Y | Y |
| 11 Davis | Y | N | N | N | N | N | N | Y |
| 12 Putnam | Y | Y | N | N | Y | N | Y | Y |
| 13 Harris | Y | Y | Y | Y | Y | N | Y | Y |
| 14 Mack | Y | Y | N | Y | Y | N | Y | Y |
| 15 Weldon | Y | Y | N | N | Y | N | Y | Y |
| 16 Foley | Y | Y | N | Y | Y | N | Y | Y |
| 17 Meek | Y | N | N | N | N | Y | Y | Y |
| 18 Ros-Lehtinen | Y | Y | N | Y | Y | N | N | Y |
| 19 Wexler | Y | N | N | N | N | Y | N | Y |
| 20 Wasserman-Schultz | Y | N | N | N | Y | Y | Y | Y |
| 21 Diaz-Balart, L. | Y | Y | N | Y | N | ? | N | Y |
| 22 Shaw | Y | Y | N | Y | N | Y | Y | Y |
| 23 Hastings | Y | N | N | Y | N | N | N | Y |
| 24 Feeney | Y | Y | N | Y | Y | N | N | Y |
| 25 Diaz-Balart, M. | Y | Y | N | Y | Y | N | Y | N |
| **GEORGIA** | | | | | | | | |
| 1 Kingston | ? | ? | ? | ? | ? | ? | ? | ? |
| 2 Bishop | Y | N | N | N | N | N | N | Y |
| 3 Marshall | Y | N | N | N | N | N | N | Y |
| 4 McKinney | Y | N | N | N | N | ? | N | N |
| 5 Lewis | Y | N | Y | N | Y | N | N | Y |
| 6 Price | Y | Y | N | Y | N | Y | Y | Y |
| 7 Linder | Y | Y | ? | ? | ? | N | Y | Y |
| 8 Westmoreland | Y | Y | N | Y | N | Y | Y | Y |
| 9 Norwood | Y | Y | N | Y | N | Y | N | Y |
| 10 Deal | Y | Y | N | N | Y | N | Y | Y |
| 11 Gingrey | Y | Y | N | N | ? | N | Y | N |
| 12 Barrow | Y | N | N | N | N | Y | Y | Y |
| 13 Scott | Y | N | N | N | N | Y | Y | Y |
| **HAWAII** | | | | | | | | |
| 1 Abercrombie | Y | N | N | Y | N | Y | Y | Y |
| 2 Case | Y | N | N | N | Y | N | Y | Y |
| **IDAHO** | | | | | | | | |
| 1 Otter | Y | Y | Y | N | Y | Y | Y | Y |
| 2 Simpson | Y | Y | N | Y | Y | N | Y | N |
| **ILLINOIS** | | | | | | | | |
| 1 Rush | Y | N | N | Y | N | Y | N | Y |
| 2 Jackson | Y | N | N | Y | N | Y | Y | Y |
| 3 Lipinski | Y | N | N | N | Y | N | Y | Y |
| 4 Gutierrez | Y | N | N | N | N | N | Y | Y |
| 5 Emanuel | Y | N | N | N | Y | Y | Y | Y |
| 6 Hyde | Y | N | N | Y | N | N | Y | N |
| 7 Davis | Y | N | N | N | N | Y | Y | Y |
| 8 Bean | Y | N | N | N | N | Y | Y | Y |
| 9 Schakowsky | Y | N | N | Y | N | Y | N | Y |
| 10 Kirk | Y | Y | N | Y | N | N | N | N |
| 11 Weller | Y | N | Y | Y | N | Y | N | Y |
| 12 Costello | Y | N | N | Y | N | Y | Y | Y |

**KEY**   Republicans   Democrats   *Independents*

| | | | |
|---|---|---|---|
| Y Voted for (yea) | X Paired against | C Voted "present" to avoid possible conflict of interest | |
| # Paired for | – Announced against | | |
| + Announced for | P Voted "present" | ? Did not vote or otherwise make a position known | |
| N Voted against (nay) | | | |

| | 324 | 325 | 326 | 327 | 328 | 329 | 330 | 331 |
|---|---|---|---|---|---|---|---|---|
| 13 **Biggert** | Y | Y | N | Y | Y | N | Y | N |
| 14 **Hastert** | | | | | | | | |
| 15 **Johnson** | Y | Y | Y | N | Y | N | Y | Y |
| 16 **Manzullo** | Y | Y | N | N | Y | N | Y | Y |
| 17 Evans | Y | N | N | N | N | Y | Y | Y |
| 18 **LaHood** | Y | Y | N | N | Y | N | Y | N |
| 19 **Shimkus** | Y | Y | N | N | Y | N | Y | N |
| **INDIANA** | | | | | | | | |
| 1 Visclosky | Y | N | N | Y | N | Y | Y | Y |
| 2 **Chocola** | Y | Y | N | N | Y | N | Y | Y |
| 3 **Souder** | Y | Y | Y | Y | Y | N | Y | Y |
| 4 **Buyer** | Y | Y | N | Y | Y | N | Y | N |
| 5 **Burton** | Y | Y | Y | Y | Y | N | Y | Y |
| 6 **Pence** | Y | Y | Y | Y | Y | N | Y | Y |
| 7 Carson | Y | N | Y | N | N | Y | Y | Y |
| 8 **Hostettler** | Y | Y | Y | Y | Y | N | Y | Y |
| 9 **Sodrel** | Y | Y | N | N | Y | N | Y | Y |
| **IOWA** | | | | | | | | |
| 1 **Nussle** | Y | Y | N | N | Y | N | Y | N |
| 2 **Leach** | Y | Y | N | Y | Y | Y | Y | N |
| 3 Boswell | Y | N | N | N | N | Y | Y | Y |
| 4 **Latham** | Y | Y | N | N | Y | N | Y | N |
| 5 **King** | Y | Y | Y | Y | Y | N | Y | Y |
| **KANSAS** | | | | | | | | |
| 1 **Moran** | Y | Y | N | N | Y | N | Y | Y |
| 2 **Ryun** | Y | Y | Y | N | Y | N | Y | Y |
| 3 Moore | Y | N | N | N | N | Y | Y | Y |
| 4 **Tiahrt** | Y | Y | N | Y | Y | N | Y | N |
| **KENTUCKY** | | | | | | | | |
| 1 **Whitfield** | Y | Y | N | Y | Y | N | Y | Y |
| 2 **Lewis** | Y | Y | N | Y | ? | N | Y | Y |
| 3 **Northup** | Y | Y | Y | N | Y | N | Y | N |
| 4 **Davis** | Y | Y | N | Y | Y | N | Y | Y |
| 5 **Rogers** | Y | Y | N | Y | Y | N | N | N |
| 6 Chandler | Y | N | N | N | N | Y | Y | Y |
| **LOUISIANA** | | | | | | | | |
| 1 **Jindal** | Y | Y | N | N | Y | N | Y | Y |
| 2 Jefferson | ? | ? | N | Y | N | Y | N | N |
| 3 Melancon | Y | N | Y | N | N | N | Y | Y |
| 4 **McCrery** | Y | Y | N | Y | Y | N | N | N |
| 5 **Alexander** | Y | Y | N | Y | Y | N | Y | Y |
| 6 **Baker** | Y | Y | N | Y | Y | N | Y | Y |
| 7 **Boustany** | Y | Y | N | N | Y | N | Y | N |
| **MAINE** | | | | | | | | |
| 1 Allen | Y | N | N | N | N | Y | Y | N |
| 2 Michaud | ? | ? | ? | ? | ? | Y | Y | Y |
| **MARYLAND** | | | | | | | | |
| 1 **Gilchrest** | Y | Y | N | Y | Y | N | Y | N |
| 2 Ruppersberger | Y | N | N | Y | N | N | Y | N |
| 3 Cardin | Y | N | N | Y | N | Y | Y | Y |
| 4 Wynn | Y | N | N | Y | N | Y | Y | Y |
| 5 Hoyer | Y | N | N | Y | N | Y | Y | Y |
| 6 **Bartlett** | Y | Y | Y | N | Y | Y | Y | N |
| 7 Cummings | Y | N | N | Y | N | Y | N | Y |
| 8 Van Hollen | Y | N | N | Y | N | Y | Y | Y |
| **MASSACHUSETTS** | | | | | | | | |
| 1 Olver | Y | N | N | Y | N | Y | N | Y |
| 2 Neal | Y | N | N | Y | N | Y | Y | Y |
| 3 McGovern | Y | N | N | Y | N | Y | N | Y |
| 4 Frank | Y | N | Y | Y | N | N | N | Y |
| 5 Meehan | Y | N | N | Y | N | Y | Y | ? |
| 6 Tierney | Y | N | N | Y | N | Y | N | Y |
| 7 Markey | Y | N | N | Y | N | Y | Y | Y |
| 8 Capuano | Y | N | N | Y | N | Y | Y | Y |
| 9 Lynch | Y | N | N | Y | N | ? | ? | Y |
| 10 Delahunt | Y | N | N | Y | N | Y | Y | N |
| **MICHIGAN** | | | | | | | | |
| 1 Stupak | Y | N | N | N | N | Y | Y | Y |
| 2 **Hoekstra** | Y | Y | N | Y | Y | N | Y | N |
| 3 **Ehlers** | Y | Y | N | Y | Y | Y | N | N |
| 4 **Camp** | Y | Y | N | Y | Y | N | Y | N |
| 5 Kildee | Y | N | N | N | N | Y | N | Y |
| 6 **Upton** | Y | Y | N | Y | Y | Y | Y | N |
| 7 **Schwarz** | Y | Y | N | Y | Y | N | Y | N |
| 8 **Rogers** | Y | Y | N | N | Y | N | Y | N |
| 9 **Knollenberg** | Y | Y | N | Y | Y | N | N | N |
| 10 **Miller** | Y | Y | N | Y | Y | N | Y | Y |
| 11 **McCotter** | Y | Y | N | Y | Y | N | Y | Y |
| 12 Levin | Y | N | N | Y | N | Y | N | Y |
| 13 Kilpatrick | + | – | N | Y | N | Y | N | N |
| 14 Conyers | Y | N | N | Y | N | Y | N | N |
| 15 Dingell | Y | N | N | Y | N | Y | N | N |

| | 324 | 325 | 326 | 327 | 328 | 329 | 330 | 331 |
|---|---|---|---|---|---|---|---|---|
| **MINNESOTA** | | | | | | | | |
| 1 **Gutknecht** | Y | Y | Y | Y | Y | Y | Y | Y |
| 2 **Kline** | Y | Y | N | Y | Y | N | Y | N |
| 3 **Ramstad** | Y | Y | N | N | Y | Y | Y | Y |
| 4 McCollum | Y | N | Y | N | N | Y | N | Y |
| 5 Sabo | Y | N | N | Y | N | Y | N | N |
| 6 **Kennedy** | Y | Y | N | N | Y | N | Y | N |
| 7 Peterson | Y | N | Y | N | N | N | Y | Y |
| 8 Oberstar | Y | N | N | Y | N | Y | N | N |
| **MISSISSIPPI** | | | | | | | | |
| 1 **Wicker** | Y | Y | N | Y | Y | N | Y | N |
| 2 Thompson | Y | N | N | Y | N | Y | Y | Y |
| 3 **Pickering** | Y | Y | N | N | Y | N | Y | Y |
| 4 Taylor | + | – | N | N | N | Y | Y | N |
| **MISSOURI** | | | | | | | | |
| 1 Clay | Y | N | Y | Y | N | Y | Y | Y |
| 2 **Akin** | Y | Y | Y | Y | Y | N | Y | Y |
| 3 Carnahan | Y | N | N | N | N | Y | Y | Y |
| 4 Skelton | Y | N | N | Y | N | Y | Y | N |
| 5 Cleaver | + | – | N | Y | N | Y | Y | Y |
| 6 **Graves** | Y | Y | N | N | Y | N | Y | Y |
| 7 **Blunt** | Y | Y | N | Y | Y | N | Y | N |
| 8 **Emerson** | Y | Y | N | N | Y | N | Y | Y |
| 9 **Hulshof** | Y | Y | N | N | Y | Y | Y | Y |
| **MONTANA** | | | | | | | | |
| AL **Rehberg** | Y | Y | N | Y | Y | N | Y | N |
| **NEBRASKA** | | | | | | | | |
| 1 **Fortenberry** | Y | Y | N | Y | Y | N | Y | Y |
| 2 **Terry** | Y | Y | N | Y | Y | N | Y | Y |
| 3 **Osborne** | Y | Y | N | N | Y | N | Y | Y |
| **NEVADA** | | | | | | | | |
| 1 Berkley | Y | N | Y | N | N | Y | Y | Y |
| 2 **Gibbons** | Y | Y | Y | N | Y | N | Y | Y |
| 3 **Porter** | Y | Y | N | N | Y | N | Y | Y |
| **NEW HAMPSHIRE** | | | | | | | | |
| 1 **Bradley** | Y | Y | Y | N | Y | N | Y | N |
| 2 **Bass** | Y | Y | N | Y | Y | N | Y | Y |
| **NEW JERSEY** | | | | | | | | |
| 1 Andrews | Y | N | N | Y | N | Y | Y | Y |
| 2 **LoBiondo** | Y | Y | Y | N | Y | N | Y | Y |
| 3 **Saxton** | Y | Y | N | Y | Y | N | Y | N |
| 4 **Smith** | Y | ? | N | Y | Y | N | Y | Y |
| 5 **Garrett** | Y | Y | Y | Y | Y | N | Y | Y |
| 6 Pallone | Y | N | N | Y | N | Y | Y | Y |
| 7 **Ferguson** | Y | Y | N | Y | Y | N | Y | Y |
| 8 Pascrell | Y | N | N | Y | N | Y | Y | Y |
| 9 Rothman | Y | N | N | Y | N | N | Y | Y |
| 10 Payne | ? | ? | Y | Y | N | Y | N | Y |
| 11 **Frelinghuysen** | Y | Y | N | Y | Y | N | Y | Y |
| 12 Holt | Y | N | N | N | N | Y | N | Y |
| 13 Menendez | Y | N | N | Y | N | N | Y | Y |
| **NEW MEXICO** | | | | | | | | |
| 1 **Wilson** | Y | Y | N | Y | Y | N | Y | N |
| 2 **Pearce** | Y | Y | N | N | Y | N | Y | N |
| 3 Udall | Y | N | Y | N | N | Y | N | Y |
| **NEW YORK** | | | | | | | | |
| 1 Bishop | Y | N | N | N | N | Y | Y | Y |
| 2 Israel | Y | N | N | Y | N | Y | Y | Y |
| 3 **King** | Y | Y | N | Y | Y | N | Y | Y |
| 4 McCarthy | Y | N | N | Y | N | Y | Y | Y |
| 5 Ackerman | Y | N | N | Y | N | Y | N | Y |
| 6 Meeks | Y | N | N | Y | N | Y | N | Y |
| 7 Crowley | Y | N | Y | Y | N | N | Y | Y |
| 8 Nadler | Y | N | Y | Y | N | Y | N | Y |
| 9 Weiner | Y | N | Y | Y | N | Y | Y | Y |
| 10 Towns | Y | N | Y | Y | N | Y | N | Y |
| 11 Owens | Y | N | N | Y | N | Y | Y | Y |
| 12 Velázquez | Y | N | N | Y | N | Y | N | Y |
| 13 **Fossella** | + | + | Y | N | Y | N | Y | Y |
| 14 Maloney | Y | N | Y | N | N | N | N | Y |
| 15 Rangel | Y | N | N | Y | N | Y | Y | Y |
| 16 Serrano | Y | N | Y | Y | N | Y | N | Y |
| 17 Engel | ? | N | N | Y | N | Y | Y | Y |
| 18 Lowey | Y | N | N | Y | N | Y | N | Y |
| 19 **Kelly** | Y | Y | N | N | Y | Y | Y | N |
| 20 **Sweeney** | ? | ? | N | Y | Y | N | N | N |
| 21 McNulty | Y | N | N | Y | N | Y | Y | Y |
| 22 Hinchey | Y | N | Y | Y | N | Y | N | Y |
| 23 **McHugh** | ? | ? | ? | ? | ? | N | Y | N |
| 24 **Boehlert** | Y | Y | N | Y | Y | N | Y | Y |
| 25 **Walsh** | Y | ? | N | Y | Y | N | Y | N |
| 26 **Reynolds** | Y | Y | N | Y | Y | N | Y | N |
| 27 Higgins | ? | ? | ? | ? | ? | Y | Y | Y |
| 28 Slaughter | Y | N | N | Y | N | Y | N | Y |
| 29 **Kuhl** | Y | Y | N | N | Y | N | Y | Y |

| | 324 | 325 | 326 | 327 | 328 | 329 | 330 | 331 |
|---|---|---|---|---|---|---|---|---|
| **NORTH CAROLINA** | | | | | | | | |
| 1 Butterfield | Y | N | N | Y | N | Y | Y | Y |
| 2 Etheridge | + | – | – | – | – | Y | Y | N |
| 3 **Jones** | ? | ? | Y | N | Y | Y | Y | Y |
| 4 Price | ? | ? | ? | ? | ? | Y | Y | N |
| 5 **Foxx** | Y | Y | Y | N | Y | N | Y | Y |
| 6 **Coble** | Y | Y | Y | N | Y | N | Y | Y |
| 7 McIntyre | Y | N | + | + | – | – | + | + |
| 8 **Hayes** | Y | Y | – | – | + | – | + | – |
| 9 **Myrick** | Y | Y | Y | Y | Y | N | Y | Y |
| 10 **McHenry** | Y | Y | Y | N | Y | N | Y | Y |
| 11 **Taylor** | Y | Y | N | Y | Y | N | Y | N |
| 12 Watt | Y | N | N | Y | N | Y | N | Y |
| 13 Miller | Y | N | N | N | N | Y | Y | Y |
| **NORTH DAKOTA** | | | | | | | | |
| AL Pomeroy | Y | N | N | N | N | Y | Y | Y |
| **OHIO** | | | | | | | | |
| 1 **Chabot** | Y | Y | N | N | N | N | Y | Y |
| 2 Vacant | | | | | | | | |
| 3 **Turner** | Y | Y | N | Y | Y | N | Y | N |
| 4 **Oxley** | Y | Y | N | Y | Y | N | N | N |
| 5 **Gillmor** | Y | Y | N | Y | Y | N | N | Y |
| 6 Strickland | Y | N | Y | N | N | Y | Y | Y |
| 7 **Hobson** | Y | Y | N | Y | Y | N | N | N |
| 8 **Boehner** | Y | Y | N | Y | Y | N | Y | N |
| 9 Kaptur | Y | N | N | N | N | Y | Y | Y |
| 10 Kucinich | Y | N | N | N | N | Y | N | Y |
| 11 Jones | Y | N | N | Y | N | Y | N | Y |
| 12 **Tiberi** | Y | Y | Y | Y | Y | N | Y | Y |
| 13 Brown | Y | N | Y | N | N | Y | Y | Y |
| 14 **LaTourette** | Y | Y | N | Y | Y | N | Y | Y |
| 15 **Pryce** | Y | Y | N | Y | Y | N | Y | N |
| 16 **Regula** | Y | Y | N | Y | Y | N | Y | N |
| 17 Ryan | Y | N | N | N | N | Y | Y | Y |
| 18 **Ney** | Y | Y | N | Y | Y | N | Y | N |
| **OKLAHOMA** | | | | | | | | |
| 1 **Sullivan** | Y | Y | N | Y | Y | N | Y | Y |
| 2 Boren | Y | N | N | N | N | Y | Y | Y |
| 3 **Lucas** | Y | Y | N | Y | Y | N | Y | Y |
| 4 **Cole** | Y | Y | N | Y | Y | N | Y | N |
| 5 **Istook** | Y | Y | N | Y | Y | N | Y | N |
| **OREGON** | | | | | | | | |
| 1 Wu | Y | N | N | N | N | Y | Y | Y |
| 2 **Walden** | Y | Y | N | N | Y | N | Y | Y |
| 3 Blumenauer | Y | N | Y | Y | N | Y | N | Y |
| 4 DeFazio | Y | N | Y | N | N | Y | Y | Y |
| 5 Hooley | Y | N | N | N | N | Y | Y | Y |
| **PENNSYLVANIA** | | | | | | | | |
| 1 Brady | Y | N | N | Y | N | Y | Y | Y |
| 2 Fattah | Y | N | N | Y | N | Y | Y | Y |
| 3 **English** | Y | Y | N | N | Y | N | Y | Y |
| 4 **Hart** | Y | Y | N | N | Y | N | Y | N |
| 5 **Peterson** | ? | ? | N | N | Y | N | N | N |
| 6 **Gerlach** | Y | Y | Y | N | Y | N | Y | Y |
| 7 **Weldon** | Y | Y | N | Y | Y | N | Y | Y |
| 8 **Fitzpatrick** | Y | Y | N | N | Y | N | Y | Y |
| 9 **Shuster** | Y | Y | N | N | Y | N | Y | Y |
| 10 **Sherwood** | Y | Y | N | N | Y | N | N | N |
| 11 Kanjorski | Y | N | N | Y | N | N | Y | N |
| 12 Murtha | ? | ? | N | Y | N | N | Y | N |
| 13 Schwartz | Y | N | N | N | N | Y | Y | Y |
| 14 Doyle | Y | N | N | Y | N | Y | Y | Y |
| 15 **Dent** | Y | Y | N | N | Y | N | Y | Y |
| 16 **Pitts** | Y | Y | Y | N | Y | Y | Y | Y |
| 17 Holden | Y | N | N | N | N | Y | Y | Y |
| 18 **Murphy** | Y | Y | N | N | Y | N | Y | N |
| 19 **Platts** | Y | Y | Y | N | Y | N | Y | Y |
| **RHODE ISLAND** | | | | | | | | |
| 1 Kennedy | Y | N | Y | Y | N | N | Y | Y |
| 2 Langevin | Y | N | N | N | N | Y | Y | Y |
| **SOUTH CAROLINA** | | | | | | | | |
| 1 **Brown** | + | + | – | + | + | N | Y | Y |
| 2 **Wilson** | Y | Y | N | Y | Y | N | Y | N |
| 3 **Barrett** | Y | Y | N | N | Y | N | Y | Y |
| 4 **Inglis** | Y | Y | N | Y | Y | N | Y | N |
| 5 Spratt | ? | ? | ? | ? | ? | Y | Y | Y |
| 6 Clyburn | ? | ? | ? | ? | ? | Y | Y | Y |
| **SOUTH DAKOTA** | | | | | | | | |
| AL Herseth | Y | N | Y | N | N | Y | Y | Y |
| **TENNESSEE** | | | | | | | | |
| 1 **Jenkins** | + | + | Y | N | Y | N | Y | Y |
| 2 **Duncan** | Y | Y | Y | N | Y | Y | Y | Y |

| | 324 | 325 | 326 | 327 | 328 | 329 | 330 | 331 |
|---|---|---|---|---|---|---|---|---|
| 3 **Wamp** | Y | Y | N | N | Y | N | Y | Y |
| 4 Davis | Y | N | N | N | N | Y | Y | Y |
| 5 Cooper | Y | N | N | Y | N | Y | Y | Y |
| 6 Gordon | Y | N | Y | N | N | Y | Y | Y |
| 7 **Blackburn** | Y | Y | N | N | Y | N | Y | N |
| 8 Tanner | Y | N | N | N | N | Y | Y | Y |
| 9 Ford | Y | N | N | N | N | Y | Y | Y |
| **TEXAS** | | | | | | | | |
| 1 **Gohmert** | Y | Y | Y | Y | Y | N | Y | Y |
| 2 **Poe** | Y | Y | Y | Y | Y | N | Y | Y |
| 3 **Johnson, S.** | Y | Y | N | Y | Y | N | Y | Y |
| 4 **Hall** | Y | Y | N | Y | Y | Y | Y | Y |
| 5 **Hensarling** | Y | Y | N | N | Y | N | Y | N |
| 6 **Barton** | Y | Y | Y | Y | Y | N | Y | N |
| 7 **Culberson** | Y | Y | N | Y | Y | N | Y | Y |
| 8 **Brady** | Y | Y | N | Y | Y | N | Y | N |
| 9 Green, A. | Y | N | N | Y | N | Y | Y | Y |
| 10 **McCaul** | Y | Y | N | N | Y | N | Y | N |
| 11 **Conaway** | Y | Y | N | Y | Y | N | Y | Y |
| 12 **Granger** | Y | Y | N | Y | Y | N | Y | N |
| 13 **Thornberry** | Y | Y | N | Y | Y | N | Y | N |
| 14 **Paul** | N | Y | Y | N | N | Y | Y | Y |
| 15 Hinojosa | Y | N | N | Y | N | + | Y | Y |
| 16 Reyes | Y | N | N | Y | N | Y | Y | Y |
| 17 Edwards | Y | N | N | N | N | N | Y | Y |
| 18 Jackson-Lee | Y | N | N | Y | N | Y | Y | Y |
| 19 **Neugebauer** | Y | Y | Y | N | Y | N | Y | Y |
| 20 Gonzalez | Y | N | N | Y | N | N | Y | Y |
| 21 **Smith** | Y | Y | N | Y | Y | N | Y | N |
| 22 **DeLay** | Y | Y | N | Y | Y | N | Y | N |
| 23 **Bonilla** | Y | Y | N | Y | Y | N | Y | N |
| 24 **Marchant** | Y | Y | N | Y | Y | N | Y | Y |
| 25 Doggett | Y | N | Y | N | N | Y | Y | Y |
| 26 **Burgess** | Y | Y | N | N | Y | N | Y | N |
| 27 Ortiz | + | – | – | + | – | – | + | + |
| 28 Cuellar | Y | N | N | N | N | Y | Y | Y |
| 29 Green, G. | Y | N | N | Y | N | N | Y | Y |
| 30 Johnson, E. | Y | N | N | Y | N | Y | N | Y |
| 31 **Carter** | Y | Y | N | Y | Y | N | Y | N |
| 32 **Sessions** | Y | Y | N | Y | Y | N | Y | N |
| **UTAH** | | | | | | | | |
| 1 **Bishop** | Y | Y | Y | Y | Y | N | Y | N |
| 2 Matheson | Y | N | Y | N | N | N | Y | Y |
| 3 **Cannon** | Y | Y | Y | Y | Y | N | Y | N |
| **VERMONT** | | | | | | | | |
| AL *Sanders* | Y | N | N | N | N | Y | N | Y |
| **VIRGINIA** | | | | | | | | |
| 1 **Davis, J.** | Y | Y | N | N | Y | N | Y | Y |
| 2 **Drake** | Y | Y | N | N | Y | N | Y | Y |
| 3 Scott | Y | N | N | Y | N | Y | N | Y |
| 4 **Forbes** | Y | Y | N | N | Y | N | Y | Y |
| 5 **Goode** | Y | Y | Y | N | Y | N | Y | Y |
| 6 **Goodlatte** | Y | Y | Y | Y | Y | N | Y | Y |
| 7 **Cantor** | Y | Y | Y | Y | Y | N | Y | N |
| 8 Moran | Y | N | N | Y | N | N | Y | Y |
| 9 Boucher | Y | N | N | Y | N | Y | N | N |
| 10 **Wolf** | Y | Y | – | Y | Y | N | Y | N |
| 11 **Davis, T.** | Y | Y | N | Y | Y | N | Y | Y |
| **WASHINGTON** | | | | | | | | |
| 1 Inslee | Y | N | N | N | N | Y | Y | Y |
| 2 Larsen | Y | N | N | Y | N | Y | N | Y |
| 3 Baird | Y | N | N | N | N | Y | N | Y |
| 4 **Hastings** | Y | Y | N | Y | Y | N | Y | N |
| 5 **McMorris** | Y | Y | N | N | Y | N | Y | N |
| 6 Dicks | Y | N | N | Y | N | Y | Y | Y |
| 7 McDermott | Y | N | N | Y | N | Y | N | N |
| 8 **Reichert** | Y | Y | N | N | Y | N | Y | N |
| 9 Smith | Y | N | N | N | N | Y | N | Y |
| **WEST VIRGINIA** | | | | | | | | |
| 1 Mollohan | Y | N | ? | ? | ? | N | Y | N |
| 2 **Capito** | Y | Y | ? | ? | ? | N | Y | N |
| 3 Rahall | Y | N | ? | ? | ? | Y | Y | N |
| **WISCONSIN** | | | | | | | | |
| 1 **Ryan** | Y | Y | N | N | Y | N | Y | N |
| 2 Baldwin | Y | N | N | Y | N | Y | N | N |
| 3 Kind | Y | N | N | N | N | Y | Y | Y |
| 4 Moore | Y | N | N | Y | N | Y | Y | Y |
| 5 **Sensenbrenner** | Y | Y | Y | N | Y | Y | Y | Y |
| 6 **Petri** | Y | Y | Y | N | Y | N | Y | Y |
| 7 Obey | Y | N | N | N | N | Y | Y | N |
| 8 **Green** | Y | Y | N | N | Y | N | Y | Y |
| **WYOMING** | | | | | | | | |
| AL **Cubin** | Y | Y | N | Y | Y | N | Y | Y |

# IN THE HOUSE | By Vote Number

**332.** HR 3057. Fiscal 2006 Foreign Operations Appropriations/Nuclear Power Plants in China. Sanders, I-Vt., amendment that would bar the Export-Import Bank from using funds in the bill to approve federal loans or loan guarantees for the construction of nuclear power plants in China. Adopted 313-114: R 139-88; D 173-26 (ND 136-15, SD 37-11); I 1-0. June 28, 2005.

**333.** HR 3057. Fiscal 2006 Foreign Operations Appropriations/Foreign Assistance Limit. Deal, R-Ga., amendment that would prohibit the State Department from using funds in the bill to provide aid to any country that has an extradition treaty with the United States but refuses to extradite individuals accused of a crime punishable by imprisonment. The restriction would not affect funds for international narcotics control and law enforcement. Adopted 294-132: R 184-43; D 109-89 (ND 80-71, SD 29-18); I 1-0. June 28, 2005.

**334.** HR 3057. Fiscal 2006 Foreign Operations Appropriations/Discretionary Spending Cut. Hefley, R-Colo., amendment that would reduce discretionary spending in the bill by 1 percent. Rejected 117-309: R 105-122; D 12-186 (ND 8-142, SD 4-44); I 0-1. June 28, 2005.

**335.** HR 3057. Fiscal 2006 Foreign Operations Appropriations/Passage. Passage of the bill that would appropriate $20.3 billion in fiscal 2006 for foreign operations and economic assistance, including $2.7 billion for programs to combat HIV/AIDS and related diseases, and $1.75 billion for the Millennium Challenge Corporation. Passed 393-32: R 199-27; D 193-5 (ND 148-2, SD 45-3); I 1-0. June 28, 2005.

**336.** HR 3058. Fiscal 2006 Transportation-Treasury-Housing Appropriations/Amtrak Routes. Brown, D-Fla., amendment that would eliminate language in the bill that would prohibit the use of federal funds for 18 specified Amtrak routes, all of which require federal subsidies of more than $30 per passenger. Adopted 269-152: R 73-151; D 195-1 (ND 148-0, SD 47-1); I 1-0. June 29, 2005.

**337.** HR 3058. Fiscal 2006 Transportation-Treasury-Housing Appropriations/Homeless Assistance Grants. Kennedy, R-Minn., amendment that would increase homeless-assistance grants by $100 million, offset with a reduction to Amtrak. Rejected 59-362: R 57-168; D 2-193 (ND 0-147, SD 2-46); I 0-1. June 29, 2005.

**338.** HR 3058. Fiscal 2006 Transportation-Treasury-Housing Appropriations/Fair Housing Programs. A. Green, D-Texas, amendment that would increase funding for Fair Housing programs by $7.7 million, offset by a cut to the IRS information systems account. Adopted 231-191: R 35-191; D 195-0 (ND 147-0, SD 48-0); I 1-0. June 29, 2005.

**339.** HR 3058. Fiscal 2006 Transportation-Treasury-Housing Appropriations/Housing Vouchers. Nadler, D-N.Y., amendment that would provide an additional $100 million for Section 8 housing vouchers, offset by a $120 million decrease to the working capital fund from the Housing and Urban Development management and administration account. Adopted 225-194: R 30-193; D 194-1 (ND 147-1, SD 47-0); I 1-0. June 29, 2005.

| | 332 | 333 | 334 | 335 | 336 | 337 | 338 | 339 |
|---|---|---|---|---|---|---|---|---|
| **ALABAMA** | | | | | | | | |
| 1 Bonner | Y | Y | Y | Y | N | N | N | N |
| 2 Everett | Y | Y | Y | Y | N | N | N | N |
| 3 Rogers | Y | Y | N | Y | N | N | N | N |
| 4 Aderholt | Y | Y | N | Y | N | N | N | N |
| 5 Cramer | N | Y | N | Y | Y | Y | Y | Y |
| 6 Bachus | Y | Y | N | Y | Y | N | N | ? |
| 7 Davis | Y | N | N | Y | Y | N | Y | Y |
| **ALASKA** | | | | | | | | |
| AL Young | Y | Y | N | Y | Y | N | N | N |
| **ARIZONA** | | | | | | | | |
| 1 Renzi | Y | N | N | Y | Y | Y | Y | Y |
| 2 Franks | Y | Y | Y | N | Y | N | N | Y |
| 3 Shadegg | Y | Y | Y | Y | N | Y | N | N |
| 4 Pastor | Y | N | N | Y | Y | N | Y | Y |
| 5 Hayworth | Y | Y | Y | N | Y | N | N | N |
| 6 Flake | Y | Y | Y | N | N | N | N | N |
| 7 Grijalva | Y | N | N | Y | N | Y | Y | Y |
| 8 Kolbe | N | N | N | Y | N | N | N | N |
| **ARKANSAS** | | | | | | | | |
| 1 Berry | Y | Y | Y | N | Y | N | Y | Y |
| 2 Snyder | N | N | N | Y | Y | N | Y | Y |
| 3 Boozman | Y | Y | N | Y | N | N | N | N |
| 4 Ross | ? | ? | ? | ? | ? | ? | ? | ? |
| **CALIFORNIA** | | | | | | | | |
| 1 Thompson | Y | N | N | Y | Y | Y | Y | Y |
| 2 Herger | Y | Y | Y | Y | N | Y | N | N |
| 3 Lungren | N | Y | Y | Y | N | N | N | N |
| 4 Doolittle | ? | ? | ? | ? | N | N | N | N |
| 5 Matsui, D. | Y | N | N | Y | N | Y | N | Y |
| 6 Woolsey | Y | N | N | Y | Y | Y | Y | Y |
| 7 Miller, George | Y | N | N | Y | N | ? | Y | Y |
| 8 Pelosi | Y | N | N | Y | Y | Y | Y | Y |
| 9 Lee | Y | N | N | Y | N | Y | Y | Y |
| 10 Tauscher | N | N | N | Y | Y | Y | Y | Y |
| 11 Pombo | Y | Y | Y | N | N | N | N | N |
| 12 Lantos | Y | Y | N | Y | N | Y | Y | Y |
| 13 Stark | Y | N | N | Y | ? | ? | ? | ? |
| 14 Eshoo | Y | N | N | Y | N | Y | Y | Y |
| 15 Honda | Y | N | N | Y | Y | Y | Y | Y |
| 16 Lofgren | N | Y | N | Y | Y | Y | Y | Y |
| 17 Farr | Y | N | N | Y | Y | Y | Y | Y |
| 18 Cardoza | Y | N | N | Y | N | Y | Y | Y |
| 19 Radanovich | N | Y | Y | Y | N | N | N | N |
| 20 Costa | Y | N | N | Y | Y | Y | Y | Y |
| 21 Nunes | Y | N | N | Y | N | N | N | N |
| 22 Thomas | N | N | N | Y | N | N | N | N |
| 23 Capps | Y | N | N | Y | N | Y | Y | Y |
| 24 Gallegly | Y | Y | Y | Y | N | N | N | N |
| 25 McKeon | Y | N | N | Y | N | Y | N | N |
| 26 Dreier | N | N | N | Y | N | N | N | N |
| 27 Sherman | Y | N | N | Y | Y | Y | Y | Y |
| 28 Berman | Y | N | N | Y | Y | N | Y | Y |
| 29 Schiff | Y | N | N | Y | N | Y | Y | Y |
| 30 Waxman | Y | N | N | Y | N | Y | Y | Y |
| 31 Becerra | Y | N | N | Y | N | Y | Y | Y |
| 32 Solis | Y | N | N | Y | Y | Y | Y | Y |
| 33 Watson | Y | N | N | Y | Y | Y | Y | Y |
| 34 Roybal-Allard | Y | N | N | Y | N | Y | Y | Y |
| 35 Waters | Y | N | ? | Y | Y | N | Y | Y |
| 36 Harman | Y | Y | N | Y | N | Y | Y | Y |
| 37 Millender-McD. | Y | Y | N | Y | Y | Y | Y | Y |
| 38 Napolitano | Y | N | N | Y | Y | Y | Y | Y |
| 39 Sánchez, Linda | Y | N | N | Y | N | Y | Y | Y |
| 40 Royce | Y | Y | Y | Y | N | N | N | N |
| 41 Lewis | N | N | N | ? | N | N | N | N |
| 42 Miller, Gary | Y | N | Y | Y | N | Y | N | N |
| 43 Baca | Y | N | N | Y | N | Y | Y | Y |
| 44 Calvert | Y | N | N | Y | N | N | N | N |
| 45 Bono | Y | Y | N | Y | N | N | N | N |
| 46 Rohrabacher | Y | Y | Y | N | N | N | N | N |
| 47 Sanchez, Loretta | Y | N | N | Y | N | Y | Y | Y |
| 48 Cox | Y | Y | Y | Y | N | ? | ? | ? |
| 49 Issa | Y | Y | Y | Y | N | N | N | N |
| 50 Cunningham | Y | Y | N | Y | N | N | N | N |
| 51 Filner | Y | Y | N | Y | N | Y | Y | Y |
| 52 Hunter | Y | Y | N | Y | N | Y | N | N |
| 53 Davis | Y | Y | N | Y | N | Y | N | Y |
| **COLORADO** | | | | | | | | |
| 1 DeGette | Y | N | N | Y | N | Y | N | Y |
| 2 Udall | Y | N | N | Y | N | Y | N | Y |
| 3 Salazar | Y | Y | N | Y | N | Y | Y | Y |
| 4 Musgrave | Y | Y | Y | Y | N | N | N | N |
| 5 Hefley | Y | Y | Y | N | N | N | N | N |
| 6 Tancredo | Y | Y | N | N | Y | N | N | N |
| 7 Beauprez | N | Y | Y | Y | N | N | Y | N |
| **CONNECTICUT** | | | | | | | | |
| 1 Larson | Y | N | N | Y | N | Y | Y | Y |
| 2 Simmons | Y | Y | N | Y | Y | N | Y | Y |
| 3 DeLauro | Y | N | N | Y | N | Y | Y | Y |
| 4 Shays | N | N | N | Y | N | N | Y | Y |
| 5 Johnson | N | Y | N | Y | Y | N | N | Y |
| **DELAWARE** | | | | | | | | |
| AL Castle | N | N | N | Y | Y | N | N | Y |
| **FLORIDA** | | | | | | | | |
| 1 Miller | Y | Y | Y | N | N | Y | N | N |
| 2 Boyd | Y | Y | N | Y | N | Y | N | Y |
| 3 Brown | Y | N | N | Y | Y | Y | Y | Y |
| 4 Crenshaw | N | N | N | Y | Y | N | N | N |
| 5 Brown-Waite | Y | Y | Y | Y | Y | N | N | N |
| 6 Stearns | Y | Y | N | Y | N | N | N | N |
| 7 Mica | N | Y | Y | Y | N | Y | N | N |
| 8 Keller | N | Y | Y | Y | N | N | N | N |
| 9 Bilirakis | N | Y | Y | Y | N | N | N | N |
| 10 Young | Y | Y | N | Y | N | N | N | N |
| 11 Davis | Y | N | N | Y | N | Y | N | Y |
| 12 Putnam | N | Y | N | Y | N | Y | N | N |
| 13 Harris | Y | Y | Y | Y | N | N | N | N |
| 14 Mack | Y | Y | Y | Y | N | N | N | N |
| 15 Weldon | N | Y | N | Y | N | N | N | N |
| 16 Foley | Y | Y | N | Y | N | N | N | ? |
| 17 Meek | N | N | N | Y | N | Y | Y | Y |
| 18 Ros-Lehtinen | N | N | N | Y | Y | Y | N | Y |
| 19 Wexler | N | N | N | Y | Y | Y | Y | Y |
| 20 Wasserman-Schultz | Y | Y | N | Y | N | Y | Y | Y |
| 21 Diaz-Balart, L. | Y | N | N | Y | ? | N | N | N |
| 22 Shaw | Y | Y | N | Y | N | N | N | N |
| 23 Hastings | Y | Y | N | Y | Y | Y | Y | Y |
| 24 Feeney | N | Y | Y | Y | N | N | N | N |
| 25 Diaz-Balart, M. | Y | N | Y | Y | ? | N | N | N |
| **GEORGIA** | | | | | | | | |
| 1 Kingston | ? | ? | ? | ? | N | N | N | N |
| 2 Bishop | Y | Y | N | Y | Y | N | Y | Y |
| 3 Marshall | Y | N | Y | Y | Y | N | Y | Y |
| 4 McKinney | Y | N | N | Y | Y | N | Y | Y |
| 5 Lewis | Y | N | N | Y | ? | ? | ? | ? |
| 6 Price | N | Y | Y | Y | N | N | N | N |
| 7 Linder | Y | Y | Y | Y | N | N | N | N |
| 8 Westmoreland | Y | Y | Y | Y | N | N | N | N |
| 9 Norwood | Y | Y | Y | Y | N | N | N | N |
| 10 Deal | Y | Y | Y | Y | N | N | N | N |
| 11 Gingrey | Y | N | Y | Y | N | N | N | N |
| 12 Barrow | Y | Y | N | Y | N | Y | N | ? |
| 13 Scott | Y | N | N | Y | ? | ? | ? | ? |
| **HAWAII** | | | | | | | | |
| 1 Abercrombie | Y | Y | N | Y | N | Y | N | Y |
| 2 Case | N | Y | N | Y | N | Y | Y | Y |
| **IDAHO** | | | | | | | | |
| 1 Otter | N | Y | N | N | N | N | N | N |
| 2 Simpson | N | Y | N | Y | N | N | N | N |
| **ILLINOIS** | | | | | | | | |
| 1 Rush | Y | N | N | Y | N | Y | Y | Y |
| 2 Jackson | Y | N | N | Y | Y | N | Y | Y |
| 3 Lipinski | Y | N | N | Y | Y | N | Y | Y |
| 4 Gutierrez | Y | N | N | Y | N | Y | Y | Y |
| 5 Emanuel | Y | N | N | Y | N | Y | Y | Y |
| 6 Hyde | Y | Y | N | Y | N | N | N | N |
| 7 Davis | Y | N | N | Y | N | Y | Y | Y |
| 8 Bean | Y | Y | N | Y | Y | N | Y | Y |
| 9 Schakowsky | Y | N | N | Y | N | Y | Y | Y |
| 10 Kirk | N | N | N | Y | N | N | N | Y |
| 11 Weller | N | Y | N | Y | N | N | N | N |
| 12 Costello | Y | Y | Y | Y | N | Y | N | Y |

| | 332 | 333 | 334 | 335 | 336 | 337 | 338 | 339 |
|---|---|---|---|---|---|---|---|---|
| 13 **Biggert** | N | N | N | Y | N | Y | Y | N |
| 14 **Hastert** | | | | | | | | |
| 15 **Johnson** | Y | Y | N | Y | N | N | N | Y |
| 16 **Manzullo** | N | Y | Y | Y | N | N | N | N |
| 17 Evans | Y | N | N | Y | Y | N | Y | Y |
| 18 **LaHood** | N | Y | N | Y | N | N | N | N |
| 19 **Shimkus** | N | Y | Y | Y | N | N | Y | N |
| **INDIANA** | | | | | | | | |
| 1 Visclosky | Y | Y | N | Y | Y | N | Y | Y |
| 2 **Chocola** | N | Y | Y | Y | N | Y | N | N |
| 3 **Souder** | Y | N | N | Y | Y | N | N | N |
| 4 **Buyer** | Y | Y | Y | Y | N | N | N | N |
| 5 **Burton** | Y | Y | Y | Y | N | N | N | N |
| 6 **Pence** | Y | Y | Y | Y | N | Y | N | N |
| 7 Carson | Y | N | N | Y | Y | N | Y | Y |
| 8 **Hostettler** | Y | Y | Y | N | N | Y | N | N |
| 9 **Sodrel** | Y | Y | N | Y | N | N | N | N |
| **IOWA** | | | | | | | | |
| 1 **Nussle** | Y | Y | N | Y | Y | N | N | ? |
| 2 **Leach** | Y | Y | N | Y | Y | N | Y | Y |
| 3 Boswell | Y | Y | N | Y | Y | N | Y | Y |
| 4 **Latham** | N | N | N | Y | Y | N | N | N |
| 5 **King** | Y | Y | Y | Y | N | N | N | N |
| **KANSAS** | | | | | | | | |
| 1 **Moran** | N | Y | Y | Y | Y | N | Y | Y |
| 2 **Ryun** | N | Y | Y | N | N | Y | N | N |
| 3 Moore | Y | Y | N | Y | Y | N | Y | Y |
| 4 **Tiahrt** | N | Y | N | Y | N | N | N | N |
| **KENTUCKY** | | | | | | | | |
| 1 **Whitfield** | N | Y | N | Y | Y | N | N | N |
| 2 **Lewis** | Y | Y | Y | Y | N | N | Y | N |
| 3 **Northup** | Y | Y | N | Y | N | N | N | N |
| 4 **Davis** | N | N | N | Y | N | N | N | N |
| 5 **Rogers** | Y | Y | N | Y | N | N | N | N |
| 6 Chandler | Y | Y | N | Y | Y | N | Y | Y |
| **LOUISIANA** | | | | | | | | |
| 1 **Jindal** | Y | Y | Y | Y | Y | Y | N | N |
| 2 Jefferson | N | N | N | Y | Y | N | Y | Y |
| 3 Melancon | Y | Y | N | Y | Y | N | Y | Y |
| 4 **McCrery** | N | N | N | Y | N | Y | N | N |
| 5 **Alexander** | N | Y | N | Y | N | N | N | N |
| 6 **Baker** | Y | Y | Y | Y | N | N | N | N |
| 7 **Boustany** | N | Y | N | Y | Y | N | N | Y |
| **MAINE** | | | | | | | | |
| 1 Allen | Y | N | N | Y | Y | N | Y | Y |
| 2 Michaud | Y | Y | N | Y | Y | N | Y | Y |
| **MARYLAND** | | | | | | | | |
| 1 **Gilchrest** | N | N | N | Y | Y | N | N | N |
| 2 Ruppersberger | N | Y | N | Y | Y | N | Y | Y |
| 3 Cardin | Y | Y | N | Y | Y | N | Y | Y |
| 4 Wynn | Y | Y | N | Y | Y | N | Y | Y |
| 5 Hoyer | Y | Y | N | Y | Y | N | Y | Y |
| 6 **Bartlett** | N | Y | Y | N | N | N | N | N |
| 7 Cummings | Y | N | N | Y | Y | N | Y | Y |
| 8 Van Hollen | Y | Y | N | Y | Y | N | Y | Y |
| **MASSACHUSETTS** | | | | | | | | |
| 1 Olver | Y | N | N | Y | Y | N | Y | Y |
| 2 Neal | Y | Y | N | Y | ? | ? | ? | ? |
| 3 McGovern | Y | N | N | Y | Y | N | Y | Y |
| 4 Frank | Y | N | N | Y | Y | N | Y | Y |
| 5 Meehan | Y | N | N | Y | Y | N | Y | Y |
| 6 Tierney | Y | N | N | Y | Y | N | Y | Y |
| 7 Markey | Y | N | N | Y | Y | N | Y | Y |
| 8 Capuano | Y | N | N | Y | Y | N | Y | Y |
| 9 Lynch | Y | Y | N | Y | Y | N | Y | Y |
| 10 Delahunt | Y | N | N | Y | Y | N | Y | Y |
| **MICHIGAN** | | | | | | | | |
| 1 Stupak | Y | Y | N | Y | Y | N | Y | Y |
| 2 **Hoekstra** | N | N | N | Y | N | N | N | N |
| 3 **Ehlers** | N | N | N | Y | Y | N | Y | N |
| 4 **Camp** | Y | Y | N | Y | Y | N | N | N |
| 5 Kildee | Y | Y | N | Y | Y | N | Y | Y |
| 6 **Upton** | N | Y | Y | Y | Y | N | N | N |
| 7 **Schwarz** | N | N | N | Y | Y | N | Y | N |
| 8 **Rogers** | Y | Y | Y | Y | Y | N | N | N |
| 9 **Knollenberg** | N | N | N | Y | N | N | N | N |
| 10 **Miller** | N | Y | N | Y | N | N | N | N |
| 11 **McCotter** | Y | Y | Y | Y | Y | N | Y | N |
| 12 Levin | N | Y | N | Y | Y | N | Y | Y |
| 13 Kilpatrick | Y | N | N | Y | Y | N | Y | Y |
| 14 Conyers | Y | N | N | Y | ? | ? | Y | Y |
| 15 Dingell | Y | N | N | Y | Y | N | Y | Y |

| | 332 | 333 | 334 | 335 | 336 | 337 | 338 | 339 |
|---|---|---|---|---|---|---|---|---|
| **MINNESOTA** | | | | | | | | |
| 1 **Gutknecht** | Y | Y | Y | Y | N | N | N | N |
| 2 **Kline** | N | N | N | Y | N | Y | N | N |
| 3 **Ramstad** | Y | Y | N | Y | N | Y | Y | Y |
| 4 McCollum | Y | Y | N | Y | Y | N | Y | Y |
| 5 Sabo | Y | N | N | Y | Y | N | Y | Y |
| 6 **Kennedy** | Y | Y | Y | Y | N | Y | Y | Y |
| 7 Peterson | Y | Y | Y | Y | Y | N | Y | Y |
| 8 Oberstar | N | N | N | Y | Y | N | Y | Y |
| **MISSISSIPPI** | | | | | | | | |
| 1 **Wicker** | N | Y | N | Y | Y | N | N | N |
| 2 Thompson | Y | Y | N | Y | Y | N | Y | Y |
| 3 **Pickering** | Y | Y | N | Y | Y | N | Y | N |
| 4 Taylor | Y | Y | Y | N | Y | N | Y | Y |
| **MISSOURI** | | | | | | | | |
| 1 Clay | Y | N | N | Y | ? | ? | ? | ? |
| 2 **Akin** | Y | Y | Y | Y | – | – | – | – |
| 3 Carnahan | Y | Y | N | Y | Y | N | Y | Y |
| 4 Skelton | Y | Y | N | Y | Y | N | Y | Y |
| 5 Cleaver | Y | N | N | Y | Y | N | Y | Y |
| 6 **Graves** | N | Y | Y | Y | N | Y | N | N |
| 7 **Blunt** | Y | N | N | Y | N | N | N | N |
| 8 **Emerson** | Y | Y | N | Y | N | N | Y | N |
| 9 **Hulshof** | N | Y | Y | N | N | N | Y | N |
| **MONTANA** | | | | | | | | |
| AL **Rehberg** | N | N | N | Y | Y | N | N | N |
| **NEBRASKA** | | | | | | | | |
| 1 **Fortenberry** | Y | Y | N | Y | Y | N | N | N |
| 2 **Terry** | Y | Y | Y | Y | N | N | N | N |
| 3 **Osborne** | Y | Y | N | Y | Y | N | N | N |
| **NEVADA** | | | | | | | | |
| 1 Berkley | Y | Y | N | Y | Y | N | Y | Y |
| 2 **Gibbons** | Y | Y | Y | N | Y | N | Y | N |
| 3 **Porter** | Y | Y | N | Y | Y | Y | N | N |
| **NEW HAMPSHIRE** | | | | | | | | |
| 1 **Bradley** | N | Y | Y | Y | N | Y | Y | Y |
| 2 **Bass** | Y | Y | Y | Y | N | N | N | N |
| **NEW JERSEY** | | | | | | | | |
| 1 Andrews | Y | Y | N | Y | Y | N | Y | Y |
| 2 **LoBiondo** | Y | Y | N | Y | Y | N | N | N |
| 3 **Saxton** | Y | Y | N | Y | Y | N | N | N |
| 4 **Smith** | Y | N | N | Y | Y | N | N | N |
| 5 **Garrett** | Y | Y | Y | Y | N | N | N | N |
| 6 Pallone | Y | Y | N | Y | Y | N | Y | Y |
| 7 **Ferguson** | Y | Y | N | Y | N | N | N | N |
| 8 Pascrell | Y | N | N | Y | Y | N | Y | Y |
| 9 Rothman | Y | Y | N | Y | Y | N | Y | Y |
| 10 Payne | Y | N | N | Y | Y | N | Y | Y |
| 11 **Frelinghuysen** | N | N | N | Y | N | N | N | N |
| 12 Holt | Y | N | N | Y | Y | N | Y | Y |
| 13 Menendez | Y | Y | N | Y | Y | N | Y | Y |
| **NEW MEXICO** | | | | | | | | |
| 1 **Wilson** | Y | Y | N | Y | Y | Y | Y | Y |
| 2 **Pearce** | N | Y | N | Y | N | Y | N | N |
| 3 Udall | Y | N | N | Y | Y | N | Y | Y |
| **NEW YORK** | | | | | | | | |
| 1 Bishop | Y | Y | N | Y | Y | N | Y | Y |
| 2 Israel | Y | Y | N | Y | Y | N | Y | Y |
| 3 **King** | N | Y | N | Y | N | N | N | N |
| 4 McCarthy | Y | Y | N | Y | Y | N | Y | Y |
| 5 Ackerman | Y | N | N | Y | Y | N | Y | Y |
| 6 Meeks | Y | N | N | Y | Y | N | Y | Y |
| 7 Crowley | N | Y | N | Y | Y | N | Y | Y |
| 8 Nadler | Y | N | N | Y | Y | N | Y | Y |
| 9 Weiner | Y | Y | N | Y | Y | N | Y | Y |
| 10 Towns | Y | N | N | Y | Y | N | Y | Y |
| 11 Owens | Y | Y | N | Y | Y | N | Y | Y |
| 12 Velázquez | Y | N | N | Y | Y | N | Y | Y |
| 13 **Fossella** | Y | Y | Y | Y | N | N | N | Y |
| 14 Maloney | Y | N | N | Y | Y | N | Y | Y |
| 15 Rangel | Y | Y | N | Y | Y | N | Y | Y |
| 16 Serrano | Y | N | N | Y | Y | N | Y | Y |
| 17 Engel | Y | Y | N | Y | Y | N | Y | Y |
| 18 Lowey | Y | N | N | Y | Y | N | Y | Y |
| 19 **Kelly** | Y | Y | N | Y | Y | N | Y | Y |
| 20 **Sweeney** | N | N | N | Y | N | N | N | N |
| 21 McNulty | Y | Y | Y | Y | Y | N | Y | Y |
| 22 Hinchey | Y | Y | N | Y | Y | N | Y | Y |
| 23 **McHugh** | Y | Y | N | Y | N | N | N | Y |
| 24 **Boehlert** | Y | Y | N | Y | N | N | N | Y |
| 25 **Walsh** | Y | N | N | Y | N | N | N | N |
| 26 **Reynolds** | Y | Y | N | Y | N | N | N | N |
| 27 Higgins | Y | Y | N | Y | Y | N | Y | Y |
| 28 Slaughter | Y | Y | N | Y | Y | N | Y | Y |
| 29 **Kuhl** | N | Y | N | Y | Y | N | N | Y |

| | 332 | 333 | 334 | 335 | 336 | 337 | 338 | 339 |
|---|---|---|---|---|---|---|---|---|
| **NORTH CAROLINA** | | | | | | | | |
| 1 Butterfield | Y | N | N | Y | Y | N | Y | Y |
| 2 Etheridge | N | N | N | Y | Y | N | Y | Y |
| 3 **Jones** | Y | Y | Y | N | N | Y | Y | Y |
| 4 Price | N | N | N | Y | Y | N | Y | Y |
| 5 **Foxx** | Y | Y | Y | Y | N | Y | N | N |
| 6 **Coble** | Y | Y | Y | Y | N | N | N | N |
| 7 McIntyre | + | + | – | + | Y | N | Y | Y |
| 8 **Hayes** | + | + | + | – | N | N | N | N |
| 9 **Myrick** | N | Y | Y | Y | N | Y | N | N |
| 10 **McHenry** | Y | Y | Y | Y | N | Y | N | N |
| 11 **Taylor** | Y | Y | N | Y | N | N | N | N |
| 12 Watt | Y | N | N | Y | Y | N | Y | Y |
| 13 Miller | N | Y | N | Y | Y | N | Y | Y |
| **NORTH DAKOTA** | | | | | | | | |
| AL Pomeroy | N | Y | N | Y | Y | N | Y | Y |
| **OHIO** | | | | | | | | |
| 1 **Chabot** | Y | Y | Y | Y | N | Y | N | N |
| 2 Vacant | | | | | | | | |
| 3 **Turner** | Y | Y | N | Y | Y | N | N | N |
| 4 **Oxley** | N | N | N | Y | N | N | N | N |
| 5 **Gillmor** | Y | Y | N | Y | N | N | N | N |
| 6 Strickland | Y | Y | N | Y | Y | N | Y | Y |
| 7 **Hobson** | N | N | N | Y | N | N | N | N |
| 8 **Boehner** | Y | Y | N | Y | N | N | N | N |
| 9 Kaptur | Y | Y | N | Y | Y | N | Y | Y |
| 10 Kucinich | Y | N | N | Y | Y | N | Y | Y |
| 11 Jones | Y | N | N | Y | Y | N | Y | Y |
| 12 **Tiberi** | Y | Y | Y | Y | Y | Y | N | N |
| 13 Brown | Y | Y | N | Y | Y | N | Y | Y |
| 14 **LaTourette** | Y | Y | N | Y | Y | N | N | N |
| 15 **Pryce** | N | N | N | Y | N | N | N | N |
| 16 **Regula** | N | N | N | Y | Y | N | N | N |
| 17 Ryan | Y | Y | N | Y | Y | N | Y | Y |
| 18 **Ney** | Y | Y | N | Y | Y | N | Y | N |
| **OKLAHOMA** | | | | | | | | |
| 1 **Sullivan** | N | Y | N | Y | N | N | N | N |
| 2 Boren | Y | Y | N | Y | Y | N | Y | Y |
| 3 **Lucas** | Y | Y | N | N | N | N | N | N |
| 4 **Cole** | N | Y | N | Y | N | N | N | N |
| 5 **Istook** | Y | Y | N | Y | N | ? | N | N |
| **OREGON** | | | | | | | | |
| 1 Wu | Y | Y | N | Y | Y | N | Y | Y |
| 2 **Walden** | Y | Y | Y | Y | Y | N | N | N |
| 3 Blumenauer | Y | N | N | Y | Y | N | Y | Y |
| 4 DeFazio | Y | Y | Y | Y | Y | N | Y | Y |
| 5 Hooley | Y | N | N | Y | Y | N | Y | Y |
| **PENNSYLVANIA** | | | | | | | | |
| 1 Brady | Y | Y | N | Y | Y | N | Y | Y |
| 2 Fattah | Y | Y | N | Y | Y | N | Y | Y |
| 3 **English** | Y | Y | N | Y | Y | N | N | N |
| 4 **Hart** | N | Y | Y | Y | Y | N | N | N |
| 5 **Peterson** | N | N | N | Y | ? | ? | ? | ? |
| 6 **Gerlach** | Y | Y | N | Y | Y | N | Y | N |
| 7 **Weldon** | Y | Y | N | Y | Y | N | N | N |
| 8 **Fitzpatrick** | Y | Y | N | Y | Y | N | Y | Y |
| 9 **Shuster** | Y | Y | Y | Y | Y | N | N | N |
| 10 **Sherwood** | N | N | N | Y | N | N | N | N |
| 11 Kanjorski | Y | Y | N | Y | Y | N | Y | Y |
| 12 Murtha | N | Y | N | Y | Y | N | Y | Y |
| 13 Schwartz | Y | Y | N | Y | Y | N | Y | N |
| 14 Doyle | N | Y | N | Y | Y | N | Y | Y |
| 15 **Dent** | Y | Y | N | Y | Y | N | Y | N |
| 16 **Pitts** | Y | Y | Y | Y | N | N | N | N |
| 17 Holden | Y | Y | N | Y | Y | N | Y | Y |
| 18 **Murphy** | N | Y | N | Y | + | N | Y | Y |
| 19 **Platts** | Y | Y | Y | Y | Y | N | Y | N |
| **RHODE ISLAND** | | | | | | | | |
| 1 Kennedy | Y | Y | N | Y | Y | N | Y | Y |
| 2 Langevin | Y | Y | N | Y | Y | N | Y | Y |
| **SOUTH CAROLINA** | | | | | | | | |
| 1 **Brown** | Y | Y | N | Y | N | N | N | N |
| 2 **Wilson** | N | Y | Y | Y | N | Y | N | N |
| 3 **Barrett** | Y | Y | Y | Y | N | Y | N | N |
| 4 **Inglis** | N | Y | Y | Y | N | N | N | N |
| 5 Spratt | N | Y | N | Y | Y | N | Y | Y |
| 6 Clyburn | Y | Y | N | Y | Y | N | Y | Y |
| **SOUTH DAKOTA** | | | | | | | | |
| AL Herseth | Y | Y | N | Y | Y | N | Y | Y |
| **TENNESSEE** | | | | | | | | |
| 1 **Jenkins** | Y | Y | Y | N | N | N | N | N |
| 2 **Duncan** | Y | Y | Y | N | N | N | N | N |

| | 332 | 333 | 334 | 335 | 336 | 337 | 338 | 339 |
|---|---|---|---|---|---|---|---|---|
| 3 **Wamp** | N | Y | N | Y | N | N | N | N |
| 4 Davis | Y | Y | N | Y | Y | Y | Y | Y |
| 5 Cooper | N | N | N | Y | N | Y | Y | Y |
| 6 Gordon | Y | Y | N | Y | Y | N | Y | Y |
| 7 **Blackburn** | Y | Y | Y | Y | N | Y | N | N |
| 8 Tanner | Y | Y | Y | N | Y | N | Y | Y |
| 9 Ford | Y | Y | N | Y | Y | N | Y | Y |
| **TEXAS** | | | | | | | | |
| 1 **Gohmert** | Y | Y | Y | Y | N | N | N | N |
| 2 **Poe** | Y | Y | Y | Y | N | Y | Y | N |
| 3 **Johnson, S.** | Y | Y | Y | Y | N | ? | ? | ? |
| 4 **Hall** | N | Y | N | Y | Y | N | N | N |
| 5 **Hensarling** | Y | Y | Y | Y | N | Y | N | N |
| 6 **Barton** | N | Y | Y | Y | N | N | N | N |
| 7 **Culberson** | Y | Y | N | Y | ? | N | N | N |
| 8 **Brady** | N | Y | Y | Y | N | Y | N | N |
| 9 Green, A. | Y | Y | N | Y | Y | N | Y | Y |
| 10 **McCaul** | Y | Y | N | Y | Y | N | Y | N |
| 11 **Conaway** | N | Y | N | Y | N | N | Y | N |
| 12 **Granger** | N | N | N | Y | N | N | N | N |
| 13 **Thornberry** | N | N | N | Y | N | Y | N | N |
| 14 **Paul** | Y | Y | Y | N | N | Y | Y | Y |
| 15 Hinojosa | Y | Y | N | Y | Y | N | Y | Y |
| 16 Reyes | Y | Y | N | Y | Y | N | Y | Y |
| 17 Edwards | N | Y | N | Y | Y | N | Y | Y |
| 18 Jackson-Lee | Y | – | N | Y | Y | N | Y | Y |
| 19 **Neugebauer** | Y | Y | Y | Y | N | Y | N | N |
| 20 Gonzalez | Y | Y | N | Y | Y | N | Y | Y |
| 21 **Smith** | Y | Y | N | Y | N | N | N | N |
| 22 **DeLay** | N | N | N | Y | N | N | N | N |
| 23 **Bonilla** | N | N | N | Y | N | N | N | N |
| 24 **Marchant** | Y | Y | Y | Y | N | N | N | N |
| 25 Doggett | Y | Y | N | Y | Y | N | Y | Y |
| 26 **Burgess** | Y | Y | Y | Y | N | Y | Y | N |
| 27 Ortiz | + | + | – | + | Y | N | Y | Y |
| 28 Cuellar | Y | Y | N | Y | Y | N | Y | Y |
| 29 Green, G. | Y | Y | Y | Y | Y | N | Y | Y |
| 30 Johnson, E. | Y | N | N | Y | Y | N | Y | Y |
| 31 **Carter** | N | N | N | Y | N | N | N | N |
| 32 **Sessions** | N | Y | Y | Y | N | Y | N | N |
| **UTAH** | | | | | | | | |
| 1 **Bishop** | Y | Y | Y | Y | N | N | N | Y |
| 2 Matheson | Y | Y | N | Y | Y | N | Y | Y |
| 3 **Cannon** | N | Y | Y | Y | N | N | N | N |
| **VERMONT** | | | | | | | | |
| AL *Sanders* | Y | Y | N | Y | Y | N | Y | Y |
| **VIRGINIA** | | | | | | | | |
| 1 **Davis, J.** | Y | Y | Y | N | Y | N | N | N |
| 2 **Drake** | Y | Y | N | Y | Y | N | N | N |
| 3 Scott | Y | N | N | Y | Y | N | Y | Y |
| 4 **Forbes** | Y | Y | Y | Y | Y | N | N | N |
| 5 **Goode** | Y | Y | Y | N | Y | N | N | N |
| 6 **Goodlatte** | N | Y | Y | N | Y | N | N | N |
| 7 **Cantor** | N | N | N | Y | N | N | N | N |
| 8 Moran | Y | Y | N | Y | Y | N | Y | Y |
| 9 Boucher | N | N | N | Y | Y | N | Y | Y |
| 10 **Wolf** | Y | Y | N | Y | N | N | N | N |
| 11 **Davis, T.** | N | N | N | Y | N | N | N | N |
| **WASHINGTON** | | | | | | | | |
| 1 Inslee | Y | Y | N | Y | Y | N | Y | Y |
| 2 Larsen | N | N | N | Y | Y | N | Y | Y |
| 3 Baird | Y | Y | N | Y | Y | N | Y | Y |
| 4 **Hastings** | Y | Y | N | Y | Y | N | N | N |
| 5 **McMorris** | N | Y | Y | Y | Y | N | N | N |
| 6 Dicks | N | Y | N | Y | Y | N | Y | Y |
| 7 McDermott | Y | N | N | Y | Y | N | Y | Y |
| 8 **Reichert** | N | Y | N | Y | N | Y | Y | Y |
| 9 Smith | N | N | N | Y | Y | N | Y | Y |
| **WEST VIRGINIA** | | | | | | | | |
| 1 Mollohan | Y | Y | N | ? | Y | N | Y | Y |
| 2 **Capito** | Y | Y | N | Y | Y | N | Y | Y |
| 3 Rahall | Y | Y | Y | N | Y | N | Y | Y |
| **WISCONSIN** | | | | | | | | |
| 1 **Ryan** | N | Y | Y | Y | N | Y | N | N |
| 2 Baldwin | Y | N | N | Y | Y | N | Y | Y |
| 3 Kind | N | Y | N | Y | Y | N | Y | Y |
| 4 Moore | Y | Y | N | Y | Y | N | Y | Y |
| 5 **Sensenbrenner** | Y | Y | Y | N | N | Y | N | N |
| 6 **Petri** | Y | Y | Y | N | N | N | N | N |
| 7 Obey | Y | N | N | Y | Y | N | Y | Y |
| 8 **Green** | Y | Y | Y | Y | Y | Y | N | Y |
| **WYOMING** | | | | | | | | |
| AL **Cubin** | N | Y | Y | N | N | Y | N | N |

# IN THE HOUSE | By Vote Number

**340.** HR 3058. Fiscal 2006 Transportation-Treasury-Housing Appropriations/HOPE VI Housing. Davis, D-Ala., amendment to increase HOPE VI housing grants by $60 million, offset by a decrease in the General Services Administration Federal Buildings Fund. Adopted 248-173: R 59-166; D 188-7 (ND 143-5, SD 45-2); I 1-0. June 29, 2005.

**341.** HR 3058. Fiscal 2006 Transportation-Treasury-Housing Appropriations/Supreme Court Funding. King, R-Iowa, amendment that would reduce by $1.5 million salaries and expenses for the U.S. Supreme Court. Rejected 42-374: R 40-184; D 2-189 (ND 0-147, SD 2-42); I 0-1. June 29, 2005.

**342.** HR 3058. Fiscal 2006 Transportation-Treasury-Housing Appropriations/Federal Judiciary Funding. Herseth, D-S.D., amendment that would increase funding for the salaries and expenses of the Courts of Appeals, district courts and other judicial services by $6.9 million, offset by a reduction in the Federal Buildings Fund. Rejected 188-232: R 10-215; D 177-17 (ND 136-13, SD 41-4); I 1-0. June 29, 2005.

**343.** HR 3058. Fiscal 2006 Transportation-Treasury-Housing Appropriations/Drug Trafficking. Hooley, D-Ore., amendment that would add $9 million to the High Intensity Drug Trafficking Areas Program, offset by a cut in Office of Management and Budget salaries and expenses. Adopted 315-103: R 124-100; D 190-3 (ND 145-3, SD 45-0); I 1-0. June 29, 2005.

**344.** HR 3058. Fiscal 2006 Transportation-Treasury-Housing Appropriations/Youth Anti-Drug Campaign. Souder, R-Ind., amendment that would increase by $25 million funding for the National Youth Anti-Drug Media Campaign, offset by a decrease in the Federal Buildings Fund. Adopted 268-151: R 136-88; D 131-63 (ND 100-49, SD 31-14); I 1-0. June 29, 2005.

**345.** HR 3058. Fiscal 2006 Transportation-Treasury-Housing Appropriations/Cuban Travel Restrictions. Davis, D-Fla., amendment that would prohibit use of funds in the bill to implement, administer or enforce administration restrictions on travel to Cuba that allow individuals to visit immediate relatives there once every three years for a maximum of two consecutive weeks. Rejected 208-211: R 32-192; D 175-19 (ND 138-11, SD 37-8); I 1-0. A "nay" was a vote in support of the president's position. June 30, 2005.

**346.** HR 3058. Fiscal 2006 Transportation-Treasury-Housing Appropriations/Cuban Educational Travel. Lee, D-Calif., amendment that would prohibit use of funds in the bill to enforce regulations preventing travel to Cuba by academic institutions. Rejected 187-233: R 20-203; D 166-30 (ND 134-16, SD 32-14); I 1-0. A "nay" was a vote in support of the president's position. June 30, 2005.

**347.** HR 3058. Fiscal 2006 Transportation-Treasury-Housing Appropriations/Flight Service Stations. Sanders, I-Vt., amendment that would prohibit use of funds in the bill for the competitive sourcing of flight service stations. The amendment would nullify a $1.9 billion contract awarded to Lockheed Martin Corp. in February. Adopted 238-177: R 48-175; D 189-2 (ND 149-0, SD 40-2); I 1-0. A "nay" was a vote in support of the president's position. June 30, 2005.

| | 340 | 341 | 342 | 343 | 344 | 345 | 346 | 347 |
|---|---|---|---|---|---|---|---|---|
| **ALABAMA** | | | | | | | | |
| 1 Bonner | Y | N | N | N | Y | N | N | Y |
| 2 Everett | N | N | N | N | Y | ? | ? | ? |
| 3 Rogers | Y | N | N | N | Y | ? | ? | ? |
| 4 Aderholt | N | N | N | N | N | N | N | N |
| 5 Cramer | Y | N | N | Y | Y | ? | ? | ? |
| 6 Bachus | ? | ? | ? | ? | ? | ? | ? | ? |
| 7 Davis | Y | N | Y | Y | Y | Y | Y | Y |
| **ALASKA** | | | | | | | | |
| AL Young | N | ? | ? | ? | ? | N | N | N |
| **ARIZONA** | | | | | | | | |
| 1 Renzi | Y | Y | N | Y | Y | N | N | N |
| 2 Franks | N | Y | N | Y | Y | N | N | N |
| 3 Shadegg | N | N | N | Y | N | N | N | N |
| 4 Pastor | Y | N | N | N | Y | Y | Y | Y |
| 5 Hayworth | Y | Y | N | Y | N | N | N | N |
| 6 Flake | N | N | N | N | N | N | N | N |
| 7 Grijalva | Y | N | Y | N | Y | Y | Y | Y |
| 8 Kolbe | N | N | N | N | N | Y | N | Y |
| **ARKANSAS** | | | | | | | | |
| 1 Berry | Y | N | Y | Y | Y | Y | Y | Y |
| 2 Snyder | Y | N | Y | Y | Y | Y | Y | Y |
| 3 Boozman | N | N | N | N | Y | ? | N | Y |
| 4 Ross | ? | ? | ? | ? | ? | ? | ? | ? |
| **CALIFORNIA** | | | | | | | | |
| 1 Thompson | Y | N | Y | Y | Y | Y | Y | Y |
| 2 Herger | N | Y | N | Y | N | Y | Y | N |
| 3 Lungren | N | N | N | Y | N | N | N | N |
| 4 Doolittle | N | N | N | N | N | N | N | N |
| 5 Matsui, D. | Y | N | Y | Y | Y | Y | Y | Y |
| 6 Woolsey | Y | N | Y | Y | Y | Y | Y | Y |
| 7 Miller, George | Y | N | Y | Y | Y | Y | Y | Y |
| 8 Pelosi | Y | N | Y | Y | N | Y | Y | Y |
| 9 Lee | Y | N | Y | Y | N | Y | Y | Y |
| 10 Tauscher | Y | N | Y | Y | Y | Y | Y | Y |
| 11 Pombo | N | Y | N | Y | N | N | N | N |
| 12 Lantos | Y | N | Y | Y | Y | Y | Y | Y |
| 13 Stark | ? | ? | ? | ? | Y | Y | Y | Y |
| 14 Eshoo | Y | N | Y | Y | Y | Y | Y | Y |
| 15 Honda | Y | N | Y | Y | Y | Y | Y | Y |
| 16 Lofgren | Y | N | Y | Y | Y | Y | Y | Y |
| 17 Farr | Y | N | Y | Y | Y | Y | Y | Y |
| 18 Cardoza | Y | N | Y | Y | N | Y | N | Y |
| 19 Radanovich | N | N | N | Y | N | N | N | N |
| 20 Costa | Y | N | Y | Y | Y | Y | N | Y |
| 21 Nunes | N | N | N | Y | N | N | N | N |
| 22 Thomas | N | ? | ? | ? | ? | N | N | N |
| 23 Capps | Y | N | Y | Y | Y | Y | Y | Y |
| 24 Gallegly | N | N | N | Y | N | N | N | N |
| 25 McKeon | N | N | N | N | N | N | N | N |
| 26 Dreier | N | N | N | Y | N | N | N | N |
| 27 Sherman | Y | N | Y | N | Y | N | Y | Y |
| 28 Berman | Y | N | Y | ? | Y | Y | Y | Y |
| 29 Schiff | Y | N | Y | Y | Y | ? | ? | ? |
| 30 Waxman | Y | N | Y | Y | Y | Y | Y | Y |
| 31 Becerra | Y | N | Y | Y | Y | Y | Y | Y |
| 32 Solis | Y | N | Y | Y | N | Y | Y | Y |
| 33 Watson | Y | N | Y | Y | N | Y | Y | Y |
| 34 Roybal-Allard | Y | N | Y | Y | N | Y | Y | Y |
| 35 Waters | Y | N | Y | Y | Y | Y | Y | Y |
| 36 Harman | Y | N | Y | Y | Y | Y | Y | Y |
| 37 Millender-McD. | Y | N | Y | Y | N | Y | Y | Y |
| 38 Napolitano | Y | N | Y | Y | Y | Y | Y | Y |
| 39 Sánchez, Linda | Y | N | Y | Y | N | Y | Y | Y |
| 40 Royce | N | N | N | N | N | N | N | N |
| 41 Lewis | N | N | N | N | N | N | N | N |
| 42 Miller, Gary | N | N | N | N | N | N | N | N |
| 43 Baca | Y | N | Y | Y | Y | Y | Y | Y |
| 44 Calvert | N | N | N | Y | N | N | N | N |
| 45 Bono | N | N | N | N | N | Y | N | N |
| 46 Rohrabacher | Y | Y | N | N | N | N | N | N |
| 47 Sanchez, Loretta | Y | N | Y | Y | Y | Y | Y | Y |
| 48 Cox | ? | N | N | N | Y | N | N | N |
| 49 Issa | N | N | N | Y | N | N | N | N |
| 50 Cunningham | N | N | N | Y | N | N | N | N |
| 51 Filner | Y | N | N | Y | Y | Y | Y | Y |
| 52 Hunter | N | N | N | N | N | N | N | N |
| 53 Davis | Y | N | Y | N | Y | N | Y | Y |
| **COLORADO** | | | | | | | | |
| 1 DeGette | Y | N | Y | N | Y | N | Y | Y |
| 2 Udall | Y | N | Y | Y | Y | Y | Y | Y |
| 3 Salazar | Y | N | Y | Y | N | N | N | Y |
| 4 Musgrave | N | Y | N | Y | N | N | N | N |
| 5 Hefley | N | N | N | Y | N | N | N | N |
| 6 Tancredo | N | N | Y | Y | Y | N | N | N |
| 7 Beauprez | Y | N | N | N | Y | N | N | N |
| **CONNECTICUT** | | | | | | | | |
| 1 Larson | Y | N | Y | N | Y | N | Y | Y |
| 2 Simmons | Y | Y | N | Y | Y | N | Y | Y |
| 3 DeLauro | Y | N | Y | N | Y | N | Y | Y |
| 4 Shays | Y | N | Y | N | Y | Y | Y | Y |
| 5 Johnson | Y | N | N | N | Y | N | Y | Y |
| **DELAWARE** | | | | | | | | |
| AL Castle | Y | N | N | Y | N | Y | N | Y |
| **FLORIDA** | | | | | | | | |
| 1 Miller | N | Y | N | N | N | N | N | N |
| 2 Boyd | Y | N | Y | Y | Y | Y | N | Y |
| 3 Brown | Y | N | Y | Y | Y | N | ? | ? |
| 4 Crenshaw | N | N | N | Y | N | N | N | N |
| 5 Brown-Waite | N | N | N | Y | N | N | N | N |
| 6 Stearns | N | N | Y | N | N | N | – | |
| 7 Mica | N | N | N | Y | N | N | N | N |
| 8 Keller | N | N | N | Y | N | N | N | N |
| 9 Bilirakis | N | N | N | Y | N | N | N | N |
| 10 Young | N | N | N | N | N | N | N | Y |
| 11 Davis | Y | N | Y | Y | Y | Y | Y | Y |
| 12 Putnam | N | N | N | Y | N | N | N | N |
| 13 Harris | Y | N | N | Y | Y | N | N | N |
| 14 Mack | N | Y | N | N | N | N | N | N |
| 15 Weldon | N | N | N | N | N | N | N | N |
| 16 Foley | N | N | N | Y | N | N | N | N |
| 17 Meek | Y | N | Y | Y | Y | Y | Y | Y |
| 18 Ros-Lehtinen | Y | N | Y | Y | N | N | N | N |
| 19 Wexler | Y | N | Y | Y | Y | Y | Y | Y |
| 20 Wasserman-Schultz | Y | N | Y | Y | Y | Y | Y | Y |
| 21 Diaz-Balart, L. | N | N | N | N | N | N | N | N |
| 22 Shaw | N | N | N | Y | N | N | N | N |
| 23 Hastings | Y | N | Y | Y | Y | Y | Y | Y |
| 24 Feeney | N | N | N | N | N | N | N | N |
| 25 Diaz-Balart, M. | N | N | N | N | N | N | N | N |
| **GEORGIA** | | | | | | | | |
| 1 Kingston | N | N | N | N | N | ? | ? | ? |
| 2 Bishop | Y | ? | ? | ? | ? | ? | ? | ? |
| 3 Marshall | Y | N | Y | Y | Y | Y | N | Y |
| 4 McKinney | Y | N | Y | Y | Y | Y | Y | Y |
| 5 Lewis | ? | ? | ? | ? | ? | Y | Y | Y |
| 6 Price | N | N | N | Y | N | N | N | N |
| 7 Linder | N | N | N | Y | N | N | N | N |
| 8 Westmoreland | Y | ? | ? | ? | ? | ? | ? | ? |
| 9 Norwood | N | N | N | Y | N | N | N | N |
| 10 Deal | N | N | N | N | N | N | N | N |
| 11 Gingrey | N | Y | N | Y | N | N | N | N |
| 12 Barrow | ? | ? | ? | ? | ? | N | N | Y |
| 13 Scott | ? | ? | ? | ? | ? | ? | ? | ? |
| **HAWAII** | | | | | | | | |
| 1 Abercrombie | Y | N | Y | Y | Y | Y | Y | Y |
| 2 Case | Y | N | Y | Y | Y | N | N | Y |
| **IDAHO** | | | | | | | | |
| 1 Otter | N | N | N | Y | N | Y | N | Y |
| 2 Simpson | N | N | Y | N | N | N | N | N |
| **ILLINOIS** | | | | | | | | |
| 1 Rush | Y | N | Y | Y | N | Y | Y | Y |
| 2 Jackson | Y | N | Y | N | Y | Y | Y | Y |
| 3 Lipinski | Y | N | Y | Y | Y | Y | Y | Y |
| 4 Gutierrez | Y | N | Y | Y | Y | Y | Y | Y |
| 5 Emanuel | Y | N | Y | Y | Y | Y | Y | Y |
| 6 Hyde | N | N | N | Y | N | N | N | N |
| 7 Davis | Y | N | Y | Y | Y | Y | Y | Y |
| 8 Bean | Y | N | Y | Y | Y | Y | Y | Y |
| 9 Schakowsky | Y | N | Y | Y | Y | Y | Y | Y |
| 10 Kirk | N | N | N | Y | N | N | N | N |
| 11 Weller | N | N | Y | N | Y | N | N | N |
| 12 Costello | Y | N | Y | Y | Y | Y | Y | Y |

**KEY**  Republicans  Democrats  *Independents*

| | | | |
|---|---|---|---|
| Y | Voted for (yea) | X | Paired against | C | Voted "present" to avoid possible conflict of interest |
| # | Paired for | – | Announced against | |
| + | Announced for | P | Voted "present" | ? | Did not vote or otherwise make a position known |
| N | Voted against (nay) | | | |

| | 340 | 341 | 342 | 343 | 344 | 345 | 346 | 347 |
|---|---|---|---|---|---|---|---|---|
| 13 **Biggert** | N | N | Y | Y | Y | Y | Y | N |
| 14 **Hastert** | | | | | | | | |
| 15 **Johnson** | N | Y | N | Y | N | Y | Y | Y |
| 16 **Manzullo** | N | N | N | Y | Y | N | N | N |
| 17 Evans | Y | N | Y | Y | N | Y | Y | Y |
| 18 **LaHood** | N | N | N | Y | Y | Y | N | Y |
| 19 **Shimkus** | N | N | N | Y | N | N | N | N |
| **INDIANA** | | | | | | | | |
| 1 Visclosky | Y | N | Y | Y | N | Y | Y | Y |
| 2 **Chocola** | Y | N | N | N | Y | N | N | N |
| 3 **Souder** | N | N | N | Y | Y | N | N | N |
| 4 **Buyer** | N | N | N | ? | Y | N | N | N |
| 5 **Burton** | Y | N | N | N | Y | N | N | N |
| 6 **Pence** | N | N | N | N | Y | N | N | N |
| 7 Carson | Y | N | N | Y | N | Y | Y | Y |
| 8 **Hostettler** | N | N | N | N | Y | Y | Y | Y |
| 9 **Sodrel** | Y | N | N | N | Y | N | N | Y |
| **IOWA** | | | | | | | | |
| 1 **Nussle** | N | N | N | Y | Y | N | N | Y |
| 2 **Leach** | Y | N | N | Y | N | Y | N | Y |
| 3 Boswell | Y | N | Y | Y | Y | Y | Y | Y |
| 4 **Latham** | N | N | N | Y | Y | N | N | Y |
| 5 **King** | N | Y | N | Y | Y | N | N | N |
| **KANSAS** | | | | | | | | |
| 1 **Moran** | Y | N | N | Y | Y | Y | Y | N |
| 2 **Ryun** | N | N | N | N | N | N | N | N |
| 3 Moore | Y | N | Y | Y | Y | Y | Y | Y |
| 4 **Tiahrt** | N | N | N | N | N | N | N | N |
| **KENTUCKY** | | | | | | | | |
| 1 **Whitfield** | N | N | N | Y | N | N | N | N |
| 2 **Lewis** | Y | Y | N | Y | Y | N | N | N |
| 3 **Northup** | N | N | N | N | N | N | N | N |
| 4 **Davis** | N | N | N | Y | Y | N | N | Y |
| 5 **Rogers** | N | N | N | N | Y | N | N | N |
| 6 Chandler | Y | N | Y | Y | Y | N | N | Y |
| **LOUISIANA** | | | | | | | | |
| 1 **Jindal** | Y | N | N | Y | N | N | N | N |
| 2 Jefferson | Y | N | Y | Y | Y | Y | Y | Y |
| 3 Melancon | Y | N | Y | Y | Y | N | N | Y |
| 4 **McCrery** | N | N | N | N | N | N | N | N |
| 5 **Alexander** | N | N | N | Y | Y | N | N | N |
| 6 **Baker** | N | N | N | N | Y | N | N | N |
| 7 **Boustany** | Y | N | N | Y | Y | N | N | N |
| **MAINE** | | | | | | | | |
| 1 Allen | Y | N | Y | Y | N | Y | Y | Y |
| 2 Michaud | N | N | N | Y | N | Y | Y | Y |
| **MARYLAND** | | | | | | | | |
| 1 **Gilchrest** | Y | N | N | Y | Y | Y | Y | N |
| 2 Ruppersberger | Y | N | Y | Y | Y | Y | Y | Y |
| 3 Cardin | Y | N | Y | Y | Y | Y | Y | Y |
| 4 Wynn | Y | N | Y | Y | N | Y | Y | Y |
| 5 Hoyer | Y | N | Y | Y | N | Y | Y | Y |
| 6 **Bartlett** | Y | N | N | N | Y | N | N | N |
| 7 Cummings | Y | N | Y | Y | Y | Y | Y | Y |
| 8 Van Hollen | Y | N | Y | Y | Y | Y | Y | Y |
| **MASSACHUSETTS** | | | | | | | | |
| 1 Olver | Y | N | Y | Y | N | Y | Y | Y |
| 2 Neal | ? | ? | ? | ? | ? | Y | Y | Y |
| 3 McGovern | Y | N | Y | Y | N | Y | Y | Y |
| 4 Frank | Y | N | N | N | N | Y | Y | Y |
| 5 Meehan | Y | N | Y | Y | Y | Y | Y | Y |
| 6 Tierney | Y | N | Y | Y | N | Y | Y | Y |
| 7 Markey | Y | N | Y | Y | N | Y | Y | Y |
| 8 Capuano | Y | N | Y | Y | N | Y | Y | Y |
| 9 Lynch | Y | N | Y | Y | Y | Y | Y | Y |
| 10 Delahunt | Y | N | Y | Y | Y | Y | Y | Y |
| **MICHIGAN** | | | | | | | | |
| 1 Stupak | Y | N | Y | Y | Y | Y | Y | Y |
| 2 **Hoekstra** | N | N | N | N | N | N | N | N |
| 3 **Ehlers** | N | N | N | N | Y | Y | N | N |
| 4 **Camp** | N | N | N | Y | Y | N | N | N |
| 5 Kildee | Y | N | Y | Y | N | Y | Y | Y |
| 6 **Upton** | Y | N | N | Y | Y | N | N | N |
| 7 **Schwarz** | N | N | N | Y | Y | N | N | Y |
| 8 **Rogers** | N | N | N | N | Y | N | N | Y |
| 9 **Knollenberg** | N | N | N | N | N | N | N | N |
| 10 **Miller** | N | N | N | N | Y | N | N | N |
| 11 **McCotter** | N | N | N | Y | Y | N | N | Y |
| 12 Levin | Y | N | Y | Y | Y | Y | Y | Y |
| 13 Kilpatrick | Y | N | N | Y | N | Y | Y | Y |
| 14 Conyers | Y | N | Y | Y | Y | Y | Y | Y |
| 15 Dingell | Y | N | Y | Y | Y | Y | Y | Y |

| | 340 | 341 | 342 | 343 | 344 | 345 | 346 | 347 |
|---|---|---|---|---|---|---|---|---|
| **MINNESOTA** | | | | | | | | |
| 1 **Gutknecht** | Y | Y | N | N | Y | N | N | N |
| 2 **Kline** | Y | N | N | Y | Y | N | N | N |
| 3 **Ramstad** | Y | N | N | Y | Y | Y | Y | N |
| 4 McCollum | Y | N | Y | Y | Y | Y | Y | Y |
| 5 Sabo | Y | N | Y | Y | N | Y | Y | Y |
| 6 **Kennedy** | Y | N | N | Y | Y | N | N | N |
| 7 Peterson | Y | N | Y | Y | Y | Y | Y | Y |
| 8 Oberstar | N | N | Y | Y | Y | Y | Y | Y |
| **MISSISSIPPI** | | | | | | | | |
| 1 **Wicker** | Y | N | N | N | N | N | N | N |
| 2 Thompson | Y | N | Y | Y | N | Y | Y | Y |
| 3 **Pickering** | Y | N | N | Y | Y | N | N | N |
| 4 Taylor | Y | Y | Y | Y | Y | Y | Y | Y |
| **MISSOURI** | | | | | | | | |
| 1 Clay | ? | N | Y | Y | N | Y | Y | Y |
| 2 **Akin** | – | Y | N | N | Y | N | N | N |
| 3 Carnahan | Y | N | Y | Y | Y | Y | N | Y |
| 4 Skelton | Y | N | Y | Y | Y | N | N | Y |
| 5 Cleaver | Y | N | Y | Y | N | Y | Y | Y |
| 6 **Graves** | Y | N | N | Y | Y | Y | Y | N |
| 7 **Blunt** | N | N | N | N | N | N | N | N |
| 8 **Emerson** | N | N | N | Y | N | Y | Y | Y |
| 9 **Hulshof** | Y | N | N | Y | Y | N | N | N |
| **MONTANA** | | | | | | | | |
| AL **Rehberg** | N | N | N | N | N | N | N | Y |
| **NEBRASKA** | | | | | | | | |
| 1 **Fortenberry** | N | N | N | Y | Y | N | N | Y |
| 2 **Terry** | Y | N | N | Y | Y | N | N | N |
| 3 **Osborne** | N | N | N | Y | Y | Y | Y | Y |
| **NEVADA** | | | | | | | | |
| 1 Berkley | Y | N | Y | Y | Y | N | N | Y |
| 2 **Gibbons** | Y | Y | N | Y | Y | N | N | Y |
| 3 **Porter** | N | N | Y | Y | Y | N | N | Y |
| **NEW HAMPSHIRE** | | | | | | | | |
| 1 **Bradley** | N | N | N | Y | N | N | N | N |
| 2 **Bass** | N | N | N | Y | Y | Y | Y | Y |
| **NEW JERSEY** | | | | | | | | |
| 1 Andrews | Y | N | Y | Y | Y | Y | N | Y |
| 2 **LoBiondo** | Y | N | N | Y | Y | N | N | Y |
| 3 **Saxton** | N | N | N | N | N | N | N | N |
| 4 **Smith** | Y | N | N | Y | Y | N | N | Y |
| 5 **Garrett** | N | N | N | N | N | Y | N | N |
| 6 Pallone | Y | N | Y | Y | Y | N | N | Y |
| 7 **Ferguson** | N | N | N | N | N | N | N | N |
| 8 Pascrell | Y | N | Y | Y | N | Y | N | Y |
| 9 Rothman | Y | N | Y | Y | Y | N | N | Y |
| 10 Payne | Y | N | Y | Y | Y | Y | Y | Y |
| 11 **Frelinghuysen** | N | N | N | N | N | N | N | N |
| 12 Holt | Y | N | Y | Y | Y | Y | Y | Y |
| 13 Menendez | Y | N | Y | Y | Y | N | N | Y |
| **NEW MEXICO** | | | | | | | | |
| 1 **Wilson** | Y | N | N | Y | Y | N | N | N |
| 2 **Pearce** | N | Y | N | N | N | N | N | N |
| 3 Udall | Y | N | Y | Y | Y | Y | Y | Y |
| **NEW YORK** | | | | | | | | |
| 1 Bishop | Y | N | Y | Y | Y | Y | Y | Y |
| 2 Israel | Y | N | Y | Y | Y | Y | Y | Y |
| 3 **King** | N | N | N | Y | Y | N | N | Y |
| 4 McCarthy | Y | N | Y | Y | Y | Y | Y | Y |
| 5 Ackerman | Y | N | Y | Y | Y | N | N | Y |
| 6 Meeks | Y | N | Y | Y | Y | Y | Y | Y |
| 7 Crowley | Y | N | Y | Y | Y | Y | Y | Y |
| 8 Nadler | Y | N | Y | Y | Y | Y | Y | Y |
| 9 Weiner | Y | N | Y | Y | Y | Y | Y | Y |
| 10 Towns | Y | N | Y | Y | N | Y | Y | Y |
| 11 Owens | Y | N | Y | Y | Y | Y | Y | Y |
| 12 Velázquez | Y | N | Y | Y | Y | Y | Y | Y |
| 13 **Fossella** | N | N | N | Y | Y | N | N | Y |
| 14 Maloney | Y | N | Y | Y | N | Y | Y | Y |
| 15 Rangel | Y | ? | N | Y | Y | Y | Y | Y |
| 16 Serrano | Y | N | Y | Y | Y | Y | Y | Y |
| 17 Engel | Y | N | Y | Y | Y | N | N | Y |
| 18 Lowey | Y | N | Y | Y | N | Y | Y | Y |
| 19 **Kelly** | Y | Y | Y | Y | Y | N | N | Y |
| 20 **Sweeney** | N | N | N | N | Y | N | N | Y |
| 21 McNulty | Y | N | Y | Y | Y | Y | Y | Y |
| 22 Hinchey | Y | N | Y | Y | Y | Y | Y | Y |
| 23 **McHugh** | N | N | N | Y | N | N | N | Y |
| 24 **Boehlert** | Y | N | N | Y | N | Y | Y | Y |
| 25 **Walsh** | N | N | N | N | N | N | N | Y |
| 26 **Reynolds** | N | N | N | N | N | N | N | Y |
| 27 Higgins | Y | ? | Y | Y | Y | Y | N | Y |
| 28 Slaughter | Y | N | Y | Y | Y | Y | Y | Y |
| 29 **Kuhl** | N | N | N | Y | Y | N | N | N |

| | 340 | 341 | 342 | 343 | 344 | 345 | 346 | 347 |
|---|---|---|---|---|---|---|---|---|
| **NORTH CAROLINA** | | | | | | | | |
| 1 Butterfield | Y | N | Y | Y | Y | Y | Y | Y |
| 2 Etheridge | Y | N | Y | Y | Y | Y | Y | Y |
| 3 **Jones** | Y | N | N | Y | Y | N | N | N |
| 4 Price | Y | N | Y | Y | Y | Y | Y | Y |
| 5 **Foxx** | N | Y | N | N | Y | N | N | N |
| 6 **Coble** | Y | N | Y | Y | Y | N | N | N |
| 7 McIntyre | Y | Y | Y | Y | Y | N | N | Y |
| 8 **Hayes** | N | N | N | N | N | N | N | N |
| 9 **Myrick** | N | Y | N | N | Y | N | N | N |
| 10 **McHenry** | N | Y | N | Y | Y | N | N | N |
| 11 **Taylor** | N | N | N | Y | N | N | N | N |
| 12 Watt | Y | ? | Y | Y | N | Y | Y | Y |
| 13 Miller | Y | N | Y | Y | Y | N | N | Y |
| **NORTH DAKOTA** | | | | | | | | |
| AL Pomeroy | Y | N | Y | Y | Y | Y | Y | Y |
| **OHIO** | | | | | | | | |
| 1 **Chabot** | N | Y | N | Y | Y | N | N | N |
| 2 Vacant | | | | | | | | |
| 3 **Turner** | Y | N | N | N | N | N | N | Y |
| 4 **Oxley** | N | N | N | Y | N | N | N | N |
| 5 **Gillmor** | N | N | N | Y | Y | N | N | N |
| 6 Strickland | Y | N | Y | Y | Y | Y | Y | Y |
| 7 **Hobson** | N | N | N | N | N | N | N | N |
| 8 **Boehner** | N | N | N | Y | Y | N | N | N |
| 9 Kaptur | Y | N | N | Y | Y | Y | Y | ? |
| 10 Kucinich | Y | N | Y | Y | N | Y | Y | Y |
| 11 Jones | Y | N | Y | Y | N | Y | Y | Y |
| 12 **Tiberi** | Y | N | N | Y | Y | Y | Y | Y |
| 13 Brown | Y | N | Y | Y | N | Y | Y | Y |
| 14 **LaTourette** | N | N | N | Y | N | N | N | Y |
| 15 **Pryce** | N | N | N | N | N | N | N | N |
| 16 **Regula** | N | N | N | N | N | N | N | Y |
| 17 Ryan | Y | N | Y | Y | N | Y | Y | Y |
| 18 **Ney** | Y | ? | N | Y | Y | Y | N | N |
| **OKLAHOMA** | | | | | | | | |
| 1 **Sullivan** | N | N | N | N | N | N | N | N |
| 2 Boren | Y | N | Y | Y | Y | Y | N | Y |
| 3 **Lucas** | N | N | N | Y | Y | N | N | N |
| 4 **Cole** | N | N | N | N | N | N | N | N |
| 5 **Istook** | N | N | N | N | ? | N | N | N |
| **OREGON** | | | | | | | | |
| 1 Wu | Y | N | Y | Y | Y | N | N | Y |
| 2 **Walden** | N | N | N | Y | Y | N | N | N |
| 3 Blumenauer | Y | N | Y | Y | N | Y | Y | Y |
| 4 DeFazio | N | N | N | Y | Y | Y | Y | Y |
| 5 Hooley | Y | N | Y | Y | Y | Y | Y | Y |
| **PENNSYLVANIA** | | | | | | | | |
| 1 Brady | Y | N | Y | Y | Y | Y | Y | Y |
| 2 Fattah | Y | N | Y | Y | Y | Y | Y | Y |
| 3 **English** | N | N | N | N | Y | N | N | Y |
| 4 **Hart** | N | Y | N | N | Y | N | N | N |
| 5 **Peterson** | ? | ? | ? | ? | ? | ? | ? | ? |
| 6 **Gerlach** | Y | N | N | Y | Y | N | N | Y |
| 7 **Weldon** | Y | N | N | Y | Y | Y | N | N |
| 8 **Fitzpatrick** | Y | N | Y | Y | Y | N | N | Y |
| 9 **Shuster** | N | Y | N | Y | N | N | N | Y |
| 10 **Sherwood** | N | N | N | Y | N | N | N | N |
| 11 Kanjorski | Y | N | Y | Y | N | Y | Y | Y |
| 12 Murtha | Y | N | Y | Y | Y | Y | Y | Y |
| 13 Schwartz | Y | N | Y | Y | Y | Y | Y | Y |
| 14 Doyle | Y | N | Y | Y | Y | Y | Y | Y |
| 15 **Dent** | Y | N | N | Y | Y | N | N | N |
| 16 **Pitts** | N | Y | N | N | Y | N | N | N |
| 17 Holden | N | N | Y | Y | Y | Y | Y | Y |
| 18 **Murphy** | Y | N | N | Y | Y | N | N | Y |
| 19 **Platts** | Y | N | N | N | Y | N | N | N |
| **RHODE ISLAND** | | | | | | | | |
| 1 Kennedy | Y | N | Y | Y | Y | Y | N | Y |
| 2 Langevin | Y | N | Y | Y | Y | Y | Y | Y |
| **SOUTH CAROLINA** | | | | | | | | |
| 1 **Brown** | Y | N | N | N | N | N | N | N |
| 2 **Wilson** | Y | Y | N | N | Y | N | N | N |
| 3 **Barrett** | Y | N | N | N | Y | N | N | N |
| 4 **Inglis** | N | N | N | N | N | N | N | N |
| 5 Spratt | Y | N | Y | Y | Y | Y | Y | Y |
| 6 Clyburn | Y | N | Y | Y | N | Y | Y | Y |
| **SOUTH DAKOTA** | | | | | | | | |
| AL Herseth | Y | N | Y | Y | Y | Y | Y | Y |
| **TENNESSEE** | | | | | | | | |
| 1 **Jenkins** | Y | N | N | Y | Y | N | N | N |
| 2 **Duncan** | Y | Y | N | Y | Y | Y | N | N |

| | 340 | 341 | 342 | 343 | 344 | 345 | 346 | 347 |
|---|---|---|---|---|---|---|---|---|
| 3 **Wamp** | N | N | N | Y | Y | N | N | N |
| 4 Davis | Y | N | N | Y | Y | Y | Y | Y |
| 5 Cooper | Y | ? | ? | ? | ? | ? | ? | ? |
| 6 Gordon | Y | N | Y | Y | Y | Y | Y | Y |
| 7 **Blackburn** | N | Y | N | Y | Y | N | N | N |
| 8 Tanner | Y | N | Y | Y | Y | Y | Y | Y |
| 9 Ford | Y | N | Y | Y | Y | Y | Y | Y |
| **TEXAS** | | | | | | | | |
| 1 **Gohmert** | Y | Y | Y | Y | Y | N | N | N |
| 2 **Poe** | N | Y | N | Y | Y | N | N | N |
| 3 **Johnson, S.** | ? | N | N | N | Y | N | N | N |
| 4 **Hall** | N | N | N | N | Y | N | N | N |
| 5 **Hensarling** | N | N | N | N | N | N | N | N |
| 6 **Barton** | N | N | N | Y | Y | N | N | N |
| 7 **Culberson** | N | N | N | N | N | N | N | N |
| 8 **Brady** | N | N | N | N | N | N | N | N |
| 9 Green, A. | Y | N | Y | Y | Y | Y | Y | Y |
| 10 **McCaul** | N | N | N | N | Y | N | N | N |
| 11 **Conaway** | N | N | N | Y | Y | N | N | Y |
| 12 **Granger** | N | N | N | N | N | N | N | N |
| 13 **Thornberry** | N | N | N | N | Y | N | N | N |
| 14 **Paul** | N | Y | N | N | N | Y | Y | N |
| 15 Hinojosa | Y | N | Y | Y | N | Y | Y | Y |
| 16 Reyes | Y | N | Y | Y | N | ? | Y | Y |
| 17 Edwards | Y | N | Y | Y | Y | Y | Y | Y |
| 18 Jackson-Lee | Y | N | Y | Y | N | Y | Y | Y |
| 19 **Neugebauer** | N | Y | N | N | Y | N | N | N |
| 20 Gonzalez | N | N | N | Y | N | Y | Y | Y |
| 21 **Smith** | N | N | Y | N | N | N | N | N |
| 22 **DeLay** | N | N | N | N | N | N | N | N |
| 23 **Bonilla** | N | N | N | N | N | N | N | N |
| 24 **Marchant** | N | N | N | N | Y | N | N | N |
| 25 Doggett | Y | N | Y | Y | N | Y | Y | Y |
| 26 **Burgess** | N | N | N | Y | N | N | N | N |
| 27 Ortiz | Y | N | Y | Y | Y | N | N | ? |
| 28 Cuellar | Y | N | Y | Y | Y | Y | N | Y |
| 29 Green, G. | N | N | Y | Y | N | Y | N | N |
| 30 Johnson, E. | Y | N | Y | Y | N | Y | Y | ? |
| 31 **Carter** | N | N | N | N | N | N | N | N |
| 32 **Sessions** | N | N | N | N | Y | N | N | N |
| **UTAH** | | | | | | | | |
| 1 **Bishop** | N | Y | N | Y | Y | N | N | N |
| 2 Matheson | Y | N | Y | Y | Y | Y | Y | Y |
| 3 **Cannon** | N | N | N | Y | Y | N | N | N |
| **VERMONT** | | | | | | | | |
| AL *Sanders* | Y | N | Y | Y | Y | Y | Y | Y |
| **VIRGINIA** | | | | | | | | |
| 1 **Davis, J.** | N | Y | N | Y | Y | N | N | N |
| 2 **Drake** | N | Y | N | Y | N | N | N | N |
| 3 Scott | Y | N | N | Y | N | Y | Y | Y |
| 4 **Forbes** | N | N | N | Y | Y | N | N | N |
| 5 **Goode** | N | Y | N | Y | N | N | N | N |
| 6 **Goodlatte** | N | N | Y | Y | Y | N | N | N |
| 7 **Cantor** | N | N | N | N | N | N | N | N |
| 8 Moran | Y | N | Y | Y | N | Y | Y | N |
| 9 Boucher | Y | N | Y | Y | N | Y | Y | Y |
| 10 **Wolf** | N | N | N | N | N | N | N | N |
| 11 **Davis, T.** | N | N | N | Y | Y | N | N | N |
| **WASHINGTON** | | | | | | | | |
| 1 Inslee | Y | N | Y | Y | Y | Y | Y | Y |
| 2 Larsen | Y | N | Y | Y | Y | Y | Y | Y |
| 3 Baird | N | N | N | Y | Y | Y | Y | Y |
| 4 **Hastings** | N | N | N | N | N | N | N | N |
| 5 **McMorris** | N | N | N | Y | Y | N | N | N |
| 6 Dicks | Y | N | Y | Y | Y | Y | Y | Y |
| 7 McDermott | Y | N | Y | Y | Y | Y | Y | Y |
| 8 **Reichert** | Y | N | N | Y | Y | N | N | N |
| 9 Smith | Y | N | Y | Y | Y | Y | Y | Y |
| **WEST VIRGINIA** | | | | | | | | |
| 1 Mollohan | Y | N | N | N | N | Y | Y | Y |
| 2 **Capito** | Y | N | N | Y | Y | N | N | Y |
| 3 Rahall | Y | N | Y | Y | Y | Y | Y | Y |
| **WISCONSIN** | | | | | | | | |
| 1 **Ryan** | N | N | N | N | Y | Y | Y | N |
| 2 Baldwin | Y | N | Y | Y | Y | Y | Y | Y |
| 3 Kind | Y | N | Y | Y | Y | Y | Y | Y |
| 4 Moore | Y | N | Y | N | Y | – | Y | Y |
| 5 **Sensenbrenner** | N | N | N | Y | Y | N | N | N |
| 6 **Petri** | Y | N | N | Y | N | N | N | N |
| 7 Obey | Y | N | Y | Y | N | Y | Y | Y |
| 8 **Green** | N | N | N | Y | Y | N | N | Y |
| **WYOMING** | | | | | | | | |
| AL **Cubin** | Y | Y | N | Y | Y | Y | N | Y |

# IN THE HOUSE | By Vote Number

**348.** **HR 3058. Fiscal 2006 Transportation-Treasury-Housing Appropriations/Cuba Economic Embargo.** Rangel, D-N.Y., amendment that would prohibit the use of funds to implement, administer or enforce the economic embargo of Cuba. Rejected 169-250: R 20-203; D 148-47 (ND 122-27, SD 26-20); I 1-0. A "nay" was a vote in support of the president's position. June 30, 2005.

**349.** **HR 3058. Fiscal 2006 Transportation-Treasury-Housing Appropriations/D.C. Firearm Laws.** Souder, R-Ind., amendment that would prohibit the use of funds in the bill to enforce District of Columbia laws requiring that a registered firearm be kept unloaded and disassembled, or with the trigger locked, unless it is kept at a place of business or used for lawful recreation. Adopted 259-161: R 209-15; D 50-145 (ND 27-122, SD 23-23); I 0-1. June 30, 2005.

**350.** **HR 3058. Fiscal 2006 Transportation-Treasury-Housing Appropriations/Eminent Domain.** Garrett, R-N.J., amendment that would prohibit the use of funds in the bill to improve or construct infrastructure support on private property obtained through the power of eminent domain for private development. Adopted 231-189: R 192-31; D 39-157 (ND 23-127, SD 16-30); I 0-1. June 30, 2005.

**351.** **HR 3058. Fiscal 2006 Transportation-Treasury-Housing Appropriations/Offshore Contracts.** DeLauro, D-Conn., amendment that would prohibit the use of funds in the bill to carry out contracts with a U.S. company that is incorporated or chartered in Bermuda, Barbados, the Cayman Islands, Antigua or Panama to avoid U.S. taxes. Rejected 190-231: R 20-203; D 169-28 (ND 137-13, SD 32-15); I 1-0. June 30, 2005.

**352.** **HR 3058. Fiscal 2006 Transportation-Treasury-Housing Appropriations/Discretionary Spending Cut.** Hefley, R-Colo., amendment that would reduce discretionary spending in the bill by 1 percent. Rejected 88-338: R 83-144; D 5-193 (ND 2-146, SD 3-47); I 0-1. June 30, 2005.

**353.** **HR 3058. Fiscal 2006 Transportation-Treasury-Housing Appropriations/Sale of Unocal Corp.** Kilpatrick, D-Mich., amendment that would prohibit the use of funds by the Treasury Department to make a favorable recommendation of the sale of Unocal Corporation to the China National Offshore Oil Corporation. Adopted 333-92: R 155-71; D 177-21 (ND 132-16, SD 45-5); I 1-0. June 30, 2005.

**354.** **HR 3058. Fiscal 2006 Transportation-Treasury-Housing Appropriations/Congressional Testimony.** Obey, D-Wis., amendment that would prohibit the use of funds in the bill to contravene an Office of Management and Budget regulation that requires administration officials to give frank and complete answers to all questions when testifying before congressional committees or communicating with members of Congress. Rejected 208-215: R 9-215; D 198-0 (ND 148-0, SD 50-0); I 1-0. June 30, 2005.

**355.** **HR 3058. Fiscal 2006 Transportation-Treasury-Housing Appropriations/Prescription Drug Costs.** Brown, D-Ohio, amendment that would prohibit the use of funds in the bill by the Council of Economic Advisers to produce an Economic Report of the President estimating that the average cost of developing and introducing a new prescription drug to the market would be $800 million or more. Rejected 141-284: R 15-212; D 125-72 (ND 100-47, SD 25-25); I 1-0. June 30, 2005.

| | 348 | 349 | 350 | 351 | 352 | 353 | 354 | 355 |
|---|---|---|---|---|---|---|---|---|
| **ALABAMA** | | | | | | | | |
| 1 Bonner | N | Y | Y | N | N | Y | N | N |
| 2 Everett | ? | ? | ? | ? | ? | ? | ? | ? |
| 3 Rogers | ? | ? | ? | ? | Y | N | N | N |
| 4 Aderholt | N | Y | Y | N | N | Y | N | N |
| 5 Cramer | ? | ? | ? | ? | N | Y | Y | N |
| 6 Bachus | ? | ? | ? | ? | Y | N | N | N |
| 7 Davis | N | Y | N | Y | N | Y | Y | N |
| **ALASKA** | | | | | | | | |
| AL Young | N | Y | Y | N | N | N | N | N |
| **ARIZONA** | | | | | | | | |
| 1 Renzi | N | Y | Y | N | N | Y | N | N |
| 2 Franks | N | Y | Y | N | Y | Y | N | N |
| 3 Shadegg | ? | Y | Y | N | Y | N | N | N |
| 4 Pastor | Y | N | N | Y | N | Y | Y | Y |
| 5 Hayworth | N | Y | Y | N | Y | Y | N | N |
| 6 Flake | Y | Y | Y | N | Y | N | N | N |
| 7 Grijalva | Y | N | N | Y | N | Y | Y | Y |
| 8 Kolbe | Y | Y | N | N | N | N | N | N |
| **ARKANSAS** | | | | | | | | |
| 1 Berry | Y | Y | Y | N | Y | N | Y | Y |
| 2 Snyder | Y | N | N | N | N | N | Y | Y |
| 3 Boozman | Y | Y | Y | N | Y | N | N | N |
| 4 Ross | ? | ? | ? | ? | ? | ? | ? | ? |
| **CALIFORNIA** | | | | | | | | |
| 1 Thompson | Y | N | N | N | N | Y | Y | N |
| 2 Herger | Y | Y | Y | N | Y | Y | N | N |
| 3 Lungren | N | Y | Y | N | Y | N | N | N |
| 4 Doolittle | N | Y | Y | N | N | Y | N | N |
| 5 Matsui, D. | Y | N | N | Y | N | Y | Y | Y |
| 6 Woolsey | Y | N | N | Y | N | Y | Y | Y |
| 7 Miller, George | Y | N | N | Y | N | Y | Y | Y |
| 8 Pelosi | Y | N | N | Y | N | Y | Y | Y |
| 9 Lee | Y | N | N | Y | N | Y | Y | Y |
| 10 Tauscher | Y | N | Y | N | Y | Y | Y | Y |
| 11 Pombo | N | Y | Y | N | N | Y | N | N |
| 12 Lantos | N | N | N | Y | N | Y | Y | Y |
| 13 Stark | Y | N | N | Y | N | N | Y | Y |
| 14 Eshoo | Y | N | N | Y | N | Y | Y | Y |
| 15 Honda | Y | N | N | Y | N | Y | Y | Y |
| 16 Lofgren | Y | N | N | N | N | N | Y | Y |
| 17 Farr | Y | N | N | Y | N | Y | Y | Y |
| 18 Cardoza | N | Y | N | Y | N | Y | Y | Y |
| 19 Radanovich | N | Y | Y | N | Y | N | N | N |
| 20 Costa | N | Y | N | Y | N | Y | Y | N |
| 21 Nunes | N | Y | Y | N | N | Y | N | N |
| 22 Thomas | N | Y | N | N | N | N | N | N |
| 23 Capps | Y | N | N | Y | N | Y | Y | Y |
| 24 Gallegly | N | Y | Y | N | N | Y | N | N |
| 25 McKeon | N | Y | Y | N | N | N | N | N |
| 26 Dreier | N | Y | Y | N | N | N | N | N |
| 27 Sherman | N | N | N | Y | N | Y | Y | Y |
| 28 Berman | N | N | N | Y | N | N | Y | Y |
| 29 Schiff | ? | ? | ? | ? | ? | ? | ? | ? |
| 30 Waxman | Y | N | N | Y | N | N | N | Y |
| 31 Becerra | Y | N | N | Y | N | Y | Y | Y |
| 32 Solis | Y | N | N | Y | N | Y | Y | Y |
| 33 Watson | Y | N | N | Y | N | Y | Y | Y |
| 34 Roybal-Allard | Y | N | N | Y | N | Y | Y | Y |
| 35 Waters | Y | N | Y | N | ? | ? | ? | ? |
| 36 Harman | Y | N | N | Y | ? | ? | ? | ? |
| 37 Millender-McD. | Y | N | N | Y | N | Y | Y | Y |
| 38 Napolitano | Y | N | N | Y | N | Y | Y | Y |
| 39 Sánchez, Linda | Y | N | N | Y | N | Y | Y | Y |
| 40 Royce | N | Y | Y | N | Y | Y | N | N |
| 41 Lewis | N | Y | N | N | N | N | N | N |
| 42 Miller, Gary | N | Y | Y | N | N | Y | N | N |
| 43 Baca | Y | N | N | Y | N | Y | Y | N |
| 44 Calvert | N | Y | Y | N | N | N | N | N |
| 45 Bono | Y | N | Y | N | N | Y | N | N |
| 46 Rohrabacher | N | Y | Y | Y | Y | Y | N | N |
| 47 Sanchez, Loretta | Y | N | Y | N | N | Y | Y | Y |
| 48 Cox | N | Y | Y | N | Y | ? | N | N |
| 49 Issa | N | Y | Y | N | N | Y | N | N |

| | 348 | 349 | 350 | 351 | 352 | 353 | 354 | 355 |
|---|---|---|---|---|---|---|---|---|
| 50 Cunningham | N | Y | Y | N | Y | N | N | N |
| 51 Filner | Y | N | N | Y | N | Y | Y | Y |
| 52 Hunter | N | Y | Y | N | Y | Y | N | N |
| 53 Davis | N | N | N | Y | N | N | Y | Y |
| **COLORADO** | | | | | | | | |
| 1 DeGette | Y | N | N | Y | N | Y | Y | N |
| 2 Udall | Y | N | N | Y | N | Y | Y | Y |
| 3 Salazar | N | Y | N | Y | N | Y | Y | N |
| 4 Musgrave | N | Y | Y | N | N | Y | N | N |
| 5 Hefley | N | Y | Y | Y | Y | Y | N | Y |
| 6 Tancredo | N | Y | Y | N | Y | Y | N | N |
| 7 Beauprez | N | Y | Y | N | N | N | N | N |
| **CONNECTICUT** | | | | | | | | |
| 1 Larson | Y | N | N | Y | N | Y | Y | Y |
| 2 Simmons | N | Y | Y | Y | N | Y | Y | Y |
| 3 DeLauro | Y | N | N | Y | N | Y | Y | Y |
| 4 Shays | N | N | N | Y | N | N | N | N |
| 5 Johnson | Y | N | N | Y | N | N | Y | N |
| **DELAWARE** | | | | | | | | |
| AL Castle | N | N | N | N | Y | N | N | N |
| **FLORIDA** | | | | | | | | |
| 1 Miller | N | Y | Y | N | Y | Y | N | N |
| 2 Boyd | N | Y | Y | N | Y | N | Y | N |
| 3 Brown | N | Y | N | Y | N | Y | Y | N |
| 4 Crenshaw | N | Y | Y | N | Y | Y | N | N |
| 5 Brown-Waite | N | Y | Y | N | Y | N | N | N |
| 6 Stearns | N | Y | N | N | Y | N | Y | N |
| 7 Mica | N | Y | Y | N | Y | Y | N | N |
| 8 Keller | N | Y | Y | N | Y | Y | N | N |
| 9 Bilirakis | N | Y | Y | N | Y | Y | N | N |
| 10 Young | N | N | Y | N | Y | N | Y | Y |
| 11 Davis | N | N | Y | N | Y | Y | Y | Y |
| 12 Putnam | N | Y | Y | N | Y | N | N | N |
| 13 Harris | N | Y | Y | N | Y | N | N | N |
| 14 Mack | N | Y | Y | N | Y | Y | N | N |
| 15 Weldon | Y | N | N | Y | N | N | N | N |
| 16 Foley | N | N | Y | N | Y | N | N | N |
| 17 Meek | N | Y | N | Y | N | Y | Y | Y |
| 18 Ros-Lehtinen | N | Y | Y | N | Y | N | N | N |
| 19 Wexler | N | N | N | Y | N | Y | Y | Y |
| 20 Wasserman-Schultz | N | N | N | Y | N | Y | Y | Y |
| 21 Diaz-Balart, L. | N | Y | Y | N | Y | N | N | N |
| 22 Shaw | N | Y | Y | N | N | N | N | N |
| 23 Hastings | N | N | N | Y | N | Y | Y | Y |
| 24 Feeney | N | Y | Y | N | Y | N | N | N |
| 25 Diaz-Balart, M. | N | Y | Y | N | Y | Y | N | N |
| **GEORGIA** | | | | | | | | |
| 1 Kingston | ? | ? | ? | ? | ? | ? | ? | ? |
| 2 Bishop | ? | ? | ? | Y | N | Y | Y | N |
| 3 Marshall | N | Y | Y | N | Y | N | Y | N |
| 4 McKinney | Y | N | N | Y | N | Y | Y | Y |
| 5 Lewis | Y | N | N | Y | N | Y | Y | Y |
| 6 Price | N | Y | Y | N | Y | N | N | N |
| 7 Linder | N | Y | Y | N | Y | N | N | N |
| 8 Westmoreland | ? | ? | ? | ? | Y | Y | N | N |
| 9 Norwood | N | Y | Y | N | Y | Y | N | N |
| 10 Deal | N | Y | Y | N | Y | N | N | N |
| 11 Gingrey | N | Y | Y | N | Y | N | N | N |
| 12 Barrow | N | Y | Y | N | Y | Y | Y | Y |
| 13 Scott | ? | ? | ? | ? | N | Y | Y | Y |
| **HAWAII** | | | | | | | | |
| 1 Abercrombie | Y | N | Y | N | Y | N | Y | N |
| 2 Case | N | N | N | Y | N | Y | Y | Y |
| **IDAHO** | | | | | | | | |
| 1 Otter | Y | Y | Y | N | Y | Y | N | Y |
| 2 Simpson | N | Y | N | N | N | Y | Y | N |
| **ILLINOIS** | | | | | | | | |
| 1 Rush | Y | N | N | Y | N | Y | Y | Y |
| 2 Jackson | Y | N | N | Y | N | Y | Y | Y |
| 3 Lipinski | N | N | N | Y | N | Y | Y | Y |
| 4 Gutierrez | N | N | N | Y | N | Y | Y | Y |
| 5 Emanuel | N | N | N | Y | N | Y | Y | Y |
| 6 Hyde | N | Y | Y | N | N | Y | N | N |
| 7 Davis | Y | N | N | Y | N | Y | Y | Y |
| 8 Bean | Y | N | N | Y | N | Y | Y | Y |
| 9 Schakowsky | Y | N | N | Y | N | Y | Y | Y |
| 10 Kirk | N | N | N | N | N | Y | Y | N |
| 11 Weller | N | Y | Y | N | N | Y | N | N |
| 12 Costello | Y | Y | Y | N | Y | Y | Y | Y |

**KEY**    **Republicans**    Democrats    *Independents*

| | | | |
|---|---|---|---|
| **Y** | Voted for (yea) | **X** | Paired against |
| **#** | Paired for | **–** | Announced against |
| **+** | Announced for | **P** | Voted "present" |
| **N** | Voted against (nay) | **C** | Voted "present" to avoid possible conflict of interest |
| | | **?** | Did not vote or otherwise make a position known |

| | 348 | 349 | 350 | 351 | 352 | 353 | 354 | 355 |
|---|---|---|---|---|---|---|---|---|
| 13 **Biggert** | Y | Y | Y | N | N | N | N | N |
| 14 **Hastert** | | | | | | | | |
| 15 **Johnson** | Y | Y | Y | N | N | N | N | N |
| 16 **Manzullo** | Y | Y | Y | N | Y | Y | N | Y |
| 17 Evans | ? | N | N | Y | N | Y | Y | Y |
| 18 **LaHood** | Y | Y | Y | N | N | Y | N | N |
| 19 **Shimkus** | N | Y | Y | N | Y | Y | N | N |
| INDIANA | | | | | | | | |
| 1 Visclosky | Y | N | N | Y | N | Y | Y | Y |
| 2 **Chocola** | N | Y | Y | N | Y | N | N | N |
| 3 **Souder** | N | Y | Y | N | N | Y | Y | N |
| 4 **Buyer** | N | Y | Y | N | Y | Y | N | N |
| 5 **Burton** | N | Y | Y | N | Y | Y | N | Y |
| 6 **Pence** | N | Y | Y | N | Y | Y | N | N |
| 7 Carson | Y | N | N | Y | N | Y | Y | Y |
| 8 **Hostettler** | N | Y | Y | N | Y | Y | N | N |
| 9 **Sodrel** | N | Y | Y | N | N | Y | N | N |
| IOWA | | | | | | | | |
| 1 **Nussle** | N | Y | Y | N | N | Y | N | N |
| 2 **Leach** | Y | N | Y | N | N | N | Y | N |
| 3 Boswell | Y | Y | N | N | N | Y | Y | Y |
| 4 **Latham** | N | Y | N | N | N | N | N | N |
| 5 **King** | N | Y | Y | N | Y | Y | N | Y |
| KANSAS | | | | | | | | |
| 1 **Moran** | Y | Y | Y | Y | N | Y | N | N |
| 2 **Ryun** | N | Y | Y | N | Y | Y | N | N |
| 3 Moore | Y | N | N | N | N | Y | Y | N |
| 4 **Tiahrt** | N | Y | + | N | N | Y | Y | N |
| KENTUCKY | | | | | | | | |
| 1 **Whitfield** | N | Y | Y | N | N | Y | N | N |
| 2 **Lewis** | N | Y | Y | N | Y | Y | N | N |
| 3 **Northup** | N | Y | Y | Y | N | Y | N | Y |
| 4 **Davis** | N | Y | Y | N | N | N | N | N |
| 5 **Rogers** | N | Y | Y | N | N | Y | N | N |
| 6 Chandler | N | Y | Y | Y | N | Y | Y | Y |
| LOUISIANA | | | | | | | | |
| 1 **Jindal** | N | Y | Y | N | Y | N | N | N |
| 2 Jefferson | Y | Y | N | N | N | Y | Y | N |
| 3 Melancon | N | Y | Y | N | N | Y | Y | N |
| 4 **McCrery** | N | Y | Y | N | N | N | N | N |
| 5 **Alexander** | N | Y | Y | N | N | N | N | N |
| 6 **Baker** | N | Y | Y | N | N | N | N | N |
| 7 **Boustany** | N | Y | Y | N | N | N | N | N |
| MAINE | | | | | | | | |
| 1 Allen | Y | N | N | Y | N | Y | Y | Y |
| 2 Michaud | Y | Y | N | Y | N | Y | Y | Y |
| MARYLAND | | | | | | | | |
| 1 **Gilchrest** | N | N | Y | N | N | N | N | N |
| 2 Ruppersberger | Y | N | Y | Y | N | Y | Y | Y |
| 3 Cardin | N | N | N | Y | N | Y | Y | Y |
| 4 Wynn | Y | N | N | Y | N | Y | Y | Y |
| 5 Hoyer | Y | N | N | Y | N | Y | Y | Y |
| 6 **Bartlett** | N | Y | Y | N | Y | N | N | Y |
| 7 Cummings | Y | N | N | Y | N | Y | Y | Y |
| 8 Van Hollen | Y | N | N | Y | N | Y | Y | Y |
| MASSACHUSETTS | | | | | | | | |
| 1 Olver | Y | N | N | Y | N | Y | Y | Y |
| 2 Neal | Y | N | N | Y | N | Y | Y | Y |
| 3 McGovern | Y | N | N | Y | N | Y | Y | N |
| 4 Frank | Y | N | N | Y | N | Y | Y | N |
| 5 Meehan | Y | N | N | Y | N | Y | Y | Y |
| 6 Tierney | Y | N | N | Y | N | Y | Y | Y |
| 7 Markey | Y | N | N | Y | N | Y | Y | N |
| 8 Capuano | Y | N | N | Y | N | Y | Y | N |
| 9 Lynch | Y | N | Y | Y | N | Y | Y | Y |
| 10 Delahunt | Y | N | N | Y | N | N | Y | Y |
| MICHIGAN | | | | | | | | |
| 1 Stupak | Y | Y | N | Y | N | Y | Y | Y |
| 2 **Hoekstra** | N | Y | Y | N | Y | N | N | Y |
| 3 **Ehlers** | N | Y | N | N | N | N | N | N |
| 4 **Camp** | N | Y | Y | N | N | Y | N | N |
| 5 Kildee | Y | N | N | Y | N | Y | Y | Y |
| 6 **Upton** | Y | Y | Y | Y | N | N | Y | N |
| 7 **Schwarz** | N | Y | N | N | N | Y | N | N |
| 8 **Rogers** | N | Y | Y | N | Y | Y | N | N |
| 9 **Knollenberg** | N | Y | N | N | N | N | N | N |
| 10 **Miller** | N | Y | Y | N | N | Y | N | N |
| 11 **McCotter** | N | Y | Y | N | N | Y | N | N |
| 12 Levin | Y | N | N | Y | N | N | Y | Y |
| 13 Kilpatrick | Y | N | N | Y | N | Y | Y | Y |
| 14 Conyers | Y | N | Y | Y | N | Y | Y | Y |
| 15 Dingell | Y | Y | N | Y | N | Y | Y | N |
| MINNESOTA | | | | | | | | |
| 1 **Gutknecht** | N | Y | Y | N | Y | Y | N | Y |
| 2 **Kline** | N | Y | Y | N | N | Y | N | N |
| 3 **Ramstad** | Y | N | Y | N | N | Y | Y | N |
| 4 McCollum | Y | N | N | Y | N | Y | Y | Y |
| 5 Sabo | Y | N | N | Y | N | Y | Y | Y |
| 6 **Kennedy** | N | Y | Y | N | N | Y | N | N |
| 7 Peterson | Y | Y | Y | Y | N | Y | Y | N |
| 8 Oberstar | Y | Y | N | Y | N | Y | Y | Y |
| MISSISSIPPI | | | | | | | | |
| 1 **Wicker** | N | Y | Y | N | N | Y | N | N |
| 2 Thompson | Y | N | Y | Y | N | Y | Y | N |
| 3 **Pickering** | N | Y | Y | N | N | Y | N | N |
| 4 Taylor | Y | Y | Y | Y | Y | Y | Y | Y |
| MISSOURI | | | | | | | | |
| 1 Clay | Y | N | Y | Y | N | Y | Y | N |
| 2 **Akin** | N | Y | Y | N | Y | Y | N | N |
| 3 Carnahan | N | N | N | Y | N | Y | Y | Y |
| 4 Skelton | N | Y | N | Y | N | Y | Y | N |
| 5 Cleaver | Y | N | N | Y | N | Y | Y | N |
| 6 **Graves** | N | Y | Y | N | Y | N | N | N |
| 7 **Blunt** | N | Y | Y | N | N | N | N | N |
| 8 **Emerson** | Y | Y | Y | N | N | Y | N | Y |
| 9 **Hulshof** | N | Y | Y | N | N | N | N | N |
| MONTANA | | | | | | | | |
| AL **Rehberg** | N | Y | Y | N | N | Y | N | N |
| NEBRASKA | | | | | | | | |
| 1 **Fortenberry** | N | Y | Y | N | N | Y | N | N |
| 2 **Terry** | N | Y | Y | N | Y | Y | N | N |
| 3 **Osborne** | Y | Y | Y | N | N | Y | N | N |
| NEVADA | | | | | | | | |
| 1 Berkley | N | N | N | Y | N | Y | Y | Y |
| 2 **Gibbons** | N | Y | Y | N | Y | Y | N | Y |
| 3 **Porter** | N | Y | Y | N | N | Y | N | N |
| NEW HAMPSHIRE | | | | | | | | |
| 1 **Bradley** | N | Y | Y | Y | N | Y | N | N |
| 2 **Bass** | N | Y | Y | Y | Y | Y | N | N |
| NEW JERSEY | | | | | | | | |
| 1 Andrews | N | N | N | Y | Y | Y | Y | N |
| 2 **LoBiondo** | N | Y | Y | N | N | Y | N | N |
| 3 **Saxton** | N | Y | Y | N | N | Y | N | N |
| 4 **Smith** | N | Y | Y | Y | N | Y | N | N |
| 5 **Garrett** | N | Y | Y | N | Y | N | N | N |
| 6 Pallone | N | N | Y | Y | N | Y | Y | Y |
| 7 **Ferguson** | N | N | Y | N | N | Y | N | N |
| 8 Pascrell | N | N | N | Y | N | Y | Y | N |
| 9 Rothman | N | N | N | Y | N | Y | Y | N |
| 10 Payne | Y | N | N | Y | N | Y | Y | Y |
| 11 **Frelinghuysen** | N | N | Y | N | N | N | N | N |
| 12 Holt | N | N | N | Y | N | Y | Y | N |
| 13 Menendez | N | N | N | Y | N | Y | Y | N |
| NEW MEXICO | | | | | | | | |
| 1 **Wilson** | N | Y | Y | N | N | Y | N | N |
| 2 **Pearce** | N | Y | Y | N | N | Y | N | N |
| 3 Udall | Y | N | N | Y | N | Y | Y | Y |
| NEW YORK | | | | | | | | |
| 1 Bishop | Y | N | N | Y | N | Y | Y | Y |
| 2 Israel | Y | N | N | Y | N | Y | Y | Y |
| 3 **King** | N | N | N | N | N | N | N | N |
| 4 McCarthy | Y | N | N | Y | N | Y | Y | Y |
| 5 Ackerman | N | N | N | Y | N | Y | Y | Y |
| 6 Meeks | Y | N | N | Y | N | Y | Y | N |
| 7 Crowley | Y | N | N | Y | N | Y | Y | Y |
| 8 Nadler | Y | N | N | Y | N | Y | Y | Y |
| 9 Weiner | Y | N | N | Y | N | Y | Y | Y |
| 10 Towns | Y | N | N | Y | N | Y | Y | N |
| 11 Owens | Y | N | N | Y | N | Y | Y | Y |
| 12 Velázquez | Y | N | N | Y | N | Y | Y | Y |
| 13 **Fossella** | N | Y | Y | N | Y | Y | N | N |
| 14 Maloney | Y | N | N | Y | N | Y | Y | Y |
| 15 Rangel | Y | N | N | Y | N | Y | Y | Y |
| 16 Serrano | Y | N | N | Y | N | Y | Y | Y |
| 17 Engel | N | N | N | Y | N | Y | Y | N |
| 18 Lowey | Y | N | N | Y | N | Y | Y | Y |
| 19 **Kelly** | N | Y | Y | N | N | Y | N | N |
| 20 **Sweeney** | N | Y | Y | N | N | Y | N | N |
| 21 McNulty | Y | N | Y | Y | N | Y | Y | Y |
| 22 Hinchey | Y | N | Y | Y | N | Y | Y | Y |
| 23 **McHugh** | N | Y | Y | N | N | Y | N | N |
| 24 **Boehlert** | N | Y | N | N | N | N | N | N |
| 25 **Walsh** | N | Y | N | N | N | N | N | N |
| 26 **Reynolds** | N | Y | N | N | N | Y | N | N |
| 27 Higgins | N | Y | Y | Y | N | Y | Y | Y |
| 28 Slaughter | Y | N | Y | Y | N | Y | Y | Y |
| 29 **Kuhl** | N | Y | Y | N | N | Y | N | N |
| NORTH CAROLINA | | | | | | | | |
| 1 Butterfield | N | N | N | N | N | Y | Y | Y |
| 2 Etheridge | N | N | N | N | N | Y | Y | N |
| 3 **Jones** | N | Y | Y | Y | Y | Y | Y | Y |
| 4 Price | Y | N | N | N | N | N | Y | N |
| 5 **Foxx** | N | Y | Y | N | Y | Y | N | N |
| 6 **Coble** | N | Y | Y | N | Y | Y | N | N |
| 7 McIntyre | N | Y | Y | Y | N | Y | Y | N |
| 8 **Hayes** | N | Y | N | Y | N | N | N | N |
| 9 **Myrick** | N | Y | Y | N | Y | Y | N | N |
| 10 **McHenry** | N | Y | Y | N | Y | Y | N | N |
| 11 **Taylor** | N | Y | Y | N | N | Y | N | N |
| 12 Watt | Y | N | N | N | N | Y | Y | Y |
| 13 Miller | N | N | N | N | N | Y | Y | Y |
| NORTH DAKOTA | | | | | | | | |
| AL Pomeroy | Y | Y | Y | N | N | Y | Y | Y |
| OHIO | | | | | | | | |
| 1 **Chabot** | N | Y | Y | N | Y | Y | N | N |
| 2 Vacant | | | | | | | | |
| 3 **Turner** | N | Y | N | N | N | Y | N | N |
| 4 **Oxley** | N | Y | N | N | N | N | N | N |
| 5 **Gillmor** | N | Y | Y | ? | N | Y | N | N |
| 6 Strickland | Y | Y | N | Y | N | Y | Y | Y |
| 7 **Hobson** | N | Y | N | N | N | Y | N | N |
| 8 **Boehner** | N | Y | Y | N | N | N | N | N |
| 9 Kaptur | Y | N | N | Y | N | Y | Y | N |
| 10 Kucinich | Y | N | N | Y | N | Y | Y | Y |
| 11 Jones | Y | N | N | Y | N | Y | Y | Y |
| 12 **Tiberi** | Y | Y | Y | N | N | Y | N | N |
| 13 Brown | Y | N | N | Y | N | Y | Y | Y |
| 14 **LaTourette** | N | Y | N | N | N | Y | N | N |
| 15 **Pryce** | N | Y | Y | N | N | N | N | N |
| 16 **Regula** | N | Y | N | N | N | Y | N | N |
| 17 Ryan | Y | Y | N | Y | N | Y | Y | Y |
| 18 **Ney** | N | Y | Y | N | N | Y | N | N |
| OKLAHOMA | | | | | | | | |
| 1 **Sullivan** | N | Y | Y | N | N | Y | ? | N |
| 2 Boren | Y | Y | Y | N | N | Y | Y | N |
| 3 **Lucas** | N | Y | Y | N | N | Y | N | N |
| 4 **Cole** | N | Y | Y | N | N | N | N | N |
| 5 **Istook** | N | Y | Y | N | N | N | N | N |
| OREGON | | | | | | | | |
| 1 Wu | N | Y | N | Y | N | Y | Y | N |
| 2 **Walden** | N | Y | Y | N | N | Y | N | N |
| 3 Blumenauer | Y | N | N | N | N | N | Y | Y |
| 4 DeFazio | Y | Y | Y | Y | N | Y | Y | Y |
| 5 Hooley | Y | N | Y | N | N | Y | Y | N |
| PENNSYLVANIA | | | | | | | | |
| 1 Brady | Y | N | N | Y | N | Y | Y | Y |
| 2 Fattah | Y | N | N | Y | N | Y | Y | Y |
| 3 **English** | N | Y | N | N | N | Y | N | N |
| 4 **Hart** | N | Y | Y | N | Y | Y | N | N |
| 5 **Peterson** | ? | ? | ? | ? | ? | ? | ? | ? |
| 6 **Gerlach** | N | Y | Y | N | N | Y | N | N |
| 7 **Weldon** | N | Y | Y | N | N | N | N | N |
| 8 **Fitzpatrick** | N | Y | Y | Y | N | Y | N | N |
| 9 **Shuster** | N | Y | Y | N | N | Y | ? | N |
| 10 **Sherwood** | N | Y | N | Y | N | N | ? | N |
| 11 Kanjorski | Y | Y | N | Y | N | Y | Y | N |
| 12 Murtha | N | Y | N | N | N | N | Y | N |
| 13 Schwartz | Y | N | N | Y | N | Y | Y | N |
| 14 Doyle | Y | N | N | Y | N | Y | Y | N |
| 15 **Dent** | N | Y | Y | N | N | Y | N | N |
| 16 **Pitts** | N | Y | Y | N | Y | Y | N | N |
| 17 Holden | N | Y | N | Y | N | Y | Y | N |
| 18 **Murphy** | N | Y | Y | N | N | Y | N | N |
| 19 **Platts** | N | Y | Y | Y | N | Y | N | N |
| RHODE ISLAND | | | | | | | | |
| 1 Kennedy | N | N | N | Y | N | Y | Y | Y |
| 2 Langevin | Y | N | N | Y | N | Y | Y | Y |
| SOUTH CAROLINA | | | | | | | | |
| 1 **Brown** | N | Y | Y | N | N | Y | N | N |
| 2 **Wilson** | N | Y | Y | N | Y | N | N | N |
| 3 **Barrett** | N | Y | Y | N | Y | Y | N | N |
| 4 **Inglis** | N | Y | N | N | Y | Y | N | N |
| 5 Spratt | N | N | N | N | N | Y | Y | N |
| 6 Clyburn | Y | N | Y | Y | N | Y | Y | N |
| SOUTH DAKOTA | | | | | | | | |
| AL Herseth | Y | Y | Y | Y | N | Y | Y | Y |
| TENNESSEE | | | | | | | | |
| 1 **Jenkins** | N | Y | Y | Y | Y | Y | N | N |
| 2 **Duncan** | N | Y | Y | Y | Y | Y | N | N |
| 3 **Wamp** | N | Y | Y | Y | N | Y | N | N |
| 4 Davis | Y | Y | Y | Y | Y | Y | Y | N |
| 5 Cooper | ? | ? | ? | ? | N | N | Y | N |
| 6 Gordon | Y | Y | Y | Y | N | Y | Y | N |
| 7 **Blackburn** | N | Y | Y | N | Y | Y | N | N |
| 8 Tanner | Y | Y | Y | N | Y | Y | Y | N |
| 9 Ford | Y | Y | N | Y | N | Y | Y | Y |
| TEXAS | | | | | | | | |
| 1 **Gohmert** | N | Y | Y | N | Y | Y | N | N |
| 2 **Poe** | N | Y | Y | N | Y | Y | N | N |
| 3 **Johnson, S.** | N | Y | Y | N | Y | Y | N | N |
| 4 **Hall** | N | Y | Y | N | N | N | N | N |
| 5 **Hensarling** | N | Y | Y | N | Y | N | N | N |
| 6 **Barton** | N | Y | Y | N | Y | N | N | N |
| 7 **Culberson** | N | Y | Y | N | N | Y | N | N |
| 8 **Brady** | N | Y | Y | N | Y | N | N | N |
| 9 Green, A. | Y | N | N | Y | N | Y | Y | Y |
| 10 **McCaul** | N | Y | Y | N | N | Y | N | N |
| 11 **Conaway** | N | Y | Y | N | N | N | N | N |
| 12 **Granger** | N | Y | N | N | N | N | N | N |
| 13 **Thornberry** | N | Y | Y | N | Y | N | N | N |
| 14 **Paul** | Y | Y | Y | Y | Y | N | Y | Y |
| 15 Hinojosa | Y | N | N | Y | N | Y | Y | Y |
| 16 Reyes | Y | Y | N | Y | N | Y | Y | N |
| 17 Edwards | Y | Y | N | Y | N | Y | Y | Y |
| 18 Jackson-Lee | Y | N | Y | Y | N | Y | Y | Y |
| 19 **Neugebauer** | N | Y | Y | N | Y | N | N | N |
| 20 Gonzalez | Y | N | N | Y | N | Y | Y | N |
| 21 **Smith** | N | Y | Y | N | N | N | N | N |
| 22 **DeLay** | N | Y | Y | N | N | Y | N | N |
| 23 **Bonilla** | N | Y | Y | N | N | N | N | N |
| 24 **Marchant** | N | Y | Y | N | N | Y | N | N |
| 25 Doggett | Y | N | N | Y | N | N | Y | Y |
| 26 **Burgess** | N | Y | Y | N | N | N | N | N |
| 27 Ortiz | N | Y | N | Y | N | Y | Y | Y |
| 28 Cuellar | N | Y | Y | Y | N | Y | Y | N |
| 29 Green, G. | N | Y | N | N | N | Y | Y | Y |
| 30 Johnson, E. | Y | N | N | Y | N | Y | Y | Y |
| 31 **Carter** | N | Y | Y | N | N | N | N | N |
| 32 **Sessions** | N | Y | Y | N | Y | N | N | N |
| UTAH | | | | | | | | |
| 1 **Bishop** | N | Y | Y | N | N | Y | N | N |
| 2 Matheson | Y | Y | Y | N | N | Y | Y | N |
| 3 **Cannon** | N | Y | Y | N | Y | N | N | N |
| VERMONT | | | | | | | | |
| AL *Sanders* | Y | N | N | Y | N | Y | Y | Y |
| VIRGINIA | | | | | | | | |
| 1 **Davis, J.** | N | Y | Y | N | Y | Y | N | N |
| 2 **Drake** | N | Y | Y | N | N | Y | N | N |
| 3 Scott | Y | N | N | N | N | Y | Y | N |
| 4 **Forbes** | N | Y | Y | N | N | Y | N | N |
| 5 **Goode** | N | Y | Y | N | N | Y | N | N |
| 6 **Goodlatte** | N | Y | Y | N | N | Y | N | N |
| 7 **Cantor** | N | Y | Y | N | N | N | N | N |
| 8 Moran | Y | N | N | N | N | N | Y | Y |
| 9 Boucher | Y | Y | N | Y | N | Y | Y | N |
| 10 **Wolf** | N | N | N | N | N | Y | N | N |
| 11 **Davis, T.** | N | N | N | N | N | N | N | N |
| WASHINGTON | | | | | | | | |
| 1 Inslee | Y | N | N | Y | N | N | Y | N |
| 2 Larsen | Y | N | N | Y | N | N | Y | Y |
| 3 Baird | Y | Y | N | Y | N | N | Y | N |
| 4 **Hastings** | N | Y | N | N | N | N | N | N |
| 5 **McMorris** | N | Y | Y | N | Y | N | N | N |
| 6 Dicks | Y | N | N | N | N | N | Y | N |
| 7 McDermott | Y | N | N | Y | N | N | Y | Y |
| 8 **Reichert** | N | Y | N | N | N | Y | N | Y |
| 9 Smith | Y | N | N | Y | N | N | Y | N |
| WEST VIRGINIA | | | | | | | | |
| 1 Mollohan | Y | Y | Y | Y | N | Y | Y | Y |
| 2 **Capito** | N | Y | Y | N | N | Y | N | N |
| 3 Rahall | Y | Y | N | Y | N | Y | Y | N |
| WISCONSIN | | | | | | | | |
| 1 **Ryan** | Y | Y | Y | N | Y | N | N | N |
| 2 Baldwin | Y | N | N | Y | N | Y | Y | Y |
| 3 Kind | Y | Y | N | Y | N | Y | Y | N |
| 4 Moore | Y | N | N | Y | N | Y | Y | N |
| 5 **Sensenbrenner** | N | Y | Y | N | Y | Y | N | N |
| 6 **Petri** | N | Y | Y | N | Y | N | N | N |
| 7 Obey | Y | P | N | Y | N | Y | Y | ? |
| 8 **Green** | N | Y | Y | Y | N | Y | N | N |
| WYOMING | | | | | | | | |
| AL **Cubin** | N | Y | Y | N | Y | Y | N | N |

# IN THE HOUSE | By Vote Number

**356.** HR 3058. Fiscal 2006 Transportation-Treasury-Housing Appropriations/Travel Service Program. Velázquez, D-N.Y., amendment that would prohibit use of funds in the bill for the General Services Administration to carry out the eTravel Service program. Adopted 233-192: R 39-187; D 193-5 (ND 143-5, SD 50-0); I 1-0. June 30, 2005.

**357.** HR 3058. Fiscal 2006 Transportation-Treasury-Housing Appropriations/Federal Job Outsourcing. Van Hollen, D-Md., amendment that would prohibit use of funds in the bill to implement a May 29, 2003, Office of Management and Budget rule streamlining the outsourcing of work by federal agencies. Adopted 222-203: R 24-202; D 197-1 (ND 147-1, SD 50-0); I 1-0. A "nay" was a vote in support of the president's position. June 30, 2005.

**358.** HR 3058. Fiscal 2006 Transportation-Treasury-Housing Appropriations/Passage. Passage of the bill that would appropriate $139.1 billion in fiscal 2006, including $66.9 billion in discretionary spending, for the departments of Housing and Urban Development, Treasury and Transportation, and related agencies. The bill includes $603 million for the District of Columbia. Passed 405-18: R 216-9; D 188-9 (ND 140-7, SD 48-2); I 1-0. June 30, 2005.

**359.** H Res 345. Suspension Motions/Previous Question. Putnam, R-Fla., motion to order the previous question (thus ending debate and possibility of amendment) on adoption of the resolution to provide for House floor consideration of bills under suspension of the rules on June 30, 2005. Motion agreed to 216-191: R 216-0; D 0-190 (ND 0-142, SD 0-48); I 0-1. (Subsequently, the rule was adopted by voice vote.) June 30, 2005.

**360.** H Res 344. Review of Sale of Unocal/Adoption. Ney, R-Ohio, motion to suspend the rules and adopt the resolution that would state if the Unocal Corporation enters into an agreement of acquisition, merger, or takeover by the China National Offshore Oil Corporation, the president should immediately start a thorough review of the action. Motion agreed to 398-15: R 216-6; D 181-9 (ND 133-8, SD 48-1); I 1-0. A two-thirds majority of those present and voting (276 in this case) is required for adoption under suspension of the rules. June 30, 2005.

**361.** H Res 340. Eminent Domain Ruling/Adoption. Sensenbrenner, R-Wis., motion to suspend the rules and adopt the resolution that would note the House of Representatives disagrees with the majority opinion in *Kelo v. City of New London* and its holdings, and agrees with the dissenting opinion in its upholding of the historical interpretation of the takings clause and its deference to the rights of individuals and their property. Motion agreed to 365-33: R 220-1; D 144-32 (ND 101-28, SD 43-4); I 1-0. A two-thirds majority of those present and voting (266 in this case) is required for adoption under suspension of the rules. June 30, 2005.

**362.** HR 3130. Fiscal 2005 Veterans' Supplemental Appropriations/Passage. Walsh, R-N.Y., motion to suspend the rules and pass the bill that would provide $975 million in supplemental fiscal 2005 funding for veterans' medical care. Motion agreed to 419-0: R 227-0; D 191-0 (ND 142-0, SD 49-0); I 1-0. A two-thirds majority of those present and voting (280 in this case) is required for passage under suspension of the rules. June 30, 2005.

| | 356 | 357 | 358 | 359 | 360 | 361 | 362 |
|---|---|---|---|---|---|---|---|
| **ALABAMA** | | | | | | | |
| 1 Bonner | N | N | Y | Y | Y | Y | Y |
| 2 Everett | ? | ? | ? | ? | ? | ? | ? |
| 3 Rogers | N | Y | Y | Y | Y | Y | Y |
| 4 Aderholt | N | N | Y | Y | Y | Y | Y |
| 5 Cramer | Y | Y | Y | ? | ? | ? | ? |
| 6 Bachus | N | N | Y | Y | Y | Y | Y |
| 7 Davis | Y | Y | Y | N | Y | Y | Y |
| **ALASKA** | | | | | | | |
| AL Young | N | N | Y | Y | Y | Y | Y |
| **ARIZONA** | | | | | | | |
| 1 Renzi | Y | N | Y | Y | Y | Y | Y |
| 2 Franks | N | N | N | Y | Y | Y | Y |
| 3 Shadegg | N | N | Y | Y | Y | Y | Y |
| 4 Pastor | Y | Y | Y | N | Y | N | Y |
| 5 Hayworth | Y | N | Y | Y | Y | Y | Y |
| 6 Flake | N | N | N | Y | Y | Y | Y |
| 7 Grijalva | Y | Y | Y | N | Y | N | Y |
| 8 Kolbe | N | N | Y | Y | Y | Y | Y |
| **ARKANSAS** | | | | | | | |
| 1 Berry | Y | Y | Y | N | Y | Y | Y |
| 2 Snyder | Y | Y | Y | N | Y | P | Y |
| 3 Boozman | ? | N | Y | Y | Y | Y | Y |
| 4 Ross | ? | ? | ? | ? | ? | ? | ? |
| **CALIFORNIA** | | | | | | | |
| 1 Thompson | Y | Y | Y | N | Y | Y | Y |
| 2 Herger | N | N | Y | Y | Y | Y | Y |
| 3 Lungren | N | N | Y | Y | N | Y | Y |
| 4 Doolittle | N | N | Y | Y | Y | Y | Y |
| 5 Matsui, D. | Y | Y | Y | N | Y | N | Y |
| 6 Woolsey | Y | Y | Y | N | Y | N | Y |
| 7 Miller, George | Y | Y | Y | N | Y | N | Y |
| 8 Pelosi | Y | Y | Y | N | ? | ? | ? |
| 9 Lee | Y | Y | Y | N | Y | N | Y |
| 10 Tauscher | Y | Y | Y | N | Y | Y | Y |
| 11 Pombo | N | N | Y | Y | Y | Y | Y |
| 12 Lantos | Y | Y | Y | N | Y | Y | Y |
| 13 Stark | Y | Y | N | N | N | N | Y |
| 14 Eshoo | Y | Y | Y | N | Y | Y | Y |
| 15 Honda | Y | Y | Y | N | Y | Y | Y |
| 16 Lofgren | Y | Y | Y | N | Y | Y | Y |
| 17 Farr | Y | Y | Y | N | Y | N | Y |
| 18 Cardoza | Y | Y | Y | N | Y | Y | Y |
| 19 Radanovich | N | N | Y | ? | Y | Y | Y |
| 20 Costa | N | N | Y | N | Y | Y | Y |
| 21 Nunes | N | N | Y | Y | Y | Y | Y |
| 22 Thomas | N | N | Y | Y | N | Y | Y |
| 23 Capps | Y | Y | Y | N | Y | Y | Y |
| 24 Gallegly | N | N | Y | Y | Y | Y | Y |
| 25 McKeon | N | N | Y | Y | Y | Y | Y |
| 26 Dreier | N | N | Y | Y | Y | Y | Y |
| 27 Sherman | Y | Y | Y | N | Y | N | Y |
| 28 Berman | Y | Y | Y | ? | ? | ? | ? |
| 29 Schiff | ? | ? | ? | ? | ? | ? | ? |
| 30 Waxman | Y | Y | Y | N | Y | N | Y |
| 31 Becerra | Y | Y | Y | N | Y | Y | Y |
| 32 Solis | Y | Y | Y | − | + | + | + |
| 33 Watson | Y | Y | Y | N | Y | N | Y |
| 34 Roybal-Allard | Y | Y | Y | N | Y | Y | Y |
| 35 Waters | ? | ? | ? | ? | ? | ? | ? |
| 36 Harman | ? | ? | ? | ? | ? | ? | ? |
| 37 Millender-McD. | Y | Y | Y | N | Y | Y | Y |
| 38 Napolitano | Y | Y | Y | N | Y | Y | Y |
| 39 Sánchez, Linda | Y | Y | Y | N | Y | Y | Y |
| 40 Royce | N | N | Y | Y | Y | Y | Y |
| 41 Lewis | N | N | Y | Y | Y | Y | Y |
| 42 Miller, Gary | N | N | Y | Y | Y | Y | Y |
| 43 Baca | Y | Y | Y | N | Y | Y | Y |
| 44 Calvert | N | N | Y | Y | Y | Y | Y |
| 45 Bono | N | N | Y | Y | Y | Y | Y |
| 46 Rohrabacher | N | N | Y | Y | Y | Y | Y |
| 47 Sanchez, Loretta | Y | Y | Y | N | Y | P | Y |
| 48 Cox | N | ? | Y | Y | ? | Y | Y |
| 49 Issa | N | N | Y | Y | Y | Y | Y |

| | 356 | 357 | 358 | 359 | 360 | 361 | 362 |
|---|---|---|---|---|---|---|---|
| 50 Cunningham | N | N | Y | Y | Y | Y | Y |
| 51 Filner | Y | Y | Y | N | Y | Y | Y |
| 52 Hunter | N | N | Y | Y | Y | Y | Y |
| 53 Davis | Y | Y | Y | N | Y | Y | Y |
| **COLORADO** | | | | | | | |
| 1 DeGette | Y | Y | Y | N | Y | N | Y |
| 2 Udall | Y | Y | Y | N | Y | N | Y |
| 3 Salazar | Y | Y | Y | N | Y | N | Y |
| 4 Musgrave | N | N | Y | ? | Y | Y | Y |
| 5 Hefley | N | N | N | Y | Y | Y | Y |
| 6 Tancredo | N | N | N | Y | Y | Y | Y |
| 7 Beauprez | N | N | Y | Y | Y | Y | Y |
| **CONNECTICUT** | | | | | | | |
| 1 Larson | Y | Y | Y | N | Y | Y | Y |
| 2 Simmons | Y | Y | Y | Y | Y | Y | Y |
| 3 DeLauro | Y | Y | Y | N | Y | Y | Y |
| 4 Shays | Y | N | Y | Y | Y | Y | Y |
| 5 Johnson | N | N | Y | Y | Y | Y | Y |
| **DELAWARE** | | | | | | | |
| AL Castle | N | N | Y | Y | Y | Y | Y |
| **FLORIDA** | | | | | | | |
| 1 Miller | N | N | Y | Y | Y | Y | Y |
| 2 Boyd | Y | Y | Y | N | Y | Y | Y |
| 3 Brown | Y | Y | Y | N | Y | N | Y |
| 4 Crenshaw | N | N | Y | Y | Y | Y | Y |
| 5 Brown-Waite | N | N | Y | Y | Y | Y | Y |
| 6 Stearns | N | N | Y | Y | Y | Y | Y |
| 7 Mica | N | N | Y | Y | Y | Y | Y |
| 8 Keller | N | Y | ? | Y | Y | Y | Y |
| 9 Bilirakis | N | N | Y | Y | Y | Y | Y |
| 10 Young | N | N | Y | Y | Y | Y | Y |
| 11 Davis | Y | Y | Y | N | Y | Y | Y |
| 12 Putnam | N | N | Y | Y | Y | Y | Y |
| 13 Harris | N | N | Y | Y | Y | Y | Y |
| 14 Mack | N | N | Y | Y | Y | Y | Y |
| 15 Weldon | N | N | Y | Y | Y | Y | Y |
| 16 Foley | N | N | Y | Y | Y | Y | Y |
| 17 Meek | Y | Y | Y | N | Y | N | Y |
| 18 Ros-Lehtinen | Y | Y | Y | Y | Y | Y | Y |
| 19 Wexler | Y | Y | Y | N | Y | Y | Y |
| 20 Wasserman-Schultz | Y | Y | Y | N | Y | Y | Y |
| 21 Diaz-Balart, L. | Y | Y | Y | Y | Y | Y | Y |
| 22 Shaw | N | N | Y | Y | Y | Y | Y |
| 23 Hastings | Y | Y | Y | N | Y | N | Y |
| 24 Feeney | N | N | Y | Y | Y | Y | Y |
| 25 Diaz-Balart, M. | N | N | Y | Y | Y | Y | Y |
| **GEORGIA** | | | | | | | |
| 1 Kingston | ? | ? | ? | ? | ? | ? | ? |
| 2 Bishop | Y | Y | Y | N | Y | Y | Y |
| 3 Marshall | Y | Y | Y | N | Y | Y | Y |
| 4 McKinney | Y | Y | Y | N | Y | N | Y |
| 5 Lewis | Y | Y | Y | N | Y | Y | Y |
| 6 Price | N | N | Y | Y | Y | Y | Y |
| 7 Linder | N | N | Y | Y | Y | Y | Y |
| 8 Westmoreland | N | N | Y | Y | Y | Y | Y |
| 9 Norwood | N | N | Y | ? | Y | Y | Y |
| 10 Deal | N | N | Y | Y | Y | Y | Y |
| 11 Gingrey | N | N | Y | Y | Y | Y | Y |
| 12 Barrow | Y | Y | Y | N | Y | Y | Y |
| 13 Scott | Y | Y | Y | N | Y | Y | Y |
| **HAWAII** | | | | | | | |
| 1 Abercrombie | Y | Y | Y | N | Y | N | Y |
| 2 Case | Y | Y | Y | N | Y | N | Y |
| **IDAHO** | | | | | | | |
| 1 Otter | N | N | N | Y | Y | Y | Y |
| 2 Simpson | N | N | Y | Y | Y | Y | Y |
| **ILLINOIS** | | | | | | | |
| 1 Rush | Y | Y | Y | N | Y | Y | Y |
| 2 Jackson | Y | Y | Y | N | Y | N | Y |
| 3 Lipinski | Y | Y | Y | N | Y | Y | Y |
| 4 Gutierrez | Y | Y | Y | N | Y | Y | Y |
| 5 Emanuel | Y | Y | Y | N | Y | Y | Y |
| 6 Hyde | N | N | Y | Y | Y | Y | Y |
| 7 Davis | Y | Y | Y | N | Y | Y | Y |
| 8 Bean | Y | Y | Y | N | Y | Y | Y |
| 9 Schakowsky | Y | Y | Y | N | Y | P | Y |
| 10 Kirk | N | N | Y | Y | N | Y | Y |
| 11 Weller | N | N | Y | Y | Y | Y | Y |
| 12 Costello | Y | Y | Y | N | Y | Y | Y |

### KEY    Republicans    Democrats    *Independents*

| Y | Voted for (yea) | X | Paired against | C | Voted "present" to avoid possible conflict of interest |
|---|---|---|---|---|---|
| # | Paired for | − | Announced against | | |
| + | Announced for | P | Voted "present" | ? | Did not vote or otherwise make a position known |
| N | Voted against (nay) | | | | |

| | 356 | 357 | 358 | 359 | 360 | 361 | 362 |
|---|---|---|---|---|---|---|---|
| 13 **Biggert** | N | N | Y | Y | Y | Y | Y |
| 14 **Hastert** | | | | | | | |
| 15 **Johnson** | Y | Y | Y | Y | Y | Y | Y |
| 16 **Manzullo** | Y | N | Y | Y | Y | Y | Y |
| 17 Evans | Y | Y | Y | N | Y | Y | Y |
| 18 **LaHood** | N | N | Y | Y | Y | Y | Y |
| 19 **Shimkus** | N | Y | Y | Y | Y | Y | Y |
| **INDIANA** | | | | | | | |
| 1 Visclosky | Y | Y | Y | N | Y | Y | Y |
| 2 **Chocola** | N | N | Y | Y | Y | Y | Y |
| 3 **Souder** | N | N | Y | Y | Y | Y | Y |
| 4 **Buyer** | N | N | Y | Y | Y | Y | Y |
| 5 **Burton** | N | N | Y | Y | Y | Y | Y |
| 6 **Pence** | N | N | Y | Y | Y | Y | Y |
| 7 Carson | Y | Y | N | N | Y | Y | Y |
| 8 **Hostettler** | N | Y | Y | Y | Y | N | Y |
| 9 **Sodrel** | N | N | Y | Y | Y | Y | Y |
| **IOWA** | | | | | | | |
| 1 **Nussle** | N | N | Y | Y | Y | Y | Y |
| 2 **Leach** | N | N | Y | Y | Y | Y | Y |
| 3 Boswell | Y | Y | Y | N | Y | Y | Y |
| 4 **Latham** | N | N | Y | Y | Y | Y | Y |
| 5 **King** | Y | N | Y | Y | Y | Y | Y |
| **KANSAS** | | | | | | | |
| 1 **Moran** | Y | N | Y | Y | Y | Y | Y |
| 2 **Ryun** | N | N | Y | Y | Y | Y | Y |
| 3 Moore | Y | Y | Y | N | Y | Y | Y |
| 4 **Tiahrt** | N | N | Y | Y | Y | Y | Y |
| **KENTUCKY** | | | | | | | |
| 1 **Whitfield** | N | N | Y | Y | Y | Y | Y |
| 2 **Lewis** | N | Y | Y | Y | Y | Y | Y |
| 3 **Northup** | N | N | Y | Y | Y | Y | Y |
| 4 **Davis** | N | N | Y | Y | Y | Y | Y |
| 5 **Rogers** | N | N | Y | ? | Y | Y | Y |
| 6 Chandler | Y | Y | Y | N | Y | Y | Y |
| **LOUISIANA** | | | | | | | |
| 1 **Jindal** | N | N | Y | Y | Y | Y | Y |
| 2 Jefferson | Y | Y | Y | N | Y | Y | Y |
| 3 Melancon | Y | Y | Y | N | Y | Y | Y |
| 4 **McCrery** | N | N | ? | Y | Y | Y | Y |
| 5 **Alexander** | N | N | Y | Y | Y | Y | Y |
| 6 **Baker** | N | N | Y | Y | Y | Y | Y |
| 7 **Boustany** | N | N | + | Y | Y | Y | Y |
| **MAINE** | | | | | | | |
| 1 Allen | Y | Y | Y | N | Y | N | Y |
| 2 Michaud | Y | Y | Y | N | Y | Y | Y |
| **MARYLAND** | | | | | | | |
| 1 **Gilchrest** | N | N | Y | Y | Y | Y | Y |
| 2 Ruppersberger | Y | Y | Y | N | Y | Y | Y |
| 3 Cardin | Y | Y | Y | ? | Y | Y | Y |
| 4 Wynn | Y | Y | Y | N | Y | N | Y |
| 5 Hoyer | Y | Y | Y | N | Y | Y | Y |
| 6 **Bartlett** | N | N | Y | Y | Y | Y | Y |
| 7 Cummings | Y | Y | Y | N | Y | Y | Y |
| 8 Van Hollen | Y | Y | Y | N | Y | Y | Y |
| **MASSACHUSETTS** | | | | | | | |
| 1 Olver | Y | Y | Y | N | Y | P | Y |
| 2 Neal | Y | Y | Y | N | Y | P | Y |
| 3 McGovern | Y | Y | Y | N | Y | Y | Y |
| 4 Frank | Y | Y | Y | N | Y | Y | Y |
| 5 Meehan | Y | Y | Y | N | Y | Y | Y |
| 6 Tierney | Y | Y | Y | N | Y | P | Y |
| 7 Markey | Y | Y | Y | N | Y | Y | Y |
| 8 Capuano | N | Y | Y | N | Y | P | Y |
| 9 Lynch | Y | Y | Y | N | Y | Y | Y |
| 10 Delahunt | Y | Y | Y | N | Y | Y | Y |
| **MICHIGAN** | | | | | | | |
| 1 Stupak | Y | Y | Y | N | Y | Y | Y |
| 2 **Hoekstra** | N | N | Y | Y | Y | Y | Y |
| 3 **Ehlers** | N | N | Y | Y | Y | Y | Y |
| 4 **Camp** | N | N | Y | Y | Y | Y | Y |
| 5 Kildee | Y | Y | Y | N | Y | Y | Y |
| 6 **Upton** | N | N | Y | Y | Y | Y | Y |
| 7 **Schwarz** | N | N | Y | Y | Y | Y | Y |
| 8 **Rogers** | N | N | Y | ? | Y | Y | Y |
| 9 **Knollenberg** | N | N | Y | Y | Y | Y | Y |
| 10 **Miller** | N | N | Y | Y | Y | Y | Y |
| 11 **McCotter** | Y | Y | Y | Y | Y | Y | Y |
| 12 Levin | Y | Y | Y | N | Y | N | Y |
| 13 Kilpatrick | Y | Y | Y | N | Y | N | Y |
| 14 Conyers | Y | Y | N | N | Y | Y | Y |
| 15 Dingell | Y | Y | Y | N | Y | N | Y |

| | 356 | 357 | 358 | 359 | 360 | 361 | 362 |
|---|---|---|---|---|---|---|---|
| **MINNESOTA** | | | | | | | |
| 1 **Gutknecht** | N | Y | Y | Y | Y | Y | Y |
| 2 **Kline** | N | N | Y | Y | Y | Y | Y |
| 3 **Ramstad** | Y | N | Y | Y | Y | Y | Y |
| 4 McCollum | Y | Y | Y | N | Y | P | Y |
| 5 Sabo | N | Y | Y | N | Y | P | Y |
| 6 **Kennedy** | N | N | Y | Y | Y | Y | Y |
| 7 Peterson | N | Y | Y | N | Y | Y | Y |
| 8 Oberstar | N | Y | Y | ? | Y | N | Y |
| **MISSISSIPPI** | | | | | | | |
| 1 **Wicker** | N | N | Y | ? | Y | Y | Y |
| 2 Thompson | Y | Y | Y | N | Y | Y | Y |
| 3 **Pickering** | Y | N | Y | Y | Y | Y | Y |
| 4 Taylor | Y | Y | N | N | Y | Y | Y |
| **MISSOURI** | | | | | | | |
| 1 Clay | Y | Y | Y | N | ? | ? | ? |
| 2 **Akin** | N | N | Y | Y | Y | Y | Y |
| 3 Carnahan | Y | Y | Y | N | Y | Y | Y |
| 4 Skelton | Y | Y | Y | N | Y | Y | Y |
| 5 Cleaver | Y | Y | Y | N | Y | Y | Y |
| 6 **Graves** | Y | N | Y | Y | Y | Y | Y |
| 7 **Blunt** | N | N | Y | Y | Y | Y | Y |
| 8 **Emerson** | N | Y | Y | Y | Y | Y | Y |
| 9 **Hulshof** | Y | N | Y | Y | Y | Y | Y |
| **MONTANA** | | | | | | | |
| AL **Rehberg** | N | N | Y | Y | Y | Y | Y |
| **NEBRASKA** | | | | | | | |
| 1 **Fortenberry** | Y | N | Y | Y | Y | Y | Y |
| 2 **Terry** | Y | N | Y | Y | Y | Y | Y |
| 3 **Osborne** | Y | N | Y | Y | Y | Y | Y |
| **NEVADA** | | | | | | | |
| 1 Berkley | Y | Y | Y | N | Y | Y | Y |
| 2 **Gibbons** | Y | N | Y | Y | Y | Y | Y |
| 3 **Porter** | Y | N | Y | Y | Y | Y | Y |
| **NEW HAMPSHIRE** | | | | | | | |
| 1 **Bradley** | N | N | Y | Y | Y | Y | Y |
| 2 **Bass** | N | N | Y | Y | Y | Y | Y |
| **NEW JERSEY** | | | | | | | |
| 1 Andrews | Y | Y | Y | N | Y | Y | Y |
| 2 **LoBiondo** | N | Y | Y | Y | Y | Y | Y |
| 3 **Saxton** | N | N | Y | Y | Y | Y | Y |
| 4 **Smith** | Y | Y | Y | ? | Y | Y | Y |
| 5 **Garrett** | N | N | Y | Y | Y | Y | Y |
| 6 Pallone | Y | Y | Y | N | Y | Y | Y |
| 7 **Ferguson** | N | N | Y | Y | Y | Y | Y |
| 8 Pascrell | Y | Y | Y | N | Y | Y | Y |
| 9 Rothman | Y | Y | Y | N | Y | N | Y |
| 10 Payne | Y | Y | Y | N | Y | N | Y |
| 11 **Frelinghuysen** | N | N | Y | Y | Y | Y | Y |
| 12 Holt | Y | Y | Y | N | Y | P | Y |
| 13 Menendez | Y | Y | Y | N | Y | Y | Y |
| **NEW MEXICO** | | | | | | | |
| 1 **Wilson** | N | N | Y | Y | Y | Y | Y |
| 2 **Pearce** | Y | N | Y | Y | Y | Y | Y |
| 3 Udall | Y | Y | Y | N | Y | Y | Y |
| **NEW YORK** | | | | | | | |
| 1 Bishop | Y | Y | Y | N | Y | Y | Y |
| 2 Israel | Y | Y | Y | N | Y | Y | Y |
| 3 **King** | Y | N | Y | Y | Y | Y | Y |
| 4 McCarthy | Y | Y | Y | N | Y | Y | Y |
| 5 Ackerman | Y | Y | Y | N | Y | P | Y |
| 6 Meeks | Y | Y | Y | N | Y | Y | Y |
| 7 Crowley | Y | Y | Y | N | Y | Y | Y |
| 8 Nadler | Y | Y | Y | N | Y | N | Y |
| 9 Weiner | Y | Y | Y | N | Y | Y | Y |
| 10 Towns | Y | Y | Y | N | Y | Y | Y |
| 11 Owens | Y | Y | Y | N | Y | Y | Y |
| 12 Velázquez | Y | Y | Y | N | Y | Y | Y |
| 13 **Fossella** | N | N | Y | Y | Y | Y | Y |
| 14 Maloney | Y | Y | Y | N | Y | Y | Y |
| 15 Rangel | Y | Y | ? | N | Y | Y | Y |
| 16 Serrano | Y | Y | Y | N | Y | Y | Y |
| 17 Engel | Y | Y | Y | N | Y | Y | Y |
| 18 Lowey | Y | Y | Y | N | Y | N | Y |
| 19 **Kelly** | Y | Y | Y | Y | Y | Y | Y |
| 20 **Sweeney** | N | N | Y | Y | Y | Y | Y |
| 21 McNulty | Y | Y | Y | N | Y | Y | Y |
| 22 Hinchey | Y | Y | Y | N | Y | Y | Y |
| 23 **McHugh** | N | Y | Y | Y | Y | Y | Y |
| 24 **Boehlert** | N | N | Y | Y | Y | Y | Y |
| 25 **Walsh** | N | N | Y | Y | Y | Y | Y |
| 26 **Reynolds** | N | N | Y | Y | Y | + | Y |
| 27 Higgins | Y | Y | Y | ? | ? | ? | ? |
| 28 Slaughter | Y | Y | Y | N | Y | Y | Y |
| 29 **Kuhl** | N | Y | Y | Y | Y | Y | Y |

| | 356 | 357 | 358 | 359 | 360 | 361 | 362 |
|---|---|---|---|---|---|---|---|
| **NORTH CAROLINA** | | | | | | | |
| 1 Butterfield | Y | Y | Y | ? | Y | Y | Y |
| 2 Etheridge | Y | Y | Y | N | Y | Y | Y |
| 3 **Jones** | N | Y | N | Y | Y | Y | Y |
| 4 Price | Y | Y | Y | N | Y | Y | Y |
| 5 **Foxx** | N | N | Y | Y | Y | Y | Y |
| 6 **Coble** | Y | N | Y | Y | Y | Y | Y |
| 7 McIntyre | Y | Y | Y | N | Y | Y | Y |
| 8 **Hayes** | N | N | Y | Y | Y | Y | Y |
| 9 **Myrick** | N | N | Y | Y | Y | Y | Y |
| 10 **McHenry** | N | N | Y | Y | Y | Y | Y |
| 11 **Taylor** | Y | N | Y | Y | Y | Y | Y |
| 12 Watt | Y | Y | Y | N | Y | P | Y |
| 13 Miller | Y | Y | Y | N | Y | N | Y |
| **NORTH DAKOTA** | | | | | | | |
| AL Pomeroy | Y | Y | Y | N | Y | Y | Y |
| **OHIO** | | | | | | | |
| 1 **Chabot** | N | N | Y | Y | Y | Y | Y |
| 2 Vacant | | | | | | | |
| 3 **Turner** | N | N | Y | Y | Y | P | Y |
| 4 **Oxley** | N | N | Y | Y | Y | Y | Y |
| 5 **Gillmor** | N | N | Y | Y | Y | Y | Y |
| 6 Strickland | Y | Y | Y | N | Y | Y | Y |
| 7 **Hobson** | N | N | Y | Y | Y | Y | Y |
| 8 **Boehner** | N | N | Y | ? | Y | Y | Y |
| 9 Kaptur | Y | Y | Y | N | Y | P | Y |
| 10 Kucinich | Y | Y | Y | N | Y | Y | Y |
| 11 Jones | Y | Y | Y | N | Y | N | Y |
| 12 **Tiberi** | N | N | Y | Y | Y | Y | Y |
| 13 Brown | Y | Y | Y | N | Y | Y | Y |
| 14 **LaTourette** | N | Y | Y | Y | Y | Y | Y |
| 15 **Pryce** | N | N | Y | Y | Y | Y | Y |
| 16 **Regula** | N | N | Y | Y | Y | Y | Y |
| 17 Ryan | Y | Y | Y | N | Y | Y | Y |
| 18 **Ney** | N | N | Y | Y | Y | Y | Y |
| **OKLAHOMA** | | | | | | | |
| 1 **Sullivan** | N | N | Y | Y | Y | Y | Y |
| 2 Boren | Y | Y | Y | N | Y | Y | Y |
| 3 **Lucas** | N | N | Y | Y | Y | Y | Y |
| 4 **Cole** | N | N | Y | Y | ? | Y | Y |
| 5 **Istook** | N | N | Y | Y | Y | Y | Y |
| **OREGON** | | | | | | | |
| 1 Wu | Y | Y | Y | N | Y | P | Y |
| 2 **Walden** | N | N | Y | Y | Y | Y | Y |
| 3 Blumenauer | Y | Y | Y | N | N | P | Y |
| 4 DeFazio | Y | Y | Y | N | Y | Y | Y |
| 5 Hooley | Y | Y | Y | N | Y | Y | Y |
| **PENNSYLVANIA** | | | | | | | |
| 1 Brady | Y | Y | Y | N | Y | Y | Y |
| 2 Fattah | Y | Y | Y | N | ? | N | Y |
| 3 **English** | N | N | Y | ? | Y | Y | Y |
| 4 **Hart** | N | N | Y | Y | Y | Y | Y |
| 5 **Peterson** | ? | ? | ? | ? | ? | ? | ? |
| 6 **Gerlach** | Y | Y | Y | Y | ? | Y | Y |
| 7 **Weldon** | Y | N | Y | Y | Y | Y | Y |
| 8 **Fitzpatrick** | Y | Y | Y | Y | Y | Y | Y |
| 9 **Shuster** | Y | N | Y | Y | Y | Y | Y |
| 10 **Sherwood** | N | N | Y | Y | Y | Y | Y |
| 11 Kanjorski | Y | Y | Y | N | Y | Y | Y |
| 12 Murtha | Y | Y | Y | N | ? | ? | ? |
| 13 Schwartz | Y | Y | Y | N | Y | Y | Y |
| 14 Doyle | Y | Y | Y | N | Y | Y | Y |
| 15 **Dent** | Y | Y | Y | Y | Y | Y | Y |
| 16 **Pitts** | N | N | Y | Y | Y | Y | Y |
| 17 Holden | Y | Y | Y | N | Y | Y | Y |
| 18 **Murphy** | N | N | Y | Y | Y | Y | Y |
| 19 **Platts** | Y | Y | Y | Y | Y | Y | Y |
| **RHODE ISLAND** | | | | | | | |
| 1 Kennedy | Y | Y | Y | N | Y | Y | Y |
| 2 Langevin | Y | Y | Y | N | Y | Y | Y |
| **SOUTH CAROLINA** | | | | | | | |
| 1 **Brown** | N | N | Y | Y | Y | Y | Y |
| 2 **Wilson** | N | N | Y | Y | Y | Y | Y |
| 3 **Barrett** | N | N | Y | Y | Y | Y | Y |
| 4 **Inglis** | N | N | Y | Y | Y | Y | Y |
| 5 Spratt | Y | Y | Y | N | Y | Y | Y |
| 6 Clyburn | Y | Y | Y | N | Y | Y | Y |
| **SOUTH DAKOTA** | | | | | | | |
| AL Herseth | Y | Y | Y | N | Y | Y | Y |
| **TENNESSEE** | | | | | | | |
| 1 **Jenkins** | N | N | Y | Y | Y | Y | Y |
| 2 **Duncan** | N | N | Y | Y | Y | Y | Y |

| | 356 | 357 | 358 | 359 | 360 | 361 | 362 |
|---|---|---|---|---|---|---|---|
| 3 **Wamp** | N | N | Y | Y | Y | Y | Y |
| 4 Davis | Y | Y | Y | N | Y | Y | Y |
| 5 Cooper | Y | Y | N | N | Y | Y | Y |
| 6 Gordon | Y | Y | Y | N | Y | Y | Y |
| 7 **Blackburn** | N | N | Y | Y | Y | Y | Y |
| 8 Tanner | Y | Y | Y | N | Y | Y | Y |
| 9 Ford | Y | Y | Y | N | Y | Y | Y |
| **TEXAS** | | | | | | | |
| 1 **Gohmert** | N | N | Y | Y | Y | Y | Y |
| 2 **Poe** | Y | N | Y | Y | Y | Y | Y |
| 3 **Johnson, S.** | N | N | Y | Y | ? | ? | Y |
| 4 **Hall** | Y | N | Y | Y | Y | Y | Y |
| 5 **Hensarling** | N | N | Y | Y | Y | Y | Y |
| 6 **Barton** | N | N | Y | Y | Y | Y | Y |
| 7 **Culberson** | N | N | Y | Y | Y | Y | Y |
| 8 **Brady** | N | N | Y | Y | Y | Y | Y |
| 9 Green, A. | Y | Y | Y | N | Y | N | Y |
| 10 **McCaul** | N | N | Y | Y | ? | ? | Y |
| 11 **Conaway** | N | N | Y | Y | Y | Y | Y |
| 12 **Granger** | N | N | Y | Y | Y | P | Y |
| 13 **Thornberry** | N | N | Y | Y | Y | Y | Y |
| 14 **Paul** | N | Y | N | ? | N | P | Y |
| 15 Hinojosa | Y | Y | Y | N | Y | Y | Y |
| 16 Reyes | Y | Y | Y | N | Y | Y | Y |
| 17 Edwards | Y | Y | Y | N | Y | Y | Y |
| 18 Jackson-Lee | Y | Y | Y | N | Y | Y | Y |
| 19 **Neugebauer** | N | N | Y | Y | Y | Y | Y |
| 20 Gonzalez | Y | Y | Y | N | Y | Y | Y |
| 21 **Smith** | N | N | Y | Y | Y | Y | Y |
| 22 **DeLay** | N | N | Y | Y | Y | Y | Y |
| 23 **Bonilla** | N | N | Y | Y | Y | Y | Y |
| 24 **Marchant** | N | N | Y | Y | Y | Y | Y |
| 25 Doggett | Y | Y | Y | N | Y | Y | Y |
| 26 **Burgess** | N | N | Y | Y | Y | Y | Y |
| 27 Ortiz | Y | Y | Y | N | Y | Y | Y |
| 28 Cuellar | Y | Y | Y | N | Y | Y | Y |
| 29 Green, G. | Y | Y | Y | N | Y | Y | Y |
| 30 Johnson, E. | Y | Y | Y | N | Y | Y | Y |
| 31 **Carter** | N | N | Y | Y | Y | Y | Y |
| 32 **Sessions** | N | N | Y | Y | Y | Y | Y |
| **UTAH** | | | | | | | |
| 1 **Bishop** | N | Y | Y | Y | Y | Y | Y |
| 2 Matheson | Y | Y | N | N | Y | Y | Y |
| 3 **Cannon** | N | N | Y | Y | Y | Y | Y |
| **VERMONT** | | | | | | | |
| AL *Sanders* | Y | Y | Y | N | Y | Y | Y |
| **VIRGINIA** | | | | | | | |
| 1 **Davis, J.** | Y | Y | Y | Y | Y | Y | Y |
| 2 **Drake** | N | N | Y | Y | Y | Y | Y |
| 3 Scott | Y | Y | Y | N | Y | Y | Y |
| 4 **Forbes** | Y | N | Y | Y | Y | Y | Y |
| 5 **Goode** | Y | N | Y | Y | Y | Y | Y |
| 6 **Goodlatte** | N | N | Y | Y | Y | Y | Y |
| 7 **Cantor** | N | N | Y | Y | Y | Y | Y |
| 8 Moran | Y | Y | Y | N | N | N | Y |
| 9 Boucher | Y | Y | Y | N | Y | Y | Y |
| 10 **Wolf** | N | N | Y | Y | Y | Y | Y |
| 11 **Davis, T.** | N | N | Y | Y | N | Y | Y |
| **WASHINGTON** | | | | | | | |
| 1 Inslee | Y | Y | Y | N | N | N | Y |
| 2 Larsen | Y | Y | Y | N | N | N | Y |
| 3 Baird | Y | Y | Y | N | N | N | Y |
| 4 **Hastings** | N | N | Y | Y | Y | Y | Y |
| 5 **McMorris** | N | N | Y | Y | Y | Y | Y |
| 6 Dicks | Y | Y | Y | N | N | N | Y |
| 7 McDermott | Y | Y | Y | N | N | N | Y |
| 8 **Reichert** | Y | N | Y | Y | Y | Y | Y |
| 9 Smith | N | N | Y | N | N | Y | Y |
| **WEST VIRGINIA** | | | | | | | |
| 1 Mollohan | Y | Y | Y | N | Y | Y | Y |
| 2 **Capito** | N | Y | Y | Y | Y | Y | Y |
| 3 Rahall | Y | Y | Y | – | Y | Y | Y |
| **WISCONSIN** | | | | | | | |
| 1 **Ryan** | N | N | Y | Y | Y | Y | Y |
| 2 Baldwin | Y | Y | N | N | Y | Y | Y |
| 3 Kind | Y | Y | N | N | Y | Y | Y |
| 4 Moore | Y | Y | Y | N | Y | Y | Y |
| 5 **Sensenbrenner** | N | N | N | Y | Y | Y | Y |
| 6 **Petri** | N | N | Y | Y | Y | Y | Y |
| 7 Obey | Y | Y | N | N | Y | Y | Y |
| 8 **Green** | N | N | Y | Y | Y | Y | Y |
| **WYOMING** | | | | | | | |
| AL **Cubin** | N | N | Y | Y | Y | Y | Y |

# IN THE HOUSE | By Vote Number

**363.** **H Con Res 168. North Korea Kidnapping Condemnation/Adoption.** Smith, R-N.J., motion to suspend the rules and adopt the concurrent resolution that would condemn and call upon the North Korean government to immediately cease and desist in the abduction and continued captivity of citizens of South Korea and Japan. Motion agreed to 362-1: R 201-1; D 160-0 (ND 122-0, SD 38-0); I 1-0. A two-thirds majority of those present and voting (242 in this case) is required for adoption under suspension of the rules. July 11, 2005.

**364.** **H Res 333. Weekend of Prayer for Darfur/Adoption.** Smith, R-N.J., motion to suspend the rules and adopt the resolution that would support a National Weekend of Prayer and Reflection for Darfur, Sudan. Motion agreed to 364-2: R 203-1; D 160-1 (ND 120-1, SD 40-0); I 1-0. A two-thirds majority of those present and voting (244 in this case) is required for adoption under suspension of the rules. July 11, 2005.

**365.** **HR 739, HR 740, HR 741, HR 742. OSHA Bills/Previous Question.** Bishop, R-Utah, motion to order the previous question (thus ending debate and possibility of amendment) on adoption of the rule (H Res 351) to provide for House floor consideration of four Occupational Safety and Health Administration (OSHA)-related bills. Motion agreed to 223-191: R 222-1; D 1-189 (ND 1-142, SD 0-47); I 0-1. July 12, 2005.

**366.** **HR 739, HR 740, HR 741, HR 742. OSHA Bills/Rule.** Adoption of the rule (H Res 351) that would provide for House consideration of four OSHA-related bills. The rule specifies that if more than one bill passes the House, the text of those bills will be combined into one measure. Adopted 224-189: R 224-0; D 0-188 (ND 0-142, SD 0-46); I 0-1. July 12, 2005.

**367.** **H Res 352. Barriers to U.S. Economic Competitiveness/Adoption.** Boustany, R-La., motion to suspend the rules and adopt the resolution that would recognize that to improve U.S. competitiveness, congressional action is needed to remove barriers — ranging from tax law and trade restrictions to health care security — to keeping and creating jobs. Motion rejected 242-177: R 225-0; D 17-176 (ND 7-139, SD 10-37); I 0-1. A two-thirds majority of those present and voting (280 in this case) is required for adoption under suspension of the rules. July 12, 2005.

**368.** **H Res 343. Women's Political Rights in Kuwait/Adoption.** Smith, R-N.J., motion to suspend the rules and adopt the resolution that would commend the government of Kuwait for providing female citizens the right to vote and hold public office and urge the full participation of Kuwaiti women in the political life of their country. Motion agreed to 420-0: R 226-0; D 193-0 (ND 146-0, SD 47-0); I 1-0. A two-thirds majority of those present and voting (280 in this case) is required for adoption under suspension of the rules. July 12, 2005.

| | 363 | 364 | 365 | 366 | 367 | 368 |
|---|---|---|---|---|---|---|
| **ALABAMA** | | | | | | |
| 1 Bonner | + | + | Y | Y | Y | Y |
| 2 Everett | ? | ? | Y | Y | Y | Y |
| 3 Rogers | Y | Y | Y | Y | Y | Y |
| 4 Aderholt | Y | Y | Y | Y | Y | Y |
| 5 Cramer | Y | Y | N | N | Y | Y |
| 6 Bachus | Y | Y | Y | Y | Y | Y |
| 7 Davis | Y | Y | N | N | N | Y |
| **ALASKA** | | | | | | |
| AL Young | Y | Y | Y | Y | Y | Y |
| **ARIZONA** | | | | | | |
| 1 Renzi | Y | Y | Y | Y | Y | Y |
| 2 Franks | Y | Y | Y | Y | Y | Y |
| 3 Shadegg | ? | ? | ? | ? | ? | ? |
| 4 Pastor | Y | Y | N | N | N | Y |
| 5 Hayworth | Y | Y | Y | Y | Y | Y |
| 6 Flake | Y | Y | Y | Y | Y | Y |
| 7 Grijalva | Y | Y | N | N | N | Y |
| 8 Kolbe | Y | Y | Y | Y | Y | Y |
| **ARKANSAS** | | | | | | |
| 1 Berry | Y | Y | N | N | N | Y |
| 2 Snyder | Y | Y | N | N | N | Y |
| 3 Boozman | ? | ? | Y | Y | Y | Y |
| 4 Ross | Y | Y | N | N | N | Y |
| **CALIFORNIA** | | | | | | |
| 1 Thompson | Y | Y | N | N | N | Y |
| 2 Herger | Y | Y | Y | Y | Y | Y |
| 3 Lungren | Y | Y | Y | Y | Y | Y |
| 4 Doolittle | Y | Y | Y | Y | Y | Y |
| 5 Matsui, D. | Y | Y | N | N | N | Y |
| 6 Woolsey | Y | Y | N | N | N | Y |
| 7 Miller, George | ? | ? | N | N | N | Y |
| 8 Pelosi | Y | Y | N | N | N | Y |
| 9 Lee | + | + | N | N | N | Y |
| 10 Tauscher | Y | Y | N | N | N | Y |
| 11 Pombo | + | + | ? | ? | ? | ? |
| 12 Lantos | Y | Y | N | N | N | Y |
| 13 Stark | Y | Y | N | N | N | Y |
| 14 Eshoo | + | + | N | N | N | Y |
| 15 Honda | Y | Y | N | N | N | Y |
| 16 Lofgren | Y | Y | N | N | N | Y |
| 17 Farr | ? | ? | N | N | N | Y |
| 18 Cardoza | Y | Y | N | N | N | Y |
| 19 Radanovich | Y | Y | Y | Y | Y | Y |
| 20 Costa | Y | Y | N | N | N | Y |
| 21 Nunes | Y | Y | Y | Y | Y | Y |
| 22 Thomas | Y | Y | Y | Y | Y | Y |
| 23 Capps | Y | Y | N | N | N | Y |
| 24 Gallegly | + | + | Y | Y | Y | Y |
| 25 McKeon | Y | Y | Y | Y | Y | Y |
| 26 Dreier | Y | Y | Y | Y | Y | Y |
| 27 Sherman | Y | Y | N | N | N | Y |
| 28 Berman | Y | Y | ? | ? | N | Y |
| 29 Schiff | Y | Y | N | N | N | Y |
| 30 Waxman | Y | Y | N | N | N | Y |
| 31 Becerra | ? | ? | N | N | N | Y |
| 32 Solis | Y | Y | N | N | N | Y |
| 33 Watson | Y | Y | N | N | N | Y |
| 34 Roybal-Allard | Y | Y | N | N | N | Y |
| 35 Waters | ? | ? | N | N | N | Y |
| 36 Harman | Y | Y | N | N | N | Y |
| 37 Millender-McD. | Y | Y | N | N | N | Y |
| 38 Napolitano | Y | Y | N | N | N | Y |
| 39 Sánchez, Linda | + | + | N | N | N | Y |
| 40 Royce | Y | Y | Y | Y | Y | Y |
| 41 Lewis | Y | Y | Y | Y | Y | Y |
| 42 Miller, Gary | Y | Y | Y | Y | Y | Y |
| 43 Baca | Y | Y | N | N | N | Y |
| 44 Calvert | Y | Y | Y | Y | Y | Y |
| 45 Bono | Y | Y | Y | Y | Y | Y |
| 46 Rohrabacher | Y | Y | Y | Y | Y | Y |
| 47 Sanchez, Loretta | Y | Y | N | N | N | Y |
| 48 Cox | Y | Y | Y | Y | Y | Y |
| 49 Issa | Y | Y | Y | Y | Y | Y |

| | 363 | 364 | 365 | 366 | 367 | 368 |
|---|---|---|---|---|---|---|
| 50 Cunningham | Y | Y | Y | Y | Y | Y |
| 51 Filner | ? | + | N | N | N | Y |
| 52 Hunter | ? | ? | Y | Y | Y | Y |
| 53 Davis | Y | Y | N | N | N | Y |
| **COLORADO** | | | | | | |
| 1 DeGette | Y | Y | N | N | N | Y |
| 2 Udall | Y | Y | N | N | N | Y |
| 3 Salazar | Y | Y | N | N | N | Y |
| 4 Musgrave | Y | Y | Y | Y | Y | Y |
| 5 Hefley | Y | Y | Y | Y | Y | Y |
| 6 Tancredo | Y | Y | Y | Y | Y | Y |
| 7 Beauprez | Y | Y | Y | Y | Y | Y |
| **CONNECTICUT** | | | | | | |
| 1 Larson | Y | Y | N | N | N | Y |
| 2 Simmons | Y | Y | Y | Y | Y | Y |
| 3 DeLauro | Y | Y | N | N | N | Y |
| 4 Shays | Y | Y | N | Y | Y | Y |
| 5 Johnson | Y | Y | Y | Y | Y | Y |
| **DELAWARE** | | | | | | |
| AL Castle | Y | Y | Y | Y | Y | Y |
| **FLORIDA** | | | | | | |
| 1 Miller | ? | ? | ? | ? | ? | ? |
| 2 Boyd | Y | Y | N | N | N | Y |
| 3 Brown | ? | ? | ? | ? | ? | ? |
| 4 Crenshaw | Y | Y | Y | Y | Y | Y |
| 5 Brown-Waite | Y | Y | Y | Y | Y | Y |
| 6 Stearns | Y | Y | Y | Y | Y | Y |
| 7 Mica | Y | Y | Y | Y | Y | Y |
| 8 Keller | Y | Y | Y | Y | Y | Y |
| 9 Bilirakis | Y | Y | Y | Y | Y | Y |
| 10 Young | Y | Y | Y | Y | Y | Y |
| 11 Davis | Y | Y | N | N | N | Y |
| 12 Putnam | Y | Y | Y | Y | Y | Y |
| 13 Harris | Y | Y | Y | Y | Y | Y |
| 14 Mack | Y | Y | Y | Y | Y | Y |
| 15 Weldon | Y | Y | Y | Y | Y | Y |
| 16 Foley | Y | Y | Y | Y | Y | Y |
| 17 Meek | Y | Y | N | N | N | Y |
| 18 Ros-Lehtinen | Y | Y | Y | Y | Y | Y |
| 19 Wexler | Y | Y | N | N | N | Y |
| 20 Wasserman-Schultz | ? | ? | N | N | N | Y |
| 21 Diaz-Balart, L. | Y | Y | Y | Y | Y | Y |
| 22 Shaw | Y | Y | Y | Y | Y | Y |
| 23 Hastings | Y | Y | N | N | N | Y |
| 24 Feeney | Y | Y | Y | Y | Y | Y |
| 25 Diaz-Balart, M. | Y | Y | Y | Y | Y | Y |
| **GEORGIA** | | | | | | |
| 1 Kingston | ? | ? | Y | Y | Y | Y |
| 2 Bishop | Y | Y | N | N | N | Y |
| 3 Marshall | Y | Y | N | N | N | Y |
| 4 McKinney | ? | Y | N | N | N | Y |
| 5 Lewis | Y | Y | N | N | N | Y |
| 6 Price | Y | Y | Y | ? | Y | Y |
| 7 Linder | Y | Y | Y | Y | Y | Y |
| 8 Westmoreland | Y | Y | Y | Y | Y | Y |
| 9 Norwood | Y | Y | Y | Y | Y | Y |
| 10 Deal | Y | Y | Y | Y | Y | Y |
| 11 Gingrey | Y | Y | Y | Y | Y | Y |
| 12 Barrow | Y | Y | N | N | Y | Y |
| 13 Scott | Y | Y | N | N | N | Y |
| **HAWAII** | | | | | | |
| 1 Abercrombie | Y | Y | – | – | – | + |
| 2 Case | Y | Y | N | N | Y | Y |
| **IDAHO** | | | | | | |
| 1 Otter | Y | Y | Y | Y | Y | Y |
| 2 Simpson | Y | Y | Y | Y | Y | Y |
| **ILLINOIS** | | | | | | |
| 1 Rush | ? | ? | N | N | N | Y |
| 2 Jackson | Y | Y | N | N | N | Y |
| 3 Lipinski | Y | Y | N | N | N | Y |
| 4 Gutierrez | + | + | N | N | N | Y |
| 5 Emanuel | Y | Y | N | N | N | Y |
| 6 Hyde | Y | Y | Y | Y | Y | Y |
| 7 Davis | Y | Y | N | N | N | Y |
| 8 Bean | Y | Y | N | N | N | Y |
| 9 Schakowsky | Y | Y | N | N | N | Y |
| 10 Kirk | Y | Y | Y | Y | Y | Y |
| 11 Weller | Y | Y | Y | Y | Y | Y |
| 12 Costello | ? | ? | N | N | N | Y |

**KEY**   Republicans   Democrats   *Independents*

| | | | | |
|---|---|---|---|---|
| Y | Voted for (yea) | X | Paired against | C   Voted "present" to avoid possible conflict of interest |
| # | Paired for | – | Announced against | |
| + | Announced for | P | Voted "present" | ?   Did not vote or otherwise make a position known |
| N | Voted against (nay) | | | |

| | 363 | 364 | 365 | 366 | 367 | 368 |
|---|---|---|---|---|---|---|
| 13 **Biggert** | Y | Y | Y | Y | Y | Y |
| 14 **Hastert** | | | | | | |
| 15 **Johnson** | + | + | Y | Y | + | Y |
| 16 **Manzullo** | Y | Y | Y | Y | Y | Y |
| 17 Evans | Y | Y | N | N | N | Y |
| 18 **LaHood** | ? | ? | Y | Y | Y | Y |
| 19 **Shimkus** | ? | ? | Y | Y | Y | Y |
| **INDIANA** | | | | | | |
| 1 Visclosky | Y | Y | N | N | N | Y |
| 2 **Chocola** | Y | Y | Y | Y | Y | Y |
| 3 **Souder** | Y | Y | Y | Y | Y | Y |
| 4 **Buyer** | Y | Y | Y | Y | Y | Y |
| 5 **Burton** | Y | Y | Y | Y | Y | Y |
| 6 **Pence** | Y | Y | Y | Y | Y | Y |
| 7 Carson | Y | Y | – | N | N | Y |
| 8 **Hostettler** | Y | Y | Y | Y | Y | Y |
| 9 **Sodrel** | Y | Y | Y | Y | Y | Y |
| **IOWA** | | | | | | |
| 1 **Nussle** | Y | Y | Y | Y | Y | Y |
| 2 **Leach** | Y | Y | Y | Y | Y | Y |
| 3 Boswell | Y | Y | N | N | N | Y |
| 4 **Latham** | Y | Y | Y | Y | Y | Y |
| 5 **King** | Y | Y | Y | Y | Y | Y |
| **KANSAS** | | | | | | |
| 1 **Moran** | Y | Y | Y | Y | Y | Y |
| 2 **Ryun** | Y | Y | Y | Y | Y | Y |
| 3 Moore | Y | Y | N | N | N | Y |
| 4 **Tiahrt** | Y | Y | Y | Y | Y | Y |
| **KENTUCKY** | | | | | | |
| 1 **Whitfield** | Y | Y | Y | Y | Y | Y |
| 2 **Lewis** | Y | Y | Y | Y | Y | Y |
| 3 **Northup** | Y | Y | Y | Y | Y | Y |
| 4 **Davis** | Y | Y | Y | Y | Y | Y |
| 5 **Rogers** | Y | Y | Y | Y | Y | Y |
| 6 Chandler | Y | Y | N | N | Y | Y |
| **LOUISIANA** | | | | | | |
| 1 **Jindal** | Y | Y | Y | Y | Y | Y |
| 2 Jefferson | Y | Y | N | N | N | Y |
| 3 Melancon | Y | Y | N | N | Y | Y |
| 4 **McCrery** | Y | Y | Y | Y | Y | Y |
| 5 **Alexander** | Y | Y | Y | Y | Y | Y |
| 6 **Baker** | ? | ? | Y | Y | Y | Y |
| 7 **Boustany** | Y | Y | Y | Y | Y | Y |
| **MAINE** | | | | | | |
| 1 Allen | Y | Y | N | N | N | Y |
| 2 Michaud | Y | Y | N | N | N | Y |
| **MARYLAND** | | | | | | |
| 1 **Gilchrest** | Y | Y | Y | Y | Y | Y |
| 2 Ruppersberger | Y | Y | N | N | N | Y |
| 3 Cardin | Y | Y | N | N | N | Y |
| 4 Wynn | Y | Y | N | N | N | Y |
| 5 Hoyer | Y | Y | N | N | N | Y |
| 6 **Bartlett** | P | Y | Y | Y | Y | Y |
| 7 Cummings | Y | Y | N | N | N | Y |
| 8 Van Hollen | Y | Y | N | N | N | Y |
| **MASSACHUSETTS** | | | | | | |
| 1 Olver | Y | Y | N | N | N | Y |
| 2 Neal | ? | ? | N | N | N | Y |
| 3 McGovern | Y | Y | N | N | N | Y |
| 4 Frank | Y | Y | N | ? | N | Y |
| 5 Meehan | Y | Y | N | N | N | Y |
| 6 Tierney | ? | ? | N | N | N | Y |
| 7 Markey | Y | Y | N | N | N | Y |
| 8 Capuano | Y | Y | N | N | N | Y |
| 9 Lynch | Y | Y | N | N | N | Y |
| 10 Delahunt | Y | Y | ? | ? | N | Y |
| **MICHIGAN** | | | | | | |
| 1 Stupak | ? | ? | N | N | N | Y |
| 2 **Hoekstra** | Y | Y | Y | Y | Y | Y |
| 3 **Ehlers** | Y | Y | + | Y | Y | Y |
| 4 **Camp** | ? | ? | Y | Y | Y | Y |
| 5 Kildee | Y | Y | N | N | N | Y |
| 6 **Upton** | Y | Y | Y | Y | Y | Y |
| 7 **Schwarz** | Y | Y | Y | Y | Y | Y |
| 8 **Rogers** | Y | Y | Y | Y | Y | Y |
| 9 **Knollenberg** | Y | Y | Y | Y | Y | Y |
| 10 **Miller** | Y | Y | Y | Y | Y | Y |
| 11 **McCotter** | Y | Y | Y | Y | Y | Y |
| 12 Levin | Y | Y | N | N | N | Y |
| 13 Kilpatrick | + | + | N | N | N | Y |
| 14 Conyers | + | + | – | – | – | + |
| 15 Dingell | Y | Y | N | N | N | Y |

| | 363 | 364 | 365 | 366 | 367 | 368 |
|---|---|---|---|---|---|---|
| **MINNESOTA** | | | | | | |
| 1 **Gutknecht** | Y | Y | Y | Y | Y | Y |
| 2 **Kline** | Y | Y | Y | Y | Y | Y |
| 3 **Ramstad** | Y | Y | Y | Y | Y | Y |
| 4 McCollum | Y | Y | N | N | N | Y |
| 5 Sabo | Y | Y | N | N | N | Y |
| 6 **Kennedy** | Y | Y | Y | Y | Y | Y |
| 7 Peterson | Y | Y | N | N | N | Y |
| 8 Oberstar | Y | Y | N | N | N | Y |
| **MISSISSIPPI** | | | | | | |
| 1 **Wicker** | Y | Y | Y | Y | Y | Y |
| 2 Thompson | Y | Y | N | N | N | Y |
| 3 **Pickering** | ? | ? | Y | Y | Y | Y |
| 4 Taylor | Y | Y | N | N | Y | Y |
| **MISSOURI** | | | | | | |
| 1 Clay | ? | ? | ? | ? | ? | ? |
| 2 **Akin** | Y | Y | Y | Y | Y | Y |
| 3 Carnahan | Y | Y | N | N | N | Y |
| 4 Skelton | Y | Y | N | N | Y | Y |
| 5 Cleaver | Y | Y | N | N | N | Y |
| 6 **Graves** | Y | Y | Y | Y | Y | Y |
| 7 **Blunt** | Y | Y | Y | Y | Y | Y |
| 8 **Emerson** | Y | Y | Y | Y | Y | Y |
| 9 **Hulshof** | ? | ? | Y | Y | Y | Y |
| **MONTANA** | | | | | | |
| AL **Rehberg** | Y | Y | Y | Y | Y | Y |
| **NEBRASKA** | | | | | | |
| 1 **Fortenberry** | Y | Y | Y | Y | Y | Y |
| 2 **Terry** | Y | Y | Y | Y | Y | Y |
| 3 **Osborne** | Y | Y | Y | Y | Y | Y |
| **NEVADA** | | | | | | |
| 1 Berkley | Y | Y | N | N | N | Y |
| 2 **Gibbons** | Y | Y | Y | Y | Y | Y |
| 3 **Porter** | Y | Y | Y | Y | Y | Y |
| **NEW HAMPSHIRE** | | | | | | |
| 1 **Bradley** | Y | Y | Y | Y | Y | Y |
| 2 **Bass** | Y | Y | Y | Y | Y | Y |
| **NEW JERSEY** | | | | | | |
| 1 Andrews | Y | Y | N | N | N | Y |
| 2 **LoBiondo** | Y | Y | Y | Y | Y | Y |
| 3 **Saxton** | Y | Y | Y | Y | Y | Y |
| 4 **Smith** | Y | Y | Y | Y | Y | Y |
| 5 **Garrett** | Y | Y | Y | Y | Y | Y |
| 6 Pallone | Y | Y | N | N | N | Y |
| 7 **Ferguson** | Y | Y | Y | Y | Y | Y |
| 8 Pascrell | Y | Y | N | N | N | Y |
| 9 Rothman | Y | Y | Y | N | N | Y |
| 10 Payne | Y | Y | N | N | N | Y |
| 11 **Frelinghuysen** | Y | Y | Y | Y | Y | Y |
| 12 Holt | + | + | N | N | N | Y |
| 13 Menendez | Y | Y | N | N | N | Y |
| **NEW MEXICO** | | | | | | |
| 1 **Wilson** | Y | Y | Y | Y | Y | Y |
| 2 **Pearce** | Y | Y | Y | Y | Y | Y |
| 3 Udall | Y | Y | N | N | N | Y |
| **NEW YORK** | | | | | | |
| 1 Bishop | Y | Y | N | N | N | Y |
| 2 Israel | Y | Y | N | N | N | Y |
| 3 **King** | Y | Y | Y | Y | Y | Y |
| 4 McCarthy | Y | Y | N | N | N | Y |
| 5 Ackerman | Y | N | N | N | N | Y |
| 6 Meeks | Y | Y | N | N | N | Y |
| 7 Crowley | Y | Y | N | N | N | Y |
| 8 Nadler | Y | Y | N | N | N | Y |
| 9 Weiner | ? | ? | N | N | N | Y |
| 10 Towns | ? | ? | N | N | N | Y |
| 11 Owens | Y | Y | N | N | N | Y |
| 12 Velázquez | Y | Y | N | N | N | Y |
| 13 **Fossella** | Y | Y | Y | Y | Y | Y |
| 14 Maloney | Y | Y | N | N | N | Y |
| 15 Rangel | Y | Y | N | N | N | Y |
| 16 Serrano | Y | Y | N | N | N | Y |
| 17 Engel | Y | Y | N | N | N | Y |
| 18 Lowey | Y | Y | N | N | N | Y |
| 19 **Kelly** | Y | Y | Y | Y | Y | Y |
| 20 **Sweeney** | ? | ? | Y | Y | Y | Y |
| 21 McNulty | Y | Y | N | N | N | Y |
| 22 Hinchey | ? | ? | N | N | N | Y |
| 23 **McHugh** | Y | Y | Y | Y | Y | Y |
| 24 **Boehlert** | Y | Y | Y | Y | Y | Y |
| 25 **Walsh** | Y | Y | Y | Y | Y | Y |
| 26 **Reynolds** | Y | Y | Y | Y | Y | Y |
| 27 Higgins | Y | Y | N | N | N | Y |
| 28 Slaughter | Y | Y | N | N | N | Y |
| 29 **Kuhl** | Y | Y | Y | Y | Y | Y |

| | 363 | 364 | 365 | 366 | 367 | 368 |
|---|---|---|---|---|---|---|
| **NORTH CAROLINA** | | | | | | |
| 1 Butterfield | Y | Y | N | N | N | Y |
| 2 Etheridge | Y | Y | N | N | N | Y |
| 3 **Jones** | Y | Y | Y | Y | Y | Y |
| 4 Price | ? | ? | N | N | N | Y |
| 5 **Foxx** | Y | + | Y | Y | Y | Y |
| 6 **Coble** | Y | Y | Y | Y | Y | Y |
| 7 McIntyre | Y | Y | N | N | N | Y |
| 8 **Hayes** | Y | Y | Y | Y | Y | Y |
| 9 **Myrick** | ? | ? | ? | ? | ? | ? |
| 10 **McHenry** | Y | Y | Y | Y | Y | Y |
| 11 **Taylor** | ? | ? | Y | Y | Y | Y |
| 12 Watt | ? | ? | N | ? | N | Y |
| 13 Miller | Y | Y | N | N | N | Y |
| **NORTH DAKOTA** | | | | | | |
| AL Pomeroy | Y | Y | N | N | N | Y |
| **OHIO** | | | | | | |
| 1 **Chabot** | Y | Y | Y | Y | Y | Y |
| 2 Vacant | | | | | | |
| 3 **Turner** | Y | Y | Y | Y | Y | Y |
| 4 **Oxley** | Y | Y | Y | Y | Y | Y |
| 5 **Gillmor** | Y | Y | Y | Y | Y | Y |
| 6 Strickland | ? | ? | N | N | N | Y |
| 7 **Hobson** | Y | Y | Y | Y | Y | Y |
| 8 **Boehner** | Y | Y | Y | Y | Y | Y |
| 9 Kaptur | Y | Y | N | N | N | Y |
| 10 Kucinich | Y | Y | N | N | N | Y |
| 11 Jones | ? | ? | ? | ? | ? | ? |
| 12 **Tiberi** | Y | Y | Y | Y | Y | Y |
| 13 Brown | Y | Y | N | N | N | Y |
| 14 **LaTourette** | Y | Y | Y | Y | Y | Y |
| 15 **Pryce** | ? | ? | Y | Y | Y | Y |
| 16 **Regula** | Y | Y | Y | Y | Y | Y |
| 17 Ryan | Y | Y | N | N | N | Y |
| 18 **Ney** | Y | Y | Y | Y | Y | Y |
| **OKLAHOMA** | | | | | | |
| 1 **Sullivan** | Y | Y | Y | Y | Y | Y |
| 2 Boren | Y | Y | N | N | Y | Y |
| 3 **Lucas** | Y | Y | Y | Y | Y | Y |
| 4 **Cole** | Y | Y | Y | Y | Y | Y |
| 5 **Istook** | Y | Y | Y | Y | Y | Y |
| **OREGON** | | | | | | |
| 1 Wu | Y | Y | N | N | N | Y |
| 2 **Walden** | Y | Y | Y | Y | Y | Y |
| 3 Blumenauer | Y | Y | N | N | N | Y |
| 4 DeFazio | ? | ? | N | N | N | Y |
| 5 Hooley | Y | Y | N | N | N | Y |
| **PENNSYLVANIA** | | | | | | |
| 1 Brady | ? | ? | N | N | N | Y |
| 2 Fattah | ? | ? | N | N | N | Y |
| 3 **English** | ? | ? | Y | Y | Y | Y |
| 4 **Hart** | Y | Y | Y | Y | Y | Y |
| 5 **Peterson** | Y | Y | Y | Y | Y | Y |
| 6 **Gerlach** | Y | Y | Y | Y | Y | Y |
| 7 **Weldon** | ? | Y | Y | Y | Y | Y |
| 8 **Fitzpatrick** | Y | Y | Y | Y | Y | Y |
| 9 **Shuster** | Y | Y | Y | Y | Y | Y |
| 10 **Sherwood** | Y | Y | Y | Y | Y | Y |
| 11 Kanjorski | Y | Y | N | N | N | Y |
| 12 Murtha | ? | ? | N | N | N | Y |
| 13 Schwartz | Y | Y | N | N | N | Y |
| 14 Doyle | Y | Y | N | N | N | Y |
| 15 **Dent** | Y | Y | Y | Y | Y | Y |
| 16 **Pitts** | Y | Y | Y | Y | Y | Y |
| 17 Holden | Y | Y | N | N | Y | Y |
| 18 **Murphy** | Y | Y | Y | Y | Y | Y |
| 19 **Platts** | Y | Y | Y | Y | Y | Y |
| **RHODE ISLAND** | | | | | | |
| 1 Kennedy | Y | Y | N | – | N | Y |
| 2 Langevin | Y | Y | N | N | N | Y |
| **SOUTH CAROLINA** | | | | | | |
| 1 **Brown** | Y | Y | Y | Y | Y | Y |
| 2 **Wilson** | Y | Y | Y | Y | Y | Y |
| 3 **Barrett** | Y | Y | Y | Y | Y | Y |
| 4 **Inglis** | Y | Y | Y | Y | Y | Y |
| 5 Spratt | ? | Y | N | N | N | Y |
| 6 Clyburn | Y | Y | N | N | N | Y |
| **SOUTH DAKOTA** | | | | | | |
| AL Herseth | Y | Y | N | N | N | Y |
| **TENNESSEE** | | | | | | |
| 1 **Jenkins** | ? | ? | Y | Y | Y | Y |
| 2 **Duncan** | Y | Y | Y | Y | Y | Y |

| | 363 | 364 | 365 | 366 | 367 | 368 |
|---|---|---|---|---|---|---|
| 3 **Wamp** | Y | Y | Y | Y | Y | Y |
| 4 Davis | Y | Y | N | N | N | Y |
| 5 Cooper | Y | Y | N | N | N | Y |
| 6 Gordon | Y | Y | N | N | N | Y |
| 7 **Blackburn** | Y | Y | Y | Y | Y | Y |
| 8 Tanner | Y | Y | N | N | Y | Y |
| 9 Ford | Y | Y | N | N | N | Y |
| **TEXAS** | | | | | | |
| 1 **Gohmert** | Y | Y | Y | Y | Y | Y |
| 2 **Poe** | Y | Y | Y | ? | Y | Y |
| 3 **Johnson, S.** | Y | Y | Y | Y | Y | Y |
| 4 **Hall** | Y | Y | Y | Y | Y | Y |
| 5 **Hensarling** | Y | Y | Y | Y | Y | Y |
| 6 **Barton** | Y | Y | Y | Y | Y | Y |
| 7 **Culberson** | Y | Y | Y | Y | Y | Y |
| 8 **Brady** | ? | Y | Y | Y | Y | Y |
| 9 Green, A. | Y | Y | N | N | N | Y |
| 10 **McCaul** | Y | Y | Y | Y | Y | Y |
| 11 **Conaway** | Y | Y | Y | Y | Y | Y |
| 12 **Granger** | Y | Y | Y | Y | Y | Y |
| 13 **Thornberry** | ? | ? | Y | Y | Y | Y |
| 14 **Paul** | N | N | Y | Y | Y | Y |
| 15 Hinojosa | + | + | – | – | – | + |
| 16 Reyes | ? | ? | N | N | N | Y |
| 17 Edwards | ? | ? | N | N | N | Y |
| 18 Jackson-Lee | ? | ? | N | N | N | Y |
| 19 **Neugebauer** | + | + | Y | Y | Y | Y |
| 20 Gonzalez | + | + | – | – | – | + |
| 21 **Smith** | Y | Y | Y | Y | Y | Y |
| 22 **DeLay** | Y | Y | ? | Y | Y | Y |
| 23 **Bonilla** | Y | Y | Y | Y | Y | Y |
| 24 **Marchant** | ? | ? | ? | Y | Y | Y |
| 25 Doggett | Y | Y | N | N | N | Y |
| 26 **Burgess** | Y | Y | Y | Y | Y | Y |
| 27 Ortiz | + | + | – | – | – | + |
| 28 Cuellar | Y | Y | N | N | Y | Y |
| 29 Green, G. | Y | Y | N | N | N | Y |
| 30 Johnson, E. | Y | Y | N | N | N | Y |
| 31 **Carter** | Y | Y | Y | Y | Y | Y |
| 32 **Sessions** | Y | Y | Y | Y | Y | Y |
| **UTAH** | | | | | | |
| 1 **Bishop** | Y | Y | Y | Y | Y | Y |
| 2 Matheson | Y | Y | N | N | Y | Y |
| 3 **Cannon** | Y | Y | Y | Y | Y | Y |
| **VERMONT** | | | | | | |
| AL *Sanders* | Y | Y | N | N | N | Y |
| **VIRGINIA** | | | | | | |
| 1 **Davis, J.** | Y | Y | Y | Y | Y | Y |
| 2 **Drake** | Y | Y | Y | Y | Y | Y |
| 3 Scott | ? | ? | N | N | N | Y |
| 4 **Forbes** | Y | Y | Y | Y | Y | Y |
| 5 **Goode** | Y | Y | Y | Y | Y | Y |
| 6 **Goodlatte** | Y | Y | Y | Y | Y | Y |
| 7 **Cantor** | Y | Y | Y | Y | Y | Y |
| 8 Moran | Y | Y | N | N | N | Y |
| 9 Boucher | Y | Y | N | N | N | Y |
| 10 **Wolf** | Y | Y | Y | Y | Y | Y |
| 11 **Davis, T.** | Y | Y | Y | Y | Y | Y |
| **WASHINGTON** | | | | | | |
| 1 Inslee | Y | Y | N | N | N | Y |
| 2 Larsen | Y | Y | N | N | N | Y |
| 3 Baird | Y | Y | N | N | N | Y |
| 4 **Hastings** | Y | Y | Y | Y | Y | Y |
| 5 **McMorris** | Y | Y | Y | Y | Y | Y |
| 6 Dicks | Y | ? | N | N | N | Y |
| 7 McDermott | Y | Y | N | N | N | Y |
| 8 **Reichert** | Y | Y | Y | Y | Y | Y |
| 9 Smith | Y | Y | N | N | N | Y |
| **WEST VIRGINIA** | | | | | | |
| 1 Mollohan | Y | Y | N | N | N | Y |
| 2 **Capito** | Y | Y | Y | Y | Y | Y |
| 3 Rahall | Y | Y | N | N | N | Y |
| **WISCONSIN** | | | | | | |
| 1 **Ryan** | Y | Y | Y | Y | Y | Y |
| 2 Baldwin | Y | Y | N | N | N | Y |
| 3 Kind | Y | Y | N | N | N | Y |
| 4 Moore | + | + | N | N | N | Y |
| 5 **Sensenbrenner** | Y | Y | Y | Y | Y | Y |
| 6 **Petri** | Y | Y | Y | Y | Y | Y |
| 7 Obey | ? | ? | ? | ? | ? | ? |
| 8 **Green** | Y | Y | Y | Y | Y | Y |
| **WYOMING** | | | | | | |
| AL **Cubin** | Y | Y | Y | Y | Y | Y |

# IN THE HOUSE | By Vote Number

**369.** HR 739. Workplace Safety Citation Appeals/Passage. Passage of the bill that would allow the Occupational Safety and Health Review Commission to make exceptions to the 15-day deadline for employers to respond to an OSHA citation. Passed 256-164: R 225-0; D 31-163 (ND 15-130, SD 16-33); I 0-1. July 12, 2005.

**370.** HR 740. Occupational Safety and Health Review Commission/Passage. Passage of the bill that would expand the membership of the Occupational Safety and Health Review Commission from three to five. Passed 234-185: R 226-0; D 8-184 (ND 2-141, SD 6-43); I 0-1. July 12, 2005.

**371.** HR 741. Occupational Safety and Health Review Commission Rulings/Passage. Passage of the bill that would require courts and judges to defer to Occupational Safety and Health Review Commission rulings when interpreting questions of law. The commission hears appeals of Occupational Safety and Health Administration violations. Passed 226-197: R 217-9; D 9-187 (ND 2-144, SD 7-43); I 0-1. July 12, 2005.

**372.** HR 742. Small Business Attorneys' Fees/Passage. Passage of the bill that would allow courts to reimburse small businesses for their attorney fees if they successfully contest an OSHA ruling. Current law permits such reimbursement only if the court finds that OSHA was not "substantially justified" in its ruling. Passed 235-187: R 218-8; D 17-178 (ND 5-140, SD 12-38); I 0-1. July 12, 2005.

**373.** HR 6. Energy Policy/Motion to Instruct. Capps, D-Calif., motion to instruct House conferees to reject the inclusion of any provisions in the conference report that would provide liability protection for manufacturers of the gasoline additive methyl tertiary butyl ether. Motion rejected 201-217: R 21-204; D 179-13 (ND 141-1, SD 38-12); I 1-0. July 14, 2005.

**374.** HR 3100. Arms Sales to China/Passage. Hyde, R-Ill., motion to suspend the rules and pass the bill that would require the president to report to Congress 180 days after the bill's enactment, and yearly thereafter, identifying European or other entities that have exported any arms or dual-use technology to China for military use since Jan. 1, 2005. Motion rejected 215-203: R 118-106; D 96-97 (ND 70-73, SD 26-24); I 1-0. A two-thirds majority of those present and voting (279 in this case) is required for passage under suspension of the rules. July 14, 2005.

| | 369 | 370 | 371 | 372 | 373 | 374 |
|---|---|---|---|---|---|---|
| **ALABAMA** | | | | | | |
| 1 Bonner | Y | Y | Y | Y | N | N |
| 2 Everett | Y | Y | Y | Y | N | Y |
| 3 Rogers | Y | Y | Y | Y | N | Y |
| 4 Aderholt | Y | Y | Y | Y | N | Y |
| 5 Cramer | Y | Y | Y | Y | N | N |
| 6 Bachus | Y | Y | Y | Y | N | Y |
| 7 Davis | N | N | N | N | Y | N |
| **ALASKA** | | | | | | |
| AL Young | Y | Y | Y | Y | N | N |
| **ARIZONA** | | | | | | |
| 1 Renzi | Y | Y | Y | Y | N | N |
| 2 Franks | Y | Y | Y | Y | N | Y |
| 3 Shadegg | ? | ? | ? | ? | N | Y |
| 4 Pastor | N | N | N | N | Y | N |
| 5 Hayworth | Y | Y | Y | Y | N | Y |
| 6 Flake | Y | Y | Y | Y | N | Y |
| 7 Grijalva | N | N | N | N | Y | Y |
| 8 Kolbe | Y | Y | Y | Y | N | N |
| **ARKANSAS** | | | | | | |
| 1 Berry | N | N | N | N | Y | N |
| 2 Snyder | N | N | N | N | Y | N |
| 3 Boozman | Y | Y | Y | Y | N | Y |
| 4 Ross | N | N | N | N | Y | Y |
| **CALIFORNIA** | | | | | | |
| 1 Thompson | N | N | N | N | Y | N |
| 2 Herger | Y | Y | Y | Y | N | Y |
| 3 Lungren | Y | Y | Y | Y | N | Y |
| 4 Doolittle | Y | Y | Y | Y | N | Y |
| 5 Matsui, D. | N | N | N | N | Y | Y |
| 6 Woolsey | N | N | N | N | Y | N |
| 7 Miller, George | N | N | N | N | Y | N |
| 8 Pelosi | N | N | N | N | Y | Y |
| 9 Lee | N | N | N | N | Y | N |
| 10 Tauscher | N | N | N | N | Y | N |
| 11 Pombo | + | + | + | + | N | Y |
| 12 Lantos | N | N | N | N | Y | Y |
| 13 Stark | N | N | N | N | Y | N |
| 14 Eshoo | N | N | N | N | Y | N |
| 15 Honda | N | N | N | N | Y | N |
| 16 Lofgren | N | N | N | N | Y | N |
| 17 Farr | N | N | N | N | Y | N |
| 18 Cardoza | N | N | N | N | Y | Y |
| 19 Radanovich | Y | Y | Y | Y | N | Y |
| 20 Costa | Y | N | N | Y | Y | Y |
| 21 Nunes | Y | Y | Y | Y | N | N |
| 22 Thomas | Y | Y | Y | Y | N | N |
| 23 Capps | N | N | N | N | + | + |
| 24 Gallegly | Y | Y | Y | Y | ? | ? |
| 25 McKeon | Y | Y | Y | Y | N | Y |
| 26 Dreier | Y | Y | Y | Y | N | N |
| 27 Sherman | N | N | N | N | Y | N |
| 28 Berman | N | N | N | N | Y | N |
| 29 Schiff | N | N | N | N | Y | N |
| 30 Waxman | N | N | N | N | Y | N |
| 31 Becerra | N | N | N | N | Y | N |
| 32 Solis | N | N | N | N | Y | N |
| 33 Watson | N | N | N | N | Y | N |
| 34 Roybal-Allard | N | N | N | N | Y | N |
| 35 Waters | N | N | N | N | Y | N |
| 36 Harman | Y | N | N | N | Y | N |
| 37 Millender-McD. | N | N | N | N | Y | N |
| 38 Napolitano | N | N | N | N | Y | N |
| 39 Sánchez, Linda | N | N | N | N | Y | N |
| 40 Royce | Y | Y | Y | Y | N | Y |
| 41 Lewis | Y | Y | Y | Y | N | Y |
| 42 Miller, Gary | Y | Y | Y | Y | N | Y |
| 43 Baca | N | N | N | N | Y | N |
| 44 Calvert | Y | Y | Y | Y | N | N |
| 45 Bono | Y | Y | Y | Y | N | Y |
| 46 Rohrabacher | Y | Y | Y | Y | Y | Y |
| 47 Sanchez, Loretta | N | N | N | N | Y | N |
| 48 Cox | ? | ? | ? | ? | N | Y |
| 49 Issa | Y | Y | Y | Y | N | Y |

| | 369 | 370 | 371 | 372 | 373 | 374 |
|---|---|---|---|---|---|---|
| 50 Cunningham | Y | Y | Y | Y | ? | ? |
| 51 Filner | N | N | N | N | Y | Y |
| 52 Hunter | Y | Y | Y | Y | N | N |
| 53 Davis | N | N | N | N | Y | N |
| **COLORADO** | | | | | | |
| 1 DeGette | N | N | N | N | Y | Y |
| 2 Udall | Y | N | N | N | Y | Y |
| 3 Salazar | Y | N | N | N | Y | Y |
| 4 Musgrave | Y | Y | Y | Y | N | Y |
| 5 Hefley | Y | Y | Y | Y | N | Y |
| 6 Tancredo | Y | Y | Y | Y | N | N |
| 7 Beauprez | Y | Y | Y | Y | N | N |
| **CONNECTICUT** | | | | | | |
| 1 Larson | N | N | N | N | Y | ? |
| 2 Simmons | Y | Y | N | Y | ? | ? |
| 3 DeLauro | N | N | N | N | Y | Y |
| 4 Shays | Y | Y | Y | N | N | N |
| 5 Johnson | Y | Y | Y | Y | N | N |
| **DELAWARE** | | | | | | |
| AL Castle | Y | Y | Y | Y | Y | Y |
| **FLORIDA** | | | | | | |
| 1 Miller | ? | ? | ? | ? | ? | ? |
| 2 Boyd | Y | Y | Y | Y | Y | Y |
| 3 Brown | ? | ? | ? | ? | Y | Y |
| 4 Crenshaw | Y | Y | Y | Y | N | N |
| 5 Brown-Waite | Y | Y | Y | Y | N | Y |
| 6 Stearns | Y | Y | Y | Y | N | N |
| 7 Mica | Y | Y | Y | Y | N | N |
| 8 Keller | Y | Y | Y | Y | N | Y |
| 9 Bilirakis | Y | Y | Y | Y | N | Y |
| 10 Young | Y | Y | Y | Y | ? | ? |
| 11 Davis | Y | N | N | Y | Y | Y |
| 12 Putnam | Y | Y | Y | Y | N | Y |
| 13 Harris | Y | Y | Y | Y | N | N |
| 14 Mack | Y | Y | Y | Y | N | Y |
| 15 Weldon | Y | Y | Y | Y | N | Y |
| 16 Foley | Y | Y | Y | Y | N | N |
| 17 Meek | N | N | N | N | Y | N |
| 18 Ros-Lehtinen | Y | Y | Y | Y | N | N |
| 19 Wexler | N | N | N | N | Y | Y |
| 20 Wasserman-Schultz | N | N | N | N | Y | Y |
| 21 Diaz-Balart, L. | Y | Y | Y | Y | N | Y |
| 22 Shaw | Y | Y | Y | Y | N | Y |
| 23 Hastings | N | N | N | N | Y | Y |
| 24 Feeney | Y | Y | Y | Y | N | Y |
| 25 Diaz-Balart, M. | Y | Y | Y | Y | N | Y |
| **GEORGIA** | | | | | | |
| 1 Kingston | Y | Y | Y | Y | N | N |
| 2 Bishop | Y | N | N | Y | Y | Y |
| 3 Marshall | Y | N | N | Y | Y | N |
| 4 McKinney | N | N | N | N | Y | N |
| 5 Lewis | N | N | N | N | Y | N |
| 6 Price | Y | Y | Y | Y | N | N |
| 7 Linder | Y | Y | Y | Y | N | N |
| 8 Westmoreland | Y | Y | Y | Y | N | N |
| 9 Norwood | Y | Y | Y | Y | N | Y |
| 10 Deal | Y | Y | Y | Y | N | Y |
| 11 Gingrey | Y | Y | Y | Y | N | Y |
| 12 Barrow | N | N | N | N | Y | N |
| 13 Scott | N | N | N | N | Y | Y |
| **HAWAII** | | | | | | |
| 1 Abercrombie | – | – | – | – | N | Y |
| 2 Case | Y | Y | Y | Y | Y | Y |
| **IDAHO** | | | | | | |
| 1 Otter | Y | Y | Y | Y | N | N |
| 2 Simpson | Y | Y | Y | Y | N | N |
| **ILLINOIS** | | | | | | |
| 1 Rush | N | N | N | N | Y | N |
| 2 Jackson | N | N | N | N | Y | N |
| 3 Lipinski | Y | N | N | N | Y | N |
| 4 Gutierrez | N | ? | N | N | + | + |
| 5 Emanuel | N | N | N | N | Y | N |
| 6 Hyde | Y | Y | Y | Y | N | Y |
| 7 Davis | N | N | N | N | Y | N |
| 8 Bean | Y | N | N | Y | Y | N |
| 9 Schakowsky | N | N | N | N | Y | N |
| 10 Kirk | Y | Y | Y | Y | N | Y |
| 11 Weller | Y | Y | Y | Y | N | Y |
| 12 Costello | N | N | N | N | Y | N |

**KEY**    Republicans    Democrats    *Independents*

| | | | |
|---|---|---|---|
| Y | Voted for (yea) | X | Paired against |
| # | Paired for | – | Announced against |
| + | Announced for | P | Voted "present" |
| N | Voted against (nay) | | |
| C | Voted "present" to avoid possible conflict of interest | | |
| ? | Did not vote or otherwise make a position known | | |

| | 369 | 370 | 371 | 372 | 373 | 374 |
|---|---|---|---|---|---|---|
| 13 **Biggert** | Y | Y | Y | Y | N | N |
| 14 **Hastert** | | | | | N | |
| 15 **Johnson** | Y | Y | Y | Y | Y | Y |
| 16 **Manzullo** | Y | Y | Y | Y | N | N |
| 17 Evans | N | N | N | N | Y | Y |
| 18 **LaHood** | Y | Y | Y | Y | N | N |
| 19 **Shimkus** | Y | Y | Y | Y | N | N |
| **INDIANA** | | | | | | |
| 1 Visclosky | N | N | N | N | Y | N |
| 2 **Chocola** | Y | Y | Y | Y | N | Y |
| 3 **Souder** | Y | Y | Y | Y | N | Y |
| 4 **Buyer** | Y | Y | Y | Y | N | Y |
| 5 **Burton** | Y | Y | Y | Y | N | Y |
| 6 **Pence** | Y | Y | Y | Y | N | Y |
| 7 Carson | N | N | N | N | ? | ? |
| 8 **Hostettler** | Y | Y | Y | Y | N | Y |
| 9 **Sodrel** | Y | Y | Y | Y | N | N |
| **IOWA** | | | | | | |
| 1 **Nussle** | Y | Y | Y | Y | N | N |
| 2 **Leach** | Y | Y | Y | Y | Y | N |
| 3 Boswell | N | N | N | N | Y | N |
| 4 **Latham** | Y | Y | Y | Y | N | N |
| 5 **King** | Y | Y | Y | Y | N | N |
| **KANSAS** | | | | | | |
| 1 **Moran** | Y | Y | Y | Y | N | N |
| 2 **Ryun** | Y | Y | Y | Y | N | N |
| 3 Moore | N | N | N | N | Y | N |
| 4 **Tiahrt** | Y | Y | Y | Y | N | N |
| **KENTUCKY** | | | | | | |
| 1 **Whitfield** | Y | Y | Y | Y | N | N |
| 2 **Lewis** | Y | Y | Y | Y | N | N |
| 3 **Northup** | Y | Y | Y | Y | N | Y |
| 4 **Davis** | Y | Y | Y | Y | N | N |
| 5 **Rogers** | Y | Y | Y | Y | N | Y |
| 6 Chandler | N | N | N | N | Y | Y |
| **LOUISIANA** | | | | | | |
| 1 **Jindal** | Y | Y | Y | Y | N | Y |
| 2 Jefferson | N | N | N | N | Y | N |
| 3 Melancon | N | N | N | N | N | Y |
| 4 **McCrery** | Y | Y | Y | Y | N | N |
| 5 **Alexander** | Y | Y | Y | Y | N | Y |
| 6 **Baker** | Y | Y | Y | Y | N | N |
| 7 **Boustany** | Y | Y | Y | Y | N | N |
| **MAINE** | | | | | | |
| 1 Allen | N | N | N | N | Y | Y |
| 2 Michaud | N | N | N | N | Y | Y |
| **MARYLAND** | | | | | | |
| 1 **Gilchrest** | Y | Y | Y | Y | N | N |
| 2 Ruppersberger | N | N | N | N | Y | N |
| 3 Cardin | ? | ? | ? | ? | ? | ? |
| 4 Wynn | Y | N | N | Y | Y | N |
| 5 Hoyer | N | N | N | N | Y | N |
| 6 **Bartlett** | Y | Y | Y | Y | N | N |
| 7 Cummings | N | N | N | N | Y | Y |
| 8 Van Hollen | N | N | N | N | Y | N |
| **MASSACHUSETTS** | | | | | | |
| 1 Olver | N | N | N | N | Y | N |
| 2 Neal | N | N | N | N | Y | Y |
| 3 McGovern | N | N | N | N | Y | N |
| 4 Frank | N | N | N | N | Y | Y |
| 5 Meehan | N | N | N | N | Y | N |
| 6 Tierney | N | N | N | N | Y | Y |
| 7 Markey | N | N | N | N | Y | Y |
| 8 Capuano | N | N | N | N | Y | N |
| 9 Lynch | N | N | N | N | Y | N |
| 10 Delahunt | N | N | N | N | Y | N |
| **MICHIGAN** | | | | | | |
| 1 Stupak | N | N | N | N | Y | Y |
| 2 **Hoekstra** | Y | Y | Y | Y | N | N |
| 3 **Ehlers** | Y | Y | Y | Y | N | N |
| 4 **Camp** | Y | Y | Y | Y | N | N |
| 5 Kildee | N | N | N | N | Y | Y |
| 6 **Upton** | Y | Y | Y | Y | N | N |
| 7 **Schwarz** | Y | Y | Y | Y | N | Y |
| 8 **Rogers** | Y | Y | Y | Y | N | Y |
| 9 **Knollenberg** | Y | Y | Y | Y | N | Y |
| 10 **Miller** | Y | Y | Y | Y | N | Y |
| 11 **McCotter** | Y | Y | Y | Y | N | Y |
| 12 Levin | N | N | N | N | Y | N |
| 13 Kilpatrick | N | N | N | N | + | + |
| 14 Conyers | – | – | – | – | Y | Y |
| 15 Dingell | N | N | N | N | Y | Y |
| **MINNESOTA** | | | | | | |
| 1 **Gutknecht** | Y | Y | Y | Y | N | N |
| 2 **Kline** | Y | Y | Y | Y | N | N |
| 3 **Ramstad** | Y | Y | Y | Y | Y | Y |
| 4 McCollum | N | N | N | N | Y | N |
| 5 Sabo | N | N | N | N | Y | N |
| 6 **Kennedy** | Y | Y | Y | Y | N | N |
| 7 Peterson | N | N | N | N | Y | Y |
| 8 Oberstar | N | N | N | N | ? | ? |
| **MISSISSIPPI** | | | | | | |
| 1 **Wicker** | Y | Y | Y | Y | N | Y |
| 2 Thompson | N | N | N | N | Y | Y |
| 3 **Pickering** | Y | Y | Y | Y | N | Y |
| 4 Taylor | Y | Y | Y | Y | Y | Y |
| **MISSOURI** | | | | | | |
| 1 Clay | N | N | N | N | Y | N |
| 2 **Akin** | Y | Y | Y | Y | N | Y |
| 3 Carnahan | N | N | N | N | Y | Y |
| 4 Skelton | Y | N | N | N | Y | N |
| 5 Cleaver | N | N | N | N | Y | Y |
| 6 **Graves** | Y | Y | Y | Y | N | Y |
| 7 **Blunt** | Y | Y | Y | Y | N | Y |
| 8 **Emerson** | Y | Y | Y | Y | N | Y |
| 9 **Hulshof** | Y | Y | Y | Y | N | N |
| **MONTANA** | | | | | | |
| AL **Rehberg** | Y | Y | Y | Y | N | N |
| **NEBRASKA** | | | | | | |
| 1 **Fortenberry** | Y | Y | Y | Y | N | Y |
| 2 **Terry** | Y | Y | Y | Y | N | Y |
| 3 **Osborne** | Y | Y | Y | Y | N | Y |
| **NEVADA** | | | | | | |
| 1 Berkley | N | N | N | N | Y | Y |
| 2 **Gibbons** | Y | Y | Y | Y | N | N |
| 3 **Porter** | Y | Y | Y | Y | N | Y |
| **NEW HAMPSHIRE** | | | | | | |
| 1 **Bradley** | Y | Y | Y | Y | Y | Y |
| 2 **Bass** | Y | Y | Y | Y | N | N |
| **NEW JERSEY** | | | | | | |
| 1 Andrews | N | N | N | N | Y | Y |
| 2 **LoBiondo** | Y | Y | N | N | Y | N |
| 3 **Saxton** | Y | Y | N | N | Y | N |
| 4 **Smith** | Y | Y | N | N | Y | Y |
| 5 **Garrett** | Y | Y | Y | Y | N | N |
| 6 Pallone | N | N | N | N | Y | N |
| 7 **Ferguson** | Y | Y | Y | Y | N | N |
| 8 Pascrell | N | N | N | N | Y | Y |
| 9 Rothman | N | N | N | N | Y | Y |
| 10 Payne | N | N | N | N | Y | N |
| 11 **Frelinghuysen** | Y | Y | Y | Y | Y | N |
| 12 Holt | N | N | N | N | Y | N |
| 13 Menendez | N | N | N | – | Y | N |
| **NEW MEXICO** | | | | | | |
| 1 **Wilson** | Y | Y | Y | Y | Y | N |
| 2 **Pearce** | Y | Y | Y | Y | N | Y |
| 3 Udall | N | N | N | N | Y | N |
| **NEW YORK** | | | | | | |
| 1 Bishop | N | N | N | N | Y | Y |
| 2 Israel | N | N | N | N | Y | N |
| 3 **King** | Y | Y | N | Y | N | Y |
| 4 McCarthy | N | N | N | N | Y | N |
| 5 Ackerman | N | N | N | N | Y | Y |
| 6 Meeks | N | N | N | N | Y | N |
| 7 Crowley | N | N | N | N | Y | Y |
| 8 Nadler | N | N | N | N | Y | Y |
| 9 Weiner | N | N | N | N | ? | ? |
| 10 Towns | ? | ? | N | N | Y | Y |
| 11 Owens | N | N | N | N | Y | Y |
| 12 Velázquez | Y | N | N | Y | Y | N |
| 13 **Fossella** | Y | Y | Y | Y | N | N |
| 14 Maloney | N | N | N | N | Y | Y |
| 15 Rangel | N | ? | N | N | Y | N |
| 16 Serrano | N | N | N | N | Y | Y |
| 17 Engel | N | N | N | N | Y | Y |
| 18 Lowey | N | N | N | N | Y | Y |
| 19 **Kelly** | Y | Y | Y | Y | Y | Y |
| 20 **Sweeney** | Y | Y | N | Y | Y | N |
| 21 McNulty | N | N | N | N | Y | Y |
| 22 Hinchey | N | N | N | N | Y | N |
| 23 **McHugh** | Y | Y | N | Y | N | N |
| 24 **Boehlert** | Y | Y | Y | N | Y | N |
| 25 **Walsh** | Y | Y | Y | Y | N | Y |
| 26 **Reynolds** | Y | Y | Y | Y | N | Y |
| 27 Higgins | N | N | N | N | Y | Y |
| 28 Slaughter | N | N | N | N | Y | N |
| 29 **Kuhl** | Y | Y | Y | Y | N | N |
| **NORTH CAROLINA** | | | | | | |
| 1 Butterfield | N | N | N | N | Y | Y |
| 2 Etheridge | N | N | N | N | Y | N |
| 3 **Jones** | Y | Y | Y | Y | N | Y |
| 4 Price | N | N | N | N | Y | N |
| 5 **Foxx** | Y | Y | Y | Y | N | Y |
| 6 **Coble** | Y | Y | Y | Y | N | N |
| 7 McIntyre | Y | N | N | N | ? | ? |
| 8 **Hayes** | Y | Y | Y | Y | N | Y |
| 9 **Myrick** | ? | ? | ? | ? | N | Y |
| 10 **McHenry** | Y | Y | Y | Y | N | Y |
| 11 **Taylor** | Y | Y | Y | Y | N | Y |
| 12 Watt | N | ? | N | N | Y | N |
| 13 Miller | N | N | N | N | Y | N |
| **NORTH DAKOTA** | | | | | | |
| AL Pomeroy | N | N | N | N | Y | N |
| **OHIO** | | | | | | |
| 1 **Chabot** | Y | Y | Y | Y | N | Y |
| 2 Vacant | | | | | | |
| 3 **Turner** | Y | Y | Y | Y | N | N |
| 4 **Oxley** | Y | Y | Y | Y | N | Y |
| 5 **Gillmor** | Y | Y | Y | Y | N | Y |
| 6 Strickland | N | N | N | N | ? | Y |
| 7 **Hobson** | Y | Y | Y | Y | N | N |
| 8 **Boehner** | Y | Y | Y | Y | N | N |
| 9 Kaptur | N | N | N | N | Y | Y |
| 10 Kucinich | N | N | N | N | Y | Y |
| 11 Jones | ? | ? | ? | ? | Y | N |
| 12 **Tiberi** | Y | Y | Y | Y | N | N |
| 13 Brown | N | N | N | N | Y | Y |
| 14 **LaTourette** | Y | Y | Y | N | N | N |
| 15 **Pryce** | Y | Y | Y | Y | N | N |
| 16 **Regula** | Y | Y | Y | Y | N | N |
| 17 Ryan | N | N | N | N | Y | Y |
| 18 **Ney** | Y | Y | Y | Y | N | Y |
| **OKLAHOMA** | | | | | | |
| 1 **Sullivan** | Y | Y | Y | Y | N | N |
| 2 Boren | Y | Y | Y | Y | N | N |
| 3 **Lucas** | Y | Y | Y | Y | N | Y |
| 4 **Cole** | Y | Y | Y | Y | N | Y |
| 5 **Istook** | Y | Y | Y | Y | N | Y |
| **OREGON** | | | | | | |
| 1 Wu | N | N | N | N | Y | Y |
| 2 **Walden** | Y | Y | Y | Y | N | Y |
| 3 Blumenauer | N | N | N | N | Y | N |
| 4 DeFazio | N | N | N | N | Y | Y |
| 5 Hooley | N | N | N | N | Y | N |
| **PENNSYLVANIA** | | | | | | |
| 1 Brady | N | N | N | N | Y | Y |
| 2 Fattah | N | N | N | N | Y | Y |
| 3 **English** | Y | Y | Y | Y | N | N |
| 4 **Hart** | Y | Y | Y | Y | N | N |
| 5 **Peterson** | Y | Y | Y | Y | N | Y |
| 6 **Gerlach** | Y | Y | Y | Y | N | Y |
| 7 **Weldon** | Y | Y | Y | N | N | Y |
| 8 **Fitzpatrick** | Y | Y | N | N | Y | Y |
| 9 **Shuster** | Y | Y | Y | Y | N | N |
| 10 **Sherwood** | Y | Y | Y | Y | N | Y |
| 11 Kanjorski | N | N | N | N | Y | Y |
| 12 Murtha | N | N | N | N | Y | N |
| 13 Schwartz | N | N | N | N | Y | Y |
| 14 Doyle | N | N | N | N | Y | Y |
| 15 **Dent** | Y | Y | Y | Y | N | Y |
| 16 **Pitts** | Y | Y | Y | Y | N | Y |
| 17 Holden | N | N | N | N | Y | Y |
| 18 **Murphy** | Y | Y | Y | Y | N | N |
| 19 **Platts** | Y | Y | Y | Y | N | Y |
| **RHODE ISLAND** | | | | | | |
| 1 Kennedy | N | N | N | N | Y | Y |
| 2 Langevin | N | N | N | N | Y | Y |
| **SOUTH CAROLINA** | | | | | | |
| 1 **Brown** | Y | Y | Y | Y | N | N |
| 2 **Wilson** | Y | Y | Y | Y | N | Y |
| 3 **Barrett** | Y | Y | Y | Y | N | Y |
| 4 **Inglis** | Y | Y | Y | Y | N | Y |
| 5 Spratt | N | N | N | N | Y | Y |
| 6 Clyburn | N | N | N | N | Y | N |
| **SOUTH DAKOTA** | | | | | | |
| AL Herseth | Y | N | N | N | Y | N |
| **TENNESSEE** | | | | | | |
| 1 **Jenkins** | Y | Y | Y | Y | N | N |
| 2 **Duncan** | Y | Y | Y | Y | N | Y |
| 3 **Wamp** | Y | Y | Y | Y | N | Y |
| 4 Davis | Y | N | Y | Y | Y | Y |
| 5 Cooper | Y | N | N | Y | Y | Y |
| 6 Gordon | Y | Y | N | N | Y | N |
| 7 **Blackburn** | Y | Y | Y | Y | N | Y |
| 8 Tanner | Y | N | N | Y | Y | Y |
| 9 Ford | Y | N | N | Y | Y | Y |
| **TEXAS** | | | | | | |
| 1 **Gohmert** | Y | Y | Y | Y | N | N |
| 2 **Poe** | Y | Y | Y | Y | N | N |
| 3 **Johnson, S.** | Y | Y | Y | Y | N | Y |
| 4 **Hall** | Y | Y | Y | Y | N | N |
| 5 **Hensarling** | Y | Y | Y | Y | N | N |
| 6 **Barton** | Y | Y | Y | Y | N | Y |
| 7 **Culberson** | Y | Y | Y | Y | N | Y |
| 8 **Brady** | Y | Y | Y | Y | N | N |
| 9 Green, A. | N | N | N | N | N | Y |
| 10 **McCaul** | Y | Y | Y | Y | N | Y |
| 11 **Conaway** | Y | Y | Y | Y | N | N |
| 12 **Granger** | Y | Y | Y | Y | N | Y |
| 13 **Thornberry** | Y | Y | Y | Y | N | N |
| 14 **Paul** | Y | Y | N | Y | N | N |
| 15 Hinojosa | – | N | N | N | N | Y |
| 16 Reyes | N | N | N | N | N | N |
| 17 Edwards | Y | N | N | Y | N | Y |
| 18 Jackson-Lee | N | N | N | N | N | Y |
| 19 **Neugebauer** | Y | Y | Y | Y | N | N |
| 20 Gonzalez | Y | N | N | Y | N | N |
| 21 **Smith** | Y | Y | Y | Y | N | N |
| 22 **DeLay** | Y | Y | Y | Y | N | Y |
| 23 **Bonilla** | Y | Y | Y | Y | N | N |
| 24 **Marchant** | Y | Y | Y | Y | N | N |
| 25 Doggett | N | N | N | N | Y | Y |
| 26 **Burgess** | Y | Y | Y | Y | N | N |
| 27 Ortiz | N | N | N | N | N | N |
| 28 Cuellar | Y | Y | Y | Y | N | N |
| 29 Green, G. | N | N | N | N | N | Y |
| 30 Johnson, E. | N | N | N | N | Y | Y |
| 31 **Carter** | Y | Y | Y | Y | N | N |
| 32 **Sessions** | Y | Y | Y | Y | N | N |
| **UTAH** | | | | | | |
| 1 **Bishop** | Y | Y | Y | Y | N | Y |
| 2 Matheson | Y | Y | Y | Y | Y | Y |
| 3 **Cannon** | Y | Y | Y | Y | N | N |
| **VERMONT** | | | | | | |
| AL *Sanders* | N | N | N | N | Y | Y |
| **VIRGINIA** | | | | | | |
| 1 **Davis, J.** | Y | Y | Y | Y | N | Y |
| 2 **Drake** | Y | Y | Y | Y | N | Y |
| 3 Scott | N | N | N | N | Y | N |
| 4 **Forbes** | Y | Y | Y | Y | N | Y |
| 5 **Goode** | Y | Y | Y | Y | N | Y |
| 6 **Goodlatte** | Y | Y | Y | Y | N | N |
| 7 **Cantor** | Y | Y | Y | Y | N | Y |
| 8 Moran | N | N | N | N | Y | N |
| 9 Boucher | N | N | N | N | Y | N |
| 10 **Wolf** | Y | Y | Y | Y | Y | Y |
| 11 **Davis, T.** | Y | Y | Y | Y | Y | N |
| **WASHINGTON** | | | | | | |
| 1 Inslee | N | N | N | N | Y | N |
| 2 Larsen | N | N | N | N | Y | N |
| 3 Baird | Y | N | N | N | Y | N |
| 4 **Hastings** | Y | Y | Y | Y | N | Y |
| 5 **McMorris** | Y | Y | Y | Y | N | Y |
| 6 Dicks | N | N | N | N | Y | N |
| 7 McDermott | N | N | N | N | Y | N |
| 8 **Reichert** | Y | Y | Y | Y | Y | N |
| 9 Smith | N | N | N | N | Y | N |
| **WEST VIRGINIA** | | | | | | |
| 1 Mollohan | Y | N | N | N | Y | Y |
| 2 **Capito** | Y | Y | Y | Y | N | Y |
| 3 Rahall | Y | N | N | N | Y | N |
| **WISCONSIN** | | | | | | |
| 1 **Ryan** | Y | Y | Y | Y | N | N |
| 2 Baldwin | N | N | N | N | Y | Y |
| 3 Kind | N | N | N | N | Y | N |
| 4 Moore | N | N | N | N | Y | Y |
| 5 **Sensenbrenner** | Y | Y | Y | Y | Y | N |
| 6 **Petri** | Y | Y | Y | Y | N | N |
| 7 Obey | ? | ? | ? | ? | ? | ? |
| 8 **Green** | Y | Y | Y | Y | Y | Y |
| **WYOMING** | | | | | | |
| AL **Cubin** | Y | Y | Y | Y | ? | ? |

## IN THE HOUSE | By Vote Number

**375.** **H Res 356. London Bombings Condemnation/Adoption.** Hyde, R-Ill., motion to suspend the rules and adopt the resolution that would condemn the London terrorist attacks on July 7, 2005, and express condolences to the families and friends of those killed in the attacks and sympathies to those injured. Motion agreed to 416-0: R 224-0; D 191-0 (ND 142-0, SD 49-0); I 1-0. A two-thirds majority of those present and voting (278 in this case) is required for adoption under suspension of the rules. July 14, 2005.

**376.** **HR 2864. Water Resources Development/Tonnage Fees.** Rohrabacher, R-Calif., amendment that would permit ports to impose container fees in addition to tonnage fees and currently allowed fees on imports. It would also expand the allowed use of collected fees to include construction, operation and maintenance of infrastructure and security services related to the port that levies the fee. Rejected 111-310: R 57-167; D 53-143 (ND 46-100, SD 7-43); I 1-0. July 14, 2005.

**377.** **HR 2864. Water Resources Development/Upper Mississippi River and Illinois Waterway System.** Flake, R-Ariz., amendment that would allow the Army Corps of Engineers to proceed with seven new locks authorized in the bill on the Mississippi and Illinois rivers only if more than an average of 35 million tons of commodities per lock are processed in 2007 through 2009. It would also require the Corps to implement an appointment system to schedule and prioritize barge traffic and prepare two reports to evaluate any project that goes forward. Rejected 105-315: R 46-179; D 59-136 (ND 51-94, SD 8-42); I 0-0. July 14, 2005.

**378.** **HR 2864. Water Resources Development/Passage.** Passage of the bill that would authorize $11.6 billion for more than 700 water resource development projects and studies by the Army Corps of Engineers for flood control, navigation, beach erosion control and environmental restoration. Certain water development projects that exceed $50 million would receive an independent review. The bill would authorize $3.4 billion for a system of new locks and dams and environmental restoration for the Upper Mississippi River and Illinois waterway system. Passed 406-14: R 211-13; D 194-1 (ND 145-0, SD 49-1); I 1-0. July 14, 2005.

**379.** **H Con Res 191. Victory in Japan Day Tribute/Adoption.** Hyde, R-Ill., motion to suspend the rules and adopt the concurrent resolution that would honor all veterans of World War II on the 60th anniversary of the war's end and call upon the public to commemorate Sept. 2, 2005, as a day of remembrance and appreciation. Motion agreed to 399-0: R 213-0; D 186-0 (ND 140-0, SD 46-0); I 0-0. A two-thirds majority of those present and voting (266 in this case) is required for adoption under suspension of the rules. July 14, 2005.

| | 375 | 376 | 377 | 378 | 379 |
|---|---|---|---|---|---|
| **ALABAMA** | | | | | |
| 1 Bonner | Y | N | N | Y | Y |
| 2 Everett | Y | N | N | Y | ? |
| 3 Rogers | Y | N | N | Y | Y |
| 4 Aderholt | Y | N | N | Y | Y |
| 5 Cramer | Y | N | N | Y | Y |
| 6 Bachus | Y | Y | N | Y | Y |
| 7 Davis | Y | N | N | Y | Y |
| **ALASKA** | | | | | |
| AL Young | Y | N | N | Y | Y |
| **ARIZONA** | | | | | |
| 1 Renzi | Y | Y | N | Y | Y |
| 2 Franks | ? | Y | Y | N | Y |
| 3 Shadegg | Y | Y | Y | N | Y |
| 4 Pastor | Y | N | N | Y | Y |
| 5 Hayworth | Y | Y | Y | Y | Y |
| 6 Flake | Y | Y | Y | N | Y |
| 7 Grijalva | Y | N | N | Y | Y |
| 8 Kolbe | Y | N | Y | Y | Y |
| **ARKANSAS** | | | | | |
| 1 Berry | Y | N | N | Y | Y |
| 2 Snyder | Y | N | N | Y | Y |
| 3 Boozman | Y | N | N | Y | Y |
| 4 Ross | Y | N | N | Y | Y |
| **CALIFORNIA** | | | | | |
| 1 Thompson | Y | N | N | Y | Y |
| 2 Herger | Y | Y | N | Y | Y |
| 3 Lungren | Y | Y | N | Y | Y |
| 4 Doolittle | Y | Y | Y | Y | Y |
| 5 Matsui, D. | Y | N | N | Y | Y |
| 6 Woolsey | Y | N | Y | Y | Y |
| 7 Miller, George | Y | N | Y | Y | Y |
| 8 Pelosi | Y | N | ? | ? | ? |
| 9 Lee | Y | N | N | Y | Y |
| 10 Tauscher | Y | N | N | Y | Y |
| 11 Pombo | Y | Y | Y | Y | Y |
| 12 Lantos | Y | N | N | Y | Y |
| 13 Stark | Y | N | Y | Y | Y |
| 14 Eshoo | Y | N | Y | Y | Y |
| 15 Honda | Y | N | Y | Y | Y |
| 16 Lofgren | Y | N | Y | Y | Y |
| 17 Farr | Y | Y | Y | Y | Y |
| 18 Cardoza | Y | N | N | Y | Y |
| 19 Radanovich | Y | N | N | Y | Y |
| 20 Costa | Y | N | N | Y | Y |
| 21 Nunes | Y | N | N | Y | Y |
| 22 Thomas | Y | N | N | Y | Y |
| 23 Capps | + | – | + | + | + |
| 24 Gallegly | ? | ? | ? | ? | ? |
| 25 McKeon | Y | N | N | Y | Y |
| 26 Dreier | Y | N | N | Y | Y |
| 27 Sherman | Y | Y | Y | Y | Y |
| 28 Berman | Y | N | N | Y | Y |
| 29 Schiff | Y | N | N | Y | Y |
| 30 Waxman | Y | N | Y | Y | Y |
| 31 Becerra | Y | N | N | Y | Y |
| 32 Solis | Y | N | N | Y | Y |
| 33 Watson | Y | N | Y | Y | Y |
| 34 Roybal-Allard | Y | N | N | Y | Y |
| 35 Waters | Y | N | Y | Y | Y |
| 36 Harman | Y | Y | Y | Y | Y |
| 37 Millender-McD. | Y | N | Y | Y | Y |
| 38 Napolitano | Y | Y | N | Y | Y |
| 39 Sánchez, Linda | Y | N | N | Y | Y |
| 40 Royce | Y | Y | Y | N | Y |
| 41 Lewis | Y | N | N | Y | Y |
| 42 Miller, Gary | Y | N | N | Y | Y |
| 43 Baca | Y | N | N | Y | Y |
| 44 Calvert | Y | Y | N | Y | Y |
| 45 Bono | Y | Y | Y | Y | Y |
| 46 Rohrabacher | Y | Y | Y | Y | Y |
| 47 Sanchez, Loretta | Y | Y | Y | Y | Y |
| 48 Cox | Y | N | N | Y | Y |
| 49 Issa | Y | Y | N | Y | Y |

| | 375 | 376 | 377 | 378 | 379 |
|---|---|---|---|---|---|
| 50 Cunningham | ? | ? | ? | ? | ? |
| 51 Filner | Y | N | N | Y | Y |
| 52 Hunter | Y | N | N | Y | Y |
| 53 Davis | Y | N | Y | Y | Y |
| **COLORADO** | | | | | |
| 1 DeGette | Y | Y | Y | Y | Y |
| 2 Udall | Y | Y | Y | Y | Y |
| 3 Salazar | Y | N | N | Y | Y |
| 4 Musgrave | Y | N | N | Y | ? |
| 5 Hefley | Y | Y | N | Y | Y |
| 6 Tancredo | Y | Y | Y | N | Y |
| 7 Beauprez | Y | N | N | Y | Y |
| **CONNECTICUT** | | | | | |
| 1 Larson | Y | Y | N | Y | Y |
| 2 Simmons | Y | N | N | Y | Y |
| 3 DeLauro | Y | Y | Y | Y | Y |
| 4 Shays | Y | N | Y | Y | Y |
| 5 Johnson | Y | N | Y | Y | Y |
| **DELAWARE** | | | | | |
| AL Castle | Y | N | Y | Y | Y |
| **FLORIDA** | | | | | |
| 1 Miller | ? | ? | ? | ? | ? |
| 2 Boyd | Y | N | N | Y | ? |
| 3 Brown | Y | N | N | Y | Y |
| 4 Crenshaw | Y | N | N | Y | Y |
| 5 Brown-Waite | Y | N | N | Y | Y |
| 6 Stearns | Y | Y | Y | N | Y |
| 7 Mica | Y | Y | N | Y | Y |
| 8 Keller | Y | N | N | Y | Y |
| 9 Bilirakis | Y | N | N | Y | ? |
| 10 Young | ? | ? | ? | ? | ? |
| 11 Davis | Y | N | N | Y | Y |
| 12 Putnam | Y | N | N | Y | Y |
| 13 Harris | Y | N | N | Y | Y |
| 14 Mack | Y | N | N | Y | Y |
| 15 Weldon | Y | N | N | Y | Y |
| 16 Foley | Y | N | N | Y | Y |
| 17 Meek | Y | N | N | Y | Y |
| 18 Ros-Lehtinen | Y | N | N | Y | Y |
| 19 Wexler | Y | N | N | Y | Y |
| 20 Wasserman-Schultz | Y | N | N | Y | Y |
| 21 Diaz-Balart, L. | Y | N | N | Y | Y |
| 22 Shaw | Y | N | N | Y | Y |
| 23 Hastings | Y | N | N | Y | Y |
| 24 Feeney | Y | Y | Y | Y | Y |
| 25 Diaz-Balart, M. | Y | N | N | Y | Y |
| **GEORGIA** | | | | | |
| 1 Kingston | Y | N | N | Y | Y |
| 2 Bishop | Y | N | N | Y | Y |
| 3 Marshall | Y | Y | Y | Y | ? |
| 4 McKinney | Y | Y | Y | Y | Y |
| 5 Lewis | Y | N | N | Y | Y |
| 6 Price | Y | N | N | Y | Y |
| 7 Linder | Y | N | N | Y | Y |
| 8 Westmoreland | Y | N | N | Y | Y |
| 9 Norwood | Y | N | N | Y | Y |
| 10 Deal | Y | N | N | Y | Y |
| 11 Gingrey | Y | N | N | Y | Y |
| 12 Barrow | Y | Y | Y | Y | Y |
| 13 Scott | Y | Y | N | Y | Y |
| **HAWAII** | | | | | |
| 1 Abercrombie | ? | Y | N | Y | Y |
| 2 Case | Y | Y | N | Y | Y |
| **IDAHO** | | | | | |
| 1 Otter | Y | Y | Y | Y | Y |
| 2 Simpson | Y | N | N | Y | Y |
| **ILLINOIS** | | | | | |
| 1 Rush | Y | N | N | Y | Y |
| 2 Jackson | Y | N | N | Y | Y |
| 3 Lipinski | Y | N | N | Y | Y |
| 4 Gutierrez | Y | N | N | Y | Y |
| 5 Emanuel | Y | N | N | Y | Y |
| 6 Hyde | Y | N | N | Y | Y |
| 7 Davis | Y | N | N | Y | Y |
| 8 Bean | Y | N | N | Y | Y |
| 9 Schakowsky | Y | N | N | Y | Y |
| 10 Kirk | Y | N | N | Y | Y |
| 11 Weller | Y | N | N | Y | Y |
| 12 Costello | Y | Y | N | Y | Y |

| | 375 | 376 | 377 | 378 | 379 |
|---|---|---|---|---|---|
| 13 Biggert | Y | N | N | Y | Y |
| 14 Hastert | Y | | | | |
| 15 Johnson | Y | N | N | Y | Y |
| 16 Manzullo | Y | N | N | Y | Y |
| 17 Evans | Y | Y | N | Y | Y |
| 18 LaHood | Y | N | N | Y | Y |
| 19 Shimkus | Y | N | N | Y | Y |
| **INDIANA** | | | | | |
| 1 Visclosky | Y | N | N | Y | Y |
| 2 Chocola | Y | N | Y | Y | Y |
| 3 Souder | Y | N | N | Y | Y |
| 4 Buyer | Y | N | Y | Y | Y |
| 5 Burton | Y | Y | Y | Y | Y |
| 6 Pence | Y | Y | Y | Y | Y |
| 7 Carson | ? | ? | ? | ? | ? |
| 8 Hostettler | Y | Y | N | Y | Y |
| 9 Sodrel | Y | Y | N | Y | Y |
| **IOWA** | | | | | |
| 1 Nussle | Y | N | N | Y | Y |
| 2 Leach | Y | N | N | Y | Y |
| 3 Boswell | Y | N | N | Y | Y |
| 4 Latham | Y | N | N | Y | Y |
| 5 King | Y | Y | N | Y | Y |
| **KANSAS** | | | | | |
| 1 Moran | Y | N | N | Y | Y |
| 2 Ryun | Y | N | N | Y | Y |
| 3 Moore | Y | N | N | Y | Y |
| 4 Tiahrt | Y | N | N | Y | Y |
| **KENTUCKY** | | | | | |
| 1 Whitfield | Y | N | N | Y | Y |
| 2 Lewis | Y | N | N | Y | Y |
| 3 Northup | Y | N | N | Y | Y |
| 4 Davis | Y | N | N | Y | Y |
| 5 Rogers | Y | N | N | Y | Y |
| 6 Chandler | Y | N | N | Y | Y |
| **LOUISIANA** | | | | | |
| 1 Jindal | Y | N | N | Y | Y |
| 2 Jefferson | Y | N | N | Y | Y |
| 3 Melancon | Y | N | N | Y | Y |
| 4 McCrery | Y | N | N | Y | Y |
| 5 Alexander | Y | N | N | Y | Y |
| 6 Baker | Y | N | N | Y | Y |
| 7 Boustany | Y | N | N | Y | Y |
| **MAINE** | | | | | |
| 1 Allen | Y | N | N | Y | Y |
| 2 Michaud | Y | N | Y | Y | Y |
| **MARYLAND** | | | | | |
| 1 Gilchrest | Y | N | N | Y | Y |
| 2 Ruppersberger | Y | N | N | Y | Y |
| 3 Cardin | ? | ? | ? | ? | ? |
| 4 Wynn | Y | N | N | Y | Y |
| 5 Hoyer | Y | N | N | Y | Y |
| 6 Bartlett | Y | Y | Y | Y | Y |
| 7 Cummings | Y | N | N | Y | Y |
| 8 Van Hollen | Y | N | Y | Y | Y |
| **MASSACHUSETTS** | | | | | |
| 1 Olver | Y | Y | Y | Y | ? |
| 2 Neal | Y | N | N | Y | Y |
| 3 McGovern | Y | Y | N | Y | Y |
| 4 Frank | Y | Y | N | Y | Y |
| 5 Meehan | Y | Y | N | Y | ? |
| 6 Tierney | Y | N | Y | Y | Y |
| 7 Markey | Y | N | Y | Y | Y |
| 8 Capuano | Y | N | N | Y | Y |
| 9 Lynch | Y | N | N | Y | Y |
| 10 Delahunt | Y | Y | N | Y | ? |
| **MICHIGAN** | | | | | |
| 1 Stupak | Y | N | N | Y | Y |
| 2 Hoekstra | Y | N | Y | Y | Y |
| 3 Ehlers | Y | N | N | Y | Y |
| 4 Camp | Y | N | N | Y | Y |
| 5 Kildee | Y | N | N | Y | Y |
| 6 Upton | Y | N | N | Y | Y |
| 7 Schwarz | Y | N | N | Y | Y |
| 8 Rogers | Y | Y | N | Y | Y |
| 9 Knollenberg | Y | N | N | Y | Y |
| 10 Miller | Y | N | N | Y | Y |
| 11 McCotter | Y | N | N | Y | Y |
| 12 Levin | Y | N | N | Y | Y |
| 13 Kilpatrick | + | + | + | + | + |
| 14 Conyers | Y | N | N | Y | Y |
| 15 Dingell | Y | Y | N | Y | Y |

| | 375 | 376 | 377 | 378 | 379 |
|---|---|---|---|---|---|
| **MINNESOTA** | | | | | |
| 1 Gutknecht | Y | Y | N | Y | Y |
| 2 Kline | Y | N | N | Y | Y |
| 3 Ramstad | Y | N | Y | Y | Y |
| 4 McCollum | Y | Y | Y | Y | Y |
| 5 Sabo | Y | Y | N | Y | Y |
| 6 Kennedy | Y | N | N | Y | Y |
| 7 Peterson | Y | Y | N | Y | Y |
| 8 Oberstar | ? | ? | ? | ? | ? |
| **MISSISSIPPI** | | | | | |
| 1 Wicker | Y | N | N | Y | Y |
| 2 Thompson | Y | N | N | Y | Y |
| 3 Pickering | Y | N | N | Y | Y |
| 4 Taylor | Y | Y | N | Y | Y |
| **MISSOURI** | | | | | |
| 1 Clay | Y | N | N | Y | Y |
| 2 Akin | Y | N | N | Y | Y |
| 3 Carnahan | Y | N | N | Y | Y |
| 4 Skelton | Y | N | N | Y | Y |
| 5 Cleaver | Y | N | N | Y | Y |
| 6 Graves | Y | N | N | Y | Y |
| 7 Blunt | Y | N | N | Y | Y |
| 8 Emerson | Y | Y | N | Y | Y |
| 9 Hulshof | Y | N | N | Y | Y |
| **MONTANA** | | | | | |
| AL Rehberg | Y | N | N | Y | Y |
| **NEBRASKA** | | | | | |
| 1 Fortenberry | Y | Y | N | Y | Y |
| 2 Terry | Y | N | N | Y | ? |
| 3 Osborne | Y | N | N | Y | ? |
| **NEVADA** | | | | | |
| 1 Berkley | Y | N | Y | Y | Y |
| 2 Gibbons | Y | N | N | Y | Y |
| 3 Porter | Y | N | N | Y | Y |
| **NEW HAMPSHIRE** | | | | | |
| 1 Bradley | Y | N | N | Y | Y |
| 2 Bass | Y | N | Y | Y | Y |
| **NEW JERSEY** | | | | | |
| 1 Andrews | Y | N | Y | Y | Y |
| 2 LoBiondo | Y | N | N | Y | Y |
| 3 Saxton | Y | N | Y | Y | ? |
| 4 Smith | Y | N | N | Y | Y |
| 5 Garrett | Y | N | Y | Y | Y |
| 6 Pallone | Y | N | Y | Y | Y |
| 7 Ferguson | Y | N | N | Y | Y |
| 8 Pascrell | Y | N | N | Y | Y |
| 9 Rothman | Y | N | Y | Y | Y |
| 10 Payne | Y | N | N | Y | Y |
| 11 Frelinghuysen | Y | N | N | Y | ? |
| 12 Holt | Y | N | Y | Y | Y |
| 13 Menendez | Y | N | Y | Y | + |
| **NEW MEXICO** | | | | | |
| 1 Wilson | Y | N | N | Y | Y |
| 2 Pearce | ? | N | N | Y | Y |
| 3 Udall | Y | Y | Y | Y | Y |
| **NEW YORK** | | | | | |
| 1 Bishop | Y | N | N | Y | Y |
| 2 Israel | Y | N | N | Y | Y |
| 3 King | Y | N | N | Y | Y |
| 4 McCarthy | Y | N | N | Y | Y |
| 5 Ackerman | Y | N | N | Y | Y |
| 6 Meeks | Y | N | N | Y | Y |
| 7 Crowley | Y | N | Y | Y | Y |
| 8 Nadler | Y | Y | N | Y | Y |
| 9 Weiner | ? | N | N | Y | Y |
| 10 Towns | Y | N | N | Y | Y |
| 11 Owens | Y | N | N | Y | Y |
| 12 Velázquez | Y | N | N | Y | Y |
| 13 Fossella | Y | N | N | Y | Y |
| 14 Maloney | Y | Y | Y | Y | Y |
| 15 Rangel | Y | N | N | Y | Y |
| 16 Serrano | Y | N | N | Y | Y |
| 17 Engel | Y | Y | N | Y | Y |
| 18 Lowey | Y | N | N | Y | Y |
| 19 Kelly | Y | N | N | Y | Y |
| 20 Sweeney | Y | N | N | Y | Y |
| 21 McNulty | Y | Y | Y | Y | Y |
| 22 Hinchey | Y | N | N | Y | ? |
| 23 McHugh | Y | N | Y | Y | Y |
| 24 Boehlert | Y | Y | N | Y | Y |
| 25 Walsh | Y | N | N | Y | Y |
| 26 Reynolds | Y | N | N | Y | Y |
| 27 Higgins | Y | N | N | Y | Y |
| 28 Slaughter | Y | N | N | Y | Y |
| 29 Kuhl | Y | N | N | Y | Y |

| | 375 | 376 | 377 | 378 | 379 |
|---|---|---|---|---|---|
| **NORTH CAROLINA** | | | | | |
| 1 Butterfield | ? | Y | N | Y | Y |
| 2 Etheridge | Y | N | N | Y | Y |
| 3 Jones | Y | Y | N | Y | Y |
| 4 Price | Y | N | N | Y | Y |
| 5 Foxx | Y | N | N | Y | Y |
| 6 Coble | Y | Y | N | Y | Y |
| 7 McIntyre | ? | ? | ? | ? | ? |
| 8 Hayes | Y | N | N | Y | Y |
| 9 Myrick | Y | Y | Y | Y | Y |
| 10 McHenry | Y | Y | Y | Y | Y |
| 11 Taylor | Y | Y | N | Y | Y |
| 12 Watt | Y | Y | N | Y | Y |
| 13 Miller | Y | N | N | Y | Y |
| **NORTH DAKOTA** | | | | | |
| AL Pomeroy | Y | N | N | Y | Y |
| **OHIO** | | | | | |
| 1 Chabot | Y | N | Y | Y | Y |
| 2 Vacant | | | | | |
| 3 Turner | Y | N | N | Y | ? |
| 4 Oxley | Y | N | N | Y | Y |
| 5 Gillmor | Y | N | N | Y | Y |
| 6 Strickland | Y | Y | N | Y | Y |
| 7 Hobson | Y | N | N | Y | ? |
| 8 Boehner | Y | N | N | Y | Y |
| 9 Kaptur | Y | Y | N | Y | Y |
| 10 Kucinich | Y | Y | Y | Y | Y |
| 11 Jones | Y | N | N | Y | Y |
| 12 Tiberi | Y | N | N | Y | ? |
| 13 Brown | Y | Y | Y | Y | Y |
| 14 LaTourette | Y | N | N | Y | Y |
| 15 Pryce | Y | N | N | Y | Y |
| 16 Regula | Y | N | N | Y | Y |
| 17 Ryan | Y | Y | N | Y | Y |
| 18 Ney | Y | N | N | Y | Y |
| **OKLAHOMA** | | | | | |
| 1 Sullivan | Y | N | N | Y | Y |
| 2 Boren | Y | N | N | Y | Y |
| 3 Lucas | Y | N | N | Y | Y |
| 4 Cole | Y | N | N | Y | Y |
| 5 Istook | Y | Y | N | Y | Y |
| **OREGON** | | | | | |
| 1 Wu | Y | N | Y | Y | Y |
| 2 Walden | Y | N | Y | Y | ? |
| 3 Blumenauer | Y | N | Y | Y | Y |
| 4 DeFazio | Y | Y | Y | Y | Y |
| 5 Hooley | Y | Y | Y | Y | Y |
| **PENNSYLVANIA** | | | | | |
| 1 Brady | Y | N | N | Y | Y |
| 2 Fattah | Y | N | N | Y | Y |
| 3 English | Y | N | N | Y | Y |
| 4 Hart | Y | N | N | Y | Y |
| 5 Peterson | Y | N | N | Y | Y |
| 6 Gerlach | Y | N | N | Y | Y |
| 7 Weldon | Y | N | N | Y | Y |
| 8 Fitzpatrick | Y | N | N | Y | Y |
| 9 Shuster | Y | Y | N | Y | Y |
| 10 Sherwood | Y | N | N | Y | Y |
| 11 Kanjorski | Y | N | N | Y | Y |
| 12 Murtha | Y | N | N | Y | Y |
| 13 Schwartz | Y | N | N | Y | Y |
| 14 Doyle | Y | Y | N | Y | Y |
| 15 Dent | Y | N | N | Y | Y |
| 16 Pitts | Y | N | N | Y | Y |
| 17 Holden | Y | N | N | Y | Y |
| 18 Murphy | Y | N | N | Y | Y |
| 19 Platts | Y | ? | N | Y | Y |
| **RHODE ISLAND** | | | | | |
| 1 Kennedy | Y | Y | Y | Y | Y |
| 2 Langevin | Y | Y | Y | Y | Y |
| **SOUTH CAROLINA** | | | | | |
| 1 Brown | Y | N | N | Y | ? |
| 2 Wilson | Y | N | Y | Y | Y |
| 3 Barrett | Y | N | Y | Y | Y |
| 4 Inglis | Y | N | N | Y | N |
| 5 Spratt | Y | N | N | Y | Y |
| 6 Clyburn | Y | N | N | Y | Y |
| **SOUTH DAKOTA** | | | | | |
| AL Herseth | Y | Y | N | Y | Y |
| **TENNESSEE** | | | | | |
| 1 Jenkins | Y | N | N | Y | Y |
| 2 Duncan | Y | Y | N | Y | Y |

| | 375 | 376 | 377 | 378 | 379 |
|---|---|---|---|---|---|
| 3 Wamp | Y | N | N | Y | Y |
| 4 Davis | Y | N | N | Y | Y |
| 5 Cooper | Y | N | Y | N | Y |
| 6 Gordon | Y | N | N | Y | ? |
| 7 Blackburn | Y | N | Y | Y | Y |
| 8 Tanner | Y | N | N | Y | Y |
| 9 Ford | Y | N | N | Y | Y |
| **TEXAS** | | | | | |
| 1 Gohmert | Y | Y | Y | Y | Y |
| 2 Poe | Y | N | N | Y | Y |
| 3 Johnson, S. | Y | Y | N | Y | Y |
| 4 Hall | Y | N | N | ? | Y |
| 5 Hensarling | Y | N | N | Y | Y |
| 6 Barton | Y | N | N | Y | Y |
| 7 Culberson | Y | N | N | Y | Y |
| 8 Brady | Y | N | N | Y | Y |
| 9 Green, A. | Y | N | N | Y | Y |
| 10 McCaul | Y | N | N | Y | Y |
| 11 Conaway | Y | N | N | Y | Y |
| 12 Granger | Y | N | N | Y | Y |
| 13 Thornberry | Y | N | N | Y | Y |
| 14 Paul | Y | Y | Y | N | Y |
| 15 Hinojosa | Y | N | N | Y | Y |
| 16 Reyes | Y | N | N | Y | Y |
| 17 Edwards | Y | N | N | Y | Y |
| 18 Jackson-Lee | Y | N | N | Y | Y |
| 19 Neugebauer | Y | N | N | Y | Y |
| 20 Gonzalez | Y | N | N | Y | Y |
| 21 Smith | Y | N | N | Y | Y |
| 22 DeLay | Y | N | N | Y | Y |
| 23 Bonilla | Y | N | N | Y | Y |
| 24 Marchant | Y | N | N | Y | Y |
| 25 Doggett | Y | Y | Y | Y | Y |
| 26 Burgess | Y | Y | N | Y | Y |
| 27 Ortiz | Y | N | N | Y | Y |
| 28 Cuellar | Y | N | N | Y | Y |
| 29 Green, G. | Y | N | N | Y | Y |
| 30 Johnson, E. | Y | N | N | Y | ? |
| 31 Carter | Y | N | N | Y | Y |
| 32 Sessions | Y | N | N | Y | Y |
| **UTAH** | | | | | |
| 1 Bishop | Y | N | N | Y | Y |
| 2 Matheson | Y | N | N | Y | Y |
| 3 Cannon | Y | N | N | Y | Y |
| **VERMONT** | | | | | |
| AL *Sanders* | Y | Y | ? | Y | ? |
| **VIRGINIA** | | | | | |
| 1 Davis, J. | Y | N | N | N | Y |
| 2 Drake | Y | N | N | Y | Y |
| 3 Scott | Y | N | N | Y | Y |
| 4 Forbes | Y | N | N | Y | Y |
| 5 Goode | Y | Y | N | Y | Y |
| 6 Goodlatte | Y | Y | N | Y | Y |
| 7 Cantor | Y | N | N | Y | Y |
| 8 Moran | Y | N | N | Y | Y |
| 9 Boucher | Y | N | N | Y | Y |
| 10 Wolf | Y | N | N | Y | Y |
| 11 Davis, T. | Y | N | N | N | Y |
| **WASHINGTON** | | | | | |
| 1 Inslee | Y | N | Y | Y | Y |
| 2 Larsen | Y | N | N | Y | Y |
| 3 Baird | Y | N | Y | Y | Y |
| 4 Hastings | Y | N | N | Y | Y |
| 5 McMorris | Y | N | N | Y | Y |
| 6 Dicks | Y | N | N | Y | Y |
| 7 McDermott | Y | Y | Y | Y | Y |
| 8 Reichert | Y | N | N | Y | Y |
| 9 Smith | Y | N | Y | Y | Y |
| **WEST VIRGINIA** | | | | | |
| 1 Mollohan | ? | N | N | Y | Y |
| 2 Capito | Y | N | N | Y | Y |
| 3 Rahall | Y | N | N | Y | Y |
| **WISCONSIN** | | | | | |
| 1 Ryan | Y | Y | Y | Y | Y |
| 2 Baldwin | Y | Y | Y | Y | Y |
| 3 Kind | Y | N | Y | Y | Y |
| 4 Moore | Y | Y | N | Y | Y |
| 5 Sensenbrenner | Y | Y | Y | Y | Y |
| 6 Petri | Y | N | Y | Y | Y |
| 7 Obey | ? | N | N | Y | Y |
| 8 Green | Y | N | Y | Y | Y |
| **WYOMING** | | | | | |
| AL Cubin | ? | ? | ? | ? | ? |

# IN THE HOUSE | By Vote Number

**380.** H Res 328. Polish Workers Strike Anniversary/Adoption.
Ros-Lehtinen, R-Fla., motion to suspend the rules and adopt the resolution that would recognize the 25th anniversary of the strikes that led to the formation of Poland's Solidarity trade union and the fall of communism in Poland. Motion agreed to 385-0: R 213-0; D 171-0 (ND 127-0, SD 44-0); I 1-0. A two-thirds majority of those present and voting (257 in this case) is required for adoption under suspension of the rules. July 18, 2005.

**381.** H Con Res 175. Tribute to Slave Trade Descendants/Adoption.
Ros-Lehtinen, R-Fla., motion to suspend the rules and adopt the concurrent resolution that would recognize the injustices suffered by African descendants of the trans-Atlantic slave trade in Latin America and the Caribbean. Motion agreed to 382-6: R 206-6; D 175-0 (ND 130-0, SD 45-0); I 1-0. A two-thirds majority of those present and voting (259 in this case) is required for adoption under suspension of the rules. July 18, 2005.

**382.** H Res 364. U.S.-India Relations/Adoption. Ros-Lehtinen, R-Fla., motion to suspend the rules and adopt the resolution that would commend the continuing improvement of relations between the United States and India. Motion agreed to 388-0: R 211-0; D 176-0 (ND 131-0, SD 45-0); I 1-0. A two-thirds majority of those present and voting (259 in this case) is required for adoption under suspension of the rules. July 18, 2005.

**383.** HR 2601. State Department Authorization/Previous Question.
Bishop, R-Utah, motion to order the previous question (thus ending debate and the possibility of amendment) on adoption of the rule (H Res 365) and a Bishop amendment to the rule. The rule would provide for House floor consideration of the bill that would authorize $20.8 billion in appropriations through fiscal 2007 for the Department of State and foreign aid programs. The Bishop amendment would clarify the debate time for certain amendments. Motion agreed to 226-196: R 224-0; D 2-195 (ND 0-148, SD 2-47); I 0-1. (Subsequently, the Bishop amendment was adopted by voice vote.) July 19, 2005.

**384.** HR 2601. State Department Authorization/Rule. Adoption of the rule (H Res 365) that would provide for House consideration of the bill that would authorize $20.8 billion in appropriations through fiscal 2007 for the Department of State and foreign aid programs. Adopted 228-190: R 225-0; D 3-189 (ND 3-141, SD 0-48); I 0-1. July 19, 2005.

**385.** HR 2601. State Department Authorization/U.N. Hyde, R-Ill., amendment that would withhold up to 50 percent of U.S. dues to the United Nations unless the secretary of State certifies by Oct. 1, 2007, that the organization has complied with 32 of 39 changes in its operations, such as more rigorous budget control, the creation of a U.N. independent oversight board and detailed financial disclosure for top U.N. officials. Adopted 226-195: R 217-6; D 9-188 (ND 3-147, SD 6-41); I 0-1. July 19, 2005.

**386.** HR 2601. State Department Authorization/Methamphetamine Precursors. Kennedy, R-Minn., amendment that would require the State Department to certify annually that the five biggest exporters and importers of certain methamphetamine precursors are fully cooperating with U.S. law enforcement to prevent diversion of those chemicals for illicit purposes. Countries that are not certified would be subject to foreign aid eligibility provisions under current law. Adopted 423-2: R 222-2; D 200-0 (ND 151-0, SD 49-0); I 1-0. July 19, 2005.

| | 380 | 381 | 382 | 383 | 384 | 385 | 386 |
|---|---|---|---|---|---|---|---|
| **ALABAMA** | | | | | | | |
| 1 Bonner | Y | Y | Y | Y | Y | Y | Y |
| 2 Everett | Y | Y | Y | Y | Y | Y | Y |
| 3 Rogers | Y | Y | Y | Y | Y | Y | Y |
| 4 Aderholt | Y | Y | Y | Y | Y | Y | Y |
| 5 Cramer | Y | Y | Y | N | N | ? | Y |
| 6 Bachus | Y | Y | Y | Y | Y | Y | Y |
| 7 Davis | Y | Y | Y | N | N | N | Y |
| **ALASKA** | | | | | | | |
| AL Young | Y | Y | Y | Y | Y | Y | Y |
| **ARIZONA** | | | | | | | |
| 1 Renzi | Y | Y | Y | Y | Y | Y | Y |
| 2 Franks | Y | Y | Y | Y | Y | Y | Y |
| 3 Shadegg | ? | ? | ? | Y | Y | Y | Y |
| 4 Pastor | Y | Y | Y | N | N | N | Y |
| 5 Hayworth | Y | Y | Y | Y | Y | Y | Y |
| 6 Flake | Y | N | Y | Y | Y | Y | N |
| 7 Grijalva | Y | Y | Y | N | N | N | Y |
| 8 Kolbe | Y | Y | Y | Y | Y | Y | Y |
| **ARKANSAS** | | | | | | | |
| 1 Berry | Y | Y | Y | N | N | N | Y |
| 2 Snyder | Y | Y | Y | N | N | N | Y |
| 3 Boozman | Y | Y | Y | Y | Y | Y | Y |
| 4 Ross | Y | Y | Y | N | N | N | Y |
| **CALIFORNIA** | | | | | | | |
| 1 Thompson | Y | Y | Y | N | N | N | Y |
| 2 Herger | Y | Y | Y | Y | Y | Y | Y |
| 3 Lungren | Y | Y | Y | Y | Y | Y | Y |
| 4 Doolittle | Y | Y | Y | Y | Y | Y | Y |
| 5 Matsui, D. | Y | Y | Y | N | N | N | Y |
| 6 Woolsey | Y | Y | Y | N | N | N | Y |
| 7 Miller, George | Y | Y | Y | N | N | N | Y |
| 8 Pelosi | Y | Y | Y | N | N | N | Y |
| 9 Lee | Y | Y | Y | N | N | N | Y |
| 10 Tauscher | Y | Y | Y | N | N | N | Y |
| 11 Pombo | Y | Y | Y | Y | Y | Y | Y |
| 12 Lantos | Y | Y | Y | N | N | N | Y |
| 13 Stark | ? | ? | ? | N | N | N | Y |
| 14 Eshoo | Y | Y | Y | N | ? | N | Y |
| 15 Honda | Y | Y | Y | N | N | N | Y |
| 16 Lofgren | Y | Y | Y | N | N | N | Y |
| 17 Farr | Y | Y | Y | N | N | N | Y |
| 18 Cardoza | Y | Y | Y | N | N | N | Y |
| 19 Radanovich | Y | Y | Y | Y | Y | Y | Y |
| 20 Costa | ? | ? | ? | N | N | N | Y |
| 21 Nunes | Y | Y | Y | Y | Y | Y | Y |
| 22 Thomas | Y | Y | Y | Y | Y | Y | Y |
| 23 Capps | Y | Y | Y | N | N | N | Y |
| 24 Gallegly | Y | Y | Y | Y | Y | Y | Y |
| 25 McKeon | Y | Y | ? | Y | Y | Y | Y |
| 26 Dreier | Y | Y | Y | Y | Y | Y | Y |
| 27 Sherman | Y | Y | Y | N | N | N | Y |
| 28 Berman | Y | Y | Y | N | N | N | Y |
| 29 Schiff | Y | Y | Y | N | N | N | Y |
| 30 Waxman | Y | Y | Y | N | N | N | Y |
| 31 Becerra | Y | Y | Y | – | – | N | Y |
| 32 Solis | Y | Y | Y | N | N | N | Y |
| 33 Watson | ? | ? | ? | N | N | N | Y |
| 34 Roybal-Allard | Y | Y | Y | N | N | N | Y |
| 35 Waters | Y | Y | Y | N | ? | N | Y |
| 36 Harman | Y | Y | Y | N | N | N | Y |
| 37 Millender-McD. | Y | Y | Y | N | N | N | Y |
| 38 Napolitano | Y | Y | Y | N | N | N | Y |
| 39 Sánchez, Linda | Y | Y | Y | N | N | N | Y |
| 40 Royce | Y | Y | Y | Y | Y | Y | Y |
| 41 Lewis | Y | Y | Y | Y | Y | Y | Y |
| 42 Miller, Gary | Y | Y | Y | Y | Y | Y | Y |
| 43 Baca | Y | Y | Y | N | N | N | Y |
| 44 Calvert | Y | Y | Y | Y | Y | Y | Y |
| 45 Bono | Y | Y | Y | Y | Y | Y | Y |
| 46 Rohrabacher | Y | Y | Y | Y | Y | Y | Y |
| 47 Sanchez, Loretta | Y | Y | Y | N | N | N | Y |
| 48 Cox | Y | Y | Y | Y | Y | ? | ? |
| 49 Issa | Y | Y | Y | Y | Y | Y | Y |
| **COLORADO** | | | | | | | |
| 50 Cunningham | Y | Y | Y | Y | Y | Y | Y |
| 51 Filner | Y | Y | Y | N | N | N | Y |
| 52 Hunter | ? | ? | Y | Y | Y | N | Y |
| 53 Davis | Y | Y | Y | N | N | N | Y |
| **COLORADO** | | | | | | | |
| 1 DeGette | Y | Y | Y | N | N | N | Y |
| 2 Udall | + | Y | Y | N | N | N | Y |
| 3 Salazar | Y | Y | Y | N | N | N | Y |
| 4 Musgrave | ? | Y | Y | Y | Y | Y | Y |
| 5 Hefley | Y | Y | Y | Y | Y | Y | Y |
| 6 Tancredo | Y | Y | Y | Y | Y | Y | ? |
| 7 Beauprez | Y | Y | Y | Y | Y | Y | Y |
| **CONNECTICUT** | | | | | | | |
| 1 Larson | Y | Y | Y | N | N | N | Y |
| 2 Simmons | Y | Y | Y | Y | Y | Y | Y |
| 3 DeLauro | Y | Y | Y | N | N | N | Y |
| 4 Shays | Y | Y | Y | Y | Y | N | Y |
| 5 Johnson | Y | Y | Y | Y | Y | Y | Y |
| **DELAWARE** | | | | | | | |
| AL Castle | Y | Y | Y | Y | Y | N | Y |
| **FLORIDA** | | | | | | | |
| 1 Miller | Y | Y | Y | Y | Y | Y | Y |
| 2 Boyd | ? | Y | Y | N | N | N | Y |
| 3 Brown | ? | ? | ? | N | N | ? | Y |
| 4 Crenshaw | Y | Y | Y | Y | Y | Y | Y |
| 5 Brown-Waite | Y | Y | Y | Y | Y | Y | Y |
| 6 Stearns | Y | Y | Y | Y | Y | Y | Y |
| 7 Mica | Y | Y | Y | Y | Y | Y | Y |
| 8 Keller | Y | Y | Y | Y | Y | Y | Y |
| 9 Bilirakis | Y | Y | Y | Y | Y | Y | Y |
| 10 Young | Y | Y | Y | Y | Y | Y | Y |
| 11 Davis | Y | Y | Y | N | N | N | Y |
| 12 Putnam | Y | Y | Y | Y | Y | Y | Y |
| 13 Harris | Y | Y | Y | Y | Y | Y | Y |
| 14 Mack | Y | Y | Y | Y | Y | Y | Y |
| 15 Weldon | Y | Y | Y | Y | Y | Y | Y |
| 16 Foley | Y | Y | Y | Y | Y | Y | Y |
| 17 Meek | Y | Y | Y | N | N | N | Y |
| 18 Ros-Lehtinen | Y | Y | Y | Y | Y | N | Y |
| 19 Wexler | Y | Y | Y | N | N | N | Y |
| 20 Wasserman-Schultz | Y | Y | Y | N | N | N | Y |
| 21 Diaz-Balart, L. | Y | Y | Y | Y | Y | Y | Y |
| 22 Shaw | Y | Y | Y | Y | Y | Y | Y |
| 23 Hastings | Y | Y | Y | N | N | N | Y |
| 24 Feeney | Y | Y | Y | Y | Y | Y | Y |
| 25 Diaz-Balart, M. | Y | Y | Y | Y | Y | Y | Y |
| **GEORGIA** | | | | | | | |
| 1 Kingston | Y | Y | Y | Y | Y | Y | Y |
| 2 Bishop | Y | Y | Y | N | N | N | Y |
| 3 Marshall | Y | Y | Y | N | N | Y | Y |
| 4 McKinney | ? | ? | ? | N | N | N | Y |
| 5 Lewis | Y | Y | Y | N | N | N | Y |
| 6 Price | Y | P | Y | Y | Y | Y | Y |
| 7 Linder | Y | Y | Y | Y | Y | Y | Y |
| 8 Westmoreland | Y | N | Y | Y | Y | Y | Y |
| 9 Norwood | Y | N | Y | Y | Y | Y | Y |
| 10 Deal | Y | N | Y | Y | Y | Y | Y |
| 11 Gingrey | Y | Y | Y | Y | Y | Y | Y |
| 12 Barrow | Y | Y | Y | N | N | N | Y |
| 13 Scott | Y | Y | Y | N | N | N | Y |
| **HAWAII** | | | | | | | |
| 1 Abercrombie | Y | Y | Y | N | N | N | Y |
| 2 Case | Y | Y | Y | N | N | N | Y |
| **IDAHO** | | | | | | | |
| 1 Otter | Y | Y | Y | Y | Y | Y | Y |
| 2 Simpson | Y | Y | Y | Y | Y | Y | Y |
| **ILLINOIS** | | | | | | | |
| 1 Rush | ? | ? | ? | N | N | N | Y |
| 2 Jackson | Y | Y | Y | N | N | N | Y |
| 3 Lipinski | Y | Y | Y | N | N | N | Y |
| 4 Gutierrez | ? | ? | ? | Y | Y | N | Y |
| 5 Emanuel | Y | Y | Y | N | N | N | Y |
| 6 Hyde | Y | Y | Y | Y | Y | Y | Y |
| 7 Davis | ? | ? | ? | N | N | N | Y |
| 8 Bean | Y | Y | Y | N | N | N | Y |
| 9 Schakowsky | ? | ? | ? | N | N | N | Y |
| 10 Kirk | Y | Y | Y | Y | Y | Y | Y |
| 11 Weller | + | + | + | Y | Y | Y | Y |
| 12 Costello | Y | Y | Y | N | N | N | Y |

| | 380 | 381 | 382 | 383 | 384 | 385 | 386 |
|---|---|---|---|---|---|---|---|
| 13 **Biggert** | Y | Y | Y | Y | Y | Y | Y |
| 14 **Hastert** | | | | | | | |
| 15 **Johnson** | + | + | + | Y | Y | Y | Y |
| 16 **Manzullo** | Y | Y | Y | Y | Y | Y | Y |
| 17 Evans | + | + | + | N | N | N | Y |
| 18 **LaHood** | Y | Y | Y | Y | Y | Y | Y |
| 19 **Shimkus** | Y | Y | Y | Y | Y | Y | Y |
| **INDIANA** | | | | | | | |
| 1 Visclosky | Y | Y | Y | N | N | N | Y |
| 2 **Chocola** | Y | Y | Y | Y | Y | Y | Y |
| 3 **Souder** | Y | Y | Y | Y | Y | Y | Y |
| 4 **Buyer** | ? | ? | ? | Y | Y | Y | Y |
| 5 **Burton** | Y | Y | Y | Y | Y | Y | Y |
| 6 **Pence** | Y | Y | Y | Y | Y | Y | Y |
| 7 Carson | Y | Y | Y | N | N | N | Y |
| 8 **Hostettler** | Y | Y | Y | Y | Y | Y | Y |
| 9 **Sodrel** | Y | Y | Y | Y | Y | Y | Y |
| **IOWA** | | | | | | | |
| 1 **Nussle** | ? | ? | ? | Y | Y | Y | Y |
| 2 **Leach** | ? | ? | ? | Y | Y | N | Y |
| 3 Boswell | ? | ? | ? | N | N | N | Y |
| 4 **Latham** | Y | Y | Y | Y | Y | Y | Y |
| 5 **King** | Y | N | Y | Y | Y | Y | Y |
| **KANSAS** | | | | | | | |
| 1 **Moran** | Y | Y | Y | Y | Y | Y | Y |
| 2 **Ryun** | + | + | + | Y | Y | Y | Y |
| 3 Moore | Y | Y | Y | N | N | N | Y |
| 4 **Tiahrt** | Y | Y | Y | Y | Y | Y | Y |
| **KENTUCKY** | | | | | | | |
| 1 **Whitfield** | Y | Y | Y | Y | Y | Y | Y |
| 2 **Lewis** | Y | Y | Y | Y | Y | Y | Y |
| 3 **Northup** | Y | Y | Y | Y | Y | Y | Y |
| 4 **Davis** | Y | Y | Y | Y | Y | Y | Y |
| 5 **Rogers** | Y | Y | Y | Y | Y | Y | Y |
| 6 Chandler | Y | Y | Y | N | N | N | Y |
| **LOUISIANA** | | | | | | | |
| 1 **Jindal** | ? | ? | ? | Y | Y | Y | Y |
| 2 Jefferson | Y | Y | Y | N | N | N | Y |
| 3 Melancon | Y | Y | Y | N | N | N | Y |
| 4 **McCrery** | Y | Y | ? | Y | Y | Y | Y |
| 5 **Alexander** | Y | Y | Y | Y | Y | Y | Y |
| 6 **Baker** | Y | Y | Y | Y | Y | Y | Y |
| 7 **Boustany** | Y | Y | Y | Y | Y | Y | Y |
| **MAINE** | | | | | | | |
| 1 Allen | Y | Y | Y | N | N | N | Y |
| 2 Michaud | Y | Y | Y | N | N | N | Y |
| **MARYLAND** | | | | | | | |
| 1 **Gilchrest** | Y | Y | Y | Y | Y | Y | Y |
| 2 Ruppersberger | Y | Y | Y | N | N | N | Y |
| 3 Cardin | Y | Y | Y | N | N | N | Y |
| 4 Wynn | Y | Y | Y | N | N | N | Y |
| 5 Hoyer | Y | Y | Y | N | N | N | Y |
| 6 **Bartlett** | Y | P | Y | Y | Y | Y | Y |
| 7 Cummings | Y | Y | Y | N | N | N | Y |
| 8 Van Hollen | Y | Y | Y | N | N | N | Y |
| **MASSACHUSETTS** | | | | | | | |
| 1 Olver | Y | Y | Y | N | N | N | Y |
| 2 Neal | ? | ? | Y | N | N | N | Y |
| 3 McGovern | Y | Y | Y | N | N | N | Y |
| 4 Frank | Y | Y | Y | N | N | N | Y |
| 5 Meehan | Y | Y | Y | N | ? | N | Y |
| 6 Tierney | Y | Y | Y | N | N | N | Y |
| 7 Markey | Y | Y | Y | N | N | N | Y |
| 8 Capuano | ? | ? | ? | N | N | N | Y |
| 9 Lynch | Y | Y | Y | N | N | N | Y |
| 10 Delahunt | Y | Y | Y | N | N | N | Y |
| **MICHIGAN** | | | | | | | |
| 1 Stupak | Y | Y | Y | N | N | N | Y |
| 2 **Hoekstra** | Y | Y | Y | Y | Y | Y | Y |
| 3 **Ehlers** | Y | Y | Y | Y | Y | Y | Y |
| 4 **Camp** | Y | Y | Y | Y | Y | Y | Y |
| 5 Kildee | Y | Y | Y | N | N | N | Y |
| 6 **Upton** | Y | Y | Y | Y | Y | Y | Y |
| 7 **Schwarz** | Y | Y | Y | Y | Y | Y | Y |
| 8 **Rogers** | Y | Y | Y | Y | Y | Y | Y |
| 9 **Knollenberg** | Y | Y | Y | Y | Y | Y | Y |
| 10 **Miller** | Y | Y | Y | Y | Y | Y | Y |
| 11 **McCotter** | Y | Y | Y | Y | Y | Y | Y |
| 12 Levin | Y | Y | Y | N | N | N | Y |
| 13 Kilpatrick | Y | Y | Y | N | N | N | Y |
| 14 Conyers | Y | Y | Y | N | N | N | Y |
| 15 Dingell | Y | Y | Y | N | N | N | Y |
| **MINNESOTA** | | | | | | | |
| 1 **Gutknecht** | Y | Y | Y | Y | Y | Y | Y |
| 2 **Kline** | Y | Y | Y | Y | Y | Y | Y |
| 3 **Ramstad** | Y | Y | Y | Y | Y | Y | Y |
| 4 McCollum | Y | Y | Y | N | N | N | Y |
| 5 Sabo | Y | Y | Y | N | N | N | Y |
| 6 **Kennedy** | Y | Y | Y | Y | Y | Y | Y |
| 7 Peterson | Y | Y | Y | N | N | N | Y |
| 8 Oberstar | Y | Y | Y | N | N | N | Y |
| **MISSISSIPPI** | | | | | | | |
| 1 **Wicker** | Y | Y | Y | Y | Y | Y | Y |
| 2 Thompson | Y | Y | Y | N | N | N | Y |
| 3 **Pickering** | Y | Y | Y | Y | Y | Y | Y |
| 4 Taylor | Y | Y | Y | N | N | Y | Y |
| **MISSOURI** | | | | | | | |
| 1 Clay | Y | Y | Y | N | N | N | Y |
| 2 **Akin** | Y | Y | Y | Y | Y | Y | Y |
| 3 Carnahan | Y | Y | Y | N | N | N | Y |
| 4 Skelton | Y | Y | Y | N | N | N | Y |
| 5 Cleaver | Y | Y | Y | N | N | N | Y |
| 6 **Graves** | Y | Y | Y | Y | Y | Y | Y |
| 7 **Blunt** | Y | Y | Y | Y | Y | Y | Y |
| 8 **Emerson** | Y | Y | Y | Y | Y | Y | Y |
| 9 **Hulshof** | Y | Y | Y | ? | Y | Y | Y |
| **MONTANA** | | | | | | | |
| AL **Rehberg** | Y | Y | Y | Y | Y | Y | Y |
| **NEBRASKA** | | | | | | | |
| 1 **Fortenberry** | Y | Y | Y | Y | Y | Y | Y |
| 2 **Terry** | Y | Y | Y | Y | Y | Y | Y |
| 3 **Osborne** | Y | Y | Y | Y | Y | Y | Y |
| **NEVADA** | | | | | | | |
| 1 Berkley | Y | Y | Y | N | N | Y | Y |
| 2 **Gibbons** | + | + | + | Y | Y | Y | Y |
| 3 **Porter** | Y | Y | Y | Y | Y | Y | Y |
| **NEW HAMPSHIRE** | | | | | | | |
| 1 **Bradley** | Y | Y | Y | Y | Y | Y | Y |
| 2 **Bass** | Y | Y | Y | Y | Y | Y | Y |
| **NEW JERSEY** | | | | | | | |
| 1 Andrews | Y | Y | Y | N | N | N | Y |
| 2 **LoBiondo** | Y | Y | Y | Y | Y | Y | Y |
| 3 **Saxton** | Y | Y | Y | Y | Y | Y | Y |
| 4 **Smith** | Y | Y | Y | Y | Y | Y | Y |
| 5 **Garrett** | Y | Y | Y | Y | Y | Y | Y |
| 6 Pallone | Y | Y | Y | N | N | N | Y |
| 7 **Ferguson** | Y | Y | Y | Y | Y | Y | Y |
| 8 Pascrell | ? | ? | ? | N | N | N | Y |
| 9 Rothman | Y | Y | Y | N | N | N | Y |
| 10 Payne | Y | Y | Y | ? | ? | ? | Y |
| 11 **Frelinghuysen** | + | + | + | + | + | + | Y |
| 12 Holt | Y | Y | Y | N | N | N | Y |
| 13 Menendez | Y | Y | Y | N | N | N | Y |
| **NEW MEXICO** | | | | | | | |
| 1 **Wilson** | Y | Y | Y | Y | Y | Y | Y |
| 2 **Pearce** | Y | Y | Y | ? | ? | Y | Y |
| 3 Udall | Y | Y | Y | N | N | N | Y |
| **NEW YORK** | | | | | | | |
| 1 Bishop | Y | Y | Y | N | N | N | Y |
| 2 Israel | Y | Y | Y | N | N | N | Y |
| 3 **King** | Y | Y | Y | Y | Y | Y | Y |
| 4 McCarthy | Y | Y | Y | N | N | N | Y |
| 5 Ackerman | Y | Y | Y | N | N | N | Y |
| 6 Meeks | Y | Y | Y | N | N | N | Y |
| 7 Crowley | + | + | + | N | N | N | Y |
| 8 Nadler | Y | Y | Y | N | N | N | Y |
| 9 Weiner | ? | ? | ? | N | N | N | Y |
| 10 Towns | ? | ? | ? | N | N | N | Y |
| 11 Owens | Y | Y | Y | N | N | N | Y |
| 12 Velázquez | Y | Y | Y | N | N | N | Y |
| 13 **Fossella** | Y | Y | Y | Y | Y | Y | Y |
| 14 Maloney | Y | Y | Y | N | N | N | Y |
| 15 Rangel | Y | Y | Y | N | N | N | Y |
| 16 Serrano | Y | Y | Y | N | N | N | Y |
| 17 Engel | Y | Y | Y | N | N | N | Y |
| 18 Lowey | Y | Y | Y | N | N | N | Y |
| 19 **Kelly** | Y | Y | Y | Y | Y | Y | Y |
| 20 **Sweeney** | ? | ? | ? | ? | ? | ? | ? |
| 21 McNulty | Y | Y | Y | N | N | N | Y |
| 22 Hinchey | Y | Y | Y | N | N | N | Y |
| 23 **McHugh** | Y | Y | Y | Y | Y | Y | Y |
| 24 **Boehlert** | Y | Y | Y | Y | Y | N | ? |
| 25 **Walsh** | Y | Y | Y | Y | Y | Y | Y |
| 26 **Reynolds** | Y | Y | Y | Y | Y | Y | Y |
| 27 Higgins | ? | ? | ? | N | N | N | Y |
| 28 Slaughter | Y | Y | Y | N | N | N | Y |
| 29 **Kuhl** | Y | Y | ? | Y | Y | Y | Y |
| **NORTH CAROLINA** | | | | | | | |
| 1 Butterfield | Y | Y | Y | N | N | N | Y |
| 2 Etheridge | + | + | + | N | N | N | Y |
| 3 **Jones** | Y | Y | Y | Y | Y | Y | Y |
| 4 Price | Y | Y | Y | N | N | N | Y |
| 5 **Foxx** | Y | Y | Y | Y | Y | Y | Y |
| 6 **Coble** | Y | Y | Y | Y | Y | Y | Y |
| 7 McIntyre | Y | Y | Y | N | - | Y | Y |
| 8 **Hayes** | Y | Y | Y | Y | Y | Y | Y |
| 9 **Myrick** | Y | Y | Y | Y | Y | Y | Y |
| 10 **McHenry** | Y | Y | Y | Y | Y | + | + |
| 11 **Taylor** | Y | Y | Y | Y | Y | Y | Y |
| 12 Watt | Y | Y | Y | N | N | N | Y |
| 13 Miller | Y | Y | Y | N | N | N | Y |
| **NORTH DAKOTA** | | | | | | | |
| AL Pomeroy | Y | Y | Y | N | N | N | Y |
| **OHIO** | | | | | | | |
| 1 **Chabot** | Y | Y | Y | Y | Y | Y | Y |
| 2 Vacant | | | | | | | |
| 3 **Turner** | Y | Y | Y | Y | Y | Y | Y |
| 4 **Oxley** | Y | Y | Y | Y | Y | Y | Y |
| 5 **Gillmor** | Y | Y | Y | Y | Y | Y | Y |
| 6 Strickland | ? | ? | ? | N | N | N | Y |
| 7 **Hobson** | Y | Y | Y | Y | Y | Y | Y |
| 8 **Boehner** | Y | Y | Y | Y | Y | Y | Y |
| 9 Kaptur | ? | ? | ? | N | N | N | Y |
| 10 Kucinich | Y | Y | Y | N | N | N | Y |
| 11 Jones | Y | Y | Y | ? | ? | N | Y |
| 12 **Tiberi** | Y | Y | Y | Y | Y | Y | Y |
| 13 Brown | Y | Y | Y | N | N | N | Y |
| 14 **LaTourette** | Y | Y | Y | Y | Y | Y | Y |
| 15 **Pryce** | ? | ? | ? | Y | Y | Y | Y |
| 16 **Regula** | Y | Y | Y | Y | Y | Y | Y |
| 17 Ryan | ? | Y | Y | N | N | N | Y |
| 18 **Ney** | Y | Y | Y | Y | Y | Y | Y |
| **OKLAHOMA** | | | | | | | |
| 1 **Sullivan** | Y | Y | Y | Y | Y | Y | Y |
| 2 Boren | Y | Y | Y | N | N | N | Y |
| 3 **Lucas** | Y | Y | Y | Y | Y | Y | Y |
| 4 **Cole** | Y | Y | Y | Y | Y | Y | Y |
| 5 **Istook** | Y | Y | Y | ? | ? | Y | Y |
| **OREGON** | | | | | | | |
| 1 Wu | Y | Y | Y | N | N | N | Y |
| 2 **Walden** | Y | Y | Y | Y | Y | Y | Y |
| 3 Blumenauer | Y | Y | Y | N | N | N | Y |
| 4 DeFazio | Y | Y | Y | N | N | N | Y |
| 5 Hooley | Y | Y | Y | N | N | N | Y |
| **PENNSYLVANIA** | | | | | | | |
| 1 Brady | ? | ? | ? | N | N | N | Y |
| 2 Fattah | ? | ? | ? | N | N | N | Y |
| 3 **English** | Y | Y | Y | Y | Y | Y | Y |
| 4 **Hart** | Y | Y | Y | Y | Y | Y | Y |
| 5 **Peterson** | Y | Y | Y | Y | Y | Y | Y |
| 6 **Gerlach** | Y | Y | Y | Y | Y | Y | Y |
| 7 **Weldon** | Y | Y | Y | Y | Y | Y | Y |
| 8 **Fitzpatrick** | Y | Y | Y | Y | Y | Y | Y |
| 9 **Shuster** | Y | Y | Y | Y | Y | Y | Y |
| 10 **Sherwood** | Y | Y | Y | Y | Y | Y | Y |
| 11 Kanjorski | Y | Y | Y | N | N | N | Y |
| 12 Murtha | Y | Y | Y | N | N | N | Y |
| 13 Schwartz | Y | Y | Y | N | N | N | Y |
| 14 Doyle | ? | Y | Y | N | N | N | Y |
| 15 **Dent** | Y | Y | Y | Y | Y | Y | Y |
| 16 **Pitts** | Y | Y | Y | Y | Y | Y | Y |
| 17 Holden | Y | Y | Y | N | N | N | Y |
| 18 **Murphy** | Y | Y | Y | Y | Y | Y | Y |
| 19 **Platts** | Y | Y | Y | Y | Y | Y | Y |
| **RHODE ISLAND** | | | | | | | |
| 1 Kennedy | Y | Y | Y | N | N | N | Y |
| 2 Langevin | Y | Y | Y | N | N | N | Y |
| **SOUTH CAROLINA** | | | | | | | |
| 1 **Brown** | Y | Y | Y | ? | ? | ? | ? |
| 2 **Wilson** | Y | Y | Y | Y | Y | + | Y |
| 3 **Barrett** | Y | Y | Y | Y | Y | Y | Y |
| 4 **Inglis** | Y | Y | Y | Y | Y | Y | Y |
| 5 Spratt | Y | Y | Y | N | N | N | Y |
| 6 Clyburn | Y | Y | Y | N | N | N | Y |
| **SOUTH DAKOTA** | | | | | | | |
| AL Herseth | Y | Y | Y | N | N | N | Y |
| **TENNESSEE** | | | | | | | |
| 1 **Jenkins** | ? | ? | ? | Y | Y | Y | Y |
| 2 **Duncan** | Y | Y | Y | Y | Y | Y | Y |
| 3 **Wamp** | Y | Y | Y | Y | Y | Y | Y |
| 4 Davis | Y | Y | Y | N | N | N | Y |
| 5 Cooper | Y | Y | Y | N | N | N | Y |
| 6 Gordon | Y | Y | Y | N | N | N | Y |
| 7 **Blackburn** | Y | Y | Y | Y | Y | Y | Y |
| 8 Tanner | Y | Y | Y | N | N | N | Y |
| 9 Ford | ? | ? | ? | N | N | N | Y |
| **TEXAS** | | | | | | | |
| 1 **Gohmert** | Y | Y | Y | Y | Y | Y | Y |
| 2 **Poe** | Y | Y | Y | Y | Y | Y | Y |
| 3 **Johnson, S.** | Y | Y | Y | Y | Y | Y | Y |
| 4 **Hall** | Y | Y | Y | Y | Y | Y | Y |
| 5 **Hensarling** | Y | Y | Y | Y | Y | Y | Y |
| 6 **Barton** | Y | Y | Y | Y | Y | Y | Y |
| 7 **Culberson** | Y | Y | Y | Y | Y | Y | Y |
| 8 **Brady** | Y | Y | Y | Y | Y | Y | Y |
| 9 Green, A. | Y | Y | Y | N | N | N | Y |
| 10 **McCaul** | Y | Y | Y | Y | Y | Y | Y |
| 11 **Conaway** | Y | Y | Y | Y | Y | Y | Y |
| 12 **Granger** | Y | Y | Y | Y | Y | Y | Y |
| 13 **Thornberry** | Y | Y | Y | Y | Y | ? | Y |
| 14 **Paul** | Y | N | Y | Y | Y | N | N |
| 15 Hinojosa | ? | ? | ? | ? | ? | ? | ? |
| 16 Reyes | ? | ? | ? | ? | ? | ? | ? |
| 17 Edwards | Y | Y | Y | N | N | N | Y |
| 18 Jackson-Lee | Y | Y | Y | N | N | N | Y |
| 19 **Neugebauer** | Y | Y | Y | Y | Y | Y | Y |
| 20 Gonzalez | Y | Y | Y | N | N | N | Y |
| 21 **Smith** | Y | Y | Y | Y | Y | Y | Y |
| 22 **DeLay** | ? | ? | ? | Y | Y | Y | Y |
| 23 **Bonilla** | Y | Y | Y | Y | Y | Y | Y |
| 24 **Marchant** | Y | Y | Y | Y | Y | Y | Y |
| 25 Doggett | Y | Y | Y | N | N | N | Y |
| 26 **Burgess** | Y | Y | Y | Y | Y | Y | Y |
| 27 Ortiz | Y | Y | Y | N | N | N | Y |
| 28 Cuellar | Y | Y | Y | N | N | Y | Y |
| 29 Green, G. | Y | Y | Y | N | N | Y | Y |
| 30 Johnson, E. | Y | Y | Y | N | N | N | Y |
| 31 **Carter** | Y | Y | Y | Y | Y | Y | Y |
| 32 **Sessions** | ? | ? | ? | Y | Y | Y | Y |
| **UTAH** | | | | | | | |
| 1 **Bishop** | Y | Y | Y | Y | Y | Y | Y |
| 2 Matheson | Y | Y | Y | N | N | N | Y |
| 3 **Cannon** | Y | Y | Y | Y | Y | Y | Y |
| **VERMONT** | | | | | | | |
| AL *Sanders* | Y | Y | Y | N | N | N | Y |
| **VIRGINIA** | | | | | | | |
| 1 **Davis, J.** | Y | Y | Y | Y | Y | Y | Y |
| 2 **Drake** | Y | Y | Y | Y | Y | Y | Y |
| 3 Scott | Y | Y | Y | N | N | N | Y |
| 4 **Forbes** | Y | Y | Y | Y | Y | Y | Y |
| 5 **Goode** | Y | Y | Y | Y | Y | Y | Y |
| 6 **Goodlatte** | Y | Y | Y | Y | Y | Y | Y |
| 7 **Cantor** | Y | Y | Y | Y | Y | Y | Y |
| 8 Moran | Y | Y | Y | N | N | N | Y |
| 9 Boucher | Y | Y | Y | N | N | N | Y |
| 10 **Wolf** | Y | Y | Y | Y | Y | Y | Y |
| 11 **Davis, T.** | Y | Y | Y | Y | Y | Y | Y |
| **WASHINGTON** | | | | | | | |
| 1 Inslee | Y | Y | Y | N | N | N | Y |
| 2 Larsen | ? | ? | ? | N | N | N | Y |
| 3 Baird | Y | Y | Y | N | N | N | Y |
| 4 **Hastings** | Y | Y | Y | Y | Y | Y | Y |
| 5 **McMorris** | Y | Y | Y | Y | Y | Y | Y |
| 6 Dicks | Y | Y | Y | N | ? | N | Y |
| 7 McDermott | Y | Y | Y | N | N | N | Y |
| 8 **Reichert** | Y | Y | Y | Y | Y | N | Y |
| 9 Smith | Y | Y | Y | N | N | N | Y |
| **WEST VIRGINIA** | | | | | | | |
| 1 Mollohan | Y | Y | Y | N | N | Y | Y |
| 2 **Capito** | Y | Y | Y | Y | Y | Y | Y |
| 3 Rahall | Y | Y | Y | N | N | N | Y |
| **WISCONSIN** | | | | | | | |
| 1 **Ryan** | Y | Y | Y | Y | Y | Y | Y |
| 2 Baldwin | Y | Y | Y | N | N | N | Y |
| 3 Kind | Y | Y | Y | N | N | N | Y |
| 4 Moore | Y | Y | Y | N | N | N | Y |
| 5 **Sensenbrenner** | Y | Y | Y | Y | Y | Y | Y |
| 6 **Petri** | Y | Y | Y | Y | Y | Y | Y |
| 7 Obey | Y | Y | Y | N | Y | N | Y |
| 8 **Green** | Y | Y | Y | Y | Y | Y | Y |
| **WYOMING** | | | | | | | |
| AL **Cubin** | Y | Y | ? | Y | Y | Y | Y |

# IN THE HOUSE | By Vote Number

**387.** HR 2601. State Department Authorization/Methamphetamines From Mexico. Hooley, D-Ore., amendment that would direct the Bureau for International Narcotics and Law Enforcement Affairs to make a priority of stemming the influx of methamphetamine from Mexico into the United States. Adopted 424-1: R 223-1; D 200-0 (ND 151-0, SD 49-0); I 1-0. July 19, 2005.

**388.** HR 2601. State Department Authorization/Extradition Requests for Afghans. Souder, R-Ind., amendment that would require a State Department report on pending U.S. extradition requests for Afghans who have committed violations of narcotics laws in the United States. Adopted 426-1: R 225-1; D 200-0 (ND 151-0, SD 49-0); I 1-0. July 19, 2005.

**389.** HR 2601. State Department Authorization/Obstetric Fistula. Smith, R-N.J., amendment that would increase access to emergency obstetrical care for women suffering from obstetric fistula and increase the fiscal 2007 authorization for new treatment centers to $7.5 million. It would provide access to family planning services and abstinence education, and make these prevention activities discretionary. Adopted 223-205: R 202-25; D 21-179 (ND 11-140, SD 10-39); I 0-1. July 19, 2005.

**390.** HR 2601. State Department Authorization/Palestinian Terrorist Attacks. King, R-Iowa, amendment that would condemn attacks on U.S. citizens by Palestinian terrorists. It would also encourage Palestinian leaders to work with Israel to end all terrorist acts on innocent individuals, regardless of citizenship. Adopted 423-0: R 222-0; D 200-0 (ND 150-0, SD 50-0); I 1-0. July 20, 2005.

**391.** HR 2601. State Department Authorization/Space-Based Weapons. Kucinich, D-Ohio, amendment that would require the president to direct the U.S. representative to the United Nations to begin negotiations for an international treaty banning space-based weapons. Rejected 124-302: R 2-223; D 121-79 (ND 109-41, SD 12-38); I 1-0. July 20, 2005.

**392.** HR 2601. State Department Authorization/Foreign Students. Lantos, D-Calif., amendment to require the State Department to develop a strategy to counter perceptions among foreign students that the United States is no longer welcoming and annually consult non-governmental organizations, university officials and other interested parties on the strategy. Adopted 373-56: R 171-56; D 201-0 (ND 151-0, SD 50-0); I 1-0. July 20, 2005.

**393.** HR 2601. State Department Authorization/Great Lakes Water. Rogers, R-Mich., amendment that would state that Congress recognizes the efforts of the Great Lakes governors and Canadian premiers in developing a common standard for decisions related to water withdrawal from the Great Lakes and urge that the management authority remain with the governors and premiers who share stewardship over the lakes. Rejected 156-273: R 154-73; D 2-199 (ND 1-150, SD 1-49); I 0-1. July 20, 2005.

| | 387 | 388 | 389 | 390 | 391 | 392 | 393 |
|---|---|---|---|---|---|---|---|
| **ALABAMA** | | | | | | | |
| 1 Bonner | Y | Y | Y | Y | N | Y | Y |
| 2 Everett | Y | Y | Y | Y | N | Y | Y |
| 3 Rogers | Y | Y | Y | Y | N | Y | Y |
| 4 Aderholt | Y | Y | Y | Y | N | Y | Y |
| 5 Cramer | Y | Y | Y | Y | N | Y | N |
| 6 Bachus | Y | Y | Y | Y | N | Y | Y |
| 7 Davis | Y | Y | N | Y | N | Y | N |
| **ALASKA** | | | | | | | |
| AL Young | Y | Y | Y | Y | N | Y | N |
| **ARIZONA** | | | | | | | |
| 1 Renzi | Y | Y | Y | Y | N | N | N |
| 2 Franks | Y | Y | Y | Y | N | N | Y |
| 3 Shadegg | Y | Y | Y | Y | N | N | N |
| 4 Pastor | Y | N | Y | Y | Y | N | N |
| 5 Hayworth | Y | Y | Y | Y | N | N | N |
| 6 Flake | Y | Y | Y | N | Y | N | N |
| 7 Grijalva | Y | N | Y | Y | Y | Y | N |
| 8 Kolbe | Y | Y | N | Y | N | Y | Y |
| **ARKANSAS** | | | | | | | |
| 1 Berry | Y | Y | Y | Y | N | Y | N |
| 2 Snyder | Y | Y | N | Y | N | Y | N |
| 3 Boozman | Y | Y | Y | Y | N | Y | Y |
| 4 Ross | Y | Y | N | Y | N | Y | N |
| **CALIFORNIA** | | | | | | | |
| 1 Thompson | Y | Y | N | Y | Y | Y | N |
| 2 Herger | Y | Y | Y | Y | N | N | Y |
| 3 Lungren | Y | Y | Y | Y | N | Y | N |
| 4 Doolittle | Y | Y | Y | Y | N | N | N |
| 5 Matsui, D. | Y | Y | N | Y | Y | Y | N |
| 6 Woolsey | Y | N | N | Y | Y | Y | N |
| 7 Miller, George | Y | Y | N | Y | Y | Y | N |
| 8 Pelosi | Y | N | N | Y | Y | Y | N |
| 9 Lee | Y | N | N | Y | Y | Y | N |
| 10 Tauscher | Y | Y | N | Y | Y | Y | N |
| 11 Pombo | Y | Y | Y | Y | N | N | N |
| 12 Lantos | Y | Y | N | Y | N | Y | N |
| 13 Stark | Y | N | N | Y | Y | Y | N |
| 14 Eshoo | Y | Y | N | Y | Y | Y | N |
| 15 Honda | Y | Y | N | Y | Y | Y | N |
| 16 Lofgren | Y | Y | N | Y | Y | Y | N |
| 17 Farr | Y | Y | N | Y | Y | Y | N |
| 18 Cardoza | Y | Y | N | Y | Y | Y | N |
| 19 Radanovich | Y | Y | Y | Y | N | N | N |
| 20 Costa | Y | Y | N | Y | Y | Y | N |
| 21 Nunes | Y | Y | Y | Y | N | N | N |
| 22 Thomas | Y | Y | Y | Y | N | N | N |
| 23 Capps | Y | Y | N | Y | Y | Y | N |
| 24 Gallegly | Y | Y | Y | Y | N | Y | Y |
| 25 McKeon | Y | Y | Y | Y | N | Y | Y |
| 26 Dreier | Y | Y | Y | Y | N | Y | N |
| 27 Sherman | Y | Y | N | Y | Y | Y | N |
| 28 Berman | Y | Y | N | Y | Y | Y | N |
| 29 Schiff | Y | Y | N | Y | N | Y | N |
| 30 Waxman | Y | N | N | Y | Y | Y | N |
| 31 Becerra | Y | Y | N | Y | Y | Y | N |
| 32 Solis | Y | Y | N | Y | Y | Y | N |
| 33 Watson | Y | Y | N | Y | Y | Y | N |
| 34 Roybal-Allard | Y | Y | N | Y | Y | Y | N |
| 35 Waters | Y | Y | N | Y | Y | Y | N |
| 36 Harman | Y | Y | N | Y | Y | Y | N |
| 37 Millender-McD. | Y | N | N | Y | Y | Y | N |
| 38 Napolitano | Y | Y | N | Y | Y | Y | N |
| 39 Sánchez, Linda | Y | Y | N | Y | Y | Y | N |
| 40 Royce | Y | Y | Y | Y | N | N | Y |
| 41 Lewis | Y | Y | Y | Y | N | Y | Y |
| 42 Miller, Gary | Y | Y | Y | Y | N | N | Y |
| 43 Baca | Y | Y | N | Y | Y | Y | N |
| 44 Calvert | Y | Y | Y | Y | N | Y | N |
| 45 Bono | Y | Y | N | Y | Y | Y | Y |
| 46 Rohrabacher | Y | Y | Y | Y | N | N | Y |
| 47 Sanchez, Loretta | Y | Y | N | Y | Y | Y | N |
| 48 Cox | ? | ? | Y | Y | N | Y | Y |
| 49 Issa | Y | Y | Y | Y | N | Y | Y |

| | 387 | 388 | 389 | 390 | 391 | 392 | 393 |
|---|---|---|---|---|---|---|---|
| 50 Cunningham | Y | Y | Y | Y | N | Y | N |
| 51 Filner | Y | Y | N | Y | Y | Y | N |
| 52 Hunter | Y | Y | Y | Y | N | Y | Y |
| 53 Davis | Y | Y | N | Y | N | Y | N |
| **COLORADO** | | | | | | | |
| 1 DeGette | Y | Y | N | Y | N | Y | N |
| 2 Udall | Y | Y | N | Y | Y | Y | N |
| 3 Salazar | Y | Y | N | Y | N | Y | N |
| 4 Musgrave | ? | Y | Y | Y | N | Y | Y |
| 5 Hefley | Y | Y | Y | Y | N | N | Y |
| 6 Tancredo | ? | ? | ? | Y | N | N | Y |
| 7 Beauprez | Y | Y | Y | Y | N | Y | Y |
| **CONNECTICUT** | | | | | | | |
| 1 Larson | Y | Y | N | Y | Y | Y | N |
| 2 Simmons | Y | Y | N | ? | N | Y | N |
| 3 DeLauro | Y | Y | N | Y | N | Y | N |
| 4 Shays | Y | Y | N | Y | Y | Y | N |
| 5 Johnson | Y | Y | N | Y | N | Y | N |
| **DELAWARE** | | | | | | | |
| AL Castle | Y | Y | N | Y | N | Y | N |
| **FLORIDA** | | | | | | | |
| 1 Miller | Y | Y | Y | Y | N | N | N |
| 2 Boyd | Y | Y | N | Y | N | Y | N |
| 3 Brown | Y | Y | N | Y | Y | Y | N |
| 4 Crenshaw | Y | Y | Y | Y | N | Y | N |
| 5 Brown-Waite | Y | Y | Y | Y | N | Y | N |
| 6 Stearns | Y | Y | Y | Y | N | Y | N |
| 7 Mica | Y | Y | Y | Y | N | Y | Y |
| 8 Keller | Y | Y | Y | Y | N | Y | Y |
| 9 Bilirakis | Y | Y | Y | Y | N | Y | N |
| 10 Young | Y | Y | Y | Y | N | N | Y |
| 11 Davis | Y | Y | N | Y | N | Y | N |
| 12 Putnam | Y | Y | Y | Y | N | Y | N |
| 13 Harris | Y | Y | Y | Y | N | Y | Y |
| 14 Mack | Y | Y | Y | Y | N | N | Y |
| 15 Weldon | Y | Y | Y | Y | N | Y | Y |
| 16 Foley | Y | Y | N | Y | N | Y | Y |
| 17 Meek | Y | Y | N | Y | N | Y | N |
| 18 Ros-Lehtinen | Y | Y | Y | Y | N | Y | Y |
| 19 Wexler | Y | Y | N | Y | Y | Y | N |
| 20 Wasserman-Schultz | Y | Y | N | Y | Y | Y | N |
| 21 Diaz-Balart, L. | Y | Y | Y | Y | N | Y | Y |
| 22 Shaw | Y | Y | Y | Y | N | N | N |
| 23 Hastings | Y | Y | N | Y | N | Y | N |
| 24 Feeney | Y | Y | Y | ? | N | Y | Y |
| 25 Diaz-Balart, M. | Y | Y | Y | Y | N | Y | Y |
| **GEORGIA** | | | | | | | |
| 1 Kingston | Y | Y | N | Y | N | N | Y |
| 2 Bishop | Y | Y | N | Y | N | Y | N |
| 3 Marshall | Y | Y | N | Y | N | Y | N |
| 4 McKinney | Y | Y | N | Y | Y | Y | N |
| 5 Lewis | Y | Y | N | Y | Y | Y | N |
| 6 Price | Y | Y | Y | Y | N | Y | Y |
| 7 Linder | Y | Y | Y | Y | N | Y | Y |
| 8 Westmoreland | Y | Y | Y | Y | N | N | Y |
| 9 Norwood | Y | Y | Y | Y | N | N | Y |
| 10 Deal | Y | Y | Y | Y | N | Y | Y |
| 11 Gingrey | Y | Y | Y | Y | N | Y | Y |
| 12 Barrow | Y | Y | N | Y | Y | Y | N |
| 13 Scott | Y | Y | N | Y | N | Y | N |
| **HAWAII** | | | | | | | |
| 1 Abercrombie | Y | Y | N | Y | Y | Y | N |
| 2 Case | Y | Y | N | Y | N | Y | N |
| **IDAHO** | | | | | | | |
| 1 Otter | Y | Y | Y | Y | N | N | Y |
| 2 Simpson | Y | Y | Y | Y | N | Y | Y |
| **ILLINOIS** | | | | | | | |
| 1 Rush | Y | Y | N | Y | ? | Y | N |
| 2 Jackson | Y | Y | N | Y | Y | Y | N |
| 3 Lipinski | Y | Y | Y | Y | N | Y | N |
| 4 Gutierrez | Y | Y | N | Y | Y | Y | N |
| 5 Emanuel | Y | N | N | Y | N | Y | N |
| 6 Hyde | Y | Y | N | Y | N | Y | Y |
| 7 Davis | Y | Y | N | Y | Y | Y | N |
| 8 Bean | Y | Y | N | Y | N | Y | N |
| 9 Schakowsky | Y | Y | N | Y | Y | Y | N |
| 10 Kirk | Y | Y | N | Y | N | Y | N |
| 11 Weller | Y | Y | Y | Y | N | Y | N |
| 12 Costello | Y | Y | Y | Y | N | Y | N |

**KEY**    **Republicans**    Democrats    *Independents*

| Y | Voted for (yea) | X | Paired against | C | Voted "present" to avoid possible conflict of interest |
|---|---|---|---|---|---|
| # | Paired for | – | Announced against | | |
| + | Announced for | P | Voted "present" | ? | Did not vote or otherwise make a position known |
| N | Voted against (nay) | | | | |

| | 387 | 388 | 389 | 390 | 391 | 392 | 393 |
|---|---|---|---|---|---|---|---|
| 13 **Biggert** | Y | Y | N | Y | N | Y | Y |
| 14 **Hastert** | | | | | | | |
| 15 **Johnson** | Y | Y | Y | Y | N | Y | N |
| 16 **Manzullo** | Y | Y | Y | Y | N | N | Y |
| 17 Evans | Y | Y | N | Y | Y | Y | N |
| 18 **LaHood** | Y | Y | Y | Y | N | Y | N |
| 19 **Shimkus** | Y | Y | Y | Y | N | Y | N |
| **INDIANA** | | | | | | | |
| 1 Visclosky | Y | Y | N | Y | Y | Y | N |
| 2 **Chocola** | Y | Y | Y | Y | N | Y | Y |
| 3 **Souder** | Y | Y | Y | Y | N | Y | Y |
| 4 **Buyer** | Y | Y | Y | Y | N | Y | Y |
| 5 **Burton** | Y | Y | Y | Y | N | Y | Y |
| 6 **Pence** | Y | Y | Y | Y | N | Y | Y |
| 7 Carson | Y | Y | N | Y | Y | Y | N |
| 8 **Hostettler** | Y | Y | Y | Y | N | N | Y |
| 9 **Sodrel** | Y | Y | Y | Y | N | Y | Y |
| **IOWA** | | | | | | | |
| 1 **Nussle** | Y | Y | Y | Y | N | N | Y |
| 2 **Leach** | Y | Y | N | Y | Y | Y | N |
| 3 Boswell | Y | Y | N | Y | Y | Y | N |
| 4 **Latham** | Y | Y | Y | Y | N | Y | Y |
| 5 **King** | Y | Y | Y | Y | N | Y | Y |
| **KANSAS** | | | | | | | |
| 1 **Moran** | Y | Y | Y | Y | N | Y | Y |
| 2 **Ryun** | Y | Y | Y | Y | N | Y | Y |
| 3 Moore | Y | Y | N | Y | N | Y | N |
| 4 **Tiahrt** | Y | Y | Y | Y | N | Y | Y |
| **KENTUCKY** | | | | | | | |
| 1 **Whitfield** | Y | Y | Y | Y | N | Y | Y |
| 2 **Lewis** | Y | Y | Y | Y | N | Y | Y |
| 3 **Northup** | Y | Y | Y | Y | N | Y | Y |
| 4 **Davis** | Y | Y | Y | + | - | N | Y |
| 5 **Rogers** | Y | Y | Y | Y | N | Y | Y |
| 6 Chandler | Y | Y | N | Y | N | Y | N |
| **LOUISIANA** | | | | | | | |
| 1 **Jindal** | Y | Y | Y | ? | ? | ? | ? |
| 2 Jefferson | Y | Y | N | Y | N | Y | N |
| 3 Melancon | Y | Y | N | Y | N | Y | N |
| 4 **McCrery** | Y | Y | Y | Y | N | Y | Y |
| 5 **Alexander** | Y | Y | Y | Y | N | Y | Y |
| 6 **Baker** | Y | Y | Y | Y | N | Y | Y |
| 7 **Boustany** | Y | Y | Y | Y | N | Y | Y |
| **MAINE** | | | | | | | |
| 1 Allen | Y | Y | N | Y | Y | Y | N |
| 2 Michaud | Y | Y | N | Y | Y | Y | N |
| **MARYLAND** | | | | | | | |
| 1 **Gilchrest** | Y | Y | N | Y | N | Y | N |
| 2 Ruppersberger | Y | Y | N | Y | Y | Y | N |
| 3 Cardin | Y | Y | N | Y | N | Y | N |
| 4 Wynn | Y | Y | N | Y | Y | Y | N |
| 5 Hoyer | Y | Y | N | Y | N | Y | N |
| 6 **Bartlett** | Y | Y | Y | Y | N | N | Y |
| 7 Cummings | Y | Y | N | Y | Y | Y | N |
| 8 Van Hollen | Y | Y | N | Y | Y | Y | N |
| **MASSACHUSETTS** | | | | | | | |
| 1 Olver | Y | Y | N | Y | Y | Y | N |
| 2 Neal | Y | Y | N | Y | Y | Y | N |
| 3 McGovern | Y | Y | N | Y | Y | Y | N |
| 4 Frank | Y | Y | N | Y | Y | Y | N |
| 5 Meehan | Y | Y | N | Y | Y | Y | N |
| 6 Tierney | Y | Y | N | Y | Y | Y | N |
| 7 Markey | Y | Y | N | Y | Y | Y | N |
| 8 Capuano | Y | Y | N | Y | Y | Y | N |
| 9 Lynch | Y | Y | N | Y | N | Y | N |
| 10 Delahunt | Y | Y | N | Y | Y | Y | N |
| **MICHIGAN** | | | | | | | |
| 1 Stupak | Y | Y | Y | Y | Y | Y | N |
| 2 **Hoekstra** | Y | Y | Y | Y | N | Y | N |
| 3 **Ehlers** | Y | Y | Y | Y | N | Y | N |
| 4 **Camp** | Y | Y | Y | Y | N | Y | N |
| 5 Kildee | Y | Y | Y | Y | N | Y | N |
| 6 **Upton** | Y | Y | Y | Y | N | Y | N |
| 7 **Schwarz** | Y | Y | N | Y | N | Y | Y |
| 8 **Rogers** | Y | Y | Y | Y | N | Y | Y |
| 9 **Knollenberg** | Y | Y | Y | Y | N | Y | Y |
| 10 **Miller** | Y | Y | Y | Y | N | Y | N |
| 11 **McCotter** | Y | Y | Y | Y | N | Y | Y |
| 12 Levin | Y | Y | N | Y | N | Y | N |
| 13 Kilpatrick | Y | Y | N | Y | Y | Y | N |
| 14 Conyers | Y | Y | N | Y | Y | Y | N |
| 15 Dingell | Y | Y | N | Y | Y | Y | N |
| **MINNESOTA** | | | | | | | |
| 1 **Gutknecht** | Y | Y | Y | Y | N | N | N |
| 2 **Kline** | Y | Y | Y | Y | N | Y | N |
| 3 **Ramstad** | Y | Y | N | Y | N | Y | N |
| 4 McCollum | Y | Y | N | Y | Y | Y | N |
| 5 Sabo | Y | Y | N | Y | Y | Y | N |
| 6 **Kennedy** | Y | Y | Y | Y | N | Y | N |
| 7 Peterson | Y | Y | Y | Y | N | Y | N |
| 8 Oberstar | Y | Y | N | Y | Y | Y | N |
| **MISSISSIPPI** | | | | | | | |
| 1 **Wicker** | Y | Y | Y | Y | N | Y | Y |
| 2 Thompson | Y | Y | N | Y | N | Y | N |
| 3 **Pickering** | Y | Y | Y | Y | N | Y | N |
| 4 Taylor | Y | Y | Y | Y | N | Y | N |
| **MISSOURI** | | | | | | | |
| 1 Clay | Y | Y | N | Y | Y | Y | N |
| 2 **Akin** | Y | Y | Y | Y | N | N | Y |
| 3 Carnahan | Y | Y | N | Y | N | Y | N |
| 4 Skelton | Y | Y | Y | Y | N | Y | N |
| 5 Cleaver | Y | Y | N | Y | Y | Y | N |
| 6 **Graves** | Y | Y | Y | Y | N | Y | Y |
| 7 **Blunt** | Y | Y | Y | Y | N | Y | Y |
| 8 **Emerson** | Y | Y | Y | Y | N | Y | Y |
| 9 **Hulshof** | Y | Y | Y | Y | N | Y | Y |
| **MONTANA** | | | | | | | |
| AL **Rehberg** | Y | Y | Y | Y | N | Y | Y |
| **NEBRASKA** | | | | | | | |
| 1 **Fortenberry** | Y | Y | Y | Y | N | Y | Y |
| 2 **Terry** | Y | Y | Y | Y | N | Y | Y |
| 3 **Osborne** | Y | Y | Y | Y | N | Y | Y |
| **NEVADA** | | | | | | | |
| 1 Berkley | Y | Y | N | Y | Y | Y | N |
| 2 **Gibbons** | Y | Y | Y | Y | N | N | Y |
| 3 **Porter** | Y | Y | Y | Y | N | Y | Y |
| **NEW HAMPSHIRE** | | | | | | | |
| 1 **Bradley** | Y | Y | N | Y | N | Y | N |
| 2 **Bass** | Y | Y | N | Y | N | Y | N |
| **NEW JERSEY** | | | | | | | |
| 1 Andrews | Y | Y | N | Y | Y | Y | N |
| 2 **LoBiondo** | Y | Y | Y | Y | N | Y | Y |
| 3 **Saxton** | Y | Y | Y | Y | N | Y | Y |
| 4 **Smith** | Y | Y | Y | Y | N | Y | N |
| 5 **Garrett** | Y | Y | Y | Y | N | N | Y |
| 6 Pallone | Y | Y | N | Y | Y | Y | N |
| 7 **Ferguson** | Y | Y | Y | Y | N | Y | N |
| 8 Pascrell | Y | Y | N | Y | Y | Y | N |
| 9 Rothman | Y | Y | N | Y | Y | Y | N |
| 10 Payne | Y | Y | N | Y | Y | Y | N |
| 11 **Frelinghuysen** | Y | Y | N | Y | N | Y | Y |
| 12 Holt | Y | Y | N | Y | Y | Y | N |
| 13 Menendez | Y | Y | N | Y | N | Y | N |
| **NEW MEXICO** | | | | | | | |
| 1 **Wilson** | Y | Y | Y | Y | N | Y | Y |
| 2 **Pearce** | Y | Y | Y | Y | N | Y | Y |
| 3 Udall | Y | Y | N | Y | Y | Y | N |
| **NEW YORK** | | | | | | | |
| 1 Bishop | Y | Y | N | Y | Y | Y | N |
| 2 Israel | Y | Y | N | Y | N | Y | N |
| 3 **King** | Y | Y | Y | Y | N | Y | Y |
| 4 McCarthy | Y | Y | N | Y | N | Y | N |
| 5 Ackerman | Y | Y | N | Y | Y | Y | N |
| 6 Meeks | Y | Y | N | Y | Y | Y | Y |
| 7 Crowley | Y | Y | N | Y | Y | Y | N |
| 8 Nadler | Y | Y | N | Y | Y | Y | N |
| 9 Weiner | Y | Y | N | Y | Y | Y | N |
| 10 Towns | Y | Y | N | Y | Y | Y | N |
| 11 Owens | Y | Y | N | Y | Y | Y | N |
| 12 Velázquez | Y | Y | N | Y | Y | Y | N |
| 13 **Fossella** | Y | Y | Y | Y | N | Y | Y |
| 14 Maloney | Y | Y | N | Y | Y | Y | N |
| 15 Rangel | Y | Y | N | Y | Y | Y | N |
| 16 Serrano | Y | Y | N | Y | Y | Y | N |
| 17 Engel | Y | Y | N | Y | Y | Y | N |
| 18 Lowey | Y | Y | N | Y | Y | Y | N |
| 19 **Kelly** | Y | Y | N | Y | N | Y | N |
| 20 **Sweeney** | ? | ? | ? | Y | N | Y | Y |
| 21 McNulty | Y | Y | N | Y | Y | Y | N |
| 22 Hinchey | Y | Y | N | Y | Y | Y | N |
| 23 **McHugh** | Y | Y | Y | Y | N | Y | Y |
| 24 **Boehlert** | Y | Y | N | Y | N | Y | Y |
| 25 **Walsh** | Y | Y | Y | Y | N | Y | Y |
| 26 **Reynolds** | Y | Y | Y | Y | N | Y | Y |
| 27 Higgins | Y | Y | N | Y | Y | Y | N |
| 28 Slaughter | Y | Y | N | + | Y | Y | N |
| 29 **Kuhl** | Y | Y | Y | Y | N | Y | Y |
| **NORTH CAROLINA** | | | | | | | |
| 1 Butterfield | Y | Y | N | Y | N | Y | N |
| 2 Etheridge | Y | Y | N | Y | N | Y | N |
| 3 **Jones** | Y | Y | Y | Y | N | N | Y |
| 4 Price | Y | Y | N | Y | Y | Y | N |
| 5 **Foxx** | Y | Y | Y | Y | N | N | N |
| 6 **Coble** | Y | Y | Y | Y | N | N | Y |
| 7 McIntyre | Y | Y | Y | Y | N | Y | N |
| 8 **Hayes** | Y | Y | Y | Y | N | Y | Y |
| 9 **Myrick** | Y | Y | Y | Y | N | N | Y |
| 10 **McHenry** | Y | Y | Y | Y | N | N | Y |
| 11 **Taylor** | Y | Y | Y | Y | N | N | N |
| 12 Watt | Y | Y | N | Y | Y | Y | N |
| 13 Miller | Y | Y | N | Y | N | Y | N |
| **NORTH DAKOTA** | | | | | | | |
| AL Pomeroy | Y | Y | N | Y | N | Y | N |
| **OHIO** | | | | | | | |
| 1 **Chabot** | Y | Y | Y | Y | N | Y | Y |
| 2 Vacant | | | | | | | |
| 3 **Turner** | Y | Y | Y | Y | N | Y | Y |
| 4 **Oxley** | Y | Y | Y | Y | N | Y | Y |
| 5 **Gillmor** | Y | Y | Y | Y | N | Y | N |
| 6 Strickland | Y | Y | N | Y | Y | Y | N |
| 7 **Hobson** | Y | Y | Y | Y | N | Y | Y |
| 8 **Boehner** | Y | Y | Y | Y | N | Y | Y |
| 9 Kaptur | Y | Y | Y | Y | Y | Y | N |
| 10 Kucinich | Y | Y | N | Y | Y | Y | N |
| 11 Jones | Y | Y | N | Y | Y | Y | N |
| 12 **Tiberi** | Y | Y | Y | Y | N | Y | Y |
| 13 Brown | Y | Y | N | Y | Y | Y | N |
| 14 **LaTourette** | Y | Y | Y | Y | N | Y | N |
| 15 **Pryce** | Y | Y | N | Y | N | Y | N |
| 16 **Regula** | Y | Y | Y | Y | N | Y | Y |
| 17 Ryan | Y | Y | N | Y | Y | Y | N |
| 18 **Ney** | Y | Y | Y | Y | N | Y | N |
| **OKLAHOMA** | | | | | | | |
| 1 **Sullivan** | Y | Y | Y | ? | ? | Y | Y |
| 2 Boren | Y | Y | Y | Y | N | Y | N |
| 3 **Lucas** | Y | Y | Y | Y | N | Y | N |
| 4 **Cole** | Y | Y | Y | Y | N | Y | Y |
| 5 **Istook** | Y | Y | Y | Y | N | Y | N |
| **OREGON** | | | | | | | |
| 1 Wu | Y | Y | N | Y | Y | Y | N |
| 2 **Walden** | Y | Y | N | Y | N | N | Y |
| 3 Blumenauer | Y | Y | N | Y | Y | Y | N |
| 4 DeFazio | Y | Y | N | Y | Y | Y | N |
| 5 Hooley | Y | Y | N | Y | Y | Y | N |
| **PENNSYLVANIA** | | | | | | | |
| 1 Brady | Y | Y | N | Y | Y | Y | N |
| 2 Fattah | Y | Y | N | Y | Y | Y | N |
| 3 **English** | Y | Y | Y | Y | N | Y | N |
| 4 **Hart** | Y | Y | Y | Y | N | Y | N |
| 5 **Peterson** | Y | Y | Y | Y | N | Y | Y |
| 6 **Gerlach** | Y | Y | N | Y | N | Y | Y |
| 7 **Weldon** | Y | Y | Y | Y | N | Y | N |
| 8 **Fitzpatrick** | Y | Y | Y | Y | N | Y | N |
| 9 **Shuster** | Y | Y | Y | Y | N | N | N |
| 10 **Sherwood** | Y | Y | Y | Y | N | Y | Y |
| 11 Kanjorski | Y | Y | N | Y | N | Y | N |
| 12 Murtha | Y | Y | Y | Y | N | Y | N |
| 13 Schwartz | Y | Y | N | Y | Y | Y | N |
| 14 Doyle | Y | Y | N | Y | Y | Y | N |
| 15 **Dent** | Y | Y | N | Y | N | Y | Y |
| 16 **Pitts** | Y | Y | Y | Y | N | Y | Y |
| 17 Holden | Y | Y | Y | Y | N | Y | N |
| 18 **Murphy** | Y | Y | Y | Y | N | Y | Y |
| 19 **Platts** | Y | Y | Y | Y | N | Y | N |
| **RHODE ISLAND** | | | | | | | |
| 1 Kennedy | Y | Y | N | Y | N | Y | N |
| 2 Langevin | Y | Y | N | Y | N | Y | N |
| **SOUTH CAROLINA** | | | | | | | |
| 1 **Brown** | ? | ? | ? | ? | ? | ? | ? |
| 2 **Wilson** | Y | Y | Y | Y | N | Y | Y |
| 3 **Barrett** | Y | Y | Y | Y | N | N | Y |
| 4 **Inglis** | Y | Y | Y | Y | N | Y | N |
| 5 Spratt | Y | Y | N | Y | N | Y | N |
| 6 Clyburn | Y | Y | N | Y | N | Y | N |
| **SOUTH DAKOTA** | | | | | | | |
| AL Herseth | Y | Y | N | Y | N | Y | N |
| **TENNESSEE** | | | | | | | |
| 1 **Jenkins** | Y | Y | Y | Y | N | N | Y |
| 2 **Duncan** | Y | Y | Y | Y | N | N | Y |
| 3 **Wamp** | Y | Y | Y | Y | N | Y | N |
| 4 Davis | Y | Y | Y | Y | N | Y | N |
| 5 Cooper | Y | Y | N | Y | N | Y | N |
| 6 Gordon | Y | Y | Y | Y | N | Y | N |
| 7 **Blackburn** | Y | Y | Y | Y | N | N | Y |
| 8 Tanner | Y | Y | N | Y | N | Y | N |
| 9 Ford | Y | Y | N | Y | N | Y | N |
| **TEXAS** | | | | | | | |
| 1 **Gohmert** | Y | Y | Y | Y | N | N | Y |
| 2 **Poe** | Y | Y | Y | Y | N | Y | Y |
| 3 **Johnson, S.** | Y | Y | Y | Y | N | N | Y |
| 4 **Hall** | Y | Y | Y | Y | N | Y | Y |
| 5 **Hensarling** | Y | Y | Y | Y | N | Y | Y |
| 6 **Barton** | Y | Y | Y | Y | N | Y | N |
| 7 **Culberson** | Y | Y | Y | Y | N | N | Y |
| 8 **Brady** | Y | Y | Y | ? | ? | ? | ? |
| 9 Green, A. | Y | Y | N | Y | Y | Y | N |
| 10 **McCaul** | Y | Y | Y | Y | N | Y | Y |
| 11 **Conaway** | Y | Y | Y | Y | N | Y | Y |
| 12 **Granger** | Y | Y | Y | Y | N | Y | Y |
| 13 **Thornberry** | Y | Y | Y | Y | N | Y | Y |
| 14 **Paul** | N | N | N | Y | N | N | Y |
| 15 Hinojosa | ? | ? | ? | ? | ? | ? | ? |
| 16 Reyes | ? | ? | ? | Y | N | Y | N |
| 17 Edwards | Y | Y | N | Y | N | Y | N |
| 18 Jackson-Lee | Y | Y | N | Y | Y | Y | N |
| 19 **Neugebauer** | Y | Y | Y | Y | N | Y | Y |
| 20 Gonzalez | Y | Y | N | Y | N | Y | N |
| 21 **Smith** | Y | Y | Y | Y | N | N | Y |
| 22 **DeLay** | Y | Y | Y | Y | N | Y | Y |
| 23 **Bonilla** | Y | Y | Y | Y | N | N | Y |
| 24 **Marchant** | Y | Y | Y | Y | N | N | Y |
| 25 Doggett | Y | Y | N | Y | Y | Y | N |
| 26 **Burgess** | Y | Y | Y | Y | N | N | Y |
| 27 Ortiz | Y | Y | Y | Y | N | Y | N |
| 28 Cuellar | Y | Y | Y | Y | N | Y | N |
| 29 Green, G. | Y | Y | N | Y | Y | Y | Y |
| 30 Johnson, E. | Y | Y | N | Y | Y | Y | N |
| 31 **Carter** | Y | Y | Y | Y | N | Y | Y |
| 32 **Sessions** | Y | Y | Y | Y | N | N | Y |
| **UTAH** | | | | | | | |
| 1 **Bishop** | ? | Y | Y | Y | N | Y | Y |
| 2 Matheson | Y | Y | N | Y | N | Y | N |
| 3 **Cannon** | Y | Y | Y | Y | N | Y | N |
| **VERMONT** | | | | | | | |
| AL *Sanders* | Y | Y | N | Y | Y | Y | N |
| **VIRGINIA** | | | | | | | |
| 1 **Davis, J.** | Y | Y | Y | Y | N | N | Y |
| 2 **Drake** | Y | Y | Y | Y | N | Y | Y |
| 3 Scott | Y | Y | N | Y | Y | Y | N |
| 4 **Forbes** | Y | Y | Y | Y | N | N | Y |
| 5 **Goode** | Y | Y | Y | Y | N | N | Y |
| 6 **Goodlatte** | Y | Y | Y | Y | N | Y | N |
| 7 **Cantor** | Y | Y | Y | Y | N | Y | Y |
| 8 Moran | Y | Y | N | Y | N | Y | N |
| 9 Boucher | Y | Y | N | Y | N | Y | N |
| 10 **Wolf** | Y | Y | Y | Y | N | Y | N |
| 11 **Davis, T.** | Y | Y | Y | Y | N | Y | N |
| **WASHINGTON** | | | | | | | |
| 1 Inslee | Y | Y | N | Y | Y | Y | N |
| 2 Larsen | Y | Y | N | Y | Y | Y | N |
| 3 Baird | Y | Y | N | Y | Y | Y | N |
| 4 **Hastings** | Y | Y | Y | Y | N | Y | Y |
| 5 **McMorris** | Y | Y | Y | + | N | Y | Y |
| 6 Dicks | Y | Y | N | Y | N | Y | N |
| 7 McDermott | Y | Y | N | Y | Y | Y | N |
| 8 **Reichert** | Y | Y | Y | Y | N | Y | Y |
| 9 Smith | Y | Y | N | Y | Y | Y | N |
| **WEST VIRGINIA** | | | | | | | |
| 1 Mollohan | Y | Y | Y | Y | N | Y | N |
| 2 **Capito** | Y | Y | Y | Y | N | Y | N |
| 3 Rahall | Y | Y | Y | Y | Y | Y | N |
| **WISCONSIN** | | | | | | | |
| 1 **Ryan** | Y | Y | Y | Y | N | Y | N |
| 2 Baldwin | Y | Y | N | Y | Y | Y | N |
| 3 Kind | Y | Y | N | Y | N | Y | N |
| 4 Moore | Y | Y | N | Y | Y | Y | N |
| 5 **Sensenbrenner** | Y | Y | Y | Y | N | Y | Y |
| 6 **Petri** | Y | Y | Y | Y | N | Y | N |
| 7 Obey | Y | Y | N | Y | Y | Y | N |
| 8 **Green** | Y | Y | Y | Y | N | Y | N |
| **WYOMING** | | | | | | | |
| AL **Cubin** | Y | Y | Y | Y | N | N | N |

# IN THE HOUSE | By Vote Number

**394.** **HR 2601. State Department Authorization/Extradition of Charles Taylor.** Watson, D-Calif., amendment that would require the United States. to seek the extradition of former Liberian President Charles Taylor to the Special Court for Sierra Leone, where he would be tried for war crimes, crimes against humanity and other violations of international humanitarian law. Adopted 422-2: R 222-2; D 199-0 (ND 150-0, SD 49-0); I 1-0. July 20, 2005.

**395.** **HR 2601. State Department Authorization/Palestinian Territories.** Berkley, D-Nev., amendment that would state that the United States should promote the emergence of a democratic Palestinian government that denounces and combats terrorism. It would specify that no more than 25 percent of the aid for the Palestinian Authority could be obligated and expended during any calendar quarter. Adopted 330-100: R 211-18; D 119-81 (ND 80-70, SD 39-11); I 0-1. July 20, 2005.

**396.** **HR 2601. State Department Authorization/Detention of International Terrorists.** Rohrabacher, R-Calif., amendment that would express the sense of Congress that the detention and lawful human interrogation of detainees at Guantánamo Bay, Cuba, is essential to U.S. defense and prosecution of the war on terrorism. Adopted 304-124: R 223-4; D 81-119 (ND 50-100, SD 31-19); I 0-1. July 20, 2005.

**397.** **HR 2601. State Department Authorization/Iraqi Forces Power Transfer.** Ros-Lehtinen, R-Fla., amendment that would state that it is U.S. policy not to withdraw U.S. forces prematurely from Iraq, but to do so only when it is clear that U.S. national security and foreign policy goals relating to a free and stable Iraq have been or are about to be achieved. Adopted 291-137: R 220-7; D 71-129 (ND 38-112, SD 33-17); I 0-1. July 20, 2005.

**398.** **HR 2601. State Department Authorization/Recommit.** Menendez, D-N.J., motion to recommit the bill to the International Relations Committee with instructions to add language asking the president to advise Congress on the benchmarks for a successful strategy in Iraq. The language would also state that it is U.S. policy to devise a plan to bring stability to Iraq so that the responsibility for Iraq's security may be transferred to the Iraqi people as soon as possible, to provide adequate equipment for U.S. troops and to provide adequate health care benefits upon their return. Motion rejected 203-227: R 2-227; D 200-0 (ND 150-0, SD 50-0); I 1-0. July 20, 2005.

**399.** **HR 2601. State Department Authorization/Passage.** Passage of the bill that would authorize $10.8 billion in fiscal 2006 and $10 billion in fiscal 2007 for the State Department, international broadcasting activities, international assistance programs and related agencies. Passed 351-78: R 216-13; D 135-64 (ND 95-54, SD 40-10); I 0-1. July 20, 2005.

**400.** **H Res 326. Elections in Azerbaijan/Adoption.** Ros-Lehtinen, R-Fla., motion to suspend the rules and adopt the resolution that would call for free and fair parliamentary elections in the Republic of Azerbaijan in November 2005. Motion agreed to 416-1: R 222-1; D 193-0 (ND 144-0, SD 49-0); I 1-0. A two-thirds majority of those present and voting (278 in this case) is required for adoption under suspension of the rules. July 20, 2005.

| | 394 | 395 | 396 | 397 | 398 | 399 | 400 |
|---|---|---|---|---|---|---|---|
| **ALABAMA** | | | | | | | |
| 1 Bonner | Y | Y | Y | Y | N | Y | Y |
| 2 Everett | Y | Y | Y | Y | N | Y | Y |
| 3 Rogers | Y | Y | Y | Y | N | Y | Y |
| 4 Aderholt | Y | Y | Y | Y | N | Y | Y |
| 5 Cramer | Y | Y | Y | Y | Y | Y | Y |
| 6 Bachus | Y | Y | Y | Y | N | Y | Y |
| 7 Davis | Y | Y | Y | Y | Y | Y | Y |
| **ALASKA** | | | | | | | |
| AL Young | Y | Y | Y | Y | N | Y | Y |
| **ARIZONA** | | | | | | | |
| 1 Renzi | Y | Y | Y | Y | N | Y | Y |
| 2 Franks | Y | Y | Y | Y | N | N | Y |
| 3 Shadegg | Y | Y | Y | Y | N | Y | Y |
| 4 Pastor | Y | N | N | N | Y | N | Y |
| 5 Hayworth | Y | Y | Y | Y | N | Y | Y |
| 6 Flake | Y | Y | Y | Y | N | N | Y |
| 7 Grijalva | Y | N | N | N | Y | N | Y |
| 8 Kolbe | Y | N | Y | Y | N | Y | Y |
| **ARKANSAS** | | | | | | | |
| 1 Berry | Y | Y | Y | Y | Y | N | Y |
| 2 Snyder | Y | N | N | N | Y | Y | Y |
| 3 Boozman | Y | Y | Y | Y | N | Y | ? |
| 4 Ross | Y | Y | Y | Y | Y | Y | Y |
| **CALIFORNIA** | | | | | | | |
| 1 Thompson | Y | Y | N | N | Y | Y | Y |
| 2 Herger | Y | Y | Y | Y | N | Y | Y |
| 3 Lungren | Y | Y | Y | Y | N | Y | Y |
| 4 Doolittle | Y | Y | Y | Y | N | Y | Y |
| 5 Matsui, D. | Y | N | N | N | Y | Y | Y |
| 6 Woolsey | Y | N | N | N | Y | N | Y |
| 7 Miller, George | Y | N | N | N | Y | N | Y |
| 8 Pelosi | Y | N | N | N | Y | N | Y |
| 9 Lee | Y | N | N | N | Y | N | Y |
| 10 Tauscher | Y | N | Y | N | Y | Y | Y |
| 11 Pombo | Y | Y | Y | Y | N | Y | Y |
| 12 Lantos | Y | Y | Y | Y | Y | Y | Y |
| 13 Stark | Y | N | N | N | Y | N | Y |
| 14 Eshoo | Y | N | N | N | Y | N | Y |
| 15 Honda | Y | N | N | N | Y | N | Y |
| 16 Lofgren | Y | N | N | N | Y | N | Y |
| 17 Farr | Y | N | N | N | Y | N | Y |
| 18 Cardoza | Y | Y | Y | Y | Y | Y | Y |
| 19 Radanovich | Y | Y | Y | Y | N | Y | Y |
| 20 Costa | Y | Y | Y | Y | Y | Y | Y |
| 21 Nunes | Y | Y | Y | Y | N | Y | Y |
| 22 Thomas | Y | Y | Y | Y | N | Y | Y |
| 23 Capps | Y | N | N | N | Y | Y | Y |
| 24 Gallegly | Y | Y | Y | Y | N | Y | Y |
| 25 McKeon | Y | Y | Y | Y | N | Y | Y |
| 26 Dreier | N | Y | Y | Y | N | Y | Y |
| 27 Sherman | Y | Y | N | Y | Y | Y | Y |
| 28 Berman | Y | N | Y | Y | Y | Y | ? |
| 29 Schiff | Y | Y | Y | Y | Y | Y | Y |
| 30 Waxman | Y | Y | N | N | Y | Y | Y |
| 31 Becerra | Y | N | N | N | Y | N | Y |
| 32 Solis | Y | N | N | N | Y | N | Y |
| 33 Watson | Y | N | N | N | Y | N | Y |
| 34 Roybal-Allard | Y | N | N | N | Y | N | Y |
| 35 Waters | ? | N | N | N | Y | N | Y |
| 36 Harman | Y | Y | N | N | Y | Y | Y |
| 37 Millender-McD. | Y | Y | N | N | Y | N | Y |
| 38 Napolitano | Y | N | N | N | Y | N | Y |
| 39 Sánchez, Linda | Y | N | N | N | Y | Y | ? |
| 40 Royce | Y | Y | Y | Y | N | Y | Y |
| 41 Lewis | Y | Y | Y | Y | N | Y | Y |
| 42 Miller, Gary | Y | Y | Y | Y | N | Y | Y |
| 43 Baca | Y | Y | N | Y | Y | Y | Y |
| 44 Calvert | Y | Y | Y | Y | N | Y | Y |
| 45 Bono | Y | Y | Y | Y | N | Y | Y |
| 46 Rohrabacher | Y | N | Y | Y | N | Y | Y |
| 47 Sanchez, Loretta | N | Y | N | Y | Y | Y | Y |
| 48 Cox | Y | Y | Y | Y | N | Y | Y |
| 49 Issa | Y | N | Y | Y | N | Y | Y |
| 50 Cunningham | Y | Y | Y | N | Y | N | Y |
| 51 Filner | Y | Y | N | N | Y | N | Y |
| 52 Hunter | Y | Y | Y | Y | N | Y | Y |
| 53 Davis | Y | Y | Y | N | Y | Y | Y |
| **COLORADO** | | | | | | | |
| 1 DeGette | Y | N | N | N | Y | Y | Y |
| 2 Udall | Y | Y | Y | Y | Y | Y | Y |
| 3 Salazar | Y | Y | Y | Y | Y | Y | Y |
| 4 Musgrave | Y | Y | Y | Y | N | Y | Y |
| 5 Hefley | Y | Y | Y | Y | N | N | Y |
| 6 Tancredo | Y | Y | Y | Y | N | N | Y |
| 7 Beauprez | Y | Y | Y | Y | N | Y | Y |
| **CONNECTICUT** | | | | | | | |
| 1 Larson | Y | Y | N | N | Y | Y | Y |
| 2 Simmons | ? | Y | Y | N | Y | Y | Y |
| 3 DeLauro | Y | N | N | N | Y | Y | Y |
| 4 Shays | Y | Y | N | Y | N | Y | Y |
| 5 Johnson | Y | Y | Y | N | Y | Y | Y |
| **DELAWARE** | | | | | | | |
| AL Castle | Y | Y | Y | Y | N | Y | Y |
| **FLORIDA** | | | | | | | |
| 1 Miller | Y | Y | Y | Y | N | N | Y |
| 2 Boyd | Y | Y | Y | Y | Y | Y | Y |
| 3 Brown | Y | Y | N | N | Y | Y | Y |
| 4 Crenshaw | Y | Y | Y | Y | N | Y | Y |
| 5 Brown-Waite | Y | Y | Y | Y | N | Y | Y |
| 6 Stearns | Y | Y | Y | Y | N | Y | Y |
| 7 Mica | Y | Y | Y | Y | N | Y | Y |
| 8 Keller | Y | Y | Y | Y | N | Y | Y |
| 9 Bilirakis | Y | Y | Y | Y | N | Y | Y |
| 10 Young | Y | Y | Y | N | N | Y | Y |
| 11 Davis | Y | Y | Y | Y | Y | Y | ? |
| 12 Putnam | Y | Y | Y | Y | N | Y | Y |
| 13 Harris | Y | Y | Y | Y | N | Y | Y |
| 14 Mack | Y | Y | Y | Y | N | Y | Y |
| 15 Weldon | Y | Y | Y | Y | N | Y | Y |
| 16 Foley | Y | Y | Y | Y | N | Y | Y |
| 17 Meek | Y | Y | Y | Y | Y | Y | Y |
| 18 Ros-Lehtinen | Y | Y | Y | Y | N | Y | Y |
| 19 Wexler | Y | N | N | N | Y | N | Y |
| 20 Wasserman-Schultz | Y | N | Y | N | Y | N | Y |
| 21 Diaz-Balart, L. | Y | Y | Y | Y | N | Y | Y |
| 22 Shaw | Y | Y | Y | Y | N | Y | Y |
| 23 Hastings | Y | Y | N | N | Y | N | Y |
| 24 Feeney | Y | Y | Y | Y | N | Y | Y |
| 25 Diaz-Balart, M. | ? | Y | Y | Y | N | Y | Y |
| **GEORGIA** | | | | | | | |
| 1 Kingston | Y | Y | Y | Y | N | Y | Y |
| 2 Bishop | Y | Y | Y | Y | Y | Y | Y |
| 3 Marshall | Y | Y | Y | Y | Y | Y | Y |
| 4 McKinney | ? | N | N | N | Y | N | Y |
| 5 Lewis | Y | N | N | N | Y | N | Y |
| 6 Price | Y | Y | Y | Y | N | Y | Y |
| 7 Linder | Y | Y | Y | Y | N | Y | ? |
| 8 Westmoreland | Y | Y | Y | Y | N | Y | Y |
| 9 Norwood | Y | Y | Y | Y | N | Y | Y |
| 10 Deal | Y | Y | Y | Y | N | Y | Y |
| 11 Gingrey | Y | Y | Y | Y | N | Y | Y |
| 12 Barrow | Y | Y | Y | Y | Y | Y | Y |
| 13 Scott | Y | Y | Y | Y | Y | Y | Y |
| **HAWAII** | | | | | | | |
| 1 Abercrombie | Y | N | N | N | Y | N | Y |
| 2 Case | Y | Y | Y | Y | Y | Y | Y |
| **IDAHO** | | | | | | | |
| 1 Otter | Y | Y | Y | Y | N | N | Y |
| 2 Simpson | Y | Y | Y | Y | N | Y | Y |
| **ILLINOIS** | | | | | | | |
| 1 Rush | Y | N | N | N | Y | N | Y |
| 2 Jackson | Y | N | N | N | Y | N | Y |
| 3 Lipinski | Y | Y | Y | Y | Y | Y | Y |
| 4 Gutierrez | Y | N | N | N | Y | N | Y |
| 5 Emanuel | Y | Y | N | Y | Y | Y | Y |
| 6 Hyde | Y | N | Y | Y | N | Y | Y |
| 7 Davis | Y | N | N | N | Y | N | Y |
| 8 Bean | Y | Y | Y | Y | Y | Y | Y |
| 9 Schakowsky | Y | N | N | N | Y | N | Y |
| 10 Kirk | Y | Y | Y | Y | N | Y | Y |
| 11 Weller | Y | Y | Y | Y | N | Y | Y |
| 12 Costello | Y | Y | Y | N | Y | Y | Y |

**KEY**    Republicans    Democrats    *Independents*

| | | | |
|---|---|---|---|
| **Y** Voted for (yea) | **X** Paired against | **C** Voted "present" to avoid possible conflict of interest | |
| **#** Paired for | **–** Announced against | | |
| **+** Announced for | **P** Voted "present" | **?** Did not vote or otherwise make a position known | |
| **N** Voted against (nay) | | | |

| | 394 | 395 | 396 | 397 | 398 | 399 | 400 |
|---|---|---|---|---|---|---|---|
| 13 **Biggert** | Y | Y | Y | Y | N | Y | Y |
| 14 **Hastert** | | | | | | | |
| 15 **Johnson** | Y | Y | Y | Y | N | Y | Y |
| 16 **Manzullo** | Y | Y | Y | Y | N | Y | Y |
| 17 Evans | Y | Y | N | N | Y | Y | Y |
| 18 **LaHood** | Y | N | Y | Y | N | Y | Y |
| 19 **Shimkus** | Y | Y | Y | Y | N | Y | Y |
| **INDIANA** | | | | | | | |
| 1 Visclosky | Y | N | N | N | Y | N | Y |
| 2 **Chocola** | Y | Y | Y | Y | N | Y | Y |
| 3 **Souder** | Y | Y | Y | Y | N | Y | Y |
| 4 **Buyer** | Y | Y | Y | Y | N | Y | Y |
| 5 **Burton** | Y | Y | Y | Y | N | Y | Y |
| 6 **Pence** | Y | Y | Y | Y | N | Y | Y |
| 7 Carson | Y | Y | Y | N | Y | Y | Y |
| 8 **Hostettler** | Y | Y | Y | N | N | Y | Y |
| 9 **Sodrel** | Y | Y | Y | Y | N | Y | Y |
| **IOWA** | | | | | | | |
| 1 **Nussle** | Y | Y | Y | Y | N | Y | Y |
| 2 **Leach** | Y | Y | N | N | N | Y | Y |
| 3 Boswell | Y | Y | Y | Y | Y | Y | Y |
| 4 **Latham** | Y | Y | Y | Y | N | Y | Y |
| 5 **King** | Y | N | Y | Y | N | Y | Y |
| **KANSAS** | | | | | | | |
| 1 **Moran** | Y | Y | Y | Y | N | Y | Y |
| 2 **Ryun** | Y | Y | Y | Y | N | Y | Y |
| 3 Moore | Y | Y | Y | Y | Y | Y | Y |
| 4 **Tiahrt** | Y | N | Y | Y | N | Y | Y |
| **KENTUCKY** | | | | | | | |
| 1 **Whitfield** | Y | Y | Y | Y | N | Y | Y |
| 2 **Lewis** | Y | Y | Y | Y | N | Y | Y |
| 3 **Northup** | Y | Y | Y | Y | N | Y | Y |
| 4 **Davis** | Y | Y | Y | Y | N | Y | Y |
| 5 **Rogers** | Y | Y | Y | Y | N | Y | Y |
| 6 Chandler | Y | Y | Y | Y | Y | Y | Y |
| **LOUISIANA** | | | | | | | |
| 1 **Jindal** | ? | Y | Y | Y | N | Y | Y |
| 2 Jefferson | Y | N | N | N | Y | Y | Y |
| 3 Melancon | Y | Y | Y | Y | Y | Y | Y |
| 4 **McCrery** | Y | N | Y | Y | N | Y | Y |
| 5 **Alexander** | Y | Y | Y | Y | N | Y | Y |
| 6 **Baker** | Y | Y | Y | Y | N | Y | Y |
| 7 **Boustany** | Y | Y | Y | Y | N | Y | Y |
| **MAINE** | | | | | | | |
| 1 Allen | Y | Y | N | N | Y | Y | Y |
| 2 Michaud | Y | Y | N | N | Y | Y | Y |
| **MARYLAND** | | | | | | | |
| 1 **Gilchrest** | Y | N | Y | Y | N | Y | Y |
| 2 Ruppersberger | Y | Y | Y | Y | Y | Y | Y |
| 3 Cardin | Y | Y | Y | Y | Y | Y | Y |
| 4 Wynn | Y | N | Y | Y | Y | Y | Y |
| 5 Hoyer | Y | Y | Y | Y | Y | Y | Y |
| 6 **Bartlett** | Y | Y | P | P | N | N | Y |
| 7 Cummings | Y | ? | ? | ? | ? | ? | ? |
| 8 Van Hollen | Y | Y | N | N | Y | Y | Y |
| **MASSACHUSETTS** | | | | | | | |
| 1 Olver | Y | N | N | N | Y | N | Y |
| 2 Neal | Y | Y | N | N | Y | N | Y |
| 3 McGovern | Y | N | N | N | Y | N | Y |
| 4 Frank | Y | N | N | N | Y | N | Y |
| 5 Meehan | Y | Y | N | N | Y | N | Y |
| 6 Tierney | Y | N | N | N | Y | N | Y |
| 7 Markey | Y | Y | N | N | Y | N | Y |
| 8 Capuano | Y | N | N | N | Y | N | Y |
| 9 Lynch | Y | N | Y | N | Y | Y | Y |
| 10 Delahunt | Y | N | N | N | Y | N | Y |
| **MICHIGAN** | | | | | | | |
| 1 Stupak | Y | Y | N | N | Y | Y | Y |
| 2 **Hoekstra** | Y | Y | Y | Y | N | Y | Y |
| 3 **Ehlers** | Y | Y | P | Y | N | Y | Y |
| 4 **Camp** | Y | Y | Y | Y | N | Y | Y |
| 5 Kildee | Y | N | Y | N | Y | Y | Y |
| 6 **Upton** | Y | Y | Y | Y | N | Y | Y |
| 7 **Schwarz** | Y | Y | Y | Y | N | Y | Y |
| 8 **Rogers** | Y | Y | Y | Y | N | Y | Y |
| 9 **Knollenberg** | Y | N | Y | Y | N | Y | ? |
| 10 **Miller** | Y | Y | Y | Y | N | Y | Y |
| 11 **McCotter** | Y | Y | Y | Y | N | Y | Y |
| 12 Levin | Y | Y | N | N | Y | N | Y |
| 13 Kilpatrick | Y | N | N | N | Y | N | Y |
| 14 Conyers | Y | N | N | N | Y | N | Y |
| 15 Dingell | Y | N | N | N | Y | Y | Y |

| | 394 | 395 | 396 | 397 | 398 | 399 | 400 |
|---|---|---|---|---|---|---|---|
| **MINNESOTA** | | | | | | | |
| 1 **Gutknecht** | Y | Y | Y | Y | N | Y | Y |
| 2 **Kline** | Y | Y | Y | Y | N | Y | Y |
| 3 **Ramstad** | Y | Y | Y | Y | N | Y | Y |
| 4 McCollum | Y | N | N | N | Y | N | Y |
| 5 Sabo | Y | N | N | N | Y | N | Y |
| 6 **Kennedy** | Y | Y | Y | Y | N | Y | Y |
| 7 Peterson | Y | Y | Y | Y | Y | Y | Y |
| 8 Oberstar | Y | N | N | N | Y | N | Y |
| **MISSISSIPPI** | | | | | | | |
| 1 **Wicker** | Y | N | Y | Y | N | Y | Y |
| 2 Thompson | Y | N | N | N | Y | Y | Y |
| 3 **Pickering** | Y | Y | Y | Y | N | Y | Y |
| 4 Taylor | Y | Y | Y | Y | Y | N | Y |
| **MISSOURI** | | | | | | | |
| 1 Clay | Y | N | N | N | Y | N | Y |
| 2 **Akin** | Y | Y | Y | Y | N | Y | Y |
| 3 Carnahan | Y | Y | Y | Y | Y | Y | Y |
| 4 Skelton | Y | Y | Y | Y | Y | Y | Y |
| 5 Cleaver | Y | N | N | N | Y | Y | Y |
| 6 **Graves** | Y | Y | Y | Y | N | Y | Y |
| 7 **Blunt** | Y | Y | Y | Y | N | Y | Y |
| 8 **Emerson** | Y | Y | Y | Y | N | Y | Y |
| 9 **Hulshof** | Y | Y | Y | Y | N | Y | Y |
| **MONTANA** | | | | | | | |
| AL **Rehberg** | Y | Y | Y | Y | N | Y | Y |
| **NEBRASKA** | | | | | | | |
| 1 **Fortenberry** | Y | Y | Y | Y | N | Y | Y |
| 2 **Terry** | Y | Y | Y | Y | N | Y | Y |
| 3 **Osborne** | Y | Y | Y | Y | N | Y | Y |
| **NEVADA** | | | | | | | |
| 1 Berkley | Y | Y | Y | Y | Y | Y | Y |
| 2 **Gibbons** | Y | Y | Y | Y | N | Y | Y |
| 3 **Porter** | Y | Y | Y | Y | N | Y | Y |
| **NEW HAMPSHIRE** | | | | | | | |
| 1 **Bradley** | Y | Y | Y | Y | N | Y | Y |
| 2 **Bass** | Y | Y | Y | Y | N | Y | ? |
| **NEW JERSEY** | | | | | | | |
| 1 Andrews | Y | Y | Y | Y | Y | Y | Y |
| 2 **LoBiondo** | Y | Y | Y | Y | N | Y | Y |
| 3 **Saxton** | Y | Y | Y | Y | N | Y | Y |
| 4 **Smith** | Y | Y | Y | Y | N | Y | Y |
| 5 **Garrett** | Y | Y | Y | Y | N | Y | Y |
| 6 Pallone | Y | Y | N | N | Y | Y | Y |
| 7 **Ferguson** | Y | Y | Y | Y | N | Y | Y |
| 8 Pascrell | Y | N | N | N | Y | Y | Y |
| 9 Rothman | Y | N | N | N | Y | Y | Y |
| 10 Payne | Y | N | N | N | Y | N | Y |
| 11 **Frelinghuysen** | Y | Y | Y | Y | N | Y | Y |
| 12 Holt | Y | Y | N | N | Y | Y | Y |
| 13 Menendez | Y | Y | Y | Y | Y | Y | Y |
| **NEW MEXICO** | | | | | | | |
| 1 **Wilson** | Y | Y | Y | Y | N | Y | Y |
| 2 **Pearce** | Y | Y | Y | Y | N | Y | Y |
| 3 Udall | Y | Y | N | N | Y | Y | Y |
| **NEW YORK** | | | | | | | |
| 1 Bishop | Y | Y | Y | Y | Y | Y | Y |
| 2 Israel | Y | Y | Y | Y | Y | Y | Y |
| 3 **King** | Y | Y | Y | Y | N | Y | Y |
| 4 McCarthy | Y | Y | Y | Y | Y | Y | Y |
| 5 Ackerman | Y | N | N | N | Y | N | ? |
| 6 Meeks | Y | N | N | N | Y | Y | Y |
| 7 Crowley | Y | Y | N | N | Y | Y | Y |
| 8 Nadler | Y | Y | N | N | Y | N | Y |
| 9 Weiner | Y | Y | N | N | Y | Y | Y |
| 10 Towns | Y | Y | Y | N | Y | Y | Y |
| 11 Owens | Y | Y | N | N | Y | N | Y |
| 12 Velázquez | Y | Y | N | N | Y | N | Y |
| 13 **Fossella** | Y | Y | Y | Y | N | Y | Y |
| 14 Maloney | Y | Y | N | N | Y | N | Y |
| 15 Rangel | Y | Y | N | N | Y | Y | Y |
| 16 Serrano | Y | N | N | N | Y | N | Y |
| 17 Engel | Y | Y | Y | Y | Y | Y | Y |
| 18 Lowey | Y | N | N | N | Y | Y | Y |
| 19 **Kelly** | Y | Y | Y | Y | N | Y | Y |
| 20 **Sweeney** | Y | Y | Y | Y | N | Y | Y |
| 21 McNulty | Y | Y | N | N | Y | N | Y |
| 22 Hinchey | Y | Y | N | N | Y | N | Y |
| 23 **McHugh** | Y | Y | Y | Y | N | Y | Y |
| 24 **Boehlert** | Y | Y | Y | Y | N | Y | Y |
| 25 **Walsh** | Y | Y | Y | Y | N | Y | Y |
| 26 **Reynolds** | Y | Y | Y | Y | N | Y | Y |
| 27 Higgins | Y | Y | Y | Y | Y | Y | ? |
| 28 Slaughter | Y | N | N | N | Y | N | Y |
| 29 **Kuhl** | Y | Y | Y | Y | N | Y | Y |

| | 394 | 395 | 396 | 397 | 398 | 399 | 400 |
|---|---|---|---|---|---|---|---|
| **NORTH CAROLINA** | | | | | | | |
| 1 Butterfield | Y | Y | Y | Y | Y | Y | Y |
| 2 Etheridge | Y | Y | Y | Y | Y | Y | Y |
| 3 **Jones** | Y | N | Y | P | Y | N | Y |
| 4 Price | Y | N | N | N | Y | Y | Y |
| 5 **Foxx** | Y | Y | Y | Y | N | Y | Y |
| 6 **Coble** | Y | Y | Y | Y | N | Y | ? |
| 7 McIntyre | Y | Y | Y | Y | Y | Y | Y |
| 8 **Hayes** | Y | N | Y | Y | N | Y | Y |
| 9 **Myrick** | Y | Y | Y | Y | N | Y | Y |
| 10 **McHenry** | Y | Y | Y | Y | N | Y | Y |
| 11 **Taylor** | Y | Y | Y | Y | N | Y | Y |
| 12 Watt | Y | N | N | N | Y | N | Y |
| 13 Miller | Y | Y | Y | N | Y | Y | Y |
| **NORTH DAKOTA** | | | | | | | |
| AL Pomeroy | Y | Y | Y | Y | Y | Y | Y |
| **OHIO** | | | | | | | |
| 1 **Chabot** | Y | Y | Y | Y | N | Y | Y |
| 2 Vacant | | | | | | | |
| 3 **Turner** | Y | N | Y | Y | N | Y | Y |
| 4 **Oxley** | Y | Y | Y | Y | N | Y | Y |
| 5 **Gillmor** | Y | Y | Y | Y | N | Y | Y |
| 6 Strickland | Y | Y | N | N | Y | Y | Y |
| 7 **Hobson** | Y | N | Y | Y | N | Y | Y |
| 8 **Boehner** | Y | Y | Y | Y | N | Y | Y |
| 9 Kaptur | Y | N | N | N | Y | Y | Y |
| 10 Kucinich | Y | N | N | N | Y | N | Y |
| 11 Jones | Y | Y | N | N | Y | Y | Y |
| 12 **Tiberi** | Y | Y | Y | Y | N | Y | Y |
| 13 Brown | Y | Y | N | N | Y | Y | Y |
| 14 **LaTourette** | Y | Y | Y | Y | N | Y | Y |
| 15 **Pryce** | Y | Y | Y | Y | N | Y | Y |
| 16 **Regula** | Y | Y | Y | Y | N | Y | Y |
| 17 Ryan | Y | N | Y | N | Y | Y | Y |
| 18 **Ney** | Y | Y | Y | Y | N | Y | Y |
| **OKLAHOMA** | | | | | | | |
| 1 **Sullivan** | Y | Y | Y | Y | N | Y | Y |
| 2 Boren | Y | Y | Y | Y | Y | Y | Y |
| 3 **Lucas** | Y | Y | Y | Y | N | Y | Y |
| 4 **Cole** | Y | Y | Y | Y | N | Y | Y |
| 5 **Istook** | Y | Y | Y | Y | N | Y | Y |
| **OREGON** | | | | | | | |
| 1 Wu | Y | Y | Y | N | Y | N | Y |
| 2 **Walden** | Y | Y | Y | Y | N | Y | Y |
| 3 Blumenauer | Y | N | N | N | Y | Y | Y |
| 4 DeFazio | Y | Y | Y | N | Y | N | Y |
| 5 Hooley | Y | Y | Y | N | Y | Y | Y |
| **PENNSYLVANIA** | | | | | | | |
| 1 Brady | Y | Y | N | N | Y | Y | Y |
| 2 Fattah | Y | Y | N | N | Y | Y | Y |
| 3 **English** | Y | Y | Y | Y | N | Y | Y |
| 4 **Hart** | Y | Y | Y | Y | N | Y | Y |
| 5 **Peterson** | Y | Y | Y | Y | N | Y | Y |
| 6 **Gerlach** | Y | Y | Y | Y | N | Y | Y |
| 7 **Weldon** | Y | Y | Y | Y | N | Y | Y |
| 8 **Fitzpatrick** | Y | Y | Y | Y | N | Y | Y |
| 9 **Shuster** | Y | Y | Y | Y | N | Y | Y |
| 10 **Sherwood** | Y | N | Y | Y | N | Y | Y |
| 11 Kanjorski | Y | N | N | N | Y | Y | Y |
| 12 Murtha | Y | N | N | N | Y | Y | Y |
| 13 Schwartz | Y | Y | Y | Y | Y | Y | Y |
| 14 Doyle | Y | N | N | N | Y | Y | Y |
| 15 **Dent** | Y | Y | Y | Y | N | Y | Y |
| 16 **Pitts** | Y | Y | Y | Y | N | Y | Y |
| 17 Holden | Y | Y | N | N | Y | Y | Y |
| 18 **Murphy** | Y | Y | Y | Y | N | Y | Y |
| 19 **Platts** | Y | Y | Y | Y | N | Y | Y |
| **RHODE ISLAND** | | | | | | | |
| 1 Kennedy | Y | Y | N | Y | Y | Y | Y |
| 2 Langevin | Y | Y | Y | Y | Y | Y | Y |
| **SOUTH CAROLINA** | | | | | | | |
| 1 **Brown** | ? | ? | ? | ? | ? | ? | ? |
| 2 **Wilson** | Y | Y | Y | Y | N | Y | Y |
| 3 **Barrett** | Y | N | Y | Y | N | Y | Y |
| 4 **Inglis** | Y | Y | Y | Y | N | Y | Y |
| 5 Spratt | Y | Y | Y | Y | Y | Y | Y |
| 6 Clyburn | Y | Y | Y | Y | Y | Y | Y |
| **SOUTH DAKOTA** | | | | | | | |
| AL Herseth | Y | Y | Y | Y | Y | Y | Y |
| **TENNESSEE** | | | | | | | |
| 1 **Jenkins** | Y | Y | Y | Y | N | Y | Y |
| 2 **Duncan** | Y | Y | Y | N | N | N | Y |

| | 394 | 395 | 396 | 397 | 398 | 399 | 400 |
|---|---|---|---|---|---|---|---|
| 3 **Wamp** | Y | Y | Y | N | N | Y | Y |
| 4 Davis | Y | Y | Y | Y | Y | Y | Y |
| 5 Cooper | Y | Y | Y | Y | Y | Y | Y |
| 6 Gordon | Y | Y | Y | Y | Y | Y | Y |
| 7 **Blackburn** | Y | Y | Y | Y | N | Y | Y |
| 8 Tanner | Y | Y | Y | Y | Y | Y | Y |
| 9 Ford | Y | Y | Y | Y | Y | Y | Y |
| **TEXAS** | | | | | | | |
| 1 **Gohmert** | Y | Y | Y | Y | N | Y | Y |
| 2 **Poe** | Y | Y | Y | Y | N | Y | Y |
| 3 **Johnson, S.** | Y | Y | Y | Y | N | Y | Y |
| 4 **Hall** | Y | Y | Y | Y | N | Y | Y |
| 5 **Hensarling** | Y | Y | Y | Y | N | Y | Y |
| 6 **Barton** | Y | Y | Y | Y | N | Y | Y |
| 7 **Culberson** | Y | Y | Y | Y | N | Y | Y |
| 8 **Brady** | ? | Y | Y | Y | N | Y | Y |
| 9 Green, A. | Y | Y | N | N | Y | Y | Y |
| 10 **McCaul** | Y | Y | Y | Y | N | Y | Y |
| 11 **Conaway** | Y | Y | Y | Y | N | Y | Y |
| 12 **Granger** | Y | Y | Y | Y | N | Y | ? |
| 13 **Thornberry** | Y | Y | Y | Y | N | Y | Y |
| 14 **Paul** | N | N | N | N | Y | N | N |
| 15 Hinojosa | ? | ? | ? | ? | ? | ? | ? |
| 16 Reyes | Y | Y | Y | Y | Y | Y | Y |
| 17 Edwards | Y | Y | Y | Y | Y | Y | Y |
| 18 Jackson-Lee | Y | Y | N | N | Y | Y | Y |
| 19 **Neugebauer** | Y | Y | Y | Y | N | Y | Y |
| 20 Gonzalez | Y | Y | N | Y | Y | Y | Y |
| 21 **Smith** | Y | Y | Y | Y | N | Y | Y |
| 22 **DeLay** | Y | Y | Y | Y | N | Y | Y |
| 23 **Bonilla** | Y | Y | Y | Y | N | Y | Y |
| 24 **Marchant** | Y | Y | Y | Y | N | Y | Y |
| 25 Doggett | Y | N | N | N | Y | N | Y |
| 26 **Burgess** | Y | Y | Y | Y | N | Y | Y |
| 27 Ortiz | Y | Y | Y | Y | Y | Y | Y |
| 28 Cuellar | Y | Y | Y | Y | Y | Y | Y |
| 29 Green, G. | Y | Y | Y | Y | Y | Y | Y |
| 30 Johnson, E. | Y | N | N | Y | Y | Y | Y |
| 31 **Carter** | Y | Y | Y | Y | N | Y | Y |
| 32 **Sessions** | Y | Y | Y | Y | N | Y | Y |
| **UTAH** | | | | | | | |
| 1 **Bishop** | Y | Y | Y | Y | N | Y | Y |
| 2 Matheson | Y | Y | Y | Y | Y | Y | Y |
| 3 **Cannon** | Y | Y | Y | Y | N | Y | Y |
| **VERMONT** | | | | | | | |
| AL *Sanders* | Y | N | N | N | Y | N | Y |
| **VIRGINIA** | | | | | | | |
| 1 **Davis, J.** | Y | Y | Y | Y | N | Y | Y |
| 2 **Drake** | Y | Y | Y | Y | N | Y | Y |
| 3 Scott | Y | Y | N | N | Y | N | Y |
| 4 **Forbes** | Y | Y | Y | Y | N | Y | Y |
| 5 **Goode** | Y | Y | Y | Y | N | N | Y |
| 6 **Goodlatte** | Y | Y | Y | Y | N | Y | Y |
| 7 **Cantor** | ? | Y | Y | Y | N | Y | Y |
| 8 Moran | Y | N | N | N | Y | N | Y |
| 9 Boucher | Y | N | N | Y | Y | Y | Y |
| 10 **Wolf** | Y | Y | Y | Y | N | Y | Y |
| 11 **Davis, T.** | Y | Y | Y | Y | N | Y | Y |
| **WASHINGTON** | | | | | | | |
| 1 Inslee | Y | N | N | N | Y | N | Y |
| 2 Larsen | Y | Y | Y | N | Y | Y | Y |
| 3 Baird | Y | N | Y | Y | Y | Y | Y |
| 4 **Hastings** | Y | Y | Y | Y | N | Y | Y |
| 5 **McMorris** | Y | Y | Y | Y | N | Y | Y |
| 6 Dicks | Y | Y | Y | Y | Y | ? | ? |
| 7 McDermott | Y | N | N | N | Y | N | Y |
| 8 **Reichert** | Y | Y | Y | Y | N | Y | Y |
| 9 Smith | Y | N | Y | N | Y | Y | ? |
| **WEST VIRGINIA** | | | | | | | |
| 1 Mollohan | Y | N | N | N | Y | Y | Y |
| 2 **Capito** | Y | Y | Y | Y | N | Y | Y |
| 3 Rahall | Y | N | N | N | Y | N | Y |
| **WISCONSIN** | | | | | | | |
| 1 **Ryan** | Y | Y | Y | Y | N | Y | Y |
| 2 Baldwin | Y | N | N | N | Y | N | Y |
| 3 Kind | Y | Y | Y | Y | Y | N | Y |
| 4 Moore | Y | N | N | N | Y | Y | Y |
| 5 **Sensenbrenner** | Y | Y | Y | Y | N | N | Y |
| 6 **Petri** | Y | Y | Y | Y | N | Y | Y |
| 7 Obey | Y | N | N | N | Y | N | Y |
| 8 **Green** | Y | Y | Y | Y | N | Y | Y |
| **WYOMING** | | | | | | | |
| AL **Cubin** | Y | Y | Y | Y | N | Y | Y |

# IN THE HOUSE | By Vote Number

**401.** HR 3199. **"Patriot Act" Reauthorization/Previous Question.**
Gingrey, R-Ga., motion to order the previous question (thus ending debate and possibility of amendment) on adoption of the rule (H Res 369) to provide for House floor consideration of the bill that would reauthorize 16 expiring provisions of the 2001 anti-terrorism law known as the Patriot Act. Motion agreed to 224-197: R 224-0; D 0-196 (ND 0-148, SD 0-48); I 0-1. July 21, 2005.

**402.** HR 3199. **"Patriot Act" Reauthorization/Rule.** Adoption of the rule (H Res 369) that would provide for House consideration of the bill that would reauthorize 16 expiring provisions of the 2001 anti-terrorism law known as the Patriot Act. Adopted 224-196: R 224-0; D 0-195 (ND 0-147, SD 0-48); I 0-1. July 21, 2005.

**403.** HR 3199. **"Patriot Act" Reauthorization/Library or Bookstore Records.** Flake, R-Ariz., amendment that would require the FBI director to personally approve a request for library or bookstore records under the business records provision of law known as the Patriot Act. Adopted 402-26: R 201-26; D 200-0 (ND 151-0, SD 49-0); I 1-0. July 21, 2005.

**404.** HR 3199. **"Patriot Act" Reauthorization/Roving Wiretaps.** Issa, R-Calif., amendment that would require authorities to notify the issuing judge of a venue change of a surveillance facility or place within 15 days or at the earliest reasonable time as determined by the court. It also would require authorities to specify the total number of electronic surveillances that have been or are being carried out. Adopted 406-21: R 205-21; D 200-0 (ND 151-0, SD 49-0); I 1-0. July 21, 2005.

**405.** HR 3199. **"Patriot Act" Reauthorization/Violence Against Rail and Mass Transit.** Capito, R-W.Va., amendment that would authorize up to 20 years in prison for individuals who commit terrorist or other violent attacks on land, water or air against railroad and mass transportation systems. It would provide a minimum sentence of 30 years if the vehicle attacked is carrying spent nuclear fuel or high-level radioactive waste, and a mandatory life sentence, with the possibility of the death penalty, if the attack results in the death of a person. Adopted 362-66: R 226-1; D 135-65 (ND 92-59, SD 43-6); I 1-0. July 21, 2005.

**406.** HR 3199. **"Patriot Act" Reauthorization/National Security Letter.** Flake, R-Ariz., amendment that would specify that the recipient of a national security letter may consult with an attorney and challenge the letter in court. It would authorize a judge to throw out the letter if complying with the request would be "unreasonable or oppressive." It would allow the letter recipient to challenge the non-disclosure requirements of the request in court. Adopted 394-32: R 197-28; D 196-4 (ND 148-3, SD 48-1); I 1-0. July 21, 2005.

**407.** HR 3199. **"Patriot Act" Reauthorization/Forfeiture of Assets.**
Delahunt, D-Mass., amendment that would raise the threshold for authorities to seize assets of suspected terrorists. It would allow assets to be seized only for those specifically accused of terrorist crimes. Adopted 418-7: R 218-7; D 199-0 (ND 151-0, SD 48-0); I 1-0. July 21, 2005.

| | 401 | 402 | 403 | 404 | 405 | 406 | 407 |
|---|---|---|---|---|---|---|---|
| **ALABAMA** | | | | | | | |
| 1 Bonner | Y | Y | Y | Y | Y | N | Y |
| 2 Everett | Y | Y | Y | N | Y | N | Y |
| 3 Rogers | Y | Y | Y | Y | Y | N | Y |
| 4 Aderholt | Y | Y | Y | Y | Y | N | Y |
| 5 Cramer | N | N | Y | Y | Y | Y | Y |
| 6 Bachus | Y | Y | N | N | Y | N | Y |
| 7 Davis | N | N | Y | Y | Y | Y | Y |
| **ALASKA** | | | | | | | |
| AL Young | Y | Y | Y | Y | Y | Y | Y |
| **ARIZONA** | | | | | | | |
| 1 Renzi | Y | Y | N | Y | Y | N | Y |
| 2 Franks | Y | Y | Y | Y | Y | N | Y |
| 3 Shadegg | Y | Y | N | Y | Y | N | Y |
| 4 Pastor | N | N | Y | N | Y | N | Y |
| 5 Hayworth | Y | Y | Y | Y | Y | N | Y |
| 6 Flake | Y | Y | Y | Y | Y | Y | Y |
| 7 Grijalva | N | N | Y | Y | N | Y | Y |
| 8 Kolbe | Y | Y | Y | Y | Y | Y | Y |
| **ARKANSAS** | | | | | | | |
| 1 Berry | N | N | Y | Y | Y | Y | Y |
| 2 Snyder | N | N | Y | Y | Y | Y | Y |
| 3 Boozman | Y | Y | Y | Y | Y | N | Y |
| 4 Ross | N | N | Y | Y | Y | Y | Y |
| **CALIFORNIA** | | | | | | | |
| 1 Thompson | N | N | Y | Y | Y | Y | Y |
| 2 Herger | Y | Y | Y | Y | Y | N | Y |
| 3 Lungren | Y | Y | Y | Y | Y | N | Y |
| 4 Doolittle | Y | Y | Y | Y | Y | N | Y |
| 5 Matsui, D. | N | N | Y | Y | Y | Y | Y |
| 6 Woolsey | N | N | Y | N | Y | N | Y |
| 7 Miller, George | N | N | Y | Y | Y | N | Y |
| 8 Pelosi | N | N | Y | Y | Y | Y | Y |
| 9 Lee | N | N | Y | Y | Y | N | Y |
| 10 Tauscher | N | N | Y | Y | Y | Y | Y |
| 11 Pombo | Y | Y | Y | Y | Y | N | Y |
| 12 Lantos | N | N | Y | Y | Y | Y | Y |
| 13 Stark | N | N | Y | Y | N | Y | Y |
| 14 Eshoo | N | N | Y | Y | Y | Y | Y |
| 15 Honda | N | N | Y | N | Y | N | Y |
| 16 Lofgren | N | N | Y | Y | Y | Y | Y |
| 17 Farr | N | N | Y | N | Y | N | Y |
| 18 Cardoza | N | N | Y | Y | Y | Y | Y |
| 19 Radanovich | Y | Y | Y | Y | Y | N | Y |
| 20 Costa | N | N | Y | Y | Y | Y | Y |
| 21 Nunes | Y | Y | Y | Y | Y | N | Y |
| 22 Thomas | Y | Y | N | Y | Y | Y | Y |
| 23 Capps | N | N | Y | Y | Y | Y | Y |
| 24 Gallegly | Y | Y | Y | Y | Y | N | Y |
| 25 McKeon | Y | Y | Y | Y | Y | N | Y |
| 26 Dreier | Y | Y | Y | Y | Y | N | Y |
| 27 Sherman | N | N | Y | Y | Y | Y | Y |
| 28 Berman | N | N | Y | Y | Y | Y | Y |
| 29 Schiff | N | N | Y | Y | Y | Y | Y |
| 30 Waxman | N | N | Y | Y | N | Y | Y |
| 31 Becerra | N | N | Y | Y | Y | Y | Y |
| 32 Solis | N | N | Y | Y | Y | Y | Y |
| 33 Watson | N | N | Y | Y | Y | N | Y |
| 34 Roybal-Allard | N | N | Y | Y | Y | Y | Y |
| 35 Waters | N | N | Y | Y | N | Y | Y |
| 36 Harman | N | N | Y | Y | Y | Y | Y |
| 37 Millender-McD. | N | N | Y | Y | Y | Y | Y |
| 38 Napolitano | N | N | Y | Y | Y | Y | Y |
| 39 Sánchez, Linda | N | N | Y | Y | N | Y | Y |
| 40 Royce | Y | Y | Y | Y | Y | Y | Y |
| 41 Lewis | Y | Y | N | Y | Y | N | Y |
| 42 Miller, Gary | Y | Y | Y | Y | Y | Y | Y |
| 43 Baca | N | N | Y | Y | Y | Y | Y |
| 44 Calvert | Y | Y | N | Y | Y | Y | Y |
| 45 Bono | Y | Y | N | N | Y | N | N |
| 46 Rohrabacher | Y | P | Y | Y | Y | N | N |
| 47 Sanchez, Loretta | N | N | Y | Y | Y | Y | Y |
| 48 Cox | Y | Y | ? | ? | ? | ? | ? |
| 49 Issa | Y | Y | Y | Y | Y | Y | Y |
| 50 Cunningham | Y | Y | Y | Y | Y | Y | Y |
| 51 Filner | N | N | Y | Y | N | Y | Y |
| 52 Hunter | Y | Y | Y | N | Y | N | N |
| 53 Davis | N | N | Y | Y | Y | Y | Y |
| **COLORADO** | | | | | | | |
| 1 DeGette | N | N | Y | Y | N | Y | Y |
| 2 Udall | N | N | Y | Y | Y | Y | Y |
| 3 Salazar | N | N | Y | Y | Y | Y | Y |
| 4 Musgrave | Y | Y | Y | Y | Y | N | Y |
| 5 Hefley | Y | Y | Y | N | Y | N | Y |
| 6 Tancredo | Y | Y | Y | Y | Y | N | Y |
| 7 Beauprez | Y | Y | Y | Y | Y | Y | Y |
| **CONNECTICUT** | | | | | | | |
| 1 Larson | N | N | Y | Y | Y | Y | Y |
| 2 Simmons | Y | Y | Y | Y | Y | N | Y |
| 3 DeLauro | Y | Y | Y | Y | Y | Y | Y |
| 4 Shays | Y | Y | Y | Y | Y | Y | Y |
| 5 Johnson | Y | Y | Y | Y | Y | ? | Y |
| **DELAWARE** | | | | | | | |
| AL Castle | Y | Y | Y | Y | Y | Y | Y |
| **FLORIDA** | | | | | | | |
| 1 Miller | Y | Y | + | Y | Y | Y | Y |
| 2 Boyd | N | N | Y | Y | Y | Y | Y |
| 3 Brown | N | N | Y | Y | Y | Y | ? |
| 4 Crenshaw | Y | Y | Y | Y | Y | N | Y |
| 5 Brown-Waite | Y | Y | Y | Y | Y | N | Y |
| 6 Stearns | Y | Y | Y | Y | Y | N | Y |
| 7 Mica | Y | Y | Y | Y | Y | ? | Y |
| 8 Keller | Y | Y | Y | Y | Y | N | Y |
| 9 Bilirakis | Y | Y | Y | Y | Y | N | Y |
| 10 Young | Y | Y | Y | Y | Y | N | Y |
| 11 Davis | N | N | Y | Y | Y | Y | Y |
| 12 Putnam | Y | Y | Y | Y | Y | N | Y |
| 13 Harris | Y | Y | Y | Y | Y | N | Y |
| 14 Mack | Y | Y | Y | Y | Y | N | Y |
| 15 Weldon | Y | Y | Y | Y | Y | N | Y |
| 16 Foley | Y | Y | Y | Y | Y | N | Y |
| 17 Meek | Y | Y | Y | Y | Y | N | Y |
| 18 Ros-Lehtinen | Y | Y | ? | Y | Y | Y | Y |
| 19 Wexler | N | N | Y | Y | Y | Y | Y |
| 20 Wasserman-Schultz | N | N | Y | Y | N | Y | Y |
| 21 Diaz-Balart, L. | Y | Y | Y | Y | Y | Y | Y |
| 22 Shaw | Y | Y | Y | Y | Y | Y | Y |
| 23 Hastings | ? | ? | ? | ? | ? | ? | ? |
| 24 Feeney | Y | Y | Y | Y | Y | N | Y |
| 25 Diaz-Balart, M. | Y | Y | Y | Y | Y | Y | Y |
| **GEORGIA** | | | | | | | |
| 1 Kingston | Y | Y | Y | Y | Y | Y | Y |
| 2 Bishop | N | N | Y | Y | Y | Y | Y |
| 3 Marshall | N | N | Y | Y | Y | Y | Y |
| 4 McKinney | N | N | Y | Y | N | N | Y |
| 5 Lewis | N | N | Y | Y | Y | N | Y |
| 6 Price | Y | Y | Y | Y | Y | N | Y |
| 7 Linder | Y | Y | N | Y | Y | N | Y |
| 8 Westmoreland | Y | Y | N | Y | Y | N | Y |
| 9 Norwood | Y | Y | Y | Y | Y | N | Y |
| 10 Deal | Y | Y | Y | Y | Y | N | Y |
| 11 Gingrey | Y | Y | Y | Y | Y | N | Y |
| 12 Barrow | N | N | Y | Y | Y | Y | Y |
| 13 Scott | N | N | Y | Y | Y | Y | Y |
| **HAWAII** | | | | | | | |
| 1 Abercrombie | N | N | Y | Y | N | Y | Y |
| 2 Case | N | N | Y | Y | Y | Y | Y |
| **IDAHO** | | | | | | | |
| 1 Otter | Y | P | Y | Y | Y | Y | Y |
| 2 Simpson | Y | Y | Y | Y | Y | Y | Y |
| **ILLINOIS** | | | | | | | |
| 1 Rush | N | N | Y | Y | N | Y | Y |
| 2 Jackson | N | N | Y | Y | N | Y | Y |
| 3 Lipinski | N | N | Y | Y | Y | Y | Y |
| 4 Gutierrez | N | ? | Y | Y | N | Y | Y |
| 5 Emanuel | N | N | Y | Y | Y | Y | Y |
| 6 Hyde | ? | ? | Y | Y | Y | N | Y |
| 7 Davis | N | N | Y | Y | N | Y | Y |
| 8 Bean | N | N | Y | Y | Y | Y | Y |
| 9 Schakowsky | N | N | Y | Y | N | Y | Y |
| 10 Kirk | Y | Y | Y | Y | Y | Y | Y |
| 11 Weller | Y | Y | Y | Y | Y | N | Y |
| 12 Costello | N | N | Y | Y | N | Y | Y |

| KEY | **Republicans** | Democrats | *Independents* | |
|---|---|---|---|---|
| Y | Voted for (yea) | X | Paired against | C Voted "present" to avoid possible conflict of interest |
| # | Paired for | – | Announced against | |
| + | Announced for | P | Voted "present" | ? Did not vote or otherwise make a position known |
| N | Voted against (nay) | | | |

| | 401 | 402 | 403 | 404 | 405 | 406 | 407 |
|---|---|---|---|---|---|---|---|
| 13 **Biggert** | Y | Y | N | N | Y | Y | Y |
| 14 **Hastert** | | | | | | | |
| 15 **Johnson** | Y | Y | Y | Y | Y | Y | Y |
| 16 **Manzullo** | Y | Y | Y | Y | Y | Y | Y |
| 17 Evans | N | N | Y | Y | Y | Y | Y |
| 18 **LaHood** | Y | Y | Y | Y | Y | N | Y |
| 19 **Shimkus** | Y | Y | Y | Y | Y | Y | Y |
| **INDIANA** | | | | | | | |
| 1 Visclosky | N | N | Y | Y | N | Y | Y |
| 2 **Chocola** | Y | Y | Y | Y | Y | Y | Y |
| 3 **Souder** | Y | Y | N | N | Y | N | Y |
| 4 **Buyer** | Y | Y | N | N | Y | Y | Y |
| 5 **Burton** | Y | Y | N | ? | Y | Y | Y |
| 6 **Pence** | Y | Y | Y | Y | Y | Y | Y |
| 7 Carson | N | N | Y | Y | N | Y | Y |
| 8 **Hostettler** | Y | Y | N | Y | Y | N | Y |
| 9 **Sodrel** | Y | Y | Y | Y | Y | Y | Y |
| **IOWA** | | | | | | | |
| 1 **Nussle** | Y | Y | Y | Y | Y | Y | Y |
| 2 **Leach** | Y | Y | Y | Y | Y | Y | Y |
| 3 Boswell | N | N | Y | Y | Y | Y | Y |
| 4 **Latham** | Y | Y | Y | Y | Y | Y | Y |
| 5 **King** | Y | Y | Y | Y | Y | Y | Y |
| **KANSAS** | | | | | | | |
| 1 **Moran** | Y | Y | Y | Y | Y | Y | Y |
| 2 **Ryun** | Y | Y | Y | Y | Y | N | Y |
| 3 Moore | N | N | Y | Y | Y | Y | Y |
| 4 **Tiahrt** | Y | Y | N | N | Y | N | Y |
| **KENTUCKY** | | | | | | | |
| 1 **Whitfield** | Y | Y | Y | Y | Y | N | Y |
| 2 **Lewis** | Y | Y | Y | Y | Y | Y | Y |
| 3 **Northup** | Y | Y | Y | Y | Y | Y | Y |
| 4 **Davis** | Y | Y | N | N | Y | Y | Y |
| 5 **Rogers** | ? | Y | Y | Y | Y | Y | Y |
| 6 Chandler | N | N | Y | Y | Y | Y | Y |
| **LOUISIANA** | | | | | | | |
| 1 **Jindal** | Y | Y | Y | Y | Y | Y | Y |
| 2 Jefferson | N | N | Y | Y | Y | Y | Y |
| 3 Melancon | N | N | Y | Y | Y | Y | Y |
| 4 **McCrery** | Y | Y | Y | Y | Y | Y | Y |
| 5 **Alexander** | Y | Y | Y | Y | Y | Y | Y |
| 6 **Baker** | Y | Y | Y | Y | Y | Y | Y |
| 7 **Boustany** | Y | Y | Y | Y | Y | Y | Y |
| **MAINE** | | | | | | | |
| 1 Allen | N | N | Y | Y | N | Y | Y |
| 2 Michaud | N | N | Y | Y | N | Y | Y |
| **MARYLAND** | | | | | | | |
| 1 **Gilchrest** | Y | Y | Y | Y | Y | Y | Y |
| 2 Ruppersberger | N | N | Y | Y | Y | Y | Y |
| 3 Cardin | N | N | Y | Y | Y | Y | Y |
| 4 Wynn | N | N | Y | Y | Y | Y | Y |
| 5 Hoyer | N | N | Y | Y | Y | Y | Y |
| 6 **Bartlett** | Y | Y | Y | Y | Y | Y | Y |
| 7 Cummings | N | N | Y | Y | N | Y | Y |
| 8 Van Hollen | N | N | Y | Y | Y | Y | Y |
| **MASSACHUSETTS** | | | | | | | |
| 1 Olver | N | N | Y | Y | N | Y | Y |
| 2 Neal | N | N | Y | Y | N | Y | Y |
| 3 McGovern | N | N | Y | Y | N | Y | Y |
| 4 Frank | N | N | Y | Y | N | Y | Y |
| 5 Meehan | N | N | Y | Y | N | Y | Y |
| 6 Tierney | N | N | Y | Y | N | Y | Y |
| 7 Markey | N | N | Y | Y | N | Y | Y |
| 8 Capuano | N | N | Y | Y | N | Y | Y |
| 9 Lynch | N | N | Y | Y | Y | Y | Y |
| 10 Delahunt | N | N | Y | Y | N | Y | Y |
| **MICHIGAN** | | | | | | | |
| 1 Stupak | N | N | Y | Y | Y | Y | Y |
| 2 **Hoekstra** | Y | Y | N | Y | Y | Y | ? |
| 3 **Ehlers** | Y | Y | Y | Y | Y | Y | Y |
| 4 **Camp** | Y | Y | Y | Y | Y | Y | Y |
| 5 Kildee | N | N | Y | Y | Y | Y | Y |
| 6 **Upton** | Y | Y | Y | Y | Y | Y | Y |
| 7 **Schwarz** | Y | Y | Y | Y | Y | Y | Y |
| 8 **Rogers** | Y | Y | N | N | Y | N | N |
| 9 **Knollenberg** | Y | Y | Y | Y | Y | Y | Y |
| 10 **Miller** | Y | Y | Y | Y | Y | Y | Y |
| 11 **McCotter** | Y | Y | Y | Y | Y | Y | Y |
| 12 Levin | N | N | Y | Y | Y | Y | Y |
| 13 Kilpatrick | N | N | Y | Y | Y | N | Y |
| 14 Conyers | N | N | Y | Y | N | N | Y |
| 15 Dingell | N | N | Y | Y | Y | Y | Y |
| **MINNESOTA** | | | | | | | |
| 1 **Gutknecht** | Y | Y | Y | Y | Y | Y | Y |
| 2 **Kline** | Y | Y | Y | Y | Y | Y | Y |
| 3 **Ramstad** | Y | Y | Y | Y | Y | Y | Y |
| 4 McCollum | N | N | Y | Y | N | Y | Y |
| 5 Sabo | N | N | Y | Y | N | Y | Y |
| 6 **Kennedy** | Y | Y | Y | Y | Y | Y | Y |
| 7 Peterson | N | N | Y | Y | Y | Y | Y |
| 8 Oberstar | N | N | Y | Y | Y | Y | Y |
| **MISSISSIPPI** | | | | | | | |
| 1 **Wicker** | Y | Y | Y | Y | Y | Y | Y |
| 2 Thompson | N | N | Y | Y | Y | Y | Y |
| 3 **Pickering** | Y | Y | Y | Y | Y | Y | Y |
| 4 Taylor | N | N | Y | Y | Y | Y | Y |
| **MISSOURI** | | | | | | | |
| 1 Clay | N | N | Y | Y | N | Y | Y |
| 2 **Akin** | Y | Y | Y | Y | Y | Y | Y |
| 3 Carnahan | N | N | Y | Y | Y | Y | Y |
| 4 Skelton | N | N | Y | Y | Y | Y | Y |
| 5 Cleaver | N | N | Y | Y | N | Y | Y |
| 6 **Graves** | Y | Y | Y | Y | Y | Y | Y |
| 7 **Blunt** | Y | Y | Y | Y | Y | Y | Y |
| 8 **Emerson** | Y | Y | Y | Y | Y | Y | Y |
| 9 **Hulshof** | Y | Y | Y | Y | Y | Y | Y |
| **MONTANA** | | | | | | | |
| AL **Rehberg** | Y | Y | Y | Y | Y | Y | Y |
| **NEBRASKA** | | | | | | | |
| 1 **Fortenberry** | Y | Y | Y | Y | Y | Y | Y |
| 2 **Terry** | Y | Y | Y | Y | Y | Y | Y |
| 3 **Osborne** | Y | Y | Y | Y | Y | Y | Y |
| **NEVADA** | | | | | | | |
| 1 Berkley | N | N | Y | Y | Y | Y | Y |
| 2 **Gibbons** | Y | Y | Y | Y | Y | Y | Y |
| 3 **Porter** | Y | Y | Y | Y | Y | Y | Y |
| **NEW HAMPSHIRE** | | | | | | | |
| 1 **Bradley** | Y | Y | Y | Y | Y | Y | Y |
| 2 **Bass** | Y | Y | Y | Y | Y | Y | Y |
| **NEW JERSEY** | | | | | | | |
| 1 Andrews | – | – | Y | Y | Y | Y | Y |
| 2 **LoBiondo** | Y | Y | Y | Y | Y | Y | Y |
| 3 **Saxton** | Y | Y | Y | Y | ? | Y | N |
| 4 **Smith** | Y | Y | Y | Y | Y | Y | Y |
| 5 **Garrett** | Y | Y | Y | Y | Y | Y | Y |
| 6 Pallone | N | N | Y | Y | Y | Y | Y |
| 7 **Ferguson** | Y | Y | Y | Y | Y | Y | Y |
| 8 Pascrell | ? | ? | Y | Y | Y | Y | Y |
| 9 Rothman | N | N | Y | Y | Y | Y | Y |
| 10 Payne | N | N | Y | Y | N | Y | Y |
| 11 **Frelinghuysen** | Y | Y | Y | Y | Y | Y | Y |
| 12 Holt | N | N | Y | Y | N | Y | Y |
| 13 Menendez | N | N | Y | Y | Y | Y | Y |
| **NEW MEXICO** | | | | | | | |
| 1 **Wilson** | Y | Y | Y | Y | Y | Y | Y |
| 2 **Pearce** | Y | Y | Y | Y | Y | Y | Y |
| 3 Udall | N | N | Y | Y | Y | Y | Y |
| **NEW YORK** | | | | | | | |
| 1 Bishop | N | N | Y | Y | Y | Y | Y |
| 2 Israel | N | N | Y | Y | Y | Y | Y |
| 3 **King** | Y | Y | Y | Y | Y | Y | Y |
| 4 McCarthy | N | N | Y | Y | Y | Y | Y |
| 5 Ackerman | N | N | Y | Y | Y | Y | Y |
| 6 Meeks | N | N | Y | Y | N | Y | Y |
| 7 Crowley | ? | ? | Y | Y | Y | Y | Y |
| 8 Nadler | N | N | Y | Y | N | Y | Y |
| 9 Weiner | N | N | Y | Y | Y | Y | Y |
| 10 Towns | N | N | Y | Y | N | Y | Y |
| 11 Owens | N | N | Y | Y | N | Y | Y |
| 12 Velázquez | N | N | Y | Y | N | Y | Y |
| 13 **Fossella** | Y | Y | Y | Y | Y | Y | Y |
| 14 Maloney | N | N | Y | Y | Y | Y | Y |
| 15 Rangel | N | N | Y | Y | N | Y | Y |
| 16 Serrano | N | N | Y | Y | N | Y | Y |
| 17 Engel | N | N | Y | Y | Y | Y | Y |
| 18 Lowey | N | N | Y | Y | Y | Y | Y |
| 19 **Kelly** | Y | Y | Y | Y | Y | Y | Y |
| 20 **Sweeney** | Y | Y | Y | Y | Y | Y | Y |
| 21 McNulty | N | N | Y | Y | N | Y | Y |
| 22 Hinchey | N | N | Y | Y | N | Y | Y |
| 23 **McHugh** | Y | Y | Y | Y | Y | Y | Y |
| 24 **Boehlert** | Y | Y | Y | Y | Y | Y | Y |
| 25 **Walsh** | Y | Y | N | Y | Y | Y | Y |
| 26 **Reynolds** | Y | Y | Y | Y | Y | Y | Y |
| 27 Higgins | N | N | Y | Y | Y | Y | Y |
| 28 Slaughter | N | N | Y | Y | N | Y | Y |
| 29 **Kuhl** | Y | Y | Y | Y | Y | Y | Y |
| **NORTH CAROLINA** | | | | | | | |
| 1 Butterfield | N | N | Y | Y | Y | Y | Y |
| 2 Etheridge | N | N | Y | Y | Y | Y | Y |
| 3 **Jones** | Y | Y | Y | Y | Y | Y | Y |
| 4 Price | N | N | Y | Y | Y | Y | Y |
| 5 **Foxx** | Y | Y | Y | Y | Y | Y | Y |
| 6 **Coble** | Y | Y | Y | Y | Y | Y | Y |
| 7 McIntyre | N | N | Y | Y | Y | Y | Y |
| 8 **Hayes** | Y | Y | Y | Y | Y | Y | N |
| 9 **Myrick** | Y | Y | N | Y | Y | Y | Y |
| 10 **McHenry** | Y | Y | Y | Y | Y | Y | Y |
| 11 **Taylor** | Y | Y | Y | Y | Y | ? | Y |
| 12 Watt | N | N | Y | Y | N | Y | Y |
| 13 Miller | N | N | Y | Y | Y | Y | Y |
| **NORTH DAKOTA** | | | | | | | |
| AL Pomeroy | N | N | Y | Y | Y | Y | Y |
| **OHIO** | | | | | | | |
| 1 **Chabot** | Y | Y | Y | Y | Y | Y | Y |
| 2 Vacant | | | | | | | |
| 3 **Turner** | Y | Y | Y | Y | Y | Y | Y |
| 4 **Oxley** | Y | Y | N | N | Y | N | Y |
| 5 **Gillmor** | Y | Y | Y | Y | Y | Y | Y |
| 6 Strickland | N | N | Y | Y | Y | Y | Y |
| 7 **Hobson** | Y | Y | Y | Y | Y | Y | Y |
| 8 **Boehner** | Y | Y | Y | Y | Y | Y | ? |
| 9 Kaptur | N | N | Y | Y | Y | Y | Y |
| 10 Kucinich | N | N | Y | Y | N | Y | Y |
| 11 Jones | N | N | Y | Y | Y | Y | Y |
| 12 **Tiberi** | Y | Y | Y | Y | Y | Y | Y |
| 13 Brown | N | N | Y | Y | N | Y | Y |
| 14 **LaTourette** | Y | Y | Y | Y | Y | Y | Y |
| 15 **Pryce** | Y | Y | Y | Y | Y | Y | Y |
| 16 **Regula** | Y | Y | Y | Y | Y | Y | Y |
| 17 Ryan | N | N | Y | Y | Y | Y | Y |
| 18 **Ney** | Y | Y | Y | Y | Y | Y | Y |
| **OKLAHOMA** | | | | | | | |
| 1 **Sullivan** | Y | Y | Y | Y | Y | Y | Y |
| 2 Boren | N | N | Y | Y | Y | Y | Y |
| 3 **Lucas** | Y | Y | Y | Y | Y | Y | Y |
| 4 **Cole** | Y | Y | N | N | Y | Y | Y |
| 5 **Istook** | Y | Y | Y | Y | Y | Y | Y |
| **OREGON** | | | | | | | |
| 1 Wu | N | N | Y | Y | Y | Y | Y |
| 2 **Walden** | Y | Y | Y | Y | Y | Y | Y |
| 3 Blumenauer | N | N | Y | Y | N | Y | Y |
| 4 DeFazio | N | N | Y | Y | Y | Y | Y |
| 5 Hooley | N | N | Y | Y | Y | Y | Y |
| **PENNSYLVANIA** | | | | | | | |
| 1 Brady | N | N | Y | Y | Y | Y | Y |
| 2 Fattah | N | N | Y | Y | Y | Y | Y |
| 3 **English** | Y | Y | Y | Y | Y | Y | Y |
| 4 **Hart** | Y | Y | Y | Y | Y | Y | Y |
| 5 **Peterson** | Y | Y | Y | Y | Y | Y | Y |
| 6 **Gerlach** | ? | Y | Y | Y | Y | Y | Y |
| 7 **Weldon** | Y | Y | Y | Y | Y | Y | Y |
| 8 **Fitzpatrick** | Y | Y | Y | Y | Y | Y | Y |
| 9 **Shuster** | Y | Y | Y | N | Y | Y | Y |
| 10 **Sherwood** | Y | Y | Y | Y | Y | Y | Y |
| 11 Kanjorski | N | N | Y | Y | Y | Y | Y |
| 12 Murtha | N | N | Y | Y | Y | Y | Y |
| 13 Schwartz | N | N | Y | Y | Y | Y | Y |
| 14 Doyle | N | N | Y | Y | Y | Y | Y |
| 15 **Dent** | Y | Y | Y | Y | Y | Y | Y |
| 16 **Pitts** | Y | Y | Y | Y | Y | Y | Y |
| 17 Holden | N | N | Y | Y | Y | Y | Y |
| 18 **Murphy** | Y | Y | Y | Y | Y | Y | Y |
| 19 **Platts** | Y | Y | Y | Y | Y | Y | Y |
| **RHODE ISLAND** | | | | | | | |
| 1 Kennedy | N | N | Y | Y | Y | Y | Y |
| 2 Langevin | N | N | Y | Y | Y | Y | Y |
| **SOUTH CAROLINA** | | | | | | | |
| 1 **Brown** | ? | ? | ? | ? | ? | ? | ? |
| 2 **Wilson** | Y | Y | Y | Y | Y | Y | Y |
| 3 **Barrett** | Y | Y | Y | Y | Y | Y | Y |
| 4 **Inglis** | Y | Y | Y | Y | Y | Y | Y |
| 5 Spratt | N | N | Y | Y | Y | Y | Y |
| 6 Clyburn | N | N | Y | Y | Y | Y | Y |
| **SOUTH DAKOTA** | | | | | | | |
| AL Herseth | N | N | Y | Y | Y | Y | Y |
| **TENNESSEE** | | | | | | | |
| 1 **Jenkins** | Y | Y | Y | Y | Y | Y | Y |
| 2 **Duncan** | Y | Y | Y | Y | Y | Y | Y |
| 3 Wamp | Y | Y | Y | Y | Y | Y | Y |
| 4 Davis | N | N | Y | Y | Y | Y | Y |
| 5 Cooper | N | N | Y | Y | Y | Y | Y |
| 6 Gordon | N | N | Y | Y | Y | Y | Y |
| 7 **Blackburn** | Y | Y | Y | Y | Y | Y | Y |
| 8 Tanner | N | N | Y | Y | Y | Y | Y |
| 9 Ford | N | N | Y | Y | Y | Y | Y |
| **TEXAS** | | | | | | | |
| 1 **Gohmert** | Y | Y | Y | Y | Y | Y | ? |
| 2 **Poe** | Y | Y | Y | Y | Y | Y | Y |
| 3 **Johnson, S.** | Y | Y | N | N | Y | N | Y |
| 4 **Hall** | Y | Y | Y | Y | Y | N | Y |
| 5 **Hensarling** | Y | Y | Y | Y | Y | Y | Y |
| 6 **Barton** | Y | Y | Y | Y | Y | N | Y |
| 7 **Culberson** | Y | Y | Y | Y | Y | Y | Y |
| 8 **Brady** | ? | Y | Y | Y | Y | Y | Y |
| 9 Green, A. | N | N | Y | Y | Y | Y | Y |
| 10 **McCaul** | Y | Y | Y | Y | Y | Y | Y |
| 11 **Conaway** | Y | Y | Y | Y | Y | Y | Y |
| 12 **Granger** | Y | Y | Y | Y | Y | Y | Y |
| 13 **Thornberry** | Y | Y | N | N | Y | N | Y |
| 14 **Paul** | Y | P | Y | Y | N | Y | Y |
| 15 Hinojosa | ? | ? | ? | ? | ? | ? | ? |
| 16 Reyes | N | N | Y | Y | Y | Y | Y |
| 17 Edwards | N | N | Y | Y | Y | Y | Y |
| 18 Jackson-Lee | N | N | Y | Y | Y | Y | Y |
| 19 **Neugebauer** | Y | Y | Y | Y | Y | Y | Y |
| 20 Gonzalez | N | N | Y | Y | Y | Y | Y |
| 21 **Smith** | Y | Y | Y | Y | Y | Y | Y |
| 22 **DeLay** | Y | Y | N | Y | Y | Y | Y |
| 23 **Bonilla** | Y | Y | N | N | Y | Y | Y |
| 24 **Marchant** | Y | Y | Y | Y | Y | Y | Y |
| 25 Doggett | N | N | Y | Y | Y | Y | Y |
| 26 **Burgess** | Y | Y | Y | Y | Y | Y | Y |
| 27 Ortiz | – | – | Y | Y | Y | Y | Y |
| 28 Cuellar | N | N | Y | Y | Y | Y | Y |
| 29 Green, G. | N | N | Y | Y | Y | Y | Y |
| 30 Johnson, E. | N | N | Y | Y | N | Y | Y |
| 31 **Carter** | Y | Y | Y | Y | Y | Y | Y |
| 32 **Sessions** | Y | Y | N | Y | Y | N | Y |
| **UTAH** | | | | | | | |
| 1 **Bishop** | Y | Y | Y | Y | Y | Y | Y |
| 2 Matheson | N | N | Y | Y | Y | Y | Y |
| 3 **Cannon** | Y | Y | Y | Y | Y | Y | Y |
| **VERMONT** | | | | | | | |
| AL *Sanders* | N | N | Y | Y | Y | Y | Y |
| **VIRGINIA** | | | | | | | |
| 1 **Davis, J.** | Y | Y | Y | Y | Y | Y | Y |
| 2 **Drake** | Y | Y | Y | Y | Y | Y | Y |
| 3 Scott | N | N | Y | Y | N | Y | Y |
| 4 **Forbes** | Y | Y | Y | Y | Y | Y | Y |
| 5 **Goode** | Y | Y | Y | Y | Y | Y | Y |
| 6 **Goodlatte** | Y | Y | Y | Y | Y | Y | Y |
| 7 **Cantor** | Y | Y | Y | N | Y | N | N |
| 8 Moran | N | N | Y | Y | Y | Y | Y |
| 9 Boucher | N | N | Y | Y | Y | Y | Y |
| 10 **Wolf** | Y | Y | Y | Y | Y | Y | Y |
| 11 **Davis, T.** | Y | Y | Y | Y | Y | Y | Y |
| **WASHINGTON** | | | | | | | |
| 1 Inslee | N | N | Y | Y | Y | Y | Y |
| 2 Larsen | N | N | Y | Y | Y | Y | Y |
| 3 Baird | N | N | Y | Y | Y | Y | Y |
| 4 **Hastings** | Y | Y | Y | Y | Y | Y | Y |
| 5 **McMorris** | Y | Y | Y | Y | Y | Y | Y |
| 6 Dicks | N | N | Y | Y | Y | Y | Y |
| 7 McDermott | N | N | Y | Y | N | Y | Y |
| 8 **Reichert** | Y | Y | Y | Y | Y | Y | Y |
| 9 Smith | N | N | Y | Y | Y | Y | Y |
| **WEST VIRGINIA** | | | | | | | |
| 1 Mollohan | N | N | Y | Y | N | Y | Y |
| 2 **Capito** | Y | Y | Y | Y | Y | Y | Y |
| 3 Rahall | N | N | Y | Y | Y | Y | Y |
| **WISCONSIN** | | | | | | | |
| 1 **Ryan** | Y | Y | Y | Y | Y | Y | Y |
| 2 Baldwin | N | N | Y | Y | N | Y | Y |
| 3 Kind | N | N | Y | Y | Y | Y | Y |
| 4 Moore | N | N | Y | Y | N | Y | Y |
| 5 **Sensenbrenner** | Y | Y | Y | Y | Y | Y | Y |
| 6 **Petri** | Y | Y | Y | Y | Y | Y | Y |
| 7 Obey | N | N | Y | Y | Y | Y | Y |
| 8 **Green** | Y | Y | Y | Y | Y | Y | Y |
| **WYOMING** | | | | | | | |
| AL **Cubin** | ? | ? | Y | Y | Y | N | N |

# IN THE HOUSE | By Vote Number

**408.** HR 3199. **"Patriot Act" Reauthorization/"Sneak and Peek" Searches.** Flake, R-Ariz., amendment that would require the Administrative Office of the Courts to report annually to Congress on the number of search warrants granted and eliminate unduly delaying a trial as a reason for delaying notification of "sneak and peek" searches. Adopted 407-21: R 206-21; D 200-0 (ND 151-0, SD 49-0); I 1-0. July 21, 2005.

**409.** HR 3199. **"Patriot Act" Reauthorization/Data-Mining Technology.** Berman, D-Calif., amendment that would require the Justice Department to report to Congress on the development and use of data-mining technology by federal departments and agencies. Adopted 261-165: R 62-165; D 198-0 (ND 151-0, SD 47-0); I 1-0. July 21, 2005.

**410.** HR 3199. **"Patriot Act" Reauthorization/Maritime Security.** Schiff, D-Calif., amendment that would make it a crime to use a vessel to smuggle terrorists or dangerous substances, including nuclear material, into the United States. It would impose criminal penalties for providing false information to a federal law enforcement officer at a port or on a vessel and would increase penalties for anyone who fraudulently gains access to a seaport. Adopted 381-45: R 225-2; D 155-43 (ND 114-37, SD 41-6); I 1-0. July 21, 2005.

**411.** HR 3199. **"Patriot Act" Reauthorization/Terrorism Financing.** Hart, R-Pa., amendment that would increase criminal penalties for anyone convicted on charges of financing terrorists to $50,000 in fines per transaction and 20 years in prison. It also would add terrorism-financing offenses to the list of crimes that constitute money laundering and would permit authorities to seize the assets of anyone who has committed terrorist acts against foreign countries or international organizations. Adopted 387-38: R 224-2; D 162-36 (ND 120-31, SD 42-5); I 1-0. July 21, 2005.

**412.** HR 3199. **"Patriot Act" Reauthorization/Seizure of Assets.** Jackson-Lee, D-Texas, amendment that would allow for the seizure of assets in the enforcement of a civil judgment against an individual or entity who has engaged in planning or perpetrating an act of domestic or international terrorism. Adopted 233-192: R 45-182; D 187-10 (ND 147-3, SD 40-7); I 1-0. July 21, 2005.

**413.** HR 3199. **"Patriot Act" Reauthorization/Recommit.** Boucher, D-Va., motion to recommit the bill to the Judiciary Committee with instructions to extend the sunsets of all 16 expiring provisions of the law known as the Patriot Act through Dec. 31, 2009. Motion rejected 209-218: R 9-218; D 199-0 (ND 151-0, SD 48-0); I 1-0. July 21, 2005.

**414.** HR 3199. **"Patriot Act" Reauthorization/Passage.** Passage of the bill that would make permanent 14 of the 16 provisions of the law known as the Patriot Act scheduled to expire at the end of this year and extend for 10 years the remaining two provisions on access to business and other records and "roving" wiretaps. The bill would permanently extend provisions that expand law enforcement's power to investigate suspected terrorists. Passed 257-171: R 214-14; D 43-156 (ND 19-132, SD 24-24); I 0-1. A "yea" was a vote in support of the president's position. July 21, 2005.

| | 408 | 409 | 410 | 411 | 412 | 413 | 414 |
|---|---|---|---|---|---|---|---|
| **ALABAMA** | | | | | | | |
| 1 Bonner | Y | N | Y | Y | N | N | Y |
| 2 Everett | Y | N | Y | Y | N | N | Y |
| 3 Rogers | Y | N | Y | Y | N | N | Y |
| 4 Aderholt | Y | Y | Y | Y | N | N | Y |
| 5 Cramer | Y | Y | Y | Y | N | Y | Y |
| 6 Bachus | Y | N | Y | Y | N | N | Y |
| 7 Davis | Y | Y | Y | Y | N | Y | Y |
| **ALASKA** | | | | | | | |
| AL Young | Y | Y | Y | Y | N | N | N |
| **ARIZONA** | | | | | | | |
| 1 Renzi | N | N | Y | Y | N | N | Y |
| 2 Franks | Y | N | Y | Y | N | N | Y |
| 3 Shadegg | N | N | N | Y | N | N | Y |
| 4 Pastor | Y | Y | Y | Y | Y | Y | N |
| 5 Hayworth | N | N | Y | Y | N | N | Y |
| 6 Flake | Y | Y | Y | Y | N | Y | N |
| 7 Grijalva | Y | Y | N | N | Y | Y | N |
| 8 Kolbe | Y | N | Y | Y | N | N | Y |
| **ARKANSAS** | | | | | | | |
| 1 Berry | Y | Y | Y | Y | Y | Y | N |
| 2 Snyder | Y | Y | Y | Y | Y | Y | N |
| 3 Boozman | Y | Y | Y | Y | N | N | Y |
| 4 Ross | Y | Y | Y | Y | Y | Y | Y |
| **CALIFORNIA** | | | | | | | |
| 1 Thompson | Y | Y | Y | Y | Y | Y | N |
| 2 Herger | Y | N | Y | Y | N | N | Y |
| 3 Lungren | Y | N | Y | Y | N | N | Y |
| 4 Doolittle | Y | N | Y | Y | N | N | Y |
| 5 Matsui, D. | Y | Y | Y | Y | Y | Y | N |
| 6 Woolsey | Y | Y | N | N | Y | Y | N |
| 7 Miller, George | Y | Y | N | N | Y | Y | N |
| 8 Pelosi | Y | Y | Y | Y | Y | Y | N |
| 9 Lee | Y | Y | N | N | Y | Y | N |
| 10 Tauscher | Y | Y | Y | Y | Y | Y | N |
| 11 Pombo | Y | N | Y | Y | N | N | Y |
| 12 Lantos | Y | Y | Y | Y | Y | Y | N |
| 13 Stark | Y | Y | N | N | Y | Y | N |
| 14 Eshoo | Y | Y | Y | Y | Y | Y | N |
| 15 Honda | Y | Y | Y | Y | Y | Y | N |
| 16 Lofgren | Y | Y | Y | N | Y | Y | N |
| 17 Farr | Y | Y | Y | Y | Y | Y | N |
| 18 Cardoza | Y | Y | Y | Y | ? | Y | N |
| 19 Radanovich | Y | N | Y | Y | N | N | Y |
| 20 Costa | Y | Y | Y | Y | Y | Y | N |
| 21 Nunes | Y | N | Y | Y | N | N | Y |
| 22 Thomas | Y | ? | ? | ? | ? | ? | ? |
| 23 Capps | Y | Y | Y | Y | Y | Y | N |
| 24 Gallegly | Y | N | Y | Y | N | N | Y |
| 25 McKeon | Y | N | Y | Y | N | N | Y |
| 26 Dreier | Y | N | Y | Y | N | N | Y |
| 27 Sherman | Y | Y | Y | Y | Y | Y | N |
| 28 Berman | Y | Y | Y | Y | Y | Y | N |
| 29 Schiff | Y | Y | Y | Y | Y | Y | N |
| 30 Waxman | Y | Y | Y | Y | Y | Y | N |
| 31 Becerra | Y | Y | Y | Y | Y | Y | N |
| 32 Solis | Y | Y | Y | N | Y | Y | N |
| 33 Watson | Y | Y | Y | Y | Y | Y | N |
| 34 Roybal-Allard | Y | Y | Y | Y | Y | Y | N |
| 35 Waters | Y | Y | N | N | Y | Y | N |
| 36 Harman | Y | Y | Y | Y | Y | Y | N |
| 37 Millender-McD. | Y | Y | N | Y | Y | Y | N |
| 38 Napolitano | Y | Y | Y | Y | Y | Y | N |
| 39 Sánchez, Linda | Y | Y | Y | N | Y | Y | N |
| 40 Royce | Y | N | Y | Y | N | N | Y |
| 41 Lewis | Y | N | Y | ? | N | N | Y |
| 42 Miller, Gary | Y | N | Y | Y | N | N | Y |
| 43 Baca | Y | Y | Y | Y | Y | Y | N |
| 44 Calvert | Y | N | Y | Y | N | N | Y |
| 45 Bono | N | N | Y | Y | N | N | Y |
| 46 Rohrabacher | Y | Y | Y | Y | N | Y | N |
| 47 Sanchez, Loretta | Y | Y | Y | N | Y | Y | N |
| 48 Cox | ? | Y | Y | Y | N | N | Y |
| 49 Issa | Y | Y | Y | Y | N | N | Y |
| 50 Cunningham | Y | Y | Y | Y | N | N | Y |
| 51 Filner | Y | Y | N | N | Y | Y | N |
| 52 Hunter | N | N | Y | Y | Y | N | Y |
| 53 Davis | Y | Y | Y | Y | Y | Y | N |
| **COLORADO** | | | | | | | |
| 1 DeGette | Y | Y | Y | Y | Y | Y | N |
| 2 Udall | Y | Y | Y | Y | Y | Y | N |
| 3 Salazar | Y | Y | Y | Y | Y | Y | N |
| 4 Musgrave | Y | N | Y | Y | N | N | Y |
| 5 Hefley | Y | N | Y | N | Y | N | Y |
| 6 Tancredo | Y | N | Y | Y | N | N | Y |
| 7 Beauprez | Y | N | Y | Y | N | N | Y |
| **CONNECTICUT** | | | | | | | |
| 1 Larson | Y | Y | Y | Y | Y | Y | N |
| 2 Simmons | Y | N | Y | Y | Y | N | Y |
| 3 DeLauro | Y | Y | Y | Y | Y | Y | N |
| 4 Shays | Y | N | Y | Y | Y | Y | N |
| 5 Johnson | Y | N | Y | Y | Y | N | Y |
| **DELAWARE** | | | | | | | |
| AL Castle | Y | N | Y | Y | Y | N | Y |
| **FLORIDA** | | | | | | | |
| 1 Miller | Y | N | Y | Y | N | N | Y |
| 2 Boyd | Y | Y | Y | Y | Y | Y | N |
| 3 Brown | Y | Y | Y | Y | Y | Y | N |
| 4 Crenshaw | Y | N | Y | Y | N | N | Y |
| 5 Brown-Waite | Y | N | Y | Y | N | N | Y |
| 6 Stearns | Y | N | Y | Y | N | N | Y |
| 7 Mica | Y | N | Y | Y | N | N | Y |
| 8 Keller | Y | N | Y | Y | N | N | Y |
| 9 Bilirakis | Y | N | Y | Y | N | N | Y |
| 10 Young | Y | N | Y | Y | N | N | Y |
| 11 Davis | Y | Y | Y | Y | Y | Y | N |
| 12 Putnam | Y | N | Y | Y | N | N | Y |
| 13 Harris | Y | Y | Y | Y | N | N | Y |
| 14 Mack | Y | Y | Y | Y | ? | N | Y |
| 15 Weldon | Y | N | Y | Y | N | N | Y |
| 16 Foley | Y | N | Y | Y | N | N | Y |
| 17 Meek | Y | Y | Y | Y | Y | Y | N |
| 18 Ros-Lehtinen | Y | Y | Y | Y | N | N | Y |
| 19 Wexler | Y | Y | Y | N | Y | Y | N |
| 20 Wasserman-Schultz | Y | Y | N | Y | Y | Y | N |
| 21 Diaz-Balart, L. | Y | N | Y | Y | N | N | Y |
| 22 Shaw | Y | N | Y | Y | N | N | Y |
| 23 Hastings | ? | ? | ? | ? | ? | ? | ? |
| 24 Feeney | Y | Y | Y | Y | N | N | Y |
| 25 Diaz-Balart, M. | Y | N | Y | Y | N | N | Y |
| **GEORGIA** | | | | | | | |
| 1 Kingston | Y | Y | Y | Y | N | N | Y |
| 2 Bishop | Y | Y | Y | Y | Y | Y | Y |
| 3 Marshall | Y | Y | Y | Y | Y | Y | Y |
| 4 McKinney | Y | Y | N | N | Y | Y | N |
| 5 Lewis | Y | Y | N | N | Y | Y | N |
| 6 Price | Y | Y | Y | N | N | N | Y |
| 7 Linder | N | N | Y | Y | N | N | Y |
| 8 Westmoreland | N | N | Y | Y | N | N | Y |
| 9 Norwood | Y | N | Y | Y | N | N | Y |
| 10 Deal | Y | N | Y | Y | N | N | Y |
| 11 Gingrey | Y | N | Y | Y | N | N | Y |
| 12 Barrow | Y | Y | Y | Y | Y | Y | N |
| 13 Scott | Y | Y | Y | Y | Y | Y | N |
| **HAWAII** | | | | | | | |
| 1 Abercrombie | Y | Y | Y | Y | Y | Y | N |
| 2 Case | Y | Y | Y | Y | Y | Y | Y |
| **IDAHO** | | | | | | | |
| 1 Otter | Y | Y | N | Y | N | Y | N |
| 2 Simpson | Y | Y | Y | Y | N | N | Y |
| **ILLINOIS** | | | | | | | |
| 1 Rush | Y | Y | Y | Y | Y | Y | N |
| 2 Jackson | Y | Y | N | Y | Y | Y | N |
| 3 Lipinski | Y | Y | Y | Y | Y | Y | Y |
| 4 Gutierrez | Y | Y | Y | N | Y | Y | N |
| 5 Emanuel | Y | Y | Y | Y | Y | Y | Y |
| 6 Hyde | Y | N | Y | Y | N | N | Y |
| 7 Davis | Y | Y | Y | Y | Y | Y | N |
| 8 Bean | Y | Y | Y | Y | Y | Y | Y |
| 9 Schakowsky | Y | Y | N | N | Y | Y | N |
| 10 Kirk | Y | N | Y | Y | ? | Y | N |
| 11 Weller | Y | N | Y | Y | N | N | Y |
| 12 Costello | Y | Y | Y | Y | Y | Y | N |

**KEY**    Republicans    Democrats    *Independents*

| | | | |
|---|---|---|---|
| Y | Voted for (yea) | X | Paired against |
| # | Paired for | − | Announced against |
| + | Announced for | P | Voted "present" |
| N | Voted against (nay) | | |

C   Voted "present" to avoid possible conflict of interest
?   Did not vote or otherwise make a position known

| | 408 | 409 | 410 | 411 | 412 | 413 | 414 |
|---|---|---|---|---|---|---|---|
| 13 **Biggert** | Y | N | Y | Y | N | N | Y |
| 14 **Hastert** | | | | | N | N | Y |
| 15 **Johnson** | Y | Y | Y | Y | Y | Y | N |
| 16 **Manzullo** | Y | N | Y | Y | N | N | N |
| 17 Evans | Y | Y | Y | Y | Y | Y | N |
| 18 **LaHood** | Y | N | Y | Y | N | N | N |
| 19 **Shimkus** | Y | N | Y | Y | N | N | Y |
| **INDIANA** | | | | | | | |
| 1 Visclosky | Y | Y | N | Y | Y | Y | N |
| 2 **Chocola** | Y | N | Y | Y | Y | N | Y |
| 3 **Souder** | N | N | Y | Y | N | N | Y |
| 4 **Buyer** | Y | N | Y | Y | N | N | Y |
| 5 **Burton** | Y | N | Y | Y | N | N | Y |
| 6 **Pence** | Y | Y | Y | Y | N | N | Y |
| 7 Carson | Y | Y | Y | N | Y | Y | N |
| 8 **Hostettler** | N | N | Y | Y | N | N | Y |
| 9 **Sodrel** | Y | N | Y | Y | N | N | Y |
| **IOWA** | | | | | | | |
| 1 **Nussle** | Y | N | Y | Y | Y | N | Y |
| 2 **Leach** | Y | Y | Y | Y | Y | Y | Y |
| 3 Boswell | Y | Y | Y | Y | Y | Y | Y |
| 4 **Latham** | Y | N | Y | Y | N | N | Y |
| 5 **King** | Y | N | Y | Y | N | N | Y |
| **KANSAS** | | | | | | | |
| 1 **Moran** | Y | N | Y | Y | N | N | Y |
| 2 **Ryun** | Y | N | Y | Y | N | N | Y |
| 3 Moore | Y | Y | Y | Y | Y | Y | N |
| 4 **Tiahrt** | N | N | Y | Y | N | N | Y |
| **KENTUCKY** | | | | | | | |
| 1 **Whitfield** | Y | N | Y | Y | Y | N | Y |
| 2 **Lewis** | Y | N | Y | Y | Y | N | Y |
| 3 **Northup** | Y | N | Y | Y | N | N | Y |
| 4 **Davis** | N | N | Y | Y | N | N | Y |
| 5 **Rogers** | Y | N | Y | Y | Y | N | Y |
| 6 Chandler | Y | Y | Y | Y | N | Y | Y |
| **LOUISIANA** | | | | | | | |
| 1 **Jindal** | Y | N | Y | Y | N | N | Y |
| 2 Jefferson | Y | ? | ? | ? | ? | Y | N |
| 3 Melancon | Y | Y | Y | Y | Y | Y | Y |
| 4 **McCrery** | Y | N | Y | Y | N | N | Y |
| 5 **Alexander** | Y | N | Y | Y | Y | N | Y |
| 6 **Baker** | Y | N | Y | Y | N | N | Y |
| 7 **Boustany** | Y | N | Y | Y | N | N | Y |
| **MAINE** | | | | | | | |
| 1 Allen | Y | Y | Y | Y | Y | Y | N |
| 2 Michaud | Y | Y | N | Y | Y | Y | N |
| **MARYLAND** | | | | | | | |
| 1 **Gilchrest** | Y | N | Y | Y | Y | N | Y |
| 2 Ruppersberger | Y | Y | Y | Y | Y | Y | Y |
| 3 Cardin | Y | Y | Y | Y | Y | Y | Y |
| 4 Wynn | Y | Y | Y | Y | Y | Y | N |
| 5 Hoyer | Y | Y | Y | Y | Y | Y | Y |
| 6 **Bartlett** | Y | Y | Y | Y | N | Y | N |
| 7 Cummings | Y | Y | Y | N | Y | Y | N |
| 8 Van Hollen | Y | Y | Y | Y | Y | Y | N |
| **MASSACHUSETTS** | | | | | | | |
| 1 Olver | Y | Y | N | Y | Y | Y | N |
| 2 Neal | Y | Y | Y | Y | Y | Y | N |
| 3 McGovern | Y | Y | N | N | Y | Y | N |
| 4 Frank | Y | Y | N | N | Y | Y | N |
| 5 Meehan | Y | Y | Y | Y | Y | Y | N |
| 6 Tierney | Y | Y | N | Y | Y | Y | N |
| 7 Markey | Y | Y | N | N | Y | Y | N |
| 8 Capuano | Y | Y | Y | N | Y | Y | N |
| 9 Lynch | Y | Y | Y | Y | Y | Y | N |
| 10 Delahunt | Y | Y | N | Y | Y | Y | N |
| **MICHIGAN** | | | | | | | |
| 1 Stupak | Y | Y | Y | Y | Y | Y | N |
| 2 **Hoekstra** | Y | N | Y | Y | N | N | Y |
| 3 **Ehlers** | Y | Y | Y | Y | N | Y | Y |
| 4 **Camp** | Y | N | Y | Y | N | N | Y |
| 5 Kildee | Y | Y | N | Y | Y | Y | N |
| 6 **Upton** | Y | Y | Y | Y | N | N | Y |
| 7 **Schwarz** | Y | Y | Y | Y | Y | N | Y |
| 8 **Rogers** | N | N | Y | Y | N | N | Y |
| 9 **Knollenberg** | N | N | Y | Y | N | N | Y |
| 10 **Miller** | Y | N | Y | Y | N | N | Y |
| 11 **McCotter** | Y | Y | Y | Y | Y | N | Y |
| 12 Levin | Y | Y | Y | Y | Y | Y | N |
| 13 Kilpatrick | Y | Y | N | Y | Y | Y | N |
| 14 Conyers | Y | Y | N | N | Y | Y | N |
| 15 Dingell | Y | Y | Y | Y | Y | Y | N |
| **MINNESOTA** | | | | | | | |
| 1 **Gutknecht** | Y | Y | Y | Y | N | N | Y |
| 2 **Kline** | Y | N | Y | Y | N | N | Y |
| 3 **Ramstad** | Y | N | Y | Y | Y | N | Y |
| 4 McCollum | Y | Y | N | Y | Y | Y | N |
| 5 Sabo | Y | Y | N | Y | Y | Y | N |
| 6 **Kennedy** | Y | Y | Y | Y | N | N | Y |
| 7 Peterson | Y | Y | Y | Y | N | Y | N |
| 8 Oberstar | Y | Y | N | Y | Y | Y | N |
| **MISSISSIPPI** | | | | | | | |
| 1 **Wicker** | Y | N | Y | Y | N | N | Y |
| 2 Thompson | Y | Y | Y | Y | Y | Y | N |
| 3 **Pickering** | Y | ? | ? | ? | ? | ? | ? |
| 4 Taylor | Y | ? | ? | ? | ? | ? | ? |
| **MISSOURI** | | | | | | | |
| 1 Clay | Y | Y | Y | N | Y | Y | N |
| 2 **Akin** | Y | N | Y | Y | N | N | Y |
| 3 Carnahan | Y | Y | Y | Y | Y | Y | Y |
| 4 Skelton | Y | Y | Y | Y | Y | Y | Y |
| 5 Cleaver | Y | Y | Y | Y | Y | Y | N |
| 6 **Graves** | Y | N | Y | Y | N | N | Y |
| 7 **Blunt** | Y | N | Y | Y | N | N | Y |
| 8 **Emerson** | Y | Y | Y | Y | N | N | Y |
| 9 **Hulshof** | Y | Y | Y | Y | N | N | Y |
| **MONTANA** | | | | | | | |
| AL **Rehberg** | Y | N | Y | Y | N | N | Y |
| **NEBRASKA** | | | | | | | |
| 1 **Fortenberry** | Y | N | Y | Y | Y | N | Y |
| 2 **Terry** | Y | N | Y | Y | Y | N | Y |
| 3 **Osborne** | Y | N | Y | Y | N | N | Y |
| **NEVADA** | | | | | | | |
| 1 Berkley | Y | Y | Y | Y | Y | Y | N |
| 2 **Gibbons** | Y | N | Y | Y | N | N | Y |
| 3 **Porter** | Y | Y | Y | Y | N | N | Y |
| **NEW HAMPSHIRE** | | | | | | | |
| 1 **Bradley** | Y | Y | Y | Y | Y | N | Y |
| 2 **Bass** | Y | N | Y | Y | Y | N | Y |
| **NEW JERSEY** | | | | | | | |
| 1 Andrews | Y | Y | Y | Y | Y | Y | Y |
| 2 **LoBiondo** | Y | N | Y | Y | Y | N | Y |
| 3 **Saxton** | Y | N | Y | Y | N | N | Y |
| 4 **Smith** | Y | Y | Y | Y | N | N | Y |
| 5 **Garrett** | Y | N | Y | Y | N | N | Y |
| 6 Pallone | Y | Y | Y | Y | Y | Y | N |
| 7 **Ferguson** | Y | N | Y | Y | N | N | Y |
| 8 Pascrell | Y | Y | Y | Y | Y | Y | N |
| 9 Rothman | Y | Y | Y | Y | Y | Y | N |
| 10 Payne | Y | Y | N | N | Y | Y | N |
| 11 **Frelinghuysen** | Y | N | Y | Y | Y | N | Y |
| 12 Holt | Y | Y | N | N | Y | Y | N |
| 13 Menendez | Y | Y | Y | Y | Y | Y | Y |
| **NEW MEXICO** | | | | | | | |
| 1 **Wilson** | Y | N | Y | Y | N | N | Y |
| 2 **Pearce** | Y | N | Y | Y | N | N | Y |
| 3 Udall | Y | Y | Y | Y | Y | Y | N |
| **NEW YORK** | | | | | | | |
| 1 Bishop | Y | Y | Y | Y | Y | Y | N |
| 2 Israel | Y | Y | Y | Y | Y | Y | N |
| 3 **King** | Y | N | Y | Y | N | N | Y |
| 4 McCarthy | Y | Y | Y | Y | Y | Y | N |
| 5 Ackerman | Y | Y | Y | Y | Y | Y | N |
| 6 Meeks | Y | Y | N | Y | Y | Y | N |
| 7 Crowley | Y | Y | Y | N | Y | Y | N |
| 8 Nadler | Y | Y | N | Y | Y | Y | N |
| 9 Weiner | Y | Y | Y | Y | Y | Y | N |
| 10 Towns | Y | Y | Y | Y | Y | Y | N |
| 11 Owens | Y | Y | N | Y | Y | Y | N |
| 12 Velázquez | Y | Y | Y | Y | Y | Y | N |
| 13 **Fossella** | Y | N | Y | Y | N | N | Y |
| 14 Maloney | Y | Y | Y | Y | Y | Y | N |
| 15 Rangel | Y | Y | Y | Y | Y | Y | N |
| 16 Serrano | Y | Y | N | N | Y | Y | N |
| 17 Engel | Y | Y | Y | Y | Y | Y | N |
| 18 Lowey | Y | Y | Y | Y | Y | Y | N |
| 19 **Kelly** | Y | N | Y | Y | N | N | Y |
| 20 **Sweeney** | Y | N | Y | Y | N | N | Y |
| 21 McNulty | Y | Y | Y | Y | Y | Y | N |
| 22 Hinchey | Y | Y | Y | Y | Y | Y | N |
| 23 **McHugh** | Y | N | Y | Y | N | N | Y |
| 24 **Boehlert** | Y | N | Y | Y | N | N | Y |
| 25 **Walsh** | Y | N | Y | Y | N | N | Y |
| 26 **Reynolds** | Y | N | Y | Y | N | N | Y |
| 27 Higgins | Y | Y | Y | Y | Y | Y | Y |
| 28 Slaughter | Y | Y | Y | Y | Y | Y | N |
| 29 **Kuhl** | Y | Y | Y | Y | N | N | Y |
| **NORTH CAROLINA** | | | | | | | |
| 1 Butterfield | Y | Y | Y | Y | Y | Y | Y |
| 2 Etheridge | Y | Y | Y | Y | Y | Y | Y |
| 3 **Jones** | Y | Y | Y | Y | Y | Y | Y |
| 4 Price | Y | Y | Y | Y | Y | Y | N |
| 5 **Foxx** | Y | N | Y | Y | N | N | Y |
| 6 **Coble** | Y | Y | Y | Y | Y | N | Y |
| 7 McIntyre | Y | Y | Y | Y | Y | Y | Y |
| 8 **Hayes** | Y | N | Y | Y | N | N | Y |
| 9 **Myrick** | Y | N | Y | Y | N | N | Y |
| 10 **McHenry** | Y | N | Y | Y | N | N | Y |
| 11 **Taylor** | Y | N | Y | Y | N | N | Y |
| 12 Watt | Y | Y | N | N | Y | Y | N |
| 13 Miller | Y | Y | Y | Y | Y | Y | Y |
| **NORTH DAKOTA** | | | | | | | |
| AL Pomeroy | Y | Y | Y | Y | Y | Y | Y |
| **OHIO** | | | | | | | |
| 1 **Chabot** | Y | N | Y | Y | N | N | Y |
| 2 Vacant | | | | | | | |
| 3 **Turner** | Y | N | Y | Y | N | N | Y |
| 4 **Oxley** | N | N | Y | Y | N | N | Y |
| 5 **Gillmor** | Y | Y | Y | Y | Y | N | Y |
| 6 Strickland | Y | Y | Y | Y | Y | Y | N |
| 7 **Hobson** | Y | N | Y | Y | Y | N | Y |
| 8 **Boehner** | Y | N | Y | Y | N | N | Y |
| 9 Kaptur | Y | Y | Y | Y | Y | Y | N |
| 10 Kucinich | Y | Y | N | N | Y | Y | N |
| 11 Jones | Y | Y | N | N | Y | Y | N |
| 12 **Tiberi** | Y | N | Y | Y | N | N | Y |
| 13 Brown | Y | Y | Y | Y | Y | Y | N |
| 14 **LaTourette** | Y | Y | Y | Y | N | N | Y |
| 15 **Pryce** | Y | N | Y | Y | N | N | Y |
| 16 **Regula** | Y | Y | Y | Y | N | N | Y |
| 17 Ryan | Y | Y | Y | Y | Y | Y | N |
| 18 **Ney** | Y | N | Y | Y | Y | N | N |
| **OKLAHOMA** | | | | | | | |
| 1 **Sullivan** | Y | N | Y | Y | N | N | Y |
| 2 Boren | Y | Y | Y | Y | Y | Y | Y |
| 3 **Lucas** | Y | N | Y | Y | N | N | N |
| 4 **Cole** | N | N | Y | Y | Y | N | Y |
| 5 **Istook** | Y | Y | Y | Y | N | N | Y |
| **OREGON** | | | | | | | |
| 1 Wu | Y | Y | Y | Y | Y | Y | N |
| 2 **Walden** | Y | Y | Y | Y | Y | N | Y |
| 3 Blumenauer | Y | Y | N | N | Y | Y | N |
| 4 DeFazio | Y | Y | Y | Y | Y | Y | N |
| 5 Hooley | Y | Y | Y | Y | Y | Y | N |
| **PENNSYLVANIA** | | | | | | | |
| 1 Brady | Y | Y | Y | Y | Y | Y | N |
| 2 Fattah | Y | Y | Y | Y | Y | Y | N |
| 3 **English** | Y | Y | Y | Y | N | N | Y |
| 4 **Hart** | Y | Y | Y | Y | N | N | Y |
| 5 **Peterson** | Y | N | Y | Y | N | N | Y |
| 6 **Gerlach** | Y | Y | Y | Y | Y | N | Y |
| 7 **Weldon** | Y | N | Y | Y | N | N | Y |
| 8 **Fitzpatrick** | Y | Y | Y | Y | Y | N | Y |
| 9 **Shuster** | N | N | Y | Y | N | N | Y |
| 10 **Sherwood** | Y | N | Y | Y | N | N | Y |
| 11 Kanjorski | Y | Y | Y | Y | N | Y | N |
| 12 Murtha | Y | Y | Y | Y | N | Y | N |
| 13 Schwartz | Y | Y | Y | Y | Y | Y | Y |
| 14 Doyle | Y | Y | Y | Y | Y | Y | N |
| 15 **Dent** | Y | N | Y | Y | Y | N | Y |
| 16 **Pitts** | Y | N | Y | Y | N | N | Y |
| 17 Holden | Y | Y | Y | Y | Y | Y | Y |
| 18 **Murphy** | Y | Y | Y | Y | N | N | Y |
| 19 **Platts** | Y | N | Y | Y | N | N | Y |
| **RHODE ISLAND** | | | | | | | |
| 1 Kennedy | Y | Y | Y | Y | Y | Y | N |
| 2 Langevin | Y | Y | Y | Y | Y | Y | N |
| **SOUTH CAROLINA** | | | | | | | |
| 1 **Brown** | ? | ? | ? | ? | ? | ? | ? |
| 2 **Wilson** | Y | N | Y | Y | N | N | Y |
| 3 **Barrett** | Y | N | Y | Y | N | N | Y |
| 4 **Inglis** | Y | Y | Y | Y | N | N | Y |
| 5 Spratt | Y | Y | Y | Y | Y | Y | Y |
| 6 Clyburn | Y | Y | Y | Y | N | Y | Y |
| **SOUTH DAKOTA** | | | | | | | |
| AL Herseth | Y | Y | Y | Y | Y | Y | Y |
| **TENNESSEE** | | | | | | | |
| 1 **Jenkins** | Y | Y | Y | Y | N | N | Y |
| 2 **Duncan** | Y | Y | Y | Y | Y | N | N |
| 3 **Wamp** | Y | Y | Y | Y | N | N | Y |
| 4 Davis | Y | Y | Y | Y | Y | Y | Y |
| 5 Cooper | Y | Y | Y | Y | N | Y | Y |
| 6 Gordon | Y | Y | Y | Y | Y | Y | Y |
| 7 **Blackburn** | Y | N | Y | Y | N | N | Y |
| 8 Tanner | Y | Y | Y | Y | Y | Y | N |
| 9 Ford | Y | Y | Y | Y | Y | Y | N |
| **TEXAS** | | | | | | | |
| 1 **Gohmert** | ? | Y | Y | Y | Y | N | Y |
| 2 **Poe** | Y | Y | Y | Y | Y | N | Y |
| 3 **Johnson, S.** | Y | N | Y | Y | N | N | Y |
| 4 **Hall** | Y | N | Y | Y | N | N | Y |
| 5 **Hensarling** | Y | Y | Y | Y | N | N | Y |
| 6 **Barton** | N | N | Y | Y | N | N | Y |
| 7 **Culberson** | Y | N | Y | Y | N | N | Y |
| 8 **Brady** | Y | N | Y | Y | Y | N | Y |
| 9 Green, A. | Y | Y | Y | Y | Y | Y | N |
| 10 **McCaul** | Y | N | Y | Y | Y | N | Y |
| 11 **Conaway** | Y | Y | Y | Y | N | N | Y |
| 12 **Granger** | Y | N | Y | Y | N | N | Y |
| 13 **Thornberry** | N | N | Y | Y | N | N | Y |
| 14 **Paul** | Y | Y | N | N | Y | Y | N |
| 15 Hinojosa | ? | ? | ? | ? | ? | ? | ? |
| 16 Reyes | Y | Y | Y | Y | Y | Y | Y |
| 17 Edwards | Y | Y | Y | Y | Y | Y | Y |
| 18 Jackson-Lee | Y | Y | N | Y | Y | Y | N |
| 19 **Neugebauer** | Y | N | Y | Y | N | N | Y |
| 20 Gonzalez | Y | Y | Y | Y | Y | Y | N |
| 21 **Smith** | Y | Y | Y | Y | N | N | Y |
| 22 **DeLay** | Y | N | Y | Y | N | N | Y |
| 23 **Bonilla** | N | N | Y | Y | N | N | Y |
| 24 **Marchant** | Y | N | Y | Y | N | N | Y |
| 25 Doggett | Y | Y | Y | Y | Y | Y | N |
| 26 **Burgess** | Y | N | Y | Y | N | N | Y |
| 27 Ortiz | Y | Y | Y | Y | Y | Y | Y |
| 28 Cuellar | Y | Y | Y | Y | Y | Y | N |
| 29 Green, G. | Y | Y | Y | Y | Y | Y | Y |
| 30 Johnson, E. | Y | Y | Y | Y | Y | Y | N |
| 31 **Carter** | Y | N | Y | Y | N | N | Y |
| 32 **Sessions** | N | N | Y | Y | N | N | Y |
| **UTAH** | | | | | | | |
| 1 **Bishop** | Y | N | Y | Y | N | N | N |
| 2 Matheson | Y | Y | Y | Y | Y | Y | N |
| 3 **Cannon** | Y | Y | Y | Y | N | N | Y |
| **VERMONT** | | | | | | | |
| AL *Sanders* | Y | Y | Y | Y | Y | Y | N |
| **VIRGINIA** | | | | | | | |
| 1 **Davis, J.** | Y | N | Y | Y | N | N | Y |
| 2 **Drake** | Y | N | Y | Y | N | N | Y |
| 3 Scott | Y | Y | N | N | N | Y | N |
| 4 **Forbes** | Y | N | Y | Y | N | N | Y |
| 5 **Goode** | Y | Y | Y | Y | N | N | Y |
| 6 **Goodlatte** | Y | Y | Y | Y | N | N | Y |
| 7 **Cantor** | N | N | Y | Y | N | N | Y |
| 8 Moran | Y | Y | Y | Y | N | Y | N |
| 9 Boucher | Y | Y | Y | Y | Y | Y | N |
| 10 **Wolf** | Y | N | Y | Y | N | N | Y |
| 11 **Davis, T.** | Y | N | Y | Y | Y | N | Y |
| **WASHINGTON** | | | | | | | |
| 1 Inslee | Y | Y | Y | Y | Y | Y | N |
| 2 Larsen | Y | Y | Y | Y | Y | Y | N |
| 3 Baird | Y | Y | Y | Y | Y | Y | N |
| 4 **Hastings** | Y | Y | Y | Y | N | N | Y |
| 5 **McMorris** | Y | N | Y | Y | N | N | Y |
| 6 Dicks | Y | Y | Y | Y | Y | Y | N |
| 7 McDermott | Y | Y | N | N | Y | Y | N |
| 8 **Reichert** | Y | N | Y | Y | N | N | Y |
| 9 Smith | Y | Y | Y | Y | Y | Y | N |
| **WEST VIRGINIA** | | | | | | | |
| 1 Mollohan | Y | Y | N | Y | Y | Y | N |
| 2 **Capito** | Y | N | Y | Y | N | N | Y |
| 3 Rahall | Y | Y | Y | Y | Y | Y | N |
| **WISCONSIN** | | | | | | | |
| 1 **Ryan** | Y | N | Y | Y | N | N | Y |
| 2 Baldwin | Y | Y | N | N | Y | Y | N |
| 3 Kind | Y | Y | Y | Y | Y | Y | N |
| 4 Moore | Y | Y | N | N | Y | Y | N |
| 5 **Sensenbrenner** | Y | Y | Y | Y | N | N | Y |
| 6 **Petri** | Y | Y | Y | N | N | N | Y |
| 7 Obey | Y | Y | Y | Y | Y | Y | N |
| 8 **Green** | Y | Y | Y | Y | N | N | Y |
| **WYOMING** | | | | | | | |
| AL **Cubin** | Y | N | Y | Y | N | N | Y |

# IN THE HOUSE | By Vote Number

**415.** **HR 3070. NASA Reauthorization/Minority-Serving Institutions.** Velázquez, D-N.Y., amendment that would create a four-year pilot program for NASA to award grants to minority-serving institutions for the development of NASA research facilities and infrastructure. Rejected 192-206: R 9-201; D 182-5 (ND 141-2, SD 41-3); I 1-0. July 22, 2005.

**416.** **HR 3070. NASA Reauthorization/Passage.** Passage of the bill that would authorize $34.7 billion for NASA — $17 billion in fiscal 2006 and $17.7 billion in fiscal 2007. It would direct NASA to manage the human space flight program with a goal of sending Americans to the moon by 2020, launch a crew exploration vehicle as close to 2010 as possible and send astronaut crews to Mars and other destinations. Passed 383-15: R 207-3; D 176-11 (ND 132-11, SD 44-0); I 0-1. July 22, 2005.

**417.** **H J Res 59. Women's Suffrage Commemoration Day/Passage.** Issa, R-Calif., motion to suspend the rules and pass the joint resolution that would express the sense of Congress that women suffragists should be revered and celebrated for working to ensure the right of women to vote in the United States. Motion agreed to 378-0: R 197-0; D 180-0 (ND 136-0, SD 44-0); I 1-0. A two-thirds majority of those present and voting (252 in this case) is required for passage under suspension of the rules. July 25, 2005.

**418.** **H Con Res 181. National Life Insurance Awareness Month/Adoption.** Issa, R-Calif., motion to suspend the rules and adopt the concurrent resolution that would support the goals and ideals of National Life Insurance Awareness Month. Motion agreed to 377-4: R 196-2; D 180-2 (ND 136-2, SD 44-0); I 1-0. A two-thirds majority of those present and voting (254 in this case) is required for adoption under suspension of the rules. July 25, 2005.

**419.** **H Res 376. Video Game Investigation/Adoption.** Upton, R-Mich., motion to suspend the rules and adopt the resolution that would urge the Federal Trade Commission to launch an investigation of the "Grand Theft Auto: San Andreas" video game and impose the strictest penalty if the game manufacturer is found guilty of deception or fraud to secure a lesser content rating. Motion agreed to 355-21: R 195-2; D 159-19 (ND 119-16, SD 40-3); I 1-0. A two-thirds majority of those present and voting (252 in this case) is required for adoption under suspension of the rules. July 25, 2005.

**420.** **HR 3200. Servicemembers' Group Life Insurance/Passage.** Buyer, R-Ind., motion to suspend the rules and pass the bill that would make permanent current law that raises the maximum federally subsidized life insurance payout to $400,000 for service members killed in the line of duty. Motion agreed to 424-0: R 224-0; D 199-0 (ND 150-0, SD 49-0); I 1-0. A two-thirds majority of those present and voting (283 in this case) is required for passage under suspension of the rules. July 26, 2005.

| | 415 | 416 | 417 | 418 | 419 | 420 |
|---|---|---|---|---|---|---|
| **ALABAMA** | | | | | | |
| 1 Bonner | N | Y | Y | Y | Y | Y |
| 2 Everett | N | Y | Y | Y | Y | Y |
| 3 Rogers | Y | Y | Y | Y | Y | Y |
| 4 Aderholt | N | Y | Y | Y | Y | Y |
| 5 Cramer | N | Y | ? | ? | ? | Y |
| 6 Bachus | N | Y | Y | Y | ? | Y |
| 7 Davis | Y | Y | Y | Y | Y | Y |
| **ALASKA** | | | | | | |
| AL Young | N | Y | Y | Y | Y | Y |
| **ARIZONA** | | | | | | |
| 1 Renzi | N | Y | Y | Y | Y | Y |
| 2 Franks | N | Y | Y | Y | Y | Y |
| 3 Shadegg | N | N | Y | Y | Y | Y |
| 4 Pastor | Y | Y | Y | Y | Y | Y |
| 5 Hayworth | N | Y | Y | Y | Y | Y |
| 6 Flake | N | N | N | N | N | Y |
| 7 Grijalva | Y | Y | Y | Y | N | Y |
| 8 Kolbe | N | Y | Y | Y | Y | Y |
| **ARKANSAS** | | | | | | |
| 1 Berry | Y | Y | Y | Y | Y | Y |
| 2 Snyder | Y | Y | Y | Y | Y | Y |
| 3 Boozman | N | Y | Y | Y | Y | Y |
| 4 Ross | Y | Y | Y | Y | Y | Y |
| **CALIFORNIA** | | | | | | |
| 1 Thompson | Y | Y | Y | Y | Y | Y |
| 2 Herger | N | Y | Y | Y | Y | Y |
| 3 Lungren | N | Y | Y | Y | Y | Y |
| 4 Doolittle | N | Y | ? | ? | ? | Y |
| 5 Matsui, D. | Y | Y | Y | Y | Y | Y |
| 6 Woolsey | Y | Y | Y | Y | N | Y |
| 7 Miller, George | Y | Y | Y | N | Y | Y |
| 8 Pelosi | Y | Y | ? | ? | ? | Y |
| 9 Lee | Y | Y | Y | Y | N | Y |
| 10 Tauscher | Y | Y | Y | Y | Y | Y |
| 11 Pombo | N | Y | Y | Y | Y | Y |
| 12 Lantos | Y | Y | Y | Y | Y | Y |
| 13 Stark | ? | ? | Y | N | N | Y |
| 14 Eshoo | Y | Y | Y | Y | Y | Y |
| 15 Honda | Y | Y | Y | Y | Y | Y |
| 16 Lofgren | Y | Y | Y | Y | Y | Y |
| 17 Farr | Y | Y | Y | Y | Y | Y |
| 18 Cardoza | ? | ? | Y | Y | Y | Y |
| 19 Radanovich | ? | ? | ? | ? | ? | Y |
| 20 Costa | N | Y | Y | Y | Y | Y |
| 21 Nunes | N | Y | Y | Y | Y | Y |
| 22 Thomas | ? | ? | Y | Y | Y | Y |
| 23 Capps | Y | Y | Y | Y | Y | Y |
| 24 Gallegly | N | Y | ? | ? | ? | Y |
| 25 McKeon | N | Y | Y | Y | Y | Y |
| 26 Dreier | N | Y | Y | Y | Y | Y |
| 27 Sherman | Y | Y | Y | Y | Y | Y |
| 28 Berman | Y | Y | ? | ? | ? | Y |
| 29 Schiff | Y | Y | + | Y | Y | Y |
| 30 Waxman | ? | ? | Y | Y | Y | Y |
| 31 Becerra | Y | Y | ? | ? | ? | Y |
| 32 Solis | Y | Y | Y | Y | Y | Y |
| 33 Watson | Y | Y | Y | Y | Y | Y |
| 34 Roybal-Allard | Y | Y | Y | Y | Y | Y |
| 35 Waters | Y | Y | Y | Y | Y | Y |
| 36 Harman | Y | Y | Y | Y | Y | Y |
| 37 Millender-McD. | Y | Y | Y | Y | Y | Y |
| 38 Napolitano | Y | Y | Y | Y | Y | Y |
| 39 Sánchez, Linda | Y | Y | Y | Y | Y | Y |
| 40 Royce | N | Y | Y | Y | Y | Y |
| 41 Lewis | N | Y | Y | Y | Y | Y |
| 42 Miller, Gary | N | Y | Y | Y | Y | Y |
| 43 Baca | Y | Y | Y | Y | Y | Y |
| 44 Calvert | N | Y | Y | Y | Y | Y |
| 45 Bono | N | Y | Y | Y | Y | Y |
| 46 Rohrabacher | N | Y | Y | Y | Y | Y |
| 47 Sanchez, Loretta | Y | Y | Y | Y | Y | Y |
| 48 Cox | N | Y | Y | Y | Y | ? |
| 49 Issa | N | Y | Y | Y | Y | Y |

| | 415 | 416 | 417 | 418 | 419 | 420 |
|---|---|---|---|---|---|---|
| 50 Cunningham | ? | ? | ? | ? | ? | Y |
| 51 Filner | Y | Y | Y | Y | Y | Y |
| 52 Hunter | N | Y | Y | Y | Y | Y |
| 53 Davis | Y | Y | Y | Y | Y | Y |
| **COLORADO** | | | | | | |
| 1 DeGette | ? | ? | Y | Y | Y | Y |
| 2 Udall | N | Y | Y | Y | Y | Y |
| 3 Salazar | Y | Y | Y | Y | Y | Y |
| 4 Musgrave | N | Y | Y | Y | Y | Y |
| 5 Hefley | N | Y | Y | Y | Y | Y |
| 6 Tancredo | N | Y | Y | Y | Y | Y |
| 7 Beauprez | N | Y | Y | Y | Y | Y |
| **CONNECTICUT** | | | | | | |
| 1 Larson | Y | Y | Y | Y | Y | Y |
| 2 Simmons | N | Y | Y | Y | Y | Y |
| 3 DeLauro | Y | Y | Y | Y | Y | Y |
| 4 Shays | N | Y | + | + | + | Y |
| 5 Johnson | N | Y | Y | Y | Y | Y |
| **DELAWARE** | | | | | | |
| AL Castle | N | Y | Y | Y | Y | ? |
| **FLORIDA** | | | | | | |
| 1 Miller | ? | ? | Y | Y | Y | Y |
| 2 Boyd | Y | Y | Y | Y | Y | Y |
| 3 Brown | Y | Y | ? | ? | ? | Y |
| 4 Crenshaw | ? | ? | Y | Y | Y | Y |
| 5 Brown-Waite | N | Y | + | + | + | Y |
| 6 Stearns | N | Y | Y | Y | Y | Y |
| 7 Mica | N | Y | Y | Y | Y | Y |
| 8 Keller | N | Y | Y | Y | Y | Y |
| 9 Bilirakis | N | Y | Y | Y | Y | Y |
| 10 Young | ? | ? | ? | ? | ? | Y |
| 11 Davis | Y | Y | Y | ? | ? | Y |
| 12 Putnam | N | Y | Y | Y | Y | Y |
| 13 Harris | N | Y | Y | Y | Y | Y |
| 14 Mack | Y | Y | Y | Y | Y | Y |
| 15 Weldon | ? | ? | + | + | + | Y |
| 16 Foley | N | Y | Y | Y | Y | Y |
| 17 Meek | Y | Y | Y | Y | Y | Y |
| 18 Ros-Lehtinen | N | Y | Y | Y | Y | Y |
| 19 Wexler | ? | ? | Y | Y | Y | Y |
| 20 Wasserman-Schultz | Y | Y | Y | Y | Y | Y |
| 21 Diaz-Balart, L. | N | Y | Y | Y | Y | Y |
| 22 Shaw | N | Y | Y | Y | Y | Y |
| 23 Hastings | ? | ? | Y | Y | N | Y |
| 24 Feeney | N | Y | ? | ? | ? | ? |
| 25 Diaz-Balart, M. | N | Y | ? | ? | ? | Y |
| **GEORGIA** | | | | | | |
| 1 Kingston | ? | ? | Y | Y | Y | Y |
| 2 Bishop | Y | Y | Y | Y | Y | Y |
| 3 Marshall | Y | Y | Y | Y | Y | Y |
| 4 McKinney | Y | Y | Y | Y | Y | Y |
| 5 Lewis | Y | Y | Y | Y | N | Y |
| 6 Price | N | Y | Y | Y | Y | Y |
| 7 Linder | – | + | + | + | + | Y |
| 8 Westmoreland | ? | ? | Y | Y | Y | Y |
| 9 Norwood | N | Y | Y | Y | Y | Y |
| 10 Deal | N | Y | Y | Y | Y | Y |
| 11 Gingrey | N | Y | Y | Y | Y | Y |
| 12 Barrow | Y | Y | Y | Y | Y | Y |
| 13 Scott | Y | Y | Y | Y | Y | Y |
| **HAWAII** | | | | | | |
| 1 Abercrombie | Y | Y | Y | Y | N | Y |
| 2 Case | Y | Y | Y | Y | Y | Y |
| **IDAHO** | | | | | | |
| 1 Otter | N | Y | Y | Y | Y | Y |
| 2 Simpson | N | Y | Y | Y | Y | Y |
| **ILLINOIS** | | | | | | |
| 1 Rush | Y | Y | ? | ? | ? | Y |
| 2 Jackson | Y | Y | Y | Y | Y | Y |
| 3 Lipinski | Y | Y | Y | Y | Y | Y |
| 4 Gutierrez | + | + | + | + | + | Y |
| 5 Emanuel | Y | Y | Y | Y | Y | Y |
| 6 Hyde | N | Y | Y | Y | Y | Y |
| 7 Davis | Y | Y | Y | Y | Y | Y |
| 8 Bean | Y | Y | ? | ? | ? | Y |
| 9 Schakowsky | Y | Y | Y | Y | Y | Y |
| 10 Kirk | N | Y | + | Y | Y | Y |
| 11 Weller | N | Y | Y | Y | Y | Y |
| 12 Costello | Y | Y | Y | ? | ? | Y |

| | 415 | 416 | 417 | 418 | 419 | 420 |
|---|---|---|---|---|---|---|
| 13 **Biggert** | N | Y | Y | Y | Y | Y |
| 14 **Hastert** | | | | | | |
| 15 **Johnson** | N | Y | Y | Y | Y | Y |
| 16 **Manzullo** | N | Y | Y | Y | Y | Y |
| 17 Evans | Y | Y | Y | Y | Y | Y |
| 18 **LaHood** | N | Y | Y | Y | Y | Y |
| 19 **Shimkus** | N | Y | Y | Y | Y | Y |
| **INDIANA** | | | | | | |
| 1 Visclosky | Y | Y | Y | Y | Y | Y |
| 2 **Chocola** | N | Y | Y | Y | Y | Y |
| 3 **Souder** | N | Y | ? | ? | ? | Y |
| 4 **Buyer** | N | Y | ? | ? | ? | Y |
| 5 **Burton** | N | Y | Y | Y | Y | Y |
| 6 **Pence** | N | Y | Y | Y | Y | Y |
| 7 Carson | Y | Y | Y | Y | Y | Y |
| 8 **Hostettler** | N | Y | ? | ? | ? | Y |
| 9 **Sodrel** | N | Y | ? | ? | ? | Y |
| **IOWA** | | | | | | |
| 1 **Nussle** | ? | ? | ? | ? | ? | Y |
| 2 **Leach** | N | Y | Y | Y | Y | Y |
| 3 Boswell | Y | Y | Y | Y | Y | Y |
| 4 **Latham** | N | Y | Y | Y | Y | Y |
| 5 **King** | N | Y | Y | Y | Y | Y |
| **KANSAS** | | | | | | |
| 1 **Moran** | N | Y | Y | Y | Y | Y |
| 2 **Ryun** | N | Y | Y | Y | Y | Y |
| 3 Moore | Y | Y | Y | Y | Y | Y |
| 4 **Tiahrt** | N | Y | Y | Y | Y | Y |
| **KENTUCKY** | | | | | | |
| 1 **Whitfield** | N | Y | Y | Y | Y | Y |
| 2 **Lewis** | N | Y | Y | Y | Y | Y |
| 3 **Northup** | N | Y | Y | Y | Y | Y |
| 4 **Davis** | N | Y | Y | Y | Y | Y |
| 5 **Rogers** | N | Y | Y | Y | Y | Y |
| 6 Chandler | Y | Y | Y | Y | Y | Y |
| **LOUISIANA** | | | | | | |
| 1 **Jindal** | Y | Y | Y | Y | Y | Y |
| 2 Jefferson | ? | ? | Y | Y | ? | Y |
| 3 Melancon | Y | Y | Y | Y | Y | Y |
| 4 **McCrery** | Y | Y | Y | Y | Y | Y |
| 5 **Alexander** | N | Y | Y | Y | Y | Y |
| 6 **Baker** | N | ? | Y | Y | Y | Y |
| 7 **Boustany** | Y | Y | Y | Y | Y | Y |
| **MAINE** | | | | | | |
| 1 Allen | Y | Y | Y | Y | Y | Y |
| 2 Michaud | Y | Y | Y | Y | Y | Y |
| **MARYLAND** | | | | | | |
| 1 **Gilchrest** | N | Y | Y | Y | Y | Y |
| 2 Ruppersberger | Y | Y | Y | Y | Y | Y |
| 3 Cardin | Y | Y | Y | Y | Y | Y |
| 4 Wynn | Y | Y | Y | Y | Y | Y |
| 5 Hoyer | Y | Y | Y | Y | Y | Y |
| 6 **Bartlett** | N | Y | Y | Y | Y | Y |
| 7 Cummings | Y | Y | Y | Y | Y | Y |
| 8 Van Hollen | Y | Y | Y | Y | Y | Y |
| **MASSACHUSETTS** | | | | | | |
| 1 Olver | Y | N | Y | Y | Y | Y |
| 2 Neal | Y | Y | ? | Y | Y | Y |
| 3 McGovern | Y | Y | Y | Y | Y | Y |
| 4 Frank | Y | N | Y | Y | N | Y |
| 5 Meehan | Y | N | Y | Y | Y | Y |
| 6 Tierney | Y | N | Y | Y | Y | Y |
| 7 Markey | Y | Y | Y | Y | Y | Y |
| 8 Capuano | Y | Y | Y | Y | Y | Y |
| 9 Lynch | Y | Y | Y | Y | Y | Y |
| 10 Delahunt | ? | ? | ? | ? | ? | Y |
| **MICHIGAN** | | | | | | |
| 1 Stupak | Y | Y | Y | Y | Y | Y |
| 2 **Hoekstra** | N | Y | Y | Y | Y | Y |
| 3 **Ehlers** | N | Y | Y | Y | Y | Y |
| 4 **Camp** | N | Y | Y | Y | Y | Y |
| 5 Kildee | Y | Y | Y | Y | Y | Y |
| 6 **Upton** | N | Y | Y | Y | Y | Y |
| 7 **Schwarz** | N | Y | Y | Y | Y | Y |
| 8 **Rogers** | N | Y | Y | Y | Y | Y |
| 9 **Knollenberg** | N | Y | Y | Y | Y | Y |
| 10 **Miller** | N | Y | ? | ? | ? | Y |
| 11 **McCotter** | N | Y | Y | Y | Y | Y |
| 12 Levin | Y | Y | Y | Y | Y | Y |
| 13 Kilpatrick | Y | Y | + | + | + | Y |
| 14 Conyers | Y | N | Y | Y | N | Y |
| 15 Dingell | Y | N | Y | Y | Y | Y |

| | 415 | 416 | 417 | 418 | 419 | 420 |
|---|---|---|---|---|---|---|
| **MINNESOTA** | | | | | | |
| 1 **Gutknecht** | N | Y | Y | Y | Y | Y |
| 2 **Kline** | N | Y | Y | Y | Y | Y |
| 3 **Ramstad** | N | Y | Y | Y | Y | Y |
| 4 McCollum | Y | Y | Y | Y | Y | Y |
| 5 Sabo | Y | N | Y | Y | Y | Y |
| 6 **Kennedy** | N | Y | Y | Y | Y | Y |
| 7 Peterson | Y | Y | Y | Y | Y | Y |
| 8 Oberstar | Y | N | Y | Y | Y | Y |
| **MISSISSIPPI** | | | | | | |
| 1 **Wicker** | N | Y | Y | Y | Y | Y |
| 2 Thompson | Y | Y | Y | Y | Y | Y |
| 3 **Pickering** | ? | ? | Y | Y | Y | Y |
| 4 Taylor | ? | ? | Y | Y | Y | Y |
| **MISSOURI** | | | | | | |
| 1 Clay | ? | ? | ? | ? | ? | Y |
| 2 **Akin** | N | Y | Y | Y | Y | Y |
| 3 Carnahan | Y | Y | Y | Y | Y | Y |
| 4 Skelton | Y | Y | Y | Y | Y | Y |
| 5 Cleaver | Y | Y | Y | Y | Y | Y |
| 6 **Graves** | N | Y | Y | Y | Y | Y |
| 7 **Blunt** | N | Y | Y | Y | Y | Y |
| 8 **Emerson** | N | Y | Y | Y | Y | Y |
| 9 **Hulshof** | N | Y | ? | ? | ? | Y |
| **MONTANA** | | | | | | |
| AL **Rehberg** | N | Y | Y | Y | Y | Y |
| **NEBRASKA** | | | | | | |
| 1 **Fortenberry** | N | Y | Y | Y | Y | Y |
| 2 **Terry** | N | Y | ? | ? | ? | Y |
| 3 **Osborne** | N | Y | Y | Y | Y | Y |
| **NEVADA** | | | | | | |
| 1 Berkley | Y | Y | Y | Y | N | Y |
| 2 **Gibbons** | N | Y | ? | ? | ? | ? |
| 3 **Porter** | N | Y | Y | Y | Y | Y |
| **NEW HAMPSHIRE** | | | | | | |
| 1 **Bradley** | N | Y | Y | Y | Y | Y |
| 2 **Bass** | N | Y | Y | Y | Y | Y |
| **NEW JERSEY** | | | | | | |
| 1 Andrews | Y | Y | Y | Y | Y | Y |
| 2 **LoBiondo** | N | Y | Y | Y | Y | Y |
| 3 **Saxton** | N | Y | Y | Y | Y | Y |
| 4 **Smith** | N | Y | Y | Y | Y | Y |
| 5 **Garrett** | N | Y | Y | Y | Y | Y |
| 6 Pallone | Y | Y | Y | Y | Y | Y |
| 7 **Ferguson** | N | Y | Y | Y | Y | Y |
| 8 Pascrell | Y | Y | Y | Y | Y | Y |
| 9 Rothman | Y | Y | ? | ? | ? | Y |
| 10 Payne | Y | Y | Y | Y | N | ? |
| 11 **Frelinghuysen** | N | Y | Y | Y | Y | Y |
| 12 Holt | + | Y | Y | Y | Y | Y |
| 13 Menendez | Y | Y | Y | Y | Y | Y |
| **NEW MEXICO** | | | | | | |
| 1 **Wilson** | N | Y | Y | Y | Y | Y |
| 2 **Pearce** | ? | Y | Y | Y | Y | Y |
| 3 Udall | Y | Y | Y | Y | Y | Y |
| **NEW YORK** | | | | | | |
| 1 Bishop | Y | Y | Y | Y | Y | Y |
| 2 Israel | Y | Y | Y | Y | Y | Y |
| 3 **King** | N | Y | ? | ? | ? | Y |
| 4 McCarthy | Y | Y | Y | Y | Y | Y |
| 5 Ackerman | Y | Y | Y | Y | Y | Y |
| 6 Meeks | Y | Y | Y | Y | Y | Y |
| 7 Crowley | Y | Y | Y | Y | Y | Y |
| 8 Nadler | Y | Y | Y | Y | Y | Y |
| 9 Weiner | Y | Y | Y | Y | Y | Y |
| 10 Towns | Y | Y | Y | Y | N | Y |
| 11 Owens | Y | Y | Y | Y | N | Y |
| 12 Velázquez | Y | Y | Y | Y | N | Y |
| 13 **Fossella** | N | Y | ? | ? | ? | Y |
| 14 Maloney | Y | Y | Y | Y | Y | Y |
| 15 Rangel | Y | Y | Y | Y | Y | Y |
| 16 Serrano | Y | Y | Y | Y | N | Y |
| 17 Engel | Y | Y | Y | Y | Y | Y |
| 18 Lowey | Y | Y | Y | Y | Y | Y |
| 19 **Kelly** | N | Y | Y | Y | Y | Y |
| 20 **Sweeney** | N | Y | ? | ? | ? | Y |
| 21 McNulty | Y | Y | Y | Y | Y | Y |
| 22 Hinchey | Y | Y | Y | Y | Y | Y |
| 23 **McHugh** | N | Y | Y | Y | Y | Y |
| 24 **Boehlert** | N | Y | Y | Y | Y | Y |
| 25 **Walsh** | Y | Y | Y | Y | Y | Y |
| 26 **Reynolds** | ? | Y | Y | Y | Y | Y |
| 27 Higgins | Y | Y | Y | Y | Y | Y |
| 28 Slaughter | Y | Y | Y | Y | Y | Y |
| 29 **Kuhl** | N | Y | Y | Y | Y | Y |

| | 415 | 416 | 417 | 418 | 419 | 420 |
|---|---|---|---|---|---|---|
| **NORTH CAROLINA** | | | | | | |
| 1 Butterfield | Y | Y | Y | Y | Y | Y |
| 2 Etheridge | Y | Y | Y | Y | Y | Y |
| 3 **Jones** | N | Y | Y | Y | Y | Y |
| 4 Price | Y | Y | Y | Y | Y | Y |
| 5 **Foxx** | N | Y | Y | Y | Y | Y |
| 6 **Coble** | N | Y | Y | Y | Y | Y |
| 7 McIntyre | Y | Y | Y | Y | Y | Y |
| 8 **Hayes** | N | Y | Y | Y | Y | Y |
| 9 **Myrick** | – | + | Y | Y | Y | Y |
| 10 **McHenry** | N | Y | Y | Y | Y | Y |
| 11 **Taylor** | – | + | Y | Y | Y | Y |
| 12 Watt | Y | Y | Y | Y | P | Y |
| 13 Miller | Y | Y | Y | Y | Y | Y |
| **NORTH DAKOTA** | | | | | | |
| AL Pomeroy | Y | Y | Y | Y | Y | Y |
| **OHIO** | | | | | | |
| 1 **Chabot** | N | Y | Y | Y | Y | Y |
| 2 Vacant | | | | | | |
| 3 **Turner** | N | Y | Y | Y | Y | Y |
| 4 **Oxley** | N | Y | Y | Y | Y | Y |
| 5 **Gillmor** | N | Y | Y | Y | Y | Y |
| 6 Strickland | Y | Y | ? | ? | ? | Y |
| 7 **Hobson** | N | Y | ? | ? | ? | Y |
| 8 **Boehner** | N | Y | Y | Y | Y | Y |
| 9 Kaptur | Y | Y | Y | Y | Y | Y |
| 10 Kucinich | Y | Y | Y | Y | Y | Y |
| 11 Jones | Y | Y | Y | Y | N | Y |
| 12 **Tiberi** | N | Y | + | + | + | Y |
| 13 Brown | Y | Y | Y | Y | Y | Y |
| 14 **LaTourette** | N | Y | Y | Y | Y | Y |
| 15 **Pryce** | N | Y | ? | ? | ? | Y |
| 16 **Regula** | N | Y | Y | Y | Y | Y |
| 17 Ryan | Y | Y | Y | Y | Y | Y |
| 18 **Ney** | Y | Y | Y | Y | Y | Y |
| **OKLAHOMA** | | | | | | |
| 1 **Sullivan** | N | Y | Y | Y | Y | Y |
| 2 Boren | ? | ? | Y | Y | Y | Y |
| 3 **Lucas** | N | Y | Y | Y | Y | Y |
| 4 **Cole** | N | Y | + | + | + | Y |
| 5 **Istook** | N | Y | ? | ? | ? | Y |
| **OREGON** | | | | | | |
| 1 Wu | Y | Y | Y | Y | Y | Y |
| 2 **Walden** | N | Y | Y | Y | Y | Y |
| 3 Blumenauer | Y | Y | Y | Y | N | Y |
| 4 DeFazio | Y | N | Y | Y | Y | Y |
| 5 Hooley | Y | Y | Y | Y | Y | Y |
| **PENNSYLVANIA** | | | | | | |
| 1 Brady | Y | Y | Y | Y | Y | Y |
| 2 Fattah | Y | Y | ? | ? | ? | Y |
| 3 **English** | N | Y | Y | Y | Y | Y |
| 4 **Hart** | N | Y | Y | Y | Y | Y |
| 5 **Peterson** | N | Y | Y | Y | Y | Y |
| 6 **Gerlach** | N | Y | Y | Y | Y | Y |
| 7 **Weldon** | N | Y | ? | ? | ? | Y |
| 8 **Fitzpatrick** | N | Y | Y | Y | Y | Y |
| 9 **Shuster** | N | Y | Y | Y | Y | Y |
| 10 **Sherwood** | N | Y | Y | Y | Y | Y |
| 11 Kanjorski | Y | Y | Y | Y | Y | Y |
| 12 Murtha | Y | Y | Y | Y | ? | Y |
| 13 Schwartz | Y | Y | Y | Y | Y | Y |
| 14 Doyle | Y | Y | Y | Y | Y | Y |
| 15 **Dent** | N | Y | Y | Y | Y | Y |
| 16 **Pitts** | N | Y | Y | Y | Y | Y |
| 17 Holden | Y | Y | Y | Y | Y | Y |
| 18 **Murphy** | N | Y | Y | Y | Y | Y |
| 19 **Platts** | N | Y | Y | Y | Y | Y |
| **RHODE ISLAND** | | | | | | |
| 1 Kennedy | Y | Y | Y | Y | Y | Y |
| 2 Langevin | Y | Y | Y | Y | Y | Y |
| **SOUTH CAROLINA** | | | | | | |
| 1 **Brown** | ? | ? | Y | Y | Y | Y |
| 2 **Wilson** | N | Y | Y | Y | Y | Y |
| 3 **Barrett** | N | Y | Y | Y | Y | Y |
| 4 **Inglis** | N | Y | Y | Y | Y | Y |
| 5 Spratt | Y | Y | Y | Y | Y | Y |
| 6 Clyburn | Y | Y | Y | Y | Y | Y |
| **SOUTH DAKOTA** | | | | | | |
| AL Herseth | Y | Y | Y | Y | Y | Y |
| **TENNESSEE** | | | | | | |
| 1 **Jenkins** | N | Y | ? | ? | ? | Y |
| 2 **Duncan** | N | Y | Y | Y | Y | Y |

| | 415 | 416 | 417 | 418 | 419 | 420 |
|---|---|---|---|---|---|---|
| 3 **Wamp** | N | Y | Y | Y | Y | Y |
| 4 Davis | Y | Y | Y | Y | Y | Y |
| 5 Cooper | + | + | + | + | Y | Y |
| 6 Gordon | N | Y | Y | Y | Y | Y |
| 7 **Blackburn** | N | N | Y | Y | Y | Y |
| 8 Tanner | N | Y | Y | Y | Y | Y |
| 9 Ford | Y | Y | ? | Y | Y | Y |
| **TEXAS** | | | | | | |
| 1 **Gohmert** | N | ? | Y | Y | Y | Y |
| 2 **Poe** | N | Y | Y | Y | Y | Y |
| 3 **Johnson, S.** | N | Y | Y | Y | Y | Y |
| 4 **Hall** | N | Y | Y | Y | Y | Y |
| 5 **Hensarling** | N | Y | Y | Y | Y | Y |
| 6 **Barton** | N | Y | Y | Y | Y | Y |
| 7 **Culberson** | N | Y | Y | Y | Y | Y |
| 8 **Brady** | ? | Y | Y | Y | Y | Y |
| 9 Green, A. | Y | Y | Y | Y | Y | Y |
| 10 **McCaul** | N | Y | Y | Y | Y | Y |
| 11 **Conaway** | N | Y | Y | Y | Y | Y |
| 12 **Granger** | N | Y | Y | Y | Y | Y |
| 13 **Thornberry** | N | Y | Y | Y | Y | Y |
| 14 **Paul** | N | ? | Y | N | N | Y |
| 15 Hinojosa | ? | ? | + | + | + | Y |
| 16 Reyes | Y | Y | ? | ? | ? | Y |
| 17 Edwards | Y | Y | Y | Y | Y | Y |
| 18 Jackson-Lee | Y | Y | Y | Y | Y | Y |
| 19 **Neugebauer** | N | Y | Y | Y | Y | Y |
| 20 Gonzalez | Y | Y | Y | Y | Y | Y |
| 21 **Smith** | N | Y | Y | Y | Y | Y |
| 22 **DeLay** | N | Y | Y | Y | Y | ? |
| 23 **Bonilla** | N | Y | Y | Y | Y | Y |
| 24 **Marchant** | N | Y | Y | Y | Y | Y |
| 25 Doggett | Y | Y | Y | Y | Y | Y |
| 26 **Burgess** | N | Y | Y | Y | Y | Y |
| 27 Ortiz | Y | Y | + | + | + | Y |
| 28 Cuellar | Y | Y | Y | Y | Y | Y |
| 29 Green, G. | Y | Y | Y | Y | Y | Y |
| 30 Johnson, E. | Y | Y | Y | Y | N | Y |
| 31 **Carter** | N | Y | Y | Y | Y | Y |
| 32 **Sessions** | N | Y | Y | Y | Y | Y |
| **UTAH** | | | | | | |
| 1 **Bishop** | ? | ? | ? | ? | ? | Y |
| 2 Matheson | Y | Y | Y | Y | Y | Y |
| 3 **Cannon** | N | Y | ? | ? | ? | Y |
| **VERMONT** | | | | | | |
| AL *Sanders* | Y | N | Y | Y | Y | Y |
| **VIRGINIA** | | | | | | |
| 1 **Davis, J.** | N | Y | Y | Y | Y | Y |
| 2 **Drake** | N | Y | Y | Y | Y | Y |
| 3 Scott | Y | Y | Y | Y | Y | Y |
| 4 **Forbes** | Y | Y | Y | Y | Y | Y |
| 5 **Goode** | N | Y | Y | Y | Y | Y |
| 6 **Goodlatte** | N | Y | Y | Y | Y | Y |
| 7 **Cantor** | N | Y | Y | Y | Y | Y |
| 8 Moran | Y | Y | Y | Y | Y | ? |
| 9 Boucher | Y | Y | Y | Y | Y | Y |
| 10 **Wolf** | N | Y | Y | Y | Y | Y |
| 11 **Davis, T.** | N | Y | Y | Y | Y | Y |
| **WASHINGTON** | | | | | | |
| 1 Inslee | Y | ? | Y | Y | Y | Y |
| 2 Larsen | Y | Y | Y | Y | Y | Y |
| 3 Baird | Y | Y | Y | Y | Y | Y |
| 4 **Hastings** | N | Y | Y | Y | Y | Y |
| 5 **McMorris** | N | Y | Y | Y | Y | Y |
| 6 Dicks | Y | Y | Y | Y | Y | Y |
| 7 McDermott | Y | N | Y | Y | N | Y |
| 8 **Reichert** | N | Y | Y | Y | Y | Y |
| 9 Smith | Y | Y | Y | Y | Y | Y |
| **WEST VIRGINIA** | | | | | | |
| 1 Mollohan | Y | Y | Y | Y | Y | Y |
| 2 **Capito** | N | Y | Y | Y | Y | Y |
| 3 Rahall | Y | Y | + | + | + | Y |
| **WISCONSIN** | | | | | | |
| 1 **Ryan** | N | Y | Y | Y | Y | Y |
| 2 Baldwin | Y | Y | Y | Y | Y | Y |
| 3 Kind | Y | Y | Y | Y | Y | Y |
| 4 Moore | Y | Y | Y | Y | Y | Y |
| 5 **Sensenbrenner** | N | Y | Y | Y | Y | Y |
| 6 **Petri** | N | Y | Y | Y | Y | Y |
| 7 Obey | Y | N | Y | Y | ? | Y |
| 8 **Green** | N | Y | Y | Y | Y | Y |
| **WYOMING** | | | | | | |
| AL **Cubin** | ? | ? | Y | Y | Y | Y |

# IN THE HOUSE | By Vote Number

**421.** HR 3283. China Trade Practices/Passage. Thomas, R-Calif., motion to suspend the rules and pass the bill that would establish mechanisms to ensure that China abides by previous trade commitments, including creating a system to monitor compliance with trade obligations on intellectual property rights, market access for U.S. goods, services and agriculture and the accounting of Chinese subsidies. Motion rejected 240-186: R 221-5; D 19-180 (ND 10-139, SD 9-41); I 0-1. A two-thirds majority of those present and voting (284 in this case) is required for passage under suspension of the rules. July 26, 2005.

**422.** HR 2361. Fiscal 2006 Interior-Environment Appropriations/Motion to Instruct. Obey, D-Wis., motion to instruct House conferees to accept the Senate language providing an additional $1.5 billion for veterans' medical care in fiscal 2005. Motion agreed to 426-0: R 225-0; D 200-0 (ND 150-0, SD 50-0); I 1-0. July 26, 2005.

**423.** HR 2977. Paul Kasten Post Office/Passage. Issa, R-Calif., motion to suspend the rules and pass the bill to designate a post office in Brockway, Mont., for Paul Kasten, a postal carrier serving eastern Montana postal routes for more than 50 years. Motion agreed to 422-0: R 224-0; D 198-0 (ND 148-0, SD 50-0); I 0-0. A two-thirds majority of those present and voting (282 in this case) is required for passage under suspension of the rules. July 26, 2005.

**424.** HR 525. Health Plans for Small Businesses/Democratic Substitute. Kind, D-Wis., substitute amendment that would require the Labor Department to establish a Small Employer Health Benefits Plan and make all employers with fewer than 100 employees during the previous calendar year eligible for coverage. The Labor Department would contract annually with state-licensed health insurers to offer health insurance within a state, and participating insurers would remain subject to the laws of the state in which they cover residents. Rejected 197-230: R 1-225; D 195-5 (ND 147-3, SD 48-2); I 1-0. July 26, 2005.

**425.** HR 525. Health Plans for Small Businesses/Recommit. Miller, D-Calif., motion to recommit the bill to the Education and Workforce Committee with instructions to maintain state health coverage for pregnancy, childbirth, child care, breast and cervical cancer screening and tests recommended by a physician, mental illness, and diabetes. Motion rejected 198-230: R 0-227; D 197-3 (ND 147-3, SD 50-0); I 1-0. July 26, 2005.

**426.** HR 525. Health Plans for Small Businesses/Passage. Passage of the bill that would allow for the creation of association health plans through which small companies could band together to buy insurance for their employees. Association health plans that cover employees in multiple states would be exempt from many individual state insurance regulations but would be regulated by the Labor Department. Passed 263-165: R 227-0; D 36-164 (ND 18-132, SD 18-32); I 0-1. A "yea" was a vote in support of the president's position. July 26, 2005.

| | 421 | 422 | 423 | 424 | 425 | 426 |
|---|---|---|---|---|---|---|
| **ALABAMA** | | | | | | |
| 1 Bonner | Y | Y | Y | N | N | Y |
| 2 Everett | Y | Y | Y | N | N | Y |
| 3 Rogers | Y | Y | Y | N | N | Y |
| 4 Aderholt | Y | Y | Y | N | N | Y |
| 5 Cramer | ? | ? | ? | ? | ? | ? |
| 6 Bachus | Y | Y | Y | N | N | Y |
| 7 Davis | N | Y | Y | Y | N | Y |
| **ALASKA** | | | | | | |
| AL Young | Y | Y | Y | N | N | Y |
| **ARIZONA** | | | | | | |
| 1 Renzi | Y | Y | Y | N | N | Y |
| 2 Franks | Y | Y | Y | N | N | Y |
| 3 Shadegg | Y | Y | Y | N | N | Y |
| 4 Pastor | N | Y | Y | Y | Y | N |
| 5 Hayworth | Y | Y | Y | N | N | Y |
| 6 Flake | Y | Y | Y | N | N | Y |
| 7 Grijalva | N | Y | Y | Y | Y | N |
| 8 Kolbe | N | Y | Y | N | N | Y |
| **ARKANSAS** | | | | | | |
| 1 Berry | Y | Y | Y | Y | Y | N |
| 2 Snyder | N | Y | Y | Y | Y | N |
| 3 Boozman | Y | Y | Y | N | N | Y |
| 4 Ross | N | Y | Y | Y | Y | N |
| **CALIFORNIA** | | | | | | |
| 1 Thompson | N | Y | Y | Y | Y | N |
| 2 Herger | Y | Y | Y | N | N | Y |
| 3 Lungren | Y | Y | Y | N | N | Y |
| 4 Doolittle | Y | Y | Y | N | N | Y |
| 5 Matsui, D. | N | Y | Y | Y | Y | N |
| 6 Woolsey | N | Y | Y | Y | Y | N |
| 7 Miller, George | N | Y | Y | Y | Y | N |
| 8 Pelosi | N | Y | Y | Y | Y | N |
| 9 Lee | N | Y | Y | Y | Y | N |
| 10 Tauscher | N | Y | Y | Y | Y | N |
| 11 Pombo | Y | Y | Y | N | N | Y |
| 12 Lantos | N | Y | Y | Y | Y | N |
| 13 Stark | N | Y | Y | Y | Y | N |
| 14 Eshoo | N | Y | Y | Y | Y | N |
| 15 Honda | N | Y | Y | Y | Y | N |
| 16 Lofgren | N | Y | Y | Y | Y | N |
| 17 Farr | N | Y | Y | Y | Y | N |
| 18 Cardoza | N | Y | Y | Y | Y | N |
| 19 Radanovich | Y | Y | Y | N | N | Y |
| 20 Costa | N | Y | Y | Y | Y | N |
| 21 Nunes | Y | Y | Y | N | N | Y |
| 22 Thomas | Y | Y | Y | N | N | Y |
| 23 Capps | N | Y | Y | Y | Y | N |
| 24 Gallegly | Y | Y | Y | N | N | Y |
| 25 McKeon | Y | Y | Y | N | N | Y |
| 26 Dreier | Y | Y | Y | N | N | Y |
| 27 Sherman | N | Y | Y | Y | Y | N |
| 28 Berman | N | Y | Y | Y | Y | N |
| 29 Schiff | N | Y | Y | Y | Y | N |
| 30 Waxman | N | Y | Y | Y | ? | ? |
| 31 Becerra | N | Y | Y | Y | Y | N |
| 32 Solis | N | Y | Y | Y | Y | N |
| 33 Watson | N | Y | Y | Y | Y | N |
| 34 Roybal-Allard | N | Y | Y | Y | Y | N |
| 35 Waters | N | Y | Y | Y | Y | N |
| 36 Harman | Y | Y | Y | Y | Y | N |
| 37 Millender-McD. | N | Y | Y | Y | Y | N |
| 38 Napolitano | N | Y | Y | Y | Y | N |
| 39 Sánchez, Linda | N | Y | Y | Y | Y | N |
| 40 Royce | Y | Y | Y | N | N | Y |
| 41 Lewis | Y | Y | Y | N | N | Y |
| 42 Miller, Gary | Y | Y | Y | N | N | Y |
| 43 Baca | N | Y | Y | Y | Y | N |
| 44 Calvert | Y | Y | Y | N | N | Y |
| 45 Bono | Y | Y | Y | N | N | Y |
| 46 Rohrabacher | Y | Y | Y | N | N | Y |
| 47 Sanchez, Loretta | N | Y | Y | Y | Y | N |
| 48 Cox | ? | ? | ? | N | N | Y |
| 49 Issa | Y | Y | Y | N | N | Y |

| | 421 | 422 | 423 | 424 | 425 | 426 |
|---|---|---|---|---|---|---|
| 50 Cunningham | Y | Y | Y | N | N | Y |
| 51 Filner | N | Y | Y | Y | Y | N |
| 52 Hunter | Y | Y | Y | N | N | Y |
| 53 Davis | N | Y | Y | Y | Y | N |
| **COLORADO** | | | | | | |
| 1 DeGette | N | Y | Y | Y | Y | N |
| 2 Udall | N | Y | Y | Y | Y | N |
| 3 Salazar | N | Y | Y | Y | Y | N |
| 4 Musgrave | Y | Y | Y | N | N | Y |
| 5 Hefley | Y | Y | Y | N | N | Y |
| 6 Tancredo | Y | Y | Y | N | N | Y |
| 7 Beauprez | Y | Y | Y | N | N | Y |
| **CONNECTICUT** | | | | | | |
| 1 Larson | N | Y | Y | Y | Y | N |
| 2 Simmons | Y | Y | Y | N | N | Y |
| 3 DeLauro | N | Y | Y | Y | Y | N |
| 4 Shays | Y | Y | Y | N | N | Y |
| 5 Johnson | Y | Y | Y | N | N | Y |
| **DELAWARE** | | | | | | |
| AL Castle | Y | Y | Y | N | N | Y |
| **FLORIDA** | | | | | | |
| 1 Miller | Y | Y | Y | N | N | Y |
| 2 Boyd | N | Y | Y | Y | Y | N |
| 3 Brown | N | Y | Y | Y | Y | N |
| 4 Crenshaw | Y | Y | Y | N | N | Y |
| 5 Brown-Waite | Y | Y | Y | N | N | Y |
| 6 Stearns | Y | ? | Y | N | N | Y |
| 7 Mica | Y | Y | Y | N | N | Y |
| 8 Keller | Y | Y | Y | N | N | Y |
| 9 Bilirakis | Y | Y | Y | N | N | Y |
| 10 Young | Y | Y | Y | N | N | Y |
| 11 Davis | N | Y | Y | Y | Y | N |
| 12 Putnam | Y | Y | Y | N | N | Y |
| 13 Harris | Y | Y | Y | N | N | Y |
| 14 Mack | Y | Y | Y | N | N | Y |
| 15 Weldon | + | + | + | N | N | Y |
| 16 Foley | Y | Y | Y | N | N | Y |
| 17 Meek | N | Y | Y | Y | Y | N |
| 18 Ros-Lehtinen | Y | Y | Y | N | N | Y |
| 19 Wexler | N | Y | Y | Y | Y | N |
| 20 Wasserman-Schultz | N | Y | Y | Y | Y | N |
| 21 Diaz-Balart, L. | Y | Y | Y | N | N | Y |
| 22 Shaw | Y | Y | Y | N | N | Y |
| 23 Hastings | N | Y | Y | Y | Y | N |
| 24 Feeney | ? | ? | ? | ? | ? | ? |
| 25 Diaz-Balart, M. | Y | Y | Y | N | N | Y |
| **GEORGIA** | | | | | | |
| 1 Kingston | Y | Y | Y | N | N | Y |
| 2 Bishop | N | Y | Y | Y | Y | Y |
| 3 Marshall | N | Y | Y | Y | Y | Y |
| 4 McKinney | N | Y | Y | Y | Y | N |
| 5 Lewis | N | Y | Y | Y | Y | N |
| 6 Price | Y | Y | Y | N | N | Y |
| 7 Linder | Y | Y | Y | N | N | Y |
| 8 Westmoreland | Y | Y | Y | ? | N | Y |
| 9 Norwood | Y | Y | Y | N | N | Y |
| 10 Deal | Y | Y | Y | N | N | Y |
| 11 Gingrey | Y | Y | Y | N | N | Y |
| 12 Barrow | Y | Y | Y | N | N | Y |
| 13 Scott | N | Y | Y | Y | Y | N |
| **HAWAII** | | | | | | |
| 1 Abercrombie | N | Y | Y | Y | Y | N |
| 2 Case | N | Y | Y | Y | Y | N |
| **IDAHO** | | | | | | |
| 1 Otter | Y | Y | Y | N | N | Y |
| 2 Simpson | Y | Y | Y | N | N | Y |
| **ILLINOIS** | | | | | | |
| 1 Rush | N | Y | Y | Y | Y | N |
| 2 Jackson | N | Y | Y | Y | Y | N |
| 3 Lipinski | N | Y | Y | Y | Y | Y |
| 4 Gutierrez | N | Y | Y | Y | Y | N |
| 5 Emanuel | N | Y | Y | Y | Y | N |
| 6 Hyde | Y | Y | Y | N | N | Y |
| 7 Davis | N | Y | Y | Y | Y | N |
| 8 Bean | N | Y | Y | Y | Y | Y |
| 9 Schakowsky | N | Y | Y | Y | Y | N |
| 10 Kirk | N | Y | Y | N | N | Y |
| 11 Weller | Y | Y | Y | N | N | Y |
| 12 Costello | N | Y | Y | Y | Y | Y |

**KEY**   Republicans   Democrats   *Independents*

| Y | Voted for (yea) | X | Paired against | C | Voted "present" to avoid possible conflict of interest |
|---|---|---|---|---|---|
| # | Paired for | – | Announced against | | |
| + | Announced for | P | Voted "present" | ? | Did not vote or otherwise make a position known |
| N | Voted against (nay) | | | | |

| | 421 | 422 | 423 | 424 | 425 | 426 |
|---|---|---|---|---|---|---|
| 13 **Biggert** | Y | Y | Y | N | N | Y |
| 14 **Hastert** | | | | | | |
| 15 **Johnson** | Y | Y | Y | N | N | Y |
| 16 **Manzullo** | Y | Y | Y | N | N | Y |
| 17 Evans | N | Y | Y | Y | N | N |
| 18 **LaHood** | Y | Y | Y | N | N | Y |
| 19 **Shimkus** | Y | Y | Y | N | N | Y |
| **INDIANA** | | | | | | |
| 1 Visclosky | N | Y | Y | Y | Y | N |
| 2 **Chocola** | Y | Y | Y | N | N | Y |
| 3 **Souder** | Y | Y | Y | N | N | Y |
| 4 **Buyer** | Y | Y | Y | N | N | Y |
| 5 **Burton** | Y | Y | Y | N | N | Y |
| 6 **Pence** | Y | Y | Y | N | N | Y |
| 7 Carson | N | Y | Y | Y | Y | N |
| 8 **Hostettler** | Y | Y | Y | N | N | Y |
| 9 **Sodrel** | Y | Y | Y | N | N | Y |
| **IOWA** | | | | | | |
| 1 **Nussle** | Y | Y | Y | N | N | Y |
| 2 **Leach** | Y | Y | Y | N | N | Y |
| 3 Boswell | Y | Y | Y | Y | Y | N |
| 4 **Latham** | Y | Y | Y | N | N | Y |
| 5 **King** | Y | Y | Y | N | N | Y |
| **KANSAS** | | | | | | |
| 1 **Moran** | Y | Y | Y | N | N | Y |
| 2 **Ryun** | Y | Y | Y | N | N | Y |
| 3 Moore | N | Y | Y | Y | Y | N |
| 4 **Tiahrt** | Y | Y | Y | N | N | Y |
| **KENTUCKY** | | | | | | |
| 1 **Whitfield** | Y | Y | Y | N | N | Y |
| 2 **Lewis** | Y | Y | Y | N | N | Y |
| 3 **Northup** | Y | Y | Y | N | N | Y |
| 4 **Davis** | Y | Y | Y | N | N | Y |
| 5 **Rogers** | Y | Y | Y | N | N | Y |
| 6 Chandler | N | Y | Y | Y | Y | N |
| **LOUISIANA** | | | | | | |
| 1 **Jindal** | Y | Y | Y | N | N | Y |
| 2 Jefferson | N | Y | Y | Y | Y | N |
| 3 Melancon | N | Y | Y | Y | Y | N |
| 4 **McCrery** | Y | Y | Y | N | N | Y |
| 5 **Alexander** | Y | Y | Y | N | N | Y |
| 6 **Baker** | Y | Y | Y | N | N | Y |
| 7 **Boustany** | Y | Y | Y | N | N | Y |
| **MAINE** | | | | | | |
| 1 Allen | N | Y | Y | Y | Y | N |
| 2 Michaud | N | Y | Y | Y | Y | N |
| **MARYLAND** | | | | | | |
| 1 **Gilchrest** | Y | Y | Y | N | N | Y |
| 2 Ruppersberger | N | Y | Y | Y | Y | N |
| 3 Cardin | N | Y | Y | Y | Y | N |
| 4 Wynn | N | Y | Y | N | N | Y |
| 5 Hoyer | N | Y | Y | Y | Y | N |
| 6 **Bartlett** | N | Y | Y | N | N | Y |
| 7 Cummings | N | Y | Y | Y | Y | N |
| 8 Van Hollen | N | Y | Y | Y | Y | N |
| **MASSACHUSETTS** | | | | | | |
| 1 Olver | N | Y | Y | Y | Y | N |
| 2 Neal | N | Y | Y | Y | Y | N |
| 3 McGovern | N | Y | Y | Y | Y | N |
| 4 Frank | N | Y | Y | Y | Y | N |
| 5 Meehan | N | Y | Y | Y | Y | N |
| 6 Tierney | N | Y | Y | Y | Y | N |
| 7 Markey | N | Y | Y | Y | Y | N |
| 8 Capuano | N | Y | Y | Y | Y | N |
| 9 Lynch | N | Y | Y | Y | Y | N |
| 10 Delahunt | N | Y | Y | Y | Y | N |
| **MICHIGAN** | | | | | | |
| 1 Stupak | N | Y | Y | Y | Y | N |
| 2 **Hoekstra** | Y | Y | Y | N | N | Y |
| 3 **Ehlers** | Y | Y | Y | N | N | Y |
| 4 **Camp** | Y | Y | Y | N | N | Y |
| 5 Kildee | N | Y | Y | Y | Y | N |
| 6 **Upton** | Y | Y | Y | N | N | Y |
| 7 **Schwarz** | Y | Y | Y | Y | N | Y |
| 8 **Rogers** | Y | Y | Y | N | N | Y |
| 9 **Knollenberg** | Y | Y | Y | N | N | Y |
| 10 **Miller** | Y | Y | Y | N | N | Y |
| 11 **McCotter** | Y | Y | Y | N | N | Y |
| 12 Levin | N | Y | Y | Y | Y | N |
| 13 Kilpatrick | N | Y | Y | Y | Y | N |
| 14 Conyers | N | Y | Y | Y | Y | N |
| 15 Dingell | N | Y | Y | Y | Y | N |

| | 421 | 422 | 423 | 424 | 425 | 426 |
|---|---|---|---|---|---|---|
| **MINNESOTA** | | | | | | |
| 1 **Gutknecht** | Y | Y | Y | N | N | Y |
| 2 **Kline** | Y | Y | Y | N | N | Y |
| 3 **Ramstad** | Y | Y | Y | N | N | Y |
| 4 McCollum | N | Y | Y | Y | Y | N |
| 5 Sabo | N | Y | Y | Y | Y | N |
| 6 **Kennedy** | Y | Y | Y | N | N | Y |
| 7 Peterson | ? | Y | Y | Y | Y | Y |
| 8 Oberstar | N | Y | ? | Y | Y | N |
| **MISSISSIPPI** | | | | | | |
| 1 **Wicker** | Y | Y | Y | N | N | Y |
| 2 Thompson | N | Y | Y | Y | Y | Y |
| 3 **Pickering** | Y | Y | Y | N | N | Y |
| 4 Taylor | Y | Y | Y | Y | Y | Y |
| **MISSOURI** | | | | | | |
| 1 Clay | N | Y | Y | Y | Y | N |
| 2 **Akin** | Y | Y | Y | N | N | Y |
| 3 Carnahan | N | Y | Y | Y | Y | N |
| 4 Skelton | Y | Y | Y | Y | Y | Y |
| 5 Cleaver | N | Y | Y | Y | Y | N |
| 6 **Graves** | Y | Y | Y | N | N | Y |
| 7 **Blunt** | Y | Y | Y | N | N | Y |
| 8 **Emerson** | Y | Y | Y | N | N | Y |
| 9 **Hulshof** | Y | Y | Y | N | N | Y |
| **MONTANA** | | | | | | |
| AL **Rehberg** | Y | Y | Y | N | N | Y |
| **NEBRASKA** | | | | | | |
| 1 **Fortenberry** | Y | Y | Y | N | N | Y |
| 2 **Terry** | Y | Y | Y | N | N | Y |
| 3 **Osborne** | Y | Y | Y | N | N | Y |
| **NEVADA** | | | | | | |
| 1 Berkley | N | Y | Y | Y | Y | N |
| 2 **Gibbons** | ? | ? | ? | ? | ? | ? |
| 3 **Porter** | Y | Y | Y | N | N | Y |
| **NEW HAMPSHIRE** | | | | | | |
| 1 **Bradley** | Y | Y | Y | N | N | Y |
| 2 **Bass** | Y | Y | Y | N | N | Y |
| **NEW JERSEY** | | | | | | |
| 1 Andrews | N | Y | Y | Y | Y | N |
| 2 **LoBiondo** | Y | Y | Y | N | N | Y |
| 3 **Saxton** | Y | Y | Y | N | N | Y |
| 4 **Smith** | Y | Y | Y | N | N | Y |
| 5 **Garrett** | Y | Y | Y | N | N | Y |
| 6 Pallone | N | Y | Y | Y | Y | N |
| 7 **Ferguson** | Y | Y | Y | N | N | Y |
| 8 Pascrell | N | Y | Y | Y | Y | N |
| 9 Rothman | N | Y | Y | Y | Y | Y |
| 10 Payne | ? | ? | ? | Y | Y | N |
| 11 **Frelinghuysen** | Y | Y | Y | N | N | Y |
| 12 Holt | N | Y | Y | Y | Y | N |
| 13 Menendez | N | Y | Y | Y | Y | N |
| **NEW MEXICO** | | | | | | |
| 1 **Wilson** | Y | Y | Y | N | N | Y |
| 2 **Pearce** | Y | Y | Y | N | N | Y |
| 3 Udall | N | Y | Y | Y | Y | N |
| **NEW YORK** | | | | | | |
| 1 Bishop | N | Y | Y | Y | Y | N |
| 2 Israel | N | Y | Y | Y | Y | Y |
| 3 **King** | Y | Y | Y | N | N | Y |
| 4 McCarthy | N | Y | Y | Y | Y | N |
| 5 Ackerman | N | Y | Y | Y | Y | N |
| 6 Meeks | N | Y | Y | Y | Y | N |
| 7 Crowley | N | Y | Y | Y | Y | N |
| 8 Nadler | N | Y | Y | Y | Y | N |
| 9 Weiner | N | Y | Y | Y | Y | N |
| 10 Towns | Y | Y | Y | Y | Y | N |
| 11 Owens | N | Y | Y | ? | Y | N |
| 12 Velázquez | N | Y | Y | N | N | Y |
| 13 **Fossella** | Y | Y | Y | N | N | Y |
| 14 Maloney | N | Y | Y | Y | Y | N |
| 15 Rangel | N | Y | Y | Y | Y | N |
| 16 Serrano | N | Y | Y | Y | Y | N |
| 17 Engel | Y | Y | Y | Y | Y | N |
| 18 Lowey | N | Y | Y | Y | Y | N |
| 19 **Kelly** | Y | Y | Y | N | N | Y |
| 20 **Sweeney** | Y | Y | Y | N | N | Y |
| 21 McNulty | N | Y | Y | Y | Y | N |
| 22 Hinchey | N | Y | Y | Y | Y | N |
| 23 **McHugh** | Y | Y | Y | N | N | Y |
| 24 **Boehlert** | Y | Y | ? | N | N | Y |
| 25 **Walsh** | Y | Y | Y | N | N | Y |
| 26 **Reynolds** | Y | Y | Y | N | N | Y |
| 27 Higgins | N | Y | Y | Y | Y | N |
| 28 Slaughter | N | Y | Y | Y | Y | N |
| 29 **Kuhl** | Y | Y | Y | N | N | Y |

| | 421 | 422 | 423 | 424 | 425 | 426 |
|---|---|---|---|---|---|---|
| **NORTH CAROLINA** | | | | | | |
| 1 Butterfield | N | Y | Y | Y | Y | N |
| 2 Etheridge | Y | Y | Y | Y | Y | N |
| 3 **Jones** | Y | Y | Y | N | N | Y |
| 4 Price | N | Y | Y | Y | Y | N |
| 5 **Foxx** | Y | Y | Y | N | N | Y |
| 6 **Coble** | Y | Y | Y | N | N | Y |
| 7 McIntyre | Y | Y | Y | N | Y | Y |
| 8 **Hayes** | Y | Y | Y | N | N | Y |
| 9 **Myrick** | Y | Y | Y | N | N | Y |
| 10 **McHenry** | Y | Y | Y | N | N | Y |
| 11 **Taylor** | Y | Y | Y | N | N | Y |
| 12 Watt | N | Y | Y | Y | Y | N |
| 13 Miller | N | Y | Y | Y | Y | N |
| **NORTH DAKOTA** | | | | | | |
| AL Pomeroy | N | Y | Y | Y | Y | N |
| **OHIO** | | | | | | |
| 1 **Chabot** | Y | Y | Y | N | N | Y |
| 2 Vacant | | | | | | |
| 3 **Turner** | Y | Y | Y | N | N | Y |
| 4 **Oxley** | Y | Y | Y | ? | ? | ? |
| 5 **Gillmor** | Y | Y | ? | N | N | Y |
| 6 Strickland | N | Y | Y | Y | Y | N |
| 7 **Hobson** | Y | Y | Y | N | N | Y |
| 8 **Boehner** | Y | Y | Y | N | N | Y |
| 9 Kaptur | N | Y | Y | Y | Y | N |
| 10 Kucinich | N | Y | Y | Y | Y | N |
| 11 Jones | N | Y | Y | Y | Y | N |
| 12 **Tiberi** | Y | Y | Y | N | N | Y |
| 13 Brown | N | Y | Y | Y | Y | N |
| 14 **LaTourette** | Y | Y | Y | N | N | Y |
| 15 **Pryce** | Y | Y | Y | N | N | Y |
| 16 **Regula** | Y | Y | Y | N | N | Y |
| 17 Ryan | N | Y | Y | Y | Y | N |
| 18 **Ney** | Y | Y | Y | N | N | Y |
| **OKLAHOMA** | | | | | | |
| 1 **Sullivan** | Y | Y | Y | N | N | Y |
| 2 Boren | Y | Y | Y | N | Y | Y |
| 3 **Lucas** | Y | Y | Y | N | N | Y |
| 4 **Cole** | Y | Y | Y | N | N | Y |
| 5 **Istook** | Y | Y | Y | N | N | Y |
| **OREGON** | | | | | | |
| 1 Wu | N | Y | Y | Y | Y | N |
| 2 **Walden** | Y | Y | Y | N | N | Y |
| 3 Blumenauer | N | Y | Y | Y | Y | N |
| 4 DeFazio | N | Y | Y | Y | Y | N |
| 5 Hooley | N | Y | Y | Y | Y | N |
| **PENNSYLVANIA** | | | | | | |
| 1 Brady | N | Y | Y | Y | Y | N |
| 2 Fattah | N | Y | Y | Y | Y | N |
| 3 **English** | Y | Y | Y | N | N | Y |
| 4 **Hart** | Y | Y | Y | N | N | Y |
| 5 **Peterson** | Y | Y | Y | N | N | Y |
| 6 **Gerlach** | Y | Y | Y | N | N | Y |
| 7 **Weldon** | Y | Y | Y | N | N | Y |
| 8 **Fitzpatrick** | Y | Y | Y | N | N | Y |
| 9 **Shuster** | Y | Y | Y | N | N | Y |
| 10 **Sherwood** | Y | Y | Y | N | N | Y |
| 11 Kanjorski | N | Y | Y | Y | Y | N |
| 12 Murtha | N | Y | Y | Y | Y | N |
| 13 Schwartz | N | Y | Y | Y | Y | N |
| 14 Doyle | N | Y | Y | Y | Y | N |
| 15 **Dent** | Y | Y | Y | N | N | Y |
| 16 **Pitts** | Y | Y | Y | N | N | Y |
| 17 Holden | N | Y | Y | Y | Y | N |
| 18 **Murphy** | Y | Y | Y | N | N | Y |
| 19 **Platts** | Y | Y | Y | N | N | Y |
| **RHODE ISLAND** | | | | | | |
| 1 Kennedy | N | Y | Y | Y | Y | N |
| 2 Langevin | N | Y | Y | Y | Y | N |
| **SOUTH CAROLINA** | | | | | | |
| 1 **Brown** | Y | Y | Y | N | N | Y |
| 2 **Wilson** | Y | Y | Y | N | N | Y |
| 3 **Barrett** | Y | Y | Y | N | N | Y |
| 4 **Inglis** | Y | Y | Y | N | N | Y |
| 5 Spratt | N | Y | Y | Y | Y | N |
| 6 Clyburn | N | Y | Y | Y | Y | N |
| **SOUTH DAKOTA** | | | | | | |
| AL Herseth | Y | Y | Y | Y | Y | Y |
| **TENNESSEE** | | | | | | |
| 1 **Jenkins** | Y | Y | Y | N | N | Y |
| 2 **Duncan** | Y | Y | Y | N | N | Y |

| | 421 | 422 | 423 | 424 | 425 | 426 |
|---|---|---|---|---|---|---|
| 3 **Wamp** | Y | Y | Y | N | N | Y |
| 4 Davis | N | Y | Y | Y | Y | Y |
| 5 Cooper | N | Y | Y | Y | Y | Y |
| 6 Gordon | Y | Y | Y | Y | Y | Y |
| 7 **Blackburn** | Y | Y | Y | N | N | Y |
| 8 Tanner | Y | Y | Y | Y | Y | N |
| 9 Ford | N | Y | Y | Y | Y | Y |
| **TEXAS** | | | | | | |
| 1 **Gohmert** | Y | Y | Y | N | N | Y |
| 2 **Poe** | Y | Y | Y | N | N | Y |
| 3 **Johnson, S.** | Y | Y | Y | N | N | Y |
| 4 **Hall** | Y | Y | Y | N | N | Y |
| 5 **Hensarling** | Y | Y | Y | N | N | Y |
| 6 **Barton** | Y | Y | Y | N | N | Y |
| 7 **Culberson** | Y | Y | Y | N | N | Y |
| 8 **Brady** | Y | Y | Y | N | N | Y |
| 9 Green, A. | N | Y | Y | Y | Y | N |
| 10 **McCaul** | Y | Y | Y | N | N | Y |
| 11 **Conaway** | Y | Y | Y | N | N | Y |
| 12 **Granger** | Y | Y | Y | N | N | Y |
| 13 **Thornberry** | Y | Y | Y | N | N | Y |
| 14 **Paul** | N | Y | Y | N | N | Y |
| 15 Hinojosa | N | Y | Y | Y | Y | N |
| 16 Reyes | N | Y | Y | Y | Y | N |
| 17 Edwards | N | Y | Y | Y | Y | Y |
| 18 Jackson-Lee | N | Y | Y | Y | Y | Y |
| 19 **Neugebauer** | Y | Y | Y | N | N | Y |
| 20 Gonzalez | N | Y | Y | Y | Y | Y |
| 21 **Smith** | Y | Y | Y | N | N | Y |
| 22 **DeLay** | Y | Y | Y | N | N | Y |
| 23 **Bonilla** | Y | Y | Y | N | N | Y |
| 24 **Marchant** | Y | Y | Y | N | N | Y |
| 25 Doggett | N | Y | Y | Y | Y | N |
| 26 **Burgess** | Y | Y | Y | N | N | Y |
| 27 Ortiz | N | Y | Y | Y | Y | Y |
| 28 Cuellar | Y | Y | Y | Y | Y | Y |
| 29 Green, G. | N | Y | Y | Y | Y | N |
| 30 Johnson, E. | N | Y | Y | Y | Y | N |
| 31 **Carter** | Y | Y | Y | N | N | Y |
| 32 **Sessions** | Y | Y | Y | N | N | Y |
| **UTAH** | | | | | | |
| 1 **Bishop** | Y | Y | Y | N | N | Y |
| 2 Matheson | Y | Y | Y | Y | Y | Y |
| 3 **Cannon** | Y | Y | Y | N | N | Y |
| **VERMONT** | | | | | | |
| AL *Sanders* | N | Y | ? | Y | Y | N |
| **VIRGINIA** | | | | | | |
| 1 **Davis, J.** | Y | Y | Y | N | N | Y |
| 2 **Drake** | Y | Y | Y | N | N | Y |
| 3 Scott | N | Y | Y | Y | Y | N |
| 4 **Forbes** | Y | Y | Y | N | N | Y |
| 5 **Goode** | Y | Y | Y | N | N | Y |
| 6 **Goodlatte** | Y | Y | Y | N | N | Y |
| 7 **Cantor** | Y | Y | Y | N | N | Y |
| 8 Moran | N | Y | Y | Y | Y | Y |
| 9 Boucher | N | Y | Y | Y | Y | N |
| 10 **Wolf** | Y | Y | Y | N | N | Y |
| 11 **Davis, T.** | Y | Y | Y | N | N | Y |
| **WASHINGTON** | | | | | | |
| 1 Inslee | Y | Y | Y | Y | Y | N |
| 2 Larsen | N | Y | Y | Y | Y | N |
| 3 Baird | N | Y | Y | Y | Y | Y |
| 4 **Hastings** | Y | Y | Y | N | N | Y |
| 5 **McMorris** | Y | Y | Y | N | N | Y |
| 6 Dicks | N | Y | ? | Y | Y | N |
| 7 McDermott | N | Y | Y | Y | Y | N |
| 8 **Reichert** | Y | Y | Y | N | N | Y |
| 9 Smith | Y | Y | Y | Y | Y | N |
| **WEST VIRGINIA** | | | | | | |
| 1 Mollohan | N | Y | Y | Y | Y | Y |
| 2 **Capito** | Y | Y | Y | N | N | Y |
| 3 Rahall | N | Y | Y | Y | Y | Y |
| **WISCONSIN** | | | | | | |
| 1 **Ryan** | Y | Y | Y | N | N | Y |
| 2 Baldwin | N | Y | Y | Y | Y | N |
| 3 Kind | Y | Y | Y | Y | Y | N |
| 4 Moore | N | Y | Y | Y | Y | N |
| 5 **Sensenbrenner** | Y | Y | Y | N | N | Y |
| 6 **Petri** | Y | Y | Y | N | N | Y |
| 7 Obey | N | Y | Y | Y | Y | N |
| 8 **Green** | Y | Y | Y | N | N | Y |
| **WYOMING** | | | | | | |
| AL **Cubin** | Y | Y | Y | N | N | Y |

# IN THE HOUSE | By Vote Number

**427.** **HR 2894. Abraham Lincoln Birthplace Post Office/Passage.** Issa, R-Calif., motion to suspend the rules and pass the bill that would designate a post office in Hodgenville, Ky., for Abraham Lincoln, who was born Feb. 12, 1809, in Hodgenville on the Sinking Spring Farm, now a national historic site. Motion agreed to 421-0: R 221-0; D 199-0 (ND 149-0, SD 50-0); I 1-0. A two-thirds majority of those present and voting (281 in this case) is required for passage under suspension of the rules. July 26, 2005.

**428.** **HR 22. Postal Service Overhaul/Postal Service Board of Governors.** Pence, R-Ind., amendment that would strike a provision in the bill that would require the next position on the Postal Service's Board of Governors to be filled by an individual with the unanimous backing of labor unions. Rejected 82-345: R 82-146; D 0-198 (ND 0-149, SD 0-49); I 0-1. July 26, 2005.

**429.** **HR 22. Postal Service Overhaul/Alternative Delivery Services.** Flake, R-Ariz., amendment that would create pilot programs for up to 20 communities to determine the feasibility of alternative mail delivery services. Rejected 51-379: R 51-177; D 0-201 (ND 0-150, SD 0-51); I 0-1. July 26, 2005.

**430.** **HR 22. Postal Service Overhaul/Passage.** Passage of the bill that would overhaul the operations of the U.S. Postal Service. The bill would replace the existing Postal Rate Commission with a Postal Regulatory Commission that has expanded regulatory powers. It would require separate rate regulation systems for market-dominant products and competitive products, including Express and Priority Mail. It would require the Treasury Department to pay postal worker retirement costs related to military service and would establish the Postal Service Retiree Health Benefits Fund. Passed 410-20: R 208-20; D 201-0 (ND 150-0, SD 51-0); I 1-0. A "nay" was a vote in support of the president's position. July 26, 2005.

**431.** **HR 3339. James T. Molloy Post Office/Passage.** Issa, R-Calif., motion to suspend the rules and pass the bill that would designate a post office in Buffalo, N.Y., for James T. Molloy, a former doorkeeper of the House. Motion agreed to 423-0: R 225-0; D 197-0 (ND 149-0, SD 48-0); I 1-0. A two-thirds majority of those present and voting (282 in this case) is required for passage under suspension of the rules. July 26, 2005.

**432.** **HR 3283. China Trade Practices/Previous Question.** Putnam, R-Fla., motion to order the previous question (thus ending debate and possibility of amendment) on adoption of the rule (H Res 387) to provide for House floor consideration of the bill that would establish mechanisms to ensure that China abides by previous trade agreement commitments. Motion agreed to 226-202: R 226-0; D 0-201 (ND 0-150, SD 0-51); I 0-1. July 27, 2005.

**433.** **HR 3283. China Trade Practices/Rule.** Adoption of the rule (H Res 387) to provide for House floor consideration of the bill that would establish mechanisms to ensure that China abides by previous trade agreement commitments. Adopted 228-200: R 228-0; D 0-199 (ND 0-150, SD 0-49); I 0-1. July 27, 2005.

| | 427 | 428 | 429 | 430 | 431 | 432 | 433 |
|---|---|---|---|---|---|---|---|
| **ALABAMA** | | | | | | | |
| 1 Bonner | Y | N | N | Y | Y | Y | Y |
| 2 Everett | Y | N | N | Y | Y | Y | Y |
| 3 Rogers | Y | N | N | Y | Y | Y | Y |
| 4 Aderholt | Y | Y | N | Y | Y | Y | Y |
| 5 Cramer | ? | N | N | Y | Y | N | N |
| 6 Bachus | Y | N | N | Y | Y | Y | Y |
| 7 Davis | Y | N | N | Y | Y | N | N |
| **ALASKA** | | | | | | | |
| AL Young | Y | N | N | Y | Y | Y | Y |
| **ARIZONA** | | | | | | | |
| 1 Renzi | Y | N | N | Y | Y | Y | Y |
| 2 Franks | Y | Y | Y | N | Y | Y | Y |
| 3 Shadegg | Y | Y | Y | N | Y | Y | Y |
| 4 Pastor | Y | N | N | Y | Y | N | N |
| 5 Hayworth | Y | Y | Y | Y | Y | Y | Y |
| 6 Flake | Y | Y | Y | N | Y | Y | Y |
| 7 Grijalva | Y | N | N | Y | Y | N | N |
| 8 Kolbe | Y | N | Y | Y | Y | Y | Y |
| **ARKANSAS** | | | | | | | |
| 1 Berry | Y | N | N | Y | Y | N | N |
| 2 Snyder | Y | N | N | Y | Y | N | N |
| 3 Boozman | Y | N | N | Y | Y | Y | Y |
| 4 Ross | Y | N | N | Y | Y | N | N |
| **CALIFORNIA** | | | | | | | |
| 1 Thompson | Y | N | N | Y | Y | N | N |
| 2 Herger | Y | Y | N | Y | Y | Y | Y |
| 3 Lungren | Y | N | Y | Y | Y | Y | Y |
| 4 Doolittle | Y | N | Y | Y | Y | Y | Y |
| 5 Matsui, D. | Y | N | N | Y | Y | N | N |
| 6 Woolsey | Y | N | N | Y | Y | N | N |
| 7 Miller, George | Y | ? | ? | ? | ? | N | N |
| 8 Pelosi | Y | N | N | Y | Y | N | N |
| 9 Lee | Y | N | N | Y | Y | N | N |
| 10 Tauscher | Y | N | N | Y | Y | N | N |
| 11 Pombo | Y | N | N | Y | Y | Y | Y |
| 12 Lantos | Y | N | N | Y | Y | N | N |
| 13 Stark | Y | N | N | Y | Y | N | N |
| 14 Eshoo | Y | N | N | Y | Y | N | N |
| 15 Honda | Y | N | N | Y | Y | N | N |
| 16 Lofgren | Y | N | N | Y | Y | N | N |
| 17 Farr | Y | N | N | Y | Y | N | N |
| 18 Cardoza | Y | N | N | Y | Y | N | N |
| 19 Radanovich | Y | N | N | Y | ? | Y | Y |
| 20 Costa | Y | N | N | Y | Y | N | N |
| 21 Nunes | Y | N | N | Y | Y | Y | Y |
| 22 Thomas | Y | N | N | Y | Y | Y | Y |
| 23 Capps | Y | N | N | Y | Y | N | N |
| 24 Gallegly | Y | N | N | Y | Y | Y | Y |
| 25 McKeon | Y | N | N | Y | Y | Y | Y |
| 26 Dreier | Y | N | N | Y | Y | Y | Y |
| 27 Sherman | Y | N | N | Y | Y | N | N |
| 28 Berman | ? | N | N | Y | Y | N | N |
| 29 Schiff | Y | N | N | Y | Y | N | N |
| 30 Waxman | ? | N | N | Y | Y | N | N |
| 31 Becerra | Y | N | N | Y | Y | N | N |
| 32 Solis | Y | N | N | Y | Y | N | N |
| 33 Watson | Y | N | N | Y | Y | N | N |
| 34 Roybal-Allard | Y | N | N | Y | Y | N | N |
| 35 Waters | Y | N | N | Y | Y | N | N |
| 36 Harman | Y | N | N | Y | Y | N | N |
| 37 Millender-McD. | Y | N | N | Y | Y | N | N |
| 38 Napolitano | Y | N | N | Y | Y | N | N |
| 39 Sánchez, Linda | Y | N | N | Y | Y | N | N |
| 40 Royce | Y | Y | Y | N | Y | Y | Y |
| 41 Lewis | Y | N | N | Y | ? | Y | Y |
| 42 Miller, Gary | Y | N | N | Y | Y | Y | Y |
| 43 Baca | Y | N | N | Y | Y | N | N |
| 44 Calvert | Y | N | N | Y | Y | Y | Y |
| 45 Bono | Y | N | N | Y | Y | Y | Y |
| 46 Rohrabacher | Y | Y | Y | Y | Y | Y | Y |
| 47 Sanchez, Loretta | Y | N | N | Y | N | N | N |
| 48 Cox | Y | Y | N | Y | Y | Y | Y |
| 49 Issa | Y | Y | N | Y | Y | ? | ? |

| | 427 | 428 | 429 | 430 | 431 | 432 | 433 |
|---|---|---|---|---|---|---|---|
| 50 Cunningham | Y | N | Y | Y | Y | Y | Y |
| 51 Filner | Y | N | Y | Y | N | N | N |
| 52 Hunter | Y | N | N | Y | Y | N | N |
| 53 Davis | Y | N | N | Y | N | N | N |
| **COLORADO** | | | | | | | |
| 1 DeGette | Y | N | N | Y | Y | N | N |
| 2 Udall | Y | N | N | Y | Y | N | N |
| 3 Salazar | Y | N | N | Y | Y | N | N |
| 4 Musgrave | Y | Y | Y | N | Y | Y | Y |
| 5 Hefley | Y | Y | N | Y | ? | Y | Y |
| 6 Tancredo | Y | N | N | Y | Y | Y | Y |
| 7 Beauprez | Y | Y | N | Y | Y | Y | Y |
| **CONNECTICUT** | | | | | | | |
| 1 Larson | Y | N | N | Y | Y | N | N |
| 2 Simmons | Y | N | N | Y | Y | Y | Y |
| 3 DeLauro | Y | N | N | Y | Y | N | N |
| 4 Shays | Y | N | N | Y | Y | Y | Y |
| 5 Johnson | Y | N | N | Y | Y | Y | Y |
| **DELAWARE** | | | | | | | |
| AL Castle | Y | N | N | Y | Y | Y | Y |
| **FLORIDA** | | | | | | | |
| 1 Miller | Y | Y | Y | Y | Y | Y | Y |
| 2 Boyd | Y | N | N | Y | Y | N | N |
| 3 Brown | Y | N | N | Y | Y | N | N |
| 4 Crenshaw | Y | N | N | Y | Y | Y | Y |
| 5 Brown-Waite | ? | N | N | Y | Y | Y | Y |
| 6 Stearns | Y | Y | Y | Y | Y | Y | Y |
| 7 Mica | Y | N | N | Y | Y | Y | Y |
| 8 Keller | Y | N | N | Y | Y | Y | Y |
| 9 Bilirakis | Y | N | N | Y | Y | Y | Y |
| 10 Young | Y | N | N | Y | Y | Y | Y |
| 11 Davis | Y | N | Y | ? | N | N | N |
| 12 Putnam | Y | N | N | Y | Y | Y | Y |
| 13 Harris | Y | N | Y | Y | Y | Y | Y |
| 14 Mack | Y | Y | Y | Y | Y | Y | Y |
| 15 Weldon | Y | Y | N | Y | Y | Y | Y |
| 16 Foley | Y | N | N | Y | Y | Y | Y |
| 17 Meek | Y | N | N | Y | Y | N | N |
| 18 Ros-Lehtinen | Y | N | N | Y | Y | Y | Y |
| 19 Wexler | Y | N | N | Y | ? | N | N |
| 20 Wasserman-Schultz | Y | N | N | Y | Y | N | N |
| 21 Diaz-Balart, L. | Y | N | N | Y | Y | Y | Y |
| 22 Shaw | Y | N | N | Y | Y | Y | Y |
| 23 Hastings | Y | N | N | Y | Y | N | N |
| 24 Feeney | ? | Y | Y | N | Y | Y | Y |
| 25 Diaz-Balart, M. | Y | N | N | Y | Y | Y | Y |
| **GEORGIA** | | | | | | | |
| 1 Kingston | Y | Y | Y | Y | Y | Y | Y |
| 2 Bishop | Y | N | N | Y | Y | N | N |
| 3 Marshall | Y | N | N | Y | ? | N | N |
| 4 McKinney | Y | N | N | Y | Y | N | ? |
| 5 Lewis | Y | N | N | Y | Y | N | N |
| 6 Price | Y | Y | N | Y | Y | Y | Y |
| 7 Linder | Y | N | Y | Y | Y | Y | Y |
| 8 Westmoreland | Y | Y | Y | Y | Y | Y | Y |
| 9 Norwood | Y | N | N | Y | Y | Y | Y |
| 10 Deal | Y | N | N | Y | Y | Y | Y |
| 11 Gingrey | Y | Y | N | Y | Y | Y | Y |
| 12 Barrow | Y | N | N | Y | Y | N | N |
| 13 Scott | Y | N | N | Y | Y | N | N |
| **HAWAII** | | | | | | | |
| 1 Abercrombie | Y | N | N | Y | Y | N | N |
| 2 Case | Y | N | N | Y | Y | N | N |
| **IDAHO** | | | | | | | |
| 1 Otter | ? | Y | Y | N | Y | Y | Y |
| 2 Simpson | Y | N | N | Y | Y | Y | Y |
| **ILLINOIS** | | | | | | | |
| 1 Rush | Y | N | N | Y | Y | N | N |
| 2 Jackson | Y | N | N | Y | N | N | N |
| 3 Lipinski | Y | N | N | Y | Y | N | N |
| 4 Gutierrez | Y | N | N | Y | Y | N | N |
| 5 Emanuel | Y | N | N | Y | Y | N | N |
| 6 Hyde | Y | Y | N | Y | Y | Y | Y |
| 7 Davis | Y | N | N | Y | Y | N | N |
| 8 Bean | Y | N | N | Y | Y | N | N |
| 9 Schakowsky | Y | N | N | Y | Y | N | N |
| 10 Kirk | Y | Y | N | Y | Y | Y | Y |
| 11 Weller | Y | N | N | Y | Y | Y | Y |
| 12 Costello | Y | N | N | Y | Y | N | N |

| | 427 | 428 | 429 | 430 | 431 | 432 | 433 |
|---|---|---|---|---|---|---|---|
| 13 **Biggert** | Y | N | N | Y | Y | Y | Y |
| 14 **Hastert** | | | | | | | |
| 15 **Johnson** | Y | N | N | Y | Y | ? | Y |
| 16 **Manzullo** | Y | N | N | Y | Y | Y | Y |
| 17 Evans | Y | N | N | Y | Y | N | N |
| 18 **LaHood** | Y | N | N | Y | Y | Y | Y |
| 19 **Shimkus** | Y | N | N | Y | Y | Y | Y |
| **INDIANA** | | | | | | | |
| 1 Visclosky | Y | N | N | Y | Y | N | N |
| 2 **Chocola** | Y | Y | Y | N | Y | Y | Y |
| 3 **Souder** | Y | N | N | Y | Y | Y | Y |
| 4 **Buyer** | Y | Y | Y | Y | Y | Y | Y |
| 5 **Burton** | Y | N | N | Y | Y | Y | Y |
| 6 **Pence** | Y | Y | Y | N | Y | Y | Y |
| 7 Carson | Y | N | N | Y | Y | N | N |
| 8 **Hostettler** | Y | Y | N | Y | Y | Y | Y |
| 9 **Sodrel** | Y | N | N | Y | Y | Y | Y |
| **IOWA** | | | | | | | |
| 1 **Nussle** | Y | N | N | N | Y | Y | Y |
| 2 **Leach** | Y | N | N | Y | Y | Y | Y |
| 3 Boswell | Y | N | N | Y | Y | N | N |
| 4 **Latham** | Y | N | N | Y | Y | Y | Y |
| 5 **King** | Y | Y | Y | Y | Y | Y | Y |
| **KANSAS** | | | | | | | |
| 1 **Moran** | Y | N | N | Y | Y | Y | Y |
| 2 **Ryun** | Y | Y | N | Y | Y | Y | Y |
| 3 Moore | Y | N | N | Y | Y | N | N |
| 4 **Tiahrt** | Y | Y | N | Y | Y | Y | Y |
| **KENTUCKY** | | | | | | | |
| 1 **Whitfield** | Y | Y | N | Y | Y | Y | Y |
| 2 **Lewis** | Y | N | N | Y | Y | Y | Y |
| 3 **Northup** | Y | N | N | Y | Y | Y | Y |
| 4 **Davis** | Y | N | N | Y | Y | Y | Y |
| 5 **Rogers** | Y | N | N | Y | Y | Y | Y |
| 6 Chandler | Y | N | N | Y | Y | N | N |
| **LOUISIANA** | | | | | | | |
| 1 **Jindal** | Y | Y | Y | Y | Y | Y | Y |
| 2 Jefferson | Y | N | N | Y | Y | N | ? |
| 3 Melancon | Y | N | N | Y | Y | N | N |
| 4 **McCrery** | Y | Y | N | Y | Y | Y | Y |
| 5 **Alexander** | Y | N | N | Y | Y | Y | Y |
| 6 **Baker** | Y | N | N | Y | Y | Y | Y |
| 7 **Boustany** | Y | Y | N | Y | Y | Y | Y |
| **MAINE** | | | | | | | |
| 1 Allen | Y | N | N | Y | Y | N | N |
| 2 Michaud | Y | N | N | Y | Y | N | N |
| **MARYLAND** | | | | | | | |
| 1 **Gilchrest** | Y | N | N | Y | Y | Y | Y |
| 2 Ruppersberger | Y | N | N | Y | Y | N | N |
| 3 Cardin | Y | N | N | Y | Y | N | N |
| 4 Wynn | Y | N | N | Y | Y | N | N |
| 5 Hoyer | Y | N | N | Y | Y | N | N |
| 6 **Bartlett** | Y | Y | Y | Y | Y | Y | Y |
| 7 Cummings | Y | N | N | Y | Y | N | N |
| 8 Van Hollen | Y | N | N | Y | Y | N | N |
| **MASSACHUSETTS** | | | | | | | |
| 1 Olver | Y | N | N | Y | Y | N | N |
| 2 Neal | Y | N | N | Y | Y | N | N |
| 3 McGovern | Y | N | N | Y | Y | N | N |
| 4 Frank | Y | N | N | Y | Y | N | N |
| 5 Meehan | Y | N | N | Y | Y | N | N |
| 6 Tierney | Y | N | N | Y | Y | N | N |
| 7 Markey | Y | N | N | Y | Y | N | N |
| 8 Capuano | Y | N | N | Y | Y | N | N |
| 9 Lynch | Y | N | N | Y | Y | N | N |
| 10 Delahunt | Y | N | N | Y | Y | N | N |
| **MICHIGAN** | | | | | | | |
| 1 Stupak | Y | N | N | Y | Y | N | N |
| 2 **Hoekstra** | Y | N | N | Y | Y | Y | Y |
| 3 **Ehlers** | Y | N | N | Y | Y | Y | Y |
| 4 **Camp** | Y | N | N | Y | Y | Y | Y |
| 5 Kildee | Y | N | N | Y | Y | N | N |
| 6 **Upton** | Y | N | N | Y | Y | Y | Y |
| 7 **Schwarz** | Y | N | N | Y | Y | Y | Y |
| 8 **Rogers** | Y | N | N | Y | Y | Y | Y |
| 9 **Knollenberg** | Y | N | N | Y | Y | Y | Y |
| 10 **Miller** | Y | N | N | Y | Y | Y | Y |
| 11 **McCotter** | Y | N | N | Y | Y | Y | Y |
| 12 Levin | Y | N | N | Y | Y | N | N |
| 13 Kilpatrick | Y | N | N | Y | Y | N | N |
| 14 Conyers | Y | N | N | Y | Y | N | N |
| 15 Dingell | Y | N | N | Y | Y | N | N |

| | 427 | 428 | 429 | 430 | 431 | 432 | 433 |
|---|---|---|---|---|---|---|---|
| **MINNESOTA** | | | | | | | |
| 1 **Gutknecht** | Y | N | N | Y | Y | Y | Y |
| 2 **Kline** | Y | N | N | Y | Y | Y | Y |
| 3 **Ramstad** | Y | N | N | Y | Y | Y | Y |
| 4 McCollum | Y | N | N | Y | Y | N | N |
| 5 Sabo | Y | N | N | Y | Y | N | N |
| 6 **Kennedy** | Y | N | N | Y | Y | Y | Y |
| 7 Peterson | Y | N | N | Y | Y | N | N |
| 8 Oberstar | Y | N | N | Y | Y | N | N |
| **MISSISSIPPI** | | | | | | | |
| 1 **Wicker** | Y | N | N | Y | Y | Y | Y |
| 2 Thompson | Y | N | N | Y | Y | N | N |
| 3 **Pickering** | Y | N | N | Y | Y | Y | Y |
| 4 Taylor | Y | N | N | Y | Y | N | N |
| **MISSOURI** | | | | | | | |
| 1 Clay | Y | N | N | Y | Y | N | N |
| 2 **Akin** | Y | Y | Y | N | Y | Y | Y |
| 3 Carnahan | Y | N | N | Y | Y | N | N |
| 4 Skelton | Y | N | N | Y | Y | N | N |
| 5 Cleaver | Y | N | N | Y | Y | N | N |
| 6 **Graves** | Y | N | N | Y | Y | Y | Y |
| 7 **Blunt** | Y | Y | N | Y | Y | Y | Y |
| 8 **Emerson** | Y | N | N | Y | Y | Y | Y |
| 9 **Hulshof** | Y | N | N | Y | Y | Y | Y |
| **MONTANA** | | | | | | | |
| AL **Rehberg** | Y | N | N | Y | Y | Y | Y |
| **NEBRASKA** | | | | | | | |
| 1 **Fortenberry** | Y | N | N | Y | Y | Y | Y |
| 2 **Terry** | Y | N | N | Y | Y | Y | Y |
| 3 **Osborne** | Y | N | N | Y | Y | Y | Y |
| **NEVADA** | | | | | | | |
| 1 Berkley | Y | N | N | Y | Y | N | N |
| 2 **Gibbons** | ? | ? | ? | ? | ? | Y | Y |
| 3 **Porter** | Y | N | N | Y | Y | Y | Y |
| **NEW HAMPSHIRE** | | | | | | | |
| 1 **Bradley** | Y | N | N | Y | Y | Y | Y |
| 2 **Bass** | Y | Y | N | Y | Y | Y | Y |
| **NEW JERSEY** | | | | | | | |
| 1 Andrews | Y | N | N | Y | Y | N | N |
| 2 **LoBiondo** | Y | N | N | Y | Y | Y | Y |
| 3 **Saxton** | Y | N | N | Y | Y | Y | Y |
| 4 **Smith** | Y | N | N | Y | Y | Y | Y |
| 5 **Garrett** | Y | Y | Y | Y | Y | Y | Y |
| 6 Pallone | Y | N | N | Y | Y | N | N |
| 7 **Ferguson** | Y | N | N | Y | Y | Y | Y |
| 8 Pascrell | Y | N | N | Y | Y | N | N |
| 9 Rothman | Y | N | N | Y | Y | N | N |
| 10 Payne | Y | N | N | Y | Y | N | N |
| 11 **Frelinghuysen** | Y | N | N | Y | Y | Y | Y |
| 12 Holt | Y | N | N | Y | Y | N | N |
| 13 Menendez | Y | N | N | Y | Y | N | N |
| **NEW MEXICO** | | | | | | | |
| 1 **Wilson** | Y | N | N | Y | Y | Y | Y |
| 2 **Pearce** | Y | N | N | Y | Y | Y | Y |
| 3 Udall | Y | N | N | Y | Y | N | N |
| **NEW YORK** | | | | | | | |
| 1 Bishop | Y | N | N | Y | Y | N | N |
| 2 Israel | Y | N | N | Y | Y | N | N |
| 3 **King** | Y | N | N | Y | Y | Y | Y |
| 4 McCarthy | Y | N | N | Y | Y | N | N |
| 5 Ackerman | Y | N | N | Y | Y | N | N |
| 6 Meeks | Y | N | N | Y | Y | N | N |
| 7 Crowley | Y | N | N | Y | Y | N | N |
| 8 Nadler | Y | N | N | Y | Y | N | N |
| 9 Weiner | Y | N | N | Y | Y | N | N |
| 10 Towns | Y | N | N | Y | Y | N | N |
| 11 Owens | Y | N | N | Y | Y | N | N |
| 12 Velázquez | Y | N | N | Y | Y | N | N |
| 13 **Fossella** | Y | N | N | Y | Y | Y | Y |
| 14 Maloney | Y | N | N | Y | Y | N | N |
| 15 Rangel | Y | N | N | Y | Y | N | N |
| 16 Serrano | Y | N | N | Y | Y | N | N |
| 17 Engel | Y | N | N | Y | Y | N | N |
| 18 Lowey | Y | N | N | Y | Y | N | N |
| 19 **Kelly** | Y | N | N | Y | Y | Y | Y |
| 20 **Sweeney** | Y | N | N | Y | Y | Y | Y |
| 21 McNulty | Y | N | N | Y | Y | N | N |
| 22 Hinchey | Y | N | N | Y | Y | N | N |
| 23 **McHugh** | Y | N | N | Y | Y | Y | Y |
| 24 **Boehlert** | Y | N | N | Y | Y | Y | Y |
| 25 **Walsh** | Y | N | N | Y | Y | Y | Y |
| 26 **Reynolds** | Y | N | N | Y | Y | Y | Y |
| 27 Higgins | Y | N | N | Y | Y | N | N |
| 28 Slaughter | Y | N | N | Y | Y | N | N |
| 29 **Kuhl** | Y | N | N | Y | Y | Y | Y |

| | 427 | 428 | 429 | 430 | 431 | 432 | 433 |
|---|---|---|---|---|---|---|---|
| **NORTH CAROLINA** | | | | | | | |
| 1 Butterfield | Y | N | N | Y | Y | N | N |
| 2 Etheridge | Y | N | N | Y | Y | N | N |
| 3 **Jones** | Y | Y | N | Y | Y | Y | Y |
| 4 Price | Y | N | N | Y | Y | N | N |
| 5 **Foxx** | Y | Y | Y | Y | Y | Y | Y |
| 6 **Coble** | Y | N | N | Y | Y | Y | Y |
| 7 McIntyre | Y | N | N | Y | Y | N | N |
| 8 **Hayes** | Y | Y | N | Y | Y | Y | Y |
| 9 **Myrick** | Y | Y | Y | Y | Y | Y | Y |
| 10 **McHenry** | ? | Y | Y | Y | Y | Y | Y |
| 11 **Taylor** | Y | N | N | Y | Y | Y | Y |
| 12 Watt | Y | N | N | Y | Y | N | N |
| 13 Miller | Y | N | N | Y | Y | N | N |
| **NORTH DAKOTA** | | | | | | | |
| AL Pomeroy | Y | N | N | Y | Y | N | N |
| **OHIO** | | | | | | | |
| 1 **Chabot** | Y | Y | N | Y | Y | Y | Y |
| 2 Vacant | | | | | | | |
| 3 **Turner** | Y | N | N | Y | Y | Y | Y |
| 4 **Oxley** | ? | ? | ? | ? | ? | Y | Y |
| 5 **Gillmor** | Y | N | N | Y | Y | Y | Y |
| 6 Strickland | Y | N | N | Y | Y | N | N |
| 7 **Hobson** | Y | N | N | Y | Y | Y | Y |
| 8 **Boehner** | Y | N | N | Y | Y | Y | Y |
| 9 Kaptur | Y | N | N | Y | Y | N | N |
| 10 Kucinich | Y | N | N | Y | Y | N | N |
| 11 Jones | Y | N | N | Y | Y | N | N |
| 12 **Tiberi** | Y | N | N | Y | Y | Y | Y |
| 13 Brown | Y | N | N | Y | Y | N | N |
| 14 **LaTourette** | ? | N | N | Y | Y | Y | Y |
| 15 **Pryce** | Y | N | N | Y | Y | Y | Y |
| 16 **Regula** | Y | N | N | Y | Y | Y | Y |
| 17 Ryan | Y | N | N | Y | Y | N | N |
| 18 **Ney** | Y | N | N | Y | Y | Y | Y |
| **OKLAHOMA** | | | | | | | |
| 1 **Sullivan** | Y | Y | Y | Y | Y | Y | Y |
| 2 Boren | Y | N | N | Y | Y | N | N |
| 3 **Lucas** | Y | N | N | Y | Y | Y | Y |
| 4 **Cole** | Y | Y | N | Y | Y | Y | Y |
| 5 **Istook** | Y | Y | N | N | Y | Y | Y |
| **OREGON** | | | | | | | |
| 1 Wu | Y | N | N | Y | Y | N | N |
| 2 **Walden** | Y | N | N | Y | Y | Y | Y |
| 3 Blumenauer | Y | N | N | Y | Y | N | N |
| 4 DeFazio | Y | N | N | Y | Y | N | N |
| 5 Hooley | Y | N | N | Y | Y | N | N |
| **PENNSYLVANIA** | | | | | | | |
| 1 Brady | Y | N | N | Y | Y | ? | ? |
| 2 Fattah | Y | N | N | Y | Y | N | N |
| 3 **English** | Y | N | N | Y | Y | Y | Y |
| 4 **Hart** | Y | N | N | Y | Y | Y | Y |
| 5 **Peterson** | ? | N | N | Y | Y | Y | Y |
| 6 **Gerlach** | Y | N | N | Y | Y | Y | Y |
| 7 **Weldon** | Y | N | N | Y | Y | Y | Y |
| 8 **Fitzpatrick** | Y | N | N | Y | Y | Y | Y |
| 9 **Shuster** | Y | N | N | Y | Y | Y | Y |
| 10 **Sherwood** | Y | N | N | Y | Y | Y | Y |
| 11 Kanjorski | Y | N | N | Y | Y | N | N |
| 12 Murtha | Y | N | N | Y | ? | N | N |
| 13 Schwartz | Y | N | N | Y | Y | N | N |
| 14 Doyle | Y | N | N | Y | Y | N | N |
| 15 **Dent** | Y | N | N | Y | Y | Y | Y |
| 16 **Pitts** | Y | Y | N | Y | Y | Y | Y |
| 17 Holden | Y | N | N | Y | Y | N | N |
| 18 **Murphy** | Y | N | N | Y | Y | ? | ? |
| 19 **Platts** | Y | N | N | Y | Y | ? | Y |
| **RHODE ISLAND** | | | | | | | |
| 1 Kennedy | Y | N | N | Y | Y | N | N |
| 2 Langevin | Y | N | N | Y | Y | N | N |
| **SOUTH CAROLINA** | | | | | | | |
| 1 **Brown** | Y | N | N | Y | Y | Y | Y |
| 2 **Wilson** | Y | Y | Y | Y | Y | Y | Y |
| 3 **Barrett** | Y | Y | Y | N | Y | Y | Y |
| 4 **Inglis** | Y | Y | Y | Y | Y | Y | Y |
| 5 Spratt | Y | N | N | Y | Y | N | N |
| 6 Clyburn | Y | N | N | Y | Y | N | N |
| **SOUTH DAKOTA** | | | | | | | |
| AL Herseth | Y | N | N | Y | Y | N | N |
| **TENNESSEE** | | | | | | | |
| 1 **Jenkins** | Y | N | N | Y | Y | Y | Y |
| 2 **Duncan** | Y | N | Y | Y | Y | Y | Y |

| | 427 | 428 | 429 | 430 | 431 | 432 | 433 |
|---|---|---|---|---|---|---|---|
| 3 **Wamp** | Y | N | N | Y | Y | Y | Y |
| 4 Davis | Y | N | N | Y | Y | N | N |
| 5 Cooper | Y | ? | N | Y | Y | N | N |
| 6 Gordon | Y | N | N | Y | Y | N | N |
| 7 **Blackburn** | Y | Y | Y | Y | Y | Y | Y |
| 8 Tanner | Y | N | N | Y | Y | N | N |
| 9 Ford | Y | N | N | Y | Y | N | N |
| **TEXAS** | | | | | | | |
| 1 **Gohmert** | Y | Y | N | N | Y | Y | Y |
| 2 **Poe** | Y | Y | Y | Y | Y | Y | Y |
| 3 **Johnson, S.** | Y | Y | Y | N | Y | Y | Y |
| 4 **Hall** | Y | Y | N | Y | Y | Y | Y |
| 5 **Hensarling** | Y | Y | Y | N | Y | Y | Y |
| 6 **Barton** | Y | N | N | Y | Y | Y | Y |
| 7 **Culberson** | Y | Y | Y | N | Y | Y | Y |
| 8 **Brady** | Y | Y | Y | Y | Y | Y | Y |
| 9 Green, A. | Y | N | N | Y | Y | N | N |
| 10 **McCaul** | Y | Y | Y | Y | Y | Y | Y |
| 11 **Conaway** | Y | Y | Y | Y | Y | Y | Y |
| 12 **Granger** | Y | Y | N | Y | Y | Y | Y |
| 13 **Thornberry** | Y | Y | N | Y | Y | Y | Y |
| 14 **Paul** | ? | Y | Y | N | Y | Y | Y |
| 15 Hinojosa | Y | – | N | Y | Y | N | N |
| 16 Reyes | Y | N | N | Y | Y | N | N |
| 17 Edwards | Y | N | N | Y | Y | N | N |
| 18 Jackson-Lee | Y | N | N | Y | Y | N | N |
| 19 **Neugebauer** | Y | Y | Y | Y | Y | Y | Y |
| 20 Gonzalez | Y | N | N | Y | Y | N | N |
| 21 **Smith** | Y | N | N | Y | Y | Y | Y |
| 22 **DeLay** | Y | Y | N | Y | Y | Y | Y |
| 23 **Bonilla** | Y | Y | N | Y | Y | Y | Y |
| 24 **Marchant** | Y | Y | N | Y | Y | Y | Y |
| 25 Doggett | Y | N | N | Y | Y | N | N |
| 26 **Burgess** | Y | Y | N | Y | Y | Y | Y |
| 27 Ortiz | Y | N | N | Y | Y | N | N |
| 28 Cuellar | Y | N | N | Y | Y | N | N |
| 29 Green, G. | Y | N | N | Y | Y | N | N |
| 30 Johnson, E. | Y | N | N | Y | Y | N | N |
| 31 **Carter** | Y | Y | Y | Y | Y | Y | Y |
| 32 **Sessions** | Y | Y | Y | Y | Y | Y | Y |
| **UTAH** | | | | | | | |
| 1 **Bishop** | Y | N | N | Y | Y | Y | Y |
| 2 Matheson | Y | N | N | Y | Y | N | N |
| 3 **Cannon** | Y | N | N | Y | Y | Y | Y |
| **VERMONT** | | | | | | | |
| AL *Sanders* | Y | N | N | Y | Y | N | N |
| **VIRGINIA** | | | | | | | |
| 1 **Davis, J.** | Y | N | N | N | Y | Y | Y |
| 2 **Drake** | Y | N | N | Y | Y | Y | Y |
| 3 Scott | Y | N | N | Y | Y | N | N |
| 4 **Forbes** | Y | N | N | Y | Y | Y | Y |
| 5 **Goode** | Y | N | N | Y | Y | Y | Y |
| 6 **Goodlatte** | Y | Y | N | Y | Y | Y | Y |
| 7 **Cantor** | Y | Y | N | Y | Y | Y | Y |
| 8 Moran | Y | N | N | Y | Y | N | N |
| 9 Boucher | Y | N | N | Y | Y | N | N |
| 10 **Wolf** | Y | N | N | Y | Y | Y | Y |
| 11 **Davis, T.** | Y | N | N | Y | Y | Y | Y |
| **WASHINGTON** | | | | | | | |
| 1 Inslee | Y | N | N | Y | Y | N | N |
| 2 Larsen | Y | N | N | Y | Y | N | N |
| 3 Baird | Y | N | N | Y | Y | N | N |
| 4 **Hastings** | Y | N | N | Y | Y | Y | Y |
| 5 **McMorris** | Y | Y | Y | Y | Y | Y | Y |
| 6 Dicks | Y | N | N | Y | Y | N | N |
| 7 McDermott | Y | N | N | Y | Y | N | N |
| 8 **Reichert** | Y | N | N | Y | Y | Y | Y |
| 9 Smith | Y | N | N | Y | Y | N | N |
| **WEST VIRGINIA** | | | | | | | |
| 1 Mollohan | Y | N | N | Y | Y | N | N |
| 2 **Capito** | Y | N | N | Y | Y | Y | Y |
| 3 Rahall | Y | N | N | Y | Y | N | N |
| **WISCONSIN** | | | | | | | |
| 1 **Ryan** | Y | N | N | Y | Y | Y | Y |
| 2 Baldwin | Y | N | N | Y | Y | N | N |
| 3 Kind | Y | N | N | Y | Y | N | N |
| 4 Moore | Y | N | N | Y | Y | N | N |
| 5 **Sensenbrenner** | Y | N | N | Y | Y | Y | Y |
| 6 **Petri** | Y | N | N | Y | Y | Y | Y |
| 7 Obey | Y | ? | N | Y | Y | N | N |
| 8 **Green** | Y | N | N | Y | Y | Y | Y |
| **WYOMING** | | | | | | | |
| AL **Cubin** | Y | N | N | Y | Y | Y | Y |

# IN THE HOUSE | By Vote Number

**434.** **S 544. Medical Error Reporting/Passage.** Deal, R-Ga., motion to suspend the rules and pass the bill that would establish a set of procedures for the voluntary and confidential reporting of medical errors to patient safety organizations that would analyze the data and develop ways to improve patient safety and reduce medical errors. Motion agreed to 428-3: R 226-3; D 201-0 (ND 150-0, SD 51-0); I 1-0. A two-thirds majority of those present and voting (288 in this case) is required for passage under suspension of the rules. July 27, 2005.

**435.** **S 45. Drug Addiction Treatment/Passage.** Deal, R-Ga., motion to suspend the rules and pass the bill that would lift the 30-patient limit on group practices for treating drug addicts with narcotic drugs in a maintenance or detoxification-treatment program. Motion agreed to 429-0: R 228-0; D 200-0 (ND 149-0, SD 51-0); I 1-0. A two-thirds majority of those present and voting (286 in this case) is required for passage under suspension of the rules. July 27, 2005.

**436.** **HR 3283. China Trade Practices/Recommit.** Cardin, D-Md., motion to recommit the bill to the Ways and Means Committee with instructions to add language that would require the U.S. trade representative to conduct an investigation, make applicable determinations and implement any necessary action on China's currency practices. Motion rejected 195-232: R 0-227; D 194-5 (ND 144-4, SD 50-1); I 1-0. July 27, 2005.

**437.** **HR 3283. China Trade Practices/Passage.** Passage of the bill that would establish mechanisms to ensure that China abides by previous trade agreement commitments, including creating a system to monitor compliance with trade obligations on intellectual property rights, market access for U.S. goods, services and agriculture and the accounting of Chinese subsidies. Passed 255-168: R 221-5; D 34-162 (ND 14-133, SD 20-29); I 0-1. July 27, 2005.

**438.** **H Res 383. Rights of Iraqi Women/Adoption.** Ros-Lehtinen, R-Fla., motion to suspend the rules and adopt the resolution that would strongly encourage Iraq to adopt a constitution that grants women equal rights. Motion agreed to 426-0: R 226-0; D 199-0 (ND 148-0, SD 51-0); I 1-0. A two-thirds majority of those present and voting (284 in this case) is required for adoption under suspension of the rules. July 27, 2005.

**439.** **H Res 384. Terrorist Attacks in Egypt/Adoption.** Ros-Lehtinen, R-Fla., motion to suspend the rules and adopt the resolution that would strongly condemn the terrorist attacks in Sharm el-Sheikh, Egypt, and other terrorist attacks against Egypt, and express condolences to the families and friends of those injured and killed in the attacks. Motion agreed to 428-0: R 229-0; D 198-0 (ND 148-0, SD 50-0); I 1-0. A two-thirds majority of those present and voting (286 in this case) is required for adoption under suspension of the rules. July 27, 2005.

| | 434 | 435 | 436 | 437 | 438 | 439 |
|---|---|---|---|---|---|---|
| **ALABAMA** | | | | | | |
| 1 Bonner | Y | Y | N | Y | Y | Y |
| 2 Everett | Y | Y | N | Y | Y | Y |
| 3 Rogers | Y | Y | N | Y | Y | Y |
| 4 Aderholt | Y | Y | N | Y | Y | Y |
| 5 Cramer | Y | Y | Y | Y | Y | Y |
| 6 Bachus | Y | Y | N | Y | Y | Y |
| 7 Davis | Y | Y | Y | Y | Y | Y |
| **ALASKA** | | | | | | |
| AL Young | Y | Y | N | Y | Y | Y |
| **ARIZONA** | | | | | | |
| 1 Renzi | Y | Y | N | Y | Y | Y |
| 2 Franks | Y | Y | N | Y | Y | Y |
| 3 Shadegg | Y | Y | N | Y | Y | Y |
| 4 Pastor | Y | Y | Y | N | Y | Y |
| 5 Hayworth | Y | Y | N | Y | Y | Y |
| 6 Flake | N | Y | N | N | Y | Y |
| 7 Grijalva | Y | Y | Y | N | Y | Y |
| 8 Kolbe | Y | Y | N | N | Y | Y |
| **ARKANSAS** | | | | | | |
| 1 Berry | Y | Y | Y | Y | Y | Y |
| 2 Snyder | Y | Y | Y | N | Y | Y |
| 3 Boozman | Y | Y | N | Y | Y | Y |
| 4 Ross | Y | Y | Y | N | Y | Y |
| **CALIFORNIA** | | | | | | |
| 1 Thompson | Y | Y | Y | Y | Y | Y |
| 2 Herger | Y | Y | N | Y | Y | Y |
| 3 Lungren | Y | Y | N | Y | Y | Y |
| 4 Doolittle | Y | Y | N | Y | Y | Y |
| 5 Matsui, D. | Y | Y | Y | Y | Y | Y |
| 6 Woolsey | Y | Y | Y | N | Y | Y |
| 7 Miller, George | Y | Y | Y | N | Y | Y |
| 8 Pelosi | Y | Y | Y | N | Y | Y |
| 9 Lee | Y | Y | Y | N | Y | Y |
| 10 Tauscher | Y | Y | Y | N | Y | Y |
| 11 Pombo | Y | Y | N | Y | Y | Y |
| 12 Lantos | Y | Y | Y | N | Y | Y |
| 13 Stark | Y | Y | Y | N | Y | Y |
| 14 Eshoo | Y | Y | Y | N | Y | Y |
| 15 Honda | Y | Y | Y | N | Y | Y |
| 16 Lofgren | Y | Y | N | N | Y | Y |
| 17 Farr | Y | Y | Y | N | Y | Y |
| 18 Cardoza | Y | Y | Y | N | Y | Y |
| 19 Radanovich | Y | Y | N | Y | Y | Y |
| 20 Costa | Y | Y | Y | N | Y | Y |
| 21 Nunes | Y | Y | N | Y | Y | Y |
| 22 Thomas | Y | Y | N | Y | Y | Y |
| 23 Capps | Y | Y | Y | N | Y | Y |
| 24 Gallegly | Y | Y | N | Y | Y | Y |
| 25 McKeon | Y | Y | N | Y | Y | Y |
| 26 Dreier | Y | Y | N | Y | Y | Y |
| 27 Sherman | Y | Y | Y | N | Y | Y |
| 28 Berman | Y | Y | Y | N | Y | Y |
| 29 Schiff | Y | Y | Y | N | Y | Y |
| 30 Waxman | Y | Y | Y | N | Y | Y |
| 31 Becerra | Y | Y | Y | N | Y | Y |
| 32 Solis | Y | Y | Y | N | Y | Y |
| 33 Watson | Y | Y | Y | N | Y | Y |
| 34 Roybal-Allard | Y | Y | Y | N | Y | Y |
| 35 Waters | Y | Y | Y | N | Y | Y |
| 36 Harman | Y | Y | Y | N | Y | Y |
| 37 Millender-McD. | Y | Y | Y | N | Y | Y |
| 38 Napolitano | Y | Y | Y | N | Y | Y |
| 39 Sánchez, Linda | Y | Y | Y | N | Y | Y |
| 40 Royce | Y | Y | N | Y | Y | Y |
| 41 Lewis | Y | Y | N | Y | Y | Y |
| 42 Miller, Gary | Y | Y | N | Y | Y | Y |
| 43 Baca | Y | Y | Y | N | Y | Y |
| 44 Calvert | Y | Y | N | Y | Y | Y |
| 45 Bono | Y | Y | N | Y | Y | Y |
| 46 Rohrabacher | Y | Y | N | Y | Y | Y |
| 47 Sanchez, Loretta | Y | Y | Y | N | Y | Y |
| 48 Cox | Y | Y | ? | ? | ? | Y |
| 49 Issa | Y | Y | N | Y | Y | Y |
| 50 Cunningham | Y | Y | N | Y | Y | Y |
| 51 Filner | Y | Y | Y | N | Y | Y |
| 52 Hunter | Y | Y | N | Y | Y | Y |
| 53 Davis | Y | Y | N | Y | Y | Y |
| **COLORADO** | | | | | | |
| 1 DeGette | Y | Y | Y | N | Y | Y |
| 2 Udall | Y | Y | Y | N | Y | Y |
| 3 Salazar | Y | Y | Y | N | Y | Y |
| 4 Musgrave | Y | Y | N | Y | Y | Y |
| 5 Hefley | Y | Y | N | Y | Y | Y |
| 6 Tancredo | Y | Y | N | Y | Y | Y |
| 7 Beauprez | Y | Y | N | Y | Y | Y |
| **CONNECTICUT** | | | | | | |
| 1 Larson | Y | Y | Y | N | Y | Y |
| 2 Simmons | Y | Y | Y | N | Y | Y |
| 3 DeLauro | Y | Y | Y | N | Y | Y |
| 4 Shays | Y | Y | N | Y | Y | Y |
| 5 Johnson | Y | Y | N | Y | Y | Y |
| **DELAWARE** | | | | | | |
| AL Castle | Y | Y | N | Y | Y | Y |
| **FLORIDA** | | | | | | |
| 1 Miller | Y | Y | N | Y | Y | Y |
| 2 Boyd | Y | Y | Y | N | Y | Y |
| 3 Brown | Y | Y | Y | Y | Y | Y |
| 4 Crenshaw | Y | Y | N | Y | Y | Y |
| 5 Brown-Waite | Y | Y | N | Y | Y | Y |
| 6 Stearns | Y | Y | N | Y | Y | Y |
| 7 Mica | Y | Y | N | Y | Y | Y |
| 8 Keller | Y | Y | N | Y | Y | Y |
| 9 Bilirakis | Y | Y | N | Y | Y | Y |
| 10 Young | Y | Y | N | Y | Y | Y |
| 11 Davis | Y | Y | Y | N | Y | Y |
| 12 Putnam | Y | Y | N | Y | Y | Y |
| 13 Harris | Y | Y | N | Y | Y | Y |
| 14 Mack | Y | Y | N | Y | Y | Y |
| 15 Weldon | Y | Y | N | Y | Y | Y |
| 16 Foley | Y | Y | N | Y | Y | Y |
| 17 Meek | Y | Y | Y | N | Y | Y |
| 18 Ros-Lehtinen | Y | Y | N | Y | Y | Y |
| 19 Wexler | Y | Y | Y | N | Y | Y |
| 20 Wasserman-Schultz | Y | Y | Y | N | Y | Y |
| 21 Diaz-Balart, L. | Y | Y | N | ? | Y | Y |
| 22 Shaw | Y | Y | N | Y | Y | Y |
| 23 Hastings | Y | Y | Y | ? | Y | Y |
| 24 Feeney | Y | Y | N | Y | Y | Y |
| 25 Diaz-Balart, M. | Y | Y | N | Y | Y | Y |
| **GEORGIA** | | | | | | |
| 1 Kingston | Y | Y | N | Y | Y | Y |
| 2 Bishop | Y | Y | Y | N | Y | Y |
| 3 Marshall | Y | Y | Y | N | Y | Y |
| 4 McKinney | Y | Y | Y | N | Y | Y |
| 5 Lewis | Y | Y | Y | N | Y | Y |
| 6 Price | Y | Y | N | Y | Y | Y |
| 7 Linder | Y | Y | N | Y | Y | Y |
| 8 Westmoreland | Y | Y | N | Y | Y | Y |
| 9 Norwood | Y | Y | N | Y | Y | Y |
| 10 Deal | Y | Y | N | Y | Y | Y |
| 11 Gingrey | Y | Y | N | Y | Y | Y |
| 12 Barrow | Y | Y | Y | Y | Y | Y |
| 13 Scott | Y | Y | Y | N | Y | Y |
| **HAWAII** | | | | | | |
| 1 Abercrombie | Y | Y | Y | N | Y | Y |
| 2 Case | Y | Y | Y | N | Y | Y |
| **IDAHO** | | | | | | |
| 1 Otter | Y | Y | N | Y | Y | Y |
| 2 Simpson | Y | Y | N | Y | Y | Y |
| **ILLINOIS** | | | | | | |
| 1 Rush | Y | Y | Y | N | Y | Y |
| 2 Jackson | Y | Y | Y | N | Y | Y |
| 3 Lipinski | Y | Y | Y | N | Y | Y |
| 4 Gutierrez | Y | Y | Y | N | Y | Y |
| 5 Emanuel | Y | Y | Y | N | Y | Y |
| 6 Hyde | Y | Y | N | Y | Y | Y |
| 7 Davis | Y | Y | Y | N | Y | Y |
| 8 Bean | Y | Y | Y | N | Y | Y |
| 9 Schakowsky | Y | Y | Y | N | Y | Y |
| 10 Kirk | Y | Y | N | Y | Y | Y |
| 11 Weller | Y | Y | N | Y | Y | Y |
| 12 Costello | Y | Y | Y | N | Y | Y |

**KEY**   Republicans   Democrats   *Independents*

| | | | |
|---|---|---|---|
| **Y** Voted for (yea) | **X** Paired against | **C** Voted "present" to avoid possible conflict of interest |
| **#** Paired for | **–** Announced against | |
| **+** Announced for | **P** Voted "present" | **?** Did not vote or otherwise make a position known |
| **N** Voted against (nay) | | |

| | 434 | 435 | 436 | 437 | 438 | 439 |
|---|---|---|---|---|---|---|
| 13 **Biggert** | Y | Y | N | Y | Y | Y |
| 14 **Hastert** | | | | | | |
| 15 **Johnson** | Y | Y | N | Y | Y | Y |
| 16 **Manzullo** | Y | Y | N | Y | Y | Y |
| 17 Evans | Y | Y | Y | N | Y | Y |
| 18 **LaHood** | Y | Y | N | Y | Y | Y |
| 19 **Shimkus** | Y | Y | N | Y | Y | Y |
| **INDIANA** | | | | | | |
| 1 Visclosky | Y | Y | Y | N | Y | Y |
| 2 **Chocola** | Y | Y | N | Y | Y | Y |
| 3 **Souder** | Y | Y | N | Y | Y | Y |
| 4 **Buyer** | Y | Y | N | Y | Y | Y |
| 5 **Burton** | Y | Y | N | Y | Y | Y |
| 6 **Pence** | Y | Y | N | Y | Y | Y |
| 7 Carson | Y | Y | Y | N | Y | Y |
| 8 **Hostettler** | Y | Y | N | Y | Y | Y |
| 9 **Sodrel** | Y | Y | N | Y | Y | Y |
| **IOWA** | | | | | | |
| 1 **Nussle** | Y | Y | N | Y | Y | Y |
| 2 **Leach** | Y | Y | N | Y | Y | Y |
| 3 Boswell | Y | Y | Y | Y | Y | Y |
| 4 **Latham** | Y | Y | N | Y | Y | Y |
| 5 **King** | Y | Y | N | Y | Y | Y |
| **KANSAS** | | | | | | |
| 1 **Moran** | Y | Y | N | Y | Y | Y |
| 2 **Ryun** | Y | Y | N | Y | Y | Y |
| 3 Moore | Y | Y | Y | N | Y | Y |
| 4 **Tiahrt** | Y | Y | N | Y | ? | Y |
| **KENTUCKY** | | | | | | |
| 1 **Whitfield** | Y | Y | N | Y | Y | Y |
| 2 **Lewis** | Y | Y | N | Y | Y | Y |
| 3 **Northup** | Y | Y | N | Y | Y | Y |
| 4 **Davis** | Y | Y | N | Y | Y | Y |
| 5 **Rogers** | Y | Y | N | Y | Y | Y |
| 6 Chandler | Y | Y | Y | N | Y | Y |
| **LOUISIANA** | | | | | | |
| 1 **Jindal** | Y | Y | N | Y | Y | Y |
| 2 Jefferson | Y | Y | Y | N | Y | ? |
| 3 Melancon | Y | Y | Y | Y | Y | Y |
| 4 **McCrery** | Y | Y | N | Y | Y | Y |
| 5 **Alexander** | Y | Y | N | Y | Y | Y |
| 6 **Baker** | Y | Y | N | Y | Y | Y |
| 7 **Boustany** | Y | Y | N | Y | Y | Y |
| **MAINE** | | | | | | |
| 1 Allen | Y | Y | Y | N | Y | Y |
| 2 Michaud | Y | Y | Y | N | Y | Y |
| **MARYLAND** | | | | | | |
| 1 **Gilchrest** | Y | Y | N | Y | Y | Y |
| 2 Ruppersberger | Y | Y | Y | N | Y | Y |
| 3 Cardin | Y | Y | Y | N | Y | Y |
| 4 Wynn | Y | Y | Y | Y | Y | Y |
| 5 Hoyer | Y | Y | Y | N | Y | Y |
| 6 **Bartlett** | Y | Y | N | N | Y | Y |
| 7 Cummings | Y | Y | ? | ? | ? | ? |
| 8 Van Hollen | Y | Y | Y | N | Y | Y |
| **MASSACHUSETTS** | | | | | | |
| 1 Olver | Y | Y | Y | N | Y | Y |
| 2 Neal | Y | Y | Y | N | Y | Y |
| 3 McGovern | Y | Y | Y | N | Y | Y |
| 4 Frank | Y | Y | Y | N | Y | Y |
| 5 Meehan | Y | Y | Y | N | Y | Y |
| 6 Tierney | Y | Y | Y | N | Y | Y |
| 7 Markey | Y | Y | Y | N | Y | Y |
| 8 Capuano | Y | Y | Y | N | Y | Y |
| 9 Lynch | Y | Y | Y | N | Y | Y |
| 10 Delahunt | Y | Y | Y | N | Y | Y |
| **MICHIGAN** | | | | | | |
| 1 Stupak | Y | Y | Y | N | Y | Y |
| 2 **Hoekstra** | Y | Y | N | Y | Y | Y |
| 3 **Ehlers** | Y | Y | N | Y | Y | Y |
| 4 **Camp** | Y | Y | N | Y | Y | Y |
| 5 Kildee | Y | Y | Y | N | Y | Y |
| 6 **Upton** | Y | Y | N | Y | Y | Y |
| 7 **Schwarz** | Y | Y | N | Y | Y | Y |
| 8 **Rogers** | Y | Y | N | Y | Y | Y |
| 9 **Knollenberg** | Y | Y | N | Y | Y | Y |
| 10 **Miller** | Y | Y | N | Y | Y | Y |
| 11 **McCotter** | Y | Y | N | Y | Y | Y |
| 12 Levin | Y | Y | Y | N | Y | Y |
| 13 Kilpatrick | Y | Y | Y | N | Y | Y |
| 14 Conyers | Y | Y | Y | N | Y | Y |
| 15 Dingell | Y | Y | Y | N | Y | Y |
| **MINNESOTA** | | | | | | |
| 1 **Gutknecht** | Y | Y | N | Y | Y | Y |
| 2 **Kline** | Y | Y | N | Y | Y | Y |
| 3 **Ramstad** | Y | Y | N | Y | Y | Y |
| 4 McCollum | Y | Y | Y | N | Y | Y |
| 5 Sabo | Y | Y | Y | N | Y | Y |
| 6 **Kennedy** | Y | Y | N | Y | Y | Y |
| 7 Peterson | Y | Y | Y | N | Y | Y |
| 8 Oberstar | Y | Y | Y | N | Y | Y |
| **MISSISSIPPI** | | | | | | |
| 1 **Wicker** | Y | Y | N | Y | Y | Y |
| 2 Thompson | Y | Y | Y | N | Y | Y |
| 3 **Pickering** | Y | Y | N | Y | Y | Y |
| 4 Taylor | Y | Y | Y | Y | Y | Y |
| **MISSOURI** | | | | | | |
| 1 Clay | Y | Y | Y | ? | Y | Y |
| 2 **Akin** | Y | Y | N | Y | Y | Y |
| 3 Carnahan | Y | Y | Y | N | Y | Y |
| 4 Skelton | Y | Y | Y | Y | Y | Y |
| 5 Cleaver | Y | Y | Y | N | Y | Y |
| 6 **Graves** | Y | Y | N | Y | Y | Y |
| 7 **Blunt** | Y | Y | N | Y | Y | Y |
| 8 **Emerson** | Y | Y | N | Y | Y | Y |
| 9 **Hulshof** | Y | Y | N | Y | Y | Y |
| **MONTANA** | | | | | | |
| AL **Rehberg** | Y | Y | N | Y | Y | Y |
| **NEBRASKA** | | | | | | |
| 1 **Fortenberry** | Y | Y | N | Y | Y | Y |
| 2 **Terry** | Y | Y | N | Y | Y | Y |
| 3 **Osborne** | Y | Y | N | Y | Y | Y |
| **NEVADA** | | | | | | |
| 1 Berkley | Y | Y | Y | N | Y | Y |
| 2 **Gibbons** | Y | Y | N | Y | Y | Y |
| 3 **Porter** | Y | Y | N | Y | Y | Y |
| **NEW HAMPSHIRE** | | | | | | |
| 1 **Bradley** | Y | Y | N | Y | Y | Y |
| 2 **Bass** | Y | Y | N | Y | Y | Y |
| **NEW JERSEY** | | | | | | |
| 1 Andrews | Y | Y | Y | N | Y | Y |
| 2 **LoBiondo** | Y | Y | N | Y | Y | Y |
| 3 **Saxton** | Y | Y | N | Y | Y | Y |
| 4 **Smith** | Y | Y | N | Y | Y | Y |
| 5 **Garrett** | Y | Y | N | Y | Y | Y |
| 6 Pallone | Y | Y | Y | N | Y | Y |
| 7 **Ferguson** | Y | Y | N | Y | Y | Y |
| 8 Pascrell | Y | Y | Y | N | Y | Y |
| 9 Rothman | Y | Y | Y | N | Y | Y |
| 10 Payne | Y | Y | Y | N | Y | Y |
| 11 **Frelinghuysen** | Y | Y | N | Y | Y | Y |
| 12 Holt | Y | Y | Y | N | Y | Y |
| 13 Menendez | Y | Y | Y | N | Y | Y |
| **NEW MEXICO** | | | | | | |
| 1 **Wilson** | Y | Y | N | Y | Y | Y |
| 2 **Pearce** | Y | Y | N | Y | Y | Y |
| 3 Udall | Y | Y | Y | N | Y | Y |
| **NEW YORK** | | | | | | |
| 1 Bishop | Y | Y | Y | N | Y | Y |
| 2 Israel | Y | Y | Y | N | Y | Y |
| 3 **King** | Y | Y | N | Y | Y | Y |
| 4 McCarthy | Y | Y | Y | N | Y | Y |
| 5 Ackerman | Y | Y | Y | Y | Y | Y |
| 6 Meeks | Y | Y | Y | N | Y | Y |
| 7 Crowley | Y | Y | Y | N | Y | Y |
| 8 Nadler | Y | Y | Y | N | Y | Y |
| 9 Weiner | Y | Y | Y | N | Y | Y |
| 10 Towns | Y | Y | Y | N | Y | Y |
| 11 Owens | Y | Y | Y | N | Y | Y |
| 12 Velázquez | Y | Y | Y | N | Y | Y |
| 13 **Fossella** | Y | Y | N | Y | Y | Y |
| 14 Maloney | Y | Y | Y | N | Y | Y |
| 15 Rangel | Y | Y | Y | N | Y | Y |
| 16 Serrano | Y | Y | Y | N | Y | Y |
| 17 Engel | Y | Y | Y | Y | Y | Y |
| 18 Lowey | Y | Y | Y | N | Y | Y |
| 19 **Kelly** | Y | Y | N | Y | Y | Y |
| 20 **Sweeney** | Y | Y | N | Y | Y | Y |
| 21 McNulty | Y | Y | Y | N | Y | Y |
| 22 Hinchey | Y | Y | Y | N | Y | Y |
| 23 **McHugh** | Y | Y | N | Y | Y | Y |
| 24 **Boehlert** | Y | Y | N | Y | Y | Y |
| 25 **Walsh** | Y | Y | N | Y | Y | Y |
| 26 **Reynolds** | Y | Y | N | Y | Y | Y |
| 27 Higgins | Y | Y | Y | Y | Y | Y |
| 28 Slaughter | Y | Y | Y | N | Y | Y |
| 29 **Kuhl** | Y | Y | N | Y | Y | Y |
| **NORTH CAROLINA** | | | | | | |
| 1 Butterfield | Y | Y | Y | Y | Y | Y |
| 2 Etheridge | Y | Y | Y | Y | Y | Y |
| 3 **Jones** | Y | Y | N | Y | Y | Y |
| 4 Price | Y | Y | Y | Y | Y | Y |
| 5 **Foxx** | N | Y | N | Y | Y | Y |
| 6 **Coble** | Y | Y | N | Y | Y | Y |
| 7 McIntyre | Y | Y | Y | Y | Y | Y |
| 8 **Hayes** | Y | Y | N | Y | Y | Y |
| 9 **Myrick** | Y | Y | N | Y | Y | Y |
| 10 **McHenry** | Y | Y | N | Y | Y | Y |
| 11 **Taylor** | Y | Y | N | Y | Y | Y |
| 12 Watt | Y | Y | Y | N | Y | Y |
| 13 Miller | Y | Y | Y | N | Y | Y |
| **NORTH DAKOTA** | | | | | | |
| AL Pomeroy | Y | Y | Y | N | Y | Y |
| **OHIO** | | | | | | |
| 1 **Chabot** | Y | Y | N | Y | Y | Y |
| 2 Vacant | | | | | | |
| 3 **Turner** | Y | Y | N | Y | Y | Y |
| 4 **Oxley** | Y | Y | N | Y | Y | Y |
| 5 **Gillmor** | Y | Y | N | Y | Y | Y |
| 6 Strickland | Y | Y | Y | N | Y | Y |
| 7 **Hobson** | Y | Y | N | Y | Y | Y |
| 8 **Boehner** | Y | Y | N | Y | Y | Y |
| 9 Kaptur | Y | Y | Y | N | Y | Y |
| 10 Kucinich | Y | Y | Y | N | Y | Y |
| 11 Jones | Y | Y | Y | N | Y | Y |
| 12 **Tiberi** | Y | Y | N | Y | Y | Y |
| 13 Brown | Y | Y | Y | N | Y | Y |
| 14 **LaTourette** | Y | Y | N | Y | Y | Y |
| 15 **Pryce** | Y | Y | N | Y | Y | Y |
| 16 **Regula** | Y | Y | N | Y | Y | Y |
| 17 Ryan | Y | Y | Y | N | Y | Y |
| 18 **Ney** | Y | Y | N | Y | Y | Y |
| **OKLAHOMA** | | | | | | |
| 1 **Sullivan** | Y | Y | N | Y | Y | Y |
| 2 Boren | Y | Y | Y | Y | Y | Y |
| 3 **Lucas** | Y | Y | N | Y | Y | Y |
| 4 **Cole** | Y | Y | N | Y | Y | Y |
| 5 **Istook** | Y | Y | N | Y | Y | Y |
| **OREGON** | | | | | | |
| 1 Wu | Y | Y | Y | Y | Y | Y |
| 2 **Walden** | Y | Y | N | Y | Y | Y |
| 3 Blumenauer | Y | ? | Y | N | Y | Y |
| 4 DeFazio | Y | Y | Y | N | Y | Y |
| 5 Hooley | Y | Y | Y | N | Y | Y |
| **PENNSYLVANIA** | | | | | | |
| 1 Brady | ? | ? | ? | ? | ? | ? |
| 2 Fattah | Y | Y | Y | N | Y | Y |
| 3 **English** | Y | Y | N | Y | Y | Y |
| 4 **Hart** | Y | Y | N | Y | Y | Y |
| 5 **Peterson** | Y | Y | N | Y | Y | Y |
| 6 **Gerlach** | Y | Y | N | Y | Y | Y |
| 7 **Weldon** | Y | Y | N | Y | Y | Y |
| 8 **Fitzpatrick** | Y | Y | N | Y | Y | Y |
| 9 **Shuster** | Y | Y | N | Y | Y | Y |
| 10 **Sherwood** | Y | Y | N | Y | Y | Y |
| 11 Kanjorski | Y | Y | Y | N | Y | Y |
| 12 Murtha | Y | Y | ? | ? | ? | ? |
| 13 Schwartz | Y | Y | Y | N | Y | Y |
| 14 Doyle | Y | Y | Y | N | Y | Y |
| 15 **Dent** | Y | Y | N | Y | Y | Y |
| 16 **Pitts** | Y | Y | N | Y | Y | Y |
| 17 Holden | Y | Y | Y | N | Y | Y |
| 18 **Murphy** | ? | ? | ? | ? | ? | ? |
| 19 **Platts** | Y | Y | N | Y | Y | Y |
| **RHODE ISLAND** | | | | | | |
| 1 Kennedy | Y | Y | Y | N | Y | Y |
| 2 Langevin | Y | Y | Y | N | Y | Y |
| **SOUTH CAROLINA** | | | | | | |
| 1 **Brown** | Y | Y | N | Y | Y | Y |
| 2 **Wilson** | Y | Y | N | Y | Y | Y |
| 3 **Barrett** | Y | Y | N | Y | Y | Y |
| 4 **Inglis** | Y | Y | N | Y | Y | Y |
| 5 Spratt | Y | Y | Y | N | Y | Y |
| 6 Clyburn | Y | Y | Y | N | Y | Y |
| **SOUTH DAKOTA** | | | | | | |
| AL Herseth | Y | Y | Y | Y | Y | Y |
| **TENNESSEE** | | | | | | |
| 1 **Jenkins** | Y | Y | ? | ? | ? | Y |
| 2 **Duncan** | Y | Y | N | Y | Y | Y |
| 3 **Wamp** | Y | Y | N | Y | Y | Y |
| 4 Davis | Y | Y | Y | N | Y | Y |
| 5 Cooper | Y | Y | Y | Y | Y | Y |
| 6 Gordon | Y | Y | Y | Y | Y | Y |
| 7 **Blackburn** | Y | Y | N | Y | Y | Y |
| 8 Tanner | Y | Y | Y | Y | Y | Y |
| 9 Ford | Y | Y | Y | Y | Y | Y |
| **TEXAS** | | | | | | |
| 1 **Gohmert** | Y | Y | N | Y | Y | Y |
| 2 **Poe** | Y | Y | N | Y | Y | Y |
| 3 **Johnson, S.** | Y | Y | N | Y | Y | Y |
| 4 **Hall** | Y | Y | N | Y | Y | Y |
| 5 **Hensarling** | Y | Y | N | Y | Y | Y |
| 6 **Barton** | Y | Y | N | Y | Y | Y |
| 7 **Culberson** | Y | Y | N | Y | Y | Y |
| 8 **Brady** | Y | Y | N | Y | Y | Y |
| 9 Green, A. | Y | Y | Y | N | Y | Y |
| 10 **McCaul** | Y | Y | N | Y | Y | Y |
| 11 **Conaway** | Y | Y | N | Y | Y | Y |
| 12 **Granger** | Y | Y | N | Y | Y | Y |
| 13 **Thornberry** | Y | Y | N | Y | Y | Y |
| 14 **Paul** | N | Y | N | N | Y | Y |
| 15 Hinojosa | Y | Y | Y | N | Y | Y |
| 16 Reyes | Y | Y | Y | ? | Y | Y |
| 17 Edwards | Y | Y | Y | N | Y | Y |
| 18 Jackson-Lee | Y | Y | Y | N | Y | Y |
| 19 **Neugebauer** | Y | Y | N | Y | Y | Y |
| 20 Gonzalez | Y | Y | Y | N | Y | Y |
| 21 **Smith** | Y | Y | N | Y | Y | Y |
| 22 **DeLay** | Y | Y | N | Y | Y | Y |
| 23 **Bonilla** | Y | Y | N | Y | Y | Y |
| 24 **Marchant** | Y | Y | N | Y | Y | Y |
| 25 Doggett | Y | Y | Y | N | Y | Y |
| 26 **Burgess** | Y | Y | N | Y | Y | Y |
| 27 Ortiz | Y | Y | Y | Y | Y | Y |
| 28 Cuellar | Y | Y | Y | Y | Y | Y |
| 29 Green, G. | Y | Y | Y | N | Y | Y |
| 30 Johnson, E. | Y | Y | Y | N | Y | Y |
| 31 **Carter** | Y | ? | N | Y | Y | Y |
| 32 **Sessions** | Y | Y | N | Y | Y | Y |
| **UTAH** | | | | | | |
| 1 **Bishop** | Y | Y | N | Y | Y | Y |
| 2 Matheson | Y | Y | Y | Y | Y | Y |
| 3 **Cannon** | Y | Y | N | Y | Y | Y |
| **VERMONT** | | | | | | |
| AL *Sanders* | Y | Y | Y | N | Y | Y |
| **VIRGINIA** | | | | | | |
| 1 **Davis, J.** | Y | Y | N | Y | Y | Y |
| 2 **Drake** | Y | Y | N | Y | Y | Y |
| 3 Scott | Y | Y | Y | N | Y | Y |
| 4 **Forbes** | Y | Y | N | Y | Y | Y |
| 5 **Goode** | Y | Y | N | Y | Y | Y |
| 6 **Goodlatte** | Y | Y | N | Y | Y | Y |
| 7 **Cantor** | Y | Y | N | Y | Y | Y |
| 8 Moran | Y | Y | N | N | Y | Y |
| 9 Boucher | Y | Y | Y | Y | Y | Y |
| 10 **Wolf** | Y | Y | N | Y | Y | Y |
| 11 **Davis, T.** | Y | Y | N | Y | Y | Y |
| **WASHINGTON** | | | | | | |
| 1 Inslee | Y | Y | Y | Y | Y | Y |
| 2 Larsen | Y | Y | N | N | Y | Y |
| 3 Baird | Y | Y | Y | N | Y | Y |
| 4 **Hastings** | Y | Y | N | Y | Y | Y |
| 5 **McMorris** | Y | Y | N | Y | Y | Y |
| 6 Dicks | Y | Y | N | Y | Y | Y |
| 7 McDermott | Y | Y | Y | N | Y | Y |
| 8 **Reichert** | Y | Y | N | Y | Y | Y |
| 9 Smith | Y | Y | N | Y | Y | Y |
| **WEST VIRGINIA** | | | | | | |
| 1 Mollohan | Y | Y | Y | N | Y | Y |
| 2 **Capito** | Y | Y | N | Y | Y | Y |
| 3 Rahall | Y | Y | Y | N | Y | Y |
| **WISCONSIN** | | | | | | |
| 1 **Ryan** | Y | Y | N | Y | Y | Y |
| 2 Baldwin | Y | Y | Y | N | Y | Y |
| 3 Kind | Y | Y | Y | Y | Y | Y |
| 4 Moore | Y | Y | Y | N | Y | Y |
| 5 **Sensenbrenner** | Y | Y | N | Y | Y | Y |
| 6 **Petri** | Y | Y | N | Y | Y | Y |
| 7 Obey | Y | Y | Y | N | Y | Y |
| 8 **Green** | Y | Y | N | Y | Y | Y |
| **WYOMING** | | | | | | |
| AL **Cubin** | Y | Y | N | Y | Y | Y |

# IN THE HOUSE | By Vote Number

**440.** **HR 5. Medical Malpractice/Previous Question.** Gingrey, R-Ga., motion to order the previous question (thus ending debate and the possibility of amendment) on adoption of the rule (H Res 385) to provide for House floor consideration of the bill that would cap the awards plaintiffs and their attorneys could receive in medical malpractice cases. Motion agreed to 226-200: R 226-0; D 0-199 (ND 0-148, SD 0-51); I 0-1. July 27, 2005.

**441.** **HR 5. Medical Malpractice/Rule.** Adoption of the rule (H Res 385) to provide for House consideration of the bill that would cap the awards plaintiffs and their attorneys could receive in medical malpractice cases. Adopted 226-200: R 225-1; D 1-198 (ND 1-147, SD 0-51); I 0-1. July 27, 2005.

**442.** **HR 3045. Central American Free Trade Agreement/Rule.** Adoption of the rule (H Res 386) to provide for House consideration of the bill that would implement a free trade agreement between the United States and Costa Rica, El Salvador, Guatemala, Honduras and Nicaragua and a separate pact with the Dominican Republic. Adopted 227-201: R 227-0; D 0-200 (ND 0-149, SD 0-51); I 0-1. July 27, 2005.

**443.** **HR 3045. Central American Free Trade Agreement/Passage.** Passage of the bill that would implement a free trade agreement between the United States and Costa Rica, El Salvador, Guatemala, Honduras and Nicaragua and a separate pact with the Dominican Republic. Passed 217-215: R 202-27; D 15-187 (ND 7-144, SD 8-43); I 0-1. A "yea" was a vote in support of the president's position. July 28, 2005 (in the session that began and the Congressional Record dated July 27, 2005).

**444.** **H Res 308. National Marina Day/Adoption.** Coble, R-N.C., motion to suspend the rules and adopt the resolution that would support the goals of National Marina Day and urge U.S. marinas to continue to provide environmentally friendly gateways to boating for Americans. Motion agreed to 385-0: R 203-0; D 181-0 (ND 137-0, SD 44-0); I 1-0. A two-thirds majority of those present and voting (257 in this case) is required for adoption under suspension of the rules. July 28, 2005 (in the session that began and the Congressional Record dated July 27, 2005).

**445.** **HR 6. Energy Policy/Conference Report.** Adoption of the conference report on the bill that would overhaul the nation's energy policy and provide for $14.6 billion in energy-related tax incentives. It would allow lawsuits involving the gasoline additive methyl tertiary butyl ether to be moved to a federal district court and require refiners to use 7.5 billion gallons of renewable fuels annually by 2012. It would grant the Federal Energy Regulatory Commission jurisdiction over reliability standards for electricity transmission networks and extend daylight-saving time by one month. Adopted (thus sent to the Senate) 275-156: R 200-31; D 75-124 (ND 41-107, SD 34-17); I 0-1. A "yea" was a vote in support of the president's position. July 28, 2005.

**446.** **HR 2361. Fiscal 2006 Interior-Environment Appropriations/Rule.** Adoption of the rule (H Res 392) to provide for House floor consideration of the conference report on the bill that would appropriate $26.2 billion in fiscal 2006 for the Department of Interior, the EPA and related agencies. Adopted 402-4: R 207-0; D 194-4 (ND 145-3, SD 49-1); I 1-0. July 28, 2005.

| | 440 | 441 | 442 | 443 | 444 | 445 | 446 |
|---|---|---|---|---|---|---|---|
| **ALABAMA** | | | | | | | |
| 1 Bonner | Y | Y | Y | Y | Y | N | Y |
| 2 Everett | Y | Y | Y | Y | Y | Y | Y |
| 3 Rogers | Y | Y | Y | Y | Y | Y | Y |
| 4 Aderholt | Y | Y | Y | Y | Y | Y | Y |
| 5 Cramer | N | N | N | N | ? | Y | Y |
| 6 Bachus | Y | Y | Y | Y | Y | Y | Y |
| 7 Davis | N | N | N | N | Y | Y | Y |
| **ALASKA** | | | | | | | |
| AL Young | Y | Y | Y | Y | Y | Y | Y |
| **ARIZONA** | | | | | | | |
| 1 Renzi | Y | Y | Y | Y | Y | Y | Y |
| 2 Franks | Y | Y | Y | Y | Y | Y | P |
| 3 Shadegg | Y | Y | Y | Y | Y | Y | Y |
| 4 Pastor | N | N | N | N | Y | Y | Y |
| 5 Hayworth | Y | Y | Y | Y | Y | Y | Y |
| 6 Flake | Y | Y | Y | Y | Y | N | P |
| 7 Grijalva | N | N | N | N | ? | N | Y |
| 8 Kolbe | Y | Y | Y | Y | Y | Y | Y |
| **ARKANSAS** | | | | | | | |
| 1 Berry | N | N | N | N | Y | Y | Y |
| 2 Snyder | N | N | N | Y | Y | Y | Y |
| 3 Boozman | Y | Y | Y | Y | Y | Y | Y |
| 4 Ross | N | N | N | N | Y | Y | Y |
| **CALIFORNIA** | | | | | | | |
| 1 Thompson | N | N | N | N | Y | N | Y |
| 2 Herger | Y | Y | Y | Y | Y | Y | Y |
| 3 Lungren | Y | Y | Y | Y | Y | Y | P |
| 4 Doolittle | Y | Y | Y | Y | Y | Y | Y |
| 5 Matsui, D. | N | N | N | N | Y | Y | Y |
| 6 Woolsey | N | N | N | N | Y | N | Y |
| 7 Miller, George | N | N | N | N | Y | N | Y |
| 8 Pelosi | N | N | N | N | Y | N | Y |
| 9 Lee | N | N | N | N | Y | N | Y |
| 10 Tauscher | N | N | N | N | Y | N | Y |
| 11 Pombo | Y | Y | Y | Y | Y | Y | Y |
| 12 Lantos | N | N | N | N | Y | N | Y |
| 13 Stark | N | N | N | N | ? | N | Y |
| 14 Eshoo | N | N | N | N | Y | N | Y |
| 15 Honda | N | N | N | N | Y | N | Y |
| 16 Lofgren | N | N | N | N | Y | N | Y |
| 17 Farr | N | N | N | N | Y | N | Y |
| 18 Cardoza | N | N | N | N | Y | Y | Y |
| 19 Radanovich | Y | Y | Y | Y | Y | Y | Y |
| 20 Costa | N | N | N | N | Y | Y | Y |
| 21 Nunes | Y | Y | Y | Y | Y | Y | Y |
| 22 Thomas | Y | Y | Y | Y | Y | Y | Y |
| 23 Capps | N | N | N | N | Y | N | Y |
| 24 Gallegly | Y | Y | Y | Y | Y | Y | Y |
| 25 McKeon | Y | Y | Y | Y | Y | Y | Y |
| 26 Dreier | Y | Y | Y | Y | Y | Y | Y |
| 27 Sherman | N | N | N | N | Y | N | Y |
| 28 Berman | N | N | N | N | Y | N | Y |
| 29 Schiff | N | N | N | N | Y | N | Y |
| 30 Waxman | N | N | N | N | Y | N | Y |
| 31 Becerra | N | N | N | N | Y | N | Y |
| 32 Solis | N | N | N | N | Y | N | Y |
| 33 Watson | N | N | N | N | Y | N | Y |
| 34 Roybal-Allard | N | N | N | N | Y | N | Y |
| 35 Waters | N | N | N | N | Y | N | Y |
| 36 Harman | N | N | N | N | Y | N | Y |
| 37 Millender-McD. | N | N | N | N | Y | N | Y |
| 38 Napolitano | N | N | N | N | Y | N | Y |
| 39 Sánchez, Linda | ? | N | N | N | Y | N | Y |
| 40 Royce | Y | Y | Y | Y | Y | N | Y |
| 41 Lewis | Y | Y | Y | Y | Y | Y | Y |
| 42 Miller, Gary | Y | Y | Y | Y | ? | Y | Y |
| 43 Baca | N | N | N | N | Y | Y | Y |
| 44 Calvert | Y | Y | Y | Y | Y | Y | Y |
| 45 Bono | Y | Y | Y | Y | Y | Y | Y |
| 46 Rohrabacher | Y | Y | Y | Y | Y | N | Y |
| 47 Sanchez, Loretta | N | N | N | N | Y | N | Y |
| 48 Cox | Y | Y | Y | Y | Y | Y | Y |
| 49 Issa | Y | Y | Y | Y | Y | Y | Y |

| | 440 | 441 | 442 | 443 | 444 | 445 | 446 |
|---|---|---|---|---|---|---|---|
| 50 Cunningham | Y | Y | Y | Y | ? | Y | Y |
| 51 Filner | N | N | N | N | Y | N | Y |
| 52 Hunter | Y | Y | Y | N | Y | Y | Y |
| 53 Davis | N | N | N | N | Y | N | Y |
| **COLORADO** | | | | | | | |
| 1 DeGette | N | N | N | N | Y | N | Y |
| 2 Udall | N | N | N | N | Y | N | Y |
| 3 Salazar | N | N | N | N | ? | Y | Y |
| 4 Musgrave | Y | Y | Y | Y | Y | Y | P |
| 5 Hefley | Y | N | Y | N | ? | Y | P |
| 6 Tancredo | Y | Y | Y | N | ? | Y | P |
| 7 Beauprez | Y | Y | Y | Y | Y | Y | Y |
| **CONNECTICUT** | | | | | | | |
| 1 Larson | N | N | N | N | Y | N | Y |
| 2 Simmons | Y | Y | Y | N | Y | Y | Y |
| 3 DeLauro | N | N | N | N | Y | N | Y |
| 4 Shays | Y | Y | Y | Y | Y | Y | Y |
| 5 Johnson | Y | Y | Y | Y | Y | Y | Y |
| **DELAWARE** | | | | | | | |
| AL Castle | Y | Y | Y | Y | Y | N | Y |
| **FLORIDA** | | | | | | | |
| 1 Miller | Y | Y | Y | Y | Y | N | P |
| 2 Boyd | N | N | N | N | Y | N | Y |
| 3 Brown | N | N | N | N | Y | N | Y |
| 4 Crenshaw | Y | Y | Y | Y | Y | Y | Y |
| 5 Brown-Waite | Y | Y | Y | Y | Y | Y | Y |
| 6 Stearns | Y | Y | Y | Y | ? | Y | Y |
| 7 Mica | Y | Y | Y | Y | Y | Y | Y |
| 8 Keller | Y | Y | Y | Y | Y | Y | Y |
| 9 Bilirakis | Y | Y | Y | Y | Y | Y | Y |
| 10 Young | Y | Y | Y | Y | ? | N | Y |
| 11 Davis | N | N | N | N | Y | N | Y |
| 12 Putnam | Y | Y | Y | Y | Y | Y | Y |
| 13 Harris | Y | Y | Y | Y | Y | Y | Y |
| 14 Mack | Y | Y | Y | Y | N | Y | Y |
| 15 Weldon | Y | Y | Y | Y | Y | N | Y |
| 16 Foley | Y | Y | Y | Y | Y | N | Y |
| 17 Meek | N | N | N | N | Y | N | Y |
| 18 Ros-Lehtinen | Y | Y | Y | Y | Y | Y | Y |
| 19 Wexler | N | N | N | N | Y | N | Y |
| 20 Wasserman-Schultz | N | N | N | N | Y | N | Y |
| 21 Diaz-Balart, L. | Y | Y | Y | Y | Y | Y | Y |
| 22 Shaw | Y | Y | Y | Y | Y | Y | Y |
| 23 Hastings | N | N | N | N | Y | N | Y |
| 24 Feeney | Y | Y | Y | Y | Y | N | Y |
| 25 Diaz-Balart, M. | Y | Y | Y | Y | Y | N | Y |
| **GEORGIA** | | | | | | | |
| 1 Kingston | Y | Y | Y | Y | Y | Y | Y |
| 2 Bishop | N | N | N | N | Y | Y | Y |
| 3 Marshall | N | N | N | N | Y | Y | Y |
| 4 McKinney | N | N | N | N | Y | N | Y |
| 5 Lewis | N | N | N | N | Y | N | Y |
| 6 Price | Y | Y | Y | Y | Y | Y | P |
| 7 Linder | Y | Y | Y | Y | Y | Y | Y |
| 8 Westmoreland | Y | Y | Y | Y | Y | Y | P |
| 9 Norwood | Y | Y | Y | N | ? | Y | Y |
| 10 Deal | Y | Y | Y | Y | Y | Y | Y |
| 11 Gingrey | Y | Y | Y | Y | Y | Y | Y |
| 12 Barrow | N | N | N | N | Y | Y | Y |
| 13 Scott | N | N | N | N | Y | Y | Y |
| **HAWAII** | | | | | | | |
| 1 Abercrombie | N | ? | N | N | Y | Y | Y |
| 2 Case | N | N | N | N | Y | N | Y |
| **IDAHO** | | | | | | | |
| 1 Otter | Y | Y | Y | N | ? | Y | P |
| 2 Simpson | Y | Y | Y | N | ? | Y | Y |
| **ILLINOIS** | | | | | | | |
| 1 Rush | N | N | N | N | Y | Y | Y |
| 2 Jackson | N | N | N | N | Y | N | Y |
| 3 Lipinski | N | N | N | N | Y | Y | Y |
| 4 Gutierrez | N | N | N | N | Y | N | Y |
| 5 Emanuel | N | N | N | N | Y | N | Y |
| 6 Hyde | Y | Y | Y | Y | Y | Y | Y |
| 7 Davis | N | N | N | N | Y | N | Y |
| 8 Bean | N | N | N | N | Y | Y | Y |
| 9 Schakowsky | N | N | N | N | Y | ? | ? |
| 10 Kirk | Y | Y | Y | Y | Y | Y | Y |
| 11 Weller | Y | Y | Y | Y | Y | Y | Y |
| 12 Costello | N | N | N | N | Y | N | Y |

**KEY**     Republicans          Democrats          *Independents*

| | | | |
|---|---|---|---|
| Y | Voted for (yea) | X | Paired against | C Voted "present" to avoid possible conflict of interest |
| # | Paired for | – | Announced against | |
| + | Announced for | P | Voted "present" | ? Did not vote or otherwise make a position known |
| N | Voted against (nay) | | | |

| | 440 | 441 | 442 | 443 | 444 | 445 | 446 |
|---|---|---|---|---|---|---|---|
| 13 **Biggert** | Y | Y | Y | Y | Y | Y | Y |
| 14 **Hastert** | | | | Y | | Y | |
| 15 **Johnson** | Y | Y | Y | Y | Y | Y | Y |
| 16 **Manzullo** | Y | Y | Y | Y | Y | Y | Y |
| 17 Evans | N | N | N | N | Y | Y | Y |
| 18 **LaHood** | Y | Y | Y | Y | Y | Y | Y |
| 19 **Shimkus** | Y | Y | Y | Y | Y | Y | Y |
| **INDIANA** | | | | | | | |
| 1 Visclosky | N | N | N | N | Y | Y | Y |
| 2 **Chocola** | Y | Y | Y | Y | Y | Y | Y |
| 3 **Souder** | Y | Y | Y | Y | Y | Y | Y |
| 4 **Buyer** | Y | Y | Y | Y | ? | Y | Y |
| 5 **Burton** | Y | Y | Y | Y | Y | Y | Y |
| 6 **Pence** | Y | Y | Y | Y | Y | Y | P |
| 7 Carson | ? | ? | ? | N | ? | Y | Y |
| 8 **Hostettler** | Y | Y | Y | N | Y | Y | Y |
| 9 **Sodrel** | Y | Y | Y | Y | Y | Y | P |
| **IOWA** | | | | | | | |
| 1 **Nussle** | Y | Y | Y | Y | Y | Y | Y |
| 2 **Leach** | ? | ? | ? | Y | Y | Y | Y |
| 3 Boswell | N | N | N | N | Y | Y | Y |
| 4 **Latham** | Y | Y | Y | Y | Y | Y | Y |
| 5 **King** | Y | Y | Y | Y | Y | Y | P |
| **KANSAS** | | | | | | | |
| 1 **Moran** | Y | Y | Y | Y | Y | Y | Y |
| 2 **Ryun** | Y | Y | Y | Y | Y | Y | Y |
| 3 Moore | N | N | N | Y | Y | Y | Y |
| 4 **Tiahrt** | Y | Y | Y | Y | Y | Y | Y |
| **KENTUCKY** | | | | | | | |
| 1 **Whitfield** | Y | Y | Y | Y | ? | Y | Y |
| 2 **Lewis** | Y | Y | Y | Y | Y | Y | Y |
| 3 **Northup** | Y | Y | Y | Y | Y | Y | Y |
| 4 **Davis** | Y | Y | Y | Y | Y | Y | Y |
| 5 **Rogers** | Y | Y | Y | Y | Y | Y | Y |
| 6 Chandler | N | N | N | N | Y | N | Y |
| **LOUISIANA** | | | | | | | |
| 1 **Jindal** | Y | Y | Y | N | Y | Y | Y |
| 2 Jefferson | N | N | N | Y | ? | Y | Y |
| 3 Melancon | N | N | N | N | Y | Y | Y |
| 4 **McCrery** | Y | Y | Y | Y | Y | Y | Y |
| 5 **Alexander** | Y | Y | Y | Y | Y | Y | Y |
| 6 **Baker** | Y | Y | Y | Y | ? | Y | Y |
| 7 **Boustany** | Y | Y | Y | N | Y | Y | Y |
| **MAINE** | | | | | | | |
| 1 Allen | N | N | N | N | Y | N | Y |
| 2 Michaud | N | N | N | N | Y | N | Y |
| **MARYLAND** | | | | | | | |
| 1 **Gilchrest** | Y | Y | Y | Y | Y | Y | Y |
| 2 Ruppersberger | N | N | N | N | Y | Y | Y |
| 3 Cardin | N | N | N | N | Y | N | Y |
| 4 Wynn | N | N | N | N | Y | Y | Y |
| 5 Hoyer | N | N | N | N | Y | Y | Y |
| 6 **Bartlett** | Y | Y | Y | Y | Y | N | P |
| 7 Cummings | N | N | N | N | Y | N | Y |
| 8 Van Hollen | N | N | N | N | Y | N | Y |
| **MASSACHUSETTS** | | | | | | | |
| 1 Olver | N | N | N | N | Y | N | Y |
| 2 Neal | N | N | N | N | Y | N | Y |
| 3 McGovern | N | N | N | N | Y | N | Y |
| 4 Frank | N | N | N | N | Y | N | Y |
| 5 Meehan | N | N | N | N | Y | N | Y |
| 6 Tierney | N | N | N | N | Y | N | Y |
| 7 Markey | N | N | N | N | ? | N | Y |
| 8 Capuano | N | N | N | N | Y | N | N |
| 9 Lynch | N | N | N | N | Y | N | Y |
| 10 Delahunt | N | N | N | N | Y | N | Y |
| **MICHIGAN** | | | | | | | |
| 1 Stupak | N | N | N | N | Y | Y | N |
| 2 **Hoekstra** | Y | Y | Y | Y | Y | Y | Y |
| 3 **Ehlers** | Y | Y | Y | Y | Y | Y | Y |
| 4 **Camp** | Y | Y | Y | Y | Y | Y | Y |
| 5 Kildee | N | N | N | N | Y | N | Y |
| 6 **Upton** | Y | Y | Y | Y | Y | Y | Y |
| 7 **Schwarz** | Y | Y | Y | Y | Y | Y | Y |
| 8 **Rogers** | Y | Y | Y | Y | Y | Y | Y |
| 9 **Knollenberg** | Y | Y | Y | Y | Y | Y | Y |
| 10 **Miller** | Y | Y | Y | N | Y | Y | Y |
| 11 **McCotter** | Y | Y | Y | N | Y | Y | Y |
| 12 Levin | N | N | N | N | Y | Y | Y |
| 13 Kilpatrick | N | N | N | N | Y | N | Y |
| 14 Conyers | N | N | N | N | Y | N | Y |
| 15 Dingell | N | N | N | N | ? | Y | N |
| **MINNESOTA** | | | | | | | |
| 1 **Gutknecht** | Y | Y | Y | N | ? | Y | P |
| 2 **Kline** | Y | Y | Y | Y | Y | Y | Y |
| 3 **Ramstad** | Y | Y | Y | Y | Y | Y | Y |
| 4 McCollum | N | N | N | N | Y | N | Y |
| 5 Sabo | N | N | N | N | Y | N | Y |
| 6 **Kennedy** | Y | Y | Y | Y | Y | Y | Y |
| 7 Peterson | N | Y | N | N | Y | Y | Y |
| 8 Oberstar | N | N | N | N | Y | Y | Y |
| **MISSISSIPPI** | | | | | | | |
| 1 **Wicker** | Y | Y | Y | Y | Y | Y | Y |
| 2 Thompson | N | N | N | N | Y | Y | Y |
| 3 **Pickering** | Y | Y | Y | Y | Y | Y | Y |
| 4 Taylor | N | N | N | N | Y | N | Y |
| **MISSOURI** | | | | | | | |
| 1 Clay | N | N | N | N | ? | N | Y |
| 2 **Akin** | Y | Y | Y | Y | Y | Y | P |
| 3 Carnahan | N | N | N | N | Y | N | Y |
| 4 Skelton | N | N | N | Y | ? | Y | Y |
| 5 Cleaver | N | N | N | N | Y | N | Y |
| 6 **Graves** | Y | Y | Y | Y | Y | Y | Y |
| 7 **Blunt** | Y | Y | Y | Y | ? | Y | Y |
| 8 **Emerson** | Y | Y | Y | Y | Y | Y | Y |
| 9 **Hulshof** | Y | Y | Y | Y | Y | Y | Y |
| **MONTANA** | | | | | | | |
| AL **Rehberg** | Y | Y | Y | N | Y | Y | Y |
| **NEBRASKA** | | | | | | | |
| 1 **Fortenberry** | Y | Y | Y | Y | Y | Y | Y |
| 2 **Terry** | Y | Y | Y | Y | Y | Y | Y |
| 3 **Osborne** | Y | Y | Y | Y | Y | Y | Y |
| **NEVADA** | | | | | | | |
| 1 Berkley | N | N | N | N | Y | N | Y |
| 2 **Gibbons** | Y | Y | Y | Y | Y | Y | Y |
| 3 **Porter** | Y | Y | Y | Y | Y | Y | Y |
| **NEW HAMPSHIRE** | | | | | | | |
| 1 **Bradley** | Y | Y | Y | Y | Y | N | Y |
| 2 **Bass** | Y | Y | Y | Y | ? | Y | Y |
| **NEW JERSEY** | | | | | | | |
| 1 Andrews | N | N | N | N | Y | N | Y |
| 2 **LoBiondo** | Y | Y | Y | N | Y | N | Y |
| 3 **Saxton** | Y | Y | Y | Y | Y | N | Y |
| 4 **Smith** | Y | Y | Y | N | Y | N | Y |
| 5 **Garrett** | Y | Y | Y | N | ? | Y | Y |
| 6 Pallone | N | N | N | N | Y | N | Y |
| 7 **Ferguson** | Y | Y | Y | Y | Y | Y | Y |
| 8 Pascrell | N | N | N | N | Y | N | Y |
| 9 Rothman | N | N | N | N | Y | N | Y |
| 10 Payne | N | N | N | N | Y | ? | ? |
| 11 **Frelinghuysen** | Y | Y | Y | Y | Y | Y | Y |
| 12 Holt | N | N | N | N | Y | N | Y |
| 13 Menendez | N | N | N | N | Y | N | Y |
| **NEW MEXICO** | | | | | | | |
| 1 **Wilson** | Y | Y | Y | Y | Y | Y | Y |
| 2 **Pearce** | Y | Y | Y | Y | Y | Y | Y |
| 3 Udall | N | N | N | N | Y | Y | Y |
| **NEW YORK** | | | | | | | |
| 1 Bishop | N | N | N | N | Y | N | Y |
| 2 Israel | N | N | N | N | Y | N | Y |
| 3 **King** | Y | Y | Y | Y | Y | Y | Y |
| 4 McCarthy | N | N | N | N | Y | N | Y |
| 5 Ackerman | N | N | N | N | Y | N | Y |
| 6 Meeks | N | N | N | Y | ? | Y | Y |
| 7 Crowley | N | N | N | N | Y | N | Y |
| 8 Nadler | N | N | N | N | Y | N | Y |
| 9 Weiner | N | N | N | N | Y | N | Y |
| 10 Towns | N | N | N | Y | ? | Y | Y |
| 11 Owens | N | N | N | N | Y | N | Y |
| 12 Velázquez | N | N | N | N | ? | N | Y |
| 13 **Fossella** | Y | Y | Y | Y | Y | Y | Y |
| 14 Maloney | N | N | N | N | Y | N | Y |
| 15 Rangel | N | N | N | N | Y | N | Y |
| 16 Serrano | N | N | N | N | Y | N | Y |
| 17 Engel | N | N | N | N | Y | N | Y |
| 18 Lowey | N | N | N | N | Y | N | Y |
| 19 **Kelly** | Y | Y | Y | Y | Y | N | Y |
| 20 **Sweeney** | Y | Y | Y | Y | Y | Y | Y |
| 21 McNulty | N | N | N | N | Y | N | Y |
| 22 Hinchey | N | N | N | N | Y | N | Y |
| 23 **McHugh** | Y | Y | Y | N | ? | Y | Y |
| 24 **Boehlert** | Y | Y | Y | Y | Y | N | Y |
| 25 **Walsh** | Y | Y | Y | Y | Y | Y | Y |
| 26 **Reynolds** | Y | Y | Y | Y | Y | Y | Y |
| 27 Higgins | N | N | N | N | Y | N | Y |
| 28 Slaughter | N | N | N | N | Y | Y | Y |
| 29 **Kuhl** | Y | Y | Y | Y | Y | Y | Y |
| **NORTH CAROLINA** | | | | | | | |
| 1 Butterfield | N | N | N | N | Y | Y | Y |
| 2 Etheridge | N | N | N | N | Y | Y | Y |
| 3 **Jones** | Y | Y | Y | N | Y | N | P |
| 4 Price | N | N | N | N | Y | N | Y |
| 5 **Foxx** | Y | Y | Y | N | Y | Y | P |
| 6 **Coble** | Y | Y | Y | N | Y | Y | Y |
| 7 McIntyre | N | N | N | N | Y | Y | Y |
| 8 **Hayes** | Y | Y | Y | Y | Y | Y | Y |
| 9 **Myrick** | Y | Y | Y | Y | Y | Y | Y |
| 10 **McHenry** | Y | Y | Y | N | Y | Y | Y |
| 11 **Taylor** | Y | Y | Y | ? | ? | Y | Y |
| 12 Watt | N | N | N | N | Y | N | Y |
| 13 Miller | N | N | N | N | Y | N | Y |
| **NORTH DAKOTA** | | | | | | | |
| AL Pomeroy | N | N | N | N | Y | Y | Y |
| **OHIO** | | | | | | | |
| 1 **Chabot** | Y | Y | Y | Y | Y | Y | Y |
| 2 Vacant | | | | | | | |
| 3 **Turner** | Y | Y | Y | Y | Y | Y | Y |
| 4 **Oxley** | Y | Y | Y | Y | ? | Y | Y |
| 5 **Gillmor** | Y | Y | Y | Y | Y | Y | Y |
| 6 Strickland | N | N | N | N | Y | Y | Y |
| 7 **Hobson** | Y | Y | Y | Y | Y | Y | Y |
| 8 **Boehner** | Y | Y | Y | Y | Y | Y | Y |
| 9 Kaptur | N | N | N | N | Y | N | Y |
| 10 Kucinich | N | N | N | N | Y | N | Y |
| 11 Jones | N | N | N | N | Y | N | Y |
| 12 **Tiberi** | Y | Y | Y | Y | Y | Y | Y |
| 13 Brown | N | N | N | N | Y | N | Y |
| 14 **LaTourette** | Y | Y | Y | Y | Y | Y | Y |
| 15 **Pryce** | Y | Y | Y | Y | Y | Y | Y |
| 16 **Regula** | Y | Y | Y | Y | Y | Y | Y |
| 17 Ryan | N | N | N | N | Y | Y | Y |
| 18 **Ney** | Y | Y | Y | N | Y | Y | Y |
| **OKLAHOMA** | | | | | | | |
| 1 **Sullivan** | Y | Y | Y | Y | Y | Y | Y |
| 2 Boren | N | N | N | N | Y | Y | Y |
| 3 **Lucas** | Y | Y | Y | Y | Y | Y | Y |
| 4 **Cole** | Y | Y | Y | Y | Y | Y | Y |
| 5 **Istook** | Y | Y | Y | Y | ? | Y | Y |
| **OREGON** | | | | | | | |
| 1 Wu | N | N | N | N | Y | N | Y |
| 2 **Walden** | Y | Y | Y | Y | Y | Y | Y |
| 3 Blumenauer | N | N | N | N | Y | N | Y |
| 4 DeFazio | N | N | N | N | Y | N | Y |
| 5 Hooley | N | N | N | N | Y | N | Y |
| **PENNSYLVANIA** | | | | | | | |
| 1 Brady | ? | ? | ? | N | Y | ? | ? |
| 2 Fattah | N | N | N | N | Y | N | Y |
| 3 **English** | Y | Y | Y | Y | Y | Y | Y |
| 4 **Hart** | Y | Y | Y | Y | Y | Y | Y |
| 5 **Peterson** | Y | Y | Y | Y | Y | Y | Y |
| 6 **Gerlach** | Y | Y | Y | Y | Y | Y | Y |
| 7 **Weldon** | Y | Y | Y | Y | Y | Y | Y |
| 8 **Fitzpatrick** | Y | Y | Y | Y | Y | N | Y |
| 9 **Shuster** | Y | Y | Y | Y | Y | Y | Y |
| 10 **Sherwood** | Y | Y | Y | Y | Y | Y | Y |
| 11 Kanjorski | N | N | N | N | Y | Y | Y |
| 12 Murtha | N | N | N | N | ? | Y | Y |
| 13 Schwartz | N | N | N | N | Y | N | Y |
| 14 Doyle | N | N | N | N | Y | Y | Y |
| 15 **Dent** | Y | Y | Y | Y | Y | Y | Y |
| 16 **Pitts** | Y | Y | Y | Y | Y | Y | Y |
| 17 Holden | N | N | N | N | ? | Y | Y |
| 18 **Murphy** | ? | ? | ? | Y | Y | Y | Y |
| 19 **Platts** | Y | Y | Y | Y | Y | Y | Y |
| **RHODE ISLAND** | | | | | | | |
| 1 Kennedy | N | N | N | N | Y | N | Y |
| 2 Langevin | N | N | N | N | Y | N | Y |
| **SOUTH CAROLINA** | | | | | | | |
| 1 **Brown** | Y | Y | Y | Y | Y | Y | Y |
| 2 **Wilson** | Y | Y | Y | Y | ? | Y | Y |
| 3 **Barrett** | Y | Y | Y | Y | Y | Y | P |
| 4 **Inglis** | Y | Y | Y | Y | Y | Y | Y |
| 5 Spratt | N | N | N | N | Y | Y | Y |
| 6 Clyburn | N | N | N | N | Y | Y | Y |
| **SOUTH DAKOTA** | | | | | | | |
| AL Herseth | N | N | N | N | Y | Y | Y |
| **TENNESSEE** | | | | | | | |
| 1 **Jenkins** | Y | Y | Y | Y | ? | Y | Y |
| 2 **Duncan** | Y | Y | Y | Y | Y | Y | Y |
| 3 **Wamp** | Y | Y | Y | Y | Y | Y | Y |
| 4 Davis | N | N | N | N | Y | Y | Y |
| 5 Cooper | N | N | N | Y | Y | N | N |
| 6 Gordon | N | N | N | N | ? | Y | Y |
| 7 **Blackburn** | Y | Y | Y | Y | Y | Y | Y |
| 8 Tanner | N | N | N | Y | Y | Y | P |
| 9 Ford | N | N | N | N | Y | Y | Y |
| **TEXAS** | | | | | | | |
| 1 **Gohmert** | Y | Y | Y | Y | Y | Y | P |
| 2 **Poe** | Y | Y | Y | Y | Y | Y | Y |
| 3 **Johnson, S.** | Y | Y | Y | Y | Y | Y | Y |
| 4 **Hall** | Y | Y | Y | Y | Y | Y | Y |
| 5 **Hensarling** | Y | Y | Y | Y | Y | Y | P |
| 6 **Barton** | Y | Y | Y | Y | Y | Y | Y |
| 7 **Culberson** | Y | Y | Y | Y | Y | Y | Y |
| 8 **Brady** | Y | Y | Y | Y | ? | Y | Y |
| 9 Green, A. | N | N | N | N | Y | Y | Y |
| 10 **McCaul** | Y | Y | Y | Y | Y | Y | Y |
| 11 **Conaway** | Y | Y | Y | Y | Y | Y | Y |
| 12 **Granger** | Y | Y | Y | Y | Y | Y | Y |
| 13 **Thornberry** | Y | Y | Y | Y | ? | Y | Y |
| 14 **Paul** | Y | Y | Y | N | Y | N | ? |
| 15 Hinojosa | N | N | N | Y | ? | Y | Y |
| 16 Reyes | N | N | N | N | ? | Y | Y |
| 17 Edwards | N | N | N | N | ? | Y | Y |
| 18 Jackson-Lee | N | N | N | N | Y | Y | Y |
| 19 **Neugebauer** | Y | Y | Y | Y | Y | Y | Y |
| 20 Gonzalez | N | N | N | N | Y | Y | Y |
| 21 **Smith** | Y | Y | Y | Y | Y | Y | Y |
| 22 **DeLay** | Y | Y | Y | Y | Y | Y | Y |
| 23 **Bonilla** | Y | Y | Y | Y | Y | Y | Y |
| 24 **Marchant** | Y | Y | Y | Y | Y | Y | Y |
| 25 Doggett | N | N | N | N | Y | N | Y |
| 26 **Burgess** | Y | Y | Y | Y | Y | Y | Y |
| 27 Ortiz | N | N | N | Y | Y | Y | Y |
| 28 Cuellar | N | N | N | Y | Y | Y | Y |
| 29 Green, G. | N | N | N | N | Y | Y | Y |
| 30 Johnson, E. | N | N | N | N | Y | Y | Y |
| 31 **Carter** | Y | Y | Y | Y | Y | Y | Y |
| 32 **Sessions** | Y | Y | Y | Y | Y | Y | Y |
| **UTAH** | | | | | | | |
| 1 **Bishop** | Y | Y | Y | Y | Y | Y | Y |
| 2 Matheson | N | N | N | Y | Y | Y | Y |
| 3 **Cannon** | Y | Y | Y | Y | Y | Y | Y |
| **VERMONT** | | | | | | | |
| AL *Sanders* | N | N | N | N | Y | N | Y |
| **VIRGINIA** | | | | | | | |
| 1 **Davis, J.** | ? | ? | ? | ? | ? | Y | Y |
| 2 **Drake** | Y | Y | Y | Y | Y | Y | Y |
| 3 Scott | N | N | N | N | Y | Y | Y |
| 4 **Forbes** | Y | Y | Y | Y | Y | Y | Y |
| 5 **Goode** | Y | Y | Y | N | ? | Y | Y |
| 6 **Goodlatte** | Y | Y | Y | Y | Y | Y | Y |
| 7 **Cantor** | Y | Y | Y | Y | Y | Y | Y |
| 8 Moran | N | N | N | Y | Y | N | Y |
| 9 Boucher | N | N | N | N | ? | Y | Y |
| 10 **Wolf** | Y | Y | Y | Y | Y | Y | Y |
| 11 **Davis, T.** | Y | Y | Y | Y | Y | Y | Y |
| **WASHINGTON** | | | | | | | |
| 1 Inslee | N | N | N | N | Y | N | Y |
| 2 Larsen | N | N | N | N | Y | Y | Y |
| 3 Baird | N | N | N | N | Y | Y | Y |
| 4 **Hastings** | Y | Y | Y | Y | Y | Y | Y |
| 5 **McMorris** | Y | Y | Y | Y | Y | Y | Y |
| 6 Dicks | N | N | N | Y | ? | Y | Y |
| 7 McDermott | N | N | N | N | Y | N | Y |
| 8 **Reichert** | Y | Y | Y | Y | Y | Y | Y |
| 9 Smith | N | N | N | N | Y | Y | Y |
| **WEST VIRGINIA** | | | | | | | |
| 1 Mollohan | N | N | N | N | Y | Y | Y |
| 2 **Capito** | Y | Y | Y | Y | Y | Y | Y |
| 3 Rahall | N | N | N | N | Y | Y | Y |
| **WISCONSIN** | | | | | | | |
| 1 **Ryan** | Y | Y | Y | Y | Y | Y | P |
| 2 Baldwin | N | N | N | N | Y | N | Y |
| 3 Kind | N | N | N | N | Y | Y | Y |
| 4 Moore | N | N | N | N | Y | N | Y |
| 5 **Sensenbrenner** | P | P | Y | Y | Y | Y | Y |
| 6 **Petri** | Y | Y | Y | Y | Y | Y | Y |
| 7 Obey | N | N | N | N | Y | N | Y |
| 8 **Green** | Y | Y | Y | Y | Y | Y | Y |
| **WYOMING** | | | | | | | |
| AL **Cubin** | Y | Y | Y | N | ? | Y | Y |

# IN THE HOUSE | By Vote Number

**447.** HR 2985. Fiscal 2006 Legislative Branch Appropriations/Rule. Adoption of the rule (H Res 396) to provide for House floor consideration of the conference report on the bill that would appropriate $3.8 billion in fiscal 2006 for legislative branch operations. Adopted 375-27: R 204-0; D 170-27 (ND 126-22, SD 44-5); I 1-0. July 28, 2005.

**448.** HR 5. Medical Malpractice/Recommit. Conyers, D-Mich., motion to recommit the bill to the House Judiciary and Energy and Commerce committees with instructions to include language that would establish an independent advisory commission on medical malpractice insurance and require plaintiff attorneys in medical malpractice cases to file a certificate of merit. Motion rejected 193-234: R 0-227; D 192-7 (ND 144-4, SD 48-3); I 1-0. July 28, 2005.

**449.** HR 5. Medical Malpractice/Passage. Passage of the bill that would cap the awards that plaintiffs and their attorneys could receive in medical malpractice cases. The bill would limit non-economic damages to $250,000 and cap punitive damages at $250,000 or double economic damages, whichever is greater. Punitive damages could only be awarded if economic damages were found. The bill would not pre-empt state damage caps but would impose federal caps on any states that do not have their own. Passed 230-194: R 216-9; D 14-184 (ND 6-141, SD 8-43); I 0-1. A "yea" was a vote in support of the president's position. July 28, 2005.

**450.** HR 2361. Fiscal 2006 Interior-Environment Appropriations/Conference Report. Adoption of the conference report on the bill that would appropriate $26.2 billion in fiscal 2006 for the Interior Department, the EPA and related agencies. It would provide $9.9 billion for the Interior Department, $7.7 billion for the EPA, $4.3 billion for the Forest Service, and $3.1 billion for the Indian Health Service. It also would provide $1.5 billion in fiscal 2005 funding for veterans' medical care, which would remain available through fiscal 2006. Adopted (thus sent to the Senate) 410-10: R 218-9; D 191-1 (ND 144-1, SD 47-0); I 1-0. July 28, 2005.

| | 447 | 448 | 449 | 450 |
|---|---|---|---|---|
| **ALABAMA** | | | | |
| 1 Bonner | Y | N | Y | Y |
| 2 Everett | Y | N | Y | Y |
| 3 Rogers | Y | N | Y | Y |
| 4 Aderholt | Y | N | Y | Y |
| 5 Cramer | Y | N | Y | ? |
| 6 Bachus | Y | N | Y | Y |
| 7 Davis | Y | Y | N | Y |
| **ALASKA** | | | | |
| AL Young | Y | N | Y | Y |
| **ARIZONA** | | | | |
| 1 Renzi | Y | N | Y | + |
| 2 Franks | P | N | Y | N |
| 3 Shadegg | Y | N | Y | Y |
| 4 Pastor | Y | Y | N | Y |
| 5 Hayworth | Y | N | Y | Y |
| 6 Flake | P | N | N | N |
| 7 Grijalva | Y | Y | N | Y |
| 8 Kolbe | Y | N | Y | Y |
| **ARKANSAS** | | | | |
| 1 Berry | Y | Y | N | Y |
| 2 Snyder | Y | Y | N | Y |
| 3 Boozman | Y | N | Y | Y |
| 4 Ross | Y | Y | N | Y |
| **CALIFORNIA** | | | | |
| 1 Thompson | Y | Y | N | Y |
| 2 Herger | Y | N | Y | Y |
| 3 Lungren | P | N | Y | Y |
| 4 Doolittle | Y | N | Y | Y |
| 5 Matsui, D. | Y | Y | N | Y |
| 6 Woolsey | Y | Y | N | Y |
| 7 Miller, George | N | Y | N | Y |
| 8 Pelosi | Y | Y | N | Y |
| 9 Lee | Y | Y | N | Y |
| 10 Tauscher | Y | Y | N | Y |
| 11 Pombo | Y | N | Y | Y |
| 12 Lantos | Y | Y | N | Y |
| 13 Stark | N | Y | N | Y |
| 14 Eshoo | Y | Y | N | Y |
| 15 Honda | Y | Y | N | Y |
| 16 Lofgren | N | Y | N | Y |
| 17 Farr | Y | Y | N | Y |
| 18 Cardoza | Y | Y | N | Y |
| 19 Radanovich | Y | N | Y | Y |
| 20 Costa | Y | Y | N | Y |
| 21 Nunes | Y | N | Y | Y |
| 22 Thomas | Y | N | Y | Y |
| 23 Capps | Y | Y | N | Y |
| 24 Gallegly | Y | N | Y | Y |
| 25 McKeon | Y | N | Y | Y |
| 26 Dreier | Y | N | Y | Y |
| 27 Sherman | Y | Y | N | Y |
| 28 Berman | Y | Y | N | Y |
| 29 Schiff | Y | Y | N | Y |
| 30 Waxman | Y | Y | N | ? |
| 31 Becerra | Y | Y | N | Y |
| 32 Solis | Y | Y | N | Y |
| 33 Watson | Y | Y | N | Y |
| 34 Roybal-Allard | Y | Y | N | Y |
| 35 Waters | Y | Y | N | Y |
| 36 Harman | Y | Y | N | Y |
| 37 Millender-McD. | Y | Y | N | Y |
| 38 Napolitano | Y | Y | N | Y |
| 39 Sánchez, Linda | Y | Y | N | Y |
| 40 Royce | Y | N | Y | Y |
| 41 Lewis | Y | N | Y | Y |
| 42 Miller, Gary | Y | N | Y | Y |
| 43 Baca | Y | Y | N | Y |
| 44 Calvert | Y | N | Y | Y |
| 45 Bono | Y | N | Y | Y |
| 46 Rohrabacher | Y | N | Y | Y |
| 47 Sanchez, Loretta | Y | Y | N | Y |
| 48 Cox | Y | N | Y | ? |
| 49 Issa | Y | N | Y | Y |
| **COLORADO** | | | | |
| 1 DeGette | Y | Y | N | Y |
| 2 Udall | Y | Y | N | Y |
| 3 Salazar | Y | Y | N | Y |
| 4 Musgrave | Y | N | Y | Y |
| 5 Hefley | P | N | Y | N |
| 6 Tancredo | P | N | Y | Y |
| 7 Beauprez | Y | N | Y | Y |
| **CONNECTICUT** | | | | |
| 1 Larson | Y | Y | N | Y |
| 2 Simmons | Y | N | Y | Y |
| 3 DeLauro | Y | Y | N | Y |
| 4 Shays | Y | N | Y | Y |
| 5 Johnson | Y | N | Y | Y |
| **DELAWARE** | | | | |
| AL Castle | Y | N | Y | Y |
| **FLORIDA** | | | | |
| 1 Miller | P | N | Y | Y |
| 2 Boyd | Y | Y | Y | Y |
| 3 Brown | Y | Y | N | Y |
| 4 Crenshaw | Y | N | Y | Y |
| 5 Brown-Waite | Y | N | Y | Y |
| 6 Stearns | Y | N | Y | Y |
| 7 Mica | Y | N | Y | Y |
| 8 Keller | Y | N | Y | Y |
| 9 Bilirakis | Y | N | Y | Y |
| 10 Young | Y | N | Y | Y |
| 11 Davis | Y | Y | N | ? |
| 12 Putnam | Y | N | Y | Y |
| 13 Harris | Y | N | Y | Y |
| 14 Mack | Y | N | Y | Y |
| 15 Weldon | Y | N | Y | Y |
| 16 Foley | Y | N | Y | Y |
| 17 Meek | Y | Y | N | Y |
| 18 Ros-Lehtinen | Y | N | Y | Y |
| 19 Wexler | Y | Y | N | Y |
| 20 Wasserman-Schultz | Y | Y | N | Y |
| 21 Diaz-Balart, L. | Y | N | Y | Y |
| 22 Shaw | Y | N | Y | Y |
| 23 Hastings | Y | Y | N | Y |
| 24 Feeney | ? | N | Y | Y |
| 25 Diaz-Balart, M. | Y | N | Y | Y |
| **GEORGIA** | | | | |
| 1 Kingston | Y | N | Y | Y |
| 2 Bishop | Y | Y | N | Y |
| 3 Marshall | Y | Y | N | Y |
| 4 McKinney | Y | Y | N | Y |
| 5 Lewis | Y | Y | N | Y |
| 6 Price | P | N | Y | Y |
| 7 Linder | Y | N | Y | Y |
| 8 Westmoreland | P | N | Y | Y |
| 9 Norwood | Y | N | Y | Y |
| 10 Deal | Y | N | Y | Y |
| 11 Gingrey | Y | N | Y | Y |
| 12 Barrow | N | Y | N | Y |
| 13 Scott | Y | Y | Y | ? |
| **HAWAII** | | | | |
| 1 Abercrombie | Y | Y | N | Y |
| 2 Case | Y | Y | N | Y |
| **IDAHO** | | | | |
| 1 Otter | P | N | Y | Y |
| 2 Simpson | Y | N | Y | Y |
| **ILLINOIS** | | | | |
| 1 Rush | Y | Y | N | Y |
| 2 Jackson | Y | Y | N | Y |
| 3 Lipinski | Y | Y | N | Y |
| 4 Gutierrez | Y | Y | N | Y |
| 5 Emanuel | Y | Y | N | Y |
| 6 Hyde | Y | N | Y | Y |
| 7 Davis | Y | Y | N | Y |
| 8 Bean | Y | Y | N | Y |
| 9 Schakowsky | ? | ? | ? | ? |
| 10 Kirk | Y | N | Y | Y |
| 11 Weller | Y | N | Y | Y |
| 12 Costello | Y | Y | N | Y |
| **Reps above 49 (col 2):** | | | | |
| 50 Cunningham | Y | N | Y | Y |
| 51 Filner | Y | Y | N | Y |
| 52 Hunter | Y | N | Y | Y |
| 53 Davis | Y | Y | N | Y |

## KEY

Republicans **Democrats** *Independents*

| | | |
|---|---|---|
| **Y** Voted for (yea) | **X** Paired against | **C** Voted "present" to avoid possible conflict of interest |
| **#** Paired for | **–** Announced against | |
| **+** Announced for | **P** Voted "present" | **?** Did not vote or otherwise make a position known |
| **N** Voted against (nay) | | |

| | 447 | 448 | 449 | 450 |
|---|---|---|---|---|
| 13 Biggert | Y | N | Y | Y |
| 14 Hastert | | | | Y |
| 15 Johnson | Y | N | N | Y |
| 16 Manzullo | Y | N | Y | Y |
| 17 Evans | Y | Y | N | Y |
| 18 LaHood | Y | N | Y | Y |
| 19 Shimkus | Y | N | Y | Y |
| **INDIANA** | | | | |
| 1 Visclosky | Y | Y | N | Y |
| 2 Chocola | Y | N | Y | Y |
| 3 Souder | Y | N | Y | Y |
| 4 Buyer | Y | N | Y | Y |
| 5 Burton | Y | N | P | Y |
| 6 Pence | P | N | Y | N |
| 7 Carson | Y | ? | ? | ? |
| 8 Hostettler | Y | N | Y | Y |
| 9 Sodrel | P | N | Y | Y |
| **IOWA** | | | | |
| 1 Nussle | Y | N | Y | Y |
| 2 Leach | Y | N | Y | Y |
| 3 Boswell | Y | Y | N | Y |
| 4 Latham | Y | N | Y | Y |
| 5 King | P | N | Y | Y |
| **KANSAS** | | | | |
| 1 Moran | Y | N | Y | Y |
| 2 Ryun | Y | N | Y | Y |
| 3 Moore | Y | Y | N | Y |
| 4 Tiahrt | Y | N | Y | Y |
| **KENTUCKY** | | | | |
| 1 Whitfield | Y | N | Y | Y |
| 2 Lewis | Y | N | Y | Y |
| 3 Northup | Y | N | Y | Y |
| 4 Davis | Y | N | Y | Y |
| 5 Rogers | Y | N | Y | Y |
| 6 Chandler | Y | Y | N | Y |
| **LOUISIANA** | | | | |
| 1 Jindal | Y | N | Y | Y |
| 2 Jefferson | Y | Y | N | Y |
| 3 Melancon | Y | Y | N | Y |
| 4 McCrery | Y | N | Y | Y |
| 5 Alexander | Y | N | Y | Y |
| 6 Baker | Y | N | Y | Y |
| 7 Boustany | Y | N | Y | Y |
| **MAINE** | | | | |
| 1 Allen | Y | Y | N | Y |
| 2 Michaud | Y | Y | N | Y |
| **MARYLAND** | | | | |
| 1 Gilchrest | Y | N | Y | Y |
| 2 Ruppersberger | Y | Y | N | Y |
| 3 Cardin | Y | Y | N | Y |
| 4 Wynn | Y | Y | N | Y |
| 5 Hoyer | Y | Y | N | Y |
| 6 Bartlett | P | N | Y | Y |
| 7 Cummings | Y | Y | N | Y |
| 8 Van Hollen | Y | Y | N | Y |
| **MASSACHUSETTS** | | | | |
| 1 Olver | N | Y | N | ? |
| 2 Neal | Y | Y | N | Y |
| 3 McGovern | Y | Y | N | Y |
| 4 Frank | N | Y | N | Y |
| 5 Meehan | N | Y | N | Y |
| 6 Tierney | N | Y | N | Y |
| 7 Markey | N | Y | N | Y |
| 8 Capuano | Y | Y | N | Y |
| 9 Lynch | Y | Y | N | ? |
| 10 Delahunt | Y | Y | N | Y |
| **MICHIGAN** | | | | |
| 1 Stupak | Y | Y | N | Y |
| 2 Hoekstra | Y | N | Y | Y |
| 3 Ehlers | Y | N | Y | Y |
| 4 Camp | Y | N | Y | Y |
| 5 Kildee | N | Y | N | Y |
| 6 Upton | Y | N | Y | Y |
| 7 Schwarz | Y | N | Y | Y |
| 8 Rogers | Y | N | Y | Y |
| 9 Knollenberg | Y | N | Y | Y |
| 10 Miller | Y | N | Y | Y |
| 11 McCotter | Y | N | Y | Y |
| 12 Levin | Y | Y | N | Y |
| 13 Kilpatrick | Y | Y | N | Y |
| 14 Conyers | N | Y | N | Y |
| 15 Dingell | Y | Y | N | N |

| | 447 | 448 | 449 | 450 |
|---|---|---|---|---|
| **MINNESOTA** | | | | |
| 1 Gutknecht | P | N | Y | Y |
| 2 Kline | Y | N | Y | Y |
| 3 Ramstad | Y | N | Y | Y |
| 4 McCollum | Y | Y | N | Y |
| 5 Sabo | Y | Y | N | Y |
| 6 Kennedy | Y | N | Y | Y |
| 7 Peterson | Y | Y | Y | Y |
| 8 Oberstar | Y | Y | N | Y |
| **MISSISSIPPI** | | | | |
| 1 Wicker | Y | N | Y | Y |
| 2 Thompson | ? | Y | N | Y |
| 3 Pickering | Y | N | Y | Y |
| 4 Taylor | N | N | Y | Y |
| **MISSOURI** | | | | |
| 1 Clay | Y | Y | N | Y |
| 2 Akin | P | N | Y | Y |
| 3 Carnahan | Y | Y | N | Y |
| 4 Skelton | Y | Y | N | Y |
| 5 Cleaver | Y | Y | N | Y |
| 6 Graves | Y | N | Y | N |
| 7 Blunt | Y | N | Y | Y |
| 8 Emerson | Y | N | Y | Y |
| 9 Hulshof | Y | N | Y | Y |
| **MONTANA** | | | | |
| AL Rehberg | Y | N | Y | Y |
| **NEBRASKA** | | | | |
| 1 Fortenberry | Y | N | Y | Y |
| 2 Terry | Y | N | N | Y |
| 3 Osborne | Y | N | Y | Y |
| **NEVADA** | | | | |
| 1 Berkley | Y | Y | N | Y |
| 2 Gibbons | Y | N | Y | Y |
| 3 Porter | Y | N | Y | Y |
| **NEW HAMPSHIRE** | | | | |
| 1 Bradley | Y | N | Y | Y |
| 2 Bass | Y | N | Y | Y |
| **NEW JERSEY** | | | | |
| 1 Andrews | Y | + | – | + |
| 2 LoBiondo | Y | N | Y | Y |
| 3 Saxton | Y | N | Y | Y |
| 4 Smith | Y | N | Y | Y |
| 5 Garrett | P | N | Y | Y |
| 6 Pallone | Y | Y | N | Y |
| 7 Ferguson | Y | N | Y | Y |
| 8 Pascrell | Y | Y | N | Y |
| 9 Rothman | Y | Y | N | Y |
| 10 Payne | ? | Y | N | Y |
| 11 Frelinghuysen | Y | N | Y | Y |
| 12 Holt | Y | Y | N | Y |
| 13 Menendez | Y | Y | N | Y |
| **NEW MEXICO** | | | | |
| 1 Wilson | Y | N | Y | Y |
| 2 Pearce | Y | N | Y | Y |
| 3 Udall | N | Y | N | Y |
| **NEW YORK** | | | | |
| 1 Bishop | Y | Y | N | Y |
| 2 Israel | N | Y | N | Y |
| 3 King | Y | N | Y | Y |
| 4 McCarthy | Y | Y | N | Y |
| 5 Ackerman | Y | Y | N | Y |
| 6 Meeks | Y | Y | N | Y |
| 7 Crowley | Y | Y | N | Y |
| 8 Nadler | Y | Y | N | Y |
| 9 Weiner | Y | Y | N | Y |
| 10 Towns | Y | Y | N | Y |
| 11 Owens | Y | Y | N | Y |
| 12 Velázquez | N | Y | N | Y |
| 13 Fossella | Y | N | Y | Y |
| 14 Maloney | Y | Y | N | Y |
| 15 Rangel | Y | Y | N | Y |
| 16 Serrano | Y | Y | N | Y |
| 17 Engel | Y | Y | N | Y |
| 18 Lowey | Y | Y | N | Y |
| 19 Kelly | Y | ? | Y | Y |
| 20 Sweeney | Y | N | Y | Y |
| 21 McNulty | Y | Y | N | Y |
| 22 Hinchey | Y | Y | N | Y |
| 23 McHugh | Y | N | Y | Y |
| 24 Boehlert | Y | N | Y | Y |
| 25 Walsh | Y | N | Y | Y |
| 26 Reynolds | ? | N | Y | Y |
| 27 Higgins | Y | Y | N | Y |
| 28 Slaughter | Y | Y | N | Y |
| 29 Kuhl | Y | N | Y | Y |

| | 447 | 448 | 449 | 450 |
|---|---|---|---|---|
| **NORTH CAROLINA** | | | | |
| 1 Butterfield | Y | Y | N | Y |
| 2 Etheridge | Y | Y | N | Y |
| 3 Jones | P | N | Y | N |
| 4 Price | Y | Y | N | Y |
| 5 Foxx | P | N | Y | Y |
| 6 Coble | Y | N | N | Y |
| 7 McIntyre | Y | Y | N | Y |
| 8 Hayes | Y | N | Y | Y |
| 9 Myrick | Y | N | Y | Y |
| 10 McHenry | Y | N | Y | Y |
| 11 Taylor | Y | N | Y | Y |
| 12 Watt | Y | Y | N | Y |
| 13 Miller | Y | Y | N | Y |
| **NORTH DAKOTA** | | | | |
| AL Pomeroy | Y | Y | Y | Y |
| **OHIO** | | | | |
| 1 Chabot | Y | N | Y | Y |
| 2 Vacant | | | | |
| 3 Turner | Y | N | Y | Y |
| 4 Oxley | Y | N | Y | Y |
| 5 Gillmor | Y | N | Y | ? |
| 6 Strickland | Y | Y | N | Y |
| 7 Hobson | Y | N | Y | Y |
| 8 Boehner | Y | N | Y | Y |
| 9 Kaptur | Y | Y | N | Y |
| 10 Kucinich | N | Y | N | Y |
| 11 Jones | Y | Y | N | Y |
| 12 Tiberi | Y | N | Y | Y |
| 13 Brown | N | Y | N | Y |
| 14 LaTourette | Y | N | Y | Y |
| 15 Pryce | Y | N | Y | Y |
| 16 Regula | Y | N | Y | Y |
| 17 Ryan | N | Y | N | Y |
| 18 Ney | Y | N | Y | Y' |
| **OKLAHOMA** | | | | |
| 1 Sullivan | Y | N | Y | Y |
| 2 Boren | Y | Y | N | Y |
| 3 Lucas | Y | N | Y | Y |
| 4 Cole | Y | N | Y | Y |
| 5 Istook | Y | N | N | Y |
| **OREGON** | | | | |
| 1 Wu | N | Y | ? | Y |
| 2 Walden | Y | N | Y | Y |
| 3 Blumenauer | Y | Y | N | Y |
| 4 DeFazio | Y | Y | N | Y |
| 5 Hooley | Y | Y | N | Y |
| **PENNSYLVANIA** | | | | |
| 1 Brady | ? | Y | N | Y |
| 2 Fattah | Y | Y | N | Y |
| 3 English | Y | N | Y | Y |
| 4 Hart | Y | N | Y | Y |
| 5 Peterson | Y | N | Y | Y |
| 6 Gerlach | Y | N | Y | Y |
| 7 Weldon | Y | N | Y | Y |
| 8 Fitzpatrick | Y | N | Y | Y |
| 9 Shuster | Y | N | Y | Y |
| 10 Sherwood | Y | N | Y | Y |
| 11 Kanjorski | Y | Y | N | Y |
| 12 Murtha | Y | N | Y | Y |
| 13 Schwartz | Y | Y | N | Y |
| 14 Doyle | Y | Y | N | Y |
| 15 Dent | Y | N | Y | Y |
| 16 Pitts | Y | N | Y | Y |
| 17 Holden | Y | N | Y | Y |
| 18 Murphy | Y | N | Y | Y |
| 19 Platts | Y | N | Y | Y |
| **RHODE ISLAND** | | | | |
| 1 Kennedy | N | Y | N | Y |
| 2 Langevin | Y | Y | N | Y |
| **SOUTH CAROLINA** | | | | |
| 1 Brown | Y | N | Y | Y |
| 2 Wilson | Y | N | Y | Y |
| 3 Barrett | P | N | Y | Y |
| 4 Inglis | Y | N | Y | Y |
| 5 Spratt | Y | Y | N | Y |
| 6 Clyburn | Y | Y | N | Y |
| **SOUTH DAKOTA** | | | | |
| AL Herseth | Y | Y | N | Y |
| **TENNESSEE** | | | | |
| 1 Jenkins | Y | N | N | Y |
| 2 Duncan | Y | N | N | N |

| | 447 | 448 | 449 | 450 |
|---|---|---|---|---|
| 3 Wamp | Y | N | Y | Y |
| 4 Davis | Y | Y | Y | Y |
| 5 Cooper | N | Y | N | Y |
| 6 Gordon | Y | N | Y | Y |
| 7 Blackburn | Y | N | Y | Y |
| 8 Tanner | P | Y | N | Y |
| 9 Ford | Y | Y | N | Y |
| **TEXAS** | | | | |
| 1 Gohmert | P | N | Y | Y |
| 2 Poe | Y | N | Y | Y |
| 3 Johnson, S. | Y | N | ? | Y |
| 4 Hall | Y | N | Y | Y |
| 5 Hensarling | P | N | Y | N |
| 6 Barton | Y | N | Y | Y |
| 7 Culberson | Y | N | Y | Y |
| 8 Brady | Y | N | Y | Y |
| 9 Green, A. | Y | Y | N | Y |
| 10 McCaul | Y | N | Y | Y |
| 11 Conaway | Y | N | Y | Y |
| 12 Granger | Y | N | Y | Y |
| 13 Thornberry | Y | N | Y | Y |
| 14 Paul | ? | ? | ? | ? |
| 15 Hinojosa | Y | Y | N | Y |
| 16 Reyes | Y | Y | N | Y |
| 17 Edwards | Y | Y | N | Y |
| 18 Jackson-Lee | N | Y | N | Y |
| 19 Neugebauer | Y | N | Y | Y |
| 20 Gonzalez | Y | Y | N | Y |
| 21 Smith | Y | N | Y | Y |
| 22 DeLay | Y | N | Y | Y |
| 23 Bonilla | Y | N | Y | Y |
| 24 Marchant | P | N | Y | Y |
| 25 Doggett | N | Y | N | Y |
| 26 Burgess | Y | N | + | Y |
| 27 Ortiz | Y | Y | N | Y |
| 28 Cuellar | Y | Y | Y | + |
| 29 Green, G. | Y | Y | N | Y |
| 30 Johnson, E. | Y | Y | N | Y |
| 31 Carter | Y | N | Y | Y |
| 32 Sessions | Y | N | Y | Y |
| **UTAH** | | | | |
| 1 Bishop | Y | N | Y | Y |
| 2 Matheson | Y | N | Y | Y |
| 3 Cannon | Y | N | Y | Y |
| **VERMONT** | | | | |
| AL *Sanders* | Y | Y | N | Y |
| **VIRGINIA** | | | | |
| 1 Davis, J. | Y | N | Y | Y |
| 2 Drake | Y | N | Y | Y |
| 3 Scott | Y | Y | N | Y |
| 4 Forbes | Y | N | Y | Y |
| 5 Goode | Y | N | Y | Y |
| 6 Goodlatte | Y | N | Y | Y |
| 7 Cantor | Y | N | Y | Y |
| 8 Moran | Y | Y | N | Y |
| 9 Boucher | Y | Y | N | Y |
| 10 Wolf | Y | N | Y | Y |
| 11 Davis, T. | Y | N | Y | Y |
| **WASHINGTON** | | | | |
| 1 Inslee | Y | Y | N | Y |
| 2 Larsen | Y | Y | N | Y |
| 3 Baird | N | Y | N | Y |
| 4 Hastings | Y | N | Y | Y |
| 5 McMorris | Y | N | Y | Y |
| 6 Dicks | Y | Y | N | Y |
| 7 McDermott | Y | Y | N | Y |
| 8 Reichert | Y | N | Y | Y |
| 9 Smith | Y | Y | N | Y |
| **WEST VIRGINIA** | | | | |
| 1 Mollohan | Y | N | N | Y |
| 2 Capito | Y | N | Y | Y |
| 3 Rahall | Y | Y | N | Y |
| **WISCONSIN** | | | | |
| 1 Ryan | P | N | Y | Y |
| 2 Baldwin | N | Y | N | Y |
| 3 Kind | Y | Y | N | Y |
| 4 Moore | Y | Y | N | Y |
| 5 Sensenbrenner | Y | P | P | Y |
| 6 Petri | Y | N | Y | N |
| 7 Obey | N | Y | N | Y |
| 8 Green | Y | N | Y | Y |
| **WYOMING** | | | | |
| AL Cubin | Y | N | Y | Y |

# IN THE HOUSE | By Vote Number

**451.** HR 2985. Fiscal 2006 Legislative Branch Appropriations/ **Conference Report.** Adoption of the conference report on the bill that would appropriate $3.8 billion in fiscal 2006 for legislative branch operations, including $1.1 billion for operations of the House of Representatives and $786 million for Senate operations. It also would require special elections if needed to replace members after a catastrophe. Adopted (thus sent to the Senate) 305-122: R 195-34; D 110-87 (ND 78-68, SD 32-19); I 0-1. July 28, 2005.

**452.** H Con Res 225. Adjournment/Adoption. Adoption of the concurrent resolution that would provide for adjournment of the House until 2 p.m., Tuesday, Sept. 6 and adjournment of the Senate until 12 p.m. on Tuesday, Sept. 6. Adopted 404-16: R 227-0; D 177-16 (ND 134-9, SD 43-7); I 0-0. July 28, 2005.

**453.** HR 3. Surface Transportation Reauthorization/Conference Report. Adoption of the conference report on the bill that would bring total authorization for federal highway, mass transit, safety and research programs, including fiscal 2004 funding, to $286.5 billion through 2009. The bill would increase the rate of return to states on their Highway Trust Fund contributions to 92 percent by fiscal 2008. It would make the Transportation Department the lead agency in the environmental review process for transportation projects. Adopted (thus sent to the Senate) 412-8: R 217-8; D 194-0 (ND 144-0, SD 50-0); I 1-0. July 29, 2005.

| | 451 | 452 | 453 |
|---|---|---|---|
| **ALABAMA** | | | |
| 1 Bonner | Y | Y | Y |
| 2 Everett | Y | Y | Y |
| 3 Rogers | Y | Y | Y |
| 4 Aderholt | Y | Y | Y |
| 5 Cramer | Y | Y | Y |
| 6 Bachus | Y | Y | Y |
| 7 Davis | Y | Y | Y |
| **ALASKA** | | | |
| AL Young | Y | Y | Y |
| **ARIZONA** | | | |
| 1 Renzi | + | + | Y |
| 2 Franks | N | Y | Y |
| 3 Shadegg | Y | Y | N |
| 4 Pastor | Y | Y | Y |
| 5 Hayworth | N | Y | Y |
| 6 Flake | N | Y | N |
| 7 Grijalva | N | Y | Y |
| 8 Kolbe | Y | Y | Y |
| **ARKANSAS** | | | |
| 1 Berry | N | Y | Y |
| 2 Snyder | N | Y | Y |
| 3 Boozman | Y | Y | Y |
| 4 Ross | N | Y | Y |
| **CALIFORNIA** | | | |
| 1 Thompson | Y | Y | Y |
| 2 Herger | Y | Y | Y |
| 3 Lungren | Y | Y | Y |
| 4 Doolittle | Y | Y | Y |
| 5 Matsui, D. | Y | Y | Y |
| 6 Woolsey | N | Y | Y |
| 7 Miller, George | N | Y | ? |
| 8 Pelosi | N | Y | Y |
| 9 Lee | N | Y | Y |
| 10 Tauscher | N | Y | Y |
| 11 Pombo | Y | Y | + |
| 12 Lantos | Y | Y | Y |
| 13 Stark | N | Y | ? |
| 14 Eshoo | Y | ? | Y |
| 15 Honda | N | Y | Y |
| 16 Lofgren | N | N | Y |
| 17 Farr | Y | Y | Y |
| 18 Cardoza | N | Y | Y |
| 19 Radanovich | Y | Y | Y |
| 20 Costa | Y | Y | Y |
| 21 Nunes | Y | Y | Y |
| 22 Thomas | Y | Y | Y |
| 23 Capps | Y | Y | + |
| 24 Gallegly | Y | Y | Y |
| 25 McKeon | Y | Y | Y |
| 26 Dreier | Y | Y | Y |
| 27 Sherman | N | N | Y |
| 28 Berman | N | Y | Y |
| 29 Schiff | Y | Y | Y |
| 30 Waxman | Y | Y | Y |
| 31 Becerra | N | Y | Y |
| 32 Solis | N | Y | Y |
| 33 Watson | Y | Y | Y |
| 34 Roybal-Allard | N | Y | Y |
| 35 Waters | Y | Y | Y |
| 36 Harman | Y | Y | Y |
| 37 Millender-McD. | Y | Y | Y |
| 38 Napolitano | Y | Y | Y |
| 39 Sánchez, Linda | Y | Y | Y |
| 40 Royce | Y | Y | N |
| 41 Lewis | Y | Y | Y |
| 42 Miller, Gary | Y | Y | Y |
| 43 Baca | Y | Y | Y |
| 44 Calvert | Y | Y | Y |
| 45 Bono | Y | Y | Y |
| 46 Rohrabacher | N | Y | Y |
| 47 Sanchez, Loretta | N | N | Y |
| 48 Cox | Y | Y | Y |
| 49 Issa | Y | Y | Y |

| | 451 | 452 | 453 |
|---|---|---|---|
| 50 Cunningham | Y | Y | Y |
| 51 Filner | Y | Y | Y |
| 52 Hunter | Y | Y | Y |
| 53 Davis | N | Y | Y |
| **COLORADO** | | | |
| 1 DeGette | N | Y | Y |
| 2 Udall | N | N | Y |
| 3 Salazar | N | Y | Y |
| 4 Musgrave | N | Y | Y |
| 5 Hefley | N | Y | Y |
| 6 Tancredo | N | Y | Y |
| 7 Beauprez | Y | Y | Y |
| **CONNECTICUT** | | | |
| 1 Larson | Y | ? | Y |
| 2 Simmons | Y | Y | Y |
| 3 DeLauro | Y | Y | Y |
| 4 Shays | N | Y | Y |
| 5 Johnson | Y | Y | Y |
| **DELAWARE** | | | |
| AL Castle | Y | Y | Y |
| **FLORIDA** | | | |
| 1 Miller | N | Y | Y |
| 2 Boyd | Y | Y | Y |
| 3 Brown | Y | Y | Y |
| 4 Crenshaw | Y | Y | Y |
| 5 Brown-Waite | N | Y | Y |
| 6 Stearns | N | Y | Y |
| 7 Mica | Y | Y | ? |
| 8 Keller | Y | Y | Y |
| 9 Bilirakis | Y | Y | Y |
| 10 Young | Y | Y | Y |
| 11 Davis | Y | Y | Y |
| 12 Putnam | Y | Y | Y |
| 13 Harris | N | Y | Y |
| 14 Mack | Y | Y | Y |
| 15 Weldon | Y | Y | Y |
| 16 Foley | Y | Y | Y |
| 17 Meek | N | Y | Y |
| 18 Ros-Lehtinen | Y | Y | Y |
| 19 Wexler | Y | Y | ? |
| 20 Wasserman-Schultz | Y | Y | Y |
| 21 Diaz-Balart, L. | Y | Y | Y |
| 22 Shaw | Y | Y | Y |
| 23 Hastings | Y | Y | Y |
| 24 Feeney | N | Y | Y |
| 25 Diaz-Balart, M. | Y | Y | Y |
| **GEORGIA** | | | |
| 1 Kingston | Y | Y | Y |
| 2 Bishop | Y | Y | Y |
| 3 Marshall | N | N | Y |
| 4 McKinney | N | Y | Y |
| 5 Lewis | N | N | Y |
| 6 Price | N | Y | Y |
| 7 Linder | Y | Y | Y |
| 8 Westmoreland | N | Y | Y |
| 9 Norwood | Y | Y | Y |
| 10 Deal | Y | Y | Y |
| 11 Gingrey | Y | Y | Y |
| 12 Barrow | N | Y | Y |
| 13 Scott | Y | Y | Y |
| **HAWAII** | | | |
| 1 Abercrombie | Y | Y | Y |
| 2 Case | Y | Y | Y |
| **IDAHO** | | | |
| 1 Otter | Y | Y | Y |
| 2 Simpson | Y | Y | Y |
| **ILLINOIS** | | | |
| 1 Rush | Y | Y | Y |
| 2 Jackson | Y | Y | Y |
| 3 Lipinski | N | Y | Y |
| 4 Gutierrez | N | Y | Y |
| 5 Emanuel | Y | Y | Y |
| 6 Hyde | Y | Y | Y |
| 7 Davis | Y | Y | Y |
| 8 Bean | N | Y | Y |
| 9 Schakowsky | ? | ? | ? |
| 10 Kirk | Y | Y | Y |
| 11 Weller | Y | Y | Y |
| 12 Costello | N | Y | Y |

| | 451 | 452 | 453 |
|---|---|---|---|
| 13 Biggert | Y | Y | Y |
| 14 Hastert | Y | | Y |
| 15 Johnson | Y | Y | Y |
| 16 Manzullo | Y | Y | Y |
| 17 Evans | Y | Y | Y |
| 18 LaHood | Y | Y | Y |
| 19 Shimkus | N | Y | Y |
| **INDIANA** | | | |
| 1 Visclosky | Y | Y | Y |
| 2 Chocola | N | Y | Y |
| 3 Souder | Y | Y | Y |
| 4 Buyer | Y | Y | Y |
| 5 Burton | Y | Y | Y |
| 6 Pence | N | Y | Y |
| 7 Carson | ? | ? | Y |
| 8 Hostettler | Y | Y | Y |
| 9 Sodrel | Y | Y | Y |
| **IOWA** | | | |
| 1 Nussle | Y | Y | Y |
| 2 Leach | Y | Y | Y |
| 3 Boswell | N | N | Y |
| 4 Latham | Y | Y | Y |
| 5 King | Y | Y | Y |
| **KANSAS** | | | |
| 1 Moran | Y | Y | Y |
| 2 Ryun | Y | Y | Y |
| 3 Moore | N | ? | Y |
| 4 Tiahrt | Y | Y | Y |
| **KENTUCKY** | | | |
| 1 Whitfield | Y | Y | Y |
| 2 Lewis | Y | Y | Y |
| 3 Northup | Y | Y | Y |
| 4 Davis | Y | Y | Y |
| 5 Rogers | Y | Y | Y |
| 6 Chandler | N | N | Y |
| **LOUISIANA** | | | |
| 1 Jindal | Y | Y | Y |
| 2 Jefferson | Y | Y | Y |
| 3 Melancon | N | Y | Y |
| 4 McCrery | Y | Y | Y |
| 5 Alexander | Y | Y | Y |
| 6 Baker | Y | Y | Y |
| 7 Boustany | Y | Y | Y |
| **MAINE** | | | |
| 1 Allen | Y | Y | Y |
| 2 Michaud | Y | Y | Y |
| **MARYLAND** | | | |
| 1 Gilchrest | Y | Y | Y |
| 2 Ruppersberger | Y | Y | Y |
| 3 Cardin | Y | Y | Y |
| 4 Wynn | Y | Y | Y |
| 5 Hoyer | Y | Y | Y |
| 6 Bartlett | Y | Y | Y |
| 7 Cummings | Y | Y | Y |
| 8 Van Hollen | N | Y | Y |
| **MASSACHUSETTS** | | | |
| 1 Olver | N | N | Y |
| 2 Neal | Y | Y | Y |
| 3 McGovern | N | Y | Y |
| 4 Frank | N | Y | Y |
| 5 Meehan | N | Y | Y |
| 6 Tierney | N | Y | Y |
| 7 Markey | N | Y | Y |
| 8 Capuano | Y | Y | Y |
| 9 Lynch | ? | ? | Y |
| 10 Delahunt | Y | Y | ? |
| **MICHIGAN** | | | |
| 1 Stupak | Y | Y | Y |
| 2 Hoekstra | Y | Y | Y |
| 3 Ehlers | Y | Y | Y |
| 4 Camp | Y | Y | Y |
| 5 Kildee | N | Y | Y |
| 6 Upton | Y | Y | Y |
| 7 Schwarz | Y | Y | ? |
| 8 Rogers | Y | Y | Y |
| 9 Knollenberg | Y | Y | Y |
| 10 Miller | Y | Y | Y |
| 11 McCotter | Y | Y | Y |
| 12 Levin | Y | Y | Y |
| 13 Kilpatrick | N | Y | Y |
| 14 Conyers | N | Y | Y |
| 15 Dingell | Y | Y | Y |

| | 451 | 452 | 453 |
|---|---|---|---|
| **MINNESOTA** | | | |
| 1 Gutknecht | N | Y | Y |
| 2 Kline | Y | Y | Y |
| 3 Ramstad | Y | Y | Y |
| 4 McCollum | N | Y | Y |
| 5 Sabo | Y | Y | Y |
| 6 Kennedy | N | Y | Y |
| 7 Peterson | N | Y | Y |
| 8 Oberstar | N | Y | Y |
| **MISSISSIPPI** | | | |
| 1 Wicker | Y | Y | Y |
| 2 Thompson | Y | Y | Y |
| 3 Pickering | Y | Y | Y |
| 4 Taylor | N | N | Y |
| **MISSOURI** | | | |
| 1 Clay | ? | Y | Y |
| 2 Akin | Y | Y | Y |
| 3 Carnahan | Y | Y | Y |
| 4 Skelton | Y | Y | Y |
| 5 Cleaver | Y | Y | Y |
| 6 Graves | N | Y | Y |
| 7 Blunt | Y | Y | Y |
| 8 Emerson | Y | Y | Y |
| 9 Hulshof | N | Y | Y |
| **MONTANA** | | | |
| AL Rehberg | Y | Y | Y |
| **NEBRASKA** | | | |
| 1 Fortenberry | Y | Y | Y |
| 2 Terry | Y | Y | Y |
| 3 Osborne | Y | Y | Y |
| **NEVADA** | | | |
| 1 Berkley | Y | Y | Y |
| 2 Gibbons | Y | Y | Y |
| 3 Porter | Y | Y | Y |
| **NEW HAMPSHIRE** | | | |
| 1 Bradley | Y | Y | Y |
| 2 Bass | Y | Y | Y |
| **NEW JERSEY** | | | |
| 1 Andrews | – | + | Y |
| 2 LoBiondo | Y | Y | Y |
| 3 Saxton | Y | Y | Y |
| 4 Smith | Y | Y | Y |
| 5 Garrett | N | Y | Y |
| 6 Pallone | N | Y | Y |
| 7 Ferguson | Y | Y | Y |
| 8 Pascrell | Y | Y | Y |
| 9 Rothman | Y | Y | Y |
| 10 Payne | Y | Y | Y |
| 11 Frelinghuysen | Y | Y | Y |
| 12 Holt | Y | Y | Y |
| 13 Menendez | N | Y | Y |
| **NEW MEXICO** | | | |
| 1 Wilson | Y | Y | Y |
| 2 Pearce | Y | Y | Y |
| 3 Udall | N | N | Y |
| **NEW YORK** | | | |
| 1 Bishop | N | Y | Y |
| 2 Israel | N | Y | Y |
| 3 King | Y | Y | Y |
| 4 McCarthy | Y | Y | Y |
| 5 Ackerman | Y | Y | Y |
| 6 Meeks | Y | Y | Y |
| 7 Crowley | Y | Y | Y |
| 8 Nadler | N | Y | Y |
| 9 Weiner | Y | Y | Y |
| 10 Towns | Y | Y | Y |
| 11 Owens | Y | Y | Y |
| 12 Velázquez | N | ? | Y |
| 13 Fossella | N | Y | Y |
| 14 Maloney | N | Y | Y |
| 15 Rangel | Y | Y | Y |
| 16 Serrano | Y | Y | Y |
| 17 Engel | Y | Y | Y |
| 18 Lowey | N | Y | Y |
| 19 Kelly | Y | Y | Y |
| 20 Sweeney | Y | Y | Y |
| 21 McNulty | Y | Y | Y |
| 22 Hinchey | N | Y | Y |
| 23 McHugh | Y | Y | Y |
| 24 Boehlert | Y | Y | Y |
| 25 Walsh | Y | Y | Y |
| 26 Reynolds | Y | Y | Y |
| 27 Higgins | Y | Y | Y |
| 28 Slaughter | N | Y | Y |
| 29 Kuhl | Y | Y | Y |

| | 451 | 452 | 453 |
|---|---|---|---|
| **NORTH CAROLINA** | | | |
| 1 Butterfield | Y | ? | Y |
| 2 Etheridge | N | Y | Y |
| 3 Jones | N | Y | N |
| 4 Price | Y | Y | Y |
| 5 Foxx | Y | Y | Y |
| 6 Coble | N | Y | Y |
| 7 McIntyre | Y | Y | Y |
| 8 Hayes | Y | Y | Y |
| 9 Myrick | Y | Y | Y |
| 10 McHenry | Y | Y | Y |
| 11 Taylor | Y | Y | Y |
| 12 Watt | Y | Y | Y |
| 13 Miller | Y | Y | Y |
| **NORTH DAKOTA** | | | |
| AL Pomeroy | N | Y | Y |
| **OHIO** | | | |
| 1 Chabot | N | Y | Y |
| 2 Vacant | | | |
| 3 Turner | Y | Y | Y |
| 4 Oxley | Y | Y | Y |
| 5 Gillmor | Y | Y | Y |
| 6 Strickland | Y | Y | Y |
| 7 Hobson | Y | Y | Y |
| 8 Boehner | Y | Y | N |
| 9 Kaptur | N | Y | Y |
| 10 Kucinich | N | Y | Y |
| 11 Jones | N | Y | Y |
| 12 Tiberi | Y | Y | Y |
| 13 Brown | N | Y | Y |
| 14 LaTourette | Y | Y | Y |
| 15 Pryce | Y | Y | Y |
| 16 Regula | Y | Y | Y |
| 17 Ryan | Y | Y | Y |
| 18 Ney | Y | Y | Y |
| **OKLAHOMA** | | | |
| 1 Sullivan | Y | Y | Y |
| 2 Boren | Y | Y | Y |
| 3 Lucas | Y | Y | Y |
| 4 Cole | Y | Y | Y |
| 5 Istook | Y | Y | Y |
| **OREGON** | | | |
| 1 Wu | N | N | Y |
| 2 Walden | Y | Y | Y |
| 3 Blumenauer | N | Y | Y |
| 4 DeFazio | N | Y | Y |
| 5 Hooley | N | Y | Y |
| **PENNSYLVANIA** | | | |
| 1 Brady | Y | Y | ? |
| 2 Fattah | Y | Y | ? |
| 3 English | Y | Y | Y |
| 4 Hart | Y | Y | Y |
| 5 Peterson | Y | Y | Y |
| 6 Gerlach | Y | Y | Y |
| 7 Weldon | Y | Y | Y |
| 8 Fitzpatrick | Y | Y | Y |
| 9 Shuster | Y | Y | Y |
| 10 Sherwood | Y | Y | Y |
| 11 Kanjorski | Y | Y | Y |
| 12 Murtha | Y | Y | Y |
| 13 Schwartz | Y | Y | Y |
| 14 Doyle | Y | Y | Y |
| 15 Dent | Y | Y | Y |
| 16 Pitts | Y | Y | ? |
| 17 Holden | Y | Y | Y |
| 18 Murphy | Y | Y | Y |
| 19 Platts | Y | Y | Y |
| **RHODE ISLAND** | | | |
| 1 Kennedy | Y | Y | Y |
| 2 Langevin | Y | Y | Y |
| **SOUTH CAROLINA** | | | |
| 1 Brown | Y | Y | Y |
| 2 Wilson | Y | Y | Y |
| 3 Barrett | Y | ? | Y |
| 4 Inglis | Y | Y | Y |
| 5 Spratt | N | Y | Y |
| 6 Clyburn | Y | Y | Y |
| **SOUTH DAKOTA** | | | |
| AL Herseth | N | Y | Y |
| **TENNESSEE** | | | |
| 1 Jenkins | Y | Y | Y |
| 2 Duncan | N | Y | Y |

| | 451 | 452 | 453 |
|---|---|---|---|
| 3 Wamp | Y | Y | Y |
| 4 Davis | Y | Y | Y |
| 5 Cooper | N | N | Y |
| 6 Gordon | N | Y | Y |
| 7 Blackburn | Y | Y | Y |
| 8 Tanner | N | Y | Y |
| 9 Ford | N | N | Y |
| **TEXAS** | | | |
| 1 Gohmert | Y | Y | Y |
| 2 Poe | Y | Y | Y |
| 3 Johnson, S. | Y | Y | ? |
| 4 Hall | Y | Y | Y |
| 5 Hensarling | N | Y | N |
| 6 Barton | Y | Y | Y |
| 7 Culberson | Y | Y | Y |
| 8 Brady | Y | Y | Y |
| 9 Green, A. | Y | Y | Y |
| 10 McCaul | Y | Y | Y |
| 11 Conaway | Y | Y | Y |
| 12 Granger | Y | Y | Y |
| 13 Thornberry | Y | Y | N |
| 14 Paul | ? | ? | ? |
| 15 Hinojosa | Y | Y | Y |
| 16 Reyes | Y | Y | Y |
| 17 Edwards | Y | Y | Y |
| 18 Jackson-Lee | Y | Y | Y |
| 19 Neugebauer | Y | Y | Y |
| 20 Gonzalez | Y | Y | Y |
| 21 Smith | Y | Y | Y |
| 22 DeLay | Y | Y | Y |
| 23 Bonilla | Y | Y | Y |
| 24 Marchant | Y | Y | Y |
| 25 Doggett | N | N | Y |
| 26 Burgess | Y | Y | Y |
| 27 Ortiz | Y | Y | Y |
| 28 Cuellar | Y | Y | Y |
| 29 Green, G. | N | Y | Y |
| 30 Johnson, E. | Y | Y | Y |
| 31 Carter | Y | Y | Y |
| 32 Sessions | Y | Y | Y |
| **UTAH** | | | |
| 1 Bishop | Y | Y | Y |
| 2 Matheson | N | N | Y |
| 3 Cannon | Y | Y | Y |
| **VERMONT** | | | |
| AL *Sanders* | N | ? | Y |
| **VIRGINIA** | | | |
| 1 Davis, J. | Y | Y | Y |
| 2 Drake | Y | Y | Y |
| 3 Scott | Y | Y | Y |
| 4 Forbes | N | Y | Y |
| 5 Goode | N | Y | Y |
| 6 Goodlatte | Y | Y | Y |
| 7 Cantor | Y | Y | Y |
| 8 Moran | Y | Y | Y |
| 9 Boucher | Y | Y | Y |
| 10 Wolf | Y | Y | Y |
| 11 Davis, T. | Y | Y | Y |
| **WASHINGTON** | | | |
| 1 Inslee | N | Y | Y |
| 2 Larsen | Y | Y | Y |
| 3 Baird | N | Y | Y |
| 4 Hastings | Y | Y | Y |
| 5 McMorris | Y | Y | Y |
| 6 Dicks | N | Y | Y |
| 7 McDermott | N | Y | Y |
| 8 Reichert | Y | Y | Y |
| 9 Smith | Y | Y | Y |
| **WEST VIRGINIA** | | | |
| 1 Mollohan | Y | Y | Y |
| 2 Capito | Y | Y | Y |
| 3 Rahall | Y | Y | Y |
| **WISCONSIN** | | | |
| 1 Ryan | Y | Y | Y |
| 2 Baldwin | N | Y | Y |
| 3 Kind | N | Y | Y |
| 4 Moore | N | Y | Y |
| 5 Sensenbrenner | Y | Y | N |
| 6 Petri | N | Y | Y |
| 7 Obey | N | Y | Y |
| 8 Green | Y | Y | Y |
| **WYOMING** | | | |
| AL Cubin | Y | Y | Y |

# IN THE HOUSE | By Vote Number

**454.** **H Res 360. V-J Day 60th Anniversary/Adoption.** Smith, R-N.J., motion to suspend the rules and adopt the resolution that would commemorate the 60th anniversary of Victory over Japan Day (V-J Day) and the end of World War II and express appreciation for the members of the armed services who served in the Pacific during the war. Motion agreed to 394-0: R 216-0; D 177-0 (ND 129-0, SD 48-0); I 1-0. A two-thirds majority of those present and voting (263 in this case) is required for adoption under suspension of the rules. Sept. 6, 2005.

**455.** **S J Res 19. Helsinki Final Act 30th Anniversary/Passage.** Smith, R-N.J., motion to suspend the rules and pass the joint resolution that would call on the president to issue a proclamation recognizing the 30th anniversary of the Helsinki Final Act signing and reassert U.S. commitment to its full implementation. Motion agreed to 393-1: R 215-1; D 177-0 (ND 130-0, SD 47-0); I 1-0. A two-thirds majority of those present and voting (263 in this case) is required for passage under suspension of the rules. Sept. 6, 2005.

**456.** **HR 3650. Federal Judiciary Emergency Special Sessions/Passage.** Sensenbrenner, R-Wis., motion to suspend the rules and pass the bill that would allow circuit courts, district courts and bankruptcy courts to hold special sessions outside their normal geographic region if no area within their jurisdiction is reasonably available because of emergency conditions. Motion agreed to 409-0: R 218-0; D 190-0 (ND 143-0, SD 47-0); I 1-0. A two-thirds majority of those present and voting (273 in this case) is required for passage under suspension of the rules. Sept. 7, 2005.

**457.** **HR 3169. Pell Grant Disaster Relief/Passage.** Keller, R-Fla., motion to suspend the rules and pass the bill that would allow the Education Department to waive the repayment requirement for Pell Grant recipients whose school attendance is interrupted because of the impact of a disaster if students were living, working or attending school in an area designated by the president to warrant major disaster assistance. Motion agreed to 412-0: R 220-0; D 191-0 (ND 144-0, SD 47-0); I 1-0. A two-thirds majority of those present and voting (275 in this case) is required for passage under suspension of the rules. Sept. 7, 2005.

**458.** **H Res 426. Suspension Motions/Previous Question.** L. Diaz-Balart, R-Fla., motion to order the previous question (thus ending debate and possibility of amendment) on adoption of the resolution (H Res 426) to provide for House floor consideration of bills under suspension of the rules on Thursday, Sept. 8, 2005. Motion agreed to 221-193: R 221-0; D 0-192 (ND 0-145, SD 0-47); I 0-1. Sept. 8, 2005.

**459.** **H Res 426. Suspension Motions/Rule.** Adoption of the resolution (H Res 426) to provide for House floor consideration of bills under suspension of the rules on Thursday, Sept. 8, 2005. Adopted 235-179: R 219-2; D 16-176 (ND 11-133, SD 5-43); I 0-1. Sept. 8, 2005.

[1] Rep. Christopher Cox, R-Calif., resigned effective Aug. 2. The last vote for which he was eligible was vote 453.

[2] Rep. Jean Schmidt, R-Ohio, was sworn in Sept. 6. The first vote for which she was eligible was vote 454.

| | 454 | 455 | 456 | 457 | 458 | 459 |
|---|---|---|---|---|---|---|
| **ALABAMA** | | | | | | |
| 1 **Bonner** | Y | Y | Y | Y | Y | Y |
| 2 **Everett** | Y | Y | Y | Y | Y | Y |
| 3 **Rogers** | Y | Y | Y | Y | Y | Y |
| 4 **Aderholt** | Y | Y | Y | Y | Y | Y |
| 5 **Cramer** | Y | Y | Y | Y | N | N |
| 6 **Bachus** | Y | Y | Y | Y | Y | Y |
| 7 Davis | Y | Y | Y | Y | N | N |
| **ALASKA** | | | | | | |
| AL **Young** | ? | ? | ? | ? | ? | ? |
| **ARIZONA** | | | | | | |
| 1 **Renzi** | Y | Y | Y | Y | Y | Y |
| 2 **Franks** | Y | Y | Y | Y | Y | Y |
| 3 **Shadegg** | Y | Y | Y | Y | Y | Y |
| 4 **Pastor** | Y | Y | Y | Y | N | N |
| 5 **Hayworth** | Y | Y | Y | Y | Y | Y |
| 6 **Flake** | Y | Y | Y | Y | Y | N |
| 7 Grijalva | Y | Y | Y | N | N | N |
| 8 **Kolbe** | Y | Y | Y | Y | Y | Y |
| **ARKANSAS** | | | | | | |
| 1 Berry | Y | Y | Y | Y | N | N |
| 2 Snyder | Y | Y | Y | Y | N | N |
| 3 **Boozman** | Y | Y | Y | Y | Y | Y |
| 4 Ross | Y | Y | Y | Y | N | N |
| **CALIFORNIA** | | | | | | |
| 1 Thompson | Y | Y | Y | Y | N | N |
| 2 **Herger** | Y | Y | Y | Y | Y | Y |
| 3 **Lungren** | Y | Y | Y | Y | Y | Y |
| 4 **Doolittle** | Y | Y | Y | Y | Y | Y |
| 5 Matsui, D. | Y | Y | Y | Y | N | N |
| 6 Woolsey | Y | Y | Y | Y | N | N |
| 7 Miller, George | Y | Y | Y | Y | N | N |
| 8 Pelosi | Y | Y | Y | Y | N | N |
| 9 Lee | Y | Y | Y | N | N | N |
| 10 Tauscher | Y | Y | Y | Y | N | N |
| 11 **Pombo** | Y | Y | Y | Y | Y | Y |
| 12 Lantos | Y | Y | Y | Y | N | N |
| 13 Stark | ? | ? | Y | N | N | N |
| 14 Eshoo | Y | Y | Y | Y | N | N |
| 15 Honda | Y | Y | Y | Y | N | N |
| 16 Lofgren | Y | Y | Y | Y | N | N |
| 17 Farr | Y | Y | Y | N | N | N |
| 18 Cardoza | Y | Y | Y | Y | N | N |
| 19 **Radanovich** | Y | Y | Y | Y | Y | Y |
| 20 Costa | Y | Y | Y | Y | N | N |
| 21 **Nunes** | Y | Y | Y | Y | Y | Y |
| 22 **Thomas** | Y | Y | Y | Y | Y | Y |
| 23 Capps | Y | Y | Y | Y | N | N |
| 24 **Gallegly** | + | + | Y | Y | Y | Y |
| 25 **McKeon** | Y | Y | Y | Y | Y | Y |
| 26 **Dreier** | Y | Y | + | + | Y | Y |
| 27 Sherman | Y | Y | Y | Y | N | N |
| 28 Berman | Y | Y | Y | Y | N | N |
| 29 Schiff | Y | Y | Y | Y | N | N |
| 30 Waxman | Y | Y | Y | Y | N | N |
| 31 Becerra | Y | Y | Y | N | N | N |
| 32 Solis | Y | Y | Y | Y | N | N |
| 33 Watson | Y | Y | Y | Y | N | N |
| 34 Roybal-Allard | Y | Y | Y | Y | N | N |
| 35 Waters | ? | ? | Y | N | N | N |
| 36 Harman | Y | Y | Y | Y | N | N |
| 37 Millender-McD. | Y | Y | Y | Y | N | N |
| 38 Napolitano | Y | Y | Y | Y | N | ? |
| 39 Sánchez, Linda | Y | Y | Y | Y | N | N |
| 40 **Royce** | Y | Y | Y | Y | Y | Y |
| 41 **Lewis** | Y | Y | Y | Y | Y | Y |
| 42 **Miller, Gary** | Y | Y | Y | Y | Y | Y |
| 43 Baca | Y | Y | Y | Y | N | N |
| 44 **Calvert** | Y | Y | Y | Y | Y | Y |
| 45 **Bono** | Y | Y | Y | Y | Y | Y |
| 46 **Rohrabacher** | Y | Y | Y | Y | Y | Y |
| 47 Sanchez, Loretta | + | + | + | + | − | − |
| 48 Vacant[1] | | | | | | |
| 49 **Issa** | Y | Y | Y | Y | Y | Y |
| 50 **Cunningham** | Y | Y | Y | Y | Y | Y |
| 51 Filner | Y | Y | Y | Y | N | N |
| 52 **Hunter** | ? | ? | Y | Y | Y | Y |
| 53 Davis | Y | Y | Y | Y | N | N |
| **COLORADO** | | | | | | |
| 1 DeGette | Y | Y | Y | Y | N | N |
| 2 Udall | Y | Y | Y | Y | N | N |
| 3 Salazar | Y | Y | Y | Y | N | N |
| 4 **Musgrave** | Y | Y | Y | Y | Y | Y |
| 5 **Hefley** | ? | ? | Y | Y | Y | Y |
| 6 **Tancredo** | ? | ? | Y | Y | Y | Y |
| 7 **Beauprez** | Y | Y | Y | Y | Y | Y |
| **CONNECTICUT** | | | | | | |
| 1 Larson | Y | Y | Y | Y | N | N |
| 2 **Simmons** | Y | Y | Y | Y | Y | Y |
| 3 DeLauro | Y | Y | Y | Y | N | N |
| 4 **Shays** | Y | Y | Y | Y | Y | Y |
| 5 **Johnson** | Y | Y | Y | Y | Y | Y |
| **DELAWARE** | | | | | | |
| AL **Castle** | Y | Y | Y | Y | Y | Y |
| **FLORIDA** | | | | | | |
| 1 **Miller** | Y | Y | Y | Y | Y | Y |
| 2 Boyd | Y | Y | Y | N | N | N |
| 3 Brown | Y | Y | Y | N | N | N |
| 4 **Crenshaw** | Y | Y | Y | Y | Y | Y |
| 5 **Brown-Waite** | Y | Y | Y | Y | Y | Y |
| 6 **Stearns** | Y | Y | Y | Y | Y | Y |
| 7 **Mica** | Y | Y | Y | Y | Y | Y |
| 8 **Keller** | Y | Y | Y | Y | Y | Y |
| 9 **Bilirakis** | + | + | Y | Y | Y | Y |
| 10 **Young** | Y | Y | Y | Y | Y | Y |
| 11 Davis | Y | Y | Y | Y | N | N |
| 12 **Putnam** | Y | Y | Y | Y | Y | Y |
| 13 **Harris** | Y | Y | Y | Y | Y | Y |
| 14 **Mack** | Y | Y | Y | Y | Y | Y |
| 15 **Weldon** | Y | Y | Y | Y | Y | Y |
| 16 **Foley** | Y | Y | Y | Y | Y | Y |
| 17 Meek | Y | Y | Y | Y | N | N |
| 18 **Ros-Lehtinen** | Y | Y | Y | Y | Y | Y |
| 19 Wexler | Y | Y | Y | Y | ? | N |
| 20 Wasserman-Schultz | Y | Y | Y | Y | N | N |
| 21 **Diaz-Balart, L.** | Y | Y | Y | Y | Y | Y |
| 22 **Shaw** | Y | Y | Y | Y | Y | Y |
| 23 Hastings | Y | Y | Y | Y | N | N |
| 24 **Feeney** | Y | Y | Y | Y | Y | Y |
| 25 **Diaz-Balart, M.** | Y | Y | Y | Y | Y | Y |
| **GEORGIA** | | | | | | |
| 1 **Kingston** | Y | Y | Y | N | Y | Y |
| 2 Bishop | Y | Y | Y | Y | N | N |
| 3 Marshall | Y | Y | Y | N | N | N |
| 4 McKinney | Y | Y | Y | N | N | N |
| 5 Lewis | Y | Y | Y | N | N | N |
| 6 **Price** | Y | Y | Y | Y | Y | Y |
| 7 **Linder** | Y | Y | Y | Y | Y | Y |
| 8 **Westmoreland** | Y | Y | Y | Y | Y | Y |
| 9 **Norwood** | Y | Y | Y | Y | Y | Y |
| 10 **Deal** | Y | Y | Y | Y | Y | Y |
| 11 **Gingrey** | Y | Y | Y | Y | Y | Y |
| 12 **Barrow** | Y | Y | Y | Y | N | N |
| 13 Scott | Y | Y | Y | N | N | N |
| **HAWAII** | | | | | | |
| 1 Abercrombie | Y | Y | Y | Y | N | N |
| 2 Case | ? | Y | Y | N | N | N |
| **IDAHO** | | | | | | |
| 1 **Otter** | Y | Y | Y | Y | Y | Y |
| 2 **Simpson** | Y | Y | Y | Y | Y | Y |
| **ILLINOIS** | | | | | | |
| 1 Rush | ? | ? | Y | N | N | N |
| 2 Jackson | Y | Y | Y | N | N | N |
| 3 Lipinski | Y | Y | Y | N | N | N |
| 4 Gutierrez | Y | Y | Y | N | N | N |
| 5 Emanuel | Y | Y | Y | Y | N | N |
| 6 **Hyde** | Y | Y | Y | Y | ? | ? |
| 7 Davis | Y | Y | Y | N | N | N |
| 8 Bean | Y | Y | Y | Y | N | N |
| 9 Schakowsky | Y | Y | Y | Y | N | N |
| 10 **Kirk** | Y | Y | Y | Y | Y | Y |
| 11 **Weller** | Y | Y | Y | Y | Y | Y |
| 12 Costello | ? | ? | ? | ? | N | N |

| KEY | Republicans | Democrats | Independents |
|---|---|---|---|

| | | |
|---|---|---|
| Y Voted for (yea) | X Paired against | C Voted "present" to avoid possible conflict of interest |
| # Paired for | − Announced against | |
| + Announced for | P Voted "present" | ? Did not vote or otherwise make a position known |
| N Voted against (nay) | | |

| | 454 | 455 | 456 | 457 | 458 | 459 |
|---|---|---|---|---|---|---|
| 13 **Biggert** | Y | Y | Y | Y | Y | Y |
| 14 **Hastert** | | | | | | |
| 15 **Johnson** | Y | Y | Y | Y | Y | Y |
| 16 **Manzullo** | Y | Y | Y | Y | Y | Y |
| 17 Evans | Y | Y | Y | Y | N | N |
| 18 **LaHood** | Y | Y | Y | Y | Y | Y |
| 19 **Shimkus** | Y | Y | Y | Y | Y | Y |
| **INDIANA** | | | | | | |
| 1 Visclosky | Y | Y | Y | Y | N | N |
| 2 **Chocola** | Y | Y | Y | Y | Y | Y |
| 3 **Souder** | Y | Y | Y | Y | Y | Y |
| 4 **Buyer** | ? | ? | ? | ? | ? | ? |
| 5 **Burton** | Y | Y | Y | Y | Y | Y |
| 6 **Pence** | Y | Y | Y | Y | Y | Y |
| 7 Carson | Y | Y | Y | Y | N | N |
| 8 **Hostettler** | Y | Y | Y | Y | Y | Y |
| 9 **Sodrel** | Y | Y | Y | Y | Y | Y |
| **IOWA** | | | | | | |
| 1 **Nussle** | Y | Y | Y | Y | Y | Y |
| 2 **Leach** | Y | Y | Y | Y | Y | Y |
| 3 Boswell | Y | Y | Y | Y | N | Y |
| 4 **Latham** | ? | ? | Y | Y | Y | Y |
| 5 **King** | Y | Y | Y | Y | Y | Y |
| **KANSAS** | | | | | | |
| 1 **Moran** | Y | Y | Y | Y | Y | Y |
| 2 **Ryun** | Y | Y | Y | Y | Y | Y |
| 3 Moore | ? | ? | Y | Y | N | Y |
| 4 **Tiahrt** | Y | Y | Y | Y | Y | Y |
| **KENTUCKY** | | | | | | |
| 1 **Whitfield** | Y | Y | Y | Y | Y | Y |
| 2 **Lewis** | Y | Y | Y | Y | Y | Y |
| 3 **Northup** | Y | Y | Y | Y | Y | Y |
| 4 **Davis** | Y | Y | Y | Y | Y | Y |
| 5 **Rogers** | Y | Y | Y | Y | Y | Y |
| 6 Chandler | Y | Y | Y | Y | N | Y |
| **LOUISIANA** | | | | | | |
| 1 **Jindal** | Y | Y | Y | Y | Y | Y |
| 2 Jefferson | Y | ? | Y | Y | N | N |
| 3 Melancon | ? | ? | ? | ? | ? | ? |
| 4 **McCrery** | ? | ? | Y | Y | ? | ? |
| 5 **Alexander** | Y | Y | Y | Y | Y | Y |
| 6 **Baker** | Y | Y | ? | ? | ? | ? |
| 7 **Boustany** | Y | Y | Y | Y | Y | Y |
| **MAINE** | | | | | | |
| 1 Allen | Y | Y | Y | Y | N | N |
| 2 Michaud | Y | Y | Y | Y | N | N |
| **MARYLAND** | | | | | | |
| 1 **Gilchrest** | Y | Y | Y | Y | Y | Y |
| 2 Ruppersberger | Y | Y | Y | Y | N | Y |
| 3 Cardin | ? | ? | Y | Y | N | Y |
| 4 Wynn | Y | Y | Y | Y | N | Y |
| 5 Hoyer | Y | Y | Y | Y | N | N |
| 6 **Bartlett** | Y | Y | Y | Y | Y | Y |
| 7 Cummings | Y | Y | Y | Y | N | N |
| 8 Van Hollen | Y | Y | Y | Y | N | N |
| **MASSACHUSETTS** | | | | | | |
| 1 Olver | ? | ? | ? | ? | ? | ? |
| 2 Neal | Y | Y | Y | Y | N | N |
| 3 McGovern | Y | Y | Y | Y | N | N |
| 4 Frank | Y | Y | Y | Y | N | N |
| 5 Meehan | Y | Y | Y | Y | N | N |
| 6 Tierney | Y | Y | Y | Y | N | N |
| 7 Markey | Y | Y | Y | Y | N | N |
| 8 Capuano | Y | Y | Y | Y | N | N |
| 9 Lynch | Y | Y | Y | Y | N | Y |
| 10 Delahunt | ? | ? | Y | Y | N | N |
| **MICHIGAN** | | | | | | |
| 1 Stupak | Y | Y | Y | Y | N | N |
| 2 **Hoekstra** | Y | Y | ? | ? | Y | Y |
| 3 **Ehlers** | Y | Y | Y | Y | Y | Y |
| 4 **Camp** | Y | Y | Y | Y | Y | Y |
| 5 Kildee | Y | Y | Y | Y | N | N |
| 6 **Upton** | Y | Y | Y | Y | Y | Y |
| 7 **Schwarz** | Y | Y | Y | Y | Y | Y |
| 8 **Rogers** | Y | Y | Y | Y | Y | Y |
| 9 **Knollenberg** | Y | Y | Y | Y | Y | Y |
| 10 **Miller** | Y | Y | Y | Y | Y | Y |
| 11 **McCotter** | Y | Y | Y | Y | Y | Y |
| 12 Levin | Y | Y | ? | Y | N | N |
| 13 Kilpatrick | Y | Y | Y | Y | N | N |
| 14 Conyers | Y | Y | Y | Y | N | N |
| 15 Dingell | Y | Y | Y | Y | N | N |

| | 454 | 455 | 456 | 457 | 458 | 459 |
|---|---|---|---|---|---|---|
| **MINNESOTA** | | | | | | |
| 1 **Gutknecht** | Y | Y | Y | Y | Y | Y |
| 2 **Kline** | Y | Y | Y | Y | Y | Y |
| 3 **Ramstad** | Y | Y | Y | Y | Y | Y |
| 4 McCollum | Y | Y | Y | Y | N | N |
| 5 Sabo | Y | Y | Y | Y | N | N |
| 6 **Kennedy** | Y | Y | Y | Y | Y | Y |
| 7 Peterson | Y | Y | Y | Y | N | N |
| 8 Oberstar | Y | Y | Y | Y | ? | ? |
| **MISSISSIPPI** | | | | | | |
| 1 **Wicker** | Y | Y | Y | Y | Y | Y |
| 2 Thompson | Y | Y | Y | Y | N | N |
| 3 **Pickering** | + | + | ? | ? | Y | Y |
| 4 Taylor | ? | ? | ? | ? | ? | ? |
| **MISSOURI** | | | | | | |
| 1 Clay | Y | Y | Y | Y | N | N |
| 2 **Akin** | Y | Y | Y | Y | Y | Y |
| 3 Carnahan | Y | Y | Y | Y | N | N |
| 4 Skelton | Y | Y | Y | Y | N | N |
| 5 Cleaver | Y | Y | Y | Y | N | N |
| 6 **Graves** | Y | Y | Y | Y | Y | Y |
| 7 **Blunt** | Y | Y | Y | Y | Y | Y |
| 8 **Emerson** | + | + | + | + | + | + |
| 9 **Hulshof** | Y | Y | Y | Y | Y | Y |
| **MONTANA** | | | | | | |
| AL **Rehberg** | Y | Y | Y | Y | Y | Y |
| **NEBRASKA** | | | | | | |
| 1 **Fortenberry** | Y | Y | Y | Y | Y | Y |
| 2 **Terry** | Y | Y | Y | Y | Y | Y |
| 3 **Osborne** | Y | Y | Y | Y | Y | Y |
| **NEVADA** | | | | | | |
| 1 Berkley | ? | ? | ? | ? | ? | ? |
| 2 **Gibbons** | Y | Y | Y | Y | Y | Y |
| 3 **Porter** | Y | Y | Y | Y | Y | Y |
| **NEW HAMPSHIRE** | | | | | | |
| 1 **Bradley** | Y | Y | Y | Y | Y | Y |
| 2 **Bass** | Y | Y | Y | Y | Y | Y |
| **NEW JERSEY** | | | | | | |
| 1 Andrews | Y | Y | Y | Y | N | N |
| 2 **LoBiondo** | Y | Y | Y | Y | Y | Y |
| 3 **Saxton** | Y | Y | Y | Y | Y | Y |
| 4 **Smith** | Y | Y | Y | Y | Y | Y |
| 5 **Garrett** | Y | Y | Y | Y | Y | Y |
| 6 Pallone | Y | Y | Y | Y | N | N |
| 7 **Ferguson** | Y | Y | Y | Y | Y | Y |
| 8 Pascrell | Y | Y | Y | Y | N | N |
| 9 Rothman | Y | Y | Y | Y | N | N |
| 10 Payne | Y | Y | Y | Y | N | N |
| 11 **Frelinghuysen** | Y | Y | Y | Y | Y | Y |
| 12 Holt | Y | Y | Y | Y | N | N |
| 13 Menendez | Y | Y | Y | Y | N | Y |
| **NEW MEXICO** | | | | | | |
| 1 **Wilson** | Y | Y | Y | Y | Y | Y |
| 2 **Pearce** | Y | Y | Y | Y | Y | Y |
| 3 Udall | Y | Y | Y | Y | N | N |
| **NEW YORK** | | | | | | |
| 1 Bishop | Y | Y | Y | Y | N | N |
| 2 Israel | Y | Y | Y | Y | N | N |
| 3 **King** | Y | Y | Y | Y | Y | Y |
| 4 McCarthy | Y | Y | Y | Y | N | N |
| 5 Ackerman | Y | Y | Y | Y | N | N |
| 6 Meeks | Y | Y | Y | Y | N | N |
| 7 Crowley | Y | Y | Y | Y | N | N |
| 8 Nadler | Y | Y | Y | Y | N | N |
| 9 Weiner | ? | ? | ? | ? | ? | ? |
| 10 Towns | Y | Y | Y | Y | N | N |
| 11 Owens | Y | Y | Y | Y | N | N |
| 12 Velázquez | Y | Y | Y | Y | N | N |
| 13 **Fossella** | Y | Y | Y | Y | Y | Y |
| 14 Maloney | + | + | + | + | ? | ? |
| 15 Rangel | Y | Y | Y | Y | N | N |
| 16 Serrano | Y | Y | Y | Y | N | N |
| 17 Engel | ? | ? | Y | Y | N | N |
| 18 Lowey | Y | Y | Y | Y | N | N |
| 19 **Kelly** | Y | Y | Y | Y | Y | Y |
| 20 **Sweeney** | Y | Y | Y | Y | Y | Y |
| 21 McNulty | Y | Y | ? | ? | N | N |
| 22 Hinchey | Y | Y | Y | Y | N | N |
| 23 **McHugh** | Y | Y | Y | Y | Y | Y |
| 24 **Boehlert** | Y | Y | Y | Y | Y | Y |
| 25 **Walsh** | Y | Y | Y | Y | Y | Y |
| 26 **Reynolds** | Y | Y | ? | Y | Y | Y |
| 27 Higgins | Y | Y | Y | Y | N | N |
| 28 Slaughter | Y | Y | Y | Y | N | N |
| 29 **Kuhl** | Y | Y | Y | Y | Y | Y |

| | 454 | 455 | 456 | 457 | 458 | 459 |
|---|---|---|---|---|---|---|
| **NORTH CAROLINA** | | | | | | |
| 1 Butterfield | Y | Y | ? | ? | ? | ? |
| 2 Etheridge | Y | Y | Y | Y | N | N |
| 3 **Jones** | Y | Y | Y | Y | Y | Y |
| 4 Price | Y | Y | Y | Y | N | N |
| 5 **Foxx** | Y | Y | Y | Y | Y | Y |
| 6 **Coble** | Y | Y | Y | Y | Y | Y |
| 7 McIntyre | Y | Y | Y | Y | N | Y |
| 8 **Hayes** | Y | Y | Y | Y | Y | Y |
| 9 **Myrick** | Y | Y | Y | Y | Y | Y |
| 10 **McHenry** | Y | Y | Y | Y | Y | Y |
| 11 **Taylor** | Y | Y | Y | Y | Y | Y |
| 12 Watt | Y | Y | Y | Y | N | N |
| 13 Miller | Y | Y | Y | Y | N | N |
| **NORTH DAKOTA** | | | | | | |
| AL Pomeroy | Y | Y | Y | Y | N | N |
| **OHIO** | | | | | | |
| 1 **Chabot** | Y | Y | Y | Y | Y | Y |
| 2 **Schmidt**[2] | Y | Y | Y | Y | Y | Y |
| 3 **Turner** | Y | Y | Y | Y | Y | Y |
| 4 **Oxley** | Y | Y | Y | Y | Y | Y |
| 5 **Gillmor** | Y | Y | Y | Y | Y | Y |
| 6 Strickland | ? | ? | Y | Y | N | N |
| 7 **Hobson** | Y | Y | Y | Y | Y | Y |
| 8 **Boehner** | Y | Y | Y | Y | Y | Y |
| 9 Kaptur | Y | Y | Y | Y | N | N |
| 10 Kucinich | Y | Y | Y | Y | N | N |
| 11 Jones | Y | Y | Y | Y | N | N |
| 12 **Tiberi** | Y | Y | Y | Y | Y | Y |
| 13 Brown | Y | Y | Y | Y | N | N |
| 14 **LaTourette** | Y | Y | Y | Y | Y | Y |
| 15 **Pryce** | Y | Y | Y | Y | Y | Y |
| 16 **Regula** | Y | Y | Y | Y | Y | Y |
| 17 Ryan | Y | Y | Y | Y | N | N |
| 18 **Ney** | Y | Y | Y | Y | Y | Y |
| **OKLAHOMA** | | | | | | |
| 1 **Sullivan** | Y | Y | Y | Y | Y | Y |
| 2 Boren | Y | Y | Y | Y | N | N |
| 3 **Lucas** | Y | Y | Y | Y | Y | Y |
| 4 **Cole** | Y | Y | Y | Y | Y | Y |
| 5 **Istook** | Y | Y | Y | Y | Y | Y |
| **OREGON** | | | | | | |
| 1 Wu | Y | Y | Y | Y | N | N |
| 2 **Walden** | Y | Y | Y | Y | Y | Y |
| 3 Blumenauer | Y | Y | Y | Y | N | N |
| 4 DeFazio | Y | Y | Y | Y | N | N |
| 5 Hooley | Y | Y | Y | Y | N | N |
| **PENNSYLVANIA** | | | | | | |
| 1 Brady | ? | ? | Y | Y | N | N |
| 2 Fattah | ? | ? | Y | Y | N | N |
| 3 **English** | Y | Y | Y | Y | Y | Y |
| 4 **Hart** | Y | Y | Y | Y | Y | Y |
| 5 **Peterson** | Y | Y | Y | Y | Y | Y |
| 6 **Gerlach** | Y | Y | Y | Y | Y | Y |
| 7 **Weldon** | Y | Y | ? | Y | Y | Y |
| 8 **Fitzpatrick** | Y | Y | Y | Y | Y | Y |
| 9 **Shuster** | Y | Y | Y | Y | Y | Y |
| 10 **Sherwood** | Y | Y | Y | Y | Y | Y |
| 11 Kanjorski | Y | Y | Y | Y | N | N |
| 12 Murtha | ? | ? | Y | Y | N | N |
| 13 Schwartz | Y | Y | Y | Y | N | N |
| 14 Doyle | Y | Y | Y | Y | N | N |
| 15 **Dent** | Y | Y | Y | Y | Y | Y |
| 16 **Pitts** | Y | Y | Y | Y | Y | Y |
| 17 Holden | Y | Y | Y | Y | N | N |
| 18 **Murphy** | Y | Y | Y | Y | Y | Y |
| 19 **Platts** | Y | Y | Y | Y | Y | Y |
| **RHODE ISLAND** | | | | | | |
| 1 Kennedy | Y | Y | Y | Y | N | N |
| 2 Langevin | Y | Y | Y | Y | N | Y |
| **SOUTH CAROLINA** | | | | | | |
| 1 **Brown** | Y | Y | Y | Y | Y | Y |
| 2 **Wilson** | Y | Y | Y | Y | Y | Y |
| 3 **Barrett** | Y | Y | Y | Y | Y | Y |
| 4 **Inglis** | Y | Y | Y | Y | Y | Y |
| 5 Spratt | Y | Y | Y | Y | N | N |
| 6 Clyburn | Y | Y | Y | Y | N | N |
| **SOUTH DAKOTA** | | | | | | |
| AL Herseth | Y | Y | Y | Y | N | N |
| **TENNESSEE** | | | | | | |
| 1 **Jenkins** | Y | Y | Y | Y | Y | Y |
| 2 **Duncan** | Y | Y | Y | Y | Y | Y |

| | 454 | 455 | 456 | 457 | 458 | 459 |
|---|---|---|---|---|---|---|
| 3 **Wamp** | Y | Y | Y | Y | Y | Y |
| 4 Davis | Y | Y | Y | Y | N | N |
| 5 Cooper | Y | Y | Y | Y | N | N |
| 6 Gordon | Y | Y | Y | Y | N | N |
| 7 **Blackburn** | Y | Y | Y | Y | Y | Y |
| 8 Tanner | Y | Y | Y | Y | N | N |
| 9 Ford | Y | Y | ? | ? | N | N |
| **TEXAS** | | | | | | |
| 1 **Gohmert** | Y | Y | Y | Y | Y | Y |
| 2 **Poe** | Y | Y | Y | Y | Y | Y |
| 3 **Johnson, S.** | Y | Y | Y | Y | Y | Y |
| 4 **Hall** | Y | Y | Y | Y | Y | Y |
| 5 **Hensarling** | Y | Y | Y | Y | Y | Y |
| 6 **Barton** | Y | Y | Y | Y | Y | Y |
| 7 **Culberson** | Y | Y | Y | Y | Y | Y |
| 8 **Brady** | ? | ? | ? | ? | ? | ? |
| 9 Green, A. | Y | Y | Y | Y | N | N |
| 10 **McCaul** | Y | Y | Y | Y | Y | Y |
| 11 **Conaway** | ? | ? | ? | ? | ? | ? |
| 12 **Granger** | Y | Y | Y | Y | Y | Y |
| 13 **Thornberry** | Y | Y | Y | Y | Y | Y |
| 14 **Paul** | Y | N | Y | Y | Y | Y |
| 15 Hinojosa | Y | Y | Y | Y | N | N |
| 16 Reyes | Y | Y | Y | Y | N | N |
| 17 Edwards | Y | Y | Y | Y | N | Y |
| 18 Jackson-Lee | Y | Y | Y | Y | N | N |
| 19 **Neugebauer** | Y | Y | Y | Y | Y | Y |
| 20 Gonzalez | Y | Y | Y | Y | N | Y |
| 21 **Smith** | Y | Y | Y | Y | Y | Y |
| 22 **DeLay** | Y | Y | Y | Y | Y | Y |
| 23 **Bonilla** | Y | Y | Y | Y | Y | Y |
| 24 **Marchant** | Y | Y | ? | ? | Y | Y |
| 25 Doggett | Y | Y | Y | Y | N | N |
| 26 **Burgess** | Y | Y | Y | Y | Y | Y |
| 27 Ortiz | Y | Y | Y | Y | N | N |
| 28 Cuellar | Y | Y | Y | Y | N | N |
| 29 Green, G. | Y | Y | Y | Y | N | N |
| 30 Johnson, E. | Y | Y | Y | Y | N | N |
| 31 **Carter** | Y | Y | Y | Y | Y | Y |
| 32 **Sessions** | ? | ? | Y | Y | Y | Y |
| **UTAH** | | | | | | |
| 1 **Bishop** | Y | Y | Y | Y | Y | Y |
| 2 Matheson | Y | Y | Y | Y | N | N |
| 3 **Cannon** | Y | Y | Y | Y | Y | Y |
| **VERMONT** | | | | | | |
| AL *Sanders* | Y | Y | Y | Y | N | N |
| **VIRGINIA** | | | | | | |
| 1 **Davis, J.** | Y | Y | Y | Y | Y | Y |
| 2 **Drake** | Y | Y | Y | Y | Y | Y |
| 3 Scott | Y | Y | Y | Y | N | N |
| 4 **Forbes** | Y | Y | Y | Y | Y | Y |
| 5 **Goode** | Y | Y | Y | Y | Y | Y |
| 6 **Goodlatte** | Y | Y | Y | Y | Y | Y |
| 7 **Cantor** | Y | Y | Y | Y | Y | Y |
| 8 Moran | Y | Y | Y | Y | N | N |
| 9 Boucher | ? | ? | Y | Y | N | N |
| 10 **Wolf** | Y | Y | Y | Y | Y | Y |
| 11 **Davis, T.** | Y | Y | Y | Y | Y | Y |
| **WASHINGTON** | | | | | | |
| 1 Inslee | + | + | Y | Y | N | N |
| 2 Larsen | Y | Y | Y | Y | N | N |
| 3 Baird | Y | Y | Y | Y | N | N |
| 4 **Hastings** | Y | Y | Y | Y | Y | Y |
| 5 **McMorris** | Y | Y | Y | Y | Y | Y |
| 6 Dicks | ? | ? | Y | Y | N | Y |
| 7 McDermott | + | + | Y | Y | N | N |
| 8 **Reichert** | Y | Y | Y | Y | Y | Y |
| 9 Smith | Y | Y | Y | Y | N | N |
| **WEST VIRGINIA** | | | | | | |
| 1 Mollohan | ? | ? | Y | Y | N | N |
| 2 **Capito** | Y | Y | Y | Y | Y | Y |
| 3 Rahall | Y | Y | Y | Y | N | N |
| **WISCONSIN** | | | | | | |
| 1 **Ryan** | Y | Y | Y | Y | Y | Y |
| 2 Baldwin | Y | Y | Y | Y | N | N |
| 3 Kind | Y | Y | Y | Y | N | N |
| 4 Moore | Y | Y | Y | Y | N | N |
| 5 **Sensenbrenner** | Y | Y | Y | Y | Y | Y |
| 6 **Petri** | Y | Y | Y | Y | Y | Y |
| 7 Obey | Y | Y | Y | Y | N | N |
| 8 **Green** | Y | Y | Y | Y | Y | Y |
| **WYOMING** | | | | | | |
| AL **Cubin** | Y | Y | Y | Y | ? | ? |

# IN THE HOUSE | By Vote Number

**460.** HR 3673. Fiscal 2005 Emergency Supplemental **Appropriations/Passage.** Lewis, R-Calif., motion to suspend the rules and pass the bill that would appropriate $51.8 billion in fiscal 2005 supplemental spending for disaster relief to areas affected by Hurricane Katrina. The bill would provide $50 billion for the Federal Emergency Management Agency, $1.4 billion for the Defense Department and $400 million for the Army Corps of Engineers. Motion agreed to 410-11: R 213-11; D 196-0 (ND 147-0, SD 49-0); I 1-0. A two-thirds majority of those present and voting (281 in this case) is required for passage under suspension of the rules. Sept. 8, 2005.

**461.** HR 3669. National Flood Insurance Program/Passage. Ney, R-Ohio, motion to suspend the rules and pass the bill that would temporarily increase to $3.5 billion, from $1.5 billion, the amount that the Federal Emergency Management Agency may borrow to pay claims under the National Flood Insurance Program that exceed collected premiums in the National Flood Insurance Fund. Motion agreed to 416-0: R 223-0; D 192-0 (ND 144-0, SD 48-0); I 1-0. A two-thirds majority of those present and voting (278 in this case) is required for passage under suspension of the rules. Sept. 8, 2005.

**462.** HR 3668. Federal Student Grant Assistance/Passage. Boustany, R-La., motion to suspend the rules and pass the bill that would allow the Education Department to waive the repayment requirement for any federal student grant assistance provided to students under Title IV of the Higher Education Act if their school attendance is interrupted because of the impact of a major disaster. To qualify for the waiver, students must have lived, worked, or attended schools in an area designated by the president as a major disaster. Motion agreed to 414-0: R 222-0; D 191-0 (ND 142-0, SD 49-0); I 1-0. A two-thirds majority of those present and voting (276 in this case) is required for passage under suspension of the rules. Sept. 8, 2005.

**463.** H Res 428. Gratitude to Foreign Individuals and Governments/ **Adoption.** Leach, R-Iowa, motion to suspend the rules and adopt the resolution that would express the sincere gratitude of the House to foreign individuals, organizations and governments that have offered material assistance and other forms of support to people affected by Hurricane Katrina. Motion agreed to 410-0: R 220-0; D 189-0 (ND 141-0, SD 48-0); I 1-0. A two-thirds majority of those present and voting (274 in this case) is required for adoption under suspension of the rules. Sept. 8, 2005.

**464.** H Res 427. September 11 Remembrance/Adoption. Leach, R-Iowa, motion to suspend the rules and adopt the resolution that would express the sense of the House on the anniversary of the Sept. 11 terrorist attacks. The resolution would extend the deepest sympathies of the House to the victims of the attacks and thank foreign leaders and citizens of all nations who assisted the United States in its fight against terrorism. Motion agreed to 402-6: R 219-0; D 182-6 (ND 135-5, SD 47-1); I 1-0. A two-thirds majority of those present and voting (272 in this case) is required for adoption under suspension of the rules. Sept. 8, 2005.

| | 460 | 461 | 462 | 463 | 464 |
|---|---|---|---|---|---|
| **ALABAMA** | | | | | |
| 1 Bonner | Y | Y | Y | Y | Y |
| 2 Everett | ? | ? | ? | ? | ? |
| 3 Rogers | Y | Y | Y | Y | Y |
| 4 Aderholt | Y | Y | Y | Y | Y |
| 5 Cramer | Y | Y | Y | Y | Y |
| 6 Bachus | Y | Y | Y | Y | Y |
| 7 Davis | Y | Y | Y | Y | |
| **ALASKA** | | | | | |
| AL Young | ? | ? | ? | ? | ? |
| **ARIZONA** | | | | | |
| 1 Renzi | Y | Y | Y | Y | Y |
| 2 Franks | Y | Y | Y | Y | Y |
| 3 Shadegg | Y | Y | Y | Y | Y |
| 4 Pastor | Y | Y | Y | Y | Y |
| 5 Hayworth | Y | Y | Y | Y | Y |
| 6 Flake | N | Y | Y | Y | Y |
| 7 Grijalva | Y | Y | Y | Y | Y |
| 8 Kolbe | Y | Y | Y | Y | Y |
| **ARKANSAS** | | | | | |
| 1 Berry | Y | Y | Y | Y | Y |
| 2 Snyder | Y | Y | Y | Y | Y |
| 3 Boozman | Y | Y | Y | Y | Y |
| 4 Ross | Y | Y | Y | Y | |
| **CALIFORNIA** | | | | | |
| 1 Thompson | Y | Y | Y | Y | Y |
| 2 Herger | Y | Y | Y | Y | Y |
| 3 Lungren | Y | Y | Y | Y | Y |
| 4 Doolittle | Y | Y | Y | Y | Y |
| 5 Matsui, D. | Y | Y | Y | Y | Y |
| 6 Woolsey | Y | Y | Y | Y | N |
| 7 Miller, George | Y | Y | Y | Y | Y |
| 8 Pelosi | Y | Y | Y | Y | Y |
| 9 Lee | Y | Y | Y | Y | N |
| 10 Tauscher | Y | Y | Y | Y | Y |
| 11 Pombo | Y | Y | Y | Y | Y |
| 12 Lantos | Y | Y | Y | Y | Y |
| 13 Stark | Y | Y | Y | Y | N |
| 14 Eshoo | Y | Y | Y | Y | Y |
| 15 Honda | Y | Y. | Y | Y | Y |
| 16 Lofgren | Y | Y | Y | Y | Y |
| 17 Farr | Y | Y | Y | Y | Y |
| 18 Cardoza | Y | Y | Y | Y | Y |
| 19 Radanovich | Y | Y | Y | Y | Y |
| 20 Costa | Y | Y | Y | Y | Y |
| 21 Nunes | Y | Y | Y | Y | Y |
| 22 Thomas | Y | Y | Y | Y | Y |
| 23 Capps | Y | Y | Y | Y | Y |
| 24 Gallegly | Y | Y | Y | Y | Y |
| 25 McKeon | Y | Y | Y | ? | ? |
| 26 Dreier | Y | Y | Y | Y | Y |
| 27 Sherman | Y | Y | Y | Y | Y |
| 28 Berman | Y | Y | Y | ? | ? |
| 29 Schiff | Y | Y | Y | Y | Y |
| 30 Waxman | Y | Y | Y | Y | Y |
| 31 Becerra | Y | Y | Y | Y | Y |
| 32 Solis | Y | Y | Y | Y | Y |
| 33 Watson | Y | Y | Y | Y | Y |
| 34 Roybal-Allard | Y | Y | Y | Y | Y |
| 35 Waters | Y | Y | Y | Y | Y |
| 36 Harman | Y | Y | Y | Y | Y |
| 37 Millender-McD. | Y | Y | Y | Y | Y |
| 38 Napolitano | Y | Y | Y | Y | Y |
| 39 Sánchez, Linda | Y | Y | Y | Y | Y |
| 40 Royce | Y | Y | Y | Y | Y |
| 41 Lewis | Y | Y | Y | Y | Y |
| 42 Miller, Gary | Y | Y | Y | ? | ? |
| 43 Baca | Y | Y | Y | Y | Y |
| 44 Calvert | Y | Y | Y | Y | Y |
| 45 Bono | Y | Y | Y | Y | Y |
| 46 Rohrabacher | Y | Y | Y | Y | Y |
| 47 Sanchez, Loretta | + | + | + | + | + |
| 48 Vacant | | | | | |
| 49 Issa | Y | ? | ? | ? | ? |

| | 460 | 461 | 462 | 463 | 464 |
|---|---|---|---|---|---|
| 50 Cunningham | Y | Y | Y | Y | Y |
| 51 Filner | Y | + | + | + | + |
| 52 Hunter | Y | Y | Y | Y | Y |
| 53 Davis | Y | Y | Y | Y | |
| **COLORADO** | | | | | |
| 1 DeGette | Y | Y | Y | Y | ? |
| 2 Udall | Y | Y | Y | Y | Y |
| 3 Salazar | Y | Y | Y | Y | Y |
| 4 Musgrave | Y | Y | Y | Y | Y |
| 5 Hefley | Y | Y | Y | Y | Y |
| 6 Tancredo | N | Y | Y | Y | Y |
| 7 Beauprez | Y | Y | Y | Y | Y |
| **CONNECTICUT** | | | | | |
| 1 Larson | Y | Y | Y | Y | Y |
| 2 Simmons | Y | Y | Y | Y | Y |
| 3 DeLauro | Y | Y | Y | Y | Y |
| 4 Shays | Y | Y | Y | Y | Y |
| 5 Johnson | Y | Y | Y | Y | Y |
| **DELAWARE** | | | | | |
| AL Castle | Y | Y | Y | Y | Y |
| **FLORIDA** | | | | | |
| 1 Miller | Y | Y | Y | Y | Y |
| 2 Boyd | Y | Y | Y | Y | Y |
| 3 Brown | Y | Y | Y | Y | Y |
| 4 Crenshaw | Y | Y | Y | Y | Y |
| 5 Brown-Waite | Y | Y | Y | Y | Y |
| 6 Stearns | Y | Y | Y | Y | Y |
| 7 Mica | Y | Y | Y | Y | Y |
| 8 Keller | Y | Y | Y | Y | Y |
| 9 Bilirakis | Y | Y | Y | Y | Y |
| 10 Young | Y | Y | Y | Y | Y |
| 11 Davis | Y | Y | Y | Y | Y |
| 12 Putnam | Y | Y | Y | Y | Y |
| 13 Harris | Y | Y | Y | Y | Y |
| 14 Mack | Y | Y | Y | Y | Y |
| 15 Weldon | Y | Y | Y | Y | Y |
| 16 Foley | Y | Y | Y | Y | Y |
| 17 Meek | Y | Y | Y | Y | Y |
| 18 Ros-Lehtinen | Y | Y | Y | Y | Y |
| 19 Wexler | Y | Y | Y | Y | Y |
| 20 Wasserman-Schultz | Y | Y | Y | Y | Y |
| 21 Diaz-Balart, L. | Y | Y | Y | Y | Y |
| 22 Shaw | Y | Y | Y | Y | Y |
| 23 Hastings | Y | Y | Y | Y | Y |
| 24 Feeney | Y | Y | Y | Y | Y |
| 25 Diaz-Balart, M. | Y | Y | Y | Y | Y |
| **GEORGIA** | | | | | |
| 1 Kingston | Y | Y | Y | Y | Y |
| 2 Bishop | Y | ? | Y | Y | Y |
| 3 Marshall | Y | Y | Y | Y | Y |
| 4 McKinney | Y | Y | Y | Y | N |
| 5 Lewis | Y | Y | Y | Y | Y |
| 6 Price | Y | Y | Y | Y | Y |
| 7 Linder | Y | Y | Y | Y | Y |
| 8 Westmoreland | N | Y | Y | Y | Y |
| 9 Norwood | Y | Y | Y | Y | Y |
| 10 Deal | Y | Y | Y | Y | Y |
| 11 Gingrey | Y | Y | Y | Y | Y |
| 12 Barrow | Y | Y | Y | Y | Y |
| 13 Scott | Y | Y | Y | Y | Y |
| **HAWAII** | | | | | |
| 1 Abercrombie | Y | Y | Y | Y | Y |
| 2 Case | Y | Y | Y | Y | Y |
| **IDAHO** | | | | | |
| 1 Otter | N | Y | Y | Y | Y |
| 2 Simpson | Y | Y | Y | Y | Y |
| **ILLINOIS** | | | | | |
| 1 Rush | Y | Y | Y | Y | Y |
| 2 Jackson | Y | Y | Y | Y | Y |
| 3 Lipinski | Y | Y | Y | Y | Y |
| 4 Gutierrez | Y | Y | Y | Y | Y |
| 5 Emanuel | Y | Y | Y | Y | Y |
| 6 Hyde | Y | Y | Y | Y | Y |
| 7 Davis | Y | Y | Y | Y | Y |
| 8 Bean | Y | Y | Y | Y | Y |
| 9 Schakowsky | Y | Y | Y | Y | Y |
| 10 Kirk | Y | Y | Y | Y | Y |
| 11 Weller | Y | Y | Y | Y | Y |
| 12 Costello | Y | Y | Y | Y | Y |

| KEY | Republicans | | Democrats | | *Independents* | |
|---|---|---|---|---|---|---|
| Y | Voted for (yea) | X | Paired against | C | Voted "present" to avoid possible conflict of interest | |
| # | Paired for | – | Announced against | | | |
| + | Announced for | P | Voted "present" | ? | Did not vote or otherwise make a position known | |
| N | Voted against (nay) | | | | | |

| | 460 | 461 | 462 | 463 | 464 |
|---|---|---|---|---|---|
| 13 Biggert | Y | Y | Y | Y | Y |
| 14 Hastert | | | | | Y |
| 15 Johnson | Y | Y | Y | Y | Y |
| 16 Manzullo | Y | Y | Y | Y | Y |
| 17 Evans | Y | Y | Y | Y | Y |
| 18 LaHood | Y | Y | Y | Y | Y |
| 19 Shimkus | Y | Y | Y | Y | Y |
| **INDIANA** | | | | | |
| 1 Visclosky | Y | Y | Y | Y | Y |
| 2 Chocola | Y | Y | Y | Y | Y |
| 3 Souder | Y | Y | Y | Y | Y |
| 4 Buyer | Y | Y | Y | Y | Y |
| 5 Burton | Y | Y | Y | Y | Y |
| 6 Pence | Y | Y | Y | Y | Y |
| 7 Carson | Y | Y | Y | Y | Y |
| 8 Hostettler | N | Y | Y | Y | Y |
| 9 Sodrel | Y | Y | Y | Y | Y |
| **IOWA** | | | | | |
| 1 Nussle | Y | Y | Y | Y | Y |
| 2 Leach | Y | Y | Y | Y | Y |
| 3 Boswell | Y | Y | Y | Y | Y |
| 4 Latham | Y | Y | Y | Y | Y |
| 5 King | N | Y | Y | Y | Y |
| **KANSAS** | | | | | |
| 1 Moran | Y | Y | Y | Y | |
| 2 Ryun | Y | Y | Y | Y | Y |
| 3 Moore | Y | Y | Y | Y | Y |
| 4 Tiahrt | Y | Y | Y | Y | |
| **KENTUCKY** | | | | | |
| 1 Whitfield | Y | Y | Y | Y | Y |
| 2 Lewis | Y | Y | Y | Y | Y |
| 3 Northup | Y | Y | Y | Y | Y |
| 4 Davis | Y | Y | Y | Y | Y |
| 5 Rogers | Y | Y | Y | Y | Y |
| 6 Chandler | Y | Y | Y | Y | Y |
| **LOUISIANA** | | | | | |
| 1 Jindal | Y | Y | Y | Y | Y |
| 2 Jefferson | Y | Y | Y | Y | Y |
| 3 Melancon | Y | Y | Y | Y | Y |
| 4 McCrery | ? | ? | ? | ? | ? |
| 5 Alexander | Y | Y | Y | Y | Y |
| 6 Baker | ? | ? | ? | ? | ? |
| 7 Boustany | Y | Y | Y | Y | Y |
| **MAINE** | | | | | |
| 1 Allen | Y | Y | Y | Y | Y |
| 2 Michaud | Y | Y | Y | Y | Y |
| **MARYLAND** | | | | | |
| 1 Gilchrest | Y | Y | Y | Y | Y |
| 2 Ruppersberger | Y | Y | Y | Y | Y |
| 3 Cardin | Y | Y | Y | Y | Y |
| 4 Wynn | Y | Y | Y | Y | Y |
| 5 Hoyer | Y | Y | Y | Y | Y |
| 6 Bartlett | Y | Y | Y | Y | Y |
| 7 Cummings | Y | Y | Y | Y | Y |
| 8 Van Hollen | Y | Y | Y | Y | Y |
| **MASSACHUSETTS** | | | | | |
| 1 Olver | ? | ? | ? | ? | ? |
| 2 Neal | Y | Y | Y | Y | Y |
| 3 McGovern | Y | Y | Y | Y | Y |
| 4 Frank | Y | Y | Y | Y | Y |
| 5 Meehan | Y | ? | ? | ? | ? |
| 6 Tierney | Y | Y | Y | Y | Y |
| 7 Markey | Y | Y | Y | Y | Y |
| 8 Capuano | Y | Y | Y | Y | Y |
| 9 Lynch | Y | Y | Y | ? | ? |
| 10 Delahunt | Y | Y | Y | Y | Y |
| **MICHIGAN** | | | | | |
| 1 Stupak | Y | Y | Y | Y | Y |
| 2 Hoekstra | Y | Y | Y | Y | Y |
| 3 Ehlers | Y | Y | Y | Y | Y |
| 4 Camp | Y | Y | Y | Y | Y |
| 5 Kildee | Y | Y | Y | Y | Y |
| 6 Upton | Y | Y | Y | Y | Y |
| 7 Schwarz | Y | Y | Y | Y | Y |
| 8 Rogers | Y | Y | Y | Y | Y |
| 9 Knollenberg | Y | Y | Y | Y | Y |
| 10 Miller | Y | Y | Y | Y | Y |
| 11 McCotter | Y | Y | Y | Y | Y |
| 12 Levin | Y | Y | Y | Y | Y |
| 13 Kilpatrick | Y | Y | Y | Y | Y |
| 14 Conyers | Y | Y | Y | Y | N |
| 15 Dingell | Y | Y | Y | Y | Y |

| | 460 | 461 | 462 | 463 | 464 |
|---|---|---|---|---|---|
| **MINNESOTA** | | | | | |
| 1 Gutknecht | Y | Y | Y | Y | Y |
| 2 Kline | Y | Y | Y | Y | Y |
| 3 Ramstad | Y | Y | Y | Y | Y |
| 4 McCollum | Y | Y | Y | Y | Y |
| 5 Sabo | Y | Y | Y | Y | Y |
| 6 Kennedy | Y | Y | Y | Y | Y |
| 7 Peterson | Y | Y | Y | Y | Y |
| 8 Oberstar | Y | Y | Y | Y | |
| **MISSISSIPPI** | | | | | |
| 1 Wicker | Y | Y | Y | Y | Y |
| 2 Thompson | Y | Y | Y | Y | Y |
| 3 Pickering | Y | Y | ? | Y | Y |
| 4 Taylor | ? | ? | ? | ? | ? |
| **MISSOURI** | | | | | |
| 1 Clay | Y | Y | Y | Y | Y |
| 2 Akin | Y | Y | Y | Y | Y |
| 3 Carnahan | Y | Y | Y | Y | Y |
| 4 Skelton | Y | Y | Y | Y | Y |
| 5 Cleaver | Y | Y | Y | Y | Y |
| 6 Graves | Y | Y | Y | Y | Y |
| 7 Blunt | Y | Y | Y | Y | Y |
| 8 Emerson | Y | Y | Y | Y | Y |
| 9 Hulshof | Y | Y | Y | Y | Y |
| **MONTANA** | | | | | |
| AL Rehberg | Y | Y | Y | Y | Y |
| **NEBRASKA** | | | | | |
| 1 Fortenberry | Y | Y | Y | Y | Y |
| 2 Terry | Y | Y | Y | Y | Y |
| 3 Osborne | Y | Y | Y | Y | Y |
| **NEVADA** | | | | | |
| 1 Berkley | ? | ? | ? | ? | ? |
| 2 Gibbons | Y | Y | Y | Y | Y |
| 3 Porter | Y | Y | Y | Y | Y |
| **NEW HAMPSHIRE** | | | | | |
| 1 Bradley | Y | Y | Y | Y | Y |
| 2 Bass | Y | Y | Y | Y | + |
| **NEW JERSEY** | | | | | |
| 1 Andrews | Y | Y | Y | Y | Y |
| 2 LoBiondo | Y | Y | Y | Y | Y |
| 3 Saxton | Y | Y | Y | Y | Y |
| 4 Smith | Y | Y | Y | Y | Y |
| 5 Garrett | N | Y | Y | Y | Y |
| 6 Pallone | Y | Y | Y | Y | Y |
| 7 Ferguson | Y | Y | Y | Y | Y |
| 8 Pascrell | Y | Y | Y | Y | Y |
| 9 Rothman | Y | Y | Y | Y | Y |
| 10 Payne | Y | Y | Y | Y | Y |
| 11 Frelinghuysen | Y | Y | Y | Y | Y |
| 12 Holt | Y | Y | Y | Y | Y |
| 13 Menendez | Y | Y | Y | Y | Y |
| **NEW MEXICO** | | | | | |
| 1 Wilson | Y | Y | Y | Y | Y |
| 2 Pearce | Y | Y | Y | Y | Y |
| 3 Udall | Y | Y | Y | Y | |
| **NEW YORK** | | | | | |
| 1 Bishop | Y | Y | Y | Y | Y |
| 2 Israel | Y | Y | Y | Y | Y |
| 3 King | Y | Y | Y | Y | Y |
| 4 McCarthy | Y | Y | Y | Y | Y |
| 5 Ackerman | Y | Y | Y | Y | Y |
| 6 Meeks | Y | Y | Y | Y | Y |
| 7 Crowley | Y | Y | ? | ? | ? |
| 8 Nadler | Y | Y | Y | Y | Y |
| 9 Weiner | Y | Y | Y | Y | Y |
| 10 Towns | Y | Y | ? | ? | ? |
| 11 Owens | Y | Y | Y | Y | Y |
| 12 Velázquez | Y | Y | Y | Y | Y |
| 13 Fossella | Y | Y | Y | Y | Y |
| 14 Maloney | ? | ? | ? | ? | ? |
| 15 Rangel | Y | Y | Y | Y | Y |
| 16 Serrano | Y | Y | Y | Y | Y |
| 17 Engel | Y | Y | Y | Y | Y |
| 18 Lowey | Y | Y | Y | Y | Y |
| 19 Kelly | Y | Y | Y | Y | Y |
| 20 Sweeney | Y | Y | Y | Y | Y |
| 21 McNulty | Y | Y | Y | Y | Y |
| 22 Hinchey | Y | Y | Y | Y | Y |
| 23 McHugh | Y | Y | Y | Y | Y |
| 24 Boehlert | Y | Y | Y | Y | Y |
| 25 Walsh | Y | Y | Y | Y | Y |
| 26 Reynolds | Y | Y | Y | Y | Y |
| 27 Higgins | Y | Y | Y | Y | Y |
| 28 Slaughter | Y | Y | Y | Y | Y |
| 29 Kuhl | Y | Y | Y | Y | Y |

| | 460 | 461 | 462 | 463 | 464 |
|---|---|---|---|---|---|
| **NORTH CAROLINA** | | | | | |
| 1 Butterfield | ? | ? | ? | ? | ? |
| 2 Etheridge | Y | Y | Y | Y | Y |
| 3 Jones | Y | Y | Y | Y | Y |
| 4 Price | Y | Y | Y | Y | Y |
| 5 Foxx | N | Y | Y | Y | Y |
| 6 Coble | Y | Y | Y | Y | Y |
| 7 McIntyre | Y | Y | Y | Y | Y |
| 8 Hayes | Y | Y | Y | Y | Y |
| 9 Myrick | Y | Y | Y | Y | Y |
| 10 McHenry | Y | Y | Y | Y | Y |
| 11 Taylor | Y | Y | Y | Y | Y |
| 12 Watt | Y | Y | Y | Y | Y |
| 13 Miller | Y | Y | Y | Y | Y |
| **NORTH DAKOTA** | | | | | |
| AL Pomeroy | Y | Y | Y | Y | Y |
| **OHIO** | | | | | |
| 1 Chabot | Y | Y | Y | Y | Y |
| 2 Schmidt | Y | Y | Y | Y | Y |
| 3 Turner | Y | Y | Y | Y | Y |
| 4 Oxley | Y | Y | Y | Y | Y |
| 5 Gillmor | Y | Y | Y | Y | Y |
| 6 Strickland | Y | Y | Y | Y | Y |
| 7 Hobson | Y | Y | Y | Y | Y |
| 8 Boehner | Y | Y | Y | Y | Y |
| 9 Kaptur | Y | ? | ? | Y | Y |
| 10 Kucinich | Y | Y | Y | Y | Y |
| 11 Jones | Y | Y | Y | Y | Y |
| 12 Tiberi | Y | Y | Y | Y | Y |
| 13 Brown | Y | Y | Y | Y | Y |
| 14 LaTourette | Y | Y | Y | Y | Y |
| 15 Pryce | Y | Y | Y | Y | Y |
| 16 Regula | Y | Y | Y | Y | Y |
| 17 Ryan | Y | Y | Y | Y | Y |
| 18 Ney | Y | Y | Y | Y | ? |
| **OKLAHOMA** | | | | | |
| 1 Sullivan | Y | Y | Y | Y | Y |
| 2 Boren | Y | Y | Y | Y | Y |
| 3 Lucas | Y | Y | Y | Y | Y |
| 4 Cole | Y | Y | Y | Y | Y |
| 5 Istook | Y | Y | Y | Y | Y |
| **OREGON** | | | | | |
| 1 Wu | Y | Y | Y | Y | Y |
| 2 Walden | Y | Y | Y | Y | Y |
| 3 Blumenauer | Y | Y | ? | ? | ? |
| 4 DeFazio | Y | Y | Y | Y | Y |
| 5 Hooley | Y | Y | Y | Y | Y |
| **PENNSYLVANIA** | | | | | |
| 1 Brady | Y | Y | Y | Y | Y |
| 2 Fattah | Y | Y | Y | Y | Y |
| 3 English | Y | Y | Y | Y | Y |
| 4 Hart | Y | Y | Y | Y | Y |
| 5 Peterson | Y | Y | Y | Y | Y |
| 6 Gerlach | Y | Y | Y | Y | Y |
| 7 Weldon | Y | Y | Y | Y | Y |
| 8 Fitzpatrick | Y | Y | Y | Y | Y |
| 9 Shuster | Y | Y | Y | Y | Y |
| 10 Sherwood | Y | Y | Y | Y | Y |
| 11 Kanjorski | Y | Y | Y | Y | Y |
| 12 Murtha | Y | Y | Y | Y | Y |
| 13 Schwartz | Y | Y | Y | Y | Y |
| 14 Doyle | Y | Y | Y | Y | Y |
| 15 Dent | Y | Y | Y | Y | Y |
| 16 Pitts | Y | Y | Y | Y | Y |
| 17 Holden | Y | Y | Y | Y | Y |
| 18 Murphy | Y | Y | Y | Y | Y |
| 19 Platts | Y | Y | Y | Y | Y |
| **RHODE ISLAND** | | | | | |
| 1 Kennedy | Y | Y | Y | Y | Y |
| 2 Langevin | Y | Y | Y | Y | Y |
| **SOUTH CAROLINA** | | | | | |
| 1 Brown | Y | Y | Y | Y | Y |
| 2 Wilson | Y | Y | Y | Y | Y |
| 3 Barrett | Y | Y | Y | Y | Y |
| 4 Inglis | N | Y | Y | Y | Y |
| 5 Spratt | Y | Y | Y | Y | Y |
| 6 Clyburn | Y | Y | Y | Y | Y |
| **SOUTH DAKOTA** | | | | | |
| AL Herseth | Y | Y | Y | Y | Y |
| **TENNESSEE** | | | | | |
| 1 Jenkins | Y | Y | Y | Y | Y |
| 2 Duncan | Y | Y | Y | Y | Y |

| | 460 | 461 | 462 | 463 | 464 |
|---|---|---|---|---|---|
| 3 Wamp | Y | Y | Y | Y | Y |
| 4 Davis | Y | Y | Y | Y | Y |
| 5 Cooper | Y | Y | Y | Y | Y |
| 6 Gordon | Y | Y | Y | Y | ? |
| 7 Blackburn | Y | Y | Y | Y | Y |
| 8 Tanner | Y | Y | Y | Y | Y |
| 9 Ford | Y | Y | Y | Y | Y |
| **TEXAS** | | | | | |
| 1 Gohmert | Y | Y | Y | Y | Y |
| 2 Poe | Y | Y | Y | Y | Y |
| 3 Johnson, S. | Y | Y | Y | Y | Y |
| 4 Hall | Y | Y | Y | Y | Y |
| 5 Hensarling | Y | Y | Y | Y | Y |
| 6 Barton | N | Y | Y | ? | ? |
| 7 Culberson | Y | Y | Y | Y | Y |
| 8 Brady | ? | ? | ? | ? | ? |
| 9 Green, A. | Y | Y | Y | Y | Y |
| 10 McCaul | Y | Y | Y | Y | Y |
| 11 Conaway | ? | ? | ? | ? | ? |
| 12 Granger | Y | Y | Y | Y | Y |
| 13 Thornberry | Y | Y | Y | Y | Y |
| 14 Paul | N | Y | Y | Y | Y |
| 15 Hinojosa | Y | Y | Y | Y | Y |
| 16 Reyes | Y | Y | Y | Y | Y |
| 17 Edwards | Y | Y | Y | Y | Y |
| 18 Jackson-Lee | Y | Y | Y | Y | Y |
| 19 Neugebauer | Y | Y | Y | Y | Y |
| 20 Gonzalez | Y | Y | Y | Y | Y |
| 21 Smith | Y | Y | Y | Y | Y |
| 22 DeLay | Y | Y | Y | Y | Y |
| 23 Bonilla | Y | Y | Y | Y | Y |
| 24 Marchant | Y | Y | Y | Y | Y |
| 25 Doggett | Y | Y | Y | Y | Y |
| 26 Burgess | Y | Y | Y | Y | Y |
| 27 Ortiz | Y | Y | Y | Y | Y |
| 28 Cuellar | Y | Y | Y | Y | Y |
| 29 Green, G. | Y | Y | Y | Y | Y |
| 30 Johnson, E. | Y | Y | Y | + | Y |
| 31 Carter | Y | Y | Y | Y | Y |
| 32 Sessions | Y | Y | Y | Y | Y |
| **UTAH** | | | | | |
| 1 Bishop | Y | Y | Y | Y | Y |
| 2 Matheson | Y | Y | Y | Y | Y |
| 3 Cannon | Y | Y | Y | Y | Y |
| **VERMONT** | | | | | |
| AL *Sanders* | Y | Y | Y | Y | Y |
| **VIRGINIA** | | | | | |
| 1 Davis, J. | Y | Y | Y | Y | Y |
| 2 Drake | Y | Y | Y | Y | Y |
| 3 Scott | Y | Y | Y | Y | Y |
| 4 Forbes | Y | Y | Y | Y | Y |
| 5 Goode | Y | Y | Y | Y | Y |
| 6 Goodlatte | Y | Y | Y | Y | Y |
| 7 Cantor | Y | Y | Y | Y | Y |
| 8 Moran | Y | Y | Y | Y | Y |
| 9 Boucher | Y | Y | Y | Y | Y |
| 10 Wolf | Y | Y | Y | Y | Y |
| 11 Davis, T. | Y | Y | Y | Y | Y |
| **WASHINGTON** | | | | | |
| 1 Inslee | Y | Y | Y | Y | Y |
| 2 Larsen | Y | Y | Y | Y | Y |
| 3 Baird | Y | Y | Y | Y | Y |
| 4 Hastings | Y | Y | Y | Y | Y |
| 5 McMorris | Y | Y | Y | Y | Y |
| 6 Dicks | Y | Y | Y | Y | Y |
| 7 McDermott | Y | Y | Y | Y | N |
| 8 Reichert | Y | Y | Y | Y | Y |
| 9 Smith | Y | Y | Y | Y | Y |
| **WEST VIRGINIA** | | | | | |
| 1 Mollohan | Y | Y | Y | Y | Y |
| 2 Capito | Y | Y | Y | Y | Y |
| 3 Rahall | Y | Y | Y | Y | Y |
| **WISCONSIN** | | | | | |
| 1 Ryan | Y | Y | Y | Y | Y |
| 2 Baldwin | Y | Y | Y | Y | Y |
| 3 Kind | Y | Y | Y | Y | Y |
| 4 Moore | Y | Y | Y | Y | Y |
| 5 Sensenbrenner | N | Y | Y | Y | Y |
| 6 Petri | Y | Y | Y | Y | Y |
| 7 Obey | Y | Y | Y | Y | Y |
| 8 Green | Y | Y | Y | Y | Y |
| **WYOMING** | | | | | |
| AL Cubin | Y | Y | Y | Y | Y |

# IN THE HOUSE | By Vote Number

**465.** **S Con Res 26. United Airlines Flight 93 Memorial/Adoption.** Shuster, R-Pa., motion to suspend the rules and adopt the concurrent resolution that would establish a panel of congressional leaders to select a Capitol memorial honoring the passengers and crew of Flight 93, which crashed in Pennsylvania on Sept. 11, 2001. Motion agreed to 403-0: R 219-0; D 183-0 (ND 135-0, SD 48-0); I 1-0. A two-thirds majority of those present and voting (269 in this case) is required for adoption under suspension of the rules. Sept. 13, 2005.

**466.** **HR 3649. Sportfishing and Recreational Boating Safety/Passage.** Shuster, R-Pa., motion to suspend the rules and pass the bill that would continue funding through fiscal 2005 for various sportfishing and recreational boating programs. Motion agreed to 401-1: R 217-1; D 183-0 (ND 135-0, SD 48-0); I 1-0. A two-thirds majority of those present and voting (268 in this case) is required for passage under suspension of the rules. Sept. 13, 2005.

**467.** **S 276. Wind Cave National Park Boundary Revision/Passage.** Fortuño, R-P.R., motion to suspend the rules and pass the bill that would authorize the Interior Department to acquire 5,675 acres of land to expand the Wind Cave National Park in South Dakota. Motion agreed to 295-106: R 111-106; D 183-0 (ND 135-0, SD 48-0); I 1-0. A two-thirds majority of those present and voting (268 in this case) is required for passage under suspension of the rules. Sept. 13, 2005.

**468.** **HR 3132. Sex Offender Registration/Mandatory Minimum Sentences.** Inglis, R-S.C., amendment that would eliminate the mandatory minimum sentences of five years in prison for failing to register as a sex offender or for making false statements during registration. Rejected 106-316: R 7-217; D 98-99 (ND 81-67, SD 17-32); I 1-0. Sept. 14, 2005.

**469.** **HR 3132. Sex Offender Registration/Hate Crimes.** Conyers, D-Mich., amendment that would broaden the categories covered by hate crimes to include crimes motivated by the victim's gender, sexual orientation or disability. The amendment would require the Justice Department to certify that bias was a motivating factor in the crime and that the state does not object to the federal government assuming jurisdiction. It also would authorize $5 million per year for fiscal 2006 and 2007 for the Justice Department to assist states and local authorities in investigating and prosecuting hate crimes. Adopted 223-199: R 30-194; D 192-5 (ND 148-0, SD 44-5); I 1-0. Sept. 14, 2005.

**470.** **HR 3132. Sex Offender Registration/Passage.** Passage of the bill that would create a national sex offender registry database and require individuals convicted of a sex crime to register before completing a prison term or within five days of being sentenced if they are not sentenced to prison. Convicted sex offenders who fail to register would face fines and five to 20 years in prison. The penalty for sexual exploitation of children would increase to 25 years to life in prison. State foster care programs would be required to check child abuse and neglect registries in all areas where prospective foster care families have lived within the past five years. Passed 371-52: R 195-29; D 175-23 (ND 130-19, SD 45-4); I 1-0. Sept. 14, 2005.

| | 465 | 466 | 467 | 468 | 469 | 470 |
|---|---|---|---|---|---|---|
| **ALABAMA** | | | | | | |
| 1 Bonner | Y | Y | N | N | N | Y |
| 2 Everett | Y | Y | N | N | N | Y |
| 3 Rogers | Y | Y | Y | N | N | Y |
| 4 Aderholt | Y | Y | Y | N | N | Y |
| 5 Cramer | Y | Y | Y | N | Y | Y |
| 6 Bachus | Y | Y | Y | N | N | Y |
| 7 Davis | Y | Y | N | N | Y | Y |
| **ALASKA** | | | | | | |
| AL Young | Y | Y | N | N | N | Y |
| **ARIZONA** | | | | | | |
| 1 Renzi | Y | Y | Y | N | N | Y |
| 2 Franks | Y | Y | N | N | N | Y |
| 3 Shadegg | Y | Y | N | N | N | N |
| 4 Pastor | Y | Y | Y | Y | Y | Y |
| 5 Hayworth | Y | Y | N | N | N | Y |
| 6 Flake | Y | N | N | N | N | N |
| 7 Grijalva | Y | Y | Y | Y | Y | Y |
| 8 Kolbe | Y | Y | Y | N | Y | Y |
| **ARKANSAS** | | | | | | |
| 1 Berry | Y | Y | Y | N | N | Y |
| 2 Snyder | Y | Y | Y | Y | Y | Y |
| 3 Boozman | Y | Y | N | N | N | Y |
| 4 Ross | Y | Y | Y | N | Y | Y |
| **CALIFORNIA** | | | | | | |
| 1 Thompson | Y | Y | Y | N | Y | Y |
| 2 Herger | Y | Y | N | N | N | Y |
| 3 Lungren | Y | Y | Y | N | Y | Y |
| 4 Doolittle | Y | Y | N | N | N | Y |
| 5 Matsui, D. | Y | Y | Y | Y | Y | Y |
| 6 Woolsey | Y | Y | Y | Y | Y | N |
| 7 Miller, George | Y | Y | Y | Y | Y | Y |
| 8 Pelosi | Y | Y | Y | Y | Y | Y |
| 9 Lee | Y | Y | Y | Y | Y | N |
| 10 Tauscher | Y | Y | Y | N | Y | Y |
| 11 Pombo | Y | Y | N | N | N | Y |
| 12 Lantos | Y | Y | Y | Y | Y | Y |
| 13 Stark | Y | Y | Y | Y | Y | N |
| 14 Eshoo | Y | Y | Y | N | Y | Y |
| 15 Honda | Y | Y | Y | Y | Y | Y |
| 16 Lofgren | Y | Y | Y | Y | Y | Y |
| 17 Farr | Y | Y | Y | Y | Y | Y |
| 18 Cardoza | Y | Y | Y | N | Y | Y |
| 19 Radanovich | Y | Y | ? | N | N | Y |
| 20 Costa | Y | Y | Y | N | Y | Y |
| 21 Nunes | Y | Y | N | N | N | Y |
| 22 Thomas | Y | Y | Y | N | N | Y |
| 23 Capps | Y | Y | Y | N | Y | Y |
| 24 Gallegly | + | + | + | N | N | Y |
| 25 McKeon | Y | Y | Y | N | N | Y |
| 26 Dreier | Y | Y | N | N | N | Y |
| 27 Sherman | Y | Y | Y | Y | Y | Y |
| 28 Berman | Y | Y | Y | Y | Y | Y |
| 29 Schiff | Y | Y | Y | N | Y | Y |
| 30 Waxman | Y | Y | Y | Y | Y | N |
| 31 Becerra | Y | Y | Y | Y | Y | Y |
| 32 Solis | Y | Y | Y | Y | Y | Y |
| 33 Watson | Y | Y | Y | Y | Y | N |
| 34 Roybal-Allard | Y | Y | Y | Y | Y | Y |
| 35 Waters | Y | Y | Y | Y | Y | Y |
| 36 Harman | Y | Y | Y | ? | ? | Y |
| 37 Millender-McD. | Y | Y | Y | Y | Y | Y |
| 38 Napolitano | Y | Y | Y | Y | Y | Y |
| 39 Sánchez, Linda | Y | Y | Y | Y | Y | Y |
| 40 Royce | Y | Y | N | ? | ? | ? |
| 41 Lewis | Y | Y | Y | N | N | Y |
| 42 Miller, Gary | Y | Y | N | N | N | Y |
| 43 Baca | Y | Y | Y | N | Y | Y |
| 44 Calvert | Y | Y | Y | N | N | Y |
| 45 Bono | Y | Y | Y | N | Y | Y |
| 46 Rohrabacher | Y | Y | N | N | N | Y |
| 47 Sanchez, Loretta | Y | Y | Y | N | Y | Y |
| 48 Vacant | | | | | | |
| 49 Issa | Y | Y | N | N | N | Y |

| | 465 | 466 | 467 | 468 | 469 | 470 |
|---|---|---|---|---|---|---|
| 50 Cunningham | Y | Y | Y | N | N | Y |
| 51 Filner | Y | Y | Y | Y | Y | Y |
| 52 Hunter | Y | Y | Y | N | N | Y |
| 53 Davis | Y | Y | Y | N | Y | Y |
| **COLORADO** | | | | | | |
| 1 DeGette | Y | Y | Y | Y | Y | Y |
| 2 Udall | Y | Y | Y | N | Y | Y |
| 3 Salazar | Y | Y | Y | N | Y | Y |
| 4 Musgrave | Y | Y | N | N | N | Y |
| 5 Hefley | Y | Y | Y | N | N | N |
| 6 Tancredo | Y | Y | N | N | N | N |
| 7 Beauprez | ? | ? | ? | ? | ? | ? |
| **CONNECTICUT** | | | | | | |
| 1 Larson | Y | Y | Y | N | Y | Y |
| 2 Simmons | Y | Y | Y | N | Y | Y |
| 3 DeLauro | Y | Y | Y | N | Y | Y |
| 4 Shays | Y | Y | Y | N | Y | Y |
| 5 Johnson | Y | Y | Y | N | Y | Y |
| **DELAWARE** | | | | | | |
| AL Castle | Y | Y | Y | N | Y | Y |
| **FLORIDA** | | | | | | |
| 1 Miller | Y | Y | N | N | N | N |
| 2 Boyd | Y | Y | Y | N | Y | Y |
| 3 Brown | Y | Y | Y | Y | Y | Y |
| 4 Crenshaw | Y | Y | N | N | N | Y |
| 5 Brown-Waite | Y | Y | N | N | N | Y |
| 6 Stearns | Y | Y | N | N | N | Y |
| 7 Mica | Y | Y | N | N | N | Y |
| 8 Keller | Y | Y | N | N | N | Y |
| 9 Bilirakis | Y | Y | Y | N | N | Y |
| 10 Young | Y | Y | N | N | N | Y |
| 11 Davis | Y | Y | N | N | Y | Y |
| 12 Putnam | Y | Y | N | N | N | Y |
| 13 Harris | Y | Y | N | N | N | Y |
| 14 Mack | Y | Y | N | N | N | Y |
| 15 Weldon | Y | Y | N | N | N | N |
| 16 Foley | Y | Y | Y | N | Y | Y |
| 17 Meek | Y | Y | Y | N | Y | Y |
| 18 Ros-Lehtinen | Y | Y | Y | N | Y | Y |
| 19 Wexler | Y | Y | Y | N | Y | Y |
| 20 Wasserman-Schultz | Y | Y | Y | Y | Y | Y |
| 21 Diaz-Balart, L. | Y | Y | Y | N | Y | Y |
| 22 Shaw | Y | Y | Y | N | N | Y |
| 23 Hastings | Y | Y | Y | Y | Y | Y |
| 24 Feeney | Y | Y | N | N | N | Y |
| 25 Diaz-Balart, M. | Y | Y | N | N | N | Y |
| **GEORGIA** | | | | | | |
| 1 Kingston | Y | Y | N | N | N | N |
| 2 Bishop | Y | Y | Y | Y | Y | Y |
| 3 Marshall | Y | Y | N | Y | Y | Y |
| 4 McKinney | Y | Y | Y | Y | Y | N |
| 5 Lewis | Y | Y | Y | Y | Y | N |
| 6 Price | Y | Y | N | N | N | N |
| 7 Linder | Y | Y | N | N | N | N |
| 8 Westmoreland | Y | Y | N | N | N | N |
| 9 Norwood | Y | Y | N | N | N | N |
| 10 Deal | Y | Y | N | N | N | N |
| 11 Gingrey | Y | Y | N | N | N | N |
| 12 Barrow | Y | Y | Y | N | Y | Y |
| 13 Scott | Y | Y | Y | N | Y | Y |
| **HAWAII** | | | | | | |
| 1 Abercrombie | Y | Y | Y | Y | Y | Y |
| 2 Case | Y | Y | Y | N | Y | Y |
| **IDAHO** | | | | | | |
| 1 Otter | Y | Y | Y | N | N | Y |
| 2 Simpson | Y | Y | Y | N | N | Y |
| **ILLINOIS** | | | | | | |
| 1 Rush | Y | Y | Y | Y | Y | Y |
| 2 Jackson | Y | Y | Y | Y | Y | Y |
| 3 Lipinski | Y | Y | Y | N | Y | Y |
| 4 Gutierrez | Y | Y | Y | N | Y | Y |
| 5 Emanuel | Y | Y | Y | N | Y | Y |
| 6 Hyde | Y | Y | Y | N | N | Y |
| 7 Davis | Y | Y | Y | Y | Y | Y |
| 8 Bean | Y | Y | Y | N | Y | Y |
| 9 Schakowsky | Y | Y | Y | Y | Y | N |
| 10 Kirk | Y | ? | Y | N | Y | Y |
| 11 Weller | Y | Y | Y | N | Y | Y |
| 12 Costello | Y | Y | Y | N | Y | Y |

| KEY | Republicans | Democrats | Independents |
|---|---|---|---|

| Y | Voted for (yea) | X | Paired against | C | Voted "present" to avoid possible conflict of interest |
|---|---|---|---|---|---|
| # | Paired for | – | Announced against | | |
| + | Announced for | P | Voted "present" | ? | Did not vote or otherwise make a position known |
| N | Voted against (nay) | | | | |

| | 465 | 466 | 467 | 468 | 469 | 470 |
|---|---|---|---|---|---|---|
| 13 **Biggert** | Y | Y | Y | N | Y | Y |
| 14 **Hastert** | | | | | | |
| 15 **Johnson** | Y | Y | Y | N | N | Y |
| 16 **Manzullo** | Y | Y | Y | N | N | Y |
| 17 Evans | Y | Y | Y | Y | Y | Y |
| 18 **LaHood** | Y | Y | N | N | Y | Y |
| 19 **Shimkus** | Y | Y | Y | N | Y | Y |
| **INDIANA** | | | | | | |
| 1 Visclosky | Y | Y | Y | N | Y | Y |
| 2 **Chocola** | Y | Y | N | N | N | Y |
| 3 **Souder** | Y | Y | Y | N | N | N |
| 4 **Buyer** | Y | Y | Y | N | N | N |
| 5 **Burton** | Y | Y | N | N | N | Y |
| 6 **Pence** | Y | Y | N | N | N | Y |
| 7 Carson | Y | Y | Y | Y | Y | Y |
| 8 **Hostettler** | Y | Y | N | N | N | Y |
| 9 **Sodrel** | Y | Y | N | N | N | Y |
| **IOWA** | | | | | | |
| 1 **Nussle** | ? | ? | ? | N | N | Y |
| 2 **Leach** | Y | Y | Y | N | Y | Y |
| 3 Boswell | Y | Y | Y | N | Y | Y |
| 4 **Latham** | Y | Y | Y | N | N | Y |
| 5 **King** | Y | Y | N | N | N | Y |
| **KANSAS** | | | | | | |
| 1 **Moran** | Y | Y | N | N | N | N |
| 2 **Ryun** | Y | Y | N | N | N | N |
| 3 Moore | Y | Y | Y | N | Y | Y |
| 4 **Tiahrt** | Y | Y | N | N | N | Y |
| **KENTUCKY** | | | | | | |
| 1 **Whitfield** | Y | Y | Y | N | N | Y |
| 2 **Lewis** | Y | Y | N | N | N | Y |
| 3 **Northup** | Y | Y | Y | N | N | Y |
| 4 **Davis** | Y | Y | Y | N | N | Y |
| 5 **Rogers** | Y | Y | Y | N | N | Y |
| 6 Chandler | Y | Y | Y | N | Y | Y |
| **LOUISIANA** | | | | | | |
| 1 **Jindal** | ? | ? | ? | N | N | Y |
| 2 Jefferson | Y | Y | Y | Y | Y | Y |
| 3 Melancon | ? | ? | ? | ? | ? | ? |
| 4 **McCrery** | Y | Y | Y | N | N | Y |
| 5 **Alexander** | Y | Y | Y | N | N | Y |
| 6 **Baker** | Y | Y | N | N | N | Y |
| 7 **Boustany** | Y | Y | Y | N | N | Y |
| **MAINE** | | | | | | |
| 1 Allen | Y | Y | Y | N | Y | Y |
| 2 Michaud | Y | Y | Y | N | Y | Y |
| **MARYLAND** | | | | | | |
| 1 **Gilchrest** | ? | ? | ? | ? | ? | + |
| 2 Ruppersberger | Y | Y | Y | N | Y | Y |
| 3 Cardin | Y | Y | Y | N | Y | Y |
| 4 Wynn | Y | Y | Y | Y | Y | Y |
| 5 Hoyer | Y | Y | Y | Y | Y | Y |
| 6 **Bartlett** | Y | Y | N | N | N | Y |
| 7 Cummings | Y | Y | Y | Y | Y | Y |
| 8 Van Hollen | Y | Y | Y | N | Y | Y |
| **MASSACHUSETTS** | | | | | | |
| 1 Olver | Y | Y | Y | Y | Y | Y |
| 2 Neal | Y | Y | Y | Y | Y | Y |
| 3 McGovern | Y | Y | Y | Y | Y | Y |
| 4 Frank | Y | Y | Y | Y | Y | Y |
| 5 Meehan | Y | Y | Y | Y | Y | Y |
| 6 Tierney | Y | Y | Y | Y | Y | Y |
| 7 Markey | Y | Y | Y | Y | Y | Y |
| 8 Capuano | Y | Y | Y | Y | Y | Y |
| 9 Lynch | Y | Y | Y | N | Y | Y |
| 10 Delahunt | Y | Y | Y | Y | Y | Y |
| **MICHIGAN** | | | | | | |
| 1 Stupak | Y | Y | Y | Y | Y | Y |
| 2 **Hoekstra** | ? | ? | ? | ? | ? | Y |
| 3 **Ehlers** | Y | Y | Y | Y | N | Y |
| 4 **Camp** | Y | ? | ? | N | N | ? |
| 5 Kildee | Y | Y | Y | Y | Y | Y |
| 6 **Upton** | Y | Y | Y | N | N | Y |
| 7 **Schwarz** | Y | Y | Y | Y | Y | Y |
| 8 **Rogers** | Y | Y | Y | N | N | Y |
| 9 **Knollenberg** | Y | Y | Y | N | N | Y |
| 10 **Miller** | Y | Y | N | N | N | Y |
| 11 **McCotter** | Y | Y | N | N | Y | Y |
| 12 Levin | Y | Y | Y | Y | Y | Y |
| 13 Kilpatrick | Y | Y | Y | Y | Y | Y |
| 14 Conyers | Y | Y | Y | Y | Y | Y |
| 15 Dingell | ? | ? | ? | Y | Y | Y |

| | 465 | 466 | 467 | 468 | 469 | 470 |
|---|---|---|---|---|---|---|
| **MINNESOTA** | | | | | | |
| 1 **Gutknecht** | Y | Y | N | N | N | Y |
| 2 **Kline** | Y | Y | N | N | N | Y |
| 3 **Ramstad** | Y | Y | Y | N | N | Y |
| 4 McCollum | Y | Y | Y | N | Y | Y |
| 5 Sabo | Y | Y | Y | Y | Y | N |
| 6 **Kennedy** | Y | Y | Y | N | N | Y |
| 7 Peterson | Y | Y | Y | N | Y | Y |
| 8 Oberstar | Y | Y | Y | Y | Y | N |
| **MISSISSIPPI** | | | | | | |
| 1 **Wicker** | Y | Y | N | N | N | Y |
| 2 Thompson | Y | Y | Y | N | Y | Y |
| 3 **Pickering** | Y | Y | Y | N | N | Y |
| 4 Taylor | Y | Y | Y | N | N | Y |
| **MISSOURI** | | | | | | |
| 1 Clay | Y | Y | Y | Y | Y | Y |
| 2 **Akin** | Y | Y | N | N | N | N |
| 3 Carnahan | Y | Y | Y | N | Y | Y |
| 4 Skelton | Y | Y | Y | N | Y | Y |
| 5 Cleaver | Y | Y | Y | Y | Y | Y |
| 6 **Graves** | Y | Y | Y | N | N | Y |
| 7 **Blunt** | Y | Y | N | N | N | N |
| 8 **Emerson** | Y | Y | Y | N | N | Y |
| 9 **Hulshof** | Y | Y | Y | N | N | Y |
| **MONTANA** | | | | | | |
| AL **Rehberg** | Y | Y | N | N | N | Y |
| **NEBRASKA** | | | | | | |
| 1 **Fortenberry** | + | + | + | N | N | Y |
| 2 **Terry** | Y | Y | N | N | N | Y |
| 3 **Osborne** | Y | Y | Y | N | N | Y |
| **NEVADA** | | | | | | |
| 1 Berkley | Y | Y | Y | N | Y | Y |
| 2 **Gibbons** | Y | Y | N | N | N | Y |
| 3 **Porter** | Y | Y | Y | N | N | Y |
| **NEW HAMPSHIRE** | | | | | | |
| 1 **Bradley** | Y | Y | Y | N | N | Y |
| 2 **Bass** | Y | Y | Y | N | Y | Y |
| **NEW JERSEY** | | | | | | |
| 1 Andrews | Y | Y | Y | N | Y | Y |
| 2 **LoBiondo** | Y | Y | Y | N | Y | Y |
| 3 **Saxton** | Y | Y | Y | N | Y | Y |
| 4 **Smith** | Y | Y | Y | N | N | Y |
| 5 **Garrett** | Y | Y | N | N | N | Y |
| 6 Pallone | Y | Y | Y | N | Y | Y |
| 7 **Ferguson** | Y | Y | Y | N | N | Y |
| 8 Pascrell | Y | Y | Y | N | Y | Y |
| 9 Rothman | Y | Y | Y | N | Y | Y |
| 10 Payne | Y | Y | Y | ? | ? | ? |
| 11 **Frelinghuysen** | Y | Y | Y | N | N | Y |
| 12 Holt | Y | Y | Y | Y | Y | N |
| 13 Menendez | Y | Y | Y | N | Y | Y |
| **NEW MEXICO** | | | | | | |
| 1 **Wilson** | Y | Y | Y | N | N | Y |
| 2 **Pearce** | Y | Y | N | N | N | Y |
| 3 Udall | Y | Y | Y | Y | Y | Y |
| **NEW YORK** | | | | | | |
| 1 Bishop | Y | Y | Y | N | Y | Y |
| 2 Israel | Y | Y | Y | N | Y | Y |
| 3 **King** | Y | Y | Y | N | N | Y |
| 4 McCarthy | Y | Y | Y | N | Y | Y |
| 5 Ackerman | Y | Y | Y | Y | Y | Y |
| 6 Meeks | ? | ? | ? | Y | Y | Y |
| 7 Crowley | Y | Y | Y | Y | Y | Y |
| 8 Nadler | ? | ? | ? | Y | Y | Y |
| 9 Weiner | ? | ? | ? | ? | ? | ? |
| 10 Towns | ? | ? | ? | Y | Y | Y |
| 11 Owens | + | + | + | Y | Y | Y |
| 12 Velázquez | ? | ? | ? | Y | Y | N |
| 13 **Fossella** | ? | ? | ? | N | N | Y |
| 14 Maloney | + | + | + | Y | Y | Y |
| 15 Rangel | Y | Y | Y | Y | Y | Y |
| 16 Serrano | ? | ? | ? | Y | Y | Y |
| 17 Engel | ? | ? | ? | Y | Y | Y |
| 18 Lowey | Y | Y | Y | N | Y | Y |
| 19 **Kelly** | Y | Y | Y | N | Y | Y |
| 20 **Sweeney** | Y | Y | N | N | N | Y |
| 21 McNulty | ? | ? | ? | N | Y | Y |
| 22 Hinchey | Y | Y | Y | Y | Y | N |
| 23 **McHugh** | ? | ? | ? | N | N | Y |
| 24 **Boehlert** | Y | Y | Y | N | Y | Y |
| 25 **Walsh** | ? | ? | ? | ? | ? | ? |
| 26 **Reynolds** | Y | Y | N | N | N | Y |
| 27 Higgins | Y | Y | Y | N | Y | Y |
| 28 Slaughter | Y | Y | Y | N | Y | Y |
| 29 **Kuhl** | Y | Y | Y | N | N | Y |

| | 465 | 466 | 467 | 468 | 469 | 470 |
|---|---|---|---|---|---|---|
| **NORTH CAROLINA** | | | | | | |
| 1 Butterfield | Y | Y | Y | Y | Y | Y |
| 2 Etheridge | Y | Y | Y | N | Y | Y |
| 3 **Jones** | Y | Y | N | N | N | N |
| 4 Price | Y | Y | Y | Y | Y | Y |
| 5 **Foxx** | Y | Y | N | N | N | Y |
| 6 **Coble** | Y | Y | N | N | N | Y |
| 7 McIntyre | Y | Y | Y | N | Y | Y |
| 8 **Hayes** | Y | Y | Y | N | N | Y |
| 9 **Myrick** | Y | Y | N | N | N | Y |
| 10 **McHenry** | Y | Y | N | N | N | Y |
| 11 **Taylor** | Y | Y | N | N | N | Y |
| 12 Watt | Y | Y | Y | Y | Y | N |
| 13 Miller | Y | Y | Y | N | Y | Y |
| **NORTH DAKOTA** | | | | | | |
| AL Pomeroy | Y | Y | Y | N | Y | Y |
| **OHIO** | | | | | | |
| 1 **Chabot** | Y | Y | N | N | N | Y |
| 2 **Schmidt** | Y | Y | N | N | N | Y |
| 3 **Turner** | Y | Y | Y | N | N | Y |
| 4 **Oxley** | Y | Y | N | N | N | Y |
| 5 **Gillmor** | Y | Y | Y | N | N | Y |
| 6 Strickland | ? | ? | ? | N | Y | Y |
| 7 **Hobson** | Y | Y | Y | N | N | Y |
| 8 **Boehner** | Y | Y | Y | N | N | Y |
| 9 Kaptur | Y | Y | Y | Y | Y | Y |
| 10 Kucinich | Y | Y | Y | Y | Y | N |
| 11 Jones | ? | ? | ? | Y | Y | N |
| 12 **Tiberi** | Y | Y | Y | N | N | Y |
| 13 Brown | Y | Y | Y | Y | Y | Y |
| 14 **LaTourette** | Y | Y | N | Y | N | Y |
| 15 **Pryce** | Y | Y | Y | N | N | Y |
| 16 **Regula** | Y | Y | Y | N | N | Y |
| 17 Ryan | Y | Y | Y | N | Y | Y |
| 18 **Ney** | Y | Y | N | N | N | Y |
| **OKLAHOMA** | | | | | | |
| 1 **Sullivan** | Y | Y | N | N | N | Y |
| 2 Boren | Y | Y | Y | N | N | Y |
| 3 **Lucas** | Y | Y | Y | N | N | Y |
| 4 **Cole** | Y | Y | Y | N | N | Y |
| 5 **Istook** | Y | Y | N | N | N | Y |
| **OREGON** | | | | | | |
| 1 Wu | Y | Y | Y | N | Y | Y |
| 2 **Walden** | Y | Y | Y | N | Y | Y |
| 3 Blumenauer | Y | Y | Y | N | Y | Y |
| 4 DeFazio | ? | ? | ? | N | Y | Y |
| 5 Hooley | ? | ? | ? | N | Y | Y |
| **PENNSYLVANIA** | | | | | | |
| 1 Brady | Y | Y | Y | N | Y | Y |
| 2 Fattah | ? | ? | ? | N | Y | Y |
| 3 **English** | Y | Y | Y | N | N | Y |
| 4 **Hart** | Y | Y | ? | N | N | Y |
| 5 **Peterson** | Y | Y | N | N | N | Y |
| 6 **Gerlach** | Y | Y | Y | N | Y | Y |
| 7 **Weldon** | Y | Y | Y | N | Y | Y |
| 8 **Fitzpatrick** | Y | Y | Y | N | Y | Y |
| 9 **Shuster** | Y | Y | Y | N | N | Y |
| 10 **Sherwood** | Y | Y | N | N | N | Y |
| 11 Kanjorski | Y | Y | Y | N | Y | Y |
| 12 Murtha | Y | Y | Y | N | Y | Y |
| 13 Schwartz | Y | Y | Y | N | Y | Y |
| 14 Doyle | Y | Y | Y | N | Y | Y |
| 15 **Dent** | Y | Y | Y | N | Y | Y |
| 16 **Pitts** | Y | Y | Y | N | N | Y |
| 17 Holden | Y | Y | Y | N | Y | Y |
| 18 **Murphy** | Y | Y | Y | N | N | Y |
| 19 **Platts** | Y | Y | Y | N | Y | Y |
| **RHODE ISLAND** | | | | | | |
| 1 Kennedy | Y | Y | Y | N | Y | Y |
| 2 Langevin | Y | Y | Y | N | Y | Y |
| **SOUTH CAROLINA** | | | | | | |
| 1 **Brown** | Y | Y | Y | N | N | Y |
| 2 **Wilson** | Y | Y | N | N | N | Y |
| 3 **Barrett** | Y | Y | N | N | N | N |
| 4 **Inglis** | Y | Y | N | Y | N | Y |
| 5 Spratt | Y | Y | Y | N | Y | Y |
| 6 Clyburn | Y | Y | Y | ? | ? | ? |
| **SOUTH DAKOTA** | | | | | | |
| AL Herseth | Y | Y | Y | N | Y | Y |
| **TENNESSEE** | | | | | | |
| 1 **Jenkins** | Y | Y | Y | N | N | Y |
| 2 **Duncan** | Y | Y | N | N | N | N |

| | 465 | 466 | 467 | 468 | 469 | 470 |
|---|---|---|---|---|---|---|
| 3 **Wamp** | Y | Y | N | N | N | N |
| 4 Davis | Y | Y | Y | N | N | Y |
| 5 Cooper | Y | Y | Y | N | Y | Y |
| 6 Gordon | Y | Y | Y | N | Y | Y |
| 7 **Blackburn** | Y | Y | N | N | N | Y |
| 8 Tanner | Y | Y | Y | N | N | Y |
| 9 Ford | Y | Y | Y | N | Y | Y |
| **TEXAS** | | | | | | |
| 1 **Gohmert** | Y | Y | N | N | N | N |
| 2 **Poe** | Y | Y | N | N | N | Y |
| 3 **Johnson, S.** | Y | Y | N | N | N | N |
| 4 **Hall** | Y | Y | N | N | N | Y |
| 5 **Hensarling** | Y | Y | N | N | N | Y |
| 6 **Barton** | Y | Y | N | ? | ? | ? |
| 7 **Culberson** | Y | Y | Y | N | N | Y |
| 8 **Brady** | Y | Y | Y | N | N | Y |
| 9 Green, A. | Y | Y | Y | Y | Y | Y |
| 10 **McCaul** | Y | Y | N | N | N | Y |
| 11 **Conaway** | Y | Y | N | N | N | N |
| 12 **Granger** | Y | Y | Y | N | N | Y |
| 13 **Thornberry** | Y | Y | N | N | N | N |
| 14 **Paul** | Y | Y | N | Y | N | N |
| 15 Hinojosa | + | + | + | N | Y | Y |
| 16 Reyes | Y | Y | Y | N | Y | Y |
| 17 Edwards | Y | Y | Y | N | Y | Y |
| 18 Jackson-Lee | Y | Y | Y | Y | Y | Y |
| 19 **Neugebauer** | Y | Y | N | N | N | Y |
| 20 Gonzalez | Y | Y | Y | N | Y | Y |
| 21 **Smith** | Y | Y | Y | N | N | Y |
| 22 **DeLay** | Y | Y | Y | N | N | Y |
| 23 **Bonilla** | Y | Y | Y | N | N | N |
| 24 **Marchant** | Y | Y | N | N | N | Y |
| 25 Doggett | Y | Y | Y | N | Y | Y |
| 26 **Burgess** | Y | Y | N | N | N | Y |
| 27 Ortiz | Y | Y | Y | N | Y | Y |
| 28 Cuellar | Y | Y | Y | N | Y | Y |
| 29 Green, G. | Y | Y | Y | N | Y | Y |
| 30 Johnson, E. | Y | Y | Y | Y | Y | Y |
| 31 **Carter** | Y | Y | N | N | N | Y |
| 32 **Sessions** | Y | Y | N | N | N | Y |
| **UTAH** | | | | | | |
| 1 **Bishop** | ? | Y | N | N | N | Y |
| 2 Matheson | Y | Y | Y | N | Y | Y |
| 3 **Cannon** | Y | Y | N | N | N | Y |
| **VERMONT** | | | | | | |
| AL *Sanders* | Y | Y | Y | Y | Y | Y |
| **VIRGINIA** | | | | | | |
| 1 **Davis, J.** | Y | Y | N | N | N | Y |
| 2 **Drake** | Y | Y | N | N | N | Y |
| 3 Scott | Y | Y | Y | Y | Y | N |
| 4 **Forbes** | Y | Y | N | N | N | Y |
| 5 **Goode** | Y | Y | N | N | N | Y |
| 6 **Goodlatte** | Y | Y | Y | N | N | Y |
| 7 **Cantor** | Y | Y | Y | N | N | Y |
| 8 Moran | ? | ? | ? | Y | Y | Y |
| 9 Boucher | Y | Y | Y | Y | Y | Y |
| 10 **Wolf** | Y | Y | Y | N | N | Y |
| 11 **Davis, T.** | Y | Y | Y | N | N | Y |
| **WASHINGTON** | | | | | | |
| 1 Inslee | Y | Y | Y | N | Y | Y |
| 2 Larsen | Y | Y | Y | Y | Y | Y |
| 3 Baird | Y | Y | Y | Y | Y | Y |
| 4 **Hastings** | Y | Y | Y | N | N | Y |
| 5 **McMorris** | Y | Y | N | N | N | Y |
| 6 Dicks | Y | Y | Y | N | Y | Y |
| 7 McDermott | Y | Y | Y | Y | Y | N |
| 8 **Reichert** | Y | Y | Y | N | Y | Y |
| 9 Smith | Y | Y | Y | Y | Y | Y |
| **WEST VIRGINIA** | | | | | | |
| 1 Mollohan | Y | Y | Y | Y | Y | N |
| 2 **Capito** | Y | Y | Y | N | N | Y |
| 3 Rahall | Y | Y | Y | Y | Y | N |
| **WISCONSIN** | | | | | | |
| 1 **Ryan** | Y | Y | N | N | N | Y |
| 2 Baldwin | Y | Y | Y | Y | Y | Y |
| 3 Kind | Y | Y | Y | N | Y | Y |
| 4 Moore | Y | Y | Y | Y | Y | Y |
| 5 **Sensenbrenner** | Y | Y | N | N | N | Y |
| 6 **Petri** | Y | Y | N | N | N | Y |
| 7 Obey | Y | Y | Y | N | Y | Y |
| 8 **Green** | Y | Y | N | N | N | Y |
| **WYOMING** | | | | | | |
| AL **Cubin** | Y | Y | N | N | N | Y |

# IN THE HOUSE | By Vote Number

**471.** **H Res 437. Hurricane Katrina Investigatory Committee/Previous Question.** Dreier, R-Calif., motion to order the previous question (thus ending debate and the possibility of amendment) on adoption of the rule (H Res 439) to provide for House floor consideration of the resolution that would create a bipartisan select committee to investigate the actions of federal, state and local governments before and after Hurricane Katrina. Motion agreed to 222-193: R 222-0; D 0-192 (ND 0-144, SD 0-48); I 0-1. Sept. 15, 2005.

**472.** **H Res 437. Hurricane Katrina Investigatory Committee/Rule.** Adoption of the rule (H Res 439) to provide for House floor consideration of the resolution that would create a bipartisan select committee to investigate the actions of federal, state and local governments before and after Hurricane Katrina. Adopted 221-193: R 221-0; D 0-192 (ND 0-144, SD 0-48); I 0-1. Sept. 15, 2005.

**473.** **HR 889. Coast Guard Reauthorization/Liquefied Natural Gas.** Markey, D-Mass., amendment that would require the Coast Guard to conduct a comprehensive security and safety review of the proposed construction, expansion or operation of a waterfront facility for transferring liquefied natural gas between ships and land. Rejected 163-254: R 7-213; D 155-41 (ND 121-27, SD 34-14); I 1-0. Sept. 15, 2005.

**474.** **HR 889. Coast Guard Reauthorization/Passage.** Passage of the bill that would authorize $8.7 billion in fiscal 2006 for the Coast Guard, including $5.6 billion for operation and maintenance, $1 billion in mandatory spending for retired pay and $1.6 billion for the Deepwater program to replace aging ships and aircraft. It would require a new implementation plan for the program. Passed 415-0: R 220-0; D 194-0 (ND 147-0, SD 47-0); I 1-0. Sept. 15, 2005.

**475.** **H Res 437. Hurricane Katrina Investigatory Committee/Adoption.** Adoption of the resolution that would establish a bipartisan select committee to investigate the government preparation and response to Hurricane Katrina. The Speaker would select 20 members to the committee, including nine Democrats appointed after consultation with the minority leader. The resolution would earmark $500,000 out of existing House accounts for the committee. Adopted 224-188: R 217-1; D 7-186 (ND 2-144, SD 5-42); I 0-1. Sept. 15, 2005.

| | 471 | 472 | 473 | 474 | 475 |
|---|---|---|---|---|---|
| **ALABAMA** | | | | | |
| 1 Bonner | Y | Y | Y | Y | Y |
| 2 Everett | Y | Y | N | Y | Y |
| 3 Rogers | Y | Y | N | Y | Y |
| 4 Aderholt | Y | Y | N | Y | Y |
| 5 Cramer | N | N | Y | Y | N |
| 6 Bachus | Y | Y | N | Y | Y |
| 7 Davis | N | N | Y | Y | N |
| **ALASKA** | | | | | |
| AL Young | Y | Y | N | Y | Y |
| **ARIZONA** | | | | | |
| 1 Renzi | Y | Y | N | Y | Y |
| 2 Franks | Y | Y | N | Y | Y |
| 3 Shadegg | Y | Y | N | Y | Y |
| 4 Pastor | N | N | Y | Y | N |
| 5 Hayworth | Y | Y | N | Y | Y |
| 6 Flake | Y | Y | N | Y | Y |
| 7 Grijalva | N | N | Y | Y | N |
| 8 Kolbe | Y | Y | N | Y | Y |
| **ARKANSAS** | | | | | |
| 1 Berry | N | N | N | Y | N |
| 2 Snyder | N | N | Y | Y | N |
| 3 Boozman | Y | Y | N | Y | Y |
| 4 Ross | N | N | N | Y | N |
| **CALIFORNIA** | | | | | |
| 1 Thompson | N | N | Y | Y | N |
| 2 Herger | Y | Y | N | Y | Y |
| 3 Lungren | Y | Y | N | Y | Y |
| 4 Doolittle | ? | Y | N | Y | Y |
| 5 Matsui, D. | N | N | Y | Y | N |
| 6 Woolsey | ? | ? | Y | Y | N |
| 7 Miller, George | N | N | Y | Y | N |
| 8 Pelosi | N | N | Y | Y | N |
| 9 Lee | N | N | Y | Y | N |
| 10 Tauscher | N | N | Y | Y | N |
| 11 Pombo | Y | Y | N | Y | Y |
| 12 Lantos | N | N | Y | Y | N |
| 13 Stark | N | N | Y | Y | N |
| 14 Eshoo | N | N | Y | Y | N |
| 15 Honda | N | N | Y | Y | N |
| 16 Lofgren | N | N | Y | Y | N |
| 17 Farr | N | N | Y | Y | N |
| 18 Cardoza | N | N | Y | Y | N |
| 19 Radanovich | Y | Y | N | Y | Y |
| 20 Costa | N | N | N | Y | N |
| 21 Nunes | Y | Y | N | Y | Y |
| 22 Thomas | Y | Y | N | Y | Y |
| 23 Capps | N | N | Y | Y | N |
| 24 Gallegly | Y | Y | N | Y | ? |
| 25 McKeon | Y | Y | N | Y | Y |
| 26 Dreier | Y | Y | N | Y | Y |
| 27 Sherman | N | N | Y | Y | N |
| 28 Berman | N | N | Y | ? | ? |
| 29 Schiff | N | N | Y | Y | N |
| 30 Waxman | N | N | Y | Y | N |
| 31 Becerra | N | N | Y | Y | N |
| 32 Solis | ? | N | Y | Y | N |
| 33 Watson | N | N | Y | Y | N |
| 34 Roybal-Allard | N | N | Y | Y | N |
| 35 Waters | N | N | Y | Y | N |
| 36 Harman | N | N | Y | Y | N |
| 37 Millender-McD. | N | N | Y | Y | N |
| 38 Napolitano | N | N | Y | Y | N |
| 39 Sánchez, Linda | N | N | Y | Y | N |
| 40 Royce | Y | Y | Y | Y | Y |
| 41 Lewis | Y | Y | N | Y | Y |
| 42 Miller, Gary | Y | Y | ? | ? | ? |
| 43 Baca | N | N | Y | Y | ? |
| 44 Calvert | Y | Y | ? | ? | ? |
| 45 Bono | Y | Y | N | Y | Y |
| 46 Rohrabacher | Y | Y | N | Y | Y |
| 47 Sanchez, Loretta | N | N | Y | Y | N |
| 48 Vacant | | | | | |
| 49 Issa | Y | Y | N | Y | Y |

| | 471 | 472 | 473 | 474 | 475 |
|---|---|---|---|---|---|
| 50 Cunningham | Y | Y | ? | ? | ? |
| 51 Filner | N | N | Y | Y | N |
| 52 Hunter | Y | Y | N | Y | Y |
| 53 Davis | N | N | Y | Y | N |
| **COLORADO** | | | | | |
| 1 DeGette | N | N | Y | Y | N |
| 2 Udall | N | N | Y | Y | N |
| 3 Salazar | N | N | N | Y | N |
| 4 Musgrave | Y | Y | N | Y | ? |
| 5 Hefley | Y | Y | N | Y | Y |
| 6 Tancredo | Y | ? | N | Y | Y |
| 7 Beauprez | ? | ? | ? | ? | ? |
| **CONNECTICUT** | | | | | |
| 1 Larson | N | N | Y | Y | N |
| 2 Simmons | Y | Y | Y | Y | Y |
| 3 DeLauro | N | N | Y | Y | N |
| 4 Shays | Y | + | Y | Y | Y |
| 5 Johnson | Y | Y | Y | Y | Y |
| **DELAWARE** | | | | | |
| AL Castle | Y | Y | N | Y | Y |
| **FLORIDA** | | | | | |
| 1 Miller | Y | + | N | Y | Y |
| 2 Boyd | N | N | Y | Y | N |
| 3 Brown | N | N | Y | Y | N |
| 4 Crenshaw | Y | Y | N | Y | Y |
| 5 Brown-Waite | Y | Y | N | Y | Y |
| 6 Stearns | Y | Y | N | Y | Y |
| 7 Mica | Y | Y | N | Y | Y |
| 8 Keller | Y | Y | N | Y | Y |
| 9 Bilirakis | Y | Y | N | Y | Y |
| 10 Young | Y | Y | N | Y | Y |
| 11 Davis | N | N | Y | Y | N |
| 12 Putnam | Y | Y | N | Y | Y |
| 13 Harris | Y | Y | N | Y | Y |
| 14 Mack | Y | Y | N | Y | Y |
| 15 Weldon | Y | Y | N | Y | Y |
| 16 Foley | Y | Y | N | Y | Y |
| 17 Meek | N | N | Y | Y | N |
| 18 Ros-Lehtinen | Y | Y | N | Y | Y |
| 19 Wexler | N | N | Y | Y | N |
| 20 Wasserman-Schultz | N | N | N | Y | N |
| 21 Diaz-Balart, L. | Y | Y | N | Y | Y |
| 22 Shaw | Y | Y | N | Y | Y |
| 23 Hastings | N | N | Y | Y | N |
| 24 Feeney | Y | Y | N | Y | Y |
| 25 Diaz-Balart, M. | Y | Y | N | Y | Y |
| **GEORGIA** | | | | | |
| 1 Kingston | Y | Y | N | Y | Y |
| 2 Bishop | N | N | N | Y | N |
| 3 Marshall | N | N | Y | Y | N |
| 4 McKinney | N | N | Y | Y | N |
| 5 Lewis | N | ? | Y | Y | N |
| 6 Price | Y | Y | N | Y | Y |
| 7 Linder | Y | Y | N | Y | Y |
| 8 Westmoreland | Y | Y | N | Y | Y |
| 9 Norwood | Y | Y | N | Y | Y |
| 10 Deal | Y | Y | N | Y | Y |
| 11 Gingrey | Y | Y | N | Y | Y |
| 12 Barrow | N | N | Y | Y | N |
| 13 Scott | N | N | Y | Y | N |
| **HAWAII** | | | | | |
| 1 Abercrombie | N | N | Y | Y | N |
| 2 Case | N | N | Y | Y | N |
| **IDAHO** | | | | | |
| 1 Otter | Y | Y | N | Y | Y |
| 2 Simpson | Y | Y | N | Y | Y |
| **ILLINOIS** | | | | | |
| 1 Rush | N | N | N | Y | N |
| 2 Jackson | N | N | Y | Y | N |
| 3 Lipinski | N | N | Y | Y | N |
| 4 Gutierrez | N | N | Y | Y | N |
| 5 Emanuel | N | N | Y | Y | N |
| 6 Hyde | Y | Y | N | Y | Y |
| 7 Davis | N | N | Y | Y | N |
| 8 Bean | N | N | N | Y | N |
| 9 Schakowsky | N | N | Y | Y | N |
| 10 Kirk | Y | Y | N | Y | Y |
| 11 Weller | Y | Y | N | Y | Y |
| 12 Costello | N | N | N | Y | N |

**KEY**    **Republicans**    Democrats    *Independents*

| | | | |
|---|---|---|---|
| **Y** Voted for (yea) | **X** Paired against | **C** Voted "present" to avoid |
| **#** Paired for | **–** Announced against | possible conflict of interest |
| **+** Announced for | **P** Voted "present" | **?** Did not vote or otherwise |
| **N** Voted against (nay) | | make a position known |

| | 471 | 472 | 473 | 474 | 475 |
|---|---|---|---|---|---|
| 13 Biggert | Y | Y | N | Y | Y |
| 14 Hastert | | | | | |
| 15 Johnson | Y | Y | N | Y | Y |
| 16 Manzullo | Y | Y | N | Y | Y |
| 17 Evans | N | N | Y | Y | N |
| 18 LaHood | Y | Y | N | Y | Y |
| 19 Shimkus | Y | Y | N | Y | Y |
| **INDIANA** | | | | | |
| 1 Visclosky | N | N | Y | Y | N |
| 2 Chocola | Y | Y | N | Y | Y |
| 3 Souder | Y | Y | N | Y | Y |
| 4 Buyer | Y | Y | N | Y | Y |
| 5 Burton | Y | Y | N | Y | Y |
| 6 Pence | Y | Y | N | Y | Y |
| 7 Carson | N | N | Y | Y | N |
| 8 Hostettler | Y | Y | N | Y | Y |
| 9 Sodrel | Y | Y | N | Y | Y |
| **IOWA** | | | | | |
| 1 Nussle | Y | Y | N | Y | Y |
| 2 Leach | Y | Y | N | Y | Y |
| 3 Boswell | N | N | N | Y | N |
| 4 Latham | Y | Y | N | Y | Y |
| 5 King | Y | Y | N | Y | Y |
| **KANSAS** | | | | | |
| 1 Moran | Y | Y | N | Y | Y |
| 2 Ryun | Y | Y | N | Y | Y |
| 3 Moore | N | N | Y | Y | N |
| 4 Tiahrt | Y | Y | N | Y | Y |
| **KENTUCKY** | | | | | |
| 1 Whitfield | Y | Y | N | Y | N |
| 2 Lewis | Y | Y | N | Y | Y |
| 3 Northup | Y | Y | N | Y | Y |
| 4 Davis | Y | Y | N | Y | Y |
| 5 Rogers | Y | Y | N | Y | Y |
| 6 Chandler | N | N | Y | Y | N |
| **LOUISIANA** | | | | | |
| 1 Jindal | ? | ? | N | Y | Y |
| 2 Jefferson | N | N | Y | Y | N |
| 3 Melancon | ? | ? | ? | ? | ? |
| 4 McCrery | Y | Y | N | Y | Y |
| 5 Alexander | Y | Y | N | Y | Y |
| 6 Baker | Y | Y | N | Y | Y |
| 7 Boustany | Y | Y | N | Y | Y |
| **MAINE** | | | | | |
| 1 Allen | N | N | Y | Y | N |
| 2 Michaud | N | N | N | Y | N |
| **MARYLAND** | | | | | |
| 1 Gilchrest | Y | Y | N | Y | Y |
| 2 Ruppersberger | N | N | N | Y | N |
| 3 Cardin | N | N | Y | Y | N |
| 4 Wynn | N | N | N | Y | N |
| 5 Hoyer | N | N | N | Y | N |
| 6 Bartlett | Y | Y | N | Y | Y |
| 7 Cummings | N | N | Y | Y | N |
| 8 Van Hollen | N | N | Y | Y | N |
| **MASSACHUSETTS** | | | | | |
| 1 Olver | N | N | ? | ? | ? |
| 2 Neal | N | N | Y | Y | N |
| 3 McGovern | N | N | Y | Y | N |
| 4 Frank | N | N | Y | Y | N |
| 5 Meehan | N | N | Y | Y | N |
| 6 Tierney | N | N | Y | Y | N |
| 7 Markey | N | N | Y | Y | N |
| 8 Capuano | N | N | Y | Y | N |
| 9 Lynch | N | N | Y | Y | N |
| 10 Delahunt | N | N | Y | Y | N |
| **MICHIGAN** | | | | | |
| 1 Stupak | N | N | Y | Y | N |
| 2 Hoekstra | Y | Y | N | Y | Y |
| 3 Ehlers | Y | Y | N | Y | Y |
| 4 Camp | Y | Y | N | Y | Y |
| 5 Kildee | N | N | Y | Y | N |
| 6 Upton | Y | Y | N | Y | Y |
| 7 Schwarz | ? | ? | Y | N | Y |
| 8 Rogers | ? | ? | ? | ? | ? |
| 9 Knollenberg | Y | Y | N | Y | Y |
| 10 Miller | Y | Y | N | Y | Y |
| 11 McCotter | Y | Y | N | Y | Y |
| 12 Levin | N | N | Y | Y | N |
| 13 Kilpatrick | N | N | Y | Y | N |
| 14 Conyers | N | N | Y | Y | N |
| 15 Dingell | N | N | Y | Y | N |

| | 471 | 472 | 473 | 474 | 475 |
|---|---|---|---|---|---|
| **MINNESOTA** | | | | | |
| 1 Gutknecht | Y | Y | N | Y | Y |
| 2 Kline | Y | Y | N | Y | Y |
| 3 Ramstad | Y | Y | N | Y | Y |
| 4 McCollum | N | N | Y | Y | N |
| 5 Sabo | N | N | Y | Y | N |
| 6 Kennedy | Y | Y | N | Y | Y |
| 7 Peterson | N | N | Y | Y | N |
| 8 Oberstar | N | N | N | Y | N |
| **MISSISSIPPI** | | | | | |
| 1 Wicker | Y | Y | N | Y | Y |
| 2 Thompson | N | N | N | Y | N |
| 3 Pickering | Y | Y | ? | ? | ? |
| 4 Taylor | N | N | Y | Y | Y |
| **MISSOURI** | | | | | |
| 1 Clay | N | N | Y | Y | N |
| 2 Akin | Y | Y | N | Y | Y |
| 3 Carnahan | N | N | Y | Y | N |
| 4 Skelton | N | N | Y | Y | N |
| 5 Cleaver | N | N | Y | Y | N |
| 6 Graves | Y | Y | N | Y | Y |
| 7 Blunt | Y | Y | N | Y | Y |
| 8 Emerson | Y | Y | N | Y | Y |
| 9 Hulshof | Y | Y | N | Y | Y |
| **MONTANA** | | | | | |
| AL Rehberg | Y | Y | N | Y | Y |
| **NEBRASKA** | | | | | |
| 1 Fortenberry | Y | Y | N | Y | Y |
| 2 Terry | Y | Y | N | Y | Y |
| 3 Osborne | Y | Y | N | Y | Y |
| **NEVADA** | | | | | |
| 1 Berkley | N | N | Y | Y | N |
| 2 Gibbons | Y | Y | N | Y | Y |
| 3 Porter | Y | Y | N | Y | Y |
| **NEW HAMPSHIRE** | | | | | |
| 1 Bradley | Y | Y | N | Y | Y |
| 2 Bass | Y | Y | N | Y | Y |
| **NEW JERSEY** | | | | | |
| 1 Andrews | N | N | Y | Y | N |
| 2 LoBiondo | Y | Y | N | Y | Y |
| 3 Saxton | Y | Y | N | Y | Y |
| 4 Smith | Y | Y | N | Y | Y |
| 5 Garrett | Y | Y | N | Y | Y |
| 6 Pallone | N | N | Y | Y | N |
| 7 Ferguson | Y | Y | N | Y | Y |
| 8 Pascrell | N | N | Y | Y | N |
| 9 Rothman | ? | ? | ? | ? | ? |
| 10 Payne | N | N | Y | Y | N |
| 11 Frelinghuysen | Y | Y | N | Y | Y |
| 12 Holt | N | N | Y | Y | N |
| 13 Menendez | N | N | Y | Y | N |
| **NEW MEXICO** | | | | | |
| 1 Wilson | Y | Y | N | Y | Y |
| 2 Pearce | Y | Y | N | Y | Y |
| 3 Udall | N | N | Y | Y | N |
| **NEW YORK** | | | | | |
| 1 Bishop | N | N | Y | Y | N |
| 2 Israel | N | N | Y | Y | N |
| 3 King | Y | Y | N | Y | N |
| 4 McCarthy | N | N | Y | Y | N |
| 5 Ackerman | N | N | Y | Y | N |
| 6 Meeks | N | N | Y | Y | N |
| 7 Crowley | N | N | Y | Y | N |
| 8 Nadler | ? | ? | ? | ? | ? |
| 9 Weiner | ? | ? | Y | Y | N |
| 10 Towns | N | N | Y | Y | N |
| 11 Owens | N | N | Y | Y | N |
| 12 Velázquez | N | N | Y | Y | N |
| 13 Fossella | Y | Y | Y | Y | Y |
| 14 Maloney | N | N | Y | Y | N |
| 15 Rangel | N | N | Y | Y | N |
| 16 Serrano | N | N | Y | Y | N |
| 17 Engel | N | N | Y | Y | N |
| 18 Lowey | N | N | Y | Y | N |
| 19 Kelly | Y | Y | N | Y | Y |
| 20 Sweeney | Y | Y | N | Y | Y |
| 21 McNulty | N | N | Y | Y | N |
| 22 Hinchey | ? | ? | Y | Y | N |
| 23 McHugh | Y | Y | N | Y | Y |
| 24 Boehlert | Y | Y | N | Y | Y |
| 25 Walsh | Y | Y | N | Y | Y |
| 26 Reynolds | Y | Y | N | Y | Y |
| 27 Higgins | N | N | Y | Y | N |
| 28 Slaughter | N | N | Y | Y | N |
| 29 Kuhl | Y | Y | N | Y | Y |

| | 471 | 472 | 473 | 474 | 475 |
|---|---|---|---|---|---|
| **NORTH CAROLINA** | | | | | |
| 1 Butterfield | N | N | Y | Y | N |
| 2 Etheridge | N | N | Y | Y | N |
| 3 Jones | Y | Y | Y | Y | Y |
| 4 Price | N | N | Y | Y | N |
| 5 Foxx | Y | Y | N | Y | Y |
| 6 Coble | Y | Y | N | Y | Y |
| 7 McIntyre | N | N | N | Y | N |
| 8 Hayes | Y | Y | N | Y | Y |
| 9 Myrick | Y | Y | N | Y | Y |
| 10 McHenry | Y | Y | N | Y | Y |
| 11 Taylor | Y | Y | ? | ? | ? |
| 12 Watt | N | N | Y | Y | N |
| 13 Miller | N | N | Y | Y | N |
| **NORTH DAKOTA** | | | | | |
| AL Pomeroy | N | N | N | Y | N |
| **OHIO** | | | | | |
| 1 Chabot | Y | Y | N | Y | Y |
| 2 Schmidt | Y | Y | N | Y | Y |
| 3 Turner | Y | Y | N | Y | Y |
| 4 Oxley | Y | Y | N | Y | Y |
| 5 Gillmor | Y | Y | N | Y | Y |
| 6 Strickland | N | N | Y | Y | N |
| 7 Hobson | Y | Y | N | Y | Y |
| 8 Boehner | Y | Y | N | Y | Y |
| 9 Kaptur | N | N | Y | Y | N |
| 10 Kucinich | N | N | Y | Y | N |
| 11 Jones | ? | ? | Y | Y | N |
| 12 Tiberi | Y | Y | N | Y | Y |
| 13 Brown | N | N | Y | Y | N |
| 14 LaTourette | Y | Y | N | Y | Y |
| 15 Pryce | Y | Y | N | Y | Y |
| 16 Regula | Y | Y | N | Y | Y |
| 17 Ryan | N | N | Y | Y | N |
| 18 Ney | Y | Y | N | Y | Y |
| **OKLAHOMA** | | | | | |
| 1 Sullivan | Y | Y | N | Y | Y |
| 2 Boren | N | N | N | Y | N |
| 3 Lucas | Y | Y | N | Y | Y |
| 4 Cole | Y | Y | N | Y | Y |
| 5 Istook | ? | ? | ? | ? | ? |
| **OREGON** | | | | | |
| 1 Wu | N | N | Y | Y | N |
| 2 Walden | Y | Y | N | Y | Y |
| 3 Blumenauer | N | N | Y | Y | N |
| 4 DeFazio | N | N | Y | Y | N |
| 5 Hooley | N | N | Y | Y | N |
| **PENNSYLVANIA** | | | | | |
| 1 Brady | N | N | Y | Y | N |
| 2 Fattah | N | N | Y | Y | N |
| 3 English | Y | Y | N | Y | Y |
| 4 Hart | Y | Y | N | Y | Y |
| 5 Peterson | Y | Y | N | Y | Y |
| 6 Gerlach | Y | Y | N | Y | Y |
| 7 Weldon | Y | Y | N | Y | Y |
| 8 Fitzpatrick | Y | Y | N | Y | Y |
| 9 Shuster | Y | Y | N | Y | Y |
| 10 Sherwood | Y | Y | N | Y | Y |
| 11 Kanjorski | N | N | N | Y | N |
| 12 Murtha | N | ? | N | Y | N |
| 13 Schwartz | N | N | Y | Y | N |
| 14 Doyle | N | N | Y | Y | N |
| 15 Dent | Y | Y | N | Y | Y |
| 16 Pitts | Y | Y | N | Y | Y |
| 17 Holden | N | N | N | Y | N |
| 18 Murphy | Y | Y | N | Y | Y |
| 19 Platts | Y | Y | N | Y | Y |
| **RHODE ISLAND** | | | | | |
| 1 Kennedy | N | N | Y | Y | N |
| 2 Langevin | N | N | Y | Y | N |
| **SOUTH CAROLINA** | | | | | |
| 1 Brown | Y | Y | N | Y | Y |
| 2 Wilson | Y | Y | N | Y | Y |
| 3 Barrett | Y | Y | N | Y | Y |
| 4 Inglis | Y | Y | N | Y | Y |
| 5 Spratt | N | N | Y | Y | N |
| 6 Clyburn | N | N | Y | Y | N |
| **SOUTH DAKOTA** | | | | | |
| AL Herseth | N | N | N | Y | N |
| **TENNESSEE** | | | | | |
| 1 Jenkins | Y | Y | N | Y | Y |
| 2 Duncan | Y | Y | N | Y | Y |

| | 471 | 472 | 473 | 474 | 475 |
|---|---|---|---|---|---|
| 3 Wamp | Y | Y | N | Y | Y |
| 4 Davis | N | N | Y | Y | Y |
| 5 Cooper | N | N | ? | ? | ? |
| 6 Gordon | N | N | Y | Y | N |
| 7 Blackburn | Y | Y | N | Y | Y |
| 8 Tanner | ? | ? | ? | ? | ? |
| 9 Ford | N | N | Y | ? | ? |
| **TEXAS** | | | | | |
| 1 Gohmert | Y | Y | N | Y | Y |
| 2 Poe | Y | Y | N | Y | Y |
| 3 Johnson, S. | Y | Y | N | Y | Y |
| 4 Hall | Y | Y | N | Y | Y |
| 5 Hensarling | Y | Y | N | Y | Y |
| 6 Barton | ? | ? | ? | ? | ? |
| 7 Culberson | Y | Y | N | Y | Y |
| 8 Brady | Y | Y | N | Y | Y |
| 9 Green, A. | N | N | N | Y | N |
| 10 McCaul | Y | Y | N | Y | Y |
| 11 Conaway | Y | Y | N | Y | Y |
| 12 Granger | Y | Y | N | Y | Y |
| 13 Thornberry | Y | Y | N | Y | Y |
| 14 Paul | Y | Y | N | Y | Y |
| 15 Hinojosa | N | N | N | Y | N |
| 16 Reyes | N | N | Y | Y | N |
| 17 Edwards | N | N | Y | Y | N |
| 18 Jackson-Lee | N | N | Y | Y | N |
| 19 Neugebauer | Y | Y | N | Y | Y |
| 20 Gonzalez | N | N | Y | Y | N |
| 21 Smith | Y | Y | N | Y | Y |
| 22 DeLay | Y | Y | N | Y | Y |
| 23 Bonilla | Y | Y | N | Y | Y |
| 24 Marchant | Y | Y | N | Y | Y |
| 25 Doggett | ? | N | Y | Y | N |
| 26 Burgess | Y | Y | N | Y | Y |
| 27 Ortiz | N | N | Y | Y | N |
| 28 Cuellar | N | N | Y | Y | N |
| 29 Green, G. | N | N | N | Y | N |
| 30 Johnson, E. | N | N | Y | Y | N |
| 31 Carter | Y | Y | N | Y | Y |
| 32 Sessions | Y | Y | N | Y | Y |
| **UTAH** | | | | | |
| 1 Bishop | ? | ? | ? | ? | ? |
| 2 Matheson | N | N | N | Y | Y |
| 3 Cannon | Y | Y | N | Y | Y |
| **VERMONT** | | | | | |
| AL Sanders | N | N | Y | Y | N |
| **VIRGINIA** | | | | | |
| 1 Davis, J. | Y | Y | N | Y | Y |
| 2 Drake | Y | Y | N | Y | Y |
| 3 Scott | N | N | Y | Y | N |
| 4 Forbes | Y | Y | N | Y | Y |
| 5 Goode | Y | Y | N | Y | Y |
| 6 Goodlatte | Y | Y | N | Y | Y |
| 7 Cantor | Y | Y | N | Y | Y |
| 8 Moran | N | N | Y | Y | N |
| 9 Boucher | N | N | Y | Y | N |
| 10 Wolf | Y | Y | N | Y | Y |
| 11 Davis, T. | Y | Y | N | Y | Y |
| **WASHINGTON** | | | | | |
| 1 Inslee | N | N | Y | Y | N |
| 2 Larsen | N | N | Y | Y | N |
| 3 Baird | N | N | Y | Y | N |
| 4 Hastings | Y | Y | N | Y | Y |
| 5 McMorris | Y | Y | N | Y | Y |
| 6 Dicks | N | N | Y | Y | N |
| 7 McDermott | N | N | Y | Y | N |
| 8 Reichert | Y | Y | N | Y | Y |
| 9 Smith | N | N | N | Y | N |
| **WEST VIRGINIA** | | | | | |
| 1 Mollohan | N | N | N | Y | N |
| 2 Capito | Y | Y | N | Y | Y |
| 3 Rahall | N | N | N | Y | N |
| **WISCONSIN** | | | | | |
| 1 Ryan | Y | Y | N | Y | Y |
| 2 Baldwin | N | N | Y | Y | N |
| 3 Kind | N | N | N | Y | N |
| 4 Moore | N | N | Y | Y | N |
| 5 Sensenbrenner | Y | Y | N | Y | Y |
| 6 Petri | Y | Y | N | Y | Y |
| 7 Obey | N | N | Y | Y | N |
| 8 Green | Y | Y | N | Y | Y |
| **WYOMING** | | | | | |
| AL Cubin | Y | Y | N | Y | Y |

# IN THE HOUSE | By Vote Number

**476.** **HR 3761. Flexibility for Displaced Workers/Passage.** Boustany, R-La., motion to suspend the rules and pass the bill that would give more flexibility for a Labor Department program that provides temporary disaster relief and training to individuals who take part in projects that assist victims of a disaster. Motion agreed to 400-0: R 215-0; D 185-0 (ND 139-0, SD 46-0); I 0-0. A two-thirds majority of those present and voting (267 in this case) is required for passage under suspension of the rules. Sept. 20, 2005.

**477.** **H Res 441. Congratulate NASA and Space Shuttle Discovery Crew/Adoption.** Calvert, R-Calif., motion to suspend the rules and adopt the resolution that would commend the NASA team and community for the recent Space Shuttle Discovery flight and recognize the achievements of the Discovery crew, including Commander Eileen Collins, the first female space shuttle commander. Motion agreed to 401-0: R 216-0; D 185-0 (ND 139-0, SD 46-0); I 0-0. A two-thirds majority of those present and voting (268 in this case) is required for adoption under suspension of the rules. Sept. 20, 2005.

**478.** **HR 250. Manufacturing Technology/Rule.** Adoption of the rule (H Res 451) that would provide for House floor consideration of the bill that would authorize $2.1 billion in fiscal 2006 through 2008 for activities designed to improve the competitiveness of the U.S. manufacturing sector, including grant programs, scientific research and education. Adopted 222-198: R 222-0; D 0-197 (ND 0-148, SD 0-49); I 0-1. Sept. 21, 2005.

**479.** **H J Res 61. Gold Star Mothers Day/Passage.** Gutknecht, R-Minn., motion to suspend the rules and pass the joint resolution that would express the support of the House of Representatives for the goals and ideals of Gold Star Mothers Day. Motion agreed to 419-0: R 222-0; D 197-0 (ND 147-0, SD 50-0); I 0-0. A two-thirds majority of those present and voting (280 in this case) is required for passage under suspension of the rules. Sept. 21, 2005.

**480.** **HR 3768. Hurricane Katrina Tax Relief/Adoption.** McCrery, R-La., motion to suspend the rules and adopt the resolution (H Res 454) that would agree to the Senate amendment, with an amendment. The bill, as modified, would provide tax breaks to Hurricane Katrina victims, including provisions to waive penalties for early withdrawal from retirement funds, increase deductions for charitable donations by individuals and businesses and allow low-income workers to maintain benefits such as the earned income tax credit. Motion agreed to 422-0: R 223-0; D 198-0 (ND 148-0, SD 50-0); I 1-0. A two-thirds majority of those present and voting (282 in this case) is required for adoption under suspension of the rules. Sept. 21, 2005.

**481.** **HR 250. Manufacturing Technology/Minority-Serving Institutions.** Jackson-Lee, D-Texas, amendment that would make funds authorized in the bill for scientific, technical research and general services available, to the maximum extent practical, to historically black colleges and universities and other minority-serving institutions. Adopted 416-8: R 216-8; D 199-0 (ND 149-0, SD 50-0); I 1-0. Sept. 21, 2005.

| | 476 | 477 | 478 | 479 | 480 | 481 |
|---|---|---|---|---|---|---|
| **ALABAMA** | | | | | | |
| 1 Bonner | Y | Y | Y | Y | Y | Y |
| 2 Everett | Y | Y | Y | Y | Y | Y |
| 3 Rogers | Y | Y | Y | Y | Y | Y |
| 4 Aderholt | Y | Y | Y | Y | Y | Y |
| 5 Cramer | Y | Y | N | Y | Y | Y |
| 6 Bachus | Y | Y | Y | Y | Y | Y |
| 7 Davis | Y | Y | N | Y | Y | Y |
| **ALASKA** | | | | | | |
| AL Young | Y | Y | Y | Y | Y | N |
| **ARIZONA** | | | | | | |
| 1 Renzi | Y | Y | Y | Y | Y | Y |
| 2 Franks | Y | Y | Y | Y | Y | Y |
| 3 Shadegg | Y | Y | Y | Y | Y | Y |
| 4 Pastor | Y | Y | N | Y | Y | Y |
| 5 Hayworth | Y | Y | Y | Y | Y | Y |
| 6 Flake | Y | Y | Y | Y | Y | Y |
| 7 Grijalva | Y | Y | N | Y | Y | Y |
| 8 Kolbe | Y | + | Y | Y | Y | Y |
| **ARKANSAS** | | | | | | |
| 1 Berry | Y | Y | N | Y | Y | Y |
| 2 Snyder | Y | Y | N | Y | Y | Y |
| 3 Boozman | Y | Y | Y | Y | Y | Y |
| 4 Ross | Y | Y | N | Y | Y | Y |
| **CALIFORNIA** | | | | | | |
| 1 Thompson | Y | Y | N | Y | Y | Y |
| 2 Herger | Y | Y | Y | Y | Y | Y |
| 3 Lungren | Y | Y | Y | Y | Y | Y |
| 4 Doolittle | ? | ? | ? | ? | ? | ? |
| 5 Matsui, D. | Y | Y | N | Y | Y | Y |
| 6 Woolsey | Y | Y | N | Y | Y | Y |
| 7 Miller, George | Y | Y | N | Y | Y | Y |
| 8 Pelosi | Y | Y | N | Y | Y | Y |
| 9 Lee | Y | Y | N | Y | Y | Y |
| 10 Tauscher | Y | Y | N | Y | Y | Y |
| 11 Pombo | Y | Y | Y | Y | Y | Y |
| 12 Lantos | Y | Y | N | Y | Y | Y |
| 13 Stark | Y | Y | N | Y | Y | Y |
| 14 Eshoo | Y | Y | N | Y | Y | Y |
| 15 Honda | Y | Y | N | Y | Y | Y |
| 16 Lofgren | Y | Y | N | Y | Y | Y |
| 17 Farr | Y | Y | N | Y | Y | Y |
| 18 Cardoza | Y | Y | N | Y | Y | Y |
| 19 Radanovich | ? | ? | Y | Y | Y | Y |
| 20 Costa | Y | Y | N | Y | Y | Y |
| 21 Nunes | Y | Y | Y | Y | Y | Y |
| 22 Thomas | Y | Y | Y | Y | Y | Y |
| 23 Capps | Y | Y | N | Y | Y | Y |
| 24 Gallegly | Y | Y | Y | Y | Y | Y |
| 25 McKeon | Y | Y | Y | Y | Y | Y |
| 26 Dreier | Y | Y | Y | Y | Y | Y |
| 27 Sherman | Y | Y | N | Y | Y | Y |
| 28 Berman | Y | Y | N | Y | Y | Y |
| 29 Schiff | Y | Y | N | Y | Y | Y |
| 30 Waxman | Y | Y | N | Y | Y | Y |
| 31 Becerra | Y | Y | N | + | Y | Y |
| 32 Solis | Y | Y | N | Y | Y | Y |
| 33 Watson | Y | Y | N | Y | Y | Y |
| 34 Roybal-Allard | Y | Y | N | Y | Y | Y |
| 35 Waters | Y | Y | N | Y | Y | Y |
| 36 Harman | Y | Y | N | Y | Y | Y |
| 37 Millender-McD. | Y | Y | N | Y | Y | Y |
| 38 Napolitano | Y | Y | N | Y | Y | Y |
| 39 Sánchez, Linda | Y | Y | N | Y | Y | Y |
| 40 Royce | Y | Y | Y | Y | Y | Y |
| 41 Lewis | Y | Y | Y | Y | Y | Y |
| 42 Miller, Gary | Y | Y | Y | Y | Y | Y |
| 43 Baca | Y | Y | N | Y | Y | Y |
| 44 Calvert | Y | Y | Y | Y | Y | Y |
| 45 Bono | Y | Y | Y | Y | Y | Y |
| 46 Rohrabacher | Y | Y | Y | Y | Y | Y |
| 47 Sanchez, Loretta | Y | Y | N | Y | Y | Y |
| 48 Vacant | | | | | | |
| 49 Issa | Y | Y | Y | Y | Y | Y |
| 50 Cunningham | Y | Y | Y | Y | Y | Y |
| 51 Filner | Y | Y | N | Y | Y | Y |
| 52 Hunter | Y | Y | Y | Y | Y | Y |
| 53 Davis | Y | Y | N | Y | Y | Y |
| **COLORADO** | | | | | | |
| 1 DeGette | Y | Y | N | Y | Y | Y |
| 2 Udall | Y | Y | N | Y | Y | Y |
| 3 Salazar | Y | Y | N | Y | Y | Y |
| 4 Musgrave | Y | Y | Y | Y | Y | Y |
| 5 Hefley | Y | Y | ? | ? | ? | ? |
| 6 Tancredo | Y | Y | Y | Y | Y | Y |
| 7 Beauprez | Y | Y | Y | Y | Y | Y |
| **CONNECTICUT** | | | | | | |
| 1 Larson | Y | Y | N | Y | Y | Y |
| 2 Simmons | Y | Y | Y | Y | Y | Y |
| 3 DeLauro | Y | Y | N | Y | Y | Y |
| 4 Shays | Y | Y | Y | Y | Y | Y |
| 5 Johnson | Y | Y | Y | Y | Y | Y |
| **DELAWARE** | | | | | | |
| AL Castle | Y | Y | Y | Y | Y | Y |
| **FLORIDA** | | | | | | |
| 1 Miller | Y | Y | Y | Y | Y | Y |
| 2 Boyd | Y | Y | N | Y | Y | Y |
| 3 Brown | ? | ? | N | Y | Y | Y |
| 4 Crenshaw | Y | Y | Y | Y | Y | Y |
| 5 Brown-Waite | Y | Y | Y | Y | Y | N |
| 6 Stearns | Y | Y | Y | Y | Y | Y |
| 7 Mica | Y | Y | Y | Y | Y | Y |
| 8 Keller | Y | Y | Y | Y | Y | Y |
| 9 Bilirakis | Y | Y | Y | Y | Y | Y |
| 10 Young | Y | Y | Y | Y | Y | Y |
| 11 Davis | ? | ? | N | Y | Y | Y |
| 12 Putnam | Y | Y | Y | Y | Y | Y |
| 13 Harris | Y | Y | Y | Y | Y | Y |
| 14 Mack | Y | Y | Y | Y | Y | Y |
| 15 Weldon | Y | Y | Y | Y | Y | Y |
| 16 Foley | Y | Y | Y | Y | Y | Y |
| 17 Meek | Y | Y | N | Y | Y | Y |
| 18 Ros-Lehtinen | ? | ? | Y | Y | Y | Y |
| 19 Wexler | Y | Y | N | Y | Y | Y |
| 20 Wasserman-Schultz | Y | Y | N | Y | Y | Y |
| 21 Diaz-Balart, L. | ? | ? | Y | Y | Y | Y |
| 22 Shaw | Y | Y | Y | Y | Y | Y |
| 23 Hastings | Y | Y | N | Y | Y | Y |
| 24 Feeney | Y | Y | Y | Y | Y | Y |
| 25 Diaz-Balart, M. | ? | ? | Y | Y | Y | Y |
| **GEORGIA** | | | | | | |
| 1 Kingston | Y | Y | Y | Y | Y | Y |
| 2 Bishop | Y | Y | N | Y | Y | Y |
| 3 Marshall | Y | ? | N | Y | Y | Y |
| 4 McKinney | ? | Y | ? | Y | Y | Y |
| 5 Lewis | Y | Y | N | Y | Y | Y |
| 6 Price | Y | Y | Y | Y | Y | Y |
| 7 Linder | Y | Y | + | + | + | Y |
| 8 Westmoreland | Y | Y | Y | Y | Y | Y |
| 9 Norwood | Y | Y | Y | Y | Y | Y |
| 10 Deal | Y | Y | Y | Y | Y | Y |
| 11 Gingrey | Y | Y | Y | Y | Y | Y |
| 12 Barrow | Y | Y | N | Y | Y | Y |
| 13 Scott | Y | Y | N | Y | Y | Y |
| **HAWAII** | | | | | | |
| 1 Abercrombie | Y | Y | N | Y | Y | Y |
| 2 Case | Y | Y | N | Y | Y | Y |
| **IDAHO** | | | | | | |
| 1 Otter | Y | Y | Y | Y | Y | Y |
| 2 Simpson | Y | Y | Y | Y | Y | Y |
| **ILLINOIS** | | | | | | |
| 1 Rush | ? | ? | N | Y | Y | Y |
| 2 Jackson | Y | Y | N | Y | Y | Y |
| 3 Lipinski | Y | Y | N | Y | Y | Y |
| 4 Gutierrez | Y | Y | N | Y | Y | Y |
| 5 Emanuel | Y | Y | N | Y | Y | Y |
| 6 Hyde | Y | Y | Y | Y | Y | Y |
| 7 Davis | Y | Y | N | Y | Y | Y |
| 8 Bean | Y | Y | N | Y | Y | Y |
| 9 Schakowsky | Y | Y | N | Y | Y | Y |
| 10 Kirk | Y | Y | Y | Y | Y | Y |
| 11 Weller | Y | Y | ? | ? | ? | ? |
| 12 Costello | Y | Y | N | Y | Y | Y |

| **KEY** | **Republicans** | Democrats | *Independents* |
|---|---|---|---|
| Y | Voted for (yea) | X Paired against | C Voted "present" to avoid possible conflict of interest |
| # | Paired for | – Announced against | |
| + | Announced for | P Voted "present" | ? Did not vote or otherwise make a position known |
| N | Voted against (nay) | | |

| | 476 | 477 | 478 | 479 | 480 | 481 |
|---|---|---|---|---|---|---|
| 13 **Biggert** | Y | Y | Y | Y | Y | Y |
| 14 **Hastert** | | | | | | |
| 15 **Johnson** | Y | Y | Y | Y | Y | Y |
| 16 **Manzullo** | ? | ? | Y | Y | Y | Y |
| 17 Evans | Y | Y | N | Y | Y | Y |
| 18 **LaHood** | Y | Y | Y | Y | Y | Y |
| 19 **Shimkus** | Y | Y | Y | Y | Y | Y |
| **INDIANA** | | | | | | |
| 1 Visclosky | Y | Y | N | Y | Y | Y |
| 2 **Chocola** | Y | Y | Y | Y | Y | Y |
| 3 **Souder** | Y | Y | Y | Y | Y | Y |
| 4 **Buyer** | Y | Y | ? | Y | Y | Y |
| 5 **Burton** | + | + | Y | Y | Y | Y |
| 6 **Pence** | Y | Y | Y | Y | Y | Y |
| 7 Carson | Y | Y | N | Y | Y | Y |
| 8 **Hostettler** | Y | Y | Y | Y | Y | Y |
| 9 **Sodrel** | Y | Y | Y | Y | Y | Y |
| **IOWA** | | | | | | |
| 1 **Nussle** | Y | Y | Y | Y | Y | Y |
| 2 **Leach** | Y | Y | Y | Y | Y | Y |
| 3 Boswell | ? | ? | ? | ? | ? | ? |
| 4 **Latham** | Y | Y | Y | Y | Y | Y |
| 5 **King** | Y | Y | Y | Y | Y | N |
| **KANSAS** | | | | | | |
| 1 **Moran** | Y | Y | Y | Y | Y | Y |
| 2 **Ryun** | Y | Y | Y | Y | Y | Y |
| 3 Moore | Y | Y | N | Y | Y | Y |
| 4 **Tiahrt** | Y | Y | Y | Y | Y | Y |
| **KENTUCKY** | | | | | | |
| 1 **Whitfield** | Y | Y | Y | Y | Y | Y |
| 2 **Lewis** | Y | Y | Y | Y | Y | Y |
| 3 **Northup** | Y | Y | Y | Y | Y | Y |
| 4 **Davis** | Y | Y | Y | Y | Y | Y |
| 5 **Rogers** | Y | Y | Y | Y | Y | Y |
| 6 Chandler | Y | Y | N | Y | Y | Y |
| **LOUISIANA** | | | | | | |
| 1 **Jindal** | Y | Y | Y | Y | Y | Y |
| 2 Jefferson | Y | Y | N | Y | Y | Y |
| 3 Melancon | Y | Y | N | Y | Y | Y |
| 4 **McCrery** | Y | Y | Y | Y | Y | Y |
| 5 **Alexander** | Y | Y | Y | Y | Y | Y |
| 6 **Baker** | ? | Y | Y | Y | Y | Y |
| 7 **Boustany** | Y | Y | Y | Y | Y | Y |
| **MAINE** | | | | | | |
| 1 Allen | Y | Y | N | Y | Y | Y |
| 2 Michaud | Y | Y | N | Y | Y | Y |
| **MARYLAND** | | | | | | |
| 1 **Gilchrest** | Y | Y | Y | Y | Y | Y |
| 2 Ruppersberger | Y | Y | N | Y | Y | Y |
| 3 Cardin | Y | Y | N | Y | Y | Y |
| 4 Wynn | Y | Y | N | Y | Y | Y |
| 5 Hoyer | Y | Y | N | Y | Y | Y |
| 6 **Bartlett** | Y | Y | Y | Y | Y | Y |
| 7 Cummings | ? | Y | N | Y | Y | Y |
| 8 Van Hollen | Y | Y | N | Y | Y | Y |
| **MASSACHUSETTS** | | | | | | |
| 1 Olver | Y | Y | N | Y | Y | Y |
| 2 Neal | Y | Y | N | Y | Y | Y |
| 3 McGovern | Y | Y | N | Y | Y | Y |
| 4 Frank | Y | Y | N | Y | Y | Y |
| 5 Meehan | Y | Y | N | Y | Y | Y |
| 6 Tierney | Y | Y | N | Y | Y | Y |
| 7 Markey | Y | Y | N | Y | Y | Y |
| 8 Capuano | Y | Y | N | Y | Y | Y |
| 9 Lynch | ? | ? | N | Y | Y | Y |
| 10 Delahunt | Y | Y | N | Y | Y | Y |
| **MICHIGAN** | | | | | | |
| 1 Stupak | Y | Y | N | Y | Y | Y |
| 2 **Hoekstra** | ? | ? | Y | Y | Y | Y |
| 3 **Ehlers** | Y | Y | Y | Y | Y | Y |
| 4 **Camp** | ? | ? | ? | ? | ? | ? |
| 5 Kildee | Y | Y | N | Y | Y | Y |
| 6 **Upton** | Y | Y | Y | Y | Y | Y |
| 7 **Schwarz** | Y | Y | Y | Y | Y | Y |
| 8 **Rogers** | Y | Y | Y | Y | Y | Y |
| 9 **Knollenberg** | Y | Y | Y | Y | Y | Y |
| 10 **Miller** | Y | Y | Y | Y | Y | Y |
| 11 **McCotter** | Y | Y | Y | Y | Y | Y |
| 12 Levin | Y | Y | N | Y | Y | Y |
| 13 Kilpatrick | Y | Y | N | Y | Y | Y |
| 14 Conyers | Y | Y | N | Y | Y | Y |
| 15 Dingell | Y | Y | N | Y | Y | Y |
| **MINNESOTA** | | | | | | |
| 1 **Gutknecht** | Y | Y | Y | Y | Y | Y |
| 2 **Kline** | Y | Y | Y | Y | Y | Y |
| 3 **Ramstad** | Y | Y | Y | Y | Y | Y |
| 4 McCollum | Y | Y | N | Y | Y | Y |
| 5 Sabo | Y | Y | N | Y | Y | Y |
| 6 **Kennedy** | Y | Y | Y | Y | Y | Y |
| 7 Peterson | Y | Y | N | Y | Y | Y |
| 8 Oberstar | Y | Y | N | Y | Y | Y |
| **MISSISSIPPI** | | | | | | |
| 1 **Wicker** | Y | Y | Y | Y | Y | Y |
| 2 Thompson | Y | Y | N | Y | Y | Y |
| 3 **Pickering** | Y | Y | Y | Y | Y | Y |
| 4 Taylor | ? | ? | N | Y | Y | Y |
| **MISSOURI** | | | | | | |
| 1 Clay | Y | Y | N | Y | Y | Y |
| 2 **Akin** | Y | Y | Y | Y | Y | Y |
| 3 Carnahan | Y | Y | N | Y | Y | Y |
| 4 Skelton | ? | Y | N | Y | Y | Y |
| 5 Cleaver | Y | Y | N | Y | Y | Y |
| 6 **Graves** | Y | Y | Y | Y | Y | Y |
| 7 **Blunt** | Y | Y | Y | Y | Y | Y |
| 8 **Emerson** | Y | Y | Y | Y | Y | Y |
| 9 **Hulshof** | Y | Y | Y | Y | Y | Y |
| **MONTANA** | | | | | | |
| AL **Rehberg** | Y | Y | Y | Y | Y | Y |
| **NEBRASKA** | | | | | | |
| 1 **Fortenberry** | Y | Y | Y | Y | Y | Y |
| 2 **Terry** | Y | Y | Y | Y | Y | Y |
| 3 **Osborne** | Y | Y | Y | Y | Y | Y |
| **NEVADA** | | | | | | |
| 1 Berkley | Y | Y | N | Y | Y | Y |
| 2 **Gibbons** | + | + | Y | Y | Y | Y |
| 3 **Porter** | Y | Y | Y | Y | Y | Y |
| **NEW HAMPSHIRE** | | | | | | |
| 1 **Bradley** | Y | Y | Y | Y | Y | Y |
| 2 **Bass** | Y | Y | Y | Y | Y | Y |
| **NEW JERSEY** | | | | | | |
| 1 Andrews | + | + | N | Y | Y | Y |
| 2 **LoBiondo** | Y | Y | Y | Y | Y | Y |
| 3 **Saxton** | Y | Y | Y | Y | Y | Y |
| 4 **Smith** | Y | Y | Y | Y | Y | Y |
| 5 **Garrett** | Y | Y | Y | Y | Y | Y |
| 6 Pallone | ? | ? | N | Y | Y | Y |
| 7 **Ferguson** | Y | Y | Y | Y | Y | Y |
| 8 Pascrell | Y | Y | N | Y | Y | Y |
| 9 Rothman | Y | Y | N | Y | Y | Y |
| 10 Payne | Y | Y | N | Y | Y | Y |
| 11 **Frelinghuysen** | Y | Y | Y | Y | Y | Y |
| 12 Holt | Y | Y | N | Y | Y | Y |
| 13 Menendez | + | + | N | Y | Y | Y |
| **NEW MEXICO** | | | | | | |
| 1 **Wilson** | Y | Y | Y | Y | Y | Y |
| 2 **Pearce** | Y | Y | Y | Y | Y | Y |
| 3 Udall | Y | Y | N | Y | Y | Y |
| **NEW YORK** | | | | | | |
| 1 Bishop | Y | Y | N | Y | Y | Y |
| 2 Israel | Y | Y | N | Y | Y | Y |
| 3 **King** | Y | Y | Y | Y | Y | Y |
| 4 McCarthy | Y | Y | N | Y | Y | Y |
| 5 Ackerman | Y | Y | N | Y | Y | Y |
| 6 Meeks | Y | Y | N | Y | Y | Y |
| 7 Crowley | Y | Y | N | Y | Y | Y |
| 8 Nadler | Y | Y | N | Y | Y | Y |
| 9 Weiner | Y | Y | N | Y | Y | Y |
| 10 Towns | ? | ? | ? | ? | ? | Y |
| 11 Owens | Y | Y | N | Y | Y | Y |
| 12 Velázquez | Y | Y | N | Y | Y | Y |
| 13 **Fossella** | Y | Y | Y | + | Y | Y |
| 14 Maloney | Y | Y | N | Y | Y | Y |
| 15 Rangel | Y | Y | N | Y | Y | Y |
| 16 Serrano | Y | Y | N | Y | Y | Y |
| 17 Engel | Y | Y | N | Y | Y | Y |
| 18 Lowey | Y | Y | N | Y | Y | Y |
| 19 **Kelly** | Y | Y | Y | Y | Y | Y |
| 20 **Sweeney** | Y | Y | Y | Y | Y | Y |
| 21 McNulty | Y | Y | N | Y | Y | Y |
| 22 Hinchey | Y | Y | N | Y | Y | Y |
| 23 **McHugh** | Y | Y | Y | Y | Y | Y |
| 24 **Boehlert** | Y | Y | Y | Y | Y | Y |
| 25 **Walsh** | Y | Y | Y | Y | Y | Y |
| 26 **Reynolds** | Y | Y | Y | Y | Y | Y |
| 27 Higgins | Y | Y | N | Y | Y | Y |
| 28 Slaughter | Y | Y | N | Y | Y | Y |
| 29 **Kuhl** | Y | Y | Y | Y | Y | Y |
| **NORTH CAROLINA** | | | | | | |
| 1 Butterfield | Y | Y | N | Y | Y | Y |
| 2 Etheridge | Y | Y | N | Y | Y | Y |
| 3 **Jones** | Y | Y | Y | Y | Y | Y |
| 4 Price | Y | Y | N | Y | Y | Y |
| 5 **Foxx** | Y | Y | Y | Y | Y | Y |
| 6 **Coble** | Y | Y | Y | Y | Y | Y |
| 7 McIntyre | Y | Y | N | Y | Y | Y |
| 8 **Hayes** | Y | Y | Y | Y | Y | Y |
| 9 **Myrick** | + | + | Y | Y | Y | Y |
| 10 **McHenry** | ? | ? | Y | Y | Y | N |
| 11 **Taylor** | Y | Y | Y | Y | Y | N |
| 12 Watt | Y | Y | N | Y | Y | Y |
| 13 Miller | Y | Y | N | Y | Y | Y |
| **NORTH DAKOTA** | | | | | | |
| AL Pomeroy | Y | ? | N | Y | Y | Y |
| **OHIO** | | | | | | |
| 1 **Chabot** | Y | Y | Y | Y | Y | Y |
| 2 **Schmidt** | Y | Y | Y | Y | Y | Y |
| 3 **Turner** | Y | Y | Y | Y | Y | Y |
| 4 **Oxley** | Y | Y | Y | Y | Y | Y |
| 5 **Gillmor** | Y | Y | Y | Y | Y | Y |
| 6 Strickland | ? | ? | N | Y | Y | Y |
| 7 **Hobson** | Y | Y | Y | Y | Y | Y |
| 8 **Boehner** | Y | Y | Y | Y | Y | Y |
| 9 Kaptur | Y | Y | N | Y | Y | Y |
| 10 Kucinich | Y | Y | N | Y | Y | Y |
| 11 Jones | Y | Y | N | Y | Y | Y |
| 12 **Tiberi** | Y | Y | Y | Y | Y | Y |
| 13 Brown | Y | Y | N | Y | Y | Y |
| 14 **LaTourette** | Y | Y | Y | Y | Y | Y |
| 15 **Pryce** | Y | Y | Y | Y | Y | Y |
| 16 **Regula** | Y | Y | Y | Y | Y | Y |
| 17 Ryan | Y | Y | N | Y | Y | Y |
| 18 **Ney** | Y | Y | Y | Y | Y | Y |
| **OKLAHOMA** | | | | | | |
| 1 **Sullivan** | Y | Y | Y | Y | Y | Y |
| 2 Boren | Y | Y | N | Y | Y | Y |
| 3 **Lucas** | Y | Y | Y | Y | Y | Y |
| 4 **Cole** | Y | Y | Y | Y | Y | Y |
| 5 **Istook** | Y | Y | Y | Y | Y | Y |
| **OREGON** | | | | | | |
| 1 Wu | Y | Y | N | Y | Y | Y |
| 2 **Walden** | Y | Y | Y | Y | Y | Y |
| 3 Blumenauer | Y | Y | N | Y | Y | Y |
| 4 DeFazio | Y | Y | N | Y | Y | Y |
| 5 Hooley | Y | Y | N | Y | Y | Y |
| **PENNSYLVANIA** | | | | | | |
| 1 Brady | Y | Y | N | Y | Y | Y |
| 2 Fattah | Y | Y | N | Y | Y | Y |
| 3 **English** | Y | Y | Y | Y | Y | Y |
| 4 **Hart** | Y | Y | Y | Y | Y | Y |
| 5 **Peterson** | Y | Y | Y | Y | Y | Y |
| 6 **Gerlach** | Y | Y | Y | Y | Y | Y |
| 7 **Weldon** | Y | Y | Y | Y | Y | Y |
| 8 **Fitzpatrick** | Y | Y | Y | Y | Y | Y |
| 9 **Shuster** | Y | Y | Y | Y | Y | Y |
| 10 **Sherwood** | Y | Y | Y | Y | Y | Y |
| 11 Kanjorski | Y | Y | N | Y | Y | Y |
| 12 Murtha | ? | ? | N | Y | Y | Y |
| 13 Schwartz | Y | Y | N | Y | Y | Y |
| 14 Doyle | Y | Y | N | Y | Y | Y |
| 15 **Dent** | Y | Y | Y | Y | Y | Y |
| 16 **Pitts** | Y | Y | Y | Y | Y | Y |
| 17 Holden | Y | Y | N | Y | Y | Y |
| 18 **Murphy** | Y | Y | Y | Y | Y | Y |
| 19 **Platts** | ? | Y | Y | Y | Y | Y |
| **RHODE ISLAND** | | | | | | |
| 1 Kennedy | Y | Y | N | Y | Y | Y |
| 2 Langevin | Y | Y | N | Y | Y | Y |
| **SOUTH CAROLINA** | | | | | | |
| 1 **Brown** | Y | Y | Y | Y | Y | Y |
| 2 **Wilson** | Y | Y | Y | Y | Y | Y |
| 3 **Barrett** | Y | Y | Y | Y | Y | Y |
| 4 **Inglis** | Y | Y | Y | Y | Y | Y |
| 5 Spratt | Y | Y | N | Y | Y | Y |
| 6 Clyburn | Y | Y | N | Y | Y | Y |
| **SOUTH DAKOTA** | | | | | | |
| AL Herseth | Y | Y | N | Y | Y | Y |
| **TENNESSEE** | | | | | | |
| 1 **Jenkins** | Y | Y | Y | Y | Y | Y |
| 2 **Duncan** | Y | Y | Y | Y | Y | Y |
| 3 **Wamp** | Y | Y | Y | Y | Y | Y |
| 4 Davis | Y | Y | N | Y | Y | Y |
| 5 Cooper | Y | Y | N | Y | Y | Y |
| 6 Gordon | Y | Y | N | Y | Y | Y |
| 7 **Blackburn** | Y | Y | Y | Y | Y | Y |
| 8 Tanner | Y | Y | N | Y | Y | Y |
| 9 Ford | ? | ? | N | Y | Y | Y |
| **TEXAS** | | | | | | |
| 1 **Gohmert** | Y | Y | Y | Y | Y | Y |
| 2 **Poe** | Y | Y | Y | Y | Y | Y |
| 3 **Johnson, S.** | Y | Y | Y | Y | Y | N |
| 4 **Hall** | Y | Y | Y | Y | Y | Y |
| 5 **Hensarling** | Y | Y | Y | Y | Y | Y |
| 6 **Barton** | Y | Y | ? | ? | ? | ? |
| 7 **Culberson** | Y | Y | Y | Y | Y | N |
| 8 **Brady** | Y | Y | Y | Y | Y | Y |
| 9 Green, A. | Y | Y | N | Y | Y | Y |
| 10 **McCaul** | Y | Y | Y | Y | Y | Y |
| 11 **Conaway** | Y | Y | Y | Y | Y | Y |
| 12 **Granger** | Y | Y | Y | Y | Y | Y |
| 13 **Thornberry** | Y | Y | Y | Y | Y | Y |
| 14 **Paul** | Y | Y | Y | Y | Y | Y |
| 15 Hinojosa | Y | Y | N | Y | Y | Y |
| 16 Reyes | Y | Y | N | Y | Y | Y |
| 17 Edwards | Y | Y | N | Y | Y | Y |
| 18 Jackson-Lee | Y | Y | N | Y | Y | Y |
| 19 **Neugebauer** | Y | Y | Y | Y | Y | Y |
| 20 Gonzalez | Y | Y | N | Y | Y | Y |
| 21 **Smith** | Y | Y | Y | Y | Y | Y |
| 22 **DeLay** | Y | Y | ? | ? | ? | ? |
| 23 **Bonilla** | Y | Y | Y | Y | Y | Y |
| 24 **Marchant** | Y | Y | Y | Y | Y | Y |
| 25 Doggett | Y | Y | N | Y | Y | Y |
| 26 **Burgess** | Y | Y | Y | Y | Y | Y |
| 27 Ortiz | Y | Y | – | + | + | + |
| 28 Cuellar | Y | Y | N | Y | Y | Y |
| 29 Green, G. | Y | Y | N | Y | Y | Y |
| 30 Johnson, E. | Y | Y | N | Y | Y | Y |
| 31 **Carter** | Y | Y | Y | Y | Y | Y |
| 32 **Sessions** | ? | ? | Y | Y | Y | N |
| **UTAH** | | | | | | |
| 1 **Bishop** | Y | Y | Y | Y | Y | Y |
| 2 Matheson | Y | Y | N | Y | Y | Y |
| 3 **Cannon** | Y | Y | Y | Y | Y | Y |
| **VERMONT** | | | | | | |
| AL *Sanders* | ? | ? | N | ? | Y | Y |
| **VIRGINIA** | | | | | | |
| 1 **Davis, J.** | Y | Y | Y | Y | Y | Y |
| 2 **Drake** | Y | Y | Y | Y | Y | Y |
| 3 Scott | Y | Y | N | Y | Y | Y |
| 4 **Forbes** | Y | Y | Y | Y | Y | Y |
| 5 **Goode** | Y | Y | Y | Y | Y | Y |
| 6 **Goodlatte** | Y | Y | Y | Y | Y | Y |
| 7 **Cantor** | Y | Y | Y | Y | Y | Y |
| 8 Moran | Y | Y | N | Y | Y | Y |
| 9 Boucher | Y | Y | N | Y | Y | Y |
| 10 **Wolf** | Y | Y | Y | Y | Y | Y |
| 11 **Davis, T.** | Y | Y | Y | Y | Y | Y |
| **WASHINGTON** | | | | | | |
| 1 Inslee | Y | Y | N | Y | Y | Y |
| 2 Larsen | Y | Y | N | Y | Y | Y |
| 3 Baird | Y | Y | N | Y | Y | Y |
| 4 **Hastings** | Y | Y | Y | Y | Y | Y |
| 5 **McMorris** | Y | Y | Y | Y | Y | Y |
| 6 Dicks | Y | Y | N | Y | Y | Y |
| 7 McDermott | Y | Y | N | Y | Y | Y |
| 8 **Reichert** | Y | Y | Y | Y | Y | Y |
| 9 Smith | Y | ? | N | Y | Y | Y |
| **WEST VIRGINIA** | | | | | | |
| 1 Mollohan | Y | Y | N | Y | Y | Y |
| 2 **Capito** | Y | Y | Y | Y | Y | Y |
| 3 Rahall | Y | Y | N | Y | Y | Y |
| **WISCONSIN** | | | | | | |
| 1 **Ryan** | Y | Y | Y | Y | Y | Y |
| 2 Baldwin | Y | Y | N | Y | Y | Y |
| 3 Kind | ? | ? | ? | ? | ? | ? |
| 4 Moore | Y | Y | N | Y | Y | Y |
| 5 **Sensenbrenner** | Y | Y | Y | Y | Y | Y |
| 6 **Petri** | Y | Y | Y | Y | Y | Y |
| 7 Obey | Y | Y | N | Y | Y | Y |
| 8 **Green** | Y | Y | Y | Y | Y | Y |
| **WYOMING** | | | | | | |
| AL **Cubin** | Y | Y | Y | Y | Y | Y |

# IN THE HOUSE | By Vote Number

**482.** HR 250. Manufacturing Technology/Manufacturing and Technology Administration. Larson, D-Conn., amendment that would establish a Manufacturing and Technology Administration within the Commerce Department. It would direct the president to appoint an under-secretary to supervise the new office. Rejected 210-213: R 10-213; D 199-0 (ND 149-0, SD 50-0); I 1-0. Sept. 21, 2005.

**483.** HR 250. Manufacturing Technology/Advanced Technological Education Program. Udall, D-Colo., amendment that would increase to $220.5 million the authorization for fiscal 2006 through 2008 for the National Science Foundation's Advanced Technological Education Program. Rejected 210-212: R 12-212; D 197-0 (ND 147-0, SD 50-0); I 1-0. Sept. 21, 2005.

**484.** HR 250. Manufacturing Technology/Recommit. Honda, D-Calif., motion to recommit the bill to the Science Committee with instructions to add language that would authorize $140 million in fiscal 2006 for the Advanced Technology Program. Motion rejected 196-226: R 0-224; D 196-1 (ND 147-1, SD 49-0); I 0-1. Sept. 21, 2005.

**485.** HR 250. Manufacturing Technology/Passage. Passage of the bill that would authorize $2.1 billion in fiscal 2006 through 2008 for activities designed to improve the competitiveness of the U.S. manufacturing sector, including grant programs, scientific research and education. The bill includes $1.3 billion in fiscal 2006 through 2008 for laboratory activities and technical research run by the National Institute of Standards and Technology. Passed 394-24: R 196-24; D 197-0 (ND 148-0, SD 49-0); I 1-0. Sept. 21, 2005.

**486.** HR 2123. Head Start Reauthorization/Rule. Adoption of the rule (H Res 455) that would provide for House floor consideration of the bill that would reauthorize the Head Start program through fiscal 2011. Adopted 221-189: R 221-0; D 0-188 (ND 0-142, SD 0-46); I 0-1. Sept. 22, 2005.

**487.** Procedural Motion/Journal. Approval of the House Journal of Wednesday Sept. 21, 2005. Approved 346-59: R 200-17; D 145-42 (ND 111-31, SD 34-11); I 1-0. Sept. 22, 2005.

| | 482 | 483 | 484 | 485 | 486 | 487 |
|---|---|---|---|---|---|---|
| **ALABAMA** | | | | | | |
| 1 Bonner | N | N | N | Y | Y | Y |
| 2 Everett | N | N | N | Y | Y | Y |
| 3 Rogers | N | N | N | Y | Y | Y |
| 4 Aderholt | N | N | N | Y | Y | Y |
| 5 Cramer | Y | Y | Y | Y | N | Y |
| 6 Bachus | N | N | N | Y | Y | Y |
| 7 Davis | Y | Y | Y | Y | N | Y |
| **ALASKA** | | | | | | |
| AL Young | N | N | N | Y | Y | Y |
| **ARIZONA** | | | | | | |
| 1 Renzi | N | Y | N | Y | Y | Y |
| 2 Franks | N | N | N | N | Y | Y |
| 3 Shadegg | N | N | N | N | Y | Y |
| 4 Pastor | Y | Y | Y | Y | N | Y |
| 5 Hayworth | N | N | N | Y | Y | Y |
| 6 Flake | N | N | N | N | Y | Y |
| 7 Grijalva | Y | Y | Y | Y | N | Y |
| 8 Kolbe | N | N | N | Y | Y | Y |
| **ARKANSAS** | | | | | | |
| 1 Berry | Y | Y | Y | Y | N | N |
| 2 Snyder | Y | Y | Y | Y | N | Y |
| 3 Boozman | N | N | N | Y | Y | Y |
| 4 Ross | Y | Y | Y | Y | N | Y |
| **CALIFORNIA** | | | | | | |
| 1 Thompson | Y | Y | Y | Y | N | N |
| 2 Herger | N | N | N | Y | Y | Y |
| 3 Lungren | N | N | N | Y | Y | Y |
| 4 Doolittle | ? | ? | ? | ? | ? | ? |
| 5 Matsui, D. | Y | Y | Y | Y | N | Y |
| 6 Woolsey | Y | Y | Y | Y | N | Y |
| 7 Miller, George | Y | Y | Y | Y | N | N |
| 8 Pelosi | Y | Y | Y | Y | N | Y |
| 9 Lee | Y | Y | Y | Y | N | Y |
| 10 Tauscher | Y | Y | Y | Y | N | Y |
| 11 Pombo | N | N | N | Y | Y | Y |
| 12 Lantos | Y | Y | Y | Y | N | Y |
| 13 Stark | Y | Y | Y | Y | N | Y |
| 14 Eshoo | Y | Y | Y | Y | N | Y |
| 15 Honda | Y | Y | Y | Y | N | Y |
| 16 Lofgren | Y | Y | Y | Y | N | Y |
| 17 Farr | Y | Y | Y | Y | N | Y |
| 18 Cardoza | Y | Y | Y | Y | N | Y |
| 19 Radanovich | N | N | N | Y | Y | Y |
| 20 Costa | Y | Y | Y | Y | N | Y |
| 21 Nunes | N | N | N | Y | Y | Y |
| 22 Thomas | N | N | N | Y | Y | Y |
| 23 Capps | Y | Y | Y | Y | N | Y |
| 24 Gallegly | N | N | N | Y | Y | Y |
| 25 McKeon | N | N | N | Y | Y | Y |
| 26 Dreier | N | N | N | Y | Y | Y |
| 27 Sherman | Y | Y | Y | Y | N | Y |
| 28 Berman | Y | Y | Y | Y | N | ? |
| 29 Schiff | Y | Y | Y | Y | N | Y |
| 30 Waxman | Y | Y | ? | Y | N | Y |
| 31 Becerra | Y | Y | Y | Y | N | N |
| 32 Solis | Y | Y | Y | Y | N | Y |
| 33 Watson | Y | Y | Y | Y | N | Y |
| 34 Roybal-Allard | Y | Y | Y | Y | N | Y |
| 35 Waters | Y | Y | Y | Y | N | Y |
| 36 Harman | Y | Y | Y | Y | N | Y |
| 37 Millender-McD. | Y | Y | Y | Y | ? | ? |
| 38 Napolitano | Y | Y | Y | Y | N | Y |
| 39 Sánchez, Linda | Y | Y | Y | Y | N | Y |
| 40 Royce | N | N | N | N | Y | Y |
| 41 Lewis | N | N | N | Y | Y | Y |
| 42 Miller, Gary | N | N | N | Y | Y | Y |
| 43 Baca | Y | Y | Y | Y | N | Y |
| 44 Calvert | N | N | N | Y | Y | Y |
| 45 Bono | N | N | N | Y | Y | Y |
| 46 Rohrabacher | N | N | N | Y | Y | Y |
| 47 Sanchez, Loretta | Y | Y | Y | Y | N | N |
| 48 Vacant | | | | | | |
| 49 Issa | N | N | N | Y | Y | Y |

| | 482 | 483 | 484 | 485 | 486 | 487 |
|---|---|---|---|---|---|---|
| 50 Cunningham | N | N | N | Y | Y | Y |
| 51 Filner | Y | Y | Y | Y | N | N |
| 52 Hunter | N | N | N | Y | Y | Y |
| 53 Davis | Y | Y | Y | N | N | Y |
| **COLORADO** | | | | | | |
| 1 DeGette | Y | Y | Y | Y | N | Y |
| 2 Udall | Y | Y | Y | Y | N | N |
| 3 Salazar | Y | Y | Y | Y | N | Y |
| 4 Musgrave | N | N | N | N | Y | Y |
| 5 Hefley | ? | ? | ? | ? | ? | ? |
| 6 Tancredo | ? | ? | ? | ? | Y | P |
| 7 Beauprez | N | N | N | Y | Y | Y |
| **CONNECTICUT** | | | | | | |
| 1 Larson | Y | Y | Y | Y | N | Y |
| 2 Simmons | Y | N | N | Y | Y | Y |
| 3 DeLauro | Y | Y | Y | Y | N | Y |
| 4 Shays | Y | Y | Y | Y | Y | Y |
| 5 Johnson | Y | N | N | Y | Y | Y |
| **DELAWARE** | | | | | | |
| AL Castle | N | N | N | Y | Y | Y |
| **FLORIDA** | | | | | | |
| 1 Miller | N | N | N | Y | Y | Y |
| 2 Boyd | Y | Y | Y | Y | N | Y |
| 3 Brown | Y | Y | Y | Y | ? | ? |
| 4 Crenshaw | N | N | N | Y | Y | Y |
| 5 Brown-Waite | N | N | N | Y | Y | Y |
| 6 Stearns | N | N | N | N | Y | Y |
| 7 Mica | N | N | N | Y | Y | Y |
| 8 Keller | N | N | N | Y | Y | Y |
| 9 Bilirakis | N | N | N | Y | Y | Y |
| 10 Young | Y | Y | Y | Y | Y | Y |
| 11 Davis | Y | Y | Y | Y | N | Y |
| 12 Putnam | N | N | N | Y | Y | Y |
| 13 Harris | N | N | N | + | Y | Y |
| 14 Mack | N | N | N | Y | Y | Y |
| 15 Weldon | N | N | N | Y | Y | Y |
| 16 Foley | N | N | N | Y | Y | Y |
| 17 Meek | Y | Y | Y | Y | N | N |
| 18 Ros-Lehtinen | N | N | N | Y | Y | Y |
| 19 Wexler | Y | Y | Y | Y | N | Y |
| 20 Wasserman-Schultz | Y | Y | Y | Y | N | Y |
| 21 Diaz-Balart, L. | N | N | N | Y | Y | Y |
| 22 Shaw | N | N | N | Y | Y | Y |
| 23 Hastings | Y | Y | Y | Y | N | Y |
| 24 Feeney | N | N | N | ? | Y | Y |
| 25 Diaz-Balart, M. | N | N | N | Y | Y | Y |
| **GEORGIA** | | | | | | |
| 1 Kingston | N | N | N | Y | Y | Y |
| 2 Bishop | Y | Y | Y | Y | N | Y |
| 3 Marshall | Y | Y | Y | Y | N | N |
| 4 McKinney | Y | Y | ? | Y | N | Y |
| 5 Lewis | Y | Y | Y | Y | N | Y |
| 6 Price | N | N | N | Y | Y | Y |
| 7 Linder | N | N | N | Y | Y | Y |
| 8 Westmoreland | N | N | N | N | Y | Y |
| 9 Norwood | N | N | N | Y | Y | Y |
| 10 Deal | N | N | N | Y | Y | Y |
| 11 Gingrey | N | N | N | Y | Y | Y |
| 12 Barrow | Y | Y | Y | Y | N | Y |
| 13 Scott | Y | Y | Y | Y | N | Y |
| **HAWAII** | | | | | | |
| 1 Abercrombie | Y | Y | Y | Y | N | Y |
| 2 Case | Y | Y | Y | Y | N | Y |
| **IDAHO** | | | | | | |
| 1 Otter | N | N | N | Y | Y | Y |
| 2 Simpson | N | N | N | Y | Y | Y |
| **ILLINOIS** | | | | | | |
| 1 Rush | Y | Y | Y | Y | ? | ? |
| 2 Jackson | Y | Y | Y | Y | N | Y |
| 3 Lipinski | Y | Y | Y | Y | N | Y |
| 4 Gutierrez | Y | Y | Y | Y | N | Y |
| 5 Emanuel | Y | Y | Y | Y | N | Y |
| 6 Hyde | N | N | N | Y | Y | Y |
| 7 Davis | Y | Y | Y | Y | ? | ? |
| 8 Bean | Y | Y | Y | + | N | Y |
| 9 Schakowsky | Y | Y | Y | Y | N | N |
| 10 Kirk | N | N | N | Y | Y | Y |
| 11 Weller | ? | ? | ? | ? | ? | ? |
| 12 Costello | Y | Y | Y | Y | N | Y |

| KEY | Republicans | Democrats | *Independents* | | |
|---|---|---|---|---|---|
| Y | Voted for (yea) | X | Paired against | C | Voted "present" to avoid possible conflict of interest |
| # | Paired for | – | Announced against | | |
| + | Announced for | P | Voted "present" | ? | Did not vote or otherwise make a position known |
| N | Voted against (nay) | | | | |

| | 482 | 483 | 484 | 485 | 486 | 487 |
|---|---|---|---|---|---|---|
| 13 **Biggert** | N | N | N | Y | Y | Y |
| 14 **Hastert** | | | | | | |
| 15 **Johnson** | N | N | N | Y | Y | Y |
| 16 **Manzullo** | N | N | N | Y | Y | Y |
| 17 Evans | Y | Y | Y | Y | N | N |
| 18 **LaHood** | N | N | N | Y | Y | Y |
| 19 **Shimkus** | N | N | N | Y | Y | Y |
| **INDIANA** | | | | | | |
| 1 Visclosky | Y | Y | Y | Y | N | N |
| 2 **Chocola** | N | N | N | Y | Y | Y |
| 3 **Souder** | N | N | N | Y | Y | Y |
| 4 **Buyer** | N | N | N | Y | Y | Y |
| 5 **Burton** | N | N | N | Y | Y | Y |
| 6 **Pence** | N | N | N | N | Y | Y |
| 7 Carson | Y | Y | Y | Y | N | Y |
| 8 **Hostettler** | N | N | N | N | Y | ? |
| 9 **Sodrel** | N | N | N | Y | Y | Y |
| **IOWA** | | | | | | |
| 1 **Nussle** | N | N | N | Y | Y | Y |
| 2 **Leach** | N | N | N | Y | Y | Y |
| 3 Boswell | ? | ? | ? | ? | ? | ? |
| 4 **Latham** | N | N | N | Y | Y | N |
| 5 **King** | N | N | N | N | Y | Y |
| **KANSAS** | | | | | | |
| 1 **Moran** | N | N | N | Y | Y | N |
| 2 **Ryun** | N | N | N | Y | Y | Y |
| 3 Moore | Y | Y | Y | Y | N | Y |
| 4 **Tiahrt** | N | N | N | Y | Y | N |
| **KENTUCKY** | | | | | | |
| 1 **Whitfield** | N | N | N | Y | Y | Y |
| 2 **Lewis** | N | N | N | Y | Y | Y |
| 3 **Northup** | N | N | N | Y | Y | Y |
| 4 **Davis** | N | N | N | + | Y | Y |
| 5 **Rogers** | N | N | N | Y | Y | Y |
| 6 Chandler | Y | Y | Y | Y | N | N |
| **LOUISIANA** | | | | | | |
| 1 **Jindal** | N | N | N | Y | Y | Y |
| 2 Jefferson | Y | Y | Y | Y | N | Y |
| 3 Melancon | Y | Y | Y | Y | N | Y |
| 4 **McCrery** | N | N | N | Y | Y | Y |
| 5 **Alexander** | N | N | N | Y | Y | Y |
| 6 **Baker** | N | N | N | Y | Y | Y |
| 7 **Boustany** | N | N | N | Y | ? | ? |
| **MAINE** | | | | | | |
| 1 Allen | Y | Y | Y | Y | N | Y |
| 2 Michaud | Y | Y | Y | Y | N | Y |
| **MARYLAND** | | | | | | |
| 1 **Gilchrest** | N | N | N | Y | Y | Y |
| 2 Ruppersberger | Y | Y | Y | Y | N | Y |
| 3 Cardin | Y | Y | Y | Y | N | Y |
| 4 Wynn | Y | Y | Y | Y | N | Y |
| 5 Hoyer | Y | Y | Y | Y | N | Y |
| 6 **Bartlett** | N | N | N | Y | Y | Y |
| 7 Cummings | Y | Y | Y | Y | N | Y |
| 8 Van Hollen | Y | Y | Y | Y | N | Y |
| **MASSACHUSETTS** | | | | | | |
| 1 Olver | Y | Y | Y | Y | N | N |
| 2 Neal | Y | Y | Y | Y | N | Y |
| 3 McGovern | Y | Y | Y | Y | N | N |
| 4 Frank | Y | Y | Y | Y | N | Y |
| 5 Meehan | Y | Y | Y | Y | N | Y |
| 6 Tierney | Y | Y | Y | Y | N | Y |
| 7 Markey | Y | Y | Y | Y | N | Y |
| 8 Capuano | Y | Y | Y | Y | N | N |
| 9 Lynch | Y | Y | Y | Y | N | Y |
| 10 Delahunt | Y | Y | Y | Y | N | Y |
| **MICHIGAN** | | | | | | |
| 1 Stupak | Y | Y | Y | Y | N | N |
| 2 **Hoekstra** | N | N | N | Y | Y | Y |
| 3 **Ehlers** | N | N | N | Y | Y | Y |
| 4 **Camp** | ? | ? | ? | ? | ? | ? |
| 5 Kildee | Y | Y | Y | Y | N | Y |
| 6 **Upton** | N | N | N | Y | Y | Y |
| 7 **Schwarz** | N | N | N | Y | Y | Y |
| 8 **Rogers** | N | N | N | Y | Y | Y |
| 9 **Knollenberg** | N | N | N | Y | Y | Y |
| 10 **Miller** | N | N | N | Y | Y | Y |
| 11 **McCotter** | N | N | N | Y | Y | N |
| 12 Levin | Y | Y | Y | Y | N | Y |
| 13 Kilpatrick | Y | Y | Y | Y | N | Y |
| 14 Conyers | Y | ? | Y | Y | ? | ? |
| 15 Dingell | Y | Y | Y | Y | N | Y |

| | 482 | 483 | 484 | 485 | 486 | 487 |
|---|---|---|---|---|---|---|
| **MINNESOTA** | | | | | | |
| 1 **Gutknecht** | N | N | N | N | Y | N |
| 2 **Kline** | N | N | N | Y | Y | Y |
| 3 **Ramstad** | N | N | N | Y | Y | N |
| 4 McCollum | Y | Y | Y | Y | N | Y |
| 5 Sabo | Y | Y | Y | Y | ? | ? |
| 6 **Kennedy** | N | Y | N | Y | Y | Y |
| 7 Peterson | Y | Y | Y | Y | ? | N |
| 8 Oberstar | Y | Y | Y | Y | N | N |
| **MISSISSIPPI** | | | | | | |
| 1 **Wicker** | N | N | N | Y | Y | Y |
| 2 Thompson | Y | Y | Y | Y | N | N |
| 3 **Pickering** | N | N | N | Y | Y | Y |
| 4 Taylor | Y | Y | Y | Y | N | N |
| **MISSOURI** | | | | | | |
| 1 Clay | Y | Y | Y | Y | N | Y |
| 2 **Akin** | N | N | N | Y | Y | Y |
| 3 Carnahan | Y | Y | Y | Y | N | Y |
| 4 Skelton | Y | Y | Y | Y | N | Y |
| 5 Cleaver | Y | Y | Y | Y | N | Y |
| 6 **Graves** | N | N | N | Y | Y | N |
| 7 **Blunt** | N | N | N | Y | Y | ? |
| 8 **Emerson** | N | N | N | Y | Y | Y |
| 9 **Hulshof** | N | N | N | Y | Y | N |
| **MONTANA** | | | | | | |
| AL **Rehberg** | N | N | N | Y | Y | Y |
| **NEBRASKA** | | | | | | |
| 1 **Fortenberry** | N | N | N | Y | Y | Y |
| 2 **Terry** | N | N | N | Y | Y | Y |
| 3 **Osborne** | N | N | N | Y | Y | Y |
| **NEVADA** | | | | | | |
| 1 Berkley | Y | Y | Y | Y | N | Y |
| 2 **Gibbons** | N | Y | N | Y | Y | Y |
| 3 **Porter** | N | Y | N | Y | Y | Y |
| **NEW HAMPSHIRE** | | | | | | |
| 1 **Bradley** | N | N | N | Y | Y | Y |
| 2 **Bass** | N | N | N | Y | Y | Y |
| **NEW JERSEY** | | | | | | |
| 1 Andrews | Y | Y | Y | Y | N | Y |
| 2 **LoBiondo** | N | N | N | Y | Y | N |
| 3 **Saxton** | N | N | N | Y | Y | Y |
| 4 **Smith** | Y | N | N | Y | Y | Y |
| 5 **Garrett** | N | N | N | N | Y | Y |
| 6 Pallone | Y | Y | Y | Y | N | Y |
| 7 **Ferguson** | N | N | N | Y | Y | Y |
| 8 Pascrell | Y | Y | Y | Y | N | Y |
| 9 Rothman | Y | Y | Y | Y | N | Y |
| 10 Payne | Y | Y | Y | Y | N | Y |
| 11 **Frelinghuysen** | N | N | N | Y | Y | Y |
| 12 Holt | Y | Y | Y | Y | N | N |
| 13 Menendez | Y | Y | Y | Y | N | Y |
| **NEW MEXICO** | | | | | | |
| 1 **Wilson** | N | Y | N | Y | Y | Y |
| 2 **Pearce** | N | N | N | Y | Y | Y |
| 3 Udall | Y | Y | Y | Y | N | N |
| **NEW YORK** | | | | | | |
| 1 Bishop | Y | Y | Y | Y | N | Y |
| 2 Israel | Y | Y | Y | Y | N | Y |
| 3 **King** | N | N | N | Y | Y | Y |
| 4 McCarthy | Y | Y | Y | Y | N | Y |
| 5 Ackerman | Y | Y | Y | Y | N | Y |
| 6 Meeks | Y | ? | Y | Y | N | Y |
| 7 Crowley | Y | Y | Y | Y | N | Y |
| 8 Nadler | Y | Y | Y | Y | N | Y |
| 9 Weiner | Y | Y | Y | Y | N | Y |
| 10 Towns | Y | Y | Y | Y | N | Y |
| 11 Owens | Y | Y | Y | Y | N | Y |
| 12 Velázquez | Y | Y | Y | Y | N | N |
| 13 **Fossella** | N | N | N | Y | Y | N |
| 14 Maloney | Y | Y | Y | Y | N | Y |
| 15 Rangel | Y | Y | Y | Y | N | Y |
| 16 Serrano | Y | Y | Y | Y | N | Y |
| 17 Engel | Y | Y | Y | Y | N | Y |
| 18 Lowey | Y | Y | Y | Y | N | Y |
| 19 **Kelly** | N | N | N | Y | Y | Y |
| 20 **Sweeney** | N | N | N | Y | Y | N |
| 21 McNulty | Y | Y | Y | Y | N | N |
| 22 Hinchey | Y | Y | Y | Y | N | Y |
| 23 **McHugh** | N | N | N | Y | Y | Y |
| 24 **Boehlert** | N | N | N | Y | Y | Y |
| 25 **Walsh** | N | N | N | Y | Y | Y |
| 26 **Reynolds** | N | N | N | Y | Y | Y |
| 27 Higgins | Y | Y | Y | Y | N | Y |
| 28 Slaughter | Y | Y | Y | Y | N | N |
| 29 **Kuhl** | N | N | N | Y | Y | Y |

| | 482 | 483 | 484 | 485 | 486 | 487 |
|---|---|---|---|---|---|---|
| **NORTH CAROLINA** | | | | | | |
| 1 Butterfield | Y | Y | Y | Y | N | Y |
| 2 Etheridge | Y | Y | Y | Y | N | Y |
| 3 **Jones** | Y | N | N | N | Y | Y |
| 4 Price | Y | Y | Y | Y | N | Y |
| 5 **Foxx** | N | N | N | N | Y | Y |
| 6 **Coble** | N | Y | N | Y | Y | Y |
| 7 McIntyre | Y | Y | Y | Y | N | Y |
| 8 **Hayes** | N | N | N | Y | Y | Y |
| 9 **Myrick** | N | N | N | N | Y | Y |
| 10 **McHenry** | N | N | N | N | Y | Y |
| 11 **Taylor** | N | N | N | Y | Y | Y |
| 12 Watt | Y | Y | Y | Y | N | Y |
| 13 Miller | Y | Y | Y | Y | N | Y |
| **NORTH DAKOTA** | | | | | | |
| AL Pomeroy | Y | Y | Y | Y | N | Y |
| **OHIO** | | | | | | |
| 1 **Chabot** | N | N | N | Y | Y | Y |
| 2 **Schmidt** | N | N | N | Y | Y | Y |
| 3 **Turner** | N | N | N | Y | Y | Y |
| 4 **Oxley** | N | N | N | Y | Y | Y |
| 5 **Gillmor** | N | N | N | Y | Y | Y |
| 6 Strickland | Y | Y | Y | Y | N | Y |
| 7 **Hobson** | N | N | N | Y | Y | Y |
| 8 **Boehner** | N | N | N | Y | Y | Y |
| 9 Kaptur | Y | Y | Y | Y | N | Y |
| 10 Kucinich | Y | Y | Y | Y | N | N |
| 11 Jones | Y | Y | Y | Y | N | Y |
| 12 **Tiberi** | N | N | N | Y | Y | N |
| 13 Brown | Y | Y | Y | Y | N | Y |
| 14 **LaTourette** | N | N | N | Y | Y | Y |
| 15 **Pryce** | N | N | N | Y | Y | Y |
| 16 **Regula** | N | N | N | Y | Y | Y |
| 17 Ryan | Y | Y | Y | Y | N | Y |
| 18 **Ney** | N | N | N | Y | Y | Y |
| **OKLAHOMA** | | | | | | |
| 1 **Sullivan** | N | N | N | Y | Y | Y |
| 2 Boren | Y | Y | Y | Y | N | Y |
| 3 **Lucas** | N | N | N | Y | Y | Y |
| 4 **Cole** | N | N | N | Y | Y | Y |
| 5 **Istook** | N | N | N | Y | Y | Y |
| **OREGON** | | | | | | |
| 1 Wu | Y | Y | Y | Y | N | N |
| 2 **Walden** | N | N | N | Y | Y | Y |
| 3 Blumenauer | Y | Y | Y | Y | N | Y |
| 4 DeFazio | Y | Y | N | Y | N | N |
| 5 Hooley | Y | Y | Y | Y | N | Y |
| **PENNSYLVANIA** | | | | | | |
| 1 Brady | Y | Y | Y | Y | N | N |
| 2 Fattah | Y | Y | Y | Y | ? | ? |
| 3 **English** | N | N | N | Y | Y | N |
| 4 **Hart** | N | N | N | Y | Y | N |
| 5 **Peterson** | Y | Y | N | Y | Y | Y |
| 6 **Gerlach** | N | N | N | Y | Y | Y |
| 7 **Weldon** | Y | N | N | Y | Y | Y |
| 8 **Fitzpatrick** | Y | Y | N | Y | Y | N |
| 9 **Shuster** | N | N | N | Y | Y | Y |
| 10 **Sherwood** | N | N | N | Y | Y | N |
| 11 Kanjorski | Y | Y | Y | Y | N | Y |
| 12 Murtha | Y | Y | Y | Y | ? | ? |
| 13 Schwartz | Y | Y | Y | Y | N | Y |
| 14 Doyle | Y | Y | Y | Y | N | Y |
| 15 **Dent** | N | N | N | Y | Y | Y |
| 16 **Pitts** | N | N | N | Y | Y | Y |
| 17 Holden | Y | Y | Y | Y | N | Y |
| 18 **Murphy** | N | N | N | Y | Y | Y |
| 19 **Platts** | Y | N | N | Y | Y | Y |
| **RHODE ISLAND** | | | | | | |
| 1 Kennedy | Y | Y | Y | Y | N | Y |
| 2 Langevin | Y | Y | Y | Y | N | Y |
| **SOUTH CAROLINA** | | | | | | |
| 1 **Brown** | N | N | N | Y | Y | Y |
| 2 **Wilson** | N | N | N | Y | Y | Y |
| 3 **Barrett** | N | N | N | N | Y | Y |
| 4 **Inglis** | N | N | N | Y | Y | Y |
| 5 Spratt | Y | Y | Y | Y | N | Y |
| 6 Clyburn | Y | Y | Y | Y | N | Y |
| **SOUTH DAKOTA** | | | | | | |
| AL Herseth | Y | Y | Y | Y | N | Y |
| **TENNESSEE** | | | | | | |
| 1 **Jenkins** | N | N | N | Y | Y | Y |
| 2 **Duncan** | N | N | N | N | Y | Y |

| | 482 | 483 | 484 | 485 | 486 | 487 |
|---|---|---|---|---|---|---|
| 3 **Wamp** | N | N | N | Y | Y | Y |
| 4 Davis | Y | Y | Y | Y | N | Y |
| 5 Cooper | Y | Y | Y | Y | N | Y |
| 6 Gordon | Y | Y | Y | Y | N | Y |
| 7 **Blackburn** | N | N | N | Y | Y | Y |
| 8 Tanner | Y | Y | Y | Y | N | N |
| 9 Ford | Y | Y | Y | Y | N | N |
| **TEXAS** | | | | | | |
| 1 **Gohmert** | N | N | N | Y | Y | Y |
| 2 **Poe** | N | N | N | Y | ? | ? |
| 3 **Johnson, S.** | N | N | N | N | Y | Y |
| 4 **Hall** | N | N | N | Y | Y | Y |
| 5 **Hensarling** | N | N | N | N | Y | Y |
| 6 **Barton** | ? | ? | ? | ? | Y | Y |
| 7 **Culberson** | N | N | N | Y | Y | Y |
| 8 **Brady** | N | N | N | Y | ? | ? |
| 9 Green, A. | Y | Y | Y | Y | N | Y |
| 10 **McCaul** | N | N | N | Y | Y | Y |
| 11 **Conaway** | N | N | N | Y | Y | Y |
| 12 **Granger** | N | N | N | Y | Y | Y |
| 13 **Thornberry** | N | N | N | Y | Y | Y |
| 14 **Paul** | N | N | N | ? | Y | ? |
| 15 Hinojosa | Y | Y | Y | Y | ? | ? |
| 16 Reyes | Y | Y | Y | Y | N | Y |
| 17 Edwards | Y | Y | Y | Y | N | ? |
| 18 Jackson-Lee | Y | Y | Y | Y | ? | ? |
| 19 **Neugebauer** | N | N | N | Y | Y | Y |
| 20 Gonzalez | Y | Y | Y | Y | N | Y |
| 21 **Smith** | N | N | N | Y | Y | Y |
| 22 **DeLay** | ? | ? | ? | ? | ? | ? |
| 23 **Bonilla** | N | N | N | Y | Y | Y |
| 24 **Marchant** | N | N | N | N | Y | Y |
| 25 Doggett | Y | Y | Y | Y | N | Y |
| 26 **Burgess** | N | N | N | Y | Y | Y |
| 27 Ortiz | + | + | + | + | − | + |
| 28 Cuellar | Y | Y | Y | Y | N | Y |
| 29 Green, G. | Y | Y | Y | Y | + | + |
| 30 Johnson, E. | Y | Y | Y | Y | N | N |
| 31 **Carter** | ? | N | N | Y | Y | Y |
| 32 **Sessions** | N | N | N | Y | Y | Y |
| **UTAH** | | | | | | |
| 1 **Bishop** | N | N | N | Y | Y | Y |
| 2 Matheson | Y | Y | Y | Y | N | N |
| 3 **Cannon** | N | N | N | Y | Y | Y |
| **VERMONT** | | | | | | |
| AL *Sanders* | Y | Y | N | Y | N | Y |
| **VIRGINIA** | | | | | | |
| 1 **Davis, J.** | N | N | N | Y | Y | Y |
| 2 **Drake** | N | N | N | Y | Y | Y |
| 3 Scott | Y | Y | Y | Y | N | Y |
| 4 **Forbes** | N | N | N | Y | Y | Y |
| 5 **Goode** | Y | N | N | Y | Y | Y |
| 6 **Goodlatte** | N | N | N | Y | Y | Y |
| 7 **Cantor** | N | N | N | Y | Y | ? |
| 8 Moran | Y | Y | Y | Y | N | Y |
| 9 Boucher | Y | Y | Y | ? | N | Y |
| 10 **Wolf** | N | N | N | Y | Y | Y |
| 11 **Davis, T.** | N | Y | N | Y | Y | Y |
| **WASHINGTON** | | | | | | |
| 1 Inslee | Y | Y | Y | Y | N | Y |
| 2 Larsen | Y | Y | Y | Y | N | N |
| 3 Baird | Y | Y | Y | Y | N | N |
| 4 **Hastings** | N | N | N | Y | Y | Y |
| 5 **McMorris** | N | N | N | Y | + | Y |
| 6 Dicks | Y | Y | Y | Y | N | Y |
| 7 McDermott | Y | Y | Y | Y | N | N |
| 8 **Reichert** | N | N | N | Y | Y | Y |
| 9 Smith | Y | Y | Y | Y | N | Y |
| **WEST VIRGINIA** | | | | | | |
| 1 Mollohan | Y | Y | Y | Y | N | Y |
| 2 **Capito** | N | N | N | Y | Y | N |
| 3 Rahall | Y | Y | Y | Y | N | Y |
| **WISCONSIN** | | | | | | |
| 1 **Ryan** | N | N | N | Y | Y | Y |
| 2 Baldwin | Y | Y | Y | Y | N | N |
| 3 Kind | ? | ? | ? | ? | N | Y |
| 4 Moore | Y | Y | Y | Y | N | Y |
| 5 **Sensenbrenner** | N | N | N | Y | Y | Y |
| 6 **Petri** | N | N | N | Y | Y | Y |
| 7 Obey | Y | Y | Y | Y | N | Y |
| 8 **Green** | N | Y | N | Y | Y | Y |
| **WYOMING** | | | | | | |
| AL **Cubin** | N | N | N | Y | Y | Y |

# IN THE HOUSE | By Vote Number

**488.** HR 2123. Head Start Reauthorization/Policy Councils. Souder, R-Ind., amendment that would allow the policy councils of the Head Start program to approve or disapprove most program planning and operation activities along with the board of directors. Rejected 153-266: R 69-152; D 83-114 (ND 64-85, SD 19-29); I 1-0. Sept. 22, 2005.

**489.** HR 2123. Head Start Reauthorization/Children with Disabilities. Stearns, R-Fla., amendment that would provide staff and teacher training concerning children with disabilities. Adopted 411-0: R 217-0; D 193-0 (ND 148-0, SD 45-0); I 1-0. Sept. 22, 2005.

**490.** HR 2123. Head Start Reauthorization/Outreach Program. Davis, D-Ill., amendment that would direct the Health and Human Services Department to conduct an outreach program to train and recruit African-American and Latino-American men to become Head Start teachers. Adopted 401-14: R 204-14; D 196-0 (ND 148-0, SD 48-0); I 1-0. Sept. 22, 2005.

**491.** HR 2123. Head Start Reauthorization/For-Profit Head Start Programs. Musgrave, R-Colo., amendment that would allow for-profit Head Start programs that spend less than 15 percent of their grant money on administration to take as profit the difference between the 15 percent and the amount they actually spend. Rejected 175-241: R 175-44; D 0-196 (ND 0-148, SD 0-48); I 0-1. Sept. 22, 2005.

**492.** HR 2123. Head Start Reauthorization/Religious Organizations. Boehner, R-Ohio, amendment that would allow faith-based charities that operate Head Start programs to consider religion as a factor in hiring decisions. Adopted 220-196: R 210-9; D 10-186 (ND 3-145, SD 7-41); I 0-1. A "yea" was a vote in support of the president's position. Sept. 22, 2005.

**493.** HR 2123. Head Start Reauthorization/Passage. Passage of the bill that would reauthorize the Head Start program through fiscal 2011. It would authorize $6.8 billion for the program in fiscal 2006. Half of all Head Start teachers would be required to have at least a bachelor's degree by 2011. The bill would authorize the Health and Human Services Department (HHS) to conduct unscheduled reviews of Head Start programs and allow HHS to contract out monitoring activities to third parties. As amended, it would allow faith-based charities that operate Head Start programs to consider religion as a factor in hiring decisions. Passed 231-184: R 208-10; D 23-173 (ND 11-137, SD 12-36); I 0-1. A "yea" was a vote in support of the president's position. Sept. 22, 2005.

| | 488 | 489 | 490 | 491 | 492 | 493 |
|---|---|---|---|---|---|---|
| **ALABAMA** | | | | | | |
| 1 Bonner | N | Y | Y | Y | Y | Y |
| 2 Everett | N | Y | Y | Y | Y | Y |
| 3 Rogers | N | Y | Y | Y | Y | Y |
| 4 Aderholt | N | Y | Y | Y | Y | Y |
| 5 Cramer | Y | Y | Y | N | N | Y |
| 6 Bachus | N | Y | Y | Y | Y | Y |
| 7 Davis | N | Y | Y | N | N | N |
| **ALASKA** | | | | | | |
| AL Young | N | Y | Y | Y | Y | Y |
| **ARIZONA** | | | | | | |
| 1 Renzi | N | Y | Y | N | Y | Y |
| 2 Franks | Y | Y | N | Y | Y | Y |
| 3 Shadegg | Y | Y | N | Y | Y | Y |
| 4 Pastor | N | Y | Y | N | N | N |
| 5 Hayworth | Y | Y | Y | Y | Y | Y |
| 6 Flake | Y | Y | Y | Y | Y | Y |
| 7 Grijalva | N | Y | Y | N | N | N |
| 8 Kolbe | N | Y | Y | Y | Y | Y |
| **ARKANSAS** | | | | | | |
| 1 Berry | N | Y | Y | N | N | N |
| 2 Snyder | N | Y | Y | N | N | N |
| 3 Boozman | Y | Y | Y | Y | Y | Y |
| 4 Ross | N | Y | Y | N | N | N |
| **CALIFORNIA** | | | | | | |
| 1 Thompson | N | Y | Y | N | N | N |
| 2 Herger | N | Y | N | N | Y | Y |
| 3 Lungren | Y | Y | Y | Y | Y | Y |
| 4 Doolittle | Y | Y | Y | Y | Y | Y |
| 5 Matsui, D. | Y | Y | Y | N | N | N |
| 6 Woolsey | N | Y | Y | N | N | N |
| 7 Miller, George | N | Y | Y | N | N | N |
| 8 Pelosi | N | Y | Y | N | N | N |
| 9 Lee | Y | Y | Y | N | N | N |
| 10 Tauscher | N | Y | Y | N | N | N |
| 11 Pombo | N | Y | Y | Y | Y | Y |
| 12 Lantos | N | Y | Y | N | N | N |
| 13 Stark | N | Y | Y | N | N | N |
| 14 Eshoo | N | Y | Y | N | N | N |
| 15 Honda | Y | Y | Y | N | N | N |
| 16 Lofgren | N | Y | Y | N | N | N |
| 17 Farr | Y | Y | Y | N | N | N |
| 18 Cardoza | N | Y | Y | N | N | N |
| 19 Radanovich | Y | Y | Y | Y | Y | Y |
| 20 Costa | N | Y | Y | N | N | N |
| 21 Nunes | Y | Y | Y | Y | Y | Y |
| 22 Thomas | N | Y | Y | Y | Y | Y |
| 23 Capps | N | Y | Y | N | N | N |
| 24 Gallegly | N | Y | Y | N | Y | Y |
| 25 McKeon | N | Y | Y | Y | Y | Y |
| 26 Dreier | Y | Y | Y | Y | Y | Y |
| 27 Sherman | N | Y | Y | N | N | N |
| 28 Berman | N | Y | Y | N | N | N |
| 29 Schiff | Y | Y | Y | N | N | N |
| 30 Waxman | N | Y | Y | N | N | N |
| 31 Becerra | Y | Y | Y | N | N | N |
| 32 Solis | N | Y | Y | N | N | N |
| 33 Watson | N | Y | Y | N | N | N |
| 34 Roybal-Allard | Y | Y | Y | N | N | N |
| 35 Waters | Y | Y | Y | N | N | N |
| 36 Harman | N | Y | Y | N | N | N |
| 37 Millender-McD. | Y | Y | Y | N | N | N |
| 38 Napolitano | Y | Y | Y | N | N | N |
| 39 Sánchez, Linda | Y | Y | Y | N | N | N |
| 40 Royce | Y | Y | Y | Y | Y | Y |
| 41 Lewis | N | Y | Y | Y | Y | Y |
| 42 Miller, Gary | N | Y | Y | Y | Y | Y |
| 43 Baca | Y | Y | Y | N | N | N |
| 44 Calvert | N | Y | Y | Y | Y | Y |
| 45 Bono | N | Y | Y | Y | Y | Y |
| 46 Rohrabacher | Y | Y | Y | Y | Y | Y |
| 47 Sanchez, Loretta | Y | Y | Y | N | N | N |
| 48 Vacant | | | | | | |
| 49 Issa | N | Y | Y | Y | Y | Y |
| 50 Cunningham | N | Y | Y | Y | Y | Y |
| 51 Filner | Y | Y | Y | N | N | N |
| 52 Hunter | N | Y | Y | Y | Y | Y |
| 53 Davis | N | Y | Y | N | N | N |
| **COLORADO** | | | | | | |
| 1 DeGette | N | Y | Y | N | N | Y |
| 2 Udall | Y | Y | Y | N | N | Y |
| 3 Salazar | N | Y | Y | N | N | Y |
| 4 Musgrave | Y | Y | Y | Y | Y | Y |
| 5 Hefley | ? | ? | ? | ? | ? | ? |
| 6 Tancredo | Y | Y | Y | Y | Y | Y |
| 7 Beauprez | N | Y | Y | N | Y | Y |
| **CONNECTICUT** | | | | | | |
| 1 Larson | Y | Y | Y | N | N | N |
| 2 Simmons | Y | Y | Y | N | N | N |
| 3 DeLauro | Y | Y | Y | N | N | N |
| 4 Shays | N | Y | Y | N | N | N |
| 5 Johnson | Y | ? | Y | N | N | Y |
| **DELAWARE** | | | | | | |
| AL Castle | N | Y | Y | N | Y | Y |
| **FLORIDA** | | | | | | |
| 1 Miller | Y | Y | Y | Y | Y | Y |
| 2 Boyd | N | Y | Y | N | N | N |
| 3 Brown | N | Y | Y | N | N | N |
| 4 Crenshaw | N | Y | Y | Y | Y | Y |
| 5 Brown-Waite | Y | Y | Y | Y | Y | Y |
| 6 Stearns | Y | Y | Y | Y | Y | Y |
| 7 Mica | Y | Y | Y | Y | Y | Y |
| 8 Keller | Y | Y | Y | Y | Y | Y |
| 9 Bilirakis | Y | Y | Y | Y | Y | Y |
| 10 Young | N | ? | Y | Y | Y | Y |
| 11 Davis | N | Y | Y | N | N | N |
| 12 Putnam | N | Y | Y | Y | Y | Y |
| 13 Harris | N | Y | Y | Y | Y | Y |
| 14 Mack | Y | Y | Y | Y | Y | Y |
| 15 Weldon | Y | Y | Y | Y | Y | Y |
| 16 Foley | N | Y | Y | Y | Y | Y |
| 17 Meek | N | Y | Y | N | N | N |
| 18 Ros-Lehtinen | N | Y | Y | N | N | N |
| 19 Wexler | N | Y | Y | N | N | N |
| 20 Wasserman-Schultz | N | Y | Y | N | N | N |
| 21 Diaz-Balart, L. | N | Y | ? | N | Y | Y |
| 22 Shaw | Y | Y | Y | Y | Y | Y |
| 23 Hastings | N | Y | Y | N | N | N |
| 24 Feeney | N | Y | Y | Y | Y | Y |
| 25 Diaz-Balart, M. | N | Y | Y | N | Y | Y |
| **GEORGIA** | | | | | | |
| 1 Kingston | N | Y | Y | Y | Y | Y |
| 2 Bishop | Y | Y | Y | N | N | N |
| 3 Marshall | Y | Y | Y | N | N | N |
| 4 McKinney | Y | Y | Y | N | N | N |
| 5 Lewis | Y | Y | Y | N | N | N |
| 6 Price | N | Y | N | Y | Y | Y |
| 7 Linder | Y | Y | Y | Y | Y | Y |
| 8 Westmoreland | N | Y | Y | Y | Y | Y |
| 9 Norwood | N | Y | Y | Y | Y | Y |
| 10 Deal | N | Y | Y | Y | Y | Y |
| 11 Gingrey | N | Y | Y | Y | Y | Y |
| 12 Barrow | N | Y | Y | N | Y | Y |
| 13 Scott | Y | Y | Y | N | N | N |
| **HAWAII** | | | | | | |
| 1 Abercrombie | N | Y | Y | N | N | N |
| 2 Case | Y | Y | Y | N | Y | Y |
| **IDAHO** | | | | | | |
| 1 Otter | Y | Y | Y | Y | Y | Y |
| 2 Simpson | N | Y | Y | Y | Y | Y |
| **ILLINOIS** | | | | | | |
| 1 Rush | N | Y | Y | N | N | N |
| 2 Jackson | N | Y | Y | N | N | N |
| 3 Lipinski | Y | Y | Y | N | N | N |
| 4 Gutierrez | Y | Y | Y | N | N | N |
| 5 Emanuel | N | Y | Y | N | N | N |
| 6 Hyde | N | Y | Y | Y | Y | Y |
| 7 Davis | Y | Y | Y | N | N | N |
| 8 Bean | N | Y | Y | N | N | Y |
| 9 Schakowsky | Y | ? | Y | N | N | N |
| 10 Kirk | N | Y | Y | Y | N | Y |
| 11 Weller | ? | ? | ? | ? | ? | ? |
| 12 Costello | Y | Y | Y | N | N | N |

**KEY**   Republicans   Democrats   *Independents*

| | | | |
|---|---|---|---|
| Y Voted for (yea) | X Paired against | C Voted "present" to avoid possible conflict of interest |
| # Paired for | – Announced against | |
| + Announced for | P Voted "present" | ? Did not vote or otherwise make a position known |
| N Voted against (nay) | | |

| | 488 | 489 | 490 | 491 | 492 | 493 |
|---|---|---|---|---|---|---|
| 13 **Biggert** | Y | Y | Y | N | Y | Y |
| 14 **Hastert** | | | | | | |
| 15 **Johnson** | Y | Y | Y | Y | Y | Y |
| 16 **Manzullo** | Y | Y | Y | Y | Y | N |
| 17 Evans | Y | Y | Y | N | N | N |
| 18 **LaHood** | N | Y | Y | N | Y | N |
| 19 **Shimkus** | N | Y | Y | N | Y | Y |
| **INDIANA** | | | | | | |
| 1 Visclosky | Y | Y | Y | N | N | N |
| 2 **Chocola** | N | Y | Y | Y | Y | Y |
| 3 **Souder** | Y | Y | Y | Y | Y | Y |
| 4 **Buyer** | ? | ? | ? | ? | ? | ? |
| 5 **Burton** | Y | Y | Y | Y | Y | Y |
| 6 **Pence** | Y | Y | Y | Y | Y | Y |
| 7 Carson | N | Y | Y | N | N | N |
| 8 **Hostettler** | Y | Y | Y | Y | Y | Y |
| 9 **Sodrel** | Y | Y | Y | Y | Y | Y |
| **IOWA** | | | | | | |
| 1 **Nussle** | N | Y | Y | Y | Y | Y |
| 2 **Leach** | N | Y | Y | N | N | N |
| 3 Boswell | ? | ? | ? | ? | ? | ? |
| 4 **Latham** | N | Y | Y | Y | Y | Y |
| 5 **King** | N | Y | N | Y | Y | Y |
| **KANSAS** | | | | | | |
| 1 **Moran** | Y | Y | Y | Y | Y | Y |
| 2 **Ryun** | Y | Y | Y | Y | Y | Y |
| 3 Moore | Y | Y | Y | N | N | N |
| 4 **Tiahrt** | Y | Y | Y | Y | Y | Y |
| **KENTUCKY** | | | | | | |
| 1 **Whitfield** | Y | Y | Y | Y | Y | Y |
| 2 **Lewis** | Y | Y | Y | Y | Y | Y |
| 3 **Northup** | N | Y | Y | Y | Y | Y |
| 4 **Davis** | N | Y | Y | Y | Y | Y |
| 5 **Rogers** | Y | Y | Y | Y | Y | Y |
| 6 Chandler | Y | Y | Y | N | Y | Y |
| **LOUISIANA** | | | | | | |
| 1 **Jindal** | N | Y | Y | Y | Y | Y |
| 2 Jefferson | Y | Y | Y | N | N | N |
| 3 Melancon | Y | ? | Y | N | N | N |
| 4 **McCrery** | N | Y | Y | Y | Y | Y |
| 5 **Alexander** | N | Y | Y | Y | Y | Y |
| 6 **Baker** | N | Y | ? | ? | ? | ? |
| 7 **Boustany** | - | + | + | + | + | + |
| **MAINE** | | | | | | |
| 1 Allen | N | Y | Y | N | N | N |
| 2 Michaud | N | Y | Y | N | N | N |
| **MARYLAND** | | | | | | |
| 1 **Gilchrest** | N | Y | Y | Y | Y | Y |
| 2 Ruppersberger | N | Y | Y | N | N | N |
| 3 Cardin | Y | Y | Y | N | N | N |
| 4 Wynn | Y | Y | Y | N | N | N |
| 5 Hoyer | N | Y | Y | N | N | N |
| 6 **Bartlett** | Y | Y | Y | Y | Y | N |
| 7 Cummings | Y | Y | Y | N | N | N |
| 8 Van Hollen | Y | Y | Y | N | N | N |
| **MASSACHUSETTS** | | | | | | |
| 1 Olver | N | Y | Y | N | N | N |
| 2 Neal | N | Y | Y | N | N | N |
| 3 McGovern | N | Y | Y | N | N | N |
| 4 Frank | N | Y | Y | N | N | N |
| 5 Meehan | N | Y | Y | N | N | N |
| 6 Tierney | N | Y | Y | N | N | N |
| 7 Markey | N | Y | Y | N | N | N |
| 8 Capuano | Y | Y | Y | N | N | N |
| 9 Lynch | Y | Y | ? | ? | ? | ? |
| 10 Delahunt | N | Y | Y | N | N | N |
| **MICHIGAN** | | | | | | |
| 1 Stupak | N | Y | Y | N | N | N |
| 2 **Hoekstra** | Y | Y | Y | Y | Y | Y |
| 3 **Ehlers** | N | Y | Y | Y | Y | Y |
| 4 **Camp** | ? | ? | ? | ? | ? | ? |
| 5 Kildee | N | Y | Y | N | N | N |
| 6 **Upton** | N | Y | Y | N | Y | Y |
| 7 **Schwarz** | N | Y | Y | N | N | Y |
| 8 **Rogers** | N | Y | Y | N | Y | Y |
| 9 **Knollenberg** | N | Y | Y | Y | Y | Y |
| 10 **Miller** | N | Y | Y | Y | Y | Y |
| 11 **McCotter** | N | Y | Y | N | Y | Y |
| 12 Levin | N | Y | Y | N | N | N |
| 13 Kilpatrick | N | Y | Y | N | N | N |
| 14 Conyers | N | Y | Y | N | N | N |
| 15 Dingell | N | Y | Y | N | N | N |

| | 488 | 489 | 490 | 491 | 492 | 493 |
|---|---|---|---|---|---|---|
| **MINNESOTA** | | | | | | |
| 1 **Gutknecht** | Y | Y | Y | Y | Y | Y |
| 2 **Kline** | N | Y | Y | Y | Y | Y |
| 3 **Ramstad** | Y | Y | Y | N | Y | Y |
| 4 McCollum | N | Y | Y | N | N | N |
| 5 Sabo | Y | Y | Y | N | N | N |
| 6 **Kennedy** | Y | Y | Y | Y | Y | Y |
| 7 Peterson | Y | Y | Y | N | Y | N |
| 8 Oberstar | Y | Y | Y | N | N | N |
| **MISSISSIPPI** | | | | | | |
| 1 **Wicker** | N | Y | Y | Y | Y | Y |
| 2 Thompson | N | Y | Y | N | N | N |
| 3 **Pickering** | N | Y | Y | Y | Y | Y |
| 4 Taylor | N | Y | Y | N | Y | Y |
| **MISSOURI** | | | | | | |
| 1 Clay | N | Y | Y | N | N | N |
| 2 **Akin** | Y | Y | Y | Y | Y | Y |
| 3 Carnahan | N | Y | Y | N | N | N |
| 4 Skelton | N | Y | Y | N | N | Y |
| 5 Cleaver | N | Y | Y | N | N | N |
| 6 **Graves** | N | Y | Y | Y | Y | Y |
| 7 **Blunt** | N | Y | N | Y | Y | Y |
| 8 **Emerson** | N | Y | Y | N | Y | Y |
| 9 **Hulshof** | Y | Y | Y | N | Y | Y |
| **MONTANA** | | | | | | |
| AL **Rehberg** | N | Y | Y | Y | Y | Y |
| **NEBRASKA** | | | | | | |
| 1 **Fortenberry** | N | Y | Y | Y | Y | Y |
| 2 **Terry** | N | Y | Y | N | Y | Y |
| 3 **Osborne** | N | Y | Y | N | Y | Y |
| **NEVADA** | | | | | | |
| 1 Berkley | N | Y | Y | N | N | N |
| 2 **Gibbons** | Y | Y | Y | Y | Y | Y |
| 3 **Porter** | N | Y | Y | N | Y | Y |
| **NEW HAMPSHIRE** | | | | | | |
| 1 **Bradley** | N | Y | Y | N | N | Y |
| 2 **Bass** | N | Y | Y | N | Y | Y |
| **NEW JERSEY** | | | | | | |
| 1 Andrews | N | Y | Y | N | N | N |
| 2 **LoBiondo** | N | Y | Y | N | Y | N |
| 3 **Saxton** | N | Y | Y | N | Y | Y |
| 4 **Smith** | Y | Y | Y | Y | Y | ? |
| 5 **Garrett** | Y | Y | Y | Y | Y | Y |
| 6 Pallone | Y | Y | Y | N | N | N |
| 7 **Ferguson** | N | Y | Y | Y | Y | Y |
| 8 Pascrell | N | Y | Y | N | N | N |
| 9 Rothman | Y | Y | Y | N | N | N |
| 10 Payne | Y | Y | Y | N | N | N |
| 11 **Frelinghuysen** | Y | Y | Y | N | Y | Y |
| 12 Holt | Y | Y | Y | N | N | N |
| 13 Menendez | Y | Y | Y | N | N | N |
| **NEW MEXICO** | | | | | | |
| 1 **Wilson** | N | Y | Y | Y | Y | Y |
| 2 **Pearce** | N | Y | Y | Y | Y | Y |
| 3 Udall | Y | Y | Y | N | N | N |
| **NEW YORK** | | | | | | |
| 1 Bishop | N | Y | Y | N | N | N |
| 2 Israel | Y | Y | Y | N | N | N |
| 3 **King** | N | Y | Y | Y | Y | Y |
| 4 McCarthy | N | Y | Y | N | N | N |
| 5 Ackerman | N | Y | Y | N | N | N |
| 6 Meeks | Y | Y | Y | N | N | N |
| 7 Crowley | Y | Y | Y | N | N | N |
| 8 Nadler | Y | Y | Y | N | N | N |
| 9 Weiner | N | Y | Y | N | N | N |
| 10 Towns | Y | Y | Y | N | N | N |
| 11 Owens | N | Y | Y | N | N | N |
| 12 Velázquez | Y | Y | Y | N | N | N |
| 13 **Fossella** | N | Y | Y | Y | Y | Y |
| 14 Maloney | Y | Y | Y | N | N | N |
| 15 Rangel | N | Y | Y | N | N | N |
| 16 Serrano | N | Y | Y | N | N | N |
| 17 Engel | Y | Y | Y | N | N | N |
| 18 Lowey | Y | Y | Y | N | N | N |
| 19 **Kelly** | N | Y | Y | N | N | Y |
| 20 **Sweeney** | N | Y | Y | N | Y | Y |
| 21 McNulty | Y | Y | Y | N | N | N |
| 22 Hinchey | N | Y | Y | N | N | N |
| 23 **McHugh** | N | Y | Y | N | Y | Y |
| 24 **Boehlert** | N | Y | Y | N | Y | Y |
| 25 **Walsh** | N | ? | Y | N | Y | Y |
| 26 **Reynolds** | N | Y | Y | Y | Y | Y |
| 27 Higgins | N | Y | Y | N | N | N |
| 28 Slaughter | N | Y | Y | N | N | N |
| 29 **Kuhl** | N | Y | Y | N | Y | Y |

| | 488 | 489 | 490 | 491 | 492 | 493 |
|---|---|---|---|---|---|---|
| **NORTH CAROLINA** | | | | | | |
| 1 Butterfield | N | Y | Y | N | N | N |
| 2 Etheridge | Y | Y | Y | N | N | N |
| 3 **Jones** | Y | Y | Y | Y | Y | N |
| 4 Price | N | Y | Y | N | N | N |
| 5 **Foxx** | Y | Y | Y | Y | Y | Y |
| 6 **Coble** | N | Y | Y | Y | Y | Y |
| 7 McIntyre | N | Y | Y | N | Y | Y |
| 8 **Hayes** | N | Y | Y | Y | Y | Y |
| 9 **Myrick** | N | ? | N | Y | Y | Y |
| 10 **McHenry** | Y | Y | N | Y | Y | Y |
| 11 **Taylor** | Y | Y | Y | Y | Y | Y |
| 12 Watt | Y | ? | Y | N | N | N |
| 13 Miller | N | Y | Y | N | N | N |
| **NORTH DAKOTA** | | | | | | |
| AL Pomeroy | N | Y | Y | N | N | N |
| **OHIO** | | | | | | |
| 1 **Chabot** | Y | Y | Y | Y | Y | Y |
| 2 **Schmidt** | N | Y | Y | Y | Y | Y |
| 3 **Turner** | N | Y | Y | Y | Y | Y |
| 4 **Oxley** | N | Y | Y | Y | Y | Y |
| 5 **Gillmor** | Y | Y | Y | Y | Y | Y |
| 6 Strickland | Y | Y | Y | N | N | N |
| 7 **Hobson** | N | Y | Y | Y | Y | Y |
| 8 **Boehner** | N | Y | Y | Y | Y | Y |
| 9 Kaptur | N | Y | Y | N | N | N |
| 10 Kucinich | N | Y | Y | N | N | N |
| 11 Jones | Y | Y | Y | N | N | N |
| 12 **Tiberi** | N | Y | Y | Y | Y | Y |
| 13 Brown | N | Y | Y | N | N | N |
| 14 **LaTourette** | N | Y | Y | N | Y | Y |
| 15 **Pryce** | N | Y | Y | Y | Y | Y |
| 16 **Regula** | N | Y | Y | N | Y | Y |
| 17 Ryan | N | Y | Y | N | N | N |
| 18 **Ney** | N | Y | Y | N | Y | Y |
| **OKLAHOMA** | | | | | | |
| 1 **Sullivan** | N | Y | Y | Y | Y | Y |
| 2 Boren | N | Y | Y | N | Y | Y |
| 3 **Lucas** | N | Y | Y | Y | Y | Y |
| 4 **Cole** | N | Y | Y | Y | Y | Y |
| 5 **Istook** | N | Y | Y | Y | Y | Y |
| **OREGON** | | | | | | |
| 1 Wu | Y | Y | Y | N | N | Y |
| 2 **Walden** | N | Y | Y | N | Y | Y |
| 3 Blumenauer | Y | Y | Y | N | N | N |
| 4 DeFazio | Y | Y | Y | N | N | N |
| 5 Hooley | N | Y | Y | N | N | N |
| **PENNSYLVANIA** | | | | | | |
| 1 Brady | N | Y | Y | N | N | N |
| 2 Fattah | N | Y | Y | N | N | N |
| 3 **English** | Y | Y | Y | Y | Y | Y |
| 4 **Hart** | N | Y | Y | N | Y | Y |
| 5 **Peterson** | N | Y | Y | ? | Y | Y |
| 6 **Gerlach** | N | Y | Y | N | Y | Y |
| 7 **Weldon** | N | Y | Y | N | Y | Y |
| 8 **Fitzpatrick** | Y | Y | Y | N | Y | Y |
| 9 **Shuster** | N | Y | Y | Y | Y | Y |
| 10 **Sherwood** | N | Y | Y | Y | N | Y |
| 11 Kanjorski | N | Y | Y | N | N | N |
| 12 Murtha | N | Y | Y | N | N | N |
| 13 Schwartz | N | Y | Y | N | N | N |
| 14 Doyle | N | Y | Y | N | N | N |
| 15 **Dent** | Y | Y | Y | N | Y | Y |
| 16 **Pitts** | N | Y | Y | Y | Y | Y |
| 17 Holden | Y | Y | Y | N | N | Y |
| 18 **Murphy** | N | Y | Y | N | Y | Y |
| 19 **Platts** | Y | Y | Y | N | Y | Y |
| **RHODE ISLAND** | | | | | | |
| 1 Kennedy | Y | Y | Y | N | N | N |
| 2 Langevin | Y | Y | Y | N | N | N |
| **SOUTH CAROLINA** | | | | | | |
| 1 **Brown** | N | Y | Y | Y | Y | Y |
| 2 **Wilson** | N | Y | Y | Y | Y | Y |
| 3 **Barrett** | N | Y | Y | Y | Y | Y |
| 4 **Inglis** | N | Y | Y | Y | Y | Y |
| 5 Spratt | N | Y | Y | N | N | N |
| 6 Clyburn | N | Y | Y | N | N | N |
| **SOUTH DAKOTA** | | | | | | |
| AL Herseth | N | Y | Y | N | N | Y |
| **TENNESSEE** | | | | | | |
| 1 **Jenkins** | N | Y | Y | Y | Y | Y |
| 2 **Duncan** | Y | Y | Y | Y | Y | N |

| | 488 | 489 | 490 | 491 | 492 | 493 |
|---|---|---|---|---|---|---|
| 3 **Wamp** | Y | Y | Y | Y | Y | Y |
| 4 Davis | N | Y | Y | N | Y | Y |
| 5 Cooper | N | Y | Y | N | N | N |
| 6 Gordon | N | Y | Y | N | N | Y |
| 7 **Blackburn** | N | Y | Y | Y | Y | Y |
| 8 Tanner | Y | Y | Y | N | N | N |
| 9 Ford | N | Y | Y | N | N | Y |
| **TEXAS** | | | | | | |
| 1 **Gohmert** | N | Y | Y | Y | ? | ? |
| 2 **Poe** | ? | ? | ? | ? | ? | ? |
| 3 **Johnson, S.** | N | Y | N | Y | Y | Y |
| 4 **Hall** | N | Y | N | Y | Y | Y |
| 5 **Hensarling** | Y | Y | Y | Y | Y | Y |
| 6 **Barton** | N | Y | Y | Y | Y | Y |
| 7 **Culberson** | Y | Y | Y | Y | Y | N |
| 8 **Brady** | ? | ? | ? | ? | ? | ? |
| 9 Green, A. | Y | Y | Y | N | N | N |
| 10 **McCaul** | N | Y | Y | Y | Y | Y |
| 11 **Conaway** | N | Y | Y | Y | Y | Y |
| 12 **Granger** | N | Y | Y | Y | Y | Y |
| 13 **Thornberry** | N | Y | Y | Y | Y | Y |
| 14 **Paul** | Y | Y | Y | Y | Y | N |
| 15 Hinojosa | ? | ? | ? | ? | ? | ? |
| 16 Reyes | N | Y | Y | N | N | N |
| 17 Edwards | N | ? | Y | N | N | Y |
| 18 Jackson-Lee | Y | Y | Y | N | N | N |
| 19 **Neugebauer** | N | Y | Y | Y | Y | Y |
| 20 Gonzalez | Y | Y | Y | N | N | N |
| 21 **Smith** | N | Y | Y | Y | Y | Y |
| 22 **DeLay** | ? | ? | ? | ? | ? | ? |
| 23 **Bonilla** | N | Y | Y | Y | Y | Y |
| 24 **Marchant** | N | Y | N | Y | Y | Y |
| 25 Doggett | N | Y | Y | N | N | N |
| 26 **Burgess** | N | Y | Y | Y | Y | Y |
| 27 Ortiz | + | + | + | - | - | - |
| 28 Cuellar | Y | Y | Y | N | N | Y |
| 29 Green, G. | + | + | + | - | - | + |
| 30 Johnson, E. | Y | Y | Y | N | N | N |
| 31 **Carter** | N | Y | N | Y | Y | Y |
| 32 **Sessions** | N | Y | N | Y | Y | Y |
| **UTAH** | | | | | | |
| 1 **Bishop** | Y | Y | Y | Y | Y | Y |
| 2 Matheson | Y | Y | Y | N | N | N |
| 3 **Cannon** | Y | Y | Y | Y | Y | Y |
| **VERMONT** | | | | | | |
| AL *Sanders* | Y | Y | Y | N | N | N |
| **VIRGINIA** | | | | | | |
| 1 **Davis, J.** | Y | Y | Y | Y | Y | Y |
| 2 **Drake** | N | Y | Y | Y | Y | Y |
| 3 Scott | Y | Y | Y | N | N | N |
| 4 **Forbes** | Y | Y | Y | Y | Y | Y |
| 5 **Goode** | Y | Y | ? | Y | Y | Y |
| 6 **Goodlatte** | N | Y | Y | Y | Y | Y |
| 7 **Cantor** | N | Y | Y | Y | Y | Y |
| 8 Moran | N | Y | Y | N | N | N |
| 9 Boucher | N | Y | Y | N | N | N |
| 10 **Wolf** | N | Y | Y | Y | Y | Y |
| 11 **Davis, T.** | N | Y | Y | Y | Y | Y |
| **WASHINGTON** | | | | | | |
| 1 Inslee | Y | Y | Y | N | N | N |
| 2 Larsen | N | Y | Y | N | N | N |
| 3 Baird | Y | Y | Y | N | N | N |
| 4 **Hastings** | ? | ? | ? | ? | ? | ? |
| 5 **McMorris** | N | Y | Y | Y | Y | Y |
| 6 Dicks | N | Y | Y | N | N | N |
| 7 McDermott | N | Y | Y | N | N | N |
| 8 **Reichert** | N | Y | Y | Y | Y | Y |
| 9 Smith | N | Y | Y | N | N | N |
| **WEST VIRGINIA** | | | | | | |
| 1 Mollohan | N | Y | Y | N | Y | Y |
| 2 **Capito** | Y | Y | Y | Y | Y | Y |
| 3 Rahall | N | Y | Y | N | N | N |
| **WISCONSIN** | | | | | | |
| 1 **Ryan** | N | Y | Y | Y | Y | Y |
| 2 Baldwin | N | Y | Y | N | N | N |
| 3 Kind | ? | ? | ? | ? | ? | ? |
| 4 Moore | Y | Y | Y | N | N | N |
| 5 **Sensenbrenner** | N | Y | Y | Y | Y | Y |
| 6 **Petri** | N | Y | Y | Y | Y | Y |
| 7 Obey | N | Y | Y | N | N | N |
| 8 **Green** | N | Y | Y | Y | Y | Y |
| **WYOMING** | | | | | | |
| AL **Cubin** | Y | Y | Y | Y | Y | Y |

# IN THE HOUSE | By Vote Number

**494.** **H J Res 66. After-School Programs/Passage.** Ehlers, R-Mich., motion to suspend the rules and pass the joint resolution that would support the goals and ideals of "Lights on Afterschool!"and call on the president to issue a proclamation requesting that communities nationwide institute after-school programs. Motion agreed to 403-0: R 222-0; D 180-0 (ND 135-0, SD 45-0); I 1-0. A two-thirds majority of those present and voting (269 in this case) is required for passage under suspension of the rules. Sept. 27, 2005.

**495.** **HR 438. Maudelle Shirek Post Office/Passage.** Brown-Waite, R-Fla., motion to suspend the rules and pass the bill that would designate a post office in Berkeley, Calif., for Maudelle Shirek, who was active in the movements for civil rights and the rights of unions and their workers. Motion rejected 190-215: R 9-212; D 180-3 (ND 138-0, SD 42-3); I 1-0. A two-thirds majority of those present and voting (270 in this case) is required for passage under suspension of the rules. Sept. 27, 2005.

**496.** **H Con Res 209. Domestic Violence Awareness Month/Adoption.** Brown-Waite, R-Fla., motion to suspend the rules and adopt the concurrent resolution that would support the goals and ideals of National Domestic Violence Awareness Month. Motion agreed to 404-0: R 221-0; D 182-0 (ND 138-0, SD 44-0); I 1-0. A two-thirds majority of those present and voting (270 in this case) is required for adoption under suspension of the rules. Sept. 27, 2005.

**497.** **HR 2360. Fiscal 2006 Homeland Security Appropriations/Motion to Instruct.** Sabo, D-Minn., motion to instruct House conferees to include language that would insist that the Homeland Security secretary delay a proposal to reorganize the department's existing preparedness functions under a new preparedness directorate while making the Federal Emergency Management Agency a separate office focused on recovery and response. Motion rejected 196-227: R 0-226; D 195-1 (ND 147-0, SD 48-1); I 1-0. Sept. 28, 2005.

**498.** **HR 3402. Justice Department Authorization/Rule.** Adoption of the rule (H Res 462) to provide for House floor consideration of the bill that would reauthorize funds for the Justice Department for fiscal 2006 through 2009. Adopted 330-89: R 224-0; D 105-89 (ND 70-75, SD 35-14); I 1-0. Sept. 28, 2005.

**499.** **HR 3402. Justice Department Reauthorization/Manager's Amendment.** Sensenbrenner, R-Wis., amendment that would authorize $7.5 million per year in fiscal 2006 through 2010 for grants to assist state and local law enforcement agencies in prosecuting child abuse cases. It also would encourage the chief justice of each U.S. District Court to respond to requests by state and local courts to make federal facilities available for the proceedings of courts whose operations have been "significantly disrupted" by hurricanes Katrina or Rita. Adopted 225-191: R 220-5; D 5-185 (ND 1-140, SD 4-45); I 0-1. Sept. 28, 2005.

| | 494 | 495 | 496 | 497 | 498 | 499 |
|---|---|---|---|---|---|---|
| **ALABAMA** | | | | | | |
| 1 Bonner | Y | N | Y | N | Y | Y |
| 2 Everett | Y | N | Y | N | Y | Y |
| 3 Rogers | Y | N | Y | N | Y | Y |
| 4 Aderholt | Y | N | Y | N | Y | Y |
| 5 Cramer | Y | N | Y | Y | Y | N |
| 6 Bachus | Y | N | Y | N | Y | Y |
| 7 Davis | Y | Y | Y | Y | Y | N |
| **ALASKA** | | | | | | |
| AL Young | Y | N | Y | N | Y | Y |
| **ARIZONA** | | | | | | |
| 1 Renzi | Y | N | Y | N | ? | Y |
| 2 Franks | Y | N | Y | N | Y | Y |
| 3 Shadegg | ? | ? | ? | N | Y | Y |
| 4 Pastor | Y | Y | Y | Y | N | N |
| 5 Hayworth | Y | N | Y | N | Y | Y |
| 6 Flake | Y | N | Y | N | Y | Y |
| 7 Grijalva | + | + | + | Y | N | N |
| 8 Kolbe | Y | N | Y | N | Y | Y |
| **ARKANSAS** | | | | | | |
| 1 Berry | Y | Y | Y | Y | Y | N |
| 2 Snyder | Y | Y | Y | Y | Y | N |
| 3 Boozman | Y | N | Y | N | Y | Y |
| 4 Ross | Y | Y | Y | Y | Y | N |
| **CALIFORNIA** | | | | | | |
| 1 Thompson | Y | Y | Y | Y | Y | N |
| 2 Herger | Y | N | Y | N | Y | Y |
| 3 Lungren | Y | N | Y | N | Y | Y |
| 4 Doolittle | Y | N | Y | N | Y | Y |
| 5 Matsui, D. | Y | Y | Y | Y | N | N |
| 6 Woolsey | Y | Y | Y | Y | N | N |
| 7 Miller, George | Y | Y | Y | Y | N | N |
| 8 Pelosi | Y | Y | Y | Y | ? | N |
| 9 Lee | Y | Y | Y | Y | N | N |
| 10 Tauscher | Y | Y | Y | Y | N | ? |
| 11 Pombo | Y | ? | Y | N | Y | Y |
| 12 Lantos | Y | Y | Y | Y | N | N |
| 13 Stark | Y | Y | Y | Y | N | N |
| 14 Eshoo | Y | Y | Y | Y | N | N |
| 15 Honda | Y | Y | Y | Y | N | N |
| 16 Lofgren | Y | Y | Y | Y | N | N |
| 17 Farr | Y | Y | Y | Y | N | N |
| 18 Cardoza | Y | Y | Y | Y | Y | N |
| 19 Radanovich | Y | N | Y | N | Y | Y |
| 20 Costa | Y | Y | Y | Y | Y | ? |
| 21 Nunes | Y | N | Y | N | Y | Y |
| 22 Thomas | Y | N | Y | N | Y | Y |
| 23 Capps | ? | Y | Y | Y | N | N |
| 24 Gallegly | Y | N | Y | N | Y | N |
| 25 McKeon | Y | N | Y | N | Y | Y |
| 26 Dreier | Y | N | Y | N | Y | Y |
| 27 Sherman | Y | Y | Y | Y | N | N |
| 28 Berman | Y | Y | Y | Y | N | N |
| 29 Schiff | Y | Y | Y | Y | N | N |
| 30 Waxman | Y | Y | Y | Y | N | N |
| 31 Becerra | Y | Y | Y | Y | N | N |
| 32 Solis | Y | Y | Y | Y | N | N |
| 33 Watson | Y | Y | Y | Y | N | N |
| 34 Roybal-Allard | Y | Y | Y | Y | N | N |
| 35 Waters | Y | Y | Y | Y | N | N |
| 36 Harman | ? | ? | ? | ? | ? | ? |
| 37 Millender-McD. | Y | Y | ? | Y | Y | N |
| 38 Napolitano | Y | Y | Y | Y | Y | N |
| 39 Sánchez, Linda | Y | Y | Y | Y | N | N |
| 40 Royce | Y | N | Y | N | Y | Y |
| 41 Lewis | Y | N | Y | N | Y | Y |
| 42 Miller, Gary | Y | N | Y | N | Y | Y |
| 43 Baca | Y | Y | Y | Y | Y | N |
| 44 Calvert | Y | N | Y | N | Y | Y |
| 45 Bono | Y | Y | Y | Y | Y | N |
| 46 Rohrabacher | Y | N | Y | N | Y | Y |
| 47 Sanchez, Loretta | Y | Y | Y | Y | N | N |
| 48 Vacant | | | | | | |
| 49 Issa | Y | N | Y | N | Y | Y |
| 50 Cunningham | Y | N | Y | N | Y | Y |
| 51 Filner | Y | Y | Y | Y | N | N |
| 52 Hunter | ? | ? | ? | ? | ? | Y |
| 53 Davis | Y | Y | Y | Y | Y | N |
| **COLORADO** | | | | | | |
| 1 DeGette | Y | Y | Y | Y | Y | N |
| 2 Udall | Y | Y | Y | Y | Y | N |
| 3 Salazar | Y | Y | Y | Y | Y | N |
| 4 Musgrave | Y | N | Y | N | Y | Y |
| 5 Hefley | Y | N | Y | N | Y | Y |
| 6 Tancredo | Y | N | Y | N | Y | ? |
| 7 Beauprez | Y | N | Y | N | Y | Y |
| **CONNECTICUT** | | | | | | |
| 1 Larson | Y | Y | Y | Y | Y | N |
| 2 Simmons | Y | N | Y | N | Y | Y |
| 3 DeLauro | Y | Y | Y | Y | Y | N |
| 4 Shays | Y | N | Y | ? | ? | Y |
| 5 Johnson | Y | Y | Y | Y | Y | N |
| **DELAWARE** | | | | | | |
| AL Castle | Y | N | Y | N | Y | Y |
| **FLORIDA** | | | | | | |
| 1 Miller | Y | N | Y | N | Y | Y |
| 2 Boyd | Y | Y | Y | Y | Y | N |
| 3 Brown | Y | Y | Y | Y | Y | N |
| 4 Crenshaw | Y | N | Y | N | Y | Y |
| 5 Brown-Waite | Y | N | Y | N | Y | Y |
| 6 Stearns | Y | N | Y | N | Y | Y |
| 7 Mica | Y | N | Y | N | Y | Y |
| 8 Keller | Y | N | Y | N | Y | Y |
| 9 Bilirakis | Y | N | Y | N | Y | Y |
| 10 Young | Y | N | Y | N | Y | Y |
| 11 Davis | ? | ? | ? | ? | ? | ? |
| 12 Putnam | Y | N | Y | N | Y | Y |
| 13 Harris | Y | N | Y | N | Y | Y |
| 14 Mack | Y | N | Y | N | Y | Y |
| 15 Weldon | Y | N | Y | N | Y | Y |
| 16 Foley | Y | N | Y | N | Y | Y |
| 17 Meek | ? | ? | ? | Y | N | N |
| 18 Ros-Lehtinen | ? | ? | N | Y | Y | Y |
| 19 Wexler | Y | Y | Y | Y | N | N |
| 20 Wasserman-Schultz | Y | Y | Y | Y | N | N |
| 21 Diaz-Balart, L. | Y | N | Y | N | Y | Y |
| 22 Shaw | Y | N | Y | N | Y | Y |
| 23 Hastings | Y | Y | Y | Y | N | N |
| 24 Feeney | Y | N | Y | N | Y | Y |
| 25 Diaz-Balart, M. | Y | N | Y | N | Y | Y |
| **GEORGIA** | | | | | | |
| 1 Kingston | Y | N | Y | N | Y | Y |
| 2 Bishop | Y | Y | Y | Y | Y | N |
| 3 Marshall | Y | Y | ? | Y | Y | N |
| 4 McKinney | ? | ? | ? | N | N | N |
| 5 Lewis | Y | Y | Y | Y | N | N |
| 6 Price | Y | N | Y | N | Y | Y |
| 7 Linder | Y | N | Y | N | Y | Y |
| 8 Westmoreland | Y | N | Y | N | Y | Y |
| 9 Norwood | Y | N | Y | N | Y | Y |
| 10 Deal | Y | N | Y | N | Y | Y |
| 11 Gingrey | Y | N | Y | N | Y | Y |
| 12 Barrow | Y | Y | Y | Y | N | Y |
| 13 Scott | Y | Y | Y | Y | Y | N |
| **HAWAII** | | | | | | |
| 1 Abercrombie | Y | Y | Y | Y | Y | N |
| 2 Case | Y | Y | Y | Y | Y | N |
| **IDAHO** | | | | | | |
| 1 Otter | Y | N | Y | N | Y | Y |
| 2 Simpson | Y | N | Y | N | Y | Y |
| **ILLINOIS** | | | | | | |
| 1 Rush | ? | ? | ? | Y | N | N |
| 2 Jackson | Y | Y | Y | Y | N | N |
| 3 Lipinski | Y | Y | Y | Y | N | N |
| 4 Gutierrez | + | + | + | + | + | + |
| 5 Emanuel | Y | Y | Y | Y | N | N |
| 6 Hyde | Y | N | Y | N | Y | Y |
| 7 Davis | Y | Y | Y | Y | N | N |
| 8 Bean | Y | Y | Y | Y | N | N |
| 9 Schakowsky | Y | Y | Y | Y | N | N |
| 10 Kirk | Y | N | Y | N | Y | Y |
| 11 Weller | + | - | + | N | Y | Y |
| 12 Costello | Y | Y | Y | Y | N | N |

| KEY | **Republicans** | Democrats | *Independents* | | |
|---|---|---|---|---|---|
| Y | Voted for (yea) | X | Paired against | C | Voted "present" to avoid possible conflict of interest |
| # | Paired for | – | Announced against | | |
| + | Announced for | P | Voted "present" | ? | Did not vote or otherwise make a position known |
| N | Voted against (nay) | | | | |

| | 494 | 495 | 496 | 497 | 498 | 499 |
|---|---|---|---|---|---|---|
| 13 **Biggert** | Y | N | Y | N | Y | Y |
| 14 **Hastert** | | | | | | |
| 15 **Johnson** | Y | N | Y | N | Y | N |
| 16 **Manzullo** | Y | N | Y | N | Y | Y |
| 17 Evans | Y | Y | Y | Y | N | N |
| 18 **LaHood** | Y | N | Y | N | Y | Y |
| 19 **Shimkus** | Y | N | Y | N | Y | Y |
| **INDIANA** | | | | | | |
| 1 Visclosky | Y | Y | Y | Y | Y | N |
| 2 **Chocola** | Y | N | Y | N | Y | Y |
| 3 **Souder** | Y | N | Y | N | Y | Y |
| 4 **Buyer** | Y | N | Y | N | Y | Y |
| 5 **Burton** | Y | N | Y | N | Y | Y |
| 6 **Pence** | Y | N | Y | N | Y | Y |
| 7 Carson | Y | Y | Y | Y | N | N |
| 8 **Hostettler** | Y | N | Y | N | Y | Y |
| 9 **Sodrel** | Y | N | Y | N | Y | Y |
| **IOWA** | | | | | | |
| 1 **Nussle** | Y | N | Y | N | Y | Y |
| 2 **Leach** | Y | Y | Y | N | Y | N |
| 3 Boswell | ? | ? | ? | ? | ? | ? |
| 4 **Latham** | Y | N | Y | N | Y | Y |
| 5 **King** | Y | N | Y | N | Y | Y |
| **KANSAS** | | | | | | |
| 1 **Moran** | Y | N | Y | N | Y | Y |
| 2 **Ryun** | Y | N | Y | N | Y | Y |
| 3 Moore | Y | Y | Y | Y | Y | N |
| 4 **Tiahrt** | Y | N | Y | N | Y | Y |
| **KENTUCKY** | | | | | | |
| 1 **Whitfield** | Y | N | Y | N | Y | Y |
| 2 **Lewis** | Y | N | Y | N | Y | Y |
| 3 **Northup** | ? | ? | ? | N | Y | Y |
| 4 **Davis** | Y | N | Y | N | Y | Y |
| 5 **Rogers** | Y | N | Y | N | Y | Y |
| 6 Chandler | Y | Y | Y | Y | Y | N |
| **LOUISIANA** | | | | | | |
| 1 **Jindal** | Y | N | Y | N | Y | Y |
| 2 Jefferson | Y | Y | Y | Y | N | N |
| 3 Melancon | ? | ? | ? | ? | ? | ? |
| 4 **McCrery** | Y | Y | Y | N | Y | Y |
| 5 **Alexander** | Y | N | Y | N | Y | ? |
| 6 **Baker** | Y | N | Y | N | Y | Y |
| 7 **Boustany** | ? | ? | ? | N | Y | Y |
| **MAINE** | | | | | | |
| 1 Allen | Y | Y | Y | Y | Y | N |
| 2 Michaud | Y | Y | Y | Y | Y | N |
| **MARYLAND** | | | | | | |
| 1 **Gilchrest** | Y | Y | Y | N | Y | Y |
| 2 Ruppersberger | Y | Y | Y | Y | Y | – |
| 3 Cardin | ? | ? | ? | Y | Y | N |
| 4 Wynn | Y | Y | Y | Y | Y | N |
| 5 Hoyer | Y | Y | Y | Y | N | N |
| 6 **Bartlett** | Y | N | Y | N | Y | Y |
| 7 Cummings | Y | Y | Y | Y | N | N |
| 8 Van Hollen | Y | Y | Y | Y | N | N |
| **MASSACHUSETTS** | | | | | | |
| 1 Olver | ? | Y | Y | Y | N | N |
| 2 Neal | Y | Y | Y | Y | N | N |
| 3 McGovern | Y | Y | Y | Y | N | N |
| 4 Frank | Y | Y | Y | Y | N | N |
| 5 Meehan | Y | Y | Y | Y | N | N |
| 6 Tierney | Y | Y | Y | Y | N | N |
| 7 Markey | Y | Y | Y | Y | N | N |
| 8 Capuano | Y | Y | Y | Y | Y | N |
| 9 Lynch | Y | Y | Y | Y | Y | N |
| 10 Delahunt | Y | Y | Y | Y | Y | N |
| **MICHIGAN** | | | | | | |
| 1 Stupak | Y | Y | Y | Y | N | N |
| 2 **Hoekstra** | Y | N | Y | N | Y | Y |
| 3 **Ehlers** | Y | N | Y | N | Y | Y |
| 4 **Camp** | Y | N | Y | N | Y | Y |
| 5 Kildee | Y | Y | Y | Y | Y | N |
| 6 **Upton** | Y | N | Y | N | Y | Y |
| 7 **Schwarz** | Y | N | Y | N | Y | Y |
| 8 **Rogers** | Y | N | Y | N | Y | Y |
| 9 **Knollenberg** | Y | N | Y | N | Y | Y |
| 10 **Miller** | Y | N | Y | N | Y | Y |
| 11 **McCotter** | Y | N | Y | N | Y | Y |
| 12 Levin | Y | Y | Y | Y | Y | N |
| 13 Kilpatrick | Y | Y | Y | Y | Y | N |
| 14 Conyers | Y | Y | Y | Y | N | N |
| 15 Dingell | Y | Y | Y | Y | Y | N |

| | 494 | 495 | 496 | 497 | 498 | 499 |
|---|---|---|---|---|---|---|
| **MINNESOTA** | | | | | | |
| 1 **Gutknecht** | Y | N | Y | N | Y | Y |
| 2 **Kline** | Y | N | Y | N | Y | Y |
| 3 **Ramstad** | Y | N | Y | N | Y | Y |
| 4 McCollum | Y | Y | Y | Y | ? | N |
| 5 Sabo | Y | Y | Y | Y | Y | N |
| 6 **Kennedy** | Y | N | Y | N | Y | Y |
| 7 Peterson | Y | Y | Y | Y | Y | N |
| 8 Oberstar | Y | Y | Y | Y | Y | N |
| **MISSISSIPPI** | | | | | | |
| 1 **Wicker** | Y | N | Y | N | Y | Y |
| 2 Thompson | Y | Y | Y | Y | N | N |
| 3 **Pickering** | Y | N | Y | N | Y | ? |
| 4 Taylor | Y | Y | Y | N | Y | Y |
| **MISSOURI** | | | | | | |
| 1 Clay | Y | Y | Y | Y | Y | N |
| 2 **Akin** | Y | N | Y | N | Y | Y |
| 3 Carnahan | Y | Y | Y | Y | Y | N |
| 4 Skelton | Y | Y | Y | Y | Y | – |
| 5 Cleaver | Y | Y | Y | Y | Y | ? |
| 6 **Graves** | Y | N | Y | N | Y | Y |
| 7 **Blunt** | Y | N | Y | N | Y | Y |
| 8 **Emerson** | Y | N | Y | N | Y | Y |
| 9 **Hulshof** | Y | N | Y | N | Y | Y |
| **MONTANA** | | | | | | |
| AL **Rehberg** | Y | N | Y | N | Y | Y |
| **NEBRASKA** | | | | | | |
| 1 **Fortenberry** | Y | N | Y | N | Y | Y |
| 2 **Terry** | Y | N | Y | N | Y | Y |
| 3 **Osborne** | Y | N | Y | N | Y | Y |
| **NEVADA** | | | | | | |
| 1 Berkley | Y | Y | Y | Y | N | ? |
| 2 **Gibbons** | Y | N | Y | N | Y | Y |
| 3 **Porter** | Y | N | Y | N | Y | Y |
| **NEW HAMPSHIRE** | | | | | | |
| 1 **Bradley** | Y | N | Y | N | Y | N |
| 2 **Bass** | Y | N | Y | N | Y | Y |
| **NEW JERSEY** | | | | | | |
| 1 Andrews | Y | Y | Y | Y | Y | N |
| 2 **LoBiondo** | Y | N | Y | N | Y | Y |
| 3 **Saxton** | Y | N | Y | N | Y | Y |
| 4 **Smith** | Y | N | Y | N | Y | Y |
| 5 **Garrett** | Y | N | Y | N | Y | Y |
| 6 Pallone | Y | Y | Y | Y | N | N |
| 7 **Ferguson** | Y | N | Y | N | Y | Y |
| 8 Pascrell | Y | Y | Y | Y | Y | N |
| 9 Rothman | Y | Y | Y | Y | Y | Y |
| 10 Payne | Y | Y | Y | Y | N | N |
| 11 **Frelinghuysen** | Y | N | Y | N | Y | Y |
| 12 Holt | Y | Y | Y | Y | N | N |
| 13 Menendez | + | ? | + | Y | N | N |
| **NEW MEXICO** | | | | | | |
| 1 **Wilson** | Y | N | Y | N | Y | Y |
| 2 **Pearce** | Y | N | Y | N | Y | Y |
| 3 Udall | Y | Y | Y | Y | N | N |
| **NEW YORK** | | | | | | |
| 1 Bishop | Y | Y | Y | Y | N | N |
| 2 Israel | Y | Y | Y | Y | N | N |
| 3 **King** | Y | N | Y | N | Y | Y |
| 4 McCarthy | Y | Y | Y | Y | N | N |
| 5 Ackerman | Y | Y | Y | Y | N | N |
| 6 Meeks | Y | Y | Y | Y | N | N |
| 7 Crowley | Y | Y | Y | Y | N | N |
| 8 Nadler | Y | Y | Y | Y | N | N |
| 9 Weiner | Y | Y | Y | Y | Y | N |
| 10 Towns | Y | Y | Y | Y | N | N |
| 11 Owens | Y | Y | Y | Y | Y | N |
| 12 Velázquez | Y | Y | Y | Y | N | N |
| 13 **Fossella** | Y | Y | Y | N | Y | Y |
| 14 Maloney | Y | Y | Y | Y | N | N |
| 15 Rangel | Y | Y | Y | Y | Y | N |
| 16 Serrano | Y | Y | Y | Y | N | N |
| 17 Engel | Y | Y | Y | Y | Y | N |
| 18 Lowey | Y | Y | Y | Y | N | N |
| 19 **Kelly** | Y | N | Y | N | Y | Y |
| 20 **Sweeney** | Y | N | Y | N | Y | Y |
| 21 McNulty | Y | Y | Y | Y | Y | N |
| 22 Hinchey | Y | Y | Y | Y | N | N |
| 23 **McHugh** | Y | N | Y | N | Y | Y |
| 24 **Boehlert** | Y | Y | Y | N | Y | Y |
| 25 **Walsh** | Y | N | Y | N | Y | Y |
| 26 **Reynolds** | Y | N | Y | N | Y | Y |
| 27 Higgins | Y | Y | Y | Y | N | N |
| 28 Slaughter | Y | Y | Y | Y | N | N |
| 29 **Kuhl** | Y | N | Y | N | Y | Y |

| | 494 | 495 | 496 | 497 | 498 | 499 |
|---|---|---|---|---|---|---|
| **NORTH CAROLINA** | | | | | | |
| 1 Butterfield | Y | Y | Y | Y | Y | N |
| 2 Etheridge | Y | Y | Y | Y | Y | N |
| 3 **Jones** | Y | N | Y | N | Y | Y |
| 4 Price | Y | Y | Y | Y | Y | N |
| 5 **Foxx** | Y | N | Y | N | Y | Y |
| 6 **Coble** | Y | N | Y | N | Y | Y |
| 7 McIntyre | Y | ? | Y | Y | N | N |
| 8 **Hayes** | Y | N | Y | N | Y | Y |
| 9 **Myrick** | Y | N | Y | N | Y | Y |
| 10 **McHenry** | Y | N | Y | N | Y | Y |
| 11 **Taylor** | Y | N | Y | N | Y | Y |
| 12 Watt | ? | ? | ? | Y | N | N |
| 13 Miller | Y | Y | Y | Y | Y | N |
| **NORTH DAKOTA** | | | | | | |
| AL Pomeroy | Y | Y | Y | Y | Y | N |
| **OHIO** | | | | | | |
| 1 **Chabot** | Y | N | Y | N | Y | Y |
| 2 **Schmidt** | Y | N | Y | N | Y | Y |
| 3 **Turner** | Y | N | Y | N | Y | Y |
| 4 **Oxley** | Y | N | Y | N | Y | Y |
| 5 **Gillmor** | Y | N | Y | N | Y | Y |
| 6 Strickland | ? | ? | ? | Y | N | N |
| 7 **Hobson** | Y | N | Y | N | Y | Y |
| 8 **Boehner** | Y | N | ? | N | Y | Y |
| 9 Kaptur | ? | Y | Y | Y | N | N |
| 10 Kucinich | Y | Y | Y | Y | N | N |
| 11 Jones | Y | Y | Y | Y | Y | N |
| 12 **Tiberi** | Y | N | Y | N | Y | Y |
| 13 Brown | Y | Y | Y | Y | Y | N |
| 14 **LaTourette** | Y | N | Y | N | Y | Y |
| 15 **Pryce** | Y | N | Y | N | Y | Y |
| 16 **Regula** | Y | N | Y | N | Y | Y |
| 17 Ryan | ? | ? | Y | Y | Y | N |
| 18 **Ney** | Y | N | Y | N | Y | Y |
| **OKLAHOMA** | | | | | | |
| 1 **Sullivan** | Y | N | Y | N | Y | Y |
| 2 Boren | Y | N | Y | Y | Y | Y |
| 3 **Lucas** | Y | N | Y | N | ? | Y |
| 4 **Cole** | Y | N | Y | N | Y | Y |
| 5 **Istook** | Y | N | Y | N | Y | Y |
| **OREGON** | | | | | | |
| 1 Wu | Y | Y | Y | Y | Y | N |
| 2 **Walden** | Y | N | Y | N | Y | Y |
| 3 Blumenauer | ? | ? | ? | ? | ? | ? |
| 4 DeFazio | Y | Y | Y | Y | N | N |
| 5 Hooley | Y | Y | Y | Y | Y | N |
| **PENNSYLVANIA** | | | | | | |
| 1 Brady | Y | Y | Y | Y | Y | N |
| 2 Fattah | ? | ? | ? | Y | N | N |
| 3 **English** | Y | N | Y | N | Y | Y |
| 4 **Hart** | Y | N | Y | N | Y | Y |
| 5 **Peterson** | Y | N | Y | N | Y | Y |
| 6 **Gerlach** | Y | N | Y | N | Y | Y |
| 7 **Weldon** | Y | N | Y | N | Y | Y |
| 8 **Fitzpatrick** | Y | N | Y | N | Y | Y |
| 9 **Shuster** | Y | N | Y | N | Y | Y |
| 10 **Sherwood** | Y | N | Y | N | Y | Y |
| 11 Kanjorski | Y | Y | Y | Y | Y | N |
| 12 Murtha | ? | ? | ? | Y | Y | N |
| 13 Schwartz | Y | Y | Y | Y | N | N |
| 14 Doyle | Y | Y | Y | Y | Y | N |
| 15 **Dent** | Y | N | Y | N | Y | Y |
| 16 **Pitts** | Y | N | Y | N | Y | Y |
| 17 Holden | Y | Y | Y | Y | Y | N |
| 18 **Murphy** | Y | N | Y | N | Y | Y |
| 19 **Platts** | Y | N | Y | N | Y | Y |
| **RHODE ISLAND** | | | | | | |
| 1 Kennedy | Y | Y | Y | Y | Y | N |
| 2 Langevin | Y | Y | Y | Y | N | N |
| **SOUTH CAROLINA** | | | | | | |
| 1 **Brown** | Y | N | Y | N | Y | Y |
| 2 **Wilson** | Y | N | Y | N | Y | Y |
| 3 **Barrett** | Y | N | Y | N | Y | Y |
| 4 **Inglis** | Y | N | Y | N | Y | Y |
| 5 Spratt | Y | Y | Y | Y | Y | N |
| 6 Clyburn | Y | Y | Y | Y | N | N |
| **SOUTH DAKOTA** | | | | | | |
| AL Herseth | Y | Y | Y | Y | Y | N |
| **TENNESSEE** | | | | | | |
| 1 **Jenkins** | Y | N | Y | N | Y | Y |
| 2 **Duncan** | Y | N | Y | N | Y | Y |

| | 494 | 495 | 496 | 497 | 498 | 499 |
|---|---|---|---|---|---|---|
| 3 **Wamp** | Y | N | Y | N | Y | Y |
| 4 Davis | Y | Y | Y | Y | Y | Y |
| 5 Cooper | Y | Y | Y | Y | Y | N |
| 6 Gordon | Y | Y | ? | Y | Y | N |
| 7 **Blackburn** | Y | N | Y | N | Y | Y |
| 8 Tanner | Y | Y | Y | Y | Y | N |
| 9 Ford | Y | Y | Y | Y | Y | N |
| **TEXAS** | | | | | | |
| 1 **Gohmert** | Y | N | Y | N | Y | Y |
| 2 **Poe** | Y | N | Y | N | Y | Y |
| 3 **Johnson, S.** | Y | N | Y | N | Y | Y |
| 4 **Hall** | Y | N | Y | N | Y | Y |
| 5 **Hensarling** | Y | N | Y | N | Y | Y |
| 6 **Barton** | Y | N | Y | N | Y | Y |
| 7 **Culberson** | ? | ? | ? | ? | ? | ? |
| 8 **Brady** | ? | ? | ? | N | Y | Y |
| 9 Green, A. | Y | Y | Y | Y | Y | N |
| 10 **McCaul** | Y | N | Y | N | Y | Y |
| 11 **Conaway** | Y | N | Y | N | Y | Y |
| 12 **Granger** | Y | N | Y | N | Y | Y |
| 13 **Thornberry** | Y | N | Y | N | Y | Y |
| 14 **Paul** | Y | N | Y | N | Y | N |
| 15 Hinojosa | + | Y | Y | Y | Y | N |
| 16 Reyes | Y | Y | Y | Y | Y | N |
| 17 Edwards | Y | Y | Y | Y | Y | N |
| 18 Jackson-Lee | Y | Y | Y | Y | Y | N |
| 19 **Neugebauer** | Y | N | Y | N | Y | Y |
| 20 Gonzalez | Y | Y | Y | Y | N | N |
| 21 **Smith** | Y | N | Y | N | Y | Y |
| 22 **DeLay** | Y | N | Y | N | Y | Y |
| 23 **Bonilla** | Y | N | Y | N | Y | Y |
| 24 **Marchant** | Y | N | Y | N | Y | Y |
| 25 Doggett | Y | Y | Y | Y | N | N |
| 26 **Burgess** | Y | N | Y | N | Y | Y |
| 27 Ortiz | Y | Y | Y | Y | Y | N |
| 28 Cuellar | Y | Y | Y | Y | Y | N |
| 29 Green, G. | Y | Y | Y | Y | Y | N |
| 30 Johnson, E. | Y | Y | Y | Y | N | N |
| 31 **Carter** | Y | N | Y | N | Y | Y |
| 32 **Sessions** | Y | N | Y | N | Y | Y |
| **UTAH** | | | | | | |
| 1 **Bishop** | Y | N | Y | N | Y | Y |
| 2 Matheson | Y | Y | Y | Y | Y | N |
| 3 **Cannon** | Y | N | Y | N | Y | Y |
| **VERMONT** | | | | | | |
| AL *Sanders* | Y | Y | Y | Y | Y | N |
| **VIRGINIA** | | | | | | |
| 1 **Davis, J.** | Y | N | Y | ? | ? | Y |
| 2 **Drake** | Y | N | Y | N | Y | Y |
| 3 Scott | Y | Y | Y | Y | Y | N |
| 4 **Forbes** | Y | N | Y | N | Y | Y |
| 5 **Goode** | Y | N | Y | N | Y | Y |
| 6 **Goodlatte** | Y | N | Y | N | Y | Y |
| 7 **Cantor** | Y | N | Y | N | Y | Y |
| 8 Moran | Y | Y | Y | Y | Y | N |
| 9 Boucher | Y | Y | Y | Y | Y | N |
| 10 **Wolf** | Y | N | Y | N | Y | Y |
| 11 **Davis, T.** | Y | Y | Y | N | Y | Y |
| **WASHINGTON** | | | | | | |
| 1 Inslee | Y | Y | Y | Y | N | N |
| 2 Larsen | Y | Y | Y | Y | Y | N |
| 3 Baird | Y | Y | Y | Y | N | N |
| 4 **Hastings** | Y | N | Y | N | Y | Y |
| 5 **McMorris** | Y | N | Y | N | Y | Y |
| 6 Dicks | Y | Y | Y | Y | Y | N |
| 7 McDermott | + | + | + | Y | N | N |
| 8 **Reichert** | Y | N | Y | N | Y | Y |
| 9 Smith | Y | Y | Y | Y | Y | N |
| **WEST VIRGINIA** | | | | | | |
| 1 Mollohan | Y | Y | Y | Y | Y | N |
| 2 **Capito** | Y | N | Y | N | Y | Y |
| 3 Rahall | Y | Y | Y | Y | Y | N |
| **WISCONSIN** | | | | | | |
| 1 **Ryan** | Y | N | Y | N | Y | Y |
| 2 Baldwin | Y | Y | Y | Y | N | N |
| 3 Kind | Y | Y | Y | Y | Y | N |
| 4 Moore | Y | Y | Y | Y | Y | N |
| 5 **Sensenbrenner** | Y | N | Y | N | Y | Y |
| 6 **Petri** | Y | N | Y | N | Y | Y |
| 7 Obey | Y | Y | Y | Y | Y | N |
| 8 **Green** | Y | N | Y | N | Y | Y |
| **WYOMING** | | | | | | |
| AL **Cubin** | Y | Y | Y | N | Y | Y |

# IN THE HOUSE | By Vote Number

**500.** **HR 3402. Justice Department Reauthorization/Recommit.**
Stupak, D-Mich., motion to recommit the bill to the Judiciary Committee with instructions to add language that would give the Justice Department authority to prosecute oil companies that engage in gas price gouging and impose fines of up to $100 million on corporations, as well as up to $1 million in fines or 10 years in prison or both for individuals. Motion rejected 195-226: R 0-226; D 194-0 (ND 145-0, SD 49-0); I 1-0. Sept. 28, 2005.

**501.** **HR 3402. Justice Department Reauthorization/Passage.** Passage of the bill that would authorize nearly $85 billion for the Justice Department, related programs and agencies for fiscal 2006 through 2009, including $24.4 billion for the FBI, $21.5 billion for the Federal Prison System and $7.3 billion for the Drug Enforcement Administration. The measure also would reauthorize provisions of the Violence Against Women Act, require the attorney general to report to Congress annually on the number of U.S. citizens or legal residents detained on suspicion of terrorism and create a privacy officer for the department. Passed 415-4: R 225-2; D 189-2 (ND 140-2, SD 49-0); I 1-0. Sept. 28, 2005.

**502.** **HR 3824. Endangered Species Act Overhaul/Rule.** Adoption of the rule (H Res 470) that would provide for House floor consideration of the bill that would overhaul the Endangered Species Act. Adopted 252-171: R 228-0; D 24-170 (ND 11-133, SD 13-37); I 0-1. Sept. 29, 2005.

**503.** **H Res 388. Cuban Human Rights/Adoption.** Boozman, R-Ark., motion to suspend the rules and adopt the resolution that would condemn human rights violations by the Cuban government and urge an international solidarity campaign to demand the immediate release of all Cuban political prisoners. Motion agreed to 393-31: R 228-1; D 164-30 (ND 119-25, SD 45-5); I 1-0. A two-thirds majority of those present and voting (283 in this case) is required for adoption under suspension of the rules. Sept. 29, 2005.

**504.** **H Con Res 245. Pledge of Allegiance/Adoption.** Sensenbrenner, R-Wis., motion to suspend the rules and adopt the concurrent resolution that would express the sense of Congress that the Supreme Court should speedily recognize the constitutional right of children to recite the pledge in school. Motion agreed to 383-31: R 226-0; D 156-31 (ND 114-26, SD 42-5); I 1-0. A two-thirds majority of those present and voting (276 in this case) is required for adoption under suspension of the rules. Sept. 29, 2005.

| | 500 | 501 | 502 | 503 | 504 |
|---|---|---|---|---|---|
| **ALABAMA** | | | | | |
| 1 Bonner | N | Y | Y | Y | Y |
| 2 Everett | N | Y | Y | Y | Y |
| 3 Rogers | N | Y | Y | Y | Y |
| 4 Aderholt | N | Y | Y | Y | Y |
| 5 Cramer | Y | Y | Y | Y | Y |
| 6 Bachus | N | Y | Y | Y | Y |
| 7 Davis | Y | Y | Y | Y | Y |
| **ALASKA** | | | | | |
| AL Young | ? | Y | Y | Y | Y |
| **ARIZONA** | | | | | |
| 1 Renzi | N | Y | Y | Y | Y |
| 2 Franks | N | Y | Y | Y | Y |
| 3 Shadegg | N | Y | Y | Y | Y |
| 4 Pastor | Y | Y | N | N | N |
| 5 Hayworth | N | Y | Y | Y | Y |
| 6 Flake | N | Y | Y | Y | Y |
| 7 Grijalva | Y | Y | N | N | N |
| 8 Kolbe | N | Y | Y | Y | Y |
| **ARKANSAS** | | | | | |
| 1 Berry | Y | Y | Y | Y | Y |
| 2 Snyder | Y | Y | N | Y | Y |
| 3 Boozman | N | Y | Y | Y | Y |
| 4 Ross | Y | Y | Y | Y | Y |
| **CALIFORNIA** | | | | | |
| 1 Thompson | Y | Y | N | Y | Y |
| 2 Herger | N | Y | Y | Y | Y |
| 3 Lungren | N | Y | Y | Y | Y |
| 4 Doolittle | N | Y | Y | Y | Y |
| 5 Matsui, D. | Y | Y | N | Y | Y |
| 6 Woolsey | Y | Y | N | N | N |
| 7 Miller, George | Y | Y | N | N | N |
| 8 Pelosi | Y | Y | N | Y | Y |
| 9 Lee | Y | Y | ? | ? | ? |
| 10 Tauscher | Y | Y | N | Y | Y |
| 11 Pombo | N | Y | Y | Y | Y |
| 12 Lantos | Y | Y | N | Y | Y |
| 13 Stark | Y | Y | N | N | N |
| 14 Eshoo | Y | Y | N | Y | Y |
| 15 Honda | Y | Y | N | N | N |
| 16 Lofgren | Y | Y | N | Y | Y |
| 17 Farr | Y | Y | N | N | N |
| 18 Cardoza | Y | Y | Y | Y | Y |
| 19 Radanovich | N | Y | Y | Y | Y |
| 20 Costa | ? | ? | Y | Y | Y |
| 21 Nunes | N | Y | Y | Y | Y |
| 22 Thomas | N | Y | Y | Y | Y |
| 23 Capps | Y | Y | N | Y | Y |
| 24 Gallegly | N | Y | Y | Y | Y |
| 25 McKeon | N | Y | Y | Y | Y |
| 26 Dreier | N | Y | Y | Y | Y |
| 27 Sherman | Y | Y | N | Y | Y |
| 28 Berman | Y | Y | N | Y | Y |
| 29 Schiff | Y | Y | N | Y | Y |
| 30 Waxman | Y | Y | N | Y | N |
| 31 Becerra | Y | Y | N | Y | Y |
| 32 Solis | Y | Y | N | Y | Y |
| 33 Watson | Y | N | N | N | N |
| 34 Roybal-Allard | Y | Y | N | Y | Y |
| 35 Waters | Y | ? | N | N | N |
| 36 Harman | ? | ? | ? | ? | ? |
| 37 Millender-McD. | Y | Y | N | Y | Y |
| 38 Napolitano | Y | Y | N | Y | Y |
| 39 Sánchez, Linda | Y | Y | N | Y | P |
| 40 Royce | N | Y | Y | Y | Y |
| 41 Lewis | N | Y | Y | Y | Y |
| 42 Miller, Gary | N | Y | Y | Y | Y |
| 43 Baca | Y | Y | Y | Y | Y |
| 44 Calvert | N | Y | Y | Y | Y |
| 45 Bono | N | Y | Y | Y | Y |
| 46 Rohrabacher | N | Y | Y | Y | Y |
| 47 Sanchez, Loretta | Y | Y | N | Y | Y |
| 48 Vacant | | | | | |
| 49 Issa | N | Y | Y | Y | + |

| | 500 | 501 | 502 | 503 | 504 |
|---|---|---|---|---|---|
| 50 Cunningham | N | Y | Y | Y | Y |
| 51 Filner | Y | Y | N | Y | Y |
| 52 Hunter | ? | ? | Y | Y | Y |
| 53 Davis | Y | Y | N | Y | Y |
| **COLORADO** | | | | | |
| 1 DeGette | Y | Y | N | Y | N |
| 2 Udall | Y | Y | N | Y | Y |
| 3 Salazar | Y | Y | Y | Y | Y |
| 4 Musgrave | N | Y | Y | Y | Y |
| 5 Hefley | N | Y | Y | Y | Y |
| 6 Tancredo | N | N | Y | Y | Y |
| 7 Beauprez | N | Y | Y | Y | Y |
| **CONNECTICUT** | | | | | |
| 1 Larson | Y | Y | N | Y | Y |
| 2 Simmons | N | Y | Y | Y | Y |
| 3 DeLauro | Y | Y | N | Y | Y |
| 4 Shays | N | Y | Y | Y | Y |
| 5 Johnson | N | Y | Y | Y | Y |
| **DELAWARE** | | | | | |
| AL Castle | N | Y | Y | Y | Y |
| **FLORIDA** | | | | | |
| 1 Miller | N | Y | Y | Y | Y |
| 2 Boyd | Y | Y | Y | Y | Y |
| 3 Brown | Y | Y | N | Y | Y |
| 4 Crenshaw | N | Y | Y | Y | Y |
| 5 Brown-Waite | N | Y | Y | Y | Y |
| 6 Stearns | N | Y | Y | Y | Y |
| 7 Mica | N | Y | Y | Y | Y |
| 8 Keller | N | Y | Y | Y | Y |
| 9 Bilirakis | N | Y | Y | Y | Y |
| 10 Young | N | Y | Y | Y | Y |
| 11 Davis | ? | ? | ? | ? | ? |
| 12 Putnam | N | Y | Y | Y | Y |
| 13 Harris | N | Y | Y | Y | Y |
| 14 Mack | N | Y | Y | Y | Y |
| 15 Weldon | N | Y | Y | Y | Y |
| 16 Foley | N | Y | Y | Y | Y |
| 17 Meek | Y | Y | N | Y | Y |
| 18 Ros-Lehtinen | Y | Y | Y | Y | Y |
| 19 Wexler | Y | Y | N | Y | Y |
| 20 Wasserman-Schultz | Y | Y | N | Y | N |
| 21 Diaz-Balart, L. | N | Y | Y | Y | Y |
| 22 Shaw | N | Y | Y | Y | Y |
| 23 Hastings | Y | Y | N | Y | N |
| 24 Feeney | N | Y | Y | Y | Y |
| 25 Diaz-Balart, M. | N | Y | Y | Y | Y |
| **GEORGIA** | | | | | |
| 1 Kingston | N | Y | Y | Y | Y |
| 2 Bishop | Y | Y | Y | Y | Y |
| 3 Marshall | Y | Y | Y | Y | Y |
| 4 McKinney | Y | Y | N | N | ? |
| 5 Lewis | Y | Y | N | N | N |
| 6 Price | N | Y | Y | Y | Y |
| 7 Linder | N | Y | Y | Y | Y |
| 8 Westmoreland | N | Y | Y | Y | Y |
| 9 Norwood | N | Y | Y | Y | Y |
| 10 Deal | N | Y | Y | Y | Y |
| 11 Gingrey | N | Y | Y | Y | Y |
| 12 Barrow | Y | Y | N | Y | Y |
| 13 Scott | Y | Y | Y | Y | Y |
| **HAWAII** | | | | | |
| 1 Abercrombie | Y | Y | Y | Y | Y |
| 2 Case | Y | Y | N | Y | Y |
| **IDAHO** | | | | | |
| 1 Otter | N | Y | Y | Y | Y |
| 2 Simpson | N | Y | Y | Y | Y |
| **ILLINOIS** | | | | | |
| 1 Rush | Y | Y | N | N | P |
| 2 Jackson | Y | Y | N | Y | Y |
| 3 Lipinski | Y | Y | N | Y | Y |
| 4 Gutierrez | + | + | – | + | ? |
| 5 Emanuel | Y | Y | N | Y | Y |
| 6 Hyde | – | + | Y | Y | Y |
| 7 Davis | Y | Y | N | N | Y |
| 8 Bean | Y | Y | N | Y | Y |
| 9 Schakowsky | Y | Y | N | N | N |
| 10 Kirk | N | Y | Y | Y | Y |
| 11 Weller | N | Y | Y | Y | Y |
| 12 Costello | Y | Y | N | Y | Y |

**KEY**   Republicans   Democrats   *Independents*

| | | | |
|---|---|---|---|
| **Y** | Voted for (yea) | **X** | Paired against |
| **#** | Paired for | **–** | Announced against |
| **+** | Announced for | **P** | Voted "present" |
| **N** | Voted against (nay) | | |

| | |
|---|---|
| **C** | Voted "present" to avoid possible conflict of interest |
| **?** | Did not vote or otherwise make a position known |

| | 500 | 501 | 502 | 503 | 504 |
|---|---|---|---|---|---|
| 13 Biggert | N | Y | Y | Y | Y |
| 14 Hastert | | | | | |
| 15 Johnson | N | Y | Y | Y | Y |
| 16 Manzullo | N | Y | Y | Y | Y |
| 17 Evans | Y | Y | N | Y | Y |
| 18 LaHood | N | Y | Y | Y | Y |
| 19 Shimkus | N | Y | Y | Y | Y |
| **INDIANA** | | | | | |
| 1 Visclosky | Y | ? | N | Y | Y |
| 2 Chocola | N | Y | Y | Y | Y |
| 3 Souder | N | Y | Y | Y | Y |
| 4 Buyer | N | Y | Y | Y | Y |
| 5 Burton | N | Y | Y | Y | Y |
| 6 Pence | N | Y | Y | Y | Y |
| 7 Carson | Y | Y | N | N | N |
| 8 Hostettler | N | Y | Y | Y | Y |
| 9 Sodrel | N | Y | Y | Y | Y |
| **IOWA** | | | | | |
| 1 Nussle | N | Y | Y | Y | Y |
| 2 Leach | N | Y | Y | Y | Y |
| 3 Boswell | ? | ? | ? | ? | ? |
| 4 Latham | N | Y | Y | Y | Y |
| 5 King | N | Y | Y | Y | Y |
| **KANSAS** | | | | | |
| 1 Moran | N | Y | Y | Y | Y |
| 2 Ryun | N | Y | Y | Y | Y |
| 3 Moore | Y | Y | N | Y | Y |
| 4 Tiahrt | N | Y | Y | Y | Y |
| **KENTUCKY** | | | | | |
| 1 Whitfield | N | Y | Y | Y | Y |
| 2 Lewis | N | Y | Y | Y | Y |
| 3 Northup | N | Y | Y | Y | Y |
| 4 Davis | N | Y | Y | Y | Y |
| 5 Rogers | N | Y | Y | Y | Y |
| 6 Chandler | Y | Y | N | Y | Y |
| **LOUISIANA** | | | | | |
| 1 Jindal | N | Y | Y | Y | Y |
| 2 Jefferson | Y | Y | N | Y | Y |
| 3 Melancon | ? | ? | Y | Y | Y |
| 4 McCrery | N | Y | Y | Y | Y |
| 5 Alexander | N | Y | Y | Y | Y |
| 6 Baker | N | Y | Y | Y | Y |
| 7 Boustany | N | Y | Y | Y | Y |
| **MAINE** | | | | | |
| 1 Allen | Y | Y | N | Y | Y |
| 2 Michaud | Y | Y | N | Y | Y |
| **MARYLAND** | | | | | |
| 1 Gilchrest | N | Y | Y | Y | Y |
| 2 Ruppersberger | + | + | N | Y | Y |
| 3 Cardin | Y | Y | N | Y | Y |
| 4 Wynn | Y | Y | N | N | Y |
| 5 Hoyer | Y | Y | N | Y | Y |
| 6 Bartlett | N | Y | Y | Y | Y |
| 7 Cummings | Y | Y | N | Y | Y |
| 8 Van Hollen | Y | Y | N | Y | Y |
| **MASSACHUSETTS** | | | | | |
| 1 Olver | Y | Y | N | Y | Y |
| 2 Neal | Y | Y | N | Y | Y |
| 3 McGovern | Y | Y | N | Y | Y |
| 4 Frank | Y | Y | N | Y | N |
| 5 Meehan | Y | N | N | Y | Y |
| 6 Tierney | Y | Y | N | Y | P |
| 7 Markey | Y | Y | N | Y | N |
| 8 Capuano | Y | Y | N | Y | P |
| 9 Lynch | Y | Y | N | Y | Y |
| 10 Delahunt | Y | Y | N | Y | Y |
| **MICHIGAN** | | | | | |
| 1 Stupak | Y | Y | N | Y | Y |
| 2 Hoekstra | N | Y | Y | Y | Y |
| 3 Ehlers | N | Y | Y | Y | Y |
| 4 Camp | N | Y | Y | Y | Y |
| 5 Kildee | Y | Y | N | Y | Y |
| 6 Upton | N | Y | Y | Y | Y |
| 7 Schwarz | N | Y | Y | Y | Y |
| 8 Rogers | N | Y | Y | Y | Y |
| 9 Knollenberg | N | Y | Y | Y | Y |
| 10 Miller | N | Y | Y | Y | Y |
| 11 McCotter | N | Y | Y | Y | Y |
| 12 Levin | Y | Y | N | Y | Y |
| 13 Kilpatrick | Y | Y | N | Y | Y |
| 14 Conyers | Y | Y | N | N | N |
| 15 Dingell | Y | Y | N | Y | Y |

| | 500 | 501 | 502 | 503 | 504 |
|---|---|---|---|---|---|
| **MINNESOTA** | | | | | |
| 1 Gutknecht | N | Y | Y | Y | Y |
| 2 Kline | N | Y | Y | Y | Y |
| 3 Ramstad | N | Y | Y | Y | Y |
| 4 McCollum | Y | Y | N | Y | Y |
| 5 Sabo | Y | Y | N | Y | Y |
| 6 Kennedy | N | Y | Y | Y | Y |
| 7 Peterson | Y | Y | Y | Y | Y |
| 8 Oberstar | Y | Y | N | Y | Y |
| **MISSISSIPPI** | | | | | |
| 1 Wicker | N | Y | Y | Y | Y |
| 2 Thompson | Y | Y | Y | N | Y |
| 3 Pickering | N | Y | Y | Y | Y |
| 4 Taylor | Y | Y | N | Y | Y |
| **MISSOURI** | | | | | |
| 1 Clay | Y | Y | N | N | Y |
| 2 Akin | N | Y | Y | Y | Y |
| 3 Carnahan | Y | Y | N | Y | Y |
| 4 Skelton | Y | Y | N | Y | Y |
| 5 Cleaver | Y | Y | N | Y | N |
| 6 Graves | N | Y | Y | Y | Y |
| 7 Blunt | N | Y | Y | Y | Y |
| 8 Emerson | N | Y | Y | Y | Y |
| 9 Hulshof | N | Y | Y | Y | Y |
| **MONTANA** | | | | | |
| AL Rehberg | N | Y | Y | Y | Y |
| **NEBRASKA** | | | | | |
| 1 Fortenberry | N | Y | Y | Y | Y |
| 2 Terry | N | Y | Y | Y | Y |
| 3 Osborne | N | Y | Y | Y | Y |
| **NEVADA** | | | | | |
| 1 Berkley | Y | Y | N | Y | Y |
| 2 Gibbons | N | Y | Y | Y | + |
| 3 Porter | N | Y | Y | Y | Y |
| **NEW HAMPSHIRE** | | | | | |
| 1 Bradley | N | Y | Y | Y | Y |
| 2 Bass | N | Y | Y | Y | Y |
| **NEW JERSEY** | | | | | |
| 1 Andrews | Y | Y | – | Y | Y |
| 2 LoBiondo | N | Y | Y | Y | Y |
| 3 Saxton | N | Y | Y | Y | Y |
| 4 Smith | N | Y | Y | Y | Y |
| 5 Garrett | N | Y | Y | Y | Y |
| 6 Pallone | Y | Y | N | Y | Y |
| 7 Ferguson | Y | Y | N | Y | Y |
| 8 Pascrell | Y | Y | N | Y | Y |
| 9 Rothman | Y | Y | N | Y | Y |
| 10 Payne | Y | Y | N | N | N |
| 11 Frelinghuysen | N | Y | Y | Y | Y |
| 12 Holt | Y | Y | N | Y | Y |
| 13 Menendez | Y | Y | N | Y | Y |
| **NEW MEXICO** | | | | | |
| 1 Wilson | N | Y | Y | Y | Y |
| 2 Pearce | N | Y | Y | Y | Y |
| 3 Udall | Y | Y | N | Y | Y |
| **NEW YORK** | | | | | |
| 1 Bishop | Y | Y | N | Y | Y |
| 2 Israel | Y | Y | N | Y | Y |
| 3 King | N | Y | Y | Y | Y |
| 4 McCarthy | Y | Y | N | Y | Y |
| 5 Ackerman | Y | Y | N | Y | N |
| 6 Meeks | Y | Y | N | N | Y |
| 7 Crowley | Y | Y | N | Y | Y |
| 8 Nadler | Y | Y | N | Y | N |
| 9 Weiner | Y | Y | N | Y | Y |
| 10 Towns | Y | Y | N | N | N |
| 11 Owens | Y | Y | N | Y | P |
| 12 Velázquez | Y | Y | N | N | N |
| 13 Fossella | N | Y | Y | Y | Y |
| 14 Maloney | Y | Y | N | Y | Y |
| 15 Rangel | Y | Y | N | Y | Y |
| 16 Serrano | Y | Y | N | N | N |
| 17 Engel | Y | Y | N | Y | Y |
| 18 Lowey | Y | Y | N | Y | Y |
| 19 Kelly | N | Y | Y | Y | Y |
| 20 Sweeney | N | Y | Y | Y | Y |
| 21 McNulty | Y | Y | N | Y | Y |
| 22 Hinchey | Y | Y | N | N | N |
| 23 McHugh | N | Y | Y | Y | Y |
| 24 Boehlert | N | Y | Y | Y | Y |
| 25 Walsh | N | Y | Y | Y | Y |
| 26 Reynolds | N | Y | Y | Y | Y |
| 27 Higgins | Y | Y | N | Y | Y |
| 28 Slaughter | Y | Y | ? | ? | ? |
| 29 Kuhl | N | Y | Y | Y | Y |

| | 500 | 501 | 502 | 503 | 504 |
|---|---|---|---|---|---|
| **NORTH CAROLINA** | | | | | |
| 1 Butterfield | Y | Y | N | Y | Y |
| 2 Etheridge | Y | Y | N | Y | Y |
| 3 Jones | N | Y | Y | Y | Y |
| 4 Price | Y | Y | N | Y | Y |
| 5 Foxx | N | Y | Y | Y | Y |
| 6 Coble | N | Y | Y | Y | Y |
| 7 McIntyre | Y | Y | N | Y | Y |
| 8 Hayes | N | Y | Y | Y | Y |
| 9 Myrick | N | Y | Y | Y | Y |
| 10 McHenry | N | Y | Y | Y | Y |
| 11 Taylor | N | Y | Y | Y | Y |
| 12 Watt | Y | Y | N | Y | P |
| 13 Miller | Y | Y | N | Y | Y |
| **NORTH DAKOTA** | | | | | |
| AL Pomeroy | Y | Y | Y | Y | Y |
| **OHIO** | | | | | |
| 1 Chabot | N | Y | Y | Y | Y |
| 2 Schmidt | N | Y | Y | Y | Y |
| 3 Turner | N | Y | Y | Y | Y |
| 4 Oxley | N | Y | Y | Y | Y |
| 5 Gillmor | N | Y | Y | Y | Y |
| 6 Strickland | Y | Y | N | Y | Y |
| 7 Hobson | N | Y | Y | Y | Y |
| 8 Boehner | N | Y | Y | Y | Y |
| 9 Kaptur | Y | Y | N | ? | Y |
| 10 Kucinich | Y | Y | N | N | Y |
| 11 Jones | Y | Y | N | N | N |
| 12 Tiberi | N | Y | Y | Y | Y |
| 13 Brown | Y | Y | N | Y | Y |
| 14 LaTourette | N | Y | Y | Y | Y |
| 15 Pryce | N | Y | Y | Y | Y |
| 16 Regula | N | Y | Y | Y | Y |
| 17 Ryan | Y | Y | N | Y | Y |
| 18 Ney | N | Y | Y | Y | Y |
| **OKLAHOMA** | | | | | |
| 1 Sullivan | N | Y | Y | Y | Y |
| 2 Boren | Y | Y | Y | Y | Y |
| 3 Lucas | N | Y | Y | Y | Y |
| 4 Cole | N | Y | Y | Y | Y |
| 5 Istook | N | Y | Y | Y | Y |
| **OREGON** | | | | | |
| 1 Wu | Y | Y | Y | Y | Y |
| 2 Walden | N | Y | Y | Y | Y |
| 3 Blumenauer | ? | ? | N | Y | N |
| 4 DeFazio | Y | Y | N | Y | N |
| 5 Hooley | Y | Y | N | Y | Y |
| **PENNSYLVANIA** | | | | | |
| 1 Brady | Y | Y | N | Y | Y |
| 2 Fattah | Y | Y | N | Y | Y |
| 3 English | N | Y | Y | Y | Y |
| 4 Hart | N | Y | Y | Y | Y |
| 5 Peterson | N | Y | Y | Y | Y |
| 6 Gerlach | N | Y | ? | Y | Y |
| 7 Weldon | N | Y | Y | Y | Y |
| 8 Fitzpatrick | N | Y | Y | Y | Y |
| 9 Shuster | N | Y | Y | Y | Y |
| 10 Sherwood | N | Y | Y | Y | Y |
| 11 Kanjorski | Y | Y | N | Y | Y |
| 12 Murtha | Y | Y | N | Y | Y |
| 13 Schwartz | Y | Y | N | Y | Y |
| 14 Doyle | Y | Y | N | Y | Y |
| 15 Dent | N | Y | Y | Y | Y |
| 16 Pitts | N | Y | Y | Y | Y |
| 17 Holden | Y | Y | N | Y | Y |
| 18 Murphy | N | Y | Y | Y | Y |
| 19 Platts | N | Y | Y | Y | Y |
| **RHODE ISLAND** | | | | | |
| 1 Kennedy | Y | Y | N | Y | Y |
| 2 Langevin | Y | Y | N | Y | Y |
| **SOUTH CAROLINA** | | | | | |
| 1 Brown | N | Y | Y | Y | Y |
| 2 Wilson | N | Y | Y | Y | Y |
| 3 Barrett | N | Y | Y | Y | Y |
| 4 Inglis | N | Y | Y | Y | Y |
| 5 Spratt | Y | Y | N | Y | Y |
| 6 Clyburn | Y | Y | N | Y | Y |
| **SOUTH DAKOTA** | | | | | |
| AL Herseth | Y | Y | Y | Y | Y |
| **TENNESSEE** | | | | | |
| 1 Jenkins | N | Y | Y | Y | Y |
| 2 Duncan | N | Y | Y | Y | Y |

| | 500 | 501 | 502 | 503 | 504 |
|---|---|---|---|---|---|
| 3 Wamp | N | Y | Y | Y | Y |
| 4 Davis | Y | Y | N | Y | Y |
| 5 Cooper | Y | Y | N | Y | Y |
| 6 Gordon | Y | Y | N | Y | Y |
| 7 Blackburn | N | Y | Y | Y | Y |
| 8 Tanner | Y | Y | N | Y | Y |
| 9 Ford | Y | Y | N | Y | Y |
| **TEXAS** | | | | | |
| 1 Gohmert | N | Y | Y | Y | Y |
| 2 Poe | N | Y | Y | Y | Y |
| 3 Johnson, S. | N | Y | Y | Y | Y |
| 4 Hall | N | Y | Y | Y | Y |
| 5 Hensarling | N | Y | Y | Y | Y |
| 6 Barton | N | Y | Y | Y | Y |
| 7 Culberson | ? | ? | ? | ? | ? |
| 8 Brady | N | Y | Y | Y | Y |
| 9 Green, A. | Y | Y | N | Y | P |
| 10 McCaul | N | Y | Y | Y | Y |
| 11 Conaway | N | Y | Y | Y | Y |
| 12 Granger | N | Y | Y | Y | Y |
| 13 Thornberry | N | Y | Y | Y | Y |
| 14 Paul | N | N | N | N | Y |
| 15 Hinojosa | Y | Y | N | Y | Y |
| 16 Reyes | Y | Y | N | Y | Y |
| 17 Edwards | Y | Y | N | Y | Y |
| 18 Jackson-Lee | Y | Y | N | N | Y |
| 19 Neugebauer | N | Y | Y | Y | Y |
| 20 Gonzalez | Y | Y | N | Y | Y |
| 21 Smith | N | Y | Y | Y | Y |
| 22 DeLay | N | Y | Y | Y | Y |
| 23 Bonilla | N | Y | Y | Y | Y |
| 24 Marchant | N | Y | Y | Y | ? |
| 25 Doggett | Y | Y | N | Y | Y |
| 26 Burgess | N | Y | Y | Y | Y |
| 27 Ortiz | Y | Y | N | Y | Y |
| 28 Cuellar | Y | Y | Y | Y | Y |
| 29 Green, G. | Y | Y | N | Y | Y |
| 30 Johnson, E. | Y | Y | N | N | N |
| 31 Carter | N | Y | Y | Y | Y |
| 32 Sessions | N | Y | Y | Y | Y |
| **UTAH** | | | | | |
| 1 Bishop | N | Y | Y | Y | Y |
| 2 Matheson | Y | Y | Y | Y | Y |
| 3 Cannon | N | Y | Y | Y | Y |
| **VERMONT** | | | | | |
| AL *Sanders* | Y | Y | N | Y | Y |
| **VIRGINIA** | | | | | |
| 1 Davis, J. | N | Y | Y | Y | Y |
| 2 Drake | N | Y | Y | Y | Y |
| 3 Scott | Y | Y | N | Y | N |
| 4 Forbes | N | Y | Y | Y | Y |
| 5 Goode | N | Y | Y | Y | Y |
| 6 Goodlatte | N | Y | Y | Y | Y |
| 7 Cantor | N | Y | Y | Y | Y |
| 8 Moran | Y | Y | N | Y | Y |
| 9 Boucher | Y | Y | N | Y | Y |
| 10 Wolf | N | Y | Y | Y | Y |
| 11 Davis, T. | N | Y | Y | Y | Y |
| **WASHINGTON** | | | | | |
| 1 Inslee | Y | Y | N | Y | Y |
| 2 Larsen | Y | Y | N | Y | Y |
| 3 Baird | Y | Y | N | Y | Y |
| 4 Hastings | N | Y | Y | Y | Y |
| 5 McMorris | N | Y | Y | Y | Y |
| 6 Dicks | Y | ? | N | Y | Y |
| 7 McDermott | Y | Y | N | N | N |
| 8 Reichert | N | Y | Y | Y | Y |
| 9 Smith | Y | Y | N | Y | Y |
| **WEST VIRGINIA** | | | | | |
| 1 Mollohan | Y | Y | N | Y | Y |
| 2 Capito | N | Y | Y | Y | Y |
| 3 Rahall | Y | Y | N | Y | Y |
| **WISCONSIN** | | | | | |
| 1 Ryan | N | Y | Y | Y | Y |
| 2 Baldwin | Y | Y | N | Y | Y |
| 3 Kind | Y | Y | N | Y | Y |
| 4 Moore | Y | Y | ? | Y | P |
| 5 Sensenbrenner | N | Y | Y | Y | Y |
| 6 Petri | N | Y | Y | Y | Y |
| 7 Obey | Y | Y | N | ? | Y |
| 8 Green | N | Y | Y | Y | Y |
| **WYOMING** | | | | | |
| AL Cubin | N | Y | Y | Y | Y |

# IN THE HOUSE | By Vote Number

**505.** **HR 3824. Endangered Species Act Overhaul/Substitute.** Miller, D-Calif., substitute amendment that would reauthorize the Endangered Species Act through 2010 and make changes to the species recovery plan process. It would require recovery plans to identify publicly owned land necessary to achieve species recovery. It would establish a program to promote voluntary habitat conservation for endangered species on privately owned land. The definition of putting a species in jeopardy would be changed to any action that directly or indirectly "makes it less likely" that a threatened or endangered species would recover, or significantly delays or increases the cost of species recovery. Rejected 206-216: R 29-198; D 176-18 (ND 138-6, SD 38-12); I 1-0. Sept. 29, 2005.

**506.** **HR 3824. Endangered Species Act Overhaul/Passage.** Passage of the bill that would overhaul and reauthorize the Endangered Species Act through 2010. It would replace the critical habitat designation with expanded authority to develop recovery plans for species that take into account areas of "special value" in conserving an endangered or threatened species. The Interior Department would be required to reimburse landowners who are not allowed to develop their land because of protections for endangered species. It also would authorize grants for private landowners to protect endangered species. Passed 229-193: R 193-34; D 36-158 (ND 15-129, SD 21-29); I 0-1. Sept. 29, 2005.

**507.** **H J Res 68. Fiscal 2006 Continuing Resolution/Passage.** Passage of the joint resolution that would provide continuing appropriations through Nov. 18 for all federal departments and agencies whose fiscal 2006 appropriations bills have not been enacted. Passed 348-65: R 219-2; D 129-62 (ND 87-54, SD 42-8); I 0-1. Sept. 29, 2005.

**508.** **H Con Res 178. Idiopathic Pulmonary Fibrosis/Adoption.** Deal, R-Ga., motion to suspend the rules and adopt the concurrent resolution that would recognize the need to increase awareness of idiopathic pulmonary fibrosis and to work to find a cure. Motion agreed to 401-0: R 218-0; D 182-0 (ND 133-0, SD 49-0); I 1-0. A two-thirds majority of those present and voting (268 in this case) is required for adoption under suspension of the rules. Sept. 29, 2005.

| | 505 | 506 | 507 | 508 |
|---|---|---|---|---|
| **ALABAMA** | | | | |
| 1 Bonner | N | Y | Y | Y |
| 2 Everett | N | Y | Y | Y |
| 3 Rogers | N | Y | Y | Y |
| 4 Aderholt | N | Y | Y | Y |
| 5 Cramer | N | Y | Y | Y |
| 6 Bachus | N | Y | Y | Y |
| 7 Davis | N | Y | Y | Y |
| **ALASKA** | | | | |
| AL Young | N | Y | Y | Y |
| **ARIZONA** | | | | |
| 1 Renzi | N | Y | Y | Y |
| 2 Franks | N | Y | Y | Y |
| 3 Shadegg | N | Y | Y | ? |
| 4 Pastor | Y | N | N | Y |
| 5 Hayworth | N | Y | Y | Y |
| 6 Flake | N | Y | Y | Y |
| 7 Grijalva | Y | N | N | Y |
| 8 Kolbe | N | Y | Y | Y |
| **ARKANSAS** | | | | |
| 1 Berry | N | Y | Y | Y |
| 2 Snyder | Y | N | Y | Y |
| 3 Boozman | N | Y | Y | Y |
| 4 Ross | N | Y | Y | Y |
| **CALIFORNIA** | | | | |
| 1 Thompson | Y | N | Y | Y |
| 2 Herger | N | Y | Y | Y |
| 3 Lungren | N | Y | Y | Y |
| 4 Doolittle | N | Y | Y | ? |
| 5 Matsui, D. | Y | N | Y | Y |
| 6 Woolsey | Y | N | N | Y |
| 7 Miller, George | Y | N | N | ? |
| 8 Pelosi | Y | N | Y | Y |
| 9 Lee | ? | ? | ? | ? |
| 10 Tauscher | Y | N | Y | Y |
| 11 Pombo | N | Y | Y | Y |
| 12 Lantos | Y | N | Y | Y |
| 13 Stark | Y | N | N | ? |
| 14 Eshoo | Y | N | Y | Y |
| 15 Honda | Y | N | N | Y |
| 16 Lofgren | Y | N | Y | ? |
| 17 Farr | Y | N | N | Y |
| 18 Cardoza | N | Y | Y | Y |
| 19 Radanovich | N | Y | Y | Y |
| 20 Costa | N | Y | Y | Y |
| 21 Nunes | N | Y | Y | Y |
| 22 Thomas | N | Y | Y | Y |
| 23 Capps | Y | N | N | Y |
| 24 Gallegly | N | Y | ? | ? |
| 25 McKeon | N | Y | Y | Y |
| 26 Dreier | N | Y | Y | Y |
| 27 Sherman | Y | N | Y | Y |
| 28 Berman | Y | N | ? | ? |
| 29 Schiff | Y | N | Y | Y |
| 30 Waxman | Y | N | Y | Y |
| 31 Becerra | Y | N | Y | Y |
| 32 Solis | Y | N | Y | Y |
| 33 Watson | Y | N | Y | Y |
| 34 Roybal-Allard | Y | N | Y | Y |
| 35 Waters | Y | N | N | Y |
| 36 Harman | ? | ? | ? | ? |
| 37 Millender-McD. | Y | N | Y | Y |
| 38 Napolitano | Y | N | Y | Y |
| 39 Sánchez, Linda | Y | N | Y | Y |
| 40 Royce | N | Y | Y | Y |
| 41 Lewis | N | Y | Y | Y |
| 42 Miller, Gary | N | Y | ? | ? |
| 43 Baca | Y | N | Y | Y |
| 44 Calvert | N | Y | Y | Y |
| 45 Bono | N | Y | Y | Y |
| 46 Rohrabacher | N | Y | Y | Y |
| 47 Sanchez, Loretta | Y | N | Y | Y |
| 48 Vacant | | | | |
| 49 Issa | N | Y | Y | Y |
| 50 Cunningham | N | Y | Y | Y |
| 51 Filner | Y | N | N | Y |
| 52 Hunter | N | Y | Y | Y |
| 53 Davis | Y | N | Y | Y |
| **COLORADO** | | | | |
| 1 DeGette | Y | N | N | Y |
| 2 Udall | Y | N | Y | Y |
| 3 Salazar | N | Y | Y | Y |
| 4 Musgrave | N | Y | Y | Y |
| 5 Hefley | N | Y | Y | Y |
| 6 Tancredo | N | Y | Y | Y |
| 7 Beauprez | N | Y | Y | Y |
| **CONNECTICUT** | | | | |
| 1 Larson | Y | N | N | Y |
| 2 Simmons | N | N | Y | Y |
| 3 DeLauro | Y | N | N | Y |
| 4 Shays | Y | N | Y | Y |
| 5 Johnson | Y | N | Y | Y |
| **DELAWARE** | | | | |
| AL Castle | Y | N | Y | Y |
| **FLORIDA** | | | | |
| 1 Miller | N | Y | Y | ? |
| 2 Boyd | Y | Y | Y | Y |
| 3 Brown | Y | N | Y | Y |
| 4 Crenshaw | N | Y | Y | Y |
| 5 Brown-Waite | N | Y | Y | Y |
| 6 Stearns | N | Y | Y | Y |
| 7 Mica | N | Y | Y | Y |
| 8 Keller | N | Y | Y | Y |
| 9 Bilirakis | N | Y | Y | Y |
| 10 Young | N | Y | Y | Y |
| 11 Davis | ? | ? | ? | ? |
| 12 Putnam | N | Y | Y | Y |
| 13 Harris | N | Y | Y | Y |
| 14 Mack | N | Y | Y | Y |
| 15 Weldon | N | Y | Y | Y |
| 16 Foley | N | N | Y | Y |
| 17 Meek | Y | N | Y | Y |
| 18 Ros-Lehtinen | N | Y | Y | ? |
| 19 Wexler | Y | N | Y | Y |
| 20 Wasserman-Schultz | Y | N | Y | Y |
| 21 Diaz-Balart, L. | N | Y | Y | Y |
| 22 Shaw | N | N | Y | Y |
| 23 Hastings | Y | N | Y | Y |
| 24 Feeney | N | Y | Y | Y |
| 25 Diaz-Balart, M. | N | Y | Y | Y |
| **GEORGIA** | | | | |
| 1 Kingston | N | Y | Y | Y |
| 2 Bishop | N | Y | Y | Y |
| 3 Marshall | Y | Y | Y | Y |
| 4 McKinney | Y | N | N | Y |
| 5 Lewis | Y | N | N | Y |
| 6 Price | N | Y | Y | Y |
| 7 Linder | N | Y | Y | Y |
| 8 Westmoreland | N | Y | Y | Y |
| 9 Norwood | N | Y | Y | Y |
| 10 Deal | N | Y | Y | Y |
| 11 Gingrey | N | Y | Y | Y |
| 12 Barrow | Y | Y | Y | Y |
| 13 Scott | N | Y | Y | ? |
| **HAWAII** | | | | |
| 1 Abercrombie | Y | Y | Y | Y |
| 2 Case | Y | N | Y | Y |
| **IDAHO** | | | | |
| 1 Otter | N | Y | Y | Y |
| 2 Simpson | N | Y | Y | Y |
| **ILLINOIS** | | | | |
| 1 Rush | Y | N | Y | Y |
| 2 Jackson | Y | N | Y | Y |
| 3 Lipinski | Y | N | Y | Y |
| 4 Gutierrez | + | – | + | + |
| 5 Emanuel | Y | N | Y | Y |
| 6 Hyde | N | Y | Y | Y |
| 7 Davis | Y | N | Y | Y |
| 8 Bean | Y | N | Y | Y |
| 9 Schakowsky | Y | N | N | Y |
| 10 Kirk | Y | N | Y | Y |
| 11 Weller | N | Y | Y | Y |
| 12 Costello | Y | Y | N | Y |

**KEY** | **Republicans** | Democrats | *Independents*

| | | | |
|---|---|---|---|
| Y | Voted for (yea) | X | Paired against |
| # | Paired for | – | Announced against |
| + | Announced for | P | Voted "present" |
| N | Voted against (nay) | | |
| | | C | Voted "present" to avoid possible conflict of interest |
| | | ? | Did not vote or otherwise make a position known |

| | 505 | 506 | 507 | 508 |
|---|---|---|---|---|
| 13 Biggert | Y | N | Y | Y |
| 14 Hastert | | | | |
| 15 Johnson | Y | N | Y | Y |
| 16 Manzullo | N | Y | Y | Y |
| 17 Evans | Y | N | Y | Y |
| 18 LaHood | N | N | Y | Y |
| 19 Shimkus | N | Y | Y | Y |
| **INDIANA** | | | | |
| 1 Visclosky | Y | N | Y | Y |
| 2 Chocola | N | Y | Y | Y |
| 3 Souder | N | Y | Y | Y |
| 4 Buyer | N | Y | ? | Y |
| 5 Burton | N | Y | Y | Y |
| 6 Pence | N | Y | Y | Y |
| 7 Carson | Y | N | N | Y |
| 8 Hostettler | N | Y | Y | Y |
| 9 Sodrel | N | Y | Y | Y |
| **IOWA** | | | | |
| 1 Nussle | N | Y | Y | Y |
| 2 Leach | Y | N | Y | Y |
| 3 Boswell | ? | ? | ? | ? |
| 4 Latham | N | Y | Y | Y |
| 5 King | N | Y | Y | Y |
| **KANSAS** | | | | |
| 1 Moran | N | Y | Y | Y |
| 2 Ryun | N | Y | Y | Y |
| 3 Moore | Y | N | Y | Y |
| 4 Tiahrt | N | Y | Y | Y |
| **KENTUCKY** | | | | |
| 1 Whitfield | N | Y | Y | Y |
| 2 Lewis | N | Y | Y | Y |
| 3 Northup | N | Y | Y | Y |
| 4 Davis | N | Y | Y | Y |
| 5 Rogers | N | Y | Y | Y |
| 6 Chandler | Y | N | Y | Y |
| **LOUISIANA** | | | | |
| 1 Jindal | N | Y | Y | Y |
| 2 Jefferson | Y | N | Y | Y |
| 3 Melancon | N | Y | Y | Y |
| 4 McCrery | N | Y | Y | Y |
| 5 Alexander | N | Y | Y | Y |
| 6 Baker | N | Y | Y | Y |
| 7 Boustany | N | Y | Y | Y |
| **MAINE** | | | | |
| 1 Allen | Y | N | Y | Y |
| 2 Michaud | Y | N | Y | Y |
| **MARYLAND** | | | | |
| 1 Gilchrest | Y | N | Y | Y |
| 2 Ruppersberger | Y | N | Y | Y |
| 3 Cardin | Y | N | Y | Y |
| 4 Wynn | Y | Y | Y | Y |
| 5 Hoyer | Y | N | Y | Y |
| 6 Bartlett | N | Y | Y | Y |
| 7 Cummings | Y | N | ? | ? |
| 8 Van Hollen | Y | N | Y | Y |
| **MASSACHUSETTS** | | | | |
| 1 Olver | Y | N | N | Y |
| 2 Neal | Y | N | N | Y |
| 3 McGovern | Y | N | N | Y |
| 4 Frank | Y | N | N | Y |
| 5 Meehan | Y | N | N | Y |
| 6 Tierney | Y | N | N | Y |
| 7 Markey | Y | N | N | Y |
| 8 Capuano | Y | N | N | Y |
| 9 Lynch | Y | N | Y | ? |
| 10 Delahunt | Y | N | ? | ? |
| **MICHIGAN** | | | | |
| 1 Stupak | Y | N | Y | Y |
| 2 Hoekstra | N | Y | Y | Y |
| 3 Ehlers | Y | N | Y | Y |
| 4 Camp | N | Y | Y | Y |
| 5 Kildee | Y | N | Y | N |
| 6 Upton | Y | N | Y | Y |
| 7 Schwarz | Y | N | Y | Y |
| 8 Rogers | N | Y | Y | Y |
| 9 Knollenberg | N | Y | Y | Y |
| 10 Miller | N | Y | Y | Y |
| 11 McCotter | N | Y | Y | Y |
| 12 Levin | Y | N | Y | Y |
| 13 Kilpatrick | Y | N | Y | + |
| 14 Conyers | Y | N | N | Y |
| 15 Dingell | Y | N | Y | Y |
| **MINNESOTA** | | | | |
| 1 Gutknecht | N | Y | Y | Y |
| 2 Kline | N | Y | Y | Y |
| 3 Ramstad | Y | N | Y | Y |
| 4 McCollum | Y | N | N | Y |
| 5 Sabo | Y | N | Y | Y |
| 6 Kennedy | N | Y | Y | Y |
| 7 Peterson | N | Y | Y | Y |
| 8 Oberstar | Y | N | N | Y |
| **MISSISSIPPI** | | | | |
| 1 Wicker | N | Y | Y | Y |
| 2 Thompson | Y | Y | Y | Y |
| 3 Pickering | N | Y | Y | Y |
| 4 Taylor | Y | Y | Y | Y |
| **MISSOURI** | | | | |
| 1 Clay | Y | N | N | Y |
| 2 Akin | N | Y | Y | Y |
| 3 Carnahan | Y | N | Y | Y |
| 4 Skelton | Y | Y | Y | Y |
| 5 Cleaver | Y | N | Y | Y |
| 6 Graves | N | Y | Y | Y |
| 7 Blunt | N | Y | Y | Y |
| 8 Emerson | N | Y | Y | ? |
| 9 Hulshof | N | Y | Y | Y |
| **MONTANA** | | | | |
| AL Rehberg | N | Y | Y | Y |
| **NEBRASKA** | | | | |
| 1 Fortenberry | N | Y | Y | Y |
| 2 Terry | N | Y | Y | Y |
| 3 Osborne | N | Y | Y | Y |
| **NEVADA** | | | | |
| 1 Berkley | Y | N | Y | Y |
| 2 Gibbons | N | Y | Y | Y |
| 3 Porter | N | Y | Y | Y |
| **NEW HAMPSHIRE** | | | | |
| 1 Bradley | Y | N | Y | Y |
| 2 Bass | Y | N | Y | Y |
| **NEW JERSEY** | | | | |
| 1 Andrews | Y | N | Y | Y |
| 2 LoBiondo | Y | N | Y | Y |
| 3 Saxton | Y | N | Y | Y |
| 4 Smith | Y | N | Y | Y |
| 5 Garrett | N | Y | Y | Y |
| 6 Pallone | Y | N | Y | Y |
| 7 Ferguson | Y | N | Y | Y |
| 8 Pascrell | Y | N | Y | Y |
| 9 Rothman | Y | N | Y | Y |
| 10 Payne | ? | ? | ? | ? |
| 11 Frelinghuysen | Y | N | Y | Y |
| 12 Holt | Y | N | N | Y |
| 13 Menendez | Y | N | Y | Y |
| **NEW MEXICO** | | | | |
| 1 Wilson | N | Y | Y | Y |
| 2 Pearce | N | Y | Y | Y |
| 3 Udall | Y | N | N | Y |
| **NEW YORK** | | | | |
| 1 Bishop | Y | N | Y | Y |
| 2 Israel | Y | N | Y | Y |
| 3 King | N | Y | Y | Y |
| 4 McCarthy | Y | N | Y | Y |
| 5 Ackerman | Y | N | Y | ? |
| 6 Meeks | Y | N | Y | Y |
| 7 Crowley | Y | N | N | Y |
| 8 Nadler | Y | N | Y | Y |
| 9 Weiner | Y | N | N | Y |
| 10 Towns | ? | ? | ? | ? |
| 11 Owens | Y | N | Y | Y |
| 12 Velázquez | Y | N | N | Y |
| 13 Fossella | N | Y | Y | Y |
| 14 Maloney | Y | N | Y | Y |
| 15 Rangel | Y | N | Y | Y |
| 16 Serrano | Y | N | Y | Y |
| 17 Engel | Y | N | Y | Y |
| 18 Lowey | Y | N | Y | Y |
| 19 Kelly | Y | N | Y | Y |
| 20 Sweeney | N | Y | Y | Y |
| 21 McNulty | Y | N | Y | ? |
| 22 Hinchey | Y | N | N | Y |
| 23 McHugh | N | Y | Y | Y |
| 24 Boehlert | Y | N | Y | Y |
| 25 Walsh | N | Y | Y | Y |
| 26 Reynolds | N | Y | Y | Y |
| 27 Higgins | Y | N | Y | Y |
| 28 Slaughter | Y | N | Y | Y |
| 29 Kuhl | N | Y | Y | Y |
| **NORTH CAROLINA** | | | | |
| 1 Butterfield | Y | N | Y | Y |
| 2 Etheridge | Y | N | Y | Y |
| 3 Jones | N | Y | Y | Y |
| 4 Price | Y | N | Y | Y |
| 5 Foxx | N | Y | Y | Y |
| 6 Coble | N | Y | Y | Y |
| 7 McIntyre | N | Y | N | Y |
| 8 Hayes | N | Y | Y | Y |
| 9 Myrick | N | Y | Y | Y |
| 10 McHenry | N | Y | Y | Y |
| 11 Taylor | N | Y | Y | Y |
| 12 Watt | Y | N | N | Y |
| 13 Miller | Y | N | Y | Y |
| **NORTH DAKOTA** | | | | |
| AL Pomeroy | Y | Y | Y | Y |
| **OHIO** | | | | |
| 1 Chabot | N | Y | Y | Y |
| 2 Schmidt | N | Y | Y | Y |
| 3 Turner | N | Y | Y | Y |
| 4 Oxley | N | Y | Y | Y |
| 5 Gillmor | N | Y | Y | Y |
| 6 Strickland | Y | N | Y | Y |
| 7 Hobson | ? | ? | ? | ? |
| 8 Boehner | N | Y | Y | Y |
| 9 Kaptur | Y | N | Y | Y |
| 10 Kucinich | Y | N | N | Y |
| 11 Jones | Y | N | N | Y |
| 12 Tiberi | N | Y | Y | Y |
| 13 Brown | Y | N | Y | Y |
| 14 LaTourette | N | Y | Y | Y |
| 15 Pryce | N | Y | Y | Y |
| 16 Regula | N | Y | Y | Y |
| 17 Ryan | Y | N | N | Y |
| 18 Ney | N | Y | Y | Y |
| **OKLAHOMA** | | | | |
| 1 Sullivan | N | Y | Y | Y |
| 2 Boren | N | Y | Y | Y |
| 3 Lucas | N | Y | Y | Y |
| 4 Cole | N | Y | Y | Y |
| 5 Istook | N | Y | Y | Y |
| **OREGON** | | | | |
| 1 Wu | Y | N | N | Y |
| 2 Walden | N | Y | Y | Y |
| 3 Blumenauer | Y | N | N | Y |
| 4 DeFazio | Y | N | N | Y |
| 5 Hooley | Y | N | Y | Y |
| **PENNSYLVANIA** | | | | |
| 1 Brady | Y | N | N | Y |
| 2 Fattah | + | - | ? | ? |
| 3 English | N | Y | ? | Y |
| 4 Hart | N | Y | Y | Y |
| 5 Peterson | Y | Y | Y | Y |
| 6 Gerlach | Y | N | Y | Y |
| 7 Weldon | Y | N | Y | Y |
| 8 Fitzpatrick | Y | N | Y | Y |
| 9 Shuster | N | Y | Y | Y |
| 10 Sherwood | N | Y | Y | Y |
| 11 Kanjorski | Y | N | N | Y |
| 12 Murtha | Y | Y | Y | Y |
| 13 Schwartz | Y | N | Y | Y |
| 14 Doyle | Y | N | N | Y |
| 15 Dent | N | Y | Y | Y |
| 16 Pitts | N | Y | Y | Y |
| 17 Holden | Y | Y | Y | Y |
| 18 Murphy | N | Y | Y | Y |
| 19 Platts | Y | N | Y | Y |
| **RHODE ISLAND** | | | | |
| 1 Kennedy | Y | N | N | Y |
| 2 Langevin | Y | N | N | Y |
| **SOUTH CAROLINA** | | | | |
| 1 Brown | N | Y | Y | Y |
| 2 Wilson | N | Y | Y | Y |
| 3 Barrett | N | Y | Y | Y |
| 4 Inglis | Y | Y | Y | Y |
| 5 Spratt | Y | N | Y | Y |
| 6 Clyburn | Y | N | Y | Y |
| **SOUTH DAKOTA** | | | | |
| AL Herseth | N | Y | Y | Y |
| **TENNESSEE** | | | | |
| 1 Jenkins | N | Y | Y | Y |
| 2 Duncan | N | Y | Y | Y |
| 3 Wamp | N | Y | Y | Y |
| 4 Davis | Y | Y | Y | Y |
| 5 Cooper | Y | N | Y | Y |
| 6 Gordon | Y | N | Y | Y |
| 7 Blackburn | N | Y | Y | Y |
| 8 Tanner | Y | Y | Y | Y |
| 9 Ford | Y | Y | N | Y |
| **TEXAS** | | | | |
| 1 Gohmert | N | Y | Y | Y |
| 2 Poe | N | Y | Y | Y |
| 3 Johnson, S. | N | Y | Y | Y |
| 4 Hall | N | Y | Y | Y |
| 5 Hensarling | N | Y | Y | Y |
| 6 Barton | N | Y | Y | Y |
| 7 Culberson | ? | ? | ? | ? |
| 8 Brady | N | Y | ? | Y |
| 9 Green, A. | Y | N | Y | Y |
| 10 McCaul | N | Y | Y | Y |
| 11 Conaway | N | Y | Y | Y |
| 12 Granger | N | Y | Y | Y |
| 13 Thornberry | N | Y | Y | Y |
| 14 Paul | ? | ? | ? | ? |
| 15 Hinojosa | Y | Y | Y | Y |
| 16 Reyes | Y | N | Y | Y |
| 17 Edwards | N | Y | Y | Y |
| 18 Jackson-Lee | Y | N | Y | Y |
| 19 Neugebauer | N | Y | Y | Y |
| 20 Gonzalez | Y | N | Y | Y |
| 21 Smith | N | Y | Y | Y |
| 22 DeLay | N | Y | Y | ? |
| 23 Bonilla | N | Y | Y | Y |
| 24 Marchant | N | Y | Y | Y |
| 25 Doggett | Y | N | Y | Y |
| 26 Burgess | N | Y | Y | Y |
| 27 Ortiz | N | Y | Y | Y |
| 28 Cuellar | N | Y | Y | Y |
| 29 Green, G. | Y | N | Y | Y |
| 30 Johnson, E. | Y | N | Y | Y |
| 31 Carter | N | Y | Y | Y |
| 32 Sessions | N | Y | Y | Y |
| **UTAH** | | | | |
| 1 Bishop | N | Y | Y | Y |
| 2 Matheson | Y | Y | Y | Y |
| 3 Cannon | N | Y | Y | Y |
| **VERMONT** | | | | |
| AL *Sanders* | Y | N | N | Y |
| **VIRGINIA** | | | | |
| 1 Davis, J. | N | Y | Y | Y |
| 2 Drake | N | Y | Y | Y |
| 3 Scott | Y | N | N | Y |
| 4 Forbes | N | Y | Y | Y |
| 5 Goode | N | Y | Y | Y |
| 6 Goodlatte | N | Y | Y | Y |
| 7 Cantor | N | Y | Y | Y |
| 8 Moran | Y | N | N | Y |
| 9 Boucher | Y | N | N | Y |
| 10 Wolf | Y | N | Y | Y |
| 11 Davis, T. | Y | N | Y | Y |
| **WASHINGTON** | | | | |
| 1 Inslee | Y | N | Y | Y |
| 2 Larsen | Y | N | Y | Y |
| 3 Baird | Y | N | Y | Y |
| 4 Hastings | N | Y | Y | Y |
| 5 McMorris | N | Y | Y | Y |
| 6 Dicks | Y | N | Y | Y |
| 7 McDermott | Y | N | N | Y |
| 8 Reichert | N | Y | Y | Y |
| 9 Smith | Y | N | Y | Y |
| **WEST VIRGINIA** | | | | |
| 1 Mollohan | Y | Y | Y | Y |
| 2 Capito | N | Y | Y | Y |
| 3 Rahall | Y | N | Y | Y |
| **WISCONSIN** | | | | |
| 1 Ryan | N | Y | N | Y |
| 2 Baldwin | Y | N | N | Y |
| 3 Kind | Y | N | N | Y |
| 4 Moore | Y | N | N | Y |
| 5 Sensenbrenner | N | Y | Y | Y |
| 6 Petri | Y | Y | ? | ? |
| 7 Obey | Y | N | N | Y |
| 8 Green | N | Y | N | Y |
| **WYOMING** | | | | |
| AL Cubin | N | Y | Y | Y |

# IN THE HOUSE | By Vote Number

**509.** **S 1786. Airport Emergency Grants/Passage.** Mica, R-Fla., motion to suspend the rules and pass the bill that would authorize the Transportation Department to provide emergency grants to certain airports in Louisiana, Mississippi, Alabama and Texas that were damaged by hurricanes Katrina and Rita. Motion agreed to 420-0: R 225-0; D 194-0 (ND 144-0, SD 50-0); I 1-0. A two-thirds majority of those present and voting (280 in this case) is required for passage under suspension of the rules. Oct. 6, 2005.

**510.** **H Res 276. Pancreatic Cancer Awareness Month/Adoption.** Duncan, R-Tenn., motion to suspend the rules and adopt the resolution that would support the goals and ideals of Pancreatic Cancer Awareness Month, to be designated for November. Motion agreed to 415-0: R 220-0; D 194-0 (ND 144-0, SD 50-0); I 1-0. A two-thirds majority of those present and voting (277 in this case) is required for adoption under suspension of the rules. Oct. 6, 2005.

**511.** **HR 3894. Hurricane Katrina Section 8 Housing Relief/Passage.** Baker, R-La., motion to suspend the rules and pass the bill that would direct the Housing and Urban Development Department to waive eligibility requirements for the Section 8 housing voucher program for anyone who resided in a federal disaster area and whose residence became uninhabitable as a result of Hurricane Katrina. Motion agreed to 418-0: R 223-0; D 194-0 (ND 144-0, SD 50-0); I 1-0. A two-thirds majority of those present and voting (279 in this case) is required for passage under suspension of the rules. Oct. 6, 2005.

**512.** **HR 2360. Fiscal 2006 Homeland Security Appropriations/Conference Report.** Adoption of the conference report on the bill that would appropriate $31.9 billion in fiscal 2006 for the Homeland Security Department and related agencies. The bill includes $6 billion for customs and border protection; $5.9 billion for the Transportation Security Administration, including fees; $7.8 billion for the Coast Guard; $1.2 billion for the Secret Service and $2.6 billion for response and recovery efforts conducted by the Federal Emergency Management Agency. Adopted (thus sent to the Senate) 347-70: R 223-2; D 124-67 (ND 83-58, SD 41-9); I 0-1. Oct. 6, 2005.

**513.** **HR 3895. Rural Housing Hurricane Katrina Relief/Passage.** Baker, R-La., motion to suspend the rules and pass the bill that would allow the Agricultural Department, in the event of a presidentially declared natural disaster, to convert rural rental assistance into urban and rural housing vouchers. Motion agreed to 335-81: R 149-76; D 185-5 (ND 136-4, SD 49-1); I 1-0. A two-thirds majority of those present and voting (278 in this case) is required for passage under suspension of the rules. Oct. 6, 2005.

**514.** **HR 3896. CDBG Hurricane Katrina Relief/Passage.** Baker, R-La., motion to suspend the rules and pass the bill that would direct the Housing and Urban Development Department to suspend Community Development Block Grant caps for fiscal 2005 through 2008 for communities directly affected by hurricanes Katrina and Rita. Motion agreed to 415-0: R 224-0; D 190-0 (ND 140-0, SD 50-0); I 1-0. A two-thirds majority of those present and voting (277 in this case) is required for passage under suspension of the rules. Oct. 6, 2005.

| | 509 | 510 | 511 | 512 | 513 | 514 |
|---|---|---|---|---|---|---|
| **ALABAMA** | | | | | | |
| 1 Bonner | Y | Y | Y | Y | Y | Y |
| 2 Everett | Y | Y | Y | Y | Y | Y |
| 3 Rogers | Y | Y | Y | Y | Y | Y |
| 4 Aderholt | Y | Y | Y | Y | Y | Y |
| 5 Cramer | Y | Y | Y | Y | Y | Y |
| 6 Bachus | Y | Y | Y | Y | Y | Y |
| 7 Davis | Y | Y | Y | Y | Y | Y |
| **ALASKA** | | | | | | |
| AL Young | Y | Y | Y | ? | ? | ? |
| **ARIZONA** | | | | | | |
| 1 Renzi | Y | Y | Y | Y | Y | Y |
| 2 Franks | Y | Y | Y | Y | N | Y |
| 3 Shadegg | Y | Y | Y | Y | Y | Y |
| 4 Pastor | Y | Y | Y | N | Y | Y |
| 5 Hayworth | Y | Y | Y | Y | Y | Y |
| 6 Flake | Y | Y | Y | N | Y | Y |
| 7 Grijalva | Y | Y | Y | N | N | Y |
| 8 Kolbe | Y | Y | Y | Y | Y | N |
| **ARKANSAS** | | | | | | |
| 1 Berry | Y | Y | Y | N | Y | Y |
| 2 Snyder | Y | Y | Y | Y | Y | Y |
| 3 Boozman | Y | Y | Y | N | Y | Y |
| 4 Ross | Y | Y | Y | Y | Y | Y |
| **CALIFORNIA** | | | | | | |
| 1 Thompson | Y | Y | Y | Y | Y | Y |
| 2 Herger | Y | Y | Y | Y | N | Y |
| 3 Lungren | Y | Y | Y | Y | Y | Y |
| 4 Doolittle | Y | Y | Y | N | Y | Y |
| 5 Matsui, D. | Y | Y | Y | Y | Y | Y |
| 6 Woolsey | Y | Y | Y | N | Y | Y |
| 7 Miller, George | Y | Y | Y | N | Y | Y |
| 8 Pelosi | Y | Y | Y | Y | Y | Y |
| 9 Lee | Y | Y | Y | N | Y | Y |
| 10 Tauscher | Y | Y | Y | Y | Y | Y |
| 11 Pombo | Y | Y | Y | Y | Y | Y |
| 12 Lantos | Y | Y | Y | Y | Y | Y |
| 13 Stark | Y | Y | Y | ? | ? | ? |
| 14 Eshoo | Y | Y | Y | Y | Y | Y |
| 15 Honda | Y | Y | Y | N | Y | Y |
| 16 Lofgren | Y | Y | Y | Y | Y | Y |
| 17 Farr | Y | Y | Y | Y | Y | Y |
| 18 Cardoza | Y | Y | Y | Y | Y | Y |
| 19 Radanovich | Y | Y | Y | Y | Y | Y |
| 20 Costa | Y | ? | Y | Y | Y | Y |
| 21 Nunes | Y | ? | Y | Y | Y | Y |
| 22 Thomas | Y | Y | Y | Y | Y | Y |
| 23 Capps | Y | Y | Y | N | Y | Y |
| 24 Gallegly | Y | Y | Y | Y | Y | Y |
| 25 McKeon | Y | Y | Y | Y | Y | Y |
| 26 Dreier | Y | Y | Y | Y | Y | Y |
| 27 Sherman | Y | Y | Y | Y | Y | Y |
| 28 Berman | Y | Y | Y | Y | Y | Y |
| 29 Schiff | Y | Y | Y | Y | Y | Y |
| 30 Waxman | Y | Y | Y | N | Y | Y |
| 31 Becerra | Y | Y | Y | N | Y | Y |
| 32 Solis | Y | Y | Y | Y | Y | Y |
| 33 Watson | ? | ? | ? | ? | ? | ? |
| 34 Roybal-Allard | Y | Y | Y | Y | Y | Y |
| 35 Waters | Y | Y | Y | N | Y | Y |
| 36 Harman | Y | Y | Y | Y | Y | Y |
| 37 Millender-McD. | Y | Y | Y | Y | Y | Y |
| 38 Napolitano | Y | Y | Y | N | Y | Y |
| 39 Sánchez, Linda | Y | Y | Y | Y | Y | Y |
| 40 Royce | ? | ? | ? | ? | ? | ? |
| 41 Lewis | Y | ? | Y | N | Y | Y |
| 42 Miller, Gary | Y | Y | Y | N | Y | Y |
| 43 Baca | Y | Y | Y | N | Y | Y |
| 44 Calvert | Y | Y | Y | Y | Y | Y |
| 45 Bono | Y | Y | Y | Y | Y | Y |
| 46 Rohrabacher | Y | Y | Y | Y | N | Y |
| 47 Sanchez, Loretta | Y | Y | Y | Y | Y | |
| 48 Vacant | | | | | | |
| 49 Issa | Y | Y | Y | Y | Y | Y |
| 50 Cunningham | Y | Y | Y | Y | Y | Y |
| 51 Filner | Y | Y | Y | N | Y | Y |
| 52 Hunter | Y | Y | Y | Y | N | Y |
| 53 Davis | Y | Y | Y | Y | Y | Y |
| **COLORADO** | | | | | | |
| 1 DeGette | Y | Y | Y | N | Y | Y |
| 2 Udall | Y | Y | Y | Y | Y | Y |
| 3 Salazar | Y | Y | Y | Y | Y | Y |
| 4 Musgrave | Y | Y | Y | Y | Y | Y |
| 5 Hefley | Y | Y | Y | Y | Y | Y |
| 6 Tancredo | Y | Y | Y | Y | Y | Y |
| 7 Beauprez | Y | Y | Y | Y | Y | Y |
| **CONNECTICUT** | | | | | | |
| 1 Larson | Y | Y | Y | N | Y | Y |
| 2 Simmons | Y | Y | Y | Y | Y | Y |
| 3 DeLauro | Y | Y | Y | N | Y | Y |
| 4 Shays | Y | Y | Y | Y | Y | Y |
| 5 Johnson | Y | Y | Y | Y | Y | Y |
| **DELAWARE** | | | | | | |
| AL Castle | Y | Y | Y | Y | Y | Y |
| **FLORIDA** | | | | | | |
| 1 Miller | Y | Y | Y | Y | Y | Y |
| 2 Boyd | Y | Y | Y | Y | Y | Y |
| 3 Brown | Y | Y | Y | N | Y | Y |
| 4 Crenshaw | Y | Y | Y | Y | N | Y |
| 5 Brown-Waite | Y | Y | Y | Y | N | Y |
| 6 Stearns | Y | Y | Y | Y | N | Y |
| 7 Mica | Y | Y | Y | Y | Y | Y |
| 8 Keller | Y | Y | Y | Y | Y | Y |
| 9 Bilirakis | Y | Y | Y | Y | Y | Y |
| 10 Young | Y | Y | Y | Y | N | Y |
| 11 Davis | Y | Y | Y | Y | Y | Y |
| 12 Putnam | Y | Y | Y | Y | N | Y |
| 13 Harris | Y | Y | Y | Y | Y | Y |
| 14 Mack | Y | Y | Y | Y | Y | Y |
| 15 Weldon | Y | Y | Y | Y | Y | Y |
| 16 Foley | Y | Y | Y | Y | Y | Y |
| 17 Meek | Y | Y | Y | Y | Y | Y |
| 18 Ros-Lehtinen | Y | Y | Y | Y | Y | Y |
| 19 Wexler | Y | Y | Y | N | Y | Y |
| 20 Wasserman-Schultz | Y | Y | Y | N | Y | Y |
| 21 Diaz-Balart, L. | Y | Y | Y | Y | Y | Y |
| 22 Shaw | Y | Y | Y | Y | Y | Y |
| 23 Hastings | ? | ? | ? | ? | ? | ? |
| 24 Feeney | Y | Y | Y | Y | Y | Y |
| 25 Diaz-Balart, M. | Y | Y | Y | Y | Y | Y |
| **GEORGIA** | | | | | | |
| 1 Kingston | Y | Y | Y | Y | N | Y |
| 2 Bishop | Y | Y | Y | Y | Y | Y |
| 3 Marshall | Y | Y | Y | Y | Y | Y |
| 4 McKinney | Y | Y | Y | N | Y | Y |
| 5 Lewis | Y | Y | Y | Y | Y | Y |
| 6 Price | Y | Y | Y | Y | Y | Y |
| 7 Linder | ? | ? | ? | Y | Y | Y |
| 8 Westmoreland | Y | Y | Y | Y | Y | Y |
| 9 Norwood | Y | Y | Y | Y | Y | Y |
| 10 Deal | Y | Y | Y | Y | Y | Y |
| 11 Gingrey | Y | Y | Y | Y | Y | Y |
| 12 Barrow | Y | Y | Y | Y | Y | Y |
| 13 Scott | Y | Y | Y | Y | Y | Y |
| **HAWAII** | | | | | | |
| 1 Abercrombie | Y | Y | Y | N | Y | Y |
| 2 Case | Y | Y | Y | Y | Y | Y |
| **IDAHO** | | | | | | |
| 1 Otter | Y | Y | Y | Y | N | Y |
| 2 Simpson | Y | Y | Y | Y | Y | Y |
| **ILLINOIS** | | | | | | |
| 1 Rush | Y | Y | Y | N | Y | Y |
| 2 Jackson | Y | Y | Y | N | Y | Y |
| 3 Lipinski | Y | Y | Y | N | Y | Y |
| 4 Gutierrez | Y | Y | Y | N | Y | Y |
| 5 Emanuel | Y | Y | Y | Y | Y | Y |
| 6 Hyde | Y | Y | Y | Y | Y | Y |
| 7 Davis | Y | Y | Y | Y | Y | Y |
| 8 Bean | Y | Y | Y | Y | Y | Y |
| 9 Schakowsky | Y | Y | Y | N | Y | Y |
| 10 Kirk | Y | Y | ? | Y | N | Y |
| 11 Weller | Y | Y | Y | Y | Y | Y |
| 12 Costello | Y | Y | Y | N | Y | Y |

| KEY | Republicans | Democrats | *Independents* |
|---|---|---|---|

| | | |
|---|---|---|
| Y Voted for (yea) | X Paired against | C Voted "present" to avoid possible conflict of interest |
| # Paired for | – Announced against | |
| + Announced for | P Voted "present" | ? Did not vote or otherwise make a position known |
| N Voted against (nay) | | |

| | 509 | 510 | 511 | 512 | 513 | 514 |
|---|---|---|---|---|---|---|
| 13 **Biggert** | Y | Y | Y | Y | Y | Y |
| 14 **Hastert** | | | | | | |
| 15 **Johnson** | Y | Y | Y | Y | Y | Y |
| 16 **Manzullo** | Y | Y | Y | Y | Y | Y |
| 17 Evans | Y | Y | Y | ? | ? | ? |
| 18 **LaHood** | Y | Y | Y | Y | N | Y |
| 19 **Shimkus** | Y | Y | Y | Y | Y | Y |
| **INDIANA** | | | | | | |
| 1 Visclosky | Y | Y | Y | Y | Y | Y |
| 2 **Chocola** | Y | Y | Y | Y | Y | Y |
| 3 **Souder** | Y | Y | Y | Y | Y | Y |
| 4 **Buyer** | Y | Y | Y | Y | Y | Y |
| 5 **Burton** | Y | Y | Y | Y | Y | Y |
| 6 **Pence** | Y | Y | Y | Y | Y | Y |
| 7 Carson | Y | Y | Y | Y | Y | Y |
| 8 **Hostettler** | Y | Y | Y | Y | Y | Y |
| 9 **Sodrel** | Y | Y | Y | Y | Y | Y |
| **IOWA** | | | | | | |
| 1 **Nussle** | Y | Y | Y | Y | Y | Y |
| 2 **Leach** | Y | Y | Y | Y | Y | Y |
| 3 Boswell | ? | ? | ? | ? | ? | ? |
| 4 **Latham** | Y | Y | Y | Y | N | Y |
| 5 **King** | Y | Y | Y | Y | Y | Y |
| **KANSAS** | | | | | | |
| 1 **Moran** | Y | Y | Y | Y | N | Y |
| 2 **Ryun** | Y | Y | Y | Y | Y | Y |
| 3 Moore | Y | Y | Y | Y | Y | Y |
| 4 **Tiahrt** | Y | Y | Y | Y | N | Y |
| **KENTUCKY** | | | | | | |
| 1 **Whitfield** | ? | ? | ? | Y | N | Y |
| 2 **Lewis** | Y | Y | Y | Y | N | Y |
| 3 **Northup** | Y | Y | Y | Y | N | Y |
| 4 **Davis** | Y | Y | Y | Y | Y | Y |
| 5 **Rogers** | Y | Y | Y | Y | N | Y |
| 6 Chandler | Y | Y | Y | Y | Y | Y |
| **LOUISIANA** | | | | | | |
| 1 **Jindal** | Y | Y | Y | Y | Y | Y |
| 2 Jefferson | Y | Y | Y | Y | Y | Y |
| 3 Melancon | Y | Y | Y | Y | Y | Y |
| 4 **McCrery** | Y | Y | Y | Y | Y | Y |
| 5 **Alexander** | Y | Y | Y | Y | Y | Y |
| 6 **Baker** | Y | Y | Y | Y | Y | Y |
| 7 **Boustany** | Y | Y | Y | Y | Y | Y |
| **MAINE** | | | | | | |
| 1 Allen | Y | Y | Y | N | Y | Y |
| 2 Michaud | Y | Y | Y | N | Y | Y |
| **MARYLAND** | | | | | | |
| 1 **Gilchrest** | Y | Y | Y | Y | Y | Y |
| 2 Ruppersberger | Y | Y | Y | Y | Y | Y |
| 3 Cardin | Y | Y | Y | Y | Y | Y |
| 4 Wynn | Y | Y | Y | Y | Y | Y |
| 5 Hoyer | Y | Y | Y | Y | Y | Y |
| 6 **Bartlett** | Y | Y | Y | Y | N | Y |
| 7 Cummings | Y | Y | Y | Y | Y | Y |
| 8 Van Hollen | Y | Y | Y | Y | Y | Y |
| **MASSACHUSETTS** | | | | | | |
| 1 Olver | ? | ? | ? | ? | ? | ? |
| 2 Neal | Y | Y | Y | N | ? | ? |
| 3 McGovern | Y | Y | Y | N | Y | Y |
| 4 Frank | Y | Y | Y | N | Y | Y |
| 5 Meehan | Y | Y | Y | N | Y | Y |
| 6 Tierney | Y | Y | Y | N | Y | Y |
| 7 Markey | Y | Y | Y | N | Y | Y |
| 8 Capuano | Y | Y | Y | N | Y | Y |
| 9 Lynch | Y | Y | Y | N | Y | Y |
| 10 Delahunt | ? | ? | ? | ? | ? | ? |
| **MICHIGAN** | | | | | | |
| 1 Stupak | Y | Y | Y | Y | Y | Y |
| 2 **Hoekstra** | Y | Y | Y | Y | N | Y |
| 3 **Ehlers** | Y | Y | Y | Y | N | Y |
| 4 **Camp** | Y | Y | Y | Y | Y | Y |
| 5 Kildee | Y | Y | Y | Y | Y | Y |
| 6 **Upton** | Y | Y | Y | Y | N | Y |
| 7 **Schwarz** | ? | ? | ? | ? | ? | ? |
| 8 **Rogers** | Y | Y | Y | Y | Y | Y |
| 9 **Knollenberg** | Y | Y | Y | Y | N | Y |
| 10 **Miller** | Y | Y | Y | Y | N | Y |
| 11 **McCotter** | Y | Y | Y | Y | Y | Y |
| 12 Levin | Y | Y | Y | Y | Y | Y |
| 13 Kilpatrick | Y | Y | Y | Y | Y | Y |
| 14 Conyers | Y | Y | Y | N | Y | Y |
| 15 Dingell | Y | Y | Y | Y | Y | Y |

| | 509 | 510 | 511 | 512 | 513 | 514 |
|---|---|---|---|---|---|---|
| **MINNESOTA** | | | | | | |
| 1 **Gutknecht** | Y | Y | Y | Y | N | Y |
| 2 **Kline** | Y | Y | Y | Y | N | Y |
| 3 **Ramstad** | Y | Y | Y | Y | Y | Y |
| 4 McCollum | Y | Y | Y | N | Y | Y |
| 5 Sabo | Y | Y | Y | Y | Y | Y |
| 6 **Kennedy** | Y | Y | Y | Y | Y | Y |
| 7 Peterson | Y | Y | Y | Y | N | Y |
| 8 Oberstar | Y | Y | Y | N | Y | Y |
| **MISSISSIPPI** | | | | | | |
| 1 **Wicker** | Y | Y | Y | Y | Y | Y |
| 2 Thompson | Y | Y | Y | Y | Y | Y |
| 3 **Pickering** | Y | Y | Y | Y | Y | Y |
| 4 Taylor | Y | Y | Y | Y | Y | Y |
| **MISSOURI** | | | | | | |
| 1 Clay | Y | Y | Y | N | Y | Y |
| 2 **Akin** | Y | Y | Y | Y | Y | Y |
| 3 Carnahan | Y | Y | Y | Y | Y | Y |
| 4 Skelton | Y | Y | Y | Y | Y | Y |
| 5 Cleaver | Y | Y | Y | Y | Y | Y |
| 6 **Graves** | Y | Y | Y | Y | Y | Y |
| 7 **Blunt** | Y | Y | Y | Y | Y | Y |
| 8 **Emerson** | Y | Y | Y | Y | N | Y |
| 9 **Hulshof** | Y | Y | Y | Y | Y | Y |
| **MONTANA** | | | | | | |
| AL **Rehberg** | Y | Y | Y | Y | N | Y |
| **NEBRASKA** | | | | | | |
| 1 **Fortenberry** | Y | Y | Y | Y | Y | Y |
| 2 **Terry** | Y | Y | Y | Y | Y | Y |
| 3 **Osborne** | Y | Y | Y | Y | Y | Y |
| **NEVADA** | | | | | | |
| 1 Berkley | Y | Y | Y | Y | Y | Y |
| 2 **Gibbons** | Y | Y | Y | Y | Y | Y |
| 3 **Porter** | Y | Y | Y | Y | Y | Y |
| **NEW HAMPSHIRE** | | | | | | |
| 1 **Bradley** | Y | Y | Y | Y | Y | Y |
| 2 **Bass** | Y | Y | Y | Y | Y | Y |
| **NEW JERSEY** | | | | | | |
| 1 Andrews | Y | Y | Y | N | Y | Y |
| 2 **LoBiondo** | Y | + | Y | Y | Y | Y |
| 3 **Saxton** | Y | Y | Y | Y | N | Y |
| 4 **Smith** | Y | Y | Y | Y | Y | Y |
| 5 **Garrett** | Y | Y | Y | Y | Y | Y |
| 6 Pallone | Y | Y | Y | N | Y | Y |
| 7 **Ferguson** | Y | Y | Y | Y | Y | Y |
| 8 Pascrell | Y | Y | Y | Y | Y | Y |
| 9 Rothman | ? | ? | ? | ? | ? | ? |
| 10 Payne | ? | ? | ? | ? | ? | ? |
| 11 **Frelinghuysen** | Y | Y | Y | Y | N | Y |
| 12 Holt | Y | Y | Y | N | Y | Y |
| 13 Menendez | Y | Y | Y | N | Y | Y |
| **NEW MEXICO** | | | | | | |
| 1 **Wilson** | Y | Y | Y | Y | Y | Y |
| 2 **Pearce** | Y | Y | Y | Y | Y | Y |
| 3 Udall | Y | Y | Y | Y | Y | Y |
| **NEW YORK** | | | | | | |
| 1 Bishop | Y | Y | Y | Y | Y | Y |
| 2 Israel | Y | Y | Y | Y | Y | Y |
| 3 **King** | Y | Y | Y | Y | Y | Y |
| 4 McCarthy | Y | Y | Y | Y | Y | Y |
| 5 Ackerman | Y | Y | Y | Y | Y | Y |
| 6 Meeks | Y | Y | Y | Y | Y | Y |
| 7 Crowley | ? | ? | ? | ? | ? | ? |
| 8 Nadler | Y | Y | Y | N | Y | Y |
| 9 Weiner | Y | Y | Y | Y | Y | Y |
| 10 Towns | Y | Y | Y | Y | Y | Y |
| 11 Owens | Y | Y | Y | N | Y | Y |
| 12 Velázquez | Y | Y | Y | N | Y | Y |
| 13 **Fossella** | Y | Y | Y | Y | Y | Y |
| 14 Maloney | Y | Y | Y | N | Y | Y |
| 15 Rangel | Y | Y | Y | Y | Y | Y |
| 16 Serrano | Y | Y | Y | Y | Y | Y |
| 17 Engel | Y | Y | Y | Y | Y | Y |
| 18 Lowey | Y | Y | Y | Y | Y | Y |
| 19 **Kelly** | Y | Y | Y | Y | Y | Y |
| 20 **Sweeney** | Y | Y | Y | Y | N | Y |
| 21 McNulty | Y | Y | Y | Y | Y | Y |
| 22 Hinchey | Y | Y | Y | N | Y | Y |
| 23 **McHugh** | Y | Y | Y | Y | N | Y |
| 24 **Boehlert** | Y | Y | Y | Y | Y | Y |
| 25 **Walsh** | Y | Y | Y | Y | Y | Y |
| 26 **Reynolds** | Y | Y | Y | Y | Y | Y |
| 27 Higgins | Y | Y | Y | Y | Y | Y |
| 28 Slaughter | Y | Y | Y | N | Y | Y |
| 29 **Kuhl** | Y | Y | Y | Y | N | Y |

| | 509 | 510 | 511 | 512 | 513 | 514 |
|---|---|---|---|---|---|---|
| **NORTH CAROLINA** | | | | | | |
| 1 Butterfield | Y | Y | Y | Y | Y | Y |
| 2 Etheridge | Y | Y | Y | Y | Y | Y |
| 3 **Jones** | Y | Y | Y | Y | N | Y |
| 4 Price | Y | Y | Y | Y | Y | Y |
| 5 **Foxx** | Y | Y | Y | Y | Y | Y |
| 6 **Coble** | Y | Y | Y | Y | N | Y |
| 7 McIntyre | Y | Y | Y | Y | Y | Y |
| 8 **Hayes** | Y | Y | Y | Y | Y | Y |
| 9 **Myrick** | Y | Y | Y | Y | N | Y |
| 10 **McHenry** | Y | Y | Y | Y | N | Y |
| 11 **Taylor** | Y | Y | Y | Y | N | Y |
| 12 Watt | Y | Y | Y | N | Y | Y |
| 13 Miller | Y | Y | Y | Y | Y | Y |
| **NORTH DAKOTA** | | | | | | |
| AL Pomeroy | Y | Y | Y | Y | Y | Y |
| **OHIO** | | | | | | |
| 1 **Chabot** | Y | Y | Y | Y | N | Y |
| 2 **Schmidt** | Y | Y | Y | Y | N | Y |
| 3 **Turner** | Y | Y | Y | Y | Y | Y |
| 4 **Oxley** | Y | Y | Y | Y | Y | Y |
| 5 **Gillmor** | Y | Y | ? | Y | Y | Y |
| 6 Strickland | Y | Y | Y | ? | ? | ? |
| 7 **Hobson** | Y | Y | Y | Y | N | Y |
| 8 **Boehner** | Y | Y | Y | Y | Y | Y |
| 9 Kaptur | Y | Y | Y | Y | Y | Y |
| 10 Kucinich | Y | Y | Y | N | Y | Y |
| 11 Jones | Y | Y | Y | N | Y | Y |
| 12 **Tiberi** | Y | Y | Y | Y | Y | Y |
| 13 Brown | Y | Y | Y | Y | Y | Y |
| 14 **LaTourette** | Y | Y | Y | Y | Y | Y |
| 15 **Pryce** | Y | Y | Y | Y | Y | Y |
| 16 **Regula** | Y | Y | Y | Y | N | Y |
| 17 Ryan | Y | Y | Y | Y | Y | Y |
| 18 **Ney** | Y | Y | Y | Y | Y | Y |
| **OKLAHOMA** | | | | | | |
| 1 **Sullivan** | Y | ? | Y | Y | Y | Y |
| 2 Boren | Y | Y | Y | Y | Y | Y |
| 3 **Lucas** | Y | Y | Y | Y | Y | Y |
| 4 **Cole** | Y | Y | Y | Y | Y | Y |
| 5 **Istook** | Y | Y | Y | Y | Y | Y |
| **OREGON** | | | | | | |
| 1 Wu | Y | Y | Y | N | Y | Y |
| 2 **Walden** | Y | Y | Y | Y | Y | Y |
| 3 Blumenauer | Y | Y | Y | N | Y | Y |
| 4 DeFazio | Y | Y | Y | Y | Y | Y |
| 5 Hooley | Y | Y | Y | Y | Y | Y |
| **PENNSYLVANIA** | | | | | | |
| 1 Brady | Y | Y | Y | N | Y | Y |
| 2 Fattah | Y | Y | Y | N | Y | Y |
| 3 **English** | Y | Y | Y | Y | N | Y |
| 4 **Hart** | Y | Y | Y | Y | Y | Y |
| 5 **Peterson** | Y | Y | Y | Y | N | Y |
| 6 **Gerlach** | Y | Y | Y | Y | Y | Y |
| 7 **Weldon** | Y | Y | Y | Y | Y | Y |
| 8 **Fitzpatrick** | Y | Y | Y | Y | Y | Y |
| 9 **Shuster** | Y | Y | Y | Y | Y | Y |
| 10 **Sherwood** | Y | Y | Y | Y | N | Y |
| 11 Kanjorski | Y | Y | Y | Y | Y | Y |
| 12 Murtha | Y | Y | Y | Y | N | Y |
| 13 Schwartz | Y | Y | Y | Y | Y | Y |
| 14 Doyle | Y | Y | Y | N | Y | Y |
| 15 **Dent** | Y | Y | Y | Y | Y | Y |
| 16 **Pitts** | Y | Y | Y | Y | Y | Y |
| 17 Holden | Y | Y | Y | Y | Y | Y |
| 18 **Murphy** | Y | Y | Y | Y | Y | Y |
| 19 **Platts** | Y | Y | Y | Y | Y | Y |
| **RHODE ISLAND** | | | | | | |
| 1 Kennedy | Y | Y | Y | Y | Y | Y |
| 2 Langevin | Y | Y | Y | Y | Y | Y |
| **SOUTH CAROLINA** | | | | | | |
| 1 **Brown** | Y | Y | Y | Y | N | Y |
| 2 **Wilson** | Y | Y | Y | Y | Y | ? |
| 3 **Barrett** | Y | Y | Y | Y | Y | Y |
| 4 **Inglis** | Y | Y | Y | ? | ? | ? |
| 5 Spratt | Y | Y | Y | Y | Y | Y |
| 6 Clyburn | Y | Y | Y | Y | Y | Y |
| **SOUTH DAKOTA** | | | | | | |
| AL Herseth | Y | Y | Y | Y | Y | Y |
| **TENNESSEE** | | | | | | |
| 1 **Jenkins** | Y | Y | Y | Y | N | Y |
| 2 **Duncan** | Y | Y | Y | Y | Y | Y |

| | 509 | 510 | 511 | 512 | 513 | 514 |
|---|---|---|---|---|---|---|
| 3 **Wamp** | Y | Y | Y | Y | N | Y |
| 4 Davis | Y | Y | Y | Y | Y | Y |
| 5 Cooper | Y | Y | Y | N | Y | Y |
| 6 Gordon | Y | Y | Y | Y | Y | Y |
| 7 **Blackburn** | Y | Y | Y | Y | N | Y |
| 8 Tanner | Y | Y | Y | Y | Y | Y |
| 9 Ford | Y | Y | Y | N | Y | Y |
| **TEXAS** | | | | | | |
| 1 **Gohmert** | Y | Y | Y | Y | N | Y |
| 2 **Poe** | ? | ? | ? | ? | ? | ? |
| 3 **Johnson, S.** | Y | ? | Y | Y | N | Y |
| 4 **Hall** | Y | Y | Y | Y | Y | Y |
| 5 **Hensarling** | Y | Y | Y | Y | Y | Y |
| 6 **Barton** | Y | Y | Y | Y | Y | Y |
| 7 **Culberson** | Y | Y | Y | Y | Y | Y |
| 8 **Brady** | Y | Y | Y | Y | Y | Y |
| 9 Green, A. | Y | Y | Y | Y | Y | Y |
| 10 **McCaul** | Y | Y | Y | Y | Y | Y |
| 11 **Conaway** | Y | Y | Y | Y | Y | Y |
| 12 **Granger** | Y | Y | Y | Y | N | Y |
| 13 **Thornberry** | Y | Y | Y | Y | N | Y |
| 14 **Paul** | Y | Y | Y | N | Y | Y |
| 15 Hinojosa | Y | Y | Y | Y | Y | Y |
| 16 Reyes | Y | Y | Y | Y | Y | Y |
| 17 Edwards | Y | Y | Y | Y | Y | Y |
| 18 Jackson-Lee | Y | Y | Y | Y | Y | Y |
| 19 **Neugebauer** | Y | Y | Y | Y | N | Y |
| 20 Gonzalez | Y | Y | Y | Y | Y | Y |
| 21 **Smith** | Y | Y | Y | Y | Y | Y |
| 22 **DeLay** | Y | Y | Y | Y | Y | Y |
| 23 **Bonilla** | Y | Y | Y | Y | N | Y |
| 24 **Marchant** | Y | Y | Y | Y | N | Y |
| 25 Doggett | Y | Y | Y | Y | Y | Y |
| 26 **Burgess** | Y | Y | Y | Y | Y | Y |
| 27 Ortiz | Y | Y | Y | Y | Y | Y |
| 28 Cuellar | Y | Y | Y | Y | Y | Y |
| 29 Green, G. | Y | Y | Y | Y | Y | Y |
| 30 Johnson, E. | Y | Y | Y | Y | Y | Y |
| 31 **Carter** | Y | Y | Y | Y | N | Y |
| 32 **Sessions** | Y | Y | Y | Y | Y | Y |
| **UTAH** | | | | | | |
| 1 **Bishop** | Y | Y | Y | Y | Y | Y |
| 2 Matheson | Y | Y | Y | Y | Y | Y |
| 3 **Cannon** | Y | Y | Y | Y | N | Y |
| **VERMONT** | | | | | | |
| AL *Sanders* | Y | Y | Y | N | Y | Y |
| **VIRGINIA** | | | | | | |
| 1 **Davis, J.** | Y | Y | Y | Y | N | Y |
| 2 **Drake** | Y | Y | Y | Y | Y | Y |
| 3 Scott | Y | Y | Y | Y | Y | Y |
| 4 **Forbes** | Y | Y | Y | Y | N | Y |
| 5 **Goode** | Y | Y | Y | Y | N | Y |
| 6 **Goodlatte** | Y | Y | Y | Y | N | Y |
| 7 **Cantor** | Y | Y | Y | Y | N | Y |
| 8 Moran | Y | Y | Y | Y | N | Y |
| 9 Boucher | Y | Y | Y | Y | Y | Y |
| 10 **Wolf** | Y | Y | Y | Y | Y | Y |
| 11 **Davis, T.** | Y | Y | Y | Y | Y | Y |
| **WASHINGTON** | | | | | | |
| 1 Inslee | Y | Y | Y | Y | Y | Y |
| 2 Larsen | Y | Y | Y | Y | Y | Y |
| 3 Baird | Y | Y | Y | Y | Y | Y |
| 4 **Hastings** | Y | Y | Y | Y | Y | Y |
| 5 **McMorris** | Y | Y | Y | Y | Y | Y |
| 6 Dicks | Y | Y | Y | Y | Y | Y |
| 7 McDermott | Y | Y | Y | N | Y | Y |
| 8 **Reichert** | Y | Y | Y | Y | Y | Y |
| 9 Smith | Y | Y | Y | Y | Y | Y |
| **WEST VIRGINIA** | | | | | | |
| 1 Mollohan | Y | Y | Y | Y | Y | Y |
| 2 **Capito** | Y | Y | Y | Y | Y | Y |
| 3 Rahall | Y | Y | Y | Y | Y | Y |
| **WISCONSIN** | | | | | | |
| 1 **Ryan** | Y | Y | Y | Y | N | Y |
| 2 Baldwin | Y | Y | Y | N | Y | Y |
| 3 Kind | Y | Y | Y | N | Y | Y |
| 4 Moore | Y | Y | Y | Y | Y | Y |
| 5 **Sensenbrenner** | Y | Y | Y | Y | N | Y |
| 6 **Petri** | Y | Y | Y | Y | N | Y |
| 7 Obey | Y | Y | Y | N | N | Y |
| 8 **Green** | Y | Y | Y | Y | Y | Y |
| **WYOMING** | | | | | | |
| AL **Cubin** | Y | Y | Y | Y | N | Y |

# IN THE HOUSE | By Vote Number

**515.** **HR 3893. Oil Refinery Construction/Rule.** Adoption of the rule (H Res 481) that would provide for House floor consideration of the bill that would allow state governors to opt into a streamlined regulatory process for refinery expansion and construction projects. Adopted 216-201: R 216-5; D 0-195 (ND 0-145, SD 0-50); I 0-1. Oct. 7, 2005.

**516.** **Procedural Motion/Journal.** Approval of the House Journal of Thursday, Oct. 6, 2005. Approved 348-63: R 203-16; D 144-47 (ND 103-41, SD 41-6); I 1-0. Oct. 7, 2005.

**517.** **HR 3893. Oil Refinery Construction/Democratic Substitute.** Stupak, D-Mich., substitute amendment that would outlaw gasoline price gouging in a time of a presidentially declared energy emergency, authorize the Federal Trade Commission to impose fines for price gouging, and authorize the Energy Department to construct new refineries or open closed refineries to create a strategic refinery reserve that would have a capacity equaling 5 percent of the daily U.S. demand for gasoline, home heating oil and other refined petroleum products. Rejected 199-222: R 2-222; D 196-0 (ND 146-0, SD 50-0); I 1-0. Oct. 7, 2005.

**518.** **HR 3893. Oil Refinery Construction/Recommit.** Bishop, D-N.Y., motion to recommit the bill to the Energy and Commerce Committee with instructions to add language that would provide for stricter penalties dealing with gasoline price gouging, outlaw market manipulation and empower state attorneys general to enforce the law. Motion rejected 200-222: R 3-222; D 196-0 (ND 146-0, SD 50-0); I 1-0. Oct. 7, 2005.

**519.** **HR 3893. Oil Refinery Construction/Passage.** Passage of the bill that would allow state governors to opt into a streamlined regulatory process for refinery expansion and construction projects. It would require the president to designate federal sites for new oil refineries and allow the federal government to pay new refineries for the costs of significant delays due to lawsuits and government regulations. Price gouging on gasoline would be banned in times of emergencies. The bill also would direct the Federal Trade Commission to investigate price gouging after Hurricane Katrina. It would specify that the federal government could provide loan guarantees for the Alaska natural gas pipeline up to two years after enactment, unless the state of Alaska has a contractual agreement to complete construction of the pipeline. Passed 212-210: R 212-13; D 0-196 (ND 0-146, SD 0-50); I 0-1. Oct. 7, 2005.

**520.** **H Con Res 248. Simon Wiesenthal Tribute/Adoption.** Smith, R-N.J., motion to suspend the rules and adopt the resolution that would honor the life and work of Simon Wiesenthal to memorialize the victims of the Holocaust and to bring the perpetrators of crimes against humanity to justice. Motion agreed to 354-0: R 187-0; D 166-0 (ND 120-0, SD 46-0); I 1-0. A two-thirds majority of those present and voting (236 in this case) is required for adoption under suspension of the rules. Oct. 7, 2005.

| | 515 | 516 | 517 | 518 | 519 | 520 |
|---|---|---|---|---|---|---|
| **ALABAMA** | | | | | | |
| 1 Bonner | Y | Y | N | N | Y | Y |
| 2 Everett | Y | Y | N | N | Y | ? |
| 3 Rogers | Y | Y | N | N | Y | Y |
| 4 Aderholt | Y | Y | N | N | Y | Y |
| 5 Cramer | N | Y | Y | Y | N | Y |
| 6 Bachus | Y | Y | N | N | Y | ? |
| 7 Davis | N | Y | Y | Y | N | Y |
| **ALASKA** | | | | | | |
| AL Young | ? | ? | N | N | Y | Y |
| **ARIZONA** | | | | | | |
| 1 Renzi | Y | Y | N | N | Y | Y |
| 2 Franks | Y | Y | N | N | Y | Y |
| 3 Shadegg | Y | Y | N | N | Y | Y |
| 4 Pastor | N | Y | Y | Y | N | Y |
| 5 Hayworth | Y | Y | N | N | Y | Y |
| 6 Flake | Y | Y | N | N | Y | Y |
| 7 Grijalva | N | Y | Y | Y | N | Y |
| 8 Kolbe | Y | Y | N | N | Y | Y |
| **ARKANSAS** | | | | | | |
| 1 Berry | N | N | Y | Y | N | Y |
| 2 Snyder | N | Y | Y | Y | N | Y |
| 3 Boozman | Y | Y | N | N | Y | Y |
| 4 Ross | N | Y | Y | Y | N | Y |
| **CALIFORNIA** | | | | | | |
| 1 Thompson | N | N | Y | Y | N | Y |
| 2 Herger | Y | Y | N | N | Y | Y |
| 3 Lungren | Y | Y | N | N | Y | Y |
| 4 Doolittle | Y | Y | N | N | Y | Y |
| 5 Matsui, D. | N | Y | Y | Y | N | Y |
| 6 Woolsey | N | Y | Y | Y | N | Y |
| 7 Miller, George | N | N | Y | Y | N | Y |
| 8 Pelosi | N | Y | Y | Y | N | Y |
| 9 Lee | N | Y | Y | Y | N | Y |
| 10 Tauscher | N | N | Y | Y | N | Y |
| 11 Pombo | Y | Y | N | N | Y | ? |
| 12 Lantos | N | Y | Y | Y | N | Y |
| 13 Stark | N | N | Y | Y | N | ? |
| 14 Eshoo | N | Y | Y | Y | N | ? |
| 15 Honda | N | Y | Y | Y | N | Y |
| 16 Lofgren | N | Y | Y | Y | N | Y |
| 17 Farr | N | Y | Y | Y | N | Y |
| 18 Cardoza | N | Y | Y | Y | N | Y |
| 19 Radanovich | Y | Y | N | N | Y | Y |
| 20 Costa | N | Y | Y | Y | N | Y |
| 21 Nunes | Y | Y | N | N | Y | Y |
| 22 Thomas | Y | Y | N | N | Y | Y |
| 23 Capps | N | Y | Y | Y | N | + |
| 24 Gallegly | Y | Y | N | N | Y | Y |
| 25 McKeon | Y | Y | N | N | Y | Y |
| 26 Dreier | Y | Y | N | N | Y | Y |
| 27 Sherman | N | Y | Y | Y | N | Y |
| 28 Berman | N | Y | Y | Y | N | Y |
| 29 Schiff | N | Y | Y | Y | N | Y |
| 30 Waxman | N | Y | Y | Y | N | Y |
| 31 Becerra | N | Y | Y | Y | N | Y |
| 32 Solis | N | Y | Y | Y | N | Y |
| 33 Watson | N | N | Y | Y | N | ? |
| 34 Roybal-Allard | N | Y | Y | Y | N | Y |
| 35 Waters | N | N | Y | Y | N | ? |
| 36 Harman | N | Y | Y | Y | N | Y |
| 37 Millender-McD. | N | Y | Y | Y | N | Y |
| 38 Napolitano | N | Y | Y | Y | N | Y |
| 39 Sánchez, Linda | N | Y | Y | Y | N | Y |
| 40 Royce | ? | ? | ? | ? | ? | ? |
| 41 Lewis | Y | ? | N | N | Y | Y |
| 42 Miller, Gary | Y | Y | N | N | Y | Y |
| 43 Baca | N | Y | Y | Y | N | Y |
| 44 Calvert | Y | Y | N | N | Y | Y |
| 45 Bono | Y | Y | N | N | Y | Y |
| 46 Rohrabacher | Y | Y | N | N | Y | Y |
| 47 Sanchez, Loretta | N | N | Y | Y | N | Y |
| 48 Vacant | | | | | | |
| 49 Issa | Y | Y | N | N | Y | Y |

| | 515 | 516 | 517 | 518 | 519 | 520 |
|---|---|---|---|---|---|---|
| 50 Cunningham | Y | Y | N | N | Y | Y |
| 51 Filner | N | N | Y | Y | N | + |
| 52 Hunter | Y | Y | N | N | Y | Y |
| 53 Davis | N | Y | Y | Y | N | Y |
| **COLORADO** | | | | | | |
| 1 DeGette | N | Y | Y | Y | N | Y |
| 2 Udall | N | N | Y | Y | N | Y |
| 3 Salazar | N | Y | Y | Y | N | Y |
| 4 Musgrave | Y | Y | N | N | Y | ? |
| 5 Hefley | Y | N | N | N | Y | Y |
| 6 Tancredo | Y | N | N | N | Y | Y |
| 7 Beauprez | ? | ? | ? | ? | ? | ? |
| **CONNECTICUT** | | | | | | |
| 1 Larson | N | N | Y | Y | N | + |
| 2 Simmons | + | + | N | N | Y | Y |
| 3 DeLauro | N | Y | Y | Y | N | ? |
| 4 Shays | N | Y | Y | Y | N | Y |
| 5 Johnson | Y | Y | N | N | Y | Y |
| **DELAWARE** | | | | | | |
| AL Castle | N | Y | N | N | N | Y |
| **FLORIDA** | | | | | | |
| 1 Miller | Y | Y | N | N | Y | Y |
| 2 Boyd | N | Y | Y | Y | N | Y |
| 3 Brown | N | Y | Y | Y | N | Y |
| 4 Crenshaw | Y | Y | N | N | Y | Y |
| 5 Brown-Waite | Y | Y | N | N | Y | ? |
| 6 Stearns | Y | Y | N | N | Y | Y |
| 7 Mica | Y | Y | N | N | Y | + |
| 8 Keller | Y | Y | N | N | Y | Y |
| 9 Bilirakis | Y | Y | N | N | Y | Y |
| 10 Young | Y | Y | N | N | Y | Y |
| 11 Davis | N | Y | Y | Y | N | ? |
| 12 Putnam | Y | Y | N | N | Y | Y |
| 13 Harris | Y | Y | N | N | Y | Y |
| 14 Mack | Y | Y | N | N | Y | Y |
| 15 Weldon | Y | Y | N | N | Y | Y |
| 16 Foley | Y | Y | N | N | Y | Y |
| 17 Meek | N | Y | Y | Y | N | Y |
| 18 Ros-Lehtinen | Y | Y | N | N | Y | Y |
| 19 Wexler | N | ? | Y | Y | N | Y |
| 20 Wasserman-Schultz | N | Y | Y | Y | N | Y |
| 21 Diaz-Balart, L. | Y | Y | N | N | Y | Y |
| 22 Shaw | Y | Y | N | N | Y | Y |
| 23 Hastings | ? | ? | ? | ? | ? | ? |
| 24 Feeney | Y | Y | N | N | Y | ? |
| 25 Diaz-Balart, M. | Y | Y | N | N | Y | Y |
| **GEORGIA** | | | | | | |
| 1 Kingston | Y | Y | N | N | Y | Y |
| 2 Bishop | N | Y | Y | Y | N | Y |
| 3 Marshall | N | N | Y | Y | N | Y |
| 4 McKinney | N | Y | Y | Y | N | Y |
| 5 Lewis | N | Y | Y | Y | N | Y |
| 6 Price | Y | Y | N | N | Y | Y |
| 7 Linder | Y | ? | N | N | Y | ? |
| 8 Westmoreland | Y | Y | N | N | Y | ? |
| 9 Norwood | ? | ? | ? | ? | ? | ? |
| 10 Deal | ? | ? | ? | ? | ? | ? |
| 11 Gingrey | Y | Y | N | N | Y | Y |
| 12 Barrow | N | N | Y | Y | N | Y |
| 13 Scott | N | Y | Y | Y | N | Y |
| **HAWAII** | | | | | | |
| 1 Abercrombie | N | Y | Y | Y | N | Y |
| 2 Case | N | Y | Y | Y | N | Y |
| **IDAHO** | | | | | | |
| 1 Otter | Y | Y | N | N | Y | Y |
| 2 Simpson | Y | Y | N | N | Y | Y |
| **ILLINOIS** | | | | | | |
| 1 Rush | N | Y | Y | Y | N | Y |
| 2 Jackson | N | Y | Y | Y | N | Y |
| 3 Lipinski | N | Y | Y | Y | N | Y |
| 4 Gutierrez | N | Y | Y | Y | N | + |
| 5 Emanuel | N | Y | Y | Y | N | Y |
| 6 Hyde | Y | Y | N | N | Y | Y |
| 7 Davis | N | Y | Y | Y | N | Y |
| 8 Bean | N | Y | Y | Y | N | Y |
| 9 Schakowsky | N | N | Y | Y | N | Y |
| 10 Kirk | Y | Y | N | N | Y | Y |
| 11 Weller | Y | N | N | N | Y | Y |
| 12 Costello | N | N | Y | Y | N | Y |

**KEY**    **Republicans**    Democrats    *Independents*

| | | | | |
|---|---|---|---|---|
| **Y** Voted for (yea) | **X** Paired against | **C** Voted "present" to avoid possible conflict of interest |
| **#** Paired for | **–** Announced against | |
| **+** Announced for | **P** Voted "present" | **?** Did not vote or otherwise make a position known |
| **N** Voted against (nay) | | |

| | 515 | 516 | 517 | 518 | 519 | 520 |
|---|---|---|---|---|---|---|
| 13 **Biggert** | Y | Y | N | N | Y | Y |
| 14 **Hastert** | | | | N | Y | |
| 15 **Johnson** | N | Y | N | N | N | + |
| 16 **Manzullo** | Y | Y | N | N | Y | Y |
| 17 Evans | N | N | Y | Y | N | Y |
| 18 **LaHood** | Y | Y | N | N | N | ? |
| 19 **Shimkus** | Y | Y | N | N | Y | Y |
| **INDIANA** | | | | | | |
| 1 Visclosky | N | N | Y | Y | N | Y |
| 2 **Chocola** | Y | Y | N | N | Y | Y |
| 3 **Souder** | Y | Y | N | N | Y | Y |
| 4 **Buyer** | Y | Y | N | N | Y | Y |
| 5 **Burton** | Y | Y | N | N | Y | Y |
| 6 **Pence** | Y | Y | N | N | Y | + |
| 7 Carson | N | Y | Y | Y | N | ? |
| 8 **Hostettler** | Y | Y | N | N | Y | Y |
| 9 **Sodrel** | Y | Y | N | N | Y | Y |
| **IOWA** | | | | | | |
| 1 **Nussle** | Y | Y | N | N | Y | ? |
| 2 **Leach** | N | Y | N | N | N | Y |
| 3 Boswell | ? | ? | ? | ? | ? | ? |
| 4 **Latham** | Y | N | N | N | Y | Y |
| 5 **King** | Y | Y | N | N | Y | Y |
| **KANSAS** | | | | | | |
| 1 **Moran** | Y | N | N | N | Y | ? |
| 2 **Ryun** | Y | Y | N | N | Y | Y |
| 3 Moore | N | Y | Y | Y | N | Y |
| 4 **Tiahrt** | Y | Y | N | N | Y | Y |
| **KENTUCKY** | | | | | | |
| 1 **Whitfield** | Y | N | N | N | Y | Y |
| 2 **Lewis** | Y | Y | N | N | Y | Y |
| 3 **Northup** | Y | Y | N | N | Y | Y |
| 4 **Davis** | Y | N | N | N | Y | Y |
| 5 **Rogers** | Y | Y | N | N | Y | Y |
| 6 Chandler | N | N | Y | Y | N | Y |
| **LOUISIANA** | | | | | | |
| 1 **Jindal** | Y | Y | N | N | Y | Y |
| 2 Jefferson | N | Y | Y | Y | N | Y |
| 3 Melancon | N | ? | Y | Y | N | Y |
| 4 **McCrery** | Y | Y | N | N | Y | Y |
| 5 **Alexander** | Y | Y | N | N | Y | Y |
| 6 **Baker** | Y | Y | N | N | Y | Y |
| 7 **Boustany** | Y | Y | N | N | Y | Y |
| **MAINE** | | | | | | |
| 1 Allen | N | Y | Y | Y | N | Y |
| 2 Michaud | N | Y | Y | Y | N | Y |
| **MARYLAND** | | | | | | |
| 1 **Gilchrest** | Y | Y | N | N | Y | Y |
| 2 Ruppersberger | N | Y | Y | Y | N | Y |
| 3 Cardin | N | Y | Y | Y | N | Y |
| 4 Wynn | N | Y | Y | Y | N | Y |
| 5 Hoyer | N | Y | Y | Y | N | Y |
| 6 **Bartlett** | Y | Y | N | N | Y | Y |
| 7 Cummings | N | Y | Y | Y | N | Y |
| 8 Van Hollen | N | Y | Y | Y | N | Y |
| **MASSACHUSETTS** | | | | | | |
| 1 Olver | ? | ? | ? | ? | ? | ? |
| 2 Neal | ? | ? | ? | ? | ? | ? |
| 3 McGovern | N | Y | Y | Y | N | Y |
| 4 Frank | N | Y | Y | Y | N | Y |
| 5 Meehan | N | Y | Y | Y | N | ? |
| 6 Tierney | N | Y | Y | Y | N | Y |
| 7 Markey | N | N | Y | Y | N | Y |
| 8 Capuano | N | N | Y | Y | N | Y |
| 9 Lynch | N | N | Y | Y | N | ? |
| 10 Delahunt | ? | ? | ? | ? | ? | ? |
| **MICHIGAN** | | | | | | |
| 1 Stupak | N | N | Y | Y | N | ? |
| 2 **Hoekstra** | Y | Y | N | N | Y | Y |
| 3 **Ehlers** | Y | Y | N | N | Y | Y |
| 4 **Camp** | Y | Y | N | N | Y | Y |
| 5 Kildee | N | Y | Y | Y | N | Y |
| 6 **Upton** | Y | Y | N | N | Y | Y |
| 7 **Schwarz** | ? | ? | ? | ? | ? | ? |
| 8 **Rogers** | Y | Y | N | N | Y | Y |
| 9 **Knollenberg** | Y | Y | N | N | Y | Y |
| 10 **Miller** | Y | Y | N | N | Y | Y |
| 11 **McCotter** | Y | N | N | N | Y | Y |
| 12 Levin | N | Y | Y | Y | N | Y |
| 13 Kilpatrick | N | Y | Y | Y | N | Y |
| 14 Conyers | N | Y | Y | Y | N | Y |
| 15 Dingell | N | Y | Y | Y | N | Y |
| **MINNESOTA** | | | | | | |
| 1 **Gutknecht** | Y | N | N | N | Y | Y |
| 2 **Kline** | Y | Y | N | N | Y | Y |
| 3 **Ramstad** | Y | N | N | N | Y | Y |
| 4 McCollum | N | Y | Y | Y | N | Y |
| 5 Sabo | N | N | Y | Y | N | ? |
| 6 **Kennedy** | Y | N | N | N | Y | Y |
| 7 Peterson | N | Y | Y | Y | N | ? |
| 8 Oberstar | N | N | Y | Y | N | Y |
| **MISSISSIPPI** | | | | | | |
| 1 **Wicker** | Y | Y | N | N | Y | ? |
| 2 Thompson | N | N | Y | Y | N | Y |
| 3 **Pickering** | Y | Y | N | N | Y | Y |
| 4 Taylor | N | N | Y | Y | N | Y |
| **MISSOURI** | | | | | | |
| 1 Clay | ? | ? | Y | Y | N | Y |
| 2 **Akin** | Y | Y | N | N | Y | Y |
| 3 Carnahan | N | Y | Y | Y | N | Y |
| 4 Skelton | N | Y | Y | Y | N | Y |
| 5 Cleaver | N | Y | Y | Y | N | + |
| 6 **Graves** | Y | N | N | N | Y | ? |
| 7 **Blunt** | Y | Y | N | N | Y | Y |
| 8 **Emerson** | Y | Y | N | N | Y | Y |
| 9 **Hulshof** | Y | Y | N | N | Y | Y |
| **MONTANA** | | | | | | |
| AL **Rehberg** | Y | Y | N | N | Y | Y |
| **NEBRASKA** | | | | | | |
| 1 **Fortenberry** | Y | Y | N | N | Y | Y |
| 2 **Terry** | Y | Y | N | N | Y | ? |
| 3 **Osborne** | Y | Y | N | N | Y | ? |
| **NEVADA** | | | | | | |
| 1 Berkley | N | Y | Y | Y | N | Y |
| 2 **Gibbons** | Y | Y | N | N | Y | Y |
| 3 **Porter** | Y | Y | N | N | Y | Y |
| **NEW HAMPSHIRE** | | | | | | |
| 1 **Bradley** | Y | Y | N | N | N | Y |
| 2 **Bass** | Y | Y | N | N | Y | Y |
| **NEW JERSEY** | | | | | | |
| 1 Andrews | N | ? | Y | Y | N | Y |
| 2 **LoBiondo** | Y | N | N | Y | N | Y |
| 3 **Saxton** | Y | Y | N | N | N | Y |
| 4 **Smith** | Y | Y | N | N | N | Y |
| 5 **Garrett** | Y | Y | N | N | Y | Y |
| 6 Pallone | N | Y | Y | Y | N | Y |
| 7 **Ferguson** | Y | Y | N | N | Y | Y |
| 8 Pascrell | N | Y | Y | Y | N | ? |
| 9 Rothman | N | Y | Y | Y | N | Y |
| 10 Payne | ? | ? | ? | ? | ? | ? |
| 11 **Frelinghuysen** | Y | Y | N | N | Y | ? |
| 12 Holt | N | N | Y | Y | N | Y |
| 13 Menendez | N | Y | Y | Y | N | Y |
| **NEW MEXICO** | | | | | | |
| 1 **Wilson** | Y | Y | N | N | Y | Y |
| 2 **Pearce** | Y | Y | N | N | Y | Y |
| 3 Udall | N | N | Y | Y | N | Y |
| **NEW YORK** | | | | | | |
| 1 Bishop | N | Y | Y | Y | N | Y |
| 2 Israel | N | N | Y | Y | N | ? |
| 3 **King** | Y | Y | N | N | Y | ? |
| 4 McCarthy | N | N | Y | Y | N | ? |
| 5 Ackerman | N | N | Y | Y | N | Y |
| 6 Meeks | N | Y | Y | Y | N | Y |
| 7 Crowley | N | Y | Y | Y | N | Y |
| 8 Nadler | N | Y | Y | Y | N | Y |
| 9 Weiner | N | Y | Y | Y | N | Y |
| 10 Towns | N | N | Y | Y | N | Y |
| 11 Owens | N | Y | Y | Y | N | Y |
| 12 Velázquez | N | N | Y | Y | N | Y |
| 13 **Fossella** | Y | N | N | N | Y | Y |
| 14 Maloney | N | N | Y | Y | N | Y |
| 15 Rangel | N | Y | Y | Y | N | Y |
| 16 Serrano | N | Y | Y | Y | N | Y |
| 17 Engel | N | Y | Y | Y | N | Y |
| 18 Lowey | N | Y | Y | Y | N | Y |
| 19 **Kelly** | Y | Y | N | N | Y | Y |
| 20 **Sweeney** | Y | N | N | Y | Y | Y |
| 21 McNulty | N | N | Y | Y | N | Y |
| 22 Hinchey | N | N | Y | Y | N | Y |
| 23 **McHugh** | Y | Y | N | N | Y | Y |
| 24 **Boehlert** | N | Y | N | N | N | Y |
| 25 **Walsh** | Y | Y | N | N | Y | ? |
| 26 **Reynolds** | Y | Y | N | N | Y | Y |
| 27 Higgins | N | Y | Y | Y | N | Y |
| 28 Slaughter | N | N | Y | Y | N | Y |
| 29 **Kuhl** | Y | Y | N | N | Y | Y |
| **NORTH CAROLINA** | | | | | | |
| 1 Butterfield | N | Y | Y | Y | N | Y |
| 2 Etheridge | N | Y | Y | Y | N | Y |
| 3 **Jones** | Y | Y | N | N | N | Y |
| 4 Price | N | Y | Y | Y | N | Y |
| 5 **Foxx** | Y | Y | N | N | Y | ? |
| 6 **Coble** | Y | Y | N | N | Y | ? |
| 7 McIntyre | N | Y | Y | Y | N | Y |
| 8 **Hayes** | Y | Y | N | N | Y | Y |
| 9 **Myrick** | Y | Y | N | N | Y | Y |
| 10 **McHenry** | Y | Y | N | N | Y | Y |
| 11 **Taylor** | Y | Y | N | N | Y | ? |
| 12 Watt | N | Y | Y | Y | N | Y |
| 13 Miller | N | Y | Y | Y | N | Y |
| **NORTH DAKOTA** | | | | | | |
| AL Pomeroy | N | Y | Y | Y | N | Y |
| **OHIO** | | | | | | |
| 1 **Chabot** | Y | Y | N | N | Y | Y |
| 2 **Schmidt** | Y | Y | N | N | Y | Y |
| 3 **Turner** | Y | Y | N | N | Y | Y |
| 4 **Oxley** | Y | Y | N | N | Y | ? |
| 5 **Gillmor** | Y | Y | N | N | Y | ? |
| 6 Strickland | N | N | Y | Y | N | Y |
| 7 **Hobson** | Y | Y | N | N | Y | Y |
| 8 **Boehner** | Y | Y | N | N | Y | Y |
| 9 Kaptur | N | Y | Y | Y | N | Y |
| 10 Kucinich | N | N | Y | Y | N | Y |
| 11 Jones | N | Y | Y | Y | N | Y |
| 12 **Tiberi** | Y | Y | N | N | Y | ? |
| 13 Brown | N | Y | Y | Y | N | Y |
| 14 **LaTourette** | Y | Y | N | N | Y | Y |
| 15 **Pryce** | Y | Y | N | N | Y | Y |
| 16 **Regula** | Y | Y | N | N | Y | Y |
| 17 Ryan | N | Y | Y | Y | N | Y |
| 18 **Ney** | Y | Y | N | N | Y | ? |
| **OKLAHOMA** | | | | | | |
| 1 **Sullivan** | Y | Y | N | N | Y | Y |
| 2 Boren | N | Y | Y | Y | N | Y |
| 3 **Lucas** | Y | Y | N | N | Y | Y |
| 4 **Cole** | Y | Y | N | N | Y | Y |
| 5 **Istook** | Y | Y | N | N | Y | Y |
| **OREGON** | | | | | | |
| 1 Wu | N | N | Y | Y | N | Y |
| 2 **Walden** | Y | Y | N | N | Y | Y |
| 3 Blumenauer | N | Y | Y | Y | N | Y |
| 4 DeFazio | N | N | Y | Y | N | ? |
| 5 Hooley | N | Y | Y | Y | N | ? |
| **PENNSYLVANIA** | | | | | | |
| 1 Brady | N | N | Y | Y | N | Y |
| 2 Fattah | N | Y | Y | Y | N | Y |
| 3 **English** | Y | N | N | N | Y | Y |
| 4 **Hart** | Y | Y | N | N | Y | Y |
| 5 **Peterson** | Y | Y | N | N | Y | ? |
| 6 **Gerlach** | Y | Y | N | N | Y | Y |
| 7 **Weldon** | Y | Y | N | ? | N | Y |
| 8 **Fitzpatrick** | ? | ? | N | N | N | Y |
| 9 **Shuster** | Y | N | N | N | Y | Y |
| 10 **Sherwood** | Y | Y | N | N | Y | Y |
| 11 Kanjorski | N | Y | Y | Y | N | Y |
| 12 Murtha | N | Y | Y | Y | N | ? |
| 13 Schwartz | N | Y | Y | Y | N | Y |
| 14 Doyle | N | Y | Y | Y | N | Y |
| 15 **Dent** | Y | Y | N | N | Y | Y |
| 16 **Pitts** | Y | Y | N | N | Y | Y |
| 17 Holden | N | Y | Y | Y | N | Y |
| 18 **Murphy** | Y | Y | N | N | Y | Y |
| 19 **Platts** | Y | Y | N | N | Y | Y |
| **RHODE ISLAND** | | | | | | |
| 1 Kennedy | N | Y | Y | Y | N | Y |
| 2 Langevin | N | Y | Y | Y | N | Y |
| **SOUTH CAROLINA** | | | | | | |
| 1 **Brown** | Y | Y | N | N | Y | Y |
| 2 **Wilson** | Y | Y | N | N | Y | Y |
| 3 **Barrett** | Y | Y | N | N | Y | Y |
| 4 **Inglis** | Y | Y | N | N | Y | Y |
| 5 Spratt | N | Y | Y | Y | N | Y |
| 6 Clyburn | N | Y | Y | Y | N | ? |
| **SOUTH DAKOTA** | | | | | | |
| AL Herseth | N | Y | Y | Y | N | Y |
| **TENNESSEE** | | | | | | |
| 1 **Jenkins** | Y | Y | N | N | Y | ? |
| 2 **Duncan** | Y | Y | N | N | Y | Y |
| 3 **Wamp** | Y | Y | N | N | Y | ? |
| 4 Davis | N | Y | Y | Y | N | ? |
| 5 Cooper | N | Y | Y | Y | N | Y |
| 6 Gordon | N | Y | Y | Y | N | Y |
| 7 **Blackburn** | Y | Y | N | N | Y | ? |
| 8 Tanner | N | Y | Y | Y | N | Y |
| 9 Ford | N | Y | Y | Y | N | Y |
| **TEXAS** | | | | | | |
| 1 **Gohmert** | Y | Y | N | N | Y | Y |
| 2 **Poe** | + | + | - | N | Y | Y |
| 3 **Johnson, S.** | Y | Y | N | N | Y | Y |
| 4 **Hall** | Y | Y | N | N | Y | Y |
| 5 **Hensarling** | Y | Y | N | N | Y | Y |
| 6 **Barton** | Y | Y | N | N | Y | Y |
| 7 **Culberson** | Y | Y | N | N | Y | Y |
| 8 **Brady** | Y | Y | N | N | Y | ? |
| 9 Green, A. | N | Y | Y | Y | N | Y |
| 10 **McCaul** | Y | Y | N | N | Y | Y |
| 11 **Conaway** | Y | Y | N | N | Y | Y |
| 12 **Granger** | Y | Y | N | N | Y | ? |
| 13 **Thornberry** | Y | Y | N | N | Y | Y |
| 14 **Paul** | Y | Y | N | N | ? | Y |
| 15 Hinojosa | N | Y | Y | Y | N | Y |
| 16 Reyes | N | Y | Y | Y | N | Y |
| 17 Edwards | N | ? | Y | Y | N | Y |
| 18 Jackson-Lee | N | Y | Y | Y | N | Y |
| 19 **Neugebauer** | Y | Y | N | N | Y | Y |
| 20 Gonzalez | N | Y | Y | Y | N | Y |
| 21 **Smith** | Y | Y | N | N | Y | Y |
| 22 **DeLay** | Y | Y | N | N | Y | Y |
| 23 **Bonilla** | Y | Y | N | N | Y | Y |
| 24 **Marchant** | Y | Y | N | N | Y | ? |
| 25 Doggett | N | Y | Y | Y | N | Y |
| 26 **Burgess** | Y | Y | N | N | Y | Y |
| 27 Ortiz | N | Y | Y | Y | N | Y |
| 28 Cuellar | N | Y | Y | Y | N | Y |
| 29 Green, G. | N | Y | Y | Y | N | Y |
| 30 Johnson, E. | N | Y | Y | Y | N | Y |
| 31 **Carter** | Y | Y | N | N | Y | Y |
| 32 **Sessions** | Y | Y | N | N | Y | Y |
| **UTAH** | | | | | | |
| 1 **Bishop** | Y | Y | N | N | Y | Y |
| 2 Matheson | N | N | Y | Y | N | Y |
| 3 **Cannon** | Y | Y | N | N | Y | Y |
| **VERMONT** | | | | | | |
| AL *Sanders* | N | Y | Y | Y | N | Y |
| **VIRGINIA** | | | | | | |
| 1 **Davis, J.** | Y | Y | N | N | Y | ? |
| 2 **Drake** | Y | Y | N | N | Y | Y |
| 3 Scott | N | Y | Y | Y | N | Y |
| 4 **Forbes** | Y | Y | N | N | Y | Y |
| 5 **Goode** | Y | Y | N | N | Y | ? |
| 6 **Goodlatte** | Y | Y | N | N | Y | Y |
| 7 **Cantor** | Y | Y | N | N | Y | Y |
| 8 Moran | N | Y | Y | Y | N | Y |
| 9 Boucher | N | Y | Y | Y | N | ? |
| 10 **Wolf** | Y | Y | N | N | Y | Y |
| 11 **Davis, T.** | Y | Y | N | N | Y | Y |
| **WASHINGTON** | | | | | | |
| 1 Inslee | N | Y | Y | Y | N | Y |
| 2 Larsen | N | N | Y | Y | N | Y |
| 3 Baird | N | N | Y | Y | N | Y |
| 4 **Hastings** | Y | Y | N | N | Y | Y |
| 5 **McMorris** | Y | Y | N | N | Y | Y |
| 6 Dicks | N | Y | Y | Y | N | ? |
| 7 McDermott | N | N | Y | Y | N | ? |
| 8 **Reichert** | Y | Y | N | N | Y | Y |
| 9 Smith | N | Y | Y | Y | N | Y |
| **WEST VIRGINIA** | | | | | | |
| 1 Mollohan | N | Y | Y | Y | N | Y |
| 2 **Capito** | Y | Y | N | N | Y | Y |
| 3 Rahall | N | Y | Y | Y | N | Y |
| **WISCONSIN** | | | | | | |
| 1 **Ryan** | Y | Y | N | N | Y | Y |
| 2 Baldwin | N | N | Y | Y | N | Y |
| 3 Kind | N | Y | Y | Y | N | Y |
| 4 Moore | N | Y | Y | Y | N | Y |
| 5 **Sensenbrenner** | Y | Y | N | N | Y | Y |
| 6 **Petri** | Y | Y | N | N | Y | Y |
| 7 Obey | N | Y | Y | Y | N | Y |
| 8 **Green** | Y | Y | N | N | Y | + |
| **WYOMING** | | | | | | |
| AL **Cubin** | Y | Y | N | N | Y | Y |

# IN THE HOUSE | By Vote Number

**521.** **Procedural Motion/Journal.** Approval of the House Journal of Friday, October 7, 2005. Approved 317-52: R 188-17; D 129-35 (ND 96-28, SD 33-7); I 0-0. Oct. 17, 2005.

**522.** **H Res 457. National Chemistry Week/Adoption.** Smith, R-Texas, motion to suspend the rules and adopt the resolution that would support the goals of National Chemistry Week. Motion agreed to 366-2: R 202-2; D 164-0 (ND 124-0, SD 40-0); I 0-0. A two-thirds majority of those present and voting (246 in this case) is required for adoption under suspension of the rules. Oct. 17, 2005.

**523.** **H Res 491. Cyber Security Awareness Month/Adoption.** Smith, R-Texas, motion to suspend the rules and adopt the resolution that would express support for the goals and ideals of National Cyber Security Awareness Month. Motion agreed to 354-13: R 192-13; D 162-0 (ND 123-0, SD 39-0); I 0-0. A two-thirds majority of those present and voting (245 in this case) is required for adoption under suspension of the rules. Oct. 17, 2005.

**524.** **HR 554. Food Industry Lawsuits/Rule.** Adoption of the rule (H Res 494) that would provide for House floor consideration of the bill that would prohibit lawsuits in federal or state courts against restaurants, food manufacturers and distributors based on claims that the food contributed to the plaintiff's obesity or weight gain. Adopted 310-114: R 228-0; D 81-114 (ND 50-96, SD 31-18); I 1-0. Oct. 18, 2005.

**525.** **HR 1409. Orphan Assistance in Developing Countries/Passage.** Hyde, R-Ill., motion to suspend the rules and pass the bill that would establish a special adviser within the U.S. Agency for International Development who would be responsible for reviewing and approving all assistance provided by the agency to orphans and vulnerable children in developing countries. Motion agreed to 415-9: R 219-9; D 195-0 (ND 146-0, SD 49-0); I 1-0. A two-thirds majority of those present and voting (283 in this case) is required for passage under suspension of the rules. Oct. 18, 2005.

**526.** **H Res 492. Earthquake Victims Condolence/Adoption.** Hyde, R-Ill., motion to suspend the rules and adopt the resolution that would mourn the loss of life and suffering caused by the earthquake that occurred in Pakistan and India on Oct. 8, 2005. Motion agreed to 423-0: R 227-0; D 195-0 (ND 146-0, SD 49-0); I 1-0. A two-thirds majority of those present and voting (282 in this case) is required for adoption under suspension of the rules. Oct. 18, 2005.

**527.** **HR 3549. William F. Clinger Post Office/Passage.** Porter, R-Nev., motion to suspend the rules and pass the bill that would designate a post office in Warren, Pa., for William F. Clinger, R-Pa. (1979-97), who represented Pennsylvania in the House for nine successive terms and was chairman of the Government Reform and Oversight Committee in the 104th Congress. Motion agreed to 422-1: R 228-0; D 193-1 (ND 144-1, SD 49-0); I 1-0. A two-thirds majority of those present and voting (282 in this case) is required for passage under suspension of the rules. Oct. 18, 2005.

**528.** **HR 3853. Willie Vaughn Post Office/Passage.** Porter, R-Nev., motion to suspend the rules and pass the bill that would designate a post office in Parkdale, Ark., for Willie Vaughn, a church, civic and community leader in Parkdale. Motion agreed to 421-0: R 227-0; D 193-0 (ND 144-0, SD 49-0); I 1-0. A two-thirds majority of those present and voting (281 in this case) is required for passage under suspension of the rules. Oct. 18, 2005.

| | 521 | 522 | 523 | 524 | 525 | 526 | 527 | 528 |
|---|---|---|---|---|---|---|---|---|
| **ALABAMA** | | | | | | | | |
| 1 Bonner | Y | Y | Y | Y | Y | Y | Y | Y |
| 2 Everett | Y | Y | Y | Y | Y | Y | Y | Y |
| 3 Rogers | Y | Y | Y | Y | Y | Y | Y | Y |
| 4 Aderholt | Y | Y | Y | Y | Y | Y | Y | Y |
| 5 Cramer | Y | Y | Y | Y | Y | Y | Y | Y |
| 6 Bachus | Y | Y | Y | Y | Y | Y | Y | Y |
| 7 Davis | Y | Y | Y | Y | Y | Y | Y | Y |
| **ALASKA** | | | | | | | | |
| AL Young | Y | Y | Y | Y | Y | Y | Y | Y |
| **ARIZONA** | | | | | | | | |
| 1 Renzi | Y | Y | Y | Y | Y | Y | Y | Y |
| 2 Franks | Y | Y | Y | Y | Y | Y | Y | Y |
| 3 Shadegg | Y | N | N | Y | N | Y | Y | Y |
| 4 Pastor | N | Y | Y | N | Y | Y | Y | Y |
| 5 Hayworth | Y | Y | Y | Y | Y | Y | Y | Y |
| 6 Flake | Y | N | N | Y | N | Y | Y | Y |
| 7 Grijalva | – | + | + | – | + | + | + | + |
| 8 Kolbe | Y | Y | Y | Y | Y | Y | Y | Y |
| **ARKANSAS** | | | | | | | | |
| 1 Berry | Y | Y | Y | Y | Y | Y | Y | Y |
| 2 Snyder | Y | Y | Y | Y | Y | Y | Y | Y |
| 3 Boozman | Y | Y | Y | Y | Y | Y | Y | Y |
| 4 Ross | Y | Y | Y | Y | Y | Y | Y | Y |
| **CALIFORNIA** | | | | | | | | |
| 1 Thompson | N | Y | Y | Y | Y | Y | Y | Y |
| 2 Herger | Y | Y | Y | Y | Y | Y | Y | Y |
| 3 Lungren | Y | Y | Y | Y | Y | Y | Y | Y |
| 4 Doolittle | Y | Y | Y | Y | ? | Y | Y | Y |
| 5 Matsui, D. | Y | Y | Y | N | Y | Y | Y | Y |
| 6 Woolsey | Y | Y | Y | N | Y | Y | Y | Y |
| 7 Miller, George | Y | Y | Y | N | Y | Y | Y | Y |
| 8 Pelosi | Y | Y | Y | N | Y | Y | Y | Y |
| 9 Lee | Y | Y | Y | N | Y | Y | Y | Y |
| 10 Tauscher | Y | Y | Y | N | Y | Y | Y | Y |
| 11 Pombo | Y | ? | Y | Y | Y | Y | Y | Y |
| 12 Lantos | Y | Y | Y | N | Y | Y | Y | Y |
| 13 Stark | ? | ? | ? | N | Y | Y | ? | Y |
| 14 Eshoo | Y | Y | Y | N | Y | Y | Y | Y |
| 15 Honda | Y | Y | Y | N | Y | Y | Y | Y |
| 16 Lofgren | Y | Y | Y | N | Y | Y | Y | Y |
| 17 Farr | Y | Y | Y | N | Y | Y | Y | Y |
| 18 Cardoza | Y | Y | Y | N | Y | Y | Y | Y |
| 19 Radanovich | Y | Y | Y | Y | Y | Y | Y | Y |
| 20 Costa | Y | Y | Y | Y | Y | Y | Y | Y |
| 21 Nunes | Y | Y | Y | Y | Y | Y | Y | Y |
| 22 Thomas | Y | Y | Y | Y | Y | Y | Y | Y |
| 23 Capps | Y | Y | Y | N | Y | Y | Y | Y |
| 24 Gallegly | + | + | + | Y | Y | Y | Y | Y |
| 25 McKeon | ? | ? | ? | Y | Y | Y | Y | Y |
| 26 Dreier | Y | Y | Y | Y | Y | Y | Y | Y |
| 27 Sherman | Y | Y | Y | N | Y | Y | Y | Y |
| 28 Berman | Y | Y | Y | N | Y | Y | Y | Y |
| 29 Schiff | ? | ? | ? | ? | ? | ? | ? | ? |
| 30 Waxman | Y | Y | Y | N | Y | Y | Y | Y |
| 31 Becerra | + | + | + | N | Y | Y | Y | Y |
| 32 Solis | Y | Y | Y | N | Y | Y | Y | Y |
| 33 Watson | Y | Y | Y | N | Y | Y | Y | Y |
| 34 Roybal-Allard | ? | ? | ? | ? | ? | ? | ? | ? |
| 35 Waters | N | Y | Y | N | Y | Y | Y | Y |
| 36 Harman | ? | ? | ? | Y | Y | Y | Y | Y |
| 37 Millender-McD. | Y | Y | Y | N | Y | Y | Y | Y |
| 38 Napolitano | Y | Y | Y | N | Y | Y | Y | Y |
| 39 Sánchez, Linda | Y | Y | Y | Y | Y | Y | Y | Y |
| 40 Royce | Y | Y | Y | Y | Y | Y | Y | Y |
| 41 Lewis | Y | Y | Y | Y | Y | Y | Y | Y |
| 42 Miller, Gary | Y | Y | Y | Y | Y | Y | Y | Y |
| 43 Baca | Y | Y | Y | Y | Y | Y | Y | Y |
| 44 Calvert | ? | ? | ? | Y | Y | Y | Y | Y |
| 45 Bono | Y | Y | Y | Y | Y | Y | Y | Y |
| 46 Rohrabacher | Y | Y | Y | Y | Y | Y | Y | Y |
| 47 Sanchez, Loretta | N | Y | Y | Y | Y | Y | Y | Y |
| 48 Vacant | | | | | | | | |
| 49 Issa | Y | Y | Y | Y | Y | Y | Y | Y |
| 50 Cunningham | Y | Y | Y | Y | Y | Y | Y | Y |
| 51 Filner | N | Y | Y | N | Y | Y | Y | Y |
| 52 Hunter | Y | Y | Y | Y | Y | Y | Y | Y |
| 53 Davis | Y | Y | Y | Y | Y | Y | Y | Y |
| **COLORADO** | | | | | | | | |
| 1 DeGette | Y | Y | Y | Y | Y | Y | Y | Y |
| 2 Udall | N | Y | Y | N | Y | Y | Y | Y |
| 3 Salazar | Y | Y | Y | Y | Y | Y | Y | Y |
| 4 Musgrave | Y | Y | Y | Y | Y | Y | Y | Y |
| 5 Hefley | N | Y | Y | Y | Y | Y | Y | Y |
| 6 Tancredo | P | Y | Y | Y | Y | Y | Y | Y |
| 7 Beauprez | Y | Y | Y | Y | Y | Y | Y | Y |
| **CONNECTICUT** | | | | | | | | |
| 1 Larson | Y | Y | Y | N | Y | Y | Y | Y |
| 2 Simmons | Y | Y | Y | Y | Y | Y | Y | Y |
| 3 DeLauro | Y | Y | Y | N | Y | Y | Y | Y |
| 4 Shays | Y | Y | Y | Y | Y | Y | Y | Y |
| 5 Johnson | Y | Y | Y | Y | Y | Y | Y | Y |
| **DELAWARE** | | | | | | | | |
| AL Castle | Y | Y | Y | Y | Y | Y | Y | Y |
| **FLORIDA** | | | | | | | | |
| 1 Miller | Y | Y | Y | Y | Y | Y | Y | Y |
| 2 Boyd | Y | Y | Y | Y | Y | Y | Y | Y |
| 3 Brown | ? | ? | ? | N | Y | Y | Y | Y |
| 4 Crenshaw | Y | Y | Y | Y | Y | Y | Y | Y |
| 5 Brown-Waite | Y | Y | Y | N | Y | Y | Y | Y |
| 6 Stearns | Y | Y | N | Y | N | Y | Y | Y |
| 7 Mica | Y | Y | Y | Y | Y | Y | Y | Y |
| 8 Keller | ? | ? | ? | ? | ? | ? | ? | ? |
| 9 Bilirakis | Y | Y | Y | Y | Y | Y | Y | Y |
| 10 Young | Y | Y | Y | Y | Y | Y | Y | Y |
| 11 Davis | ? | ? | ? | ? | ? | ? | ? | ? |
| 12 Putnam | Y | Y | Y | Y | Y | Y | Y | Y |
| 13 Harris | ? | ? | ? | Y | Y | Y | Y | Y |
| 14 Mack | Y | Y | Y | Y | Y | Y | Y | Y |
| 15 Weldon | Y | Y | Y | Y | Y | Y | Y | Y |
| 16 Foley | Y | Y | Y | Y | Y | Y | Y | Y |
| 17 Meek | Y | Y | Y | N | Y | Y | Y | Y |
| 18 Ros-Lehtinen | ? | ? | ? | Y | Y | Y | Y | Y |
| 19 Wexler | Y | Y | Y | N | Y | Y | Y | Y |
| 20 Wasserman-Schultz | ? | ? | ? | Y | Y | Y | Y | Y |
| 21 Diaz-Balart, L. | ? | ? | ? | Y | Y | Y | Y | Y |
| 22 Shaw | Y | Y | Y | Y | Y | Y | Y | Y |
| 23 Hastings | N | Y | Y | N | Y | Y | Y | Y |
| 24 Feeney | ? | ? | ? | Y | Y | Y | Y | Y |
| 25 Diaz-Balart, M. | Y | Y | Y | Y | Y | Y | Y | Y |
| **GEORGIA** | | | | | | | | |
| 1 Kingston | Y | Y | Y | ? | ? | ? | ? | ? |
| 2 Bishop | Y | Y | Y | Y | Y | Y | Y | Y |
| 3 Marshall | N | Y | Y | Y | Y | Y | Y | Y |
| 4 McKinney | Y | Y | Y | N | Y | Y | Y | Y |
| 5 Lewis | N | Y | Y | ? | ? | ? | ? | ? |
| 6 Price | Y | Y | Y | Y | Y | Y | Y | Y |
| 7 Linder | Y | Y | Y | Y | Y | Y | Y | Y |
| 8 Westmoreland | Y | Y | Y | Y | N | Y | Y | Y |
| 9 Norwood | Y | Y | N | Y | Y | Y | Y | Y |
| 10 Deal | Y | Y | Y | Y | Y | Y | Y | Y |
| 11 Gingrey | Y | Y | Y | Y | Y | Y | Y | Y |
| 12 Barrow | ? | ? | ? | Y | Y | Y | Y | Y |
| 13 Scott | Y | Y | Y | Y | Y | Y | Y | Y |
| **HAWAII** | | | | | | | | |
| 1 Abercrombie | N | Y | Y | N | Y | Y | N | Y |
| 2 Case | ? | ? | ? | Y | Y | Y | Y | Y |
| **IDAHO** | | | | | | | | |
| 1 Otter | Y | Y | Y | Y | Y | Y | Y | Y |
| 2 Simpson | Y | Y | Y | Y | Y | Y | Y | Y |
| **ILLINOIS** | | | | | | | | |
| 1 Rush | ? | ? | ? | N | Y | Y | Y | Y |
| 2 Jackson | Y | Y | Y | N | Y | Y | Y | Y |
| 3 Lipinski | Y | Y | Y | N | Y | Y | Y | Y |
| 4 Gutierrez | + | + | ? | Y | Y | Y | Y | Y |
| 5 Emanuel | Y | Y | Y | Y | Y | Y | Y | Y |
| 6 Hyde | Y | Y | Y | Y | Y | Y | Y | Y |
| 7 Davis | Y | Y | Y | N | Y | Y | Y | Y |
| 8 Bean | Y | Y | Y | Y | Y | Y | Y | Y |
| 9 Schakowsky | Y | Y | Y | N | Y | Y | Y | Y |
| 10 Kirk | + | Y | Y | Y | Y | Y | Y | Y |
| 11 Weller | N | Y | Y | Y | Y | Y | Y | Y |
| 12 Costello | N | Y | Y | N | Y | Y | Y | Y |

| KEY | Republicans | Democrats | *Independents* |
|---|---|---|---|

| | | |
|---|---|---|
| **Y** Voted for (yea) | **X** Paired against | **C** Voted "present" to avoid possible conflict of interest |
| **#** Paired for | **–** Announced against | |
| **+** Announced for | **P** Voted "present" | **?** Did not vote or otherwise make a position known |
| **N** Voted against (nay) | | |

| | 521 | 522 | 523 | 524 | 525 | 526 | 527 | 528 |
|---|---|---|---|---|---|---|---|---|
| 13 **Biggert** | ? | ? | ? | Y | Y | Y | Y | Y |
| 14 **Hastert** | | | | | | | | |
| 15 **Johnson** | Y | Y | Y | Y | Y | Y | Y | Y |
| 16 **Manzullo** | Y | Y | Y | Y | Y | Y | Y | Y |
| 17 Evans | Y | Y | Y | N | Y | Y | Y | Y |
| 18 **LaHood** | ? | ? | ? | Y | Y | Y | Y | Y |
| 19 **Shimkus** | Y | Y | N | Y | Y | Y | Y | Y |
| **INDIANA** | | | | | | | | |
| 1 Visclosky | ? | ? | ? | N | Y | Y | Y | Y |
| 2 **Chocola** | Y | Y | Y | Y | Y | Y | Y | Y |
| 3 **Souder** | Y | Y | Y | Y | Y | Y | Y | Y |
| 4 **Buyer** | Y | Y | Y | Y | Y | Y | Y | Y |
| 5 **Burton** | Y | Y | Y | Y | Y | Y | Y | Y |
| 6 **Pence** | Y | Y | Y | Y | Y | Y | Y | Y |
| 7 Carson | Y | Y | Y | Y | Y | Y | Y | Y |
| 8 **Hostettler** | Y | Y | Y | Y | Y | Y | Y | Y |
| 9 **Sodrel** | Y | Y | Y | Y | Y | Y | Y | Y |
| **IOWA** | | | | | | | | |
| 1 **Nussle** | N | Y | Y | Y | Y | Y | Y | Y |
| 2 **Leach** | Y | Y | Y | Y | Y | Y | Y | Y |
| 3 Boswell | ? | ? | ? | ? | ? | ? | ? | ? |
| 4 **Latham** | N | Y | Y | Y | Y | Y | Y | Y |
| 5 **King** | + | + | ? | Y | Y | Y | Y | Y |
| **KANSAS** | | | | | | | | |
| 1 **Moran** | N | Y | Y | Y | Y | Y | Y | Y |
| 2 **Ryun** | + | + | + | Y | Y | Y | Y | Y |
| 3 Moore | Y | Y | Y | Y | Y | Y | Y | Y |
| 4 **Tiahrt** | Y | Y | ? | Y | Y | Y | Y | Y |
| **KENTUCKY** | | | | | | | | |
| 1 **Whitfield** | Y | Y | Y | Y | Y | Y | Y | Y |
| 2 **Lewis** | Y | Y | Y | Y | Y | Y | Y | Y |
| 3 **Northup** | Y | Y | Y | Y | Y | Y | Y | Y |
| 4 **Davis** | N | Y | Y | Y | Y | Y | Y | Y |
| 5 **Rogers** | + | + | + | Y | Y | Y | Y | Y |
| 6 Chandler | N | Y | Y | Y | Y | Y | Y | Y |
| **LOUISIANA** | | | | | | | | |
| 1 **Jindal** | Y | Y | Y | Y | Y | Y | Y | Y |
| 2 Jefferson | Y | Y | Y | N | Y | Y | Y | Y |
| 3 Melancon | Y | Y | Y | Y | Y | Y | Y | Y |
| 4 **McCrery** | Y | Y | Y | Y | Y | Y | Y | Y |
| 5 **Alexander** | ? | ? | ? | Y | Y | Y | Y | Y |
| 6 **Baker** | Y | Y | Y | Y | Y | Y | Y | Y |
| 7 **Boustany** | Y | Y | Y | Y | Y | Y | Y | Y |
| **MAINE** | | | | | | | | |
| 1 Allen | Y | Y | Y | N | Y | Y | Y | Y |
| 2 Michaud | Y | Y | Y | Y | Y | Y | Y | Y |
| **MARYLAND** | | | | | | | | |
| 1 **Gilchrest** | Y | Y | Y | Y | Y | Y | Y | Y |
| 2 Ruppersberger | Y | Y | Y | Y | Y | Y | Y | Y |
| 3 Cardin | ? | ? | ? | N | Y | Y | Y | Y |
| 4 Wynn | Y | Y | Y | Y | Y | Y | Y | Y |
| 5 Hoyer | Y | Y | Y | Y | Y | Y | Y | Y |
| 6 **Bartlett** | Y | Y | Y | Y | Y | Y | Y | Y |
| 7 Cummings | Y | Y | Y | N | Y | Y | Y | Y |
| 8 Van Hollen | Y | Y | Y | Y | Y | Y | Y | Y |
| **MASSACHUSETTS** | | | | | | | | |
| 1 Olver | N | Y | ? | N | Y | Y | Y | Y |
| 2 Neal | ? | ? | ? | Y | Y | Y | Y | Y |
| 3 McGovern | ? | ? | ? | N | Y | Y | Y | Y |
| 4 Frank | Y | Y | Y | Y | Y | Y | Y | Y |
| 5 Meehan | Y | Y | Y | N | Y | Y | Y | Y |
| 6 Tierney | Y | Y | Y | N | Y | Y | Y | Y |
| 7 Markey | N | Y | Y | N | Y | Y | Y | Y |
| 8 Capuano | N | Y | Y | N | Y | Y | Y | Y |
| 9 Lynch | Y | Y | Y | Y | Y | Y | Y | Y |
| 10 Delahunt | Y | Y | Y | N | Y | Y | Y | Y |
| **MICHIGAN** | | | | | | | | |
| 1 Stupak | N | Y | Y | N | Y | Y | Y | Y |
| 2 **Hoekstra** | Y | Y | Y | Y | Y | Y | Y | Y |
| 3 **Ehlers** | Y | Y | Y | Y | Y | Y | Y | Y |
| 4 **Camp** | Y | Y | Y | Y | Y | Y | Y | Y |
| 5 Kildee | Y | Y | Y | Y | Y | Y | Y | Y |
| 6 **Upton** | Y | Y | N | Y | Y | Y | Y | Y |
| 7 **Schwarz** | Y | Y | Y | Y | Y | Y | Y | Y |
| 8 **Rogers** | Y | Y | Y | Y | Y | Y | Y | Y |
| 9 **Knollenberg** | Y | Y | Y | Y | Y | Y | Y | Y |
| 10 **Miller** | Y | Y | Y | Y | Y | Y | Y | Y |
| 11 **McCotter** | ? | ? | ? | Y | Y | Y | Y | Y |
| 12 Levin | Y | Y | Y | N | Y | Y | Y | Y |
| 13 Kilpatrick | + | + | + | N | Y | Y | Y | Y |
| 14 Conyers | Y | Y | Y | Y | Y | Y | Y | Y |
| 15 Dingell | Y | Y | Y | Y | Y | Y | Y | Y |
| **MINNESOTA** | | | | | | | | |
| 1 **Gutknecht** | Y | Y | Y | Y | Y | Y | Y | Y |
| 2 **Kline** | Y | Y | Y | Y | Y | Y | Y | Y |
| 3 **Ramstad** | N | Y | Y | Y | Y | Y | Y | Y |
| 4 McCollum | N | Y | Y | N | Y | Y | Y | Y |
| 5 Sabo | N | Y | Y | N | Y | Y | Y | Y |
| 6 **Kennedy** | N | Y | Y | Y | Y | Y | Y | Y |
| 7 Peterson | N | Y | Y | Y | Y | Y | Y | Y |
| 8 Oberstar | N | Y | Y | N | Y | Y | Y | Y |
| **MISSISSIPPI** | | | | | | | | |
| 1 **Wicker** | Y | Y | Y | Y | Y | Y | Y | Y |
| 2 Thompson | Y | Y | Y | N | Y | Y | Y | Y |
| 3 **Pickering** | ? | ? | ? | Y | Y | Y | Y | Y |
| 4 Taylor | N | Y | Y | Y | Y | Y | Y | Y |
| **MISSOURI** | | | | | | | | |
| 1 Clay | Y | Y | Y | N | Y | Y | Y | Y |
| 2 **Akin** | Y | Y | Y | Y | Y | Y | Y | Y |
| 3 Carnahan | Y | Y | Y | N | Y | Y | Y | Y |
| 4 Skelton | Y | Y | Y | Y | Y | Y | Y | Y |
| 5 Cleaver | Y | Y | Y | N | Y | Y | Y | Y |
| 6 **Graves** | Y | Y | Y | Y | Y | Y | Y | Y |
| 7 **Blunt** | Y | Y | Y | Y | Y | Y | Y | ? |
| 8 **Emerson** | Y | Y | Y | Y | Y | Y | Y | Y |
| 9 **Hulshof** | Y | Y | Y | Y | Y | Y | Y | Y |
| **MONTANA** | | | | | | | | |
| AL **Rehberg** | Y | Y | Y | Y | Y | Y | Y | Y |
| **NEBRASKA** | | | | | | | | |
| 1 **Fortenberry** | Y | Y | Y | Y | Y | Y | Y | Y |
| 2 **Terry** | ? | ? | ? | Y | Y | Y | Y | Y |
| 3 **Osborne** | Y | Y | Y | Y | Y | Y | Y | Y |
| **NEVADA** | | | | | | | | |
| 1 Berkley | Y | Y | Y | Y | Y | Y | Y | Y |
| 2 **Gibbons** | + | + | + | Y | Y | Y | Y | Y |
| 3 **Porter** | Y | Y | Y | Y | Y | Y | Y | Y |
| **NEW HAMPSHIRE** | | | | | | | | |
| 1 **Bradley** | Y | Y | Y | Y | Y | Y | Y | Y |
| 2 **Bass** | Y | Y | Y | Y | Y | Y | Y | Y |
| **NEW JERSEY** | | | | | | | | |
| 1 Andrews | Y | Y | Y | – | + | + | + | + |
| 2 **LoBiondo** | N | Y | Y | Y | Y | Y | Y | Y |
| 3 **Saxton** | Y | ? | Y | Y | Y | Y | Y | Y |
| 4 **Smith** | Y | Y | Y | Y | Y | Y | Y | Y |
| 5 **Garrett** | Y | Y | Y | Y | Y | Y | Y | Y |
| 6 Pallone | Y | Y | Y | N | Y | Y | Y | Y |
| 7 **Ferguson** | Y | Y | N | Y | Y | Y | Y | Y |
| 8 Pascrell | + | + | + | N | Y | Y | Y | Y |
| 9 Rothman | Y | Y | Y | N | Y | Y | Y | Y |
| 10 Payne | Y | Y | Y | N | Y | Y | Y | Y |
| 11 **Frelinghuysen** | Y | Y | Y | Y | Y | Y | Y | Y |
| 12 Holt | Y | Y | Y | N | Y | Y | Y | Y |
| 13 Menendez | + | + | Y | Y | Y | Y | Y | Y |
| **NEW MEXICO** | | | | | | | | |
| 1 **Wilson** | Y | Y | Y | Y | Y | Y | Y | Y |
| 2 **Pearce** | Y | Y | Y | Y | Y | Y | Y | Y |
| 3 Udall | N | Y | Y | N | Y | Y | Y | Y |
| **NEW YORK** | | | | | | | | |
| 1 Bishop | Y | Y | Y | Y | Y | Y | Y | Y |
| 2 Israel | Y | Y | Y | Y | Y | Y | Y | Y |
| 3 **King** | Y | Y | Y | Y | Y | Y | Y | Y |
| 4 McCarthy | N | Y | Y | N | Y | Y | Y | Y |
| 5 Ackerman | Y | Y | Y | N | Y | Y | Y | Y |
| 6 Meeks | ? | ? | ? | N | Y | Y | Y | Y |
| 7 Crowley | Y | Y | Y | N | Y | Y | Y | Y |
| 8 Nadler | Y | Y | Y | N | Y | Y | Y | Y |
| 9 Weiner | Y | Y | Y | N | Y | Y | Y | Y |
| 10 Towns | ? | ? | ? | N | Y | Y | Y | Y |
| 11 Owens | Y | Y | Y | N | Y | Y | Y | Y |
| 12 Velázquez | N | Y | Y | N | Y | Y | Y | Y |
| 13 **Fossella** | N | Y | Y | Y | Y | Y | Y | Y |
| 14 Maloney | Y | Y | Y | N | Y | Y | Y | Y |
| 15 Rangel | ? | ? | ? | Y | Y | Y | Y | Y |
| 16 Serrano | Y | Y | Y | Y | Y | Y | Y | Y |
| 17 Engel | ? | ? | ? | N | Y | Y | Y | Y |
| 18 Lowey | Y | Y | Y | N | Y | Y | Y | Y |
| 19 **Kelly** | Y | Y | Y | Y | Y | Y | Y | Y |
| 20 **Sweeney** | N | Y | Y | Y | Y | Y | Y | Y |
| 21 McNulty | Y | Y | Y | N | Y | Y | Y | Y |
| 22 Hinchey | Y | Y | Y | N | Y | Y | Y | Y |
| 23 **McHugh** | Y | Y | Y | Y | Y | Y | Y | Y |
| 24 **Boehlert** | Y | Y | Y | Y | Y | Y | Y | Y |
| 25 **Walsh** | Y | Y | Y | Y | Y | Y | Y | Y |
| 26 **Reynolds** | Y | ? | Y | Y | Y | Y | Y | Y |
| 27 Higgins | Y | Y | Y | Y | Y | Y | Y | Y |
| 28 Slaughter | Y | Y | Y | N | Y | Y | Y | Y |
| 29 **Kuhl** | Y | Y | Y | Y | Y | Y | Y | Y |
| **NORTH CAROLINA** | | | | | | | | |
| 1 Butterfield | ? | ? | ? | N | Y | Y | Y | Y |
| 2 Etheridge | N | Y | Y | N | Y | Y | Y | Y |
| 3 **Jones** | Y | Y | N | Y | Y | Y | Y | Y |
| 4 Price | Y | Y | ? | N | Y | Y | Y | Y |
| 5 **Foxx** | Y | Y | Y | Y | Y | Y | Y | Y |
| 6 **Coble** | Y | Y | Y | Y | Y | Y | Y | Y |
| 7 McIntyre | Y | Y | Y | Y | Y | Y | Y | Y |
| 8 **Hayes** | Y | Y | Y | Y | Y | Y | Y | Y |
| 9 **Myrick** | Y | Y | Y | Y | Y | Y | Y | Y |
| 10 **McHenry** | Y | Y | Y | Y | Y | Y | Y | Y |
| 11 **Taylor** | Y | Y | Y | Y | Y | Y | Y | Y |
| 12 Watt | ? | ? | ? | N | Y | Y | Y | Y |
| 13 Miller | Y | Y | Y | N | Y | Y | Y | Y |
| **NORTH DAKOTA** | | | | | | | | |
| AL Pomeroy | Y | Y | Y | Y | Y | Y | Y | Y |
| **OHIO** | | | | | | | | |
| 1 **Chabot** | Y | Y | Y | Y | Y | Y | Y | Y |
| 2 **Schmidt** | Y | Y | Y | Y | Y | Y | Y | Y |
| 3 **Turner** | Y | Y | Y | Y | Y | Y | Y | Y |
| 4 **Oxley** | + | + | + | Y | Y | Y | Y | Y |
| 5 **Gillmor** | Y | Y | Y | Y | Y | Y | Y | Y |
| 6 Strickland | ? | ? | ? | N | Y | Y | Y | Y |
| 7 **Hobson** | Y | Y | Y | Y | Y | Y | Y | Y |
| 8 **Boehner** | Y | Y | Y | Y | Y | Y | Y | Y |
| 9 Kaptur | Y | Y | Y | N | Y | Y | Y | Y |
| 10 Kucinich | N | Y | Y | N | Y | Y | Y | Y |
| 11 Jones | ? | ? | ? | N | Y | Y | Y | Y |
| 12 **Tiberi** | N | Y | Y | Y | Y | Y | Y | Y |
| 13 Brown | Y | Y | Y | N | Y | Y | Y | Y |
| 14 **LaTourette** | Y | Y | Y | Y | Y | Y | Y | Y |
| 15 **Pryce** | Y | Y | Y | Y | Y | Y | Y | Y |
| 16 **Regula** | Y | Y | Y | Y | Y | Y | Y | Y |
| 17 Ryan | Y | Y | Y | N | Y | Y | Y | Y |
| 18 **Ney** | Y | Y | Y | Y | Y | Y | Y | Y |
| **OKLAHOMA** | | | | | | | | |
| 1 **Sullivan** | ? | ? | ? | Y | Y | Y | Y | Y |
| 2 Boren | Y | Y | Y | Y | Y | Y | Y | Y |
| 3 **Lucas** | Y | Y | Y | Y | Y | Y | Y | Y |
| 4 **Cole** | Y | Y | Y | Y | Y | Y | Y | Y |
| 5 **Istook** | ? | ? | ? | Y | Y | Y | Y | Y |
| **OREGON** | | | | | | | | |
| 1 Wu | N | Y | Y | Y | Y | Y | Y | Y |
| 2 **Walden** | Y | Y | N | Y | Y | Y | Y | Y |
| 3 Blumenauer | + | + | + | N | Y | Y | Y | Y |
| 4 DeFazio | ? | ? | ? | Y | Y | Y | Y | Y |
| 5 Hooley | Y | Y | Y | Y | Y | Y | Y | Y |
| **PENNSYLVANIA** | | | | | | | | |
| 1 Brady | ? | ? | ? | N | Y | Y | Y | Y |
| 2 Fattah | N | Y | Y | N | Y | Y | Y | ? |
| 3 **English** | N | Y | Y | Y | Y | Y | Y | Y |
| 4 **Hart** | N | Y | Y | Y | Y | Y | Y | Y |
| 5 **Peterson** | Y | Y | Y | Y | Y | Y | Y | Y |
| 6 **Gerlach** | + | + | + | Y | Y | Y | Y | Y |
| 7 **Weldon** | Y | Y | Y | Y | Y | Y | Y | Y |
| 8 **Fitzpatrick** | N | Y | Y | Y | Y | Y | Y | Y |
| 9 **Shuster** | N | Y | Y | Y | N | Y | Y | Y |
| 10 **Sherwood** | Y | Y | Y | Y | Y | Y | Y | Y |
| 11 Kanjorski | N | Y | Y | N | Y | Y | Y | Y |
| 12 Murtha | Y | Y | ? | N | Y | Y | Y | ? |
| 13 Schwartz | Y | Y | Y | Y | Y | Y | Y | Y |
| 14 Doyle | Y | Y | Y | Y | Y | Y | Y | Y |
| 15 **Dent** | Y | Y | Y | Y | Y | Y | Y | Y |
| 16 **Pitts** | Y | Y | Y | Y | Y | Y | Y | Y |
| 17 Holden | N | Y | Y | N | Y | Y | Y | Y |
| 18 **Murphy** | Y | Y | Y | Y | Y | Y | Y | Y |
| 19 **Platts** | Y | Y | Y | Y | Y | Y | Y | Y |
| **RHODE ISLAND** | | | | | | | | |
| 1 Kennedy | + | + | + | Y | Y | Y | Y | Y |
| 2 Langevin | Y | Y | Y | Y | Y | Y | Y | Y |
| **SOUTH CAROLINA** | | | | | | | | |
| 1 **Brown** | Y | Y | Y | Y | Y | Y | Y | Y |
| 2 **Wilson** | Y | Y | Y | Y | Y | Y | Y | Y |
| 3 **Barrett** | Y | Y | Y | Y | Y | Y | Y | Y |
| 4 **Inglis** | Y | Y | Y | Y | Y | Y | Y | Y |
| 5 Spratt | Y | Y | Y | N | Y | Y | Y | Y |
| 6 Clyburn | Y | Y | Y | N | Y | Y | Y | Y |
| **SOUTH DAKOTA** | | | | | | | | |
| AL Herseth | Y | Y | Y | Y | Y | Y | Y | Y |
| **TENNESSEE** | | | | | | | | |
| 1 **Jenkins** | Y | Y | Y | Y | Y | Y | Y | Y |
| 2 **Duncan** | Y | Y | Y | Y | Y | Y | Y | Y |
| 3 **Wamp** | Y | Y | Y | Y | Y | Y | Y | Y |
| 4 Davis | Y | Y | Y | Y | Y | Y | Y | Y |
| 5 Cooper | Y | Y | Y | Y | Y | Y | Y | Y |
| 6 Gordon | Y | Y | Y | Y | Y | Y | Y | Y |
| 7 **Blackburn** | Y | Y | Y | Y | Y | Y | Y | Y |
| 8 Tanner | Y | Y | Y | Y | Y | Y | Y | Y |
| 9 Ford | ? | ? | ? | N | Y | Y | Y | Y |
| **TEXAS** | | | | | | | | |
| 1 **Gohmert** | Y | Y | Y | Y | N | Y | Y | Y |
| 2 **Poe** | Y | Y | Y | Y | Y | Y | Y | Y |
| 3 **Johnson, S.** | Y | Y | Y | Y | N | Y | Y | Y |
| 4 **Hall** | Y | Y | Y | Y | Y | Y | Y | Y |
| 5 **Hensarling** | Y | Y | N | Y | Y | Y | Y | Y |
| 6 **Barton** | Y | Y | N | Y | Y | Y | Y | Y |
| 7 **Culberson** | Y | Y | Y | Y | Y | Y | Y | Y |
| 8 **Brady** | Y | Y | Y | Y | Y | Y | Y | Y |
| 9 Green, A. | Y | Y | Y | N | Y | Y | Y | Y |
| 10 **McCaul** | Y | Y | Y | Y | Y | Y | Y | Y |
| 11 **Conaway** | Y | Y | Y | Y | Y | Y | Y | Y |
| 12 **Granger** | Y | Y | Y | Y | Y | Y | Y | Y |
| 13 **Thornberry** | Y | Y | Y | Y | Y | Y | Y | Y |
| 14 **Paul** | Y | Y | N | Y | N | Y | Y | Y |
| 15 Hinojosa | Y | Y | Y | Y | Y | Y | Y | Y |
| 16 Reyes | ? | ? | ? | Y | Y | Y | Y | Y |
| 17 Edwards | Y | Y | Y | Y | Y | Y | Y | Y |
| 18 Jackson-Lee | + | + | + | Y | Y | Y | Y | Y |
| 19 **Neugebauer** | Y | Y | Y | Y | Y | Y | Y | Y |
| 20 Gonzalez | Y | Y | Y | Y | Y | Y | Y | Y |
| 21 **Smith** | Y | Y | ? | Y | Y | Y | Y | Y |
| 22 **DeLay** | Y | Y | Y | Y | Y | Y | Y | Y |
| 23 **Bonilla** | Y | Y | Y | Y | Y | Y | Y | Y |
| 24 **Marchant** | Y | Y | Y | Y | Y | Y | Y | Y |
| 25 Doggett | Y | Y | Y | N | Y | Y | Y | Y |
| 26 **Burgess** | Y | Y | Y | Y | Y | Y | Y | Y |
| 27 Ortiz | Y | Y | Y | Y | Y | Y | Y | Y |
| 28 Cuellar | Y | Y | Y | Y | Y | Y | Y | Y |
| 29 Green, G. | N | Y | Y | Y | Y | Y | Y | Y |
| 30 Johnson, E. | Y | Y | Y | N | Y | Y | Y | Y |
| 31 **Carter** | Y | Y | Y | Y | Y | Y | Y | Y |
| 32 **Sessions** | Y | Y | N | Y | Y | Y | Y | Y |
| **UTAH** | | | | | | | | |
| 1 **Bishop** | Y | Y | Y | Y | Y | Y | Y | Y |
| 2 Matheson | N | Y | Y | Y | Y | Y | Y | Y |
| 3 **Cannon** | Y | Y | Y | Y | Y | Y | Y | Y |
| **VERMONT** | | | | | | | | |
| AL *Sanders* | ? | ? | ? | Y | Y | Y | Y | Y |
| **VIRGINIA** | | | | | | | | |
| 1 **Davis, J.** | Y | Y | Y | Y | Y | Y | Y | Y |
| 2 **Drake** | Y | Y | Y | Y | Y | Y | Y | Y |
| 3 Scott | Y | Y | Y | Y | Y | Y | Y | Y |
| 4 **Forbes** | Y | Y | Y | Y | Y | Y | Y | Y |
| 5 **Goode** | ? | ? | ? | Y | Y | Y | Y | Y |
| 6 **Goodlatte** | Y | Y | Y | Y | Y | Y | Y | Y |
| 7 **Cantor** | Y | Y | Y | Y | Y | Y | Y | Y |
| 8 Moran | ? | ? | ? | Y | Y | Y | Y | Y |
| 9 Boucher | ? | ? | ? | Y | Y | Y | Y | Y |
| 10 **Wolf** | Y | Y | Y | Y | Y | Y | Y | Y |
| 11 **Davis, T.** | Y | Y | Y | Y | Y | Y | Y | Y |
| **WASHINGTON** | | | | | | | | |
| 1 Inslee | Y | Y | Y | N | Y | Y | Y | Y |
| 2 Larsen | Y | Y | Y | Y | Y | Y | Y | Y |
| 3 Baird | N | Y | Y | N | Y | Y | Y | Y |
| 4 **Hastings** | Y | Y | Y | Y | Y | Y | Y | Y |
| 5 **McMorris** | Y | Y | Y | Y | Y | Y | Y | Y |
| 6 Dicks | Y | Y | Y | Y | Y | Y | Y | Y |
| 7 McDermott | N | Y | Y | N | Y | Y | Y | Y |
| 8 **Reichert** | Y | Y | Y | Y | Y | Y | Y | Y |
| 9 Smith | Y | Y | Y | Y | Y | Y | Y | Y |
| **WEST VIRGINIA** | | | | | | | | |
| 1 Mollohan | Y | Y | Y | N | Y | Y | Y | Y |
| 2 **Capito** | N | Y | Y | Y | Y | Y | Y | Y |
| 3 Rahall | Y | Y | Y | N | Y | Y | Y | Y |
| **WISCONSIN** | | | | | | | | |
| 1 **Ryan** | Y | Y | Y | Y | Y | Y | Y | Y |
| 2 Baldwin | N | Y | Y | N | Y | Y | Y | Y |
| 3 Kind | Y | Y | Y | Y | Y | Y | Y | Y |
| 4 Moore | Y | Y | Y | N | Y | Y | Y | Y |
| 5 **Sensenbrenner** | Y | Y | Y | Y | Y | Y | Y | Y |
| 6 **Petri** | Y | Y | Y | Y | Y | Y | Y | Y |
| 7 Obey | Y | Y | Y | N | Y | Y | Y | Y |
| 8 **Green** | Y | Y | Y | Y | Y | Y | Y | Y |
| **WYOMING** | | | | | | | | |
| AL **Cubin** | Y | Y | Y | Y | Y | Y | Y | Y |

# IN THE HOUSE | By Vote Number

**529.** **HR 554. Food Industry Lawsuits/Lawsuits by Food Manufacturers.** Jackson-Lee, D-Texas, amendment that would prohibit food manufacturers, vendors or trade associations from filing lawsuits against any individual due to that person's consumption of food that has led to weight gain, obesity or related health problems. Rejected 67-357: R 0-227; D 66-130 (ND 53-95, SD 13-35); I 1-0. Oct. 19, 2005.

**530.** **HR 554. Food Industry Lawsuits/Lawsuits for Children.** Filner, D-Calif., amendment that would allow lawsuits for obesity-related injuries of children age 8 and under against chain outlets with at least 20 stores that have marketed food to children under age 8. Rejected 129-298: R 1-227; D 127-71 (ND 105-44, SD 22-27); I 1-0. Oct. 19, 2005.

**531.** **HR 554. Food Industry Lawsuits/State Consumer Protection Laws.** Scott, D-Va., amendment that would exempt from the bill an action brought by a state agency to enforce state consumer protection laws concerning mislabeling or other unfair and deceptive trade practices. Rejected 192-234: R 6-221; D 185-13 (ND 145-4, SD 40-9); I 1-0. Oct. 19, 2005.

**532.** **HR 554. Food Industry Lawsuits/Dietary Supplement Makers.** Waxman, D-Calif., amendment that would allow lawsuits against dietary supplement makers for damages because of obesity, weight gain or related health problems. Rejected 177-247: R 5-221; D 171-26 (ND 137-11, SD 34-15); I 1-0. Oct. 19, 2005.

**533.** **HR 554. Food Industry Lawsuits/Passage.** Passage of the bill that would prohibit lawsuits in federal or state courts against restaurants, food manufacturers or distributors based on claims that the food contributed to the plaintiff's obesity or weight gain. Suits would be allowed if the defendant knowingly violated federal or state laws governing the labeling, advertising or selling of food products. Passed 306-120: R 226-1; D 80-118 (ND 49-100, SD 31-18); I 0-1. A "yea" was a vote in support of the president's position. Oct. 19, 2005.

**534.** **S 397. Gun Liability/Passage.** Passage of the bill that would bar certain civil lawsuits against manufacturers, distributors, dealers and importers of firearms and ammunition, principally those lawsuits aimed at making them liable for gun violence. Trade groups also would be protected, and all pending legal action against gunmakers would be dismissed. The bill would also, with certain exceptions, make it unlawful for licensed gun importers, manufacturers or dealers to sell, deliver or transfer handguns without a secure gun storage or safety device. Passed (thus cleared for the president) 283-144: R 223-4; D 59-140 (ND 31-118, SD 28-22); I 1-0. A "yea" was a vote in support of the president's position. Oct. 20, 2005.

**535.** **HR 2744. Fiscal 2006 Agriculture Appropriations/Motion to Instruct.** DeLauro, D-Conn., motion to instruct House conferees to include language that would agree to a Senate provision that would block use of funds in the bill from being used to close or relocate state Farm Service Agency offices unless the Agriculture Department reports that such closures are necessary and cost effective. It also would instruct conferees to agree to a new provision that would prohibit a state agency from using federal funds for administrative costs related to Food Stamp Program operations that are contracted to a private entity. Motion rejected 209-216: R 12-215; D 196-1 (ND 147-1, SD 49-0); I 1-0. Oct. 20, 2005.

| | 529 | 530 | 531 | 532 | 533 | 534 | 535 |
|---|---|---|---|---|---|---|---|
| **ALABAMA** | | | | | | | |
| 1 Bonner | N | N | N | N | Y | Y | N |
| 2 Everett | N | N | N | N | Y | Y | N |
| 3 Rogers | N | N | N | N | Y | Y | N |
| 4 Aderholt | N | N | N | N | Y | Y | N |
| 5 Cramer | N | N | N | N | Y | Y | Y |
| 6 Bachus | N | N | N | N | Y | Y | N |
| 7 Davis | N | N | Y | N | Y | Y | Y |
| **ALASKA** | | | | | | | |
| AL Young | N | N | N | N | Y | Y | N |
| **ARIZONA** | | | | | | | |
| 1 Renzi | N | N | N | N | Y | Y | N |
| 2 Franks | N | N | N | N | Y | Y | N |
| 3 Shadegg | N | N | N | N | Y | Y | N |
| 4 Pastor | Y | Y | Y | Y | N | N | Y |
| 5 Hayworth | N | N | N | N | Y | Y | N |
| 6 Flake | N | N | N | N | Y | Y | N |
| 7 Grijalva | Y | Y | Y | Y | N | N | Y |
| 8 Kolbe | N | N | N | N | Y | Y | N |
| **ARKANSAS** | | | | | | | |
| 1 Berry | N | N | Y | Y | Y | Y | Y |
| 2 Snyder | N | N | Y | Y | N | N | Y |
| 3 Boozman | N | N | N | N | Y | Y | N |
| 4 Ross | N | N | Y | Y | Y | Y | Y |
| **CALIFORNIA** | | | | | | | |
| 1 Thompson | N | N | N | N | Y | Y | Y |
| 2 Herger | N | N | N | N | Y | Y | N |
| 3 Lungren | N | N | N | N | Y | Y | N |
| 4 Doolittle | N | N | N | N | Y | Y | N |
| 5 Matsui, D. | N | Y | Y | Y | N | N | Y |
| 6 Woolsey | Y | Y | Y | Y | N | N | Y |
| 7 Miller, George | N | Y | Y | Y | N | N | Y |
| 8 Pelosi | Y | Y | Y | Y | N | N | Y |
| 9 Lee | Y | Y | Y | Y | N | N | Y |
| 10 Tauscher | N | N | Y | Y | Y | N | Y |
| 11 Pombo | N | N | N | N | Y | Y | N |
| 12 Lantos | N | Y | Y | Y | N | N | Y |
| 13 Stark | Y | Y | Y | Y | N | N | ? |
| 14 Eshoo | N | Y | Y | Y | N | N | Y |
| 15 Honda | Y | Y | Y | Y | N | N | Y |
| 16 Lofgren | N | Y | Y | Y | N | N | Y |
| 17 Farr | Y | Y | Y | Y | N | N | Y |
| 18 Cardoza | N | N | Y | N | Y | Y | Y |
| 19 Radanovich | N | N | N | N | Y | Y | N |
| 20 Costa | N | N | Y | Y | Y | Y | Y |
| 21 Nunes | N | N | N | N | Y | Y | N |
| 22 Thomas | N | N | N | N | Y | Y | N |
| 23 Capps | N | Y | Y | Y | N | N | Y |
| 24 Gallegly | N | N | N | N | Y | Y | N |
| 25 McKeon | N | N | N | N | Y | Y | N |
| 26 Dreier | N | N | N | N | Y | Y | N |
| 27 Sherman | N | Y | Y | Y | N | N | Y |
| 28 Berman | N | Y | Y | Y | N | N | Y |
| 29 Schiff | N | Y | Y | Y | N | N | Y |
| 30 Waxman | N | Y | Y | Y | N | N | Y |
| 31 Becerra | N | Y | Y | Y | N | N | Y |
| 32 Solis | Y | Y | Y | Y | N | N | Y |
| 33 Watson | Y | Y | Y | Y | N | N | Y |
| 34 Roybal-Allard | ? | ? | ? | ? | ? | ? | ? |
| 35 Waters | Y | Y | Y | Y | N | N | Y |
| 36 Harman | N | N | Y | Y | Y | N | Y |
| 37 Millender-McD. | N | Y | Y | Y | N | N | Y |
| 38 Napolitano | Y | Y | Y | Y | N | N | Y |
| 39 Sánchez, Linda | Y | Y | Y | Y | N | N | Y |
| 40 Royce | N | N | N | N | Y | Y | N |
| 41 Lewis | N | N | N | N | Y | Y | N |
| 42 Miller, Gary | N | N | N | N | Y | Y | N |
| 43 Baca | N | Y | Y | Y | Y | N | Y |
| 44 Calvert | N | N | N | N | Y | Y | N |
| 45 Bono | N | N | N | N | Y | Y | N |
| 46 Rohrabacher | N | N | Y | N | Y | Y | N |
| 47 Sanchez, Loretta | N | N | Y | Y | Y | Y | Y |
| 48 Vacant | | | | | | | |
| 49 Issa | N | N | N | N | Y | Y | N |

| | 529 | 530 | 531 | 532 | 533 | 534 | 535 |
|---|---|---|---|---|---|---|---|
| 50 Cunningham | N | N | N | N | Y | Y | N |
| 51 Filner | Y | Y | Y | Y | N | N | Y |
| 52 Hunter | N | N | N | N | Y | Y | N |
| 53 Davis | N | Y | Y | Y | N | N | Y |
| **COLORADO** | | | | | | | |
| 1 DeGette | N | N | Y | Y | N | N | Y |
| 2 Udall | N | N | Y | Y | Y | N | Y |
| 3 Salazar | N | N | Y | Y | Y | Y | Y |
| 4 Musgrave | N | Y | N | N | Y | + | N |
| 5 Hefley | N | N | N | N | Y | Y | N |
| 6 Tancredo | N | N | N | N | Y | Y | N |
| 7 Beauprez | N | N | N | N | Y | Y | N |
| **CONNECTICUT** | | | | | | | |
| 1 Larson | Y | Y | Y | Y | N | N | Y |
| 2 Simmons | N | N | N | N | Y | Y | Y |
| 3 DeLauro | N | Y | Y | Y | N | N | Y |
| 4 Shays | N | N | N | N | Y | Y | Y |
| 5 Johnson | N | N | N | N | Y | Y | Y |
| **DELAWARE** | | | | | | | |
| AL Castle | N | N | N | N | Y | N | N |
| **FLORIDA** | | | | | | | |
| 1 Miller | N | N | N | N | Y | Y | N |
| 2 Boyd | N | N | N | N | Y | Y | Y |
| 3 Brown | N | Y | Y | Y | N | Y | Y |
| 4 Crenshaw | N | N | N | N | Y | Y | N |
| 5 Brown-Waite | N | N | N | Y | Y | Y | N |
| 6 Stearns | N | N | N | N | Y | Y | N |
| 7 Mica | N | N | N | N | Y | Y | N |
| 8 Keller | ? | ? | ? | ? | ? | ? | ? |
| 9 Bilirakis | N | N | N | N | Y | Y | N |
| 10 Young | N | N | N | N | Y | Y | N |
| 11 Davis | ? | ? | ? | ? | ? | ? | ? |
| 12 Putnam | N | N | N | N | Y | Y | N |
| 13 Harris | N | N | N | N | Y | Y | N |
| 14 Mack | N | N | N | N | Y | Y | N |
| 15 Weldon | N | N | N | N | Y | Y | N |
| 16 Foley | N | N | N | N | Y | Y | N |
| 17 Meek | N | Y | Y | Y | N | N | Y |
| 18 Ros-Lehtinen | N | N | N | N | Y | Y | N |
| 19 Wexler | Y | Y | Y | Y | N | N | Y |
| 20 Wasserman-Schultz | Y | N | Y | Y | N | N | Y |
| 21 Diaz-Balart, L. | N | N | N | N | Y | Y | N |
| 22 Shaw | N | N | N | N | Y | Y | N |
| 23 Hastings | N | Y | Y | Y | N | N | Y |
| 24 Feeney | ? | N | N | N | Y | Y | N |
| 25 Diaz-Balart, M. | N | N | N | N | Y | Y | N |
| **GEORGIA** | | | | | | | |
| 1 Kingston | N | N | N | N | Y | Y | N |
| 2 Bishop | N | N | Y | Y | Y | Y | Y |
| 3 Marshall | N | N | N | N | Y | Y | N |
| 4 McKinney | Y | Y | Y | Y | N | N | Y |
| 5 Lewis | ? | ? | ? | ? | ? | N | Y |
| 6 Price | N | N | N | N | Y | Y | N |
| 7 Linder | N | N | N | N | Y | Y | N |
| 8 Westmoreland | N | N | N | N | Y | Y | N |
| 9 Norwood | N | N | N | N | Y | Y | N |
| 10 Deal | N | N | N | N | Y | Y | N |
| 11 Gingrey | N | N | N | N | Y | Y | N |
| 12 Barrow | N | N | N | N | Y | Y | Y |
| 13 Scott | N | N | Y | N | Y | Y | Y |
| **HAWAII** | | | | | | | |
| 1 Abercrombie | N | Y | Y | Y | N | N | Y |
| 2 Case | N | N | Y | N | N | N | Y |
| **IDAHO** | | | | | | | |
| 1 Otter | N | N | N | N | Y | Y | N |
| 2 Simpson | N | N | ? | ? | Y | Y | N |
| **ILLINOIS** | | | | | | | |
| 1 Rush | Y | Y | Y | Y | N | N | Y |
| 2 Jackson | Y | Y | Y | Y | N | N | Y |
| 3 Lipinski | N | Y | Y | Y | N | N | Y |
| 4 Gutierrez | Y | Y | Y | Y | N | N | Y |
| 5 Emanuel | N | Y | Y | Y | N | N | Y |
| 6 Hyde | N | N | N | N | Y | Y | N |
| 7 Davis | N | Y | Y | Y | N | N | Y |
| 8 Bean | N | N | Y | Y | Y | Y | Y |
| 9 Schakowsky | Y | Y | Y | Y | N | N | Y |
| 10 Kirk | N | N | N | N | Y | Y | N |
| 11 Weller | N | N | N | N | Y | Y | N |
| 12 Costello | N | Y | Y | Y | N | Y | Y |

### KEY

| Republicans | Democrats | *Independents* |
|---|---|---|

| | | |
|---|---|---|
| Y Voted for (yea) | X Paired against | C Voted "present" to avoid possible conflict of interest |
| # Paired for | – Announced against | |
| + Announced for | P Voted "present" | ? Did not vote or otherwise make a position known |
| N Voted against (nay) | | |

| | 529 | 530 | 531 | 532 | 533 | 534 | 535 |
|---|---|---|---|---|---|---|---|
| 13 **Biggert** | N | N | N | N | Y | Y | N |
| 14 **Hastert** | | | | | | | |
| 15 **Johnson** | N | N | N | N | Y | Y | Y |
| 16 **Manzullo** | N | N | N | N | Y | Y | N |
| 17 Evans | N | Y | Y | Y | N | N | Y |
| 18 **LaHood** | N | N | N | N | Y | Y | N |
| 19 **Shimkus** | N | N | N | N | Y | Y | N |
| **INDIANA** | | | | | | | |
| 1 Visclosky | Y | N | Y | Y | N | N | Y |
| 2 **Chocola** | N | N | N | N | Y | Y | N |
| 3 **Souder** | N | N | N | N | Y | Y | N |
| 4 **Buyer** | N | N | N | N | Y | Y | N |
| 5 **Burton** | N | N | N | N | Y | Y | N |
| 6 **Pence** | N | N | N | N | Y | Y | N |
| 7 Carson | Y | Y | Y | Y | N | N | Y |
| 8 **Hostettler** | N | N | N | N | Y | Y | N |
| 9 **Sodrel** | N | N | N | N | Y | Y | N |
| **IOWA** | | | | | | | |
| 1 **Nussle** | N | N | N | N | Y | Y | N |
| 2 **Leach** | N | N | N | N | Y | Y | Y |
| 3 Boswell | ? | ? | ? | ? | ? | ? | ? |
| 4 **Latham** | N | N | N | N | Y | Y | N |
| 5 **King** | N | N | N | N | Y | Y | N |
| **KANSAS** | | | | | | | |
| 1 **Moran** | N | N | N | N | Y | Y | N |
| 2 **Ryun** | N | N | N | N | Y | Y | N |
| 3 Moore | N | N | Y | Y | Y | N | Y |
| 4 **Tiahrt** | N | N | N | N | Y | Y | N |
| **KENTUCKY** | | | | | | | |
| 1 **Whitfield** | N | N | N | N | Y | Y | Y |
| 2 **Lewis** | N | N | N | N | Y | Y | Y |
| 3 **Northup** | N | N | N | N | Y | Y | N |
| 4 **Davis** | N | N | N | N | Y | Y | N |
| 5 **Rogers** | N | N | N | N | Y | Y | N |
| 6 Chandler | N | Y | Y | Y | N | Y | Y |
| **LOUISIANA** | | | | | | | |
| 1 **Jindal** | N | N | N | N | Y | Y | N |
| 2 Jefferson | N | Y | Y | Y | N | N | Y |
| 3 Melancon | N | N | N | Y | Y | Y | Y |
| 4 **McCrery** | N | N | N | N | Y | Y | N |
| 5 **Alexander** | N | N | N | N | Y | Y | N |
| 6 **Baker** | N | N | N | N | Y | Y | N |
| 7 **Boustany** | N | N | N | N | Y | Y | N |
| **MAINE** | | | | | | | |
| 1 Allen | N | N | Y | Y | N | N | Y |
| 2 Michaud | N | N | Y | Y | Y | Y | Y |
| **MARYLAND** | | | | | | | |
| 1 **Gilchrest** | N | N | N | N | Y | Y | N |
| 2 Ruppersberger | N | N | Y | Y | Y | N | Y |
| 3 Cardin | N | Y | Y | Y | N | N | Y |
| 4 Wynn | Y | N | Y | Y | Y | N | Y |
| 5 Hoyer | N | Y | Y | Y | N | N | Y |
| 6 **Bartlett** | N | N | N | N | Y | Y | N |
| 7 Cummings | Y | Y | Y | Y | N | N | Y |
| 8 Van Hollen | N | Y | Y | Y | N | N | Y |
| **MASSACHUSETTS** | | | | | | | |
| 1 Olver | N | Y | Y | Y | N | N | Y |
| 2 Neal | N | N | Y | Y | N | N | Y |
| 3 McGovern | N | Y | Y | Y | N | N | Y |
| 4 Frank | N | N | Y | Y | N | N | Y |
| 5 Meehan | Y | Y | Y | Y | N | N | Y |
| 6 Tierney | N | Y | Y | Y | N | N | Y |
| 7 Markey | Y | Y | Y | Y | N | N | Y |
| 8 Capuano | Y | Y | Y | Y | N | N | Y |
| 9 Lynch | N | N | Y | Y | Y | N | Y |
| 10 Delahunt | Y | Y | Y | Y | N | N | Y |
| **MICHIGAN** | | | | | | | |
| 1 Stupak | N | Y | Y | Y | Y | Y | Y |
| 2 **Hoekstra** | N | N | N | N | Y | Y | N |
| 3 **Ehlers** | N | N | N | N | Y | Y | N |
| 4 **Camp** | N | N | N | N | Y | Y | Y |
| 5 Kildee | N | Y | Y | Y | N | N | Y |
| 6 **Upton** | N | N | N | N | Y | Y | N |
| 7 **Schwarz** | N | N | N | N | Y | Y | N |
| 8 **Rogers** | N | N | N | N | Y | Y | N |
| 9 **Knollenberg** | N | N | N | N | Y | Y | N |
| 10 **Miller** | N | N | N | N | Y | Y | N |
| 11 **McCotter** | N | N | N | N | Y | Y | N |
| 12 Levin | N | Y | Y | Y | N | N | Y |
| 13 Kilpatrick | Y | Y | Y | Y | N | N | Y |
| 14 Conyers | N | Y | Y | Y | N | N | Y |
| 15 Dingell | ? | Y | Y | Y | Y | Y | Y |
| **MINNESOTA** | | | | | | | |
| 1 **Gutknecht** | N | N | N | N | Y | Y | N |
| 2 **Kline** | N | N | N | N | Y | Y | N |
| 3 **Ramstad** | N | N | N | N | Y | Y | N |
| 4 McCollum | N | N | Y | Y | N | N | Y |
| 5 Sabo | N | Y | Y | Y | N | N | Y |
| 6 **Kennedy** | N | N | N | N | Y | Y | N |
| 7 Peterson | N | N | N | N | Y | Y | Y |
| 8 Oberstar | N | Y | Y | Y | N | N | Y |
| **MISSISSIPPI** | | | | | | | |
| 1 **Wicker** | N | N | N | N | Y | Y | N |
| 2 Thompson | Y | Y | Y | Y | N | N | Y |
| 3 **Pickering** | N | N | N | N | Y | Y | N |
| 4 Taylor | N | N | Y | N | Y | Y | Y |
| **MISSOURI** | | | | | | | |
| 1 Clay | Y | Y | Y | Y | Y | N | Y |
| 2 **Akin** | N | N | N | N | Y | Y | N |
| 3 Carnahan | Y | Y | Y | Y | N | N | Y |
| 4 Skelton | N | N | Y | Y | Y | Y | Y |
| 5 Cleaver | Y | Y | Y | Y | N | N | Y |
| 6 **Graves** | N | N | N | N | Y | Y | N |
| 7 **Blunt** | N | N | N | N | Y | Y | N |
| 8 **Emerson** | N | N | N | N | Y | Y | N |
| 9 **Hulshof** | N | N | N | N | Y | Y | N |
| **MONTANA** | | | | | | | |
| AL **Rehberg** | N | N | N | N | Y | Y | N |
| **NEBRASKA** | | | | | | | |
| 1 **Fortenberry** | N | N | N | N | Y | Y | N |
| 2 **Terry** | N | N | N | N | Y | Y | N |
| 3 **Osborne** | N | N | N | N | Y | Y | N |
| **NEVADA** | | | | | | | |
| 1 Berkley | Y | N | Y | Y | Y | Y | Y |
| 2 **Gibbons** | N | N | N | N | Y | Y | N |
| 3 **Porter** | N | N | N | N | Y | Y | N |
| **NEW HAMPSHIRE** | | | | | | | |
| 1 **Bradley** | N | N | N | N | Y | Y | N |
| 2 **Bass** | N | N | N | N | Y | Y | N |
| **NEW JERSEY** | | | | | | | |
| 1 Andrews | N | Y | Y | Y | N | N | Y |
| 2 **LoBiondo** | N | N | N | N | Y | Y | N |
| 3 **Saxton** | N | N | N | N | Y | Y | N |
| 4 **Smith** | N | N | N | N | Y | Y | N |
| 5 **Garrett** | N | N | N | N | Y | Y | N |
| 6 Pallone | Y | Y | Y | Y | N | N | Y |
| 7 **Ferguson** | N | N | N | N | Y | Y | N |
| 8 Pascrell | Y | N | Y | Y | N | N | Y |
| 9 Rothman | N | N | Y | Y | N | N | Y |
| 10 Payne | Y | Y | Y | Y | N | N | Y |
| 11 **Frelinghuysen** | N | N | N | N | Y | Y | N |
| 12 Holt | N | Y | Y | Y | N | N | Y |
| 13 Menendez | N | Y | Y | Y | Y | N | Y |
| **NEW MEXICO** | | | | | | | |
| 1 **Wilson** | N | N | N | N | Y | Y | N |
| 2 **Pearce** | N | N | N | N | Y | Y | N |
| 3 Udall | N | Y | Y | Y | N | N | Y |
| **NEW YORK** | | | | | | | |
| 1 Bishop | N | Y | Y | Y | N | N | Y |
| 2 Israel | N | Y | Y | Y | N | N | Y |
| 3 **King** | N | N | N | N | Y | Y | N |
| 4 McCarthy | N | Y | Y | Y | N | N | Y |
| 5 Ackerman | N | Y | Y | Y | N | N | Y |
| 6 Meeks | N | Y | Y | Y | Y | N | Y |
| 7 Crowley | Y | Y | Y | Y | N | N | Y |
| 8 Nadler | Y | Y | Y | Y | N | N | Y |
| 9 Weiner | N | Y | Y | Y | N | N | Y |
| 10 Towns | N | N | Y | Y | Y | N | Y |
| 11 Owens | Y | Y | Y | Y | N | N | Y |
| 12 Velázquez | N | Y | Y | Y | N | N | Y |
| 13 **Fossella** | N | N | N | N | Y | Y | N |
| 14 Maloney | N | Y | Y | ? | N | N | Y |
| 15 Rangel | N | Y | Y | Y | N | N | Y |
| 16 Serrano | Y | Y | Y | Y | N | N | Y |
| 17 Engel | N | Y | Y | Y | N | N | Y |
| 18 Lowey | N | Y | Y | Y | N | N | Y |
| 19 **Kelly** | N | N | N | N | Y | Y | N |
| 20 **Sweeney** | N | N | N | Y | Y | Y | N |
| 21 McNulty | Y | Y | Y | Y | Y | N | Y |
| 22 Hinchey | Y | Y | Y | Y | N | N | Y |
| 23 **McHugh** | N | N | N | N | Y | Y | N |
| 24 **Boehlert** | N | N | N | N | Y | Y | N |
| 25 **Walsh** | N | N | N | N | Y | Y | N |
| 26 **Reynolds** | N | N | N | N | Y | Y | N |
| 27 Higgins | Y | Y | Y | Y | Y | Y | Y |
| 28 Slaughter | Y | Y | Y | Y | Y | N | Y |
| 29 **Kuhl** | N | N | N | N | Y | Y | N |
| **NORTH CAROLINA** | | | | | | | |
| 1 Butterfield | Y | Y | Y | Y | N | Y | Y |
| 2 Etheridge | N | Y | Y | Y | N | N | Y |
| 3 **Jones** | N | N | N | N | Y | Y | Y |
| 4 Price | N | Y | Y | Y | N | N | Y |
| 5 **Foxx** | N | N | N | N | Y | Y | N |
| 6 **Coble** | N | N | N | N | Y | Y | N |
| 7 McIntyre | N | N | Y | Y | Y | Y | Y |
| 8 **Hayes** | N | N | N | N | Y | Y | N |
| 9 **Myrick** | - | - | - | - | + | Y | ? |
| 10 **McHenry** | N | N | N | N | Y | Y | N |
| 11 **Taylor** | N | N | N | N | Y | Y | N |
| 12 Watt | Y | Y | Y | Y | N | N | Y |
| 13 Miller | N | Y | Y | Y | N | N | Y |
| **NORTH DAKOTA** | | | | | | | |
| AL Pomeroy | N | N | Y | Y | Y | Y | Y |
| **OHIO** | | | | | | | |
| 1 **Chabot** | N | N | N | N | Y | Y | N |
| 2 **Schmidt** | N | N | N | N | Y | Y | N |
| 3 **Turner** | N | N | N | N | Y | Y | N |
| 4 **Oxley** | N | N | N | N | Y | Y | N |
| 5 **Gillmor** | N | N | N | N | Y | Y | N |
| 6 Strickland | N | N | Y | Y | N | Y | Y |
| 7 **Hobson** | N | N | N | N | Y | Y | N |
| 8 **Boehner** | N | N | N | N | Y | Y | N |
| 9 Kaptur | N | Y | Y | Y | N | Y | Y |
| 10 Kucinich | Y | Y | Y | Y | N | N | Y |
| 11 Jones | Y | Y | Y | Y | N | N | Y |
| 12 **Tiberi** | N | N | N | N | Y | Y | N |
| 13 Brown | Y | Y | Y | Y | N | N | Y |
| 14 **LaTourette** | N | N | N | N | Y | Y | N |
| 15 **Pryce** | N | N | N | N | ? | Y | N |
| 16 **Regula** | N | N | N | N | Y | Y | N |
| 17 Ryan | N | Y | Y | Y | Y | Y | Y |
| 18 **Ney** | N | N | N | N | Y | Y | N |
| **OKLAHOMA** | | | | | | | |
| 1 **Sullivan** | N | N | N | N | Y | Y | Y |
| 2 Boren | N | N | N | N | Y | Y | Y |
| 3 **Lucas** | N | N | N | N | Y | Y | N |
| 4 **Cole** | N | N | N | N | Y | Y | N |
| 5 **Istook** | N | N | N | N | Y | Y | N |
| **OREGON** | | | | | | | |
| 1 Wu | N | Y | Y | Y | Y | N | Y |
| 2 **Walden** | N | N | N | N | Y | Y | N |
| 3 Blumenauer | N | Y | Y | Y | N | N | Y |
| 4 DeFazio | Y | N | Y | N | Y | Y | Y |
| 5 Hooley | N | N | Y | Y | Y | N | Y |
| **PENNSYLVANIA** | | | | | | | |
| 1 Brady | Y | Y | Y | Y | N | N | Y |
| 2 Fattah | Y | Y | Y | Y | N | N | Y |
| 3 **English** | N | N | N | N | Y | Y | N |
| 4 **Hart** | N | N | N | N | Y | Y | N |
| 5 **Peterson** | N | N | N | N | Y | Y | N |
| 6 **Gerlach** | N | N | N | N | Y | Y | N |
| 7 **Weldon** | N | N | N | N | Y | Y | N |
| 8 **Fitzpatrick** | N | N | Y | Y | Y | Y | N |
| 9 **Shuster** | N | N | N | N | Y | Y | N |
| 10 **Sherwood** | N | N | N | N | Y | Y | N |
| 11 Kanjorski | N | Y | Y | N | N | Y | Y |
| 12 Murtha | N | N | Y | N | N | Y | Y |
| 13 Schwartz | N | Y | Y | Y | N | N | Y |
| 14 Doyle | N | Y | Y | Y | Y | N | Y |
| 15 **Dent** | N | N | N | N | Y | Y | N |
| 16 **Pitts** | N | N | N | N | Y | Y | N |
| 17 Holden | N | N | Y | N | Y | Y | Y |
| 18 **Murphy** | N | N | N | N | Y | Y | N |
| 19 **Platts** | N | N | N | N | Y | Y | N |
| **RHODE ISLAND** | | | | | | | |
| 1 Kennedy | N | Y | Y | Y | N | N | Y |
| 2 Langevin | Y | N | Y | Y | Y | N | Y |
| **SOUTH CAROLINA** | | | | | | | |
| 1 **Brown** | N | N | N | N | Y | Y | N |
| 2 **Wilson** | N | N | N | N | Y | Y | N |
| 3 **Barrett** | N | N | N | N | Y | Y | N |
| 4 **Inglis** | N | N | N | N | Y | Y | N |
| 5 Spratt | N | N | Y | N | Y | Y | Y |
| 6 Clyburn | N | N | Y | Y | Y | N | Y |
| **SOUTH DAKOTA** | | | | | | | |
| AL Herseth | N | N | Y | N | Y | Y | Y |
| **TENNESSEE** | | | | | | | |
| 1 **Jenkins** | N | N | N | N | Y | Y | N |
| 2 **Duncan** | N | N | Y | N | Y | Y | N |
| 3 **Wamp** | N | N | N | N | Y | Y | N |
| 4 Davis | N | N | N | N | Y | Y | Y |
| 5 Cooper | N | N | Y | N | Y | Y | Y |
| 6 Gordon | N | N | N | N | Y | Y | Y |
| 7 **Blackburn** | N | N | N | N | Y | Y | N |
| 8 Tanner | N | N | N | N | Y | Y | Y |
| 9 Ford | N | N | Y | Y | Y | Y | Y |
| **TEXAS** | | | | | | | |
| 1 **Gohmert** | N | N | N | N | Y | Y | N |
| 2 **Poe** | N | N | N | N | Y | Y | N |
| 3 **Johnson, S.** | N | N | N | N | Y | Y | N |
| 4 **Hall** | N | N | N | N | Y | Y | N |
| 5 **Hensarling** | N | N | N | N | Y | Y | N |
| 6 **Barton** | N | N | N | N | Y | Y | N |
| 7 **Culberson** | N | N | N | N | Y | Y | N |
| 8 **Brady** | N | N | N | N | Y | Y | N |
| 9 Green, A. | Y | Y | Y | Y | N | N | Y |
| 10 **McCaul** | N | N | N | N | Y | Y | N |
| 11 **Conaway** | N | N | N | N | Y | Y | N |
| 12 **Granger** | N | N | N | N | Y | Y | N |
| 13 **Thornberry** | N | N | N | N | Y | Y | N |
| 14 **Paul** | N | N | Y | N | N | N | N |
| 15 Hinojosa | Y | N | Y | Y | Y | Y | Y |
| 16 Reyes | N | N | Y | Y | Y | Y | Y |
| 17 Edwards | ? | N | N | N | Y | Y | Y |
| 18 Jackson-Lee | Y | Y | Y | N | N | N | Y |
| 19 **Neugebauer** | N | N | N | N | Y | Y | N |
| 20 Gonzalez | N | Y | Y | Y | N | N | Y |
| 21 **Smith** | N | N | N | N | Y | Y | N |
| 22 **DeLay** | N | N | N | N | Y | ? | ? |
| 23 **Bonilla** | N | N | N | N | Y | Y | N |
| 24 **Marchant** | N | N | N | ? | Y | Y | N |
| 25 Doggett | Y | Y | Y | Y | N | N | Y |
| 26 **Burgess** | N | N | N | N | Y | Y | N |
| 27 Ortiz | N | N | Y | Y | Y | Y | Y |
| 28 Cuellar | N | Y | Y | N | Y | Y | Y |
| 29 Green, G. | Y | Y | Y | Y | Y | Y | Y |
| 30 Johnson, E. | Y | Y | Y | Y | N | N | Y |
| 31 **Carter** | N | N | N | N | Y | Y | N |
| 32 **Sessions** | N | N | N | N | Y | Y | N |
| **UTAH** | | | | | | | |
| 1 **Bishop** | N | N | N | N | Y | Y | N |
| 2 Matheson | N | N | N | N | Y | Y | Y |
| 3 **Cannon** | N | N | N | N | Y | Y | N |
| **VERMONT** | | | | | | | |
| AL *Sanders* | Y | Y | Y | Y | N | Y | Y |
| **VIRGINIA** | | | | | | | |
| 1 **Davis, J.** | N | N | N | N | Y | Y | N |
| 2 **Drake** | N | N | N | N | Y | Y | N |
| 3 Scott | Y | Y | Y | Y | N | N | Y |
| 4 **Forbes** | N | N | N | N | Y | Y | N |
| 5 **Goode** | N | N | N | N | Y | Y | N |
| 6 **Goodlatte** | N | N | N | N | Y | Y | N |
| 7 **Cantor** | N | N | N | N | Y | Y | N |
| 8 Moran | N | Y | Y | Y | Y | N | ? |
| 9 Boucher | N | N | Y | Y | Y | Y | Y |
| 10 **Wolf** | N | N | N | Y | Y | Y | N |
| 11 **Davis, T.** | N | N | N | Y | Y | Y | N |
| **WASHINGTON** | | | | | | | |
| 1 Inslee | N | N | Y | Y | N | N | Y |
| 2 Larsen | N | N | Y | Y | Y | Y | Y |
| 3 Baird | N | N | Y | N | Y | Y | Y |
| 4 **Hastings** | N | N | N | N | Y | Y | N |
| 5 **McMorris** | N | N | N | N | Y | Y | N |
| 6 Dicks | N | Y | Y | Y | Y | N | Y |
| 7 McDermott | Y | Y | Y | Y | N | N | Y |
| 8 **Reichert** | N | N | N | N | Y | Y | N |
| 9 Smith | N | N | Y | Y | Y | N | N |
| **WEST VIRGINIA** | | | | | | | |
| 1 Mollohan | N | Y | Y | Y | N | Y | Y |
| 2 **Capito** | N | N | N | N | Y | Y | N |
| 3 Rahall | N | Y | Y | Y | N | Y | Y |
| **WISCONSIN** | | | | | | | |
| 1 **Ryan** | N | N | N | N | Y | Y | N |
| 2 Baldwin | N | Y | Y | Y | N | N | Y |
| 3 Kind | N | N | Y | Y | Y | Y | Y |
| 4 Moore | Y | Y | Y | Y | N | N | Y |
| 5 **Sensenbrenner** | N | N | N | N | Y | Y | N |
| 6 **Petri** | N | N | N | N | Y | Y | N |
| 7 Obey | Y | Y | Y | Y | Y | Y | Y |
| 8 **Green** | N | N | N | N | Y | Y | N |
| **WYOMING** | | | | | | | |
| AL **Cubin** | N | N | N | N | Y | Y | N |

# IN THE HOUSE | By Vote Number

**536.** **HR 3675. Fraud in Emergencies/Passage.** Stearns, R-Fla., motion to suspend the rules and pass the bill that would increase civil penalties to $22,000 per violation for individuals or companies that commit unfair or deceptive acts that exploit the popular reaction to disasters and national emergencies. Motion agreed to 399-3: R 216-3; D 182-0 (ND 139-0, SD 43-0); I 1-0. A two-thirds majority of those present and voting (268 in this case) is required for passage under suspension of the rules. Oct. 25, 2005.

**537.** **H Con Res 269. White House Fellows Program/Adoption.** Schmidt, R-Ohio, motion to suspend the rules and adopt the concurrent resolution that would recognize the 40th anniversary of the White House Fellows Program and the contributions of the fellows to their communities, the United States and the world. Motion agreed to 401-0: R 218-0; D 182-0 (ND 139-0, SD 43-0); I 1-0. A two-thirds majority of those present and voting (268 in this case) is required for adoption under suspension of the rules. Oct. 25, 2005.

**538.** **HR 3256. James Grove Fulton Post Office/Passage.** Schmidt, R-Ohio, motion to suspend the rules and pass the bill that would designate a post office in Pittsburgh, Pa., for James Grove Fulton, R-Pa. (1945-71), who served in the House for 13 full terms, including more than two terms as the ranking member of the then-Science and Astronautics Committee. Motion agreed to 396-1: R 215-0; D 180-1 (ND 137-1, SD 43-0); I 1-0. A two-thirds majority of those present and voting (265 in this case) is required for passage under suspension of the rules. Oct. 25, 2005.

**539.** **HR 1461. Government-Sponsored Enterprises/Rule.** Adoption of the rule (H Res 509) that would provide for House floor consideration of the bill that would overhaul the regulation of government-sponsored enterprises, including Fannie Mae, Freddie Mac and the 12 Federal Home Loan Banks. Adopted 220-196: R 220-1; D 0-194 (ND 0-148, SD 0-46); I 0-1. Oct. 26, 2005.

**540.** **Procedural Motion/Journal.** Approval of the House Journal of Tuesday, October 25, 2005. Approved 349-62: R 199-19; D 149-43 (ND 113-35, SD 36-8); I 1-0. Oct. 26, 2005.

**541.** **HR 1461. Government-Sponsored Enterprises/Manager's Amendment.** Oxley, R-Ohio, amendment that would sunset the affordable housing fund in the bill after five years and require Fannie Mae and Freddie Mac to allocate 3.5 percent of their profits for the fund in the first two years and 5 percent in the final three years. Priority for funds in the first two years would go to areas affected by hurricanes Katrina and Rita. It also would prohibit the use of funds in the bill for purposes such as political activities, lobbying, travel expenses or providing advice on tax returns. Adopted 210-205: R 208-13; D 2-191 (ND 1-146, SD 1-45); I 0-1. Oct. 26, 2005.

**542.** **HR 1461. Government-Sponsored Enterprises/Minimum Capital Levels.** Leach, R-Iowa, amendment that would allow the new regulator that would be created under the bill — the Federal Housing Finance Agency — to establish a minimum capital level for Fannie Mae, Freddie Mac or any Federal Home Loan Bank if it is needed for the long-term viability of any of the institutions. Rejected 36-378: R 31-190; D 5-187 (ND 3-143, SD 2-44); I 0-1. Oct. 26, 2005.

| | 536 | 537 | 538 | 539 | 540 | 541 | 542 |
|---|---|---|---|---|---|---|---|
| **ALABAMA** | | | | | | | |
| 1 Bonner | Y | Y | Y | Y | Y | Y | N |
| 2 Everett | Y | Y | Y | Y | Y | Y | N |
| 3 Rogers | Y | Y | Y | Y | Y | Y | N |
| 4 Aderholt | Y | Y | Y | Y | Y | Y | N |
| 5 Cramer | Y | Y | Y | N | Y | N | N |
| 6 Bachus | Y | Y | Y | Y | Y | Y | N |
| 7 Davis | Y | Y | Y | N | Y | N | N |
| **ALASKA** | | | | | | | |
| AL Young | Y | Y | Y | Y | Y | Y | N |
| **ARIZONA** | | | | | | | |
| 1 Renzi | Y | Y | Y | Y | Y | Y | N |
| 2 Franks | Y | Y | Y | Y | Y | Y | Y |
| 3 Shadegg | Y | Y | Y | Y | Y | Y | Y |
| 4 Pastor | Y | Y | Y | N | N | N | N |
| 5 Hayworth | Y | Y | Y | Y | Y | Y | N |
| 6 Flake | N | Y | Y | Y | Y | Y | Y |
| 7 Grijalva | Y | Y | Y | N | N | N | N |
| 8 Kolbe | Y | Y | Y | Y | Y | Y | N |
| **ARKANSAS** | | | | | | | |
| 1 Berry | Y | Y | Y | N | N | N | N |
| 2 Snyder | Y | Y | Y | N | Y | N | N |
| 3 Boozman | Y | Y | Y | Y | Y | Y | N |
| 4 Ross | Y | Y | Y | N | N | N | N |
| **CALIFORNIA** | | | | | | | |
| 1 Thompson | Y | Y | Y | N | N | N | N |
| 2 Herger | Y | Y | Y | Y | Y | Y | Y |
| 3 Lungren | Y | Y | Y | Y | Y | Y | Y |
| 4 Doolittle | Y | Y | Y | Y | Y | Y | N |
| 5 Matsui, D. | Y | Y | Y | N | Y | N | N |
| 6 Woolsey | Y | Y | Y | N | N | N | N |
| 7 Miller, George | Y | Y | Y | N | N | N | N |
| 8 Pelosi | Y | Y | Y | N | N | N | N |
| 9 Lee | Y | Y | Y | N | N | N | N |
| 10 Tauscher | Y | Y | Y | N | N | N | N |
| 11 Pombo | Y | Y | ? | Y | Y | Y | N |
| 12 Lantos | Y | Y | Y | N | Y | N | N |
| 13 Stark | Y | Y | Y | N | N | N | N |
| 14 Eshoo | Y | Y | Y | N | Y | N | N |
| 15 Honda | ? | ? | Y | N | N | N | N |
| 16 Lofgren | Y | Y | Y | N | Y | N | N |
| 17 Farr | Y | Y | Y | N | Y | N | N |
| 18 Cardoza | | | | | | | |
| 19 Radanovich | Y | Y | Y | Y | Y | Y | N |
| 20 Costa | Y | Y | Y | N | Y | N | N |
| 21 Nunes | Y | Y | Y | Y | Y | Y | N |
| 22 Thomas | Y | Y | Y | N | Y | N | N |
| 23 Capps | Y | Y | Y | N | N | N | N |
| 24 Gallegly | Y | Y | Y | Y | Y | Y | N |
| 25 McKeon | Y | Y | Y | Y | Y | Y | N |
| 26 Dreier | Y | Y | Y | Y | Y | Y | N |
| 27 Sherman | Y | Y | Y | N | Y | N | ? |
| 28 Berman | Y | Y | Y | N | Y | N | N |
| 29 Schiff | Y | Y | Y | N | Y | N | N |
| 30 Waxman | Y | Y | Y | N | N | N | N |
| 31 Becerra | Y | Y | Y | N | N | N | N |
| 32 Solis | Y | Y | Y | N | N | N | N |
| 33 Watson | Y | Y | Y | N | N | N | N |
| 34 Roybal-Allard | ? | ? | ? | ? | ? | ? | ? |
| 35 Waters | Y | Y | ? | N | N | N | N |
| 36 Harman | Y | Y | Y | N | Y | N | N |
| 37 Millender-McD. | Y | Y | Y | N | N | N | N |
| 38 Napolitano | Y | Y | Y | N | N | N | N |
| 39 Sánchez, Linda | Y | Y | Y | N | Y | N | N |
| 40 Royce | Y | Y | Y | Y | Y | Y | Y |
| 41 Lewis | Y | Y | Y | Y | Y | Y | N |
| 42 Miller, Gary | Y | Y | Y | Y | Y | Y | N |
| 43 Baca | Y | Y | Y | N | Y | N | N |
| 44 Calvert | Y | Y | Y | Y | Y | Y | N |
| 45 Bono | Y | Y | Y | Y | Y | Y | N |
| 46 Rohrabacher | Y | Y | Y | Y | Y | Y | Y |
| 47 Sanchez, Loretta | Y | Y | Y | N | N | N | N |
| 48 Vacant | | | | | | | |
| 49 Issa | Y | Y | Y | Y | Y | Y | N |
| 50 Cunningham | Y | Y | Y | Y | Y | Y | N |
| 51 Filner | Y | Y | Y | N | N | N | N |
| 52 Hunter | Y | Y | Y | Y | Y | Y | N |
| 53 Davis | Y | Y | Y | N | Y | N | N |
| **COLORADO** | | | | | | | |
| 1 DeGette | Y | Y | Y | N | Y | N | N |
| 2 Udall | Y | Y | Y | N | N | N | N |
| 3 Salazar | Y | Y | Y | N | Y | N | N |
| 4 Musgrave | Y | Y | Y | Y | Y | Y | Y |
| 5 Hefley | Y | Y | Y | Y | N | Y | N |
| 6 Tancredo | Y | Y | Y | Y | P | Y | N |
| 7 Beauprez | Y | Y | Y | Y | Y | Y | N |
| **CONNECTICUT** | | | | | | | |
| 1 Larson | Y | Y | Y | N | N | N | N |
| 2 Simmons | Y | Y | Y | Y | N | Y | N |
| 3 DeLauro | Y | Y | Y | N | N | N | N |
| 4 Shays | Y | Y | Y | Y | Y | Y | Y |
| 5 Johnson | Y | Y | Y | Y | Y | Y | Y |
| **DELAWARE** | | | | | | | |
| AL Castle | Y | Y | Y | Y | Y | Y | Y |
| **FLORIDA** | | | | | | | |
| 1 Miller | Y | Y | ? | Y | Y | Y | N |
| 2 Boyd | Y | Y | Y | N | Y | N | N |
| 3 Brown | ? | ? | ? | N | Y | N | N |
| 4 Crenshaw | Y | Y | Y | Y | Y | Y | N |
| 5 Brown-Waite | ? | ? | ? | ? | ? | ? | ? |
| 6 Stearns | Y | Y | Y | Y | Y | Y | N |
| 7 Mica | Y | Y | Y | Y | Y | Y | N |
| 8 Keller | Y | Y | ? | Y | Y | Y | N |
| 9 Bilirakis | Y | Y | Y | Y | Y | Y | N |
| 10 Young | ? | ? | ? | ? | ? | Y | N |
| 11 Davis | Y | Y | Y | N | N | N | N |
| 12 Putnam | Y | Y | Y | Y | Y | Y | N |
| 13 Harris | Y | Y | Y | Y | Y | Y | N |
| 14 Mack | Y | Y | Y | Y | Y | Y | N |
| 15 Weldon | Y | Y | Y | Y | Y | Y | N |
| 16 Foley | ? | ? | ? | ? | ? | ? | ? |
| 17 Meek | ? | ? | ? | ? | ? | ? | ? |
| 18 Ros-Lehtinen | ? | ? | ? | ? | ? | ? | ? |
| 19 Wexler | ? | ? | ? | ? | ? | ? | ? |
| 20 Wasserman-Schultz | ? | ? | ? | ? | ? | N | N |
| 21 Diaz-Balart, L. | ? | ? | ? | ? | ? | ? | ? |
| 22 Shaw | ? | ? | ? | ? | ? | ? | ? |
| 23 Hastings | Y | Y | Y | N | N | N | N |
| 24 Feeney | Y | Y | Y | Y | Y | Y | N |
| 25 Diaz-Balart, M. | ? | ? | ? | ? | ? | ? | ? |
| **GEORGIA** | | | | | | | |
| 1 Kingston | Y | Y | Y | Y | Y | Y | Y |
| 2 Bishop | Y | Y | Y | ? | ? | ? | ? |
| 3 Marshall | Y | Y | Y | N | Y | N | N |
| 4 McKinney | Y | Y | Y | N | N | N | N |
| 5 Lewis | Y | Y | Y | N | N | N | N |
| 6 Price | Y | Y | Y | Y | Y | Y | N |
| 7 Linder | Y | Y | Y | Y | Y | Y | N |
| 8 Westmoreland | Y | Y | Y | Y | Y | Y | N |
| 9 Norwood | Y | Y | Y | Y | Y | Y | N |
| 10 Deal | Y | Y | Y | Y | Y | Y | N |
| 11 Gingrey | ? | ? | ? | Y | Y | Y | N |
| 12 Barrow | Y | Y | Y | N | N | N | N |
| 13 Scott | Y | Y | Y | N | N | N | N |
| **HAWAII** | | | | | | | |
| 1 Abercrombie | Y | Y | N | N | N | N | N |
| 2 Case | Y | Y | Y | N | Y | N | N |
| **IDAHO** | | | | | | | |
| 1 Otter | Y | Y | Y | N | N | N | N |
| 2 Simpson | Y | Y | Y | Y | Y | Y | N |
| **ILLINOIS** | | | | | | | |
| 1 Rush | Y | Y | Y | N | N | N | N |
| 2 Jackson | Y | Y | Y | N | N | N | N |
| 3 Lipinski | Y | Y | Y | N | N | N | N |
| 4 Gutierrez | + | + | + | N | N | N | N |
| 5 Emanuel | Y | Y | Y | ? | Y | ? | ? |
| 6 Hyde | Y | Y | Y | Y | Y | Y | N |
| 7 Davis | Y | Y | Y | N | N | N | N |
| 8 Bean | Y | Y | Y | N | Y | N | N |
| 9 Schakowsky | Y | Y | Y | N | N | N | N |
| 10 Kirk | Y | Y | Y | Y | Y | Y | N |
| 11 Weller | Y | Y | Y | N | Y | N | N |
| 12 Costello | Y | Y | Y | N | N | N | N |

| KEY | Republicans | Democrats | *Independents* |
|---|---|---|---|
| Y Voted for (yea) | X Paired against | | C Voted "present" to avoid possible conflict of interest |
| # Paired for | – Announced against | | |
| + Announced for | P Voted "present" | | ? Did not vote or otherwise make a position known |
| N Voted against (nay) | | | |

| | 536 | 537 | 538 | 539 | 540 | 541 | 542 |
|---|---|---|---|---|---|---|---|
| 13 **Biggert** | Y | Y | Y | Y | Y | Y | N |
| 14 **Hastert** | | | | | | Y | |
| 15 **Johnson** | Y | Y | Y | Y | Y | N | N |
| 16 **Manzullo** | Y | ? | ? | Y | Y | Y | N |
| 17 Evans | ? | Y | Y | N | Y | N | N |
| 18 **LaHood** | Y | Y | Y | Y | Y | Y | N |
| 19 **Shimkus** | Y | Y | Y | Y | Y | Y | N |
| **INDIANA** | | | | | | | |
| 1 Visclosky | ? | ? | ? | N | N | N | N |
| 2 **Chocola** | Y | Y | Y | Y | Y | Y | Y |
| 3 **Souder** | Y | Y | Y | Y | Y | Y | N |
| 4 **Buyer** | Y | Y | Y | Y | Y | Y | N |
| 5 **Burton** | Y | Y | Y | Y | Y | Y | N |
| 6 **Pence** | Y | Y | Y | Y | Y | Y | Y |
| 7 Carson | + | + | + | N | P | N | N |
| 8 **Hostettler** | Y | Y | Y | Y | Y | Y | Y |
| 9 **Sodrel** | Y | Y | Y | Y | Y | Y | N |
| **IOWA** | | | | | | | |
| 1 **Nussle** | Y | Y | Y | Y | Y | Y | Y |
| 2 **Leach** | Y | Y | Y | Y | ? | N | Y |
| 3 Boswell | ? | ? | ? | ? | ? | ? | ? |
| 4 **Latham** | Y | Y | Y | Y | N | Y | Y |
| 5 **King** | Y | Y | Y | Y | Y | Y | Y |
| **KANSAS** | | | | | | | |
| 1 **Moran** | Y | Y | Y | Y | N | Y | N |
| 2 **Ryun** | Y | Y | Y | Y | Y | Y | N |
| 3 Moore | Y | Y | Y | N | N | N | N |
| 4 **Tiahrt** | Y | Y | Y | Y | Y | Y | N |
| **KENTUCKY** | | | | | | | |
| 1 **Whitfield** | Y | Y | Y | Y | Y | ? | ? |
| 2 **Lewis** | Y | Y | Y | Y | Y | Y | N |
| 3 **Northup** | Y | Y | Y | Y | Y | Y | N |
| 4 **Davis** | Y | Y | Y | Y | N | Y | N |
| 5 **Rogers** | Y | Y | Y | Y | Y | Y | N |
| 6 Chandler | Y | Y | Y | N | N | N | N |
| **LOUISIANA** | | | | | | | |
| 1 **Jindal** | Y | Y | Y | Y | Y | Y | N |
| 2 Jefferson | Y | Y | Y | N | Y | N | N |
| 3 Melancon | Y | Y | Y | N | Y | N | N |
| 4 **McCrery** | Y | Y | Y | Y | Y | Y | N |
| 5 **Alexander** | Y | Y | Y | Y | Y | Y | N |
| 6 **Baker** | Y | Y | Y | Y | Y | Y | N |
| 7 **Boustany** | Y | Y | Y | Y | Y | Y | N |
| **MAINE** | | | | | | | |
| 1 Allen | Y | Y | Y | N | Y | N | N |
| 2 Michaud | Y | Y | Y | N | Y | N | N |
| **MARYLAND** | | | | | | | |
| 1 **Gilchrest** | Y | Y | Y | Y | Y | N | Y |
| 2 Ruppersberger | Y | Y | Y | N | Y | N | N |
| 3 Cardin | Y | Y | Y | N | Y | N | N |
| 4 Wynn | Y | Y | Y | N | Y | N | Y |
| 5 Hoyer | Y | Y | Y | N | Y | N | N |
| 6 **Bartlett** | Y | Y | Y | Y | Y | Y | N |
| 7 Cummings | Y | Y | Y | N | Y | N | N |
| 8 Van Hollen | Y | Y | Y | N | Y | N | N |
| **MASSACHUSETTS** | | | | | | | |
| 1 Olver | Y | Y | Y | N | N | N | N |
| 2 Neal | Y | Y | Y | N | Y | N | N |
| 3 McGovern | Y | Y | Y | N | Y | N | N |
| 4 Frank | Y | Y | Y | N | Y | N | N |
| 5 Meehan | Y | Y | Y | N | Y | N | N |
| 6 Tierney | Y | Y | Y | N | Y | N | N |
| 7 Markey | Y | Y | Y | N | Y | N | ? |
| 8 Capuano | Y | Y | Y | N | N | N | N |
| 9 Lynch | Y | Y | Y | N | Y | N | N |
| 10 Delahunt | Y | Y | Y | N | Y | N | N |
| **MICHIGAN** | | | | | | | |
| 1 Stupak | Y | Y | Y | N | N | N | N |
| 2 **Hoekstra** | Y | Y | Y | Y | Y | Y | N |
| 3 **Ehlers** | Y | Y | Y | Y | Y | N | Y |
| 4 **Camp** | Y | Y | Y | Y | Y | Y | N |
| 5 Kildee | Y | Y | Y | N | Y | N | N |
| 6 **Upton** | Y | Y | Y | Y | Y | Y | N |
| 7 **Schwarz** | Y | Y | Y | Y | Y | Y | N |
| 8 **Rogers** | Y | Y | Y | Y | Y | Y | N |
| 9 **Knollenberg** | Y | Y | Y | Y | Y | Y | N |
| 10 **Miller** | Y | Y | Y | Y | Y | Y | N |
| 11 **McCotter** | Y | Y | Y | Y | N | Y | N |
| 12 Levin | Y | Y | Y | N | Y | N | N |
| 13 Kilpatrick | Y | Y | Y | N | Y | N | N |
| 14 Conyers | Y | Y | Y | N | Y | N | N |
| 15 Dingell | Y | Y | Y | N | Y | N | Y |

| | 536 | 537 | 538 | 539 | 540 | 541 | 542 |
|---|---|---|---|---|---|---|---|
| **MINNESOTA** | | | | | | | |
| 1 **Gutknecht** | Y | Y | Y | Y | N | Y | Y |
| 2 **Kline** | Y | Y | Y | Y | Y | Y | N |
| 3 **Ramstad** | Y | Y | Y | Y | N | N | N |
| 4 McCollum | Y | Y | Y | N | Y | N | N |
| 5 Sabo | Y | Y | Y | N | N | N | N |
| 6 **Kennedy** | Y | Y | Y | N | N | N | N |
| 7 Peterson | Y | ? | Y | N | N | N | N |
| 8 Oberstar | Y | Y | Y | N | N | N | N |
| **MISSISSIPPI** | | | | | | | |
| 1 **Wicker** | Y | Y | Y | Y | Y | Y | N |
| 2 Thompson | Y | Y | Y | N | N | N | N |
| 3 **Pickering** | Y | Y | Y | Y | Y | Y | N |
| 4 Taylor | Y | Y | Y | N | N | Y | Y |
| **MISSOURI** | | | | | | | |
| 1 Clay | Y | Y | Y | N | Y | N | N |
| 2 **Akin** | Y | Y | Y | Y | Y | Y | N |
| 3 Carnahan | Y | Y | Y | N | Y | N | N |
| 4 Skelton | Y | Y | Y | N | Y | N | N |
| 5 Cleaver | Y | Y | Y | N | Y | N | N |
| 6 **Graves** | Y | Y | Y | Y | N | Y | N |
| 7 **Blunt** | Y | Y | Y | Y | Y | Y | N |
| 8 **Emerson** | Y | Y | Y | Y | Y | Y | N |
| 9 **Hulshof** | ? | ? | ? | Y | Y | Y | N |
| **MONTANA** | | | | | | | |
| AL **Rehberg** | Y | Y | Y | Y | Y | Y | N |
| **NEBRASKA** | | | | | | | |
| 1 **Fortenberry** | Y | Y | Y | Y | Y | Y | N |
| 2 **Terry** | Y | Y | Y | Y | Y | Y | N |
| 3 **Osborne** | Y | Y | Y | Y | Y | Y | N |
| **NEVADA** | | | | | | | |
| 1 Berkley | Y | Y | Y | N | Y | N | N |
| 2 **Gibbons** | Y | Y | Y | Y | Y | Y | N |
| 3 **Porter** | Y | Y | Y | Y | Y | Y | N |
| **NEW HAMPSHIRE** | | | | | | | |
| 1 **Bradley** | Y | Y | Y | Y | Y | N | N |
| 2 **Bass** | Y | Y | Y | Y | Y | Y | N |
| **NEW JERSEY** | | | | | | | |
| 1 Andrews | + | + | + | N | Y | N | N |
| 2 **LoBiondo** | Y | Y | Y | Y | N | Y | N |
| 3 **Saxton** | Y | Y | Y | Y | Y | Y | N |
| 4 **Smith** | Y | Y | Y | Y | Y | N | N |
| 5 **Garrett** | Y | Y | Y | Y | Y | Y | Y |
| 6 Pallone | Y | Y | Y | N | Y | N | N |
| 7 **Ferguson** | Y | Y | Y | Y | Y | Y | N |
| 8 Pascrell | Y | Y | Y | N | Y | N | N |
| 9 Rothman | Y | Y | Y | N | Y | N | N |
| 10 Payne | ? | ? | ? | N | Y | N | N |
| 11 **Frelinghuysen** | Y | Y | Y | Y | Y | Y | N |
| 12 Holt | Y | Y | Y | N | N | N | N |
| 13 Menendez | Y | Y | Y | N | Y | N | N |
| **NEW MEXICO** | | | | | | | |
| 1 **Wilson** | Y | Y | Y | Y | Y | Y | N |
| 2 **Pearce** | Y | Y | Y | Y | Y | Y | N |
| 3 Udall | Y | Y | Y | N | N | N | N |
| **NEW YORK** | | | | | | | |
| 1 Bishop | Y | Y | Y | N | Y | N | N |
| 2 Israel | Y | Y | Y | N | Y | N | N |
| 3 **King** | Y | Y | Y | Y | Y | Y | N |
| 4 McCarthy | Y | Y | Y | N | Y | N | N |
| 5 Ackerman | Y | Y | Y | N | Y | N | N |
| 6 Meeks | Y | Y | Y | N | Y | N | N |
| 7 Crowley | Y | Y | Y | N | Y | N | N |
| 8 Nadler | Y | Y | Y | N | Y | N | N |
| 9 Weiner | Y | Y | Y | N | Y | N | N |
| 10 Towns | Y | Y | Y | N | Y | ? | N |
| 11 Owens | Y | Y | Y | N | Y | N | N |
| 12 Velázquez | Y | Y | Y | N | N | N | N |
| 13 **Fossella** | Y | Y | Y | Y | N | Y | N |
| 14 Maloney | Y | Y | ? | N | Y | N | N |
| 15 Rangel | Y | Y | Y | N | Y | N | N |
| 16 Serrano | Y | Y | Y | N | Y | N | N |
| 17 Engel | Y | Y | Y | N | Y | N | N |
| 18 Lowey | Y | Y | Y | N | Y | N | N |
| 19 **Kelly** | Y | Y | Y | Y | Y | Y | N |
| 20 **Sweeney** | Y | Y | Y | Y | N | N | N |
| 21 McNulty | Y | Y | Y | N | N | N | N |
| 22 Hinchey | Y | Y | Y | N | Y | N | N |
| 23 **McHugh** | Y | Y | Y | Y | Y | N | N |
| 24 **Boehlert** | Y | Y | Y | Y | Y | Y | N |
| 25 **Walsh** | Y | Y | Y | Y | Y | Y | N |
| 26 **Reynolds** | ? | ? | ? | ? | ? | ? | ? |
| 27 Higgins | ? | ? | ? | N | Y | N | N |
| 28 Slaughter | Y | Y | Y | N | N | N | N |
| 29 **Kuhl** | Y | Y | Y | Y | Y | Y | N |

| | 536 | 537 | 538 | 539 | 540 | 541 | 542 |
|---|---|---|---|---|---|---|---|
| **NORTH CAROLINA** | | | | | | | |
| 1 Butterfield | Y | Y | Y | N | Y | N | N |
| 2 Etheridge | Y | Y | Y | N | Y | N | N |
| 3 **Jones** | Y | Y | Y | Y | Y | Y | N |
| 4 Price | Y | Y | Y | N | Y | N | N |
| 5 **Foxx** | Y | Y | Y | Y | Y | Y | N |
| 6 **Coble** | Y | Y | Y | Y | Y | Y | N |
| 7 McIntyre | Y | Y | Y | N | Y | N | N |
| 8 **Hayes** | Y | Y | Y | Y | Y | Y | N |
| 9 **Myrick** | Y | Y | Y | Y | Y | Y | N |
| 10 **McHenry** | Y | Y | Y | Y | Y | Y | N |
| 11 **Taylor** | Y | Y | Y | Y | Y | Y | Y |
| 12 Watt | Y | Y | Y | N | Y | N | N |
| 13 Miller | Y | Y | Y | N | Y | N | N |
| **NORTH DAKOTA** | | | | | | | |
| AL Pomeroy | Y | Y | Y | N | Y | N | N |
| **OHIO** | | | | | | | |
| 1 **Chabot** | Y | Y | Y | Y | Y | Y | N |
| 2 **Schmidt** | Y | Y | Y | Y | Y | Y | N |
| 3 **Turner** | Y | Y | Y | Y | Y | Y | N |
| 4 **Oxley** | Y | Y | Y | Y | Y | Y | N |
| 5 **Gillmor** | Y | Y | Y | Y | Y | Y | Y |
| 6 Strickland | ? | ? | ? | N | N | N | N |
| 7 **Hobson** | Y | Y | Y | Y | Y | Y | N |
| 8 **Boehner** | Y | Y | Y | Y | Y | Y | N |
| 9 Kaptur | Y | Y | Y | N | Y | N | N |
| 10 Kucinich | Y | Y | Y | N | N | N | N |
| 11 Jones | Y | Y | Y | N | N | N | N |
| 12 **Tiberi** | Y | Y | Y | Y | N | Y | N |
| 13 Brown | Y | Y | Y | N | Y | N | N |
| 14 **LaTourette** | Y | Y | Y | Y | Y | Y | N |
| 15 **Pryce** | Y | Y | Y | Y | Y | Y | N |
| 16 **Regula** | Y | Y | Y | Y | Y | Y | N |
| 17 Ryan | Y | Y | Y | N | Y | N | N |
| 18 **Ney** | Y | Y | Y | Y | Y | Y | N |
| **OKLAHOMA** | | | | | | | |
| 1 **Sullivan** | Y | Y | Y | Y | Y | Y | N |
| 2 Boren | Y | Y | Y | N | Y | N | N |
| 3 **Lucas** | Y | Y | Y | Y | Y | Y | N |
| 4 **Cole** | Y | Y | Y | Y | Y | Y | N |
| 5 **Istook** | Y | Y | Y | Y | Y | Y | N |
| **OREGON** | | | | | | | |
| 1 Wu | Y | Y | Y | N | N | N | N |
| 2 **Walden** | Y | Y | Y | Y | Y | Y | N |
| 3 Blumenauer | Y | Y | Y | N | Y | N | N |
| 4 DeFazio | Y | Y | Y | N | N | N | N |
| 5 Hooley | Y | Y | Y | N | Y | N | N |
| **PENNSYLVANIA** | | | | | | | |
| 1 Brady | Y | Y | Y | N | N | N | N |
| 2 Fattah | ? | ? | ? | N | Y | N | N |
| 3 **English** | Y | Y | Y | Y | N | Y | N |
| 4 **Hart** | Y | Y | Y | Y | N | Y | N |
| 5 **Peterson** | Y | Y | Y | Y | Y | Y | N |
| 6 **Gerlach** | Y | Y | Y | Y | Y | Y | N |
| 7 **Weldon** | Y | Y | Y | Y | Y | Y | N |
| 8 **Fitzpatrick** | Y | Y | Y | Y | N | Y | N |
| 9 **Shuster** | Y | Y | Y | Y | N | Y | N |
| 10 **Sherwood** | Y | Y | Y | Y | Y | Y | N |
| 11 Kanjorski | Y | Y | Y | N | Y | N | N |
| 12 Murtha | Y | Y | ? | N | Y | N | N |
| 13 Schwartz | Y | Y | Y | N | Y | N | N |
| 14 Doyle | Y | Y | Y | N | Y | N | N |
| 15 **Dent** | Y | Y | Y | Y | Y | Y | N |
| 16 **Pitts** | Y | Y | Y | Y | Y | Y | N |
| 17 Holden | Y | Y | Y | N | Y | N | N |
| 18 **Murphy** | Y | Y | Y | Y | Y | Y | N |
| 19 **Platts** | Y | Y | Y | ? | ? | ? | ? |
| **RHODE ISLAND** | | | | | | | |
| 1 Kennedy | Y | Y | Y | N | Y | N | N |
| 2 Langevin | Y | Y | Y | N | Y | N | N |
| **SOUTH CAROLINA** | | | | | | | |
| 1 **Brown** | Y | Y | Y | Y | Y | Y | N |
| 2 **Wilson** | Y | Y | Y | Y | Y | Y | N |
| 3 **Barrett** | Y | Y | Y | Y | Y | Y | N |
| 4 **Inglis** | Y | Y | Y | Y | Y | Y | N |
| 5 Spratt | Y | Y | Y | N | Y | N | N |
| 6 Clyburn | Y | Y | Y | N | Y | N | N |
| **SOUTH DAKOTA** | | | | | | | |
| AL Herseth | Y | Y | Y | N | Y | N | N |
| **TENNESSEE** | | | | | | | |
| 1 **Jenkins** | Y | Y | Y | Y | Y | Y | N |
| 2 **Duncan** | Y | Y | Y | Y | Y | Y | Y |

| | 536 | 537 | 538 | 539 | 540 | 541 | 542 |
|---|---|---|---|---|---|---|---|
| 3 **Wamp** | Y | Y | Y | Y | Y | Y | Y |
| 4 Davis | Y | Y | Y | N | Y | N | N |
| 5 Cooper | Y | Y | Y | N | Y | N | Y |
| 6 Gordon | Y | Y | Y | N | Y | N | N |
| 7 **Blackburn** | Y | Y | Y | Y | Y | Y | Y |
| 8 Tanner | Y | Y | Y | N | N | N | N |
| 9 Ford | ? | ? | ? | N | Y | N | N |
| **TEXAS** | | | | | | | |
| 1 **Gohmert** | Y | Y | Y | Y | Y | Y | N |
| 2 **Poe** | Y | Y | Y | Y | Y | Y | N |
| 3 **Johnson, S.** | Y | Y | Y | Y | Y | Y | N |
| 4 **Hall** | Y | Y | Y | Y | Y | Y | N |
| 5 **Hensarling** | Y | Y | Y | Y | Y | Y | Y |
| 6 **Barton** | Y | Y | Y | Y | Y | Y | N |
| 7 **Culberson** | Y | Y | Y | Y | Y | Y | N |
| 8 **Brady** | ? | ? | ? | Y | Y | Y | N |
| 9 Green, A. | Y | Y | Y | N | Y | N | N |
| 10 **McCaul** | Y | Y | Y | Y | Y | Y | N |
| 11 **Conaway** | N | Y | Y | Y | Y | Y | N |
| 12 **Granger** | Y | Y | Y | Y | Y | Y | N |
| 13 **Thornberry** | Y | Y | Y | Y | Y | Y | N |
| 14 **Paul** | N | Y | Y | Y | Y | Y | Y |
| 15 Hinojosa | Y | Y | Y | N | Y | N | N |
| 16 Reyes | ? | ? | ? | ? | ? | ? | ? |
| 17 Edwards | ? | ? | ? | N | Y | N | N |
| 18 Jackson-Lee | ? | ? | ? | N | Y | N | N |
| 19 **Neugebauer** | Y | Y | Y | Y | Y | Y | N |
| 20 Gonzalez | Y | Y | Y | N | Y | N | N |
| 21 **Smith** | Y | Y | Y | Y | Y | Y | N |
| 22 **DeLay** | Y | Y | Y | Y | Y | Y | N |
| 23 **Bonilla** | Y | Y | Y | Y | Y | Y | N |
| 24 **Marchant** | Y | Y | Y | Y | Y | Y | N |
| 25 Doggett | Y | Y | Y | N | Y | N | N |
| 26 **Burgess** | Y | Y | Y | Y | Y | Y | N |
| 27 Ortiz | Y | Y | Y | N | Y | N | N |
| 28 Cuellar | Y | Y | Y | N | Y | N | N |
| 29 Green, G. | Y | Y | Y | N | ? | N | N |
| 30 Johnson, E. | Y | Y | Y | N | Y | N | N |
| 31 **Carter** | Y | Y | Y | Y | Y | Y | N |
| 32 **Sessions** | Y | Y | Y | Y | Y | Y | N |
| **UTAH** | | | | | | | |
| 1 **Bishop** | Y | Y | Y | Y | Y | Y | N |
| 2 Matheson | Y | Y | Y | N | N | N | N |
| 3 **Cannon** | Y | Y | Y | Y | Y | ? | N |
| **VERMONT** | | | | | | | |
| AL *Sanders* | Y | Y | Y | N | Y | N | N |
| **VIRGINIA** | | | | | | | |
| 1 **Davis, J.** | Y | Y | Y | Y | Y | Y | N |
| 2 **Drake** | Y | Y | Y | Y | Y | Y | N |
| 3 Scott | Y | Y | Y | N | Y | N | N |
| 4 **Forbes** | Y | Y | Y | Y | Y | Y | N |
| 5 **Goode** | Y | Y | Y | Y | Y | Y | N |
| 6 **Goodlatte** | Y | Y | Y | Y | Y | Y | N |
| 7 **Cantor** | Y | Y | Y | Y | Y | Y | N |
| 8 Moran | Y | Y | Y | N | ? | ? | ? |
| 9 Boucher | Y | Y | Y | N | Y | N | N |
| 10 **Wolf** | Y | Y | Y | Y | Y | Y | N |
| 11 **Davis, T.** | Y | Y | Y | Y | Y | Y | N |
| **WASHINGTON** | | | | | | | |
| 1 Inslee | Y | Y | Y | N | Y | N | N |
| 2 Larsen | Y | Y | Y | N | N | N | N |
| 3 Baird | Y | Y | Y | N | N | N | N |
| 4 **Hastings** | Y | Y | Y | Y | Y | Y | N |
| 5 **McMorris** | Y | Y | Y | Y | Y | Y | N |
| 6 Dicks | Y | Y | Y | N | Y | N | Y |
| 7 McDermott | Y | Y | Y | N | N | N | N |
| 8 **Reichert** | Y | Y | Y | Y | Y | Y | N |
| 9 Smith | Y | Y | Y | N | Y | N | N |
| **WEST VIRGINIA** | | | | | | | |
| 1 Mollohan | Y | Y | Y | N | Y | N | N |
| 2 **Capito** | Y | Y | Y | Y | Y | Y | N |
| 3 Rahall | Y | Y | Y | N | Y | N | N |
| **WISCONSIN** | | | | | | | |
| 1 **Ryan** | Y | Y | Y | Y | Y | Y | Y |
| 2 Baldwin | Y | Y | Y | N | N | N | N |
| 3 Kind | Y | Y | Y | N | Y | N | N |
| 4 Moore | Y | Y | Y | N | Y | N | N |
| 5 **Sensenbrenner** | Y | Y | Y | Y | Y | Y | N |
| 6 **Petri** | Y | Y | Y | Y | Y | N | Y |
| 7 Obey | Y | Y | Y | N | Y | N | N |
| 8 **Green** | Y | Y | Y | Y | Y | Y | N |
| **WYOMING** | | | | | | | |
| AL **Cubin** | Y | Y | Y | Y | Y | Y | N |

# IN THE HOUSE | By Vote Number

**543.** HR 1461. Government-Sponsored Enterprises/Systemic Risk.
Royce, R-Calif., amendment that would authorize the new regulator to require Fannie Mae or Freddie Mac to sell or acquire assets or liabilities, if an asset or liability is deemed to be a potential systemic risk to the housing market, the capital markets or the financial system. Rejected 73-346: R 70-153; D 3-192 (ND 1-147, SD 2-45); I 0-1. Oct. 26, 2005.

**544.** HR 1461. Government-Sponsored Enterprises/U.S. Treasury Borrowing. Paul, R-Texas, amendment that would eliminate the ability of Fannie Mae, Freddie Mac and the Federal Home Loan Bank Board to borrow from the U.S. Treasury. Rejected 47-371: R 47-176; D 0-194 (ND 0-147, SD 0-47); I 0-1. Oct. 26, 2005.

**545.** HR 1461. Government-Sponsored Enterprises/Loan Limit. Garrett, R-N.J., amendment that would strike language in the bill that would increase by 50 percent the maximum mortgages Fannie Mae and Freddie Mac can buy in areas with high home prices. Rejected 57-358: R 53-168; D 4-189 (ND 2-145, SD 2-44); I 0-1. Oct. 26, 2005.

**546.** HR 1461. Government-Sponsored Enterprises/Recommit. Frank, D-Mass., motion to recommit the bill to the Financial Services Committee with instructions to add language clarifying that housing must be among a nonprofit organization's primary purposes and that recipients of money from the affordable housing fund may participate in any voter registration or get-out-the-vote-activity conducted on a nonpartisan basis. Motion rejected 200-220: R 3-220; D 196-0 (ND 148-0, SD 48-0); I 1-0. Oct. 26, 2005.

**547.** HR 1461. Government-Sponsored Enterprises/Passage. Passage of the bill that would overhaul the regulation of government-sponsored enterprises, including Fannie Mae, Freddie Mac and the 12 Federal Home Loan Banks. The bill would create a new independent agency, the Federal Housing Finance Agency, to regulate Fannie Mae, Freddie Mac and the Federal Home Loan Bank System. It also would establish an affordable housing fund. Passed 331-90: R 209-15; D 122-74 (ND 90-58, SD 32-16); I 0-1. A "nay" was a vote in support of the president's position. Oct. 26, 2005.

**548.** H J Res 65. Base Closure and Realignment Commission/Passage.
Passage of the joint resolution that would disapprove the recommendations of the Base Realignment and Closure Commission for the fifth round of base closures and realignments. Rejected 85-324: R 34-183; D 51-140 (ND 35-109, SD 16-31); I 0-1. A "nay" was a vote in support of the president's position. Oct. 27, 2005.

| | 543 | 544 | 545 | 546 | 547 | 548 |
|---|---|---|---|---|---|---|
| **ALABAMA** | | | | | | |
| 1 Bonner | N | N | N | N | Y | N |
| 2 Everett | N | N | N | N | Y | N |
| 3 Rogers | N | N | N | N | Y | N |
| 4 Aderholt | N | N | N | N | Y | N |
| 5 Cramer | N | N | N | Y | Y | N |
| 6 Bachus | N | N | N | N | Y | N |
| 7 Davis | N | N | N | Y | Y | N |
| **ALASKA** | | | | | | |
| AL Young | N | Y | N | N | Y | N |
| **ARIZONA** | | | | | | |
| 1 Renzi | N | N | N | N | Y | N |
| 2 Franks | Y | Y | Y | N | Y | N |
| 3 Shadegg | Y | Y | Y | N | N | N |
| 4 Pastor | N | N | N | Y | N | N |
| 5 Hayworth | Y | N | N | N | Y | N |
| 6 Flake | Y | Y | Y | N | N | N |
| 7 Grijalva | N | N | N | Y | N | N |
| 8 Kolbe | Y | N | Y | N | Y | N |
| **ARKANSAS** | | | | | | |
| 1 Berry | N | N | N | Y | Y | N |
| 2 Snyder | N | N | N | Y | Y | N |
| 3 Boozman | N | N | N | N | Y | N |
| 4 Ross | N | N | N | Y | Y | N |
| **CALIFORNIA** | | | | | | |
| 1 Thompson | N | N | N | Y | Y | – |
| 2 Herger | N | N | N | N | Y | N |
| 3 Lungren | Y | N | N | N | Y | N |
| 4 Doolittle | N | N | N | N | Y | Y |
| 5 Matsui, D. | N | N | N | Y | Y | N |
| 6 Woolsey | N | N | N | Y | N | N |
| 7 Miller, George | N | N | N | Y | N | N |
| 8 Pelosi | N | N | ? | Y | N | N |
| 9 Lee | N | N | N | Y | N | N |
| 10 Tauscher | N | N | N | Y | Y | ? |
| 11 Pombo | N | N | N | N | Y | N |
| 12 Lantos | N | N | N | Y | N | N |
| 13 Stark | N | N | N | Y | N | N |
| 14 Eshoo | N | N | N | Y | Y | N |
| 15 Honda | N | N | N | Y | N | N |
| 16 Lofgren | N | N | N | Y | N | N |
| 17 Farr | N | N | N | Y | Y | N |
| 18 Cardoza | Y | N | N | Y | Y | Y |
| 19 Radanovich | Y | N | Y | N | Y | N |
| 20 Costa | N | N | N | Y | Y | N |
| 21 Nunes | N | N | N | N | Y | N |
| 22 Thomas | N | N | N | N | Y | N |
| 23 Capps | N | N | N | Y | N | N |
| 24 Gallegly | N | N | N | N | Y | Y |
| 25 McKeon | N | N | N | N | Y | N |
| 26 Dreier | Y | N | N | N | Y | N |
| 27 Sherman | N | ? | N | Y | Y | Y |
| 28 Berman | N | N | N | Y | N | N |
| 29 Schiff | N | N | N | Y | Y | N |
| 30 Waxman | N | N | N | N | N | N |
| 31 Becerra | N | N | N | Y | Y | N |
| 32 Solis | N | N | N | Y | N | N |
| 33 Watson | N | N | N | Y | N | N |
| 34 Roybal-Allard | ? | ? | ? | ? | ? | ? |
| 35 Waters | N | N | N | Y | N | N |
| 36 Harman | N | N | N | Y | Y | N |
| 37 Millender-McD. | N | N | N | Y | N | N |
| 38 Napolitano | N | N | N | Y | Y | N |
| 39 Sánchez, Linda | N | N | N | Y | N | N |
| 40 Royce | Y | Y | Y | N | Y | N |
| 41 Lewis | N | N | N | N | Y | N |
| 42 Miller, Gary | N | N | N | N | Y | N |
| 43 Baca | N | N | N | Y | Y | N |
| 44 Calvert | N | N | N | N | Y | N |
| 45 Bono | N | N | N | N | Y | N |
| 46 Rohrabacher | Y | Y | N | N | Y | N |
| 47 Sanchez, Loretta | N | N | N | Y | Y | N |
| 48 Vacant | | | | | | |
| 49 Issa | N | N | N | N | Y | N |
| 50 Cunningham | N | N | N | N | Y | ? |
| 51 Filner | N | N | N | Y | Y | N |
| 52 Hunter | Y | N | N | N | Y | N |
| 53 Davis | N | N | N | Y | Y | N |
| **COLORADO** | | | | | | |
| 1 DeGette | N | N | N | Y | N | Y |
| 2 Udall | N | N | N | Y | Y | N |
| 3 Salazar | N | N | N | Y | Y | N |
| 4 Musgrave | Y | N | Y | N | N | N |
| 5 Hefley | N | N | N | N | Y | N |
| 6 Tancredo | Y | Y | Y | N | N | N |
| 7 Beauprez | Y | N | N | N | Y | N |
| **CONNECTICUT** | | | | | | |
| 1 Larson | N | N | N | Y | Y | Y |
| 2 Simmons | N | N | N | N | Y | ? |
| 3 DeLauro | N | N | N | Y | Y | Y |
| 4 Shays | Y | Y | N | Y | Y | Y |
| 5 Johnson | N | N | N | N | Y | N |
| **DELAWARE** | | | | | | |
| AL Castle | N | N | Y | N | Y | N |
| **FLORIDA** | | | | | | |
| 1 Miller | N | Y | N | N | Y | Y |
| 2 Boyd | N | N | N | Y | Y | N |
| 3 Brown | N | N | N | Y | Y | N |
| 4 Crenshaw | N | N | N | N | Y | N |
| 5 Brown-Waite | ? | ? | ? | ? | ? | ? |
| 6 Stearns | Y | N | Y | N | N | N |
| 7 Mica | N | N | N | N | Y | N |
| 8 Keller | N | N | N | N | Y | N |
| 9 Bilirakis | N | N | N | N | Y | N |
| 10 Young | N | N | N | N | Y | N |
| 11 Davis | N | N | ? | Y | Y | N |
| 12 Putnam | N | N | N | N | Y | N |
| 13 Harris | N | N | Y | N | Y | ? |
| 14 Mack | N | Y | N | N | N | ? |
| 15 Weldon | Y | N | Y | N | Y | N |
| 16 Foley | ? | ? | ? | ? | ? | ? |
| 17 Meek | ? | ? | N | Y | N | N |
| 18 Ros-Lehtinen | ? | ? | ? | Y | ? | ? |
| 19 Wexler | ? | ? | ? | ? | ? | ? |
| 20 Wasserman-Schultz | N | N | N | Y | N | N |
| 21 Diaz-Balart, L. | ? | ? | ? | ? | ? | ? |
| 22 Shaw | ? | ? | ? | ? | ? | ? |
| 23 Hastings | N | N | N | Y | N | N |
| 24 Feeney | Y | Y | N | N | Y | N |
| 25 Diaz-Balart, M. | ? | ? | ? | ? | ? | ? |
| **GEORGIA** | | | | | | |
| 1 Kingston | Y | Y | N | N | Y | N |
| 2 Bishop | ? | ? | ? | ? | ? | N |
| 3 Marshall | N | N | ? | Y | Y | N |
| 4 McKinney | N | N | N | Y | N | N |
| 5 Lewis | N | N | N | Y | N | Y |
| 6 Price | N | Y | N | N | Y | N |
| 7 Linder | N | Y | N | N | Y | N |
| 8 Westmoreland | Y | Y | Y | N | Y | N |
| 9 Norwood | Y | Y | N | N | Y | N |
| 10 Deal | Y | Y | Y | N | Y | N |
| 11 Gingrey | N | N | N | N | Y | N |
| 12 Barrow | N | N | N | Y | Y | Y |
| 13 Scott | N | N | N | Y | Y | N |
| **HAWAII** | | | | | | |
| 1 Abercrombie | N | N | N | Y | N | Y |
| 2 Case | N | N | N | Y | Y | N |
| **IDAHO** | | | | | | |
| 1 Otter | Y | Y | Y | N | N | N |
| 2 Simpson | N | N | N | N | N | N |
| **ILLINOIS** | | | | | | |
| 1 Rush | N | N | Y | Y | Y | Y |
| 2 Jackson | N | N | N | Y | Y | Y |
| 3 Lipinski | N | N | N | Y | Y | N |
| 4 Gutierrez | N | N | N | Y | N | N |
| 5 Emanuel | ? | ? | ? | ? | ? | Y |
| 6 Hyde | N | N | N | N | Y | N |
| 7 Davis | N | N | N | Y | Y | Y |
| 8 Bean | N | N | Y | Y | Y | N |
| 9 Schakowsky | N | N | N | Y | N | Y |
| 10 Kirk | Y | N | N | N | Y | N |
| 11 Weller | N | N | N | N | Y | N |
| 12 Costello | N | N | N | Y | Y | N |

| | 543 | 544 | 545 | 546 | 547 | 548 |
|---|---|---|---|---|---|---|
| 13 **Biggert** | N | N | N | N | Y | N |
| 14 **Hastert** | | | | | | |
| 15 **Johnson** | N | N | N | N | Y | Y |
| 16 **Manzullo** | Y | Y | N | N | Y | Y |
| 17 Evans | N | N | N | Y | Y | Y |
| 18 **LaHood** | N | N | N | N | Y | Y |
| 19 **Shimkus** | N | N | N | N | Y | N |
| **INDIANA** | | | | | | |
| 1 Visclosky | N | N | N | Y | N | N |
| 2 **Chocola** | Y | Y | Y | N | N | N |
| 3 **Souder** | N | N | N | N | Y | N |
| 4 **Buyer** | N | N | N | N | Y | N |
| 5 **Burton** | N | Y | N | N | Y | N |
| 6 **Pence** | Y | Y | Y | N | Y | N |
| 7 Carson | N | N | N | Y | N | N |
| 8 **Hostettler** | Y | Y | Y | N | Y | Y |
| 9 **Sodrel** | N | N | Y | N | Y | N |
| **IOWA** | | | | | | |
| 1 **Nussle** | Y | Y | Y | N | Y | Y |
| 2 **Leach** | Y | Y | Y | Y | N | Y |
| 3 Boswell | ? | ? | ? | ? | ? | ? |
| 4 **Latham** | N | N | N | N | Y | N |
| 5 **King** | Y | N | Y | N | Y | N |
| **KANSAS** | | | | | | |
| 1 **Moran** | N | N | N | N | Y | N |
| 2 **Ryun** | N | N | N | N | Y | N |
| 3 Moore | N | N | N | Y | Y | N |
| 4 **Tiahrt** | Y | N | Y | N | Y | N |
| **KENTUCKY** | | | | | | |
| 1 **Whitfield** | ? | ? | ? | ? | ? | N |
| 2 **Lewis** | N | N | N | N | Y | N |
| 3 **Northup** | N | N | N | N | Y | N |
| 4 **Davis** | N | N | N | N | Y | N |
| 5 **Rogers** | N | N | N | N | Y | N |
| 6 Chandler | N | N | N | Y | Y | N |
| **LOUISIANA** | | | | | | |
| 1 **Jindal** | N | N | Y | N | Y | Y |
| 2 Jefferson | N | N | N | Y | Y | N |
| 3 Melancon | N | N | N | Y | Y | N |
| 4 **McCrery** | N | N | Y | N | Y | N |
| 5 **Alexander** | N | N | Y | N | Y | N |
| 6 **Baker** | N | N | Y | N | Y | N |
| 7 **Boustany** | N | N | Y | N | Y | N |
| **MAINE** | | | | | | |
| 1 Allen | N | N | N | Y | Y | Y |
| 2 Michaud | N | N | N | Y | Y | N |
| **MARYLAND** | | | | | | |
| 1 **Gilchrest** | N | N | N | N | Y | N |
| 2 Ruppersberger | N | N | N | Y | Y | N |
| 3 Cardin | N | N | N | Y | Y | N |
| 4 Wynn | N | N | N | Y | Y | N |
| 5 Hoyer | N | N | N | Y | Y | N |
| 6 **Bartlett** | Y | Y | Y | N | Y | N |
| 7 Cummings | N | N | N | Y | Y | N |
| 8 Van Hollen | N | N | N | Y | Y | N |
| **MASSACHUSETTS** | | | | | | |
| 1 Olver | N | N | N | Y | N | N |
| 2 Neal | N | N | N | Y | Y | N |
| 3 McGovern | N | N | N | Y | N | N |
| 4 Frank | N | N | N | Y | N | N |
| 5 Meehan | N | N | N | Y | Y | N |
| 6 Tierney | N | N | N | Y | Y | N |
| 7 Markey | N | N | N | Y | N | N |
| 8 Capuano | N | N | N | Y | N | N |
| 9 Lynch | N | N | N | Y | Y | Y |
| 10 Delahunt | N | N | Y | Y | Y | Y |
| **MICHIGAN** | | | | | | |
| 1 Stupak | N | N | N | Y | Y | Y |
| 2 **Hoekstra** | Y | Y | N | N | Y | N |
| 3 **Ehlers** | Y | N | N | N | Y | N |
| 4 **Camp** | N | N | N | N | Y | N |
| 5 Kildee | N | N | N | Y | Y | N |
| 6 **Upton** | Y | N | N | N | Y | N |
| 7 **Schwarz** | N | N | N | N | Y | N |
| 8 **Rogers** | N | N | N | N | Y | N |
| 9 **Knollenberg** | N | N | N | N | Y | N |
| 10 **Miller** | N | N | N | N | Y | N |
| 11 **McCotter** | N | N | N | N | Y | N |
| 12 Levin | N | N | N | Y | Y | N |
| 13 Kilpatrick | N | N | N | Y | N | N |
| 14 Conyers | N | N | N | Y | N | N |
| 15 Dingell | N | N | N | Y | N | N |
| **MINNESOTA** | | | | | | |
| 1 **Gutknecht** | Y | N | Y | N | Y | N |
| 2 **Kline** | Y | N | N | N | Y | N |
| 3 **Ramstad** | Y | N | N | Y | N | N |
| 4 McCollum | N | N | N | Y | N | N |
| 5 Sabo | N | N | N | Y | N | N |
| 6 **Kennedy** | Y | N | N | N | Y | N |
| 7 Peterson | N | N | N | Y | Y | N |
| 8 Oberstar | N | N | N | Y | N | N |
| **MISSISSIPPI** | | | | | | |
| 1 **Wicker** | N | N | N | N | Y | Y |
| 2 Thompson | N | N | N | Y | Y | N |
| 3 **Pickering** | N | N | N | N | Y | Y |
| 4 Taylor | Y | N | Y | Y | Y | Y |
| **MISSOURI** | | | | | | |
| 1 Clay | N | N | N | Y | N | Y |
| 2 **Akin** | Y | Y | Y | N | Y | Y |
| 3 Carnahan | N | N | N | Y | Y | Y |
| 4 Skelton | N | N | N | Y | Y | N |
| 5 Cleaver | N | N | N | Y | N | N |
| 6 **Graves** | N | N | N | N | Y | N |
| 7 **Blunt** | Y | N | N | N | Y | N |
| 8 **Emerson** | N | N | N | N | Y | Y |
| 9 **Hulshof** | N | N | N | N | Y | Y |
| **MONTANA** | | | | | | |
| AL **Rehberg** | N | N | N | N | Y | N |
| **NEBRASKA** | | | | | | |
| 1 **Fortenberry** | Y | N | N | N | Y | N |
| 2 **Terry** | N | N | N | N | Y | N |
| 3 **Osborne** | N | N | N | N | Y | N |
| **NEVADA** | | | | | | |
| 1 Berkley | N | N | N | Y | Y | N |
| 2 **Gibbons** | N | N | N | N | Y | N |
| 3 **Porter** | N | N | N | N | Y | N |
| **NEW HAMPSHIRE** | | | | | | |
| 1 **Bradley** | N | N | N | N | Y | N |
| 2 **Bass** | N | N | N | N | Y | N |
| **NEW JERSEY** | | | | | | |
| 1 Andrews | N | N | N | Y | Y | Y |
| 2 **LoBiondo** | N | N | N | N | Y | N |
| 3 **Saxton** | Y | N | N | N | Y | N |
| 4 **Smith** | Y | N | N | N | Y | Y |
| 5 **Garrett** | Y | Y | Y | N | N | N |
| 6 Pallone | N | N | N | Y | Y | Y |
| 7 **Ferguson** | Y | N | N | N | Y | N |
| 8 Pascrell | N | N | N | Y | Y | Y |
| 9 Rothman | N | N | N | Y | Y | Y |
| 10 Payne | N | N | N | Y | N | ? |
| 11 **Frelinghuysen** | N | N | N | N | Y | N |
| 12 Holt | N | N | N | Y | Y | Y |
| 13 Menendez | N | N | N | Y | Y | Y |
| **NEW MEXICO** | | | | | | |
| 1 **Wilson** | N | N | N | N | Y | Y |
| 2 **Pearce** | N | N | N | N | Y | N |
| 3 Udall | N | N | N | Y | Y | Y |
| **NEW YORK** | | | | | | |
| 1 Bishop | N | N | N | Y | Y | N |
| 2 Israel | N | N | N | Y | N | N |
| 3 **King** | N | N | N | N | Y | N |
| 4 McCarthy | N | N | N | Y | Y | N |
| 5 Ackerman | N | N | N | Y | N | N |
| 6 Meeks | N | N | N | Y | N | N |
| 7 Crowley | N | N | N | Y | N | Y |
| 8 Nadler | N | N | N | Y | N | N |
| 9 Weiner | N | N | N | Y | N | N |
| 10 Towns | N | N | N | Y | N | N |
| 11 Owens | N | N | N | Y | N | N |
| 12 Velázquez | N | N | N | Y | N | N |
| 13 **Fossella** | N | N | N | N | Y | N |
| 14 Maloney | N | N | N | Y | N | N |
| 15 Rangel | N | N | N | Y | N | ? |
| 16 Serrano | N | N | N | Y | N | N |
| 17 Engel | N | N | N | Y | Y | N |
| 18 Lowey | N | N | N | Y | Y | N |
| 19 **Kelly** | N | N | N | N | Y | N |
| 20 **Sweeney** | N | N | N | N | Y | N |
| 21 McNulty | N | N | N | Y | N | N |
| 22 Hinchey | N | N | N | Y | N | N |
| 23 **McHugh** | N | N | N | N | Y | N |
| 24 **Boehlert** | N | N | N | N | Y | N |
| 25 **Walsh** | N | N | N | N | Y | N |
| 26 **Reynolds** | N | N | N | N | Y | N |
| 27 Higgins | N | N | N | Y | Y | N |
| 28 Slaughter | N | N | N | Y | Y | N |
| 29 **Kuhl** | N | N | N | N | Y | N |
| **NORTH CAROLINA** | | | | | | |
| 1 Butterfield | N | N | N | Y | Y | N |
| 2 Etheridge | N | N | N | Y | Y | N |
| 3 **Jones** | Y | Y | Y | N | Y | N |
| 4 Price | N | N | N | Y | N | N |
| 5 **Foxx** | Y | Y | N | N | Y | N |
| 6 **Coble** | N | N | N | N | Y | N |
| 7 McIntyre | N | N | N | Y | Y | N |
| 8 **Hayes** | N | N | N | N | Y | N |
| 9 **Myrick** | N | Y | N | N | Y | N |
| 10 **McHenry** | Y | Y | N | N | Y | N |
| 11 **Taylor** | Y | N | N | N | Y | N |
| 12 Watt | N | N | N | Y | N | N |
| 13 Miller | N | N | N | Y | N | N |
| **NORTH DAKOTA** | | | | | | |
| AL Pomeroy | N | N | N | Y | Y | N |
| **OHIO** | | | | | | |
| 1 **Chabot** | Y | N | N | N | Y | N |
| 2 **Schmidt** | N | N | N | N | Y | N |
| 3 **Turner** | N | N | N | N | Y | N |
| 4 **Oxley** | N | N | N | N | Y | Y |
| 5 **Gillmor** | Y | N | N | N | Y | N |
| 6 Strickland | N | N | N | Y | Y | N |
| 7 **Hobson** | N | N | N | N | Y | Y |
| 8 **Boehner** | N | Y | N | N | Y | N |
| 9 Kaptur | N | N | N | Y | N | N |
| 10 Kucinich | N | N | N | Y | N | N |
| 11 Jones | N | N | N | Y | N | N |
| 12 **Tiberi** | N | N | N | N | Y | N |
| 13 Brown | N | N | N | Y | Y | Y |
| 14 **LaTourette** | N | N | N | N | Y | N |
| 15 **Pryce** | N | N | N | N | Y | N |
| 16 **Regula** | Y | N | N | N | Y | N |
| 17 Ryan | N | N | N | Y | Y | N |
| 18 **Ney** | N | N | N | N | Y | N |
| **OKLAHOMA** | | | | | | |
| 1 **Sullivan** | N | N | N | N | Y | N |
| 2 Boren | N | N | N | Y | Y | N |
| 3 **Lucas** | N | N | N | N | Y | N |
| 4 **Cole** | N | N | N | N | Y | N |
| 5 **Istook** | N | Y | Y | N | Y | N |
| **OREGON** | | | | | | |
| 1 Wu | N | N | N | Y | Y | N |
| 2 **Walden** | N | N | N | N | Y | N |
| 3 Blumenauer | N | N | N | Y | Y | N |
| 4 DeFazio | N | N | N | Y | Y | N |
| 5 Hooley | N | N | N | Y | Y | N |
| **PENNSYLVANIA** | | | | | | |
| 1 Brady | N | N | N | Y | N | Y |
| 2 Fattah | N | N | N | Y | N | Y |
| 3 **English** | N | N | Y | N | Y | N |
| 4 **Hart** | N | N | N | N | Y | N |
| 5 **Peterson** | N | N | N | N | Y | N |
| 6 **Gerlach** | N | N | N | N | Y | Y |
| 7 **Weldon** | N | N | N | N | Y | N |
| 8 **Fitzpatrick** | N | N | N | N | Y | Y |
| 9 **Shuster** | N | N | N | N | Y | N |
| 10 **Sherwood** | Y | N | N | N | Y | N |
| 11 Kanjorski | N | N | N | Y | N | N |
| 12 Murtha | N | N | N | Y | Y | Y |
| 13 Schwartz | N | N | N | Y | Y | Y |
| 14 Doyle | N | N | N | Y | N | N |
| 15 **Dent** | N | N | N | N | Y | Y |
| 16 **Pitts** | Y | Y | Y | N | Y | N |
| 17 Holden | N | N | N | Y | Y | N |
| 18 **Murphy** | N | N | N | N | Y | N |
| 19 **Platts** | Y | Y | Y | N | N | N |
| **RHODE ISLAND** | | | | | | |
| 1 Kennedy | N | N | N | Y | N | N |
| 2 Langevin | N | N | N | Y | Y | N |
| **SOUTH CAROLINA** | | | | | | |
| 1 **Brown** | N | N | N | N | Y | Y |
| 2 **Wilson** | N | N | N | N | Y | N |
| 3 **Barrett** | N | N | Y | N | Y | N |
| 4 **Inglis** | Y | Y | N | N | Y | N |
| 5 Spratt | N | N | N | Y | Y | N |
| 6 Clyburn | N | N | N | Y | N | N |
| **SOUTH DAKOTA** | | | | | | |
| AL Herseth | N | N | N | Y | Y | N |
| **TENNESSEE** | | | | | | |
| 1 **Jenkins** | N | N | N | N | Y | Y |
| 2 **Duncan** | Y | Y | Y | N | Y | N |
| 3 **Wamp** | N | N | N | N | Y | N |
| 4 Davis | N | N | N | Y | Y | N |
| 5 Cooper | Y | N | Y | Y | N | Y |
| 6 Gordon | N | N | N | Y | Y | Y |
| 7 **Blackburn** | Y | Y | Y | N | N | N |
| 8 Tanner | N | N | N | Y | Y | N |
| 9 Ford | N | N | N | Y | Y | Y |
| **TEXAS** | | | | | | |
| 1 **Gohmert** | Y | Y | Y | N | Y | ? |
| 2 **Poe** | N | N | N | N | Y | Y |
| 3 **Johnson, S.** | N | N | ? | N | Y | N |
| 4 **Hall** | Y | N | N | N | Y | ? |
| 5 **Hensarling** | Y | Y | Y | N | Y | N |
| 6 **Barton** | N | Y | Y | N | Y | N |
| 7 **Culberson** | Y | N | Y | N | Y | N |
| 8 **Brady** | N | N | N | N | Y | N |
| 9 Green, A. | N | N | N | Y | N | Y |
| 10 **McCaul** | N | N | N | N | Y | Y |
| 11 **Conaway** | N | N | N | N | Y | N |
| 12 **Granger** | N | N | N | N | Y | N |
| 13 **Thornberry** | N | N | N | N | Y | N |
| 14 **Paul** | Y | Y | Y | N | N | Y |
| 15 Hinojosa | N | N | N | Y | Y | Y |
| 16 Reyes | ? | ? | ? | ? | ? | ? |
| 17 Edwards | N | N | N | Y | Y | Y |
| 18 Jackson-Lee | N | N | N | Y | N | N |
| 19 **Neugebauer** | N | N | N | N | Y | N |
| 20 Gonzalez | N | N | N | Y | Y | N |
| 21 **Smith** | N | N | N | N | Y | N |
| 22 **DeLay** | Y | N | N | N | Y | Y |
| 23 **Bonilla** | N | N | N | N | Y | N |
| 24 **Marchant** | N | N | N | N | Y | N |
| 25 Doggett | N | N | N | Y | Y | N |
| 26 **Burgess** | N | N | Y | N | Y | N |
| 27 Ortiz | N | N | N | Y | Y | Y |
| 28 Cuellar | N | N | N | Y | Y | P |
| 29 Green, G. | N | N | N | Y | N | Y |
| 30 Johnson, E. | N | N | N | Y | N | Y |
| 31 **Carter** | N | N | Y | N | Y | N |
| 32 **Sessions** | N | N | N | N | Y | N |
| **UTAH** | | | | | | |
| 1 **Bishop** | N | N | ? | N | Y | N |
| 2 Matheson | N | N | N | Y | Y | N |
| 3 **Cannon** | N | N | N | N | Y | N |
| **VERMONT** | | | | | | |
| AL *Sanders* | N | N | N | Y | N | N |
| **VIRGINIA** | | | | | | |
| 1 **Davis, J.** | N | N | Y | N | Y | Y |
| 2 **Drake** | N | N | N | N | Y | Y |
| 3 Scott | N | N | N | Y | N | Y |
| 4 **Forbes** | N | N | N | N | Y | Y |
| 5 **Goode** | Y | Y | N | N | Y | N |
| 6 **Goodlatte** | N | N | N | N | Y | N |
| 7 **Cantor** | N | N | N | N | Y | N |
| 8 Moran | N | N | N | Y | Y | Y |
| 9 Boucher | N | N | N | Y | Y | N |
| 10 **Wolf** | N | N | N | N | Y | N |
| 11 **Davis, T.** | N | N | N | N | Y | Y |
| **WASHINGTON** | | | | | | |
| 1 Inslee | N | N | N | Y | N | N |
| 2 Larsen | N | N | N | Y | Y | N |
| 3 Baird | N | N | N | Y | Y | N |
| 4 **Hastings** | N | N | N | N | Y | N |
| 5 **McMorris** | N | N | N | N | Y | N |
| 6 Dicks | N | N | N | Y | Y | N |
| 7 McDermott | N | N | N | Y | N | N |
| 8 **Reichert** | N | N | N | N | Y | N |
| 9 Smith | N | N | N | Y | Y | N |
| **WEST VIRGINIA** | | | | | | |
| 1 Mollohan | N | N | N | Y | Y | Y |
| 2 **Capito** | N | N | N | N | Y | N |
| 3 Rahall | N | N | N | Y | Y | N |
| **WISCONSIN** | | | | | | |
| 1 **Ryan** | Y | Y | Y | N | Y | N |
| 2 Baldwin | N | N | N | Y | Y | N |
| 3 Kind | N | N | N | Y | Y | N |
| 4 Moore | N | N | N | Y | Y | Y |
| 5 **Sensenbrenner** | Y | Y | Y | N | Y | ? |
| 6 **Petri** | Y | N | Y | N | Y | N |
| 7 Obey | N | N | N | Y | Y | ? |
| 8 **Green** | N | N | Y | N | Y | N |
| **WYOMING** | | | | | | |
| AL **Cubin** | N | N | N | N | Y | N |

# IN THE HOUSE | By Vote Number

**549.** **HR 3945. Hurricane Katrina Financial Services Relief/Passage.**
Baker, R-La., motion to suspend the rules and pass the bill that would require Federal Reserve banks to waive or rebate any transaction fees for wire transfer services to insured depository institutions or credit unions that are headquartered in an area declared a disaster after Hurricane Katrina. Motion agreed to 411-0: R 216-0; D 194-0 (ND 146-0, SD 48-0); I 1-0. A two-thirds majority of those present and voting (274 in this case) is required for passage under suspension of the rules. Oct. 27, 2005.

**550.** **H Res 368. Vice President of the U.N. General Assembly/Adoption.** Chabot, R-Ohio, motion to suspend the rules and adopt the resolution that would congratulate Ambassador Dan Gillerman, Israel's permanent representative to the United Nations, and the Israeli government and people on Gillerman's election as vice president of the 60th U.N. General Assembly. Motion agreed to 407-0: R 215-0; D 191-0 (ND 144-0, SD 47-0); I 1-0. A two-thirds majority of those present and voting (272 in this case) is required for adoption under suspension of the rules. Oct. 27, 2005.

**551.** **HR 420. "Meritless" Lawsuits/Democratic Substitute.** Schiff, D-Calif., substitute amendment that would require mandatory sanctions against attorneys who file frivolous civil lawsuits, including payment of costs and attorney fees. Attorneys would be allowed to appeal. It would prevent a court from sealing or otherwise restricting access to a court record unless the court finds that such a restriction is justified. Rejected 184-226: R 1-215; D 182-11 (ND 137-9, SD 45-2); I 1-0. Oct. 27, 2005.

**552.** **HR 420. "Meritless" Lawsuits/Recommit.** Barrow, D-Ga., motion to recommit the bill to the Judiciary Committee with instructions to add language that would exempt from the bill claims against "disaster profiteering businesses." Motion rejected 196-217: R 1-217; D 194-0 (ND 147-0, SD 47-0); I 1-0. Oct. 27, 2005.

**553.** **HR 420. "Meritless" Lawsuits/Passage.** Passage of the bill that would increase federal sanctions on attorneys who file "meritless" civil lawsuits. It would restore mandatory sanctions against such attorneys instead of giving judges the discretion to implement sanctions. The bill would strike a "safe harbor" provision in existing law that allows attorneys to avoid sanctions by withdrawing or correcting questionable claims. Passed 228-184: R 212-5; D 16-178 (ND 5-142, SD 11-36); I 0-1. A "yea" was a vote in support of the president's position. Oct. 27, 2005.

**554.** **HR 3057. Fiscal 2006 Foreign Operations Appropriations/Motion to Instruct.** Lowey, D-N.Y., motion to instruct House conferees to include language that would agree to a Senate provision allowing for $3 billion to combat HIV/AIDS, tuberculosis and malaria, including $500 million for a U.S. contribution to the Global Fund to Fight AIDS, Tuberculosis and Malaria. Motion agreed to 259-147: R 69-145; D 189-2 (ND 145-0, SD 44-2); I 1-0. Oct. 27, 2005.

| | 549 | 550 | 551 | 552 | 553 | 554 |
|---|---|---|---|---|---|---|
| **ALABAMA** | | | | | | |
| 1 Bonner | Y | Y | N | N | Y | N |
| 2 Everett | Y | Y | N | N | Y | N |
| 3 Rogers | Y | Y | N | N | Y | N |
| 4 Aderholt | Y | Y | N | N | Y | Y |
| 5 Cramer | Y | Y | Y | Y | Y | Y |
| 6 Bachus | Y | Y | N | N | Y | Y |
| 7 Davis | Y | Y | Y | Y | N | Y |
| **ALASKA** | | | | | | |
| AL Young | Y | Y | N | N | Y | N |
| **ARIZONA** | | | | | | |
| 1 Renzi | Y | Y | N | N | Y | N |
| 2 Franks | Y | Y | N | N | Y | N |
| 3 Shadegg | Y | Y | N | N | Y | N |
| 4 Pastor | Y | Y | Y | Y | N | Y |
| 5 Hayworth | Y | Y | N | N | Y | N |
| 6 Flake | Y | Y | N | N | Y | N |
| 7 Grijalva | Y | Y | Y | Y | N | Y |
| 8 Kolbe | Y | Y | N | N | Y | Y |
| **ARKANSAS** | | | | | | |
| 1 Berry | Y | Y | Y | Y | N | Y |
| 2 Snyder | Y | Y | N | Y | N | Y |
| 3 Boozman | Y | Y | N | N | Y | N |
| 4 Ross | Y | Y | Y | Y | N | Y |
| **CALIFORNIA** | | | | | | |
| 1 Thompson | Y | Y | Y | Y | N | Y |
| 2 Herger | Y | Y | N | N | Y | Y |
| 3 Lungren | Y | Y | N | N | Y | Y |
| 4 Doolittle | Y | Y | N | N | Y | N |
| 5 Matsui, D. | Y | Y | Y | Y | N | Y |
| 6 Woolsey | Y | Y | Y | Y | N | Y |
| 7 Miller, George | Y | Y | Y | Y | N | Y |
| 8 Pelosi | Y | Y | Y | Y | N | Y |
| 9 Lee | Y | Y | Y | Y | N | Y |
| 10 Tauscher | ? | ? | ? | ? | ? | ? |
| 11 Pombo | Y | Y | N | N | Y | Y |
| 12 Lantos | Y | Y | Y | Y | N | Y |
| 13 Stark | Y | Y | Y | Y | N | Y |
| 14 Eshoo | Y | Y | Y | Y | N | Y |
| 15 Honda | Y | Y | Y | Y | N | Y |
| 16 Lofgren | Y | Y | Y | Y | N | Y |
| 17 Farr | Y | Y | Y | Y | N | Y |
| 18 Cardoza | Y | Y | Y | Y | Y | Y |
| 19 Radanovich | Y | Y | N | N | Y | N |
| 20 Costa | Y | Y | Y | Y | N | Y |
| 21 Nunes | Y | Y | N | N | Y | N |
| 22 Thomas | Y | Y | N | N | Y | N |
| 23 Capps | Y | Y | Y | Y | N | Y |
| 24 Gallegly | Y | Y | N | N | Y | ? |
| 25 McKeon | Y | Y | N | N | Y | Y |
| 26 Dreier | Y | Y | N | N | Y | N |
| 27 Sherman | Y | Y | Y | Y | N | Y |
| 28 Berman | Y | Y | Y | Y | N | Y |
| 29 Schiff | Y | Y | Y | Y | N | Y |
| 30 Waxman | Y | Y | Y | Y | N | Y |
| 31 Becerra | Y | Y | Y | Y | N | Y |
| 32 Solis | Y | Y | Y | Y | N | Y |
| 33 Watson | Y | Y | Y | Y | N | Y |
| 34 Roybal-Allard | ? | ? | ? | ? | ? | ? |
| 35 Waters | Y | Y | Y | Y | N | Y |
| 36 Harman | Y | Y | Y | Y | N | Y |
| 37 Millender-McD. | Y | Y | Y | Y | N | Y |
| 38 Napolitano | Y | Y | Y | Y | N | Y |
| 39 Sánchez, Linda | Y | Y | Y | Y | N | Y |
| 40 Royce | Y | Y | N | N | Y | N |
| 41 Lewis | Y | Y | N | N | Y | N |
| 42 Miller, Gary | Y | Y | Y | Y | N | N |
| 43 Baca | Y | Y | Y | Y | N | Y |
| 44 Calvert | Y | Y | N | N | Y | N |
| 45 Bono | Y | Y | N | N | Y | N |
| 46 Rohrabacher | Y | Y | N | N | Y | N |
| 47 Sanchez, Loretta | Y | Y | Y | N | Y | Y |
| 48 Vacant | | | | | | |
| 49 Issa | Y | Y | N | N | Y | N |

| | 549 | 550 | 551 | 552 | 553 | 554 |
|---|---|---|---|---|---|---|
| 50 Cunningham | ? | ? | N | N | Y | Y |
| 51 Filner | Y | Y | Y | Y | N | Y |
| 52 Hunter | Y | Y | N | N | Y | N |
| 53 Davis | Y | Y | Y | Y | N | Y |
| **COLORADO** | | | | | | |
| 1 DeGette | Y | Y | N | N | Y | Y |
| 2 Udall | Y | Y | Y | Y | N | Y |
| 3 Salazar | Y | Y | Y | Y | N | Y |
| 4 Musgrave | Y | Y | N | N | Y | N |
| 5 Hefley | Y | Y | N | N | Y | N |
| 6 Tancredo | Y | Y | N | N | Y | N |
| 7 Beauprez | Y | Y | N | N | Y | N |
| **CONNECTICUT** | | | | | | |
| 1 Larson | Y | Y | Y | Y | N | Y |
| 2 Simmons | ? | ? | ? | ? | ? | ? |
| 3 DeLauro | Y | Y | Y | Y | N | Y |
| 4 Shays | Y | Y | N | N | Y | Y |
| 5 Johnson | Y | Y | N | N | Y | Y |
| **DELAWARE** | | | | | | |
| AL Castle | Y | Y | N | N | Y | ? |
| **FLORIDA** | | | | | | |
| 1 Miller | Y | Y | N | N | Y | N |
| 2 Boyd | Y | Y | Y | Y | Y | Y |
| 3 Brown | Y | Y | Y | Y | N | Y |
| 4 Crenshaw | Y | Y | N | N | Y | N |
| 5 Brown-Waite | ? | ? | ? | ? | ? | ? |
| 6 Stearns | Y | Y | N | N | Y | N |
| 7 Mica | Y | Y | N | N | Y | N |
| 8 Keller | Y | Y | N | N | Y | N |
| 9 Bilirakis | Y | Y | N | N | Y | N |
| 10 Young | Y | Y | N | N | Y | N |
| 11 Davis | Y | Y | Y | Y | N | Y |
| 12 Putnam | Y | Y | N | N | Y | N |
| 13 Harris | ? | ? | ? | ? | ? | ? |
| 14 Mack | ? | ? | ? | ? | ? | ? |
| 15 Weldon | Y | Y | N | N | Y | N |
| 16 Foley | ? | ? | ? | ? | ? | ? |
| 17 Meek | Y | Y | Y | Y | N | Y |
| 18 Ros-Lehtinen | ? | ? | ? | ? | ? | ? |
| 19 Wexler | ? | ? | ? | ? | ? | ? |
| 20 Wasserman-Schultz | ? | ? | ? | N | Y | Y |
| 21 Diaz-Balart, L. | ? | ? | ? | ? | ? | ? |
| 22 Shaw | ? | ? | ? | ? | ? | ? |
| 23 Hastings | ? | ? | ? | ? | ? | ? |
| 24 Feeney | Y | Y | N | N | Y | N |
| 25 Diaz-Balart, M. | ? | ? | ? | ? | ? | ? |
| **GEORGIA** | | | | | | |
| 1 Kingston | Y | Y | N | N | Y | N |
| 2 Bishop | Y | Y | Y | Y | N | Y |
| 3 Marshall | Y | Y | Y | Y | Y | Y |
| 4 McKinney | Y | Y | Y | Y | N | Y |
| 5 Lewis | Y | Y | Y | Y | N | Y |
| 6 Price | Y | Y | N | N | Y | N |
| 7 Linder | Y | Y | N | N | Y | N |
| 8 Westmoreland | Y | Y | N | N | Y | N |
| 9 Norwood | Y | Y | N | N | Y | N |
| 10 Deal | Y | Y | N | N | Y | N |
| 11 Gingrey | Y | Y | ? | N | Y | N |
| 12 Barrow | Y | Y | Y | Y | N | Y |
| 13 Scott | Y | Y | Y | Y | Y | Y |
| **HAWAII** | | | | | | |
| 1 Abercrombie | Y | Y | Y | Y | N | Y |
| 2 Case | Y | Y | Y | Y | Y | Y |
| **IDAHO** | | | | | | |
| 1 Otter | Y | Y | N | N | Y | N |
| 2 Simpson | Y | Y | N | N | Y | N |
| **ILLINOIS** | | | | | | |
| 1 Rush | Y | Y | Y | Y | N | Y |
| 2 Jackson | Y | Y | Y | Y | N | Y |
| 3 Lipinski | Y | Y | Y | Y | N | Y |
| 4 Gutierrez | Y | Y | Y | Y | N | Y |
| 5 Emanuel | Y | Y | Y | Y | N | Y |
| 6 Hyde | Y | Y | N | N | Y | Y |
| 7 Davis | Y | Y | Y | Y | N | Y |
| 8 Bean | Y | Y | Y | Y | Y | Y |
| 9 Schakowsky | Y | Y | Y | Y | N | Y |
| 10 Kirk | Y | Y | N | N | Y | Y |
| 11 Weller | Y | Y | N | N | Y | Y |
| 12 Costello | Y | Y | Y | Y | N | Y |

**KEY**   Republicans   Democrats   *Independents*

| Y | Voted for (yea) | X | Paired against | C | Voted "present" to avoid possible conflict of interest |
|---|---|---|---|---|---|
| # | Paired for | – | Announced against | | |
| + | Announced for | P | Voted "present" | ? | Did not vote or otherwise make a position known |
| N | Voted against (nay) | | | | |

| | 549 | 550 | 551 | 552 | 553 | 554 |
|---|---|---|---|---|---|---|
| 13 **Biggert** | Y | Y | N | N | Y | Y |
| 14 **Hastert** | | | | | | |
| 15 Johnson | Y | Y | Y | Y | Y | Y |
| 16 **Manzullo** | Y | Y | N | N | N | Y |
| 17 Evans | Y | Y | Y | Y | N | Y |
| 18 **LaHood** | Y | Y | N | N | Y | Y |
| 19 **Shimkus** | Y | Y | N | N | Y | Y |
| **INDIANA** | | | | | | |
| 1 Visclosky | Y | Y | Y | Y | N | Y |
| 2 **Chocola** | Y | Y | N | N | Y | Y |
| 3 **Souder** | Y | Y | N | N | Y | N |
| 4 **Buyer** | Y | Y | N | N | Y | N |
| 5 **Burton** | Y | Y | N | N | Y | N |
| 6 **Pence** | Y | Y | N | N | Y | N |
| 7 Carson | Y | Y | Y | Y | N | Y |
| 8 **Hostettler** | Y | Y | N | N | Y | N |
| 9 **Sodrel** | Y | Y | N | N | Y | N |
| **IOWA** | | | | | | |
| 1 **Nussle** | Y | Y | N | N | Y | Y |
| 2 **Leach** | Y | Y | N | N | Y | Y |
| 3 Boswell | ? | ? | ? | ? | ? | ? |
| 4 **Latham** | Y | Y | N | N | Y | Y |
| 5 **King** | Y | Y | N | N | Y | N |
| **KANSAS** | | | | | | |
| 1 **Moran** | Y | Y | N | N | Y | N |
| 2 **Ryun** | Y | Y | N | N | Y | N |
| 3 Moore | Y | Y | Y | Y | N | Y |
| 4 **Tiahrt** | Y | Y | N | N | Y | N |
| **KENTUCKY** | | | | | | |
| 1 **Whitfield** | ? | Y | N | N | Y | Y |
| 2 **Lewis** | Y | Y | N | N | Y | N |
| 3 **Northup** | Y | Y | N | N | Y | Y |
| 4 **Davis** | Y | Y | N | N | Y | N |
| 5 **Rogers** | Y | Y | N | N | Y | N |
| 6 Chandler | Y | Y | Y | Y | N | Y |
| **LOUISIANA** | | | | | | |
| 1 **Jindal** | Y | Y | N | N | Y | N |
| 2 Jefferson | Y | Y | Y | Y | N | Y |
| 3 Melancon | Y | Y | Y | Y | N | Y |
| 4 **McCrery** | Y | Y | N | N | Y | N |
| 5 **Alexander** | Y | Y | N | N | Y | N |
| 6 **Baker** | Y | Y | N | N | Y | N |
| 7 **Boustany** | Y | Y | N | N | Y | N |
| **MAINE** | | | | | | |
| 1 Allen | Y | Y | N | Y | N | Y |
| 2 Michaud | Y | Y | Y | Y | N | Y |
| **MARYLAND** | | | | | | |
| 1 **Gilchrest** | Y | Y | N | N | Y | Y |
| 2 Ruppersberger | Y | Y | Y | Y | N | Y |
| 3 Cardin | Y | Y | Y | Y | N | Y |
| 4 Wynn | Y | Y | Y | Y | N | Y |
| 5 Hoyer | Y | Y | Y | Y | N | Y |
| 6 **Bartlett** | Y | Y | N | N | Y | N |
| 7 Cummings | Y | Y | Y | Y | N | Y |
| 8 Van Hollen | Y | Y | Y | Y | N | Y |
| **MASSACHUSETTS** | | | | | | |
| 1 Olver | Y | Y | Y | Y | N | Y |
| 2 Neal | Y | ? | Y | Y | N | Y |
| 3 McGovern | Y | Y | Y | Y | N | Y |
| 4 Frank | Y | Y | Y | Y | N | Y |
| 5 Meehan | Y | Y | Y | Y | N | Y |
| 6 Tierney | Y | Y | Y | Y | N | Y |
| 7 Markey | Y | Y | Y | Y | N | Y |
| 8 Capuano | Y | Y | Y | Y | N | Y |
| 9 Lynch | Y | Y | Y | Y | N | ? |
| 10 Delahunt | Y | Y | Y | Y | N | Y |
| **MICHIGAN** | | | | | | |
| 1 Stupak | Y | Y | Y | Y | N | Y |
| 2 **Hoekstra** | Y | Y | N | N | Y | N |
| 3 **Ehlers** | Y | Y | N | N | Y | Y |
| 4 **Camp** | Y | Y | N | N | Y | N |
| 5 Kildee | Y | Y | Y | Y | N | Y |
| 6 **Upton** | Y | Y | N | N | Y | Y |
| 7 **Schwarz** | Y | Y | N | N | Y | Y |
| 8 **Rogers** | Y | Y | N | N | Y | N |
| 9 **Knollenberg** | Y | Y | N | N | Y | Y |
| 10 **Miller** | Y | Y | N | N | Y | N |
| 11 **McCotter** | Y | Y | N | N | Y | Y |
| 12 Levin | Y | Y | Y | Y | N | Y |
| 13 Kilpatrick | Y | Y | Y | Y | N | Y |
| 14 Conyers | Y | Y | Y | Y | N | Y |
| 15 Dingell | Y | Y | Y | Y | N | Y |

| | 549 | 550 | 551 | 552 | 553 | 554 |
|---|---|---|---|---|---|---|
| **MINNESOTA** | | | | | | |
| 1 **Gutknecht** | Y | Y | N | N | Y | N |
| 2 **Kline** | Y | Y | N | N | Y | N |
| 3 **Ramstad** | Y | Y | N | N | Y | Y |
| 4 McCollum | Y | Y | Y | Y | N | Y |
| 5 Sabo | Y | Y | Y | Y | N | Y |
| 6 **Kennedy** | Y | Y | N | N | Y | N |
| 7 Peterson | Y | Y | N | Y | Y | Y |
| 8 Oberstar | Y | Y | Y | Y | N | Y |
| **MISSISSIPPI** | | | | | | |
| 1 **Wicker** | Y | Y | N | N | Y | Y |
| 2 Thompson | Y | Y | Y | Y | N | Y |
| 3 **Pickering** | Y | Y | N | N | Y | N |
| 4 Taylor | Y | Y | Y | Y | Y | N |
| **MISSOURI** | | | | | | |
| 1 Clay | Y | Y | Y | Y | N | Y |
| 2 **Akin** | Y | Y | N | N | Y | N |
| 3 Carnahan | Y | Y | Y | Y | N | Y |
| 4 Skelton | Y | Y | Y | Y | N | Y |
| 5 Cleaver | Y | Y | Y | Y | N | Y |
| 6 **Graves** | Y | Y | N | N | ? | N |
| 7 **Blunt** | Y | Y | ? | ? | ? | ? |
| 8 **Emerson** | Y | Y | N | N | Y | Y |
| 9 **Hulshof** | Y | Y | N | N | Y | Y |
| **MONTANA** | | | | | | |
| AL **Rehberg** | Y | Y | N | N | Y | N |
| **NEBRASKA** | | | | | | |
| 1 **Fortenberry** | Y | Y | N | N | Y | N |
| 2 **Terry** | Y | Y | N | N | N | N |
| 3 **Osborne** | Y | Y | N | N | Y | Y |
| **NEVADA** | | | | | | |
| 1 Berkley | Y | Y | Y | Y | N | Y |
| 2 **Gibbons** | Y | Y | N | N | Y | N |
| 3 **Porter** | Y | Y | N | N | Y | N |
| **NEW HAMPSHIRE** | | | | | | |
| 1 **Bradley** | Y | Y | N | N | Y | N |
| 2 **Bass** | Y | Y | N | N | Y | N |
| **NEW JERSEY** | | | | | | |
| 1 Andrews | Y | Y | N | Y | N | Y |
| 2 **LoBiondo** | Y | Y | N | N | Y | Y |
| 3 **Saxton** | Y | Y | N | N | Y | Y |
| 4 **Smith** | Y | Y | N | N | Y | ? |
| 5 **Garrett** | Y | ? | N | N | Y | N |
| 6 Pallone | Y | Y | Y | Y | N | Y |
| 7 **Ferguson** | Y | Y | N | N | Y | Y |
| 8 Pascrell | Y | Y | Y | Y | N | Y |
| 9 Rothman | Y | Y | Y | Y | N | Y |
| 10 Payne | ? | ? | Y | Y | N | Y |
| 11 **Frelinghuysen** | Y | Y | N | N | Y | N |
| 12 Holt | Y | Y | Y | Y | N | Y |
| 13 Menendez | Y | Y | Y | Y | N | Y |
| **NEW MEXICO** | | | | | | |
| 1 **Wilson** | Y | Y | N | N | Y | Y |
| 2 **Pearce** | Y | Y | N | N | Y | N |
| 3 Udall | Y | Y | Y | Y | N | Y |
| **NEW YORK** | | | | | | |
| 1 Bishop | Y | Y | Y | Y | N | Y |
| 2 Israel | Y | Y | Y | Y | N | Y |
| 3 **King** | Y | Y | N | N | N | Y |
| 4 McCarthy | Y | Y | Y | Y | N | Y |
| 5 Ackerman | Y | Y | Y | Y | N | Y |
| 6 Meeks | Y | Y | ? | Y | N | Y |
| 7 Crowley | Y | Y | Y | Y | N | Y |
| 8 Nadler | Y | Y | N | Y | N | Y |
| 9 Weiner | Y | Y | Y | Y | N | Y |
| 10 Towns | Y | Y | Y | Y | N | Y |
| 11 Owens | Y | Y | Y | Y | N | Y |
| 12 Velázquez | Y | Y | Y | Y | N | ? |
| 13 **Fossella** | Y | Y | N | N | Y | Y |
| 14 Maloney | Y | Y | Y | Y | N | Y |
| 15 Rangel | Y | Y | Y | Y | N | Y |
| 16 Serrano | Y | Y | Y | Y | N | Y |
| 17 Engel | Y | Y | Y | Y | N | Y |
| 18 Lowey | Y | Y | Y | Y | N | Y |
| 19 **Kelly** | Y | Y | N | N | Y | N |
| 20 **Sweeney** | Y | Y | N | N | Y | Y |
| 21 McNulty | Y | Y | Y | Y | N | Y |
| 22 Hinchey | Y | Y | Y | Y | N | Y |
| 23 **McHugh** | Y | Y | N | N | Y | Y |
| 24 **Boehlert** | Y | Y | N | N | Y | Y |
| 25 **Walsh** | Y | Y | N | N | Y | N |
| 26 **Reynolds** | Y | Y | N | N | Y | Y |
| 27 Higgins | Y | Y | Y | Y | N | Y |
| 28 Slaughter | Y | Y | Y | Y | N | Y |
| 29 **Kuhl** | Y | Y | N | N | Y | Y |

| | 549 | 550 | 551 | 552 | 553 | 554 |
|---|---|---|---|---|---|---|
| **NORTH CAROLINA** | | | | | | |
| 1 Butterfield | Y | Y | Y | Y | N | Y |
| 2 Etheridge | Y | Y | Y | Y | N | Y |
| 3 **Jones** | Y | Y | N | N | Y | N |
| 4 Price | Y | Y | Y | Y | N | Y |
| 5 **Foxx** | Y | Y | N | N | Y | N |
| 6 **Coble** | Y | Y | N | N | Y | N |
| 7 McIntyre | Y | Y | Y | Y | N | Y |
| 8 **Hayes** | Y | Y | N | N | Y | N |
| 9 **Myrick** | Y | Y | N | N | Y | N |
| 10 **McHenry** | Y | Y | N | N | Y | N |
| 11 **Taylor** | Y | Y | N | N | Y | N |
| 12 Watt | Y | Y | Y | Y | N | Y |
| 13 Miller | Y | Y | Y | Y | N | Y |
| **NORTH DAKOTA** | | | | | | |
| AL Pomeroy | Y | Y | Y | Y | N | Y |
| **OHIO** | | | | | | |
| 1 **Chabot** | Y | Y | N | N | Y | N |
| 2 **Schmidt** | Y | Y | N | N | Y | N |
| 3 **Turner** | Y | Y | N | N | Y | Y |
| 4 **Oxley** | Y | Y | N | N | Y | N |
| 5 **Gillmor** | Y | Y | N | N | Y | Y |
| 6 Strickland | Y | Y | Y | Y | N | Y |
| 7 **Hobson** | Y | Y | N | N | Y | Y |
| 8 **Boehner** | Y | Y | N | N | Y | N |
| 9 Kaptur | Y | Y | Y | Y | N | Y |
| 10 Kucinich | Y | Y | N | Y | N | Y |
| 11 Jones | Y | Y | N | Y | N | Y |
| 12 **Tiberi** | Y | Y | N | N | Y | N |
| 13 Brown | Y | Y | Y | Y | N | Y |
| 14 **LaTourette** | Y | Y | N | N | Y | Y |
| 15 **Pryce** | Y | Y | N | N | Y | Y |
| 16 **Regula** | Y | Y | N | N | Y | Y |
| 17 Ryan | Y | Y | Y | Y | N | Y |
| 18 **Ney** | Y | Y | N | N | Y | Y |
| **OKLAHOMA** | | | | | | |
| 1 **Sullivan** | Y | Y | N | N | Y | N |
| 2 Boren | Y | Y | Y | Y | Y | Y |
| 3 **Lucas** | Y | Y | N | N | Y | N |
| 4 **Cole** | Y | Y | N | N | Y | N |
| 5 **Istook** | Y | Y | N | N | Y | N |
| **OREGON** | | | | | | |
| 1 Wu | Y | Y | Y | Y | N | Y |
| 2 **Walden** | Y | Y | N | N | Y | N |
| 3 Blumenauer | Y | Y | Y | Y | N | Y |
| 4 DeFazio | Y | Y | Y | Y | N | Y |
| 5 Hooley | Y | Y | Y | Y | N | Y |
| **PENNSYLVANIA** | | | | | | |
| 1 Brady | Y | Y | Y | Y | N | Y |
| 2 Fattah | Y | Y | Y | Y | N | Y |
| 3 **English** | Y | Y | N | N | Y | Y |
| 4 **Hart** | Y | Y | N | N | Y | N |
| 5 **Peterson** | Y | Y | N | N | Y | N |
| 6 **Gerlach** | Y | Y | N | N | Y | Y |
| 7 **Weldon** | Y | Y | N | N | Y | Y |
| 8 **Fitzpatrick** | Y | Y | N | N | N | Y |
| 9 **Shuster** | Y | Y | N | N | Y | N |
| 10 **Sherwood** | Y | Y | N | N | Y | Y |
| 11 Kanjorski | Y | Y | Y | Y | N | Y |
| 12 Murtha | Y | Y | Y | Y | N | Y |
| 13 Schwartz | Y | Y | Y | Y | N | Y |
| 14 Doyle | Y | Y | Y | Y | N | Y |
| 15 **Dent** | Y | Y | N | N | Y | Y |
| 16 **Pitts** | Y | Y | N | N | Y | N |
| 17 Holden | Y | Y | Y | Y | Y | Y |
| 18 **Murphy** | Y | Y | N | N | Y | N |
| 19 **Platts** | Y | Y | N | N | Y | Y |
| **RHODE ISLAND** | | | | | | |
| 1 Kennedy | Y | Y | Y | Y | N | Y |
| 2 Langevin | Y | Y | Y | Y | N | Y |
| **SOUTH CAROLINA** | | | | | | |
| 1 **Brown** | Y | Y | N | N | Y | N |
| 2 **Wilson** | Y | Y | N | N | Y | N |
| 3 **Barrett** | Y | Y | N | N | Y | N |
| 4 **Inglis** | Y | Y | N | N | Y | N |
| 5 Spratt | Y | Y | Y | Y | N | Y |
| 6 Clyburn | Y | Y | ? | ? | ? | ? |
| **SOUTH DAKOTA** | | | | | | |
| AL Herseth | Y | Y | Y | Y | N | Y |
| **TENNESSEE** | | | | | | |
| 1 **Jenkins** | Y | Y | N | N | Y | N |
| 2 **Duncan** | Y | Y | N | N | Y | N |

| | 549 | 550 | 551 | 552 | 553 | 554 |
|---|---|---|---|---|---|---|
| 3 **Wamp** | Y | Y | N | N | Y | N |
| 4 Davis | Y | Y | Y | Y | Y | Y |
| 5 Cooper | Y | Y | Y | Y | N | Y |
| 6 Gordon | Y | Y | Y | Y | Y | Y |
| 7 **Blackburn** | Y | Y | N | N | Y | N |
| 8 Tanner | Y | Y | Y | Y | Y | Y |
| 9 Ford | Y | Y | Y | Y | N | ? |
| **TEXAS** | | | | | | |
| 1 **Gohmert** | ? | ? | N | N | Y | N |
| 2 **Poe** | Y | Y | N | N | Y | N |
| 3 **Johnson, S.** | Y | Y | N | N | Y | N |
| 4 **Hall** | ? | ? | ? | ? | ? | ? |
| 5 **Hensarling** | Y | Y | N | N | Y | N |
| 6 **Barton** | Y | Y | N | N | Y | N |
| 7 **Culberson** | Y | ? | N | N | Y | N |
| 8 **Brady** | Y | Y | N | N | Y | N |
| 9 Green, A. | Y | Y | Y | Y | N | Y |
| 10 **McCaul** | Y | Y | N | N | Y | N |
| 11 **Conaway** | Y | Y | N | N | Y | Y |
| 12 **Granger** | Y | Y | N | N | Y | ? |
| 13 **Thornberry** | Y | Y | N | N | Y | N |
| 14 **Paul** | Y | Y | N | N | Y | N |
| 15 Hinojosa | Y | Y | Y | Y | N | Y |
| 16 Reyes | ? | ? | ? | ? | ? | ? |
| 17 Edwards | Y | Y | Y | Y | Y | Y |
| 18 Jackson-Lee | Y | Y | Y | Y | N | Y |
| 19 **Neugebauer** | Y | Y | N | N | Y | N |
| 20 Gonzalez | Y | Y | Y | Y | N | Y |
| 21 **Smith** | Y | Y | N | N | Y | N |
| 22 **DeLay** | Y | Y | N | N | Y | N |
| 23 **Bonilla** | Y | Y | N | N | Y | N |
| 24 **Marchant** | Y | Y | ? | N | Y | N |
| 25 Doggett | Y | Y | Y | Y | N | Y |
| 26 **Burgess** | Y | Y | N | N | Y | N |
| 27 Ortiz | Y | Y | Y | Y | N | Y |
| 28 Cuellar | Y | Y | Y | Y | Y | Y |
| 29 Green, G. | Y | Y | Y | Y | N | Y |
| 30 Johnson, E. | Y | Y | Y | Y | N | Y |
| 31 **Carter** | Y | Y | N | N | Y | N |
| 32 **Sessions** | Y | Y | N | N | Y | N |
| **UTAH** | | | | | | |
| 1 **Bishop** | Y | Y | N | N | Y | N |
| 2 Matheson | Y | Y | Y | Y | Y | Y |
| 3 **Cannon** | Y | Y | N | N | Y | N |
| **VERMONT** | | | | | | |
| AL *Sanders* | Y | Y | Y | Y | N | Y |
| **VIRGINIA** | | | | | | |
| 1 **Davis, J.** | Y | Y | N | N | Y | N |
| 2 **Drake** | Y | Y | N | N | Y | N |
| 3 Scott | Y | Y | Y | Y | N | Y |
| 4 **Forbes** | Y | Y | N | N | Y | N |
| 5 **Goode** | Y | Y | N | N | Y | N |
| 6 **Goodlatte** | Y | Y | N | N | Y | N |
| 7 **Cantor** | Y | Y | N | N | Y | N |
| 8 Moran | Y | Y | Y | Y | N | Y |
| 9 Boucher | Y | Y | Y | Y | N | Y |
| 10 **Wolf** | Y | Y | N | N | Y | Y |
| 11 **Davis, T.** | Y | Y | N | N | Y | Y |
| **WASHINGTON** | | | | | | |
| 1 Inslee | Y | Y | Y | Y | N | Y |
| 2 Larsen | Y | Y | Y | Y | N | Y |
| 3 Baird | Y | Y | Y | Y | N | Y |
| 4 **Hastings** | Y | Y | N | N | Y | N |
| 5 **McMorris** | Y | Y | N | N | Y | N |
| 6 Dicks | Y | ? | Y | Y | N | Y |
| 7 McDermott | Y | Y | Y | Y | N | Y |
| 8 **Reichert** | Y | Y | N | N | Y | Y |
| 9 Smith | Y | Y | Y | Y | N | Y |
| **WEST VIRGINIA** | | | | | | |
| 1 Mollohan | Y | Y | Y | Y | N | Y |
| 2 **Capito** | Y | Y | N | N | Y | Y |
| 3 Rahall | Y | Y | Y | Y | N | Y |
| **WISCONSIN** | | | | | | |
| 1 **Ryan** | Y | Y | N | N | Y | Y |
| 2 Baldwin | Y | Y | Y | Y | N | Y |
| 3 Kind | Y | Y | Y | Y | N | Y |
| 4 Moore | Y | Y | Y | Y | N | Y |
| 5 **Sensenbrenner** | ? | ? | ? | ? | ? | ? |
| 6 **Petri** | Y | Y | N | N | Y | N |
| 7 Obey | ? | ? | ? | ? | ? | ? |
| 8 **Green** | Y | Y | N | N | Y | N |
| **WYOMING** | | | | | | |
| AL **Cubin** | Y | Y | N | N | Y | N |

# IN THE HOUSE | By Vote Number

**555.** **HR 2744. Fiscal 2006 Agriculture Appropriations/Conference Report.** Adoption of the conference report on the bill that would appropriate $101 billion in fiscal 2006 for the Department of Agriculture, the Food and Drug Administration (FDA) and related agencies. The bill would provide $40.7 billion for the food stamp program, $12.7 billion for child nutrition, $25.7 billion for the Commodity Credit Corporation, $5.3 billion for the Women, Infants and Children program and $1.5 billion for the FDA. Adopted (thus sent to the Senate) 318-63: R 163-41; D 154-22 (ND 114-18, SD 40-4); I 1-0. Oct. 28, 2005.

**556.** **H Res 523. Condemnation Against Iran President/Adoption.** Adoption of the resolution that would condemn Iranian President Mahmoud Ahmadinejad's threats against Israel and nations that support Israel. Adopted 383-0: R 204-0; D 178-0 (ND 135-0, SD 43-0); I 1-0. Oct. 28, 2005.

**557.** **HR 3548. Heinz Ahlmeyer Jr. Post Office/Passage.** Gutknecht, R-Minn, motion to suspend the rules and pass the bill that would designate a post office in Pearl River, N.Y., for Heinz Ahlmeyer Jr., who was killed in action in Vietnam. Motion agreed to 390-0: R 214-0; D 175-0 (ND 131-0, SD 44-0); I 1-0. A two-thirds majority of those present and voting (260 in this case) is required for passage under suspension of the rules. Nov. 1, 2005.

**558.** **HR 3989. Albert Harold Quie Post Office/Passage.** Gutknecht, R-Minn, motion to suspend the rules and pass the bill that would designate a post office in Dennison, Minn., for Albert Harold Quie, R-Minn. (1958-79), who served 10 full terms in the House and one term as governor. Motion agreed to 391-1: R 213-0; D 177-1 (ND 132-1, SD 45-0); I 1-0. A two-thirds majority of those present and voting (262 in this case) is required for passage under suspension of the rules. Nov. 1, 2005.

**559.** **HR 1606. Online Freedom of Speech/Passage.** Miller, R-Mich., motion to suspend the rules and pass the bill that would exempt the Internet, including blogs and e-mail, from being considered a form of public communication subject to Federal Election Commission regulation and disclosure requirements. Motion rejected 225-182: R 179-38; D 46-143 (ND 34-108, SD 12-35); I 0-1. A two-thirds majority of those present and voting (272 in this case) is required for passage under suspension of the rules. Nov. 2, 2005.

**560.** **HR 4061. Veterans' Affairs Information Technology/Passage.** Buyer, R-Ind., motion to suspend the rules and pass the bill that would reorganize the information technology (IT) division of the Department of Veterans Affairs (VA) and give the VA chief information officer authority over all IT resources, budget and personnel. Motion agreed to 408-0: R 218-0; D 189-0 (ND 142-0, SD 47-0); I 1-0. A two-thirds majority of those present and voting (272 in this case) is required for passage under suspension of the rules. Nov. 2, 2005.

**561.** **HR 1691. John H. Bradley Outpatient Clinic/Passage.** Buyer, R-Ind., motion to suspend the rules and pass the bill that would designate a Veterans Affairs Department outpatient clinic in Appleton, Wis., for John H. Bradley, one of six Marines who raised a U.S. flag on the top of Mt. Suribachi at Iwo Jima. Motion agreed to 407-0: R 218-0; D 188-0 (ND 141-0, SD 47-0); I 1-0. A two-thirds majority of those present and voting (272 in this case) is required for passage under suspension of the rules. Nov. 2, 2005.

| | 555 | 556 | 557 | 558 | 559 | 560 | 561 |
|---|---|---|---|---|---|---|---|
| **ALABAMA** | | | | | | | |
| 1 Bonner | Y | Y | Y | Y | Y | Y | Y |
| 2 Everett | Y | Y | Y | Y | Y | Y | Y |
| 3 Rogers | Y | Y | Y | Y | Y | Y | Y |
| 4 Aderholt | Y | Y | Y | Y | Y | Y | Y |
| 5 Cramer | Y | Y | Y | Y | Y | Y | Y |
| 6 Bachus | Y | Y | Y | Y | Y | Y | Y |
| 7 Davis | Y | Y | Y | Y | N | Y | Y |
| **ALASKA** | | | | | | | |
| AL Young | Y | Y | Y | Y | ? | ? | ? |
| **ARIZONA** | | | | | | | |
| 1 Renzi | Y | Y | Y | Y | Y | Y | Y |
| 2 Franks | N | Y | Y | Y | Y | Y | Y |
| 3 Shadegg | ? | ? | Y | Y | Y | Y | Y |
| 4 Pastor | Y | Y | Y | Y | N | Y | Y |
| 5 Hayworth | N | Y | Y | Y | Y | Y | Y |
| 6 Flake | N | Y | Y | Y | Y | Y | Y |
| 7 Grijalva | Y | Y | Y | Y | N | Y | Y |
| 8 Kolbe | Y | Y | Y | Y | Y | Y | Y |
| **ARKANSAS** | | | | | | | |
| 1 Berry | Y | Y | Y | Y | N | Y | Y |
| 2 Snyder | Y | Y | Y | Y | N | Y | Y |
| 3 Boozman | Y | Y | Y | Y | Y | Y | Y |
| 4 Ross | Y | Y | Y | Y | Y | Y | Y |
| **CALIFORNIA** | | | | | | | |
| 1 Thompson | Y | Y | Y | Y | Y | Y | Y |
| 2 Herger | Y | Y | Y | Y | Y | Y | Y |
| 3 Lungren | Y | Y | Y | Y | Y | Y | Y |
| 4 Doolittle | Y | Y | Y | Y | Y | Y | Y |
| 5 Matsui, D. | Y | Y | Y | Y | N | Y | Y |
| 6 Woolsey | Y | Y | Y | Y | N | Y | Y |
| 7 Miller, George | Y | Y | Y | Y | N | Y | Y |
| 8 Pelosi | ? | ? | Y | Y | N | Y | Y |
| 9 Lee | N | Y | Y | Y | N | Y | Y |
| 10 Tauscher | ? | ? | Y | Y | N | Y | Y |
| 11 Pombo | Y | Y | + | + | + | + | + |
| 12 Lantos | Y | Y | Y | Y | N | Y | Y |
| 13 Stark | ? | ? | Y | Y | ? | ? | ? |
| 14 Eshoo | + | + | Y | Y | Y | Y | Y |
| 15 Honda | N | Y | Y | Y | N | Y | Y |
| 16 Lofgren | Y | Y | Y | Y | N | Y | Y |
| 17 Farr | Y | Y | Y | Y | N | Y | Y |
| 18 Cardoza | Y | Y | Y | Y | Y | Y | Y |
| 19 Radanovich | Y | Y | Y | Y | ? | ? | Y |
| 20 Costa | Y | Y | Y | Y | Y | Y | Y |
| 21 Nunes | + | + | Y | Y | Y | Y | Y |
| 22 Thomas | Y | Y | Y | Y | Y | Y | Y |
| 23 Capps | Y | Y | Y | Y | N | Y | Y |
| 24 Gallegly | + | + | + | + | N | Y | Y |
| 25 McKeon | ? | ? | Y | Y | Y | Y | Y |
| 26 Dreier | Y | Y | Y | Y | Y | Y | Y |
| 27 Sherman | Y | Y | Y | Y | N | Y | Y |
| 28 Berman | ? | Y | ? | Y | Y | Y | Y |
| 29 Schiff | Y | Y | Y | Y | N | Y | Y |
| 30 Waxman | Y | Y | Y | Y | N | Y | Y |
| 31 Becerra | + | + | Y | Y | N | Y | Y |
| 32 Solis | Y | Y | Y | Y | N | Y | Y |
| 33 Watson | Y | Y | Y | Y | N | Y | Y |
| 34 Roybal-Allard | ? | ? | ? | ? | ? | ? | ? |
| 35 Waters | Y | Y | Y | Y | N | Y | Y |
| 36 Harman | Y | Y | Y | Y | ? | ? | Y |
| 37 Millender-McD. | ? | Y | Y | Y | N | Y | Y |
| 38 Napolitano | ? | ? | Y | Y | N | Y | Y |
| 39 Sánchez, Linda | Y | Y | Y | Y | N | Y | Y |
| 40 Royce | N | Y | Y | Y | Y | Y | Y |
| 41 Lewis | Y | Y | Y | Y | Y | Y | Y |
| 42 Miller, Gary | ? | ? | ? | ? | Y | Y | Y |
| 43 Baca | Y | Y | Y | Y | Y | Y | Y |
| 44 Calvert | ? | ? | Y | Y | Y | Y | Y |
| 45 Bono | N | Y | Y | Y | Y | Y | Y |
| 46 Rohrabacher | N | Y | ? | ? | Y | Y | Y |
| 47 Sanchez, Loretta | Y | Y | Y | Y | N | Y | Y |
| 48 Vacant | | | | | | | |
| 49 Issa | Y | Y | Y | Y | Y | Y | Y |

| | 555 | 556 | 557 | 558 | 559 | 560 | 561 |
|---|---|---|---|---|---|---|---|
| 50 **Cunningham** | Y | Y | Y | Y | Y | Y | Y |
| 51 **Filner** | Y | Y | Y | N | Y | Y | Y |
| 52 **Hunter** | Y | Y | Y | Y | Y | Y | Y |
| 53 Davis | Y | Y | Y | N | N | Y | Y |
| **COLORADO** | | | | | | | |
| 1 DeGette | Y | Y | Y | Y | N | Y | Y |
| 2 Udall | Y | Y | + | + | Y | Y | Y |
| 3 Salazar | Y | Y | Y | Y | Y | Y | Y |
| 4 Musgrave | Y | Y | Y | Y | Y | Y | Y |
| 5 Hefley | N | Y | Y | Y | N | Y | Y |
| 6 Tancredo | N | Y | Y | Y | N | Y | Y |
| 7 Beauprez | Y | Y | Y | Y | Y | Y | Y |
| **CONNECTICUT** | | | | | | | |
| 1 Larson | Y | Y | Y | Y | N | Y | Y |
| 2 Simmons | N | Y | Y | Y | N | Y | Y |
| 3 DeLauro | Y | Y | Y | Y | N | Y | Y |
| 4 Shays | N | Y | ? | ? | N | Y | Y |
| 5 Johnson | Y | Y | Y | Y | N | Y | Y |
| **DELAWARE** | | | | | | | |
| AL Castle | Y | Y | Y | N | Y | Y | Y |
| **FLORIDA** | | | | | | | |
| 1 Miller | Y | Y | Y | Y | + | – | + |
| 2 Boyd | Y | Y | Y | Y | Y | Y | Y |
| 3 Brown | Y | Y | ? | ? | N | Y | Y |
| 4 Crenshaw | Y | Y | Y | Y | Y | Y | Y |
| 5 Brown-Waite | ? | ? | ? | ? | ? | ? | ? |
| 6 Stearns | N | Y | Y | Y | Y | Y | Y |
| 7 Mica | Y | Y | Y | Y | Y | Y | Y |
| 8 Keller | Y | Y | Y | Y | Y | Y | Y |
| 9 Bilirakis | N | Y | Y | Y | Y | Y | Y |
| 10 Young | Y | Y | Y | Y | Y | Y | Y |
| 11 Davis | ? | ? | ? | ? | N | Y | Y |
| 12 Putnam | Y | Y | Y | Y | Y | Y | Y |
| 13 Harris | ? | ? | Y | Y | Y | Y | Y |
| 14 Mack | Y | Y | Y | Y | Y | Y | Y |
| 15 Weldon | Y | Y | Y | Y | Y | Y | Y |
| 16 Foley | Y | Y | ? | ? | Y | Y | Y |
| 17 Meek | ? | ? | Y | Y | N | Y | Y |
| 18 Ros-Lehtinen | Y | Y | Y | Y | Y | Y | Y |
| 19 Wexler | Y | Y | Y | N | Y | Y | Y |
| 20 Wasserman-Schultz | Y | Y | Y | Y | N | Y | Y |
| 21 Diaz-Balart, L. | ? | ? | Y | Y | Y | Y | Y |
| 22 Shaw | ? | ? | Y | Y | Y | Y | Y |
| 23 Hastings | Y | Y | ? | ? | ? | ? | ? |
| 24 Feeney | N | Y | Y | Y | Y | Y | Y |
| 25 Diaz-Balart, M. | ? | ? | Y | Y | Y | Y | Y |
| **GEORGIA** | | | | | | | |
| 1 Kingston | ? | ? | Y | Y | Y | Y | Y |
| 2 Bishop | Y | Y | Y | Y | Y | Y | Y |
| 3 Marshall | Y | Y | Y | Y | ? | ? | Y |
| 4 McKinney | Y | ? | Y | Y | N | Y | Y |
| 5 Lewis | N | Y | Y | Y | N | Y | Y |
| 6 Price | N | Y | Y | Y | Y | Y | Y |
| 7 Linder | + | + | Y | Y | Y | Y | Y |
| 8 Westmoreland | ? | ? | Y | Y | Y | Y | Y |
| 9 Norwood | Y | Y | ? | ? | ? | ? | ? |
| 10 Deal | Y | Y | Y | Y | Y | Y | Y |
| 11 Gingrey | Y | Y | Y | Y | Y | Y | Y |
| 12 Barrow | Y | Y | Y | Y | Y | Y | Y |
| 13 Scott | Y | Y | Y | Y | Y | Y | Y |
| **HAWAII** | | | | | | | |
| 1 Abercrombie | Y | Y | Y | N | Y | Y | Y |
| 2 Case | Y | Y | Y | N | Y | Y | Y |
| **IDAHO** | | | | | | | |
| 1 Otter | N | Y | Y | Y | Y | Y | Y |
| 2 Simpson | Y | Y | Y | Y | Y | Y | Y |
| **ILLINOIS** | | | | | | | |
| 1 Rush | Y | Y | ? | ? | N | Y | Y |
| 2 Jackson | Y | Y | ? | ? | N | Y | Y |
| 3 Lipinski | Y | Y | Y | Y | N | Y | Y |
| 4 Gutierrez | + | + | + | + | N | Y | Y |
| 5 Emanuel | Y | Y | Y | Y | N | Y | Y |
| 6 Hyde | Y | Y | + | + | – | + | + |
| 7 Davis | Y | Y | Y | Y | N | Y | Y |
| 8 Bean | N | Y | Y | Y | Y | Y | Y |
| 9 Schakowsky | N | Y | Y | Y | N | Y | Y |
| 10 Kirk | N | Y | Y | Y | N | Y | Y |
| 11 Weller | Y | Y | Y | Y | Y | Y | Y |
| 12 Costello | Y | Y | ? | ? | N | Y | Y |

**KEY**  Republicans  Democrats  *Independents*

| | | | |
|---|---|---|---|
| Y | Voted for (yea) | X | Paired against |
| # | Paired for | – | Announced against |
| + | Announced for | P | Voted "present" |
| N | Voted against (nay) | | |

| | |
|---|---|
| C | Voted "present" to avoid possible conflict of interest |
| ? | Did not vote or otherwise make a position known |

| | 555 | 556 | 557 | 558 | 559 | 560 | 561 |
|---|---|---|---|---|---|---|---|
| 13 **Biggert** | N | Y | Y | Y | Y | Y | Y |
| 14 **Hastert** | | | | | | | |
| 15 **Johnson** | Y | Y | Y | Y | N | Y | Y |
| 16 **Manzullo** | Y | Y | Y | Y | Y | Y | Y |
| 17 Evans | Y | Y | Y | Y | N | Y | Y |
| 18 **LaHood** | Y | Y | Y | Y | N | Y | Y |
| 19 **Shimkus** | Y | Y | Y | Y | Y | Y | Y |
| **INDIANA** | | | | | | | |
| 1 Visclosky | Y | Y | Y | Y | N | Y | Y |
| 2 **Chocola** | N | Y | Y | Y | Y | Y | Y |
| 3 **Souder** | Y | Y | Y | Y | Y | Y | Y |
| 4 **Buyer** | Y | Y | Y | Y | Y | Y | Y |
| 5 **Burton** | Y | Y | Y | Y | Y | Y | Y |
| 6 **Pence** | N | Y | Y | Y | Y | Y | Y |
| 7 Carson | Y | Y | Y | Y | N | Y | Y |
| 8 **Hostettler** | N | Y | Y | Y | Y | Y | Y |
| 9 **Sodrel** | Y | Y | Y | Y | Y | Y | Y |
| **IOWA** | | | | | | | |
| 1 **Nussle** | Y | Y | Y | Y | Y | Y | Y |
| 2 **Leach** | Y | Y | Y | Y | N | Y | Y |
| 3 Boswell | ? | ? | ? | ? | ? | ? | ? |
| 4 **Latham** | Y | Y | Y | Y | Y | Y | Y |
| 5 **King** | Y | Y | Y | Y | Y | Y | Y |
| **KANSAS** | | | | | | | |
| 1 **Moran** | Y | Y | Y | Y | Y | Y | Y |
| 2 **Ryun** | Y | Y | Y | Y | Y | Y | Y |
| 3 Moore | Y | Y | Y | Y | N | Y | Y |
| 4 **Tiahrt** | + | + | Y | Y | Y | Y | Y |
| **KENTUCKY** | | | | | | | |
| 1 **Whitfield** | N | Y | Y | Y | Y | Y | Y |
| 2 **Lewis** | Y | Y | Y | Y | Y | Y | Y |
| 3 **Northup** | Y | Y | Y | Y | Y | Y | Y |
| 4 **Davis** | Y | Y | Y | Y | Y | Y | Y |
| 5 **Rogers** | Y | Y | Y | Y | Y | Y | Y |
| 6 Chandler | Y | Y | Y | Y | Y | Y | Y |
| **LOUISIANA** | | | | | | | |
| 1 **Jindal** | Y | Y | Y | Y | Y | Y | Y |
| 2 Jefferson | ? | ? | Y | Y | N | Y | Y |
| 3 Melancon | Y | Y | Y | Y | Y | Y | Y |
| 4 **McCrery** | Y | Y | Y | Y | Y | Y | Y |
| 5 **Alexander** | Y | Y | Y | Y | Y | Y | Y |
| 6 **Baker** | ? | ? | Y | Y | Y | Y | Y |
| 7 **Boustany** | Y | Y | Y | Y | Y | Y | Y |
| **MAINE** | | | | | | | |
| 1 Allen | Y | Y | Y | Y | N | Y | Y |
| 2 Michaud | Y | Y | Y | Y | N | Y | Y |
| **MARYLAND** | | | | | | | |
| 1 **Gilchrest** | Y | Y | Y | Y | N | Y | Y |
| 2 Ruppersberger | Y | Y | Y | Y | N | Y | Y |
| 3 Cardin | Y | Y | Y | Y | N | Y | Y |
| 4 Wynn | Y | Y | ? | ? | Y | Y | Y |
| 5 Hoyer | Y | Y | ? | ? | Y | Y | Y |
| 6 **Bartlett** | Y | Y | Y | Y | Y | Y | Y |
| 7 Cummings | Y | Y | ? | ? | N | Y | Y |
| 8 Van Hollen | Y | Y | Y | Y | N | Y | Y |
| **MASSACHUSETTS** | | | | | | | |
| 1 Olver | Y | Y | Y | Y | N | Y | Y |
| 2 Neal | Y | Y | Y | Y | N | Y | Y |
| 3 McGovern | Y | Y | Y | Y | N | Y | Y |
| 4 Frank | Y | Y | Y | Y | N | Y | Y |
| 5 Meehan | Y | Y | Y | Y | N | Y | Y |
| 6 Tierney | Y | Y | Y | Y | N | Y | Y |
| 7 Markey | Y | Y | Y | Y | N | Y | Y |
| 8 Capuano | N | Y | ? | ? | Y | Y | Y |
| 9 Lynch | ? | Y | Y | Y | N | Y | Y |
| 10 Delahunt | Y | Y | Y | Y | N | Y | Y |
| **MICHIGAN** | | | | | | | |
| 1 Stupak | Y | Y | Y | Y | N | Y | Y |
| 2 **Hoekstra** | Y | Y | Y | Y | Y | Y | Y |
| 3 **Ehlers** | Y | Y | Y | Y | Y | Y | Y |
| 4 **Camp** | Y | Y | Y | Y | Y | Y | Y |
| 5 Kildee | Y | Y | Y | Y | N | Y | Y |
| 6 **Upton** | Y | Y | Y | Y | N | Y | Y |
| 7 **Schwarz** | Y | Y | Y | Y | N | Y | Y |
| 8 **Rogers** | Y | Y | Y | Y | Y | Y | Y |
| 9 **Knollenberg** | Y | Y | Y | Y | Y | Y | Y |
| 10 **Miller** | Y | Y | Y | Y | Y | Y | Y |
| 11 **McCotter** | Y | Y | Y | Y | Y | Y | Y |
| 12 Levin | Y | Y | Y | Y | N | Y | Y |
| 13 Kilpatrick | Y | Y | Y | Y | N | Y | Y |
| 14 Conyers | N | Y | Y | Y | Y | Y | Y |
| 15 Dingell | Y | Y | ? | ? | N | Y | Y |
| **MINNESOTA** | | | | | | | |
| 1 **Gutknecht** | Y | Y | Y | Y | Y | Y | Y |
| 2 **Kline** | Y | Y | Y | Y | Y | Y | Y |
| 3 **Ramstad** | N | Y | Y | Y | N | Y | Y |
| 4 McCollum | N | Y | ? | ? | ? | ? | ? |
| 5 Sabo | Y | Y | Y | Y | ? | ? | ? |
| 6 **Kennedy** | Y | Y | Y | Y | Y | Y | Y |
| 7 Peterson | Y | Y | Y | Y | Y | Y | Y |
| 8 Oberstar | Y | Y | Y | Y | N | Y | Y |
| **MISSISSIPPI** | | | | | | | |
| 1 **Wicker** | Y | ? | Y | Y | Y | Y | Y |
| 2 Thompson | Y | Y | ? | ? | N | Y | Y |
| 3 **Pickering** | Y | Y | Y | Y | Y | Y | Y |
| 4 Taylor | Y | Y | Y | Y | N | Y | Y |
| **MISSOURI** | | | | | | | |
| 1 Clay | Y | Y | Y | Y | Y | Y | Y |
| 2 **Akin** | Y | Y | Y | Y | Y | Y | Y |
| 3 Carnahan | Y | Y | Y | Y | N | Y | Y |
| 4 Skelton | Y | Y | Y | Y | N | Y | Y |
| 5 Cleaver | Y | Y | Y | Y | N | Y | Y |
| 6 **Graves** | Y | Y | Y | Y | Y | Y | Y |
| 7 **Blunt** | ? | ? | Y | Y | Y | Y | Y |
| 8 **Emerson** | Y | Y | Y | Y | N | Y | Y |
| 9 **Hulshof** | Y | Y | Y | Y | Y | Y | Y |
| **MONTANA** | | | | | | | |
| AL **Rehberg** | N | Y | Y | Y | Y | Y | Y |
| **NEBRASKA** | | | | | | | |
| 1 **Fortenberry** | Y | Y | Y | Y | Y | Y | Y |
| 2 **Terry** | Y | Y | ? | ? | Y | Y | Y |
| 3 **Osborne** | Y | Y | Y | Y | N | Y | Y |
| **NEVADA** | | | | | | | |
| 1 Berkley | Y | Y | Y | Y | N | Y | Y |
| 2 **Gibbons** | N | Y | Y | Y | Y | Y | Y |
| 3 **Porter** | Y | Y | Y | Y | Y | Y | Y |
| **NEW HAMPSHIRE** | | | | | | | |
| 1 **Bradley** | N | Y | Y | Y | N | Y | Y |
| 2 **Bass** | N | Y | Y | Y | N | Y | Y |
| **NEW JERSEY** | | | | | | | |
| 1 Andrews | N | Y | + | + | N | Y | Y |
| 2 **LoBiondo** | Y | Y | Y | Y | N | Y | Y |
| 3 **Saxton** | Y | Y | Y | Y | N | Y | Y |
| 4 **Smith** | Y | Y | Y | Y | N | Y | Y |
| 5 **Garrett** | N | Y | Y | Y | Y | Y | Y |
| 6 Pallone | Y | Y | Y | Y | N | Y | Y |
| 7 **Ferguson** | N | Y | Y | Y | Y | Y | Y |
| 8 Pascrell | Y | Y | Y | Y | N | Y | Y |
| 9 Rothman | Y | Y | Y | Y | N | Y | Y |
| 10 Payne | N | Y | Y | Y | N | Y | Y |
| 11 **Frelinghuysen** | Y | Y | Y | Y | N | Y | Y |
| 12 Holt | Y | Y | Y | Y | N | Y | Y |
| 13 Menendez | Y | Y | Y | Y | – | + | + |
| **NEW MEXICO** | | | | | | | |
| 1 **Wilson** | Y | Y | Y | Y | N | Y | Y |
| 2 **Pearce** | Y | Y | ? | ? | ? | ? | ? |
| 3 Udall | Y | Y | Y | Y | N | Y | Y |
| **NEW YORK** | | | | | | | |
| 1 Bishop | Y | Y | Y | Y | N | Y | Y |
| 2 Israel | N | Y | Y | Y | N | Y | Y |
| 3 **King** | Y | Y | Y | Y | ? | ? | ? |
| 4 McCarthy | Y | Y | Y | Y | N | Y | Y |
| 5 Ackerman | Y | Y | Y | Y | ? | ? | ? |
| 6 Meeks | Y | Y | Y | Y | N | Y | Y |
| 7 Crowley | Y | Y | Y | Y | N | Y | Y |
| 8 Nadler | N | Y | Y | Y | N | Y | Y |
| 9 Weiner | Y | Y | Y | Y | N | Y | Y |
| 10 Towns | ? | ? | Y | Y | N | Y | ? |
| 11 Owens | N | Y | Y | Y | N | Y | Y |
| 12 Velázquez | ? | ? | Y | Y | N | Y | Y |
| 13 **Fossella** | N | Y | Y | Y | Y | Y | Y |
| 14 Maloney | Y | Y | + | + | N | Y | Y |
| 15 Rangel | Y | Y | Y | Y | N | Y | Y |
| 16 Serrano | Y | Y | Y | Y | N | Y | Y |
| 17 Engel | N | Y | Y | Y | N | Y | Y |
| 18 Lowey | Y | Y | Y | Y | N | Y | Y |
| 19 **Kelly** | Y | Y | Y | Y | Y | Y | Y |
| 20 **Sweeney** | N | Y | Y | Y | Y | Y | Y |
| 21 McNulty | Y | Y | Y | Y | N | Y | Y |
| 22 Hinchey | Y | Y | ? | Y | N | Y | Y |
| 23 **McHugh** | Y | Y | Y | Y | Y | Y | Y |
| 24 **Boehlert** | ? | ? | Y | Y | N | Y | Y |
| 25 **Walsh** | Y | Y | Y | Y | N | Y | Y |
| 26 **Reynolds** | Y | Y | Y | Y | Y | Y | Y |
| 27 Higgins | Y | Y | Y | Y | N | Y | Y |
| 28 Slaughter | ? | ? | Y | Y | N | Y | Y |
| 29 **Kuhl** | Y | Y | Y | Y | Y | Y | Y |
| **NORTH CAROLINA** | | | | | | | |
| 1 Butterfield | Y | Y | Y | Y | N | Y | Y |
| 2 Etheridge | Y | Y | Y | Y | – | + | + |
| 3 **Jones** | – | + | Y | Y | Y | Y | Y |
| 4 Price | Y | Y | Y | Y | N | Y | Y |
| 5 **Foxx** | Y | Y | Y | Y | Y | Y | Y |
| 6 **Coble** | Y | Y | Y | Y | N | Y | Y |
| 7 McIntyre | Y | Y | Y | Y | N | Y | Y |
| 8 **Hayes** | Y | Y | Y | Y | Y | Y | Y |
| 9 **Myrick** | Y | Y | Y | Y | Y | Y | Y |
| 10 **McHenry** | Y | Y | Y | Y | Y | Y | Y |
| 11 **Taylor** | Y | Y | Y | Y | Y | Y | Y |
| 12 Watt | Y | Y | Y | Y | N | Y | Y |
| 13 Miller | Y | Y | Y | Y | N | Y | Y |
| **NORTH DAKOTA** | | | | | | | |
| AL Pomeroy | Y | Y | Y | Y | N | Y | Y |
| **OHIO** | | | | | | | |
| 1 **Chabot** | Y | Y | Y | Y | Y | Y | Y |
| 2 **Schmidt** | Y | Y | Y | Y | N | Y | Y |
| 3 **Turner** | Y | Y | Y | Y | N | Y | Y |
| 4 **Oxley** | Y | Y | + | + | ? | ? | ? |
| 5 **Gillmor** | Y | Y | Y | Y | N | Y | Y |
| 6 Strickland | Y | Y | Y | ? | Y | Y | Y |
| 7 **Hobson** | Y | Y | Y | Y | N | Y | Y |
| 8 **Boehner** | Y | Y | Y | Y | Y | Y | Y |
| 9 Kaptur | Y | Y | Y | Y | N | Y | Y |
| 10 Kucinich | N | Y | Y | Y | N | Y | Y |
| 11 Jones | Y | Y | Y | Y | N | Y | Y |
| 12 **Tiberi** | Y | Y | Y | Y | Y | Y | Y |
| 13 Brown | Y | Y | Y | Y | Y | Y | Y |
| 14 **LaTourette** | ? | Y | Y | Y | N | Y | Y |
| 15 **Pryce** | Y | Y | Y | Y | ? | Y | Y |
| 16 **Regula** | Y | Y | Y | Y | N | Y | Y |
| 17 Ryan | Y | Y | Y | Y | Y | Y | Y |
| 18 **Ney** | + | + | Y | Y | Y | Y | Y |
| **OKLAHOMA** | | | | | | | |
| 1 **Sullivan** | Y | Y | Y | Y | Y | Y | Y |
| 2 Boren | Y | Y | Y | Y | Y | Y | Y |
| 3 **Lucas** | Y | Y | Y | Y | Y | Y | Y |
| 4 **Cole** | Y | Y | Y | Y | Y | Y | Y |
| 5 **Istook** | Y | Y | ? | ? | Y | Y | Y |
| **OREGON** | | | | | | | |
| 1 Wu | ? | Y | Y | Y | N | Y | Y |
| 2 **Walden** | Y | Y | Y | Y | N | Y | Y |
| 3 Blumenauer | N | Y | Y | Y | Y | Y | Y |
| 4 DeFazio | N | Y | Y | Y | N | Y | Y |
| 5 Hooley | Y | Y | Y | Y | N | Y | Y |
| **PENNSYLVANIA** | | | | | | | |
| 1 Brady | Y | Y | Y | Y | ? | ? | ? |
| 2 Fattah | Y | Y | Y | Y | Y | Y | Y |
| 3 **English** | Y | Y | Y | Y | Y | Y | Y |
| 4 **Hart** | Y | Y | Y | Y | Y | Y | Y |
| 5 **Peterson** | Y | Y | Y | Y | Y | Y | Y |
| 6 **Gerlach** | Y | Y | Y | Y | Y | Y | Y |
| 7 **Weldon** | Y | Y | Y | Y | N | Y | Y |
| 8 **Fitzpatrick** | Y | Y | Y | Y | Y | Y | Y |
| 9 **Shuster** | Y | Y | Y | Y | Y | Y | Y |
| 10 **Sherwood** | Y | Y | Y | Y | Y | Y | Y |
| 11 Kanjorski | Y | Y | Y | Y | N | Y | Y |
| 12 Murtha | Y | Y | ? | ? | Y | Y | Y |
| 13 Schwartz | Y | Y | Y | Y | N | Y | Y |
| 14 Doyle | Y | Y | ? | ? | N | Y | Y |
| 15 **Dent** | Y | Y | Y | Y | Y | Y | Y |
| 16 **Pitts** | N | Y | Y | Y | Y | Y | Y |
| 17 Holden | Y | Y | Y | Y | N | Y | Y |
| 18 **Murphy** | Y | Y | Y | Y | Y | Y | Y |
| 19 **Platts** | Y | Y | Y | Y | N | Y | Y |
| **RHODE ISLAND** | | | | | | | |
| 1 Kennedy | Y | Y | Y | Y | Y | Y | Y |
| 2 Langevin | Y | Y | Y | Y | N | Y | Y |
| **SOUTH CAROLINA** | | | | | | | |
| 1 **Brown** | Y | Y | Y | Y | Y | Y | Y |
| 2 **Wilson** | Y | Y | Y | Y | Y | Y | Y |
| 3 **Barrett** | N | Y | Y | Y | Y | Y | Y |
| 4 **Inglis** | Y | Y | Y | Y | Y | Y | Y |
| 5 Spratt | Y | Y | ? | ? | N | Y | Y |
| 6 Clyburn | ? | ? | Y | Y | N | Y | Y |
| **SOUTH DAKOTA** | | | | | | | |
| AL Herseth | N | Y | ? | ? | Y | Y | Y |
| **TENNESSEE** | | | | | | | |
| 1 **Jenkins** | Y | Y | ? | ? | Y | Y | Y |
| 2 **Duncan** | N | Y | Y | Y | Y | Y | Y |
| 3 **Wamp** | Y | Y | Y | Y | N | Y | Y |
| 4 Davis | Y | Y | ? | Y | Y | Y | Y |
| 5 Cooper | N | Y | Y | Y | N | Y | Y |
| 6 Gordon | Y | Y | Y | Y | N | Y | Y |
| 7 **Blackburn** | N | Y | Y | Y | Y | Y | Y |
| 8 Tanner | Y | Y | Y | Y | N | Y | Y |
| 9 Ford | ? | ? | ? | ? | N | Y | Y |
| **TEXAS** | | | | | | | |
| 1 **Gohmert** | Y | Y | Y | Y | Y | Y | Y |
| 2 **Poe** | Y | Y | Y | Y | Y | Y | Y |
| 3 **Johnson, S.** | Y | Y | Y | Y | Y | Y | Y |
| 4 **Hall** | Y | Y | ? | ? | ? | ? | ? |
| 5 **Hensarling** | N | Y | Y | Y | Y | Y | Y |
| 6 **Barton** | Y | Y | Y | Y | Y | Y | Y |
| 7 **Culberson** | Y | Y | Y | Y | Y | Y | Y |
| 8 **Brady** | Y | Y | Y | Y | Y | Y | Y |
| 9 Green, A. | Y | Y | Y | Y | N | Y | Y |
| 10 **McCaul** | Y | Y | Y | Y | Y | Y | Y |
| 11 **Conaway** | Y | Y | Y | Y | Y | Y | Y |
| 12 **Granger** | Y | Y | Y | Y | Y | Y | Y |
| 13 **Thornberry** | Y | Y | Y | Y | Y | Y | Y |
| 14 **Paul** | N | P | Y | Y | Y | Y | Y |
| 15 Hinojosa | Y | Y | Y | Y | N | Y | Y |
| 16 Reyes | ? | ? | Y | Y | ? | ? | ? |
| 17 Edwards | Y | Y | Y | Y | N | Y | Y |
| 18 Jackson-Lee | N | Y | Y | Y | N | Y | Y |
| 19 **Neugebauer** | Y | Y | Y | Y | Y | Y | Y |
| 20 Gonzalez | Y | Y | Y | Y | N | Y | Y |
| 21 **Smith** | ? | ? | Y | Y | Y | Y | Y |
| 22 **DeLay** | Y | Y | ? | ? | Y | Y | Y |
| 23 **Bonilla** | Y | Y | Y | Y | Y | Y | Y |
| 24 **Marchant** | N | Y | Y | Y | Y | Y | Y |
| 25 Doggett | Y | Y | Y | Y | N | Y | Y |
| 26 **Burgess** | Y | Y | Y | Y | Y | Y | Y |
| 27 Ortiz | + | + | Y | Y | N | Y | Y |
| 28 Cuellar | Y | Y | Y | Y | Y | Y | Y |
| 29 Green, G. | Y | Y | Y | Y | N | Y | Y |
| 30 Johnson, E. | Y | Y | Y | Y | N | Y | Y |
| 31 **Carter** | Y | Y | Y | Y | Y | Y | Y |
| 32 **Sessions** | Y | Y | Y | Y | Y | Y | Y |
| **UTAH** | | | | | | | |
| 1 **Bishop** | Y | Y | Y | Y | Y | Y | Y |
| 2 Matheson | Y | Y | Y | Y | Y | Y | Y |
| 3 **Cannon** | Y | Y | Y | Y | Y | Y | Y |
| **VERMONT** | | | | | | | |
| AL *Sanders* | Y | Y | Y | Y | N | Y | Y |
| **VIRGINIA** | | | | | | | |
| 1 **Davis, J.** | + | + | Y | Y | Y | Y | Y |
| 2 **Drake** | ? | ? | Y | Y | Y | Y | Y |
| 3 Scott | Y | Y | Y | Y | N | Y | Y |
| 4 **Forbes** | Y | Y | Y | Y | Y | Y | Y |
| 5 **Goode** | Y | Y | Y | Y | Y | Y | Y |
| 6 **Goodlatte** | Y | Y | Y | Y | Y | Y | Y |
| 7 **Cantor** | Y | Y | Y | Y | Y | Y | Y |
| 8 Moran | Y | Y | Y | Y | N | Y | Y |
| 9 Boucher | Y | Y | Y | Y | Y | Y | Y |
| 10 **Wolf** | Y | Y | Y | Y | N | Y | Y |
| 11 **Davis, T.** | N | Y | Y | Y | Y | Y | Y |
| **WASHINGTON** | | | | | | | |
| 1 Inslee | N | Y | Y | Y | N | Y | Y |
| 2 Larsen | Y | Y | Y | Y | N | Y | Y |
| 3 Baird | Y | Y | Y | Y | N | Y | Y |
| 4 **Hastings** | Y | Y | Y | Y | Y | Y | Y |
| 5 **McMorris** | Y | Y | Y | Y | Y | Y | Y |
| 6 Dicks | Y | Y | Y | Y | N | Y | Y |
| 7 McDermott | – | + | Y | Y | N | Y | Y |
| 8 **Reichert** | Y | Y | Y | Y | Y | Y | Y |
| 9 Smith | Y | Y | Y | Y | Y | Y | Y |
| **WEST VIRGINIA** | | | | | | | |
| 1 Mollohan | Y | Y | Y | Y | N | Y | Y |
| 2 **Capito** | Y | Y | Y | Y | Y | Y | Y |
| 3 Rahall | Y | Y | Y | Y | Y | Y | Y |
| **WISCONSIN** | | | | | | | |
| 1 **Ryan** | N | Y | Y | Y | Y | Y | Y |
| 2 Baldwin | Y | Y | Y | Y | N | Y | Y |
| 3 Kind | ? | ? | Y | Y | Y | Y | Y |
| 4 Moore | Y | Y | Y | Y | N | Y | Y |
| 5 **Sensenbrenner** | ? | ? | Y | Y | Y | Y | Y |
| 6 **Petri** | N | Y | Y | Y | N | Y | Y |
| 7 Obey | ? | ? | Y | Y | N | Y | Y |
| 8 **Green** | N | Y | Y | Y | Y | Y | Y |
| **WYOMING** | | | | | | | |
| AL **Cubin** | Y | Y | ? | ? | ? | ? | ? |

# IN THE HOUSE | By Vote Number

**562.** **Iraq War Investigation/Appeal Ruling of the Chair.** Walsh, R-N.Y., motion to table (kill) the Pelosi, D-Calif., appeal of the ruling of the chair that the Pelosi resolution did not qualify as a question of privilege as it relates to the safety and efficiency of the House. The Pelosi resolution would ask the Republican leadership and the chairmen of the committees of jurisdiction to conduct an investigation into possible abuses in the Iraq War. Motion agreed to 220-191: R 219-0; D 1-190 (ND 0-144, SD 1-46); I 0-1. Nov. 3, 2005.

**563.** **HR 4128. Eminent Domain/Rule.** Adoption of the rule (H Res 527) that would provide for House floor consideration of the bill that would prohibit state and local governments that receive federal economic development funds from using eminent domain to seize land for economic development purposes. Adopted 401-11: R 219-0; D 181-11 (ND 135-10, SD 46-1); I 1-0. Nov. 3, 2005.

**564.** **HR 4128. Eminent Domain/Court Action.** Nadler, D-N.Y., amendment that would permit a property owner to go to court before any property is taken to challenge a government's use of eminent domain to seize their property. It would strike provisions that would prohibit state and local governments that violate the restrictions in the bill from receiving federal economic development funds for two fiscal years. Rejected 63-355: R 1-222; D 62-132 (ND 56-92, SD 6-40); I 0-1. Nov. 3, 2005.

**565.** **HR 4128. Eminent Domain/Economic Development Definition.** Moran, D-Va., amendment that would define economic development as the use of property for commercial for-profit enterprises, or where the primary purpose is to increase tax revenue or the tax base. Rejected 49-368: R 1-221; D 48-146 (ND 42-106, SD 6-40); I 0-1. Nov. 3, 2005.

**566.** **HR 4128. Eminent Domain/Harmful Uses of Land.** Turner, R-Ohio, amendment that would specify harmful uses of land that would constitute a threat to public health and safety. It would permit the use of eminent domain in such cases. Rejected 56-357: R 28-192; D 28-164 (ND 24-123, SD 4-41); I 0-1. Nov. 3, 2005.

**567.** **HR 4128. Eminent Domain/Sense of Congress.** Watt, D-N.C., amendment that would strike all sections of the bill and retain only a provision expressing the sense of Congress that recognizes the importance of property rights and states that the Supreme Court's decision in *Kelo v. City of New London* may lead to abuses of eminent domain power. Rejected 44-371: R 0-221; D 44-149 (ND 40-107, SD 4-42); I 0-1. Nov. 3, 2005.

**568.** **HR 4128. Eminent Domain/Passage.** Passage of the bill that would prohibit state and local governments that receive federal economic development funds from using eminent domain to seize land for economic development purposes. Any private property owner who suffers injury as a result of such actions by a state or local government would be able to bring a lawsuit against the government or seek a temporary restraining order or a preliminary injunction. State and local governments that violate the restrictions in the bill could be barred from receiving federal economic development funds for two years. Passed 376-38: R 218-2; D 157-36 (ND 116-32, SD 41-4); I 1-0. Nov. 3, 2005.

| | 562 | 563 | 564 | 565 | 566 | 567 | 568 |
|---|---|---|---|---|---|---|---|
| **ALABAMA** | | | | | | | |
| 1 Bonner | Y | Y | N | N | N | N | Y |
| 2 Everett | Y | Y | N | N | N | N | Y |
| 3 Rogers | Y | Y | N | N | N | N | Y |
| 4 Aderholt | Y | Y | Y | N | N | N | Y |
| 5 Cramer | N | Y | N | N | N | N | Y |
| 6 Bachus | Y | Y | N | N | N | N | + |
| 7 Davis | N | Y | N | N | N | N | Y |
| **ALASKA** | | | | | | | |
| AL Young | Y | Y | N | N | N | N | Y |
| **ARIZONA** | | | | | | | |
| 1 Renzi | Y | Y | N | N | N | N | Y |
| 2 Franks | Y | Y | N | N | N | N | Y |
| 3 Shadegg | Y | Y | N | N | N | N | Y |
| 4 Pastor | N | N | Y | N | N | Y | N |
| 5 Hayworth | Y | Y | N | N | N | N | Y |
| 6 Flake | Y | Y | N | N | N | N | Y |
| 7 Grijalva | N | N | Y | N | N | Y | N |
| 8 Kolbe | Y | Y | N | N | N | N | Y |
| **ARKANSAS** | | | | | | | |
| 1 Berry | N | Y | N | N | N | N | Y |
| 2 Snyder | N | Y | N | N | N | N | Y |
| 3 Boozman | Y | Y | N | N | N | N | Y |
| 4 Ross | N | Y | N | N | N | N | Y |
| **CALIFORNIA** | | | | | | | |
| 1 Thompson | N | Y | Y | N | N | N | Y |
| 2 Herger | Y | Y | N | N | N | N | Y |
| 3 Lungren | Y | Y | N | N | N | N | Y |
| 4 Doolittle | Y | Y | N | N | N | N | Y |
| 5 Matsui, D. | N | Y | Y | N | Y | Y | Y |
| 6 Woolsey | N | Y | Y | Y | Y | Y | N |
| 7 Miller, George | N | Y | Y | N | Y | Y | N |
| 8 Pelosi | N | Y | Y | Y | N | Y | N |
| 9 Lee | N | Y | N | N | N | N | Y |
| 10 Tauscher | N | Y | N | N | N | N | Y |
| 11 Pombo | ? | ? | ? | ? | ? | ? | + |
| 12 Lantos | N | Y | N | N | N | N | Y |
| 13 Stark | N | Y | N | N | N | Y | N |
| 14 Eshoo | N | Y | N | Y | N | N | Y |
| 15 Honda | N | Y | N | N | N | Y | Y |
| 16 Lofgren | N | Y | N | N | N | Y | Y |
| 17 Farr | N | Y | Y | N | N | N | Y |
| 18 Cardoza | N | Y | N | N | N | N | Y |
| 19 Radanovich | Y | Y | N | N | N | N | Y |
| 20 Costa | N | Y | N | N | N | N | Y |
| 21 Nunes | Y | Y | N | N | N | N | Y |
| 22 Thomas | Y | Y | N | N | N | N | Y |
| 23 Capps | N | Y | N | N | N | N | Y |
| 24 Gallegly | Y | Y | N | N | N | N | Y |
| 25 McKeon | Y | Y | N | N | N | N | Y |
| 26 Dreier | Y | Y | N | N | N | N | Y |
| 27 Sherman | N | Y | N | Y | N | N | Y |
| 28 Berman | N | Y | N | N | N | N | Y |
| 29 Schiff | ? | ? | ? | ? | ? | ? | ? |
| 30 Waxman | N | Y | N | Y | N | Y | N |
| 31 Becerra | N | Y | N | N | N | N | Y |
| 32 Solis | N | Y | Y | N | N | N | Y |
| 33 Watson | N | Y | N | N | N | N | Y |
| 34 Roybal-Allard | ? | ? | ? | ? | ? | ? | ? |
| 35 Waters | N | Y | N | N | N | N | Y |
| 36 Harman | N | Y | N | N | N | N | Y |
| 37 Millender-McD. | N | Y | N | N | N | N | Y |
| 38 Napolitano | N | Y | N | N | N | N | Y |
| 39 Sánchez, Linda | N | Y | N | N | N | N | Y |
| 40 Royce | Y | Y | N | N | N | N | Y |
| 41 Lewis | Y | Y | N | N | N | N | Y |
| 42 Miller, Gary | Y | Y | N | N | N | N | Y |
| 43 Baca | N | Y | N | N | N | N | Y |
| 44 Calvert | Y | Y | N | N | N | N | Y |
| 45 Bono | Y | Y | N | N | N | N | Y |
| 46 Rohrabacher | Y | Y | N | N | N | N | Y |
| 47 Sanchez, Loretta | N | Y | N | N | N | Y | Y |
| 48 Vacant | | | | | | | |
| 49 Issa | Y | Y | N | N | N | N | Y |
| 50 Cunningham | Y | Y | N | N | N | N | Y |
| 51 Filner | N | Y | N | N | N | N | Y |
| 52 Hunter | Y | Y | N | N | N | ? | Y |
| 53 Davis | N | Y | N | N | N | N | Y |
| **COLORADO** | | | | | | | |
| 1 DeGette | N | Y | Y | Y | Y | Y | N |
| 2 Udall | N | Y | N | N | Y | N | Y |
| 3 Salazar | N | Y | N | N | N | N | Y |
| 4 Musgrave | Y | Y | N | N | N | N | Y |
| 5 Hefley | Y | Y | N | N | N | N | Y |
| 6 Tancredo | Y | Y | N | N | N | N | Y |
| 7 Beauprez | Y | Y | N | N | Y | N | Y |
| **CONNECTICUT** | | | | | | | |
| 1 Larson | N | Y | Y | Y | Y | Y | N |
| 2 Simmons | Y | Y | N | N | N | N | Y |
| 3 DeLauro | N | Y | N | N | N | N | Y |
| 4 Shays | Y | Y | N | N | N | N | Y |
| 5 Johnson | Y | Y | N | N | N | N | Y |
| **DELAWARE** | | | | | | | |
| AL Castle | Y | Y | N | N | N | N | Y |
| **FLORIDA** | | | | | | | |
| 1 Miller | Y | Y | N | N | N | N | Y |
| 2 Boyd | ? | ? | ? | ? | ? | ? | ? |
| 3 Brown | N | Y | Y | N | N | N | Y |
| 4 Crenshaw | Y | Y | N | N | N | N | Y |
| 5 Brown-Waite | ? | ? | ? | ? | ? | ? | ? |
| 6 Stearns | Y | Y | N | N | N | N | Y |
| 7 Mica | Y | Y | N | N | N | N | Y |
| 8 Keller | Y | Y | N | N | N | N | Y |
| 9 Bilirakis | Y | Y | N | N | N | N | Y |
| 10 Young | Y | Y | N | N | Y | N | Y |
| 11 Davis | ? | ? | ? | ? | ? | ? | ? |
| 12 Putnam | Y | Y | N | N | N | N | Y |
| 13 Harris | Y | Y | N | N | N | ? | Y |
| 14 Mack | Y | Y | N | N | N | N | Y |
| 15 Weldon | Y | Y | N | N | N | N | Y |
| 16 Foley | Y | Y | N | N | N | N | Y |
| 17 Meek | N | Y | N | N | N | N | Y |
| 18 Ros-Lehtinen | Y | Y | N | N | N | N | Y |
| 19 Wexler | N | Y | N | N | N | N | Y |
| 20 Wasserman-Schultz | N | Y | N | N | N | N | Y |
| 21 Diaz-Balart, L. | Y | Y | N | N | N | N | Y |
| 22 Shaw | Y | Y | N | N | N | N | Y |
| 23 Hastings | ? | ? | ? | ? | ? | ? | ? |
| 24 Feeney | Y | Y | N | ? | N | N | Y |
| 25 Diaz-Balart, M. | Y | Y | N | N | N | N | Y |
| **GEORGIA** | | | | | | | |
| 1 Kingston | Y | Y | N | N | N | N | Y |
| 2 Bishop | N | Y | N | N | Y | N | Y |
| 3 Marshall | Y | Y | N | N | N | N | Y |
| 4 McKinney | N | Y | Y | N | N | N | Y |
| 5 Lewis | N | Y | ? | ? | ? | ? | ? |
| 6 Price | Y | Y | N | N | N | N | Y |
| 7 Linder | Y | Y | N | N | N | N | Y |
| 8 Westmoreland | Y | Y | N | N | N | N | Y |
| 9 Norwood | ? | ? | ? | ? | ? | ? | ? |
| 10 Deal | Y | Y | N | N | N | N | Y |
| 11 Gingrey | Y | Y | N | N | N | N | Y |
| 12 Barrow | N | Y | N | N | N | N | Y |
| 13 Scott | N | Y | N | N | N | N | Y |
| **HAWAII** | | | | | | | |
| 1 Abercrombie | N | Y | Y | N | N | N | Y |
| 2 Case | N | Y | Y | Y | Y | Y | N |
| **IDAHO** | | | | | | | |
| 1 Otter | Y | Y | N | N | N | N | Y |
| 2 Simpson | Y | Y | N | N | N | N | Y |
| **ILLINOIS** | | | | | | | |
| 1 Rush | N | Y | N | N | N | N | Y |
| 2 Jackson | N | Y | N | Y | Y | Y | N |
| 3 Lipinski | N | Y | N | N | N | N | Y |
| 4 Gutierrez | N | Y | N | N | N | N | Y |
| 5 Emanuel | N | Y | Y | Y | N | Y | Y |
| 6 Hyde | Y | Y | N | N | N | N | Y |
| 7 Davis | N | Y | N | N | N | N | Y |
| 8 Bean | N | Y | N | N | N | N | Y |
| 9 Schakowsky | N | Y | Y | Y | Y | Y | N |
| 10 Kirk | Y | Y | N | N | N | N | Y |
| 11 Weller | Y | Y | N | Y | N | N | Y |
| 12 Costello | N | Y | N | N | N | N | Y |

**KEY**  Republicans   Democrats   *Independents*

| | | | |
|---|---|---|---|
| Y | Voted for (yea) | X | Paired against |
| # | Paired for | – | Announced against |
| + | Announced for | P | Voted "present" |
| N | Voted against (nay) | C | Voted "present" to avoid possible conflict of interest |
| | | ? | Did not vote or otherwise make a position known |

| | 562 | 563 | 564 | 565 | 566 | 567 | 568 |
|---|---|---|---|---|---|---|---|
| 13 **Biggert** | Y | Y | N | N | N | N | Y |
| 14 **Hastert** | | | | | | | |
| 15 **Johnson** | Y | Y | N | N | N | N | Y |
| 16 **Manzullo** | Y | Y | N | N | N | N | Y |
| 17 Evans | N | Y | N | N | N | N | Y |
| 18 **LaHood** | Y | Y | N | N | N | N | Y |
| 19 **Shimkus** | Y | Y | N | N | N | N | Y |
| **INDIANA** | | | | | | | |
| 1 Visclosky | N | Y | N | N | N | Y | N |
| 2 **Chocola** | Y | Y | N | N | Y | N | Y |
| 3 **Souder** | Y | Y | N | N | Y | N | Y |
| 4 **Buyer** | Y | Y | ? | ? | ? | ? | ? |
| 5 **Burton** | Y | Y | N | N | N | N | Y |
| 6 **Pence** | Y | Y | N | N | N | N | Y |
| 7 Carson | N | Y | N | Y | N | Y | Y |
| 8 **Hostettler** | Y | Y | N | N | N | N | Y |
| 9 **Sodrel** | Y | Y | N | N | N | N | Y |
| **IOWA** | | | | | | | |
| 1 **Nussle** | Y | Y | N | N | N | N | Y |
| 2 **Leach** | Y | Y | N | N | N | N | Y |
| 3 Boswell | ? | ? | ? | ? | ? | ? | ? |
| 4 **Latham** | Y | Y | N | N | N | N | Y |
| 5 **King** | Y | Y | N | N | N | N | Y |
| **KANSAS** | | | | | | | |
| 1 **Moran** | Y | Y | N | N | N | N | Y |
| 2 **Ryun** | Y | Y | N | N | N | N | Y |
| 3 Moore | N | Y | N | N | N | N | Y |
| 4 **Tiahrt** | + | + | – | – | – | – | + |
| **KENTUCKY** | | | | | | | |
| 1 **Whitfield** | Y | Y | N | N | N | N | Y |
| 2 **Lewis** | Y | Y | N | N | N | N | Y |
| 3 **Northup** | Y | Y | N | N | N | N | Y |
| 4 **Davis** | Y | Y | N | N | N | N | Y |
| 5 **Rogers** | Y | Y | N | N | N | N | Y |
| 6 Chandler | N | Y | N | N | N | N | Y |
| **LOUISIANA** | | | | | | | |
| 1 **Jindal** | Y | Y | N | N | N | N | Y |
| 2 Jefferson | N | Y | N | Y | N | N | Y |
| 3 Melancon | N | Y | N | N | N | N | Y |
| 4 **McCrery** | Y | Y | N | N | N | N | Y |
| 5 **Alexander** | Y | Y | N | N | N | N | Y |
| 6 **Baker** | Y | Y | N | N | Y | N | Y |
| 7 **Boustany** | Y | Y | N | N | N | N | Y |
| **MAINE** | | | | | | | |
| 1 Allen | N | Y | N | N | N | N | Y |
| 2 Michaud | N | Y | N | N | N | N | Y |
| **MARYLAND** | | | | | | | |
| 1 **Gilchrest** | Y | Y | N | N | N | N | Y |
| 2 Ruppersberger | N | Y | N | N | N | N | Y |
| 3 Cardin | N | Y | N | N | N | N | Y |
| 4 Wynn | N | Y | N | Y | Y | Y | N |
| 5 Hoyer | N | Y | Y | N | N | N | Y |
| 6 **Bartlett** | Y | Y | N | N | N | N | Y |
| 7 Cummings | ? | Y | N | N | N | N | Y |
| 8 Van Hollen | N | Y | N | N | N | N | Y |
| **MASSACHUSETTS** | | | | | | | |
| 1 Olver | N | N | Y | Y | N | Y | N |
| 2 Neal | N | Y | Y | Y | Y | Y | N |
| 3 McGovern | N | Y | N | Y | Y | N | Y |
| 4 Frank | N | Y | N | N | N | N | Y |
| 5 Meehan | N | Y | N | N | N | N | Y |
| 6 Tierney | N | Y | N | N | Y | N | Y |
| 7 Markey | N | Y | Y | Y | N | Y | Y |
| 8 Capuano | N | Y | Y | Y | Y | Y | N |
| 9 Lynch | N | Y | N | N | N | N | Y |
| 10 Delahunt | N | Y | Y | Y | Y | Y | Y |
| **MICHIGAN** | | | | | | | |
| 1 Stupak | N | Y | N | N | N | N | Y |
| 2 **Hoekstra** | Y | Y | N | N | N | N | Y |
| 3 **Ehlers** | Y | Y | N | N | Y | N | ? |
| 4 **Camp** | Y | Y | N | N | N | N | Y |
| 5 Kildee | N | Y | Y | N | N | N | Y |
| 6 **Upton** | Y | Y | N | N | N | N | Y |
| 7 **Schwarz** | Y | Y | N | N | N | N | Y |
| 8 **Rogers** | Y | Y | N | N | N | N | Y |
| 9 **Knollenberg** | Y | Y | N | N | N | N | Y |
| 10 **Miller** | Y | Y | N | N | Y | N | Y |
| 11 **McCotter** | Y | Y | N | N | N | N | Y |
| 12 Levin | N | Y | Y | Y | N | Y | N |
| 13 Kilpatrick | N | Y | N | N | N | N | Y |
| 14 Conyers | N | Y | N | N | N | N | Y |
| 15 Dingell | N | Y | Y | Y | ? | Y | N |

| | 562 | 563 | 564 | 565 | 566 | 567 | 568 |
|---|---|---|---|---|---|---|---|
| **MINNESOTA** | | | | | | | |
| 1 **Gutknecht** | Y | Y | N | N | N | N | Y |
| 2 **Kline** | Y | Y | N | N | N | N | Y |
| 3 **Ramstad** | Y | Y | N | N | N | N | Y |
| 4 McCollum | N | Y | Y | N | N | N | Y |
| 5 Sabo | N | N | Y | Y | N | Y | N |
| 6 **Kennedy** | Y | Y | N | N | N | N | Y |
| 7 Peterson | N | Y | N | N | N | N | Y |
| 8 Oberstar | N | Y | Y | N | N | N | Y |
| **MISSISSIPPI** | | | | | | | |
| 1 **Wicker** | Y | Y | N | N | Y | N | Y |
| 2 Thompson | N | Y | N | N | N | N | Y |
| 3 **Pickering** | Y | Y | N | N | Y | N | Y |
| 4 Taylor | N | N | N | N | N | N | Y |
| **MISSOURI** | | | | | | | |
| 1 Clay | N | Y | N | N | N | Y | Y |
| 2 **Akin** | Y | Y | N | N | N | N | Y |
| 3 Carnahan | N | Y | N | N | N | N | Y |
| 4 Skelton | N | Y | N | N | N | N | Y |
| 5 Cleaver | N | Y | Y | Y | N | Y | N |
| 6 **Graves** | Y | Y | N | N | N | N | Y |
| 7 **Blunt** | Y | Y | N | N | Y | N | Y |
| 8 **Emerson** | Y | Y | N | N | N | N | Y |
| 9 **Hulshof** | Y | Y | N | N | N | N | Y |
| **MONTANA** | | | | | | | |
| AL **Rehberg** | Y | Y | N | N | N | N | Y |
| **NEBRASKA** | | | | | | | |
| 1 **Fortenberry** | Y | Y | N | N | Y | N | Y |
| 2 **Terry** | Y | Y | N | N | N | N | Y |
| 3 **Osborne** | Y | Y | N | N | N | N | Y |
| **NEVADA** | | | | | | | |
| 1 Berkley | N | Y | N | N | N | N | Y |
| 2 **Gibbons** | Y | Y | N | N | N | N | Y |
| 3 **Porter** | Y | Y | N | N | N | N | Y |
| **NEW HAMPSHIRE** | | | | | | | |
| 1 **Bradley** | Y | Y | N | N | N | N | Y |
| 2 **Bass** | Y | Y | N | N | N | N | Y |
| **NEW JERSEY** | | | | | | | |
| 1 Andrews | N | Y | N | N | N | N | Y |
| 2 **LoBiondo** | Y | Y | N | N | N | N | Y |
| 3 **Saxton** | Y | Y | N | N | N | ? | Y |
| 4 **Smith** | Y | Y | N | N | N | N | Y |
| 5 **Garrett** | Y | Y | N | N | N | N | Y |
| 6 Pallone | N | Y | N | N | N | N | Y |
| 7 **Ferguson** | Y | Y | N | N | N | N | Y |
| 8 Pascrell | N | Y | N | N | Y | N | Y |
| 9 Rothman | N | N | Y | Y | Y | Y | N |
| 10 Payne | N | Y | Y | Y | N | Y | Y |
| 11 **Frelinghuysen** | Y | Y | N | N | N | N | Y |
| 12 Holt | N | N | Y | Y | N | N | Y |
| 13 Menendez | N | Y | N | N | N | N | Y |
| **NEW MEXICO** | | | | | | | |
| 1 **Wilson** | Y | Y | N | N | N | N | Y |
| 2 **Pearce** | Y | Y | N | N | N | N | Y |
| 3 Udall | N | Y | N | N | N | N | Y |
| **NEW YORK** | | | | | | | |
| 1 Bishop | N | Y | Y | N | N | N | Y |
| 2 Israel | N | Y | N | N | N | N | Y |
| 3 **King** | ? | ? | N | N | N | N | Y |
| 4 McCarthy | N | ? | N | N | N | N | Y |
| 5 Ackerman | N | Y | Y | N | N | Y | N |
| 6 Meeks | N | Y | Y | N | N | N | N |
| 7 Crowley | N | Y | N | N | N | N | Y |
| 8 Nadler | N | N | Y | Y | N | Y | N |
| 9 Weiner | N | Y | Y | Y | N | N | Y |
| 10 Towns | ? | ? | Y | N | N | N | Y |
| 11 Owens | N | Y | Y | N | N | N | Y |
| 12 Velázquez | N | Y | N | N | N | N | Y |
| 13 **Fossella** | Y | Y | N | N | N | N | Y |
| 14 Maloney | N | Y | Y | N | N | N | Y |
| 15 Rangel | N | Y | Y | Y | N | Y | Y |
| 16 Serrano | ? | Y | Y | N | N | N | Y |
| 17 Engel | N | Y | Y | Y | N | N | Y |
| 18 Lowey | N | Y | Y | Y | N | Y | N |
| 19 **Kelly** | Y | Y | N | N | Y | N | Y |
| 20 **Sweeney** | Y | Y | N | N | Y | N | Y |
| 21 McNulty | N | Y | N | N | N | N | Y |
| 22 Hinchey | N | Y | Y | Y | N | Y | N |
| 23 **McHugh** | Y | Y | N | N | N | N | Y |
| 24 **Boehlert** | Y | Y | N | N | Y | N | N |
| 25 **Walsh** | Y | Y | N | N | N | N | Y |
| 26 **Reynolds** | Y | Y | N | N | N | N | Y |
| 27 Higgins | N | Y | N | N | N | N | Y |
| 28 Slaughter | N | Y | Y | Y | N | Y | Y |
| 29 **Kuhl** | Y | Y | N | N | N | N | Y |

| | 562 | 563 | 564 | 565 | 566 | 567 | 568 |
|---|---|---|---|---|---|---|---|
| **NORTH CAROLINA** | | | | | | | |
| 1 Butterfield | – | + | N | N | N | N | Y |
| 2 Etheridge | N | Y | N | N | N | N | Y |
| 3 **Jones** | Y | Y | N | N | N | N | Y |
| 4 Price | N | Y | N | Y | N | N | Y |
| 5 **Foxx** | Y | Y | N | N | N | N | Y |
| 6 **Coble** | Y | Y | N | N | N | N | Y |
| 7 McIntyre | N | Y | N | N | N | N | Y |
| 8 **Hayes** | Y | Y | N | N | N | N | Y |
| 9 **Myrick** | Y | Y | N | N | N | N | Y |
| 10 **McHenry** | Y | Y | N | N | N | N | Y |
| 11 **Taylor** | Y | Y | N | N | N | N | Y |
| 12 Watt | N | Y | Y | Y | N | Y | N |
| 13 Miller | N | Y | Y | Y | Y | Y | N |
| **NORTH DAKOTA** | | | | | | | |
| AL Pomeroy | N | Y | N | N | N | N | Y |
| **OHIO** | | | | | | | |
| 1 **Chabot** | ? | ? | N | N | Y | N | Y |
| 2 **Schmidt** | Y | Y | N | N | Y | N | Y |
| 3 **Turner** | Y | Y | N | N | Y | N | N |
| 4 **Oxley** | Y | Y | N | N | Y | N | Y |
| 5 **Gillmor** | Y | Y | N | N | N | N | Y |
| 6 Strickland | N | Y | N | N | N | N | Y |
| 7 **Hobson** | Y | Y | N | N | Y | N | Y |
| 8 **Boehner** | Y | Y | N | N | N | N | Y |
| 9 Kaptur | N | Y | Y | N | N | N | Y |
| 10 Kucinich | N | Y | N | N | N | N | Y |
| 11 Jones | N | N | N | N | N | N | Y |
| 12 **Tiberi** | Y | Y | N | N | Y | N | Y |
| 13 Brown | N | Y | Y | N | N | N | Y |
| 14 **LaTourette** | Y | Y | N | N | Y | N | Y |
| 15 **Pryce** | Y | Y | N | N | Y | N | Y |
| 16 **Regula** | Y | Y | N | N | Y | N | Y |
| 17 Ryan | N | Y | Y | N | N | N | Y |
| 18 **Ney** | Y | Y | N | N | N | N | Y |
| **OKLAHOMA** | | | | | | | |
| 1 **Sullivan** | Y | Y | ? | ? | ? | ? | ? |
| 2 Boren | N | Y | N | N | N | N | Y |
| 3 **Lucas** | Y | Y | N | N | N | N | Y |
| 4 **Cole** | Y | Y | N | N | N | N | Y |
| 5 **Istook** | ? | ? | N | N | N | N | Y |
| **OREGON** | | | | | | | |
| 1 Wu | N | N | N | N | N | N | Y |
| 2 **Walden** | Y | Y | N | N | N | N | Y |
| 3 Blumenauer | N | Y | Y | Y | Y | Y | N |
| 4 DeFazio | N | Y | N | N | N | N | Y |
| 5 Hooley | N | Y | Y | Y | N | N | Y |
| **PENNSYLVANIA** | | | | | | | |
| 1 Brady | ? | ? | N | Y | N | Y | N |
| 2 Fattah | N | Y | Y | Y | N | Y | N |
| 3 **English** | Y | Y | N | N | N | N | Y |
| 4 **Hart** | Y | Y | N | N | N | N | Y |
| 5 **Peterson** | Y | Y | N | N | N | N | Y |
| 6 **Gerlach** | Y | Y | N | N | Y | N | Y |
| 7 **Weldon** | ? | Y | N | N | N | N | Y |
| 8 **Fitzpatrick** | Y | Y | N | N | N | N | Y |
| 9 **Shuster** | Y | Y | N | N | N | N | Y |
| 10 **Sherwood** | Y | Y | N | N | N | N | Y |
| 11 Kanjorski | N | Y | Y | Y | Y | Y | Y |
| 12 Murtha | N | Y | N | Y | N | N | Y |
| 13 Schwartz | N | Y | Y | Y | N | Y | N |
| 14 Doyle | N | Y | N | N | N | N | Y |
| 15 **Dent** | Y | Y | N | N | N | N | Y |
| 16 **Pitts** | Y | Y | N | N | N | N | Y |
| 17 Holden | N | Y | N | N | N | N | Y |
| 18 **Murphy** | Y | Y | N | N | N | N | Y |
| 19 **Platts** | Y | Y | N | N | N | N | Y |
| **RHODE ISLAND** | | | | | | | |
| 1 Kennedy | N | Y | Y | Y | Y | N | Y |
| 2 Langevin | N | Y | N | N | Y | N | Y |
| **SOUTH CAROLINA** | | | | | | | |
| 1 **Brown** | Y | Y | N | N | N | N | Y |
| 2 **Wilson** | Y | Y | N | N | N | N | Y |
| 3 **Barrett** | Y | Y | N | N | N | N | Y |
| 4 **Inglis** | Y | Y | N | N | N | N | Y |
| 5 Spratt | N | Y | N | N | N | N | Y |
| 6 Clyburn | N | Y | N | N | N | N | Y |
| **SOUTH DAKOTA** | | | | | | | |
| AL Herseth | N | Y | N | N | N | N | Y |
| **TENNESSEE** | | | | | | | |
| 1 **Jenkins** | Y | Y | N | N | N | N | Y |
| 2 **Duncan** | Y | Y | N | N | N | N | Y |

| | 562 | 563 | 564 | 565 | 566 | 567 | 568 |
|---|---|---|---|---|---|---|---|
| 3 **Wamp** | Y | Y | N | N | N | N | Y |
| 4 Davis | N | Y | N | N | N | N | Y |
| 5 Cooper | N | Y | N | N | N | N | Y |
| 6 Gordon | N | Y | N | N | N | N | Y |
| 7 **Blackburn** | Y | Y | N | N | N | N | Y |
| 8 Tanner | N | Y | N | N | N | N | Y |
| 9 Ford | N | Y | N | N | N | N | Y |
| **TEXAS** | | | | | | | |
| 1 **Gohmert** | Y | Y | N | N | N | N | Y |
| 2 **Poe** | Y | Y | N | N | N | N | Y |
| 3 **Johnson, S.** | Y | Y | N | N | N | N | Y |
| 4 **Hall** | ? | ? | N | N | N | N | Y |
| 5 **Hensarling** | Y | Y | N | N | N | N | Y |
| 6 **Barton** | Y | Y | N | N | N | N | Y |
| 7 **Culberson** | Y | Y | N | N | N | N | Y |
| 8 **Brady** | Y | Y | N | N | ? | N | Y |
| 9 Green, A. | N | Y | N | N | – | N | Y |
| 10 **McCaul** | Y | ? | N | N | N | N | Y |
| 11 **Conaway** | Y | Y | N | N | N | N | Y |
| 12 **Granger** | Y | Y | N | N | Y | N | Y |
| 13 **Thornberry** | Y | Y | N | N | N | N | Y |
| 14 **Paul** | Y | Y | N | N | N | N | Y |
| 15 Hinojosa | N | Y | N | N | N | N | Y |
| 16 Reyes | N | Y | N | N | N | N | Y |
| 17 Edwards | N | Y | N | N | N | N | Y |
| 18 Jackson-Lee | N | Y | N | N | N | N | Y |
| 19 **Neugebauer** | Y | Y | N | N | N | N | Y |
| 20 Gonzalez | N | Y | N | N | N | N | Y |
| 21 **Smith** | Y | Y | N | N | N | N | Y |
| 22 **DeLay** | Y | Y | N | N | N | N | Y |
| 23 **Bonilla** | Y | Y | N | N | N | N | Y |
| 24 **Marchant** | Y | Y | N | N | N | N | Y |
| 25 Doggett | N | Y | N | N | N | N | Y |
| 26 **Burgess** | Y | Y | N | N | N | N | Y |
| 27 Ortiz | N | Y | – | – | – | – | + |
| 28 Cuellar | N | Y | N | N | N | N | Y |
| 29 Green, G. | N | Y | N | N | Y | N | Y |
| 30 Johnson, E. | N | Y | N | N | N | N | Y |
| 31 **Carter** | Y | Y | N | N | N | N | Y |
| 32 **Sessions** | Y | Y | N | N | N | N | Y |
| **UTAH** | | | | | | | |
| 1 **Bishop** | ? | ? | N | N | ? | N | Y |
| 2 Matheson | N | Y | N | N | N | N | Y |
| 3 **Cannon** | Y | Y | N | N | N | N | Y |
| **VERMONT** | | | | | | | |
| AL *Sanders* | N | Y | N | N | N | N | Y |
| **VIRGINIA** | | | | | | | |
| 1 **Davis, J.** | Y | Y | N | N | Y | N | Y |
| 2 **Drake** | Y | Y | N | N | N | N | Y |
| 3 Scott | N | Y | Y | Y | N | Y | N |
| 4 **Forbes** | Y | Y | N | N | N | N | Y |
| 5 **Goode** | Y | Y | N | N | N | N | Y |
| 6 **Goodlatte** | Y | Y | N | N | N | N | Y |
| 7 **Cantor** | Y | Y | N | N | N | N | Y |
| 8 Moran | N | Y | Y | Y | Y | Y | N |
| 9 Boucher | N | Y | N | N | N | N | ? |
| 10 **Wolf** | Y | Y | N | N | N | N | ? |
| 11 **Davis, T.** | Y | Y | N | N | Y | N | Y |
| **WASHINGTON** | | | | | | | |
| 1 Inslee | N | Y | N | N | N | N | Y |
| 2 Larsen | N | Y | N | N | N | N | Y |
| 3 Baird | N | Y | N | Y | N | N | Y |
| 4 **Hastings** | Y | Y | N | N | N | N | Y |
| 5 **McMorris** | ? | ? | ? | ? | ? | ? | ? |
| 6 Dicks | N | Y | Y | N | N | N | Y |
| 7 McDermott | N | N | Y | N | Y | Y | N |
| 8 **Reichert** | Y | Y | N | N | N | N | Y |
| 9 Smith | N | Y | N | Y | N | N | Y |
| **WEST VIRGINIA** | | | | | | | |
| 1 Mollohan | N | Y | N | N | N | N | Y |
| 2 **Capito** | Y | Y | N | N | N | N | Y |
| 3 Rahall | N | Y | N | N | N | N | Y |
| **WISCONSIN** | | | | | | | |
| 1 **Ryan** | Y | Y | N | N | N | N | Y |
| 2 Baldwin | N | Y | N | N | N | N | Y |
| 3 Kind | N | Y | N | N | N | N | Y |
| 4 Moore | N | Y | N | N | N | N | Y |
| 5 **Sensenbrenner** | Y | Y | N | N | N | N | Y |
| 6 **Petri** | Y | Y | N | N | N | N | Y |
| 7 Obey | N | Y | N | N | N | N | Y |
| 8 **Green** | Y | Y | N | N | N | N | Y |
| **WYOMING** | | | | | | | |
| AL **Cubin** | Y | Y | N | N | N | N | Y |

# IN THE HOUSE | By Vote Number

**569.** **HR 3057. Fiscal 2006 Foreign Operations Appropriations/ Conference Report.** Adoption of the conference report on the bill that would provide $21 billion in fiscal 2006 for foreign operations and related programs, including $2.8 billion to fight HIV/AIDS, tuberculosis and malaria; $1.8 billion for the Millennium Challenge Corporation; and $1.6 billion for the Child Survival and Health Programs Fund. Adopted (thus sent to the Senate) 358-39: R 179-32; D 178-7 (ND 137-3, SD 41-4); I 1-0. Nov. 4, 2005.

**570.** **H Con Res 260. Nostra Aetate Tribute/Adoption.** Poe, R-Texas, motion to suspend the rules and adopt the concurrent resolution that would recognize the 40th anniversary of Nostra Aetate, the Second Vatican Council's Declaration on the Relation of the Church to Non-Christian Religions, and also recognize the religious diversity of the United States and the world. Motion agreed to 349-0: R 202-0; D 146-0 (ND 104-0, SD 42-0); I 1-0. A two-thirds majority of those present and voting (233 in this case) is required for adoption under suspension of the rules. Nov. 7, 2005.

**571.** **HR 1973. Water for the Poor/Passage.** Poe, R-Texas, motion to suspend the rules and pass the bill that would authorize unspecified sums to provide safe water and sanitation to people in developing countries. Motion agreed to 319-34: R 170-34; D 148-0 (ND 106-0, SD 42-0); I 1-0. A two-thirds majority of those present and voting (236 in this case) is required for passage under suspension of the rules. Nov. 7, 2005.

**572.** **H Res 444. Ovarian Cancer Awareness Month/Adoption.** Upton, R-Mich., motion to suspend the rules and adopt the resolution that would support the goals and ideals of National Ovarian Cancer Awareness Month in September. Motion agreed to 348-0: R 201-0; D 146-0 (ND 105-0, SD 41-0); I 1-0. A two-thirds majority of those present and voting (232 in this case) is required for adoption under suspension of the rules. Nov. 7, 2005.

**573.** **HR 3010. Fiscal 2006 Labor-HHS-Education Appropriations/ Appeal Ruling of the Chair.** Regula, R-Ohio, motion to table (kill) the Obey, D-Wis., appeal of the ruling of the chair against the Regula point of order against the Obey motion. The Obey motion would instruct House conferees to agree to various Senate provisions including $8.1 billion for avian flu preparation and $5.1 billion for the Low Income Home Energy Assistance Program, offset by reducing tax cuts for the wealthy. Motion agreed to 218-173: R 218-0; D 0-172 (ND 0-125, SD 0-47); I 0-1. Nov. 8, 2005.

**574.** **H Res 38. Israel and the OECD/Adoption.** Ros-Lehtinen, R-Fla., motion to suspend the rules and adopt the resolution that would express the sense of the House that the U.S. government should support the accession of Israel to the Organization for Economic Co-Operation and Development. Motion agreed to 391-0: R 219-0; D 171-0 (ND 123-0, SD 48-0); I 1-0. A two-thirds majority of those present and voting (261 in this case) is required for adoption under suspension of the rules. Nov. 8, 2005.

| | 569 | 570 | 571 | 572 | 573 | 574 |
|---|---|---|---|---|---|---|
| **ALABAMA** | | | | | | |
| 1 Bonner | Y | Y | Y | Y | Y | Y |
| 2 Everett | Y | Y | Y | Y | Y | Y |
| 3 Rogers | Y | Y | Y | Y | Y | Y |
| 4 Aderholt | Y | Y | Y | Y | Y | Y |
| 5 Cramer | Y | Y | Y | Y | N | Y |
| 6 Bachus | Y | Y | Y | Y | Y | Y |
| 7 Davis | Y | Y | Y | Y | N | Y |
| **ALASKA** | | | | | | |
| AL Young | Y | Y | Y | Y | Y | Y |
| **ARIZONA** | | | | | | |
| 1 Renzi | Y | Y | Y | Y | Y | Y |
| 2 Franks | N | Y | N | ? | Y | Y |
| 3 Shadegg | Y | Y | N | Y | Y | Y |
| 4 Pastor | Y | Y | Y | Y | N | Y |
| 5 Hayworth | Y | Y | Y | Y | Y | Y |
| 6 Flake | N | Y | N | Y | Y | Y |
| 7 Grijalva | Y | Y | Y | Y | N | Y |
| 8 Kolbe | Y | Y | Y | Y | Y | Y |
| **ARKANSAS** | | | | | | |
| 1 Berry | N | Y | Y | Y | N | Y |
| 2 Snyder | Y | Y | Y | Y | N | Y |
| 3 Boozman | Y | Y | Y | Y | Y | Y |
| 4 Ross | Y | Y | Y | Y | N | Y |
| **CALIFORNIA** | | | | | | |
| 1 Thompson | Y | Y | Y | Y | N | Y |
| 2 Herger | Y | Y | N | Y | Y | Y |
| 3 Lungren | Y | Y | Y | Y | Y | Y |
| 4 Doolittle | Y | Y | Y | Y | Y | Y |
| 5 Matsui, D. | Y | Y | Y | Y | N | Y |
| 6 Woolsey | Y | Y | Y | Y | N | Y |
| 7 Miller, George | Y | Y | Y | Y | N | Y |
| 8 Pelosi | Y | Y | Y | Y | N | Y |
| 9 Lee | Y | + | + | + | ? | ? |
| 10 Tauscher | Y | Y | Y | Y | N | Y |
| 11 Pombo | – | Y | Y | Y | Y | Y |
| 12 Lantos | Y | ? | Y | Y | N | Y |
| 13 Stark | N | ? | ? | ? | N | Y |
| 14 Eshoo | Y | Y | Y | Y | N | Y |
| 15 Honda | Y | Y | Y | Y | N | Y |
| 16 Lofgren | Y | Y | Y | Y | N | Y |
| 17 Farr | Y | Y | Y | Y | N | Y |
| 18 Cardoza | Y | Y | Y | Y | N | Y |
| 19 Radanovich | Y | Y | Y | Y | Y | Y |
| 20 Costa | Y | Y | Y | Y | N | Y |
| 21 Nunes | + | Y | Y | Y | Y | Y |
| 22 Thomas | Y | Y | Y | Y | Y | Y |
| 23 Capps | Y | Y | Y | Y | N | Y |
| 24 Gallegly | + | Y | Y | Y | Y | Y |
| 25 McKeon | Y | Y | Y | Y | Y | Y |
| 26 Dreier | Y | Y | Y | Y | Y | Y |
| 27 Sherman | Y | ? | ? | ? | ? | ? |
| 28 Berman | Y | ? | ? | ? | ? | ? |
| 29 Schiff | + | Y | Y | Y | N | Y |
| 30 Waxman | Y | Y | Y | Y | N | Y |
| 31 Becerra | + | + | + | + | N | Y |
| 32 Solis | Y | + | + | + | – | + |
| 33 Watson | Y | Y | Y | Y | N | Y |
| 34 Roybal-Allard | + | Y | Y | Y | N | Y |
| 35 Waters | Y | ? | ? | ? | ? | ? |
| 36 Harman | Y | Y | Y | Y | N | Y |
| 37 Millender-McD. | Y | ? | ? | ? | ? | ? |
| 38 Napolitano | Y | Y | Y | Y | N | Y |
| 39 Sánchez, Linda | Y | ? | ? | ? | N | Y |
| 40 Royce | Y | Y | Y | Y | Y | Y |
| 41 Lewis | Y | Y | Y | Y | Y | Y |
| 42 Miller, Gary | ? | Y | N | Y | Y | Y |
| 43 Baca | Y | ? | ? | ? | N | Y |
| 44 Calvert | ? | Y | Y | Y | Y | Y |
| 45 Bono | Y | Y | Y | Y | Y | Y |
| 46 Rohrabacher | N | Y | Y | Y | Y | Y |
| 47 Sanchez, Loretta | Y | Y | Y | Y | N | Y |
| 48 Vacant | | | | | | |
| 49 Issa | ? | Y | Y | Y | Y | Y |

| | 569 | 570 | 571 | 572 | 573 | 574 |
|---|---|---|---|---|---|---|
| 50 Cunningham | Y | Y | Y | Y | Y | Y |
| 51 Filner | + | Y | Y | Y | N | Y |
| 52 Hunter | Y | Y | Y | Y | Y | Y |
| 53 Davis | Y | Y | Y | Y | N | Y |
| **COLORADO** | | | | | | |
| 1 DeGette | Y | Y | Y | Y | N | ? |
| 2 Udall | Y | Y | Y | Y | N | Y |
| 3 Salazar | Y | Y | Y | Y | N | Y |
| 4 Musgrave | Y | Y | N | Y | Y | Y |
| 5 Hefley | N | Y | Y | Y | Y | Y |
| 6 Tancredo | N | Y | N | Y | Y | Y |
| 7 Beauprez | Y | Y | Y | Y | Y | Y |
| **CONNECTICUT** | | | | | | |
| 1 Larson | Y | Y | Y | ? | N | Y |
| 2 Simmons | Y | Y | Y | Y | Y | Y |
| 3 DeLauro | Y | Y | Y | Y | N | Y |
| 4 Shays | Y | Y | Y | Y | Y | Y |
| 5 Johnson | Y | ? | ? | ? | Y | ? |
| **DELAWARE** | | | | | | |
| AL Castle | Y | Y | Y | Y | Y | Y |
| **FLORIDA** | | | | | | |
| 1 Miller | N | Y | N | Y | Y | Y |
| 2 Boyd | ? | Y | Y | Y | N | Y |
| 3 Brown | Y | ? | ? | ? | N | Y |
| 4 Crenshaw | Y | ? | ? | ? | ? | ? |
| 5 Brown-Waite | ? | ? | ? | ? | ? | ? |
| 6 Stearns | N | Y | N | Y | Y | Y |
| 7 Mica | Y | Y | Y | Y | Y | Y |
| 8 Keller | N | Y | Y | Y | Y | Y |
| 9 Bilirakis | Y | Y | Y | Y | Y | Y |
| 10 Young | Y | ? | ? | ? | ? | ? |
| 11 Davis | ? | Y | Y | Y | N | Y |
| 12 Putnam | Y | Y | Y | Y | Y | Y |
| 13 Harris | Y | ? | ? | ? | ? | ? |
| 14 Mack | Y | Y | Y | Y | Y | Y |
| 15 Weldon | Y | ? | Y | Y | Y | Y |
| 16 Foley | Y | Y | Y | Y | Y | Y |
| 17 Meek | Y | Y | Y | Y | N | Y |
| 18 Ros-Lehtinen | Y | Y | Y | Y | Y | Y |
| 19 Wexler | Y | Y | Y | Y | N | Y |
| 20 Wasserman-Schultz | Y | Y | Y | Y | N | Y |
| 21 Diaz-Balart, L. | Y | Y | Y | Y | Y | Y |
| 22 Shaw | Y | Y | Y | Y | Y | Y |
| 23 Hastings | ? | ? | ? | ? | ? | ? |
| 24 Feeney | Y | Y | N | Y | Y | Y |
| 25 Diaz-Balart, M. | Y | Y | Y | Y | Y | Y |
| **GEORGIA** | | | | | | |
| 1 Kingston | Y | Y | Y | Y | Y | Y |
| 2 Bishop | Y | Y | Y | Y | N | Y |
| 3 Marshall | Y | Y | Y | ? | N | Y |
| 4 McKinney | Y | ? | ? | ? | N | Y |
| 5 Lewis | Y | Y | Y | Y | N | Y |
| 6 Price | Y | Y | N | Y | Y | Y |
| 7 Linder | Y | Y | Y | Y | Y | Y |
| 8 Westmoreland | N | Y | N | Y | ? | ? |
| 9 Norwood | – | + | – | + | + | + |
| 10 Deal | Y | Y | N | Y | Y | Y |
| 11 Gingrey | Y | Y | Y | Y | Y | Y |
| 12 Barrow | Y | Y | Y | Y | N | Y |
| 13 Scott | Y | Y | Y | Y | N | Y |
| **HAWAII** | | | | | | |
| 1 Abercrombie | Y | Y | Y | Y | N | Y |
| 2 Case | Y | ? | ? | ? | N | Y |
| **IDAHO** | | | | | | |
| 1 Otter | N | Y | Y | Y | Y | Y |
| 2 Simpson | Y | Y | Y | Y | Y | Y |
| **ILLINOIS** | | | | | | |
| 1 Rush | Y | ? | ? | ? | N | Y |
| 2 Jackson | Y | Y | Y | Y | N | Y |
| 3 Lipinski | Y | ? | ? | ? | N | Y |
| 4 Gutierrez | + | ? | ? | ? | N | Y |
| 5 Emanuel | Y | Y | Y | Y | N | Y |
| 6 Hyde | Y | Y | Y | Y | Y | Y |
| 7 Davis | Y | Y | Y | Y | N | Y |
| 8 Bean | Y | Y | Y | Y | N | Y |
| 9 Schakowsky | Y | Y | Y | Y | N | Y |
| 10 Kirk | Y | + | + | + | Y | Y |
| 11 Weller | Y | Y | Y | Y | N | Y |
| 12 Costello | Y | Y | Y | Y | N | Y |

**KEY**    Republicans    Democrats    *Independents*

| | | |
|---|---|---|
| **Y** Voted for (yea) | **X** Paired against | **C** Voted "present" to avoid possible conflict of interest |
| **#** Paired for | **–** Announced against | |
| **+** Announced for | **P** Voted "present" | **?** Did not vote or otherwise make a position known |
| **N** Voted against (nay) | | |

| | 569 | 570 | 571 | 572 | 573 | 574 |
|---|---|---|---|---|---|---|
| 13 **Biggert** | Y | Y | Y | Y | Y | Y |
| 14 **Hastert** | | | | | | |
| 15 **Johnson** | Y | Y | Y | Y | Y | Y |
| 16 **Manzullo** | Y | Y | Y | Y | Y | Y |
| 17 Evans | Y | Y | Y | Y | N | Y |
| 18 **LaHood** | Y | ? | ? | ? | Y | Y |
| 19 **Shimkus** | Y | ? | ? | ? | Y | Y |
| **INDIANA** | | | | | | |
| 1 Visclosky | Y | Y | Y | Y | N | Y |
| 2 **Chocola** | Y | ? | Y | Y | Y | Y |
| 3 **Souder** | Y | ? | ? | ? | ? | Y |
| 4 **Buyer** | ? | Y | Y | Y | Y | Y |
| 5 **Burton** | Y | Y | Y | Y | Y | Y |
| 6 **Pence** | Y | Y | N | Y | Y | Y |
| 7 Carson | Y | Y | Y | Y | N | Y |
| 8 **Hostettler** | N | Y | N | Y | Y | Y |
| 9 **Sodrel** | Y | Y | N | Y | Y | Y |
| **IOWA** | | | | | | |
| 1 **Nussle** | Y | Y | Y | Y | Y | Y |
| 2 **Leach** | Y | ? | ? | ? | Y | Y |
| 3 Boswell | ? | ? | ? | ? | ? | ? |
| 4 **Latham** | Y | Y | Y | Y | Y | Y |
| 5 **King** | Y | Y | N | Y | Y | Y |
| **KANSAS** | | | | | | |
| 1 **Moran** | N | Y | Y | Y | Y | Y |
| 2 **Ryun** | N | Y | Y | Y | Y | Y |
| 3 Moore | Y | Y | Y | Y | N | Y |
| 4 **Tiahrt** | + | Y | Y | Y | Y | Y |
| **KENTUCKY** | | | | | | |
| 1 **Whitfield** | Y | ? | ? | ? | ? | ? |
| 2 **Lewis** | Y | + | + | + | Y | Y |
| 3 **Northup** | Y | Y | Y | Y | Y | Y |
| 4 **Davis** | Y | Y | N | Y | Y | Y |
| 5 **Rogers** | Y | Y | Y | Y | Y | Y |
| 6 Chandler | Y | Y | Y | Y | N | Y |
| **LOUISIANA** | | | | | | |
| 1 **Jindal** | Y | Y | Y | Y | Y | Y |
| 2 Jefferson | Y | Y | Y | Y | N | Y |
| 3 Melancon | N | Y | Y | Y | N | Y |
| 4 **McCrery** | Y | Y | Y | Y | Y | Y |
| 5 **Alexander** | Y | Y | Y | Y | Y | Y |
| 6 **Baker** | ? | Y | Y | Y | Y | Y |
| 7 **Boustany** | Y | ? | ? | ? | Y | Y |
| **MAINE** | | | | | | |
| 1 Allen | Y | Y | Y | Y | N | Y |
| 2 Michaud | Y | Y | Y | Y | N | Y |
| **MARYLAND** | | | | | | |
| 1 **Gilchrest** | Y | Y | Y | Y | Y | Y |
| 2 Ruppersberger | Y | Y | Y | Y | N | Y |
| 3 Cardin | Y | ? | ? | ? | N | Y |
| 4 Wynn | Y | Y | Y | Y | N | Y |
| 5 Hoyer | ? | Y | Y | Y | N | Y |
| 6 **Bartlett** | N | Y | N | Y | Y | Y |
| 7 Cummings | Y | ? | Y | Y | ? | ? |
| 8 Van Hollen | Y | Y | Y | Y | N | Y |
| **MASSACHUSETTS** | | | | | | |
| 1 Olver | Y | Y | Y | Y | N | Y |
| 2 Neal | Y | ? | ? | ? | N | Y |
| 3 McGovern | Y | Y | Y | Y | N | Y |
| 4 Frank | Y | Y | Y | Y | N | Y |
| 5 Meehan | Y | Y | Y | Y | N | Y |
| 6 Tierney | Y | Y | Y | Y | N | Y |
| 7 Markey | Y | Y | Y | Y | N | Y |
| 8 Capuano | Y | ? | ? | ? | N | Y |
| 9 Lynch | Y | Y | Y | Y | N | Y |
| 10 Delahunt | Y | Y | Y | Y | N | Y |
| **MICHIGAN** | | | | | | |
| 1 Stupak | Y | ? | ? | ? | N | Y |
| 2 **Hoekstra** | Y | ? | ? | ? | Y | Y |
| 3 **Ehlers** | Y | Y | Y | Y | Y | Y |
| 4 **Camp** | Y | Y | Y | Y | Y | Y |
| 5 Kildee | Y | Y | Y | Y | N | Y |
| 6 **Upton** | Y | Y | Y | Y | Y | Y |
| 7 **Schwarz** | Y | ? | ? | ? | Y | Y |
| 8 **Rogers** | Y | Y | Y | Y | Y | Y |
| 9 **Knollenberg** | Y | Y | Y | Y | Y | Y |
| 10 **Miller** | Y | Y | N | Y | Y | Y |
| 11 **McCotter** | Y | Y | Y | Y | Y | Y |
| 12 Levin | Y | Y | Y | Y | N | Y |
| 13 Kilpatrick | Y | + | + | + | − | + |
| 14 Conyers | Y | ? | ? | ? | ? | ? |
| 15 Dingell | Y | Y | Y | Y | ? | ? |

| | 569 | 570 | 571 | 572 | 573 | 574 |
|---|---|---|---|---|---|---|
| **MINNESOTA** | | | | | | |
| 1 **Gutknecht** | N | + | + | + | + | + |
| 2 **Kline** | Y | Y | Y | Y | Y | Y |
| 3 **Ramstad** | Y | Y | Y | Y | Y | Y |
| 4 McCollum | Y | Y | Y | Y | N | Y |
| 5 Sabo | Y | Y | Y | Y | N | Y |
| 6 **Kennedy** | Y | Y | Y | Y | Y | Y |
| 7 Peterson | Y | Y | Y | Y | N | Y |
| 8 Oberstar | Y | Y | Y | Y | N | Y |
| **MISSISSIPPI** | | | | | | |
| 1 **Wicker** | Y | Y | Y | Y | Y | Y |
| 2 Thompson | ? | Y | Y | Y | N | Y |
| 3 **Pickering** | Y | Y | Y | Y | Y | Y |
| 4 Taylor | N | Y | Y | Y | N | Y |
| **MISSOURI** | | | | | | |
| 1 Clay | Y | Y | Y | Y | N | Y |
| 2 **Akin** | Y | Y | Y | Y | Y | Y |
| 3 Carnahan | Y | Y | Y | Y | N | Y |
| 4 Skelton | Y | Y | Y | Y | N | + |
| 5 Cleaver | Y | Y | Y | Y | N | Y |
| 6 **Graves** | N | Y | Y | Y | Y | Y |
| 7 **Blunt** | Y | Y | Y | Y | Y | Y |
| 8 **Emerson** | + | Y | Y | Y | Y | Y |
| 9 **Hulshof** | N | ? | ? | ? | Y | Y |
| **MONTANA** | | | | | | |
| AL **Rehberg** | Y | Y | Y | Y | Y | Y |
| **NEBRASKA** | | | | | | |
| 1 **Fortenberry** | Y | Y | Y | Y | Y | Y |
| 2 **Terry** | Y | ? | ? | ? | Y | Y |
| 3 **Osborne** | + | Y | Y | Y | Y | Y |
| **NEVADA** | | | | | | |
| 1 Berkley | Y | Y | Y | Y | N | Y |
| 2 **Gibbons** | N | + | + | + | Y | Y |
| 3 **Porter** | Y | Y | Y | Y | Y | Y |
| **NEW HAMPSHIRE** | | | | | | |
| 1 **Bradley** | Y | Y | Y | Y | Y | Y |
| 2 **Bass** | Y | Y | Y | Y | Y | Y |
| **NEW JERSEY** | | | | | | |
| 1 Andrews | Y | + | + | + | − | + |
| 2 **LoBiondo** | Y | Y | Y | Y | Y | Y |
| 3 **Saxton** | Y | Y | Y | Y | Y | Y |
| 4 **Smith** | Y | Y | Y | Y | Y | Y |
| 5 **Garrett** | Y | Y | N | Y | Y | Y |
| 6 Pallone | Y | ? | ? | ? | ? | ? |
| 7 **Ferguson** | Y | Y | Y | Y | Y | Y |
| 8 Pascrell | Y | + | + | + | − | + |
| 9 Rothman | Y | Y | Y | Y | N | Y |
| 10 Payne | Y | ? | ? | ? | ? | ? |
| 11 **Frelinghuysen** | Y | Y | Y | Y | Y | Y |
| 12 Holt | Y | Y | Y | Y | N | Y |
| 13 Menendez | Y | Y | Y | Y | N | Y |
| **NEW MEXICO** | | | | | | |
| 1 **Wilson** | Y | Y | Y | Y | Y | Y |
| 2 **Pearce** | Y | Y | Y | Y | Y | Y |
| 3 Udall | Y | Y | Y | Y | N | Y |
| **NEW YORK** | | | | | | |
| 1 Bishop | Y | ? | ? | ? | N | Y |
| 2 Israel | Y | ? | ? | ? | N | Y |
| 3 **King** | Y | Y | Y | Y | Y | Y |
| 4 McCarthy | Y | ? | ? | ? | N | Y |
| 5 Ackerman | Y | ? | ? | ? | ? | ? |
| 6 Meeks | Y | ? | ? | ? | ? | ? |
| 7 Crowley | Y | ? | ? | ? | ? | ? |
| 8 Nadler | Y | Y | Y | Y | N | Y |
| 9 Weiner | Y | Y | Y | Y | N | Y |
| 10 Towns | Y | ? | ? | ? | ? | ? |
| 11 Owens | Y | + | + | + | − | + |
| 12 Velázquez | Y | ? | ? | ? | ? | ? |
| 13 **Fossella** | Y | Y | Y | Y | Y | Y |
| 14 Maloney | Y | Y | Y | Y | N | Y |
| 15 Rangel | Y | ? | ? | ? | N | Y |
| 16 Serrano | Y | ? | ? | ? | ? | ? |
| 17 Engel | Y | Y | Y | Y | N | Y |
| 18 Lowey | Y | Y | Y | Y | N | Y |
| 19 **Kelly** | Y | Y | Y | Y | Y | Y |
| 20 **Sweeney** | Y | Y | Y | Y | Y | Y |
| 21 McNulty | Y | Y | Y | Y | N | Y |
| 22 Hinchey | ? | ? | ? | ? | ? | ? |
| 23 **McHugh** | Y | Y | Y | Y | Y | Y |
| 24 **Boehlert** | ? | Y | Y | Y | Y | Y |
| 25 **Walsh** | Y | Y | Y | Y | Y | Y |
| 26 **Reynolds** | Y | Y | Y | Y | Y | Y |
| 27 Higgins | Y | Y | Y | Y | N | Y |
| 28 Slaughter | Y | + | + | + | N | Y |
| 29 **Kuhl** | Y | Y | Y | Y | Y | Y |

| | 569 | 570 | 571 | 572 | 573 | 574 |
|---|---|---|---|---|---|---|
| **NORTH CAROLINA** | | | | | | |
| 1 Butterfield | Y | Y | Y | Y | N | Y |
| 2 Etheridge | Y | Y | Y | Y | N | Y |
| 3 **Jones** | N | Y | N | Y | ? | Y |
| 4 Price | Y | ? | ? | ? | N | Y |
| 5 **Foxx** | Y | Y | N | Y | Y | Y |
| 6 **Coble** | Y | Y | N | Y | Y | Y |
| 7 McIntyre | Y | Y | Y | Y | N | Y |
| 8 **Hayes** | N | Y | N | Y | Y | Y |
| 9 **Myrick** | Y | Y | Y | Y | Y | Y |
| 10 **McHenry** | Y | Y | N | Y | Y | Y |
| 11 **Taylor** | Y | ? | ? | ? | Y | Y |
| 12 Watt | Y | Y | Y | Y | N | Y |
| 13 Miller | Y | Y | Y | Y | N | Y |
| **NORTH DAKOTA** | | | | | | |
| AL Pomeroy | Y | ? | ? | ? | N | Y |
| **OHIO** | | | | | | |
| 1 **Chabot** | Y | Y | Y | Y | Y | Y |
| 2 **Schmidt** | Y | Y | Y | Y | Y | Y |
| 3 **Turner** | Y | Y | Y | Y | Y | Y |
| 4 **Oxley** | Y | Y | Y | Y | Y | Y |
| 5 **Gillmor** | Y | Y | Y | Y | Y | Y |
| 6 Strickland | Y | ? | ? | ? | N | Y |
| 7 **Hobson** | Y | Y | Y | Y | Y | Y |
| 8 **Boehner** | Y | Y | Y | Y | Y | Y |
| 9 Kaptur | Y | Y | Y | Y | N | Y |
| 10 Kucinich | Y | Y | Y | Y | N | Y |
| 11 Jones | Y | ? | ? | ? | ? | ? |
| 12 **Tiberi** | Y | Y | Y | Y | Y | Y |
| 13 Brown | Y | + | + | + | N | Y |
| 14 **LaTourette** | Y | Y | Y | Y | Y | Y |
| 15 **Pryce** | Y | Y | Y | Y | Y | Y |
| 16 **Regula** | Y | Y | Y | Y | Y | Y |
| 17 Ryan | Y | Y | Y | Y | N | Y |
| 18 **Ney** | Y | Y | Y | Y | Y | Y |
| **OKLAHOMA** | | | | | | |
| 1 **Sullivan** | ? | Y | Y | Y | Y | Y |
| 2 Boren | Y | Y | Y | Y | N | Y |
| 3 **Lucas** | N | Y | Y | Y | Y | Y |
| 4 **Cole** | Y | Y | Y | Y | Y | Y |
| 5 **Istook** | Y | ? | ? | ? | Y | Y |
| **OREGON** | | | | | | |
| 1 Wu | Y | Y | Y | Y | N | Y |
| 2 **Walden** | Y | Y | Y | Y | Y | Y |
| 3 Blumenauer | Y | Y | Y | Y | N | Y |
| 4 DeFazio | N | Y | Y | Y | N | Y |
| 5 Hooley | Y | Y | Y | Y | N | Y |
| **PENNSYLVANIA** | | | | | | |
| 1 Brady | ? | Y | Y | Y | ? | ? |
| 2 Fattah | Y | Y | Y | Y | N | Y |
| 3 **English** | Y | Y | Y | Y | Y | Y |
| 4 **Hart** | Y | Y | Y | Y | Y | Y |
| 5 **Peterson** | Y | Y | Y | Y | Y | Y |
| 6 **Gerlach** | Y | Y | Y | Y | Y | Y |
| 7 **Weldon** | Y | ? | Y | Y | Y | Y |
| 8 **Fitzpatrick** | Y | Y | Y | Y | Y | Y |
| 9 **Shuster** | Y | Y | Y | Y | Y | Y |
| 10 **Sherwood** | Y | Y | Y | Y | Y | Y |
| 11 Kanjorski | Y | Y | Y | Y | N | Y |
| 12 Murtha | Y | ? | ? | ? | N | Y |
| 13 Schwartz | Y | Y | Y | Y | N | Y |
| 14 Doyle | Y | ? | ? | ? | ? | ? |
| 15 **Dent** | Y | Y | Y | Y | Y | Y |
| 16 **Pitts** | Y | Y | Y | Y | Y | Y |
| 17 Holden | Y | ? | ? | ? | N | Y |
| 18 **Murphy** | Y | Y | Y | Y | Y | Y |
| 19 **Platts** | Y | Y | Y | Y | Y | Y |
| **RHODE ISLAND** | | | | | | |
| 1 Kennedy | Y | Y | Y | Y | N | Y |
| 2 Langevin | Y | Y | Y | Y | N | Y |
| **SOUTH CAROLINA** | | | | | | |
| 1 **Brown** | Y | Y | Y | Y | ? | ? |
| 2 **Wilson** | Y | Y | Y | ? | Y | Y |
| 3 **Barrett** | Y | Y | Y | Y | Y | Y |
| 4 **Inglis** | Y | Y | Y | Y | Y | Y |
| 5 Spratt | Y | Y | Y | Y | N | Y |
| 6 Clyburn | Y | Y | Y | Y | N | Y |
| **SOUTH DAKOTA** | | | | | | |
| AL Herseth | Y | Y | Y | Y | N | Y |
| **TENNESSEE** | | | | | | |
| 1 **Jenkins** | N | ? | ? | ? | Y | Y |
| 2 **Duncan** | N | Y | N | Y | Y | Y |

| | 569 | 570 | 571 | 572 | 573 | 574 |
|---|---|---|---|---|---|---|
| 3 **Wamp** | Y | Y | Y | Y | Y | Y |
| 4 Davis | Y | ? | ? | ? | ? | ? |
| 5 Cooper | Y | Y | Y | Y | N | Y |
| 6 Gordon | Y | ? | ? | ? | N | Y |
| 7 **Blackburn** | Y | Y | Y | Y | Y | Y |
| 8 Tanner | N | Y | Y | Y | N | Y |
| 9 Ford | ? | ? | ? | ? | N | Y |
| **TEXAS** | | | | | | |
| 1 **Gohmert** | Y | Y | Y | Y | Y | Y |
| 2 **Poe** | ? | Y | Y | Y | + | Y |
| 3 **Johnson, S.** | Y | Y | N | ? | Y | Y |
| 4 **Hall** | Y | Y | Y | Y | Y | Y |
| 5 **Hensarling** | N | Y | N | Y | Y | Y |
| 6 **Barton** | Y | Y | Y | Y | Y | Y |
| 7 **Culberson** | Y | Y | Y | Y | Y | Y |
| 8 **Brady** | ? | Y | Y | Y | Y | Y |
| 9 Green, A. | Y | Y | Y | Y | N | Y |
| 10 **McCaul** | Y | Y | Y | Y | Y | Y |
| 11 **Conaway** | Y | Y | N | Y | Y | Y |
| 12 **Granger** | Y | Y | Y | Y | Y | Y |
| 13 **Thornberry** | Y | Y | Y | Y | Y | Y |
| 14 **Paul** | N | Y | N | Y | Y | ? |
| 15 Hinojosa | Y | Y | Y | Y | N | Y |
| 16 Reyes | Y | ? | ? | ? | N | Y |
| 17 Edwards | Y | Y | Y | Y | N | Y |
| 18 Jackson-Lee | Y | Y | Y | Y | N | Y |
| 19 **Neugebauer** | Y | Y | N | Y | Y | Y |
| 20 Gonzalez | Y | Y | Y | Y | N | Y |
| 21 **Smith** | Y | Y | Y | Y | Y | Y |
| 22 **DeLay** | Y | Y | Y | Y | Y | Y |
| 23 **Bonilla** | Y | Y | Y | Y | Y | Y |
| 24 **Marchant** | Y | ? | ? | ? | ? | ? |
| 25 Doggett | Y | Y | Y | Y | N | Y |
| 26 **Burgess** | Y | Y | Y | Y | Y | Y |
| 27 Ortiz | + | Y | Y | Y | N | Y |
| 28 Cuellar | Y | Y | Y | Y | N | Y |
| 29 Green, G. | Y | Y | Y | Y | N | Y |
| 30 Johnson, E. | Y | Y | Y | Y | N | Y |
| 31 **Carter** | Y | Y | Y | Y | Y | Y |
| 32 **Sessions** | Y | Y | Y | Y | Y | Y |
| **UTAH** | | | | | | |
| 1 **Bishop** | Y | Y | Y | Y | Y | Y |
| 2 Matheson | Y | Y | Y | Y | N | Y |
| 3 **Cannon** | Y | Y | Y | Y | Y | Y |
| **VERMONT** | | | | | | |
| AL *Sanders* | Y | Y | Y | Y | N | Y |
| **VIRGINIA** | | | | | | |
| 1 **Davis, J.** | N | Y | Y | Y | Y | Y |
| 2 **Drake** | Y | Y | Y | Y | Y | Y |
| 3 Scott | Y | ? | ? | ? | N | Y |
| 4 **Forbes** | Y | Y | Y | Y | Y | Y |
| 5 **Goode** | N | Y | N | Y | Y | Y |
| 6 **Goodlatte** | N | Y | Y | Y | Y | Y |
| 7 **Cantor** | Y | ? | ? | ? | Y | Y |
| 8 Moran | Y | Y | Y | Y | − | Y |
| 9 Boucher | Y | Y | Y | Y | N | Y |
| 10 **Wolf** | Y | Y | Y | Y | Y | Y |
| 11 **Davis, T.** | Y | Y | Y | Y | Y | Y |
| **WASHINGTON** | | | | | | |
| 1 Inslee | Y | Y | Y | Y | N | Y |
| 2 Larsen | Y | Y | Y | Y | N | Y |
| 3 Baird | Y | Y | Y | Y | N | Y |
| 4 **Hastings** | Y | Y | Y | Y | Y | Y |
| 5 **McMorris** | ? | Y | Y | Y | Y | Y |
| 6 Dicks | ? | Y | Y | Y | N | Y |
| 7 McDermott | Y | Y | Y | Y | N | Y |
| 8 **Reichert** | Y | Y | Y | Y | Y | Y |
| 9 Smith | Y | Y | Y | Y | N | Y |
| **WEST VIRGINIA** | | | | | | |
| 1 Mollohan | Y | Y | Y | Y | N | Y |
| 2 **Capito** | Y | Y | Y | Y | Y | Y |
| 3 Rahall | N | Y | Y | Y | N | Y |
| **WISCONSIN** | | | | | | |
| 1 **Ryan** | + | + | + | + | Y | Y |
| 2 Baldwin | Y | Y | Y | Y | N | Y |
| 3 Kind | ? | Y | Y | Y | N | Y |
| 4 Moore | Y | Y | Y | Y | N | Y |
| 5 **Sensenbrenner** | N | Y | N | Y | Y | Y |
| 6 **Petri** | N | Y | N | Y | Y | Y |
| 7 Obey | Y | Y | Y | Y | N | Y |
| 8 **Green** | N | Y | Y | Y | Y | Y |
| **WYOMING** | | | | | | |
| AL **Cubin** | N | Y | Y | Y | Y | Y |

# IN THE HOUSE | By Vote Number

**575.** **H Res 302. Employers of National Guard and Reserve Forces/Adoption.** Johnson, R-Texas., motion to suspend the rules and adopt the resolution that would recognize and support employers of National Guard and other reserve forces for their strong support of U.S. goals and struggles in the war on terrorism. Motion agreed to 395-0: R 221-0; D 173-0 (ND 125-0, SD 48-0); I 1-0. A two-thirds majority of those present and voting (264 in this case) is required for adoption under suspension of the rules. Nov. 8, 2005.

**576.** **HR 3770. Grant W. Green Post Office/Passage.** Westmoreland, R-Ga., motion to suspend the rules and pass the bill that would designate a post office in Knox, Ind., for Grant W. Green, who was a postal worker for 50 years, serving from 1920 to 1970. Motion agreed to 393-1: R 221-0; D 171-1 (ND 123-1, SD 48-0); I 1-0. A two-thirds majority of those present and voting (263 in this case) is required for passage under suspension of the rules. Nov. 8, 2005.

**577.** **HR 2419. Fiscal 2006 Energy-Water Appropriations/Rule.** Adoption of the rule (H Res 539) that would provide for House floor consideration of the conference report on the bill that would appropriate $30.5 billion in fiscal 2006 for energy and water development projects. Adopted 412-2: R 220-1; D 191-1 (ND 142-1, SD 49-0); I 1-0. Nov. 9, 2005.

**578.** **HR 2862. Fiscal 2006 Commerce-Justice-Science Appropriations/Rule.** Adoption of the rule (H Res 538) that would provide for House floor consideration of the conference report on the bill that would appropriate $61.8 billion in fiscal 2006 for the departments of Commerce, Justice and State, and various science and other related agencies. Adopted 410-0: R 220-0; D 189-0 (ND 142-0, SD 47-0); I 1-0. Nov. 9, 2005.

**579.** **HR 1751. Court Security/Rule.** Adoption of the rule (H Res 540) that would provide for House floor consideration of the bill that would increase federal penalties for the assault, murder or kidnapping of judges or their immediate family members. Adopted 412-0: R 221-0; D 190-0 (ND 142-0, SD 48-0); I 1-0. Nov. 9, 2005.

**580.** **HR 2419. Fiscal 2006 Energy-Water Appropriations/Conference Report.** Adoption of the conference report on the bill that would provide $30.5 billion in fiscal 2006 for energy and water development projects, including $24.3 billion for the Energy Department, $5.4 billion for the Army Corps of Engineers and $1.1 billion for Interior Department water projects. Adopted (thus sent to the Senate) 399-17: R 209-12; D 189-5 (ND 140-5, SD 49-0); I 1-0. Nov. 9, 2005.

| | 575 | 576 | 577 | 578 | 579 | 580 |
|---|---|---|---|---|---|---|
| **ALABAMA** | | | | | | |
| 1 Bonner | Y | Y | Y | Y | Y | Y |
| 2 Everett | Y | Y | Y | Y | Y | Y |
| 3 Rogers | Y | Y | Y | Y | Y | Y |
| 4 Aderholt | Y | Y | Y | Y | Y | Y |
| 5 Cramer | Y | Y | Y | Y | Y | Y |
| 6 Bachus | Y | Y | Y | Y | Y | Y |
| 7 Davis | Y | Y | Y | Y | Y | |
| **ALASKA** | | | | | | |
| AL Young | Y | Y | Y | Y | Y | Y |
| **ARIZONA** | | | | | | |
| 1 Renzi | Y | Y | Y | Y | Y | Y |
| 2 Franks | Y | Y | Y | Y | Y | Y |
| 3 Shadegg | Y | Y | Y | Y | Y | Y |
| 4 Pastor | Y | Y | Y | Y | Y | Y |
| 5 Hayworth | Y | Y | Y | Y | Y | Y |
| 6 Flake | Y | Y | Y | Y | Y | N |
| 7 Grijalva | Y | Y | Y | Y | Y | Y |
| 8 Kolbe | Y | Y | Y | Y | Y | Y |
| **ARKANSAS** | | | | | | |
| 1 Berry | Y | Y | Y | Y | Y | Y |
| 2 Snyder | Y | Y | Y | Y | Y | Y |
| 3 Boozman | Y | Y | Y | Y | Y | Y |
| 4 Ross | Y | Y | Y | Y | Y | Y |
| **CALIFORNIA** | | | | | | |
| 1 Thompson | Y | Y | Y | Y | Y | Y |
| 2 Herger | Y | Y | Y | Y | Y | Y |
| 3 Lungren | Y | Y | Y | Y | Y | Y |
| 4 Doolittle | Y | Y | Y | Y | Y | Y |
| 5 Matsui, D. | Y | Y | Y | Y | Y | Y |
| 6 Woolsey | Y | Y | Y | Y | Y | Y |
| 7 Miller, George | Y | Y | Y | Y | Y | Y |
| 8 Pelosi | Y | Y | Y | Y | Y | Y |
| 9 Lee | ? | ? | Y | Y | Y | Y |
| 10 Tauscher | Y | Y | Y | Y | Y | Y |
| 11 Pombo | Y | Y | Y | Y | Y | Y |
| 12 Lantos | Y | Y | Y | Y | Y | Y |
| 13 Stark | Y | Y | Y | ? | Y | Y |
| 14 Eshoo | Y | Y | Y | Y | Y | Y |
| 15 Honda | Y | Y | Y | Y | Y | Y |
| 16 Lofgren | ? | Y | Y | Y | Y | Y |
| 17 Farr | Y | Y | Y | Y | Y | Y |
| 18 Cardoza | Y | Y | Y | Y | Y | Y |
| 19 Radanovich | Y | Y | Y | Y | Y | Y |
| 20 Costa | Y | Y | Y | Y | Y | Y |
| 21 Nunes | Y | Y | Y | Y | Y | Y |
| 22 Thomas | Y | Y | Y | Y | Y | Y |
| 23 Capps | Y | Y | Y | Y | Y | Y |
| 24 Gallegly | Y | Y | Y | Y | Y | Y |
| 25 McKeon | Y | Y | Y | Y | Y | Y |
| 26 Dreier | Y | Y | Y | Y | Y | Y |
| 27 Sherman | ? | ? | Y | Y | Y | Y |
| 28 Berman | ? | ? | ? | ? | ? | Y |
| 29 Schiff | Y | Y | Y | Y | Y | Y |
| 30 Waxman | Y | Y | Y | Y | Y | Y |
| 31 Becerra | Y | Y | Y | Y | Y | Y |
| 32 Solis | + | + | + | + | + | + |
| 33 Watson | Y | Y | Y | Y | Y | Y |
| 34 Roybal-Allard | Y | Y | Y | Y | Y | Y |
| 35 Waters | ? | ? | Y | Y | Y | Y |
| 36 Harman | Y | Y | Y | Y | Y | Y |
| 37 Millender-McD. | ? | ? | ? | ? | ? | ? |
| 38 Napolitano | Y | ? | Y | Y | Y | Y |
| 39 Sánchez, Linda | Y | Y | Y | Y | Y | Y |
| 40 Royce | Y | Y | Y | Y | Y | Y |
| 41 Lewis | Y | Y | Y | Y | Y | Y |
| 42 Miller, Gary | Y | Y | Y | Y | Y | Y |
| 43 Baca | Y | Y | Y | Y | Y | Y |
| 44 Calvert | Y | Y | Y | Y | Y | Y |
| 45 Bono | Y | Y | Y | Y | Y | Y |
| 46 Rohrabacher | Y | Y | Y | Y | Y | Y |
| 47 Sanchez, Loretta | Y | Y | Y | Y | Y | Y |
| 48 Vacant | | | | | | |
| 49 Issa | Y | Y | Y | Y | Y | Y |
| 50 Cunningham | Y | Y | Y | Y | Y | Y |
| 51 Filner | Y | Y | Y | Y | Y | Y |
| 52 Hunter | Y | Y | Y | Y | Y | Y |
| 53 Davis | Y | Y | Y | Y | Y | Y |
| **COLORADO** | | | | | | |
| 1 DeGette | Y | Y | Y | Y | Y | Y |
| 2 Udall | Y | Y | Y | Y | Y | Y |
| 3 Salazar | Y | Y | Y | Y | Y | Y |
| 4 Musgrave | Y | Y | Y | Y | Y | Y |
| 5 Hefley | Y | Y | Y | Y | Y | N |
| 6 Tancredo | Y | Y | Y | Y | Y | N |
| 7 Beauprez | Y | Y | Y | Y | Y | Y |
| **CONNECTICUT** | | | | | | |
| 1 Larson | Y | Y | Y | Y | Y | Y |
| 2 Simmons | Y | Y | Y | Y | Y | Y |
| 3 DeLauro | Y | Y | Y | Y | Y | Y |
| 4 Shays | Y | Y | Y | Y | Y | Y |
| 5 Johnson | Y | Y | Y | Y | Y | Y |
| **DELAWARE** | | | | | | |
| AL Castle | Y | Y | Y | Y | Y | Y |
| **FLORIDA** | | | | | | |
| 1 Miller | Y | Y | Y | Y | Y | N |
| 2 Boyd | Y | Y | Y | Y | Y | Y |
| 3 Brown | ? | ? | Y | Y | Y | Y |
| 4 Crenshaw | Y | Y | Y | Y | Y | Y |
| 5 Brown-Waite | ? | ? | ? | ? | ? | ? |
| 6 Stearns | Y | Y | Y | Y | Y | N |
| 7 Mica | Y | Y | Y | Y | Y | Y |
| 8 Keller | Y | Y | Y | Y | Y | Y |
| 9 Bilirakis | Y | Y | Y | Y | Y | Y |
| 10 Young | ? | ? | ? | ? | ? | ? |
| 11 Davis | Y | Y | ? | ? | ? | ? |
| 12 Putnam | Y | Y | Y | Y | Y | Y |
| 13 Harris | ? | ? | Y | Y | Y | Y |
| 14 Mack | Y | Y | Y | Y | Y | Y |
| 15 Weldon | Y | Y | Y | Y | Y | Y |
| 16 Foley | Y | Y | Y | Y | Y | Y |
| 17 Meek | Y | Y | Y | Y | Y | Y |
| 18 Ros-Lehtinen | Y | Y | Y | Y | Y | Y |
| 19 Wexler | Y | Y | Y | Y | Y | Y |
| 20 Wasserman-Schultz | Y | Y | Y | Y | Y | Y |
| 21 Diaz-Balart, L. | Y | Y | ? | ? | Y | Y |
| 22 Shaw | Y | Y | Y | Y | Y | Y |
| 23 Hastings | ? | ? | ? | ? | ? | ? |
| 24 Feeney | Y | Y | Y | Y | Y | Y |
| 25 Diaz-Balart, M. | Y | Y | Y | Y | Y | Y |
| **GEORGIA** | | | | | | |
| 1 Kingston | Y | Y | Y | Y | Y | Y |
| 2 Bishop | Y | Y | Y | Y | Y | Y |
| 3 Marshall | Y | Y | Y | Y | Y | Y |
| 4 McKinney | Y | Y | Y | Y | Y | Y |
| 5 Lewis | Y | Y | Y | Y | Y | Y |
| 6 Price | Y | Y | Y | Y | Y | Y |
| 7 Linder | Y | Y | Y | Y | Y | Y |
| 8 Westmoreland | ? | ? | Y | Y | Y | Y |
| 9 Norwood | + | + | + | + | + | – |
| 10 Deal | Y | Y | Y | Y | Y | Y |
| 11 Gingrey | Y | Y | Y | Y | Y | Y |
| 12 Barrow | Y | Y | Y | Y | Y | Y |
| 13 Scott | Y | Y | Y | Y | Y | Y |
| **HAWAII** | | | | | | |
| 1 Abercrombie | Y | N | Y | Y | Y | Y |
| 2 Case | Y | Y | Y | Y | Y | Y |
| **IDAHO** | | | | | | |
| 1 Otter | Y | Y | Y | Y | Y | Y |
| 2 Simpson | Y | Y | Y | Y | Y | Y |
| **ILLINOIS** | | | | | | |
| 1 Rush | Y | Y | Y | Y | Y | Y |
| 2 Jackson | Y | Y | Y | Y | Y | Y |
| 3 Lipinski | Y | Y | Y | Y | Y | Y |
| 4 Gutierrez | Y | Y | Y | Y | Y | Y |
| 5 Emanuel | Y | Y | Y | ? | ? | Y |
| 6 Hyde | Y | Y | Y | Y | Y | Y |
| 7 Davis | Y | Y | Y | Y | Y | Y |
| 8 Bean | Y | Y | Y | Y | Y | Y |
| 9 Schakowsky | Y | Y | Y | Y | Y | Y |
| 10 Kirk | Y | Y | Y | Y | Y | Y |
| 11 Weller | Y | Y | Y | Y | Y | Y |
| 12 Costello | Y | Y | Y | Y | Y | Y |

| KEY | Republicans | Democrats | Independents |
|---|---|---|---|

| | | |
|---|---|---|
| Y Voted for (yea) | X Paired against | C Voted "present" to avoid possible conflict of interest |
| # Paired for | – Announced against | |
| + Announced for | P Voted "present" | ? Did not vote or otherwise make a position known |
| N Voted against (nay) | | |

| | 575 | 576 | 577 | 578 | 579 | 580 |
|---|---|---|---|---|---|---|
| 13 **Biggert** | Y | Y | Y | Y | Y | Y |
| 14 **Hastert** | | | | | | |
| 15 **Johnson** | Y | Y | Y | Y | Y | Y |
| 16 **Manzullo** | Y | Y | Y | Y | Y | Y |
| 17 Evans | Y | Y | Y | Y | Y | Y |
| 18 **LaHood** | Y | Y | Y | Y | Y | Y |
| 19 **Shimkus** | Y | Y | Y | Y | Y | Y |
| **INDIANA** | | | | | | |
| 1 Visclosky | Y | Y | Y | Y | Y | Y |
| 2 **Chocola** | Y | Y | Y | Y | Y | Y |
| 3 **Souder** | Y | Y | Y | Y | Y | Y |
| 4 **Buyer** | Y | Y | Y | Y | Y | Y |
| 5 **Burton** | Y | Y | Y | Y | Y | Y |
| 6 **Pence** | Y | Y | Y | Y | Y | Y |
| 7 Carson | Y | Y | Y | Y | Y | Y |
| 8 **Hostettler** | Y | Y | Y | Y | Y | N |
| 9 **Sodrel** | Y | Y | Y | Y | Y | Y |
| **IOWA** | | | | | | |
| 1 **Nussle** | Y | Y | Y | Y | Y | Y |
| 2 **Leach** | Y | Y | Y | Y | Y | Y |
| 3 Boswell | ? | ? | ? | ? | ? | ? |
| 4 **Latham** | Y | Y | Y | Y | Y | Y |
| 5 **King** | Y | Y | Y | Y | Y | Y |
| **KANSAS** | | | | | | |
| 1 **Moran** | Y | Y | Y | Y | Y | Y |
| 2 **Ryun** | Y | Y | Y | Y | Y | Y |
| 3 Moore | Y | Y | Y | Y | Y | Y |
| 4 **Tiahrt** | Y | Y | Y | Y | Y | Y |
| **KENTUCKY** | | | | | | |
| 1 **Whitfield** | ? | ? | Y | Y | Y | Y |
| 2 **Lewis** | Y | Y | Y | Y | Y | Y |
| 3 **Northup** | Y | Y | Y | Y | Y | Y |
| 4 **Davis** | Y | Y | Y | Y | Y | Y |
| 5 **Rogers** | Y | Y | Y | Y | Y | Y |
| 6 Chandler | Y | Y | Y | Y | Y | Y |
| **LOUISIANA** | | | | | | |
| 1 **Jindal** | Y | Y | Y | Y | Y | Y |
| 2 Jefferson | Y | Y | Y | ? | Y | Y |
| 3 Melancon | Y | Y | Y | Y | Y | Y |
| 4 **McCrery** | Y | Y | Y | Y | Y | Y |
| 5 **Alexander** | Y | Y | Y | Y | Y | Y |
| 6 **Baker** | Y | Y | Y | Y | Y | Y |
| 7 **Boustany** | Y | Y | Y | Y | Y | Y |
| **MAINE** | | | | | | |
| 1 Allen | Y | Y | Y | Y | Y | Y |
| 2 Michaud | Y | Y | Y | Y | Y | Y |
| **MARYLAND** | | | | | | |
| 1 **Gilchrest** | Y | Y | Y | Y | Y | Y |
| 2 Ruppersberger | Y | Y | Y | Y | Y | Y |
| 3 Cardin | Y | Y | Y | Y | Y | Y |
| 4 Wynn | Y | Y | Y | Y | Y | Y |
| 5 Hoyer | Y | Y | Y | Y | Y | Y |
| 6 **Bartlett** | Y | Y | Y | Y | Y | Y |
| 7 Cummings | ? | ? | Y | Y | Y | Y |
| 8 Van Hollen | Y | Y | Y | Y | Y | Y |
| **MASSACHUSETTS** | | | | | | |
| 1 Olver | Y | Y | Y | Y | Y | Y |
| 2 Neal | Y | Y | Y | Y | Y | Y |
| 3 McGovern | Y | Y | Y | Y | Y | Y |
| 4 Frank | Y | Y | Y | Y | Y | Y |
| 5 Meehan | Y | Y | Y | Y | Y | Y |
| 6 Tierney | Y | Y | Y | Y | Y | Y |
| 7 Markey | Y | Y | Y | Y | Y | Y |
| 8 Capuano | Y | Y | Y | Y | Y | Y |
| 9 Lynch | Y | Y | Y | Y | Y | Y |
| 10 Delahunt | Y | Y | Y | Y | Y | Y |
| **MICHIGAN** | | | | | | |
| 1 Stupak | Y | Y | Y | Y | Y | Y |
| 2 **Hoekstra** | Y | Y | Y | Y | Y | Y |
| 3 **Ehlers** | Y | Y | Y | Y | Y | Y |
| 4 **Camp** | Y | Y | Y | Y | Y | Y |
| 5 Kildee | Y | Y | Y | Y | Y | Y |
| 6 **Upton** | Y | Y | Y | Y | Y | Y |
| 7 **Schwarz** | Y | Y | Y | Y | Y | Y |
| 8 **Rogers** | Y | Y | Y | Y | Y | Y |
| 9 **Knollenberg** | Y | Y | Y | Y | Y | Y |
| 10 **Miller** | Y | Y | Y | Y | Y | Y |
| 11 **McCotter** | Y | Y | Y | Y | Y | Y |
| 12 Levin | Y | Y | Y | Y | Y | Y |
| 13 Kilpatrick | + | + | ? | ? | ? | Y |
| 14 Conyers | ? | ? | Y | Y | Y | Y |
| 15 Dingell | ? | ? | Y | Y | Y | Y |
| **MINNESOTA** | | | | | | |
| 1 **Gutknecht** | + | + | Y | Y | Y | Y |
| 2 **Kline** | Y | Y | Y | Y | Y | Y |
| 3 **Ramstad** | Y | Y | Y | Y | Y | Y |
| 4 McCollum | Y | Y | Y | Y | Y | Y |
| 5 Sabo | Y | Y | Y | Y | Y | Y |
| 6 **Kennedy** | Y | Y | Y | Y | Y | Y |
| 7 Peterson | Y | Y | Y | Y | Y | Y |
| 8 Oberstar | Y | Y | Y | Y | Y | Y |
| **MISSISSIPPI** | | | | | | |
| 1 **Wicker** | Y | Y | Y | Y | Y | Y |
| 2 Thompson | Y | Y | Y | Y | Y | Y |
| 3 **Pickering** | Y | Y | Y | Y | Y | Y |
| 4 Taylor | Y | Y | Y | Y | Y | Y |
| **MISSOURI** | | | | | | |
| 1 Clay | Y | Y | Y | Y | Y | Y |
| 2 **Akin** | Y | Y | Y | Y | Y | Y |
| 3 Carnahan | Y | Y | Y | Y | Y | Y |
| 4 Skelton | Y | + | Y | Y | Y | Y |
| 5 Cleaver | Y | Y | Y | Y | Y | Y |
| 6 **Graves** | Y | Y | Y | Y | Y | Y |
| 7 **Blunt** | Y | Y | Y | Y | Y | Y |
| 8 **Emerson** | Y | Y | Y | Y | Y | Y |
| 9 **Hulshof** | Y | Y | Y | Y | Y | Y |
| **MONTANA** | | | | | | |
| AL **Rehberg** | Y | Y | Y | Y | Y | Y |
| **NEBRASKA** | | | | | | |
| 1 **Fortenberry** | Y | Y | Y | Y | Y | Y |
| 2 **Terry** | Y | Y | Y | Y | Y | Y |
| 3 **Osborne** | Y | Y | Y | Y | Y | Y |
| **NEVADA** | | | | | | |
| 1 Berkley | Y | Y | N | Y | Y | N |
| 2 **Gibbons** | Y | Y | Y | Y | Y | N |
| 3 **Porter** | Y | Y | N | Y | Y | N |
| **NEW HAMPSHIRE** | | | | | | |
| 1 **Bradley** | Y | Y | Y | Y | Y | Y |
| 2 **Bass** | Y | Y | Y | Y | Y | Y |
| **NEW JERSEY** | | | | | | |
| 1 Andrews | + | + | Y | Y | Y | N |
| 2 **LoBiondo** | Y | Y | Y | Y | Y | Y |
| 3 **Saxton** | Y | Y | Y | Y | Y | Y |
| 4 **Smith** | Y | Y | Y | Y | Y | Y |
| 5 **Garrett** | Y | Y | Y | Y | Y | Y |
| 6 Pallone | ? | ? | Y | Y | Y | Y |
| 7 **Ferguson** | Y | Y | Y | Y | Y | Y |
| 8 Pascrell | + | + | Y | Y | Y | Y |
| 9 Rothman | Y | Y | Y | Y | Y | Y |
| 10 Payne | ? | ? | Y | Y | Y | Y |
| 11 **Frelinghuysen** | Y | Y | Y | Y | Y | Y |
| 12 Holt | Y | Y | Y | Y | Y | Y |
| 13 Menendez | Y | Y | Y | Y | Y | Y |
| **NEW MEXICO** | | | | | | |
| 1 **Wilson** | Y | Y | Y | Y | Y | Y |
| 2 **Pearce** | Y | Y | Y | Y | Y | Y |
| 3 Udall | Y | Y | Y | Y | Y | Y |
| **NEW YORK** | | | | | | |
| 1 Bishop | Y | Y | Y | Y | Y | N |
| 2 Israel | Y | Y | Y | Y | Y | Y |
| 3 **King** | Y | Y | Y | Y | Y | Y |
| 4 McCarthy | Y | Y | Y | Y | Y | Y |
| 5 Ackerman | ? | ? | Y | Y | ? | Y |
| 6 Meeks | ? | ? | Y | Y | Y | ? |
| 7 Crowley | ? | ? | Y | Y | Y | Y |
| 8 Nadler | Y | Y | Y | Y | Y | Y |
| 9 Weiner | Y | Y | Y | Y | Y | Y |
| 10 Towns | ? | ? | Y | Y | Y | Y |
| 11 Owens | + | + | Y | Y | Y | Y |
| 12 Velázquez | ? | ? | Y | Y | Y | Y |
| 13 **Fossella** | Y | Y | ? | ? | ? | Y |
| 14 Maloney | Y | Y | Y | Y | Y | Y |
| 15 Rangel | Y | Y | Y | Y | Y | Y |
| 16 Serrano | ? | ? | Y | Y | Y | Y |
| 17 Engel | Y | Y | Y | Y | Y | Y |
| 18 Lowey | Y | Y | Y | Y | Y | Y |
| 19 **Kelly** | Y | Y | Y | Y | Y | Y |
| 20 **Sweeney** | Y | Y | ? | ? | ? | ? |
| 21 McNulty | Y | Y | Y | Y | Y | Y |
| 22 Hinchey | ? | ? | Y | Y | Y | Y |
| 23 **McHugh** | Y | Y | Y | Y | Y | Y |
| 24 **Boehlert** | Y | Y | Y | Y | Y | Y |
| 25 **Walsh** | Y | Y | ? | ? | ? | Y |
| 26 **Reynolds** | Y | Y | Y | Y | Y | Y |
| 27 Higgins | Y | Y | Y | Y | Y | Y |
| 28 Slaughter | Y | Y | Y | Y | Y | ? |
| 29 **Kuhl** | Y | Y | Y | Y | Y | Y |
| **NORTH CAROLINA** | | | | | | |
| 1 Butterfield | Y | Y | Y | Y | Y | Y |
| 2 Etheridge | Y | Y | Y | Y | Y | Y |
| 3 **Jones** | Y | Y | Y | Y | Y | Y |
| 4 Price | Y | Y | Y | Y | Y | Y |
| 5 **Foxx** | Y | Y | Y | Y | Y | Y |
| 6 **Coble** | Y | Y | Y | Y | Y | Y |
| 7 McIntyre | Y | Y | Y | Y | Y | Y |
| 8 **Hayes** | + | + | Y | Y | Y | Y |
| 9 **Myrick** | Y | Y | Y | Y | Y | Y |
| 10 **McHenry** | Y | Y | Y | Y | Y | Y |
| 11 **Taylor** | Y | Y | Y | Y | Y | Y |
| 12 Watt | Y | Y | Y | Y | Y | Y |
| 13 Miller | Y | Y | Y | Y | Y | Y |
| **NORTH DAKOTA** | | | | | | |
| AL Pomeroy | Y | Y | Y | Y | Y | Y |
| **OHIO** | | | | | | |
| 1 **Chabot** | Y | Y | Y | Y | Y | Y |
| 2 **Schmidt** | Y | Y | Y | Y | Y | Y |
| 3 **Turner** | Y | Y | ? | ? | ? | ? |
| 4 **Oxley** | Y | Y | Y | Y | Y | + |
| 5 **Gillmor** | Y | Y | Y | Y | Y | Y |
| 6 Strickland | Y | Y | ? | ? | ? | ? |
| 7 **Hobson** | Y | Y | Y | Y | Y | Y |
| 8 **Boehner** | Y | Y | Y | Y | Y | Y |
| 9 Kaptur | Y | Y | Y | Y | Y | Y |
| 10 Kucinich | Y | Y | Y | Y | Y | N |
| 11 Jones | ? | ? | ? | ? | ? | Y |
| 12 **Tiberi** | Y | Y | Y | Y | Y | Y |
| 13 Brown | Y | Y | Y | Y | Y | Y |
| 14 **LaTourette** | Y | Y | Y | Y | Y | Y |
| 15 **Pryce** | Y | Y | Y | Y | Y | Y |
| 16 **Regula** | Y | Y | Y | Y | Y | Y |
| 17 Ryan | Y | Y | Y | Y | Y | Y |
| 18 **Ney** | Y | Y | Y | Y | Y | Y |
| **OKLAHOMA** | | | | | | |
| 1 **Sullivan** | Y | Y | Y | Y | Y | Y |
| 2 Boren | Y | Y | Y | Y | Y | Y |
| 3 **Lucas** | Y | Y | Y | Y | Y | Y |
| 4 **Cole** | Y | Y | Y | Y | Y | Y |
| 5 **Istook** | Y | Y | Y | Y | Y | Y |
| **OREGON** | | | | | | |
| 1 Wu | Y | Y | Y | Y | Y | Y |
| 2 **Walden** | Y | Y | Y | Y | Y | Y |
| 3 Blumenauer | Y | Y | ? | Y | Y | Y |
| 4 DeFazio | Y | Y | Y | Y | Y | Y |
| 5 Hooley | Y | Y | Y | Y | Y | Y |
| **PENNSYLVANIA** | | | | | | |
| 1 Brady | ? | ? | Y | Y | Y | Y |
| 2 Fattah | Y | Y | Y | Y | Y | Y |
| 3 **English** | Y | Y | Y | Y | Y | Y |
| 4 **Hart** | Y | Y | Y | Y | Y | Y |
| 5 **Peterson** | Y | Y | Y | Y | Y | Y |
| 6 **Gerlach** | Y | Y | Y | Y | Y | Y |
| 7 **Weldon** | Y | Y | Y | Y | Y | Y |
| 8 **Fitzpatrick** | Y | Y | Y | Y | Y | Y |
| 9 **Shuster** | Y | Y | Y | Y | Y | Y |
| 10 **Sherwood** | Y | Y | Y | Y | Y | Y |
| 11 Kanjorski | Y | Y | Y | Y | Y | Y |
| 12 Murtha | Y | Y | Y | Y | Y | Y |
| 13 Schwartz | Y | Y | Y | Y | Y | Y |
| 14 Doyle | Y | Y | Y | Y | Y | Y |
| 15 **Dent** | Y | Y | Y | Y | Y | Y |
| 16 **Pitts** | Y | Y | Y | Y | Y | Y |
| 17 Holden | Y | Y | Y | Y | Y | Y |
| 18 **Murphy** | Y | Y | Y | Y | Y | Y |
| 19 **Platts** | Y | Y | Y | Y | Y | Y |
| **RHODE ISLAND** | | | | | | |
| 1 Kennedy | Y | Y | Y | Y | Y | Y |
| 2 Langevin | Y | Y | Y | Y | Y | Y |
| **SOUTH CAROLINA** | | | | | | |
| 1 **Brown** | Y | Y | Y | Y | Y | Y |
| 2 **Wilson** | Y | Y | Y | Y | Y | Y |
| 3 **Barrett** | Y | Y | Y | Y | Y | Y |
| 4 **Inglis** | Y | Y | Y | Y | Y | Y |
| 5 Spratt | Y | Y | Y | Y | Y | Y |
| 6 Clyburn | Y | Y | Y | Y | Y | Y |
| **SOUTH DAKOTA** | | | | | | |
| AL Herseth | Y | Y | Y | Y | Y | Y |
| **TENNESSEE** | | | | | | |
| 1 **Jenkins** | Y | Y | Y | ? | Y | Y |
| 2 **Duncan** | Y | Y | Y | Y | Y | N |
| 3 **Wamp** | Y | Y | Y | Y | Y | Y |
| 4 Davis | ? | ? | Y | Y | Y | Y |
| 5 Cooper | Y | Y | Y | Y | Y | Y |
| 6 Gordon | Y | Y | Y | Y | Y | Y |
| 7 **Blackburn** | Y | Y | Y | Y | Y | Y |
| 8 Tanner | Y | Y | Y | Y | Y | Y |
| 9 Ford | Y | Y | Y | Y | Y | Y |
| **TEXAS** | | | | | | |
| 1 **Gohmert** | Y | Y | Y | Y | Y | Y |
| 2 **Poe** | Y | Y | Y | Y | Y | Y |
| 3 **Johnson, S.** | Y | Y | Y | Y | Y | Y |
| 4 **Hall** | Y | Y | Y | Y | Y | Y |
| 5 **Hensarling** | Y | Y | Y | Y | Y | Y |
| 6 **Barton** | Y | Y | Y | Y | Y | Y |
| 7 **Culberson** | Y | Y | Y | Y | Y | Y |
| 8 **Brady** | Y | Y | Y | Y | Y | Y |
| 9 Green, A. | Y | Y | Y | Y | Y | Y |
| 10 **McCaul** | Y | Y | Y | Y | Y | Y |
| 11 **Conaway** | Y | Y | ? | ? | ? | ? |
| 12 **Granger** | Y | Y | Y | Y | Y | Y |
| 13 **Thornberry** | Y | Y | Y | Y | Y | Y |
| 14 **Paul** | Y | Y | Y | Y | Y | ? |
| 15 Hinojosa | Y | Y | Y | Y | Y | Y |
| 16 Reyes | Y | Y | Y | Y | Y | Y |
| 17 Edwards | Y | Y | Y | Y | Y | Y |
| 18 Jackson-Lee | Y | Y | Y | Y | Y | Y |
| 19 **Neugebauer** | Y | Y | Y | Y | Y | Y |
| 20 Gonzalez | Y | Y | Y | ? | ? | Y |
| 21 **Smith** | Y | Y | Y | Y | Y | Y |
| 22 **DeLay** | Y | Y | Y | Y | Y | Y |
| 23 **Bonilla** | Y | Y | Y | Y | Y | Y |
| 24 **Marchant** | ? | ? | Y | Y | Y | Y |
| 25 Doggett | Y | Y | Y | Y | Y | Y |
| 26 **Burgess** | Y | Y | Y | Y | Y | Y |
| 27 Ortiz | Y | Y | Y | Y | Y | Y |
| 28 Cuellar | Y | Y | Y | Y | Y | Y |
| 29 Green, G. | Y | Y | Y | Y | Y | Y |
| 30 Johnson, E. | Y | Y | Y | Y | Y | Y |
| 31 **Carter** | Y | Y | Y | Y | Y | Y |
| 32 **Sessions** | Y | Y | Y | Y | Y | ? |
| **UTAH** | | | | | | |
| 1 **Bishop** | Y | Y | Y | Y | Y | Y |
| 2 Matheson | Y | Y | Y | Y | Y | N |
| 3 **Cannon** | Y | Y | Y | Y | Y | Y |
| **VERMONT** | | | | | | |
| AL *Sanders* | Y | Y | Y | Y | Y | Y |
| **VIRGINIA** | | | | | | |
| 1 **Davis, J.** | Y | Y | Y | Y | ? | Y |
| 2 **Drake** | Y | Y | Y | Y | Y | Y |
| 3 Scott | Y | Y | Y | Y | Y | Y |
| 4 **Forbes** | Y | Y | Y | Y | Y | Y |
| 5 **Goode** | Y | Y | Y | Y | Y | Y |
| 6 **Goodlatte** | Y | Y | Y | Y | Y | Y |
| 7 **Cantor** | Y | Y | Y | Y | Y | Y |
| 8 Moran | Y | Y | Y | Y | Y | Y |
| 9 Boucher | Y | Y | Y | Y | Y | Y |
| 10 **Wolf** | Y | Y | Y | Y | Y | Y |
| 11 **Davis, T.** | Y | Y | Y | Y | Y | Y |
| **WASHINGTON** | | | | | | |
| 1 Inslee | Y | Y | Y | Y | Y | Y |
| 2 Larsen | Y | Y | Y | Y | Y | Y |
| 3 Baird | Y | Y | Y | Y | Y | Y |
| 4 **Hastings** | Y | Y | Y | Y | Y | Y |
| 5 **McMorris** | Y | Y | Y | Y | Y | Y |
| 6 Dicks | Y | Y | Y | Y | Y | Y |
| 7 McDermott | Y | Y | Y | Y | Y | Y |
| 8 **Reichert** | Y | Y | Y | Y | Y | Y |
| 9 Smith | Y | Y | Y | Y | Y | Y |
| **WEST VIRGINIA** | | | | | | |
| 1 Mollohan | Y | Y | Y | Y | Y | Y |
| 2 **Capito** | Y | Y | Y | Y | Y | Y |
| 3 Rahall | Y | Y | Y | Y | Y | Y |
| **WISCONSIN** | | | | | | |
| 1 **Ryan** | Y | Y | Y | Y | Y | Y |
| 2 Baldwin | Y | Y | Y | Y | Y | Y |
| 3 Kind | Y | Y | Y | Y | Y | Y |
| 4 Moore | Y | Y | Y | Y | Y | Y |
| 5 **Sensenbrenner** | Y | Y | Y | Y | Y | N |
| 6 **Petri** | Y | Y | Y | Y | Y | Y |
| 7 Obey | Y | Y | Y | Y | Y | Y |
| 8 **Green** | Y | Y | Y | Y | Y | N |
| **WYOMING** | | | | | | |
| AL **Cubin** | Y | Y | Y | Y | Y | Y |

# IN THE HOUSE | By Vote Number

**581.** HR 2862. Fiscal 2006 Commerce-Justice-Science Appropriations/ **Conference Report.** Adoption of the conference report on the bill that would provide $61.8 billion, including $57.9 billion in discretionary spending, in fiscal 2006 for the departments of Commerce, Justice and State, as well as various science and other related agencies. It would provide $21.7 billion for Justice, $6.6 billion for Commerce, $9.7 billion for the State Department and international broadcasting agencies, $16.5 billion for NASA and $5.6 billion for the National Science Foundation. Adopted (thus sent to the Senate) 397-19: R 211-9; D 185-10 (ND 138-8, SD 47-2); I 1-0. Nov. 9, 2005.

**582.** S 1894. **Access to Foster Care/Passage.** Herger, R-Calif., motion to suspend the rules and pass the bill that would clarify that federal foster care payments could be made to private, for-profit — as well as nonprofit — therapeutic foster care agencies. Motion agreed to 408-1: R 218-0; D 189-1 (ND 142-1, SD 47-0); I 1-0. A two-thirds majority of those present and voting (273 in this case) is required for passage under suspension of the rules. Nov. 9, 2005.

**583.** HR 1751. **Court Security/Penalty for Killing Federal Officers.** Scott, D-Va., amendment to eliminate the death penalty authorized in the bill for individuals convicted of killing federal public safety officers, and instead allow a sentence of up to life in prison for the same crime. Rejected 97-325: R 5-218; D 91-107 (ND 82-67, SD 9-40); I 1-0. Nov. 9, 2005.

**584.** HR 1751. **Court Security/Recommit.** Higgins, D-N.Y., motion to recommit the bill to the Judiciary Committee with instructions to add language to impose stricter criminal and civil penalties on corporations that intentionally overcharge the federal government for the provision of goods and services in response to a presidentially declared major disaster, emergency or military action, including in Iraq and Afghanistan. Motion rejected 201-221: R 2-221; D 198-0 (ND 149-0, SD 49-0); I 1-0. Nov. 9, 2005.

**585.** HR 1751. **Court Security/Passage.** Passage of the bill that would increase federal penalties for the assault, murder or kidnapping of judges or their immediate family members. It would make it a federal crime to kill or assault public safety officers or other court personnel. The bill would bar the possession of dangerous weapons, in addition to guns, in federal courts. It would give presiding judges in federal appellate or circuit courts the authority to allow news media to photograph, broadcast, televise or electronically record court proceedings. Passed 375-45: R 221-1; D 153-44 (ND 108-40, SD 45-4); I 1-0. Nov. 9, 2005.

| | 581 | 582 | 583 | 584 | 585 |
|---|---|---|---|---|---|
| **ALABAMA** | | | | | |
| 1 Bonner | Y | Y | N | N | Y |
| 2 Everett | Y | Y | N | N | Y |
| 3 Rogers | Y | Y | N | N | Y |
| 4 Aderholt | Y | Y | N | N | Y |
| 5 Cramer | Y | Y | N | Y | Y |
| 6 Bachus | Y | Y | N | N | Y |
| 7 Davis | Y | Y | N | Y | Y |
| **ALASKA** | | | | | |
| AL Young | Y | Y | N | N | Y |
| **ARIZONA** | | | | | |
| 1 Renzi | Y | Y | N | N | Y |
| 2 Franks | Y | Y | N | N | Y |
| 3 Shadegg | Y | Y | N | N | Y |
| 4 Pastor | Y | Y | Y | Y | Y |
| 5 Hayworth | Y | Y | N | N | Y |
| 6 Flake | N | Y | N | N | Y |
| 7 Grijalva | Y | Y | N | Y | N |
| 8 Kolbe | Y | Y | N | N | Y |
| **ARKANSAS** | | | | | |
| 1 Berry | Y | Y | N | Y | Y |
| 2 Snyder | Y | Y | N | Y | Y |
| 3 Boozman | Y | Y | N | N | Y |
| 4 Ross | Y | Y | N | Y | Y |
| **CALIFORNIA** | | | | | |
| 1 Thompson | Y | Y | N | Y | Y |
| 2 Herger | Y | Y | N | N | Y |
| 3 Lungren | Y | Y | N | N | Y |
| 4 Doolittle | Y | Y | N | N | Y |
| 5 Matsui, D. | Y | Y | N | Y | Y |
| 6 Woolsey | Y | Y | Y | Y | N |
| 7 Miller, George | Y | Y | Y | Y | N |
| 8 Pelosi | Y | Y | Y | Y | N |
| 9 Lee | Y | Y | Y | Y | N |
| 10 Tauscher | Y | Y | N | Y | Y |
| 11 Pombo | Y | Y | N | N | Y |
| 12 Lantos | Y | Y | Y | Y | Y |
| 13 Stark | Y | Y | Y | Y | N |
| 14 Eshoo | Y | Y | N | Y | Y |
| 15 Honda | Y | ? | Y | Y | Y |
| 16 Lofgren | Y | Y | N | Y | Y |
| 17 Farr | Y | Y | Y | Y | Y |
| 18 Cardoza | Y | Y | N | Y | Y |
| 19 Radanovich | Y | Y | N | N | Y |
| 20 Costa | Y | Y | N | Y | Y |
| 21 Nunes | Y | Y | N | N | Y |
| 22 Thomas | Y | Y | N | N | Y |
| 23 Capps | Y | Y | N | Y | Y |
| 24 Gallegly | Y | Y | N | N | Y |
| 25 McKeon | Y | Y | N | N | Y |
| 26 Dreier | Y | Y | N | N | Y |
| 27 Sherman | Y | Y | N | Y | Y |
| 28 Berman | Y | Y | Y | Y | Y |
| 29 Schiff | Y | Y | N | Y | Y |
| 30 Waxman | Y | Y | Y | Y | N |
| 31 Becerra | Y | Y | Y | Y | Y |
| 32 Solis | + | + | Y | Y | N |
| 33 Watson | Y | Y | Y | Y | Y |
| 34 Roybal-Allard | Y | Y | Y | Y | Y |
| 35 Waters | Y | ? | Y | Y | N |
| 36 Harman | Y | Y | N | Y | Y |
| 37 Millender-McD. | ? | ? | Y | Y | Y |
| 38 Napolitano | Y | Y | N | Y | Y |
| 39 Sánchez, Linda | Y | Y | Y | Y | Y |
| 40 Royce | Y | Y | N | N | Y |
| 41 Lewis | Y | Y | N | N | Y |
| 42 Miller, Gary | Y | Y | N | N | Y |
| 43 Baca | Y | Y | N | Y | Y |
| 44 Calvert | Y | Y | N | N | Y |
| 45 Bono | Y | Y | N | N | Y |
| 46 Rohrabacher | Y | Y | N | N | Y |
| 47 Sanchez, Loretta | Y | Y | Y | Y | Y |
| 48 Vacant | | | | | |
| 49 Issa | Y | Y | N | N | Y |

| | 581 | 582 | 583 | 584 | 585 |
|---|---|---|---|---|---|
| 50 Cunningham | Y | Y | N | N | Y |
| 51 Filner | Y | Y | Y | Y | N |
| 52 Hunter | Y | Y | N | N | Y |
| 53 Davis | Y | Y | N | Y | Y |
| **COLORADO** | | | | | |
| 1 DeGette | Y | Y | Y | Y | Y |
| 2 Udall | Y | Y | Y | Y | Y |
| 3 Salazar | Y | Y | N | Y | Y |
| 4 Musgrave | Y | Y | N | N | Y |
| 5 Hefley | N | Y | N | N | Y |
| 6 Tancredo | N | ? | N | N | Y |
| 7 Beauprez | Y | Y | N | N | Y |
| **CONNECTICUT** | | | | | |
| 1 Larson | Y | Y | N | Y | Y |
| 2 Simmons | Y | Y | N | N | Y |
| 3 DeLauro | Y | Y | N | Y | Y |
| 4 Shays | Y | Y | N | Y | Y |
| 5 Johnson | Y | Y | N | N | Y |
| **DELAWARE** | | | | | |
| AL Castle | ? | Y | N | N | Y |
| **FLORIDA** | | | | | |
| 1 Miller | Y | Y | N | N | Y |
| 2 Boyd | Y | Y | N | Y | Y |
| 3 Brown | Y | Y | N | Y | Y |
| 4 Crenshaw | Y | Y | N | Y | Y |
| 5 Brown-Waite | ? | ? | ? | ? | ? |
| 6 Stearns | Y | Y | N | Y | Y |
| 7 Mica | Y | Y | N | N | Y |
| 8 Keller | Y | Y | N | N | Y |
| 9 Bilirakis | Y | Y | N | N | Y |
| 10 Young | ? | ? | ? | ? | ? |
| 11 Davis | ? | ? | ? | ? | ? |
| 12 Putnam | Y | Y | N | N | Y |
| 13 Harris | Y | Y | N | N | Y |
| 14 Mack | Y | Y | N | N | Y |
| 15 Weldon | Y | Y | N | N | Y |
| 16 Foley | Y | Y | N | N | Y |
| 17 Meek | Y | Y | N | Y | Y |
| 18 Ros-Lehtinen | Y | Y | N | N | Y |
| 19 Wexler | Y | Y | N | Y | Y |
| 20 Wasserman-Schultz | Y | Y | Y | Y | Y |
| 21 Diaz-Balart, L. | Y | Y | N | N | Y |
| 22 Shaw | Y | Y | N | N | Y |
| 23 Hastings | ? | ? | ? | ? | ? |
| 24 Feeney | Y | Y | N | N | Y |
| 25 Diaz-Balart, M. | Y | Y | N | N | Y |
| **GEORGIA** | | | | | |
| 1 Kingston | Y | Y | N | N | Y |
| 2 Bishop | Y | Y | N | Y | Y |
| 3 Marshall | Y | Y | N | Y | Y |
| 4 McKinney | Y | Y | Y | Y | N |
| 5 Lewis | Y | Y | Y | Y | N |
| 6 Price | Y | Y | N | N | + |
| 7 Linder | Y | Y | N | N | Y |
| 8 Westmoreland | Y | Y | N | N | Y |
| 9 Norwood | + | + | - | - | + |
| 10 Deal | Y | Y | N | N | Y |
| 11 Gingrey | Y | Y | N | N | Y |
| 12 Barrow | Y | Y | N | Y | Y |
| 13 Scott | Y | Y | N | Y | Y |
| **HAWAII** | | | | | |
| 1 Abercrombie | Y | Y | Y | Y | Y |
| 2 Case | Y | Y | N | Y | Y |
| **IDAHO** | | | | | |
| 1 Otter | N | Y | N | N | Y |
| 2 Simpson | Y | Y | N | N | Y |
| **ILLINOIS** | | | | | |
| 1 Rush | Y | Y | Y | Y | N |
| 2 Jackson | Y | Y | Y | Y | N |
| 3 Lipinski | Y | Y | Y | Y | Y |
| 4 Gutierrez | Y | Y | Y | Y | Y |
| 5 Emanuel | Y | Y | Y | Y | Y |
| 6 Hyde | Y | Y | N | N | Y |
| 7 Davis | Y | Y | Y | Y | N |
| 8 Bean | Y | Y | N | Y | Y |
| 9 Schakowsky | Y | Y | Y | Y | N |
| 10 Kirk | Y | Y | N | N | Y |
| 11 Weller | Y | Y | N | N | Y |
| 12 Costello | Y | Y | N | Y | Y |

| KEY | Republicans | Democrats | *Independents* |
|---|---|---|---|

| | | |
|---|---|---|
| Y Voted for (yea) | X Paired against | C Voted "present" to avoid possible conflict of interest |
| # Paired for | – Announced against | |
| + Announced for | P Voted "present" | ? Did not vote or otherwise make a position known |
| N Voted against (nay) | | |

| | 581 | 582 | 583 | 584 | 585 |
|---|---|---|---|---|---|
| 13 Biggert | Y | Y | N | N | Y |
| 14 Hastert | | | | | |
| 15 Johnson | Y | Y | N | N | Y |
| 16 Manzullo | Y | Y | N | N | Y |
| 17 Evans | Y | Y | Y | Y | Y |
| 18 LaHood | Y | Y | N | N | Y |
| 19 Shimkus | Y | Y | N | N | Y |
| **INDIANA** | | | | | |
| 1 Visclosky | Y | Y | N | Y | Y |
| 2 Chocola | Y | Y | N | N | Y |
| 3 Souder | Y | Y | N | N | Y |
| 4 Buyer | Y | Y | N | N | Y |
| 5 Burton | Y | Y | N | N | Y |
| 6 Pence | + | + | − | − | + |
| 7 Carson | Y | Y | Y | Y | N |
| 8 Hostettler | N | Y | N | N | Y |
| 9 Sodrel | Y | Y | N | N | Y |
| **IOWA** | | | | | |
| 1 Nussle | Y | Y | N | N | Y |
| 2 Leach | Y | Y | N | Y | Y |
| 3 Boswell | ? | ? | ? | ? | ? |
| 4 Latham | Y | Y | N | N | Y |
| 5 King | Y | Y | N | N | Y |
| **KANSAS** | | | | | |
| 1 Moran | Y | Y | N | N | Y |
| 2 Ryun | Y | Y | N | N | Y |
| 3 Moore | Y | Y | N | Y | Y |
| 4 Tiahrt | Y | Y | N | N | Y |
| **KENTUCKY** | | | | | |
| 1 Whitfield | Y | Y | N | N | Y |
| 2 Lewis | Y | Y | N | N | Y |
| 3 Northup | Y | Y | N | N | Y |
| 4 Davis | Y | Y | N | N | Y |
| 5 Rogers | Y | Y | N | N | Y |
| 6 Chandler | Y | Y | N | Y | Y |
| **LOUISIANA** | | | | | |
| 1 Jindal | Y | Y | N | N | Y |
| 2 Jefferson | Y | Y | N | Y | Y |
| 3 Melancon | Y | ? | N | Y | Y |
| 4 McCrery | Y | Y | N | N | Y |
| 5 Alexander | Y | Y | N | N | Y |
| 6 Baker | Y | Y | N | N | Y |
| 7 Boustany | Y | Y | N | N | Y |
| **MAINE** | | | | | |
| 1 Allen | Y | Y | Y | Y | Y |
| 2 Michaud | Y | Y | Y | Y | N |
| **MARYLAND** | | | | | |
| 1 Gilchrest | Y | Y | N | N | Y |
| 2 Ruppersberger | Y | Y | N | Y | Y |
| 3 Cardin | Y | Y | N | Y | Y |
| 4 Wynn | Y | Y | N | Y | Y |
| 5 Hoyer | Y | Y | N | Y | Y |
| 6 Bartlett | Y | Y | Y | N | Y |
| 7 Cummings | Y | Y | Y | Y | N |
| 8 Van Hollen | Y | Y | Y | Y | Y |
| **MASSACHUSETTS** | | | | | |
| 1 Olver | Y | Y | Y | Y | N |
| 2 Neal | Y | Y | Y | Y | Y |
| 3 McGovern | Y | Y | Y | Y | N |
| 4 Frank | Y | Y | Y | Y | Y |
| 5 Meehan | Y | Y | Y | Y | Y |
| 6 Tierney | N | Y | Y | Y | Y |
| 7 Markey | Y | Y | Y | Y | Y |
| 8 Capuano | N | Y | Y | Y | Y |
| 9 Lynch | Y | Y | Y | Y | Y |
| 10 Delahunt | Y | Y | Y | Y | N |
| **MICHIGAN** | | | | | |
| 1 Stupak | Y | Y | N | N | Y |
| 2 Hoekstra | Y | Y | Y | N | Y |
| 3 Ehlers | Y | Y | N | N | Y |
| 4 Camp | Y | Y | N | N | Y |
| 5 Kildee | Y | Y | N | Y | N |
| 6 Upton | Y | Y | N | N | Y |
| 7 Schwarz | Y | Y | N | N | Y |
| 8 Rogers | Y | Y | N | N | Y |
| 9 Knollenberg | Y | Y | N | N | Y |
| 10 Miller | Y | Y | N | N | Y |
| 11 McCotter | Y | Y | N | N | Y |
| 12 Levin | Y | Y | Y | Y | Y |
| 13 Kilpatrick | Y | Y | Y | Y | N |
| 14 Conyers | N | Y | Y | Y | N |
| 15 Dingell | Y | Y | Y | Y | Y |

| | 581 | 582 | 583 | 584 | 585 |
|---|---|---|---|---|---|
| **MINNESOTA** | | | | | |
| 1 Gutknecht | Y | Y | N | N | Y |
| 2 Kline | Y | Y | N | N | Y |
| 3 Ramstad | Y | Y | N | N | Y |
| 4 McCollum | Y | Y | Y | Y | ? |
| 5 Sabo | Y | Y | Y | Y | N |
| 6 Kennedy | Y | Y | N | N | Y |
| 7 Peterson | Y | Y | N | Y | Y |
| 8 Oberstar | Y | Y | Y | Y | N |
| **MISSISSIPPI** | | | | | |
| 1 Wicker | Y | Y | N | N | Y |
| 2 Thompson | Y | Y | N | Y | Y |
| 3 Pickering | Y | Y | N | N | Y |
| 4 Taylor | N | Y | N | Y | Y |
| **MISSOURI** | | | | | |
| 1 Clay | Y | Y | Y | Y | N |
| 2 Akin | Y | Y | N | N | Y |
| 3 Carnahan | Y | Y | N | N | Y |
| 4 Skelton | Y | Y | N | N | Y |
| 5 Cleaver | Y | Y | Y | Y | Y |
| 6 Graves | Y | Y | N | N | Y |
| 7 Blunt | Y | Y | N | N | Y |
| 8 Emerson | Y | ? | N | N | Y |
| 9 Hulshof | Y | Y | N | N | Y |
| **MONTANA** | | | | | |
| AL Rehberg | Y | Y | N | N | Y |
| **NEBRASKA** | | | | | |
| 1 Fortenberry | Y | Y | N | N | Y |
| 2 Terry | Y | Y | N | N | Y |
| 3 Osborne | Y | Y | N | N | Y |
| **NEVADA** | | | | | |
| 1 Berkley | Y | Y | N | Y | Y |
| 2 Gibbons | Y | Y | N | N | Y |
| 3 Porter | Y | Y | N | N | Y |
| **NEW HAMPSHIRE** | | | | | |
| 1 Bradley | Y | Y | N | N | Y |
| 2 Bass | Y | Y | N | N | Y |
| **NEW JERSEY** | | | | | |
| 1 Andrews | Y | Y | N | N | Y |
| 2 LoBiondo | Y | Y | N | N | Y |
| 3 Saxton | Y | Y | N | N | Y |
| 4 Smith | Y | Y | Y | N | Y |
| 5 Garrett | Y | Y | N | N | Y |
| 6 Pallone | Y | Y | N | Y | Y |
| 7 Ferguson | Y | Y | N | N | Y |
| 8 Pascrell | Y | Y | N | Y | Y |
| 9 Rothman | Y | Y | N | Y | Y |
| 10 Payne | Y | Y | Y | Y | N |
| 11 Frelinghuysen | Y | Y | N | N | Y |
| 12 Holt | Y | Y | Y | Y | Y |
| 13 Menendez | Y | Y | N | Y | Y |
| **NEW MEXICO** | | | | | |
| 1 Wilson | Y | Y | N | N | Y |
| 2 Pearce | Y | Y | N | N | Y |
| 3 Udall | Y | Y | N | Y | Y |
| **NEW YORK** | | | | | |
| 1 Bishop | Y | Y | N | Y | Y |
| 2 Israel | Y | Y | N | Y | Y |
| 3 King | Y | Y | N | N | Y |
| 4 McCarthy | Y | Y | Y | Y | Y |
| 5 Ackerman | Y | Y | Y | Y | Y |
| 6 Meeks | ? | ? | Y | Y | Y |
| 7 Crowley | Y | Y | Y | Y | Y |
| 8 Nadler | Y | Y | Y | Y | N |
| 9 Weiner | Y | Y | N | Y | Y |
| 10 Towns | Y | Y | Y | Y | Y |
| 11 Owens | Y | Y | Y | Y | N |
| 12 Velázquez | N | Y | Y | Y | Y |
| 13 Fossella | Y | Y | N | N | Y |
| 14 Maloney | Y | Y | Y | Y | Y |
| 15 Rangel | Y | Y | Y | Y | Y |
| 16 Serrano | Y | Y | Y | Y | Y |
| 17 Engel | Y | Y | Y | Y | Y |
| 18 Lowey | Y | Y | Y | Y | Y |
| 19 Kelly | Y | Y | N | N | Y |
| 20 Sweeney | ? | ? | ? | ? | ? |
| 21 McNulty | Y | Y | Y | Y | Y |
| 22 Hinchey | Y | Y | Y | Y | N |
| 23 McHugh | Y | Y | N | N | Y |
| 24 Boehlert | Y | Y | N | N | Y |
| 25 Walsh | Y | Y | N | N | Y |
| 26 Reynolds | Y | Y | N | N | Y |
| 27 Higgins | Y | ? | N | Y | Y |
| 28 Slaughter | Y | Y | Y | Y | Y |
| 29 Kuhl | Y | Y | N | N | Y |

| | 581 | 582 | 583 | 584 | 585 |
|---|---|---|---|---|---|
| **NORTH CAROLINA** | | | | | |
| 1 Butterfield | Y | Y | N | Y | Y |
| 2 Etheridge | Y | Y | N | Y | Y |
| 3 Jones | N | Y | N | N | Y |
| 4 Price | Y | Y | N | Y | Y |
| 5 Foxx | Y | Y | N | N | Y |
| 6 Coble | Y | Y | N | N | Y |
| 7 McIntyre | Y | Y | N | Y | Y |
| 8 Hayes | Y | Y | N | N | Y |
| 9 Myrick | Y | Y | N | N | Y |
| 10 McHenry | Y | Y | N | N | Y |
| 11 Taylor | Y | Y | N | N | Y |
| 12 Watt | Y | Y | Y | Y | N |
| 13 Miller | Y | Y | N | Y | Y |
| **NORTH DAKOTA** | | | | | |
| AL Pomeroy | Y | Y | N | Y | Y |
| **OHIO** | | | | | |
| 1 Chabot | Y | Y | N | N | Y |
| 2 Schmidt | Y | Y | N | N | Y |
| 3 Turner | ? | ? | N | N | Y |
| 4 Oxley | + | + | N | N | Y |
| 5 Gillmor | Y | Y | N | N | Y |
| 6 Strickland | ? | ? | ? | ? | ? |
| 7 Hobson | Y | Y | N | N | Y |
| 8 Boehner | Y | Y | N | N | Y |
| 9 Kaptur | Y | Y | N | Y | Y |
| 10 Kucinich | Y | Y | Y | Y | N |
| 11 Jones | Y | Y | Y | Y | N |
| 12 Tiberi | Y | Y | N | N | Y |
| 13 Brown | Y | Y | N | Y | Y |
| 14 LaTourette | Y | Y | N | N | Y |
| 15 Pryce | Y | Y | N | N | Y |
| 16 Regula | Y | Y | N | N | Y |
| 17 Ryan | Y | Y | Y | Y | Y |
| 18 Ney | Y | Y | N | N | Y |
| **OKLAHOMA** | | | | | |
| 1 Sullivan | Y | Y | N | N | Y |
| 2 Boren | Y | Y | N | Y | Y |
| 3 Lucas | Y | Y | N | N | Y |
| 4 Cole | Y | Y | N | N | Y |
| 5 Istook | Y | Y | N | N | Y |
| **OREGON** | | | | | |
| 1 Wu | Y | Y | N | Y | Y |
| 2 Walden | Y | Y | N | N | Y |
| 3 Blumenauer | Y | Y | Y | Y | Y |
| 4 DeFazio | Y | Y | N | Y | Y |
| 5 Hooley | Y | Y | N | Y | Y |
| **PENNSYLVANIA** | | | | | |
| 1 Brady | Y | Y | N | Y | Y |
| 2 Fattah | Y | Y | Y | Y | Y |
| 3 English | Y | Y | N | N | Y |
| 4 Hart | Y | Y | N | N | Y |
| 5 Peterson | Y | Y | N | N | Y |
| 6 Gerlach | Y | Y | N | N | Y |
| 7 Weldon | Y | Y | N | N | Y |
| 8 Fitzpatrick | Y | Y | N | N | Y |
| 9 Shuster | Y | Y | N | N | Y |
| 10 Sherwood | Y | Y | N | N | Y |
| 11 Kanjorski | Y | Y | N | Y | Y |
| 12 Murtha | Y | Y | N | Y | Y |
| 13 Schwartz | Y | Y | N | Y | Y |
| 14 Doyle | Y | Y | N | Y | Y |
| 15 Dent | Y | Y | N | N | Y |
| 16 Pitts | Y | Y | N | N | Y |
| 17 Holden | Y | Y | N | Y | Y |
| 18 Murphy | Y | Y | N | N | Y |
| 19 Platts | Y | Y | N | N | Y |
| **RHODE ISLAND** | | | | | |
| 1 Kennedy | Y | Y | N | Y | Y |
| 2 Langevin | Y | Y | N | Y | Y |
| **SOUTH CAROLINA** | | | | | |
| 1 Brown | Y | Y | N | N | Y |
| 2 Wilson | Y | Y | N | N | Y |
| 3 Barrett | Y | Y | N | N | Y |
| 4 Inglis | Y | Y | N | N | Y |
| 5 Spratt | Y | Y | N | Y | Y |
| 6 Clyburn | Y | Y | Y | Y | Y |
| **SOUTH DAKOTA** | | | | | |
| AL Herseth | Y | Y | N | Y | Y |
| **TENNESSEE** | | | | | |
| 1 Jenkins | Y | Y | N | N | Y |
| 2 Duncan | N | Y | N | N | Y |

| | 581 | 582 | 583 | 584 | 585 |
|---|---|---|---|---|---|
| 3 Wamp | Y | Y | N | N | Y |
| 4 Davis | Y | Y | N | N | Y |
| 5 Cooper | Y | Y | N | Y | Y |
| 6 Gordon | Y | Y | N | Y | Y |
| 7 Blackburn | Y | Y | N | N | Y |
| 8 Tanner | Y | Y | N | Y | Y |
| 9 Ford | Y | Y | N | Y | Y |
| **TEXAS** | | | | | |
| 1 Gohmert | Y | ? | N | N | Y |
| 2 Poe | Y | Y | N | N | Y |
| 3 Johnson, S. | Y | Y | N | N | Y |
| 4 Hall | Y | Y | N | N | Y |
| 5 Hensarling | Y | Y | N | N | Y |
| 6 Barton | Y | Y | N | N | Y |
| 7 Culberson | Y | Y | N | N | Y |
| 8 Brady | Y | Y | N | N | Y |
| 9 Green, A. | Y | Y | Y | Y | Y |
| 10 McCaul | Y | Y | N | N | Y |
| 11 Conaway | ? | ? | ? | ? | ? |
| 12 Granger | Y | Y | N | N | Y |
| 13 Thornberry | Y | Y | N | N | Y |
| 14 Paul | N | Y | N | N | N |
| 15 Hinojosa | Y | Y | N | Y | Y |
| 16 Reyes | Y | Y | N | Y | Y |
| 17 Edwards | Y | Y | N | Y | Y |
| 18 Jackson-Lee | Y | Y | Y | Y | Y |
| 19 Neugebauer | Y | Y | N | N | Y |
| 20 Gonzalez | Y | Y | N | Y | Y |
| 21 Smith | Y | Y | N | N | Y |
| 22 DeLay | Y | Y | N | N | Y |
| 23 Bonilla | Y | Y | N | N | Y |
| 24 Marchant | Y | Y | N | N | Y |
| 25 Doggett | N | Y | N | Y | Y |
| 26 Burgess | Y | Y | N | N | Y |
| 27 Ortiz | Y | ? | N | Y | Y |
| 28 Cuellar | Y | Y | N | Y | Y |
| 29 Green, G. | Y | Y | N | Y | Y |
| 30 Johnson, E. | Y | Y | Y | Y | Y |
| 31 Carter | Y | Y | N | N | Y |
| 32 Sessions | ? | ? | ? | ? | ? |
| **UTAH** | | | | | |
| 1 Bishop | Y | Y | N | N | Y |
| 2 Matheson | N | Y | N | Y | Y |
| 3 Cannon | Y | Y | N | N | Y |
| **VERMONT** | | | | | |
| AL *Sanders* | Y | Y | Y | Y | Y |
| **VIRGINIA** | | | | | |
| 1 Davis, J. | Y | Y | N | N | Y |
| 2 Drake | Y | Y | N | N | Y |
| 3 Scott | Y | Y | Y | Y | N |
| 4 Forbes | Y | Y | N | N | Y |
| 5 Goode | Y | Y | N | N | Y |
| 6 Goodlatte | Y | Y | N | N | Y |
| 7 Cantor | Y | Y | N | N | Y |
| 8 Moran | Y | Y | N | Y | Y |
| 9 Boucher | Y | Y | N | Y | Y |
| 10 Wolf | Y | Y | N | N | Y |
| 11 Davis, T. | Y | Y | N | N | Y |
| **WASHINGTON** | | | | | |
| 1 Inslee | Y | Y | N | Y | Y |
| 2 Larsen | Y | Y | N | Y | Y |
| 3 Baird | Y | Y | N | Y | Y |
| 4 Hastings | Y | Y | N | N | Y |
| 5 McMorris | Y | Y | N | N | Y |
| 6 Dicks | Y | Y | N | Y | Y |
| 7 McDermott | N | Y | Y | Y | N |
| 8 Reichert | Y | Y | N | N | Y |
| 9 Smith | Y | Y | Y | Y | Y |
| **WEST VIRGINIA** | | | | | |
| 1 Mollohan | Y | Y | N | Y | N |
| 2 Capito | Y | Y | N | N | Y |
| 3 Rahall | Y | Y | N | Y | Y |
| **WISCONSIN** | | | | | |
| 1 Ryan | Y | Y | N | N | Y |
| 2 Baldwin | N | Y | Y | Y | N |
| 3 Kind | Y | Y | N | Y | Y |
| 4 Moore | N | Y | Y | Y | N |
| 5 Sensenbrenner | Y | Y | N | N | Y |
| 6 Petri | Y | Y | N | N | Y |
| 7 Obey | N | Y | Y | Y | N |
| 8 Green | N | Y | N | N | Y |
| **WYOMING** | | | | | |
| AL Cubin | Y | Y | N | N | Y |

# IN THE HOUSE | By Vote Number

**586.** **HR 1564. Yakima-Tieton Irrigation District/Passage.** Musgrave, R-Colo., motion to suspend the rules and pass the bill that would transfer nine acres of federal land and several buildings to the Yakima-Tieton Irrigation District in Washington. Motion agreed to 420-0: R 226-0; D 193-0 (ND 144-0, SD 49-0); I 1-0. A two-thirds majority of those present and voting (280 in this case) is required for passage under suspension of the rules. Nov. 15, 2005.

**587.** **HR 323. Bob Hope Memorial Library/Passage.** Musgrave, R-Colo., motion to suspend the rules and pass the bill that would redesignate the Ellis Island Library, which is part of the Ellis Island Immigration Museum, as the Bob Hope Memorial Library. Motion agreed to 419-0: R 226-0; D 192-0 (ND 143-0, SD 49-0); I 1-0. A two-thirds majority of those present and voting (280 in this case) is required for passage under suspension of the rules. Nov. 15, 2005.

**588.** **HR 856. Federal Youth Coordination/Passage.** Osborne, R-Neb., motion to suspend the rules and pass the bill that would establish a Federal Youth Development Council to allow for better communication among federal agencies serving youth, assess the needs of disadvantaged youth and report on youth programs. Motion agreed to 353-62: R 163-62; D 189-0 (ND 140-0, SD 49-0); I 1-0. A two-thirds majority of those present and voting (277 in this case) is required for passage under suspension of the rules. Nov. 15, 2005.

**589.** **HR 1065. U.S. Boxing Commission/Rule.** Adoption of the rule (H Res 553) that would provide for House floor consideration of the bill that would create a federal boxing commission within the Commerce Department to regulate professional boxing. Adopted 366-56: R 224-1; D 141-55 (ND 107-40, SD 34-15); I 1-0. Nov. 16, 2005.

**590.** **HR 1790. Child Medication in Schools/Passage.** Kline, R-Minn., motion to suspend the rules and pass the bill that would require states, as a condition of receiving federal education funds, to prohibit schools from requiring a child to be medicated as a condition of attending school or receiving services. Motion agreed to 407-12: R 221-1; D 185-11 (ND 137-10, SD 48-1); I 1-0. A two-thirds majority of those present and voting (280 in this case) is required for passage under suspension of the rules. Nov. 16, 2005.

**591.** **H Res 547. Disapprove 9th Circuit Court Ruling/Adoption.** Sensenbrenner, R-Wis., motion to suspend the rules and adopt the resolution that would express the sense of the House that parents have a "fundamental right" to direct their children's education and that the 9th Circuit Court of Appeals' ruling in *Fields v. Palmdale School District* would undermine that right. Motion agreed to 320-91: R 225-0; D 94-91 (ND 61-78, SD 33-13); I 1-0. A two-thirds majority of those present and voting (274 in this case) is required for adoption under suspension of the rules. Nov. 16, 2005.

| | 586 | 587 | 588 | 589 | 590 | 591 |
|---|---|---|---|---|---|---|
| **ALABAMA** | | | | | | |
| 1 Bonner | Y | Y | Y | Y | Y | Y |
| 2 Everett | Y | Y | Y | Y | Y | Y |
| 3 Rogers | Y | Y | Y | Y | Y | Y |
| 4 Aderholt | Y | Y | Y | Y | Y | Y |
| 5 Cramer | Y | Y | Y | Y | Y | Y |
| 6 Bachus | Y | Y | Y | Y | Y | Y |
| 7 Davis | Y | Y | Y | Y | Y | Y |
| **ALASKA** | | | | | | |
| AL Young | Y | Y | Y | Y | Y | Y |
| **ARIZONA** | | | | | | |
| 1 Renzi | Y | Y | Y | Y | Y | Y |
| 2 Franks | Y | Y | N | Y | Y | Y |
| 3 Shadegg | Y | Y | N | Y | Y | Y |
| 4 Pastor | Y | Y | Y | N | Y | N |
| 5 Hayworth | Y | Y | N | Y | Y | Y |
| 6 Flake | Y | Y | N | Y | Y | Y |
| 7 Grijalva | Y | Y | Y | Y | Y | N |
| 8 Kolbe | Y | Y | Y | Y | Y | Y |
| **ARKANSAS** | | | | | | |
| 1 Berry | Y | Y | Y | N | Y | Y |
| 2 Snyder | Y | Y | Y | Y | Y | P |
| 3 Boozman | Y | Y | Y | Y | Y | Y |
| 4 Ross | Y | Y | Y | Y | Y | Y |
| **CALIFORNIA** | | | | | | |
| 1 Thompson | Y | Y | Y | Y | Y | N |
| 2 Herger | Y | Y | N | Y | Y | Y |
| 3 Lungren | Y | Y | Y | Y | Y | Y |
| 4 Doolittle | Y | Y | Y | Y | Y | Y |
| 5 Matsui, D. | Y | Y | Y | Y | Y | N |
| 6 Woolsey | Y | Y | Y | N | Y | N |
| 7 Miller, George | Y | Y | ? | Y | N | N |
| 8 Pelosi | Y | Y | Y | Y | Y | P |
| 9 Lee | Y | Y | Y | N | Y | N |
| 10 Tauscher | Y | Y | Y | Y | Y | N |
| 11 Pombo | Y | Y | Y | Y | Y | Y |
| 12 Lantos | Y | Y | Y | ? | ? | Y |
| 13 Stark | ? | ? | ? | ? | ? | ? |
| 14 Eshoo | Y | Y | Y | Y | Y | P |
| 15 Honda | Y | Y | Y | N | Y | N |
| 16 Lofgren | Y | P | Y | Y | Y | P |
| 17 Farr | Y | Y | Y | Y | Y | N |
| 18 Cardoza | Y | Y | Y | Y | Y | Y |
| 19 Radanovich | Y | Y | Y | Y | Y | Y |
| 20 Costa | Y | Y | Y | Y | Y | Y |
| 21 Nunes | Y | Y | Y | Y | Y | Y |
| 22 Thomas | Y | Y | Y | Y | Y | Y |
| 23 Capps | Y | Y | Y | Y | Y | N |
| 24 Gallegly | Y | Y | Y | Y | Y | Y |
| 25 McKeon | Y | Y | Y | Y | Y | Y |
| 26 Dreier | Y | Y | Y | Y | Y | Y |
| 27 Sherman | Y | Y | Y | N | Y | N |
| 28 Berman | Y | Y | Y | Y | Y | N |
| 29 Schiff | Y | Y | Y | Y | Y | N |
| 30 Waxman | Y | Y | Y | N | Y | N |
| 31 Becerra | Y | Y | Y | Y | Y | N |
| 32 Solis | Y | Y | Y | Y | Y | N |
| 33 Watson | Y | Y | Y | Y | N | N |
| 34 Roybal-Allard | Y | Y | Y | Y | Y | N |
| 35 Waters | Y | Y | Y | N | Y | N |
| 36 Harman | Y | Y | Y | Y | Y | N |
| 37 Millender-McD. | Y | Y | Y | Y | Y | N |
| 38 Napolitano | Y | Y | Y | Y | Y | N |
| 39 Sánchez, Linda | Y | Y | Y | Y | Y | N |
| 40 Royce | Y | Y | N | Y | Y | Y |
| 41 Lewis | Y | Y | Y | Y | Y | Y |
| 42 Miller, Gary | Y | Y | N | Y | Y | Y |
| 43 Baca | Y | Y | Y | Y | Y | Y |
| 44 Calvert | Y | Y | Y | Y | Y | Y |
| 45 Bono | Y | Y | Y | Y | Y | Y |
| 46 Rohrabacher | Y | Y | N | Y | Y | Y |
| 47 Sanchez, Loretta | Y | Y | Y | Y | Y | Y |
| 48 Vacant | | | | | | |
| 49 Issa | Y | Y | Y | Y | Y | Y |
| 50 Cunningham | ? | ? | ? | ? | ? | ? |
| 51 Filner | | | | | | |
| 52 Hunter | Y | Y | Y | ? | Y | Y |
| 53 Davis | Y | Y | Y | Y | N | N |
| **COLORADO** | | | | | | |
| 1 DeGette | Y | Y | Y | Y | Y | N |
| 2 Udall | Y | Y | Y | Y | Y | Y |
| 3 Salazar | Y | Y | Y | Y | Y | Y |
| 4 Musgrave | Y | Y | N | Y | Y | Y |
| 5 Hefley | Y | Y | N | Y | Y | Y |
| 6 Tancredo | Y | Y | N | Y | Y | Y |
| 7 Beauprez | Y | Y | N | Y | Y | Y |
| **CONNECTICUT** | | | | | | |
| 1 Larson | Y | Y | Y | Y | Y | Y |
| 2 Simmons | Y | Y | Y | Y | ? | Y |
| 3 DeLauro | Y | Y | Y | Y | Y | Y |
| 4 Shays | Y | Y | Y | Y | Y | Y |
| 5 Johnson | Y | Y | Y | Y | Y | Y |
| **DELAWARE** | | | | | | |
| AL Castle | Y | Y | Y | Y | Y | Y |
| **FLORIDA** | | | | | | |
| 1 Miller | Y | Y | N | Y | Y | Y |
| 2 Boyd | Y | Y | Y | Y | Y | Y |
| 3 Brown | Y | Y | Y | Y | Y | Y |
| 4 Crenshaw | Y | Y | N | Y | Y | Y |
| 5 Brown-Waite | Y | Y | Y | N | Y | Y |
| 6 Stearns | Y | Y | N | Y | Y | Y |
| 7 Mica | Y | Y | Y | Y | Y | Y |
| 8 Keller | Y | Y | Y | Y | Y | Y |
| 9 Bilirakis | Y | Y | N | Y | Y | Y |
| 10 Young | Y | Y | N | Y | Y | Y |
| 11 Davis | Y | Y | Y | ? | ? | ? |
| 12 Putnam | Y | Y | Y | Y | Y | Y |
| 13 Harris | Y | Y | Y | Y | ? | Y |
| 14 Mack | Y | Y | N | Y | Y | Y |
| 15 Weldon | Y | Y | Y | Y | Y | Y |
| 16 Foley | Y | Y | Y | Y | Y | Y |
| 17 Meek | Y | Y | Y | N | Y | Y |
| 18 Ros-Lehtinen | Y | Y | Y | Y | Y | Y |
| 19 Wexler | ? | ? | ? | Y | Y | N |
| 20 Wasserman-Schultz | Y | Y | Y | Y | Y | N |
| 21 Diaz-Balart, L. | Y | Y | Y | Y | Y | Y |
| 22 Shaw | Y | Y | Y | Y | Y | Y |
| 23 Hastings | Y | Y | Y | N | Y | N |
| 24 Feeney | Y | Y | Y | Y | Y | Y |
| 25 Diaz-Balart, M. | Y | Y | Y | Y | Y | Y |
| **GEORGIA** | | | | | | |
| 1 Kingston | Y | Y | N | Y | Y | Y |
| 2 Bishop | Y | Y | Y | Y | Y | Y |
| 3 Marshall | Y | Y | Y | Y | Y | Y |
| 4 McKinney | Y | Y | N | N | Y | N |
| 5 Lewis | Y | Y | N | Y | Y | N |
| 6 Price | Y | Y | N | Y | Y | Y |
| 7 Linder | Y | Y | N | Y | Y | Y |
| 8 Westmoreland | Y | Y | N | Y | Y | Y |
| 9 Norwood | Y | Y | Y | Y | Y | Y |
| 10 Deal | Y | Y | Y | Y | Y | Y |
| 11 Gingrey | Y | Y | N | Y | P | Y |
| 12 Barrow | Y | Y | Y | Y | Y | Y |
| 13 Scott | Y | Y | N | Y | Y | Y |
| **HAWAII** | | | | | | |
| 1 Abercrombie | Y | Y | Y | Y | Y | N |
| 2 Case | Y | Y | Y | Y | Y | N |
| **IDAHO** | | | | | | |
| 1 Otter | Y | Y | Y | Y | Y | Y |
| 2 Simpson | Y | Y | Y | Y | Y | Y |
| **ILLINOIS** | | | | | | |
| 1 Rush | Y | Y | Y | Y | Y | N |
| 2 Jackson | Y | Y | Y | Y | N | Y |
| 3 Lipinski | Y | Y | Y | Y | Y | Y |
| 4 Gutierrez | + | + | + | N | N | Y |
| 5 Emanuel | Y | Y | Y | Y | Y | Y |
| 6 Hyde | Y | Y | Y | Y | Y | Y |
| 7 Davis | Y | Y | Y | N | Y | N |
| 8 Bean | Y | Y | Y | Y | Y | Y |
| 9 Schakowsky | Y | Y | ? | Y | Y | N |
| 10 Kirk | Y | Y | Y | Y | Y | Y |
| 11 Weller | Y | Y | Y | Y | Y | Y |
| 12 Costello | Y | Y | Y | N | Y | Y |

| KEY | Republicans | Democrats | *Independents* |
|---|---|---|---|
| Y Voted for (yea) | X Paired against | C Voted "present" to avoid possible conflict of interest |
| # Paired for | – Announced against | |
| + Announced for | P Voted "present" | ? Did not vote or otherwise make a position known |
| N Voted against (nay) | | |

| | 586 | 587 | 588 | 589 | 590 | 591 |
|---|---|---|---|---|---|---|
| 13 **Biggert** | Y | Y | Y | Y | Y | P |
| 14 **Hastert** | | | | | | |
| 15 **Johnson** | Y | Y | Y | Y | Y | Y |
| 16 **Manzullo** | Y | Y | N | Y | Y | Y |
| 17 Evans | Y | Y | Y | Y | Y | Y |
| 18 **LaHood** | Y | Y | Y | Y | Y | Y |
| 19 **Shimkus** | Y | Y | Y | Y | Y | Y |
| **INDIANA** | | | | | | |
| 1 Visclosky | Y | Y | Y | Y | Y | Y |
| 2 **Chocola** | Y | Y | N | Y | Y | Y |
| 3 **Souder** | Y | Y | Y | Y | Y | Y |
| 4 **Buyer** | Y | Y | Y | Y | Y | Y |
| 5 **Burton** | Y | Y | N | Y | Y | Y |
| 6 **Pence** | Y | Y | N | Y | Y | Y |
| 7 Carson | Y | Y | Y | N | Y | N |
| 8 **Hostettler** | Y | Y | N | Y | Y | Y |
| 9 **Sodrel** | Y | Y | N | Y | Y | Y |
| **IOWA** | | | | | | |
| 1 **Nussle** | Y | Y | Y | Y | Y | Y |
| 2 **Leach** | Y | Y | Y | Y | Y | Y |
| 3 Boswell | ? | ? | ? | ? | ? | ? |
| 4 **Latham** | Y | Y | Y | Y | Y | Y |
| 5 **King** | Y | Y | Y | Y | Y | Y |
| **KANSAS** | | | | | | |
| 1 **Moran** | Y | Y | Y | Y | Y | Y |
| 2 **Ryun** | Y | Y | N | Y | Y | Y |
| 3 Moore | Y | Y | Y | Y | Y | Y |
| 4 **Tiahrt** | Y | Y | N | Y | Y | Y |
| **KENTUCKY** | | | | | | |
| 1 **Whitfield** | Y | Y | Y | Y | Y | Y |
| 2 **Lewis** | Y | Y | Y | Y | Y | Y |
| 3 **Northup** | Y | Y | Y | Y | Y | Y |
| 4 **Davis** | Y | Y | N | Y | Y | Y |
| 5 **Rogers** | Y | Y | Y | Y | Y | Y |
| 6 Chandler | Y | Y | Y | Y | Y | Y |
| **LOUISIANA** | | | | | | |
| 1 **Jindal** | Y | Y | N | Y | Y | Y |
| 2 Jefferson | Y | Y | Y | N | Y | Y |
| 3 Melancon | Y | Y | Y | N | Y | Y |
| 4 **McCrery** | Y | Y | Y | Y | Y | Y |
| 5 **Alexander** | Y | Y | Y | Y | Y | Y |
| 6 **Baker** | Y | Y | Y | Y | Y | Y |
| 7 **Boustany** | Y | Y | Y | Y | Y | Y |
| **MAINE** | | | | | | |
| 1 Allen | Y | Y | Y | Y | Y | P |
| 2 Michaud | Y | Y | Y | Y | Y | Y |
| **MARYLAND** | | | | | | |
| 1 **Gilchrest** | Y | Y | Y | Y | Y | Y |
| 2 Ruppersberger | Y | Y | Y | Y | Y | Y |
| 3 Cardin | Y | Y | Y | Y | Y | Y |
| 4 Wynn | Y | Y | Y | Y | Y | Y |
| 5 Hoyer | Y | Y | Y | Y | Y | N |
| 6 **Bartlett** | Y | Y | N | Y | Y | Y |
| 7 Cummings | Y | Y | Y | Y | Y | Y |
| 8 Van Hollen | Y | Y | Y | Y | Y | N |
| **MASSACHUSETTS** | | | | | | |
| 1 Olver | Y | Y | Y | N | N | N |
| 2 Neal | Y | Y | Y | N | Y | Y |
| 3 McGovern | Y | Y | Y | Y | Y | N |
| 4 Frank | Y | Y | Y | Y | N | N |
| 5 Meehan | Y | Y | Y | Y | Y | N |
| 6 Tierney | Y | Y | Y | N | Y | N |
| 7 Markey | Y | Y | Y | Y | Y | N |
| 8 Capuano | Y | Y | Y | N | Y | P |
| 9 Lynch | Y | Y | Y | Y | Y | Y |
| 10 Delahunt | Y | Y | Y | N | Y | N |
| **MICHIGAN** | | | | | | |
| 1 Stupak | Y | Y | Y | Y | Y | Y |
| 2 **Hoekstra** | Y | Y | Y | Y | Y | Y |
| 3 **Ehlers** | Y | Y | Y | Y | Y | Y |
| 4 **Camp** | Y | Y | Y | Y | Y | Y |
| 5 Kildee | Y | Y | Y | Y | Y | Y |
| 6 **Upton** | Y | Y | Y | Y | Y | Y |
| 7 **Schwarz** | Y | Y | Y | Y | Y | Y |
| 8 **Rogers** | Y | Y | Y | Y | Y | Y |
| 9 **Knollenberg** | Y | Y | Y | Y | Y | Y |
| 10 **Miller** | Y | Y | Y | Y | Y | Y |
| 11 **McCotter** | Y | Y | Y | Y | Y | Y |
| 12 Levin | Y | Y | Y | Y | Y | N |
| 13 Kilpatrick | Y | Y | Y | Y | Y | Y |
| 14 Conyers | Y | Y | ? | N | Y | N |
| 15 Dingell | Y | Y | Y | Y | N | N |
| **MINNESOTA** | | | | | | |
| 1 **Gutknecht** | Y | Y | Y | Y | Y | Y |
| 2 **Kline** | Y | Y | Y | Y | Y | Y |
| 3 **Ramstad** | Y | Y | Y | Y | Y | Y |
| 4 McCollum | Y | Y | Y | Y | Y | P |
| 5 Sabo | Y | Y | Y | N | Y | P |
| 6 **Kennedy** | Y | Y | Y | Y | Y | Y |
| 7 Peterson | Y | Y | Y | Y | Y | Y |
| 8 Oberstar | Y | Y | Y | Y | Y | N |
| **MISSISSIPPI** | | | | | | |
| 1 **Wicker** | Y | Y | Y | Y | Y | Y |
| 2 Thompson | Y | Y | Y | N | Y | Y |
| 3 **Pickering** | Y | Y | Y | Y | Y | Y |
| 4 Taylor | ? | ? | ? | ? | ? | ? |
| **MISSOURI** | | | | | | |
| 1 Clay | Y | Y | Y | N | Y | N |
| 2 **Akin** | Y | Y | N | Y | Y | Y |
| 3 Carnahan | Y | Y | Y | Y | Y | Y |
| 4 Skelton | Y | Y | Y | Y | Y | Y |
| 5 Cleaver | Y | Y | Y | N | Y | N |
| 6 **Graves** | Y | Y | Y | Y | Y | Y |
| 7 **Blunt** | Y | Y | Y | Y | Y | Y |
| 8 **Emerson** | Y | Y | Y | Y | Y | Y |
| 9 **Hulshof** | Y | Y | Y | Y | Y | Y |
| **MONTANA** | | | | | | |
| AL **Rehberg** | Y | Y | Y | Y | Y | Y |
| **NEBRASKA** | | | | | | |
| 1 **Fortenberry** | Y | Y | Y | Y | Y | Y |
| 2 **Terry** | Y | Y | Y | Y | Y | Y |
| 3 **Osborne** | Y | Y | Y | Y | Y | Y |
| **NEVADA** | | | | | | |
| 1 Berkley | Y | Y | Y | Y | N | Y |
| 2 **Gibbons** | Y | Y | Y | Y | Y | Y |
| 3 **Porter** | Y | Y | Y | Y | Y | Y |
| **NEW HAMPSHIRE** | | | | | | |
| 1 **Bradley** | Y | Y | Y | Y | Y | Y |
| 2 **Bass** | Y | Y | Y | Y | Y | Y |
| **NEW JERSEY** | | | | | | |
| 1 Andrews | + | + | + | N | Y | N |
| 2 **LoBiondo** | Y | Y | Y | Y | Y | Y |
| 3 **Saxton** | Y | Y | Y | Y | Y | Y |
| 4 **Smith** | Y | Y | Y | Y | Y | Y |
| 5 **Garrett** | Y | Y | N | Y | N | Y |
| 6 Pallone | Y | Y | Y | N | Y | N |
| 7 **Ferguson** | Y | Y | Y | + | + | + |
| 8 Pascrell | Y | Y | Y | Y | Y | Y |
| 9 Rothman | Y | Y | Y | N | Y | Y |
| 10 Payne | Y | Y | Y | N | Y | N |
| 11 **Frelinghuysen** | Y | Y | Y | Y | Y | Y |
| 12 Holt | Y | Y | Y | Y | Y | N |
| 13 Menendez | Y | Y | Y | N | Y | Y |
| **NEW MEXICO** | | | | | | |
| 1 **Wilson** | Y | Y | Y | Y | Y | Y |
| 2 **Pearce** | Y | Y | Y | Y | Y | Y |
| 3 Udall | Y | Y | Y | N | Y | N |
| **NEW YORK** | | | | | | |
| 1 Bishop | Y | Y | Y | Y | Y | Y |
| 2 Israel | Y | Y | Y | Y | Y | N |
| 3 **King** | Y | Y | Y | Y | Y | Y |
| 4 McCarthy | Y | Y | Y | Y | Y | Y |
| 5 Ackerman | Y | Y | Y | N | Y | N |
| 6 Meeks | Y | Y | Y | Y | Y | N |
| 7 Crowley | Y | Y | Y | Y | Y | N |
| 8 Nadler | Y | Y | Y | N | Y | N |
| 9 Weiner | Y | Y | Y | Y | Y | Y |
| 10 Towns | Y | Y | Y | N | Y | Y |
| 11 Owens | Y | Y | Y | Y | Y | N |
| 12 Velázquez | Y | Y | Y | N | Y | N |
| 13 **Fossella** | Y | Y | Y | Y | Y | Y |
| 14 Maloney | Y | Y | Y | Y | Y | N |
| 15 Rangel | Y | Y | Y | N | Y | N |
| 16 Serrano | Y | Y | Y | N | Y | N |
| 17 Engel | Y | Y | Y | Y | Y | P |
| 18 Lowey | Y | Y | Y | Y | Y | N |
| 19 **Kelly** | Y | Y | Y | Y | Y | Y |
| 20 **Sweeney** | Y | Y | Y | Y | Y | Y |
| 21 McNulty | ? | ? | ? | ? | ? | ? |
| 22 Hinchey | Y | Y | Y | N | Y | N |
| 23 **McHugh** | Y | Y | Y | Y | Y | Y |
| 24 **Boehlert** | Y | Y | Y | Y | Y | Y |
| 25 **Walsh** | Y | Y | Y | Y | Y | Y |
| 26 **Reynolds** | Y | Y | Y | Y | Y | Y |
| 27 Higgins | Y | Y | Y | Y | Y | Y |
| 28 Slaughter | Y | Y | ? | N | Y | N |
| 29 **Kuhl** | Y | Y | Y | Y | Y | Y |
| **NORTH CAROLINA** | | | | | | |
| 1 Butterfield | Y | Y | Y | Y | Y | Y |
| 2 Etheridge | Y | Y | Y | Y | Y | Y |
| 3 **Jones** | Y | Y | N | Y | Y | Y |
| 4 Price | Y | Y | Y | Y | Y | N |
| 5 **Foxx** | Y | Y | N | Y | Y | Y |
| 6 **Coble** | Y | Y | N | Y | Y | Y |
| 7 McIntyre | Y | Y | Y | Y | Y | Y |
| 8 **Hayes** | Y | Y | Y | Y | Y | Y |
| 9 **Myrick** | Y | Y | N | Y | Y | Y |
| 10 **McHenry** | Y | Y | N | Y | Y | Y |
| 11 **Taylor** | Y | Y | Y | Y | Y | Y |
| 12 Watt | Y | Y | Y | N | Y | P |
| 13 Miller | Y | Y | Y | Y | Y | N |
| **NORTH DAKOTA** | | | | | | |
| AL Pomeroy | Y | Y | Y | Y | Y | Y |
| **OHIO** | | | | | | |
| 1 **Chabot** | Y | Y | Y | Y | Y | Y |
| 2 **Schmidt** | Y | Y | Y | Y | Y | Y |
| 3 **Turner** | Y | Y | Y | Y | Y | Y |
| 4 **Oxley** | Y | Y | Y | Y | Y | Y |
| 5 **Gillmor** | Y | Y | Y | Y | Y | Y |
| 6 Strickland | Y | Y | Y | Y | Y | Y |
| 7 **Hobson** | Y | Y | Y | Y | Y | Y |
| 8 **Boehner** | Y | Y | Y | Y | Y | Y |
| 9 Kaptur | Y | Y | Y | Y | Y | Y |
| 10 Kucinich | Y | Y | Y | N | Y | Y |
| 11 Jones | Y | Y | Y | Y | N | N |
| 12 **Tiberi** | Y | Y | Y | Y | Y | Y |
| 13 Brown | Y | Y | Y | Y | Y | Y |
| 14 **LaTourette** | Y | Y | Y | Y | Y | Y |
| 15 **Pryce** | Y | Y | Y | Y | Y | Y |
| 16 **Regula** | Y | Y | Y | Y | Y | Y |
| 17 Ryan | Y | Y | Y | Y | Y | Y |
| 18 **Ney** | Y | Y | Y | Y | Y | Y |
| **OKLAHOMA** | | | | | | |
| 1 **Sullivan** | Y | Y | Y | Y | Y | Y |
| 2 Boren | Y | Y | Y | Y | Y | Y |
| 3 **Lucas** | Y | Y | Y | Y | Y | Y |
| 4 **Cole** | Y | Y | Y | Y | Y | Y |
| 5 **Istook** | Y | Y | N | Y | Y | Y |
| **OREGON** | | | | | | |
| 1 Wu | Y | Y | Y | N | Y | Y |
| 2 **Walden** | Y | Y | Y | Y | Y | Y |
| 3 Blumenauer | Y | Y | Y | Y | Y | N |
| 4 DeFazio | Y | Y | Y | Y | Y | Y |
| 5 Hooley | Y | Y | Y | Y | Y | Y |
| **PENNSYLVANIA** | | | | | | |
| 1 Brady | Y | Y | Y | Y | Y | N |
| 2 Fattah | Y | Y | Y | Y | Y | Y |
| 3 **English** | Y | Y | Y | Y | Y | Y |
| 4 **Hart** | Y | Y | Y | Y | Y | Y |
| 5 **Peterson** | Y | Y | Y | Y | Y | Y |
| 6 **Gerlach** | Y | Y | Y | Y | Y | Y |
| 7 **Weldon** | Y | Y | Y | Y | Y | Y |
| 8 **Fitzpatrick** | Y | Y | Y | Y | Y | Y |
| 9 **Shuster** | Y | Y | Y | Y | Y | Y |
| 10 **Sherwood** | Y | Y | Y | Y | Y | Y |
| 11 Kanjorski | Y | Y | Y | Y | Y | N |
| 12 Murtha | ? | ? | ? | Y | Y | N |
| 13 Schwartz | Y | Y | Y | Y | Y | Y |
| 14 Doyle | Y | Y | Y | Y | Y | N |
| 15 **Dent** | Y | Y | Y | Y | Y | Y |
| 16 **Pitts** | Y | Y | N | Y | Y | Y |
| 17 Holden | Y | Y | Y | Y | Y | Y |
| 18 **Murphy** | Y | Y | Y | Y | Y | Y |
| 19 **Platts** | Y | Y | Y | Y | Y | Y |
| **RHODE ISLAND** | | | | | | |
| 1 Kennedy | Y | Y | Y | N | Y | N |
| 2 Langevin | Y | Y | Y | Y | Y | N |
| **SOUTH CAROLINA** | | | | | | |
| 1 **Brown** | Y | Y | Y | Y | Y | Y |
| 2 **Wilson** | Y | Y | N | Y | Y | Y |
| 3 **Barrett** | Y | Y | N | Y | Y | Y |
| 4 **Inglis** | Y | Y | N | Y | Y | Y |
| 5 Spratt | Y | Y | Y | Y | Y | Y |
| 6 Clyburn | Y | Y | Y | Y | Y | Y |
| **SOUTH DAKOTA** | | | | | | |
| AL Herseth | Y | Y | Y | Y | Y | Y |
| **TENNESSEE** | | | | | | |
| 1 **Jenkins** | ? | ? | ? | ? | ? | ? |
| 2 **Duncan** | Y | Y | Y | Y | Y | Y |
| 3 **Wamp** | Y | Y | Y | Y | Y | Y |
| 4 Davis | Y | Y | Y | N | Y | Y |
| 5 Cooper | Y | Y | Y | N | Y | Y |
| 6 Gordon | Y | Y | Y | Y | Y | Y |
| 7 **Blackburn** | Y | Y | N | Y | Y | Y |
| 8 Tanner | Y | Y | Y | Y | Y | Y |
| 9 Ford | Y | Y | Y | Y | Y | Y |
| **TEXAS** | | | | | | |
| 1 **Gohmert** | Y | Y | Y | Y | Y | Y |
| 2 **Poe** | Y | Y | N | Y | Y | Y |
| 3 **Johnson, S.** | Y | Y | N | Y | Y | Y |
| 4 **Hall** | Y | Y | Y | Y | Y | Y |
| 5 **Hensarling** | Y | Y | N | Y | Y | Y |
| 6 **Barton** | Y | Y | Y | Y | Y | Y |
| 7 **Culberson** | Y | Y | N | Y | Y | Y |
| 8 **Brady** | Y | Y | Y | Y | Y | Y |
| 9 Green, A. | Y | Y | Y | Y | Y | P |
| 10 **McCaul** | Y | Y | Y | Y | Y | Y |
| 11 **Conaway** | Y | Y | N | Y | Y | Y |
| 12 **Granger** | ? | ? | ? | Y | Y | Y |
| 13 **Thornberry** | Y | Y | Y | Y | Y | Y |
| 14 **Paul** | Y | Y | N | Y | Y | Y |
| 15 Hinojosa | Y | Y | Y | Y | Y | Y |
| 16 Reyes | Y | Y | Y | Y | Y | Y |
| 17 Edwards | Y | Y | Y | Y | Y | Y |
| 18 Jackson-Lee | Y | Y | Y | N | Y | Y |
| 19 **Neugebauer** | Y | Y | N | Y | Y | Y |
| 20 Gonzalez | Y | Y | Y | Y | Y | N |
| 21 **Smith** | Y | Y | Y | Y | Y | Y |
| 22 **DeLay** | Y | Y | N | Y | Y | Y |
| 23 **Bonilla** | Y | Y | Y | Y | Y | Y |
| 24 **Marchant** | Y | Y | N | Y | Y | Y |
| 25 Doggett | Y | Y | Y | Y | Y | N |
| 26 **Burgess** | Y | Y | Y | Y | Y | Y |
| 27 Ortiz | Y | Y | Y | Y | Y | Y |
| 28 Cuellar | Y | Y | Y | Y | Y | Y |
| 29 Green, G. | Y | Y | Y | Y | Y | Y |
| 30 Johnson, E. | Y | Y | Y | Y | Y | N |
| 31 **Carter** | Y | Y | ? | Y | Y | Y |
| 32 **Sessions** | Y | Y | N | Y | Y | Y |
| **UTAH** | | | | | | |
| 1 **Bishop** | Y | Y | N | Y | ? | Y |
| 2 Matheson | Y | Y | Y | Y | Y | Y |
| 3 **Cannon** | Y | Y | Y | Y | Y | Y |
| **VERMONT** | | | | | | |
| AL *Sanders* | Y | Y | Y | Y | Y | Y |
| **VIRGINIA** | | | | | | |
| 1 **Davis, J.** | Y | Y | N | Y | Y | Y |
| 2 **Drake** | Y | Y | N | Y | Y | Y |
| 3 Scott | Y | Y | Y | N | N | N |
| 4 **Forbes** | Y | Y | Y | Y | Y | Y |
| 5 **Goode** | Y | Y | N | Y | Y | Y |
| 6 **Goodlatte** | Y | Y | Y | Y | Y | Y |
| 7 **Cantor** | Y | Y | Y | Y | Y | Y |
| 8 Moran | Y | Y | Y | Y | Y | N |
| 9 Boucher | Y | Y | Y | Y | Y | N |
| 10 **Wolf** | Y | Y | Y | Y | Y | Y |
| 11 **Davis, T.** | Y | Y | Y | Y | Y | Y |
| **WASHINGTON** | | | | | | |
| 1 Inslee | Y | Y | Y | Y | Y | N |
| 2 Larsen | Y | Y | Y | Y | Y | N |
| 3 Baird | Y | Y | Y | Y | N | N |
| 4 **Hastings** | Y | Y | Y | Y | Y | Y |
| 5 **McMorris** | Y | Y | Y | Y | Y | Y |
| 6 Dicks | Y | Y | Y | Y | Y | Y |
| 7 McDermott | Y | Y | Y | N | N | N |
| 8 **Reichert** | ? | ? | ? | ? | ? | ? |
| 9 Smith | Y | Y | Y | Y | Y | Y |
| **WEST VIRGINIA** | | | | | | |
| 1 Mollohan | ? | ? | ? | Y | Y | Y |
| 2 **Capito** | Y | Y | Y | Y | Y | Y |
| 3 Rahall | Y | Y | Y | Y | Y | Y |
| **WISCONSIN** | | | | | | |
| 1 **Ryan** | Y | Y | N | Y | Y | Y |
| 2 Baldwin | Y | Y | Y | N | Y | Y |
| 3 Kind | Y | Y | Y | Y | Y | Y |
| 4 Moore | Y | Y | Y | Y | Y | N |
| 5 **Sensenbrenner** | Y | Y | N | Y | Y | Y |
| 6 **Petri** | Y | Y | Y | Y | Y | Y |
| 7 Obey | Y | Y | Y | N | Y | Y |
| 8 **Green** | Y | Y | N | Y | Y | Y |
| **WYOMING** | | | | | | |
| AL **Cubin** | Y | Y | Y | Y | Y | Y |

# IN THE HOUSE | By Vote Number

**592.** **HR 1065. United States Boxing Commission/Passage.** Passage of the bill that would create a federal boxing commission within the Commerce Department to regulate professional boxing. Rejected 190-233: R 43-183; D 146-50 (ND 116-32, SD 30-18); I 1-0. Nov. 16, 2005.

**593.** **H Con Res 230. Enforcing Intellectual Property Rights/Adoption.** Shaw, R-Fla., motion to suspend the rules and adopt the concurrent resolution that would express the sense of Congress that Russia should provide adequate and effective protection of intellectual property rights, or risk losing its eligibility to participate in the Generalized System of Preferences. Motion agreed to 421-2: R 224-2; D 196-0 (ND 148-0, SD 48-0); I 1-0. A two-thirds majority of those present and voting (282 in this case) is required for adoption under suspension of the rules. Nov. 16, 2005.

**594.** **H Con Res 268. Internet Corporation for Assigned Names and Numbers/Adoption.** Upton, R-Mich., motion to suspend the rules and adopt the concurrent resolution that would express the sense of Congress that the authoritative root zone server should remain physically located in the United States, with the Commerce Department maintaining oversight of the Internet Corporation for Assigned Names and Numbers. Motion agreed to 423-0: R 225-0; D 197-0 (ND 148-0, SD 49-0); I 1-0. A two-thirds majority of those present and voting (282 in this case) is required for adoption under suspension of the rules. Nov. 16, 2005.

**595.** **H Res 558, H J Res 72. Fiscal 2006 Continuing Resolution/Rule.** Adoption of the rule (H Res 558) that would provide for House floor consideration of the joint resolution that would provide continuing appropriations through Dec. 17 for all federal departments and agencies whose fiscal 2006 appropriations bills have not been enacted. Adopted 407-21: R 229-0; D 177-21 (ND 132-17, SD 45-4); I 1-0. Nov. 17, 2005.

**596.** **H Res 559, HR 3010. Fiscal 2006 Labor-HHS-Education Appropriations/Rule.** Adoption of the rule (H Res 559) that would provide for House floor consideration of the conference report on the bill that would appropriate $601.7 billion, including $142.5 billion in discretionary spending, in fiscal 2006 for the departments of Labor, Health and Human Services and Education, and for other various agencies and programs. Adopted 244-185: R 227-2; D 17-182 (ND 9-140, SD 8-42); I 0-1. Nov. 17, 2005.

**597.** **H Res 500. 60th Anniversary of Flight 19 Rescue/Adoption.** J. Davis, R-Va., motion to suspend the rules and adopt the resolution which would recognize the 60th anniversary of the disappearance of the five naval Avenger torpedo bombers of Flight 19 and the naval Mariner rescue aircraft sent to search for Flight 19. Motion agreed to 420-2: R 222-2; D 197-0 (ND 148-0, SD 49-0); I 1-0. A two-thirds majority of those present and voting (282 in this case) is required for adoption under suspension of the rules. Nov. 17, 2005.

| | 592 | 593 | 594 | 595 | 596 | 597 |
|---|---|---|---|---|---|---|
| **ALABAMA** | | | | | | |
| 1 Bonner | N | Y | Y | Y | Y | Y |
| 2 Everett | N | Y | Y | Y | Y | Y |
| 3 Rogers | N | Y | Y | Y | N | Y |
| 4 Aderholt | N | Y | Y | Y | Y | Y |
| 5 Cramer | Y | Y | Y | Y | Y | Y |
| 6 Bachus | N | Y | Y | Y | Y | Y |
| 7 Davis | Y | Y | Y | Y | N | Y |
| **ALASKA** | | | | | | |
| AL Young | N | Y | Y | Y | N | Y |
| **ARIZONA** | | | | | | |
| 1 Renzi | N | Y | Y | Y | Y | Y |
| 2 Franks | N | Y | Y | Y | Y | Y |
| 3 Shadegg | N | Y | Y | Y | Y | Y |
| 4 Pastor | N | Y | Y | Y | N | Y |
| 5 Hayworth | N | Y | Y | Y | Y | Y |
| 6 Flake | N | Y | Y | Y | Y | Y |
| 7 Grijalva | Y | Y | Y | N | N | Y |
| 8 Kolbe | N | Y | ? | Y | Y | + |
| **ARKANSAS** | | | | | | |
| 1 Berry | N | Y | Y | Y | N | Y |
| 2 Snyder | N | Y | Y | Y | N | Y |
| 3 Boozman | N | Y | Y | Y | Y | Y |
| 4 Ross | N | Y | Y | Y | N | Y |
| **CALIFORNIA** | | | | | | |
| 1 Thompson | Y | Y | Y | Y | N | Y |
| 2 Herger | N | Y | Y | Y | Y | Y |
| 3 Lungren | Y | Y | Y | Y | Y | Y |
| 4 Doolittle | N | Y | Y | Y | Y | Y |
| 5 Matsui, D. | Y | Y | Y | Y | N | Y |
| 6 Woolsey | Y | Y | Y | Y | N | Y |
| 7 Miller, George | Y | Y | Y | N | N | Y |
| 8 Pelosi | Y | Y | Y | Y | N | Y |
| 9 Lee | Y | Y | Y | N | N | Y |
| 10 Tauscher | Y | Y | Y | Y | N | Y |
| 11 Pombo | N | Y | Y | ? | Y | Y |
| 12 Lantos | ? | ? | ? | Y | N | Y |
| 13 Stark | ? | ? | ? | ? | ? | Y |
| 14 Eshoo | Y | Y | Y | Y | N | Y |
| 15 Honda | Y | Y | Y | N | N | Y |
| 16 Lofgren | Y | Y | Y | Y | N | Y |
| 17 Farr | Y | Y | Y | Y | N | Y |
| 18 Cardoza | N | Y | Y | Y | N | Y |
| 19 Radanovich | N | Y | Y | Y | Y | Y |
| 20 Costa | N | Y | Y | Y | N | Y |
| 21 Nunes | N | Y | Y | Y | Y | Y |
| 22 Thomas | N | Y | Y | Y | Y | Y |
| 23 Capps | Y | Y | Y | Y | N | Y |
| 24 Gallegly | N | Y | Y | Y | Y | Y |
| 25 McKeon | N | Y | Y | Y | Y | Y |
| 26 Dreier | N | Y | Y | Y | Y | Y |
| 27 Sherman | Y | Y | Y | Y | N | Y |
| 28 Berman | Y | Y | Y | Y | N | Y |
| 29 Schiff | Y | Y | Y | Y | N | Y |
| 30 Waxman | Y | Y | Y | Y | N | Y |
| 31 Becerra | Y | Y | Y | N | N | Y |
| 32 Solis | Y | Y | Y | Y | N | Y |
| 33 Watson | Y | Y | Y | Y | N | Y |
| 34 Roybal-Allard | Y | Y | Y | Y | N | Y |
| 35 Waters | Y | Y | Y | Y | N | Y |
| 36 Harman | Y | Y | Y | Y | N | Y |
| 37 Millender-McD. | Y | Y | Y | Y | N | Y |
| 38 Napolitano | Y | Y | Y | Y | N | Y |
| 39 Sánchez, Linda | Y | Y | Y | Y | N | Y |
| 40 Royce | N | Y | Y | Y | Y | Y |
| 41 Lewis | N | Y | Y | Y | Y | Y |
| 42 Miller, Gary | N | Y | Y | Y | Y | Y |
| 43 Baca | Y | Y | Y | Y | N | Y |
| 44 Calvert | N | Y | Y | Y | Y | Y |
| 45 Bono | N | Y | Y | Y | Y | Y |
| 46 Rohrabacher | N | Y | Y | Y | Y | + |
| 47 Sanchez, Loretta | Y | Y | Y | Y | N | Y |
| 48 Vacant | | | | | | |
| 49 Issa | Y | Y | Y | Y | Y | Y |
| 50 Cunningham | ? | ? | ? | Y | Y | Y |
| 51 Filner | Y | Y | Y | Y | N | Y |
| 52 Hunter | N | Y | Y | Y | Y | Y |
| 53 Davis | Y | Y | Y | Y | N | Y |
| **COLORADO** | | | | | | |
| 1 DeGette | Y | Y | Y | Y | Y | ? |
| 2 Udall | Y | Y | Y | N | N | Y |
| 3 Salazar | N | Y | Y | Y | N | Y |
| 4 Musgrave | N | Y | Y | Y | Y | Y |
| 5 Hefley | N | Y | Y | Y | Y | Y |
| 6 Tancredo | N | Y | Y | Y | Y | Y |
| 7 Beauprez | N | Y | Y | Y | Y | Y |
| **CONNECTICUT** | | | | | | |
| 1 Larson | Y | Y | Y | Y | N | Y |
| 2 Simmons | Y | Y | Y | Y | Y | Y |
| 3 DeLauro | Y | Y | Y | Y | N | Y |
| 4 Shays | Y | Y | Y | Y | Y | Y |
| 5 Johnson | Y | Y | Y | Y | Y | Y |
| **DELAWARE** | | | | | | |
| AL Castle | Y | Y | Y | Y | Y | Y |
| **FLORIDA** | | | | | | |
| 1 Miller | N | Y | Y | Y | Y | Y |
| 2 Boyd | Y | Y | Y | Y | N | Y |
| 3 Brown | Y | Y | Y | Y | N | Y |
| 4 Crenshaw | N | Y | Y | Y | Y | Y |
| 5 Brown-Waite | N | Y | Y | Y | Y | Y |
| 6 Stearns | Y | Y | Y | Y | Y | Y |
| 7 Mica | N | Y | Y | Y | Y | Y |
| 8 Keller | N | Y | Y | Y | Y | Y |
| 9 Bilirakis | N | Y | Y | Y | Y | Y |
| 10 Young | Y | Y | Y | Y | Y | Y |
| 11 Davis | ? | ? | ? | Y | Y | Y |
| 12 Putnam | N | Y | Y | Y | Y | Y |
| 13 Harris | N | Y | Y | Y | Y | Y |
| 14 Mack | N | Y | Y | Y | Y | Y |
| 15 Weldon | Y | Y | Y | Y | Y | Y |
| 16 Foley | N | Y | Y | Y | Y | Y |
| 17 Meek | N | Y | Y | Y | N | Y |
| 18 Ros-Lehtinen | ? | Y | Y | Y | Y | Y |
| 19 Wexler | Y | Y | Y | ? | N | Y |
| 20 Wasserman-Schultz | N | Y | Y | Y | N | Y |
| 21 Diaz-Balart, L. | Y | Y | Y | Y | Y | Y |
| 22 Shaw | N | Y | ? | Y | Y | Y |
| 23 Hastings | N | Y | Y | N | N | Y |
| 24 Feeney | N | Y | Y | Y | Y | Y |
| 25 Diaz-Balart, M. | N | Y | Y | Y | Y | Y |
| **GEORGIA** | | | | | | |
| 1 Kingston | N | Y | Y | Y | Y | Y |
| 2 Bishop | N | Y | Y | Y | Y | Y |
| 3 Marshall | N | Y | Y | Y | N | Y |
| 4 McKinney | Y | Y | Y | Y | N | Y |
| 5 Lewis | Y | Y | Y | Y | N | Y |
| 6 Price | N | Y | Y | Y | Y | Y |
| 7 Linder | N | Y | Y | Y | Y | Y |
| 8 Westmoreland | N | Y | Y | Y | Y | Y |
| 9 Norwood | N | Y | Y | Y | Y | Y |
| 10 Deal | N | Y | Y | Y | Y | Y |
| 11 Gingrey | N | Y | Y | Y | Y | Y |
| 12 Barrow | N | Y | Y | Y | N | Y |
| 13 Scott | Y | Y | Y | Y | N | Y |
| **HAWAII** | | | | | | |
| 1 Abercrombie | Y | Y | Y | Y | N | Y |
| 2 Case | N | Y | Y | Y | N | Y |
| **IDAHO** | | | | | | |
| 1 Otter | N | Y | Y | Y | Y | Y |
| 2 Simpson | N | Y | Y | Y | Y | Y |
| **ILLINOIS** | | | | | | |
| 1 Rush | Y | Y | Y | Y | N | Y |
| 2 Jackson | Y | Y | Y | N | N | Y |
| 3 Lipinski | Y | Y | Y | Y | N | Y |
| 4 Gutierrez | Y | Y | Y | Y | N | Y |
| 5 Emanuel | Y | Y | Y | Y | N | Y |
| 6 Hyde | Y | Y | Y | Y | Y | Y |
| 7 Davis | Y | Y | Y | Y | N | Y |
| 8 Bean | N | Y | Y | Y | N | Y |
| 9 Schakowsky | Y | Y | Y | Y | N | Y |
| 10 Kirk | Y | Y | Y | Y | Y | N |
| 11 Weller | N | Y | Y | Y | Y | Y |
| 12 Costello | N | Y | Y | Y | N | Y |

**KEY**    Republicans    Democrats    *Independents*

| | |
|---|---|
| Y Voted for (yea) | X Paired against |
| # Paired for | – Announced against |
| + Announced for | P Voted "present" |
| N Voted against (nay) | C Voted "present" to avoid possible conflict of interest |
| | ? Did not vote or otherwise make a position known |

| | 592 | 593 | 594 | 595 | 596 | 597 |
|---|---|---|---|---|---|---|
| 13 **Biggert** | N | Y | Y | Y | Y | Y |
| 14 **Hastert** | | | | | | |
| 15 **Johnson** | N | Y | Y | Y | Y | ? |
| 16 **Manzullo** | N | Y | Y | Y | Y | Y |
| 17 Evans | Y | Y | Y | Y | N | Y |
| 18 **LaHood** | N | Y | Y | Y | Y | Y |
| 19 **Shimkus** | Y | Y | Y | Y | Y | Y |
| **INDIANA** | | | | | | |
| 1 Visclosky | Y | Y | Y | Y | N | Y |
| 2 **Chocola** | N | Y | Y | Y | Y | Y |
| 3 **Souder** | N | Y | Y | Y | Y | Y |
| 4 **Buyer** | Y | Y | Y | Y | Y | Y |
| 5 **Burton** | N | Y | Y | Y | Y | Y |
| 6 **Pence** | N | Y | Y | Y | Y | Y |
| 7 Carson | N | Y | Y | Y | N | Y |
| 8 **Hostettler** | N | Y | Y | Y | Y | Y |
| 9 **Sodrel** | N | Y | Y | Y | Y | Y |
| **IOWA** | | | | | | |
| 1 **Nussle** | N | Y | Y | Y | Y | Y |
| 2 **Leach** | N | Y | Y | Y | Y | Y |
| 3 Boswell | ? | ? | ? | ? | ? | ? |
| 4 **Latham** | N | Y | Y | Y | Y | Y |
| 5 **King** | N | Y | Y | Y | Y | Y |
| **KANSAS** | | | | | | |
| 1 **Moran** | Y | Y | Y | Y | Y | Y |
| 2 **Ryun** | N | Y | Y | Y | Y | Y |
| 3 Moore | Y | Y | Y | Y | N | Y |
| 4 **Tiahrt** | N | Y | Y | Y | Y | Y |
| **KENTUCKY** | | | | | | |
| 1 **Whitfield** | Y | Y | Y | Y | Y | Y |
| 2 **Lewis** | N | Y | Y | Y | Y | Y |
| 3 **Northup** | N | Y | Y | Y | Y | Y |
| 4 **Davis** | N | Y | Y | Y | Y | Y |
| 5 **Rogers** | Y | Y | Y | Y | Y | Y |
| 6 Chandler | Y | Y | Y | Y | N | Y |
| **LOUISIANA** | | | | | | |
| 1 **Jindal** | N | Y | Y | Y | Y | Y |
| 2 Jefferson | Y | Y | Y | Y | N | Y |
| 3 Melancon | N | Y | Y | Y | N | Y |
| 4 **McCrery** | N | Y | Y | Y | Y | ? |
| 5 **Alexander** | N | Y | Y | Y | Y | Y |
| 6 **Baker** | N | Y | Y | Y | Y | Y |
| 7 **Boustany** | N | Y | Y | Y | Y | Y |
| **MAINE** | | | | | | |
| 1 Allen | Y | Y | Y | Y | N | Y |
| 2 Michaud | Y | Y | Y | Y | N | Y |
| **MARYLAND** | | | | | | |
| 1 **Gilchrest** | Y | Y | Y | Y | Y | Y |
| 2 Ruppersberger | Y | Y | Y | Y | N | Y |
| 3 Cardin | Y | Y | Y | Y | N | Y |
| 4 Wynn | Y | Y | Y | Y | N | Y |
| 5 Hoyer | Y | Y | Y | Y | N | Y |
| 6 **Bartlett** | N | Y | Y | Y | Y | Y |
| 7 Cummings | Y | Y | Y | Y | N | Y |
| 8 Van Hollen | Y | Y | Y | Y | N | Y |
| **MASSACHUSETTS** | | | | | | |
| 1 Olver | Y | Y | Y | Y | N | Y |
| 2 Neal | Y | Y | Y | Y | N | Y |
| 3 McGovern | Y | Y | Y | Y | N | Y |
| 4 Frank | N | Y | Y | N | N | Y |
| 5 Meehan | Y | Y | Y | Y | N | Y |
| 6 Tierney | N | Y | Y | Y | N | Y |
| 7 Markey | Y | Y | Y | N | N | Y |
| 8 Capuano | N | Y | Y | Y | N | Y |
| 9 Lynch | Y | Y | Y | Y | N | Y |
| 10 Delahunt | Y | Y | Y | Y | N | Y |
| **MICHIGAN** | | | | | | |
| 1 Stupak | Y | Y | Y | N | N | Y |
| 2 **Hoekstra** | N | Y | Y | Y | Y | Y |
| 3 **Ehlers** | Y | Y | Y | Y | Y | Y |
| 4 **Camp** | N | Y | Y | Y | Y | Y |
| 5 Kildee | Y | Y | Y | Y | N | Y |
| 6 **Upton** | Y | Y | Y | Y | Y | Y |
| 7 **Schwarz** | Y | Y | Y | Y | Y | Y |
| 8 **Rogers** | N | Y | Y | Y | Y | Y |
| 9 **Knollenberg** | N | Y | Y | Y | Y | Y |
| 10 **Miller** | N | Y | Y | Y | Y | Y |
| 11 **McCotter** | N | Y | Y | Y | Y | Y |
| 12 Levin | Y | Y | Y | Y | N | Y |
| 13 Kilpatrick | Y | Y | Y | Y | N | Y |
| 14 Conyers | Y | Y | Y | N | N | Y |
| 15 Dingell | Y | Y | Y | Y | N | Y |
| **MINNESOTA** | | | | | | |
| 1 **Gutknecht** | Y | Y | Y | Y | Y | Y |
| 2 **Kline** | N | Y | Y | Y | Y | Y |
| 3 **Ramstad** | N | Y | Y | Y | Y | Y |
| 4 McCollum | Y | Y | Y | Y | N | Y |
| 5 Sabo | Y | Y | Y | Y | N | Y |
| 6 **Kennedy** | N | Y | Y | Y | Y | Y |
| 7 Peterson | N | Y | Y | Y | N | Y |
| 8 Oberstar | Y | Y | Y | Y | Y | Y |
| **MISSISSIPPI** | | | | | | |
| 1 **Wicker** | N | Y | Y | Y | Y | Y |
| 2 Thompson | Y | Y | Y | Y | N | Y |
| 3 **Pickering** | Y | Y | Y | Y | Y | Y |
| 4 Taylor | ? | ? | ? | Y | N | Y |
| **MISSOURI** | | | | | | |
| 1 Clay | Y | Y | Y | Y | N | Y |
| 2 **Akin** | N | Y | Y | Y | Y | Y |
| 3 Carnahan | Y | Y | Y | Y | N | Y |
| 4 Skelton | Y | Y | Y | Y | N | Y |
| 5 Cleaver | N | Y | Y | Y | N | Y |
| 6 **Graves** | N | Y | Y | Y | Y | Y |
| 7 **Blunt** | Y | Y | Y | Y | Y | Y |
| 8 **Emerson** | N | Y | Y | Y | Y | Y |
| 9 **Hulshof** | N | Y | Y | Y | Y | Y |
| **MONTANA** | | | | | | |
| AL **Rehberg** | N | Y | Y | Y | Y | Y |
| **NEBRASKA** | | | | | | |
| 1 **Fortenberry** | Y | Y | Y | Y | Y | Y |
| 2 **Terry** | N | Y | Y | Y | Y | Y |
| 3 **Osborne** | Y | Y | Y | Y | Y | Y |
| **NEVADA** | | | | | | |
| 1 Berkley | Y | Y | Y | Y | N | Y |
| 2 **Gibbons** | Y | Y | Y | Y | Y | Y |
| 3 **Porter** | Y | Y | Y | Y | Y | Y |
| **NEW HAMPSHIRE** | | | | | | |
| 1 **Bradley** | N | Y | Y | Y | Y | Y |
| 2 **Bass** | Y | Y | Y | Y | Y | Y |
| **NEW JERSEY** | | | | | | |
| 1 Andrews | N | Y | Y | N | N | Y |
| 2 **LoBiondo** | N | Y | Y | Y | Y | Y |
| 3 **Saxton** | N | Y | Y | Y | Y | Y |
| 4 **Smith** | Y | Y | Y | Y | Y | Y |
| 5 **Garrett** | N | Y | Y | Y | Y | Y |
| 6 Pallone | N | Y | Y | Y | N | Y |
| 7 **Ferguson** | N | Y | Y | Y | Y | Y |
| 8 Pascrell | Y | Y | Y | Y | N | Y |
| 9 Rothman | N | Y | Y | Y | N | Y |
| 10 Payne | N | Y | Y | Y | N | Y |
| 11 **Frelinghuysen** | N | Y | Y | Y | Y | Y |
| 12 Holt | N | Y | Y | Y | N | Y |
| 13 Menendez | N | Y | Y | Y | N | Y |
| **NEW MEXICO** | | | | | | |
| 1 **Wilson** | N | Y | Y | Y | Y | Y |
| 2 **Pearce** | N | Y | Y | Y | Y | Y |
| 3 Udall | N | Y | Y | N | N | Y |
| **NEW YORK** | | | | | | |
| 1 Bishop | Y | Y | Y | Y | N | Y |
| 2 Israel | Y | Y | Y | Y | N | Y |
| 3 **King** | Y | Y | Y | Y | Y | Y |
| 4 McCarthy | Y | Y | Y | Y | N | Y |
| 5 Ackerman | Y | Y | Y | Y | N | Y |
| 6 Meeks | Y | Y | Y | Y | N | Y |
| 7 Crowley | Y | Y | Y | N | N | Y |
| 8 Nadler | N | Y | Y | Y | N | ? |
| 9 Weiner | Y | Y | Y | Y | N | Y |
| 10 Towns | Y | Y | Y | Y | N | Y |
| 11 Owens | Y | Y | Y | Y | N | Y |
| 12 Velázquez | Y | Y | Y | Y | N | Y |
| 13 **Fossella** | N | Y | Y | Y | Y | Y |
| 14 Maloney | Y | Y | Y | Y | N | Y |
| 15 Rangel | Y | Y | Y | Y | N | Y |
| 16 Serrano | Y | Y | Y | Y | Y | Y |
| 17 Engel | Y | Y | Y | Y | N | Y |
| 18 Lowey | Y | Y | Y | Y | N | Y |
| 19 **Kelly** | N | Y | Y | Y | Y | Y |
| 20 **Sweeney** | N | Y | Y | Y | Y | Y |
| 21 McNulty | Y | Y | Y | Y | N | Y |
| 22 Hinchey | Y | Y | Y | Y | N | Y |
| 23 **McHugh** | N | Y | Y | Y | Y | Y |
| 24 **Boehlert** | N | Y | Y | Y | Y | Y |
| 25 **Walsh** | N | Y | Y | Y | Y | Y |
| 26 **Reynolds** | N | Y | Y | Y | Y | Y |
| 27 Higgins | Y | Y | Y | Y | N | Y |
| 28 Slaughter | Y | Y | Y | Y | N | Y |
| 29 **Kuhl** | N | Y | Y | Y | Y | Y |
| **NORTH CAROLINA** | | | | | | |
| 1 Butterfield | Y | Y | Y | Y | N | Y |
| 2 Etheridge | N | Y | Y | Y | N | Y |
| 3 **Jones** | N | N | Y | Y | Y | Y |
| 4 Price | Y | Y | Y | Y | N | Y |
| 5 **Foxx** | N | Y | Y | Y | Y | ? |
| 6 **Coble** | N | Y | Y | Y | Y | Y |
| 7 McIntyre | Y | Y | Y | Y | N | Y |
| 8 **Hayes** | N | Y | Y | Y | Y | Y |
| 9 **Myrick** | N | Y | Y | Y | Y | Y |
| 10 **McHenry** | N | Y | Y | Y | Y | Y |
| 11 **Taylor** | N | Y | Y | Y | Y | Y |
| 12 Watt | N | Y | Y | Y | N | Y |
| 13 Miller | Y | Y | Y | Y | Y | Y |
| **NORTH DAKOTA** | | | | | | |
| AL Pomeroy | Y | Y | Y | Y | N | Y |
| **OHIO** | | | | | | |
| 1 **Chabot** | N | Y | Y | Y | Y | ? |
| 2 **Schmidt** | N | Y | Y | Y | Y | Y |
| 3 **Turner** | N | Y | Y | Y | Y | Y |
| 4 **Oxley** | N | Y | Y | Y | Y | Y |
| 5 **Gillmor** | Y | Y | Y | Y | Y | Y |
| 6 Strickland | Y | Y | Y | Y | N | Y |
| 7 **Hobson** | N | Y | Y | Y | Y | Y |
| 8 **Boehner** | N | Y | Y | Y | Y | Y |
| 9 Kaptur | N | Y | Y | Y | N | Y |
| 10 Kucinich | Y | Y | Y | N | N | Y |
| 11 Jones | N | Y | Y | Y | N | Y |
| 12 **Tiberi** | N | Y | Y | Y | Y | Y |
| 13 Brown | Y | Y | Y | Y | N | Y |
| 14 **LaTourette** | N | Y | Y | Y | Y | Y |
| 15 **Pryce** | Y | Y | Y | Y | Y | Y |
| 16 **Regula** | N | Y | Y | Y | Y | Y |
| 17 Ryan | Y | Y | Y | Y | N | Y |
| 18 **Ney** | N | Y | Y | Y | Y | Y |
| **OKLAHOMA** | | | | | | |
| 1 **Sullivan** | N | Y | Y | Y | Y | Y |
| 2 Boren | Y | Y | Y | Y | N | Y |
| 3 **Lucas** | N | Y | Y | Y | Y | Y |
| 4 **Cole** | N | Y | Y | Y | Y | Y |
| 5 **Istook** | N | Y | Y | Y | Y | Y |
| **OREGON** | | | | | | |
| 1 Wu | N | Y | Y | N | Y | Y |
| 2 **Walden** | Y | Y | Y | Y | Y | Y |
| 3 Blumenauer | N | Y | Y | Y | N | Y |
| 4 DeFazio | N | Y | Y | N | N | Y |
| 5 Hooley | Y | Y | Y | Y | N | Y |
| **PENNSYLVANIA** | | | | | | |
| 1 Brady | Y | Y | Y | Y | N | Y |
| 2 Fattah | Y | Y | Y | Y | N | Y |
| 3 **English** | N | Y | Y | Y | Y | Y |
| 4 **Hart** | N | Y | Y | Y | Y | Y |
| 5 **Peterson** | N | Y | Y | Y | Y | Y |
| 6 **Gerlach** | Y | Y | Y | Y | Y | Y |
| 7 **Weldon** | N | Y | Y | Y | Y | Y |
| 8 **Fitzpatrick** | Y | Y | Y | Y | Y | Y |
| 9 **Shuster** | N | Y | Y | Y | Y | Y |
| 10 **Sherwood** | N | Y | Y | Y | Y | Y |
| 11 Kanjorski | N | Y | Y | Y | Y | Y |
| 12 Murtha | N | Y | Y | Y | Y | Y |
| 13 Schwartz | Y | Y | Y | Y | N | Y |
| 14 Doyle | Y | Y | Y | Y | N | Y |
| 15 **Dent** | N | Y | Y | Y | Y | Y |
| 16 **Pitts** | Y | Y | Y | Y | Y | Y |
| 17 Holden | Y | Y | Y | Y | N | Y |
| 18 **Murphy** | N | Y | Y | Y | Y | Y |
| 19 **Platts** | N | Y | Y | Y | Y | Y |
| **RHODE ISLAND** | | | | | | |
| 1 Kennedy | Y | Y | Y | Y | N | Y |
| 2 Langevin | Y | Y | Y | Y | N | Y |
| **SOUTH CAROLINA** | | | | | | |
| 1 **Brown** | N | Y | Y | Y | Y | Y |
| 2 **Wilson** | N | Y | Y | Y | Y | Y |
| 3 **Barrett** | N | Y | Y | Y | Y | Y |
| 4 **Inglis** | N | Y | Y | Y | Y | Y |
| 5 Spratt | Y | Y | Y | Y | N | Y |
| 6 Clyburn | Y | Y | Y | Y | N | Y |
| **SOUTH DAKOTA** | | | | | | |
| AL Herseth | Y | Y | Y | Y | N | Y |
| **TENNESSEE** | | | | | | |
| 1 **Jenkins** | ? | ? | ? | Y | Y | Y |
| 2 **Duncan** | N | Y | Y | Y | Y | Y |
| 3 **Wamp** | N | Y | Y | Y | Y | Y |
| 4 Davis | N | Y | Y | Y | N | Y |
| 5 Cooper | N | Y | Y | N | N | Y |
| 6 Gordon | N | Y | Y | Y | Y | Y |
| 7 **Blackburn** | N | Y | Y | Y | Y | Y |
| 8 Tanner | N | Y | Y | Y | N | Y |
| 9 Ford | N | Y | Y | N | N | ? |
| **TEXAS** | | | | | | |
| 1 **Gohmert** | N | Y | Y | Y | Y | N |
| 2 **Poe** | N | Y | Y | Y | Y | Y |
| 3 **Johnson, S.** | N | Y | Y | Y | Y | Y |
| 4 **Hall** | Y | Y | Y | Y | Y | Y |
| 5 **Hensarling** | N | Y | Y | Y | Y | Y |
| 6 **Barton** | Y | Y | Y | Y | ? | Y |
| 7 **Culberson** | N | ? | Y | Y | Y | Y |
| 8 **Brady** | N | Y | Y | Y | Y | Y |
| 9 Green, A. | N | Y | Y | Y | N | Y |
| 10 **McCaul** | N | Y | Y | Y | Y | Y |
| 11 **Conaway** | N | Y | Y | Y | Y | Y |
| 12 **Granger** | N | Y | Y | Y | Y | Y |
| 13 **Thornberry** | N | Y | Y | Y | Y | Y |
| 14 **Paul** | N | N | Y | Y | Y | Y |
| 15 Hinojosa | Y | Y | Y | Y | Y | Y |
| 16 Reyes | Y | Y | Y | Y | N | Y |
| 17 Edwards | ? | ? | Y | Y | N | Y |
| 18 Jackson-Lee | Y | Y | Y | N | N | Y |
| 19 **Neugebauer** | N | Y | Y | Y | Y | Y |
| 20 Gonzalez | Y | Y | Y | Y | N | Y |
| 21 **Smith** | N | Y | Y | Y | Y | ? |
| 22 **DeLay** | N | Y | Y | Y | Y | Y |
| 23 **Bonilla** | N | Y | Y | Y | Y | Y |
| 24 **Marchant** | N | Y | Y | Y | Y | Y |
| 25 Doggett | Y | Y | Y | Y | N | Y |
| 26 **Burgess** | Y | Y | Y | Y | Y | Y |
| 27 Ortiz | Y | Y | Y | Y | N | Y |
| 28 Cuellar | N | Y | Y | Y | Y | Y |
| 29 Green, G. | Y | Y | Y | Y | N | Y |
| 30 Johnson, E. | N | Y | Y | Y | N | Y |
| 31 **Carter** | N | Y | Y | Y | Y | Y |
| 32 **Sessions** | N | Y | Y | Y | Y | Y |
| **UTAH** | | | | | | |
| 1 **Bishop** | N | Y | Y | Y | Y | Y |
| 2 Matheson | Y | Y | Y | Y | N | Y |
| 3 **Cannon** | N | Y | Y | Y | Y | Y |
| **VERMONT** | | | | | | |
| AL *Sanders* | Y | Y | Y | Y | N | Y |
| **VIRGINIA** | | | | | | |
| 1 **Davis, J.** | N | Y | Y | Y | Y | Y |
| 2 **Drake** | N | Y | Y | Y | Y | Y |
| 3 Scott | Y | Y | Y | Y | N | Y |
| 4 **Forbes** | N | Y | Y | Y | Y | Y |
| 5 **Goode** | N | Y | Y | Y | Y | Y |
| 6 **Goodlatte** | N | Y | Y | Y | Y | Y |
| 7 **Cantor** | N | Y | Y | Y | Y | Y |
| 8 Moran | Y | Y | Y | ? | ? | ? |
| 9 Boucher | Y | Y | Y | Y | N | Y |
| 10 **Wolf** | N | Y | Y | Y | Y | Y |
| 11 **Davis, T.** | Y | Y | Y | Y | Y | Y |
| **WASHINGTON** | | | | | | |
| 1 Inslee | Y | Y | Y | Y | N | Y |
| 2 Larsen | N | Y | Y | Y | N | Y |
| 3 Baird | Y | Y | Y | Y | N | Y |
| 4 **Hastings** | N | Y | Y | Y | Y | Y |
| 5 **McMorris** | N | Y | Y | Y | Y | Y |
| 6 Dicks | Y | Y | Y | Y | N | Y |
| 7 McDermott | N | Y | Y | Y | N | Y |
| 8 **Reichert** | ? | ? | ? | Y | Y | Y |
| 9 Smith | Y | Y | Y | Y | Y | Y |
| **WEST VIRGINIA** | | | | | | |
| 1 Mollohan | N | Y | Y | Y | Y | Y |
| 2 **Capito** | N | Y | Y | Y | Y | Y |
| 3 Rahall | N | Y | Y | Y | N | Y |
| **WISCONSIN** | | | | | | |
| 1 **Ryan** | N | Y | Y | Y | Y | Y |
| 2 Baldwin | Y | Y | Y | Y | N | Y |
| 3 Kind | Y | Y | Y | Y | Y | Y |
| 4 Moore | Y | Y | Y | Y | N | Y |
| 5 **Sensenbrenner** | N | Y | Y | Y | Y | Y |
| 6 **Petri** | N | Y | Y | Y | Y | Y |
| 7 Obey | Y | Y | Y | Y | N | Y |
| 8 **Green** | N | Y | Y | Y | Y | Y |
| **WYOMING** | | | | | | |
| AL **Cubin** | Y | Y | Y | Y | Y | Y |

# IN THE HOUSE | By Vote Number

**598.** **HR 3010. Fiscal 2006 Labor-HHS-Education Appropriations/Conference Report.** Adoption of the conference report on the bill that would appropriate $601.7 billion, including $142.5 billion in discretionary spending, for the Labor, Health and Human Services (HHS) and Education departments and related agencies in fiscal 2006. It would provide $63.5 billion for the Education Department, $14.8 billion for the Labor Department and $474.1 billion for Health and Human Services. Rejected 209-224: R 209-22; D 0-201 (ND 0-150, SD 0-51); I 0-1. Nov. 17, 2005.

**599.** **H J Res 72. Fiscal 2006 Continuing Resolution/Passage.** Passage of the joint resolution that would provide continuing appropriations through Dec. 17 for all federal departments and agencies whose fiscal 2006 appropriations bills have not been enacted. Passed 413-16: R 230-0; D 182-16 (ND 135-13, SD 47-3); I 1-0. Nov. 17, 2005.

**600.** **HR 4241. Budget Reconciliation/Question of Consideration.** Question of whether the House should consider the rule (H Res 560) to provide for House floor consideration of the bill that would make changes to programs for a net savings of approximately $49.9 billion over five years. Agreed to consider 224-198: R 224-1; D 0-196 (ND 0-145, SD 0-51); I 0-1. Nov. 17, 2005.

**601.** **HR 4241. Budget Reconciliation/Passage.** Passage of the bill that would make changes to programs for a net savings of $49.9 billion over five years. It would reduce subsidies to lenders of student loans, reduce aid to states to enforce child support payments, reduce federal spending on Medicaid and repeal a law that sends anti-dumping trade penalties to aggrieved corporations instead of to the U.S. Treasury. It would provide $2.5 billion in Medicaid and other assistance to Hurricane Katrina victims. Passed 217-215: R 217-14; D 0-200 (ND 0-149, SD 0-51); I 0-1. A "yea" was a vote in support of the president's position. Nov. 18, 2005 (in the session that began and the Congressional Record dated Nov. 17, 2005).

**602.** **H Res 546. Condemn Terrorist Attacks in Jordan/Adoption.** Ros-Lehtinen, R-Fla., motion to suspend the rules and adopt the resolution that would condemn the Nov. 9 terrorist attacks in Amman, Jordan, and express the condolences of the House of Representatives to the families and friends of those killed in the attacks. Motion agreed to 409-0: R 217-0; D 191-0 (ND 143-0, SD 48-0); I 1-0. A two-thirds majority of those present and voting (273 in this case) is required for adoption under suspension of the rules. Nov. 18, 2005 (in the session that began and the Congressional Record dated Nov. 17, 2005).

| | 598 | 599 | 600 | 601 | 602 |
|---|---|---|---|---|---|
| **ALABAMA** | | | | | |
| 1 Bonner | Y | Y | Y | Y | Y |
| 2 Everett | Y | Y | Y | Y | Y |
| 3 Rogers | N | Y | Y | Y | Y |
| 4 Aderholt | Y | Y | Y | Y | Y |
| 5 Cramer | N | Y | N | N | Y |
| 6 Bachus | Y | Y | Y | Y | Y |
| 7 Davis | N | Y | N | N | Y |
| **ALASKA** | | | | | |
| AL Young | Y | Y | Y | Y | Y |
| **ARIZONA** | | | | | |
| 1 Renzi | N | Y | Y | Y | Y |
| 2 Franks | Y | Y | Y | Y | Y |
| 3 Shadegg | Y | Y | Y | Y | Y |
| 4 Pastor | N | Y | N | N | Y |
| 5 Hayworth | Y | Y | Y | Y | Y |
| 6 Flake | Y | Y | Y | Y | Y |
| 7 Grijalva | N | N | N | N | Y |
| 8 Kolbe | Y | Y | Y | Y | Y |
| **ARKANSAS** | | | | | |
| 1 Berry | N | Y | N | N | Y |
| 2 Snyder | N | Y | N | N | Y |
| 3 Boozman | Y | Y | Y | Y | Y |
| 4 Ross | N | Y | N | N | Y |
| **CALIFORNIA** | | | | | |
| 1 Thompson | N | N | N | N | Y |
| 2 Herger | Y | Y | Y | Y | Y |
| 3 Lungren | Y | Y | Y | Y | Y |
| 4 Doolittle | Y | Y | Y | Y | Y |
| 5 Matsui, D. | N | Y | N | N | Y |
| 6 Woolsey | N | Y | N | N | Y |
| 7 Miller, George | N | Y | N | N | Y |
| 8 Pelosi | N | Y | N | N | Y |
| 9 Lee | N | Y | N | N | Y |
| 10 Tauscher | N | Y | N | N | Y |
| 11 Pombo | Y | Y | Y | Y | Y |
| 12 Lantos | N | Y | N | N | Y |
| 13 Stark | N | Y | N | N | ? |
| 14 Eshoo | N | Y | N | N | Y |
| 15 Honda | N | Y | N | N | Y |
| 16 Lofgren | N | N | N | N | Y |
| 17 Farr | N | Y | N | N | Y |
| 18 Cardoza | N | Y | N | N | Y |
| 19 Radanovich | Y | Y | ? | Y | ? |
| 20 Costa | N | Y | N | N | Y |
| 21 Nunes | N | Y | Y | Y | Y |
| 22 Thomas | N | Y | Y | Y | Y |
| 23 Capps | N | Y | N | N | Y |
| 24 Gallegly | Y | Y | Y | Y | Y |
| 25 McKeon | Y | Y | Y | Y | Y |
| 26 Dreier | Y | Y | Y | Y | Y |
| 27 Sherman | N | Y | N | N | Y |
| 28 Berman | N | Y | N | N | Y |
| 29 Schiff | N | Y | N | N | Y |
| 30 Waxman | N | Y | N | N | Y |
| 31 Becerra | N | N | N | N | Y |
| 32 Solis | N | Y | N | N | Y |
| 33 Watson | N | Y | N | N | Y |
| 34 Roybal-Allard | N | Y | N | N | Y |
| 35 Waters | N | Y | N | N | Y |
| 36 Harman | N | Y | N | N | Y |
| 37 Millender-McD. | N | Y | N | N | Y |
| 38 Napolitano | N | Y | N | N | Y |
| 39 Sánchez, Linda | N | Y | N | N | Y |
| 40 Royce | Y | Y | Y | Y | Y |
| 41 Lewis | Y | Y | Y | Y | Y |
| 42 Miller, Gary | Y | Y | Y | Y | Y |
| 43 Baca | N | Y | N | N | Y |
| 44 Calvert | Y | Y | Y | Y | Y |
| 45 Bono | Y | Y | Y | Y | Y |
| 46 Rohrabacher | Y | Y | Y | Y | Y |
| 47 Sanchez, Loretta | N | Y | N | N | Y |
| 48 Vacant | | | | | |
| 49 Issa | Y | Y | Y | Y | Y |

| | 598 | 599 | 600 | 601 | 602 |
|---|---|---|---|---|---|
| 50 Cunningham | Y | Y | Y | Y | Y |
| 51 Filner | N | Y | N | N | Y |
| 52 Hunter | Y | Y | Y | Y | Y |
| 53 Davis | N | Y | N | N | Y |
| **COLORADO** | | | | | |
| 1 DeGette | N | Y | N | N | Y |
| 2 Udall | N | Y | N | N | Y |
| 3 Salazar | N | Y | N | N | Y |
| 4 Musgrave | Y | Y | Y | Y | Y |
| 5 Hefley | Y | Y | Y | Y | ? |
| 6 Tancredo | Y | Y | Y | Y | ? |
| 7 Beauprez | Y | Y | Y | Y | Y |
| **CONNECTICUT** | | | | | |
| 1 Larson | N | Y | N | N | Y |
| 2 Simmons | N | Y | N | N | Y |
| 3 DeLauro | N | Y | N | N | Y |
| 4 Shays | Y | Y | Y | N | Y |
| 5 Johnson | N | Y | Y | N | Y |
| **DELAWARE** | | | | | |
| AL Castle | N | Y | Y | Y | Y |
| **FLORIDA** | | | | | |
| 1 Miller | Y | Y | Y | Y | Y |
| 2 Boyd | N | Y | N | N | Y |
| 3 Brown | N | Y | N | N | Y |
| 4 Crenshaw | Y | Y | Y | Y | Y |
| 5 Brown-Waite | Y | Y | Y | Y | Y |
| 6 Stearns | N | Y | Y | Y | Y |
| 7 Mica | Y | Y | Y | Y | Y |
| 8 Keller | Y | Y | Y | Y | Y |
| 9 Bilirakis | Y | Y | Y | Y | Y |
| 10 Young | Y | Y | ? | Y | Y |
| 11 Davis | N | Y | N | N | Y |
| 12 Putnam | Y | Y | Y | Y | Y |
| 13 Harris | Y | Y | Y | Y | Y |
| 14 Mack | Y | Y | Y | Y | Y |
| 15 Weldon | Y | Y | Y | Y | Y |
| 16 Foley | Y | Y | Y | Y | Y |
| 17 Meek | N | Y | N | N | Y |
| 18 Ros-Lehtinen | Y | Y | Y | Y | Y |
| 19 Wexler | N | Y | N | N | Y |
| 20 Wasserman-Schultz | N | Y | N | N | Y |
| 21 Diaz-Balart, L. | Y | Y | Y | Y | Y |
| 22 Shaw | Y | Y | Y | Y | Y |
| 23 Hastings | N | N | N | N | Y |
| 24 Feeney | Y | Y | Y | Y | Y |
| 25 Diaz-Balart, M. | Y | Y | Y | Y | Y |
| **GEORGIA** | | | | | |
| 1 Kingston | Y | Y | Y | Y | Y |
| 2 Bishop | N | Y | N | N | Y |
| 3 Marshall | N | Y | N | N | ? |
| 4 McKinney | N | Y | N | N | Y |
| 5 Lewis | N | Y | N | N | Y |
| 6 Price | Y | Y | Y | Y | Y |
| 7 Linder | Y | Y | Y | Y | Y |
| 8 Westmoreland | Y | Y | Y | Y | Y |
| 9 Norwood | Y | Y | Y | Y | Y |
| 10 Deal | Y | Y | Y | Y | Y |
| 11 Gingrey | Y | Y | Y | Y | Y |
| 12 Barrow | N | Y | N | N | Y |
| 13 Scott | N | Y | N | N | Y |
| **HAWAII** | | | | | |
| 1 Abercrombie | N | Y | N | N | Y |
| 2 Case | N | Y | N | N | Y |
| **IDAHO** | | | | | |
| 1 Otter | N | Y | Y | Y | Y |
| 2 Simpson | Y | Y | Y | Y | Y |
| **ILLINOIS** | | | | | |
| 1 Rush | N | Y | N | N | Y |
| 2 Jackson | N | N | N | N | Y |
| 3 Lipinski | N | Y | N | N | Y |
| 4 Gutierrez | N | Y | N | N | Y |
| 5 Emanuel | N | Y | N | N | Y |
| 6 Hyde | Y | Y | ? | Y | Y |
| 7 Davis | N | Y | N | N | Y |
| 8 Bean | N | Y | N | N | ? |
| 9 Schakowsky | N | Y | N | N | Y |
| 10 Kirk | N | Y | Y | Y | Y |
| 11 Weller | Y | Y | Y | Y | Y |
| 12 Costello | N | Y | N | N | Y |

| KEY | Republicans | | Democrats | Independents | |
|---|---|---|---|---|---|
| Y | Voted for (yea) | X | Paired against | C | Voted "present" to avoid possible conflict of interest |
| # | Paired for | – | Announced against | | |
| + | Announced for | P | Voted "present" | ? | Did not vote or otherwise make a position known |
| N | Voted against (nay) | | | | |

| | 598 | 599 | 600 | 601 | 602 |
|---|---|---|---|---|---|
| 13 Biggert | Y | Y | Y | Y | Y |
| 14 Hastert | Y | | Y | Y | Y |
| 15 Johnson | Y | Y | Y | N | Y |
| 16 Manzullo | Y | Y | Y | Y | Y |
| 17 Evans | N | Y | N | N | Y |
| 18 LaHood | Y | Y | Y | Y | Y |
| 19 Shimkus | Y | Y | Y | Y | Y |
| **INDIANA** | | | | | |
| 1 Visclosky | N | Y | N | N | Y |
| 2 Chocola | Y | Y | Y | Y | Y |
| 3 Souder | Y | Y | Y | Y | Y |
| 4 Buyer | Y | Y | Y | Y | Y |
| 5 Burton | Y | Y | Y | Y | Y |
| 6 Pence | Y | Y | Y | Y | Y |
| 7 Carson | N | Y | N | N | Y |
| 8 Hostettler | Y | Y | Y | Y | Y |
| 9 Sodrel | Y | Y | Y | Y | Y |
| **IOWA** | | | | | |
| 1 Nussle | Y | Y | Y | Y | Y |
| 2 Leach | N | Y | Y | N | Y |
| 3 Boswell | ? | ? | ? | ? | ? |
| 4 Latham | Y | Y | Y | Y | ? |
| 5 King | Y | Y | Y | Y | Y |
| **KANSAS** | | | | | |
| 1 Moran | N | Y | Y | Y | Y |
| 2 Ryun | Y | Y | Y | Y | Y |
| 3 Moore | N | Y | N | N | Y |
| 4 Tiahrt | Y | Y | Y | Y | Y |
| **KENTUCKY** | | | | | |
| 1 Whitfield | Y | Y | Y | Y | Y |
| 2 Lewis | Y | Y | Y | Y | Y |
| 3 Northup | Y | Y | Y | Y | Y |
| 4 Davis | Y | Y | Y | Y | Y |
| 5 Rogers | Y | Y | Y | Y | Y |
| 6 Chandler | N | Y | N | N | Y |
| **LOUISIANA** | | | | | |
| 1 Jindal | Y | Y | Y | Y | Y |
| 2 Jefferson | N | Y | N | N | Y |
| 3 Melancon | N | Y | N | N | Y |
| 4 McCrery | Y | Y | Y | Y | Y |
| 5 Alexander | Y | Y | Y | Y | Y |
| 6 Baker | Y | Y | Y | Y | ? |
| 7 Boustany | Y | Y | Y | Y | Y |
| **MAINE** | | | | | |
| 1 Allen | N | Y | N | N | Y |
| 2 Michaud | N | Y | N | N | Y |
| **MARYLAND** | | | | | |
| 1 Gilchrest | Y | Y | Y | Y | Y |
| 2 Ruppersberger | N | Y | N | N | Y |
| 3 Cardin | N | Y | ? | N | Y |
| 4 Wynn | N | Y | N | N | Y |
| 5 Hoyer | N | Y | N | N | Y |
| 6 Bartlett | Y | Y | Y | Y | Y |
| 7 Cummings | N | Y | N | N | Y |
| 8 Van Hollen | N | Y | N | N | Y |
| **MASSACHUSETTS** | | | | | |
| 1 Olver | N | Y | N | N | Y |
| 2 Neal | N | Y | N | N | Y |
| 3 McGovern | N | Y | N | N | Y |
| 4 Frank | N | N | N | N | Y |
| 5 Meehan | N | N | N | N | Y |
| 6 Tierney | N | N | N | N | Y |
| 7 Markey | N | Y | N | N | Y |
| 8 Capuano | N | N | N | N | Y |
| 9 Lynch | N | Y | N | N | Y |
| 10 Delahunt | N | Y | N | N | Y |
| **MICHIGAN** | | | | | |
| 1 Stupak | N | N | N | N | Y |
| 2 Hoekstra | Y | Y | ? | Y | Y |
| 3 Ehlers | Y | Y | Y | Y | Y |
| 4 Camp | Y | Y | Y | Y | Y |
| 5 Kildee | N | Y | N | N | Y |
| 6 Upton | Y | Y | Y | Y | Y |
| 7 Schwarz | Y | Y | Y | Y | Y |
| 8 Rogers | Y | Y | Y | Y | Y |
| 9 Knollenberg | Y | Y | Y | Y | Y |
| 10 Miller | Y | Y | Y | Y | Y |
| 11 McCotter | Y | Y | Y | Y | Y |
| 12 Levin | N | Y | N | N | Y |
| 13 Kilpatrick | N | Y | N | N | Y |
| 14 Conyers | N | N | N | N | Y |
| 15 Dingell | N | N | N | N | Y |

| | 598 | 599 | 600 | 601 | 602 |
|---|---|---|---|---|---|
| **MINNESOTA** | | | | | |
| 1 Gutknecht | Y | Y | Y | Y | Y |
| 2 Kline | Y | Y | Y | Y | Y |
| 3 Ramstad | N | Y | Y | N | ? |
| 4 McCollum | N | Y | N | N | Y |
| 5 Sabo | N | Y | N | N | Y |
| 6 Kennedy | Y | Y | Y | Y | Y |
| 7 Peterson | N | Y | N | N | Y |
| 8 Oberstar | N | Y | N | N | Y |
| **MISSISSIPPI** | | | | | |
| 1 Wicker | Y | Y | Y | Y | Y |
| 2 Thompson | N | Y | N | N | Y |
| 3 Pickering | N | Y | Y | Y | Y |
| 4 Taylor | N | Y | N | N | Y |
| **MISSOURI** | | | | | |
| 1 Clay | N | Y | N | N | ? |
| 2 Akin | Y | Y | Y | Y | Y |
| 3 Carnahan | N | ? | N | N | Y |
| 4 Skelton | N | Y | N | N | Y |
| 5 Cleaver | N | Y | N | N | Y |
| 6 Graves | Y | Y | Y | Y | Y |
| 7 Blunt | Y | Y | Y | Y | Y |
| 8 Emerson | N | Y | Y | Y | Y |
| 9 Hulshof | Y | Y | Y | Y | Y |
| **MONTANA** | | | | | |
| AL Rehberg | Y | Y | Y | Y | Y |
| **NEBRASKA** | | | | | |
| 1 Fortenberry | Y | Y | ? | Y | Y |
| 2 Terry | Y | Y | Y | Y | Y |
| 3 Osborne | Y | Y | Y | Y | Y |
| **NEVADA** | | | | | |
| 1 Berkley | N | Y | N | N | Y |
| 2 Gibbons | N | Y | Y | Y | Y |
| 3 Porter | Y | Y | Y | Y | Y |
| **NEW HAMPSHIRE** | | | | | |
| 1 Bradley | Y | Y | Y | Y | Y |
| 2 Bass | Y | Y | Y | Y | Y |
| **NEW JERSEY** | | | | | |
| 1 Andrews | N | Y | N | N | Y |
| 2 LoBiondo | Y | Y | Y | Y | Y |
| 3 Saxton | Y | Y | Y | Y | Y |
| 4 Smith | Y | Y | Y | N | Y |
| 5 Garrett | Y | Y | Y | Y | Y |
| 6 Pallone | N | Y | N | N | Y |
| 7 Ferguson | Y | Y | Y | Y | Y |
| 8 Pascrell | N | Y | N | N | Y |
| 9 Rothman | N | Y | N | N | Y |
| 10 Payne | N | Y | N | N | Y |
| 11 Frelinghuysen | Y | Y | Y | Y | Y |
| 12 Holt | N | Y | N | N | Y |
| 13 Menendez | N | Y | N | N | Y |
| **NEW MEXICO** | | | | | |
| 1 Wilson | N | Y | Y | N | Y |
| 2 Pearce | Y | Y | Y | Y | Y |
| 3 Udall | N | Y | N | N | Y |
| **NEW YORK** | | | | | |
| 1 Bishop | N | Y | N | N | Y |
| 2 Israel | N | Y | N | N | Y |
| 3 King | Y | Y | Y | Y | Y |
| 4 McCarthy | N | Y | N | N | Y |
| 5 Ackerman | N | Y | N | N | Y |
| 6 Meeks | N | Y | N | N | Y |
| 7 Crowley | N | Y | N | N | Y |
| 8 Nadler | N | Y | N | N | Y |
| 9 Weiner | N | Y | N | N | Y |
| 10 Towns | N | ? | ? | ? | ? |
| 11 Owens | N | Y | N | N | Y |
| 12 Velázquez | N | Y | N | N | Y |
| 13 Fossella | Y | Y | Y | Y | Y |
| 14 Maloney | N | Y | N | N | Y |
| 15 Rangel | N | Y | N | N | ? |
| 16 Serrano | N | Y | N | N | Y |
| 17 Engel | N | Y | ? | N | Y |
| 18 Lowey | N | Y | N | N | Y |
| 19 Kelly | Y | Y | Y | Y | Y |
| 20 Sweeney | Y | Y | Y | Y | Y |
| 21 McNulty | N | Y | N | N | Y |
| 22 Hinchey | N | Y | N | N | Y |
| 23 McHugh | Y | Y | Y | Y | ? |
| 24 Boehlert | Y | Y | Y | Y | Y |
| 25 Walsh | Y | Y | Y | Y | Y |
| 26 Reynolds | Y | Y | Y | Y | Y |
| 27 Higgins | N | Y | N | N | Y |
| 28 Slaughter | N | Y | N | N | Y |
| 29 Kuhl | Y | Y | Y | Y | Y |

| | 598 | 599 | 600 | 601 | 602 |
|---|---|---|---|---|---|
| **NORTH CAROLINA** | | | | | |
| 1 Butterfield | N | Y | N | N | Y |
| 2 Etheridge | N | Y | N | N | Y |
| 3 Jones | Y | Y | Y | N | ? |
| 4 Price | N | Y | N | N | Y |
| 5 Foxx | Y | Y | Y | Y | Y |
| 6 Coble | Y | Y | Y | Y | Y |
| 7 McIntyre | N | Y | N | N | Y |
| 8 Hayes | Y | Y | Y | Y | Y |
| 9 Myrick | Y | Y | Y | Y | Y |
| 10 McHenry | Y | Y | Y | Y | Y |
| 11 Taylor | Y | Y | Y | Y | Y |
| 12 Watt | N | Y | N | N | Y |
| 13 Miller | N | Y | N | N | Y |
| **NORTH DAKOTA** | | | | | |
| AL Pomeroy | N | Y | N | N | Y |
| **OHIO** | | | | | |
| 1 Chabot | Y | Y | Y | Y | Y |
| 2 Schmidt | Y | Y | Y | Y | Y |
| 3 Turner | Y | Y | Y | Y | Y |
| 4 Oxley | Y | Y | Y | Y | ? |
| 5 Gillmor | Y | Y | Y | Y | Y |
| 6 Strickland | N | Y | N | N | Y |
| 7 Hobson | Y | Y | Y | Y | Y |
| 8 Boehner | Y | Y | Y | Y | ? |
| 9 Kaptur | N | Y | N | N | Y |
| 10 Kucinich | N | N | N | N | Y |
| 11 Jones | N | Y | N | N | Y |
| 12 Tiberi | Y | Y | Y | Y | Y |
| 13 Brown | N | Y | N | N | Y |
| 14 LaTourette | Y | Y | Y | Y | Y |
| 15 Pryce | Y | Y | Y | Y | Y |
| 16 Regula | Y | Y | Y | Y | Y |
| 17 Ryan | N | Y | ? | N | Y |
| 18 Ney | Y | Y | Y | Y | Y |
| **OKLAHOMA** | | | | | |
| 1 Sullivan | Y | Y | Y | Y | Y |
| 2 Boren | N | Y | N | N | Y |
| 3 Lucas | Y | Y | Y | Y | Y |
| 4 Cole | Y | Y | Y | Y | Y |
| 5 Istook | Y | Y | Y | Y | Y |
| **OREGON** | | | | | |
| 1 Wu | N | N | N | N | Y |
| 2 Walden | Y | Y | ? | Y | Y |
| 3 Blumenauer | N | Y | N | N | Y |
| 4 DeFazio | N | N | N | N | Y |
| 5 Hooley | N | Y | N | N | Y |
| **PENNSYLVANIA** | | | | | |
| 1 Brady | N | Y | N | N | Y |
| 2 Fattah | N | Y | N | N | Y |
| 3 English | Y | Y | Y | Y | Y |
| 4 Hart | Y | Y | Y | Y | Y |
| 5 Peterson | Y | Y | Y | Y | Y |
| 6 Gerlach | Y | Y | Y | N | Y |
| 7 Weldon | Y | Y | Y | Y | Y |
| 8 Fitzpatrick | N | Y | Y | Y | Y |
| 9 Shuster | Y | Y | Y | Y | Y |
| 10 Sherwood | Y | Y | Y | Y | Y |
| 11 Kanjorski | N | Y | N | N | ? |
| 12 Murtha | N | Y | N | N | Y |
| 13 Schwartz | N | Y | N | N | Y |
| 14 Doyle | N | Y | N | N | Y |
| 15 Dent | Y | Y | Y | Y | Y |
| 16 Pitts | Y | Y | Y | Y | Y |
| 17 Holden | N | Y | N | N | Y |
| 18 Murphy | N | Y | Y | N | Y |
| 19 Platts | Y | Y | Y | Y | Y |
| **RHODE ISLAND** | | | | | |
| 1 Kennedy | N | Y | N | N | Y |
| 2 Langevin | N | Y | N | N | Y |
| **SOUTH CAROLINA** | | | | | |
| 1 Brown | Y | Y | Y | Y | Y |
| 2 Wilson | Y | Y | Y | Y | Y |
| 3 Barrett | Y | Y | Y | Y | Y |
| 4 Inglis | Y | Y | Y | Y | Y |
| 5 Spratt | N | Y | N | N | Y |
| 6 Clyburn | N | Y | N | N | Y |
| **SOUTH DAKOTA** | | | | | |
| AL Herseth | N | Y | N | N | Y |
| **TENNESSEE** | | | | | |
| 1 Jenkins | Y | Y | Y | Y | Y |
| 2 Duncan | Y | Y | Y | Y | Y |

| | 598 | 599 | 600 | 601 | 602 |
|---|---|---|---|---|---|
| 3 Wamp | Y | Y | Y | Y | Y |
| 4 Davis | N | Y | N | N | Y |
| 5 Cooper | N | N | N | N | Y |
| 6 Gordon | N | Y | N | N | Y |
| 7 Blackburn | Y | Y | Y | Y | Y |
| 8 Tanner | N | Y | N | N | Y |
| 9 Ford | N | N | N | N | Y |
| **TEXAS** | | | | | |
| 1 Gohmert | Y | Y | Y | Y | Y |
| 2 Poe | Y | Y | Y | Y | Y |
| 3 Johnson, S. | Y | Y | Y | Y | Y |
| 4 Hall | Y | Y | Y | Y | ? |
| 5 Hensarling | Y | Y | Y | Y | Y |
| 6 Barton | Y | Y | Y | Y | Y |
| 7 Culberson | Y | Y | Y | Y | Y |
| 8 Brady | Y | Y | Y | Y | Y |
| 9 Green, A. | N | Y | N | N | Y |
| 10 McCaul | Y | Y | Y | Y | Y |
| 11 Conaway | Y | Y | Y | Y | Y |
| 12 Granger | Y | Y | Y | Y | Y |
| 13 Thornberry | Y | Y | Y | Y | Y |
| 14 Paul | N | Y | Y | N | ? |
| 15 Hinojosa | N | Y | N | N | Y |
| 16 Reyes | N | Y | N | N | Y |
| 17 Edwards | N | ? | N | N | Y |
| 18 Jackson-Lee | N | Y | N | N | Y |
| 19 Neugebauer | Y | Y | Y | Y | Y |
| 20 Gonzalez | N | Y | N | N | Y |
| 21 Smith | Y | Y | Y | Y | Y |
| 22 DeLay | Y | Y | Y | Y | Y |
| 23 Bonilla | Y | Y | Y | Y | Y |
| 24 Marchant | Y | Y | Y | Y | Y |
| 25 Doggett | N | Y | N | N | Y |
| 26 Burgess | Y | Y | Y | Y | Y |
| 27 Ortiz | N | Y | N | N | Y |
| 28 Cuellar | N | Y | N | N | Y |
| 29 Green, G. | N | Y | N | N | Y |
| 30 Johnson, E. | N | Y | N | N | ? |
| 31 Carter | Y | Y | Y | Y | Y |
| 32 Sessions | Y | Y | Y | Y | Y |
| **UTAH** | | | | | |
| 1 Bishop | Y | Y | Y | | Y |
| 2 Matheson | N | Y | N | N | Y |
| 3 Cannon | Y | Y | Y | Y | Y |
| **VERMONT** | | | | | |
| AL Sanders | N | Y | N | N | Y |
| **VIRGINIA** | | | | | |
| 1 Davis, J. | Y | Y | Y | Y | ? |
| 2 Drake | Y | Y | Y | Y | Y |
| 3 Scott | N | Y | N | N | Y |
| 4 Forbes | Y | Y | Y | Y | Y |
| 5 Goode | Y | Y | Y | Y | Y |
| 6 Goodlatte | Y | Y | Y | Y | Y |
| 7 Cantor | Y | Y | Y | Y | Y |
| 8 Moran | N | Y | N | N | Y |
| 9 Boucher | N | Y | N | N | Y |
| 10 Wolf | Y | Y | Y | Y | Y |
| 11 Davis, T. | Y | Y | Y | Y | Y |
| **WASHINGTON** | | | | | |
| 1 Inslee | N | Y | N | N | Y |
| 2 Larsen | N | Y | N | N | Y |
| 3 Baird | N | Y | N | N | Y |
| 4 Hastings | Y | Y | Y | Y | Y |
| 5 McMorris | Y | Y | Y | Y | Y |
| 6 Dicks | N | Y | N | N | ? |
| 7 McDermott | N | Y | N | N | Y |
| 8 Reichert | Y | Y | Y | Y | Y |
| 9 Smith | N | Y | N | N | Y |
| **WEST VIRGINIA** | | | | | |
| 1 Mollohan | N | Y | ? | N | Y |
| 2 Capito | Y | Y | Y | Y | Y |
| 3 Rahall | N | Y | N | N | Y |
| **WISCONSIN** | | | | | |
| 1 Ryan | Y | Y | Y | Y | Y |
| 2 Baldwin | N | Y | N | N | Y |
| 3 Kind | N | Y | N | N | Y |
| 4 Moore | N | Y | N | N | Y |
| 5 Sensenbrenner | Y | Y | Y | Y | Y |
| 6 Petri | Y | Y | Y | Y | Y |
| 7 Obey | N | Y | N | N | Y |
| 8 Green | Y | Y | Y | Y | Y |
| **WYOMING** | | | | | |
| AL Cubin | Y | Y | Y | Y | Y |

## IN THE HOUSE | By Vote Number

**603.** **Quorum Call.*** 417 members responded. Nov. 18, 2005.

**604.** **HR 2528. Fiscal 2006 Military Construction-VA Appropriations/ Conference Report.** Adoption of the conference report on the bill that would provide $82.6 billion in fiscal 2006 for the Department of Veterans Affairs, military construction and military housing. The bill would provide $22.5 billion for veterans' medical services, $6.2 billion for military construction, $4 billion for military family housing and $1.5 billion for the latest round of base closures. Adopted (thus sent to the Senate) 427-0: R 227-0; D 199-0 (ND 148-0, SD 51-0); I 1-0. Nov. 18, 2005.

**605.** **HR 3058. Fiscal 2006 Transportation-Treasury-Housing Appropriations/Conference Report.** Adoption of the conference report on the bill that would appropriate $137.6 billion in fiscal 2006, including $65.9 billion in discretionary spending, for the departments of Housing and Urban Development (HUD), Treasury, and Transportation, and related agencies. It would provide $34 billion for HUD, $34.7 billion for the Federal Highway Administration, $13.8 billion for the Federal Aviation Administration, $11.7 billion for the Treasury Department and $5.8 billion for the judiciary. It also includes $603 million for the District of Columbia. Adopted (thus sent to the Senate) 392-31: R 204-21; D 187-10 (ND 137-9, SD 50-1); I 1-0. Nov. 18, 2005.

**606.** **H Res 563. Immediate Iraq Withdrawal/Consideration of Rule.** Adoption of the resolution (H Res 563) that would waive the two-thirds vote requirement for same-day consideration of any rule to provide for House floor consideration of a resolution relating to U.S. forces in Iraq, or any outstanding conference reports on fiscal 2006 appropriations bills, a conference report on the bill (HR 3199) that would reauthorize the law known as the Patriot Act, a bill or joint resolution relating to flood insurance, or a fiscal 2006 tax reconciliation measure. Adopted 211-204: R 211-6; D 0-197 (ND 0-147, SD 0-50); I 0-1. Nov. 18, 2005.

**607.** **H Res 571. Immediate Iraq Withdrawal/Rule.** Adoption of the rule (H Res 572) that would provide for House floor consideration of the resolution that would express the sense of the House of Representatives that deployment of U.S. forces in Iraq should be terminated immediately. Adopted 210-202: R 210-5; D 0-196 (ND 0-147, SD 0-49); I 0-1. Nov. 18, 2005.

**608.** **H Res 571. Immediate Iraq Withdrawal/Adoption.** Adoption of the resolution that would express the sense of the House of Representatives that deployment of U.S. forces in Iraq should be terminated immediately. Rejected 3-403: R 0-215; D 3-187 (ND 1-140, SD 2-47); I 0-1. Nov. 18, 2005.

| | 604 | 605 | 606 | 607 | 608 |
|---|---|---|---|---|---|
| **ALABAMA** | | | | | |
| 1 Bonner | Y | Y | Y | Y | N |
| 2 Everett | Y | Y | Y | Y | N |
| 3 Rogers | Y | Y | Y | Y | N |
| 4 Aderholt | Y | Y | Y | Y | N |
| 5 Cramer | Y | Y | N | N | N |
| 6 Bachus | Y | Y | Y | Y | N |
| 7 Davis | Y | Y | N | ? | ? |
| **ALASKA** | | | | | |
| AL Young | Y | N | Y | ? | ? |
| **ARIZONA** | | | | | |
| 1 Renzi | Y | Y | Y | Y | N |
| 2 Franks | Y | N | Y | Y | N |
| 3 Shadegg | Y | N | ? | ? | ? |
| 4 Pastor | Y | Y | N | N | N |
| 5 Hayworth | Y | Y | Y | Y | N |
| 6 Flake | Y | N | ? | ? | ? |
| 7 Grijalva | Y | Y | N | N | N |
| 8 Kolbe | Y | Y | Y | Y | N |
| **ARKANSAS** | | | | | |
| 1 Berry | Y | Y | N | N | N |
| 2 Snyder | Y | Y | N | N | N |
| 3 Boozman | Y | Y | Y | Y | N |
| 4 Ross | Y | Y | N | N | N |
| **CALIFORNIA** | | | | | |
| 1 Thompson | Y | Y | N | N | N |
| 2 Herger | Y | Y | Y | Y | N |
| 3 Lungren | Y | Y | Y | Y | N |
| 4 Doolittle | Y | Y | Y | Y | N |
| 5 Matsui, D. | Y | Y | N | N | N |
| 6 Woolsey | Y | Y | N | N | N |
| 7 Miller, George | Y | Y | N | N | N |
| 8 Pelosi | Y | Y | N | N | N |
| 9 Lee | Y | Y | N | N | N |
| 10 Tauscher | Y | Y | N | N | N |
| 11 Pombo | Y | Y | Y | Y | N |
| 12 Lantos | Y | Y | N | N | N |
| 13 Stark | Y | N | N | N | N |
| 14 Eshoo | Y | Y | N | N | N |
| 15 Honda | Y | Y | N | N | N |
| 16 Lofgren | Y | Y | N | N | N |
| 17 Farr | Y | Y | N | N | N |
| 18 Cardoza | Y | Y | N | N | N |
| 19 Radanovich | Y | Y | Y | Y | N |
| 20 Costa | Y | Y | N | N | N |
| 21 Nunes | Y | Y | Y | Y | N |
| 22 Thomas | Y | Y | Y | Y | N |
| 23 Capps | Y | Y | N | N | N |
| 24 Gallegly | Y | Y | ? | ? | ? |
| 25 McKeon | Y | Y | Y | Y | N |
| 26 Dreier | Y | Y | Y | Y | N |
| 27 Sherman | Y | Y | N | N | N |
| 28 Berman | + | + | - | - | - |
| 29 Schiff | Y | Y | N | N | N |
| 30 Waxman | Y | Y | N | N | N |
| 31 Becerra | Y | Y | N | N | N |
| 32 Solis | Y | Y | N | N | N |
| 33 Watson | Y | Y | N | N | N |
| 34 Roybal-Allard | Y | Y | N | N | N |
| 35 Waters | Y | N | N | N | N |
| 36 Harman | Y | Y | N | N | N |
| 37 Millender-McD. | Y | Y | N | N | N |
| 38 Napolitano | Y | Y | N | N | N |
| 39 Sánchez, Linda | Y | Y | N | N | N |
| 40 Royce | Y | Y | Y | Y | N |
| 41 Lewis | Y | Y | Y | Y | N |
| 42 Miller, Gary | Y | Y | ? | ? | ? |
| 43 Baca | Y | Y | N | N | N |
| 44 Calvert | Y | Y | Y | Y | N |
| 45 Bono | Y | Y | Y | Y | N |
| 46 Rohrabacher | Y | Y | Y | Y | N |
| 47 Sanchez, Loretta | Y | Y | N | N | N |
| 48 Vacant | | | | | |
| 49 Issa | Y | Y | Y | Y | N |

| | 604 | 605 | 606 | 607 | 608 |
|---|---|---|---|---|---|
| 50 Cunningham | Y | Y | ? | ? | ? |
| 51 Filner | Y | Y | N | N | N |
| 52 Hunter | Y | Y | Y | Y | N |
| 53 Davis | Y | Y | N | N | N |
| **COLORADO** | | | | | |
| 1 DeGette | Y | Y | N | N | N |
| 2 Udall | Y | Y | N | N | N |
| 3 Salazar | Y | Y | N | N | N |
| 4 Musgrave | Y | Y | Y | Y | N |
| 5 Hefley | Y | N | Y | Y | N |
| 6 Tancredo | Y | N | Y | Y | N |
| 7 Beauprez | Y | Y | ? | ? | ? |
| **CONNECTICUT** | | | | | |
| 1 Larson | Y | Y | N | N | N |
| 2 Simmons | Y | Y | Y | Y | N |
| 3 DeLauro | Y | Y | N | N | N |
| 4 Shays | Y | Y | Y | Y | N |
| 5 Johnson | Y | Y | Y | Y | N |
| **DELAWARE** | | | | | |
| AL Castle | Y | N | Y | Y | N |
| **FLORIDA** | | | | | |
| 1 Miller | Y | N | Y | Y | N |
| 2 Boyd | Y | Y | ? | ? | ? |
| 3 Brown | Y | Y | N | N | N |
| 4 Crenshaw | Y | Y | Y | Y | N |
| 5 Brown-Waite | Y | Y | Y | Y | N |
| 6 Stearns | Y | Y | Y | Y | N |
| 7 Mica | Y | Y | Y | Y | N |
| 8 Keller | Y | Y | Y | Y | N |
| 9 Bilirakis | Y | Y | Y | Y | N |
| 10 Young | Y | Y | Y | Y | N |
| 11 Davis | Y | Y | N | N | N |
| 12 Putnam | Y | Y | Y | Y | N |
| 13 Harris | Y | ? | Y | Y | N |
| 14 Mack | Y | Y | Y | Y | N |
| 15 Weldon | Y | Y | Y | Y | N |
| 16 Foley | Y | Y | Y | Y | N |
| 17 Meek | Y | Y | N | N | N |
| 18 Ros-Lehtinen | Y | Y | Y | Y | N |
| 19 Wexler | Y | Y | N | N | Y |
| 20 Wasserman-Schultz | Y | Y | N | N | N |
| 21 Diaz-Balart, L. | Y | Y | Y | Y | N |
| 22 Shaw | Y | Y | Y | Y | N |
| 23 Hastings | Y | Y | N | N | N |
| 24 Feeney | Y | ? | Y | Y | N |
| 25 Diaz-Balart, M. | Y | Y | Y | Y | N |
| **GEORGIA** | | | | | |
| 1 Kingston | Y | Y | Y | Y | N |
| 2 Bishop | Y | Y | N | N | N |
| 3 Marshall | Y | Y | N | N | N |
| 4 McKinney | Y | Y | N | N | Y |
| 5 Lewis | Y | Y | N | N | N |
| 6 Price | Y | N | Y | Y | N |
| 7 Linder | Y | Y | Y | Y | N |
| 8 Westmoreland | Y | Y | Y | Y | N |
| 9 Norwood | Y | Y | Y | Y | N |
| 10 Deal | Y | Y | Y | Y | N |
| 11 Gingrey | Y | Y | Y | Y | N |
| 12 Barrow | Y | Y | N | N | N |
| 13 Scott | Y | Y | N | N | N |
| **HAWAII** | | | | | |
| 1 Abercrombie | Y | Y | N | N | N |
| 2 Case | Y | Y | N | N | N |
| **IDAHO** | | | | | |
| 1 Otter | Y | Y | Y | Y | N |
| 2 Simpson | Y | Y | N | N | N |
| **ILLINOIS** | | | | | |
| 1 Rush | Y | Y | N | N | N |
| 2 Jackson | Y | Y | N | N | N |
| 3 Lipinski | Y | Y | N | N | N |
| 4 Gutierrez | Y | Y | N | N | N |
| 5 Emanuel | Y | Y | N | N | N |
| 6 Hyde | Y | Y | Y | Y | N |
| 7 Davis | Y | Y | N | N | N |
| 8 Bean | Y | Y | N | N | N |
| 9 Schakowsky | Y | Y | N | N | N |
| 10 Kirk | Y | Y | Y | Y | N |
| 11 Weller | Y | Y | Y | Y | N |
| 12 Costello | Y | N | N | N | N |

**KEY**    **Republicans**    Democrats    *Independents*

| | | |
|---|---|---|
| Y   Voted for (yea) | X   Paired against | C   Voted "present" to avoid possible conflict of interest |
| #   Paired for | –   Announced against | |
| +   Announced for | P   Voted "present" | ?   Did not vote or otherwise make a position known |
| N   Voted against (nay) | | |

*CQ does not include quorum calls in its vote charts.

| | 604 | 605 | 606 | 607 | 608 |
|---|---|---|---|---|---|
| 13 Biggert | Y | Y | Y | Y | N |
| 14 Hastert | | | | Y | N |
| 15 Johnson | Y | Y | Y | Y | N |
| 16 Manzullo | Y | Y | Y | Y | N |
| 17 Evans | Y | Y | N | N | N |
| 18 LaHood | Y | Y | ? | ? | ? |
| 19 Shimkus | Y | Y | Y | Y | N |
| **INDIANA** | | | | | |
| 1 Visclosky | Y | Y | N | N | N |
| 2 Chocola | Y | Y | Y | Y | N |
| 3 Souder | Y | Y | Y | Y | N |
| 4 Buyer | Y | Y | Y | Y | N |
| 5 Burton | Y | Y | Y | Y | N |
| 6 Pence | Y | Y | Y | Y | N |
| 7 Carson | Y | Y | N | N | N |
| 8 Hostettler | Y | Y | N | N | N |
| 9 Sodrel | Y | Y | Y | Y | N |
| **IOWA** | | | | | |
| 1 Nussle | Y | Y | Y | Y | N |
| 2 Leach | Y | Y | N | N | N |
| 3 Boswell | ? | ? | ? | ? | ? |
| 4 Latham | Y | Y | Y | Y | N |
| 5 King | Y | Y | Y | Y | N |
| **KANSAS** | | | | | |
| 1 Moran | Y | Y | ? | ? | ? |
| 2 Ryun | Y | Y | Y | Y | N |
| 3 Moore | Y | Y | N | N | N |
| 4 Tiahrt | Y | Y | Y | Y | N |
| **KENTUCKY** | | | | | |
| 1 Whitfield | Y | Y | Y | Y | N |
| 2 Lewis | Y | Y | Y | Y | N |
| 3 Northup | Y | Y | Y | ? | – |
| 4 Davis | Y | Y | Y | Y | N |
| 5 Rogers | Y | Y | Y | Y | N |
| 6 Chandler | Y | Y | N | N | N |
| **LOUISIANA** | | | | | |
| 1 Jindal | Y | Y | ? | ? | ? |
| 2 Jefferson | Y | Y | N | N | N |
| 3 Melancon | Y | Y | N | N | N |
| 4 McCrery | Y | Y | Y | Y | N |
| 5 Alexander | Y | Y | Y | Y | N |
| 6 Baker | Y | Y | Y | Y | N |
| 7 Boustany | Y | N | Y | Y | N |
| **MAINE** | | | | | |
| 1 Allen | Y | Y | N | N | N |
| 2 Michaud | Y | Y | N | N | N |
| **MARYLAND** | | | | | |
| 1 Gilchrest | Y | Y | N | N | N |
| 2 Ruppersberger | Y | Y | N | N | N |
| 3 Cardin | Y | ? | N | N | N |
| 4 Wynn | Y | Y | N | N | N |
| 5 Hoyer | Y | Y | N | N | N |
| 6 Bartlett | Y | Y | N | Y | N |
| 7 Cummings | Y | Y | N | N | N |
| 8 Van Hollen | Y | Y | N | N | N |
| **MASSACHUSETTS** | | | | | |
| 1 Olver | Y | Y | N | N | N |
| 2 Neal | Y | Y | N | N | N |
| 3 McGovern | Y | Y | N | N | N |
| 4 Frank | Y | Y | N | N | N |
| 5 Meehan | Y | Y | N | N | N |
| 6 Tierney | Y | Y | N | N | N |
| 7 Markey | Y | Y | N | N | N |
| 8 Capuano | Y | Y | N | N | P |
| 9 Lynch | Y | Y | N | N | N |
| 10 Delahunt | Y | Y | N | N | N |
| **MICHIGAN** | | | | | |
| 1 Stupak | Y | Y | N | N | N |
| 2 Hoekstra | Y | Y | Y | Y | N |
| 3 Ehlers | Y | Y | Y | Y | N |
| 4 Camp | Y | Y | Y | ? | ? |
| 5 Kildee | Y | Y | N | N | N |
| 6 Upton | Y | Y | Y | Y | N |
| 7 Schwarz | Y | Y | Y | Y | N |
| 8 Rogers | Y | Y | Y | Y | N |
| 9 Knollenberg | Y | Y | Y | Y | N |
| 10 Miller | Y | Y | Y | Y | N |
| 11 McCotter | Y | Y | Y | Y | N |
| 12 Levin | Y | Y | N | N | N |
| 13 Kilpatrick | Y | Y | N | N | N |
| 14 Conyers | Y | Y | N | N | N |
| 15 Dingell | Y | Y | N | N | N |

| | 604 | 605 | 606 | 607 | 608 |
|---|---|---|---|---|---|
| **MINNESOTA** | | | | | |
| 1 Gutknecht | Y | Y | Y | Y | N |
| 2 Kline | Y | Y | Y | Y | N |
| 3 Ramstad | Y | Y | Y | Y | N |
| 4 McCollum | Y | Y | N | N | N |
| 5 Sabo | Y | Y | N | N | N |
| 6 Kennedy | Y | Y | Y | Y | N |
| 7 Peterson | Y | Y | N | N | N |
| 8 Oberstar | Y | N | N | N | N |
| **MISSISSIPPI** | | | | | |
| 1 Wicker | Y | Y | Y | Y | N |
| 2 Thompson | Y | Y | N | N | N |
| 3 Pickering | Y | Y | Y | Y | N |
| 4 Taylor | Y | Y | N | N | N |
| **MISSOURI** | | | | | |
| 1 Clay | Y | Y | N | N | P |
| 2 Akin | Y | Y | Y | Y | N |
| 3 Carnahan | Y | Y | N | N | N |
| 4 Skelton | Y | Y | N | N | N |
| 5 Cleaver | Y | Y | N | N | N |
| 6 Graves | Y | Y | Y | Y | N |
| 7 Blunt | Y | Y | Y | Y | N |
| 8 Emerson | Y | Y | Y | Y | N |
| 9 Hulshof | Y | Y | Y | Y | N |
| **MONTANA** | | | | | |
| AL Rehberg | Y | Y | Y | Y | N |
| **NEBRASKA** | | | | | |
| 1 Fortenberry | + | + | Y | Y | N |
| 2 Terry | Y | Y | Y | Y | N |
| 3 Osborne | Y | Y | Y | Y | N |
| **NEVADA** | | | | | |
| 1 Berkley | Y | Y | N | N | N |
| 2 Gibbons | Y | Y | Y | Y | N |
| 3 Porter | Y | Y | Y | Y | N |
| **NEW HAMPSHIRE** | | | | | |
| 1 Bradley | Y | Y | Y | Y | N |
| 2 Bass | Y | Y | Y | Y | N |
| **NEW JERSEY** | | | | | |
| 1 Andrews | Y | Y | N | N | N |
| 2 LoBiondo | Y | Y | Y | Y | N |
| 3 Saxton | Y | Y | Y | Y | N |
| 4 Smith | Y | Y | Y | Y | N |
| 5 Garrett | Y | Y | Y | Y | N |
| 6 Pallone | Y | Y | N | N | N |
| 7 Ferguson | Y | Y | Y | Y | N |
| 8 Pascrell | Y | Y | N | N | N |
| 9 Rothman | Y | Y | N | N | N |
| 10 Payne | Y | Y | N | N | N |
| 11 Frelinghuysen | Y | Y | Y | Y | N |
| 12 Holt | Y | + | N | N | N |
| 13 Menendez | Y | Y | N | N | N |
| **NEW MEXICO** | | | | | |
| 1 Wilson | Y | Y | Y | Y | N |
| 2 Pearce | Y | Y | Y | Y | N |
| 3 Udall | Y | Y | N | N | N |
| **NEW YORK** | | | | | |
| 1 Bishop | Y | Y | N | N | N |
| 2 Israel | Y | Y | N | N | N |
| 3 King | Y | Y | Y | Y | N |
| 4 McCarthy | Y | Y | N | N | N |
| 5 Ackerman | Y | Y | N | N | N |
| 6 Meeks | Y | Y | N | N | N |
| 7 Crowley | Y | Y | N | N | N |
| 8 Nadler | Y | Y | N | N | P |
| 9 Weiner | Y | Y | N | N | N |
| 10 Towns | ? | ? | ? | ? | ? |
| 11 Owens | Y | Y | N | N | P |
| 12 Velázquez | Y | N | N | N | N |
| 13 Fossella | Y | Y | ? | ? | ? |
| 14 Maloney | Y | Y | N | N | N |
| 15 Rangel | Y | Y | N | N | N |
| 16 Serrano | Y | Y | N | N | Y |
| 17 Engel | Y | Y | N | N | N |
| 18 Lowey | Y | Y | N | N | N |
| 19 Kelly | Y | Y | Y | Y | N |
| 20 Sweeney | Y | Y | Y | Y | N |
| 21 McNulty | Y | Y | N | N | N |
| 22 Hinchey | Y | Y | N | N | P |
| 23 McHugh | Y | Y | Y | Y | N |
| 24 Boehlert | Y | Y | N | N | N |
| 25 Walsh | Y | Y | Y | Y | N |
| 26 Reynolds | Y | Y | Y | Y | N |
| 27 Higgins | Y | Y | N | N | N |
| 28 Slaughter | Y | Y | N | N | N |
| 29 Kuhl | Y | Y | Y | Y | N |

| | 604 | 605 | 606 | 607 | 608 |
|---|---|---|---|---|---|
| **NORTH CAROLINA** | | | | | |
| 1 Butterfield | Y | Y | N | N | N |
| 2 Etheridge | Y | Y | N | N | N |
| 3 Jones | Y | N | N | N | N |
| 4 Price | Y | Y | N | N | N |
| 5 Foxx | Y | Y | Y | Y | N |
| 6 Coble | Y | Y | Y | Y | N |
| 7 McIntyre | Y | Y | N | N | N |
| 8 Hayes | Y | Y | Y | Y | N |
| 9 Myrick | Y | Y | Y | Y | N |
| 10 McHenry | Y | Y | Y | Y | N |
| 11 Taylor | Y | Y | Y | Y | N |
| 12 Watt | Y | Y | N | N | N |
| 13 Miller | Y | Y | N | N | N |
| **NORTH DAKOTA** | | | | | |
| AL Pomeroy | Y | Y | N | N | N |
| **OHIO** | | | | | |
| 1 Chabot | Y | Y | Y | Y | N |
| 2 Schmidt | Y | Y | Y | Y | N |
| 3 Turner | Y | Y | Y | Y | N |
| 4 Oxley | Y | Y | Y | Y | N |
| 5 Gillmor | Y | Y | Y | Y | N |
| 6 Strickland | Y | Y | N | N | N |
| 7 Hobson | Y | Y | Y | Y | N |
| 8 Boehner | Y | Y | Y | Y | N |
| 9 Kaptur | Y | Y | N | N | N |
| 10 Kucinich | Y | N | N | N | N |
| 11 Jones | Y | Y | N | N | N |
| 12 Tiberi | Y | Y | Y | Y | N |
| 13 Brown | Y | Y | N | N | N |
| 14 LaTourette | Y | N | Y | Y | N |
| 15 Pryce | Y | Y | Y | Y | N |
| 16 Regula | Y | Y | Y | Y | N |
| 17 Ryan | Y | Y | N | N | N |
| 18 Ney | Y | Y | Y | Y | N |
| **OKLAHOMA** | | | | | |
| 1 Sullivan | Y | Y | Y | Y | N |
| 2 Boren | Y | Y | N | N | N |
| 3 Lucas | Y | Y | Y | Y | N |
| 4 Cole | Y | Y | Y | Y | N |
| 5 Istook | Y | Y | Y | Y | N |
| **OREGON** | | | | | |
| 1 Wu | Y | Y | N | N | N |
| 2 Walden | Y | Y | Y | Y | N |
| 3 Blumenauer | Y | Y | N | N | N |
| 4 DeFazio | Y | Y | N | N | N |
| 5 Hooley | Y | Y | N | N | N |
| **PENNSYLVANIA** | | | | | |
| 1 Brady | Y | Y | N | N | N |
| 2 Fattah | Y | Y | N | N | N |
| 3 English | Y | Y | Y | Y | N |
| 4 Hart | Y | Y | Y | Y | N |
| 5 Peterson | Y | Y | ? | ? | ? |
| 6 Gerlach | Y | Y | Y | Y | N |
| 7 Weldon | Y | Y | Y | Y | N |
| 8 Fitzpatrick | Y | Y | Y | Y | N |
| 9 Shuster | Y | N | Y | Y | N |
| 10 Sherwood | Y | Y | Y | Y | N |
| 11 Kanjorski | Y | Y | N | N | N |
| 12 Murtha | Y | Y | N | N | N |
| 13 Schwartz | Y | Y | N | N | N |
| 14 Doyle | Y | Y | N | N | N |
| 15 Dent | Y | Y | Y | Y | N |
| 16 Pitts | Y | Y | Y | Y | N |
| 17 Holden | Y | Y | N | N | N |
| 18 Murphy | Y | Y | Y | Y | N |
| 19 Platts | Y | Y | Y | Y | N |
| **RHODE ISLAND** | | | | | |
| 1 Kennedy | Y | Y | N | N | N |
| 2 Langevin | Y | Y | N | N | N |
| **SOUTH CAROLINA** | | | | | |
| 1 Brown | Y | Y | Y | Y | N |
| 2 Wilson | Y | Y | Y | Y | N |
| 3 Barrett | Y | Y | Y | Y | N |
| 4 Inglis | Y | Y | Y | Y | N |
| 5 Spratt | Y | Y | N | N | N |
| 6 Clyburn | Y | Y | N | N | N |
| **SOUTH DAKOTA** | | | | | |
| AL Herseth | Y | Y | N | N | N |
| **TENNESSEE** | | | | | |
| 1 Jenkins | Y | Y | Y | Y | N |
| 2 Duncan | Y | N | Y | Y | N |

| | 604 | 605 | 606 | 607 | 608 |
|---|---|---|---|---|---|
| 3 Wamp | Y | Y | Y | Y | N |
| 4 Davis | Y | Y | N | N | N |
| 5 Cooper | Y | Y | N | N | N |
| 6 Gordon | Y | Y | N | N | N |
| 7 Blackburn | Y | Y | Y | Y | N |
| 8 Tanner | Y | Y | N | N | N |
| 9 Ford | Y | Y | N | N | N |
| **TEXAS** | | | | | |
| 1 Gohmert | Y | Y | Y | Y | N |
| 2 Poe | Y | N | Y | Y | N |
| 3 Johnson, S. | Y | Y | Y | Y | N |
| 4 Hall | ? | ? | ? | ? | ? |
| 5 Hensarling | Y | Y | Y | Y | N |
| 6 Barton | Y | N | Y | Y | N |
| 7 Culberson | Y | Y | Y | Y | N |
| 8 Brady | Y | Y | Y | Y | N |
| 9 Green, A. | Y | Y | N | N | N |
| 10 McCaul | Y | Y | Y | Y | N |
| 11 Conaway | Y | Y | Y | Y | N |
| 12 Granger | Y | Y | Y | Y | N |
| 13 Thornberry | Y | Y | Y | Y | N |
| 14 Paul | ? | ? | ? | ? | ? |
| 15 Hinojosa | Y | Y | N | N | N |
| 16 Reyes | Y | Y | N | N | N |
| 17 Edwards | Y | Y | N | N | N |
| 18 Jackson-Lee | Y | Y | N | N | N |
| 19 Neugebauer | Y | Y | Y | Y | N |
| 20 Gonzalez | Y | Y | N | N | N |
| 21 Smith | Y | Y | Y | Y | N |
| 22 DeLay | Y | Y | Y | Y | N |
| 23 Bonilla | Y | Y | Y | Y | N |
| 24 Marchant | Y | N | Y | Y | N |
| 25 Doggett | Y | Y | N | N | N |
| 26 Burgess | Y | Y | Y | Y | N |
| 27 Ortiz | Y | Y | N | N | N |
| 28 Cuellar | Y | Y | N | N | N |
| 29 Green, G. | Y | Y | N | N | N |
| 30 Johnson, E. | Y | N | N | N | N |
| 31 Carter | Y | Y | Y | Y | N |
| 32 Sessions | Y | Y | Y | Y | N |
| **UTAH** | | | | | |
| 1 Bishop | Y | Y | Y | Y | N |
| 2 Matheson | Y | N | N | N | N |
| 3 Cannon | Y | Y | Y | Y | N |
| **VERMONT** | | | | | |
| AL Sanders | Y | Y | N | N | N |
| **VIRGINIA** | | | | | |
| 1 Davis, J. | Y | Y | Y | Y | N |
| 2 Drake | Y | Y | Y | Y | N |
| 3 Scott | Y | Y | N | N | N |
| 4 Forbes | Y | Y | Y | Y | N |
| 5 Goode | Y | Y | Y | Y | N |
| 6 Goodlatte | Y | Y | Y | Y | N |
| 7 Cantor | Y | Y | Y | Y | N |
| 8 Moran | Y | Y | N | N | N |
| 9 Boucher | Y | Y | N | N | N |
| 10 Wolf | Y | Y | Y | Y | N |
| 11 Davis, T. | Y | Y | Y | Y | N |
| **WASHINGTON** | | | | | |
| 1 Inslee | Y | Y | N | N | N |
| 2 Larsen | Y | Y | N | N | N |
| 3 Baird | Y | Y | N | N | N |
| 4 Hastings | Y | Y | Y | Y | N |
| 5 McMorris | Y | Y | Y | Y | N |
| 6 Dicks | Y | Y | N | N | N |
| 7 McDermott | Y | N | N | N | P |
| 8 Reichert | Y | Y | Y | Y | N |
| 9 Smith | Y | Y | N | N | N |
| **WEST VIRGINIA** | | | | | |
| 1 Mollohan | Y | Y | N | N | N |
| 2 Capito | Y | Y | Y | Y | N |
| 3 Rahall | Y | Y | N | N | N |
| **WISCONSIN** | | | | | |
| 1 Ryan | Y | N | Y | Y | N |
| 2 Baldwin | Y | Y | N | N | N |
| 3 Kind | Y | Y | ? | ? | ? |
| 4 Moore | Y | Y | N | N | N |
| 5 Sensenbrenner | Y | N | Y | Y | N |
| 6 Petri | Y | N | Y | Y | N |
| 7 Obey | Y | Y | N | N | N |
| 8 Green | Y | N | Y | Y | N |
| **WYOMING** | | | | | |
| AL Cubin | Y | Y | Y | Y | N |

## IN THE HOUSE | By Vote Number

**609.** **H Res 438. Anti-Israel Resolutions/Adoption.** Ros-Lehtinen, R-Fla., motion to suspend the rules and adopt the resolution that would state that the House of Representatives urges U.N. member states to stop supporting resolutions that unfairly castigate Israel. Motion agreed to 400-1: R 219-1; D 180-0 (ND 137-0, SD 43-0); I 1-0. A two-thirds majority of those present and voting (268 in this case) is required for adoption under suspension of the rules. Dec. 6, 2005.

**610.** **H Res 535. Yitzhak Rabin Commemoration/Adoption.** Ros-Lehtinen, R-Fla., motion to suspend the rules and adopt the resolution that would honor the late Yitzhak Rabin, former Israeli prime minister, for his contributions to the country and express condolences on the 10th anniversary of his death. Motion agreed to 399-0: R 219-0; D 179-0 (ND 136-0, SD 43-0); I 1-0. A two-thirds majority of those present and voting (266 in this case) is required for adoption under suspension of the rules. Dec. 6, 2005.

**611.** **H Res 479. 50th Anniversary of Hungarian Revolution/Adoption.** Gallegly, R-Calif., motion to suspend the rules and adopt the resolution that would commend the people of Hungary as they mark the 50th anniversary of the 1956 Hungarian Revolution, which set the stage for the ultimate collapse of communism in 1989 throughout central and eastern Europe. Motion agreed to 395-0: R 217-0; D 177-0 (ND 136-0, SD 41-0); I 1-0. A two-thirds majority of those present and voting (264 in this case) is required for adoption under suspension of the rules. Dec. 6, 2005.

**612.** **S 467. Terrorism Risk Insurance Extension/Passage.** Oxley, R-Ohio, motion to suspend the rules and pass the bill, as amended, that would reauthorize the federal terrorism insurance program through Dec. 31, 2007. It would increase the "trigger" level from the current $5 million aggregate industry insured losses to $50 million in 2006 and $100 million in 2007. The bill also would extend the $100 billion annual cap on covered losses. Motion agreed to 371-49: R 178-46; D 192-3 (ND 146-2, SD 46-1); I 1-0. A two-thirds majority of those present and voting (280 in this case) is required for passage under suspension of the rules. A "nay" was a vote in support of the president's position. Dec. 7, 2005.

**613.** **HR 4096. Alternative Minimum Tax Relief/Passage.** Reynolds, R-N.Y., motion to suspend the rules and pass the bill that would extend for one year, through 2006, the higher exemption levels for the alternative minimum tax, adjusted for inflation. Motion agreed to 414-4: R 225-0; D 188-4 (ND 143-3, SD 45-1); I 1-0. A two-thirds majority of those present and voting (279 in this case) is required for passage under suspension of the rules. Dec. 7, 2005.

| | 609 | 610 | 611 | 612 | 613 |
|---|---|---|---|---|---|
| **ALABAMA** | | | | | |
| 1 Bonner | Y | Y | Y | Y | Y |
| 2 Everett | Y | Y | Y | Y | Y |
| 3 Rogers | Y | Y | Y | Y | Y |
| 4 Aderholt | Y | Y | Y | N | Y |
| 5 Cramer | ? | ? | ? | Y | Y |
| 6 Bachus | Y | Y | Y | Y | Y |
| 7 Davis | Y | Y | Y | Y | Y |
| **ALASKA** | | | | | |
| AL Young | Y | Y | Y | Y | Y |
| **ARIZONA** | | | | | |
| 1 Renzi | Y | Y | Y | Y | Y |
| 2 Franks | Y | Y | Y | N | Y |
| 3 Shadegg | Y | Y | Y | N | Y |
| 4 Pastor | Y | Y | Y | Y | Y |
| 5 Hayworth | Y | Y | Y | Y | Y |
| 6 Flake | Y | Y | Y | N | Y |
| 7 Grijalva | Y | Y | Y | Y | Y |
| 8 Kolbe | Y | Y | Y | N | Y |
| **ARKANSAS** | | | | | |
| 1 Berry | Y | Y | Y | Y | Y |
| 2 Snyder | Y | Y | Y | Y | Y |
| 3 Boozman | Y | Y | Y | Y | Y |
| 4 Ross | Y | Y | Y | Y | Y |
| **CALIFORNIA** | | | | | |
| 1 Thompson | Y | Y | Y | Y | Y |
| 2 Herger | Y | Y | Y | Y | Y |
| 3 Lungren | Y | Y | Y | Y | Y |
| 4 Doolittle | ? | ? | ? | N | Y |
| 5 Matsui, D. | Y | Y | Y | Y | Y |
| 6 Woolsey | Y | Y | Y | Y | Y |
| 7 Miller, George | Y | Y | Y | Y | Y |
| 8 Pelosi | Y | Y | Y | Y | ? |
| 9 Lee | Y | Y | Y | Y | Y |
| 10 Tauscher | Y | Y | Y | Y | Y |
| 11 Pombo | Y | Y | Y | Y | Y |
| 12 Lantos | Y | Y | Y | Y | Y |
| 13 Stark | Y | Y | Y | Y | Y |
| 14 Eshoo | Y | Y | Y | Y | Y |
| 15 Honda | Y | Y | Y | Y | ? |
| 16 Lofgren | Y | Y | Y | Y | Y |
| 17 Farr | Y | Y | Y | Y | Y |
| 18 Cardoza | Y | Y | Y | Y | Y |
| 19 Radanovich | Y | Y | Y | Y | Y |
| 20 Costa | Y | Y | Y | Y | Y |
| 21 Nunes | Y | Y | Y | Y | Y |
| 22 Thomas | Y | Y | Y | Y | Y |
| 23 Capps | + | + | + | Y | Y |
| 24 Gallegly | Y | Y | Y | Y | Y |
| 25 McKeon | Y | Y | Y | Y | Y |
| 26 Dreier | Y | Y | Y | Y | Y |
| 27 Sherman | Y | Y | Y | Y | Y |
| 28 Berman | Y | Y | Y | Y | Y |
| 29 Schiff | Y | Y | Y | Y | Y |
| 30 Waxman | Y | Y | Y | Y | Y |
| 31 Becerra | Y | Y | Y | Y | Y |
| 32 Solis | Y | Y | Y | Y | Y |
| 33 Watson | Y | Y | Y | Y | Y |
| 34 Roybal-Allard | Y | Y | Y | Y | Y |
| 35 Waters | Y | Y | Y | Y | ? |
| 36 Harman | Y | Y | Y | Y | Y |
| 37 Millender-McD. | Y | Y | Y | Y | Y |
| 38 Napolitano | Y | Y | Y | Y | Y |
| 39 Sánchez, Linda | Y | Y | Y | Y | Y |
| 40 Royce | Y | Y | Y | N | Y |
| 41 Lewis | Y | Y | Y | Y | Y |
| 42 Miller, Gary | Y | Y | Y | Y | Y |
| 43 Baca | Y | Y | Y | Y | Y |
| 44 Calvert | Y | Y | Y | Y | Y |
| 45 Bono | Y | Y | Y | Y | Y |
| 46 Rohrabacher | Y | Y | Y | N | Y |
| 47 Sanchez, Loretta | Y | Y | Y | Y | |
| 48 Vacant | | | | | |
| 49 Issa | Y | Y | Y | Y | Y |

| | 609 | 610 | 611 | 612 | 613 |
|---|---|---|---|---|---|
| 50 Vacant* | | | | | |
| 51 Filner | Y | Y | Y | Y | Y |
| 52 Hunter | Y | Y | Y | Y | Y |
| 53 Davis | Y | Y | Y | Y | Y |
| **COLORADO** | | | | | |
| 1 DeGette | Y | Y | Y | Y | Y |
| 2 Udall | Y | Y | Y | Y | Y |
| 3 Salazar | Y | Y | Y | Y | Y |
| 4 Musgrave | Y | Y | Y | Y | Y |
| 5 Hefley | Y | Y | Y | Y | Y |
| 6 Tancredo | Y | Y | Y | N | Y |
| 7 Beauprez | Y | Y | Y | Y | Y |
| **CONNECTICUT** | | | | | |
| 1 Larson | Y | Y | Y | Y | Y |
| 2 Simmons | ? | ? | ? | Y | Y |
| 3 DeLauro | Y | Y | Y | Y | Y |
| 4 Shays | Y | Y | Y | Y | Y |
| 5 Johnson | Y | Y | Y | Y | Y |
| **DELAWARE** | | | | | |
| AL Castle | Y | Y | Y | Y | Y |
| **FLORIDA** | | | | | |
| 1 Miller | Y | Y | Y | N | Y |
| 2 Boyd | Y | Y | ? | Y | Y |
| 3 Brown | ? | ? | ? | Y | Y |
| 4 Crenshaw | Y | Y | Y | Y | Y |
| 5 Brown-Waite | ? | ? | ? | ? | ? |
| 6 Stearns | Y | Y | Y | Y | Y |
| 7 Mica | Y | Y | Y | Y | Y |
| 8 Keller | Y | Y | Y | Y | Y |
| 9 Bilirakis | Y | Y | Y | Y | Y |
| 10 Young | Y | Y | Y | Y | Y |
| 11 Davis | ? | ? | ? | ? | Y |
| 12 Putnam | Y | Y | Y | N | Y |
| 13 Harris | Y | Y | Y | Y | Y |
| 14 Mack | Y | Y | Y | N | Y |
| 15 Weldon | Y | Y | Y | N | Y |
| 16 Foley | Y | Y | Y | Y | Y |
| 17 Meek | Y | Y | Y | Y | Y |
| 18 Ros-Lehtinen | Y | Y | Y | Y | Y |
| 19 Wexler | ? | ? | ? | ? | ? |
| 20 Wasserman-Schultz | Y | ? | ? | Y | Y |
| 21 Diaz-Balart, L. | Y | Y | Y | Y | Y |
| 22 Shaw | Y | Y | Y | Y | Y |
| 23 Hastings | Y | Y | Y | Y | Y |
| 24 Feeney | Y | Y | Y | N | Y |
| 25 Diaz-Balart, M. | ? | ? | ? | Y | Y |
| **GEORGIA** | | | | | |
| 1 Kingston | Y | Y | Y | Y | Y |
| 2 Bishop | Y | Y | Y | Y | Y |
| 3 Marshall | Y | Y | Y | Y | Y |
| 4 McKinney | ? | Y | Y | Y | Y |
| 5 Lewis | Y | Y | Y | Y | Y |
| 6 Price | Y | Y | Y | Y | Y |
| 7 Linder | Y | Y | Y | Y | Y |
| 8 Westmoreland | Y | Y | Y | N | Y |
| 9 Norwood | Y | Y | Y | Y | Y |
| 10 Deal | Y | Y | Y | Y | Y |
| 11 Gingrey | Y | Y | Y | Y | Y |
| 12 Barrow | Y | Y | Y | Y | Y |
| 13 Scott | Y | Y | Y | Y | ? |
| **HAWAII** | | | | | |
| 1 Abercrombie | Y | Y | Y | Y | Y |
| 2 Case | Y | Y | Y | Y | Y |
| **IDAHO** | | | | | |
| 1 Otter | Y | Y | Y | N | Y |
| 2 Simpson | Y | Y | Y | Y | Y |
| **ILLINOIS** | | | | | |
| 1 Rush | Y | Y | Y | Y | Y |
| 2 Jackson | Y | Y | Y | Y | Y |
| 3 Lipinski | Y | Y | Y | Y | Y |
| 4 Gutierrez | + | + | + | Y | Y |
| 5 Emanuel | Y | Y | Y | Y | Y |
| 6 Hyde | Y | Y | Y | Y | Y |
| 7 Davis | Y | Y | Y | Y | Y |
| 8 Bean | Y | Y | Y | Y | Y |
| 9 Schakowsky | Y | Y | Y | Y | Y |
| 10 Kirk | Y | Y | Y | Y | Y |
| 11 Weller | Y | Y | Y | Y | Y |
| 12 Costello | Y | Y | Y | N | N |

*Rep. Randy "Duke" Cunningham, R-Calif., resigned effective Dec. 1, 2005. The last vote for which he was eligible was vote 608.

| | 609 | 610 | 611 | 612 | 613 |
|---|---|---|---|---|---|
| 13 Biggert | Y | Y | Y | Y | Y |
| 14 Hastert | | | | | |
| 15 Johnson | Y | Y | Y | Y | Y |
| 16 Manzullo | Y | Y | Y | Y | Y |
| 17 Evans | Y | Y | Y | Y | Y |
| 18 LaHood | Y | Y | Y | Y | Y |
| 19 Shimkus | Y | Y | Y | Y | Y |
| **INDIANA** | | | | | |
| 1 Visclosky | Y | Y | Y | Y | Y |
| 2 Chocola | Y | Y | Y | Y | Y |
| 3 Souder | Y | Y | Y | Y | Y |
| 4 Buyer | Y | Y | Y | Y | Y |
| 5 Burton | Y | Y | Y | Y | Y |
| 6 Pence | Y | Y | Y | ? | ? |
| 7 Carson | + | + | + | Y | Y |
| 8 Hostettler | Y | Y | Y | Y | Y |
| 9 Sodrel | Y | Y | Y | Y | Y |
| **IOWA** | | | | | |
| 1 Nussle | Y | Y | Y | Y | Y |
| 2 Leach | Y | Y | Y | Y | Y |
| 3 Boswell | Y | Y | Y | Y | Y |
| 4 Latham | Y | Y | Y | Y | Y |
| 5 King | Y | Y | Y | Y | Y |
| **KANSAS** | | | | | |
| 1 Moran | Y | Y | Y | Y | Y |
| 2 Ryun | Y | Y | Y | Y | Y |
| 3 Moore | Y | Y | Y | Y | Y |
| 4 Tiahrt | Y | Y | Y | Y | Y |
| **KENTUCKY** | | | | | |
| 1 Whitfield | Y | Y | Y | Y | Y |
| 2 Lewis | Y | Y | Y | Y | Y |
| 3 Northup | Y | Y | Y | Y | Y |
| 4 Davis | Y | Y | Y | Y | Y |
| 5 Rogers | Y | Y | Y | Y | Y |
| 6 Chandler | Y | Y | Y | Y | Y |
| **LOUISIANA** | | | | | |
| 1 Jindal | Y | Y | Y | Y | Y |
| 2 Jefferson | Y | Y | Y | Y | Y |
| 3 Melancon | Y | Y | Y | Y | Y |
| 4 McCrery | Y | Y | Y | Y | Y |
| 5 Alexander | Y | Y | Y | Y | Y |
| 6 Baker | Y | Y | Y | Y | Y |
| 7 Boustany | Y | Y | Y | Y | Y |
| **MAINE** | | | | | |
| 1 Allen | Y | Y | Y | Y | Y |
| 2 Michaud | Y | Y | Y | Y | Y |
| **MARYLAND** | | | | | |
| 1 Gilchrest | Y | Y | ? | Y | Y |
| 2 Ruppersberger | Y | Y | Y | Y | Y |
| 3 Cardin | Y | Y | Y | Y | Y |
| 4 Wynn | Y | Y | Y | Y | Y |
| 5 Hoyer | Y | Y | Y | Y | Y |
| 6 Bartlett | Y | Y | Y | N | Y |
| 7 Cummings | Y | Y | Y | Y | Y |
| 8 Van Hollen | Y | Y | Y | Y | Y |
| **MASSACHUSETTS** | | | | | |
| 1 Olver | ? | ? | ? | Y | Y |
| 2 Neal | Y | Y | Y | Y | Y |
| 3 McGovern | Y | Y | Y | Y | Y |
| 4 Frank | ? | ? | ? | Y | Y |
| 5 Meehan | Y | Y | Y | Y | Y |
| 6 Tierney | ? | ? | ? | Y | Y |
| 7 Markey | Y | Y | Y | Y | Y |
| 8 Capuano | Y | Y | Y | Y | Y |
| 9 Lynch | Y | Y | Y | Y | Y |
| 10 Delahunt | Y | Y | Y | Y | Y |
| **MICHIGAN** | | | | | |
| 1 Stupak | Y | Y | Y | Y | Y |
| 2 Hoekstra | Y | Y | Y | Y | Y |
| 3 Ehlers | Y | Y | Y | Y | Y |
| 4 Camp | Y | Y | Y | Y | Y |
| 5 Kildee | Y | Y | Y | Y | Y |
| 6 Upton | Y | Y | Y | Y | Y |
| 7 Schwarz | Y | Y | Y | Y | Y |
| 8 Rogers | Y | Y | Y | Y | Y |
| 9 Knollenberg | Y | Y | Y | Y | Y |
| 10 Miller | Y | Y | Y | Y | Y |
| 11 McCotter | Y | Y | Y | Y | Y |
| 12 Levin | Y | Y | Y | Y | Y |
| 13 Kilpatrick | Y | Y | Y | Y | Y |
| 14 Conyers | Y | Y | Y | Y | Y |
| 15 Dingell | Y | Y | Y | Y | Y |

| | 609 | 610 | 611 | 612 | 613 |
|---|---|---|---|---|---|
| **MINNESOTA** | | | | | |
| 1 Gutknecht | Y | Y | Y | N | Y |
| 2 Kline | Y | Y | Y | Y | Y |
| 3 Ramstad | Y | Y | Y | Y | Y |
| 4 McCollum | Y | Y | Y | Y | Y |
| 5 Sabo | Y | Y | Y | Y | N |
| 6 Kennedy | Y | Y | Y | Y | Y |
| 7 Peterson | Y | Y | Y | N | N |
| 8 Oberstar | Y | Y | Y | Y | Y |
| **MISSISSIPPI** | | | | | |
| 1 Wicker | Y | Y | Y | Y | Y |
| 2 Thompson | Y | Y | Y | Y | Y |
| 3 Pickering | Y | Y | Y | Y | Y |
| 4 Taylor | Y | Y | Y | N | Y |
| **MISSOURI** | | | | | |
| 1 Clay | ? | ? | ? | ? | ? |
| 2 Akin | Y | Y | Y | N | Y |
| 3 Carnahan | Y | Y | Y | Y | Y |
| 4 Skelton | Y | Y | Y | Y | Y |
| 5 Cleaver | Y | Y | Y | Y | Y |
| 6 Graves | Y | Y | Y | Y | Y |
| 7 Blunt | Y | Y | Y | Y | Y |
| 8 Emerson | Y | Y | Y | Y | Y |
| 9 Hulshof | Y | Y | Y | Y | Y |
| **MONTANA** | | | | | |
| AL Rehberg | Y | Y | Y | Y | Y |
| **NEBRASKA** | | | | | |
| 1 Fortenberry | Y | Y | Y | Y | Y |
| 2 Terry | Y | Y | Y | Y | Y |
| 3 Osborne | Y | Y | Y | Y | Y |
| **NEVADA** | | | | | |
| 1 Berkley | Y | Y | Y | Y | Y |
| 2 Gibbons | Y | Y | Y | Y | Y |
| 3 Porter | Y | Y | Y | Y | Y |
| **NEW HAMPSHIRE** | | | | | |
| 1 Bradley | Y | Y | Y | Y | Y |
| 2 Bass | Y | Y | Y | Y | Y |
| **NEW JERSEY** | | | | | |
| 1 Andrews | Y | Y | Y | + | + |
| 2 LoBiondo | Y | Y | Y | Y | Y |
| 3 Saxton | Y | Y | Y | Y | Y |
| 4 Smith | Y | Y | Y | Y | Y |
| 5 Garrett | Y | Y | Y | Y | Y |
| 6 Pallone | Y | Y | Y | Y | Y |
| 7 Ferguson | Y | Y | Y | Y | Y |
| 8 Pascrell | Y | Y | Y | Y | Y |
| 9 Rothman | Y | Y | Y | Y | Y |
| 10 Payne | Y | Y | Y | Y | Y |
| 11 Frelinghuysen | Y | Y | Y | Y | Y |
| 12 Holt | Y | Y | Y | Y | Y |
| 13 Menendez | Y | Y | Y | Y | Y |
| **NEW MEXICO** | | | | | |
| 1 Wilson | Y | Y | Y | Y | Y |
| 2 Pearce | Y | Y | Y | Y | Y |
| 3 Udall | Y | Y | Y | Y | Y |
| **NEW YORK** | | | | | |
| 1 Bishop | Y | Y | Y | Y | Y |
| 2 Israel | Y | Y | Y | Y | Y |
| 3 King | Y | Y | Y | Y | Y |
| 4 McCarthy | Y | Y | Y | Y | Y |
| 5 Ackerman | Y | Y | Y | Y | Y |
| 6 Meeks | Y | Y | Y | Y | Y |
| 7 Crowley | Y | Y | Y | Y | Y |
| 8 Nadler | Y | Y | Y | Y | Y |
| 9 Weiner | ? | ? | ? | Y | Y |
| 10 Towns | Y | Y | Y | Y | Y |
| 11 Owens | Y | Y | Y | Y | Y |
| 12 Velázquez | Y | Y | Y | Y | Y |
| 13 Fossella | Y | Y | Y | Y | Y |
| 14 Maloney | Y | Y | Y | Y | Y |
| 15 Rangel | Y | Y | Y | Y | Y |
| 16 Serrano | Y | Y | Y | Y | Y |
| 17 Engel | Y | Y | Y | Y | Y |
| 18 Lowey | Y | Y | Y | Y | Y |
| 19 Kelly | Y | Y | Y | Y | Y |
| 20 Sweeney | ? | ? | ? | ? | ? |
| 21 McNulty | Y | Y | Y | Y | Y |
| 22 Hinchey | ? | ? | ? | Y | Y |
| 23 McHugh | Y | Y | Y | Y | Y |
| 24 Boehlert | Y | Y | Y | Y | Y |
| 25 Walsh | Y | Y | Y | Y | Y |
| 26 Reynolds | Y | Y | Y | Y | Y |
| 27 Higgins | Y | Y | Y | Y | Y |
| 28 Slaughter | Y | Y | Y | Y | Y |
| 29 Kuhl | Y | Y | Y | Y | Y |

| | 609 | 610 | 611 | 612 | 613 |
|---|---|---|---|---|---|
| **NORTH CAROLINA** | | | | | |
| 1 Butterfield | Y | Y | Y | Y | Y |
| 2 Etheridge | Y | Y | Y | Y | Y |
| 3 Jones | Y | Y | Y | N | Y |
| 4 Price | Y | Y | Y | Y | Y |
| 5 Foxx | Y | Y | Y | N | Y |
| 6 Coble | Y | Y | Y | Y | Y |
| 7 McIntyre | Y | Y | Y | Y | Y |
| 8 Hayes | Y | Y | Y | Y | Y |
| 9 Myrick | Y | Y | Y | N | Y |
| 10 McHenry | Y | Y | Y | Y | Y |
| 11 Taylor | ? | ? | ? | Y | Y |
| 12 Watt | Y | Y | Y | ? | ? |
| 13 Miller | Y | Y | Y | Y | Y |
| **NORTH DAKOTA** | | | | | |
| AL Pomeroy | Y | Y | Y | Y | Y |
| **OHIO** | | | | | |
| 1 Chabot | Y | Y | Y | N | Y |
| 2 Schmidt | Y | Y | Y | Y | Y |
| 3 Turner | Y | Y | Y | Y | Y |
| 4 Oxley | Y | ? | ? | Y | Y |
| 5 Gillmor | Y | Y | Y | Y | Y |
| 6 Strickland | Y | Y | Y | Y | Y |
| 7 Hobson | Y | Y | Y | Y | Y |
| 8 Boehner | Y | Y | ? | ? | Y |
| 9 Kaptur | ? | ? | ? | Y | Y |
| 10 Kucinich | Y | Y | Y | Y | Y |
| 11 Jones | + | + | + | Y | Y |
| 12 Tiberi | Y | Y | Y | Y | Y |
| 13 Brown | Y | + | + | Y | Y |
| 14 LaTourette | Y | Y | Y | Y | Y |
| 15 Pryce | Y | Y | Y | Y | Y |
| 16 Regula | Y | Y | Y | Y | Y |
| 17 Ryan | Y | Y | Y | Y | Y |
| 18 Ney | Y | Y | Y | Y | Y |
| **OKLAHOMA** | | | | | |
| 1 Sullivan | Y | Y | Y | Y | Y |
| 2 Boren | Y | Y | Y | Y | Y |
| 3 Lucas | Y | Y | Y | Y | Y |
| 4 Cole | Y | Y | Y | Y | Y |
| 5 Istook | Y | Y | Y | Y | Y |
| **OREGON** | | | | | |
| 1 Wu | Y | Y | Y | Y | Y |
| 2 Walden | Y | Y | Y | Y | Y |
| 3 Blumenauer | Y | Y | Y | Y | Y |
| 4 DeFazio | Y | Y | Y | Y | Y |
| 5 Hooley | Y | Y | Y | Y | Y |
| **PENNSYLVANIA** | | | | | |
| 1 Brady | Y | Y | Y | Y | Y |
| 2 Fattah | Y | Y | Y | Y | Y |
| 3 English | Y | Y | Y | Y | Y |
| 4 Hart | Y | Y | Y | Y | Y |
| 5 Peterson | Y | Y | Y | Y | Y |
| 6 Gerlach | Y | Y | Y | + | + |
| 7 Weldon | Y | Y | Y | Y | Y |
| 8 Fitzpatrick | Y | Y | Y | Y | Y |
| 9 Shuster | Y | Y | Y | Y | Y |
| 10 Sherwood | Y | Y | Y | Y | Y |
| 11 Kanjorski | Y | Y | Y | Y | Y |
| 12 Murtha | ? | ? | ? | ? | Y |
| 13 Schwartz | + | + | + | Y | Y |
| 14 Doyle | Y | Y | Y | Y | Y |
| 15 Dent | Y | Y | Y | Y | Y |
| 16 Pitts | Y | Y | Y | N | Y |
| 17 Holden | Y | Y | Y | Y | Y |
| 18 Murphy | Y | Y | Y | Y | Y |
| 19 Platts | Y | Y | Y | Y | Y |
| **RHODE ISLAND** | | | | | |
| 1 Kennedy | Y | Y | Y | Y | Y |
| 2 Langevin | Y | Y | Y | Y | Y |
| **SOUTH CAROLINA** | | | | | |
| 1 Brown | Y | Y | Y | Y | Y |
| 2 Wilson | Y | Y | Y | Y | Y |
| 3 Barrett | Y | Y | Y | N | Y |
| 4 Inglis | Y | Y | Y | Y | Y |
| 5 Spratt | Y | Y | Y | Y | Y |
| 6 Clyburn | Y | Y | Y | Y | Y |
| **SOUTH DAKOTA** | | | | | |
| AL Herseth | Y | Y | Y | Y | Y |
| **TENNESSEE** | | | | | |
| 1 Jenkins | Y | Y | Y | Y | Y |
| 2 Duncan | Y | Y | Y | N | Y |

| | 609 | 610 | 611 | 612 | 613 |
|---|---|---|---|---|---|
| 3 Wamp | Y | Y | Y | Y | Y |
| 4 Davis | Y | Y | Y | Y | Y |
| 5 Cooper | Y | Y | Y | Y | Y |
| 6 Gordon | Y | Y | Y | Y | Y |
| 7 Blackburn | + | Y | Y | N | Y |
| 8 Tanner | Y | Y | Y | Y | Y |
| 9 Ford | ? | ? | ? | Y | Y |
| **TEXAS** | | | | | |
| 1 Gohmert | Y | Y | Y | N | Y |
| 2 Poe | Y | Y | Y | N | Y |
| 3 Johnson, S. | Y | Y | Y | N | Y |
| 4 Hall | Y | Y | Y | Y | Y |
| 5 Hensarling | Y | Y | Y | N | Y |
| 6 Barton | Y | Y | Y | N | Y |
| 7 Culberson | Y | Y | Y | N | Y |
| 8 Brady | Y | Y | Y | N | Y |
| 9 Green, A. | Y | Y | Y | Y | Y |
| 10 McCaul | Y | Y | Y | Y | Y |
| 11 Conaway | Y | Y | Y | N | Y |
| 12 Granger | Y | Y | Y | N | Y |
| 13 Thornberry | Y | Y | Y | N | Y |
| 14 Paul | N | Y | Y | N | Y |
| 15 Hinojosa | Y | Y | Y | Y | Y |
| 16 Reyes | ? | ? | ? | ? | ? |
| 17 Edwards | Y | Y | Y | Y | Y |
| 18 Jackson-Lee | Y | Y | Y | Y | Y |
| 19 Neugebauer | Y | Y | Y | Y | Y |
| 20 Gonzalez | Y | Y | Y | Y | Y |
| 21 Smith | Y | Y | Y | Y | Y |
| 22 DeLay | Y | Y | Y | N | Y |
| 23 Bonilla | Y | Y | Y | Y | Y |
| 24 Marchant | Y | Y | Y | Y | Y |
| 25 Doggett | Y | Y | Y | Y | Y |
| 26 Burgess | Y | Y | Y | N | Y |
| 27 Ortiz | Y | Y | Y | Y | Y |
| 28 Cuellar | Y | Y | Y | Y | Y |
| 29 Green, G. | Y | Y | Y | Y | Y |
| 30 Johnson, E. | Y | Y | Y | Y | Y |
| 31 Carter | Y | Y | Y | N | Y |
| 32 Sessions | Y | Y | Y | Y | Y |
| **UTAH** | | | | | |
| 1 Bishop | Y | Y | Y | Y | Y |
| 2 Matheson | Y | Y | Y | Y | Y |
| 3 Cannon | Y | Y | Y | Y | Y |
| **VERMONT** | | | | | |
| AL Sanders | Y | Y | Y | Y | Y |
| **VIRGINIA** | | | | | |
| 1 Davis, J. | Y | Y | Y | N | Y |
| 2 Drake | Y | Y | Y | Y | Y |
| 3 Scott | Y | Y | Y | Y | N |
| 4 Forbes | Y | Y | Y | N | Y |
| 5 Goode | Y | Y | Y | Y | Y |
| 6 Goodlatte | Y | Y | Y | Y | Y |
| 7 Cantor | Y | ? | ? | Y | Y |
| 8 Moran | ? | ? | ? | Y | Y |
| 9 Boucher | Y | Y | Y | Y | Y |
| 10 Wolf | Y | Y | Y | Y | Y |
| 11 Davis, T. | Y | Y | Y | Y | Y |
| **WASHINGTON** | | | | | |
| 1 Inslee | Y | Y | Y | Y | Y |
| 2 Larsen | ? | ? | ? | Y | Y |
| 3 Baird | Y | Y | Y | Y | Y |
| 4 Hastings | Y | Y | Y | N | Y |
| 5 McMorris | Y | Y | Y | Y | Y |
| 6 Dicks | Y | Y | Y | Y | Y |
| 7 McDermott | Y | Y | Y | Y | Y |
| 8 Reichert | Y | Y | Y | Y | Y |
| 9 Smith | Y | Y | Y | Y | Y |
| **WEST VIRGINIA** | | | | | |
| 1 Mollohan | Y | Y | Y | Y | Y |
| 2 Capito | Y | Y | Y | Y | Y |
| 3 Rahall | Y | Y | Y | Y | Y |
| **WISCONSIN** | | | | | |
| 1 Ryan | Y | Y | Y | N | Y |
| 2 Baldwin | Y | Y | Y | Y | Y |
| 3 Kind | Y | Y | Y | Y | Y |
| 4 Moore | Y | Y | Y | Y | Y |
| 5 Sensenbrenner | Y | Y | Y | N | Y |
| 6 Petri | Y | Y | Y | N | Y |
| 7 Obey | Y | Y | Y | Y | Y |
| 8 Green | + | + | + | Y | Y |
| **WYOMING** | | | | | |
| AL Cubin | ? | ? | ? | Y | Y |

# IN THE HOUSE | By Vote Number

**614.** **H Con Res 196. Federal Flight Deck Officer Program/Adoption.** Pearce, R-N.M., motion to suspend the rules and adopt the concurrent resolution that would recognize volunteer pilots in the Federal Flight Deck Officer Program and applaud them for taking a stand against terrorism. Motion agreed to 413-2: R 221-0; D 191-2 (ND 145-2, SD 46-0); I 1-0. A two-thirds majority of those present and voting (277 in this case) is required for adoption under suspension of the rules. Dec. 7, 2005.

**615.** **HR 3010. Fiscal 2006 Labor-HHS-Education Appropriations/ Appeal Ruling of the Chair.** Regula, R-Ohio., motion to table (kill) the Obey, D-Wis., appeal of the ruling of the chair against the Regula point of order against the Obey motion to instruct House conferees on the grounds that the provisions in the motion exceed the scope of the conference. The Obey motion would instruct House conferees to include language that would appropriate $4.2 billion for the Low Income Home Energy Assistance Program, with $2 billion of the total designated as emergency funding. Motion agreed to 226-196: R 226-0; D 0-195 (ND 0-146, SD 0-49); I 0-1. Dec. 7, 2005.

**616.** **HR 4340. United States-Bahrain Free Trade Agreement/Passage.** Passage of the bill that would implement a trade agreement between the United States and Bahrain. It would provide immediate duty-free access for 98 percent of U.S. agricultural exports and phase out tariffs on the remaining products within 10 years. It also would provide immediate duty-free access on all of Bahrain's agricultural exports to the United States. Passed 327-95: R 212-13; D 115-81 (ND 82-65, SD 33-16); I 0-1. A "yea" was a vote in support of the president's position. Dec. 7, 2005.

**617.** **HR 4388. Tax Breaks Extensions/Passage.** McCrery, R-La., motion to suspend the rules and pass the bill that would extend for one year various expiring tax provisions including one that would allow military combat pay to continue to be counted for purposes of calculating the earned income tax credit. Motion agreed to 423-0: R 226-0; D 196-0 (ND 147-0, SD 49-0); I 1-0. A two-thirds majority of those present and voting (282 in this case) is required for passage under suspension of the rules. Dec. 7, 2005.

**618.** **HR 4440. Gulf Zone Tax Relief/Passage.** McCrery, R-La., motion to suspend the rules and pass the bill that would provide tax benefits for areas of Alabama, Louisiana and Mississippi affected by Hurricane Katrina. It would provide authority for tax-exempt bonds to help rebuild infrastructure, authorize additional credits for low-income housing and authorize federal guarantees for up to $3 billion in bonds to aid local governments that cannot meet certain financing requirements. Motion agreed to 415-4: R 223-3; D 191-1 (ND 144-1, SD 47-0); I 1-0. A two-thirds majority of those present and voting (280 in this case) is required for passage under suspension of the rules. Dec. 7, 2005.

| | 614 | 615 | 616 | 617 | 618 |
|---|---|---|---|---|---|
| **ALABAMA** | | | | | |
| 1 Bonner | Y | Y | Y | Y | Y |
| 2 Everett | Y | Y | N | Y | Y |
| 3 Rogers | Y | Y | N | Y | Y |
| 4 Aderholt | Y | Y | Y | Y | Y |
| 5 Cramer | Y | N | Y | Y | Y |
| 6 Bachus | Y | Y | Y | Y | Y |
| 7 Davis | Y | N | Y | Y | Y |
| **ALASKA** | | | | | |
| AL Young | Y | Y | Y | Y | Y |
| **ARIZONA** | | | | | |
| 1 Renzi | Y | Y | Y | Y | Y |
| 2 Franks | Y | Y | Y | Y | Y |
| 3 Shadegg | Y | Y | Y | Y | Y |
| 4 Pastor | Y | N | N | Y | Y |
| 5 Hayworth | Y | Y | Y | Y | Y |
| 6 Flake | Y | Y | Y | Y | Y |
| 7 Grijalva | Y | N | N | Y | Y |
| 8 Kolbe | Y | Y | Y | Y | Y |
| **ARKANSAS** | | | | | |
| 1 Berry | Y | N | N | Y | Y |
| 2 Snyder | Y | N | Y | Y | Y |
| 3 Boozman | Y | Y | Y | Y | Y |
| 4 Ross | Y | N | Y | Y | Y |
| **CALIFORNIA** | | | | | |
| 1 Thompson | Y | N | Y | Y | Y |
| 2 Herger | Y | Y | Y | Y | Y |
| 3 Lungren | Y | Y | Y | Y | Y |
| 4 Doolittle | Y | Y | Y | Y | Y |
| 5 Matsui, D. | Y | N | Y | Y | Y |
| 6 Woolsey | Y | N | N | Y | Y |
| 7 Miller, George | Y | N | Y | Y | Y |
| 8 Pelosi | ? | ? | ? | ? | ? |
| 9 Lee | Y | N | N | Y | Y |
| 10 Tauscher | Y | N | Y | Y | Y |
| 11 Pombo | Y | Y | Y | Y | Y |
| 12 Lantos | Y | N | N | Y | Y |
| 13 Stark | N | N | N | Y | Y |
| 14 Eshoo | Y | N | Y | Y | Y |
| 15 Honda | Y | N | Y | Y | Y |
| 16 Lofgren | Y | N | Y | Y | Y |
| 17 Farr | Y | N | Y | Y | Y |
| 18 Cardoza | Y | N | Y | Y | Y |
| 19 Radanovich | Y | Y | Y | Y | Y |
| 20 Costa | Y | N | Y | Y | Y |
| 21 Nunes | Y | Y | Y | Y | Y |
| 22 Thomas | Y | Y | Y | Y | Y |
| 23 Capps | Y | N | Y | Y | Y |
| 24 Gallegly | Y | Y | Y | Y | Y |
| 25 McKeon | Y | Y | Y | Y | Y |
| 26 Dreier | Y | Y | Y | Y | Y |
| 27 Sherman | Y | N | Y | Y | Y |
| 28 Berman | Y | N | Y | Y | Y |
| 29 Schiff | Y | N | Y | Y | Y |
| 30 Waxman | Y | N | Y | Y | Y |
| 31 Becerra | Y | N | Y | Y | Y |
| 32 Solis | Y | N | N | Y | Y |
| 33 Watson | Y | N | Y | Y | Y |
| 34 Roybal-Allard | Y | N | Y | Y | Y |
| 35 Waters | Y | N | N | Y | Y |
| 36 Harman | Y | N | Y | Y | Y |
| 37 Millender-McD. | Y | N | N | Y | Y |
| 38 Napolitano | Y | – | N | Y | Y |
| 39 Sánchez, Linda | Y | N | N | Y | Y |
| 40 Royce | Y | Y | ? | Y | Y |
| 41 Lewis | Y | Y | Y | Y | Y |
| 42 Miller, Gary | Y | Y | Y | Y | Y |
| 43 Baca | Y | N | N | Y | Y |
| 44 Calvert | Y | Y | Y | Y | Y |
| 45 Bono | Y | Y | Y | Y | Y |
| 46 Rohrabacher | Y | Y | Y | Y | Y |
| 47 Sanchez, Loretta | Y | N | Y | Y | Y |
| 48 Vacant | | | | | |
| 49 Issa | Y | Y | Y | Y | Y |
| 50 Vacant | | | | | |
| 51 Filner | Y | N | N | Y | Y |
| 52 Hunter | Y | Y | Y | Y | Y |
| 53 Davis | Y | N | Y | Y | Y |
| **COLORADO** | | | | | |
| 1 DeGette | Y | N | N | Y | Y |
| 2 Udall | Y | N | N | Y | Y |
| 3 Salazar | Y | N | Y | Y | Y |
| 4 Musgrave | Y | Y | Y | Y | Y |
| 5 Hefley | Y | Y | Y | Y | Y |
| 6 Tancredo | Y | Y | Y | Y | Y |
| 7 Beauprez | Y | Y | Y | Y | Y |
| **CONNECTICUT** | | | | | |
| 1 Larson | Y | N | Y | Y | Y |
| 2 Simmons | Y | Y | Y | Y | Y |
| 3 DeLauro | Y | N | N | Y | Y |
| 4 Shays | Y | Y | Y | Y | Y |
| 5 Johnson | Y | Y | Y | Y | Y |
| **DELAWARE** | | | | | |
| AL Castle | Y | Y | Y | Y | Y |
| **FLORIDA** | | | | | |
| 1 Miller | Y | Y | Y | Y | Y |
| 2 Boyd | Y | N | Y | Y | Y |
| 3 Brown | Y | N | N | Y | Y |
| 4 Crenshaw | Y | Y | Y | Y | Y |
| 5 Brown-Waite | ? | ? | ? | ? | ? |
| 6 Stearns | Y | Y | Y | Y | Y |
| 7 Mica | Y | Y | Y | Y | Y |
| 8 Keller | Y | Y | Y | Y | Y |
| 9 Bilirakis | Y | Y | Y | Y | Y |
| 10 Young | Y | Y | Y | Y | Y |
| 11 Davis | ? | ? | ? | ? | ? |
| 12 Putnam | Y | Y | Y | Y | Y |
| 13 Harris | Y | Y | Y | Y | Y |
| 14 Mack | Y | Y | Y | Y | Y |
| 15 Weldon | Y | Y | Y | Y | Y |
| 16 Foley | Y | Y | Y | Y | Y |
| 17 Meek | Y | N | Y | Y | Y |
| 18 Ros-Lehtinen | Y | Y | Y | Y | Y |
| 19 Wexler | ? | ? | ? | ? | ? |
| 20 Wasserman-Schultz | Y | N | Y | Y | Y |
| 21 Diaz-Balart, L. | Y | Y | Y | Y | Y |
| 22 Shaw | Y | Y | Y | Y | Y |
| 23 Hastings | Y | N | N | Y | Y |
| 24 Feeney | Y | Y | Y | Y | Y |
| 25 Diaz-Balart, M. | Y | Y | Y | Y | Y |
| **GEORGIA** | | | | | |
| 1 Kingston | Y | Y | Y | Y | Y |
| 2 Bishop | Y | N | Y | Y | Y |
| 3 Marshall | Y | N | Y | Y | Y |
| 4 McKinney | Y | N | N | Y | Y |
| 5 Lewis | Y | N | Y | Y | Y |
| 6 Price | Y | Y | Y | Y | Y |
| 7 Linder | Y | Y | Y | Y | Y |
| 8 Westmoreland | Y | Y | Y | Y | Y |
| 9 Norwood | Y | Y | Y | Y | Y |
| 10 Deal | Y | Y | Y | Y | Y |
| 11 Gingrey | Y | Y | Y | Y | Y |
| 12 Barrow | Y | N | Y | Y | Y |
| 13 Scott | Y | N | Y | Y | Y |
| **HAWAII** | | | | | |
| 1 Abercrombie | Y | N | N | Y | Y |
| 2 Case | Y | N | Y | Y | Y |
| **IDAHO** | | | | | |
| 1 Otter | Y | Y | Y | Y | Y |
| 2 Simpson | Y | Y | Y | Y | Y |
| **ILLINOIS** | | | | | |
| 1 Rush | Y | N | Y | Y | Y |
| 2 Jackson | Y | N | N | Y | Y |
| 3 Lipinski | Y | N | N | Y | Y |
| 4 Gutierrez | Y | N | N | Y | + |
| 5 Emanuel | Y | N | Y | Y | Y |
| 6 Hyde | Y | Y | Y | Y | Y |
| 7 Davis | Y | N | Y | Y | Y |
| 8 Bean | Y | N | Y | Y | Y |
| 9 Schakowsky | Y | N | N | Y | Y |
| 10 Kirk | Y | Y | Y | Y | Y |
| 11 Weller | Y | Y | Y | Y | Y |
| 12 Costello | Y | N | N | Y | Y |

| | | 614 | 615 | 616 | 617 | 618 |
|---|---|---|---|---|---|---|
| 13 | Biggert | Y | Y | Y | Y | Y |
| 14 | Hastert | | | | | |
| 15 | Johnson | Y | Y | Y | Y | Y |
| 16 | Manzullo | Y | Y | Y | Y | Y |
| 17 | Evans | Y | N | N | Y | Y |
| 18 | LaHood | Y | Y | Y | Y | Y |
| 19 | Shimkus | Y | Y | Y | Y | Y |
| **INDIANA** | | | | | | |
| 1 | Visclosky | Y | N | N | Y | Y |
| 2 | Chocola | Y | Y | Y | Y | Y |
| 3 | Souder | Y | Y | Y | Y | Y |
| 4 | Buyer | Y | Y | Y | Y | Y |
| 5 | Burton | Y | Y | Y | Y | Y |
| 6 | Pence | ? | ? | ? | ? | ? |
| 7 | Carson | Y | N | N | Y | Y |
| 8 | Hostettler | Y | Y | N | Y | Y |
| 9 | Sodrel | Y | Y | Y | Y | Y |
| **IOWA** | | | | | | |
| 1 | Nussle | Y | Y | Y | Y | Y |
| 2 | Leach | Y | Y | Y | Y | Y |
| 3 | Boswell | Y | N | Y | Y | Y |
| 4 | Latham | Y | Y | Y | Y | Y |
| 5 | King | Y | Y | Y | Y | Y |
| **KANSAS** | | | | | | |
| 1 | Moran | Y | Y | Y | Y | Y |
| 2 | Ryun | Y | Y | Y | Y | Y |
| 3 | Moore | Y | N | Y | Y | Y |
| 4 | Tiahrt | Y | Y | Y | Y | Y |
| **KENTUCKY** | | | | | | |
| 1 | Whitfield | Y | Y | Y | Y | Y |
| 2 | Lewis | Y | Y | Y | Y | Y |
| 3 | Northup | Y | Y | Y | Y | Y |
| 4 | Davis | Y | Y | Y | Y | Y |
| 5 | Rogers | Y | Y | Y | Y | Y |
| 6 | Chandler | Y | N | Y | Y | Y |
| **LOUISIANA** | | | | | | |
| 1 | Jindal | Y | Y | Y | Y | Y |
| 2 | Jefferson | Y | N | Y | Y | Y |
| 3 | Melancon | Y | N | Y | Y | Y |
| 4 | McCrery | Y | Y | Y | Y | Y |
| 5 | Alexander | Y | Y | Y | Y | Y |
| 6 | Baker | Y | Y | Y | Y | Y |
| 7 | Boustany | Y | Y | Y | Y | Y |
| **MAINE** | | | | | | |
| 1 | Allen | Y | N | Y | Y | Y |
| 2 | Michaud | Y | N | N | Y | Y |
| **MARYLAND** | | | | | | |
| 1 | Gilchrest | Y | Y | Y | Y | Y |
| 2 | Ruppersberger | Y | N | Y | Y | Y |
| 3 | Cardin | Y | N | Y | Y | Y |
| 4 | Wynn | Y | N | Y | Y | Y |
| 5 | Hoyer | Y | N | Y | Y | Y |
| 6 | Bartlett | Y | Y | Y | Y | Y |
| 7 | Cummings | Y | N | Y | Y | Y |
| 8 | Van Hollen | Y | N | Y | Y | Y |
| **MASSACHUSETTS** | | | | | | |
| 1 | Olver | Y | N | N | Y | Y |
| 2 | Neal | Y | N | Y | Y | Y |
| 3 | McGovern | Y | N | N | Y | Y |
| 4 | Frank | Y | N | Y | Y | Y |
| 5 | Meehan | Y | N | N | Y | Y |
| 6 | Tierney | Y | N | N | Y | Y |
| 7 | Markey | Y | N | Y | Y | Y |
| 8 | Capuano | Y | N | N | Y | Y |
| 9 | Lynch | Y | N | N | Y | Y |
| 10 | Delahunt | Y | N | Y | Y | Y |
| **MICHIGAN** | | | | | | |
| 1 | Stupak | Y | N | N | Y | Y |
| 2 | Hoekstra | Y | Y | Y | Y | Y |
| 3 | Ehlers | Y | Y | Y | Y | Y |
| 4 | Camp | Y | Y | Y | Y | Y |
| 5 | Kildee | Y | N | N | Y | Y |
| 6 | Upton | Y | Y | Y | Y | Y |
| 7 | Schwarz | Y | Y | Y | Y | Y |
| 8 | Rogers | Y | Y | Y | Y | Y |
| 9 | Knollenberg | Y | Y | Y | Y | Y |
| 10 | Miller | Y | Y | Y | Y | Y |
| 11 | McCotter | Y | Y | Y | Y | Y |
| 12 | Levin | Y | N | Y | Y | Y |
| 13 | Kilpatrick | Y | N | N | Y | Y |
| 14 | Conyers | Y | N | N | Y | Y |
| 15 | Dingell | Y | N | Y | Y | Y |

| | | 614 | 615 | 616 | 617 | 618 |
|---|---|---|---|---|---|---|
| **MINNESOTA** | | | | | | |
| 1 | Gutknecht | Y | Y | Y | Y | Y |
| 2 | Kline | Y | Y | Y | Y | Y |
| 3 | Ramstad | Y | Y | Y | Y | Y |
| 4 | McCollum | Y | N | N | Y | Y |
| 5 | Sabo | Y | N | N | Y | Y |
| 6 | Kennedy | Y | Y | Y | Y | Y |
| 7 | Peterson | Y | N | Y | Y | Y |
| 8 | Oberstar | Y | N | N | Y | Y |
| **MISSISSIPPI** | | | | | | |
| 1 | Wicker | Y | Y | Y | Y | Y |
| 2 | Thompson | Y | N | N | Y | Y |
| 3 | Pickering | Y | Y | Y | Y | Y |
| 4 | Taylor | ? | N | N | Y | Y |
| **MISSOURI** | | | | | | |
| 1 | Clay | ? | ? | ? | ? | ? |
| 2 | Akin | Y | Y | Y | Y | Y |
| 3 | Carnahan | Y | N | Y | Y | Y |
| 4 | Skelton | Y | N | Y | Y | Y |
| 5 | Cleaver | Y | N | Y | Y | Y |
| 6 | Graves | Y | Y | Y | Y | Y |
| 7 | Blunt | Y | Y | Y | Y | Y |
| 8 | Emerson | Y | Y | Y | Y | Y |
| 9 | Hulshof | Y | Y | Y | Y | Y |
| **MONTANA** | | | | | | |
| AL | Rehberg | Y | Y | Y | Y | Y |
| **NEBRASKA** | | | | | | |
| 1 | Fortenberry | Y | Y | Y | Y | Y |
| 2 | Terry | Y | Y | Y | Y | Y |
| 3 | Osborne | Y | Y | Y | Y | Y |
| **NEVADA** | | | | | | |
| 1 | Berkley | Y | N | Y | Y | N |
| 2 | Gibbons | Y | Y | Y | Y | N |
| 3 | Porter | Y | Y | Y | Y | N |
| **NEW HAMPSHIRE** | | | | | | |
| 1 | Bradley | Y | Y | Y | Y | Y |
| 2 | Bass | Y | Y | Y | Y | Y |
| **NEW JERSEY** | | | | | | |
| 1 | Andrews | + | - | - | + | + |
| 2 | LoBiondo | Y | Y | Y | Y | N |
| 3 | Saxton | Y | Y | Y | Y | Y |
| 4 | Smith | Y | Y | Y | Y | Y |
| 5 | Garrett | Y | Y | Y | Y | Y |
| 6 | Pallone | Y | N | N | Y | Y |
| 7 | Ferguson | Y | Y | Y | Y | Y |
| 8 | Pascrell | Y | N | Y | Y | Y |
| 9 | Rothman | Y | N | N | Y | Y |
| 10 | Payne | Y | N | N | Y | Y |
| 11 | Frelinghuysen | Y | Y | Y | Y | Y |
| 12 | Holt | Y | N | N | Y | Y |
| 13 | Menendez | Y | N | N | Y | Y |
| **NEW MEXICO** | | | | | | |
| 1 | Wilson | Y | Y | Y | Y | Y |
| 2 | Pearce | Y | Y | Y | Y | Y |
| 3 | Udall | Y | N | Y | Y | Y |
| **NEW YORK** | | | | | | |
| 1 | Bishop | Y | N | Y | Y | Y |
| 2 | Israel | Y | N | Y | Y | Y |
| 3 | King | Y | Y | Y | Y | Y |
| 4 | McCarthy | + | N | Y | Y | Y |
| 5 | Ackerman | Y | N | Y | Y | Y |
| 6 | Meeks | Y | N | Y | Y | Y |
| 7 | Crowley | Y | N | Y | Y | Y |
| 8 | Nadler | Y | - | - | + | + |
| 9 | Weiner | Y | N | Y | Y | Y |
| 10 | Towns | Y | N | Y | Y | Y |
| 11 | Owens | Y | N | N | Y | Y |
| 12 | Velázquez | Y | N | Y | Y | Y |
| 13 | Fossella | Y | Y | Y | Y | Y |
| 14 | Maloney | Y | N | Y | Y | Y |
| 15 | Rangel | Y | N | Y | Y | Y |
| 16 | Serrano | Y | N | N | Y | Y |
| 17 | Engel | Y | N | Y | Y | Y |
| 18 | Lowey | Y | N | Y | Y | Y |
| 19 | Kelly | Y | Y | Y | Y | Y |
| 20 | Sweeney | ? | Y | Y | Y | Y |
| 21 | McNulty | Y | N | Y | Y | Y |
| 22 | Hinchey | Y | N | N | Y | Y |
| 23 | McHugh | Y | Y | Y | Y | Y |
| 24 | Boehlert | Y | Y | Y | Y | Y |
| 25 | Walsh | Y | Y | Y | Y | Y |
| 26 | Reynolds | Y | Y | Y | Y | Y |
| 27 | Higgins | Y | N | N | Y | Y |
| 28 | Slaughter | Y | N | N | Y | ? |
| 29 | Kuhl | Y | Y | Y | Y | Y |

| | | 614 | 615 | 616 | 617 | 618 |
|---|---|---|---|---|---|---|
| **NORTH CAROLINA** | | | | | | |
| 1 | Butterfield | Y | N | Y | Y | Y |
| 2 | Etheridge | Y | N | Y | Y | Y |
| 3 | Jones | Y | Y | N | Y | Y |
| 4 | Price | Y | N | Y | Y | Y |
| 5 | Foxx | Y | Y | Y | Y | Y |
| 6 | Coble | Y | Y | N | Y | Y |
| 7 | McIntyre | Y | N | N | Y | Y |
| 8 | Hayes | Y | Y | Y | Y | Y |
| 9 | Myrick | Y | Y | Y | Y | Y |
| 10 | McHenry | Y | Y | Y | Y | Y |
| 11 | Taylor | Y | Y | N | Y | Y |
| 12 | Watt | ? | N | N | Y | Y |
| 13 | Miller | Y | N | N | Y | Y |
| **NORTH DAKOTA** | | | | | | |
| AL | Pomeroy | Y | N | Y | Y | Y |
| **OHIO** | | | | | | |
| 1 | Chabot | Y | Y | Y | Y | Y |
| 2 | Schmidt | Y | Y | Y | Y | Y |
| 3 | Turner | Y | Y | Y | Y | Y |
| 4 | Oxley | Y | Y | Y | Y | Y |
| 5 | Gillmor | Y | Y | Y | Y | Y |
| 6 | Strickland | Y | N | N | Y | Y |
| 7 | Hobson | Y | Y | Y | Y | Y |
| 8 | Boehner | Y | Y | Y | Y | Y |
| 9 | Kaptur | Y | N | Y | Y | Y |
| 10 | Kucinich | Y | N | N | Y | Y |
| 11 | Jones | Y | N | Y | Y | Y |
| 12 | Tiberi | Y | Y | Y | Y | Y |
| 13 | Brown | Y | N | N | Y | Y |
| 14 | LaTourette | Y | Y | Y | Y | Y |
| 15 | Pryce | Y | Y | Y | Y | Y |
| 16 | Regula | Y | Y | Y | Y | Y |
| 17 | Ryan | Y | N | N | Y | Y |
| 18 | Ney | Y | Y | Y | Y | Y |
| **OKLAHOMA** | | | | | | |
| 1 | Sullivan | Y | Y | Y | Y | Y |
| 2 | Boren | Y | N | Y | Y | Y |
| 3 | Lucas | Y | Y | Y | Y | Y |
| 4 | Cole | + | Y | Y | Y | Y |
| 5 | Istook | Y | Y | Y | Y | Y |
| **OREGON** | | | | | | |
| 1 | Wu | N | N | Y | Y | Y |
| 2 | Walden | Y | Y | Y | Y | Y |
| 3 | Blumenauer | Y | N | Y | Y | Y |
| 4 | DeFazio | Y | N | N | Y | Y |
| 5 | Hooley | Y | N | Y | Y | Y |
| **PENNSYLVANIA** | | | | | | |
| 1 | Brady | Y | N | N | Y | Y |
| 2 | Fattah | Y | N | N | Y | Y |
| 3 | English | Y | Y | Y | Y | Y |
| 4 | Hart | Y | Y | Y | Y | Y |
| 5 | Peterson | Y | Y | Y | Y | Y |
| 6 | Gerlach | + | Y | Y | Y | Y |
| 7 | Weldon | Y | Y | Y | Y | Y |
| 8 | Fitzpatrick | Y | Y | Y | Y | Y |
| 9 | Shuster | Y | Y | Y | Y | Y |
| 10 | Sherwood | Y | Y | Y | Y | Y |
| 11 | Kanjorski | Y | N | N | Y | Y |
| 12 | Murtha | Y | N | N | Y | Y |
| 13 | Schwartz | Y | N | N | Y | Y |
| 14 | Doyle | Y | N | N | Y | Y |
| 15 | Dent | Y | Y | Y | Y | Y |
| 16 | Pitts | Y | Y | Y | Y | Y |
| 17 | Holden | Y | N | N | Y | Y |
| 18 | Murphy | Y | Y | Y | Y | Y |
| 19 | Platts | Y | Y | Y | Y | Y |
| **RHODE ISLAND** | | | | | | |
| 1 | Kennedy | Y | N | Y | Y | Y |
| 2 | Langevin | Y | N | Y | Y | Y |
| **SOUTH CAROLINA** | | | | | | |
| 1 | Brown | Y | Y | Y | Y | Y |
| 2 | Wilson | Y | Y | Y | Y | Y |
| 3 | Barrett | Y | Y | N | Y | Y |
| 4 | Inglis | Y | Y | Y | Y | Y |
| 5 | Spratt | Y | N | Y | Y | Y |
| 6 | Clyburn | Y | N | N | Y | Y |
| **SOUTH DAKOTA** | | | | | | |
| AL | Herseth | Y | N | Y | Y | Y |
| **TENNESSEE** | | | | | | |
| 1 | Jenkins | Y | Y | Y | Y | Y |
| 2 | Duncan | Y | Y | Y | Y | Y |

| | | 614 | 615 | 616 | 617 | 618 |
|---|---|---|---|---|---|---|
| 3 | Wamp | Y | Y | Y | Y | Y |
| 4 | Davis | Y | N | Y | Y | Y |
| 5 | Cooper | Y | N | Y | Y | Y |
| 6 | Gordon | Y | N | Y | Y | Y |
| 7 | Blackburn | Y | Y | Y | Y | Y |
| 8 | Tanner | Y | N | Y | Y | Y |
| 9 | Ford | Y | N | Y | Y | Y |
| **TEXAS** | | | | | | |
| 1 | Gohmert | Y | Y | Y | Y | Y |
| 2 | Poe | Y | Y | Y | Y | Y |
| 3 | Johnson, S. | ? | Y | Y | Y | Y |
| 4 | Hall | Y | Y | Y | Y | Y |
| 5 | Hensarling | Y | Y | Y | Y | Y |
| 6 | Barton | Y | Y | Y | Y | Y |
| 7 | Culberson | Y | Y | Y | Y | Y |
| 8 | Brady | Y | Y | Y | Y | Y |
| 9 | Green, A. | Y | N | N | Y | Y |
| 10 | McCaul | Y | Y | Y | Y | Y |
| 11 | Conaway | Y | Y | Y | Y | Y |
| 12 | Granger | Y | Y | Y | Y | Y |
| 13 | Thornberry | Y | Y | Y | Y | Y |
| 14 | Paul | Y | N | Y | N | Y |
| 15 | Hinojosa | Y | N | Y | Y | Y |
| 16 | Reyes | ? | N | Y | Y | Y |
| 17 | Edwards | Y | N | Y | Y | Y |
| 18 | Jackson-Lee | Y | N | Y | Y | Y |
| 19 | Neugebauer | Y | Y | Y | Y | Y |
| 20 | Gonzalez | Y | N | Y | Y | Y |
| 21 | Smith | Y | Y | Y | Y | Y |
| 22 | DeLay | Y | Y | Y | Y | Y |
| 23 | Bonilla | Y | Y | Y | Y | Y |
| 24 | Marchant | Y | Y | Y | Y | Y |
| 25 | Doggett | Y | N | Y | Y | Y |
| 26 | Burgess | Y | Y | Y | Y | Y |
| 27 | Ortiz | Y | N | Y | Y | Y |
| 28 | Cuellar | Y | N | Y | Y | Y |
| 29 | Green, G. | Y | N | N | Y | Y |
| 30 | Johnson, E. | Y | N | N | Y | ? |
| 31 | Carter | Y | Y | Y | Y | Y |
| 32 | Sessions | Y | Y | Y | Y | Y |
| **UTAH** | | | | | | |
| 1 | Bishop | Y | N | Y | Y | Y |
| 2 | Matheson | Y | N | Y | Y | Y |
| 3 | Cannon | Y | Y | Y | Y | Y |
| **VERMONT** | | | | | | |
| AL | *Sanders* | Y | N | N | Y | Y |
| **VIRGINIA** | | | | | | |
| 1 | Davis, J. | Y | N | Y | Y | Y |
| 2 | Drake | Y | Y | Y | Y | Y |
| 3 | Scott | Y | N | N | Y | ? |
| 4 | Forbes | Y | Y | Y | Y | Y |
| 5 | Goode | Y | Y | Y | Y | Y |
| 6 | Goodlatte | Y | Y | Y | Y | Y |
| 7 | Cantor | Y | Y | Y | Y | Y |
| 8 | Moran | Y | N | Y | Y | Y |
| 9 | Boucher | Y | N | N | Y | Y |
| 10 | Wolf | Y | Y | Y | Y | Y |
| 11 | Davis, T. | Y | Y | Y | Y | Y |
| **WASHINGTON** | | | | | | |
| 1 | Inslee | Y | N | Y | Y | Y |
| 2 | Larsen | Y | N | Y | Y | Y |
| 3 | Baird | Y | N | Y | Y | Y |
| 4 | Hastings | ? | ? | ? | ? | ? |
| 5 | McMorris | Y | Y | Y | Y | Y |
| 6 | Dicks | Y | N | Y | Y | Y |
| 7 | McDermott | Y | N | Y | Y | Y |
| 8 | Reichert | Y | Y | Y | Y | Y |
| 9 | Smith | Y | N | Y | Y | Y |
| **WEST VIRGINIA** | | | | | | |
| 1 | Mollohan | Y | N | N | Y | Y |
| 2 | Capito | ? | Y | Y | Y | Y |
| 3 | Rahall | Y | N | N | Y | Y |
| **WISCONSIN** | | | | | | |
| 1 | Ryan | Y | Y | Y | Y | Y |
| 2 | Baldwin | Y | N | N | Y | Y |
| 3 | Kind | Y | N | Y | Y | Y |
| 4 | Moore | Y | N | Y | Y | Y |
| 5 | Sensenbrenner | Y | Y | Y | Y | Y |
| 6 | Petri | Y | Y | Y | Y | Y |
| 7 | Obey | Y | N | N | Y | Y |
| 8 | Green | Y | Y | Y | Y | Y |
| **WYOMING** | | | | | | |
| AL | Cubin | Y | Y | Y | Y | Y |

# IN THE HOUSE | By Vote Number

**619.** **HR 4297. Fiscal 2006 Tax Reconciliation/Democratic Substitute.** Rangel, D-N.Y., substitute amendment that would extend for one year many expiring provisions such as the deduction for state and local retail sales taxes, the deduction for college tuition expenses, tax incentives for the District of Columbia and Indian reservations, the 15-year depreciation period for leasehold and restaurant improvements, qualified zone academy bonds and the Brownfields cleanup tax incentive. The amendment would also eliminate all individual minimum tax liability for incomes below $200,000 in the case of joint returns and below $100,000 in all other cases for taxable year 2006. Rejected 192-239: R 2-226; D 189-13 (ND 141-10, SD 48-3); I 1-0. Dec. 8, 2005.

**620.** **HR 4297. Fiscal 2006 Tax Reconciliation/Recommit.** Rangel, D-N.Y., motion to recommit the bill to the Ways and Means Committee with instructions to strike language related to the capital gains and dividend tax breaks as well as add a new section to the bill dealing with tax relief for the alternative minimum tax. Motion rejected 193-235: R 0-226; D 192-9 (ND 145-5, SD 47-4); I 1-0. Dec. 8, 2005.

**621.** **HR 4297. Fiscal 2006 Tax Reconciliation/Passage.** Passage of bill that would provide $56.1 billion to extend a series of tax cuts set to expire between 2005 and 2010. It would extend for two years, through 2010, reduced tax rates on capital gains and dividends. It would extend, for two years, a tax provision that allows small businesses to write off more than $100,000 in capital investments in the year they are made. It would allow for a one-year extension of the college tuition deduction, the research and experimentation tax credit, and the state and local sales tax deduction in states without income taxes. Passed 234-197: R 225-3; D 9-193 (ND 1-150, SD 8-43); I 0-1. A "yea" is a vote in support of the president's position. Dec. 8, 2005.

**622.** **H Res 591. Ethics and the Medicare Drug Benefit Vote/Motion to Table.** Putnam, R-Fla., motion to table (kill) the Pelosi, D-Calif., privileged resolution that would denounce a "culture of corruption" by Republican leaders who have held open votes — particularly on the 2003 Medicare drug benefit bill — beyond a reasonable time "for the sole purpose of circumventing the will of the House." Motion agreed to 219-188: R 218-0; D 1-187 (ND 1-139, SD 0-48); I 0-1. Dec. 8, 2005.

| | | 619 | 620 | 621 | 622 |
|---|---|---|---|---|---|
| **ALABAMA** | | | | | |
| 1 | Bonner | N | N | Y | Y |
| 2 | Everett | N | N | Y | ? |
| 3 | Rogers | N | N | Y | Y |
| 4 | Aderholt | N | N | Y | Y |
| 5 | Cramer | Y | N | Y | N |
| 6 | Bachus | N | N | Y | Y |
| 7 | Davis | Y | Y | N | N |
| **ALASKA** | | | | | |
| AL | Young | N | N | Y | Y |
| **ARIZONA** | | | | | |
| 1 | Renzi | N | N | Y | Y |
| 2 | Franks | N | N | + | Y |
| 3 | Shadegg | N | N | Y | Y |
| 4 | Pastor | Y | Y | N | N |
| 5 | Hayworth | N | N | Y | Y |
| 6 | Flake | N | N | Y | Y |
| 7 | Grijalva | Y | Y | N | N |
| 8 | Kolbe | N | N | Y | Y |
| **ARKANSAS** | | | | | |
| 1 | Berry | Y | Y | N | N |
| 2 | Snyder | Y | Y | N | N |
| 3 | Boozman | N | ? | Y | Y |
| 4 | Ross | Y | Y | N | N |
| **CALIFORNIA** | | | | | |
| 1 | Thompson | Y | Y | N | N |
| 2 | Herger | N | N | Y | Y |
| 3 | Lungren | N | N | Y | Y |
| 4 | Doolittle | N | N | Y | Y |
| 5 | Matsui, D. | Y | Y | N | N |
| 6 | Woolsey | Y | Y | N | ? |
| 7 | Miller, George | Y | Y | N | N |
| 8 | Pelosi | Y | Y | N | N |
| 9 | Lee | Y | Y | N | N |
| 10 | Tauscher | Y | Y | N | N |
| 11 | Pombo | N | N | Y | Y |
| 12 | Lantos | Y | Y | N | N |
| 13 | Stark | Y | Y | N | N |
| 14 | Eshoo | Y | Y | N | N |
| 15 | Honda | Y | Y | N | N |
| 16 | Lofgren | Y | Y | N | N |
| 17 | Farr | Y | Y | N | N |
| 18 | Cardoza | Y | Y | N | N |
| 19 | Radanovich | N | N | Y | Y |
| 20 | Costa | Y | Y | N | N |
| 21 | Nunes | N | N | Y | Y |
| 22 | Thomas | N | N | Y | Y |
| 23 | Capps | Y | Y | N | N |
| 24 | Gallegly | N | N | Y | Y |
| 25 | McKeon | N | N | Y | Y |
| 26 | Dreier | N | N | Y | Y |
| 27 | Sherman | Y | Y | N | N |
| 28 | Berman | Y | Y | N | N |
| 29 | Schiff | Y | Y | N | N |
| 30 | Waxman | Y | Y | N | N |
| 31 | Becerra | Y | Y | N | N |
| 32 | Solis | Y | Y | N | N |
| 33 | Watson | Y | Y | N | N |
| 34 | Roybal-Allard | Y | Y | N | N |
| 35 | Waters | Y | Y | N | ? |
| 36 | Harman | Y | Y | N | N |
| 37 | Millender-McD. | Y | Y | N | N |
| 38 | Napolitano | Y | Y | N | N |
| 39 | Sánchez, Linda | Y | Y | N | N |
| 40 | Royce | N | N | Y | Y |
| 41 | Lewis | N | N | Y | Y |
| 42 | Miller, Gary | N | N | Y | Y |
| 43 | Baca | Y | Y | N | N |
| 44 | Calvert | N | N | Y | Y |
| 45 | Bono | N | N | Y | Y |
| 46 | Rohrabacher | N | N | Y | Y |
| 47 | Sanchez, Loretta | Y | Y | N | N |
| 48 | Campbell* | N | N | Y | Y |
| 49 | Issa | N | N | Y | Y |
| 50 | Vacant | | | | |
| 51 | Filner | Y | Y | N | N |
| 52 | Hunter | N | N | Y | Y |
| 53 | Davis | Y | Y | N | N |
| **COLORADO** | | | | | |
| 1 | DeGette | Y | Y | N | N |
| 2 | Udall | Y | Y | N | N |
| 3 | Salazar | Y | Y | N | N |
| 4 | Musgrave | N | N | Y | Y |
| 5 | Hefley | N | N | Y | Y |
| 6 | Tancredo | N | N | Y | Y |
| 7 | Beauprez | N | N | Y | Y |
| **CONNECTICUT** | | | | | |
| 1 | Larson | Y | Y | N | N |
| 2 | Simmons | N | N | Y | Y |
| 3 | DeLauro | Y | Y | N | N |
| 4 | Shays | N | N | Y | Y |
| 5 | Johnson | N | N | Y | Y |
| **DELAWARE** | | | | | |
| AL | Castle | N | N | Y | Y |
| **FLORIDA** | | | | | |
| 1 | Miller | N | N | Y | Y |
| 2 | Boyd | Y | Y | N | ? |
| 3 | Brown | Y | Y | N | N |
| 4 | Crenshaw | N | N | Y | Y |
| 5 | Brown-Waite | ? | ? | ? | ? |
| 6 | Stearns | N | N | Y | Y |
| 7 | Mica | N | N | Y | Y |
| 8 | Keller | N | N | Y | Y |
| 9 | Bilirakis | N | N | Y | Y |
| 10 | Young | N | N | Y | Y |
| 11 | Davis | Y | Y | N | N |
| 12 | Putnam | N | N | Y | Y |
| 13 | Harris | N | N | Y | Y |
| 14 | Mack | N | N | Y | Y |
| 15 | Weldon | N | N | Y | Y |
| 16 | Foley | N | N | Y | Y |
| 17 | Meek | Y | Y | N | N |
| 18 | Ros-Lehtinen | N | N | Y | Y |
| 19 | Wexler | Y | Y | N | N |
| 20 | Wasserman-Schultz | Y | Y | N | N |
| 21 | Diaz-Balart, L. | N | N | Y | Y |
| 22 | Shaw | N | N | Y | Y |
| 23 | Hastings | Y | Y | N | N |
| 24 | Feeney | N | N | Y | Y |
| 25 | Diaz-Balart, M. | N | N | Y | Y |
| **GEORGIA** | | | | | |
| 1 | Kingston | N | N | Y | Y |
| 2 | Bishop | Y | Y | N | N |
| 3 | Marshall | Y | Y | N | N |
| 4 | McKinney | Y | Y | N | N |
| 5 | Lewis | Y | Y | N | N |
| 6 | Price | N | N | Y | Y |
| 7 | Linder | N | N | Y | Y |
| 8 | Westmoreland | N | N | Y | Y |
| 9 | Norwood | N | N | Y | Y |
| 10 | Deal | N | N | Y | Y |
| 11 | Gingrey | N | N | Y | Y |
| 12 | Barrow | N | Y | Y | N |
| 13 | Scott | Y | Y | N | N |
| **HAWAII** | | | | | |
| 1 | Abercrombie | Y | Y | N | Y |
| 2 | Case | Y | Y | N | N |
| **IDAHO** | | | | | |
| 1 | Otter | N | N | Y | Y |
| 2 | Simpson | N | N | Y | Y |
| **ILLINOIS** | | | | | |
| 1 | Rush | Y | Y | N | N |
| 2 | Jackson | Y | Y | N | N |
| 3 | Lipinski | Y | Y | N | N |
| 4 | Gutierrez | Y | Y | N | N |
| 5 | Emanuel | Y | Y | N | N |
| 6 | Hyde | N | N | Y | ? |
| 7 | Davis | Y | Y | N | N |
| 8 | Bean | N | N | Y | N |
| 9 | Schakowsky | Y | Y | N | N |
| 10 | Kirk | N | N | Y | Y |
| 11 | Weller | N | N | Y | Y |
| 12 | Costello | N | Y | N | N |

| KEY | Republicans | Democrats | *Independents* |
|---|---|---|---|

| | | | |
|---|---|---|---|
| Y | Voted for (yea) | X Paired against | C Voted "present" to avoid possible conflict of interest |
| # | Paired for | – Announced against | |
| + | Announced for | P Voted "present" | ? Did not vote or otherwise make a position known |
| N | Voted against (nay) | | |

\* Rep. John Campbell, R-Calif., was sworn in Dec. 7, 2005. The first vote for which he was eligible was vote 619.

| | | 619 | 620 | 621 | 622 |
|---|---|---|---|---|---|
| 13 | Biggert | N | N | Y | Y |
| 14 | Hastert | | | Y | Y |
| 15 | Johnson | N | N | Y | Y |
| 16 | Manzullo | N | N | Y | Y |
| 17 | Evans | Y | Y | N | N |
| 18 | LaHood | N | N | Y | Y |
| 19 | Shimkus | N | N | Y | Y |
| **INDIANA** | | | | | |
| 1 | Visclosky | N | Y | N | N |
| 2 | Chocola | N | N | Y | ? |
| 3 | Souder | N | N | Y | Y |
| 4 | Buyer | N | N | Y | ? |
| 5 | Burton | N | N | Y | Y |
| 6 | Pence | N | N | Y | Y |
| 7 | Carson | Y | Y | N | N |
| 8 | Hostettler | N | N | Y | Y |
| 9 | Sodrel | N | N | Y | Y |
| **IOWA** | | | | | |
| 1 | Nussle | N | N | Y | Y |
| 2 | Leach | Y | N | N | Y |
| 3 | Boswell | Y | Y | N | N |
| 4 | Latham | N | N | Y | Y |
| 5 | King | N | N | Y | Y |
| **KANSAS** | | | | | |
| 1 | Moran | N | N | Y | Y |
| 2 | Ryun | N | N | Y | Y |
| 3 | Moore | Y | Y | N | N |
| 4 | Tiahrt | N | N | Y | Y |
| **KENTUCKY** | | | | | |
| 1 | Whitfield | N | N | Y | Y |
| 2 | Lewis | N | N | Y | Y |
| 3 | Northup | N | N | Y | Y |
| 4 | Davis | N | N | Y | Y |
| 5 | Rogers | N | N | Y | Y |
| 6 | Chandler | Y | Y | N | N |
| **LOUISIANA** | | | | | |
| 1 | Jindal | N | N | Y | Y |
| 2 | Jefferson | Y | Y | N | N |
| 3 | Melancon | Y | Y | N | N |
| 4 | McCrery | N | N | Y | Y |
| 5 | Alexander | N | N | Y | Y |
| 6 | Baker | N | N | Y | Y |
| 7 | Boustany | N | N | Y | Y |
| **MAINE** | | | | | |
| 1 | Allen | Y | Y | N | N |
| 2 | Michaud | Y | Y | N | N |
| **MARYLAND** | | | | | |
| 1 | Gilchrest | N | N | Y | Y |
| 2 | Ruppersberger | Y | Y | N | N |
| 3 | Cardin | Y | Y | N | N |
| 4 | Wynn | Y | Y | N | N |
| 5 | Hoyer | Y | Y | N | N |
| 6 | Bartlett | N | N | Y | Y |
| 7 | Cummings | Y | Y | N | N |
| 8 | Van Hollen | Y | Y | N | N |
| **MASSACHUSETTS** | | | | | |
| 1 | Olver | Y | Y | N | N |
| 2 | Neal | Y | Y | N | N |
| 3 | McGovern | Y | Y | N | N |
| 4 | Frank | Y | Y | N | N |
| 5 | Meehan | Y | Y | N | N |
| 6 | Tierney | Y | Y | N | N |
| 7 | Markey | Y | ? | N | N |
| 8 | Capuano | Y | Y | N | N |
| 9 | Lynch | Y | Y | N | N |
| 10 | Delahunt | Y | Y | N | N |
| **MICHIGAN** | | | | | |
| 1 | Stupak | Y | Y | N | N |
| 2 | Hoekstra | N | N | Y | Y |
| 3 | Ehlers | N | N | Y | Y |
| 4 | Camp | N | N | Y | Y |
| 5 | Kildee | Y | Y | N | N |
| 6 | Upton | N | N | N | Y |
| 7 | Schwarz | N | N | Y | Y |
| 8 | Rogers | N | N | Y | Y |
| 9 | Knollenberg | N | N | Y | Y |
| 10 | Miller | N | N | Y | Y |
| 11 | McCotter | N | N | Y | Y |
| 12 | Levin | Y | Y | N | N |
| 13 | Kilpatrick | Y | Y | N | N |
| 14 | Conyers | Y | Y | N | N |
| 15 | Dingell | Y | Y | N | N |

| | | 619 | 620 | 621 | 622 |
|---|---|---|---|---|---|
| **MINNESOTA** | | | | | |
| 1 | Gutknecht | N | N | Y | Y |
| 2 | Kline | N | N | Y | Y |
| 3 | Ramstad | N | N | Y | Y |
| 4 | McCollum | N | Y | N | N |
| 5 | Sabo | N | Y | N | N |
| 6 | Kennedy | N | N | Y | Y |
| 7 | Peterson | N | N | N | N |
| 8 | Oberstar | N | Y | N | N |
| **MISSISSIPPI** | | | | | |
| 1 | Wicker | N | N | Y | Y |
| 2 | Thompson | Y | Y | N | N |
| 3 | Pickering | N | N | Y | Y |
| 4 | Taylor | Y | N | N | N |
| **MISSOURI** | | | | | |
| 1 | Clay | Y | Y | N | N |
| 2 | Akin | N | N | Y | Y |
| 3 | Carnahan | Y | Y | N | N |
| 4 | Skelton | Y | Y | N | N |
| 5 | Cleaver | Y | Y | N | N |
| 6 | Graves | N | N | Y | Y |
| 7 | Blunt | N | N | Y | Y |
| 8 | Emerson | N | N | Y | Y |
| 9 | Hulshof | N | N | Y | Y |
| **MONTANA** | | | | | |
| AL | Rehberg | N | N | Y | Y |
| **NEBRASKA** | | | | | |
| 1 | Fortenberry | N | N | Y | Y |
| 2 | Terry | N | N | Y | Y |
| 3 | Osborne | N | N | Y | Y |
| **NEVADA** | | | | | |
| 1 | Berkley | Y | Y | N | N |
| 2 | Gibbons | N | N | Y | Y |
| 3 | Porter | N | N | Y | Y |
| **NEW HAMPSHIRE** | | | | | |
| 1 | Bradley | N | N | Y | Y |
| 2 | Bass | N | N | Y | Y |
| **NEW JERSEY** | | | | | |
| 1 | Andrews | Y | Y | N | N |
| 2 | LoBiondo | N | N | Y | Y |
| 3 | Saxton | N | N | Y | Y |
| 4 | Smith | N | ? | Y | Y |
| 5 | Garrett | N | N | Y | Y |
| 6 | Pallone | Y | Y | N | N |
| 7 | Ferguson | N | N | Y | Y |
| 8 | Pascrell | Y | Y | N | ? |
| 9 | Rothman | Y | Y | N | N |
| 10 | Payne | Y | Y | N | N |
| 11 | Frelinghuysen | N | N | Y | Y |
| 12 | Holt | Y | Y | N | N |
| 13 | Menendez | Y | Y | N | ? |
| **NEW MEXICO** | | | | | |
| 1 | Wilson | Y | N | Y | Y |
| 2 | Pearce | N | N | Y | Y |
| 3 | Udall | Y | Y | N | N |
| **NEW YORK** | | | | | |
| 1 | Bishop | Y | Y | N | N |
| 2 | Israel | Y | Y | N | N |
| 3 | King | N | N | Y | Y |
| 4 | McCarthy | Y | Y | N | N |
| 5 | Ackerman | Y | Y | N | N |
| 6 | Meeks | Y | Y | N | N |
| 7 | Crowley | Y | Y | N | N |
| 8 | Nadler | Y | Y | N | N |
| 9 | Weiner | Y | Y | N | N |
| 10 | Towns | Y | Y | N | N |
| 11 | Owens | Y | Y | N | N |
| 12 | Velázquez | Y | Y | N | N |
| 13 | Fossella | N | N | Y | Y |
| 14 | Maloney | Y | Y | N | N |
| 15 | Rangel | Y | Y | N | N |
| 16 | Serrano | Y | Y | N | N |
| 17 | Engel | Y | Y | N | N |
| 18 | Lowey | Y | Y | N | N |
| 19 | Kelly | N | N | Y | Y |
| 20 | Sweeney | N | N | Y | Y |
| 21 | McNulty | Y | Y | N | ? |
| 22 | Hinchey | Y | Y | N | N |
| 23 | McHugh | N | N | Y | Y |
| 24 | Boehlert | N | N | Y | Y |
| 25 | Walsh | N | N | Y | Y |
| 26 | Reynolds | N | N | Y | Y |
| 27 | Higgins | Y | Y | N | N |
| 28 | Slaughter | Y | Y | N | N |
| 29 | Kuhl | N | N | Y | Y |

| | | 619 | 620 | 621 | 622 |
|---|---|---|---|---|---|
| **NORTH CAROLINA** | | | | | |
| 1 | Butterfield | Y | Y | N | N |
| 2 | Etheridge | Y | Y | N | ? |
| 3 | Jones | N | N | Y | ? |
| 4 | Price | Y | Y | N | N |
| 5 | Foxx | N | N | Y | Y |
| 6 | Coble | N | N | Y | ? |
| 7 | McIntyre | Y | N | Y | N |
| 8 | Hayes | N | N | Y | ? |
| 9 | Myrick | N | N | Y | Y |
| 10 | McHenry | N | N | Y | Y |
| 11 | Taylor | N | N | Y | Y |
| 12 | Watt | Y | Y | N | N |
| 13 | Miller | Y | Y | N | N |
| **NORTH DAKOTA** | | | | | |
| AL | Pomeroy | Y | Y | N | N |
| **OHIO** | | | | | |
| 1 | Chabot | N | N | Y | Y |
| 2 | Schmidt | N | N | Y | Y |
| 3 | Turner | N | N | Y | Y |
| 4 | Oxley | N | N | Y | Y |
| 5 | Gillmor | N | N | Y | Y |
| 6 | Strickland | Y | Y | N | N |
| 7 | Hobson | N | N | Y | Y |
| 8 | Boehner | N | N | Y | Y |
| 9 | Kaptur | Y | Y | N | N |
| 10 | Kucinich | Y | Y | N | N |
| 11 | Jones | Y | Y | N | N |
| 12 | Tiberi | N | N | Y | Y |
| 13 | Brown | Y | Y | N | N |
| 14 | LaTourette | N | N | Y | Y |
| 15 | Pryce | N | N | Y | Y |
| 16 | Regula | N | N | Y | Y |
| 17 | Ryan | Y | Y | N | N |
| 18 | Ney | N | N | Y | Y |
| **OKLAHOMA** | | | | | |
| 1 | Sullivan | N | N | Y | ? |
| 2 | Boren | N | N | Y | N |
| 3 | Lucas | N | N | Y | Y |
| 4 | Cole | N | N | Y | Y |
| 5 | Istook | N | N | Y | Y |
| **OREGON** | | | | | |
| 1 | Wu | Y | Y | N | N |
| 2 | Walden | N | N | Y | ? |
| 3 | Blumenauer | Y | Y | N | ? |
| 4 | DeFazio | Y | Y | N | ? |
| 5 | Hooley | Y | Y | N | N |
| **PENNSYLVANIA** | | | | | |
| 1 | Brady | Y | Y | N | N |
| 2 | Fattah | Y | Y | N | N |
| 3 | English | N | N | Y | Y |
| 4 | Hart | N | N | Y | Y |
| 5 | Peterson | N | N | Y | ? |
| 6 | Gerlach | N | N | Y | Y |
| 7 | Weldon | N | N | Y | Y |
| 8 | Fitzpatrick | N | N | Y | Y |
| 9 | Shuster | N | N | Y | Y |
| 10 | Sherwood | N | N | Y | Y |
| 11 | Kanjorski | N | N | N | N |
| 12 | Murtha | N | N | N | N |
| 13 | Schwartz | Y | Y | N | N |
| 14 | Doyle | Y | Y | N | ? |
| 15 | Dent | N | N | Y | Y |
| 16 | Pitts | N | N | Y | Y |
| 17 | Holden | N | N | Y | ? |
| 18 | Murphy | N | N | Y | Y |
| 19 | Platts | N | N | Y | Y |
| **RHODE ISLAND** | | | | | |
| 1 | Kennedy | Y | Y | N | N |
| 2 | Langevin | Y | Y | N | N |
| **SOUTH CAROLINA** | | | | | |
| 1 | Brown | N | N | Y | Y |
| 2 | Wilson | N | N | Y | Y |
| 3 | Barrett | N | N | Y | Y |
| 4 | Inglis | N | N | Y | Y |
| 5 | Spratt | Y | Y | N | N |
| 6 | Clyburn | Y | Y | N | N |
| **SOUTH DAKOTA** | | | | | |
| AL | Herseth | Y | Y | N | N |
| **TENNESSEE** | | | | | |
| 1 | Jenkins | N | N | Y | Y |
| 2 | Duncan | N | N | Y | Y |

| | | 619 | 620 | 621 | 622 |
|---|---|---|---|---|---|
| 3 | Wamp | N | N | Y | Y |
| 4 | Davis | Y | Y | Y | N |
| 5 | Cooper | Y | Y | Y | N |
| 6 | Gordon | Y | Y | Y | N |
| 7 | Blackburn | N | N | Y | Y |
| 8 | Tanner | Y | Y | Y | N |
| 9 | Ford | Y | Y | N | N |
| **TEXAS** | | | | | |
| 1 | Gohmert | N | N | Y | Y |
| 2 | Poe | N | N | Y | Y |
| 3 | Johnson, S. | N | N | Y | Y |
| 4 | Hall | N | N | Y | Y |
| 5 | Hensarling | N | N | Y | Y |
| 6 | Barton | N | N | Y | Y |
| 7 | Culberson | N | N | Y | Y |
| 8 | Brady | N | N | Y | Y |
| 9 | Green, A. | Y | Y | N | N |
| 10 | McCaul | N | N | Y | Y |
| 11 | Conaway | N | N | Y | Y |
| 12 | Granger | N | N | Y | Y |
| 13 | Thornberry | N | N | Y | Y |
| 14 | Paul | N | N | Y | ? |
| 15 | Hinojosa | Y | Y | N | N |
| 16 | Reyes | Y | Y | N | N |
| 17 | Edwards | Y | Y | N | N |
| 18 | Jackson-Lee | Y | Y | N | N |
| 19 | Neugebauer | N | N | Y | Y |
| 20 | Gonzalez | Y | Y | N | N |
| 21 | Smith | N | N | Y | Y |
| 22 | DeLay | N | N | Y | Y |
| 23 | Bonilla | N | N | Y | Y |
| 24 | Marchant | N | N | Y | Y |
| 25 | Doggett | Y | Y | N | N |
| 26 | Burgess | N | N | Y | Y |
| 27 | Ortiz | Y | Y | N | N |
| 28 | Cuellar | Y | Y | Y | N |
| 29 | Green, G. | Y | Y | N | ? |
| 30 | Johnson, E. | Y | Y | N | N |
| 31 | Carter | N | N | Y | Y |
| 32 | Sessions | N | N | Y | Y |
| **UTAH** | | | | | |
| 1 | Bishop | N | N | Y | Y |
| 2 | Matheson | N | N | N | N |
| 3 | Cannon | N | N | Y | Y |
| **VERMONT** | | | | | |
| AL | *Sanders* | Y | Y | N | N |
| **VIRGINIA** | | | | | |
| 1 | Davis, J. | N | N | Y | Y |
| 2 | Drake | N | N | Y | Y |
| 3 | Scott | Y | Y | N | N |
| 4 | Forbes | N | N | Y | Y |
| 5 | Goode | N | N | Y | Y |
| 6 | Goodlatte | N | N | Y | Y |
| 7 | Cantor | N | N | Y | Y |
| 8 | Moran | Y | Y | N | N |
| 9 | Boucher | Y | Y | N | N |
| 10 | Wolf | N | N | Y | Y |
| 11 | Davis, T. | N | N | Y | Y |
| **WASHINGTON** | | | | | |
| 1 | Inslee | Y | Y | N | N |
| 2 | Larsen | Y | Y | N | N |
| 3 | Baird | Y | Y | N | N |
| 4 | Hastings | ? | ? | ? | ? |
| 5 | McMorris | N | N | Y | Y |
| 6 | Dicks | Y | Y | N | N |
| 7 | McDermott | Y | Y | N | ? |
| 8 | Reichert | N | N | Y | Y |
| 9 | Smith | Y | Y | N | N |
| **WEST VIRGINIA** | | | | | |
| 1 | Mollohan | Y | Y | N | N |
| 2 | Capito | N | N | Y | Y |
| 3 | Rahall | Y | Y | N | N |
| **WISCONSIN** | | | | | |
| 1 | Ryan | N | N | Y | Y |
| 2 | Baldwin | Y | Y | N | N |
| 3 | Kind | Y | Y | N | ? |
| 4 | Moore | Y | Y | N | N |
| 5 | Sensenbrenner | N | N | Y | Y |
| 6 | Petri | N | N | Y | Y |
| 7 | Obey | Y | Y | N | N |
| 8 | Green | N | N | Y | Y |
| **WYOMING** | | | | | |
| AL | Cubin | N | N | Y | Y |

# IN THE HOUSE | By Vote Number

**623.** H Res 487. Korean-American Day/Adoption. Cannon, R-Utah, motion to suspend the rules and adopt the resolution that would support the goals and ideals of Korean-American Day and urge all Americans to observe the day in appreciation of the contributions that Korean-Americans have made to the United States. Motion agreed to 405-0: R 215-0; D 189-0 (ND 142-0, SD 47-0); I 1-0. A two-thirds majority of those present and voting (270 in this case) is required for adoption under suspension of the rules. Dec. 13, 2005.

**624.** S 1047. Presidential Coin/Passage. Oxley, R-Ohio, motion to suspend the rules and pass the bill that would authorize the U.S. Mint to issue a redesigned $1 coin to commemorate U.S. presidents, a series of $10 gold bullion coins to honor first ladies and a new $50 gold bullion coin. It also would authorize the redesign of the penny in 2009 to commemorate the 200th anniversary of President Abraham Lincoln's birth. Motion agreed to 291-113: R 103-111; D 187-2 (ND 141-1, SD 46-1); I 1-0. A two-thirds majority of those present and voting (270 in this case) is required for passage under suspension of the rules. Dec. 13, 2005.

**625.** HR 3422. Small Public Housing Authority/Passage. Oxley, R-Ohio, motion to suspend the rules and pass the bill that would exempt qualified small public housing authorities from the requirement of preparing an annual housing agency plan. Motion agreed to 387-2: R 203-2; D 183-0 (ND 137-0, SD 46-0); I 1-0. A two-thirds majority of those present and voting (260 in this case) is required for passage under suspension of the rules. Dec. 13, 2005.

**626.** HR 3199. "Patriot Act" Reauthorization/Recommit. Conyers, D-Mich., motion to recommit the bill to the Judiciary Committee with instructions to replace the text of the conference report on the bill with the Senate-passed version of the bill. Motion rejected 202-224: R 5-221; D 196-3 (ND 146-2, SD 50-1); I 1-0. Dec. 14, 2005.

**627.** HR 3199. "Patriot Act" Reauthorization/Conference Report. Adoption of the conference report on the bill that would make permanent 14 of the 16 provisions of the anti-terrorism law known as the Patriot Act set to expire at the end of the year, and extend for four years two provisions on access to business and other records and "roving" wiretaps. The measure would allow recipients of "national security letters" demanding information to consult with lawyers and to challenge the letters in court. Adopted (thus sent to the Senate) 251-174: R 207-18; D 44-155 (ND 22-127, SD 22-28); I 0-1. A "yea" is a vote in support of the president's position. Dec. 14, 2005.

**628.** HR 3010. Fiscal 2006 Labor-HHS-Education Appropriations/ Conference Report. Adoption of the conference report on the bill that would appropriate $601.6 billion, including $142.5 billion in discretionary spending, for the Labor, Health and Human Services, and Education departments and related agencies in fiscal 2006. It would provide $63.5 billion for the Education Department, $14.8 billion for the Labor Department and $474.1 billion for Health and Human Services, including $28.6 billion for the National Institutes of Health. Adopted (thus sent to the Senate) 215-213: R 215-12; D 0-200 (ND 0-149, SD 0-51); I 0-1. Dec. 14, 2005.

**629.** HR 2863. Fiscal 2006 Defense Appropriations/Motion to Close Conference. Young, R-Fla., motion to close portions of the conference on the bill that would appropriate funding for Defense programs for fiscal 2006. Motion agreed to 415-9: R 225-0; D 189-9 (ND 141-8, SD 48-1); I 1-0. Dec. 14, 2005.

| | 623 | 624 | 625 | 626 | 627 | 628 | 629 |
|---|---|---|---|---|---|---|---|
| **ALABAMA** | | | | | | | |
| 1 Bonner | ? | ? | ? | N | Y | Y | Y |
| 2 Everett | ? | ? | ? | N | Y | Y | Y |
| 3 Rogers | Y | Y | Y | N | Y | Y | Y |
| 4 Aderholt | Y | Y | Y | N | Y | Y | Y |
| 5 Cramer | Y | Y | Y | Y | Y | N | Y |
| 6 Bachus | ? | ? | ? | N | Y | Y | Y |
| 7 Davis | Y | Y | Y | Y | N | Y | N |
| **ALASKA** | | | | | | | |
| AL Young | Y | N | Y | N | N | Y | Y |
| **ARIZONA** | | | | | | | |
| 1 Renzi | Y | Y | Y | N | Y | N | Y |
| 2 Franks | Y | N | Y | N | Y | Y | Y |
| 3 Shadegg | Y | N | Y | N | Y | Y | Y |
| 4 Pastor | Y | Y | Y | Y | N | N | Y |
| 5 Hayworth | ? | ? | ? | N | Y | Y | Y |
| 6 Flake | Y | N | Y | N | Y | Y | Y |
| 7 Grijalva | Y | Y | Y | Y | N | N | Y |
| 8 Kolbe | Y | N | Y | N | Y | Y | Y |
| **ARKANSAS** | | | | | | | |
| 1 Berry | Y | Y | Y | Y | N | N | Y |
| 2 Snyder | Y | Y | Y | Y | N | N | Y |
| 3 Boozman | Y | N | Y | N | Y | Y | Y |
| 4 Ross | Y | Y | Y | Y | N | Y | N |
| **CALIFORNIA** | | | | | | | |
| 1 Thompson | Y | Y | Y | Y | N | N | Y |
| 2 Herger | Y | N | Y | N | Y | Y | Y |
| 3 Lungren | Y | N | Y | N | Y | Y | Y |
| 4 Doolittle | Y | N | Y | N | Y | Y | Y |
| 5 Matsui, D. | Y | Y | Y | Y | N | N | Y |
| 6 Woolsey | Y | Y | Y | Y | N | N | N |
| 7 Miller, George | Y | Y | Y | Y | N | N | Y |
| 8 Pelosi | Y | Y | Y | Y | N | N | Y |
| 9 Lee | Y | Y | Y | Y | N | N | N |
| 10 Tauscher | Y | Y | Y | Y | N | N | Y |
| 11 Pombo | Y | Y | Y | N | Y | Y | Y |
| 12 Lantos | Y | Y | Y | Y | N | N | Y |
| 13 Stark | Y | Y | Y | Y | N | N | N |
| 14 Eshoo | Y | Y | Y | Y | N | N | Y |
| 15 Honda | Y | Y | Y | Y | N | N | Y |
| 16 Lofgren | Y | Y | Y | Y | N | N | Y |
| 17 Farr | Y | Y | Y | Y | N | N | Y |
| 18 Cardoza | Y | Y | Y | Y | N | N | Y |
| 19 Radanovich | Y | Y | Y | N | ? | Y | Y |
| 20 Costa | Y | Y | Y | Y | N | Y | + |
| 21 Nunes | Y | Y | Y | N | Y | Y | Y |
| 22 Thomas | Y | Y | Y | N | Y | Y | Y |
| 23 Capps | Y | Y | Y | Y | N | N | Y |
| 24 Gallegly | + | + | + | N | Y | Y | Y |
| 25 McKeon | Y | Y | Y | N | Y | Y | Y |
| 26 Dreier | Y | Y | Y | N | Y | Y | Y |
| 27 Sherman | Y | Y | Y | Y | N | N | Y |
| 28 Berman | Y | Y | Y | Y | N | N | Y |
| 29 Schiff | Y | Y | Y | Y | N | N | Y |
| 30 Waxman | Y | Y | Y | Y | N | N | Y |
| 31 Becerra | Y | Y | Y | Y | N | N | Y |
| 32 Solis | Y | Y | ? | Y | N | N | Y |
| 33 Watson | Y | Y | Y | Y | N | N | Y |
| 34 Roybal-Allard | Y | Y | Y | Y | N | N | Y |
| 35 Waters | Y | Y | ? | Y | N | N | Y |
| 36 Harman | Y | Y | Y | Y | N | N | Y |
| 37 Millender-McD. | Y | Y | Y | Y | N | N | Y |
| 38 Napolitano | Y | Y | Y | Y | N | N | Y |
| 39 Sánchez, Linda | Y | Y | ? | Y | N | N | Y |
| 40 Royce | Y | N | Y | N | Y | Y | Y |
| 41 Lewis | Y | Y | ? | N | Y | Y | Y |
| 42 Miller, Gary | Y | N | Y | N | Y | Y | Y |
| 43 Baca | Y | Y | Y | Y | N | Y | Y |
| 44 Calvert | ? | ? | ? | N | Y | Y | Y |
| 45 Bono | Y | N | Y | N | Y | Y | Y |
| 46 Rohrabacher | Y | N | Y | N | Y | Y | Y |
| 47 Sanchez, Loretta | Y | Y | Y | Y | N | N | Y |
| 48 Campbell | Y | N | Y | N | Y | Y | Y |
| 49 Issa | Y | Y | Y | N | Y | Y | Y |
| 50 Vacant | | | | | | | |
| 51 Filner | Y | Y | Y | N | N | N | Y |
| 52 Hunter | Y | N | Y | N | Y | Y | Y |
| 53 Davis | Y | Y | Y | Y | N | N | Y |
| **COLORADO** | | | | | | | |
| 1 DeGette | ? | ? | ? | ? | ? | ? | Y |
| 2 Udall | + | + | + | Y | N | N | Y |
| 3 Salazar | Y | Y | Y | Y | N | N | Y |
| 4 Musgrave | Y | N | Y | N | Y | Y | Y |
| 5 Hefley | Y | N | Y | N | Y | Y | Y |
| 6 Tancredo | Y | Y | Y | N | Y | Y | Y |
| 7 Beauprez | Y | N | Y | N | Y | Y | Y |
| **CONNECTICUT** | | | | | | | |
| 1 Larson | Y | Y | Y | Y | N | N | Y |
| 2 Simmons | Y | Y | Y | N | N | Y | Y |
| 3 DeLauro | Y | Y | Y | Y | N | N | Y |
| 4 Shays | Y | Y | Y | Y | Y | N | Y |
| 5 Johnson | Y | Y | ? | N | Y | N | Y |
| **DELAWARE** | | | | | | | |
| AL Castle | Y | Y | Y | N | Y | N | Y |
| **FLORIDA** | | | | | | | |
| 1 Miller | Y | N | Y | N | Y | Y | Y |
| 2 Boyd | Y | Y | Y | Y | Y | N | Y |
| 3 Brown | ? | ? | ? | Y | N | N | Y |
| 4 Crenshaw | Y | Y | Y | N | Y | Y | Y |
| 5 Brown-Waite | Y | Y | Y | N | Y | Y | Y |
| 6 Stearns | Y | Y | Y | N | Y | Y | Y |
| 7 Mica | Y | Y | Y | N | Y | Y | Y |
| 8 Keller | Y | Y | Y | N | Y | Y | Y |
| 9 Bilirakis | Y | N | Y | N | Y | Y | Y |
| 10 Young | Y | N | Y | N | Y | Y | Y |
| 11 Davis | ? | ? | ? | Y | Y | N | Y |
| 12 Putnam | Y | Y | N | N | Y | Y | Y |
| 13 Harris | ? | ? | ? | N | Y | Y | Y |
| 14 Mack | Y | N | Y | N | Y | Y | Y |
| 15 Weldon | Y | N | Y | N | Y | Y | Y |
| 16 Foley | Y | Y | Y | N | Y | Y | Y |
| 17 Meek | Y | Y | Y | Y | N | N | Y |
| 18 Ros-Lehtinen | ? | ? | ? | ? | ? | ? | Y |
| 19 Wexler | Y | Y | Y | Y | N | N | Y |
| 20 Wasserman-Schultz | Y | Y | Y | Y | N | N | Y |
| 21 Diaz-Balart, L. | Y | Y | Y | N | Y | Y | Y |
| 22 Shaw | Y | Y | ? | N | Y | Y | Y |
| 23 Hastings | Y | Y | Y | Y | N | N | Y |
| 24 Feeney | Y | N | Y | N | Y | ? | Y |
| 25 Diaz-Balart, M. | + | - | + | - | + | + | + |
| **GEORGIA** | | | | | | | |
| 1 Kingston | Y | N | Y | N | Y | Y | Y |
| 2 Bishop | Y | Y | Y | Y | Y | N | Y |
| 3 Marshall | Y | Y | Y | Y | N | N | N |
| 4 McKinney | Y | Y | Y | Y | N | N | N |
| 5 Lewis | Y | Y | Y | Y | N | N | Y |
| 6 Price | Y | N | ? | N | Y | Y | Y |
| 7 Linder | Y | Y | Y | N | Y | Y | Y |
| 8 Westmoreland | Y | N | Y | N | Y | Y | ? |
| 9 Norwood | Y | N | Y | N | Y | Y | Y |
| 10 Deal | Y | Y | ? | N | Y | Y | Y |
| 11 Gingrey | Y | N | Y | N | Y | Y | Y |
| 12 Barrow | Y | Y | Y | Y | Y | N | Y |
| 13 Scott | Y | Y | Y | Y | N | Y | |
| **HAWAII** | | | | | | | |
| 1 Abercrombie | Y | Y | Y | Y | N | N | ? |
| 2 Case | Y | Y | Y | Y | N | N | Y |
| **IDAHO** | | | | | | | |
| 1 Otter | Y | N | Y | Y | N | Y | Y |
| 2 Simpson | Y | Y | Y | N | Y | Y | ? |
| **ILLINOIS** | | | | | | | |
| 1 Rush | Y | Y | Y | Y | N | N | Y |
| 2 Jackson | Y | Y | Y | Y | N | N | Y |
| 3 Lipinski | Y | Y | Y | Y | Y | N | Y |
| 4 Gutierrez | Y | Y | Y | Y | N | N | Y |
| 5 Emanuel | Y | Y | Y | Y | N | N | Y |
| 6 Hyde | + | - | + | - | + | + | + |
| 7 Davis | Y | Y | Y | Y | N | N | Y |
| 8 Bean | Y | Y | Y | Y | Y | N | Y |
| 9 Schakowsky | Y | Y | Y | Y | N | N | Y |
| 10 Kirk | Y | Y | Y | N | Y | Y | Y |
| 11 Weller | Y | Y | Y | N | Y | Y | Y |
| 12 Costello | ? | ? | ? | N | N | N | Y |

**KEY** — Republicans — Democrats — *Independents*

| | | | |
|---|---|---|---|
| Y | Voted for (yea) | X | Paired against |
| # | Paired for | – | Announced against |
| + | Announced for | P | Voted "present" |
| N | Voted against (nay) | C | Voted "present" to avoid possible conflict of interest |
| | | ? | Did not vote or otherwise make a position known |

| | 623 | 624 | 625 | 626 | 627 | 628 | 629 |
|---|---|---|---|---|---|---|---|
| 13 **Biggert** | Y | Y | Y | N | Y | Y | Y |
| 14 **Hastert** | | | | | Y | Y | |
| 15 **Johnson** | Y | N | Y | Y | N | Y | Y |
| 16 **Manzullo** | Y | Y | Y | N | N | Y | Y |
| 17 Evans | Y | Y | Y | Y | N | N | Y |
| 18 **LaHood** | Y | Y | Y | N | Y | Y | Y |
| 19 **Shimkus** | Y | Y | Y | N | Y | Y | Y |
| **INDIANA** | | | | | | | |
| 1 Visclosky | Y | Y | Y | Y | N | N | Y |
| 2 **Chocola** | Y | N | Y | N | Y | Y | Y |
| 3 **Souder** | Y | N | Y | N | Y | Y | Y |
| 4 **Buyer** | Y | N | Y | N | Y | Y | Y |
| 5 **Burton** | Y | N | Y | N | Y | Y | Y |
| 6 **Pence** | Y | N | Y | N | Y | Y | Y |
| 7 Carson | Y | Y | Y | Y | N | N | Y |
| 8 **Hostettler** | Y | Y | Y | N | Y | Y | Y |
| 9 **Sodrel** | Y | N | Y | N | Y | Y | Y |
| **IOWA** | | | | | | | |
| 1 **Nussle** | Y | Y | Y | N | Y | Y | Y |
| 2 **Leach** | Y | Y | Y | Y | Y | Y | Y |
| 3 Boswell | Y | Y | Y | Y | Y | N | Y |
| 4 **Latham** | Y | Y | Y | N | Y | Y | Y |
| 5 **King** | Y | N | Y | N | Y | Y | Y |
| **KANSAS** | | | | | | | |
| 1 **Moran** | Y | Y | Y | N | Y | Y | Y |
| 2 **Ryun** | Y | N | Y | N | Y | Y | Y |
| 3 Moore | Y | Y | Y | Y | Y | N | Y |
| 4 **Tiahrt** | Y | N | Y | N | Y | Y | Y |
| **KENTUCKY** | | | | | | | |
| 1 **Whitfield** | Y | N | Y | N | Y | Y | Y |
| 2 **Lewis** | Y | N | Y | N | Y | Y | Y |
| 3 **Northup** | Y | Y | Y | N | Y | Y | Y |
| 4 **Davis** | Y | N | Y | N | Y | Y | Y |
| 5 **Rogers** | Y | Y | Y | N | Y | Y | Y |
| 6 Chandler | Y | Y | Y | Y | Y | N | Y |
| **LOUISIANA** | | | | | | | |
| 1 **Jindal** | Y | N | Y | N | Y | Y | Y |
| 2 Jefferson | Y | Y | ? | Y | N | N | Y |
| 3 Melancon | Y | Y | Y | Y | Y | N | Y |
| 4 **McCrery** | Y | N | Y | N | Y | Y | Y |
| 5 **Alexander** | Y | N | Y | N | Y | Y | Y |
| 6 **Baker** | Y | Y | Y | N | Y | Y | Y |
| 7 **Boustany** | Y | Y | Y | N | Y | Y | Y |
| **MAINE** | | | | | | | |
| 1 Allen | Y | Y | Y | Y | N | N | Y |
| 2 Michaud | Y | Y | Y | Y | N | N | Y |
| **MARYLAND** | | | | | | | |
| 1 **Gilchrest** | Y | Y | Y | N | Y | Y | Y |
| 2 Ruppersberger | Y | Y | Y | Y | Y | N | Y |
| 3 Cardin | Y | Y | Y | Y | Y | N | Y |
| 4 Wynn | ? | ? | ? | Y | N | N | Y |
| 5 Hoyer | Y | Y | Y | Y | Y | N | Y |
| 6 **Bartlett** | Y | N | Y | N | N | Y | Y |
| 7 Cummings | Y | Y | Y | Y | N | N | Y |
| 8 Van Hollen | Y | Y | Y | Y | N | N | Y |
| **MASSACHUSETTS** | | | | | | | |
| 1 Olver | Y | Y | Y | Y | N | N | N |
| 2 Neal | Y | Y | Y | Y | N | N | Y |
| 3 McGovern | Y | Y | Y | Y | N | N | Y |
| 4 Frank | Y | Y | Y | Y | N | N | Y |
| 5 Meehan | Y | Y | Y | Y | N | N | Y |
| 6 Tierney | Y | Y | Y | Y | N | N | Y |
| 7 Markey | Y | Y | Y | Y | N | N | Y |
| 8 Capuano | Y | Y | Y | Y | N | N | Y |
| 9 Lynch | Y | Y | Y | Y | N | N | Y |
| 10 Delahunt | Y | Y | Y | Y | N | N | Y |
| **MICHIGAN** | | | | | | | |
| 1 Stupak | Y | Y | Y | Y | N | N | Y |
| 2 **Hoekstra** | Y | Y | Y | N | Y | Y | Y |
| 3 **Ehlers** | Y | Y | Y | N | N | Y | Y |
| 4 **Camp** | Y | N | Y | N | Y | Y | Y |
| 5 Kildee | Y | Y | Y | Y | N | N | Y |
| 6 **Upton** | Y | N | Y | N | Y | Y | Y |
| 7 **Schwarz** | Y | Y | Y | N | Y | Y | Y |
| 8 **Rogers** | Y | Y | Y | N | Y | Y | Y |
| 9 **Knollenberg** | Y | Y | ? | N | Y | Y | Y |
| 10 **Miller** | Y | N | Y | N | Y | Y | Y |
| 11 **McCotter** | Y | N | Y | N | Y | Y | Y |
| 12 Levin | Y | Y | Y | Y | N | N | Y |
| 13 Kilpatrick | Y | Y | Y | Y | N | N | Y |
| 14 Conyers | Y | Y | Y | Y | N | N | Y |
| 15 Dingell | Y | Y | Y | Y | N | N | Y |

| | 623 | 624 | 625 | 626 | 627 | 628 | 629 |
|---|---|---|---|---|---|---|---|
| **MINNESOTA** | | | | | | | |
| 1 **Gutknecht** | Y | Y | Y | N | Y | Y | Y |
| 2 **Kline** | Y | N | Y | N | Y | Y | Y |
| 3 **Ramstad** | Y | Y | Y | N | Y | N | Y |
| 4 McCollum | Y | Y | Y | Y | N | N | Y |
| 5 Sabo | ? | ? | ? | Y | N | N | Y |
| 6 **Kennedy** | Y | N | Y | N | Y | Y | Y |
| 7 Peterson | Y | Y | Y | Y | N | N | Y |
| 8 Oberstar | Y | Y | Y | Y | N | N | Y |
| **MISSISSIPPI** | | | | | | | |
| 1 **Wicker** | Y | N | Y | N | Y | Y | Y |
| 2 Thompson | Y | Y | Y | Y | N | N | Y |
| 3 **Pickering** | Y | Y | Y | N | Y | Y | Y |
| 4 Taylor | Y | Y | Y | Y | Y | N | Y |
| **MISSOURI** | | | | | | | |
| 1 Clay | Y | Y | Y | Y | N | N | Y |
| 2 **Akin** | Y | N | Y | N | Y | Y | Y |
| 3 Carnahan | Y | Y | Y | Y | Y | N | Y |
| 4 Skelton | Y | Y | Y | Y | Y | N | Y |
| 5 Cleaver | Y | Y | Y | Y | N | N | Y |
| 6 **Graves** | Y | Y | Y | N | Y | Y | Y |
| 7 **Blunt** | Y | N | Y | N | Y | Y | Y |
| 8 **Emerson** | Y | Y | Y | N | Y | Y | Y |
| 9 **Hulshof** | Y | Y | Y | N | Y | Y | Y |
| **MONTANA** | | | | | | | |
| AL **Rehberg** | ? | Y | Y | N | Y | Y | Y |
| **NEBRASKA** | | | | | | | |
| 1 **Fortenberry** | + | + | Y | N | Y | Y | Y |
| 2 **Terry** | Y | N | Y | N | Y | Y | Y |
| 3 **Osborne** | Y | Y | Y | N | Y | Y | Y |
| **NEVADA** | | | | | | | |
| 1 Berkley | Y | Y | Y | Y | N | N | Y |
| 2 **Gibbons** | Y | Y | Y | N | Y | N | Y |
| 3 **Porter** | Y | Y | Y | N | Y | Y | Y |
| **NEW HAMPSHIRE** | | | | | | | |
| 1 **Bradley** | Y | Y | Y | N | Y | Y | Y |
| 2 **Bass** | Y | Y | Y | N | Y | Y | Y |
| **NEW JERSEY** | | | | | | | |
| 1 Andrews | Y | Y | Y | Y | Y | N | Y |
| 2 **LoBiondo** | Y | N | Y | N | Y | Y | Y |
| 3 **Saxton** | Y | N | Y | N | Y | Y | Y |
| 4 **Smith** | Y | Y | Y | N | Y | Y | Y |
| 5 **Garrett** | Y | N | Y | N | Y | Y | Y |
| 6 Pallone | Y | Y | Y | Y | N | N | Y |
| 7 **Ferguson** | Y | Y | Y | N | Y | Y | Y |
| 8 Pascrell | Y | Y | Y | Y | N | N | Y |
| 9 Rothman | Y | Y | Y | Y | Y | N | Y |
| 10 Payne | Y | Y | Y | ? | N | N | Y |
| 11 **Frelinghuysen** | Y | Y | Y | N | Y | Y | Y |
| 12 Holt | Y | Y | Y | Y | N | N | Y |
| 13 Menendez | Y | Y | Y | Y | N | N | Y |
| **NEW MEXICO** | | | | | | | |
| 1 **Wilson** | Y | Y | Y | N | Y | N | Y |
| 2 **Pearce** | Y | Y | Y | N | Y | Y | Y |
| 3 Udall | Y | Y | Y | Y | N | N | Y |
| **NEW YORK** | | | | | | | |
| 1 Bishop | Y | Y | Y | Y | N | N | Y |
| 2 Israel | Y | Y | Y | Y | N | N | Y |
| 3 **King** | Y | Y | Y | N | Y | Y | Y |
| 4 McCarthy | Y | Y | ? | Y | Y | N | Y |
| 5 Ackerman | Y | Y | Y | Y | N | N | Y |
| 6 Meeks | Y | Y | Y | Y | N | N | Y |
| 7 Crowley | Y | Y | Y | Y | N | N | Y |
| 8 Nadler | Y | Y | Y | Y | N | N | Y |
| 9 Weiner | ? | ? | ? | Y | N | N | Y |
| 10 Towns | Y | Y | Y | Y | N | N | Y |
| 11 Owens | Y | Y | Y | Y | N | N | Y |
| 12 Velázquez | Y | Y | Y | Y | N | N | Y |
| 13 **Fossella** | Y | Y | Y | N | Y | Y | Y |
| 14 Maloney | Y | Y | Y | Y | N | N | Y |
| 15 Rangel | Y | Y | ? | Y | N | N | Y |
| 16 Serrano | Y | Y | Y | Y | N | N | Y |
| 17 Engel | Y | Y | Y | Y | N | N | Y |
| 18 Lowey | Y | Y | Y | Y | N | N | Y |
| 19 **Kelly** | Y | Y | Y | N | Y | Y | Y |
| 20 **Sweeney** | Y | N | Y | N | N | Y | Y |
| 21 McNulty | Y | Y | Y | Y | N | N | Y |
| 22 Hinchey | ? | ? | Y | Y | N | N | N |
| 23 **McHugh** | Y | Y | Y | N | Y | Y | Y |
| 24 **Boehlert** | Y | Y | Y | N | Y | Y | Y |
| 25 **Walsh** | Y | Y | Y | N | Y | Y | Y |
| 26 **Reynolds** | ? | ? | ? | N | Y | Y | Y |
| 27 Higgins | Y | Y | Y | Y | Y | N | Y |
| 28 Slaughter | Y | Y | Y | Y | N | N | Y |
| 29 **Kuhl** | Y | N | Y | N | Y | Y | Y |

| | 623 | 624 | 625 | 626 | 627 | 628 | 629 |
|---|---|---|---|---|---|---|---|
| **NORTH CAROLINA** | | | | | | | |
| 1 Butterfield | Y | Y | Y | Y | N | N | Y |
| 2 Etheridge | Y | Y | Y | Y | Y | N | Y |
| 3 **Jones** | Y | N | Y | N | N | N | Y |
| 4 Price | Y | Y | Y | Y | N | N | Y |
| 5 **Foxx** | Y | N | N | N | Y | Y | Y |
| 6 **Coble** | Y | N | ? | N | Y | Y | Y |
| 7 McIntyre | Y | Y | Y | Y | Y | N | Y |
| 8 **Hayes** | Y | N | Y | N | Y | Y | Y |
| 9 **Myrick** | Y | N | Y | N | Y | Y | Y |
| 10 **McHenry** | Y | N | Y | N | Y | Y | Y |
| 11 **Taylor** | Y | N | Y | N | N | Y | Y |
| 12 Watt | Y | Y | Y | Y | N | N | ? |
| 13 Miller | Y | Y | Y | Y | Y | N | Y |
| **NORTH DAKOTA** | | | | | | | |
| AL Pomeroy | Y | Y | Y | Y | Y | N | Y |
| **OHIO** | | | | | | | |
| 1 **Chabot** | Y | N | Y | N | Y | Y | Y |
| 2 **Schmidt** | Y | N | Y | N | Y | Y | Y |
| 3 **Turner** | Y | N | Y | N | Y | Y | Y |
| 4 **Oxley** | Y | Y | ? | N | Y | Y | Y |
| 5 **Gillmor** | Y | Y | Y | N | Y | Y | Y |
| 6 Strickland | Y | N | Y | Y | N | N | Y |
| 7 **Hobson** | Y | Y | Y | N | Y | Y | Y |
| 8 **Boehner** | Y | Y | Y | N | Y | Y | Y |
| 9 Kaptur | Y | Y | Y | Y | N | N | Y |
| 10 Kucinich | Y | Y | Y | Y | N | N | N |
| 11 Jones | Y | Y | Y | Y | N | N | Y |
| 12 **Tiberi** | Y | N | Y | N | Y | Y | Y |
| 13 Brown | Y | Y | Y | Y | N | N | Y |
| 14 **LaTourette** | Y | Y | Y | N | Y | Y | Y |
| 15 **Pryce** | Y | Y | Y | N | Y | Y | Y |
| 16 **Regula** | Y | Y | Y | N | Y | Y | Y |
| 17 Ryan | Y | Y | Y | Y | N | N | Y |
| 18 **Ney** | Y | Y | Y | N | N | Y | Y |
| **OKLAHOMA** | | | | | | | |
| 1 **Sullivan** | Y | N | Y | N | Y | Y | Y |
| 2 Boren | Y | Y | Y | Y | Y | N | Y |
| 3 **Lucas** | Y | Y | Y | N | Y | Y | Y |
| 4 **Cole** | Y | ? | Y | N | Y | Y | Y |
| 5 **Istook** | Y | N | Y | N | Y | Y | Y |
| **OREGON** | | | | | | | |
| 1 Wu | Y | Y | Y | Y | N | N | Y |
| 2 **Walden** | Y | Y | Y | N | Y | Y | Y |
| 3 Blumenauer | Y | Y | Y | Y | N | N | N |
| 4 DeFazio | Y | Y | Y | Y | N | N | N |
| 5 Hooley | Y | Y | Y | Y | N | N | Y |
| **PENNSYLVANIA** | | | | | | | |
| 1 Brady | Y | Y | Y | Y | N | N | Y |
| 2 Fattah | Y | Y | Y | Y | N | N | Y |
| 3 **English** | Y | Y | Y | N | Y | Y | Y |
| 4 **Hart** | Y | N | Y | N | Y | Y | Y |
| 5 **Peterson** | Y | N | Y | N | + | Y | Y |
| 6 **Gerlach** | Y | Y | Y | N | Y | N | Y |
| 7 **Weldon** | Y | Y | Y | N | Y | Y | Y |
| 8 **Fitzpatrick** | Y | Y | Y | N | N | N | Y |
| 9 **Shuster** | Y | N | Y | N | Y | Y | Y |
| 10 **Sherwood** | Y | Y | Y | N | Y | Y | Y |
| 11 Kanjorski | Y | Y | Y | Y | N | N | Y |
| 12 Murtha | Y | Y | ? | Y | N | N | Y |
| 13 Schwartz | Y | Y | Y | Y | Y | N | Y |
| 14 Doyle | Y | Y | Y | Y | N | N | Y |
| 15 **Dent** | Y | Y | Y | N | Y | Y | Y |
| 16 **Pitts** | Y | N | Y | N | Y | Y | Y |
| 17 Holden | Y | Y | Y | Y | Y | N | Y |
| 18 **Murphy** | Y | N | Y | N | Y | Y | Y |
| 19 **Platts** | Y | ? | ? | N | Y | N | Y |
| **RHODE ISLAND** | | | | | | | |
| 1 Kennedy | Y | Y | Y | Y | N | N | Y |
| 2 Langevin | Y | Y | Y | Y | N | N | Y |
| **SOUTH CAROLINA** | | | | | | | |
| 1 **Brown** | Y | Y | Y | N | Y | Y | Y |
| 2 **Wilson** | Y | Y | Y | N | Y | Y | Y |
| 3 **Barrett** | Y | N | Y | N | Y | Y | Y |
| 4 **Inglis** | Y | Y | Y | N | Y | Y | Y |
| 5 Spratt | Y | Y | Y | Y | Y | N | Y |
| 6 Clyburn | ? | ? | ? | Y | N | N | Y |
| **SOUTH DAKOTA** | | | | | | | |
| AL Herseth | Y | Y | Y | Y | Y | N | Y |
| **TENNESSEE** | | | | | | | |
| 1 **Jenkins** | Y | Y | ? | N | Y | Y | Y |
| 2 **Duncan** | Y | N | Y | N | N | Y | Y |

| | 623 | 624 | 625 | 626 | 627 | 628 | 629 |
|---|---|---|---|---|---|---|---|
| 3 **Wamp** | Y | N | Y | N | Y | Y | Y |
| 4 Davis | Y | Y | Y | Y | Y | N | Y |
| 5 Cooper | Y | Y | Y | Y | Y | N | Y |
| 6 Gordon | Y | Y | Y | Y | N | N | Y |
| 7 **Blackburn** | Y | N | N | N | Y | Y | Y |
| 8 Tanner | Y | Y | Y | Y | N | N | ? |
| 9 Ford | ? | ? | ? | Y | N | N | Y |
| **TEXAS** | | | | | | | |
| 1 **Gohmert** | Y | N | Y | N | Y | Y | Y |
| 2 **Poe** | Y | N | Y | ? | ? | Y | Y |
| 3 **Johnson, S.** | Y | Y | Y | N | Y | Y | Y |
| 4 **Hall** | Y | N | Y | N | Y | Y | Y |
| 5 **Hensarling** | Y | N | Y | N | Y | Y | Y |
| 6 **Barton** | Y | Y | Y | N | Y | Y | Y |
| 7 **Culberson** | Y | N | Y | N | Y | Y | Y |
| 8 **Brady** | Y | Y | Y | N | Y | Y | Y |
| 9 Green, A. | Y | Y | Y | Y | N | N | Y |
| 10 **McCaul** | Y | Y | Y | N | Y | Y | Y |
| 11 **Conaway** | Y | N | Y | N | Y | Y | Y |
| 12 **Granger** | Y | N | Y | N | Y | Y | Y |
| 13 **Thornberry** | Y | N | Y | N | Y | Y | Y |
| 14 **Paul** | Y | N | Y | Y | N | N | Y |
| 15 Hinojosa | Y | Y | Y | Y | N | N | Y |
| 16 Reyes | Y | Y | Y | Y | Y | N | Y |
| 17 Edwards | Y | Y | Y | N | Y | N | Y |
| 18 Jackson-Lee | Y | Y | Y | Y | N | N | Y |
| 19 **Neugebauer** | Y | N | Y | N | Y | Y | Y |
| 20 Gonzalez | Y | Y | Y | Y | N | N | Y |
| 21 **Smith** | Y | Y | Y | N | Y | Y | Y |
| 22 **DeLay** | Y | N | Y | N | Y | Y | Y |
| 23 **Bonilla** | Y | N | Y | N | Y | Y | Y |
| 24 **Marchant** | Y | Y | Y | N | Y | Y | Y |
| 25 Doggett | Y | Y | Y | Y | N | N | Y |
| 26 **Burgess** | Y | N | Y | N | Y | Y | Y |
| 27 Ortiz | Y | Y | Y | Y | + | N | Y |
| 28 Cuellar | Y | Y | Y | Y | Y | N | Y |
| 29 Green, G. | Y | Y | Y | Y | N | N | Y |
| 30 Johnson, E. | Y | N | Y | Y | N | N | Y |
| 31 **Carter** | Y | N | Y | N | Y | Y | Y |
| 32 **Sessions** | Y | N | Y | N | Y | Y | Y |
| **UTAH** | | | | | | | |
| 1 **Bishop** | Y | N | Y | N | N | Y | ? |
| 2 Matheson | Y | Y | Y | Y | Y | N | Y |
| 3 **Cannon** | Y | N | Y | N | Y | Y | Y |
| **VERMONT** | | | | | | | |
| AL *Sanders* | Y | Y | Y | Y | N | N | Y |
| **VIRGINIA** | | | | | | | |
| 1 **Davis, J.** | Y | N | Y | N | Y | Y | Y |
| 2 **Drake** | Y | N | Y | N | Y | Y | Y |
| 3 Scott | Y | Y | Y | Y | N | N | Y |
| 4 **Forbes** | Y | N | Y | N | Y | Y | Y |
| 5 **Goode** | ? | ? | ? | N | Y | Y | Y |
| 6 **Goodlatte** | Y | N | Y | N | Y | Y | Y |
| 7 **Cantor** | Y | Y | ? | N | Y | Y | Y |
| 8 Moran | Y | Y | Y | Y | N | N | Y |
| 9 Boucher | Y | Y | Y | Y | N | N | Y |
| 10 **Wolf** | Y | Y | Y | N | Y | Y | Y |
| 11 **Davis, T.** | Y | N | ? | N | Y | Y | Y |
| **WASHINGTON** | | | | | | | |
| 1 Inslee | Y | Y | Y | Y | N | N | Y |
| 2 Larsen | Y | Y | Y | Y | N | N | Y |
| 3 Baird | Y | Y | Y | Y | N | N | Y |
| 4 **Hastings** | Y | Y | Y | N | Y | Y | Y |
| 5 **McMorris** | Y | N | Y | N | Y | Y | Y |
| 6 Dicks | Y | Y | Y | Y | N | N | Y |
| 7 McDermott | + | + | ? | + | – | – | Y |
| 8 **Reichert** | Y | Y | Y | N | Y | Y | Y |
| 9 Smith | Y | Y | Y | Y | N | N | Y |
| **WEST VIRGINIA** | | | | | | | |
| 1 Mollohan | Y | Y | Y | Y | N | N | Y |
| 2 **Capito** | Y | Y | Y | N | Y | Y | Y |
| 3 Rahall | Y | Y | Y | Y | N | N | Y |
| **WISCONSIN** | | | | | | | |
| 1 **Ryan** | Y | N | Y | N | Y | Y | Y |
| 2 Baldwin | Y | Y | Y | Y | N | N | Y |
| 3 Kind | ? | ? | ? | Y | N | N | Y |
| 4 Moore | Y | Y | Y | Y | N | N | Y |
| 5 **Sensenbrenner** | Y | N | Y | N | Y | Y | Y |
| 6 **Petri** | Y | Y | Y | N | Y | Y | Y |
| 7 Obey | Y | Y | Y | Y | N | N | Y |
| 8 **Green** | Y | N | Y | N | Y | Y | Y |
| **WYOMING** | | | | | | | |
| AL **Cubin** | ? | ? | ? | N | Y | Y | Y |

# IN THE HOUSE | By Vote Number

**630.** **HR 2863. Fiscal 2006 Defense Appropriations/Motion to Instruct.** Murtha, D-Pa., motion to instruct House conferees to include Senate-passed language that would establish the U.S. Army Field Manual on Intelligence Interrogation as the uniform standard for interrogating persons detained by the Department of Defense, and prohibit cruel, inhuman or degrading treatment of any prisoner detained by the U.S. government. Motion agreed to 308-122: R 107-121; D 200-1 (ND 150-0, SD 50-1); I 1-0. A "nay" was a vote was a vote in support of the president's position. Dec. 14, 2005.

**631.** **H Res 599. Ocean Policy Task Force/Adoption.** Hastings, R-Wash., motion to suspend the rules and adopt the resolution that would establish a House Task Force on Ocean Policy to make recommendations on the final report of the U.S. Commission on Ocean Policy and report these recommendations to the House. Motion rejected 103-327: R 93-134; D 10-192 (ND 9-142, SD 1-50); I 0-1. A two-thirds majority of those present and voting (287 in this case) is required for adoption under suspension of the rules. Dec. 14, 2005.

**632.** **HR 972. Trafficking Victims Protection Reauthorization/Passage.** Smith, R-N.J., motion to suspend the rules and pass the bill that would reauthorize the Trafficking Victims Protection Act of 2000. It would authorize $15 million in fiscal 2006 to remain available until spent for the FBI to investigate severe forms of trafficking and $18 million per year in fiscal 2006-07 for investigations by Immigration and Customs Enforcement in the Homeland Security Department. Motion agreed to 426-0: R 225-0; D 201-0 (ND 151-0, SD 50-0); I 0-0. A two-thirds majority of those present and voting (284 in this case) is required for passage under suspension of the rules. Dec. 14, 2005.

**633.** **HR 2830. Pension Overhaul/Rule.** Adoption of the rule (H Res 602) to provide for House floor consideration of the bill that would overhaul federal pension laws. Adopted 226-199: R 224-1; D 2-197 (ND 1-149, SD 1-48); I 0-1. Dec. 15, 2005.

**634.** **HR 2830. Pension Overhaul/Recommit.** Miller, D-Calif., motion to recommit the bill to the Education and the Workforce and Ways and Means committees with instructions to substitute the text of a Democratic bill that would make it harder for companies to declare bankruptcy or eliminate workers' pensions, and include relief for struggling airlines and multi-employer plans. Motion rejected 200-227: R 0-226; D 199-1 (ND 149-1, SD 50-0); I 1-0. Dec. 15, 2005.

**635.** **HR 2830. Pension Overhaul/Passage.** Passage of the bill that would overhaul federal pension law and increase the premiums companies pay to the Pension Benefit Guaranty Corporation to $30 per participant from $19. It would establish a premium for employers who terminate their pension plans on an involuntary basis. It also would require employers to make sufficient contributions to meet a 100 percent funding target. Passed 294-132: R 224-1; D 70-130 (ND 49-101, SD 21-29); I 0-1. Dec. 15, 2005.

**636.** **HR 4437. Border Security/Rule.** Adoption of the rule (H Res 610) that would provide for House floor consideration of the bill to increase security at the international border and at ports of entry into the United States. Adopted 220-206: R 219-7; D 1-198 (ND 1-148, SD 0-50); I 0-1. Dec. 15, 2005.

| | 630 | 631 | 632 | 633 | 634 | 635 | 636 |
|---|---|---|---|---|---|---|---|
| **ALABAMA** | | | | | | | |
| 1 Bonner | N | N | Y | Y | N | Y | Y |
| 2 Everett | N | N | Y | Y | N | Y | Y |
| 3 Rogers | N | Y | Y | Y | N | Y | Y |
| 4 Aderholt | N | N | Y | Y | N | Y | Y |
| 5 Cramer | Y | N | Y | N | Y | Y | Y |
| 6 Bachus | Y | N | Y | N | Y | Y | Y |
| 7 Davis | Y | N | Y | N | Y | N | N |
| **ALASKA** | | | | | | | |
| AL Young | N | Y | Y | Y | N | Y | Y |
| **ARIZONA** | | | | | | | |
| 1 Renzi | N | N | Y | Y | N | Y | Y |
| 2 Franks | N | N | Y | Y | N | Y | Y |
| 3 Shadegg | N | N | Y | Y | N | Y | Y |
| 4 Pastor | Y | N | Y | N | Y | Y | N |
| 5 Hayworth | N | N | Y | Y | N | Y | N |
| 6 Flake | Y | N | Y | Y | N | Y | Y |
| 7 Grijalva | Y | N | Y | N | Y | N | N |
| 8 Kolbe | Y | Y | Y | Y | N | Y | N |
| **ARKANSAS** | | | | | | | |
| 1 Berry | Y | N | Y | N | Y | Y | N |
| 2 Snyder | Y | N | Y | N | Y | Y | N |
| 3 Boozman | Y | N | Y | Y | Y | Y | N |
| 4 Ross | Y | N | Y | N | Y | Y | N |
| **CALIFORNIA** | | | | | | | |
| 1 Thompson | Y | N | Y | N | Y | N | N |
| 2 Herger | N | N | Y | Y | N | Y | Y |
| 3 Lungren | N | N | Y | Y | N | Y | Y |
| 4 Doolittle | N | N | Y | Y | N | Y | Y |
| 5 Matsui, D. | Y | N | Y | N | Y | N | N |
| 6 Woolsey | Y | N | Y | N | Y | N | N |
| 7 Miller, George | Y | N | Y | N | Y | N | N |
| 8 Pelosi | Y | N | Y | N | Y | N | N |
| 9 Lee | Y | N | Y | N | Y | N | N |
| 10 Tauscher | Y | N | Y | N | Y | Y | N |
| 11 Pombo | Y | N | Y | Y | N | Y | Y |
| 12 Lantos | Y | N | Y | N | Y | N | N |
| 13 Stark | Y | N | Y | N | Y | N | N |
| 14 Eshoo | Y | N | Y | N | Y | N | N |
| 15 Honda | Y | N | Y | N | Y | N | N |
| 16 Lofgren | Y | N | Y | N | Y | N | N |
| 17 Farr | Y | N | Y | N | Y | N | N |
| 18 Cardoza | Y | Y | Y | N | Y | N | N |
| 19 Radanovich | N | N | Y | Y | N | Y | Y |
| 20 Costa | + | N | Y | N | Y | N | N |
| 21 Nunes | N | N | Y | Y | N | Y | Y |
| 22 Thomas | Y | N | Y | N | Y | N | Y |
| 23 Capps | Y | N | Y | N | Y | N | N |
| 24 Gallegly | N | N | Y | Y | N | Y | Y |
| 25 McKeon | N | N | Y | Y | N | Y | Y |
| 26 Dreier | N | Y | Y | Y | N | Y | Y |
| 27 Sherman | Y | N | Y | N | Y | N | N |
| 28 Berman | Y | N | Y | N | Y | N | N |
| 29 Schiff | Y | N | Y | N | Y | N | N |
| 30 Waxman | Y | N | Y | N | Y | N | N |
| 31 Becerra | Y | N | Y | N | Y | N | N |
| 32 Solis | Y | N | Y | N | Y | N | N |
| 33 Watson | Y | N | Y | N | Y | N | N |
| 34 Roybal-Allard | Y | N | Y | N | Y | N | N |
| 35 Waters | Y | N | Y | N | ? | ? | ? |
| 36 Harman | Y | N | Y | N | Y | Y | N |
| 37 Millender-McD. | Y | N | Y | N | Y | N | N |
| 38 Napolitano | Y | N | Y | N | Y | N | N |
| 39 Sánchez, Linda | Y | N | Y | N | Y | N | N |
| 40 Royce | N | N | Y | Y | N | Y | Y |
| 41 Lewis | N | N | Y | Y | N | Y | Y |
| 42 Miller, Gary | N | N | Y | Y | N | Y | Y |
| 43 Baca | Y | N | Y | N | Y | N | N |
| 44 Calvert | N | N | Y | Y | N | Y | Y |
| 45 Bono | N | N | Y | Y | N | Y | Y |
| 46 Rohrabacher | N | N | Y | Y | N | Y | Y |
| 47 Sanchez, Loretta | Y | N | Y | N | Y | N | N |
| 48 Campbell | N | N | Y | Y | N | Y | Y |
| 49 Issa | Y | N | Y | N | Y | Y | Y |

| | 630 | 631 | 632 | 633 | 634 | 635 | 636 |
|---|---|---|---|---|---|---|---|
| 50 Vacant | | | | | | | |
| 51 Filner | Y | N | Y | N | Y | N | N |
| 52 Hunter | N | Y | Y | N | Y | N | ? |
| 53 Davis | Y | N | Y | N | Y | N | N |
| **COLORADO** | | | | | | | |
| 1 DeGette | Y | N | Y | N | Y | N | N |
| 2 Udall | Y | N | Y | N | Y | N | N |
| 3 Salazar | Y | N | Y | N | Y | N | N |
| 4 Musgrave | N | N | Y | Y | N | Y | Y |
| 5 Hefley | N | N | Y | N | Y | N | Y |
| 6 Tancredo | Y | N | Y | N | Y | N | Y |
| 7 Beauprez | Y | N | Y | Y | N | Y | Y |
| **CONNECTICUT** | | | | | | | |
| 1 Larson | Y | N | Y | N | Y | N | N |
| 2 Simmons | Y | Y | Y | Y | N | Y | Y |
| 3 DeLauro | Y | N | Y | N | Y | N | N |
| 4 Shays | Y | Y | Y | Y | N | Y | Y |
| 5 Johnson | Y | Y | Y | Y | N | Y | Y |
| **DELAWARE** | | | | | | | |
| AL Castle | Y | Y | Y | Y | N | Y | N |
| **FLORIDA** | | | | | | | |
| 1 Miller | N | N | Y | Y | N | Y | Y |
| 2 Boyd | Y | N | Y | N | Y | N | N |
| 3 Brown | Y | N | Y | N | Y | N | N |
| 4 Crenshaw | N | N | Y | Y | N | Y | Y |
| 5 Brown-Waite | N | N | Y | Y | N | Y | Y |
| 6 Stearns | N | N | Y | Y | N | Y | Y |
| 7 Mica | N | Y | Y | Y | N | Y | Y |
| 8 Keller | Y | N | Y | Y | N | Y | Y |
| 9 Bilirakis | N | Y | Y | Y | N | Y | Y |
| 10 Young | N | N | Y | Y | N | Y | Y |
| 11 Davis | Y | N | ? | ? | ? | ? | ? |
| 12 Putnam | Y | Y | Y | Y | N | Y | Y |
| 13 Harris | Y | Y | Y | Y | N | Y | Y |
| 14 Mack | Y | Y | Y | N | Y | N | Y |
| 15 Weldon | Y | Y | Y | Y | N | Y | Y |
| 16 Foley | Y | N | Y | Y | N | Y | Y |
| 17 Meek | Y | N | Y | N | Y | N | N |
| 18 Ros-Lehtinen | Y | Y | Y | Y | N | Y | Y |
| 19 Wexler | Y | N | Y | N | Y | N | N |
| 20 Wasserman-Schultz | Y | N | Y | N | Y | N | N |
| 21 Diaz-Balart, L. | Y | Y | Y | Y | N | ? | Y |
| 22 Shaw | Y | Y | Y | Y | N | Y | Y |
| 23 Hastings | Y | N | Y | N | Y | N | N |
| 24 Feeney | N | N | Y | Y | N | Y | Y |
| 25 Diaz-Balart, M. | + | + | + | + | - | + | + |
| **GEORGIA** | | | | | | | |
| 1 Kingston | N | Y | Y | Y | N | Y | Y |
| 2 Bishop | Y | N | Y | N | Y | Y | N |
| 3 Marshall | N | N | Y | N | Y | Y | N |
| 4 McKinney | Y | N | Y | N | Y | N | N |
| 5 Lewis | Y | N | Y | N | Y | N | N |
| 6 Price | N | N | Y | Y | N | Y | Y |
| 7 Linder | N | N | Y | Y | N | Y | Y |
| 8 Westmoreland | N | N | Y | Y | N | Y | Y |
| 9 Norwood | N | N | Y | Y | N | Y | Y |
| 10 Deal | N | N | Y | Y | N | Y | Y |
| 11 Gingrey | N | N | Y | Y | N | Y | Y |
| 12 Barrow | Y | N | Y | N | Y | Y | N |
| 13 Scott | Y | N | Y | N | Y | Y | N |
| **HAWAII** | | | | | | | |
| 1 Abercrombie | Y | Y | Y | N | Y | N | N |
| 2 Case | Y | Y | Y | N | Y | Y | Y |
| **IDAHO** | | | | | | | |
| 1 Otter | Y | N | Y | Y | N | Y | Y |
| 2 Simpson | N | Y | Y | Y | N | Y | Y |
| **ILLINOIS** | | | | | | | |
| 1 Rush | Y | N | Y | N | Y | N | N |
| 2 Jackson | Y | N | Y | N | Y | N | N |
| 3 Lipinski | Y | N | Y | N | Y | Y | N |
| 4 Gutierrez | Y | N | Y | N | Y | N | N |
| 5 Emanuel | Y | N | Y | N | Y | N | N |
| 6 Hyde | + | - | + | + | - | + | + |
| 7 Davis | Y | N | Y | N | Y | N | N |
| 8 Bean | Y | N | Y | N | Y | Y | N |
| 9 Schakowsky | Y | N | Y | N | Y | N | N |
| 10 Kirk | Y | Y | Y | Y | N | Y | Y |
| 11 Weller | Y | Y | Y | Y | N | Y | Y |
| 12 Costello | Y | N | Y | N | Y | Y | N |

| | 630 | 631 | 632 | 633 | 634 | 635 | 636 |
|---|---|---|---|---|---|---|---|
| 13 **Biggert** | Y | Y | Y | Y | N | Y | Y |
| 14 **Hastert** | | | | | | | |
| 15 **Johnson** | Y | Y | Y | Y | N | Y | Y |
| 16 **Manzullo** | Y | N | Y | Y | N | Y | Y |
| 17 Evans | Y | N | Y | N | Y | N | N |
| 18 **LaHood** | N | N | Y | Y | N | Y | Y |
| 19 **Shimkus** | Y | N | Y | Y | N | Y | Y |
| **INDIANA** | | | | | | | |
| 1 Visclosky | Y | N | Y | N | Y | N | N |
| 2 **Chocola** | Y | N | Y | Y | N | Y | Y |
| 3 **Souder** | N | Y | Y | Y | N | Y | ? |
| 4 **Buyer** | N | N | ? | Y | N | Y | Y |
| 5 **Burton** | N | N | Y | Y | N | Y | Y |
| 6 **Pence** | N | N | Y | Y | N | Y | Y |
| 7 Carson | Y | N | Y | N | Y | N | N |
| 8 **Hostettler** | N | N | Y | Y | N | Y | Y |
| 9 **Sodrel** | Y | N | Y | Y | N | Y | Y |
| **IOWA** | | | | | | | |
| 1 **Nussle** | Y | N | Y | Y | N | Y | Y |
| 2 **Leach** | Y | Y | Y | Y | N | Y | N |
| 3 Boswell | Y | N | Y | N | Y | Y | N |
| 4 **Latham** | Y | Y | Y | Y | N | Y | Y |
| 5 **King** | N | N | Y | Y | N | Y | Y |
| **KANSAS** | | | | | | | |
| 1 **Moran** | Y | N | Y | Y | N | Y | Y |
| 2 **Ryun** | N | N | Y | Y | N | Y | Y |
| 3 Moore | Y | N | Y | N | Y | Y | N |
| 4 **Tiahrt** | N | N | Y | Y | N | Y | Y |
| **KENTUCKY** | | | | | | | |
| 1 **Whitfield** | Y | Y | Y | Y | N | Y | Y |
| 2 **Lewis** | N | Y | Y | Y | N | Y | Y |
| 3 **Northup** | Y | N | Y | Y | N | Y | Y |
| 4 **Davis** | Y | N | Y | Y | N | Y | Y |
| 5 **Rogers** | N | Y | Y | Y | N | Y | Y |
| 6 Chandler | Y | N | Y | N | Y | Y | N |
| **LOUISIANA** | | | | | | | |
| 1 **Jindal** | N | N | Y | Y | N | Y | Y |
| 2 Jefferson | Y | N | Y | N | Y | N | N |
| 3 Melancon | Y | Y | Y | N | Y | Y | N |
| 4 **McCrery** | Y | Y | Y | Y | N | Y | Y |
| 5 **Alexander** | Y | N | Y | Y | N | Y | Y |
| 6 **Baker** | N | N | Y | Y | N | Y | Y |
| 7 **Boustany** | Y | N | Y | Y | N | Y | Y |
| **MAINE** | | | | | | | |
| 1 Allen | Y | Y | Y | N | Y | N | N |
| 2 Michaud | Y | Y | Y | N | Y | N | N |
| **MARYLAND** | | | | | | | |
| 1 **Gilchrest** | Y | Y | Y | Y | N | ? | Y |
| 2 Ruppersberger | Y | Y | Y | N | Y | N | N |
| 3 Cardin | Y | Y | Y | N | Y | N | N |
| 4 Wynn | Y | N | Y | N | Y | Y | N |
| 5 Hoyer | Y | N | Y | N | Y | N | N |
| 6 **Bartlett** | Y | Y | Y | Y | N | Y | Y |
| 7 Cummings | Y | N | Y | N | Y | N | N |
| 8 Van Hollen | Y | Y | Y | N | Y | N | N |
| **MASSACHUSETTS** | | | | | | | |
| 1 Olver | Y | N | Y | N | Y | N | N |
| 2 Neal | Y | N | Y | N | Y | N | N |
| 3 McGovern | Y | N | Y | N | Y | N | N |
| 4 Frank | Y | N | Y | N | Y | N | N |
| 5 Meehan | Y | N | Y | N | Y | N | N |
| 6 Tierney | Y | N | Y | N | Y | N | N |
| 7 Markey | Y | N | Y | N | Y | N | N |
| 8 Capuano | Y | N | Y | N | Y | Y | N |
| 9 Lynch | Y | N | Y | N | Y | Y | N |
| 10 Delahunt | Y | N | Y | N | Y | N | N |
| **MICHIGAN** | | | | | | | |
| 1 Stupak | Y | N | Y | N | Y | Y | N |
| 2 **Hoekstra** | N | Y | Y | Y | N | Y | Y |
| 3 **Ehlers** | Y | Y | Y | Y | N | Y | Y |
| 4 **Camp** | Y | N | Y | Y | N | Y | Y |
| 5 Kildee | Y | N | Y | N | Y | Y | N |
| 6 **Upton** | Y | Y | Y | Y | N | Y | Y |
| 7 **Schwarz** | Y | Y | Y | Y | N | Y | Y |
| 8 **Rogers** | N | Y | Y | Y | N | Y | Y |
| 9 **Knollenberg** | Y | N | Y | Y | N | Y | Y |
| 10 **Miller** | Y | Y | Y | Y | N | Y | Y |
| 11 **McCotter** | Y | N | Y | Y | N | Y | Y |
| 12 Levin | Y | N | Y | N | Y | N | N |
| 13 Kilpatrick | Y | N | Y | N | Y | Y | N |
| 14 Conyers | Y | N | Y | N | Y | Y | N |
| 15 Dingell | Y | N | Y | N | Y | Y | N |

| | 630 | 631 | 632 | 633 | 634 | 635 | 636 |
|---|---|---|---|---|---|---|---|
| **MINNESOTA** | | | | | | | |
| 1 **Gutknecht** | Y | N | Y | Y | N | Y | Y |
| 2 **Kline** | Y | N | Y | Y | N | Y | Y |
| 3 **Ramstad** | Y | Y | Y | Y | N | Y | Y |
| 4 McCollum | Y | N | Y | N | Y | N | N |
| 5 Sabo | Y | N | Y | N | Y | N | N |
| 6 **Kennedy** | Y | N | Y | Y | N | Y | Y |
| 7 Peterson | Y | N | Y | N | Y | Y | N |
| 8 Oberstar | Y | N | Y | Y | Y | Y | N |
| **MISSISSIPPI** | | | | | | | |
| 1 **Wicker** | N | N | Y | Y | N | Y | Y |
| 2 Thompson | Y | N | Y | N | Y | N | N |
| 3 **Pickering** | Y | N | Y | Y | - | + | Y |
| 4 Taylor | Y | N | Y | N | Y | N | N |
| **MISSOURI** | | | | | | | |
| 1 Clay | Y | N | Y | N | Y | Y | N |
| 2 **Akin** | N | Y | Y | Y | N | Y | Y |
| 3 Carnahan | Y | N | Y | N | Y | N | N |
| 4 Skelton | Y | N | Y | N | Y | N | N |
| 5 Cleaver | Y | N | Y | N | Y | Y | N |
| 6 **Graves** | N | N | Y | Y | N | Y | Y |
| 7 **Blunt** | N | Y | Y | Y | N | Y | Y |
| 8 **Emerson** | Y | N | Y | Y | N | Y | Y |
| 9 **Hulshof** | Y | N | Y | Y | N | Y | Y |
| **MONTANA** | | | | | | | |
| AL **Rehberg** | N | Y | Y | Y | N | Y | Y |
| **NEBRASKA** | | | | | | | |
| 1 **Fortenberry** | Y | Y | Y | Y | N | Y | Y |
| 2 **Terry** | N | N | Y | Y | N | Y | Y |
| 3 **Osborne** | Y | Y | Y | Y | N | Y | Y |
| **NEVADA** | | | | | | | |
| 1 Berkley | Y | N | Y | - | Y | N | N |
| 2 **Gibbons** | Y | N | Y | Y | N | Y | Y |
| 3 **Porter** | Y | N | Y | Y | N | Y | Y |
| **NEW HAMPSHIRE** | | | | | | | |
| 1 **Bradley** | Y | Y | Y | Y | N | Y | Y |
| 2 **Bass** | Y | Y | Y | Y | N | Y | Y |
| **NEW JERSEY** | | | | | | | |
| 1 Andrews | Y | N | Y | N | Y | Y | N |
| 2 **LoBiondo** | Y | N | Y | Y | N | Y | Y |
| 3 **Saxton** | Y | Y | Y | Y | N | Y | Y |
| 4 **Smith** | Y | Y | Y | Y | N | Y | Y |
| 5 **Garrett** | N | N | Y | Y | N | Y | Y |
| 6 Pallone | Y | N | Y | N | Y | N | N |
| 7 **Ferguson** | Y | ? | ? | Y | N | Y | Y |
| 8 Pascrell | Y | N | Y | N | Y | Y | N |
| 9 Rothman | Y | N | Y | N | Y | Y | N |
| 10 Payne | Y | N | Y | N | Y | N | N |
| 11 **Frelinghuysen** | N | Y | Y | Y | N | Y | Y |
| 12 Holt | Y | N | Y | N | Y | N | N |
| 13 Menendez | Y | N | Y | N | Y | Y | N |
| **NEW MEXICO** | | | | | | | |
| 1 **Wilson** | Y | Y | Y | Y | N | Y | N |
| 2 **Pearce** | N | N | Y | Y | ? | Y | Y |
| 3 Udall | Y | N | Y | N | Y | N | N |
| **NEW YORK** | | | | | | | |
| 1 Bishop | Y | N | Y | N | Y | N | N |
| 2 Israel | Y | N | Y | N | Y | Y | N |
| 3 **King** | N | Y | Y | Y | N | Y | Y |
| 4 McCarthy | Y | N | Y | N | Y | Y | N |
| 5 Ackerman | Y | N | Y | N | Y | N | N |
| 6 Meeks | Y | N | Y | N | Y | Y | N |
| 7 Crowley | Y | N | Y | N | Y | N | N |
| 8 Nadler | Y | N | Y | N | Y | N | N |
| 9 Weiner | Y | N | Y | N | Y | N | N |
| 10 Towns | Y | N | Y | N | Y | N | N |
| 11 Owens | Y | N | Y | N | Y | N | N |
| 12 Velázquez | Y | N | Y | N | Y | N | N |
| 13 **Fossella** | N | Y | Y | ? | N | Y | Y |
| 14 Maloney | Y | N | Y | N | Y | N | N |
| 15 Rangel | Y | N | Y | N | Y | N | N |
| 16 Serrano | Y | N | Y | N | Y | N | N |
| 17 Engel | Y | N | Y | N | Y | Y | N |
| 18 Lowey | Y | N | Y | N | Y | N | N |
| 19 **Kelly** | Y | Y | Y | Y | N | Y | Y |
| 20 **Sweeney** | Y | Y | Y | Y | N | Y | Y |
| 21 McNulty | Y | N | Y | N | Y | Y | N |
| 22 Hinchey | Y | N | Y | N | Y | N | N |
| 23 **McHugh** | Y | Y | Y | ? | N | Y | Y |
| 24 **Boehlert** | Y | Y | Y | Y | N | Y | Y |
| 25 **Walsh** | Y | Y | Y | Y | N | Y | Y |
| 26 **Reynolds** | Y | Y | Y | Y | N | Y | Y |
| 27 Higgins | Y | N | Y | N | Y | Y | N |
| 28 Slaughter | Y | N | Y | N | Y | N | N |
| 29 **Kuhl** | Y | N | Y | Y | N | Y | Y |

| | 630 | 631 | 632 | 633 | 634 | 635 | 636 |
|---|---|---|---|---|---|---|---|
| **NORTH CAROLINA** | | | | | | | |
| 1 Butterfield | Y | N | Y | N | Y | N | N |
| 2 Etheridge | Y | N | Y | N | Y | N | N |
| 3 **Jones** | Y | Y | Y | Y | N | Y | Y |
| 4 Price | Y | N | Y | N | Y | N | N |
| 5 **Foxx** | N | N | Y | Y | N | Y | Y |
| 6 **Coble** | N | N | Y | Y | N | Y | Y |
| 7 McIntyre | Y | N | Y | N | Y | Y | N |
| 8 **Hayes** | N | N | Y | Y | N | Y | Y |
| 9 **Myrick** | N | Y | Y | Y | N | Y | Y |
| 10 **McHenry** | N | N | Y | Y | N | Y | Y |
| 11 **Taylor** | N | N | Y | Y | N | Y | Y |
| 12 Watt | Y | N | Y | N | Y | N | N |
| 13 Miller | Y | N | Y | N | Y | N | N |
| **NORTH DAKOTA** | | | | | | | |
| AL Pomeroy | Y | N | Y | N | Y | N | N |
| **OHIO** | | | | | | | |
| 1 **Chabot** | N | N | Y | Y | N | Y | Y |
| 2 **Schmidt** | N | N | Y | Y | N | Y | Y |
| 3 **Turner** | N | N | Y | Y | N | Y | Y |
| 4 **Oxley** | N | N | Y | Y | N | Y | Y |
| 5 **Gillmor** | N | Y | Y | Y | N | Y | Y |
| 6 Strickland | Y | N | Y | N | Y | Y | N |
| 7 **Hobson** | N | Y | Y | Y | N | Y | Y |
| 8 **Boehner** | N | Y | Y | Y | N | Y | Y |
| 9 Kaptur | Y | N | Y | N | Y | N | N |
| 10 Kucinich | Y | N | Y | N | Y | Y | N |
| 11 Jones | Y | N | Y | N | Y | N | N |
| 12 **Tiberi** | Y | N | Y | Y | N | Y | Y |
| 13 Brown | Y | N | Y | N | Y | Y | N |
| 14 **LaTourette** | Y | N | Y | Y | N | Y | Y |
| 15 **Pryce** | Y | Y | Y | Y | N | Y | Y |
| 16 **Regula** | Y | Y | Y | Y | N | Y | Y |
| 17 Ryan | Y | N | Y | N | Y | Y | N |
| 18 **Ney** | N | N | Y | Y | N | Y | Y |
| **OKLAHOMA** | | | | | | | |
| 1 **Sullivan** | N | N | Y | Y | N | Y | Y |
| 2 Boren | Y | N | Y | N | Y | Y | N |
| 3 **Lucas** | N | N | Y | Y | N | Y | Y |
| 4 **Cole** | N | N | Y | Y | N | Y | Y |
| 5 **Istook** | N | N | ? | Y | N | Y | Y |
| **OREGON** | | | | | | | |
| 1 Wu | Y | N | Y | N | Y | Y | N |
| 2 **Walden** | Y | Y | Y | Y | N | Y | Y |
| 3 Blumenauer | Y | N | Y | N | Y | N | N |
| 4 DeFazio | Y | N | Y | N | Y | N | N |
| 5 Hooley | Y | N | Y | N | Y | Y | N |
| **PENNSYLVANIA** | | | | | | | |
| 1 Brady | Y | N | Y | N | Y | Y | N |
| 2 Fattah | Y | N | Y | N | Y | Y | N |
| 3 **English** | Y | Y | Y | Y | N | Y | Y |
| 4 **Hart** | N | N | Y | Y | N | Y | Y |
| 5 **Peterson** | N | N | Y | Y | N | Y | Y |
| 6 **Gerlach** | Y | Y | Y | Y | N | Y | Y |
| 7 **Weldon** | Y | Y | Y | Y | N | Y | Y |
| 8 **Fitzpatrick** | Y | N | Y | ? | N | Y | Y |
| 9 **Shuster** | N | Y | Y | Y | N | Y | Y |
| 10 **Sherwood** | Y | Y | Y | Y | N | Y | Y |
| 11 Kanjorski | Y | N | Y | N | Y | N | N |
| 12 Murtha | Y | N | Y | N | Y | N | N |
| 13 Schwartz | Y | N | Y | N | Y | N | N |
| 14 Doyle | Y | N | Y | N | Y | N | N |
| 15 **Dent** | Y | Y | Y | Y | N | Y | Y |
| 16 **Pitts** | Y | N | Y | Y | N | Y | Y |
| 17 Holden | Y | N | Y | N | Y | Y | N |
| 18 **Murphy** | Y | N | Y | Y | N | Y | Y |
| 19 **Platts** | Y | Y | Y | Y | N | Y | Y |
| **RHODE ISLAND** | | | | | | | |
| 1 Kennedy | Y | N | Y | N | Y | N | N |
| 2 Langevin | Y | N | Y | N | Y | N | N |
| **SOUTH CAROLINA** | | | | | | | |
| 1 **Brown** | N | N | Y | Y | N | Y | Y |
| 2 **Wilson** | N | N | Y | Y | N | Y | Y |
| 3 **Barrett** | N | N | Y | Y | N | Y | Y |
| 4 **Inglis** | Y | N | Y | Y | N | Y | Y |
| 5 Spratt | Y | N | Y | N | Y | N | N |
| 6 Clyburn | Y | N | Y | N | Y | N | N |
| **SOUTH DAKOTA** | | | | | | | |
| AL Herseth | Y | N | Y | N | Y | Y | N |
| **TENNESSEE** | | | | | | | |
| 1 **Jenkins** | Y | Y | Y | Y | N | Y | Y |
| 2 **Duncan** | Y | Y | Y | Y | N | Y | Y |

| | 630 | 631 | 632 | 633 | 634 | 635 | 636 |
|---|---|---|---|---|---|---|---|
| 3 **Wamp** | Y | Y | Y | Y | N | Y | Y |
| 4 Davis | Y | N | Y | N | Y | Y | N |
| 5 Cooper | Y | N | Y | N | Y | Y | N |
| 6 Gordon | Y | N | Y | N | Y | Y | N |
| 7 **Blackburn** | N | N | Y | Y | N | Y | Y |
| 8 Tanner | Y | N | Y | N | Y | Y | N |
| 9 Ford | Y | N | Y | N | Y | Y | N |
| **TEXAS** | | | | | | | |
| 1 **Gohmert** | N | N | Y | Y | N | Y | Y |
| 2 **Poe** | N | N | Y | Y | N | Y | Y |
| 3 **Johnson, S.** | N | N | Y | Y | N | Y | Y |
| 4 **Hall** | N | N | Y | Y | N | Y | Y |
| 5 **Hensarling** | N | N | Y | Y | N | Y | Y |
| 6 **Barton** | N | Y | Y | Y | N | Y | Y |
| 7 **Culberson** | N | N | Y | Y | N | Y | Y |
| 8 **Brady** | N | N | Y | Y | N | Y | Y |
| 9 Green, A. | Y | N | Y | N | Y | N | N |
| 10 **McCaul** | Y | Y | Y | Y | N | Y | Y |
| 11 **Conaway** | N | N | Y | Y | N | Y | Y |
| 12 **Granger** | N | N | Y | Y | N | Y | Y |
| 13 **Thornberry** | N | N | Y | Y | N | Y | Y |
| 14 **Paul** | Y | N | Y | N | N | Y | Y |
| 15 Hinojosa | Y | N | Y | N | Y | N | N |
| 16 Reyes | Y | N | Y | N | Y | N | N |
| 17 Edwards | Y | N | Y | N | Y | Y | N |
| 18 Jackson-Lee | Y | N | Y | N | Y | N | N |
| 19 **Neugebauer** | N | N | Y | Y | N | Y | Y |
| 20 Gonzalez | Y | N | Y | N | Y | N | N |
| 21 **Smith** | N | Y | Y | Y | N | Y | Y |
| 22 **DeLay** | N | Y | Y | Y | N | Y | Y |
| 23 **Bonilla** | N | N | Y | Y | N | Y | Y |
| 24 **Marchant** | N | N | Y | Y | N | Y | Y |
| 25 Doggett | Y | N | Y | N | Y | N | N |
| 26 **Burgess** | N | Y | Y | Y | N | Y | Y |
| 27 Ortiz | Y | N | Y | N | Y | N | N |
| 28 Cuellar | Y | N | Y | Y | Y | Y | N |
| 29 Green, G. | Y | N | Y | N | Y | Y | N |
| 30 Johnson, E. | Y | N | Y | N | Y | N | N |
| 31 **Carter** | N | N | Y | Y | N | Y | Y |
| 32 **Sessions** | N | N | Y | Y | N | Y | Y |
| **UTAH** | | | | | | | |
| 1 **Bishop** | N | Y | Y | Y | N | Y | Y |
| 2 Matheson | Y | N | Y | N | N | Y | N |
| 3 **Cannon** | N | Y | Y | Y | N | Y | Y |
| **VERMONT** | | | | | | | |
| AL *Sanders* | Y | N | ? | N | Y | N | N |
| **VIRGINIA** | | | | | | | |
| 1 **Davis, J.** | Y | N | Y | Y | N | Y | Y |
| 2 **Drake** | N | N | Y | Y | N | Y | Y |
| 3 Scott | Y | N | Y | N | Y | N | N |
| 4 **Forbes** | Y | N | Y | Y | N | Y | Y |
| 5 **Goode** | N | N | Y | Y | N | Y | Y |
| 6 **Goodlatte** | Y | N | Y | Y | N | Y | Y |
| 7 **Cantor** | N | N | Y | Y | N | Y | Y |
| 8 Moran | Y | N | Y | N | Y | N | N |
| 9 Boucher | Y | N | Y | ? | Y | N | N |
| 10 **Wolf** | Y | Y | Y | Y | N | Y | Y |
| 11 **Davis, T.** | Y | Y | Y | Y | N | Y | Y |
| **WASHINGTON** | | | | | | | |
| 1 Inslee | Y | Y | Y | N | Y | Y | N |
| 2 Larsen | Y | N | Y | N | Y | Y | N |
| 3 Baird | Y | N | Y | N | Y | N | N |
| 4 **Hastings** | N | Y | Y | Y | N | Y | Y |
| 5 **McMorris** | Y | N | Y | Y | N | Y | Y |
| 6 Dicks | Y | N | Y | N | Y | N | N |
| 7 McDermott | Y | N | Y | N | Y | N | N |
| 8 **Reichert** | Y | N | Y | Y | N | Y | Y |
| 9 Smith | Y | N | Y | N | Y | Y | N |
| **WEST VIRGINIA** | | | | | | | |
| 1 Mollohan | Y | N | Y | N | Y | N | N |
| 2 **Capito** | Y | Y | Y | Y | N | Y | Y |
| 3 Rahall | Y | N | Y | N | Y | Y | N |
| **WISCONSIN** | | | | | | | |
| 1 **Ryan** | Y | N | Y | Y | N | Y | Y |
| 2 Baldwin | Y | N | Y | N | Y | N | N |
| 3 Kind | Y | N | Y | N | Y | Y | N |
| 4 Moore | Y | N | Y | N | Y | N | N |
| 5 **Sensenbrenner** | Y | Y | Y | Y | N | Y | Y |
| 6 **Petri** | Y | Y | Y | Y | N | Y | Y |
| 7 Obey | Y | N | Y | N | Y | N | N |
| 8 **Green** | Y | N | Y | Y | N | Y | Y |
| **WYOMING** | | | | | | | |
| AL **Cubin** | N | Y | Y | Y | N | Y | Y |

# IN THE HOUSE | By Vote Number

**637.** **H Res 579. Christmas Symbols and Traditions/Adoption.** Porter, R-Nev., motion to suspend the rules and adopt the resolution that would recognize the importance of the symbols and traditions of Christmas and strongly disapprove of attempts to ban references to Christmas. Motion agreed to 401-22: R 228-0; D 172-22 (ND 128-16, SD 44-6); I 1-0. A two-thirds majority of those present and voting (282 in this case) is required for adoption under suspension of the rules. Dec. 15, 2005.

**638.** **H Con Res 315. American Jewish History Month/Adoption.** Porter, R-Nev., motion to suspend the rules and adopt the concurrent resolution that would urge the president to issue an annual proclamation calling for the observance of an American Jewish History Month in January. Motion agreed to 423-0: R 225-0; D 197-0 (ND 148-0, SD 49-0); I 1-0. A two-thirds majority of those present and voting (282 in this case) is required for adoption under suspension of the rules. Dec. 15, 2005.

**639.** **HR 4437. Border Security/Removal Process.** Jackson-Lee, D-Texas, amendment that would direct the Homeland Security Department to create a program under which certain illegal immigrants undergoing expedited removal could be released to the custody of an individual or group who would monitor them and ensure that they make required court appearances. Rejected 162-252: R 0-218; D 161-34 (ND 128-17, SD 33-17); I 1-0. Dec. 15, 2005.

**640.** **HR 4437. Border Security/Security Fencing.** Hunter, R-Calif., amendment that would require the construction of security fencing, including lights and cameras, along certain ports of entry along the U.S.-Mexico border. Adopted 260-159: R 211-12; D 49-146 (ND 28-117, SD 21-29); I 0-1. Dec. 15, 2005.

**641.** **H Con Res 312. Russia and NGOs/Adoption.** Smith, R-N.J., motion to suspend the rules and adopt the concurrent resolution that would state that Congress urges the Russian government to withdraw draft legislation that would have the effect of severely restricting the activities of non-governmental organizations in Russia. Motion agreed to 405-15: R 211-12; D 193-3 (ND 145-2, SD 48-1); I 1-0. A two-thirds majority of those present and voting (280 in this case) is required for adoption under suspension of the rules. Dec. 15, 2005.

**642.** **HR 1815. Fiscal 2006 Defense Authorization/Motion to Close Conference.** Drake, R-Va., motion to close portions of the conference on the bill that would authorize funding for defense programs for fiscal 2006. Motion agreed to 409-12: R 221-0; D 187-12 (ND 138-10, SD 49-2); I 1-0. Dec. 16, 2005.

**643.** **HR 1815. Fiscal 2006 Defense Authorization/Motion to Instruct.** Skelton, D-Mo., motion to instruct House conferees to include Senate-passed language that would require the Defense secretary and the director of National Intelligence to submit a report within 60 days of the bill's enactment on clandestine U.S. detention facilities abroad. Motion agreed to 228-187: R 31-186; D 196-1 (ND 147-0, SD 49-1); I 1-0. Dec. 16, 2005.

**644.** **H Res 612. Commitment to Iraq Victory/Previous Question.** Dreier, R-Calif., motion to order the previous question (thus ending debate and the possibility of amendment) on adoption of the rule (H Res 619) for House floor consideration of the resolution that would express the commitment of the House of Representatives to achieving victory in Iraq. Motion agreed to 221-200: R 221-0; D 0-199 (ND 0-148, SD 0-51); I 0-1. Dec. 16, 2005.

| | 637 | 638 | 639 | 640 | 641 | 642 | 643 | 644 |
|---|---|---|---|---|---|---|---|---|
| **ALABAMA** | | | | | | | | |
| 1 Bonner | Y | Y | N | Y | Y | Y | N | Y |
| 2 Everett | Y | Y | N | Y | Y | Y | N | Y |
| 3 Rogers | Y | Y | N | Y | Y | Y | N | Y |
| 4 Aderholt | Y | Y | N | Y | Y | Y | N | Y |
| 5 Cramer | Y | Y | N | Y | Y | Y | Y | N |
| 6 Bachus | Y | Y | N | Y | Y | Y | N | Y |
| 7 Davis | Y | Y | N | N | Y | Y | Y | N |
| **ALASKA** | | | | | | | | |
| AL Young | Y | Y | ? | ? | ? | Y | N | Y |
| **ARIZONA** | | | | | | | | |
| 1 Renzi | Y | Y | N | Y | Y | Y | N | Y |
| 2 Franks | Y | Y | N | Y | Y | Y | N | Y |
| 3 Shadegg | Y | Y | N | Y | Y | Y | N | Y |
| 4 Pastor | Y | Y | Y | N | Y | Y | Y | N |
| 5 Hayworth | Y | Y | N | Y | Y | Y | N | Y |
| 6 Flake | Y | Y | Y | Y | Y | Y | N | Y |
| 7 Grijalva | Y | Y | Y | N | Y | Y | Y | N |
| 8 Kolbe | Y | Y | N | Y | Y | Y | N | Y |
| **ARKANSAS** | | | | | | | | |
| 1 Berry | Y | Y | N | Y | Y | Y | N | Y |
| 2 Snyder | Y | Y | N | N | Y | Y | Y | N |
| 3 Boozman | Y | Y | N | Y | Y | Y | N | Y |
| 4 Ross | Y | Y | N | Y | Y | Y | Y | N |
| **CALIFORNIA** | | | | | | | | |
| 1 Thompson | Y | Y | N | N | Y | Y | Y | N |
| 2 Herger | Y | ? | N | Y | Y | Y | N | Y |
| 3 Lungren | Y | Y | N | Y | Y | Y | N | Y |
| 4 Doolittle | Y | Y | N | Y | Y | Y | N | Y |
| 5 Matsui, D. | Y | Y | Y | N | Y | Y | Y | Y |
| 6 Woolsey | N | Y | Y | N | Y | N | Y | N |
| 7 Miller, George | N | Y | N | Y | Y | N | Y | N |
| 8 Pelosi | Y | Y | Y | N | Y | Y | Y | N |
| 9 Lee | N | Y | Y | N | Y | N | Y | N |
| 10 Tauscher | Y | Y | Y | N | Y | Y | Y | N |
| 11 Pombo | Y | Y | N | Y | Y | Y | N | Y |
| 12 Lantos | Y | Y | N | Y | Y | Y | Y | N |
| 13 Stark | N | Y | N | N | Y | N | Y | N |
| 14 Eshoo | Y | Y | Y | N | Y | Y | Y | N |
| 15 Honda | N | Y | N | N | Y | Y | Y | N |
| 16 Lofgren | Y | Y | N | Y | Y | Y | Y | N |
| 17 Farr | Y | Y | N | N | Y | Y | Y | N |
| 18 Cardoza | Y | Y | N | Y | Y | Y | Y | N |
| 19 Radanovich | Y | Y | N | N | Y | N | N | Y |
| 20 Costa | Y | Y | N | Y | Y | Y | Y | N |
| 21 Nunes | Y | Y | N | Y | Y | Y | N | Y |
| 22 Thomas | Y | Y | ? | Y | Y | Y | N | Y |
| 23 Capps | N | Y | Y | N | Y | Y | Y | N |
| 24 Gallegly | Y | Y | N | Y | Y | Y | N | Y |
| 25 McKeon | Y | Y | N | Y | Y | Y | N | Y |
| 26 Dreier | Y | Y | N | Y | Y | Y | N | Y |
| 27 Sherman | Y | Y | Y | N | Y | Y | Y | N |
| 28 Berman | Y | Y | Y | N | Y | Y | Y | N |
| 29 Schiff | Y | Y | N | Y | Y | Y | + | Y |
| 30 Waxman | Y | Y | Y | N | Y | Y | Y | N |
| 31 Becerra | Y | Y | N | Y | Y | Y | Y | N |
| 32 Solis | Y | Y | Y | N | Y | Y | Y | N |
| 33 Watson | Y | Y | N | N | Y | Y | Y | N |
| 34 Roybal-Allard | Y | Y | N | Y | Y | Y | Y | N |
| 35 Waters | ? | ? | ? | ? | ? | N | Y | N |
| 36 Harman | N | Y | N | N | Y | Y | Y | N |
| 37 Millender-McD. | Y | Y | Y | N | Y | Y | Y | N |
| 38 Napolitano | Y | Y | Y | N | Y | ? | ? | ? |
| 39 Sánchez, Linda | Y | Y | Y | N | Y | Y | Y | N |
| 40 Royce | Y | Y | N | Y | Y | Y | N | Y |
| 41 Lewis | Y | Y | N | Y | Y | Y | N | Y |
| 42 Miller, Gary | Y | Y | N | Y | Y | Y | N | Y |
| 43 Baca | Y | Y | N | Y | Y | Y | Y | N |
| 44 Calvert | Y | Y | N | Y | Y | Y | N | Y |
| 45 Bono | Y | Y | N | Y | Y | Y | N | Y |
| 46 Rohrabacher | Y | Y | N | Y | Y | Y | N | Y |
| 47 Sanchez, Loretta | Y | Y | N | Y | Y | Y | Y | N |
| 48 Campbell | Y | Y | N | Y | Y | Y | N | Y |
| 49 Issa | Y | Y | N | Y | Y | Y | N | Y |

| | 637 | 638 | 639 | 640 | 641 | 642 | 643 | 644 |
|---|---|---|---|---|---|---|---|---|
| 50 Vacant | | | | | | | | |
| 51 Filner | Y | Y | Y | N | Y | Y | Y | N |
| 52 Hunter | Y | ? | N | Y | Y | Y | N | Y |
| 53 Davis | Y | Y | Y | N | Y | Y | Y | N |
| **COLORADO** | | | | | | | | |
| 1 DeGette | N | Y | Y | N | Y | Y | Y | N |
| 2 Udall | Y | Y | Y | N | Y | Y | Y | N |
| 3 Salazar | Y | Y | Y | N | Y | Y | Y | N |
| 4 Musgrave | Y | Y | N | Y | Y | Y | N | Y |
| 5 Hefley | Y | Y | N | Y | Y | Y | N | Y |
| 6 Tancredo | Y | Y | N | Y | Y | Y | N | Y |
| 7 Beauprez | Y | Y | N | Y | Y | Y | N | Y |
| **CONNECTICUT** | | | | | | | | |
| 1 Larson | Y | Y | N | Y | Y | Y | Y | N |
| 2 Simmons | Y | Y | Y | Y | Y | Y | Y | Y |
| 3 DeLauro | Y | Y | Y | N | Y | Y | Y | N |
| 4 Shays | Y | Y | Y | Y | Y | Y | Y | Y |
| 5 Johnson | Y | Y | N | Y | Y | Y | N | Y |
| **DELAWARE** | | | | | | | | |
| AL Castle | Y | Y | N | Y | Y | Y | Y | Y |
| **FLORIDA** | | | | | | | | |
| 1 Miller | Y | Y | N | Y | Y | Y | N | Y |
| 2 Boyd | Y | Y | N | Y | Y | Y | Y | N |
| 3 Brown | Y | Y | Y | N | ? | Y | Y | N |
| 4 Crenshaw | Y | Y | N | Y | Y | Y | N | Y |
| 5 Brown-Waite | Y | Y | N | Y | Y | Y | N | Y |
| 6 Stearns | Y | Y | N | Y | Y | Y | N | Y |
| 7 Mica | Y | Y | N | Y | Y | Y | N | Y |
| 8 Keller | Y | Y | N | Y | Y | Y | N | Y |
| 9 Bilirakis | Y | Y | N | Y | Y | Y | N | Y |
| 10 Young | Y | Y | N | Y | Y | Y | N | Y |
| 11 Davis | ? | ? | ? | ? | ? | Y | Y | N |
| 12 Putnam | Y | Y | N | Y | Y | – | Y | Y |
| 13 Harris | Y | Y | N | Y | Y | Y | N | Y |
| 14 Mack | Y | Y | N | Y | Y | Y | N | Y |
| 15 Weldon | Y | Y | N | Y | Y | Y | N | Y |
| 16 Foley | Y | Y | N | Y | Y | Y | Y | Y |
| 17 Meek | Y | Y | Y | N | Y | Y | Y | N |
| 18 Ros-Lehtinen | Y | Y | N | Y | Y | Y | N | Y |
| 19 Wexler | N | Y | Y | N | Y | Y | Y | N |
| 20 Wasserman-Schultz | N | Y | Y | N | Y | Y | Y | N |
| 21 Diaz-Balart, L. | Y | Y | N | Y | Y | Y | N | Y |
| 22 Shaw | Y | Y | N | Y | Y | Y | N | Y |
| 23 Hastings | N | Y | N | N | Y | Y | Y | N |
| 24 Feeney | Y | Y | ? | Y | Y | Y | ? | Y |
| 25 Diaz-Balart, M. | + | + | – | – | + | + | – | + |
| **GEORGIA** | | | | | | | | |
| 1 Kingston | Y | Y | N | Y | Y | Y | N | Y |
| 2 Bishop | Y | Y | Y | Y | Y | Y | Y | N |
| 3 Marshall | Y | Y | N | Y | Y | Y | Y | N |
| 4 McKinney | Y | Y | N | Y | N | N | Y | N |
| 5 Lewis | N | Y | N | Y | Y | Y | Y | N |
| 6 Price | Y | Y | N | Y | Y | Y | N | Y |
| 7 Linder | Y | Y | N | Y | Y | Y | N | Y |
| 8 Westmoreland | Y | Y | N | Y | Y | Y | N | Y |
| 9 Norwood | Y | Y | N | Y | Y | Y | N | Y |
| 10 Deal | Y | ? | N | Y | Y | Y | N | Y |
| 11 Gingrey | Y | Y | N | Y | Y | Y | N | Y |
| 12 Barrow | Y | Y | N | Y | Y | Y | Y | N |
| 13 Scott | Y | Y | Y | Y | Y | Y | Y | N |
| **HAWAII** | | | | | | | | |
| 1 Abercrombie | Y | Y | Y | N | N | Y | Y | N |
| 2 Case | Y | Y | N | Y | Y | Y | Y | N |
| **IDAHO** | | | | | | | | |
| 1 Otter | Y | Y | N | N | N | N | Y | Y |
| 2 Simpson | Y | Y | N | Y | Y | Y | N | Y |
| **ILLINOIS** | | | | | | | | |
| 1 Rush | N | Y | Y | N | N | Y | Y | N |
| 2 Jackson | Y | Y | Y | N | Y | Y | Y | N |
| 3 Lipinski | Y | Y | Y | Y | Y | Y | Y | N |
| 4 Gutierrez | Y | Y | Y | N | Y | Y | Y | N |
| 5 Emanuel | + | + | + | – | + | Y | Y | N |
| 6 Hyde | + | + | – | + | + | + | – | + |
| 7 Davis | Y | Y | Y | N | Y | Y | Y | N |
| 8 Bean | Y | Y | N | Y | Y | Y | Y | N |
| 9 Schakowsky | N | Y | Y | N | Y | Y | Y | N |
| 10 Kirk | Y | Y | N | Y | ? | Y | – | Y |
| 11 Weller | Y | Y | N | Y | Y | Y | N | Y |
| 12 Costello | Y | Y | N | Y | Y | Y | Y | N |

**KEY**    Republicans    Democrats    *Independents*

| | | | |
|---|---|---|---|
| **Y** Voted for (yea) | **X** Paired against | **C** Voted "present" to avoid possible conflict of interest |
| **#** Paired for | **–** Announced against | |
| **+** Announced for | **P** Voted "present" | **?** Did not vote or otherwise make a position known |
| **N** Voted against (nay) | | |

| | 637 | 638 | 639 | 640 | 641 | 642 | 643 | 644 |
|---|---|---|---|---|---|---|---|---|
| 13 **Biggert** | Y | Y | N | Y | Y | Y | N | Y |
| 14 **Hastert** | | | | | | | | |
| 15 **Johnson** | Y | Y | N | Y | Y | Y | N | Y |
| 16 **Manzullo** | Y | Y | N | Y | Y | Y | N | Y |
| 17 Evans | Y | Y | Y | N | Y | Y | Y | N |
| 18 **LaHood** | Y | Y | ? | ? | ? | ? | ? | ? |
| 19 **Shimkus** | Y | Y | N | Y | Y | Y | N | Y |
| **INDIANA** | | | | | | | | |
| 1 Visclosky | Y | Y | N | N | Y | Y | Y | N |
| 2 **Chocola** | Y | Y | N | Y | Y | Y | N | Y |
| 3 **Souder** | Y | Y | N | Y | Y | Y | N | Y |
| 4 **Buyer** | Y | Y | N | Y | Y | Y | N | Y |
| 5 **Burton** | Y | Y | N | Y | Y | Y | N | Y |
| 6 **Pence** | Y | Y | N | Y | Y | Y | N | Y |
| 7 Carson | Y | Y | Y | N | Y | Y | Y | N |
| 8 **Hostettler** | Y | Y | N | Y | Y | Y | N | Y |
| 9 **Sodrel** | Y | Y | N | Y | Y | Y | N | Y |
| **IOWA** | | | | | | | | |
| 1 **Nussle** | Y | Y | N | Y | Y | Y | N | Y |
| 2 **Leach** | Y | Y | N | Y | Y | Y | Y | Y |
| 3 Boswell | Y | Y | Y | Y | Y | Y | Y | N |
| 4 **Latham** | Y | Y | N | Y | Y | Y | N | Y |
| 5 **King** | Y | Y | N | Y | Y | Y | N | Y |
| **KANSAS** | | | | | | | | |
| 1 **Moran** | Y | Y | N | Y | Y | Y | Y | Y |
| 2 **Ryun** | Y | Y | N | Y | Y | Y | N | Y |
| 3 Moore | Y | Y | Y | Y | Y | Y | Y | N |
| 4 **Tiahrt** | Y | Y | N | Y | Y | Y | N | Y |
| **KENTUCKY** | | | | | | | | |
| 1 **Whitfield** | Y | Y | N | Y | Y | Y | Y | Y |
| 2 **Lewis** | Y | Y | N | Y | Y | Y | N | Y |
| 3 **Northup** | Y | Y | N | Y | Y | Y | N | Y |
| 4 **Davis** | Y | Y | N | Y | Y | Y | Y | Y |
| 5 **Rogers** | Y | Y | N | Y | Y | Y | N | Y |
| 6 Chandler | Y | Y | N | Y | Y | Y | Y | N |
| **LOUISIANA** | | | | | | | | |
| 1 **Jindal** | Y | Y | N | Y | Y | Y | N | Y |
| 2 Jefferson | Y | Y | Y | N | Y | Y | Y | N |
| 3 Melancon | Y | Y | N | Y | Y | Y | Y | N |
| 4 **McCrery** | Y | Y | N | Y | Y | Y | N | Y |
| 5 **Alexander** | Y | Y | N | Y | Y | Y | N | Y |
| 6 **Baker** | Y | Y | N | Y | Y | Y | N | Y |
| 7 **Boustany** | Y | Y | N | Y | Y | Y | N | Y |
| **MAINE** | | | | | | | | |
| 1 Allen | Y | Y | Y | N | Y | Y | Y | N |
| 2 Michaud | Y | Y | Y | N | Y | Y | Y | N |
| **MARYLAND** | | | | | | | | |
| 1 **Gilchrest** | Y | Y | N | Y | Y | Y | Y | Y |
| 2 Ruppersberger | Y | Y | Y | Y | Y | Y | Y | N |
| 3 Cardin | Y | Y | Y | N | Y | Y | Y | N |
| 4 Wynn | Y | Y | Y | N | Y | Y | Y | N |
| 5 Hoyer | Y | Y | Y | N | Y | Y | Y | N |
| 6 **Bartlett** | Y | Y | N | Y | Y | Y | Y | Y |
| 7 Cummings | Y | Y | Y | N | Y | Y | Y | N |
| 8 Van Hollen | Y | Y | N | Y | Y | Y | Y | N |
| **MASSACHUSETTS** | | | | | | | | |
| 1 Olver | Y | Y | Y | N | Y | N | Y | N |
| 2 Neal | Y | Y | Y | N | Y | Y | Y | N |
| 3 McGovern | Y | Y | Y | N | Y | Y | Y | N |
| 4 Frank | Y | Y | Y | N | Y | Y | Y | N |
| 5 Meehan | Y | Y | Y | N | Y | Y | Y | N |
| 6 Tierney | Y | ? | Y | N | Y | Y | Y | N |
| 7 Markey | Y | Y | Y | N | Y | Y | Y | N |
| 8 Capuano | Y | Y | Y | N | Y | Y | Y | N |
| 9 Lynch | Y | Y | ? | ? | Y | Y | Y | N |
| 10 Delahunt | Y | Y | N | Y | Y | Y | Y | N |
| **MICHIGAN** | | | | | | | | |
| 1 Stupak | Y | Y | N | Y | Y | Y | Y | N |
| 2 **Hoekstra** | Y | Y | N | Y | Y | Y | N | Y |
| 3 **Ehlers** | Y | Y | N | N | Y | Y | Y | Y |
| 4 **Camp** | Y | Y | N | Y | Y | Y | N | Y |
| 5 Kildee | Y | Y | Y | N | Y | Y | Y | N |
| 6 **Upton** | Y | Y | N | Y | Y | Y | Y | Y |
| 7 **Schwarz** | Y | Y | N | Y | Y | Y | N | Y |
| 8 **Rogers** | Y | Y | ? | Y | Y | Y | N | Y |
| 9 **Knollenberg** | Y | Y | N | Y | Y | Y | N | Y |
| 10 **Miller** | Y | Y | N | Y | Y | Y | N | Y |
| 11 **McCotter** | Y | Y | N | Y | Y | Y | Y | Y |
| 12 Levin | Y | Y | Y | N | Y | Y | Y | N |
| 13 Kilpatrick | Y | Y | Y | N | Y | Y | Y | N |
| 14 Conyers | Y | Y | Y | N | Y | Y | Y | N |
| 15 Dingell | Y | Y | Y | N | Y | Y | Y | N |

| | 637 | 638 | 639 | 640 | 641 | 642 | 643 | 644 |
|---|---|---|---|---|---|---|---|---|
| **MINNESOTA** | | | | | | | | |
| 1 **Gutknecht** | Y | Y | N | Y | N | Y | N | Y |
| 2 **Kline** | Y | Y | N | Y | Y | Y | N | Y |
| 3 **Ramstad** | Y | Y | N | Y | Y | Y | N | Y |
| 4 McCollum | Y | Y | Y | N | Y | Y | Y | N |
| 5 Sabo | Y | Y | Y | N | Y | Y | Y | N |
| 6 **Kennedy** | Y | Y | N | Y | Y | Y | N | Y |
| 7 Peterson | Y | Y | N | Y | Y | Y | Y | N |
| 8 Oberstar | Y | Y | Y | N | Y | Y | Y | N |
| **MISSISSIPPI** | | | | | | | | |
| 1 **Wicker** | Y | Y | N | Y | Y | Y | N | Y |
| 2 Thompson | Y | Y | Y | N | Y | Y | Y | N |
| 3 **Pickering** | Y | Y | N | Y | Y | Y | N | Y |
| 4 Taylor | Y | Y | N | Y | Y | Y | Y | N |
| **MISSOURI** | | | | | | | | |
| 1 Clay | Y | Y | ? | ? | Y | Y | Y | N |
| 2 **Akin** | Y | Y | N | Y | Y | Y | ? | Y |
| 3 Carnahan | Y | Y | Y | N | Y | Y | Y | N |
| 4 Skelton | Y | Y | N | Y | Y | Y | Y | N |
| 5 Cleaver | N | Y | Y | N | Y | Y | Y | N |
| 6 **Graves** | Y | Y | N | Y | Y | Y | N | Y |
| 7 **Blunt** | Y | Y | N | Y | Y | Y | N | Y |
| 8 **Emerson** | Y | Y | N | Y | Y | Y | Y | Y |
| 9 **Hulshof** | Y | Y | N | Y | Y | Y | Y | Y |
| **MONTANA** | | | | | | | | |
| AL **Rehberg** | Y | Y | N | Y | Y | Y | N | Y |
| **NEBRASKA** | | | | | | | | |
| 1 **Fortenberry** | Y | Y | N | Y | Y | Y | N | Y |
| 2 **Terry** | Y | Y | N | Y | Y | Y | N | Y |
| 3 **Osborne** | Y | Y | N | Y | Y | Y | N | Y |
| **NEVADA** | | | | | | | | |
| 1 Berkley | Y | Y | Y | Y | Y | Y | Y | N |
| 2 **Gibbons** | Y | Y | N | Y | Y | Y | Y | Y |
| 3 **Porter** | Y | Y | N | Y | Y | Y | Y | Y |
| **NEW HAMPSHIRE** | | | | | | | | |
| 1 **Bradley** | Y | Y | N | Y | Y | Y | N | Y |
| 2 **Bass** | Y | Y | N | Y | Y | Y | N | Y |
| **NEW JERSEY** | | | | | | | | |
| 1 Andrews | Y | Y | Y | N | Y | Y | Y | N |
| 2 **LoBiondo** | Y | Y | N | Y | Y | Y | N | Y |
| 3 **Saxton** | Y | Y | ? | Y | N | Y | N | Y |
| 4 **Smith** | Y | Y | N | Y | Y | Y | Y | Y |
| 5 **Garrett** | Y | Y | N | Y | Y | Y | N | Y |
| 6 Pallone | Y | Y | Y | N | Y | Y | Y | N |
| 7 **Ferguson** | Y | Y | N | Y | Y | Y | N | Y |
| 8 Pascrell | Y | Y | Y | N | Y | Y | Y | N |
| 9 Rothman | Y | Y | Y | N | Y | Y | Y | N |
| 10 Payne | N | Y | Y | N | Y | ? | ? | ? |
| 11 **Frelinghuysen** | Y | Y | N | Y | Y | Y | N | Y |
| 12 Holt | P | Y | Y | N | Y | Y | Y | N |
| 13 Menendez | Y | Y | Y | N | Y | Y | Y | N |
| **NEW MEXICO** | | | | | | | | |
| 1 **Wilson** | Y | Y | N | N | Y | Y | N | Y |
| 2 **Pearce** | Y | Y | N | N | Y | ? | ? | ? |
| 3 Udall | Y | Y | Y | N | Y | Y | Y | N |
| **NEW YORK** | | | | | | | | |
| 1 Bishop | Y | Y | Y | Y | Y | Y | Y | N |
| 2 Israel | P | Y | Y | Y | Y | Y | Y | N |
| 3 **King** | Y | Y | N | Y | Y | Y | N | Y |
| 4 McCarthy | Y | Y | + | + | + | + | + | - |
| 5 Ackerman | N | Y | Y | N | Y | Y | Y | N |
| 6 Meeks | Y | Y | ? | ? | Y | Y | Y | N |
| 7 Crowley | Y | Y | Y | N | Y | Y | Y | N |
| 8 Nadler | Y | Y | Y | N | Y | Y | Y | N |
| 9 Weiner | Y | Y | Y | N | Y | Y | Y | N |
| 10 Towns | Y | Y | Y | N | Y | Y | Y | N |
| 11 Owens | P | Y | Y | N | Y | Y | Y | N |
| 12 Velázquez | Y | Y | Y | N | Y | Y | Y | N |
| 13 **Fossella** | Y | Y | N | Y | Y | Y | N | Y |
| 14 Maloney | Y | Y | Y | Y | Y | Y | Y | N |
| 15 Rangel | Y | Y | Y | N | Y | Y | Y | N |
| 16 Serrano | Y | Y | Y | N | Y | Y | Y | N |
| 17 Engel | Y | Y | Y | N | Y | Y | Y | N |
| 18 Lowey | P | Y | Y | N | Y | Y | Y | N |
| 19 **Kelly** | Y | Y | N | Y | Y | Y | Y | Y |
| 20 **Sweeney** | Y | Y | ? | ? | ? | ? | ? | ? |
| 21 McNulty | Y | Y | Y | N | Y | Y | Y | N |
| 22 Hinchey | Y | Y | Y | Y | Y | N | Y | N |
| 23 **McHugh** | Y | Y | N | Y | Y | Y | N | Y |
| 24 **Boehlert** | Y | Y | N | N | Y | Y | Y | Y |
| 25 **Walsh** | Y | Y | N | Y | Y | Y | N | Y |
| 26 **Reynolds** | Y | Y | N | N | Y | Y | N | Y |
| 27 Higgins | Y | Y | Y | Y | Y | Y | Y | N |
| 28 Slaughter | Y | Y | Y | N | Y | Y | Y | N |
| 29 **Kuhl** | Y | Y | N | Y | Y | Y | N | Y |

| | 637 | 638 | 639 | 640 | 641 | 642 | 643 | 644 |
|---|---|---|---|---|---|---|---|---|
| **NORTH CAROLINA** | | | | | | | | |
| 1 Butterfield | Y | Y | Y | N | Y | Y | Y | N |
| 2 Etheridge | Y | Y | Y | Y | Y | Y | Y | N |
| 3 **Jones** | Y | Y | N | Y | N | Y | Y | Y |
| 4 Price | Y | Y | Y | N | Y | Y | Y | N |
| 5 **Foxx** | Y | Y | N | Y | Y | Y | N | Y |
| 6 **Coble** | Y | Y | N | Y | N | Y | N | Y |
| 7 McIntyre | Y | Y | N | Y | Y | Y | Y | N |
| 8 **Hayes** | Y | Y | N | Y | Y | Y | N | Y |
| 9 **Myrick** | Y | Y | N | Y | Y | Y | N | Y |
| 10 **McHenry** | Y | Y | N | Y | Y | Y | N | Y |
| 11 **Taylor** | Y | Y | N | Y | N | Y | N | Y |
| 12 Watt | Y | Y | Y | N | Y | Y | Y | N |
| 13 Miller | Y | Y | Y | Y | Y | Y | Y | N |
| **NORTH DAKOTA** | | | | | | | | |
| AL Pomeroy | Y | Y | N | Y | Y | Y | Y | N |
| **OHIO** | | | | | | | | |
| 1 **Chabot** | Y | Y | N | Y | Y | Y | Y | Y |
| 2 **Schmidt** | Y | Y | N | Y | Y | Y | N | Y |
| 3 **Turner** | Y | Y | N | Y | Y | Y | N | Y |
| 4 **Oxley** | Y | Y | N | Y | Y | Y | N | Y |
| 5 **Gillmor** | Y | Y | N | Y | Y | Y | N | Y |
| 6 Strickland | Y | Y | Y | N | Y | Y | Y | N |
| 7 **Hobson** | Y | Y | N | Y | Y | Y | N | Y |
| 8 **Boehner** | Y | Y | N | Y | Y | Y | N | Y |
| 9 Kaptur | Y | Y | Y | N | Y | Y | Y | N |
| 10 Kucinich | Y | Y | Y | N | N | N | Y | N |
| 11 Jones | Y | Y | Y | N | Y | Y | Y | N |
| 12 **Tiberi** | Y | Y | N | Y | Y | Y | N | Y |
| 13 Brown | Y | Y | Y | N | Y | Y | Y | N |
| 14 **LaTourette** | Y | Y | N | Y | Y | Y | N | Y |
| 15 **Pryce** | Y | Y | N | Y | Y | Y | N | Y |
| 16 **Regula** | Y | Y | N | Y | Y | Y | N | Y |
| 17 Ryan | Y | Y | Y | Y | Y | Y | Y | N |
| 18 **Ney** | Y | Y | N | Y | Y | Y | N | Y |
| **OKLAHOMA** | | | | | | | | |
| 1 **Sullivan** | Y | Y | N | Y | Y | Y | N | Y |
| 2 Boren | Y | Y | N | Y | Y | Y | Y | N |
| 3 **Lucas** | Y | Y | N | Y | Y | Y | N | Y |
| 4 **Cole** | Y | Y | N | Y | Y | Y | N | Y |
| 5 **Istook** | Y | Y | N | Y | Y | ? | ? | ? |
| **OREGON** | | | | | | | | |
| 1 Wu | Y | Y | Y | N | Y | Y | Y | N |
| 2 **Walden** | Y | Y | N | Y | Y | Y | Y | Y |
| 3 Blumenauer | N | Y | Y | N | Y | N | Y | N |
| 4 DeFazio | Y | Y | Y | N | Y | N | Y | N |
| 5 Hooley | Y | Y | Y | Y | Y | Y | Y | N |
| **PENNSYLVANIA** | | | | | | | | |
| 1 Brady | Y | Y | Y | N | Y | Y | Y | N |
| 2 Fattah | Y | Y | Y | N | Y | Y | Y | N |
| 3 **English** | Y | Y | N | Y | Y | Y | N | Y |
| 4 **Hart** | Y | Y | N | Y | Y | Y | N | Y |
| 5 **Peterson** | Y | Y | N | Y | Y | Y | N | Y |
| 6 **Gerlach** | Y | Y | N | Y | Y | Y | Y | Y |
| 7 **Weldon** | Y | Y | N | Y | N | Y | N | Y |
| 8 **Fitzpatrick** | Y | Y | N | Y | Y | Y | Y | Y |
| 9 **Shuster** | Y | Y | N | Y | Y | Y | N | Y |
| 10 **Sherwood** | Y | Y | N | Y | Y | Y | N | Y |
| 11 Kanjorski | Y | Y | N | Y | Y | Y | Y | N |
| 12 Murtha | Y | Y | Y | Y | ? | Y | Y | N |
| 13 Schwartz | P | Y | Y | N | Y | Y | Y | N |
| 14 Doyle | Y | Y | Y | N | Y | Y | Y | N |
| 15 **Dent** | Y | Y | N | Y | Y | Y | N | Y |
| 16 **Pitts** | Y | Y | N | Y | Y | Y | N | Y |
| 17 Holden | Y | Y | N | Y | Y | Y | Y | N |
| 18 **Murphy** | Y | Y | N | Y | Y | Y | N | Y |
| 19 **Platts** | Y | Y | N | Y | Y | Y | Y | Y |
| **RHODE ISLAND** | | | | | | | | |
| 1 Kennedy | Y | Y | Y | N | Y | Y | Y | N |
| 2 Langevin | Y | Y | Y | N | Y | Y | Y | N |
| **SOUTH CAROLINA** | | | | | | | | |
| 1 **Brown** | Y | Y | N | Y | Y | Y | N | Y |
| 2 **Wilson** | Y | Y | N | Y | Y | Y | N | Y |
| 3 **Barrett** | Y | Y | N | Y | Y | + | - | + |
| 4 **Inglis** | Y | Y | N | Y | Y | Y | Y | Y |
| 5 Spratt | Y | Y | Y | Y | Y | Y | Y | N |
| 6 Clyburn | Y | Y | Y | N | Y | Y | Y | N |
| **SOUTH DAKOTA** | | | | | | | | |
| AL Herseth | Y | Y | N | Y | Y | Y | Y | N |
| **TENNESSEE** | | | | | | | | |
| 1 **Jenkins** | Y | Y | N | Y | N | Y | N | Y |
| 2 **Duncan** | Y | Y | N | Y | N | Y | N | Y |

| | 637 | 638 | 639 | 640 | 641 | 642 | 643 | 644 |
|---|---|---|---|---|---|---|---|---|
| 3 **Wamp** | Y | Y | N | Y | N | Y | N | Y |
| 4 Davis | Y | Y | N | Y | Y | Y | Y | N |
| 5 Cooper | Y | Y | Y | N | Y | Y | Y | N |
| 6 Gordon | Y | Y | N | Y | Y | Y | Y | N |
| 7 **Blackburn** | Y | Y | N | Y | Y | Y | N | Y |
| 8 Tanner | Y | Y | N | Y | Y | Y | Y | N |
| 9 Ford | Y | Y | Y | N | Y | Y | Y | N |
| **TEXAS** | | | | | | | | |
| 1 **Gohmert** | Y | Y | N | Y | Y | Y | N | Y |
| 2 **Poe** | Y | Y | N | Y | Y | Y | N | Y |
| 3 **Johnson, S.** | Y | Y | N | Y | Y | Y | N | Y |
| 4 **Hall** | Y | Y | N | Y | Y | Y | N | Y |
| 5 **Hensarling** | Y | Y | N | Y | Y | Y | N | Y |
| 6 **Barton** | Y | Y | - | + | + | + | - | + |
| 7 **Culberson** | Y | Y | N | Y | Y | Y | N | Y |
| 8 **Brady** | Y | Y | N | Y | Y | Y | N | Y |
| 9 Green, A. | Y | Y | Y | N | Y | Y | Y | N |
| 10 **McCaul** | Y | Y | N | Y | Y | Y | N | Y |
| 11 **Conaway** | Y | Y | N | N | Y | Y | N | Y |
| 12 **Granger** | Y | Y | N | N | Y | Y | N | Y |
| 13 **Thornberry** | Y | Y | N | Y | Y | Y | N | Y |
| 14 **Paul** | Y | Y | N | N | N | Y | Y | Y |
| 15 Hinojosa | Y | Y | Y | N | Y | Y | Y | N |
| 16 Reyes | Y | Y | Y | N | Y | Y | Y | N |
| 17 Edwards | Y | Y | N | Y | Y | Y | ? | N |
| 18 Jackson-Lee | Y | Y | Y | N | Y | Y | Y | N |
| 19 **Neugebauer** | Y | Y | N | Y | Y | Y | N | Y |
| 20 Gonzalez | Y | + | Y | N | Y | Y | Y | N |
| 21 **Smith** | Y | Y | N | Y | Y | Y | N | Y |
| 22 **DeLay** | Y | Y | ? | Y | Y | Y | N | Y |
| 23 **Bonilla** | Y | Y | N | N | Y | Y | N | Y |
| 24 **Marchant** | Y | Y | N | Y | Y | Y | N | Y |
| 25 Doggett | Y | Y | Y | N | Y | Y | Y | N |
| 26 **Burgess** | Y | Y | N | Y | Y | Y | N | Y |
| 27 Ortiz | Y | Y | Y | N | Y | Y | Y | N |
| 28 Cuellar | Y | Y | Y | N | Y | Y | Y | N |
| 29 Green, G. | Y | Y | Y | N | Y | Y | Y | N |
| 30 Johnson, E. | Y | Y | Y | N | Y | Y | Y | N |
| 31 **Carter** | Y | Y | N | Y | Y | Y | N | Y |
| 32 **Sessions** | Y | Y | N | Y | Y | Y | N | Y |
| **UTAH** | | | | | | | | |
| 1 **Bishop** | Y | Y | N | Y | Y | Y | N | Y |
| 2 Matheson | Y | Y | N | Y | Y | Y | Y | N |
| 3 **Cannon** | Y | Y | N | ? | Y | Y | N | Y |
| **VERMONT** | | | | | | | | |
| AL *Sanders* | Y | Y | Y | N | Y | Y | Y | N |
| **VIRGINIA** | | | | | | | | |
| 1 **Davis, J.** | Y | Y | N | Y | Y | + | + | + |
| 2 **Drake** | Y | Y | N | Y | Y | Y | N | Y |
| 3 Scott | N | Y | Y | N | Y | Y | Y | N |
| 4 **Forbes** | Y | Y | N | Y | Y | Y | N | Y |
| 5 **Goode** | Y | Y | N | Y | Y | Y | N | Y |
| 6 **Goodlatte** | Y | Y | N | Y | Y | Y | N | Y |
| 7 **Cantor** | Y | Y | ? | Y | Y | Y | N | Y |
| 8 Moran | N | Y | Y | N | Y | Y | Y | N |
| 9 Boucher | Y | Y | Y | Y | Y | Y | Y | N |
| 10 **Wolf** | Y | Y | N | Y | Y | Y | Y | Y |
| 11 **Davis, T.** | Y | Y | N | Y | Y | Y | N | Y |
| **WASHINGTON** | | | | | | | | |
| 1 Inslee | Y | Y | Y | N | Y | Y | Y | N |
| 2 Larsen | Y | Y | Y | N | Y | Y | Y | N |
| 3 Baird | Y | Y | Y | N | Y | Y | Y | N |
| 4 **Hastings** | Y | Y | N | Y | Y | Y | N | Y |
| 5 **McMorris** | Y | Y | N | Y | Y | Y | N | Y |
| 6 Dicks | Y | Y | Y | N | Y | Y | Y | N |
| 7 McDermott | N | Y | Y | N | Y | N | Y | N |
| 8 **Reichert** | Y | Y | N | Y | Y | Y | N | Y |
| 9 Smith | Y | Y | N | Y | Y | Y | Y | N |
| **WEST VIRGINIA** | | | | | | | | |
| 1 Mollohan | Y | Y | Y | N | Y | Y | Y | N |
| 2 **Capito** | Y | Y | N | Y | Y | Y | N | Y |
| 3 Rahall | Y | Y | Y | N | Y | Y | Y | N |
| **WISCONSIN** | | | | | | | | |
| 1 **Ryan** | Y | Y | N | Y | Y | Y | N | Y |
| 2 Baldwin | Y | Y | Y | N | Y | Y | Y | N |
| 3 Kind | Y | Y | Y | Y | Y | Y | Y | N |
| 4 Moore | N | Y | Y | N | Y | Y | Y | N |
| 5 **Sensenbrenner** | Y | Y | N | Y | N | Y | N | Y |
| 6 **Petri** | Y | Y | N | Y | Y | Y | Y | Y |
| 7 Obey | Y | Y | Y | N | Y | Y | Y | N |
| 8 **Green** | Y | Y | N | Y | Y | Y | N | Y |
| **WYOMING** | | | | | | | | |
| AL **Cubin** | Y | Y | N | Y | Y | Y | N | Y |

# IN THE HOUSE | By Vote Number

**645.** **H Res 612. Commitment to Iraq Victory/Rule.** Adoption of the rule (H Res 619) that would provide for House floor consideration of the resolution that would express the commitment of the House of Representatives to achieving victory in Iraq. Adopted 217-202: R 217-3; D 0-198 (ND 0-147, SD 0-51); I 0-1. Dec. 16, 2005.

**646.** **HR 4437. Border Security/Rule.** Adoption of the rule (H Res 621) that would provide for House floor consideration of the bill that would increase security at international borders and at ports of entry into the United States. Adopted 216-203: R 213-8; D 3-194 (ND 3-143, SD 0-51); I 0-1. Dec. 16, 2005.

**647.** **H Con Res 294. Condemn Prison Camps in China/Adoption.** Smith, R-N.J., motion to suspend the rules and adopt the concurrent resolution that would call on the international community to condemn the Laogai, the system of forced labor prison camps in China, as a tool for suppression maintained by the Chinese government. Motion agreed to 413-1: R 216-1; D 196-0 (ND 146-0, SD 50-0); I 1-0. A two-thirds majority of those present and voting (276 in this case) is required for adoption under suspension of the rules. Dec. 16, 2005.

**648.** **H Res 612. Commitment to Iraq Victory/Adoption.** Adoption of the resolution that would state the commitment of the House of Representatives to achieving victory in Iraq. Adopted 279-109: R 220-0; D 59-108 (ND 28-92, SD 31-16); I 0-1. Dec. 16, 2005.

**649.** **H Res 409. Operation Murambatsvina Condemnation/Adoption.** Smith, R-N.J., motion to suspend the rules and adopt the resolution that would condemn Operation Murambatsvina as a major humanitarian catastrophe caused by the Zimbabwean government's callousness toward its own people, disregard for the rule of law, and lack of planning to move families and businesses to more desirable locations. Motion agreed to 421-1: R 221-1; D 199-0 (ND 148-0, SD 51-0); I 1-0. A two-thirds majority of those present and voting (282 in this case) is required for adoption under suspension of the rules. Dec. 16, 2005.

**650.** **H Res 575. Palestinian Elections/Adoption.** Ros-Lehtinen, R-Fla., motion to suspend the rules and adopt the resolution that would assert that organizations that carry out terrorist acts, such as Hamas, should not be allowed to participate in Palestinian elections until they recognize Israel, disarm and cease terrorist activities. Motion agreed to 397-17: R 217-1; D 179-16 (ND 132-12, SD 47-4); I 1-0. A two-thirds majority of those present and voting (276 in this case) is required for adoption under suspension of the rules. Dec. 16, 2005.

**651.** **H Res 534. Iraqi Judiciary/Adoption.** Ros-Lehtinen, R-Fla., motion to suspend the rules and adopt the resolution that would recognize the importance of the Iraqi judiciary. Motion agreed to 408-1: R 213-1; D 194-0 (ND 143-0, SD 51-0); I 1-0. A two-thirds majority of those present and voting (273 in this case) is required for adoption under suspension of the rules. Dec. 16, 2005.

**652.** **S 1932. Budget Reconciliation/Motion to Instruct.** Spratt, D-S.C., motion to instruct House conferees to eliminate House provisions that would reduce eligibility for food stamps and funding for child support enforcement, repeal the Byrd amendment in the House-passed bill and accept the Senate-passed language eliminating the stabilization fund for Medicare Advantage payments. Motion agreed to 246-175: R 46-175; D 199-0 (ND 148-0, SD 51-0); I 1-0. Dec. 16, 2005.

| | 645 | 646 | 647 | 648 | 649 | 650 | 651 | 652 |
|---|---|---|---|---|---|---|---|---|
| **ALABAMA** | | | | | | | | |
| 1 Bonner | Y | Y | Y | Y | Y | Y | Y | N |
| 2 Everett | Y | Y | Y | Y | Y | Y | Y | N |
| 3 Rogers | Y | Y | Y | Y | Y | Y | Y | N |
| 4 Aderholt | Y | Y | Y | Y | Y | Y | Y | N |
| 5 Cramer | N | N | Y | Y | Y | Y | Y | Y |
| 6 Bachus | Y | Y | Y | Y | Y | Y | ? | N |
| 7 Davis | N | N | Y | Y | Y | Y | Y | Y |
| **ALASKA** | | | | | | | | |
| AL Young | Y | Y | Y | Y | Y | Y | Y | N |
| **ARIZONA** | | | | | | | | |
| 1 Renzi | Y | Y | Y | Y | Y | Y | Y | N |
| 2 Franks | Y | Y | Y | Y | Y | Y | Y | N |
| 3 Shadegg | Y | Y | Y | Y | Y | Y | Y | N |
| 4 Pastor | N | N | Y | N | Y | Y | Y | Y |
| 5 Hayworth | Y | N | Y | Y | Y | Y | Y | N |
| 6 Flake | Y | Y | Y | Y | Y | Y | Y | N |
| 7 Grijalva | N | N | Y | N | Y | Y | Y | Y |
| 8 Kolbe | Y | N | Y | Y | Y | P | Y | ? |
| **ARKANSAS** | | | | | | | | |
| 1 Berry | N | N | Y | Y | Y | Y | Y | Y |
| 2 Snyder | N | N | Y | Y | Y | Y | Y | Y |
| 3 Boozman | Y | Y | Y | Y | Y | Y | Y | N |
| 4 Ross | N | N | Y | Y | Y | Y | Y | Y |
| **CALIFORNIA** | | | | | | | | |
| 1 Thompson | N | N | Y | P | Y | Y | Y | Y |
| 2 Herger | Y | Y | Y | Y | Y | Y | Y | N |
| 3 Lungren | Y | Y | Y | Y | Y | Y | Y | N |
| 4 Doolittle | Y | Y | Y | Y | ? | Y | Y | N |
| 5 Matsui, D. | N | N | Y | P | Y | Y | Y | Y |
| 6 Woolsey | N | N | Y | N | Y | Y | Y | Y |
| 7 Miller, George | N | N | Y | N | Y | ? | Y | Y |
| 8 Pelosi | N | N | Y | N | Y | Y | Y | Y |
| 9 Lee | N | N | Y | N | N | Y | N | Y |
| 10 Tauscher | N | N | Y | P | Y | Y | Y | Y |
| 11 Pombo | Y | Y | Y | Y | Y | Y | Y | N |
| 12 Lantos | N | N | Y | P | Y | Y | ? | Y |
| 13 Stark | N | N | ? | N | Y | N | Y | Y |
| 14 Eshoo | N | N | Y | P | Y | Y | Y | Y |
| 15 Honda | N | N | Y | N | Y | Y | Y | Y |
| 16 Lofgren | N | N | Y | P | Y | Y | Y | Y |
| 17 Farr | N | N | Y | Y | Y | Y | Y | Y |
| 18 Cardoza | N | N | Y | Y | Y | Y | Y | Y |
| 19 Radanovich | Y | Y | Y | Y | Y | Y | ? | N |
| 20 Costa | N | N | Y | Y | Y | Y | Y | Y |
| 21 Nunes | Y | Y | Y | Y | Y | Y | Y | N |
| 22 Thomas | Y | Y | Y | Y | Y | Y | Y | N |
| 23 Capps | N | N | Y | N | Y | Y | Y | Y |
| 24 Gallegly | Y | Y | Y | Y | Y | Y | Y | N |
| 25 McKeon | Y | Y | Y | Y | Y | Y | Y | N |
| 26 Dreier | Y | Y | Y | Y | Y | Y | Y | N |
| 27 Sherman | N | N | Y | P | Y | Y | Y | Y |
| 28 Berman | N | N | Y | Y | Y | Y | Y | Y |
| 29 Schiff | N | N | Y | P | Y | Y | Y | Y |
| 30 Waxman | N | N | Y | N | Y | Y | Y | Y |
| 31 Becerra | N | N | Y | N | Y | P | Y | Y |
| 32 Solis | N | N | Y | N | Y | Y | Y | Y |
| 33 Watson | N | N | Y | N | Y | N | Y | Y |
| 34 Roybal-Allard | N | N | Y | N | Y | Y | Y | Y |
| 35 Waters | N | N | Y | N | Y | N | Y | Y |
| 36 Harman | N | N | Y | P | Y | Y | Y | Y |
| 37 Millender-McD. | N | N | Y | N | Y | Y | Y | Y |
| 38 Napolitano | ? | ? | ? | ? | ? | ? | ? | ? |
| 39 Sánchez, Linda | N | N | Y | N | Y | Y | Y | Y |
| 40 Royce | Y | Y | Y | Y | Y | Y | Y | N |
| 41 Lewis | Y | Y | ? | Y | Y | Y | Y | N |
| 42 Miller, Gary | Y | Y | Y | Y | Y | Y | Y | N |
| 43 Baca | N | N | Y | N | Y | Y | Y | Y |
| 44 Calvert | Y | Y | Y | Y | Y | Y | Y | N |
| 45 Bono | Y | Y | Y | Y | Y | Y | Y | N |
| 46 Rohrabacher | Y | Y | Y | Y | Y | Y | Y | N |
| 47 Sanchez, Loretta | N | N | Y | P | Y | Y | Y | Y |
| 48 Campbell | Y | Y | Y | Y | Y | Y | Y | N |
| 49 Issa | Y | Y | Y | Y | Y | Y | Y | N |
| 50 Vacant | | | | | | | | |
| 51 Filner | N | N | Y | N | Y | Y | Y | Y |
| 52 Hunter | Y | Y | Y | Y | Y | Y | Y | N |
| 53 Davis | N | N | Y | Y | Y | Y | Y | Y |
| **COLORADO** | | | | | | | | |
| 1 DeGette | N | N | Y | N | Y | Y | Y | Y |
| 2 Udall | N | N | Y | Y | Y | Y | Y | Y |
| 3 Salazar | N | N | Y | Y | Y | Y | Y | Y |
| 4 Musgrave | Y | Y | Y | Y | Y | Y | Y | N |
| 5 Hefley | Y | N | Y | Y | Y | Y | Y | N |
| 6 Tancredo | Y | Y | Y | Y | Y | Y | Y | N |
| 7 Beauprez | Y | Y | Y | Y | Y | Y | Y | N |
| **CONNECTICUT** | | | | | | | | |
| 1 Larson | N | N | Y | N | Y | Y | Y | Y |
| 2 Simmons | Y | Y | Y | Y | Y | Y | Y | Y |
| 3 DeLauro | N | N | Y | N | Y | Y | Y | Y |
| 4 Shays | Y | N | Y | Y | Y | Y | Y | Y |
| 5 Johnson | Y | Y | Y | Y | Y | Y | Y | N |
| **DELAWARE** | | | | | | | | |
| AL Castle | Y | Y | Y | Y | Y | Y | Y | Y |
| **FLORIDA** | | | | | | | | |
| 1 Miller | Y | Y | Y | Y | Y | Y | ? | N |
| 2 Boyd | N | N | Y | P | Y | Y | Y | Y |
| 3 Brown | N | N | Y | N | Y | Y | Y | Y |
| 4 Crenshaw | Y | Y | Y | Y | Y | Y | Y | N |
| 5 Brown-Waite | Y | Y | Y | Y | Y | Y | Y | N |
| 6 Stearns | Y | Y | Y | Y | Y | Y | Y | N |
| 7 Mica | Y | Y | Y | Y | Y | Y | ? | N |
| 8 Keller | Y | Y | Y | Y | Y | Y | Y | N |
| 9 Bilirakis | Y | Y | Y | Y | Y | Y | Y | N |
| 10 Young | Y | Y | Y | Y | Y | Y | Y | ? |
| 11 Davis | N | N | Y | Y | Y | Y | Y | Y |
| 12 Putnam | Y | Y | Y | Y | Y | Y | Y | N |
| 13 Harris | Y | Y | Y | Y | Y | Y | Y | N |
| 14 Mack | Y | Y | Y | Y | Y | Y | Y | N |
| 15 Weldon | Y | Y | Y | Y | Y | Y | Y | N |
| 16 Foley | Y | Y | Y | Y | Y | Y | Y | Y |
| 17 Meek | N | N | Y | P | Y | Y | Y | Y |
| 18 Ros-Lehtinen | Y | Y | Y | Y | Y | Y | Y | N |
| 19 Wexler | N | N | Y | N | Y | Y | Y | Y |
| 20 Wasserman-Schultz | N | N | Y | N | Y | Y | Y | Y |
| 21 Diaz-Balart, L. | Y | Y | Y | Y | Y | Y | Y | N |
| 22 Shaw | Y | Y | Y | Y | Y | Y | Y | N |
| 23 Hastings | N | N | Y | N | Y | Y | Y | Y |
| 24 Feeney | Y | Y | Y | Y | Y | Y | Y | N |
| 25 Diaz-Balart, M. | + | + | + | + | + | + | + | − |
| **GEORGIA** | | | | | | | | |
| 1 Kingston | Y | Y | Y | Y | Y | Y | Y | N |
| 2 Bishop | N | N | Y | Y | Y | Y | Y | Y |
| 3 Marshall | N | N | Y | Y | Y | Y | Y | Y |
| 4 McKinney | N | N | Y | N | Y | N | Y | Y |
| 5 Lewis | N | N | Y | N | Y | N | Y | Y |
| 6 Price | Y | Y | Y | Y | Y | Y | Y | N |
| 7 Linder | Y | Y | Y | Y | Y | Y | Y | N |
| 8 Westmoreland | Y | Y | Y | Y | Y | Y | Y | N |
| 9 Norwood | Y | Y | Y | Y | Y | Y | Y | N |
| 10 Deal | Y | Y | Y | Y | Y | Y | Y | N |
| 11 Gingrey | Y | Y | Y | Y | Y | Y | Y | N |
| 12 Barrow | N | N | Y | Y | Y | Y | Y | Y |
| 13 Scott | N | N | Y | Y | Y | Y | Y | Y |
| **HAWAII** | | | | | | | | |
| 1 Abercrombie | N | N | Y | N | Y | N | Y | Y |
| 2 Case | N | N | Y | Y | Y | Y | Y | Y |
| **IDAHO** | | | | | | | | |
| 1 Otter | Y | Y | Y | Y | Y | Y | Y | Y |
| 2 Simpson | Y | Y | Y | Y | Y | Y | Y | Y |
| **ILLINOIS** | | | | | | | | |
| 1 Rush | N | N | Y | N | Y | Y | Y | Y |
| 2 Jackson | N | N | Y | N | Y | Y | Y | Y |
| 3 Lipinski | N | N | Y | Y | Y | Y | Y | Y |
| 4 Gutierrez | N | N | Y | N | P | Y | Y | Y |
| 5 Emanuel | N | N | Y | P | Y | Y | Y | Y |
| 6 Hyde | + | + | + | ? | ? | ? | ? | ? |
| 7 Davis | N | N | Y | N | Y | Y | Y | Y |
| 8 Bean | N | N | Y | Y | Y | Y | Y | Y |
| 9 Schakowsky | N | N | Y | N | Y | Y | Y | Y |
| 10 Kirk | Y | Y | Y | Y | Y | Y | Y | N |
| 11 Weller | Y | Y | Y | Y | Y | Y | Y | N |
| 12 Costello | N | N | Y | Y | Y | Y | Y | Y |

**KEY**  Republicans  Democrats  *Independents*

| | | | |
|---|---|---|---|
| **Y** Voted for (yea) | **X** Paired against | **C** Voted "present" to avoid possible conflict of interest |
| **#** Paired for | **−** Announced against | |
| **+** Announced for | **P** Voted "present" | **?** Did not vote or otherwise make a position known |
| **N** Voted against (nay) | | |

| | 645 | 646 | 647 | 648 | 649 | 650 | 651 | 652 |
|---|---|---|---|---|---|---|---|---|
| 13 **Biggert** | Y | Y | Y | Y | Y | Y | Y | N |
| 14 **Hastert** | | Y | | | | | | |
| 15 **Johnson** | Y | Y | Y | Y | Y | Y | Y | Y |
| 16 **Manzullo** | Y | Y | Y | Y | Y | Y | Y | N |
| 17 Evans | N | N | Y | N | Y | Y | Y | Y |
| 18 **LaHood** | ? | ? | ? | ? | ? | ? | ? | ? |
| 19 **Shimkus** | Y | Y | Y | Y | Y | Y | Y | Y |
| **INDIANA** | | | | | | | | |
| 1 Visclosky | N | N | Y | N | Y | Y | Y | Y |
| 2 **Chocola** | Y | Y | Y | Y | Y | Y | ? | N |
| 3 **Souder** | Y | Y | Y | Y | Y | Y | Y | N |
| 4 **Buyer** | Y | Y | Y | Y | Y | Y | Y | N |
| 5 **Burton** | Y | Y | Y | Y | Y | Y | Y | N |
| 6 **Pence** | Y | Y | Y | Y | Y | Y | Y | N |
| 7 Carson | N | N | Y | P | Y | Y | Y | Y |
| 8 **Hostettler** | Y | Y | Y | Y | Y | Y | Y | N |
| 9 **Sodrel** | Y | Y | Y | Y | Y | Y | Y | N |
| **IOWA** | | | | | | | | |
| 1 **Nussle** | Y | Y | Y | Y | Y | Y | Y | N |
| 2 **Leach** | N | N | Y | P | Y | P | Y | Y |
| 3 Boswell | N | N | Y | Y | Y | Y | Y | Y |
| 4 **Latham** | Y | Y | Y | Y | Y | Y | Y | N |
| 5 **King** | Y | Y | Y | Y | Y | Y | Y | N |
| **KANSAS** | | | | | | | | |
| 1 **Moran** | Y | Y | Y | Y | Y | Y | Y | N |
| 2 **Ryun** | Y | Y | Y | Y | Y | Y | Y | N |
| 3 Moore | N | N | Y | Y | Y | Y | Y | Y |
| 4 **Tiahrt** | Y | Y | Y | Y | Y | Y | Y | N |
| **KENTUCKY** | | | | | | | | |
| 1 **Whitfield** | Y | Y | Y | Y | Y | Y | Y | N |
| 2 **Lewis** | Y | Y | Y | Y | Y | Y | Y | N |
| 3 **Northup** | Y | Y | Y | Y | Y | Y | Y | N |
| 4 **Davis** | Y | Y | Y | Y | Y | Y | Y | N |
| 5 **Rogers** | Y | Y | Y | Y | Y | Y | Y | N |
| 6 Chandler | N | N | Y | Y | Y | Y | Y | Y |
| **LOUISIANA** | | | | | | | | |
| 1 **Jindal** | Y | Y | Y | Y | Y | Y | Y | N |
| 2 Jefferson | N | N | Y | Y | Y | Y | Y | Y |
| 3 Melancon | N | N | Y | Y | Y | Y | Y | Y |
| 4 **McCrery** | Y | Y | Y | Y | Y | Y | Y | N |
| 5 **Alexander** | Y | Y | Y | Y | Y | Y | Y | N |
| 6 **Baker** | Y | Y | Y | Y | Y | Y | Y | N |
| 7 **Boustany** | Y | Y | Y | Y | Y | Y | Y | N |
| **MAINE** | | | | | | | | |
| 1 Allen | N | N | Y | N | Y | Y | Y | Y |
| 2 Michaud | N | N | Y | P | Y | Y | Y | Y |
| **MARYLAND** | | | | | | | | |
| 1 **Gilchrest** | Y | Y | ? | Y | Y | Y | Y | Y |
| 2 Ruppersberger | N | N | Y | Y | Y | Y | Y | Y |
| 3 Cardin | N | N | Y | N | Y | Y | Y | Y |
| 4 Wynn | N | N | Y | N | Y | Y | Y | Y |
| 5 Hoyer | N | N | Y | P | Y | Y | Y | Y |
| 6 **Bartlett** | Y | Y | Y | Y | Y | Y | Y | N |
| 7 Cummings | N | N | Y | N | Y | Y | Y | Y |
| 8 Van Hollen | N | N | Y | P | Y | Y | Y | Y |
| **MASSACHUSETTS** | | | | | | | | |
| 1 Olver | N | N | Y | N | Y | Y | Y | Y |
| 2 Neal | N | N | ? | N | Y | Y | Y | Y |
| 3 McGovern | N | N | Y | N | Y | Y | Y | Y |
| 4 Frank | N | N | Y | N | Y | Y | Y | Y |
| 5 Meehan | N | N | Y | N | Y | Y | Y | Y |
| 6 Tierney | N | N | Y | N | Y | Y | Y | Y |
| 7 Markey | N | N | Y | N | Y | Y | Y | Y |
| 8 Capuano | N | N | Y | N | Y | P | Y | Y |
| 9 Lynch | N | N | Y | N | Y | Y | Y | Y |
| 10 Delahunt | N | N | Y | N | Y | Y | ? | Y |
| **MICHIGAN** | | | | | | | | |
| 1 Stupak | N | N | Y | N | Y | Y | Y | Y |
| 2 **Hoekstra** | Y | Y | ? | Y | Y | Y | Y | N |
| 3 **Ehlers** | Y | Y | Y | Y | Y | Y | Y | N |
| 4 **Camp** | Y | Y | Y | Y | Y | Y | Y | N |
| 5 Kildee | N | N | Y | N | Y | Y | Y | Y |
| 6 **Upton** | Y | N | Y | Y | Y | Y | Y | Y |
| 7 **Schwarz** | Y | Y | Y | Y | Y | Y | Y | Y |
| 8 **Rogers** | Y | Y | Y | Y | Y | Y | Y | N |
| 9 **Knollenberg** | Y | Y | Y | Y | Y | Y | Y | N |
| 10 **Miller** | Y | Y | Y | Y | Y | Y | Y | Y |
| 11 **McCotter** | Y | Y | Y | Y | Y | Y | Y | Y |
| 12 Levin | N | N | Y | N | Y | Y | Y | Y |
| 13 Kilpatrick | N | N | Y | N | Y | N | Y | Y |
| 14 Conyers | N | N | Y | N | Y | Y | Y | Y |
| 15 Dingell | N | N | Y | N | Y | N | Y | Y |

| | 645 | 646 | 647 | 648 | 649 | 650 | 651 | 652 |
|---|---|---|---|---|---|---|---|---|
| **MINNESOTA** | | | | | | | | |
| 1 **Gutknecht** | Y | Y | Y | Y | Y | P | Y | N |
| 2 **Kline** | Y | Y | Y | Y | Y | Y | Y | N |
| 3 **Ramstad** | Y | Y | Y | Y | Y | Y | Y | Y |
| 4 McCollum | N | N | Y | N | Y | Y | Y | Y |
| 5 Sabo | N | N | Y | N | Y | Y | Y | Y |
| 6 **Kennedy** | Y | Y | Y | Y | Y | Y | Y | N |
| 7 Peterson | N | Y | Y | Y | Y | Y | Y | Y |
| 8 Oberstar | N | N | Y | N | Y | Y | Y | Y |
| **MISSISSIPPI** | | | | | | | | |
| 1 **Wicker** | Y | Y | Y | Y | Y | Y | Y | N |
| 2 Thompson | N | N | Y | N | Y | Y | Y | Y |
| 3 **Pickering** | Y | Y | Y | Y | Y | Y | Y | N |
| 4 Taylor | N | N | Y | Y | Y | Y | Y | Y |
| **MISSOURI** | | | | | | | | |
| 1 Clay | N | N | Y | N | Y | Y | Y | Y |
| 2 **Akin** | Y | Y | Y | Y | Y | Y | Y | N |
| 3 Carnahan | N | N | Y | Y | Y | Y | Y | Y |
| 4 Skelton | N | N | Y | Y | Y | Y | Y | Y |
| 5 Cleaver | N | N | Y | N | Y | Y | Y | Y |
| 6 **Graves** | Y | Y | Y | Y | Y | Y | Y | N |
| 7 **Blunt** | Y | Y | Y | Y | Y | Y | Y | N |
| 8 **Emerson** | Y | Y | Y | Y | Y | Y | Y | Y |
| 9 **Hulshof** | Y | Y | Y | Y | Y | Y | Y | N |
| **MONTANA** | | | | | | | | |
| AL **Rehberg** | Y | Y | Y | Y | Y | Y | Y | Y |
| **NEBRASKA** | | | | | | | | |
| 1 **Fortenberry** | Y | Y | Y | Y | Y | Y | Y | N |
| 2 **Terry** | Y | Y | Y | Y | Y | Y | Y | N |
| 3 **Osborne** | Y | Y | Y | Y | Y | Y | Y | N |
| **NEVADA** | | | | | | | | |
| 1 Berkley | N | N | Y | Y | Y | Y | Y | Y |
| 2 **Gibbons** | Y | Y | Y | Y | Y | Y | Y | N |
| 3 **Porter** | Y | Y | Y | Y | Y | Y | Y | N |
| **NEW HAMPSHIRE** | | | | | | | | |
| 1 **Bradley** | Y | Y | Y | Y | Y | Y | Y | N |
| 2 **Bass** | Y | Y | Y | Y | Y | Y | Y | N |
| **NEW JERSEY** | | | | | | | | |
| 1 Andrews | N | N | Y | P | Y | Y | Y | Y |
| 2 **LoBiondo** | Y | Y | Y | Y | Y | Y | Y | Y |
| 3 **Saxton** | Y | Y | Y | Y | Y | Y | Y | Y |
| 4 **Smith** | Y | Y | Y | Y | Y | Y | Y | Y |
| 5 **Garrett** | Y | Y | Y | Y | Y | Y | Y | N |
| 6 Pallone | N | N | Y | N | Y | Y | Y | Y |
| 7 **Ferguson** | Y | Y | Y | Y | Y | Y | Y | N |
| 8 Pascrell | N | N | Y | N | Y | Y | Y | Y |
| 9 Rothman | N | N | Y | N | Y | Y | Y | Y |
| 10 Payne | ? | ? | ? | ? | ? | ? | ? | ? |
| 11 **Frelinghuysen** | Y | Y | Y | Y | Y | Y | Y | N |
| 12 Holt | N | N | Y | N | Y | Y | Y | Y |
| 13 Menendez | N | N | Y | N | Y | Y | Y | Y |
| **NEW MEXICO** | | | | | | | | |
| 1 **Wilson** | Y | Y | Y | Y | Y | Y | Y | Y |
| 2 **Pearce** | ? | ? | ? | Y | Y | Y | Y | N |
| 3 Udall | N | N | Y | N | Y | Y | Y | Y |
| **NEW YORK** | | | | | | | | |
| 1 Bishop | N | N | Y | P | Y | Y | Y | Y |
| 2 Israel | N | N | Y | Y | Y | Y | Y | Y |
| 3 **King** | Y | Y | Y | Y | Y | Y | Y | N |
| 4 McCarthy | - | - | + | + | + | + | + | + |
| 5 Ackerman | N | N | Y | N | Y | Y | Y | Y |
| 6 Meeks | N | N | Y | N | Y | Y | Y | Y |
| 7 Crowley | N | N | Y | N | Y | Y | Y | Y |
| 8 Nadler | N | N | Y | N | Y | Y | Y | Y |
| 9 Weiner | N | N | Y | N | Y | Y | Y | Y |
| 10 Towns | N | N | Y | N | Y | Y | Y | Y |
| 11 Owens | N | N | Y | P | Y | Y | Y | Y |
| 12 Velázquez | N | N | Y | N | Y | Y | Y | Y |
| 13 **Fossella** | Y | Y | Y | Y | Y | Y | Y | N |
| 14 Maloney | N | N | Y | P | Y | Y | Y | Y |
| 15 Rangel | N | N | Y | N | Y | Y | ? | Y |
| 16 Serrano | N | N | Y | N | Y | Y | Y | Y |
| 17 Engel | N | N | Y | P | Y | Y | Y | Y |
| 18 Lowey | N | N | Y | P | Y | Y | Y | Y |
| 19 **Kelly** | Y | Y | Y | Y | Y | Y | Y | Y |
| 20 **Sweeney** | ? | ? | ? | ? | ? | ? | ? | Y |
| 21 McNulty | N | Y | Y | P | Y | Y | Y | Y |
| 22 Hinchey | N | N | Y | N | Y | Y | Y | Y |
| 23 **McHugh** | Y | Y | Y | Y | Y | Y | Y | Y |
| 24 **Boehlert** | Y | Y | Y | Y | Y | Y | Y | Y |
| 25 **Walsh** | Y | Y | ? | Y | Y | Y | Y | N |
| 26 **Reynolds** | Y | Y | Y | Y | Y | Y | Y | N |
| 27 Higgins | N | N | Y | Y | Y | Y | Y | Y |
| 28 Slaughter | N | N | Y | P | Y | Y | Y | Y |
| 29 **Kuhl** | Y | Y | Y | Y | Y | Y | Y | Y |

| | 645 | 646 | 647 | 648 | 649 | 650 | 651 | 652 |
|---|---|---|---|---|---|---|---|---|
| **NORTH CAROLINA** | | | | | | | | |
| 1 Butterfield | N | N | Y | P | Y | Y | Y | Y |
| 2 Etheridge | N | N | Y | Y | Y | Y | Y | Y |
| 3 **Jones** | N | Y | Y | Y | Y | Y | Y | Y |
| 4 Price | N | N | Y | N | Y | Y | Y | Y |
| 5 **Foxx** | Y | Y | Y | Y | Y | Y | Y | N |
| 6 **Coble** | Y | Y | Y | Y | Y | Y | Y | Y |
| 7 McIntyre | N | N | Y | Y | Y | Y | Y | Y |
| 8 **Hayes** | Y | Y | Y | Y | Y | Y | Y | Y |
| 9 **Myrick** | Y | Y | Y | Y | Y | Y | Y | N |
| 10 **McHenry** | Y | Y | Y | Y | Y | Y | Y | N |
| 11 **Taylor** | Y | Y | Y | Y | Y | Y | Y | N |
| 12 Watt | N | N | ? | N | Y | N | Y | Y |
| 13 Miller | N | N | Y | N | Y | Y | Y | Y |
| **NORTH DAKOTA** | | | | | | | | |
| AL Pomeroy | N | N | Y | Y | Y | Y | Y | Y |
| **OHIO** | | | | | | | | |
| 1 **Chabot** | Y | N | Y | Y | Y | Y | Y | N |
| 2 **Schmidt** | Y | Y | Y | Y | Y | Y | Y | N |
| 3 **Turner** | Y | Y | Y | Y | Y | Y | Y | N |
| 4 **Oxley** | Y | Y | Y | Y | Y | Y | Y | N |
| 5 **Gillmor** | Y | Y | Y | Y | Y | Y | Y | Y |
| 6 Strickland | N | N | Y | N | Y | Y | Y | Y |
| 7 **Hobson** | Y | Y | Y | Y | Y | Y | Y | N |
| 8 **Boehner** | Y | Y | Y | Y | Y | Y | Y | N |
| 9 Kaptur | N | N | Y | P | Y | Y | Y | Y |
| 10 Kucinich | N | N | Y | N | Y | N | Y | Y |
| 11 Jones | N | - | Y | N | Y | Y | Y | Y |
| 12 **Tiberi** | Y | Y | Y | Y | Y | Y | Y | N |
| 13 Brown | N | N | Y | N | Y | Y | Y | Y |
| 14 **LaTourette** | Y | Y | Y | Y | Y | Y | Y | N |
| 15 **Pryce** | Y | Y | Y | Y | Y | Y | Y | N |
| 16 **Regula** | Y | Y | Y | Y | Y | Y | Y | Y |
| 17 Ryan | N | N | Y | N | Y | Y | Y | Y |
| 18 **Ney** | Y | Y | Y | Y | Y | Y | Y | Y |
| **OKLAHOMA** | | | | | | | | |
| 1 **Sullivan** | Y | Y | Y | Y | Y | Y | Y | N |
| 2 Boren | N | N | Y | Y | Y | Y | Y | Y |
| 3 **Lucas** | Y | Y | Y | Y | Y | Y | Y | N |
| 4 **Cole** | Y | Y | Y | Y | Y | Y | + | N |
| 5 **Istook** | ? | ? | ? | ? | ? | ? | ? | ? |
| **OREGON** | | | | | | | | |
| 1 Wu | N | N | Y | N | Y | Y | Y | Y |
| 2 **Walden** | Y | Y | Y | Y | Y | Y | Y | N |
| 3 Blumenauer | N | N | Y | N | Y | N | Y | Y |
| 4 DeFazio | N | N | Y | P | Y | Y | Y | Y |
| 5 Hooley | N | N | Y | P | Y | Y | Y | Y |
| **PENNSYLVANIA** | | | | | | | | |
| 1 Brady | N | N | Y | N | Y | Y | Y | Y |
| 2 Fattah | N | N | Y | N | Y | Y | Y | Y |
| 3 **English** | Y | Y | Y | Y | Y | Y | Y | N |
| 4 **Hart** | ? | Y | Y | Y | Y | Y | Y | N |
| 5 **Peterson** | Y | Y | Y | Y | Y | Y | Y | N |
| 6 **Gerlach** | Y | Y | Y | Y | Y | Y | Y | Y |
| 7 **Weldon** | Y | Y | Y | Y | Y | Y | Y | Y |
| 8 **Fitzpatrick** | Y | Y | Y | Y | Y | Y | Y | Y |
| 9 **Shuster** | Y | Y | Y | Y | Y | Y | Y | N |
| 10 **Sherwood** | Y | Y | Y | Y | Y | Y | Y | N |
| 11 Kanjorski | N | N | Y | N | Y | Y | Y | Y |
| 12 Murtha | N | N | Y | N | Y | Y | Y | Y |
| 13 Schwartz | ? | N | Y | N | Y | Y | Y | Y |
| 14 Doyle | N | N | Y | N | Y | Y | Y | Y |
| 15 **Dent** | Y | Y | Y | Y | Y | Y | Y | Y |
| 16 **Pitts** | Y | Y | Y | Y | Y | Y | Y | N |
| 17 Holden | N | N | Y | Y | Y | Y | Y | Y |
| 18 **Murphy** | Y | Y | Y | Y | Y | Y | Y | N |
| 19 **Platts** | Y | Y | Y | Y | Y | Y | Y | Y |
| **RHODE ISLAND** | | | | | | | | |
| 1 Kennedy | N | N | Y | Y | Y | Y | Y | Y |
| 2 Langevin | N | N | Y | Y | Y | Y | Y | Y |
| **SOUTH CAROLINA** | | | | | | | | |
| 1 **Brown** | Y | Y | Y | Y | Y | Y | Y | N |
| 2 **Wilson** | Y | Y | Y | Y | Y | Y | Y | N |
| 3 **Barrett** | + | + | + | + | + | + | + | - |
| 4 **Inglis** | Y | Y | Y | Y | Y | Y | Y | N |
| 5 Spratt | N | N | Y | Y | Y | Y | Y | Y |
| 6 Clyburn | N | N | Y | N | Y | Y | Y | Y |
| **SOUTH DAKOTA** | | | | | | | | |
| AL Herseth | N | N | Y | Y | Y | Y | Y | Y |
| **TENNESSEE** | | | | | | | | |
| 1 **Jenkins** | Y | Y | Y | Y | Y | Y | Y | N |
| 2 **Duncan** | Y | Y | Y | Y | Y | Y | Y | N |

| | 645 | 646 | 647 | 648 | 649 | 650 | 651 | 652 |
|---|---|---|---|---|---|---|---|---|
| 3 **Wamp** | Y | Y | Y | Y | Y | Y | Y | N |
| 4 Davis | N | N | Y | Y | Y | Y | Y | Y |
| 5 Cooper | N | N | Y | Y | Y | Y | Y | Y |
| 6 Gordon | N | N | Y | Y | Y | Y | Y | Y |
| 7 **Blackburn** | Y | ? | Y | Y | Y | Y | Y | N |
| 8 Tanner | N | N | Y | Y | Y | Y | Y | Y |
| 9 Ford | N | N | Y | Y | Y | Y | Y | Y |
| **TEXAS** | | | | | | | | |
| 1 **Gohmert** | Y | Y | Y | Y | Y | Y | Y | N |
| 2 **Poe** | Y | Y | Y | Y | Y | Y | Y | N |
| 3 **Johnson, S.** | Y | Y | Y | Y | Y | Y | ? | N |
| 4 **Hall** | Y | Y | Y | Y | Y | Y | Y | N |
| 5 **Hensarling** | Y | Y | Y | Y | Y | Y | Y | N |
| 6 **Barton** | + | + | + | + | + | + | + | - |
| 7 **Culberson** | Y | Y | Y | Y | Y | Y | Y | N |
| 8 **Brady** | Y | Y | Y | Y | Y | Y | ? | N |
| 9 Green, A. | N | N | Y | N | Y | Y | Y | Y |
| 10 **McCaul** | Y | Y | Y | Y | Y | Y | Y | N |
| 11 **Conaway** | Y | Y | Y | Y | Y | Y | Y | N |
| 12 **Granger** | Y | Y | Y | Y | Y | Y | Y | N |
| 13 **Thornberry** | Y | Y | Y | Y | Y | Y | Y | N |
| 14 **Paul** | N | N | N | P | N | N | N | N |
| 15 Hinojosa | N | N | Y | Y | Y | Y | Y | Y |
| 16 Reyes | N | N | Y | Y | Y | Y | Y | Y |
| 17 Edwards | N | N | Y | Y | Y | Y | Y | Y |
| 18 Jackson-Lee | N | N | Y | N | Y | Y | Y | Y |
| 19 **Neugebauer** | Y | Y | Y | Y | Y | Y | Y | N |
| 20 Gonzalez | N | N | Y | Y | Y | Y | Y | Y |
| 21 **Smith** | Y | Y | Y | Y | Y | Y | Y | N |
| 22 **DeLay** | Y | Y | Y | Y | Y | Y | Y | N |
| 23 **Bonilla** | Y | Y | Y | Y | Y | Y | Y | N |
| 24 **Marchant** | Y | Y | Y | Y | Y | Y | Y | N |
| 25 Doggett | N | N | Y | N | Y | Y | Y | Y |
| 26 **Burgess** | Y | Y | Y | Y | Y | Y | Y | N |
| 27 Ortiz | N | N | Y | Y | Y | Y | Y | Y |
| 28 Cuellar | N | N | Y | Y | Y | Y | Y | Y |
| 29 Green, G. | N | N | Y | Y | Y | Y | Y | Y |
| 30 Johnson, E. | N | N | Y | P | Y | N | Y | Y |
| 31 **Carter** | Y | Y | Y | Y | Y | Y | Y | N |
| 32 **Sessions** | Y | Y | Y | Y | Y | Y | Y | N |
| **UTAH** | | | | | | | | |
| 1 **Bishop** | Y | Y | Y | Y | Y | Y | Y | N |
| 2 Matheson | N | N | Y | Y | Y | Y | Y | Y |
| 3 **Cannon** | Y | Y | Y | Y | Y | Y | Y | N |
| **VERMONT** | | | | | | | | |
| AL *Sanders* | N | N | Y | N | Y | Y | Y | Y |
| **VIRGINIA** | | | | | | | | |
| 1 **Davis, J.** | + | + | + | + | + | + | + | - |
| 2 **Drake** | Y | Y | Y | Y | Y | Y | Y | N |
| 3 Scott | N | N | Y | N | Y | Y | Y | Y |
| 4 **Forbes** | Y | Y | Y | Y | Y | Y | Y | N |
| 5 **Goode** | Y | Y | Y | Y | Y | Y | Y | N |
| 6 **Goodlatte** | Y | Y | Y | Y | Y | Y | Y | N |
| 7 **Cantor** | Y | Y | Y | Y | Y | Y | Y | N |
| 8 Moran | N | N | Y | N | Y | N | Y | Y |
| 9 Boucher | N | N | Y | Y | Y | Y | Y | Y |
| 10 **Wolf** | Y | Y | Y | Y | Y | Y | Y | N |
| 11 **Davis, T.** | Y | Y | Y | Y | Y | Y | Y | Y |
| **WASHINGTON** | | | | | | | | |
| 1 Inslee | N | N | Y | N | Y | Y | Y | Y |
| 2 Larsen | N | N | Y | P | Y | Y | Y | Y |
| 3 Baird | N | N | Y | P | Y | Y | Y | Y |
| 4 **Hastings** | Y | Y | Y | Y | Y | Y | Y | N |
| 5 **McMorris** | Y | Y | Y | Y | Y | Y | Y | N |
| 6 Dicks | N | N | Y | Y | Y | Y | Y | Y |
| 7 McDermott | N | N | Y | N | Y | N | + | Y |
| 8 **Reichert** | Y | Y | Y | Y | Y | Y | Y | Y |
| 9 Smith | N | N | Y | Y | Y | Y | Y | Y |
| **WEST VIRGINIA** | | | | | | | | |
| 1 Mollohan | N | N | Y | N | Y | Y | Y | Y |
| 2 **Capito** | Y | Y | Y | Y | Y | Y | Y | Y |
| 3 Rahall | N | N | Y | N | Y | N | Y | Y |
| **WISCONSIN** | | | | | | | | |
| 1 **Ryan** | Y | Y | Y | Y | Y | Y | Y | N |
| 2 Baldwin | N | N | Y | N | Y | Y | Y | Y |
| 3 Kind | N | N | Y | Y | Y | Y | Y | Y |
| 4 Moore | N | ? | Y | N | Y | P | Y | Y |
| 5 **Sensenbrenner** | Y | Y | Y | Y | Y | Y | Y | N |
| 6 **Petri** | Y | Y | Y | Y | Y | Y | Y | N |
| 7 Obey | N | N | Y | N | Y | N | Y | Y |
| 8 **Green** | Y | Y | Y | Y | Y | Y | Y | N |
| **WYOMING** | | | | | | | | |
| AL **Cubin** | Y | Y | Y | Y | Y | Y | Y | N |

# IN THE HOUSE | By Vote Number

**653.** **HR 4437. Border Security/Diversity Visa Program.** Goodlatte, R-Va., amendment that would eliminate the diversity visa program, which makes available 50,000 permanent resident visas annually, drawn from a random selection of entries from people who meet eligibility requirements from countries with low rates of immigration into the United States. Adopted 273-148: R 215-6; D 57-142 (ND 32-116, SD 25-26); I 1-0. Dec. 16, 2005.

**654.** **HR 4437. Border Security/Legal Immigration Status.** Stearns, R-Fla., amendment that would prohibit the Homeland Security and Justice departments and courts from granting any kind of legal immigration status to an alien until all the relevant criminal records databases and terrorist watch lists are checked. Adopted 420-0: R 220-0; D 199-0 (ND 148-0, SD 51-0); I 1-0. Dec. 16, 2005.

**655.** **HR 4437. Border Security/Illegal Entry.** Sensenbrenner, R-Wis., amendment that would strike language in the bill that would increase the maximum sentence for illegal presence or illegal entry into the United States to one year and a day. Rejected 164-257: R 156-65; D 8-191 (ND 3-145, SD 5-46); I 0-1 . Dec. 16, 2005.

**656.** **HR 4437. Border Security/Illegal Immigrants.** Norwood, R-Ga., amendment that would require the Homeland Security Department to provide training at no cost to local and state law enforcement, authorize $1 billion each year for the State Criminal Alien Assistance Program and require the department to submit for entry into the National Crime Information Database the names of certain categories of aliens. Adopted 237-180: R 207-11; D 30-168 (ND 13-134, SD 17-34); I 0-1. Dec. 16, 2005.

**657.** **HR 4437. Border Security/Penalties for Unauthorized Aliens.** Westmoreland, R-Ga., amendment that would cap the monetary penalties for hiring or employing unauthorized aliens at $7,500 for first time offenses, $15,000 for second offenses, and $40,000 for all subsequent offenses. It would provide an exemption for initial good faith violations and a safe harbor for contractors if their subcontractor hires an unauthorized alien. Adopted 247-170: R 217-2; D 30-167 (ND 10-137, SD 20-30); I 0-1. Dec. 16, 2005.

**658.** **HR 4437. Border Security/Increase Fines on Businesses.** Gonzalez, D-Texas, amendment that would increase the fines on businesses for knowingly hiring unauthorized aliens to $50,000, and provide that proceeds be shared with state and local governments to help cover the costs associated with providing services to undocumented immigrants. Rejected 87-332: R 0-219; D 86-113 (ND 69-79, SD 17-34); I 1-0. Dec. 16, 2005.

**659.** **HR 4437. Border Security/Deportation of Illegal Immigrants.** Sullivan, R-Okla., amendment that would expand deportation for illegal immigrants who cannot prove that they have been in the United States for longer than one year to be applicable nationwide. It also would require federal authorities to detain all illegal immigrants reported to the Homeland Security Department by state and local authorities and require all non-citizens to be processed through the UH-VISIT system. Rejected 163-251: R 139-77; D 24-173 (ND 7-139, SD 17-34); I 0-1. Dec. 16, 2005.

| | 653 | 654 | 655 | 656 | 657 | 658 | 659 |
|---|---|---|---|---|---|---|---|
| **ALABAMA** | | | | | | | |
| 1 Bonner | Y | Y | Y | Y | Y | N | Y |
| 2 Everett | Y | Y | Y | Y | Y | N | Y |
| 3 Rogers | Y | Y | N | Y | Y | N | Y |
| 4 Aderholt | Y | Y | Y | Y | Y | N | Y |
| 5 Cramer | Y | Y | N | Y | Y | N | Y |
| 6 Bachus | Y | Y | Y | Y | Y | N | Y |
| 7 Davis | N | Y | N | N | N | N | N |
| **ALASKA** | | | | | | | |
| AL Young | Y | Y | Y | N | ? | ? | ? |
| **ARIZONA** | | | | | | | |
| 1 Renzi | Y | Y | N | Y | Y | N | Y |
| 2 Franks | Y | Y | N | Y | Y | N | Y |
| 3 Shadegg | Y | Y | Y | Y | Y | N | N |
| 4 Pastor | N | Y | N | N | N | N | N |
| 5 Hayworth | Y | Y | N | Y | N | N | N |
| 6 Flake | Y | Y | Y | N | Y | N | N |
| 7 Grijalva | N | Y | N | N | N | N | N |
| 8 Kolbe | ? | ? | ? | ? | ? | ? | ? |
| **ARKANSAS** | | | | | | | |
| 1 Berry | Y | Y | Y | Y | Y | N | Y |
| 2 Snyder | Y | Y | N | N | N | N | N |
| 3 Boozman | Y | Y | Y | Y | Y | N | Y |
| 4 Ross | Y | Y | N | Y | N | N | Y |
| **CALIFORNIA** | | | | | | | |
| 1 Thompson | Y | Y | N | N | N | Y | N |
| 2 Herger | Y | Y | N | Y | N | Y | Y |
| 3 Lungren | Y | Y | Y | Y | Y | N | Y |
| 4 Doolittle | Y | Y | Y | Y | Y | N | Y |
| 5 Matsui, D. | N | Y | N | N | N | Y | N |
| 6 Woolsey | N | Y | N | ? | N | N | N |
| 7 Miller, George | N | Y | N | N | N | N | N |
| 8 Pelosi | N | Y | N | N | N | N | N |
| 9 Lee | N | Y | N | N | N | N | N |
| 10 Tauscher | N | Y | N | N | N | N | N |
| 11 Pombo | Y | Y | Y | Y | Y | N | Y |
| 12 Lantos | N | Y | N | N | N | Y | N |
| 13 Stark | N | Y | N | N | N | Y | N |
| 14 Eshoo | N | Y | N | N | N | Y | N |
| 15 Honda | N | Y | N | N | N | Y | N |
| 16 Lofgren | N | Y | N | N | N | Y | N |
| 17 Farr | N | Y | N | N | N | Y | N |
| 18 Cardoza | Y | Y | N | N | Y | N | Y |
| 19 Radanovich | Y | Y | Y | Y | Y | N | Y |
| 20 Costa | Y | Y | N | N | Y | N | Y |
| 21 Nunes | Y | Y | Y | Y | Y | N | N |
| 22 Thomas | Y | Y | Y | Y | Y | N | Y |
| 23 Capps | N | Y | N | N | N | Y | N |
| 24 Gallegly | Y | Y | N | Y | Y | N | Y |
| 25 McKeon | Y | Y | N | Y | Y | N | Y |
| 26 Dreier | Y | Y | Y | Y | Y | N | Y |
| 27 Sherman | Y | Y | N | N | N | Y | N |
| 28 Berman | Y | Y | N | N | N | Y | N |
| 29 Schiff | N | Y | N | N | N | Y | N |
| 30 Waxman | Y | Y | N | N | N | Y | Y |
| 31 Becerra | N | Y | N | N | N | Y | N |
| 32 Solis | N | Y | N | N | N | N | N |
| 33 Watson | N | Y | N | N | N | Y | N |
| 34 Roybal-Allard | N | Y | N | N | N | Y | N |
| 35 Waters | N | Y | N | N | N | N | N |
| 36 Harman | N | Y | N | N | N | N | N |
| 37 Millender-McD. | N | Y | N | N | N | N | N |
| 38 Napolitano | ? | ? | ? | ? | ? | ? | ? |
| 39 Sánchez, Linda | N | Y | N | N | N | Y | N |
| 40 Royce | Y | Y | Y | Y | Y | N | Y |
| 41 Lewis | Y | Y | Y | Y | Y | N | ? |
| 42 Miller, Gary | Y | Y | Y | Y | Y | N | Y |
| 43 Baca | N | Y | N | N | N | N | N |
| 44 Calvert | Y | Y | Y | Y | Y | N | Y |
| 45 Bono | Y | Y | Y | Y | Y | N | Y |
| 46 Rohrabacher | Y | Y | Y | Y | Y | N | Y |
| 47 Sanchez, Loretta | N | Y | N | N | N | N | N |
| 48 Campbell | Y | Y | Y | Y | Y | N | Y |
| 49 Issa | Y | Y | Y | Y | Y | N | N |
| 50 Vacant | | | | | | | |
| 51 Filner | N | Y | N | N | N | N | N |
| 52 Hunter | Y | Y | Y | Y | Y | N | Y |
| 53 Davis | N | Y | N | N | N | Y | N |
| **COLORADO** | | | | | | | |
| 1 DeGette | N | Y | N | N | N | Y | N |
| 2 Udall | Y | Y | Y | N | Y | N | N |
| 3 Salazar | N | Y | N | N | N | Y | N |
| 4 Musgrave | Y | Y | Y | Y | Y | N | Y |
| 5 Hefley | Y | Y | Y | Y | Y | N | Y |
| 6 Tancredo | Y | Y | Y | Y | Y | N | Y |
| 7 Beauprez | Y | Y | Y | Y | Y | N | Y |
| **CONNECTICUT** | | | | | | | |
| 1 Larson | N | Y | N | N | N | Y | N |
| 2 Simmons | Y | Y | Y | Y | Y | N | N |
| 3 DeLauro | N | Y | N | N | N | Y | N |
| 4 Shays | Y | Y | Y | Y | Y | N | Y |
| 5 Johnson | Y | Y | Y | Y | Y | N | Y |
| **DELAWARE** | | | | | | | |
| AL Castle | Y | Y | Y | N | Y | N | N |
| **FLORIDA** | | | | | | | |
| 1 Miller | Y | Y | N | Y | Y | N | Y |
| 2 Boyd | Y | Y | N | Y | N | N | Y |
| 3 Brown | N | Y | N | N | N | N | N |
| 4 Crenshaw | Y | Y | Y | Y | Y | N | Y |
| 5 Brown-Waite | Y | Y | Y | Y | Y | N | Y |
| 6 Stearns | Y | Y | N | Y | Y | N | Y |
| 7 Mica | Y | Y | Y | Y | Y | N | Y |
| 8 Keller | Y | Y | Y | Y | Y | N | Y |
| 9 Bilirakis | Y | Y | Y | Y | Y | N | Y |
| 10 Young | ? | ? | ? | ? | ? | ? | ? |
| 11 Davis | Y | Y | N | N | N | N | N |
| 12 Putnam | Y | Y | Y | Y | Y | N | Y |
| 13 Harris | Y | Y | Y | Y | Y | N | Y |
| 14 Mack | Y | Y | Y | Y | Y | N | Y |
| 15 Weldon | Y | Y | Y | Y | Y | N | Y |
| 16 Foley | Y | Y | Y | Y | Y | N | N |
| 17 Meek | N | Y | N | N | N | N | N |
| 18 Ros-Lehtinen | N | Y | N | N | N | N | N |
| 19 Wexler | N | Y | N | N | N | Y | N |
| 20 Wasserman-Schultz | N | Y | N | N | N | N | N |
| 21 Diaz-Balart, L. | N | Y | N | N | N | N | N |
| 22 Shaw | Y | Y | Y | Y | Y | N | Y |
| 23 Hastings | N | Y | N | N | N | N | N |
| 24 Feeney | Y | Y | Y | Y | Y | N | N |
| 25 Diaz-Balart, M. | - | + | + | - | + | - | - |
| **GEORGIA** | | | | | | | |
| 1 Kingston | Y | Y | Y | Y | Y | N | Y |
| 2 Bishop | N | Y | N | N | Y | N | Y |
| 3 Marshall | Y | Y | N | Y | Y | Y | Y |
| 4 McKinney | N | Y | N | N | N | N | N |
| 5 Lewis | N | Y | N | N | N | N | N |
| 6 Price | Y | Y | N | Y | Y | N | Y |
| 7 Linder | Y | Y | Y | Y | Y | N | Y |
| 8 Westmoreland | Y | Y | Y | Y | Y | N | Y |
| 9 Norwood | Y | Y | Y | Y | Y | N | Y |
| 10 Deal | Y | Y | Y | Y | Y | N | Y |
| 11 Gingrey | Y | Y | Y | Y | Y | N | Y |
| 12 Barrow | Y | Y | Y | N | N | Y | Y |
| 13 Scott | Y | Y | N | N | N | N | N |
| **HAWAII** | | | | | | | |
| 1 Abercrombie | N | Y | N | N | N | N | N |
| 2 Case | Y | Y | N | N | N | Y | Y |
| **IDAHO** | | | | | | | |
| 1 Otter | Y | Y | N | Y | Y | N | Y |
| 2 Simpson | Y | Y | Y | Y | Y | N | Y |
| **ILLINOIS** | | | | | | | |
| 1 Rush | N | Y | N | N | N | Y | N |
| 2 Jackson | N | Y | N | N | Y | N | N |
| 3 Lipinski | Y | Y | N | N | N | Y | N |
| 4 Gutierrez | N | Y | N | N | N | N | N |
| 5 Emanuel | Y | Y | N | N | N | Y | N |
| 6 Hyde | ? | ? | ? | ? | ? | ? | ? |
| 7 Davis | N | Y | N | N | N | N | N |
| 8 Bean | Y | Y | N | N | N | N | Y |
| 9 Schakowsky | N | Y | N | N | N | Y | N |
| 10 Kirk | Y | Y | Y | Y | Y | N | Y |
| 11 Weller | Y | ? | Y | Y | Y | N | N |
| 12 Costello | Y | Y | N | N | N | N | N |

| | 653 | 654 | 655 | 656 | 657 | 658 | 659 |
|---|---|---|---|---|---|---|---|
| 13 **Biggert** | Y | Y | Y | Y | Y | N | N |
| 14 **Hastert** | | | | | | | |
| 15 **Johnson** | Y | Y | Y | Y | Y | N | N |
| 16 **Manzullo** | Y | Y | Y | Y | Y | N | Y |
| 17 Evans | N | Y | N | N | N | Y | N |
| 18 **LaHood** | ? | ? | ? | ? | ? | ? | ? |
| 19 **Shimkus** | Y | Y | Y | Y | Y | N | Y |
| **INDIANA** | | | | | | | |
| 1 Visclosky | Y | Y | N | N | N | N | N |
| 2 **Chocola** | Y | Y | Y | Y | Y | N | Y |
| 3 **Souder** | Y | Y | Y | Y | P | N | N |
| 4 **Buyer** | Y | Y | Y | Y | Y | N | Y |
| 5 **Burton** | Y | Y | Y | Y | Y | N | N |
| 6 **Pence** | Y | Y | Y | Y | Y | N | N |
| 7 Carson | N | Y | N | N | N | N | N |
| 8 **Hostettler** | Y | Y | Y | Y | Y | N | Y |
| 9 **Sodrel** | Y | Y | N | Y | Y | N | N |
| **IOWA** | | | | | | | |
| 1 **Nussle** | Y | Y | Y | Y | Y | N | Y |
| 2 **Leach** | N | Y | Y | Y | Y | N | N |
| 3 Boswell | N | Y | N | Y | Y | N | Y |
| 4 **Latham** | Y | Y | Y | Y | Y | N | Y |
| 5 **King** | Y | Y | N | Y | Y | N | Y |
| **KANSAS** | | | | | | | |
| 1 **Moran** | Y | Y | Y | Y | Y | N | Y |
| 2 **Ryun** | Y | Y | Y | Y | Y | N | Y |
| 3 Moore | Y | Y | Y | N | N | N | N |
| 4 **Tiahrt** | Y | Y | Y | Y | Y | N | N |
| **KENTUCKY** | | | | | | | |
| 1 **Whitfield** | Y | Y | N | Y | Y | N | Y |
| 2 **Lewis** | Y | Y | N | Y | Y | N | Y |
| 3 **Northup** | Y | Y | Y | Y | Y | N | N |
| 4 **Davis** | Y | Y | Y | Y | Y | N | Y |
| 5 **Rogers** | N | Y | N | Y | Y | N | Y |
| 6 Chandler | Y | Y | N | Y | Y | N | Y |
| **LOUISIANA** | | | | | | | |
| 1 **Jindal** | Y | Y | Y | Y | Y | N | Y |
| 2 Jefferson | N | Y | N | N | N | N | N |
| 3 Melancon | Y | Y | N | N | N | Y | Y |
| 4 **McCrery** | Y | Y | Y | Y | Y | N | Y |
| 5 **Alexander** | Y | Y | Y | Y | Y | N | Y |
| 6 **Baker** | Y | Y | Y | Y | Y | N | Y |
| 7 **Boustany** | Y | Y | Y | Y | Y | N | N |
| **MAINE** | | | | | | | |
| 1 Allen | N | Y | N | N | N | N | N |
| 2 Michaud | Y | Y | N | N | N | N | N |
| **MARYLAND** | | | | | | | |
| 1 **Gilchrest** | Y | Y | Y | Y | Y | N | N |
| 2 Ruppersberger | Y | Y | N | N | N | N | N |
| 3 Cardin | N | Y | N | N | N | N | N |
| 4 Wynn | N | Y | N | N | Y | N | N |
| 5 Hoyer | N | Y | N | N | N | N | N |
| 6 **Bartlett** | Y | Y | Y | Y | Y | N | Y |
| 7 Cummings | N | Y | N | N | N | Y | N |
| 8 Van Hollen | N | Y | N | N | N | Y | N |
| **MASSACHUSETTS** | | | | | | | |
| 1 Olver | N | Y | N | N | N | N | N |
| 2 Neal | N | Y | N | N | N | N | N |
| 3 McGovern | N | Y | N | N | N | Y | N |
| 4 Frank | N | Y | N | N | N | N | N |
| 5 Meehan | N | Y | N | N | N | N | N |
| 6 Tierney | N | Y | N | N | N | Y | N |
| 7 Markey | N | Y | N | N | N | N | N |
| 8 Capuano | N | Y | N | N | N | Y | N |
| 9 Lynch | N | Y | N | N | N | N | N |
| 10 Delahunt | N | Y | N | N | N | N | N |
| **MICHIGAN** | | | | | | | |
| 1 Stupak | N | Y | N | N | N | N | N |
| 2 **Hoekstra** | Y | Y | Y | Y | Y | N | N |
| 3 **Ehlers** | Y | Y | Y | N | Y | N | N |
| 4 **Camp** | Y | Y | Y | Y | Y | N | N |
| 5 Kildee | N | Y | N | N | N | N | N |
| 6 **Upton** | Y | Y | Y | Y | Y | N | N |
| 7 **Schwarz** | Y | Y | Y | Y | Y | N | N |
| 8 **Rogers** | Y | Y | N | Y | Y | N | Y |
| 9 **Knollenberg** | Y | Y | Y | Y | Y | N | N |
| 10 **Miller** | Y | Y | N | Y | Y | N | N |
| 11 **McCotter** | Y | Y | N | Y | Y | N | P |
| 12 Levin | N | Y | N | N | N | N | N |
| 13 Kilpatrick | N | Y | N | N | N | Y | N |
| 14 Conyers | N | Y | N | N | N | Y | N |
| 15 Dingell | N | Y | N | N | N | N | N |

| | 653 | 654 | 655 | 656 | 657 | 658 | 659 |
|---|---|---|---|---|---|---|---|
| **MINNESOTA** | | | | | | | |
| 1 **Gutknecht** | Y | Y | Y | Y | Y | N | Y |
| 2 **Kline** | Y | Y | Y | Y | Y | N | Y |
| 3 **Ramstad** | Y | Y | N | Y | Y | N | Y |
| 4 McCollum | N | Y | N | N | N | Y | N |
| 5 Sabo | N | Y | N | N | N | N | N |
| 6 **Kennedy** | Y | Y | Y | Y | Y | N | Y |
| 7 Peterson | Y | Y | N | Y | Y | N | Y |
| 8 Oberstar | N | Y | N | N | N | N | N |
| **MISSISSIPPI** | | | | | | | |
| 1 **Wicker** | Y | Y | Y | Y | Y | N | Y |
| 2 Thompson | N | Y | N | N | N | Y | N |
| 3 **Pickering** | Y | Y | Y | Y | Y | N | Y |
| 4 Taylor | Y | Y | N | Y | Y | N | Y |
| **MISSOURI** | | | | | | | |
| 1 Clay | N | Y | N | N | N | Y | N |
| 2 **Akin** | Y | Y | Y | Y | Y | N | N |
| 3 Carnahan | N | Y | N | N | N | Y | N |
| 4 Skelton | Y | Y | N | N | N | N | Y |
| 5 Cleaver | N | Y | N | N | N | Y | N |
| 6 **Graves** | Y | Y | N | Y | Y | N | Y |
| 7 **Blunt** | Y | Y | Y | Y | Y | N | Y |
| 8 **Emerson** | Y | Y | Y | Y | Y | N | Y |
| 9 **Hulshof** | Y | Y | Y | Y | Y | N | Y |
| **MONTANA** | | | | | | | |
| AL **Rehberg** | Y | Y | N | Y | Y | N | N |
| **NEBRASKA** | | | | | | | |
| 1 **Fortenberry** | Y | Y | Y | Y | Y | N | Y |
| 2 **Terry** | Y | Y | Y | N | Y | N | N |
| 3 **Osborne** | Y | Y | Y | Y | Y | N | Y |
| **NEVADA** | | | | | | | |
| 1 Berkley | N | Y | N | N | Y | N | N |
| 2 **Gibbons** | Y | Y | N | Y | Y | N | Y |
| 3 **Porter** | Y | Y | N | Y | Y | N | Y |
| **NEW HAMPSHIRE** | | | | | | | |
| 1 **Bradley** | Y | Y | Y | Y | Y | N | Y |
| 2 **Bass** | Y | Y | Y | Y | Y | N | N |
| **NEW JERSEY** | | | | | | | |
| 1 Andrews | N | Y | N | N | N | Y | N |
| 2 **LoBiondo** | Y | Y | N | Y | Y | N | Y |
| 3 **Saxton** | Y | Y | N | Y | Y | N | Y |
| 4 **Smith** | Y | Y | N | Y | Y | N | N |
| 5 **Garrett** | Y | Y | Y | Y | Y | N | Y |
| 6 Pallone | N | Y | N | N | N | Y | N |
| 7 **Ferguson** | Y | Y | N | Y | Y | N | N |
| 8 Pascrell | N | Y | N | N | N | Y | N |
| 9 Rothman | N | Y | N | N | N | N | ? |
| 10 Payne | ? | ? | ? | ? | ? | ? | ? |
| 11 **Frelinghuysen** | Y | Y | Y | N | Y | N | N |
| 12 Holt | N | Y | N | N | N | N | N |
| 13 Menendez | N | Y | N | N | N | Y | N |
| **NEW MEXICO** | | | | | | | |
| 1 **Wilson** | Y | Y | Y | N | Y | N | N |
| 2 **Pearce** | Y | Y | Y | Y | Y | N | N |
| 3 Udall | Y | Y | N | N | N | Y | N |
| **NEW YORK** | | | | | | | |
| 1 Bishop | N | Y | N | Y | N | Y | N |
| 2 Israel | N | Y | N | Y | N | Y | N |
| 3 **King** | Y | Y | Y | Y | Y | N | N |
| 4 McCarthy | – | + | + | – | – | – | – |
| 5 Ackerman | N | Y | N | N | N | Y | N |
| 6 Meeks | N | Y | N | N | N | N | N |
| 7 Crowley | N | Y | N | N | N | Y | N |
| 8 Nadler | N | Y | N | N | N | N | N |
| 9 Weiner | N | Y | N | N | N | N | N |
| 10 Towns | N | Y | N | N | N | Y | N |
| 11 Owens | N | Y | N | N | N | Y | N |
| 12 Velázquez | N | Y | N | N | N | Y | N |
| 13 **Fossella** | Y | Y | Y | Y | Y | N | N |
| 14 Maloney | N | Y | N | N | N | Y | N |
| 15 Rangel | N | Y | N | N | N | N | N |
| 16 Serrano | N | Y | N | N | N | N | N |
| 17 Engel | N | Y | N | N | N | Y | N |
| 18 Lowey | N | Y | N | N | N | N | N |
| 19 **Kelly** | Y | Y | Y | Y | Y | N | Y |
| 20 **Sweeney** | Y | Y | N | Y | Y | N | Y |
| 21 McNulty | N | Y | N | N | N | N | N |
| 22 Hinchey | N | Y | N | N | N | N | N |
| 23 **McHugh** | Y | Y | N | Y | Y | N | ? |
| 24 **Boehlert** | Y | Y | Y | Y | Y | N | N |
| 25 **Walsh** | Y | Y | Y | Y | Y | N | N |
| 26 **Reynolds** | Y | Y | Y | Y | Y | – | Y |
| 27 Higgins | N | Y | N | N | Y | N | N |
| 28 Slaughter | N | Y | N | N | N | N | N |
| 29 **Kuhl** | Y | Y | N | Y | Y | N | N |

| | 653 | 654 | 655 | 656 | 657 | 658 | 659 |
|---|---|---|---|---|---|---|---|
| **NORTH CAROLINA** | | | | | | | |
| 1 Butterfield | N | Y | N | N | N | N | N |
| 2 Etheridge | N | Y | N | N | Y | N | N |
| 3 **Jones** | Y | Y | N | ? | Y | N | Y |
| 4 Price | N | Y | N | N | N | N | N |
| 5 **Foxx** | Y | Y | N | Y | Y | N | N |
| 6 **Coble** | Y | Y | Y | Y | Y | N | Y |
| 7 McIntyre | Y | Y | N | Y | Y | N | Y |
| 8 **Hayes** | Y | Y | Y | Y | Y | N | Y |
| 9 **Myrick** | Y | Y | Y | Y | Y | N | Y |
| 10 **McHenry** | Y | Y | N | Y | Y | N | Y |
| 11 **Taylor** | Y | Y | N | Y | Y | N | Y |
| 12 Watt | N | Y | N | N | N | N | N |
| 13 Miller | N | Y | N | N | N | Y | N |
| **NORTH DAKOTA** | | | | | | | |
| AL Pomeroy | N | Y | N | N | ? | Y | N |
| **OHIO** | | | | | | | |
| 1 **Chabot** | Y | Y | Y | Y | Y | N | Y |
| 2 **Schmidt** | Y | Y | N | Y | Y | N | Y |
| 3 **Turner** | Y | Y | Y | Y | Y | N | N |
| 4 **Oxley** | Y | Y | Y | ? | Y | N | N |
| 5 **Gillmor** | Y | Y | Y | Y | Y | N | N |
| 6 Strickland | Y | Y | N | N | N | N | N |
| 7 **Hobson** | Y | Y | Y | Y | Y | N | N |
| 8 **Boehner** | Y | Y | N | Y | Y | N | Y |
| 9 Kaptur | N | Y | N | N | N | N | N |
| 10 Kucinich | N | Y | N | N | N | Y | N |
| 11 Jones | N | Y | N | N | N | N | N |
| 12 **Tiberi** | Y | Y | Y | Y | Y | N | Y |
| 13 Brown | Y | Y | N | N | N | Y | N |
| 14 **LaTourette** | Y | Y | N | Y | Y | N | N |
| 15 **Pryce** | Y | Y | Y | ? | Y | N | Y |
| 16 **Regula** | Y | Y | Y | Y | Y | N | N |
| 17 Ryan | N | Y | N | N | N | Y | N |
| 18 **Ney** | Y | Y | N | Y | Y | N | Y |
| **OKLAHOMA** | | | | | | | |
| 1 **Sullivan** | Y | Y | N | Y | Y | N | Y |
| 2 Boren | Y | Y | N | Y | Y | N | Y |
| 3 **Lucas** | Y | Y | N | Y | Y | N | Y |
| 4 **Cole** | Y | Y | Y | Y | Y | N | + |
| 5 **Istook** | ? | ? | ? | ? | ? | ? | ? |
| **OREGON** | | | | | | | |
| 1 Wu | N | Y | N | N | N | Y | N |
| 2 **Walden** | Y | Y | Y | Y | Y | N | Y |
| 3 Blumenauer | N | Y | N | N | N | N | N |
| 4 DeFazio | Y | Y | N | Y | N | Y | N |
| 5 Hooley | Y | Y | N | Y | N | Y | N |
| **PENNSYLVANIA** | | | | | | | |
| 1 Brady | N | Y | N | N | N | Y | N |
| 2 Fattah | N | Y | N | N | N | Y | N |
| 3 **English** | Y | Y | Y | Y | Y | N | Y |
| 4 **Hart** | Y | Y | N | Y | Y | N | Y |
| 5 **Peterson** | Y | Y | Y | Y | Y | N | Y |
| 6 **Gerlach** | Y | Y | N | Y | Y | N | N |
| 7 **Weldon** | Y | Y | N | Y | Y | N | N |
| 8 **Fitzpatrick** | Y | Y | N | Y | Y | N | N |
| 9 **Shuster** | Y | Y | N | Y | Y | N | Y |
| 10 **Sherwood** | Y | Y | Y | Y | Y | N | Y |
| 11 Kanjorski | N | Y | N | N | N | N | N |
| 12 Murtha | N | Y | N | N | N | N | N |
| 13 Schwartz | Y | Y | N | N | N | Y | N |
| 14 Doyle | N | Y | N | N | N | N | N |
| 15 **Dent** | Y | Y | N | Y | Y | N | Y |
| 16 **Pitts** | Y | Y | Y | Y | Y | N | Y |
| 17 Holden | Y | Y | N | Y | N | N | Y |
| 18 **Murphy** | Y | Y | Y | Y | Y | N | Y |
| 19 **Platts** | Y | Y | N | Y | Y | N | Y |
| **RHODE ISLAND** | | | | | | | |
| 1 Kennedy | N | Y | N | N | N | N | ? |
| 2 Langevin | N | Y | N | N | N | N | N |
| **SOUTH CAROLINA** | | | | | | | |
| 1 **Brown** | Y | Y | Y | Y | Y | N | Y |
| 2 **Wilson** | Y | Y | N | Y | Y | N | Y |
| 3 **Barrett** | + | + | – | + | + | – | + |
| 4 **Inglis** | Y | Y | Y | Y | Y | N | Y |
| 5 Spratt | Y | Y | Y | Y | Y | N | N |
| 6 Clyburn | N | Y | N | N | N | Y | N |
| **SOUTH DAKOTA** | | | | | | | |
| AL Herseth | Y | Y | N | Y | N | Y | Y |
| **TENNESSEE** | | | | | | | |
| 1 **Jenkins** | Y | Y | Y | Y | Y | N | Y |
| 2 **Duncan** | Y | Y | N | Y | Y | N | Y |

| | 653 | 654 | 655 | 656 | 657 | 658 | 659 |
|---|---|---|---|---|---|---|---|
| 3 **Wamp** | Y | Y | Y | Y | Y | N | Y |
| 4 Davis | Y | Y | N | Y | Y | N | Y |
| 5 Cooper | Y | Y | N | Y | Y | Y | Y |
| 6 Gordon | Y | Y | N | N | Y | N | Y |
| 7 **Blackburn** | Y | Y | Y | Y | Y | N | Y |
| 8 Tanner | Y | Y | N | Y | Y | Y | Y |
| 9 Ford | Y | Y | N | Y | Y | N | Y |
| **TEXAS** | | | | | | | |
| 1 **Gohmert** | Y | Y | N | Y | Y | N | Y |
| 2 **Poe** | Y | Y | N | Y | Y | N | Y |
| 3 **Johnson, S.** | Y | Y | Y | Y | Y | N | Y |
| 4 **Hall** | Y | Y | Y | Y | Y | N | Y |
| 5 **Hensarling** | Y | Y | Y | Y | Y | N | N |
| 6 **Barton** | + | + | + | + | + | – | + |
| 7 **Culberson** | Y | Y | N | Y | Y | N | Y |
| 8 **Brady** | Y | Y | Y | Y | Y | N | Y |
| 9 Green, A. | N | Y | N | N | N | Y | N |
| 10 **McCaul** | Y | Y | Y | Y | Y | N | Y |
| 11 **Conaway** | Y | Y | N | Y | Y | N | Y |
| 12 **Granger** | Y | Y | Y | Y | Y | N | N |
| 13 **Thornberry** | Y | Y | Y | Y | Y | N | N |
| 14 **Paul** | Y | Y | Y | Y | Y | N | Y |
| 15 Hinojosa | N | Y | N | N | N | N | N |
| 16 Reyes | N | Y | N | N | N | Y | N |
| 17 Edwards | Y | Y | Y | Y | Y | N | Y |
| 18 Jackson-Lee | N | Y | N | N | N | Y | N |
| 19 **Neugebauer** | Y | Y | N | Y | Y | N | Y |
| 20 Gonzalez | N | Y | N | N | N | Y | N |
| 21 **Smith** | Y | Y | Y | Y | Y | N | Y |
| 22 **DeLay** | Y | Y | Y | Y | Y | N | N |
| 23 **Bonilla** | Y | Y | Y | Y | Y | N | N |
| 24 **Marchant** | Y | Y | N | Y | Y | N | Y |
| 25 Doggett | N | Y | N | N | N | N | N |
| 26 **Burgess** | Y | Y | Y | Y | Y | N | N |
| 27 Ortiz | N | Y | N | N | N | Y | N |
| 28 Cuellar | Y | Y | N | N | N | N | N |
| 29 Green, G. | Y | Y | N | N | N | Y | N |
| 30 Johnson, E. | N | Y | N | N | N | Y | N |
| 31 **Carter** | Y | Y | N | Y | Y | N | N |
| 32 **Sessions** | Y | Y | Y | Y | Y | N | Y |
| **UTAH** | | | | | | | |
| 1 **Bishop** | Y | Y | Y | Y | Y | N | Y |
| 2 Matheson | Y | Y | Y | Y | Y | N | Y |
| 3 **Cannon** | N | Y | Y | N | Y | N | N |
| **VERMONT** | | | | | | | |
| AL *Sanders* | Y | Y | N | N | N | Y | N |
| **VIRGINIA** | | | | | | | |
| 1 **Davis, J.** | + | + | + | + | + | – | + |
| 2 **Drake** | Y | Y | N | Y | Y | N | Y |
| 3 Scott | N | Y | N | N | N | N | N |
| 4 **Forbes** | Y | Y | N | Y | Y | N | Y |
| 5 **Goode** | Y | Y | N | Y | Y | N | Y |
| 6 **Goodlatte** | Y | Y | N | Y | Y | N | Y |
| 7 **Cantor** | Y | Y | Y | Y | Y | N | Y |
| 8 Moran | Y | Y | N | N | – | N | N |
| 9 Boucher | Y | Y | N | Y | N | Y | N |
| 10 **Wolf** | Y | Y | N | Y | Y | N | N |
| 11 **Davis, T.** | Y | Y | N | Y | Y | N | N |
| **WASHINGTON** | | | | | | | |
| 1 Inslee | N | Y | N | N | N | N | N |
| 2 Larsen | N | Y | N | N | N | N | N |
| 3 Baird | Y | Y | N | N | N | N | N |
| 4 **Hastings** | Y | Y | Y | Y | Y | N | N |
| 5 **McMorris** | Y | Y | Y | Y | Y | N | N |
| 6 Dicks | Y | Y | N | N | N | N | N |
| 7 McDermott | N | Y | N | N | N | Y | N |
| 8 **Reichert** | Y | Y | Y | Y | Y | N | N |
| 9 Smith | N | Y | N | N | N | Y | N |
| **WEST VIRGINIA** | | | | | | | |
| 1 Mollohan | N | Y | N | N | N | N | N |
| 2 **Capito** | Y | Y | Y | Y | Y | N | Y |
| 3 Rahall | N | Y | N | N | N | Y | N |
| **WISCONSIN** | | | | | | | |
| 1 **Ryan** | Y | Y | Y | N | Y | N | N |
| 2 Baldwin | N | Y | N | N | N | N | N |
| 3 Kind | Y | Y | N | N | N | N | N |
| 4 Moore | N | Y | N | N | N | N | N |
| 5 **Sensenbrenner** | Y | Y | Y | Y | Y | N | N |
| 6 **Petri** | Y | Y | Y | Y | Y | N | N |
| 7 Obey | Y | Y | N | N | N | Y | N |
| 8 **Green** | Y | Y | Y | Y | Y | N | N |
| **WYOMING** | | | | | | | |
| AL **Cubin** | Y | Y | Y | Y | Y | N | Y |

# IN THE HOUSE | By Vote Number

**660.** **HR 4437. Border Security/Recommit.** Reyes, D-Texas, motion to recommit the bill to the Homeland Security and Judiciary committees with instructions to substitute language that would require the Department of Homeland Security to develop a comprehensive security strategy for all U.S. borders and ports, provide increased personnel including 12,000 additional Border Patrol agents, and provide 100,000 additional detention beds. Motion rejected 198-221: R 0-219; D 197-2 (ND 148-1, SD 49-1); I 1-0. Dec. 16, 2005.

**661.** **HR 4437. Border Security/Passage.** Passage of the bill that would tighten border security and increase enforcement of immigration laws. It would designate unlawful presence, in addition to illegal migration, as a criminal, rather than a civil, offense. It also would increase penalties for a variety of immigration-related crimes. It would create a mandatory program under which all employers would have to verify employees' work eligibility with the federal government. As amended, it would require the construction of security fencing, including lights and cameras, along certain ports of entry along the U.S.-Mexico border. Passed 239-182: R 203-17; D 36-164 (ND 20-129, SD 16-35); I 0-1. A "yea" was a vote in support of the president's position. Dec. 16, 2005.

**662.** **H Res 598. Lebanese Prime Minister Assassination/Adoption.** Ros-Lehtinen, R-Fla., motion to suspend the rules and adopt the resolution that would condemn the Syrian government for hindering and failing to fully cooperate in a timely manner with the U.N. investigation of the assassination of former Lebanese Prime Minister Rafik Hariri. Motion agreed to 404-5: R 214-1; D 189-4 (ND 140-3, SD 49-1); I 1-0. A two-thirds majority of those present and voting (273 in this case) is required for adoption under suspension of the rules. Dec. 16, 2005.

**663.** **H Res 623. Suspension Motions/Rule.** Adoption of the rule (H Res 623) to provide for House floor consideration of bills under suspension of the rules on Saturday, Nov. 17, 2005. Adopted 213-190: R 212-0; D 1-189 (ND 1-140, SD 0-49); I 0-1. Dec. 17, 2005.

**664.** **HR 2520. Cord Blood Stem Cell Research/Passage.** Deal, R-Ga., motion to suspend the rules and agree to the Senate amendment to the bill that would create a new federal program to collect and store umbilical cord blood stem cells. The bill also would reauthorize and expand the current bone marrow registry program. Motion agreed to 413-0: R 216-0; D 196-0 (ND 145-0, SD 51-0); I 1-0. A two-thirds majority of those present and voting (276 in this case) is required for passage under suspension of the rules. Dec. 17, 2005.

**665.** **HR 1815. Fiscal 2006 Defense Authorization/Conference Report.** Adoption of the conference report on the bill that would authorize $441.5 billion for defense programs and $50 billion for military operations in Iraq and Afghanistan. The bill includes $77 billion for weapons procurement, $108.9 billion for personnel and $12.2 billion for military construction and family housing. It would also authorize $6.6 billion for Hurricane Katrina relief, $130 million for flu preparedness and $40 million for Pakistan earthquake relief. It would prohibit cruel, inhuman or degrading treatment of any prisoner detained by the U.S. government. Adopted (thus sent to the Senate) 374-41: R 218-1; D 155-40 (ND 109-36, SD 46-4); I 1-0. Dec. 19, 2005 (in the session that began and the Congressional Record dated Dec. 18, 2005).

| | 660 | 661 | 662 | 663 | 664 | 665 |
|---|---|---|---|---|---|---|
| **ALABAMA** | | | | | | |
| 1 Bonner | N | Y | Y | Y | Y | Y |
| 2 Everett | N | Y | Y | Y | Y | Y |
| 3 Rogers | N | Y | Y | Y | Y | Y |
| 4 Aderholt | N | Y | Y | Y | Y | Y |
| 5 Cramer | Y | Y | Y | N | Y | Y |
| 6 Bachus | N | Y | Y | Y | Y | Y |
| 7 Davis | Y | N | Y | N | Y | Y |
| **ALASKA** | | | | | | |
| AL Young | ? | ? | ? | Y | Y | Y |
| **ARIZONA** | | | | | | |
| 1 Renzi | N | Y | Y | Y | Y | Y |
| 2 Franks | N | Y | Y | Y | Y | Y |
| 3 Shadegg | N | Y | Y | Y | Y | Y |
| 4 Pastor | Y | N | Y | ? | Y | Y |
| 5 Hayworth | N | N | Y | Y | Y | Y |
| 6 Flake | N | Y | Y | Y | Y | Y |
| 7 Grijalva | Y | N | Y | N | Y | N |
| 8 Kolbe | ? | ? | ? | ? | ? | ? |
| **ARKANSAS** | | | | | | |
| 1 Berry | Y | Y | Y | N | Y | Y |
| 2 Snyder | Y | N | Y | N | Y | Y |
| 3 Boozman | N | Y | Y | N | Y | Y |
| 4 Ross | Y | Y | Y | N | Y | Y |
| **CALIFORNIA** | | | | | | |
| 1 Thompson | Y | N | Y | N | Y | Y |
| 2 Herger | N | Y | Y | Y | Y | Y |
| 3 Lungren | N | Y | Y | Y | Y | Y |
| 4 Doolittle | N | Y | Y | Y | Y | Y |
| 5 Matsui, D. | Y | N | Y | N | Y | Y |
| 6 Woolsey | Y | N | Y | N | Y | N |
| 7 Miller, George | Y | N | Y | N | Y | N |
| 8 Pelosi | Y | N | Y | N | Y | Y |
| 9 Lee | Y | N | Y | N | Y | N |
| 10 Tauscher | Y | N | Y | N | Y | Y |
| 11 Pombo | N | Y | Y | Y | Y | Y |
| 12 Lantos | Y | N | N | N | Y | Y |
| 13 Stark | Y | N | Y | N | Y | N |
| 14 Eshoo | Y | N | Y | N | Y | Y |
| 15 Honda | Y | N | Y | N | Y | Y |
| 16 Lofgren | Y | N | Y | N | Y | Y |
| 17 Farr | Y | N | ? | N | Y | Y |
| 18 Cardoza | Y | N | Y | ? | Y | Y |
| 19 Radanovich | N | N | ? | Y | ? | Y |
| 20 Costa | Y | N | Y | N | Y | Y |
| 21 Nunes | N | N | Y | Y | Y | Y |
| 22 Thomas | N | Y | Y | Y | Y | Y |
| 23 Capps | Y | N | Y | N | Y | Y |
| 24 Gallegly | N | Y | Y | Y | Y | Y |
| 25 McKeon | N | Y | Y | Y | Y | Y |
| 26 Dreier | N | Y | Y | Y | Y | Y |
| 27 Sherman | Y | N | Y | N | Y | Y |
| 28 Berman | Y | N | ? | N | Y | Y |
| 29 Schiff | Y | N | Y | N | Y | Y |
| 30 Waxman | Y | N | Y | N | Y | Y |
| 31 Becerra | Y | N | Y | – | + | Y |
| 32 Solis | Y | N | Y | N | Y | Y |
| 33 Watson | Y | N | Y | ? | Y | N |
| 34 Roybal-Allard | Y | N | Y | N | Y | ? |
| 35 Waters | Y | N | Y | ? | Y | ? |
| 36 Harman | Y | N | Y | N | Y | ? |
| 37 Millender-McD. | Y | N | Y | N | Y | Y |
| 38 Napolitano | ? | ? | ? | N | Y | Y |
| 39 Sánchez, Linda | Y | N | Y | N | Y | Y |
| 40 Royce | N | Y | Y | Y | Y | Y |
| 41 Lewis | N | Y | Y | Y | Y | Y |
| 42 Miller, Gary | N | Y | Y | Y | Y | Y |
| 43 Baca | Y | N | Y | ? | ? | Y |
| 44 Calvert | N | Y | Y | Y | Y | Y |
| 45 Bono | N | Y | Y | Y | Y | Y |
| 46 Rohrabacher | N | Y | Y | Y | Y | Y |
| 47 Sanchez, Loretta | Y | N | Y | N | Y | Y |
| 48 Campbell | N | Y | Y | Y | Y | Y |
| 49 Issa | N | Y | Y | Y | Y | Y |

| | 660 | 661 | 662 | 663 | 664 | 665 |
|---|---|---|---|---|---|---|
| 50 Vacant | | | | | | |
| 51 Filner | Y | N | Y | N | Y | N |
| 52 Hunter | N | Y | Y | Y | Y | Y |
| 53 Davis | Y | N | Y | N | Y | Y |
| **COLORADO** | | | | | | |
| 1 DeGette | Y | N | Y | N | Y | Y |
| 2 Udall | Y | Y | Y | N | Y | Y |
| 3 Salazar | Y | Y | Y | N | Y | Y |
| 4 Musgrave | N | Y | Y | Y | Y | Y |
| 5 Hefley | N | Y | Y | Y | Y | ? |
| 6 Tancredo | N | Y | Y | Y | Y | Y |
| 7 Beauprez | N | Y | Y | Y | Y | Y |
| **CONNECTICUT** | | | | | | |
| 1 Larson | Y | N | Y | N | Y | Y |
| 2 Simmons | N | Y | Y | Y | Y | Y |
| 3 DeLauro | Y | N | Y | N | Y | Y |
| 4 Shays | N | Y | Y | Y | Y | Y |
| 5 Johnson | N | Y | Y | Y | Y | Y |
| **DELAWARE** | | | | | | |
| AL Castle | N | Y | Y | Y | Y | Y |
| **FLORIDA** | | | | | | |
| 1 Miller | N | Y | Y | Y | Y | Y |
| 2 Boyd | Y | N | Y | N | Y | Y |
| 3 Brown | Y | N | Y | N | Y | Y |
| 4 Crenshaw | N | Y | Y | Y | Y | Y |
| 5 Brown-Waite | N | Y | Y | Y | Y | Y |
| 6 Stearns | N | Y | Y | + | Y | Y |
| 7 Mica | N | Y | Y | Y | Y | Y |
| 8 Keller | N | Y | Y | Y | Y | Y |
| 9 Bilirakis | N | Y | Y | Y | Y | Y |
| 10 Young | ? | ? | ? | ? | Y | Y |
| 11 Davis | Y | N | Y | N | Y | Y |
| 12 Putnam | N | Y | Y | Y | Y | Y |
| 13 Harris | N | Y | Y | Y | Y | Y |
| 14 Mack | N | Y | Y | Y | Y | Y |
| 15 Weldon | N | Y | Y | Y | Y | Y |
| 16 Foley | N | Y | Y | Y | Y | Y |
| 17 Meek | Y | N | Y | N | Y | Y |
| 18 Ros-Lehtinen | N | N | Y | Y | Y | Y |
| 19 Wexler | Y | N | Y | ? | Y | Y |
| 20 Wasserman-Schultz | Y | N | Y | N | Y | Y |
| 21 Diaz-Balart, L. | N | N | Y | Y | Y | Y |
| 22 Shaw | N | Y | Y | Y | Y | Y |
| 23 Hastings | Y | N | Y | N | Y | N |
| 24 Feeney | N | Y | Y | Y | Y | Y |
| 25 Diaz-Balart, M. | – | – | ? | ? | Y | Y |
| **GEORGIA** | | | | | | |
| 1 Kingston | N | Y | Y | Y | Y | Y |
| 2 Bishop | Y | N | Y | N | Y | Y |
| 3 Marshall | Y | Y | Y | N | Y | Y |
| 4 McKinney | Y | N | N | N | Y | N |
| 5 Lewis | Y | N | Y | N | Y | N |
| 6 Price | N | Y | Y | Y | Y | + |
| 7 Linder | N | Y | Y | Y | Y | Y |
| 8 Westmoreland | N | Y | ? | Y | Y | Y |
| 9 Norwood | N | Y | Y | Y | Y | Y |
| 10 Deal | N | Y | Y | Y | Y | Y |
| 11 Gingrey | N | Y | Y | Y | Y | Y |
| 12 Barrow | Y | N | Y | N | Y | Y |
| 13 Scott | Y | N | Y | N | Y | Y |
| **HAWAII** | | | | | | |
| 1 Abercrombie | Y | N | P | N | Y | Y |
| 2 Case | N | Y | Y | N | Y | Y |
| **IDAHO** | | | | | | |
| 1 Otter | N | Y | Y | Y | Y | Y |
| 2 Simpson | N | Y | Y | Y | Y | Y |
| **ILLINOIS** | | | | | | |
| 1 Rush | Y | N | Y | N | Y | N |
| 2 Jackson | Y | N | Y | N | Y | N |
| 3 Lipinski | Y | Y | Y | N | Y | Y |
| 4 Gutierrez | Y | N | Y | N | Y | ? |
| 5 Emanuel | Y | N | Y | N | Y | ? |
| 6 Hyde | ? | ? | ? | ? | ? | ? |
| 7 Davis | Y | N | Y | N | Y | N |
| 8 Bean | Y | Y | Y | N | Y | Y |
| 9 Schakowsky | Y | N | Y | N | Y | N |
| 10 Kirk | N | Y | Y | Y | Y | Y |
| 11 Weller | N | Y | Y | Y | Y | Y |
| 12 Costello | Y | N | Y | N | Y | Y |

**KEY**  Republicans   Democrats   *Independents*

| | | |
|---|---|---|
| **Y** Voted for (yea) | **X** Paired against | **C** Voted "present" to avoid possible conflict of interest |
| **#** Paired for | **–** Announced against | |
| **+** Announced for | **P** Voted "present" | **?** Did not vote or otherwise make a position known |
| **N** Voted against (nay) | | |

| | 660 | 661 | 662 | 663 | 664 | 665 |
|---|---|---|---|---|---|---|
| 13 **Biggert** | N | Y | Y | Y | Y | Y |
| 14 **Hastert** | | Y | | | | Y |
| 15 **Johnson** | N | Y | Y | Y | Y | Y |
| 16 **Manzullo** | N | Y | Y | Y | ? | Y |
| 17 Evans | Y | N | Y | N | Y | Y |
| 18 **LaHood** | ? | ? | ? | Y | Y | Y |
| 19 **Shimkus** | N | Y | Y | Y | Y | Y |
| **INDIANA** | | | | | | |
| 1 Visclosky | Y | Y | Y | N | Y | Y |
| 2 **Chocola** | N | Y | Y | Y | Y | Y |
| 3 **Souder** | N | N | Y | Y | Y | Y |
| 4 **Buyer** | N | Y | Y | Y | Y | Y |
| 5 **Burton** | N | Y | Y | Y | Y | Y |
| 6 **Pence** | N | Y | Y | Y | Y | Y |
| 7 Carson | Y | N | Y | N | Y | Y |
| 8 **Hostettler** | N | Y | Y | Y | ? | ? |
| 9 **Sodrel** | N | Y | Y | Y | Y | Y |
| **IOWA** | | | | | | |
| 1 **Nussle** | ? | Y | ? | Y | Y | Y |
| 2 **Leach** | N | N | Y | Y | Y | Y |
| 3 Boswell | Y | Y | Y | N | Y | Y |
| 4 **Latham** | N | Y | Y | Y | Y | Y |
| 5 **King** | N | Y | Y | Y | Y | Y |
| **KANSAS** | | | | | | |
| 1 **Moran** | N | Y | Y | Y | Y | Y |
| 2 **Ryun** | N | Y | Y | Y | Y | Y |
| 3 Moore | Y | Y | Y | N | Y | Y |
| 4 **Tiahrt** | N | Y | Y | Y | Y | Y |
| **KENTUCKY** | | | | | | |
| 1 **Whitfield** | N | Y | Y | Y | Y | Y |
| 2 **Lewis** | N | Y | Y | Y | Y | Y |
| 3 **Northup** | N | Y | Y | Y | Y | Y |
| 4 **Davis** | N | Y | Y | Y | Y | Y |
| 5 **Rogers** | N | Y | Y | Y | Y | Y |
| 6 Chandler | Y | Y | Y | N | Y | Y |
| **LOUISIANA** | | | | | | |
| 1 **Jindal** | N | Y | Y | Y | Y | Y |
| 2 Jefferson | ? | N | Y | N | Y | Y |
| 3 Melancon | Y | Y | Y | N | Y | Y |
| 4 **McCrery** | N | Y | Y | ? | Y | Y |
| 5 **Alexander** | N | Y | Y | Y | Y | Y |
| 6 **Baker** | N | Y | ? | Y | Y | Y |
| 7 **Boustany** | N | Y | Y | Y | Y | Y |
| **MAINE** | | | | | | |
| 1 Allen | Y | N | Y | N | Y | Y |
| 2 Michaud | Y | N | Y | N | Y | Y |
| **MARYLAND** | | | | | | |
| 1 **Gilchrest** | N | Y | Y | ? | Y | Y |
| 2 Ruppersberger | Y | N | Y | N | Y | Y |
| 3 Cardin | Y | N | Y | N | Y | Y |
| 4 Wynn | Y | N | Y | N | Y | Y |
| 5 Hoyer | Y | N | Y | ? | Y | Y |
| 6 **Bartlett** | N | N | Y | Y | Y | Y |
| 7 Cummings | Y | N | Y | ? | Y | Y |
| 8 Van Hollen | Y | N | Y | N | Y | Y |
| **MASSACHUSETTS** | | | | | | |
| 1 Olver | Y | N | Y | N | Y | N |
| 2 Neal | Y | N | Y | N | Y | Y |
| 3 McGovern | Y | N | Y | N | Y | N |
| 4 Frank | Y | N | Y | N | Y | N |
| 5 Meehan | Y | N | Y | N | Y | Y |
| 6 Tierney | Y | N | Y | N | Y | N |
| 7 Markey | Y | N | ? | N | Y | N |
| 8 Capuano | Y | N | Y | N | Y | Y |
| 9 Lynch | Y | N | Y | N | Y | Y |
| 10 Delahunt | Y | N | Y | N | Y | Y |
| **MICHIGAN** | | | | | | |
| 1 Stupak | Y | N | Y | N | Y | Y |
| 2 **Hoekstra** | N | Y | Y | Y | Y | Y |
| 3 **Ehlers** | N | Y | Y | ? | ? | Y |
| 4 **Camp** | N | Y | Y | Y | Y | Y |
| 5 Kildee | Y | N | Y | N | Y | Y |
| 6 **Upton** | N | Y | Y | Y | Y | Y |
| 7 **Schwarz** | N | Y | Y | Y | Y | Y |
| 8 **Rogers** | N | Y | Y | Y | Y | Y |
| 9 **Knollenberg** | N | Y | Y | Y | Y | Y |
| 10 **Miller** | N | Y | Y | Y | Y | Y |
| 11 **McCotter** | N | Y | Y | Y | Y | Y |
| 12 Levin | Y | N | Y | N | Y | Y |
| 13 Kilpatrick | Y | N | ? | N | Y | N |
| 14 Conyers | Y | N | Y | N | Y | N |
| 15 Dingell | Y | N | Y | N | Y | Y |

| | 660 | 661 | 662 | 663 | 664 | 665 |
|---|---|---|---|---|---|---|
| **MINNESOTA** | | | | | | |
| 1 **Gutknecht** | N | Y | Y | Y | Y | Y |
| 2 **Kline** | N | Y | Y | Y | Y | Y |
| 3 **Ramstad** | N | Y | Y | Y | Y | Y |
| 4 McCollum | Y | N | Y | N | Y | Y |
| 5 Sabo | Y | N | Y | N | Y | Y |
| 6 **Kennedy** | N | Y | Y | Y | Y | Y |
| 7 Peterson | Y | Y | Y | N | Y | Y |
| 8 Oberstar | Y | N | Y | N | Y | N |
| **MISSISSIPPI** | | | | | | |
| 1 **Wicker** | N | Y | Y | Y | Y | Y |
| 2 Thompson | Y | N | Y | N | Y | Y |
| 3 **Pickering** | N | Y | Y | Y | Y | Y |
| 4 Taylor | Y | Y | Y | N | Y | Y |
| **MISSOURI** | | | | | | |
| 1 Clay | Y | N | Y | ? | Y | ? |
| 2 **Akin** | N | Y | Y | ? | ? | Y |
| 3 Carnahan | Y | N | Y | N | Y | Y |
| 4 Skelton | Y | Y | Y | N | Y | Y |
| 5 Cleaver | Y | N | Y | N | Y | Y |
| 6 **Graves** | N | Y | Y | Y | Y | Y |
| 7 **Blunt** | N | Y | Y | Y | Y | Y |
| 8 **Emerson** | N | Y | Y | Y | Y | Y |
| 9 **Hulshof** | N | Y | Y | Y | Y | Y |
| **MONTANA** | | | | | | |
| AL **Rehberg** | N | Y | Y | Y | Y | Y |
| **NEBRASKA** | | | | | | |
| 1 **Fortenberry** | N | Y | Y | Y | Y | Y |
| 2 **Terry** | N | Y | Y | Y | Y | Y |
| 3 **Osborne** | N | Y | Y | Y | Y | Y |
| **NEVADA** | | | | | | |
| 1 Berkley | Y | N | Y | N | Y | Y |
| 2 **Gibbons** | N | Y | Y | Y | Y | Y |
| 3 **Porter** | N | Y | Y | Y | Y | Y |
| **NEW HAMPSHIRE** | | | | | | |
| 1 **Bradley** | N | Y | Y | Y | Y | Y |
| 2 **Bass** | N | Y | Y | Y | Y | Y |
| **NEW JERSEY** | | | | | | |
| 1 Andrews | Y | N | Y | N | Y | Y |
| 2 **LoBiondo** | N | Y | Y | Y | Y | Y |
| 3 **Saxton** | N | Y | Y | Y | Y | Y |
| 4 **Smith** | N | N | Y | Y | Y | Y |
| 5 **Garrett** | N | Y | Y | Y | Y | Y |
| 6 Pallone | Y | N | Y | N | Y | Y |
| 7 **Ferguson** | N | Y | Y | Y | Y | Y |
| 8 Pascrell | Y | N | Y | N | Y | Y |
| 9 Rothman | Y | N | Y | Y | Y | Y |
| 10 Payne | Y | N | Y | N | Y | N |
| 11 **Frelinghuysen** | N | Y | Y | Y | Y | Y |
| 12 Holt | Y | N | Y | N | Y | Y |
| 13 Menendez | Y | N | Y | N | Y | Y |
| **NEW MEXICO** | | | | | | |
| 1 **Wilson** | N | N | Y | Y | Y | Y |
| 2 **Pearce** | N | N | Y | Y | Y | Y |
| 3 Udall | Y | N | Y | N | Y | Y |
| **NEW YORK** | | | | | | |
| 1 Bishop | Y | N | Y | N | Y | Y |
| 2 Israel | Y | N | Y | N | Y | Y |
| 3 **King** | N | Y | Y | Y | Y | Y |
| 4 McCarthy | + | – | + | – | + | Y |
| 5 Ackerman | Y | N | Y | N | Y | Y |
| 6 Meeks | Y | N | Y | N | Y | Y |
| 7 Crowley | Y | N | Y | N | Y | Y |
| 8 Nadler | Y | N | Y | N | Y | N |
| 9 Weiner | Y | N | Y | N | Y | Y |
| 10 Towns | Y | N | Y | N | Y | N |
| 11 Owens | Y | N | Y | N | Y | N |
| 12 Velázquez | Y | N | Y | N | Y | N |
| 13 **Fossella** | N | Y | Y | Y | ? | Y |
| 14 Maloney | Y | N | Y | N | Y | Y |
| 15 Rangel | Y | N | Y | N | Y | N |
| 16 Serrano | Y | N | Y | N | Y | N |
| 17 Engel | Y | N | Y | N | Y | Y |
| 18 Lowey | Y | N | Y | N | Y | Y |
| 19 **Kelly** | N | Y | Y | Y | Y | Y |
| 20 **Sweeney** | N | Y | Y | Y | Y | Y |
| 21 McNulty | Y | N | Y | N | Y | N |
| 22 Hinchey | Y | N | Y | N | Y | N |
| 23 **McHugh** | N | Y | Y | Y | Y | Y |
| 24 **Boehlert** | N | Y | Y | Y | Y | Y |
| 25 **Walsh** | N | Y | Y | Y | Y | Y |
| 26 **Reynolds** | N | Y | Y | Y | Y | Y |
| 27 Higgins | Y | Y | Y | N | Y | Y |
| 28 Slaughter | Y | N | Y | N | ? | Y |
| 29 **Kuhl** | N | Y | Y | Y | Y | Y |

| | 660 | 661 | 662 | 663 | 664 | 665 |
|---|---|---|---|---|---|---|
| **NORTH CAROLINA** | | | | | | |
| 1 Butterfield | Y | N | Y | N | Y | Y |
| 2 Etheridge | Y | N | Y | N | Y | Y |
| 3 **Jones** | N | Y | Y | Y | Y | ? |
| 4 Price | Y | N | Y | N | Y | Y |
| 5 **Foxx** | N | Y | Y | Y | Y | Y |
| 6 **Coble** | N | Y | Y | Y | Y | Y |
| 7 McIntyre | Y | Y | Y | N | Y | Y |
| 8 **Hayes** | N | Y | Y | Y | Y | Y |
| 9 **Myrick** | N | Y | Y | ? | ? | ? |
| 10 **McHenry** | N | Y | Y | Y | Y | Y |
| 11 **Taylor** | N | Y | Y | Y | Y | Y |
| 12 Watt | Y | N | Y | N | Y | N |
| 13 Miller | Y | N | Y | N | Y | Y |
| **NORTH DAKOTA** | | | | | | |
| AL Pomeroy | Y | Y | Y | N | Y | Y |
| **OHIO** | | | | | | |
| 1 **Chabot** | N | Y | Y | Y | Y | Y |
| 2 **Schmidt** | N | Y | Y | Y | Y | Y |
| 3 **Turner** | N | N | Y | Y | Y | Y |
| 4 **Oxley** | N | Y | ? | Y | Y | Y |
| 5 **Gillmor** | N | Y | Y | Y | Y | Y |
| 6 Strickland | Y | Y | Y | N | Y | Y |
| 7 **Hobson** | N | N | Y | Y | Y | Y |
| 8 **Boehner** | N | N | Y | Y | Y | Y |
| 9 Kaptur | Y | N | N | N | Y | Y |
| 10 Kucinich | Y | N | Y | N | Y | N |
| 11 Jones | Y | N | Y | N | Y | N |
| 12 **Tiberi** | N | N | Y | Y | Y | Y |
| 13 Brown | Y | N | Y | N | Y | Y |
| 14 **LaTourette** | N | Y | Y | Y | Y | Y |
| 15 **Pryce** | N | Y | Y | Y | Y | Y |
| 16 **Regula** | N | Y | Y | Y | Y | Y |
| 17 Ryan | Y | N | Y | N | Y | Y |
| 18 **Ney** | N | Y | Y | Y | Y | Y |
| **OKLAHOMA** | | | | | | |
| 1 **Sullivan** | N | Y | Y | Y | Y | Y |
| 2 Boren | Y | Y | Y | N | Y | Y |
| 3 **Lucas** | N | Y | Y | Y | Y | Y |
| 4 **Cole** | N | + | Y | Y | Y | Y |
| 5 **Istook** | ? | ? | ? | ? | ? | ? |
| **OREGON** | | | | | | |
| 1 Wu | Y | N | Y | N | Y | Y |
| 2 **Walden** | N | Y | ? | Y | Y | Y |
| 3 Blumenauer | Y | N | Y | N | Y | N |
| 4 DeFazio | Y | Y | Y | N | Y | Y |
| 5 Hooley | Y | N | Y | N | Y | Y |
| **PENNSYLVANIA** | | | | | | |
| 1 Brady | Y | N | Y | N | Y | Y |
| 2 Fattah | Y | N | Y | N | Y | Y |
| 3 **English** | N | Y | Y | Y | Y | Y |
| 4 **Hart** | N | Y | Y | Y | Y | Y |
| 5 **Peterson** | N | Y | Y | Y | Y | Y |
| 6 **Gerlach** | N | Y | Y | Y | Y | Y |
| 7 **Weldon** | N | Y | Y | ? | Y | Y |
| 8 **Fitzpatrick** | N | Y | Y | Y | Y | Y |
| 9 **Shuster** | N | Y | Y | Y | Y | Y |
| 10 **Sherwood** | N | Y | Y | Y | Y | Y |
| 11 Kanjorski | Y | Y | Y | N | Y | Y |
| 12 Murtha | Y | N | ? | N | ? | Y |
| 13 Schwartz | Y | N | Y | N | Y | Y |
| 14 Doyle | Y | N | Y | N | Y | Y |
| 15 **Dent** | N | Y | Y | Y | Y | Y |
| 16 **Pitts** | N | Y | Y | Y | Y | Y |
| 17 Holden | Y | Y | Y | N | Y | Y |
| 18 **Murphy** | N | Y | Y | Y | Y | Y |
| 19 **Platts** | N | Y | Y | ? | Y | Y |
| **RHODE ISLAND** | | | | | | |
| 1 Kennedy | Y | N | Y | N | Y | Y |
| 2 Langevin | Y | N | Y | N | Y | Y |
| **SOUTH CAROLINA** | | | | | | |
| 1 **Brown** | N | Y | Y | Y | Y | Y |
| 2 **Wilson** | N | Y | Y | Y | Y | Y |
| 3 **Barrett** | – | + | + | Y | Y | Y |
| 4 **Inglis** | N | Y | Y | Y | Y | Y |
| 5 Spratt | Y | N | Y | ? | Y | Y |
| 6 Clyburn | Y | N | Y | N | Y | Y |
| **SOUTH DAKOTA** | | | | | | |
| AL Herseth | Y | Y | Y | N | Y | Y |
| **TENNESSEE** | | | | | | |
| 1 **Jenkins** | N | Y | Y | Y | Y | Y |
| 2 **Duncan** | N | Y | Y | Y | Y | Y |

| | 660 | 661 | 662 | 663 | 664 | 665 |
|---|---|---|---|---|---|---|
| 3 **Wamp** | N | Y | Y | Y | Y | Y |
| 4 Davis | Y | Y | Y | N | Y | Y |
| 5 Cooper | Y | N | Y | N | Y | Y |
| 6 Gordon | Y | Y | Y | N | Y | Y |
| 7 **Blackburn** | N | Y | Y | Y | Y | Y |
| 8 Tanner | Y | Y | Y | N | Y | Y |
| 9 Ford | Y | Y | ? | N | Y | Y |
| **TEXAS** | | | | | | |
| 1 **Gohmert** | N | Y | Y | Y | Y | Y |
| 2 **Poe** | N | Y | Y | Y | Y | Y |
| 3 **Johnson, S.** | N | Y | Y | Y | Y | ? |
| 4 **Hall** | N | Y | Y | Y | Y | Y |
| 5 **Hensarling** | N | Y | Y | Y | Y | Y |
| 6 **Barton** | – | + | + | + | + | Y |
| 7 **Culberson** | N | Y | Y | Y | Y | Y |
| 8 **Brady** | N | Y | Y | Y | Y | Y |
| 9 Green, A. | Y | N | Y | N | Y | Y |
| 10 **McCaul** | N | Y | Y | Y | Y | Y |
| 11 **Conaway** | N | Y | Y | Y | Y | Y |
| 12 **Granger** | N | Y | Y | Y | Y | Y |
| 13 **Thornberry** | N | Y | Y | Y | Y | Y |
| 14 **Paul** | N | Y | N | Y | ? | N |
| 15 Hinojosa | Y | N | Y | N | Y | Y |
| 16 Reyes | Y | N | Y | N | Y | ? |
| 17 Edwards | Y | Y | Y | N | Y | Y |
| 18 Jackson-Lee | Y | N | Y | N | Y | Y |
| 19 **Neugebauer** | N | Y | Y | Y | Y | Y |
| 20 Gonzalez | Y | N | Y | N | Y | Y |
| 21 **Smith** | N | Y | Y | Y | Y | Y |
| 22 **DeLay** | N | Y | Y | Y | Y | Y |
| 23 **Bonilla** | N | Y | Y | Y | Y | Y |
| 24 **Marchant** | N | Y | Y | Y | Y | Y |
| 25 Doggett | Y | N | Y | N | Y | Y |
| 26 **Burgess** | N | Y | Y | Y | Y | Y |
| 27 Ortiz | Y | N | Y | N | Y | Y |
| 28 Cuellar | Y | N | Y | N | Y | Y |
| 29 Green, G. | Y | N | Y | N | Y | Y |
| 30 Johnson, E. | Y | N | Y | N | Y | Y |
| 31 **Carter** | N | Y | Y | Y | Y | Y |
| 32 **Sessions** | N | Y | Y | Y | Y | Y |
| **UTAH** | | | | | | |
| 1 **Bishop** | N | Y | Y | Y | Y | Y |
| 2 Matheson | Y | Y | Y | N | Y | Y |
| 3 **Cannon** | N | Y | Y | Y | Y | Y |
| **VERMONT** | | | | | | |
| AL *Sanders* | Y | N | Y | N | Y | Y |
| **VIRGINIA** | | | | | | |
| 1 **Davis, J.** | – | + | + | + | + | ? |
| 2 **Drake** | N | Y | Y | Y | Y | Y |
| 3 Scott | Y | N | Y | N | Y | Y |
| 4 **Forbes** | N | Y | Y | Y | Y | Y |
| 5 **Goode** | N | Y | Y | Y | Y | Y |
| 6 **Goodlatte** | N | Y | Y | Y | Y | Y |
| 7 **Cantor** | N | Y | Y | Y | Y | Y |
| 8 Moran | Y | N | Y | N | Y | Y |
| 9 Boucher | Y | Y | Y | N | Y | Y |
| 10 **Wolf** | N | Y | Y | Y | Y | Y |
| 11 **Davis, T.** | N | Y | Y | ? | Y | Y |
| **WASHINGTON** | | | | | | |
| 1 Inslee | Y | N | Y | N | Y | Y |
| 2 Larsen | Y | Y | Y | N | Y | Y |
| 3 Baird | Y | N | Y | N | Y | N |
| 4 **Hastings** | N | N | Y | Y | Y | Y |
| 5 **McMorris** | N | Y | Y | Y | Y | Y |
| 6 Dicks | Y | N | Y | N | Y | Y |
| 7 McDermott | Y | N | N | N | Y | N |
| 8 **Reichert** | N | Y | Y | Y | Y | Y |
| 9 Smith | Y | N | Y | N | Y | Y |
| **WEST VIRGINIA** | | | | | | |
| 1 Mollohan | Y | N | Y | N | Y | Y |
| 2 **Capito** | N | Y | Y | Y | Y | Y |
| 3 Rahall | Y | N | Y | N | Y | Y |
| **WISCONSIN** | | | | | | |
| 1 **Ryan** | N | Y | Y | Y | Y | Y |
| 2 Baldwin | Y | N | Y | N | Y | N |
| 3 Kind | Y | N | Y | N | Y | Y |
| 4 Moore | Y | N | Y | N | Y | Y |
| 5 **Sensenbrenner** | N | Y | Y | Y | Y | Y |
| 6 **Petri** | N | Y | Y | Y | Y | Y |
| 7 Obey | Y | N | Y | N | Y | Y |
| 8 **Green** | N | Y | Y | Y | Y | Y |
| **WYOMING** | | | | | | |
| AL **Cubin** | N | Y | Y | ? | Y | Y |

# IN THE HOUSE | By Vote Number

**666.** **HR 2863. Fiscal 2006 Defense Appropriations/Rule.** Adoption of the rule (H Res 639) to provide for House floor consideration of the conference report on the bill that would appropriate $453.5 billion in fiscal 2006 for defense, including $50 billion for operations in Iraq and Afghanistan. Adopted 214-201: R 198-21; D 16-179 (ND 7-138, SD 9-41); I 0-1. Dec. 19, 2005 (in the session that began and the Congressional Record dated Dec. 18, 2005).

**667.** **H Con Res 284. Egyptian Elections/Adoption.** Ros-Lehtinen, R-Fla., motion to suspend the rules and adopt the concurrent resolution to express the sense of Congress recognizing the importance of the Egyptian presidential election held Sept. 7, 2005, as a first step toward greater openness and political changes in that country. Motion agreed to 388-22: R 214-3; D 173-19 (ND 128-16, SD 45-3); I 1-0. A two-thirds majority of those present and voting (274 in this case) is required for adoption under suspension of the rules. Dec. 19, 2005 (in the session that began and the Congressional Record dated Dec. 18, 2005).

**668.** **HR 2863. Fiscal 2006 Defense Appropriations/Recommit.** Obey, D-Wis., motion to recommit the conference report on the bill to the Appropriations Committee with instructions to eliminate the legislation's across-the-board spending cuts. Motion rejected 183-231: R 1-218; D 181-13 (ND 135-9, SD 46-4); I 1-0. Dec. 19, 2005 (in the session that began and the Congressional Record dated Dec. 18, 2005).

**669.** **HR 2863. Fiscal 2006 Defense Appropriations/Conference Report.** Adoption of the conference report on the bill that would appropriate $453.5 billion for defense spending, including $50 billion for operations in Iraq and Afghanistan. The total includes $123.6 billion for operations and maintenance, $76.5 billion for procurement and $72.1 billion for research and development. It would require a 1 percent across-the-board cut to all fiscal 2006 discretionary spending except Veterans Administration funding that was added to the legislation. It would provide $29 billion for disaster assistance to hurricane-damaged areas and $3.8 billion for flu preparedness. It would allow oil and gas leasing in the Arctic National Wildlife Refuge. Adopted (thus sent to the Senate) 308-106: R 202-16; D 106-89 (ND 65-80, SD 41-9); I 0-1. Dec. 19, 2005 (in the session that began and the Congressional Record dated Dec. 18, 2005).

**670.** **S 1932. Budget Reconciliation/Conference Report.** Adoption of the conference report on the bill that would make changes to programs for a net savings of $38.8 billion over five years. The total includes savings of roughly $12.7 billion from the student loan program, $1.5 billion from aid to states to enforce child support payments and $4.8 billion from Medicaid. The bill would provide $2.1 billion in hurricane assistance, authorize an additional $1 billion for low-income energy assistance and provide $7.3 billion to avoid a scheduled Medicare reimbursement cut to physicians. Adopted (thus sent to the Senate) 212-206: R 212-9; D 0-196 (ND 0-146, SD 0-50); I 0-1. A "yea" was a vote in support of the president's position. Dec. 19, 2005 (in the session that began and the Congressional Record dated Dec. 18, 2005).

**671.** **H Con Res 275. Education Curriculum in Saudi Arabia/Adoption.** Ros-Lehtinen, R-Fla., motion to suspend the rules and adopt the concurrent resolution that would urge the Saudi Arabian government to revise its textbooks and education curriculum to promote tolerance and peaceful coexistence with others, develop civil society and encourage functionality in the global economy. Motion agreed to 351-1: R 175-1; D 175-0 (ND 128-0, SD 47-0); I 1-0. A two-thirds majority of those present and voting (235 in this case) is required for adoption under suspension of the rules. Dec. 19, 2005 (in the session that began and the Congressional Record dated Dec. 18, 2005).

| | 666 | 667 | 668 | 669 | 670 | 671 |
|---|---|---|---|---|---|---|
| **ALABAMA** | | | | | | |
| 1 Bonner | Y | Y | N | Y | Y | Y |
| 2 Everett | Y | Y | N | Y | Y | ? |
| 3 Rogers | Y | Y | N | Y | Y | Y |
| 4 Aderholt | Y | Y | N | Y | Y | Y |
| 5 Cramer | Y | Y | Y | Y | N | Y |
| 6 Bachus | Y | Y | N | Y | Y | Y |
| 7 Davis | N | Y | Y | Y | N | Y |
| **ALASKA** | | | | | | |
| AL Young | Y | Y | N | Y | Y | Y |
| **ARIZONA** | | | | | | |
| 1 Renzi | Y | Y | N | Y | Y | Y |
| 2 Franks | Y | Y | N | Y | Y | Y |
| 3 Shadegg | Y | Y | N | Y | Y | ? |
| 4 Pastor | N | N | Y | N | N | Y |
| 5 Hayworth | Y | Y | N | Y | Y | Y |
| 6 Flake | Y | Y | N | Y | N | ? |
| 7 Grijalva | N | Y | Y | N | N | Y |
| 8 Kolbe | ? | ? | ? | ? | ? | ? |
| **ARKANSAS** | | | | | | |
| 1 Berry | N | Y | Y | Y | N | Y |
| 2 Snyder | N | Y | Y | Y | N | Y |
| 3 Boozman | Y | Y | N | Y | Y | Y |
| 4 Ross | N | Y | Y | Y | N | Y |
| **CALIFORNIA** | | | | | | |
| 1 Thompson | N | Y | Y | N | N | Y |
| 2 Herger | Y | Y | N | Y | Y | Y |
| 3 Lungren | Y | Y | N | Y | Y | Y |
| 4 Doolittle | Y | Y | N | Y | Y | Y |
| 5 Matsui, D. | N | Y | Y | Y | N | Y |
| 6 Woolsey | N | Y | Y | N | N | Y |
| 7 Miller, George | N | N | Y | N | N | Y |
| 8 Pelosi | N | Y | Y | Y | N | Y |
| 9 Lee | N | N | Y | N | N | Y |
| 10 Tauscher | N | Y | Y | Y | N | Y |
| 11 Pombo | Y | Y | N | Y | Y | Y |
| 12 Lantos | N | Y | Y | Y | N | Y |
| 13 Stark | N | Y | ? | N | N | Y |
| 14 Eshoo | N | Y | Y | N | N | Y |
| 15 Honda | N | Y | Y | N | N | Y |
| 16 Lofgren | N | Y | Y | N | N | Y |
| 17 Farr | N | Y | Y | N | N | Y |
| 18 Cardoza | N | Y | N | Y | N | ? |
| 19 Radanovich | ? | ? | ? | ? | ? | ? |
| 20 Costa | N | Y | Y | Y | N | Y |
| 21 Nunes | Y | Y | N | Y | Y | Y |
| 22 Thomas | Y | Y | N | Y | Y | Y |
| 23 Capps | N | Y | Y | N | N | Y |
| 24 Gallegly | Y | Y | N | Y | Y | Y |
| 25 McKeon | Y | Y | N | Y | Y | ? |
| 26 Dreier | Y | Y | N | Y | Y | Y |
| 27 Sherman | N | Y | Y | Y | N | Y |
| 28 Berman | N | Y | Y | Y | N | Y |
| 29 Schiff | N | Y | Y | Y | N | Y |
| 30 Waxman | N | Y | Y | N | N | Y |
| 31 Becerra | N | Y | Y | N | N | Y |
| 32 Solis | N | Y | Y | N | N | Y |
| 33 Watson | N | Y | Y | N | N | Y |
| 34 Roybal-Allard | ? | ? | ? | ? | ? | ? |
| 35 Waters | N | N | Y | N | N | ? |
| 36 Harman | ? | ? | ? | ? | ? | ? |
| 37 Millender-McD. | N | Y | Y | N | N | Y |
| 38 Napolitano | N | Y | Y | N | N | Y |
| 39 Sánchez, Linda | N | Y | Y | N | N | Y |
| 40 Royce | Y | Y | N | Y | Y | Y |
| 41 Lewis | Y | Y | N | Y | Y | Y |
| 42 Miller, Gary | ? | ? | ? | ? | ? | ? |
| 43 Baca | ? | ? | ? | ? | ? | ? |
| 44 Calvert | Y | Y | N | Y | Y | ? |
| 45 Bono | Y | Y | N | Y | Y | Y |
| 46 Rohrabacher | Y | Y | N | Y | Y | Y |
| 47 Sanchez, Loretta | N | Y | Y | N | N | Y |
| 48 Campbell | Y | Y | N | Y | Y | Y |
| 49 Issa | Y | Y | N | Y | Y | ? |

| | 666 | 667 | 668 | 669 | 670 | 671 |
|---|---|---|---|---|---|---|
| 50 Vacant | | | | | | |
| 51 Filner | N | Y | Y | N | N | Y |
| 52 Hunter | Y | Y | N | Y | Y | ? |
| 53 Davis | N | Y | Y | Y | N | Y |
| **COLORADO** | | | | | | |
| 1 DeGette | N | Y | Y | N | N | Y |
| 2 Udall | N | Y | Y | N | N | Y |
| 3 Salazar | N | Y | Y | Y | N | Y |
| 4 Musgrave | Y | Y | N | Y | Y | Y |
| 5 Hefley | ? | ? | ? | ? | Y | Y |
| 6 Tancredo | Y | Y | N | Y | Y | Y |
| 7 Beauprez | Y | Y | N | Y | Y | Y |
| **CONNECTICUT** | | | | | | |
| 1 Larson | N | Y | Y | Y | N | ? |
| 2 Simmons | N | Y | N | Y | Y | Y |
| 3 DeLauro | N | Y | Y | Y | N | Y |
| 4 Shays | N | Y | N | N | Y | Y |
| 5 Johnson | N | Y | N | N | Y | ? |
| **DELAWARE** | | | | | | |
| AL Castle | N | Y | N | N | Y | Y |
| **FLORIDA** | | | | | | |
| 1 Miller | Y | Y | N | Y | Y | ? |
| 2 Boyd | N | Y | Y | Y | N | Y |
| 3 Brown | N | Y | Y | Y | N | Y |
| 4 Crenshaw | Y | Y | N | Y | Y | Y |
| 5 Brown-Waite | Y | Y | N | Y | Y | Y |
| 6 Stearns | Y | Y | N | Y | Y | Y |
| 7 Mica | Y | Y | N | Y | Y | Y |
| 8 Keller | Y | Y | N | Y | Y | Y |
| 9 Bilirakis | Y | Y | N | Y | Y | Y |
| 10 Young | Y | Y | N | Y | Y | Y |
| 11 Davis | N | Y | Y | Y | N | Y |
| 12 Putnam | Y | Y | N | Y | Y | Y |
| 13 Harris | Y | Y | N | Y | Y | Y |
| 14 Mack | Y | Y | N | Y | Y | Y |
| 15 Weldon | Y | Y | N | Y | Y | Y |
| 16 Foley | Y | Y | N | Y | Y | Y |
| 17 Meek | N | Y | Y | Y | N | Y |
| 18 Ros-Lehtinen | Y | Y | N | Y | Y | Y |
| 19 Wexler | N | Y | Y | N | N | Y |
| 20 Wasserman-Schultz | N | Y | Y | Y | N | Y |
| 21 Diaz-Balart, L. | Y | ? | N | Y | Y | ? |
| 22 Shaw | Y | Y | N | Y | Y | Y |
| 23 Hastings | N | ? | Y | N | N | Y |
| 24 Feeney | Y | Y | ? | Y | Y | ? |
| 25 Diaz-Balart, M. | Y | ? | N | Y | Y | ? |
| **GEORGIA** | | | | | | |
| 1 Kingston | Y | Y | N | Y | Y | Y |
| 2 Bishop | Y | Y | N | Y | N | Y |
| 3 Marshall | N | ? | Y | Y | N | Y |
| 4 McKinney | N | N | Y | N | N | ? |
| 5 Lewis | N | Y | Y | N | N | Y |
| 6 Price | + | Y | N | Y | Y | Y |
| 7 Linder | Y | Y | N | Y | Y | Y |
| 8 Westmoreland | Y | Y | N | Y | Y | Y |
| 9 Norwood | Y | Y | N | Y | Y | Y |
| 10 Deal | Y | Y | N | Y | Y | Y |
| 11 Gingrey | Y | Y | N | Y | Y | Y |
| 12 Barrow | Y | Y | Y | Y | N | Y |
| 13 Scott | N | Y | Y | Y | N | Y |
| **HAWAII** | | | | | | |
| 1 Abercrombie | N | Y | Y | Y | N | P |
| 2 Case | N | Y | Y | N | N | Y |
| **IDAHO** | | | | | | |
| 1 Otter | Y | Y | N | Y | Y | Y |
| 2 Simpson | Y | Y | N | Y | Y | Y |
| **ILLINOIS** | | | | | | |
| 1 Rush | N | Y | Y | N | N | Y |
| 2 Jackson | N | N | Y | N | N | Y |
| 3 Lipinski | N | Y | Y | Y | N | Y |
| 4 Gutierrez | ? | ? | ? | ? | ? | ? |
| 5 Emanuel | ? | ? | ? | ? | ? | ? |
| 6 Hyde | ? | ? | ? | ? | ? | ? |
| 7 Davis | N | Y | Y | N | N | Y |
| 8 Bean | N | Y | Y | Y | N | Y |
| 9 Schakowsky | N | Y | Y | N | N | Y |
| 10 Kirk | Y | Y | N | Y | N | Y |
| 11 Weller | Y | Y | N | Y | Y | Y |
| 12 Costello | N | Y | Y | Y | N | Y |

**KEY**  Republicans  Democrats  *Independents*

| | | | |
|---|---|---|---|
| Y | Voted for (yea) | X Paired against | C Voted "present" to avoid possible conflict of interest |
| # | Paired for | – Announced against | |
| + | Announced for | P Voted "present" | ? Did not vote or otherwise make a position known |
| N | Voted against (nay) | | |

| | 666 | 667 | 668 | 669 | 670 | 671 |
|---|---|---|---|---|---|---|
| 13 **Biggert** | N | Y | N | Y | Y | Y |
| 14 **Hastert** | Y | Y | N | Y | Y | |
| 15 **Johnson** | N | Y | N | N | N | Y |
| 16 **Manzullo** | Y | Y | N | Y | Y | Y |
| 17 Evans | N | Y | Y | Y | N | Y |
| 18 **LaHood** | Y | Y | N | Y | Y | Y |
| 19 **Shimkus** | Y | Y | N | Y | Y | Y |
| **INDIANA** | | | | | | |
| 1 Visclosky | N | Y | Y | Y | N | Y |
| 2 **Chocola** | Y | Y | N | Y | Y | ? |
| 3 **Souder** | Y | Y | N | Y | Y | Y |
| 4 **Buyer** | Y | Y | N | Y | N | ? |
| 5 **Burton** | Y | Y | N | P | Y | ? |
| 6 **Pence** | Y | Y | N | Y | Y | Y |
| 7 Carson | N | Y | Y | Y | N | Y |
| 8 **Hostettler** | ? | ? | ? | ? | ? | ? |
| 9 **Sodrel** | Y | Y | N | Y | Y | Y |
| **IOWA** | | | | | | |
| 1 **Nussle** | Y | Y | N | Y | Y | Y |
| 2 **Leach** | N | Y | Y | N | N | ? |
| 3 Boswell | N | Y | Y | N | N | Y |
| 4 **Latham** | Y | Y | N | Y | Y | Y |
| 5 **King** | Y | Y | N | Y | Y | Y |
| **KANSAS** | | | | | | |
| 1 **Moran** | Y | Y | N | Y | Y | ? |
| 2 **Ryun** | Y | Y | N | Y | Y | Y |
| 3 Moore | N | Y | Y | Y | N | Y |
| 4 **Tiahrt** | Y | Y | N | Y | Y | Y |
| **KENTUCKY** | | | | | | |
| 1 **Whitfield** | Y | Y | N | Y | Y | Y |
| 2 **Lewis** | Y | Y | N | Y | Y | Y |
| 3 **Northup** | Y | Y | N | Y | Y | Y |
| 4 **Davis** | Y | Y | N | Y | Y | Y |
| 5 **Rogers** | Y | Y | N | Y | Y | Y |
| 6 Chandler | N | Y | Y | Y | N | Y |
| **LOUISIANA** | | | | | | |
| 1 **Jindal** | Y | Y | N | Y | Y | Y |
| 2 Jefferson | N | Y | N | Y | N | Y |
| 3 Melancon | Y | Y | N | Y | N | Y |
| 4 **McCrery** | Y | Y | N | Y | Y | ? |
| 5 **Alexander** | Y | Y | N | Y | Y | Y |
| 6 **Baker** | Y | Y | N | Y | Y | ? |
| 7 **Boustany** | Y | Y | N | Y | Y | Y |
| **MAINE** | | | | | | |
| 1 Allen | N | Y | Y | Y | N | Y |
| 2 Michaud | N | Y | Y | N | N | Y |
| **MARYLAND** | | | | | | |
| 1 **Gilchrest** | N | Y | N | Y | Y | Y |
| 2 Ruppersberger | N | Y | Y | Y | N | Y |
| 3 Cardin | N | Y | Y | N | N | ? |
| 4 Wynn | N | N | Y | Y | N | Y |
| 5 Hoyer | N | Y | Y | Y | N | Y |
| 6 **Bartlett** | N | Y | N | Y | Y | Y |
| 7 Cummings | N | Y | Y | N | N | Y |
| 8 Van Hollen | N | Y | Y | N | N | Y |
| **MASSACHUSETTS** | | | | | | |
| 1 Olver | N | Y | Y | N | N | Y |
| 2 Neal | N | Y | Y | Y | N | ? |
| 3 McGovern | N | Y | + | – | N | Y |
| 4 Frank | N | Y | Y | N | N | Y |
| 5 Meehan | N | Y | Y | Y | N | Y |
| 6 Tierney | N | Y | Y | N | N | Y |
| 7 Markey | N | Y | Y | N | N | Y |
| 8 Capuano | N | Y | Y | Y | N | Y |
| 9 Lynch | N | Y | Y | Y | N | ? |
| 10 Delahunt | N | Y | Y | N | N | ? |
| **MICHIGAN** | | | | | | |
| 1 Stupak | N | Y | Y | N | N | Y |
| 2 **Hoekstra** | Y | Y | N | N | Y | ? |
| 3 **Ehlers** | N | Y | N | N | Y | Y |
| 4 **Camp** | Y | Y | N | Y | Y | Y |
| 5 Kildee | N | Y | Y | N | N | Y |
| 6 **Upton** | Y | Y | N | Y | Y | Y |
| 7 **Schwarz** | N | Y | N | Y | Y | Y |
| 8 **Rogers** | Y | Y | N | Y | Y | Y |
| 9 **Knollenberg** | Y | Y | N | Y | Y | Y |
| 10 **Miller** | Y | Y | N | Y | Y | Y |
| 11 **McCotter** | Y | Y | N | Y | Y | Y |
| 12 Levin | N | Y | Y | Y | N | Y |
| 13 Kilpatrick | N | N | Y | N | N | Y |
| 14 Conyers | N | N | Y | N | N | Y |
| 15 Dingell | N | Y | Y | N | N | Y |

| | 666 | 667 | 668 | 669 | 670 | 671 |
|---|---|---|---|---|---|---|
| **MINNESOTA** | | | | | | |
| 1 **Gutknecht** | Y | Y | N | Y | Y | Y |
| 2 **Kline** | Y | Y | N | Y | Y | Y |
| 3 **Ramstad** | N | Y | N | N | Y | Y |
| 4 McCollum | N | Y | Y | N | N | Y |
| 5 Sabo | N | Y | Y | N | N | Y |
| 6 **Kennedy** | Y | Y | N | Y | Y | Y |
| 7 Peterson | N | Y | N | Y | N | Y |
| 8 Oberstar | N | Y | Y | N | N | Y |
| **MISSISSIPPI** | | | | | | |
| 1 **Wicker** | Y | Y | N | Y | Y | Y |
| 2 Thompson | N | Y | Y | Y | N | Y |
| 3 **Pickering** | Y | Y | N | Y | Y | Y |
| 4 Taylor | Y | Y | N | Y | N | Y |
| **MISSOURI** | | | | | | |
| 1 Clay | ? | ? | Y | Y | N | Y |
| 2 **Akin** | Y | Y | N | Y | Y | Y |
| 3 Carnahan | N | Y | Y | Y | N | Y |
| 4 Skelton | N | Y | Y | Y | N | Y |
| 5 Cleaver | N | ? | Y | Y | N | Y |
| 6 **Graves** | Y | Y | N | Y | Y | ? |
| 7 **Blunt** | Y | Y | N | Y | Y | ? |
| 8 **Emerson** | Y | Y | N | Y | Y | Y |
| 9 **Hulshof** | Y | Y | N | Y | Y | ? |
| **MONTANA** | | | | | | |
| AL **Rehberg** | Y | Y | N | Y | Y | Y |
| **NEBRASKA** | | | | | | |
| 1 **Fortenberry** | Y | N | N | Y | Y | Y |
| 2 **Terry** | Y | Y | N | Y | Y | Y |
| 3 **Osborne** | N | Y | N | Y | Y | Y |
| **NEVADA** | | | | | | |
| 1 Berkley | N | Y | Y | Y | N | Y |
| 2 **Gibbons** | Y | Y | N | Y | Y | Y |
| 3 **Porter** | Y | Y | N | Y | Y | Y |
| **NEW HAMPSHIRE** | | | | | | |
| 1 **Bradley** | Y | Y | N | Y | Y | Y |
| 2 **Bass** | N | Y | N | N | Y | Y |
| **NEW JERSEY** | | | | | | |
| 1 Andrews | N | Y | Y | N | N | Y |
| 2 **LoBiondo** | N | Y | N | N | Y | Y |
| 3 **Saxton** | Y | Y | N | P | Y | Y |
| 4 **Smith** | N | Y | N | N | N | Y |
| 5 **Garrett** | Y | Y | N | Y | Y | Y |
| 6 Pallone | N | Y | Y | N | N | Y |
| 7 **Ferguson** | Y | Y | N | Y | Y | Y |
| 8 Pascrell | Y | Y | Y | Y | N | Y |
| 9 Rothman | N | Y | Y | N | N | Y |
| 10 Payne | N | N | Y | N | N | Y |
| 11 **Frelinghuysen** | Y | Y | N | Y | Y | Y |
| 12 Holt | N | Y | Y | N | N | Y |
| 13 Menendez | N | Y | Y | N | N | Y |
| **NEW MEXICO** | | | | | | |
| 1 **Wilson** | Y | Y | N | Y | N | Y |
| 2 **Pearce** | Y | Y | N | Y | Y | ? |
| 3 Udall | N | Y | Y | N | N | Y |
| **NEW YORK** | | | | | | |
| 1 Bishop | N | Y | Y | Y | N | Y |
| 2 Israel | N | Y | Y | Y | N | Y |
| 3 **King** | Y | Y | N | Y | Y | Y |
| 4 McCarthy | N | Y | Y | Y | N | Y |
| 5 Ackerman | N | Y | Y | N | N | ? |
| 6 Meeks | N | Y | Y | N | N | Y |
| 7 Crowley | N | Y | Y | Y | N | ? |
| 8 Nadler | N | Y | Y | N | N | Y |
| 9 Weiner | N | Y | Y | N | N | Y |
| 10 Towns | N | Y | Y | N | N | Y |
| 11 Owens | N | Y | Y | N | N | Y |
| 12 Velázquez | N | Y | Y | N | N | ? |
| 13 **Fossella** | Y | Y | N | Y | Y | ? |
| 14 Maloney | N | Y | Y | N | N | Y |
| 15 Rangel | N | Y | Y | N | N | ? |
| 16 Serrano | N | Y | Y | N | N | Y |
| 17 Engel | N | Y | Y | N | N | Y |
| 18 Lowey | N | Y | Y | N | N | Y |
| 19 **Kelly** | Y | Y | N | N | Y | Y |
| 20 **Sweeney** | Y | Y | N | Y | Y | Y |
| 21 McNulty | N | Y | Y | N | N | ? |
| 22 Hinchey | N | N | Y | N | N | Y |
| 23 **McHugh** | Y | Y | N | Y | N | ? |
| 24 **Boehlert** | N | Y | N | Y | Y | Y |
| 25 **Walsh** | Y | Y | N | Y | N | Y |
| 26 **Reynolds** | Y | Y | N | Y | Y | Y |
| 27 Higgins | N | Y | Y | Y | N | Y |
| 28 Slaughter | N | Y | Y | N | N | ? |
| 29 **Kuhl** | Y | Y | N | Y | Y | Y |

| | 666 | 667 | 668 | 669 | 670 | 671 |
|---|---|---|---|---|---|---|
| **NORTH CAROLINA** | | | | | | |
| 1 Butterfield | N | Y | Y | Y | N | Y |
| 2 Etheridge | N | Y | Y | Y | N | Y |
| 3 **Jones** | ? | ? | ? | ? | ? | ? |
| 4 Price | N | Y | Y | Y | N | Y |
| 5 **Foxx** | Y | Y | N | Y | Y | Y |
| 6 **Coble** | Y | Y | N | Y | Y | ? |
| 7 McIntyre | N | Y | Y | Y | N | Y |
| 8 **Hayes** | Y | Y | N | Y | Y | ? |
| 9 **Myrick** | ? | ? | ? | ? | ? | ? |
| 10 **McHenry** | Y | Y | N | Y | Y | Y |
| 11 **Taylor** | Y | N | N | Y | Y | P |
| 12 Watt | N | Y | Y | N | N | Y |
| 13 Miller | N | Y | Y | Y | N | Y |
| **NORTH DAKOTA** | | | | | | |
| AL Pomeroy | N | Y | Y | Y | N | Y |
| **OHIO** | | | | | | |
| 1 **Chabot** | Y | Y | N | Y | Y | Y |
| 2 **Schmidt** | Y | Y | N | Y | Y | Y |
| 3 **Turner** | Y | Y | N | Y | Y | Y |
| 4 **Oxley** | Y | Y | N | Y | Y | Y |
| 5 **Gillmor** | Y | Y | N | Y | Y | Y |
| 6 Strickland | N | Y | Y | Y | N | Y |
| 7 **Hobson** | Y | Y | N | Y | Y | Y |
| 8 **Boehner** | Y | Y | N | Y | Y | Y |
| 9 Kaptur | N | Y | Y | Y | N | Y |
| 10 Kucinich | N | N | Y | N | N | Y |
| 11 Jones | N | Y | Y | N | N | Y |
| 12 **Tiberi** | Y | Y | N | Y | Y | Y |
| 13 Brown | N | Y | Y | Y | N | ? |
| 14 **LaTourette** | Y | Y | N | Y | N | ? |
| 15 **Pryce** | Y | Y | N | Y | Y | ? |
| 16 **Regula** | Y | Y | N | Y | Y | Y |
| 17 Ryan | N | Y | Y | Y | N | Y |
| 18 **Ney** | Y | Y | N | Y | N | Y |
| **OKLAHOMA** | | | | | | |
| 1 **Sullivan** | Y | Y | N | Y | Y | Y |
| 2 Boren | Y | Y | Y | Y | N | Y |
| 3 **Lucas** | Y | Y | N | Y | Y | Y |
| 4 **Cole** | Y | Y | N | Y | Y | Y |
| 5 **Istook** | ? | ? | ? | ? | ? | ? |
| **OREGON** | | | | | | |
| 1 Wu | N | Y | Y | N | N | Y |
| 2 **Walden** | Y | Y | N | Y | Y | Y |
| 3 Blumenauer | N | N | Y | N | N | Y |
| 4 DeFazio | N | N | Y | Y | N | Y |
| 5 Hooley | N | Y | Y | Y | N | Y |
| **PENNSYLVANIA** | | | | | | |
| 1 Brady | Y | Y | N | Y | N | Y |
| 2 Fattah | N | Y | Y | Y | N | Y |
| 3 **English** | Y | Y | N | Y | Y | Y |
| 4 **Hart** | Y | Y | N | Y | Y | Y |
| 5 **Peterson** | Y | Y | N | Y | Y | ? |
| 6 **Gerlach** | N | Y | N | Y | Y | Y |
| 7 **Weldon** | Y | Y | N | Y | Y | Y |
| 8 **Fitzpatrick** | N | Y | N | N | Y | Y |
| 9 **Shuster** | Y | Y | N | Y | Y | Y |
| 10 **Sherwood** | Y | Y | N | Y | Y | ? |
| 11 Kanjorski | Y | Y | N | Y | N | Y |
| 12 Murtha | Y | Y | N | Y | N | ? |
| 13 Schwartz | N | Y | Y | Y | N | Y |
| 14 Doyle | Y | Y | Y | Y | N | ? |
| 15 **Dent** | Y | Y | N | Y | Y | Y |
| 16 **Pitts** | Y | Y | N | Y | Y | ? |
| 17 Holden | Y | Y | N | Y | N | Y |
| 18 **Murphy** | Y | Y | N | Y | Y | Y |
| 19 **Platts** | N | Y | N | Y | Y | Y |
| **RHODE ISLAND** | | | | | | |
| 1 Kennedy | N | Y | Y | Y | N | Y |
| 2 Langevin | N | Y | Y | Y | N | Y |
| **SOUTH CAROLINA** | | | | | | |
| 1 **Brown** | Y | Y | N | Y | Y | Y |
| 2 **Wilson** | Y | Y | N | Y | Y | Y |
| 3 **Barrett** | Y | Y | N | Y | Y | Y |
| 4 **Inglis** | Y | Y | N | Y | Y | Y |
| 5 Spratt | N | Y | Y | Y | N | Y |
| 6 Clyburn | N | Y | Y | Y | N | Y |
| **SOUTH DAKOTA** | | | | | | |
| AL Herseth | N | Y | Y | Y | N | Y |
| **TENNESSEE** | | | | | | |
| 1 **Jenkins** | Y | Y | N | Y | Y | ? |
| 2 **Duncan** | Y | Y | N | Y | Y | Y |

| | 666 | 667 | 668 | 669 | 670 | 671 |
|---|---|---|---|---|---|---|
| 3 **Wamp** | Y | Y | N | Y | Y | Y |
| 4 Davis | Y | Y | Y | Y | N | Y |
| 5 Cooper | N | Y | Y | N | N | Y |
| 6 Gordon | N | Y | Y | Y | N | Y |
| 7 **Blackburn** | Y | Y | N | Y | Y | Y |
| 8 Tanner | N | Y | Y | Y | N | Y |
| 9 Ford | N | Y | Y | Y | N | Y |
| **TEXAS** | | | | | | |
| 1 **Gohmert** | Y | Y | N | Y | Y | Y |
| 2 **Poe** | Y | Y | N | Y | Y | Y |
| 3 **Johnson, S.** | ? | ? | ? | ? | ? | ? |
| 4 **Hall** | Y | Y | N | Y | Y | ? |
| 5 **Hensarling** | Y | Y | N | Y | Y | Y |
| 6 **Barton** | Y | Y | N | Y | Y | ? |
| 7 **Culberson** | Y | Y | N | Y | Y | Y |
| 8 **Brady** | Y | Y | N | Y | Y | ? |
| 9 Green, A. | N | Y | Y | Y | N | Y |
| 10 **McCaul** | Y | Y | N | Y | Y | Y |
| 11 **Conaway** | Y | Y | N | Y | Y | Y |
| 12 **Granger** | Y | Y | N | Y | Y | ? |
| 13 **Thornberry** | Y | Y | N | Y | Y | ? |
| 14 **Paul** | Y | N | N | N | N | N |
| 15 Hinojosa | N | Y | Y | Y | N | ? |
| 16 Reyes | ? | ? | ? | ? | ? | ? |
| 17 Edwards | N | Y | Y | Y | N | Y |
| 18 Jackson-Lee | N | N | Y | Y | N | Y |
| 19 **Neugebauer** | Y | Y | N | Y | Y | Y |
| 20 Gonzalez | N | Y | Y | Y | N | Y |
| 21 **Smith** | Y | Y | N | Y | Y | Y |
| 22 **DeLay** | Y | Y | N | Y | Y | Y |
| 23 **Bonilla** | Y | ? | N | Y | Y | ? |
| 24 **Marchant** | Y | Y | N | Y | Y | Y |
| 25 Doggett | N | Y | Y | N | N | Y |
| 26 **Burgess** | Y | Y | N | Y | Y | Y |
| 27 Ortiz | Y | Y | Y | Y | N | ? |
| 28 Cuellar | Y | Y | Y | Y | N | Y |
| 29 Green, G. | Y | Y | Y | Y | N | Y |
| 30 Johnson, E. | N | N | Y | N | N | Y |
| 31 **Carter** | Y | Y | N | Y | Y | ? |
| 32 **Sessions** | Y | Y | N | Y | Y | Y |
| **UTAH** | | | | | | |
| 1 **Bishop** | Y | Y | N | Y | Y | Y |
| 2 Matheson | N | Y | Y | Y | N | Y |
| 3 **Cannon** | Y | Y | N | Y | Y | Y |
| **VERMONT** | | | | | | |
| AL *Sanders* | N | Y | Y | N | N | Y |
| **VIRGINIA** | | | | | | |
| 1 **Davis, J.** | ? | ? | ? | ? | ? | ? |
| 2 **Drake** | Y | Y | N | Y | Y | Y |
| 3 Scott | N | Y | Y | N | N | Y |
| 4 **Forbes** | Y | Y | N | Y | Y | ? |
| 5 **Goode** | Y | Y | N | Y | Y | Y |
| 6 **Goodlatte** | Y | Y | N | Y | Y | Y |
| 7 **Cantor** | Y | Y | N | Y | Y | Y |
| 8 Moran | N | Y | Y | Y | N | Y |
| 9 Boucher | N | Y | Y | Y | N | Y |
| 10 **Wolf** | Y | Y | N | Y | Y | Y |
| 11 **Davis, T.** | Y | Y | N | Y | Y | Y |
| **WASHINGTON** | | | | | | |
| 1 Inslee | N | Y | Y | N | N | Y |
| 2 Larsen | N | Y | Y | Y | N | Y |
| 3 Baird | N | N | Y | N | N | Y |
| 4 **Hastings** | Y | Y | N | Y | Y | Y |
| 5 **McMorris** | Y | Y | N | Y | Y | Y |
| 6 Dicks | N | Y | Y | Y | N | Y |
| 7 McDermott | N | Y | Y | N | N | Y |
| 8 **Reichert** | N | Y | N | Y | Y | Y |
| 9 Smith | N | Y | Y | N | N | Y |
| **WEST VIRGINIA** | | | | | | |
| 1 Mollohan | Y | Y | N | Y | N | Y |
| 2 **Capito** | Y | Y | N | Y | Y | Y |
| 3 Rahall | N | N | Y | Y | N | Y |
| **WISCONSIN** | | | | | | |
| 1 **Ryan** | Y | Y | N | Y | Y | ? |
| 2 Baldwin | N | Y | Y | N | N | Y |
| 3 Kind | N | Y | Y | Y | N | Y |
| 4 Moore | N | Y | Y | N | N | Y |
| 5 **Sensenbrenner** | Y | Y | N | Y | Y | Y |
| 6 **Petri** | Y | Y | N | N | Y | ? |
| 7 Obey | N | N | Y | N | N | ? |
| 8 **Green** | Y | Y | N | Y | Y | Y |
| **WYOMING** | | | | | | |
| AL **Cubin** | Y | Y | N | Y | Y | Y |

# House Roll Call Index by Subject

# SENATE
# ROLL CALL
# VOTES

# Senate Roll Call Index
# By Bill Number

## SENATE BILLS

**S 5,** S-5
**S 250,** S-11
**S 256,** S-7, S-9, S-10, S-11
**S 306,** S-6
**S 397,** S-41, S-42, S-43
**S 600,** S-17
**S 1042,** S-39, S-40, S-60,
  S-61, S-62, S-63,
  S-64
**S 1307,** S-34
**S 1783,** S-64
**S 1932,** S-56, S-57, S-58,
  S-59, S-69, S-70

**S Con Res 18,** S-12, S-13,
  S-14, S-15, S-16
**S Con Res 25,** S-18

**S J Res 4,** S-8
**S J Res 20,** S-45

**S Res 38,** S-5
**S Res 95,** S-17
**S Res 193,** S-35
**S Res 207,** S-40
**S Res 233,** S-43
**S Res 234,** S-43

**Treaty Doc 108-6,** S-48

## HOUSE BILLS

**H Con Res 95,** S-22

**H J Res 52,** S-38
**H J Res 68,** S-49
**H J Res 72,** S-68

**HR 3,** S-22, S-23, S-24,
  S-25, S-43
**HR 6,** S-28, S-29, S-30,
  S-31, S32, S-42
**HR 1268,** S-18, S-19, S-20,
  S-21, S-23
**HR 1815,** S-70
**HR 2020,** S-64, S-65, S-66,
  S-67
**HR 2360,** S-35, S-36, S-37
**HR 2361,** S-32, S-33, S-34,
  S-42
**HR 2419,** S-34, S-63
**HR 2528,** S-47
**HR 2744,** S-47, S-56
**HR 2862,** S-45, S-46, S-64
**HR 2863,** S-49, S-50, S-70,
  S-71
**HR 2985,** S-42
**HR 3010,** S-53, S-54, S-55,
  S-68
**HR 3045,** S-41
**HR 3057,** S-38, S-39, S-62
**HR 3058,** S-51, S-52
**HR 3199,** S-69
**HR 3673,** S-43

# IN THE SENATE | By Vote Number

**1. Electoral Vote Count.** Rep. Stephanie Tubbs Jones, D-Ohio, and Sen. Barbara Boxer, D-Calif., objection to the certification of the Ohio electoral votes to protest voting irregularities in that state. Rejected 1-74: R 0-38; D 1-35 (ND 1-32, SD 0-3); I 0-1. Jan. 6, 2005.

**2. Rice Nomination/Confirmation.** Confirmation of President Bush's nomination of Condoleezza Rice to be secretary of State. Confirmed 85-13: R 53-0; D 32-12 (ND 28-12, SD 4-0); I 0-1. A "yea" was a vote in support of the president's position. Jan. 25, 2005.

**3. Gonzales Nomination/Confirmation.** Confirmation of President Bush's nomination of Alberto R. Gonzales of Texas to be attorney general. Confirmed 60-36: R 54-0; D 6-35 (ND 3-34, SD 3-1); I 0-1. A "yea" was a vote in support of the president's position. Feb. 3, 2005.

| | 1 | 2 | 3 | | 1 | 2 | 3 |
|---|---|---|---|---|---|---|---|
| **ALABAMA** | | | | **MONTANA** | | | |
| Shelby | ? | Y | Y | Baucus | N | Y | ? |
| Sessions | N | Y | Y | Burns | ? | + | + |
| **ALASKA** | | | | **NEBRASKA** | | | |
| Stevens | N | Y | Y | Hagel | N | Y | Y |
| Murkowski | ? | Y | Y | Nelson | N | Y | Y |
| **ARIZONA** | | | | **NEVADA** | | | |
| McCain | - | Y | Y | Reid | N | Y | N |
| Kyl | - | Y | Y | Ensign | ? | Y | Y |
| **ARKANSAS** | | | | **NEW HAMPSHIRE** | | | |
| Lincoln | N | Y | N | Gregg | N | ? | Y |
| Pryor | N | Y | Y | Sununu | N | Y | Y |
| **CALIFORNIA** | | | | **NEW JERSEY** | | | |
| Feinstein | ? | Y | N | Corzine | ? | Y | N |
| Boxer | Y | N | N | Lautenberg | N | N | N |
| **COLORADO** | | | | **NEW MEXICO** | | | |
| Allard | N | Y | Y | Domenici | N | Y | Y |
| Salazar | N | Y | Y | Bingaman | ? | Y | N |
| **CONNECTICUT** | | | | **NEW YORK** | | | |
| Dodd | N | Y | N | Schumer | N | Y | N |
| Lieberman | N | Y | Y | Clinton | N | Y | N |
| **DELAWARE** | | | | **NORTH CAROLINA** | | | |
| Biden | N | Y | N | Dole | N | Y | Y |
| Carper | N | Y | N | Burr | N | Y | Y |
| **FLORIDA** | | | | **NORTH DAKOTA** | | | |
| Nelson | N | Y | Y | Conrad | N | Y | ? |
| Martinez | ? | Y | Y | Dorgan | N | Y | N |
| **GEORGIA** | | | | **OHIO** | | | |
| Chambliss | N | Y | Y | DeWine | N | Y | Y |
| Isakson | N | Y | Y | Voinovich | N | Y | Y |
| **HAWAII** | | | | **OKLAHOMA** | | | |
| Inouye | N | Y | - | Inhofe | - | Y | Y |
| Akaka | ? | N | N | Coburn | N | Y | Y |
| **IDAHO** | | | | **OREGON** | | | |
| Craig | ? | Y | Y | Wyden | N | Y | N |
| Crapo | N | Y | Y | Smith | N | Y | Y |
| **ILLINOIS** | | | | **PENNSYLVANIA** | | | |
| Durbin | N | N | N | Specter | N | Y | Y |
| Obama | N | Y | N | Santorum | N | Y | Y |
| **INDIANA** | | | | **RHODE ISLAND** | | | |
| Lugar | ? | Y | Y | Reed | N | N | N |
| Bayh | ? | N | N | Chafee | ? | Y | Y |
| **IOWA** | | | | **SOUTH CAROLINA** | | | |
| Grassley | N | Y | Y | Graham | N | Y | Y |
| Harkin | N | N | N | DeMint | N | Y | Y |
| **KANSAS** | | | | **SOUTH DAKOTA** | | | |
| Brownback | N | Y | Y | Johnson | N | Y | N |
| Roberts | N | Y | Y | Thune | N | Y | Y |
| **KENTUCKY** | | | | **TENNESSEE** | | | |
| McConnell | N | Y | Y | Frist | ? | Y | Y |
| Bunning | - | Y | Y | Alexander | N | Y | Y |
| **LOUISIANA** | | | | **TEXAS** | | | |
| Landrieu | ? | Y | Y | Hutchison | ? | Y | Y |
| Vitter | - | Y | Y | Cornyn | N | Y | Y |
| **MAINE** | | | | **UTAH** | | | |
| Snowe | N | Y | Y | Hatch | N | Y | Y |
| Collins | N | Y | Y | Bennett | N | Y | Y |
| **MARYLAND** | | | | **VERMONT** | | | |
| Sarbanes | N | Y | N | Leahy | N | Y | N |
| Mikulski | N | Y | N | Jeffords | N | N | N |
| **MASSACHUSETTS** | | | | **VIRGINIA** | | | |
| Kennedy | N | N | N | Warner | N | Y | Y |
| Kerry | ? | N | N | Allen | ? | Y | Y |
| **MICHIGAN** | | | | **WASHINGTON** | | | |
| Levin | N | N | N | Murray | ? | Y | N |
| Stabenow | N | Y | N | Cantwell | N | Y | N |
| **MINNESOTA** | | | | **WEST VIRGINIA** | | | |
| Dayton | N | N | N | Byrd | N | N | N |
| Coleman | N | Y | Y | Rockefeller | N | Y | N |
| **MISSISSIPPI** | | | | **WISCONSIN** | | | |
| Cochran | N | Y | Y | Kohl | N | Y | ? |
| Lott | N | Y | Y | Feingold | N | Y | N |
| **MISSOURI** | | | | **WYOMING** | | | |
| Bond | N | Y | Y | Thomas | ? | Y | Y |
| Talent | N | Y | Y | Enzi | N | Y | Y |

**KEY**  Republicans  Democrats  *Independents*

| | | | |
|---|---|---|---|
| **Y** Voted for (yea) | **X** Paired against | **C** Voted "present" to avoid possible conflict of interest |
| **#** Paired for | **-** Announced against | |
| **+** Announced for | **P** Voted "present" | **?** Did not vote or otherwise make a position known |
| **N** Voted against (nay) | | |

# IN THE SENATE | By Vote Number

**4. S Res 38. Iraqi Elections/Adoption.** Adoption of the resolution that would commend the people of Iraq on the Jan. 30, 2005, elections, express support for the establishment of a fully democratic Iraqi government, and condemn "all acts of violence and intimidation" committed by insurgents. Adopted 93-0: R 49-0; D 43-0 (ND 39-0, SD 4-0); I 1-0. Feb. 7, 2005.

**5. S 5. Class Action Overhaul/State Attorneys General.** Specter, R-Pa., motion to table (kill) the Pryor, D-Ark., amendment that would exempt class action suits brought by state attorneys general from the provisions of the bill. Motion agreed to 60-39: R 54-0; D 6-38 (ND 5-35, SD 1-3); I 0-1. Feb. 9, 2005.

**6. S 5. Class Action Overhaul/Civil Rights and Labor Cases.** Kennedy, D-Mass., amendment that would exclude civil rights class action suits and class action claims for lost wages and overtime from the bill's provisions. Rejected 40-59: R 0-54; D 39-5 (ND 35-5, SD 4-0); I 1-0. Feb. 9, 2005.

**7. S 5. Class Action Overhaul/Judicial Discretion.** Feinstein, D-Calif., amendment that would give federal judges additional discretion in deciding which state consumer protection laws to apply in class action suits where plaintiffs are from multiple states. Rejected 38-61: R 1-53; D 37-7 (ND 34-6, SD 3-1); I 0-1. Feb. 9, 2005.

**8. S 5. Class Action Overhaul/Time Limit.** Feingold, D-Wis., amendment that would place a 60-day limit on the amount of time federal judges have to consider whether to send class action cases back to state courts. Rejected 37-61: R 0-53; D 36-8 (ND 33-7, SD 3-1); I 1-0. Feb. 10, 2005.

**9. S 5. Class Action Overhaul/Passage.** Passage of the bill that would give federal courts jurisdiction over class action cases involving at least 100 plaintiffs if at least $5 million was at stake and two-thirds of the plaintiffs lived in different states. It would require judges to review all non-cash settlements, such as coupons for goods and services, and limit attorney's fees paid in such settlements. It also would prohibit federal judges from approving a net loss settlement without finding that the loss was outweighed by non-monetary benefits. Passed 72-26: R 53-0; D 18-26 (ND 16-24, SD 2-2); I 1-0. A "yea" was a vote in support of the president's position. Feb. 10, 2005.

| | 4 | 5 | 6 | 7 | 8 | 9 |
|---|---|---|---|---|---|---|
| **ALABAMA** | | | | | | |
| Shelby | Y | Y | N | N | N | Y |
| Sessions | Y | Y | N | N | N | Y |
| **ALASKA** | | | | | | |
| Stevens | Y | Y | N | N | N | Y |
| Murkowski | ? | Y | N | N | N | Y |
| **ARIZONA** | | | | | | |
| McCain | Y | Y | N | N | N | Y |
| Kyl | Y | Y | N | N | N | Y |
| **ARKANSAS** | | | | | | |
| Lincoln | Y | Y | Y | N | Y | Y |
| Pryor | Y | N | Y | Y | Y | N |
| **CALIFORNIA** | | | | | | |
| Feinstein | Y | N | N | Y | Y | Y |
| Boxer | Y | N | Y | Y | Y | N |
| **COLORADO** | | | | | | |
| Allard | Y | Y | N | N | N | Y |
| Salazar | Y | N | Y | Y | Y | Y |
| **CONNECTICUT** | | | | | | |
| Dodd | Y | Y | N | N | N | Y |
| Lieberman | Y | N | Y | N | N | Y |
| **DELAWARE** | | | | | | |
| Biden | Y | N | Y | Y | Y | N |
| Carper | Y | Y | N | N | Y | Y |
| **FLORIDA** | | | | | | |
| Nelson | Y | N | Y | Y | Y | Y |
| Martinez | Y | Y | N | N | N | Y |
| **GEORGIA** | | | | | | |
| Chambliss | Y | Y | N | N | N | Y |
| Isakson | Y | Y | N | N | N | Y |
| **HAWAII** | | | | | | |
| Inouye | Y | N | Y | Y | Y | N |
| Akaka | ? | N | Y | Y | Y | N |
| **IDAHO** | | | | | | |
| Craig | Y | Y | N | N | N | Y |
| Crapo | Y | Y | N | N | N | Y |
| **ILLINOIS** | | | | | | |
| Durbin | Y | N | Y | Y | Y | N |
| Obama | Y | N | Y | Y | Y | Y |
| **INDIANA** | | | | | | |
| Lugar | Y | Y | N | N | ? | Y |
| Bayh | Y | N | Y | N | N | Y |
| **IOWA** | | | | | | |
| Grassley | Y | Y | N | N | N | Y |
| Harkin | Y | N | Y | Y | Y | N |
| **KANSAS** | | | | | | |
| Brownback | Y | Y | N | N | N | Y |
| Roberts | Y | Y | N | N | N | Y |
| **KENTUCKY** | | | | | | |
| McConnell | Y | Y | N | N | N | Y |
| Bunning | Y | Y | N | N | N | Y |
| **LOUISIANA** | | | | | | |
| Landrieu | Y | N | Y | Y | N | Y |
| Vitter | + | Y | N | N | N | Y |
| **MAINE** | | | | | | |
| Snowe | Y | Y | N | N | N | Y |
| Collins | Y | Y | N | N | N | Y |
| **MARYLAND** | | | | | | |
| Sarbanes | Y | N | Y | Y | Y | N |
| Mikulski | Y | N | Y | Y | Y | N |
| **MASSACHUSETTS** | | | | | | |
| Kennedy | Y | N | Y | Y | Y | N |
| Kerry | Y | N | Y | Y | Y | N |
| **MICHIGAN** | | | | | | |
| Levin | Y | N | Y | Y | Y | N |
| Stabenow | Y | N | Y | Y | Y | N |
| **MINNESOTA** | | | | | | |
| Dayton | Y | N | Y | Y | Y | N |
| Coleman | Y | Y | N | N | N | Y |
| **MISSISSIPPI** | | | | | | |
| Cochran | Y | Y | N | N | N | Y |
| Lott | Y | Y | N | N | N | Y |
| **MISSOURI** | | | | | | |
| Bond | Y | Y | N | N | N | Y |
| Talent | Y | Y | N | N | N | Y |

| | 4 | 5 | 6 | 7 | 8 | 9 |
|---|---|---|---|---|---|---|
| **MONTANA** | | | | | | |
| Baucus | Y | N | Y | Y | Y | N |
| Burns | + | Y | N | N | N | Y |
| **NEBRASKA** | | | | | | |
| Hagel | Y | Y | N | N | N | Y |
| Nelson | Y | Y | N | N | N | Y |
| **NEVADA** | | | | | | |
| Reid | Y | N | Y | Y | Y | N |
| Ensign | ? | Y | N | N | N | Y |
| **NEW HAMPSHIRE** | | | | | | |
| Gregg | Y | Y | N | N | N | Y |
| Sununu | Y | ? | ? | ? | ? | ? |
| **NEW JERSEY** | | | | | | |
| Corzine | Y | N | Y | Y | Y | N |
| Lautenberg | Y | N | Y | Y | Y | N |
| **NEW MEXICO** | | | | | | |
| Domenici | Y | Y | N | N | N | Y |
| Bingaman | Y | N | Y | Y | Y | Y |
| **NEW YORK** | | | | | | |
| Schumer | Y | N | Y | Y | Y | N |
| Clinton | Y | N | Y | Y | Y | N |
| **NORTH CAROLINA** | | | | | | |
| Dole | Y | Y | N | N | N | Y |
| Burr | Y | Y | N | N | N | Y |
| **NORTH DAKOTA** | | | | | | |
| Conrad | Y | N | Y | Y | Y | Y |
| Dorgan | Y | N | Y | Y | Y | Y |
| **OHIO** | | | | | | |
| DeWine | ? | Y | N | N | N | Y |
| Voinovich | Y | Y | N | N | N | Y |
| **OKLAHOMA** | | | | | | |
| Inhofe | Y | Y | N | N | N | Y |
| Coburn | Y | Y | N | N | N | Y |
| **OREGON** | | | | | | |
| Wyden | Y | N | Y | Y | Y | N |
| Smith | Y | Y | N | N | N | Y |
| **PENNSYLVANIA** | | | | | | |
| Specter | Y | Y | N | N | N | Y |
| Santorum | Y | Y | N | N | N | ? |
| **RHODE ISLAND** | | | | | | |
| Reed | Y | N | Y | Y | Y | Y |
| Chafee | Y | Y | N | N | N | Y |
| **SOUTH CAROLINA** | | | | | | |
| Graham | Y | Y | N | N | N | Y |
| DeMint | Y | Y | N | N | N | Y |
| **SOUTH DAKOTA** | | | | | | |
| Johnson | Y | N | Y | Y | Y | Y |
| Thune | Y | Y | N | N | N | Y |
| **TENNESSEE** | | | | | | |
| Frist | Y | Y | N | N | N | Y |
| Alexander | Y | Y | N | N | N | Y |
| **TEXAS** | | | | | | |
| Hutchison | ? | Y | N | N | N | Y |
| Cornyn | Y | Y | N | N | N | Y |
| **UTAH** | | | | | | |
| Hatch | Y | Y | N | N | N | Y |
| Bennett | Y | Y | N | N | N | Y |
| **VERMONT** | | | | | | |
| Leahy | Y | N | Y | Y | Y | N |
| Jeffords | Y | N | Y | N | Y | N |
| **VIRGINIA** | | | | | | |
| Warner | Y | Y | N | N | N | Y |
| Allen | Y | Y | N | N | N | Y |
| **WASHINGTON** | | | | | | |
| Murray | Y | N | Y | Y | Y | N |
| Cantwell | Y | N | Y | Y | N | Y |
| **WEST VIRGINIA** | | | | | | |
| Byrd | Y | N | Y | Y | Y | N |
| Rockefeller | Y | N | Y | Y | Y | Y |
| **WISCONSIN** | | | | | | |
| Kohl | Y | Y | N | N | N | Y |
| Feingold | Y | N | Y | Y | Y | N |
| **WYOMING** | | | | | | |
| Thomas | Y | Y | N | N | N | Y |
| Enzi | Y | Y | N | N | N | Y |

**KEY**   Republicans   Democrats   *Independents*

| | | |
|---|---|---|
| Y   Voted for (yea) | X   Paired against | C   Voted "present" to avoid possible conflict of interest |
| #   Paired for | –   Announced against | |
| +   Announced for | P   Voted "present" | ?   Did not vote or otherwise make a position known |
| N   Voted against (nay) | | |

# IN THE SENATE | By Vote Number

**10.** **Chertoff Nomination/Confirmation.** Confirmation of President Bush's nomination of Michael Chertoff to be secretary of Homeland Security. Confirmed 98-0: R 54-0; D 43-0 (ND 39-0, SD 4-0); I 1-0. A "yea" was a vote in support of the president's position. Feb. 15, 2005.

**11.** **S 306. Genetic Non-Discrimination/Passage.** Passage of a bill that would ban employers and health insurers from discriminating based on an individual's genetic profile. Employers would be barred from using genetic information in employment decisions, and insurers would be prohibited from using genetic information to deny coverage or set or adjust premiums. Passed 98-0: R 54-0; D 43-0 (ND 39-0, SD 4-0); I 1-0. Feb. 17, 2005.

| | 10 | 11 | | | 10 | 11 |
|---|---|---|---|---|---|---|
| **ALABAMA** | | | | **MONTANA** | | |
| Shelby | Y | Y | | Baucus | ? | Y |
| Sessions | Y | Y | | Burns | Y | Y |
| **ALASKA** | | | | **NEBRASKA** | | |
| Stevens | Y | Y | | Hagel | Y | Y |
| Murkowski | Y | Y | | Nelson | Y | Y |
| **ARIZONA** | | | | **NEVADA** | | |
| McCain | Y | Y | | Reid | Y | Y |
| Kyl | Y | Y | | Ensign | Y | Y |
| **ARKANSAS** | | | | **NEW HAMPSHIRE** | | |
| Lincoln | Y | Y | | Gregg | Y | Y |
| Pryor | Y | Y | | Sununu | Y | Y |
| **CALIFORNIA** | | | | **NEW JERSEY** | | |
| Feinstein | Y | Y | | Corzine | Y | Y |
| Boxer | Y | Y | | Lautenberg | Y | Y |
| **COLORADO** | | | | **NEW MEXICO** | | |
| Allard | Y | Y | | Domenici | Y | Y |
| Salazar | Y | Y | | Bingaman | Y | Y |
| **CONNECTICUT** | | | | **NEW YORK** | | |
| Dodd | Y | Y | | Schumer | Y | Y |
| Lieberman | Y | Y | | Clinton | Y | Y |
| **DELAWARE** | | | | **NORTH CAROLINA** | | |
| Biden | Y | + | | Dole | Y | Y |
| Carper | Y | Y | | Burr | Y | Y |
| **FLORIDA** | | | | **NORTH DAKOTA** | | |
| Nelson | Y | Y | | Conrad | Y | Y |
| Martinez | Y | Y | | Dorgan | Y | Y |
| **GEORGIA** | | | | **OHIO** | | |
| Chambliss | Y | Y | | DeWine | Y | Y |
| Isakson | Y | Y | | Voinovich | Y | Y |
| **HAWAII** | | | | **OKLAHOMA** | | |
| Inouye | Y | Y | | Inhofe | Y | Y |
| Akaka | Y | Y | | Coburn | Y | Y |
| **IDAHO** | | | | **OREGON** | | |
| Craig | Y | Y | | Wyden | Y | Y |
| Crapo | Y | Y | | Smith | Y | Y |
| **ILLINOIS** | | | | **PENNSYLVANIA** | | |
| Durbin | Y | Y | | Specter | ? | ? |
| Obama | Y | Y | | Santorum | Y | Y |
| **INDIANA** | | | | **RHODE ISLAND** | | |
| Lugar | Y | Y | | Reed | Y | Y |
| Bayh | Y | Y | | Chafee | Y | Y |
| **IOWA** | | | | **SOUTH CAROLINA** | | |
| Grassley | Y | Y | | Graham | Y | Y |
| Harkin | Y | Y | | DeMint | Y | Y |
| **KANSAS** | | | | **SOUTH DAKOTA** | | |
| Brownback | Y | Y | | Johnson | Y | Y |
| Roberts | Y | Y | | Thune | Y | Y |
| **KENTUCKY** | | | | **TENNESSEE** | | |
| McConnell | Y | Y | | Frist | Y | Y |
| Bunning | Y | Y | | Alexander | Y | Y |
| **LOUISIANA** | | | | **TEXAS** | | |
| Landrieu | Y | Y | | Hutchison | Y | Y |
| Vitter | Y | Y | | Cornyn | Y | Y |
| **MAINE** | | | | **UTAH** | | |
| Snowe | Y | Y | | Hatch | Y | Y |
| Collins | Y | Y | | Bennett | Y | Y |
| **MARYLAND** | | | | **VERMONT** | | |
| Sarbanes | Y | Y | | Leahy | Y | Y |
| Mikulski | Y | Y | | Jeffords | Y | Y |
| **MASSACHUSETTS** | | | | **VIRGINIA** | | |
| Kennedy | Y | Y | | Warner | Y | Y |
| Kerry | Y | Y | | Allen | Y | Y |
| **MICHIGAN** | | | | **WASHINGTON** | | |
| Levin | Y | Y | | Murray | Y | Y |
| Stabenow | Y | Y | | Cantwell | Y | Y |
| **MINNESOTA** | | | | **WEST VIRGINIA** | | |
| Dayton | Y | Y | | Byrd | Y | Y |
| Coleman | Y | Y | | Rockefeller | Y | Y |
| **MISSISSIPPI** | | | | **WISCONSIN** | | |
| Cochran | Y | Y | | Kohl | Y | Y |
| Lott | Y | Y | | Feingold | Y | Y |
| **MISSOURI** | | | | **WYOMING** | | |
| Bond | Y | Y | | Thomas | Y | Y |
| Talent | Y | Y | | Enzi | Y | Y |

**KEY**   Republicans   Democrats   *Independents*

| | | | |
|---|---|---|---|
| Y | Voted for (yea) | X | Paired against |
| # | Paired for | – | Announced against |
| + | Announced for | P | Voted "present" |
| N | Voted against (nay) | C | Voted "present" to avoid possible conflict of interest |
| | | ? | Did not vote or otherwise make a position known |

# IN THE SENATE | By Vote Number

**12.** **S 256. Bankruptcy Overhaul/Safe Harbor.** Sessions, R-Ala., amendment that would clarify that the bill's "safe harbor" provision would apply to low-income veterans, debtors who have medical conditions, or those called or ordered to active duty. It would require such individuals to satisfy all the procedural requirements of a means test used by bankruptcy judges to determine whether debtors have the ability to repay some or all of their debts. Adopted 63-32: R 52-0; D 11-31 (ND 9-29, SD 2-2); I 0-1. March 1, 2005.

**13.** **S 256. Bankruptcy Overhaul/Means Test Exemptions.** Durbin, D-Ill., amendment that would exempt members of the armed forces, veterans and spouses of service members who die in military service from application of the bill's means test provisions. It also would allow such individuals to claim a minimum homestead exemption of $75,000 or choose the exemption in the state in which they file, whichever is higher. Rejected 38-58: R 1-52; D 36-6 (ND 32-6, SD 4-0); I 1-0. March 1, 2005.

**14.** **S 256. Bankruptcy Overhaul/Elderly Homestead Exemption.** Feingold, D-Wis., amendment that would create a federal homestead exemption of $75,000 for debtors over the age of 62. Rejected 40-59: R 0-55; D 40-3 (ND 36-3, SD 4-0); I 0-1. March 2, 2005.

**15.** **S 256. Bankruptcy Overhaul/Credit Cards.** Akaka, D-Hawaii, amendment that would require credit card companies to issue a warning notification on monthly statements stating that a minimum payment will increase the amount of interest paid and the time it will take to repay the outstanding balance. It would require companies to disclose the amount required for the consumer to pay off the outstanding balance in three years, if no further advances are made. It also would require credit card companies to provide a toll-free number for consumers to receive information about credit counseling and debt management assistance. Rejected 40-59: R 1-54; D 38-5 (ND 34-5, SD 4-0); I 1-0. March 2, 2005.

**16.** **S 256. Bankruptcy Overhaul/Medical Expenses.** Kennedy, D-Mass., amendment that would exempt debtors from the means test if their financial troubles were caused by medical expenses. Rejected 39-58: R 0-54; D 38-4 (ND 34-4, SD 4-0); I 1-0. March 2, 2005.

**17.** **S 256. Bankruptcy Overhaul/Medical Homestead Exemption.** Kennedy, D-Mass., amendment that would provide a homestead exemption of at least $150,000 of the equity in the property the debtor uses as a primary residence if the bankruptcy stems from medical expenses. Rejected 39-58: R 0-54; D 38-4 (ND 34-4, SD 4-0); I 1-0. March 2, 2005.

**18.** **S 256. Bankruptcy Overhaul/Caregivers Exemption.** Corzine, D-N.J., amendment that would exempt from the means test individuals who have incurred substantial medical debt on behalf of dependent or non-dependent family members, such as a parent or grandparent, or who have experienced a reduction in employment status while caring for such a family member. Rejected 37-60: R 0-54; D 37-5 (ND 33-5, SD 4-0); I 0-1. March 2, 2005.

| | 12 | 13 | 14 | 15 | 16 | 17 | 18 |
|---|---|---|---|---|---|---|---|
| **ALABAMA** | | | | | | | |
| Shelby | Y | N | N | N | N | N | N |
| Sessions | Y | N | N | N | N | N | N |
| **ALASKA** | | | | | | | |
| Stevens | Y | N | N | N | N | N | N |
| Murkowski | Y | N | N | N | N | N | N |
| **ARIZONA** | | | | | | | |
| McCain | Y | N | N | N | N | N | N |
| Kyl | Y | N | N | N | N | N | N |
| **ARKANSAS** | | | | | | | |
| Lincoln | Y | Y | Y | Y | Y | Y | Y |
| Pryor | N | Y | Y | Y | Y | Y | Y |
| **CALIFORNIA** | | | | | | | |
| Feinstein | Y | Y | Y | Y | Y | Y | Y |
| Boxer | N | Y | Y | Y | Y | Y | Y |
| **COLORADO** | | | | | | | |
| Allard | Y | N | N | N | N | N | N |
| Salazar | N | Y | Y | Y | Y | Y | Y |
| **CONNECTICUT** | | | | | | | |
| Dodd | N | Y | Y | Y | ? | Y | Y |
| Lieberman | N | Y | Y | Y | Y | Y | Y |
| **DELAWARE** | | | | | | | |
| Biden | Y | N | N | N | N | ? | ? |
| Carper | Y | N | N | N | N | N | N |
| **FLORIDA** | | | | | | | |
| Nelson | Y | Y | Y | Y | Y | Y | Y |
| Martinez | Y | N | N | N | N | N | N |
| **GEORGIA** | | | | | | | |
| Chambliss | Y | N | N | N | N | N | N |
| Isakson | Y | N | N | N | N | N | N |
| **HAWAII** | | | | | | | |
| Inouye | ? | ? | ? | ? | ? | ? | ? |
| Akaka | N | Y | Y | Y | Y | Y | Y |
| **IDAHO** | | | | | | | |
| Craig | Y | N | N | N | N | N | N |
| Crapo | Y | N | N | N | N | N | N |
| **ILLINOIS** | | | | | | | |
| Durbin | N | Y | Y | Y | Y | Y | Y |
| Obama | N | Y | Y | Y | Y | Y | Y |
| **INDIANA** | | | | | | | |
| Lugar | Y | N | N | N | N | N | N |
| Bayh | N | Y | Y | Y | Y | Y | Y |
| **IOWA** | | | | | | | |
| Grassley | Y | N | N | N | N | N | N |
| Harkin | N | Y | Y | Y | Y | Y | Y |
| **KANSAS** | | | | | | | |
| Brownback | Y | N | N | N | N | N | N |
| Roberts | Y | N | N | N | N | N | N |
| **KENTUCKY** | | | | | | | |
| McConnell | Y | N | N | N | N | N | N |
| Bunning | Y | N | N | N | N | N | N |
| **LOUISIANA** | | | | | | | |
| Landrieu | N | Y | Y | Y | Y | Y | Y |
| Vitter | Y | N | N | N | N | N | N |
| **MAINE** | | | | | | | |
| Snowe | Y | N | N | N | N | N | N |
| Collins | Y | N | N | N | N | N | N |
| **MARYLAND** | | | | | | | |
| Sarbanes | N | Y | Y | Y | Y | Y | Y |
| Mikulski | N | Y | Y | Y | Y | Y | Y |
| **MASSACHUSETTS** | | | | | | | |
| Kennedy | N | Y | Y | Y | Y | Y | Y |
| Kerry | N | Y | Y | Y | Y | Y | Y |
| **MICHIGAN** | | | | | | | |
| Levin | N | Y | Y | Y | Y | Y | Y |
| Stabenow | N | Y | Y | Y | Y | Y | Y |
| **MINNESOTA** | | | | | | | |
| Dayton | ? | ? | Y | Y | Y | Y | Y |
| Coleman | ? | ? | N | N | N | N | N |
| **MISSISSIPPI** | | | | | | | |
| Cochran | Y | N | N | N | N | N | N |
| Lott | Y | N | N | N | N | N | N |
| **MISSOURI** | | | | | | | |
| Bond | Y | N | N | N | N | N | N |
| Talent | Y | N | N | N | N | N | N |
| **MONTANA** | | | | | | | |
| Baucus | Y | N | Y | N | Y | Y | Y |
| Burns | Y | N | N | N | N | N | N |
| **NEBRASKA** | | | | | | | |
| Hagel | Y | N | N | N | N | N | N |
| Nelson | Y | N | N | N | N | N | N |
| **NEVADA** | | | | | | | |
| Reid | N | Y | Y | Y | Y | Y | Y |
| Ensign | Y | N | N | N | N | N | N |
| **NEW HAMPSHIRE** | | | | | | | |
| Gregg | Y | N | N | N | N | N | N |
| Sununu | Y | N | N | N | N | N | N |
| **NEW JERSEY** | | | | | | | |
| Corzine | N | Y | Y | Y | Y | Y | Y |
| Lautenberg | N | Y | Y | Y | Y | Y | Y |
| **NEW MEXICO** | | | | | | | |
| Domenici | Y | N | N | N | N | N | N |
| Bingaman | N | Y | Y | Y | Y | N | N |
| **NEW YORK** | | | | | | | |
| Schumer | N | Y | Y | Y | Y | Y | Y |
| Clinton | N | Y | Y | Y | Y | Y | Y |
| **NORTH CAROLINA** | | | | | | | |
| Dole | Y | N | N | N | N | N | N |
| Burr | Y | N | N | N | N | N | N |
| **NORTH DAKOTA** | | | | | | | |
| Conrad | Y | Y | Y | Y | Y | Y | Y |
| Dorgan | N | Y | Y | Y | Y | Y | Y |
| **OHIO** | | | | | | | |
| DeWine | Y | N | N | N | N | N | N |
| Voinovich | Y | N | N | N | N | N | N |
| **OKLAHOMA** | | | | | | | |
| Inhofe | Y | N | N | N | N | N | N |
| Coburn | Y | N | N | N | N | N | N |
| **OREGON** | | | | | | | |
| Wyden | N | Y | Y | Y | Y | Y | Y |
| Smith | Y | N | N | N | N | N | N |
| **PENNSYLVANIA** | | | | | | | |
| Specter | Y | Y | N | N | N | N | N |
| Santorum | Y | N | N | N | ? | ? | ? |
| **RHODE ISLAND** | | | | | | | |
| Reed | N | Y | Y | Y | Y | Y | Y |
| Chafee | Y | N | N | N | N | N | N |
| **SOUTH CAROLINA** | | | | | | | |
| Graham | Y | N | N | N | N | N | N |
| DeMint | Y | N | N | N | N | N | N |
| **SOUTH DAKOTA** | | | | | | | |
| Johnson | Y | N | N | N | N | N | N |
| Thune | Y | N | N | N | N | N | N |
| **TENNESSEE** | | | | | | | |
| Frist | Y | N | N | N | N | N | N |
| Alexander | Y | N | N | N | N | N | N |
| **TEXAS** | | | | | | | |
| Hutchison | Y | N | N | N | N | N | N |
| Cornyn | ? | ? | N | N | N | N | N |
| **UTAH** | | | | | | | |
| Hatch | Y | N | N | N | N | N | N |
| Bennett | Y | N | N | N | N | N | N |
| **VERMONT** | | | | | | | |
| Leahy | N | Y | Y | Y | Y | Y | Y |
| Jeffords | N | Y | N | Y | Y | Y | Y |
| **VIRGINIA** | | | | | | | |
| Warner | ? | N | N | N | N | N | N |
| Allen | Y | N | N | N | N | N | N |
| **WASHINGTON** | | | | | | | |
| Murray | N | Y | Y | Y | Y | Y | Y |
| Cantwell | N | Y | Y | Y | Y | Y | Y |
| **WEST VIRGINIA** | | | | | | | |
| Byrd | Y | N | Y | Y | Y | Y | Y |
| Rockefeller | N | Y | Y | Y | Y | Y | Y |
| **WISCONSIN** | | | | | | | |
| Kohl | Y | Y | Y | Y | Y | Y | Y |
| Feingold | N | Y | Y | Y | Y | Y | Y |
| **WYOMING** | | | | | | | |
| Thomas | Y | N | N | N | N | N | N |
| Enzi | Y | N | N | N | N | N | N |

**KEY**   Republicans   Democrats   *Independents*

| | | |
|---|---|---|
| **Y** Voted for (yea) | **X** Paired against | **C** Voted "present" to avoid possible conflict of interest |
| **#** Paired for | **−** Announced against | |
| **+** Announced for | **P** Voted "present" | **?** Did not vote or otherwise make a position known |
| **N** Voted against (nay) | | |

## IN THE SENATE | By Vote Number

**19.** **S J Res 4. Agriculture Department Rule Disapproval/Passage.**
Passage of the joint resolution that would block a proposed Agriculture Department regulation that would ease restrictions on Canadian beef. Passed 52-46: R 13-42; D 38-4 (ND 37-1, SD 1-3); I 1-0. A "nay" was a vote in support of the president's position. March 3, 2005.

**20.** **S 256. Bankruptcy Overhaul/Interest Rates.** Dayton, D-Minn., amendment that would set a 30 percent ceiling on interest rates for loans or credit cards. Rejected 24-74: R 0-55; D 23-19 (ND 22-16, SD 1-3); I 1-0. March 3, 2005.

**21.** **S 256. Bankruptcy Overhaul/Identity Theft Exemption.** Nelson, D-Fla., amendment that would exempt identity theft victims from the bill's means test provisions and amend the bankruptcy code to include definitions of identity theft and identity theft victims. Rejected 37-61: R 0-55; D 36-6 (ND 32-6, SD 4-0); I 1-0. March 3, 2005.

**22.** **S 256. Bankruptcy Overhaul/Predatory Lending.** Durbin, D-Ill., amendment that would prohibit high cost mortgage lenders from collecting on their claims in bankruptcy court if they extend credit in violation of the Truth in Lending Act. Rejected 40-58: R 1-54; D 38-4 (ND 34-4, SD 4-0); I 1-0. March 3, 2005.

**23.** **S 256. Bankruptcy Overhaul/Asset Protection Trusts.** Schumer, D-N.Y., amendment that would prohibit debtors from transferring more than $125,000 in assets into an asset protection trust within the 10-year period prior to filing bankruptcy. Rejected 39-56: R 1-53; D 37-3 (ND 33-3, SD 4-0); I 1-0. March 3, 2005.

**24.** **S 256. Bankruptcy Overhaul/Wage and Benefit Payments.**
Rockefeller, D-W.Va., amendment that would allow employees to recover up to $15,000 in back pay or other compensation owed to them and entitle retirees to payment equal to the cost of buying health insurance for a period of 18 months if an employer reduces retiree health care benefits as part of a bankruptcy plan. Rejected 40-54: R 2-51; D 37-3 (ND 33-3, SD 4-0); I 1-0. March 3, 2005.

**25.** **S 256. Bankruptcy Overhaul/Corporate Fraud.** Durbin, D-Ill., amendment that would increase from one to four years the period of time during which a bankruptcy court can recapture assets of corporate executives who make fraudulent transfers. It also would give employees and retirees a priority unsecured claim in bankruptcy for the value of company stock held for their benefit in an employee pension plan, unless the beneficiary had the option to invest the assets in another way. Rejected 40-54: R 0-53; D 39-1 (ND 35-1, SD 4-0); I 1-0. March 3, 2005.

| | 19 | 20 | 21 | 22 | 23 | 24 | 25 |
|---|---|---|---|---|---|---|---|
| **ALABAMA** | | | | | | | |
| Shelby | Y | N | N | N | N | N | N |
| Sessions | Y | N | N | N | N | N | N |
| **ALASKA** | | | | | | | |
| Stevens | N | N | N | N | N | N | N |
| Murkowski | N | N | N | N | N | N | N |
| **ARIZONA** | | | | | | | |
| McCain | N | N | N | N | N | N | N |
| Kyl | N | N | N | N | N | N | N |
| **ARKANSAS** | | | | | | | |
| Lincoln | N | N | Y | Y | Y | Y | Y |
| Pryor | N | Y | Y | Y | Y | Y | Y |
| **CALIFORNIA** | | | | | | | |
| Feinstein | Y | Y | Y | Y | Y | Y | Y |
| Boxer | Y | Y | Y | Y | ? | ? | ? |
| **COLORADO** | | | | | | | |
| Allard | N | N | N | N | N | N | N |
| Salazar | Y | Y | Y | Y | Y | Y | Y |
| **CONNECTICUT** | | | | | | | |
| Dodd | Y | Y | Y | Y | Y | Y | Y |
| Lieberman | Y | Y | Y | Y | Y | Y | Y |
| **DELAWARE** | | | | | | | |
| Biden | Y | N | N | Y | N | Y | N |
| Carper | Y | N | N | N | N | N | Y |
| **FLORIDA** | | | | | | | |
| Nelson | N | N | Y | Y | Y | Y | Y |
| Martinez | N | N | N | N | N | N | N |
| **GEORGIA** | | | | | | | |
| Chambliss | N | N | N | N | N | N | N |
| Isakson | N | N | N | N | N | N | N |
| **HAWAII** | | | | | | | |
| Inouye | ? | ? | ? | ? | ? | ? | ? |
| Akaka | Y | Y | Y | Y | Y | Y | Y |
| **IDAHO** | | | | | | | |
| Craig | Y | N | N | N | N | N | N |
| Crapo | Y | N | N | N | N | N | N |
| **ILLINOIS** | | | | | | | |
| Durbin | Y | N | Y | Y | Y | Y | Y |
| Obama | Y | N | Y | Y | Y | Y | Y |
| **INDIANA** | | | | | | | |
| Lugar | N | N | N | N | N | N | N |
| Bayh | Y | Y | Y | Y | Y | Y | Y |
| **IOWA** | | | | | | | |
| Grassley | N | N | N | N | N | N | N |
| Harkin | Y | Y | Y | Y | Y | Y | Y |
| **KANSAS** | | | | | | | |
| Brownback | N | N | N | N | N | N | N |
| Roberts | N | N | N | N | N | N | N |
| **KENTUCKY** | | | | | | | |
| McConnell | N | N | N | N | N | N | N |
| Bunning | N | N | N | N | N | N | N |
| **LOUISIANA** | | | | | | | |
| Landrieu | Y | N | Y | Y | Y | Y | Y |
| Vitter | N | N | N | N | N | N | N |
| **MAINE** | | | | | | | |
| Snowe | N | N | N | N | N | N | N |
| Collins | N | N | N | Y | N | Y | N |
| **MARYLAND** | | | | | | | |
| Sarbanes | Y | N | Y | Y | Y | Y | Y |
| Mikulski | Y | Y | Y | Y | Y | Y | Y |
| **MASSACHUSETTS** | | | | | | | |
| Kennedy | Y | Y | Y | Y | Y | Y | Y |
| Kerry | Y | N | Y | Y | Y | Y | Y |
| **MICHIGAN** | | | | | | | |
| Levin | Y | Y | Y | Y | Y | Y | Y |
| Stabenow | Y | Y | Y | Y | Y | Y | Y |
| **MINNESOTA** | | | | | | | |
| Dayton | Y | Y | Y | Y | Y | Y | Y |
| Coleman | N | N | N | N | N | N | N |
| **MISSISSIPPI** | | | | | | | |
| Cochran | N | N | N | N | N | N | N |
| Lott | N | N | N | N | N | N | N |
| **MISSOURI** | | | | | | | |
| Bond | N | N | N | N | N | N | N |
| Talent | N | N | N | N | N | N | N |

| | 19 | 20 | 21 | 22 | 23 | 24 | 25 |
|---|---|---|---|---|---|---|---|
| **MONTANA** | | | | | | | |
| Baucus | Y | N | Y | Y | Y | Y | Y |
| Burns | Y | N | N | N | N | N | N |
| **NEBRASKA** | | | | | | | |
| Hagel | N | N | N | N | N | N | N |
| Nelson | Y | N | N | N | N | N | N |
| **NEVADA** | | | | | | | |
| Reid | Y | N | Y | Y | Y | Y | Y |
| Ensign | Y | N | N | N | N | N | N |
| **NEW HAMPSHIRE** | | | | | | | |
| Gregg | N | N | N | N | N | N | N |
| Sununu | N | N | N | N | N | N | N |
| **NEW JERSEY** | | | | | | | |
| Corzine | Y | Y | Y | Y | ? | ? | ? |
| Lautenberg | Y | Y | Y | Y | Y | Y | Y |
| **NEW MEXICO** | | | | | | | |
| Domenici | Y | N | N | N | N | N | N |
| Bingaman | Y | N | N | Y | Y | Y | Y |
| **NEW YORK** | | | | | | | |
| Schumer | Y | Y | Y | Y | Y | Y | Y |
| Clinton | Y | Y | Y | Y | Y | Y | Y |
| **NORTH CAROLINA** | | | | | | | |
| Dole | N | N | N | N | N | N | N |
| Burr | N | N | N | N | N | N | N |
| **NORTH DAKOTA** | | | | | | | |
| Conrad | Y | Y | Y | Y | Y | Y | Y |
| Dorgan | Y | Y | Y | Y | Y | Y | Y |
| **OHIO** | | | | | | | |
| DeWine | N | N | N | N | N | N | N |
| Voinovich | N | N | N | N | N | N | N |
| **OKLAHOMA** | | | | | | | |
| Inhofe | Y | N | N | N | - | ? | ? |
| Coburn | Y | N | N | N | N | N | N |
| **OREGON** | | | | | | | |
| Wyden | Y | N | N | Y | Y | Y | Y |
| Smith | Y | N | N | N | N | N | N |
| **PENNSYLVANIA** | | | | | | | |
| Specter | N | N | N | N | N | ? | ? |
| Santorum | N | N | N | N | N | N | N |
| **RHODE ISLAND** | | | | | | | |
| Reed | Y | N | Y | Y | Y | Y | Y |
| Chafee | N | N | N | Y | N | N | N |
| **SOUTH CAROLINA** | | | | | | | |
| Graham | N | N | N | N | N | N | N |
| DeMint | N | N | N | N | N | N | N |
| **SOUTH DAKOTA** | | | | | | | |
| Johnson | Y | N | N | N | N | Y | Y |
| Thune | Y | N | N | N | N | N | N |
| **TENNESSEE** | | | | | | | |
| Frist | N | N | N | N | N | N | N |
| Alexander | N | N | N | N | N | N | N |
| **TEXAS** | | | | | | | |
| Hutchison | N | N | N | N | N | N | N |
| Cornyn | N | N | N | N | N | N | N |
| **UTAH** | | | | | | | |
| Hatch | N | N | N | N | N | N | N |
| Bennett | N | N | N | N | N | N | N |
| **VERMONT** | | | | | | | |
| Leahy | Y | N | Y | Y | Y | Y | Y |
| Jeffords | Y | Y | Y | Y | Y | Y | Y |
| **VIRGINIA** | | | | | | | |
| Warner | N | N | N | N | N | N | N |
| Allen | N | N | N | N | N | N | N |
| **WASHINGTON** | | | | | | | |
| Murray | Y | Y | Y | Y | Y | Y | Y |
| Cantwell | Y | N | Y | Y | Y | Y | Y |
| **WEST VIRGINIA** | | | | | | | |
| Byrd | Y | Y | Y | Y | Y | Y | Y |
| Rockefeller | N | Y | Y | Y | Y | Y | Y |
| **WISCONSIN** | | | | | | | |
| Kohl | Y | N | Y | Y | Y | Y | Y |
| Feingold | ? | ? | ? | ? | ? | ? | ? |
| **WYOMING** | | | | | | | |
| Thomas | Y | N | N | N | N | N | N |
| Enzi | Y | N | N | N | N | N | N |

**KEY**    Republicans    Democrats    *Independents*

| | | |
|---|---|---|
| Y Voted for (yea) | X Paired against | C Voted "present" to avoid possible conflict of interest |
| # Paired for | - Announced against | |
| + Announced for | P Voted "present" | ? Did not vote or otherwise make a position known |
| N Voted against (nay) | | |

# IN THE SENATE | By Vote Number

**26.** **S 256. Bankruptcy Overhaul/Minimum Wage.** Kennedy, D-Mass., amendment that would raise the minimum wage from $5.15 an hour to $7.25 an hour over 26 months. Rejected 46-49: R 4-49; D 41-0 (ND 37-0, SD 4-0); I 1-0. March 7, 2005.

**27.** **S 256. Bankruptcy Overhaul/Minimum Wage.** Santorum, R-Pa., amendment that would raise the minimum wage from $5.15 to $6.25 over 18 months in two increments of 55 cents. It also would provide several tax cuts for small businesses. Rejected 38-61: R 38-17; D 0-43 (ND 0-39, SD 0-4); I 0-1. March 7, 2005.

**28.** **S 256. Bankruptcy Overhaul/Violent Protesters.** Schumer, D-N.Y., amendment that would prohibit violent protesters, such as anti-abortion activists, from escaping court-ordered fines or judgments by filing for bankruptcy protection. It would bar such debtors from discharging debts, such as damages, court fines, penalties, citations or attorney fees, incurred from acts of violence or potential acts of violence. Rejected 46-53: R 4-51; D 41-2 (ND 37-2, SD 4-0); I 1-0. March 8, 2005.

**29.** **S 256. Bankruptcy Overhaul/Cloture.** Motion to invoke cloture (thus limiting debate) on the bill that would revise bankruptcy laws to make it easier for courts to move debtors from Chapter 7 of the bankruptcy code, which allows most debts to be discharged, to Chapter 13, which requires a reorganization of debts under a repayment. Motion agreed to 69-31: R 55-0; D 14-30 (ND 10-30, SD 4-0); I 0-1. Three-fifths of the total Senate (60) is required to invoke cloture. March 8, 2005.

**30.** **S 256. Bankruptcy Overhaul/Small Business Provisions.** Feingold, D-Wis., amendment that would strike certain small business-related bankruptcy provisions in the bill, including the 300-day deadline for small businesses seeking to reorganize under Chapter 11. Rejected 41-59: R 0-55; D 40-4 (ND 36-4, SD 4-0); I 1-0. March 8, 2005.

**31.** **S 256. Bankruptcy Overhaul/Median Income.** Durbin, D-Ill., amendment that would clarify that the means test would not apply to debtors whose incomes fell below the median. Rejected 42-58: R 0-55; D 41-3 (ND 37-3, SD 4-0); I 1-0. March 9, 2005.

**32.** **S 256. Bankruptcy Overhaul/Employee Wage Priority.** Harkin, D-Iowa, amendment that would strike the 180-day limit on the accrual period for the employee wage priority to protect the back pay and severance for workers whose employers are in bankruptcy. Rejected 48-52: R 3-52; D 44-0 (ND 40-0, SD 4-0); I 1-0. March 9, 2005.

| | 26 | 27 | 28 | 29 | 30 | 31 | 32 |
|---|---|---|---|---|---|---|---|
| **ALABAMA** | | | | | | | |
| Shelby | N | Y | N | Y | N | N | N |
| Sessions | N | Y | N | Y | N | N | N |
| **ALASKA** | | | | | | | |
| Stevens | N | Y | N | Y | N | N | N |
| Murkowski | N | Y | N | Y | N | N | N |
| **ARIZONA** | | | | | | | |
| McCain | N | Y | N | Y | N | N | N |
| Kyl | N | Y | N | Y | N | N | N |
| **ARKANSAS** | | | | | | | |
| Lincoln | Y | N | Y | Y | Y | Y | Y |
| Pryor | Y | N | Y | N | Y | Y | Y |
| **CALIFORNIA** | | | | | | | |
| Feinstein | Y | N | Y | N | Y | Y | Y |
| Boxer | Y | N | Y | N | Y | Y | Y |
| **COLORADO** | | | | | | | |
| Allard | N | N | N | Y | N | N | N |
| Salazar | Y | N | Y | Y | Y | Y | Y |
| **CONNECTICUT** | | | | | | | |
| Dodd | Y | N | Y | N | Y | Y | Y |
| Lieberman | Y | N | Y | Y | Y | Y | Y |
| **DELAWARE** | | | | | | | |
| Biden | Y | N | Y | Y | N | Y | Y |
| Carper | Y | N | Y | Y | N | N | Y |
| **FLORIDA** | | | | | | | |
| Nelson | Y | N | Y | Y | Y | Y | Y |
| Martinez | N | Y | N | Y | N | N | N |
| **GEORGIA** | | | | | | | |
| Chambliss | N | N | N | Y | N | N | N |
| Isakson | N | N | N | Y | N | N | N |
| **HAWAII** | | | | | | | |
| Inouye | Y | N | Y | N | Y | Y | Y |
| Akaka | Y | N | Y | N | Y | Y | Y |
| **IDAHO** | | | | | | | |
| Craig | N | Y | N | Y | N | N | N |
| Crapo | N | Y | N | Y | N | N | N |
| **ILLINOIS** | | | | | | | |
| Durbin | Y | N | Y | N | Y | Y | Y |
| Obama | Y | N | Y | N | Y | Y | Y |
| **INDIANA** | | | | | | | |
| Lugar | N | Y | N | Y | N | N | N |
| Bayh | Y | N | Y | N | Y | N | N |
| **IOWA** | | | | | | | |
| Grassley | N | Y | N | Y | N | N | N |
| Harkin | Y | N | Y | N | Y | Y | Y |
| **KANSAS** | | | | | | | |
| Brownback | N | Y | N | Y | N | N | N |
| Roberts | N | Y | N | Y | N | N | N |
| **KENTUCKY** | | | | | | | |
| McConnell | N | Y | N | Y | N | N | N |
| Bunning | N | Y | N | Y | N | N | N |
| **LOUISIANA** | | | | | | | |
| Landrieu | Y | N | Y | Y | Y | Y | Y |
| Vitter | N | N | N | Y | N | N | N |
| **MAINE** | | | | | | | |
| Snowe | N | Y | Y | Y | N | N | Y |
| Collins | N | N | Y | N | N | Y | N |
| **MARYLAND** | | | | | | | |
| Sarbanes | Y | N | Y | N | Y | Y | Y |
| Mikulski | ? | ? | Y | N | Y | Y | Y |
| **MASSACHUSETTS** | | | | | | | |
| Kennedy | Y | N | Y | Y | Y | Y | Y |
| Kerry | Y | N | Y | N | Y | Y | Y |
| **MICHIGAN** | | | | | | | |
| Levin | Y | N | Y | Y | Y | Y | Y |
| Stabenow | Y | N | Y | Y | Y | Y | Y |
| **MINNESOTA** | | | | | | | |
| Dayton | Y | N | Y | N | Y | Y | Y |
| Coleman | Y | Y | N | Y | N | N | N |
| **MISSISSIPPI** | | | | | | | |
| Cochran | N | N | N | Y | N | N | N |
| Lott | N | N | N | Y | N | N | N |
| **MISSOURI** | | | | | | | |
| Bond | N | N | N | Y | N | N | N |
| Talent | N | Y | N | Y | N | N | N |
| **MONTANA** | | | | | | | |
| Baucus | ? | N | Y | N | Y | Y | Y |
| Burns | N | Y | N | Y | N | N | N |
| **NEBRASKA** | | | | | | | |
| Hagel | N | Y | N | Y | N | N | N |
| Nelson | Y | N | N | Y | N | N | Y |
| **NEVADA** | | | | | | | |
| Reid | Y | N | Y | N | Y | Y | Y |
| Ensign | ? | Y | N | Y | N | N | N |
| **NEW HAMPSHIRE** | | | | | | | |
| Gregg | N | N | N | Y | N | N | N |
| Sununu | N | N | N | Y | N | N | N |
| **NEW JERSEY** | | | | | | | |
| Corzine | Y | N | ? | N | Y | Y | Y |
| Lautenberg | Y | N | Y | N | Y | Y | Y |
| **NEW MEXICO** | | | | | | | |
| Domenici | Y | Y | N | Y | N | N | N |
| Bingaman | Y | N | Y | N | Y | Y | Y |
| **NEW YORK** | | | | | | | |
| Schumer | Y | N | Y | N | Y | Y | Y |
| Clinton | Y | N | Y | N | Y | Y | Y |
| **NORTH CAROLINA** | | | | | | | |
| Dole | N | Y | N | Y | N | N | N |
| Burr | N | N | N | Y | N | N | N |
| **NORTH DAKOTA** | | | | | | | |
| Conrad | ? | N | Y | Y | Y | Y | Y |
| Dorgan | Y | N | Y | N | Y | Y | Y |
| **OHIO** | | | | | | | |
| DeWine | Y | Y | N | Y | N | N | N |
| Voinovich | N | Y | N | Y | N | N | N |
| **OKLAHOMA** | | | | | | | |
| Inhofe | N | N | N | Y | N | N | N |
| Coburn | N | N | N | Y | N | N | N |
| **OREGON** | | | | | | | |
| Wyden | Y | N | Y | N | Y | Y | Y |
| Smith | N | Y | N | Y | N | N | N |
| **PENNSYLVANIA** | | | | | | | |
| Specter | ? | Y | Y | Y | N | N | Y |
| Santorum | N | Y | N | Y | N | N | N |
| **RHODE ISLAND** | | | | | | | |
| Reed | Y | N | Y | N | Y | Y | Y |
| Chafee | Y | N | Y | N | Y | N | N |
| **SOUTH CAROLINA** | | | | | | | |
| Graham | N | Y | N | Y | N | N | N |
| DeMint | N | N | N | Y | N | N | N |
| **SOUTH DAKOTA** | | | | | | | |
| Johnson | Y | N | Y | N | Y | N | Y |
| Thune | N | Y | N | Y | N | N | N |
| **TENNESSEE** | | | | | | | |
| Frist | N | Y | N | Y | N | N | N |
| Alexander | N | N | N | Y | N | N | N |
| **TEXAS** | | | | | | | |
| Hutchison | N | Y | N | Y | N | N | N |
| Cornyn | N | N | N | Y | N | N | N |
| **UTAH** | | | | | | | |
| Hatch | N | Y | N | Y | N | N | N |
| Bennett | N | Y | N | Y | N | N | N |
| **VERMONT** | | | | | | | |
| Leahy | Y | N | Y | N | Y | Y | Y |
| Jeffords | Y | N | Y | N | Y | Y | Y |
| **VIRGINIA** | | | | | | | |
| Warner | N | Y | N | Y | N | N | N |
| Allen | N | Y | N | Y | N | N | N |
| **WASHINGTON** | | | | | | | |
| Murray | Y | N | Y | N | Y | Y | Y |
| Cantwell | Y | N | Y | N | Y | Y | Y |
| **WEST VIRGINIA** | | | | | | | |
| Byrd | Y | N | Y | N | Y | Y | Y |
| Rockefeller | Y | N | Y | N | Y | Y | Y |
| **WISCONSIN** | | | | | | | |
| Kohl | Y | N | Y | Y | Y | Y | Y |
| Feingold | Y | N | Y | N | Y | Y | Y |
| **WYOMING** | | | | | | | |
| Thomas | N | Y | N | Y | N | N | N |
| Enzi | N | Y | N | Y | N | N | N |

# IN THE SENATE | By Vote Number

**33.** **S 256. Bankruptcy Overhaul/Disallowance of Claims.** Boxer, D-Calif., amendment that would not allow creditors to file a bankruptcy claim if the claim was based on the extension of credit to an individual age 21 or younger who, at the time the credit was extended, did not have a parental or spousal co-signer, had an income level below the poverty line, and already had six or more unsecured credit cards. Rejected 40-60: R 1-54; D 38-6 (ND 35-5, SD 3-1); I 1-0. March 9, 2005.

**34.** **S 256. Bankruptcy Overhaul/Family-Related Provisions.** Dodd, D-Conn., amendment that would alter the means test to provide greater flexibility when calculating a debtor's ability to pay, and broaden allowable monthly expenses to ensure that parents had the resources to support their children throughout bankruptcy. It also would allow debtors to keep personal property found in or around the home, excluding cars, and ensure that support payments and tax refunds do not become the property of the bankruptcy estate. Rejected 42-58: R 0-55; D 41-3 (ND 37-3, SD 4-0); I 1-0. March 9, 2005.

**35.** **S 256. Bankruptcy Overhaul/Homestead Exemption Cap.** Kennedy, D-Mass., amendment that would place a $300,000 cap on the bill's homestead exemption. Rejected 47-53: R 5-50; D 41-3 (ND 38-2, SD 3-1); I 1-0. March 9, 2005.

**36.** **S 256. Bankruptcy Overhaul/Means Test Exemption.** Kennedy, D-Mass., amendment that would exempt debtors from the means test if they failed to receive alimony or child support in any consecutive 12-month period in the two years before filing a bankruptcy petition and the amount exceeded 35 percent of the debtor's household income. Rejected 41-58: R 1-54; D 39-4 (ND 35-4, SD 4-0); I 1-0. March 10, 2005.

**37.** **S 256. Bankruptcy Overhaul/Current Monthly Income.** Kennedy, D-Mass., amendment that would change the bill's definition of current monthly income to specifically exclude income from a debtor's former job and income from any activity the debtor can no longer engage in due to disability. Rejected 41-58: R 0-55; D 40-3 (ND 36-3, SD 4-0); I 1-0. March 10, 2005.

**38.** **S 256. Bankruptcy Overhaul/Unsecured Creditors.** Akaka, D-Hawaii, amendment that would disallow an unsecured creditor's claim in bankruptcy if the creditor did not have a policy of waiving additional interest for all debtors who participate in a debt management plan administered by a nonprofit budget and credit counseling agency. Rejected 38-61: R 0-55; D 37-6 (ND 33-6, SD 4-0); I 1-0. March 10, 2005.

| | 33 | 34 | 35 | 36 | 37 | 38 |
|---|---|---|---|---|---|---|
| **ALABAMA** | | | | | | |
| Shelby | N | N | N | N | N | N |
| Sessions | N | N | N | N | N | N |
| **ALASKA** | | | | | | |
| Stevens | N | N | N | N | N | N |
| Murkowski | N | N | N | N | N | N |
| **ARIZONA** | | | | | | |
| McCain | N | N | N | N | N | N |
| Kyl | N | N | N | N | N | N |
| **ARKANSAS** | | | | | | |
| Lincoln | Y | Y | Y | Y | Y | Y |
| Pryor | Y | Y | Y | Y | Y | Y |
| **CALIFORNIA** | | | | | | |
| Feinstein | Y | Y | Y | Y | Y | Y |
| Boxer | Y | Y | Y | Y | Y | Y |
| **COLORADO** | | | | | | |
| Allard | N | N | N | N | N | N |
| Salazar | Y | Y | Y | Y | Y | Y |
| **CONNECTICUT** | | | | | | |
| Dodd | Y | Y | Y | Y | Y | Y |
| Lieberman | Y | Y | Y | Y | Y | Y |
| **DELAWARE** | | | | | | |
| Biden | Y | N | Y | N | Y | N |
| Carper | N | N | Y | N | Y | N |
| **FLORIDA** | | | | | | |
| Nelson | N | Y | N | Y | Y | Y |
| Martinez | N | N | N | N | N | N |
| **GEORGIA** | | | | | | |
| Chambliss | N | N | N | N | N | N |
| Isakson | N | N | N | N | N | N |
| **HAWAII** | | | | | | |
| Inouye | Y | Y | Y | Y | Y | Y |
| Akaka | Y | Y | Y | Y | Y | Y |
| **IDAHO** | | | | | | |
| Craig | N | N | N | N | N | N |
| Crapo | N | N | N | N | N | N |
| **ILLINOIS** | | | | | | |
| Durbin | Y | Y | Y | Y | Y | Y |
| Obama | Y | Y | Y | Y | Y | Y |
| **INDIANA** | | | | | | |
| Lugar | N | N | N | N | N | N |
| Bayh | N | Y | Y | Y | Y | Y |
| **IOWA** | | | | | | |
| Grassley | N | N | N | N | N | N |
| Harkin | Y | Y | Y | Y | Y | Y |
| **KANSAS** | | | | | | |
| Brownback | N | N | N | N | N | N |
| Roberts | N | N | N | N | N | N |
| **KENTUCKY** | | | | | | |
| McConnell | N | N | N | N | N | N |
| Bunning | N | N | N | N | N | N |
| **LOUISIANA** | | | | | | |
| Landrieu | Y | Y | Y | Y | Y | Y |
| Vitter | N | N | N | N | N | N |
| **MAINE** | | | | | | |
| Snowe | N | N | Y | N | N | N |
| Collins | N | N | Y | N | N | N |
| **MARYLAND** | | | | | | |
| Sarbanes | Y | Y | Y | Y | Y | Y |
| Mikulski | Y | Y | Y | Y | Y | Y |
| **MASSACHUSETTS** | | | | | | |
| Kennedy | Y | Y | Y | Y | Y | Y |
| Kerry | Y | Y | Y | Y | Y | Y |
| **MICHIGAN** | | | | | | |
| Levin | Y | Y | Y | Y | Y | Y |
| Stabenow | Y | Y | Y | Y | Y | Y |
| **MINNESOTA** | | | | | | |
| Dayton | Y | Y | Y | Y | Y | Y |
| Coleman | N | N | N | N | N | N |
| **MISSISSIPPI** | | | | | | |
| Cochran | N | N | N | N | N | N |
| Lott | N | N | N | N | N | N |
| **MISSOURI** | | | | | | |
| Bond | N | N | N | N | N | N |
| Talent | N | N | N | N | N | N |

| | 33 | 34 | 35 | 36 | 37 | 38 |
|---|---|---|---|---|---|---|
| **MONTANA** | | | | | | |
| Baucus | N | Y | N | Y | Y | N |
| Burns | N | N | N | N | N | N |
| **NEBRASKA** | | | | | | |
| Hagel | N | N | N | N | N | N |
| Nelson | N | N | N | N | N | N |
| **NEVADA** | | | | | | |
| Reid | Y | Y | Y | Y | Y | Y |
| Ensign | N | N | N | N | N | N |
| **NEW HAMPSHIRE** | | | | | | |
| Gregg | N | N | N | N | N | N |
| Sununu | N | N | N | N | N | N |
| **NEW JERSEY** | | | | | | |
| Corzine | Y | Y | Y | Y | Y | Y |
| Lautenberg | Y | Y | Y | Y | Y | Y |
| **NEW MEXICO** | | | | | | |
| Domenici | N | N | N | N | N | N |
| Bingaman | Y | Y | Y | N | N | N |
| **NEW YORK** | | | | | | |
| Schumer | Y | Y | Y | Y | Y | Y |
| Clinton | Y | Y | Y | ? | ? | ? |
| **NORTH CAROLINA** | | | | | | |
| Dole | N | N | N | N | N | N |
| Burr | N | N | N | N | N | N |
| **NORTH DAKOTA** | | | | | | |
| Conrad | Y | Y | Y | Y | Y | Y |
| Dorgan | Y | Y | Y | Y | Y | Y |
| **OHIO** | | | | | | |
| DeWine | N | N | Y | N | N | N |
| Voinovich | N | N | N | N | N | N |
| **OKLAHOMA** | | | | | | |
| Inhofe | N | N | N | N | N | N |
| Coburn | N | N | N | N | N | N |
| **OREGON** | | | | | | |
| Wyden | Y | Y | Y | Y | Y | Y |
| Smith | N | N | N | N | N | N |
| **PENNSYLVANIA** | | | | | | |
| Specter | N | N | N | N | N | N |
| Santorum | N | N | N | N | N | N |
| **RHODE ISLAND** | | | | | | |
| Reed | Y | Y | Y | Y | Y | Y |
| Chafee | Y | N | Y | N | N | N |
| **SOUTH CAROLINA** | | | | | | |
| Graham | N | N | N | N | N | N |
| DeMint | N | N | N | N | N | N |
| **SOUTH DAKOTA** | | | | | | |
| Johnson | N | Y | N | Y | Y | N |
| Thune | N | N | N | N | N | N |
| **TENNESSEE** | | | | | | |
| Frist | N | N | N | N | N | N |
| Alexander | N | N | N | N | N | N |
| **TEXAS** | | | | | | |
| Hutchison | N | N | N | N | N | N |
| Cornyn | N | N | N | N | N | N |
| **UTAH** | | | | | | |
| Hatch | N | N | N | N | N | N |
| Bennett | N | N | N | N | N | N |
| **VERMONT** | | | | | | |
| Leahy | Y | Y | Y | Y | Y | Y |
| Jeffords | Y | Y | Y | Y | Y | Y |
| **VIRGINIA** | | | | | | |
| Warner | N | N | N | N | N | N |
| Allen | N | N | N | N | N | N |
| **WASHINGTON** | | | | | | |
| Murray | Y | Y | Y | Y | Y | Y |
| Cantwell | Y | Y | Y | Y | Y | Y |
| **WEST VIRGINIA** | | | | | | |
| Byrd | Y | Y | Y | Y | Y | Y |
| Rockefeller | Y | Y | Y | Y | Y | Y |
| **WISCONSIN** | | | | | | |
| Kohl | Y | Y | Y | Y | Y | Y |
| Feingold | Y | Y | Y | Y | Y | Y |
| **WYOMING** | | | | | | |
| Thomas | N | N | N | N | N | N |
| Enzi | N | N | N | N | N | N |

**KEY**   Republicans   Democrats   *Independents*

| | | | | | |
|---|---|---|---|---|---|
| Y | Voted for (yea) | X | Paired against | C | Voted "present" to avoid possible conflict of interest |
| # | Paired for | – | Announced against | | |
| + | Announced for | P | Voted "present" | ? | Did not vote or otherwise make a position known |
| N | Voted against (nay) | | | | |

# IN THE SENATE | By Vote Number

**39.** **S 256. Bankruptcy Overhaul/Conflict of Interest.** Leahy, D-Vt., amendment that would prohibit investment bankers from acting as financial advisers to debtor companies filing for bankruptcy if they have advised those same companies within five years of the company's bankruptcy. Rejected 44-55: R 5-50; D 38-5 (ND 35-4, SD 2-2); I 1-0. March 10, 2005.

**40.** **S 256. Bankruptcy Overhaul/Disabled Veterans.** Durbin, D-Ill., amendment that would exempt disabled veterans from the means test if their debts were incurred primarily when they were on active duty or performing homeland defense duties. Adopted 99-0: R 55-0; D 43-0 (ND 39-0, SD 4-0); I 1-0. March 10, 2005.

**41.** **S 256. Bankruptcy Overhaul/Asset Protection Trusts.** Schumer, D-N.Y., amendment to the Talent, R-Mo., amendment. The Schumer amendment would strike language in the underlying amendment that would require bankruptcy courts to show that the owner of an asset protection trust had the intent of defrauding creditors and employees. The Talent amendment would allow bankruptcy courts to access assets in such trusts up to 10 years before the owner filed a bankruptcy petition. Rejected 43-56: R 1-54; D 41-2 (ND 37-2, SD 4-0); I 1-0. March 10, 2005.

**42.** **S 256. Bankruptcy Overhaul/Asset Protection Trusts.** Talent, R-Mo., amendment that would allow bankruptcy courts to access assets in asset protection trusts up to 10 years before the owner filed a bankruptcy petition. It also would require courts to show that the owner of such a trust had the intent of defrauding creditors and employees. Adopted 73-26: R 55-0; D 18-25 (ND 15-24, SD 3-1); I 0-1. March 10, 2005.

**43.** **S 250. Vocational-Technical Education/Passage.** Passage of the bill that would reauthorize the Carl D. Perkins Vocational and Technical Education Act, which provides federal grants to states to develop and support vocational training programs. It would set the within-state allotment at a minimum of 85 percent and remove spending caps on non-traditional programs such as prisoner retraining. It would eliminate the Tech-Prep demonstration program. Passed 99-0: R 55-0; D 43-0 (ND 39-0, SD 4-0); I 1-0. March 10, 2005.

**44.** **S 256. Bankruptcy Overhaul/Passage.** Passage of the bill that would create a means test tied to the median incomes of individual states to determine whether personal bankruptcy filers were able to repay some or all of their debts. Those deemed able to pay would be pushed into Chapter 13 bankruptcy, which results in a court-ordered repayment plan; those with insufficient assets would be allowed to file under Chapter 7, which erases debts after the forfeiture of certain assets. The bill would exempt disabled veterans from the means test if their debts were incurred primarily when they were on active duty or performing homeland defense duties. It also would make a number of debts non-dischargeable, including student loans, child support, alimony and luxury payments over $500 made within three months of a bankruptcy filing. Passed 74-25: R 55-0; D 18-25 (ND 14-25, SD 4-0); I 1-0. March 10, 2005.

| | 39 | 40 | 41 | 42 | 43 | 44 |
|---|---|---|---|---|---|---|
| **ALABAMA** | | | | | | |
| Shelby | N | Y | N | Y | Y | Y |
| Sessions | N | Y | N | Y | Y | Y |
| **ALASKA** | | | | | | |
| Stevens | N | Y | N | Y | Y | Y |
| Murkowski | N | Y | N | Y | Y | Y |
| **ARIZONA** | | | | | | |
| McCain | N | Y | N | Y | Y | Y |
| Kyl | N | Y | N | Y | Y | Y |
| **ARKANSAS** | | | | | | |
| Lincoln | N | Y | Y | Y | Y | Y |
| Pryor | Y | Y | Y | Y | Y | Y |
| **CALIFORNIA** | | | | | | |
| Feinstein | Y | Y | Y | N | Y | N |
| Boxer | Y | Y | Y | N | Y | N |
| **COLORADO** | | | | | | |
| Allard | N | Y | N | Y | Y | Y |
| Salazar | Y | Y | Y | Y | Y | Y |
| **CONNECTICUT** | | | | | | |
| Dodd | Y | Y | Y | Y | Y | N |
| Lieberman | Y | Y | Y | N | Y | Y |
| **DELAWARE** | | | | | | |
| Biden | Y | Y | Y | Y | Y | Y |
| Carper | Y | Y | N | N | Y | Y |
| **FLORIDA** | | | | | | |
| Nelson | Y | Y | Y | Y | Y | Y |
| Martinez | N | Y | N | Y | Y | Y |
| **GEORGIA** | | | | | | |
| Chambliss | N | Y | N | Y | Y | Y |
| Isakson | N | Y | N | Y | Y | Y |
| **HAWAII** | | | | | | |
| Inouye | Y | Y | Y | N | Y | Y |
| Akaka | Y | Y | Y | N | Y | N |
| **IDAHO** | | | | | | |
| Craig | N | Y | N | Y | Y | Y |
| Crapo | N | Y | N | Y | Y | Y |
| **ILLINOIS** | | | | | | |
| Durbin | Y | Y | Y | N | Y | N |
| Obama | Y | Y | Y | N | Y | N |
| **INDIANA** | | | | | | |
| Lugar | N | Y | N | Y | Y | Y |
| Bayh | N | Y | Y | N | Y | N |
| **IOWA** | | | | | | |
| Grassley | N | Y | N | Y | Y | Y |
| Harkin | Y | Y | Y | Y | Y | N |
| **KANSAS** | | | | | | |
| Brownback | N | Y | N | Y | Y | Y |
| Roberts | N | Y | N | Y | Y | Y |
| **KENTUCKY** | | | | | | |
| McConnell | N | Y | N | Y | Y | Y |
| Bunning | N | Y | N | Y | Y | Y |
| **LOUISIANA** | | | | | | |
| Landrieu | Y | Y | Y | N | Y | Y |
| Vitter | N | Y | Y | Y | Y | Y |
| **MAINE** | | | | | | |
| Snowe | Y | Y | N | Y | Y | Y |
| Collins | Y | Y | N | Y | Y | Y |
| **MARYLAND** | | | | | | |
| Sarbanes | Y | Y | Y | N | Y | N |
| Mikulski | Y | Y | Y | N | Y | N |
| **MASSACHUSETTS** | | | | | | |
| Kennedy | Y | Y | Y | N | Y | N |
| Kerry | Y | Y | Y | N | Y | N |
| **MICHIGAN** | | | | | | |
| Levin | Y | Y | Y | N | Y | N |
| Stabenow | N | Y | Y | N | Y | Y |
| **MINNESOTA** | | | | | | |
| Dayton | Y | Y | Y | Y | Y | N |
| Coleman | N | Y | N | Y | Y | Y |
| **MISSISSIPPI** | | | | | | |
| Cochran | N | Y | N | Y | Y | Y |
| Lott | N | Y | N | Y | Y | Y |
| **MISSOURI** | | | | | | |
| Bond | N | Y | N | Y | Y | Y |
| Talent | N | Y | N | Y | Y | Y |

| | 39 | 40 | 41 | 42 | 43 | 44 |
|---|---|---|---|---|---|---|
| **MONTANA** | | | | | | |
| Baucus | N | Y | N | Y | Y | Y |
| Burns | N | Y | N | Y | Y | Y |
| **NEBRASKA** | | | | | | |
| Hagel | N | Y | N | Y | Y | Y |
| Nelson | Y | Y | N | Y | Y | Y |
| **NEVADA** | | | | | | |
| Reid | Y | Y | Y | N | Y | Y |
| Ensign | N | Y | N | Y | Y | Y |
| **NEW HAMPSHIRE** | | | | | | |
| Gregg | N | Y | N | Y | Y | Y |
| Sununu | N | Y | N | Y | Y | Y |
| **NEW JERSEY** | | | | | | |
| Corzine | Y | Y | Y | Y | Y | N |
| Lautenberg | Y | Y | Y | N | Y | N |
| **NEW MEXICO** | | | | | | |
| Domenici | N | Y | N | Y | Y | Y |
| Bingaman | Y | Y | Y | Y | Y | Y |
| **NEW YORK** | | | | | | |
| Schumer | Y | Y | Y | N | Y | N |
| Clinton | ? | ? | ? | ? | ? | ? |
| **NORTH CAROLINA** | | | | | | |
| Dole | N | Y | N | Y | Y | Y |
| Burr | N | Y | N | Y | Y | Y |
| **NORTH DAKOTA** | | | | | | |
| Conrad | Y | Y | Y | Y | Y | Y |
| Dorgan | Y | Y | Y | Y | Y | N |
| **OHIO** | | | | | | |
| DeWine | N | Y | N | Y | Y | Y |
| Voinovich | Y | Y | N | Y | Y | Y |
| **OKLAHOMA** | | | | | | |
| Inhofe | N | Y | N | Y | Y | Y |
| Coburn | N | Y | N | Y | Y | Y |
| **OREGON** | | | | | | |
| Wyden | Y | Y | Y | N | Y | N |
| Smith | N | Y | N | Y | Y | Y |
| **PENNSYLVANIA** | | | | | | |
| Specter | Y | Y | Y | Y | Y | Y |
| Santorum | N | Y | N | Y | Y | Y |
| **RHODE ISLAND** | | | | | | |
| Reed | Y | Y | Y | N | Y | N |
| Chafee | N | Y | Y | Y | Y | Y |
| **SOUTH CAROLINA** | | | | | | |
| Graham | N | Y | N | Y | Y | Y |
| DeMint | N | Y | N | Y | Y | Y |
| **SOUTH DAKOTA** | | | | | | |
| Johnson | Y | Y | Y | Y | Y | Y |
| Thune | N | Y | N | Y | Y | Y |
| **TENNESSEE** | | | | | | |
| Frist | N | Y | N | Y | Y | Y |
| Alexander | N | Y | N | Y | Y | Y |
| **TEXAS** | | | | | | |
| Hutchison | N | Y | N | Y | Y | Y |
| Cornyn | N | Y | N | Y | Y | Y |
| **UTAH** | | | | | | |
| Hatch | N | Y | N | Y | Y | Y |
| Bennett | N | Y | N | Y | Y | Y |
| **VERMONT** | | | | | | |
| Leahy | Y | Y | Y | N | Y | N |
| Jeffords | Y | Y | N | N | Y | Y |
| **VIRGINIA** | | | | | | |
| Warner | N | Y | N | Y | Y | Y |
| Allen | N | Y | N | Y | Y | Y |
| **WASHINGTON** | | | | | | |
| Murray | Y | Y | Y | N | Y | N |
| Cantwell | Y | Y | Y | Y | Y | N |
| **WEST VIRGINIA** | | | | | | |
| Byrd | Y | Y | Y | N | Y | Y |
| Rockefeller | Y | Y | Y | N | Y | Y |
| **WISCONSIN** | | | | | | |
| Kohl | Y | Y | Y | Y | Y | Y |
| Feingold | Y | Y | Y | N | Y | N |
| **WYOMING** | | | | | | |
| Thomas | N | Y | N | Y | Y | Y |
| Enzi | N | Y | N | Y | Y | Y |

**KEY**    Republicans    Democrats    *Independents*

| | | |
|---|---|---|
| Y   Voted for (yea) | X   Paired against | C   Voted "present" to avoid possible conflict of interest |
| #   Paired for | −   Announced against | |
| +   Announced for | P   Voted "present" | ?   Did not vote or otherwise make a position known |
| N   Voted against (nay) | | |

# IN THE SENATE | By Vote Number

**45.** S Con Res 18. Fiscal 2006 Budget Resolution/Education Funding.
Bingaman, D-N.M., amendment that would increase education funding for fiscal 2006 by $4.75 billion, restoring it to fiscal 2005 levels, and reduce the federal deficit by $4.75 billion. It would be offset by a $9.5 billion reduction in tax cuts. Rejected 44-49: R 3-49; D 40-0 (ND 36-0, SD 4-0); I 1-0. March 14, 2005.

**46.** S Con Res 18. Fiscal 2006 Budget Resolution/Social Security Solvency. Graham, R-S.C., amendment that would express the sense of the Senate that the president, Congress and the American people should work together to enact legislation that would achieve a solvent and permanently sustainable Social Security system. Adopted 100-0: R 55-0; D 44-0 (ND 40-0, SD 4-0); I 1-0. March 15, 2005.

**47.** S Con Res 18. Fiscal 2006 Budget Resolution/Social Security Solvency. Conrad, D-N.D., amendment that would make the consideration of new tax cuts or net mandatory spending that would increase the deficit subject to a 60-vote point of order unless Congress had restored the solvency of Social Security for 75 years. Rejected 45-55: R 0-55; D 44-0 (ND 40-0, SD 4-0); I 1-0. March 15, 2005.

**48.** S Con Res 18. Fiscal 2006 Budget Resolution/Social Security Benefit Cuts. DeMint, R-S.C., amendment that would express the sense of the Senate that Congress should reject any Social Security plan that requires deep benefit cuts or a massive increase in debt, and that a failure to act on Social Security would result in massive debt, deep benefit cuts and tax increases. Adopted 56-43: R 53-2; D 3-40 (ND 2-38, SD 1-2); I 0-1. March 15, 2005.

**49.** S Con Res 18. Fiscal 2006 Budget Resolution/Social Security.
Nelson, D-Fla., amendment that would express the sense of the Senate that Congress should reject any Social Security plan that requires deep benefit cuts or a massive increase in debt. It also would urge Congress to take action to address Social Security solvency. Rejected 50-50: R 5-50; D 44-0 (ND 40-0, SD 4-0); I 1-0. March 15, 2005.

**50.** S Con Res 18. Fiscal 2006 Budget Resolution/First-Responder Funding. Stabenow, D-Mich., amendment that would increase funding for first-responder programs by $1.6 billion in fiscal 2006 and reduce the federal deficit by $1.6 billion. It would be offset by a $3.2 billion reduction in tax reconciliation provisions. Rejected 46-54: R 1-54; D 44-0 (ND 40-0, SD 4-0); I 1-0. March 15, 2005.

**51.** S Con Res 18. Fiscal 2006 Budget Resolution/Amtrak Funding. Byrd, D-W.Va., amendment that would allow $1.04 billion in additional fiscal 2006 funding for Amtrak and increase the fiscal 2006 discretionary spending limit by $1.04 billion. The spending would be offset by revenue increases. Rejected 46-52: R 4-51; D 41-1 (ND 38-1, SD 3-0); I 1-0. March 16, 2005.

**52.** S Con Res 18. Fiscal 2006 Budget Resolution/ANWR Oil Drilling.
Cantwell, D-Wash., amendment that would strike language in the resolution that would give procedural protection to legislation authorizing oil drilling in part of the Arctic National Wildlife Refuge (ANWR) in Alaska. Rejected 49-51: R 7-48; D 41-3 (ND 38-2, SD 3-1); I 1-0. A "nay" was a vote in support of the president's position. March 16, 2005.

| State / Senator | 45 | 46 | 47 | 48 | 49 | 50 | 51 | 52 |
|---|---|---|---|---|---|---|---|---|
| **ALABAMA** | | | | | | | | |
| Shelby | N | Y | N | Y | N | N | N | N |
| Sessions | N | Y | N | Y | N | N | N | N |
| **ALASKA** | | | | | | | | |
| Stevens | N | Y | N | Y | N | N | N | N |
| Murkowski | N | Y | N | Y | N | N | N | N |
| **ARIZONA** | | | | | | | | |
| McCain | ? | Y | N | Y | N | N | N | Y |
| Kyl | N | Y | N | Y | N | N | N | N |
| **ARKANSAS** | | | | | | | | |
| Lincoln | Y | Y | Y | N | Y | Y | Y | Y |
| Pryor | Y | Y | Y | N | Y | Y | ? | Y |
| **CALIFORNIA** | | | | | | | | |
| Feinstein | Y | Y | Y | N | Y | Y | Y | Y |
| Boxer | Y | Y | Y | N | Y | Y | Y | Y |
| **COLORADO** | | | | | | | | |
| Allard | N | Y | N | Y | N | N | N | N |
| Salazar | Y | Y | Y | N | Y | Y | Y | Y |
| **CONNECTICUT** | | | | | | | | |
| Dodd | Y | Y | Y | N | Y | Y | Y | Y |
| Lieberman | Y | Y | Y | N | Y | Y | Y | Y |
| **DELAWARE** | | | | | | | | |
| Biden | Y | Y | Y | N | Y | Y | Y | Y |
| Carper | Y | Y | Y | N | Y | Y | Y | Y |
| **FLORIDA** | | | | | | | | |
| Nelson | Y | Y | Y | Y | Y | Y | N | Y |
| Martinez | N | Y | N | Y | N | N | N | N |
| **GEORGIA** | | | | | | | | |
| Chambliss | N | Y | N | Y | N | N | N | N |
| Isakson | N | Y | N | Y | N | N | N | N |
| **HAWAII** | | | | | | | | |
| Inouye | Y | Y | Y | N | Y | Y | Y | Y |
| Akaka | Y | Y | Y | N | Y | Y | Y | N |
| **IDAHO** | | | | | | | | |
| Craig | N | Y | N | Y | N | N | N | N |
| Crapo | N | Y | N | Y | N | N | N | N |
| **ILLINOIS** | | | | | | | | |
| Durbin | Y | Y | Y | N | Y | Y | Y | Y |
| Obama | Y | Y | Y | N | Y | Y | Y | Y |
| **INDIANA** | | | | | | | | |
| Lugar | N | Y | N | Y | N | N | N | N |
| Bayh | Y | Y | Y | N | Y | Y | Y | Y |
| **IOWA** | | | | | | | | |
| Grassley | N | Y | N | Y | N | N | N | N |
| Harkin | ? | Y | Y | N | Y | Y | Y | Y |
| **KANSAS** | | | | | | | | |
| Brownback | N | Y | N | Y | N | N | N | N |
| Roberts | ? | Y | N | Y | N | N | N | N |
| **KENTUCKY** | | | | | | | | |
| McConnell | N | Y | N | Y | N | N | N | N |
| Bunning | N | Y | N | Y | N | N | N | N |
| **LOUISIANA** | | | | | | | | |
| Landrieu | Y | Y | Y | ? | Y | Y | Y | N |
| Vitter | N | Y | N | Y | N | N | N | N |
| **MAINE** | | | | | | | | |
| Snowe | N | Y | N | Y | N | Y | Y | Y |
| Collins | N | Y | N | Y | Y | N | Y | Y |
| **MARYLAND** | | | | | | | | |
| Sarbanes | Y | Y | Y | N | Y | Y | Y | Y |
| Mikulski | Y | Y | Y | N | Y | Y | Y | Y |
| **MASSACHUSETTS** | | | | | | | | |
| Kennedy | Y | Y | Y | N | Y | Y | Y | Y |
| Kerry | Y | Y | Y | N | Y | Y | Y | Y |
| **MICHIGAN** | | | | | | | | |
| Levin | Y | Y | Y | N | Y | Y | Y | Y |
| Stabenow | Y | Y | Y | N | Y | Y | Y | Y |
| **MINNESOTA** | | | | | | | | |
| Dayton | Y | Y | Y | N | Y | Y | Y | Y |
| Coleman | Y | Y | N | Y | N | N | N | Y |
| **MISSISSIPPI** | | | | | | | | |
| Cochran | N | Y | N | Y | N | N | N | N |
| Lott | N | Y | N | Y | N | N | N | N |
| **MISSOURI** | | | | | | | | |
| Bond | N | Y | N | Y | N | N | N | N |
| Talent | N | Y | N | Y | N | N | N | N |

| State / Senator | 45 | 46 | 47 | 48 | 49 | 50 | 51 | 52 |
|---|---|---|---|---|---|---|---|---|
| **MONTANA** | | | | | | | | |
| Baucus | Y | Y | Y | N | Y | Y | Y | Y |
| Burns | N | Y | N | Y | N | N | N | N |
| **NEBRASKA** | | | | | | | | |
| Hagel | N | Y | N | Y | N | N | N | N |
| Nelson | Y | Y | Y | Y | Y | Y | Y | Y |
| **NEVADA** | | | | | | | | |
| Reid | Y | Y | Y | N | Y | Y | Y | Y |
| Ensign | N | Y | N | Y | N | N | N | N |
| **NEW HAMPSHIRE** | | | | | | | | |
| Gregg | N | Y | N | Y | N | N | N | N |
| Sununu | N | Y | N | Y | N | N | N | N |
| **NEW JERSEY** | | | | | | | | |
| Corzine | ? | Y | Y | N | Y | Y | Y | Y |
| Lautenberg | Y | Y | Y | N | Y | Y | Y | Y |
| **NEW MEXICO** | | | | | | | | |
| Domenici | N | Y | N | Y | N | N | N | N |
| Bingaman | Y | Y | Y | N | Y | Y | Y | Y |
| **NEW YORK** | | | | | | | | |
| Schumer | Y | Y | Y | N | Y | Y | Y | Y |
| Clinton | ? | Y | Y | N | Y | Y | Y | Y |
| **NORTH CAROLINA** | | | | | | | | |
| Dole | N | Y | N | Y | N | N | N | N |
| Burr | N | Y | N | Y | N | N | N | N |
| **NORTH DAKOTA** | | | | | | | | |
| Conrad | Y | Y | Y | N | Y | Y | Y | Y |
| Dorgan | Y | Y | Y | N | Y | Y | Y | Y |
| **OHIO** | | | | | | | | |
| DeWine | Y | Y | Y | N | Y | N | Y | Y |
| Voinovich | N | Y | N | Y | N | N | N | N |
| **OKLAHOMA** | | | | | | | | |
| Inhofe | N | Y | N | Y | N | N | N | N |
| Coburn | N | Y | N | Y | N | N | N | N |
| **OREGON** | | | | | | | | |
| Wyden | Y | Y | Y | N | Y | Y | Y | Y |
| Smith | N | Y | N | Y | N | N | N | Y |
| **PENNSYLVANIA** | | | | | | | | |
| Specter | N | Y | N | Y | N | Y | N | Y |
| Santorum | N | Y | N | Y | N | N | N | N |
| **RHODE ISLAND** | | | | | | | | |
| Reed | Y | Y | Y | N | Y | Y | ? | Y |
| Chafee | Y | Y | N | Y | N | Y | Y | Y |
| **SOUTH CAROLINA** | | | | | | | | |
| Graham | ? | Y | N | Y | N | N | N | N |
| DeMint | N | Y | N | Y | N | N | N | N |
| **SOUTH DAKOTA** | | | | | | | | |
| Johnson | Y | Y | Y | N | Y | Y | Y | Y |
| Thune | N | Y | N | Y | N | N | N | N |
| **TENNESSEE** | | | | | | | | |
| Frist | N | Y | N | Y | N | N | N | N |
| Alexander | N | Y | N | Y | N | N | N | N |
| **TEXAS** | | | | | | | | |
| Hutchison | N | Y | N | Y | N | N | N | N |
| Cornyn | N | Y | N | Y | N | N | N | N |
| **UTAH** | | | | | | | | |
| Hatch | N | Y | N | Y | N | N | N | N |
| Bennett | N | Y | N | Y | N | N | N | N |
| **VERMONT** | | | | | | | | |
| Leahy | ? | Y | Y | N | Y | Y | Y | Y |
| Jeffords | Y | Y | Y | N | Y | Y | Y | Y |
| **VIRGINIA** | | | | | | | | |
| Warner | N | Y | N | Y | N | N | N | N |
| Allen | N | Y | N | Y | N | N | N | N |
| **WASHINGTON** | | | | | | | | |
| Murray | Y | Y | Y | N | Y | Y | Y | Y |
| Cantwell | Y | Y | Y | N | Y | Y | Y | Y |
| **WEST VIRGINIA** | | | | | | | | |
| Byrd | Y | Y | Y | Y | Y | Y | Y | Y |
| Rockefeller | Y | Y | Y | N | Y | Y | Y | Y |
| **WISCONSIN** | | | | | | | | |
| Kohl | Y | Y | Y | N | Y | Y | Y | Y |
| Feingold | Y | Y | Y | N | Y | Y | Y | Y |
| **WYOMING** | | | | | | | | |
| Thomas | N | Y | N | Y | N | N | N | N |
| Enzi | N | Y | N | Y | N | N | N | N |

**KEY**    **Republicans**    Democrats    *Independents*

| | | |
|---|---|---|
| Y   Voted for (yea) | X   Paired against | C   Voted "present" to avoid possible conflict of interest |
| #   Paired for | −   Announced against | |
| +   Announced for | P   Voted "present" | ?   Did not vote or otherwise make a position known |
| N   Voted against (nay) | | |

# IN THE SENATE | By Vote Number

**53.** S Con Res 18. Fiscal 2006 Budget Resolution/PAYGO Rules.
Feingold, D-Wis., amendment that would restore pay-as-you-go (PAYGO) rules, which would create a 60-vote point of order against any direct spending or revenue legislation that would increase the on-budget deficit or cause an on-budget deficit. Tax cuts and new entitlement spending would have to be offset with revenue increases or spending cuts. Rejected 50-50: R 5-50 D 44-0 (ND 40-0, SD 4-0); I 1-0. March 16, 2005.

**54.** S Con Res 18. Fiscal 2006 Budget Resolution/Veterans' Health Care Funding. Ensign, R-Nev., amendment that would increase fiscal 2006 health care funding for veterans by $410 million. It would be offset by a reduction in foreign aid funding. Adopted 96-4: R 51-4; D 44-0 (ND 40-0, SD 4-0); I 1-0. March 16, 2005.

**55.** S Con Res 18. Fiscal 2006 Budget Resolution/Veterans' Health Care and Deficit Reduction. Akaka, D-Hawaii, amendment that would increase funding for veterans health care by $2.8 billion for fiscal 2006 and reduce the deficit by $2.8 billion. Rejected 47-53: R 2-53; D 44-0 (ND 40-0, SD 4-0); I 1-0. March 16, 2005.

**56.** S Con Res 18. Fiscal 2006 Budget Resolution/Health and Education Funding. Specter, R-Pa., amendment that would increase fiscal 2006 funding for the National Institutes of Health by $1.5 billion and education funding by $500 million. It would be offset by a $2 billion cut in the allowances account. Adopted 63-37: R 18-37; D 44-0 (ND 40-0, SD 4-0); I 1-0. March 16, 2005.

**57.** S Con Res 18. Fiscal 2006 Budget Resolution/Medicaid. Gregg, R-N.H., amendment that would express the sense of the Senate that the Health and Human Services secretary, working with a bipartisan group of governors and stakeholders, should make recommendations for changes to Medicaid. It also would express the sense of the Senate that the Finance Committee should report a reconciliation bill that allows Medicaid savings to be shared by federal and state governments, emphasizes state flexibility through voluntary options for states and would not cause Medicaid recipients to lose coverage. Rejected 49-51: R 49-6; D 0-44 (ND 0-40, SD 0-4); I 0-1. March 17, 2005.

**58.** S Con Res 18. Fiscal 2006 Budget Resolution/Medicaid Cuts. Smith, R-Ore., amendment that would strip out reconciliation instructions to the Finance Committee to reduce its outlays by $15 billion over five years that would likely result in a cut of $14 billion to Medicaid. It also would set up a reserve fund for the creation of a 23-member Bipartisan Medicaid Commission to study Medicaid before any cuts are made. Adopted 52-48: R 7-48; D 44-0 (ND 40-0, SD 4-0); I 1-0. March 17, 2005.

**59.** S Con Res 18. Fiscal 2006 Budget Resolution/Tax Cuts. Carper, D-Del., amendment that would strike language in the resolution that would give reconciliation protection to tax cuts. Rejected 49-51: R 5-50; D 43-1 (ND 39-1, SD 4-0); I 1-0. March 17, 2005.

**60.** S Con Res 18. Fiscal 2006 Budget Resolution/Prescription Drug Prices. Snowe, R-Maine, amendment that would insert language that would allow the secretary of Health and Human Services to negotiate with drug manufacturers for lower drug prices under Medicare. Rejected 49-50: R 6-48; D 42-2 (ND 39-1, SD 3-1); I 1-0. March 17, 2005.

| State / Senator | 53 | 54 | 55 | 56 | 57 | 58 | 59 | 60 |
|---|---|---|---|---|---|---|---|---|
| **ALABAMA** | | | | | | | | |
| Shelby | N | Y | N | Y | Y | N | N | N |
| Sessions | N | Y | N | N | Y | N | N | N |
| **ALASKA** | | | | | | | | |
| Stevens | N | Y | N | Y | Y | N | N | N |
| Murkowski | N | Y | N | N | Y | N | N | N |
| **ARIZONA** | | | | | | | | |
| McCain | Y | Y | N | N | Y | N | Y | Y |
| Kyl | N | Y | N | N | Y | N | N | N |
| **ARKANSAS** | | | | | | | | |
| Lincoln | Y | Y | Y | Y | N | Y | Y | Y |
| Pryor | Y | Y | Y | Y | N | Y | Y | Y |
| **CALIFORNIA** | | | | | | | | |
| Feinstein | Y | Y | Y | Y | N | Y | Y | Y |
| Boxer | Y | Y | Y | Y | N | Y | Y | Y |
| **COLORADO** | | | | | | | | |
| Allard | N | N | N | N | Y | N | N | N |
| Salazar | Y | Y | Y | Y | N | Y | Y | Y |
| **CONNECTICUT** | | | | | | | | |
| Dodd | Y | Y | Y | Y | N | Y | Y | Y |
| Lieberman | Y | Y | Y | Y | N | Y | Y | Y |
| **DELAWARE** | | | | | | | | |
| Biden | Y | Y | Y | Y | N | Y | Y | Y |
| Carper | Y | Y | Y | Y | N | Y | Y | Y |
| **FLORIDA** | | | | | | | | |
| Nelson | Y | Y | Y | Y | N | Y | Y | Y |
| Martinez | N | Y | N | N | Y | N | N | N |
| **GEORGIA** | | | | | | | | |
| Chambliss | N | Y | N | N | Y | N | N | N |
| Isakson | N | Y | N | N | Y | N | N | N |
| **HAWAII** | | | | | | | | |
| Inouye | Y | Y | Y | Y | N | Y | Y | Y |
| Akaka | Y | Y | Y | Y | N | Y | Y | Y |
| **IDAHO** | | | | | | | | |
| Craig | N | Y | N | Y | N | N | N | N |
| Crapo | N | Y | N | Y | Y | N | N | N |
| **ILLINOIS** | | | | | | | | |
| Durbin | Y | Y | Y | Y | N | Y | Y | Y |
| Obama | Y | Y | Y | Y | N | Y | Y | Y |
| **INDIANA** | | | | | | | | |
| Lugar | N | N | N | Y | Y | N | N | N |
| Bayh | Y | Y | Y | Y | N | Y | Y | Y |
| **IOWA** | | | | | | | | |
| Grassley | N | Y | N | Y | Y | N | N | N |
| Harkin | Y | Y | Y | Y | N | Y | Y | Y |
| **KANSAS** | | | | | | | | |
| Brownback | N | Y | N | Y | Y | N | N | Y |
| Roberts | N | Y | N | N | Y | N | N | N |
| **KENTUCKY** | | | | | | | | |
| McConnell | N | Y | N | N | Y | N | N | N |
| Bunning | N | Y | N | N | Y | N | N | N |
| **LOUISIANA** | | | | | | | | |
| Landrieu | Y | Y | Y | Y | N | Y | Y | Y |
| Vitter | N | Y | N | N | Y | N | N | N |
| **MAINE** | | | | | | | | |
| Snowe | Y | Y | N | Y | N | Y | Y | Y |
| Collins | Y | Y | N | Y | N | Y | Y | Y |
| **MARYLAND** | | | | | | | | |
| Sarbanes | Y | Y | Y | Y | N | Y | Y | Y |
| Mikulski | Y | Y | Y | Y | N | Y | Y | Y |
| **MASSACHUSETTS** | | | | | | | | |
| Kennedy | Y | Y | Y | Y | N | Y | Y | Y |
| Kerry | Y | Y | Y | Y | N | Y | Y | Y |
| **MICHIGAN** | | | | | | | | |
| Levin | Y | Y | Y | Y | N | Y | Y | Y |
| Stabenow | Y | Y | Y | Y | N | Y | Y | Y |
| **MINNESOTA** | | | | | | | | |
| Dayton | Y | Y | Y | Y | N | Y | Y | Y |
| Coleman | N | N | Y | Y | N | Y | N | N |
| **MISSISSIPPI** | | | | | | | | |
| Cochran | N | Y | N | N | Y | N | N | N |
| Lott | N | Y | N | N | Y | N | N | N |
| **MISSOURI** | | | | | | | | |
| Bond | N | Y | N | N | Y | N | N | N |
| Talent | N | Y | N | Y | Y | N | N | N |
| **MONTANA** | | | | | | | | |
| Baucus | Y | Y | Y | Y | N | Y | N | N |
| Burns | N | Y | N | N | Y | N | N | N |
| **NEBRASKA** | | | | | | | | |
| Hagel | N | Y | N | N | Y | N | N | N |
| Nelson | Y | Y | Y | Y | N | Y | N | N |
| **NEVADA** | | | | | | | | |
| Reid | Y | Y | Y | Y | N | Y | Y | Y |
| Ensign | N | Y | N | N | Y | N | N | N |
| **NEW HAMPSHIRE** | | | | | | | | |
| Gregg | N | Y | N | N | Y | N | N | N |
| Sununu | N | Y | N | N | Y | N | N | N |
| **NEW JERSEY** | | | | | | | | |
| Corzine | Y | Y | Y | Y | N | Y | Y | Y |
| Lautenberg | Y | Y | Y | Y | N | Y | Y | Y |
| **NEW MEXICO** | | | | | | | | |
| Domenici | N | Y | N | N | Y | N | N | N |
| Bingaman | Y | Y | Y | Y | N | Y | Y | Y |
| **NEW YORK** | | | | | | | | |
| Schumer | Y | Y | Y | Y | N | Y | Y | Y |
| Clinton | Y | Y | Y | Y | N | Y | Y | Y |
| **NORTH CAROLINA** | | | | | | | | |
| Dole | N | Y | N | Y | Y | N | N | N |
| Burr | N | Y | N | Y | Y | N | N | N |
| **NORTH DAKOTA** | | | | | | | | |
| Conrad | Y | Y | Y | Y | N | Y | Y | Y |
| Dorgan | Y | Y | Y | Y | N | Y | Y | Y |
| **OHIO** | | | | | | | | |
| DeWine | N | Y | N | Y | N | Y | N | N |
| Voinovich | Y | N | N | N | Y | N | Y | ? |
| **OKLAHOMA** | | | | | | | | |
| Inhofe | N | Y | N | N | Y | N | N | N |
| Coburn | N | Y | N | N | Y | N | N | N |
| **OREGON** | | | | | | | | |
| Wyden | Y | Y | Y | Y | N | Y | Y | Y |
| Smith | N | Y | N | N | N | Y | N | N |
| **PENNSYLVANIA** | | | | | | | | |
| Specter | N | Y | N | Y | Y | N | N | N |
| Santorum | N | Y | N | Y | Y | N | N | N |
| **RHODE ISLAND** | | | | | | | | |
| Reed | Y | Y | Y | Y | N | Y | Y | Y |
| Chafee | Y | N | Y | Y | N | Y | Y | Y |
| **SOUTH CAROLINA** | | | | | | | | |
| Graham | N | Y | N | N | Y | N | N | Y |
| DeMint | N | Y | N | N | Y | N | N | N |
| **SOUTH DAKOTA** | | | | | | | | |
| Johnson | Y | Y | Y | Y | N | Y | Y | Y |
| Thune | N | Y | N | Y | N | N | N | N |
| **TENNESSEE** | | | | | | | | |
| Frist | N | Y | N | N | Y | N | N | N |
| Alexander | N | Y | N | Y | N | N | N | N |
| **TEXAS** | | | | | | | | |
| Hutchison | N | Y | N | N | Y | N | N | N |
| Cornyn | N | Y | N | N | Y | N | N | N |
| **UTAH** | | | | | | | | |
| Hatch | N | Y | N | N | Y | N | N | N |
| Bennett | N | Y | N | N | Y | N | N | N |
| **VERMONT** | | | | | | | | |
| Leahy | Y | Y | Y | Y | N | Y | Y | Y |
| *Jeffords* | Y | Y | Y | Y | N | Y | Y | Y |
| **VIRGINIA** | | | | | | | | |
| Warner | N | Y | N | N | Y | N | N | N |
| Allen | N | Y | N | Y | N | N | N | N |
| **WASHINGTON** | | | | | | | | |
| Murray | Y | Y | Y | Y | N | Y | Y | Y |
| Cantwell | Y | Y | Y | Y | N | Y | Y | Y |
| **WEST VIRGINIA** | | | | | | | | |
| Byrd | Y | Y | Y | Y | N | Y | Y | Y |
| Rockefeller | Y | Y | Y | Y | N | Y | Y | Y |
| **WISCONSIN** | | | | | | | | |
| Kohl | Y | Y | Y | Y | N | Y | Y | Y |
| Feingold | Y | Y | Y | Y | N | Y | Y | Y |
| **WYOMING** | | | | | | | | |
| Thomas | N | Y | N | N | Y | N | N | N |
| Enzi | N | Y | N | N | Y | N | N | N |

**KEY**      Republicans      Democrats      *Independents*

| | | |
|---|---|---|
| **Y** Voted for (yea) | **X** Paired against | **C** Voted "present" to avoid possible conflict of interest |
| **#** Paired for | **–** Announced against | |
| **+** Announced for | **P** Voted "present" | **?** Did not vote or otherwise make a position known |
| **N** Voted against (nay) | | |

# IN THE SENATE | By Vote Number

**61.** **S Con Res 18. Fiscal 2006 Budget Resolution/Perkins Loans.** Harkin, D-Iowa, amendment that would reinstate two provisions of the tax code and use $7.46 billion to increase funding under the Perkins Vocational and Technical Education Act and the remainder to reduce the deficit. Rejected 44-56: R 1-54; D 42-2 (ND 38-2, SD 4-0); I 1-0. March 17, 2005.

**62.** **S Con Res 18. Fiscal 2006 Budget Resolution/Reserve Fund.** Landrieu, D-La., amendment that would add language to create a deficit-neutral reserve fund if legislation is passed that would provide a 50 percent tax credit for employers who continue to pay the salaries of National Guard and Reserve members called to active duty. Adopted 100-0: R 55-0; D 44-0 (ND 40-0, SD 4-0); I 1-0. March 17, 2005.

**63.** **S Con Res 18. Fiscal 2006 Budget Resolution/Offshore Companies.** Dorgan, D-N.D., amendment that would repeal tax incentives for domestic companies that move their manufacturing plants to offshore locations; it would use the resulting revenue to reduce the federal deficit by $3.2 billion from 2006 to 2010. Rejected 40-59: R 0-54; D 40-4 (ND 37-3, SD 3-1); I 0-1. March 17, 2005.

**64.** **S Con Res 18. Fiscal 2006 Budget Resolution/Homeland Security Grants.** Lieberman, D-Conn., amendment that would increase fiscal 2006 funding for the Community and Regional Development account by $715 million and for the Administration of Justice account by $140 million. It would stipulate that the funding be used for first-responder programs, port security grants and border patrol agents. It would be offset by a cut in the Allowances account. Adopted 63-37: R 18-37; D 44-0 (ND 39-1, SD 4-0); I 1-0. March 17, 2005.

**65.** **S Con Res 18. Fiscal 2006 Budget Resolution/Community Development Block Grants.** Sarbanes, D-Md., amendment that would restore $1.9 billion in cuts to the block grant program and other programs proposed for elimination, restoring funding to fiscal 2005 levels. It would be offset by striking $1.8 billion from the reconciliation instruction's tax cut figure. Rejected 49-51: R 4-51; D 44-0 (ND 40-0, SD 4-0); I 1-0. March 17, 2005.

**66.** **S Con Res 18. Fiscal 2006 Budget Resolution/Community Development Block Grant Program.** Coleman, R-Minn., amendment that would restore funding for the block grants and other programs to fiscal 2005 levels. It would be offset by cuts to the Allowances account. Adopted 68-31: R 24-31; D 43-0 (ND 39-0, SD 4-0); I 1-0. March 17, 2005.

**67.** **S Con Res 18. Fiscal 2006 Budget Resolution/Emergency Spending.** Cochran, R-Miss., amendment that would strike language giving the president the authority to designate funding as emergency spending. Adopted 73-26: R 32-22; D 40-4 (ND 36-4, SD 4-0); I 1-0. March 17, 2005.

**68.** **S Con Res 18. Fiscal 2006 Budget Resolution/Education Funding.** Kennedy, D-Mass., amendment that would increase the discretionary spending limit in the budget by $5.4 billion to $848.8 billion to restore education program cuts and increase the maximum Pell Grant award to $4,500. It would decrease the five-year tax cut reconciliation instruction figure by $5.4 billion. Adopted 51-49: R 6-49; D 44-0 (ND 40-0, SD 4-0); I 1-0. March 17, 2005.

| | 61 | 62 | 63 | 64 | 65 | 66 | 67 | 68 |
|---|---|---|---|---|---|---|---|---|
| **ALABAMA** | | | | | | | | |
| Shelby | N | Y | N | N | N | N | Y | N |
| Sessions | N | Y | N | N | N | N | N | N |
| **ALASKA** | | | | | | | | |
| Stevens | N | Y | N | N | N | N | Y | N |
| Murkowski | N | Y | N | Y | N | Y | Y | N |
| **ARIZONA** | | | | | | | | |
| McCain | N | Y | N | N | N | N | N | N |
| Kyl | N | Y | ? | N | N | N | N | N |
| **ARKANSAS** | | | | | | | | |
| Lincoln | Y | Y | Y | Y | Y | Y | Y | Y |
| Pryor | Y | Y | N | Y | Y | Y | Y | Y |
| **CALIFORNIA** | | | | | | | | |
| Feinstein | Y | Y | Y | Y | Y | Y | Y | Y |
| Boxer | Y | Y | Y | Y | Y | Y | Y | Y |
| **COLORADO** | | | | | | | | |
| Allard | N | Y | N | N | N | N | Y | N |
| Salazar | Y | Y | Y | Y | Y | Y | Y | Y |
| **CONNECTICUT** | | | | | | | | |
| Dodd | Y | Y | Y | Y | Y | Y | N | Y |
| Lieberman | Y | Y | Y | Y | Y | ? | N | Y |
| **DELAWARE** | | | | | | | | |
| Biden | Y | Y | Y | Y | Y | Y | Y | Y |
| Carper | Y | Y | Y | Y | Y | Y | Y | Y |
| **FLORIDA** | | | | | | | | |
| Nelson | Y | Y | Y | Y | Y | Y | Y | Y |
| Martinez | N | Y | N | Y | N | Y | N | N |
| **GEORGIA** | | | | | | | | |
| Chambliss | N | Y | N | N | N | Y | Y | N |
| Isakson | N | Y | N | Y | N | Y | Y | N |
| **HAWAII** | | | | | | | | |
| Inouye | Y | Y | Y | Y | Y | Y | Y | Y |
| Akaka | Y | Y | Y | Y | Y | Y | Y | Y |
| **IDAHO** | | | | | | | | |
| Craig | N | Y | N | N | N | N | Y | N |
| Crapo | N | Y | N | N | N | N | N | N |
| **ILLINOIS** | | | | | | | | |
| Durbin | Y | Y | Y | Y | Y | Y | Y | Y |
| Obama | Y | Y | Y | Y | Y | Y | Y | Y |
| **INDIANA** | | | | | | | | |
| Lugar | N | Y | N | Y | N | Y | N | N |
| Bayh | Y | Y | Y | Y | Y | Y | Y | Y |
| **IOWA** | | | | | | | | |
| Grassley | N | Y | N | N | N | N | N | N |
| Harkin | Y | Y | Y | Y | Y | Y | Y | Y |
| **KANSAS** | | | | | | | | |
| Brownback | N | Y | N | N | N | N | Y | N |
| Roberts | N | Y | N | Y | N | N | Y | N |
| **KENTUCKY** | | | | | | | | |
| McConnell | N | Y | N | N | N | N | Y | N |
| Bunning | N | Y | N | N | N | N | Y | N |
| **LOUISIANA** | | | | | | | | |
| Landrieu | Y | Y | Y | Y | Y | Y | Y | Y |
| Vitter | N | Y | N | Y | N | Y | N | N |
| **MAINE** | | | | | | | | |
| Snowe | N | Y | N | Y | N | Y | Y | Y |
| Collins | N | Y | N | Y | N | Y | Y | Y |
| **MARYLAND** | | | | | | | | |
| Sarbanes | Y | Y | Y | Y | Y | Y | Y | Y |
| Mikulski | Y | Y | Y | Y | Y | Y | Y | Y |
| **MASSACHUSETTS** | | | | | | | | |
| Kennedy | Y | Y | Y | Y | Y | Y | Y | Y |
| Kerry | Y | Y | Y | Y | Y | Y | Y | Y |
| **MICHIGAN** | | | | | | | | |
| Levin | Y | Y | Y | Y | Y | Y | Y | Y |
| Stabenow | Y | Y | Y | Y | Y | Y | Y | Y |
| **MINNESOTA** | | | | | | | | |
| Dayton | Y | Y | Y | Y | Y | Y | Y | Y |
| Coleman | N | Y | N | Y | Y | Y | Y | Y |
| **MISSISSIPPI** | | | | | | | | |
| Cochran | N | Y | N | N | N | N | Y | N |
| Lott | N | Y | N | N | N | N | Y | N |
| **MISSOURI** | | | | | | | | |
| Bond | N | Y | N | N | N | Y | Y | N |
| Talent | N | Y | N | Y | N | Y | Y | N |

| | 61 | 62 | 63 | 64 | 65 | 66 | 67 | 68 |
|---|---|---|---|---|---|---|---|---|
| **MONTANA** | | | | | | | | |
| Baucus | N | Y | N | Y | Y | Y | Y | Y |
| Burns | N | Y | N | N | N | Y | Y | N |
| **NEBRASKA** | | | | | | | | |
| Hagel | N | Y | N | N | N | N | N | N |
| Nelson | N | Y | N | Y | Y | Y | Y | Y |
| **NEVADA** | | | | | | | | |
| Reid | Y | Y | Y | Y | Y | Y | Y | Y |
| Ensign | N | Y | N | N | N | N | N | N |
| **NEW HAMPSHIRE** | | | | | | | | |
| Gregg | N | Y | N | N | N | N | N | N |
| Sununu | N | Y | N | N | N | N | N | N |
| **NEW JERSEY** | | | | | | | | |
| Corzine | Y | Y | Y | Y | Y | Y | Y | Y |
| Lautenberg | Y | Y | Y | Y | Y | Y | Y | Y |
| **NEW MEXICO** | | | | | | | | |
| Domenici | N | Y | N | N | N | Y | Y | N |
| Bingaman | Y | Y | Y | Y | Y | Y | Y | Y |
| **NEW YORK** | | | | | | | | |
| Schumer | Y | Y | Y | Y | Y | Y | N | Y |
| Clinton | Y | Y | Y | Y | Y | Y | Y | Y |
| **NORTH CAROLINA** | | | | | | | | |
| Dole | N | Y | N | Y | N | Y | Y | N |
| Burr | N | Y | N | N | N | N | Y | N |
| **NORTH DAKOTA** | | | | | | | | |
| Conrad | Y | Y | Y | Y | Y | Y | Y | Y |
| Dorgan | Y | Y | Y | Y | Y | Y | Y | Y |
| **OHIO** | | | | | | | | |
| DeWine | N | Y | N | Y | Y | Y | Y | Y |
| Voinovich | N | Y | N | N | N | Y | Y | N |
| **OKLAHOMA** | | | | | | | | |
| Inhofe | N | Y | N | N | N | N | N | N |
| Coburn | N | Y | N | N | N | N | N | N |
| **OREGON** | | | | | | | | |
| Wyden | Y | Y | Y | Y | Y | Y | Y | Y |
| Smith | N | Y | N | N | N | Y | Y | N |
| **PENNSYLVANIA** | | | | | | | | |
| Specter | N | Y | N | N | N | Y | Y | N |
| Santorum | N | Y | N | N | N | Y | ? | N |
| **RHODE ISLAND** | | | | | | | | |
| Reed | Y | Y | Y | Y | Y | Y | Y | Y |
| Chafee | Y | Y | N | Y | Y | Y | Y | Y |
| **SOUTH CAROLINA** | | | | | | | | |
| Graham | N | Y | N | N | N | N | N | N |
| DeMint | N | Y | N | N | N | N | N | N |
| **SOUTH DAKOTA** | | | | | | | | |
| Johnson | Y | Y | Y | Y | Y | Y | Y | Y |
| Thune | N | Y | N | Y | N | Y | Y | N |
| **TENNESSEE** | | | | | | | | |
| Frist | N | Y | N | N | N | N | Y | N |
| Alexander | N | Y | N | N | N | N | N | N |
| **TEXAS** | | | | | | | | |
| Hutchison | N | Y | N | N | N | N | Y | N |
| Cornyn | N | Y | N | N | N | N | N | N |
| **UTAH** | | | | | | | | |
| Hatch | N | Y | N | N | N | N | Y | N |
| Bennett | N | Y | N | N | N | N | Y | N |
| **VERMONT** | | | | | | | | |
| Leahy | Y | Y | Y | Y | Y | Y | Y | Y |
| Jeffords | Y | Y | N | Y | Y | Y | Y | Y |
| **VIRGINIA** | | | | | | | | |
| Warner | N | Y | N | Y | N | Y | Y | N |
| Allen | N | Y | N | N | N | Y | Y | N |
| **WASHINGTON** | | | | | | | | |
| Murray | Y | Y | Y | Y | Y | Y | Y | Y |
| Cantwell | Y | Y | N | Y | Y | Y | Y | Y |
| **WEST VIRGINIA** | | | | | | | | |
| Byrd | Y | Y | Y | Y | Y | Y | Y | Y |
| Rockefeller | Y | Y | Y | Y | Y | Y | Y | Y |
| **WISCONSIN** | | | | | | | | |
| Kohl | Y | Y | Y | Y | Y | Y | Y | Y |
| Feingold | Y | Y | Y | Y | Y | Y | Y | Y |
| **WYOMING** | | | | | | | | |
| Thomas | N | Y | N | N | N | N | N | N |
| Enzi | N | Y | N | N | N | N | N | N |

**KEY**  Republicans  Democrats  *Independents*

| | | | |
|---|---|---|---|
| Y | Voted for (yea) | X Paired against | C Voted "present" to avoid possible conflict of interest |
| # | Paired for | − Announced against | |
| + | Announced for | P Voted "present" | ? Did not vote or otherwise make a position known |
| N | Voted against (nay) | | |

# IN THE SENATE | By Vote Number

**69.** **S Con Res 18. Fiscal 2006 Budget Resolution/Agriculture Cuts.**
Baucus, D-Mont., amendment that would strike language in the resolution that would instruct the Agriculture Committee to cut mandatory spending for agriculture programs by $2.8 billion between 2006 and 2010. Rejected 46-54: R 1-54; D 44-0 (ND 40-0, SD 4-0); I 1-0. March 17, 2005.

**70.** **S Con Res 18. Fiscal 2006 Budget Resolution/Community Oriented Policing Services.** Biden, D-Del., amendment that would increase the discretionary spending limit by $1 billion and decrease the five-year tax cut reconciliation instruction figure by $2 billion. It would increase funding for the Office of Community Oriented Policing Services by $1 billion and use $1 billion to reduce the deficit. Rejected 45-55: R 0-55; D 44-0 (ND 40-0, SD 4-0); I 1-0. March 17, 2005.

**71.** **S Con Res 18. Fiscal 2006 Budget Resolution/Surface Transportation Funding.** Byrd, D-W.Va., amendment that would increase revenue by $13.8 billion and use it to increase spending for surface transportation projects. It also would add a section designating $34.7 billion in outlays for highways in fiscal 2006 and $7.1 billion for public transit. Rejected 45-54: R 0-54; D 44-0 (ND 40-0, SD 4-0); I 1-0. March 17, 2005.

**72.** **S Con Res 18. Fiscal 2006 Budget Resolution/Surface Transportation Adjustments.** Talent, R-Mo., amendment that would alter language in the section on adjustment for surface transportation to make it possible to consider all available transportation funding options. Adopted 81-19: R 36-19; D 44-0 (ND 40-0, SD 4-0); I 1-0. March 17, 2005.

**73.** **S Con Res 18. Fiscal 2006 Budget Resolution/Social Security Benefits Tax.** Conrad, D-N.D., amendment that would express the sense of the Senate that the tax cuts assumed in the resolution include the repeal of the 1993 income tax increase on Social Security benefits. Adopted 94-6: R 49-6; D 44-0 (ND 40-0, SD 4-0); I 1-0. March 17, 2005.

**74.** **S Con Res 18. Fiscal 2006 Budget Resolution/Social Security Benefit Tax.** Bunning, R-Ky., amendment that would repeal the 1993 tax increase on Social Security benefits and increase the five-year tax cut reconciliation instruction figure by $63.9 billion. Adopted 55-45: R 50-5; D 5-39 (ND 3-37, SD 2-2); I 0-1. March 17, 2005.

**75.** **S Con Res 18. Fiscal 2006 Budget Resolution/Family Planning Programs.** Clinton, D-N.Y., amendment that would reduce the five-year tax cut reconciliation instructions by $198 million and increase the discretionary spending limit in the budget by $36 million. It also would express the sense of the Senate that $1 billion should be used for family planning programs, such as teen pregnancy prevention. Rejected 47-53: R 3-52; D 43-1 (ND 39-1, SD 4-0); I 1-0. March 17, 2005.

| | 69 | 70 | 71 | 72 | 73 | 74 | 75 |
|---|---|---|---|---|---|---|---|
| **ALABAMA** | | | | | | | |
| Shelby | N | N | N | Y | Y | Y | N |
| Sessions | N | N | N | N | Y | Y | N |
| **ALASKA** | | | | | | | |
| Stevens | N | N | N | Y | N | Y | N |
| Murkowski | N | N | N | Y | Y | Y | N |
| **ARIZONA** | | | | | | | |
| McCain | N | N | N | N | Y | Y | N |
| Kyl | N | N | N | N | N | Y | N |
| **ARKANSAS** | | | | | | | |
| Lincoln | Y | Y | Y | Y | Y | N | Y |
| Pryor | Y | Y | Y | Y | Y | N | Y |
| **CALIFORNIA** | | | | | | | |
| Feinstein | Y | Y | Y | Y | Y | N | Y |
| Boxer | Y | Y | Y | Y | Y | N | Y |
| **COLORADO** | | | | | | | |
| Allard | N | N | N | N | Y | N | N |
| Salazar | Y | Y | Y | Y | Y | Y | Y |
| **CONNECTICUT** | | | | | | | |
| Dodd | Y | Y | Y | Y | Y | N | Y |
| Lieberman | Y | Y | Y | Y | Y | N | Y |
| **DELAWARE** | | | | | | | |
| Biden | Y | Y | Y | Y | Y | N | Y |
| Carper | Y | Y | Y | Y | Y | N | Y |
| **FLORIDA** | | | | | | | |
| Nelson | Y | Y | Y | Y | Y | Y | Y |
| Martinez | N | N | N | Y | Y | Y | N |
| **GEORGIA** | | | | | | | |
| Chambliss | N | N | N | Y | Y | Y | N |
| Isakson | N | N | N | Y | Y | Y | N |
| **HAWAII** | | | | | | | |
| Inouye | Y | Y | Y | Y | Y | N | Y |
| Akaka | Y | Y | Y | Y | Y | N | Y |
| **IDAHO** | | | | | | | |
| Craig | N | N | N | Y | Y | Y | N |
| Crapo | N | N | N | Y | Y | Y | N |
| **ILLINOIS** | | | | | | | |
| Durbin | Y | Y | Y | Y | Y | N | Y |
| Obama | Y | Y | Y | Y | Y | N | Y |
| **INDIANA** | | | | | | | |
| Lugar | N | N | N | N | N | Y | N |
| Bayh | Y | Y | Y | Y | Y | N | Y |
| **IOWA** | | | | | | | |
| Grassley | N | N | N | Y | Y | Y | N |
| Harkin | Y | Y | Y | Y | Y | N | Y |
| **KANSAS** | | | | | | | |
| Brownback | N | N | N | Y | Y | Y | N |
| Roberts | N | N | N | Y | Y | Y | N |
| **KENTUCKY** | | | | | | | |
| McConnell | N | N | N | Y | Y | Y | N |
| Bunning | N | N | N | Y | N | Y | N |
| **LOUISIANA** | | | | | | | |
| Landrieu | Y | Y | Y | Y | Y | N | Y |
| Vitter | N | N | N | Y | Y | Y | N |
| **MAINE** | | | | | | | |
| Snowe | N | N | N | Y | Y | N | Y |
| Collins | N | N | N | Y | Y | Y | Y |
| **MARYLAND** | | | | | | | |
| Sarbanes | Y | Y | Y | Y | Y | N | Y |
| Mikulski | Y | Y | Y | Y | Y | N | Y |
| **MASSACHUSETTS** | | | | | | | |
| Kennedy | Y | Y | Y | Y | Y | N | Y |
| Kerry | Y | Y | Y | Y | Y | N | Y |
| **MICHIGAN** | | | | | | | |
| Levin | Y | Y | Y | Y | Y | N | Y |
| Stabenow | Y | Y | Y | Y | Y | N | Y |
| **MINNESOTA** | | | | | | | |
| Dayton | Y | Y | Y | Y | Y | N | Y |
| Coleman | N | N | N | Y | Y | Y | N |
| **MISSISSIPPI** | | | | | | | |
| Cochran | N | N | N | Y | Y | Y | N |
| Lott | N | N | N | Y | Y | Y | N |
| **MISSOURI** | | | | | | | |
| Bond | N | N | N | Y | Y | Y | N |
| Talent | N | N | N | Y | Y | Y | N |

| | 69 | 70 | 71 | 72 | 73 | 74 | 75 |
|---|---|---|---|---|---|---|---|
| **MONTANA** | | | | | | | |
| Baucus | Y | Y | Y | Y | Y | N | Y |
| Burns | N | N | N | Y | Y | Y | N |
| **NEBRASKA** | | | | | | | |
| Hagel | N | N | N | N | Y | Y | N |
| Nelson | Y | Y | Y | Y | Y | Y | Y |
| **NEVADA** | | | | | | | |
| Reid | Y | Y | Y | Y | Y | N | Y |
| Ensign | N | N | N | N | Y | Y | N |
| **NEW HAMPSHIRE** | | | | | | | |
| Gregg | N | N | N | Y | Y | Y | N |
| Sununu | N | N | N | Y | Y | Y | N |
| **NEW JERSEY** | | | | | | | |
| Corzine | Y | Y | Y | Y | Y | N | Y |
| Lautenberg | Y | Y | Y | Y | Y | N | Y |
| **NEW MEXICO** | | | | | | | |
| Domenici | N | N | N | Y | Y | Y | N |
| Bingaman | Y | Y | Y | Y | Y | N | Y |
| **NEW YORK** | | | | | | | |
| Schumer | Y | Y | Y | Y | Y | N | Y |
| Clinton | Y | Y | Y | Y | Y | N | Y |
| **NORTH CAROLINA** | | | | | | | |
| Dole | N | N | N | Y | Y | Y | N |
| Burr | N | N | N | Y | Y | Y | N |
| **NORTH DAKOTA** | | | | | | | |
| Conrad | Y | Y | Y | Y | Y | N | Y |
| Dorgan | Y | Y | Y | Y | Y | N | Y |
| **OHIO** | | | | | | | |
| DeWine | N | N | N | Y | Y | Y | N |
| Voinovich | N | N | N | Y | N | N | N |
| **OKLAHOMA** | | | | | | | |
| Inhofe | N | N | N | Y | Y | Y | N |
| Coburn | N | N | N | N | Y | Y | N |
| **OREGON** | | | | | | | |
| Wyden | Y | Y | Y | Y | Y | N | Y |
| Smith | N | N | N | Y | Y | Y | N |
| **PENNSYLVANIA** | | | | | | | |
| Specter | N | N | N | Y | Y | Y | N |
| Santorum | N | N | N | Y | Y | Y | N |
| **RHODE ISLAND** | | | | | | | |
| Reed | Y | Y | Y | Y | Y | N | Y |
| Chafee | N | N | N | Y | Y | N | Y |
| **SOUTH CAROLINA** | | | | | | | |
| Graham | N | N | N | Y | Y | Y | N |
| DeMint | N | N | N | Y | Y | Y | N |
| **SOUTH DAKOTA** | | | | | | | |
| Johnson | Y | Y | Y | Y | Y | Y | Y |
| Thune | N | N | N | Y | Y | Y | N |
| **TENNESSEE** | | | | | | | |
| Frist | N | N | N | Y | Y | Y | N |
| Alexander | N | N | N | Y | Y | Y | N |
| **TEXAS** | | | | | | | |
| Hutchison | N | N | N | Y | Y | Y | N |
| Cornyn | N | N | ? | Y | Y | Y | N |
| **UTAH** | | | | | | | |
| Hatch | N | N | N | Y | Y | Y | N |
| Bennett | N | N | N | Y | Y | Y | N |
| **VERMONT** | | | | | | | |
| Leahy | Y | Y | Y | Y | Y | N | Y |
| Jeffords | Y | Y | Y | Y | Y | N | Y |
| **VIRGINIA** | | | | | | | |
| Warner | N | N | N | Y | Y | Y | N |
| Allen | N | N | N | Y | Y | Y | N |
| **WASHINGTON** | | | | | | | |
| Murray | Y | Y | Y | Y | Y | N | Y |
| Cantwell | Y | Y | Y | Y | Y | N | Y |
| **WEST VIRGINIA** | | | | | | | |
| Byrd | Y | Y | Y | Y | Y | N | Y |
| Rockefeller | Y | Y | Y | Y | Y | N | Y |
| **WISCONSIN** | | | | | | | |
| Kohl | Y | Y | Y | Y | Y | N | Y |
| Feingold | Y | Y | Y | Y | Y | N | Y |
| **WYOMING** | | | | | | | |
| Thomas | N | N | N | Y | Y | Y | N |
| Enzi | N | N | N | N | Y | Y | N |

**KEY**   Republicans   Democrats   *Independents*

| | | |
|---|---|---|
| **Y** Voted for (yea) | **X** Paired against | **C** Voted "present" to avoid possible conflict of interest |
| **#** Paired for | **–** Announced against | |
| **+** Announced for | **P** Voted "present" | **?** Did not vote or otherwise make a position known |
| **N** Voted against (nay) | | |

## IN THE SENATE | By Vote Number

**76.** S Con Res 18. Fiscal 2006 Budget Resolution/Debt Limit.
Lautenberg, D-N.J., amendment that would strike reconciliation instructions in the budget related to the debt limit. Rejected 45-54: R 1-53; D 43-1 (ND 39-1, SD 4-0); I 1-0. March 17, 2005.

**77.** S Con Res 18. Fiscal 2006 Budget Resolution/News Packages. Boxer, D-Calif., amendment that would establish a point of order in the Senate against any appropriations bill if it allows funds to be provided for "prepackaged news stories" that do not have a disclaimer stating "Paid for by the United States Government" running throughout the presentation. Rejected 44-54: R 0-54; D 43-0 (ND 39-0, SD 4-0); I 1-0. March 17, 2005.

**78.** S Con Res 18. Fiscal 2006 Budget Resolution/Tribal Program Funding. Dorgan, D-N.D., amendment that would decrease the five-year tax cut reconciliation instruction figure by $3.2 billion and increase the discretionary spending limit in the budget by $1 billion. The funds would be used to increase spending for tribal programs and reduce the deficit. Rejected 45-55: R 0-55; D 44-0 (ND 40-0, SD 4-0); I 1-0. March 17, 2005.

**79.** S Con Res 18. Fiscal 2006 Budget Resolution/Special Education Funding. Dayton, D-Minn., amendment that would create a reserve fund that would provide $71.3 billion for special education programs under the Individuals with Disabilities Education Act. It would be offset by a $73.8 billion cut in the five-year tax cut reconciliation instruction figure. It also would reduce the deficit by $2.5 billion. Rejected 37-63: R 1-54; D 35-9 (ND 32-8, SD 3-1); I 1-0. March 17, 2005.

**80.** S Con Res 18. Fiscal 2006 Budget Resolution/Technology Funding. Levin, D-Mich., amendment that would express the sense of the Senate that the Appropriations Committee should make every effort to provide funding for the Advanced Technology Program in fiscal 2006. Adopted 53-46: R 9-45; D 43-1 (ND 39-1, SD 4-0); I 1-0. March 17, 2005.

**81.** S Con Res 18. Fiscal 2006 Budget Resolution/Adoption. Adoption of the concurrent resolution that would set broad spending and revenue targets over the next five years. The resolution would allow up to $848.8 billion in discretionary spending for fiscal 2006 and call for $17 billion in cuts in mandatory spending over five years. It also would give procedural protection to legislation authorizing oil drilling in part of the Arctic National Wildlife Refuge (ANWR) in Alaska. Adopted 51-49: R 51-4; D 0-44 (ND 0-40, SD 0-4); I 0-1. March 17, 2005.

| | 76 | 77 | 78 | 79 | 80 | 81 | | 76 | 77 | 78 | 79 | 80 | 81 |
|---|---|---|---|---|---|---|---|---|---|---|---|---|---|
| **ALABAMA** | | | | | | | **MONTANA** | | | | | | |
| Shelby | N | N | N | N | Y | Y | Baucus | Y | Y | Y | Y | Y | N |
| Sessions | N | N | N | N | N | Y | Burns | N | ? | N | N | N | Y |
| **ALASKA** | | | | | | | **NEBRASKA** | | | | | | |
| Stevens | N | N | N | N | N | Y | Hagel | N | N | N | N | N | Y |
| Murkowski | N | N | N | N | N | Y | Nelson | N | Y | Y | N | Y | N |
| **ARIZONA** | | | | | | | **NEVADA** | | | | | | |
| McCain | Y | N | N | N | N | Y | Reid | Y | Y | Y | Y | Y | N |
| Kyl | N | N | N | N | N | Y | Ensign | N | N | N | N | N | Y |
| **ARKANSAS** | | | | | | | **NEW HAMPSHIRE** | | | | | | |
| Lincoln | Y | Y | Y | Y | Y | N | Gregg | N | N | N | N | N | Y |
| Pryor | Y | Y | Y | Y | Y | N | Sununu | N | N | N | N | N | Y |
| **CALIFORNIA** | | | | | | | **NEW JERSEY** | | | | | | |
| Feinstein | Y | Y | Y | Y | Y | N | Corzine | Y | Y | Y | Y | Y | N |
| Boxer | Y | Y | Y | Y | Y | N | Lautenberg | Y | Y | Y | Y | Y | N |
| **COLORADO** | | | | | | | **NEW MEXICO** | | | | | | |
| Allard | N | N | N | N | N | Y | Domenici | N | N | N | N | N | Y |
| Salazar | Y | Y | Y | N | Y | N | Bingaman | Y | Y | Y | N | Y | N |
| **CONNECTICUT** | | | | | | | **NEW YORK** | | | | | | |
| Dodd | Y | Y | Y | N | Y | N | Schumer | Y | Y | Y | Y | Y | N |
| Lieberman | Y | Y | Y | Y | Y | N | Clinton | Y | ? | Y | Y | Y | N |
| **DELAWARE** | | | | | | | **NORTH CAROLINA** | | | | | | |
| Biden | Y | Y | Y | Y | Y | N | Dole | N | N | N | N | N | Y |
| Carper | Y | Y | Y | N | Y | N | Burr | N | N | N | N | N | Y |
| **FLORIDA** | | | | | | | **NORTH DAKOTA** | | | | | | |
| Nelson | Y | Y | Y | Y | Y | N | Conrad | Y | Y | Y | Y | Y | N |
| Martinez | N | N | N | N | N | Y | Dorgan | Y | Y | Y | Y | Y | N |
| **GEORGIA** | | | | | | | **OHIO** | | | | | | |
| Chambliss | ? | N | N | N | N | Y | DeWine | N | N | N | N | Y | N |
| Isakson | N | N | N | N | N | Y | Voinovich | N | N | N | N | Y | N |
| **HAWAII** | | | | | | | **OKLAHOMA** | | | | | | |
| Inouye | Y | Y | Y | Y | Y | N | Inhofe | N | N | N | N | N | Y |
| Akaka | Y | Y | Y | Y | Y | N | Coburn | N | N | N | N | N | Y |
| **IDAHO** | | | | | | | **OREGON** | | | | | | |
| Craig | N | N | N | N | N | Y | Wyden | Y | Y | Y | Y | Y | N |
| Crapo | N | N | N | N | N | Y | Smith | N | N | N | N | N | Y |
| **ILLINOIS** | | | | | | | **PENNSYLVANIA** | | | | | | |
| Durbin | Y | Y | Y | Y | Y | N | Specter | N | N | N | N | Y | Y |
| Obama | Y | Y | Y | Y | Y | N | Santorum | N | N | N | ? | Y | Y |
| **INDIANA** | | | | | | | **RHODE ISLAND** | | | | | | |
| Lugar | N | N | N | N | N | Y | Reed | Y | Y | Y | Y | Y | N |
| Bayh | Y | Y | Y | Y | Y | N | Chafee | N | N | N | Y | N | N |
| **IOWA** | | | | | | | **SOUTH CAROLINA** | | | | | | |
| Grassley | N | N | N | N | N | Y | Graham | N | N | N | N | N | Y |
| Harkin | Y | Y | Y | Y | Y | N | DeMint | N | N | N | N | N | Y |
| **KANSAS** | | | | | | | **SOUTH DAKOTA** | | | | | | |
| Brownback | N | N | N | N | N | Y | Johnson | Y | Y | Y | Y | Y | N |
| Roberts | N | N | N | N | N | Y | Thune | N | N | N | N | N | Y |
| **KENTUCKY** | | | | | | | **TENNESSEE** | | | | | | |
| McConnell | N | N | N | N | N | Y | Frist | N | N | N | N | N | Y |
| Bunning | N | N | N | N | N | Y | Alexander | N | N | N | N | N | Y |
| **LOUISIANA** | | | | | | | **TEXAS** | | | | | | |
| Landrieu | Y | Y | Y | Y | Y | N | Hutchison | N | N | N | N | N | Y |
| Vitter | N | N | N | N | N | Y | Cornyn | N | N | N | N | N | Y |
| **MAINE** | | | | | | | **UTAH** | | | | | | |
| Snowe | N | N | N | N | N | N | Hatch | N | N | N | N | N | Y |
| Collins | N | N | N | N | N | N | Bennett | N | N | N | N | N | Y |
| **MARYLAND** | | | | | | | **VERMONT** | | | | | | |
| Sarbanes | Y | Y | Y | Y | Y | N | Leahy | Y | Y | Y | Y | Y | N |
| Mikulski | Y | Y | Y | Y | Y | N | Jeffords | Y | Y | Y | Y | Y | N |
| **MASSACHUSETTS** | | | | | | | **VIRGINIA** | | | | | | |
| Kennedy | Y | Y | Y | Y | Y | N | Warner | N | N | N | N | Y | Y |
| Kerry | Y | Y | Y | Y | Y | N | Allen | N | N | N | N | Y | Y |
| **MICHIGAN** | | | | | | | **WASHINGTON** | | | | | | |
| Levin | Y | Y | Y | Y | Y | N | Murray | Y | Y | Y | Y | Y | N |
| Stabenow | Y | Y | Y | Y | Y | N | Cantwell | Y | Y | Y | Y | Y | N |
| **MINNESOTA** | | | | | | | **WEST VIRGINIA** | | | | | | |
| Dayton | Y | Y | Y | Y | Y | N | Byrd | Y | Y | Y | Y | Y | N |
| Coleman | N | N | N | N | Y | Y | Rockefeller | Y | Y | Y | Y | Y | N |
| **MISSISSIPPI** | | | | | | | **WISCONSIN** | | | | | | |
| Cochran | N | N | N | N | N | Y | Kohl | Y | Y | Y | N | Y | N |
| Lott | N | N | N | N | N | Y | Feingold | Y | Y | Y | N | N | N |
| **MISSOURI** | | | | | | | **WYOMING** | | | | | | |
| Bond | N | N | N | N | N | Y | Thomas | N | N | N | N | N | Y |
| Talent | N | N | N | N | N | Y | Enzi | N | N | N | N | N | Y |

**KEY**    **Republicans**    Democrats    *Independents*

| | | | |
|---|---|---|---|
| Y | Voted for (yea) | X | Paired against |
| # | Paired for | − | Announced against |
| + | Announced for | P | Voted "present" |
| N | Voted against (nay) | | |

C   Voted "present" to avoid possible conflict of interest
?   Did not vote or otherwise make a position known

# IN THE SENATE | By Vote Number

**82.** **S Res 95. Pope John Paul II Tribute/Adoption.** Adoption of the resolution that would pay tribute to Pope John Paul II, who died April 2, 2005, and state that the Congress joins the world in mourning his death. Adopted 98-0: R 54-0; D 43-0 (ND 39-0, SD 4-0); I 1-0. April 5, 2005.

**83.** **S 600. Fiscal 2006 State Department Authorization/"Mexico City" Policy.** Boxer, D-Calif., amendment that would repeal the "Mexico City" policy, which bars U.S. aid to international family planning organizations that perform or promote abortions, even if they use their own funds to do so. Under the amendment, organizations could receive U.S. aid if they used their own funds to provide health or medical services that do not violate federal law or the laws of the country in which they are being provided. Adopted 52-46: R 8-46; D 43-0 (ND 39-0, SD 4-0); I 1-0. A "nay" was a vote in support of the president's position. April 5, 2005.

**84.** **S 600. Fiscal 2006 State Department Authorization/U.N. Peacekeepers.** Biden, D-Del., amendment to the Lugar, R-Ind., amendment. The Biden amendment would cap U.S. contributions for U.N. peacekeeping at 27.1 percent for calendar year 2005 through 2007. The Lugar amendment would delete a permanent 27.1 percent cap provided in the bill. Rejected 40-57: R 0-54; D 39-3 (ND 35-3, SD 4-0); I 1-0. (Subsequently, the Lugar amendment was adopted by voice vote.) A "nay" was a vote in support of the president's position. April 6, 2005.

**85.** **S 600. Fiscal 2006 State Department Authorization/Television Broadcasting to Cuba.** Lugar, R-Ind., motion to table (kill) the Dorgan, D-N.D., amendment that would reduce funding for international broadcasting operations from $641 million to $620 million in fiscal 2006 and prohibit the use of funds for television broadcasts to Cuba. It also would bar broadcasting capital improvement funds for this purpose. Motion agreed to 65-35: R 53-2; D 12-32 (ND 11-29, SD 1-3); I 0-1. April 6, 2005.

**86.** **S 600. Fiscal 2006 State Department Authorization/Tariffs on Chinese Imports.** Lugar, R-Ind., motion to table (kill) the Schumer, D-N.Y., amendment that would impose a 27.5 percent duty on Chinese imports 180 days after enactment of the bill if China does not allow its currency to appreciate relative to the value of the U.S dollar. It would allow the president to delay implementation of the tariffs and permit their removal if he certified that China had agreed to revalue its currency upward to at, or near, fair market value. Motion rejected 33-67: R 26-29; D 7-37 (ND 7-33, SD 0-4); I 0-1. April 6, 2005.

| | 82 | 83 | 84 | 85 | 86 | | | 82 | 83 | 84 | 85 | 86 |
|---|---|---|---|---|---|---|---|---|---|---|---|---|
| **ALABAMA** | | | | | | | **MONTANA** | | | | | |
| Shelby | Y | N | N | Y | N | | Baucus | Y | Y | N | N | Y |
| Sessions | Y | N | N | Y | N | | Burns | Y | N | N | Y | Y |
| **ALASKA** | | | | | | | **NEBRASKA** | | | | | |
| Stevens | Y | Y | N | Y | Y | | Hagel | Y | N | N | Y | Y |
| Murkowski | Y | Y | N | Y | Y | | Nelson | Y | Y | N | Y | Y |
| **ARIZONA** | | | | | | | **NEVADA** | | | | | |
| McCain | Y | N | N | Y | N | | Reid | Y | Y | Y | Y | N |
| Kyl | Y | N | N | Y | Y | | Ensign | Y | N | N | Y | Y |
| **ARKANSAS** | | | | | | | **NEW HAMPSHIRE** | | | | | |
| Lincoln | Y | Y | Y | N | N | | Gregg | Y | N | N | Y | Y |
| Pryor | Y | Y | Y | N | N | | Sununu | Y | N | N | N | Y |
| **CALIFORNIA** | | | | | | | **NEW JERSEY** | | | | | |
| Feinstein | Y | Y | Y | N | Y | | Corzine | Y | Y | Y | N | N |
| Boxer | Y | Y | Y | N | N | | Lautenberg | Y | Y | Y | Y | N |
| **COLORADO** | | | | | | | **NEW MEXICO** | | | | | |
| Allard | ? | ? | N | Y | Y | | Domenici | Y | N | N | Y | N |
| Salazar | Y | Y | Y | Y | N | | Bingaman | Y | Y | Y | N | N |
| **CONNECTICUT** | | | | | | | **NEW YORK** | | | | | |
| Dodd | Y | Y | Y | N | N | | Schumer | Y | Y | Y | Y | N |
| Lieberman | Y | Y | Y | Y | N | | Clinton | Y | Y | Y | Y | N |
| **DELAWARE** | | | | | | | **NORTH CAROLINA** | | | | | |
| Biden | Y | Y | Y | Y | N | | Dole | Y | N | N | Y | N |
| Carper | Y | Y | Y | N | Y | | Burr | Y | N | N | Y | N |
| **FLORIDA** | | | | | | | **NORTH DAKOTA** | | | | | |
| Nelson | Y | Y | Y | Y | N | | Conrad | Y | Y | Y | N | N |
| Martinez | Y | N | N | Y | N | | Dorgan | Y | Y | Y | N | N |
| **GEORGIA** | | | | | | | **OHIO** | | | | | |
| Chambliss | Y | N | N | Y | N | | DeWine | Y | N | N | Y | N |
| Isakson | Y | N | N | Y | N | | Voinovich | Y | N | N | Y | N |
| **HAWAII** | | | | | | | **OKLAHOMA** | | | | | |
| Inouye | Y | Y | Y | N | N | | Inhofe | Y | N | N | Y | N |
| Akaka | Y | Y | Y | N | N | | Coburn | Y | N | N | Y | N |
| **IDAHO** | | | | | | | **OREGON** | | | | | |
| Craig | Y | N | N | Y | Y | | Wyden | Y | Y | Y | N | Y |
| Crapo | Y | N | ? | Y | N | | Smith | Y | Y | N | Y | Y |
| **ILLINOIS** | | | | | | | **PENNSYLVANIA** | | | | | |
| Durbin | Y | Y | Y | N | N | | Specter | Y | N | N | Y | N |
| Obama | Y | Y | Y | N | N | | Santorum | Y | N | N | Y | N |
| **INDIANA** | | | | | | | **RHODE ISLAND** | | | | | |
| Lugar | Y | N | N | Y | Y | | Reed | Y | Y | Y | N | N |
| Bayh | Y | Y | Y | Y | N | | Chafee | Y | Y | Y | N | Y |
| **IOWA** | | | | | | | **SOUTH CAROLINA** | | | | | |
| Grassley | Y | N | N | Y | Y | | Graham | Y | N | N | Y | N |
| Harkin | Y | Y | Y | N | N | | DeMint | Y | N | N | Y | N |
| **KANSAS** | | | | | | | **SOUTH DAKOTA** | | | | | |
| Brownback | Y | N | N | Y | Y | | Johnson | Y | Y | Y | N | N |
| Roberts | Y | N | N | Y | Y | | Thune | Y | N | N | Y | N |
| **KENTUCKY** | | | | | | | **TENNESSEE** | | | | | |
| McConnell | Y | N | N | Y | Y | | Frist | Y | N | N | Y | Y |
| Bunning | Y | N | N | Y | N | | Alexander | Y | N | N | Y | Y |
| **LOUISIANA** | | | | | | | **TEXAS** | | | | | |
| Landrieu | Y | Y | Y | N | N | | Hutchison | Y | N | N | Y | N |
| Vitter | Y | N | N | Y | N | | Cornyn | Y | N | N | Y | N |
| **MAINE** | | | | | | | **UTAH** | | | | | |
| Snowe | Y | Y | Y | N | Y | | Hatch | Y | N | N | Y | N |
| Collins | Y | Y | N | Y | Y | | Bennett | Y | N | N | Y | Y |
| **MARYLAND** | | | | | | | **VERMONT** | | | | | |
| Sarbanes | Y | Y | Y | Y | N | | Leahy | Y | Y | Y | N | N |
| Mikulski | Y | Y | Y | N | N | | Jeffords | Y | Y | Y | N | N |
| **MASSACHUSETTS** | | | | | | | **VIRGINIA** | | | | | |
| Kennedy | ? | ? | Y | N | N | | Warner | Y | Y | N | Y | N |
| Kerry | Y | Y | Y | N | N | | Allen | Y | N | N | Y | N |
| **MICHIGAN** | | | | | | | **WASHINGTON** | | | | | |
| Levin | Y | Y | Y | N | N | | Murray | Y | Y | Y | N | N |
| Stabenow | Y | Y | Y | N | N | | Cantwell | Y | Y | Y | N | Y |
| **MINNESOTA** | | | | | | | **WEST VIRGINIA** | | | | | |
| Dayton | Y | Y | ? | N | N | | Byrd | Y | Y | N | N | N |
| Coleman | Y | N | N | Y | Y | | Rockefeller | Y | Y | ? | N | N |
| **MISSISSIPPI** | | | | | | | **WISCONSIN** | | | | | |
| Cochran | Y | N | N | Y | Y | | Kohl | Y | Y | Y | N | N |
| Lott | Y | N | N | Y | Y | | Feingold | Y | Y | Y | N | N |
| **MISSOURI** | | | | | | | **WYOMING** | | | | | |
| Bond | Y | N | N | Y | Y | | Thomas | Y | N | N | Y | N |
| Talent | Y | N | N | Y | N | | Enzi | Y | N | N | Y | N |

**KEY**  Republicans  Democrats  *Independents*

| | | | |
|---|---|---|---|
| Y | Voted for (yea) | X Paired against | C Voted "present" to avoid possible conflict of interest |
| # | Paired for | – Announced against | ? Did not vote or otherwise make a position known |
| + | Announced for | P Voted "present" | |
| N | Voted against (nay) | | |

# IN THE SENATE | By Vote Number

**87.** **Crotty Nomination/Confirmation.** Confirmation of President Bush's nomination of Paul A. Crotty of New York to be U.S. district judge for the Southern District of New York. Confirmed 95-0: R 53-0; D 41-0 (ND 37-0, SD 4-0); I 1-0. A "yea" was a vote in support of the president's position. April 11, 2005.

**88.** **S Con Res 25. Airbus Subsidies/Adoption.** Adoption of the concurrent resolution that would express the sense of the Congress that European governments should reject a pending launch aid application by the airplane manufacturer Airbus for the A350 aircraft and any future models. It also would urge the U.S. Trade Representative to request a World Trade Organization dispute resolution panel if no immediate agreement is reached and if there is no progress toward a comprehensive bilateral agreement covering all government subsidies of the large aircraft sector. Adopted 96-0: R 53-0; D 42-0 (ND 38-0, SD 4-0); I 1-0. April 11, 2005.

**89.** **HR 1268. Fiscal 2005 Supplemental Appropriations/Veterans' Health Care Funding.** Murray, D-Wash., motion to waive the Budget Act with respect to the Cochran, R-Miss., point of order against the Murray amendment. The Murray amendment would increase funding for the Veterans Affairs Department by $1.98 billion and designate it as emergency spending. It would stipulate that $840 million be used for veterans' regional health networks; $610 million be used to address the needs of service members deployed in Iraq and Afghanistan; and $525 million be used to provide mental health care and treatment. Motion rejected 46-54: R 1-54; D 44-0 (ND 40-0, SD 4-0); I 1-0. A three-fifths majority vote (60) of the total Senate is required to waive the Budget Act. (Subsequently, the chair upheld the point of order, and the emergency designation was stricken.) April 12, 2005.

**90.** **HR 1268. Fiscal 2005 Supplemental Appropriations/Veterans' Health Care Funding.** Murray, D-Wash., motion to waive the Budget Act with respect to the Cochran, R-Miss., point of order against the Murray amendment, modified to remove the emergency designation. Motion rejected 46-54: R 1-54; D 44-0 (ND 40-0, SD 4-0); I 1-0. A three-fifths majority vote (60) of the total Senate is required to waive the Budget Act. (Subsequently, the chair upheld the point of order, and the amendment fell.) April 12, 2005.

**91.** **HR 1268. Fiscal 2005 Supplemental Appropriations/Salary Reimbursement for Federal Employees.** Stevens, R-Alaska, motion to table (kill) the Durbin, D-Ill., amendment that would require that federal employees who take a leave without pay to perform certain services as a member of the uniformed service or the National Guard, be reimbursed for the difference between their salary and the pay and allowances they receive while on duty. Motion rejected 39-61: R 39-16; D 0-44 (ND 0-40, SD 0-4); I 0-1. (Subsequently, the amendment was adopted by voice vote.) April 13, 2005.

| | 87 | 88 | 89 | 90 | 91 |
|---|---|---|---|---|---|
| **ALABAMA** | | | | | |
| Shelby | Y | Y | N | N | Y |
| Sessions | Y | Y | N | N | Y |
| **ALASKA** | | | | | |
| Stevens | Y | Y | N | N | Y |
| Murkowski | ? | ? | N | N | Y |
| **ARIZONA** | | | | | |
| McCain | Y | Y | N | N | Y |
| Kyl | Y | Y | N | N | Y |
| **ARKANSAS** | | | | | |
| Lincoln | Y | Y | Y | Y | N |
| Pryor | Y | Y | Y | Y | N |
| **CALIFORNIA** | | | | | |
| Feinstein | Y | Y | Y | Y | N |
| Boxer | Y | Y | Y | Y | N |
| **COLORADO** | | | | | |
| Allard | Y | Y | N | N | Y |
| Salazar | Y | Y | Y | Y | N |
| **CONNECTICUT** | | | | | |
| Dodd | Y | Y | Y | Y | N |
| Lieberman | Y | Y | Y | Y | N |
| **DELAWARE** | | | | | |
| Biden | Y | Y | Y | Y | N |
| Carper | Y | Y | Y | Y | N |
| **FLORIDA** | | | | | |
| Nelson | Y | Y | Y | Y | N |
| Martinez | Y | Y | N | N | N |
| **GEORGIA** | | | | | |
| Chambliss | Y | Y | N | N | Y |
| Isakson | Y | Y | N | N | Y |
| **HAWAII** | | | | | |
| Inouye | Y | Y | Y | Y | N |
| Akaka | Y | Y | Y | Y | N |
| **IDAHO** | | | | | |
| Craig | Y | Y | N | N | Y |
| Crapo | Y | Y | N | N | Y |
| **ILLINOIS** | | | | | |
| Durbin | Y | Y | Y | Y | N |
| Obama | Y | Y | Y | Y | N |
| **INDIANA** | | | | | |
| Lugar | Y | Y | N | N | Y |
| Bayh | Y | Y | Y | Y | N |
| **IOWA** | | | | | |
| Grassley | Y | Y | N | N | Y |
| Harkin | ? | ? | Y | Y | N |
| **KANSAS** | | | | | |
| Brownback | Y | Y | N | N | Y |
| Roberts | Y | Y | N | N | Y |
| **KENTUCKY** | | | | | |
| McConnell | Y | Y | N | N | Y |
| Bunning | Y | Y | N | N | Y |
| **LOUISIANA** | | | | | |
| Landrieu | Y | Y | Y | Y | N |
| Vitter | Y | Y | N | N | Y |
| **MAINE** | | | | | |
| Snowe | Y | Y | N | N | N |
| Collins | Y | Y | N | N | N |
| **MARYLAND** | | | | | |
| Sarbanes | Y | Y | Y | Y | N |
| Mikulski | Y | Y | Y | Y | N |
| **MASSACHUSETTS** | | | | | |
| Kennedy | Y | Y | Y | Y | N |
| Kerry | Y | Y | Y | Y | N |
| **MICHIGAN** | | | | | |
| Levin | Y | Y | Y | Y | N |
| Stabenow | Y | Y | Y | Y | N |
| **MINNESOTA** | | | | | |
| Dayton | Y | Y | Y | Y | N |
| Coleman | Y | Y | N | N | N |
| **MISSISSIPPI** | | | | | |
| Cochran | Y | Y | N | N | Y |
| Lott | Y | Y | N | N | Y |
| **MISSOURI** | | | | | |
| Bond | Y | Y | N | N | Y |
| Talent | Y | Y | N | N | Y |
| **MONTANA** | | | | | |
| Baucus | Y | Y | Y | Y | N |
| Burns | Y | Y | N | N | Y |
| **NEBRASKA** | | | | | |
| Hagel | Y | Y | N | N | Y |
| Nelson | Y | Y | Y | Y | N |
| **NEVADA** | | | | | |
| Reid | Y | Y | Y | Y | N |
| Ensign | Y | Y | N | N | Y |
| **NEW HAMPSHIRE** | | | | | |
| Gregg | Y | Y | N | N | Y |
| Sununu | Y | Y | N | N | Y |
| **NEW JERSEY** | | | | | |
| Corzine | Y | Y | Y | Y | N |
| Lautenberg | ? | ? | Y | Y | N |
| **NEW MEXICO** | | | | | |
| Domenici | Y | Y | N | N | N |
| Bingaman | Y | Y | Y | Y | N |
| **NEW YORK** | | | | | |
| Schumer | Y | Y | Y | Y | N |
| Clinton | Y | Y | Y | Y | N |
| **NORTH CAROLINA** | | | | | |
| Dole | Y | Y | N | N | N |
| Burr | Y | Y | N | N | Y |
| **NORTH DAKOTA** | | | | | |
| Conrad | Y | Y | Y | Y | N |
| Dorgan | + | Y | Y | Y | N |
| **OHIO** | | | | | |
| DeWine | Y | Y | N | N | Y |
| Voinovich | Y | Y | N | N | Y |
| **OKLAHOMA** | | | | | |
| Inhofe | Y | Y | N | N | Y |
| Coburn | Y | Y | N | N | Y |
| **OREGON** | | | | | |
| Wyden | Y | Y | Y | Y | N |
| Smith | Y | Y | Y | Y | N |
| **PENNSYLVANIA** | | | | | |
| Specter | Y | Y | N | N | Y |
| Santorum | Y | Y | N | N | Y |
| **RHODE ISLAND** | | | | | |
| Reed | Y | Y | N | N | N |
| Chafee | Y | Y | N | N | N |
| **SOUTH CAROLINA** | | | | | |
| Graham | Y | Y | N | N | Y |
| DeMint | Y | Y | N | N | Y |
| **SOUTH DAKOTA** | | | | | |
| Johnson | Y | Y | N | N | N |
| Thune | Y | Y | N | N | N |
| **TENNESSEE** | | | | | |
| Frist | Y | Y | N | N | Y |
| Alexander | Y | Y | N | N | Y |
| **TEXAS** | | | | | |
| Hutchison | Y | Y | N | N | N |
| Cornyn | Y | Y | N | N | Y |
| **UTAH** | | | | | |
| Hatch | Y | Y | N | N | Y |
| Bennett | Y | Y | N | N | Y |
| **VERMONT** | | | | | |
| Leahy | Y | Y | Y | Y | N |
| Jeffords | Y | Y | Y | Y | N |
| **VIRGINIA** | | | | | |
| Warner | Y | Y | N | N | N |
| Allen | Y | Y | N | N | N |
| **WASHINGTON** | | | | | |
| Murray | Y | Y | Y | Y | N |
| Cantwell | Y | Y | Y | Y | N |
| **WEST VIRGINIA** | | | | | |
| Byrd | Y | Y | Y | Y | N |
| Rockefeller | Y | Y | Y | Y | N |
| **WISCONSIN** | | | | | |
| Kohl | Y | Y | Y | Y | N |
| Feingold | Y | Y | Y | Y | N |
| **WYOMING** | | | | | |
| Thomas | Y | Y | N | N | N |
| Enzi | ? | ? | N | N | N |

**KEY**    Republicans    Democrats    *Independents*

| | | |
|---|---|---|
| Y   Voted for (yea) | X   Paired against | C   Voted "present" to avoid possible conflict of interest |
| #   Paired for | –   Announced against | ?   Did not vote or otherwise make a position known |
| +   Announced for | P   Voted "present" | |
| N   Voted against (nay) | | |

# IN THE SENATE | By Vote Number

**92.** **HR 1268. Fiscal 2005 Supplemental Appropriations/Military Death Benefits.** Stevens, R-Alaska, motion to table (kill) the Kerry, D-Mass., amendment that would increase the military death benefit from $12,420 to $100,000 for all military members who died on active duty on or after Oct. 7, 2001, not just those serving in combat. Motion rejected 25-75: R 25-30; D 0-44 (ND 0-40, SD 0-4); I 0-1. (Subsequently, the amendment was adopted by voice vote.) April 13, 2005.

**93.** **HR 1268. Fiscal 2005 Supplemental Appropriations/Prison Construction.** Byrd, D-W.Va., amendment that would delete $36 million from the bill's appropriation for military construction earmarked to pay for a new maximum security prison at Guantánamo, Cuba. Rejected 27-71: R 1-54; D 25-17 (ND 23-15, SD 2-2); I 1-0. April 13, 2005.

**94.** **HR 1268. Fiscal 2005 Supplemental Appropriations/Immigration Debate.** Cornyn, R-Texas, amendment that would express the sense of the Senate that Congress should not delay enactment of the supplemental appropriations bill by conducting a debate about immigration overhaul while the measure is pending on the Senate floor. Adopted 61-38: R 48-7; D 13-30 (ND 10-29, SD 3-1); I 0-1. April 13, 2005.

**95.** **HR 1268. Fiscal 2005 Supplemental Appropriations/News Packages.** Byrd, D-W.Va., amendment that would prohibit a federal agency, unless otherwise authorized by existing law, to use funds in the bill or any other act to produce a "prepackaged news" story, unless it includes a clear notification within the text or audio that it was prepared or funded by that agency. Adopted 98-0: R 54-0; D 43-0 (ND 39-0, SD 4-0); I 1-0. April 14, 2005.

| | 92 | 93 | 94 | 95 |
|---|---|---|---|---|
| **ALABAMA** | | | | |
| Shelby | Y | N | Y | Y |
| Sessions | Y | N | Y | Y |
| **ALASKA** | | | | |
| Stevens | Y | N | Y | Y |
| Murkowski | N | N | Y | Y |
| **ARIZONA** | | | | |
| McCain | N | N | Y | Y |
| Kyl | N | N | Y | Y |
| **ARKANSAS** | | | | |
| Lincoln | N | Y | Y | Y |
| Pryor | N | Y | Y | Y |
| **CALIFORNIA** | | | | |
| Feinstein | N | Y | Y | Y |
| Boxer | N | Y | Y | Y |
| **COLORADO** | | | | |
| Allard | Y | N | Y | Y |
| Salazar | N | N | Y | Y |
| **CONNECTICUT** | | | | |
| Dodd | N | N | N | Y |
| Lieberman | N | N | N | Y |
| **DELAWARE** | | | | |
| Biden | N | Y | N | Y |
| Carper | N | Y | N | Y |
| **FLORIDA** | | | | |
| Nelson | N | N | N | Y |
| Martinez | N | N | Y | Y |
| **GEORGIA** | | | | |
| Chambliss | N | N | Y | Y |
| Isakson | N | N | N | Y |
| **HAWAII** | | | | |
| Inouye | N | Y | N | Y |
| Akaka | N | Y | N | Y |
| **IDAHO** | | | | |
| Craig | N | N | N | Y |
| Crapo | N | N | N | Y |
| **ILLINOIS** | | | | |
| Durbin | N | N | N | Y |
| Obama | N | N | N | Y |
| **INDIANA** | | | | |
| Lugar | N | N | Y | Y |
| Bayh | N | N | N | Y |
| **IOWA** | | | | |
| Grassley | Y | N | N | Y |
| Harkin | N | Y | N | Y |
| **KANSAS** | | | | |
| Brownback | N | N | Y | Y |
| Roberts | N | N | Y | Y |
| **KENTUCKY** | | | | |
| McConnell | Y | N | Y | Y |
| Bunning | Y | N | Y | Y |
| **LOUISIANA** | | | | |
| Landrieu | N | N | Y | Y |
| Vitter | N | N | Y | Y |
| **MAINE** | | | | |
| Snowe | N | N | N | Y |
| Collins | N | N | Y | Y |
| **MARYLAND** | | | | |
| Sarbanes | N | Y | N | ? |
| Mikulski | N | Y | N | Y |
| **MASSACHUSETTS** | | | | |
| Kennedy | N | ? | N | Y |
| Kerry | N | N | N | Y |
| **MICHIGAN** | | | | |
| Levin | N | Y | N | Y |
| Stabenow | N | Y | N | Y |
| **MINNESOTA** | | | | |
| Dayton | N | ? | ? | Y |
| Coleman | N | N | Y | Y |
| **MISSISSIPPI** | | | | |
| Cochran | Y | N | Y | Y |
| Lott | Y | N | Y | Y |
| **MISSOURI** | | | | |
| Bond | Y | N | Y | Y |
| Talent | N | N | Y | Y |
| **MONTANA** | | | | |
| Baucus | N | Y | N | Y |
| Burns | Y | N | Y | Y |
| **NEBRASKA** | | | | |
| Hagel | N | N | Y | Y |
| Nelson | N | N | Y | Y |
| **NEVADA** | | | | |
| Reid | N | Y | N | Y |
| Ensign | N | N | Y | Y |
| **NEW HAMPSHIRE** | | | | |
| Gregg | N | N | Y | Y |
| Sununu | N | N | Y | Y |
| **NEW JERSEY** | | | | |
| Corzine | N | N | N | Y |
| Lautenberg | N | Y | N | Y |
| **NEW MEXICO** | | | | |
| Domenici | Y | N | Y | Y |
| Bingaman | N | N | N | Y |
| **NEW YORK** | | | | |
| Schumer | N | N | Y | Y |
| Clinton | N | N | Y | Y |
| **NORTH CAROLINA** | | | | |
| Dole | Y | N | Y | Y |
| Burr | Y | N | Y | Y |
| **NORTH DAKOTA** | | | | |
| Conrad | N | N | N | Y |
| Dorgan | N | Y | N | Y |
| **OHIO** | | | | |
| DeWine | N | N | N | Y |
| Voinovich | Y | N | N | Y |
| **OKLAHOMA** | | | | |
| Inhofe | Y | N | Y | ? |
| Coburn | N | N | Y | Y |
| **OREGON** | | | | |
| Wyden | N | Y | Y | Y |
| Smith | N | N | Y | Y |
| **PENNSYLVANIA** | | | | |
| Specter | N | Y | Y | Y |
| Santorum | Y | N | Y | Y |
| **RHODE ISLAND** | | | | |
| Reed | N | Y | N | Y |
| Chafee | N | N | Y | Y |
| **SOUTH CAROLINA** | | | | |
| Graham | N | N | Y | Y |
| DeMint | Y | N | Y | Y |
| **SOUTH DAKOTA** | | | | |
| Johnson | N | Y | N | Y |
| Thune | N | N | Y | Y |
| **TENNESSEE** | | | | |
| Frist | Y | N | Y | Y |
| Alexander | N | N | Y | Y |
| **TEXAS** | | | | |
| Hutchison | N | N | Y | Y |
| Cornyn | Y | N | Y | Y |
| **UTAH** | | | | |
| Hatch | Y | N | Y | Y |
| Bennett | Y | N | Y | Y |
| **VERMONT** | | | | |
| Leahy | N | Y | N | Y |
| *Jeffords* | N | Y | N | Y |
| **VIRGINIA** | | | | |
| Warner | Y | N | N | Y |
| Allen | N | N | Y | Y |
| **WASHINGTON** | | | | |
| Murray | N | N | Y | Y |
| Cantwell | N | N | Y | Y |
| **WEST VIRGINIA** | | | | |
| Byrd | N | Y | Y | Y |
| Rockefeller | N | Y | N | Y |
| **WISCONSIN** | | | | |
| Kohl | N | Y | N | Y |
| Feingold | N | Y | N | Y |
| **WYOMING** | | | | |
| Thomas | Y | N | Y | Y |
| Enzi | Y | N | Y | Y |

**KEY**  **Republicans**   Democrats   *Independents*

| | | | | | |
|---|---|---|---|---|---|
| Y | Voted for (yea) | X | Paired against | C | Voted "present" to avoid possible conflict of interest |
| # | Paired for | − | Announced against | | |
| + | Announced for | P | Voted "present" | ? | Did not vote or otherwise make a position known |
| N | Voted against (nay) | | | | |

# IN THE SENATE | By Vote Number

**96.** HR 1268. Fiscal 2005 Supplemental Appropriations/Overseas Military Funding. Byrd, D-W.Va., amendment that would express the sense of the Senate that any funds for ongoing military operations overseas, including those in Afghanistan and Iraq, should be included in the president's annual budget request and urge the president to detail cost estimates for ongoing overseas military operations by Sept. 1, 2005. Adopted 61-31: R 21-31; D 39-0 (ND 36-0, SD 3-0); I 1-0. April 18, 2005.

**97.** HR 1268. Fiscal 2005 Supplemental Appropriations/Cloture. Motion to invoke cloture (thus limiting debate) on the Chambliss, R-Ga., amendment that would create a "blue card" program that would grant foreign workers temporary legal status if an employer could show they unsuccessfully tried to recruit and hire U.S. workers. Motion rejected 21-77: R 19-36; D 2-40 (ND 1-37, SD 1-3); I 0-1. Three-fifths of the total Senate (60) is required to invoke cloture. April 19, 2005.

**98.** HR 1268. Fiscal 2005 Supplemental Appropriations/Cloture. Motion to invoke cloture (thus limiting debate) on the Craig, R-Idaho, amendment that would grant certain agricultural workers who are in the country illegally temporary resident status and put them on the path toward permanent resident status if they meet specified employment and residency requirements. Motion rejected 53-45: R 15-40; D 37-5 (ND 33-5, SD 4-0); I 1-0. Three-fifths of the total Senate (60) is required to invoke cloture. April 19, 2005.

**99.** Procedural Motion/Require Attendance. Frist, R-Tenn., motion to instruct the sergeant at arms to request the attendance of absent senators. Motion agreed to 91-7: R 54-1; D 36-6 (ND 32-6, SD 4-0); I 1-0. April 19, 2005.

**100.** Procedural Motion/Recess. Frist, R-Tenn., motion to recess until 5 p.m. on Tuesday, April 19, 2005. Motion agreed to 56-42: R 55-0; D 1-41 (ND 1-37, SD 0-4); I 0-1. April 19, 2005.

**101.** HR 1268. Fiscal 2005 Supplemental Appropriation/Cloture. Motion to invoke cloture (thus limiting debate) on the Mikulski, D-Md., amendment that would exempt returning seasonal workers from the national H-2B visa cap of 66,000 if they have already successfully participated in the program. Motion agreed to 83-17: R 39-16; D 43-1 (ND 39-1, SD 4-0); I 1-0. Three-fifths of the total Senate (60) is required to invoke cloture. April 19, 2005.

**102.** HR 1268. Fiscal 2005 Supplemental Appropriations/Seasonal Workers. Mikulski, D-Md., amendment that would exempt returning seasonal workers from the national H-2B visa cap of 66,000 if they have already successfully participated in the program. It also would require employers to pay an anti-fraud fee of $150 on each H-2B petition and require the Department of Homeland Security to certify that the foreign employee is a returning worker. Adopted 94-6: R 51-4; D 42-2 (ND 39-1, SD 3-1); I 1-0. April 19, 2005.

**103.** HR 1268. Fiscal 2005 Supplemental Appropriations/Cloture. Motion to invoke cloture (thus limiting debate) on the bill that would appropriate $80.7 billion in fiscal 2005 supplemental spending for military operations and reconstruction in Iraq and Afghanistan and for disaster assistance to victims of the December 2004 tsunami in South Asia. Motion agreed to 100-0: R 55-0; D 44-0 (ND 40-0, SD 4-0); I 1-0. April 19, 2005.

| | 96 | 97 | 98 | 99 | 100 | 101 | 102 | 103 |
|---|---|---|---|---|---|---|---|---|
| **ALABAMA** | | | | | | | | |
| Shelby | N | N | N | Y | Y | N | N | Y |
| Sessions | N | N | N | Y | Y | N | N | Y |
| **ALASKA** | | | | | | | | |
| Stevens | Y | Y | N | Y | Y | Y | Y | Y |
| Murkowski | N | N | N | Y | Y | Y | Y | Y |
| **ARIZONA** | | | | | | | | |
| McCain | Y | N | Y | Y | Y | Y | Y | Y |
| Kyl | N | Y | N | Y | Y | Y | Y | Y |
| **ARKANSAS** | | | | | | | | |
| Lincoln | Y | N | Y | N | Y | N | Y | Y |
| Pryor | Y | N | Y | N | Y | N | Y | Y |
| **CALIFORNIA** | | | | | | | | |
| Feinstein | Y | N | N | N | Y | N | Y | Y |
| Boxer | Y | N | Y | N | N | N | Y | Y |
| **COLORADO** | | | | | | | | |
| Allard | N | Y | N | Y | Y | Y | Y | Y |
| Salazar | Y | Y | Y | Y | Y | N | Y | Y |
| **CONNECTICUT** | | | | | | | | |
| Dodd | Y | N | N | N | Y | N | Y | Y |
| Lieberman | Y | N | Y | Y | Y | N | Y | Y |
| **DELAWARE** | | | | | | | | |
| Biden | ? | N | Y | Y | N | Y | Y | Y |
| Carper | Y | N | Y | N | Y | N | Y | Y |
| **FLORIDA** | | | | | | | | |
| Nelson | Y | N | Y | N | Y | N | N | Y |
| Martinez | N | N | Y | Y | Y | Y | Y | Y |
| **GEORGIA** | | | | | | | | |
| Chambliss | N | Y | N | Y | Y | Y | Y | Y |
| Isakson | N | N | N | Y | Y | Y | Y | Y |
| **HAWAII** | | | | | | | | |
| Inouye | Y | N | Y | N | Y | N | Y | Y |
| Akaka | Y | N | Y | N | Y | N | Y | Y |
| **IDAHO** | | | | | | | | |
| Craig | Y | N | Y | Y | Y | Y | Y | Y |
| Crapo | Y | N | N | Y | Y | Y | Y | Y |
| **ILLINOIS** | | | | | | | | |
| Durbin | ? | ? | ? | ? | ? | Y | Y | Y |
| Obama | ? | ? | ? | ? | ? | Y | Y | Y |
| **INDIANA** | | | | | | | | |
| Lugar | N | N | Y | Y | Y | Y | Y | Y |
| Bayh | Y | N | Y | N | Y | N | Y | Y |
| **IOWA** | | | | | | | | |
| Grassley | N | Y | N | Y | N | Y | Y | Y |
| Harkin | Y | N | Y | N | Y | N | Y | Y |
| **KANSAS** | | | | | | | | |
| Brownback | N | N | N | Y | N | Y | N | Y |
| Roberts | N | N | N | Y | Y | N | Y | Y |
| **KENTUCKY** | | | | | | | | |
| McConnell | ? | N | N | Y | N | Y | N | Y |
| Bunning | N | N | N | Y | Y | N | Y | Y |
| **LOUISIANA** | | | | | | | | |
| Landrieu | ? | Y | Y | N | Y | N | Y | Y |
| Vitter | N | N | N | Y | Y | N | N | Y |
| **MAINE** | | | | | | | | |
| Snowe | Y | N | Y | Y | Y | Y | Y | Y |
| Collins | Y | Y | N | Y | Y | Y | Y | Y |
| **MARYLAND** | | | | | | | | |
| Sarbanes | Y | N | Y | N | Y | N | Y | Y |
| Mikulski | Y | N | Y | N | N | Y | Y | Y |
| **MASSACHUSETTS** | | | | | | | | |
| Kennedy | Y | N | Y | N | Y | N | Y | Y |
| Kerry | ? | N | Y | Y | N | Y | Y | Y |
| **MICHIGAN** | | | | | | | | |
| Levin | Y | N | Y | N | Y | N | Y | Y |
| Stabenow | Y | N | Y | N | Y | N | Y | Y |
| **MINNESOTA** | | | | | | | | |
| Dayton | Y | N | Y | Y | N | Y | Y | Y |
| Coleman | Y | N | Y | Y | Y | Y | Y | Y |
| **MISSISSIPPI** | | | | | | | | |
| Cochran | N | Y | N | Y | Y | N | Y | Y |
| Lott | N | Y | N | Y | Y | N | Y | Y |
| **MISSOURI** | | | | | | | | |
| Bond | ? | Y | N | Y | Y | Y | Y | Y |
| Talent | Y | N | N | Y | Y | Y | Y | Y |
| **MONTANA** | | | | | | | | |
| Baucus | Y | N | Y | N | N | Y | Y | Y |
| Burns | ? | Y | Y | Y | Y | Y | Y | Y |
| **NEBRASKA** | | | | | | | | |
| Hagel | Y | N | Y | Y | Y | Y | Y | Y |
| Nelson | Y | N | Y | N | Y | N | Y | Y |
| **NEVADA** | | | | | | | | |
| Reid | Y | N | Y | N | Y | N | Y | Y |
| Ensign | N | N | N | Y | Y | N | Y | Y |
| **NEW HAMPSHIRE** | | | | | | | | |
| Gregg | N | Y | N | Y | Y | Y | Y | Y |
| Sununu | Y | Y | N | Y | Y | Y | Y | Y |
| **NEW JERSEY** | | | | | | | | |
| Corzine | Y | N | Y | N | Y | N | Y | Y |
| Lautenberg | Y | N | Y | N | Y | N | Y | Y |
| **NEW MEXICO** | | | | | | | | |
| Domenici | N | N | Y | Y | Y | Y | Y | Y |
| Bingaman | Y | N | Y | N | Y | N | Y | Y |
| **NEW YORK** | | | | | | | | |
| Schumer | Y | N | Y | N | Y | N | Y | Y |
| Clinton | Y | N | Y | N | Y | N | Y | Y |
| **NORTH CAROLINA** | | | | | | | | |
| Dole | N | Y | N | Y | Y | Y | Y | Y |
| Burr | N | Y | N | Y | Y | Y | Y | Y |
| **NORTH DAKOTA** | | | | | | | | |
| Conrad | Y | N | N | Y | N | Y | Y | Y |
| Dorgan | Y | N | N | N | Y | N | Y | Y |
| **OHIO** | | | | | | | | |
| DeWine | N | N | Y | Y | Y | Y | Y | Y |
| Voinovich | Y | N | Y | Y | Y | Y | Y | Y |
| **OKLAHOMA** | | | | | | | | |
| Inhofe | N | N | N | Y | N | N | N | Y |
| Coburn | Y | N | N | Y | Y | Y | Y | Y |
| **OREGON** | | | | | | | | |
| Wyden | Y | N | Y | N | Y | N | Y | Y |
| Smith | Y | N | Y | Y | Y | Y | Y | Y |
| **PENNSYLVANIA** | | | | | | | | |
| Specter | Y | N | Y | Y | Y | Y | Y | Y |
| Santorum | N | Y | N | Y | Y | Y | Y | Y |
| **RHODE ISLAND** | | | | | | | | |
| Reed | Y | N | Y | N | Y | N | Y | Y |
| Chafee | Y | N | Y | Y | Y | Y | Y | Y |
| **SOUTH CAROLINA** | | | | | | | | |
| Graham | N | Y | N | Y | Y | Y | Y | Y |
| DeMint | N | Y | N | Y | Y | Y | Y | Y |
| **SOUTH DAKOTA** | | | | | | | | |
| Johnson | Y | N | Y | N | Y | N | Y | Y |
| Thune | Y | N | N | Y | Y | Y | Y | Y |
| **TENNESSEE** | | | | | | | | |
| Frist | N | N | N | Y | Y | N | Y | Y |
| Alexander | N | N | N | Y | Y | N | Y | Y |
| **TEXAS** | | | | | | | | |
| Hutchison | Y | N | N | Y | Y | N | Y | Y |
| Cornyn | N | N | N | Y | Y | N | Y | Y |
| **UTAH** | | | | | | | | |
| Hatch | Y | N | Y | Y | Y | Y | Y | Y |
| Bennett | Y | N | Y | Y | Y | Y | Y | Y |
| **VERMONT** | | | | | | | | |
| Leahy | Y | N | N | Y | N | Y | Y | Y |
| Jeffords | Y | N | Y | N | Y | N | Y | Y |
| **VIRGINIA** | | | | | | | | |
| Warner | Y | Y | Y | Y | Y | Y | Y | Y |
| Allen | Y | N | N | N | Y | Y | Y | Y |
| **WASHINGTON** | | | | | | | | |
| Murray | Y | N | Y | N | Y | N | Y | Y |
| Cantwell | Y | N | Y | N | N | N | Y | Y |
| **WEST VIRGINIA** | | | | | | | | |
| Byrd | Y | N | Y | N | N | N | N | Y |
| Rockefeller | Y | N | N | Y | N | Y | Y | Y |
| **WISCONSIN** | | | | | | | | |
| Kohl | Y | N | Y | Y | Y | Y | Y | Y |
| Feingold | Y | N | Y | N | N | N | Y | Y |
| **WYOMING** | | | | | | | | |
| Thomas | N | Y | N | Y | Y | Y | Y | Y |
| Enzi | N | N | N | Y | Y | Y | Y | Y |

**KEY** — Republicans — Democrats — *Independents*

| | | | |
|---|---|---|---|
| Y | Voted for (yea) | X | Paired against |
| # | Paired for | – | Announced against |
| + | Announced for | P | Voted "present" |
| N | Voted against (nay) | C | Voted "present" to avoid possible conflict of interest |
| | | ? | Did not vote or otherwise make a position known |

# IN THE SENATE | By Vote Number

**104.** HR 1268. Fiscal 2005 Supplemental Appropriations/Iraq Embassy **Funding.** Cochran, R-Miss., motion to table (kill) the Coburn, R-Okla., amendment that would reduce appropriations for the security, construction and maintenance of U.S. embassies from $592 million to $106 million, effectively cutting funding for the construction of a new U.S. embassy in Iraq. Motion agreed to 54-45: R 29-26; D 25-19 (ND 23-17, SD 2-2); I 0-0. A "yea" was a vote in support of the president's position. April 20, 2005.

**105.** HR 1268. Fiscal 2005 Supplemental Appropriations/Border **Security Funding.** Byrd, D-W.Va., amendment that would increase funding for immigration and customs enforcement at the Homeland Security Department by $389.6 million and reduce funding for diplomatic and consular programs at the State Department by $400 million. It would provide for the hiring of additional border patrol agents and fund the operation of unmanned aerial vehicles along the southwest U.S.-Mexico border. Adopted 65-34: R 21-34; D 44-0 (ND 40-0, SD 4-0); I 0-0. April 20, 2005.

**106.** HR 1268. Fiscal 2005 Supplemental Appropriations/Navy Aircraft **Carriers.** Warner, R-Va., amendment that would bar funds appropriated or made available in the bill from being obligated or spent to reduce the number of active Navy aircraft carriers to less than 12 until certain conditions are met. It also would require funding to be made available to the Navy for the repair and maintenance of the *USS John F. Kennedy*. Adopted 58-38: R 24-31; D 34-7 (ND 30-7, SD 4-0); I 0-0. April 20, 2005.

**107.** Negroponte Nomination/Confirmation. Confirmation of President Bush's nomination of John D. Negroponte of New York to be director of national intelligence. Confirmed 98-2: R 55-0; D 42-2 (ND 38-2, SD 4-0); I 1-0. A "yea" was a vote in support of the president's position. April 21, 2005.

**108.** HR 1268. Fiscal 2005 Supplemental Appropriations/Humvees **Funding.** Bayh, D-Ind., amendment that would appropriate an additional $213 million to the army for the procurement of up-armored high mobility multipurpose-wheeled vehicles, known as Humvees. Adopted 61-39: R 17-38; D 43-1 (ND 39-1, SD 4-0); I 1-0. April 21, 2005.

**109.** HR 1268. Fiscal 2005 Supplemental Appropriations/Passage. Passage of the bill that would appropriate $81.3 billion in fiscal 2005 supplemental spending for military operations and reconstruction in Iraq and Afghanistan, and for disaster assistance to victims of the December 2004 tsunami in South Asia. The bill would provide $17.5 billion for military personnel, $37.4 billion for operations and maintenance, and $16.1 billion for procurement. It also would provide $907.3 million for tsunami relief and recovery, and $592 million for the security, construction and maintenance of U.S. embassies, such as one in Iraq. Passed 99-0: R 55-0; D 43-0 (ND 39-0, SD 4-0); I 1-0. April 21, 2005.

| | 104 | 105 | 106 | 107 | 108 | 109 |
|---|---|---|---|---|---|---|
| **ALABAMA** | | | | | | |
| Shelby | Y | N | N | Y | N | Y |
| Sessions | N | Y | N | Y | N | Y |
| **ALASKA** | | | | | | |
| Stevens | Y | N | Y | N | N | Y |
| Murkowski | Y | N | N | Y | N | Y |
| **ARIZONA** | | | | | | |
| McCain | Y | N | N | Y | Y | Y |
| Kyl | N | Y | N | Y | N | Y |
| **ARKANSAS** | | | | | | |
| Lincoln | N | Y | Y | Y | Y | Y |
| Pryor | N | Y | Y | Y | Y | Y |
| **CALIFORNIA** | | | | | | |
| Feinstein | Y | Y | Y | Y | Y | Y |
| Boxer | N | Y | Y | Y | Y | Y |
| **COLORADO** | | | | | | |
| Allard | Y | N | N | Y | N | Y |
| Salazar | Y | Y | Y | Y | Y | Y |
| **CONNECTICUT** | | | | | | |
| Dodd | N | Y | Y | Y | Y | Y |
| Lieberman | Y | Y | Y | Y | Y | Y |
| **DELAWARE** | | | | | | |
| Biden | Y | Y | Y | Y | Y | Y |
| Carper | N | Y | Y | Y | Y | Y |
| **FLORIDA** | | | | | | |
| Nelson | Y | Y | Y | Y | Y | Y |
| Martinez | Y | N | Y | Y | Y | Y |
| **GEORGIA** | | | | | | |
| Chambliss | N | Y | Y | Y | N | Y |
| Isakson | N | Y | Y | Y | N | Y |
| **HAWAII** | | | | | | |
| Inouye | Y | Y | Y | Y | N | ? |
| Akaka | Y | Y | Y | Y | Y | Y |
| **IDAHO** | | | | | | |
| Craig | N | Y | Y | Y | N | Y |
| Crapo | N | Y | N | Y | N | Y |
| **ILLINOIS** | | | | | | |
| Durbin | Y | Y | Y | Y | Y | Y |
| Obama | N | Y | Y | Y | Y | Y |
| **INDIANA** | | | | | | |
| Lugar | Y | N | N | Y | N | Y |
| Bayh | N | Y | Y | Y | Y | Y |
| **IOWA** | | | | | | |
| Grassley | Y | N | N | Y | N | Y |
| Harkin | N | Y | Y | N | Y | Y |
| **KANSAS** | | | | | | |
| Brownback | N | N | Y | Y | N | Y |
| Roberts | Y | Y | N | Y | N | Y |
| **KENTUCKY** | | | | | | |
| McConnell | Y | N | N | Y | N | Y |
| Bunning | N | Y | N | Y | N | Y |
| **LOUISIANA** | | | | | | |
| Landrieu | Y | Y | Y | Y | Y | Y |
| Vitter | N | Y | Y | Y | N | Y |
| **MAINE** | | | | | | |
| Snowe | Y | Y | Y | Y | Y | Y |
| Collins | N | N | Y | Y | Y | Y |
| **MARYLAND** | | | | | | |
| Sarbanes | N | Y | Y | Y | Y | Y |
| Mikulski | Y | Y | Y | Y | Y | Y |
| **MASSACHUSETTS** | | | | | | |
| Kennedy | N | Y | ? | Y | Y | Y |
| Kerry | Y | Y | Y | Y | Y | Y |
| **MICHIGAN** | | | | | | |
| Levin | Y | Y | Y | Y | Y | Y |
| Stabenow | Y | Y | Y | Y | Y | Y |
| **MINNESOTA** | | | | | | |
| Dayton | Y | Y | Y | Y | Y | Y |
| Coleman | Y | N | Y | Y | Y | Y |
| **MISSISSIPPI** | | | | | | |
| Cochran | Y | N | N | Y | N | Y |
| Lott | N | N | Y | Y | Y | Y |
| **MISSOURI** | | | | | | |
| Bond | Y | N | N | Y | N | Y |
| Talent | Y | Y | Y | Y | Y | Y |
| **MONTANA** | | | | | | |
| Baucus | Y | Y | Y | Y | Y | Y |
| Burns | Y | N | N | Y | Y | Y |
| **NEBRASKA** | | | | | | |
| Hagel | Y | N | Y | Y | N | Y |
| Nelson | N | Y | Y | Y | Y | Y |
| **NEVADA** | | | | | | |
| Reid | Y | Y | Y | Y | Y | Y |
| Ensign | N | N | Y | Y | N | Y |
| **NEW HAMPSHIRE** | | | | | | |
| Gregg | N | Y | N | Y | N | Y |
| Sununu | N | Y | N | Y | N | Y |
| **NEW JERSEY** | | | | | | |
| Corzine | Y | Y | Y | Y | Y | Y |
| Lautenberg | Y | Y | Y | Y | Y | Y |
| **NEW MEXICO** | | | | | | |
| Domenici | Y | Y | N | Y | N | Y |
| Bingaman | Y | Y | Y | Y | Y | Y |
| **NEW YORK** | | | | | | |
| Schumer | N | Y | Y | Y | Y | Y |
| Clinton | N | Y | Y | Y | Y | Y |
| **NORTH CAROLINA** | | | | | | |
| Dole | Y | N | Y | Y | N | Y |
| Burr | N | N | Y | Y | N | Y |
| **NORTH DAKOTA** | | | | | | |
| Conrad | N | Y | ? | Y | Y | Y |
| Dorgan | N | Y | Y | Y | Y | Y |
| **OHIO** | | | | | | |
| DeWine | Y | N | Y | Y | Y | Y |
| Voinovich | Y | N | N | Y | Y | Y |
| **OKLAHOMA** | | | | | | |
| Inhofe | N | Y | Y | Y | N | Y |
| Coburn | N | Y | Y | Y | N | Y |
| **OREGON** | | | | | | |
| Wyden | N | Y | N | N | Y | Y |
| Smith | Y | N | N | Y | N | Y |
| **PENNSYLVANIA** | | | | | | |
| Specter | Y | N | N | Y | N | Y |
| Santorum | Y | Y | N | Y | Y | Y |
| **RHODE ISLAND** | | | | | | |
| Reed | Y | Y | Y | Y | Y | Y |
| Chafee | N | N | N | Y | Y | Y |
| **SOUTH CAROLINA** | | | | | | |
| Graham | N | Y | Y | Y | N | Y |
| DeMint | N | N | N | Y | N | Y |
| **SOUTH DAKOTA** | | | | | | |
| Johnson | Y | Y | Y | Y | Y | Y |
| Thune | N | Y | Y | Y | Y | Y |
| **TENNESSEE** | | | | | | |
| Frist | Y | N | N | Y | N | Y |
| Alexander | Y | N | N | Y | Y | Y |
| **TEXAS** | | | | | | |
| Hutchison | Y | Y | N | Y | Y | Y |
| Cornyn | N | Y | Y | Y | N | Y |
| **UTAH** | | | | | | |
| Hatch | N | N | Y | Y | N | Y |
| Bennett | Y | N | N | Y | N | Y |
| **VERMONT** | | | | | | |
| Leahy | Y | Y | Y | Y | Y | Y |
| *Jeffords* | ? | ? | ? | Y | Y | Y |
| **VIRGINIA** | | | | | | |
| Warner | Y | N | Y | Y | N | Y |
| Allen | N | Y | Y | Y | Y | Y |
| **WASHINGTON** | | | | | | |
| Murray | Y | Y | Y | Y | Y | Y |
| Cantwell | Y | Y | Y | Y | Y | Y |
| **WEST VIRGINIA** | | | | | | |
| Byrd | N | Y | ? | Y | Y | Y |
| Rockefeller | Y | Y | N | Y | Y | Y |
| **WISCONSIN** | | | | | | |
| Kohl | N | Y | N | Y | Y | Y |
| Feingold | N | Y | N | Y | Y | Y |
| **WYOMING** | | | | | | |
| Thomas | N | N | N | Y | N | Y |
| Enzi | N | N | N | Y | N | Y |

**KEY**   Republicans   Democrats   *Independents*

| | | |
|---|---|---|
| Y   Voted for (yea) | X   Paired against | C   Voted "present" to avoid possible conflict of interest |
| #   Paired for | –   Announced against | |
| +   Announced for | P   Voted "present" | ?   Did not vote or otherwise make a position known |
| N   Voted against (nay) | | |

# IN THE SENATE | By Vote Number

**110.** **HR 3. Surface Transportation Reauthorization/Cloture.** Motion to invoke cloture (thus limiting debate) on the motion to proceed to the bill that would authorize $283.9 billion for federal-aid highway, mass transit, safety and research programs through fiscal 2009. Motion agreed to 94-6: R 49-6; D 44-0 (ND 40-0, SD 4-0); I 1-0. Three-fifths of the total Senate (60) is required to invoke cloture. April 26, 2005.

**111.** **Seabright Nomination/Confirmation.** Confirmation of President Bush's nomination of J. Michael Seabright of Hawaii to be U.S. district judge for the District of Hawaii. Confirmed 98-0: R 55-0; D 42-0 (ND 38-0, SD 4-0); I 1-0. A "yea" was a vote in support of the president's position. April 27, 2005.

**112.** **Procedural Motion/Recess.** Frist, R-Tenn., motion to recess until 2 p.m. on Thursday, April 28, 2005. Motion agreed to 98-1: R 55-0; D 42-1 (ND 38-1, SD 4-0); I 1-0. April, 28, 2005.

**113.** **HR 3. Surface Transportation Reauthorization/Stormwater Mitigation.** Warner, R-Va., motion to table (kill) the Bond, R-Mo., amendment to the Inhofe, R-Okla., substitute amendment. The Bond amendment would strike a section that would require every state to set aside 2 percent of its surface transportation funds and associated equity bonus funding to be used for stormwater mitigation activities. The substitute amendment would authorize $283.9 billion for federal-aid highway, mass transit, safety and research programs through fiscal 2009 and guarantee that every state receives at least 92 cents in funding for every dollar in gas taxes it pays into the Highway Trust Fund. Motion agreed to 51-49: R 9-46; D 41-3 (ND 38-2, SD 3-1); I 1-0. April 28, 2005.

**114.** **H Con Res 95. Fiscal 2006 Budget Resolution/Conference Report.** Adoption of the conference report on the concurrent resolution that would set broad spending and revenue targets for five years, limit discretionary spending to $843 billion in fiscal 2006, and provide instructions for reconciliation bills that would achieve $70 billion in tax cuts and $34.7 billion in savings to mandatory programs, including $10 billion in Medicaid savings. Adopted 52-47: R 52-3; D 0-43 (ND 0-39, SD 0-4); I 0-1. April 28, 2005.

**115.** **Johnson Nomination/Cloture.** Motion to invoke cloture (thus limiting debate) on the nomination of Stephen L. Johnson of Maryland to be the EPA administrator. Motion agreed to 61-37: R 54-0; D 7-36 (ND 6-33, SD 1-3); I 0-1. Three-fifths of the total Senate (60) is required to invoke cloture. (Subsequently, the nomination was confirmed by voice vote.) April 29, 2005 (in the session that began and the Congressional Record dated April 28, 2005).

| | 110 | 111 | 112 | 113 | 114 | 115 | | | 110 | 111 | 112 | 113 | 114 | 115 |
|---|---|---|---|---|---|---|---|---|---|---|---|---|---|---|
| **ALABAMA** | | | | | | | | **MONTANA** | | | | | | |
| Shelby | Y | Y | Y | N | Y | Y | | Baucus | Y | ? | ? | Y | N | Y |
| Sessions | Y | Y | Y | N | Y | Y | | Burns | Y | Y | Y | N | Y | Y |
| **ALASKA** | | | | | | | | **NEBRASKA** | | | | | | |
| Stevens | Y | Y | Y | N | Y | Y | | Hagel | Y | Y | Y | N | Y | Y |
| Murkowski | Y | Y | Y | N | Y | Y | | Nelson | Y | Y | Y | Y | N | Y |
| **ARIZONA** | | | | | | | | **NEVADA** | | | | | | |
| McCain | N | Y | Y | Y | Y | Y | | Reid | Y | Y | Y | Y | N | N |
| Kyl | N | Y | Y | N | Y | Y | | Ensign | Y | Y | Y | Y | Y | Y |
| **ARKANSAS** | | | | | | | | **NEW HAMPSHIRE** | | | | | | |
| Lincoln | Y | Y | Y | Y | N | N | | Gregg | N | Y | N | Y | Y | Y |
| Pryor | Y | Y | Y | Y | N | N | | Sununu | N | Y | N | Y | Y | Y |
| **CALIFORNIA** | | | | | | | | **NEW JERSEY** | | | | | | |
| Feinstein | Y | Y | Y | Y | N | Y | | Corzine | Y | Y | Y | Y | N | N |
| Boxer | Y | Y | Y | Y | N | N | | Lautenberg | Y | Y | Y | Y | N | N |
| **COLORADO** | | | | | | | | **NEW MEXICO** | | | | | | |
| Allard | Y | Y | Y | N | Y | Y | | Domenici | Y | Y | Y | N | Y | Y |
| Salazar | Y | Y | Y | Y | N | N | | Bingaman | Y | Y | Y | Y | N | N |
| **CONNECTICUT** | | | | | | | | **NEW YORK** | | | | | | |
| Dodd | Y | Y | Y | Y | N | N | | Schumer | Y | Y | Y | Y | N | N |
| Lieberman | Y | Y | Y | Y | ? | ? | | Clinton | Y | Y | N | Y | N | N |
| **DELAWARE** | | | | | | | | **NORTH CAROLINA** | | | | | | |
| Biden | Y | ? | Y | Y | N | N | | Dole | Y | Y | Y | N | Y | Y |
| Carper | Y | Y | Y | Y | N | N | | Burr | Y | Y | Y | N | Y | Y |
| **FLORIDA** | | | | | | | | **NORTH DAKOTA** | | | | | | |
| Nelson | Y | Y | Y | Y | N | Y | | Conrad | Y | Y | Y | N | N | N |
| Martinez | Y | Y | Y | N | Y | Y | | Dorgan | Y | Y | Y | N | N | N |
| **GEORGIA** | | | | | | | | **OHIO** | | | | | | |
| Chambliss | Y | Y | Y | N | Y | Y | | DeWine | Y | Y | Y | N | N | Y |
| Isakson | Y | Y | Y | N | Y | Y | | Voinovich | Y | Y | Y | N | N | Y |
| **HAWAII** | | | | | | | | **OKLAHOMA** | | | | | | |
| Inouye | Y | Y | Y | Y | N | N | | Inhofe | Y | Y | Y | N | Y | Y |
| Akaka | Y | Y | Y | Y | N | N | | Coburn | Y | Y | Y | N | Y | Y |
| **IDAHO** | | | | | | | | **OREGON** | | | | | | |
| Craig | Y | Y | Y | N | Y | Y | | Wyden | Y | Y | Y | Y | N | N |
| Crapo | Y | Y | Y | N | Y | Y | | Smith | Y | Y | Y | Y | Y | Y |
| **ILLINOIS** | | | | | | | | **PENNSYLVANIA** | | | | | | |
| Durbin | Y | Y | Y | Y | N | N | | Specter | Y | Y | Y | N | Y | Y |
| Obama | Y | Y | Y | Y | N | N | | Santorum | Y | Y | Y | N | Y | Y |
| **INDIANA** | | | | | | | | **RHODE ISLAND** | | | | | | |
| Lugar | Y | Y | Y | N | Y | Y | | Reed | Y | Y | Y | Y | N | N |
| Bayh | Y | Y | Y | Y | N | N | | Chafee | Y | Y | Y | Y | N | Y |
| **IOWA** | | | | | | | | **SOUTH CAROLINA** | | | | | | |
| Grassley | Y | Y | Y | N | Y | Y | | Graham | Y | Y | Y | N | Y | Y |
| Harkin | Y | Y | Y | Y | N | N | | DeMint | Y | Y | Y | N | Y | Y |
| **KANSAS** | | | | | | | | **SOUTH DAKOTA** | | | | | | |
| Brownback | Y | Y | Y | N | Y | Y | | Johnson | Y | Y | Y | N | Y | Y |
| Roberts | Y | Y | Y | N | Y | Y | | Thune | Y | Y | Y | N | Y | Y |
| **KENTUCKY** | | | | | | | | **TENNESSEE** | | | | | | |
| McConnell | Y | Y | Y | N | Y | Y | | Frist | Y | Y | Y | N | Y | Y |
| Bunning | Y | Y | Y | N | Y | Y | | Alexander | Y | Y | Y | Y | Y | Y |
| **LOUISIANA** | | | | | | | | **TEXAS** | | | | | | |
| Landrieu | Y | Y | Y | N | N | N | | Hutchison | N | Y | Y | N | Y | Y |
| Vitter | Y | Y | Y | N | Y | Y | | Cornyn | N | Y | Y | N | Y | Y |
| **MAINE** | | | | | | | | **UTAH** | | | | | | |
| Snowe | Y | Y | Y | N | Y | Y | | Hatch | Y | Y | Y | Y | Y | Y |
| Collins | Y | Y | Y | N | Y | Y | | Bennett | Y | Y | Y | Y | Y | Y |
| **MARYLAND** | | | | | | | | **VERMONT** | | | | | | |
| Sarbanes | Y | Y | Y | Y | N | N | | Leahy | Y | Y | Y | Y | N | Y |
| Mikulski | Y | Y | Y | Y | N | N | | Jeffords | Y | Y | Y | Y | N | N |
| **MASSACHUSETTS** | | | | | | | | **VIRGINIA** | | | | | | |
| Kennedy | Y | Y | Y | Y | N | N | | Warner | Y | Y | Y | Y | Y | Y |
| Kerry | Y | Y | Y | Y | N | N | | Allen | Y | Y | Y | N | Y | Y |
| **MICHIGAN** | | | | | | | | **WASHINGTON** | | | | | | |
| Levin | Y | Y | Y | Y | N | N | | Murray | Y | Y | Y | Y | N | N |
| Stabenow | Y | Y | Y | Y | N | N | | Cantwell | Y | Y | Y | Y | N | N |
| **MINNESOTA** | | | | | | | | **WEST VIRGINIA** | | | | | | |
| Dayton | Y | Y | Y | Y | N | N | | Byrd | Y | Y | Y | N | N | Y |
| Coleman | Y | Y | Y | Y | Y | Y | | Rockefeller | Y | Y | Y | N | N | N |
| **MISSISSIPPI** | | | | | | | | **WISCONSIN** | | | | | | |
| Cochran | Y | Y | Y | N | Y | Y | | Kohl | Y | Y | Y | N | N | N |
| Lott | Y | Y | Y | N | Y | ? | | Feingold | Y | Y | Y | N | N | Y |
| **MISSOURI** | | | | | | | | **WYOMING** | | | | | | |
| Bond | Y | Y | Y | N | Y | Y | | Thomas | Y | Y | Y | N | Y | Y |
| Talent | Y | Y | Y | N | Y | Y | | Enzi | Y | Y | Y | N | Y | Y |

**KEY**    **Republicans**    Democrats    *Independents*

| | | | |
|---|---|---|---|
| Y | Voted for (yea) | X | Paired against |
| # | Paired for | – | Announced against |
| + | Announced for | P | Voted "present" |
| N | Voted against (nay) | C | Voted "present" to avoid possible conflict of interest |
| | | ? | Did not vote or otherwise make a position known |

# IN THE SENATE | By Vote Number

**116.** **HR 3. Surface Transportation Reauthorization/Minority Contractors.** Talent, R-Mo., amendment to the Inhofe, R-Okla., substitute amendment. The Talent amendment would direct the Transportation secretary to notify state and local governments that receive federal funds of a new law providing that once certain minority-owned small businesses are certified at the federal level they do not have be re-certified at the state and local level to compete for federal contracts such as federal highway projects. The substitute would authorize $283.9 billion for federal-aid highway, mass transit, safety and research programs in fiscal 2004 through 2009 and guarantee that every state receives at least 92 cents in funding for every dollar in gas taxes it pays into the Highway Trust Fund. Adopted 89-0: R 49-0; D 39-0 (ND 35-0, SD 4-0); I 1-0. May 9, 2005.

**117.** **HR 1268. Fiscal 2005 Supplemental Appropriations/Adoption.** Adoption of the conference report on the bill that would appropriate $82 billion in fiscal 2005 supplemental spending for military operations and reconstruction in Iraq and Afghanistan and for disaster assistance to victims of the December 2004 tsunami in South Asia. It also would establish national driver's license standards, stiffen asylum requirements and speed completion of a fence on the U.S.-Mexico border. Adopted (thus cleared for the president) 100-0: R 55-0; D 44-0 (ND 40-0, SD 4-0); I 1-0. May 10, 2005.

**118.** **HR 3. Surface Transportation Reauthorization/Substitute.** Inhofe, R-Okla., motion to waive the Budget Act with respect to the Gregg, R-N.H., point of order against the Inhofe substitute amendment. The substitute would authorize $295 billion for federal-aid highway, mass transit, safety and research programs from fiscal 2004 through 2009. The funding total includes $234 billion for highway programs and $54 billion for public transportation programs. Motion agreed to 76-22: R 33-21; D 42-1 (ND 38-1, SD 4-0); I 1-0. A three-fifths majority (60) of the total Senate is required to waive the Budget Act. May 11, 2005.

**119.** **HR 3. Surface Transportation Reauthorization/Contractor Campaign Contributions.** Inhofe, R-Okla., motion to table (kill) the Corzine, D-N.J., amendment to the Inhofe substitute amendment. The Corzine amendment would allow states to enact laws limiting political campaign contributions by contractors for transportation contracts awarded by the state, without losing federal transportation funding. Motion agreed to 57-40: R 48-5; D 8-35 (ND 7-32, SD 1-3); I 1-0. May 11, 2005.

| | 116 | 117 | 118 | 119 | | | 116 | 117 | 118 | 119 |
|---|---|---|---|---|---|---|---|---|---|---|
| **ALABAMA** | | | | | | **MONTANA** | | | | |
| Shelby | Y | Y | Y | Y | | Baucus | Y | Y | Y | Y |
| Sessions | Y | Y | N | Y | | Burns | Y | Y | Y | Y |
| **ALASKA** | | | | | | **NEBRASKA** | | | | |
| Stevens | Y | Y | Y | Y | | Hagel | Y | Y | N | Y |
| Murkowski | ? | Y | Y | Y | | Nelson | Y | Y | Y | Y |
| **ARIZONA** | | | | | | **NEVADA** | | | | |
| McCain | ? | Y | N | N | | Reid | Y | Y | Y | Y |
| Kyl | ? | Y | N | Y | | Ensign | Y | Y | N | Y |
| **ARKANSAS** | | | | | | **NEW HAMPSHIRE** | | | | |
| Lincoln | Y | Y | Y | N | | Gregg | Y | Y | N | N |
| Pryor | Y | Y | Y | N | | Sununu | Y | Y | N | Y |
| **CALIFORNIA** | | | | | | **NEW JERSEY** | | | | |
| Feinstein | Y | Y | Y | N | | Corzine | Y | Y | Y | N |
| Boxer | Y | Y | Y | N | | Lautenberg | Y | Y | Y | N |
| **COLORADO** | | | | | | **NEW MEXICO** | | | | |
| Allard | Y | Y | N | Y | | Domenici | Y | Y | Y | ? |
| Salazar | Y | Y | Y | N | | Bingaman | Y | Y | Y | N |
| **CONNECTICUT** | | | | | | **NEW YORK** | | | | |
| Dodd | Y | Y | Y | N | | Schumer | Y | Y | Y | N |
| Lieberman | Y | Y | Y | N | | Clinton | Y | Y | Y | N |
| **DELAWARE** | | | | | | **NORTH CAROLINA** | | | | |
| Biden | ? | Y | Y | N | | Dole | Y | Y | Y | Y |
| Carper | Y | Y | Y | N | | Burr | Y | Y | Y | Y |
| **FLORIDA** | | | | | | **NORTH DAKOTA** | | | | |
| Nelson | Y | Y | Y | N | | Conrad | Y | Y | Y | Y |
| Martinez | Y | Y | Y | Y | | Dorgan | ? | Y | Y | Y |
| **GEORGIA** | | | | | | **OHIO** | | | | |
| Chambliss | Y | Y | N | Y | | DeWine | Y | Y | Y | Y |
| Isakson | Y | Y | N | Y | | Voinovich | Y | Y | Y | Y |
| **HAWAII** | | | | | | **OKLAHOMA** | | | | |
| Inouye | Y | Y | Y | N | | Inhofe | Y | Y | Y | Y |
| Akaka | Y | Y | Y | N | | Coburn | Y | Y | N | Y |
| **IDAHO** | | | | | | **OREGON** | | | | |
| Craig | Y | Y | N | Y | | Wyden | Y | Y | Y | N |
| Crapo | Y | Y | Y | Y | | Smith | Y | Y | Y | Y |
| **ILLINOIS** | | | | | | **PENNSYLVANIA** | | | | |
| Durbin | Y | Y | Y | N | | Specter | Y | Y | Y | Y |
| Obama | Y | Y | Y | N | | Santorum | Y | Y | Y | Y |
| **INDIANA** | | | | | | **RHODE ISLAND** | | | | |
| Lugar | Y | Y | Y | Y | | Reed | Y | Y | Y | N |
| Bayh | Y | Y | N | Y | | Chafee | Y | Y | Y | N |
| **IOWA** | | | | | | **SOUTH CAROLINA** | | | | |
| Grassley | Y | Y | Y | Y | | Graham | Y | Y | N | Y |
| Harkin | ? | Y | Y | N | | DeMint | Y | Y | N | Y |
| **KANSAS** | | | | | | **SOUTH DAKOTA** | | | | |
| Brownback | Y | Y | N | Y | | Johnson | Y | Y | Y | N |
| Roberts | Y | Y | Y | Y | | Thune | Y | Y | Y | Y |
| **KENTUCKY** | | | | | | **TENNESSEE** | | | | |
| McConnell | Y | Y | N | Y | | Frist | Y | Y | N | Y |
| Bunning | Y | Y | Y | Y | | Alexander | ? | Y | Y | Y |
| **LOUISIANA** | | | | | | **TEXAS** | | | | |
| Landrieu | Y | Y | Y | Y | | Hutchison | Y | Y | N | Y |
| Vitter | Y | Y | Y | Y | | Cornyn | Y | Y | N | Y |
| **MAINE** | | | | | | **UTAH** | | | | |
| Snowe | Y | Y | Y | N | | Hatch | Y | Y | Y | Y |
| Collins | Y | Y | Y | N | | Bennett | Y | Y | Y | Y |
| **MARYLAND** | | | | | | **VERMONT** | | | | |
| Sarbanes | ? | Y | Y | N | | Leahy | Y | Y | Y | N |
| Mikulski | Y | Y | Y | N | | Jeffords | Y | Y | Y | Y |
| **MASSACHUSETTS** | | | | | | **VIRGINIA** | | | | |
| Kennedy | Y | Y | Y | N | | Warner | Y | Y | Y | Y |
| Kerry | Y | Y | Y | N | | Allen | Y | Y | Y | Y |
| **MICHIGAN** | | | | | | **WASHINGTON** | | | | |
| Levin | Y | Y | Y | N | | Murray | Y | Y | Y | Y |
| Stabenow | Y | Y | Y | N | | Cantwell | Y | Y | Y | N |
| **MINNESOTA** | | | | | | **WEST VIRGINIA** | | | | |
| Dayton | ? | Y | ? | ? | | Byrd | Y | Y | Y | Y |
| Coleman | Y | Y | ? | ? | | Rockefeller | Y | Y | Y | N |
| **MISSISSIPPI** | | | | | | **WISCONSIN** | | | | |
| Cochran | ? | Y | Y | Y | | Kohl | Y | Y | Y | N |
| Lott | Y | Y | Y | Y | | Feingold | Y | Y | N | N |
| **MISSOURI** | | | | | | **WYOMING** | | | | |
| Bond | Y | Y | Y | Y | | Thomas | Y | Y | N | Y |
| Talent | Y | Y | Y | Y | | Enzi | ? | Y | N | Y |

**KEY**  Republicans  Democrats  *Independents*

| | | | |
|---|---|---|---|
| Y | Voted for (yea) | X | Paired against |
| # | Paired for | – | Announced against |
| + | Announced for | P | Voted "present" |
| N | Voted against (nay) | | |

| | |
|---|---|
| C | Voted "present" to avoid possible conflict of interest |
| ? | Did not vote or otherwise make a position known |

# IN THE SENATE | By Vote Number

**120.** **HR 3. Surface Transportation Reauthorization/Motorcycle Safety Programs.** Lautenberg, D-N.J., amendment to the Inhofe, R-Okla., substitute amendment. The Lautenberg amendment would stipulate that, beginning in fiscal 2008, funding for motorcycle safety training programs in states without helmet laws would come from the state's share of federal highway funds. Rejected 28-69: R 6-47; D 22-21 (ND 21-18, SD 1-3); I 0-1. May 11, 2005.

**121.** **HR 3. Surface Transportation Reauthorization/Pedestrian and Bicycle Safety.** Harkin, D-Iowa, amendment to the Inhofe, R-Okla., substitute amendment. The Harkin amendment would direct the Transportation secretary to promote a goal of increasing the percentage of pedestrian and bicycle trips relative to motorized trips, while reducing accidents involving bicyclists and pedestrians by 10 percent. It would encourage local action on bicycle and pedestrian safety. Rejected 44-53: R 4-49; D 40-3 (ND 36-3, SD 4-0); I 0-1. May 11, 2005.

**122.** **HR 3. Surface Transportation Reauthorization/Cloture.** Motion to invoke cloture (thus limiting debate) on the Inhofe, R-Okla., substitute amendment that would authorize $295 billion for federal aid highway, mass transit, safety and research programs from fiscal 2004 through 2009. The funding total includes $234 billion for highway programs and $54 billion for public transportation programs. Motion agreed to 92-7: R 47-7; D 44-0 (ND 40-0, SD 4-0); I 1-0. Three-fifths of the total Senate (60) is required to invoke cloture. May 12, 2005.

| | 120 | 121 | 122 | | | 120 | 121 | 122 |
|---|---|---|---|---|---|---|---|---|
| **ALABAMA** | | | | | **MONTANA** | | | |
| Shelby | N | N | Y | | Baucus | N | N | Y |
| Sessions | N | N | Y | | Burns | N | N | Y |
| **ALASKA** | | | | | **NEBRASKA** | | | |
| Stevens | N | N | Y | | Hagel | N | N | Y |
| Murkowski | N | N | Y | | Nelson | N | N | Y |
| **ARIZONA** | | | | | **NEVADA** | | | |
| McCain | N | N | N | | Reid | Y | Y | Y |
| Kyl | N | N | N | | Ensign | N | Y | Y |
| **ARKANSAS** | | | | | **NEW HAMPSHIRE** | | | |
| Lincoln | N | Y | Y | | Gregg | N | N | N |
| Pryor | N | Y | Y | | Sununu | N | N | N |
| **CALIFORNIA** | | | | | **NEW JERSEY** | | | |
| Feinstein | Y | Y | Y | | Corzine | Y | Y | Y |
| Boxer | Y | Y | Y | | Lautenberg | Y | Y | Y |
| **COLORADO** | | | | | **NEW MEXICO** | | | |
| Allard | N | N | Y | | Domenici | ? | ? | Y |
| Salazar | N | Y | Y | | Bingaman | N | Y | Y |
| **CONNECTICUT** | | | | | **NEW YORK** | | | |
| Dodd | Y | Y | Y | | Schumer | N | Y | Y |
| Lieberman | Y | Y | Y | | Clinton | N | Y | Y |
| **DELAWARE** | | | | | **NORTH CAROLINA** | | | |
| Biden | Y | Y | Y | | Dole | Y | N | Y |
| Carper | N | Y | Y | | Burr | N | N | Y |
| **FLORIDA** | | | | | **NORTH DAKOTA** | | | |
| Nelson | N | Y | Y | | Conrad | N | N | Y |
| Martinez | Y | N | N | | Dorgan | N | Y | Y |
| **GEORGIA** | | | | | **OHIO** | | | |
| Chambliss | N | N | Y | | DeWine | Y | N | Y |
| Isakson | N | N | Y | | Voinovich | N | N | Y |
| **HAWAII** | | | | | **OKLAHOMA** | | | |
| Inouye | Y | Y | Y | | Inhofe | N | N | Y |
| Akaka | Y | Y | Y | | Coburn | N | N | Y |
| **IDAHO** | | | | | **OREGON** | | | |
| Craig | N | N | Y | | Wyden | Y | Y | Y |
| Crapo | N | N | Y | | Smith | N | N | Y |
| **ILLINOIS** | | | | | **PENNSYLVANIA** | | | |
| Durbin | Y | Y | Y | | Specter | N | N | Y |
| Obama | N | Y | Y | | Santorum | N | N | ? |
| **INDIANA** | | | | | **RHODE ISLAND** | | | |
| Lugar | N | N | Y | | Reed | N | Y | Y |
| Bayh | N | Y | Y | | Chafee | Y | N | Y |
| **IOWA** | | | | | **SOUTH CAROLINA** | | | |
| Grassley | N | N | Y | | Graham | N | N | Y |
| Harkin | Y | Y | Y | | DeMint | N | N | Y |
| **KANSAS** | | | | | **SOUTH DAKOTA** | | | |
| Brownback | N | N | Y | | Johnson | N | Y | Y |
| Roberts | N | N | Y | | Thune | N | N | Y |
| **KENTUCKY** | | | | | **TENNESSEE** | | | |
| McConnell | N | N | Y | | Frist | Y | N | Y |
| Bunning | N | N | Y | | Alexander | N | N | Y |
| **LOUISIANA** | | | | | **TEXAS** | | | |
| Landrieu | Y | Y | Y | | Hutchison | N | N | N |
| Vitter | N | N | Y | | Cornyn | N | N | N |
| **MAINE** | | | | | **UTAH** | | | |
| Snowe | N | Y | Y | | Hatch | N | N | Y |
| Collins | N | Y | Y | | Bennett | N | N | Y |
| **MARYLAND** | | | | | **VERMONT** | | | |
| Sarbanes | Y | Y | Y | | Leahy | N | Y | Y |
| Mikulski | Y | Y | Y | | Jeffords | N | N | Y |
| **MASSACHUSETTS** | | | | | **VIRGINIA** | | | |
| Kennedy | Y | Y | Y | | Warner | Y | Y | Y |
| Kerry | N | Y | Y | | Allen | N | N | Y |
| **MICHIGAN** | | | | | **WASHINGTON** | | | |
| Levin | Y | Y | Y | | Murray | Y | Y | Y |
| Stabenow | N | Y | Y | | Cantwell | Y | Y | Y |
| **MINNESOTA** | | | | | **WEST VIRGINIA** | | | |
| Dayton | ? | ? | Y | | Byrd | Y | Y | Y |
| Coleman | ? | ? | Y | | Rockefeller | Y | Y | Y |
| **MISSISSIPPI** | | | | | **WISCONSIN** | | | |
| Cochran | N | N | Y | | Kohl | N | Y | Y |
| Lott | N | N | Y | | Feingold | N | Y | Y |
| **MISSOURI** | | | | | **WYOMING** | | | |
| Bond | N | N | Y | | Thomas | N | N | Y |
| Talent | N | N | Y | | Enzi | N | N | Y |

**KEY**    Republicans    Democrats    *Independents*

| | | | |
|---|---|---|---|
| Y | Voted for (yea) | X Paired against | C Voted "present" to avoid possible conflict of interest |
| # | Paired for | – Announced against | |
| + | Announced for | P Voted "present" | ? Did not vote or otherwise make a position known |
| N | Voted against (nay) | | |

# IN THE SENATE | By Vote Number

**123.** **HR 3. Surface Transportation Reauthorization/Seat Belts.** Allen, R-Va., amendment to the Inhofe, R-Okla., substitute amendment. The Allen amendment would revise the Occupant Protection Incentive Grant program to base grant awards on an 85 percent safety belt use rate in the preceding calendar year. It would strike the requirement that to receive funds under the program, states must either have a primary safety belt law in effect, or have a safety belt use rate of 90 percent. The substitute amendment would bring the total authorization for federal-aid highway, mass transit, safety and research programs, including fiscal 2004 funds, to $295 billion through 2009. The funding total includes $234 billion for highway programs and $54 billion for public transportation programs. Rejected 14-86: R 11-44; D 3-41 (ND 2-38, SD 1-3); I 0-1. May 17, 2005.

**124.** **HR 3. Surface Transportation Reauthorization/Funding Reduction.** Sessions, R-Ala., amendment to the Inhofe, R-Okla., substitute amendment. The Sessions amendment would reduce funding for certain programs by $10.7 billion, including a $5 billion cut for mass transit, a $4 billion cut for the congestion mitigation and air quality improvement program, and a $1.1 billion cut for surface transportation enhancement projects. Rejected 16-84: R 16-39; D 0-44 (ND 0-40, SD 0-4); I 0-1. May 17, 2005.

**125.** **HR 3. Surface Transportation Reauthorization/Passage.** Passage of the bill that would bring the total authorization for federal-aid highway, mass transit, safety and research programs, including fiscal 2004 funds, to $295 billion through 2009. The bill includes $234 billion for highway programs and $54 billion for public transportation programs. It would increase the rate of return to states on their Highway Trust Fund contributions to 92 percent by 2009. Passed 89-11: R 46-9; D 42-2 (ND 38-2, SD 4-0); I 1-0. A "nay" was a vote in support of the president's position. (Before passage, the Senate adopted the Inhofe substitute by voice vote.) May 17, 2005.

| | 123 | 124 | 125 | | | 123 | 124 | 125 |
|---|---|---|---|---|---|---|---|---|
| **ALABAMA** | | | | | **MONTANA** | | | |
| Shelby | N | N | Y | | Baucus | Y | N | Y |
| Sessions | N | Y | Y | | Burns | N | N | Y |
| **ALASKA** | | | | | **NEBRASKA** | | | |
| Stevens | N | N | Y | | Hagel | N | Y | Y |
| Murkowski | N | N | Y | | Nelson | N | N | Y |
| **ARIZONA** | | | | | **NEVADA** | | | |
| McCain | N | Y | N | | Reid | N | N | Y |
| Kyl | Y | Y | N | | Ensign | Y | N | Y |
| **ARKANSAS** | | | | | **NEW HAMPSHIRE** | | | |
| Lincoln | N | N | Y | | Gregg | Y | Y | N |
| Pryor | N | N | Y | | Sununu | Y | Y | N |
| **CALIFORNIA** | | | | | **NEW JERSEY** | | | |
| Feinstein | N | N | Y | | Corzine | N | N | Y |
| Boxer | N | N | Y | | Lautenberg | N | N | Y |
| **COLORADO** | | | | | **NEW MEXICO** | | | |
| Allard | N | N | Y | | Domenici | N | N | Y |
| Salazar | N | N | Y | | Bingaman | N | N | Y |
| **CONNECTICUT** | | | | | **NEW YORK** | | | |
| Dodd | N | N | Y | | Schumer | N | N | Y |
| Lieberman | N | N | Y | | Clinton | N | N | Y |
| **DELAWARE** | | | | | **NORTH CAROLINA** | | | |
| Biden | N | N | Y | | Dole | N | N | Y |
| Carper | N | N | Y | | Burr | N | Y | Y |
| **FLORIDA** | | | | | **NORTH DAKOTA** | | | |
| Nelson | Y | N | Y | | Conrad | N | N | Y |
| Martinez | N | N | Y | | Dorgan | N | N | Y |
| **GEORGIA** | | | | | **OHIO** | | | |
| Chambliss | N | N | Y | | DeWine | N | N | Y |
| Isakson | N | N | Y | | Voinovich | N | N | Y |
| **HAWAII** | | | | | **OKLAHOMA** | | | |
| Inouye | N | N | Y | | Inhofe | N | N | Y |
| Akaka | N | N | Y | | Coburn | N | Y | Y |
| **IDAHO** | | | | | **OREGON** | | | |
| Craig | N | N | Y | | Wyden | N | N | Y |
| Crapo | N | N | Y | | Smith | N | N | Y |
| **ILLINOIS** | | | | | **PENNSYLVANIA** | | | |
| Durbin | N | N | Y | | Specter | N | N | Y |
| Obama | N | N | Y | | Santorum | N | N | Y |
| **INDIANA** | | | | | **RHODE ISLAND** | | | |
| Lugar | Y | N | Y | | Reed | N | N | Y |
| Bayh | N | N | Y | | Chafee | N | N | Y |
| **IOWA** | | | | | **SOUTH CAROLINA** | | | |
| Grassley | N | N | Y | | Graham | N | Y | N |
| Harkin | N | N | Y | | DeMint | N | Y | N |
| **KANSAS** | | | | | **SOUTH DAKOTA** | | | |
| Brownback | N | Y | N | | Johnson | N | N | Y |
| Roberts | N | N | Y | | Thune | N | N | Y |
| **KENTUCKY** | | | | | **TENNESSEE** | | | |
| McConnell | N | N | Y | | Frist | N | Y | Y |
| Bunning | N | N | Y | | Alexander | Y | N | Y |
| **LOUISIANA** | | | | | **TEXAS** | | | |
| Landrieu | N | N | Y | | Hutchison | N | Y | N |
| Vitter | Y | N | Y | | Cornyn | N | Y | N |
| **MAINE** | | | | | **UTAH** | | | |
| Snowe | Y | N | Y | | Hatch | N | N | Y |
| Collins | Y | N | Y | | Bennett | N | N | Y |
| **MARYLAND** | | | | | **VERMONT** | | | |
| Sarbanes | N | N | Y | | Leahy | N | N | Y |
| Mikulski | N | N | Y | | Jeffords | N | N | Y |
| **MASSACHUSETTS** | | | | | **VIRGINIA** | | | |
| Kennedy | N | N | Y | | Warner | N | N | Y |
| Kerry | N | N | Y | | Allen | Y | N | Y |
| **MICHIGAN** | | | | | **WASHINGTON** | | | |
| Levin | N | N | Y | | Murray | N | N | Y |
| Stabenow | N | N | Y | | Cantwell | N | N | Y |
| **MINNESOTA** | | | | | **WEST VIRGINIA** | | | |
| Dayton | N | N | Y | | Byrd | N | N | Y |
| Coleman | N | N | Y | | Rockefeller | N | N | Y |
| **MISSISSIPPI** | | | | | **WISCONSIN** | | | |
| Cochran | N | N | Y | | Kohl | N | N | N |
| Lott | N | N | Y | | Feingold | Y | N | N |
| **MISSOURI** | | | | | **WYOMING** | | | |
| Bond | Y | N | Y | | Thomas | N | Y | Y |
| Talent | N | N | Y | | Enzi | N | Y | Y |

**KEY**    **Republicans**    Democrats    *Independents*

| | | | | | | |
|---|---|---|---|---|---|---|
| Y | Voted for (yea) | X | Paired against | C | Voted "present" to avoid possible conflict of interest | |
| # | Paired for | – | Announced against | | | |
| + | Announced for | P | Voted "present" | ? | Did not vote or otherwise make a position known | |
| N | Voted against (nay) | | | | | |

# IN THE SENATE | By Vote Number

**126.** **Procedural Motion/Require Attendance.** Frist, R-Tenn., motion to instruct the sergeant at arms to request the attendance of absent senators. Motion agreed to 90-1: R 49-1; D 40-0 (ND 37-0, SD 3-0); I 1-0. May 23, 2005.

**127.** **Owen Nomination/Cloture.** Motion to invoke cloture (thus limiting debate) on President Bush's nomination of Priscilla R. Owen of Texas to be a judge for the U.S. Court of Appeals for the 5th Circuit. Motion agreed to 81-18: R 55-0; D 26-17 (ND 23-16, SD 3-1); I 0-1. Three-fifths of the total Senate (60) is required to invoke cloture. May 24, 2005.

**128.** **Owen Nomination/Confirmation.** Confirmation of President Bush's nomination of Priscilla R. Owen of Texas to be a judge for the U.S. Court of Appeals for the 5th Circuit. Confirmed 55-43: R 53-1; D 2-41 (ND 1-38, SD 1-3); I 0-1. A "yea" was a vote in support of the president's position. May 25, 2005.

**129.** **Bolton Nomination/Cloture.** Motion to invoke cloture (thus limiting debate) on President Bush's nomination of John R. Bolton of Maryland to be the permanent U.S. representative to the United Nations. Motion rejected 56-42: R 53-1; D 3-40 (ND 1-38, SD 2-2); I 0-1. Three-fifths of the total Senate (60) is required to invoke cloture. A "yea" was a vote in support of the president's position. May 26, 2005.

| | 126 | 127 | 128 | 129 | | 126 | 127 | 128 | 129 |
|---|---|---|---|---|---|---|---|---|---|
| **ALABAMA** | | | | | **MONTANA** | | | | |
| Shelby | Y | Y | Y | Y | Baucus | Y | Y | N | N |
| Sessions | Y | Y | Y | Y | Burns | Y | Y | Y | Y |
| **ALASKA** | | | | | **NEBRASKA** | | | | |
| Stevens | Y | Y | P | Y | Hagel | Y | Y | Y | Y |
| Murkowski | ? | Y | Y | Y | Nelson | Y | Y | N | Y |
| **ARIZONA** | | | | | **NEVADA** | | | | |
| McCain | Y | Y | Y | Y | Reid | Y | Y | N | N |
| Kyl | Y | Y | Y | Y | Ensign | Y | Y | Y | Y |
| **ARKANSAS** | | | | | **NEW HAMPSHIRE** | | | | |
| Lincoln | ? | N | N | N | Gregg | ? | Y | Y | Y |
| Pryor | Y | Y | N | Y | Sununu | Y | Y | Y | Y |
| **CALIFORNIA** | | | | | **NEW JERSEY** | | | | |
| Feinstein | Y | Y | N | N | Corzine | Y | N | N | N |
| Boxer | Y | N | N | N | Lautenberg | Y | N | N | N |
| **COLORADO** | | | | | **NEW MEXICO** | | | | |
| Allard | Y | Y | Y | Y | Domenici | Y | Y | Y | Y |
| Salazar | Y | Y | N | N | Bingaman | Y | Y | N | N |
| **CONNECTICUT** | | | | | **NEW YORK** | | | | |
| Dodd | Y | N | N | N | Schumer | Y | Y | N | N |
| Lieberman | Y | Y | N | N | Clinton | Y | Y | N | N |
| **DELAWARE** | | | | | **NORTH CAROLINA** | | | | |
| Biden | Y | N | N | N | Dole | Y | Y | Y | Y |
| Carper | Y | Y | N | N | Burr | Y | Y | Y | Y |
| **FLORIDA** | | | | | **NORTH DAKOTA** | | | | |
| Nelson | Y | Y | N | N | Conrad | Y | Y | N | N |
| Martinez | Y | Y | Y | Y | Dorgan | Y | N | N | N |
| **GEORGIA** | | | | | **OHIO** | | | | |
| Chambliss | Y | Y | Y | Y | DeWine | Y | Y | Y | Y |
| Isakson | Y | Y | Y | Y | Voinovich | Y | Y | Y | Y |
| **HAWAII** | | | | | **OKLAHOMA** | | | | |
| Inouye | ? | ? | – | ? | Inhofe | Y | Y | Y | Y |
| Akaka | Y | Y | N | N | Coburn | Y | Y | Y | Y |
| **IDAHO** | | | | | **OREGON** | | | | |
| Craig | Y | Y | Y | Y | Wyden | Y | Y | N | N |
| Crapo | Y | Y | Y | Y | Smith | Y | Y | Y | Y |
| **ILLINOIS** | | | | | **PENNSYLVANIA** | | | | |
| Durbin | Y | Y | N | N | Specter | Y | Y | Y | ? |
| Obama | Y | N | N | N | Santorum | Y | Y | Y | Y |
| **INDIANA** | | | | | **RHODE ISLAND** | | | | |
| Lugar | Y | Y | Y | Y | Reed | Y | N | N | N |
| Bayh | Y | Y | N | N | Chafee | Y | Y | N | Y |
| **IOWA** | | | | | **SOUTH CAROLINA** | | | | |
| Grassley | Y | Y | Y | Y | Graham | Y | Y | Y | Y |
| Harkin | Y | Y | N | N | DeMint | Y | Y | Y | Y |
| **KANSAS** | | | | | **SOUTH DAKOTA** | | | | |
| Brownback | Y | Y | Y | Y | Johnson | Y | Y | N | N |
| Roberts | Y | Y | Y | Y | Thune | Y | Y | Y | Y |
| **KENTUCKY** | | | | | **TENNESSEE** | | | | |
| McConnell | Y | Y | Y | Y | Frist | Y | Y | Y | N |
| Bunning | Y | Y | Y | Y | Alexander | Y | Y | Y | Y |
| **LOUISIANA** | | | | | **TEXAS** | | | | |
| Landrieu | Y | Y | Y | Y | Hutchison | Y | Y | Y | Y |
| Vitter | Y | Y | Y | Y | Cornyn | + | Y | Y | Y |
| **MAINE** | | | | | **UTAH** | | | | |
| Snowe | Y | Y | Y | Y | Hatch | Y | Y | Y | Y |
| Collins | Y | Y | Y | Y | Bennett | Y | Y | Y | Y |
| **MARYLAND** | | | | | **VERMONT** | | | | |
| Sarbanes | Y | N | N | N | Leahy | Y | Y | N | N |
| Mikulski | Y | Y | N | N | Jeffords | Y | N | N | N |
| **MASSACHUSETTS** | | | | | **VIRGINIA** | | | | |
| Kennedy | ? | N | N | N | Warner | Y | Y | Y | Y |
| Kerry | Y | N | N | N | Allen | N | Y | Y | Y |
| **MICHIGAN** | | | | | **WASHINGTON** | | | | |
| Levin | Y | N | N | N | Murray | Y | N | N | N |
| Stabenow | Y | N | N | N | Cantwell | Y | N | N | N |
| **MINNESOTA** | | | | | **WEST VIRGINIA** | | | | |
| Dayton | ? | N | N | N | Byrd | Y | Y | Y | N |
| Coleman | Y | Y | Y | Y | Rockefeller | Y | Y | N | N |
| **MISSISSIPPI** | | | | | **WISCONSIN** | | | | |
| Cochran | ? | Y | Y | Y | Kohl | Y | Y | N | N |
| Lott | ? | Y | Y | Y | Feingold | Y | N | N | N |
| **MISSOURI** | | | | | **WYOMING** | | | | |
| Bond | Y | Y | Y | Y | Thomas | Y | Y | Y | Y |
| Talent | Y | Y | Y | Y | Enzi | Y | Y | Y | Y |

**KEY**    Republicans    Democrats    *Independents*

| | | | |
|---|---|---|---|
| **Y** Voted for (yea) | **X** Paired against | **C** Voted "present" to avoid possible conflict of interest |
| **#** Paired for | **–** Announced against | |
| **+** Announced for | **P** Voted "present" | **?** Did not vote or otherwise make a position known |
| **N** Voted against (nay) | | |

# IN THE SENATE | By Vote Number

**130. Brown Nomination/Cloture.** Motion to invoke cloture (thus limiting debate) on President Bush's nomination of Janice R. Brown of California to be a judge for the U.S. Court of Appeals for the District of Columbia Circuit. Motion agreed to 65-32: R 55-0; D 10-32 (ND 7-31, SD 3-1); I 0-0. Three-fifths of the total Senate (60) is required to invoke cloture. June 7, 2005.

**131. Brown Nomination/Confirmation.** Confirmation of President Bush's nomination of Janice R. Brown of California to be a judge for the U.S. Court of Appeals for the District of Columbia Circuit. Confirmed 56-43: R 55-0; D 1-43 (ND 1-39, SD 0-4); I 0-0. A "yea" was a vote in support of the president's position. June 8, 2005.

**132. Pryor Nomination/Cloture.** Motion to invoke cloture (thus limiting debate) on President Bush's nomination of William H. Pryor Jr. of Alabama to be a judge for the U.S. Court of Appeals for the 11th Circuit. Motion agreed to 67-32: R 55-0; D 12-32 (ND 9-31, SD 3-1); I 0-0. Three-fifths of the total Senate (60) is required to invoke cloture. June 8, 2005.

**133. Pryor Nomination/Confirmation.** Confirmation of President Bush's nomination of William H. Pryor Jr. of Alabama to be a judge for the U.S. Court of Appeals for the 11th Circuit. Confirmed 53-45: R 51-3; D 2-42 (ND 2-38, SD 0-4); I 0-0. A "yea" was a vote in support of the president's position. June 9, 2005.

**134. Griffin Nomination/Confirmation.** Confirmation of President Bush's nomination of Richard A. Griffin of Michigan to be a judge for the U.S. Court of Appeals for the 6th Circuit. Confirmed 95-0: R 53-0; D 42-0 (ND 38-0, SD 4-0); I 0-0. A "yea" was a vote in support of the president's position. June 9, 2005.

**135. McKeague Nomination/Confirmation.** Confirmation of President Bush's nomination of David W. McKeague of Michigan to be a judge for the U.S. Court of Appeals for the 6th Circuit. Confirmed 96-0: R 53-0; D 43-0 (ND 39-0, SD 4-0); I 0-0. A "yea" was a vote in support of the president's position. June 9, 2005.

| | 130 | 131 | 132 | 133 | 134 | 135 | | | 130 | 131 | 132 | 133 | 134 | 135 |
|---|---|---|---|---|---|---|---|---|---|---|---|---|---|---|
| **ALABAMA** | | | | | | | | **MONTANA** | | | | | | |
| Shelby | Y | Y | Y | Y | Y | Y | | Baucus | N | N | N | N | Y | Y |
| Sessions | Y | Y | Y | Y | Y | Y | | Burns | Y | Y | Y | Y | Y | Y |
| **ALASKA** | | | | | | | | **NEBRASKA** | | | | | | |
| Stevens | Y | Y | Y | Y | Y | Y | | Hagel | Y | Y | Y | Y | Y | Y |
| Murkowski | Y | Y | Y | ? | ? | ? | | Nelson | Y | Y | Y | Y | Y | Y |
| **ARIZONA** | | | | | | | | **NEVADA** | | | | | | |
| McCain | Y | Y | Y | Y | Y | Y | | Reid | N | N | N | N | Y | Y |
| Kyl | Y | Y | Y | Y | Y | Y | | Ensign | Y | Y | Y | Y | Y | Y |
| **ARKANSAS** | | | | | | | | **NEW HAMPSHIRE** | | | | | | |
| Lincoln | N | N | N | N | Y | Y | | Gregg | Y | Y | Y | Y | Y | Y |
| Pryor | Y | N | Y | N | Y | Y | | Sununu | Y | Y | Y | Y | Y | Y |
| **CALIFORNIA** | | | | | | | | **NEW JERSEY** | | | | | | |
| Feinstein | N | N | N | N | Y | Y | | Corzine | N | N | N | N | Y | Y |
| Boxer | N | N | N | N | Y | Y | | Lautenberg | ? | N | N | N | Y | Y |
| **COLORADO** | | | | | | | | **NEW MEXICO** | | | | | | |
| Allard | Y | Y | Y | Y | Y | Y | | Domenici | Y | Y | Y | Y | Y | Y |
| Salazar | Y | N | Y | Y | Y | Y | | Bingaman | N | N | N | N | Y | Y |
| **CONNECTICUT** | | | | | | | | **NEW YORK** | | | | | | |
| Dodd | N | N | N | N | Y | Y | | Schumer | N | N | N | N | Y | Y |
| Lieberman | Y | N | Y | N | Y | Y | | Clinton | N | N | N | N | Y | Y |
| **DELAWARE** | | | | | | | | **NORTH CAROLINA** | | | | | | |
| Biden | N | N | N | N | + | + | | Dole | Y | Y | Y | Y | Y | Y |
| Carper | Y | N | Y | N | Y | Y | | Burr | Y | Y | Y | Y | Y | Y |
| **FLORIDA** | | | | | | | | **NORTH DAKOTA** | | | | | | |
| Nelson | Y | N | Y | N | Y | Y | | Conrad | N | N | N | N | Y | Y |
| Martinez | Y | Y | Y | Y | Y | Y | | Dorgan | N | N | N | N | Y | Y |
| **GEORGIA** | | | | | | | | **OHIO** | | | | | | |
| Chambliss | Y | Y | Y | Y | Y | Y | | DeWine | Y | Y | Y | Y | Y | Y |
| Isakson | Y | Y | Y | Y | Y | Y | | Voinovich | Y | Y | Y | Y | Y | Y |
| **HAWAII** | | | | | | | | **OKLAHOMA** | | | | | | |
| Inouye | Y | N | Y | N | Y | Y | | Inhofe | Y | Y | Y | Y | Y | Y |
| Akaka | N | N | N | N | Y | Y | | Coburn | Y | Y | Y | Y | Y | Y |
| **IDAHO** | | | | | | | | **OREGON** | | | | | | |
| Craig | Y | Y | Y | Y | Y | Y | | Wyden | N | N | N | N | Y | Y |
| Crapo | Y | Y | Y | Y | Y | Y | | Smith | Y | Y | Y | Y | Y | Y |
| **ILLINOIS** | | | | | | | | **PENNSYLVANIA** | | | | | | |
| Durbin | N | N | N | N | Y | Y | | Specter | Y | Y | Y | Y | Y | Y |
| Obama | N | N | N | N | ? | Y | | Santorum | Y | Y | Y | Y | Y | Y |
| **INDIANA** | | | | | | | | **RHODE ISLAND** | | | | | | |
| Lugar | Y | Y | Y | Y | Y | Y | | Reed | N | N | N | N | Y | Y |
| Bayh | N | N | N | N | Y | Y | | Chafee | Y | Y | Y | N | Y | Y |
| **IOWA** | | | | | | | | **SOUTH CAROLINA** | | | | | | |
| Grassley | Y | Y | Y | Y | Y | Y | | Graham | Y | Y | Y | Y | Y | Y |
| Harkin | N | N | N | N | Y | Y | | DeMint | Y | Y | Y | Y | Y | Y |
| **KANSAS** | | | | | | | | **SOUTH DAKOTA** | | | | | | |
| Brownback | Y | Y | Y | Y | Y | Y | | Johnson | N | N | Y | N | Y | Y |
| Roberts | Y | Y | Y | Y | Y | Y | | Thune | Y | Y | Y | Y | Y | Y |
| **KENTUCKY** | | | | | | | | **TENNESSEE** | | | | | | |
| McConnell | Y | Y | Y | Y | Y | Y | | Frist | Y | Y | Y | Y | Y | Y |
| Bunning | Y | Y | Y | Y | Y | Y | | Alexander | Y | Y | Y | Y | ? | ? |
| **LOUISIANA** | | | | | | | | **TEXAS** | | | | | | |
| Landrieu | Y | N | Y | N | Y | Y | | Hutchison | Y | Y | Y | Y | Y | Y |
| Vitter | Y | Y | Y | Y | Y | Y | | Cornyn | Y | Y | Y | Y | Y | Y |
| **MAINE** | | | | | | | | **UTAH** | | | | | | |
| Snowe | Y | Y | Y | N | Y | Y | | Hatch | Y | Y | Y | Y | Y | Y |
| Collins | Y | Y | Y | N | Y | Y | | Bennett | Y | Y | Y | Y | Y | Y |
| **MARYLAND** | | | | | | | | **VERMONT** | | | | | | |
| Sarbanes | N | N | N | N | Y | Y | | Leahy | N | N | N | N | Y | Y |
| Mikulski | N | N | N | N | Y | Y | | Jeffords | ? | ? | ? | ? | ? | ? |
| **MASSACHUSETTS** | | | | | | | | **VIRGINIA** | | | | | | |
| Kennedy | N | N | N | N | Y | Y | | Warner | Y | Y | Y | Y | Y | Y |
| Kerry | N | N | N | N | Y | Y | | Allen | Y | Y | Y | Y | Y | Y |
| **MICHIGAN** | | | | | | | | **WASHINGTON** | | | | | | |
| Levin | N | N | N | N | Y | Y | | Murray | N | N | N | N | Y | Y |
| Stabenow | N | N | N | N | Y | Y | | Cantwell | N | N | N | N | Y | Y |
| **MINNESOTA** | | | | | | | | **WEST VIRGINIA** | | | | | | |
| Dayton | N | N | N | N | Y | Y | | Byrd | Y | N | Y | N | Y | Y |
| Coleman | Y | Y | Y | Y | Y | Y | | Rockefeller | N | N | N | N | Y | Y |
| **MISSISSIPPI** | | | | | | | | **WISCONSIN** | | | | | | |
| Cochran | Y | Y | Y | Y | Y | Y | | Kohl | ? | N | N | N | Y | Y |
| Lott | Y | Y | Y | Y | Y | Y | | Feingold | N | N | N | N | Y | Y |
| **MISSOURI** | | | | | | | | **WYOMING** | | | | | | |
| Bond | Y | Y | Y | Y | Y | Y | | Thomas | Y | Y | Y | Y | Y | Y |
| Talent | Y | Y | Y | Y | Y | Y | | Enzi | Y | Y | Y | Y | Y | Y |

**KEY** Republicans   Democrats   *Independents*

| | | | |
|---|---|---|---|
| Y | Voted for (yea) | X | Paired against | C | Voted "present" to avoid possible conflict of interest |
| # | Paired for | – | Announced against | |
| + | Announced for | P | Voted "present" | ? | Did not vote or otherwise make a position known |
| N | Voted against (nay) | | | |

# IN THE SENATE | By Vote Number

**136.** **Griffith Nomination/Confirmation.** Confirmation of President Bush's nomination of Thomas B. Griffith of Utah to be a judge for the U.S. Court of Appeals for the District of Columbia Circuit. Confirmed 73-24: R 53-0; D 20-24 (ND 17-23, SD 3-1); I 0-0. A "yea" was a vote in support of the president's position. June 14, 2005.

**137.** **HR 6. Energy Policy/Ethanol Liability.** Domenici, R-N.M., motion to table (kill) the Boxer, D-Calif., amendment to the Domenici amendment. The Boxer amendment would strike a provision in the underlying amendment that would provide liability protection for ethanol manufacturers. The Domenici amendment would require refiners to annually use 8 billion gallons of renewable fuels by 2012, grant liability protection for ethanol manufacturers, phase out the use of gasoline additive methyl tertiary butyl ether and eliminate the oxygen content requirement for reformulated gasoline. Motion agreed to 59-38: R 45-9; D 14-28 (ND 11-27, SD 3-1); I 0-1. June 14, 2005.

**138.** **HR 6. Energy Policy/Ethanol Mandate.** Domenici, R-N.M., motion to table (kill) the Schumer, D-N.Y., amendment to the Domenici amendment. The Schumer amendment would strike a section in the underlying amendment that would require refiners to annually use 8 billion gallons of renewable fuels, most likely ethanol, by 2012. Motion agreed to 69-28: R 39-14; D 30-14 (ND 26-14, SD 4-0); I 0-0. June 15, 2005.

**139.** **HR 6. Energy Policy/Renewable Fuel Mandate.** Domenici, R-N.M., amendment that would require refiners to annually use 8 billion gallons of renewable fuels by 2012, grant liability protection for ethanol manufacturers, phase out the use of the gasoline additive methyl tertiary butyl ether and eliminate the oxygen content requirement for reformulated gasoline. Adopted 70-26: R 38-14; D 32-12 (ND 28-12, SD 4-0); I 0-0. June 15, 2005.

**140.** **HR 6. Energy Policy/Foreign Oil Dependence.** Cantwell, D-Wash., amendment that would call on the president to develop and implement measures to reduce 40 percent foreign petroleum imports projected for 2025. It also would require the president to submit an annual report to Congress that would assess the progress made toward achieving that goal. Rejected 47-53: R 3-52; D 43-1 (ND 39-1, SD 4-0); I 1-0. June 16, 2005.

**141.** **HR 6. Energy Policy/Electric Utilities.** Bingaman, D-N.M., amendment that would mandate that at least 10 percent of the electricity sold by electric utilities by 2020 must be produced from renewable energy sources, beginning with a minimum annual standard of 2.5 percent for calendar years 2008 through 2011. Adopted 52-48: R 9-46; D 42-2 (ND 38-2, SD 4-0); I 1-0. June 16, 2005.

| | 136 | 137 | 138 | 139 | 140 | 141 |
|---|---|---|---|---|---|---|
| **ALABAMA** | | | | | | |
| Shelby | Y | Y | Y | N | N | N |
| Sessions | Y | Y | Y | N | N | N |
| **ALASKA** | | | | | | |
| Stevens | Y | Y | ? | ? | N | N |
| Murkowski | Y | Y | ? | ? | N | N |
| **ARIZONA** | | | | | | |
| McCain | Y | N | N | N | N | N |
| Kyl | Y | Y | N | N | N | N |
| **ARKANSAS** | | | | | | |
| Lincoln | Y | Y | Y | Y | Y | Y |
| Pryor | Y | Y | Y | Y | Y | Y |
| **CALIFORNIA** | | | | | | |
| Feinstein | Y | – | N | N | Y | Y |
| Boxer | N | N | N | N | Y | Y |
| **COLORADO** | | | | | | |
| Allard | Y | Y | N | N | N | N |
| Salazar | N | Y | Y | Y | Y | Y |
| **CONNECTICUT** | | | | | | |
| Dodd | Y | N | N | Y | Y | Y |
| Lieberman | Y | N | N | N | Y | Y |
| **DELAWARE** | | | | | | |
| Biden | Y | N | Y | Y | Y | Y |
| Carper | Y | N | Y | Y | Y | Y |
| **FLORIDA** | | | | | | |
| Nelson | Y | N | Y | Y | Y | Y |
| Martinez | Y | Y | Y | Y | N | N |
| **GEORGIA** | | | | | | |
| Chambliss | Y | Y | Y | N | N | N |
| Isakson | Y | Y | Y | N | N | N |
| **HAWAII** | | | | | | |
| Inouye | Y | N | Y | Y | Y | Y |
| Akaka | N | N | Y | Y | Y | Y |
| **IDAHO** | | | | | | |
| Craig | Y | Y | Y | N | N | N |
| Crapo | Y | Y | Y | ? | N | N |
| **ILLINOIS** | | | | | | |
| Durbin | Y | N | Y | Y | Y | Y |
| Obama | Y | N | Y | Y | Y | Y |
| **INDIANA** | | | | | | |
| Lugar | Y | Y | Y | Y | N | N |
| Bayh | N | Y | Y | Y | Y | Y |
| **IOWA** | | | | | | |
| Grassley | Y | Y | Y | Y | N | N |
| Harkin | N | Y | Y | Y | Y | Y |
| **KANSAS** | | | | | | |
| Brownback | Y | Y | Y | Y | N | N |
| Roberts | Y | Y | Y | N | N | N |
| **KENTUCKY** | | | | | | |
| McConnell | Y | Y | Y | Y | N | N |
| Bunning | Y | Y | Y | Y | N | N |
| **LOUISIANA** | | | | | | |
| Landrieu | N | Y | Y | Y | Y | Y |
| Vitter | Y | Y | Y | Y | N | N |
| **MAINE** | | | | | | |
| Snowe | Y | N | N | Y | Y | Y |
| Collins | Y | N | N | Y | Y | Y |
| **MARYLAND** | | | | | | |
| Sarbanes | N | N | Y | Y | Y | Y |
| Mikulski | N | N | N | Y | Y | Y |
| **MASSACHUSETTS** | | | | | | |
| Kennedy | N | N | N | N | Y | Y |
| Kerry | N | N | Y | Y | Y | Y |
| **MICHIGAN** | | | | | | |
| Levin | Y | N | Y | Y | Y | Y |
| Stabenow | N | Y | Y | Y | N | Y |
| **MINNESOTA** | | | | | | |
| Dayton | N | N | Y | Y | Y | Y |
| Coleman | Y | Y | Y | Y | N | Y |
| **MISSISSIPPI** | | | | | | |
| Cochran | Y | Y | Y | Y | N | N |
| Lott | Y | Y | N | N | N | N |
| **MISSOURI** | | | | | | |
| Bond | Y | Y | Y | Y | N | N |
| Talent | Y | Y | Y | Y | N | N |
| **MONTANA** | | | | | | |
| Baucus | Y | Y | Y | Y | N | N |
| Burns | Y | Y | Y | Y | N | N |
| **NEBRASKA** | | | | | | |
| Hagel | Y | Y | Y | Y | N | N |
| Nelson | Y | Y | Y | Y | Y | Y |
| **NEVADA** | | | | | | |
| Reid | Y | N | Y | Y | Y | Y |
| Ensign | Y | N | N | N | N | N |
| **NEW HAMPSHIRE** | | | | | | |
| Gregg | Y | N | N | N | N | N |
| Sununu | Y | N | N | N | N | N |
| **NEW JERSEY** | | | | | | |
| Corzine | N | ? | N | N | Y | Y |
| Lautenberg | N | N | N | N | Y | Y |
| **NEW MEXICO** | | | | | | |
| Domenici | Y | Y | Y | Y | N | N |
| Bingaman | Y | N | Y | Y | Y | Y |
| **NEW YORK** | | | | | | |
| Schumer | Y | N | N | N | Y | Y |
| Clinton | N | N | N | N | N | Y |
| **NORTH CAROLINA** | | | | | | |
| Dole | Y | Y | Y | N | N | N |
| Burr | Y | Y | Y | N | N | N |
| **NORTH DAKOTA** | | | | | | |
| Conrad | Y | Y | Y | Y | Y | Y |
| Dorgan | Y | Y | Y | Y | Y | Y |
| **OHIO** | | | | | | |
| DeWine | Y | ? | Y | Y | N | N |
| Voinovich | Y | Y | Y | Y | N | N |
| **OKLAHOMA** | | | | | | |
| Inhofe | Y | Y | N | N | N | N |
| Coburn | Y | Y | N | N | N | N |
| **OREGON** | | | | | | |
| Wyden | N | N | N | N | Y | Y |
| Smith | Y | Y | Y | Y | N | Y |
| **PENNSYLVANIA** | | | | | | |
| Specter | ? | N | N | N | Y | Y |
| Santorum | ? | N | N | N | N | N |
| **RHODE ISLAND** | | | | | | |
| Reed | N | N | N | N | Y | Y |
| Chafee | Y | N | N | Y | Y | Y |
| **SOUTH CAROLINA** | | | | | | |
| Graham | Y | Y | Y | N | N | N |
| DeMint | Y | Y | Y | N | N | N |
| **SOUTH DAKOTA** | | | | | | |
| Johnson | N | Y | Y | Y | Y | Y |
| Thune | Y | Y | Y | Y | N | N |
| **TENNESSEE** | | | | | | |
| Frist | Y | Y | Y | N | N | N |
| Alexander | Y | Y | Y | N | N | N |
| **TEXAS** | | | | | | |
| Hutchison | Y | Y | Y | Y | N | N |
| Cornyn | Y | Y | Y | Y | N | N |
| **UTAH** | | | | | | |
| Hatch | Y | Y | Y | Y | N | N |
| Bennett | Y | Y | Y | Y | N | N |
| **VERMONT** | | | | | | |
| Leahy | N | N | N | N | Y | Y |
| *Jeffords* | ? | N | ? | ? | Y | Y |
| **VIRGINIA** | | | | | | |
| Warner | Y | N | N | N | N | N |
| Allen | Y | Y | Y | N | N | N |
| **WASHINGTON** | | | | | | |
| Murray | N | N | Y | Y | Y | Y |
| Cantwell | N | N | Y | Y | Y | Y |
| **WEST VIRGINIA** | | | | | | |
| Byrd | N | N | Y | Y | Y | N |
| Rockefeller | N | Y | N | N | Y | Y |
| **WISCONSIN** | | | | | | |
| Kohl | Y | Y | Y | Y | Y | Y |
| Feingold | N | N | N | N | Y | Y |
| **WYOMING** | | | | | | |
| Thomas | Y | Y | Y | N | N | N |
| Enzi | Y | Y | Y | N | N | N |

**KEY**   Republicans   Democrats   *Independents*

| | | |
|---|---|---|
| Y Voted for (yea) | X Paired against | C Voted "present" to avoid possible conflict of interest |
| # Paired for | – Announced against | |
| + Announced for | P Voted "present" | ? Did not vote or otherwise make a position known |
| N Voted against (nay) | | |

# IN THE SENATE | By Vote Number

**142. Bolton Nomination/Cloture.** Motion to invoke cloture (thus limiting debate) on President Bush's nomination of John R. Bolton to be the permanent U.S. representative to the United Nations. Motion rejected 54-38: R 51-1; D 3-36 (ND 1-34, SD 2-2); I 0-1. Three-fifths of the total Senate (60) is required to invoke cloture. June 20, 2005.

**143. HR 6. Energy Policy/Outer Continental Shelf Inventory.** Martinez, R-Fla., amendment that would strike a section in the bill directing the Interior Department to make an assessment of oil and natural gas resources in the Outer Continental Shelf. Rejected 44-52: R 12-42; D 31-10 (ND 30-7, SD 1-3); I 1-0. June 21, 2005.

**144. HR 6. Energy Policy/Climate Change.** Hagel, R-Neb., amendment that would direct the Energy secretary to lead an interagency process to implement a national climate change strategy and authorize such sums as necessary for projects using technologies that reduce greenhouse gases. It would establish an interagency working group to promote exports of greenhouse gas-reducing technology to developing countries. Adopted 66-29: R 47-7; D 19-22 (ND 16-21, SD 3-1); I 0-0. June 21, 2005.

**145. HR 6. Energy Policy/Diesel Emissions.** Voinovich, R-Ohio, amendment that would authorize $1 billion over five years to establish voluntary national and state-level grant and loan programs to promote the reduction of diesel emissions. Adopted 92-1: R 53-1; D 39-0 (ND 35-0, SD 4-0); I 0-0. June 21, 2005.

**146. HR 6. Energy Policy/Liquefied Natural Gas Terminals.** Domenici, R-N.M., motion to table (kill) the Feinstein, D-Calif., amendment that would prohibit the Federal Energy Regulatory Commission from approving an application for a liquefied natural gas terminal located on shore or in state waters without the approval of the state's governor. Motion agreed to 52-45: R 44-10; D 8-34 (ND 6-32, SD 2-2); I 0-1. June 22, 2005.

**147. HR 6. Energy Policy/Gas Prices.** Domenici, R-N.M., motion to table (kill) the Schumer, D-N.Y., amendment that would express the sense of the Senate that the president should challenge the Organization of Petroleum Exporting Countries to immediately increase oil production, and require that 1 million barrels of oil a day be released from the Strategic Petroleum Reserve for 30 days after the bill's enactment. Motion agreed to 57-39: R 51-3; D 6-35 (ND 5-32, SD 1-3); I 0-1. June 22, 2005.

| | 142 | 143 | 144 | 145 | 146 | 147 | | 142 | 143 | 144 | 145 | 146 | 147 |
|---|---|---|---|---|---|---|---|---|---|---|---|---|---|
| **ALABAMA** | | | | | | | **MONTANA** | | | | | | |
| Shelby | Y | N | Y | Y | Y | Y | Baucus | N | N | Y | Y | Y | Y |
| **Sessions** | Y | N | Y | Y | N | Y | **Burns** | ? | N | Y | Y | Y | Y |
| **ALASKA** | | | | | | | **NEBRASKA** | | | | | | |
| Stevens | Y | N | Y | Y | Y | Y | Hagel | Y | N | Y | Y | Y | Y |
| **Murkowski** | Y | N | Y | Y | Y | Y | Nelson | Y | N | Y | Y | Y | N |
| **ARIZONA** | | | | | | | **NEVADA** | | | | | | |
| McCain | Y | Y | N | Y | Y | Y | Reid | N | Y | Y | Y | N | N |
| Kyl | Y | N | Y | Y | Y | Y | **Ensign** | Y | N | Y | Y | Y | Y |
| **ARKANSAS** | | | | | | | **NEW HAMPSHIRE** | | | | | | |
| Lincoln | N | N | Y | Y | Y | N | Gregg | Y | N | N | Y | Y | Y |
| Pryor | Y | N | Y | Y | Y | N | Sununu | Y | Y | N | Y | N | Y |
| **CALIFORNIA** | | | | | | | **NEW JERSEY** | | | | | | |
| Feinstein | N | Y | Y | Y | N | N | Corzine | N | Y | N | Y | N | N |
| Boxer | N | Y | N | Y | N | N | Lautenberg | N | Y | N | ? | N | N |
| **COLORADO** | | | | | | | **NEW MEXICO** | | | | | | |
| Allard | Y | N | Y | Y | Y | Y | Domenici | Y | N | Y | Y | Y | Y |
| Salazar | N | N | Y | Y | Y | N | Bingaman | N | N | Y | Y | Y | Y |
| **CONNECTICUT** | | | | | | | **NEW YORK** | | | | | | |
| Dodd | N | Y | N | Y | N | N | Schumer | N | Y | Y | Y | N | N |
| Lieberman | N | Y | N | Y | N | N | Clinton | N | Y | Y | Y | N | N |
| **DELAWARE** | | | | | | | **NORTH CAROLINA** | | | | | | |
| Biden | N | Y | N | Y | N | N | Dole | Y | Y | Y | Y | Y | Y |
| Carper | N | N | N | Y | N | N | Burr | Y | Y | Y | Y | Y | Y |
| **FLORIDA** | | | | | | | **NORTH DAKOTA** | | | | | | |
| Nelson | N | Y | Y | Y | N | N | Conrad | N | N | Y | ? | ? | ? |
| **Martinez** | Y | Y | Y | Y | N | Y | Dorgan | N | ? | ? | ? | Y | N |
| **GEORGIA** | | | | | | | **OHIO** | | | | | | |
| Chambliss | Y | N | Y | Y | Y | Y | DeWine | Y | N | Y | Y | Y | Y |
| Isakson | Y | N | Y | Y | Y | Y | Voinovich | N | N | Y | Y | Y | Y |
| **HAWAII** | | | | | | | **OKLAHOMA** | | | | | | |
| Inouye | N | Y | N | Y | N | ? | Inhofe | Y | N | Y | Y | Y | Y |
| Akaka | N | Y | N | Y | N | N | Coburn | Y | N | Y | Y | Y | Y |
| **IDAHO** | | | | | | | **OREGON** | | | | | | |
| Craig | Y | N | Y | Y | Y | Y | Wyden | N | Y | N | Y | N | N |
| Crapo | Y | N | Y | Y | Y | Y | **Smith** | Y | Y | Y | Y | N | N |
| **ILLINOIS** | | | | | | | **PENNSYLVANIA** | | | | | | |
| Durbin | N | Y | N | Y | N | N | Specter | Y | N | Y | Y | Y | N |
| Obama | N | Y | N | Y | N | N | Santorum | Y | N | Y | Y | Y | Y |
| **INDIANA** | | | | | | | **RHODE ISLAND** | | | | | | |
| Lugar | Y | N | Y | Y | Y | Y | Reed | N | Y | N | Y | N | N |
| Bayh | N | Y | Y | Y | N | Y | Chafee | Y | Y | N | Y | N | Y |
| **IOWA** | | | | | | | **SOUTH CAROLINA** | | | | | | |
| Grassley | Y | N | Y | Y | Y | Y | Graham | Y | Y | Y | Y | Y | Y |
| Harkin | N | Y | N | Y | N | N | DeMint | Y | Y | Y | Y | Y | Y |
| **KANSAS** | | | | | | | **SOUTH DAKOTA** | | | | | | |
| Brownback | Y | N | Y | Y | Y | Y | Johnson | ? | ? | ? | ? | ? | ? |
| Roberts | Y | N | Y | Y | Y | Y | Thune | ? | ? | ? | ? | ? | ? |
| **KENTUCKY** | | | | | | | **TENNESSEE** | | | | | | |
| McConnell | Y | N | Y | Y | Y | Y | Frist | Y | N | Y | Y | Y | Y |
| Bunning | Y | N | N | Y | Y | Y | Alexander | Y | N | Y | Y | Y | Y |
| **LOUISIANA** | | | | | | | **TEXAS** | | | | | | |
| Landrieu | Y | N | Y | Y | N | Y | Hutchison | Y | N | Y | Y | Y | Y |
| **Vitter** | Y | N | Y | Y | N | Y | Cornyn | Y | N | Y | Y | Y | Y |
| **MAINE** | | | | | | | **UTAH** | | | | | | |
| Snowe | Y | Y | N | Y | N | N | Hatch | Y | N | Y | Y | Y | Y |
| Collins | Y | Y | N | Y | N | N | Bennett | Y | N | Y | Y | Y | Y |
| **MARYLAND** | | | | | | | **VERMONT** | | | | | | |
| Sarbanes | N | Y | N | Y | N | N | Leahy | N | Y | N | Y | N | N |
| Mikulski | N | Y | Y | Y | N | N | Jeffords | N | Y | ? | ? | N | N |
| **MASSACHUSETTS** | | | | | | | **VIRGINIA** | | | | | | |
| Kennedy | N | Y | N | Y | N | N | Warner | Y | N | Y | Y | Y | Y |
| Kerry | ? | ? | ? | ? | N | N | Allen | Y | N | Y | Y | Y | Y |
| **MICHIGAN** | | | | | | | **WASHINGTON** | | | | | | |
| Levin | ? | Y | Y | Y | N | N | Murray | N | Y | Y | Y | N | Y |
| Stabenow | N | Y | Y | Y | N | N | Cantwell | N | Y | N | Y | N | Y |
| **MINNESOTA** | | | | | | | **WEST VIRGINIA** | | | | | | |
| Dayton | N | Y | Y | Y | N | N | Byrd | N | N | N | Y | N | N |
| **Coleman** | + | Y | Y | Y | Y | N | Rockefeller | N | Y | Y | Y | N | N |
| **MISSISSIPPI** | | | | | | | **WISCONSIN** | | | | | | |
| Cochran | Y | N | Y | Y | Y | Y | Kohl | ? | Y | N | Y | Y | N |
| Lott | Y | N | Y | Y | Y | Y | Feingold | ? | Y | N | Y | N | N |
| **MISSOURI** | | | | | | | **WYOMING** | | | | | | |
| Bond | Y | N | Y | Y | Y | Y | Thomas | Y | N | Y | Y | Y | Y |
| Talent | Y | N | Y | Y | Y | Y | Enzi | Y | N | Y | Y | N | Y |

**KEY**   Republicans   Democrats   *Independents*

| | | | | |
|---|---|---|---|---|
| Y | Voted for (yea) | X | Paired against | C  Voted "present" to avoid possible conflict of interest |
| # | Paired for | – | Announced against | |
| + | Announced for | P | Voted "present" | ?  Did not vote or otherwise make a position known |
| N | Voted against (nay) | | | |

# IN THE SENATE | By Vote Number

**148.** **HR 6. Energy Policy/Climate Change.** McCain, R-Ariz., amendment that would cap greenhouse gas emissions at 2000 levels by 2010. It would provide for the trading of emission allowances and reductions through a government-provided greenhouse gas database that would contain an inventory of emissions and a registry of reductions. Rejected 38-60: R 6-49; D 31-11 (ND 30-8, SD 1-3); I 1-0. A "nay" was a vote in support of the president's position. June 22, 2005.

**149.** **HR 6. Energy Policy/Climate Change.** Inhofe, R-Okla., motion to table (kill) the Bingaman, D-N.M., amendment that would express the sense of the Senate that Congress should enact a national program of mandatory, market-based limits and incentives on greenhouse gas emissions that slow, stop and reverse their growth at a rate that would not harm the economy significantly, and would encourage comparable action by other nations. Motion rejected 44-53: R 42-12; D 2-40 (ND 2-36, SD 0-4); I 0-1. (Subsequently, the amendment was adopted by voice vote.) A "yea" was a vote in support of the president's position. June 22, 2005.

**150.** **HR 6. Energy Policy/Wind Power Projects.** Alexander, R-Tenn., amendment that would bar subsidies for all wind power projects within 20 miles of highly scenic areas and federal land, including national parks, lakeshores and wildlife refuges. Environmental impact statements for all projects within 20 miles of such areas would be required and communities would be given six months notice before a project is permitted. Rejected 32-63: R 31-23; D 1-40 (ND 0-37, SD 1-3); I 0-0. June 22, 2005.

**151.** **HR 6. Energy Policy/Climate Change.** Kerry, D-Mass., amendment that would express the sense of the Senate that the United States should act to reduce the health, environmental and economic risks posed by global climate change and foster sustained economic growth through new technologies by engaging in international negotiations under the United Nations Framework Convention of Climate Change. Rejected 46-49: R 7-47; D 39-2 (ND 37-0, SD 2-2); I 0-0. June 22, 2005.

**152.** **HR 6. Energy Policy/Cloture.** Domenici, R-N.M., motion to invoke cloture on the bill that would overhaul the nation's energy policy and provide for approximately $18 billion in energy-related tax incentives. It would require refiners to annually use 8 billion gallons of renewable fuels by 2012, grant liability protection for ethanol manufacturers and phase out the use of the gasoline additive methyl tertiary butyl ether. Motion agreed to 92-4: R 53-1; D 38-3 (ND 34-3, SD 4-0); I 1-0. Three-fifths of the total Senate (60) is required to invoke cloture. June 23, 2005.

| | 148 | 149 | 150 | 151 | 152 | | | 148 | 149 | 150 | 151 | 152 |
|---|---|---|---|---|---|---|---|---|---|---|---|---|
| **ALABAMA** | | | | | | | **MONTANA** | | | | | |
| Shelby | N | Y | N | N | Y | | Baucus | N | Y | N | Y | Y |
| Sessions | N | Y | Y | N | Y | | Burns | N | Y | Y | N | Y |
| **ALASKA** | | | | | | | **NEBRASKA** | | | | | |
| Stevens | N | Y | Y | N | Y | | Hagel | N | Y | N | N | Y |
| Murkowski | N | Y | Y | N | Y | | Nelson | N | Y | N | Y | Y |
| **ARIZONA** | | | | | | | **NEVADA** | | | | | |
| McCain | Y | N | Y | Y | N | | Reid | Y | N | N | Y | Y |
| Kyl | N | Y | Y | N | Y | | Ensign | N | Y | Y | N | Y |
| **ARKANSAS** | | | | | | | **NEW HAMPSHIRE** | | | | | |
| Lincoln | N | N | Y | Y | Y | | Gregg | Y | N | Y | Y | Y |
| Pryor | N | N | N | N | Y | | Sununu | N | Y | Y | N | Y |
| **CALIFORNIA** | | | | | | | **NEW JERSEY** | | | | | |
| Feinstein | Y | N | N | Y | Y | | Corzine | Y | N | N | Y | N |
| Boxer | N | N | N | Y | Y | | Lautenberg | Y | N | N | Y | N |
| **COLORADO** | | | | | | | **NEW MEXICO** | | | | | |
| Allard | N | Y | N | N | Y | | Domenici | N | N | Y | N | Y |
| Salazar | Y | N | N | Y | Y | | Bingaman | Y | N | N | Y | Y |
| **CONNECTICUT** | | | | | | | **NEW YORK** | | | | | |
| Dodd | Y | N | N | Y | Y | | Schumer | Y | N | N | Y | Y |
| Lieberman | Y | N | N | Y | Y | | Clinton | Y | N | N | Y | Y |
| **DELAWARE** | | | | | | | **NORTH CAROLINA** | | | | | |
| Biden | Y | N | N | Y | Y | | Dole | N | Y | N | N | Y |
| Carper | Y | N | N | Y | Y | | Burr | N | Y | Y | N | Y |
| **FLORIDA** | | | | | | | **NORTH DAKOTA** | | | | | |
| Nelson | Y | N | N | Y | Y | | Conrad | ? | ? | ? | ? | ? |
| Martinez | N | Y | Y | N | Y | | Dorgan | ? | ? | ? | ? | ? |
| **GEORGIA** | | | | | | | **OHIO** | | | | | |
| Chambliss | N | Y | N | N | Y | | DeWine | N | N | Y | N | Y |
| Isakson | N | Y | N | N | Y | | Voinovich | N | Y | Y | N | Y |
| **HAWAII** | | | | | | | **OKLAHOMA** | | | | | |
| Inouye | Y | N | N | Y | Y | | Inhofe | N | Y | N | N | Y |
| Akaka | Y | N | N | Y | Y | | Coburn | N | Y | N | N | Y |
| **IDAHO** | | | | | | | **OREGON** | | | | | |
| Craig | N | Y | N | N | Y | | Wyden | Y | N | N | Y | Y |
| Crapo | N | Y | N | N | Y | | Smith | N | Y | N | Y | Y |
| **ILLINOIS** | | | | | | | **PENNSYLVANIA** | | | | | |
| Durbin | Y | N | N | Y | N | | Specter | N | N | N | N | Y |
| Obama | Y | N | N | Y | Y | | Santorum | N | Y | N | N | Y |
| **INDIANA** | | | | | | | **RHODE ISLAND** | | | | | |
| Lugar | Y | N | Y | Y | Y | | Reed | Y | N | N | Y | Y |
| Bayh | Y | N | N | Y | Y | | Chafee | Y | N | N | Y | Y |
| **IOWA** | | | | | | | **SOUTH CAROLINA** | | | | | |
| Grassley | N | Y | N | N | Y | | Graham | N | N | Y | N | Y |
| Harkin | N | N | N | Y | Y | | DeMint | N | Y | Y | N | Y |
| **KANSAS** | | | | | | | **SOUTH DAKOTA** | | | | | |
| Brownback | N | Y | Y | N | Y | | Johnson | Y | N | N | Y | Y |
| Roberts | N | Y | N | N | Y | | Thune | N | Y | N | N | Y |
| **KENTUCKY** | | | | | | | **TENNESSEE** | | | | | |
| McConnell | N | Y | Y | N | Y | | Frist | N | Y | Y | N | Y |
| Bunning | N | Y | Y | N | Y | | Alexander | N | N | Y | N | Y |
| **LOUISIANA** | | | | | | | **TEXAS** | | | | | |
| Landrieu | N | N | Y | N | Y | | Hutchison | N | Y | N | N | Y |
| Vitter | N | Y | Y | N | Y | | Cornyn | N | Y | N | N | Y |
| **MAINE** | | | | | | | **UTAH** | | | | | |
| Snowe | Y | N | N | Y | Y | | Hatch | N | Y | N | N | Y |
| Collins | Y | N | N | Y | Y | | Bennett | N | Y | N | N | Y |
| **MARYLAND** | | | | | | | **VERMONT** | | | | | |
| Sarbanes | Y | N | N | Y | Y | | Leahy | Y | N | N | Y | Y |
| Mikulski | Y | N | N | Y | Y | | *Jeffords* | Y | N | ? | ? | Y |
| **MASSACHUSETTS** | | | | | | | **VIRGINIA** | | | | | |
| Kennedy | Y | N | N | Y | Y | | Warner | N | N | Y | N | Y |
| Kerry | Y | N | N | Y | Y | | Allen | N | Y | Y | N | Y |
| **MICHIGAN** | | | | | | | **WASHINGTON** | | | | | |
| Levin | N | N | N | Y | Y | | Murray | Y | N | N | Y | Y |
| Stabenow | Y | N | N | Y | Y | | Cantwell | Y | N | N | Y | Y |
| **MINNESOTA** | | | | | | | **WEST VIRGINIA** | | | | | |
| Dayton | N | N | ? | ? | ? | | Byrd | N | N | N | Y | Y |
| Coleman | N | - | - | - | + | | Rockefeller | Y | N | N | Y | Y |
| **MISSISSIPPI** | | | | | | | **WISCONSIN** | | | | | |
| Cochran | N | Y | Y | N | Y | | Kohl | Y | N | N | Y | Y |
| Lott | N | Y | Y | N | Y | | Feingold | N | N | N | Y | Y |
| **MISSOURI** | | | | | | | **WYOMING** | | | | | |
| Bond | N | Y | N | N | Y | | Thomas | N | Y | N | N | Y |
| Talent | N | Y | Y | N | Y | | Enzi | N | Y | N | N | Y |

**KEY**   Republicans   Democrats   *Independents*

| | | | | |
|---|---|---|---|---|
| Y | Voted for (yea) | X | Paired against | C Voted "present" to avoid possible conflict of interest |
| # | Paired for | – | Announced against | |
| + | Announced for | P | Voted "present" | ? Did not vote or otherwise make a position known |
| N | Voted against (nay) | | | |

# IN THE SENATE | By Vote Number

**153.** HR 6. **Energy Policy/Coastal Impact Assistance Program.** Vitter, R-La., motion to waive the Budget Act with respect to the Gregg, R-N.H., point of order against the Domenici, R-N.M., amendment. The Domenici amendment would provide $250 million per year for fiscal 2007 through 2010 from existing royalties to six coastal states that have offshore oil and gas facilities. Motion agreed to 69-26: R 32-21; D 36-5 (ND 32-5, SD 4-0); I 1-0. A three-fifths majority (60) of the total Senate is required to waive the Budget Act. (Subsequently, the amendment was adopted by voice vote.) June 23, 2005.

**154.** HR 6. **Energy Policy/Medical Isotope Production.** Schumer, D-N.Y., amendment that would strike a provision related to the production of medical isotopes. Adopted 52-46: R 15-39; D 37-6 (ND 36-3, SD 1-3); I 0-1. June 23, 2005.

**155.** HR 6. **Energy Policy/Federal Loan Guarantees.** Sununu, R-N.H., amendment that would strike a provision that would provide incentives in the form of loan guarantees for the development of innovative technology such as those used in nuclear power plants. Rejected 21-76: R 9-44; D 12-31 (ND 12-27, SD 0-4); I 0-1. June 23, 2005.

**156.** HR 6. **Energy Policy/Fuel Economy Standards.** Bond, R-Mo., amendment that would require the Transportation secretary to consider several factors, including technological feasibility and economic practicability, when determining the Corporate Average Fuel (CAFE) Economy standards. It would direct the secretary to issue an environmental assessment of the effects of increased fuel efficiency standards on the environment and would authorize $5 million annually from fiscal 2006 through 2010 for it. Adopted 64-31: R 46-7; D 18-23 (ND 15-22, SD 3-1); I 0-1. June 23, 2005.

**157.** HR 6. **Energy Policy/Fuel Economy Standards.** Durbin, D-Ill., amendment that would mandate phased increases in the CAFE standards. Passenger vehicles made before 2008 would have to average 25 miles per gallon. The standard would gradually increase to 40 mpg by model year 2016. Non-passenger vehicles made before 2008 would have to average 17 mpg. By model year 2016, the standard would rise to an average of 27.5 mpg. Rejected 28-67: R 5-48; D 22-19 (ND 21-16, SD 1-3); I 1-0. A "nay" was a vote in support of the president's position. June 23, 2005.

| | 153 | 154 | 155 | 156 | 157 |
|---|---|---|---|---|---|
| **ALABAMA** | | | | | |
| Shelby | Y | N | N | Y | N |
| Sessions | Y | N | N | Y | N |
| **ALASKA** | | | | | |
| Stevens | ? | N | N | Y | N |
| Murkowski | Y | N | N | Y | N |
| **ARIZONA** | | | | | |
| McCain | N | Y | Y | N | N |
| Kyl | N | Y | Y | Y | N |
| **ARKANSAS** | | | | | |
| Lincoln | Y | N | N | Y | N |
| Pryor | Y | N | N | Y | N |
| **CALIFORNIA** | | | | | |
| Feinstein | Y | Y | N | N | Y |
| Boxer | Y | Y | Y | N | + |
| **COLORADO** | | | | | |
| Allard | N | N | Y | Y | N |
| Salazar | Y | Y | N | Y | N |
| **CONNECTICUT** | | | | | |
| Dodd | Y | Y | N | ? | Y |
| Lieberman | Y | Y | N | N | Y |
| **DELAWARE** | | | | | |
| Biden | Y | Y | N | N | N |
| Carper | Y | N | N | Y | Y |
| **FLORIDA** | | | | | |
| Nelson | Y | Y | N | N | Y |
| Martinez | Y | Y | N | Y | N |
| **GEORGIA** | | | | | |
| Chambliss | N | N | N | Y | N |
| Isakson | N | N | N | Y | N |
| **HAWAII** | | | | | |
| Inouye | Y | Y | N | ? | ? |
| Akaka | Y | Y | N | N | Y |
| **IDAHO** | | | | | |
| Craig | Y | N | N | Y | N |
| Crapo | N | N | N | Y | N |
| **ILLINOIS** | | | | | |
| Durbin | Y | Y | Y | N | Y |
| Obama | Y | Y | N | N | Y |
| **INDIANA** | | | | | |
| Lugar | N | Y | N | Y | Y |
| Bayh | Y | Y | N | Y | N |
| **IOWA** | | | | | |
| Grassley | Y | N | N | Y | N |
| Harkin | N | Y | Y | N | Y |
| **KANSAS** | | | | | |
| Brownback | Y | N | N | Y | N |
| Roberts | Y | N | N | Y | N |
| **KENTUCKY** | | | | | |
| McConnell | N | N | N | Y | N |
| Bunning | N | N | N | Y | N |
| **LOUISIANA** | | | | | |
| Landrieu | Y | N | N | Y | N |
| Vitter | Y | Y | N | Y | N |
| **MAINE** | | | | | |
| Snowe | Y | Y | Y | N | Y |
| Collins | N | Y | Y | N | Y |
| **MARYLAND** | | | | | |
| Sarbanes | Y | Y | Y | N | Y |
| Mikulski | Y | Y | Y | Y | N |
| **MASSACHUSETTS** | | | | | |
| Kennedy | Y | Y | Y | N | Y |
| Kerry | Y | Y | N | N | N |
| **MICHIGAN** | | | | | |
| Levin | Y | Y | N | Y | N |
| Stabenow | Y | Y | N | Y | N |
| **MINNESOTA** | | | | | |
| Dayton | ? | Y | N | Y | Y |
| Coleman | + | N | N | Y | N |
| **MISSISSIPPI** | | | | | |
| Cochran | Y | N | N | Y | N |
| Lott | Y | Y | N | ? | ? |
| **MISSOURI** | | | | | |
| Bond | Y | N | N | Y | N |
| Talent | Y | N | N | Y | N |
| **MONTANA** | | | | | |
| Baucus | Y | N | N | Y | N |
| Burns | N | N | N | Y | N |
| **NEBRASKA** | | | | | |
| Hagel | Y | N | N | Y | N |
| Nelson | Y | Y | N | Y | N |
| **NEVADA** | | | | | |
| Reid | Y | Y | N | N | Y |
| Ensign | Y | Y | ? | Y | N |
| **NEW HAMPSHIRE** | | | | | |
| Gregg | N | Y | Y | N | N |
| Sununu | N | Y | Y | N | N |
| **NEW JERSEY** | | | | | |
| Corzine | Y | Y | Y | N | Y |
| Lautenberg | Y | Y | Y | N | Y |
| **NEW MEXICO** | | | | | |
| Domenici | Y | ? | ? | ? | ? |
| Bingaman | Y | ? | ? | ? | ? |
| **NEW YORK** | | | | | |
| Schumer | Y | Y | N | Y | N |
| Clinton | Y | Y | N | N | N |
| **NORTH CAROLINA** | | | | | |
| Dole | Y | N | N | Y | N |
| Burr | Y | N | N | Y | N |
| **NORTH DAKOTA** | | | | | |
| Conrad | ? | Y | N | Y | N |
| Dorgan | ? | Y | N | Y | N |
| **OHIO** | | | | | |
| DeWine | Y | N | N | Y | N |
| Voinovich | Y | N | N | Y | N |
| **OKLAHOMA** | | | | | |
| Inhofe | N | N | N | Y | N |
| Coburn | N | N | N | Y | N |
| **OREGON** | | | | | |
| Wyden | N | Y | Y | N | Y |
| Smith | Y | N | Y | Y | N |
| **PENNSYLVANIA** | | | | | |
| Specter | N | Y | N | Y | N |
| Santorum | N | Y | N | Y | N |
| **RHODE ISLAND** | | | | | |
| Reed | Y | Y | Y | N | Y |
| Chafee | N | N | N | N | Y |
| **SOUTH CAROLINA** | | | | | |
| Graham | Y | N | N | Y | N |
| DeMint | N | N | Y | Y | N |
| **SOUTH DAKOTA** | | | | | |
| Johnson | Y | N | N | Y | N |
| Thune | Y | N | N | Y | N |
| **TENNESSEE** | | | | | |
| Frist | Y | N | N | Y | N |
| Alexander | Y | Y | N | Y | N |
| **TEXAS** | | | | | |
| Hutchison | Y | N | N | Y | N |
| Cornyn | Y | Y | N | Y | N |
| **UTAH** | | | | | |
| Hatch | Y | N | N | Y | N |
| Bennett | Y | N | N | Y | N |
| **VERMONT** | | | | | |
| Leahy | N | Y | N | N | Y |
| Jeffords | Y | N | N | N | Y |
| **VIRGINIA** | | | | | |
| Warner | Y | N | N | Y | N |
| Allen | Y | N | N | Y | N |
| **WASHINGTON** | | | | | |
| Murray | Y | Y | N | N | Y |
| Cantwell | Y | Y | N | N | Y |
| **WEST VIRGINIA** | | | | | |
| Byrd | N | Y | N | Y | N |
| Rockefeller | Y | Y | N | N | Y |
| **WISCONSIN** | | | | | |
| Kohl | Y | Y | N | Y | N |
| Feingold | N | Y | Y | Y | N |
| **WYOMING** | | | | | |
| Thomas | N | N | N | Y | N |
| Enzi | N | N | N | Y | N |

**KEY**   Republicans   Democrats   *Independents*

| | | |
|---|---|---|
| **Y** Voted for (yea) | **X** Paired against | **C** Voted "present" to avoid possible conflict of interest |
| **#** Paired for | **–** Announced against | |
| **+** Announced for | **P** Voted "present" | **?** Did not vote or otherwise make a position known |
| **N** Voted against (nay) | | |

# IN THE SENATE | By Vote Number

**158. HR 6. Energy Policy/Passage.** Passage of the bill that would overhaul the nation's energy policy and provide for about $18 billion in energy-related tax incentives. It would require refiners to use 8 billion gallons of renewable fuels per year by 2012, grant liability protection for ethanol manufacturers and phase out the use of the gasoline additive methyl tertiary butyl ether. It also would direct the Energy secretary to lead an interagency process to implement a national climate change strategy and authorize funding for projects using technologies that reduce greenhouse gases. Passed 85-12: R 49-5; D 35-7 (ND 32-6, SD 3-1); I 1-0. A "yea" was a vote in support of the president's position. June 28, 2005.

**159. HR 2361. Fiscal 2006 Interior-Environment Appropriations/ Indian Health Funding.** Coburn, R-Okla., motion to waive the Budget Act with respect to the Burns, R-Mont., point of order against the Coburn amendment. The Coburn amendment would reduce funding for land acquisition by $121 million, to $33 million, and transfer the money to the Indian Health Service. Motion rejected 17-75: R 10-41; D 7-33 (ND 7-29, SD 0-4); I 0-1. A three-fifths majority (60) of the total Senate is required to waive the Budget Act. (Subsequently, the chair upheld the point of order, and the amendment fell.) June 28, 2005.

**160. HR 2361. Fiscal 2006 Interior-Environment Appropriations/ Conference Report Language.** Coburn, R-Okla., amendment that would require that any limitation, directive or earmark be included in the bill's conference report to give both chambers the opportunity to vote on all provisions. Rejected 33-59: R 13-38; D 20-20 (ND 18-18, SD 2-2); I 0-1. June 28, 2005.

**161. HR 2361 Fiscal 2006 Interior-Environment Appropriations/ Pesticide Testing.** Burns, R-Mont., amendment that would direct the EPA administrator to conduct a review of all third-party intentional human dosing studies. It also would direct the administrator to issue a final rule within 180 days of enactment that addresses the application of ethical standards to third-party studies involving intentional human dosing to identify or quantify toxic effects. Adopted 57-40: R 49-4; D 8-35 (ND 5-34, SD 3-1); I 0-1. June 29, 2005.

**162. HR 2361. Fiscal 2006 Interior-Environment Appropriations/ Pesticide Testing.** Boxer, D-Calif., amendment that would prohibit the EPA administrator from using fiscal 2006 funds to accept, consider or rely on third-party intentional human studies on the effects of pesticides or to conduct intentional human dosing studies of pesticides. Adopted 60-37: R 16-37; D 43-0 (ND 39-0, SD 4-0); I 1-0. June 29, 2005.

| | 158 | 159 | 160 | 161 | 162 | | 158 | 159 | 160 | 161 | 162 |
|---|---|---|---|---|---|---|---|---|---|---|---|
| **ALABAMA** | | | | | | **MONTANA** | | | | | |
| Shelby | Y | N | Y | Y | N | Baucus | Y | N | N | Y | Y |
| Sessions | + | N | Y | Y | N | Burns | Y | N | N | Y | N |
| **ALASKA** | | | | | | **NEBRASKA** | | | | | |
| Stevens | Y | Y | N | Y | N | Hagel | Y | N | N | Y | N |
| Murkowski | Y | Y | N | Y | Y | Nelson | Y | Y | Y | Y | Y |
| **ARIZONA** | | | | | | **NEVADA** | | | | | |
| McCain | N | Y | Y | Y | Y | Reid | Y | Y | N | N | Y |
| Kyl | N | Y | Y | Y | Y | Ensign | Y | N | Y | Y | Y |
| **ARKANSAS** | | | | | | **NEW HAMPSHIRE** | | | | | |
| Lincoln | Y | N | N | Y | Y | Gregg | N | N | N | Y | N |
| Pryor | Y | N | N | Y | Y | Sununu | N | N | Y | Y | N |
| **CALIFORNIA** | | | | | | **NEW JERSEY** | | | | | |
| Feinstein | Y | N | Y | N | Y | Corzine | N | N | Y | N | Y |
| Boxer | Y | N | Y | N | Y | Lautenberg | N | N | N | N | Y |
| **COLORADO** | | | | | | **NEW MEXICO** | | | | | |
| Allard | Y | N | N | Y | N | Domenici | Y | N | N | Y | N |
| Salazar | Y | N | N | N | Y | Bingaman | Y | N | Y | N | Y |
| **CONNECTICUT** | | | | | | **NEW YORK** | | | | | |
| Dodd | ? | ? | ? | N | Y | Schumer | N | N | Y | N | Y |
| Lieberman | ? | ? | ? | ? | ? | Clinton | Y | N | Y | N | Y |
| **DELAWARE** | | | | | | **NORTH CAROLINA** | | | | | |
| Biden | Y | N | Y | N | Y | Dole | Y | ? | ? | Y | N |
| Carper | Y | N | N | N | Y | Burr | Y | ? | ? | Y | N |
| **FLORIDA** | | | | | | **NORTH DAKOTA** | | | | | |
| Nelson | N | N | Y | N | Y | Conrad | Y | Y | N | Y | Y |
| Martinez | N | N | N | Y | N | Dorgan | Y | Y | Y | Y | Y |
| **GEORGIA** | | | | | | **OHIO** | | | | | |
| Chambliss | Y | N | N | Y | N | DeWine | Y | N | N | Y | N |
| Isakson | Y | N | Y | Y | Y | Voinovich | Y | N | N | Y | N |
| **HAWAII** | | | | | | **OKLAHOMA** | | | | | |
| Inouye | Y | N | N | N | Y | Inhofe | Y | Y | Y | Y | N |
| Akaka | Y | Y | Y | N | Y | Coburn | Y | Y | Y | Y | Y |
| **IDAHO** | | | | | | **OREGON** | | | | | |
| Craig | Y | N | N | Y | N | Wyden | N | Y | N | Y | Y |
| Crapo | Y | N | N | Y | N | Smith | Y | N | N | Y | Y |
| **ILLINOIS** | | | | | | **PENNSYLVANIA** | | | | | |
| Durbin | Y | N | N | N | Y | Specter | Y | Y | Y | N | Y |
| Obama | Y | N | N | N | Y | Santorum | Y | N | N | Y | N |
| **INDIANA** | | | | | | **RHODE ISLAND** | | | | | |
| Lugar | Y | N | Y | ? | ? | Reed | N | N | N | N | Y |
| Bayh | Y | N | Y | N | Y | Chafee | Y | N | N | N | Y |
| **IOWA** | | | | | | **SOUTH CAROLINA** | | | | | |
| Grassley | Y | N | N | Y | N | Graham | Y | ? | ? | Y | Y |
| Harkin | Y | N | N | N | Y | DeMint | Y | ? | ? | Y | N |
| **KANSAS** | | | | | | **SOUTH DAKOTA** | | | | | |
| Brownback | Y | Y | N | Y | N | Johnson | Y | N | N | N | Y |
| Roberts | Y | N | N | Y | N | Thune | Y | Y | N | Y | Y |
| **KENTUCKY** | | | | | | **TENNESSEE** | | | | | |
| McConnell | Y | N | N | Y | N | Frist | Y | N | Y | Y | N |
| Bunning | Y | N | N | Y | N | Alexander | Y | N | Y | Y | N |
| **LOUISIANA** | | | | | | **TEXAS** | | | | | |
| Landrieu | Y | N | Y | Y | Y | Hutchison | Y | N | N | Y | Y |
| Vitter | Y | N | N | Y | N | Cornyn | Y | N | Y | Y | N |
| **MAINE** | | | | | | **UTAH** | | | | | |
| Snowe | Y | N | N | N | Y | Hatch | Y | N | N | Y | N |
| Collins | Y | N | N | N | Y | Bennett | Y | N | N | ? | ? |
| **MARYLAND** | | | | | | **VERMONT** | | | | | |
| Sarbanes | Y | N | N | N | Y | Leahy | Y | N | N | N | Y |
| Mikulski | Y | N | N | N | Y | Jeffords | Y | N | N | N | Y |
| **MASSACHUSETTS** | | | | | | **VIRGINIA** | | | | | |
| Kennedy | Y | Y | N | N | Y | Warner | Y | N | N | Y | Y |
| Kerry | Y | N | Y | N | Y | Allen | Y | N | N | Y | N |
| **MICHIGAN** | | | | | | **WASHINGTON** | | | | | |
| Levin | Y | N | Y | N | Y | Murray | Y | N | N | N | Y |
| Stabenow | Y | N | Y | N | Y | Cantwell | Y | N | Y | N | Y |
| **MINNESOTA** | | | | | | **WEST VIRGINIA** | | | | | |
| Dayton | Y | N | Y | N | Y | Byrd | Y | ? | ? | Y | Y |
| Coleman | Y | N | N | Y | N | Rockefeller | Y | ? | ? | N | Y |
| **MISSISSIPPI** | | | | | | **WISCONSIN** | | | | | |
| Cochran | Y | N | N | Y | N | Kohl | Y | N | Y | N | Y |
| Lott | Y | N | N | Y | N | Feingold | N | N | Y | N | Y |
| **MISSOURI** | | | | | | **WYOMING** | | | | | |
| Bond | Y | N | N | Y | N | Thomas | Y | N | N | Y | N |
| Talent | Y | N | N | Y | N | Enzi | Y | Y | N | Y | N |

| **KEY** | **Republicans** | Democrats | *Independents* | | | | |
|---|---|---|---|

| Y | Voted for (yea) | X | Paired against | C | Voted "present" to avoid possible conflict of interest |
|---|---|---|---|---|---|
| # | Paired for | − | Announced against | | |
| + | Announced for | P | Voted "present" | ? | Did not vote or otherwise make a position known |
| N | Voted against (nay) | | | | |

# IN THE SENATE | By Vote Number

**163.** HR 2361. Fiscal 2006 Interior-Environment Appropriations/ **Indian Health Care.** Dorgan, D-N.D., motion to waive the Budget Act with respect to the Burns, R-Mont., point of order against the Dorgan amendment. The Dorgan amendment would require the Federal Reserve banks to transfer $1 billion in fiscal 2006 from surplus funds to the general fund of the Treasury for Indian health care services. A three-fifths majority (60) of the total Senate is required to waive the Budget Act. (Subsequently, the chair upheld the point of order, and the amendment fell.) Motion rejected 47-51: R 3-51; D 43-0 (ND 39-0, SD 4-0); I 1-0. June 29, 2005.

**164.** HR 2361. Fiscal 2006 Interior-Environment Appropriations/ **Tongass National Forest.** Sununu, R-N.H., amendment that would prohibit the use of funds to plan, design, study or construct new roads in the Tongass National Forest in Alaska for the purpose of harvesting timber by private companies or individuals. Rejected 39-59: R 3-51; D 35-8 (ND 34-5, SD 1-3); I 1-0. June 29, 2005.

**165.** HR 2361. Fiscal 2006 Interior-Environment Appropriations/ **Veterans' Health Care Funding.** Santorum, R-Pa., amendment to the Murray, D-Wash., amendment. The Santorum amendment would appropriate $1.5 billion in supplemental fiscal 2005 funding to the Department of Veterans Affairs for medical services provided by the Veterans Health Administration (VHA). The Murray amendment would appropriate $1.42 billion in supplemental fiscal 2005 funding for the same purpose. Adopted 96-0: R 52-0; D 43-0 (ND 39-0, SD 4-0); I 1-0. June 29, 2005.

**166.** HR 2361. Fiscal 2006 Interior-Environment Appropriations/ **Veterans' Health Care Funding.** Murray, D-Wash., amendment, as amended, that would provide $1.5 billion in fiscal 2005 supplemental appropriations to the Department of Veterans Affairs for medical services provided by the VHA. Adopted 96-0: R 52-0; D 43-0 (ND 39-0, SD 4-0); I 1-0. June 29, 2005.

**167.** HR 2361 . Fiscal 2006 Interior-Environment Appropriations/ **Family Travel to Cuba.** Dorgan, D-N.D., motion to suspend the rule against legislating on an appropriations bill with respect to the Dorgan amendment. The Dorgan amendment would require the Treasury secretary to issue a general license to individuals subject to U.S. jurisdiction and their immediate families to travel to Cuba to visit immediate family for humanitarian reasons. Motion rejected 60-35: R 20-31; D 39-4 (ND 36-3, SD 3-1); I 1-0. A two-thirds majority of those present and voting (64 in this case) is required to suspend the rule. (Subsequently, a point of order was made and the amendment fell.) A "yea" was a vote in support of the president's position. June 29, 2005.

| | 163 | 164 | 165 | 166 | 167 |
|---|---|---|---|---|---|
| **ALABAMA** | | | | | |
| Shelby | N | N | Y | Y | N |
| Sessions | N | N | Y | Y | N |
| **ALASKA** | | | | | |
| Stevens | N | N | Y | Y | N |
| Murkowski | N | N | Y | Y | N |
| **ARIZONA** | | | | | |
| McCain | N | Y | ? | ? | ? |
| Kyl | N | N | Y | Y | Y |
| **ARKANSAS** | | | | | |
| Lincoln | Y | N | Y | Y | Y |
| Pryor | Y | N | Y | Y | Y |
| **CALIFORNIA** | | | | | |
| Feinstein | Y | Y | Y | Y | Y |
| Boxer | Y | Y | Y | Y | Y |
| **COLORADO** | | | | | |
| Allard | N | N | Y | Y | N |
| Salazar | Y | Y | Y | Y | Y |
| **CONNECTICUT** | | | | | |
| Dodd | Y | Y | Y | Y | Y |
| Lieberman | ? | ? | ? | ? | ? |
| **DELAWARE** | | | | | |
| Biden | Y | Y | Y | Y | Y |
| Carper | Y | Y | Y | Y | Y |
| **FLORIDA** | | | | | |
| Nelson | Y | Y | Y | Y | N |
| Martinez | N | N | ? | ? | X |
| **GEORGIA** | | | | | |
| Chambliss | N | N | Y | Y | N |
| Isakson | N | N | Y | Y | N |
| **HAWAII** | | | | | |
| Inouye | Y | N | Y | Y | Y |
| Akaka | Y | N | Y | Y | Y |
| **IDAHO** | | | | | |
| Craig | N | N | Y | Y | Y |
| Crapo | N | N | Y | Y | Y |
| **ILLINOIS** | | | | | |
| Durbin | Y | Y | Y | Y | Y |
| Obama | Y | Y | Y | Y | Y |
| **INDIANA** | | | | | |
| Lugar | N | N | Y | Y | Y |
| Bayh | Y | Y | Y | Y | Y |
| **IOWA** | | | | | |
| Grassley | N | N | Y | Y | N |
| Harkin | Y | Y | Y | Y | Y |
| **KANSAS** | | | | | |
| Brownback | N | N | Y | Y | N |
| Roberts | N | N | Y | Y | Y |
| **KENTUCKY** | | | | | |
| McConnell | N | N | Y | Y | N |
| Bunning | N | N | Y | Y | N |
| **LOUISIANA** | | | | | |
| Landrieu | Y | N | Y | Y | Y |
| Vitter | N | N | Y | Y | N |
| **MAINE** | | | | | |
| Snowe | N | N | Y | Y | N |
| Collins | N | N | Y | Y | Y |
| **MARYLAND** | | | | | |
| Sarbanes | Y | Y | Y | Y | Y |
| Mikulski | Y | Y | Y | Y | Y |
| **MASSACHUSETTS** | | | | | |
| Kennedy | Y | Y | Y | Y | Y |
| Kerry | Y | Y | Y | Y | Y |
| **MICHIGAN** | | | | | |
| Levin | Y | Y | Y | Y | Y |
| Stabenow | Y | Y | Y | Y | Y |
| **MINNESOTA** | | | | | |
| Dayton | Y | Y | Y | Y | Y |
| Coleman | Y | N | Y | N | N |
| **MISSISSIPPI** | | | | | |
| Cochran | N | N | Y | Y | N |
| Lott | N | N | Y | Y | N |
| **MISSOURI** | | | | | |
| Bond | N | N | Y | Y | Y |
| Talent | N | N | Y | Y | Y |
| **MONTANA** | | | | | |
| Baucus | Y | N | Y | Y | Y |
| Burns | N | N | Y | Y | N |
| **NEBRASKA** | | | | | |
| Hagel | N | N | Y | Y | Y |
| Nelson | Y | N | Y | Y | Y |
| **NEVADA** | | | | | |
| Reid | Y | Y | Y | Y | N |
| Ensign | N | N | Y | Y | N |
| **NEW HAMPSHIRE** | | | | | |
| Gregg | N | N | Y | Y | N |
| Sununu | N | Y | Y | Y | Y |
| **NEW JERSEY** | | | | | |
| Corzine | Y | Y | Y | Y | N |
| Lautenberg | Y | Y | Y | Y | N |
| **NEW MEXICO** | | | | | |
| Domenici | N | N | Y | Y | N |
| Bingaman | Y | Y | Y | Y | Y |
| **NEW YORK** | | | | | |
| Schumer | Y | Y | Y | Y | Y |
| Clinton | Y | Y | Y | Y | Y |
| **NORTH CAROLINA** | | | | | |
| Dole | N | N | Y | Y | N |
| Burr | N | N | Y | Y | N |
| **NORTH DAKOTA** | | | | | |
| Conrad | Y | Y | Y | Y | Y |
| Dorgan | Y | Y | Y | Y | Y |
| **OHIO** | | | | | |
| DeWine | N | N | Y | Y | Y |
| Voinovich | N | N | Y | Y | N |
| **OKLAHOMA** | | | | | |
| Inhofe | N | N | Y | Y | N |
| Coburn | N | N | Y | Y | # |
| **OREGON** | | | | | |
| Wyden | Y | Y | Y | Y | Y |
| Smith | Y | Y | Y | Y | Y |
| **PENNSYLVANIA** | | | | | |
| Specter | N | N | Y | Y | N |
| Santorum | N | N | Y | Y | N |
| **RHODE ISLAND** | | | | | |
| Reed | Y | Y | Y | Y | Y |
| Chafee | N | Y | Y | Y | Y |
| **SOUTH CAROLINA** | | | | | |
| Graham | N | N | Y | Y | N |
| DeMint | N | N | Y | Y | N |
| **SOUTH DAKOTA** | | | | | |
| Johnson | Y | Y | Y | Y | Y |
| Thune | N | Y | Y | Y | Y |
| **TENNESSEE** | | | | | |
| Frist | N | N | Y | Y | N |
| Alexander | N | N | Y | Y | N |
| **TEXAS** | | | | | |
| Hutchison | N | N | Y | Y | N |
| Cornyn | N | N | Y | Y | N |
| **UTAH** | | | | | |
| Hatch | N | N | Y | Y | N |
| Bennett | ? | ? | ? | ? | ? |
| **VERMONT** | | | | | |
| Leahy | Y | Y | Y | Y | Y |
| Jeffords | Y | Y | Y | Y | Y |
| **VIRGINIA** | | | | | |
| Warner | N | N | Y | Y | Y |
| Allen | N | N | Y | Y | N |
| **WASHINGTON** | | | | | |
| Murray | Y | Y | Y | Y | Y |
| Cantwell | Y | Y | Y | Y | Y |
| **WEST VIRGINIA** | | | | | |
| Byrd | Y | N | Y | Y | Y |
| Rockefeller | Y | Y | Y | Y | Y |
| **WISCONSIN** | | | | | |
| Kohl | Y | Y | Y | Y | Y |
| Feingold | Y | Y | Y | Y | Y |
| **WYOMING** | | | | | |
| Thomas | N | N | Y | Y | N |
| Enzi | N | N | Y | Y | Y |

**KEY**  Republicans  Democrats  *Independents*

| | | |
|---|---|---|
| Y Voted for (yea) | X Paired against | C Voted "present" to avoid possible conflict of interest |
| # Paired for | – Announced against | |
| + Announced for | P Voted "present" | ? Did not vote or otherwise make a position known |
| N Voted against (nay) | | |

# IN THE SENATE | By Vote Number

**168.** **HR 2361. Fiscal 2006 Interior-Environment Appropriations/ Passage.** Passage of the bill that would provide $26.3 billion in fiscal 2006 for the Department of Interior and related agencies, including $9.9 billion for the Interior Department, $7.8 billion for the EPA and $4.1 billion for the Forest Service. It also would provide $1.5 billion in emergency fiscal 2005 funding for medical services provided by the Veterans Health Administration. Passed 94-0: R 50-0; D 43-0 (ND 39-0, SD 4-0); I 1-0. June 29, 2005.

**169.** **S 1307. Central American Free Trade Agreement/Motion to Proceed.** Frist, R-Tenn., motion to proceed to consideration of a bill that would implement a free trade agreement between the United States and Costa Rica, El Salvador, Guatemala, Honduras, Nicaragua and the Dominican Republic. Motion agreed to 61-34: R 46-5; D 14-29 (ND 12-27, SD 2-2); I 1-0. June 29, 2005.

**170.** **S 1307. Central American Free Trade Agreement/Passage.** Passage of the bill that would implement a free trade agreement between the United States and Costa Rica, El Salvador, Guatemala, Honduras, Nicaragua and a separate pact with the Dominican Republic. It also would eliminate customs duties on all originating goods traded among the participating nations within 10 days. Passed 54-45: R 43-12; D 10-33 (ND 7-32, SD 3-1); I 1-0. A "yea" was a vote in support of the president's position. June 30, 2005.

**171.** **HR 2419. Fiscal 2006 Energy and Water Appropriations/Nuclear Weapons Funding.** Feinstein, D-Calif., amendment that would prohibit the use of funds in the bill for any purpose related to the Robust Nuclear Earth Penetrator. It would stipulate that the funds appropriated for this purpose be used to reduce the national debt. Rejected 43-53: R 3-50; D 39-3 (ND 36-2, SD 3-1); I 1-0. A "nay" was a vote in support of the president's position. July 1, 2005 (in the session that began and the Congressional Record dated June 30, 2005).

**172.** **HR 2419. Fiscal 2006 Energy and Water Appropriations/Passage.** Passage of the bill that would provide $31.2 billion in fiscal 2006 for energy and water development projects, including $5.3 billion for the Army Corps of Engineers and $25 billion for the Energy Department. It also would provide $577 million for the Yucca Mountain nuclear waste repository. Passed 92-3: R 50-3; D 41-0 (ND 37-0, SD 4-0); I 1-0. July 1, 2005 (in the session that began and the Congressional Record dated June 30, 2005).

| | 168 | 169 | 170 | 171 | 172 | | | 168 | 169 | 170 | 171 | 172 |
|---|---|---|---|---|---|---|---|---|---|---|---|---|
| **ALABAMA** | | | | | | | **MONTANA** | | | | | |
| Shelby | Y | Y | N | N | Y | | Baucus | Y | Y | N | Y | Y |
| Sessions | Y | Y | Y | N | Y | | Burns | Y | Y | N | N | Y |
| **ALASKA** | | | | | | | **NEBRASKA** | | | | | |
| Stevens | Y | Y | Y | N | Y | | Hagel | Y | Y | Y | N | Y |
| Murkowski | Y | Y | Y | N | Y | | Nelson | Y | Y | Y | N | Y |
| **ARIZONA** | | | | | | | **NEVADA** | | | | | |
| McCain | ? | Y | Y | N | N | | Reid | Y | N | N | Y | Y |
| Kyl | Y | Y | Y | N | Y | | Ensign | Y | Y | Y | N | Y |
| **ARKANSAS** | | | | | | | **NEW HAMPSHIRE** | | | | | |
| Lincoln | Y | Y | Y | Y | Y | | Gregg | ? | ? | Y | N | Y |
| Pryor | Y | Y | Y | Y | Y | | Sununu | Y | Y | Y | N | N |
| **CALIFORNIA** | | | | | | | **NEW JERSEY** | | | | | |
| Feinstein | Y | Y | Y | Y | Y | | Corzine | Y | N | N | Y | Y |
| Boxer | Y | N | N | Y | Y | | Lautenberg | Y | N | N | Y | Y |
| **COLORADO** | | | | | | | **NEW MEXICO** | | | | | |
| Allard | Y | Y | Y | N | Y | | Domenici | Y | Y | Y | Y | Y |
| Salazar | Y | N | N | Y | Y | | Bingaman | Y | Y | Y | Y | Y |
| **CONNECTICUT** | | | | | | | **NEW YORK** | | | | | |
| Dodd | Y | Y | N | Y | Y | | Schumer | Y | N | N | Y | Y |
| Lieberman | ? | ? | ? | ? | ? | | Clinton | Y | N | N | Y | Y |
| **DELAWARE** | | | | | | | **NORTH CAROLINA** | | | | | |
| Biden | Y | N | N | Y | Y | | Dole | Y | Y | Y | N | Y |
| Carper | Y | Y | Y | Y | Y | | Burr | Y | Y | Y | N | Y |
| **FLORIDA** | | | | | | | **NORTH DAKOTA** | | | | | |
| Nelson | Y | N | Y | N | Y | | Conrad | Y | Y | N | Y | Y |
| Martinez | ? | ? | Y | N | Y | | Dorgan | Y | N | N | Y | Y |
| **GEORGIA** | | | | | | | **OHIO** | | | | | |
| Chambliss | Y | Y | Y | N | Y | | DeWine | Y | Y | Y | N | Y |
| Isakson | Y | Y | Y | N | Y | | Voinovich | Y | Y | Y | Y | Y |
| **HAWAII** | | | | | | | **OKLAHOMA** | | | | | |
| Inouye | Y | N | N | Y | Y | | Inhofe | Y | Y | Y | N | Y |
| Akaka | Y | N | N | Y | Y | | Coburn | ? | ? | Y | N | N |
| **IDAHO** | | | | | | | **OREGON** | | | | | |
| Craig | Y | Y | N | N | Y | | Wyden | Y | Y | Y | N | Y |
| Crapo | Y | Y | N | N | Y | | Smith | Y | Y | Y | N | Y |
| **ILLINOIS** | | | | | | | **PENNSYLVANIA** | | | | | |
| Durbin | Y | N | N | Y | Y | | Specter | Y | Y | N | ? | ? |
| Obama | Y | N | N | Y | Y | | Santorum | Y | Y | Y | N | Y |
| **INDIANA** | | | | | | | **RHODE ISLAND** | | | | | |
| Lugar | Y | Y | Y | N | Y | | Reed | Y | N | N | Y | Y |
| Bayh | Y | N | N | N | ? | | Chafee | Y | Y | Y | Y | Y |
| **IOWA** | | | | | | | **SOUTH CAROLINA** | | | | | |
| Grassley | Y | Y | Y | N | Y | | Graham | Y | Y | N | N | Y |
| Harkin | Y | Y | N | Y | Y | | DeMint | Y | Y | Y | N | Y |
| **KANSAS** | | | | | | | **SOUTH DAKOTA** | | | | | |
| Brownback | Y | Y | Y | N | Y | | Johnson | Y | Y | N | Y | Y |
| Roberts | Y | Y | Y | N | Y | | Thune | Y | N | N | N | Y |
| **KENTUCKY** | | | | | | | **TENNESSEE** | | | | | |
| McConnell | Y | Y | Y | N | Y | | Frist | Y | Y | N | N | Y |
| Bunning | Y | Y | Y | ? | ? | | Alexander | Y | Y | Y | N | Y |
| **LOUISIANA** | | | | | | | **TEXAS** | | | | | |
| Landrieu | Y | N | N | Y | Y | | Hutchison | Y | Y | Y | N | Y |
| Vitter | Y | N | N | N | Y | | Cornyn | Y | Y | Y | N | Y |
| **MAINE** | | | | | | | **UTAH** | | | | | |
| Snowe | Y | N | N | N | Y | | Hatch | Y | Y | Y | N | Y |
| Collins | Y | Y | N | Y | Y | | Bennett | ? | ? | Y | N | Y |
| **MARYLAND** | | | | | | | **VERMONT** | | | | | |
| Sarbanes | Y | N | N | Y | Y | | Leahy | Y | Y | N | Y | Y |
| Mikulski | Y | N | N | ? | ? | | *Jeffords* | Y | Y | Y | Y | Y |
| **MASSACHUSETTS** | | | | | | | **VIRGINIA** | | | | | |
| Kennedy | Y | N | N | Y | Y | | Warner | Y | Y | Y | N | Y |
| Kerry | Y | N | N | Y | Y | | Allen | Y | Y | Y | N | Y |
| **MICHIGAN** | | | | | | | **WASHINGTON** | | | | | |
| Levin | Y | N | N | Y | Y | | Murray | Y | Y | Y | Y | Y |
| Stabenow | Y | N | N | Y | Y | | Cantwell | Y | Y | Y | Y | Y |
| **MINNESOTA** | | | | | | | **WEST VIRGINIA** | | | | | |
| Dayton | Y | N | N | Y | Y | | Byrd | Y | N | N | Y | Y |
| Coleman | Y | Y | Y | N | Y | | Rockefeller | Y | N | N | Y | Y |
| **MISSISSIPPI** | | | | | | | **WISCONSIN** | | | | | |
| Cochran | Y | Y | Y | N | Y | | Kohl | Y | N | N | Y | Y |
| Lott | Y | Y | Y | N | Y | | Feingold | Y | N | N | Y | Y |
| **MISSOURI** | | | | | | | **WYOMING** | | | | | |
| Bond | Y | Y | Y | N | Y | | Thomas | Y | N | N | N | Y |
| Talent | Y | Y | Y | N | Y | | Enzi | Y | N | N | N | Y |

**KEY**   Republicans   Democrats   *Independents*

| | | |
|---|---|---|
| **Y** Voted for (yea) | **X** Paired against | **C** Voted "present" to avoid possible conflict of interest |
| **#** Paired for | **–** Announced against | |
| **+** Announced for | **P** Voted "present" | **?** Did not vote or otherwise make a position known |
| **N** Voted against (nay) | | |

# IN THE SENATE | By Vote Number

**173. S Res 193. London Bombings/Adoption.** Adoption of the resolution that would express the deepest sympathies and condolences to the people of the United Kingdom in the aftermath of the July 7, 2005, terrorist attacks in London. Adopted 76-0: R 41-0; D 34-0 (ND 34-0, SD 0-0); I 1-0. July 11, 2005.

**174. HR 2360. Fiscal 2006 Homeland Security Appropriations/ Veterans' Health Care.** Murray, D-Wash., amendment that would provide $1.5 billion in fiscal 2005 supplemental appropriations to the Department of Veterans Affairs for medical services provided by the Veterans Health Administration. Adopted 95-0: R 51-0; D 43-0 (ND 39-0, SD 4-0); I 1-0. July 12, 2005.

**175. HR 2360. Fiscal 2006 Homeland Security Appropriations/First-Responders.** Collins, R-Maine, amendment that would change the distribution of certain first-responder grants and guarantee that each state receive a minimum of 0.55 percent of total funding for such grants. States with larger populations and higher population densities would receive a higher guaranteed amount on a sliding scale; the remaining funds would be distributed based on the relative threat of terrorist attack faced by an area. Adopted 71-26: R 42-11; D 28-15 (ND 26-13, SD 2-2); I 1-0. A "nay" was a vote in support of the president's position. July 12, 2005.

**176. HR 2360. Fiscal 2006 Homeland Security Appropriations/First-Responders.** Feinstein, D-Calif., amendment that would change the distribution of certain first-responder grants and guarantee that each state receive 0.25 percent of the total available funding. It would direct the Homeland Security secretary to allocate the remainder of the funds based on a risk assessment carried out by the department. Rejected 32-65: R 13-40; D 19-24 (ND 17-22, SD 2-2); I 0-1. July 12, 2005.

**177. HR 2360. Fiscal 2006 Homeland Security Appropriations/First-Responders.** Dodd, D-Conn., motion to waive the Budget Act with respect to the Gregg, R-N.H., point of order against the Dodd amendment. The Dodd amendment would increase funding for emergency first-responders and transit, rail, truck and port security programs by approximately $16 billion. Motion rejected 36-60: R 0-53; D 35-7 (ND 33-6, SD 2-1); I 1-0. A three-fifths majority (60) of the total Senate is required to waive the Budget Act. (Subsequently, the chair upheld the point of order, and the amendment fell.) July 13, 2005.

**178. HR 2360. Fiscal 2006 Homeland Security Appropriations/First-Responders.** Akaka, D-Hawaii, motion to waive the Budget Act with respect to the Gregg, R-N.H., point of order against the Akaka amendment. The Akaka amendment would add $487 million for state and local first-responder grant programs. Motion rejected 42-55: R 0-54; D 41-1 (ND 38-1, SD 3-0); I 1-0. A three-fifths majority (60) of the total Senate is required to waive the Budget Act. (Subsequently, the chair upheld the point of order, and the amendment fell.) July 13, 2005.

| | 173 | 174 | 175 | 176 | 177 | 178 |
|---|---|---|---|---|---|---|
| **ALABAMA** | | | | | | |
| Shelby | Y | Y | Y | N | N | N |
| Sessions | + | + | Y | N | N | N |
| **ALASKA** | | | | | | |
| Stevens | Y | Y | Y | N | N | N |
| Murkowski | ? | Y | Y | N | N | N |
| **ARIZONA** | | | | | | |
| McCain | ? | Y | Y | Y | N | N |
| Kyl | Y | Y | N | Y | N | N |
| **ARKANSAS** | | | | | | |
| Lincoln | + | Y | Y | N | Y | Y |
| Pryor | + | Y | Y | N | Y | Y |
| **CALIFORNIA** | | | | | | |
| Feinstein | Y | Y | N | Y | Y | Y |
| Boxer | + | Y | N | Y | Y | Y |
| **COLORADO** | | | | | | |
| Allard | Y | Y | Y | N | Y | N |
| Salazar | Y | Y | Y | N | Y | Y |
| **CONNECTICUT** | | | | | | |
| Dodd | Y | Y | Y | N | Y | Y |
| Lieberman | Y | Y | Y | N | Y | Y |
| **DELAWARE** | | | | | | |
| Biden | Y | Y | Y | N | Y | Y |
| Carper | Y | Y | Y | N | N | Y |
| **FLORIDA** | | | | | | |
| Nelson | ? | Y | N | Y | N | Y |
| Martinez | ? | Y | N | Y | N | N |
| **GEORGIA** | | | | | | |
| Chambliss | ? | Y | Y | N | N | N |
| Isakson | Y | Y | Y | N | N | N |
| **HAWAII** | | | | | | |
| Inouye | Y | Y | Y | N | Y | Y |
| Akaka | Y | Y | Y | N | Y | Y |
| **IDAHO** | | | | | | |
| Craig | Y | Y | Y | N | N | N |
| Crapo | Y | Y | Y | N | N | N |
| **ILLINOIS** | | | | | | |
| Durbin | Y | Y | N | Y | Y | Y |
| Obama | ? | Y | N | Y | Y | Y |
| **INDIANA** | | | | | | |
| Lugar | Y | Y | Y | N | N | N |
| Bayh | ? | Y | Y | N | Y | Y |
| **IOWA** | | | | | | |
| Grassley | Y | Y | Y | N | N | N |
| Harkin | Y | Y | Y | N | N | Y |
| **KANSAS** | | | | | | |
| Brownback | Y | Y | Y | N | N | N |
| Roberts | Y | Y | Y | N | N | N |
| **KENTUCKY** | | | | | | |
| McConnell | Y | Y | Y | N | N | N |
| Bunning | Y | Y | Y | N | N | N |
| **LOUISIANA** | | | | | | |
| Landrieu | ? | Y | N | Y | ? | ? |
| Vitter | Y | Y | N | Y | N | N |
| **MAINE** | | | | | | |
| Snowe | Y | Y | Y | N | N | N |
| Collins | Y | Y | Y | N | N | N |
| **MARYLAND** | | | | | | |
| Sarbanes | Y | Y | N | Y | Y | Y |
| Mikulski | ? | ? | ? | ? | ? | ? |
| **MASSACHUSETTS** | | | | | | |
| Kennedy | Y | Y | N | Y | Y | Y |
| Kerry | Y | Y | N | Y | Y | Y |
| **MICHIGAN** | | | | | | |
| Levin | Y | Y | Y | Y | Y | Y |
| Stabenow | Y | Y | Y | Y | Y | Y |
| **MINNESOTA** | | | | | | |
| Dayton | ? | Y | Y | N | Y | Y |
| Coleman | Y | Y | Y | N | N | N |
| **MISSISSIPPI** | | | | | | |
| Cochran | ? | Y | Y | N | N | N |
| Lott | ? | ? | ? | ? | ? | ? |
| **MISSOURI** | | | | | | |
| Bond | Y | Y | Y | N | N | N |
| Talent | Y | Y | Y | N | N | N |

| | 173 | 174 | 175 | 176 | 177 | 178 |
|---|---|---|---|---|---|---|
| **MONTANA** | | | | | | |
| Baucus | ? | Y | Y | N | N | N |
| Burns | Y | Y | Y | N | N | N |
| **NEBRASKA** | | | | | | |
| Hagel | Y | Y | Y | N | N | N |
| Nelson | Y | Y | Y | N | N | Y |
| **NEVADA** | | | | | | |
| Reid | Y | Y | Y | N | Y | Y |
| Ensign | Y | Y | Y | Y | N | N |
| **NEW HAMPSHIRE** | | | | | | |
| Gregg | Y | Y | N | N | N | N |
| Sununu | Y | Y | Y | N | N | N |
| **NEW JERSEY** | | | | | | |
| Corzine | Y | Y | N | Y | Y | Y |
| Lautenberg | Y | Y | N | Y | Y | Y |
| **NEW MEXICO** | | | | | | |
| Domenici | Y | Y | Y | N | N | N |
| Bingaman | Y | Y | Y | N | N | Y |
| **NEW YORK** | | | | | | |
| Schumer | Y | Y | Y | N | Y | Y |
| Clinton | Y | Y | N | Y | Y | Y |
| **NORTH CAROLINA** | | | | | | |
| Dole | Y | Y | Y | N | N | N |
| Burr | Y | Y | Y | N | N | N |
| **NORTH DAKOTA** | | | | | | |
| Conrad | Y | Y | Y | N | N | N |
| Dorgan | Y | Y | Y | N | N | Y |
| **OHIO** | | | | | | |
| DeWine | Y | Y | Y | N | N | N |
| Voinovich | Y | Y | Y | N | N | N |
| **OKLAHOMA** | | | | | | |
| Inhofe | ? | Y | Y | Y | N | N |
| Coburn | Y | Y | Y | Y | N | N |
| **OREGON** | | | | | | |
| Wyden | Y | Y | Y | N | Y | Y |
| Smith | ? | Y | Y | N | N | N |
| **PENNSYLVANIA** | | | | | | |
| Specter | Y | Y | Y | N | N | N |
| Santorum | Y | Y | N | N | N | N |
| **RHODE ISLAND** | | | | | | |
| Reed | Y | Y | Y | N | Y | Y |
| Chafee | Y | Y | Y | N | N | N |
| **SOUTH CAROLINA** | | | | | | |
| Graham | Y | Y | Y | N | N | N |
| DeMint | Y | Y | Y | N | N | N |
| **SOUTH DAKOTA** | | | | | | |
| Johnson | Y | Y | Y | N | Y | Y |
| Thune | ? | ? | ? | ? | ? | N |
| **TENNESSEE** | | | | | | |
| Frist | Y | Y | Y | N | N | N |
| Alexander | + | + | Y | N | N | N |
| **TEXAS** | | | | | | |
| Hutchison | ? | Y | N | Y | N | N |
| Cornyn | ? | Y | N | Y | N | N |
| **UTAH** | | | | | | |
| Hatch | Y | Y | N | N | N | N |
| Bennett | Y | Y | Y | N | N | N |
| **VERMONT** | | | | | | |
| Leahy | Y | Y | N | Y | Y | Y |
| Jeffords | Y | Y | Y | N | Y | Y |
| **VIRGINIA** | | | | | | |
| Warner | Y | Y | N | Y | N | N |
| Allen | Y | Y | N | Y | N | N |
| **WASHINGTON** | | | | | | |
| Murray | Y | Y | Y | Y | Y | Y |
| Cantwell | Y | Y | Y | Y | Y | Y |
| **WEST VIRGINIA** | | | | | | |
| Byrd | Y | Y | N | N | Y | Y |
| Rockefeller | Y | Y | Y | N | Y | Y |
| **WISCONSIN** | | | | | | |
| Kohl | Y | Y | Y | N | Y | Y |
| Feingold | Y | Y | Y | N | Y | Y |
| **WYOMING** | | | | | | |
| Thomas | ? | Y | Y | N | N | N |
| Enzi | Y | Y | Y | N | N | N |

**KEY**   Republicans   Democrats   *Independents*

| | | |
|---|---|---|
| Y  Voted for (yea) | X  Paired against | C  Voted "present" to avoid possible conflict of interest |
| #  Paired for | −  Announced against | |
| +  Announced for | P  Voted "present" | ?  Did not vote or otherwise make a position known |
| N  Voted against (nay) | | |

# IN THE SENATE | By Vote Number

**179.** HR 2360. Fiscal 2006 Homeland Security Appropriations/Border Security. Ensign, R-Nev., amendment to the Ensign amendment. The second-degree amendment would allow the transfer of $367.6 million to Customs and Border Protection to hire an additional 1,000 border agents. The underlying amendment would require the transfer of such funds for this purpose. Rejected 38-60: R 36-18; D 2-41 (ND 2-37, SD 0-4); I 0-1. (Subsequently, the underlying Ensign amendment was rejected by voice vote.) July 14, 2005.

**180.** HR 2360. Fiscal 2006 Homeland Security Appropriations/Air Cargo Security. Schumer, D-N.Y., motion to waive the Budget Act with respect to the Gregg, R-N.H., point of order against the Schumer amendment. The Schumer amendment would appropriate approximately $302 million for aviation security programs. Motion rejected 45-53: R 2-52; D 42-1 (ND 38-1, SD 4-0); I 1-0. A three-fifths majority (60) of the total Senate is required to waive the Budget Act. (Subsequently, the chair upheld the point of order, and the amendment fell.) July 14, 2005.

**181.** HR 2360. Fiscal 2006 Homeland Security Appropriations/Truck Security. Schumer, D-N.Y., motion to waive the Budget Act with respect to the Gregg, R-N.H., point of order against the Schumer amendment. The Schumer amendment would appropriate $70 million to the Transportation Security Administration to identify and track shipments by truck of hazardous materials using global positioning system (GPS) technology. Motion rejected 36-62: R 0-54; D 35-8 (ND 33-6, SD 2-2); I 1-0. A three-fifths majority (60) of the total Senate is required to waive the Budget Act. (Subsequently, the chair upheld the point of order, and the amendment fell.) July 14, 2005.

**182.** HR 2360. Fiscal 2006 Homeland Security Appropriations/Immigration and Customs Enforcement. McCain, R-Ariz., amendment that would increase funding for immigration and customs enforcement by about $200 million to add 5,760 detention beds and hire more personnel. It would be offset by a reduction for state and local programs. Rejected 42-56: R 35-19; D 6-37 (ND 6-33, SD 0-4); I 1-0. July 14, 2005.

**183.** HR 2360. Fiscal 2006 Homeland Security Appropriations/Interoperable Communications Equipment. Stabenow, D-Mich., motion to waive the Budget Act with respect to the Gregg, R-N.H., point of order against the Stabenow amendment. The Stabenow amendment would appropriate $5 billion for interoperable communications equipment grants and designate it as emergency spending. Motion rejected 35-63: R 0-54; D 34-9 (ND 31-8, SD 3-1); I 1-0. A three-fifths majority (60) of the total Senate is required to waive the Budget Act. (Subsequently, the chair upheld the point of order, and the emergency designation was stricken. The amendment was then rejected by voice vote.) July 14, 2005.

**184.** HR 2360. Fiscal 2006 Homeland Security Appropriations/Rail and Transit Security. Byrd, D-W.Va., motion to waive the Budget Act with respect to the Gregg, R-N.H., point of order against the Byrd amendment. The Byrd amendment would appropriate $1.2 billion for transit security grants and $265 million for intercity rail transportation. Motion rejected 43-55: R 0-54; D 42-1 (ND 38-1, SD 4-0); I 1-0. A three-fifths majority (60) of the total Senate is required to waive the Budget Act. (Subsequently, the chair upheld the point of order, and the amendment fell.) July 14, 2005.

| | 179 | 180 | 181 | 182 | 183 | 184 |
|---|---|---|---|---|---|---|
| **ALABAMA** | | | | | | |
| Shelby | Y | N | N | N | N | N |
| Sessions | Y | N | N | Y | N | N |
| **ALASKA** | | | | | | |
| Stevens | N | N | N | N | N | N |
| Murkowski | Y | N | N | N | N | N |
| **ARIZONA** | | | | | | |
| McCain | Y | N | N | Y | N | N |
| Kyl | Y | N | N | N | N | N |
| **ARKANSAS** | | | | | | |
| Lincoln | N | Y | N | N | Y | Y |
| Pryor | N | Y | N | N | Y | Y |
| **CALIFORNIA** | | | | | | |
| Feinstein | N | Y | N | Y | Y | Y |
| Boxer | N | Y | Y | Y | Y | Y |
| **COLORADO** | | | | | | |
| Allard | Y | N | N | N | N | N |
| Salazar | Y | Y | Y | Y | Y | Y |
| **CONNECTICUT** | | | | | | |
| Dodd | N | Y | Y | Y | Y | Y |
| Lieberman | N | Y | Y | N | Y | Y |
| **DELAWARE** | | | | | | |
| Biden | N | Y | Y | N | Y | Y |
| Carper | N | Y | Y | N | N | Y |
| **FLORIDA** | | | | | | |
| Nelson | N | Y | Y | N | N | Y |
| Martinez | Y | N | N | Y | N | N |
| **GEORGIA** | | | | | | |
| Chambliss | Y | N | N | Y | N | N |
| Isakson | Y | N | N | Y | N | N |
| **HAWAII** | | | | | | |
| Inouye | N | Y | N | N | N | Y |
| Akaka | N | Y | Y | N | Y | Y |
| **IDAHO** | | | | | | |
| Craig | Y | N | N | Y | N | N |
| Crapo | Y | N | N | Y | N | N |
| **ILLINOIS** | | | | | | |
| Durbin | N | Y | Y | N | Y | Y |
| Obama | N | Y | Y | Y | Y | Y |
| **INDIANA** | | | | | | |
| Lugar | N | N | N | Y | N | N |
| Bayh | N | Y | Y | Y | Y | Y |
| **IOWA** | | | | | | |
| Grassley | Y | N | N | Y | N | N |
| Harkin | N | Y | Y | N | Y | Y |
| **KANSAS** | | | | | | |
| Brownback | Y | N | N | N | N | N |
| Roberts | Y | N | N | N | N | N |
| **KENTUCKY** | | | | | | |
| McConnell | Y | N | N | Y | N | N |
| Bunning | Y | N | N | Y | N | N |
| **LOUISIANA** | | | | | | |
| Landrieu | N | Y | N | Y | Y | Y |
| Vitter | N | N | N | Y | N | N |
| **MAINE** | | | | | | |
| Snowe | N | Y | N | N | N | N |
| Collins | N | N | N | N | N | N |
| **MARYLAND** | | | | | | |
| Sarbanes | N | Y | Y | N | Y | Y |
| Mikulski | ? | ? | ? | ? | ? | ? |
| **MASSACHUSETTS** | | | | | | |
| Kennedy | N | Y | Y | N | Y | Y |
| Kerry | N | Y | Y | N | Y | Y |
| **MICHIGAN** | | | | | | |
| Levin | N | Y | Y | N | Y | Y |
| Stabenow | N | Y | Y | N | Y | Y |
| **MINNESOTA** | | | | | | |
| Dayton | N | Y | Y | N | Y | Y |
| Coleman | N | N | N | N | N | N |
| **MISSISSIPPI** | | | | | | |
| Cochran | N | N | N | N | N | N |
| Lott | ? | ? | ? | ? | ? | ? |
| **MISSOURI** | | | | | | |
| Bond | N | N | N | N | N | N |
| Talent | N | N | N | N | N | N |
| **MONTANA** | | | | | | |
| Baucus | N | Y | N | N | Y | Y |
| Burns | Y | N | N | Y | N | N |
| **NEBRASKA** | | | | | | |
| Hagel | Y | N | N | Y | N | N |
| Nelson | N | Y | N | N | N | Y |
| **NEVADA** | | | | | | |
| Reid | N | Y | Y | N | Y | Y |
| Ensign | Y | N | N | Y | N | N |
| **NEW HAMPSHIRE** | | | | | | |
| Gregg | N | N | N | N | N | N |
| Sununu | Y | N | N | N | N | N |
| **NEW JERSEY** | | | | | | |
| Corzine | N | Y | Y | N | Y | Y |
| Lautenberg | N | Y | Y | N | Y | Y |
| **NEW MEXICO** | | | | | | |
| Domenici | Y | N | N | Y | N | N |
| Bingaman | Y | Y | Y | Y | N | Y |
| **NEW YORK** | | | | | | |
| Schumer | N | Y | Y | N | Y | Y |
| Clinton | N | Y | Y | N | Y | Y |
| **NORTH CAROLINA** | | | | | | |
| Dole | Y | N | N | Y | N | N |
| Burr | Y | N | N | Y | N | N |
| **NORTH DAKOTA** | | | | | | |
| Conrad | N | N | N | N | N | N |
| Dorgan | N | Y | N | N | N | Y |
| **OHIO** | | | | | | |
| DeWine | N | N | N | N | N | N |
| Voinovich | N | N | N | N | N | N |
| **OKLAHOMA** | | | | | | |
| Inhofe | N | N | N | N | N | N |
| Coburn | Y | N | N | Y | N | N |
| **OREGON** | | | | | | |
| Wyden | N | Y | Y | N | N | Y |
| Smith | N | N | N | N | N | N |
| **PENNSYLVANIA** | | | | | | |
| Specter | N | N | N | N | N | N |
| Santorum | N | N | N | Y | N | N |
| **RHODE ISLAND** | | | | | | |
| Reed | N | Y | Y | N | Y | Y |
| Chafee | N | N | N | N | N | N |
| **SOUTH CAROLINA** | | | | | | |
| Graham | Y | N | N | Y | N | N |
| DeMint | Y | N | N | N | N | N |
| **SOUTH DAKOTA** | | | | | | |
| Johnson | N | Y | Y | N | Y | Y |
| Thune | Y | N | N | Y | N | N |
| **TENNESSEE** | | | | | | |
| Frist | Y | N | N | Y | N | N |
| Alexander | N | N | N | N | N | N |
| **TEXAS** | | | | | | |
| Hutchison | Y | Y | N | Y | N | N |
| Cornyn | Y | N | N | Y | N | N |
| **UTAH** | | | | | | |
| Hatch | Y | N | N | Y | N | N |
| Bennett | Y | N | N | Y | N | N |
| **VERMONT** | | | | | | |
| Leahy | N | Y | Y | N | Y | Y |
| Jeffords | N | Y | Y | Y | Y | Y |
| **VIRGINIA** | | | | | | |
| Warner | Y | N | N | Y | N | N |
| Allen | Y | N | N | Y | N | N |
| **WASHINGTON** | | | | | | |
| Murray | N | Y | Y | N | Y | Y |
| Cantwell | N | Y | Y | N | Y | Y |
| **WEST VIRGINIA** | | | | | | |
| Byrd | N | Y | Y | N | Y | Y |
| Rockefeller | N | Y | Y | N | Y | Y |
| **WISCONSIN** | | | | | | |
| Kohl | N | Y | Y | N | Y | Y |
| Feingold | N | Y | Y | N | N | Y |
| **WYOMING** | | | | | | |
| Thomas | Y | N | N | N | N | N |
| Enzi | Y | N | N | N | N | N |

| KEY | Republicans | Democrats | *Independents* | | |
|---|---|---|---|---|---|
| Y | Voted for (yea) | X | Paired against | C | Voted "present" to avoid possible conflict of interest |
| # | Paired for | – | Announced against | | |
| + | Announced for | P | Voted "present" | ? | Did not vote or otherwise make a position known |
| N | Voted against (nay) | | | | |

# IN THE SENATE | By Vote Number

**185.** HR 2360. Fiscal 2006 Homeland Security Appropriations/Rail and Transit Security. Gregg, R-N.H., amendment that would provide an additional $100 million for transportation and infrastructure grants, and increase intercity bus security grants to $15 million. It would be offset by cuts to state and local aid accounts. Rejected 46-52: R 45-9; D 1-42 (ND 1-38, SD 0-4); I 0-1. July 14, 2005.

**186.** HR 2360. Fiscal 2006 Homeland Security Appropriations/Transit Security. Shelby, R-Ala., motion to waive the Budget Act with respect to the Gregg, R-N.H., point of order against the Shelby amendment. The Shelby amendment would appropriate $1.5 billion for discretionary transportation and infrastructure grants, of which $1.2 billion would be for transit security grants. Motion rejected 53-45: R 9-45; D 43-0 (ND 39-0, SD 4-0); I 1-0. A three-fifths majority (60) of the total Senate is required to waive the Budget Act. (Subsequently, the chair upheld the point of order, and the amendment fell.) July 14, 2005.

**187.** HR 2360. Fiscal 2006 Homeland Security Appropriations/ Disclosure of Classified Information. Frist, R-Tenn., amendment that would bar any federal officeholder who refers to a classified FBI report on the Senate floor or makes a statement based on FBI agent comments that is then used as terrorist propaganda from having access to such information. Rejected 32-65: R 32-21; D 0-43 (ND 0-39, SD 0-4); I 0-1. July 14, 2005.

**188.** HR 2360. Fiscal 2006 Homeland Security Appropriations/ Disclosure of Classified Information. Reid, D-Nev., amendment that would bar federal employees from holding security clearances for access to classified information if they disclose, or have disclosed, classified information, including the identity of a covert CIA agent to an unauthorized person. Rejected 44-53: R 0-53; D 43-0 (ND 39-0, SD 4-0); I 1-0. July 14, 2005.

**189.** HR 2360. Fiscal 2006 Homeland Security Appropriations/Passage. Passage of the bill that would provide $31.9 billion in fiscal 2006 for the Homeland Security Department, including $7.9 billion for the Coast Guard, $6 billion for border security, $5.1 billion for the Transportation Security Administration, not including assumed fees, and $3.8 billion for investigating and enforcing immigration and customs laws. Each state would receive a minimum of 0.55 percent of total funding for first-responder grants. Passed 96-1: R 52-1; D 43-0 (ND 39-0, SD 4-0); I 1-0. July 14, 2005.

| | 185 | 186 | 187 | 188 | 189 |
|---|---|---|---|---|---|
| **ALABAMA** | | | | | |
| Shelby* | N | Y | N | N | Y |
| Sessions | Y | N | N | N | Y |
| **ALASKA** | | | | | |
| Stevens | Y | N | Y | N | Y |
| Murkowski | Y | N | N | N | Y |
| **ARIZONA** | | | | | |
| McCain | Y | N | N | N | Y |
| Kyl | Y | N | Y | N | Y |
| **ARKANSAS** | | | | | |
| Lincoln | N | Y | N | Y | Y |
| Pryor | N | Y | N | Y | Y |
| **CALIFORNIA** | | | | | |
| Feinstein | N | Y | N | Y | Y |
| Boxer | N | Y | N | Y | Y |
| **COLORADO** | | | | | |
| Allard | Y | N | Y | N | Y |
| Salazar | N | Y | N | Y | Y |
| **CONNECTICUT** | | | | | |
| Dodd | N | Y | N | Y | Y |
| Lieberman | N | Y | N | Y | Y |
| **DELAWARE** | | | | | |
| Biden | N | Y | N | Y | Y |
| Carper | N | Y | N | Y | Y |
| **FLORIDA** | | | | | |
| Nelson | N | Y | N | Y | Y |
| Martinez | Y | N | Y | N | Y |
| **GEORGIA** | | | | | |
| Chambliss | Y | N | N | N | Y |
| Isakson | Y | N | Y | N | Y |
| **HAWAII** | | | | | |
| Inouye | N | Y | N | Y | Y |
| Akaka | N | Y | N | Y | Y |
| **IDAHO** | | | | | |
| Craig | Y | N | Y | N | Y |
| Crapo | Y | N | Y | N | Y |
| **ILLINOIS** | | | | | |
| Durbin | N | Y | N | Y | Y |
| Obama | N | Y | N | Y | Y |
| **INDIANA** | | | | | |
| Lugar | Y | N | N | N | Y |
| Bayh | N | Y | N | Y | Y |
| **IOWA** | | | | | |
| Grassley | Y | N | Y | N | Y |
| Harkin | N | Y | N | Y | Y |
| **KANSAS** | | | | | |
| Brownback | Y | N | N | N | Y |
| Roberts | Y | N | N | N | Y |
| **KENTUCKY** | | | | | |
| McConnell | Y | N | Y | N | Y |
| Bunning | Y | N | Y | N | Y |
| **LOUISIANA** | | | | | |
| Landrieu | N | Y | N | Y | Y |
| Vitter | Y | N | Y | N | Y |
| **MAINE** | | | | | |
| Snowe | Y | N | N | N | Y |
| Collins | N | N | N | N | Y |
| **MARYLAND** | | | | | |
| Sarbanes | N | Y | N | Y | Y |
| Mikulski | ? | ? | ? | ? | ? |
| **MASSACHUSETTS** | | | | | |
| Kennedy | N | Y | N | Y | Y |
| Kerry | N | Y | N | Y | Y |
| **MICHIGAN** | | | | | |
| Levin | N | Y | N | Y | Y |
| Stabenow | N | Y | N | Y | Y |
| **MINNESOTA** | | | | | |
| Dayton | N | Y | N | Y | Y |
| Coleman | N | Y | Y | N | Y |
| **MISSISSIPPI** | | | | | |
| Cochran | Y | N | Y | N | Y |
| Lott | ? | ? | ? | ? | ? |
| **MISSOURI** | | | | | |
| Bond | Y | N | Y | N | Y |
| Talent | N | Y | N | N | Y |
| **MONTANA** | | | | | |
| Baucus | N | Y | N | Y | Y |
| Burns | Y | N | Y | N | Y |
| **NEBRASKA** | | | | | |
| Hagel | Y | N | N | N | Y |
| Nelson | N | Y | N | Y | Y |
| **NEVADA** | | | | | |
| Reid | N | Y | N | Y | Y |
| Ensign | Y | N | Y | N | Y |
| **NEW HAMPSHIRE** | | | | | |
| Gregg | Y | N | N | N | Y |
| Sununu | Y | N | N | N | Y |
| **NEW JERSEY** | | | | | |
| Corzine | N | Y | N | Y | Y |
| Lautenberg | N | Y | N | Y | Y |
| **NEW MEXICO** | | | | | |
| Domenici | Y | N | Y | N | Y |
| Bingaman | N | Y | N | Y | Y |
| **NEW YORK** | | | | | |
| Schumer | N | Y | N | Y | Y |
| Clinton | N | Y | N | Y | Y |
| **NORTH CAROLINA** | | | | | |
| Dole | N | Y | Y | N | Y |
| Burr | Y | N | Y | N | Y |
| **NORTH DAKOTA** | | | | | |
| Conrad | Y | Y | N | Y | Y |
| Dorgan | N | Y | N | Y | Y |
| **OHIO** | | | | | |
| DeWine | Y | Y | N | N | Y |
| Voinovich | Y | N | N | N | Y |
| **OKLAHOMA** | | | | | |
| Inhofe | N | N | Y | N | Y |
| Coburn | Y | N | Y | N | N |
| **OREGON** | | | | | |
| Wyden | N | Y | N | Y | Y |
| Smith | Y | N | Y | N | Y |
| **PENNSYLVANIA** | | | | | |
| Specter | Y | Y | Y | N | Y |
| Santorum | Y | N | Y | N | Y |
| **RHODE ISLAND** | | | | | |
| Reed | N | Y | N | Y | Y |
| Chafee | N | Y | N | N | Y |
| **SOUTH CAROLINA** | | | | | |
| Graham | Y | N | N | N | Y |
| DeMint | N | N | + | - | + |
| **SOUTH DAKOTA** | | | | | |
| Johnson | N | Y | N | Y | Y |
| Thune | N | N | N | N | Y |
| **TENNESSEE** | | | | | |
| Frist | Y | N | Y | N | Y |
| Alexander | Y | N | Y | N | Y |
| **TEXAS** | | | | | |
| Hutchison | Y | N | Y | N | Y |
| Cornyn | Y | N | Y | N | Y |
| **UTAH** | | | | | |
| Hatch | Y | Y | Y | N | Y |
| Bennett | Y | Y | Y | N | Y |
| **VERMONT** | | | | | |
| Leahy | N | Y | N | Y | Y |
| Jeffords | N | Y | N | Y | Y |
| **VIRGINIA** | | | | | |
| Warner | Y | N | N | N | Y |
| Allen | Y | N | N | N | Y |
| **WASHINGTON** | | | | | |
| Murray | N | Y | N | Y | Y |
| Cantwell | N | Y | N | Y | Y |
| **WEST VIRGINIA** | | | | | |
| Byrd | N | Y | N | Y | Y |
| Rockefeller | N | Y | N | Y | Y |
| **WISCONSIN** | | | | | |
| Kohl | N | Y | N | Y | Y |
| Feingold | N | Y | N | Y | Y |
| **WYOMING** | | | | | |
| Thomas | Y | N | N | N | Y |
| Enzi | Y | N | Y | N | Y |

**KEY**    Republicans    Democrats    *Independents*

| | | |
|---|---|---|
| **Y** Voted for (yea) | **X** Paired against | **C** Voted "present" to avoid possible conflict of interest |
| **#** Paired for | **−** Announced against | |
| **+** Announced for | **P** Voted "present" | **?** Did not vote or otherwise make a position known |
| **N** Voted against (nay) | | |

*Sen. Richard C. Shelby, R-Ala., received unanimous consent July 18 to switch from "yea" to "nay" on vote 187, taken on July 14. The switch did not affect the outcome. The corrected tally is given above.

# IN THE SENATE | By Vote Number

**190.** **Crawford Nomination/Confirmation.** Confirmation of President Bush's nomination of Lester M. Crawford of Maryland to be commissioner of the Food and Drug Administration. Confirmed 78-16: R 49-3; D 28-13 (ND 25-13, SD 3-0); I 1-0. A "yea" was a vote in support of the president's position. July 18, 2005.

**191.** **H J Res 52. Myanmar Sanctions/Passage.** Passage of the joint resolution that would extend for one year import restrictions on products from Myanmar, formerly known as Burma, until the president certifies that the Myanmar government has made significant progress toward practicing democracy and ending human rights violations. Passed (thus cleared for the president) 97-1: R 54-1; D 42-0 (ND 39-0, SD 3-0); I 1-0. July 19, 2005.

**192.** **HR 3057. Fiscal 2006 Foreign Operations Appropriation/Nuclear Power Plants in China.** Coburn, R-Okla., amendment that would prohibit the Export-Import Bank from approving federal loans or loan guarantees for the construction of nuclear power plants in China. Rejected 37-62: R 14-41; D 23-20 (ND 23-17, SD 0-3); I 0-1. July 19, 2005.

**193.** **HR 3057. Fiscal 2006 Foreign Operations Appropriations/USAID Funding.** Coburn, R-Okla., amendment that would prohibit the use of funds in the bill for entertainment expenses of the U.S. Agency for International Development. Adopted 59-40: R 51-4; D 8-35 (ND 8-32, SD 0-3); I 0-1. July 19, 2005.

**194.** **HR 3057. Fiscal 2006 Foreign Operations Appropriations/ Television Broadcasting to Cuba.** Dorgan, D-N.D., amendment that would reduce funding for international broadcasting operations by $20 million for broadcasting to Cuba and increase Peace Corps funding by that amount. It would prohibit the use of funds for television broadcasts to Cuba and bar the use of capital improvement funds for this purpose. Rejected 33-66: R 2-53; D 30-13 (ND 28-12, SD 2-1); I 1-0. July 19, 2005.

**195.** **HR 3057. Fiscal 2006 Foreign Operations Appropriations/ International Adoption.** Landrieu, D-La., amendment that would reaffirm congressional funding commitment to the founding principle of the Hague Convention related to intercountry adoption and affirm the benefits of international adoption. Adopted 98-0: R 55-0; D 42-0 (ND 38-0, SD 4-0); I 1-0. July 20, 2005.

| | 190 | 191 | 192 | 193 | 194 | 195 |
|---|---|---|---|---|---|---|
| **ALABAMA** | | | | | | |
| Shelby | Y | Y | N | Y | N | Y |
| Sessions | Y | Y | Y | Y | Y | Y |
| **ALASKA** | | | | | | |
| Stevens | Y | Y | N | Y | N | Y |
| Murkowski | ? | Y | N | Y | N | Y |
| **ARIZONA** | | | | | | |
| McCain | ? | Y | N | Y | N | Y |
| Kyl | Y | Y | N | Y | N | Y |
| **ARKANSAS** | | | | | | |
| Lincoln | ? | Y | N | N | Y | Y |
| Pryor | Y | Y | N | N | Y | Y |
| **CALIFORNIA** | | | | | | |
| Feinstein | Y | Y | N | N | Y | Y |
| Boxer | N | Y | Y | N | Y | Y |
| **COLORADO** | | | | | | |
| Allard | Y | Y | Y | Y | N | Y |
| Salazar | Y | Y | Y | Y | N | Y |
| **CONNECTICUT** | | | | | | |
| Dodd | ? | Y | N | N | Y | Y |
| Lieberman | Y | Y | N | N | N | Y |
| **DELAWARE** | | | | | | |
| Biden | Y | Y | N | N | Y | Y |
| Carper | Y | Y | N | N | Y | Y |
| **FLORIDA** | | | | | | |
| Nelson | Y | Y | N | N | N | Y |
| Martinez | Y | Y | Y | N | N | Y |
| **GEORGIA** | | | | | | |
| Chambliss | Y | Y | N | Y | N | Y |
| Isakson | Y | Y | N | Y | N | Y |
| **HAWAII** | | | | | | |
| Inouye | Y | Y | Y | N | Y | Y |
| Akaka | Y | Y | N | N | Y | Y |
| **IDAHO** | | | | | | |
| Craig | Y | Y | N | Y | N | Y |
| Crapo | Y | Y | N | Y | N | Y |
| **ILLINOIS** | | | | | | |
| Durbin | N | Y | Y | N | Y | Y |
| Obama | N | Y | Y | N | Y | Y |
| **INDIANA** | | | | | | |
| Lugar | Y | Y | N | Y | N | Y |
| Bayh | Y | Y | Y | Y | N | Y |
| **IOWA** | | | | | | |
| Grassley | N | Y | N | Y | N | Y |
| Harkin | Y | Y | Y | N | Y | Y |
| **KANSAS** | | | | | | |
| Brownback | Y | Y | Y | Y | N | Y |
| Roberts | Y | Y | N | Y | N | Y |
| **KENTUCKY** | | | | | | |
| McConnell | Y | Y | N | Y | N | Y |
| Bunning | Y | Y | N | Y | N | Y |
| **LOUISIANA** | | | | | | |
| Landrieu | Y | ? | ? | ? | ? | Y |
| Vitter | N | Y | N | Y | N | Y |
| **MAINE** | | | | | | |
| Snowe | N | Y | Y | Y | N | Y |
| Collins | Y | Y | Y | Y | Y | Y |
| **MARYLAND** | | | | | | |
| Sarbanes | Y | Y | Y | N | N | Y |
| Mikulski | N | Y | Y | N | Y | Y |
| **MASSACHUSETTS** | | | | | | |
| Kennedy | Y | Y | Y | N | Y | Y |
| Kerry | Y | Y | N | N | N | Y |
| **MICHIGAN** | | | | | | |
| Levin | Y | Y | Y | N | Y | Y |
| Stabenow | N | Y | Y | Y | Y | Y |
| **MINNESOTA** | | | | | | |
| Dayton | N | Y | Y | Y | Y | Y |
| Coleman | Y | Y | N | Y | N | Y |
| **MISSISSIPPI** | | | | | | |
| Cochran | Y | Y | N | Y | N | Y |
| Lott | Y | Y | N | Y | N | Y |
| **MISSOURI** | | | | | | |
| Bond | Y | Y | N | Y | N | Y |
| Talent | Y | Y | Y | Y | N | Y |

| | 190 | 191 | 192 | 193 | 194 | 195 |
|---|---|---|---|---|---|---|
| **MONTANA** | | | | | | |
| Baucus | N | Y | N | N | Y | Y |
| Burns | Y | Y | N | Y | N | Y |
| **NEBRASKA** | | | | | | |
| Hagel | Y | Y | N | N | N | Y |
| Nelson | Y | Y | N | N | N | Y |
| **NEVADA** | | | | | | |
| Reid | Y | Y | N | N | N | Y |
| Ensign | Y | Y | Y | Y | N | Y |
| **NEW HAMPSHIRE** | | | | | | |
| Gregg | Y | Y | Y | Y | Y | Y |
| Sununu | Y | Y | Y | Y | Y | Y |
| **NEW JERSEY** | | | | | | |
| Corzine | ? | Y | N | N | N | Y |
| Lautenberg | N | Y | N | N | N | Y |
| **NEW MEXICO** | | | | | | |
| Domenici | Y | Y | N | Y | N | Y |
| Bingaman | Y | Y | N | Y | N | Y |
| **NEW YORK** | | | | | | |
| Schumer | N | Y | Y | N | N | Y |
| Clinton | N | Y | Y | N | N | Y |
| **NORTH CAROLINA** | | | | | | |
| Dole | Y | Y | N | Y | N | Y |
| Burr | Y | Y | N | Y | N | Y |
| **NORTH DAKOTA** | | | | | | |
| Conrad | Y | Y | Y | Y | Y | Y |
| Dorgan | N | Y | Y | Y | Y | Y |
| **OHIO** | | | | | | |
| DeWine | Y | Y | N | Y | N | Y |
| Voinovich | Y | Y | N | N | N | Y |
| **OKLAHOMA** | | | | | | |
| Inhofe | Y | Y | Y | Y | N | Y |
| Coburn | ? | Y | Y | Y | Y | Y |
| **OREGON** | | | | | | |
| Wyden | Y | Y | Y | Y | Y | Y |
| Smith | Y | Y | Y | Y | N | Y |
| **PENNSYLVANIA** | | | | | | |
| Specter | Y | Y | N | Y | N | Y |
| Santorum | Y | Y | N | Y | N | Y |
| **RHODE ISLAND** | | | | | | |
| Reed | Y | Y | N | Y | N | Y |
| Chafee | Y | Y | N | N | N | Y |
| **SOUTH CAROLINA** | | | | | | |
| Graham | Y | Y | N | Y | N | Y |
| DeMint | Y | Y | N | Y | N | Y |
| **SOUTH DAKOTA** | | | | | | |
| Johnson | Y | Y | Y | Y | Y | Y |
| Thune | Y | Y | Y | Y | N | Y |
| **TENNESSEE** | | | | | | |
| Frist | Y | Y | N | Y | N | Y |
| Alexander | Y | Y | N | Y | N | Y |
| **TEXAS** | | | | | | |
| Hutchison | Y | Y | N | Y | N | Y |
| Cornyn | Y | Y | N | Y | N | Y |
| **UTAH** | | | | | | |
| Hatch | Y | Y | N | Y | N | Y |
| Bennett | Y | Y | N | Y | N | Y |
| **VERMONT** | | | | | | |
| Leahy | Y | Y | Y | N | Y | Y |
| Jeffords | Y | Y | Y | Y | N | Y |
| **VIRGINIA** | | | | | | |
| Warner | Y | Y | N | Y | N | Y |
| Allen | Y | Y | N | Y | N | Y |
| **WASHINGTON** | | | | | | |
| Murray | N | Y | N | N | Y | Y |
| Cantwell | N | Y | N | N | Y | Y |
| **WEST VIRGINIA** | | | | | | |
| Byrd | Y | Y | Y | Y | Y | ? |
| Rockefeller | Y | ? | N | N | Y | ? |
| **WISCONSIN** | | | | | | |
| Kohl | Y | Y | N | N | Y | Y |
| Feingold | Y | Y | Y | N | Y | Y |
| **WYOMING** | | | | | | |
| Thomas | Y | Y | N | Y | N | Y |
| Enzi | Y | N | Y | Y | N | Y |

**KEY** — Republicans — Democrats — *Independents*

| | | | |
|---|---|---|---|
| Y | Voted for (yea) | X | Paired against |
| # | Paired for | – | Announced against |
| + | Announced for | P | Voted "present" |
| N | Voted against (nay) | C | Voted "present" to avoid possible conflict of interest |
| | | ? | Did not vote or otherwise make a position known |

# IN THE SENATE | By Vote Number

**196.** **HR 3057. Fiscal 2006 Foreign Operations Appropriations/ Extradition Refusal.** Chambliss, R-Ga., amendment that would prohibit the State Department from providing assistance to any country that has refused to extradite individuals charged with committing certain crimes in the United States, regardless of their citizenship. Adopted 86-12: R 52-3; D 34-9 (ND 30-9, SD 4-0); I 0-1. July 20, 2005.

**197.** **HR 3057. Fiscal 2006 Foreign Operations Appropriations/Passage.** Passage of the bill that would appropriate $31.8 billion in fiscal 2006 for foreign operations and the State Department. It would appropriate $9.7 billion for the State Department and related agencies, and $22.1 billion for foreign aid programs, including $2.9 billion for programs to combat HIV/AIDS and related diseases, and $1.8 billion for the Millennium Challenge Corporation. Passed 98-1: R 54-0; D 43-1 (ND 39-1, SD 4-0); I 1-0. July 20, 2005.

**198.** **Dorr Nomination/Confirmation.** Confirmation of President Bush's nomination of Thomas C. Dorr as undersecretary of Agriculture for rural development. Confirmed 62-38: R 55-0; D 7-37 (ND 5-35, SD 2-2); I 0-1. A "yea" was a vote in support of the president's position. (Subsequently, Dorr was confirmed by voice vote as a member of the board of directors of the Commodity Credit Corporation.) July 21, 2005.

**199.** **S 1042. Fiscal 2006 Defense Authorization/Vehicle Armor.** Warner, R-Va., amendment that would authorize an additional $105 million to the Army and $340.4 million to the Marine Corps for the procurement of various high-mobility vehicles and add-on armor protection. It would be offset by a reduction of $445.4 million for the Iraq Freedom Fund. Adopted 100-0: R 55-0; D 44-0 (ND 40-0, SD 4-0); I 1-0. July 21, 2005.

**200.** **S 1042. Fiscal 2006 Defense Authorization/Non-Proliferation Programs.** Lugar, R-Ind., amendment that would remove certain restrictions on provisions of the Cooperative Threat Reduction Assistance program, including the removal of certifications the president must make for countries receiving assistance under it. Adopted 78-19: R 34-19; D 43-0 (ND 39-0, SD 4-0); I 1-0. July 21, 2005.

| | 196 | 197 | 198 | 199 | 200 |
|---|---|---|---|---|---|
| **ALABAMA** | | | | | |
| Shelby | Y | Y | Y | Y | N |
| Sessions | Y | Y | Y | Y | N |
| **ALASKA** | | | | | |
| Stevens | Y | Y | Y | Y | Y |
| Murkowski | Y | Y | Y | Y | Y |
| **ARIZONA** | | | | | |
| McCain | Y | Y | Y | Y | Y |
| Kyl | Y | Y | Y | Y | N |
| **ARKANSAS** | | | | | |
| Lincoln | Y | Y | Y | Y | Y |
| Pryor | Y | Y | Y | Y | Y |
| **CALIFORNIA** | | | | | |
| Feinstein | Y | Y | N | Y | Y |
| Boxer | Y | Y | N | Y | + |
| **COLORADO** | | | | | |
| Allard | Y | Y | Y | Y | N |
| Salazar | Y | Y | Y | Y | Y |
| **CONNECTICUT** | | | | | |
| Dodd | Y | Y | N | Y | Y |
| Lieberman | Y | Y | Y | Y | Y |
| **DELAWARE** | | | | | |
| Biden | Y | Y | N | Y | Y |
| Carper | Y | Y | N | Y | Y |
| **FLORIDA** | | | | | |
| Nelson | Y | Y | N | Y | Y |
| Martinez | Y | Y | Y | Y | Y |
| **GEORGIA** | | | | | |
| Chambliss | Y | Y | Y | Y | N |
| Isakson | Y | Y | Y | Y | N |
| **HAWAII** | | | | | |
| Inouye | Y | Y | Y | Y | Y |
| Akaka | N | Y | Y | Y | Y |
| **IDAHO** | | | | | |
| Craig | Y | Y | Y | Y | Y |
| Crapo | Y | Y | Y | Y | Y |
| **ILLINOIS** | | | | | |
| Durbin | Y | Y | N | Y | Y |
| Obama | Y | Y | N | Y | Y |
| **INDIANA** | | | | | |
| Lugar | N | Y | Y | Y | Y |
| Bayh | Y | Y | N | Y | Y |
| **IOWA** | | | | | |
| Grassley | Y | Y | Y | Y | N |
| Harkin | Y | Y | N | Y | Y |
| **KANSAS** | | | | | |
| Brownback | Y | Y | Y | Y | Y |
| Roberts | Y | Y | Y | Y | N |
| **KENTUCKY** | | | | | |
| McConnell | Y | Y | Y | Y | Y |
| Bunning | Y | Y | Y | Y | N |
| **LOUISIANA** | | | | | |
| Landrieu | Y | Y | N | Y | Y |
| Vitter | Y | Y | Y | Y | N |
| **MAINE** | | | | | |
| Snowe | Y | Y | Y | Y | Y |
| Collins | Y | Y | Y | Y | Y |
| **MARYLAND** | | | | | |
| Sarbanes | N | Y | N | Y | Y |
| Mikulski | N | Y | N | Y | Y |
| **MASSACHUSETTS** | | | | | |
| Kennedy | N | Y | N | Y | Y |
| Kerry | Y | Y | N | Y | Y |
| **MICHIGAN** | | | | | |
| Levin | Y | Y | N | Y | Y |
| Stabenow | Y | Y | N | Y | Y |
| **MINNESOTA** | | | | | |
| Dayton | N | Y | N | Y | Y |
| Coleman | Y | Y | Y | Y | Y |
| **MISSISSIPPI** | | | | | |
| Cochran | Y | Y | Y | Y | ? |
| Lott | Y | Y | Y | Y | Y |
| **MISSOURI** | | | | | |
| Bond | Y | Y | Y | Y | Y |
| Talent | Y | Y | Y | Y | N |
| **MONTANA** | | | | | |
| Baucus | Y | Y | N | Y | Y |
| Burns | Y | Y | Y | Y | Y |
| **NEBRASKA** | | | | | |
| Hagel | N | Y | Y | Y | Y |
| Nelson | Y | Y | Y | Y | Y |
| **NEVADA** | | | | | |
| Reid | Y | Y | N | Y | Y |
| Ensign | Y | Y | Y | Y | N |
| **NEW HAMPSHIRE** | | | | | |
| Gregg | Y | Y | Y | Y | Y |
| Sununu | Y | Y | Y | Y | Y |
| **NEW JERSEY** | | | | | |
| Corzine | Y | Y | N | Y | Y |
| Lautenberg | Y | Y | N | Y | Y |
| **NEW MEXICO** | | | | | |
| Domenici | Y | Y | Y | Y | Y |
| Bingaman | Y | Y | N | Y | Y |
| **NEW YORK** | | | | | |
| Schumer | Y | Y | N | Y | Y |
| Clinton | Y | Y | N | Y | Y |
| **NORTH CAROLINA** | | | | | |
| Dole | Y | Y | Y | Y | N |
| Burr | Y | Y | Y | Y | N |
| **NORTH DAKOTA** | | | | | |
| Conrad | Y | Y | N | Y | Y |
| Dorgan | Y | Y | N | Y | Y |
| **OHIO** | | | | | |
| DeWine | Y | Y | Y | Y | Y |
| Voinovich | N | Y | Y | Y | Y |
| **OKLAHOMA** | | | | | |
| Inhofe | Y | N | Y | Y | N |
| Coburn | Y | Y | Y | Y | Y |
| **OREGON** | | | | | |
| Wyden | Y | Y | N | Y | Y |
| Smith | Y | Y | Y | Y | Y |
| **PENNSYLVANIA** | | | | | |
| Specter | Y | Y | Y | Y | Y |
| Santorum | Y | Y | Y | Y | N |
| **RHODE ISLAND** | | | | | |
| Reed | N | Y | N | Y | Y |
| Chafee | Y | Y | Y | Y | Y |
| **SOUTH CAROLINA** | | | | | |
| Graham | Y | Y | Y | Y | Y |
| DeMint | Y | Y | Y | Y | N |
| **SOUTH DAKOTA** | | | | | |
| Johnson | Y | Y | N | Y | Y |
| Thune | Y | Y | Y | Y | Y |
| **TENNESSEE** | | | | | |
| Frist | Y | Y | Y | Y | ? |
| Alexander | Y | Y | Y | Y | Y |
| **TEXAS** | | | | | |
| Hutchison | Y | Y | Y | Y | Y |
| Cornyn | Y | Y | Y | Y | N |
| **UTAH** | | | | | |
| Hatch | Y | Y | Y | Y | Y |
| Bennett | Y | Y | Y | Y | Y |
| **VERMONT** | | | | | |
| Leahy | N | Y | N | Y | Y |
| Jeffords | N | Y | N | Y | Y |
| **VIRGINIA** | | | | | |
| Warner | Y | Y | Y | Y | N |
| Allen | Y | Y | Y | Y | Y |
| **WASHINGTON** | | | | | |
| Murray | Y | Y | N | Y | Y |
| Cantwell | Y | Y | N | Y | Y |
| **WEST VIRGINIA** | | | | | |
| Byrd | ? | Y | N | Y | Y |
| Rockefeller | ? | ? | N | Y | Y |
| **WISCONSIN** | | | | | |
| Kohl | Y | Y | N | Y | Y |
| Feingold | N | Y | N | Y | Y |
| **WYOMING** | | | | | |
| Thomas | Y | Y | Y | Y | Y |
| Enzi | Y | Y | Y | Y | Y |

**KEY**   Republicans   Democrats   *Independents*

| Y | Voted for (yea) | X | Paired against | C | Voted "present" to avoid possible conflict of interest |
|---|---|---|---|---|---|
| # | Paired for | – | Announced against | | |
| + | Announced for | P | Voted "present" | ? | Did not vote or otherwise make a position known |
| N | Voted against (nay) | | | | |

# IN THE SENATE | By Vote Number

**201.** **S Res 207. Americans with Disabilities Act Anniversary/Adoption.**
Adoption of the resolution that would commemorate the 15th anniversary of the enactment of the Americans with Disabilities Act of 1990 and salute those who contributed to it. Adopted 87-0: R 47-0; D 39-0 (ND 35-0, SD 4-0); I 1-0. July 25, 2005.

**202.** **S 1042. Fiscal 2006 Defense Authorization/Terrorist Financing.**
Collins, R-Maine, amendment that would strengthen penalties for U.S. parent companies and their employees that do business with terrorist nations. It would increase the statutory limit in civil penalties under the International Emergency Economic Powers Act from $10,000 to $250,000 and from $50,000 to $500,000 for willful violations. It also would grant the Treasury Department subpoena power. Adopted 98-0: R 54-0; D 43-0 (ND 39-0, SD 4-0); I 1-0. July 26, 2005.

**203.** **S 1042. Fiscal 2006 Defense Authorization/Terrorist Financing.**
Lautenberg, D-N.J., amendment that would make certain foreign subsidiaries controlled by U.S. parent companies subject to sanctions under the International Emergency Economic Powers Act if they engage in business with terrorist nations. It also would require all firms subject to U.S. law to annually disclose an ownership stake of more than 10 percent in companies that are engaged in transactions that violate the terrorist financing law. Rejected 47-51: R 3-51; D 43-0 (ND 39-0, SD 4-0); I 1-0. July 26, 2005.

**204.** **S 1042. Fiscal 2006 Defense Authorization/Support of Youth Organizations.** Frist, R-Tenn., amendment that would stipulate that a federal agency cannot provide less support to youth organizations than the agency has in the past, except under certain special circumstances. It also would stipulate that the Defense secretary should provide at least the same level of support for a national or world Boy Scouts Jamboree as the department has provided in the past. Adopted 98-0: R 54-0; D 43-0 (ND 39-0, SD 4-0); I 1-0. July 26, 2005.

**205.** **S 1042. Fiscal 2006 Defense Authorization/Cloture.** McConnell, R-Ky., motion to invoke cloture on the bill that would authorize $441.6 billion for defense programs and another $50 billion for military action in Iraq and Afghanistan for fiscal 2006. Motion rejected 50-48: R 47-7; D 3-40 (ND 2-37, SD 1-3); I 0-1. Three-fifths of the total Senate (60) is required to invoke cloture. July 26, 2005.

| | 201 | 202 | 203 | 204 | 205 | | | 201 | 202 | 203 | 204 | 205 |
|---|---|---|---|---|---|---|---|---|---|---|---|---|
| **ALABAMA** | | | | | | | **MONTANA** | | | | | |
| Shelby | Y | Y | N | Y | Y | | Baucus | Y | Y | Y | Y | N |
| Sessions | Y | Y | N | Y | Y | | Burns | Y | Y | N | Y | Y |
| **ALASKA** | | | | | | | **NEBRASKA** | | | | | |
| Stevens | Y | Y | N | Y | Y | | Hagel | Y | Y | N | Y | Y |
| Murkowski | Y | Y | N | Y | Y | | Nelson | Y | Y | Y | Y | Y |
| **ARIZONA** | | | | | | | **NEVADA** | | | | | |
| McCain | Y | Y | N | Y | N | | Reid | Y | Y | Y | Y | N |
| Kyl | ? | Y | Y | Y | Y | | Ensign | Y | Y | Y | Y | Y |
| **ARKANSAS** | | | | | | | **NEW HAMPSHIRE** | | | | | |
| Lincoln | Y | Y | Y | Y | N | | Gregg | Y | Y | N | Y | Y |
| Pryor | Y | Y | Y | Y | N | | Sununu | Y | Y | N | Y | Y |
| **CALIFORNIA** | | | | | | | **NEW JERSEY** | | | | | |
| Feinstein | Y | Y | Y | Y | N | | Corzine | ? | Y | Y | Y | N |
| Boxer | Y | Y | Y | Y | N | | Lautenberg | Y | Y | Y | Y | N |
| **COLORADO** | | | | | | | **NEW MEXICO** | | | | | |
| Allard | Y | Y | N | Y | Y | | Domenici | Y | Y | N | Y | Y |
| Salazar | Y | Y | Y | Y | N | | Bingaman | Y | Y | Y | Y | N |
| **CONNECTICUT** | | | | | | | **NEW YORK** | | | | | |
| Dodd | Y | Y | Y | Y | N | | Schumer | Y | Y | Y | Y | N |
| Lieberman | Y | Y | Y | Y | N | | Clinton | Y | Y | Y | Y | N |
| **DELAWARE** | | | | | | | **NORTH CAROLINA** | | | | | |
| Biden | ? | Y | Y | Y | N | | Dole | Y | Y | N | Y | Y |
| Carper | Y | Y | Y | Y | N | | Burr | Y | Y | Y | Y | Y |
| **FLORIDA** | | | | | | | **NORTH DAKOTA** | | | | | |
| Nelson | Y | Y | Y | Y | Y | | Conrad | Y | Y | Y | Y | N |
| Martinez | ? | Y | N | Y | Y | | Dorgan | Y | Y | Y | Y | N |
| **GEORGIA** | | | | | | | **OHIO** | | | | | |
| Chambliss | ? | Y | N | Y | Y | | DeWine | Y | Y | N | Y | Y |
| Isakson | Y | Y | N | Y | Y | | Voinovich | Y | Y | N | Y | Y |
| **HAWAII** | | | | | | | **OKLAHOMA** | | | | | |
| Inouye | Y | Y | Y | Y | N | | Inhofe | Y | Y | N | Y | Y |
| Akaka | Y | Y | Y | Y | N | | Coburn | Y | Y | N | Y | Y |
| **IDAHO** | | | | | | | **OREGON** | | | | | |
| Craig | ? | ? | ? | ? | ? | | Wyden | Y | Y | Y | Y | N |
| Crapo | Y | Y | N | Y | Y | | Smith | Y | Y | N | Y | Y |
| **ILLINOIS** | | | | | | | **PENNSYLVANIA** | | | | | |
| Durbin | Y | Y | Y | Y | N | | Specter | Y | Y | N | Y | Y |
| Obama | Y | Y | Y | Y | N | | Santorum | ? | Y | N | Y | Y |
| **INDIANA** | | | | | | | **RHODE ISLAND** | | | | | |
| Lugar | Y | Y | N | Y | Y | | Reed | Y | Y | Y | Y | N |
| Bayh | ? | Y | Y | Y | N | | Chafee | Y | Y | Y | Y | N |
| **IOWA** | | | | | | | **SOUTH CAROLINA** | | | | | |
| Grassley | Y | Y | N | Y | Y | | Graham | Y | Y | N | Y | N |
| Harkin | Y | Y | Y | Y | N | | DeMint | Y | Y | N | Y | Y |
| **KANSAS** | | | | | | | **SOUTH DAKOTA** | | | | | |
| Brownback | Y | Y | N | Y | Y | | Johnson | Y | Y | Y | Y | N |
| Roberts | Y | Y | N | Y | Y | | Thune | Y | Y | N | Y | N |
| **KENTUCKY** | | | | | | | **TENNESSEE** | | | | | |
| McConnell | Y | Y | N | Y | Y | | Frist | ? | Y | Y | Y | Y |
| Bunning | Y | Y | N | Y | Y | | Alexander | Y | Y | N | Y | Y |
| **LOUISIANA** | | | | | | | **TEXAS** | | | | | |
| Landrieu | Y | Y | Y | Y | N | | Hutchison | Y | Y | N | Y | Y |
| Vitter | Y | Y | N | Y | Y | | Cornyn | Y | Y | N | Y | Y |
| **MAINE** | | | | | | | **UTAH** | | | | | |
| Snowe | Y | Y | N | Y | N | | Hatch | Y | Y | N | Y | Y |
| Collins | Y | Y | N | Y | N | | Bennett | ? | Y | N | Y | Y |
| **MARYLAND** | | | | | | | **VERMONT** | | | | | |
| Sarbanes | Y | Y | Y | Y | N | | Leahy | Y | Y | Y | Y | N |
| Mikulski | Y | Y | Y | Y | N | | *Jeffords* | Y | Y | Y | Y | N |
| **MASSACHUSETTS** | | | | | | | **VIRGINIA** | | | | | |
| Kennedy | ? | Y | Y | Y | N | | Warner | Y | Y | N | Y | Y |
| Kerry | Y | Y | Y | Y | N | | Allen | Y | Y | N | Y | Y |
| **MICHIGAN** | | | | | | | **WASHINGTON** | | | | | |
| Levin | Y | Y | Y | Y | N | | Murray | Y | Y | Y | Y | N |
| Stabenow | Y | Y | Y | Y | N | | Cantwell | Y | Y | Y | Y | N |
| **MINNESOTA** | | | | | | | **WEST VIRGINIA** | | | | | |
| Dayton | Y | Y | Y | Y | N | | Byrd | Y | Y | Y | Y | N |
| Coleman | Y | Y | N | Y | Y | | Rockefeller | ? | ? | ? | ? | ? |
| **MISSISSIPPI** | | | | | | | **WISCONSIN** | | | | | |
| Cochran | ? | Y | N | Y | Y | | Kohl | Y | Y | Y | Y | N |
| Lott | Y | Y | N | Y | N | | Feingold | Y | Y | Y | Y | N |
| **MISSOURI** | | | | | | | **WYOMING** | | | | | |
| Bond | Y | Y | N | Y | Y | | Thomas | Y | Y | N | Y | Y |
| Talent | Y | Y | N | Y | Y | | Enzi | Y | Y | N | Y | Y |

**KEY**   Republicans   Democrats   *Independents*

| | | | | |
|---|---|---|---|---|
| **Y** | Voted for (yea) | **X** | Paired against | **C** Voted "present" to avoid possible conflict of interest |
| **#** | Paired for | **–** | Announced against | |
| **+** | Announced for | **P** | Voted "present" | **?** Did not vote or otherwise make a position known |
| **N** | Voted against (nay) | | | |

# IN THE SENATE | By Vote Number

**206.** **S 397. Gun Liability/Cloture.** McConnell, R-Ky., motion to invoke cloture (thus limiting debate) on the motion to proceed to the bill that would prohibit civil liability actions from being brought in any state or federal court against manufacturers, distributors, dealers and importers of firearms and ammunition resulting from the misuse of their products by others. Motion agreed to 66-32: R 53-1; D 13-30 (ND 9-30, SD 4-0); I 0-1. Three-fifths of the total Senate (60) is required to invoke cloture. July 26, 2005.

**207.** **S 397. Gun Liability/Safety Locks.** Kohl, D-Wis., amendment that would add a section to the bill that would, with certain exceptions, make it unlawful for licensed gun importers, manufacturers or dealers to sell, deliver or transfer handguns without a secure gun storage or safety device. It also would establish penalties for non-compliance, including a six-month suspension of a license, the revocation of a license or a $2,500 fine. Adopted 70-30: R 25-30; D 44-0 (ND 40-0, SD 4-0); I 1-0. July 28, 2005.

**208.** **S 397. Gun Liability/Civil Liability.** Craig, R-Idaho, motion to table (kill) the Levin, D-Mich., amendment that would add a section to the bill allowing civil liability action against all gun dealers and manufacturers who commit reckless or grossly negligent practices that contribute to a death or injury. Motion agreed to 62-37: R 50-4; D 12-32 (ND 9-31, SD 3-1); I 0-1. July 28, 2005.

**209.** **HR 3045. Central American Free Trade Agreement/Passage.** Passage of the bill that would implement a free trade agreement between the United States and Costa Rica, El Salvador, Guatemala, Honduras, Nicaragua and a separate pact with the Dominican Republic. Passed (thus cleared for the president) 55-45: R 43-12; D 11-33 (ND 8-32, SD 3-1); I 1-0. July 28, 2005.

| | 206 | 207 | 208 | 209 | | | 206 | 207 | 208 | 209 |
|---|---|---|---|---|---|---|---|---|---|---|
| **ALABAMA** | | | | | | **MONTANA** | | | | |
| Shelby | Y | N | Y | N | | Baucus | Y | Y | Y | N |
| Sessions | Y | N | Y | Y | | Burns | Y | N | Y | N |
| **ALASKA** | | | | | | **NEBRASKA** | | | | |
| Stevens | Y | Y | Y | Y | | Hagel | Y | Y | Y | Y |
| Murkowski | Y | Y | Y | Y | | Nelson | Y | Y | Y | Y |
| **ARIZONA** | | | | | | **NEVADA** | | | | |
| McCain | Y | Y | Y | Y | | Reid | Y | Y | Y | N |
| Kyl | Y | N | Y | Y | | Ensign | Y | N | Y | Y |
| **ARKANSAS** | | | | | | **NEW HAMPSHIRE** | | | | |
| Lincoln | Y | Y | Y | Y | | Gregg | Y | Y | Y | Y |
| Pryor | Y | Y | Y | Y | | Sununu | Y | Y | Y | Y |
| **CALIFORNIA** | | | | | | **NEW JERSEY** | | | | |
| Feinstein | N | Y | N | Y | | Corzine | N | Y | N | N |
| Boxer | N | Y | N | N | | Lautenberg | N | Y | N | N |
| **COLORADO** | | | | | | **NEW MEXICO** | | | | |
| Allard | Y | N | Y | Y | | Domenici | Y | Y | ? | Y |
| Salazar | Y | Y | Y | N | | Bingaman | N | Y | N | Y |
| **CONNECTICUT** | | | | | | **NEW YORK** | | | | |
| Dodd | N | Y | N | N | | Schumer | N | Y | N | N |
| Lieberman | N | Y | N | Y | | Clinton | N | Y | N | N |
| **DELAWARE** | | | | | | **NORTH CAROLINA** | | | | |
| Biden | N | Y | N | N | | Dole | Y | N | Y | Y |
| Carper | N | Y | N | Y | | Burr | Y | N | Y | Y |
| **FLORIDA** | | | | | | **NORTH DAKOTA** | | | | |
| Nelson | Y | Y | N | Y | | Conrad | Y | Y | Y | N |
| Martinez | Y | N | Y | Y | | Dorgan | Y | Y | Y | N |
| **GEORGIA** | | | | | | **OHIO** | | | | |
| Chambliss | Y | N | Y | Y | | DeWine | N | Y | N | Y |
| Isakson | Y | N | Y | Y | | Voinovich | Y | Y | Y | Y |
| **HAWAII** | | | | | | **OKLAHOMA** | | | | |
| Inouye | N | Y | N | N | | Inhofe | Y | N | Y | Y |
| Akaka | N | Y | N | N | | Coburn | Y | N | Y | Y |
| **IDAHO** | | | | | | **OREGON** | | | | |
| Craig | ? | N | Y | N | | Wyden | N | Y | N | Y |
| Crapo | Y | N | Y | N | | Smith | Y | Y | Y | Y |
| **ILLINOIS** | | | | | | **PENNSYLVANIA** | | | | |
| Durbin | N | Y | N | N | | Specter | Y | Y | Y | N |
| Obama | N | Y | N | N | | Santorum | Y | Y | Y | Y |
| **INDIANA** | | | | | | **RHODE ISLAND** | | | | |
| Lugar | Y | Y | N | Y | | Reed | N | Y | N | N |
| Bayh | N | Y | N | N | | Chafee | Y | Y | N | Y |
| **IOWA** | | | | | | **SOUTH CAROLINA** | | | | |
| Grassley | Y | Y | Y | Y | | Graham | Y | N | Y | Y |
| Harkin | N | Y | N | N | | DeMint | Y | N | Y | Y |
| **KANSAS** | | | | | | **SOUTH DAKOTA** | | | | |
| Brownback | Y | Y | Y | Y | | Johnson | Y | Y | Y | N |
| Roberts | Y | Y | Y | Y | | Thune | Y | N | Y | N |
| **KENTUCKY** | | | | | | **TENNESSEE** | | | | |
| McConnell | Y | Y | Y | Y | | Frist | Y | Y | Y | Y |
| Bunning | Y | N | Y | Y | | Alexander | Y | N | Y | Y |
| **LOUISIANA** | | | | | | **TEXAS** | | | | |
| Landrieu | Y | Y | Y | N | | Hutchison | Y | Y | Y | Y |
| Vitter | Y | N | Y | N | | Cornyn | Y | N | Y | Y |
| **MAINE** | | | | | | **UTAH** | | | | |
| Snowe | Y | Y | Y | N | | Hatch | Y | N | Y | Y |
| Collins | Y | Y | Y | N | | Bennett | Y | N | Y | Y |
| **MARYLAND** | | | | | | **VERMONT** | | | | |
| Sarbanes | N | Y | N | N | | Leahy | N | Y | N | Y |
| Mikulski | N | Y | N | N | | Jeffords | N | Y | N | Y |
| **MASSACHUSETTS** | | | | | | **VIRGINIA** | | | | |
| Kennedy | N | Y | N | N | | Warner | Y | Y | N | Y |
| Kerry | N | Y | N | N | | Allen | Y | N | Y | Y |
| **MICHIGAN** | | | | | | **WASHINGTON** | | | | |
| Levin | N | Y | N | N | | Murray | N | Y | N | Y |
| Stabenow | N | Y | N | N | | Cantwell | N | Y | N | Y |
| **MINNESOTA** | | | | | | **WEST VIRGINIA** | | | | |
| Dayton | N | Y | N | N | | Byrd | Y | Y | Y | N |
| Coleman | Y | Y | Y | Y | | Rockefeller | ? | Y | Y | N |
| **MISSISSIPPI** | | | | | | **WISCONSIN** | | | | |
| Cochran | Y | N | Y | Y | | Kohl | Y | Y | N | N |
| Lott | Y | N | Y | Y | | Feingold | N | Y | N | N |
| **MISSOURI** | | | | | | **WYOMING** | | | | |
| Bond | Y | N | Y | Y | | Thomas | Y | N | Y | N |
| Talent | Y | N | Y | Y | | Enzi | Y | N | Y | N |

**KEY**   Republicans   Democrats   *Independents*

| | | | | | |
|---|---|---|---|---|---|
| Y | Voted for (yea) | X | Paired against | C | Voted "present" to avoid possible conflict of interest |
| # | Paired for | – | Announced against | | |
| + | Announced for | P | Voted "present" | ? | Did not vote or otherwise make a position known |
| N | Voted against (nay) | | | | |

# IN THE SENATE | By Vote Number

**210. HR 2361. Fiscal 2006 Interior-Environment Appropriations/ Conference Report.** Adoption of the conference report on the bill that would appropriate $26.2 billion in fiscal 2006 for the Interior Department, the EPA and related agencies. It would provide $9.9 billion for the Interior Department, $7.7 billion for the EPA, $4.3 billion for the Forest Service and $3.1 billion for the Indian Health Service. It also would provide $1.5 billion in fiscal 2005 funding for veterans' medical care. Adopted (thus cleared for the president) 99-1: R 54-1; D 44-0 (ND 40-0, SD 4-0); I 1-0. July 29, 2005.

**211. HR 2985. Fiscal 2006 Legislative Branch Appropriations/ Conference Report.** Adoption of the conference report on the bill that would appropriate $3.8 billion in fiscal 2006 for legislative branch operations, including $1.1 billion for operations of the House of Representatives and $786 million for Senate operations. It also would require states to hold special elections within 49 days in the event that more than 100 lawmakers are killed or incapacitated. Adopted (thus cleared for the president) 96-4: R 52-3; D 43-1 (ND 39-1, SD 4-0); I 1-0. July 29, 2005.

**212. HR 6. Energy Policy/Conference Report.** Domenici, R-N.M., motion to waive the Budget Act with respect to the Feingold, D-Wis., point of order against the conference report on the bill that would overhaul the nation's energy policy and provide for $14.6 billion in energy-related tax incentives. Motion agreed to 71-29: R 46-9; D 25-19 (ND 22-18, SD 3-1); I 0-1. A three-fifths majority (60) of the total Senate is required to waive the Budget Act. July 29, 2005.

**213. HR 6. Energy Policy/Conference Report.** Adoption of the conference report on the bill that would overhaul the nation's energy policy and provide for $14.6 billion in energy-related tax incentives. It would allow lawsuits involving the gasoline additive methyl tertiary butyl ether (MTBE) to be moved to federal district court and require refiners to use 7.5 billion gallons of renewable fuels annually by 2012. It would grant the Federal Energy Regulatory Commission jurisdiction over reliability standards for electricity transmission networks and extend daylight-saving time by one month. Adopted (thus cleared for the president) 74-26: R 49-6; D 25-19 (ND 22-18, SD 3-1); I 0-1. A "yea" was a vote in support of the president's position. July 29, 2005.

**214. S 397. Gun Liability/Child Victims.** Craig, R-Idaho, amendment that would insert language to clarify that nothing in the bill would limit the right of individuals under the age of 17 to recover damages authorized under federal or state law in a civil action suit that meets the existing exceptions in the bill. Adopted 72-26: R 52-2; D 20-23 (ND 16-23, SD 4-0); I 0-1. July 29, 2005.

| | 210 | 211 | 212 | 213 | 214 |
|---|---|---|---|---|---|
| **ALABAMA** | | | | | |
| Shelby | Y | Y | Y | Y | Y |
| Sessions | Y | Y | Y | Y | Y |
| **ALASKA** | | | | | |
| Stevens | Y | Y | Y | Y | Y |
| Murkowski | Y | Y | Y | Y | Y |
| **ARIZONA** | | | | | |
| McCain | Y | Y | N | N | Y |
| Kyl | Y | Y | N | N | Y |
| **ARKANSAS** | | | | | |
| Lincoln | Y | Y | Y | Y | Y |
| Pryor | Y | Y | Y | Y | Y |
| **CALIFORNIA** | | | | | |
| Feinstein | Y | Y | Y | N | N |
| Boxer | Y | Y | N | N | N |
| **COLORADO** | | | | | |
| Allard | Y | Y | Y | Y | Y |
| Salazar | Y | Y | Y | Y | Y |
| **CONNECTICUT** | | | | | |
| Dodd | Y | Y | Y | N | N |
| Lieberman | Y | Y | Y | Y | Y |
| **DELAWARE** | | | | | |
| Biden | Y | Y | N | N | – |
| Carper | Y | Y | N | N | N |
| **FLORIDA** | | | | | |
| Nelson | Y | Y | N | N | Y |
| Martinez | Y | Y | N | N | Y |
| **GEORGIA** | | | | | |
| Chambliss | Y | Y | N | Y | Y |
| Isakson | Y | Y | N | Y | Y |
| **HAWAII** | | | | | |
| Inouye | Y | Y | Y | N | N |
| Akaka | Y | Y | Y | N | N |
| **IDAHO** | | | | | |
| Craig | Y | Y | Y | Y | Y |
| Crapo | Y | Y | Y | Y | Y |
| **ILLINOIS** | | | | | |
| Durbin | Y | Y | Y | N | N |
| Obama | Y | Y | Y | N | N |
| **INDIANA** | | | | | |
| Lugar | Y | Y | Y | Y | Y |
| Bayh | Y | Y | N | Y | Y |
| **IOWA** | | | | | |
| Grassley | Y | Y | Y | Y | Y |
| Harkin | Y | Y | Y | N | N |
| **KANSAS** | | | | | |
| Brownback | Y | Y | Y | Y | Y |
| Roberts | Y | Y | Y | Y | Y |
| **KENTUCKY** | | | | | |
| McConnell | Y | Y | Y | Y | Y |
| Bunning | Y | Y | Y | Y | Y |
| **LOUISIANA** | | | | | |
| Landrieu | Y | Y | Y | Y | Y |
| Vitter | Y | Y | Y | Y | Y |
| **MAINE** | | | | | |
| Snowe | Y | Y | Y | Y | Y |
| Collins | Y | Y | Y | Y | Y |
| **MARYLAND** | | | | | |
| Sarbanes | Y | Y | N | N | N |
| Mikulski | Y | Y | Y | N | N |
| **MASSACHUSETTS** | | | | | |
| Kennedy | Y | Y | N | N | N |
| Kerry | Y | Y | N | N | N |
| **MICHIGAN** | | | | | |
| Levin | Y | Y | Y | Y | Y |
| Stabenow | Y | Y | Y | Y | Y |
| **MINNESOTA** | | | | | |
| Dayton | Y | Y | Y | N | N |
| Coleman | Y | Y | Y | Y | Y |
| **MISSISSIPPI** | | | | | |
| Cochran | Y | Y | Y | Y | Y |
| Lott | Y | Y | Y | Y | Y |
| **MISSOURI** | | | | | |
| Bond | Y | Y | Y | Y | Y |
| Talent | Y | Y | Y | Y | Y |
| **MONTANA** | | | | | |
| Baucus | Y | Y | Y | Y | Y |
| Burns | Y | Y | Y | Y | Y |
| **NEBRASKA** | | | | | |
| Hagel | Y | Y | Y | Y | Y |
| Nelson | Y | Y | Y | Y | Y |
| **NEVADA** | | | | | |
| Reid | Y | Y | N | N | Y |
| Ensign | Y | N | Y | Y | Y |
| **NEW HAMPSHIRE** | | | | | |
| Gregg | Y | Y | N | N | Y |
| Sununu | Y | Y | N | N | ? |
| **NEW JERSEY** | | | | | |
| Corzine | Y | Y | N | N | N |
| Lautenberg | Y | Y | N | N | N |
| **NEW MEXICO** | | | | | |
| Domenici | Y | Y | Y | Y | Y |
| Bingaman | Y | Y | Y | Y | Y |
| **NEW YORK** | | | | | |
| Schumer | Y | Y | N | N | N |
| Clinton | Y | Y | N | N | N |
| **NORTH CAROLINA** | | | | | |
| Dole | Y | Y | Y | Y | Y |
| Burr | Y | Y | Y | Y | Y |
| **NORTH DAKOTA** | | | | | |
| Conrad | Y | N | Y | Y | Y |
| Dorgan | Y | Y | Y | Y | Y |
| **OHIO** | | | | | |
| DeWine | Y | Y | Y | Y | N |
| Voinovich | Y | Y | Y | Y | Y |
| **OKLAHOMA** | | | | | |
| Inhofe | Y | N | Y | Y | Y |
| Coburn | N | N | Y | Y | Y |
| **OREGON** | | | | | |
| Wyden | Y | Y | N | N | N |
| Smith | Y | Y | Y | N | N |
| **PENNSYLVANIA** | | | | | |
| Specter | Y | Y | Y | Y | Y |
| Santorum | Y | Y | Y | Y | Y |
| **RHODE ISLAND** | | | | | |
| Reed | Y | Y | N | N | N |
| Chafee | Y | Y | N | N | N |
| **SOUTH CAROLINA** | | | | | |
| Graham | Y | Y | Y | Y | Y |
| DeMint | Y | Y | Y | Y | Y |
| **SOUTH DAKOTA** | | | | | |
| Johnson | Y | Y | Y | Y | Y |
| Thune | Y | Y | Y | Y | ? |
| **TENNESSEE** | | | | | |
| Frist | Y | Y | Y | Y | Y |
| Alexander | Y | Y | Y | Y | Y |
| **TEXAS** | | | | | |
| Hutchison | Y | Y | Y | Y | Y |
| Cornyn | Y | Y | N | Y | Y |
| **UTAH** | | | | | |
| Hatch | Y | Y | Y | Y | Y |
| Bennett | Y | Y | Y | Y | Y |
| **VERMONT** | | | | | |
| Leahy | Y | Y | N | N | N |
| Jeffords | Y | Y | N | N | N |
| **VIRGINIA** | | | | | |
| Warner | Y | Y | Y | Y | Y |
| Allen | Y | Y | Y | Y | Y |
| **WASHINGTON** | | | | | |
| Murray | Y | Y | N | N | Y |
| Cantwell | Y | Y | Y | Y | Y |
| **WEST VIRGINIA** | | | | | |
| Byrd | Y | Y | Y | Y | Y |
| Rockefeller | Y | Y | Y | Y | Y |
| **WISCONSIN** | | | | | |
| Kohl | Y | Y | N | Y | Y |
| Feingold | Y | Y | N | N | N |
| **WYOMING** | | | | | |
| Thomas | Y | Y | Y | Y | Y |
| Enzi | Y | Y | Y | Y | Y |

**KEY**   Republicans   Democrats   *Independents*

| | | |
|---|---|---|
| Y Voted for (yea) | X Paired against | C Voted "present" to avoid possible conflict of interest |
| # Paired for | – Announced against | |
| + Announced for | P Voted "present" | ? Did not vote or otherwise make a position known |
| N Voted against (nay) | | |

# IN THE SENATE | By Vote Number

**215.** **S 397. Gun Liability/Child Victims.** Lautenberg, D-N.J., amendment that would exempt lawsuits involving injuries to individuals age 17 and under from the bill's definition of qualified civil liability action. Rejected 35-64: R 2-52; D 32-12 (ND 31-9, SD 1-3); I 1-0. July 29, 2005.

**216.** **S 397. Gun Liability/Armor-Piercing Ammunition.** Craig, R-Idaho, amendment that would require the attorney general to commission a study to determine whether a uniform standard for the testing of projectiles against body armor is feasible. It also would increase the penalties for violent or drug trafficking crimes in which the perpetrator uses or possesses armor-piercing ammunition to a minimum of 15 years imprisonment. Adopted 87-11: R 53-0; D 33-11 (ND 29-11, SD 4-0); I 1-0. July 29, 2005.

**217.** **S 397. Gun Liability/Armor-Piercing Ammunition.** Kennedy, D-Mass., amendment that would expand the current ban on armor-piercing handgun ammunition by adding a performance standard to the current content-based standard and by prohibiting certain ammunition for sniper rifles and assault weapons. Rejected 31-64: R 1-50; D 30-13 (ND 29-10, SD 1-3); I 0-1. July 29, 2005.

**218.** **S 397. Gun Liability/Substitute.** Reed, D-R.I., substitute amendment that would bar certain civil lawsuits against manufacturers, distributors, dealers and importers of firearms and ammunition, principally those lawsuits aimed at making them liable for gun violence. The substitute would block municipalities from suing for damages caused by firearms but would allow individuals to sue. Rejected 33-63: R 2-50; D 30-13 (ND 29-10, SD 1-3); I 1-0. July 29, 2005.

**219.** **S 397. Gun Liability/Passage.** Passage of the bill that would bar certain civil lawsuits against manufacturers, distributors, dealers and importers of firearms and ammunition, principally those lawsuits aimed at making them liable for gun violence. Trade groups also would be protected, and all pending legal action against gunmakers would be dismissed. It also would, with certain exceptions, make it unlawful for licensed gun importers, manufacturers or dealers to sell, deliver or transfer handguns without a secure gun storage or safety device. Passed 65-31: R 50-2; D 14-29 (ND 10-29, SD 4-0); I 1-0. A "yea" was a vote in support of the president's position. July 29, 2005.

**220.** **HR 3. Surface Transportation Reauthorization/Conference Report.** Adoption of the conference report on the bill that would bring total authorization for federal aid highway, mass transit, safety and research programs, including fiscal 2004 funding, to $286.5 billion through 2009. The bill would increase the rate of return to states on their Highway Trust Fund contributions to 92 percent by fiscal 2008. It would make the Transportation Department the lead agency in the environmental review process for transportation projects. Adopted (thus cleared for the president) 91-4: R 48-4; D 42-0 (ND 38-0, SD 4-0); I 1-0. July 29, 2005.

| | 215 | 216 | 217 | 218 | 219 | 220 | | 215 | 216 | 217 | 218 | 219 | 220 |
|---|---|---|---|---|---|---|---|---|---|---|---|---|---|
| **ALABAMA** | | | | | | | **MONTANA** | | | | | | |
| Shelby | N | Y | N | N | Y | Y | Baucus | N | Y | N | N | Y | Y |
| Sessions | N | Y | N | N | Y | Y | Burns | N | Y | N | N | Y | Y |
| **ALASKA** | | | | | | | **NEBRASKA** | | | | | | |
| Stevens | N | Y | N | N | Y | Y | Hagel | N | Y | N | N | Y | Y |
| Murkowski | N | Y | N | N | Y | Y | Nelson | N | Y | N | N | Y | Y |
| **ARIZONA** | | | | | | | **NEVADA** | | | | | | |
| McCain | N | Y | N | N | Y | N | Reid | N | Y | N | N | Y | Y |
| Kyl | N | Y | N | N | Y | N | Ensign | N | Y | N | N | Y | Y |
| **ARKANSAS** | | | | | | | **NEW HAMPSHIRE** | | | | | | |
| Lincoln | N | Y | N | N | Y | Y | Gregg | N | Y | N | N | Y | N |
| Pryor | N | Y | N | N | Y | Y | Sununu | ? | ? | ? | ? | ? | ? |
| **CALIFORNIA** | | | | | | | **NEW JERSEY** | | | | | | |
| Feinstein | Y | Y | + | + | – | + | Corzine | Y | N | Y | Y | N | Y |
| Boxer | Y | N | Y | Y | N | + | Lautenberg | Y | N | Y | Y | N | Y |
| **COLORADO** | | | | | | | **NEW MEXICO** | | | | | | |
| Allard | N | Y | N | N | Y | Y | Domenici | N | Y | N | N | Y | Y |
| Salazar | N | Y | N | N | Y | Y | Bingaman | Y | Y | N | Y | N | Y |
| **CONNECTICUT** | | | | | | | **NEW YORK** | | | | | | |
| Dodd | Y | Y | Y | Y | N | Y | Schumer | Y | Y | Y | Y | N | Y |
| Lieberman | Y | N | Y | N | N | Y | Clinton | Y | Y | Y | Y | N | Y |
| **DELAWARE** | | | | | | | **NORTH CAROLINA** | | | | | | |
| Biden | Y | Y | Y | Y | N | Y | Dole | N | Y | N | N | Y | Y |
| Carper | Y | Y | Y | Y | N | Y | Burr | N | Y | N | N | Y | Y |
| **FLORIDA** | | | | | | | **NORTH DAKOTA** | | | | | | |
| Nelson | Y | Y | Y | Y | Y | Y | Conrad | N | Y | N | N | Y | Y |
| Martinez | N | Y | N | N | Y | Y | Dorgan | N | Y | N | N | Y | Y |
| **GEORGIA** | | | | | | | **OHIO** | | | | | | |
| Chambliss | N | Y | N | N | Y | Y | DeWine | Y | Y | N | Y | N | Y |
| Isakson | N | Y | N | N | Y | Y | Voinovich | N | Y | N | N | Y | Y |
| **HAWAII** | | | | | | | **OKLAHOMA** | | | | | | |
| Inouye | Y | Y | Y | Y | N | Y | Inhofe | N | Y | N | N | Y | Y |
| Akaka | Y | N | Y | N | N | Y | Coburn | N | Y | N | N | Y | Y |
| **IDAHO** | | | | | | | **OREGON** | | | | | | |
| Craig | N | Y | N | N | Y | Y | Wyden | Y | N | Y | Y | N | Y |
| Crapo | N | Y | N | N | Y | Y | Smith | N | Y | ? | – | + | + |
| **ILLINOIS** | | | | | | | **PENNSYLVANIA** | | | | | | |
| Durbin | Y | Y | Y | Y | N | Y | Specter | N | Y | N | N | Y | Y |
| Obama | Y | Y | Y | Y | N | Y | Santorum | N | Y | N | N | Y | Y |
| **INDIANA** | | | | | | | **RHODE ISLAND** | | | | | | |
| Lugar | N | Y | N | N | Y | Y | Reed | N | Y | N | Y | N | Y |
| Bayh | Y | Y | Y | Y | N | Y | Chafee | Y | Y | Y | Y | N | Y |
| **IOWA** | | | | | | | **SOUTH CAROLINA** | | | | | | |
| Grassley | N | Y | N | N | Y | Y | Graham | N | Y | N | N | Y | Y |
| Harkin | Y | Y | Y | Y | N | Y | DeMint | N | Y | N | N | Y | Y |
| **KANSAS** | | | | | | | **SOUTH DAKOTA** | | | | | | |
| Brownback | N | Y | N | N | Y | Y | Johnson | N | Y | N | N | Y | Y |
| Roberts | N | + | – | – | + | + | Thune | N | Y | N | N | Y | Y |
| **KENTUCKY** | | | | | | | **TENNESSEE** | | | | | | |
| McConnell | N | Y | N | N | Y | Y | Frist | N | Y | N | N | Y | Y |
| Bunning | N | Y | N | N | Y | Y | Alexander | N | Y | N | N | Y | Y |
| **LOUISIANA** | | | | | | | **TEXAS** | | | | | | |
| Landrieu | N | Y | N | N | Y | Y | Hutchison | N | Y | N | N | Y | Y |
| Vitter | N | Y | N | N | Y | Y | Cornyn | N | Y | ? | N | Y | N |
| **MAINE** | | | | | | | **UTAH** | | | | | | |
| Snowe | N | Y | N | N | Y | Y | Hatch | N | Y | N | N | Y | Y |
| Collins | N | Y | N | N | Y | Y | Bennett | N | Y | N | N | Y | Y |
| **MARYLAND** | | | | | | | **VERMONT** | | | | | | |
| Sarbanes | Y | N | Y | Y | N | Y | Leahy | Y | Y | N | Y | N | Y |
| Mikulski | Y | Y | Y | Y | N | Y | Jeffords | Y | Y | N | Y | N | Y |
| **MASSACHUSETTS** | | | | | | | **VIRGINIA** | | | | | | |
| Kennedy | Y | N | Y | Y | N | Y | Warner | N | Y | N | N | Y | Y |
| Kerry | Y | Y | Y | Y | N | Y | Allen | N | Y | N | N | Y | Y |
| **MICHIGAN** | | | | | | | **WASHINGTON** | | | | | | |
| Levin | Y | N | Y | Y | N | Y | Murray | Y | Y | Y | Y | N | Y |
| Stabenow | Y | Y | Y | Y | N | Y | Cantwell | Y | Y | Y | Y | N | Y |
| **MINNESOTA** | | | | | | | **WEST VIRGINIA** | | | | | | |
| Dayton | Y | Y | Y | Y | N | Y | Byrd | N | Y | N | Y | N | Y |
| Coleman | N | Y | N | N | Y | Y | Rockefeller | N | Y | Y | N | Y | Y |
| **MISSISSIPPI** | | | | | | | **WISCONSIN** | | | | | | |
| Cochran | N | Y | N | N | Y | Y | Kohl | Y | Y | Y | Y | N | Y |
| Lott | N | Y | N | N | Y | Y | Feingold | Y | N | Y | Y | N | Y |
| **MISSOURI** | | | | | | | **WYOMING** | | | | | | |
| Bond | N | Y | N | N | Y | Y | Thomas | N | Y | N | N | Y | Y |
| Talent | N | Y | N | N | Y | Y | Enzi | N | Y | N | N | Y | Y |

**KEY**    Republicans    Democrats    *Independents*

| | | | |
|---|---|---|---|
| Y | Voted for (yea) | X | Paired against | C | Voted "present" to avoid possible conflict of interest |
| # | Paired for | – | Announced against | |
| + | Announced for | P | Voted "present" | ? | Did not vote or otherwise make a position known |
| N | Voted against (nay) | | | |

# IN THE SENATE | By Vote Number

**221.** **S Res 233. Condolences for Hurricane Victims/Adoption.** Adoption of the resolution that would express the nation's condolences to the victims of Hurricane Katrina and commit to providing the necessary resources to the affected states for relief, recovery and rebuilding efforts. Adopted 94-0: R 52-0; D 41-0 (ND 38-0, SD 3-0); I 1-0. Sept. 6, 2005.

**222.** **S Res 234. Rehnquist Tribute/Adoption.** Adoption of the resolution that would pay tribute to the late William H. Rehnquist, chief justice of the Supreme Court, who died Sept. 3. Adopted 95-0: R 54-0; D 40-0 (ND 37-0, SD 3-0); I 1-0. Sept. 7, 2005.

**223.** **HR 3673. Fiscal 2005 Emergency Supplemental Appropriations/ Passage.** Passage of the bill that would appropriate $51.8 billion in fiscal 2005 supplemental spending for disaster relief to areas affected by Hurricane Katrina. The bill would provide $50 billion for the Federal Emergency Management Agency, $1.4 billion for the Defense Department and $400 million for the Army Corps of Engineers. Passed (thus cleared for the president) 97-0: R 52-0; D 44-0 (ND 40-0, SD 4-0); I 1-0. Sept. 8, 2005.

| | 221 | 222 | 223 | | | 221 | 222 | 223 |
|---|---|---|---|---|---|---|---|---|
| **ALABAMA** | | | | | **MONTANA** | | | |
| Shelby | Y | Y | Y | | Baucus | Y | Y | Y |
| Sessions | Y | Y | Y | | Burns | Y | Y | Y |
| **ALASKA** | | | | | **NEBRASKA** | | | |
| Stevens | Y | Y | ? | | Hagel | Y | Y | Y |
| Murkowski | Y | Y | Y | | Nelson | Y | Y | Y |
| **ARIZONA** | | | | | **NEVADA** | | | |
| McCain | Y | Y | Y | | Reid | Y | Y | Y |
| Kyl | Y | Y | Y | | Ensign | Y | Y | Y |
| **ARKANSAS** | | | | | **NEW HAMPSHIRE** | | | |
| Lincoln | Y | Y | Y | | Gregg | Y | Y | Y |
| Pryor | Y | Y | Y | | Sununu | Y | Y | Y |
| **CALIFORNIA** | | | | | **NEW JERSEY** | | | |
| Feinstein | Y | Y | Y | | Corzine | Y | ? | Y |
| Boxer | Y | Y | Y | | Lautenberg | Y | Y | Y |
| **COLORADO** | | | | | **NEW MEXICO** | | | |
| Allard | ? | Y | Y | | Domenici | Y | Y | Y |
| Salazar | Y | Y | Y | | Bingaman | Y | Y | Y |
| **CONNECTICUT** | | | | | **NEW YORK** | | | |
| Dodd | Y | Y | Y | | Schumer | Y | Y | Y |
| Lieberman | Y | Y | Y | | Clinton | Y | Y | Y |
| **DELAWARE** | | | | | **NORTH CAROLINA** | | | |
| Biden | Y | ? | Y | | Dole | Y | Y | Y |
| Carper | Y | Y | Y | | Burr | Y | Y | Y |
| **FLORIDA** | | | | | **NORTH DAKOTA** | | | |
| Nelson | Y | Y | Y | | Conrad | Y | Y | Y |
| Martinez | Y | Y | Y | | Dorgan | Y | Y | Y |
| **GEORGIA** | | | | | **OHIO** | | | |
| Chambliss | Y | Y | Y | | DeWine | Y | Y | Y |
| Isakson | Y | Y | Y | | Voinovich | Y | Y | Y |
| **HAWAII** | | | | | **OKLAHOMA** | | | |
| Inouye | + | Y | ? | | Inhofe | Y | Y | Y |
| Akaka | Y | Y | Y | | Coburn | Y | Y | Y |
| **IDAHO** | | | | | **OREGON** | | | |
| Craig | Y | Y | Y | | Wyden | Y | Y | Y |
| Crapo | Y | Y | Y | | Smith | Y | Y | Y |
| **ILLINOIS** | | | | | **PENNSYLVANIA** | | | |
| Durbin | Y | Y | Y | | Specter | ? | Y | Y |
| Obama | Y | Y | Y | | Santorum | Y | Y | Y |
| **INDIANA** | | | | | **RHODE ISLAND** | | | |
| Lugar | Y | Y | Y | | Reed | Y | Y | Y |
| Bayh | Y | Y | Y | | Chafee | Y | Y | Y |
| **IOWA** | | | | | **SOUTH CAROLINA** | | | |
| Grassley | Y | Y | Y | | Graham | Y | Y | Y |
| Harkin | Y | Y | Y | | DeMint | Y | Y | Y |
| **KANSAS** | | | | | **SOUTH DAKOTA** | | | |
| Brownback | Y | Y | Y | | Johnson | Y | Y | Y |
| Roberts | Y | Y | Y | | Thune | Y | Y | Y |
| **KENTUCKY** | | | | | **TENNESSEE** | | | |
| McConnell | Y | Y | Y | | Frist | Y | Y | Y |
| Bunning | Y | Y | Y | | Alexander | Y | Y | Y |
| **LOUISIANA** | | | | | **TEXAS** | | | |
| Landrieu | ? | ? | Y | | Hutchison | Y | Y | Y |
| Vitter | + | ? | ? | | Cornyn | Y | Y | Y |
| **MAINE** | | | | | **UTAH** | | | |
| Snowe | Y | Y | Y | | Hatch | Y | Y | Y |
| Collins | Y | Y | Y | | Bennett | Y | Y | Y |
| **MARYLAND** | | | | | **VERMONT** | | | |
| Sarbanes | Y | Y | Y | | Leahy | Y | Y | Y |
| Mikulski | Y | Y | Y | | Jeffords | Y | Y | Y |
| **MASSACHUSETTS** | | | | | **VIRGINIA** | | | |
| Kennedy | Y | Y | Y | | Warner | Y | Y | Y |
| Kerry | Y | Y | Y | | Allen | Y | Y | Y |
| **MICHIGAN** | | | | | **WASHINGTON** | | | |
| Levin | Y | Y | Y | | Murray | Y | Y | Y |
| Stabenow | Y | Y | Y | | Cantwell | Y | Y | Y |
| **MINNESOTA** | | | | | **WEST VIRGINIA** | | | |
| Dayton | Y | Y | Y | | Byrd | Y | Y | Y |
| Coleman | Y | Y | Y | | Rockefeller | ? | ? | Y |
| **MISSISSIPPI** | | | | | **WISCONSIN** | | | |
| Cochran | Y | Y | Y | | Kohl | Y | Y | Y |
| Lott | Y | Y | Y | | Feingold | Y | Y | Y |
| **MISSOURI** | | | | | **WYOMING** | | | |
| Bond | Y | Y | Y | | Thomas | Y | Y | Y |
| Talent | Y | Y | Y | | Enzi | Y | Y | Y |

**KEY**    Republicans    Democrats    *Independents*

| | | | |
|---|---|---|---|
| Y | Voted for (yea) | X Paired against | C Voted "present" to avoid possible conflict of interest |
| # | Paired for | – Announced against | |
| + | Announced for | P Voted "present" | ? Did not vote or otherwise make a position known |
| N | Voted against (nay) | | |

# IN THE SENATE | By Vote Number

**224.** **S J Res 20. EPA Rule Disapproval/Motion to Proceed.** Inhofe, R-Okla., motion to proceed to consideration of a joint resolution that would provide for congressional disapproval of an EPA rule that removes coal and oil-fired electric generating units from the list of major sources of hazardous air pollutants as defined by the Clean Air Act. Motion agreed to 92-0: R 50-0; D 41-0 (ND 37-0, SD 4-0); I 1-0. Sept. 12, 2005.

**225.** **S J Res 20. EPA Rule Disapproval/Passage.** Passage of a joint resolution that would provide for congressional disapproval of an EPA rule that removes coal and oil-fired electric generating units from the list of major sources of hazardous air pollutants as defined by the Clean Air Act. Rejected 47-51: R 9-45; D 37-6 (ND 34-5, SD 3-1); I 1-0. A "nay" was a vote in support of the president's position. Sept. 13, 2005.

**226.** **HR 2862. Fiscal 2006 Commerce-Justice-Science Appropriations/ Law Enforcement Programs.** Biden, D-Del., motion to waive the Budget Act with respect to the Gregg, R-N.H., point of order against the emergency designation of the Biden amendment. The Biden amendment would increase funding for the Community Oriented Policing Services program by $1 billion; the National Center for Missing and Exploited Children by $10 million; and the Office of Violence Against Women by $9 million, and designate the increases as emergency spending. Motion rejected 41-56: R 1-53; D 39-3 (ND 35-3, SD 4-0); I 1-0. A three-fifths majority (60) of the total Senate is required to waive the Budget Act. (Subsequently, the chair upheld the point of order, and the emergency designation was stricken. The amendment fell after a second budgetary point of order was upheld.) Sept. 13, 2005.

**227.** **HR 2862. Fiscal 2006 Commerce-Justice-Science Appropriations/ Interoperable Communications Funding.** Stabenow, D-Mich., motion to waive the Budget Act with respect to the Gregg, R-N.H., point of order against the Stabenow amendment. The Stabenow amendment would increase funding for interoperable communications equipment grants by $5 billion. Motion rejected 40-58: R 0-54; D 39-4 (ND 35-4, SD 4-0); I 1-0. A three-fifths majority vote (60) of the total Senate is required to waive the Budget Act. (Subsequently, the chair upheld the point of order and the amendment fell.) Sept. 14, 2005.

**228.** **HR 2862. Fiscal 2006 Commerce-Justice-Science Appropriations/ Special Committee.** Dorgan, D-N.D., motion to suspend the rule against legislating on an appropriations bill with respect to the Dorgan amendment, which would establish a special Senate committee to investigate the awarding and carrying out of contracts in Afghanistan and Iraq. Motion rejected 44-53: R 0-53; D 43-0 (ND 39-0, SD 4-0); I 1-0. A two-thirds majority of those present and voting (65 in this case) is required to suspend the rule. (Subsequently, the amendment fell on a previous point of order.) Sept. 14, 2005.

**229.** **HR 2862. Fiscal 2006 Commerce-Justice-Science Appropriations/ Hurricane Katrina Commission.** Dorgan, D-N.D., motion to suspend the rule against legislating on an appropriations bill with respect to the Clinton, D-N.Y., amendment. The Clinton amendment would establish an independent commission to examine the federal, state and local response to Hurricane Katrina and make immediate corrective measures to improve future responses. Motion rejected 44-54: R 0-54; D 43-0 (ND 39-0, SD 4-0); I 1-0. A two-thirds majority of those present and voting (66 in this case) is required to suspend the rule. (Subsequently, the amendment fell on a previous point of order.) Sept. 14, 2005.

| | 224 | 225 | 226 | 227 | 228 | 229 | | | 224 | 225 | 226 | 227 | 228 | 229 |
|---|---|---|---|---|---|---|---|---|---|---|---|---|---|---|
| **ALABAMA** | | | | | | | | **MONTANA** | | | | | | |
| Shelby | Y | N | N | N | N | N | | Baucus | Y | N | Y | Y | Y | Y |
| Sessions | Y | N | N | N | N | N | | Burns | ? | N | N | N | N | N |
| **ALASKA** | | | | | | | | **NEBRASKA** | | | | | | |
| Stevens | Y | N | N | N | N | N | | Hagel | Y | N | N | N | N | N |
| Murkowski | Y | N | N | N | N | N | | Nelson | Y | N | N | N | Y | Y |
| **ARIZONA** | | | | | | | | **NEVADA** | | | | | | |
| McCain | Y | Y | N | N | N | N | | Reid | Y | Y | Y | Y | Y | Y |
| Kyl | Y | N | N | N | N | N | | Ensign | Y | N | N | N | N | N |
| **ARKANSAS** | | | | | | | | **NEW HAMPSHIRE** | | | | | | |
| Lincoln | Y | Y | Y | Y | Y | Y | | Gregg | Y | Y | N | N | N | N |
| Pryor | Y | N | Y | Y | Y | Y | | Sununu | Y | Y | N | N | N | N |
| **CALIFORNIA** | | | | | | | | **NEW JERSEY** | | | | | | |
| Feinstein | Y | Y | Y | Y | Y | Y | | Corzine | Y | Y | ? | ? | ? | ? |
| Boxer | Y | Y | Y | Y | Y | Y | | Lautenberg | Y | Y | Y | Y | Y | Y |
| **COLORADO** | | | | | | | | **NEW MEXICO** | | | | | | |
| Allard | Y | N | N | N | N | N | | Domenici | Y | N | N | N | N | N |
| Salazar | Y | Y | Y | Y | Y | Y | | Bingaman | Y | Y | Y | Y | Y | Y |
| **CONNECTICUT** | | | | | | | | **NEW YORK** | | | | | | |
| Dodd | Y | Y | Y | Y | Y | Y | | Schumer | Y | Y | Y | Y | Y | Y |
| Lieberman | Y | Y | Y | Y | Y | Y | | Clinton | Y | Y | Y | Y | Y | Y |
| **DELAWARE** | | | | | | | | **NORTH CAROLINA** | | | | | | |
| Biden | Y | Y | Y | Y | Y | Y | | Dole | Y | N | N | N | N | N |
| Carper | Y | Y | Y | N | Y | Y | | Burr | Y | N | N | N | N | N |
| **FLORIDA** | | | | | | | | **NORTH DAKOTA** | | | | | | |
| Nelson | Y | Y | Y | Y | Y | Y | | Conrad | Y | N | N | N | Y | Y |
| Martinez | ? | N | N | N | N | N | | Dorgan | Y | N | Y | Y | Y | Y |
| **GEORGIA** | | | | | | | | **OHIO** | | | | | | |
| Chambliss | ? | N | N | N | N | N | | DeWine | Y | N | N | N | N | N |
| Isakson | Y | N | N | N | N | N | | Voinovich | Y | N | N | N | N | N |
| **HAWAII** | | | | | | | | **OKLAHOMA** | | | | | | |
| Inouye | ? | Y | Y | Y | Y | Y | | Inhofe | Y | N | N | N | N | N |
| Akaka | Y | Y | Y | Y | Y | Y | | Coburn | Y | N | N | N | N | N |
| **IDAHO** | | | | | | | | **OREGON** | | | | | | |
| Craig | Y | N | N | N | N | N | | Wyden | Y | Y | Y | Y | Y | Y |
| Crapo | Y | N | N | N | N | N | | Smith | Y | Y | N | N | N | N |
| **ILLINOIS** | | | | | | | | **PENNSYLVANIA** | | | | | | |
| Durbin | Y | Y | Y | Y | Y | Y | | Specter | Y | Y | N | N | N | N |
| Obama | Y | Y | Y | Y | Y | Y | | Santorum | Y | N | N | N | N | N |
| **INDIANA** | | | | | | | | **RHODE ISLAND** | | | | | | |
| Lugar | Y | N | N | N | N | N | | Reed | Y | Y | Y | Y | Y | Y |
| Bayh | Y | Y | Y | Y | Y | Y | | Chafee | Y | Y | N | N | N | N |
| **IOWA** | | | | | | | | **SOUTH CAROLINA** | | | | | | |
| Grassley | Y | N | N | N | N | N | | Graham | Y | N | N | N | N | N |
| Harkin | Y | Y | Y | Y | Y | Y | | DeMint | + | N | N | N | N | N |
| **KANSAS** | | | | | | | | **SOUTH DAKOTA** | | | | | | |
| Brownback | Y | N | N | N | N | N | | Johnson | Y | Y | N | Y | Y | Y |
| Roberts | ? | N | N | N | N | N | | Thune | Y | N | N | N | N | N |
| **KENTUCKY** | | | | | | | | **TENNESSEE** | | | | | | |
| McConnell | Y | N | N | N | N | N | | Frist | Y | N | N | N | N | N |
| Bunning | Y | N | N | N | N | N | | Alexander | Y | N | N | N | N | N |
| **LOUISIANA** | | | | | | | | **TEXAS** | | | | | | |
| Landrieu | Y | Y | Y | Y | Y | Y | | Hutchison | Y | N | N | N | N | N |
| Vitter | Y | N | ? | ? | ? | ? | | Cornyn | Y | N | N | N | N | N |
| **MAINE** | | | | | | | | **UTAH** | | | | | | |
| Snowe | Y | Y | N | N | N | N | | Hatch | Y | ? | N | N | N | N |
| Collins | Y | Y | N | N | N | N | | Bennett | Y | N | N | N | N | N |
| **MARYLAND** | | | | | | | | **VERMONT** | | | | | | |
| Sarbanes | Y | Y | Y | Y | Y | Y | | Leahy | Y | Y | Y | Y | Y | Y |
| Mikulski | Y | Y | Y | Y | Y | Y | | Jeffords | Y | Y | Y | Y | Y | Y |
| **MASSACHUSETTS** | | | | | | | | **VIRGINIA** | | | | | | |
| Kennedy | Y | Y | Y | Y | Y | Y | | Warner | Y | N | N | N | ? | N |
| Kerry | ? | Y | Y | Y | Y | Y | | Allen | Y | N | N | N | N | N |
| **MICHIGAN** | | | | | | | | **WASHINGTON** | | | | | | |
| Levin | Y | Y | Y | Y | Y | Y | | Murray | Y | Y | Y | Y | Y | Y |
| Stabenow | Y | Y | Y | Y | Y | Y | | Cantwell | Y | Y | Y | Y | Y | Y |
| **MINNESOTA** | | | | | | | | **WEST VIRGINIA** | | | | | | |
| Dayton | Y | Y | Y | Y | Y | Y | | Byrd | Y | N | Y | Y | Y | Y |
| Coleman | Y | Y | N | N | N | N | | Rockefeller | ? | ? | ? | Y | Y | Y |
| **MISSISSIPPI** | | | | | | | | **WISCONSIN** | | | | | | |
| Cochran | Y | N | N | N | N | N | | Kohl | Y | Y | Y | Y | Y | Y |
| Lott | Y | N | N | N | N | N | | Feingold | Y | Y | Y | N | Y | Y |
| **MISSOURI** | | | | | | | | **WYOMING** | | | | | | |
| Bond | Y | N | N | N | N | N | | Thomas | Y | N | N | N | N | N |
| Talent | Y | N | Y | N | N | N | | Enzi | Y | N | N | N | N | N |

**KEY** Republicans  Democrats  *Independents*

| | | | | | |
|---|---|---|---|---|---|
| Y | Voted for (yea) | X | Paired against | C | Voted "present" to avoid possible conflict of interest |
| # | Paired for | – | Announced against | | |
| + | Announced for | P | Voted "present" | ? | Did not vote or otherwise make a position known |
| N | Voted against (nay) | | | | |

# IN THE SENATE | By Vote Number

**230.** HR 2862. Fiscal 2006 Commerce-Justice-Science Appropriations/ **Advanced Technology Program.** Shelby, R-Ala., motion to table (kill) the Coburn, R-Okla., amendment that would eliminate funding for the Advanced Technology Program and increase funding for the National Oceanic and Atmospheric Administration by $4.9 million, Community Oriented Policing Services by $72 million and state and local law enforcement assistance by $48 million. Motion agreed to 68-29: R 28-25; D 39-4 (ND 35-4, SD 4-0); I 1-0. Sept. 14, 2005.

**231.** HR 2862. Fiscal 2006 Commerce-Justice-Science Appropriations/ **Trade Promotion Authority Enforcement.** Grassley, R-Iowa, amendment that would require that funds appropriated in the bill be used in a manner consistent with the Bipartisan Trade Promotion Authority Act of 2002. Adopted 99-0: R 55-0; D 43-0 (ND 39-0, SD 4-0); I 1-0. Sept. 15, 2005.

**232.** HR 2862. Fiscal 2006 Commerce-Justice-Science Appropriations/ **Trade Negotiating Restrictions.** Dorgan, D-N.D., amendment that would prohibit the U.S. trade representative from using funds appropriated in the bill to change or establish any trade agreement that would alter U.S. law relating to national security import restrictions or remedies to domestic firms harmed by the trade practices of foreign competitors. Rejected 39-60: R 8-47; D 31-12 (ND 28-11, SD 3-1); I 0-1. Sept. 15, 2005.

**233.** HR 2862. Fiscal 2006 Commerce-Justice-Science Appropriations/ **Small Business Emergency Relief.** Snowe, R-Maine, amendment that would provide $595 million in disaster aid to victims of Hurricane Katrina through modified Small Business Administration programs for small-business owners, homeowners and renters. The funds would be designated as emergency spending. Adopted 96-0: R 52-0; D 43-0 (ND 39-0, SD 4-0); I 1-0. Sept. 15, 2005.

**234.** HR 2862. Fiscal 2006 Commerce-Justice-Science Appropriations/ **Financial Relief for Hurricane Katrina Victims.** Lieberman, D-Conn., motion to suspend the rule against legislating on an appropriations bill with respect to the Lieberman amendment. The Lieberman amendment would allow for up to 52 weeks of unemployment benefits for an individual as a result of a major disaster and provide other relief. Motion rejected 43-52: R 1-51; D 41-1 (ND 38-1, SD 3-0); I 1-0. A two-thirds majority of those present and voting (64 in this case) is required to suspend the rule. (Subsequently the amendment fell on a point of order.) Sept. 15, 2005.

**235.** HR 2862. Fiscal 2006 Commerce-Justice-Science Appropriations/ **Passage.** Passage of the bill that would provide $52.4 billion in fiscal 2006, including $48.6 billion in discretionary funds, for the Commerce and Justice departments, as well as agencies such as NASA. It would provide $21.2 billion for the Justice Department, $7.2 billion for the Commerce Department and related agencies and $16.4 billion for NASA. Passed 91-4: R 48-4; D 42-0 (ND 39-0, SD 3-0); I 1-0. Sept. 15, 2005.

| | 230 | 231 | 232 | 233 | 234 | 235 |
|---|---|---|---|---|---|---|
| **ALABAMA** | | | | | | |
| Shelby | Y | Y | Y | Y | N | Y |
| Sessions | Y | Y | N | Y | N | Y |
| **ALASKA** | | | | | | |
| Stevens | N | Y | N | Y | N | Y |
| Murkowski | ? | Y | N | Y | N | Y |
| **ARIZONA** | | | | | | |
| McCain | N | Y | N | Y | N | Y |
| Kyl | N | Y | N | Y | N | Y |
| **ARKANSAS** | | | | | | |
| Lincoln | Y | Y | N | Y | Y | Y |
| Pryor | Y | Y | Y | Y | Y | Y |
| **CALIFORNIA** | | | | | | |
| Feinstein | Y | Y | N | Y | Y | Y |
| Boxer | Y | Y | Y | Y | Y | Y |
| **COLORADO** | | | | | | |
| Allard | Y | Y | N | Y | N | Y |
| Salazar | Y | Y | Y | Y | Y | Y |
| **CONNECTICUT** | | | | | | |
| Dodd | Y | Y | Y | Y | Y | Y |
| Lieberman | Y | Y | N | Y | Y | Y |
| **DELAWARE** | | | | | | |
| Biden | Y | Y | Y | Y | Y | Y |
| Carper | Y | Y | N | Y | Y | Y |
| **FLORIDA** | | | | | | |
| Nelson | Y | Y | Y | Y | Y | Y |
| Martinez | N | Y | N | Y | N | Y |
| **GEORGIA** | | | | | | |
| Chambliss | N | Y | N | Y | N | Y |
| Isakson | N | Y | N | Y | N | Y |
| **HAWAII** | | | | | | |
| Inouye | Y | Y | Y | Y | Y | Y |
| Akaka | Y | Y | Y | Y | Y | Y |
| **IDAHO** | | | | | | |
| Craig | N | Y | Y | Y | N | Y |
| Crapo | Y | Y | N | Y | N | Y |
| **ILLINOIS** | | | | | | |
| Durbin | Y | Y | N | Y | Y | Y |
| Obama | Y | Y | N | Y | Y | Y |
| **INDIANA** | | | | | | |
| Lugar | Y | Y | N | Y | N | Y |
| Bayh | Y | Y | Y | Y | Y | Y |
| **IOWA** | | | | | | |
| Grassley | N | Y | N | Y | N | Y |
| Harkin | N | Y | Y | Y | Y | Y |
| **KANSAS** | | | | | | |
| Brownback | N | Y | N | Y | N | Y |
| Roberts | Y | Y | N | Y | N | Y |
| **KENTUCKY** | | | | | | |
| McConnell | N | Y | N | Y | N | Y |
| Bunning | Y | Y | N | Y | N | Y |
| **LOUISIANA** | | | | | | |
| Landrieu | Y | Y | Y | Y | ? | ? |
| Vitter | ? | Y | N | ? | ? | ? |
| **MAINE** | | | | | | |
| Snowe | N | Y | Y | Y | N | Y |
| Collins | N | Y | Y | Y | N | Y |
| **MARYLAND** | | | | | | |
| Sarbanes | Y | Y | Y | Y | Y | Y |
| Mikulski | Y | Y | Y | Y | Y | Y |
| **MASSACHUSETTS** | | | | | | |
| Kennedy | Y | Y | Y | Y | Y | Y |
| Kerry | Y | Y | Y | Y | Y | Y |
| **MICHIGAN** | | | | | | |
| Levin | Y | Y | Y | Y | Y | Y |
| Stabenow | Y | Y | Y | Y | Y | Y |
| **MINNESOTA** | | | | | | |
| Dayton | Y | Y | Y | Y | Y | Y |
| Coleman | N | Y | N | Y | N | Y |
| **MISSISSIPPI** | | | | | | |
| Cochran | Y | Y | N | Y | N | Y |
| Lott | N | Y | N | ? | ? | ? |
| **MISSOURI** | | | | | | |
| Bond | Y | Y | Y | Y | N | Y |
| Talent | N | Y | N | Y | N | Y |
| **MONTANA** | | | | | | |
| Baucus | Y | Y | N | Y | Y | Y |
| Burns | Y | Y | N | Y | N | Y |
| **NEBRASKA** | | | | | | |
| Hagel | Y | Y | N | Y | N | Y |
| Nelson | Y | Y | N | Y | N | Y |
| **NEVADA** | | | | | | |
| Reid | Y | Y | Y | Y | N | Y |
| Ensign | N | Y | N | Y | N | Y |
| **NEW HAMPSHIRE** | | | | | | |
| Gregg | Y | Y | N | Y | N | Y |
| Sununu | N | Y | N | Y | N | Y |
| **NEW JERSEY** | | | | | | |
| Corzine | ? | ? | ? | ? | ? | ? |
| Lautenberg | Y | Y | Y | Y | Y | Y |
| **NEW MEXICO** | | | | | | |
| Domenici | Y | Y | N | Y | N | Y |
| Bingaman | Y | Y | Y | Y | Y | Y |
| **NEW YORK** | | | | | | |
| Schumer | Y | Y | N | Y | Y | Y |
| Clinton | Y | Y | Y | Y | Y | Y |
| **NORTH CAROLINA** | | | | | | |
| Dole | Y | Y | N | Y | N | Y |
| Burr | N | Y | N | Y | N | Y |
| **NORTH DAKOTA** | | | | | | |
| Conrad | N | Y | Y | Y | Y | Y |
| Dorgan | N | Y | Y | Y | Y. | Y |
| **OHIO** | | | | | | |
| DeWine | Y | Y | N | Y | N | Y |
| Voinovich | Y | Y | N | Y | N | Y |
| **OKLAHOMA** | | | | | | |
| Inhofe | N | Y | N | Y | N | N |
| Coburn | N | Y | Y | Y | N | N |
| **OREGON** | | | | | | |
| Wyden | Y | Y | N | Y | Y | Y |
| Smith | Y | Y | N | Y | N | Y |
| **PENNSYLVANIA** | | | | | | |
| Specter | Y | Y | Y | Y | N | Y |
| Santorum | N | Y | N | Y | N | Y |
| **RHODE ISLAND** | | | | | | |
| Reed | Y | Y | N | Y | Y | Y |
| Chafee | Y | Y | N | Y | N | Y |
| **SOUTH CAROLINA** | | | | | | |
| Graham | N | Y | Y | Y | N | Y |
| DeMint | N | Y | N | Y | N | Y |
| **SOUTH DAKOTA** | | | | | | |
| Johnson | Y | Y | Y | Y | Y | Y |
| Thune | N | Y | N | + | - | + |
| **TENNESSEE** | | | | | | |
| Frist | Y | Y | N | Y | N | Y |
| Alexander | Y | Y | N | Y | N | Y |
| **TEXAS** | | | | | | |
| Hutchison | Y | Y | N | Y | N | Y |
| Cornyn | Y | Y | N | Y | N | Y |
| **UTAH** | | | | | | |
| Hatch | Y | Y | N | Y | N | Y |
| Bennett | Y | Y | N | Y | N | Y |
| **VERMONT** | | | | | | |
| Leahy | Y | Y | Y | Y | Y | Y |
| Jeffords | Y | Y | N | Y | Y | Y |
| **VIRGINIA** | | | | | | |
| Warner | Y | Y | N | Y | N | Y |
| Allen | Y | Y | N | Y | N | Y |
| **WASHINGTON** | | | | | | |
| Murray | Y | Y | N | Y | Y | Y |
| Cantwell | Y | Y | N | Y | Y | Y |
| **WEST VIRGINIA** | | | | | | |
| Byrd | Y | Y | Y | Y | Y | Y |
| Rockefeller | Y | Y | Y | Y | Y | Y |
| **WISCONSIN** | | | | | | |
| Kohl | Y | Y | N | Y | Y | Y |
| Feingold | N | Y | Y | Y | Y | Y |
| **WYOMING** | | | | | | |
| Thomas | N | Y | N | Y | N | N |
| Enzi | Y | Y | N | Y | N | N |

**KEY**  Republicans  Democrats  *Independents*

| | | | |
|---|---|---|---|
| **Y** Voted for (yea) | **X** Paired against | **C** Voted "present" to avoid possible conflict of interest |
| **#** Paired for | **−** Announced against | |
| **+** Announced for | **P** Voted "present" | **?** Did not vote or otherwise make a position known |
| **N** Voted against (nay) | | |

# IN THE SENATE | By Vote Number

**236.** HR 2744. Fiscal 2006 Agriculture Appropriations/Japanese Beef Importation. Nelson, D-Neb., amendment that would prohibit the Agriculture Department from using funds in the bill to develop a final rule to allow the importation of beef from Japan unless the president certifies to Congress that Japan has granted open access for U.S. beef and beef products. Adopted 72-26: R 31-24; D 40-2 (ND 36-2, SD 4-0); I 1-0. Sept. 20, 2005.

**237.** HR 2744. Fiscal 2006 Agriculture Appropriations/Horse Slaughtering Ban. Ensign, R-Nev., amendment that would prohibit the use of funds in the bill to pay the salaries or expenses of personnel to inspect horses being sent to slaughter for human consumption. Adopted 69-28: R 35-20; D 33-8 (ND 32-6, SD 1-2); I 1-0. Sept. 20, 2005.

**238.** HR 2744. Fiscal 2006 Agriculture Appropriations/Sunshine Report Language. Coburn, R-Okla., amendment that would require any limitation, directive or earmark contained in the House or Senate report accompanying the bill to be included in the conference report to be considered as approved by both chambers. Adopted 55-39: R 32-21; D 23-17 (ND 21-15, SD 2-2); I 0-1. Sept. 21, 2005.

**239.** HR 2744. Fiscal 2006 Agriculture Appropriations/Nutrition Education. Bingaman, D-N.M., amendment that would increase funding for Team Nutrition programs by $10 million with an offset of $10 million from the Common Computer Environment program. Adopted 66-29: R 25-29; D 40-0 (ND 36-0, SD 4-0); I 1-0. Sept. 21, 2005.

**240.** HR 2744. Fiscal 2006 Agriculture Appropriations/Prevented Planting Payments. Dayton, D-Minn., amendment that would modify the timetable for the Prevented Planting Payment program for one year to help farmers in areas that have been declared agriculture disasters in calendar 2005 by the president or Agriculture secretary, with an increase in funding by $1 million offset by a reduction in departmental travel expenses. Rejected 47-52: R 3-52; D 43-0 (ND 39-0, SD 4-0); I 1-0. Sept. 22, 2005.

**241.** HR 2744. Fiscal 2006 Agriculture Appropriations/Passage. Passage of the bill that would provide $100.7 billion in fiscal 2006 for the Agriculture Department, the Food and Drug Administration and related agencies, including $17.3 billion in discretionary spending. The bill includes $40.7 billion for the food stamp program, $25.7 billion for the Commodity Credit Corporation and $12.4 billion for school meal programs. Passed 97-2: R 53-2; D 43-0 (ND 39-0, SD 4-0); I 1-0. Sept. 22, 2005.

**242.** HR 2528. Fiscal 2006 Military Construction-VA Appropriations/Counseling Service Funding. Akaka, D-Hawaii, amendment that would shift $10 million from a Veterans Affairs Department (VA) information technology program to a readjustment counseling program for veterans. Rejected 48-50: R 4-50; D 43-0 (ND 39-0, SD 4-0); I 1-0. Sept. 22, 2005.

**243.** HR 2528. Fiscal 2006 Military Construction-VA Appropriations/Passage. Passage of the bill that would provide $83 billion in fiscal 2006 for the VA and military construction, including $46.4 billion for discretionary spending. It would provide $70.7 billion for the VA, $12 billion for military construction and $2 billion in emergency spending to address a shortfall in veterans' health care funding. Passed 98-0: R 54-0; D 43-0 (ND 39-0, SD 4-0); I 1-0. Sept. 22, 2005.

| | 236 | 237 | 238 | 239 | 240 | 241 | 242 | 243 |
|---|---|---|---|---|---|---|---|---|
| **ALABAMA** | | | | | | | | |
| Shelby | Y | N | N | Y | N | Y | N | Y |
| Sessions | Y | N | Y | Y | N | Y | N | Y |
| **ALASKA** | | | | | | | | |
| Stevens | N | Y | N | N | N | Y | N | Y |
| Murkowski | N | Y | Y | Y | N | Y | N | Y |
| **ARIZONA** | | | | | | | | |
| McCain | N | Y | Y | N | N | Y | N | Y |
| Kyl | N | Y | Y | N | N | Y | N | Y |
| **ARKANSAS** | | | | | | | | |
| Lincoln | Y | N | N | Y | Y | Y | Y | Y |
| Pryor | Y | N | N | Y | Y | Y | Y | Y |
| **CALIFORNIA** | | | | | | | | |
| Feinstein | Y | Y | Y | Y | Y | Y | Y | Y |
| Boxer | Y | Y | Y | Y | Y | Y | Y | Y |
| **COLORADO** | | | | | | | | |
| Allard | N | N | N | N | N | Y | N | Y |
| Salazar | N | N | Y | Y | Y | Y | Y | Y |
| **CONNECTICUT** | | | | | | | | |
| Dodd | Y | Y | Y | Y | Y | Y | Y | Y |
| Lieberman | Y | Y | Y | Y | Y | Y | Y | Y |
| **DELAWARE** | | | | | | | | |
| Biden | Y | Y | Y | Y | Y | Y | Y | Y |
| Carper | Y | Y | N | Y | Y | Y | Y | Y |
| **FLORIDA** | | | | | | | | |
| Nelson | Y | Y | Y | Y | Y | Y | Y | Y |
| Martinez | N | Y | Y | N | N | Y | ? | + |
| **GEORGIA** | | | | | | | | |
| Chambliss | Y | Y | N | N | N | Y | N | Y |
| Isakson | N | Y | N | N | N | Y | N | Y |
| **HAWAII** | | | | | | | | |
| Inouye | N | Y | ? | ? | Y | Y | Y | Y |
| Akaka | Y | Y | Y | Y | Y | Y | Y | Y |
| **IDAHO** | | | | | | | | |
| Craig | Y | N | Y | N | N | Y | N | Y |
| Crapo | Y | N | Y | N | N | Y | N | Y |
| **ILLINOIS** | | | | | | | | |
| Durbin | Y | Y | Y | Y | Y | Y | Y | Y |
| Obama | Y | Y | Y | Y | Y | Y | Y | Y |
| **INDIANA** | | | | | | | | |
| Lugar | N | Y | Y | Y | N | Y | N | Y |
| Bayh | Y | Y | Y | Y | Y | Y | Y | Y |
| **IOWA** | | | | | | | | |
| Grassley | N | N | N | Y | Y | Y | N | Y |
| Harkin | Y | Y | N | Y | Y | Y | Y | Y |
| **KANSAS** | | | | | | | | |
| Brownback | Y | N | Y | N | N | Y | N | Y |
| Roberts | Y | N | Y | N | N | Y | N | Y |
| **KENTUCKY** | | | | | | | | |
| McConnell | N | Y | Y | Y | N | Y | N | Y |
| Bunning | N | Y | N | N | N | Y | N | Y |
| **LOUISIANA** | | | | | | | | |
| Landrieu | Y | ? | Y | Y | Y | Y | Y | Y |
| Vitter | Y | Y | N | N | N | Y | N | Y |
| **MAINE** | | | | | | | | |
| Snowe | Y | Y | Y | Y | N | Y | Y | Y |
| Collins | Y | Y | Y | Y | N | Y | Y | Y |
| **MARYLAND** | | | | | | | | |
| Sarbanes | Y | Y | N | Y | Y | Y | Y | Y |
| Mikulski | Y | Y | ? | ? | Y | Y | Y | Y |
| **MASSACHUSETTS** | | | | | | | | |
| Kennedy | Y | Y | N | Y | Y | Y | Y | Y |
| Kerry | Y | Y | Y | Y | Y | Y | Y | Y |
| **MICHIGAN** | | | | | | | | |
| Levin | Y | Y | Y | Y | Y | Y | Y | Y |
| Stabenow | Y | Y | Y | Y | Y | Y | Y | Y |
| **MINNESOTA** | | | | | | | | |
| Dayton | Y | Y | Y | Y | Y | Y | Y | Y |
| Coleman | Y | Y | N | Y | Y | Y | N | Y |
| **MISSISSIPPI** | | | | | | | | |
| Cochran | N | N | N | N | N | Y | N | Y |
| Lott | N | Y | N | N | N | Y | N | Y |
| **MISSOURI** | | | | | | | | |
| Bond | Y | N | N | N | N | Y | N | Y |
| Talent | Y | N | Y | Y | N | Y | N | Y |
| **MONTANA** | | | | | | | | |
| Baucus | Y | N | N | Y | Y | Y | Y | Y |
| Burns | Y | N | Y | N | N | Y | N | Y |
| **NEBRASKA** | | | | | | | | |
| Hagel | N | Y | N | N | N | Y | N | Y |
| Nelson | Y | Y | Y | Y | Y | Y | Y | Y |
| **NEVADA** | | | | | | | | |
| Reid | Y | Y | N | Y | Y | Y | Y | Y |
| Ensign | Y | Y | Y | N | N | Y | N | N |
| **NEW HAMPSHIRE** | | | | | | | | |
| Gregg | N | Y | N | N | N | Y | N | Y |
| Sununu | N | Y | Y | N | N | N | N | Y |
| **NEW JERSEY** | | | | | | | | |
| Corzine | ? | ? | ? | ? | ? | ? | ? | ? |
| Lautenberg | Y | Y | N | Y | Y | Y | Y | Y |
| **NEW MEXICO** | | | | | | | | |
| Domenici | Y | N | ? | ? | N | Y | N | Y |
| Bingaman | Y | N | Y | Y | Y | Y | Y | Y |
| **NEW YORK** | | | | | | | | |
| Schumer | Y | Y | Y | Y | Y | Y | Y | Y |
| Clinton | Y | Y | Y | Y | Y | Y | Y | Y |
| **NORTH CAROLINA** | | | | | | | | |
| Dole | N | Y | N | Y | N | Y | N | Y |
| Burr | N | Y | Y | N | N | Y | N | Y |
| **NORTH DAKOTA** | | | | | | | | |
| Conrad | Y | N | N | Y | Y | Y | Y | Y |
| Dorgan | Y | N | N | Y | Y | Y | Y | Y |
| **OHIO** | | | | | | | | |
| DeWine | Y | Y | N | Y | N | Y | N | Y |
| Voinovich | Y | N | N | N | N | Y | N | Y |
| **OKLAHOMA** | | | | | | | | |
| Inhofe | Y | N | N | N | N | Y | N | Y |
| Coburn | Y | N | Y | N | N | Y | N | Y |
| **OREGON** | | | | | | | | |
| Wyden | Y | Y | N | Y | Y | Y | N | Y |
| Smith | Y | Y | N | Y | N | Y | N | Y |
| **PENNSYLVANIA** | | | | | | | | |
| Specter | Y | Y | Y | Y | N | Y | Y | Y |
| Santorum | Y | Y | Y | Y | N | Y | N | Y |
| **RHODE ISLAND** | | | | | | | | |
| Reed | Y | Y | N | Y | Y | Y | Y | Y |
| Chafee | N | Y | Y | Y | Y | Y | Y | Y |
| **SOUTH CAROLINA** | | | | | | | | |
| Graham | Y | Y | Y | N | N | Y | N | Y |
| DeMint | Y | Y | N | Y | N | Y | N | Y |
| **SOUTH DAKOTA** | | | | | | | | |
| Johnson | Y | N | N | Y | Y | Y | Y | Y |
| Thune | Y | N | N | Y | Y | Y | N | Y |
| **TENNESSEE** | | | | | | | | |
| Frist | N | Y | N | N | N | Y | N | Y |
| Alexander | N | Y | Y | N | N | Y | N | Y |
| **TEXAS** | | | | | | | | |
| Hutchison | Y | N | Y | N | N | Y | N | Y |
| Cornyn | Y | N | Y | N | N | Y | N | Y |
| **UTAH** | | | | | | | | |
| Hatch | N | N | N | N | N | Y | N | Y |
| Bennett | N | N | N | N | N | Y | N | Y |
| **VERMONT** | | | | | | | | |
| Leahy | Y | Y | N | Y | Y | Y | Y | Y |
| Jeffords | Y | Y | N | Y | Y | Y | Y | Y |
| **VIRGINIA** | | | | | | | | |
| Warner | Y | Y | N | Y | N | Y | N | Y |
| Allen | Y | Y | N | Y | N | N | Y | |
| **WASHINGTON** | | | | | | | | |
| Murray | Y | Y | Y | Y | Y | Y | Y | Y |
| Cantwell | Y | Y | Y | Y | Y | Y | Y | Y |
| **WEST VIRGINIA** | | | | | | | | |
| Byrd | Y | Y | N | Y | Y | Y | Y | Y |
| Rockefeller | ? | ? | ? | ? | Y | Y | Y | Y |
| **WISCONSIN** | | | | | | | | |
| Kohl | Y | Y | Y | Y | Y | Y | Y | Y |
| Feingold | Y | Y | Y | Y | Y | Y | Y | Y |
| **WYOMING** | | | | | | | | |
| Thomas | Y | N | Y | N | N | Y | N | Y |
| Enzi | Y | N | ? | N | N | Y | N | Y |

**KEY**   Republicans   Democrats   *Independents*

| | | | |
|---|---|---|---|
| **Y** Voted for (yea) | **X** Paired against | **C** Voted "present" to avoid possible conflict of interest |
| **#** Paired for | **–** Announced against | |
| **+** Announced for | **P** Voted "present" | **?** Did not vote or otherwise make a position known |
| **N** Voted against (nay) | | |

# IN THE SENATE | By Vote Number

**244.** **Treaty Doc 108-6. Customs Simplification Treaty/Adoption.**
Adoption of the resolution of ratification of the Protocol of Amendment to the International Convention on Simplification and Harmonization of Customs Procedures that would require participants to implement standardized customs procedures, continuously modernize customs procedures and provide transparency in administrative and judicial reviews of customs decisions. Adopted (thus consenting to ratification) 87-0: R 48-0; D 38-0 (ND 36-0, SD 2-0); I 1-0. A two-thirds majority of those present and voting (58 in this case) is required for adoption of resolutions of ratification. Sept. 26, 2005.

**245.** **Roberts Nomination/Confirmation.** Confirmation of President Bush's nomination of John G. Roberts Jr. of Maryland to be chief justice of the United States. Confirmed 78-22: R 55-0; D 22-22 (ND 18-22, SD 4-0); I 1-0. A "yea" was a vote in support of the president's position. Sept. 29, 2005.

| | 244 | 245 | | | 244 | 245 |
|---|---|---|---|---|---|---|
| **ALABAMA** | | | | **MONTANA** | | |
| Shelby | Y | Y | | Baucus | Y | Y |
| Sessions | Y | Y | | Burns | Y | Y |
| **ALASKA** | | | | **NEBRASKA** | | |
| Stevens | Y | Y | | Hagel | ? | Y |
| Murkowski | Y | Y | | Nelson | Y | Y |
| **ARIZONA** | | | | **NEVADA** | | |
| McCain | Y | Y | | Reid | Y | N |
| Kyl | Y | Y | | Ensign | Y | Y |
| **ARKANSAS** | | | | **NEW HAMPSHIRE** | | |
| Lincoln | Y | Y | | Gregg | Y | Y |
| Pryor | Y | Y | | Sununu | Y | Y |
| **CALIFORNIA** | | | | **NEW JERSEY** | | |
| Feinstein | Y | N | | Corzine | ? | N |
| Boxer | Y | N | | Lautenberg | Y | N |
| **COLORADO** | | | | **NEW MEXICO** | | |
| Allard | Y | Y | | Domenici | Y | Y |
| Salazar | Y | Y | | Bingaman | Y | Y |
| **CONNECTICUT** | | | | **NEW YORK** | | |
| Dodd | Y | Y | | Schumer | Y | N |
| Lieberman | Y | Y | | Clinton | Y | N |
| **DELAWARE** | | | | **NORTH CAROLINA** | | |
| Biden | ? | N | | Dole | Y | Y |
| Carper | Y | Y | | Burr | ? | Y |
| **FLORIDA** | | | | **NORTH DAKOTA** | | |
| Nelson | + | Y | | Conrad | Y | Y |
| Martinez | + | Y | | Dorgan | Y | Y |
| **GEORGIA** | | | | **OHIO** | | |
| Chambliss | Y | Y | | DeWine | Y | Y |
| Isakson | Y | Y | | Voinovich | Y | Y |
| **HAWAII** | | | | **OKLAHOMA** | | |
| Inouye | Y | N | | Inhofe | Y | Y |
| Akaka | Y | N | | Coburn | Y | Y |
| **IDAHO** | | | | **OREGON** | | |
| Craig | Y | Y | | Wyden | Y | Y |
| Crapo | Y | Y | | Smith | Y | Y |
| **ILLINOIS** | | | | **PENNSYLVANIA** | | |
| Durbin | Y | N | | Specter | Y | Y |
| Obama | Y | N | | Santorum | Y | Y |
| **INDIANA** | | | | **RHODE ISLAND** | | |
| Lugar | Y | Y | | Reed | Y | N |
| Bayh | Y | N | | Chafee | Y | Y |
| **IOWA** | | | | **SOUTH CAROLINA** | | |
| Grassley | Y | Y | | Graham | Y | Y |
| Harkin | ? | N | | DeMint | Y | Y |
| **KANSAS** | | | | **SOUTH DAKOTA** | | |
| Brownback | ? | Y | | Johnson | Y | Y |
| Roberts | Y | Y | | Thune | Y | Y |
| **KENTUCKY** | | | | **TENNESSEE** | | |
| McConnell | Y | Y | | Frist | Y | Y |
| Bunning | Y | Y | | Alexander | Y | Y |
| **LOUISIANA** | | | | **TEXAS** | | |
| Landrieu | ? | Y | | Hutchison | ? | Y |
| Vitter | + | Y | | Cornyn | + | Y |
| **MAINE** | | | | **UTAH** | | |
| Snowe | Y | Y | | Hatch | Y | Y |
| Collins | Y | Y | | Bennett | Y | Y |
| **MARYLAND** | | | | **VERMONT** | | |
| Sarbanes | Y | N | | Leahy | Y | Y |
| Mikulski | Y | N | | Jeffords | Y | Y |
| **MASSACHUSETTS** | | | | **VIRGINIA** | | |
| Kennedy | Y | N | | Warner | Y | Y |
| Kerry | Y | N | | Allen | Y | Y |
| **MICHIGAN** | | | | **WASHINGTON** | | |
| Levin | Y | Y | | Murray | Y | Y |
| Stabenow | ? | N | | Cantwell | Y | N |
| **MINNESOTA** | | | | **WEST VIRGINIA** | | |
| Dayton | Y | N | | Byrd | Y | Y |
| Coleman | Y | Y | | Rockefeller | Y | Y |
| **MISSISSIPPI** | | | | **WISCONSIN** | | |
| Cochran | Y | Y | | Kohl | Y | Y |
| Lott | Y | Y | | Feingold | Y | Y |
| **MISSOURI** | | | | **WYOMING** | | |
| Bond | Y | Y | | Thomas | Y | Y |
| Talent | Y | Y | | Enzi | Y | Y |

**KEY**   **Republicans**   Democrats   *Independents*

| | | | | | |
|---|---|---|---|---|---|
| Y | Voted for (yea) | X | Paired against | C | Voted "present" to avoid possible conflict of interest |
| # | Paired for | – | Announced against | | |
| + | Announced for | P | Voted "present" | ? | Did not vote or otherwise make a position known |
| N | Voted against (nay) | | | | |

# IN THE SENATE | By Vote Number

**246.** **H J Res 68. Fiscal 2006 Continuing Resolution/Community Services Block Grant Funding.** Harkin, D-Iowa, amendment that would continue funding for the Community Services Block Grant at no less than the fiscal 2005 level. Rejected 39-53: R 0-53; D 38-0 (ND 34-0, SD 4-0); I 1-0. Sept. 30, 2005.

**247.** **HR 2863. Fiscal 2006 Defense Appropriations/Defense Authorization.** Judgment of the Senate on the germaneness of the Warner, R-Va., amendment that would authorize funding for defense programs in fiscal 2006, plus another $50 billion for military operations in Iraq and Afghanistan. Ruled not germane 49-50: R 17-38; D 31-12 (ND 28-11, SD 3-1); I 1-0. Oct. 5, 2005.

**248.** **HR 2863. Fiscal 2006 Defense Appropriations/Armored Vehicle Funding.** Bayh, D-Ind., motion to waive the Budget Act with respect to the Stevens, R-Alaska, point of order against the Bayh amendment. The Bayh amendment would increase funding by $360.8 million for the procurement of armored Tactical Wheeled Vehicles for use in Iraq and Afghanistan, or to reconstitute certain facilities at Fort Polk, La. Motion rejected 56-43: R 13-42; D 42-1 (ND 38-1, SD 4-0); I 1-0. A three-fifths majority vote (60) of the total Senate is required to waive the Budget Act. (Subsequently, the chair upheld the point of order, and the amendment fell.) Oct. 5, 2005.

**249.** **HR 2863. Fiscal 2006 Defense Appropriations/Detainee Standards.** McCain, R-Ariz., amendment that would establish the U.S. Army Field Manual on Intelligence Interrogation as the uniform standard for interrogating persons detained by the Department of Defense, and prohibit cruel, inhuman or degrading treatment of any prisoner detained by the U.S. government. Adopted 90-9: R 46-9; D 43-0 (ND 39-0, SD 4-0); I 1-0. A "nay" was a vote in support of the president's position. Oct. 5, 2005.

**250.** **HR 2863. Fiscal 2006 Defense Appropriations/Low Income Heating Funding.** Kerry, D-Mass., motion to waive the Budget Act with respect to the Stevens, R-Alaska, point of order against the emergency designation of the Kerry amendment. The Kerry amendment would appropriate $3.1 billion for the Low Income Home Energy Assistance Program and designate it as emergency spending. Motion rejected 50-49: R 9-46; D 40-3 (ND 36-3, SD 4-0); I 1-0. A three-fifths majority vote (60) of the total Senate is required to waive the Budget Act. (Subsequently, the chair upheld the point of order, and the emergency designation was stricken. The amendment later fell on a second budget point of order.) Oct. 5, 2005.

| | 246 | 247 | 248 | 249 | 250 |
|---|---|---|---|---|---|
| **ALABAMA** | | | | | |
| Shelby | N | N | N | Y | N |
| Sessions | N | Y | N | N | N |
| **ALASKA** | | | | | |
| Stevens | N | N | N | N | N |
| Murkowski | N | N | N | Y | N |
| **ARIZONA** | | | | | |
| McCain | N | N | N | Y | N |
| Kyl | N | N | N | Y | N |
| **ARKANSAS** | | | | | |
| Lincoln | Y | Y | Y | Y | Y |
| Pryor | Y | Y | Y | Y | Y |
| **CALIFORNIA** | | | | | |
| Feinstein | Y | N | Y | Y | Y |
| Boxer | Y | Y | Y | Y | Y |
| **COLORADO** | | | | | |
| Allard | N | N | N | N | N |
| Salazar | Y | Y | Y | Y | Y |
| **CONNECTICUT** | | | | | |
| Dodd | Y | Y | Y | Y | Y |
| Lieberman | Y | Y | Y | Y | Y |
| **DELAWARE** | | | | | |
| Biden | ? | Y | Y | Y | Y |
| Carper | Y | Y | Y | Y | N |
| **FLORIDA** | | | | | |
| Nelson | Y | Y | Y | Y | Y |
| Martinez | N | N | N | Y | N |
| **GEORGIA** | | | | | |
| Chambliss | N | Y | N | Y | N |
| Isakson | N | N | N | Y | N |
| **HAWAII** | | | | | |
| Inouye | Y | N | N | Y | N |
| Akaka | Y | Y | Y | Y | Y |
| **IDAHO** | | | | | |
| Craig | N | N | N | Y | N |
| Crapo | N | N | N | Y | N |
| **ILLINOIS** | | | | | |
| Durbin | Y | Y | Y | Y | Y |
| Obama | Y | Y | Y | Y | Y |
| **INDIANA** | | | | | |
| Lugar | N | Y | N | Y | N |
| Bayh | Y | Y | Y | Y | Y |
| **IOWA** | | | | | |
| Grassley | N | N | N | Y | N |
| Harkin | Y | N | Y | Y | Y |
| **KANSAS** | | | | | |
| Brownback | N | N | N | Y | N |
| Roberts | N | N | N | N | N |
| **KENTUCKY** | | | | | |
| McConnell | N | N | N | Y | N |
| Bunning | N | N | N | Y | N |
| **LOUISIANA** | | | | | |
| Landrieu | Y | N | Y | Y | Y |
| Vitter | ? | N | N | Y | N |
| **MAINE** | | | | | |
| Snowe | N | Y | Y | Y | Y |
| Collins | N | Y | Y | Y | Y |
| **MARYLAND** | | | | | |
| Sarbanes | Y | Y | Y | Y | Y |
| Mikulski | ? | N | Y | Y | Y |
| **MASSACHUSETTS** | | | | | |
| Kennedy | Y | Y | Y | Y | Y |
| Kerry | Y | Y | Y | Y | Y |
| **MICHIGAN** | | | | | |
| Levin | Y | Y | Y | Y | Y |
| Stabenow | Y | Y | Y | Y | Y |
| **MINNESOTA** | | | | | |
| Dayton | Y | Y | Y | Y | Y |
| Coleman | N | N | Y | Y | Y |
| **MISSISSIPPI** | | | | | |
| Cochran | N | N | N | N | N |
| Lott | N | N | N | Y | N |
| **MISSOURI** | | | | | |
| Bond | N | N | N | N | N |
| Talent | N | Y | Y | Y | Y |
| **MONTANA** | | | | | |
| Baucus | Y | Y | Y | Y | Y |
| Burns | N | N | N | Y | N |
| **NEBRASKA** | | | | | |
| Hagel | N | Y | N | Y | N |
| Nelson | Y | Y | Y | Y | N |
| **NEVADA** | | | | | |
| Reid | Y | Y | Y | Y | Y |
| Ensign | N | Y | N | Y | N |
| **NEW HAMPSHIRE** | | | | | |
| Gregg | ? | N | N | Y | N |
| Sununu | N | N | N | Y | N |
| **NEW JERSEY** | | | | | |
| Corzine | ? | ? | ? | ? | ? |
| Lautenberg | Y | Y | Y | Y | Y |
| **NEW MEXICO** | | | | | |
| Domenici | N | N | N | Y | N |
| Bingaman | Y | Y | Y | Y | Y |
| **NEW YORK** | | | | | |
| Schumer | Y | Y | Y | Y | Y |
| Clinton | Y | Y | Y | Y | Y |
| **NORTH CAROLINA** | | | | | |
| Dole | N | Y | N | Y | N |
| Burr | N | N | N | Y | N |
| **NORTH DAKOTA** | | | | | |
| Conrad | Y | N | Y | Y | Y |
| Dorgan | Y | N | Y | Y | Y |
| **OHIO** | | | | | |
| DeWine | N | N | Y | Y | N |
| Voinovich | N | N | Y | Y | N |
| **OKLAHOMA** | | | | | |
| Inhofe | N | Y | N | N | N |
| Coburn | N | N | N | Y | N |
| **OREGON** | | | | | |
| Wyden | Y | N | Y | Y | Y |
| Smith | N | N | N | Y | N |
| **PENNSYLVANIA** | | | | | |
| Specter | N | N | Y | Y | Y |
| Santorum | N | N | N | Y | Y |
| **RHODE ISLAND** | | | | | |
| Reed | Y | Y | Y | Y | Y |
| Chafee | N | Y | Y | Y | Y |
| **SOUTH CAROLINA** | | | | | |
| Graham | N | Y | N | Y | N |
| DeMint | N | N | N | Y | N |
| **SOUTH DAKOTA** | | | | | |
| Johnson | Y | Y | Y | Y | Y |
| Thune | N | Y | N | Y | N |
| **TENNESSEE** | | | | | |
| Frist | N | N | N | Y | N |
| Alexander | N | N | N | Y | N |
| **TEXAS** | | | | | |
| Hutchison | N | N | N | Y | N |
| Cornyn | N | Y | N | N | N |
| **UTAH** | | | | | |
| Hatch | N | N | N | Y | N |
| Bennett | N | N | N | Y | N |
| **VERMONT** | | | | | |
| Leahy | Y | N | Y | Y | Y |
| Jeffords | Y | Y | Y | Y | Y |
| **VIRGINIA** | | | | | |
| Warner | N | N | N | Y | N |
| Allen | N | Y | N | Y | N |
| **WASHINGTON** | | | | | |
| Murray | ? | N | Y | Y | Y |
| Cantwell | Y | Y | Y | Y | Y |
| **WEST VIRGINIA** | | | | | |
| Byrd | ? | N | Y | Y | Y |
| Rockefeller | ? | Y | Y | Y | Y |
| **WISCONSIN** | | | | | |
| Kohl | Y | N | Y | Y | Y |
| Feingold | Y | Y | Y | Y | Y |
| **WYOMING** | | | | | |
| Thomas | N | N | N | Y | N |
| Enzi | N | N | N | Y | N |

**KEY**    Republicans    Democrats    *Independents*

| | | |
|---|---|---|
| Y  Voted for (yea) | X  Paired against | C  Voted "present" to avoid possible conflict of interest |
| #  Paired for | −  Announced against | |
| +  Announced for | P  Voted "present" | ?  Did not vote or otherwise make a position known |
| N  Voted against (nay) | | |

# IN THE SENATE | By Vote Number

**251.** **HR 2863. Fiscal 2006 Defense Appropriations/Veterans' Health Care Funding.** Stabenow, D-Mich., motion to waive the Budget Act with respect to the Stevens, R-Alaska, point of order against the Stabenow amendment. The Stabenow amendment would establish a formula that would adjust health care funding for veterans to account for changes in population and inflation. Motion rejected 48-51: R 5-50; D 42-1 (ND 38-1, SD 4-0); I 1-0. A three-fifths majority vote (60) of the total Senate is required to waive the Budget Act. (Subsequently, the chair upheld the point of order, and the amendment fell.) Oct. 5, 2005.

**252.** **HR 2863. Fiscal 2006 Defense Appropriations/Cloture.** Frist, R-Tenn., motion to invoke cloture (thus limiting debate) on the bill that would provide $445.4 billion in defense spending, including $50 billion in bridge funding for continued military operations in Iraq and Afghanistan. Motion agreed to 95-4: R 55-0; D 39-4 (ND 35-4, SD 4-0); I 1-0. Three-fifths of the total Senate (60) is required to invoke cloture. Oct. 5, 2005.

**253.** **HR 2863. Fiscal 2006 Defense Appropriations/Web-Based Travel Program.** Stevens, R-Alaska, motion to table (kill) the Coburn, R-Okla., amendment that would prohibit use of funds in the bill for a Web-based travel system being developed by the Pentagon. Motion agreed to 65-32: R 37-16; D 27-16 (ND 25-14, SD 2-2); I 1-0. Oct. 6, 2005.

**254.** **HR 2863. Fiscal 2006 Defense Appropriations/Passage.** Passage of the bill that would provide $445.4 billion for fiscal 2006 military operations, including $390 billion in discretionary spending. The total also includes $50 billion in bridge funding for continued military operations in Iraq and Afghanistan. The bill would provide $95.7 billion for personnel, $75.8 billion for procurement and $125 billion for operations and maintenance. Passed 97-0: R 53-0; D 43-0 (ND 39-0, SD 4-0); I 1-0. Oct. 7, 2005.

| | 251 | 252 | 253 | 254 | | 251 | 252 | 253 | 254 |
|---|---|---|---|---|---|---|---|---|---|
| **ALABAMA** | | | | | **MONTANA** | | | | |
| Shelby | N | Y | Y | Y | Baucus | Y | Y | Y | Y |
| Sessions | N | Y | N | Y | Burns | N | Y | Y | Y |
| **ALASKA** | | | | | **NEBRASKA** | | | | |
| Stevens | N | Y | Y | Y | Hagel | N | Y | Y | Y |
| Murkowski | N | Y | Y | Y | Nelson | Y | Y | Y | Y |
| **ARIZONA** | | | | | **NEVADA** | | | | |
| McCain | N | Y | N | Y | Reid | Y | N | Y | Y |
| Kyl | N | Y | N | Y | Ensign | N | Y | Y | Y |
| **ARKANSAS** | | | | | **NEW HAMPSHIRE** | | | | |
| Lincoln | Y | Y | N | Y | Gregg | N | Y | N | ? |
| Pryor | Y | Y | Y | Y | Sununu | N | Y | N | Y |
| **CALIFORNIA** | | | | | **NEW JERSEY** | | | | |
| Feinstein | Y | Y | Y | Y | Corzine | ? | ? | ? | Y |
| Boxer | Y | N | N | Y | Lautenberg | Y | Y | Y | Y |
| **COLORADO** | | | | | **NEW MEXICO** | | | | |
| Allard | N | Y | ? | Y | Domenici | N | Y | N | Y |
| Salazar | Y | Y | Y | Y | Bingaman | Y | N | N | Y |
| **CONNECTICUT** | | | | | **NEW YORK** | | | | |
| Dodd | Y | Y | N | Y | Schumer | Y | Y | Y | Y |
| Lieberman | Y | Y | Y | Y | Clinton | Y | Y | Y | Y |
| **DELAWARE** | | | | | **NORTH CAROLINA** | | | | |
| Biden | Y | Y | Y | Y | Dole | N | Y | N | Y |
| Carper | Y | Y | Y | Y | Burr | N | Y | N | Y |
| **FLORIDA** | | | | | **NORTH DAKOTA** | | | | |
| Nelson | Y | Y | N | Y | Conrad | Y | Y | Y | Y |
| Martinez | N | Y | Y | Y | Dorgan | Y | Y | Y | Y |
| **GEORGIA** | | | | | **OHIO** | | | | |
| Chambliss | N | Y | Y | Y | DeWine | N | Y | Y | Y |
| Isakson | N | Y | Y | Y | Voinovich | N | Y | Y | Y |
| **HAWAII** | | | | | **OKLAHOMA** | | | | |
| Inouye | N | Y | Y | Y | Inhofe | N | Y | N | Y |
| Akaka | Y | Y | Y | Y | Coburn | N | Y | N | Y |
| **IDAHO** | | | | | **OREGON** | | | | |
| Craig | N | Y | Y | Y | Wyden | Y | Y | N | Y |
| Crapo | N | Y | Y | Y | Smith | N | Y | Y | Y |
| **ILLINOIS** | | | | | **PENNSYLVANIA** | | | | |
| Durbin | Y | Y | N | Y | Specter | Y | Y | Y | Y |
| Obama | Y | Y | N | Y | Santorum | N | Y | Y | Y |
| **INDIANA** | | | | | **RHODE ISLAND** | | | | |
| Lugar | N | Y | Y | Y | Reed | Y | Y | Y | Y |
| Bayh | Y | Y | N | Y | Chafee | Y | Y | Y | Y |
| **IOWA** | | | | | **SOUTH CAROLINA** | | | | |
| Grassley | N | Y | N | Y | Graham | N | Y | N | Y |
| Harkin | Y | Y | Y | Y | DeMint | N | Y | N | Y |
| **KANSAS** | | | | | **SOUTH DAKOTA** | | | | |
| Brownback | N | Y | N | Y | Johnson | Y | Y | Y | Y |
| Roberts | N | Y | Y | Y | Thune | Y | Y | N | Y |
| **KENTUCKY** | | | | | **TENNESSEE** | | | | |
| McConnell | N | Y | Y | Y | Frist | N | Y | Y | Y |
| Bunning | N | Y | Y | + | Alexander | N | Y | Y | Y |
| **LOUISIANA** | | | | | **TEXAS** | | | | |
| Landrieu | Y | Y | Y | Y | Hutchison | N | Y | Y | Y |
| Vitter | N | Y | Y | Y | Cornyn | N | Y | Y | Y |
| **MAINE** | | | | | **UTAH** | | | | |
| Snowe | Y | Y | N | Y | Hatch | N | Y | + | Y |
| Collins | Y | Y | Y | Y | Bennett | N | Y | Y | Y |
| **MARYLAND** | | | | | **VERMONT** | | | | |
| Sarbanes | Y | Y | Y | Y | Leahy | Y | Y | Y | ? |
| Mikulski | Y | Y | Y | Y | Jeffords | Y | Y | Y | Y |
| **MASSACHUSETTS** | | | | | **VIRGINIA** | | | | |
| Kennedy | Y | Y | Y | Y | Warner | N | Y | Y | Y |
| Kerry | Y | Y | N | Y | Allen | N | Y | Y | Y |
| **MICHIGAN** | | | | | **WASHINGTON** | | | | |
| Levin | Y | N | Y | Y | Murray | Y | Y | Y | Y |
| Stabenow | Y | Y | N | Y | Cantwell | Y | Y | N | Y |
| **MINNESOTA** | | | | | **WEST VIRGINIA** | | | | |
| Dayton | Y | Y | N | Y | Byrd | Y | Y | N | Y |
| Coleman | N | Y | Y | Y | Rockefeller | Y | Y | Y | Y |
| **MISSISSIPPI** | | | | | **WISCONSIN** | | | | |
| Cochran | N | Y | Y | Y | Kohl | Y | Y | N | Y |
| Lott | N | Y | Y | Y | Feingold | Y | Y | N | Y |
| **MISSOURI** | | | | | **WYOMING** | | | | |
| Bond | N | Y | Y | Y | Thomas | N | Y | N | Y |
| Talent | N | Y | Y | Y | Enzi | N | Y | Y | Y |

| KEY | Republicans | Democrats | *Independents* | |
|---|---|---|---|---|
| Y Voted for (yea) | | X Paired against | | C Voted "present" to avoid possible conflict of interest |
| # Paired for | | – Announced against | | |
| + Announced for | | P Voted "present" | | ? Did not vote or otherwise make a position known |
| N Voted against (nay) | | | | |

# IN THE SENATE | By Vote Number

**255.** HR 3058. Fiscal 2006 Transportation-Treasury-Housing Appropriations/HUD Authority. Bond, R-Mo., amendment that would clarify the authority of the Housing and Urban Development (HUD) Department to recover losses from owners of multifamily houses who are intentionally withholding assets from rent receipts on Federal Housing Administration loans. It would allow the agency to recover double damages from individuals, groups or heirs who have violated HUD project agreements. Adopted 93-0: R 52-0; D 40-0 (ND 36-0, SD 4-0); I 1-0. Oct. 17, 2005.

**256.** HR 3058. Fiscal 2006 Transportation-Treasury-Housing Appropriations/Congressional Pay Raise. Kyl, R-Ariz., amendment that would prevent members of Congress from receiving their automatic yearly pay increase in fiscal 2006. Adopted 92-6: R 52-2; D 40-3 (ND 36-3, SD 4-0); I 0-1. Oct. 18, 2005.

**257.** HR 3058. Fiscal 2006 Transportation-Treasury-Housing Appropriations/Minimum Wage Increase. Kennedy, D-Mass., motion to waive the Budget Act with respect to the Bond, R-Mo., point of order against the Kennedy amendment. The Kennedy amendment would increase the minimum hourly wage to $5.70 six months after the bill's enactment and to $6.25 one year after enactment. Motion rejected 47-51: R 4-51; D 42-0 (ND 38-0, SD 4-0); I 1-0. A three-fifths majority vote (60) of the total Senate is required to waive the Budget Act. (Subsequently, the chair upheld the point of order, and the amendment fell.) Oct. 19, 2005.

**258.** HR 3058. Fiscal 2006 Transportation-Treasury-Housing Appropriations/Minimum Wage Increase. Enzi, R-Wyo., motion to waive the Budget Act with respect to the Kennedy, D-Mass., point of order against an Enzi amendment. The Enzi amendment would increase the minimum hourly wage to $5.70 six months after enactment and to $6.25 eighteen months after enactment. It also would exempt businesses with gross annual sales of under $1 million; permit private-sector workers to participate in biweekly flex-hour programs; exclude tips from the minimum wage rates paid to restaurant workers; and provide tax benefits for small-business owners. Motion rejected 42-57: R 42-13; D 0-43 (ND 0-39, SD 0-4); I 0-1. A three-fifths majority vote (60) of the total Senate is required to waive the Budget Act. (Subsequently, the chair upheld the point of order, and the amendment fell.) Oct. 19, 2005.

**259.** HR 3058. Fiscal 2006 Transportation-Treasury-Housing Appropriations/Independent Investigation. Dorgan, D-N.D., motion to suspend the rule against legislating on an appropriations bill with respect to the Dorgan amendment. The Dorgan amendment would establish a special committee to investigate waste, fraud and abuse in the awarding and performing of contracts in Iraq and Afghanistan, and for the reconstruction of damage done by hurricanes Katrina and Rita. Motion rejected 44-54: R 0-54; D 43-0 (ND 39-0, SD 4-0); I 1-0. A two-thirds majority of those present and voting (66 in this case) is required to suspend the rule. Oct. 19, 2005.

| | 255 | 256 | 257 | 258 | 259 |
|---|---|---|---|---|---|
| **ALABAMA** | | | | | |
| Shelby | Y | Y | N | Y | N |
| Sessions | Y | Y | N | Y | N |
| **ALASKA** | | | | | |
| Stevens | Y | Y | N | Y | N |
| Murkowski | Y | Y | N | Y | N |
| **ARIZONA** | | | | | |
| McCain | ? | Y | N | Y | N |
| Kyl | Y | Y | N | Y | N |
| **ARKANSAS** | | | | | |
| Lincoln | Y | Y | Y | N | Y |
| Pryor | Y | Y | Y | N | Y |
| **CALIFORNIA** | | | | | |
| Feinstein | Y | Y | Y | N | Y |
| Boxer | Y | Y | Y | N | Y |
| **COLORADO** | | | | | |
| Allard | Y | Y | N | N | N |
| Salazar | Y | Y | Y | N | Y |
| **CONNECTICUT** | | | | | |
| Dodd | Y | Y | Y | N | Y |
| Lieberman | Y | Y | Y | N | Y |
| **DELAWARE** | | | | | |
| Biden | ? | Y | Y | N | Y |
| Carper | Y | Y | Y | N | Y |
| **FLORIDA** | | | | | |
| Nelson | Y | Y | Y | N | Y |
| Martinez | Y | Y | N | Y | N |
| **GEORGIA** | | | | | |
| Chambliss | Y | ? | N | N | N |
| Isakson | Y | Y | N | N | N |
| **HAWAII** | | | | | |
| Inouye | Y | N | ? | ? | ? |
| Akaka | Y | Y | Y | N | Y |
| **IDAHO** | | | | | |
| Craig | Y | Y | N | Y | N |
| Crapo | Y | Y | N | Y | N |
| **ILLINOIS** | | | | | |
| Durbin | Y | Y | Y | N | Y |
| Obama | Y | Y | Y | N | Y |
| **INDIANA** | | | | | |
| Lugar | Y | N | N | Y | N |
| Bayh | Y | Y | Y | N | Y |
| **IOWA** | | | | | |
| Grassley | Y | Y | N | Y | N |
| Harkin | ? | Y | Y | N | Y |
| **KANSAS** | | | | | |
| Brownback | Y | Y | N | Y | N |
| Roberts | Y | Y | N | Y | N |
| **KENTUCKY** | | | | | |
| McConnell | Y | Y | N | Y | N |
| Bunning | Y | Y | N | Y | N |
| **LOUISIANA** | | | | | |
| Landrieu | Y | Y | Y | N | Y |
| Vitter | ? | Y | N | N | N |
| **MAINE** | | | | | |
| Snowe | Y | Y | N | Y | N |
| Collins | Y | Y | N | Y | N |
| **MARYLAND** | | | | | |
| Sarbanes | Y | N | Y | N | Y |
| Mikulski | Y | Y | Y | N | Y |
| **MASSACHUSETTS** | | | | | |
| Kennedy | Y | Y | Y | N | Y |
| Kerry | Y | Y | Y | N | Y |
| **MICHIGAN** | | | | | |
| Levin | Y | Y | Y | N | Y |
| Stabenow | Y | Y | Y | N | Y |
| **MINNESOTA** | | | | | |
| Dayton | Y | Y | Y | N | Y |
| Coleman | Y | Y | N | Y | N |
| **MISSISSIPPI** | | | | | |
| Cochran | Y | Y | N | Y | N |
| Lott | Y | Y | N | N | N |
| **MISSOURI** | | | | | |
| Bond | Y | N | N | Y | N |
| Talent | Y | Y | N | Y | N |

| | 255 | 256 | 257 | 258 | 259 |
|---|---|---|---|---|---|
| **MONTANA** | | | | | |
| Baucus | Y | Y | Y | N | Y |
| Burns | Y | Y | N | Y | ? |
| **NEBRASKA** | | | | | |
| Hagel | Y | Y | N | Y | N |
| Nelson | Y | Y | Y | N | Y |
| **NEVADA** | | | | | |
| Reid | Y | Y | Y | N | Y |
| Ensign | Y | Y | N | Y | N |
| **NEW HAMPSHIRE** | | | | | |
| Gregg | Y | Y | N | N | N |
| Sununu | Y | Y | N | N | N |
| **NEW JERSEY** | | | | | |
| Corzine | ? | ? | + | N | Y |
| Lautenberg | ? | Y | Y | N | Y |
| **NEW MEXICO** | | | | | |
| Domenici | Y | Y | N | Y | N |
| Bingaman | Y | N | Y | N | Y |
| **NEW YORK** | | | | | |
| Schumer | Y | Y | Y | N | Y |
| Clinton | Y | Y | Y | N | Y |
| **NORTH CAROLINA** | | | | | |
| Dole | Y | Y | N | Y | N |
| Burr | Y | Y | N | N | N |
| **NORTH DAKOTA** | | | | | |
| Conrad | Y | Y | Y | N | Y |
| Dorgan | Y | Y | Y | N | Y |
| **OHIO** | | | | | |
| DeWine | Y | Y | Y | Y | N |
| Voinovich | Y | Y | Y | N | N |
| **OKLAHOMA** | | | | | |
| Inhofe | Y | Y | N | N | N |
| Coburn | Y | Y | N | N | N |
| **OREGON** | | | | | |
| Wyden | Y | Y | Y | N | Y |
| Smith | Y | Y | N | Y | N |
| **PENNSYLVANIA** | | | | | |
| Specter | Y | Y | Y | N | Y |
| Santorum | Y | Y | Y | Y | N |
| **RHODE ISLAND** | | | | | |
| Reed | Y | Y | Y | N | Y |
| Chafee | Y | Y | Y | N | N |
| **SOUTH CAROLINA** | | | | | |
| Graham | Y | Y | N | Y | N |
| DeMint | + | Y | N | N | N |
| **SOUTH DAKOTA** | | | | | |
| Johnson | Y | Y | Y | N | Y |
| Thune | Y | Y | N | Y | N |
| **TENNESSEE** | | | | | |
| Frist | Y | Y | N | Y | N |
| Alexander | Y | Y | N | Y | N |
| **TEXAS** | | | | | |
| Hutchison | Y | Y | N | Y | N |
| Cornyn | Y | Y | N | N | N |
| **UTAH** | | | | | |
| Hatch | Y | Y | N | Y | N |
| Bennett | Y | Y | N | Y | N |
| **VERMONT** | | | | | |
| Leahy | Y | Y | Y | N | Y |
| Jeffords | Y | N | Y | N | Y |
| **VIRGINIA** | | | | | |
| Warner | Y | Y | N | Y | N |
| Allen | Y | Y | N | Y | N |
| **WASHINGTON** | | | | | |
| Murray | Y | Y | Y | N | Y |
| Cantwell | Y | Y | Y | N | Y |
| **WEST VIRGINIA** | | | | | |
| Byrd | Y | Y | Y | N | Y |
| Rockefeller | Y | Y | Y | N | Y |
| **WISCONSIN** | | | | | |
| Kohl | Y | Y | Y | N | Y |
| Feingold | Y | Y | Y | N | Y |
| **WYOMING** | | | | | |
| Thomas | Y | Y | N | Y | N |
| Enzi | Y | Y | N | Y | N |

**KEY**    Republicans    Democrats    *Independents*

| | | | |
|---|---|---|---|
| Y | Voted for (yea) | X | Paired against |
| # | Paired for | – | Announced against |
| + | Announced for | P | Voted "present" |
| N | Voted against (nay) | | |

| | |
|---|---|
| C | Voted "present" to avoid possible conflict of interest |
| ? | Did not vote or otherwise make a position known |

# IN THE SENATE | By Vote Number

**260.** HR 3058. **Fiscal 2006 Transportation-Treasury-Housing Appropriations/Bar Funds for Earmark Projects.** Bond, R-Mo., motion to table (kill) Coburn, R-Okla., amendment that would prohibit use of funds in the bill from for several earmarked projects, including the Joslyn Art Museum in Omaha, Neb.; the Stand Up for Animals shelter in Westerly, R.I.; and the Seattle Art Museum's sculpture park in Seattle, Wash. Motion agreed to 86-13: R 43-12; D 42-1 (ND 38-1, SD 4-0); I 1-0. Oct. 20, 2005.

**261.** HR 3058. **Fiscal 2006 Transportation-Treasury-Housing Appropriations/LIHEAP.** Reed, D-R.I., motion to waive the Budget Act with respect to the Bond, R-Mo., point of order against the Reed amendment. The Reed amendment would provide an additional $3.1 billion in emergency funding for the Low-Income Home Energy Assistance Program (LIHEAP). Motion rejected 53-46: R 11-44; D 41-2 (ND 37-2, SD 4-0); I 1-0. A three-fifths majority vote (60) of the total Senate is required to waive the Budget Act. (Subsequently, the chair upheld the point of order, and the amendment fell.) Oct. 20, 2005.

**262.** HR 3058. **Fiscal 2006 Transportation-Treasury-Housing Appropriations/Bridge Funding.** Coburn, R-Okla., amendment that would transfer $125 million in funding from the Ketchikan-Gravina and Knik Arm bridge projects in Alaska to the reconstruction of the Twin Spans Bridge connecting New Orleans and Slidell, La. It would place remaining Alaska bridge funds into a general highway fund for Alaska. Rejected 15-82: R 11-43; D 4-38 (ND 3-35, SD 1-3); I 0-1. (By unanimous consent, the Senate agreed to raise the majority requirement for adoption of the Coburn amendment to 60 votes.) Oct. 20, 2005.

**263.** HR 3058. **Fiscal 2006 Transportation-Treasury-Housing Appropriations/Bridge Funding.** Stevens, R-Alaska, amendment that would prevent any new bridge projects funded by the surface transportation law from going forward until the reconstruction of the Twin Spans Bridge connecting New Orleans and Slidell, La., is fully funded through non-emergency accounts. Rejected 33-61: R 30-22; D 3-38 (ND 2-35, SD 1-3); I 0-1. (By unanimous consent, the Senate agreed to raise the majority requirement for adoption of the Stevens amendment to 60 votes.) Oct. 20, 2005.

**264.** HR 3058. **Fiscal 2006 Transportation-Treasury-Housing Appropriations/Passage.** Passage of the bill that would provide $141.6 billion in fiscal 2006, including $65.8 billion in discretionary spending for the departments of Housing and Urban Development, Treasury, and Transportation and for related agencies. It would provide $40.2 billion in highway spending, $34.8 billion for the Department of Housing and Urban Development and $14.3 billion for the Federal Aviation Administration. It also would provide $1.5 billion for Amtrak and $593 million in federal funds for the District of Columbia. Passed 93-1: R 53-0; D 39-1 (ND 35-1, SD 4-0); I 1-0. Oct. 20, 2005.

| | 260 | 261 | 262 | 263 | 264 |
|---|---|---|---|---|---|
| **ALABAMA** | | | | | |
| Shelby | Y | N | N | Y | Y |
| Sessions | N | N | Y | Y | Y |
| **ALASKA** | | | | | |
| Stevens | Y | N | N | Y | Y |
| Murkowski | Y | N | N | Y | Y |
| **ARIZONA** | | | | | |
| McCain | N | N | ? | ? | ? |
| Kyl | N | N | Y | Y | Y |
| **ARKANSAS** | | | | | |
| Lincoln | Y | Y | N | N | Y |
| Pryor | Y | Y | N | N | Y |
| **CALIFORNIA** | | | | | |
| Feinstein | Y | Y | N | N | Y |
| Boxer | Y | Y | N | N | Y |
| **COLORADO** | | | | | |
| Allard | Y | N | Y | Y | Y |
| Salazar | Y | Y | N | Y | Y |
| **CONNECTICUT** | | | | | |
| Dodd | Y | Y | N | N | Y |
| Lieberman | Y | Y | N | N | Y |
| **DELAWARE** | | | | | |
| Biden | Y | Y | N | N | Y |
| Carper | Y | N | N | N | Y |
| **FLORIDA** | | | | | |
| Nelson | Y | Y | N | N | Y |
| Martinez | Y | N | N | Y | Y |
| **GEORGIA** | | | | | |
| Chambliss | Y | N | N | Y | Y |
| Isakson | Y | N | N | Y | Y |
| **HAWAII** | | | | | |
| Inouye | Y | Y | N | N | ? |
| Akaka | Y | Y | N | N | Y |
| **IDAHO** | | | | | |
| Craig | Y | N | N | N | Y |
| Crapo | Y | N | N | N | Y |
| **ILLINOIS** | | | | | |
| Durbin | Y | Y | N | N | Y |
| Obama | Y | Y | N | N | Y |
| **INDIANA** | | | | | |
| Lugar | Y | Y | N | N | Y |
| Bayh | Y | Y | Y | Y | N |
| **IOWA** | | | | | |
| Grassley | Y | N | N | N | Y |
| Harkin | Y | Y | N | N | Y |
| **KANSAS** | | | | | |
| Brownback | Y | N | N | Y | Y |
| Roberts | Y | N | N | N | Y |
| **KENTUCKY** | | | | | |
| McConnell | Y | N | N | Y | Y |
| Bunning | Y | N | N | Y | Y |
| **LOUISIANA** | | | | | |
| Landrieu | Y | Y | Y | Y | Y |
| Vitter | Y | N | Y | Y | Y |
| **MAINE** | | | | | |
| Snowe | Y | Y | N | N | Y |
| Collins | Y | Y | N | N | Y |
| **MARYLAND** | | | | | |
| Sarbanes | Y | Y | N | N | Y |
| Mikulski | Y | Y | N | N | Y |
| **MASSACHUSETTS** | | | | | |
| Kennedy | Y | Y | N | N | Y |
| Kerry | Y | Y | N | N | Y |
| **MICHIGAN** | | | | | |
| Levin | Y | Y | N | N | Y |
| Stabenow | Y | Y | N | N | Y |
| **MINNESOTA** | | | | | |
| Dayton | Y | Y | N | N | Y |
| Coleman | Y | Y | N | Y | Y |
| **MISSISSIPPI** | | | | | |
| Cochran | Y | N | N | N | Y |
| Lott | Y | N | N | N | Y |
| **MISSOURI** | | | | | |
| Bond | Y | N | N | N | Y |
| Talent | N | Y | N | N | Y |

| | 260 | 261 | 262 | 263 | 264 |
|---|---|---|---|---|---|
| **MONTANA** | | | | | |
| Baucus | Y | Y | N | ? | ? |
| Burns | Y | N | N | N | Y |
| **NEBRASKA** | | | | | |
| Hagel | N | N | N | N | Y |
| Nelson | Y | N | N | N | Y |
| **NEVADA** | | | | | |
| Reid | Y | Y | N | N | Y |
| Ensign | N | N | N | N | Y |
| **NEW HAMPSHIRE** | | | | | |
| Gregg | Y | N | N | N | Y |
| Sununu | N | Y | Y | Y | ? |
| **NEW JERSEY** | | | | | |
| Corzine | ? | ? | ? | ? | ? |
| Lautenberg | Y | Y | N | N | Y |
| **NEW MEXICO** | | | | | |
| Domenici | Y | N | N | N | Y |
| Bingaman | Y | Y | N | N | Y |
| **NEW YORK** | | | | | |
| Schumer | Y | Y | ? | ? | ? |
| Clinton | Y | Y | N | N | Y |
| **NORTH CAROLINA** | | | | | |
| Dole | Y | N | N | Y | Y |
| Burr | N | N | Y | Y | Y |
| **NORTH DAKOTA** | | | | | |
| Conrad | Y | Y | Y | N | Y |
| Dorgan | Y | Y | N | N | Y |
| **OHIO** | | | | | |
| DeWine | Y | Y | N | Y | Y |
| Voinovich | Y | N | N | N | Y |
| **OKLAHOMA** | | | | | |
| Inhofe | Y | N | N | Y | Y |
| Coburn | N | N | Y | Y | Y |
| **OREGON** | | | | | |
| Wyden | Y | Y | N | N | Y |
| Smith | Y | Y | N | N | Y |
| **PENNSYLVANIA** | | | | | |
| Specter | Y | Y | N | N | Y |
| Santorum | Y | Y | N | N | Y |
| **RHODE ISLAND** | | | | | |
| Reed | Y | Y | N | N | Y |
| Chafee | Y | Y | N | Y | Y |
| **SOUTH CAROLINA** | | | | | |
| Graham | N | N | Y | Y | Y |
| DeMint | N | N | Y | Y | Y |
| **SOUTH DAKOTA** | | | | | |
| Johnson | Y | Y | N | N | Y |
| Thune | Y | N | N | N | Y |
| **TENNESSEE** | | | | | |
| Frist | Y | N | N | Y | Y |
| Alexander | Y | N | N | N | Y |
| **TEXAS** | | | | | |
| Hutchison | Y | N | N | N | Y |
| Cornyn | Y | N | N | N | Y |
| **UTAH** | | | | | |
| Hatch | Y | N | N | Y | Y |
| Bennett | Y | N | N | Y | Y |
| **VERMONT** | | | | | |
| Leahy | Y | Y | N | N | Y |
| *Jeffords* | Y | Y | N | N | Y |
| **VIRGINIA** | | | | | |
| Warner | Y | N | N | Y | Y |
| Allen | N | N | Y | Y | Y |
| **WASHINGTON** | | | | | |
| Murray | Y | Y | N | N | Y |
| Cantwell | Y | Y | N | N | Y |
| **WEST VIRGINIA** | | | | | |
| Byrd | Y | Y | N | N | Y |
| Rockefeller | Y | Y | N | N | Y |
| **WISCONSIN** | | | | | |
| Kohl | Y | Y | N | N | Y |
| Feingold | N | Y | Y | Y | Y |
| **WYOMING** | | | | | |
| Thomas | Y | N | N | ? | Y |
| Enzi | Y | N | N | ? | Y |

**KEY**   Republicans   Democrats   *Independents*

| | | |
|---|---|---|
| **Y** Voted for (yea) | **X** Paired against | **C** Voted "present" to avoid possible conflict of interest |
| **#** Paired for | **–** Announced against | |
| **+** Announced for | **P** Voted "present" | **?** Did not vote or otherwise make a position known |
| **N** Voted against (nay) | | |

# IN THE SENATE | By Vote Number

**265. Sandoval Nomination/Confirmation.** Confirmation of President Bush's nomination of Brian Sandoval of Nevada to be a judge for the U.S. District Court for the District of Nevada. Confirmed 89-0: R 52-0; D 36-0 (ND 33-0, SD 3-0); I 1-0. A "yea" was a vote in support of the president's position. Oct. 24, 2005.

**266. Mattice Nomination/Confirmation.** Confirmation of President Bush's nomination of Harry Sandlin Mattice Jr. of Tennessee to be a judge for the U.S. District Court for the Eastern District of Tennessee. Confirmed 91-0: R 52-0; D 38-0 (ND 35-0, SD 3-0); I 1-0. A "yea" was a vote in support of the president's position. Oct. 24, 2005.

**267. HR 3010. Fiscal 2006 Labor-HHS-Education Appropriations/ Patient Identifiers.** Durbin, D-Ill., amendment that would require the secretary of Health and Human Services (HHS) to submit a report to Congress by June 30, 2006, outlining a plan for discontinuing the use of Social Security numbers as numerical patient identifiers for Medicare and Medicaid recipients and the costs of implementing the plan. Adopted 98-0: R 54-0; D 43-0 (ND 39-0, SD 4-0); I 1-0. Oct. 25, 2005.

**268. HR 3010. Fiscal 2006 Labor-HHS-Education Appropriations/ Pell Grant Increase.** Kennedy, D-Mass., motion to waive the Budget Act with respect to the Specter, R-Pa., point of order against the Kennedy amendment. The Kennedy amendment would add $836 million for Pell Grants, increasing the maximum Pell Grant for the 2006-07 award year to $4,250. Motion rejected 48-51: R 6-49; D 41-2 (ND 38-1, SD 3-1); I 1-0. A three-fifths majority vote (60) of the total Senate is required to waive the Budget Act. (Subsequently, the chair upheld the point of order, and the amendment fell.) Oct. 25, 2005.

**269. HR 3010. Fiscal 2006 Labor-HHS-Education Appropriations/ Title I Funding.** Byrd, D-W.Va., motion to waive the Budget Act with respect to the Specter, R-Pa., point of order against the Byrd amendment. The Byrd amendment would add $5 billion for Title I of the Elementary and Secondary Education Act, split evenly between targeted grants and finance incentives. Motion rejected 44-51: R 3-50; D 40-1 (ND 37-1, SD 3-0); I 1-0. A three-fifths majority vote (60) of the total Senate is required to waive the Budget Act. (Subsequently, the chair upheld the point of order, and the amendment fell.) Oct. 26, 2005.

**270. HR 3010. Fiscal 2006 Labor-HHS-Education Appropriations/ LIHEAP.** Reed, D-R.I., motion to waive the Budget Act with respect to the Crapo, R-Idaho, point of order against the Reed amendment. The Reed amendment would provide an additional $2.9 billion in emergency funding for the Low-Income Home Energy Assistance Program (LIHEAP). Motion rejected 54-43: R 12-41; D 41-2 (ND 37-2, SD 4-0); I 1-0. A three-fifths majority vote (60) of the total Senate is required to waive the Budget Act. (Subsequently, the chair upheld the point of order, and the amendment fell.) Oct. 26, 2005.

**271. HR 3010. Fiscal 2006 Labor-HHS-Education Appropriations/ LIHEAP.** Gregg, R-N.H., amendment that would provide an additional $1.3 billion for LIHEAP, offset with a 0.92 percent across-the-board cut in budget authority in the bill. Rejected 46-53: R 46-9; D 0-43 (ND 0-39, SD 0-4); I 0-1. Oct. 26, 2005.

| | 265 | 266 | 267 | 268 | 269 | 270 | 271 |
|---|---|---|---|---|---|---|---|
| **ALABAMA** | | | | | | | |
| Shelby | Y | Y | ? | N | N | N | Y |
| Sessions | ? | ? | Y | N | N | ? | Y |
| **ALASKA** | | | | | | | |
| Stevens | Y | Y | Y | N | N | N | Y |
| Murkowski | Y | Y | Y | N | N | ? | Y |
| **ARIZONA** | | | | | | | |
| McCain | ? | ? | Y | N | N | N | Y |
| Kyl | Y | Y | Y | N | N | N | Y |
| **ARKANSAS** | | | | | | | |
| Lincoln | Y | Y | Y | Y | Y | Y | N |
| Pryor | Y | Y | Y | Y | Y | Y | N |
| **CALIFORNIA** | | | | | | | |
| Feinstein | ? | Y | Y | Y | Y | Y | N |
| Boxer | Y | Y | Y | Y | Y | Y | N |
| **COLORADO** | | | | | | | |
| Allard | Y | Y | Y | N | N | N | Y |
| Salazar | Y | Y | Y | Y | Y | Y | N |
| **CONNECTICUT** | | | | | | | |
| Dodd | Y | Y | Y | Y | Y | Y | N |
| Lieberman | Y | Y | Y | Y | Y | Y | N |
| **DELAWARE** | | | | | | | |
| Biden | ? | ? | Y | Y | Y | Y | N |
| Carper | Y | Y | Y | Y | Y | N | N |
| **FLORIDA** | | | | | | | |
| Nelson | ? | ? | Y | N | ? | Y | N |
| Martinez | Y | Y | Y | N | ? | N | Y |
| **GEORGIA** | | | | | | | |
| Chambliss | Y | Y | Y | N | N | N | Y |
| Isakson | Y | Y | Y | N | N | N | Y |
| **HAWAII** | | | | | | | |
| Inouye | ? | ? | Y | Y | Y | Y | N |
| Akaka | Y | Y | Y | Y | Y | Y | N |
| **IDAHO** | | | | | | | |
| Craig | Y | Y | Y | N | N | N | Y |
| Crapo | Y | Y | Y | N | N | N | Y |
| **ILLINOIS** | | | | | | | |
| Durbin | Y | Y | Y | Y | Y | Y | N |
| Obama | ? | Y | Y | Y | Y | Y | N |
| **INDIANA** | | | | | | | |
| Lugar | Y | Y | Y | N | Y | Y | Y |
| Bayh | Y | Y | Y | Y | Y | Y | N |
| **IOWA** | | | | | | | |
| Grassley | Y | Y | Y | N | N | N | Y |
| Harkin | Y | Y | Y | Y | Y | Y | N |
| **KANSAS** | | | | | | | |
| Brownback | Y | Y | Y | N | N | N | Y |
| Roberts | Y | Y | Y | N | N | N | Y |
| **KENTUCKY** | | | | | | | |
| McConnell | Y | Y | Y | N | N | N | Y |
| Bunning | Y | Y | Y | N | N | N | Y |
| **LOUISIANA** | | | | | | | |
| Landrieu | Y | Y | Y | Y | Y | Y | N |
| Vitter | Y | Y | Y | N | N | N | N |
| **MAINE** | | | | | | | |
| Snowe | Y | Y | Y | Y | Y | Y | N |
| Collins | Y | Y | Y | Y | Y | Y | N |
| **MARYLAND** | | | | | | | |
| Sarbanes | Y | Y | Y | Y | Y | Y | N |
| Mikulski | Y | Y | Y | Y | Y | Y | N |
| **MASSACHUSETTS** | | | | | | | |
| Kennedy | ? | ? | Y | Y | Y | Y | N |
| Kerry | Y | Y | Y | Y | Y | Y | N |
| **MICHIGAN** | | | | | | | |
| Levin | Y | Y | Y | Y | Y | Y | N |
| Stabenow | Y | Y | Y | Y | Y | Y | N |
| **MINNESOTA** | | | | | | | |
| Dayton | Y | Y | Y | Y | ? | Y | N |
| Coleman | Y | Y | Y | Y | N | Y | N |
| **MISSISSIPPI** | | | | | | | |
| Cochran | Y | Y | Y | N | N | N | Y |
| Lott | Y | Y | Y | N | N | N | Y |
| **MISSOURI** | | | | | | | |
| Bond | Y | Y | Y | N | N | N | Y |
| Talent | Y | Y | Y | N | N | Y | N |

| | 265 | 266 | 267 | 268 | 269 | 270 | 271 |
|---|---|---|---|---|---|---|---|
| **MONTANA** | | | | | | | |
| Baucus | Y | Y | Y | Y | Y | Y | N |
| Burns | Y | Y | Y | N | N | N | Y |
| **NEBRASKA** | | | | | | | |
| Hagel | Y | Y | Y | N | N | N | Y |
| Nelson | Y | Y | Y | Y | Y | N | N |
| **NEVADA** | | | | | | | |
| Reid | Y | Y | Y | Y | Y | Y | N |
| Ensign | Y | Y | Y | N | N | N | Y |
| **NEW HAMPSHIRE** | | | | | | | |
| Gregg | Y | Y | Y | N | N | N | Y |
| Sununu | Y | Y | Y | N | N | Y | Y |
| **NEW JERSEY** | | | | | | | |
| Corzine | ? | ? | ? | Y | ? | ? | ? |
| Lautenberg | Y | Y | Y | Y | Y | Y | N |
| **NEW MEXICO** | | | | | | | |
| Domenici | Y | Y | Y | N | N | N | Y |
| Bingaman | Y | Y | Y | Y | Y | Y | N |
| **NEW YORK** | | | | | | | |
| Schumer | Y | Y | Y | Y | Y | Y | N |
| Clinton | Y | Y | Y | Y | Y | Y | N |
| **NORTH CAROLINA** | | | | | | | |
| Dole | Y | Y | Y | N | N | N | Y |
| Burr | Y | Y | Y | N | N | N | Y |
| **NORTH DAKOTA** | | | | | | | |
| Conrad | Y | Y | Y | N | N | Y | N |
| Dorgan | Y | Y | Y | Y | Y | Y | N |
| **OHIO** | | | | | | | |
| DeWine | Y | Y | Y | N | N | Y | Y |
| Voinovich | Y | Y | Y | N | N | Y | Y |
| **OKLAHOMA** | | | | | | | |
| Inhofe | Y | Y | Y | N | N | N | Y |
| Coburn | Y | Y | Y | N | N | N | Y |
| **OREGON** | | | | | | | |
| Wyden | ? | ? | Y | Y | Y | Y | N |
| Smith | ? | ? | Y | N | N | Y | N |
| **PENNSYLVANIA** | | | | | | | |
| Specter | Y | Y | Y | N | N | N | Y |
| Santorum | Y | Y | Y | N | N | N | Y |
| **RHODE ISLAND** | | | | | | | |
| Reed | Y | Y | Y | Y | Y | Y | N |
| Chafee | Y | Y | Y | N | N | Y | N |
| **SOUTH CAROLINA** | | | | | | | |
| Graham | Y | Y | Y | N | N | N | Y |
| DeMint | Y | Y | Y | N | N | N | Y |
| **SOUTH DAKOTA** | | | | | | | |
| Johnson | Y | Y | Y | N | N | N | Y |
| Thune | Y | Y | Y | N | N | N | Y |
| **TENNESSEE** | | | | | | | |
| Frist | Y | Y | Y | N | N | N | Y |
| Alexander | Y | Y | Y | N | N | N | Y |
| **TEXAS** | | | | | | | |
| Hutchison | Y | Y | Y | N | N | N | Y |
| Cornyn | Y | Y | Y | N | N | N | Y |
| **UTAH** | | | | | | | |
| Hatch | Y | Y | Y | N | N | N | Y |
| Bennett | Y | Y | Y | N | N | N | Y |
| **VERMONT** | | | | | | | |
| Leahy | Y | Y | Y | Y | Y | Y | N |
| *Jeffords* | Y | Y | Y | Y | Y | Y | N |
| **VIRGINIA** | | | | | | | |
| Warner | Y | Y | Y | N | ? | N | Y |
| Allen | Y | Y | Y | N | N | N | Y |
| **WASHINGTON** | | | | | | | |
| Murray | Y | Y | Y | Y | Y | Y | N |
| Cantwell | Y | Y | Y | Y | Y | Y | N |
| **WEST VIRGINIA** | | | | | | | |
| Byrd | Y | Y | Y | Y | Y | Y | N |
| Rockefeller | Y | Y | Y | Y | Y | Y | N |
| **WISCONSIN** | | | | | | | |
| Kohl | Y | Y | Y | Y | Y | Y | N |
| Feingold | Y | Y | Y | Y | Y | Y | N |
| **WYOMING** | | | | | | | |
| Thomas | Y | Y | Y | N | N | N | Y |
| Enzi | Y | Y | Y | N | N | N | Y |

**KEY**  Republicans  Democrats  *Independents*

| | | |
|---|---|---|
| Y Voted for (yea) | X Paired against | C Voted "present" to avoid possible conflict of interest |
| # Paired for | – Announced against | |
| + Announced for | P Voted "present" | ? Did not vote or otherwise make a position known |
| N Voted against (nay) | | |

# IN THE SENATE | By Vote Number

**272.** HR 3010. Fiscal 2006 Labor-HHS-Education Appropriations/ **Head Start.** Dodd, D-Conn., motion to waive the Budget Act with respect to the Specter, R-Pa., point of order against Dodd amendment. The Dodd amendment would add $153 million for Head Start programs. Motion rejected 47-52: R 5-50; D 41-2 (ND 37-2, SD 4-0); I 1-0. A three-fifths majority vote (60) of the total Senate is required to waive the Budget Act. (Subsequently, the chair upheld the point of order, and the amendment fell.) Oct. 26, 2005.

**273.** HR 3010. Fiscal 2006 Labor-HHS-Education Appropriations/ **Special Education Funding.** Clinton, D-N.Y., motion to waive the Budget Act with respect to the Specter, R-Pa., point of order against Clinton amendment. The Clinton amendment would provide $4 billion in additional funding for state-administered federal grants for disabled and special education students. Motion rejected 46-53: R 4-51; D 41-2 (ND 37-2, SD 4-0); I 1-0. A three-fifths majority vote (60) of the total Senate is required to waive the Budget Act. (Subsequently, the chair upheld the point of order, and the amendment fell.) Oct. 26, 2005.

**274.** HR 3010. Fiscal 2006 Labor-HHS-Education Appropriations/ **AIDS Drug Assistance.** Coburn, R-Okla., amendment that would transfer $60 million in funding from construction and renovation of the Centers for Disease Control and Prevention complex to the AIDS Drug Assistance Program. Rejected 14-85: R 10-45; D 4-39 (ND 4-35, SD 0-4); I 0-1. Oct. 26, 2005.

**275.** HR 3010. Fiscal 2006 Labor-HHS-Education Appropriations/ **Cloture.** Motion to invoke cloture (thus limiting debate) on bill, that would provide $604.4 billion in 2006 for the Labor, Health and Human Services, and Education departments and related agencies, including $141.7 billion in discretionary funding. Motion agreed to 97-0: R 54-0; D 42-0 (ND 38-0, SD 4-0); I 1-0. Three-fifths of the total Senate (60) is required to invoke cloture. Oct. 27, 2005.

**276.** **Smoak Nomination/Confirmation.** Confirmation of President Bush's nomination of John R. Smoak of Florida to be a judge for the U.S. District Court for the Northern District of Florida. Confirmed 97-0: R 55-0; D 41-0 (ND 37-0, SD 4-0); I 1-0. A "yea" was a vote in support of the president's position. Oct. 27, 2005.

**277.** **Neilson Nomination/Confirmation.** Confirmation of President Bush's nomination of Susan Neilson of Michigan to be a judge for the U.S. Court of Appeals for the 6th Circuit. Confirmed 97-0: R 55-0; D 41-0 (ND 37-0, SD 4-0); I 1-0. A "yea" was a vote in support of the president's position. Oct. 27, 2005.

**278.** HR 3010. Fiscal 2006 Labor-HHS-Education Appropriations/AIDS **Drug Assistance.** Harkin, D-Iowa, motion to waive the Budget Act with respect to the Specter, R-Pa., point of order against Bingaman, D-N.M., amendment. The Bingaman amendment would provide an additional $74 million for the AIDS Drug Assistance Program. Motion rejected 46-50: R 6-48; D 39-2 (ND 36-1, SD 3-1); I 1-0. A three-fifths majority vote (60) of the total Senate is required to waive the Budget Act. (Subsequently, the chair upheld the point of order, and the amendment fell.) Oct. 27, 2005.

| | 272 | 273 | 274 | 275 | 276 | 277 | 278 |
|---|---|---|---|---|---|---|---|
| **ALABAMA** | | | | | | | |
| Shelby | N | N | N | Y | Y | Y | N |
| Sessions | N | N | N | Y | Y | Y | N |
| **ALASKA** | | | | | | | |
| Stevens | N | N | N | Y | Y | Y | N |
| Murkowski | N | N | N | Y | Y | Y | N |
| **ARIZONA** | | | | | | | |
| McCain | N | N | Y | Y | Y | Y | N |
| Kyl | N | N | N | Y | Y | Y | N |
| **ARKANSAS** | | | | | | | |
| Lincoln | Y | Y | N | Y | Y | Y | Y |
| Pryor | Y | Y | N | Y | Y | Y | Y |
| **CALIFORNIA** | | | | | | | |
| Feinstein | Y | Y | N | Y | Y | Y | Y |
| Boxer | Y | Y | N | Y | Y | Y | Y |
| **COLORADO** | | | | | | | |
| Allard | N | N | N | Y | Y | Y | N |
| Salazar | Y | Y | N | Y | Y | Y | Y |
| **CONNECTICUT** | | | | | | | |
| Dodd | Y | Y | N | Y | Y | Y | Y |
| Lieberman | Y | Y | N | Y | Y | Y | Y |
| **DELAWARE** | | | | | | | |
| Biden | Y | Y | N | Y | Y | Y | Y |
| Carper | Y | Y | N | Y | Y | Y | N |
| **FLORIDA** | | | | | | | |
| Nelson | Y | Y | N | Y | Y | Y | Y |
| Martinez | N | N | N | Y | Y | Y | N |
| **GEORGIA** | | | | | | | |
| Chambliss | N | N | N | Y | Y | Y | N |
| Isakson | N | N | N | Y | Y | Y | N |
| **HAWAII** | | | | | | | |
| Inouye | Y | Y | N | Y | ? | ? | ? |
| Akaka | Y | Y | N | Y | Y | Y | Y |
| **IDAHO** | | | | | | | |
| Craig | N | N | N | Y | Y | Y | N |
| Crapo | N | N | N | Y | Y | Y | N |
| **ILLINOIS** | | | | | | | |
| Durbin | Y | Y | N | Y | Y | Y | Y |
| Obama | Y | Y | N | Y | Y | Y | Y |
| **INDIANA** | | | | | | | |
| Lugar | Y | Y | Y | Y | Y | Y | N |
| Bayh | Y | Y | N | Y | Y | Y | Y |
| **IOWA** | | | | | | | |
| Grassley | N | N | Y | N | Y | Y | N |
| Harkin | Y | Y | N | Y | Y | Y | Y |
| **KANSAS** | | | | | | | |
| Brownback | N | N | N | Y | Y | Y | N |
| Roberts | N | N | N | Y | Y | Y | N |
| **KENTUCKY** | | | | | | | |
| McConnell | N | N | N | Y | Y | Y | N |
| Bunning | N | N | N | Y | Y | Y | N |
| **LOUISIANA** | | | | | | | |
| Landrieu | Y | Y | N | Y | Y | Y | Y |
| Vitter | N | N | N | Y | Y | Y | N |
| **MAINE** | | | | | | | |
| Snowe | Y | Y | N | Y | Y | Y | Y |
| Collins | Y | Y | N | Y | Y | Y | Y |
| **MARYLAND** | | | | | | | |
| Sarbanes | Y | Y | N | Y | Y | Y | Y |
| Mikulski | Y | Y | N | Y | Y | Y | Y |
| **MASSACHUSETTS** | | | | | | | |
| Kennedy | Y | Y | N | Y | Y | Y | Y |
| Kerry | Y | Y | N | Y | Y | Y | Y |
| **MICHIGAN** | | | | | | | |
| Levin | Y | Y | N | Y | Y | Y | Y |
| Stabenow | Y | Y | Y | Y | Y | Y | Y |
| **MINNESOTA** | | | | | | | |
| Dayton | Y | Y | Y | Y | Y | Y | Y |
| Coleman | N | N | N | Y | Y | Y | N |
| **MISSISSIPPI** | | | | | | | |
| Cochran | N | N | N | Y | Y | Y | N |
| Lott | N | N | N | ? | Y | Y | N |
| **MISSOURI** | | | | | | | |
| Bond | N | N | N | Y | Y | Y | N |
| Talent | N | N | N | Y | Y | Y | Y |
| **MONTANA** | | | | | | | |
| Baucus | Y | Y | N | Y | Y | Y | Y |
| Burns | N | N | N | Y | Y | Y | N |
| **NEBRASKA** | | | | | | | |
| Hagel | N | N | N | Y | Y | Y | N |
| Nelson | N | Y | N | Y | Y | Y | N |
| **NEVADA** | | | | | | | |
| Reid | Y | Y | N | Y | Y | Y | Y |
| Ensign | N | N | Y | Y | Y | Y | N |
| **NEW HAMPSHIRE** | | | | | | | |
| Gregg | N | N | N | Y | Y | Y | N |
| Sununu | N | N | N | Y | Y | Y | N |
| **NEW JERSEY** | | | | | | | |
| Corzine | ? | ? | ? | ? | ? | ? | ? |
| Lautenberg | Y | Y | N | Y | Y | Y | Y |
| **NEW MEXICO** | | | | | | | |
| Domenici | N | N | N | Y | Y | Y | N |
| Bingaman | Y | Y | N | Y | Y | Y | Y |
| **NEW YORK** | | | | | | | |
| Schumer | Y | Y | N | Y | Y | Y | Y |
| Clinton | Y | Y | N | Y | Y | Y | Y |
| **NORTH CAROLINA** | | | | | | | |
| Dole | N | N | N | Y | Y | Y | N |
| Burr | N | N | N | Y | Y | Y | ? |
| **NORTH DAKOTA** | | | | | | | |
| Conrad | N | N | N | Y | Y | Y | N |
| Dorgan | Y | N | N | Y | Y | Y | Y |
| **OHIO** | | | | | | | |
| DeWine | N | Y | N | Y | Y | Y | Y |
| Voinovich | N | N | N | Y | Y | Y | N |
| **OKLAHOMA** | | | | | | | |
| Inhofe | N | N | N | Y | Y | Y | N |
| Coburn | N | N | Y | Y | Y | Y | N |
| **OREGON** | | | | | | | |
| Wyden | Y | Y | N | Y | Y | Y | Y |
| Smith | N | N | N | Y | Y | Y | N |
| **PENNSYLVANIA** | | | | | | | |
| Specter | N | N | N | Y | Y | Y | N |
| Santorum | N | N | N | Y | Y | Y | N |
| **RHODE ISLAND** | | | | | | | |
| Reed | Y | Y | N | Y | Y | Y | Y |
| Chafee | Y | Y | Y | Y | Y | Y | Y |
| **SOUTH CAROLINA** | | | | | | | |
| Graham | N | N | N | Y | Y | Y | N |
| DeMint | N | N | N | Y | Y | Y | N |
| **SOUTH DAKOTA** | | | | | | | |
| Johnson | Y | Y | N | Y | Y | Y | Y |
| Thune | N | N | N | Y | Y | Y | N |
| **TENNESSEE** | | | | | | | |
| Frist | N | N | N | Y | Y | Y | N |
| Alexander | N | N | N | Y | Y | Y | N |
| **TEXAS** | | | | | | | |
| Hutchison | N | N | N | Y | Y | Y | N |
| Cornyn | N | N | Y | Y | Y | Y | N |
| **UTAH** | | | | | | | |
| Hatch | N | N | N | Y | Y | Y | N |
| Bennett | N | N | N | Y | Y | Y | N |
| **VERMONT** | | | | | | | |
| Leahy | Y | Y | N | Y | Y | Y | Y |
| Jeffords | Y | Y | N | Y | Y | Y | Y |
| **VIRGINIA** | | | | | | | |
| Warner | N | N | N | Y | Y | Y | N |
| Allen | N | N | N | Y | Y | Y | N |
| **WASHINGTON** | | | | | | | |
| Murray | Y | Y | N | Y | Y | Y | Y |
| Cantwell | Y | Y | N | Y | Y | Y | Y |
| **WEST VIRGINIA** | | | | | | | |
| Byrd | Y | Y | N | Y | Y | Y | Y |
| Rockefeller | Y | Y | N | ? | ? | ? | ? |
| **WISCONSIN** | | | | | | | |
| Kohl | Y | Y | N | Y | Y | Y | Y |
| Feingold | Y | Y | Y | Y | Y | Y | Y |
| **WYOMING** | | | | | | | |
| Thomas | N | N | N | Y | Y | Y | N |
| Enzi | N | N | N | Y | Y | Y | N |

**KEY**  Republicans  Democrats  *Independents*

| | | |
|---|---|---|
| **Y** Voted for (yea) | **X** Paired against | **C** Voted "present" to avoid possible conflict of interest |
| **#** Paired for | **–** Announced against | |
| **+** Announced for | **P** Voted "present" | **?** Did not vote or otherwise make a position known |
| **N** Voted against (nay) | | |

# IN THE SENATE | By Vote Number

**279.** HR 3010. Fiscal 2006 Labor-HHS-Education Appropriations/ **Learning Centers.** Boxer, D-Calif., motion to waive the Budget Act with respect to the Specter, R-Pa., point of order against Boxer amendment. The Boxer amendment would provide an additional $51.9 million for after-school programs under the 21st Century Community Learning Centers, part of the 2001 education overhaul law. Motion rejected 41-56: R 0-55; D 40-1 (ND 36-1, SD 4-0); I 1-0. A three-fifths majority vote (60) of the total Senate is required to waive the Budget Act. (Subsequently, the chair upheld the point of order, and the amendment fell.) Oct. 27, 2005.

**280.** HR 3010. Fiscal 2006 Labor-HHS-Education Appropriations/ **e-Language System Distribution.** Ensign, R-Nev., amendment that would prohibit funds in the bill from being used to develop or distribute the Education Department's e-Language Learning System. Rejected 41-56: R 35-20; D 6-35 (ND 6-31, SD 0-4); I 0-1. Oct. 27, 2005.

**281.** HR 3010. Fiscal 2006 Labor-HHS-Education Appropriations/ **Passage.** Passage of the bill that would provide $604.4 billion in fiscal 2006 for the Labor, Health and Human Services (HHS), and Education departments and related agencies, including $141.7 billion in discretionary spending. The bill includes $15 billion for the Labor Department; $476.2 billion for HHS, and $63.7 billion for the Education Department. It would shift $3.3 billion in mandatory Supplemental Security Income payments from fiscal 2006 to fiscal 2007. Passed 94-3: R 53-2; D 40-1 (ND 36-1, SD 4-0); I 1-0. Oct. 27, 2005.

| | 279 | 280 | 281 | | | 279 | 280 | 281 |
|---|---|---|---|---|---|---|---|---|
| **ALABAMA** | | | | | **MONTANA** | | | |
| Shelby | N | Y | Y | | Baucus | Y | N | Y |
| Sessions | N | Y | Y | | Burns | N | N | Y |
| **ALASKA** | | | | | **NEBRASKA** | | | |
| Stevens | N | N | Y | | Hagel | N | N | Y |
| Murkowski | N | N | Y | | Nelson | N | Y | Y |
| **ARIZONA** | | | | | **NEVADA** | | | |
| McCain | N | N | Y | | Reid | Y | N | Y |
| Kyl | N | Y | Y | | Ensign | N | Y | N |
| **ARKANSAS** | | | | | **NEW HAMPSHIRE** | | | |
| Lincoln | Y | N | Y | | Gregg | N | Y | Y |
| Pryor | Y | N | Y | | Sununu | N | Y | Y |
| **CALIFORNIA** | | | | | **NEW JERSEY** | | | |
| Feinstein | Y | N | Y | | Corzine | ? | ? | ? |
| Boxer | Y | N | Y | | Lautenberg | Y | N | Y |
| **COLORADO** | | | | | **NEW MEXICO** | | | |
| Allard | N | Y | Y | | Domenici | N | N | Y |
| Salazar | Y | N | Y | | Bingaman | Y | N | Y |
| **CONNECTICUT** | | | | | **NEW YORK** | | | |
| Dodd | Y | N | Y | | Schumer | Y | Y | Y |
| Lieberman | Y | N | Y | | Clinton | Y | N | Y |
| **DELAWARE** | | | | | **NORTH CAROLINA** | | | |
| Biden | Y | N | Y | | Dole | N | Y | Y |
| Carper | Y | N | Y | | Burr | N | Y | Y |
| **FLORIDA** | | | | | **NORTH DAKOTA** | | | |
| Nelson | Y | N | Y | | Conrad | Y | N | N |
| Martinez | N | Y | Y | | Dorgan | Y | Y | Y |
| **GEORGIA** | | | | | **OHIO** | | | |
| Chambliss | N | Y | Y | | DeWine | N | N | Y |
| Isakson | N | Y | Y | | Voinovich | N | N | Y |
| **HAWAII** | | | | | **OKLAHOMA** | | | |
| Inouye | ? | ? | ? | | Inhofe | N | Y | N |
| Akaka | Y | N | Y | | Coburn | N | Y | Y |
| **IDAHO** | | | | | **OREGON** | | | |
| Craig | N | Y | Y | | Wyden | Y | Y | Y |
| Crapo | N | Y | Y | | Smith | N | Y | Y |
| **ILLINOIS** | | | | | **PENNSYLVANIA** | | | |
| Durbin | Y | N | Y | | Specter | N | N | Y |
| Obama | Y | N | Y | | Santorum | N | Y | Y |
| **INDIANA** | | | | | **RHODE ISLAND** | | | |
| Lugar | N | N | Y | | Reed | Y | N | Y |
| Bayh | Y | Y | Y | | Chafee | N | N | Y |
| **IOWA** | | | | | **SOUTH CAROLINA** | | | |
| Grassley | N | Y | Y | | Graham | N | Y | Y |
| Harkin | Y | N | Y | | DeMint | N | Y | Y |
| **KANSAS** | | | | | **SOUTH DAKOTA** | | | |
| Brownback | N | Y | Y | | Johnson | Y | N | Y |
| Roberts | N | Y | Y | | Thune | N | Y | Y |
| **KENTUCKY** | | | | | **TENNESSEE** | | | |
| McConnell | N | N | Y | | Frist | N | N | Y |
| Bunning | N | N | Y | | Alexander | N | N | Y |
| **LOUISIANA** | | | | | **TEXAS** | | | |
| Landrieu | Y | N | Y | | Hutchison | N | Y | Y |
| Vitter | N | Y | Y | | Cornyn | N | Y | Y |
| **MAINE** | | | | | **UTAH** | | | |
| Snowe | N | Y | Y | | Hatch | N | Y | Y |
| Collins | N | N | Y | | Bennett | N | Y | Y |
| **MARYLAND** | | | | | **VERMONT** | | | |
| Sarbanes | Y | N | Y | | Leahy | Y | N | Y |
| Mikulski | Y | N | Y | | *Jeffords* | Y | N | Y |
| **MASSACHUSETTS** | | | | | **VIRGINIA** | | | |
| Kennedy | Y | N | Y | | Warner | N | Y | Y |
| Kerry | Y | N | Y | | Allen | N | Y | Y |
| **MICHIGAN** | | | | | **WASHINGTON** | | | |
| Levin | Y | N | Y | | Murray | Y | N | Y |
| Stabenow | Y | N | Y | | Cantwell | Y | N | Y |
| **MINNESOTA** | | | | | **WEST VIRGINIA** | | | |
| Dayton | Y | N | Y | | Byrd | Y | N | Y |
| Coleman | N | N | Y | | Rockefeller | ? | ? | ? |
| **MISSISSIPPI** | | | | | **WISCONSIN** | | | |
| Cochran | N | N | Y | | Kohl | Y | Y | Y |
| Lott | N | Y | Y | | Feingold | Y | N | Y |
| **MISSOURI** | | | | | **WYOMING** | | | |
| Bond | N | N | Y | | Thomas | N | N | Y |
| Talent | N | Y | Y | | Enzi | N | Y | Y |

| KEY | Republicans | Democrats | *Independents* | |
|---|---|---|---|---|
| Y | Voted for (yea) | X | Paired against | C | Voted "present" to avoid possible conflict of interest |
| # | Paired for | – | Announced against | |
| + | Announced for | P | Voted "present" | ? | Did not vote or otherwise make a position known |
| N | Voted against (nay) | | | |

# IN THE SENATE | By Vote Number

**282.** **HR 2744. Fiscal 2006 Agriculture Appropriations/Conference Report.** Adoption of the conference report on the bill that would appropriate $101 billion in fiscal 2006 for the Department of Agriculture, the Food and Drug Administration (FDA) and related agencies. The bill would provide $40.7 billion for the food stamp program, $12.7 billion for child nutrition, $25.7 billion for the Commodity Credit Corporation, $5.3 billion for the Women, Infants and Children program, and $1.5 billion for the FDA. Adopted (thus cleared for the president) 81-18: R 45-10; D 35-8 (ND 31-8, SD 4-0); I 1-0. Nov. 3, 2005.

**283.** **S 1932. Budget Reconciliation/PAYGO Rules.** Conrad, D-N.D., motion to waive the Budget Act with respect to the Gregg, R-N.H., point of order against the Conrad amendment. The Conrad amendment would restore pay-as-you-go (PAYGO) rules, which would create a 60-vote point of order against any direct spending or revenue legislation that would increase the on-budget deficit or cause an on-budget deficit, until Sept. 30, 2010. Tax cuts and new entitlement spending would have to be offset with revenue increases or spending cuts. Motion rejected 50-49: R 6-49; D 43-0 (ND 39-0, SD 4-0); I 1-0. A three-fifths majority vote (60) of the total Senate is required to waive the Budget Act. (Subsequently, the chair upheld the point of order, and the amendment fell.) Nov. 3, 2005.

**284.** **S 1932. Budget Reconciliation/Private School Aid.** Ensign, R-Nev., motion to waive the Budget Act with respect to the Enzi, R-Wyo., point of order against the Ensign amendment to the Enzi amendment. The Ensign amendment would allow federal funds to go to states, which would have to send checks to schools that receive Katrina evacuees. Non-public schools would be required to obtain permission from parents of displaced children before they could use the government money. The Enzi amendment would provide $1.2 billion in financial assistance for displaced students attending public, private or religious schools, $450 million in grants to schools in the Gulf Coast region, and $900 million to reduce loan origination fees for college students to 2 percent. Motion rejected 31-68: R 31-24; D 0-43 (ND 0-39, SD 0-4); I 0-1. A three-fifths majority vote (60) of the total Senate is required to waive the Budget Act. (Subsequently, the chair upheld the point of order, and the Ensign amendment fell. The Enzi amendment was adopted by voice vote.) Nov. 3, 2005.

**285.** **S 1932. Budget Reconciliation/Emergency Health Care for Katrina Victims.** Lincoln, D-Ark., motion to waive the Budget Act with respect to the Gregg, R-N.H., point of order against the Lincoln amendment. The Lincoln amendment would grant access to Medicaid to Hurricane Katrina victims for five months; provide full federal funding for Medicaid in Louisiana, Mississippi and Alabama for one year and provide other health assistance for the hurricane victims. It would be paid for with unspent Federal Emergency Management Agency funds. Motion rejected 48-51: R 4-51; D 43-0 (ND 39-0, SD 4-0); I 1-0. A three-fifths majority vote (60) of the total Senate is required to waive the Budget Act. (Subsequently, the chair upheld the point of order, and the amendment fell.) Nov. 3, 2005.

**286.** **S 1932. Budget Reconciliation/Discretionary Spending Cap.** Inhofe, R-Okla., motion to waive the Budget Act with respect to the Cochran, R-Miss., point of order against the Inhofe amendment. The Inhofe amendment would cap non-defense, non-trust fund spending at fiscal 2006 levels beginning in fiscal 2007. The Senate could waive the cap and increase spending with a two-thirds majority vote. Motion rejected 32-67: R 32-23; D 0-43 (ND 0-39, SD 0-4); I 0-1. A three-fifths majority vote (60) of the total Senate is required to waive the Budget Act. (Subsequently, the chair upheld the point of order, and the amendment fell.) Nov. 3, 2005.

| | 282 | 283 | 284 | 285 | 286 | | | 282 | 283 | 284 | 285 | 286 |
|---|---|---|---|---|---|---|---|---|---|---|---|---|
| **ALABAMA** | | | | | | | **MONTANA** | | | | | |
| Shelby | Y | N | Y | N | Y | | Baucus | N | Y | N | Y | N |
| Sessions | Y | N | Y | N | Y | | Burns | N | N | N | N | Y |
| **ALASKA** | | | | | | | **NEBRASKA** | | | | | |
| Stevens | Y | N | N | N | N | | Hagel | Y | N | Y | N | Y |
| Murkowski | Y | N | N | N | N | | Nelson | Y | Y | N | Y | N |
| **ARIZONA** | | | | | | | **NEVADA** | | | | | |
| McCain | N | Y | Y | N | Y | | Reid | Y | Y | N | Y | N |
| Kyl | N | N | Y | N | Y | | Ensign | N | N | Y | N | Y |
| **ARKANSAS** | | | | | | | **NEW HAMPSHIRE** | | | | | |
| Lincoln | Y | Y | N | Y | N | | Gregg | Y | N | Y | N | N |
| Pryor | Y | Y | N | Y | N | | Sununu | N | N | Y | N | Y |
| **CALIFORNIA** | | | | | | | **NEW JERSEY** | | | | | |
| Feinstein | Y | Y | N | Y | N | | Corzine | ? | ? | ? | ? | ? |
| Boxer | Y | Y | N | Y | N | | Lautenberg | Y | Y | N | Y | N |
| **COLORADO** | | | | | | | **NEW MEXICO** | | | | | |
| Allard | Y | N | Y | N | Y | | Domenici | Y | N | N | N | N |
| Salazar | Y | Y | N | Y | N | | Bingaman | Y | Y | N | Y | N |
| **CONNECTICUT** | | | | | | | **NEW YORK** | | | | | |
| Dodd | N | Y | N | Y | N | | Schumer | Y | Y | N | Y | N |
| Lieberman | Y | Y | N | Y | N | | Clinton | Y | Y | N | Y | N |
| **DELAWARE** | | | | | | | **NORTH CAROLINA** | | | | | |
| Biden | Y | Y | N | Y | N | | Dole | Y | N | Y | N | Y |
| Carper | Y | Y | N | Y | N | | Burr | Y | N | N | N | N |
| **FLORIDA** | | | | | | | **NORTH DAKOTA** | | | | | |
| Nelson | Y | Y | N | Y | N | | Conrad | Y | Y | N | Y | N |
| Martinez | Y | N | Y | N | Y | | Dorgan | N | Y | N | Y | N |
| **GEORGIA** | | | | | | | **OHIO** | | | | | |
| Chambliss | Y | N | N | N | Y | | DeWine | Y | N | Y | N | N |
| Isakson | Y | N | N | N | N | | Voinovich | Y | Y | Y | Y | N |
| **HAWAII** | | | | | | | **OKLAHOMA** | | | | | |
| Inouye | Y | Y | N | Y | N | | Inhofe | Y | N | Y | N | Y |
| Akaka | Y | Y | N | Y | N | | Coburn | N | Y | N | Y | N |
| **IDAHO** | | | | | | | **OREGON** | | | | | |
| Craig | Y | N | Y | N | Y | | Wyden | Y | Y | N | Y | N |
| Crapo | Y | N | Y | N | Y | | Smith | Y | N | N | N | N |
| **ILLINOIS** | | | | | | | **PENNSYLVANIA** | | | | | |
| Durbin | Y | Y | N | Y | N | | Specter | Y | Y | N | N | N |
| Obama | Y | Y | N | Y | N | | Santorum | Y | N | Y | N | N |
| **INDIANA** | | | | | | | **RHODE ISLAND** | | | | | |
| Lugar | Y | N | N | N | N | | Reed | Y | Y | N | Y | N |
| Bayh | N | Y | N | Y | N | | Chafee | Y | Y | N | N | N |
| **IOWA** | | | | | | | **SOUTH CAROLINA** | | | | | |
| Grassley | N | N | Y | N | Y | | Graham | Y | N | Y | N | Y |
| Harkin | N | Y | N | Y | N | | DeMint | Y | N | Y | N | Y |
| **KANSAS** | | | | | | | **SOUTH DAKOTA** | | | | | |
| Brownback | Y | N | N | N | Y | | Johnson | N | Y | N | Y | N |
| Roberts | Y | N | N | N | N | | Thune | N | N | Y | N | Y |
| **KENTUCKY** | | | | | | | **TENNESSEE** | | | | | |
| McConnell | Y | N | Y | N | Y | | Frist | Y | N | Y | N | Y |
| Bunning | Y | N | Y | N | Y | | Alexander | Y | N | Y | N | Y |
| **LOUISIANA** | | | | | | | **TEXAS** | | | | | |
| Landrieu | Y | Y | N | Y | N | | Hutchison | Y | N | N | Y | Y |
| Vitter | Y | N | Y | Y | Y | | Cornyn | Y | N | Y | N | Y |
| **MAINE** | | | | | | | **UTAH** | | | | | |
| Snowe | Y | Y | Y | Y | N | | Hatch | Y | N | Y | N | N |
| Collins | Y | Y | N | N | N | | Bennett | Y | N | N | N | N |
| **MARYLAND** | | | | | | | **VERMONT** | | | | | |
| Sarbanes | Y | Y | N | Y | N | | Leahy | Y | Y | N | Y | N |
| Mikulski | Y | Y | N | Y | N | | Jeffords | Y | Y | N | Y | N |
| **MASSACHUSETTS** | | | | | | | **VIRGINIA** | | | | | |
| Kennedy | Y | Y | N | Y | N | | Warner | Y | N | N | N | N |
| Kerry | N | Y | N | Y | N | | Allen | Y | N | Y | N | Y |
| **MICHIGAN** | | | | | | | **WASHINGTON** | | | | | |
| Levin | Y | Y | N | Y | N | | Murray | Y | Y | N | Y | N |
| Stabenow | Y | Y | N | Y | N | | Cantwell | Y | Y | N | Y | N |
| **MINNESOTA** | | | | | | | **WEST VIRGINIA** | | | | | |
| Dayton | Y | Y | N | Y | N | | Byrd | Y | Y | N | Y | N |
| Coleman | Y | N | Y | N | N | | Rockefeller | Y | Y | N | Y | N |
| **MISSISSIPPI** | | | | | | | **WISCONSIN** | | | | | |
| Cochran | Y | N | N | N | N | | Kohl | Y | Y | N | Y | N |
| Lott | Y | N | N | N | N | | Feingold | N | Y | N | Y | N |
| **MISSOURI** | | | | | | | **WYOMING** | | | | | |
| Bond | Y | N | N | N | N | | Thomas | N | N | N | N | Y |
| Talent | Y | N | N | N | N | | Enzi | N | N | N | N | N |

**KEY**    Republicans    Democrats    *Independents*

| | | | |
|---|---|---|---|
| **Y** | Voted for (yea) | **X** | Paired against |
| **#** | Paired for | **–** | Announced against |
| **+** | Announced for | **P** | Voted "present" |
| **N** | Voted against (nay) | | |

| | |
|---|---|
| **C** | Voted "present" to avoid possible conflict of interest |
| **?** | Did not vote or otherwise make a position known |

# IN THE SENATE | By Vote Number

**287.** **S 1932. Budget Reconciliation/Medicare Part B Premiums.**
Nelson, D-Fla., amendment that would prevent an increase in monthly Part B premiums for Medicare recipients that might result from a boost in payments to doctors. It would be offset with rebate payments by drug companies for Medicaid programs administered by health maintenance organizations (HMOs). Rejected 49-50: R 5-50; D 43-0 (ND 39-0, SD 4-0); I 1-0. Nov. 3, 2005.

**288.** **S 1932. Budget Reconciliation/ANWR Oil and Gas Leasing.**
Cantwell, D-Wash., amendment that would strike language from the underlying bill permitting oil and gas leasing in Alaska's Arctic National Wildlife Refuge (ANWR). Rejected 48-51: R 7-48; D 40-3 (ND 37-2, SD 3-1); I 1-0. A "nay" was a vote in support of the president's position. Nov. 3, 2005.

**289.** **S 1932. Budget Reconciliation/ANWR Exports.** Wyden, D-Ore., amendment that would prohibit any oil or gas produced from leases in ANWR from being sold outside the United States. Adopted 83-16: R 40-15; D 42-1 (ND 39-0, SD 3-1); I 1-0. Nov. 3, 2005.

**290.** **S 1932. Budget Reconciliation/Farm Programs.** Grassley, R-Iowa, motion to waive the Budget Act with respect to the Chambliss, R-Ga., point of order against the Grassley amendment. The Grassley amendment would cap farm commodity program payments at $250,000 a year for married couples and $125,000 for individuals and delay the onset of the 2.5 percent across-the-board reduction in farm program payments by one year until 2007. Motion rejected 46-53: R 19-36; D 27-16 (ND 27-12, SD 0-4); I 0-1. A three-fifths majority vote (60) of the total Senate is required to waive the Budget Act. (Subsequently, the chair upheld the point of order, and the amendment fell.) Nov. 3, 2005.

**291.** **S 1932. Budget Reconciliation/Medicaid FMAP.** Bingaman, D-N.M., amendment that would prevent the Medicaid federal medical assistance percentage (FMAP) from falling below 0.1 in for Delaware and Michigan, 0.3 for Kentucky and 0.5 for any other state in fiscal 2006. The amendment also would extend prescription drug rebates to Medicaid recipients enrolled in HMOs or preferred provider organizations. Adopted 54-45: R 10-45; D 43-0 (ND 39-0, SD 4-0); I 1-0. Nov. 3, 2005.

**292.** **S 1932. Budget Reconciliation/Amtrak Funding.** Lott, R-Miss., amendment that would partially restructure Amtrak and authorize more than $12 billion over six years through fiscal 2011 for operations, capital improvements and rail security. Adopted 93-6: R 49-6; D 43-0 (ND 39-0, SD 4-0); I 1-0. Nov. 3, 2005.

| | 287 | 288 | 289 | 290 | 291 | 292 | | | 287 | 288 | 289 | 290 | 291 | 292 |
|---|---|---|---|---|---|---|---|---|---|---|---|---|---|---|
| **ALABAMA** | | | | | | | | **MONTANA** | | | | | | |
| Shelby | N | N | Y | N | N | Y | | Baucus | Y | Y | Y | N | Y | Y |
| Sessions | N | N | N | N | N | N | | Burns | Y | N | Y | N | N | Y |
| **ALASKA** | | | | | | | | **NEBRASKA** | | | | | | |
| Stevens | N | N | Y | N | N | Y | | Hagel | N | N | Y | Y | N | Y |
| Murkowski | N | N | Y | N | Y | Y | | Nelson | Y | Y | Y | Y | Y | Y |
| **ARIZONA** | | | | | | | | **NEVADA** | | | | | | |
| McCain | N | Y | Y | N | N | Y | | Reid | Y | Y | Y | Y | Y | Y |
| Kyl | N | N | N | N | N | Y | | Ensign | N | N | Y | Y | N | N |
| **ARKANSAS** | | | | | | | | **NEW HAMPSHIRE** | | | | | | |
| Lincoln | Y | Y | Y | N | Y | Y | | Gregg | N | N | N | N | N | N |
| Pryor | Y | Y | Y | N | Y | Y | | Sununu | N | N | N | Y | N | N |
| **CALIFORNIA** | | | | | | | | **NEW JERSEY** | | | | | | |
| Feinstein | Y | Y | Y | N | Y | Y | | Corzine | ? | ? | ? | ? | ? | ? |
| Boxer | Y | Y | Y | N | Y | Y | | Lautenberg | Y | Y | Y | Y | Y | Y |
| **COLORADO** | | | | | | | | **NEW MEXICO** | | | | | | |
| Allard | N | N | N | Y | N | Y | | Domenici | N | N | Y | N | Y | Y |
| Salazar | Y | Y | Y | Y | Y | Y | | Bingaman | Y | Y | Y | Y | Y | Y |
| **CONNECTICUT** | | | | | | | | **NEW YORK** | | | | | | |
| Dodd | Y | Y | Y | N | Y | Y | | Schumer | Y | Y | Y | Y | Y | Y |
| Lieberman | Y | Y | Y | N | Y | Y | | Clinton | Y | Y | Y | Y | Y | Y |
| **DELAWARE** | | | | | | | | **NORTH CAROLINA** | | | | | | |
| Biden | Y | Y | Y | N | Y | Y | | Dole | N | N | Y | N | N | Y |
| Carper | Y | Y | Y | N | Y | Y | | Burr | N | N | N | N | N | Y |
| **FLORIDA** | | | | | | | | **NORTH DAKOTA** | | | | | | |
| Nelson | Y | Y | Y | N | Y | Y | | Conrad | Y | Y | Y | Y | Y | Y |
| Martinez | N | N | Y | N | N | Y | | Dorgan | Y | Y | Y | Y | Y | Y |
| **GEORGIA** | | | | | | | | **OHIO** | | | | | | |
| Chambliss | N | N | N | N | N | Y | | DeWine | Y | Y | Y | Y | Y | Y |
| Isakson | N | N | Y | N | N | Y | | Voinovich | N | N | Y | N | N | N |
| **HAWAII** | | | | | | | | **OKLAHOMA** | | | | | | |
| Inouye | Y | N | Y | N | Y | Y | | Inhofe | N | N | N | N | Y | Y |
| Akaka | Y | N | Y | N | Y | Y | | Coburn | N | N | N | N | N | Y |
| **IDAHO** | | | | | | | | **OREGON** | | | | | | |
| Craig | N | N | N | N | N | Y | | Wyden | Y | Y | Y | N | Y | Y |
| Crapo | N | N | N | N | N | Y | | Smith | N | Y | Y | N | N | Y |
| **ILLINOIS** | | | | | | | | **PENNSYLVANIA** | | | | | | |
| Durbin | Y | Y | Y | Y | Y | Y | | Specter | N | N | Y | N | N | Y |
| Obama | Y | Y | Y | Y | Y | Y | | Santorum | N | N | Y | N | N | Y |
| **INDIANA** | | | | | | | | **RHODE ISLAND** | | | | | | |
| Lugar | N | N | Y | Y | N | Y | | Reed | Y | Y | Y | Y | Y | Y |
| Bayh | Y | Y | Y | Y | Y | Y | | Chafee | N | Y | Y | Y | Y | Y |
| **IOWA** | | | | | | | | **SOUTH CAROLINA** | | | | | | |
| Grassley | N | N | Y | Y | N | Y | | Graham | N | N | N | N | N | Y |
| Harkin | Y | Y | Y | Y | Y | Y | | DeMint | N | N | N | N | N | N |
| **KANSAS** | | | | | | | | **SOUTH DAKOTA** | | | | | | |
| Brownback | N | N | N | Y | N | Y | | Johnson | Y | Y | Y | Y | Y | Y |
| Roberts | N | N | Y | N | N | Y | | Thune | N | N | Y | Y | N | Y |
| **KENTUCKY** | | | | | | | | **TENNESSEE** | | | | | | |
| McConnell | N | N | Y | N | N | Y | | Frist | N | N | Y | N | N | Y |
| Bunning | N | N | N | N | N | Y | | Alexander | N | N | N | N | N | N |
| **LOUISIANA** | | | | | | | | **TEXAS** | | | | | | |
| Landrieu | Y | N | Y | N | Y | Y | | Hutchison | N | N | N | N | Y | Y |
| Vitter | N | N | Y | N | N | Y | | Cornyn | N | N | N | N | Y | Y |
| **MAINE** | | | | | | | | **UTAH** | | | | | | |
| Snowe | Y | Y | Y | Y | Y | Y | | Hatch | N | N | N | N | N | Y |
| Collins | Y | Y | Y | Y | Y | Y | | Bennett | N | N | N | N | N | Y |
| **MARYLAND** | | | | | | | | **VERMONT** | | | | | | |
| Sarbanes | Y | Y | Y | Y | Y | Y | | Leahy | Y | Y | Y | N | Y | Y |
| Mikulski | Y | Y | Y | Y | Y | Y | | Jeffords | Y | Y | Y | N | Y | Y |
| **MASSACHUSETTS** | | | | | | | | **VIRGINIA** | | | | | | |
| Kennedy | Y | Y | Y | Y | Y | Y | | Warner | N | N | Y | N | N | Y |
| Kerry | Y | Y | Y | Y | Y | Y | | Allen | N | N | N | N | N | Y |
| **MICHIGAN** | | | | | | | | **WASHINGTON** | | | | | | |
| Levin | Y | Y | Y | Y | Y | Y | | Murray | Y | Y | Y | Y | Y | Y |
| Stabenow | Y | Y | Y | Y | Y | Y | | Cantwell | Y | Y | Y | Y | Y | Y |
| **MINNESOTA** | | | | | | | | **WEST VIRGINIA** | | | | | | |
| Dayton | Y | Y | Y | Y | Y | Y | | Byrd | Y | Y | Y | Y | Y | Y |
| Coleman | N | Y | Y | N | N | Y | | Rockefeller | Y | Y | Y | N | Y | Y |
| **MISSISSIPPI** | | | | | | | | **WISCONSIN** | | | | | | |
| Cochran | N | N | Y | N | N | Y | | Kohl | Y | Y | Y | N | Y | Y |
| Lott | N | N | Y | N | N | Y | | Feingold | Y | Y | Y | Y | Y | Y |
| **MISSOURI** | | | | | | | | **WYOMING** | | | | | | |
| Bond | N | N | Y | N | N | Y | | Thomas | N | N | Y | N | N | Y |
| Talent | Y | N | Y | N | N | Y | | Enzi | N | N | Y | N | N | Y |

**KEY**    **Republicans**    Democrats    *Independents*

| | | | | |
|---|---|---|---|---|
| Y | Voted for (yea) | X | Paired against | C   Voted "present" to avoid possible conflict of interest |
| # | Paired for | – | Announced against | |
| + | Announced for | P | Voted "present" | ?   Did not vote or otherwise make a position known |
| N | Voted against (nay) | | | |

# IN THE SENATE | By Vote Number

**293.** **S 1932. Budget Reconciliation/Broadcast Spectrum.** McCain, R-Ariz., amendment that would move the date when broadcasters must relinquish certain segments of the broadcast spectrum forward by one year to April 7, 2008. Rejected 30-69: R 9-46; D 20-23 (ND 19-20, SD 1-3); I 1-0. Nov. 3, 2005.

**294.** **S 1932. Budget Reconciliation/Medicare Dual Eligibility.** Murray, D-Wash., motion to waive the Budget Act with respect to the Gregg, R-N.H., point of order against the Murray amendment. The Murray amendment would provide an extra six months for Medicaid patients who are also seniors to enroll in the new Medicare prescription drug program. Motion rejected 43-56: R 0-55; D 42-1 (ND 38-1, SD 4-0); I 1-0. A three-fifths majority vote (60) of the total Senate is required to waive the Budget Act. (Subsequently, the chair upheld the point of order, and the amendment fell.) Nov. 3, 2005.

**295.** **S 1932. Budget Reconciliation/Non-Immigrant Visa Fee.** Byrd, D-W.Va., amendment that would strike the section of the bill related to immigrant visas and insert language that would impose a fee of $1,500 on employers filing L1 visa request for a non-immigrant employer. Rejected 14-85: R 3-52; D 10-33 (ND 9-30, SD 1-3); I 1-0. Nov. 3, 2005.

**296.** **S 1932. Budget Reconciliation/Reconciliation Consideration.** Byrd, D-W.Va., motion to waive the Budget Act with respect to the Gregg, R-N.H., point of order against the Byrd amendment. The Byrd amendment would suspend the 20-hour time limit on debate for any reconciliation bill that would increase the deficit. Motion rejected 44-55: R 0-55; D 43-0 (ND 39-0, SD 4-0); I 1-0. A three-fifths majority vote (60) of the total Senate is required to waive the Budget Act. (Subsequently, the chair upheld the point of order, and the amendment fell.) Nov. 3, 2005.

**297.** **S 1932. Budget Reconciliation/Prescription Drug Enrollment.** Lautenberg, D-N.J., motion to waive the Budget Act with respect to the Gregg, R-N.H., point of order against the Lautenberg amendment. The Lautenberg amendment would require applicants for Medicare Advantage prescription drug plans to sign a certification prior to enrollment stating that they understand that the plan may contain a potential coverage gap. Motion rejected 43-56: R 0-55; D 43-0 (ND 39-0, SD 4-0); I 0-1. A three-fifths majority vote (60) of the total Senate is required to waive the Budget Act. (Subsequently, the chair upheld the point of order, and the amendment fell.) Nov. 3, 2005.

**298.** **S 1932. Budget Reconciliation/ANWR Revenue Split.** Cantwell, D-Wash., amendment that would ensure that 50 percent of revenues from oil and natural gas leasing and production in ANWR be paid to the state of Alaska and 50 percent to the U.S. Treasury. If the state of Alaska brings a civil suit against the federal government to secure more than 50 percent, oil and gas production would cease until a non-appealable decision is handed down. Rejected 48-51: R 6-49; D 41-2 (ND 37-2, SD 4-0); I 1-0. Nov. 3, 2005.

| | 293 | 294 | 295 | 296 | 297 | 298 |
|---|---|---|---|---|---|---|
| **ALABAMA** | | | | | | |
| Shelby | N | N | N | N | N | N |
| Sessions | N | N | Y | N | N | N |
| **ALASKA** | | | | | | |
| Stevens | N | N | N | N | N | N |
| Murkowski | N | N | N | N | N | N |
| **ARIZONA** | | | | | | |
| McCain | Y | N | N | N | N | Y |
| Kyl | Y | N | N | N | N | N |
| **ARKANSAS** | | | | | | |
| Lincoln | N | Y | N | Y | Y | Y |
| Pryor | N | Y | N | Y | Y | Y |
| **CALIFORNIA** | | | | | | |
| Feinstein | Y | Y | N | Y | Y | Y |
| Boxer | Y | Y | N | Y | Y | Y |
| **COLORADO** | | | | | | |
| Allard | N | N | N | N | N | N |
| Salazar | Y | Y | N | Y | Y | Y |
| **CONNECTICUT** | | | | | | |
| Dodd | Y | Y | Y | Y | Y | Y |
| Lieberman | Y | Y | N | Y | Y | Y |
| **DELAWARE** | | | | | | |
| Biden | Y | Y | N | Y | Y | Y |
| Carper | Y | Y | N | Y | Y | Y |
| **FLORIDA** | | | | | | |
| Nelson | Y | Y | Y | Y | Y | Y |
| Martinez | N | N | N | N | N | N |
| **GEORGIA** | | | | | | |
| Chambliss | N | N | N | N | N | N |
| Isakson | N | N | N | N | N | N |
| **HAWAII** | | | | | | |
| Inouye | N | Y | N | Y | Y | N |
| Akaka | N | Y | Y | Y | Y | N |
| **IDAHO** | | | | | | |
| Craig | N | N | N | N | N | N |
| Crapo | N | N | N | N | N | N |
| **ILLINOIS** | | | | | | |
| Durbin | N | Y | Y | Y | Y | Y |
| Obama | N | Y | N | Y | Y | Y |
| **INDIANA** | | | | | | |
| Lugar | N | N | N | N | N | N |
| Bayh | Y | Y | N | Y | Y | Y |
| **IOWA** | | | | | | |
| Grassley | N | N | N | N | N | N |
| Harkin | Y | Y | N | Y | Y | Y |
| **KANSAS** | | | | | | |
| Brownback | N | N | N | N | N | N |
| Roberts | N | N | N | N | N | N |
| **KENTUCKY** | | | | | | |
| McConnell | N | N | N | N | N | N |
| Bunning | N | N | N | N | N | N |
| **LOUISIANA** | | | | | | |
| Landrieu | N | Y | Y | Y | Y | Y |
| Vitter | N | N | Y | N | N | N |
| **MAINE** | | | | | | |
| Snowe | N | N | N | N | N | Y |
| Collins | Y | N | N | N | N | Y |
| **MARYLAND** | | | | | | |
| Sarbanes | N | Y | N | Y | Y | Y |
| Mikulski | Y | Y | N | Y | Y | Y |
| **MASSACHUSETTS** | | | | | | |
| Kennedy | Y | Y | N | Y | Y | Y |
| Kerry | Y | Y | N | Y | Y | Y |
| **MICHIGAN** | | | | | | |
| Levin | Y | Y | N | Y | Y | Y |
| Stabenow | Y | Y | Y | Y | Y | Y |
| **MINNESOTA** | | | | | | |
| Dayton | N | Y | Y | Y | Y | Y |
| Coleman | N | N | N | N | N | Y |
| **MISSISSIPPI** | | | | | | |
| Cochran | N | N | N | N | N | N |
| Lott | N | N | N | N | N | N |
| **MISSOURI** | | | | | | |
| Bond | N | N | N | N | N | N |
| Talent | N | N | N | N | N | N |

| | 293 | 294 | 295 | 296 | 297 | 298 |
|---|---|---|---|---|---|---|
| **MONTANA** | | | | | | |
| Baucus | N | Y | N | Y | Y | Y |
| Burns | N | N | N | N | N | N |
| **NEBRASKA** | | | | | | |
| Hagel | N | N | N | N | N | N |
| Nelson | N | N | N | Y | Y | Y |
| **NEVADA** | | | | | | |
| Reid | N | Y | N | Y | Y | Y |
| Ensign | Y | N | N | N | N | N |
| **NEW HAMPSHIRE** | | | | | | |
| Gregg | N | N | N | N | N | N |
| Sununu | Y | N | N | N | N | N |
| **NEW JERSEY** | | | | | | |
| Corzine | ? | ? | ? | ? | ? | ? |
| Lautenberg | Y | Y | N | Y | Y | Y |
| **NEW MEXICO** | | | | | | |
| Domenici | N | N | N | N | N | N |
| Bingaman | N | Y | N | Y | Y | Y |
| **NEW YORK** | | | | | | |
| Schumer | Y | Y | N | Y | Y | Y |
| Clinton | Y | Y | N | Y | Y | Y |
| **NORTH CAROLINA** | | | | | | |
| Dole | N | N | N | N | N | N |
| Burr | N | N | N | N | N | N |
| **NORTH DAKOTA** | | | | | | |
| Conrad | N | Y | N | Y | Y | Y |
| Dorgan | Y | Y | Y | Y | Y | Y |
| **OHIO** | | | | | | |
| DeWine | N | N | N | N | N | Y |
| Voinovich | N | N | N | N | N | N |
| **OKLAHOMA** | | | | | | |
| Inhofe | N | N | Y | N | N | N |
| Coburn | Y | N | N | N | N | N |
| **OREGON** | | | | | | |
| Wyden | N | Y | N | Y | Y | Y |
| Smith | N | N | N | N | N | N |
| **PENNSYLVANIA** | | | | | | |
| Specter | N | N | N | N | N | N |
| Santorum | N | N | N | N | N | N |
| **RHODE ISLAND** | | | | | | |
| Reed | N | Y | N | Y | Y | Y |
| Chafee | N | N | N | N | N | Y |
| **SOUTH CAROLINA** | | | | | | |
| Graham | Y | N | N | N | N | N |
| DeMint | Y | N | N | N | N | N |
| **SOUTH DAKOTA** | | | | | | |
| Johnson | N | Y | N | Y | Y | Y |
| Thune | N | N | N | N | N | N |
| **TENNESSEE** | | | | | | |
| Frist | N | N | N | N | N | N |
| Alexander | N | N | N | N | N | N |
| **TEXAS** | | | | | | |
| Hutchison | N | N | N | N | N | N |
| Cornyn | N | N | N | N | N | N |
| **UTAH** | | | | | | |
| Hatch | N | N | N | N | N | N |
| Bennett | N | N | N | N | N | N |
| **VERMONT** | | | | | | |
| Leahy | N | Y | N | Y | Y | Y |
| Jeffords | Y | Y | N | Y | N | Y |
| **VIRGINIA** | | | | | | |
| Warner | N | N | N | N | N | N |
| Allen | N | N | N | N | N | N |
| **WASHINGTON** | | | | | | |
| Murray | N | Y | N | Y | Y | Y |
| Cantwell | N | Y | N | Y | Y | Y |
| **WEST VIRGINIA** | | | | | | |
| Byrd | N | Y | N | Y | Y | Y |
| Rockefeller | Y | Y | Y | Y | Y | Y |
| **WISCONSIN** | | | | | | |
| Kohl | N | Y | N | Y | Y | Y |
| Feingold | Y | Y | Y | Y | Y | Y |
| **WYOMING** | | | | | | |
| Thomas | N | N | N | N | N | N |
| Enzi | N | N | N | N | N | N |

**KEY**     Republicans     Democrats     *Independents*

| | | |
|---|---|---|
| Y  Voted for (yea) | X  Paired against | C  Voted "present" to avoid possible conflict of interest |
| #  Paired for | −  Announced against | |
| +  Announced for | P  Voted "present" | ?  Did not vote or otherwise make a position known |
| N  Voted against (nay) | | |

# IN THE SENATE | By Vote Number

**299.** **S 1932. Budget Reconciliation/Drug Rebates.** Schumer, D-N.Y., amendment to strike provisions in the bill that would increase the manufacturer's rebate on generic drugs from 11 percent to 17 percent. Rejected 49-50: R 5-50; D 43-0 (ND 39-0, SD 4-0); I 1-0. Nov. 3, 2005.

**300.** **S 1932. Budget Reconciliation/Targeted Case Management.** Reed, D-R.I., amendment that would strike the section of the bill that would prohibit Medicaid reimbursements for "targeted case management" services, including assessment activities for foster care services, in cases when a third party could provide coverage. Rejected 46-52: R 2-52; D 43-0 (ND 39-0, SD 4-0); I 1-0. Nov. 3, 2005.

**301.** **S 1932. Budget Reconciliation/FHA Assets.** Reed, D-R.I., amendment that would strike language in the bill that would change the process of a Federal Housing Administration program that issues grants to rehabilitate multifamily properties or sells those properties at below-market prices, subject the program to appropriations and authorize $100 million in fiscal 2006 for asset disposition. Rejected 48-51: R 4-51; D 43-0 (ND 39-0, SD 4-0); I 1-0. Nov. 3, 2005.

**302.** **S 1932. Budget Reconciliation/Drug Price Negotiations.** Snowe, R-Maine, motion to waive the Budget Act with respect to the Grassley R-Iowa, point of order against the Snowe amendment. The Snowe amendment would authorize the secretary of Health and Human Services to negotiate prices for prescription drugs under Medicare. It also would specify that such authority may not be used to set prices. Motion rejected 51-48: R 9-46; D 41-2 (ND 37-2, SD 4-0); I 1-0. A three-fifths majority vote (60) of the total Senate is required to waive the Budget Act. (Subsequently, the chair upheld the point of order, and the amendment fell.) Nov. 3, 2005.

**303.** **S 1932. Budget Reconciliation/Passage.** Passage of a bill that would make changes to mandatory programs for a net savings of approximately $35 billion over five years, including cuts in the growth of Medicare and Medicaid. It would provide $2.6 billion in education aid, including $1.7 billion for Hurricane Katrina victims; prohibit export of any oil or gas produced from leases in Alaska's Arctic National Wildlife Refuge; and authorize more than $12 billion over six years for Amtrak. Passed 52-47: R 50-5; D 2-41 (ND 1-38, SD 1-3); I 0-1. A " yea" was a vote in support of the president's position. Nov. 3, 2005.

| | 299 | 300 | 301 | 302 | 303 | | 299 | 300 | 301 | 302 | 303 |
|---|---|---|---|---|---|---|---|---|---|---|---|
| **ALABAMA** | | | | | | **MONTANA** | | | | | |
| Shelby | N | N | N | N | Y | Baucus | Y | Y | Y | N | N |
| Sessions | N | N | N | N | Y | Burns | N | N | N | N | Y |
| **ALASKA** | | | | | | **NEBRASKA** | | | | | |
| Stevens | N | N | N | N | Y | Hagel | N | N | N | N | Y |
| Murkowski | N | N | N | N | Y | Nelson | Y | Y | Y | N | Y |
| **ARIZONA** | | | | | | **NEVADA** | | | | | |
| McCain | Y | N | N | Y | Y | Reid | Y | Y | Y | Y | N |
| Kyl | N | N | N | N | Y | Ensign | N | N | N | N | Y |
| **ARKANSAS** | | | | | | **NEW HAMPSHIRE** | | | | | |
| Lincoln | Y | Y | Y | Y | N | Gregg | N | N | N | N | Y |
| Pryor | Y | Y | Y | Y | N | Sununu | N | N | N | N | Y |
| **CALIFORNIA** | | | | | | **NEW JERSEY** | | | | | |
| Feinstein | Y | Y | Y | Y | N | Corzine | ? | ? | ? | ? | ? |
| Boxer | Y | Y | Y | Y | N | Lautenberg | Y | Y | Y | Y | N |
| **COLORADO** | | | | | | **NEW MEXICO** | | | | | |
| Allard | N | N | N | N | Y | Domenici | N | N | N | N | Y |
| Salazar | Y | Y | Y | Y | N | Bingaman | Y | Y | Y | Y | N |
| **CONNECTICUT** | | | | | | **NEW YORK** | | | | | |
| Dodd | Y | Y | Y | Y | N | Schumer | Y | Y | Y | Y | N |
| Lieberman | Y | Y | Y | Y | N | Clinton | Y | Y | Y | Y | N |
| **DELAWARE** | | | | | | **NORTH CAROLINA** | | | | | |
| Biden | Y | Y | Y | Y | N | Dole | N | N | N | N | Y |
| Carper | Y | Y | Y | Y | N | Burr | N | N | N | N | Y |
| **FLORIDA** | | | | | | **NORTH DAKOTA** | | | | | |
| Nelson | Y | Y | Y | Y | N | Conrad | Y | Y | Y | Y | N |
| Martinez | N | N | N | N | Y | Dorgan | Y | Y | Y | Y | N |
| **GEORGIA** | | | | | | **OHIO** | | | | | |
| Chambliss | N | N | N | N | Y | DeWine | N | Y | Y | Y | N |
| Isakson | N | N | N | N | Y | Voinovich | N | N | N | N | Y |
| **HAWAII** | | | | | | **OKLAHOMA** | | | | | |
| Inouye | Y | Y | Y | Y | N | Inhofe | N | N | N | N | Y |
| Akaka | Y | Y | Y | Y | N | Coburn | N | ? | N | Y | Y |
| **IDAHO** | | | | | | **OREGON** | | | | | |
| Craig | N | N | N | N | Y | Wyden | Y | Y | Y | Y | N |
| Crapo | N | N | N | N | Y | Smith | N | N | N | N | Y |
| **ILLINOIS** | | | | | | **PENNSYLVANIA** | | | | | |
| Durbin | Y | Y | Y | Y | N | Specter | Y | Y | Y | Y | Y |
| Obama | Y | Y | Y | Y | N | Santorum | N | N | N | N | Y |
| **INDIANA** | | | | | | **RHODE ISLAND** | | | | | |
| Lugar | N | N | N | N | Y | Reed | Y | Y | Y | Y | N |
| Bayh | Y | Y | Y | Y | N | Chafee | N | Y | Y | Y | N |
| **IOWA** | | | | | | **SOUTH CAROLINA** | | | | | |
| Grassley | N | N | N | N | Y | Graham | N | N | N | Y | Y |
| Harkin | Y | Y | Y | Y | N | DeMint | N | N | N | N | Y |
| **KANSAS** | | | | | | **SOUTH DAKOTA** | | | | | |
| Brownback | N | N | N | Y | Y | Johnson | Y | Y | Y | Y | N |
| Roberts | N | N | N | N | Y | Thune | N | N | N | N | Y |
| **KENTUCKY** | | | | | | **TENNESSEE** | | | | | |
| McConnell | N | N | N | N | Y | Frist | N | N | N | N | Y |
| Bunning | N | N | N | N | Y | Alexander | N | N | N | N | Y |
| **LOUISIANA** | | | | | | **TEXAS** | | | | | |
| Landrieu | Y | Y | Y | Y | Y | Hutchison | N | N | N | N | Y |
| Vitter | N | N | N | N | Y | Cornyn | N | N | N | N | Y |
| **MAINE** | | | | | | **UTAH** | | | | | |
| Snowe | Y | N | N | Y | N | Hatch | N | N | N | N | Y |
| Collins | Y | N | N | Y | N | Bennett | N | N | N | N | Y |
| **MARYLAND** | | | | | | **VERMONT** | | | | | |
| Sarbanes | Y | Y | Y | Y | N | Leahy | Y | Y | Y | Y | N |
| Mikulski | Y | Y | Y | Y | N | Jeffords | Y | Y | Y | Y | N |
| **MASSACHUSETTS** | | | | | | **VIRGINIA** | | | | | |
| Kennedy | Y | Y | Y | Y | N | Warner | N | N | N | N | Y |
| Kerry | Y | Y | Y | Y | N | Allen | Y | N | N | N | Y |
| **MICHIGAN** | | | | | | **WASHINGTON** | | | | | |
| Levin | Y | Y | Y | Y | N | Murray | Y | Y | Y | Y | N |
| Stabenow | Y | Y | Y | Y | N | Cantwell | Y | Y | Y | Y | N |
| **MINNESOTA** | | | | | | **WEST VIRGINIA** | | | | | |
| Dayton | Y | Y | Y | Y | N | Byrd | Y | Y | Y | Y | N |
| Coleman | N | N | N | N | N | Rockefeller | Y | Y | Y | Y | N |
| **MISSISSIPPI** | | | | | | **WISCONSIN** | | | | | |
| Cochran | N | N | N | N | Y | Kohl | Y | Y | Y | Y | N |
| Lott | N | N | N | N | Y | Feingold | Y | Y | Y | Y | N |
| **MISSOURI** | | | | | | **WYOMING** | | | | | |
| Bond | N | N | Y | N | Y | Thomas | N | N | N | N | Y |
| Talent | N | N | N | N | Y | Enzi | N | N | N | N | Y |

**KEY**    **Republicans**    Democrats    *Independents*

| | | | | | |
|---|---|---|---|---|---|
| Y | Voted for (yea) | X | Paired against | C | Voted "present" to avoid possible conflict of interest |
| # | Paired for | – | Announced against | | |
| + | Announced for | P | Voted "present" | ? | Did not vote or otherwise make a position known |
| N | Voted against (nay) | | | | |

# IN THE SENATE | By Vote Number

**304.** **S 1042. Fiscal 2006 Defense Authorization/Retirement Benefits for Rocky Flats Employees.** Allard, R-Colo., amendment that would authorize $15 million to provide health, medical and life insurance benefits for employees of the Energy Department's Rocky Flats, Colo., Environmental Technology Site even if their retirement goes into effect before Dec. 15, 2006. Rejected 38-53: R 13-40; D 24-13 (ND 22-11, SD 2-2); I 1-0. Nov. 7, 2005.

**305.** **S 1042. Fiscal 2006 Defense Authorization/Armed Forces Network.** Inhofe, R-Okla., amendment that would express the sense of the Senate commending the Armed Forces Network and state that censorship on the network is unacceptable. It also would allow the Defense secretary to create an ombudsman's office for the radio network. Adopted 55-43: R 52-0; D 3-42 (ND 2-39, SD 1-3); I 0-1. Nov. 8, 2005.

**306.** **S 1042. Fiscal 2006 Defense Authorization/Armed Forces Network.** Harkin, D-Iowa, amendment that would require the Defense secretary to establish an ombudsman's office to conduct programming reviews of the Armed Forces Network, and field questions and concerns from listeners. It also would call for political balance in Armed Forces Network programming. Rejected 44-54: R 0-54; D 43-0 (ND 39-0, SD 4-0); I 1-0. Nov. 8, 2005.

**307.** **S 1042. Fiscal 2006 Defense Authorization/Survivor Benefits.** Nelson, D-Fla., amendment that would eliminate the requirement that widows and orphans of deceased or fully disabled military personnel who receive pensions under the Defense Department's Survivor Benefits Plan have those benefits reduced dollar for dollar by the amount received from the Department of Veterans Affairs Dependency and Indemnity Compensation program. Adopted 92-6: R 48-6; D 43-0 (ND 39-0, SD 4-0); I 1-0. Nov. 8, 2005.

**308.** **S 1042. Fiscal 2006 Defense Authorization/BRAC Sites.** Snowe, R-Maine, amendment that would require the Defense Department to grant a free transfer of lands to local communities when bases are closed under the Base Realignment and Closure (BRAC) process, rather than requiring communities to pay the Defense Department fair market value for the land. Rejected 36-62: R 14-40; D 21-22 (ND 18-21, SD 3-1); I 1-0. Nov. 8, 2005.

**309.** **S 1042. Fiscal 2006 Defense Authorization/Detainee Abuse.** Levin, D-Mich., amendment that would create an independent bipartisan commission to examine detainee abuse at U.S. military prisons around the world. Rejected 43-55: R 0-54; D 42-1 (ND 39-0, SD 3-1); I 1-0. A "nay" was a vote in support of the president's position. Nov. 8, 2005.

| | 304 | 305 | 306 | 307 | 308 | 309 | | | 304 | 305 | 306 | 307 | 308 | 309 |
|---|---|---|---|---|---|---|---|---|---|---|---|---|---|---|
| **ALABAMA** | | | | | | | | **MONTANA** | | | | | | |
| Shelby | N | Y | N | Y | N | N | | Baucus | Y | N | Y | Y | N | Y |
| Sessions | N | Y | N | N | N | N | | Burns | Y | Y | N | Y | N | N |
| **ALASKA** | | | | | | | | **NEBRASKA** | | | | | | |
| Stevens | N | Y | N | Y | N | N | | Hagel | N | Y | N | Y | Y | N |
| Murkowski | Y | Y | N | Y | N | N | | Nelson | N | Y | Y | Y | N | N |
| **ARIZONA** | | | | | | | | **NEVADA** | | | | | | |
| McCain | ? | ? | ? | ? | ? | ? | | Reid | N | N | Y | Y | N | Y |
| Kyl | N | Y | N | Y | N | N | | Ensign | N | Y | N | Y | N | N |
| **ARKANSAS** | | | | | | | | **NEW HAMPSHIRE** | | | | | | |
| Lincoln | N | N | Y | Y | Y | Y | | Gregg | N | Y | N | Y | N | N |
| Pryor | Y | N | Y | Y | Y | Y | | Sununu | N | Y | N | Y | Y | N |
| **CALIFORNIA** | | | | | | | | **NEW JERSEY** | | | | | | |
| Feinstein | Y | N | Y | Y | N | Y | | Corzine | ? | ? | ? | ? | ? | ? |
| Boxer | Y | N | Y | Y | N | Y | | Lautenberg | Y | N | Y | Y | Y | Y |
| **COLORADO** | | | | | | | | **NEW MEXICO** | | | | | | |
| Allard | Y | Y | N | N | N | N | | Domenici | Y | Y | N | Y | N | N |
| Salazar | Y | N | Y | Y | N | Y | | Bingaman | Y | N | Y | Y | N | Y |
| **CONNECTICUT** | | | | | | | | **NEW YORK** | | | | | | |
| Dodd | N | N | Y | Y | Y | Y | | Schumer | N | N | Y | Y | Y | Y |
| Lieberman | Y | N | Y | Y | N | Y | | Clinton | N | N | Y | Y | Y | Y |
| **DELAWARE** | | | | | | | | **NORTH CAROLINA** | | | | | | |
| Biden | ? | N | Y | Y | Y | Y | | Dole | N | Y | N | Y | N | N |
| Carper | N | N | Y | Y | N | Y | | Burr | N | Y | N | Y | N | N |
| **FLORIDA** | | | | | | | | **NORTH DAKOTA** | | | | | | |
| Nelson | N | N | Y | Y | N | Y | | Conrad | Y | N | Y | Y | Y | Y |
| Martinez | N | Y | N | Y | N | N | | Dorgan | ? | N | Y | Y | Y | Y |
| **GEORGIA** | | | | | | | | **OHIO** | | | | | | |
| Chambliss | N | Y | N | Y | N | N | | DeWine | Y | Y | N | Y | N | N |
| Isakson | N | Y | N | Y | N | N | | Voinovich | N | Y | N | Y | N | N |
| **HAWAII** | | | | | | | | **OKLAHOMA** | | | | | | |
| Inouye | ? | N | Y | Y | Y | Y | | Inhofe | N | Y | N | N | N | N |
| Akaka | N | N | Y | Y | N | Y | | Coburn | N | Y | N | N | N | N |
| **IDAHO** | | | | | | | | **OREGON** | | | | | | |
| Craig | Y | Y | N | Y | N | N | | Wyden | Y | N | Y | Y | Y | Y |
| Crapo | Y | Y | N | Y | N | N | | Smith | N | Y | N | Y | Y | N |
| **ILLINOIS** | | | | | | | | **PENNSYLVANIA** | | | | | | |
| Durbin | Y | N | Y | Y | Y | Y | | Specter | Y | Y | N | Y | N | N |
| Obama | Y | N | Y | Y | Y | Y | | Santorum | N | Y | N | Y | N | N |
| **INDIANA** | | | | | | | | **RHODE ISLAND** | | | | | | |
| Lugar | N | Y | N | Y | N | N | | Reed | N | N | Y | Y | N | Y |
| Bayh | ? | N | Y | Y | Y | Y | | Chafee | N | Y | N | Y | N | N |
| **IOWA** | | | | | | | | **SOUTH CAROLINA** | | | | | | |
| Grassley | N | Y | N | Y | N | N | | Graham | Y | Y | N | Y | N | N |
| Harkin | Y | N | Y | Y | Y | Y | | DeMint | Y | Y | N | N | N | N |
| **KANSAS** | | | | | | | | **SOUTH DAKOTA** | | | | | | |
| Brownback | N | Y | N | Y | N | N | | Johnson | Y | N | Y | Y | N | Y |
| Roberts | N | Y | N | Y | Y | N | | Thune | N | Y | N | Y | N | N |
| **KENTUCKY** | | | | | | | | **TENNESSEE** | | | | | | |
| McConnell | N | Y | | N | N | N | | Frist | N | Y | N | Y | N | N |
| Bunning | N | Y | N | Y | N | N | | Alexander | Y | Y | N | Y | N | N |
| **LOUISIANA** | | | | | | | | **TEXAS** | | | | | | |
| Landrieu | Y | N | Y | Y | Y | Y | | Hutchison | N | Y | N | Y | N | N |
| Vitter | N | Y | N | Y | Y | N | | Cornyn | N | Y | N | Y | N | N |
| **MAINE** | | | | | | | | **UTAH** | | | | | | |
| Snowe | N | Y | N | Y | Y | N | | Hatch | – | Y | N | Y | N | N |
| Collins | N | Y | N | Y | Y | N | | Bennett | N | Y | N | Y | N | N |
| **MARYLAND** | | | | | | | | **VERMONT** | | | | | | |
| Sarbanes | Y | N | Y | Y | N | Y | | Leahy | Y | N | Y | Y | N | Y |
| Mikulski | Y | N | Y | Y | Y | Y | | Jeffords | Y | N | Y | Y | Y | Y |
| **MASSACHUSETTS** | | | | | | | | **VIRGINIA** | | | | | | |
| Kennedy | ? | N | Y | Y | N | Y | | Warner | N | Y | N | Y | N | N |
| Kerry | Y | N | Y | Y | Y | Y | | Allen | N | Y | N | Y | N | N |
| **MICHIGAN** | | | | | | | | **WASHINGTON** | | | | | | |
| Levin | N | N | Y | Y | N | Y | | Murray | Y | N | Y | Y | Y | Y |
| Stabenow | ? | N | Y | Y | Y | Y | | Cantwell | Y | N | Y | Y | Y | Y |
| **MINNESOTA** | | | | | | | | **WEST VIRGINIA** | | | | | | |
| Dayton | Y | N | Y | Y | N | Y | | Byrd | N | N | Y | Y | N | Y |
| Coleman | N | Y | N | Y | N | N | | Rockefeller | N | N | Y | Y | N | Y |
| **MISSISSIPPI** | | | | | | | | **WISCONSIN** | | | | | | |
| Cochran | N | Y | N | Y | N | N | | Kohl | Y | N | Y | Y | Y | Y |
| Lott | N | Y | N | Y | N | N | | Feingold | Y | N | Y | Y | N | Y |
| **MISSOURI** | | | | | | | | **WYOMING** | | | | | | |
| Bond | Y | Y | N | Y | Y | N | | Thomas | N | Y | N | Y | N | N |
| Talent | Y | Y | N | Y | N | N | | Enzi | N | Y | N | Y | N | N |

**KEY** **Republicans** Democrats *Independents*

| | | | | | | |
|---|---|---|---|---|---|---|
| Y | Voted for (yea) | X | Paired against | C | Voted "present" to avoid possible conflict of interest | |
| # | Paired for | – | Announced against | | | |
| + | Announced for | P | Voted "present" | ? | Did not vote or otherwise make a position known | |
| N | Voted against (nay) | | | | | |

# IN THE SENATE | By Vote Number

**310.** **S 1042. Fiscal 2006 Defense Authorization/Management Study.**
Byrd, D-W.Va., amendment that would authorize a feasibility study on creating a deputy secretary of Defense for management to oversee the spending and financial management at the Defense Department. Adopted 97-0: R 54-0; D 42-0 (ND 38-0, SD 4-0); I 1-0. Nov. 8, 2005.

**311.** **S 1042. Fiscal 2006 Defense Authorization/Cooperative Threat Reduction Funding.** Reed, D-R.I., amendment that would move $50 million from missile defense accounts to the Cooperative Threat Reduction program. Rejected 37-60: R 2-52; D 34-8 (ND 30-8, SD 4-0); I 1-0. Nov. 8, 2005.

**312.** **S 1042. Fiscal 2006 Defense Authorization/Prayer at Service Academies.** Inhofe, R-Okla., amendment that would grant the superintendent of each institution the authority for setting rules for offering non-denominational, voluntary prayer at the U.S. military service academies. Adopted 99-0: R 55-0; D 43-0 (ND 39-0, SD 4-0); I 1-0. Nov. 9, 2005.

**313.** **S 1042. Fiscal 2006 Defense Authorization/Tear Gas.** Ensign, R-Nev., amendment that would state that it is U.S. policy that tear gas and other non-lethal riot-control agents are not chemical weapons and that they should be permitted for use by the military in combat situations. Adopted 98-1: R 55-0; D 42-1 (ND 38-1, SD 4-0); I 1-0. Nov. 9, 2005.

**314.** **S 1042. Fiscal 2006 Defense Authorization/Reserve Retirement.** Chambliss, R-Ga., amendment that would create a formula for reducing the eligibility age for reservists to receive retiree benefits based on the amount of time served in an active-duty capacity. Reservists would be able to receive retirement pay no earlier than age 50. Adopted 99-0: R 55-0; D 43-0 (ND 39-0, SD 4-0); I 1-0. Nov. 9, 2005.

**315.** **S 1042. Fiscal 2006 Defense Authorization/Reserve Retirement.** Durbin, D-Ill., amendment that would create a formula for reducing the eligibility age for reservists to receive retiree benefits based on the amount of time served in an active-duty capacity. Rejected 40-59: R 0-55; D 39-4 (ND 35-4, SD 4-0); I 1-0. Nov. 9, 2005.

| | 310 | 311 | 312 | 313 | 314 | 315 |
|---|---|---|---|---|---|---|
| **ALABAMA** | | | | | | |
| Shelby | Y | N | Y | Y | Y | N |
| Sessions | Y | N | Y | Y | Y | N |
| **ALASKA** | | | | | | |
| Stevens | Y | N | Y | Y | Y | N |
| Murkowski | Y | N | Y | Y | Y | N |
| **ARIZONA** | | | | | | |
| McCain | ? | ? | Y | Y | Y | N |
| Kyl | Y | N | Y | Y | Y | N |
| **ARKANSAS** | | | | | | |
| Lincoln | Y | Y | Y | Y | Y | Y |
| Pryor | Y | Y | Y | Y | Y | Y |
| **CALIFORNIA** | | | | | | |
| Feinstein | Y | Y | Y | Y | Y | Y |
| Boxer | Y | Y | Y | Y | Y | Y |
| **COLORADO** | | | | | | |
| Allard | Y | N | Y | Y | Y | N |
| Salazar | Y | N | Y | Y | Y | Y |
| **CONNECTICUT** | | | | | | |
| Dodd | Y | Y | Y | Y | Y | Y |
| Lieberman | Y | N | Y | Y | Y | Y |
| **DELAWARE** | | | | | | |
| Biden | Y | Y | Y | Y | Y | Y |
| Carper | Y | Y | Y | Y | Y | N |
| **FLORIDA** | | | | | | |
| Nelson | Y | Y | Y | Y | Y | Y |
| Martinez | Y | N | Y | Y | Y | N |
| **GEORGIA** | | | | | | |
| Chambliss | Y | N | N | Y | Y | N |
| Isakson | Y | N | N | Y | Y | N |
| **HAWAII** | | | | | | |
| Inouye | Y | N | Y | Y | Y | Y |
| Akaka | Y | N | Y | Y | Y | Y |
| **IDAHO** | | | | | | |
| Craig | Y | N | Y | Y | Y | N |
| Crapo | Y | N | Y | Y | Y | N |
| **ILLINOIS** | | | | | | |
| Durbin | Y | Y | Y | Y | Y | Y |
| Obama | Y | Y | Y | Y | Y | Y |
| **INDIANA** | | | | | | |
| Lugar | Y | Y | Y | Y | Y | N |
| Bayh | Y | N | Y | Y | Y | Y |
| **IOWA** | | | | | | |
| Grassley | Y | N | Y | Y | Y | N |
| Harkin | Y | Y | Y | N | Y | Y |
| **KANSAS** | | | | | | |
| Brownback | Y | N | Y | Y | Y | N |
| Roberts | Y | N | Y | Y | Y | N |
| **KENTUCKY** | | | | | | |
| McConnell | Y | N | Y | Y | Y | N |
| Bunning | Y | N | Y | Y | Y | N |
| **LOUISIANA** | | | | | | |
| Landrieu | Y | Y | Y | Y | Y | Y |
| Vitter | Y | N | Y | Y | Y | N |
| **MAINE** | | | | | | |
| Snowe | Y | N | Y | Y | Y | N |
| Collins | Y | N | Y | Y | Y | N |
| **MARYLAND** | | | | | | |
| Sarbanes | Y | Y | Y | Y | Y | Y |
| Mikulski | Y | Y | Y | Y | Y | Y |
| **MASSACHUSETTS** | | | | | | |
| Kennedy | Y | Y | Y | Y | Y | Y |
| Kerry | Y | Y | Y | Y | Y | Y |
| **MICHIGAN** | | | | | | |
| Levin | Y | Y | Y | Y | Y | Y |
| Stabenow | Y | Y | Y | Y | Y | Y |
| **MINNESOTA** | | | | | | |
| Dayton | Y | N | Y | Y | Y | Y |
| Coleman | Y | N | Y | Y | Y | N |
| **MISSISSIPPI** | | | | | | |
| Cochran | Y | N | Y | Y | Y | N |
| Lott | Y | N | Y | Y | Y | N |
| **MISSOURI** | | | | | | |
| Bond | Y | N | Y | Y | Y | N |
| Talent | Y | N | Y | Y | Y | N |
| **MONTANA** | | | | | | |
| Baucus | Y | N | Y | Y | Y | N |
| Burns | Y | N | Y | Y | Y | N |
| **NEBRASKA** | | | | | | |
| Hagel | Y | N | Y | Y | Y | N |
| Nelson | Y | N | Y | Y | Y | N |
| **NEVADA** | | | | | | |
| Reid | Y | Y | Y | Y | Y | Y |
| Ensign | Y | N | Y | Y | Y | N |
| **NEW HAMPSHIRE** | | | | | | |
| Gregg | Y | N | Y | Y | Y | N |
| Sununu | Y | N | Y | Y | Y | N |
| **NEW JERSEY** | | | | | | |
| Corzine | ? | ? | ? | ? | ? | ? |
| Lautenberg | ? | ? | Y | Y | Y | Y |
| **NEW MEXICO** | | | | | | |
| Domenici | Y | N | Y | Y | Y | N |
| Bingaman | Y | Y | Y | Y | Y | Y |
| **NEW YORK** | | | | | | |
| Schumer | Y | Y | Y | Y | Y | Y |
| Clinton | Y | Y | Y | Y | Y | Y |
| **NORTH CAROLINA** | | | | | | |
| Dole | Y | N | Y | Y | Y | N |
| Burr | Y | N | Y | Y | Y | N |
| **NORTH DAKOTA** | | | | | | |
| Conrad | Y | Y | Y | Y | Y | N |
| Dorgan | Y | Y | Y | Y | Y | N |
| **OHIO** | | | | | | |
| DeWine | Y | N | Y | Y | Y | N |
| Voinovich | Y | N | Y | Y | Y | N |
| **OKLAHOMA** | | | | | | |
| Inhofe | Y | N | Y | Y | Y | N |
| Coburn | Y | N | Y | Y | Y | N |
| **OREGON** | | | | | | |
| Wyden | Y | Y | Y | Y | Y | Y |
| Smith | Y | N | Y | Y | Y | N |
| **PENNSYLVANIA** | | | | | | |
| Specter | Y | N | Y | Y | Y | N |
| Santorum | Y | N | Y | Y | Y | N |
| **RHODE ISLAND** | | | | | | |
| Reed | Y | Y | Y | Y | Y | Y |
| Chafee | Y | Y | Y | Y | Y | Y |
| **SOUTH CAROLINA** | | | | | | |
| Graham | Y | N | Y | Y | Y | N |
| DeMint | Y | N | Y | Y | Y | N |
| **SOUTH DAKOTA** | | | | | | |
| Johnson | Y | Y | Y | Y | Y | Y |
| Thune | Y | N | Y | Y | Y | N |
| **TENNESSEE** | | | | | | |
| Frist | Y | N | Y | Y | Y | N |
| Alexander | Y | N | Y | Y | Y | N |
| **TEXAS** | | | | | | |
| Hutchison | Y | N | Y | Y | Y | N |
| Cornyn | Y | N | Y | Y | Y | N |
| **UTAH** | | | | | | |
| Hatch | Y | N | Y | Y | Y | N |
| Bennett | Y | N | Y | Y | Y | N |
| **VERMONT** | | | | | | |
| Leahy | Y | Y | Y | Y | Y | Y |
| Jeffords | Y | Y | Y | Y | Y | Y |
| **VIRGINIA** | | | | | | |
| Warner | Y | N | Y | Y | Y | N |
| Allen | Y | N | Y | Y | Y | N |
| **WASHINGTON** | | | | | | |
| Murray | Y | Y | Y | Y | Y | Y |
| Cantwell | Y | Y | Y | Y | Y | Y |
| **WEST VIRGINIA** | | | | | | |
| Byrd | Y | Y | Y | Y | Y | Y |
| Rockefeller | Y | Y | Y | Y | Y | Y |
| **WISCONSIN** | | | | | | |
| Kohl | Y | Y | Y | Y | Y | Y |
| Feingold | Y | Y | Y | Y | Y | Y |
| **WYOMING** | | | | | | |
| Thomas | Y | N | Y | Y | Y | N |
| Enzi | Y | N | Y | Y | Y | N |

**KEY**   Republicans    Democrats    *Independents*

| | | | |
|---|---|---|---|
| Y | Voted for (yea) | X | Paired against |
| # | Paired for | – | Announced against |
| + | Announced for | P | Voted "present" |
| N | Voted against (nay) | | |

C Voted "present" to avoid possible conflict of interest

? Did not vote or otherwise make a position known

# IN THE SENATE | By Vote Number

**316.** **S 1042. Fiscal 2006 Defense Authorization/Contracting Investigation.** Dorgan, D-N.D., amendment that would establish a special Senate committee to investigate the awarding and carrying out of contracts in Afghanistan and Iraq. Rejected 44-53: R 1-53; D 42-0 (ND 38-0, SD 4-0); I 1-0. Nov. 10, 2005.

**317.** **S 1042. Fiscal 2006 Defense Authorization/C-17 Cargo Planes.** Talent, R-Mo., amendment that would permit the Air Force to enter into contracts for advanced procurement for up to 42 C-17 Globemaster III cargo planes. Adopted 89-8: R 48-6; D 40-2 (ND 36-2, SD 4-0); I 1-0. Nov. 10, 2005.

**318.** **S 1042. Fiscal 2006 Defense Authorization/Reports on Detainee Camps.** Kerry, D-Mass., amendment that would require the Defense secretary and the director of National Intelligence to submit reports within 60 days of the bill's enactment on clandestine U.S. detention facilities abroad. Adopted 82-9: R 39-9; D 42-0 (ND 38-0, SD 4-0); I 1-0. Nov. 10, 2005.

**319.** **S 1042. Fiscal 2006 Defense Authorization/Habeas Corpus and Guantánamo Bay.** Graham, R-S.C., substitute amendment to the Graham amendment. The substitute amendment would make the underlying amendment effective one day after the bill's enactment. The underlying amendment would deny non-citizens held at Guantánamo Bay, Cuba, habeas corpus access to U.S. civilian courts to contest their detention or conviction. It would allow one appellate court review of any military tribunal decision to detain prisoners under Defense Department procedure. It also would require the Defense Secretary to submit a report to Congress detailing review procedures at Guantánamo Bay. Adopted 49-42: R 44-4; D 5-37 (ND 4-34, SD 1-3); I 0-1. Nov. 10, 2005.

**320.** **HR 3057. Fiscal 2006 Foreign Operations Appropriations/ Conference Report.** Adoption of the conference report on the bill that would provide $21 billion in fiscal 2006 for foreign operations and related programs, including $2.8 billion to fight HIV/AIDS, tuberculosis and malaria; $1.8 billion for the Millennium Challenge Corporation; and $1.6 billion for the Child Survival and Health Programs Fund. Adopted (thus cleared for the president) 91-0: R 48-0; D 42-0 (ND 38-0, SD 4-0); I 1-0. Nov. 10, 2005.

| | 316 | 317 | 318 | 319 | 320 |
|---|---|---|---|---|---|
| **ALABAMA** | | | | | |
| Shelby | N | Y | Y | Y | Y |
| Sessions | N | N | N | Y | Y |
| **ALASKA** | | | | | |
| Stevens | N | Y | N | Y | Y |
| Murkowski | N | Y | Y | Y | Y |
| **ARIZONA** | | | | | |
| McCain | N | N | Y | Y | Y |
| Kyl | N | N | N | Y | Y |
| **ARKANSAS** | | | | | |
| Lincoln | Y | Y | Y | N | Y |
| Pryor | Y | Y | Y | N | Y |
| **CALIFORNIA** | | | | | |
| Feinstein | Y | Y | Y | N | Y |
| Boxer | Y | Y | Y | N | Y |
| **COLORADO** | | | | | |
| Allard | N | N | Y | Y | Y |
| Salazar | Y | Y | Y | N | Y |
| **CONNECTICUT** | | | | | |
| Dodd | Y | Y | Y | N | Y |
| Lieberman | Y | Y | Y | Y | Y |
| **DELAWARE** | | | | | |
| Biden | Y | Y | Y | N | Y |
| Carper | Y | Y | Y | N | Y |
| **FLORIDA** | | | | | |
| Nelson | Y | Y | Y | N | Y |
| Martinez | N | Y | N | Y | Y |
| **GEORGIA** | | | | | |
| Chambliss | N | Y | N | Y | Y |
| Isakson | N | Y | N | Y | Y |
| **HAWAII** | | | | | |
| Inouye | ? | ? | ? | ? | ? |
| Akaka | Y | Y | Y | N | Y |
| **IDAHO** | | | | | |
| Craig | N | Y | Y | Y | Y |
| Crapo | N | Y | Y | Y | Y |
| **ILLINOIS** | | | | | |
| Durbin | Y | Y | Y | N | Y |
| Obama | Y | Y | Y | N | Y |
| **INDIANA** | | | | | |
| Lugar | N | Y | ? | ? | ? |
| Bayh | Y | Y | Y | N | Y |
| **IOWA** | | | | | |
| Grassley | N | Y | Y | Y | Y |
| Harkin | Y | Y | Y | N | Y |
| **KANSAS** | | | | | |
| Brownback | N | Y | Y | Y | Y |
| Roberts | N | Y | Y | Y | Y |
| **KENTUCKY** | | | | | |
| McConnell | N | Y | Y | Y | Y |
| Bunning | N | Y | Y | Y | Y |
| **LOUISIANA** | | | | | |
| Landrieu | Y | Y | Y | Y | Y |
| Vitter | N | Y | N | Y | Y |
| **MAINE** | | | | | |
| Snowe | N | Y | Y | Y | Y |
| Collins | N | Y | Y | Y | Y |
| **MARYLAND** | | | | | |
| Sarbanes | Y | Y | Y | N | Y |
| Mikulski | Y | Y | Y | N | Y |
| **MASSACHUSETTS** | | | | | |
| Kennedy | Y | Y | Y | N | Y |
| Kerry | Y | Y | Y | N | Y |
| **MICHIGAN** | | | | | |
| Levin | Y | Y | Y | N | Y |
| Stabenow | Y | Y | Y | N | Y |
| **MINNESOTA** | | | | | |
| Dayton | Y | Y | Y | N | Y |
| Coleman | N | Y | Y | Y | Y |
| **MISSISSIPPI** | | | | | |
| Cochran | N | Y | Y | Y | Y |
| Lott | N | Y | Y | Y | Y |
| **MISSOURI** | | | | | |
| Bond | N | Y | Y | Y | Y |
| Talent | N | Y | Y | Y | Y |
| **MONTANA** | | | | | |
| Baucus | Y | Y | Y | N | Y |
| Burns | N | Y | Y | Y | Y |
| **NEBRASKA** | | | | | |
| Hagel | N | Y | ? | ? | ? |
| Nelson | Y | Y | Y | Y | Y |
| **NEVADA** | | | | | |
| Reid | Y | Y | Y | N | Y |
| Ensign | N | Y | Y | Y | Y |
| **NEW HAMPSHIRE** | | | | | |
| Gregg | N | Y | Y | Y | Y |
| Sununu | N | N | Y | N | Y |
| **NEW JERSEY** | | | | | |
| Corzine | ? | ? | ? | ? | ? |
| Lautenberg | Y | Y | Y | N | Y |
| **NEW MEXICO** | | | | | |
| Domenici | N | Y | ? | ? | ? |
| Bingaman | Y | Y | Y | N | Y |
| **NEW YORK** | | | | | |
| Schumer | Y | Y | Y | N | Y |
| Clinton | Y | Y | Y | N | Y |
| **NORTH CAROLINA** | | | | | |
| Dole | N | Y | Y | Y | Y |
| Burr | N | Y | N | Y | Y |
| **NORTH DAKOTA** | | | | | |
| Conrad | Y | Y | Y | Y | Y |
| Dorgan | Y | Y | Y | N | Y |
| **OHIO** | | | | | |
| DeWine | N | Y | Y | Y | Y |
| Voinovich | N | Y | Y | Y | Y |
| **OKLAHOMA** | | | | | |
| Inhofe | N | Y | Y | Y | Y |
| Coburn | N | Y | Y | Y | Y |
| **OREGON** | | | | | |
| Wyden | Y | Y | Y | N | Y |
| Smith | N | Y | Y | N | Y |
| **PENNSYLVANIA** | | | | | |
| Specter | N | Y | Y | N | Y |
| Santorum | N | Y | ? | ? | ? |
| **RHODE ISLAND** | | | | | |
| Reed | Y | Y | Y | N | Y |
| Chafee | Y | Y | Y | N | Y |
| **SOUTH CAROLINA** | | | | | |
| Graham | N | Y | Y | Y | Y |
| DeMint | N | Y | N | Y | Y |
| **SOUTH DAKOTA** | | | | | |
| Johnson | Y | Y | Y | N | Y |
| Thune | N | Y | Y | Y | Y |
| **TENNESSEE** | | | | | |
| Frist | N | Y | Y | Y | Y |
| Alexander | ? | ? | ? | ? | ? |
| **TEXAS** | | | | | |
| Hutchison | N | Y | Y | Y | Y |
| Cornyn | N | Y | Y | Y | Y |
| **UTAH** | | | | | |
| Hatch | N | Y | Y | Y | Y |
| Bennett | N | Y | Y | Y | Y |
| **VERMONT** | | | | | |
| Leahy | Y | Y | Y | N | Y |
| Jeffords | Y | Y | Y | N | Y |
| **VIRGINIA** | | | | | |
| Warner | N | Y | Y | Y | Y |
| Allen | N | Y | Y | Y | Y |
| **WASHINGTON** | | | | | |
| Murray | Y | Y | Y | N | Y |
| Cantwell | Y | Y | Y | N | Y |
| **WEST VIRGINIA** | | | | | |
| Byrd | Y | Y | Y | N | Y |
| Rockefeller | Y | Y | Y | N | Y |
| **WISCONSIN** | | | | | |
| Kohl | Y | N | Y | N | Y |
| Feingold | Y | Y | Y | N | Y |
| **WYOMING** | | | | | |
| Thomas | N | N | ? | ? | ? |
| Enzi | N | Y | ? | ? | ? |

**KEY**    Republicans    Democrats    *Independents*

| | | |
|---|---|---|
| Y Voted for (yea) | X Paired against | C Voted "present" to avoid possible conflict of interest |
| # Paired for | − Announced against | ? Did not vote or otherwise make a position known |
| + Announced for | P Voted "present" | |
| N Voted against (nay) | | |

# IN THE SENATE | By Vote Number

**321.** HR 2419. Fiscal 2006 Energy-Water Appropriations/Conference **Report.** Adoption of the conference report on the bill that would provide $30.5 billion in fiscal 2006 for energy and water development projects, including $24.3 billion for the Energy Department, $5.4 billion for the Army Corps of Engineers and $1.1 billion for Interior Department water projects. Adopted (thus cleared for the president) 84-4: R 48-2; D 35-2 (ND 31-2, SD 4-0); I 1-0. Nov. 14, 2005.

**322.** S 1042. Fiscal 2006 Defense Authorization/Iraq Withdrawal.
Levin, D-Mich., amendment that would state that U.S. military forces should not stay in Iraq indefinitely and require the president to report to Congress within 30 days of the bill's enactment with a timetable for withdrawal and a campaign plan, including dates, outlining phased redeployment of U.S. troops from Iraq. Rejected 40-58: R 1-53; D 38-5 (ND 36-3, SD 2-2); I 1-0. Nov. 15, 2005.

**323.** S 1042. Fiscal 2006 Defense Authorization/Iraq Withdrawal.
Warner, R-Va., amendment that would require the president to submit an unclassified report to Congress on U.S. policy and operations in Iraq 90 days after enactment and every three months thereafter. It would also state that 2006 should be a period of significant transition to Iraqi sovereignty, that U.S. forces should not remain in Iraq any longer than necessary, and that the Bush administration needs to explain to Congress and the American public the strategy for completing the Iraq mission. Adopted 79-19: R 41-13; D 37-6 (ND 33-6, SD 4-0); I 1-0. Nov. 15, 2005.

**324.** S 1042. Fiscal 2006 Defense Authorization/Habeas Corpus.
Bingaman, D-N.M., amendment to the Graham, R-S.C., amendment. The Bingaman amendment would grant detainees and enemy combatants the right to petition for habeas corpus in the U.S. Circuit Court of Appeals for the District of Columbia, provided a review tribunal has been conducted. The Graham amendment would deny non-citizens held at Guantánamo Bay, Cuba, habeas corpus access to U.S. civilian courts to contest their detention or conviction. It would allow one appellate court review of any military tribunal decision to detain prisoners under Defense Department procedure. It also would require the Defense secretary to submit a report to Congress detailing procedures at Guantánamo Bay. Rejected 44-54: R 4-50; D 39-4 (ND 35-4, SD 4-0); I 1-0. Nov. 15, 2005.

**325.** S 1042. Fiscal 2006 Defense Authorization/Habeas Corpus.
Graham, R-S.C., amendment to the Graham amendment. The second-degree amendment would prevent Combatant Status Review Tribunals from considering statements obtained under undue coercion. It also would establish a "designated civilian official," appointed by the president with the advice and consent of the Senate, to oversee the release of detainees. Adopted 84-14: R 53-1; D 30-13 (ND 26-13, SD 4-0); I 1-0. (Subsequently, the underlying Graham amendment, as modified, was adopted by voice vote.) Nov. 15, 2005.

| | 321 | 322 | 323 | 324 | 325 | | 321 | 322 | 323 | 324 | 325 |
|---|---|---|---|---|---|---|---|---|---|---|---|
| **ALABAMA** | | | | | | **MONTANA** | | | | | |
| Shelby | Y | N | Y | N | Y | Baucus | Y | Y | Y | Y | N |
| Sessions | Y | N | N | N | Y | Burns | + | N | Y | N | Y |
| **ALASKA** | | | | | | **NEBRASKA** | | | | | |
| Stevens | Y | N | Y | N | Y | Hagel | Y | N | Y | N | Y |
| Murkowski | ? | N | Y | N | Y | Nelson | Y | N | Y | N | Y |
| **ARIZONA** | | | | | | **NEVADA** | | | | | |
| McCain | ? | N | N | N | Y | Reid | Y | Y | Y | Y | Y |
| Kyl | Y | N | N | N | Y | Ensign | Y | N | Y | N | Y |
| **ARKANSAS** | | | | | | **NEW HAMPSHIRE** | | | | | |
| Lincoln | Y | Y | Y | Y | Y | Gregg | Y | N | Y | N | Y |
| Pryor | Y | N | Y | Y | Y | Sununu | N | N | Y | Y | Y |
| **CALIFORNIA** | | | | | | **NEW JERSEY** | | | | | |
| Feinstein | Y | Y | Y | Y | Y | Corzine | ? | ? | ? | ? | ? |
| Boxer | ? | Y | Y | Y | Y | Lautenberg | Y | Y | Y | Y | N |
| **COLORADO** | | | | | | **NEW MEXICO** | | | | | |
| Allard | Y | N | Y | N | Y | Domenici | Y | N | Y | N | Y |
| Salazar | Y | Y | Y | Y | Y | Bingaman | Y | Y | Y | Y | N |
| **CONNECTICUT** | | | | | | **NEW YORK** | | | | | |
| Dodd | Y | Y | Y | Y | Y | Schumer | N | Y | Y | Y | Y |
| Lieberman | Y | N | Y | N | Y | Clinton | ? | Y | Y | Y | Y |
| **DELAWARE** | | | | | | **NORTH CAROLINA** | | | | | |
| Biden | ? | Y | Y | Y | N | Dole | Y | N | Y | N | Y |
| Carper | Y | Y | Y | Y | Y | Burr | ? | N | N | N | Y |
| **FLORIDA** | | | | | | **NORTH DAKOTA** | | | | | |
| Nelson | Y | N | Y | Y | Y | Conrad | Y | N | N | N | Y |
| Martinez | Y | N | Y | N | Y | Dorgan | Y | Y | Y | Y | Y |
| **GEORGIA** | | | | | | **OHIO** | | | | | |
| Chambliss | Y | N | N | N | Y | DeWine | Y | N | Y | N | Y |
| Isakson | Y | N | N | N | Y | Voinovich | Y | N | Y | N | Y |
| **HAWAII** | | | | | | **OKLAHOMA** | | | | | |
| Inouye | Y | Y | Y | Y | Y | Inhofe | Y | N | N | N | Y |
| Akaka | Y | Y | Y | Y | Y | Coburn | N | N | N | N | Y |
| **IDAHO** | | | | | | **OREGON** | | | | | |
| Craig | Y | N | Y | N | Y | Wyden | Y | Y | Y | Y | Y |
| Crapo | Y | N | Y | N | Y | Smith | Y | N | Y | Y | Y |
| **ILLINOIS** | | | | | | **PENNSYLVANIA** | | | | | |
| Durbin | Y | Y | Y | Y | N | Specter | Y | N | Y | N | Y |
| Obama | Y | Y | Y | Y | Y | Santorum | Y | N | Y | N | Y |
| **INDIANA** | | | | | | **RHODE ISLAND** | | | | | |
| Lugar | Y | N | Y | N | Y | Reed | Y | Y | Y | Y | Y |
| Bayh | ? | Y | Y | N | Y | Chafee | Y | Y | Y | Y | Y |
| **IOWA** | | | | | | **SOUTH CAROLINA** | | | | | |
| Grassley | Y | N | Y | N | Y | Graham | Y | N | N | N | Y |
| Harkin | Y | Y | N | Y | N | DeMint | Y | N | N | N | Y |
| **KANSAS** | | | | | | **SOUTH DAKOTA** | | | | | |
| Brownback | Y | N | Y | N | Y | Johnson | Y | Y | Y | Y | Y |
| Roberts | Y | N | Y | N | Y | Thune | Y | N | N | N | Y |
| **KENTUCKY** | | | | | | **TENNESSEE** | | | | | |
| McConnell | Y | N | Y | N | Y | Frist | Y | N | Y | N | Y |
| Bunning | Y | N | N | N | Y | Alexander | Y | – | + | – | + |
| **LOUISIANA** | | | | | | **TEXAS** | | | | | |
| Landrieu | Y | Y | Y | Y | Y | Hutchison | Y | N | Y | N | Y |
| Vitter | Y | N | N | N | Y | Cornyn | + | N | Y | N | Y |
| **MAINE** | | | | | | **UTAH** | | | | | |
| Snowe | Y | N | Y | N | Y | Hatch | Y | N | Y | N | Y |
| Collins | Y | N | Y | N | Y | Bennett | Y | N | Y | N | Y |
| **MARYLAND** | | | | | | **VERMONT** | | | | | |
| Sarbanes | Y | Y | Y | Y | N | Leahy | Y | N | Y | N | N |
| Mikulski | Y | Y | Y | Y | Y | Jeffords | Y | Y | Y | Y | Y |
| **MASSACHUSETTS** | | | | | | **VIRGINIA** | | | | | |
| Kennedy | ? | Y | N | Y | N | Warner | Y | N | Y | N | Y |
| Kerry | Y | Y | N | Y | Y | Allen | Y | N | Y | N | Y |
| **MICHIGAN** | | | | | | **WASHINGTON** | | | | | |
| Levin | Y | Y | Y | Y | Y | Murray | Y | Y | Y | Y | Y |
| Stabenow | Y | Y | Y | Y | Y | Cantwell | Y | Y | Y | Y | Y |
| **MINNESOTA** | | | | | | **WEST VIRGINIA** | | | | | |
| Dayton | Y | Y | Y | Y | N | Byrd | ? | Y | N | Y | N |
| Coleman | Y | N | Y | N | Y | Rockefeller | Y | Y | Y | Y | N |
| **MISSISSIPPI** | | | | | | **WISCONSIN** | | | | | |
| Cochran | Y | N | Y | N | Y | Kohl | Y | Y | Y | Y | Y |
| Lott | Y | N | Y | N | Y | Feingold | N | Y | Y | Y | N |
| **MISSOURI** | | | | | | **WYOMING** | | | | | |
| Bond | Y | N | Y | N | Y | Thomas | Y | N | Y | N | Y |
| Talent | Y | N | Y | N | Y | Enzi | Y | N | Y | N | Y |

**KEY**   Republicans   Democrats   *Independents*

| | | |
|---|---|---|
| **Y** Voted for (yea) | **X** Paired against | **C** Voted "present" to avoid possible conflict of interest |
| **#** Paired for | **–** Announced against | |
| **+** Announced for | **P** Voted "present" | **?** Did not vote or otherwise make a position known |
| **N** Voted against (nay) | | |

# IN THE SENATE | By Vote Number

**326.** **S 1042. Fiscal 2006 Defense Authorization/Passage.** Passage of the bill that would authorize $491.6 billion for fiscal 2006 defense spending, including a $50 billion bridge supplemental for war costs in Iraq and Afghanistan; $109.2 billion for military personnel; $78.2 billion for procurement; $69.8 billion for research, development, testing and evaluation; and $1.6 billion for Energy department non-proliferation programs. Passed 98-0: R 54-0; D 43-0 (ND 39-0, SD 4-0); I 1-0. Nov. 15, 2005.

**327.** **S 1783. Pension Overhaul/Airline Pilot Annuity Benefits.** Akaka, D-Hawaii, amendment that would calculate the actuarial value of monthly life annuity benefits beginning at age 60 for airline pilots. Adopted 58-41: R 16-39; D 41-2 (ND 37-2, SD 4-0); I 1-0. Nov. 16, 2005.

**328.** **S 1783. Pension Overhaul/Passage.** Passage of the bill that would overhaul pension funding rules by requiring companies to use a modified yield curve to determine their plan's funding status and to fund 100 percent of their pension obligations. Companies with underfunded plans would have seven years to make up any underfunding. Annual per-employee premiums would increase to $30 from $19 starting in 2006. Passed 97-2: R 55-0; D 41-2 (ND 37-2, SD 4-0); I 1-0. Nov. 16, 2005.

**329.** **HR 2862. Fiscal 2006 Commerce-Justice-Science Appropriations/Conference Report.** Adoption of the conference report on the bill that would provide $61.8 billion, including $57.9 billion in discretionary funding, in fiscal 2006 for the departments of Commerce, Justice and State, as well as various science and other related agencies. It would provide $21.7 billion for Justice, $6.6 billion for Commerce and $9.7 billion for the State Department and international broadcasting agencies. It also would appropriate $16.5 billion for NASA and $5.6 billion for the National Science Foundation. Adopted (thus cleared for the president) 94-5: R 53-2; D 40-3 (ND 36-3, SD 4-0); I 1-0. Nov. 16, 2005.

**330.** **S 2020. Fiscal 2006 Tax Reconciliation/2005 Tax Cut Extension.** Conrad, D-N.D., motion to waive the Budget Act with respect to the Grassley, R-Iowa, point of order against the Conrad amendment. The Conrad amendment would extend only the tax cuts that expire in 2005, offsetting the cost by altering other tax provisions. Motion rejected 44-55: R 2-53; D 41-2 (ND 38-1, SD 3-1); I 1-0. A three-fifths majority vote (60) of the total Senate is required to waive the Budget Act. (Subsequently, the chair upheld the point of order, and the amendment fell.) Nov. 17, 2005.

**331.** **S 2020. Fiscal 2006 Tax Reconciliation/Windfall Profits.** Dorgan, D-N.D., motion to waive the Budget Act with respect to the Grassley, R-Iowa, point of order against the Dorgan amendment. The Dorgan amendment would impose a temporary 50 percent tax on oil company profits from the sale of crude oil. Funds from the tax would be used to provide a consumer tax credit for petroleum products. Motion rejected 35-64: R 0-55; D 34-9 (ND 33-6, SD 1-3); I 1-0. A three-fifths majority vote (60) of the total Senate is required to waive the Budget Act. (Subsequently, the chair upheld the point of order, and the amendment fell.) Nov. 17, 2005.

| | 326 | 327 | 328 | 329 | 330 | 331 |
|---|---|---|---|---|---|---|
| **ALABAMA** | | | | | | |
| Shelby | Y | N | Y | Y | N | N |
| Sessions | Y | N | Y | Y | N | N |
| **ALASKA** | | | | | | |
| Stevens | Y | N | Y | Y | N | N |
| Murkowski | Y | N | Y | Y | N | N |
| **ARIZONA** | | | | | | |
| McCain | Y | N | Y | Y | N | N |
| Kyl | Y | N | Y | Y | N | N |
| **ARKANSAS** | | | | | | |
| Lincoln | Y | Y | Y | Y | Y | N |
| Pryor | Y | Y | Y | Y | Y | Y |
| **CALIFORNIA** | | | | | | |
| Feinstein | Y | Y | Y | Y | Y | Y |
| Boxer | Y | Y | Y | Y | Y | Y |
| **COLORADO** | | | | | | |
| Allard | Y | N | Y | Y | N | N |
| Salazar | Y | Y | Y | Y | Y | N |
| **CONNECTICUT** | | | | | | |
| Dodd | Y | Y | Y | Y | Y | Y |
| Lieberman | Y | Y | Y | Y | Y | Y |
| **DELAWARE** | | | | | | |
| Biden | Y | Y | Y | Y | Y | Y |
| Carper | Y | Y | Y | Y | Y | N |
| **FLORIDA** | | | | | | |
| Nelson | Y | Y | Y | Y | Y | Y |
| Martinez | Y | N | Y | Y | N | N |
| **GEORGIA** | | | | | | |
| Chambliss | Y | Y | Y | Y | N | N |
| Isakson | Y | Y | Y | Y | N | N |
| **HAWAII** | | | | | | |
| Inouye | Y | Y | Y | Y | Y | Y |
| Akaka | Y | Y | Y | Y | Y | Y |
| **IDAHO** | | | | | | |
| Craig | Y | N | Y | Y | N | N |
| Crapo | Y | N | Y | Y | N | N |
| **ILLINOIS** | | | | | | |
| Durbin | Y | Y | Y | Y | Y | Y |
| Obama | Y | Y | Y | Y | Y | Y |
| **INDIANA** | | | | | | |
| Lugar | Y | Y | Y | Y | N | N |
| Bayh | Y | Y | Y | Y | Y | Y |
| **IOWA** | | | | | | |
| Grassley | Y | N | Y | Y | N | N |
| Harkin | Y | Y | Y | Y | Y | Y |
| **KANSAS** | | | | | | |
| Brownback | Y | N | Y | Y | N | N |
| Roberts | Y | N | Y | Y | N | N |
| **KENTUCKY** | | | | | | |
| McConnell | Y | N | Y | Y | N | N |
| Bunning | Y | N | Y | Y | N | N |
| **LOUISIANA** | | | | | | |
| Landrieu | Y | Y | Y | Y | Y | Y |
| Vitter | Y | N | Y | Y | N | N |
| **MAINE** | | | | | | |
| Snowe | Y | N | Y | Y | N | N |
| Collins | Y | N | Y | Y | N | N |
| **MARYLAND** | | | | | | |
| Sarbanes | Y | Y | Y | Y | Y | Y |
| Mikulski | Y | Y | Y | Y | Y | Y |
| **MASSACHUSETTS** | | | | | | |
| Kennedy | Y | Y | Y | Y | Y | Y |
| Kerry | Y | Y | Y | Y | Y | Y |
| **MICHIGAN** | | | | | | |
| Levin | Y | Y | N | Y | Y | Y |
| Stabenow | Y | Y | N | Y | Y | Y |
| **MINNESOTA** | | | | | | |
| Dayton | Y | Y | Y | N | Y | Y |
| Coleman | Y | Y | Y | Y | N | N |
| **MISSISSIPPI** | | | | | | |
| Cochran | Y | N | Y | Y | N | N |
| Lott | Y | N | Y | Y | N | N |
| **MISSOURI** | | | | | | |
| Bond | Y | Y | Y | Y | N | N |
| Talent | Y | Y | Y | Y | N | N |
| **MONTANA** | | | | | | |
| Baucus | Y | N | Y | N | Y | N |
| Burns | Y | N | Y | Y | N | N |
| **NEBRASKA** | | | | | | |
| Hagel | Y | N | Y | Y | N | N |
| Nelson | Y | Y | Y | Y | N | N |
| **NEVADA** | | | | | | |
| Reid | Y | Y | Y | Y | Y | Y |
| Ensign | Y | N | Y | Y | N | N |
| **NEW HAMPSHIRE** | | | | | | |
| Gregg | Y | N | Y | Y | N | N |
| Sununu | Y | N | Y | Y | N | N |
| **NEW JERSEY** | | | | | | |
| Corzine | ? | ? | ? | ? | ? | ? |
| Lautenberg | Y | Y | Y | Y | Y | Y |
| **NEW MEXICO** | | | | | | |
| Domenici | Y | N | Y | Y | N | N |
| Bingaman | Y | Y | Y | Y | Y | Y |
| **NEW YORK** | | | | | | |
| Schumer | Y | Y | Y | Y | Y | Y |
| Clinton | Y | Y | Y | Y | Y | Y |
| **NORTH CAROLINA** | | | | | | |
| Dole | Y | Y | Y | N | N | N |
| Burr | Y | Y | Y | Y | N | N |
| **NORTH DAKOTA** | | | | | | |
| Conrad | Y | Y | Y | N | Y | Y |
| Dorgan | Y | Y | Y | Y | Y | Y |
| **OHIO** | | | | | | |
| DeWine | Y | Y | Y | Y | N | N |
| Voinovich | Y | N | Y | Y | N | N |
| **OKLAHOMA** | | | | | | |
| Inhofe | Y | N | Y | Y | N | N |
| Coburn | Y | N | N | N | N | N |
| **OREGON** | | | | | | |
| Wyden | Y | Y | Y | Y | Y | Y |
| Smith | Y | N | Y | Y | N | N |
| **PENNSYLVANIA** | | | | | | |
| Specter | Y | Y | Y | Y | N | N |
| Santorum | Y | Y | Y | Y | N | N |
| **RHODE ISLAND** | | | | | | |
| Reed | Y | Y | Y | Y | Y | Y |
| Chafee | Y | Y | Y | Y | Y | N |
| **SOUTH CAROLINA** | | | | | | |
| Graham | Y | N | Y | Y | N | N |
| DeMint | Y | N | Y | Y | N | N |
| **SOUTH DAKOTA** | | | | | | |
| Johnson | Y | Y | Y | Y | Y | Y |
| Thune | Y | N | Y | Y | N | N |
| **TENNESSEE** | | | | | | |
| Frist | Y | N | Y | Y | N | N |
| Alexander | + | N | Y | Y | N | N |
| **TEXAS** | | | | | | |
| Hutchison | Y | Y | Y | Y | N | N |
| Cornyn | Y | N | Y | Y | N | N |
| **UTAH** | | | | | | |
| Hatch | Y | Y | Y | Y | N | N |
| Bennett | Y | Y | Y | Y | N | N |
| **VERMONT** | | | | | | |
| Leahy | Y | Y | Y | Y | Y | Y |
| Jeffords | Y | Y | Y | Y | Y | Y |
| **VIRGINIA** | | | | | | |
| Warner | Y | Y | Y | N | N | N |
| Allen | Y | N | Y | Y | N | N |
| **WASHINGTON** | | | | | | |
| Murray | Y | Y | Y | Y | Y | Y |
| Cantwell | Y | Y | Y | Y | Y | N |
| **WEST VIRGINIA** | | | | | | |
| Byrd | I | Y | Y | Y | Y | Y |
| Rockefeller | Y | N | Y | Y | Y | Y |
| **WISCONSIN** | | | | | | |
| Kohl | Y | Y | Y | Y | Y | Y |
| Feingold | Y | Y | Y | Y | Y | Y |
| **WYOMING** | | | | | | |
| Thomas | Y | N | Y | N | N | N |
| Enzi | Y | N | Y | Y | N | N |

**KEY**    Republicans    Democrats    *Independents*

| | | |
|---|---|---|
| **Y** Voted for (yea) | **X** Paired against | **C** Voted "present" to avoid possible conflict of interest |
| **#** Paired for | **–** Announced against | |
| **+** Announced for | **P** Voted "present" | **?** Did not vote or otherwise make a position known |
| **N** Voted against (nay) | | |

# IN THE SENATE | By Vote Number

**332.** **S 2020. Fiscal 2006 Tax Reconciliation/Oil Company Tax Credits.** Feinstein, D-Calif., motion to waive the Budget Act with respect to the Grassley, R-Iowa, point of order against the Feinstein amendment. The Feinstein amendment would repeal tax deductions granted to major integrated oil companies for intangible drilling and exploration costs. Motion rejected 48-51: R 12-43; D 35-8 (ND 32-7, SD 3-1); I 1-0. A three-fifths majority vote (60) of the total Senate is required to waive the Budget Act. (Subsequently, the chair upheld the point of order, and the amendment fell.) Nov. 17, 2005.

**333.** **S 2020. Fiscal 2006 Tax Reconciliation/Top Tax Rate.** Feinstein, D-Calif., motion to waive the Budget Act with respect to the Grassley, R-Iowa, point of order against the Feinstein amendment. The Feinstein amendment would reinstate a 39.6 percent tax rate for individuals with annual incomes of more than $1 million. It also would repeal lower dividend and capital gains tax rates for those individuals until the federal budget is balanced. Motion rejected 40-59: R 1-54; D 38-5 (ND 35-4, SD 3-1); I 1-0. A three-fifths majority vote (60) of the total Senate is required to waive the Budget Act. (Subsequently, the chair upheld the point of order, and the amendment fell.) Nov. 17, 2005.

**334.** **S 2020. Fiscal 2006 Tax Reconciliation/Price Gouging.** Cantwell, D-Wash., motion to waive the Budget Act with respect to the Stevens, R-Alaska, point of order against the Cantwell amendment. The Cantwell amendment would make price gouging on energy products, services or markets a federal crime. Motion rejected 57-42: R 13-42; D 43-0 (ND 39-0, SD 4-0); I 1-0. A three-fifths majority vote (60) of the total Senate is required to waive the Budget Act. (Subsequently, the chair upheld the point of order, and the amendment fell.) Nov. 17, 2005.

**335.** **S 2020. Fiscal 2006 Tax Reconciliation/Physician Senators.** Lott, R-Miss., motion to waive the Budget Act with respect to the Voinovich, R-Ohio, point of order against the Lott amendment. The Lott amendment would allow senators who are physicians to continue their medical practice while serving in the Senate, provided they do not charge more than the amount necessary to cover practice expenses. Motion rejected 51-47: R 47-8; D 4-38 (ND 3-35, SD 1-3); I 0-1. A three-fifths majority vote (60) of the total Senate is required to waive the Budget Act. (Subsequently, the chair upheld the point of order, and the amendment fell.) Nov. 17, 2005.

**336.** **S 2020. Fiscal 2006 Tax Reconciliation/Insurance for Children.** Grassley, R-Iowa, motion to waive the Budget Act with respect to the Durbin, D-Ill., point of order against the Grassley amendment. The Grassley amendment would express the sense of the Senate that current tax policy should be continued to help insure children. Motion rejected 53-45: R 52-2; D 1-42 (ND 1-38, SD 0-4); I 0-1. A three-fifths majority vote (60) of the total Senate is required to waive the Budget Act. (Subsequently, the chair upheld the point of order, and the amendment fell.) Nov. 17, 2005.

**337.** **S 2020. Fiscal 2006 Tax Reconciliation/State Children's Health Insurance Program.** Durbin, D-Ill., motion to waive the Budget Act with respect to the Grassley, R-Iowa, point of order against the Durbin amendment. The Durbin amendment would express the sense of the Senate that the Senate should not extend the 15 percent dividend and capital-gains tax rates for high-income taxpayers until the federal government provides funding to state and local entities to enroll children in the State Children's Health Insurance Program. Motion rejected 43-55: R 0-54; D 42-1 (ND 39-0, SD 3-1); I 1-0. A three-fifths majority vote (60) of the total Senate is required to waive the Budget Act. (Subsequently, the chair upheld the point of order, and the amendment fell.) Nov. 17, 2005.

| State / Senator | 332 | 333 | 334 | 335 | 336 | 337 |
|---|---|---|---|---|---|---|
| **ALABAMA** | | | | | | |
| Shelby | N | N | N | N | Y | N |
| Sessions | N | N | N | Y | Y | N |
| **ALASKA** | | | | | | |
| Stevens | N | N | N | Y | Y | N |
| Murkowski | N | N | N | N | Y | N |
| **ARIZONA** | | | | | | |
| McCain | Y | N | N | Y | Y | N |
| Kyl | N | N | N | Y | Y | N |
| **ARKANSAS** | | | | | | |
| Lincoln | Y | Y | Y | N | N | Y |
| Pryor | Y | Y | Y | N | N | Y |
| **CALIFORNIA** | | | | | | |
| Feinstein | Y | Y | Y | N | N | Y |
| Boxer | Y | Y | Y | N | N | Y |
| **COLORADO** | | | | | | |
| Allard | N | N | N | Y | Y | N |
| Salazar | N | Y | Y | N | N | Y |
| **CONNECTICUT** | | | | | | |
| Dodd | Y | Y | Y | N | N | Y |
| Lieberman | Y | Y | Y | N | N | Y |
| **DELAWARE** | | | | | | |
| Biden | Y | Y | Y | N | N | Y |
| Carper | Y | Y | Y | Y | N | Y |
| **FLORIDA** | | | | | | |
| Nelson | Y | Y | Y | N | N | Y |
| Martinez | N | N | N | Y | Y | N |
| **GEORGIA** | | | | | | |
| Chambliss | N | N | N | N | Y | N |
| Isakson | N | N | N | Y | Y | N |
| **HAWAII** | | | | | | |
| Inouye | Y | Y | Y | ? | N | Y |
| Akaka | Y | Y | Y | N | N | Y |
| **IDAHO** | | | | | | |
| Craig | N | N | N | Y | Y | N |
| Crapo | N | N | N | Y | Y | N |
| **ILLINOIS** | | | | | | |
| Durbin | Y | Y | Y | N | N | Y |
| Obama | Y | Y | Y | Y | N | Y |
| **INDIANA** | | | | | | |
| Lugar | N | N | N | Y | Y | N |
| Bayh | Y | Y | Y | N | N | Y |
| **IOWA** | | | | | | |
| Grassley | N | N | N | Y | Y | N |
| Harkin | Y | Y | Y | N | N | Y |
| **KANSAS** | | | | | | |
| Brownback | N | N | N | Y | Y | N |
| Roberts | N | N | N | N | Y | N |
| **KENTUCKY** | | | | | | |
| McConnell | N | N | N | Y | Y | N |
| Bunning | N | N | N | N | Y | N |
| **LOUISIANA** | | | | | | |
| Landrieu | N | N | Y | Y | N | Y |
| Vitter | N | N | N | Y | Y | N |
| **MAINE** | | | | | | |
| Snowe | Y | N | Y | Y | Y | N |
| Collins | Y | N | Y | Y | Y | N |
| **MARYLAND** | | | | | | |
| Sarbanes | Y | Y | Y | N | N | Y |
| Mikulski | Y | Y | Y | N | N | Y |
| **MASSACHUSETTS** | | | | | | |
| Kennedy | Y | Y | Y | N | N | Y |
| Kerry | Y | Y | Y | N | N | Y |
| **MICHIGAN** | | | | | | |
| Levin | N | Y | Y | N | N | Y |
| Stabenow | Y | Y | Y | N | N | Y |
| **MINNESOTA** | | | | | | |
| Dayton | Y | Y | Y | Y | N | Y |
| Coleman | Y | N | Y | Y | Y | N |
| **MISSISSIPPI** | | | | | | |
| Cochran | N | N | N | Y | Y | N |
| Lott | N | N | N | Y | ? | ? |
| **MISSOURI** | | | | | | |
| Bond | N | N | N | Y | Y | N |
| Talent | Y | N | Y | Y | Y | N |
| **MONTANA** | | | | | | |
| Baucus | N | N | Y | N | N | Y |
| Burns | N | N | N | Y | Y | N |
| **NEBRASKA** | | | | | | |
| Hagel | N | N | N | Y | Y | N |
| Nelson | N | N | N | Y | Y | N |
| **NEVADA** | | | | | | |
| Reid | Y | Y | Y | N | N | Y |
| Ensign | N | N | N | Y | Y | N |
| **NEW HAMPSHIRE** | | | | | | |
| Gregg | Y | N | N | Y | Y | N |
| Sununu | Y | N | N | Y | Y | N |
| **NEW JERSEY** | | | | | | |
| Corzine | ? | ? | ? | ? | ? | ? |
| Lautenberg | Y | Y | Y | N | N | Y |
| **NEW MEXICO** | | | | | | |
| Domenici | N | N | N | Y | Y | N |
| Bingaman | N | N | Y | N | N | Y |
| **NEW YORK** | | | | | | |
| Schumer | Y | Y | Y | N | N | Y |
| Clinton | Y | Y | Y | N | N | Y |
| **NORTH CAROLINA** | | | | | | |
| Dole | N | N | N | Y | Y | N |
| Burr | Y | N | N | Y | Y | N |
| **NORTH DAKOTA** | | | | | | |
| Conrad | N | Y | Y | N | N | Y |
| Dorgan | N | Y | Y | N | N | Y |
| **OHIO** | | | | | | |
| DeWine | Y | N | Y | Y | N | N |
| Voinovich | N | N | N | N | Y | N |
| **OKLAHOMA** | | | | | | |
| Inhofe | N | N | N | Y | Y | N |
| Coburn | N | N | N | Y | Y | N |
| **OREGON** | | | | | | |
| Wyden | Y | Y | Y | N | N | Y |
| Smith | N | N | Y | Y | Y | N |
| **PENNSYLVANIA** | | | | | | |
| Specter | Y | N | Y | Y | N | Y |
| Santorum | N | N | Y | Y | Y | N |
| **RHODE ISLAND** | | | | | | |
| Reed | Y | Y | Y | N | N | Y |
| Chafee | Y | Y | Y | Y | N | N |
| **SOUTH CAROLINA** | | | | | | |
| Graham | N | N | Y | Y | Y | N |
| DeMint | Y | N | N | Y | Y | N |
| **SOUTH DAKOTA** | | | | | | |
| Johnson | Y | Y | Y | N | N | Y |
| Thune | N | N | Y | Y | N | N |
| **TENNESSEE** | | | | | | |
| Frist | N | N | N | N | Y | N |
| Alexander | N | N | N | N | Y | N |
| **TEXAS** | | | | | | |
| Hutchison | N | N | Y | Y | Y | N |
| Cornyn | N | N | N | Y | Y | N |
| **UTAH** | | | | | | |
| Hatch | N | N | N | Y | Y | N |
| Bennett | N | N | N | Y | Y | N |
| **VERMONT** | | | | | | |
| Leahy | Y | Y | Y | N | N | Y |
| Jeffords | Y | Y | Y | N | N | Y |
| **VIRGINIA** | | | | | | |
| Warner | N | N | N | N | Y | N |
| Allen | N | N | N | Y | Y | N |
| **WASHINGTON** | | | | | | |
| Murray | Y | Y | Y | N | N | Y |
| Cantwell | Y | Y | Y | N | N | Y |
| **WEST VIRGINIA** | | | | | | |
| Byrd | Y | Y | Y | N | N | Y |
| Rockefeller | Y | Y | Y | N | N | Y |
| **WISCONSIN** | | | | | | |
| Kohl | Y | Y | Y | N | N | Y |
| Feingold | Y | Y | Y | N | N | Y |
| **WYOMING** | | | | | | |
| Thomas | N | N | N | N | Y | N |
| Enzi | N | N | N | Y | Y | N |

**KEY**   Republicans   Democrats   *Independents*

| | |
|---|---|
| Y Voted for (yea) | X Paired against |
| # Paired for | – Announced against |
| + Announced for | P Voted "present" |
| N Voted against (nay) | |

C Voted "present" to avoid possible conflict of interest

? Did not vote or otherwise make a position known

# IN THE SENATE | By Vote Number

**338.** **S 2020. Fiscal 2006 Tax Reconciliation/Child Poverty Elimination Fund.** Kennedy, D-Mass., motion to waive the Budget Act with respect to the Grassley, R-Iowa, point of order against the Kennedy amendment. The Kennedy amendment would create a child poverty elimination trust fund with the goal of reducing child poverty within a decade. The new program would be funded by an additional 1 percent tax on people with incomes above $500,000, or $1 million for married couples. Motion rejected 36-62: R 0-54; D 35-8 (ND 33-6, SD 2-2); I 1-0. A three-fifths majority vote (60) of the total Senate is required to waive the Budget Act. (Subsequently, the chair upheld the point of order, and the amendment fell.) Nov. 17, 2005.

**339.** **S 2020. Fiscal 2006 Tax Reconciliation/LIHEAP.** Reed, D-R.I., motion to waive the Budget Act with respect to the Grassley, R-Iowa, point of order against the Reed amendment. The Reed amendment would fund the Low-Income Home Energy Assistance Program (LIHEAP) by imposing a one-year temporary tax on oil company profits from the sale of crude oil. Motion rejected 50-48: R 9-45; D 40-3 (ND 37-2, SD 3-1); I 1-0. A three-fifths majority vote (60) of the total Senate is required to waive the Budget Act. (Subsequently, the chair upheld the point of order, and the amendment fell.) Nov. 17, 2005.

**340.** **S 2020. Fiscal 2006 Tax Reconciliation/PAYGO.** Feingold, D-Wis., motion to waive the Budget Act with respect to the Grassley, R-Iowa, point of order against the Feingold amendment. The Feingold amendment would restore pay-as-you-go (PAYGO) rules, which would create a 60-vote point of order against any direct spending or revenue legislation that would increase the on-budget deficit or cause an on-budget deficit. Tax cuts and new entitlement spending would have to be offset with revenue increases or spending cuts. The amendment would sunset Sept. 30, 2010. Motion rejected 50-48: R 6-48; D 43-0 (ND 39-0, SD 4-0); I 1-0. A three-fifths majority vote (60) of the total Senate is required to waive the Budget Act. (Subsequently, the chair upheld the point of order, and the amendment fell.) Nov. 17, 2005.

**341.** **S 2020. Fiscal 2006 Tax Reconciliation/Windfall Oil Profits.** Schumer, D-N.Y., motion to waive the Budget Act with respect to the Grassley, R-Iowa, point of order against the Schumer amendment. The Schumer amendment would impose a temporary tax on oil company profits from the sale of crude oil. The funds would be used to provide every taxpayer with a $100 non-refundable tax credit for 2005 for each person in their household. Motion rejected 33-65: R 0-54; D 32-11 (ND 31-8, SD 1-3); I 1-0. A three-fifths majority vote (60) of the total Senate is required to waive the Budget Act. (Subsequently, the chair upheld the point of order, and the amendment fell.) Nov. 17, 2005.

**342.** **S 2020. Fiscal 2006 Tax Reconciliation/Medicare Enrollment.** Nelson, D-Fla., motion to waive the Budget Act with respect to the Grassley, R-Iowa, point of order against the Nelson, D-Fla., amendment. The Nelson amendment would extend the initial enrollment period for the Medicare prescription drug benefit by six months, through the end of 2006. Motion rejected 51-47: R 7-47; D 43-0 (ND 39-0, SD 4-0); I 1-0. A three-fifths majority vote (60) of the total Senate is required to waive the Budget Act. (Subsequently, the chair upheld the point of order, and the amendment fell.) Nov. 17, 2005.

| | 338 | 339 | 340 | 341 | 342 | | | 338 | 339 | 340 | 341 | 342 |
|---|---|---|---|---|---|---|---|---|---|---|---|---|
| **ALABAMA** | | | | | | | **MONTANA** | | | | | |
| Shelby | N | N | N | N | N | | Baucus | N | Y | Y | N | Y |
| Sessions | N | N | N | N | N | | Burns | N | N | N | N | N |
| **ALASKA** | | | | | | | **NEBRASKA** | | | | | |
| Stevens | N | N | N | N | N | | Hagel | N | N | N | N | N |
| Murkowski | N | N | N | N | N | | Nelson | N | N | Y | N | Y |
| **ARIZONA** | | | | | | | **NEVADA** | | | | | |
| McCain | N | N | Y | N | N | | Reid | Y | Y | Y | Y | Y |
| Kyl | N | N | N | N | N | | Ensign | N | N | N | N | N |
| **ARKANSAS** | | | | | | | **NEW HAMPSHIRE** | | | | | |
| Lincoln | N | Y | Y | N | Y | | Gregg | N | Y | N | N | N |
| Pryor | N | Y | Y | N | Y | | Sununu | N | Y | N | N | N |
| **CALIFORNIA** | | | | | | | **NEW JERSEY** | | | | | |
| Feinstein | Y | Y | Y | Y | Y | | Corzine | ? | ? | ? | ? | ? |
| Boxer | Y | Y | Y | Y | Y | | Lautenberg | Y | Y | Y | Y | Y |
| **COLORADO** | | | | | | | **NEW MEXICO** | | | | | |
| Allard | N | N | N | N | N | | Domenici | N | N | N | N | N |
| Salazar | N | Y | Y | N | Y | | Bingaman | Y | N | Y | N | Y |
| **CONNECTICUT** | | | | | | | **NEW YORK** | | | | | |
| Dodd | Y | Y | Y | Y | Y | | Schumer | Y | Y | Y | Y | Y |
| Lieberman | Y | Y | Y | Y | Y | | Clinton | Y | Y | Y | Y | Y |
| **DELAWARE** | | | | | | | **NORTH CAROLINA** | | | | | |
| Biden | N | Y | Y | N | Y | | Dole | N | N | N | N | N |
| Carper | N | Y | Y | N | Y | | Burr | N | N | N | N | N |
| **FLORIDA** | | | | | | | **NORTH DAKOTA** | | | | | |
| Nelson | Y | Y | Y | Y | Y | | Conrad | Y | Y | Y | N | Y |
| Martinez | N | N | N | N | Y | | Dorgan | Y | Y | Y | Y | Y |
| **GEORGIA** | | | | | | | **OHIO** | | | | | |
| Chambliss | N | N | N | N | N | | DeWine | N | N | N | N | N |
| Isakson | N | N | N | N | N | | Voinovich | N | Y | Y | N | Y |
| **HAWAII** | | | | | | | **OKLAHOMA** | | | | | |
| Inouye | Y | Y | Y | Y | Y | | Inhofe | N | N | N | N | N |
| Akaka | Y | Y | Y | Y | Y | | Coburn | N | N | Y | N | N |
| **IDAHO** | | | | | | | **OREGON** | | | | | |
| Craig | N | N | N | N | N | | Wyden | Y | Y | Y | Y | Y |
| Crapo | N | N | N | N | N | | Smith | N | N | N | N | N |
| **ILLINOIS** | | | | | | | **PENNSYLVANIA** | | | | | |
| Durbin | Y | Y | Y | Y | Y | | Specter | N | Y | N | N | Y |
| Obama | Y | Y | Y | Y | Y | | Santorum | N | N | N | N | N |
| **INDIANA** | | | | | | | **RHODE ISLAND** | | | | | |
| Lugar | N | N | N | N | N | | Reed | Y | Y | Y | Y | Y |
| Bayh | Y | Y | Y | Y | Y | | Chafee | N | Y | N | N | Y |
| **IOWA** | | | | | | | **SOUTH CAROLINA** | | | | | |
| Grassley | N | N | N | N | N | | Graham | N | N | N | N | N |
| Harkin | Y | Y | Y | Y | Y | | DeMint | N | N | N | N | N |
| **KANSAS** | | | | | | | **SOUTH DAKOTA** | | | | | |
| Brownback | N | N | N | N | N | | Johnson | Y | Y | Y | Y | Y |
| Roberts | N | N | N | N | N | | Thune | N | Y | N | N | N |
| **KENTUCKY** | | | | | | | **TENNESSEE** | | | | | |
| McConnell | N | N | N | N | N | | Frist | N | N | N | N | N |
| Bunning | N | N | N | N | N | | Alexander | N | N | N | N | N |
| **LOUISIANA** | | | | | | | **TEXAS** | | | | | |
| Landrieu | Y | N | Y | N | Y | | Hutchison | N | N | N | N | N |
| Vitter | N | N | N | N | N | | Cornyn | N | N | N | N | N |
| **MAINE** | | | | | | | **UTAH** | | | | | |
| Snowe | N | Y | N | N | Y | | Hatch | N | N | N | N | N |
| Collins | N | Y | Y | N | N | | Bennett | N | N | N | N | N |
| **MARYLAND** | | | | | | | **VERMONT** | | | | | |
| Sarbanes | Y | Y | Y | Y | Y | | Leahy | Y | Y | Y | Y | Y |
| Mikulski | Y | Y | Y | Y | Y | | Jeffords | Y | Y | Y | Y | Y |
| **MASSACHUSETTS** | | | | | | | **VIRGINIA** | | | | | |
| Kennedy | Y | Y | Y | Y | Y | | Warner | N | N | N | N | N |
| Kerry | Y | Y | Y | Y | Y | | Allen | N | N | N | N | N |
| **MICHIGAN** | | | | | | | **WASHINGTON** | | | | | |
| Levin | Y | Y | Y | Y | Y | | Murray | Y | Y | Y | Y | Y |
| Stabenow | Y | Y | Y | Y | Y | | Cantwell | N | Y | Y | N | Y |
| **MINNESOTA** | | | | | | | **WEST VIRGINIA** | | | | | |
| Dayton | Y | Y | Y | Y | Y | | Byrd | Y | Y | Y | Y | Y |
| Coleman | N | Y | N | N | N | | Rockefeller | Y | Y | Y | Y | Y |
| **MISSISSIPPI** | | | | | | | **WISCONSIN** | | | | | |
| Cochran | N | N | N | N | N | | Kohl | Y | Y | Y | Y | Y |
| Lott | ? | ? | ? | ? | ? | | Feingold | Y | Y | Y | Y | Y |
| **MISSOURI** | | | | | | | **WYOMING** | | | | | |
| Bond | N | N | N | N | N | | Thomas | N | N | N | N | N |
| Talent | N | N | N | N | N | | Enzi | N | N | N | N | N |

**KEY**    **Republicans**    Democrats    *Independents*

| | | | |
|---|---|---|---|
| Y | Voted for (yea) | X | Paired against |
| # | Paired for | – | Announced against |
| + | Announced for | P | Voted "present" |
| N | Voted against (nay) | | |

| | |
|---|---|
| C | Voted "present" to avoid possible conflict of interest |
| ? | Did not vote or otherwise make a position known |

# IN THE SENATE | By Vote Number

**343.** **S 2020. Fiscal 2006 Tax Reconciliation/Veterans.** Boxer, D-Calif., motion to waive the Budget Act with respect to the Grassley, R-Iowa, point of order against the Boxer amendment. The Boxer amendment would provide an additional $500 million per year for the next five years for mental health services for veterans. It would be offset by deferring tax cuts for those making $1 million per year. Motion rejected 43-55: R 1-53; D 41-2 (ND 37-2, SD 4-0); I 1-0. A three-fifths majority vote (60) of the total Senate is required to waive the Budget Act. (Subsequently, the chair upheld the point of order, and the amendment fell.) Nov. 17, 2005.

**344.** **S 2020. Fiscal 2006 Tax Reconciliation/Combat Pay.** Kerry, D-Mass., motion to waive the Budget Act with respect to the Grassley, R-Iowa, point of order against the Kerry amendment. The Kerry amendment would extend through 2007 the inclusion of combat pay in earned income. It also would accelerate so-called marriage penalty tax relief for the earned-income tax credit and extend the effective dates of leasing provisions of the American Jobs Creation Act. Motion rejected 55-43: R 11-43; D 43-0 (ND 39-0, SD 4-0); I 1-0. A three-fifths majority vote (60) of the total Senate is required to waive the Budget Act. (Subsequently, the chair upheld the point of order, and the amendment fell.) Nov. 17, 2005.

**345.** **S 2020. Fiscal 2006 Tax Reconciliation/Farmers Tax Credit.** Dayton, D-Minn., motion to waive the Budget Act with respect to the Grassley, R-Iowa, point of order against the Dayton amendment. The Dayton amendment would provide a refundable tax credit for farmers equal to the lesser of 30 percent of their energy costs for 2005, or $3,000. It would increase taxes on foreign oil and gas income for U.S. energy companies through modifications to foreign-tax credit rules. Motion rejected 47-51: R 3-51; D 43-0 (ND 39-0, SD 4-0); I 1-0. A three-fifths majority vote (60) of the total Senate is required to waive the Budget Act. (Subsequently, the chair upheld the point of order, and the amendment fell.) Nov. 17, 2005.

**346.** **S 2020. Fiscal 2006 Tax Reconciliation/Child Tax Credit.** Harkin, D-Iowa, motion to waive the Budget Act with respect to the Grassley, R-Iowa, point of order against the Harkin amendment. The Harkin amendment would reinstate the personal exemption phase-out and phase-out of itemized deductions provisions of the tax code, and would use those revenues to lower the income threshold for calculating the child tax credit from $10,000 to $9,000. Motion rejected 42-56: R 0-54; D 41-2 (ND 37-2, SD 4-0); I 1-0. A three-fifths majority vote (60) of the total Senate is required to waive the Budget Act. (Subsequently, the chair upheld the point of order, and the amendment fell.) Nov. 17, 2005.

**347.** **S 2020. Fiscal 2006 Tax Reconciliation/Passage.** Passage of bill that would extend a series of tax cuts set to expire between 2005 and 2010, including the college tuition deduction and the state and local sales tax deduction in states without income taxes. It would extend through 2006 protections for middle-class taxpayers from alternative-minimum tax liability, and include $7 billion in tax incentives to encourage reconstruction along the hurricane-damaged Gulf Coast, along with a new tax deduction for charitable giving by taxpayers who do not itemize. Passed 64-33: R 49-4; D 15-28 (ND 11-28, SD 4-0); I 0-1. Nov. 18, 2005 (in the session that began and the Congressional Record dated Nov. 17, 2005).

| | 343 | 344 | 345 | 346 | 347 |
|---|---|---|---|---|---|
| **ALABAMA** | | | | | |
| Shelby | N | N | N | N | ? |
| Sessions | N | N | N | N | Y |
| **ALASKA** | | | | | |
| Stevens | N | N | N | N | Y |
| Murkowski | N | N | N | N | Y |
| **ARIZONA** | | | | | |
| McCain | N | Y | N | N | Y |
| Kyl | N | N | N | N | Y |
| **ARKANSAS** | | | | | |
| Lincoln | Y | Y | Y | Y | Y |
| Pryor | Y | Y | Y | Y | Y |
| **CALIFORNIA** | | | | | |
| Feinstein | Y | Y | Y | Y | Y |
| Boxer | Y | Y | Y | Y | N |
| **COLORADO** | | | | | |
| Allard | N | N | N | N | Y |
| Salazar | Y | Y | Y | Y | Y |
| **CONNECTICUT** | | | | | |
| Dodd | Y | Y | Y | Y | N |
| Lieberman | Y | Y | Y | Y | Y |
| **DELAWARE** | | | | | |
| Biden | Y | Y | Y | Y | N |
| Carper | Y | Y | Y | Y | Y |
| **FLORIDA** | | | | | |
| Nelson | Y | Y | Y | Y | Y |
| Martinez | N | N | N | N | Y |
| **GEORGIA** | | | | | |
| Chambliss | N | N | N | N | Y |
| Isakson | N | N | N | N | Y |
| **HAWAII** | | | | | |
| Inouye | Y | Y | Y | Y | N |
| Akaka | Y | Y | Y | Y | N |
| **IDAHO** | | | | | |
| Craig | N | N | N | N | N |
| Crapo | N | N | N | N | N |
| **ILLINOIS** | | | | | |
| Durbin | Y | Y | Y | Y | N |
| Obama | Y | Y | Y | Y | N |
| **INDIANA** | | | | | |
| Lugar | N | N | N | N | Y |
| Bayh | Y | Y | Y | Y | N |
| **IOWA** | | | | | |
| Grassley | N | N | N | N | Y |
| Harkin | Y | Y | Y | Y | N |
| **KANSAS** | | | | | |
| Brownback | N | N | N | N | Y |
| Roberts | N | N | N | N | Y |
| **KENTUCKY** | | | | | |
| McConnell | N | N | N | N | Y |
| Bunning | N | N | N | N | Y |
| **LOUISIANA** | | | | | |
| Landrieu | Y | Y | Y | Y | Y |
| Vitter | N | N | N | N | Y |
| **MAINE** | | | | | |
| Snowe | N | Y | N | N | Y |
| Collins | N | Y | N | N | Y |
| **MARYLAND** | | | | | |
| Sarbanes | Y | Y | Y | Y | N |
| Mikulski | Y | Y | Y | Y | N |
| **MASSACHUSETTS** | | | | | |
| Kennedy | Y | Y | Y | Y | N |
| Kerry | Y | Y | Y | Y | N |
| **MICHIGAN** | | | | | |
| Levin | Y | Y | Y | Y | N |
| Stabenow | Y | Y | Y | Y | N |
| **MINNESOTA** | | | | | |
| Dayton | Y | Y | Y | Y | Y |
| Coleman | N | Y | Y | N | Y |
| **MISSISSIPPI** | | | | | |
| Cochran | N | N | N | N | Y |
| Lott | ? | ? | ? | ? | ? |
| **MISSOURI** | | | | | |
| Bond | N | N | N | N | Y |
| Talent | N | Y | Y | N | Y |
| **MONTANA** | | | | | |
| Baucus | N | Y | Y | N | Y |
| Burns | N | N | Y | N | Y |
| **NEBRASKA** | | | | | |
| Hagel | N | N | N | N | Y |
| Nelson | N | Y | Y | N | Y |
| **NEVADA** | | | | | |
| Reid | Y | Y | Y | Y | N |
| Ensign | N | N | N | N | Y |
| **NEW HAMPSHIRE** | | | | | |
| Gregg | N | N | N | N | Y |
| Sununu | N | N | N | N | Y |
| **NEW JERSEY** | | | | | |
| Corzine | ? | ? | ? | ? | ? |
| Lautenberg | Y | Y | Y | Y | N |
| **NEW MEXICO** | | | | | |
| Domenici | N | N | N | N | Y |
| Bingaman | Y | Y | Y | Y | Y |
| **NEW YORK** | | | | | |
| Schumer | Y | Y | Y | Y | Y |
| Clinton | Y | Y | Y | Y | Y |
| **NORTH CAROLINA** | | | | | |
| Dole | N | Y | N | N | Y |
| Burr | N | N | N | N | N |
| **NORTH DAKOTA** | | | | | |
| Conrad | Y | Y | Y | Y | N |
| Dorgan | Y | Y | Y | Y | N |
| **OHIO** | | | | | |
| DeWine | N | Y | N | N | Y |
| Voinovich | N | N | N | N | N |
| **OKLAHOMA** | | | | | |
| Inhofe | N | N | N | N | Y |
| Coburn | N | N | N | N | Y |
| **OREGON** | | | | | |
| Wyden | Y | Y | Y | Y | N |
| Smith | Y | N | N | N | Y |
| **PENNSYLVANIA** | | | | | |
| Specter | N | Y | N | N | Y |
| Santorum | N | Y | N | N | Y |
| **RHODE ISLAND** | | | | | |
| Reed | Y | Y | Y | Y | N |
| Chafee | N | Y | N | N | N |
| **SOUTH CAROLINA** | | | | | |
| Graham | N | N | N | N | Y |
| DeMint | N | N | N | N | Y |
| **SOUTH DAKOTA** | | | | | |
| Johnson | Y | Y | Y | Y | Y |
| Thune | N | N | N | N | Y |
| **TENNESSEE** | | | | | |
| Frist | N | N | N | N | Y |
| Alexander | N | N | N | N | Y |
| **TEXAS** | | | | | |
| Hutchison | N | Y | N | N | Y |
| Cornyn | N | N | N | N | Y |
| **UTAH** | | | | | |
| Hatch | N | N | N | N | Y |
| Bennett | N | N | N | N | Y |
| **VERMONT** | | | | | |
| Leahy | Y | Y | Y | Y | N |
| *Jeffords* | Y | Y | Y | Y | N |
| **VIRGINIA** | | | | | |
| Warner | N | N | N | N | Y |
| Allen | N | N | N | N | Y |
| **WASHINGTON** | | | | | |
| Murray | Y | Y | Y | Y | N |
| Cantwell | Y | Y | Y | Y | Y |
| **WEST VIRGINIA** | | | | | |
| Byrd | Y | Y | Y | Y | N |
| Rockefeller | Y | Y | Y | Y | N |
| **WISCONSIN** | | | | | |
| Kohl | Y | Y | Y | Y | N |
| Feingold | Y | Y | Y | Y | N |
| **WYOMING** | | | | | |
| Thomas | N | N | N | N | Y |
| Enzi | N | N | N | N | Y |

**KEY**   Republicans   Democrats   *Independents*

| | | |
|---|---|---|
| **Y** Voted for (yea) | **X** Paired against | **C** Voted "present" to avoid possible conflict of interest |
| **#** Paired for | **–** Announced against | |
| **+** Announced for | **P** Voted "present" | **?** Did not vote or otherwise make a position known |
| **N** Voted against (nay) | | |

# IN THE SENATE | By Vote Number

**348.** H J Res 72. Fiscal 2006 Continuing Resolution/Community Services Block Grant Funding. Harkin, D-Iowa, amendment that would increase the amount appropriated for the Community Services Block Grant, ensuring that its funding for Oct. 1, 2005, through Dec. 17, 2005, would continue at no less than the fiscal 2005 level. Rejected 46-50: R 4-50; D 41-0 (ND 37-0, SD 4-0); I 1-0. (Subsequently, the joint resolution was passed by voice vote.) Nov. 18, 2005.

**349.** HR 3010. Fiscal 2006 Labor-HHS-Education Appropriations/ LIHEAP. Specter, R-Pa., motion to instruct conferees to insist that $2.2 billion be available for the Low Income Home Energy Heating Assistance Program (LIHEAP), with the funding designated as emergency spending. Motion agreed to 66-28: R 30-24; D 35-4 (ND 33-2, SD 2-2); I 1-0. Nov. 18, 2005.

**350.** HR 3010. Fiscal 2006 Labor-HHS-Education Appropriations/ NIH Funding. Durbin, D-Ill., motion to instruct conferees to insist that the conference report retain the $1 billion increase for the National Institutes of Health (NIH) called for in the Senate-passed bill. Motion agreed to 58-36: R 18-36; D 39-0 (ND 35-0, SD 4-0); I 1-0. Nov. 18, 2005.

| | 348 | 349 | 350 | | | 348 | 349 | 350 |
|---|---|---|---|---|---|---|---|---|
| **ALABAMA** | | | | | **MONTANA** | | | |
| Shelby | N | Y | N | | Baucus | Y | Y | Y |
| Sessions | N | N | N | | Burns | N | Y | N |
| **ALASKA** | | | | | **NEBRASKA** | | | |
| Stevens | N | Y | N | | Hagel | N | Y | N |
| Murkowski | N | Y | N | | Nelson | Y | + | + |
| **ARIZONA** | | | | | **NEVADA** | | | |
| McCain | N | N | N | | Reid | Y | Y | Y |
| Kyl | N | N | N | | Ensign | N | ? | ? |
| **ARKANSAS** | | | | | **NEW HAMPSHIRE** | | | |
| Lincoln | Y | N | Y | | Gregg | N | N | N |
| Pryor | Y | N | Y | | Sununu | N | Y | N |
| **CALIFORNIA** | | | | | **NEW JERSEY** | | | |
| Feinstein | Y | Y | Y | | Corzine | ? | ? | ? |
| Boxer | Y | Y | Y | | Lautenberg | Y | Y | Y |
| **COLORADO** | | | | | **NEW MEXICO** | | | |
| Allard | N | N | N | | Domenici | N | Y | N |
| Salazar | Y | Y | Y | | Bingaman | Y | Y | Y |
| **CONNECTICUT** | | | | | **NEW YORK** | | | |
| Dodd | Y | Y | Y | | Schumer | Y | Y | Y |
| Lieberman | Y | Y | Y | | Clinton | Y | Y | Y |
| **DELAWARE** | | | | | **NORTH CAROLINA** | | | |
| Biden | Y | ? | ? | | Dole | N | Y | N |
| Carper | Y | N | Y | | Burr | N | Y | Y |
| **FLORIDA** | | | | | **NORTH DAKOTA** | | | |
| Nelson | Y | Y | Y | | Conrad | Y | Y | Y |
| Martinez | N | Y | N | | Dorgan | Y | Y | Y |
| **GEORGIA** | | | | | **OHIO** | | | |
| Chambliss | N | N | Y | | DeWine | N | Y | Y |
| Isakson | N | N | Y | | Voinovich | N | Y | N |
| **HAWAII** | | | | | **OKLAHOMA** | | | |
| Inouye | ? | ? | ? | | Inhofe | N | N | N |
| Akaka | Y | Y | Y | | Coburn | N | Y | N |
| **IDAHO** | | | | | **OREGON** | | | |
| Craig | N | N | N | | Wyden | Y | Y | Y |
| Crapo | N | N | N | | Smith | ? | Y | Y |
| **ILLINOIS** | | | | | **PENNSYLVANIA** | | | |
| Durbin | Y | Y | Y | | Specter | Y | Y | Y |
| Obama | Y | Y | Y | | Santorum | N | Y | N |
| **INDIANA** | | | | | **RHODE ISLAND** | | | |
| Lugar | N | Y | Y | | Reed | Y | N | Y |
| Bayh | Y | Y | Y | | Chafee | Y | N | Y |
| **IOWA** | | | | | **SOUTH CAROLINA** | | | |
| Grassley | N | Y | N | | Graham | N | N | N |
| Harkin | Y | Y | Y | | DeMint | N | N | N |
| **KANSAS** | | | | | **SOUTH DAKOTA** | | | |
| Brownback | N | N | N | | Johnson | Y | Y | Y |
| Roberts | N | N | Y | | Thune | N | Y | N |
| **KENTUCKY** | | | | | **TENNESSEE** | | | |
| McConnell | N | N | N | | Frist | N | Y | N |
| Bunning | N | N | N | | Alexander | N | N | Y |
| **LOUISIANA** | | | | | **TEXAS** | | | |
| Landrieu | Y | Y | Y | | Hutchison | N | Y | Y |
| Vitter | N | N | N | | Cornyn | N | N | Y |
| **MAINE** | | | | | **UTAH** | | | |
| Snowe | Y | Y | Y | | Hatch | N | Y | N |
| Collins | Y | Y | Y | | Bennett | N | Y | N |
| **MARYLAND** | | | | | **VERMONT** | | | |
| Sarbanes | Y | Y | Y | | Leahy | Y | Y | Y |
| Mikulski | Y | Y | Y | | *Jeffords* | Y | Y | Y |
| **MASSACHUSETTS** | | | | | **VIRGINIA** | | | |
| Kennedy | Y | Y | Y | | Warner | N | Y | Y |
| Kerry | Y | Y | Y | | Allen | N | N | Y |
| **MICHIGAN** | | | | | **WASHINGTON** | | | |
| Levin | Y | Y | Y | | Murray | Y | Y | Y |
| Stabenow | + | + | + | | Cantwell | Y | Y | Y |
| **MINNESOTA** | | | | | **WEST VIRGINIA** | | | |
| Dayton | Y | Y | Y | | Byrd | Y | Y | Y |
| Coleman | N | Y | Y | | Rockefeller | Y | Y | Y |
| **MISSISSIPPI** | | | | | **WISCONSIN** | | | |
| Cochran | N | Y | N | | Kohl | Y | Y | Y |
| Lott | N | N | N | | Feingold | Y | Y | Y |
| **MISSOURI** | | | | | **WYOMING** | | | |
| Bond | N | Y | N | | Thomas | N | N | N |
| Talent | N | Y | N | | Enzi | N | N | N |

| KEY | Republicans | Democrats | *Independents* | |
|---|---|---|---|---|
| Y | Voted for (yea) | X | Paired against | C | Voted "present" to avoid possible conflict of interest |
| # | Paired for | – | Announced against | |
| + | Announced for | P | Voted "present" | ? | Did not vote or otherwise make a position known |
| N | Voted against (nay) | | | |

# IN THE SENATE | By Vote Number

**351.** **S 1932. Budget Reconciliation/Motion to Instruct.** Carper, D-Del., motion to instruct conferees to insist that the conference report not include any provisions related to the Temporary Assistance for Needy Families (TANF) program, particularly those that would increase work hours for single mothers or cut child care funding. Motion agreed to 64-27: R 24-27; D 39-0 (ND 35-0, SD 4-0); I 1-0. Dec. 14, 2005.

**352.** **S 1932. Budget Reconciliation/Motion to Instruct.** Baucus, D-Mont., motion to instruct conferees to insist that the conference report not contain any provisions that would increase Medicaid beneficiary cost-sharing or otherwise increase costs for Medicaid recipients. Motion agreed to 75-16: R 35-16; D 39-0 (ND 35-0, SD 4-0); I 1-0. Dec. 14, 2005.

**353.** **S 1932. Budget Reconciliation/Motion to Instruct.** Harkin, D-Iowa, motion to instruct conferees to insist that the conference report not contain cuts to any federal food assistance programs, including the federal food stamp program. Motion agreed to 66-26: R 26-26; D 39-0 (ND 35-0, SD 4-0); I 1-0. Dec. 14, 2005.

**354.** **S 1932. Budget Reconciliation/Motion to Instruct.** DeWine, R-Ohio, motion to instruct conferees to insist that the conference report not include any provisions to repeal the Continued Dumping and Subsidies Offset Act. Motion agreed to 71-20: R 30-20; D 40-0 (ND 36-0, SD 4-0); I 1-0. Dec. 15, 2005.

**355.** **S 1932. Budget Reconciliation/Motion to Instruct.** Kohl, D-Wis., motion to instruct conferees not to include in the conference report any provision that would reduce states' access to funding for the child support programs under existing Social Security law. Motion agreed to 75-16: R 34-16; D 40-0 (ND 36-0, SD 4-0); I 1-0. Dec. 15, 2005.

**356.** **S 1932. Budget Reconciliation/Motion to Instruct.** Kennedy, D-Mass., motion to instruct conferees to insist that the conference report include provisions to increase need-based financial aid for college tuition. Motion agreed to 83-8: R 42-8; D 40-0 (ND 36-0, SD 4-0); I 1-0. Dec. 15, 2005.

**357.** **S 1932. Budget Reconciliation/Motion to Instruct.** Reed, D-R.I., motion to instruct conferees to insist that the conference report include $2.9 billion for the Low-Income Home Energy Assistance Program. Motion agreed to 63-28: R 23-27; D 39-1 (ND 35-1, SD 4-0); I 1-0. Dec. 15, 2005.

**358.** **HR 3199. "Patriot Act" Reauthorization/Cloture.** Motion to invoke cloture (thus limiting debate) on the conference report accompanying the bill that would make permanent 14 of the 16 provisions of the law known as the Patriot Act (PL 107-56) set to expire at the end of the year, and extend for four years the provisions on access to business and other records and "roving" wiretaps. Motion rejected 52-47: R 50-5; D 2-41 (ND 2-37, SD 0-4); I 0-1. Three-fifths of the total Senate (60) is required to invoke cloture. A "yea" was a vote in support of the president's position. Dec. 16, 2005.

| | 351 | 352 | 353 | 354 | 355 | 356 | 357 | 358 | | 351 | 352 | 353 | 354 | 355 | 356 | 357 | 358 |
|---|---|---|---|---|---|---|---|---|---|---|---|---|---|---|---|---|---|
| **ALABAMA** | | | | | | | | | **MONTANA** | | | | | | | | |
| Shelby | N | N | N | Y | Y | Y | N | Y | Baucus | Y | Y | Y | Y | Y | Y | Y | N |
| Sessions | N | N | N | Y | Y | Y | N | Y | Burns | Y | Y | Y | Y | Y | Y | Y | Y |
| **ALASKA** | | | | | | | | | **NEBRASKA** | | | | | | | | |
| Stevens | Y | Y | Y | Y | Y | Y | Y | Y | Hagel | N | N | Y | N | N | N | N | N |
| Murkowski | Y | Y | Y | N | Y | Y | Y | N | Nelson | Y | Y | Y | Y | Y | Y | N | Y |
| **ARIZONA** | | | | | | | | | **NEVADA** | | | | | | | | |
| McCain | ? | ? | ? | N | Y | Y | Y | Y | Reid | Y | Y | Y | Y | Y | Y | Y | N |
| Kyl | Y | Y | N | N | Y | N | Y | N | Ensign | N | N | N | N | N | Y | N | Y |
| **ARKANSAS** | | | | | | | | | **NEW HAMPSHIRE** | | | | | | | | |
| Lincoln | Y | Y | Y | Y | Y | Y | Y | N | Gregg | N | Y | N | N | N | N | N | Y |
| Pryor | Y | Y | Y | Y | Y | Y | Y | N | Sununu | N | N | N | N | N | N | N | Y |
| **CALIFORNIA** | | | | | | | | | **NEW JERSEY** | | | | | | | | |
| Feinstein | Y | Y | Y | Y | Y | Y | Y | N | Corzine | Y | Y | Y | Y | Y | Y | Y | N |
| Boxer | + | + | + | + | + | + | + | N | Lautenberg | Y | Y | Y | Y | Y | Y | Y | N |
| **COLORADO** | | | | | | | | | **NEW MEXICO** | | | | | | | | |
| Allard | N | N | N | N | Y | N | Y | N | Domenici | ? | ? | N | Y | Y | Y | Y | Y |
| Salazar | Y | Y | Y | Y | Y | Y | Y | N | Bingaman | Y | Y | Y | Y | Y | Y | Y | N |
| **CONNECTICUT** | | | | | | | | | **NEW YORK** | | | | | | | | |
| Dodd | ? | ? | ? | ? | ? | ? | ? | ? | Schumer | Y | Y | Y | Y | Y | Y | Y | N |
| Lieberman | + | + | + | Y | Y | Y | Y | N | Clinton | Y | Y | Y | Y | Y | Y | Y | N |
| **DELAWARE** | | | | | | | | | **NORTH CAROLINA** | | | | | | | | |
| Biden | ? | ? | ? | ? | ? | ? | N | N | Dole | Y | Y | Y | Y | Y | Y | Y | N |
| Carper | Y | Y | Y | Y | Y | Y | Y | N | Burr | N | N | Y | Y | N | N | Y | Y |
| **FLORIDA** | | | | | | | | | **NORTH DAKOTA** | | | | | | | | |
| Nelson | Y | Y | Y | Y | Y | Y | Y | N | Conrad | Y | Y | Y | Y | Y | Y | Y | N |
| Martinez | N | Y | Y | Y | N | Y | Y | Y | Dorgan | Y | Y | Y | Y | Y | Y | Y | N |
| **GEORGIA** | | | | | | | | | **OHIO** | | | | | | | | |
| Chambliss | ? | ? | ? | ? | ? | ? | ? | Y | DeWine | Y | Y | Y | Y | Y | Y | Y | Y |
| Isakson | N | N | N | ? | ? | ? | ? | Y | Voinovich | Y | N | Y | Y | Y | Y | Y | N |
| **HAWAII** | | | | | | | | | **OKLAHOMA** | | | | | | | | |
| Inouye | Y | Y | Y | Y | Y | Y | Y | N | Inhofe | N | N | N | N | N | N | N | Y |
| Akaka | Y | Y | Y | Y | Y | Y | Y | N | Coburn | N | N | N | Y | Y | N | N | Y |
| **IDAHO** | | | | | | | | | **OREGON** | | | | | | | | |
| Craig | N | Y | N | Y | Y | Y | N | N | Wyden | Y | Y | Y | Y | Y | Y | Y | N |
| Crapo | N | Y | N | Y | Y | Y | Y | Y | Smith | Y | Y | Y | Y | Y | Y | Y | Y |
| **ILLINOIS** | | | | | | | | | **PENNSYLVANIA** | | | | | | | | |
| Durbin | Y | Y | Y | Y | Y | Y | Y | N | Specter | Y | Y | Y | Y | Y | Y | Y | N |
| Obama | Y | Y | Y | Y | Y | Y | Y | N | Santorum | Y | Y | Y | + | ? | ? | + | Y |
| **INDIANA** | | | | | | | | | **RHODE ISLAND** | | | | | | | | |
| Lugar | Y | Y | Y | N | Y | Y | Y | Y | Reed | Y | Y | Y | Y | Y | Y | Y | N |
| Bayh | Y | Y | Y | Y | Y | Y | Y | N | Chafee | Y | Y | Y | N | Y | Y | Y | N |
| **IOWA** | | | | | | | | | **SOUTH CAROLINA** | | | | | | | | |
| Grassley | Y | Y | Y | N | Y | Y | Y | Y | Graham | ? | ? | ? | ? | ? | ? | ? | Y |
| Harkin | Y | Y | Y | Y | Y | Y | Y | N | DeMint | N | N | N | N | N | N | N | Y |
| **KANSAS** | | | | | | | | | **SOUTH DAKOTA** | | | | | | | | |
| Brownback | N | Y | Y | N | N | Y | N | Y | Johnson | Y | Y | Y | Y | Y | Y | Y | Y |
| Roberts | Y | Y | Y | N | Y | Y | N | Y | Thune | Y | Y | Y | Y | Y | Y | Y | Y |
| **KENTUCKY** | | | | | | | | | **TENNESSEE** | | | | | | | | |
| McConnell | N | Y | N | N | N | Y | N | Y | Frist | Y | Y | Y | Y | Y | Y | Y | Y |
| Bunning | N | N | N | Y | N | Y | N | Y | Alexander | Y | Y | N | N | Y | N | Y | N |
| **LOUISIANA** | | | | | | | | | **TEXAS** | | | | | | | | |
| Landrieu | Y | Y | Y | Y | Y | Y | Y | N | Hutchison | Y | Y | N | Y | Y | Y | N | Y |
| Vitter | N | Y | N | + | ? | ? | ? | Y | Cornyn | N | N | N | Y | Y | Y | N | Y |
| **MAINE** | | | | | | | | | **UTAH** | | | | | | | | |
| Snowe | Y | Y | Y | Y | Y | Y | Y | Y | Hatch | Y | Y | Y | Y | Y | N | Y | N |
| Collins | Y | Y | Y | Y | Y | Y | Y | Y | Bennett | Y | Y | Y | Y | Y | N | Y | N |
| **MARYLAND** | | | | | | | | | **VERMONT** | | | | | | | | |
| Sarbanes | Y | Y | Y | Y | Y | Y | Y | N | Leahy | Y | Y | Y | Y | Y | Y | Y | N |
| Mikulski | Y | Y | Y | Y | Y | Y | Y | N | Jeffords | Y | Y | Y | Y | Y | Y | Y | N |
| **MASSACHUSETTS** | | | | | | | | | **VIRGINIA** | | | | | | | | |
| Kennedy | Y | Y | Y | Y | Y | Y | Y | N | Warner | Y | Y | Y | Y | Y | Y | Y | Y |
| Kerry | Y | Y | Y | Y | Y | Y | Y | N | Allen | N | N | N | Y | N | Y | N | Y |
| **MICHIGAN** | | | | | | | | | **WASHINGTON** | | | | | | | | |
| Levin | Y | Y | Y | Y | Y | Y | Y | N | Murray | Y | Y | Y | Y | Y | Y | Y | N |
| Stabenow | Y | Y | Y | Y | Y | Y | Y | N | Cantwell | ? | ? | ? | ? | ? | ? | ? | N |
| **MINNESOTA** | | | | | | | | | **WEST VIRGINIA** | | | | | | | | |
| Dayton | Y | Y | Y | Y | Y | Y | Y | N | Byrd | Y | Y | Y | Y | Y | Y | Y | N |
| Coleman | Y | Y | Y | Y | Y | Y | Y | Y | Rockefeller | Y | Y | Y | Y | Y | Y | Y | N |
| **MISSISSIPPI** | | | | | | | | | **WISCONSIN** | | | | | | | | |
| Cochran | N | Y | N | N | N | Y | N | Y | Kohl | Y | Y | Y | Y | Y | Y | Y | N |
| Lott | N | N | N | Y | N | Y | N | Y | Feingold | Y | Y | Y | Y | Y | Y | Y | N |
| **MISSOURI** | | | | | | | | | **WYOMING** | | | | | | | | |
| Bond | N | Y | N | N | N | N | N | Y | Thomas | N | Y | N | N | Y | Y | N | Y |
| Talent | N | Y | Y | Y | Y | Y | Y | Y | Enzi | N | Y | N | Y | Y | Y | N | Y |

**KEY**   Republicans   Democrats   *Independents*

| | | |
|---|---|---|
| **Y** Voted for (yea) | **X** Paired against | **C** Voted "present" to avoid possible conflict of interest |
| **#** Paired for | **−** Announced against | **?** Did not vote or otherwise make a position known |
| **+** Announced for | **P** Voted "present" | |
| **N** Voted against (nay) | | |

# IN THE SENATE | By Vote Number

**359.** **HR 2863. Fiscal 2006 Defense Appropriations/Motion to Proceed.** Frist, R-Tenn., motion to proceed to consideration of the conference report on the bill that would appropriate $453.5 billion for defense spending in fiscal 2006, including $50 billion for operations in Iraq and Afghanistan. It also would require a 1 percent across-the-board cut to all fiscal 2006 discretionary spending except Veterans Administration funding that was added to the legislation. It would provide $29 billion for disaster assistance to hurricane-damaged areas and $3.8 billion for flu preparedness. It would allow oil and gas leasing in the Arctic National Wildlife Refuge. Motion agreed to 94-1: R 53-0; D 41-0 (ND 37-0, SD 4-0); I 0-1. Dec. 19, 2005.

**360.** **HR 1815. Fiscal 2006 Defense Authorization/Motion to Proceed.** Frist, R-Tenn., motion to proceed to consideration of the conference report on the bill that would authorize $441.5 billion for defense programs and $50 billion for military operations in Iraq and Afghanistan. Motion agreed to 95-0: R 53-0; D 41-0 (ND 37-0, SD 4-0); I 1-0. Dec. 19, 2005.

**361.** **S 1932. Budget Reconciliation/Motion to Proceed.** Frist, R-Tenn., motion to proceed to consideration of the conference report on the bill that would make changes to programs for a net savings in the federal budget of $38.8 billion over five years. Motion agreed to 86-9: R 52-1; D 34-7 (ND 30-7, SD 4-0); I 0-1. Dec. 19, 2005.

**362.** **S 1932. Budget Reconciliation/Budget Act Waiver.** Gregg, R-N.H., motion to waive the Budget Act with respect to the Conrad, D-N.D., points of order against two reporting provisions and Medicaid liability provisions in the conference report on the bill that would make changes to programs for a net savings in the federal budget of $38.8 billion over five years. Motion rejected 52-48: R 52-3; D 0-44 (ND 0-40, SD 0-4); I 0-1. A three-fifths majority vote (60) of the total Senate is required to waive the Budget Act. (Subsequently, the chair upheld the points of order, and the provisions were struck.) Dec. 21, 2005.

**363.** **S 1932. Budget Reconciliation/Concur With House Amendment.** Gregg, R-N.H., motion to concur in the House amendment with a Senate amendment on the bill that would make changes to programs for a net savings of $38.8 billion over five years. The Senate amendment would strike two reporting provisions and language that would allow for a Medicaid liability provision regarding hospitals that deny treatment to low-income individuals unable to pay. Motion agreed to, with Vice President Cheney casting a "yea" vote to break the tie, 50-50: R 50-5; D 0-44 (ND 0-40, SD 0-4); I 0-1. A "yea" was a vote in support of the president's position. Dec. 21, 2005.

| | 359 | 360 | 361 | 362 | 363 | | 359 | 360 | 361 | 362 | 363 |
|---|---|---|---|---|---|---|---|---|---|---|---|
| **ALABAMA** | | | | | | **MONTANA** | | | | | |
| Shelby | Y | Y | Y | Y | Y | Baucus | Y | Y | Y | N | N |
| Sessions | Y | Y | Y | Y | Y | Burns | Y | Y | Y | Y | Y |
| **ALASKA** | | | | | | **NEBRASKA** | | | | | |
| Stevens | Y | Y | Y | Y | Y | Hagel | Y | Y | Y | Y | Y |
| Murkowski | Y | Y | Y | Y | Y | Nelson | Y | Y | Y | N | N |
| **ARIZONA** | | | | | | **NEVADA** | | | | | |
| McCain | ? | ? | ? | Y | Y | Reid | Y | Y | Y | N | N |
| Kyl | Y | Y | Y | Y | Y | Ensign | Y | Y | Y | Y | Y |
| **ARKANSAS** | | | | | | **NEW HAMPSHIRE** | | | | | |
| Lincoln | Y | Y | Y | N | N | Gregg | Y | Y | Y | Y | Y |
| Pryor | Y | Y | Y | N | N | Sununu | Y | Y | Y | Y | Y |
| **CALIFORNIA** | | | | | | **NEW JERSEY** | | | | | |
| Feinstein | Y | Y | Y | N | N | Corzine | ? | ? | ? | N | N |
| Boxer | Y | Y | Y | N | N | Lautenberg | Y | Y | Y | N | N |
| **COLORADO** | | | | | | **NEW MEXICO** | | | | | |
| Allard | Y | Y | Y | Y | Y | Domenici | Y | Y | Y | Y | Y |
| Salazar | Y | Y | Y | N | N | Bingaman | Y | Y | Y | N | N |
| **CONNECTICUT** | | | | | | **NEW YORK** | | | | | |
| Dodd | ? | ? | ? | N | N | Schumer | Y | Y | Y | N | N |
| Lieberman | Y | Y | Y | N | N | Clinton | Y | Y | N | N | N |
| **DELAWARE** | | | | | | **NORTH CAROLINA** | | | | | |
| Biden | ? | ? | ? | N | N | Dole | Y | Y | Y | Y | Y |
| Carper | Y | Y | Y | N | N | Burr | ? | ? | ? | Y | Y |
| **FLORIDA** | | | | | | **NORTH DAKOTA** | | | | | |
| Nelson | Y | Y | Y | N | N | Conrad | Y | Y | Y | N | N |
| Martinez | Y | Y | Y | Y | Y | Dorgan | Y | Y | Y | N | N |
| **GEORGIA** | | | | | | **OHIO** | | | | | |
| Chambliss | Y | Y | Y | Y | Y | DeWine | Y | Y | Y | N | N |
| Isakson | Y | Y | Y | Y | Y | Voinovich | Y | Y | Y | Y | Y |
| **HAWAII** | | | | | | **OKLAHOMA** | | | | | |
| Inouye | Y | Y | Y | N | N | Inhofe | Y | Y | Y | Y | Y |
| Akaka | Y | Y | Y | N | N | Coburn | Y | Y | Y | Y | Y |
| **IDAHO** | | | | | | **OREGON** | | | | | |
| Craig | Y | Y | Y | Y | Y | Wyden | Y | Y | Y | N | N |
| Crapo | Y | Y | Y | Y | Y | Smith | Y | Y | Y | N | N |
| **ILLINOIS** | | | | | | **PENNSYLVANIA** | | | | | |
| Durbin | Y | Y | N | N | N | Specter | Y | Y | Y | Y | Y |
| Obama | Y | Y | N | N | N | Santorum | Y | Y | Y | Y | Y |
| **INDIANA** | | | | | | **RHODE ISLAND** | | | | | |
| Lugar | Y | Y | Y | Y | Y | Reed | Y | Y | Y | N | N |
| Bayh | Y | Y | Y | N | N | Chafee | Y | Y | Y | N | N |
| **IOWA** | | | | | | **SOUTH CAROLINA** | | | | | |
| Grassley | Y | Y | Y | Y | Y | Graham | Y | Y | Y | Y | Y |
| Harkin | Y | Y | N | N | N | DeMint | Y | Y | Y | Y | Y |
| **KANSAS** | | | | | | **SOUTH DAKOTA** | | | | | |
| Brownback | Y | Y | Y | Y | Y | Johnson | Y | Y | Y | N | N |
| Roberts | Y | Y | Y | Y | Y | Thune | Y | Y | Y | Y | Y |
| **KENTUCKY** | | | | | | **TENNESSEE** | | | | | |
| McConnell | Y | Y | Y | Y | Y | Frist | Y | Y | Y | Y | Y |
| Bunning | Y | Y | Y | Y | Y | Alexander | Y | Y | Y | Y | Y |
| **LOUISIANA** | | | | | | **TEXAS** | | | | | |
| Landrieu | Y | Y | Y | N | N | Hutchison | Y | Y | Y | Y | Y |
| Vitter | Y | Y | Y | Y | Y | Cornyn | Y | Y | Y | Y | Y |
| **MAINE** | | | | | | **UTAH** | | | | | |
| Snowe | Y | Y | N | N | N | Hatch | Y | Y | Y | Y | Y |
| Collins | Y | Y | Y | N | N | Bennett | Y | Y | Y | Y | Y |
| **MARYLAND** | | | | | | **VERMONT** | | | | | |
| Sarbanes | Y | Y | Y | N | N | Leahy | Y | Y | Y | N | N |
| Mikulski | Y | Y | Y | N | N | Jeffords | N | Y | N | N | N |
| **MASSACHUSETTS** | | | | | | **VIRGINIA** | | | | | |
| Kennedy | Y | Y | Y | N | N | Warner | Y | Y | Y | Y | Y |
| Kerry | Y | Y | N | N | N | Allen | Y | Y | Y | Y | Y |
| **MICHIGAN** | | | | | | **WASHINGTON** | | | | | |
| Levin | Y | Y | Y | N | N | Murray | Y | Y | N | N | N |
| Stabenow | Y | Y | Y | N | N | Cantwell | Y | Y | N | N | N |
| **MINNESOTA** | | | | | | **WEST VIRGINIA** | | | | | |
| Dayton | Y | Y | Y | N | N | Byrd | Y | Y | Y | N | N |
| Coleman | Y | Y | Y | Y | Y | Rockefeller | Y | Y | Y | N | N |
| **MISSISSIPPI** | | | | | | **WISCONSIN** | | | | | |
| Cochran | Y | Y | Y | Y | Y | Kohl | Y | Y | Y | N | N |
| Lott | Y | Y | Y | Y | Y | Feingold | Y | Y | N | N | N |
| **MISSOURI** | | | | | | **WYOMING** | | | | | |
| Bond | Y | Y | Y | Y | Y | Thomas | Y | Y | Y | Y | Y |
| Talent | Y | Y | Y | Y | Y | Enzi | Y | Y | Y | Y | Y |

**KEY**   **Republicans**   Democrats   *Independents*

| | | |
|---|---|---|
| Y Voted for (yea) | X Paired against | C Voted "present" to avoid possible conflict of interest |
| # Paired for | − Announced against | |
| + Announced for | P Voted "present" | ? Did not vote or otherwise make a position known |
| N Voted against (nay) | | |

# IN THE SENATE | By Vote Number

**364.** **HR 2863. Fiscal 2006 Defense Appropriations/Cloture.** Motion to invoke cloture (thus limiting debate) on the conference report on the bill that would appropriate $453.5 billion for defense spending, including $50 billion for operations in Iraq and Afghanistan. Motion rejected 56-44: R 52-3; D 4-40 (ND 3-37, SD 1-3); I 0-1. Three-fifths of the total Senate (60) is required to invoke cloture. A "yea" was a vote in support of the president's position. Dec. 21, 2005.

**365.** **HR 2863. Fiscal 2006 Defense Appropriations/Enrolling Resolution.** Adoption of the concurrent resolution (S Con Res 74) that would instruct the Clerk of the House to strike certain provisions from the conference report accompanying the bill. Those provisions would allow oil drilling in the Arctic National Wildlife Refuge and provide additional funding for hurricane recovery and other purposes. Adopted 48-45: R 7-44; D 40-1 (ND 37-0, SD 3-1); I 1-0. Dec. 21, 2005.

**366.** **HR 2863. Fiscal 2006 Defense Appropriations/Conference Report.** Adoption of the conference report on the bill that would appropriate $453.5 billion for Defense spending, including $50 billion for operations in Iraq and Afghanistan. The total includes $123.6 billion for operations and maintenance, $76.5 billion for procurement and $72.1 billion for research and development. It would require a 1 percent across-the-board cut to all fiscal 2006 discretionary spending except Veterans Administration funding that was added to the legislation. It would provide $29 billion for disaster assistance to hurricane-damaged areas and $3.8 billion for flu preparedness. Adopted (thus cleared for the president, pending House adoption of S Con Res 74) 93-0: R 51-0; D 41-0 (ND 37-0, SD 4-0); I 1-0. (Subsequently, the House adopted S Con Res 74 by voice vote Dec. 22.) Dec. 21, 2005.

| | 364 | 365 | 366 | | | 364 | 365 | 366 |
|---|---|---|---|---|---|---|---|---|
| **ALABAMA** | | | | | **MONTANA** | | | |
| Shelby | Y | N | Y | | Baucus | N | Y | Y |
| Sessions | Y | N | Y | | Burns | Y | N | Y |
| **ALASKA** | | | | | **NEBRASKA** | | | |
| Stevens | Y | N | Y | | Hagel | Y | N | Y |
| Murkowski | Y | N | Y | | Nelson | Y | Y | Y |
| **ARIZONA** | | | | | **NEVADA** | | | |
| McCain | Y | ? | ? | | Reid | N | Y | Y |
| Kyl | Y | N | Y | | Ensign | Y | N | Y |
| **ARKANSAS** | | | | | **NEW HAMPSHIRE** | | | |
| Lincoln | N | Y | Y | | Gregg | Y | ? | ? |
| Pryor | N | Y | Y | | Sununu | Y | N | Y |
| **CALIFORNIA** | | | | | **NEW JERSEY** | | | |
| Feinstein | N | Y | Y | | Corzine | N | ? | ? |
| Boxer | N | Y | Y | | Lautenberg | N | Y | Y |
| **COLORADO** | | | | | **NEW MEXICO** | | | |
| Allard | Y | N | Y | | Domenici | Y | N | Y |
| Salazar | N | Y | Y | | Bingaman | N | Y | Y |
| **CONNECTICUT** | | | | | **NEW YORK** | | | |
| Dodd | N | ? | ? | | Schumer | N | Y | Y |
| Lieberman | N | Y | Y | | Clinton | N | Y | Y |
| **DELAWARE** | | | | | **NORTH CAROLINA** | | | |
| Biden | N | Y | Y | | Dole | Y | N | Y |
| Carper | N | Y | Y | | Burr | Y | N | Y |
| **FLORIDA** | | | | | **NORTH DAKOTA** | | | |
| Nelson | N | Y | Y | | Conrad | N | Y | Y |
| Martinez | Y | N | Y | | Dorgan | N | Y | Y |
| **GEORGIA** | | | | | **OHIO** | | | |
| Chambliss | Y | N | Y | | DeWine | N | Y | Y |
| Isakson | Y | N | Y | | Voinovich | Y | N | Y |
| **HAWAII** | | | | | **OKLAHOMA** | | | |
| Inouye | Y | Y | Y | | Inhofe | Y | N | Y |
| Akaka | Y | Y | Y | | Coburn | Y | N | Y |
| **IDAHO** | | | | | **OREGON** | | | |
| Craig | Y | N | Y | | Wyden | N | Y | Y |
| Crapo | Y | N | Y | | Smith | Y | Y | Y |
| **ILLINOIS** | | | | | **PENNSYLVANIA** | | | |
| Durbin | N | Y | Y | | Specter | Y | Y | Y |
| Obama | N | Y | Y | | Santorum | Y | N | Y |
| **INDIANA** | | | | | **RHODE ISLAND** | | | |
| Lugar | Y | Y | Y | | Reed | N | Y | Y |
| Bayh | N | Y | Y | | Chafee | N | ? | ? |
| **IOWA** | | | | | **SOUTH CAROLINA** | | | |
| Grassley | Y | N | Y | | Graham | Y | N | Y |
| Harkin | N | ? | ? | | DeMint | Y | – | ? |
| **KANSAS** | | | | | **SOUTH DAKOTA** | | | |
| Brownback | Y | N | Y | | Johnson | N | Y | Y |
| Roberts | Y | N | Y | | Thune | Y | N | Y |
| **KENTUCKY** | | | | | **TENNESSEE** | | | |
| McConnell | Y | N | Y | | Frist | N | N | Y |
| Bunning | Y | N | Y | | Alexander | Y | N | Y |
| **LOUISIANA** | | | | | **TEXAS** | | | |
| Landrieu | Y | N | Y | | Hutchison | Y | N | Y |
| Vitter | Y | N | Y | | Cornyn | Y | N | Y |
| **MAINE** | | | | | **UTAH** | | | |
| Snowe | Y | Y | Y | | Hatch | Y | N | Y |
| Collins | Y | Y | Y | | Bennett | Y | N | Y |
| **MARYLAND** | | | | | **VERMONT** | | | |
| Sarbanes | N | Y | Y | | Leahy | N | Y | Y |
| Mikulski | N | Y | Y | | Jeffords | N | Y | Y |
| **MASSACHUSETTS** | | | | | **VIRGINIA** | | | |
| Kennedy | N | Y | Y | | Warner | Y | N | Y |
| Kerry | N | Y | Y | | Allen | Y | N | Y |
| **MICHIGAN** | | | | | **WASHINGTON** | | | |
| Levin | N | Y | Y | | Murray | N | Y | Y |
| Stabenow | N | Y | Y | | Cantwell | N | Y | Y |
| **MINNESOTA** | | | | | **WEST VIRGINIA** | | | |
| Dayton | N | Y | Y | | Byrd | N | Y | Y |
| Coleman | Y | Y | Y | | Rockefeller | N | Y | Y |
| **MISSISSIPPI** | | | | | **WISCONSIN** | | | |
| Cochran | Y | N | Y | | Kohl | N | Y | Y |
| Lott | Y | N | Y | | Feingold | N | Y | Y |
| **MISSOURI** | | | | | **WYOMING** | | | |
| Bond | Y | N | Y | | Thomas | Y | N | Y |
| Talent | Y | N | Y | | Enzi | Y | N | Y |

**KEY**  Republicans  Democrats  *Independents*

| | | | |
|---|---|---|---|
| Y | Voted for (yea) | X | Paired against |
| # | Paired for | – | Announced against |
| + | Announced for | P | Voted "present" |
| N | Voted against (nay) | | |

C  Voted "present" to avoid possible conflict of interest
?  Did not vote or otherwise make a position known

# Senate Roll Call Index by Subject

## SENATE VOTES